MW01013027

PRINCIPLES AND PRACTICE OF

FORENSIC PSYCHIATRY

PRINCIPLES AND PRACTICE OF

FORENSIC PSYCHIATRY

edited by

RICHARD ROSNER

CHARLES L. SCOTT

CRC Press is an imprint of the
Taylor & Francis Group, an **informa** business

CRC Press
Taylor & Francis Group
6000 Broken Sound Parkway NW, Suite 300
Boca Raton, FL 33487-2742

Version Date: 20161109

International Standard Book Number-13: 978-1-4822-6228-5 (Pack - Book and Ebook)

Visit the Taylor & Francis Web site at
http://www.taylorandfrancis.com

and the CRC Press Web site at
http://www.crcpress.com

Printed and bound by CPI Group (UK) Ltd, Croydon, CR0 4YY

This book is dedicated to the memory of M. Bernice Horner Rosner

Contents

Preface to the first edition

Principles and Practice of Forensic Psychiatry is the most ambitious publication to date of the volumes edited for the Tri-State Chapter of the American Academy of Psychiatry and the Law (AAPL). The Tri-State Chapter is the first and largest of the AAPL chapters. It draws upon the academy's resources in Connecticut, New Jersey, and New York. The Chapter provides more than 50 hours of formal training in forensic psychiatry each year through its two-semester course on forensic psychiatry and its January weekend program devoted to a specific single theme in the field. Having produced seven prior books, all in the series *Critical Issues in American Psychiatry and the Law*, the current volume is a natural extension of the Tri-State Chapter's educational work.

The literature in forensic psychiatry in the United States has grown, especially since the creation of AAPL in 1969. There are books to serve as introductions to forensic psychiatry for general psychiatrists, as research reports and monographs on specialized single topics, as compendia of legal cases and materials, and as advanced surveys of one or several major themes in psychiatry and the law. However, until the present volume, none of the existing books has been specifically designed to review the entire field of forensic psychiatry at a level consistent with the needs of subspecialists.

The American Psychiatric Association recently decided to recognize forensic psychiatry as a subspecialty and to petition the American Board of Psychiatry and Neurology (ABPN) to offer an examination for certification in "added qualifications in forensic psychiatry." The ABPN requested, and was granted, authorization from the American Board of Medical Specialties to proceed with the development and implementation of such a subspecialty examination. The increased professional recognition of forensic psychiatry makes greater the need for the present volume.

Principles and Practice of Forensic Psychiatry is designed as a foundation work in the field. Among the intended audience are (1) fellows in a fifth-postgraduate-year fellowship program in forensic psychiatry; (2) forensic psychiatrists preparing for the subspecialty examinations of the American Board of Forensic Psychiatry or the forthcoming "added qualifications in forensic psychiatry" examination of the ABPN; and (3) forensic psychiatric practitioners who want a convenient, one-volume reference book to assist them in their work. Forensic psychologists, forensic clinical psychiatric social workers, mental health administrators, and attorneys will also find the current volume to be valuable. The editors and authors have sought to set forth areas of general agreement (wherever possible) and to describe as fairly as is feasible the major contending views on those topics that lack consensus.

The current book attempts to be encyclopedic in scope. The AAPL and the American Academy of Forensic Sciences have endorsed the Accreditation Council on Fellowships in Forensic Psychiatry (ACFFP) and its standards for education and training in psychiatry and the law. The ACFFP Standards (AAPL 1982) set forth the main areas in the didactic core curriculum of forensic psychiatry as

1. Legal Regulation of Psychiatry
2. Criminal Forensic Psychiatry
3. Civil Forensic Psychiatry, including Family Law and Domestic Relations
4. Correctional Psychiatry
5. Special Issues in Forensic Psychiatry
6. Basic Issues in Law
7. Landmark Cases in Mental Health Law

It is in the sense of addressing all of these main topics identified by the ACFFP that this book is meant to be comprehensive.

Each author was asked to employ the uniform conceptual framework for the analysis of problems in forensic psychiatry that was introduced in the Tri-State Chapter's first book (Rosner 1982):

1. Identify the specific psychiatric-legal issue(s).
2. Identify the specific psychiatric-legal criteria that are used to decide the issue(s).
3. Identify the specific clinical data that are directly relevant to the psychiatric-legal criteria.
4. Set forth and explain the specific reasoning processes to be used to apply the data to the criteria to decide the issue(s).

Individual authors have adhered to this framework in their chapters to a greater or lesser degree, depending on their subject matter. It provides a uniform reference for approaching the otherwise almost dauntingly diverse contents of the field of forensic psychiatry.

Part 1, History and Practice of Forensic Psychiatry, introduces the reader to the conceptual framework of the field, the definition of forensic psychiatry, such practicalities as report writing and courtroom testimony, current educational and ethical standards, issues in administration, potential abuse of psychiatry, the death penalty, psychological autopsies, criminal profiling, competence assessments, and the history of forensic psychiatry.

Part 2, Legal Regulation of Psychiatric Practice, addresses informed consent, psychiatric hospitalization, outpatient civil commitment, the right to treatment, the right to refuse treatment, confidentiality and testimonial privilege, the duty to protect third parties, treatment boundaries, sexual misconduct by therapists, and the impaired physician.

Part 3, Forensic Evaluation and Treatment in the Criminal Justice System, considers criminal competencies, criminal responsibility, trauma-induced psychiatric disorders, and postconviction dispositional evaluations.

Part 4, Civil Law, examines psychiatric malpractice, psychiatric disability determinations, personal injury litigation, trauma-induced psychiatric disorders, evaluation of neurotoxicity, testamentary capacity, guardianships, and issues at the end of life.

Part 5, Family Law and Domestic Relations, reviews child custody, abused children, abused elders, juvenile delinquency, children in need of supervision, confidentiality, trauma-induced psychiatric disorders, fetal and infant issues, juvenile suicide, psychiatric hospitalization of minors, and adolescent violence.

Part 6, Correctional Psychiatry, focuses on the history of correctional psychiatry, standards for correctional mental health services, the structure of correctional mental health services, administrative issues, suicide prevention, inmate riots, and the ethics of correctional psychiatry.

Part 7, Special Clinical Issues in Forensic Psychiatry, explores malingering, antisocial personality disorder, dangerousness, causes and treatments of violent behaviors, epilepsy and brain disease, neuropsychiatric aspects of forensic psychiatry, psychological assessment, cultural and ethnic minorities, hypnosis, multiple personality disorder, amnesia, amytal, polygraphy, geriatric forensic psychiatry, torture, brainwashing, terrorism, AIDS (acquired immunodeficiency syndrome), and sexual offenders.

The Tri-State Chapter of the American Academy of Psychiatry and the Law offers *Principles and Practice of Forensic Psychiatry* as its latest educational contribution for students and practitioners.

ACKNOWLEDGMENT

The idea for this book originated with Robert Weinstock, MD, who presumed on 30 years of friendship with the editor to urge that a comprehensive textbook of forensic psychiatry be planned and implemented as a project of the Tri-State Chapter of the American Academy of Psychiatry and the Law.

REFERENCES

American Academy of Psychiatry and the Law (AAPL). 1982. *The Bulletin of AAPL* 10(4):281–283.

Rosner R. 1982. *Critical Issues in American Psychiatry and the Law*. Springfield, IL: Charles C Thomas Company, 5–11.

Principles and Practice of Forensic Psychiatry was edited for the American Academy of Psychiatry and the Law Tri-State Chapter.

Preface to the second edition

Principles and Practice of Forensic Psychiatry, Second Edition, was authorized by, and edited for, the Tri-State Chapter of the American Academy of Psychiatry and the Law (Tri-State AAPL). With one exception, every chapter in the book is an updated, revised, and expanded version of what appeared in the original edition, or is completely new. The one exception is the first chapter, which has been described as a "classic" statement of the Tri-State Chapter's approach to forensic psychiatry.

The Tri-State AAPL was conceived at the 1975 Boston, Massachusetts meeting of the national organization. There was initial skepticism among senior practitioners about the prospects for a local chapter of AAPL because a prior New York forensic psychiatry educational group, the Isaac Ray Society, had failed to thrive. There was initial opposition from national AAPL because of concern that local chapters might become competitors for members and dues. It was decided to poll by mail all of the AAPL members in New York State to determine if there was interest in the formation of a local forensic psychiatry society; the results of the poll indicated strong support. An organizational meeting was held, to which all New York State members of AAPL were invited. At that meeting, it was determined to call the new society the New York State Membership Group of AAPL because national AAPL had indicated that the then-bylaws of AAPL did not permit the creation of official chapters. The initial organizational meeting also generated a slate of candidates for elective office in the new society, and a mail ballot was sent to all New York State AAPL members; the election yielded the first officers of the new society. It was decided that there would be no membership dues, and that all AAPL members residing or working in New York State would automatically be members of the New York State Membership Group of AAPL.

The interest of AAPL members in New Jersey and Connecticut in participating in the educational programs of the New York State Membership Group led to a motion to expand the society. A mail ballot was sent to all AAPL members in New Jersey and Connecticut, inquiring if they wished to join a Tri-State Membership Group of AAPL; the results of the poll indicated firm support, and the society was expanded accordingly. In subsequent elections, care was taken to ensure that at least one representative from New Jersey and one representative from Connecticut were officers of the society.

The success of the Tri-State Membership Group led to a request that national AAPL authorize the creation of local chapters. An AAPL Task Force on Chapters was appointed and recommended that an appropriate bylaws modification be developed and submitted for ratification to the AAPL membership. On May 4, 1980, following approval of the new bylaw authorizing local chapters, AAPL authorized the Tri-State Membership Group to be re-named and recognized as AAPL's first official chapter: the Tri-State Chapter of AAPL.

The educational core of Tri-State AAPL has been its annual one-day educational program each January and its annual two-semester course on forensic psychiatry. As an outgrowth of those training programs, Tri-State authorized the publication of a number of books, all in the series *Critical Issues in American Psychiatry and the Law.* It is a source of great satisfaction to present the latest book authorized by Tri-State AAPL, the second edition of *Principles and Practice of Forensic Psychiatry.*

ACKNOWLEDGMENTS

Once again, Robert Weinstock, MD, has been the driving force behind this publication project. It was he who presumed on 40 years of friendship to oblige the editor to plan and implement this book.

Abraham Halpern, MD, has earned special citation for generously volunteering to read and edit the entire text for spelling, grammar, and legal citations.

FURTHER READING

Rosner R. ed. 1982. *Critical Issues in American Psychiatry and the Law.* Springfield, IL: Charles C Thomas.

Rosner R. ed. 1985. *Critical Issues in American Psychiatry and the Law.* 2 vols. New York: Plenum.

Rosner R. ed. 1994. *Principles and Practice of Forensic Psychiatry.* London, England: Chapman and Hall; republished by Edward Arnold, London, 1998.

Rosner R and Harmon R. 1989. *Correctional Psychiatry.* New York: Plenum.

Rosner R and Harmon R. 1989. *Criminal Court Consultation*. New York: Plenum.
Rosner R and Schwartz H. eds. 1987. *Geriatric Psychiatry and the Law*. New York: Plenum.
Rosner R and Schwartz H. eds. 1989. *Juvenile Psychiatry and the Law*. New York: Plenum.
Rosner R and Weinstock R. eds. 1990. *Ethical Practice in Psychiatry and the Law*. New York: Plenum.

The second edition of *Principles and Practice of Forensic Psychiatry* was edited for the Tri-State Chapter of the American Academy of Psychiatry and the Law.

Preface to the third edition

Principles and Practice of Forensic Psychiatry, Third Edition, was authorized by, and edited for, the Tri-State Chapter of the American Academy of Psychiatry and the Law (Tri-State AAPL). This third edition provides substantial revisions and additions to the second edition, and offers the reader the most current knowledge on a vast array of over 100 topics in the field of forensic psychiatry. With one exception, each chapter is either an updated version of what appeared in the original edition or is completely new. The one exception is the first chapter titled "A Conceptual Framework for Forensic Psychiatry," which has been described as a "classic" statement of the Tri-State Chapter's approach to forensic psychiatry. The Tri-State Chapter is the first and largest of the American Academy of Psychiatry and the Law (AAPL) Chapters.

As was the goal of prior editions, this third edition strives to be encyclopedic in scope and a foundation work in the field. Because of the significant expansion in the breadth and detail of material covered, this edition provides a practical source of information for a wide-ranging audience. Among the intended audience are (1) general psychiatry residents who are required to have exposure to a range of forensic psychiatric topics in their general training, (2) forensic psychiatry fellows in a fifth-postgraduate-year fellowship program in forensic psychiatry, (3) forensic psychiatrists preparing for the subspecialty examinations of the American Board of Psychiatry and Neurology's Added Qualifications in Forensic Psychiatry Examination, and (4) forensic psychiatric practitioners who want a convenient, one-volume reference book to assist them in their work. In addition, forensic psychologists, forensic clinical psychiatric social workers, mental health administrators, attorneys, and judges will find the current volume to be valuable. Although the information provided within this text is not meant to suggest a single standard of forensic psychiatric evaluation or treatment, the provided material will likely assist providers and practitioners in applying updated information as relevant to individual evaluations, policy development, expert witness testimony, and treatment planning.

Each author was asked to employ the uniform conceptual framework for the analysis of problems in forensic psychiatry that was introduced in the Tri-State Chapter's first book (Rosner 1982):

1. Identify the specific psychiatric-legal issue(s).
2. Identify the specific psychiatric-legal criteria that are used to decide the issue(s).
3. Identify the specific clinical data that are directly relevant to the psychiatric-legal criteria.
4. Set forth and explain the specific reasoning processes to be used to apply the data to the criteria to decide the issue(s).

Individual authors have adhered to this framework in their chapters to a greater or lesser degree, depending on their subject matter. It provides a uniform reference for approaching the otherwise almost dauntingly diverse contents of the field of forensic psychiatry.

This edition has expanded from nine to eleven sections, reflecting the growth of the forensic field. Part 1, History and Practice of Forensic Psychiatry, introduces the reader to the conceptual framework of the field, the definition of forensic psychiatry, history of forensic psychiatry, such practicalities as report writing and courtroom testimony, current educational and ethical standards and foundations of professional ethics, liability of the forensic psychiatry, death penalty, psychological autopsies, and competence assessments.

Part 2, Legal Regulation of Psychiatric Practice, addresses informed consent, psychiatric hospitalization, assisted outpatient commitment, the right to treatment, treatment refusal in psychiatric practice, confidentiality and testimonial privilege, the duty to protect third parties, treatment boundaries in psychiatric practice, and the impaired physician. Two newly added chapters to this section review laws related to physician prescribing of controlled substances and court oversight in psychotropic prescribing of youth in custody.

Part 3, Forensic Evaluation and Treatment in the Criminal Justice System, includes seven chapters addressing a range of evaluations for individuals facing criminal charges. Original chapters added to this section highlight emerging trends in jail diversion and speciality courts, treatment approaches for trial competency restoration, and the role of forensic evaluators in presentencing evaluations.

Part 4, Civil Law, examines psychiatric malpractice, psychiatric disability determinations, workers' compensation, personal injury litigation, sexual harassment and gender discrimination, civil competencies, and issues related to death and dying.

Part 5, Family Law and Domestic Relations, reviews child custody, termination of parental rights, abused children, juvenile delinquency, posttraumatic stress disorder in children and adolescents, forensic aspects of suicide and homicide in children and adolescents, the child witness, neuropsychological assessment of children and adolescents, and juvenile sexual offenders. Important additions to this section from prior editions include juvenile competence to stand trial and remediation, evaluations of youth culpability, and forensic aspects of childhood bullying.

Part 6, Correctional Psychiatry, focuses on the history of correctional psychiatry, standards for correctional mental health services, the structure of correctional mental health services, administrative issues, suicide prevention, inmate riots, and the ethics of correctional psychiatry. This third edition provides new chapters related to conducting psychiatric research and the use of psychopharmacology in a correctional setting.

Part 7, Aggression and Violence, is a completely new section to this edition that expands topics from other sections in prior editions. This section highlights the assessment and treatment of aggression, the assessment and treatment of antisocial personality disorder and psychopathy, terrorism, and stalking. Important and timely additions in this section include mental illness and firearms, individuals who commit mass murder, cyberstalking, and women who are violent.

Part 8, Psychological and Neuroimaging Assessments, is the second completely new section that recognizes the relevance of psychological testing and neuroimaging in conducting forensic evaluations. This section provides a practical overview to the use of psychological testing, with specific chapters highlighting the use of psychological testing in malingering assessments, sex offender risk assessments, and violence risk assessments. In addition, chapters highlighting the use of neuropsychological testing and neuroimaging in forensic psychiatric evaluations are provided.

Part 9, Special Topics in Forensic Psychiatry, includes a wide range of important topics in forensic psychiatry, such as the assessment of malingering, amnesia, cultural issues, geriatric evaluees, use of torture, terrorism, and issues related to health care and the courts. Newly added topics to this section include gender issues in forensic psychiatry, starting a forensic psychiatric practice, social science and forensic psychiatry, social media and the Internet, and community-based assessment and treatment of justice-involved individuals with mental illness.

Part 10, Basic Issues in Law, provides a useful overview for readers on the foundations of American law and the court system, philosophy of the law, criminal and civil procedure, theories of legal punishment, forensic research and the Internet, tort law and the psychiatrist, and judicial review of the constitution.

Part 11, Landmark Cases in Forensic Psychiatry, offers an extremely helpful summary of key civil and criminal law cases that involve a range of mental health issues, forensic assessments, and the provision of mental health care.

In summary, the third edition of *Principles and Practice of Forensic Psychiatry* provides an extensive overview of a wide range of topics designed to assist the forensic practitioner in maintaining currency in the field of forensic psychiatry.

The third edition of *Principles and Practice of Forensic Psychiatry* was edited for the Tri-State Chapter of the American Academy of Psychiatry and the Law. The editors are appreciative that the Tri-State Chapter of the American Academy of Psychiatry and the Law offers *Principles and Practice of Forensic Psychiatry* as its latest educational contribution for students and practitioners.

REFERENCE

Rosner R. ed. 1982. *Critical Issues in American Psychiatry and the Law.* Springfield, IL: Charles C Thomas.

Officers of the Tri-State Chapter at the time of this publication are as follows:

Medical Director and Founding President	Richard Rosner MD	*Councillors*
President	Manuel Lopez-Leon MD	Ziv Cohen MD
Vice President	Bipin Subedi MD	Jeremy Colley MD
Secretary	Susan Gray MD	Sundeep Randhawa MD
Treasurer	Robert L. Goldstein MD JD	Frank Tedeschi MD
		Emily Urbina MD
		Jonathan Weiss MD

Acknowledgments

As with the first and second editions, Robert Weinstock, MD, deserves special recognition as a major driving force for the third edition of this book. His encouragement and friendship to both editors provided inspiration and motivation for this project. In addition, David Spagnolo and Hillary Brown of the University of California, Davis, Division of Psychiatry and the Law, are greatly appreciated for all of their organizational skills and efforts in preparing this book for submission.

Editors

Richard Rosner, MD, is a Distinguished Life Fellow of the American Psychiatric Association, a Fellow of the American College of Psychiatrists, a Distinguished Fellow of the American Academy of Forensic Sciences, and a Fellow of the American Society for Adolescent Psychiatry. He is a clinical professor in both the Department of Psychiatry and the Department of Child and Adolescent Psychiatry at the New York University School of Medicine. Rosner served as the first and only Associate Commissioner for Forensic Psychiatry of the Department of Mental Health, Mental Retardation, and Alcoholism Services of the City of New York. He is a former medical director of the Forensic Psychiatry Clinic for the New York Criminal Court and Supreme Court (First Judicial District) of Bellevue Hospital Center, New York. He co-founded and is a former director of the Forensic Psychiatry Fellowship Program at New York University Medical Center. Rosner is a recipient of the Isaac Ray Award of the American Psychiatric Association. He is a former president of the following professional organizations: the American Academy of Psychiatry and the Law, the American Academy of Forensic Sciences, the Association of Directors of Forensic Psychiatry Fellowships, the Accreditation Council on Fellowships in Forensic Psychiatry, the American Board of Forensic Psychiatry, Inc., and the American Society for Adolescent Psychiatry. Rosner was the founding president and is the current medical director of the Tri-State Chapter of the American Academy of Psychiatry and the Law.

Charles L. Scott, MD, is chief of the Division of Psychiatry and the Law, Forensic Psychiatry Fellowship Training Director, and professor of Clinical Psychiatry at the University of California, Davis, Medical Center in Sacramento, California. He is board certified in Forensic Psychiatry, General Psychiatry, Child and Adolescent Psychiatry, and Addiction Psychiatry. Scott is a past president of the American Academy of Psychiatry and the Law and is also past president of the Association of Directors of Forensic Psychiatry Fellowships. He has served as a member of the American Academy of Psychiatry and the Law national task force to develop guidelines for the evaluation of criminal responsibility and competency to stand trial. He is also one of four national American Academy of Psychiatry and the Law Forensic Psychiatry Review Course faculty instructors, and in 2008 received the American Academy of Psychiatry and the Law award as the most outstanding forensic psychiatry fellowship program instructor in the United States. Scott has served as a forensic psychiatric consultant to jails, prisons, maximum security forensic inpatient units, California Department of State Hospitals, and to the National Football League, providing training on violence risk assessment for National Football League counselors. He has been an editor and co-editor of four books related to forensic psychiatry and has published articles and book chapters in the areas of risk assessment of violence and aggression, the death penalty, juvenile violence, and mental health law. His research interests include the relationship of substance use to aggression among criminal defendants and the quality of forensic evaluations of criminal responsibility. He lectures nationally on the topics of malingering, violence risk assessment, juvenile violence, substance use and violence, the assessment of sex offenders, correctional psychiatry, the *Diagnostic and Statistical Manual of Mental Disorders* (fifth edition) and the law, and malpractice issues in mental health.

Contributors

A.G. Ahmed
Division of Forensic Psychiatry, Division of Addiction and Mental Health
University of Ottawa
Ottawa, Canada

George David Annas
Department of Psychiatry
State University of New York Upstate Medical University
Syracuse, New York

Peter Ash
Psychiatry and Behavioral Sciences
Psychiatry and Law Service
Emory University
Atlanta, Georgia

Peter N. Barboriak
Central Regional Hospital
University of North Carolina School of Medicine
Chapel Hill, North Carolina

Amy Barnhorst
Department of Psychiatry and Behavioral Sciences
University of California, Davis
Davis, California

Eraka Bath
Department of Psychiatry
UCLA Neuropsychiatric Institute
Los Angeles, California

Mace Beckson
Department of Psychiatry and Biobehavioral Sciences
David Geffen School of Medicine at UCLA
Los Angeles, California

Alan L. Berman
Department of Psychiatry and Behavioral Sciences
Johns Hopkins School of Medicine
Baltimore, Maryland

Roger J. Bernstein
Criminal Defense Lawyer
New York, New York

Stephen B. Billick
Department of Psychiatry
New York University School of Medicine
New York, New York

Kate Bolton Bonnici
Department of English
University of California
Los Angeles, California

Daniel Bonnici
Department of Psychiatry
Kaiser Permanente, Southern California
Los Angeles, California

Kyle Brauer Boone
California School of Forensic Studies
Alliant International University
Alhambra, California

Dominique Bourget
Integrated Forensic Psychiatric Program
Royal Mental Health Centre
University of Ottawa
Ottawa, Canada

John Bradford
Forensic Psychiatry Royal College of Physicians and Surgeons of Canada
University of Ottawa
Ottawa, Canada

and

Department of Psychiatry
University of Alberta
Edmonton, Canada

Samuel Jan Brakel
DePaul University College of Law
Chicago, Illinois

Melody C. Brown
San Juan Capistrano, California

Alec Buchanan
Department of Psychiatry
Yale University
New Haven, Connecticut

James B. Buck
McCrea & Buck, LLC
Denver, Colorado

Kathryn A. Burns
Ohio Department of Rehabilitation and Correction
and
Department of Psychiatry
Ohio State University
Columbus, Ohio

and

Department of Psychiatry
Case Western Reserve University
Cleveland, Ohio

Harold J. Bursztajn
Harvard Medical School
Program in Psychiatry and the Law
and
Beth Israel Deaconess Medical Center
Boston, Massachusetts

Philip J. Candilis
Saint Elizabeths Hospital
and
Department of Behavioral Health
George Washington University School of Medicine and Health Sciences
and
Howard University College of Medicine
Washington, DC

Vincenzo Carannante
Shipman & Goodwin, L.L.P.
Hartford, Connecticut

Cathleen A. Cerny
Case Western Reserve University
Cleveland, Ohio

Kang Choi
Child and Adolescent Psychiatry Fellow
University of California Irvine Medical Center
Orange, California

J. Richard Ciccone
University of Rochester Medical Center
Rochester, New York

Steven J. Ciric
Department of Psychiatry
New York University School of Medicine
New York, New York

Fred Cohen
SUNY at Albany
School of Criminal Justice
Syracuse, New York

Jeremy Colley
New York University School of Medicine
New York, New York

Paul D. Cooper
Treece Alfey Musat P.C.
Denver, Colorado

William Connor Darby
Semel Institute for Neuroscience and Human Behavior
University of California, Los Angeles
Los Angeles, California

Gregory Davis
Department of Psychiatry
New York University School of Medicine
New York, New York

Sanford L. Drob
Fielding University
Santa Barbara, California

Eric Y. Drogin
Department of Psychiatry
Harvard Medical School
Boston, Massachusetts

Suzanne M. Dupée
Department of Psychiatry and Human Behavior
University of California, Irvine
Irvine, California

Joel A. Dvoskin
College of Medicine
University of Arizona
Tucson, Arizona

Gregg Dwyer
Department of Psychiatry and Behavioral Sciences
Medical University of South Carolina
Charleston, South Carolina

M. Carmela Epright
Professor of Philosophy
Furman University
Greenville, South Carolina

Brian A. Falls
Program in Psychiatry and the Law
Harvard Medical School
and
Beth Israel Deaconess Medical Center
Boston, Massachusetts

and

Private Practice
Austin, Texas

J. Paul Fedoroff
Institute of Mental Health Research
Department of Psychiatry
University of Ottawa
Ottawa, Canada

Alan R. Felthous
Department of Psychiatry
Saint Louis University School of Medicine
Saint Louis, Missouri

Jessica Ferranti
Division of Psychiatry and the Law
University of California, Davis Medical Center
Sacramento, California

Howard Forman
Department of Psychiatry and Behavioral Sciences
Albert Einstein College of Medicine
Bronx, New York

Bradley W. Freeman
Department of Psychiatry
Vanderbilt University School of Medicine
Nashville, Tennessee

Richard L. Frierson
Department of Neuropsychiatry and Behavioral Science
University of South Carolina School of Medicine
Columbia, South Carolina

Thomas Garrick
Department of Psychiatry and Biobehavioral Sciences
University of California, Los Angeles
Los Angeles, California

Jeffrey L. Geller
University of Massachusetts Medical School
Worcester, Massachusetts

Michael Gendel
Colorado Physician Health Program
University of Colorado
Denver, Colorado

Liza H. Gold
Department of Psychiatry
Georgetown University School of Medicine
Washington, DC

Robert Lloyd Goldstein
College of Physicians and Surgeons
Columbia University
New York, New York

Kelly Goodness
Clinical and Legal Psychologist
Independent Practice
Keller, Texas

Sanjiv Gulati
Department of Psychiatry
University of Ottawa
Ottawa, Canada

John Gunn
Institute of Psychiatry
King's College London
London, United Kingdom

Richard C.W. Hall
Department of Medical Education
University of Central Florida College of Medicine
Orlando, Florida

and

Department of Psychiatry
University of South Florida
Tampa, Florida

Ryan C.W. Hall
Department of Medical Education
University of Central Florida College of Medicine
and
Barry University
Dwayne O. Andreas School of Law
Orlando, Florida

and

Department of Psychiatry
University of South Florida
Tampa, Florida

Susan Hatters-Friedman
Department of Psychological Medicine
Auckland Regional Forensic Psychiatry Services
Auckland, New Zealand

and

Department of Psychiatry
Case Western Reserve University
Cleveland, Ohio

J. Michael Heinlen
Thompson & Knight
Dallas, Texas

James W. Hicks
Department of Psychiatry
New York University School of Medicine
New York, New York

Steven K. Hoge
Columbia-Cornell Forensic Psychiatry Fellowship
Columbia University Medical Center
New York, New York

Brian Holoyda
Division of Psychiatry and the Law
University of California, Davis Medical Center
Sacramento, California

Cory Jaques
Juvenile Justice Mental Health Program
Los Angeles County Department of Mental Health
Los Angeles, California

Joshua C.W. Jones
Department of Psychiatry
University of Rochester Medical Center
Rochester, New York

and

Peninsula Behavioral Health
Port Angeles, Washington

Alan Wayne Jones
Department of Clinical Pharmacology
University of Linköping
Linköping, Sweden

Claudia Kachigian
Department of Psychiatry
Saint Louis University School of Medicine
Saint Louis, Missouri

Praveen R. Kambam
Department of Psychiatry and Biobehavioral Sciences
University of California, Los Angeles
Los Angeles, California

Andrew R. Kaufman
SUNY Upstate Medical University
Syracuse, New York

Ann M. Killenbeck
University of Arkansas School of Law
Fayetteville, Arkansas

Andrew Kim
Department of Psychiatry and Biobehavioral Sciences
David Geffen School of Medicine at UCLA
Los Angeles, California

James L. Knoll
SUNY Upstate Medical University
Syracuse, New York

J. Steven Lamberti
Schizophrenia Treatment Research Laboratory
University of Rochester Medical Center
Rochester, New York

Eugene Lee
University of Arkansas for Medical Sciences
Little Rock, Arkansas

Li-Wen Lee
Columbia University College of Physicians and Surgeons
New York, New York

Gregory B. Leong
Department of Psychiatry and Behavioral Sciences
University of Southern California
Los Angeles, California

and

Department of Psychiatry and Human Behavior
University of California, Irvine
Irvine, California

Giovana de Amorim Levin
Edgeland Clinic
Winnipeg, Canada

Alison J. Lynch
Disability Rights
Brooklyn, New York

Anthony Maden
Department of Medicine
Imperial College of London
London, United Kingdom

Ann C. Marcotte
Department of Psychiatry
Columbia University College of Physicians and Surgeons
New York, New York

Barbara McDermott
Division of Psychiatry and the Law
University of California, Davis Medical Center
Sacramento, California

Jeffrey L. Metzner
Department of Psychiatry
University of Colorado School of Medicine
Denver, Colorado

John Monahan
University of Virginia School of Law
Charlottesville, Virginia

Megan M. Mroczkowski
Department of Psychiatry
Columbia University Medical Center
New York, New York

Lisa Murphy
Sexual Behaviours Clinic
Integrated Forensic Program
The Royal Ottowa Mental Health Centre
Ottawa, Canada

Mohan Nair
UCLA Medical Center
Los Angeles, California

Erin M. Nelson
Department of Psychiatry
University of Arizona College of Medicine
Phoenix, Arizona

Ariana Nesbit
Department of Psychiatry
Harvard Medical School
Cambridge, Massachusetts

William Newman
Saint Louis University Hospital
Saint Louis, Missouri

Stephen G. Noffsinger
Case Western Reserve University School of Medicine
and
University Hospitals of Cleveland
Cleveland, Ohio

and

University of Akron School of Law
Akron, Ohio

Michael A. Norko
Department of Psychiatry
Yale University
New Haven, Connecticut

Paul J. O'Leary
Department of Psychiatry
University of South Alabama
Mobile, Alabama
and
Department of Psychiatry
University of Birmingham School of Medicine
Birmingham, Alabama

Randy K. Otto
Department of Mental Health Law and Policy
University of South Florida
Tampa, Florida

Howard Owens
Department of Psychiatry
New York University School of Medicine
New York, New York

Leidy S. Partida
School of Criminology, Criminal Justice, and Emergency Management
California State University
Long Beach, California

Michael L. Perlin
International Mental Disability Law Reform Project
New York Law School
New York, New York
and
Mental Disability Law and Policy Associates
Trenton, New Jersey

Amy Phenix
Private Practice
Morro Bay, California

Laura J. Phillips
Department of Psychiatry and Behavioral Sciences
Albert Einstein College of Medicine
Bronx, New York

Jennifer L. Piel
VA Puget Sound Health Care System
and
Department of Psychiatry and Behavioral Sciences
University of Washington
Seattle, Washington

Debra A. Pinals
Program in Psychiatry, Law, and Ethics
Department of Psychiatry
University of Michigan
Ann Arbor, Michigan

Steven E. Pitt
Department of Psychiatry
University of Arizona College of Medicine
Phoenix, Arizona

Marvin Thomas Prosono
Department of Sociology and Anthropology
Missouri State University
Springfield, Missouri

Cameron Quanbeck
Cordilleras Mental Health Center
Department of Psychiatry
and
San Mateo County Health System
San Mateo, California

Andrew J. Rader
Bunnell, Woulfe, Kirschbaum, Keller, McIntyre & Gregoire
Boca Raton, Florida

Patricia R. Recupero
Warren Alpert Medical School of Brown University
and
Butler Hospital
Providence, Rhode Island

Rusty Reeves
Department of Psychiatry
Robert Wood Johnson Medical School
Rutgers University
and
Rutgers University Correctional Health Care
Piscataway, New Jersey

Daniel J. Reid
Paladin International, LLC
Paladin Special Operations Branch, LLC
Littleton, Colorado

William H. Reid
Texas Tech University Health Sciences Center
Lubbock, Texas

David Reiss
West London Mental Health NHS Trust
Imperial College London
London, United Kingdom

Phillip J. Resnick
Case Western Reserve University School of Medicine
and
University Hospitals Case Medical Center
and
Case Western Reserve University School of Law
Cleveland, Ohio

Meryl B. Rome
Private Practice
Boca Raton, Florida

Richard Rosner
Department of Psychiatry
Department of Child and Adolescent Psychiatry
School of Medicine
New York University
New York, New York

Merrill Rotter
Department of Psychiatry and Behavioral Sciences
Albert Einstein College of Medicine
Bronx, New York

Eileen P. Ryan
Department of Psychiatry and Neurobehavioral Sciences
University of Virginia School of Medicine
and
Commonwealth Center for Children and Adolescents
Staunton, Virginia

Robert L. Sadoff
Division of Forensic Psychiatry
Perelman School of Medicine
University of Pennsylvania
Philadelphia, Pennsylvania

Robert A. Schug
School of Criminology, Criminal Justice, and Emergency Management
California State University
Long Beach, California

Charles L. Scott
Division of Psychiatry and the Law
University of California, Davis Medical Center
Sacramento, California

Sanjay Shah
Department of Psychiatry and Behavioral Sciences
Emory University
Atlanta, Georgia

Shawn Sidhu
Department of Psychiatry and Behavioral Sciences
University of New Mexico School of Medicine
Albuquerque, New Mexico

Robert I. Simon
Department of Psychiatry
Georgetown University School of Medicine
Washington, DC
and
Department of Psychiatry
Suburban Hospital, Johns Hopkins Medicine
Bethesda, Maryland

Alexander I.F. Simpson
Department of Psychiatry
University of Toronto
and
Centre for Addiction and Mental Health
Toronto, Canada

Joseph R. Simpson
Department of Psychiatry
University of Southern California Keck School of Medicine
Los Angeles, California

Jennifer L. Skeem
Goldman School of Public Policy
University of California, San Francisco
Berkeley, California

Delaney Smith
Department of Psychiatry
Ohio State University College of Medicine
Columbus, Ohio

Gregory Sokolov
Department of Psychiatry and Behavioral Sciences
University of California, Davis
Sacramento, California

Renee M. Sorrentino
Institute for Sexual Wellness
Harvard Medical School
Boston, Massachusetts

Chris E. Stout
Center for Global Initiatives
College of Medicine
University of Illinois at Chicago
Chicago, Illinois

Holly E. Tabernik
Department of Psychiatry and Health Behavior
Georgia Regents University
Augusta, Georgia

Gen Tanaka
Harvard Medical School South Shore Psychiatry Residency Program
and
Veterans Affairs Boston Healthcare Center
Brockton, Massachusetts

Kenneth Tardiff
Weill Cornell Medical College
New York Presbyterian Hospital
New York, New York

Frank K. Tedeschi
Department of Child and Adolescent Psychiatry
New York University School of Medicine
New York, New York

Christopher R. Thompson
Department of Psychiatry and Biobehavioral Sciences
David Geffen School of Medicine at UCLA
Los Angeles, California

Gary Tsai
Medical Director and Science Officer, Substance Abuse Prevention and Control
County of Los Angeles Department of Public Health
Los Angeles, California

Douglas E. Tucker
Department of Psychiatry
University of California, San Francisco
San Francisco, California

Michael J. Vitacco
Department of Psychiatry and Health Behavior
Georgia Regents University
Augusta, Georgia

Kyle C. Walker
Department of Psychiatry
Bridgewater State Hospital
Bridgewater, Massachusetts

Bruce B. Way
Department of Psychiatry and Behavioral Sciences
SUNY Upstate Medical University
Syracuse, New York

Naomi Weinstein
Mental Hygiene Legal Service
Appellate Division, First Judicial Department
New York, New York

Robert Weinstock
Department of Psychiatry and Biobehavioral Sciences
University of California, Los Angeles
Los Angeles, California

Robert L. Weisman
University of Rochester Medical Center
Rochester, New York

Robert Wettstein
Department of Psychiatry
University of Pittsburgh School of Medicine
Pittsburgh, Pennsylvania

PART 1

History and Practice of Forensic Psychiatry

ROBERT WEINSTOCK AND GREGORY B. LEONG

1

A conceptual framework for forensic psychiatry

RICHARD ROSNER

INTRODUCTION

The third edition of this volume begins with a particular conceptual framework applicable to all problems in the field. This framework is designed to organize the extraordinarily wide range of factors that must be considered in the approach to forensic psychiatry, so as to make rational analysis systematic, uniform, and more likely to be effective.

The number of specific psychiatric–legal issues to consider is itself large. As set forth in the *Standards for Fellowship Programs in Forensic Psychiatry* (Rosner 1982a), they include the following:

- *Civil forensic psychiatry* including, at minimum, conservators and guardianships, child custody determinations, parental competence, termination of parental rights, child abuse, child neglect, psychiatric disability determinations (e.g., for social security, workers' compensation, private insurance coverage), testamentary capacity, psychiatric negligence and malpractice, personal injury litigation issues.
- *Criminal forensic psychiatry* including, at minimum, competence to stand trial, competence to enter a plea, testimonial capacity, voluntariness of confessions, insanity defense(s), diminished capacity, sentencing considerations, release of persons who have been acquitted by reason of insanity.
- *Legal regulation of psychiatry* including, at minimum, civil involuntary commitment, voluntary hospitalization, confidentiality, right to treatment, right to refuse treatment, informed consent, professional liability, ethical guidelines.

Similar areas are included in the more recent requirements of the Accreditation Council for Graduate Medical Education (see Chapter 7). There are many psychiatric–legal issues that forensic psychiatrists are asked to address, and my proposed model is a way to conceptualize these issues so that an opinion can be rendered.

For every psychiatric-legal issue, a variety of legal contexts exist in which the issue may occur. In the United States, there are 50 state jurisdictions, plus the District of Columbia, and federal and military jurisdictions. For each of those 53 jurisdictions, there is a separate set of legislated statutes, a separate sheet of judge-made case law, and a separate set of administrative codes. As a result, the legal criteria that define a psychiatric–legal issue and establish the basis for its resolution are disparate and diverse.

A result of the multiplicity of issues, jurisdictions, and legal criteria is that there is no such entity as a general forensic psychiatric assessment. Rather, there is only a series of specific psychiatric–legal assessments, each focusing on one psychiatric–legal issue occurring in one legal context and determined by one set of legal criteria.

These legal considerations are in addition to the array of complex clinical phenomena that are the subject matter of psychiatry. The clinical materials are more diverse than is usually encountered in therapeutic practice because they address more than current, immediately accessible data. In some instances, the past is the issue; for example, what was the mental state of a defendant at the time that he or she confessed to the police? In other instances, the future is the issue; for example, which of two competing custodial parents is likely to be the better caregiver of an infant child as the child grows and develops to adulthood? In some instances, there is no one immediately available to examine, for example, in determining the mental state of the deceased person at the time that he or she signed his or her alleged last will and testament.

Compounding all of these matters is the need to present the practitioner's psychiatric–legal opinion as the result of a process of reasoned deliberation that is comprehensible and convincing to the majority of rational legal decision makers. It is not sufficient to offer a sincere belief; what is required is logically compelling knowledge. In clinical practice, when a patient's relative asks, "Will he recover, doctor?" it may be appropriate to respond, "I certainly hope so and I will do everything that I reasonably can do toward that goal." However, that would most likely be an inadequate answer in a legal setting, where a reply supported by scientific facts and statistical projections might be what is expected. These more sophisticated facts must be presented in a systematic well-reasoned manner. It is not enough to know the materials; they must be organized in a logical, relevant, coherent fashion.

There are simply too many factors to be considered without a method for their more manageable organization. In much the same manner that all physicians are trained to organize the diversity of clinical phenomena so as to make them more amenable to rational assessment, forensic psychiatrists are trained to organize the diversity of psychiatric legal phenomena to facilitate their consideration.

For the clinical practitioner, the conceptual framework is some variation of identification, chief complaint, history of the present illness, pertinent past history, laboratory test data, differential diagnoses, and medical diagnostic impression. For the forensic psychiatric practitioner, the four-step conceptual framework is issue, legal criteria, relevant data, and reasoning process:

1. *Issue*: What is the specific psychiatric–legal issue to be considered?
2. *Legal criteria*: In the jurisdiction in which this specific psychiatric–legal issue must be resolved, what are the legally defined terms and criteria that will be used for its resolution?
3. *Relevant data*: Exactly what information (such as part of what might be collected by a clinician following the traditional clinical framework for data organization) is there that is specifically pertinent to the legal criteria that will be used to resolve the specific psychiatric–legal issue?
4. *Reasoning process*: How can the available relevant data be applied to the legal criteria so as to yield a rationally convincing psychiatric–legal opinion?

Among the virtues of a conceptual framework are that it facilitates: (a) the approach to the forensic psychiatric task to be accomplished; (b) communication among colleagues insofar as all colleagues are familiar with and use the same framework for the consideration of the forensic psychiatric work to be done; (c) the identification of areas that are unclear (e.g., the precise legal criteria for the specific issue); (d) the drawing of attention to areas that are incompletely addressed (e.g., the full range of clinical and factual data that are pertinent to the specific legal criteria); and (e) the determination of what are the bases of disagreements between different forensic psychiatrists (e.g., disagreements about the legal issue, about the legal criteria, about the relevant data, and about the reasoning processes).

It may be useful to give examples of how this approach is of practical value (Rosner 1982b,c,d, 1985, 1987, 1990). Suppose that a forensic psychiatrist is contacted by an attorney and is asked to provide an evaluation and report regarding a defendant. The forensic psychiatrist should ask the attorney exactly which psychiatric–legal issue or issues are to be addressed. Although the defendant is only one person, many distinguishable issues may be involved. The attorney may want an evaluation and opinion about a possible insanity defense, or about the defendant's mental competence to waive his or her *Miranda* rights at the time of a supposedly voluntary and knowing confession, or about the defendant's current competence to stand trial, or about the defendant's future competence to abide by the terms of probation.

If the forensic psychiatrist does not know exactly which issue to consider, there is no way to proceed with the evaluation. Pursuing the wrong issue would waste time and money and would jeopardize the outcome of the defendant's case. It is incumbent upon the forensic psychiatrist to clarify for the lawyer that there is no such thing as a general forensic psychiatric examination, and that the lawyer must specify which issue is to be the focus of the psychiatric–legal evaluation. If need be, several issues can be separately addressed, but each must be understood to be a distinguishable concern.

The forensic psychiatrist must also obtain from the lawyer the exact legal criteria, as established by statute, case law, and administrative code, that determine the specific issue in the jurisdiction that will hear the case. It may be easier to explain this point by analogy to the variable criteria that have been used at different times to make psychiatric diagnoses. Clinicians know that the American Psychiatric Association has employed several different manuals of diagnostic criteria over the course of time. To say that someone suffers from some type of schizophrenia according to the first (American Psychiatric Association 1952), second (American Psychiatric Association 1968), third (American Psychiatric Association 1980), third revised (American Psychiatric Association 1987), fourth (American Psychiatric Association 1994), fourth text revision (American Psychiatric Association 2000), fifth (American Psychiatric Association 2013), and forthcoming editions of the *Diagnostic and Statistical Manual of Mental Disorders* of the American Psychiatric Association is to say different things about that person depending on which set of diagnostic criteria is used.

It is possible that a person might be regarded as suffering from some form of schizophrenia according to one set of diagnostic criteria used at one time, but not according to a different set of diagnostic criteria used at a different time. In addition, the criteria used for clinical diagnoses may differ from nation to nation, although some standardization is achieved in those nations that agree to use the World Health Organization's periodically revised *International Classification of Diseases* (*ICD*). The clinical diagnosis is determined by the criteria used to make the diagnosis.

In an analogous manner, the legal criteria used to determine an issue have varied over time within any single place of jurisdiction, just as the clinical diagnostic criteria have varied over time within the United States. In addition, the legal criteria vary from place of jurisdiction (e.g., New York) to place of jurisdiction (e.g., Washington, DC) at the same time, depending on which legal place of jurisdiction is hearing the case. It is uncommon for a forensic psychiatrist to have to be concerned with which legal criteria were used in the past, but it is both routine and of great importance to be concerned with which legal criteria are used in the specific place of jurisdiction that will hear the case.

A forensic psychiatrist must ask the attorney who wishes to retain him or her exactly which legal criteria are to be used to determine the specific psychiatric–legal issue in the jurisdiction that will hear the case. For example, the legal criteria to determine whether or not a defendant is not guilty by reason of insanity (NGRI) may vary from one jurisdiction to another. In one jurisdiction, the criteria for NGRI may address only whether or not the defendant was able to appreciate the nature and quality of his or her act, whereas in another jurisdiction that criteria may be supplemented by whether or not the defendant was able to conform his or her conduct to the requirements of the law. A defendant who might be found guilty in the first jurisdiction might be found NGRI in the second jurisdiction. A forensic psychiatrist practicing in two adjacent states might reach a different decision about the same case, depending on the location of the trial.

At minimum, the specific psychiatric–legal issue and the specific legal criteria will establish the time frame containing the relevant psychiatric data. The forensic psychiatrist may have to obtain data about the past, present, or future. Is the time frame an assessment of the defendant's mental state at the (past) time of the alleged offense for a potential NGRI defense? Is it an assessment of the defendant's mental state at the (not quite so past) time of his or her confession to the police so as to challenge the validity of the confession? Is the time frame the defendant's current mental state for a determination of his or her competence to stand trial? Is it the defendant's future mental state so as to determine if he or she will be able to comply with the conditions of possible probation?

Importantly, the legal criteria will often set forth exactly what kinds of information a person must have had (past), has (present), or will need to have (future) in order to resolve the specific psychiatric–legal issue. For NGRI, in some jurisdictions, the person must have had (past) knowledge of what he or she was doing and must have had (past) knowledge that what he or she was doing was legally wrong. For competence to stand trial, in some jurisdictions, the defendant must have (present) knowledge of the charges against him or her, and must have (present) knowledge of the nature of the legal proceedings against him or her. These criteria direct the forensic psychiatrist to make specific inquiries regarding the defendant's knowledge, and appreciation of that knowledge, at the relevant time period.

Often the legal criteria will also set forth the exact mental capacities a person must have had (past), has (present), or will need to have (future) to resolve the specific psychiatric–legal issue. For NGRI, in some jurisdictions, the person must have had the (past) capacity to conform his or her conduct to the requirements of the law. For competence to stand trial, in some jurisdictions, the person must have the (present) capacity to cooperate with an attorney in his or her own defense. These criteria direct the forensic psychiatrist to make specific inquiries regarding the defendant's non-informational mental abilities at the relevant time period.

The use of the forensic psychiatric conceptual framework can assist the practitioner in locating potential weaknesses in the case being developed. It may be that the attorney has been insufficiently specific regarding the exact psychiatric legal issue to be explored. It may be that the legal criteria are not set forth with clarity and exactitude. It may be that relevant data are lacking. It may be that the practitioner's reasoning processes have been less than logical.

A lack of training in logic may underlie the difficulty that some forensic psychiatrists may have in explaining the reasoning processes that are the bases of their psychiatric–legal opinions. In general, the structure of psychiatric–legal reasoning is familiar: The first step is the assertion of a law or law-like proposition. The second step is the assertion of a factual proposition. The third step is a deductive inference from those two propositions. For example, (a) humans are the only rational bipedal animals; (b) Socrates is a rational bipedal animal; (c) therefore, Socrates is human. If we apply this method to a psychiatric–legal example, we can see how the reasoning process works:

1. Persons who are competent to stand trial have the capacity to understand the charges against them, the capacity to understand the nature of the court proceedings against them, and the capacity to cooperate with an attorney in their own defense.
2. John Doe has the capacity to understand the charges against him, the capacity to understand the nature of the court proceedings against him, and the capacity to cooperate with his attorney in his own defense.
3. Therefore, John Doe is competent to stand trial.

Once the structure of the reasoning process is set forth, it is relatively easy to apply in the formulation of any psychiatric–legal opinion.

This structured reasoning process also reveals potential sources of legal challenge during cross-examination. An opposing attorney may challenge the truth of either of the two major premises, or may challenge the validity of the deductive inference. All premises may be challenged and all deductive inferences may be challenged; the question is whether or not such challenges will be successful. A soundly reasoned opinion is more likely to be successfully sustained than an opinion that is not based on sound reasoning.

This review of the reasoning process that must sustain a psychiatric–legal opinion demonstrates why it is so important to be certain of the specific legal criteria that determine the issue. The first premise is the statement of the specific legal criteria (i.e., the law or law-like proposition); the second premise is the summation of the available information that pertinently bears on the legal criteria (i.e., the factual proposition). If the first premise is wrong—that is, if the legal criteria used are incorrect—then the opinion is unsupported logically. If the second premise is wrong—that is, if the available data are not relevant to the legal criteria—then the opinion is unsupported logically.

It is also possible that the two premises are correct and the deductive inference is wrong. For example, (a) all humans are rational bipedal animals; (b) Socrates is a rational bipedal animal; (c) therefore, Socrates likes chocolate.

A horrible example of such faulty deductive inference making in forensic psychiatry might be as follows:

1. Persons who are capable of understanding the charges against them, capable of understanding the nature of the court proceedings against them, and capable of cooperating in their own defense are competent to stand trial.
2. Richard Roe understands the charges against him, understands the court proceedings against him, and is able to cooperate in his own defense.
3. Therefore, Richard Roe was legally sane (and legally responsible) at the time when he committed the offense.

The conceptual framework for forensic psychiatry will assist a competent practitioner of forensic psychiatry in the cogent organization and presentation of the rational processes that are the foundation of his or her psychiatric–legal opinion. Just as the conceptual framework used by medical practitioners is not a guarantee that they will reach the correct diagnoses, the conceptual framework used by forensic psychiatrists is not a foolproof technique for reaching psychiatric–legal opinions. Rather, each is a tool for the organization of large quantities of complex data. In skilled hands, a tool will produce quality goods; in unskilled hands, a tool will produce shoddy results.

REFERENCES

American Psychiatric Association (APA). 1952. *Diagnostic and Statistical Manual of Mental Disorders*, 1st edition. Arlington, VA: APA.

American Psychiatric Association (APA). 1968. *Diagnostic and Statistical Manual of Mental Disorders*, 2nd edition. Arlington, VA: APA.

American Psychiatric Association (APA). 1980. *Diagnostic and Statistical Manual of Mental Disorders*. 3rd edition. Arlington, VA: APA.

American Psychiatric Association (APA). 1987. *Diagnostic and Statistical Manual of Mental Disorders*. 3rd revised edition. Arlington, VA: APA.

American Psychiatric Association (APA). 1994. *Diagnostic and Statistical Manual of Mental Disorders*. 4th edition. Arlington, VA: APA.

American Psychiatric Association (APA). 2000. *Diagnostic and Statistical Manual of Mental Disorders*. 4th edition, text revision. Arlington, VA: APA.

American Psychiatric Association (APA). 2013. *Diagnostic and Statistical Manual of Mental Disorders*. 5th edition. Arlington, VA: APA.

Rosner, R. 1982a. Accreditation of fellowship programs in forensic psychiatry: The development of the final report on standards. *Bulletin of the American Academy of Psychiatry and the Law* 10(4):281–283.

Rosner R. 1982b. A conceptual model for forensic psychiatry. In *Critical Issues in American Psychiatry and the Law*, edited by R Rosner, Springfield, IL: Charles Thomas Company, 5–11.

Rosner R. 1982c. Medical disability compensation: A practicum. In *Critical Issues in American Psychiatry and the Law*, edited by R Rosner, Springfield, IL: Charles Thomas Company, 71–81.

Rosner R. 1982d. Misguided loyalty, therapeutic grandiosity and scientific ignorance: Limitations on psychiatric contributions to family law and juvenile justice. In *Critical Issues in American Psychiatry and the Law*, edited by R Rosner, Springfield, IL: Charles Thomas Company, 161–170.

Rosner R. 1985. Legal regulation of psychiatry and forensic psychiatry: Clarifying categories for clinicians. In *Critical Issues in American Psychiatry and the Law*, 2 vols, edited by R Rosner, New York: Plenum, 3–17.

Rosner R. 1987. Psychiatric assessment of competence to choose to die: Proposed criteria. In *Geriatric Psychiatry and the Law*, edited by R Rosner, and H Schwartz, New York: Plenum, 81–89.

Rosner R. 1990. Forensic psychiatry: A subspecialty. In *Ethical Practice in Psychiatry and the Law*, edited by R Rosner and R Weinstock, New York: Plenum, 19–29.

2

Defining forensic psychiatry: Roles and responsibilities

ROBERT WEINSTOCK, GREGORY B. LEONG, JENNIFER L. PIEL, AND WILLIAM CONNOR DARBY

INTRODUCTION

Forensic psychiatry operates at the interface of two disparate disciplines: law and psychiatry. Although most cases in forensic psychiatry practice engender no significant conflicts, functioning at the interface of these two disciplines can lead to confusion, challenging ethical dilemmas, or both. Forensic psychiatry received official recognition as a medical subspecialty by the American Board of Medical Specialties (ABMS) with the American Board of Psychiatry and Neurology (ABPN) granting its first forensic psychiatry certification in 1994. However, much work had been done prior to ABMS subspecialty recognition on defining the proper roles and responsibilities of forensic psychiatrists.

The modern era of forensic psychiatry might be considered to have started around the time of the establishment of the American Academy of Psychiatry and the Law (AAPL) in 1969. Pollack, who had established one of the earliest (if not the first) post-residency forensic psychiatry fellowship at the University of Southern California in 1965, stated "Forensic psychiatry is limited to the application of psychiatry to evaluations for legal purposes. Psychiatric evaluation of the patient is directed primarily to legal issues in which he is involved, and consultation is concerned primarily with the ends of the legal system, justice, rather than the therapeutic objectives of the medical system" (Pollack 1974). Pollack further distinguished forensic psychiatry from the broader category of psychiatry and law that he "considered the broad, general field in which psychiatric theories, concepts, principles, and practice are applied to any and all legal matters" (Pollack 1974). Although concerned with legal issues or legal patients, community psychiatric involvements in his opinion "lean toward the traditional ends of psychiatry, that is, toward healing or otherwise helping the patient."

Similar distinctions have been made between forensic psychiatry and the legal regulation of psychiatry (Rosner 1985). Rosner believes forensic psychiatrists function outside of their role as physicians and that this is ethical so long as they make it clear to others that they are not the evaluee's personal physician. Rosner makes an analogy between the forensic psychiatric role and the psychiatrist bargaining with a car dealer, without considering the salesperson's interests.

In contrast, the philosopher Foot argues that forensic psychiatrists in their professional role are hired specifically because of their being psychiatrists, and therefore can be seen as retaining their professional responsibilities (Foot 1990). They are also clearly using psychiatric and medical skills when conducting a forensic psychiatric evaluation. Several contemporary forensic psychiatrists believe that society expects some retention of medical values when physicians participate in the legal system (Weinstock et al. 1990; Candilis et al. 2001; Weinstock 2015).

Diamond (1992) also thought that forensic psychiatrists should not blindly accept all legal ends in their professional role. Diamond believed that the forensic psychiatrist has a fiduciary responsibility to the legal system, i.e., doing what is best in terms of professional judgment rather than merely acceding to the demands of the evaluee, attorney, or any other interested party. In his opinion—much like a psychiatrist owes a fiduciary responsibility to a patient to do only that which the psychiatrist believes in his or her professional judgment is best, rather than merely doing what the patient demands—the relationship between psychiatry and the law should also be fiduciary. According to Diamond (1992), "the psychiatrist is no mere technician to be used by the law as the law sees fit, nor is the science, art, and definitions of psychiatry and psychology to be redefined and manipulated by the law as it wishes." In his opinion, the psychiatric expert should not merely deliver information without any regard for negative consequences.

Appelbaum (1997) bases the ethics of forensic psychiatry on the principles of truth telling, respect for persons, and promoting justice. Griffith (1998) proposes a narrative approach that takes the power differential and cultural considerations into account and examines the narrative of individuals of the nondominant culture. Candilis and colleagues (2001) integrate these approaches with a robust conception of professional integrity. They favor principles infused with the historical narrative of medicine as a healing profession that includes traditional medical values and an individual's personal narrative. Candilis and colleagues (2001), Weinstock and colleagues (2001), and Weinstock (2015) consider the need to balance conflicting responsibilities. In the forensic context, Weinstock agrees the duty to the legal system is primary, but that it needs to be balanced by a secondary duty to the evaluee that in some situations can become the dominant consideration. Such a circumstance could require a forensic psychiatrist to withdraw from a case if ethical concerns preclude a search for truth.

AAPL has defined forensic psychiatry as follows (AAPL 2005):

> Forensic psychiatry is a subspecialty of psychiatry in which scientific and clinical expertise is applied to legal contexts involving civil, criminal, correctional, regulatory or legislative matters, and in specialized clinical consultations in areas such as risk assessment or employment. These guidelines apply to psychiatrists practicing in a forensic role.

Unlike previous versions, this definition does not take a position on the goals and values of forensic psychiatry. The definition lists the differing contexts and functions of a forensic psychiatrist with an emphasis on the legal context of forensic psychiatric practice. However, forensic psychiatry has generally come to include and encompass all the issues and functions at the interface of psychiatry and law, including the legal regulation of contexts surrounding psychiatric practice, as reviewed by this textbook.

Neither lawyers nor the courts should determine the guidelines and ethical principles of how forensic psychiatry is to be practiced. The courts can decide what is legal, but not what is professionally responsible or ethical for forensic psychiatry.

Ethical guidelines and requirements can and do sometimes exceed what the law demands. The psychiatric profession can consider unethical, and provide sanctions for, behavior the courts consider permissible. Although the AAPL guidelines are aspirational in the sense that they are not enforced per se, they can be enforced when they flush out the meaning of guidelines of the American Psychiatric Association (APA) or state medical boards. Most guidelines are not intrinsically aspirational and can be and sometimes are enforced if other organizations choose to do so (Candilis et al. 2014).

FORENSIC EVALUATIONS

An AAPL essential ethics guideline involves informing the evaluee in any forensic psychiatric interview of the limitations of confidentiality along with for whom and for what purpose the interview is being conducted. This requirement differs from a clinical evaluation performed for a patient's benefit in which confidentiality is expected and generally is maintained. However, even in the clinical setting, confidentiality limits should be explained when they appear potentially relevant. There may be some exceptions, however, in situations of serious suicidal or homicidal danger. In such scenarios, it may be important for the treating physician to hear this information without interrupting to advise on the limits of confidentiality in order to prevent actions that could result in serious bodily harm or death to the patient or a third party. Some may think the limits of confidentiality should always be explained at the outset of treatment, but a comprehensive list would be very long and unnecessarily frighten patients who are unlikely to ever encounter any such exceptions. Psychiatric ethics guidelines permit such discretion though psychologist guidelines do not (American Psychological Association 2010).

In conducting forensic evaluations, it is of crucial importance to acquire adequate data on which to base professional opinions. For example, in the criminal setting, not only the discovery information, but the evaluee's current and past psychiatric, medical, and other records, interviews of relevant parties, and/or access to information held by the prosecution in a criminal case or both sides in a civil case not included in the discovery information, may be important to arrive at a professional opinion. In such cases, the forensic psychiatrist should request this information. For the civil setting a similar set of data from both the plaintiff and defendant may be needed in order to perform an adequate evaluation.

Because of the legal purpose of the forensic interview, an evaluee has rational reasons to exaggerate, manufacture, or minimize symptoms; therefore, whenever possible there should be corroborating data for the evaluaee's self-report (see Chapter 74 on Malingering). Such data also should be obtained not only for a thorough but objective evaluation, but also to prepare for a potential cross-examination. A careful evaluation is necessary, and an adequate evaluation requires time. Superficial evaluations can miss pathology or contradictory data. Although AAPL's ethical guidelines eliminated the requirement of impartiality in 1995 as it was not realistically achievable, the AAPL guidelines retain the need to strive for objectivity. Striving for objectivity includes the need to search for data that might contradict the forensic psychiatrist's initial opinion, biases, or both. "Honesty" has been substituted for "impartiality" in AAPL's ethical guidelines.

Diamond (1956) called attention to the fact that seriously mentally disordered persons commonly deny their illness. Simulation of sanity can be just as great a problem as simulation of mental illness, though the forensic psychiatrist may be less likely to be alert to detect faking good (dissimulation) than faking bad (simulation). An evaluee's emotional need not to be thought crazy may outweigh his or her legal self-interest. Denial of mental illness also contributes to this and may not be intentional.

There is a clear risk in forensic psychiatry of confusing professional expertise with biases about moral issues or a biased choice of one of many interpretations of the legal criteria. To quote Pollack (1974), "in forensic psychiatry, the expert applies his material to social ends, all of which are intimately related to moral values." Because psychiatric material can be largely subjective, interwoven with social variables, and influenced by a variety of cultural factors, what is presented as psychiatric data and opinion may easily disguise and conceal underlying value judgments. Although forensic psychiatrists are experts in psychiatry, they are likely to be neither experts in morality nor experts in the meaning and intent of legal terms and judicial opinions.

ROLE OF THE FORENSIC PSYCHIATRIST

Pollack was a proponent of what has been the dominant approach in modern forensic psychiatry, at least in most theoretical discussions. Diamond, however, was a proponent of an alternative but equally legitimate approach that may in reality informally be the dominant position of forensic psychiatrists, at least as reflected in surveys (Weinstock et al. 1991). Most forensic psychiatrists do not see themselves as functioning totally outside of their medical and psychiatric roles. They use their medical and psychiatric skills and techniques in the forensic role. They also can be perceived as functioning in a medical role by those they evaluate despite any disclaimers and because they conduct a psychiatric assessment. Even if an evaluee understands the specific role of the forensic psychiatrist, slippage can occur with the evaluee coming to view the forensic psychiatrist in an increasing therapeutic role, especially if the psychiatrist is empathic. Forensic psychiatrists should be sensitive to slippage of the initial warning.

In order to illustrate the proper role of forensic psychiatrists, Diamond and Pollack's views will be contrasted. They both were highly respected contemporaries with many differing views who wrote extensively on this issue during the dawn of the modern era of forensic psychiatry. Their positions are still matters of contention today. Both Diamond and Pollack agreed that forensic psychiatry applies psychiatric theories and practices to people and their legal issues for legal purposes. However, they differed insofar as Pollack thought the ends are legal ends. Diamond thought forensic psychiatrists should retain their medical and psychiatric ends in the forensic role and work toward making the legal system more therapeutic and less vengeful. This concept has a legal counterpart in the concept of therapeutic jurisprudence (Stolle et al. 2000).

Pollack wanted the forensic psychiatrist to ascertain social policy considerations and try to determine the intent of the courts and legislators. He made this attempt in the common situations in which the legal criteria are unspecified, unclear, or ambiguous. Both Pollack and Diamond thought that forensic psychiatrists have an obligation to present and expose their reasoning so that a trier of fact could understand the basis for their opinion, detect any biases, and disagree if necessary. Pollack would not try to expand or modify a legal concept in his forensic psychiatric capacity. He would try to overcome biases, including what he considered the psychiatrist's usual "therapeutic bias." He would attempt to give an impartial objective opinion in his role as consultant to the legal system (Pollack 1974) and not participate in cases in which his bias was strong.

Although Diamond agreed that his reasoning should be exposed, in contrast, he would interpret ambiguities in the legal criteria to be consistent with the values of the medical profession, but would be totally honest about doing so. That strategy may be less effective today because appellate courts are more conservative.

Diamond, himself, chose to be an expert witness solely for the defense in criminal cases. However, he would only participate in cases in which an effort would be made by the defense attorney to present the whole psychiatric truth. In most cases, he would refuse to participate after being consulted, because he did not think an honest opinion would help the side that wanted to hire him, or he did not want to be part of a legal strategy that would hide relevant information. Although he wanted to help a defendant, truth and honesty were even higher values.

Diamond interpreted legal ambiguities in a manner consistent with his view of his fiduciary responsibility. Although he had a bias in favor of a defendant's welfare, he accepted the biases of others who favor law and order and the protection of society. However, in his opinion, honesty was crucial. Although few forensic psychiatrists would go so far as to never participate for the prosecution in any criminal case, many forensic psychiatrists agree with other aspects of Diamond's approach or share his concerns about not facilitating a death penalty sentence (Weinstock et al. 1992) or, in some special situations, assisting an organization or company they think has no redeeming social value (Weinstock 2015). Many evaluators care how their testimony will be used in death penalty or other cases. Other practitioners may have qualms about helping a killer avoid punishment.

Diamond considered impartiality and objectivity impossible (Diamond 1959) and thought that the honest forensic psychiatrist should acknowledge the absence of both. Even if forensic psychiatrists start out truly impartial, the desire to defend their opinions and have their team prevail turns forensic psychiatrists into biased adversaries as the case proceeds. Though some commentators state witnesses on the stand must do their best to impartially preserve the truth (Halleck et al. 1984), Diamond considered impartiality impossible even if witnesses are totally truthful from their own subjective standpoint. The truth can have many alternative perspectives. Katz (1992) recommends "disciplined subjectivity" as a more realistic goal instead of impartiality or objectivity. Honesty in Diamond's (1990) opinion is what separates the honest advocate from a "hired gun." Although the more scientific aspects of psychiatry might be relatively objective, much of psychiatry remains subjective. Furthermore, our interpretation of the legal issue and application of psychiatric data to it are especially subjective.

Despite these considerations, forensic psychiatrists frequently are asked to indicate how often they have testified for the different sides in a legal case. Federal courts require such disclosure, which can be problematic insomuch that the information obtained can be misleading. Sometimes, those who are found to testify equally for the prosecution and defense may create an illusion that this balance reflects lack of bias, when in reality it reflects extreme dishonesty. For example, "hired guns" make a record of testifying on both sides because they are willing to testify for whichever side pays their fee regardless of their actual opinion or the merits of the case. Claims of impartiality can reflect dishonesty or lack of self-insight. Alternatively, principled though biased professionals who testify primarily for one side can be honest. The U.S. Supreme Court in *Ake v. Oklahoma* (1985) recognized bias and even advocacy implicitly by stating that defendants in capital cases needed an expert to assist defense counsel.

Many forensic psychiatrists in civil cases testify primarily for the plaintiff or defense. Although most insurance companies wish to have an "independent" medical examiner to prevent their wasting resources on indefensible cases, that sometimes is not the case. Some forensic psychiatrists contend that a number of insurance companies do not want to hire forensic psychiatrists who ever have testified against them for the plaintiff's side, and choose not to take such cases for fear they will not be hired by these companies in the future. Additionally and more concerning, some forensic psychiatrists may distort their opinions in order to please the party hiring them. For example, some insurance companies regret issuing policies that have lost the company money. For example, they now may want not to pay legitimate claims for physician policies covering disability in a specific subspecialty (e.g., an anesthesiologist with a substance use disorder). Insurance companies might want a forensic psychiatrist to say that the only reason the anesthesiologist cannot practice the specialty is medical board prohibition when the reality is the main reason the physician should not practice anesthesiology is the ready access to drugs previously diverted for personal abuse. Hopefully, most forensic psychiatrists would not distort their opinion just to please the insurance company. Some who do may be "hired guns."

Testifying for one side only does not necessarily imply being a hired gun. Many who testify for only one side in such cases probably choose a side most consonant with their values or biases, and are probably essentially honest. Sometimes only one side refers cases. Honest testimony out of interest in the issues but with only minor or negligible biases usually leads to some record of testifying for both sides, even if not equally distributed. If doing work solely for one side for whatever reason, honest experts should find many cases with facts not supporting the side retaining them. Nonetheless, in spite of any unintended bias based on retention by one side or the other, AAPL's ethical guidelines hold that the forensic psychiatrist has an ethical obligation for honesty and to strive for objectivity.

Most forensic psychiatrists are unlikely to make the best case possible for unsupportable opinions. Honesty requires informing the hiring attorney as soon as possible if a review of all the materials does not support a helpful opinion. The attorney then can either drop the case or look for other experts who see the case differently. Making the best case for a side regardless of stronger contradictory facts is an approach appropriate and ethical for attorneys. However, this is a defining difference that highlights the contrast between the role of the attorney and the role of an expert witness, and legal and forensic psychiatric ethics. Unlike attorneys whose ethics permit distortions, supporting the use of any permissible tactic for their client so long as they do not lie, an expert witness takes an oath to "tell the whole truth." It is ethical to highlight and emphasize the strong parts of a case, though such emphasis should not lead to distortion to the level of confidence in an opinion or a denial of uncertainty despite pressures from attorneys to appear certain. The acceptable dividing line, however, sometimes is unclear. The legal system unfortunately facilitates a perception of a misleading level of certainty by calling a preponderance of evidence "reasonable medical certainty." The integrity of the psychiatric expert should prevent distorting a case in order to please an attorney.

Forensic psychiatrists can consult with attorneys about the forensic psychiatric merits of a case and strategy as well as provide expert testimony. Although no oath is taken when consulting with attorneys, the primary reason to separate roles is it does not look good to a jury for the expert to then appear to be advocating for a particular result. But testifying experts can give advice to attorneys and advocate for their opinion.

General philosophies can represent preferences for how a specific forensic psychiatrist wishes to function, but they may have exceptions. Despite Pollack's philosophy, he himself refused to participate in capital cases after that of Sirhan Sirhan (who assassinated Senator Robert F. Kennedy) (Curran and Pollack 1985). He apparently agreed with Diamond that forensic psychiatrists should refuse to participate in cases in which they do not agree with the legal system's goals. More recently Weinstock (2015) shares this view. However, unlike Diamond and Weinstock, Pollack believed he needed to be prepared to support either side if he became involved in a case. Diamond believed he could support only one side, though only if he could do so with total honesty because total disclosure of the facts supported his position. Weinstock (2015) believes this applies only in some unusual situations in which secondary duties such as nonmaleficence overcome the primary forensic duty.

Unfortunately, not all forensic psychiatrists are as open and honest as Pollack and Diamond. They may intentionally create false impressions and a few may even be willing to be "hired guns" (Diamond 1990). They may make the best case possible for a weak opinion regardless of their actual findings and conclusions in order to be hired for this case and others by the attorney. Or they may be so committed to a cause that they will misrepresent the data to support their cause. This role may be appropriate for an attorney, but not for an expert witness who, unlike an attorney, takes an oath to tell the whole truth and not present a one-sided version to help "win" the case as attorneys sometimes do.

An example of differing approaches and biases is shown in the contrasting interpretation by Pollack and Diamond of the *M'Naghten* insanity defense as used in California. Pollack's interpretation tended to favor the prosecution, while Diamond's clearly favored the defense. Pollack described social policy considerations as requiring that "knowing" the nature and quality of the act in an insanity defense is broader than a simplistic, atomistic, childish level of comprehension, but does not encompass the maximum breadth, scope, and maturity of fullest comprehension (Pollack 1974). Diamond, in contrast, interpreted "know" to mean appreciate, comprehend, or realize the act's full meaning. Some jurisdictions have adopted the word "appreciate" instead of "know" to indicate a broader view of the word "know."

Diamond opined that a literal interpretation of *M'Naghten* would either encourage perjury or force the psychiatrist to "become a puppet doctor, used by the law to further the primitive and vengeful goals demanded of our society." He thought that if a literal sense of "know" is employed, "just about almost every defendant, no matter how mentally ill, no matter how far advanced his psychosis, knows the difference between right and wrong in the literal sense" and the psychiatrist becomes an expeditor of the death penalty (Diamond 1961). Diamond preferred not to resort to semantics and to an arbitrary all-or-none insanity defense but preferred to focus on the *mens rea* defense of "diminished capacity." He played an important role in the development of this defense, and in this process changed the interpretation of the law. That defense later was substantially weakened primarily by returning to English common law definitions of terms like "premeditation" and "malice" in the current defense of "diminished actuality."

RESPONSIBILITIES OF THE FORENSIC PSYCHIATRIST

Controversy exists regarding to whom the forensic psychiatrist owes a duty. This problem in part is due to the fact that a traditional doctor–patient relationship does not apply. Stone (1992) states that psychiatry enters an ethical morass when it leaves the clinical situation, such as in managed care or in forensic psychiatry. According to Appelbaum (1990, 1997), forensic psychiatrists lose the primacy of the duties of beneficence and nonmaleficence owed by treating physicians to their patients. Instead the duties of truth and respect for persons, and the goal of justice achieve primacy in the legal system. Stone (1984) does not believe "truth" solves forensic psychiatry's problems such as the good clinician seducing a patient into false trust. Surveys of forensic psychiatrists indicate that an overwhelming majority still believe that traditional medical values play a role in the functioning of forensic psychiatrists (Weinstock et al. 1991). Despite the survey findings, controversy exists in the profession regarding this issue (Weinstock et al. 1990; Weinstock 2015). In modern times, even treating psychiatrists owe a responsibility to society as well as to the patient, such as reporting suspected child and elder abuse. Most consistent with survey results, it is reasonable to view the forensic psychiatrist similar to the treating psychiatrist as having multiple agency responsibilities, such as to the courts, society, the retaining attorney, and the evaluee, regardless of who requests the psychiatric consultation.

The difference in responsibilities is probably best characterized as a difference in priority or primacy. That is, the forensic psychiatrist, unlike the treating psychiatrist, gives primacy to answering the legal question and specific forensic duties like truth and respect for persons (Appelbaum 1997). However, secondary medical responsibilities remain. These in some instances can be so important that they can become determinative of ethical action (Candilis et al. 2001; Weinstock 2001, 2015). In some death penalty roles, the conflict between primary forensic duties and secondary medical responsibilities most appropriately may require nonparticipation. Dialectical principlism (Weinstock 2015) presents as a method to determine the most ethical course of action for oneself.

Although controversy still exists, survey results best support a position of multiple agency and multiple responsibility for a forensic psychiatrist. Even though some forensic psychiatrists believe they owe a duty and responsibility only to the person who pays their fee if they make their role and allegiances clear at least once to an evaluee, survey results imply that this position may actually be held by only a minority of forensic psychiatrists. Furthermore, slippage of a warning may occur if the forensic psychiatrist is a good clinician who inspires trust. Although frequently claimed, it is unclear why a forensic psychiatrist should owe a duty solely to the person paying the fee when even treating psychiatrists do not have the luxury of such a simple, single allegiance. Thus, multiple responsibilities have become a part of all psychiatric practice.

It is important not to hold the profession of forensic psychiatry responsible for unpopular legal decisions that may result from many factors. Sometimes the decisions are unpopular but valid, or the judicial system may limit the evidence an expert is permitted to introduce. Unpopular insanity acquittals have led to changes in the law and undeserved negative press for forensic psychiatry. Sometimes forensic psychiatrists unfairly are blamed for problems presented by the adversary legal system and for the "battle of experts." Psychiatrists have legitimate differences of opinion. The "battle of experts" exists for all expert witnesses in all disciplines and is by no means unique to forensic psychiatry. Sometimes there is a risk of blaming the entire profession of forensic psychiatry when the public dislikes a decision or the testimony of a particular expert. Newspapers and politicians use such scapegoating for personal advantage. Sometimes the entire profession is blamed for the actions of a few "hired guns."

Stone (1984) expressed concern about the jury's confusion caused by a psychiatrist taking an oath to tell the whole truth yet in reality being expected by the legal system to make the best case possible for the retaining side. Stone proposes that psychiatrists be introduced in court as partisans similar to attorneys who take no oath. Stone argues that the rationalization that cross-examination will bring out the whole truth is self-deceptive, since such cross-examinations may never occur (e.g., pretrial settlement of the case). He is skeptical that forensic psychiatrists really tell the whole truth. Stone advocates honesty about what really is occurring. What is the "whole truth" is debatable, and the legal system limits how much of it can be told even if the forensic psychiatrist tries to do so. Additionally, Stone's criticisms apply to all expert witnesses and even the adversary system, and his recommendations show no sign of being adopted by any profession. Also controversial is the degree of the psychiatrist's obligation to clarify limits of his or her opinion (aside from any possible tactical advantage in doing so) or whether such clarification can be rationalized as left for cross-examination that may not occur or be done well, despite the admonition in the AAPL ethics guidelines to affirmatively state the limitations of an opinion if there is no personal examination. Katz (1992) considers acknowledgment of uncertainty as a crucial responsibility of the forensic psychiatrist.

PRESENT STATUS OF FORENSIC PSYCHIATRY

Weinstock (2015) has developed the approach of "dialectical principlism" as a method to analyze and resolve ethics dilemmas. It entails prioritizing duties according to role and then balancing them along with ethics principles and personal, societal, and cultural values.

Although controversy exists regarding some aspects of the proper role and responsibilities for forensic psychiatrists, many issues have found a general consensus in definitions and ethics guidelines. The AAPL ethics guidelines present an important ethical foundation. But those wanting to find the most ethical solution to a dilemma beyond minimum guidelines can use the method of dialectical principlism (Weinstock 2015). This method can help us determine the most ethical course of action for ourselves. It also can improve the public perception of, and credibility of, our field.

Forensic psychiatry fellowships teach the special knowledge necessary to apply psychiatry to legal issues. General residency training in psychiatry even supplemented with formal legal education is insufficient, because most law schools do not emphasize psychiatric issues or their application to the law. Specialized training is needed in forensic psychiatry covering an evolving and specialized body of knowledge, even for psychiatrists with law degrees.

Forensic psychiatry is a large subspecialty as evidenced by this textbook. The vastness of the knowledge base, both clinical and legal, creates challenges for the forensic psychiatrist to act responsibly. Claims of expertise in areas where the psychiatrist does not have special knowledge or training despite this specialization being relevant, can raise questions about whether general forensic psychiatrists should undertake evaluations in subspecialty areas. Cases involving children, the elderly, or psychosomatic problems are routinely seen by general psychiatrists and are not exclusive to those with specialized training. Questions remain whether this is acceptable practice if specialists are available.

Alternatively, it could be argued that any psychiatrist could do the assessment if sufficiently knowledgeable about the specific issues pertinent to the case. Careful evaluation of the relevant data is important considering the serious implications to the parties involved. A healthy skepticism regarding all the data supplied by either side of the legal conflict is necessary. Offering psychiatric–legal opinions on legal issues without trying to ascertain the jurisdictional legal criteria are two prime examples of irresponsible professional behavior. It is therefore incumbent on forensic psychiatrists to be informed about psychiatry, law, and ethics, in order to appropriately fulfil their professional roles and responsibilities. That is especially important when those without forensic training or expertise undertake a forensic evaluation, but also applies when those with forensic training undertake a case without relevant psychiatric expertise or knowledge of the legal criteria in the relevant jurisdiction.

When we perform our roles properly, forensic psychiatrists can assist the legal system in its effort to foster justice as well as promote a favorable impression of ourselves and our profession. (See Chapter 8, Forensic Psychiatric Ethics, for additional exploration of these topics.)

REFERENCES

Ake v. Oklahoma, 470 U.S. 68 (1985).

American Academy of Psychiatry and the Law. 2005. *Ethics Guidelines for the Practice of Forensic Psychiatry* (adopted May 2005). http://aapl.org/ethics.htm, accessed April 28, 2015.

American Psychological Association. 2010. *Ethical Principles of Psychologists and Code of Conduct.* Washington, DC: American Psychological Association.

Appelbaum PS. 1990. The parable of the forensic psychiatrist: Ethics and the problem of doing harm. *International Journal of Law and Psychiatry* 13:249–259.

Appelbaum PS. 1997. A theory of ethics for forensic psychiatry. *Journal of the American Academy of Psychiatry and the Law* 25:233–247.

Candilis PJ, Dike CC, Meyer CJ, Myers WC, and Weinstock R. 2014. Should AAPL enforce its ethics? Challenges and solutions. *Journal of the American Academy of Psychiatry and the Law* 47:322–330.

Candilis PL, Martinez R, and Dorning C. 2001. Principles and narrative in forensic psychiatry: Toward a robust view of professional role. *Journal of the American Academy of Psychiatry and the Law* 29:167–173.

Curran WL and Pollack S. 1985. Mental health justice: Ethical issues of interdisciplinary cooperation. In *Forensic Psychiatry and Psychology: Perspectives and*

Standards for Interdisciplinary Practice, edited by WJ Curran, AL McGarry, and SA Shah, Philadelphia: F. A. Davis, 61–73.

Diamond BL. 1956. The simulation of sanity. *Journal of Social Therapy* 2:158–165.

Diamond BL. 1959. The fallacy of the impartial expert. *Archives of Criminal Psychodynamics* 3:221–236.

Diamond BL. 1961. Criminal responsibility of the mentally ill. *Stanford Law Review* 14:59–86.

Diamond BL. 1990. The psychiatrist expert witness: Honest advocate or "hired gun"? In *Ethical Practice in Psychiatry and the Law*, edited by R. Rosner and R. Weinstock, New York: Plenum Press, 75–84.

Diamond BL. 1992. The forensic psychiatrist: Consultant vs. activist in legal doctrine. *Bulletin of the American Academy of Psychiatry and the Law* 20:119–131.

Foot P. 1990. Ethics and the death penalty: Participation by forensic psychiatrists in capital trials. In *Ethical Practice in Psychiatry and the Law*, edited by R. Rosner and R. Weinstock, New York: Plenum Press, 207–217.

Griffith EEH. 1998. Ethics in forensic psychiatry: A response to Stone and Appelbaum. *Journal of the American Academy of Psychiatry and the Law* 26:171–184.

Halleck SL, Appelbaum P, Rappeport JR, and Dix G. 1984. *Psychiatry in the Sentencing Process*. Washington, DC: American Psychiatric Press.

Katz J. 1992. The fallacy of the impartial expert revisited. *Bulletin of the American Academy of Psychiatry and the Law* 20:141–152.

Pollack S. 1974. *Forensic Psychiatry in Criminal Law*. Los Angeles: University of Southern California.

Rosner R. 1985. Legal regulation of psychiatry and forensic psychiatry: Clarifying categories for physicians. In *Critical Issues in American Psychiatry and the Law*, 2 vols., edited by R. Rosner, New York: Plenum Press, 19–29.

Stolle DP, Winnick B, and Wexler DB. 2000. *Practicing Therapeutic Jurisprudence*. Durham, NC: Carolina Academic Press.

Stone AA. 1984. The ethics of forensic psychiatry: A view from the ivory tower. In *Law, Psychiatry and Morality*. edited by AA Stone, Washington, DC: American Psychiatric Press.

Stone AA. 1992. Paper presented as part of a panel on controversial ethical issues in forensic psychiatry. *23rd Annual Meeting of the American Academy of Psychiatry and the Law*, Boston, October 16, 1992.

Weinstock R. 2001. Commentary: A broadened conception of forensic psychiatric ethics. *Journal of the American Academy of Psychiatry and the Law* 29:180–185.

Weinstock R. 2015. Dialectical principlism: An approach to finding our most ethical action. *Journal of the American Academy of Psychiatry and the Law* 43:10–20.

Weinstock R, Leong GB, and Silva JA. 1990. The role of traditional medical ethics in forensic psychiatry. In *Ethical Practice in Psychiatry and the Law*, edited by R. Rosner and R. Weinstock, New York: Plenum Press, 31–51.

Weinstock R, Leong GB, and Silva JA. 1991. Opinions by AAPL forensic psychiatrists on controversial ethical guidelines: A survey. *Bulletin of the American Academy of Psychiatry and the Law* 19:237–248; erratum 19, 393.

Weinstock R, Leong GB, and Silva JA. 1992. The death penalty and Bernard Diamond's approach to forensic psychiatry. *Bulletin of the American Academy of Psychiatry and the Law* 20:197–210.

3

History of forensic psychiatry

MARVIN THOMAS PROSONO

An inquiry into the formal recognition of forensic psychiatry as a medical subspecialty places heavy demands on historical reconstruction. It is not sufficient to engage the history of forensic psychiatry simply as a subtext of the greater history of psychiatry. This approach has been taken by most of the standard histories of psychiatry (Alexander and Selesnick 1966; Zilboorg 1967; Ackerknecht 1968), which portray psychiatry either as foreordained by the inevitable march of science or as crusading against the inertia of entrenched superstition and ignorance. Medical specialties have generally evolved alongside the natural sciences, although psychiatry has not precisely followed this path making its history more difficult to reconstruct (Marx 1970, 595). The history of forensic psychiatry can be traced through the dual emergence of psychiatric and legal discourse and practice as these have mutually developed and intersected over the centuries. This chapter follows the history of that intersection through the ancient, medieval, and modem periods after first considering the nature of the complex intellectual problems involved in constructing such a history.

Drawing a boundary around the activity of forensic psychiatrists is problematic because all psychiatric activity may contain an element of "forensicity." Park Dietz provided the following quote in regard to this concept of "forensicity."* It is an even greater challenge to trace back the activities preceding those now systematically performed by forensic psychiatrists. Psychiatry as a medical specialty did not exist much before the late eighteenth or early nineteenth century, and the widespread employment of physician/experts in courts of law in the West does not have a pedigree that is much older. Foucault (1972, 179) has commented that what preceded psychiatry could not be characterized as a discipline but rather was a "discursive practice" that consisted of a commentary on various physical and mental afflictions as understood at the time.

* [I]n an era in which virtually every psychiatrist must take cognizance of certain medicolegal principles, an argument could be made that "forensicity" is a continuous variable distributed unevenly over the entire population of psychiatrists (Dietz 1978, 13).

In sociological terms, the forensic psychiatrist is a medical professional called upon to participate in the establishment of legal decisions, particularly those decisions affecting the status of persons, further validating the decision-making process with their scientific and professional credentials (Prosono 1990). The task of the social historian is to construct an account of this form of social action and the concerns that gave rise to it; however, there are a number of technical obstacles that preclude any perfect reconstruction of the past (Mead 1980). Continuities, discontinuities, appearances, disappearances and reappearances, things maintained, modified, or abandoned (Foucault 1972) characterize a "discursive practice" such as that of forensic psychiatry and its predecessors in social action.

Two concerns are implicitly embedded in this history. First, there are the ancient and enduring problems of human motivation and intention. All legal systems have had to grapple with the problem of deciding competency and accountability. Second, in order to decide such questions there must be decision makers. In courts of law, judges and juries are the ultimate decision makers: judges deciding questions of law; juries, in the Anglo-American system of jurisprudence, deciding questions of fact. Matters of insanity or incompetence have routinely been described as questions of fact, with decision makers assisted, especially in modem contexts, by a highly professionalized group of experts. The history of forensic psychiatry is, in effect, the history of the intersection of the enduring legal and social problems of establishing competency and imputing responsibility, and both the professionalization of medicine and the specialization of psychiatry.†

ANCIENT PERIOD

Imhotep (circa 3000 BC), grand vizier and chief architect to the Egyptian Pharaoh Djoser, was "the first great man combining the sciences of law and medicine; he might, if you

† Appendix 3.1 summarizes the important dates and events in the evolution of forensic psychiatry.

wish, be described as the first medicolegal expert" (Smith 1951, 600). In Imhotep we find the undifferentiated roles of priest/physician/statesman/architect, although we should be wary about placing too much credence in the accomplishments of a figure who may be entirely a myth.

According to some authorities, ancient Babylonia provides us with evidence of the first murder trial and the first expert witness, in that case a midwife (Smith 1951, 600; Ackerknecht 1976, 1225). One of the first instances of the consideration of intent in the weighing of personal responsibility is found in the scriptures of the ancient Hebrews.* Deuteronomy 19:1–13 describes the logic for establishing "refuge cities" in which someone who had killed through sheer accident would be safe from capture by avenging relatives. The ancient Hebrew law understood the status of an act as determined by the intent of the actor. Thus, the notion of an evil mind entered into Western law (see Platt and Diamond 1966). The importance of intention for judging human action was already evident in the Babylonian legal system as set forth in the Code of Hammurabi, although this system of law was especially harsh, death being the sole punishment for violations of law. Such an approach can be found in much primitive law, which takes little or no account of an actor's intention. Kelsen has termed this "absolute responsibility (liability)" (Kelsen 1946, 65).

The ancient Greeks left the resolution of many conflicts to "private law," meaning that the parties to a dispute would be left to decide it among themselves. There was little need or opportunity for the rendering of expert or forensic opinion, other than isolated instances such as a physician substantiating the pre-existence of a defect in a slave who had been sold. When questions of mental competence arose, there is no evidence that physicians were used as experts among the Greeks in any modern sense (Rosen 1968, 136).

The Greek philosopher Plato saw the human soul as divided between the rational and irrational, the rational soul distinguishing human beings from lower or animal nature (Zilboorg 1967, 52). Because human beings are free to choose, more severe punishments should be imposed for those "harms committed with some degree of calculation" (Platt and Diamond 1966, 1229). Plato's great disciple, Aristotle, recognized the importance of knowledge in the imputation of responsibility: "A person is morally responsible if, with knowledge of the circumstances and in the absence of external compulsion, he deliberately chooses to commit a specific act" (cited in Platt and Diamond 1966, 1229).

These early approaches have had a significant impact on all subsequent discussions of the problem of responsibility. They presage the tension among those who would excuse the insane from responsibility for criminal acts only when there is evidence of a total loss of reason (analogous to the behavior of a "wild beast"), those who would allow such excuse when the only apparent mental impairment is a cognitive one, and others who ask whether there existed "an irresistible impulse" or whether the act was a "product" of the disease or impairment.

The heritage of Western medicine derives from Greece, and Hippocrates is considered the father of that medical tradition. He insisted that diseases were of natural origin and could be both understood and treated as manifestations of the natural order (Ackerknecht 1968, 10). Possessing a "clinical intuition," Hippocrates suggested that various physical diseases alleviated "madness" or "mania," anticipating by some 2300 years the malarial treatment of mental disease resulting from syphilis (Zilboorg 1967, 48).

Ptolemaic and Roman Egypt are of interest because of the existence of a *demosios iatros*, or public physician (Amundsen and Ferngren 1978, 338 et seq.). Although certain kinds of knowledge were exploited by Ptolemaic courts such as the expert opinion of land surveyors, physicians were not summoned to court to give expert opinion (Amundsen and Ferngren 1978, 340).

Among ancient legal systems, Roman law was certainly the most comprehensive and sophisticated. Like its Greek predecessor, Roman legal process did not employ physicians as experts (Sesto 1956, 33), although midwives, land surveyors (*agrimensores*), and handwriting experts were used in a forensic capacity (Amundsen and Ferngren 1979, 48). A iudex, or judge, had very wide discretion in gathering and considering evidence and took the counsel of *adsessores*, who were wise men learned in jurisprudence; however, there is no evidence that either on a regular or exceptional basis were *adsessores* members of professions whose knowledge could help decide questions of fact (Amundsen and Ferngren 1979, 46).†

Yet Roman law did recognize that those who committed acts without malicious intent should not be held accountable for those acts. The *Twelve Tables*, one of the earliest Roman codifications, made provision for a system of guardianship of the insane, usually placing the person and his or her possessions under the care of paternal relatives. The *Lex Aquila* in the third century BC provided: "[A] man who, without negligence or malice, but by some accident, causes damage, goes unpunished" (quoted in Platt and Diamond 1966, 1230). Under the *Lex Cornelia* (first century BC), children, because of the innocence of their intentions, and the insane, because of the nature of their misfortune, were excused from punishment (Platt and Diamond 1966, 1230).

* Platt and Diamond trace the "modern law of criminal responsibility" to the conflicting meanings given to the phrase "knowledge of good and evil," which figure in the Book of Genesis and the story of Adam and Eve and the forbidden fruit. The phrase "knowledge of good and evil" has been interpreted to mean perfect wisdom as well as moral capacity, and the ensuing confusion has been preserved, according to these authors, in modem law (Platt and Diamond 1966, 1227 et seq.).

† In cases where a curator is to be appointed to discharge the affairs of one who is considered insane, the praetor [a public official] is urged to investigate the case most thoroughly "since many people feign madness or insanity" so that they may evade their civil obligations (citing Digesta 27, 10, 6 [Ulpian]) (Amundsen and Ferngren 1978, 43).

On the subject of the insane, Roman law deals primarily with questions of guardianship and is not plagued by the almost single-minded concern with criminality one finds in modern sources. The question of intention, while important in the ancient literature, is overshadowed by issues of custody, protection, and status. This difference in emphasis flows from the approach that the Romans took toward the behavior of those who were deemed deviant or insane. The sometimes devastating result of their irrational behavior could be remitted by compensation to the victims paid by the guardian of the insane. Payment of money could act as a remedy even in a case of murder if the relatives of the victim (or the owner of the victim, in the case of a slave) would agree to such payment instead of some form of physical retribution. Roman law was not exceptional in this respect, somewhat the same kind of system obtaining in Anglo-Saxon and Danish England (Walker 1968).

Roman medicine reached its apogee in the person of Galen (AD 130–200) who, like Hippocrates, was a scientific positivist, rejecting soothsayers in favor of anatomists (Zilboorg 1967 [1941], 87). He saw the brain as the seat of thought, but posited two irrational souls, one in the heart and the other in the liver. Unfortunately, Galen became enshrined as a medical authority even though most of the dissections he performed were limited to pigs and dogs. Many medical riddles (such as the circulation of the blood) remained unsolved for over 1300 years until the authority of Galen was overthrown.

MEDIEVAL PERIOD

The Middle Ages (approximately the sixth through the sixteenth centuries) was a period of scientific retrenchment during which the traditions of Rome and theology of Christianity held sway throughout most of Europe. In AD 528 the Emperor Justinian ordered a review and codification of the enormous corpus of Roman legislation (Sandars 1970). The Code of Justinian, or the *Corpus Iuris Civilis** (distinguishing it from canon or church law), made provision for the insane. Likened to one "absent, asleep or even dead," a person who became insane was protected from loss of property or position but was not considered capable of making a will, transacting any business, or held responsible for wrongdoing. Roman law followed the principle that "an insane person, like an infant not yet capable of understanding, usually before the age of 7 or 8, was incapable of malicious intent and the will to insult" (Van Ommeren 1961, 6).

The Roman Catholic Church, once established in Europe, relied on Roman law to answer many practical questions relating to insanity. How was matrimonial consent affected by insanity? Could the insane receive the sacraments of the church? Could a priest who became insane continue in his role? Should divorce be permitted if one of the partners became insane? How could it be determined that insanity was not being feigned in order to obtain a divorce? Secular authorities also had to contend with similarly difficult questions. How was it possible to detect a lawbreaker who feigned madness to avoid punishment? What were the rights of the madman who was in remission? Who would act as guardian to such a person? Two questions arise in any historical consideration of forensic psychiatry: How was it decided that any particular individual was mad or insane—that is, how was insanity recognized, and who was given the responsibility of determining the presence of insanity when it became an issue? No evidence seems to exist demonstrating that physicians were used as experts in the resolution of any of these questions during the medieval period.

The Italian city of Bologna may have been the first to establish a system of medical expertise that was used in what we would call criminal investigation (Simili 1973).† In Germany, the medieval city of Freiburg im Breisgau gave barbers/surgeons the responsibility of playing a forensic role at a time when academic medicine remained aloof from the problems of the mundane world (Volk and Warlo 1973). In their research, Volk and Warlo (1973, 101) found that "scientific forensic medicine was preceded for centuries by an empirical prescientific form that was motivated by the practical demands of the courts" but that before the appearance of Paolo Zacchia‡ medical experts had not been utilized by courts. The ruling councils of fourteenth-century Venice relied on the *Corpus Iuris Civilis* (or the traditions of the Roman law) when faced with the problem of excusing behavior because of insanity. Once again we find that physicians did not assist the decision makers. Although physicians were called upon to testify concerning physical elements in a crime, they were not asked to testify when insanity was the issue. "This is not surprising. Insanity was

* *The Institutes of Justinian*, with English introduction, translation, and notes by the late Thomas Collett Sandars, M.A. 1970 (originally published 1922).

† Bologna is by no means the only one of the medieval Italian cities that incorporated into their laws detailed rules for medical experts. Such rules are also found, e.g., in the city statutes of Padua (1316), Genoa (14th century), Mirandola (1386), Bassano (1389), Florence (1415), Verona (1450), Brescia (1470), Milan (1840), Ferrara (1506), Genoa and Urbino (1556). These cities that played such a tremendous role in the genesis of modern economics. Political thought and art, must therefore also be regarded as among the most influential factors in the establishment of legal medicine (Ackerknecht in Burns 1977, 251).

‡ The first complete edition of Paolo Zacchia's monumental work [Questiones MedicoLegales] was printed in 1654 in Rome. At that time the author was Proto medicus of the Papal State and medical advisor of the Rota, the High Court of the Roman Catholic Church (Karplus 1973, 125). This work of Zacchia's was considered the finest exposition and synthesis of medicolegal questions for many years after its writing and illustrates the sophistication that had developed in medicolegal thinking by the middle of the seventeenth century. [Paolo Zacchia] ... may be rightly considered the founder of the medical jurisprudence of insanity (Zilboorg 1944, 508).

traditionally a community judgment, not a medical one" (Ruggiero 1982, 111).

In England, tests of legal insanity were developed and became part of the legal tradition of the common law. Henry de Bracton was an early and formative influence on the development of these tests. Occupying the position of chief justiciary of the highest English court, and author of one of the first substantial treatises on English law, *On the Laws and Customs of England*[*] (ca. 1256), Bracton has been identified with the "wild beast test" (Bracton, Henry de. 1977). This legal test of insanity demanded that in order for the insane to avoid criminal responsibility, a kind of fury or wildness must characterize the individual or the act. Platt and Diamond (1965), however, have demonstrated that Bracton's use of the concept of wild beast (brutus) was not in any way intended to compare the insane with wild beasts but was making the point that the insane, like animals, were not capable of forming the requisite intent to commit crime, much as a child would be incapable of forming such intent. When a decision on the insanity of an accused was an issue in an English criminal proceeding, the matter was given over to the judgment of the king. A royal pardon could be sought to release the insane from responsibility, a procedure also used to excuse those who killed by accident or in self-defense (Walker 1968, vol. 1, 24).

In England, the statute known as *Praerogativa Regis*[†] drew an important distinction between those who were termed "natural fools," congenitally abnormal, and those who were "*non compos mentis*," or whose symptoms of illness appeared after birth. The condition "*non compos mentis*" included a wide range of psychiatric disorders and, unlike that of "natural fool," was amenable to temporary or even permanent recovery (Neugebauer 1978, 159).[‡] How was it decided and by whom that an individual fell into one or another of these categories? Juries known as inquisitions were established to examine persons who might fall within the terms of the statute. The Court of Chancery empowered the sheriff and other public officials to make an investigation not only into the mental status of questionable persons but also the possessions and property they held. Like the pattern in the rest of medieval Europe, physicians were not involved in these determinations; a finding of incompetence or congenital insanity was in medieval England (as it was in medieval Venice) a "community judgment" (Neugebauer 1978).

One of the darker aspects of this "community judgment" during the medieval period was the practice of witch-hunting. From the fifteenth through the seventeenth centuries, thousands upon thousands of persons were tried on the charge of practicing witchcraft. The *Malleus Maleficarum* (or *Witches' Hammer)* written by two Dominican friars, Sprenger and Kraemer, set out the argument for the existence of witches, the manner by which they could be identified, and the procedures for properly trying them. A noteworthy appearance of a physician as an expert in an English court was made by Sir Thomas Browne (Finch 1950). Browne, author of the *Religio Medici*, a book of religious contemplation, participated in the witchcraft trial of two women in 1664 at Bury St. Edmonds, testifying that the devil might work through the madness of the women; thus, Browne appeared to support the independent existence of witchcraft and madness simultaneously.[§]

The physician Johann Weyer (1515–1588), possibly the first physician to devote the major part of his professional attention to psychiatric illnesses, is viewed by many as the voice of reason standing against the spirit of the time (Diamond 1961; Alexander and Selesnick 1966; Zilboorg 1967; Mora 1991). Alternatively, the witchcraft trials are portrayed by some as the true forerunner of the law/psychiatry interface. The psychiatrist Thomas Szasz (1920–2012) made a widely publicized career characterizing psychiatry as a modem version of witch-hunting. Although Szasz credited Weyer with recognizing that witchcraft was too often used as a diagnosis for what otherwise must have been madness, Szasz criticized Weyer for his belief in the existence of witches (Szasz 1970). For Szasz, however humane their motives may be, physicians who participate in the legal process assist in bringing medicine into the service of the law and of the forces of social control (see also Szasz 1974).

MODERN PERIOD

One commentator has traced the origins of modern forensic medicine to 1507 and the penal code drawn up by the Bishop of Bamberg, leading to the requirement placed in the

[*] Bracton, Henry de. 1977. *De Legibus et Consuetudinibus Angliae. On the Laws and Customs of England*, 4 vols. Translated with revisions and notes by Samuel E. Thorne. Cambridge, MA: Harvard University Press.

[†] The king's right is distinctly stated in the document known as Praerogativa Regis, which we believe to come from the early years of Edward 1 (1272-1307). The same document seems to be the oldest that gives us any clear information about a wardship of lunatics. The king is to provide that the lunatic and his family are properly maintained out of the income of his estate, and the residue is to be handed over to him upon his restoration to sanity, or, should he die without having recovered his wits, is to be administered by the ordinary for the good of his soul; but the kings is to make nothing to his own use (Pollack and Maitland 1968, 481).

[‡] "Whether a man was an idiot or a madman was a matter of local knowledge, and they [the petty jury] were therefore the obvious people to ask [concerning the mental state of an accused]" (Walker 1968, 24). In the seventeenth century, Lord Coke in Beverley's Case, 4 Co. 123b, 76 Eng. Rep. 1118 (K.B. 1603), made further clarifications to the distinctions between "idiots" or natural fools and "lunatics" and generally summarized the laws of England regarding insanity to his time (Brakel and Ruck 1971, 2-3).

[§] Some biographers of Browne, asserting that his testimony led to the convictions, have deplored his part in the proceedings (Finch 1950, 215).

Constituto Carolina of the Emperor Charles V that "required evidence of medical men in all cases where their testimony could enlighten the judge or assist investigation in such cases as personal injury, murder and pretended pregnancy" (Gerber 1961, 197). Erwin Ackerknecht finds the first reference to the medical expert in the courts of Paris of 1511 (Eigen 1985, vol. 2, 38). Whichever may be the case, the beginning of the sixteenth century apparently marks the recognition by legal authorities that forensic medical expertise was not only useful but indispensable.

What characterizes the transition to the modem period is the evolution of medical and legal theories concerning the behavior of the insane, the tests through which insanity has come to be recognized, and methods for the treatment of psychiatric illnesses. Older humoral or demonological theories were abandoned (sometimes without clear replacement), the commonsense tests for idiocy or lunacy were set aside, and the treatment accorded those defined as mad or lunatic changed from family guardianship to care in an asylum and then to maintenance on psychoactive medication.

Medical men slowly expanded on the distinctions made by the *Praerogativa Regis* between those born natural fools and those who became mentally impaired after birth. Thomas Willis (1621–1675) produced his own taxonomy of mental disorders, one of the most significant of which was melancholia, because the delusions under which a melancholic labored might be transitory. Willis distinguished between a "universal type" of melancholia in which the affliction affected all aspects of mental process and a "particular type" that would leave the judgment of an individual unaffected except in one or two areas (Jackson 1983, 176).

Matthew Hale (1609–1676), an English jurist who ultimately became lord chief justice and authored the *History of the Pleas of the* Crown (first published posthumously in 1736), may have been the first to use the term "partial insanity," a concept close to Willis' "particular type." In contrast to what he saw as "partial insanity," under which category he placed melancholia, Hale posited a "perfect madness" or "total alienation of the mind." Such a distinction was particularly significant because melancholia was a frequent basis for allegations of insanity (Jackson 1983, 173). Hale believed that it was an individual's state of mind and not the nature of his or her acts that was important in determining whether legal insanity could be used as a criminal defense (Mora 1976, 1419). In so positing, Hale was merely reiterating the logic of the English law commentators Bracton (d. 1268) and Coke (1552–1634), both of whom recognized that in order for a crime to exist there needed to be a *mens rea*, or an evil mind or guilty intent, along with an *actus* reus, or evil deed (Hermann 1983). Coke was of the opinion that the ends of punishment were not served by inflicting it upon those who were incapable of reason or understanding because such punishment could not serve as an example to others (Platt and Diamond 1965, 359; Blackstone 1979, vol. 4, 25).

The various tests of insanity to determine the presence or absence of an evil mind or criminal intent in Anglo-American law evolved through a series of important criminal cases beginning in the eighteenth century.* One of the first of those cases was *Rex v. Arnold*, 16 How. St. Tr. 695 (1724), Judge Robert Tracy presiding. Edward Arnold was tried for the attempted murder of Lord Onslow. The case has been interpreted as a precedent for the "wild beast test" in that "in order to be excused from criminal responsibility as insane, the accused must not know what he is doing, 'no more than an infant, a brute, or a wild beast'" (Judge Tracy quoted in Hermann 1983); however, it is clear that there are many different tests embedded in the instructions that Judge Tracy gave to the jury, such as a test of abstract moral judgment ("distinguish between good and evil").

"The trial of Earl Ferrers in 1760 marks the first recorded instance of 'psychiatric' testimony offered in the criminal trial" (Eigen 1985, vol. 2, 37). In a fit of rage, the Earl had shot and killed his steward, *Rex v. Ferrers*, How. St. Tr. 886 (1760). Dr. John Monro, physician superintendent of Bethlem (commonly known as Bedlam), testified as an expert witness. Dr. Monro was examined by the accused Earl Ferrers himself, who conducted his own defense in accordance with the English law of the time. The Earl was left in the difficult position of having to prove his own insanity; however, he conducted so sagacious a defense that his plea was not believed and he was found guilty and executed.

The standard of a total deprivation of reason was successfully challenged in 1800 in the case of *Rex v. Hadfield* (1800) 27 St. Tr. 1281. Hadfield had been a soldier attached to the Duke of York in the last years of the eighteenth century. While fighting, he had sustained severe head wounds, which led to his discharge from the army and resulted in permanent insanity punctuated by delusions of the world's imminent end and his role as its savior. To accomplish the world's salvation, Hadfield attempted to assassinate King George Ill so that he, himself, would be executed and thus save the world through his martyrdom. "Hadfield used a firearm, and came within a few inches of wounding, if not killing, George III" (Walker 1968, 74). Hadfield was disarmed, seized, and ultimately brought to trial. Unlike the unfortunate Earl Ferrers, Hadfield had counsel and was represented by the superlative jurist Thomas Erskine who managed to win an acquittal. Erskine recast the insanity defense in terms of disease process, a shift from the older insistence on tests of cognitive understanding or moral knowledge. It was no longer only the presence or absence of reason, but the presence of delusion or a deranged state of mind, which the jury was to take into account (Quen 1968, 45).

* It should be noted that the English common law tradition is known for its reliance on the precedent created by case law. Other European traditions that follow Roman or civil law (or variants of the Napoleonic code) do not assign the same importance to the precedents set by judicial decision-making in any particular case. Rather, statutes set out the law and judges (and less often juries) are bound only by the statute or code law and not by what other judges have determined to be the law in similar cases already decided.

> *Delusion,* therefore, where there is no frenzy or raving madness, is the true character of insanity; and where it cannot be predicated of a man standing for life or death for a crime, he ought not, in my opinion, to be acquitted ... I must convince you, not only that the unhappy prisoner was a lunatic, within my own definition of lunacy, but that the act in question was the *immediate, unqualified offspring of the disease* ... to deliver a lunatic from responsibility to *criminal* justice, above all, in a case of such atrocity as the present, the relation between the disease and the act should be apparent. (Thomas Erskine quoted in Hunter and Macalpine 1963, 571)

In 1812, John Bellingham was executed for the murder of Spencer Percevale, first lord of the Treasury and chancellor of the Exchequer. Although an insanity defense was raised, the decision in Hadfield's case was ignored and a knowledge of right and wrong test was employed. In 1840, Edward Oxford (*R. v. Oxford* [1840] 9 C.&P. 525) attempted to assassinate Queen Victoria. His subsequent insanity plea was successful. The Bellingham decision (*R. v. Bellingham* [1812] O.B.S.P. case 433) was explicitly disclaimed. "Lord Chief Justice Denman reaffirmed [in the Oxford decision] the primacy of the question of the determining or responsible factor for the act: the disease or the individual?" (Quen 1968, 46). A pattern seems to emerge from the eighteenth- and nineteenth-century cases: those who succeed in the commission of crime fail in their insanity plea; those who attempt a crime and fail, succeed in their insanity plea.

The case that definitely breaks this pattern, if there is a pattern, and establishes a rule that has been maintained by most American jurisdictions until the present day, is M'Naghten's case, 10 Cl & Fin. 200, 8 Engl. Rep. 718 (1843). Daniel M'Naghten, believing the man he shot in the back was Sir Robert Peel, the British prime minister, mistakenly assassinated Edward Drummond, private secretary to Peel. M'Naghten suffered from an elaborate set of delusions involving his persecution by the British government and the Vatican, among others. The ensuing trial is noteworthy for the number of physicians who were called as expert witnesses (nine in all), although two did not examine M'Naghten. They opined that no doubt existed as to his insanity even though M'Naghten might have been able to conduct his life along rational lines and understand the difference between right and wrong.

M'Naghten was found not guilty by reason of insanity after the case had been stopped by the judges. The two physicians called by the prosecution, although they had interviewed M'Naghten, never appeared or testified at the trial. Two of the defense experts (Winslow and Philips), although they never met M'Naghten and knew him solely by observing him in court, testified that he was insane, agreeing with the opinion of their colleagues appearing for the defense. On the strength of the medical testimony, Judge Tindal stopped the trial and charged the jury that returned with a verdict of not guilty by reason of insanity. This decision left Queen Victoria, her government, and the public in a state of uneasiness over the relatively undefined nature of that mental condition that would permit an insanity plea to succeed.

After the trial, the chancellor of the House of Lords addressed the House on the law of England regarding the responsibility of the insane and offered to call a convention of English judges. Three months later 15 judges of the Queen's Bench assembled for the purpose of clarifying the law (Quen 1968, 48). To these judges, the House of Lords addressed five questions. In part, the answers they gave to these questions have come to be called the M'Naghten Rules. These rules are still utilized in many jurisdictions in the United States. (For a discussion of current insanity tests, see Part 3, "Forensic Evaluation and Treatment in the Criminal Justice System.") Probably the most significant part of these rules for the further development of forensic psychiatry is that found in the answers to the second and third questions. These questions sought guidance on the instructions to be given to a jury and the terms into which these instructions should be cast:

> That the jury ought to be told in all cases that every man is presumed to be sane, and to possess a sufficient degree of reason to be responsible for his crimes, until the contrary be proved to their satisfaction; and that to establish a defense on the ground of insanity, *it must be clearly proved that, at the time of committing of the act, the party accused was labouring [sic] under such a defect of reason, from disease of the mind, as not to know the nature and quality of the act he was doing, or, if he did know it, that he did not know what he was doing was wrong.* [Emphasis added] (Trial of Daniel M'Naughton, 1843 In: *Modern State Trials.* Revised by William C. Townsend, 1850, quoted in Hunter and Macalpine 1963, 921)

Besides establishing and limiting the legal conditions under which psychiatric expert witnesses would have to testify (and under which they testify to this day in many English-speaking jurisdictions), the decision in this case and the answers to the subsequent questions reveal an interesting and unexpected influence. If the *M'Naghten* case can be seen as an essential ratification of the presence of physicians in courts as experts on insanity, that ratification was achieved in no small part by the work of an American physician, Isaac Ray.

FORENSIC PSYCHIATRY IN THE UNITED STATES

The legal treatment of the insane in colonial America was consistent with the treatment they received during most of European history. Determinations of insanity continued to be made by civil authorities, not by physicians (Deutsch 1949, 40; see also Grob 1973). Compared with the growth of mental asylums in Europe, American institutions devoted to the care and treatment of the mentally ill arose slowly and needed theoretical justifications from abroad. Based somewhat on its English predecessor, Bethlem (also known as Bethlehem or Bedlam), the Pennsylvania hospital, was opened in 1752.* Benjamin Franklin was among the men who founded it, and they had as one of their objectives the admittance of mental patients (Dain 1976, 1182). In a petition drawn up by Franklin for the provincial Assembly in 1751, he states:

> That with the Numbers of People, the number of Persons distempered in Mind and deprived of their rational Faculties, hath greatly increased in this Province.
>
> That some of them going at large are a Terror to their neighbors, who are daily apprehensive of the Violences they may commit ...
>
> That few or none of them are so sensible of their Condition, as to submit voluntarily to treatment that their respective Cases requires, and therefore continue in the same deplorable state during their Lives; whereas it has been found, by the existence of many Years, that above two Thirds of the Mad People received into Bethlehem Hospital, and there treated properly, have been cured. (Franklin, quoted in Deutsch 1949, 59)

By 1844 a large network of public and private asylums existed in the United States.† In that year, 13 superintendents of mental asylums founded the Association of Medical Superintendents of American Institutions for the Insane (AMSAII). One of the founding members of that association was Isaac Ray, who became the superintendent of Maine Insane Hospital in 1841 and later superintendent of the Butler Hospital in Providence, Rhode Island. At age 31, Ray wrote A *Treatise on the Medical Jurisprudence of Insanity* (1838),‡ one of the first systematic studies in English of the law/psychiatry interface.

The element in Ray's thinking that seems to have had the most profound effect on developments both within law and psychiatry is the notion of "moral insanity," a concept introduced by James Cowles Prichard, nineteenth-century English physician and scholar.§ Ray was critical of the English tests of insanity because they were too concerned with cognitive function, ignoring the role of emotion and the impact of mental disease on "moral" functioning:

> In legal contexts the term "moral insanity" implied an inability to conform to the moral dictates of society—as a consequence of disease, not depravity, and despite the absence of traditionally accepted signs of mental disturbance. The morally insane offender might seem to be quite rational in conversation, even intelligent, be able to solve problems and be subject to no delusions or sensory misconceptions—yet still be mentally ill. (Rosenberg 1968, 68)

Ray's treatise followed the work of the reformers Vincenzo Chiarugi, Philippe Pinel, and William Tuke, who through religious or ideological optimism attempted to cure the insane by either softening the atmosphere of the mental institution (Pinel supposedly struck off their chains) or taking them out of destructive environments into the countryside. "Moral treatment" consisted of kindness, understanding, and what resembled a type of behavior modification therapy.

By the middle of the nineteenth century, the notion of moral insanity gained additional support among those who followed the phrenologists Gall and Spurzheim. These men had attempted to connect particular mental faculties to particular sites within the brain. Thus, following on this logic, it would be possible for a person to be totally lucid and in apprehension of the difference between right and wrong and yet commit felonious acts because the part of the brain in charge of moral control might be diseased. During the trial of Charles Guiteau, the assassin of President Garfield, discussed later in this chapter, the various psychiatric and neurological experts who appeared debated whether "moral insanity" was a viable medical notion.

For alienists (as early psychiatrists were known) the debate over the issue of moral insanity had a significant impact. The work Ray had done affected the outcome of the M'Naghten trial and became an influence on English and American legal usage:

> Alexander Cockburn, counsel for the defense [M'Naghten's defense], followed the lead of Lord Erskine [defense counsel in Hadfield's case] and attempted to establish a more flexible test

* The idea of the Pennsylvania Hospital originated with Dr. Thomas Bond, a man who had been disowned by the Friends in 1742 for taking an oath. Having visited England later, he was impressed with the care provided the mentally ill at Bethlehem Hospital (Deutsch 1949, 17).

† The following is a list of the location of some of the early American mental hospitals and their dates of establishment: Philadelphia, Pennsylvania. 1752; Williamsburg, Virginia (first state-supported mental asylum), 1774; New York Hospital, New York, 1791; Frankford, Pennsylvania, 1817; Boston, Massachusetts, 1818; Hartford, Connecticut, 1824; Lexington, Kentucky, 1824.

‡ Five years before M'Naghten's trial, an American doctor, Isaac Ray, had published what was to become one of the most influential books of the nineteenth century on the subject [insanity and the law]: *A Treatise on the Medical Jurisprudence of Insanity* (1838), and in the year before the trial the learned, though not very original, Prichard (who was to become a Commissioner for Lunacy in 1845), had published a similar work (Walker 1968, 89).

§ Tighe characterizes the notion of "moral insanity" as "the single most controversial concept in the emerging discipline of American forensic psychiatry" (Tighe 1983, 12).

> of exculpable insanity. He made extensive and almost exclusive reference to the work of the American physician, Isaac Ray, in his attempt to demonstrate that legally exculpable insanity should include more than disease of the intellect. (Quen 1968, 47)

In spite of Ray's influence on the *M'Naghten* decision, that influence was undone in great part by the House of Lords and its panel of judges, which "clarified" the *M'Naghten* decision so as to enshrine a knowledge test of mental competence in criminal procedure. Ray was attempting to have the law recognize the "wide range of mental disorders which primarily affected an individual's emotional and volitional capacities" which would affect imputations of responsibility (Tighe 1983, 30). However, the law was reluctant to make such an acknowledgment. Ray credited such resistance to jurists' ignorance, poor education, and lack of experience with the insane. To remedy this state of affairs, Ray worked to educate both the legal and medical communities to what he saw as the correct approach to psychiatric forensic problems. In 1866 Ray was put into contact with Judge Doe of the New Hampshire Supreme Court upon the latter's seeking medical opinion in a case before his court. Thus began a six-year correspondence between the two men that had a profound effect on the direction that medical jurisprudence was to take in the United States. This correspondence gives an intimate and detailed picture of the collaboration between Ray and Doe as they sought to have the question of insanity recognized as a question of science and not of law. "The resulting rule of law, established in *State v. Pike* and subsequently known as the 'New Hampshire rule,' has been proposed from time to time for wider adoption both in this country and in England" (Reik 1953, 183).

The New Hampshire Rule, or "product rule," states that a test of insanity ought to determine if the act in question was the "product" of a mental disease or defect, more closely reflecting Isaac Ray's desire to avoid cognitive tests of insanity such as the M'Naghten Rule. This "product rule" was adopted in the District of Columbia in 1954 and called the Durham Rule (*Durham v. United States*, 214 F.2d 862 [D.C. Cir. 1954]) but was later overturned in the case *U.S. v. Brawner*, 471 F.2d 969 (D.C. Cir. 1972), which replaced it with the rule enunciated in the American Law Institute's (ALI) Model Penal Code. Quoting from that model code, the following appears in the *Brawner* decision:

> A person is not responsible for criminal conduct if at the time of such conduct as a result of mental disease or defect he lacks substantial capacity either to appreciate the criminality [wrongfulness] of his conduct or to conform his conduct to the requirements of the law. *U.S. v. Brawner*, 471 F.2d 979 (D.C. Cir. 1972)

An "irresistible impulse" test first using the word *impulse* was employed in *Commonwealth v. Rogers*, 48 Mass 500 (Massachusetts 1844). The most influential early case to add this concept to *M'Naghten* was *Parsons v. State*, 2 80 854 (Alabama 1887), which referred to mental disease as causing a loss of power to choose between right and wrong, destroying free agency at the time of the alleged criminal act. A similar test was utilized in a federal court in *Davis v. United States*, 165 U.S. 373 (1897), which referred to the will or governing power of the mind being so destroyed that a defendant's actions are no longer subject to his will but are beyond his control. Although the New Hampshire Rule or "irresistible impulse test" currently is not relied on anywhere as the sole test, similar tests are often used in conjunction with the M'Naghten Rules or are incorporated in the volitional prong of the ALI insanity test. A form of the "irresistible impulse" test is the "policeman at the elbow" test.

Much controversy arose soon after physicians began testifying as psychiatric experts because their testimony often betrayed fundamental disagreements within the profession over the nature of mental disease. These disagreements seemed to suggest that either the expert was failing to make an objective evaluation (and many motives could be adduced for such failure, such as the personal or religious values of the expert, or the payment received from a party in the case) or the expertise itself was faulty. During the meetings of the AMSAII, references were made with greater regularity to the discomfort of its members over the contradictory testimony given by physicians and the attacks made during cross-examination on the credibility of expert witnesses as the nineteenth century advanced (Tighe 1983, 112).

Probably the most important battles fought in a courtroom in the late nineteenth century over these issues occurred during the trial of Charles Guiteau, the assassin of President Garfield. On July 2, 1881, Guiteau approached Garfield at Union Station in Washington, DC, and shot him as horrified Secretary of State James G. Blaine looked on. (Garfield did not die until September 19, 1881.) The motive for this slaying is not clear, but supposedly Guiteau had been disappointed in not having been appointed to a diplomatic post in France. Some of the most eminent men from the worlds of psychiatry and neurology appeared to testify at the trial (Rosenberg 1968).*

* Among these experts were Charles H. Nichols, superintendent of the Bloomingdale Asylum in New York; Charles Folsom of Harvard and the McLean Asylum in Boston; Edward C. Spitzka, neurologist; Fordyce Barker, professor of medicine and president of the New York Academy of Medicine; Allen McLane Hamilton, alienist; John Gray, superintendent of Utica Asylum in New York and editor of the *American Journal of Insanity*; William W. Godding, superintendent of the Government Hospital for the Insane in Washington, D.C.; James H. McBride, superintendent of the Asylum for Insane in Milwaukee, Wisconsin. This list is not exhaustive.

The conflicts that occurred during the trial, centering as they did on the concept of moral insanity, brought the tensions within psychiatry and between psychiatry and the emerging specialty of neurology into the open. John Gray, superintendent of Utica Asylum, vigorously opposed the idea of moral insanity. The neurologist Edward Spitzka defended it on the basis that brain disease could be selective in its manifestations. Gray, who had many years of experience treating the insane, did not believe it was possible for an individual to be insane in only part of his or her mind. Spitzka was rallying for reform of the insanity defense and wished to see the law recognize the recent advances that had been made in medical science. Much was made at the trial of the hereditary nature of insanity, a notion that had gained much favor toward the end of the nineteenth century.

All arguments proved futile. Garfield had been a popular president, and his assassin could not have gone unpunished. This case seems to fall within the pattern described earlier for eighteenth- and early nineteenth-century English cases. Those who succeed in their deadly aims are found guilty regardless of any pleas that might be made. Guiteau was indeed found guilty and was executed in 1882.

For forensic psychiatric practice, the Guiteau trial had two important results. The first is that by focusing the light of public attention on the insanity defense, much dissatisfaction was raised in the minds of the involved professionals and the public at large over the role that medical experts were playing in courtroom proceedings. (Almost exactly one hundred years later, in 1982, the trial of John Hinckley, who had made an unsuccessful attempt on the life of President Reagan, caused a similar reaction.) Second, the mandatory use of the hypothetical question* during the trial caused further frustration among the experts. These two results, coupled with the professional rivalries that were exacerbated by conflicting testimony, helped to precipitate various attempts at reform, which have occupied many in the legal and psychiatric professions in one form or another to this day.

As a response to the ongoing professional debate and attempts at reform, there emerged various medico-legal societies in the larger cities of the United States:

> The founding of the New York Medico-Legal Society in 1867 signalled the beginning of a new era in medico-legal relations. In this new era the still struggling sub-specialty of medical jurisprudence of insanity was transformed into a "science" as the physicians and attorneys interested in it became caught up in the general process of professionalization that was changing medical and legal practice at the end of the nineteenth century. (Tighe 1983, 182)

The New York Medico-Legal Society continues in an attenuated form to this day. The Society of Medical Jurisprudence in New York, which was incorporated on March 7, 1883, claims to be the oldest society of its type in the United States. The society continues to be composed of attorneys and physicians and provides a forum for outstanding individuals from various professions whose concern is the advancement of medical jurisprudence.

Not only do organizations seem to appear and disappear from the professional landscape, but energetic and forceful individuals who formed the backbone of the early forensic organizations came from a variety of professional backgrounds. For instance, Clark Bell, an attorney and founder and editor of the *Medico-Legal Journal*, described as "the first American journal devoted exclusively to medical jurisprudence" (Tighe 1983, 185), was either president or secretary of the New York Medico-Legal Society from approximately 1872 to 1918. Bell saw the major role of the society as an educational one, bringing together legal and medical people who could engage in "mutual education" as well as in educating the general public (Tighe 1983, 187). The society also engaged in vigorous attempts at reform of the system of expert testimony and the revision of notions of criminal responsibility.

In 1909,† after a National Conference on Criminal Law and Criminology was held at Northwestern University Law School, a committee was formed under the chairmanship of the law professor Edwin Keedy to reform the law of insanity. Keedy enlisted eminent attorneys, judges, and psychiatrists to serve on this committee, which was to focus on tests of responsibility, the forms in which verdicts were cast, and expert testimony. Lack of agreement among the disparate professional elements involved meant that little was accomplished in the way of reform (Tighe 1983, 314).

As the chairman of the committee, Keedy exemplified the position of the legal profession. "According to Keedy the medical expert's only task was to give the jury technical

* It had been the practice in American courts of law for attorneys to be required to pose questions to expert witnesses only as hypothetical questions. Legal tradition construed an expert opinion on the actual facts of any particular case as an invasion of the province of the jury whose most important function was to decide such questions of fact. This practice led to the creative phrasing of questions beginning with the word "suppose" and recreating in almost every detail the case being tried except for the actual names, dates, and other identifying information. (See Kidd 1915, for an attempt in one American jurisdiction to correct this practice as part of larger evidence reforms.)

† In this same year (1909), William Healy, a British-born psychiatrist who had graduated from the University of Chicago Medical School, became the director of the Psychopathic Institute of the Cook County (Chicago) Juvenile Court, which had been opened in 1899 as the first court of its kind. The Psychopathic Institute was also the earliest such court clinic in the United States. Some of the most prominent forensic psychiatrists, such as Jonas Rappeport in Baltimore and Richard Rosner in New York, worked in such court-related psychiatric institutions.

assistance in evaluating a defendant's mental state" (Tighe 1983, 361). This model of psychiatric expert testimony contrasted sharply with the one that was supported by the psychiatrists, especially Adolph Meyer and William A. White. These psychiatrists wished to have the concepts of medical and legal insanity integrated, and the jury determination of insanity replaced by psychiatric determinations. Such a model of the expert's role in the courtroom contradicted basic rules of evidence and legal procedure. Trial by jury is a right protected by the Constitution of the United States. All witnesses may be cross-examined and all facts in question must be put to the jury for determination.

Further, psychiatrists such as William A. White (and later Karl Menninger) attacked the principles upon which criminal law and criminal procedure were predicated. They argued that punishment for crime often prevented the rehabilitation it sought to achieve, that such punishment merely expressed the need for revenge, and that legal decision making in such matters ought to be surrendered entirely to scientists. The arguments of psychoanalysts such as White and Menninger gained influence as psychoanalysis gained prestige.

Psychiatrist Bernard Diamond was instrumental in the development of the diminished capacity defense in California. Diminished capacity permitted gradations of punishment by finding gradations of guilt. It allowed the psychiatrist to explain why a defendant committed a crime often using psychodynamic terminology. In California, two separate trials are held: one to establish guilt or innocence and another afterward to determine sanity or insanity (Diamond 1961, 74). Until *People v. Wells*, 33 Cal.2d 330 (1949), psychiatrists were excluded from testifying until the second stage of the bifurcated trial. *People v. Wells* established that mental illness could negate the *mens rea* (criminal intent) required to convict for a crime and evidence supporting such negation could be introduced at the primary trial.

Diamond testified in another, later case, *People v. Gorshen*, 51 Cal.2d 716 (1959), which permitted testimony and opinions regarding specific intent in the absence of legal insanity:

> The essence of my [Diamond's] testimony was that Gorshen killed, not because he was insane, but rather as a defense against insanity. Although he knew right from wrong in the sense of *M'Naghten*, although he appeared to have premeditated, deliberated, and to have had the requisite criminal intent of malice, that he was, nevertheless, not a free agent. That he was suffering from an uncontrollable compulsion, the consequence of mental disease. (Diamond 1961, 79)

The California Supreme Court on appeal accepted the argument made by Diamond and other psychiatrists filing *amici curiae* briefs in the *Gorshen* case. It allowed that a showing of "mental abnormality not amounting to legal insanity" could provide evidence that the defendant did not possess the specific mental state required for conviction of a crime but still could be found guilty of a lesser-included crime. However, in response to the furor over the trial of Dan White, the assassin of San Francisco Mayor George Moscone and Supervisor Harvey Milk, the California legislature has undermined most of Diamond's efforts by eliminating diminished capacity as a defense. Nevertheless, the diminished capacity defense has been utilized in some other states. A *mens rea* defense of diminished actuality was retained in California (Weinstock et al. 1996).

During his long and distinguished career, Diamond also supported an approach to forensic psychiatry in which the psychiatrist in criminal trials would become an advocate, testifying with total honesty solely for the defense. (See Diamond [1985] for a characterization of this approach, which Diamond contrasts with the approach of the late Seymour Pollack, a forensic psychiatrist who established one of the earliest U.S. forensic training programs at the University of Southern California.)

In terms of forensic psychiatry, the status of psychiatrist as expert had already been achieved prior to the Freudian "revolution." Nevertheless, the movement away from interpreting insanity solely as a chemico-physiological imbalance or a hereditary degeneration, to the view that dysfunctional mental states and attendant behavioral manifestations arose from environmental and familial influences, opened every aspect of social and psychological life to the scrutiny of the psychiatrist. Psychiatric expertise began to be sought in an ever-widening range of situations. Such an increase in the perimeter of the psychiatrist's jurisdiction and responsibility is a continuing theme within medical jurisprudence; however, recent developments have moved psychiatry back toward the biological.

Forensic psychiatry failed to professionalize during its early history not merely because the pioneers and reformers were overzealous or scattered in their energies, which, in fact, they were. On the one hand, figures such as Isaac Ray (a physician), Clark Bell (attorney), and Edwin Keedy (attorney) were striving to organize across professional lines—that is, by including physicians from a variety of specialties and attorneys in their struggles. On the other hand, the task of such reformers was made doubly difficult since they were attempting to achieve meaningful substantive reform in the area of their specialization without having first formally specialized and/or professionalized it. Thus, the boundaries of the specialty were unclear and the centers of power were diffuse.

Although the formation of the medicolegal societies of the nineteenth and early twentieth centuries provides evidence that movement toward formal organization had begun, the major player in this respect continued to be AMSAII. Through its journal, the *American Journal of Insanity* founded in 1844, AMSAII played an important role in educating the growing psychiatric community to the importance of understanding legal issues.

At its annual meeting in Washington, DC, in 1892, AMSAII changed its name to the American Medico-Psychological Association (AMPA) and adopted a new constitution. This change recognized the changed shape of the psychiatric profession inasmuch as the medical superintendent no longer dominated professional affairs. Standing committees did the major work of AMSAII and AMPA. In 1882 a committee on the "criminal responsibility of the insane" was added (Barton 1987, 88–89). Neither AMSAII, nor its successor, AMPA, was distinguished by vigorous activity on the national scene. It did not provide dynamic leadership for the growth of a subspecialty in forensic psychiatry, let alone the psychiatric profession generally, until after World War I.

In 1921, the AMPA again changed its name to the American Psychiatric Association (APA) and by that time had 1000 members (Barton 1987). Adolf Meyer, a leader in the specialty before and after the First World War, assisted in promoting research in psychiatry and spurred changes in medical education to include greater attention to psychiatry. The emergence of forensic psychiatry could not have occurred without the widening exposure of physicians to education in psychiatry both in their undergraduate and graduate medical education. The addition of psychiatry to the medical school curriculum was slow in coming. Even by the late 1930s, psychiatry had not been added as a mandatory part of the curriculum at institutions such as the medical school of the University of California, San Francisco, which had only one psychiatrist on its faculty at the time. Forensic psychiatry was also absent from medical school curricula.

Except for the medico-legal societies described above, forensic psychiatry was not represented by any formal organization; however, there was movement in the APA with respect to the recognition of the growing importance of forensic issues:

> In 1925 the first report of the new Committee on Legal Aspects of Psychiatry of the American Psychiatric Association was published. Dr. Karl Menninger submitted the reports as chairman. It marked a true turning point in the history of the problem [the interface of law and psychiatry], and Karl Menninger's name must rightly occupy an honorable place among the pioneers of an important and difficult task. (Zilboorg 1944, 579)

This committee had contacts with the Section on Criminal Law and Criminology of the American Bar Association.

In 1934, a section of forensic psychiatry was initiated by the APA under the chairmanship of William Alanson White, who had been president of the APA (1924–1925) and was one of the most vocal critics from the psychiatric community of the criminal justice system. By the end of World War II, the general unresponsiveness of the APA to the growing problems surrounding the practice of psychiatry became patent and had been observed by William Menninger. He and a group called the "young turks" went on to form the Group for the Advancement of Psychiatry (GAP) in 1946 to restructure the APA because of their perception that the APA had been less than responsive in supporting the military during World War II. In fact, major changes in the APA structure were effected through the urging of GAP members, including the establishment of an office of medical director (Barton 1987, 118).

The Council on Psychiatry and Law (CPL) of the APA emerged during 1979–1980 out of the Council on Governmental Policy and Law when Alan Stone was APA president. The CPL has been very active in formulating policy proposals for its parent body. Participating with other groups, the CPL breaks up into smaller groups as needs warrant; for instance, the Insanity Defense Work Group developed an APA statement on the insanity defense in December 1982. The APA recommended elimination of the volitional prong of the insanity defense, but use of the word "appreciate" instead of the more cognitive word "know" appeared to minimize the effect of the change. It was prompted by the public furor that arose over the insanity verdict in the case of John Hinckley, who had attempted to assassinate President Reagan. The American Medical Association (AMA) had recommended abolition of the insanity defense and its replacement by a *mens rea* defense, and the APA statement was seen by many as a political move to stem antipsychiatric public sentiment. H. Keith Brodie, MD, president of the APA, who signed the foreword to the APA statement, characterized it as follows: "This is the first comprehensive position statement on the insanity defense to be developed and adopted by APA" (APA 1984, 4). Considering the age of the APA and its antecedent organizations, this characterization reveals much about activity within the APA and the caution it has shown in taking formal positions on forensic issues.*

However, it is not from any reforms within the APA itself or action on the part of any of its committees that the formal organization of forensic psychiatry has arisen. Rather, this subspecialty came into existence through the efforts of psychiatrists particularly interested in forensics who maintained professional relationships with law schools and forensic organizations. Through the 1950s, 1960s, and 1970s, law schools became interested in having psychiatrists on their faculties. Psychiatrists such as Bernard Diamond at the University of California, Berkeley; Jay Katz at Yale Law School; Alan Stone at Harvard Law School; and Andrew

* Since 1952, the APA has given the Isaac Ray Award to an individual who has made an outstanding contribution to "forensic psychiatry or to the psychiatric aspects of jurisprudence." Since 1967, the APA joined by the American Academy of Psychiatry and Law in 1982 as cosponsor) has given the Manfred Guttmacher Award for outstanding contributions to the literature of forensic psychiatry.

Watson at the University of Michigan Law School are all examples of this trend. Ultimately, training programs in forensic psychiatry arose. One of the earliest and most notable was the program developed by Seymour Pollack at the University of Southern California. The Western Psychiatric Institute in Pittsburgh is another important center of forensic psychiatric training and activity.*

Probably the most important organization to give attention to the relations of psychiatry and law has been the American Academy of Psychiatry and Law (AAPL). Jonas Robitscher, lawyer and psychiatrist, characterizes the formal inception of AAPL in 1969 in the following fashion:

> This formal group [AAPL] was the outgrowth of an informal group of about 15, mainly directors of forensic psychiatry fellowship training programs, who had met in connection with the American Psychiatric Association meeting in Boston in 1968. This new group now [1972] has about 250 members, all interested in some phase of legal psychiatry.... The by-laws of AAPL list six aims: to exchange ideas and experience among forensic psychiatrists in North America; to elevate the standards of study and practice in this field; to develop training programs for psychiatrists desirous of acquiring skills in forensic psychiatry; to take leadership in initiating and monitoring research in the field; to improve relationships between psychiatrists on the one hand and attorneys, legislators, jurists, and penologists on the other; and to take leadership in informing the public of the needs of those involved with the law and the contributions available from psychiatry. (Robitscher 1972, 316 [921])

AAPL is a thriving and vibrant professional organization that publishes a newsletter (in January, April, and September) and quarterly journal (*Journal of the American Academy of Psychiatry and the Law*), and sponsors an annual meeting. Under the direction of Jonas Rappeport as founding medical director, AAPL became the largest forensic psychiatric organization in the United States. There are chapters of AAPL throughout the United States with the first chapter organized by Richard Rosner in the New York area, known as the Tri-State Chapter. AAPL maintains an active liaison with the American Academy of Forensic Sciences (AAFS). AAPL adopted ethical guidelines in 1987, which have undergone revision. The last revision was in 2005.

The AAFS founded in 1948 (as the American Medicolegal Congress) is composed of experts from diverse disciplines including, but not limited to, psychiatry, pathology, toxicology, anthropology, engineering, and ballistics. Individuals active within the AAFS have made major contributions to the furtherance of the professionalization and specialization of forensic psychiatry. Chief among such contributors was Maier Tuchler, a psychiatrist with extensive experience in forensics, who worked assiduously to form a certifying body for forensic psychiatry.† Apparently an idea for such a certifying body had first been proposed by Lowell Sterling in the early 1950s when he was chairman of the psychiatry section of AAFS. Such a proposal was also made in the mid-1950s by Ralph Banay, a psychiatrist active in the world of criminalistics, and editor of the *Journal of Correctional Medicine and Social Therapy*. However, an earlier movement forming specialty boards had occurred in the 1930s‡ and resistance had arisen later within the medical community to what was seen as overspecialization.

When AAPL was approached to cosponsor a forensic board with the AAFS, some of the original founders of AAPL looked upon attempts at certification with skepticism. These attempts created dissension in what otherwise was a "healthy organization" and generated the fear that certification might ultimately lead away from the educational mission of AAPL, and create elites within the organization. These objections ultimately subsided when it was realized that AAPL would not be the certifying body itself but rather only a sponsoring agency.

The way ultimately opened for the formal organization of a board in June 1976, with the participation of the AAFS, AAPL, liaison with the APA and the AMA, and financing from the Legal Enforcement Assistance Administration (LEAA). The first members of the American Board of Forensic Psychiatry§ (ABFP) were all highly experienced in forensic psychiatry, were involved in teaching, and had been certified by the American Board of Psychiatry and Neurology (ABPN).

* For an excellent (although somewhat dated) discussion of the changes taking place within forensic psychiatry see Robitscher (1972).

† I am indebted to and would like to express my appreciation of the late psychiatrist Stanley Prentice, for allowing me access to materials he prepared in advance of writing a history of the American Board of Forensic Psychiatry. Those materials were invaluable in creating my own encapsulated history of the American Board of Forensic Psychiatry.

‡ The ABA [American Board of Anesthesiology] was one of nine boards established between the years 1933 and 1938, a period which saw the flowering of the specialty board movement in the United States, the others being the American Board of Pediatrics (1933), of Orthopedic Surgery (1935), of Psychiatry and Neurology (1935), of Radiology (1935), of Urology (1935), of Internal Medicine (1936), of Pathology (1936), and of Surgery (1937) (Little 1981, 317).

§ The first board of directors of the American Board of Forensic Psychiatry were: Walter Bromberg, MD; Bernard Diamond, MD; Zigmond Lebensohn, MD; Herbert Modlin, MD; Joseph Paterson, D.Crim., Irwin Peff, MD; Seymour Pollack, MD; Stanley Portnow, MD; Jonas Rappeport, MD; Robert Sadoff, MD; John Torrens, MD; and Maier Tuchler, MD.

It had been decided by the founders of the ABFP that no members would be "grandfathered" into certification—that is, even those psychiatrists who organized the ABFP would have to sit for the certifying examination. The board required that psychiatrists (limited to those practicing in the United States and Canada) wishing to be certified in forensic psychiatry also be certified by ABPN. In addition, five years of post-residency experience was required, with substantial involvement in forensic work. (Consideration was given for time spent in forensic fellowship training programs. One year of credit was given for a law degree.) Two examinations had to be successfully passed: one written, given during the annual meeting of the APA, and one oral, given during the annual meeting of the AAPL. Candidates needed to pass the written examination before taking the oral. Mechanisms were in place for retaking examinations that were not passed and for appealing board decisions. Richard Rosner was instrumental in the creation of standards for accrediting fellowship programs in forensic psychiatry as well as the development of the Accreditation Council on Fellowships in Forensic Psychiatry (ACFFP). Its processes were implemented in 1988, and the first programs were accredited in 1989. The Accreditation Council was supported financially by AAFS and was given administrative support by AAPL. Both organizations became cosponsors.

Neither the mechanisms established by the American Board of Forensic Psychiatry for certifying forensic psychiatrists nor the accreditation procedures of the Accreditation Council on Fellowships in Forensic Psychiatry are now used. After some years of struggle and negotiation, a decision was made by the American Board of Medical Specialties to recognize forensic psychiatry as a full-fledged psychiatric subspecialty. Qualifying examinations are no longer conducted under the auspices of the ABFP but are administered by the American Board of Psychiatry and Neurology. Such formal recognition has had an impact not only on the credential that forensic psychiatrists come to obtain but also on the nature of their postgraduate education.

In 1996, the Accreditation Council for Graduate Medical Education (ACGME) developed standards for certification in forensic psychiatry relying heavily on those developed by the ACFFPF. The ACGME began accrediting programs in 1997 and as of 2015 there are 40 such programs throughout the United States. When the ABPN began certifying forensic psychiatrists by examination, there were no approved ACGME fellowship programs. Thus, the requirements for taking the first examination could have been fulfilled by attending any one of a number of "nonapproved" post-residency programs or through a number of years practicing extensively in the field. In 1999, the "practice track" was eliminated. Since 2001, only completion of a fellowship program in forensic psychiatry at an ACGME-approved program is accepted as fulfilling the requirements for examination. Recertification examinations began in 2003 for those previously certified in forensic psychiatry. Of course, board certification in psychiatry is required before attempting qualification in the subspecialty of forensic psychiatry. From 1994 through 1999, 1310 board certified psychiatrists were qualified in forensic psychiatry by the American Board of Psychiatry and Neurology. At this point, the ABPN has routinized the process of awarding certification in forensic psychiatry and regular examinations are given to applicants who complete ACGME certified fellowship programs. Since 2014, following the initial certification and any recertification in forensic psychiatry, continuous maintenance of certification is required to retain the certification. This process like in other medical specialties requires more than just an examination.

After traveling a circuitous and difficult path, forensic psychiatry has emerged out of a history extending back to the beginning of civilization in the West. This emergence has not been smooth; there have been many breaks and bumps in the trail. It is only within the last 250 years that physicians or psychiatrists have been asked into courts to act as expert witnesses. Although there have been many attempts made to reorganize or reform the nature of the social action performed by forensic psychiatrists, those attempts have only had limited success. For instance, there is much dissatisfaction with the M'Naghten Rules, but many states retain them despite much psychiatric opposition. Some jurisdictions in recent years have even returned to *M'Naghten* from the ALI test in response to unpopular trial verdicts and public clamor. Although new challenges will undoubtedly confront forensic psychiatry, the next chapter of this history will be written by a subspecialty that has gained formal recognition and which is well positioned to meet those challenges.

Appendix 3.1 Important dates in the history of forensic psychiatry

	(Dates BC are approximate)
3000 BC	Imhotep combines the role of priest/physician/statesman and scientist.
1850 BC	First murder trial in Babylonia in which an expert witness (midwife) appears.
1800 BC	Code of Hammurabi makes early recognition of importance of intent in criminal law but punishes most crimes with death.
1200 BC	Hebrew law establishes the intent of actor when establishing guilt for murder.
460 BC	Birth of Hippocrates (died 377 BC).

(Continued)

Appendix 3.1 (*Continued*) Important dates in the history of forensic psychiatry

	(Dates BC are approximate)
450 BC	Twelve Tables of Roman Law refers to the legal incapacities of children and the insane; provided for guardianship of fools by family or paternal relatives.
	Lex Aquila in Roman law does not hold a man accountable for damage to property when caused without negligence or malice.
	Lex Cornelia punishes those who injured the personality of victim or lowered esteem in which victim was held but exempted children and the insane when they committed such injury.
AD 130	Birth of Galen (died AD 201).
AD 528	Code of Justinian likens the insane person to someone who was absent, asleep, or dead, although the insane did keep their property and their offices. When considering crime, the insane were excused as were children who could not form the requisite intent.
AD 1256	Henry de Bracton writes *On the Laws and Customs of England,* a discussion of the "wild beast test."
AD 1272	Enactment of *Praerogativa Regis* or King's Right in the reign of Edward 1. Established system whereby the king conserved the property of an individual who became insane after birth; however, the property of congenital fools reverted entirely upon the king. Special commissions were held to determine mental status and property rights.
AD 1292	City of Bologna establishes the first expert medical investigatory service in Europe.
AD 1302	One of the first recorded medico-legal autopsies performed in Bologna.
AD 1487	First possible publication date of the *Malleus Maleficarum,* or *Witches Hammer,* written by two Dominican friars as a handbook for witch-hunters.
AD 1648	Wardships such as those established by the *Praerogativa Regis* are transferred to the English Court of Chancery (where they are still heard today).
AD 1664	Sir Thomas Browne testifies in the trial of two women for witchcraft.
AD 1681	Thomas Willis publishes his *Opera Omnia,* which describes various cerebral diseases and a host of psychiatric disorders.
AD 1724	Arnold case.
AD 1736	Publication of Matthew Hale's *History of the Pleas of the Crown.*
AD 1752	Pennsylvania Hospital opens in Philadelphia with one of its expressed intents ministering to those with mental diseases; first hospital of its kind in colonial America.
AD 1760	Trial of Earl Ferrers; first criminal trial in which physician appears as expert witness in English law on issue of mental state.
AD 1800	Hadfield case.
AD 1810	Benjamin Rush delivers a lecture entitled "Lecture on the Medical Jurisprudence of the Mind."
AD 1812	Bellingham case.
	Benjamin Rush writes *Medical Inquiries and Observations on the Diseases of the Mind.*
AD 1838	Isaac Ray writes *A Treatise on the Medical Jurisprudence of Insanity.*
AD 1840	*Oxford* case.
AD 1843	*M'Naghten* case.
AD 1844	First issue of the *American Journal of Insanity.* Founding of the Association of Medical Superintendents of American Institutions for the Insane.
	Commonwealth v. Rogers: first use of irresistible impulse.
AD 1847	Founding of the American Medical Association.
AD 1849	First American treatise on neurology, *An Inquiry Concerning the Diseases and Functions of the Brain and Spinal Cord,* written by Amariah Brigham.
AD 1867	Founding of the New York Medico-Legal Society.
AD 1872	John Ordronaux is appointed first commissioner of lunacy in New York State.
AD 1877	Founding of Massachusetts Medico-Legal Society.
AD 1881	Trial of Charles Guiteau for assassination of President Garfield.
AD 1883	Founding of the Society of Medical Jurisprudence of New York City.
AD 1884	Founding of the Philadelphia Society of Medical Jurisprudence.
AD 1885	Founding of the Rhode Island Medico-Legal Society.
AD 1886	Founding of the Chicago Medico-Legal Society.

(*Continued*)

Appendix 3.1 (*Continued*) Important dates in the history of forensic psychiatry

(Dates BC are approximate)	
AD 1887	*Parsons v. State.*
AD 1890	Founding of the Denver Medico-Legal Society.
AD 1892	AMSAII changes its name to American Medico-Psychological Association.
AD 1897	*Davis v. United States.*
AD 1900	Publication of Sigmund Freud's *Interpretation of Dreams.*
AD 1909	National Conference on Criminal Law and Criminology held at Northwestern University Law School; attorney Edward Keedy forms committee to reform insanity law.
	First psychiatric court clinic established in Chicago at Juvenile Court by William Healy.
AD 1921	American Medico-Psychological Association changes its name to American Psychiatric Association; the *American Journal of Insanity* changes its name to the *American Journal of Psychiatry.*
AD 1925	Karl Menninger as its chairperson submits the first report of the Committee on Legal Aspects of Psychiatry of the American Psychiatric Association.
AD 1933	Founding of American Board of Medical Specialties (at first named Advisory Board for Medical Specialties).
AD 1934	William Alanson White chairs the first section on forensic psychiatry initiated by APA.
AD 1935	Founding of American Board of Psychiatry and Neurology.
AD 1946	William Menninger founds Group for the Advancement of Psychiatry.
AD 1948	Founding of American Academy of Forensic Sciences (as American Medico-legal Congress).
AD 1949	*People v. Wells.*
AD 1952	First Isaac Ray Award presented by the American Psychiatric Association to Winfred Overholser, superintendent of St Elizabeth's Hospital; award is made to an individual who has made outstanding contributions to the field of forensic psychiatry.
AD 1954	*Durham* case: crime a "product" of mental disease or defect (Durham acquitted).
AD 1959	*People v. Gorshen.*
AD 1967	Manfred S. Guttmacher Award established by American Psychiatric Association to honor outstanding contributions to forensic psychiatry; first presented in 1972.
AD 1969	Founding of American Academy of Psychiatry and the Law.
AD 1972	*Brawner* case: Durham Rule abandoned; ALI rule adopted.
AD 1976	Founding of American Board of Forensic Psychiatry.
AD 1982	*Barefoot v. Estelle* (1982) 463 U.S. 880: Supreme Court of the United States found that psychiatrists are competent to testify to the question of future dangerousness of an individual convicted of capital crime and sentenced to die; American Psychiatric Association joined defense as *amicus curiae* in opposing this outcome.
AD 1987	AAPL adopts ethical guidelines.
AD 1988	Accreditation Council on Fellowships in Forensic Psychiatry implements its processes.
AD 1989	First programs accredited by Accreditation Council on Fellowships in Forensic Psychiatry.
AD 1992	The American Board of Psychiatry and Neurology first recognizes forensic psychiatry as an area of subspecialization.
AD 1993	American Board of Psychiatry and Neurology and American Board of Medical Specialties are preparing to formally establish forensic psychiatry as a subspecialty and administer appropriate examinations.
AD 1994	American Board of Psychiatry and Neurology gives its first examinations for added qualifications in forensic psychiatry.
AD 1996	The ACGME establishes standards for accreditation for training in forensic psychiatry.
AD 1997	The ACGME accredits its first fellowships in forensic psychiatry.
	The name for certification in forensic psychiatry was changed by the American Board of Psychiatry and Neurology to certification in the subspecialty of forensic psychiatry.
AD 1999	Last certification examination of forensic psychiatrists who did not graduate from any forensic psychiatry fellowship program.
AD 2001	Last certification examination of forensic psychiatrists who graduated from a non-ACGME approved program in forensic psychiatry.
AD 2003	First recertification examination for those previously certified in forensic psychiatry by the American Board of Psychiatry and Neurology.

REFERENCES

Ackerknecht EH. 1968. *A Short History of Psychiatry.* New York and London: Hafner. (First published in 1959)

Ackerknecht EH. 1976. Midwives as experts in court. *Bulletin of the New York Academy of Medicine* 52(10):1224–1228.

Alexander FG and ST Selesnick. 1966. *The History of Psychiatry: An Evaluation of Psychiatric Thought and Practice from Prehistoric Times to the Present.* New York: Harper and Row.

American Academy of Psychiatry and the Law. *Ethics Guidelines for the Practice of Forensic Psychiatry,* adopted May 2005. http://aapl.org/ethics.htm, accessed March 23, 2015.

American Psychiatric Association. 1984. *Issues in Forensic Psychiatry.* Washington, DC: American Psychiatric Press.

Amundsen DW and GB Ferngren. 1978. The forensic role of physicians in Ptolemaic and Roman Egypt. *Bulletin of the History of Medicine* 52(3):336–353.

Amundsen DW and GB Ferngren. 1979. The forensic role of physicians in Roman law. *Bulletin of the History of Medicine* 53(l):39–56.

Barton WE. 1987. *The History and Influence of the American Psychiatric Association.* Washington, DC: American Psychiatric Press.

Blackstone W. 1979. *Commentaries on the Laws of England.* 4 vols. Chicago: University of Chicago Press. (First published in 1769)

Bracton Hde. 1977. *De Legibus et Consuetudinibus Angliae. On the Laws and Customs of England.* 4 vols., Samuel E. Thorne, trans. Cambridge, MA: Harvard University Press.

Dain N. 1976. From colonial America to bicentennial America: Two centuries of vicissitudes in the institutional care of mental patients. *Bulletin of the New York Academy of Medicine* 52(10):1179–1196.

Deutsch A. 1949. *The Mentally Ill in America. A History of Their Care and Treatment from Colonial Times.* New York: Columbia University Press. (First published in 1937)

Diamond B. 1961. Criminal responsibility of the mentally ill. *Stanford Law Review* 14:59–86.

Diamond B. 1985. Reasonable medical certainty, diagnostic thresholds, and definitions of mental illness in the legal context. *Bulletin of the American Academy of Psychiatry and the Law* 13(2):121–128.

Dietz P. 1978. Forensic and non-forensic psychiatrists: An empirical comparison. *Bulletin of the American Academy of Psychiatry and the Law* VI(l):13–22.

Eigen JP. 1985. Intentionality and insanity: What the eighteenth century juror heard. In *The Anatomy of Madness. Essays in the History of Psychiatry.* Vol 2, edited by WF Bynum, R Porter, and M Shepherd, London and New York: Tavistock Publications, 34–51.

Finch JS. 1950. *Sir Thomas Browne. A Doctor's Life of Science and Faith.* New York: Henry Schuman.

Foucault M. 1972. *The Archeology of Knowledge.* New York: Harper Torchbooks. (First published in 1969)

Gerber SR. 1961. Expert medical testimony and the medical expert. In *Medical Facts for Legal Truth,* edited by O Schroeder, Jr., Cincinnati: W. H. Anderson, 195–212.

Grob GN. 1973. *Mental Institutions in America. Social Policy to 1875.* New York: Free Press.

Hermann DHJ. 1983. *The Insanity Defense. Philosophical, Historical and Legal Perspectives.* Springfield, IL: Charles C Thomas.

Hunter R and I Macalpine. 1963. *Three Hundred Years of Psychiatry. 1535–1860. A History Presented in Selected English Texts.* London: Oxford University Press.

Jackson SW. 1983. Melancholia and partial insanity. *Journal of the History of the Behavioral Sciences* 19:173–184.

Karplus H. 1973. Medical ethics in Paolo Zacchia's Questiones Medico-Legales. In *International Symposium on Society, Medicine and Law,* edited by H Karplus, Jerusalem and Amsterdam: Elsevier, 125–133.

Kelsen H. 1946. *General Theory of Law and State,* Anders Weberg, trans. Cambridge, MA: Harvard University Press. (First published in 1945)

Marx O. 1970. What is the history of psychiatry? *American Journal of Orthopsychiatry* 40(4):593–605.

Mead GH. 1980. *The Philosophy of the Present.* Chicago: University of Chicago Press. (First published in 1932)

Mora G. 1976. 1976 anniversaries. *American Journal of Psychiatry* 133(12):1419–1425.

Mora G, gen. (ed.) 1991. *Witches, Devils and Doctors in the Renaissance. Johann Weyer, De praestigiis daemonum.* Binghamton, NY: Medieval and Renaissance Texts and Studies.

Neugebauer R. 1978. Treatment of the mentally ill in medieval and early modem England: A reappraisal. *Journal of the History of the Behavioral Sciences* 14(2):158–169.

Platt A and BL Diamond. 1965. The origins and development of the wild beast concept of mental illness and its relation to theories of criminal responsibility. *Journal of the History of the Behavioral Sciences* 1(4):355–367.

Platt A and BL Diamond. 1966. The origins of the "right and wrong" test of criminal responsibility and its subsequent development in the United States: An historical survey. *California Law Review* 54(3):1227–1260.

Prosono M. 1990. The Professionalization of Expertise in the Case of Forensic Psychiatry: A Study of Emergence and Quest for Legitimacy. Unpublished dissertation in sociology presented to the graduate division of the University of California, San Francisco.

Quen J. 1968. An historical view of the M'Naghten trial. *Bulletin of the History of Medicine* XLII(l):43–51.

Ray I. 1962. *A Treatise on the Medical Jurisprudence of Insanity.* Cambridge, MA: Harvard University Press. (First published in 1838)

Reik LE. 1953. The Doe-Ray correspondence: A pioneer collaboration in the jurisprudence of mental disease. *Yale Law Review* 63(2):183–196.

Robitscher J. 1972. The new face of legal psychiatry. *American Journal of Psychiatry* 129(3):315–321.

Rosen G. 1968. *Madness in Society: Chapters in the Historical Sociology of Mental Illness*. Chicago and London: University of Chicago Press.

Rosenberg CE. 1968. *The Trial of the Assassin Guiteau: Psychiatry and the Law in the Gilded Age*. Chicago and London: University of Chicago Press.

Ruggiero G. 1982. Excusable murder: Insanity and reason and early Renaissance Venice. *Journal of Social History* 16(l):109–119.

Sandars, TC. 1970. *The Institutes of Justinian: with English Introduction, Translation, and Notes*. Westport, CT: Greenwood Press. (First published in 1922)

Sesto GJ. 1956. *Guardians of the Mentally Ill in Ecclesiastical Trials: A Dissertation*. Washington, DC: Catholic University of America Press.

Simili A. 1973. The beginnings of forensic medicine in Bologna (with two unpublished documents). In *International Symposium on Society, Medicine and Law. Jerusalem, March 1972,* edited by H Karplus, Amsterdam: Elsevier, 91–100.

Smith SS. 1951. The history and development of forensic medicine. *British Medical Journal* 4707:599–607.

Szasz T. 1970. *The Manufacture of Madness*. New York: Dell.

Szasz T. 1974. *The Myth of Mental Illness*. New York: Harper and Row. (First published in 1951)

Tighe JA. 1983. A Question of Responsibility: The Development of American Forensic Psychiatry, 1838–1930. Unpublished dissertation in American civilization presented to the graduate faculties of the University of Pennsylvania.

Van Ommeren RWM. 1961. *Mental Illness Affecting Matrimonial Consent. A Dissertation*. Washington, DC: Catholic University of America Press.

Volk P and HJ Warlo. 1973. The role of medical experts in court proceedings in the medieval town. In *International Symposium on Society, Medicine and Law, Jerusalem,* edited by H Karplus, Amsterdam: Elsevier, 101–116.

Walker N. 1968. *Crime and Insanity in England*. 2 vols., Edinburgh: University Press.

Weinstock R, GB Leong, and J Arturo Silva. 1996. California's diminished capacity defense: Evolution and transformation. *Bulletin of the American Academy of Psychiatry and the Law* 24(3):347–366.

Zilboorg G. 1944. Legal aspects of psychiatry. In *One Hundred Years of American Psychiatry,* edited by JK Hall, G Zilboorg, HA Bunker, New York: Columbia University Press, 507–584.

Zilboorg G. 1967. *A History of Medical Psychology*. New York: Norton. (First published in 1941)

SUGGESTED READING

Eigen JP. 1995. *Witnessing Insanity. Madness and Mad-Doctors in the English Court*. New Haven: Yale University Press.

Foucault M. 1972. *Madness and Civilization. A History of Insanity in the Age of Reason*. New York: Vintage Books. (First published in 1961)

Foucault M. 1979. *Discipline and Punish. The Birth of the Prison*. New York: Vintage Books. (First published in 1975)

Kriegman G, R Gardner, and D Wilfred Abse. (eds.) 1975. *American Psychiatry: Past, Present, and Future*. Charlottesville: University Press of Virginia.

Nemec J. 1969. *International Bibliography of Medicolegal Serials, 1736–1967*. Washington, DC: U.S. Department of Health, Education, and Welfare, Public Health Service, National Institutes of Health, National Library of Medicine.

Rieber RW. (ed.) 1981. *Milestones in the History of Forensic Psychology and Psychiatry: A Book of Readings*. New York: DeCapo Press.

Riese H. (ed.) 1978. *Historical Explorations in Medicine and Psychiatry*. New York: Springer.

Rosner R. (ed.) 1982. *Critical Issues in American Psychiatry and the Law*. Springfield, IL: Charles C Thomas.

Rosner R. (ed.) 1985. *Critical Issues in American Psychiatry and the Law*. vol. 2. New York: Plenum.

4

Forensic psychiatric report writing

MICHAEL A. NORKO AND ALEC BUCHANAN

INTRODUCTION

The written report occupies a focal point in contemporary forensic mental health practice, demonstrating in tangible form the skills and efforts of the expert and providing the most common form of communication of evaluation results to the legal system (Griffith et al. 2010; Norko and Buchanan 2011; Buchanan and Norko 2013). Report writing is important because at stake are the significant interests of the litigants (Wills 2011) as well as the reputation of the evaluator.

The written report appeared in American jurisprudence in the mid-nineteenth century, during a time in which adversarial expert psychiatric testimony was becoming both more commonplace and more suspect (Weiss et al. 2011). Isaac Ray argued in 1873 that the use of written expert opinions allowed the expert to better convey the reasons for his opinions in a logical and coherent manner (Weiss et al. 2011), which remains one of the major objectives of the written report. Attempts in the early twentieth century to legally regulate expert reports were far less successful than the work of professional organizations in improving the quality of reports. The latter includes the efforts of the American Board of Forensic Psychiatry (ABFP) and the American Academy of Psychiatry and the Law (AAPL) to establish guidelines about report preparation, content, and structure (Weiss et al. 2011).

Scholarly contributions over the past 40 years have articulated multiple purposes for the written forensic report: to effectively communicate information, including narrative forms, to legal audiences; to prepare for trial or deposition testimony; to facilitate mental health treatment for an evaluee; to document that the evaluation was conducted properly; and to provide a mechanism for the evaluation and improvement of clinical and forensic practice (Weiss et al. 2011).

Context—Professionalism

Because forensic reports are prepared by mental health professionals, the work of conducting evaluations and documenting them is appropriately contextualized within the realm of professionalism. A proper forensic report is not simply a documented mental health evaluation (Griffith and Baranoski 2007). It requires an appreciation of the complicated interplay of multiple, and often competing, forces in medicine, law, and society (Norko and Buchanan 2011). Three overlapping domains of professionalism are considered here: confidentiality, ethics, and humanism.

CONFIDENTIALITY

The notice given to an evaluee about the limits of confidentiality in a forensic evaluation are based on the distinctions between the professional roles of treater and forensic evaluator, which are most often seen as conflicting roles in contemporary practice (Appelbaum 1997; Strasburger et al. 1997). It is presumed that individuals will ordinarily tend to view members of helping professions as therapeutic agents, when in fact the work of the forensic expert may or may not be helpful to an evaluee. Therefore, forensic evaluators give notice to evaluees at the start of an evaluation about how the therapeutic relationship, with its expected confidentiality, is not applicable to the evaluation at hand (AAPL 2005). Documentation of this notice and the evaluee's comprehension is an expected component of written forensic reports in the United States (see, for example, the report structure adopted by the ABFP in Silva et al. 2003, 34). Although such notice and its documentation can become routinized, the mental health professional must remain cognizant of many subtleties and complexities about confidentiality in forensic practice, including the technicalities and continued vagaries of the Health Insurance Portability and Accountability Act (HIPAA) requirements as they relate to forensic practice (Zonana 2011).

ETHICS

Honesty and striving for objectivity are pillars of the AAPL Ethics Guidelines (AAPL 2005). Scholars have expressed a range of ideas about truth-telling in forensic practice: psychiatrists have no truth to offer in court (Stone 1984); truth-telling has objective and subjective components (Appelbaum

1997); truth-telling requires cultural considerations (Griffith 1998); truth-telling is conveyed through narrative authenticity (Candilis et al. 2001; Griffith 2005); and truth in forensic settings requires a postmodern understanding of subjectivities and various cultural contexts (Martinez and Candilis 2011). Some discussions of forensic ethics have distinguished forensic and clinical practice (Appelbaum 1997; Strasburger et al. 1997), and others have placed forensic ethics within the broader historical perspectives of medical ethics (see Chapter 8; O'Grady 2011; Weinstock 2013) or attempted to reconcile these approaches via the concept of robust professionalism (Martinez and Candilis 2005, 2011). Within this latter approach, Martinez and Candilis have identified four ethics principles to guide forensic report writing: respect for persons; respect for privacy and confidentiality; respect for consent processes; and commitment to honesty and striving for objectivity (Martinez and Candilis 2011, 64–65).

HUMANISM

Resnick and Soliman have described humanity as one of the four principles of good report writing (Resnick and Soliman 2011, 2012). It is important to grasp that forensic reports are not detached, technical descriptions; they are stories about people requiring narrative constructs (Griffith and Baranoski 2007). The challenge is to do justice to the several, and sometimes competing, narrative voices that are part of the circumstances under investigation in a forensic report (Griffith et al. 2011; Buchanan and Norko 2011b, 2013).

Griffith et al. have articulated several reasons for including all relevant expository narratives in a report: doing so allows each person to be heard in the report and demonstrates that the expert considered fully the significant accounts available; it demonstrates respect for persons; and it avoids accusations that reports contradictory to the expert's conclusions were excluded, distinguishing "the ethical expert from the hired gun" (Griffith et al. 2011, 71). Buchanan and Norko have noted the challenges faced by the report writer in navigating and arbitrating the potential tensions and frank inconsistencies among multiple narratives while producing a report that is more clarifying than confounding (Buchanan and Norko 2013).

Respect for persons is a recurring and prominent theme in discussions of the ethics of forensic practice. It is tied to concerns for privacy and confidentiality, informed consent, and narrative authenticity. Respect for persons may sometimes, though, compete with the strict requirements of confidentiality. This occurs, for example, when deciding whether to seek the evaluee's consent to obtain important collateral information from individuals known to the evaluee who do not possess confidential or protected information about the evaluee (Buchanan and Norko 2013). There is no generally agreed solution to this dilemma, requiring report writers to make their own determinations. It may be helpful for the report writer to consider the ideals of compassion (Candilis et al. 2001; Griffith 2005; Norko 2005) and dignity (Buchanan 2014, 2015) in assessing the appropriateness of alternate approaches to the evaluee. The former is "an approach to justice that allows us to attend to and engage the humanity of all the subjects of our evaluations" (Norko 2005, 388), including the multiple aspects of their suffering (Candilis et al. 2001). The latter extends our concern and respect for persons deeper than the boundaries of consent, confidentiality, and autonomy through an established principle of medicine and human rights (Buchanan 2014, 2015).

A related consideration is the demonstration of empathy toward the evaluee. Appelbaum sees an appropriate use of "forensic empathy" in efforts to achieve "awareness of the perspectives and experiences of interviewees" (Appelbaum 2010, 44). Evaluators are cautioned against the use of "reflective empathy" that expresses therapeutic concern for the evaluee, which militates against the notice of the limits of confidentiality given to the evaluee (Shuman 1993, 298; Brodsky and Wilson 2013). Brodsky and Wilson have argued, however, that modest expressions of empathy convey humanity, respect for the person, and a recognition of the evaluee's emotional reality without precluding objectivity (Brodsky and Wilson 2013).

PREPARATION FOR REPORT WRITING

The forensic expert should adopt a consistent and purposeful approach to preparation for writing a report (Wills 2011). In their initial contact with the retaining party, experts must determine whether they possess the requisite knowledge, skills, training, and experience to answer the forensic question at hand (AAPL 2005). The expert must have sufficient time to conduct the evaluation thoroughly, and must be able to meet any jurisdictional requirements for expert testimony (Wills 2011). The expert also needs to consider any potential barriers to ethics concerns such as objectivity, honesty, and respect for persons (Wills 2011; Resnick and Soliman 2012). Wills recommends the use of checklists for these initial determinations (Wills 2011).

Actual report preparation begins with gathering and cataloging the available data and identifying missing data that should be requested or identified in the report as missing if unavailable (Resnick and Soliman 2012). The choice of format for the report will depend on the purpose of the report and its intended audience (Reid 2011). The preparation of an outline sufficiently detailed for the case is a useful next step, with headings and subheadings that are appropriate to the legal questions posed (Resnick and Soliman 2012). The outline of the opinion section is particularly important and should allow the writer to determine the strength of data supporting the opinion and the relative importance of these data elements, data that do not support the conclusion, and whether they suggest revisions to the opinion or concessions to be conveyed and explained (Wills 2008, 2011; Resnick and Soliman 2012). This prioritizing prepares the expert to present the strongest evidence supporting the opinion first, and to reformulate or omit the weakest evidence (Wills 2011; Resnick and Soliman 2012).

REPORT CONTENT

Structure

There is a reasonable consensus in the literature about the important elements to be included in forensic reports, as well as their general order (Griffith et al. 2010), although no single format is required for all forensic reports (Wettstein 2010b). Depending on the level of detail ascribed to each section, report structure can be outlined in as little as three sections (introduction, data, and conclusions) or as many as 11 sections, as was done by the American Board of Forensic Psychiatry in the 1980s (see Silva et al. 2003).

Although the precise structure and headings of the report will vary with the purpose of the report (Reid 2011; Resnick and Soliman 2011), a general outline for the report can be described as follows (Silva et al. 2003; Buchanan and Norko 2011a).

Introductory material includes identification of the agent requesting the evaluation and the person evaluated; the purpose of the evaluation, including the questions to be addressed; the circumstances of the request; sources of information used in the report, including dates and duration of all interviews conducted; the notice of confidentiality given to the evaluee; and a list of any documents appended to the report.

The data section or body of the report includes relevant background information (e.g., social and developmental history, educational and employment history, relationship and sexual history, past psychiatric and medical history, family history, legal history); description of the events in question from the available sources, including the evaluee; mental status examination findings; and findings from psychological and other testing.

The conclusion section contains the evaluator's opinion about the referral questions and the reasoning supporting the conclusions reached. Depending on the type of the report, it may or may not include a formal diagnostic assessment.

Draftsmanship

Resnick and Soliman note four principles for good report writing: clarity, simplicity, brevity, and humanity (Resnick and Soliman 2011, 2012). The last of these has been described above. Clarity consists in "good formatting adequate information, appropriate word choices, good grammar, and clear attribution" (Resnick and Soliman 2012, 415). Their recommendations are outlined in Table 4.1. Attention to these principles is useful in achieving Ackerman's guidance to write "in a manner that increases the likelihood that [the report] will be read in its entirety" (Ackerman 2006, 60).

Common types of reports

CRIMINAL

There are several types of criminal forensic reports, each with its own particular question(s) to be addressed, which informs the structure and content of the report. It is important that the evaluator clearly understand what is required, as the research literature demonstrates that criminal reports commonly address the wrong or extraneous matters (Ciccone and Jones 2011). AAPL Guidelines provide a rich resource for the evaluation of competence to stand trial (Mossman et al. 2007, with guidance regarding the written report on pages S48–S51) and criminal responsibility (AAPL 2014, where the report is discussed on pages S26–S28).

Criminal reports include the following categories:

- Competency—to stand trial, to confess, to represent oneself in court, to be executed
- Criminal responsibility—not guilty by reason of insanity, extreme emotional disturbance, *mens rea*

Table 4.1 Principles of report writing

Clarity	Format report pages for ease of readability
	Make report self-sufficient (provide or summarize all necessary information)
	Identify sources of all information
	Avoid ambiguity
	Use correct verb tense and appropriate word choices
	Clarify inconsistent data
Simplicity	Avoid unnecessary complexity, jargon, formality, multisyllable words, and meaningless introductory phrases
	Use common words
	Describe medications named
	Avoid emphasis such as bold letters, italics, and underlining
	Avoid conclusory words such as "clearly" or "obviously"
Brevity	Plan the report to determine what is necessary
	Omit unnecessary words, sentences, paragraphs, data, and conclusions
	Edit ruthlessly to achieve briefest report that addresses the legal issue
Humanity	Refer to people by their names, not as impersonal nouns such as "defendant"
	Use quotations to give voice to persons interviewed and demonstrate attention to each person's perspective
	Avoid pejorative language

- Dangerousness determination after insanity acquittal—for disposition, locus of care, special management concerns
- Presentence evaluation—presence of mental disorder and need/value of treatment (Ciccone and Jones 2011)

The specific questions to be addressed in these evaluations are described in state and federal law, and the evaluator needs to be familiar with statutory requirements. The contents of reports for federal court are detailed in 18 USC §4247, and there are unique elements in U.S.C. for these various types of evaluation (Johnson et al. 2011).

Each of the above, except the competency evaluations, will generally include a description of the offense (alleged or adjudicated); this description is required in criminal responsibility evaluations. The competency evaluations are generally evaluations of present state of mind and court-relevant functional abilities. Evaluation of competency to confess is an exception, as this is usually conducted retrospectively in response to an attempt to suppress confession evidence. Diagnostic formulations are generally not necessary in competency reports, but a diagnosis will usually be provided as part of the other types of criminal evaluations.

Report writers should avoid including the defendant's account of the offense in the same section as the mental status examination, even though both sets of data are derived from the interviews. The former is historical data, which will also be informed by collateral interviews. The latter describes present findings of the evaluator's formal examination of the evaluee.

In criminal evaluations, malingering must be considered by the evaluator, as the potential for conviction and punishment create external incentives for false presentations by the evaluee. Data and opinion about malingering should be segregated to the appropriate sections of the report.

The conclusion or opinion section of the report will specifically address the legal questions and the evaluator's reasoning in reaching the conclusions. It is here that the report writer explains "to the legal system how the specific manifestations of the mental illness affect or affected the subjects thinking, judgment, and behavior" (Ciccone and Jones 2011, 110).

CIVIL

There are many types of civil forensic evaluations that a forensic mental health professional might conduct (Recupero and Price 2011; AAPL 2015), each with its own special considerations for report writing. These include medical malpractice, psychic harm/trauma, employment-related evaluations (disability, fitness for duty, workers' compensation), civil commitment (including sex offender commitment), psychological autopsy, child custody, and numerous competence evaluations.

In medical malpractice cases, the expert will need to describe the standard of care applicable to the case in order to opine about a breach of the duty owed to the patient. This may require exploration of clinical practice guidelines, academic literature, accreditation and regulatory body standards, different schools of thought about treatment recommendations, common law, case law, and state statute (Meyer et al. 2010; Recupero and Price 2011).

A special element in psychic harm cases is the need to discuss what treatment the evaluee needs, with its projected costs and prognosis. As in malpractice evaluations, an opinion about causation of the injury is an important part of the report. Attention to prior functioning, the presence of personality disorders, and malingering is also vital to these evaluations (Ciccone and Jones 2010; Recupero and Price 2011).

Psychiatric disability reports address different questions depending on the entity requesting the evaluation and the circumstances (e.g., social security, workers' compensation, private insurance). In workers' compensation reports, evaluators need to attend to jurisdiction-specific criteria for disability. The rating of impairment, however, is most often derived from the American Medical Association's *Guides to the Evaluation of Permanent Impairment* (Gold et al. 2008; Granacher 2011). The *Guide* has two chapters relevant to forensic psychiatry—one on brain-based conditions producing impairment, the other on mental and behavioral disorders. Fitness-for-duty evaluations require comparison of the evaluee's function to the specific requirements of the job description, as well as to assessment of alternative causation and pre-existing conditions (Gold 2010). Special considerations are required in reports on professionals' fitness for duty or competence to practice, which may be conducted on behalf of state medical boards, health-care organizations, or a physician responding to investigation (Anfang et al. 2005; Janofsky 2011).

One of the notable distinctions about civil commitment evaluations is that they are often conducted by treating psychiatrists, and this exception is noted in the AAPL Ethical Guidelines (AAPL 2005; Pinals et al. 2011). Another notable exception is that the civil commitment "report" is usually made in the form of a petition or court-provided template, and sometimes is not required in favor of testimony alone. The evaluator generally needs to opine about the presence of mental illness (as defined in the jurisdiction) and the nexus between the illness and the jurisdiction's criteria for civil commitment (usually harm to self or others, or grave disability; Pinals et al. 2011; Pinals and Mossman 2012).

Sex offender commitment reports are a variant of civil commitment reports by virtue of the decisions of the U.S. Supreme Court confirming the civil nature of these proceedings. It is possible, however, to conceptualize these evaluations as criminal in practice, as in the AAPL Practice Guideline on the Forensic Assessment (AAPL 2015). The criteria for commitment addressed in the report will adhere closely to the wording of the relevant statute or case law in the jurisdiction (Pinals et al. 2011).

Child custody reports are very complicated in that they require interviews of each parent (or other caregiver) and each child, and evaluation of the interactions between them. The expert must also document the background histories of each of these individuals, which creates the need for unique organizational structures that help the reader make sense of a large amount of data (Ash 2011, table 12.1). The multiple sources of data present challenges to the report writer in giving voice to the narratives of the various, and often competing, parties, including the child (Steinberg and Fromm 2012). The evaluator makes custody recommendations according to jurisdiction-specific tests, which are usually some variant of "best interests of the child." (See Ash 2011, table 12.2, for a list of factors comprising the evaluation of best interests.) The child custody evaluation is also unusual in that the evaluator often offers a plan for custody and its related contingencies, which when well-crafted may lead to the settlement of highly contested matters (Ash 2011).

Competence reports address questions specific to a particular capacity or task, of which there are many examples (see Recupero and Price 2011, table 9.2). There may be jurisdiction-specific criteria in statute or case law for the various capacity determinations. For some of these, such as guardianship, there may be templates developed by the state for the report structure (Recupero and Price 2011). The American Bar Association and American Psychological Association (ABA and APA 2009) have outlined nine elements of capacity assessments, which should be addressed in competence reports:

1. Legal standard(s) to be applied
2. Functional elements related to the standards
3. Diagnosis(es) related to the functional impairments
4. Cognitive functioning
5. Relevant psychiatric or emotional factors
6. The evaluee's values related to the decisions at hand
7. The risk of the situation at hand
8. Means available to enhance capacity
9. Clinical judgment of capacity

The inclusion of diagnoses may be necessary and appropriate to many civil and criminal reports. The forensic evaluator also needs to bear in mind that describing the phenomenology of the psychological and behavioral circumstances (and the effect of these on the evaluee's functioning as it relates to the legal question) is generally more important for medico-legal purposes than enumerating the diagnoses per se (Allnutt and Chaplow 2000).

SPECIAL ISSUES

Psychological testing

The findings of any psychological testing conducted by a colleague are summarized in the data section of the report. The full report may be appended to the report, or submitted separately by the consulting psychologist. The forensic psychiatrist who is skilled in the administration of some psychological tests or assessment instruments, which has recently been encouraged as a way to strengthen forensic practice (Scott 2013), may do more than summarize the results in the report. The psychiatrist in that situation needs to know the limits of any test employed as well as its psychometric properties (Baranoski 2011). Psychological testing results can be used to identify levels of capacity or dysfunction, clarify diagnoses, assess malingering, buttress the forensic opinion, and identify areas of weakness in an evaluation requiring further data collection or other considerations (Baranoski 2011). Conflicts between the psychological findings and emerging psychiatric opinion need to be resolved before preparation of the report (Baranoski 2011).

Reasonable medical certainty

Although it is common for forensic mental health psychiatrists to offer opinions in written reports and testimony to a reasonable degree of medical certainty, this is a term without a precise definition—either in the law or in psychiatry. The term is commonly used to mean more likely than not, but some courts have required a standard approaching complete certainty (Leong et al. 2011). Jonas Rappeport described it as "that level of certainty which a physician would use in making a similar clinical judgment" (Rappeport 1985, 9). Leong and colleagues have attempted a synthesis of explanation of the term from the views of Seymour Pollack, Bernard Diamond, and Jonas Rappeport: "collection of an adequate database to answer the forensic psychiatric question at issue, considering the validity and reliability of the various data points (including vigilance for data distortion due to malingering, dissimulation, and/or exaggeration of history or symptoms), and arrival at the forensic psychiatric opinion through a reasoning process that includes consideration of alternative hypotheses and the reasons behind the ranking of the opinions considered" (Leong et al. 2011, 232). Report writers are advised to consider what they mean by using this term in any particular case and how they might answer questions about its use in their report. Buchanan and Norko have noted that it remains to be seen whether a consistent definition for this term can be attained. They suggest that the way forward may entail future descriptive research and the efforts of professional organizations to articulate guidelines addressing the level of confidence indicated by the term and the best way of describing it in reports and testimony (Buchanan and Norko 2011b).

Malingering

The *DSM-5* notes that malingering should be "strongly suspected" in any combination of four factors, each of which is commonly encountered in forensic practice: medico-legal context; discrepancy between claimed stress or disability and objective findings; lack of cooperation during a diagnostic evaluation; and antisocial personality disorder (APA 2013, 727). The evaluation of malingering is an important element of many types of criminal and civil forensic reports where the evaluee may be feigning symptoms or dysfunction (Scott and McDermott 2011). Malingering must be differentiated from factitious disorder, conversion disorder, and other somatoform disorders (Scott and McDermott 2011). As noted above, psychological testing can be a useful adjunct to clinical interview and review of records in assessing malingering (Baranoski 2011). Ethics considerations about confidentiality warnings to evaluees when malingering is suspected can present challenges for the accurate collection of data. Scott and McDermott note that evaluators take different approaches to such warnings. They offer the suggestion of advising the evaluee that it is important to answer questions as accurately as possible (Scott and McDermott 2011, 244).

Quality improvement

There is relatively little research available on the quality of forensic reports (Wettstein 2005, 2010a; Goodman-Delahunty and Dhami 2012), but recent efforts in this direction may demonstrate a welcome trend (Robinson and Acklin 2010; Nguyen et al. 2011; Duits et al. 2012; Fuger et al. 2014). Studies generally demonstrate that essential elements are often missing in various types of forensic reports (Wettstein 2005; Robinson and Acklin 2010). Work to improve the quality of forensic reports is challenging, with a major barrier being the need to define the quality of forensic evaluations (Wettstein 2005). Efforts in that direction have involved analysis of content elements of reports against a checklist or evaluation instrument (Witt 2010; Duits et al. 2012). Fuger and colleagues recommend self-monitoring against such checklists as a way to improve the quality of reports (Fuger et al. 2014). The literature is mixed as to whether short-term training improves report quality (Robinson and Acklin 2010). Other methods suggested for improving the quality of forensic reports are peer review, credentialing, system-wide assessments, and feedback from users (Wettstein 2005; Nguyen et al. 2011; Duits et al. 2012; Buchanan et al. 2016).

Research needs

Improvement in forensic report writing is thus an area ripe for empiric research, including the effects of training and professional guidelines on report quality. Further developments in synthesizing professional ethics and the effectiveness of various methods of conveying narratives are also open to future research (Buchanan and Norko 2013). Advances in defining quality in forensic reports will benefit from more sophisticated analysis utilizing information and decision-making theories (Goodman-Delahunty and Dhami 2012). These approaches put our field on notice that not all information in a report will be considered by triers of fact and other decision makers, and that decision makers rely on simple and heuristic strategies that do not entail a rational weighing of all the available information (Goodman-Delahunty and Dhami 2012). The implications of this literature for forensic practice and report writing are profound. Yet there is no existing research on how information representation in forensic reports influences legal decision making. Future study is needed to investigate what information should be included, the placement and emphasis of information, and the optimal length of reports (Goodman-Delahunty and Dhami 2012).

SUMMARY

The care with which an expert prepares a forensic report reflects on the care with which the evaluation was performed and is directly related to the utility and success of the expert's contribution to the legal matter at hand. The evaluator also demonstrates professionalism in the report by attention to confidentiality, ethics, and humanism. Careful preparation for the evaluation and the writing of the report are critical to the quality and effectiveness of the final report. There is general consensus in the literature about the structure and content of various types of reports, although evaluators should exhibit flexibility in tailoring each report to the needs of the individual case. The evaluator reflects knowledge of the appropriate legal questions, standards, and jurisdictional laws in the way in which the report is constructed and the opinions justified. Experts may wish to investigate the use of checklists to improve the quality of their own reports. Many aspects of the effect of the information and the manner in which it is presented in reports upon legal decision making are currently untested empirically, and forensic psychiatrists are encouraged to participate in, and stay abreast of, such future research efforts.

SUMMARY KEY POINTS

- The written report is a central element of forensic practice and its most visible benchmark.
- The report should reveal the highest levels of professionalism in the execution of the work.
- Good reports require thorough evaluation and careful preparation.
- Report structures and content follow generally accepted formats but are tailored to the legal needs of individual cases.
- Quality improvement in report writing involves training, self-monitoring, peer review, professional guideline development and future research.

REFERENCES

Ackerman MJ. 2006. Forensic report writing. *Journal of Clinical Psychology* 62:59–72.

Allnutt SH and D Chaplow. 2000. General principles of forensic report writing. *Australian and New Zealand Journal of Psychiatry* 34:980–987.

American Academy of Psychiatry and the Law (AAPL). 2005. *Ethics Guidelines for the Practice of Forensic Psychiatry*. Bloomfield, CT: AAPL.

American Academy of Psychiatry and the Law (AAPL). 2014. Practice guideline: Forensic psychiatric evaluation of defendants raising the insanity defense. *Journal of the American Academy of Psychiatry and the Law* 42(4 Supplement):S1–S76.

American Academy of Psychiatry and the Law (AAPL). 2015. AAPL practice guideline for the forensic assessment *Journal of the American Academy of Psychiatry and the Law* 43(2 Supplement):S3–S53.

American Bar Association (ABA) and American Psychological Association (APA). 2009. *Assessment of Older Adults with Diminished Capacity: A Handbook for Psychologists*. http://www.apa.org/pi/aging/programs/assessment/capacity-psychologist-handbook.pdf, accessed October 28, 2014.

American Psychiatric Association (APA). 2013. *Diagnostic and Statistical Manual of Mental Disorders*, 5th edition. Arlington, VA: APA.

Anfang SA, LR Faulkner, JA Fromson, and MH Gendel. 2005. The American Psychiatric Association's resource document on guidelines for psychiatric fitness-for-duty evaluations of physicians. *Journal of the American Academy of Psychiatry and the Law* 33:85–88.

Appelbaum KL. 2010. The art of forensic report writing. *Journal of the American Academy of Psychiatry and the Law* 38:43–45.

Appelbaum P. 1997. Ethics in evolution: The incompatibility of clinical and forensic functions. *American Journal of Psychiatry* 154:445–446.

Ash P. 2011. Child custody. In *The Psychiatric Report: Principles and Practice in Forensic Writing*, edited by A Buchanan and M Norko, Cambridge, UK: Cambridge University Press, 158–171.

Baranoski M. 2011. Incorporating psychological testing. In *The Psychiatric Report: Principles and Practice in Forensic Writing*, edited by A Buchanan and M Norko, Cambridge, UK: Cambridge University Press, 201–213.

Brodsky SL and JK Wilson. 2013. Empathy in forensic evaluations: A systematic reconsideration. *Behavioral Sciences and the Law* 31:192–202.

Buchanan A and M Norko. 2011a. Structure and content. In *The Psychiatric Report: Principles and Practice in Forensic Writing*, edited by A Buchanan and M Norko, Cambridge, UK: Cambridge University Press, 93–97.

Buchanan A and M Norko. 2011b. Conclusion. In *The Psychiatric Report: Principles and Practice in Forensic Writing*, edited by A Buchanan and M Norko, Cambridge, UK: Cambridge University Press, 264–269.

Buchanan A and M Norko. 2013. The forensic evaluation and report: An agenda for research. *Journal of the American Academy of Psychiatry and the Law* 41:359–365.

Buchanan A. 2014. Respect of dignity as an ethical principle in forensic psychiatry. Commentary on not just welfare over justice: Ethics in forensic consultation. *Legal and Criminal Psychology* 19:30–32.

Buchanan A. 2015. Respect for dignity and forensic psychiatry. *International Journal of Law and Psychiatry* 4:12–17.

Buchanan A, M Norko, M Baranoski, and H Zonana. 2016. A consultation and supervision model for developing the forensic opinion. *Journal of the American Academy of Psychiatry and the Law* 44, in press.

Candilis PJ, R Martinez, and C Dording. 2001. Principles and narrative in forensic psychiatry: Toward a robust view of professional role. *Journal of the American Academy of Psychiatry and the Law* 29:167–173.

Ciccone JR and J Jones. 2010. Personal injury litigation and forensic psychiatric assessment. In *The American Psychiatric Publishing Textbook of Forensic Psychiatry*, edited by RI Simon and LH Gold, Washington, DC: American Psychiatric Publishing, 261–282.

Ciccone JR and Joshua Jones. 2011. Criminal litigation. In *The Psychiatric Report: Principles and Practice in Forensic Writing*, edited by A Buchanan and M Norko, Cambridge, UK: Cambridge University Press, 98–111.

Duits N, S van der Hoorn, M Wiznitzer, RM Wettstein, and E de Beurs. 2012. Quality improvement of forensic mental health evaluations and reports of youth in the Netherlands. *International Journal of Law and Psychiatry* 35:440–444.

Fuger KD, MW Acklin, AH Nguyen, LA Ignacio, and WN Gowensmith. 2014. Quality of criminal responsibility reports submitted to the Hawaii judiciary. *International Journal of Law and Psychiatry* 37:272–280.

Gold LH, SA Anfang, AM Drukteinis, JL Metzner, M Price, BW Wall, L Wylonis, and HV Zonana. 2008. AAPL practice guideline for the forensic evaluation of psychiatric disability. *Journal of the American Academy of Psychiatry and the Law* 36:S1–S50.

Gold LH. 2010. The workplace. In *The American Psychiatric Publishing Textbook of Forensic Psychiatry*, edited by RI Simon and LH Gold, Washington, DC: American Psychiatric Publishing, 303–334.

Goodman-Delahunty J and MK Dhami. 2012. A forensic examination of court reports. *Australian Psychologist* 48:32–40.

Granacher RP. 2011. Employment: Disability and fitness. In *The Psychiatric Report: Principles and Practice in Forensic Writing*, edited by A Buchanan and M Norko, Cambridge, UK: Cambridge University Press, 172–185.

Griffith EEH. 1998. Ethics in forensic psychiatry: A cultural response to Stone and Appelbaum. *Journal of the American Academy of Psychiatry and the Law* 26:171–184.

Griffith EEH. 2005. Personal narrative and an African-American perspective on medical ethics. *Journal of the American Academy of Psychiatry and the Law* 33:371–381.

Griffith EEH and MV Baranoski. 2007. Commentary: The place of performative writing in forensic psychiatry. *Journal of the American Academy of Psychiatry* 35:27–31.

Griffith EEH, A Stankovic, and M Baranoski. 2010. Conceptualizing the forensic psychiatry report as performative narrative. *Journal of the American Academy of Psychiatry and the Law* 38:32–42.

Griffith, EEH, A Stankovic, and MV Baranoski. 2011. Writing a narrative. In *The Psychiatric Report: Principles and Practice in Forensic Writing,* edited by A Buchanan and M Norko, Cambridge, UK: Cambridge University Press, 68–80.

Janofsky JS. 2011. Competency to practice and licensing. In *The Psychiatric Report: Principles and Practice in Forensic Writing,* edited by A Buchanan and M Norko, Cambridge, UK: Cambridge University Press, 145–157.

Johnson S, E Elbogen, and A Kuroski-Mazzei. 2011. Writing for the US Federal Courts. In *The Psychiatric Report: Principles and Practice in Forensic Writing,* edited by A Buchanan and M Norko, Cambridge, UK: Cambridge University Press, 187–200.

Leong GB, JA Silva, and R Weinstock. 2011. Reasonable medical certainty. In *The Psychiatric Report: Principles and Practice in Forensic Writing,* edited by A Buchanan and M Norko, Cambridge, UK: Cambridge University Press, 214–223.

Martinez R and PJ Candilis. 2005. Commentary: Toward a unified theory of personal and professional ethics. *Journal of the American Academy of Psychiatry and the Law* 33:382–385.

Martinez R and PJ Candilis. 2011. Ethics. In *The Psychiatric Report: Principles and Practice in Forensic Writing,* edited by A Buchanan and M Norko, Cambridge, UK: Cambridge University Press, 56–67.

Meyer DJ, RI Simon, and DW Shuman. 2010. Professional liability in psychiatric practice and requisite standards of care. In *The American Psychiatric Publishing Textbook of Forensic Psychiatry,* edited by RI Simon and LH Gold, Washington, DC: American Psychiatric Publishing, 207–226.

Mossman D, SG Noffsinger, P Ash et al. 2007. AAPL practice guideline for the forensic psychiatric evaluation of competence to stand trial. *Journal of the American Academy of Psychiatry and the Law* 35:S3–S72.

Norko MA. 2005. Commentary: Compassion at the core of forensic ethics. *Journal of the American Academy of Psychiatry and the Law* 33:386–389.

Norko MA and A Buchanan. 2011 Introduction. In *The Psychiatric Report: Principles and Practice in Forensic Writing,* edited by A Buchanan and M Norko, Cambridge, UK: Cambridge University Press, 1–9.

Nguyen AH, Mw Acklin, K Fuger, WN Gowensmith, and LA Ignacio. 2011. Freedom in paradise; quality of conditional release reports submitted to the Hawaii judiciary. *International Journal of Law and Psychiatry* 34:341–348.

O'Grady J. 2011. Psychiatry and ethics in UK criminal sentencing. In *The Psychiatric Report: Principles and Practice in Forensic Writing,* edited by A Buchanan and M Norko, Cambridge, UK: Cambridge University Press, 254–263.

Pinals DA, GD Glancy, and L-W Grace Lee. 2011. Civil and sex-offender commitment. In *The Psychiatric Report: Principles and Practice in Forensic Writing,* edited by Alec Buchanan and Michael Norko, Cambridge, UK: Cambridge University Press, 128–144.

Pinals DA and D Mossman. 2012. *Evaluation for Civil Commitment. Report Writing and Testimony.* Oxford: Oxford University Press, 175–203.

Rappeport JR. 1985. Reasonable medical certainty. *Bulletin of the American Academy of Psychiatry and the Law* 13:5–15.

Recupero PR and M Price. 2011. Civil litigation. In *The Psychiatric Report: Principles and Practice in Forensic Writing,* edited by A Buchanan and M Norko, Cambridge, UK: Cambridge University Press, 112–127.

Reid WH. 2011. Writing reports for lawyers and courts. *Journal of Psychiatric Practice* 17:355–359.

Resnick PJ and S Soliman. 2011. Draftsmanship. In *The Psychiatric Report: Principles and Practice in Forensic Writing,* edited by A Buchanan and M Norko, Cambridge, UK: Cambridge University Press, 81–92.

Resnick PJ and S Soliman. 2012. Planning, writing, and editing forensic psychiatric reports. *International Journal of Law and Psychiatry* 35:412–417.

Robinson R and MW Acklin. 2010. Fitness in paradise; quality of forensic reports submitted to the Hawaii judiciary. *International Journal of Law and Psychiatry* 33:131–137.

Scott C and B McDermott. 2011. Malingering. In *The Psychiatric Report: Principles and Practice in Forensic Writing,* edited by A Buchanan and M Norko, Cambridge, UK: Cambridge University Press, 240–253.

Scott C. 2013. Believing doesn't make it so: Forensic education and the search for truth. *Journal of the American Academy of Psychiatry and the Law* 41:18–32.

Shuman DW. 1993. The use of empathy in forensic examinations. *Ethics and Behavior* 3:289–302.

Silva JA, R Weinstock, and GB. Leong. 2003. Forensic psychiatric report writing. In *Principles and Practice of Forensic Psychiatry,* 2nd edition, edited by R. Rosner, London: Arnold, 31–36.

Steinberg A and L Fromm. 2012. The use of narrative and persuasion in the child forensic psychiatric report and testimony. *Journal of Psychiatry and Law* 40:23–41.

Stone AA. 1984. The ethical boundaries of forensic psychiatry: A view from the ivory tower. *Bulletin of the American Academy of Psychiatry and the Law* 12:209–219.

Strasburger LH, TG Gutheil, and A Brodsky. 1997. On wearing two hats; role conflict in serving as both psychotherapist and expert witness. *American Journal of Psychiatry* 154:448–456.

Weinstock R. 2013. The forensic report—An inevitable nexus for resolving ethics dilemmas. *Journal of the American Academy of Psychiatry and the Law* 41:366–373.

Weiss KJ, RM Wettstein, RL Sadoff, JA Silva, and MA Norko. 2011. In *The Psychiatric Report: Principles and Practice in Forensic Writing*, edited by A Buchanan and M Norko, Cambridge, UK: Cambridge University Press, 11–21.

Wettstein RM. 2005. Quality and quality improvement in forensic mental health evaluations. *Journal of the American Academy of Psychiatry and the Law* 33:158–175.

Wettstein RM. 2010a. Conceptualizing the forensic psychiatry report. *Journal of the American Academy of Psychiatry and the Law* 38:46–48.

Wettstein RM. 2010b. The forensic examination and report. In *The American Psychiatric Publishing Textbook of Forensic Psychiatry*, 2nd edition, edited by RI Simon and LH Gold, Washington, DC: American Psychiatric Publishing, 175–203.

Wills C. 2008. The CHESS method of forensic opinion formulation; striving to checkmate bias. *Journal of the American Academy of Psychiatry and the Law* 36:535–540.

Wills C. 2011. Preparation. In *The Psychiatric Report: Principles and Practice in Forensic Writing*, edited by A Buchanan and M Norko, Cambridge, UK: Cambridge University Press, 22–34.

Witt P.H. 2010. Forensic report checklist. *Open Access Journal of Forensic Psychology* 2:233–240. http://www.oajfp.com/#!blank-8/wu9om, accessed June 29, 2016.

Zonana H. 2011. Confidentiality and record keeping. In *The Psychiatric Report: Principles and Practice in Forensic Writing*, edited by A Buchanan and M Norko Cambridge, UK: Cambridge University Press, 35–55.

5

Guidelines for courtroom testimony

PHILLIP J. RESNICK AND JENNIFER L. PIEL

INTRODUCTION

The role of the expert witness is to educate the court about matters that are beyond the layperson's understanding. A key role for forensic psychiatrists is to provide expert testimony at depositions, trials, hearings, and administrative proceedings. Medical and mental health specialists are the most common category of experts to testify in federal civil trials, making up more than 40 percent of experts (Kafka et al. 2002). Psychiatrists make up nearly 4 percent of testifying experts in civil cases, more than any other specialty, except surgeons. Similarly, in criminal trials, psychiatrists have a vital role in a variety of evaluations such as competency to stand trial and criminal responsibility. In *Ake v. Oklahoma* (1985, 83), the U.S. Supreme Court discussed the "pivotal role" that psychiatry has come to play in criminal proceedings: "to conduct a professional examination on issues relevant to the defense, help to determine whether the insanity defense is viable, to present testimony, and to assist in preparing the cross-examination of the state's psychiatric witness."

TYPES OF WITNESS

All psychiatrists have expertise in the field of psychiatry, but the mere act of testifying does not mean the psychiatrist is an expert witness. There are two types of witnesses: fact (percipient) and expert. *Fact witnesses* state their direct observations. For example, a psychiatrist who saw a patient for psychological symptoms after an automobile accident might be asked to testify about the presenting complaints, number of visits, and any medications prescribed. A psychiatrist is not ordinarily asked to give opinions when serving as a fact witness. In a small minority of jurisdictions, however, the court may ask a treating psychiatrist to state an opinion. The psychiatrist should then be qualified as an expert witness and may seek an expert witness fee from the party who sought the opinion (Hirsch 1975). The opinions of treating psychiatrists may be given high credibility by the court because they are not the views of hired witnesses.

Expert witnesses have "special knowledge" of the subject on which testimony is to be given. The knowledge must be viewed as not normally possessed by the average person and beyond direct observation. Experts may express opinions that have legal significance, such as causation for a litigant's psychological harm or mental skills required to be competent to stand trial. In practice, psychiatric expert witnesses may function to make the judge aware of the facts, as well as their conclusions about symptoms, causation, and prognosis.

TRUTH, ADVOCACY, AND ETHICS

In the United States and England, trials are conducted within the adversary model—that is, the attorneys are advocates of the causes they represent. Despite the adversarial nature of the legal process, testifying psychiatric experts should resist acting as an advocate for a party to the case (American Academy of Psychiatry and the Law 2005). Two models have been proposed regarding the role of advocacy from testifying experts: the advocate for truth model and the honest advocate model (Gutheil 2009). In an *advocate-for-truth model*, the expert strives for objectivity and absolute truth in delivering testimony. In the *honest-advocate model*, the expert may be a persuasive advocate after coming to his or her opinion, but remain truthful in delivery of information. In contrast, a consulting (nontestifying) expert may assist legal counsel with the preparation of their case (Martindale and Gould 2011).

It is a fallacy to assume that a psychiatric witness can be completely impartial. Regardless of whether one is employed by the court or by an attorney, the psychiatrist usually starts out with an impartial attitude. Once experts form an opinion, however, it is only human for them to identify themselves with that opinion and to hope for the success of the side that supports their conclusions (Diamond 1959; Candilis et al. 2007). Experts may advocate for their opinions. However, once on the witness stand, experts must do their best to impartially preserve the truth and their professional integrity. Relevant information may not be kept secret (Candilis et al. 2007).

Blatant advocacy is easily recognized and reduces the credibility of the expert witness; subtle advocacy or bias (which could include unconscious bias) is the more difficult problem (Goldyne 2007). Zusman and Simon (1983) reviewed examinations of plaintiffs about psychological damage resulting from the 1972 collapse of the Buffalo Creek dam. They attributed differences in psychiatric opinions to the interview settings, the examiners' training and orientation, and identification with the attorneys who employed them. Psychiatrists must guard against any sense of loyalty to the retaining attorney that would cause them to shift their thinking from that of an objective expert witness to that of an advocate (Gutheil and Simon 2004).

A psychiatrist's diagnoses and conclusions regarding legal issues are considered only as opinions. Juries are instructed to decide for themselves how much weight to give the testimony of each witness. Even when it is uncontradicted, the jury has the right to disregard psychiatric opinion evidence. The trier of fact makes the ultimate decisions about disputed issues, such as criminal responsibility or liability for malpractice.

The expert should not go beyond the available data or the scholarly foundations of his or her testimony (Gutheil 2009). Ethical psychiatric experts can enhance their credibility by appropriately acknowledging facts of the case which are unfavorable to their opinion, the limitations of their opinion, and hypothetical situations under which their opinion would be different.

PREPARATION FOR TESTIMONY

When approached to form an opinion for a legal case, psychiatrists should request the specific legal issue and legal standard in writing by the attorney. In a criminal case, the attorney, for example, may wish an opinion about competency to stand trial, sanity at the time of the act, or psychiatric factors for mitigation of the penalty. Legal standards vary by jurisdiction. Before accepting any legal referral, psychiatrists should be certain that there is no actual conflict of interest or even an appearance of conflict of interest. Fees should also be clearly understood.

Before beginning an evaluation for legal purposes, the psychiatrist has an absolute obligation to inform the evaluee about any limitations of confidentiality and to specify those persons who will receive copies of any report. Psychiatrist–patient confidentiality by treating psychiatrists may or may not be respected in court. A treating psychiatrist may request an opportunity to explain to the judge in chambers why certain information may be irrelevant to the issue at hand and should remain confidential. The judge, however, is the final decision maker. The psychiatrist who complies with a judge's direction to reveal information is immune from criminal and civil liability. Should the psychiatrist fail to comply, the psychiatrist may be held in contempt of court.

DEPOSITIONS

A deposition is a sworn oral statement for legal purposes, usually taken outside of court. Depositions are of two types: evidence and discovery. *Evidence depositions* are taken to preserve testimony in the event that a witness will not be available at the trial. This type of deposition adheres to the usual trial procedures of direct and cross-examination, and is often videotaped for viewing at the trial. In a videotaped deposition, the psychiatrist should think of the camera as a friend. Each question and answer should be treated as a separate item because the deposition may be edited before it is shown at trial. Turning away from the camera is glaringly obvious on videotape.

Discovery depositions are designed to gather information prior to trials. Almost all questions are asked by opposing counsel. This type of deposition plays an important role in civil litigation. The psychiatric expert should thoroughly prepare for a discovery deposition because it is likely to have a significant impact on settlement negotiations. Over 90% of cases settle before trial.

During a discovery deposition, the attorney's goals are to learn the facts and opinions of the opposing witness, assess strengths and weaknesses, and gather ammunition for cross-examination at trial. The attorney may ask broad questions to encourage rambling answers that might reveal new facts. The expert witness should not volunteer any information not called for in the questions. The psychiatric expert should listen carefully to each question asked during the deposition. It is helpful to pause for a moment after the question is asked to give it careful consideration, and to allow time for other attorneys to object (Gutheil 2009). The expert witness should request the written record or audio or video recording of the deposition for future review and planning of trial testimony. One's deposition should be reviewed prior to trial to refresh the expert's memory. Attorneys often seek to impeach the expert's credibility by showing differences between deposition and trial testimony.

COURT TESTIMONY

Psychiatric expert witnesses first undergo direct examination by the attorney who called them. This consists of nonleading questions to obtain the witness's opinions and reasoning without interference.

Cross-examination is conducted by the adversary attorney to test the credibility of the testimony. Redirect examination—sometimes called rehabilitation—allows the retaining attorney to repair damage and clarify points from cross-examination. Re-cross-examination is limited to issues raised in the redirect examination.

DIRECT EXAMINATION

Qualifications

At the beginning of the direct examination, the credentials of the expert are elicited. The retaining attorney asks questions to demonstrate the witness's credibility and to qualify the witness as an expert. Ordinarily, any licensed physician will be recognized as an expert witness. Qualifications should include schools attended, internship, residency training, academic titles, hospital affiliations, board certifications, and honors. The expert's publications that are especially relevant to the case at hand should be mentioned. It is preferable to have the attorney elicit these qualifications through several questions to avoid the appearance of immodesty (Usdin 1977). After eliciting the expert's qualifications, the attorney proffers the witness as an expert. The opposing attorney may accept the witness's qualifications; alternatively, the opposing counsel may challenge the witness's background or methodologies for his or her opinion in a process called *voir dire* ("to speak the truth"). Ultimately, the judge decides whether the witness may testify as an expert.

Credibility

It is critical for the expert witness to establish credibility with the jury. Credibility may be divided into three components: (1) expertise, including the witness's credentials, training, and experience; (2) trustworthiness, including sincerity, the appearance of objectivity, and lack of partisanship; and (3) dynamism—that is, the style of delivery during testimony (Bank and Poythress 1982).

Trustworthiness may be more important than credentials in achieving credibility (Appelbaum and Anatol 1974). People judge one another on the basis of traits that may have no relation to actual trustworthiness, such as physical characteristics (Spellman and Teeney 2010). Wearing conservative executive-style clothing increases the psychiatrist's credibility in court. Male psychiatrists should wear dark suits. Solid colors enhance credibility, whereas pinstripes confer greater authority (Malloy 1988). Female psychiatrists appear most credible if they wear solid-colored suits with skirts that fall below the knee. Conservative dresses with contrasting blazers are also effective (Malloy 1996). Both male and female witnesses should avoid jewelry or anything ostentatious. Local customs should be considered in making decisions about what to wear to court.

The expert witness's style of speech has considerable impact on the expert's credibility (Lubet and Boals 2009). In controlled studies of mock testimony, *powerful* speech was found to be more convincing and credible than *powerless* speech (Conley et al. 1978). Powerful speakers are straightforward and give more one-word answers than powerless speakers. Used by persons with low power and status vis-à-vis the court, powerless speech tends to make more frequent use of the following (Erickson et al. 1978):

1. Intensifiers (so, very, surely): I surely did.
2. Hedges (kind of, I think, I guess).
3. Especially formal grammar.
4. Hesitation forms (uh, well, you know).
5. Gestures (using the hands to point while saying "over there").
6. Questioning forms (rising, question intonation in declarative contexts).
7. Excessive politeness (please, thank you, sir).

Opinion with reasonable medical certainty

After listing their qualifications, experts are next asked to describe their clinical examination and the background materials that were reviewed. It is most efficient if the witness can refer to the first page of their report for the exact dates and length of examinations and a complete list of documents reviewed.

Witnesses are then asked whether they have formed an opinion regarding the contested issue. Psychiatrists should render their opinions to a reasonable degree of medical certainty (Leong et al. 2011). The exact definition of "reasonable medical certainty" varies from one jurisdiction to another (Miller 2006). In most states, it simply means more probable than not. Psychiatrists should ask the retaining attorney to explain the exact meaning of the phrase in a particular case if they are not certain.

In law, there is a distinction between the words *possibility* and *probability.* The law considers anything possible. However, something is not probable unless it is more likely than not. In other words, when mathematically expressed, its chances are 51% or greater (Hirsch et al. 1979). The expert should be aware that "reasonable certainty" is simply the minimum level of confidence required to express an opinion in court. It is possible for the expert who is more confident to say so (Lubet and Boals 2009).

When experts are asked whether they have formed an opinion with reasonable medical certainty, they should reply with only a "yes" or a "no." According to courtroom ritual, the witness may not offer an actual opinion until asked. The witness is then asked to explain the basis for the opinion—that is, the underlying data and step-by-step logic used to reach the conclusion. Narrative direct testimony has been found to be effective in conveying information to the trier of fact (Commons et al. 2010). The presentation should be punctuated by some questions, however, since prolonged, uninterrupted narrative may become tiresome.

Hypothetical questions

Hypothetical questions may be put to the expert witness on direct or cross-examination. Traditionally, an expert could express an opinion only if it were based on personal knowledge, a hypothetical, or a combination of these. Accordingly, attorneys used hypothetical questions to focus the jury to the key facts that supported the expert's opinion. Hypothetical questions permit the jury to know the premises that underlie the expert's opinion, enabling proper evaluation of its weight.

The modern approach, including the Federal Rules of Evidence (703, 704), has liberalized the sources of information that experts may rely upon in formulating their opinion. It is not improper for an expert witness to give an opinion without having performed a personal examination. However, the psychiatrist must have made an effort to perform a personal examination when appropriate based on the nature of the case. Both in the psychiatric report and on the witness stand, experts should state that their conclusions are limited because of the inability to perform a clinical psychiatric evaluation. The only limitation on the supporting data used by experts is that it be the type reasonably relied on by experts in forming opinions.

Hypothetical questions are used by retaining attorneys to elicit information or predictions based on underlying interpretations of facts. During cross-examination, hypothetical questions may introduce evidence that was previously unavailable to the expert witness. The appearance of a closed mind about new data suggests partisanship. One fair answer is, "I would need to re-evaluate the subject based on the new information." Opposing counsel may use hypothetical questions to make the expert assume facts that are incongruent with their conclusions or opinions (Brodsky et al. 2012). Although theoretically sound, in practice hypothetical questions often prove cumbersome and confusing to juries. The record for length was set in a 1907 Massachusetts "will" contest with a 20,000-word hypothetical question that took several hours to read. The answer was, "I don't know" (MacDonald 1976).

Suggestions regarding direct examination

During the pretrial conference, the attorney and the expert witness should plan to explicate those issues on direct examination that are most likely to be attacked during cross-examination. This provides an opportunity to fully explain problematic areas to the jury, without the constraints of cross-examination. In any event, redirect examination should allow the expert witness to explain issues that were cut short during cross-examination.

Answers to specific questions should be relatively short, clear, and stated in simple language. If answers are overqualified, boredom can cause the jury to lose interest. Generally speaking, the "homier" the analogy, the better it is. While attempting to stay within these guidelines, expert witnesses must still behave naturally for their own personalities. A stilted performance will detract from the witness's appearance of sincerity.

Psychiatrists should use demonstrative evidence if possible. Demonstrative evidence should be distinguished from substantive evidence, which include objects or materials that played a role in the incident at issue (e.g., murder weapon, x-ray). Demonstrative evidence may be referenced by the expert without formal admission into evidence. However, legal counsel may proffer it as part of the witness's testimony so that it can be taken into the jury deliberation room. Visual aids useful to psychiatrists may include charts or graphs, lists of key points of the expert's opinion, and video recordings. A graph showing a decrement in IQ, for example, may facilitate the jury's understanding of the seriousness of a head injury.

Expert witnesses should ordinarily look at the jury and direct their remarks to them. Eye contact will help the psychiatrist assess the jury's understanding of what the expert is saying and enhance the expert's credibility. The expert witness should never talk down to jurors—if jurors feel patronized, they will not accept what the witness is saying.

The expert witness must not become, or even appear to become, an adversary. The appearance of impartiality is best achieved when the witness treats both lawyers (on direct and cross-examination) with the same professional courtesy and distance (Curran et al. 1980).

Psychiatrists should not use professional jargon in court because it is likely to be misunderstood, not understood, or made to look ridiculous. It is preferable to use equivalent words, such as mood for affect, even if they are not perfect synonyms. Emerson observed that "eloquence is the power to translate a truth into language perfectly intelligible to the person to whom you speak" (Emerson 1876).

The following example of psychiatric testimony contains jargon: "The patient showed marked psychomotor retardation and considerable inhibition of speech. Some ideas of reference were implied, although no frank delusion formation was evident." This could be expressed in lay language as follows: "His movements were slow and his voice was low and monotonous. He spoke little and volunteered nothing. He felt that certain people were referring to him when they spoke with each other privately, but he did not show any clear-cut delusions about this—just vague ideas that he was the subject of other people's conversations" (Davidson 1965).

Nothing alienates a jury more quickly than a psychiatric expert witness who appears arrogant. An attorney may ask expert witnesses whether they have ever been wrong; experts should reply "yes," assuming it is true. While testifying, witnesses should attempt to display dignity, confidence, and humility.

Ordinarily, the expert witness should not attempt to be humorous; a trial is a serious matter. Self-deprecating humor is the safest type. An extremely experienced witness may attempt to use humor as a way of coping with an overzealous cross-examiner, but this is certainly not recommended for the novice.

The expert witness's answers should not go beyond the questions in direct or cross-examination. Volunteering additional information may open up new areas for cross-examination, which could be highly damaging. Similarly, psychiatric expert witnesses should be familiar with the ultimate issue rule. Historically, courts limited experts from testifying as to the ultimate issue, or the specific question that is before the trier of fact. This has largely been rejected for most types of expert testimony in Federal Rule of Evidence 704. Under Rule 704(b), however, an expert may not testify in federal court to the ultimate issue when a criminal defendant claims a mental state defense. Many state courts do allow testimony on ultimate issues related to mental state or culpability.

It is usually best for psychiatric expert witnesses not to volunteer their theoretical orientation. A theoretical school can easily be attacked on cross-examination.

Expert witnesses should not say that they have an impression, feeling, or speculation (Boccaccini 2002). If the psychiatrist believes that something is more probable than not, the same information can be communicated by calling it a professional opinion.

The expert witness should never mention the presence of a defendant's insurance company in a civil trial. In most jurisdictions, this is viewed as prejudicial because it may encourage the jury to increase the amount of money awarded to the plaintiff. Consequently, mention of an insurance company could lead to a mistrial.

Whether expert witnesses should mention counterarguments to their own position during direct examination is open to controversy. The opposing attorney will be more than happy to raise negative points during cross-examination. One approach is to directly address the counterarguments or negative points. This highlights the expert's fairness and allows the retaining attorney to present the information in the light most favorable to the attorney's client. If no rebuttal is expected, persuasive impact is reduced by bringing up counterarguments. This may, however, raise ethical issues about whether the witness is then "telling the whole truth."

Table 5.1 Common areas of cross examination

1. Qualifications
2. Compensation
3. Hired gun
4. Professional reputation
5. Professional/philosophical bias
   - Types of cases in expert role
   - Views on treatment versus punishment
   - Views on crime and punishment
6. Personal bias
   - Victim of crime
   - Relationship with attorney
   - Relationship with litigant
   - Race/culture/gender
7. Knowledge of relevant facts
8. Knowledge of relevant legal standard
9. Knowledge of relevant literature
10. Methods used in forming opinion
11. Inconsistencies
    - Internal inconsistencies from the witness
    - Inconsistencies with other documents/testimony
12. Soundness of opinion
13. Skeletons in the closet

CROSS-EXAMINATION

Areas of attack

Cross-examination is the questioning of a witness by a party other than the one who called the witness. Cross-examination is limited to the scope of testimony from direct examination, but this may be liberally construed. The purpose of cross-examination is either to discredit or clarify testimony already given.

The cross-examiner may seek to discredit adversary testimony by showing the witness to be a fool, a liar, and a nitwit. The goal of cross-examination is not to convince witnesses of their errors, but to point out a case's weakness that might not be evident to the trier of fact.

The cross-examiner may seek to attack the expert witness in the following areas: *credentials*, *bias*, *adequacy*, and *validity* (Table 5.1). The credentials of an expert witness may be attacked by showing a lack of experience or education. A cross-examining attorney may bring out the fact that an opposing expert witness has not achieved board certification or has required more than one attempt to do so.

The amount of testimonial experience may also be used to discredit an expert. The cross-examiner may imply that the witness is inexperienced and unknowledgeable because of limited testimonial experience. Conversely, if a witness does have substantial testimonial experience, the cross-examiner may try to show the witness to be a professional "hired gun." If the witness is asked whether or not he or she is a professional witness, one good answer is, "my profession is the practice of psychiatry. It just so happens that I am frequently asked to testify on psychiatric issues."

Bias in the expert witness may be demonstrated by showing a history of having always been employed by one side. The appearance of bias or personal interest is decreased when witnesses are able to say that they have testified on behalf of both prosecution and defense, or have testified on behalf of both plaintiffs and defendants in civil cases. A cross-examining attorney may also attempt to show bias by questioning about fees or pretrial conferences. The expert should not try to avoid answering these questions. If asked how much one has been paid for one's testimony, the expert may reply, "I'm not being paid for my testimony. I'm been paid for my time, like the other professional people in the courtroom." Similarly, the expert should not feel embarrassed about admitting to having a pretrial conference with an attorney, because this is necessary to prepare for testimony.

The psychiatrist's examination may be attacked as being inadequate. Issues such as examination length, privacy, or obtaining corroborating information may be questioned. A brief examination may be portrayed as being inadequate to "fully understand" a complex matter. A cross-examiner may attempt to demonstrate inconsistencies between police accounts and the defendant's account given to the psychiatrist. Marked inconsistencies may make the psychiatrist look gullible and make the defendant look guilty. A cross-examiner may seek to demean the psychiatric examination by asking, "Do you mean to say that all you did was talk to the plaintiff?" A good response is to say that psychiatrists have special training in evaluating mood, thought organization, and speech patterns of persons with mental illness. The routine mental status examination may be described as a series of tests to assess such items as memory, concentration, abstract thinking, and judgment.

The validity and reliability of all clinical examinations may be attacked. Faust (2011) described the limited reliability of psychiatric examinations. Research demonstrated that different theoretical backgrounds predispose psychiatrists to reach different conclusions based on the same data. There is no scientific evidence indicating the validity of a retrospective diagnosis. Attempts should not be made to defend the science of psychiatry; rather, the expert should state that he or she is confident of his or her opinion in this particular case. The cross-examiner may point out inconsistencies within an expert's report, between the expert's current testimony and previous testimony, and between testimony and published articles. Experts should be aware that attorneys may search the Web or subscription Internet databases for an expert's professional biography, publications, and even prior testimony (Coggins 2005).

Psychiatric expert witnesses should be aware that transference feelings toward cross-examiners, opposing experts, or judges may diminish the effectiveness of their testimony. The primary danger is overadvocacy. If a witness becomes partisan, the witness is likely to become overextended, emotional, and defensive, thereby losing credibility.

Types of cross-examiners

The expert witness should be prepared to encounter three particular types of cross-examiners (Bromberg 1969). The first is the "country" lawyer who claims to know nothing. He or she stumbles over technical words, and seeks to oversimplify human actions and reduce the psychiatrist's explanations to meaningless gobbledygook for the jury. A good response for the psychiatrist is to "one down" the attorney. For example, the psychiatrist might say, "I understand what you mean about big words; I often have difficulty understanding legal terms." This gambit places the expert witness back on the same level as the jury.

The second type of cross-examiner is the "unctuous" lawyer who is excessively polite. He or she apologizes for taking up the doctor's valuable time and refers to the witness as a "man of science." By concealing certain information, such a cross-examiner may proceed to set the psychiatrist up for a devastating blow toward the end of his or her testimony. Thus, it is particularly important for the experts not to let their guard down when the cross-examiner is especially friendly or flattering.

Finally, the "blustery" cross-examiner works toward immediate destruction of credibility and attempts to bully the witness by making reference to the psychiatrist's fee and loyalty to the retaining attorney. By remaining calm, the expert's polite demeanour will look favorable to the jury.

Suggestions regarding cross-examination

An expert witness should never be a smart aleck or argue with a cross-examiner. The jury will ordinarily identify with the witness; but if the witness acts smart, the jury will take the side of the cross-examiner in the belief that he or she is just doing his or her job.

Psychiatrists should not be defensive during cross-examination. Witnesses need not be apologetic if cross-examiners do not agree with their opinions. It gives the cross-examiner a distinct advantage when witnesses lose their temper because it makes any witness look overinvolved to the jury.

The expert witness should never guess at an answer; it is better to say that one either does not know or does not remember. An expert witness is not expected to have a quick, knowledgeable reply to every question.

During cross-examination, the expert should graciously concede points and admit the obvious. For example, when asked, "Dr., isn't it possible…," the expert should reply, "Of course it is possible." However, the expert may then go on to point out why it is unlikely. Refusing to concede an obvious point causes the expert to look either foolish or hostile. After the expert's testimony has concluded, and neither attorney has any further questions, the judge will dismiss the expert. The psychiatric expert should then leave the courtroom. The expert should not stop to consult with the retaining attorney, or linger to see the remainder of the trial. These activities suggest too much interest in the final outcome of the trial (Gutheil 2009).

The psychiatric witness should be aware that any files that are taken to the stand may be scrutinized by the cross-examining attorney; the witness may even request a recess to review them in detail. Consequently, if the psychiatrist does not wish to be cross-examined on certain information, it should not be taken to the witness stand.

The expert witness should be wary of acknowledging any book as an authority (Imwinkelried 2012). Once a book is acknowledged, the witness may be cross-examined on all of its contents. Instead, the psychiatrist might indicate that his or her knowledge comes from many sources, including training and experience, rather than any single textbook. Before responding to any question about a quote, the expert witness should insist on seeing it in context.

The cross-examiner may ask the expert witness's opinion of opposing expert witnesses. It is unbecoming to engage in personal attacks, even if one has a low opinion of an opposing witness. It is better for experts to simply state whether they disagree with the opposing expert on this occasion.

CONTROL IN THE COURTROOM

A good cross-examiner will seek to control the witness. However, there are several ways in which the witness can exert some control during cross-examination.

The witness may pause before answering a question, which serves to break the rhythm of the cross-examiner's questioning (Boccaccini 2002). It also allows the retaining attorney time to make an objection. The witness may further disrupt the flow of a cross-examiner's attack by refraining from answering any question that includes a minor error.

The expert witness should take opportunities to break eye contact with the cross-examining attorney in order to direct answers toward the jury. This serves to further establish the expert's role as an educator, as opposed to someone who is merely being questioned. The experienced expert may use cross-examination as an opportunity to reiterate opinions given during direct examination.

The expert should try to give full opinions during cross-examination. If interrupted, the expert should attempt to complete his or her answer. When the cross-examiner attempts to limit answers, the jury is given the impression that the attorney is trying to conceal something. When the expert is cut off before completing an answer, it should serve as a signal to the retaining attorney to explicate that area on redirect examination. In an effort to more tightly control the expert, the cross-examiner may demand only "yes" or "no" answers. The expert should listen closely to each question, and determine whether or not the whole truth will be conveyed by a "yes" or "no" answer. If it cannot, an appropriate answer might be "that question cannot truthfully be answered 'yes' or 'no'" (Gutheil 2009).

The expert should be alert to a pattern of questioning designed to elicit only "yes" answers. This technique, which is commonly used by salespersons, makes it more difficult for the expert to say "no" when the occasion arises. A cross-examiner may misquote an expert's report or earlier testimony. This type of error should be pointed out. It may be an innocent mistake, or a deliberate attempt to distort testimony. If an expert is badgered, the witness may turn to the judge and say that he or she has answered the question as well as he or she can. However, this option is best reserved for only extreme situations.

Finally, the expert should not appear vanquished if a point must be conceded. The witness should avoid conveying any nonverbal communication of defeat to the jury (Brodsky 2004).

RIGHTS OF WITNESSES

The expert witness has several rights in court (Danner 1983):

1. If the expert is unclear about how he or she should answer a question, or whether he or she must answer the question posed, the expert may ask the judge.
2. The expert may ask the judge whether the material asked for is privileged.
3. The expert may refuse to answer questions that he or she does not understand. The expert may also ask examining counsel to clarify or repeat the question.
4. The expert may state that he or she does not know the answer to a question.
5. The expert may ask the judge whether he or she can qualify the answer when a "yes" or "no" answer is requested.
6. The expert has a right to complete his or her answer, and should protest if interrupted.
7. The expert may refer to written records to refresh his or her recollection.

SUMMARY

The legal process should not intimidate the expert witness. The psychiatric expert possesses greater expertise in matters of mental health than the other courtroom participants. No professional undergoes more intense scrutiny than the psychiatrist who testifies in court. It takes courage of conscience for psychiatric experts to tell a retaining attorney that their opinion will not be helpful. The expert witness must be able to endure seeing his or her opinions deliberately distorted by a cross-examiner one day, and incorrectly reported by the press the next day. However, the expert who is knowledgeable, well prepared, and thinks well on his or her feet may find the courtroom experience an enjoyable challenge.

SUMMARY KEY POINTS

- The judge determines whether the witness has the necessary knowledge, skill, experience, training, and/or education to testify as an expert witness.
- Expert witnesses should prepare for testimony by reviewing their opinion, evaluation of the litigant, any deposition transcript or recording, and participating in pretrial meetings with legal counsel.
- Expert witnesses must articulate the basis for their opinion(s).
- On cross-examination, opposing counsel may seek to discredit the witness on topics of credentials, fees, bias, and methods used to formulate his or her opinion. Expert witnesses may be impeached on the bases of inconsistent statements.
- Expert witnesses have rights in court and can seek guidance from the judge on many procedural topics.

REFERENCES

Ake v. Oklahoma, 470 U.S. 68 (1985).

American Academy of Psychiatry and the Law (AAPL). 2005. *Ethics Guidelines for the Practice of Forensic Psychiatry.* Bloomfield, CT: AAPL. http://www.aapl.org/ethics.htm.

Appelbaum RL and K Anatol. 1974: *Strategies for Persuasive Communication.* Columbus, OH: Charles E. Merrill.

Bank SC and NG Poythress. 1982. The elements of persuasion in expert testimony. *Journal of Psychiatry and Law* 10:173–204.

Boccaccini MT. 2002. What do we really know about witness preparation? *Behavioral Science and the Law* 20:161–189.

Brodsky SL 2004. *Coping with Cross Examination and Other Pathways to Effective Testimony.* Washington, DC: American Psychological Association, 112–117.

Brodsky SL, C Titcomb, DM Sams, K Dickson, and Y. Brenda. 2012. Hypothetical constructs, hypothetical questions, and the expert witness. *International Journal of Law and Psychiatry* 35(5–6):354–361.

Bromberg W. 1969. Psychiatrists in court: The psychiatrist's view. *American Journal of Psychiatry* 125:49–50.

Candilis PJ, R Weinstock, and R. Martinez. 2007: *Foresic Ethics and the Expert Witness.* New York: Springer, 44, 88.

Coggins TL. 2005. Legal, factual, and other internet sites for attorneys and others. *Richmond Journal of Law and Technology* 12:17.

Commons ML, TG Gutheil, and JT Hilliard. 2010. On humanizing the expert witness: A proposed narrative approach to expert witness qualification. *Journal of the American Academy of Psychiatry and the Law* 38(3):302–304.

Conley JM, WM Obar, and EA Lind. 1978. The power of language: Presentational style in the courtroom. *Duke Law Journal* 78:1375–1399.

Curran WJ, AL McGarry, and CS Petty. 1980. *Modern Legal Medicine, Psychiatry and Forensic Science.* Philadelphia: F.A. Davis.

Danner D. 1983. *Expert Witness Checklists.* Rochester, NY: The Lawyers' Cooperative.

Davidson HA. 1965. *Forensic Psychiatry,* 2nd edition. New York: Ronald Press.

Diamond, B. 1959. The fallacy of the impartial witness. *Archives of Criminal Psychodynamics* 3:221–236.

Emerson, RW. 1876. Eloquence. *Letters and Social Aims.* Boston: Osgood & Co.

Erickson B, EA Lind, BC Johnson, and WM O'Barr. 1978. Speech style and impression formation in a court setting: The effects of "Powerful" and "Powerless" speech. *Journal of Experimental Social Psychology* 14:266–279.

Faust D. 2011. *Coping with Psychiatric and Psychological Testimony,* 6th edition. New York: Oxford University Press, 783–801.

Goldyne AJ. 2007. Minimizing the influence of unconscious bias in evaluations: A practical guide. *Journal of the American Academy of Psychiatry and the Law* 35:60–66.

Gutheil T. 2009. *The Psychiatrist as Expert Witness,* 2nd edition. Washington, DC: American Psychiatric Publishing, 1–10, 13–22, 57–72, 73–90.

Gutheil TG and RI Simon. 2004. Avoiding bias in expert testimony. *Psychiatric Annals* 34:258–270.

Hirsch C, RC Morris, and AR Moritz. 1979. *Handbook of Legal Medicine.* 5th edition. St. Louis: Mosby.

Hirsch HL. 1975. Physician as witness—Rights, duties, and obligations. *Journal of Legal Medicine* 3:40–43.

Imwinkelried EJ. 2012. Rationalization and limitation: The use of learned treatises to impeach opposing expert witnesses. *Vermont Law Review,* 36:63–80.

Kafka C, M Dunn, MJ Johnson, J Cecil, and D Miletich. 2002. Judges and attorney experiences, practices, and concerns regarding expert testimony in federal civil trials. *Psychology, Public Policy and Law* 8(3):309–322.

Leong GB, JA Silva, and R Weinstock. 2011. Reasonable medical certainty, In *The Psychiatric Report: Principles and Practice of Forensic Writing,* edited by A. Buchanan and M. A. Norko, New York: Cambridge University Press, 214–223.

Lubet S and EI Boals. 2009. *Expert Testimony: A Guide for Expert Witnesses and the Lawyers Who Examine Them.* Boulder, CO: National Institute of Trial Advocacy.

MacDonald JM. 1976. *Psychiatry and the Criminal.* Springfield, IL: Charles C Thomas.

Malloy JT. 1988. *New Dress for Success.* New York: Warner Books.

Malloy JT. 1996. *New Women's Dress for Success.* New York: Warner Books.

Martindale DA and JW Gould. 2011. Ethics in forensic practice. In *Handbook of Psychology, Vol. 11, Forensic Psychology,* 2nd edition, edited by RK Otto. New York: Wiley, 37–61.

Miller RD. 2006. Reasonable medical certainty: A rose by any other name, *Journal of Psychiatry and Law* 34:273–289.

Spellman BA and ER Teeney. 2010. Credible testimony in and out of court. *Psychonomic Bulletin and Review* 17:168–173.

Usdin G. 1977. Psychiatric participation in court. *Psychiatric Annals* 4:42–51.

Zusman L and Simon J. 1983. Differences in repeated psychiatric examinations of litigants to a lawsuit. *American Journal of Psychiatry* 140:1300–1304.

6

Practical issues in forensic psychiatric practice

ROBERT L. SADOFF

INTRODUCTION

The practice of forensic psychiatry can provide a satisfying and rewarding experience. However, it can also be very frustrating unless one pays attention to details that may significantly affect the work of forensic psychiatrists. Aside from all of the substantive materials that need to be incorporated in the practice of good psychiatry in legal contexts, forensic psychiatrists must also be good practicing clinicians.

An important difference between forensic psychiatry and general psychiatry is that forensic psychiatrists are investigators whose assessment must include information beyond the clinical examination—that is, all data relevant to the legal issue at hand. For example, in criminal cases forensic psychiatrists should obtain, at a minimum, the police investigation reports, the crime scene forensic data, witness statements, and the defendant's confession when available. In civil cases, forensic psychiatrists should review medical records of prior injuries, operations, or other traumatic experiences, as well as observations of others who have been involved in the care and treatment of the plaintiff. In sum, for forensic psychiatrists the clinical examination is necessary (when possible) but not sufficient for a complete and comprehensive assessment.

In discussing practical issues for forensic psychiatrists, it may be instructive to describe two different cases, one criminal and one civil, pointing out various areas that require observation and clarification.

CRIMINAL CASE

The first step in any case is the initial contact by the attorney to the psychiatrist. When a public defender or a private criminal defense lawyer requests consultation on a criminal case, several questions must be raised and issues clarified at that initial communication in order to avoid subsequent problems. First, the psychiatrist should ascertain the nature of the charges and the location of the defendant. Is the defendant at large—that is, on bail, or confined in a particular institution? The attorney should then be asked to give a brief synopsis of the case and the reason for seeking psychiatric consultation. If satisfied that it is the type of case on which the psychiatrist wishes to consult, then more information is obtained from the attorney (Sadoff and Dattilio 2008).

All available records should be provided at the initial mailing. The psychiatrist should be aware that various discovery rules in different jurisdictions may limit the immediate availability of some discovery material. What is important for valid assessments are the police investigation reports, the statement of the defendant if one has been made, and statements of other witnesses.

The timing of the examination of the defendant, depending on the nature of the case, may be an issue. If there is a delay between the crime and the request for psychiatric consultation, then there may be no urgency. However, some cases depend on a very early examination of the defendant, as close to the time of the commission of the alleged offense as possible. This may involve the psychiatrist traveling to the jail in the evening or on a weekend. Psychiatrists may also wish to conduct early interviews with other people such as the spouse, family members, and neighbors in order to obtain a clear picture of the event in question.

With respect to fees, the psychiatrist should clarify the requested fees with the attorney during the initial telephone call. In private criminal cases, working for the defense, a retainer fee is usually sent with the materials prior to the examination. For public defenders or prosecutors, billing procedures usually preclude retainer fees. However, the hourly fee should be agreed upon at the outset to avoid any later confusion. Some prosecutors and public defenders require contracts with their expert witnesses, and some forensic psychiatrists want that as well for their records so that there are no misunderstandings.

Depending on the wish of the psychiatrist or attorney, the defense attorney may be present at the initial examination. If the psychiatrist is examining for the defense, the presence of the attorney can help to introduce the psychiatrist to the defendant and to avoid problems where the defendant may not be certain whether to speak to the psychiatrist. It may ease entry to the institution by having the attorney present, or by calling ahead to ensure admission. Generally, a court order or letter of introduction is required for admission to various facilities.

All prisons have security measures to ensure safety and may require a search of the psychiatrist before entering secure facilities. It is essential that the psychiatrist knows not to bring contraband into these facilities. All knives, matches, and gum should be left in the car or in the office. Recording devices, cellphones, and beepers are usually not allowed. The patient's records, a notebook, and pen or pencil for taking notes are allowed. Some facilities require the psychiatrist to lock away wallets, purses, keys, or other items in a safety locker before admission.

Examining the defendant

When meeting the defendant, it is important to reveal the identity of the psychiatrist, whom the psychiatrist represents, and what will be done with the information obtained from the defendant. This is essential, especially when working for the prosecution, so the defendant understands that the psychiatrist is not working for the defendant's attorney or to help the defendant and that what is told to the psychiatrist may be presented in a court of law and can be used against the defendant. It is also important to indicate to the defendant for what purpose the psychiatrist is seeing the defendant—that is, competency to stand trial, criminal responsibility, or evaluation for sentencing, including the possibility of the death penalty. In addition to being important ethically, without telling the defendant the purpose of the examination, the psychiatrist's testimony may later be restricted or may serve as a basis for appeal if there is a conviction (*Estelle v. Smith* 1981).

In some cases, defense attorneys may wish to be present when the psychiatrist is examining for the prosecution. That appears to be the right of the defendant in most jurisdictions, unless the court orders that no one else is to be present during the examination. In some cases, when the defense attorney is not present, the court may order the examination to be audio or video recorded. In some jurisdictions, the defendant need not cooperate with the prosecution psychiatrist (Purdons; *Commonwealth v. Campo* 1978; *Commonwealth v. Glenn* 1974). The defendant may be ordered to be present during the examination, but may not be ordered to speak to the prosecution psychiatrist. Thus, the examination may be limited or restricted, and that fact should be carefully noted in any written report. However, in some jurisdictions the defense may not put forward an insanity defense if the defendant does not cooperate with the prosecution psychiatrist as the defendant did with the defense psychiatrist (*New Jersey Statutes* 2CA–5C).

It should be noted here that it is unethical for a forensic psychiatrist to examine a defendant for the prosecution before an attorney has been appointed or retained (American Academy of Psychiatry and the Law 2005).

It is important to take a thorough and comprehensive history during the examination of the defendant. Sometimes, multiple examinations will be required before an opinion can be given. Occasionally, special testing such as psychological and/or neuropsychological testing, and neurological examination with electroencephalography (EEG), magnetic resonance imaging (MRI), or computed axial tomography (CAT) is needed. Where memory is impaired, a sodium amytal or hypnotic interview may be helpful. In such cases where hypnosis or amytal is utilized, the procedure should be video recorded. During such examinations, one should not lead the defendant or make undue suggestions to the individual whose memory is impaired. Such leading questions or suggestible influence will detract from the effectiveness of the examination and may result in an invalid conclusion.

Preparation of the report

The forensic psychiatrist should receive and review all discovery materials and all information that is necessary for forming an opinion regarding the defendant's competency, criminal responsibility, and/or disposition before rendering a report. Sometimes the court orders a report before all discovery has been obtained. In that case, the psychiatrist should indicate it is a preliminary report based on the order of the court, without the availability of all records that are known to exist. At the bottom of the report, the psychiatrist may write, "When other information is obtained or made available to me, I will review it, and if it affects my opinion, I will prepare an addendum or modification to this preliminary report." In that way, the psychiatrist duly satisfies the demand of the court while recognizing that limitations on the psychiatric opinion(s) may occur as a result of the rules of law within that jurisdiction. The psychiatrist also keeps the door open for additional materials that may or may not change the opinion(s) and result in an addendum to the report.

Some jurisdictions have an open discovery rule, whereby all information is freely given by both the prosecution and defense. In other jurisdictions, attorneys withhold information until the judge orders the release of the data. In one case, for example, the prosecution expert's report was not given until the morning he testified. It was very difficult to try to read through the 67 pages of his report in the few moments before the court opened and the expert took the stand. That appears to be an unnecessary burden and a deprivation of courtesy between and among the principals in the courtroom. How much better it would be if everyone had time to review, digest, appraise, and analyze the reports of other experts so that the examination and cross-examination can be as effective as possible. This "game playing" is a reflection of the adversarial nature of the proceeding. Some jurisdictions have eliminated that problem by having a much more cooperative approach, even within the adversarial system. Nevertheless, the forensic psychiatrist must be aware of the particular rules within each jurisdiction, as these may vary. One must not be caught off guard by assuming that the rules are similar everywhere.

Preparation of the expert witness

The preparation of the psychiatrist as an expert witness is essential. The psychiatrist should never go into the courtroom without first preparing with the attorney. One must not only prepare for the questions that will be asked on direct examination but must also anticipate the cross-examination.

Preparation also includes telling the attorney what the responses will be to various cross-examination questions. This is done so the attorney is prepared to rehabilitate on redirect. Sometimes, the response to a good cross-examination question will weaken the effectiveness of direct testimony. Some attorneys prefer their experts to argue with the cross-examining attorney to defend their weakened position. However, it is better for the attorney calling the expert into court to rehabilitate on redirect, rather than to expect the expert to be the one to deny information or to argue points on cross-examination. One should be an advocate for the attorney's position, because a case should not be accepted if the psychiatrist does not support that position, but not an adversary in the traditional sense.

The most important characteristic of the expert witness is credibility. Without credibility, there is no effective testimony. Cross-examination questions are often asked that go to the credibility of the expert witness. If the expert does not respond in a believable manner, the jury will have no faith in the expert and will discount other substantive opinions given.

It is important in criminal cases, when working for the defense, to receive in advance one's fee for time in court. "The check is the key to the courtroom door." The credibility of the expert is also enhanced by having received the fee in advance, as the expert is not dependent on the outcome of the case in order to receive the fee. On cross-examination, experts are often asked if they have been paid for their testimony. The response is that experts are paid for their time, and not for the testimony. Experts should not apologize for receiving an adequate fee for the time in court. The fee is always paid on an hourly basis, but in courtroom work there may be a minimum of four hours for a half-day or eight hours for a full day if the testimony goes into the afternoon session. The psychiatrist is not able to determine how many hours will be spent in court, and thus cannot schedule patients accurately. Therefore, it is advisable to clear at least a half day or perhaps a whole day, depending on the nature of the case, and then to charge the attorney accordingly. The fee should come from the attorney and not the client. The expert is the agent of the attorney, aiding the attorney who helps the client. Whatever arrangement is made between attorney and client is of no concern to the psychiatrist. The contract is with the attorney, not the client or defendant.

It is important for expert witnesses to know that they are not responsible for the ultimate verdict. Psychiatrists neither win nor lose the case: they are but one cog in the great wheel of justice, and should not boast upon winning a case, nor should they fear being blamed for losing one.

Testifying in court is a skill and an art. Experts must be well prepared with the facts and details of the case. It is helpful to have the materials that were reviewed listed in the report so that the expert can turn to the report and read off the materials that helped support the opinion given. Experts should have those materials available in a logical sequence in order to turn directly to the materials and not appear to be fumbling with papers on the witness stand. A disorderly stance only diminishes the image of the psychiatrist as a true professional in the eyes of the jury.

It is important to respond to cross-examination questions in a professional manner and usually with direct, short answers. Good attorneys usually do not ask "why" questions on cross-examination, since that would open the door for psychiatrists to explain the rationale for their conclusions. Usually, the cross-examination questions require short responses such as "yes" or "no." However, psychiatrists should not be bound to a "yes" or "no" answer if doing so would confuse the jury or make the testimony unclear. Experts can usually appeal to the judge to be allowed to answer the question and then offer a clarification. Nevertheless, if restricted to a "yes" or "no" answer, an expert must rely on the skill of the attorney calling the expert to rehabilitate on redirect by asking the expert to clarify the answer given on cross-examination. Psychiatrists must recall that this is a battle between lawyers and not between and among the experts. Psychiatrists may disagree with colleagues without being disagreeable. Expert psychiatrists should never indicate that colleagues are lying or incompetent, but rather disagree with their findings. A colleague may have conducted a more thorough investigation or have a different database, thus reaching a different conclusion.

CIVIL CASE

When called by the plaintiff's attorney in a civil case, the forensic psychiatrist should ascertain initially the nature of the case (e.g., competency, personal injury, toxic tort, malpractice, domestic relations matter) and determine whether the case is within the psychiatrist's expertise. It may be that the psychiatrist consulted is not a child psychiatrist or does not have sufficient experience with psychopharmacology or with the use of electroshock therapy, and the case may hinge on specific expertise in any of these areas. It is incumbent upon the professional to refer the attorney to the proper experts who could give the most effective assessment and testimony, if needed, in such a case.

In malpractice cases, it is important to determine initially who the defendants are and whether there would be any conflict of interest if the psychiatrist became involved either in a medical malpractice case for damages, or in a psychiatric malpractice case for liability and damages. It may be best to refer the plaintiff's attorney in some psychiatric malpractice cases to colleagues a fair distance away or in another jurisdiction in order to avoid any conflict of interest. If the psychiatrist agrees to accept a case for a civil defense attorney in a psychiatric malpractice case in which the defendant is known to the expert, all such prior contact must be revealed at the outset. Defense attorneys may need to decide whether to allow the psychiatrist to become involved, as any prior contact may affect the case on cross-examination. Would the expert have a particular bias in helping a "friend" in court?

Fees

In civil cases, fees are established at the initial contact, and a retainer fee is requested and obtained with the materials sent by the plaintiff's attorney prior to the examination. Defense attorneys representing insurance companies may or may not be in a position to offer retainer fees. Psychiatrists should ascertain that fact at the outset.

Some psychiatrists prefer examining plaintiffs without first looking at records in order to preserve "neutrality." They do not wish to be influenced by the findings of others or by previous records before examination. That appears to be a difficulty in forensic cases, because one really needs to know the issues before exploring in a blind manner. The examination questions need to be focused on issues relevant to the particular case. Therefore, all available data should be requested at the outset. During the examination, one may be alerted to records that had not been previously obtained, and should insist on receiving them before proceeding further.

It is usually important for the psychiatrist to discuss the findings of the examination with the attorney before preparing a report. The attorney should be given the expert's preliminary opinions and should be told what additional information is required before a report can be written. The attorney may advise the psychiatrist not to prepare a report, e.g., if the attorney does not consider the psychiatric opinions helpful. In most jurisdictions, if the plaintiff's attorney is not going to utilize the psychiatrist at trial, the psychiatrist may not be identified as an expert and no report need be required or turned over to the defense attorney. However, all defense examinations are known to the plaintiff's attorney, and reports, helpful or not, are usually required.

Preparation of the report

It is important to include all relevant information in the expert psychiatric report. An attorney occasionally may ask, in a civil case, whether certain information about prior accidents or injuries may be left out of a report in order not to "prejudice" the case. This is not a good idea because a total evaluation includes all relevant information, especially prior injuries. If the attorney insists on having a report without this information, it is best not to prepare a report.

However, in criminal cases there are rules of evidence that may preclude placing certain information in the final report. For example, history of previous criminal behavior may be left out if the report is going to be shown to the jury. Juries are not to be told of prior criminal activity, as that could prejudice the jury in the particular case. Thus, there are rules that one must follow, and one should not be constrained about removing information that may be harmful to the individual examined, if the court agrees and orders that the information be deleted.

May a report, once prepared, ever be modified or changed at the request of the attorney? This is a very sensitive issue that affects all forensic psychiatrists. If, upon request, the forensic psychiatrist deems the changes to be necessary, and if the changes would not adversely affect the opinion, the psychiatrist may make the changes and send a revised report to the attorney. The psychiatrist should clearly indicate that this is a revised version of a previous report. Occasionally, the attorney would not wish to have the report so marked as revised, but would rather present only one report that includes the revisions and discard the original report. In those cases, it is appropriate to label the original report a preliminary report.

It is usual for good attorneys, on cross-examination, to ask if the expert has ever prepared an earlier version of the report submitted. In answering such a question, the psychiatrist must be truthful and explain why the changes were made. If the psychiatrist does not have a copy of the original preliminary report, there may be some implication made on cross-examination that the psychiatrist had something to hide by discarding the earlier version. Thus, it is important to retain early reports to indicate what changes were made and for what reasons.

It is essential that the expert does not lie at the request of the attorney and indicate that there was no preliminary report when, in fact, there was. There may have been several preliminary reports that had been revised several times. That fact, if questioned, should be made known to the jury as a matter reflecting credibility, truthfulness, and integrity. In addition, to lie in court about an earlier version of the report would be perjury—a felony punishable by fine or prison. The best way to avoid such a problem in court is to prepare only one report after full consultation with the attorney about the material to be included and the structure of the report.

In most jurisdictions, draft reports are currently not discoverable.

Examination of the plaintiff

The psychiatrist working for the plaintiff's attorney may see the plaintiff several times before rendering an opinion or writing a report. When working for the defense attorney, the psychiatrist may have only one shot at the examination and should make the most of it. Thus, it is suggested that ample time be allowed for such an examination.

Occasionally, the plaintiff's attorney will wish to be present during the examination by a defense-appointed psychiatrist. This has become a matter of controversy and debate among psychiatrists and forensic psychiatrists. Many psychiatrists without forensic experience do not enjoy the prospect of conducting such an examination in the presence of third parties. They argue that others present in the examining room dilute the traditional one-on-one relationship and the examination is conducted in less than ideal circumstances. Some psychiatrists refuse to examine an individual in the presence of others. However, many forensic psychiatrists understand the needs of plaintiffs to have representation during every stage of their proceedings. The examination by a defense psychiatrist may be a traumatic experience for the plaintiff, who may be comforted by having an ally in the room (Sadoff 2011). That person may be the attorney, a paralegal, or a representative of the plaintiff's law firm. The examining psychiatrist may require that person to sit behind the examinee and not give cues or signals during the examination.

Interruptions of the examination should not be tolerated unless the attorney representing the plaintiff feels that the question asked is intrusive, inappropriate, or irrelevant. There usually are no serious problems having the plaintiff's attorney present, taking notes, listening, and observing. However, there are times when plaintiffs' attorneys wish to record the examination session. The forensic psychiatrist may agree or refuse to have the session either audio or video recorded unless the examiner is able to obtain a copy of the recording and/or a copy of the transcript of the audio recording. Some forensic psychiatrists video record every examination they conduct. Of course, the recording of the interview itself can introduce distortions to the database (Falls et al. 2014).

Preparation for trial

As noted previously for criminal cases, pretrial preparation is absolutely necessary in civil cases and should occur prior to the psychiatrist entering the courtroom. The psychiatrist should know precisely what questions are to be asked on direct, and should be able to anticipate cross-examination questions. The psychiatrist should then discuss his or her responses to such anticipated questions with the attorney, so that the attorney is also prepared.

On occasion, there will be information that has not been provided to the expert. This may be a letter, a report, or even a deposition. In some cases, the expert has not had the time or availability to interview various people involved in the case. Very often, when working for the defense in a criminal case, the expert does not interview the arresting officers or members of the victim's family. That fact may be brought to light under good cross-examination to show the jury how "incomplete" the psychiatrist's investigation has been. When asked if individuals had been interviewed, the best response is a factual "no." If given the opportunity, one may explain why such examinations were not conducted, as due to limitations of time, resources, or availability, or even the unwillingness on the part of the other witnesses to be interviewed.

When the cross-examination involves showing the psychiatrist a document that was never reviewed, it is prudent for the expert, when surprised in such a manner on the witness stand, not to offer the opinion, "Yes, it automatically changes my opinion," but to indicate that the document reveals new information that has not previously been reviewed. The psychiatrist may wish to take some time to review that document and its impact on the opinion before reaching a conclusion to be offered to the jury.

ESTABLISHING A PRACTICE OF FORENSIC PSYCHIATRY

It is impossible to address all the practical points needed to avoid problems in the practice of forensic psychiatry. Salient practical advice that confronts forensic psychiatrists on a daily basis is offered herein in condensed form (Dattilio and Sadoff 2007). However, prudent forensic psychiatrists will have supplemented their education with a fellowship in forensic psychiatry before embarking on a career in this increasingly complex subspecialty of psychiatry. Since 2001 psychiatrists have to complete a forensic psychiatry fellowship accredited by the Accreditation Council for Graduate Medical Education (ACGME) before they are allowed to take the examination for board certification in forensic psychiatry. A current list of accredited Forensic Psychiatry Fellowship Programs can be found on the American Academy of Psychiatry and the Law (AAPL) website (http://aapl.org). One does not need board certification in forensic psychiatry to practice as a forensic psychiatrist, but it does add to the credibility of the individual as an expert witness.

Psychiatrists who do not wish to take a fellowship in forensic psychiatry should in the alternative enlist a practicing forensic psychiatrist as a mentor or consult with a leader in the field. Certainly, aspiring forensic psychiatrists should read the literature and be familiar with the leading cases that affect the functions of the forensic psychiatrist. It is not always easy to get started in the field in an area saturated with competent forensic psychiatrists. However, aspiring forensic experts can give lectures to lawyers' groups and can work in clinics and other forensically oriented facilities where their skills will become known to attorneys who may wish to avail themselves of such services. Writing articles for attorneys is also a means by which to become identified as a prospective expert.

It is not recommended to advertise one's wares or skills in legal journals or daily newspapers. Commercial expert witness groups that charge fees and provide experts to attorneys around the country should also be avoided. On cross-examination, one can easily be exposed as belonging to such a "factory" or "mill," as they are called. However, there are legitimate professional advisory groups that do provide forensic services to attorneys. One may affiliate with such a group and be available for consultation when needed. It would be unwise, however, to become involved in a group where membership fees are paid in order to have one's name on a list of potential experts.

It is also wise not to offer one's skills by soliciting to consult on a particular case. It is better to wait for the attorney to call the expert. However, it is proper for psychiatrists to let their colleagues know that they are interested in taking cases with legal ramifications. Working on the medical–legal committee of one's local medical society is another means of exposure for subsequent consultations. By and large, the best means of identifying oneself as a forensic expert is to express an interest, take a fellowship in an accredited program, and work under the tutelage of competent and experienced forensic experts.

There have been a number of changes in the field of forensic psychiatry in the past decade. The rise of managed care has stimulated further interest in forensic psychiatry because it tends to be "managed care free." The membership of the AAPL that began in 1969 with eight original members had over 1900 members as of January 2015. Most psychiatrists practicing forensic psychiatry are not full time in the field, but also maintain a private treatment practice. It is important for practicing psychiatrists to be aware of potential conflicts of interest when their patient becomes involved in a legal matter. In most cases, it is unwise and a potential conflict for a treating psychiatrist to act also as the expert witness for his or her patient. Claims of bias to help one's patient will be brought, as well as the difficulty of being able to strive to reach an objective opinion, as required by the AAPL ethics guidelines, that is essential in the ethics of forensic psychiatry. Furthermore, testifying for a patient who does not do well in court may reflect on the subsequent treatment of the patient and the therapeutic alliance necessary for successful therapy (Strasburger et al. 1997).

Another potential problem for practicing psychiatrists is scheduling. The demands of forensic psychiatry may preclude a psychiatrist from regular sessions with particular patients. The judge may require the psychiatrist to be in court during a regularly scheduled patient time. That can be quite disruptive to patients who depend upon regularity of sessions because of their own schedule.

There are some cases that should be avoided by the private practicing forensic psychiatrist. These include evaluating police officers or security guards for clearance to carry a gun. This is a no-win situation. If the psychiatrist clears a guard or a police officer to carry a gun and that person later misuses the weapon, the psychiatrist will be blamed for incomplete assessment and making a recommendation that was improper. If, however, the psychiatrist determines the guard or the officer to be at a special risk for carrying a weapon, such persons may sue the psychiatrist for depriving them of making a livelihood (Sadoff 1998).

Similarly, examining sex offenders to determine whether they are "dangerous" may also have peril for the forensic psychiatrist (Sadoff 1998).

Ethical questions may arise when a forensic psychiatrist is asked to evaluate a prisoner on death row who has become acutely mentally ill. What is the role of the psychiatrist in recommending treatment or providing treatment for inmates in order to alleviate their mental condition so that they can then be put to death? The American Medical Association has taken the position that it is unethical to treat inmates to make them competent to be executed. However, it is ethical to treat an inmate incompetent to be executed to relieve suffering or maintain prison security, even if that is likely to make the inmate competent to be executed (American Medical Association 2000).

Finally, due to the recent proliferation of psychiatrists carrying out forensic work, the American Psychiatric Association and the AAPL have developed peer review committees to assess and evaluate the appropriateness of forensic assessments and testimony.

SUMMARY

The practice of forensic psychiatry is rewarding and exciting, but may also be frustrating and very difficult for the uninitiated. It is strongly recommended that anyone who is seriously interested in practicing forensic psychiatry take a fellowship training year or work with a competent, respected forensic psychiatrist as a mentor. Read the literature and follow the rules to avoid obvious pitfalls. Never work on a forensic case unless an attorney is involved. Occasionally, plaintiffs or clients will call, indicating that they are going *pro se* without an attorney. It is much more difficult to work with individuals who do not have the guidance of an attorney in this very complicated area. The more one knows, the better protected one is. There is much to know in a substantive manner, but one also needs to know the practical issues that affect all forensic psychiatrists.

ACKNOWLEDGMENTS

I am indebted to Julie B. Sadoff, Esquire, for her careful reading of the manuscript and her helpful suggestions with respect to legal issues.

REFERENCES

American Academy of Psychiatry and the Law: Ethical Guidelines for the Practice of Forensic Psychiatry (adopted May 2005), http://aapl.org/ethics.htm, accessed April 5, 2015.

American Medical Association Council on Ethical and Judicial Affairs: Opinion 2.06—Capital Punishment, issued June 1980, most recently updated June 2000, http://www.ama-assn.org/ama/pub/physician-resources/medical-ethics/code-medical-ethics/opinion206.page?, accessed April 19, 2015.

Commonwealth v. Campo, 480Pa.516,391 A.2d1005 (1978).

Commonwealth v. Glenn, 459Pa. 545,330 A.2d 535 (1974).

Dattilio FM and RL Sadoff. 2007. *Mental Health Experts: Roles and Qualifications for Court*, 2nd edition, Mechanicsburg, PA: PBI Press.

Estelle v. Smith, 451 U.S. 454 (1981).

Falls BA, OS Haque, and HJ Bursztajn. 2014. Audiovisual recording the forensic psychiatric interview. *Presented at the 45th Annual Meeting of the American Academy of Psychiatry and the Law*, Chicago, IL, October 23–26, 2014.

New Jersey Statutes 2CA-5C.

Purdons Statutes for Pennsylvania 101 PA code section 21.14.

Sadoff RL. 1998. The practice of forensic psychiatry: perils, problems and pitfalls. *Journal of the American Academy of Psychiatry and the Law* 26:305–314.

Sadoff RL. 2011. *Ethical Issues in Forensic Psychiatry: Minimizing Harm*. London: Wiley-Blackwell.

Sadoff RL and FM Dattilio. 2008. *Crime and Mental Illness: A Guide to Courtroom Practice*. Mechanicsburg, PA: PBI Press.

Strasburger LH, TG Gutheil, and A Brodsky. 1997. On wearing two hats: Role conflict in serving as both psychotherapist and expert witness. *American Journal of Psychiatry* 154:448–456.

SUGGESTED READING

Appelbaum PS and TG Gutheil. 2007. *Clinical Handbook of Psychiatry and the Law*, 4th edition. Philadelphia: Lippincott, Williams and Wilkins.

Beck JC. 1990. *Confidentiality Versus the Duty to Protect: Foreseeable Harm in the Practice of Psychiatry*. Washington, DC: American Psychiatric Press.

Benedek EP, P Ash, and CL Scott. eds. 2010. *Principles and Practice of Child and Adolescent Forensic Mental Health*. Washington, DC: American Psychiatric Publishing.

Brodsky SL. 1999. *The Expert Expert Witness: More Maims and Guidelines for Testifying in Court*. Washington, DC: American Psychological Association.

Drogin EY, FM Dattilio, RL Sadoff, and TG Gutheil. 2011. *Handbook of Forensic Assessment: Psychological and Psychiatric Perspectives*. Hoboken, NJ: Wiley.

Gutheil TG. 2009. *The Psychiatrist as Expert Witness*, 2nd edition. Arlington, VA: American Psychiatric Publishing.

Simon RI and LH Gold. eds. 2010. *The American Psychiatric Publishing Textbook of Forensic Psychiatry*, 2nd edition. Washington, DC: American Psychiatric Publishing.

Slovenko R. 2002. *Psychiatry in Law/Law in Psychiatry*. New York: Brunner-Routledge.

Stone AA. 1984. *Law, Psychiatry, and Morality: Essays and Analysis*. Washington, DC: American Psychiatric Press.

7

Education and training in forensic psychiatry

RUSTY REEVES, RICHARD ROSNER, JOHN GUNN, DAVID REISS, AND DOMINIQUE BOURGET

INTRODUCTION

Since the early 1980s, education and certification in forensic psychiatry have grown more uniform and systematic in the United States, the United Kingdom, and Canada. Although many forensic psychiatrists continue to practice without formal training in the subspecialty, formal training and certification in forensic psychiatry is the preferred route into forensic psychiatry. In this chapter, the authors, who are educators and practitioners, describe the educational programs and methods of certification in their respective countries. A reader curious about education and certification in any other country should contact its national psychiatric association or national association for psychiatry and the law.

UNITED STATES

Education

The Accreditation Council for Graduate Medical Education (ACGME) is the accrediting body for all graduate medical education programs in the United States. In 1997, the ACGME began to accredit fellowships in forensic psychiatry. As of the 2014–2015 academic year, the ACGME had approved 40 programs with a total of 66 trainee positions as meeting its criteria for accreditation in forensic psychiatry (ACGME 2014a).

In the more than 10 years since the previous version of this chapter was written (Reeves and Rosner 2003, 52–55), the basic requirements for training in forensic psychiatry remain unchanged (ACGME 2013). The ACGME still requires that the training period in forensic psychiatry be 12 months, and that training occur after completion of a psychiatry residency program accredited by the ACGME. The program must be administratively attached to and sponsored by a residency program in psychiatry that is accredited by the ACGME. An assignment to a participating institution must include a program letter of agreement. Major changes to the program require approval by the sponsoring institution's Graduate Medical Education Committee, and then by the ACGME's Psychiatric Residency Review Committee (RRC).

The program director organizes and manages the activities of the educational program in all institutions that participate in the program. The program director and physician faculty must be certified by the American Board of Psychiatry and Neurology (ABPN) in the specialty of forensic psychiatry, or have qualifications in forensic psychiatry that are acceptable to the RRC.

Fellows' educational experiences must include at least 6 months of evaluating and managing patients in corrections, working with professionals in both forensic and community settings, reviewing written records, preparing written reports, providing testimony, and providing consultations to general psychiatric services on issues related to the legal regulation of psychiatric practice. The didactic curriculum must include all topics for which fellows must demonstrate competence in knowledge, such as the legal system, civil law, criminal law, and relevance of legal documents.

The ACGME requires that the program integrate into the curriculum, and the fellows demonstrate, six ACGME-required competencies: patient care and procedural skills, medical knowledge, practice-based learning and improvement, interpersonal skills, professionalism, and systems-based practice.

New for all medical specialties, and effective July 2015 for forensic psychiatry, the ACGME further requires each resident achieve "milestones" within the above-mentioned six competencies. According to the ACGME, a milestone is a "significant point in development." In forensic psychiatry, for example, under the "Patient Care" competency, a forensic fellow is expected to achieve the milestone of providing psychiatric care in a forensic setting that "consistently manages security concerns, dual agency, and the potential for conflicts with therapeutic efforts" (ACGME 2014b). Milestones are demonstrated progressively by residents and fellows from the beginning of their education to the unsupervised practice of their specialties. In forensic psychiatry, these milestones are assessed on a semi-annual basis. The ACGME requires reporting of achievement of milestones beginning in November or December 2015. The above are but a few of the ACGME requirements for education in forensic psychiatry. A summative evaluation for each fellow is completed at the end of the program to ensure fellows are able to practice independently. The entire list of requirements can be found on the ACGME's website (http://www.acgme.org).

The Association of Directors of Forensic Psychiatry Fellowships (ADFPF), a council of the American Academy of Psychiatry and the Law (AAPL), works to ensure quality education in forensic psychiatry along with providing a venue for forensic program directors to exchange ideas and remain up-to-date with developments relevant to training in forensic psychiatry. The ADFPF assisted in the creation of the above-mentioned milestones required by the ACGME. The ADFPF meets twice a year, at the annual AAPL meeting and at the annual American Psychiatric Association (APA) meeting.

Certification

The ABPN is the organization responsible for offering certification examinations in psychiatry and neurology. The ABPN is a member of the American Board of Medical Specialties (ABMS), an organization of 24 approved medical specialty boards. The ABPN in 1994 began to offer a certification examination in forensic psychiatry.

In order to take the ABPN forensic exam, an applicant must first be certified by the ABPN in psychiatry (ABPN 2014a). Applicants are required to submit documentation of successful completion of 1 year of ACGME-approved residency training in forensic psychiatry. The ABPN's initial certification examination in the subspecialty of forensic psychiatry is a 200-item, multiple-choice, 4-hour computerized test that assesses candidates' knowledge in legal regulation of psychiatry, civil law, criminal law, death penalty, legal systems and basic law, children and families, special diagnostic and treatment issues, special procedures in forensic psychiatry, special consultations and investigations, risk assessment, and forensic psychiatry practice issues (ABPN 2014a).

ABPN certificates for forensic psychiatrists are valid for 10 years; thereafter, successful completion of maintenance of certification (i.e., recertification) examinations is required to sustain ABPN forensic certification. The recertification examination is a 150-item, multiple-choice, 3-hour computerized test. In a welcome development for 2015, the ABPN offers combined maintenance of certification examinations in specialty and/or subspecialty examinations. The combined maintenance of certification examination in psychiatry and forensic psychiatry is a 5-hour and 15-minute examination with 100 questions in psychiatry, and 100 questions in forensic psychiatry. It also is possible to take a combined examination in two subspecialties.

Since 2007, admission to the recertification examination has required prerequisites. The process of completion of these prerequisites is called Maintenance of Certification (MOC) (ABPN 2014b). The ABPN has established MOC to encourage lifelong professional learning among its certified psychiatrists. MOC includes accumulation of sufficient Continuing Medical Education credits, and completion of self-assessment (SA), and performance-in-practice (PIP) activities. While understanding the necessary MOC activities may be confusing, completion of the activities is not daunting. Any CME, SA, or PIP activities completed apply to all specialties/subspecialties in which a physician is certified. Thus, a psychiatrist does not have to double the number of MOC activities in order to be certified in both psychiatry and forensic psychiatry. As of September 2, 2014, the ABPN from 1994 to 2013 had issued 2125 certificates in forensic psychiatry, of which 1455 were current (Vollmer, ABPN, personal communication, 2014). The above represents a summary of ABPN requirements with a full list of requirements available from the ABPN (http://www.abpn.com).

UNITED KINGDOM

International standards

Within the European Union all medical training is not yet harmonized between member countries, resulting in professional frustration about this barrier to potential movement between countries in some specialties, including forensic psychiatry. Only the United Kingdom, Germany, Sweden, and Finland have specialized training in forensic psychiatry at present, but this pattern is likely to spread.

The United Kingdom is in a strong position to control standards in forensic psychiatry because its state monopoly National Health Service, together with the professional monopoly of the Royal College of Psychiatrists, can control appointments in the specialty. As forensic psychiatry has until recently been a shortage specialty at the consultant level, there continues to be some slippage, and de facto general psychiatrists take on a limited amount of forensic work.

Education

Numerous recent changes have taken place to the structure and regulation of U.K. medical training, some changes in accordance with European Union medical directives. The Postgraduate Medical Education and Training Board, created April 2003, was combined with the General Medical Council (GMC) on April 1, 2010. With these changes, the GMC now regulates all postgraduate medical training, setting appropriate requirements. In England, Health Education England, established June 2012, has 13 Local Education and Training Boards (LETBs, working from April 1, 2013) that are area-based committees responsible for National Health Service (NHS) staff education and training. Local deans' offices, which previously had responsibility for NHS medical staff training in England, continue to perform this function in Northern Ireland, Scotland, and Wales. The "Shape of Training" report (Greenaway 2013) has recommended changes to postgraduate education and training that should, if implemented, still produce specialists but result in more generalist doctors working in broad specialties. These changes will not be finally determined until subsequent to the 2015 general election, and the implications for forensic psychiatry are not yet clear.

The United Kingdom's Royal College of Psychiatrists (RCPsych) runs a "Membership" examination (MRCPsych) for psychiatrists who have completed basic specialist training (equivalent to general psychiatry residency training in the United States). A psychiatrist must pass papers A and B as well as the Clinical Assessment of Skills and Competency (CASC) of this examination before being allowed to enter higher specialist training in one of the U.K.-recognized psychiatric subspecialties (see below). Paper B and the CASC contain questions on forensic psychiatry for all trainees to answer. Passing the MRCPsych is similar to passing the ABPN certification examination in general psychiatry in the United States, but it is more than just a qualification and gives immediate access to professional and educational activities within the Royal College of Psychiatrists.

A placement (rotation in the United States) in forensic psychiatry, usually of 6 months' duration, is a noncompulsory option in basic specialist training. These have to meet RCPsych specified standards, including a job description, timetable, and satisfactory clinical supervision, as well as having specific training experiences including consultations at prisons, hospitals, secure units, remand centers, and other establishments. Trainees are encouraged to write shadow reports for discussion with their consultants, as well as to be instructed in the principles of forensic psychiatry and medico-legal work.

After the completion of basic specialist training, and the passing of the MRCPsych, a psychiatrist who wishes to specialize in forensic psychiatry may enter higher specialist training. Forensic psychiatry is one of six areas of higher specialist training, with the others being general (adult) psychiatry, old age psychiatry, child and adolescent psychiatry, psychiatry of learning disability, and psychotherapy. Entry to this training is through U.K.-wide competitive interview.

For all medical postgraduate training schemes, the GMC approves curricula and assessment systems, although these are designed by the royal colleges. To complete forensic psychiatry higher training, trainees must follow and achieve a detailed competency-based curriculum, which details the intended learning outcomes for advanced specialist training. The RCPsych writes the training curricula through Faculty Education and Curriculum Committees which report to an overarching Curriculum Committee. The GMC has responsibility for quality assurance to ensure that regulatory requirements are met: it inspects training programs, publishes its findings, reviews reports from the training organizers as well as the medical royal colleges, and conducts annual national surveys of trainees and trainers.

The forensic trainee must learn how to manage offender patients in all relevant settings, including prisons, the community, specialist hostels, and hospitals, especially secure hospitals. Trainees move through a variety of different services to satisfactorily develop these competencies. Most trainees undertake some additional private work, and medico-legal experience may be acquired in all settings. Every detained patient in the United Kingdom, as well as those on Community Treatment Orders, has a periodic right to apply to a Mental Health Tribunal for review of the detention/order, which is exercised by the majority. There is, therefore, an emphasis on medico-legal work for these hearings. Criminal court work is a relatively small proportion of a forensic psychiatrist's workload, involving mainly some sentencing decisions.

Certification

Completion of forensic psychiatry training usually takes 3 years and results in the award of a Certificate of Completion of Training (CCT), which is essential for appointment to an NHS consultant post. A surprisingly small proportion of the knowledge and skills that are required to undertake the role of a British consultant forensic psychiatrist is mandatory, but the emphasis is on clinical work. There is no exit examination in any of the higher psychiatric specialties. Rather, every trainee in forensic psychiatry is annually evaluated by the scheme organizer and the LETB or dean's office, to determine whether the trainee is allowed to progress to the next year and, ultimately, to be awarded a CCT.

CANADA

Education

Historically, Canadian forensic psychiatry fellowship programs were accredited by the U.S. Accreditation Council on Fellowships in Forensic Psychiatry (ACFFP). In 1997, when the ACGME replaced the ACFFP, Canadian postgraduate medical programs were no longer able to receive accreditation (Reeves et al. 2007).

These developments did not deter the evolution and practice of forensic psychiatry in Canada. Even though forensic psychiatry was not formally accredited or recognized as distinct from the practice of general psychiatry, forensic psychiatry developed with a strong community of psychiatrists devoted to their practice. In 1996, the Education Committee of the Canadian Academy of Psychiatry and the Law (CAPL) developed a standardized Forensic Psychiatry Training Curriculum. A revised curriculum was formally endorsed by CAPL in 2004 (O'Shaughnessy 2004).

On September 29, 2009, the Council of the Royal College of Physicians and Surgeons of Canada (RCPSC) recognized forensic psychiatry as a subspecialty in psychiatry (Bourget and Chaimowitz 2010, 158–162). The RCPSC is the professional body that develops specialty-training requirements and accredits residency programs in Canada.

Prior to entering subspecialty training, residents must have completed 5 years of residency in general psychiatry, in accordance with the General Objectives of Training and Specialty Training Requirements in Psychiatry, and successfully completed the RCPSC examination in psychiatry or equivalent (Royal College of Physicians and Surgeons of Canada 2003). This stems from the principle that forensic psychiatry arises from and requires a thorough grounding in general psychiatry.

There are currently five accredited forensic psychiatry residency training programs in Canada, and several others have initiated the process toward accreditation. Each program is headed by a program director (PD), responsible for the overall conduct of the residency program. Moving toward accreditation has brought about significant changes in the way forensic psychiatry is now taught across the country. Standardization of training is one of the main results. The RCPSC has established "Minimum Training Requirements," which include a period of no less than 12 months of approved residency training commencing after successful completion of specialty training in psychiatry. The year is divided into 13 four-week blocks that include 6–9 blocks of core training.

Core training involves clinical exposure and typically includes assessments for fitness to stand trial and criminal responsibility (and relevant mitigating factors), and risk assessments. This takes place in various settings, such as inpatient and outpatient units, mental health courts, or detention centers. Core training is also concerned with provision of treatment to mentally ill offenders. In addition to core training, the resident must complete four to seven blocks of selective training that include at least two content areas drawn from the following: child and adolescent forensic psychiatry, civil psychiatry, correctional psychiatry, sexual behaviors, risk assessments, and forensic research. Mandatory and selective training may be undertaken as discrete rotations or longitudinal experiences, which is often felt to be ideal, given that cases often take some time before reaching the next stage of resolution.

Upon acceptance into the specialty program, trainees are assigned a supervisor who acts as an advisor to the trainee and ensures that opportunities to meet the optimal training requirements are made available to the trainee. Throughout their training, trainees are evaluated through evaluation reports, review of their written reports, and constructive critiques of testimony offered during the course of training. At the end of training, the PD submits a final report to the RCPSC, with regard to each trainee having completed residency training.

Now that the RCPSC recognizes forensic psychiatry as a distinct subspecialty of psychiatry, training programs are eager to deliver the best quality of teaching and to prepare the next generation of forensic psychiatrists. One of the biggest challenges thus far has been the securing of funding for post-general residency positions. As forensic psychiatry is a new subspecialty, there was no tradition to fund these programs. Nevertheless, the first trainees began accredited training in July 2012.

Certification

The RCPSC is responsible for certification examinations for Canadian physicians in various specialties and subspecialties. After successful completion of the forensic training, candidates submit their applications to the RCPSC to determine their eligibility to take the certification examination. The RCPSC has granted a temporary period to allow candidates without a formal training year and already engaged in the practice of forensic psychiatry, via the Practice Eligibility Route, to request an assessment of their credentials for examination eligibility.

The certification examination format currently consists of a 3-hour-long written examination of approximately 40 short answer development questions. The first cohort took the examination on September 26, 2013. This cohort included a large number of psychiatrists already practicing in the subspecialty.

The certification delivered by the RCPSC attests to the completion of specialty training requirements in an accredited program. This holds true for all Canadian provinces except Quebec. The medical profession in Canada is granted a significant degree of authority by provincial law, and the province of Quebec has its own regulating body. While most provinces recognized the competence of the RCPSC for certification, Quebec took years to harmonize its own examination with that of the RCPSC. However, subspecialties in psychiatry have not yet been recognized in Quebec, so RCPSC certification cannot be used by forensic psychiatrists in Quebec in their title at this time.

SUMMARY

The United States, the United Kingdom, and Canada have standardized training in forensic psychiatry through accreditation by authoritative professional organizations. A forensic psychiatry fellowship as offered in these countries provides an intense and systematic education in forensic psychiatry, with exposure to the field's diversity, and close supervision from experienced and certified practitioners. At the end of training, the physician has been certified by his or her supervisors to independently practice forensic psychiatry. Board certification in forensic psychiatry in the United States and Canada offers additional assurance that a physician meets a level of competence in the field.

REFERENCES

Accreditation Council for Graduate Medical Education (ACGME). 2013. *ACGME Program Requirements for Graduate Medical Education in Forensic Psychiatry*. http://www.acgme.org, accessed September 2, 2014.

Accreditation Council for Graduate Medical Education (ACGME). 2014a. *Number of Accredited Programs for the Current Academic Year (2014–2015) United States*. https://apps.acgme.org/ads/public, accessed June 27, 2016.

Accreditation Council for Graduate Medical Education (ACGME). 2014b. *The Forensic Psychiatry Milestone Project: A Joint Initiative of the Accreditation Council for Graduate Medical Education and the American Board of Psychiatry and Neurology*. http://www.acgme.org, accessed October 27, 2014.

American Board of Psychiatry and Neurology (ABPN). 2014a. http://www.abpn.com/cert_fp.html, accessed September 21, 2014.

American Board of Psychiatry and Neurology (ABPN). 2014b. http://www.abpn.com/moc_fp.asp, accessed September 21, 2014.

Bourget D and G Chaimowitz. 2010. Forensic psychiatry in Canada: A journey on the road to specialty. *Journal of the American Academy of Psychiatry and the Law* 38(2):158–162.

Greenaway D. 2013. *Shape of Training: Securing the Future of Excellent Medical Care. Final Report of the Independent Review Led by Professor David Greenaway. General Medical Council*. http://www.shapeoftraining.co.uk, accessed October 27, 2014.

O'Shaughnessy R. 2004. Forensic psychiatry curriculum. *Canadian Academy of Psychiatry and Law*. Unpublished.

Reeves D, R Rosner, D Bourget, and J Gunn. 2007. Training and education for mental health professionals. In *International Handbook on Psychopathic Disorders and the Law*, Vol. II, edited by A Felthous and S Henning, West Sussex, England: Wiley, 505–518.

Reeves R and R Rosner. 2003. Education and training in forensic psychiatry. In *Principles and Practice of Forensic Psychiatry*, 2nd edition. edited by R Rosner, London: Arnold, 52–55.

Royal College of Physicians and Surgeons of Canada. 2003. *Objectives of Training and Specialty Training Requirements in Psychiatry*. Ottawa, Ontario, Canada: Royal College of Physicians and Surgeons of Canada.

8

Forensic psychiatric ethics

ROBERT WEINSTOCK, WILLIAM CONNOR DARBY, PHILIP J. CANDILIS, GREGORY B. LEONG, AND JENNIFER L. PIEL

INTRODUCTION

Forensic psychiatry operates at the interface of two disparate disciplines—law and psychiatry—with differing objectives, philosophies, values, approaches, and methods. Psychiatry, a branch of medicine, endeavors to improve mental health and to help patients. Historically, Hippocratic physicians saw their duties primarily to individual patients. However, the responsibilities of physicians both ethically and legally have been extended in modern times to society as a whole. Medical ethics incorporates deontological (adherence to duties), utilitarian or consequentialist, and virtue ethics. In contrast, the law operates with justice, retribution, containment, and deterrence as its goals. Dilemmas can occur when ethical and legal considerations conflict and some ethical values may be compromised.

Although ethical conflicts do not occur in most ordinary situations at the interface of law and psychiatry, conflicts between principles, roles, duties, rules, systems, and stakeholders have the potential to create dilemmas in forensic psychiatry. In these relatively uncommon situations, there may be no clear, unequivocally relevant rule or ethics guideline to follow that does not impinge on some other competing consideration (Childress 1997). Moreover, no universally dominant consideration exists as to necessarily outweigh all others in every situation. Thus, the context in these special circumstances will be essential in determining the most ethical action.

Professional ethics guidelines in forensic psychiatry provide sufficient assistance in most contexts to help practitioners address and resolve what to do. But no set of ethical guidelines can address every possible contingency. Although ethical guidelines are extremely helpful, there often is not one clear answer and several can be acceptable when ethics dilemmas arise. As a result, forensic psychiatrists must be able to perform their own analyses in ethically complex cases.

ETHICAL FOUNDATIONS AND ALAN STONE'S CRITIQUE

Stone (1984), in a paper originally presented at the American Academy of Psychiatry and the Law (AAPL), stimulated much concern and debate by positing that the ethical requirements and boundaries of a healing profession become unclear once psychiatrists leave the therapeutic realm. Four problem areas can be distilled from Stone:

1. The basic boundary problem of whether psychiatry has anything to offer the law
2. The potential for psychiatrists to try to help a patient by twisting rules of justice and fairness
3. The potential for the psychiatrist to deceive a patient in order to serve justice and fairness
4. The power of the adversarial legal system to both seduce and abuse psychiatrists in ways that demean the profession

Stone cautioned that physicians lose their ethical boundaries when they give other factors such as justice, advancement of science, or political causes greater weight than helping patients or doing no harm. In his opinion, psychiatrists cannot simply adjust to the adversarial system and still remain true to their calling as physicians.

Stone also stated that juries do not clearly understand the partisan role of forensic psychiatrists, or that when forensic psychiatrists testify they "should be understood as having attempted to present the best case possible" (Stone 1984) for the retaining party. Stone argues that until there is candor, it will not be possible to "sweep the ethical problems of psychiatry under the rug of intelligible adversarial ethics." However, these problems are not unique to forensic psychiatry—they can arise for all expert witnesses who testify under an adversarial system. If changes were to be made, they would necessarily involve the entire adversarial process and its use of expert witnesses, because most issues do not pertain solely to forensic psychiatry.

Stone identifies another potential pitfall, the problem of reconciling deterministic psychiatric theories with a legal system based on free will. For instance, Moore (1984) contends that mind–brain confusion in American forensic psychiatry goes back at least to Isaac Ray, who thought that if mental disease is physical, the power to choose is extinguished and the actor is *ipso facto* not responsible. According to Moore, the law—in contrast to science—uses the language of action and reason with possible physical causes of mental illness therefore irrelevant to whether the law should excuse a behavior.

In a 2014 study, Appelbaum and Scurich (2014) explored how the introduction of behavioral genetic evidence could affect the perception of criminal responsibility. The data from their representative U.S. sample suggest that a genetic predisposition to violence did not alter decisions regarding degree of criminal responsibility or mitigate sentencing. These findings differed from a study of state criminal court judges whose hypothetical sentences were significantly reduced when there was evidence attributing a defendant's psychopathy to genetic causes (Aspinwall et al. 2012).

Such problems of role confusion exist even in the realm of treatment psychiatry and are not exclusive to forensic psychiatry. Society has progressively thrust conflicting responsibilities on treatment psychiatrists. For example, in child or elder abuse, other requirements and concerns may take precedence over patient welfare (Weinstock et al. 1991), especially in those jurisdictions in which reporting can lead to prosecution of a patient (*People v. Stritzinger,* 1983). In California, psychiatrists can be placed in a position to testify against their patients. Therefore, the ethical boundaries of treating as well as forensic psychiatrists sometimes may be obscured and not clearly demarcated. Thus, although forensic psychiatry deals with unique considerations inherent to functioning at the interface of law and psychiatry, the need to balance conflicting factors is common to most psychiatric roles.

ETHICAL PRINCIPLES RELEVANT TO FORENSIC PSYCHIATRY

Appelbaum (1990) wrote, "Psychiatrists operate outside the medical framework when they enter the forensic realm, and the ethical principles by which their behavior is justified are simply not the same." He contends that the principles of beneficence and nonmaleficence lose their primacy to the principles of truth in the forensic setting. Although ethical conflicts sometimes can arise, Appelbaum (1984) contends that forensic psychiatrists should present both the subjective and objective truth.

AAPL in its ethics guidelines (AAPL ethics guideline 2005) has similar concerns in requiring honesty and striving for objectivity. Psychiatrists should not stop with a convenient subjective truth as soon as they collect some evidence that substantiates it even if they are persuaded by that. They should go beyond their initial subjective, honest belief and strive to reach an objective truth by collecting as much evidence as they can, including evidence that may contradict their initial impression. Objective truth requires making evident any limitations on their conclusions. In order to strive for the most objective opinion, efforts should be made to become as familiar with the relevant literature as possible. In addition to the current AAPL ethics guideline necessitating an effort to strive for objectivity, the AAPL guidelines also require honesty. But, an honest opinion with little to substantiate it is insufficient. A careful search for and review of evidence could result in the subjective truth approaching the objective truth.

Appelbaum (1997) considers respect for persons as the second moral rule guiding forensic psychiatric ethics after that of truth-telling. He alerts forensic psychiatrists to a major risk that "subjects of forensic evaluations will assume that an evaluating psychiatrist is playing a therapeutic role and, therefore, that the usual ethics of the clinical setting apply." Evaluees may believe that, as physicians, forensic psychiatrists are there to help or at the very least do no harm to them, and may subsequently think it is safe to speak freely. According to Appelbaum, while "allowing subjects to hold such beliefs might be an effective means of gathering information, it is inherently deceptive and exploitative, and fails to respect subjects as persons." That ethical concern applies regardless of what the law permits.

Additionally, according to Appelbaum (1997), forensic psychiatrists "cannot avoid the obligation of determining whether the actions they are being asked to perform in fact promote justice." For example, assisting in abusive interrogation or torture of prisoners would fail that test. Overall, the primary duty of forensic psychiatrists according to Appelbaum is to assist the legal system to promote justice. But realistically there are limits to which forensic psychiatrists are allowed to impose their views of justice on the legal system. Also, forensic psychiatrists like all citizens have duties to behave nonmaleficently, even though some maleficence may be a consequence of some forensic roles.

Appelbaum states that violating moral rules is an inevitable consequence of the complexity of life, and resolving such conflicts "requires balancing, among other morally relevant factors, the nature of each imperative, the benefits and harms likely to flow from its violation, and the alternative means of achieving the desired end." He states that although moral ideals are desirable rather than required, morals rules are required of individuals. Professional ethics can transform a moral ideal into a moral rule. An example is the requirement of physicians to relieve pain, which is only an ideal for the general public. According to Appelbaum, the moral ideals that should be converted into moral rules are those values that society wants the profession to promote. Society gives professions certain privileges in exchange for certain duties and the expectation for self-regulation. Differences between the ethics of differing professions should reflect society's expectation of the profession.

Appelbaum (1997) supports a principled approach and recognizes a need to balance conflicting duties when complex ethical problems arise. He cautions, "if forensic psychiatrists persuade themselves that they maintain a residual duty—of a professional nature—to benefit and not to harm evaluees, they are likely to communicate that to their subjects." There is a risk of engendering inappropriate trust when the forensic psychiatrist is on the side opposite the person being evaluated. An evaluee could be misled into thinking the forensic evaluation is a quasi-therapeutic encounter. In the process of mutual deception, the subject could be betrayed and potentially seriously harmed.

In Appelbaum's view, that is an advantage of deriving the ethics of forensic psychiatry from the pursuit of justice and not health, thereby sending a clear message regarding the distinction between the forensic and therapeutic roles. Some authors have proposed ways of analyzing this conflict (Rosner 1990; Candilis et al. 2007; Weinstock 2015).

The retention of traditional Hippocratic medical values as a consideration in forensic ethics is consistent with the findings from surveys of forensic psychiatrists. The highest-rated potential new ethical guideline in a survey of forensic psychiatrists was shown to be one that considered medical and psychiatric ethics as a factor when performing a forensic evaluation (Weinstock et al. 1991). A way to retain Hippocratic ethics while conceptualizing conflicting legal duties can be to see forensic psychiatrists as having multiple agency responsibilities similar to all other psychiatrists, especially those who consult to another system like a hospital, managed care organization, prison, school, or government agency with its own inherent rules and priorities. For all psychiatric roles, however, there is generally no simple, single duty that will always trump all other considerations.

In the judicial system there may already be an assumption that traditional medical ethics remains a consideration for all roles assumed by physicians, so eschewing medical ethics completely may in fact mislead judges and juries who may interpret the physician role more traditionally than the expert who rejects medical values.

Truth-telling can harm a patient even in the treatment setting, such as when the treater makes a diagnosis of antisocial personality or malingering. Thus, harm is not unique to forensic psychiatry. It is simply more frequent in some forensic roles. Fostering justice and truth-telling, however, have more primacy than patient welfare in most forensic settings. The opposite priority may be true in the treatment setting, or at minimum hold equal value.

Like Hundert (1990), Weinstock et al. (1990) have posited that traditional medical ethics should still play a role and be a factor in the process of balancing conflicting values. Weinstock (2015) develops the balancing method further.

Primacy, though, does not mean that the primary duty must always outweigh all secondary considerations. For instance, in unusual situations, the secondary duty can be especially serious, despite the presumptive primary duty, and even become determinative of the most ethical course of action. For example, in the treatment context, societal obligations outweigh the primary duty to patient welfare in instances like child and elder abuse. These are conditions that must be reported. Conversely, in the forensic context, performing pre-arraignment assessments and treating prisoners to restore competence to be executed are unethical because the responsibility to an individual trumps the primary role of assisting the legal system—recognized as an ethical guideline by both APA and AAPL. In cases like these, the serious damage that results from violating a secondary duty makes that duty predominant. Because of these conflicting values as well as misunderstandings about the adversarial process, forensic psychiatry has developed ethical guidelines specific to the situations they commonly encounter.

However, practitioners should not necessarily be sanctioned for behavior in which no clear guidelines exist and there is serious disagreement as to what is the most ethical action. AAPL's ethics committees can advise practitioners in difficult situations, and there may be legitimate differing opinions. Clinical ethics committees may be less helpful because they may view situations from a treatment perspective and balance the conflicting considerations differently. It remains for those practicing forensic psychiatry to analyze options from a variety of ethical perspectives and advance beyond any single, simplistic rule to the exclusion of all other considerations.

Griffith (1998, 2005) advanced the discussion of forensic ethics significantly by emphasizing the importance of cultural factors in forensic cases, and specifically highlighting dominant and nondominant group dynamics. Griffith argues that these cultural considerations often are given insufficient attention in ethics analyses. He requires a sensitivity to such issues as the frequent lack of respect for African Americans seeking justice, and for nondominant personal narratives as a whole, including dominance and political facets. Even if such sensitivity does not result in an assessment helpful to a defendant, nondominant cultural issues should be understood fully and any systemic unfairness acknowledged in the assessment. In Griffith's opinion, these are important reasons for psychiatrists from nondominant cultures, who are more likely to be sensitive to these issues, to remain in court.

Candilis et al. (2001, 2007) propose a robust view of the forensic role that integrates both the principled and narrative approaches. Central to their concept is professional integrity (or wholeness) tied to the community and its values, and reflects a community expectation of a broader more physician-based approach from its forensic experts. This approach recognizes the profession's own historical narrative and the internal set of duties, values, and ideals that are essential for professional identity. These values resist the vagaries of social and situational forces that may call for experts to put institutional values over those of vulnerable individuals.

This unified or integrative approach contrasts with views of professional ethics that see forensic work defined only as an agency of justice and the courts. Developing a professionalism that protects vulnerable persons and values instead, allows for a broader view of professional integrity that acknowledges personal and traditional physician-based values.

Candilis et al. (2007) use Griffith's narrative ethics as a tool to augment the classic principlist approach espoused by Appelbaum and described and developed by Beauchamp and Childress (2013) in the clinical context. Principles, according to Candilis et al. (2001), still work at the theoretical level to create a framework for appropriate action, but require narrative to provide the detail found in the motives and intentions of individual experts and evaluees. Alone, principles in their opinion are inadequate to give guidance in complex forensic situations. Narrative operationalizes theory in a practical manner, describing the individual's unique path to the forensic encounter. It is a way to overcome Stone's silence on cultural narrative and Appelbaum's justice-laden approach. Consequently, forensic experts can take the evaluee's narrative into account, recognize their own personal biases in a case, and advocate for the profession's integrity when it comes under pressure from the judicial system. This "robust professionalism" in the views of Candilis et al. (2001) defends strongly against the practice of the "hired gun."

Ciccone and Clements (2001) fear ethics becoming arbitrary with narrative alone. They prefer an applied ethics approach entailing a probabilistic inductive theory of ethics and a systems epistemology-like context ethics. Norko (2005) considers compassion as relevant in forensic work and ethics.

Weinstock (2001) addresses the need to balance conflicting values, and conceptualizes consultation in forensic psychiatry as different in its specifics but not different conceptually from consultation to other systems such as managed care with values that differ from those of treatment. Even in research roles, a physician has duties to science but has ethical duties to remove a patient from a study if there is a serious risk of harm. Balancing conflicting considerations is a central element of dialectical principlism.

DIALECTICAL PRINCIPLISM

Dialectical principlism (Weinstock 2015) is a method of ethical analysis that provides a specific framework to enable balancing conflicting roles, duties, and principles. In dialectical principlism, "dialectical" describes the process by which apparently contradictory and competing considerations including principles can be synthesized into a coherent whole to help guide our action. Principles are interpreted in the broadest sense of the term. They may include, for example, the principle of fostering justice, answering the legal question honestly and as objectively as possible, the four principles of biomedical ethics—beneficence, nonmaleficence, autonomy, and justice (Beauchamp and Childress 2013)—meeting societal expectations, and following our personal values.

When faced with an ethical dilemma under the dialectical principlism model, it is essential to consider the specific context to determine which duties and principles are primary and which are secondary. After identifying the competing duties and principles, practitioners should then prioritize, weigh, and balance them. In the forensic role, the primary duty and relevant principles are to foster justice and answer the legal question honestly, truthfully, and as objectively as possible. Primary duties have special weight in the balancing process which ordinarily outweigh and thereby trump secondary duties. An unusually strong secondary duty in some contexts, however, could outweigh the presumptively primary one and become determinative.

For example, the secondary principle of nonmaleficence may outweigh the primary principle of fostering justice if asked by the prosecution to present only aggravating circumstances at the penalty phase of a capital case to help them obtain a death sentence. In this instance, the most ethical action may be to reject the prosecution's case at the penalty phase because the secondary duty to not do harm—death in this scenario—outweighs the primary duty to foster justice.

Conflicts among principles and duties are balanced in a manner that impinges as little as possible on each other (Childress 1997). Finally, the weighted principles are applied to the context in question. Those with little weight and importance in the situation may be deemed negligible and subsequently not be factored into the final decisional equation.

Intent is central in dialectical principlism. This approach is designed to help practitioners find the most ethical course of action rather than to penalize or get professionals into trouble. Intent is notoriously difficult for licensing or administrative bodies to determine but is more relevant for us as a tool of self-examination. It is consequently aspirational, because violations of intent cannot generally be enforced without mind reading.

The discomfort arising from challenging cases can be a signal of serious conflicting ethical considerations, and potentially a dilemma. Dialectical principlism accepts this unease as legitimate and appropriate and provides a framework to help experts determine the most ethical conclusion possible.

NO MEANINGFUL DISTINCTION BETWEEN ETHICS AND MORALS

Sometimes professional ethics have been distinguished from personal morals. However, such a distinction can be confusing because the terms "ethical" and "moral" generally have been used interchangeably. In the professional realm, "ethics" is the term usually used, while in religion, "moral" is the predominant term, though both are generally interchangeable. Sometimes problems are labelled "moral" when organizations choose not to address them but know that some members have strong ethical views on the issue in question (e.g., some death penalty roles). Sometimes legitimate differences of opinion exist about whether specific ethical concerns should apply to the entire profession. Diamond (personal communication, April 25, 1988) distinguished between organizational ethics and personal ethics. Personal ethics can be more stringent than organizational ethics, and can be held by individuals or groups for personal reasons, but not shared by other practitioners. They may be strongly held but should not be forced on all professionals if there is a good ethical foundation for alternative approaches. They can nonetheless be powerful guides to clinical practice.

Dyer (1988) has distinguished between ethical guidelines that function in a punitive role and guidelines for good practice by the concerned psychiatrist—these are not enforceable but are aspirational and intended to be considered by psychiatrists trying to behave most ethically. For example, some of AAPL's ethical guidelines are inherently aspirational because they are impossible to enforce, such as the requirement to strive to be objective. Most of AAPL's ethical guidelines, however, are capable of being enforced should anybody wish to do so. They are aspirational only in the sense that AAPL does not enforce them. Though nobody else enforces them per se, they are relevant insofar as they elucidate guidelines of other organizations like the American Psychiatric Association (APA) who enforce many forensic issues that fall within their framework (Candilis et al. 2014). Although ethical guidelines are extremely helpful, there often is not one clear answer, and several actions may be acceptable when ethics dilemmas arise.

TRADITIONAL HIPPOCRATIC ETHICS

A guiding principle for medicine has been *primum non nocere*, or "first, do no harm." This principle is not part of the Hippocratic Oath, although the oath does enjoin the physician from using medicine to harm patients (or anyone) depending on the translation (Weinstock et al. 1990). There is evidence that *primum non nocere* was first introduced by Thomas Inman in 1860 (Sokol 2013). In the *Epidemics* authored by Hippocrates and his group, there is a similar statement: "As to diseases, make a habit of two things—to help, or at least to do no harm" (Hippocrates translated 1923), even though *primum non nocere* is nowhere in the Hippocratic Oath. This principle is also not specifically stated in the current American Medical Association (AMA) Principles of Medical Ethics. It does, however, still function "to establish physicians as a moral community (with) delineated obligations and responsibilities specific to the medical profession" (American Medical News 2000). The general public also perceives this as a dominant, fundamental ethical principle guiding medical practice. The Hippocratic Oath in modified forms still is recited in many medical school graduations. The Oath was modified to permit surgery, omit the need to swear by Apollo, eliminate the bans on charging for medical education, as well as eliminate the bans forbidding abortion, euthanasia, and interestingly, sex with patients (Hulkower 2009/2010); and it reiterates the primary duty to patients in a treatment role, though this is not the case in a forensic role.

Hippocratic ethics made a resurgence when medicine was introduced into medieval Europe, probably due to its similarities to the Catholic confessional, with its paternalism and secrecy. Current medical ethical codifications date back to Thomas Percival, who in the late eighteenth century wrote his *Medical Ethics* that presented a scheme for professional conduct with many features in common with the Hippocratic Oath. It became a model for ethical codes in the United States, even though it was not adopted as an approach in England. The United Kingdom has relied more on the honor of physicians, believing rules cannot cover all contingencies (Candilis et al. 2007). Similarly, in the legal area, the United Kingdom relies more on respect for physicians and does not have privilege laws. In 1847 a dispute among several schools of physicians in the United States led orthodox practitioners to found the AMA, which adopted a Code of Ethics patterned after Percival.

AMA PRINCIPLES OF MEDICAL ETHICS

In its introductions to the Principles, the AMA states:

> The medical profession has long subscribed to a body of ethical statements developed primarily for the benefit of the patient. As a member of this profession, a physician must recognize responsibility to patients first and foremost, as well as to society, to other health professionals, and to self. The following Principles adopted by the American Medical Association are not laws, but standards of conduct, which define the essentials of honorable behavior for the physician. (AMA 2001)

THE DEVELOPMENT OF AAPL ETHICS GUIDELINES

AAPL has developed an important set of ethics guidelines for the practice of forensic psychiatry. Although not enforced by AAPL, they can be used to flush out the meaning of guidelines that are part of the APA framework, because the APA guidelines are enforced through the APA local district branches, and many of the guidelines pertain to forensic psychiatric practice. In the commentary section of the ethics guidelines, it states:

> [T]he ethics committee may issue opinions on general or hypothetical questions but will not issue opinions on the ethical conduct of specific forensic psychiatrists or about actual cases. The Academy, through its Ethics Committee, or in any other way suitable, is available to the local or national committees on ethics of the American Psychiatric Association, to state licensing boards or to ethics committees of psychiatric organizations in other countries to aid them in their adjudication of complaints of unethical conduct or the development of guidelines of ethical conduct as they relate to forensic psychiatric issues. (AAPL 2005)

The AAPL ethics committee has recently resumed consulting with the APA ethics committee and the local district branches on ethics questions they may have pertaining to forensic psychiatry without giving an opinion on the ethics case itself. For instance, in the past when a forensic psychiatrist was accused of being rude, questions of how to assess for rudeness surfaced. The ethics committee responded that it was important to distinguish between actual rudeness via name-calling and being demeaning versus misperceived rudeness such as probing areas the person might prefer not to discuss, being skeptical of information provided, and wanting to obtain corroborating evidence. The latter examples are an essential part of a forensic examination in which certain information may be crucial for a meaningful assessment, and the possibility of malingering must be evaluated. These are not examples of rudeness. Forensic assessments in that regard differ from ordinary treatment assessments in which information can be obtained later in treatment, and malingering, while possible, is less common. Such distinctions were helpful and demonstrate how the AAPL ethics committee can assist the APA ethics committee in issues that arise in the forensic realm.

The first AAPL ethics guidelines were adopted in 1987, and there have been significant changes over the years, with the last revision adopted in 2005. The original ethics guidelines required forensic psychiatrists to be both unbiased and objective, which Diamond (1959) argued would be impossible for anyone to achieve. As he stated, all of us have our biases. For example, in criminal cases some identify with the prosecution. They want those breaking the law to be locked up, in order to be punished and because they could be dangerous and reoffend. Some alternatively identify with the defense and want to rescue those accused. They may offer reasons to side with the defendant such as concern for inadequate representation by an overworked public defender, for lacking mental health treatment resources for a chronic illness, or for suffering abuse or neglect as children. Hopefully, most of us are not set inflexibly on the extremes of this continuum, but it is clear that we all have our biases. It is neither helpful nor honest to pretend they do not exist. The challenge as forensic psychiatrists is to try to overcome our inevitable biases to reach as objective an opinion as possible.

Similarly, in the civil area, some of us are biased in favor of plaintiffs who may have suffered a severe injury that interferes with their functioning. We may feel they need help, and a wealthy insurance company can afford to pay regardless of whether legal technicalities are met. We may be prone to believe what plaintiffs tell us uncritically. On the other side, we may not want to reward malingering by giving plaintiffs advantages they do not deserve. Also, malingering costs all of society by increases in insurance rates. We may believe little of what plaintiffs tell us and think there almost always is gross exaggeration if not downright malingering. Most of us again likely lie at different points in that continuum which may be subject to change depending on time and circumstance.

Diamond then went on to say that in the unlikely event we have no bias at all in a case, once we reach an opinion we will want to advocate for our opinion and be biased in favor of the opinion we had reached. Diamond thought objectivity itself also was an impossible feat.

AAPL in revising this part of the ethical guidelines agreed that bias was inevitable because it is not volitional. It is true for all who do forensic work though not all organizations or practitioners are insightful or honest enough to admit it. AAPL replaced the requirement of being unbiased with a requirement to be honest—analogous to the Appelbaum requirement for truth-telling. But AAPL did not agree with Diamond about the impossibility of objectivity. Instead, AAPL thought it important for forensic psychiatrists to work to overcome biases resulting in the ethics guideline for striving for objectivity and to reach an objective opinion nonetheless.

AAPL ETHICS GUIDELINES (LAST REVISED 2005)

The main sections of the AAPL ethics guidelines are reprinted as follows:

1. *Preamble*: The American Academy of Psychiatry and the Law (AAPL) is dedicated to the highest standards of practice in forensic psychiatry. Recognizing the unique aspects of this practice, which is at the interface of the professions of psychiatry and the law, the Academy presents these guidelines for the ethical practice of forensic psychiatry.
2. *Confidentiality*: Respect for the individual's right of privacy and the maintenance of confidentiality should be major concerns when performing forensic evaluations. Psychiatrists should maintain confidentiality to the extent possible, given the legal context. Special attention should be paid to the evaluee's understanding of medical confidentiality. A forensic evaluation requires notice to the evaluee and to collateral sources of reasonably anticipated limitations on confidentiality. Information or reports derived from a forensic evaluation are subject to the rules of confidentiality that apply to the particular evaluation, and any disclosure should be restricted accordingly.
3. *Consent*: At the outset of a face-to-face evaluation, notice should be given to the evaluee of the nature and purpose of the evaluation and the limits of its confidentiality. The informed consent of the person undergoing the forensic evaluation should be obtained when necessary and feasible. If the evaluee is not competent to give consent, the evaluator should follow the appropriate laws of the jurisdiction.
4. *Honesty and Striving for Objectivity*: When psychiatrists function as experts within the legal process, they should adhere to the principle of honesty and should strive for objectivity. Although they may be retained by one

party to a civil or criminal matter, psychiatrists should adhere to these principles when conducting evaluations, applying clinical data to legal criteria, and expressing opinions.

5. *Qualifications*: Expertise in the practice of forensic psychiatry should be claimed only in areas of actual knowledge, skills, training, and experience.

The AAPL ethics guidelines have a commentary on each section that elaborates and provides supplementary information. Below are some important forensic issues excerpted from the commentary section.

In the preamble the commentary includes:

> Psychiatrists in a forensic role are called upon to practice in a manner that balances competing duties to the individual and to society. In doing so, they should be bound by underlying ethical principles of respect for persons, honesty, justice, and social responsibility. However, when a treatment relationship exists, such as in correctional settings, the usual physician-patient duties apply.

In the commentary on confidentiality section it includes:

> At the beginning of a forensic evaluation, care should be taken to explicitly inform the evaluee that the psychiatrist is not the evaluee's 'doctor.' Psychiatrists have a continuing obligation to be sensitive to the fact that although a warning has been given, the evaluee may develop the belief that there is a treatment relationship. Psychiatrists should take precautions to ensure that they do not release confidential information to unauthorized persons.

The consent section of the commentary includes the following:

> Absent a court order, psychiatrists should not perform forensic evaluations for the prosecution or the government on persons who have not consulted with legal counsel when such persons are: known to be charged with criminal acts; under investigation for criminal or quasi-criminal conduct; held in government custody or detention; or being interrogated for criminal or quasi-criminal conduct, hostile acts against a government, or immigration violations. Examinations related to rendering medical care or treatment, such as evaluations for civil commitment or risk assessments for management or discharge planning, are not precluded by these restrictions. As is true for any physician, psychiatrists practicing in a forensic role should not participate in torture.
>
> Consent to treatment in a jail or prison or in other criminal justice settings is different from consent for a forensic evaluation.

In the honesty and striving for objectivity section the commentary includes the following:

> Honesty, objectivity and the adequacy of the clinical evaluation may be called into question when an expert opinion is offered without a personal examination. For certain evaluations (such as record reviews for malpractice cases), a personal examination is not required. In all other forensic evaluations, if, after appropriate effort, it is not feasible to conduct a personal examination, an opinion may nonetheless be rendered on the basis of other information. Under these circumstances, it is the responsibility of psychiatrists to make earnest efforts to ensure that their statements, opinions and any reports or testimony based on those opinions, clearly state that there was no personal examination and note any resulting limitations to their opinions.
>
> Contingency fees undermine honesty and efforts to attain objectivity and should not be accepted. Retainer fees, however, do not create the same problems in regard to honesty and efforts to attain objectivity and, therefore, may be accepted.
>
> Psychiatrists who take on a forensic role for patients they are treating may adversely affect the therapeutic relationship with them. Forensic evaluations usually require interviewing corroborative sources, exposing information to public scrutiny, or subjecting evaluees and the treatment itself to potentially damaging cross-examination. The forensic evaluation and the credibility of the practitioner may also be undermined by conflicts inherent in the differing clinical and forensic roles. Treating psychiatrists should therefore generally avoid acting as an expert witness for their patients or performing evaluations of their patients for legal purposes.
>
> Treating psychiatrists appearing as "fact" witnesses should be sensitive to the unnecessary disclosure of private information or the possible misinterpretation of testimony as "expert" opinion. In situations when the dual role is required or unavoidable (such as Workers' Compensation, disability evaluations, civil commitment, or guardianship hearings), sensitivity to differences between clinical and legal obligations remains important.

AAPL also has a section on Questions and Answers (revised in 2013) that further flushes out the meaning of the guidelines. The Questions and Answers as well as the guidelines with the full commentary can be accessed at http://aapl.org/ethics.htm.

AAPL's guidelines were developed specifically for forensic psychiatry and address important, relevant issues. However, they exclude or are vague regarding issues for which consensus could not be obtained. They represent guidelines for good practice, though in reality most AAPL guidelines have reached a level of general agreement and as such represent a consensus as to what is required for ethical practice. The AAPL guidelines are aspirational and not enforced as such but can help clarify ethical questions and positions to enable assessment of actions of a forensic psychiatrist by the state medical boards or the local APA district branches enforcing the APA ethics Annotations. In this way, the AAPL ethics guidelines can be enforced. Ethics complaints are referred to the APA district branch, which has the option to consider them, or to another analogous body for foreign members. AAPL members who belong only to the American Academy of Child and Adolescent Psychiatry have ethical complaints against them referred to that organization, which in turn refers complaints to state licensing boards.

The APA district branch ethics committees, who actually conduct ethics investigation hearings involving APA members accused of an ethics violation, increasingly consider the AAPL guidelines to clarify APA Annotations. The high response rate in surveys, and the fact that an overwhelming majority of forensic psychiatrists in surveys indicate they have encountered ethical problems, belies any aspersions that forensic psychiatrists are unconcerned about, or insensitive to, ethical problems.

A survey of AAPL members (Weinstock et al. 1991) showed support (in decreasing order) for the following additional guidelines that are not currently part of the official guidelines:

1. Medical and psychiatric ethics remain a consideration when performing a forensic evaluation.
2. The forensic psychiatrist should not distort data.
3. Sex between a forensic psychiatrist and an evaluee is unethical so long as the case remains in litigation.
4. Because of the seriousness of the matter, an opinion should not be given in a death penalty case without a personal examination regardless of whether court decisions hold such testimony permissible.
5. As a physician, a forensic psychiatrist owes some responsibility both to an evaluee and society, regardless of who pays the fee.

PRINCIPLES OF MEDICAL ETHICS WITH ANNOTATIONS ESPECIALLY APPLICABLE TO PSYCHIATRY RELEVANT TO FORENSIC PSYCHIATRY

The APA has developed Annotations that were revised to include the latest version of the AMA Principles of Medical Ethics (American Psychiatric Association 2013). They elaborate on issues and situations especially applicable and relevant to psychiatric practice.

In reference to the APA Annotations, Appelbaum (1992) has stated that the Annotations suffer insofar as "they are generated on an ad hoc basis, as an issue rises to the surface in the APA rather than in a systematic effort to elaborate an ethical code." Although many are relevant, they are not specifically directed to the forensic setting. Moreover, as mentioned by Appelbaum, some rules are "so general as to create no boundaries at all." Nonetheless, many of the Annotations are relevant to forensic psychiatry.

The existing Annotations are enforced through the APA district branches. They are important for all psychiatrists, and ignorance is not a legitimate excuse. An allegation of an ethics violation against an APA member is investigated by the local district branch of the APA, which holds hearings and recommends sanctions if an ethical violation is found. Sanctions include admonishment, reprimand, suspension, and expulsion from the APA. Expulsions and more than very brief suspensions also are reported to the National Practitioners Data Bank since September 1, 1990. The Data Bank contains records of medical professionals, psychotherapists, and dentists who have been successfully sued (even if settled), whose licenses have been revoked or suspended, or who have been sanctioned by a hospital, medical group, or health plan with a peer review system (with privileges suspended or removed). In addition, the Ethics Committee of the APA district branches can report offending member psychiatrists to state licensing boards. If a member resigns while the case is under investigation, this fact can be made public in an APA publication if the allegation is serious.

The section numbers in the Annotations correspond to those numbers of the AMA Principles. Relevant annotations that address forensic psychiatric issues are as follows:

Section 1

Annotation 4 prohibits physician participation in a legally authorized execution. This section had been interpreted solely as prohibiting administering lethal injections. The AMA has already passed resolutions affirming that it is unethical for physicians, regardless of their personal views of capital punishment, to participate in legally authorized executions, except to certify death. They have stated that involvement short of the death penalty process itself is ethical. They even say the controversial testimony about aggravating circumstances at the penalty phase of a capital trial is ethical, as is the testimony of mitigating circumstances. They do not consider it ethical to treat someone for the purpose of making them competent to be executed. But it is ethical to treat them to relieve suffering or maintain prison security even if that is likely to result in a prisoner becoming competent to be executed. The intent of the psychiatrist is the determining factor here.

Section 2

Annotation 1 states that sexual activity with a current or former patient is unethical because of the inherent inequality in the doctor–patient relationship that may lead to exploitation. Annotation 2 states that the psychiatrist should diligently guard against exploiting information furnished by the patient and should not use the power afforded to him or her to influence the patient in ways not directly relevant to treatment goals. Annotation 3 states that psychiatrists who practice outside their areas of expertise should be considered to be practicing unethically. Annotation 4 states that in situations in which psychiatrists, because of mental illness, jeopardize the welfare of their patients and their own reputations and practices, it is ethical and even encouraged for another psychiatrist to intercede. Annotation 5 states that like all medical services, psychiatric services are dispensed in the context of a contractual arrangement with the patient binding on the physician as well as on the patient, and the provisions of such a contract should be established explicitly. Annotation 7 states that it is unacceptable to engage in fee splitting—that is, providing supervision or administration to other physicians or nonmedical people for a percentage of their fees or gross income. It is ethical though in a team of practitioners or a multidisciplinary team to receive income for administration, research, education, or consultation if based on a mutually agreed upon set fee or salary open to renegotiation as time demand changes.

Section 3

Annotation 1 indicates that when illegal activities bear directly upon practice, it would be self-evident that such a psychiatrist would be ethically unsuited to practice. Protesting social injustice probably would not bear on either the psychiatrist's image or his or her ability to treat patients ethically and competently. Although no prior assurance about any illegal activity could be given, it is conceivable that an individual could violate a law in such circumstances without being guilty of unethical professional behavior.

Section 4

Annotation 1 requires the protection of patient records, even the identification of the person as a patient. Annotations 2 and 5 involve confidentiality and its limitations and the exercise of caution when disclosing sensitive patient information. Annotation 5 states that the disclosure of sensitive material like fantasy material and sexual orientation is usually unnecessary. Annotation 3 requires adequate disguise to protect anonymity in teaching and writing. Annotation 4 includes a duty in consultations to alert any nonphysician consultant to the duty of confidentiality.

Annotation 6 directly is applicable to forensic psychiatry and states that if individuals are examined for security purposes, determining suitability for certain jobs, or determining legal competence, the nature, purpose, and lack of confidentiality of the examination must be explained at the onset to the examinee. Although Annotation 6 does not specifically cover all forensic examinations, AAPL ethical guidelines require such explanations whenever lack of confidentiality is involved. Annotation 9 applies if psychiatrists are ordered by the court to reveal patient confidences. They may comply or ethically hold the right to dissent within the framework of the law. If in doubt, they should respect the right of the patient to confidentiality and unimpaired treatment and should reserve the right to raise the question of adequate need for disclosure. If case disclosure is required by the court, then the right to disclose only information relevant to the legal question at hand may be requested.

Annotation 13 states that "psychiatric evaluations of any person charged with criminal acts prior to access to, or availability of, legal counsel should not be performed except for rendering of care for the sole purpose of medical treatment." This is also an AAPL requirement in the commentary under section III Consent in the AAPL ethics guidelines. Annotation 14 states that sexual involvement between faculty members or supervisors and trainees or students may be unethical because an abuse of power can occur that takes advantage of inequalities in the working relationship.

Section 6

Annotation 2 states that it is ethical to refuse to provide psychiatric treatment to anyone who cannot be diagnosed in the psychiatrist's opinion with a mental illness amenable to psychiatric treatment.

Section 7

Annotation 3 refers to public figures or others who have disclosed information about themselves through the public media. It says it is ethical to share with the public opinions about psychiatric issues in general under such circumstances. But it is unethical to express an opinion about such an individual without a personal examination and proper authorization for such a statement. Annotation 4 concludes that a personal examination of the patient is required prior to certifying a patient for involuntary treatment. Annotation 5 states psychiatrists should not participate in torture.

Section 8

This section states that when caring for patients, responsibility to the patient is paramount. Annotation 1 clarifies that relationships with outside organizations can affect patient care. Annotation 2 says when these conflicts exist, psychiatrists must resolve them in a way believed to benefit patients. Annotation 3 states when these relationships conflict with patient needs, the patient or decision maker should be informed. Annotation 4 states when patients are informed of treatment options in order to promote an informed treatment decision, the options presented should include those not available from the psychiatrist or affiliated organization.

OPINIONS OF THE APA ETHICS COMMITTEE ON THE PRINCIPLES OF MEDICAL ETHICS RELEVANT TO FORENSIC PSYCHIATRY

Some published Opinions of the APA Ethics Committee on the Principles of Medical Ethics also are relevant (American Psychiatric Association 2013, 2014). The Opinions relevant to forensic psychiatry are listed under G followed by a number and then by a letter. The number refers to the corresponding principle of medical ethics. Below are some of the Opinions apropos to the practice of forensic psychiatry.

Section 1

Opinion G1b makes it clear that giving a lethal dose of a sedative to a prisoner in a legal execution is unethical because a physician is a healer, not a killer. Opinion G1c clarifies that it is ethical to provide a competency examination before the execution of a felon so long as the prisoner is fully informed of the purpose of the examination and has legal representation. Opinion G1d states it would be highly questionable to evaluate a family member who is a plaintiff in a lawsuit, because it is highly likely the relationship would influence the psychiatrist as well as the relative's presentation. Also, any attempt to testify would be vulnerable to challenge. Providing competent medical service would be too difficult in this situation. Opinion G1e clarifies that the same ethical principles apply in a diagnostic/consultative relationship. An example is an evaluation for an insurance company.

Section 4

Opinion G4a states it is not ethical for a hospital employee to perform a competency of a patient for the purpose of assisting his or her hospital employer to collect patient charges, because of a conflict of interest. Opinion G4b clarifies that developing a speculative psychological profile for someone who committed gruesome mass homicides is not unethical. If a psychiatrist believes the profile is that of one of his or her patients, he or she should strongly urge the patient to go to the police, perhaps with the assistance of an attorney. If the patient refuses, the psychiatrist can notify the police. If the attacks are past history, the guidelines advise only encouraging a patient to turn himself or herself over to the authorities, but it may be prudent to tell the patient to retain an attorney first so that his or her legal rights and welfare will not be ignored. Opinion G4c clarifies that it is ethical to render an opinion for an insurance company regarding the suicide of a patient based on a record review despite having no opportunity to examine the patient. Section Opinion G4d raises the issue of a psychiatrist who treated a member of a murdered prominent family, testified in court, and was later asked by a television company to be a consultant for a movie about the killing. The Opinions state it does not foster a good image but can be ethical if nothing new and no new insights other than those made public at the trial are revealed. It is unclear whether this admonition applies, though, to a nontreating forensic psychiatrist, but it is likely to apply to information not released in open court. Opinion G4e clarifies that it is ethical to evaluate a prisoner for the state and determine that the prisoner requires involuntary hospitalization if a proper psychiatric examination is performed and the nature, purpose, and lack of confidentiality of the exam are explained. Opinion G4f clarifies that it is unethical for a treating psychiatrist to participate in adversarial evaluations of their convicted sex offender patients around questions of whether they should later be screened for possible involuntary civil commitment as sexually violent predators, unless at the outset of treatment the dual relationship to them and the prison system were explained, and it was explained that their records could later be used to determine whether they later will be civilly committed as sexually violent predators.

Section 7

Opinion G7a states that consulting to the Catholic Diocese about marriage annulments regarding the competence of church members to request such an annulment is ethical without a personal examination with only a review of reports and other information. Requiring consultants always to conduct a personal examination if asked by various medical, social, and rehabilitative agencies for opinions would be impractical and would prevent their obtaining the benefits of psychiatric consultation. Opinion G7b discusses testifying for the state in a criminal case about the competency of the defendant based on medical records without examining the defendant or having his or her approval to render an opinion. The Opinion states that Section 7, Annotation 3, was developed to protect public figures from psychiatric speculation harmful to public figures and the psychiatric profession, and not to protect criminal defendants. This opinion, however, could be interpreted as not necessitating the more stringent requirement of AAPL's ethical guidelines. AAPL requires a personal examination if at all possible and creates an affirmative obligation to indicate the limitations of any opinion if given without such a personal examination.

One problem with the APA Annotations and Opinions is that they do not cover any issues in any systematic way and are not based on any underlying ethical principles other than the AMA Principles of Medical Ethics. They also are not specifically directed toward forensic psychiatry. They respond only to inquiries about actual cases (Appelbaum 1992). The APA lacks direct jurisdiction over the ethical improprieties of nonmembers, but their guidelines still are relevant for court and licensing board actions and are relevant to all who practice forensic psychiatry whether or not they are APA or AAPL members.

RELEVANT ETHICAL GUIDELINES OF OTHER PROFESSIONAL ORGANIZATIONS

The American Academy of Forensic Sciences (AAFS) also has an enforceable code of ethics, important even if limited in scope. The code precludes professional or personal conduct adverse to the best interests and purposes of AAFS that includes the following: misrepresentation of education, training, experience, area of expertise, or one or more criteria for membership; material misrepresentation of data upon which an expert opinion is based; and making public statements appearing to represent the position of AAFS without first obtaining the specific permission of the board of directors. Distortion of data addressed by AAFS is not specifically addressed by AAPL, but could be considered under the section on honesty (see AAPL guidelines). AAPL's Section V on qualifications does specifically address the need for accurate presentation of qualifications and experience. It is less clear whether these issues are covered by the APA Annotations, unless Section 2, referring to dealing honestly with patients and colleagues, would also be interpreted to include courtroom testimony, or Section 7 regarding a responsibility to participate in activities contributing to an improved community would apply. Section 1 on competent medical service is also relevant.

Other related organizations have developed ethical criteria for forensic participation. These include the American Psychological Association and the National Organization for Forensic Social Work (American Psychological Association 2010; National Organization for Forensic Social Work 2011).

CONTROVERSIAL ETHICAL ISSUES

An ethics survey of forensic psychiatrists showed almost all had encountered ethical problems in their forensic work. The "hired gun" problem was considered to be the greatest ethical problem (Weinstock 1986, 1988). However, without knowing the forensic psychiatrist's motives, it is difficult to distinguish honest bias, sometimes even unconscious, from that of a "hired gun." Moreover, it is too easy sometimes for forensic psychiatrists who consider their position "right" to confuse an honest difference of opinion with the problem of the expert on the other side being a "hired gun." AAPL has developed systematic ethics guidelines for the practice of forensic psychiatry. The principles were first developed by Jonas Rappeport, and refined, modified, and developed by Henry Weinstein, the section on honesty and striving for objectivity revised by Weinstock in the 1995 revision.

AAPL has been criticized for not enforcing its own ethical guidelines (Halpern 1990; Appelbaum 1992). Instead, it relies on the APA for enforcement. Forensic psychiatry's recognition as a subspecialty arguably makes medical ethics even more relevant. AAPL has developed procedures for peer review of transcripts of psychiatric testimony, because there is controversy regarding whether such issues should or would be covered in ethical guidelines (Weinstock et al. 1991; Appelbaum 1992). AAPL's ethical guidelines supplement the APA Annotations. Peer review enables additional professional self-regulation. However, because it is currently voluntary, such peer review is likely to be avoided by those most in need of it. Despite the criticisms, the ethical guidelines nevertheless are a very important development. They were initially passed in 1987, and last revised in 2005.

Some issues in forensic psychiatry remain controversial. The death penalty, for example, produces conflict in forensic psychiatry, as it does generally in American society, with the additional factor of the forensic psychiatrist being a physician. All other Western democracies have abolished the death penalty. In capital cases, the legal system often asks forensic psychiatrists to examine defendants and evaluate various legal issues, including various competencies, mental state at the time of the offense, dangerousness, and aggravating and mitigating circumstances. It can be argued in one extreme that psychiatric assessments of these forensic issues are shared by both capital and noncapital cases and do not differ. At the other extreme, some psychiatrists question the ethical propriety of providing consultation to the prosecution at any stage of a capital case (Leong et al. 2000). There are many intermediate positions.

Although there is some correlation between a psychiatrist's personal views of the death penalty and their professional views about the proper role of the forensic psychiatrist in such cases, the two are not the same. It is possible to oppose capital punishment as a citizen but to participate in the process short of the actual killing because the psychiatrist believes it does not violate professional ethics. It is not the psychiatrist's professional role to question current law, the opinion is sufficiently removed from the killing process, and such a view is supported by current professional ethical guidelines. Forensic psychiatrists who support the death penalty as a citizen can still believe it violates their view of appropriate professional medical ethics to participate in some or all forensic roles. Forensic psychiatrists who oppose the death penalty also can choose to participate honestly in cases in which they think their involvement could be helpful, even if the opposite result sometimes occurs (Diamond 1990, 1992; Foot 1990). The APA has taken a position against treating defendants incompetent to be executed if the purpose is to make them competent to be executed.

ETHICAL PRACTICE

According to the theory of virtue ethics, ethical guidelines and even knowing what is right does not necessarily lead to doing the right thing. It is necessary to wish to be ethical. Knowledge will not necessarily affect the behavior of the "hired gun." However, it is often difficult to know whether a forensic psychiatrist truly has an idiosyncratic belief, has been insensitive, or has been dishonest. Ethics committees could be placed in an untenable position of having to determine the intent of an alleged offending action. Forensic psychiatrists should not unfairly be blamed for the problems of the adversarial legal system.

Guidelines can help clarify what is ethical. However, the best insurer of ethical conduct must be the integrity of the professional persons themselves who, in forensic psychiatry, face the challenge of confronting and balancing many conflicting values. These challenges are not unique to forensic psychiatry, but are more complex than in the relatively uncomplicated treatment context, and are unique insofar as the interface is with the legal system. These challenges can provide some of the enjoyment of being a forensic psychiatrist. However, organizations that do enforce ethics requirements and provide sanctions should be aware of the complex balancing of values involved in forensic psychiatric practice. Sanctions should not be imposed if there is no general consensus, and legitimate differences of opinion about a specific ethics dilemma could apply.

REFERENCES

American Academy of Psychiatry and the Law (AAPL). 2005. *Ethics Guidelines for the Practice of Forensic Psychiatry*. http://aapl.org/ethics.htm, accessed April 27, 2015.

American Academy of Psychiatry and the Law. 2013. *Questions and Answers*. http://aapl.org/ethics.htm, accessed April 27, 2015.

American Medical Association (AMA). 2001. *Principles of Medical Ethics*. Chicago, IL: AMA.

American Medical News. 2000, May 1. *Employer Health Exams; Relevance of Hippocratic Oath*. Chicago, IL: American Medical Association.

American Psychiatric Association (APA). 2013. *The Principles of Medical Ethics with Annotations Especially Applicable to Psychiatry*. Washington, DC: APA.

American Psychiatric Association (APA). 2014. *Opinions of the Ethics Committee on the Principles of Medical Ethics with Annotations Especially Applicable to Psychiatry*. Washington, DC: APA.

American Psychological Association. 2010. *Ethical Principles of Psychologists and Code of Conduct*. Washington, DC: American Psychological Association.

Appelbaum PS. 1984. Psychiatric ethics in the courtroom. *Bulletin of the American Academy of Psychiatry and the Law* 12:225–231.

Appelbaum PS. 1990. The parable of the forensic psychiatrist: Ethics and the problem of doing harm. *International Journal of Law and Psychiatry* 13:249–259.

Appelbaum PS. 1992. Forensic psychiatry: The need for self-regulation. *Bulletin of the American Academy of Psychiatry and the Law* 20:153–162.

Appelbaum PS. 1997. A theory of ethics for forensic psychiatry. *Journal of the American Academy of Psychiatry and the Law* 25:233–247.

Appelbaum PS and N Scurich. 2014. Evidence on the adjudication of criminal behavior. *Journal of the American Academy of Psychiatry and the Law* 42:91–100.

Aspinwall LG, TR Brown, and J Tabery. 2012. The double-edged sword: Does biomechanism increase or decrease judges' sentencing of psychopaths? *Science* 337:846–849.

Beauchamp TL and JF Childress. 2013. *Principles of Biomedical Ethics*. 7th edition. New York: Oxford University Press.

Candilis PJ, CC Dike, CJ Meyer, WC Myers, and R Weinstock. 2014. Should AAPL enforce its ethics? Challenges and solutions. *Journal of the American Academy of Psychiatry and the Law* 47:322–330.

Candilis PL, R Martinez, and C Dorning. 2001. Principles and narrative in forensic psychiatry: Toward a robust view of professional role. *Journal of the American Academy of Psychiatry and the Law* 29:167–173.

Candilis PJ, R Weinstock, and R Martinez. 2007. *Forensic Ethics and the Expert Witness*. New York: Springer.

Childress JF. 1997. *Practical Reasoning in Bioethics*. Bloomington: Indiana University Press.

Ciccone JR and C Clements. 2001. Commentary: Forensic psychiatry and ethics—The voyage continues. *Journal of the American Academy of Psychiatry and the Law* 29:174–179.

Diamond BL. 1959. The fallacy of the impartial expert. *Archives Criminal Psychodynamics* 3:221–235.

Diamond BL. 1990. The psychiatrist expert witness: Honest advocate or "hired gun"? In *Ethical Practice in Psychiatry and the Law*, edited by R Rosner and R Weinstock, New York: Plenum Press, 75–84.

Diamond BL. 1992. The forensic psychiatrist: Consultant v. activist in legal doctrine. *Bulletin of the American Academy of Psychiatry and the Law* 20:119–132.

Dyer AR. 1988. *Psychiatry and Ethics*. Washington, DC: American Psychiatric Press.

Foot P. 1990. Ethics and the death penalty: Participation by forensic psychiatrists in capital trials. In *Ethical Practice in Psychiatry and the Law*, edited by R Rosner and R Weinstock, New York: Plenum Press, 207–217.

Griffith EEH. 1998. Ethics in forensic psychiatry: A response to Stone and Appelbaum. *Journal of the American Academy of Psychiatry and the Law* 26:171–184.

Griffith EEH. 2005. Personal narrative and an African American perspective on medical ethics. *Journal of the American Academy of Psychiatry and the Law* 33:371–381.

Halpern AL. 1990. Adjudication of AAPL ethical complaints: A proposal. In *Ethical Practice in Psychiatry and the Law*, edited by R Rosner and R Weinstock, New York: Plenum Press, 171–174.

Hippocrates. 1923. *Epidemics*, Book 1, Section 11, vol. 1. W.H.S. Jones, trans. Cambridge, MA: Loeb Classical Library, Harvard University Press, 165.

Hulkower R. 2009/2010. The history of the Hippocratic Oath: Outdated, inauthentic and yet still relevant. *Einstein Journal of Biology and Medicine* 25/26(1):41–44.

Hundert EM. 1990. Competing medical and legal ethical values: Balancing problems of the forensic psychiatrist. In *Ethical Practice in Psychiatry and the Law*, edited by R Rosner and R Weinstock, New York: Plenum Press, 53–72.

Leong GB, JA Silva, R Weinstock, and L Ganzini, 2000. Survey of forensic psychiatrists on evaluation and treatment of prisoners on death row. *Journal of the American Academy of Psychiatry and the Law* 28:427–432.

Moore MS. 1984. *Law and Psychiatry: Rethinking the Relationship*. New York: Cambridge University Press.

National Organization of Forensic Social Work Code of Ethics, revised November 16, 2011. http://nofsw.org/wp-content/uploads/2014/03/NOSFW-Code-of-Ethics-Changes-2-16-12.pdf, accessed July 10, 2016.

Norko MA. 2005. Commentary: Compassion at the core of forensic psychiatric ethics. *Journal of the American Academy of Psychiatry and the Law* 33:386–389.

Rosner R. 1990. Forensic psychiatry: A subspecialty. In *Ethical Practice in Psychiatry and the Law*, edited by R Rosner and R Weinstock, New York: Plenum Press, 19–29.

Sokol DK. 2013. First do no harm revisited. *British Medical Journal* 347:f6246.

Stone AA. 1984. Forensic psychiatry: A view from the ivory tower. *Journal of the American Academy of Psychiatry and the Law* 12:209–19.

Weinstock R. 1986. Ethical concerns expressed by forensic psychiatrists. *Journal of Forensic Sciences* 31:596–602.

Weinstock R. 1988. Controversial ethical issues in forensic psychiatry: A survey. *Journal of Forensic Sciences* 33:176–186.

Weinstock R. 2001. Commentary: A broadened conception of forensic psychiatric ethics. *Journal of the American Academy of Psychiatry and the Law* 29:180–185.

Weinstock R. 2015. Dialectical principlism: An approach to finding our most ethical action. *Journal of the American Academy of Psychiatry and the Law* 43:10–20.

Weinstock R, GB Leong, and JA Silva. 1990. The role of traditional medical ethics in forensic psychiatry. In *Ethical Practice in Psychiatry and the Law*, edited by R Rosner and R Weinstock, New York: Plenum Press, 31–51.

Weinstock R, GB Leong, and JA Silva. 1991. Opinions by AAPL forensic psychiatrists on controversial ethical guidelines: A survey. *Bulletin of the American Academy of Psychiatry and the Law* 19:237–248; erratum 19, 393.

9

What makes it right: Foundations for professional ethics

RICHARD ROSNER*

INTRODUCTION

One of the hallmarks of a profession is that its members share an ethical code, setting out the conduct that they regard, collectively, as acceptable. The professions are, however, unlikely to set forth its foundation—that is, what makes it right. The following is meant to stimulate thought about this gap.

A professional ethical code is an example of normative ethics, the study of the standards used for the ethical evaluation of conduct. A justification of a professional ethical code is an example of meta-ethics, the study of the meaning of ethical terms, such as "right." It is possible, but unsatisfying, to have an ethical code that is not justified, a normative ethics that is not connected to meta-ethics.

The leading nonjustifying explanations of all ethical codes are ethical relativism and subjectivism; the main justifications for ethical codes are (1) divine commandment, (2) natural law, (3) traditional folk ways, (4) consequentialism, (5) deontology, and (6) feminist ethics.

The two nonjustifying explanations for ethical codes are ethical relativism and subjectivism/emotivism.

ETHICAL RELATIVISM

Ethical relativism starts from the position that there are many ethical codes, often disagreeing about what is right. For ethical relativists, a specific professional ethical code is right because the members of its specific profession internally regard it as so. The Catholic clergy, for example, may agree that abortion is wrong, but ethical relativism states that all that makes it wrong for them is their internal agreement; obstetricians and gynecologists may agree that abortion is right, but similarly, it is only right for them because of their internal agreement. In ethical relativism, there is no external, objective standard of wrong and right and no method of adjudicating between them.

Among the criticisms of ethical relativism is that it is based on unsound reasoning. An alternative position is that it is possible that one of the ethical justifying theories is correct, but that no one yet knows this. There was once a time, for example, when some people thought that the sun moved around the earth (geocentrism) and some other people thought that the earth moved around the sun (heliocentrism). It would have been possible, but wrong, to conclude that neither theory was right. Some critics of ethical relativism suggest parallels for ethical theory, while others suggest that an as-yet-unknown correct ethical theory will emerge in future, even if no existing one is correct (Frankena 1973, 109–110; Rachels 2003, 16–31).

SUBJECTIVISM/EMOTIVISM

In its twentieth-century formulation, subjectivism is called emotivism, regarding ethical statements merely as expressions of subjective emotional states. Saying, for example, that "Abortion is bad!" or "Abortion is good!" is regarded as tantamount to saying "Abortion: phooey!" or "Abortion: hooray!" Such expressions also function as imperatives—that is, ordering people to refrain from acting in a certain way ("phooey" = do not get an abortion) or to act ("hooray" = get an abortion). For ethical subjectivists, there is no justification for any ethical code and no objective standard for evaluation; disagreements about whether an act or principle is right are like disagreements about whether a particular aesthetic style is beautiful.

Critics of ethical subjectivism find it unsatisfying because (1) it precludes a role for rationality in ethical decision making and (2) it makes emotional manipulation, such as

* This chapter is reprinted with permission from John Wiley & Sons, Ltd. from Richard Rosner's part of the following article: Grounds A, Gunn J, Myers WC, Rosner R, and Busch KG. 2010. Contemplating common ground in the professional ethics of forensic psychiatry. *Criminal Behaviour and Mental Health* 20(5):307–322.

advertising or propaganda, a legitimate means of influencing ethical codes (Rachels 2003, 32–47). The six justifying explanations for ethical codes are (1) divine commandment, (2) natural law, (3) traditional folk ways, (4) consequentialism, (5) deontology, and (6) feminist ethics.

DIVINE COMMAND

According to this view, popular among Christian, Muslim, and Jewish fundamentalists, something is right because God commanded it. The justification for the Ten Commandments, for example, is that God commanded obedience to them.

Critics of this theory say that it makes God's commands arbitrary. In one commandment, for example, God says: "honour your father and your mother." Is it God's command itself that makes it right for us to honor our parents? If it is, then, had God ordered us to dishonor them, then that behavior would be right. The suggestion that God's commands are purely arbitrary is rarely comfortable for religious people; they are likely to suggest an alternative, e.g., that in His wisdom, God knows what is right for us. If this latter view is correct, however, then it is not God's command per se that makes something right (Frankena 1973, 28–30; Rachels 2003, 48–53).

NATURAL LAW

The classic statement of this ethical theory lies with St Thomas Aquinas, in Europe's Middle Ages. Greatly oversimplified, it holds that God endowed us with the rational capacity to derive ethical rules from observations of the empirical facts of the world we live in. For natural law ethicists, there is a necessary connection between reason and what is right. Such an ethical code is not arbitrary and must benefit the persons who subscribe to it. Natural law ethicists might, for example, observe the fact that human genitalia enable human reproduction and conclude that it is ethical to use them for reproductive ends, but not for nonreproductive ends (e.g., for pleasure).

Critics of this approach say that the theory is not logically sound—"natural facts" do not lead to "natural oughts"—and that different persons looking at the same facts may come to different conclusions. To pursue the genitalia example, others might observe that human genitalia enable both reproduction and pleasure and conclude that it is ethical to use them for both (Rachels 2003, 53–62).

TRADITION

According to this view, an ethical code is right because people who adhere to it have always regarded it as right. The Hippocratic Oath recites one ethical code of physicians. In this theory, what makes it right would be that Western doctors have accepted it for over 2000 years.

Critics of traditional ethics state that this theory precludes advances in ethical codes, as change could not be justified if tradition alone made a code right. Slavery and female disenfranchisement have been, and in some cultures still are, traditionally thus regarded as right. Traditional ethics fixes ethics forever, preventing the growth and development of ethical standards for human conduct (Rachels 2003, 18).

CONSEQUENTIALISM (UTILITARIANISM)

Called utilitarianism in nineteenth-century England, consequentialism holds that what makes an ethical code right is that compliance with it produces the greatest good for the greatest number of persons. For consequentialist ethicists, there is a necessary connection between goodness and rightness, and the ends justify the means. Given two or more different courses of action, the course that produces the most good for the most people is the right one.

Critics of consequentialism state that it may conflict with justice and individual rights (Frankena 1973, 34–43; Rachels 2003, 91–116).

DEONTOLOGY

This view asserts that something other than desirable consequences makes an ethical code right. Kant was its most famous exponent. According to him, some things are contingently or hypothetically right (because they lead to a desired outcome in fact) and some categorically right (because right in themselves). Kant called his criterion of being right "the categorical imperative." It can be formulated as a criterion to act always so that the maxim of your action can be a universal and eternal rule for everyone, or the converse of this. If you pay your debts, for example, the maxim of your action is that it is right to pay debts, and the permanent and universal rule is that everyone should always pay their debts; this is a non-self-defeating maxim that can be followed. If, by contrast, you steal from others, the maxim of your action is that it is right to steal, but if this maxim were to be made into an enduring rule for everyone, society would self-destruct, making it a self-defeating maxim that cannot be followed.

Critics of deontology say that it may lead to incompatible ethical rules in irresolvable conflict, e.g., having one rule always to tell the truth and another never to endanger human life. What do you do in occupied Holland if you are hiding Anne Frank and her family when the Nazis knock on the door and ask if you know where they are (Frankena 1973, 23–33; Rachels 2003, 117–140)?

FEMINIST ETHICS

Most ethical theorists in the Western tradition have been men. Twentieth-century feminists argued that there are sufficient female–male differences that a feminist ethics is required. Men, they suggest, are interested in abstract and impersonal principles, as just described, while they are interested in caring and personal relationships.

SUMMARY

My view is that there is a gap in professional ethical codes in their failure to offer grounding for the ethical precepts that they offer. Although there are no explanations and no justifications that are beyond criticism, it may be that the drafters of professional ethical codes are avoidant of revealing the lack of meta-ethical foundations for their normative ethical prescriptions.

Critics note that this theory is not as detailed or complete as the others; if so, this may be due to its relatively recent origin (Rachels, 2003, 160–172).

REFERENCES

Frankena W. 1973. *Ethics*, 2nd edition. Englewood Cliffs, NJ: Prentice Hall.

Rachels J. 2003. *The Elements of Moral Philosophy*, 4th edition. New York: McGraw-Hill.

10

Liability of the forensic psychiatrist

DANIEL BONNICI, KATE BOLTON BONNICI, ROBERT WEINSTOCK, AND THOMAS GARRICK

INTRODUCTION

Potential legal causes of action against psychiatrists practicing in a general clinical context include medical malpractice, other types of negligence, intentional torts, federal civil rights law (statutory causes of action), and medical board complaints. Forensic psychiatrists operate within a narrower ambit than general psychiatrists, with different employers and different tasks. Because forensic psychiatrists have a particular and proscribed role, some of the liability concerns inherent in a broader clinical psychiatric practice are constrained. Because forensic psychiatrists are functioning as psychiatrists and not attorneys, they are not liable for not knowing the law. However, forensic psychiatrists should become aware of existing legal theories and causes of action, usually by consulting with an attorney about the laws in the place the alleged action occurred, as laws and legal criteria can vary widely by jurisdiction. In considering questions of legal liability for medical malpractice and negligence claims arising out of medical practice, which generally involve questions of fact, one must first resolve the following questions: (1) Who is the forensic client? (2) What is the forensic task? and (3) Is the psychiatrist immune from liability or prosecution?

OVERVIEW OF LEGAL LIABILITY

Broadly stated, the elements of negligence include a duty of care on the part of the defendant, breach of said duty, and such breach of duty must directly and proximately cause harm. Medical malpractice involves a legal claim similar to negligence, but requires an existing physician–patient relationship, and physicians are held to a "professional" standard. Less common causes of action include intentional torts such as defamation and intentional infliction of emotional distress. Defamation may be loosely defined as any statement (written or oral) that harms a person's reputation. Intentional infliction of emotional distress arises when a party acts intentionally or recklessly, with conduct that is extreme or outrageous, and the conduct causes severe emotional distress.

Medical board complaints constitute an additional area of concern for general and forensic psychiatrists. Recent data suggest that while malpractice claims against psychiatrists remain relatively low compared to other specialties, psychiatrists incur a higher proportion of medical board complaints filed against them (Reich and Schatzberg 2014).

WHO IS THE FORENSIC CLIENT?

Forensic psychiatrists practice in a variety of roles, including treating patients, completing court evaluations, providing independent medical evaluations, consulting, and teaching. Forensic psychiatrists may treat patients in a clinical setting, including prisons, where liability would be similar to general psychiatrists who are not forensically trained. Distinct liability issues arise depending on the given role. With regard to specifically forensic work, third parties may ask forensic psychiatrists to evaluate patients for a variety of reasons. Forensic psychiatrists may perform workers' compensation evaluations, mental state evaluations, and insurance-based evaluations. One growing field in both forensic psychiatry and other medical fields is the independent medical evaluation (IME), the development of which is generating new case law and additional avenues for lawsuits (Gold and Davidson 2007). In IMEs, discussed below, some duties arise to the third party who hires the psychiatrist, along with certain limited duties to the examinee.

Forensic psychiatrists also provide evaluations and testimony in both civil and criminal court cases, often at the request of the court. In such cases, psychiatric experts may be hired by attorneys representing one side in a dispute (theoretically more akin to an IME) or contracted by order of the court (which offers additional legal protections). Last, forensic psychiatrists provide consultations to psychiatrists or other medical professionals on issues that may arise in clinical practice. Forensic psychiatrists may consult with other psychiatrists or physicians regarding the legal regulation of psychiatry, consult with professional societies, or consult with hospitals or medical staffs in peer review situations and/or on ethics committees (Willick et al. 2003). Determination of the forensic client, e.g., third-party, court, party to litigation, or other medical professional, is a critical first step in considering liability and legal consequences, because this relationship—alongside the task to be performed—undergirds the construction (or nonexistence) of a legally operative obligation, violation, or omission.

Duty and the absence of a physician–patient relationship

The question of with whom the forensic psychiatrist has a relationship determines what governing duty is involved and to whom such duty is owed. Traditionally, courts have narrowed the scope of duty in forensic work by focusing on whether a doctor–patient relationship existed (similar to what is required for malpractice liability for psychiatrists functioning in a treatment capacity), as determined by the specific facts of each case. Courts have frequently discussed physician–patient relationships in contractual terms, observing, as in *Osborne v. Frazor* (1968) that the relationship "is basically contractual and wholly voluntary, created by agreement, express or implied, and by its terms may be general or limited." As well, in *Lyons v. Grether* (1977), determination of the relationship "is a question of fact, turning on a determination of whether the patient entrusted his treatment to the physician and the physician accepted the case."

In *Davis v. Tirrell*, a 1981 case, the Supreme Court of New York dismissed an action by parents on behalf of their minor child arising out of an examination into whether the child was "handicapped" for a school report given to a third party. The parents later claimed that the evaluation should have been privileged health information. The court found that there was no plan to diagnose for treatment, nor to treat, and so no physician–patient relationship existed. However, the court noted that the student and his parents "sincerely believed" that a patient–physician relationship existed and "could have asserted their claim of privilege on the proceeding before the hearing examiner, and their failure to do so could be considered either as a waiver of the privilege or as a recognition that no physician–patient relationship existed." According to the court, due to the absence of a physician–patient relationship, the action was due to be dismissed.

IMEs: limited duty to patient?

In *Felton v. Shaeffer* (1991), the California Court of Appeals held that an independent medical examiner for an industrial medical center conducting a pre-employment physical examination had no duty to an examinee concerning the accuracy of a medical report. In that case, a prospective employee presented with elevated blood pressure after not taking his medication on the day of the exam. The doctor erroneously reported that he was not compliant with his antihypertensive medication and could make "no decision" on his suitability. The court found that there was no physician–patient relationship and so no duty existed to the examinee. The court found no actionable negligence, nor a viable medical malpractice claim, because no doctor–patient relationship existed. The court did point out that the duty was owed to the third party who contracted with the physician, but that "relationship" was not involved in the case.

In IMEs, even when there is no duty to treat or to diagnose correctly, there appears to be a gaining consensus among state courts that there is a duty to *not* cause harm in the exam itself. In *Mero v. Sadoff* (1995), the California court expanded on dicta from *Felton v. Schaeffer*. In *Mero*, an orthopedic evaluation during a workers' compensation evaluation included the patient being placed in "an apparatus" which caused "a total collapse and deterioration of the spinal fusion at L5 performed in May of 1990 ... severe, permanent and disabling injuries as w[e]ll as great mental and physical pain, suffering and emotional distress." The court held that "even in the absence of a physician–patient relationship, a physician has liability to an examinee for negligence or professional malpractice for injuries incurred during the examination itself."

Additionally, in *Greenberg v. Perkins* (1993) the Colorado Supreme Court found that the trial court erred in stating that the doctor owed no duty to the patient because no doctor–patient relationship existed. In that case, Dr. Greenberg ordered a "functional capacity exam" (a physical exam) as part of his court-ordered evaluation, ultimately leading to worsening of an injury. The court found that Dr. Greenberg should have known such an exam carried significant risks, and he therefore owed a (limited) duty of care to the patient.

In *Martinez v. Lewis* (1998), the Colorado court further explains this duty with facts specific to a forensic psychiatry evaluation. In that case, the psychiatrist owed no duty to the patient for alleged misdiagnosis. Ms. Martinez was in a motor vehicle accident and claimed she contracted both psychiatric and neurologic conditions as a result. Her insurance company contracted with Dr. Lewis to evaluate the patient for such claims. After his evaluation, which included computerized tests, a patient interview, and a review of relevant records, he identified that the patient was "malingering." In holding that Dr. Lewis owed no duty of care to Ms. Martinez, the Colorado Supreme Court pointed out that the patient was not seeking treatment from Dr. Lewis, that no harm or injury was alleged from the examination itself, nor was he alleged to have made misrepresentations to the public. Therefore, he owed no additional duty to the patient.

More recently, in *Harris v. Kreutzer* (2006) the Supreme Court of Virginia held that a psychologist who performed an IME under the relevant Virginia statute was considered a health-care provider and had a limited doctor–patient relationship with the "patient" and was subject to the medical malpractice standard in that case. The limited relationship included a duty not to harm the patient during the evaluation but did not include a duty to diagnose or to treat.

Duty to a third party?

Even if there is no physician–patient relationship, a duty of care may run from the forensic psychiatrist to the third party who engaged the psychiatrist's services. For example, in *Hafner v. Beck* (1995), the Arizona court held that a forensic psychologist had a duty to the third party who contracted with her, but not to the person she examined. In that case, Ms. Hafner was evaluated by Dr. Beck for a workers' compensation claim. Dr. Beck completed an evaluation and concluded that the patient had no psychological injury and required no psychological treatment. The court concluded that Dr. Beck owed no duty of care to the patient, reasoning that "[i]f an IME practitioner's evaluations, opinions, and reports could lead not only to vehement disagreement with and vigorous cross-examination of the practitioner in the claims or litigation process, but also to his or her potential liability for negligence, the resulting chilling effect could be severe." The court noted as well that "assuming that Beck's conduct fell below the standard of care for psychologists, it was a breach of duty owed to [the insurance company], not to Hafner."

WHAT IS THE FORENSIC TASK?

The second question to consider in the context of possible legal liability for the more common categories of negligence and medical malpractice is the nature of the forensic task being performed. The specific task is relevant because different duties are owed to different parties in different circumstances.

The two principle forensic tasks include consultation and testimony. A consultation may include an examination and/or review of other sources of information regarding the person evaluated. Certain consultations may not involve an examination and would entail fewer duties. Peer reviews, ethics consultations, and postmortem suicide evaluations may only include post-hoc chart reviews, but also could involve significant financial and emotional considerations. The American Academy of Psychiatry and the Law (AAPL) ethics guidelines (2005) and the American Medical Association (AMA) (1999) opinion 10.03 should be followed even in these cases. These include striving for objectivity, maintaining confidentiality, and adhering to the principle of obtaining informed consent (when applicable).

Expert opinion testimony in a judicial proceeding is the other major category of forensic work and would generally occur after an evaluation in civil or criminal capacities. Examples include evaluations of sanity of criminal defendants for the purposes of both appropriateness for trial or culpability, and evaluating fitness for parenting in child custody cases.

INTENTIONAL TORTS

Intentional torts, including but not limited to fraud (such as the intentional misrepresentation of qualifications for the purpose of employment), intentional infliction of emotional distress, defamation, and physical and sexual assault/battery, generally do not require a threshold physician–patient relationship and so remain possible legal causes of action arising out of interactions with patients in a forensic setting.

Theoretically, a forensic psychiatrist could be sued for intentional infliction of emotional distress if an evaluation was conducted in a manner intentionally designed to be emotionally damaging. Likewise, a forensic psychiatrist who intentionally misrepresents his or her qualifications for the purpose of obtaining employment could be sued by his or her employer. Intentional torts are generally not covered by medical malpractice insurance.

CLAIMS ARISING UNDER FEDERAL CIVIL RIGHTS LAW

Federal civil rights law, codified in the U.S.C. and commonly referred to as Section 1983, governs claims for violation of federal civil rights in involuntary treatment, and is triggered by the removal of particular rights. Section 1983 claims have been used against psychiatrists and may be raised in state court cases (*Jensen v. Lane County* 2000).

Most states have additional state laws concerning involuntary treatment in a hospital setting (e.g., the Lanterman–Petris–Short Act in California, California Welfare and Institutions Code Section 5000 et. seq.). Additionally, forms of assisted outpatient treatment like "Kendra's Law" (NY Ment. Hyg. §9.60) in New York and, more recently, "Laura's Law" (Cal. Welf. & Inst. Code §5345 et. seq.) in California that allow for a variety of mandated outpatient treatment options could generate legal challenges from patients.

Tarasoff duties

In many states, psychiatrists and other mental health professionals have duties specifically related to protecting or warning nonpatient individuals when specific viable threats are made against them. After 1974, a landmark pair of cases in California, *Tarasoff v. Regents of University of California I and II* (1974 and 1976), initiated a new area of potential legal liability. In those cases, Tatiana Tarasoff's murder by an individual who had made specific threats against her to her psychologist imposed upon psychiatrists and psychotherapists a new "duty to warn" potential victims of violence in the 1974 ruling and, replaced by a new "duty to protect" potential victims in the 1976 ruling, though a duty to warn could be one way to satisfy the duty to protect. California has since modified these requirements several times, most recently, returning to solely a "duty to protect."

In any event, both warning the individual and notifying police in California will satisfy the duty and will provide absolute immunity from a possible negligence claim in the event a patient carries out his or her threats (Weinstock et al. 2014). A recent review suggests that because of the wide range of state statutes and common law, mental health professionals are not always aware of the relevant duties in their own states (Johnson et al. 2014). *Tarasoff*-type laws (in those states that have them), therefore, provide additional avenues for general and forensic psychiatrist liability.

In *People v. Clark* (1990, Section 6(b), 12), a California case, the court held that a forensic psychologist who disclosed statements (in a *Tarasoff*-type warning) that a defendant making threats to kill individuals was at worst harmless error. The court reasoned that the forensic mental health evaluator's duty as a "psychotherapist" was properly applied under *Tarasoff* as to "avert danger to others." That case involved an evaluation of a defendant who had murdered the husband of a former therapist and severely injured his former therapist who had previously ended therapy. The defendant wanted to "show her how much she had hurt him, and decided to do so by causing her to suffer similar emotional pain" by killing her husband. He later told a forensic psychologist retained by defense counsel that he had thoughts of hiring someone to kill his former therapist's brother and his ex-wife's employer. The psychologist applied a *Tarasoff* warning, the contents of which were admitted into the case at trial. The court mentions but does not elaborate specifically upon waiver of the attorney–client privilege in the case. On appeal, the court contends that even if admission of the contents of the *Tarasoff* warning was done in error it was "not prejudicial" and "Defendant's statements to Dr. Weinberger were a minor aspect of the overwhelming evidence of aggravating factors reflected in the circumstances of the crime itself."

In a more recent California case, *Elijah W. v. Superior Court* (2013), the Court of Appeals held that a forensic evaluation could be accomplished by a forensic psychologist who would "respect lawyer–client privilege" and would "not report client information concerning child abuse/neglect or a so-called *Tarasoff* threat to authorities." At issue in the case was the choice of attorney to hire a psychologist who would waive the requirements of mandated reporting and notify the attorney alone of any reports of abuse or threats made against an identifiable victim. The court held that "when a psychotherapist is appointed … to assist defense counsel, he or she is obligated to maintain the confidentiality of the client's communications not only by the psychotherapist–patient privilege but also by the lawyer–client privilege."

COMPLAINTS TO MEDICAL BOARDS AND PROFESSIONAL ASSOCIATIONS

General psychiatrists have an above average rate of claims filed against them to state medical boards (Reich and Schatzberg 2014). As well, patients generally have fewer barriers to filing claims to state medical boards than to courts of law. All U.S. members of AAPL are required to be members of either the American Psychiatric Association (APA) or the American Academy of Child and Adolescent Psychiatrists (AACAP).

If a complaint is filed with AAPL against a forensic psychiatrist for violations of ethical codes, the complaint is forwarded to either the local APA branch for possible censure or to AACAP who generally refers such cases to state medical boards. AACAP has no enforcement mechanism (Binder 2002).

Additionally, courts have allowed associations to discipline their members. The court in *Budwin v. American Psychological Association* (1994) held that witness immunity did not protect a forensic psychologist in a board-related action. In a pair of cases from the Seventh Circuit, the court held that appellant physicians could be suspended from their respective medical associations for violations of their ethical codes specifically relevant to expert witness testimony they provided (*Austin v. American Association of Neurological Surgeons* 2001; *Bradner v. American Academy of Orthopaedic Surgeons* 2014).

LEGAL IMMUNITY

Witness immunity

Witness immunity is a common-law protection at issue in a landmark case by the Supreme Court in 1983, which has often been cited in cases involving forensic psychiatrists. Witness immunity offers protections for statements made in performing witness testimony. The Supreme Court in *Briscoe v. Lahue* (1983) held that witness immunity applied to government officials. Its reasoning was twofold: first, witnesses may be reluctant to testify if they fear a retaliatory lawsuit by an aggrieved party and, second, they may be inclined to distort their testimony in fear of a retaliatory suit. In that case, a police officer testified about the likelihood a defendant's fingerprints matched those found at a crime scene. The officer testified to a higher likelihood than other organizations, including the FBI. The defendant filed a civil claim against the witness officer, which was dismissed, and the matter was appealed all the way up to the Supreme Court. The Court cited common law and the intent of Section 1983 in support of its ruling, suggesting that witness immunity served the public interest.

In *Dalton v. Miller* (1999), the Colorado Supreme Court held that quasi-judicial immunity (discussed below) did not apply in the facts of that case. An insurance company hired a psychologist to determine whether they should continue to insure the plaintiff. The court held that quasi-judicial immunity did not apply because the examiner was not court appointed but was hired by one side of a dispute. However, the doctrine of witness immunity applied to both video-taped deposition testimony to be used at trial as well as a written report for trial. In this case, the court remanded to the lower court for a determination of whether the exam itself caused harm for which witness immunity did not apply (citing *Greenberg v. Perkins*).

In *Murphy v. A.A. Mathews* (1992), the Missouri Supreme Court held that an accounting firm hired by one party for valuation of a claim was not allowed witness immunity as a professional firm that had agreed to provide litigation-related services for compensation and that the professional firm was negligent in providing those services. The Court differentiated the facts of this case from *Briscoe v. LaHue* for three reasons: (1) that the claims were "outside the realm of defamation," (2) it did "not involve an adverse witness," and (3) the claim was "limited to litigation support services, not testimony." Potentially the reasoning in this case could apply to psychiatric expert witnesses.

Additionally, the court cited *James v. Brown*, a 1982 Texas Supreme Court case involving psychiatrists who testified that a patient was incompetent, as persuasive. The Texas Supreme Court in that case rejected blanket witness immunity for the psychiatrists, but noted that their communications to the court, regardless of how negligently made, could not serve as the basis for a defamation action. That court did leave open "other remedies at law" including "negligent misdiagnosis–medical malpractice."

Judicial and quasi-judicial immunity

Judicial immunity provides protections for state actors, barring civil actions against them in judicial proceedings. *Budwin v. American Psychological Association* (1994) describes quasi-judicial immunity as a doctrine that "bars civil actions against judges for acts performed in the exercise of their judicial functions and… applies to all judicial determinations… no matter how erroneous or even malicious or corrupt they may be… and has been extended to neutral third parties including psychologists." In that case involving child custody, a psychologist made false representations about performing specific play therapy with a child that the psychologist had not performed. Notably, the court ruled that quasi-judicial immunity did not prevent the American Psychological Association from disciplining the psychologist.

In California, *Silberg v. Anderson* (1990) laid out a test for "privilege for publication." They must be communications made in a judicial or quasi-judicial proceeding, by litigants or other participants authorized by law, to achieve the objects of the litigation and that have some connection or logical relation to the action. The case involved a divorce proceeding in which an attorney hired a "neutral" third-party psychologist who interviewed each member of a family. The father was cast in a negative light, and ultimately he was not pleased with the outcome of the proceedings. He alleged that the psychologist had a prior relationship to the mother and made claims against both his former spouse's attorney and his attorney for breach of contract, negligence, and "intentional tort." The Court said that quasi-judicial immunity did not apply to activities outside of court if the expert was hired by one of the parties to the case. However, if the expert was hired by the court, quasi-judicial immunity would apply.

Also in California, the California appellate court in 2008 decided *Lambert v. Carneghi* (2008) which held that the "litigation privilege" did not apply to an expert witness being employed by one party. In the case, a home fire completely destroyed Lambert's home which was covered by fire insurance. The parties could not agree on a valuation of the home, so according to the California Insurance Code, one appraiser was hired by each party and a retired judge as an umpire. The Lamberts claimed that the umpire was not educated appropriately and "demonstrated a fundamental misunderstanding" of replacement costs, and that their appraiser failed to clarify the meaning of the term "replacement cost." They filed suit against both appraisers and on appeal the court upheld the demurrer to the appraiser hired by the insurance company but that the demurrer granted to their own expert was in error. The court held that privilege bars suit against opposing experts and experts hired jointly but not experts hired by themselves. The court discounted arguments that the application of privilege would promote truthful testimony and would promote finality of judgments, and that fewer experts would be willing to become involved if they could later be sued by the part who retained them. Instead they held that the litigation privilege does not apply to prevent a party from suing his or her own expert witness, even if that suit is based upon the expert's testimony. The Supreme Court of California denied cert and declined to hear the case. Most disturbing in this case is that the court gave no credence to the ethical requirement for experts in areas like forensic psychiatry to strive to reach an objective opinion (AAPL Ethics Guidelines 2005), even if that did not help the retaining attorney win his case. Although this case did not involve forensic psychiatrists, it would be quite disturbing if this reasoning was extended to forensic psychiatry. In essence it could find forensic psychiatrists liable to suits from retaining attorneys for giving honest opinions that do not help attorneys with their cases, or for giving honest answers in cross-examination. It could pressure forensic psychiatrists into being "hired guns" to help attorneys win cases out of fear of being sued by a retaining attorney.

In *Politi v. Tyler* (2000), a Vermont case, a psychologist was not granted quasi-judicial immunity. The specific facts of the case suggested that a forensic expert was hired by the parties themselves and was not court appointed. The court cited the contractual language and payment structure for distinguishing the psychologists' claims of being court appointed. Of note, a dissenting opinion viewed the facts differently and believed that the trial court did, in fact, order a forensic evaluation. The dissent cited a hearing to "determine who pays the cost of such evaluation and may order a party, the parties, or the court or some combination thereof to pay" and ultimately in a hand written note "hearing held. Forensic evaluation will be done… Counsel to let us know within a week who to engage for a forensic evaluation." Despite claims that judicial immunity is decided "as a matter of law" specific facts of this case led the Court to conclude that this was not a "court ordered" evaluation and, thus, quasi-judicial immunity did not apply. The court held that witness immunity did apply for statements "made on the witness stand" but not for the malpractice claim based on actions "in conducting a forensic evaluation and preparing a report."

SUMMARY

Overall, legal claims made against psychiatrists are less frequent than in other medical specialties and lower still for forensic psychiatrists. The above outlines potential avenues for lawsuits against forensic psychiatrists. Medical board claims, though, are filed against psychiatrists at a higher rate than other specialties, and no specific data are available for rates of claims against forensic psychiatrists in their forensic practice. Additional legal protections may apply to forensic psychiatrists in their forensic practice based on limited physician–patient relationships. The forensic psychiatrist should be aware of increasing exploration into lawsuits against IME practitioners based on the relationship that could develop in a forensic evaluation. Forensic psychiatrists might consider frank discussions and even providing documentation to their examinees that explicitly delineates the relationship of their forensic clients (Weinstock and Garrick 1995). Multiple factors are considered by courts in determining when a physician–patient relationship exists.

Additionally, some state licensing boards call forensic psychiatric practice the practice of medicine and discipline psychiatrists accordingly, even if out of state. The AMA says there is a limited doctor–patient relationship in performing IME evaluations.

Binder provides a list of guidelines for risk management techniques, which we add (with bracketed modification to reflect current recording practices) here as helpful, including the following (Binder 2002):

1. Not specifying a likely result or opinion and/or advertising how your services will achieve that result
2. Arranging fees and expenses, including retainers, at the outset of consultation
3. Maintaining strict records, including [audio and/or video recording]
4. Conducting interviews when appropriate
5. Keeping the attorney informed of your opinion as it develops
6. Not overstating your opinions
7. Not taking cases beyond your ability and expertise
8. Preserving the attorney's and client's confidence, as specified in the legal proceedings in which you are involved

As in all contexts involving possible liability, forensic psychiatrists should be aware of and clearly demarcate the exact parameters of their employment, and should seek legal counsel should legal liability become an issue.

REFERENCES

American Medical Association opinion 10.03, 1999.

American Academy of Psychiatry and the Law, Ethics Guidelines for the Practice of Forensic Psychiatry (adopted May 2005).

Austin v. American Association of Neurological Surgeons 253 F.3d 967 (7th Cir. 2001).

Binder R. 2002. Liability for the psychiatric expert witness. *American Journal of Psychiatry* 159:1819–1825.

Brandner v. American Academy of Orthopaedic Surgeons 760 F.3d 267 (7th Cir. 2014).

Briscoe v. Lahue, 460 U.S. 325 (1983).

Budwin v. American Psychological Association, 24 Cal. App. 4th 875, 29 Cal. Rptr. 2d 453 (1994).

Cal. Welf. & Inst. Code § 5345 et. seq. (2002).

Dalton v. Miller (Col. App. 1999). 984 P.2d. 666.

Davis v. Tirrell, 443 N.Y.S.2d 136 (1981).

Elijah W. v. Superior Court, 216 Cal. App. 4th 140, 156 Cal. Rptr. 3d 592 (2013).

Felton v. Shaeffer, 229 Cal. App. 3d 229, 279 Cal. Rptr. 713 (1991).

Gold LH and JE Davidson. 2007. Do you understand your risk? Liability and third-party evaluations in civil litigation. *Journal of the American Academy of Psychiatry and the Law* 35:200–210.

Greenberg v. Perkins, 845 P.2d 530 (1993).

Hafner v. Beck, 185 Ariz. 389, 916 P.2d 1105 at 1107, 1109 (1995).

Harris v. Kreutzer, 271 Va, 188, 624 S.E.2d 24 (2006).

James v. Brown, 637 S.W.2d 914 at 919 (1982).

Jensen v. Lane County 222 F.3d 570 (9th Cir. 2000).

Johnson R, G Persad, and D Sisti. 2014. The Tarasoff rule: The implications of interstate variation and gaps in professional training. *Journal of the American Academy of Psychiatry and the Law* 42:469–477.

Lambert v. Carneghi, 158 Cal. App. 4th 1120, 70 Cal. Rptr. 3d 626 (2008).

Lanterman Petris and Short Law, California West's Ann. Cal. Welf. & Inst. Code Section 5000.

Lyons v. Grether 218 Va. 630, 239 S.E.2d 103 (1977).

Martinez v. Lewis, 969 P.2d 913, 98 CJ C.A.R. 6097 (1998).

Mero v. Sadoff, 31 Cal. App. 4th 1466, 37 Cal. Rptr. 2d 769 (1995).

Murphy v. A.A. Mathews, 841 S.W.2d 671 (1992).

NY Ment. Hyg. § 9.60.

Osborne v. Frazor, 58 Tenn. App. 15, 425 S.W.2d 768 (1968).

People v. Clark, 50 Cal. 3d 583, 268 Cal. Rptr. 399, 789 P.2d 127 (1990).

Politi v. Tyler 751 A.2d 788, 170 Vt. 428 (Vermont 2000).

Reich J and Schatzberg A. 2014. An empirical data comparison of regulatory agency and malpractice legal problems for psychiatrists. *Annals of Clinical Psychiatry* May; 26(2):91–96.

Silberg v. Anderson 50 Cal. 3d 205, 266 Cal. Rptr. 638, 786 P.2d 365 (1990).

Tarasoff v. Regents of University of California 13 Cal. 3d 177, 118 Cal. Rptr. 129, 529 P.2d 553 (Cal. 1974).

Tarasoff v. Regents of University of California 17 Cal. 3d 425, 131 Cal. Rptr. 14, 551 P.2d 334 (Cal. 1976).

Weinstock R and Garrick T. 1995. Is liability possible for forensic psychiatrists? *Bulletin of the American Academy of Psychiatry and the Law* 23(2):183–193.

Weinstock R, Bonnici D, Seroussi A, and Leong GB. 2014. No duty to warn in California; now unambiguously solely a duty to protect. *Journal of the American Academy of Psychiatry and the Law* 42(1):101–108.

Willick D, Weinstock R, and Garrick T. 2003. Liability of the forensic psychiatrist. In *Principles and Practice of Forensic Psychiatry*, 2nd edition, edited by R Rosner, Boca Raton, FL: CRC Press, 73–78.

11

The death penalty

MICHAEL L. PERLIN AND ALISON J. LYNCH

INTRODUCTION

There have been three generations of death penalty law in the United States. The first, from the founding of the nation until the Supreme Court's 1972 decision in *Furman v. Georgia*, striking down all then-existing death penalty laws as violative of the Eighth Amendment's ban on cruel and unusual punishment, was marked by standardless imposition of the penalty with little thought given to the individual circumstances of the crime or the criminal. The second, the four years between the Court's decision in *Furman* and its 1976 decision in *Gregg v. Georgia*, finding constitutional the penalty as redrafted in certain states, was marked by a flurry of activity in state legislatures. The third, ongoing and encompassing all death penalty developments since *Gregg*, has been marked by a constant tinkering with the *Gregg* standards, and the development of a cluster of sub-issues to which the Court has returned again and again in its efforts to determine whether state policies meet constitutional muster. Among this cluster are several areas of specific and important interest to forensic psychiatrists, and it is these areas on which we focus in this chapter:

- Predictions of dangerousness
- The role of mitigation evidence
- Competency to be executed, as that concept applies to
  - Juveniles
  - Persons with intellectual disabilities
  - Persons with mental illness

On the related question of the right of defendants who are facing the death penalty to oppose involuntary medication to render them competent to be executed, see Chapter 57.

FUTURE DANGEROUSNESS

In an effort to ensure the "worst of the worst" receive death sentences, many jurisdictions encourage jurors to consider the danger a defendant will pose to society in the future by including "future dangerousness" as an aggravating factor (Vann 2011). The inclusion of this factor, however, assumes the existence of three important facts-not-in-evidence: that mental health professionals can accurately predict dangerousness, that defense counsel can effectively cross-examine state experts on this issue, and that jurors can competently assess this sort of testimony. A review of the case law and the professional literature makes it clear that none of these questions can be answered affirmatively.

On mental health professionals' predictions of dangerousness

In *Jurek v. Texas,* the Supreme Court upheld the constitutionality of a state statutory scheme requiring, inter alia, that the jury determine, beyond a reasonable doubt, whether there was a "probability that the defendant would commit criminal acts of violence that would constitute a continuing threat to society" (Tex. Crim. Proc. Art. §37.071(2)(b)(1), 1976). On this issue, the controlling plurality opinion established its guidelines as to such a "dangerousness" finding:

> What is essential is that the jury has before it all possible relevant information about the individual defendant whose fate it must determine. Texas law clearly assures that all such evidence will be adduced. (Jurek 1976, 274)

The decision in *Jurek* was immediately criticized as "appalling" (Black 1976, 8), and as "difficult to reconcile" with the Court's recognition in *Gregg v. Georgia* that "the concept of human dignity underlying the Eighth Amendment demands a principled application of the death penalty" (Harvard Law Review 1976, 71). This aspect of the opinion was specifically seen as flawed by vagueness and prejudicially misleading to the defendant (Scofield 1980; Green 1984). *Jurek* was partially overruled by *Abdul-Kabir v. Quarterman* (2007), but nothing in that decision has had much of an impact on the questions under consideration in this chapter (Perlin 2013, 20).

The significance of barefoot

Although psychiatric testimony was not at the core of the *Jurek* opinion, that issue emerged clearly and explicitly several terms later in the severely criticized opinion of *Barefoot v. Estelle*. After Barefoot was convicted of murdering a Texas police officer, two psychiatrists (who had never examined the defendant) testified in response to hypothetical questions at the penalty phase, stating that the defendant "would probably commit further acts of violence and represent a continuing threat to society" (*Barefoot v. Estelle* 1983, 884). The jury accepted this testimony and imposed the death penalty.

In affirming a subsequent opinion denying the defendant's application for a writ of habeas corpus, the Supreme Court summarized the defendant's claim on the psychiatric issue:

> First, it is urged that psychiatrists, individually and as a group, are incompetent to predict with an acceptable degree of reliability that a particular criminal will commit other crimes in the future, and so represent a danger to the community. Second, it is said that in any event, psychiatrists should not be permitted to testify about future dangerousness in response to hypothetical questions and without having examined the defendant personally. Third, it is argued that in the particular circumstances in this case the testimony of the psychiatrists was so unreliable that the sentence should be set aside. (*Barefoot v. Estelle* 1983, 896)

The Court first rejected the argument that psychiatrists could not reliably predict future dangerousness in this context, noting that it made "little sense" to exclude *only* psychiatrists from the "entire universe of persons who might have an opinion on this issue" (*Barefoot v. Estelle* 1983, 896), and that the defendant's argument would also "call into question those other contexts in which predictions of future behavior are constantly made" (*Barefoot v. Estelle* 1983, 898). In the course of this argument, the Court rejected the views presented by the American Psychiatric Association as *amicus* that (1) such testimony was invalid due to "fundamentally low reliability" and (2) long-term predictions of future dangerousness were essentially lay determinations that should be based on "predictive statistical or actuarial information that is fundamentally nonmedical in nature" (Brief Amicus Curiae 1983, 14).

Justice Blackmun dissented (for himself, and Justices Brennan and Marshall), rejecting the Court's views on the psychiatric issue:

> In a capital case, the specious testimony of a psychiatrist, colored in the eyes of an impressionable untouchability of a medical specialist's words, equates with death itself. (*Barefoot v. Estelle* 1983, 916)

Relying on the American Psychiatric Association's *amicus* brief, he concluded that such "baseless" testimony cannot be reconciled with the Constitution's "paramount concern for reliability in capital sentencing" (*Barefoot v. Estelle* 1983, 917).

Role of jurors

The majority assumed that jurors will be able to adequately assess this testimony. It noted pointedly:

> Petitioner's entire argument, as well as that of Justice Blackmun's dissent, is founded on the premise that a jury will not be able to separate the wheat from the chaff. We do not share in this low evaluation of the adversary process. (*Barefoot v. Estelle* 1983, 901 n. 7)

The uncontroverted facts paint a dismal picture and show how misguided the majority was. Violence risk assessment errors continue at capital sentencing (Cunningham and Reidy 1999; Tanner 2005). At the best, future dangerousness determinations are "wildly speculative" (Berry 2010, 907). One study concluded jurors making a prediction of future violence—the factor that is the jurors' "overriding concern" (Ramana 2011, 369) or "predominant consideration" (Blume et al. 2001, 404)—were wrong 97% of the time, showing only "chance-level" performance of capital juries in predicting future dangerousness (Vann 2011, 1273 n. 141).

Barefoot is especially troubling because research shows future dangerousness plays a part in almost all jury determinations to impose a death sentence (Vann 2011, 1274 n. 141). By way of example, between 1995 and 2006, "future violence was alleged as a non-statutory aggravating factor in [77]% of the federal capital prosecutions" and a "death [sentence] occurred in over 80% of the federal cases where the jury found that future prison violence was likely," because such predictions are "alarmingly unreliable" (Shapiro 2008, 147).

MITIGATION

Contemporaneous death penalty statutes require findings of what are called "mitigating" and "aggravating" factors. This is ostensibly done to ensure that the death penalty is reserved for only the vilest of crimes and the worst offender—ones for which there is no reasonable excuse or justification (Mandery 2003; Smith 2012). Among the mitigators is evidence of a showing that the defendant was under the influence of extreme mental or emotional disturbance or that the capacity of the defendant to appreciate the criminality of his conduct or to conform his conduct to the requirements of law was substantially impaired.

The verdict must be death if the jury unanimously finds at least one aggravating circumstance and no mitigating circumstance or if the jury unanimously finds one or more aggravating circumstances that outweigh any mitigating circumstances (e.g., 42 Pa. C.S.A. §9711(c)(4),

2010). The verdict must be a sentence of life imprisonment in all other cases.

In determining the degree to which mitigation based on mental disorder is proper, these are factors that must be considered in each case:

1. Whether the offender's suffering evidences expiation or inspires compassion
2. Whether the offender's cognitive and/or volitional impairment at the time he or she committed the crime affected his or her responsibility for his or her actions, and thereby diminished society's need for revenge
3. Whether the offender, subjectively analyzed, was less affected than the mentally normal offender by the deterrent threat of capital punishment at the time he or she committed the crime
4. Whether the exemplary value of capitally punishing the offender, as objectively perceived by reasonable persons, would be attenuated by the difficulty those persons would have identifying with the executed offender (Liebman and Shepard 1978, 818).

In *Lockett v. Ohio*, the Supreme Court substantially widened the scope of mitigating evidence allowed at the penalty phase of a capital case (*Lockett v. Ohio* 1978, 604). Four years later, the Court expanded on this rule in *Eddings v. Oklahoma*, holding that the sentencing authority must consider any and all relevant mitigating evidence (*Eddings v. Oklahoma* 1982, 114). There, the Court concluded that the sentencer must consider all mitigating evidence and then weigh it against the aggravating circumstances (*Eddings v. Oklahoma* 1982, 113). Read together, *Lockett* and *Eddings* thus "require the courts to admit into evidence, and to consider, *any* claim raised by the defendant in mitigation" (Showalter and Bonnie 1984, 161). Then, in *Penry v. Lynaugh*, the Supreme Court held that evidence as to the defendant's mental retardation was relevant to his culpability and that without such information jurors could not express their "reasoned moral response" in determining the appropriateness of the death penalty. There, the court found that assessment of the defendant's retardation would aid the jurors in determining whether the commission of the crime was "deliberate" (*Penry v. Lynaugh* 1989, 321). Also, in attempting to grapple with questions of future dangerousness or of the presence of provocation (both questions mandatory under the Texas state sentencing scheme), jurors were required to have a "vehicle" to consider whether the defendant's background and childhood should have mitigated the penalty imposed (*Penry v. Lynaugh* 1989, 322). Without such testimony, the jury could not appropriately express its "reasoned moral response" on the evidence in question (*Penry v. Lynaugh* 1989, 328).

Subsequent decisions have reconfirmed the Court's commitment to this approach. By way of example, in *Porter v. McCollum*, the Supreme Court reversed an Eleventh Circuit decision that had reversed a grant of habeas corpus, in a case in which the state court had not considered expert testimony for purposes of nonstatutory mitigation and "unreasonably discounted the evidence of [the defendant's] childhood abuse and military service" (*Porter* 2009, 455).

IMPOSITION OF DEATH PENALTY ON SPECIAL POPULATIONS

Introduction

The issues involved in psychiatric participation in capital punishment decision making raise a series of intractable (Ward 1986, 100) operational problems for mental health professionals in cases involving juveniles and defendants with mental disabilities: the responsibility of psychiatrists to construe appropriately the key terms in operative statutes, assessment of the appropriate standard of proof; reliability of diagnoses; and possibility of regression between evaluation and execution (Radelet and Barnard 1986, 43). They also raise core ethical problems that have not yet been resolved.

Juveniles

In 2005, the Supreme Court decided in *Roper v. Simmons* that the state cannot execute an individual who commits a crime before the age of 18. The Court relied on objective factors, including the "evolving standards of decency" in the United States. Most significantly, it examined scientific evidence pertaining to the juvenile brain. The justices took into account factors such as "juveniles' immature judgment, susceptibility to negative peer influences, and transitory personality development" (Feld 2008) in finding that these age-appropriate developmental markers diminished their criminal responsibility. Therefore, the Court found, juveniles did not deserve the most serious sentence that can be imposed on adults.

Although *Roper* was praised as a decision based on reason and objective factors, the written decision of the Court provides little social science evidence as support; however, many of the amicus briefs written in support of abolishing the juvenile death penalty provide ample references to developmental psychology and neuroscience that illustrate the differences in juvenile brains (Feld 2008). Additionally, the decision still allowed for the imposition of life without parole, which social scientists and researchers denounced (Flynn 2008). This decision left many questioning whether it went far enough in demonstrating the law's understanding of the developmental differences of juveniles (Flynn 2008).

Defendants with mental illness: *Ford v. Wainwright*

Eight years after Alvin Ford's murder conviction, he developed delusions and hallucinations, and his letters revealed "an increasingly pervasive delusion that he had become the target of a complex conspiracy, involving the [Ku Klux] Klan and ... others, designed to force him to commit suicide"

(*Ford v. Wainwright* 1986, 400). His treating psychiatrist concluded that the defendant suffered from a "major mental disorder severe enough to substantially affect [defendant's] present ability to assist in the defense of his life" (*Ford v. Wainwright* 1986, 402). Ford's lawyer then invoked Florida procedures governing the determination of competency of an inmate sentenced to death, and, after brief meetings, three state-appointed psychiatrists all found him to have sufficient capacity to be executed under state law.

In the only portion of any of the four separate opinions in the *Ford* case to command a majority of the Court, Justice Marshall concluded that the Eighth Amendment did prohibit the imposition of the death penalty on an insane prisoner (*Ford v. Wainwright* 1986, 405). In coming to its determination, the Court must take into account objective evidence of contemporary values before determining whether a particular punishment comports with the fundamental human dignity that the Amendment protects (*Ford v. Wainwright*, 406, citing the plurality opinion in *Coker v. Georgia* 1977, 597).

On the question of what procedures were appropriate in such a case, the Court was sufficiently fragmented that no opinion commanded a majority. In a four-Justice opinion, Justice Marshall concluded that a *de novo* evidentiary hearing on Ford's sanity was required, unless the state-court trier of fact has after a full hearing reliably found the relevant facts. In cases such as the one before the Court where fact-finding procedures must aspire to a heightened standard of reliability, the ascertainment of a prisoner's sanity as a lawful predicate to execution calls for no less stringent standards than those demanded in any other aspect of a capital proceeding, a standard particularly demanding in light of the reality that the present state of the mental sciences is at best a hazardous guess, however conscientious (*Ford v. Wainwright* 1986, 412).

The opinion left it to the state to develop appropriate procedures to enforce the constitutional restriction upon its execution of sentences, noting that it was not suggesting that only a full trial on the issue of sanity will suffice to protect the federal interests (*Ford v. Wainwright* 1986, 416).

The dissenting justices reasoned that the Eighth Amendment did not create a substantive right not to be executed while insane (e.g., *Ford v. Wainwright* 1986, 427 [O'Connor, J., concurring in part and dissenting in part]) and that Florida's procedures were "fully consistent with the common law heritage and current practice on which the Court purports to rely" [*Ford v. Wainwright* 1986, 431, Rehnquist, J., dissenting]), and that the majority decision might lead to the advancement of entirely spurious claims of insanity.

IN THE AFTERMATH OF *FORD*: THE MEANING OF *PANETTI*

The Supreme Court returned to this question two decades later in the case of Scott Panetti. Panetti, who had been convicted of capital murder in the slayings of his estranged wife's parents, had been hospitalized numerous times for serious psychiatric disorders (*Panetti v. Quarterman* 2007, 936) Notwithstanding his "bizarre," "scary," and "trance-like" behavior, he was found competent to stand trial and competent to waive counsel. He was convicted despite his defense of insanity and sentenced to death. After his direct appeals and initial petition of habeas corpus were rejected, Panetti filed a subsequent habeas writ petition, alleging that he did not understand the reasons for his pending execution (*Panetti v. Quarterman* 2007, 935). This petition was rejected, the court concluding that the test for competency to be executed "requires the petitioner know no more than the fact of his impending execution and the factual predicate for the execution" (*Panetti v. Quarterman* 2007, 942). The Fifth Circuit affirmed—finding that the fact-finding procedures on which the trial court relied were "not adequate for reaching reasonably correct results" or, at a minimum, resulted in a process that appeared to be "seriously inadequate for the ascertainment of the truth" (*Panetti v. Quarterman* 2007, 954), and the Supreme Court granted certiorari.

The Court reversed in a 5–4 decision, and in the course of its opinion, significantly elaborated on its *Ford* opinion in two dimensions: as to the procedures that are to be afforded to a defendant seeking to assert a *Ford* claim, and as to the substance of the *Ford* standard.

On the first matter, it found error below in the trial court's failure to provide the defendant an adequate opportunity to submit expert evidence in response to the report filed by the court-appointed experts, thus depriving him of his "constitutionally adequate opportunity to be heard" (*Panetti v. Quarterman* 2007, 950). On the second, it carefully elaborated on and clarified the *Ford* decision. It reviewed the testimony that demonstrated the defendant's "fixed delusion" system, and quoted with approval expert testimony that had pointed out that "an unmedicated individual suffering from schizophrenia can 'at times' hold an ordinary conversation and that 'it depends [whether the discussion concerns the individual's] fixed delusional system'" (*Panetti v. Quarterman* 2007, 955). Here, it rejected the Court of Appeals' interpretation of the *Ford* standard.

This narrow test, the Supreme Court concluded, unconstitutionally foreclosed the defendant from establishing incompetency by the means that Panetti sought to employ in the case at bar: by making a showing that his mental illness "obstruct[ed] a rational understanding of the State's reason for his execution" (*Panetti v. Quarterman* 2007, 956) In this case, the Court found, the Fifth Circuit improperly treated a prisoner's delusional belief system "as irrelevant if the prisoner knows that the State has identified his crimes as the reason for his execution." Nowhere, the Court continued, did *Ford* indicate that "delusions are irrelevant to 'comprehen[sion]' or 'aware [ness]' if they so impair the prisoner's concept of reality that he cannot reach a rational understanding of the reason for the execution." If anything, the court continued, "the *Ford* majority suggests the opposite" (*Panetti v. Quarterman* 2007, 958). There was no support in *Ford* ("or anywhere else"), the Court added, for the proposition that "a prisoner is automatically foreclosed from demonstrating incompetency once a court has found he can identify the stated reason for his execution" (*Panetti v. Quarterman* 2007, 959).

Among the questions to be explored in greater depth on remand was "the extent to which severe delusions may render a subject's perception of reality so distorted that he should be deemed incompetent," citing here to an aspect of the amicus brief by the American Psychological Association that had discussed ways in which mental health experts can inform competency determinations (*Panetti v. Quarterman* 2007, 962).

Defendants with intellectual disabilities

ATKINS V. VIRGINIA

[Author's note: For a discussion of pre-*Atkins* law, see Perlin and Cucolo 2016, §12-4.2.1, at 17-81 to 17-85.]

Atkins had been convicted of capital murder. In the penalty phase, the defense called a forensic psychologist, who testified that Atkins was "mildly mentally retarded" (with an IQ of 59) (*Atkins v. Virginia* 2002, p. 309). The jury convicted Atkins and sentenced him to death; after that sentence was set aside (for unrelated reasons), the same witness testified at the rehearing. At this time, the state called its own witness in rebuttal, who testified that the defendant was not retarded, that he was "of average intelligence, at least" (*Atkins v. Virginia* 2002, 309). The jury again sentenced Atkins to death, and this sentence was affirmed by the Virginia Supreme Court (*Atkins v. Virginia* 2002, 310).

In weighing the case, the Supreme Court pointed out that its inquiry should be guided by "objective factors," and that, in assessing these factors, the "clearest and most reliable objective evidence of contemporary values is the legislation enacted by the country's legislatures" (*Atkins v. Virginia* 2002, 312). As part of this inquiry, it noted the significant changes since it decided *Penry* in 1989 when only two states banned the execution of persons with mental retardation; in the intervening 13 years, at least another 16 (and the federal government) enacted similar laws (*Atkins v. Virginia* 2002, 314–315).

Further, the Court perceived that this consensus "unquestionably reflects widespread judgment about the relative culpability of mentally retarded offenders and the relationship between mental retardation and the penological purposes served by the death penalty" (*Atkins v. Virginia* 2002, 317).

Mental retardation, the Court found, involves "not only subaverage intellectual functioning, but also significant limitations in adaptive skills such as communication, self-care, and self-direction that became manifest before age 18" (*Atkins v. Virginia* 2002, 317). It continued in the same vein:

> Mentally retarded persons frequently know the difference between right and wrong and are competent to stand trial. Because of their impairments, however, by definition they have diminished capacities to understand and process information, to communicate, to abstract from mistakes and learn from experience, to engage in logical reasoning, to control impulses, and to understand the reactions of others. There is no evidence that they are more likely to engage in criminal conduct than others, but there is abundant evidence that they often act on impulse rather than pursuant to a premeditated plan, and that in group settings they are followers rather than leaders. Their deficiencies do not warrant an exemption from criminal sanctions, but they do diminish their personal culpability. (*Atkins v. Virginia* 2002, 318)

In light of these deficiencies, the Court found that its death penalty jurisprudence provided two reasons "consistent with the legislative consensus that the mentally retarded should be categorically excluded from execution" (*Atkins v. Virginia* 2002, 318):

> First, there is a serious question as to whether either justification that we have recognized as a basis for the death penalty applies to mentally retarded offenders. *Gregg v. Georgia* identified "retribution and deterrence of capital crimes by prospective offenders" as the social purposes served by the death penalty. Unless the imposition of the death penalty on a mentally retarded person "measurably contributes to one or both of these goals, it 'is nothing more than the purposeless and needless imposition of pain and suffering,' and hence an unconstitutional punishment." (*Atkins v. Virginia* 2002, 319)

The reduced capacity of mentally retarded offenders provided an additional justification for a categorical rule making such offenders ineligible for the death penalty. The Court went on to note that there was an "enhanced" risk of improperly imposed death penalty in cases involving defendants with mental retardation because of the possibility of false confessions, as well as "the lesser ability of mentally retarded defendants to make a persuasive showing of mitigation in the face of prosecutorial evidence of one or more aggravating factors" (*Atkins v. Virginia* 2002, 320). The Court also stressed several additional interrelated issues: the difficulties that persons with mental retardation may have in being able to give meaningful assistance to their counsel, their status as "typically poor witnesses," and the ways in which their demeanor "may create an unwarranted impression of lack of remorse for their crimes" (*Atkins v. Virginia* 2002, 321).

Here the Court acknowledged an important difficulty: "reliance on mental retardation as a mitigating factor can be a two-edged sword that may enhance the likelihood that the aggravating factor of future dangerousness will be found by the jury," raising the specter that "mentally retarded defendants in the aggregate face a special risk of wrongful execution" (*Atkins v. Virginia* 2002, 321). Thus, the Court concluded, "Construing and applying the Eighth Amendment in the light of our 'evolving standards of decency,' we therefore conclude that such punishment is excessive and that the Constitution 'places a substantive restriction on the State's power to take the life' of a mentally retarded offender" (*Atkins v. Virginia* 2002, 321).

HALL V. FLORIDA

The Supreme Court's holding in *Atkins v. Virginia* was subsequently clarified, modified, and expanded in *Hall v. Florida*. *Hall* made it clear that inquiries into a defendant's intellectual disability (for purposes of determining whether he or she is potentially subject to the death penalty) cannot be limited to a bare numerical "reading" of an IQ score.

Under Florida law, if a defendant's IQ was 70 or under, he or she was deemed intellectually disabled; if, however, his or her IQ measured 71 or above, all further inquiries into intellectual disability—for purposes of determining whether *Atkins* would apply—were foreclosed (*Hall v. Florida* 2014, 1990). *Hall* declared this rule unconstitutional as it created an "unacceptable risk" that persons with intellectual disabilities would be executed (*Hall v. Florida* 2014, 1990).

Hall was sentenced to death. Later, because of an intervening Supreme Court decision that capital defendants must be permitted to present nonstatutory mitigating evidence in death penalty proceedings (*Hitchcock v. Dugger* 1987), he was resentenced. At this resentencing hearing, he presented "substantial and unchallenged evidence" of his intellectual disability (*Hall v. Florida* 2014, 1990). The jury resentenced him to death, and this recommendation was accepted by the sentencing court (*Hall v. Florida* 2014, 481–482).

Following the Supreme Court's decision in *Atkins*, Hall was unsuccessful in seeking the application of that case. On further appeal, in a 5–4 decision, per Justice Kennedy, the Court began by restating its rationale from *Atkins*: that "no legitimate penological purpose is served by executing a person with intellectual disabilities" (*Hall v. Florida* 2014, 1992, citing *Atkins*, pp. 317, 320). After returning to its *Atkins* language on the rationales of punishment, the Court added that the prohibition on such executions is required "to protect the integrity of the trial process" (*Hall v. Florida* 2014, 1993), noting that this population faces "'a special risk of wrongful execution'" because "they are more likely to give false confessions, are often poor witnesses, and are less able to give meaningful assistance to their counsel" (*Hall v. Florida* 2014, 1993). The question before the Court was thus how intellectual disability needed to be defined for purposes of executability.

Justice Kennedy began this section of the opinion by noting that it was proper to consult the "medical community's opinions" on this issue (*Hall v. Florida* 2014, 1993). He then returned to *Atkins*, pointing out that, in that decision, the Court noted that the medical community defined intellectual disability according to three criteria: "significantly subaverage intellectual functioning, deficits in adaptive functioning (the inability to learn basic skills and adjust behavior to changing circumstances), and onset of these deficits during the developmental period" (*Hall v. Florida* 2014, 1994, citing *Atkins*, p. 308 n. 3, and *amicus curiae* brief of the American Psychological Association). The first two of these criteria were central, he said, as they had "long been" the defining characteristic of intellectual disability (*Hall v. Florida* 2014, 11).

Because, under Florida law, the standard error of measurement (SEM) was ignored, and a bright-line rule that any person with an IQ measured over 70 was not intellectually disabled was created, thus barring the defendant from introducing any other evidence that would show that "his faculties are limited" (*Hall v. Florida* 2014, 1994), state sentencing courts cannot consider "even substantial and weighty evidence of intellectual disability as measured and made manifest by the defendant's failure or inability to adapt to his social and cultural environment, including medical histories, behavioral records, school tests and reports, and testimony regarding past behavior and family circumstances" (*Hall v. Florida* 2014, 1994). This is so even though the medical community accepts that all of this evidence can be probative of intellectual disability, including for individuals who have an IQ test score above 70 (*Hall v. Florida* 2014, 1994).

Thus, the Court concluded, Florida's rule disregarded "established medical practice" in two interrelated ways:

> It takes an IQ score as final and conclusive evidence of a defendant's intellectual capacity, when experts in the field would consider other evidence. It also relies on a purportedly scientific measurement of the defendant's abilities, his IQ score, while refusing to recognize that the score is, on its own terms, imprecise. (*Hall v. Florida* 2014, 1994)

This rule is contrary to all professional judgment, the Court found: "The professionals who design, administer, and interpret IQ tests have agreed, for years now, that IQ test scores should be read not as a single fixed number but as a range." The SEM reflects the reality that "an individual's intellectual functioning cannot be reduced to a single numerical score" (*Hall v. Florida* 2014, 1994). Were the states to have complete autonomy to define intellectual disability as they wished, "the Court's decision in *Atkins* could become a nullity, and the Eighth Amendment's protection of human dignity would not become a reality" (*Hall v. Florida* 2014, 1999).

Again, in declaring the Florida rule unconstitutional, the Court stressed that it was informed by the views of medical experts, whose opinions "inform … but [do] not control ultimate legal determinations," underscoring that neither Florida nor its supporting *amici* "point to a *single* medical professional who supports this cutoff," and that Florida's rule "goes against unanimous professional consensus," noting again that "intellectual disability is a condition, not a number," and that it was not "sound to view a single factor as dispositive of a conjunctive and interrelated assessment" (*Hall v. Florida* 2014, 2000). Justice Alito dissented, critiquing the majority opinion as being based on "the views of *a small professional elite*" (*Hall v. Florida* 2014, 2005).

It is likely that *Hall* will clarify some of the confusion that has arisen in the 12 years since *Atkins* was decided as to who is to be considered "intellectually disabled" for purposes of death penalty eligibility. The majority opinion makes it crystal-clear that a "number only" IQ assessment violates the Eighth Amendment, and its opinion reflects a careful consideration of prevailing—and unanimous—professional wisdom.

In his recent blog post about *Hall*, John Parry—for many years editor-in-chief of the *Mental and Physical Disability Law Reporter*—comes to this thoughtful conclusion:

> First, the 5–4 majority opinion reprioritizes the relative importance of the two major rationales used to justify the ban on executing persons with intellectual disabilities established in *Atkins* ... This shift in emphasis substantially increases the possibility that in the future, defendants with other types of severe mental disorders may be constitutionally protected from being executed. Second, even if "contemporary values" change and a majority of Americans come to believe that executing persons with intellectual disabilities should be permitted, *Hall* has embraced a persuasive independent constitutional basis for upholding *Atkins*. (Parry 2014)

SUMMARY

Death penalty jurisprudence remains in flux. The cases discussed in this chapter reveal a pattern on the Supreme Court's part that suggest that further tinkering with the issues discussed here—future dangerousness predictions, mitigation, execution competency—will continue in the future. It is essential that forensic psychiatrists understand the Court's rationales in these cases, and incorporate those understandings into their evaluations and testimony.

REFERENCES

42 PA. C.S.A. §9711 (c) (1) (iii) (2010).

Abdul-Kabir v. Quarterman, 550 U.S. 233 (2007).

Atkins v. Virginia, 536 U.S. 304 (2002).

Barefoot v. Estelle, 463 U.S. 880 (1983).

Berry W. 2010. Ending death by dangerousness: A path to the de facto abolition of the death penalty. *Arizona Law Review* 52:889.

Black C. 1976. Due process for death: *Jurek v. Texas*. *Catholic University Law Review* 26:1.

Blume JH, SP Garvey, and SL Johnson. 2001. Future dangerousness in capital cases: Always "at issue." *Cornell Law Review* 86:397.

Brief Amicus Curiae for the American Psychiatric Association, No. 82–6080, 1982. *Barefoot v. Estelle*, 463 U.S. 880 (1983).

Coker v. Georgia, 433 U.S. 584, 597 (1977).

Cunningham MD and TJ Reidy. 1999. Don't confuse me with the facts: Common errors in violence risk assessment at capital sentencing. *Criminal Justice and Behavior* 26:20.

Eddings v. Oklahoma, 455 US. 104 (1982).

Feld B. 2008. A slower form of death: Implications of *Roper v. Simmons* for juveniles sentenced to life without parole. *Notre Dame Journal of Law, Ethics and Public Policy* 22:9.

Flynn E. 2008. Dismantling the felony-murder rule: Juvenile deterrence and retribution post-*Roper v. Simmons*. *University of Pennsylvania Law Review*, 156:1049.

Ford v. Wainwright, 477 U.S. 399 (1986).

Furman v. Georgia, 408 U.S. 238 (1972).

Green W. 1984. Capital punishment, psychiatric experts, and predictions of dangerousness. *Capital University Law Review* 13:533.

Gregg v. Georgia, 428 U.S. 153 (1976).

Hall v. Florida, 134 S. Ct. 1986 (2014).

Hall v. Florida, 614 So. 2d 473, 481–82 (Fla. 1993).

Harvard Law Review. 1976. The Supreme Court, 1975 Term. *Harvard Law Review* 90:58.

Hitchcock v. Dugger, 481 U.S. 393 (1987).

Jurek v. Texas, 428 U.S. 262 (1976).

Liebman JS and MJ Shepard. 1978. Guiding capital sentencing discretion beyond the "Boiler Plate": Mental disorder as a mitigating factor. *Georgetown Law Journal* 66:757.

Lockett v. Ohio, 438 U.S. 586 (1978).

Mandery EJ. 2003. Federalism and the death penalty. *Albany Law Review* 66:809.

Panetti v. Quarterman, 2008 WL 2338498 (W.D. Tex. 2008).

Panetti v. Quarterman, 551 U.S. 930 (2007).

Panetti v. Quarterman, No. 08-70015 (5th Cir. December 17, 2008).

Parry, J. http://www.mentaldisabilitylawreflections.com/reflections-blog/archives/06-2014, accessed June 29, 2016.

Penry v. Lynaugh, 492 U.S. 302 (1989).

Perlin M. 2013. *Mental Disability and the Death Penalty: The Shame of the States*. Lanham, MD: Rowman and Littlefield.

Perlin M and Cucolo HE. 2016. *Mental Disability Law: Civil and Criminal*. 3rd edition. Newark, NJ: Lexis-Nexis Press.

Porter v. McCollum, 558 U.S. 30 (2009).
Radelet M and G Bernard. 1986. Ethics and the psychiatric determination of competency to be executed. *Bulletin of the American Academy of Psychiatry and the Law* 14:37.
Ramana R. 2011. Living and dying with a double-edged sword: Mental health evidence in the tenth circuit's capital cases. *Denver University Law Review* 88:339.
Roper v. Simmons, 543 U.S. 551 (2005).
Scofield GR. 1980. Due process in the United States Supreme Court and the death of the Texas capital murder statute. *American Journal of Criminal Law* 8:1.
Shapiro M. 2008. An overdose of dangerousness: How "Future Dangerousness" catches the least culpable capital defendants and undermines the rationale for the executions it supports. *American Journal of Criminal Law* 35:145.
Showalter CR and R Bonnie. 1984. Psychiatrists and capital sentencing: Risks and responsibilities in a unique legal setting. *Bulletin of the American Academy of Psychiatry and the Law* 12:159.
Smith RJ. 2012. The geography of the death penalty and its ramifications. *Boston University Law Review* 92:227.
Tanner JM. 2005. "Continuing Threat" to whom?: Risk assessment in Virginia capital sentencing hearings. *Capital Defense Journal* 17:381.
Tex. Crim. Proc. Art. § 37.071(2) (b) (1) (1976).
Vann LS. 2011. History repeats itself: The post-*Furman* return to arbitrariness in capital punishment. *University of Richmond Law Review* 45:1255.
Ward B. 1986. Competency for execution: Problems in law and psychiatry. *Florida State University Law Review* 14:35.

12

Competence assessments

JENNIFER L. PIEL, GREGORY B. LEONG, AND ROBERT WEINSTOCK

INTRODUCTION

Forensic psychiatrists are commonly asked to evaluate mental competency for a specific activity. The skills and knowledge needed for specific competencies are context dependent and specific to the function or activity being evaluated. Accordingly, someone may be competent for one purpose yet incompetent for another. Competence also can vary as a person's underlying condition changes, or circumstances occur that challenge a person's capabilities. The forensic psychiatrist is tasked with assessing whether the individual has the requisite threshold levels of mental abilities to perform the activity in question. This chapter explores the concept of competence assessment, generally. Several subsequent chapters focus on specific types of competence assessments.

STANDARDS

Psychiatrists assist the court by providing information about an evaluee's unique mental abilities and limitations. Courts often take the recommendation of the forensic evaluator, but the ultimate determination of competence requires social value judgments left to the court to determine. In this manner, mental health providers may use the term "capacity" to distinguish that competence is a legal determination. Capacity refers to whether an individual can do the things required of the legal competency in question (Drogin and Barrett 2010). As the terms "capacity" and "competency" are often used interchangeably in the law, so are both terms used in this chapter.

It is important for the forensic evaluator to understand the legally significant activity and the functional skills required for the activity. For some competencies, statutory criteria outline the threshold skills or requirements for a person to be competent for the specific activity. Case law may also establish jurisdictional requirements for a competency or give guidance to statutory language on the subject. By way of illustration, all 50 states have adopted standards that are consonant with *Dusky v. United States* (1960) for competence to stand trial evaluations (Mossman et al. 2007).

Forensic evaluators should familiarize themselves with any relevant statutes, cases, or administrative regulations in the jurisdiction of the evaluation. Where no standard is articulated in the law, forensic evaluators must familiarize themselves with the objectives and functional skills required of the activity. Professional commentary on the competence such as practice guidelines or scholarly articles may additionally be useful to evaluators in determining the requisite knowledge and skills for any particular competence assessment.

CONCEPTUAL MODELS FOR COMPETENCE ASSESSMENT

Grisso (1986, 2003) conceptualizes a model of key characteristics relevant for competence assessments: functional, contextual, causal, interactive, judgmental, and dispositional. Functional abilities relate to a person's specific knowledge, beliefs, or understanding necessary to accomplish a given task. Some authors have broken this down into discrete subcategories, such as cognitive functioning, psychiatric or emotional functioning, and everyday functioning (ABA/APA 2008). This is relevant because some capacities, such as the capacity to enter into a business contract, may focus primarily on cognitive skills. However, other capacities, such as end-of-life decisions, may require cognitive and emotional skills. By way of illustration, a person with Alzheimer's disease may have diminished cognitive skills but may be able to express long-standing values that underlie their decisions (Karel et al. 2007). An individual may lack capacity to consent to treatment or research, but nevertheless retain capacity to appoint a proxy decision maker, most commonly someone with whom the evaluee has had a close relationship for years (Kim et al. 2011).

In Grisso's model, the fact that there are so many types of competence assessments speaks to the role of context as an important variable. Assessments of a person's competence require information about the evaluee's ability to function in a specific area. Causal inferences are useful to relate abilities or deficits to a specific cause and to make future prognostications. For example, if a person's Alzheimer's disorder is the basis for his or her incapacity to make a medical decision, the diagnosis provides useful information about the person's prognosis and likely symptoms and future abilities. An interactive characteristic focuses on the person's abilities to meet demands in interactions with others or demands posed by a specific situation. The judgment component concerns whether the evaluee's deficit skills warrant a finding of legal incompetence. Finally, disposition refers to the consequences to a person upon a determination of legal incompetence.

Appelbaum and Gutheil (2007) distinguish between standards for general and for specific competence. General competence questions are raised when it is believed that a person is unable to make decisions about a wide range of affairs. A finding of incompetence can lead to a person being placed on a guardianship or conservatorship. Specific competence refers to the ability to perform a specific function. A person may be competent to function in one area but not in another, because differing capacities and abilities may be required. Making this distinction itself can be an important contribution by a forensic psychiatrist consulting with general physicians and psychiatrists.

A person who is assessed as generally incompetent is considered so for all legal purposes—that is, a global incompetence. However, such a person may be *de facto* competent for a specific purpose, and this fact should be brought to the court's attention. For example, a person not competent to handle his or her money, or make decisions about psychotropic medication, may be competent to decide whether to have his or her leg amputated for medical reasons. People on guardianships in most jurisdictions generally are considered legally incompetent for all purposes. Conservatorships in some states are more limited than guardianships, and may be for incompetence in some specified general areas but not others. In cases of actual or *de facto* competence in a limited area for a person adjudicated as legally or *de jure* incompetent, the person's consent should be obtained in addition to that of a conservator or guardian if practical considerations preclude a court hearing. If a person improves and general competency is restored, courts should be petitioned to rescind the guardianship or conservatorship. This situation is similar to that of adolescents and children who may be legally incompetent because of immaturity for most purposes, solely because of their age. In fact, they may be able to make more competent decisions than many adults in some circumstances, despite being considered legally incompetent. However, unlike the disabled adult, the law may refuse to recognize a minor as competent for some purposes despite the reality or facts of a situation, probably because of the perception of immaturity of juveniles.

The sliding-scale model has been utilized for competence to give informed consent (Roth et al. 1977; Withers et al. 2008), and may be instructive for other types of competence assessments. Differing thresholds may depend on the factors in a specific case, such as the risks and benefits of a decision and the reasonableness of an evaluee's choice. A high threshold tends to be utilized for competency if a person is prepared to make an unreasonable choice or a choice with significant risks. Rather than using unreasonable outcome *per se* as a criterion, such differing thresholds suggest that a more stringent attempt should be made to search for a deficit in the ability to weigh relevant information if an evaluee's choices are too unreasonable or risky. A person's choice should at least be understandable in order to be competent, even though it may be unwise. Many irrational elements enter into decisions by normal competent individuals (Brock and Wartman 1990). Values inevitably enter into any determination of reasonableness, but varying thresholds are most consistent with commonsense approaches to this issue.

Although the sliding-scale concept has most commonly been utilized in civil competence assessments (such as medical decision making), it can also be applicable in the criminal area. Criteria for competence to stand trial can be interpreted in varying ways depending on the seriousness of the offense or the unreasonableness of the defendant's wishes regarding a trial (Buchanan 2006). A serious offense or complex legal case may require a greater degree of ability of a defendant to understand the charges against him or her and to provide assistance to his or her attorney. Depression must be seriously considered as making a defendant incompetent to stand trial in the case of serious felonies if it leads to a wish for a strategy to be found guilty and perhaps even a wish for the death penalty. A lower threshold is probably necessary to stand trial for less serious crimes. Sliding-scale criteria probably are frequently utilized but usually are not so conceptualized in the criminal area.

In recent years there has been increasing research on the neuroscience of decision making. With an aging population and more emphasis on decision-making skills in persons with mental illness, further study may provide new frameworks for looking at specific capacities. Stormoen et al. (2014), for example, identified that multiple factors are involved in medical decision making among persons with cognitive impairment, but assessment of verbal knowledge was the best predictor of competency for medical decision making. In their study, reading speed (consisting of ability to read rapidly and understand text) was the most predictive single measure of capacity to make medical decisions. Cáceda et al. (2014) looked at paradigms, such as the prisoner's dilemma and gamble theory, as additional means to inform decision-making patterns.

By their nature, many capacity assessments will reveal factors that support each side of a capacity assessment. The American Bar Association articulated a balancing-of-factors approach in the Model Rules of Professional Conduct (ABA 2009). It identified the evaluee's ability to articulate reasoning toward a decision, variability of state of mind, ability to appreciate consequences of a decision, the fairness of a decision, and whether the decision is consistent with known preferences or values of the evaluee.

Value judgments of the evaluator are implicit in each of these models. For example, different evaluators may give differing value and weight to autonomy, beneficence, paternalism, civil liberties, and social protection. Values are involved in establishing the cut-off line for abilities, which divides competence from incompetence (Faden and Beauchamp 1986). An evaluee's choices at the end of life may be contrary to what the evaluator would choose for himself or herself, for instance, but the evaluator is tasked with assessing the evaluee's skills, values, and beliefs. Accordingly, values enter into priorities and into determinations of how people ought to live, what people ought to be able to do, what value to give patient welfare, and what value to give to an individual's choice and preferences.

Objectivity denotes an evaluator's independence from significant interference due to bias. Such bias can come from the evaluator in the form of personal value judgments or from contextual factors, such as having a preexisting relationship with the evaluee or referring source for the evaluation (Heilbrun et al. 2014, 78). Although bias is an inevitable part of competence assessments, the forensic evaluators should report honestly and strive toward objectivity (AAPL Ethics Guideline 2005) in applying the requisite legal standard.

Further, value judgments should be distinguished from professional opinions and scientific data. For example, many judges and juries believe that children should be raised by conventional parents. Even though there is no empirical justification for this opinion, it still could affect the outcome of a parental fitness (capacity) hearing. Biases of the forensic psychiatrist should not be misrepresented as scientific data with reasonable medical certainty. Efforts should be made to obtain data supporting any such belief with an ethical responsibility to strive for objectivity.

TYPES OF COMPETENCE ASSESSMENTS

As mentioned, there are many different types of specific competence with varying criteria distinct for the relevant area of functioning. Although most assessments are present-day evaluations, forensic evaluators should be mindful that they could be asked to perform retrospective evaluations (e.g., determining whether someone was competent when he or she executed a will) or prospective (e.g., in guardianship proceedings, whether the evaluee's disabilities are expected to limit their future decision making). As there are numerous situations in which a person's competence to perform an activity is questioned, an exhaustive list is not provided here. Table 12.1 provides an illustrative list of criminal and civil competencies.

Several of these specific areas and their criteria are discussed in other chapters of this book.

Table 12.1 Examples of criminal and civil competencies

Examples of criminal competencies	Examples of civil competencies
Stand trial	Parent
Enter plea	Informed consent for treatment/treatment refusals
Testify	Consent for voluntary hospitalization
Waive counsel	Care for oneself/guardianship
Be sentenced	Consent for research
Waive appeals	Enter a contract
Waive *Miranda* rights	Marry, engage in sexual relationship, divorce
Confess	Vote
Refuse insanity defense	Drive
Be executed	Testamentary capacity, handle financial affairs, make a gift
	Testimonial in civil case
	Professional competency

COMMON ERRORS IN COMPETENCE ASSESSMENTS

A number of scholars have written on the evaluation and format of reports for various competence assessments. Mossman et al. (2007), for example, provide a comprehensive guide to competence to stand trial evaluations that includes ethical and cultural considerations and practical information on the assessment, formulating the opinion, and the written report. Important also is recognizing common errors made by forensic evaluators in assessing competence. Identified here are several common errors in competence assessments.

Failure to answer the question

In contrast to general clinical psychiatric evaluations, forensic evaluators need to define and answer the specific question asked. In civil competence assessment, this can be challenging because the person requesting the evaluation may not recognize a distinction, for example, between global incompetence and incompetence to make a medical decision. A competency assessment should not be a clinical assessment. Instead, the competency assessment should be tailored to the requisite knowledge and skills necessary for the competency in question.

Equating diagnosis with incompetency

A psychiatric diagnosis is not synonymous with incompetence or impairment. Only the manner in which the mental disorder interferes with functioning in a specified context is relevant to an assessment of incompetence.

However, diagnoses that include a severity description may be determinative. The *Diagnostic and Statistical Manual of Mental Disorders* (*DSM-5*) Neurocognitive Disorders are illustrative, as they are divided into Major and Mild Neurocognitive Disorders based, at least in part, on levels of functioning. Accordingly, certain diagnoses, such as Major Neurocognitive Disorder, may carry more weight in explaining incompetence (Weinstock et al. 2015). The law specifies the legal criteria, which differ depending on the type of competence evaluated. Oftentimes, incompetence is legally required to be the result of mental disease or defect.

Overreliance on assessment instruments

Many psychological test instruments (often questionnaires) have been developed for specific competencies and are increasingly being used in competence assessments (Nicholson and Norwood 2000). These instruments can be useful to an evaluator by assisting the evaluator in recognizing and focusing on commonly identified skills or criteria for a given competency. Because assessment tools are not individualized to a person or situation, these instruments produce objectivity and reliability. However, on this same basis, an evaluator who relies too heavily on an assessment tool may miss what is essential in a specific case. Although assessment instruments are useful in supporting a formulation of an evaluee, they are best used as one aspect of the forensic assessment, in addition (for example) to an interview and review of collateral material.

BIAS

The biases of an examiner also can influence the interpretation of terms utilized in the legal criteria. The most honest and effective approach is to be open about the data and also the abilities evaluated, as well as to explain which legal criteria were used and how they were interpreted. A competence assessment should indicate what areas of functioning were evaluated, how they were evaluated, and what factors were considered relevant and why. Simple conclusory statements should be avoided as they can conceal hidden value judgments and can disguise such value judgments as psychiatric expertise. As mentioned above, it is the examiner's responsibility to take measures to minimize bias by striving toward an objective assessment and opinion.

Failure to consider evaluee effort, deception, and malingering

Given the legal context of many competence assessments, forensic evaluators performing this type of work should consider whether the evaluee is putting forth effort in responding to the evaluator's assessment. In cases when the evaluee does not answer questions, for example, the evaluator should consider whether this is volitional. The forensic evaluator should also consider whether the evaluee is distorting (exaggerating or minimizing) symptoms, or malingering, as a possible explanation for his or her presentation and impaired functioning. As with other types of forensic assessments, collateral information, psychological testing, and careful interview can minimize evaluator error.

Using technical language

Psychiatry as a field has numerous technical terms, from terms to describe symptoms to diagnoses to treatment modalities. These terms may not be understood by persons without specific training in mental health. It is useful for the forensic psychiatrist to use language that is reasonably understandable to the audience. This could include, for instance, other medical providers or evaluators, a judge, attorneys, and the parties to the legal case. Minimizing the use of technical language—or jargon—helps reduce misinterpretation by others (Fuhrmann and Zibbell 2012, 181).

Opinion without support

In opining on the competence raised, the forensic evaluator should address the specific knowledge and functional tasks of the particular evaluee and provide supporting evidence for the skills in question. As above, it is not uncommon for an evaluator to equate diagnosis with impairment. Basic conclusory statements should be avoided because they can conceal hidden value judgments and can disguise such value judgments as psychiatric expertise. A helpful expert opinion lays out the relevant functional abilities and comments on how an evaluee's mental condition affects the evaluee's requisite abilities. It is useful to specify all the reasoning and criteria so that areas of agreement and disagreement can be determined.

SUMMARY

Forensic psychiatrists are especially suited for assessing a person's mental status and its potential for interfering with a specific area of functioning. If general psychiatrists are asked to make such assessments, forensic psychiatrists can provide consultation to them. Although different models and assessment tools may be utilized by the evaluator, the key focus should be on whether the individual has the requisite functional knowledge and skills to perform the specific legal competence. Minor technical disagreements should be differentiated from psychiatric data pertinent to the legal criteria. It is important to be clear about the differing aspects of competence to most readily assist the court and prevent attorneys from obfuscating the many areas of reliable and valid noncontroversial data.

REFERENCES

American Bar Association Commission on Law and Aging and American Psychological Association. 2008. *Assessment of Older Adults with Diminished Capacity: A Handbook for Psychologists*. Washington, DC: American Bar Association and American Psychological Association.

American Academy of Psychiatry and the Law. 2005. *Ethics Guidelines for the Practice of Forensic Psychiatry* (adopted May 2005). http://aapl.org/ethics.htm, accessed November 12, 2014.

American Bar Association. 2009. *Model Rules of Professional Conduct, Rule 1.4, comment 6*. Washington, DC: American Bar Association.

Appelbaum PS and TG Gutheil. 2007. *Clinical Handbook of Psychiatry and the Law*, 4th edition. Baltimore: Lippincott, Williams and Wilkins.

Brock D and S Wartman. 1990. When competent patients make irrational choices. *New England Journal of Medicine* 322:1595–1599.

Buchanan A. 2006. Competence to stand trial and the seriousness of the charge. *Journal of the American Academy of Psychiatry and the Law* 34:458–465.

Cáceda R, CB Nemeroff, and PD Harvey. 2014. Toward an understanding of decision making in severe mental illness. *Journal of Neuropsychiatry and Clinical Neurosciences* 26(3):196–213.

Drogin EY and CL Barrett. 2010. *Evaluation for Guardianship*. New York: Oxford University Press.

Dusky v. United States, 362 U.S. 402 (1960).

Faden RR and TL Beauchamp. 1986. *A History of Informed Consent*. New York: Oxford University Press.

Fuhrmann G and RA Zibbell. 2012. *Evaluation of Child Custody*. New York: Oxford University Press.

Grisso T. 1986. *Evaluating Competencies: Forensic Assessment and Instruments*. New York: Plenum.

Grisso T. 2003. *Evaluating Competencies: Forensic Assessment and Instruments*, 2nd edition. New York: Kluwer Academic/Plenum.

Heilbrun K, D DeMatteo, SB Holliday, and C LaDuke. 2014. *Forensic mental health assessment: A casebook*, 2nd edition. New York: Oxford University Press.

Karel MJ, J Moye, A Back, and AR Azar. 2007. Three methods of assessing values for advance care planning comparing persons with and without dementia. *Journal of Aging and Health* 19:123–151.

Kim SY, JH Karlawish, HM Kim, IF Wall, AL Bozoki, and PS Appelbaum. 2011. Preservation of the capacity to appoint a proxy decision-maker: Implications for dementia research. *Archives of General Psychiatry* 68(2):214–220.

Mossman D, SG Noffsinger, P Ash et al. 2007. AAPL practice guideline for the forensic psychiatric evaluation of competence to stand trial. *Journal of the American Academy of Psychiatry and the Law* 35(Supplement):S3–S72.

Nicholson RA and S Norwood. 2000. The quality of forensic psychological assessments, reports and testimony: Acknowledging the gap between promise and practice. *Law and Human Behavior* 24:9–44.

Roth LH, L Meisel, and CW Lidz. 1977. Tests of competence to consent to treatment. *American Journal of Psychiatry* 134:279–284.

Stormoen S, O Almkvist, M Eriksdotter, E Sundström, and IM Tallberg. 2014. Cognitive predictors of medical decision-making capacity in mild cognitive impairment and Alzheimer's disease. *International Journal of Geriatric Psychiatry* 29(12):1304–1311.

Weinstock R, J Piel, and GB Leong. 2015. *DSM-5* and Civil Competencies. In *DSM-5 and the Law: Changes and Challenges*, edited by C. Scott, New York: Oxford University Press, 152–176.

Withers E, DP Sklar, and CS Crandall. 2008. Impairment and severity: How ED physicians decide to override an impaired patient's refusal. *American Journal of Emergency Medicine* 26(7):803–807.

13

Psychological autopsy and postmortem toxicology in forensic psychiatry

ANDREW KIM, MACE BECKSON, ALAN WAYNE JONES, AND ALAN L. BERMAN

INTRODUCTION

The Centers for Disease Control and Prevention (CDC) defines "suicide" as "death caused by self-directed injurious behavior with any intent to die as a result of the behavior" (CDC 2014). This definition thus implicates the thoughts and behaviors of the decedent, which may be unclear from the evidence available to the medical examiner investigating an unwitnessed, nonnatural death. In these cases, the decedent's mental state, as well as underlying precipitants and risk factors, become matters of legal significance on which the opinion of a forensic expert is often sought.

In 1957, to address such matters, the Los Angeles County Coroner, Theodore Curphey, MD, contracted with Dr. Edwin Shneidman and his colleagues at the Los Angeles Suicide Prevention Center to provide behavioral science consultation with respect to manner of death determinations in "equivocal" cases, where it was unclear whether the death was intentionally self-inflicted (Botello et al. 2013). Shneidman devised a protocol, christened the "psychological autopsy," to help investigators "make a reasonable determination of what was in the mind of the decedent vis-à-vis his or her own death" (Shneidman 1994, 75). As one high-profile example, investigators employed Shneidman's protocol in examining Marilyn Monroe's death from a barbiturate overdose in 1962 and concluded it was the result of a "probable suicide" (Botello et al. 2013).

The psychological autopsy consists of a systematic retrospective investigation of the decedent's state of mind at the time of death to determine (to the highest degree of certainty possible) whether the decedent was suicidal and, if so, what distal and proximal risk factors contributed to that suicide risk. In the psychological autopsy, the subject of the investigation has died and is unavailable for personal examination. Therefore, proxy informants, in addition to contemporaneous documentation, provide important data regarding the decedent.

In coroner's death determinations, the psychological autopsy is sought to elucidate the "manner of death" (or "mode of death"). Manner of death is distinguished from "cause of death," which refers to the immediate, mechanistic factors that terminated life, e.g., blunt force trauma to the head, myocardial infarction, etc. In contrast, manner of death captures the broader circumstances, typically certified as "natural," "accidental," "suicide," or "homicide" (the so-called "NASH" categories). A case is deemed "equivocal" when uncertainty arises as to the applicable NASH category. Without further clarification, the manner is left "undetermined" by the medical examiner.

The psychological autopsy also investigates the "motive" and the "intent" associated with the suicide. "Motive" encompasses the decedent's internal calculus of the reasons and circumstances supporting a decision to die by suicide, taking into account the current and prospective stressors and resources (Scott et al. 2006). "Intent" has been defined as the aim or goal to end one's life, including the conscious awareness and expectancy that the method used will cause death (Berman 2005). Implicit in intent, "mental capacity" refers to the decedent's ability to arrive rationally at the decision to die by suicide, considering such factors as intoxication, cognitive impairment, reality testing, and "sanity" (Scott et al. 2006).

This chapter will discuss the psychological autopsy with respect to applications; methodologies and limitations; interpretation and integration of toxicological results; ethical considerations; admissibility in court; and practical considerations for providing testimony.

APPLICATIONS

From its origins in assisting the Coroner, applications of the psychological autopsy have since spread into the courtroom and beyond. In research settings, the psychological autopsy has helped expand the knowledge base for suicide risk factors and suicide prevention.

In litigation, the psychological autopsy may be utilized where the manner of death is relevant to criminal culpability or civil liability. In criminal cases involving suspected homicide, a psychological autopsy may support or refute a criminal defense that the decedent's death was self-inflicted, as opposed to the result of foul play (Ogloff and Otto 1993). It has also been used to establish criminal responsibility for a known suicide. In *Jackson v. State*, the victim was a 17-year-old girl who died by gunshot wound after years of abuse by her mother, who had forged the victim's birth certificate and forced her to work as a nude dancer (553 So. 2d 719 [Fla. 4th DCA 1989]). The criminal investigation established that the victim died by suicide, but a psychological autopsy was admitted into evidence against her mother to support charges of child abuse, procuring sexual performance by a child, and forgery (Harris 1990).

Litigation over the denial of life insurance benefits often involves psychological autopsies. Where the policy at issue contains a suicide exclusion clause, payment of benefits to beneficiaries is denied when a self-inflicted death occurs within a specified time period from the start of the policy. Though intended to protect insurers against subterfuge by a newly insured person, public sentiment and policy tend to favor the beneficiaries of life insurance policies so as not to compound the beneficiaries' loss with the denial of benefits (Schuman 1993). Accordingly, the insurance company has the burden of proving a death was a suicide, and it may obtain a psychological autopsy to meet this burden. Correspondingly, the intended beneficiaries may seek a psychological autopsy to bolster their claim that the decedent's death was not a suicide. In *Evans v. Provident Life Ins. Co.*, the Kansas Supreme Court affirmed the admission of a psychological autopsy report opining that an insured decedent was suicidal at the time of his death (815 P.2d 550 [Kan. 1991]).

Even where manner of death is not equivocal, civil cases may still invoke a psychological autopsy to obtain a cross-sectional assessment of a decedent's mental state and suicide risk prior to death. In malpractice actions against psychotherapists, a psychological autopsy may be proffered to opine on the foreseeability of a decedent's suicide and thereby show proximate causation. Parties may also seek a psychological autopsy in wrongful death litigation involving possible "suicide-by-cop," product liability claims, workers' compensation claims, and military benefits awards to surviving families.

In research settings, the purpose of the psychological autopsy is not to determine whether suicide occurred, but rather to understand why it occurs. It is a practical and widely used approach to studying distal, proximal, and contributory suicide risk factors, i.e., underlying and acute psychological and situational preconditions to suicide. Because of the statistical rarity of suicide, e.g., 20.6 males and 5.5 females per 100,000 U.S. population in 2012 (Drapeau and McIntosh 2014), longitudinal studies requiring large sample sizes would be impractical. However, the case-control study design provides an alternative approach by comparing known suicide cases to matched control samples, such as known accidental deaths. Psychological autopsy studies utilizing this design have elucidated several risk factors associated with suicide, such as history of substance use disorders, depressive disorders, and prior suicide attempt, thereby enhancing clinical suicide risk assessment and prevention measures, as well as informing policy (Yoshimasu et al. 2008).

METHODOLOGY

Since its inception, various protocols have been developed to establish a structure for the psychological autopsy (e.g., Ebert 1987; Snider et al. 2006; Knoll 2009). Common to these protocols is the targeted gathering of evidence, typically from review of available records (e.g., autopsy reports, postmortem toxicology reports, suicide notes, journals, correspondences, insurance policies, and wills, as well as psychiatric, medical, pharmacy, employment, military, legal, and academic records) and interviews of family survivors and acquaintances (i.e., knowledgeable observers). These approaches facilitate the systematic collection of psychological, psychiatric, medical, and social data, including first-person accounts of the decedent's developmental history, character, coping style, and last days of life, such that "conclusions can be drawn as to the intention of the decedent, therefore the decedent's role in effecting his/her own death" (Berman 2005, 365). However, no single approach has emerged as the standard protocol for the conduct of a psychological autopsy, and the selection, interpretation, and weighting of each source of evidence remain largely a matter of evaluator discretion, leading to inter-rater variability. This lack of a standardized protocol has raised concerns as to the psychological autopsy's reliability and validity (Pouliot and De Leo 2006).

One response to such concerns has been to create structured rating instruments addressing the range of factors to be considered in the psychological autopsy. The CDC developed the "Empirical Criteria for the Determination of Suicide" (ECDS) by selecting those factors that best correlated empirically with self-infliction and suicidal intention: autopsy evidence; toxicology; witness statements; investigatory evidence (e.g., police reports, scene photos); psychological evidence (e.g., observed behavior, personality, and lifestyle); evidence that decedent recognized high-potential lethality of means; recent and sudden change in decedent emotions; serious depression or mental disorder in decedent; indications of desire to die, anticipation of impending death, or expressions of farewell (e.g., verbally or via a suicide note); expressions of hopelessness; actual or threatened stressful events or losses; instability in immediate family; recent interpersonal conflicts; and history of poor physical health (Jobes et al. 1991). These factors are organized into a 16-item instrument, with each item categorized as evidence of self-infliction, intention, or both. If a case achieves a score of three or more on both the self-infliction and intention scales (indicating there were at least three factors evidencing self-infliction and at least three factors evidencing intention), then it is deemed a suicide. A lower score on either scale is interpreted as an accidental death. The ECDS was subjected to a validation study that applied the protocol to a blinded set of cases that had previously been certified as suicide or accidental. The ECDS correctly identified 100% of the known suicides and 82.75% of the accidents (Jobes et al. 1991).

Despite its elegance, the use of the ECDS is not without qualifications. It was not intended to obviate the investigator's clinical decision making, and it excludes traditional suicide risk factors, such as previous suicide threats or attempts, measures to prevent rescue, rehearsal of suicidal behavior, and preparations for death (Jobes et al. 1991). Moreover, the ECDS does not calculate probabilistic suicide risk. Rather, it was designed to provide medical examiners with a standardized instrument to help distinguish a suicide death from an accidental death for purposes of improving the accuracy of epidemiological data. To this extent, the ECDS may be overly deterministic, especially for forensic settings where more is required than merely sorting suicides from accidental deaths. The ECDS scoring system may also come across as conclusory, such that in litigation settings, expert opinion relying on the instrument may invite exclusion where testimony on an ultimate issue is barred.

An alternative protocol was developed based on a survey of suicidologist–forensic experts who considered the following areas of inquiry to be essential: documentation/records; site of death; demographics; recent symptoms/behaviors; precipitants to death; psychiatric history; physical health; substance abuse; family history; firearm history; attachments/social supports; emotional reactivity; lifestyle/character; and access to care (Snider et al. 2006). The "Semi-Structured Interview for Psychological Autopsy" systematizes the survivor interview along four domains: precipitants/stressors; motivation; lethality; and intentionality (Werlang and Botega 2003).

Though these protocols do offer a conceptual structure for the collection of autopsy data, true standardization remains unrealized. Most conspicuously, no decision rules govern what type or amount of evidence is sufficient to rule in or rule out suicide as the manner of death. However, standardized data points and domains have been defined (Snider et al. 2006), affording some assurance of reliability. At any rate, the lack of standardization is not unique to psychological autopsies and is common to many protocols in the behavioral sciences, including the typical psychiatric interview. Provided the psychological autopsy focuses on the degree of suicide risk, as opposed to whether the death was actually a suicide, it avoids overstepping into an ultimate issue that is reserved for the finder of fact.

RESOLVING INCONSISTENCIES IN THE EVIDENCE

The psychological autopsy frequently involves consideration of inconsistent or contradictory evidence (indeed, ambiguity is likely what prompted the psychological autopsy to be conducted in the first place). In manner of death determinations, medical examiners have variable access to information typically found in coroner's investigator reports, police investigation reports, medical records, and pharmacy records. Through discovery, the forensic expert may have a much larger database than that previously available to the medical examiner. Despite, or perhaps because of, an increased access to sources, the forensic expert commonly confronts inconsistencies in the evidence that may or may not be resolvable. Where such inconsistencies cannot be reconciled, the expert witness may offer alternative opinions based on competing versions of the facts.

One potential source of inconsistencies is the survivor interview. A survivor's recollection of the circumstances surrounding the relevant death is fraught with inherent bias, both conscious and unconscious, which may arise out of the survivor's feelings of guilt, anger, or shame, or out of personal interest in the outcome of the psychological autopsy. However, survivors provide key pieces of information about the decedent's personal history, which can provide specific observations and temporal information pertaining to circumstances shortly before death. Accordingly, while performing the interviews, the forensic expert should exercise judgment in assessing the interviewee's credibility and assigning commensurate weight to the information elicited. Such evidence should be integrated with that gleaned from other sources, particularly the death scene, physical autopsy, postmortem toxicology, and observations of other informants who had significant contact with the decedent in the days and weeks prior to death. Use of these supplemental sources offers some assurance that the ultimate interpretations will be valid (Beskow et al. 1990).

POSTMORTEM TOXICOLOGY

Another source of evidence requiring careful interpretation is the postmortem toxicology results. The role of intoxicants is often central in determining the decedent's intent at the time of death, both with respect to mental capacity and lethality. If drug or alcohol use is suspected, the psychological autopsy should address whether the decedent was too intoxicated to have formed intent and whether the suicide was by drug overdose. Thus, it is useful for the forensic expert to have some working knowledge of basic toxicology. It is also important to be aware of misconceptions and pitfalls, e.g., so-called "lethal" levels of drugs; use of postmortem toxicology results to estimate antemortem concentrations or drug dosage; and the routine and uncritical use of toxicology textbooks or tables to determine cause of death (e.g., see Berman et al. 2003; Palmer 2010; Gill et al. 2013). Discussion with an experienced forensic toxicologist and/or forensic pathologist, review of corresponding expert reports, and/or review of the relevant scientific literature will also assist the forensic expert in understanding the case.

The most challenging part of postmortem forensic toxicology is interpreting the results and explaining what they mean to nonspecialists, such as legal professionals and juries (Drummer et al. 2013). This requires a broad knowledge of the pharmacology and toxicology of licit and illicit drugs, their mechanism of action in the body, and their potential for causing intoxication and death. Tables of therapeutic, toxic, and fatal concentrations of drugs are available, although these should be used cautiously (Schulz et al. 2012). The notion of "lethal drug levels" or some concentration threshold that leads to incapacitation and death is hard to defend, because so much depends on the dose taken, route of administration, development of tolerance, body weight, and the nature of any concomitantly ingested substances. Development of tolerance is especially important with regard to toxicity of opioid drugs (Davis 2014). Certain drug combinations are more dangerous than others, such as when ethanol is taken with sedative-hypnotics (barbiturates or benzodiazepines) or when selective serotonin reuptake inhibitor (SSRI) antidepressants are taken with the painkiller tramadol, which may cause a life-threatening "serotonin syndrome" (Pilgrim et al. 2010).

The validity of the toxicological results is contingent upon the appropriate selection and collection of specimens for toxicological analysis. In the postmortem context, blood is the most important specimen for analysis, because the concentrations of drugs present in the blood typically are a direct reflection of the concentrations reaching the brain. Depending on the concentrations of centrally acting drugs in blood, tentative conclusions can be drawn about toxicity and potential lethality. However, the results of toxicological analysis are susceptible to several sources of error, ranging from the way the specimen is collected to the interpretation of assay results.

Sampling site and handling of the blood specimen can have significant effects on the reliability of the analytical results. The preferred source of blood for postmortem analytical toxicology is from a peripheral sampling site, such as a femoral vein. The worst possible source is from the chest cavity, because of the risk of contamination from drugs unabsorbed in the stomach or at higher concentrations in lung and liver than in the blood (Kugelberg and Jones 2007). Biological fluids taken for toxicological analysis should be preserved with sodium or potassium fluoride (1%–2%) and then refrigerated or frozen (Drummer 2010). Fluoride ions act as enzyme inhibitors, which help to prevent bacterial metabolism of glucose into ethanol, especially if the body is decomposed or microorganisms have spread from the gut into the blood. Because of the risk of alcohol being produced in the body after death, a realistic cut-off concentration should be used when reporting a positive blood alcohol concentration (BAC) at autopsy, e.g., 0.01 gram %. However, there is much to recommend use of a higher cutoff, such as 0.02 gram %, especially in traumatic deaths (Kugelberg and Jones 2007).

A positive BAC should be confirmed by analysis of ethanol in alternative specimens, such as stomach contents, urine, and/or vitreous humor. The sugar content of urine voided by healthy individuals is negligible, so there is no substrate for postmortem synthesis of ethanol. Given the anatomic separation, there is low likelihood of bacteria spreading from the gut to the eye and introducing newly synthesized ethanol to the vitreous humor. Analysis of biomarkers of ethanol ingestion, such as the nonoxidative metabolites ethyl glucuronide (EtG) and ethyl sulfate (EtS), can also help to ascertain if ethanol is the product of postmortem fermentation (Maenhout et al. 2013). Both EtG and EtS are produced when ethanol undergoes metabolism in the liver, so their presence in postmortem blood specimens indicates that the decedent had probably ingested alcohol while alive (Krabseth et al. 2014).

To analyze drugs and their metabolites in the circulatory system, whole blood is utilized in postmortem forensic toxicology, whereas plasma or serum is utilized in clinical pharmacology and therapeutic drug monitoring programs. Because many drugs bind to plasma proteins, the concentrations in plasma or serum are higher than in red cells and in whole blood. Unfortunately, this difference is often ignored, making it difficult to compare postmortem drug concentrations with therapeutic drug concentrations. For example, plasma-to-blood distribution ratios are 1.15:1 for ethanol, 1.8:1 for diazepam, and 2:1 for tetrahydrocannabinol (THC), the major psychoactive drug in marijuana.

Another factor to consider is the phenomenon of "postmortem redistribution," which refers to movement of drugs out of body tissue depots and into the blood after death (Pélissier-Alicot et al. 2003). Concentrations of drugs sequestered in body organs and tissues are higher than those in peripheral blood. Consequently, redistribution after death results in higher postmortem central (e.g., heart) blood concentrations that may overestimate the actual blood concentrations at the time of death. The extent of postmortem redistribution is gauged by comparing heart blood concentration to femoral blood concentration. High heart-to-femoral ratios suggest that postmortem redistribution has occurred (Han et al. 2012).

Other valuable biological specimens in postmortem toxicology include hair, fingernails, and urine. Hair strands are particularly useful when subjected to segmental analysis, which allows the creation of an approximate timeline of drug intake during life (Barbosa et al. 2013). The trace analysis of drugs in hair strands can be used to verify the decedent's compliance with medications, such as antidepressants or antipsychotics (Barbosa et al. 2013). Hair is a viable specimen even if the body is decomposed and blood specimens too contaminated for sampling and proper analysis. Both hair and nails are obtainable from exhumed bodies, allowing detection of drug intake long after death.

Urine specimens are readily available at autopsy for analysis in large volumes, with concentrations of drugs and metabolites that are higher than in blood samples, and with longer time windows for detection. However, the composition of urine is variable depending on fluid intake and state of hydration. Some urine samples are more dilute than others (some authors suggest normalizing drug test results according to creatinine concentration), and the urinary pH affects drug concentrations, especially the excretion of basic drugs. A positive postmortem urine drug test furnishes proof that particular drugs were used but does not establish exactly when they were used; whether the decedent was acutely intoxicated at the time of death; or the specific degree of drug-related impairment experienced by the decedent at the time of death. Moreover, postmortem urine drug concentrations cannot be extrapolated to determine the dosage of the drugs consumed or the drug concentrations in the blood at the time of death.

The results of postmortem toxicology are indispensable to the psychological autopsy, because they provide important information as to cause of death (e.g., acute poisoning) as well as the decedent's mental state at the time. However, the forensic expert should be aware of common sources of error in the collection and processing of specimens and in the interpretation of the analytical results. Such awareness will help ensure that reliable toxicological evidence is used for the findings and opinions set forth in the psychological autopsy.

ETHICAL CONSIDERATIONS IN SURVIVOR INTERVIEWS

Care must also be taken to protect the interests of the survivors during the psychological autopsy. Out of respect for the bereavement process, and to minimize survivors' tendency to idealize their loved one in the early stages of grief, the investigator should allow 2 to 6 months to elapse before contacting survivors (Beskow et al. 1990). The investigator should respect categorically any refusal to participate or request to withdraw from participation. Informed consent should be obtained, with the advisement that the interview is not intended to be therapeutic. Therapeutic effects of the survivor interviews may be inevitable, as survivors often experience them as cathartic, allowing ventilation of difficult feelings about the decedent and his or her death. Survivors may participate in order to contribute to the state of knowledge concerning suicide risk and prevention, thereby sublimating feelings of grief, anger, or abandonment, and salvaging some greater good from personal tragedy (Wong et al. 2010).

The interviewer should neither disavow nor deliberately avoid these salutary benefits, but should keep them from clouding the purpose of the evaluation or confusing the interviewee. The risk is that the interviewee will mistake the interview for treatment and perhaps even identify the interviewer as a therapist, leading to disclosures that are either outside the intended scope of the interview or affirmatively counter to the interests of the interviewee (e.g., if an insurance beneficiary admits a belief that the death was in fact a suicide). Nevertheless, the interviewer should be alert to any mental health needs that become apparent during the interview. The interviewer stands in a position in such cases to recommend that the interviewee seek psychological counseling, while consistently maintaining a forensic, as opposed to therapeutic, stance during the encounter.

REPORT WRITING

The investigation culminates in a detailed written psychological autopsy report, which should state the purpose of the evaluation and present the psychiatric–legal question (e.g., "Did the decedent possess a mental state consistent with suicide at the time of death?"). A discussion of the cause of death, including findings from the scene investigation, witness statements, physical autopsy, and toxicology report, should be included before entering into a detailed but concise synthesis of relevant biographical information about the decedent, including major active psychosocial stressors, relationship status, mental health history, and impressions from survivor interviews. The report should pay particular attention to life events in the days, weeks, and months immediately preceding death. In accordance with the American Academy of Psychiatry and the Law's "Ethical Guidelines for the Practice of Forensic Psychiatry," the forensic expert should acknowledge that a personal examination of the decedent was not conducted (Ogloff and Otto 1993). If an instrument such as the ECDS is used, a brief discussion of the relevant protocol and associated reliability and validity data should be included.

At the end, the report includes a summary of the behaviors and mental state of the decedent at the time of death and whether they were consistent with suicide. The expert should address "factors descriptive of high intentionality, which include conscious awareness of consequences; goal of cessation; expectation of fatal outcome; implementation of a method of high lethality; minimal rescuability or precautions; premeditation [i.e., planning]; and communications [of intent]" (Berman 2005, 369). The report should provide a probabilistic assessment of suicide risk (e.g., mildly, moderately, or severely elevated) at the time of death. The level of certainty should be commensurate with the setting in which the opinion is offered, with a confidential report to the coroner countenancing a slightly wider range of certainty than expert testimony in court. In formal legal proceedings, the forensic opinion should be offered with a "reasonable degree of medical certainty" (or "medical probability," depending on the legal jurisdiction), which is generally equivalent to "more likely than not." The forensic expert should not overstate the level of confidence in the assessment or create a misleading impression of certainty about suicide (Berman 2005).

ADMISSIBILITY AND TESTIMONY

If the psychological autopsy will be offered as expert opinion evidence in a contested legal matter, it must satisfy the requirements of legal admissibility, which in the United States, depending on the jurisdiction, is governed by one of two evidentiary standards. The older *Frye* standard, still observed in a number of states, uses the criterion of "general acceptance" in the field (*Frye v. United States*, 293 F. 1013 [D.C. Cir. 1923]). Under the newer *Daubert* standard, used in federal courts and adopted by many states, the court must find that the expert is properly qualified and that the opinion will assist the finder of fact (*Daubert v. Merrell Dow Pharm., Inc.*, 509 U.S. 579, 1993).

To qualify as an expert, the proffered witness must possess the "knowledge, skill, experience, training, or education" to offer understanding and insights above what would be obvious to the layperson (Federal Rules of Evidence 702). The forensic expert should be prepared to discuss his or her qualifications in mental health and suicidology, as well as in the conduct and analysis of the psychological autopsy. Thus, before undertaking a psychological autopsy, the forensic expert would be well served to obtain additional knowledge, training, and/or experience in suicidology and psychological autopsy, as well as basic aspects of the coroner investigation.

Whether the psychological autopsy will assist the finder of fact hinges on "a preliminary assessment of whether the reasoning or methodology underlying the testimony is scientifically valid" (*Daubert*, 509 U.S. at 12). To determine scientific validity, *Daubert* set forth a nonexhaustive list of factors for consideration, including testability, peer review, known error rate, standardization, and general acceptance (*Daubert*, 509 U.S. at 12–13). Generally, the *Daubert* standard favors admission of scientific opinion evidence, commonly shifting discretion to the finder-of-fact to determine weight and credibility.

The forensic expert nevertheless should be prepared to defend the use of the psychological autopsy in terms of its general acceptance in the field, the validity of its techniques and practices, or both. That defense may include a frank acknowledgement of the psychological autopsy's limitations, including the lack of a standardized protocol, the absence of consensus on terminology, and the inability to determine with certainty that the death was a suicide. That said, the psychological autopsy is no less valid than other forensic mental state evaluations, such as for criminal insanity or testamentary capacity. Moreover, the psychological autopsy has for decades been used and generally accepted as the state of the art in the postmortem assessment of mental state. Furthermore, the psychological autopsy has been subjected to peer review, inasmuch as several hundred research reports relying on the psychological autopsy have been published in peer-reviewed journals. Finally, though the decedent has usually not been examined personally, such direct access to the decedent's thoughts is not necessary for the forensic expert to arrive at an opinion on the decedent's mental state to a reasonable degree of medical certainty after careful analysis of the available evidence in its totality (Jacobs and Klein-Benheim 1995).

SUMMARY

The psychological autopsy is a forensic retrospective investigation and assessment, which serves as a powerful tool to assess the likelihood that a sudden, unexplained death is a suicide, as well as to understand the factors that contributed to the suicide. With its systematic approach to examining the psychological and contextual circumstances preceding suicide, the psychological autopsy has assisted in analyzing equivocal death cases and has helped survivors understand the decedent's behavior. Additionally, it has been used in a variety of legal, quality improvement, and research contexts. Despite potential criticism with respect to methodology, courts have frequently found the psychological autopsy to be scientifically valid and helpful to the finder of fact in legal settings. Though unable to make a definitive determination that any particular death was a suicide (which would go to the ultimate issue in litigation), the psychological autopsy can make a probabilistic assessment of suicide risk and can provide useful insights to coroners, courts, researchers, and survivors.

REFERENCES

Barbosa J, J Faria, F Carvalho, M Pedro, O Queirós, R Moreira, and RJ Dinis-Oliveira. 2013. Hair as an alternative matrix in bioanalysis. *Bioanalysis* 8:895–914.

Berman AL. 2005. Psychological autopsy. In *Encyclopedia of Forensic and Legal Medicine*, 2 vols., edited by J Payne-James, R Byard, T Corey, C Henderson, Amsterdam: Elsevier Academic Press, 364–371.

Berman AL, G Shepherd, and MM Silverman. 2003. The LSARS-II: Lethality of suicide attempt rating scale—Updated. *Suicide and Life-Threatening Behavior* 33:261–276.

Beskow J, B Runeson, and U Åsgård. 1990. Psychological autopsies: Methods and ethics. *Suicide and Life-Threatening Behavior* 20:307–323.

Botello T, T Noguchi, L Sathyavagiswaran, LE Weinberger, and BH Gross. 2013. Evolution of the psychological autopsy: Fifty years of experience at the Los Angeles County chief medical examiner-coroner's office. *Journal of Forensic Sciences* 58:924–926.

Centers for Disease Control and Prevention (CDC). 2014. Definitions: Self-directed Violence. http://www.cdc.gov/violenceprevention/suicide/definitions.html, accessed February 4, 2014.

Daubert v. Merrell Dow Pharm., Inc., 509 U.S. 579 (1993).

Davis GG. 2014. National association of medical examiners position paper: Recommendations for the investigation, diagnosis and certification of deaths related to opioid drugs. *Journal of Medical Toxicology* 10:100–106.

Drapeau CW and JL McIntosh. 2014. U.S.A. Suicide: 2012 Official Final Data. http://www.suicidology.org/Portals/14/docs/Resources/FactSheets/2012datapgsv1d.pdf, accessed November 11, 2014.

Drummer OH. 2010. Forensic toxicology. *EXS* 100:579–603.

Drummer OH, B Kennedy, L Bugeja, JE Ibrahim, and J Ozanne-Smith. 2013. Interpretation of postmortem forensic toxicology results for injury prevention research. *Injury Prevention* 19:284–289.

Ebert BW. 1987. Guide to conducting a psychological autopsy. *Professional Psychology: Research and Practice* 18:52–56.

Evans v. Provident Life Ins. Co., 815 P.2d 550 (Kan. 1991).

Fed. R. Evid. 702.

Frye v. United States, 293 F. 1013 (D.C. Cir. 1923).

Gill JR, PT Lin, and L Nelson. 2013. Reliability of postmortem fentanyl concentrations in determining the cause of death. *Journal of Medical Toxicology* 9:34–41.

Han E, E Kim, H Hong, S Jeong, J Kim, S In, H Chung, and S Lee. 2012. Evaluation of postmortem redistribution phenomena for commonly encountered drugs. *Forensic Science International* 219:265–271.

Harris AA. 1990. The psychological autopsy: A retrospective study of suicide. *Stetson Law Review* 20:289–308.

Jackson v. State, 553 So. 2d 719 (Fla. 4th DCA 1989).

Jacobs D and M Klein-Benheim. 1995. The psychological autopsy: A useful tool for determining the proximate causation in suicide cases. *Bulletin of the American Academy of Psychiatry and the Law* 23:165–182.

Jobes DA, JO Casey, AL Berman, and DG Wright. 1991. Empirical criteria for the determination of suicide manner of death. *Journal of Forensic Science* 36:244–256.

Knoll JL. 2009. The psychological autopsy, part II: Toward a standardized protocol. *Journal of Psychiatric Practice* 15:52–59.

Krabseth H, J Mørland, and G Høiseth. 2014. Assistance of ethyl glucuronide and ethyl sulfate in the interpretation of postmortem ethanol findings. *International Journal of Legal Medicine* 128:765–770.

Kugelberg F and AW Jones. 2007. Interpreting results of ethanol analysis in postmortem specimens: A review of the literature. *Forensic Science International* 265:10–29.

Maenhout TM, ML De Buyzere, and JR Delanghe. 2013. Non-oxidative ethanol metabolites as a measure of alcohol intake. *Clinica Chimica Acta* 415:322–329.

Ogloff JP and RK Otto. 1993. Psychological autopsy: Clinical and legal perspectives. *Saint Louis University Law Journal* 37:608–646.

Palmer RB. 2010. Fentanyl in postmortem forensic toxicology. *Clinical Toxicology* 48:771–784.

Pélissier-Alicot A-L, J-M Gaulier, P Champsaur, and P Marquet. 2003. Mechanisms underlying postmortem redistribution of drugs: A review. *Journal of Analytical Toxicology* 27(8):533–544.

Pilgrim JL, D Gerostamoulos, and OH Drummer. 2010. Deaths involving serotonergic drugs. *Forensic Science International* 198:110–117.

Pouliot L and D De Leo. 2006. Critical issues in psychological autopsy studies. *Suicide and Life Threatening Behavior* 36:491–510.

Schulz M, S Iwersen-Bergmann, H Andresen, and A Schmoldt. 2012. Therapeutic and toxic blood concentrations of nearly 1000 drugs and other xenobiotics. *Critical Care* 16:R136.

Schuman G. 1993. Suicide and the life insurance contract: Was the insured sane or insane? That is the question—Or is it? *Tort and Insurance Law Journal* 28:745–777.

Scott C, E Swartz, and K Warburton. 2006. The psychological autopsy: Solving the mysteries of death. *Psychiatric Clinics of North America* 29:805–822.

Shneidman ES. 1994. The psychological autopsy. *American Psychologist* 49:75–76.

Snider JE, S Hane, and AL Berman. 2006. Standardizing the psychological autopsy: Addressing the Daubert standard. *Suicide and Life-Threatening Behavior* 36:511–517.

Werlang BG and NJ Botega. 2003. A semi-structured interview for psychological autopsy in suicide cases. *Revista Brasileira de Psiquiatria* 25:212–219.

Wong PWC, WSC Chin, PSL Beh, FWS Yau, PSF Yip, and K Hawton. 2010. Research participation experiences of informants of suicide and control cases. *Crisis* 31:238–246.

Yoshimasu K, C Kiyohara, and K Miyashita. 2008. Suicidal risk factors and completed suicide: Meta-analyses based on psychological autopsy studies. *Environmental Health and Preventative Medicine* 13:243–256.

PART 2

Legal Regulation of Psychiatric Practice

CHRISTOPHER R. THOMPSON

14

Informed consent and competence

PRAVEEN R. KAMBAM

INTRODUCTION

> Every human being of adult years and sound mind has a right to determine what shall be done with his own body.
>
> Justice Benjamin Cardozo
> *Schloendorff v. Society of New York Hospital*, 1914, 93

Justice Cardozo's well-known quote illustrates the long-established right to self-determination of competent patients. That is, they should be free to make informed treatment decisions for themselves. Although this principle is seemingly straightforward, especially in a society such as the United States where a significant emphasis on individual rights exists, its translation into clinical practice is more complicated.

Attorney Paul Gebhard is credited with the first use of the legal term "informed consent" in a 1957 California medical malpractice case (Pace 1997), though underpinnings of the modern-day concept of informed consent have been cited throughout history (Faden and Beauchamp 1986). The Court in that case, *Salgo v. Leland Stanford Junior University Board of Trustees*, held that a physician cannot withhold any facts from a patient that are necessary to form the basis of an intelligent consent. Since then, the informed consent doctrine has evolved, influenced by new case law, ethical considerations, and changing standards of clinical practice (Meisel and Kabnick 1980).

Informed consent is particularly germane to the profession of psychiatry, a field with somewhat conflicting positions related to informed consent. In the psychoanalytic tradition, on which many psychotherapies are based, extensive disclosure by a psychiatrist is minimized, and patient efforts to obtain information about treatment may be interpreted as resistance. But, psychiatrists historically have utilized discussion-based interventions, rooted in a therapeutic relationship. These interventions often acknowledge patients' autonomy and personal responsibility for treatment decisions. In this regard, psychiatrists are more accustomed to issues related to informed consent and may place greater weight on patient autonomy than physicians in other specialties. As consultants to other medical specialties or services, psychiatrists often are called upon to assess capacity to consent to or refuse treatment, and therefore are relatively comfortable weighing and balancing the competing concerns underlying competency disputes.

LEGAL STANDARDS OF INFORMED CONSENT

In early court cases that focused on bodily integrity, like *Schloendorff*, the failure of a physician to obtain patient consent could result in the physician's committing the intentional tort of battery. However, a "battery standard" seemed inappropriate to apply to physicians not intending to harm patients and did not adequately incorporate the importance of patient knowledge and autonomy. Therefore, courts instead began to utilize a "negligence standard" that respected the importance of patient autonomy more.

PHYSICIAN-BASED STANDARDS

The Salgo case

Martin Salgo was a 55-year-old man with spinal cord injury who experienced lower body paralysis from a translumbar aortography. He claimed that he had not been informed of the risks of the diagnostic procedure beforehand. In *Salgo*, the court ruled that physicians may be liable if they withhold any facts that are "necessary to form the basis of an intelligent consent" to the proposed treatment. The court emphasized that the patient's right to consent required full disclosure of the relevant facts necessary to make an informed decision.

The professional standard or reasonable medical practitioner standard

Three years later in *Natanson v. Kline* (1960), a Kansas court delineated required elements of disclosure by establishing what has come to be known as the "professional standard" or the "reasonable medical practitioner standard." After suffering severely disabling burns from cobalt irradiation following a mastectomy, Irma Natanson claimed to have been inadequately informed of the risks of the treatment. The court held that the required elements of disclosure included the nature of the patient's illness, the nature of the proposed treatment and its likelihood of success, the risks of untoward outcomes, and the availability of alternative modes of treatment. The court limited the amount of information required to be disclosed to what a reasonable medical practitioner would disclose under similar medical circumstances.

The reasonable practitioner standard gives physicians discretion in determining what information to provide to patients and, by defining the legal standard of care in reference to the actions of other physicians, assumes that a consensus exists within the medical field as to what constitutes appropriate disclosure. This standard has been criticized as focusing too much on the physician rather than on the goal of informed consent (i.e., patient autonomy). The reasonable medical practitioner standard still exists in roughly half of the states.

PATIENT-BASED STANDARDS

The reasonable person standard

In 1972, the U.S. Court of Appeals for the District of Columbia, in *Canterbury v. Spence*, heard a case that involved Jerry Canterbury, a 19-year-old man who became partially paralyzed as a result of complications that occurred during thoracic spine surgery. His physicians failed to warn him of any risk of paralysis from the procedure. The Court rejected a physician-based standard and proposed that standards of disclosure be based on what a "reasonable person" would find material to clinical decision making.

The *Canterbury* ruling replaced the physician-based standard with one that focused on patients' autonomy to weigh for themselves the risks and benefits of a proposed treatment. In other words, this "objective patient-based standard" considered what information a typical patient would need to know in order to understand the medical decision at hand. Only risks potentially affecting the decision making of a hypothetical reasonable person would be considered material.

The reasonable person standard assumes that all patients weigh benefits and risks similarly, and does not tailor the informed consent process to the individual needs of the particular patient who actually will undergo the proposed treatment. As a result, this objective standard shields physicians from the whims of individual patients, probably in an effort to balance expansion of the patient's right to reasonable disclosure with concerns about expansion of malpractice liability (President's Commission 1982). The reasonable person standard, which exists in roughly half of the states, can be viewed as a middle position, existing somewhere in between the extreme positions of allowing physicians to disclose whatever they consider material and requiring disclosure of all information relevant to that particular patient's decision, regardless of how idiosyncratic that information may be (Appelbaum and Gutheil 2007, 127).

Subjective patient-based standard

In 1979, the Oklahoma Supreme Court established a "subjective standard" in *Scott v. Bradford*. In this case, Norma Jo Scott underwent a hysterectomy because of uterine fibroids. After the procedure, she began having incontinence because a fistula formed between her bladder and vagina. The patient claimed that she was never informed of this potential complication of the surgery. The Court held that a physician must disclose a "material risk" of a proposed treatment, defining "material risk" as one that would "be likely to affect a patient's decision." This subjective patient-based standard did not offer physicians the protection that the reasonable person standard afforded them. That is, if a material risk was not disclosed, a physician could be held liable if that particular individual patient would have declined the proposed treatment had it been disclosed.

Although the subjective standard gives significant deference to patient autonomy, it is challenging to implement and imposes upon physicians a disclosure requirement that is potentially based on individual patient whims and hindsight bias. Because of these difficulties, the subjective patient-based standard is not utilized in most jurisdictions, with only Oklahoma and Oregon requiring disclosure that resembles a subjective informed consent standard.

INFLUENCES ON THE EVOLUTION OF INFORMED CONSENT

The legal doctrine of informed consent and its application to clinical practice have evolved in the United States in the context of a variety of social, historical, and cultural forces (Katz 1984a; Faden and Beauchamp 1986; Appelbaum et al. 1987). During the twentieth century, a paternalistic model of physician-driven decision making began to shift to a more patient-centered model of care. In a culture that became less deferential to authority figures, the former model of uncontested physician power eroded, with lawsuits, research, and even statements from physicians highlighting this model's excessive cost and harm to patients.

An important precedent in the twentieth century was the development of the Nuremberg Code, which established informed consent requirements for human research (later reflected in consent requirements for treatment).

The changing structure of our health-care delivery systems also had significant influence on the evolution of informed consent. In the 1980s, rising health-care costs led economic stakeholders to question physicians' decision making in the name of cost containment. Time constraints, heightened by increased time and resources that were required to be devoted to paperwork, precertifications, and utilization management, have limited the opportunity for discussion and reflection in doctor–patient encounters.

The rise of medical consumerism—the notion that patients are consumers of services and as such, have the ability to choose what services they receive and from whom to receive such services—has increased demands for information and patient participation in decision making (Rodwin 1994). With the advent of the Internet, a rapid explosion of health and health care-related websites—accessible via portable technology—has drastically altered the manner by which patients can gather information to make medical decisions (Cohen et al. 2010; Parikh 2013).

Last, mirroring broader cultural changes, the American public's level of trust of its physicians has declined and now is among the lowest in industrialized countries (Blendon et al. 2014).

COMPONENTS OF INFORMED CONSENT

To consent to a proposed treatment, the informed consent doctrine requires that a patient's consent be "informed" and voluntarily given (i.e., free of coercion) and that the patient be competent to make the medical decision. Thus, three fundamental components of informed consent exist: information (disclosure), voluntariness, and competence.

Information (disclosure)

Appropriate disclosure of information to the patient is central to the process of informed consent. Elements required to be disclosed were articulated in the *Natanson* case and, in modern clinical practice, typically include potential benefits and indications of a treatment, risks of adverse outcomes, and alternatives, including no treatment (Meisel et al. 1977). Naturally, questions arise regarding what type and amount of information is legally sufficient, the answers to which are reflected in the varying state standards for informed consent discussed above.

Voluntariness

To be voluntary, consent must be free of duress, fraud, or coercion. When extreme, examples of duress and coercion seem relatively clear; however, they often can be more subtle and less straightforward. The psychiatrist must refrain from using coercion but can employ an appropriate level of persuasion in attempting to influence patient behavior positively and advocate for an appropriate treatment. Malcolm (1992, 241) defined coercion as a situation in which the psychiatrist aims "to manipulate the patient by introducing extraneous elements which have the effect of undermining the patient's ability to reason," and persuasion as a situation in which the psychiatrist aims "to utilize the patient's reasoning ability to arrive at a desired result." Applebaum and Gutheil (2007, 127) note that the subtlest forms of coercion exist in all interpersonal relationships and probably should not be considered by the legal system—instead, only illegitimate forms of pressure constitute coercion that may void a patient's consent.

Certain elements of the psychiatrist–patient relationship, patient regression during illness, and impacts of institutionalization all may make coercion more likely. In *Kaimowitz v. Michigan Department of Mental Health* (1973), the Court found that it would be impossible for an involuntarily hospitalized psychiatric patient to make an "uncoerced" decision when the patient's release from the hospital might depend on consenting to experimental psychosurgery. The Court opined that part of the reason for this is that such a patient lives in an inherently coercive institutional environment.

Competence

Patients must be competent to consent. From a legal standpoint, adults are presumed to be competent unless adjudicated otherwise, whereas minors are presumed to be incompetent regardless of their actual capacity. Of note, "incompetence" is a legal determination and refers to a court's adjudication, and "incapacity" refers to a clinician-determined functional inability (Mishkin 1989). Such *de jure* competence (or incompetence) usually refers to global or general competence. Despite the presumption of *de jure* competence, adult patients may in fact (de facto) lack competence to make specific treatment decisions. Here, psychiatrists may be consulted to evaluate a patient's capacity to refuse or accept a specific treatment. Some advocate the use of the term "decisional capacity" to avoid confusion surrounding the term "competence" (and to distinguish from competence to perform an act or series of acts, such as parenting).

STANDARDS FOR COMPETENCE

Roth et al. (1977) summarized the criteria by which competence assessments are made. These criteria are that the patient (a) actually evidences a choice, (b) evidences a choice that the clinician believes will lead to a reasonable outcome, (c) appears to apply rational reasoning to the decision-making process, (d) has the ability to understand the information that has been disclosed, and (e) actually understands that information. Appelbaum and Roth (1982a,b) emphasized appreciation of information, over and above understanding of information, as an important criterion in competence assessment.

Taken together, the above competence assessment criteria encompass four fundamental standards for determining competence in decision making. In order of increasing capacity required, these activities are communication of a choice; understanding relevant information provided; appreciation of the situation and its consequences; and rational decision making (Appelbaum et al. 1987, 84–87). Communication of a choice requires indication of a preferred option with enough stability in this decision for a proposed treatment to be implemented. Understanding the relevant information provided requires a factual understanding of the elements of the informational component of informed consent. Appreciation of the situation and its consequences requires a patient to possess insight into his or her condition and the likely consequences of treatment options, as applied to the patient's specific situation. Finally, rational decision making or reasoning requires a rational process of information manipulation related to the proposed treatment option.

CHOOSING STANDARDS FOR COMPETENCE

Because competence is not a medically determinable state, it represents a certain threshold of functioning at which we, as a society, are willing to allow a person to make a particular decision. Because this threshold balances patient autonomy, third-party interests, and state interests, it reflects societal policy considerations.

Similarly, models for selection of criteria by which a patient's decisional capacity will be judged reflect the principle that, as the consequences of a patient's decision to consent to or refuse treatment become more serious, the criteria for assessing capacity should become more stringent. Roth et al. (1977) formulated a model selecting criteria using a risk–benefit ratio of treatment based on the risk inherent in the treatment decision. Drane (1985) revised this model into a sliding scale. The President's Commission for the Study of Ethical Problems in Medicine and Biomedical and Behavioral Research (1982) recommended linking the criteria chosen to assess capacity and the consequences of the patient's potential decision. In another version of the sliding scale, Grisso and Appelbaum (1998) employ the model of a balance scale, with autonomy at one end and protection at the other. The patient's decision-making capacities add to the autonomy end, while increasing risk in the decision adds to the protection end. Although variably stringent criteria inherent in a sliding-scale model could be abused because the evaluator is the one who sets the standard used to determine incapacity, the model also allows for clinically appropriate balancing between the promotion of health and autonomy.

In such sliding scale models, the standards of competence that are less restrictive or most protective of the patient's autonomy (e.g., evidencing a choice) would be employed in certain very low-risk decisions. Alternatively, in certain very high-risk decisions, the highest form of understanding, appreciation, would be employed (Appelbaum and Roth 1982a; Drane 1985; Grisso and Appelbaum 1998).

STANDARDIZED ASSESSMENT INSTRUMENTS

Although decisional capacity is most often assessed through a clinical interview, several standardized instruments are available to aid in assessing competence to consent to treatment. Such structured instruments provide a framework to ensure that relevant issues are covered, and may be especially helpful in difficult cases or cases likely to be resolved in court.

In a review, Dunn et al. (2006) identified nine instruments that assessed communication of choice, understanding, appreciation, and reasoning. The authors found the *MacArthur Competence Assessment Tool–Treatment* (MacCAT-T) possessed the most empirical support. The MacCAT-T takes approximately 20 minutes to complete and includes a chart review and a semistructured interview (which incorporates information specific to the patient's situation), resulting in scores in each of the four fundamental domains of competence assessment (Grisso et al. 1997).

Although the Mini-Mental State Examination (MMSE) was not developed to identify incompetence, it may have some utility in identifying patients at the low and high ends of the range of capacity. For example, scores less than 19 on the MMSE have been found to correlate with clinical judgments of incapacity (Etchells et al. 1999; Kim and Caine 2002).

THE PROCESS MODEL OF INFORMED CONSENT

Obtaining informed consent is sometimes conceptualized as a specific, time-limited event. For example, the treating physician comes to the bedside and discloses information to a patient, who acknowledges understanding it and then signs a form documenting his or her consent. In this "event model" the signing of a consent form is all too often substituted for a truly informed consent process. Even though physicians and patients may view the primary purpose of a consent form as protection of doctors from lawsuits (Harris et al. 1982), a signed, generic consent form, in and of itself, rarely provides adequate legal protection against malpractice claims of failure to obtain informed consent.

Lidz et al. (1988) proposed that instead of an event model, informed consent should be conceptualized as a "process model." Here, informed consent is viewed as an ongoing process or dialogue between physician and patient, which continues throughout the course of treatment. A physician presents information to a patient in a discussion-like format, tailored to the patient's needs, sophistication, and level of intelligence (Stanley 1983). In the process model, the patient has an opportunity to ask questions and understand the rationale behind the proposed treatment options, and is given adequate time for consideration and consultation with family and friends, if applicable. Additionally, the level of uncertainty related to the mental health diagnosis, treatment, and prognosis is shared by the physician with the patient.

EXCEPTIONS TO INFORMED CONSENT

There are five generally recognized exceptions to informed consent. Incompetence is the most obvious exception. Because patients must be competent in order to give informed consent, they cannot provide it if they lack decisional capacity. If a patient is incompetent to consent, a physician can attempt to obtain substitute consent from a court-appointed guardian for medical decision making or from next of kin. Of note, a patient's decisional capacity may change during the treatment process as a result of treatment

(Appelbaum and Roth 1981), as a result of the natural evolution of the patient's mental disorder (Roth 1985), or as the nature of the treatment decision facing the patient changes (Schwartz and Blank 1986).

The second exception is emergency medical situations. When there is an imminent danger of serious harm to an incapacitated patient or others, treatment (limited to that which is necessary to address the imminently dangerous condition) may be given until the emergency passes. As a matter of law, the patient's consent to treatment is implied during an emergency when consent cannot be obtained. However, what constitutes a medical emergency is somewhat less clear in psychiatry than in general medicine or surgery.

Patient waivers are the third exception to informed consent requirements. The right to informed consent belongs to the patient. As such, a patient may waive the right to information and/or the right to consent.

Therapeutic privilege is the fourth exception. Therapeutic privilege is the doctrine by which the physician may withhold information from a patient when to provide it would be so clearly detrimental to the patient that the disclosure would be antitherapeutic. This exception is especially applicable if the information to be conveyed would cause a high degree of psychological distress and, as a result, impair the patient's decision-making capacity. Because therapeutic privilege can easily be abused, courts have allowed this exception in very limited circumstances. It is clearly not intended to allow physicians to withhold information simply because of their belief that the provision of such information would lead to the patient's refusing treatment. Indeed, in *Canterbury*, the court noted that therapeutic privilege was limited "lest the privilege devour the disclosure rule itself."

The final exception is involuntary treatment without informed consent based on statutory provisions that exist in some states. Here, a patient's refusal of treatment (and autonomy) is overridden by judicial, clinical, or administrative decision because of counterbalancing policy goals.

CLINICAL APPLICATIONS

Consultations to other medical services

Treatment refusal by hospitalized patients on general medical or surgical services commonly results in a psychiatric consultation request for competence assessment. Concerns that a consenting patient may lack capacity also can lead to consultation requests, though this occurs less frequently. When performing the consultation, it is often necessary for the consulting psychiatrist to remind the referring physician that although the consultant renders an opinion regarding the patient's decisional capacity and may opine as to the likely outcome were a competence hearing to be conducted, only the court can declare individuals legally incompetent. Additionally, though the psychiatric consultant may evaluate the patient's decisional capacity and recommend interventions that may enhance that capacity, it remains the patient's treating physician's obligation to obtain the patient's consent for the proposed treatment.

During decisional-capacity assessments, elements of the psychiatric interview sufficient to establish the patient's mental status should be performed. Because competence is influenced by alterations in the patient's mental status and responses to treatment, it is sometimes helpful to evaluate the patient serially (Schwartz and Blank 1986).

The psychiatric consultant should assess the evaluee for overlooked general medical conditions (e.g., delirium) that may impact decisional capacity and, if present, provide recommendations for their further workup and treatment. Because decisional-capacity assessment is task specific, it is helpful to obtain the relevant information about the nature of the proposed treatment from the referring physician. Appelbaum and Roth (1981) have emphasized the importance of clarifying with the referring physician the nature and extent of the information that actually has been presented to the patient, because it would be impossible to assess the patient's understanding without knowing the nature of the disclosure that has been made. At times, ascertaining the meaning of the patient's consent or refusal may facilitate a psychodynamically informed intervention that could enhance the patient's decisional capacity.

Minors

Informed consent requirements for minors are different than for adults. In contrast to adults, minors are presumed incompetent by law. This legal tradition reflects the perspective that an individual under the age of majority (which is, in most cases, 18 years old) cannot adequately appreciate the ramifications of refusing or accepting treatment, and therefore, such decisions are better left to those legally responsible for the minor. Indeed, some of the challenges that treating clinicians in these situations face arise because authority to make medical decisions stems from a third party, not the minor patient himself or herself. Although the responsible third party provides informed permission for treatment, minors should be included in the decision-making process at a developmentally appropriate level, and assent should be sought and obtained when possible.

Potential exceptions to informed consent for minors include (a) emergency situations; (b) emancipated minors (minors no longer receiving parental guidance or financial support); (c) mature minors; (d) specific consent statutes (e.g., treatment for substance abuse, sexually transmitted illnesses, contraception, etc.); and (e) foster care exceptions. Specific-consent statute exceptions aim to encourage desired treatment in specific situations where requiring parental or guardian consent may discourage such treatment.

Geriatric populations

Competence issues surrounding end-of-life decisions, nursing home placement, protracted periods of incapacity generated by dementing illnesses, and testamentary capacity are all issues that arise commonly when treating the elderly and nursing home patients, the number of whom are growing rapidly. Psychiatrists may encounter patients with various degrees of cognitive impairment, including those with a legal guardian. In addition to cognitive limitations, physical impairments (e.g., presbycusis, visual deficits, etc.) may present challenges to patients' comprehension of information. Therefore, the informed consent process should include providing information individually tailored to each patient's level of understanding and requiring confirmation of each patient's comprehension of the delivered information. Christensen et al. (1995) found that older patients who were particularly vulnerable to potential incompetence included those with lower vocabulary levels, lower educational levels, chronic or acute medical illness, and cognitive impairment. The authors suggested that clinicians and researchers be especially diligent in obtaining and assessing informed consent from older individuals with these characteristics.

The Patient Self-Determination Act (PSDA), passed by Congress in 1990, supports the participation of competent elderly patients in medical decision making through the use of advance directives, which consist of instructional directives and proxy directives that designate health-care decision-making surrogates. Many questions have been raised about the validity of advance instructional directives, particularly because of the difficulty in being fully informed of and appreciating the future medical contingencies that may exist at the time the directive is actually employed. Although proxy decision makers are theoretically important for extending patient autonomy, studies have demonstrated that surrogates have poor predictive abilities to exercise substituted judgment, even after advance directive instructions are discussed (Teno et al. 1994; Covinsky et al. 2000). Even though some authors question the primacy of advance directives and advocate "best interest" judgments (Dresser and Whitehouse 1994; Tonelli 1996), case law still supports the exercise of substituted judgment.

Voluntary hospitalization

Whether patients need to be competent to consent to voluntary psychiatric admission is unclear. However, many states require that patients give written informed consent for voluntary admission. In *Zinermon v. Burch* (1990), the U.S. Supreme Court seemed to suggest that in such states, patients may require screening for competence in order to voluntarily admit themselves to a psychiatric hospital. Although the impact of the *Zinermon* case on clinical practice has been limited, concerns about potential impacts led the American Psychiatric Association (APA) to establish the "Task Force on Consent to Voluntary Hospitalization." The recommendations of the task force, which were approved by the APA's Board of Trustees in 1992, included one that suggested that clinicians conduct a brief clinical assessment of the patient (based on the requirement that the patient understand that he or she was being admitted to a psychiatric hospital) and evaluate whether the patient expressed agreement with the admission through verbal, written, or behavioral actions (APA 1993).

A clinical practice that violates the spirit of informed consent is the use of the threat of commitment to coerce a patient into a voluntary admission (Schwartz and Roth 1989). This may occur when a patient is clearly in need of psychiatric hospitalization but does not meet the criteria for involuntary admission. Even though the clinician may be wary of the clinical and legal consequences of discharging the patient from the emergency room (Rachlin and Schwartz 1986), informed consent requires voluntariness (i.e., the absence of coercion) and a disclosure of treatment options; therefore, this practice may void consent for hospitalization.

Research

Psychiatric clinical researchers face the challenge of obtaining informed consent from participants with potentially diminished mental abilities and impaired decision making. Ethical and practical challenges abound in obtaining informed consent for psychiatric research (Pinals and Appelbaum 2000; Gupta and Kharawala 2012; Gupta 2013). One unique challenge facing researchers is the task of minimizing "therapeutic misconception" (i.e., the failure to understand the difference between research participation and treatment). Research involving subjects with impairments in capacity to consent can increase this challenge (National Institutes of Health, Office of Extramural Research 2009).

Researchers must strike a balance between the goals of promoting scientific advancement, minimizing study subjects' risks, and maximizing the subjects' autonomy. The National Bioethics Advisory Commission (1998) has provided some guidance to researchers by issuing a report regarding informed consent, capacity, and surrogate decision making when engaging in research involving persons with mental disorders that may affect decision-making capacity.

"Extraordinary" treatments

Some state courts and legislatures have deemed several psychiatric treatments "extraordinary." As such, these treatments require special review or procedures beyond that of a treating physician unilaterally determining whether a patient's consent is adequate. These treatments variously have included sterilization, psychosurgery, electroconvulsive therapy (ECT), and treatment with antipsychotic medication. For example, in *In re Branning* (1996), an Illinois appellate court ruled that guardians cannot consent to ECT for their wards without the ward's specifically being found incompetent to make such a treatment decision. In *Matter of A.M.P.* (1999), another Illinois appellate decision, the Court held that parents of a 16-year-old could not consent to ECT for their child (who was noncommunicative, psychotic, and failing other treatments) without judicial review.

Psychotherapy

Statutes and case law generally do not provide clear guidance on whether or not informed consent for psychotherapy is legally required. However, the ethical guidelines of the American Psychological Association (2010, 13) explicitly require it, and those of the American Psychiatric Association (2013) implicitly require it.

There may be several reasons that the typical elements of the informed consent doctrine are not consistently required of psychotherapy. A partial explanation may involve concerns that informed consent may undermine transference and be duplicative of the extensive disclosure inherent in the psychoanalytically based approaches of many psychotherapies (Robitscher 1978). Additionally, clinicians may be uncomfortable disclosing the uncertainty of predicting the benefits of, risks of, and prognosis in psychotherapy (Katz 1984b). Another explanation is that psychotherapy is not viewed as a procedure or intervention with significant risks. Finally, malpractice claims involving psychotherapy historically have had limited success, though recently the size of monetary awards in "recovered memory" litigation has grown (Beahrs and Gutheil 2001), and failure to inform about medication treatment options (as opposed to psychotherapy) has been grounds for lawsuits in the past (Malcolm 1986).

Despite these explanations, it seems reasonable for clinicians to engage in some level of discussion with psychotherapy patients regarding the nature and extent of treatment, alternatives to treatment, and, when relevant, potential limitations to confidentiality. After all, psychotherapeutic interventions are recommended to patients as treatment options, with particular indications, benefits, and alternatives, and they come with significant personal costs (emotional and financial) and a variety of potential adverse consequences (negative transference reactions, regression, depression, etc.). Therefore, the spirit of the informed consent doctrine, which promotes patient autonomy, would seem to be applicable here.

CONCLUSION

The doctrines of informed consent and competence arise from the ethical and legal principles of respect for patient autonomy balanced with beneficence. Clinically, the doctrines foster collaboration and a therapeutic alliance between psychiatrist and patient. Though questions remain about specific definitions and applications of some of the core principles of the informed consent doctrine, it behooves psychiatrists to become familiar with its theoretical underpinnings, which inform society's goals for maintaining and refining an appropriate system of informed consent.

KEY SUMMARY POINTS

- The three fundamental components of informed consent are information (disclosure), voluntariness, and competence.
- The professional standard or reasonable medical practitioner standard of informed consent limits the amount of information a physician is required to disclose to a patient to that which a reasonable medical practitioner would disclose under similar medical circumstances.
- The reasonable person standard of informed consent requires that a physician disclose information that a typical patient would need to know or consider material to the medical decision at hand.
- The four fundamental standards for determining competence in decision making, in order of increasing capacity required, are (1) communication of a choice, (2) understanding relevant information provided, (3) appreciation of the situation and its consequences, and (4) rational decision making.
- Incompetence is a legal determination and refers to a court's adjudication; incapacity refers to a clinician-determined functional inability.
- Exceptions to the requirement of informed consent are (1) incompetence; (2) emergency medical situations; (3) patient waivers; (4) therapeutic privilege; and (5) involuntary treatment based on statutory, state-specific provisions.

ACKNOWLEDGMENT

Acknowledgment is given to Harold I. Schwartz and David M. Mack. This chapter is loosely based on their previous chapter.

REFERENCES

American Psychiatric Association (APA). 1993. *Consent to Voluntary Hospitalization*. Washington, DC: APA.

American Psychiatric Association (APA). 2013. *The Principles of Medical Ethics with Annotations Especially Applicable to Psychiatry*. Washington, DC: APA.

American Psychological Association (APA). 2010. *Ethical Principles of Psychologists and Code of Conduct with 2010 Amendments*. Washington, DC: APA.

Appelbaum PS and TG Gutheil. 2007. *Clinical Handbook of Psychiatry and the Law*. Philadelphia: Lippincott Williams and Wilkins.

Appelbaum PS, CW Lidz, and A Meisel. 1987. *Informed Consent: Legal Theory and Clinical Practice*. New York: Oxford University Press.

Appelbaum PS and LH Roth. 1981. Clinical issues in the assessment of competency. *American Journal of Psychiatry* 138:1462–1467.

Appelbaum PS and LH Roth. 1982a. Treatment refusals in the medical hospitals. In *Report of the President's Commission for the Study of Ethical Problems in Medicine and Biomedical and Behavioral Research*. Volume Two, Appendix D. Washington, DC: US Government Printing Office, 411–477.

Appelbaum PS and LH Roth. 1982b. Competency to consent to research: A psychiatric overview. *Archives of General Psychiatry* 39:951–958.

Beahrs JO and TG Gutheil. 2001. Informed consent in psychotherapy. *American Journal of Psychiatry* 158:4–10.

Blendon RJ, JM Benson, and JO Hero. 2014. Public trust in physicians—U.S. medicine in international perspective. *New England Journal of Medicine* 371:1570–1572.

Canterbury v. Spence, 464 F2d 772, 787 (1972).

Christensen K, A Haroun, LJ Schneiderman, and DV Jeste. 1995. Decision-making capacity for informed consent in the older population. *Bulletin of the American Academy of Psychiatry and the Law* 23(3):353–365.

Cohen SB, KD Grote, WE Pietraszek, and F Laflamme. 2010. Increasing consumerism in healthcare through intelligent information technology. *American Journal of Managed Care* 16(12):SP37–SP43.

Covinsky KE, JD Fuller, K Yaffe et al. 2000. Communication and decision-making in seriously ill patients: Findings of the SUPPORT project. *Journal of the American Geriatric Society* 48:S187–S193.

Drane JF. 1985. The many faces of competency. *Hastings Center Report* 15:17–21.

Dresser R and PJ Whitehouse. 1994. The incompetent patient on the slippery slope. *Hastings Center Report* 4:6–12.

Dunn LB, MA Nowrangi, BW Palmer et al. 2006. Assessing decisional capacity for clinical research or treatment: A review of instruments. *American Journal of Psychiatry* 163:1323–1334.

Etchells E, P Darzins, M Silberfeld et al. 1999. Assessment of patient capacity to consent to treatment. *Journal of General Internal Medicine* 14:27–34.

Faden RR and TL Beauchamp. 1986. *A History and Theory of Informed Consent*. New York: Oxford University Press.

Grisso T and PS Appelbaum. 1998. *Assessing Competence to Consent to Treatment*. New York: Oxford University Press.

Grisso T, PS Appelbaum, and C Hill-Fotouhi. 1997. The MacCAT-T: A clinical tool to assess patients' capacities to make treatment decisions. *Psychiatric Services* 48:1415–1419.

Gupta UC. 2013. Informed consent in clinical research: Revisiting few concepts and areas. *Perspectives in Clinical Research* 4(1):26–32.

Gupta UC and S Kharawala. 2012. Informed consent in psychiatry clinical research: A conceptual review of issues, challenges, and recommendations. *Perspectives in Clinical Research* 3(1):8–15.

Harris L, JM Boyle, and PJ Bromsetin. 1982. Views of informed consent and decision making: Parallel surveys of physicians and the public. In *President's Commission for the Study of Ethical Problems in Medicine and Biomedical and Behavioral Research: Making Health Care Decisions: The Ethical and Legal Implications of Informed Consent in the Patient–Practitioner Relationship, Volume Two: Appendices, Empirical Studies of Informed Consent*. Washington, DC: Superintendent of Documents.

In re Branning (State v. Branning), 285 Ill. App. 3d 405 (1996).

Kaimowitz v. Michigan Department of Mental Health for the State of Michigan, Cir. Ct. of Wayne County, Michigan, civil action no. 73-19434-AW (1973).

Katz J. 1984a. *The Silent World of Doctor and Patient*. New York: Free Press.

Katz J. 1984b. Why doctors don't disclose uncertainty. *Hastings Center Report* 14:35–44.

Kim SYH and ED Caine. 2002. Utility and limits of the Mini Mental State Examination in evaluating consent capacity in Alzheimer's disease. *Psychiatric Services* 53:1322–1324.

Lidz CW, PS Appelbaum, and A Meisel. 1988. Two models of implementing informed consent. *Archives of Internal Medicine* 148:1385–1389.

Malcolm JG. 1986. Treatment choices and informed consent in psychotherapy: Implications of the *Osheroff* case for the profession. *Journal of Psychiatry and the Law* 14:9–106.

Malcolm JG. 1992. Informed consent in the practice of psychiatry. In *American Psychiatric Press Review of Clinical Psychiatry and the Law*, 3 vols., edited by RI Simon, Washington, DC: American Psychiatric Press, 223–281.

Matter of A.M.P. 303 Ill. App. 3d 907 (1999).

Meisel A and L Kabnick. 1980. Informed consent to medical treatment: An analysis of recent legislation. *University of Pittsburgh Law Review* 41:407–564.

Meisel A, LH Roth, and CW Lidz. 1977. Toward a model of the legal doctrine of informed consent. *American Journal of Psychiatry* 134:285–289.

Mishkin B. 1989. Determining the capacity for making health care decisions. In *Issues in Geriatric Psychiatry (Advances in Psychosomatic Medicine)*, 19 vols., edited by N Billig and PV Rabins, Basel, Switzerland: S Karger, 151–166.

Natanson v. Kline, 300 P.2d 1093, 1104, 1106 (1960).

National Bioethics Advisory Commission. 1998. *Research Involving Persons with Mental Disorders That May Affect Decision Making Capacity, Vol. I, Report and Recommendations of the National Bioethics Advisory Commission*. Rockville, MD: National Bioethics Advisory Commission.

National Institutes of Health, Office of Extramural Research. 2009. *Research Involving Individuals with Questionable Capacity to Consent: Points to Consider.* http://grants.nih.gov/grants/policy/questionablecapacity.htm, accessed October 8, 2014.

Pace E. 1997. P. G. Gebhard, 69, Developer of the Term "Informed Consent." *New York Times.* http://www.nytimes.com/1997/08/26/us/p-g-gebhard-69-developer-of-the-term-informed-consent.html, accessed October 8, 2014.

Parikh RB. 2013. The empowered patient: Consumerism in American medicine. *Virtual Mentor, American Medical Association Journal of Ethics* 15(11):923–925.

Patient Self-Determination Act. 1990. Public Law 101-158; 42 U.S.C. Sections 1395cc, 1396.

Pinals DA and PS Appelbaum. 2000. The history and current status of competency and informed consent in psychiatric research. *Israel Journal of Psychiatry and Related Sciences* 37:82–94.

President's Commission for the Study of Ethical Problems in Medicine and Biomedical and Behavioral Research. 1982. *Making Health Care Decisions: The Ethical and Legal Implications of Informed Consent in the Patient–Practitioner Relationship. Volume One: Report.* Washington, DC: Superintendent of Documents.

Rachlin S and HI Schwartz. 1986. Unforeseeable liability for patients' violent acts. *Hospital and Community Psychiatry* 37:725–731.

Robitscher J. 1978. Informed consent for psychoanalysis. *Journal of Psychiatry and Law* 6:363–370.

Rodwin MA. 1994. Patient accountability and the quality of care: Lessons from medical consumerism and the patients' rights, women's health and disability rights movements. *American Journal of Law and Medicine* 20:147–167.

Roth LH. 1985. Informed consent and its applicability for psychiatry. In *Psychiatry*, Vol 3, edited by R Michels, J Cavenar, and HKH Brodie et al. Philadelphia: J.B. Lippincott, 1–17.

Roth LK, A Meisel, and CW Lidz. 1977. Tests of competency to consent to treatment. *American Journal of Psychiatry* 134:279–284.

Salgo v. Leland Stanford Junior University Board of Trustees, 154 Cal. App. 2d 560 (1957).

Schloendorff v. Society of New York Hospital, 211 N.Y. 125, 105 N.E. 92 (1914).

Schwartz HI and K Blank. 1986. Shifting competency during hospitalization: A model for informed consent decisions. *Hospital and Community Psychiatry* 37:1256–1260.

Schwartz HI and LH Roth. 1989. Informed consent and competency in psychiatric practice. In *Review of Psychiatry*, 8 vols., edited by A Tasman, RE Hales, and AJ Frances, Washington, DC: American Psychiatric Press, 409–431.

Scott v. Bradford, 606 P.2d 554 (1979).

Stanley B. 1983. Senile dementia and informed consent. *Behavioral Sciences and the Law* 1:57–71.

Teno JM, J Lynn, RS Phillips et al. 1994. Do formal advance directives affect resuscitation decisions and the use of resources for seriously ill patients? *Journal of Clinical Ethics* 5:23–30.

Tonelli MR. 1996. Pulling the plug on living wills: A critical analysis of advance directives. *Chest* 110:816–822.

Zinermon v. Burch, 494 U.S. 113, 110 S. Ct. 975, 108 L. Ed. 2d 100 (1990).

15

Hospitalization: Voluntary and involuntary

JOSEPH R. SIMPSON AND VINCENZO CARANNANTE

INTRODUCTION

Psychiatry is a rarity among the medical specialties, in that therapeutic interventions such as hospitalization and the administration of medications can, under certain circumstances, be provided to patients against their will and over their objection. (The ability of physicians in the field of public health to confine and treat patients with certain communicable diseases such as tuberculosis is perhaps the only analogue in another medical specialty.) Finding the balance between honoring the rights of the individual citizen to liberty and freedom, and protecting the citizen's own safety and the safety of others, is the challenge faced by any system that allows for involuntary psychiatric confinement and treatment. To understand the issues at stake, it is useful to begin by examining the fundamental concepts by which society, through its government, claims the authority to place a person in a psychiatric hospital.

THE LEGAL FOUNDATIONS OF CIVIL COMMITMENTS

In the United States, forcing someone to enter a facility to undergo treatment is considered a relatively significant curtailment of his or her rights. Each state has its own laws with respect to civil commitment. However, in all cases, a state's right to enact civil commitment laws is derived from two basic legal doctrines: *parens patriae* and police power. *Parens patriae* is the legal doctrine whereby the state acts as the metaphorical parent of its constituents and has the duty and right to act on behalf of or in the best interests of those who do not have the capacity to take actions in their own best interests as a result of age, illness, or other infirmity. A state's "police power" derives from the government's interest to protect its citizens from others and to maintain order in the interest of public safety. Traditional commitment statutes generally attempt to capture the essence of these two powers and are used for those with mental illness who are a danger to themselves, others, or both (Feuerstein et al. 2005).

The history of psychiatric hospitalization in America dates back to the 1750s. Pennsylvania Hospital was opened in Philadelphia in 1752 and featured a dedicated unit for mentally ill patients. In 1773, the Eastern State Hospital in Williamsburg, Virginia, was founded for housing people who were then commonly referred to as "lunatics." New York Hospital, founded in 1791, opened a separate building designated "Lunatic Asylum" in 1808 (Shorter 1997). Several other dedicated hospitals or asylums were started along the Eastern Seaboard in the early nineteenth century, including the Friends Asylum in Frankford, Pennsylvania; the Bloomingdale Asylum in New York; the McLean Asylum in Charlestown, Massachusetts; and the Hartford Retreat (later, The Institute of Living), in Hartford, Connecticut. By 1861, there were 48 asylums in the United States, with a total census of 8500 patients (Katz 1989).

This relatively small number of patients reflects the fact that in the eighteenth and nineteenth centuries, most patients with mental illness did not find their way to asylums. Rather, they were cared for by family members at home or were placed in almshouses or jails. In the 1840s and 1850s, the reformer Dorothea Dix exposed the deplorable conditions endured by many such patients. Her work culminated in the founding of numerous new mental hospitals; 20 states improved their capability of caring for the mentally ill by either building or enlarging their mental hospitals (Brakel et al. 1985).

These early institutions were influenced by European innovations in the treatment of mental illness (Shorter 1997). Although humanitarian motives catalyzed the establishment of the asylums, and "moral [French for 'mental'] treatment" was important to psychiatrists of the day, commitment procedures reflected the paternalistic state of medicine at that time. Patients were admitted to and detained at the hospital on the basis of a doctor's judgment regarding their need for treatment. A patient's only means of challenging his or her confinement was the rarely used "writ of habeas corpus" (Gutheil and Appelbaum 2000). There were few laws or regulations governing admission to a mental hospital. Brakel et al. (1985) cite a New York law enacted in

1788 that authorized two or more judges to direct constables to detain and confine persons, who "by lunacy or otherwise, are furiously mad or are so far disordered in their senses that they may be dangerous to be permitted to go abroad." During much of the nineteenth century, commitment "was predicated only on a mentally ill person requiring care.... Admission was made simple, essentially left in the hands of family members and physicians whenever possible. Hospitalizations were involuntary and treatment was coerced, since it was presumed that all mentally ill patients had compromised reason to the extent that they were unable to request (or refuse) care on their own behalf" (Anfang and Appelbaum 2006, 210).

However, by the middle of the nineteenth century, court decisions and legislative changes established some minimal safeguards of the rights of patients and potential patients. In the 1845 case entitled *Matter of Josiah Oakes*, Oakes was confined at Mclean Asylum in Massachusetts. He invoked the common-law right of habeas corpus in order to challenge his detention. The Massachusetts Supreme Court found that the U.S. Constitution prohibited arbitrary detention without adequate justification. The court stated that "the restraint can continue as long as the necessity [for the patient's and others' safety] continues. This is the limitation and the proper limitation." This case represented an early delineation of the proper criteria for involuntary hospitalization and was one of the first to consider commitment for treatment, as opposed to merely as a means of protecting society from a potentially violent patient (Brakel et al. 1985).

In 1860, Mrs. E. P. W. Packard was confined to the Illinois State Hospital on the petition of her husband. An Illinois statute at the time stated, "[m]arried women and infants, who, in the judgment of the medical superintendent are evidently insane and distracted, may be received and detained at the request of the husband...without the evidence of insanity and distraction required in other cases." After her release 3 years later, her efforts were instrumental in the reform of commitment legislation in her state, which passed a law mandating a jury trial in civil commitments (Brakel et al. 1985).

Through the reforms that began in the mid-nineteenth century, the American legal system recognized for the first time the liberty interests of patients in mental hospitals. Over time, concerns about potential abuses of commitment by unscrupulous relatives and/or physicians led to the adoption of procedural safeguards such as judicial hearings and jury trials for commitment, which were imported from the criminal justice system (Anfang and Appelbaum 2006). However, the basis for hospitalization continued to flow from the doctrine of *parens patriae* (i.e., the patient's need for treatment).

Over the first half of the twentieth century, the censuses of state hospitals swelled, reaching a nationwide total of approximately 500,000 patients in the 1950s (Fisher et al. 2001). Beginning in the 1960s, a number of factors converged, setting in motion the process that became known as "deinstitutionalization," which culminated in the virtual emptying of the nation's state hospitals. One of the many factors in this decades-long transformation was a tightening of commitment standards. States responded to the concerns voiced by advocates for civil liberties by revamping their laws, focusing on stricter dangerousness criteria which offered patients even greater procedural protections. The evolution from *parens patriae* to "police power" as the basis for involuntary commitment can be seen in a series of landmark cases and statutes from the 1960s and 1970s.

With this backdrop, states began to shift away from the traditional "need for treatment" standard to a narrower set of circumstances defined by "dangerousness" to self or others (Testa and West 2010). Although self-danger as a basis for commitment was justified by an appeal to *parens patriae* principles, it was limited to more urgent, life-threatening situations. Commitment of those dangerous to others was seen as a pure exercise of the state's police powers. Dangerousness as the sole ground for civil commitment was first adopted by the District of Columbia in 1964 and then by California, the most populous state and frequently a bellwether for the rest of the nation. California's 1969 Lanterman–Petris–Short Act—which only permitted civil commitment of those who were imminently dangerous to themselves or to others, or who were so "gravely disabled" as to be unable to meet their minimal needs for survival (a variant of danger to self)—quickly became a model adopted by many other states. "Need for treatment" was no longer a substantive factor for civil commitment. Court decisions embraced the "dangerousness model" and need for tighter procedural standards, led by a federal district court decision in *Lessard v. Schmidt* (1972). That court criticized earlier vague "need for treatment" statutes, and subsequent decisions in other states endorsed a constitutional rationale for the belief that the state can intervene only when the lives of the patient or others are in danger (Anfang and Appelbaum 2006). One by one, nearly every state revised its commitment laws and followed suit. Eventually, the prevailing standard for civil commitment in the United States required the presence of dangerousness as a result of mental disease (Testa and West 2010).

OTHER LANDMARK CASES AND LEGISLATIVE ENACTMENTS THAT HAVE SHAPED THE CIVIL COMMITMENT LANDSCAPE

Lake v. Cameron

In 1966, the U.S. Court of Appeals for the District of Columbia decided an important legal case that emphasized dangerousness as the key criteria for involuntary hospitalizations. (See *Lake v. Cameron*, 364 F.2d 657, 1966.) Catherine Lake, a woman with mental illness, had been hospitalized against her will at St. Elizabeth's psychiatric hospital for many years, despite not showing any evidence of dangerousness to herself or anyone else. Lake wished to be set free and petitioned the Court of Appeals for her release

(Testa and West 2010; *Lake v. Cameron*, 364 F.2d 657, 1966). The Court ruled that all patients who were not dangerous should not be confined if a less restrictive alternative were available. "To this day, because of this ruling, psychiatrists who complete emergency evaluations are required by law to recommend the least restrictive level of treatment that will meet the needs of non-dangerous psychiatric patients" (Testa and West 2010).

Jackson v. Indiana

Although *Jackson v. Indiana* concerned a criminal matter rather than civil commitment, it is still considered a landmark case in the civil commitment arena. In this case, a trial court committed a deaf-mute defendant to a mental hospital after he was charged with two criminal offenses and was found incompetent to stand trial. (See *Jackson v. Indiana*, 406 U.S. 715, 1972.) The case was eventually appealed to the U.S. Supreme Court, who vacated Jackson's commitment on the grounds that the defendant was denied equal protection and due process, as guaranteed by the Fourteenth Amendment. The Court pointed out:

> Jackson was not afforded any formal commitment proceedings addressed to his ability to function in society, or to society's interest in his restraint, or to the State's ability to aid him in attaining competency through custodial care or compulsory treatment, the ostensible purpose of the commitment. At the least, due process requires that the nature and duration of commitment bear some reasonable relation to the purpose for which the individual is committed. We hold, consequently, that a person charged by a State with a criminal offense who is committed solely on account of his incapacity to proceed to trial cannot be held more than the reasonable period of time necessary to determine whether there is a substantial probability that he will attain that capacity in the foreseeable future. (*Jackson v. Indiana*, 406 U.S. 715, 738–739, 1972)

As a result of this case, many states enacted laws that limit the amount of time a person may be committed on the basis of incompetence to stand trial.

O'Connor v. Donaldson

In *O'Connor v. Donaldson*, the U.S. Supreme Court held that a "State cannot constitutionally confine without more a nondangerous individual who is capable of surviving safely in freedom by himself or with the help of willing and responsible family members or friends" (*O'Connor v. Donaldson*, 422 U.S. 563, 576, 1975). Courts have interpreted this case in two different manners. Namely, either that a finding of dangerousness is constitutionally required to justify involuntary hospitalization (Stromberg, 1982), or that the nondangerous mentally ill cannot constitutionally be confined without the provision of meaningful treatment. The Supreme Court has not provided further clarification of this specific issue and, thus, this has been left to the individual states to resolve.

Addington v. Texas

In *Addington v. Texas*, the U.S. Supreme Court shed light on, and set forth the acceptable evidentiary standards for, commitment proceedings. (See *Addington v. Texas*, 441 U.S. 418, 1979.) After considering the "preponderance of the evidence" (i.e., more likely than not), "proof beyond a reasonable doubt," and "clear and convincing" (an intermediate standard between preponderance and the higher "beyond a reasonable doubt" standard used in criminal cases) evidentiary standards, the Court ruled that the "clear and convincing" standard should be applied to commitment proceedings. The Supreme Court held that applying the "clear and convincing" standard provided an acceptable balance between providing individuals with adequate due process protections and not making it unduly burdensome to have an individual committed.

Parham v. J.R.

In *Parham v. J. R.*, the Supreme Court balanced the protection of the rights of minors undergoing commitment with an endorsement of medical decision making. (See *Parham v. J.R.*, 442 U.S. 584 1979.) In this case, the U.S. Supreme Court held that a postadmission hearing was not necessary to protect a minor's interests. Instead, the justices found that a neutral fact finder, such as a physician, could determine whether or not the commitment was appropriate, after a complete review of the reasons for the minor's hospitalization. The Court preferred this method to full-blown legal proceedings and believed that a traditional medical evaluation was preferable to a more formal adversarial hearing. In fact, the Court found that turning to the judicial system rather than a "trained specialist" on such matters "can turn rational decision making into an unmanageable enterprise." (See *Parham v. J.R.*, 442 U.S. 584, 608, 1979.)

The *Olmstead* case and the Americans with Disabilities Act

The Americans with Disabilities Act (ADA) was signed into law on July 26, 1990, by President George H.W. Bush. The ADA requires that "no qualified individual with a disability shall, by reason of such disability, be excluded from participation in or be denied the benefits of the services, programs, or activities of a public entity, or be subjected to discrimination by any such entity" (42 U.S.C. §12132). Courts and federal agencies that interpret and implement the ADA have repeatedly stated that the ADA requires that services for persons with disabilities be provided "in the most integrated setting" and that parties "make reasonable modifications in policies, practices, or procedures when the modifications are necessary to avoid discrimination on the basis of disability, unless the public entity can demonstrate that making the modifications would fundamentally alter the nature of the service, program, or activity" (28 C.F.R. §35.130(b)).

The seminal case with respect to the ADA and balancing providing treatment to individuals in the "most integrated setting" with the limitations on a state's resources is *Olmstead v. L.C. by Zimring, 527 U.S. 581* (1999). In *Olmstead,* the U.S. Supreme Court was presented with the case of two women, both of whom had mental illness and developmental disabilities, who were admitted voluntarily to the psychiatric unit in a state-operated hospital. Following their treatment and after their providers concluded that they were ready to be discharged to community-based programs, they continued to be confined to the hospital for several years because of the unavailability of community-based treatment resources. As a result, the two women filed suit under the ADA, so that they could be released from the hospital. In summary, the Court held that public entities, such as state hospitals, must provide community-based services to persons with disabilities when (1) such services are appropriate; (2) the affected persons do not oppose community-based treatment; and (3) community-based services can be reasonably accommodated, taking into account the resources available to the public entity and the needs of others who are receiving disability services from the entity. It is important to note, however, that the Court's ruling came in four separate opinions and, thus, its holding, interpretation, and the implementation thereof are not entirely clear. For example, five of the Supreme Court justices opined that holding a patient for an unreasonable or unnecessary length of time after the person is ready for discharge constitutes discrimination under the ADA. However, one of the justices argued that a program with a waiting list that moves at "a reasonable pace" would be sufficient, and another justice stated that "a state may not be forced to create a community-treatment program where none exists." As Appelbaum (1999) notes, the impact of *Olmstead* remains unclear. Accordingly, while the Court held that individuals have the right to obtain appropriate treatment in the community, the Court seemed reluctant to force states to develop community-based treatment programs.

Zinermon v. Burch

In this case, Darrell Burch, while allegedly psychotic and disoriented, signed forms requesting admission to, and treatment at, a Florida state mental hospital, in apparent compliance with state statutory requirements for "voluntary" admission to such facilities. After his release, he filed suit against his health-care providers for violating his Fourteenth Amendment (i.e., due process) rights. Specifically, he claimed that they violated state law by admitting him as a voluntary patient when they knew or should have known that he was incompetent to give informed consent to his admission and that their failure to initiate Florida's involuntary placement procedure denied him constitutionally guaranteed procedural safeguards. (See *Zinermon v. Burch*, 494 U.S. 113, 1990.) The Court held that the hospital should have allowed the option of voluntary admission only to patients who were competent to consent to such an admission. Though the Court's decision stressed the importance of "voluntariness" for voluntary admissions and held that appropriate procedural safeguards must be in place to protect a patient's liberty interest, it did not specifically set forth what those procedural safeguards need to be.

RECENT DEVELOPMENTS

The proverbial pendulum has swung back somewhat from the strict dangerousness standards of 30 to 40 years ago. Families of patients with mental illness objected to commitment criteria that made it exceedingly difficult for their loved ones to receive treatment (Dunham 1985). For example, the growth of the homeless population in recent decades is considered by many to have been an unintended consequence of the high threshold for involuntary admission in most states' commitment laws. In Washington State, a highly publicized double murder by a man who had been denied voluntary admission to a state hospital just hours earlier led to calls to change the state's commitment scheme (Durham and LaFond 1985). Washington had passed one of the most narrow commitment statutes in the country in 1973. In 1979 it was significantly relaxed to allow for the involuntary hospitalization of anyone who exhibited a severe deterioration in his or her condition (Durham and LaFond, 1985, 1988). Similar revisions followed in other states. A number of states have expanded their dangerousness criteria by eliminating the requirement for evidence of a specific overt act indicating dangerousness or the requirement that the patient poses a risk of imminent danger. In many states, revised commitment criteria now allow for the involuntary hospitalization of patients who would suffer significant deterioration in their condition if not imminently treated.

The controversies surrounding involuntary psychiatric treatment have by no means subsided. In the past 15 years, a number of mass shootings, many of them committed by people with known or suspected mental disorders, have sparked re-examination of our nation's mental health system, including the laws governing commitment. Many of these high-profile tragedies took place at schools or colleges or involved students as victims. Examples include Columbine High School in Littleton, Colorado, in 1999; Virginia Polytechnic Institute and State University (Virginia Tech) in 2007; Sandy Hook Elementary School in Newtown, Connecticut, in 2012; and a neighborhood in Santa Barbara, California, frequented by college students (Isla Vista) in 2014. Others occurred at public gathering places, including a political event in Tucson, Arizona, in

2011 and a movie premiere in Aurora, Colorado, in 2012. Some of the perpetrators had been evaluated previously by psychiatrists. In the incident at Virginia Tech, the gunman had been psychiatrically hospitalized on an emergency basis and had subsequently been ordered by the court to attend outpatient treatment.

Although mass killings by people with mental illness are extremely rare and account for a miniscule percentage of the nation's homicides, their devastating collective impact, and the possibility of preventing them through early detection and treatment, understandably have led to suggestions that current involuntary commitment standards are too restrictive, causing some people with mental illness to "fall through the cracks" (Neary 2014).

PSYCHIATRIC HOSPITALIZATION: LAWS, PROCESSES, AND PROCEDURES

The specific criteria, procedures, and legal standards pertaining to psychiatric hospitalization are determined by the laws of the state or equivalent jurisdiction (e.g., District of Columbia, Puerto Rico) where the hospital is located. However, the outlines of the system governing hospitalization are broadly similar in most jurisdictions.

Involuntary hospitalization

In most states there are two mechanisms for hospitalizing a patient who is not willing to enter on a voluntary basis. Short-term hospitalization can be accomplished via an emergency certification, typically completed by a physician or other qualified professional, such as a clinical psychologist or psychiatric nurse. Emergency certification is not reviewed by any court or other entity prior to the patient's admission. Emergency detentions are always of limited duration, generally on the order of 2 to 5 days, although the specific length varies by jurisdiction, as does the question of whether weekends or holidays count toward the detention time. At the conclusion of the time allotted for emergency certification, one of three things happens: the patient is released; he or she signs in as a voluntary patient; or the hospital seeks a formal commitment.

A formal commitment can be sought on an outpatient, a voluntary inpatient, or a patient who has been detained via emergency certification. The patient is entitled to due process protections, including the right to representation, a hearing, and an appeal. Again, the specific legal standards and procedures followed vary somewhat by jurisdiction, as does the maximum duration of the commitment. Typical initial formal commitments last on the order of 14 days. For more severely mentally ill patients, longer-term commitment (e.g., placement on guardianship or conservatorship for up to a year) can be sought either at the outset or the conclusion of one or more shorter commitments. In some jurisdictions, the initial hearing on commitment is performed at the hospital, with a neutral referee (appointed by the county) and a patient advocate (also employed by the county) assigned to argue the patient's case for release. Initial hearings in some jurisdictions, as well as appeals of initial determinations (and when longer periods of commitment are sought) are conducted before a judge, with many or all of the trappings of a civil proceeding present. These may include attorneys for both parties, a transcript generated by a court reporter, and proceedings subject to the rules of evidence.

Voluntary hospitalization

In almost every state, a voluntary psychiatric admission is treated differently than a standard medical admission. Most state statutes allow for the hospital to continue to detain a voluntary patient for a certain amount of time after they request to be discharged (Garakani et al. 2014). Unlike the case for patients in medical units, where obtaining a discharge against medical advice (AMA) is typically a relatively simple matter of signing a waiver, gathering one's belongings, and walking out, a voluntary psychiatric patient must notify hospital staff of their request for discharge. In over 30 states, this must be done in writing. The hospital treatment team is then allowed to continue the hospitalization for a period ranging from 4 hours up to 5 days, depending on the state; in some jurisdictions, only business or court days are counted. In some states, the continuation of the admission is contingent on the hospital's application for an involuntary commitment. In others, this is not required. Garakani et al. (2014) have pointed out the need to provide a truly informed consent process for patients at the time of their admission, particularly given the potential for delay in discharge after the patient's request, as well as the potential for conversion of the stay to involuntary status.

SUMMARY KEY POINTS

- Psychiatry is rare among the medical specialties in its ability to hospitalize patients and treat them against their will.
- The legal regulation of hospital psychiatry has evolved from a highly paternalistic, physician-centered model to a system that incorporates a variety of due process protections in an effort to balance the liberty interests of the patient with the safety interest of the patient and the community.
- Procedures for involuntary hospitalization and medication treatment are governed by statute and case law in all jurisdictions.
- In nearly all states, procedures for voluntary admission to and discharge from a psychiatric hospital are distinct from those that apply to admission to and discharge from a medical hospital.

REFERENCES

Addington v. Texas, 441 U.S. 418 (1979).

Anfang SA and P Appelbaum. 2006. Civil commitment—The American experience. *Israel Journal of Psychiatry and Related Sciences* 43:209–218.

Appelbaum PS. 1999. Law and psychiatry: Least restrictive alternative revisited: Olmstead's uncertain mandate for community-based care. *Psychiatric Services* 50:1271–1280.

Brakel SJ, J Parry, and BA Weiner. 1985. *The Mentally Disabled and the Law*. Chicago: American Bar Foundation.

Dunham AC. 1985. APA's Model Law: Protecting the patient's ultimate interests. *Hospital and Community Psychiatry* 36:973–975.

Durham ML and JQ LaFond. 1985. The empirical consequences and policy implications of broadening the statutory criteria for civil commitment. *Yale Law and Policy Review* 3:395–446.

Durham ML and JQ LaFond. 1988. A search for the missing premise of involuntary therapeutic commitment: Effective treatment of the mentally ill. *Rutgers Law Review* 40:303–370.

Feuerstein S, F Fortunati, CA Morgan, V Coric, H Temporini, and S Southwick. 2005. Civil commitment: A power granted to physicians by society. *Psychiatry (Edgmont)* 2(8):53–54.

Fisher WH, PJ Barreira, JL Geller, AW White, AK Lincoln, and M Sudders. 2001. Long-stay patients in state psychiatric hospitals at the end of the 20th century. *Psychiatric Services* 52:1051–1056.

Garakani A, E Shalenberg, SC Burstin, RW Brendel, and JM Appel. 2014. Voluntary psychiatric hospitalization and patient-driven requests for discharge: A statutory review and analysis of implications for the capacity to consent to voluntary hospitalization. *Harvard Review of Psychiatry* 22(4):241–249.

Gutheil TG and PS. Appelbaum. 2000. *Clinical Handbook of Psychiatry and the Law*, 3rd edition. Baltimore: Williams and Wilkins.

Jackson v. Indiana, 406 U.S. 715 (1972).

Katz SE. 1989. Hospitalization and the mental health service system. In *Comprehensive Textbook of Psychiatry*, 5th edition, edited by HI Kaplan and Sadock BJ, Baltimore: Williams and Wilkins, 2083–2090.

Lake v. Cameron, 364 F.2d 657 (1966).

Lessard v. Schmidt, 349 F. Supp. 1078 (E.D. Wis. 1972).

Matter of Josiah Oakes, 8 Law Rep. 123 (Mass. 1845).

Neary B. 2014. ACLU questions involuntary commitment changes. http://www.washingtontimes.com/news/2014/feb/3/aclu-questions-involuntary-commitment-changes/?page=all#pagebreak, accessed September 28, 2014.

O'Connor v. Donaldson, 422 U.S. 563 (1975).

Olmstead v. L.C., 527 U.S. 581 (1999).

Parham v. J.R., 42 U.S. 584 (1979).

Shorter E. 1997. *A History of Psychiatry: From the Era of the Asylum to the Age of Prozac*. New York: John Wiley & Sons.

Stromberg CD. 1982. Developments concerning the legal criteria for civil commitment: Who are we looking for? In *Psychiatry: The American Psychiatric Association Annual Review* Vol. 1. edited by L Grinspoon, Washington D.C.: American Psychiatric Publishing, 334–350.

Testa M and West SG. 2010. Civil commitment in the United States. *Psychiatry* 7(10):30–40.

Zinermon v. Burch, 494 U.S. 113 (1990).

16

Assisted outpatient treatment and outpatient commitment

GARY TSAI AND CAMERON QUANBECK

INTRODUCTION

Although civil commitment is most often thought of as an inpatient intervention, outpatient commitment (OPC), also known as assisted outpatient treatment (AOT), is another form of civil commitment that mandates adherence to mental health treatment in the community. The common goal of this intervention is to prevent relapse, hospital and criminal justice recidivism, homelessness, and other poor outcomes related to lack of treatment. Court-ordered outpatient psychiatric care is among the most contested and misunderstood issues in mental health law (Brooks 2007, 219; Dale 2010, 271). Yet, given an increasing awareness of the limitations of current mental health-care delivery, there has been a growing interest in exploring its use as a tool to improve treatment adherence in the least restrictive setting possible.

Since the onset of deinstitutionalization in the 1950s, when there were over 558,000 psychiatric hospital beds nationwide, there has been a greater than 90% reduction in available beds, according to the National Association of State Mental Health Program Directors. As of 2010, there are now less than 45,000 psychiatric beds nationwide (Torrey et al. 2012, 5). The reasons for this shift in care were multifactorial, including poor treatment and conditions in mental asylums, the emergence of effective antipsychotic medications, budgetary concerns, and concerns about the *parens patriae* aspect of commitment.

Though the goal of transitioning the care of former mental asylum residents to less restrictive settings such as community mental health clinics was noble, necessary resources to provide treatment in the community never fully materialized (Goldman et al. 1983). Additionally, the expectation that individuals released from psychiatric hospitals would voluntarily seek treatment in the community was overly optimistic for a variety of reasons, including a lack of community resources and the now well-established finding that a significant proportion of persons with serious mental illness lack insight into their psychiatric condition (Husted 1999, 33). Research has demonstrated that a significant percentage of patients (40%–50%) with serious mental illnesses suffer from deficits in insight. Those with impairments in insight have difficulty realizing that (1) they are suffering from psychiatric illness; (2) the symptoms they are experiencing (e.g., delusions, hallucinations, mania) are part of the mental illness; and (3) they likely would benefit from psychiatric treatment (Pini et al. 2001, 124; Dell'Osso et al. 2002, 315; Pini et al. 2003, 355; Cairns et al. 2005, 384). The neurological term for this phenomenon is anosognosia. Advanced neuroimaging techniques, including functional magnetic resonance imaging (Cooke et al. 2008, 40; Bedford et al. 2012, 106; van Der Meer et al. 2013, 1288) and positron emission tomography (Faget-Agius et al. 2012, 297), demonstrate that individuals with poor insight have dysfunctional neuronal circuits predominantly involving the frontal and parietal lobes.

The result of this has been that many individuals with impaired insight—particularly those with more serious mental illnesses, such as psychotic conditions—have had difficulty accessing care in either community mental health centers or inpatient facilities, and have ended up cycling between the criminal justice system, hospitals, and homelessness. Researchers have noted that the large numbers of homeless individuals who are mentally ill suggest that current outpatient mental health services are not meeting the needs of this group (McNiel and Binder 2005, 699). At any given point in time, approximately 40%–50% of cases of serious mental illness in the United States are untreated (Regier et al. 1993, 85; Kessler et al. 2001, 988; Wang et al. 2005, 629; Olfson et al. 2010, 831).

As psychiatric hospital beds have become scarce, there has been increased pressure on public mental health systems to employ more effective interventions in the ambulatory setting. At the same time, it has become clear that a certain subset of individuals with serious mental illness either cannot or will not adhere to traditional outpatient models of care. As a result, policymakers are discussing how best to engage this population in treatment. These discussions have included the merits of OPC/AOT, including the issues involving legality, eligibility criteria, and its current evidence base (in terms of effectiveness and cost savings) (Swartz et al. 1999, 1968; Appelbaum 2001, 347; Schopp 2003, 33; Swanson et al. 2013, 1423).

HISTORY AND LEGAL CONSIDERATIONS

In the 1960s, a greater emphasis on safeguarding civil liberties led to decreasing public support for the state's commitment authority. Previously, state hospitals employed a conditional release procedure whereby patients who were deemed ready for a trial release from the hospital were given a pass to leave the premises prior to their formal discharge (Miller 1987). However, if clinicians made the determination that patients needed to return to the hospital, superintendents had the authority to recommit these individuals to the state hospital.

Due process reforms in the 1970s led to the 1975 U.S. Supreme Court landmark decision *O'Connor v. Donaldson*, in which inpatient commitment was restricted to individuals who were found to be both dangerous and mentally ill. Civil commitment standards essentially were changed from a "need-for-treatment" to "imminent dangerousness," and many states subsequently tightened their inpatient commitment criteria in response to this landmark ruling. Following these modifications, some mental health providers noted that the combination of narrowed treatment criteria and underfunded community mental health services was contributing to "revolving door" recidivism (King 1995, 254). In instances such as these, chronically ill people who generally do not seek treatment voluntarily are only treated when allowable according to legal commitment standards. However, many are stabilized only to the point where they no longer meet the inpatient commitment standards and are subsequently released, only to resume this cycle by ceasing to take their medications once they leave the structured confines of a hospital (Appelbaum 2001, 348; Kress 2006, 573).

In the 1980s, there was a push to expand the state's role in the management of the chronically mentally ill and to once again lower commitment standards. In 1983, North Carolina became the first state to enact preventive outpatient commitment statutes, in which traditional OPC standards were broadened to include individuals who did not meet inpatient commitment criteria (Stefan 1987, 288). The rationale for this was to intervene in the lives of individuals with chronic recidivism prior to their becoming irretrievably ensnared in the aforementioned "revolving door." Preventive outpatient commitment laws have since expanded to include 45 states in the United States. As of the writing of this chapter, the only states without preventive outpatient commitment laws were Connecticut, Maryland, Massachusetts, New Mexico, and Tennessee.

OUTPATIENT COMMITMENT: RATIONALE AND CRITICISMS

Coercion in psychiatric care remains a controversial tactic, and the debate regarding the practice has shifted from the inpatient to outpatient setting, as the majority of mental health-care delivery has transitioned from institutions to the community (Munetz et al. 2003, 173). Courts have consistently upheld the right of individuals to make lawful decisions about most aspects of their lives, free from intrusion. The legal doctrine of informed consent outlines that individuals should be able to express and understand the complexities of a given choice and rationally manipulate the components of that decision in order to comprehend and compare alternative options (Appelbaum et al. 1987, 3). However, the issue of fully informed consent in psychiatric practice is complex, particularly given deficits in executive functioning and reasoning that frequently accompany serious mental illness.

The MacArthur Foundation competence studies divided competence into four different variables: choice, understanding, reasoning, and appreciation (Appelbaum and Grisso 1995, 105; Grisso and Appelbaum 1995a, 1034, 1995b, 149). These studies found that as a whole, psychiatrically hospitalized patients were at greater risk for deficits in decision making when compared to medically hospitalized patients, but also found that these impairments were, at times, temporary and improved with treatment. Although some individuals regain their decision-making capacity after successful treatment (Turkington et al. 2002, 523; Rittmannsberger et al. 2004, 174), a portion of individuals persistently lacks capacity despite treatment.

Researchers have found that over half of individuals with schizophrenia experienced deficits in the understanding, reasoning, and appreciation aspects of these standards, indicating impaired decision-making capacity (Grisso et al. 1995, 127). Given the growing research suggesting a neurobiological basis for this lack of self-awareness (Lysaker et al. 1997, 297; Keefe 1998, Young et al. 1998, 44; Mohamed et al. 1999, 525; Flashman et al. 2000, 1167), which most commonly implicates dysfunctional circuits in the right parietal and frontal lobes (which affect executive functioning) (Raffard et al. 2008a, 511), the pathologic biology of schizophrenia may prevent certain individuals with this condition from being able to make informed decisions. Research has supported the notion that insight is complex and exists in varying degrees, from complete denial of diagnosis, to vague recognition, to full appreciation of illness (Marková and Berrios 1995, 367).

Critiques of coercive treatment in general, and OPC in particular, typically involve several key issues. One is a "rights-based" argument, founded on the principle of self-determination and the view that involuntary treatment is a violation of one's civil liberties (Hoge and Grottole 2000, 165; Lamb and Weinberger 2013, 290). Those espousing this perspective frequently contend that seriously mentally ill individuals should have the freedom to decide whether or not to accept treatment unless they are legally deemed incompetent or pose a clear danger to themselves or others (Schopp 2003, 33), and that coercive treatment will discourage individuals from seeking mental health care voluntarily in the future (Allen and Smith 2001, 342). Because the legal definition of competence differs from the clinical definition of capacity, there are important clinical implications to this more narrowly defined interpretation of the circumstances under which involuntary psychiatric care should be provided.

Proponents of OPC often opine that self-determination in the context of impaired decision-making capacity is arguably impossible, and that these instances—a relatively common scenario in acute psychiatric settings—highlight the need for court-ordered outpatient treatment and the fine line between patient autonomy and beneficence (Torrey and Zdanowicz 2001, 337). In light of a growing body of evidence that earlier diagnosis and treatment of psychosis lead to improved prognosis (Bottlender et al. 2003, 37; Craig et al. 2004, 1067; Perkins et al. 2005, 1798; Malla et al. 2005, 881; Raffard et al. 2008b, 597), allowing psychiatric patients to refuse care in these scenarios can "empower" the symptoms of the condition rather than empowering the patient. Indeed, the association between lack of insight and schizophrenia has been linked to medication nonadherence, severe positive psychotic symptoms, psychiatric hospitalizations, comorbid depression, poor occupational functioning, homelessness, substance use, and poorer overall prognosis (Lysaker et al. 1994, 307, 2002, 142; Smith et al. 1999, 102; Löffler et al. 2003, 105; Mintz et al. 2003, 75; Rittmannsberger et al. 2004, 174; Olfson et al. 2006, 205). Ironically, some observers have noted that mandated outpatient treatment may actually lead to decreased involuntary care by decreasing the need for other mandatory interventions that are provided in more restrictive settings (Zanni and Stavis 2007, 31; Link et al. 2011, 504).

Interestingly, studies that have focused on perceived coercion among the consumers who are directly impacted by mandated outpatient treatment orders have been mixed. A self-report study analyzing perceived coercion with OPC found that persons subjected to mandated treatment reported higher levels of perceived coercion, which was directly proportional to the duration of their mandate (Swartz et al. 2002, 214). This study also suggested that perceived coercion was independently associated with several clinical characteristics, most notably severe symptoms, anosognosia, and substance use. Conversely, results of interviews with consumers with schizophrenia or related disorders indicate that 62% regarded mandated outpatient care as effective, and 55% reported that they felt such interventions were fair (Swartz et al. 2004, 780). Overall, these individuals tended to believe that OPC was beneficial and in their best interests, particularly participants who were less symptomatic, possessed better insight, and adopted a more biopsychosocial view of their own condition. Other studies have yielded similar results when psychiatric patients who received involuntary treatment were asked about their views on their coerced treatment, with a majority indicating that in retrospect, they agreed such treatment was in their best interests (Schwartz et al. 1988, 1049; Greenberg et al. 1996, 513).

A similar analysis was performed comparing the views of coercion in OPC among four stakeholder groups: consumers with schizophrenia and related disorders, their family members, treating clinicians, and members of the general public (Swartz et al. 2003, 1139). In each stakeholder group, avoiding inpatient hospitalization and interpersonal violence, and maintaining good interpersonal relationships were prioritized over concern about coercion with OPC. The results of this study suggest that the perceived coercion of mandated outpatient treatment may be a more tolerable alternative than other negative outcomes.

Resource-based arguments also are cited both in support of and against mandated outpatient treatment. Opponents of OPC commonly hold a utilitarian perspective that investing resources into services that provide the greatest good for the greatest number of people is the preferred course of action. As a result, they espouse ensuring that voluntary mental health services are available to the masses before targeting a minority of those with severe mental illness with involuntary interventions. In this case, the specific rationale is often that removing barriers to voluntary mental health services would accomplish the same objectives as OPC and would make expanding involuntary interventions unnecessary (Brown 2003, 7; Winick 2003, 107). In one California study, an infusion of resources into the public mental health system, which contributed to an improvement in access and quality of mental health care, was followed by a decrease in the number of petitions for involuntary 14-day holds, though the number of petitions for involuntary 72-hour holds was unchanged (Bruckner et al. 2010, 1008). There is also concern that investing resources in OPC will result in a reduction in voluntary services, though some research challenges this belief. New York State's AOT implementation ultimately led to greater access to intensive services for both voluntary and involuntary patients (Swanson et al. 2010, 992).

Conversely, the growing evidence supporting the neurobiological basis of anosognosia has led to recognition of an expanding chasm in access to care. That is, those who are more psychiatrically stable are able to accept care voluntarily, while those who are unable to recognize their illness are refusing voluntary care and placing themselves at greater risk of succumbing to the various negative outcomes of serious mental illness. Thus, the resource-based argument commonly cited in support of OPC is that the high costs of recidivism for both the mental health and criminal justice systems (Swanson et al. 2013, 1430) are ultimately unsustainable and inequitable, and that devoting resources to the minority of high-utilizing, recidivist patients may be a more appropriate and efficient allocation of limited mental health resources.

OUTPATIENT COMMITMENT STATUTES

All OPC programs target severely mentally ill adults who have a history of recidivism and refusing voluntary treatment, and attempt to engage and stabilize this population in the community by providing comprehensive services via a multidisciplinary treatment team. Although a majority of state legislatures have OPC statutes, the eligibility criteria, utilization, and systematic implementation of these programs vary significantly. Some states have OPC statutes with standards written so narrowly that they are unusable and OPC is nonexistent (Stettin et al., 2014, 1). Some experts have observed that there are several challenges to overcome before OPC can be widely and successfully implemented: (1) statutes must be accompanied by sufficient resources to provide the necessary intensive outpatient services, and (2) widespread support is needed among the community mental health providers who will be directly involved in clinical care within these programs (Miller 1988, 99). As mentioned previously OPC/AOT programs' roles within the mental health community continue to be controversial. Additionally, many states that have passed OPC legislation have not provided additional revenue to fund these programs and have not made implementation a statewide requirement, instead allowing local authorities to make decisions about implementation (or lack thereof).

In distinct contrast to comparable programs in other states, New York's is one of the few that allocated sufficient funds for their AOT program (through Kendra's Law). As a result, New York's OPC process is one of the most comprehensive in terms of implementation, infrastructure, and oversight (Swartz 2009, 1) and has served as a model for other states (Petrila and Christy 2008, 21).

As illustrated in Figure 16.1 and described in a report by the New York State Office of Mental Health (Swartz et al. 2009, 5), New York's AOT program consists of four phases: referral, investigation/assessment, service delivery, and monitoring. In the initial phase, referrals from the community or local hospital/correctional facility can be made to the AOT Coordinator, who performs a preliminary investigation to determine if the program's eligibility criteria are met (see bottom of Figure 16.1).

Eligible cases are then transferred to the AOT Case Review Panel for additional vetting in order to assess needs and collaborate with the referred individual in order to devise a treatment plan. Participants may agree to accept services and sign an enhanced voluntary service (EVS) agreement. Within New York, there is procedural variability in that some counties will replace a court order with the EVS, while others require that a court order be filed with the EVS. If a court order is necessary, the AOT team will petition the court to issue a court-ordered treatment plan. This plan consists of intensive, multidisciplinary care, including case management or Assertive Community Treatment (ACT), medication, and housing support, and other court-mandated services to help ensure the individual's stability

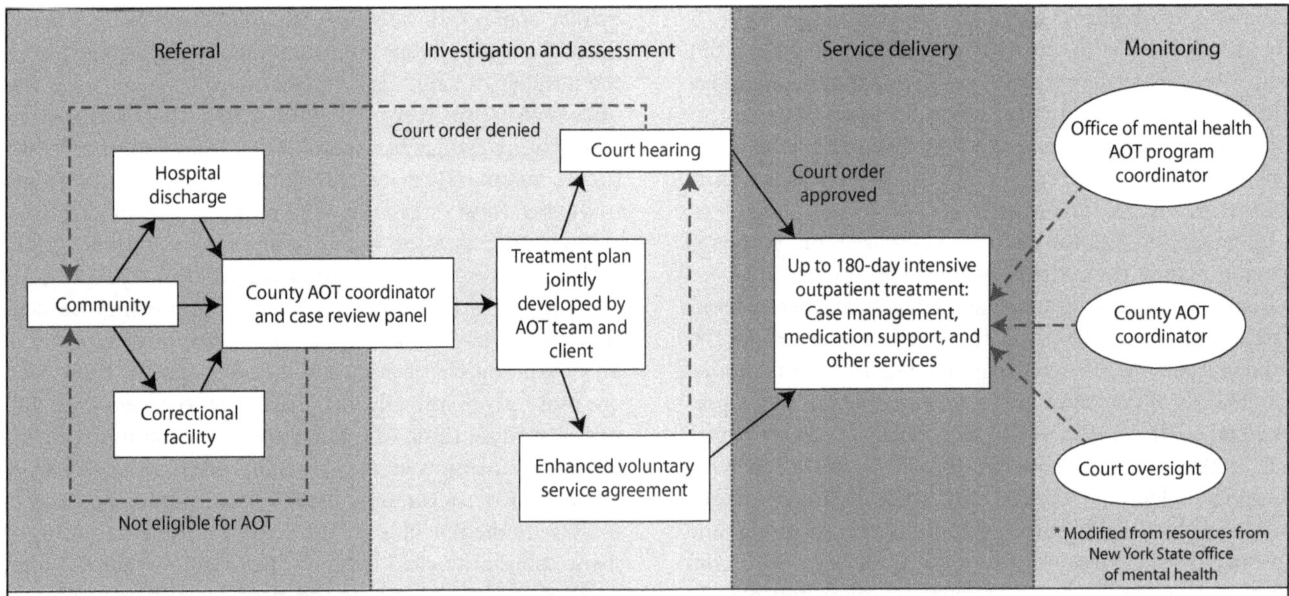

New York AOT eligibility criteria (New York Mental Hygiene Law, Section 9.60)

1. At least 18 years old and suffering from mental illness.
2. Clinical determination needs to indicate that they are unlikely to survive safely in the community without supervision.
3. History of lack of compliance with treatment for mental illness that has significantly contributed to at least two hospitalizations or incarcerations within the last 36 months, or one or more acts of serious violent behavior in the last 48 months.
4. Unlikely to voluntarily participate in outpatient treatment that would enable him or her to live safely in the community.
5. Considering treatment history and current behavior, is in need of assisted outpatient treatment in order to prevent a relapse or deterioration which would likely result in serious harm to self/others.
6. Likely to benefit from assisted outpatient treatment.
7. Previously executed health care proxies shall be taken into account by the court in determining the written treatment plan.

Figure 16.1 New York—assisted outpatient treatment process and eligibility criteria.

in the community. Upon issuance, court-ordered treatment plans may be in force up to 6 months and are eligible for renewal for successive periods of up to 1 year.

During the hearing, evidence from the petitioner and patient are presented to establish whether or not there is clear and convincing evidence that the AOT eligibility criteria are met and that the intervention is the least restrictive alternative available to the patient. The hearing process provides an important opportunity for "procedural justice," including a fair and just decision-making process, the active involvement of all participants, and benevolence on the part of authority figures (McKenna et al. 2001, 573). Research has shown that the perception of procedural justice may mitigate feelings of coercion and improve therapeutic outcomes in terms of individuals' enhanced acceptance of and engagement with treatment processes (Tyler 1992, 437; Nicholson et al. 1996, 201; Winick 1997, 30, 2003, 107; Cascardi et al. 2000, 731; Poythress et al. 2002, 529).

When patients under court order do not engage with treatment despite efforts by the treatment team to achieve compliance, the New York AOT statute allows for the patient to be transported to a local evaluating facility for assessment for up to 72 hours in order to determine if the individual meets the criteria for inpatient hospitalization. If the criteria for involuntary hospitalization are not met, the patient must be released immediately. Although this intervention incentivizes treatment compliance to a certain extent, the mechanism for achieving this compliance has been attributed to the power of the court, a term known as "therapeutic jurisprudence" or the "black robe effect." Therapeutic jurisprudence has been described as a therapeutically oriented judicial process whereby the judge plays an active role in leading a team-based approach to the treatment process (Monahan et al. 2001, 1200; Watson et al. 2001, 478). The successes of mental health and drug court models, which have relied on therapeutic jurisprudence to influence treatment compliance, have supported the effectiveness of this judicial leverage. On a "paternalism spectrum," therapeutic jurisprudence seems to lie somewhere between voluntary psychiatric care and conservatorships/guardianships, and is viewed by some as an important tool for encouraging treatment adherence in instances of compromised decision-making capacity (Monahan et al. 2003, 35).

According to a 2009 program evaluation report by the New York State Office of Mental Health (Swartz et al. 2009, 50), the AOT statute's requirements have led to improved access and coordination of services, enhanced accountability in mental health systems, and improved collaboration between the mental health and court systems. In spite of initial concerns that the AOT eligibility criteria may have been overly broad and ensnared those who did not require AOT services, an analysis found that only about 2% of the severely mentally ill service populations in New York were recipients of AOT services. Thus, although OPC orders were applied only in a small fraction of cases, the benefits of implementation extended to voluntary mental health patients by way of the resulting program enhancements required by the AOT program.

CURRENT RESEARCH

The evidence base for OPC and AOT has grown in quantity, quality, and geographic generalizability over the past several decades. As a result, there has been increasing interest and controversy surrounding this intervention. Early studies were largely anecdotal and had mixed results. Even though one of the first studies of court-ordered outpatient treatment found the intervention to be effective at reducing hospital readmissions in North Carolina, and therefore a viable, less restrictive alternative to involuntary hospitalization (Hiday and Goodman 1982, 81), a survey of clinicians' opinions (in a different Congressional district in North Carolina) found that many did not feel it was helpful (Miller and Fiddleman 1984, 147). A study of OPC in Tennessee also demonstrated that although recipients of mandated outpatient treatment showed a reduction in hospital readmission rates, a comparison with control groups revealed that these results were not attributable to the court intervention (Bursten 1986, 1257).

Subsequent research in Washington, DC (Zanni and DeVeau 1986, 941), found decreased rates of hospital readmissions and reduced lengths of stay, with similar results replicated in Ohio (Munetz et al. 1996, 1251) and Arizona (Van Putten et al. 1988, 953). Patients in the Ohio study who received OPC experienced significant reductions in psychiatric emergency room visits, hospitalizations, and lengths of stay, in addition to greater levels of participation in outpatient appointments after their discharge. In the Arizona study, there was also a significant increase in the percentage of patients who voluntarily engaged with their community mental health center 6 months after OPC.

To date, there have been only two randomized controlled trials of outpatient commitment in the United States and one such study in the United Kingdom. A 1994 study evaluated the effectiveness of a 3-year OPC pilot program at Bellevue Hospital in New York City, randomly assigning 142 participants to either a court-ordered treatment group with access to enhanced mental health services or a control group with access only to the enhanced services (Steadman et al. 2001, 330). After analyzing post-discharge follow-up interviews at 1, 5, and 11 months, investigators found no significant differences between the two groups on the major outcome measures of rehospitalizations, arrests, quality of life, symptomatology, treatment nonadherence, and perceived level of coercion. A key limitation of this study was that there was no enforcement of the court order and no procedure in place to respond to nonadherent individuals under court-ordered treatment, which likely diluted the differences between the two groups. Additionally, violent patients were omitted from the study because of ethical concerns, compromising the study's generalizability.

Similar limitations plagued the Oxford Community Treatment Order Evaluation Trial (OCTET), a randomized controlled trial of community treatment orders in the United Kingdom (Burns et al. 2013, 1627). In this analysis, 336 patients were assigned to either the experimental community treatment order (CTO) group or a "Section 17 leave" group, which served as the control condition. "Section 17 leave" refers to a well-established conditional release practice whereby hospitalized patients are authorized to leave the premises, provided they comply with outpatient treatment. They can be readmitted to the hospital without any additional legal processes should they become nonadherent to treatment in the community. Unlike OPC orders in the United States, which are issued by a court, clinicians issue CTOs in the United Kingdom. Therefore, both groups were required to receive compulsory, intensive supervision in the community, though forced outpatient treatment for patients was not authorized. At 12 months, there were no significant differences in outcomes, which included hospital readmissions, duration of hospitalizations, community stability, and clinical and social functioning.

However, researchers have highlighted important design challenges of the OCTET study (Swanson and Swartz 2014, 808). First, the experimental CTO group was not under court order and therefore avoided the impact of therapeutic jurisprudence and the "black robe effect," which is cited by OPC proponents as an important benefit of mandated outpatient care. Second, although the study has been used to compare voluntary interventions with OPC, the control group also did not receive a truly voluntary intervention, given the coercive influence of conditional release practices. These design limitations limit the generalizability of the OCTET study, and critical questions about the effectiveness of OPC compared to voluntary interventions are not answered.

The North Carolina randomized controlled trial analyzed 331 involuntarily hospitalized patients awaiting discharge, assigning them to either a group that was released to standard case management and outpatient treatment or a group under an outpatient commitment order (Swartz et al. 2001a, 325). Patients in the control group could not be placed under outpatient commitment for a period of 1 year. When the duration of OPC was not taken into account, outcomes for the OPC group did not differ significantly from those for the control group. However, extended mandated outpatient treatment was associated with 57% fewer hospitalizations when compared with the control group's hospitalizations. Individuals in the OPC group also averaged significantly shorter lengths of stay (20 days shorter). Additionally, patients who engaged with three or more outpatient service contacts per month and received sustained OPC were significantly less likely to be violent than those in the control group (24% versus 48%, respectively). Criminal victimization also significantly decreased in the treatment group (24% of the OPC group experienced victimization compared to 42% of the control group). Overall, the authors of this study concluded that a court order was not an adequate substitute for effective treatment, but that mandated outpatient treatment could lead to enhanced outcomes when sustained and combined with intensive outpatient services.

Subsequent outpatient commitment studies replicated many of these positive clinical outcomes, namely decreased psychiatric inpatient admissions and lengths of stay (Rohland et al. 2000, 383; Frank et al. 2005, 867), reduced rates of homelessness (Compton et al. 2003, 27), reduced violence and victimization (Swanson et al. 2000, 327; Appelbaum 2001, 347; Hiday et al. 2002, 1403; Frank et al. 2005, 867), and improved treatment adherence (Swanson et al. 1997, 8; Swartz et al. 2001b, 583). Evidence that mandated outpatient treatment can reduce criminal behaviors (Erickson 2005, 627; Gilbert et al. 2010, 996; Segal 2012, 1454) led the Office of Justice Programs, an agency of the U.S. Department of Justice, to designate AOT "an effective crime prevention intervention" (AOT 2012).

Analyses of Medicaid claims and state reports on 3576 patients involved in New York's AOT program yielded similar results (Swartz et al. 2010, 976). Compared to periods of time prior to the initiation of an AOT court order, AOT participants experienced a 25% reduction in psychiatric hospitalizations and over a 30% decrease in inpatient admissions after the AOT orders were renewed for 6 months. Significant declines in inpatient lengths of stay also were evident, with the average pre-AOT duration of hospital admission lasting approximately 18 days, compared to 11 days during the first 6 months of the court order and 10 days during subsequent months of mandated outpatient care. Greater access to medications and comprehensive mental health services, such as Assertive Community Treatment or intensive case management, also were evident. A number of studies have consistently supported the observation that OPC is most effective when sustained longer than 6 months and combined with intensive community-based services (Swartz et al. 1999, 1973; Swanson et al. 2003, 473; Wagner et al. 2003, 145; Van Dorn et al. 2010, 982).

Although the existing scientific literature suggests that OPC is associated with certain improved treatment outcomes, some have questioned whether these improved outcomes are related to the influences of the court order itself or the intensive outpatient treatment that accompanies OPC. A 2001 RAND meta-analysis found that involuntary OPC can be effective at reducing negative outcomes such as psychiatric relapse, violent behavior, and criminal recidivism among people with severe mental illness, but only when combined with enhanced, community-based mental health services (Ridgely et al. 2001, 98). Consequently, the authors of this study attributed the resulting benefits to enhanced services and monitoring, noting "While there may exist a subgroup of people with severe mental illness for whom a court order acts as leverage to enhance treatment compliance, the best studies suggest that the effectiveness of outpatient commitment is linked to the provision of intensive services. Whether court orders have any effect at all in the absence of intensive treatment is an unanswered question." Critics of the RAND study have noted that its conclusion questioning the benefit of the court order contradicts the authors' acknowledgement that court orders may be beneficial for a select population of individuals.

In summary, the evidence base generally supports the effectiveness of mandated outpatient treatment when appropriately implemented, targeted, and funded. Research has persuasively shown that OPC can lead to improved treatment outcomes, with success contingent upon the availability of intensive mental health services and the duration of the court order.

COST ANALYSES OF TREATMENT NONADHERENCE AND ASSISTED OUTPATIENT TREATMENT

Given the considerable human, societal, and financial costs of recidivism and untreated serious mental illness (Insel 2008, 663), successful efforts to decrease hospitalizations and criminal justice recidivism can result in significant economic benefits. In a study that quantified the excess annual costs associated with persons with schizophrenia in the United States (Wu et al. 2005, 1122), investigators used administrative claims data for both privately ($N = 1090$) and publicly (Medicaid, $N = 14{,}074$) insured patients. Annual, direct, non-health-care costs were estimated for law enforcement, homeless shelters, and research/training related to schizophrenia and then added to indirect projected costs for unemployment, reduced workplace productivity, premature mortality from suicide, and family caregiving. Overall, the 2002 U.S. cost of schizophrenia was estimated to be $62.7 billion, with $22.7 billion attributable to direct health-care costs, $7.6 billion to direct, non-health-care costs (including $2.64 billion in annual law enforcement costs), and $32.4 billion to indirect costs.

Persons with serious mental illness who do not adhere to their prescribed medication regimens in the community are at high risk of relapse and requiring acute psychiatric care, which is the most expensive type of mental health treatment. Currently, the average length of stay for acute psychiatric hospitalization is 5–6 days (Glick et al. 2011, 207). However, this length of stay is often inadequate to stabilize psychiatric crises and can lead to readmission (Boaz et al. 2013, 1225). Given the scarcity of psychiatric hospital beds across the nation, adherence to psychotropic medications is critical in preventing rehospitalization. Studies measuring adherence in those with serious mental illness indicate that this phenomenon is common. In a study of Medicaid beneficiaries with schizophrenia, pharmacy records demonstrated that 40% of patients were either nonadherent or partially adherent to their medication regimens. Those who were nonadherent incurred significantly more hospital costs than those who were adherent (Gilmer et al. 2004, 694).

A similar study of patients with schizophrenia in California found that even small gaps in medication adherence (i.e., 1–10 days) increased risk of hospitalization (odds ratio 1.98), and larger gaps (11–30 days and beyond) increased hospitalization risk further (odds ratio 2.81 and 3.96, respectively). In a retrospective analysis of 1500 individuals with schizophrenia who had been prescribed antipsychotics and then were followed for 12 months after the initial prescribing, those with a "medication gap" of greater than 30 days were 4.7 times more likely to be hospitalized than those who had a medication gap of 0–10 days. The risk of hospitalization for patients with a "medication possession ratio" (MPR) (i.e., percentage of days with prescription antipsychotic available for consumption) of less than 70% were significantly more likely to be hospitalized than those who obtained medication more consistently, with the risk of hospitalization decreasing 16.9% for every 10% increase in "medication possession" (Kozma and Weiden 2009, 36).

A study examining rehospitalization costs for Medicaid recipients who relapse because of nonadherence estimated annual costs to be $1.479 billion (Sun et al. 2007, 2305). Even small increases in medication continuity could result in significant cost savings in inpatient care costs for the national Medicaid system (Marcus and Olfson 2008, 177). A 3-year study of 1906 persons with schizophrenia found that antipsychotic nonadherence was associated with poorer functional outcomes and greater risks of hospitalization, use of emergency services, arrests, violence, victimization, and drug- and alcohol-related problems (Ascher-Svanum et al. 2006, 453).

Research has demonstrated that psychotropic nonadherence has similar deleterious effects for those with bipolar disorder. In a study of individuals with bipolar disorder with predominantly manic or mixed symptoms, a higher MPR significantly reduced total mental health expenditures, with a reduction in expenditure of $123 to $439 per one-point increase in MPR (Gianfrancesco et al. 2008, 1358). A study of patients with bipolar disorder discharged to the community found that those with an MPR of at least 0.75 had significantly lower risks of hospitalization (Hassan and Lage 2009, 358), and persons with bipolar disorder with MPRs of 0.8 and 0.9 were able to remain in the community and avoid rehospitalization and emergency services (Lage and Hassan 2009, 4). Irregular medication use is one of the strongest predictors of hospital use and cost among those with serious mental illness, and leads to hospital costs four times greater for these individuals than for those who take psychotropic medications regularly (Svarstad et al. 2001, 810). Clearly, the cost savings potential for interventions that improve treatment compliance and decrease recidivism are impressive.

In response to increasing interest and questions from policymakers, perhaps as a result of growing evidence of the merits of mandated outpatient treatment, researchers recently have attempted to evaluate the cost-effectiveness of this intervention. Investigators conducted a comprehensive analysis of the net costs of AOT programs in New York City and five surrounding counties by reviewing 36 months of observational data for 634 AOT participants and 255 recipients of voluntary intensive outpatient treatment (Swanson et al. 2013, 1423). Costs for the program were calculated from claims data that focused primarily on criminal justice and legal spending, expenditures for mental health and other medical treatment, and program administration costs. During the first 12 months after mandated outpatient treatment was initiated, hospitalizations decreased markedly, with modest declines sustained through the subsequent 12 months after the program's initiation. Utilization of psychiatric emergency and crisis services, and criminal justice involvement were also reduced. As costs for hospitalizations and other encounters declined, spending on outpatient care increased. When the entire sample was analyzed, total net costs declined by approximately 45% in the first year after the initiation of court-ordered treatment, followed by an additional 13% reduction in the second year. The data suggested that the reductions in net costs were attributable to shifting patterns of service provision, from repeated inpatient contacts to regular outpatient encounters. Based on these results, the authors concluded that states can reduce overall services costs for individuals with severe mental illness, provided that the geographic area was willing and able to invest the necessary resources to adequately fund an OPC program and intensive outpatient services.

These findings were corroborated in a cost-analysis study conducted in North Carolina (Swartz and Swanson 2013, 7). In this study, net costs were calculated from data from a prior randomized controlled trial by the same researchers (Swartz et al. 2001a, 325). Updated service unit prices for inpatient and outpatient services, arrests and days of incarceration, civil court costs, and administrative overhead were included in the analysis. Although total annual costs were approximately $3000 higher for the OPC group than the control group ($46,510 versus $43,516, respectively), when mandated outpatient treatment orders were extended for over 6 months, the total costs decreased by about 40% (or $17,594). These results suggest that the implementation of OPC programs could be cost-neutral if the funding and infrastructure for intensive outpatient services was available, and that this intervention could lead to cost savings if court orders for community-based services were extended beyond 6 months.

Finally, comparable outcomes were found in an AOT program in Nevada County, California, a small, rural community with a population of 100,000 (Tsai 2012, 16). When hospitalizations and incarcerations were compared in the same population both pre- and post-AOT over a period of 31 months, court-ordered participants experienced significant reductions in psychiatric hospitalization days (61% decrease) and incarceration days (97% decrease). As a result, Nevada County realized a net savings of 45% after implementing their OPC program, returning $1.81 for every $1 invested into the program.

SUMMARY

Clinical and legal interventions have been proposed to address the complex challenge of engaging in treatment individuals with serious mental illness and a history of recidivism. Given the poor outcomes associated with lack of treatment and the impaired decision-making capacity that impacts some people with serious mental illness, outpatient commitment has been suggested as a reasonable option to provide necessary care in the least restrictive setting possible.

However, opponents of court-ordered outpatient treatment have expressed concern about the consequences of its widespread implementation. Research has provided some clarity about the concerns, benefits, and economic considerations of OPC. Evidence from a variety of settings, including New York, North Carolina, and California generally has supported the notion that this intervention is effective when appropriately funded, implemented, and applied. Additionally, New York's AOT program was found to improve the mental health system as a whole, both for AOT participants and for voluntary recipients of services, presumably because of improved accountability and collaboration between state agencies, and the enhanced services that are required by mandated outpatient treatment. Although the limitations of mental health systems are multifaceted, and outpatient commitment is not a panacea for these shortcomings, AOT has proved to be a useful tool for engaging a certain subset of people with serious mental illness.

SUMMARY KEY POINTS

- Outpatient commitment, also known as assisted outpatient treatment, involves court-ordered, intensive, community-based mental health services that target individuals with a history of recidivism and treatment nonadherence.
- The intervention is controversial. Opponents cite concerns about undermining self-determination, damaging therapeutic relationships (and subsequent decreased voluntary engagement in treatment in the future), and siphoning resources away from voluntary services. Proponents note that some individuals who lack insight into their mental illness lack the capacity to accept care voluntarily and require involuntary interventions to prevent poor outcomes. They also note that OPC is community based and a less restrictive alternative than other potential interventions or outcomes (e.g., hospitalization, incarceration).
- A balanced assessment of the evidence generally supports the notion that OPC is effective and that it is associated with reduced hospitalizations, reduced criminalization and victimization, improved engagement with outpatient treatment, and cost savings from reduced recidivism.
- Appropriate funding, the availability of intensive community-based services, and the duration of the court order are factors influencing whether OPC can be implemented effectively.

REFERENCES

Allen M and V Smith. 2001. Opening Pandora's box: The practical and legal dangers of involuntary outpatient commitment. *Psychiatric Services* 52(3):342–346.

AOT (Assisted Outpatient Treatment). 2012. https://www.crimesolutions.gov/ProgramDetails.aspx?ID=228, accessed March 26, 2012.

Appelbaum P. 2001. Thinking carefully about outpatient commitment. *Psychiatric Services* 52(3):347–350.

Appelbaum P and T Grisso. 1995. The MacArthur treatment competence study I: Mental illness and competence to consent to treatment. *Law and Human Behavior* 19:105–126.

Appelbaum P, C Lidz, and A Meisel. 1987. *Informed Consent: Legal Theory and Clinical Practice*. Fair Lawn, NJ: Oxford University Press.

Ascher-Svanum H, D Faries, B Zhu, F Ernst, M Swartz, and J Swanson. 2006. Medication adherence and long-term functional outcomes in the treatment of schizophrenia in usual care. *Journal of Clinical Psychiatry* 67(3):453–460.

Bedford N, S Surguladze, V Giampetro, M Brammer, and A David. 2012. Self-evaluation in schizophrenia: An fMRI study with implications for the understanding of insight. *BioMed Central Psychiatry* 12:106.

Boaz T, M Becker, R Andel, R Van Dorn, J Choi, and M Sikirica. 2013. Risk factors for early readmission to acute care for persons with schizophrenia taking antipsychotic medications. *Psychiatric Services* 64(12):1225–1229.

Bottlender R, T Sato, M Jäger, U Wegener, J Wittmann, A Strauss, and H-J Möller. 2003. The impact of the duration of untreated psychosis prior to first psychotic admission on the 15-year outcome in schizophrenia. *Schizophrenia Research* 62(1–2):37–44.

Brooks R. 2007. Psychiatrists' opinions about involuntary civil commitment: Results of a national survey. *Journal of the American Academy of Psychiatry and the Law* 35(2):219–228.

Brown J. 2003. Is involuntary outpatient commitment a remedy for community mental health service failure? *Ethical Human Sciences and Services* 5(1):7–20.

Bruckner T, J Yoon, T Brown, and N Adams. 2010. Involuntary civil commitments after the implementation of California's mental health services act. *Psychiatric Services* 61(10):1006–1011.

Burns T, J Rugkåsa, A Molodynski, J Dawson, K Yeeles, M Vazquez-Montes, M Voysey, J Sinclair, and S Priebe. 2013. Community treatment orders for patients with psychosis (OCTET): A randomised controlled trial. *Lancet* 381(9878):1627–1633.

Bursten B. 1986. Posthospital mandatory outpatient treatment. *American Journal of Psychiatry* 143(10):1255–1258.

Cairns R, C Maddock, A Buchanan, A David, Pr Hayward, G Richardson, G Szmukler, and M Hotopf. 2005. Prevalence and predictors of mental incapacity in psychiatric in-patients. *British Journal of Psychiatry* 187:379–385.

Cascardi M, N Poythress, and A Hall. 2000. Procedural justice in the context of civil commitment: An analogue study. *Behavioral Sciences and the Law* 18(6):731–740.

Compton S, J Swanson, H Wagner, M Swartz, B Burns, and E Elbogen. 2003. Involuntary outpatient commitment and homelessness in persons with severe mental illness. *Mental Health Services Research* 5(1):27–38.

Cooke M, D Fannon, E Kuipers, E Peters, S Williams, and V Kumari. 2008. Neurological basis of poor insight in psychosis: Avoxel-based MRI study. *Schizophrenia Research* 103(1–3):40–51.

Craig T, P Garety, P Power, N Rahaman, S Colbert, M Fornells-Ambrojo, and G Dunn. 2004. The Lambeth Early Onset (LEO) Team: Randomised controlled trial of the effectiveness of specialised care for early psychosis. *British Medical Journal* 329(7474):1067.

Dale E. 2010. Is supervised community treatment ethically justifiable? *Journal of Medical Ethics* 36(5):271–274.

Dell'Osso L, S Pini, G Cassano, C Mastrocinque, R Seckinger, M Saettoni, A Papasogli, S Yale, and X Amador. 2002. Insight into illness in patients with mania, mixed mania, bipolar depression and major depression with psychotic features. *Bipolar Disorder* 4(5):315–322.

Erickson S. 2005. A retrospective examination of outpatient commitment in New York. *Behavioral Sciences and the Law* 23(5):627–645.

Faget-Agius C, L Boyer, R Padovani, R Richieri, O Mundler, C Lançon, and E Guedj. 2012. Schizophrenia with preserved insight is associated with increased perfusion of the precuneus. *Journal of Psychiatry and Neuroscience* 37(5):297–304.

Flashman LA, TW McAllister, NC Andreasen, and AJ Saykin. 2000. Smaller brain size associated with unawareness of illness in patients with schizophrenia. *American Journal of Psychiatry* 157:1167–1169.

Frank D, J Perry, D Kean, M Sigman, and K Geagea. 2005. Effects of compulsory treatment orders on time to hospital readmission. *Psychiatric Services* 56(7):867–869.

Gianfrancesco F, M Sajatovic, K Rajagopalan, and R-H Wang. 2008. Antipsychotic treatment adherence and associated mental health care use among individuals with bipolar disorder. *Clinical Therapeutics* 30(7):1358–1374.

Gilbert A, L Moser, R Van Dorn, J Swanson, C Wilder, P Robbins, K Keator, H Steadman, and M Swartz. 2010. Reductions in arrest under assisted outpatient treatment in New York. *Psychiatric Services* 61(10):996–999.

Gilmer T, CR Dolder, JP Lacro, DP Folsom, L Lindamer, P Garcia, and DV Jeste. 2004. Adherence to treatment with antipsychotic medication and health care costs among Medicaid beneficiaries with schizophrenia. *American Journal of Psychiatry* 161(4):692–699.

Glick I, S Sharfstein, and H Schwartz. 2011. Inpatient psychiatric care in the 21st century: The need for reform. *Psychiatric Services* 62(2):206–209.

Goldman H, N Adams, and C Taube. 1983. Deinstitutionalization: The data demythologized. *Hospital and Community Psychiatry* 24:129–134.

Greenberg W, L Moore-Duncan, and R Herron. 1996. Patients' attitudes toward having been forcibly medicated. *Bulletin of the American Academy of Psychiatry and the Law* 24:513–524.

Grisso T, and P Appelbaum. 1995a. Comparison of standards for assessing patients' capacities to make treatment decisions. *American Journal of Psychiatry* 152:1033–1037.

Grisso T and P Appelbaum. 1995b. The MacArthur treatment competence study III: Abilities of patients to consent to psychiatric and medical treatment. *Law and Human Behavior* 19:149–174.

Grisso T, P Appelbaum, E Mulvey, and K Fletcher. 1995. The MacArthur treatment competence study II: Measures of abilities related to competence to consent to treatment. *Law and Human Behavior* 19:127–148.

Hassan M and M Lage. 2009. Risk of rehospitalization among bipolar disorder patients who are nonadherent to antipsychotic therapy after hospital discharge. *American Journal of Health-System Pharmacy* 66(4):358–365.

Hiday V and R Goodman. 1982. The least restrictive alternative to involuntary hospitalization, outpatient commitment: Its use and effectiveness. *Journal of Psychiatry and Law* 10:81–96.

Hiday V, M Swartz, J Swanson, R Borum, and H Wagner. 2002. Impact of outpatient commitment on victimization of people with severe mental illness. *American Journal of Psychiatry* 159(8):1403–1411.

Hoge MA and E Grottole. 2000. The case against outpatient commitment. *Journal of the American Academy of Psychiatry and the Law* 28(2):165–170.

Husted J. 1999. Insight in severe mental illness: Implications for treatment decisions. *Journal of the American Academy of Psychiatry and the Law* 27(1):33–49.

Insel T. 2008. Assessing the economic costs of serious mental illness. *American Journal of Psychiatry* 165(6):663–665.

Keefe R. 1998. *The Neurobiology of Disturbances of the Self: Autonoetic Agnosia in Schizophrenia*. New York: Oxford University Press.

Kessler R, P Berglund, M Bruce, J Koch, E Laska, P Leaf, R Manderscheid, R Rosenheck, E Walters, and P Wang. 2001. The prevalence and correlates of untreated serious mental illness. *Health Services Research* 36:987–1007.

King E. 1995. Outpatient civil commitment in North Carolina: Constitutional and policy concerns. *Law and Contemporary Problems* 58(2):251–282.

Kozma C and P Weiden. 2009. Partial compliance with antipsychotics increases mental health hospitalizations in schizophrenic patients: Analysis of a national managed care database. *American Health and Drug Benefits* 2(1):31–38.

Kress, K. 2006. Rotting with their rights on: Why the criteria for ending commitment or restraint of liberty need not be the same as the criteria for initiating commitment or restraint of liberty, and how the restraint may sometimes justifiably continue after its prerequisites are no longer satisfied. *Behavioral Sciences and the Law* 24(4):573–598.

Lage, M and M Hassan. 2009. The relationship between antipsychotic medication adherence and patient outcomes among individuals diagnosed with bipolar disorder: A retrospective study. *Annals of General Psychiatry* 8:7.

Lamb HR and L Weinberger. 2013. Some perspectives on criminalization. *Journal of the American Academy of Psychiatry and the Law* 41(2):287–293.

Link, B, M Epperson, B Perron, D Castille, and L Yang. 2011. Arrest outcomes associated with outpatient commitment in New York State. *Psychiatric Services* 62(5):504–508.

Löffler W, R Kilian, M Toumi, and MC Angermeyer. 2003. Schizophrenic patients' subjective reasons for compliance and noncompliance with neuroleptic treatment. *Pharmacopsychiatry* 36(3):105–112.

Lysaker P, M Bell, R Milstein, G Bryson, and J Beam-Goulet. 1994. Insight and psychosocial treatment compliance in schizophrenia. *Psychiatry* 57(4):307–315.

Lysaker P, M Bell, G Bryson, and E Kaplan. 1997. Neurocognitive function and insight in schizophrenia: Support for an association with impairments in executive function but not with impairments in global function. *Acta Psychiatrica Scandinavica* 97:297–301.

Lysaker P, G Bryson, and M Bell. 2002. Insight and work performance in schizophrenia. *Journal of Nervous and Mental Disease* 190(3):142–146.

Malla A, R Norman, and R Joober. 2005. First-episode psychosis, early-intervention, and outcome: What have we learned? *Canadian Journal of Psychiatry* 50(14): 881–891.

Marcus S and M Olfson. 2008. Outpatient antipsychotic treatment and inpatient costs of schizophrenia. *Schizophrenia Bulletin* 34(1):173–180.

Marková IS and GE Berrios. 1995. Insight in clinical psychiatry revisited. *Comprehensive Psychiatry* 36(5):367–376.

McKenna B, A Simpson, J Coverdale, and T Laidlaw. 2001. An analysis of procedural justice during psychiatric hospital admission. *International Journal of Law and Psychiatry* 24(6):573–581.

McNiel D and R Binder. 2005. Psychiatric emergency service use and homelessness, mental disorder, and violence. *Psychiatric Services* 56(6):699–704.

Miller R. 1987. *Involuntary Civil Commitment of the Mentally Ill in the Post-reform Era*. Springfield, IL: Charles C Thomas.

Miller R. 1988. Outpatient civil commitment of the mentally ill: An overview and an update. *Behavioral Sciences and the Law* 6(1):99–118.

Miller R and P Fiddleman. 1984. Outpatient commitment: Treatment in the least restrictive environment? *Hospital and Community Psychiatry* 35(2):147–151.

Mintz A, K Dobson, and D Romney. 2003. Insight in schizophrenia: A meta-analysis. *Schizophrenia Research* 61(1):75–88.

Mohamed S, S Fleming, D Penn, and W Spaulding. 1999. Insight in schizophrenia: Its relationship to measures of executive functions. *Journal of Nervous and Mental Disease* 187:525–531.

Monahan J, R Bonnie, P Appelbaum, P Hyde, H Steadman, and M Swartz. 2001. Mandated community treatment: Beyond outpatient commitment. *Psychiatric Services* 52(9):1198–1205.

Monahan J, M Schwartz, and R Bonnie. 2003. Mandated treatment in the community for people with mental disorders. *Health Affairs (Millwood)* 22(5):28–38.

Munetz MR, PA Galon, and FJ Frese. 2003. The ethics of mandatory community treatment. *Journal of the American Academy of Psychiatry and the Law* 31(2):173–183.

Munetz MR, T Grande, J Kleist, and GA Peterson. 1996. The effectiveness of outpatient civil commitment. *Psychiatric Services* 47(11):1251–1253.

Nicholson R, C Ekenstam, and S Norwood. 1996. Coercion and the outcome of psychiatric hospitalization. *International Journal of Law and Psychiatry* 19:201–217.

Olfson M, S Marcus, and J Doshi. 2010. Continuity of care after inpatient discharge of patients with schizophrenia in the Medicaid program: A retrospective longitudinal cohort analysis. *Journal of Clinical Psychiatry* 71:831–838.

Olfson M, S Marcus, J Wilk, and J West. 2006. Awareness of illness and non-adherence to antipsychotic medications among persons with schizophrenia. *Psychiatric Services* 57:205–211.

Perkins D, H Gu, K Boteva, and J Lieberman. 2005. Relationship between duration of untreated psychosis and outcome in first-episode schizophrenia: A critical review and meta-analysis. *American Journal of Psychiatry* 162(10):1785–1804.

Petrila J and A Christy. 2008. Florida's outpatient commitment law: A lesson in failed reform? *Psychiatric Services* 59(1):21–23.

Pini S, G Cassano, L Dell'Osso, and X Amador. 2001. Insight into illness in schizophrenia, schizoaffective disorder, and mood disorders with psychotic features. *American Journal of Psychiatry* 158(1):122–125.

Pini S, L Dell'Osso, X Amador, C Mastrocinque, M Saettoni, and G Cassano. 2003. Awareness of illness in patients with bipolar I disorder with or without comorbid anxiety disorders. *Australian and New Zealand Journal of Psychiatry* 37(3):355–361.

Poythress N, J Petrila, A McGaha, and R Boothroyd. 2002. Perceived coercion and procedural justice in the Broward mental health court. *International Journal of Law and Psychiatry* 25:517–533.

Raffard S, S Bayard, D Capdevielle, F Garcia, JP Boulenger, and MC Gely-Nargeot. 2008a. Lack of insight in schizophrenia: A review. *Encephale* 34(5):511–516.

Raffard S, S Bayard, D Capdevielle, F Garcia, JP Boulenger, and MC Gely-Nargeot. 2008b. Lack of insight in schizophrenia: A review. Part I: Theoretical concept, clinical aspects and Amador's model. *Encephale* 34(6):597–605.

Regier D, W Narrow, D Rae, R Manderscheid, B Locke, and F Goodwin. 1993. The de facto mental and addictive disorders service system. Epidemiologic Catchment Area prospective 1-year prevalence rates of disorders and services. *Archives of General Psychiatry* 50(2):85–94.

Ridgely MS, R Borum, and J Petrila. 2001, *The Effectiveness of Involuntary Outpatient Treatment: Empirical Evidence and the Experience of Eight States.* Santa Monica, CA: RAND Corporation.

Rittmannsberger H, T Pachinger, P Keppelmüller, and J Wancata. 2004. Medication adherence among psychotic patients before admission to inpatient treatment. *Psychiatric Services* 55(2):174–179.

Rohland B, J Rohrer, and C Richards. 2000. The long-term effect of outpatient commitment on service use. *Administration and Policy in Mental Health and Mental Health Services Research* 27(6):383–394.

Schopp R. 2003. Outpatient civil commitment: A dangerous charade or a component of a comprehensive institution of civil commitment? *Psychology, Public Policy, and Law* 9(1–2):33–69.

Schwartz H, W Vingiano, and CB Perez. 1988. Autonomy and the right to refuse treatment: Patients' attitudes after involuntary medication. *Hospital and Community Psychiatry* 39:1049–1054.

Segal S. 2012. Civil commitment law, mental health services, and US homicide rates. *Social Psychiatry and Psychiatric Epidemiology* 47(9):1449–1458.

Smith T, J Hull, M Goodman, A Hedayat-Harris, D Willson, L Israel, and R Munich. 1999. The relative influences of symptoms, insight, and neurocognition on social adjustment in schizophrenia and schizoaffective disorder. *Journal of Nervous and Mental Disease* 187(2):102–108.

Steadman H, K Gounis, D Dennis, K Hopper, B Roche, M Swartz, and P Robbins. 2001. Assessing the New York City involuntary outpatient commitment pilot program. *Psychiatric Services* 52(3):330–336.

Stefan S. 1987. Preventive commitment: The concept and its pitfalls. *Mental and Physical Disability Law Reporter* 11(4):288–302.

Stettin B, J Geller, K Ragosta, K Cohen, and J Ghowrwal. 2014, *Mental Health Commitment Laws: A Survey of the States,* Research from the Treatment Advocacy Center.

http://www.tacreports.org/storage/documents/2014-state-survey-abridged.pdf, accessed August 11, 2014.

Sun S, G Liu, D Christensen, and A Fu. 2007. Review and analysis of hospitalization costs associated with antipsychotic nonadherence in the treatment of schizophrenia in the United States. *Current Medical Research and Opinion* 23(10):2305–2312.

Svarstad B, T Shireman, and J Sweeney. 2001. Using drug claims data to assess the relationship of medication adherence with hospitalization and costs. *Psychiatric Services* 52(6):805–811.

Swanson J and M Swartz. 2014. Why the evidence for outpatient commitment is good enough. *Psychiatric Services* 65(6):808–811.

Swanson J, M Swartz, R Borum, V Hiday, H Wagner, and B Burns. 2000. Involuntary out-patient commitment and reduction of violent behaviour in persons with severe mental illness. *British Journal of Psychiatry* 176:324–331.

Swanson J, M Swartz, E Elbogen, H Wagner, and B Burns. 2003. Effects of involuntary outpatient commitment on subjective quality of life in persons with severe mental illness. *Behavioral Sciences and the Law* 21(4):473–491.

Swanson J, M Swartz, L George, B Burns, V Hiday, R Borum, and H Wagner. 1997. Interpreting the effectiveness of involuntary outpatient commitment: A conceptual model. *Journal of American Academy of Psychiatry* 25(1):5–16.

Swanson J, R Van Dorn, M Swartz, A Cislo, C Wilder, L Moser, A Gilbert, and T McGuire. 2010. Robbing Peter to pay Paul: Did New York State's outpatient commitment program crowd out voluntary service recipients? *Psychiatric Services* 61(10):988–995.

Swanson J, R Van Dorn, M Swartz, P Robbins, H Steadman, T McGuire, and J Monahan. 2013. The cost of assisted outpatient treatment: Can it save states money? *American Journal of Psychiatry* 170(12):1423–1432.

Swartz M, J Swanson, H Steadman, P Robbins, and J Monahan. 2009. *New York State Assisted Outpatient Treatment Program Evaluation*. Durham, NC: Duke University School of Medicine.

Swartz M and J Swanson. 2013. Economic grand rounds: Can states implement involuntary outpatient commitment within existing state budgets? *Psychiatric Services* 64(1):7–9.

Swartz M, J Swanson, V Hiday, H Wagner, B Burns, and R Borum. 2001a. A randomized controlled trial of outpatient commitment in North Carolina. *Psychiatric Service* 52(3):325–329.

Swartz M, J Swanson, H Wagner, B Burns, and V Hiday. 2001b. Effects of involuntary outpatient commitment and depot antipsychotics on treatment adherence in persons with severe mental illness. *Journal of Nervous and Mental* Disease 189(9):583–592.

Swartz M, J Swanson, H Wagner, B Burns, V Hiday, and R Borum. 1999. Can involuntary outpatient commitment reduce hospital recidivism?: Findings from a randomized trial with severely mentally ill individuals. *American Journal of Psychiatry* 156(12):1968–1975.

Swartz M, J Swanson, H Wagner, M Hannon, B Burns, and M Shumway. 2003. Assessment of four stakeholder groups' preferences concerning outpatient commitment for persons with schizophrenia. *American Journal of Psychiatry* 160(6):1139–1146.

Swartz M, H Wagner, J Swanson, and E Elbogen. 2004. Consumers' perceptions of the fairness and effectiveness of mandated community treatment and related pressures. *Psychiatric Services* 55(7):780–785.

Swartz M, H Wagner, J Swanson, V Hiday, and B Burns. 2002. The perceived coerciveness of involuntary outpatient commitment: Findings from an experimental study. *Journal of the American Academy of Psychiatry and the Law* 30(2):207–217.

Swartz M, C Wilder, J Swanson, R Van Dorn, P Robbins, H Steadman, L Moser, A Gilbert, and J Monahan. 2010. Assessing outcomes for consumers in New York's assisted outpatient treatment program. *Psychiatric Services* 61(10):976–981.

Torrey E, D Fuller, J Geller, C Jacobs, and K Ragosta. 2012. *No Room at the Inn: Trends and Consequences of Closing Public Psychiatric Hospitals*, Treatment Advocacy Center. http://tacreports.org/storage/documents/no_room_at_the_inn-2012.pdf, accessed August 9, 2014.

Torrey E and M Zdanowicz. 2001. Outpatient commitment: What, why, and for whom. *Psychiatric Services* 52(3):337–341.

Tsai G. 2012. Assisted outpatient treatment: Preventive, recovery-based care for the most seriously mentally ill. *American Journal of Psychiatry: The Resident's Journal* 7(6):16–18.

Turkington D, D Kingdon, and T Turner. 2002. Effectiveness of a brief cognitive-behavioural therapy intervention in the treatment of schizophrenia. *British Journal of Psychiatry* 180:523–527.

Tyler T. 1992. The psychological consequences of judicial procedures: Implications for civil commitment hearings. *Southern Methodist University Law Review* (1992):433–448.

van der Meer L, A de Vos, A Stiekema, G Pijnenborg, M-J van Tol, W Nolen, A Davis, and A Aleman. 2013. Insight in schizophrenia: Involvement of self-reflection networks? *Schizophrenia Bulletin* 39(6):1288–1295.

Van Dorn R, J Swanson, M Swartz, C Wilder, L Moser, A Gilbert, A Cislo, and P Robbins. 2010. Continuing medication and hospitalization outcomes after assisted outpatient treatment in New York. *Psychiatric Services* 61(10):982–987.

Van Putten R, J Santiago, and M Berren. 1988. Involuntary outpatient commitment in Arizona: A retrospective study. *Hospital and Community Psychiatry* 39(9):953–958.

Wagner H, M Swartz, J Swanson, and B Burns. 2003. Does involuntary outpatient commitment lead to more intensive treatment? *Psychology, Public Policy, and Law* 9(1–2):145–158.

Wang P, M Lane, M Olfson, H Pincus, K Wells, and R Kessler. 2005. Twelve month use of mental health services in the United States. *Archives of General Psychiatry* 62(6):629–640.

Watson A, P Hanrahan, D Luchins, and A Lurigio. 2001. Mental health courts and the complex issue of mentally ill offenders. *Psychiatric Services* 52(4):477–481.

Winick B. 1997. Mandatory treatment: An examination of therapeutic jurisprudence. *New Directions for Mental Health Services* 75:27–34.

Winick B. 2003. Outpatient commitment: A therapeutic jurisprudence analysis. *Psychology, Public Policy, and Law* 9(1–2):107–144.

Wu E, H Birnbaum, L Shi, D Ball, R Kessler, M Moulis, and J Aggarwal. 2005. The economic burden of schizophrenia in the United States in 2002. *Journal of Clinical Psychiatry* 66(9):1122–1129.

Young D, K Zakzanis, C Bailey, R Davila, J Griese, G Sartory, and A Thom. 1998. Further parameters of insight and neuropsychological deficit in schizophrenia and other chronic mental disease. *Journal of Nervous and Mental Disease* 186:44–50.

Zanni GR and L DeVeau. 1986. A research note on the use of outpatient commitment. *Hospital and Community Psychiatry* 37:941–942.

Zanni GR and PF Stavis. 2007. The effectiveness and ethical justification of psychiatric outpatient commitment. *American Journal of Bioethics* 7(11):31–41.

17

The right to treatment

JEFFREY L. GELLER

INTRODUCTION

The right to treatment was born in the early 1960s, its progenitor the decades of parlous neglect of patients in America's public psychiatric institutions through the mid-twentieth century. Kenneth Appel, MD, chairperson of the mental hospitals committee of the Group for the Advancement of Psychiatry, proclaimed in 1947, "Automobiles get better attention than most mental patients today. The grass surrounding the state hospitals receives more care and consideration than the patients inside" (Deutsch 1948, 98). In his 1958 presidential address to the American Psychiatric Association (APA), Harry Solomon indicated that "the large mental hospital is antiquated, outmoded, and rapidly becoming obsolete. We can build them but we cannot staff them…they are bankrupt beyond remedy" (Solomon 1958, 7).

Much of the right-to-treatment litigation has focused on establishing standards of care and concomitant staffing patterns. In the 1940s, the APA maintained that there should be no less than one psychiatrist for every 150 hospitalized patients, one graduate nurse for every 40 patients, and one attendant for every 8 patients, but no state hospital of the day met all the APA's standards (Deutsch 1948).

The history of the right to treatment is that of a moral position casting about for legal grounding. The right to treatment has been variously based on the Eighth Amendment (cruel and unusual punishment), the Fourteenth Amendment (both the Due Process and the Equal Protection Clauses), the "quid pro quo" rationale (i.e., treatment is due to civilly committed patients in exchange for enforced confinement), and the "least restrictive alternative" doctrine ("deprivations of liberty solely because of dangers to ill persons themselves should not go beyond what is necessary for their protection") (*Lake v. Cameron* 1966, 660). Further, courts have struggled with clearly defining *treatment*, differentiating between *treatment* and *habilitation*, and distinguishing between the rights and needs of persons with mental illness and those with developmental disabilities.

INSTITUTIONAL TREATMENT

The early years: 1960–1974

The right to treatment was articulated initially by Morton Birnbaum, a lawyer and physician, who argued in 1960:

> If the right to treatment were to be recognized, our substantive constitutional law would then include the concepts that if a person is involuntarily institutionalized in a mental institution because he is sufficiently mentally ill to require institutionalization for care and treatment, he needs, and is entitled to, adequate medical treatment; that an institution that involuntarily institutionalizes the mentally ill without giving them adequate medical treatment for their mental illness is a mental prison; and that substantive due process of law does not allow a mentally ill person who has committed no crime to be deprived of his liberty by indefinitely institutionalizing him in a mental prison. (Birnbaum 1960, 503)

The first tests of Birnbaum's theory were in criminal committees. In *Rouse v. Cameron* (1966), Judge Bazelon found that a District of Columbia statute mandated treatment for a patient committed after a finding of not guilty by reason of insanity. Judge Bazelon postulated, however, that there could be constitutional violations in confinement without treatment, noting the Eighth and Fourteenth Amendments. He further remarked that the "hospital need not show that the treatment will cure or improve him, but only that there is a bona fide effort to do so" (*Rouse v. Cameron* 1966, 456). In *Nason v. Superintendent of Bridgewater State Hospital* (1968), the Supreme Judicial Court of Massachusetts found a constitutional right to treatment for a patient found incompetent to stand trial and whose further court proceedings required his return to competence. This court grounded its decision in the Due Process Clause of the Fourteenth Amendment.

The right to treatment was first applied to civilly committed patients in *Wyatt v. Stickney* (1971), initially a U.S. District Court case (eventually affirmed by the Eleventh Circuit Court of Appeals), which challenged the deplorable conditions in the Alabama state hospitals. In a series of far-reaching decisions, Judge Johnson adopted the theory articulated in *Rouse v. Cameron*. In the third *Wyatt* decision, Judge Johnson indicated that Alabama had failed to provide "(1) a humane psychological and physical environment; (2) qualified staff in numbers sufficient to administer adequate treatment; and (3) individualized treatment plans" (*Wyatt v. Stickney* 1972, 375). The court delineated "Minimum Constitutional Standards for Adequate Treatment of the Mentally Ill" for each of these three areas, outlining in great detail the minimal standards that the state would be required to meet. The staffing standards are of particular interest.

Other courts adopted Judge Bazelon's analysis and findings, applying them to institutions for the "mentally retarded." In *New York State Association for Retarded Children v. Rockefeller* (1973), the so-called "Willowbrook case," the court found that institutionalized mentally retarded persons had a right to protection from harm but no clear right to treatment. To this point, no case had been heard by the U.S. Supreme Court.

U.S. Supreme Court: 1975–1982

During this time period, the U.S. Supreme Court had three major opportunities to determine that a "right to treatment" existed, but declined to do so. In *O'Connor v. Donaldson* (1975), Justice Stewart, writing for the majority of the Supreme Court, indicated that

> There is no reason now to decide whether mentally ill persons dangerous to themselves or to others have a right to treatment...this case raises a single, relatively simple but nonetheless important question concerning every man's constitutional right to liberty. (*O'Connor v. Donaldson* 1975, 573)

Rather, the Court found:

> A state cannot constitutionally confine without more a non-dangerous individual who is capable of surviving safely in freedom by himself or with the help of willing and responsible family members or friends. (Ibid., 576)

To emphasize the absence of a finding of a right to treatment, in a concurring opinion Chief Justice Burger held:

> no other basis for equating an involuntarily committed mental patient's unquestioned constitutional right not to be confined without due process of law with a constitutional right to treatment. (*O'Connor v. Donaldson* 1975, 587–588, emphasis in original)

However, although Chief Justice Burger's opinion appears to reject the concept of a right to treatment, the majority opinion, while failing to find such a right, does not explicitly reject it either. In fact, the use of the phrase "without more" has been interpreted by some to mean that nondangerous individuals cannot be hospitalized involuntarily *without treatment*. Hence, lower courts could, and have, considered the right in subsequent litigation.

Having failed explicitly to find a right to treatment for the mentally ill, the Supreme Court turned its attention to the mentally retarded. In *Halderman v. Pennhurst State School and Hospital* (1977), the U.S. District Court held:

> that when a state involuntarily commits retarded persons, it must provide them a reasonable opportunity to acquire and maintain those life skills necessary to cope as effectively as their capacities permit.

The Supreme Court again did not find a constitutional basis for a right to treatment or habilitation, but rather determined in this case that the Developmental Disabilities Assistance and Bill of Rights Act (an act establishing a federal–state grant program) did not guarantee to institutionalized mentally retarded persons any such rights (*Pennhurst State School and Hospital v. Halderman* 1981).

In *Youngberg v. Romeo* (1982), the Supreme Court did finally address the substantive due process rights of mentally retarded persons involuntarily committed to institutions. The Court specifically addressed whether such persons had rights under the Fourteenth Amendment to "(i) safe conditions of confinement; (ii) freedom from bodily restraint; and (iii) training or 'habilitation'" (*Youngberg v. Romeo* 1982, 309). The Court opined:

> Respondent has constitutionally protected liberty interests under the Due Process Clause of the Fourteenth Amendment to reasonably safe conditions of confinement, freedom from unreasonable bodily restraints, and such minimally adequate training as reasonably may be required by their interests.... And in determining what is "reasonable," courts must show deference to the judgment exercised by a qualified professional, whose decision is presumptively valid. (*Youngberg v. Romeo* 1982, 307)

The "training" aspect of this case appeared to particularly interest members of the Court. Justice Blackmun, in a concurring opinion, articulated that the level of training should be "that habilitation or training necessary to *preserve* those basic self-care skills he possessed when he first entered Pennhurst" (*Youngberg v. Romeo* 1982, 327, emphasis in original). On the other hand, in his concurring opinion, Chief Justice Burger wrote:

> I would hold flatly that respondent has no constitutional right to training, or "habitation," per se.... I agree with the court that some amount of self-care instruction may be necessary to avoid unreasonable infringement of a mentally retarded person's interests in safety and freedom from restraint, but it seems clear to me that the Constitution does not otherwise place an affirmative duty on the state to provide any particular kind of training or habilitation – even such as might be encompassed under the essentially standardless rubric "minimally adequate training" to which the Court refers. (Ibid., 329–330)

Immediately post-*Youngberg*: 1983–1990

The Supreme Court did much less than those who championed the right-to-treatment cause would have hoped. Even before the Supreme Court issued decisions regarding these cases, psychiatrists with particular expertise in these matters were doubtful of the usefulness of the judicial process for ensuring this right. Stone (1975) argued, "The right to treatment cannot come from complicated judicial discourse about civil rights and about civil liberties." Roth (1977) lamented, "I do not believe that the so-called right-to-treatment laws will ever provide the help that physicians hoped they would in ensuring that patients receive needed and effective treatment."

The "right to treatment" continued to struggle throughout this period. Litigation in federal court attempting to broaden *Youngberg* is best exemplified by the long struggle between Morton Birnbaum and the state of New York, which began as *Woe v. Matthews* (1976) and ended as *Foe v. Cuomo* (1989). The major advances in the right to treatment in the 1980s occurred pursuant to the Civil Rights of Institutionalized Persons Act (CRIPA) of 1980. This act authorizes the U.S. government to institute a civil action against any state whose officials, employees, or those acting on their behalf are "subjecting persons residing in or confined to an institution to egregious or flagrant conditions which deprive such persons of any rights, privileges, or immunities secured or protected by the Constitution or laws of the United States causing such persons to suffer grievous harm" (Civil Rights of Institutionalized Persons Act, 42 U.S.C. Sec. 1997 et seq.). Under this authority, the Civil Rights Division of the U.S. Justice Department has been able to bring the right to treatment substantially closer to a reality for thousands of individuals in state psychiatric hospitals and in developmental disabilities/mental retardation facilities. It has done so by applying the standards of *Youngberg*, and has accomplished its end largely through the vehicle of consent decrees. One can ascertain the progress that made by comparing the staffing parameters of the *Wyatt* case, the first consent decree in 1984 (*United States v. Indiana* 1984), with a consent decree initiated in the late 1980s (*United States v. Hawaii* 1991).

ADA and *Wyatt*: 1990–2003

The Americans with Disabilities Act (ADA), passed on July 26, 1990, establishes "a clear and comprehensive prohibition of discrimination on the basis of disability." The Act has four major components: Title I applies to employment; Title II to public services; Title III to accommodations required of private entities; and Title IV to telecommunication services. Enforcement entities vary by Title. Title I is enforced by the Equal Employment Opportunity Commission (EEOC); Titles II–IV are enforced by specific government agencies, such as Department of Housing and Urban Development's enforcing of public housing; and the U.S. Department of Justice's (USDOJ's) enforcing all areas of Titles II–IV not enforced by any other federal agency (Wylonis 1999). Title II is of greatest interest in the area of "right to treatment," in that this title covers state and local government services and therefore includes state and county psychiatric hospitals (ADA 1990).

The part of Title II most pertinent to the right to treatment is contained in Section 12132, which indicates, "no qualified individual with a disability shall, by reason of such disability, be excluded from participation in or be denied the benefits of the services, programs, or activities of a public entity, or be subject to discrimination by any such entity." The "integration regulation," one of many regulations that were required to be promulgated to operationalize this Act, states, "A public entity shall administer services, programs, and activities in the most integrated setting appropriate to the needs of qualified individuals with disabilities" (28 C.F.R. 35.130(d)). The "reasonable-modifications" regulation states that public entities must make "reasonable modifications" in order not to discriminate "'on the basis of disability." However, these public entities are not required to "fundamentally alter" the nature of their programs (28 C.F.R. 35.130(b)(7)).

Although the ADA addresses public institutions, it generally was not viewed as a way to improve services within state and county psychiatric hospitals, but rather as a way to force states to transition patients out of these institutions. The ADA has been a vehicle that has helped to further the now five-decade-old movement of patients from institutional to noninstitutional settings, which are collectively generally referred to as "in the community" (Geller 2000a).

With regard to the *Wyatt* case, on January 20, 2000, all parties reached a settlement agreement; a fairness hearing was held on May 4, 2000, and a decision was reached on July 13, 2000. The settlement agreement endorsed by the court included the following components:

1. Accreditation: All mental illness facilities must maintain Joint Commission on Accreditation of Health-Care Organizations (JCAHO) accreditation.
2. Advocacy programs: All mental illness facilities must maintain an advocacy staff to educate patients about rights, investigate complaints of rights violations, and monitor conditions of facilities and certified community programs.
3. Census reduction: Specific target census reductions were set, but no facility closures were required.
4. Community placement: Facilities were required to develop and implement a plan for "out-placements" and concurrently increase community-based placements and services.
5. Public education: States were required to institute a comprehensive, state-wide plan to enhance the public's appreciation for the abilities, needs, and rights of persons with mental illness.
6. Quality improvement: Facilities must maintain adherence to current policy and procedures and continue Continuous Quality Improvement Systems.
7. Safety and protection: Facilities must respond in a timely manner to allegations of abuse and neglect with trained employees using standard procedures.
8. Treatment and habilitation: Alabama Disabilities Advocacy Program can have input into individualized treatment plans, and consultants will be hired to address special needs populations (e.g., the dually diagnosed mental illness/mental retardation, organic/brain injured, physically handicapped, HIV/AIDS, self-injurious, others) and to review and make recommendations concerning the use of seclusion and restraint (*Wyatt v. Sawyer* 2000).

Although the 2000 settlement agreement in the *Wyatt* case specifically addresses conditions in the state facilities of Alabama, it also addresses institutional downsizing, expansion of community services, and the monitoring of some of these community services. This settlement agreement was scheduled to end when all parties agreed that Alabama had completed "certain obligation undertaken in the agreement" (*Wyatt v. Sawyer* 2000). On December 5, 2003, Judge Myron Thompson held a fairness hearing. In this hearing, he determined that the state had complied with the 2000 settlement agreement. As a result, the *Wyatt* case was terminated after over 30 years of ongoing litigation. Mental health professionals and their professional organizations will continue to monitor with great interest if and how treatment for those with serious mental illness is actually advanced through this and other litigation.

As a footnote to this era, it is worth noting that CRIPA is still active law in the United States, although new wrinkles have appeared. States are continuing to enter into settlement agreements with "Plans for Continuous Improvement." Newer agreements generally proffer somewhat different requirements than earlier consent decrees. In 1999, Hawaii changed course in its efforts to improve Hawaii State Hospital, announcing its intent to alter the nature of the hospital by modifying it into a "secure rehabilitation facility" (Act 119, 1999 State of Hawaii Legislature). In 2000, amid litigation, Florida announced (*Johnson v. Murphy* 1987) that it would close the state hospital that was the subject of a suit (Krueger 2000) and did, in fact, close that hospital in 2002.

The end of *Wyatt* to the present

The *Wyatt* case, which ended in 2003 after over 30 years of litigation, serves as an example of judicial oversight and continued monitoring as a means to verify states' compliance in improving the conditions in their facilities. With regard to institutional treatment since *Wyatt*, although the ADA helped promote "community treatment," reformers' focus currently remains on conditions within these institutions. According to Fisher et al. (2009), a major focus of mental health policy over the past 50 years has been closing state psychiatric hospitals. There has been a 95% reduction in the country's state hospital population. Despite this, over 200 state hospitals remain operational in the United States (Fisher et al. 2009). One study found that 50 long-term state hospital beds per 100,000 population are needed (Torrey et al. 2008). However, in 2010 only 14.1 beds per 100,000 population were available (Torrey et al. 2012). Lamb and Weinberger (2013) reported that a significant number of individuals who may otherwise meet criteria for acute psychiatric hospitalization are, instead, incarcerated, possibly because of the dearth of state hospital beds. "Deinstitutionalization" legislation has helped facilitate the release of many individuals from state hospitals but has also demonstrated that community mental health systems are not perfectly equipped to help ensure a smooth transition from institution to community for these individuals. (Deinstitutionalization legislation obviously increased the number of individuals in the community who required ongoing mental health treatment.) In fact, many observers have noted that state hospitals may be necessary entities to provide care to specific subsets of the "seriously mentally ill" population (e.g., forensic committees). As a result, 2003–2013 may represent the first decade since the start of deinstitutionalization during which there has not been a continuous flow of patients out of state hospitals.

The ADA was amended in 2008 with the passage of the ADA Amendments Act (ADAAA), which became effective on January 1, 2009. The ADAAA was a response to multiple decisions by the U.S. Supreme Court that had interpreted the ADA's original text. The ADAAA explicitly overrode those decisions and rejected portions of the regulations published by the EEOC. Although this Act kept the same definition of disability as the original ADA (i.e., "physical or mental impairment that substantially limits one or more major life activities of such individual…"), it changed the manner in which certain statutory terms, such as "'substantially limits," should be interpreted. It also expanded the definition of "'major life activities." In effect, it both broadened and clarified the definition of "disability," with likely implications on the number of individuals covered by the ADA (ADAAA Summary and Resources 2009). An increase in the number of individuals covered by the ADA may lead to an increased funding requirement to continue current programs' compliance with the ADA.

CRIPA remains active 30 years after its introduction. However, its future impact on state institutions is unclear. It has been reported (Geller and Lee 2013) that the "findings letters" generated by the DOJ in psychiatric hospital CRIPA cases, which usually contain recommended remedial measures for state institutions, "were often cut and pasted from one Findings Letter to another, with limited variation in the recommendation." As of January 2009, the last month that President George W. Bush was in office, the Department of Justice had a total of six settlement agreements in various states across the country, including Hawaii, Washington, South Carolina, Connecticut, California, and Tennessee (Shapiro 2009). Last-minute settlement agreements do not necessarily reflect meaningful progress, but do offer the opportunity to foster change. As of the end of fiscal year 2011–2012, the special litigation section of the Civil Rights Division of the DOJ, which enforces CRIPA, "had active CRIPA matters and cases involving 163 facilities in 32 states, the District of Columbia, the Commonwealths of Puerto Rico and the Northern Mariana Islands, and the Territories of Guam and the Virgin Islands" (DOJ 2011).

When discussing institutional treatment, it is important to remember that it does not just occur in the United States, but also in multiple other nations. Over the past decade, the World Health Organization (WHO) has published educational materials on mental health and human rights violations. The WHO has discussed the absence of community mental health treatment services and its impact on the ongoing institutionalization of those with mental illness. In 2008, the United Nations Convention on the Rights of Persons with Disabilities (CRPD) was developed and was considered a "major step forward in promoting and protecting the rights of people with mental disabilities" (WHO 2007).

COMMUNITY TREATMENT

The right to treatment in the community initially was based on the right to treatment in the "least restrictive alternative" (LRA), a doctrine first articulated in mental health cases by Judge David Bazelon in *Lake v. Cameron* (1966). That landmark case prohibited commitment if less "restrictive" treatment alternatives were possible. Although LRA is a convoluted concept at best (Hoffman and Foust 1977; Gutheil et al. 1983; Munetz and Geller 1993; Fisher et al. 1995), it has provided the basis for extending the right to treatment through both state statutes and the federal courts.

Most states have statutes conferring a right to appropriate treatment and services, and many states have statutes that explicitly address a right to treatment in the LRA (Beis 1984; Brakel et al. 1985). In *Dixon v. Weinberger* (1975), a case involving the patients of Saint Elizabeth's Hospital in the District of Columbia, the court, in basing its decision on statutory grounds (the District of Columbia Hospitalization of the Mentally Ill Act), found that patients were guaranteed a right to treatment and that this right was no less than a right to treatment in the LRA. Unfortunately, throughout most of its existence, the *Dixon* case has resulted in considerably more process than outcome (Armstrong 1979; *Dixon v. Sullivan* 1989; Advocates welcome agreement… 2000). Through a consent order in late winter of 2000, however, it was hoped that returning the mental health system to the District (by ending the receivership) would hasten compliance with the 25-year-old court decision (*Dixon v. Miller* 2000; Miller 2000).

In Arizona, the Superior Court of Arizona ruled in *Arnold v. Sarn* (1985, 40) that pursuant to state statute, the Arizona Department of Health Services, the Arizona State Hospital, and the Maricopa County Board of Supervisors were obligated to provide "a continuum of care" through a "unified and cohesive system of community mental health care that is well integrated." This "continuum" was defined by the court as including case management, residential services, day treatment, outreach, medications, outpatient counseling, crisis stabilization, mobile crisis services, socialization, recreation, work adjustment, and transportation. Santiago (Santiago et al. 1986; Santiago 1987) cogently summarized this process in Arizona through the mid-1980s.

The plaintiff class and the state of Arizona and Maricopa County entered into a supplemental agreement in December 1998. As a result of this agreement, the defendants are required to complete a "needs assessment" on a sample of class members; determine the services necessary to meet these needs and the methodology to create these services; develop interim and long-term plans for the operation of clinical teams; and create standards and conduct performance reviews (*Arnold v. ADHS* 1998). By August 1999, a study of the mental health services needs of class members had been completed by the Human Services Research Institute of Cambridge, Massachusetts (Personal communication, H. Stephen Leff to Ronald Smith, August 6, 1999). The 2000 Independent Audit Report of the Office of the Monitor found that "only modest substantive progress has been made in the areas of assessment, service planning, service provision, or adequate monitoring by the clinical teams" (*Arnold v. Sarn* 2000, I) and refers to these results as "disheartening." In 2004, an audit released by the Office of the Monitor revealed that Arizona was out-of-compliance with requirements set forth in *Arnold v. Sarn* (Senate Research 2009). Fast forward to 2010; because of the state's budget crisis, the Superior Court of the State of Arizona issued an order regarding joint stipulation to stay litigation in the case during the fiscal budget crisis (O'Connor 2010). This resulted in a freeze in funding for the Office of the Monitor, which had been the only mechanism by which to evaluate the state's compliance. Following the end of the stay, an agreement was entered into May 2012. As of 2013, the 30-year-old *Arnold v. ADHS* (Sarn) case remains open.

One of the most far-reaching cases to date, in terms of its outcome, has been *Brewster v. Dukakis* (1976). Plaintiffs brought an action against the Commonwealth of Massachusetts claiming violations of state statutes and federal entitlements and asserting their right to be treated in the LRA. Two years later, a consent decree was signed (*Brewster v. Dukakis* 1978) that mandated a "comprehensive community mental health and retardation system to include no less than residential environments; non-residential treatment, training, and support programs; and management services to coordinate and monitor the network of environments and programs." The consent decree focused on those persons of western Massachusetts who had been, were, or could be patients at the Northampton State Hospital. Although the overall outcomes have been mixed (Geller et al. 1990a,b; Geller 1991a), some achievements have been remarkable. A decade after the consent decree was signed, every patient in the hospital on the day of the signing had been discharged at least once (Geller et al. 1990). In the area covered by the consent decree, the Commonwealth of Massachusetts managed to establish the best-funded community residential system in the United States (Geller and Fisher 1991). And 10 years after the decree took effect, the attorney who brought the suit concluded, "By most accounts, few persons are still institutionalized in western Massachusetts or are at risk of hospitalization as a result of a lack of an appropriate, less restrictive alternative" (Schwartz and Costanzo 1987, 1400).

Currently, the major changes in community-based treatment are being fuelled by courts' applications of the ADA to persons in psychiatric institutions. Prior to the first case heard by the U.S. Supreme Court, there were a series of cases in lower federal courts that essentially found that persons with mental illnesses must receive care and treatment in community settings where professional judgment finds such treatment to be appropriate (Petrila 1999). An interesting example of such cases is *Kathleen S. v. Department of Public Welfare* (1998, 1999), a Pennsylvania case that focused on the closing of Haverford State Hospital. The thrust of the case was: Which, if any, patients could be transferred to Norristown State Hospital (another Pennsylvania state hospital)? The court divided the patients into three subclasses and found the following:

- Those identified by the state as appropriate for community placement now—placement immediately.
- Those identified by the state as "placeable" during the next three years—place all within 1.5 years.
- Those identified by the state as not "placeable" and requiring hospital level of care—transfer to Norristown State Hospital, but conduct independent evaluations by a psychologist or psychiatrist within 6 months to determine appropriateness for community treatment.

The state appealed the decision. The ultimate outcome was a settlement agreement between the two parties that made no changes for the first subclass, extended the date for the second subclass by 3 months, and indicated that all members of the third subclass identified as appropriate for community services would receive them no later than 6 months after the "determination of appropriateness" deadline. This case not only supported the right to community-based care and treatment, but established quite ambitious time frames for the state to accomplish this objective.

The case of *Olmstead v. L.C.* (1999) is the hallmark U.S. Supreme Court decision to date on the application of the ADA to persons in state hospitals. The case involved two women with mental retardation—one of whom also had schizophrenia and the other of whom was diagnosed with a personality disorder—who were being kept in a Georgia state hospital despite the fact that treatment professionals had concluded each could be appropriately treated in community-based programs. The Supreme Court, in a 6–3 decision, found that for any person with a mental disability, community-based treatment rather than institutional placement is required of the states when: "(1) the state's treatment professionals have determined that community placement is appropriate; (2) the transfer from institutional care to a less restrictive setting is not opposed by the affected individual; and (3) the community placement can be reasonably accommodated, taking into account the resources available to the state and the needs of others with mental disabilities" (*Olmstead v. L.C.* 1999, 607). The majority found that the "unjustified isolation...[of persons with mental disabilities] is properly regarded as discrimination based on disability" (*Olmstead v. L.C.* 1999, 597). This finding is rooted in the majority's opinion that "institutional placement of persons who can handle and benefit from community settings perpetuates unwarranted assumptions that persons so isolated are incapable or unworthy of participating in community life" (*Olmstead v. L.C.* 1999, 600) and that institutional confinement "severely diminishes the everyday life activities of individuals, including family relations, social contacts, work options, economic independence, educational advancement, and cultural enrichment" (*Olmstead v. L.C.* 1999, 601).

In the past, commentators have noted that the decision is "vague," "weak," and "fractured" (Herbert and Young 1999). Others have remarked that "the decision is unlikely to precipitate the widespread creation of community-based services for persons with mental disabilities" (Appelbaum 1999). After the *Olmstead v. L.C* case, there were a number of lawsuits challenging institutionalization of individuals with psychiatric, physical, and/or developmental disabilities. The DOJ has participated in, filed, or joined "*Olmstead* suits" in 21 states (Bagenstos 2012). In 2009, the Department of Justice's Civil Rights Division decided to enhance enforcement of the Supreme Court's decision in *Olmstead v. L.C.* President Barack Obama introduced "The Year of Community Living" and directed the Administration to increase enforcement efforts (Office of the Press Secretary, The White House, 2009). In 2010, the Department of Justice settled a long-running dispute with the state of Georgia in the *Olmstead* case. The state agreed to spend $77 million over the next 2 years to set up community-based care for up to several thousand people with mental illness and disabilities who then lived in state institutions (Shapiro 2010). Funding has been just one of the obstacles preventing the *Olmstead* decision from fully realizing its presumptive intended effects regarding community treatment. In 2012, Assistant Attorney General Thomas E. Perez stated, "More than a decade after *Olmstead*, many individuals across the country who can live in the community and want to live in the community remain unnecessarily institutionalized."

The Affordable Care Act (ACA) also may improve funding and access to community treatment. The ACA reportedly will allow an additional 32 million individuals to obtain mental health or substance use disorder (MH/SUD) benefits. Beginning in 2014, the ACA requires all new small group and individual private market plans to cover MH/SUD services as part of the health-care law's "Essential Health Benefits" category, and insurers are required to cover mental health benefits at the same level as medical and surgical benefits. This builds on parity requirements set forth in the 2008 Mental Health Parity and Addiction Equity Act (MHPAEA). The MHPAEA specifies that "the financial requirements and treatment limitations imposed on mental health and substance use disorder benefits cannot be more restrictive than the predominant financial requirements and treatment limitations that apply to substantially all medical and surgical benefits" (U.S. Department of Labor 2013). In addition, under the ACA, insurers will no longer be allowed to deny individuals coverage because of pre-existing mental health conditions. The ADA, MHPAEA, and ACA are legislative vehicles designed to benefit a number of individuals, including those with physical or mental disabilities. It is not yet clear if the goals of these pieces of legislation will be realized.

SUMMARY

Where is the "right to treatment" at this point? Perhaps its status can best be described as "evolving." To whatever degree services in community settings are improved, the number of individuals who are in institutions, but would be appropriate for care and treatment outside of institutions, continues to expand. A court decision stirred the winds of change by finding that an individual can make claims simultaneously under the ADA and under law governing Social Security Disability Insurance (Broadman 2000). Meanwhile, Alberta Lessard, the plaintiff named in *Lessard v. Schmidt* (1972)—a case that addresses the bases for and procedures of civil commitment—has failed several times over the years to obtain care and treatment from the public psychiatric system in Milwaukee. This is because, in a system of downsized acute inpatient treatment, "they said I wasn't sick enough," said Ms. Lessard (Mental-illness ruling hinders patients 2000).

Although there is significant activity around the right to treatment, a universal definition of the term is not agreed on. The concept "least restrictive alternative" was never adequately defined (Munetz and Geller 1993); the concept "most integrated setting" uses new language but is equally inadequately defined. If an individual has a right to "community-based services," do we not need to define "'services" and "community" (Geller 1991b, 2000b)? Until such definitions are clear, and until such services are uniformly a reality, the right to treatment remains what, in current parlance, could be referred to as an "unfunded mandate"; this "right" remains simply an unfulfilled promise for persons who would be the beneficiaries of it. When the entities that govern the judicial and funding processes are simultaneously the enforcers of said policies, there are bound to be barriers to progress. Challenges remain related to altering state mental health systems in an effort to improve/increase the right to treatment through judicial means (without addressing funding); developing viable implementation strategies; and defining scope of coverage (Feng 2012). These challenges ensure that this will continue to be an arduous process.

SUMMARY KEY POINTS

- The right to treatment has been variously based on the Eighth Amendment (proscription against cruel and unusual punishment), the Fourteenth Amendment (both the Due Process and the Equal Protection Clauses), the "quid pro quo" rationale (i.e., treatment is due to civilly committed patients in exchange for enforced confinement), and the "least restrictive alternative" doctrine ("deprivations of liberty solely because of dangers to ill persons themselves should not go beyond what is necessary for their protection") (*Lake v. Cameron* 1966, 660).
- A large portion of right-to-treatment litigation has focused on establishing standards of care and

concomitant staffing patterns in treatment facilities. In addition, legislative and judicial actions have contributed to the deinstitutionalization of patients and led to the adoption of "least restrictive alternatives" for patients.

- The U.S. Supreme Court has yet to provide a definitive ruling that guarantees and clarifies the "right to treatment," "least restrictive alternative," or "community-based services."

REFERENCES

Act 119, 1999 State of Hawaii Legislature.

Americans with Disabilities Act, Public Law 101-336, 104 stat. 327, July 26, 1990 (42 U.S.C., sec 12101 et seq).

Americans with Disabilities Act Amendments Act of 2008, Public law 110-325, S.3406.

Americans with Disabilities Act Amendments Act of 2008. Summary and Resources from the Southeast DBTAC, January 2009.

Appelbaum PS. 1999. Least restrictive alternative revisited: Olmstead's uncertain mandate for community-based care. *Psychiatric Services* 50:1271–1272, 1280.

Armstrong B. 1979. St. Elizabeths Hospital: Case study of a court order. *Hospital and Community Psychiatry* 30:42–46.

Arnold v. ADHS, ASH and Maricopa Board of Arizona Supervisors, No. C-432355 (Ariz. Super. Ct. Maricopa Cty., December 10, 1998).

Arnold v. Sarn, No. C-432355 (Ariz. Super. Ct. Maricopa Cty., May 29, 1985).

Arnold v. Sarn Independent Review. Office of the Court Monitor, No. C-432355 (Ariz. Super. Ct., June, 2000).

Bagenstos S. 2012. The past and future of deinstitutionalization litigation. *Cardozo Law Review* 34(1):1–51.

Bazelon Center for Mental Health Law. 2000. Advocates welcome agreement to name new "transitional" receiver for Districts mental health system. *News for Release*, March 1.

Beis EB. 1984. *Mental Health and Law*. Rockville, MD: Aspen.

Birnbaum M. 1960. The right to treatment. *American Bar Association Journal* 46:499–505.

Brakel SJ, J Parry, and BA Weiner. 1985. *The Mentally Disabled and the Law*, 3rd edition. Chicago: American Bar Foundation.

Brewster v. Dukakis, Civil Action 76-4423-17, C.D. Mass. (filed December 15, 1976).

Brewster v. Dukakis, Civil Action 76-4423-F (E.D. Mass. December 6, 1978).

Broadman R. 2000. Americans with Disabilities Act. *Journal of the American Academy of Psychiatry and the Law* 28:236–237.

Civil Rights of Institutionalized Persons Act, 42 U.S.C. Sec. 1997 et seq.

28 Code of Federal Regulations 35.130(b)(7) (1998).

28 Code of Federal Regulations 35.130(d) (1998).

Department of Justice. 2011. *Department of Justice Activities Under the Civil Rights of Institutionalized Persons Act Fiscal Year 2011*. http://www.justice.gov/crt/about/spl/documents/split_cripa11.pdf, accessed December, 23, 2013.

Deutsch A. 1948. *The Shame of the States*. New York: Harcourt, Brace.

Dixon v. Miller, Consent Order, U.S. Dist. Ct. for the District of Columbia, C.A. No. 74-285. (March 6, 2000).

Dixon v. Sullivan, Civil Action 74-285 (AR) (D.D.C. 1989).

Dixon v. Weinberger, 405 F. Supp. 974 (D.D.C. 1975).

Feng S. 2012. Madness and mayhem: Reforming the mental health care system in Arizona. *Arizona Law Review* 54: 541–566.

Fisher WH, JL Geller, and JA Pandiani. 2009. The changing role of the state psychiatric hospital. *Health Affairs* 28(3):676–684. http://content.healthaffairs.org/content/28/3/676.long, accessed December 19, 2013.

Fisher WH, JL Geller, CL White, and F Altaffer. 1995. Serving the seriously mentally ill in the "least restrictive alternative": Issues from a federal court consent decree. *Administration and Policy in Mental Health* 22:423–436.

Foe v. Cuomo, 892 F. 2d 196 (2d Cir. 1989).

Geller JL. 1991a. "Any place but the state hospital." Examining the assumptions of the benefits of admission diversion. *Hospital and Community Psychiatry* 42:145–152.

Geller JL. 1991b. Defining the meaning of "in the community." *Hospital and Community Psychiatry* 42:1197.

Geller JL. 2000a. The last half-century of psychiatric services as reflected in Psychiatric Services. *Psychiatric Services* 51:41–67.

Geller JL. 2000b. American "community" psychiatry. *Lancet* 356(Suppl. Dec):540.

Geller JL and WH Fisher. 1991. Reply to "Community-based care in western Massachusetts" (letter to Editor). *American Journal of Psychiatry* 148:816.

Geller JL, WH Fisher, LJ Simom et al. 1990a. Second generation institutionalization II: The impact of *Brewster v. Dukakis* on correlates of community and hospital utilization. *American Journal of Psychiatry* 147:982–993.

Geller JL, Fisher WH, Wirth-Cauchon JL et al. 1990b. Second generation institutionalization I: The impact of *Brewster v. Dukakis* on state hospital case mix. *American Journal of Psychiatry* 147:982–987.

Geller JL and L Lee. 2013. United States Department of Justice findings letters in psychiatric hospitals CRIPA cases. An aid or a distraction. *Journal of American Academy Psychiatry and Law* 41(2):174–190.

Gutheil TG, PS Appelbaum, and DB Wexler. 1983. The inappropriateness of "least restrictive alternative" analysis for involuntary procedures with the institutionalized mentally ill. *Journal of Psychiatry and Law* 11:7–17.

Halderman v. Pennhurst State School and Hospital, 446 F. 2d 1295 (E.D. Pa. 1977).

Herbert PB and KA Young. 1999. The Americans with Disabilities Act and deinstitutionalization of the chronically mentally ill. *Journal of the American Academy of Psychiatry and the Law* 27:603–613.

Hoffman PB and LL Foust. 1977. Least restrictive treatment of the mentally ill: A doctrine in search of its senses. *San Diego Law Review* 14:1100–1154.

Johnson and United States v. Murphy, C.A. No. 87-369-CIV-T-24 (E) (M.D. Fla.) (Files 1987; U.S. intervention granted 1998).

Kathleen S. v. Department of Public Welfare, 10 F Supp. 2d 460 (ED Pa 1998).

Kathleen S. v. Department of Public Welfare, U.S. Dist. LEXIS 194-98 (1999).

Krueger C. 2000. Case's scope has changed over time. *St. Petersburg Times*, August 7, 1B.

Lake v. Cameron, 364 F. 2d 657 (D.C. Cir. 1966).

Lessard v. Schmidt, 349 F. Supp. 1978 (E.D. Wis. 1972).

Lamb R and L Weinberger. 2013. Some perspectives on criminalization. *Journal of American Academy of Psychiatry and Law* 41(2):287–293.

Mental-illness ruling hinders patients. 2000. *Duluth News Tribune*, August 28.

Miller B. 2000. Plan approved to restore D.C.'s control of mental health. *Washington Post*, March 7, B4.

Munetz MR and JL Geller. 1993. The least restrictive alternative in the post institutional era. *Hospital and Community Psychiatry* 44:967–973.

Nason v. Superintendent of Bridgewater State Hospital, 233 N.E. 2d 908 (Mass. 1968).

New York State Association for Retarded Children v. Rockefeller, 357 F. Supp. 752 (E.D. N.Y. 1973).

O'Connor K. 2010. *Superior Court of the State of Arizona in and for the county of Maricopa. Order Regarding Joint Stipulation to Stay Litigation During Fiscal Budget Crisis*. March 9, 2010. http://www.azdhs.gov/bhs/arnold-v-sarn/documents/arnold-v-sarn-court-order-march-2010.pdf

O'Connor v. Donaldson, 422 U.S. 563 (1975).

Office of the Press Secretary, The White House. 2009. *President Obama Commemorates Anniversary of Olmstead and Announces New Initiatives Americans with Disabilities*. http://www.whitehouse.gov/the_press_office/President-Obama-Commemorates-Anniversary-of-Olmstead-and-Announces-New-Initiatives-to-Assist-Americans-with-Disabilities/, accessed June 28, 2016.

Olmstead v. L.C. 119 S. Ct. 2176 (1999).

Pennhurst State School and Hospital v. Halderman, 451 U.S. 1 (1981).

Perez TE. 2012. *Assistant Attorney General testimony before the U.S. Senate Committee on Health, Education, Labor and Pensions*. Washington, DC. June 21. http://www.justice.gov/crt/opa/pr/speeches/2012/crt-speech-120621.html, accessed June 28, 2016.

Petrila J. 1999. The Americans with Disabilities Act and community-based treatment law. *Psychiatric Services* 50:473–474, 480.

Roth LH. 1977. Involuntary civil commitment: The right to treatment and the right to refuse treatment. *Psychiatric Annals* 7:244–257.

Rouse v. Cameron, 373 F. 2d 451 (D.C. Cir. 1966).

Santiago JM. 1987. Reforming a system of care: The Arizona experiment. *Hospital and Community Psychiatry* 38:270–273.

Santiago JM, A Gittler, A Beigel et al. 1986. Changing a state mental health system through litigation: The Arizona experiment. *American Journal of Psychiatry* 143:1575–1579.

Schwartz SJ and CE Costanzo. 1987. Compelling treatment in the community: Distorted doctrines and violated values. *Loyola of Los Angeles Law Review* 20:1329–1429.

Senate Research. 2009. *Arizona State Senate Forty-ninth Legislature, First Regular Session Program Presentation Arnold v. Sarn Caucus Report.* February 3, 2009. http://www.azsenate.gov/Committee_Program_Presentations/Arnold%20v%20Sarn_caucus%20report.pdf, accessed June 28, 2016.

Shapiro A. 2009. Settlements in Mental Health Cases Face Scrutiny. *NPR*. http://www.npr.org/templates/story/story.php?storyId=102503173, accessed June 28, 2016.

Shapiro J. 2010. A New Civil Right Looks for Stronger Enforcement. *NPR*. http://www.npr.org/2010/12/03/131786390/a-new-civil-right-lacks-enforcement, accessed June 28, 2016.

Solomon HC. 1958. The American Psychiatric Association in relation to American psychiatry. *American Journal of Psychiatry* 115:1–9.

Stone AA. 1975. Overview: The right to treatment—comments on the law and its impact. *American Journal of Psychiatry* 132:1125–1134.

Torrey EF, K Entsminger, J Geller et al. 2008. *The Shortage of Public Hospital Beds for Mentally Ill Persons*. Arlington, VA: Treatment Advocacy Center.

Torrey EF, DA Fuller, J Geller et al. 2012. *No Room at the Inn: Trends and Consequences of Closing Public Psychiatric Hospitals*. Arlington VA: Treatment Advocacy Center. http://tacreports.org/bed-study, accessed June 28, 2016.

United States v. Commonwealth of Virginia, C.A. No. 99-642-A (E.D. Va., Alexandria D.V. 1999).

United States v. Hawaii, Civil No. 91-00137 (D.A.E.) (D. Haw. Sept. 18, 1991).

United States v. Indiana et al. No. 1P84-411C (S.D. Ind. April 6, 1984).

U.S. Department of Labor, Employee Benefits Security Administration. 2013. FAQs About Affordable Care Act Implementation Part VII and Mental Health Parity

Implementation. http://www.dol.gov/ebsa/faqs/faq-aca7.html, accessed December 19, 2013.
Woe v. Matthews, 408 F. Supp. 419 (E.D. N.Y. 1976).
World Health Organization. 2007. UN Convention on the rights of persons with disabilities—A major step forward in promoting and protecting rights. Geneva. Mental Health, Human Rights and Legislation Information Sheet, Sheet 5. http://www.who.int/mental_health/policy/services/en/index.html
Wyatt v. Stickney, 325 F. Supp. 781 (M.D. Ala. 1971).
Wyatt v. Stickney, 344 F. Supp. 373 (M.D. Ala. 1972).
Wyatt v. Sawyer, 2000. U.S. Dist. LEXIS 10398 (Filed July 13, 2000).
Wylonis L. 1999. Psychiatric disability, employment and the Americans with Disabilities Act. *Psychiatric Clinics of North America* 22:147–158.
Youngberg v. Romeo, 457 U.S. 307 (1982).

18

Treatment refusal in psychiatric practice

DEBRA A. PINALS, ARIANA NESBIT, AND STEVEN K. HOGE

INTRODUCTION

Historically, individuals with mental illness have had more limited rights to refuse treatment than those without mental illness. This was primarily the case for patients committed to psychiatric facilities, but also applied to some voluntary patients (Appelbaum 1994). Until the last quarter of the twentieth century, society granted psychiatrists the authority to determine the course of treatment for committed patients and, if necessary, to administer the treatment over the patient's objection. Now, virtually every jurisdiction recognizes that all patients, regardless of their commitment status, have some rights with regard to treatment refusal. In order to understand the current legal approaches to treatment refusal, it is necessary to explore the factors that led to this dramatic change in the nature of doctor–patient relationships in psychiatric institutions. Developments in mental health case law, the evolution of the informed consent doctrine, and public perception about the quality of care delivered in psychiatric institutions all played important roles with respect to the currently recognized right to refuse treatment (Hoge et al. 1989; Perlin 1993; Appelbaum 1994; Winick 1997; Appelbaum and Gutheil 2007).

A crucial development was the shift in the legal justification for civil commitment away from paternalistic grounds—operationalized in a "need-for-treatment" criterion—to grounds rooted primarily in the police powers of the state and dangerousness-oriented criteria. When the legal standard for involuntary hospitalization was based on need for treatment, a post-commitment right to refuse treatment made no conceptual sense. However, when states adopted the new dangerousness-oriented criteria, it became possible for courts to separate the need for confinement from the need for treatment and to question why treatment was essential once the threat of harm had been minimized (Hoge et al. 1989; Appelbaum 1988, 1994; Appelbaum and Gutheil 2007). Dangerousness is generally defined as danger to others or danger to self either by suicide or by an inability to care for oneself, the so-called "grave disability" standard (Large et al. 2008). The consequences of requiring dangerousness for commitment have been discussed from numerous vantage points. For example, when dangerousness is necessary for commitment, only those who have crossed a certain risk threshold can be admitted involuntarily, while those who are less ill but deteriorating symptomatically or functionally because of medication refusal are not eligible for intensive treatment aimed at preventing risk-related behavior. Thus, when an individual is admitted involuntarily to a hospital, treatment considerations require a rapid, planned approach, especially in those cases where the patient objects to treatment.

Another major development occurred in the 1960s, when clinical and legal pressures challenged the notion that involuntarily committed patients were globally incompetent to make decisions. As patients moved out of state hospitals, committed patients were unable to successfully reintegrate into the community at least partially because of the presumption that they were incompetent to sign leases or enter into other contractual arrangements. A mental health patients' rights advocacy movement grew and won for patients greater legal equality with non-mental-health patients, who had always retained the legal presumption of competence. As a result, by the early 1970s, the presumption that committed patients were globally incompetent had virtually disappeared (Appelbaum 1994).

The presumption of competence for committed patients was a crucial development that became even more significant with the maturation of the doctrine of informed consent. From a clinical and scientific perspective, an enormous amount of research effort has been put forth in the past decade to elucidate capacities for persons with mental illness related to decision making in both treatment and research settings. This literature has further supported the notion that persons with mental illness are not, by definition, incompetent to make their own decisions. Careful examination of the patient's treatment-specific decision-making capacity is required before an individual can be deemed incompetent (Appelbaum and Gutheil 2007).

Doctors also are required by informed consent laws, case law, and ethics to describe to the patient more than just the nature of the proposed treatment. In order to obtain a valid informed consent, doctors must also disclose the risks and benefits of the treatment, alternatives to the proposed treatment, the risks and benefits of the alternative treatment, and the risk of no treatment. This expanded scope of disclosure enables individualized decision making, with the emphasis on patient autonomy to choose among various options. Thus, the doctrine of informed consent made explicit that treatment choice is inherently an individual value judgment and not an objective determination made by a physician or other authority on scientific or medical grounds. In other words, medical decision-making authority shifted dramatically from physicians to patients with the evolving informed consent doctrine. The doctrine also provided courts with a convenient analytic tool, the risk–benefit ratio, by which laypeople, judges, or other surrogate decision makers could evaluate proposed and alternative treatments (Hoge et al. 1989; Appelbaum 1994; Appelbaum and Gutheil 2007). For further discussion of informed consent, see Chapter 14.

Finally, concerns about the quality of care in psychiatric institutions also reinforced the notion that patients have a right to refuse treatment. Society had long given psychiatrists broad discretion to make treatment decisions in psychiatric institutions. This discretion was based on the presumption that treatment decisions would be in the best interests of patients and that patients would receive individualized treatment based on their specific needs. This long-standing granting of authority also applied to the use of antipsychotic medications. Because antipsychotic medications were the first effective treatment for individuals with severe mental illness, and because they were initially regarded as miracle drugs, at first, there were no reasons to question their use. However, over time, our understanding of the effects of these medications changed, and people no longer assumed that psychiatrists were always prescribing beneficently (Erickson et al. 2007; Brakel and Davis 2008). Specifically, the inherent limitations of antipsychotic medications were recognized, and it was realized that the medications were not a panacea for all mental illness. In addition, the risks of treatment were increasingly appreciated as long-term administration led to potentially irreversible tardive dyskinesia in a significant minority of patients (Slovenko 2000).

Especially in the early years of use, a common concern was that these medications were being used to sedate patients for the convenience of the staff. Even worse, some claimed that patients received these medications as punishment, and some institutions were alleged to have insufficient resources to safely and adequately monitor their patients' pharmacotherapy (Hoge et al. 1989) and that the "dangers" of antipsychotic medication were minimized (Whitaker 2002). More recently, concerns about metabolic syndrome and other serious side effects have been raised (Young et al. 2015). As these risks have been recognized, and as the concepts of patient autonomy and self-determination have made gains in psychiatric care, the right to refuse treatment has persisted, and it has become even more important to provide patients with the data necessary to make informed treatment decisions (Parsons and Kennedy 2007).

LEGAL CRITERIA

In view of the diverse factors underlying the recognition of a right to refuse treatment, it is not surprising that a variety of legal approaches have emerged that differ in defining the contours of the right and in the prescription of procedural protections (Appelbaum 1994; Pinals and Mossman 2012). Rules governing treatment refusal vary across jurisdictions. For example, definitions of what constitutes incompetence, or an emergency sufficient to override treatment refusal vary greatly. Thus, it is necessary that psychiatrists familiarize themselves with the relevant case law, statutes, and regulations related to their specific practice setting.

Legal approaches to the adjudication of treatment refusal can be categorized into two broad groups, based on whether they are driven primarily by concerns about patient rights or by concerns about the quality of patient care (Appelbaum 1994). These fundamentally different legal approaches are typified by the two initial cases in this area. In *Rogers v. Commissioner of Mental Health* (1983), the Massachusetts Supreme Judicial Court adopted a "rights-driven" model, relying on state statutes and common law principles; in contrast, in *Rennie v. Klein* (1983) the Third Circuit of the U.S. Court of Appeals found that a "treatment-driven" model satisfied U.S. constitutional requirements.

As case law in each of these areas evolved, several constitutional arguments have been made justifying a right to refuse treatment. Among these constitutional arguments are the right to free speech, based in part on the First Amendment; the right to be free of cruel and unusual punishment, based on the Eighth Amendment; the right to due process, based upon the Fourteenth Amendment; and the right to privacy, derived in a general sense from the penumbra of the First, Fourth, Fifth, and Ninth Amendments (Ciccone et al. 1990; Hermann 1990).

Rights-driven models

Rights-driven models are primarily concerned with individuals' autonomy and thus seek to protect patients' rights to determine the course of their treatment. These rights-driven models have at their core an informed consent analysis: competent patients have the right to refuse treatment, absent an emergency; only the treatment refusals of incompetent patients may be overridden. Most jurisdictions with a rights-driven model will require a formal, legal adjudication of incompetence, but some variants of this model place the determination of competence in the hands of psychiatrists or a multidisciplinary board (Appelbaum 1994; Appelbaum and Gutheil 2007).

In general, those states that hold formal judicial hearings do not place the treatment decision in the hands of clinicians, even following a determination of incompetence. Courts, such as the *Rogers* court, have feared that psychiatrists will be unable to curb past abuses because competing interests—maintaining order in the facility, discharging patients, pleasing family members—may influence their treatment decisions. Instead, in many jurisdictions, the decision-making authority for the patient is vested in a guardian. In other jurisdictions (e.g., Massachusetts and New York), the court may make the treatment decision itself. Standards for decision making may involve a variety of models (Wettstein 1999; Appelbaum and Gutheil 2007). In one of the more common prototypes, treatment decisions are made based on what is considered by an objective decision maker (e.g., the court or a guardian) to be in the best interests of the patient.

An alternative, more rigorous standard of decision making in rights-driven jurisdictions is the "substituted judgment" model. In this model, the courts attempt to approximate decisions regarding treatment based on what the patient would have wanted if competent. For example, in the *Rogers* case, the courts concluded that a substituted judgment determination requires that evidence including the following should be considered: the patient's stated preferences, experienced side effects of the medication, family preferences, prognosis with and without treatment, and any religious considerations that may have influenced the patient's treatment decisions if competent (*Rogers v. Commissioner of Mental Health* 1983). This method, although respectful of a patient's autonomy, can be difficult to implement if the patient was never competent (*Superintendent of Belchertown State School v. Saikewicz* 1977) or if there is no family or available means to ascertain the patient's preference during times when they may have been competent.

Treatment-driven models

Treatment-driven models, which view patients' right to refuse treatment as being limited to inappropriate care, have been devised by courts and legislatures. The notion that civil commitment is intended to bring about treatment—and not merely confinement—is what catalyzes the treatment-driven model of adjudicating refusal. Committed patients are entitled to refuse treatment only when it is not truly prescribed for therapeutic ends. Because the standard for overriding refusal is based on the appropriateness of the prescribed treatment, treatment-driven models place the primary authority to override refusal in the hands of professionals—such as treating psychiatrists, medical directors, independent psychiatrists, or multidisciplinary boards—who can identify misuses of medication. Moreover, because the determinations are made by clinicians, the procedures for review are often informal and do not require judicial hearings (Appelbaum 1994).

The preference for one model over the other generally depends on one's role with the treatment-refusing person. Psychiatrists generally favor treatment-driven models of adjudicating treatment refusal because they recognize the primacy of clinical decision making and therapeutic goals, and such a model reduces the risk that patients who need medications will go untreated. Administrators also favor such models because they minimize the diversion of clinical time from treatment efforts. Legal and patients' rights advocates generally object to treatment-driven models. In these models, they perceive lesser protections for the rights of committed patients, which they assert can result in disadvantage, loss of autonomy, and diminished dignity for persons with mental illness (Table 18.1).

Table 18.1 Legal approaches to the adjudication of treatment refusal

Legal approach	Prototypical legal case	Key differences
Rights-driven	*Rogers v. Commissioner of Mental Health* (1983)	Deference to judicial decision Requires affidavit and court decision
Treatment-driven	*Rennie v. Klein* (1983)	Deference to medical decision maker Often requires layered clinical reviews and permissions

Differences between state and federal courts

State and federal courts have charted different courses in deciding right-to-refuse-treatment cases, as was signaled by the *Rennie* and *Rogers* decisions. Federal courts typically have been willing to show deference to psychiatrists' judgments regarding committed patients. The U.S. Supreme Court, for example, specifically instructed the Third Circuit Court of Appeals to take the Supreme Court decision of *Youngberg v. Romeo* (1982) into consideration in deciding *Rennie v. Klein*. In *Youngberg*, a case involving a civilly committed, intellectually disabled person's right to treatment and freedom from restraint, the Supreme Court found that the exercise of professional judgment was sufficient protection of patients' rights when their liberties conflicted with therapeutic purposes.

The U.S. Supreme Court also decided a case involving the right of a prisoner with mental illness to refuse treatment, *Washington v. Harper* (1990). The Court upheld the state of Washington's regulatory scheme, a variant of the treatment-driven model that predicated override of treatment refusal on a finding that the patient met the "dangerousness standard" for commitment and needed treatment. The regulations established procedures for review, including the right to notice, a hearing before a professional panel, and lay representation. Although the decision could be read narrowly as affecting only prisoners, since then, in *United States v. Loughner* (2012), the Ninth Circuit Court of Appeals determined that *Harper* also applied to incompetent pretrial detainees who posed a risk of harm and were refusing treatment. This again demonstrated the federal courts' deference to clinical decision makers in determining treatment needs (though these cases also focused on the overarching institutional safety needs in their reasoning).

Some state courts have been willing to find greater rights for committed patients than the minimum set by the federal courts. In doing so, these courts have found that state law—statutes, common law, or state constitutions—provides additional protections beyond those mandated by the U.S. Constitution (Perlin 1993; Appelbaum 1994).

In a more recent twist on treatment refusal, the U.S. Supreme Court, in *Sell v. U.S.* (2003), also established parameters for overriding treatment refusal for the purpose of restoring an incompetent defendant's competence to stand trial. This case stands out not as reflective of a treatment-driven orientation, but it does focus on both a defendant's right to be competent when tried for a criminal matter, as well as the state's right to force treatment in order to expedite a trial process, though only in limited circumstances when a defendant is refusing treatment that would be necessary to ensure his or her competence to stand trial. The Court opined that treaters should look to alternative approaches to address treatment refusal (e.g., *Washington v. Harper* standards, local guardianship standards, etc.) before relying on the governmental interest in forcing treatment to ensure the defendant's competence to stand trial as the rationale.

Impact of the choice of model

There are several roles that the forensic psychiatrist may be called on to play with respect to the right to refuse treatment. As noted previously, the laws regulating treatment refusal and override of refusal vary based on jurisdiction, type of facility, and the legal status of the individual refusing treatment (e.g., a committed patient or a prisoner, a pretrial detainee, or an incompetent-to-stand-trial defendant); forensic psychiatrists may perform a vital function in educating treating psychiatrists about these laws. Forensic psychiatrists also may be called upon to act as consultants to treating psychiatrists in managing patients seeking to have their refusal upheld. Alternatively, forensic psychiatrists may be called on to act as expert evaluators for the individual's attorneys, hospitals, jails, prisons, or the court. Finally, psychiatrists knowledgeable about treatment refusal may be called on to help formulate policies and procedures for their hospitals, correctional facilities, and states. Because a forensic psychiatrist may assume a variety of roles with respect to a treatment-refusing patient, it is important to understand the data reflecting the impact of the choice of the model for overriding treatment decisions.

The rates of psychotropic medication refusal can range from 2% to 44% across all settings, with some studies estimating significantly higher rates of treatment refusal in forensic settings (Owiti and Bowers 2011) (though most available data are from civil settings). In nonforensic settings, studies have shown that only approximately 10% of patients will refuse treatment with antipsychotics at some point during inpatient hospitalization, with certain variations depending on patient mix (voluntary or involuntary) and other factors (Hoge et al. 1990; Appelbaum 1994; Kasper et al. 1997; Owiti and Bowers 2011). Of those patients who refused medications in civil settings, between 50% and 90% refused treatment for less than 1 week. Reasons patients cite for ultimately agreeing to medication include prior experience and discomfort with court hearings; belief that the hospital will succeed in court; pressure from family to take medication; and belief that taking medication will result in a shorter hospital stay (Russ and John 2013).

When treatment refusal is persistent (which occurs in only a very small percentage of cases), empirical reports from various jurisdictions indicate that, regardless of the model employed (rights-driven or treatment-driven), the outcome of review is the same: treatment refusal is overturned in 90%–95% of cases (Appelbaum and Hoge 1986). Although a few studies showed that override of refusal may be less frequent in treatment-driven systems (Appelbaum 1994), a study of patients in a treatment-driven jurisdiction found that treatment refusal lasted only 2.8 days, and all patients who persistently refused treatment were ultimately treated involuntarily (Kasper et al. 1997). In contrast, Hoge et al. (1990) found that, in a rights-driven setting, refusal episodes lasted about 13 days, while 23% of treatment refusers had not been treated by the end of the study period. Approximately 18% of treatment refusers were brought before a court, a venue in which their refusal was consistently overturned. That most treatment refusals that go before a decision-making body (i.e., the courts or an administrative-type review) are overturned is undoubtedly due in part to the deference to clinical opinion shown even in rights-driven, judicial models of review. Yet, one cannot conclude from these data that the model of review has no impact on practice.

Earlier studies from jurisdictions with rights-driven models of review requiring judicial determination reported considerable delays and costs in obtaining hearings, an outcome that had been feared when these models were promulgated (Veliz and James 1987; Hoge et al. 1990; Schouten and Gutheil 1990). These delays contribute to the increased length of stay seen with treatment refusers. During the interval between refusal and judicial review, refusing patients can disrupt the treatment setting, thereby impairing the quality of other patients' treatment. Although restraint prevention is more robust than when some of these studies emerged, Hoge et al. (1990) found that treatment-refusing patients required seclusion and restraint with greater frequency than other patients, a finding that was consistent with a more recent review of several related studies (Owiti and Bowers 2011).

On the other hand, judicial review mechanisms—perhaps because they are so procedurally cumbersome—seem to empower patients. For example, as described above, in one jurisdiction with a rights-driven model, only a small fraction of treatment refusers were taken to review. The majority of patients in this prospective study began to comply with treatment after some period of negotiation and discussion. In some cases, patients were successful in having the dosages of medication reduced. Nearly one-quarter of the patients had their medication discontinued, although in several cases this occurred in conjunction with discharge from the hospital (Hoge et al. 1990). It seems fair to conclude that rights-driven, judicial review does promote autonomy interests, although optimal treatment for refusing patients and fellow patients may be more readily compromised, and considerable financial expense will be incurred as a result.

Treatment-driven models of review may offer clear advantages in efficiency and clinical flexibility (Schouten and Gutheil 1990; Bloom et al. 1997). The informal procedures associated with treatment-driven models permit significantly more refusing patients to be reviewed. Although treatment-refusing patients in treatment-driven settings are just as likely to present with behavioral challenges as those in rights-driven settings, lengths of refusals may be shorter and reviews may be conducted more quickly, potentially leading to more rapid treatment and shorter hospital stays (Kasper et al. 1997).

Efficiencies gained by treatment-driven models of review may, however, come with some costs. Easy access to review may reduce some of the incentive for treating clinicians to negotiate with refusing patients and to thoroughly evaluate their concerns about medications. Treatment-driven models are also, by definition, not designed primarily to promote patient rights, and there has been concern that patients, when given less of a right to present their side to a neutral party, may not be as accepting of the outcome (Winick 1997, 384). Patients may feel that they do not have sufficient voice in a clinician-dominated process (Monahan et al. 1995). These are not necessary consequences of a treatment-driven model of review, but clinicians operating under such systems must be careful to consider the perspectives of refusing patients and to treat them with respect.

Patients who require court-ordered medication are at an increased risk for medication nonadherence after discharge, as well as for having treatment-resistant illness (Russ and John 2013). This future refusal may be related to the nature of the illness itself, symptoms of the individual's refusing treatment, or the fact that a person who refused medications once may also refuse them in the future (rather than a direct result of having had a prior court proceeding). A review of studies examining coercion in treatment and subsequent adherence to treatment found that longer-term adherence may be independent of whether coercion occurred at a certain point in time in treatment, though providing information to patients and treating patients fairly when there is a need to override their refusal often can reduce perceptions of coercion and enhance adherence (Pinals and Mossman 2012).

Psychiatric advance directives (PADs) and joint crisis plans (JCPs) are recently developed instruments that serve as vehicles whereby patients can express their views of what treatment they may or may not want to receive if they are unable to assert their preferences in the future (Campbell and Kisely 2009; Khazaal et al. 2014). In *Hargrave v. Vermont* (2003), the Second Circuit Court of Appeals found that a Vermont state law that permitted the override of durable powers of attorney, such as psychiatric advanced directives, in order to force treatment of civilly committed patients, violated the Americans with Disabilities Act. Although only applicable to Vermont and New York, the ruling raised the possibility that treatment refusal is considered an absolute right if appropriately asserted as a preference when competent. A recent study showed that, even when psychiatric advance directives are in place, there are circumstances in which clinicians still feel it is appropriate to override the patient's expressed advance wishes, especially in emergencies, when there is high risk of violence, and when the patient demonstrates lack of insight (Swanson et al. 2007). Other studies show that clinicians have more positive attitudes about PADs when they understand their provisions and limits (Elbogen et al. 2006). More research on and experience with PADs in clinical practice is needed to fully understand the impact of these tools.

GENERAL POINTS OF ASSESSMENT

Reasons for refusal

The reasons for treatment refusal must be assessed carefully. In many instances, patients' refusals of medication are based on actual side effects or other real concerns about their treatment (Owiti and Bowers 2011). Even common and relatively benign side effects, such as dry mouth and blurring of vision, which seem trivial in comparison with the beneficial effects of the medications, may lead to treatment refusal. It is necessary for clinicians to explore the practical impact and the meaning that patients impart to these side effects. Blurred vision, for example, may impair highly valued activities, such as reading or watching television. Patients also may ascribe dire meanings to the medications themselves or their side effects, which they may be reluctant to discuss with treating psychiatrists (Hoge et al. 1990; Appelbaum and Gutheil 2007; Owiti and Bowers 2011). In addition, patients may fear a loss of autonomy and pain from long-acting injectable medication (Jaeger and Rossler 2010).

Certain side effects warrant special mention. Patients may express their experience of akathisia and akinesia in idiosyncratic ways that potentially could be disregarded as being delusionally based. Some patients experience dysphoric responses to antipsychotic medication, which may lead to refusal. Many patients are embarrassed to discuss sexual dysfunction related to psychotropic medications, such as impotence, decreased libido, and retrograde ejaculation. Specific inquiry into the reasons behind treatment refusal is a necessary step before resorting to legal or administrative procedures to override the refusal (Appelbaum and Gutheil 2007).

Side effects rarely should be the basis of long-term treatment refusal. Various psychopharmacological maneuvers—for example, changing the type of antipsychotic or other psychotropic medication, dosage amounts and intervals, or adjunctive treatments—usually will ameliorate side effects. In many cases, a careful explanation of what the patient may expect with those changes may alleviate his or her concerns. Persistent treatment refusal related to side effects may be more likely when the risk–benefit ratio is narrow; for example, when a patient with significant tardive dyskinesia and a history of poor response to neuroleptics refuses medication that the treating psychiatrist thinks would be beneficial. With the introduction of newer medications, clinicians and patients have a wider range of options from which to choose in order to minimize side effects and maximize treatment opportunities (Pinals and Buckley 1999).

Treatment refusal is often illness related. Patients may refuse antipsychotic medication because of denial of their illness. Some patients will present with delusions about treatment and medication; for example, patients may believe that the medication is actually a poison. Perhaps not surprisingly, patients with less insight into their disease have higher rates of medication refusal (Droulout et al. 2003; Russ and John 2013).

Patients with illness-based reasons for refusing treatment pose the greatest clinical challenges. Even when psychiatrists, nurses, inpatient unit staff, family, and friends are intensively involved and united in support of medication, many of these patients will report that they have accepted medication only as a way to expedite discharge, and not because they have accepted an illness-based need for treatment (Hoge et al. 1990; Russ and John 2013).

Context of refusal

Methods for assessing and managing the treatment refuser may be gleaned from the context in which refusal takes place. For example, in an inpatient setting, the majority of patients who refuse medication do so shortly after admission (Hoge et al. 1990; Kasper et al. 1997). There may be many reasons for this; often, patients disagree about the need for hospitalization. Empathy, time, and space to adjust to hospitalization, along with motivational interviewing techniques and other strategies for engagement and shared decision making to foster patient-centered care, may lead to a quick end to treatment refusal (Laakso 2012).

Later in the course of hospitalization, more stable or long-term patients may refuse medication in response to specific problems on the unit or in the hospital. Patients may develop a distrust of staff. Less verbal patients may refuse treatment as a stereotypic response to physical or social distress. Finally, treatment refusal may reflect transference issues or other interpersonal difficulties. Therefore, the assessment of treatment refusal requires the broadest possible understanding of the patient's clinical circumstances (Wettstein 1999; Appelbaum and Gutheil 2007). Treatment refusal is very much context driven. The issues for the patient may be illness specific (e.g., refusal due to an eating disorder, a paranoid belief system, or a substance use disorder) and may require focused approaches that consider these issues in order to maximize treatment adherence.

Other contextual settings of treatment refusal have gained increasing attention. For example, some jurisdictions have adopted models of outpatient involuntary commitment, which often requires treatment compliance as a condition of maintaining outpatient status. This form of treatment is designed to target the issue of treatment refusal among civil outpatients and to prevent recurrent hospitalizations (Miller 1999; see also Chapter 15).

Clinicians working in correctional and forensic settings are faced with other challenges. For example and as previously noted, a pretrial defendant's right to refuse treatment has come under increasing legal and clinical scrutiny. The 1992 case of *Riggins v. Nevada* (1992) provided that treatment could be administered over the objections of a pretrial defendant only when "medically appropriate" and with "an overriding justification" for its administration. More recently in *Loughner* (2012), the Ninth Circuit Court of Appeals relied on *Harper* (1990) to help establish the mechanisms for any treatment override for pretrial defendants. As noted previously, *Sell v. United States* (2003) laid out criteria required to forcefully medicate a defendant for restoration of trial competence (see also Chapter 28). Treatment refusal by an inmate on death row who is then incompetent to be executed raises a host of other issues that are beyond the scope of this chapter but are covered in Chapter 57. Regardless of the context, clinicians working with treatment-refusing patients should consider the principles outlined above when managing such refusals and also understand any relevant case law that impacts practice. Developing a strong therapeutic alliance with the patient and an understanding of the patient's rationale for refusal may be the treating clinician's best approach.

Competence assessment

In those jurisdictions with rights-based models, careful assessment of competence to refuse medications is necessary (see Chapter 14 for a general discussion of this topic). Although most jurisdictions recognize a lack of understanding of a proposed treatment as determinative of incompetence, frequent impairments of competence will be related to deficiencies in patients' abilities to express sustained choices, rationally manipulate information, and appreciate the nature of their problem. With regard to treatment refusal, many patients who refuse treatment are likely to do so because they do not believe that they have a mental illness (Appelbaum and Hoge 1986; Hoge et al. 1990; Appelbaum and Gutheil 2007).

Appropriateness of treatment

When acting as a consultant, either to the treating psychiatrist or to the patient, the forensic psychiatrist must make an independent determination of the appropriateness of the prescribed treatment. Many episodes of refusal occur among acutely psychotic, newly admitted patients, and treatment is frequently appropriate in this clinical context. However, not all clinical scenarios are this unambiguous, and concerns about the appropriateness of treatment will increase as the risk–benefit ratio narrows. Proper evaluation requires careful attention to history, diagnosis, and assessment of psychopathology and side effects.

It is useful to begin with a thorough review of the records and history of the patient. Often, there will be a history of treatment with psychotropic medications. Documented evidence of the patient's previous response to treatment—in either past or current hospitalizations—should be carefully reviewed. Ideally, such a review will allow for a correlation between symptoms and various medication trials. Consulting psychiatrists should establish the patient's diagnosis and contributing variables that may impact treatment refusal (e.g., communication styles and deficits, cognitive limitations, etc.). The ultimate diagnosis will depend on the review of available records and the diagnostic interview. In some instances, further testing or information gathering may be necessary. Signs and symptoms of mental illness should be assessed, described, and documented carefully.

An essential component of the evaluation is the assessment of any potentially significant side effects, such as abnormal involuntary movements or metabolic syndrome. Structured instruments, such as the Abnormal Involuntary Movement Scale (AIMS), and requisite laboratory analyses should be utilized when available to assist in the quantification and documentation of side effects. Subjective complaints should be elicited and explored as described above.

Substituted judgment

In jurisdictions that rely on a substituted judgment standard for determining whether or not incompetent patients will receive antipsychotic medications, psychiatrists must look for evidence of their patient's treatment wishes when competent. Jurisdictional case law may spell out specific factors for review (e.g., *Rogers v. Commissioner of Mental Health*). In many cases, the best indication will be the patient's record of adherence to treatment during periods of wellness or times of improved functioning. Advance directives, if they exist, should be reviewed. Family members, friends, and previous inpatient and outpatient psychiatrists are also good sources of information. Understanding any potential religious objections to treatment also will be important. In jurisdictions that require the substituted judgment standard, sophisticated and careful psychiatrists will document competence assessments and medication adherence of their patients during well periods. Such documentation may prove particularly valuable in the event of a later refusal of treatment (Appelbaum and Gutheil 2007).

Reasoning process

In formulating the approach to a particular patient who is declining treatment, the dialogue with the patient must be placed in the broader and longitudinal context of the patient's treatment as a whole. Because most treatment—even for individuals who decline treatment at some point in the course of their illness—will primarily be voluntary in nature, and because interactions with physicians can play an important role in illness management, it is important to engage the patient to help understand the treatment refusal in practice. Viewing treatment refusal merely as a legal obstacle to be surmounted as quickly as possible is a common error for treating psychiatrists. The management of an episode of treatment refusal requires the varied skills of the psychiatrist: psychopharmacology, psychological management of the therapeutic alliance, and management of the milieu. Psychiatrists must not allow their feelings about the law get in the way of their acting in the best interest of the patient; indeed, many psychiatrists find legal regulation of the right to refuse treatment to be a significant intrusion into clinical matters. Although legal proceedings can create a whole host of new responsibilities and additional effort, they should not be taken lightly. Regardless of the necessity of legal or administrative proceedings, treatment refusal may be an opportunity to strengthen the treatment bond, particularly if handled with an appropriate level of engagement of, and discussion with, the patient (Appelbaum and Gutheil 2007).

When a patient is refusing treatment, ultimately, three options exist: (1) negotiation and dialogue, (2) discharge, or (3) pursuit of an override of the patient's refusal.

Negotiation and dialogue

Treatment refusal should be viewed initially as an invitation by the patient to engage in a dialogue and negotiate treatment. The psychiatrist will explore the reasons for refusal and its context. Depending on the outcome of this initial interaction, one of two questions needs to be addressed:

1. Can the patient arrive at an individualized and personal decision that will allow acceptance of the prescribed medication?
2. Are there reasonable accommodations that the treating psychiatrist can make to foster adherence?

When a patient refuses a proposed treatment, the treating psychiatrist should make an effort to engage the patient and to help him or her accept either the proposed treatment or a reasonable alternative upon which the patient and the psychiatrist agree (Patel et al. 2008). Depending on the context and staff available, the efforts of the psychiatrist should be augmented by those of the nursing and milieu staff; family members and other loved ones are also important in making efforts to help patients understand why the proposed treatment may be beneficial to them. It can be helpful to focus on how adherence to medication can help the individual achieve his or her specific goals. Strategies to engage individuals without focusing only on the medication issues can be very helpful in building trust and fostering an alliance with the patient.

Clinicians should guard against becoming entrenched in their positions regarding treatment. When doctor-patient relationships become contentious, it is important to take a step back and consider using techniques such as shared decision making and self-directed care to work with patients (Patel et al. 2008). Nevertheless, at times communications break down, and the physician and the patient may find themselves in a power struggle. Outside consultation may be helpful in navigating past such impasses. Through exploration, the treating psychiatrist may find ways to address patients' concerns about medication. Clarification of misconceptions, frank discussion of side effects, and a consistent posture of seeking to act in the best interest of the patient provide the necessary foundation for resolution. Even if the psychiatrist is unable to elicit voluntary treatment adherence in one particular instance, this approach offers the greatest promise for long-term clinical success (Appelbaum and Gutheil 2007).

Discharge

Discharge "against medical advice" may be considered in some cases when negotiation fails. This term is used more commonly in medical settings but can also be used in psychiatric settings. Clinicians may determine that it is preferable to respect the wishes of the patient rather than to pursue override of refusal. In some instances, there will be little choice. Patients who are competent (in those jurisdictions in which override of refusal requires a determination of incompetence) may be discharged or provided with other types of therapies if they are determined not to pose an unreasonable risk to themselves or others.

Discharge from the hospital should not be a rejection of the patient or an abandonment of treatment. The team should inform the patient that follow-up care, including but not limited to treatment with medication, is indicated and available (Appelbaum and Gutheil 2007).

Use of formal mechanisms to pursue override

In many instances, it will be impossible to negotiate a safe and reasonable medication regimen from a psychiatric perspective, and discharge will not be possible because of the patient's clinical condition (assuming the patient still meets criteria for commitment, appears to have significant deficits in competent decision making, or both). In general, groups of patients who are unlikely to proceed with voluntary treatment include those with very negative attitudes toward treatment and those who do not appreciate their clinical condition (Hoge et al. 1990).

Once the treating psychiatrist decides to seek override of the patient's refusal, the patient should be informed of this decision and the reasons for it. The procedures governing the review of the refusal should be explained fully, and the patient should be encouraged to participate in the process. To the extent possible, clinicians should discuss with patients what might be said about them during any adversarial proceeding. In some jurisdictions, patients will have been warned from the outset that their communications during an inpatient psychiatric hospitalization will not be confidential, to the extent that such communications are relevant to the judicial determination of treatment refusal override. For some patients, the process of adjudication can be made more therapeutic and less coercive if patients are given a mechanism by which to express their thoughts (Winick 1997, 342–344).

As mentioned previously, in the majority of cases that are formally reviewed, the refusal will be overturned. After such a ruling, patients should have the reasons for this judgment explained to them. In most instances, patients will accept medication at this point, and involuntary administration of medication will be unnecessary. An earlier study by Schwartz et al. (1988) affirmed this notion, as they found that the majority of patients who received involuntary medication eventually came to accept medication voluntarily and to acknowledge the need for treatment. Clinical experience has shown that even when medication is only available in oral forms, once an official determination to override treatment refusal has been made, many patients will no longer refuse the proposed medication. In jurisdictions that designate a decision maker on behalf of the patient (a guardian in most instances), the treating psychiatrist should obtain informed consent from this person, just as he or she would from a competent patient. Although it is not legally necessary to then obtain consent from the patient, it is desirable to continue to engage the patient in his or her treatment to the greatest possible extent, thus maintaining the therapeutic alliance. As in all clinical care, patient wishes about treatment should continue to be respected, where such wishes are reasonable and safe.

SUMMARY

Treatment refusal can be based on a number of factors. Psychiatrists must be aware of the legal mechanisms in their jurisdiction that permit the override of this refusal. At the same time, psychiatrists should continue working with patients to maximize their therapeutic alliance and subsequently improve their patients' adherence to their prescribed medication regimens. A strong working knowledge of the reasons for the treatment refusal, along with any relevant contextual factors, can be helpful in fostering discussions with patients addressing the treatment refusal.

SUMMARY KEY POINTS

- The currently recognized "right to refuse treatment" was refined in the last quarter of the twentieth century by developments in mental health case law, the evolution of the informed consent doctrine, and public perception about the quality of care delivered in psychiatric institutions.
- Legal approaches to the adjudication of treatment refusal fall into two models: rights-driven and treatment-driven (see Table 18.1).
- Reasons for refusal can be varied and may include actual side effects or other legitimate concerns about the treatment, denial of illness, or delusions about the medication.
- Goals for working with treatment-refusing patients include developing a strong therapeutic alliance, developing an understanding of the patient's rationale for refusal, and using shared-decision-making techniques in order to reach an agreement about treatment.

REFERENCES

Appelbaum PS. 1988. The right to refuse treatment: Retrospect and prospect. *American Journal of Psychiatry* 145:413–419.

Appelbaum PS. 1994. *Almost a Revolution: Mental Health Law and the Limits of Change*. New York: Oxford University Press.

Appelbaum PS and TG Gutheil. 2007. *Clinical Handbook of Psychiatry and the Law*, 4th edition. Philadelphia: Lippincott Williams and Wilkins.

Appelbaum PS and SK Hoge. 1986. The right to refuse treatment: What the research reveals. *Behavioral Sciences and the Law* 4:279–292.

Bloom J, MH Williams, C Land, MC Hornbrook, and J Mahler. 1997 Treatment refusal procedures and service utilization: A comparison of involuntarily hospitalized patients. *Journal of the American Academy of Psychiatry and the Law* 25:349–357.

Brakel SJ and JM Davis. 2008. Overriding mental health treatment refusals: How much process is "due"? *Saint Louis University Law Journal* 52:501–588.

Campbell LA and SR Kisely. 2009. Advance treatment directives for people with severe mental illness. *Cochrane Database of Systematic Reviews* 21(1):CD005963.

Ciccone JR, JF Tokoli, CD Clements, and TE Gift. 1990. Right to refuse treatment: Impact of *Rivers v. Katz*. *Bulletin of the American Academy of Psychiatry and the Law* 18:203–215.

Droulout T, F Liraud, and H Verdoux. 2003. Relationships between insight and medication adherence in subjects with psychosis. *Encephale* 29:430–437.

Elbogen EB, MS Swartz, R Van Dorn, JW Swanson, M Kim, and A Scheyett. 2006. Clinical decision making and views about psychiatric advance directives. *Psychiatric Services* 57(3):350–355.

Erickson SK, JR Ciccone, SB Schwarzkopf, JS Lamberti, and MJ Vitacco. 2007. Legal fallacies of antipsychotic drugs. *Journal of the American Academy of Psychiatry and the Law* 35(2):235–246.

Hargrave v. Vermont, 340 F.3d 27 (2d Cir 2003).

Hermann DHJ. 1990. Autonomy, self-determination, the right of involuntarily committed persons to refuse treatment, and the use of substituted judgment in medication decisions involving incompetent persons. *International Journal of Law and Psychiatry* 13:361–385.

Hoge SK, PS Appelbaum, and JG. Geller. 1989. Involuntary treatment. In *American Psychiatric Press Review of Psychiatry*. Vol. 8. edited by A. Tasman, R. E. Hales, and A. Frances, Washington, DC: American Psychiatric Press, 432–450.

Hoge SK, PS Appelbaum, T Lawlor, JC Beck, R Litman, A Greer, TG Gutheil, and E Kaplan. 1990. A prospective, multi-center study of patients' refusal of antipsychotic medications. *Archives of General Psychiatry* 47:949–956.

Jaeger M and W Rossler. 2010. Attitudes towards long-acting depot antipsychotics: A survey of patients, relatives and psychiatrists. *Psychiatry Research* 175(1–2):58–62.

Kasper JA, SK Hoge, T Feucht-Haviar, J Cortina, and B Cohen. 1997. Prospective study of patients' refusal of antipsychotic medication under a physician discretion review procedure. *American Journal of Psychiatry* 154:483–489.

Khazaal Y, R Manghi, M Delahaye, A Machado, L Penzenstadler, and A Molodynski. 2014. Psychiatric advance directives, a possible way to overcome coercion and promote empowerment. *Frontiers in Public Health* 2:37.

Laakso LJ. 2012. Motivational interviewing: Addressing ambivalence to improve medication adherence in patients with bipolar disorder. *Issues in Mental Health Nursing* 33(1):8–14.

Large MM, CJ Ryan, OB Nielssen, and RA. Hayes. 2008. The danger of dangerousness: Why we must remove the dangerousness criterion from our mental health acts. *Journal of Medical Ethics* 34(12):877–881.

Miller RD. 1999. Coerced treatment in the community. *Psychiatric Clinics of North America* 22:183–196.

Monahan J, SK Hoge, C Lidz, LH Roth, N Bennett, W Gardner, and E Mulvey. 1995. Coercion and commitment: Understanding involuntary mental hospital admission. *International Journal of Law and Psychiatry* 18:249–263.

Owiti JA and L Bowers. 2011. A narrative review of studies of refusal of psychotropic medication in acute inpatient psychiatric care. *Journal of Psychiatric and Mental Health Nursing* 18(7):637–647.

Parsons B and M Kennedy. 2007. A review of recorded information given to patients starting to take clozapine and the development of guidelines on disclosure, a key component of informed consent. *Journal of Medical Ethics* 33(10):564–567.

Patel SR, S Bakken, and C Ruland. 2008. Recent advances in shared decision making for mental health. *Current Opinion in Psychiatry* 21(6):606–612.

Perlin ML. 1993. Decoding right to refuse treatment law. *International Journal of Law and Psychiatry* 16:151–177.

Pinals DA and PF Buckley. 1999. Novel antipsychotic agents and their implications for forensic psychiatry. *Journal of the American Academy of Psychiatry and the Law* 27:7–22.

Pinals DA and D Mossman. 2012. *Evaluation for Civil Commitment.* New York: Oxford University Press.

Rennie v. Klein, 720 F.2d 266 (3rd Cir. 1983).

Riggins v. Nevada, 112 U.S. 1810 (1992).

Rogers v. Commissioner of Mental Health, 458 N.E. 2nd 308 (Mass. 1983).

Russ MJ and M John. 2013. Outcomes associated with court-ordered treatment over objection in an acute psychiatric hospital. *Journal of the American Academy of Psychiatry and the Law* 41:236–244.

Schouten R and TG Gutheil. 1990. Aftermath of the *Rogers* decision: Assessing the costs. *American Journal of Psychiatry* 147:1348–1352.

Schwartz HI, W Vingiano, and CB Perez. 1988. Autonomy and the right to refuse treatment; patients' attitudes after involuntary medication. *Hospital and Community Psychiatry* 39:1049–1054.

Sell v. U.S., 123 S. Ct. 2174 (2003).

Siegel DM, AJ Grudzinskas, and DA Pinals. 2001. Old law meets new medicine: Revisiting involuntary psychotropic medication of the criminal defendant. *Wisconsin Law Review* 2:307–380.

Slovenko R. 2000. Update on legal issues associated with tardive dyskinesia. *Journal of Clinical Psychiatry* 61(4):45–57.

Superintendent of Belchertown State School v. Saikewicz, 370 N.E.2d 417 (1977).

Swanson JW, S Van McCrary, MS Swartz, RA Van Dorn, and EB Elbogen. 2007. Overriding psychiatric advance directives: Factors associated with psychiatrists' decisions to preempt patients' advance refusal of hospitalization and medication. *Law and Human Behavior* 31(1):77–90.

United States v. Loughner, 672 F.3d 731 (9th Cir.) (2012).

Veliz J and WS James. 1987. Medicine court: *Rogers* in practice. *American Journal of Psychiatry* 144:62–67.

Washington v. Harper, 110 S.Ct. 1028 (1990).

Wettstein RM. 1999. The right to refuse psychiatric treatment. *Psychiatric Clinics of North America* 22:173–182.

Whitaker R. 2002. *Mad in America: Bad Science, Bad Medicine, and the Enduring Mistreatment of the Mentally Ill.* New York: Basic Books.

Winick BJ. 1997. *The Right to Refuse Mental Health Treatment.* Washington, DC: American Psychological Association.

Young SL, M Taylor, and SM. Lawrie. 2015. "First do no harm." A systematic review of the prevalence and management of antipsychotic adverse effects. *Journal of Psychopharmacology* 29(4):353–362.

Youngberg v. Romeo, 102 S. Ct. 2452 (1982).

19

Confidentiality and testimonial privilege

ERIC Y. DROGIN AND KYLE C. WALKER

INTRODUCTION

Confidentiality and testimonial privilege are critical factors in both psychotherapy and mental health assessment alike. Perhaps no other juxtaposition of concepts better represents the delicate interplay of clinical and legal issues that makes forensic psychiatry among the most conceptually challenging of the medical specialties. Although these two terms address what at times may seem like indistinguishable treatment of the same sensitive information, confidentiality is an essentially ethical notion, while testimonial privilege is an essentially procedural one.

This distinction is reflected in the guidance attorneys obtain from the authoritative *Black's Law Dictionary* (ed. Garner 2014), which defines "confidentiality" as "the trusting relation between two people who have an especially close bond—as between lawyer and client, guardian and ward, or spouses—with regard to the faith that is placed in the one by the other" (p. 361), and defines "testimonial privilege" as "a right not to testify based on a claim of privilege; a privilege overrides a witness's duty to disclose matters within the witness's knowledge, whether at trial or by deposition" (p. 1391). Lawyers understand—or are supposed to understand—that confidentiality is the physician's broad duty to the patient, while testimonial privilege is the way that duty is expressed in a legal forum.

Similar guidance can be gleaned from decisions rendered by the appellate courts that determine how these distinctions are applied in actual legal practice. For example, in the Ninth Circuit Court of Appeals case of *United States v. Chase* (2003), the court maintained that "confidentiality" refers to "the broad blanket of privacy" that the state sees fit to place over "the psychotherapist–patient relationship," and "testimonial privilege" refers to "the specific right of a patient to prevent the psychotherapist from testifying in court" (p. 982). Just as the courts draw distinctions, so too do they establish connections. In the New Jersey Supreme Court case of *State v. Mauti* (2012), the court confirmed the generally held principle that testimonial privilege "may be waived implicitly where a party puts a confidential communication in issue" (pp. 1223–1224).

Statutes and regulations—embodying the codified laws that the appellate courts are sometimes called on to interpret—provide concrete rules for doctors to follow and for attorneys to apply. By way of illustration, when it comes to "confidentiality" (201 KY. Admin. Regs. 9:005 2015) the state of Kentucky defers to whatever standards the American Medical Association recommends—underscoring once more the extent to which the law concedes that this is an essentially ethical concern—while defining the corresponding testimonial "privilege" as the patient's right "to refuse to disclose and to prevent any other person from disclosing" a collection of "confidential communications" made for various purposes (KY. R. Evid. 507(b), 2015).

Such deference to the medical profession's perspective on confidentiality underscores the law's tacit acknowledgement that attorneys are essentially interpreters as opposed to architects of this notion. The frequently cited *Campbell's Psychiatric Dictionary* (2004) identifies "confidentiality" as "one element of the right of the patient to privacy," and specifies that "disclosure of information gained within the therapeutic relationship without the permission of the patient is a breach of confidentiality" (p. 144). Perhaps tellingly, this same source notes "privileged communication" is information that "the physician is not allowed to divulge… without the patient's consent" (p. 521), but does not attempt to distinguish it from confidentiality in terms of its having any particularly "legal" significance.

Forensic psychiatrists encounter and accommodate the related constructs of confidentiality and testimonial privilege with every patient they treat, with every examination they conduct, with every consultation they undertake, with every record they review, with every report they write, and with every opinion they express in depositions or on the witness stand at trial. Achieving the delicate professional balance these situations require calls for mastery of the evolving clinical, ethical, and legal considerations that surface at every turn in court-related practice.

In this chapter, we examine the codified ethical guidance as well as statutory provisions and exceptions, analyzing each of these sources in a stepwise fashion with additional reference to pertinent case law and the medico-legal professional literature.

CODIFIED ETHICAL GUIDANCE

The principles of medical ethics

The Principles of Medical Ethics with Annotations Especially Applicable to Psychiatry (American Psychiatric Association 2013) was designed to address "special ethical problems in psychiatric practice that differ in coloring and degree from ethical problems in other branches of medical practice" (p. 1). Perhaps nowhere are such differences more prominent and impactful than when they concern issues of confidentiality and testimonial privilege. Even when the guidance the *Principles* offers on both topics does not directly involve court-related activities, every provision is clearly relevant to the roles and obligations of the forensic psychiatrist.

Section 4 of the *Principles* mandates generally that "a physician shall respect the rights of patients, colleagues, and other health professionals, and shall safeguard patient confidences and privacy within the constraints of the law" (p. 2).

This broad, initial treatment draws an interesting distinction between "confidences" and "privacy." If "confidences" are best regarded as discrete disclosures offered by the patient to the doctor, then distinguishing them from "privacy" encourages us to bear in mind that the latter covers such other aspects of the patient's overall medical record as diagnoses, consultations, behavioral observations, personal circumstances, and documentation generated by third parties. Simply put, it is not just the "confidences" that are likely to be confidential, and potentially there is much that could wind up being barred from disclosure in a court of law based on testimonial privilege.

The exhortation that the psychiatrist's obligation is to "safeguard" this information "within the constraints of the law" is open to variable interpretations. The most conservative view would be that the psychiatrist should not *defy* the law when attempting to preserve a patient's confidences and privacy. An attorney, judge, or licensing board might, however, read Section 4 as requiring a degree of zealous advocacy for the patient's rights that compels the psychiatrist to exhaust all antidisclosure options that lie within the *limits* of the law. Less likely, but not unimaginable, is the prospect that Section 4 will be read as being limited to those situations that the law actually *addresses*.

To date, only two appellate decisions have directly addressed the "safeguarding" obligation described in Section 4 of the *Principles*. In *Crescenzo v. Crane* (2002), the Superior Court of New Jersey referred to this portion of Section 4 as a source of guidance that would "limit a physician's ability simply to disgorge privileged records as a result of a third-party subpoena" (p. 290). In *Seebold v. Prison Health Services, Inc.* (2012), the Supreme Court of Pennsylvania mentioned in passing—in fact, only in a footnote—that a brief in this case had cited Section 4 in support of the notion that "there are many scenarios in which informing individuals who are potentially at risk of an inmate's condition would violate the inmate's privacy rights and/or the physician's ethical duty to hold personal information obtained in the doctor/patient relationship in confidence" (p. 1241). Neither of these cases provides much insight into potential interpretations of the energy and fervor with which a psychiatrist must advocate for preserving confidentiality or for preventing testimony-based disclosure in the course of legal proceedings.

Each section of the *Principles* is embellished with a number of specially crafted annotations. Perhaps not surprisingly, Section 4 has twice as many of these—14 in all—than any other section. The annotations that are specifically relevant to confidentiality and testimonial privilege (pp. 6–7) are reproduced here with our own accompanying analysis:

> Psychiatric records, including even the identification of a person as a patient, must be protected with extreme care. Confidentiality is essential to psychiatric treatment. This is based in part on the special nature of psychiatric therapy as well as on the traditional ethical relationship between physician and patient. Growing concern regarding the civil rights of patients and the possible adverse effects of computerization, duplication equipment, and data banks makes the dissemination of confidential information an increasing hazard. Because of the sensitive and private nature of the information with which the psychiatrist deals, he or she must be circumspect in the information that he or she chooses to disclose to others about a patient. The welfare of the patient must be a continuing consideration. (p. 6)

This "extreme care" provision sets a high standard, but one that hardly could be characterized as inappropriate, because the emotional, legal, and material damages that could be suffered are potentially incalculable. The "essential" nature of confidentiality to psychiatric treatment has been recognized by the legal and medical professions alike, most prominently in the case of *Jaffee v. Redmond* (1996), in which the Supreme Court of the United States, recognizing that "50 States and the District of Columbia have enacted into law some form of psychotherapist privilege" (p. 12), and observing that "the mere possibility of disclosure may impede development of the confidential relationship necessary for successful treatment" (p. 10), ultimately held that this privilege should apply in federal courts as well.

The notion of a "growing concern regarding the civil rights of patients" is a bit of an anachronism, as this has been a primary focus of mental health commentators for decades (e.g., Szasz 1962; Appelbaum 1995), but an emphasis on "the possible adverse effects" of various technological advances in data storage and sharing is as timely as it is well-placed. One of the most detailed sources for addressing the perils associated with such procedures is the American Psychological Association's "Record Keeping Guidelines" which are designed to "elaborate and provide assistance to psychologists as they attempt to establish their own record keeping policies and procedures" (2007, p. 993), in a fashion every bit as applicable to the needs of psychiatrists as to those of any other mental health professionals.

> A psychiatrist may release confidential information only with the authorization of the patient or under proper legal compulsion. The continuing duty of the psychiatrist to protect the patient includes fully apprising him/her of the connotations of waiving the privilege of privacy. This may become an issue when the patient is being investigated by a government agency, is applying for a position, or is involved in legal action. The same principles apply to the release of information concerning treatment to medical departments of government agencies, business organizations, labor unions, and insurance companies. Information gained in confidence about patients seen in student health services should not be released without the students' explicit permission. (p. 6)

The Health Insurance Portability and Accountability Act's (HIPAA; 45 CFR §164.500 et seq. 2000) mandates affect in a direct fashion what the "psychiatrist may release." As Shuman (2010) observed, "the limits of judicial discovery of protected health information are neither absent nor absolute in the forensic context" (p. 52), such that psychiatrists would do well to conduct their usual HIPAA-friendly notification procedures even when concluding that in some aspects this statute might not apply (Connell and Koocher 2003).

The "continuing duty" cited here should be seen not just as one that is projected into the future, but also as one that should have been formalized during the very earliest stages of the doctor–patient or doctor–examinee relationship. No section in these *Principles* truly enshrines and conveys the psychiatrist's obligation to establish and reinforce the service recipient's confidentiality rights at regular intervals. It is important to afford all parties an opportunity to plan ahead as psychotherapy or evaluations progress—the "connotations of waiving the privilege of privacy" must be understood from the outset, particularly when "legal action" is contemplated. It is here that the specter of testimonial privilege emerges in Section 4 for the first time. The reference to "patients seen in student health services" is somewhat reminiscent of another concern that for some reason garners no direct attention in the *Principles*—confidentiality in the supervision of medical students, residents, and other supervisees (eds. Ullmer et al. 2009).

According to the *Opinions of the Ethics Committee on the Principles of Medical Ethics with Annotations Especially Applicable to Psychiatry* (American Psychiatric Association 2016), confidentiality safeguards extend beyond the death of the patient, with an understanding that "weakening this view reduces our responsibilities to living patients who trust us to protect their confidences even after their death," and that "this is no less so if the deceased is a prominent person" (p. 26). Devotees of psychiatric history will recognize in this latter observation a reflection of the so-called "Goldwater Rule," adopted after psychiatrists were invited some five decades ago to opine in a magazine about the mental health condition of a presidential candidate (Friedman 2011).

> Clinical and other materials used in teaching and writing must be adequately disguised in order to preserve the anonymity of the individuals involved. (American Psychiatric Association 2013, 6)

This annotation does not specify whether any sort of informed consent procedure is presumed to have been undertaken with the "individuals" involved. The admonition that materials be "disguised" presumably refers to the names of the "individuals" in question, via the use of pseudonyms. Of course, another option would be to avoid any use of names whatsoever. Styling these persons as "individuals" (instead of, e.g., "patients") has a tendency to broaden—whether intentionally or not—the potential pool of persons to whom confidentiality protections are being extended.

According to the *Opinions of the Ethics Committee on the Principles of Medical Ethics with Annotations Especially Applicable to Psychiatry* (American Psychiatric Association 2016), the privacy of "persons other than the patient" who may appear in a training video "must be protected to the same degree as that of the patient" (p. 25).

Third-party considerations become particularly relevant to the forensic psychiatrist when one considers the increasing emphasis placed on the contributions of collateral sources of information in both criminal and civil cases (Kalmbach and Lyons 2006; Gold et al. 2008). Additionally—and perhaps somewhat ironically—the expansive language in this annotation serves as a reminder of the potential for *erosion* of confidentiality protections for patients, as determined on a state-by-state basis, when third parties are present during group or individual treatment (American Bar Association Commission on Domestic Violence 2007). Conducting some seminar teaching in the context of "peer review" may afford additional protections with respect to both confidentiality and testimonial privilege (Kohlberg 2002; Sharifi 2009):

> The ethical responsibility of maintaining confidentiality holds equally for the consultations in which the patient may not have been present and in which the consultee was not a physician. In such instances, the physician consultant should

> alert the consultee to his or her duty of confidentiality. (American Psychiatric Association 2013, 6)

This annotation, arguably the most ambiguously drafted piece of guidance to be found in the *Principles*, could be interpreted as asserting that it is every bit as important to maintain confidentiality when patients are not present as it is when the consultee is not a physician. Another plausible interpretation would be that in those situations in which patients are not present *and* the consultee is not a physician, psychiatrists must recognize that they bear the same confidentiality burdens as they do under the various other circumstances described in Section 4. In any event, forensic psychiatrists are best advised to maximize their commitment to confidentiality no matter which of these admonitions was actually intended. It remains unclear whether the "consultee" in this situation is the person to whom the psychiatrist is *providing* information, the person from whom the physician is obtaining information, or both. As a practical matter, it is better for forensic psychiatrists to take the broadest, most overtly patient-focused perspective and to assume that this guidance addresses both situations.

Puzzlingly, psychiatrists are being told to "alert the consultee to his or her duty of confidentiality." If "his or her" refers to the consultee, what duty truly exists for a nonphysician individual? If "his or her" refers to the psychiatrist, what is the purpose of this alert? Is it to provide some sort of reassurance that shared confidences are likely to go no further, perhaps with the goal of encouraging fuller and more detailed disclosure to the psychiatrist? Once more, the best course of action will be the one that lays out all potential obligations—those arguable as well as those established—to maximize protections and promote transparency when feasible.

> Ethically, the psychiatrist may disclose only that information which is relevant to a given situation. He or she should avoid offering speculation as fact. Sensitive information such as an individual's sexual orientation or fantasy material is usually unnecessary. (American Psychiatric Association 2013, 6)

"May" here surely means "shall." Some latitude will undoubtedly exist should the relevance in question subsequently be challenged by a licensing board or professional guild organization. For one thing, "relevant" is a legal term that does not necessarily comport with lay or other professional interpretations (Soltis et al. 2014). For another, the psychiatrist can hardly be expected to know how broadly cast is the "situation" in question—or what "situations" are likely to arise in the future. The psychiatrist's need to "avoid offering speculation as fact" is really a matter of professionalism that has little to do with confidentiality or testimonial capacity *per se*.

A murkier notion is the guidance Section 4 offers concerning "sensitive information." It is true that "sexual orientation" and "fantasy material" are "usually unnecessary." However, as a more general matter—for which sexual orientation and fantasy are offered merely as examples—"sensitive information" is as apt a way as any to describe a psychiatric patient's file and everything therein. It would have been more to the point simply to identify sexual orientation and fantasy as content either unworthy of documentation or destined for only brief mention, in light of concerns having to do with inappropriate or unforeseeably wider distribution.

> Psychiatrists are often asked to examine individuals for security purposes, to determine suitability for various jobs, and to determine legal competence. The psychiatrist must fully describe the nature and purpose and lack of confidentiality of the examination to the examinee at the beginning of the examination. (American Psychiatric Association 2013, 7)

These characterizations of various roles filled by psychiatrists—in particular by forensic psychiatrists—provide useful examples that enable doctors to place such duties in context. Specifying by way of follow-up comment that psychiatrists need to describe the "lack of confidentiality" at the outset of this particular type of examination may send an unintended message that *other* evaluative efforts do not merit similar warnings. In addition and as noted above, what remains missing is a sense that confidentiality should be revisited at critical junctures *during* the course of a forensic psychiatric evaluation—an exercise that may consist of multiple "examinations."

Because information gleaned from, and opinions generated related to, the types of services designated in this annotation are likely to be headed to the courtroom—especially concerning "legal competence"—it is worth considering discussing testimonial privilege (and the lack thereof) during these recommended descriptions. The "nature and purpose and lack of confidentiality of the examination" could refer to the nature of the examination, the purpose of the examination, and the examination's lack of confidentiality, or it could refer instead to the nature of the examination's confidentiality, the purpose of the examination's confidentiality, and the extent of the examination's lack of confidentiality. The latter approach is surely the safest, avoiding the incomplete and potentially misleading characterization of the "lack of confidentiality" as an absolute notion (e.g., "You need to know, of course, that there *is* no confidentiality").

> Careful judgment must be exercised by the psychiatrist in order to include, when appropriate, the parents or guardian in the treatment of a minor. At the same time, the psychiatrist must assure the minor proper confidentiality. (American Psychiatric Association 2013, 7)

This annotation appears to advise psychiatrists that the decision of whether or not to include parents or guardians in the treatment of children is a difficult one that merits special consideration. Conveying the "proper confidentiality" to a minor patient will require attention to two overlapping considerations: what is appropriate for the child—and to the extent relevant, for the family—for psychotherapeutic purposes, and what strictures the law provides. These limitations are jurisdiction-specific and take into account such factors as the child's age, the nature of the medical problems prompting clinical attention, and each state's construction of testimonial privilege for juvenile service recipients (Paruch 2009; Boumil et al. 2012). Semantics may have an important role to play in this passage should a psychiatrist ever be held to account for an alleged transgression: "assure" would mean that the doctor would provide the patient with information intended to underscore confidentiality rights, while "ensure" would mean that the doctor would take affirmative steps—perhaps after, as well as during treatment—to make certain that confidentiality is never breached.

> When, in the clinical judgment of the treating psychiatrist, the risk of danger is deemed to be significant, the psychiatrist may reveal confidential information disclosed by the patient. (American Psychiatric Association 2013, 7)

This brief annotation refers to circumstances that are arguably the most fraught with personal and professional danger. It alludes to the classic "duty to warn" or "duty to protect" notion most notably reflected in the Supreme Court of California case of *Tarasoff v. Regents of the University of California* (1976) and covered in detail elsewhere in this book.

The passing reference here to the "treating psychiatrist" begs the question of what sort of obligation the evaluating *forensic* psychiatrist might have—recently highlighted by the California Court of Appeal case of *Elijah W. v. Superior Court of Los Angeles County* (2013)—for mandatory reporting in the context of court-related assessment. The ruling in *Elijah W.* that the examinee "was entitled to the appointment of therapist who agreed to disclose information regarding child abuse, neglect, or threats only to minor's attorney" (p. 606) was narrowly jurisdiction-specific and cannot be relied on by doctors in other parts of the country. Given the unsettled nature of this issue, forensic psychiatrists are advised to sort out such concerns with counsel prior to the provision of services, and to make the agreed-upon conclusion a part of the informed consent process in each individual case.

> When the psychiatrist is ordered by the court to reveal the confidences entrusted to him/her by patients, he or she may comply or he/she may ethically hold the right to dissent within the framework of the law. When the psychiatrist is in doubt, the right of the patient to confidentiality and, by extension, to unimpaired treatment should be given priority. The psychiatrist should reserve the right to raise the question of adequate need for disclosure. In the event that the necessity for legal disclosure is demonstrated by the court, the psychiatrist may request the right to disclosure of only that information which is relevant to the legal question at hand. (American Psychiatric Association 2013, 7)

The clarity and salience of this annotation are perhaps unequaled not only in Section 4, but in the balance of the *Principles*. Outlined here is a logical, reasonable, and laudably patient-focused approach to navigating between the twin perils of psychotherapeutic betrayal and legal sanction. Consulting with retaining counsel in order to anticipate such concerns may make it considerably easier to establish and maintain the contemplated lines of communication with the court as successive levels of engagement are encountered (Drogin and Barrett 2013).

> With regard for the person's dignity and privacy and with truly informed consent, it is ethical to present a patient to a scientific gathering if the confidentiality of the presentation is understood and accepted by the audience. (American Psychiatric Association 2013, 7)

Unlike those situations in which courtroom involvement is predicted, the anticipation of an eventual presentation to a "scientific gathering" is not one for which the psychiatrist is expected to seek informed consent at the outset of service provision. Indeed, this is actually inadvisable when one considers the unintended "grooming" effect that this foreknowledge could have on the nature and course of psychotherapy. Perhaps more to the point than "understanding" and "acceptance" on the part of the audience is some affirmative action on its part to "ensure" confidentiality—even if this merely involves, for example, affixing one's name to a sign-up sheet that is circulated prior to the confidential portion of the presentation in question.

It is worth noting that a "scientific gathering" may be attended by numerous laypersons—not just students, assistants, and professional guild organization staff, but in some cases members of the press. Additionally, some presentations are recorded, often with pay-per-view options tied to Continuing Medical Education (CME) credit. Will the subsequently distributed material be accompanied by sufficient confidentiality warnings and attestation requirements? Such concerns should be considered well in advance of the presentation.

> It is ethical to present a patient or former patient to a public gathering or to the news media only if the patient is fully informed of enduring loss of confidentiality, is competent, and consents in writing without coercion. (American Psychiatric Association 2013, 7)

This annotation raises concerns essentially similar to the preceding concern, with a few interesting twists. For one, competency and a lack of coercion are surely no less relevant with respect to a "scientific gathering" than they would be to a "public gathering" or in the context of some sort of print or broadcast media event. These attributes should be ensured in each of these situations. Also, the "patient or former patient" designation here contrasts with the more basic "patient" designation employed in the preceding annotation. Presumably there is no reason to assume that a "former" patient (or, in particular, examinee) would not be entitled to the same treatment as a current one when a "scientific gathering" is contemplated—particularly when forensic psychiatric material is being presented (cases in which litigation is still pending are often unsuitable for such presentations). This is due not only to the examinee's interest in the outcome of court proceedings, but also counsel's interest—on the examinee's behalf—that upcoming expert witness testimony not be aired prematurely.

> When involved in funded research, the ethical psychiatrist will advise human subjects of the funding source, retain his or her freedom to reveal data and results, and follow all appropriate and current guidelines relative to human subject protection. (American Psychiatric Association 2013, 7)

Confidentiality and, to a much lesser extent, testimonial privilege issues are significant considerations in the conduct of clinical and forensic psychiatric research. The fact that they receive relatively minimal coverage in mainstream ethical codes is not a sign of disregard but instead a tacit acknowledgement of an increasingly narrow delineation of academic and practice roles. "Appropriate and current guidelines" for this topic include the *American College of Physicians Ethics Manual* (American College of Physicians Ethics, Professionalism, and Human Rights Committee 2012), which provides substantial attention to a full range of research-oriented concerns.

Ethical guidelines for the practice of forensic psychiatry

As indicated above, a forensic psychiatrist benefits from mastery of the contents of the *Principles* even when they do not directly address legal matters *per se*. There is, however, another highly regarded and oft-noted source of ethical guidance concerning confidentiality (though not testimonial privilege) that is tailor made for the concerns of the civil or criminal expert witness. The American Academy of Psychiatry and the Law (AAPL) has promulgated *Ethics Guidelines for the Practice of Forensic Psychiatry* (2005), Section II of which includes the following treatment of "Confidentiality":

> Respect for the individual's right of privacy and the maintenance of confidentiality should be major concerns when performing forensic evaluations. Psychiatrists should maintain confidentiality to the extent possible, given the legal context. Special attention should be paid to the evaluee's understanding of medical confidentiality. A forensic evaluation requires notice to the evaluee and to collateral sources of reasonably anticipated limitations on confidentiality. Information or reports derived from a forensic evaluation are subject to the rules of confidentiality that apply to the particular evaluation, and any disclosure should be restricted accordingly. (p. 1)

Here, forensic psychiatrists are informed in a crisp and accessible fashion that they should pay attention to confidentiality, that they should do all that they can with regard to whatever legal rules apply, that they should make sure that the persons they evaluate understand confidentiality and its limitations, and that the by-products of an evaluation should be kept as confidential as the evaluation itself. Use of the wording "to the extent possible" places a rather substantial burden on forensic psychiatrists, as someone seeking to turn the *Guidelines* against them could simply argue that there was *something* the doctor could legally have done that he or she did *not* attempt to do. To date, no federal or state appellate decisions have referred to Section II.

The guidance in Section II of the *Guidelines* is amplified by a "Commentary" section, reproduced here in its entirety with our own accompanying analysis:

> The practice of forensic psychiatry often presents significant problems regarding confidentiality. Psychiatrists should be aware of and alert to those issues of privacy and confidentiality presented by the particular forensic situation. Notice of reasonably anticipated limitations to confidentiality should be given to evaluees, third parties, and other appropriate individuals. (p. 1)

Although the "significant problems" this sort of work entails are not enumerated here, they are easy enough to identify. On the one hand, the very *lack* of confidentiality inherent in forensic psychiatric evaluation often makes it difficult to elicit valid and useful information when evaluees understand how their disclosures may ultimately be used against them. They may become intimidated to the point of dissimulation that seemingly resembles malingering (Rogers 2008). On the other hand, evaluees who *fail* to grasp this circumstance may become resentful and uncooperative in later stages of the process when they eventually realize—too late—that their testing and interview responses have a potentially lengthy and toxic shelf life, as addressed by the next portion of this "Commentary":

> Psychiatrists should indicate for whom they are conducting the examination and what they will do with the information obtained. At the

> beginning of a forensic evaluation, care should be taken to explicitly inform the evaluee that the psychiatrist is not the evaluee's "doctor." Psychiatrists have a continuing obligation to be sensitive to the fact that although a warning has been given, the evaluee may develop the belief that there is a treatment relationship. Psychiatrists should take precautions to ensure that they do not release confidential information to unauthorized persons. (pp. 1–2)

This guidance pinpoints the "continuing" need for confidentiality education in a fashion that is decidedly lacking in the text of the aforementioned *Principles*. The skillful forensic psychiatrist is often a seasoned psychotherapist whose clinical mien may coax the evaluee into a sense that treatment is being provided—particularly when the doctor has been sent by the evaluee's lawyer and touted as the special individual who can provide a way out of the evaluee's current legal morass. This role distinction often can be eroded by the forensic psychiatrist's ill-advised willingness to provide treatment *after* the fact, or to accept a forensic assignment when he or she was the evaluee's doctor *previously* (Strasburger et al. 1997; Drogin 2012):

> When a patient is involved in parole, probation, conditional release, or in other custodial or mandatory settings, psychiatrists should be clear about limitations on confidentiality in the treatment relationship and ensure that these limitations are communicated to the patient. Psychiatrists should be familiar with the institutional policies regarding confidentiality. When no policy exists, psychiatrists should attempt to clarify these matters with the institutional authorities and develop working guidelines. (American Academy of Psychiatry and the Law 2005, 2)

In the professional literature, relatively little attention is paid to the unique challenges that accompany forensic treatment—for example, situations in which the state forensic hospital, having determined that an evaluee was incompetent to stand trial, is now tasked with competency "restoration" on the basis of a combination of psychotherapy and medication (Samuel and Michals 2011). Under these circumstances, the advice proffered earlier by this Commentary—that one must avoid fostering "the belief that there is a treatment relationship"—is essentially stood on its head, in recognition of the simple realities of the intersection of law and medicine; however, a logically based, stepwise method of working through potential conflicts is outlined here.

STATUTORY PROVISIONS AND EXCEPTIONS

For better or for worse, American jurisprudence plays out across a panoply of 51 different state and federal jurisdictions. Fortunately, when it comes to statutory guidance, there is a broad commonality of themes, because of the similarity of issues that psychiatrists face regardless of the State in which they practice. Following is a typical example—Hawaii's "Physician–Patient Privilege" (HI.R. Evid. 504 2013), with our accompanying analysis of its various components:

1. Definitions. As used in this rule:
    a. A "patient" is a person who consults or is examined or interviewed by a physician.
    b. A "physician" is a person authorized, or reasonably believed by the patient to be authorized, to practice medicine in any state or nation.

        The "patient" and "physician" in this scheme are defined as broadly as possible. The "believed by" concept is typical of such statutes, because it would not be fair for the patient to have his or her information subject to disclosure because of a simple error in identity—particularly when one considers the parade of variously credentialed individuals the patient typically would encounter in a general or psychiatric hospital setting.
    c. A communication is "confidential" if not intended to be disclosed to third persons other than those present to further the interest of the patient in the consultation, examination, or interview, or persons reasonably necessary for the transmission of the communication, or persons who are participating in the diagnosis and treatment under the direction of the physician, including members of the patient's family.

        The key provision here is actually "intended." This reflects once again an understanding that "confidentiality" is an essentially ethical notion controlled by rules ingrained in medicine, as opposed to the law. Communications still can remain confidential when they move beyond the physician–patient dyad, as long as this comports with the overall context of treatment. For example, if a psychiatrist discusses the patient's medication with the patient's spouse, who will make sure the proper dosage is administered at the correct time, this discussion should not cause details of the patient's medical care to no longer be protected.
2. General rule of privilege. A patient has a privilege to refuse to disclose and to prevent any other person from disclosing confidential communications made for the purpose of diagnosis or treatment of the patient's physical, mental, or emotional condition, including alcohol or drug addiction, among oneself, the patient's physician, and persons who are participating in the diagnosis or treatment under the direction of the physician, including members of the patient's family.

    What was "intended" to be confidential is now safe from disclosure in the context of civil or criminal legal proceedings. The patient does not have to divulge this information in court and can keep the doctor from doing so as well. The broadly inclusive language ensures that virtually everyone normally expected to witness medically oriented disclosures will be covered.

3. Who may claim the privilege. The privilege may be claimed by the patient, the patient's guardian or conservator, or the personal representative of a deceased patient. The person who was the physician at the time of the communication is presumed to have authority to claim the privilege but only on behalf of the patient.
4. This is a critically important point in testimonial privilege. The privilege exists for the purpose of protecting patients, making it a foregone conclusion that they—or their representatives—are the ones who should be enabled to invoke it. Because doctors are the individuals most likely to have the relevant information in their possession, it seems logical and saves time for them to "claim" the privilege as well, but they are really only doing so in the patient's stead. Therefore, a better term would actually be "assert" the privilege. Exceptions include the following:
   a. Proceedings for hospitalization. There is no privilege under this rule for communications relevant to an issue in proceedings to hospitalize the patient for mental illness or substance abuse, or in proceedings for the discharge or release of a patient previously hospitalized for mental illness or substance abuse.

      This commonsensical provision is directly relevant to the day-to-day duties of clinical and forensic psychiatrists alike. Because the substance of civil commitment proceedings requires initial or at least eventual judicial oversight, raising a roadblock of testimonial privilege in these matters would be pointless.
   b. Examination by order of court. If the court orders an examination of the physical, mental, or emotional condition of a patient, whether a party or a witness, communications made in the course thereof are not privileged under this rule with respect to the particular purpose for which the examination is ordered unless the court orders otherwise.

      Forensic psychiatry gets its due here; the doctor's role is acknowledged as directly as possible. A close reading of this provision telegraphs what are essentially the "exceptions to the exception," as disclosures must pertain to a "particular purpose." For example, in the course of an examination to determine competency to stand trial, defendants may admit to having committed the crime in question. In the context of civil proceedings in a personal injury matter, plaintiffs may refer to some aspect of their private lives that would unduly prejudice a jury without having relevance to the case under consideration. A court could reasonably exclude such information.
   c. Condition an element of claim or defense. There is no privilege under this rule as to a communication relevant to the physical, mental, or emotional condition of the patient in any proceeding in which the patient relies on the condition as an element of the patient's claim or defense or, after the patient's death, in any proceeding in which any party relies on the condition as an element of the party's claim or defense.

      Seizing further on the above-noted notion of what may be the "particular purpose" of certain legal proceedings, this provision sets out in no uncertain terms the logically compelling perspective that if the patient needs to use this information, it will not be privileged. Interestingly, despite postmortem confidentiality concerns addressed by the Ethics Committee of the American Psychiatric Association (2013), anyone whose legal case focuses on the condition of a deceased individual is likely to be able to have that information entered into evidence.
   d. Proceedings against physician. There is no privilege under this rule in any administrative or judicial proceeding in which the competency, practitioner's license, or practice of the physician is at issue, provided that the identifying data of the patients whose records are admitted into evidence shall be kept confidential unless waived by the patient. The administrative agency, board, or commission may close the proceeding to the public to protect the confidentiality of the patient.

      This provision negates the possibility that the physician could lay claim to a privilege that is essentially that of the patient. It also enables governmental agencies, acting in the public interest, to review patient files in order to identify a pattern of malpractice or other malfeasance that could result in the restriction or revocation of a doctor's license. A recent *cause célèbre* in this regard was the case of *Maryland Board of Physicians v. Eist* (2011), in which a psychiatrist was ultimately unable to prevent punishment by the Board for declining to release patient records in the context of contentious divorce and child custody proceedings.
   e. Furtherance of crime or tort. There is no privilege under this rule if the services of the physician were sought, obtained, or used to enable or aid anyone to commit or plan to commit what the patient knew or reasonably should have known to be a crime or tort.
   f. Prevention of crime or tort. There is no privilege under this rule as to a communication reflecting the patient's intent to commit a criminal or tortious act that the physician reasonably believes is likely to result in death or substantial bodily harm.

Public safety concerns are a predictable source of privilege exceptions. State authorities are naturally loath to enable convicted or suspected criminals to hide behind unjustly obtained advantages. Here, also, is a correlate of the aforementioned *Tarasoff* situation, in which doctors have complied with a "duty to warn" or "duty to protect." Prosecutors seeking criminal sanctions or plaintiffs' attorneys seeking monetary compensation for their clients are allowed to introduce this sort of evidence despite its having been obtained from an otherwise protected medical record.

SUMMARY KEY POINTS

- Although they overlap in various theoretical and practical ways, confidentiality is an essentially ethical concern, while testimonial privilege is an essentially legal one.
- With respect to confidentiality, codified ethical guidance establishes that medical records must be protected with extreme care, that release of medical information requires formalized authorization, and that courts can compel release of this information on their own under certain circumstances, though the psychiatrist's professional obligations may include challenging such mandates within the limits of the law.
- Statutory provisions—confirmed by state and federal case law—provide for a testimonial privilege that may be claimed by the patient, or by the psychiatrist on the patient's behalf, concerning confidential communications that occur between the psychiatrist, the patient, and a select group of persons whose participation typically enhances diagnosis or treatment.
- A number of exceptions to testimonial privilege exist, typically regarding such subject matter as proceedings for involuntary hospitalization, court-ordered evaluations, conditions that constitute an element of a patient's legal claim or defense, and lawsuits or complaints filed against psychiatrists.

REFERENCES

201 KY. Admin. Regs. 9:005 (2015).

American Academy of Psychiatry and the Law. 2005. *Ethics Guidelines for the Practice of Forensic Psychiatry.* http://www.aapl.org/ethics.htm, accessed June 28, 2016.

American Bar Association Commission on Domestic Violence. 2007. *Summary of Domestic Violence and Sexual Abuse Advocate Confidentiality Laws.* http://www.americanbar.org/content/dam/aba/migrated/domviol/docs/Advocate ConfidentialityChart.authcheckdam.pdf

American College of Physicians Ethics, Professionalism, and Human Rights Committee. 2012. American College of Physicians ethics manual. *Annals of Internal Medicine* 23:73–104.

American Psychiatric Association (APA). 2013. *The Principles of Medical Ethics with Annotations Especially Applicable to Psychiatry.* Arlington, VA: APA.

American Psychiatric Association (APA). 2016. *Opinions of the Ethics Committee on the Principles of Medical Ethics with Annotations Especially Applicable to Psychiatry.* Arlington, VA: APA.

American Psychological Association. 2007. Record keeping guidelines. *American Psychologist* 62:993–1004.

Appelbaum PS. 1995. Civil commitment and liability for violating patients' rights. *Psychiatric Services* 46:17–18.

Boumil MM, DF Freitas, and CF Freitas. 2012. Waiver of the psychotherapist-patient privilege: Implications for child custody litigation. *Health Matrix: Journal of Law-Medicine* 22:1–31.

Campbell R. 2004. *Campbell's Psychiatric Dictionary,* 8th edition. New York: Oxford.

Connell MA and GP Koocher. 2003. HIPAA and forensic practice. *AP-LS News* 23:16–19.

Crescenzo v. Crane, 796 A.2d 283, 350 N.J.Super. 531 (2002).

Drogin EY. 2012. Determining the need for, identifying, and selecting experts. In *Coping with Psychiatric and Psychological Testimony,* 6th edition, edited by D Faust. New York: Oxford, 775–782.

Drogin EY and CL Barrett. 2013. Trial consultation. In *Handbook of Psychology.* Vol. 11, edited by IB Weiner and RK Otto. Hoboken, NJ: Wiley, 648–663.

Elijah W. v. Superior Court of Los Angeles County, 153 Cal. Rptr. 3d 606 (2013).

Friedman R. 2011. How a telescopic lens muddles psychiatric insights. *The New York Times,* 23 May, p. D5.

Garner MD (ed.). 2014. *Black's Law Dictionary,* 10th edition. St. Paul, MN: Thomson Reuters.

Gold LH, SA Anfang, AM Drukteinis, JL Metzner, M Price, BW Wall, L Wylonis, and HV Zonana. 2008. AAPL practice guideline for the forensic evaluation of psychiatric disability. *Journal of the American Academy of Psychiatry and the Law* 36:S3–S50.

Health Insurance Portability and Accountability Act, 45 CFR §164.500 et seq. (2000).

HI.R. Evid.504 (2013).

Jaffee v. Redmond, 581 U.S. 1 (1996).

Kalmbach KC and PM Lyons. 2006. Ethical issues in conducting forensic evaluations. *Applied Psychology in Criminal Justice* 2:261–290.

Kohlberg KR. 2002. The medical peer review privilege: A lynchpin for patient safety measures. *Massachusetts Bar Review* 86:158–162.

KY. R. Evid. 507(b) (2015).

Maryland State Board of Physicians v. Eist, 417 Md. 545, 11 A.3d 786 (2011).

Paruch D. 2009. The psychotherapist-patient privilege in the family court. *Northern Illinois University Law Review* 29:499–570.

Rogers R. 2008. An introduction to response styles. In *Clinical Assessment of Malingering and Deception,* 3rd edition, edited by R Rogers. New York: Guilford, 3–13.

Samuel SE and TJ Michals. 2011. Competency restoration. In *Handbook of Forensic Assessment: Psychological and Psychiatric Perspectives*, edited by EY Drogin, FM Dattilio, RL Sadoffand, and TG Gutheil. Hoboken, NJ: Wiley, 79–96.

Seebold v. Prison Health Service, Inc., 57 A.3d 1232, 618 Pa. 632 (2012).

Sharifi G. 2009. Is the door Open or Closed? Evaluating the future of the federal medical peer-review privilege. *John Marshall Law Review* 42:561–593.

Shuman DW. 2010. Introduction to the legal system. In *The American Psychiatric Publishing Textbook of Forensic Psychiatry*, 2nd edition, edited by RI Simon and LH Gold. Washington, DC: American Psychiatric Association, 43–62.

Soltis K, R Acierno, DF Gros, M Yoderand, and PW Tuerk. 2014. Post-traumatic stress disorder: Ethical and legal relevance to the Criminal Justice System. *Journal of Law, Medicine and Ethics* 42:147–152.

State v. Mauti, 208 N.J. 519, 33 A.3d 1216 (2012).

Strasburger LH, TG Gutheil, and A Brodsky. 1997. On wearing two hats: Role conflicts in serving as both psychotherapist and expert witness. *American Journal of Psychiatry* 154:488–456.

Szasz TS. 1962. Open doors or civil rights for mental patients. *Journal of Individual Psychology* 18:168–171.

Tarasoff v. Regents of the University of California, 17 Cal. 3d 425, 551 P.2d 334, 131 Cal. Rptr. 14 (Cal. 1976).

Ullmer C, DM Wolman, and MM Johns (eds.). 2009. *Resident Duty Hours: Enhancing Sleep, Supervision, and Safety.* New York: National Academies Press.

United States v. Chase, 340 F.3d 978 (2003).

20

The duty to protect

ALAN R. FELTHOUS AND CLAUDIA KACHIGIAN

INTRODUCTION

Psychiatrists and other mental health professionals can, under certain circumstances, be liable in a malpractice claim when a patient seriously harms another person. The consulting forensic psychiatrist must be familiar with relevant legal cases, statutory law, and the professional standard of practice regarding his or her duty to protect nonpatient third parties.

Depending on jurisdictional law, psychiatrists' duty to protect can necessitate risk assessments to serve three different protective mechanisms, all of which are intended to reduce the risk of the patient's killing or seriously harming another person: assessment to determine whether (1) hospitalization, involuntary if not voluntary; (2) protective disclosures or warnings; or (3) reporting in compliance with gun control law, respectively, are indicated.

These three protective legal requirements for mental health professionals developed sequentially. The duty to control and protect by hospitalization was in place "pre-*Tarasoff*." *Tarasoff*-like warnings and reportings became legal duties in many states through both common and legislative law, following the first law of its kind, the Supreme Court of California's "*Tarasoff* principle" of 1976. Recently, gun control legislation, already in effect for decades, has been expanded in a small number of states to further restrict firearm possession by mental patients deemed to be dangerous.

TARASOFF AND ITS PROGENY CASES

According to common law in the United States, one person, such as a psychiatrist or psychotherapist, is not responsible for the harmful violence that a second person, such as a patient, inflicts upon a third person, unless the first person had a special or controlling relationship with either the second or the third person (Restatement [Second] of Torts 1965). Hospital administrators and physicians were thought to have considerable control over patients and were sometimes held accountable for discharge decisions that resulted in adverse outcomes. As hospital care became more restricted in favor of community treatment programs, however, the prospect of treating outpatients who were mentally ill and potentially violent became more commonplace.

In 1974, the Supreme Court of California, in its *Tarasoff I* decision, articulated the duty to warn (*Tarasoff v. Regents of the University of California* 1974, 559). As a result of the decision, therapists in California had a legal duty to notify an identifiable victim and/or the police when a patient presented a danger of seriously harming another person and when such disclosures were the most reasonable measures to prevent violence. Several organizations, including the American Psychiatric Association, criticized this new case law (Brief of Amicus Curiae in support for Rehearing of Tarasoff 1975), so the Court reheard the case. The second decision, *Tarasoff II* (hereafter designated *Tarasoff*), in 1976, vacated *Tarasoff I*, replacing its "duty to warn" with a "duty to protect," which emphasized warnings but also allowed for other protective actions.

Through its 1976 *Tarasoff* decision, the Supreme Court of California extended liability to the world of outpatient care and, more explicitly than before, articulated a therapist's duty to protect third persons through the formulation known as the *Tarasoff* principle:

> When a psychotherapist determines, or pursuant to the standards of his profession should determine, that his patient presents a serious danger of violence to another, he incurs an obligation to use reasonable care to protect the intended victim against such danger. The discharge of this duty may require the therapist to take one or more of various steps, depending on the nature of the case. Thus, it may call for him to warn the intended victim or others likely to apprise the victim of the danger, to notify the police, or to take whatever other steps are reasonably necessary under the circumstances. (p. 431)

The *Tarasoff* decision created responsibilities and liabilities for therapists who have little actual control over their patients. In some instances, the principle could pertain to patients who could not be civilly committed. Although *Tarasoff* is the most widely known case on the duty to protect, many other courts subsequently addressed the issue of protecting third persons.

Four evolutionary periods in the clinicians' duty to warn or protect since the mid-twentieth century are recognized. In the pre-*Tarasoff* period *(1950–1974)*, any duty to protect third persons derived from a duty to control the potentially violent patient, typically through hospitalization.

More extensive liability to third persons was generally limited by (1) the nonresponsibility rule; (2) sovereign immunity; (3) the honest error in professional judgment rule (Felthous 1987); and (4) the "firefighter's rule."

In the pre-*Tarasoff* period, the common law rule of nonresponsibility was more protective against third-party liability. Clinicians were not liable for a patient's violent acts against others unless the patient was negligently discharged or poorly supervised and negligently allowed to escape from the hospital (Felthous 1987). The common law rule of nonresponsibility and its specific exceptions that permitted liability were formulated in the Restatement (Second) of Torts by the American Law Institute in 1965.

The exception most applicable to a hospital patient, especially civilly committed, was the *custodial relationship* in Section 320 that was defined by *control*:

> One who is required by law to take or who voluntarily takes the custody of another under circumstances such as to deprive the other person of his normal power of self-protection or to subject him to association with persons likely to harm him, is under a duty to exercise reasonable care so to control the conduct of [these] persons as to prevent them from intentionally harming others or so conducting themselves as to create an unreasonable risk of harm to him, if the actor:
>
> - Knows or has reason to know that he has the ability to control the conduct of the [other] person, and
> - Knows or should know of the necessity and opportunity for exercising such control. (Restatement [Second] of Torts, Section 320 1965)

Further supporting the importance of the element of control in the relationship was the *takes charge* exception to nonresponsibility of Section 319:

> One who takes charge of a ... person whom he knows or should know to be likely to cause bodily harm to others if not controlled is under a duty to exercise reasonable care to control the ... person to prevent him from doing such harm. (Restatement [Second] of Torts, Section 319 1965)

Courts consistently followed the common law rule of nonresponsibility and the takes-charge exception during the pre-*Tarasoff* period. Regardless of how "special" an outpatient relationship might have been considered, liability for violent harm inflicted on third persons could occur where the patient was controlled through hospitalization, but not through outpatient treatment (Felthous and Kachigian 2001a).

Sovereign immunity provided the second source of protection against liability for the violent harm that a patient inflicts on another. A species known as judicial immunity bars a party in a lawsuit for suing the court for an adverse judgment, and similarly, one cannot sue the government for a policy decision that resulted in harm. Because decisions to control or release a hospitalized patient were considered discretionary, a person who is injured by a discharged patient could not sue the hospital or the government clinician who discharged the patient. The clinician's inability to accurately predict future violence was implicitly respected through the recognition of the fallibility of decisions over the safe management of mental patients (Felthous and Kachigian 2001a).

Even in the pre-*Tarasoff* period, sovereign immunity was not equally protective of government clinicians in all jurisdictions. In order to ensure that victims of negligence by government employees have equal access to redress and compensation as victims of negligence in the private sector, Congress enacted the Federal Tort Claims Act (FTCA) (28 U.S.C.A. Sec. 2671) (West 1990). Some courts found clinicians' decisions to discharge to be discretionary and therefore nonliable (e.g., *McDowell v. County of Alameda* 1979), whereas others regarded such decisions as ministerial, involving "implementation of policies or regulations, and accordingly liable within the FTCA" (e.g., *Fair v. United States* 1956; *Merchants National Bank & Trust Co. of Fargo v. United States* 1967). Nonetheless, sovereign immunity provided protection against third-party liability, especially in the pre-*Tarasoff* period, but even since then in some jurisdictions (e.g., *Canon v. Thumudo* 1988).

The honest error in professional judgment rule (e.g., *Greenberg v. Barbour* 1971) provided the third pillar of protection of pre-*Tarasoff* immunity. Courts resisted sustaining liability where the only error was an honest mistake in professional judgment. For liability to exist there must have been negligence that exceeded a single, good-faith misjudgment. This principle was advanced in 1954 by the New York Appellate Court in *St. George v. State*. Other courts subsequently cited *St. George* when invoking the rule (Felthous and Kachigian 2001a).

Clinicians may not have such duty if the victim of the patient's threatened and actual violence happens to be a police officer or firefighter who was victimized while responding to an incident in the course of his or her employment (*Tilley v. Schulte* 1999). This is known as the "firefighter's rule." In the pre-*Tarasoff* period, no liability for a clinician's failure to warn a potential victim of a patient's violent threats was recognized.

The second evolutionary period was the *inception of the Tarasoff principle (1974–1980)*, wherein outpatient therapy was posited as providing enough "control" over a patient so as to impose on the therapist a duty to warn or protect under the "takes charge" exception (Section 319 of the Restatement [Second] of Torts) of the common law rule of nonresponsibility (American Law Institute 1965).

Liability through failure to control by hospitalization was essentially eliminated by California's Lanterman–Petris–Short Act (LPS Act), California's progressive mental health code, which was signed into law in 1967 and became effective in 1972. LPS provided immunity for liability related to hospital admission and discharge decisions. In other words, in order to support the dehospitalization and community mental health movements, the California legislature negated the traditional basis for liability to third persons, failure to control through hospitalization. The Supreme Court of California in *Tarasoff* invoked the immunity provision of the LPS Act in dismissing the claim of failure to hospitalize, viz "to detain" a dangerous person. After other claims were consolidated or dismissed, the remaining claim was "failure to warn of a dangerous patient." The question before the court was how liability, no longer available for failure to control by hospitalization, could be found in outpatient treatment without considering hospitalization.

From its opinion, it is clear that the court relied heavily on the just published law review article by Fleming and Maximov (1974). From this article, the court found that enough "control" exists in an outpatient psychotherapeutic relationship for the "special relation" exception to the rule of nonresponsibility, heretofore allowing liability concerning decisions to initiate or continue hospitalization, to now allow for liability concerning a claim of failure to warn of the violent acts of an outpatient (Felthous 1989).

The *period of diversification (1980–1989)* was the third evolutionary period, when courts and state legislatures adopted a wide variety of rules concerning warnings to potential third persons about the acts of potentially violent patients. These rules included the foreseeability rule, the foreseeable victim rule, the identifiable victim rule, the specificity rule, the zone of danger rule, the sovereign immunity rule, and the professional judgment rule. Some courts, on the other hand, found no duty to warn or protect. If earlier psychiatrists anticipated that the *Tarasoff* principle would be adopted by their state, by the mid-1980s it became clear that they were required to familiarize themselves with the relevant law of their own state (Felthous and Kachigian 2001a).

The fourth evolutionary period was *Retreat from Tarasoff (1990–1999)*, when appellate courts and legislatures restricted application of the *Tarasoff* principle by the following means: adoption but with limitations, rejecting a duty to warn (e.g., in Florida [*Boynton v. Burgess* 1991]) and/or a duty to control a voluntary patient (e.g., Virginia [*Nasser v. Parker* 1995], and acknowledging a duty to warn or protect but proactively circumscribing its application (e.g., Illinois [*Charleston v. Larson* 1998]) (Felthous and Kachigian 2001a). The important point is that the consulting forensic psychiatrist must become familiar with the relevant case law of the jurisdiction in which treatment being examined was rendered.

LAW FROM THE LEGISLATURES

Thirty states now have statutes that explicitly permit or establish a duty for psychiatrists to make some type of disclosure to protect those threatened by their patients. Almost all of these statutes present options for dealing with patients posing a threat (Table 20.1). Most all the statutes allow or require warning the potential victims. Other options include informing law enforcement or hospitalizing the patient. Less common options include warning the parents of a minor or other state-specific alternatives. For example, in Arizona the duty can be fulfilled by "taking any other precautions that a reasonable and prudent mental health provider would take under the circumstances." Such a law implicitly acknowledges the uniqueness of each situation and gives significant discretion to individual clinicians, but it provides precious little more guidance than the courts have done.

The *Tarasoff* statutes fall into one of the following four categories with regard to whether they establish or affirm a duty to warn: those that (1) seem to explicitly establish a duty, (2) prohibit liability except under specified circumstances, (3) seem to be permissive, and (4) take other approaches. A statute that creates a duty includes wording such as "a mental health professional *has a duty*" (emphasis added). Conditional duties are evident from wording such as "There can be no cause of action … unless …" On the other hand, the language of permissive statutes appears to allow warning, without requiring protective disclosure (e.g., "The psychiatrist *may* disclose …") (Kachigian and Felthous 2004).

LAW FROM BOTH COURTS AND LEGISLATURES

A number of states now have *both* case and statutory law that address a *Tarasoff*-like duty to warn or protect. Familiarity with relevant case law alone is insufficient for the forensic psychiatrist who consults on a "duty to protect" case in one of these jurisdictions, as is examining only the state's protective disclosure statute. Germane law may have been crafted by both the legislature and the courts and may include law governing civil commitment and privileged and confidential information. Therefore, it behooves the consultant to be somewhat knowledgeable about both statutory and judicial law pertaining to confidentiality and the duty to protect.

Sponsors and originators of *Tarasoff*-inspired protective disclosure statutes hoped for greater clarity and coherence of the duty to protect within the state's jurisprudence. A systematic review of appellate court decisions in states with such statutes in place revealed remarkable diversity in how courts applied or chose not to apply the relevant statute in *Tarasoff*-like situations. Courts' use of *Tarasoff* statutes could be broadly classified as (1) not referencing the state's *Tarasoff* statute; (2) referencing the state's statute but not using it in the court's analysis; (3) referencing the statute, using it in the court's analysis, and finding that the statute creates a duty; (4) referencing the statute, using the statute in the court's

Table 20.1 Statutory options for discharging the duty to protect

State (year referenced is year statute was first in effect)	Warn victim	and/ or	Report to police	and/ or	Hospitalize voluntarily	Attempt involuntary hospitalization	Other
Arizona							
A.R.S. §36–517.02 (1989)	Yes	—	Yes	—	Yes	Yes	Yes
California							
Cal. Civ. Code §43.92 (1985)	—	—	Yes	—	—	—	—
Colorado							
C.R.S. §13-21-117 (1986)	Yes	and	Yes	or	Yes[b]	Yes	Yes
Delaware							
16 Del. C. §5402 (1992)	Yes	and	Yes	or	Yes	Yes	—
District of Columbia[a]							
D.C. Code §7-1203.03 (1979)	Yes	or	Yes	or	—	Yes	Yes
Florida[a]							
FLA. Stat. Ann. §456.059 (2000)	Yes	or	Yes	—	—	—	—
Fla. Stat. §491.0147 (1991)	Yes	or	Yes	—	—	—	Yes
Idaho							
Idaho Code §6-1902 (1991)	Yes	—	—	—	—	—	—
Idaho Code §6-1903 (1991)	Yes	and	Yes	—	—	—	Yes
Illinois							
740 ILCS 110/11 (viii) (1990)	—	—	—	—	—	—	—
405 ILCS 5/6-103 (1991)	Yes	and	Yes	or	Yes[b]	Yes	—
Indiana							
Burns Ind. Code Ann. §34-30-16-1 (1998)	—	—	—	—	—	—	—
Burns Ind. Code Ann. §34-30-16-2 (1998)	Yes	or	Yes	or	—	Yes	Yes
Kentucky							
K.R.S. §202A.400 (1986)	Yes	and	Yes	—	—	Yes	—
Louisiana							
La.R.S. §9:2800.2 (1986)	Yes	and	Yes	—	—	—	—
Maryland							
Md. Courts and Judicial Proceedings Code Ann. §5-609 (1989)	Yes	and	Yes	or	—	Yes	Yes
Massachusetts							
ALM GL ch. 123, §1 (1989)	Yes	or	Yes	or	Yes	Yes	—
ALM GL ch. 123 §36B (1989)	—	—	—	—	—	—	—
Michigan							
MCLS §330.1946 (1989)	Yes	and	Yes	or	Yes[b]	Yes[b]	Yes
Mississippi[a]							
Miss. Code Ann. ' 41-21-97 (1991)	Yes	or	Yes	—	—	—	Yes
Montana							
Mont. Code Ann. ' 27-1-1102 (1987)	Yes	and	Yes	—	—	—	—
Nebraska							
R.R.S. Neb §38-2137 (1994)	Yes	and	Yes	—	—	—	—
New Hampshire							
RSA 329:31 (1987)	Yes	or	Yes	or	—	Yes	—
New Jersey							
N.J. Stat. §2A:62A-16 (1991)	Yes	or	Yes	or	Yes	Yes	Yes
New York[a]							
NY CLS Men Hyg §33.13(c)(7) (1985)	Yes	and	Yes	—	—	—	—
Ohio[a]							
Ohio Rev. Code Ann ' 2305.51 (Baldwin 1999)	Yes	and	Yes	or	Yes	Yes	Yes

(Continued)

Table 20.1 (*Continued*) Statutory options for discharging the duty to protect

State (year referenced is year statute was first in effect)	Warn victim	and/or	Report to police	and/or	Hospitalize voluntarily	Attempt involuntary hospitalization	Other
Oregon[a]							
ORS §179.505(12)(1973)	—	—	—	—	—	—	Yes
Rhode Island							
R.I. Gen. Laws §5-37.3-4 (1978)	Yes	or	Yes	—	—	—	Yes
Tennessee							
Tenn. Code Ann. §33-3-207 (1989)	Yes	—	—	or	Yes	Yes	Yes
Tenn. Code Ann. §33-3-206 (1989)	Yes	or	—	—	—	—	Yes
Texas[a]							
Tex. Health & Safety Code §611.004(a)(2) (1991)	—	—	Yes	—	—	—	Yes
Utah							
Utah Code Ann. §783-3-502 (1988)	Yes	and	Yes	—	—	—	—
Virginia							
Va. Code Ann. §54.1-2400.1 (1994)	Yes	or	Yes	or	—	Yes	Yes
Washington[a]							
Rev. Code Wash (ARCW) §71.05.120	Yes	and	Yes	—	—	—	—
Rev. Code Wash (ARCW) §71.05.390 (1987)	Yes	and	Yes	—	—	—	Yes
West Virginia[c]							
W. Va. Code §27-3-1(b)(5) (1977)	—	—	—	—	—	—	—
Wyoming[c]							
Wyo. Stat. §33-38-113(a)(iv) (1999)	—	—	—	—	—	—	—

[a] Provide options for dealing with patient-expressed threats, but statute is permissive; no explicit duty to warn or protect is stated.
[b] Initiation of hospitalization unspecified as voluntary or involuntary.
[c] Acknowledgment of a *Tarasoff*-like warning included only as an exception to privileged communication.

analysis, but finding that the statute does not create a duty; and (5) referencing the statute only in the context of testimonial privilege (Kachigian and Felthous 2004).

In this review, only a minority of court decisions interpreted their state statute so as to delimit the clinician's duties owed to third parties. Most court decisions concerning *Tarasoff*-like situations left the duty to protect ambiguous, and either overlooked the statute or found a common law duty to override the statute's limitations. Thus, even in states with *Tarasoff* statutes, forensic psychiatrists must keep abreast of relevant common law that may or may not be consistent with or override the statute.

Although the survey by Kachigian and Felthous demonstrated the disparate court responses to *Tarasoff* statutes, two other surveys came to contrary conclusions. From their earlier survey, Herbert and Young (2003) further confirmed that the *Tarasoff* jurisprudence lacked coherence on a national level. In a follow-up article (2003), Herbert concluded that protective disclosure law has vitiated psychotherapy. In a more recent survey and in contrast, Soulier and colleagues (2010) found *Tarasoff*-like liability appeared to be reduced where *Tarasoff* statutes with an affirmative duty were in place. Fox (2010) provided reasons why the low *Tarasoff* liability may have been inflated. If such statutes provide risk management guidance to clinicians, the concern over diverse approaches taken in the common law remains valid. Even if always necessary, and usually helpful, comparisons of statutory and judicial law are not always satisfactorily clarifying, particularly because the process can be confounded by the flux of changing public policies. Here we cite only California as one of several possible comparisons.

If court responses to *Tarasoff* protective disclosure statutes represent a third generation of *Tarasoff* jurisprudence, California now has developed a fourth in the most recently enacted amendment to its original *Tarasoff* statute. The four generations are as follows: (1) the Supreme Court of California formulated its well-known duty to protect, with warnings serving as an option for fulfilling this duty; (2) California enacted its original *Tarasoff* protective disclosure law (Cal. Civ. Code §43.92 [1986]) intended to clarify when the duty to warn exists and how it is to be discharged; (3) the *Tilley v. Schulte* (1999) decision required warning of a threat without further risk assessment and the *Ewing* cases (*Ewing v. Northridge Hospital Medical* Center 2004; *Ewing v. Goldstein* 2004) interpreted the law to require automatic warnings, in effect eliminating a duty to protect; and (4) now the amended protective disclosure law restores the *Tarasoff* principle of protection, which may be fulfilled with, but not necessarily by, warnings (Cal. Civ. Code §43.92 [2013]).

The California *Tarasoff* statute was amended in 2013 to replace "duty to warn" with "duty to protect" (Section 13.92 of the California Civil Code 2013). As before, the statute exempts a psychotherapist from the liability of her or his patient's violent behavior, "except if the patient has communicated to the psychotherapist a serious threat of physical violence against a reasonably identifiable victim or victims." Under these circumstances, there is no liability when the therapist "discharges his or her duty to protect by making reasonable efforts to communicate the threat to the victims or victims and to a law enforcement agency." The amended statute further specifies that the present amendments "only change the name of the duty referenced in this section from a duty to warn and protect to a duty to protect."

Weinstock et al. (2014) commend this current amended California *Tarasoff* statute that makes the duty solely one of protection, allowing the clinician more flexibility to make the optimal intervention in a particular case. Although notifying victims and police of the danger/threat may provide protection, clinicians can also take alternative, legally defensible measures, especially if the clinician has reason to believe that warnings could exacerbate the patient's risk. As an example, Weinstock et al. (2014) point to the *Ewing* case (*Ewing v. Goldstein* 2004; *Ewing v. Northridge Hospital Medical Center* 2004) wherein the treaters of the hospitalized daughter thought that if they warned her father that she wanted to kill him, he would more likely kill her after her discharge. In this case, it was thought the warning would increase rather than decrease the risk of someone being killed. In any event, the clinician is prudent to document the reasoned justification for her or his selected protective measure, whatever that measure might be.

The *Tarasoff* duty to protect of the Supreme Court of California was borne out of there being no duty to hospitalize, and the current *Tarasoff* statute does not establish an explicit duty to control by hospitalization. Unlike other states, California still provides immunity against liability for failure to hospitalize. Also unlike some other states, immunity for failure to protect does not inure by involuntary hospitalization of a dangerous patient in the State of California (Weinstock et al. 2014).

More complete chronologies of the evolution of the *Tarasoff* jurisprudence in California are provided by Weinstock et al. (2006, 2014).

DISTINGUISHING THE DUTY TO WARN FROM THE DUTY TO CONTROL

The *Tarasoff* Principle consolidated protective duties under a single "duty to protect." Many courts outside of California followed the Supreme Court of California's precedent in this respect. Eventually, other courts separated out a duty to warn from a duty to control, typically by extending hospitalization. Accurate understanding of a jurisdiction's jurisprudence over a clinician's protective duties requires close attention to this distinction, particularly where it delineates a clinician's obligation. Courts that have made this distinction have variously adopted and rejected a duty to warn. Courts have similarly adopted and rejected a duty to control (Felthous and Kachigian 2001b).

DOES THE DUTY TO WARN SAVE LIVES?

Soon after the Supreme Court of California's *Tarasoff* Decision, critics of this case law argued that it would endanger rather than protect others because potentially violent patients would be reluctant to enter therapy and those in therapy would hesitate to share their violent thoughts with their treatment provider (Stone 1976). In the years following *Tarasoff*, surveys of therapists provided some empirical support to these concerns (Wise 1978; Rosenhan et al. 1993). Other authors reported that legally required protective warnings have promoted the therapeutic alliance (Wulsin et al. 1983), resulted in therapists paying more attention to a patient's potential for violence and to carefully documenting (Buckner and Firestone 2000), and have not adversely affected the therapeutic relationship when warnings are discussed with the patient prior to their being made (Beck 1980). Perlin observed that "there is no reliable database of empirical evidence as to the therapeutic value of *Tarasoff* warnings or of the case's ultimate 'real life impact'" (Perlin 1992, 60). Slobogin (2006–2007) concluded that many jurisdictions have rejected a *Tarasoff*-like duty to warn because of such duties' lack of demonstrated value in reducing serious violent acts by patients.

Edwards (2010) used a fixed-effects model to examine differences in timing and duty to warn laws' relationship with intra-state rates of homicide. He concluded that "mandatory duty to warn laws cause an increase in homicides of 5%" (p. 1). A finding that homicide rates are higher in states with mandatory duty to warn laws does not prove, however, that warning identified victims or the mandatory warning laws actually cause patients or even nonpatients to commit homicide. Clearly, more research is needed to determine why states with mandatory reporting laws have higher rates of homicide, if indeed this is a replicable finding.

TYPES OF DUTY TO WARN

Four different warning practices that are based partly on the purpose and wording of the guiding law have been identified in the literature: (1) warning of the risk of violence, (2) warning of the threat of violence, (3) requested warning, and (4) criminal victims' warning mandated by statute (Felthous 2006). In "warning of the risk of violence," warning the identified potential victim is not automatically triggered by a verbal threat. Rather, the patient's verbal threat or other indication that the patient presents a risk of seriously harming another person causes the clinician to evaluate the patient further to determine whether, beyond the verbal threat itself, he or she presents an increased risk of harming the victim. Only if the clinician determines the risk to be elevated does the clinician then warn the victim of the risk, not simply the verbal threat. This is the model that is discussed and promoted in the literature and complies with the *Tarasoff* Principle (Felthous 2006), which specifies that it is the danger (not a verbal threat) that is to be disclosed.

Apart from the *Tarasoff* Principle, various *Tarasoff* statutes and court opinions do not mention risk assessment or communication of the risk. Rather, the clinician's duty appears to be triggered by the patient's expression of a verbal threat, and it is the threat, not the risk, that is to be communicated to the would-be victim. For example, although the *Tarasoff* Principle of the Supreme Court of California would mandate the would-be victim be notified of the "danger" (*Tarasoff v. Regents of the University of California* 1976, 426), until the most recent amendment to the statute, the subsequent *Tarasoff* statute would require that the victim be informed of the "threat" (Cal. Civil Code §43.92 [1986, 1970, 2013]).

The third practice is to warn a person who fears physical violence by the patient because the person requests to be warned. Typically, the requesting person was already threatened or assaulted by the patient and wants to be warned, not of the risk of violence or of any expressed threats, but that the patient is about to be released from custody, whether from a hospital, jail, or prison.

Although not legally relevant to a clinician's duty to warn or protect, clinicians, particularly those employed in a correctional or forensic institutional setting, should be aware of their state and the federal mechanism for notifying victims or witnesses upon release of an individual inmate. A person who has been criminally victimized by another can request to be notified when the offender is released from incarceration. Such notifications are made through correctional authorities or prosecutors immediately prior to the offender's release (Corcoran 2003). This is a matter of victim's rights and does not involve mental health clinicians or risk assessment (Felthous 2006).

MENTAL ILLNESS, GUNS, AND HOMICIDE

Every year, tens of thousands of people in the United States are killed with firearms. In the year 2010, 31,672 persons were killed with firearms. In 2011, 11,101 people committed homicide with firearms, a rate of 3.6 per 100,000. This represented a decrease from 2006 (12,791, 4.29 per 100,000). During this period, suicides by firearms increased from 16,883 (i.e., 5.66 per 100,000) to 19,766 (i.e., 6.3 per 100,000) (Alpers et al. 2015).

Although precise figures on the number of homicides committed by mentally ill persons with a firearm as the lethal weapon remain elusive, it appears that most homicides resulting in *Tarasoff* litigation and published legal cases involved firearms (Felthous 1989). In any event, to the extent that some may kill as a result of mental illness (Kunz et al. 2013), it seems reasonable to assume that more aggressive treatment of these individuals' mental disorders and close management would offer hope for preventing some of these homicides.

Federal and state legislatures have enacted successive laws intended to prevent criminal felons and mentally ill persons thought to be at risk for killing themselves or others from possessing firearms (see Khin Khin et al. 2013). In the wake of the horror ignited by mass killings, most recently the slaughter of children at the Sandy Hook Elementary School in Newtown, Connecticut, several states have extended this public policy to require mental health professionals to report to authorities mental patients who are thought to be at increased risk of gun violence (see Beck et al. 2013).

As of the writing of this chapter, the State of New York has the most expansive gun control law designed to keep those mentally ill persons thought to be at risk for violence from owning a gun (New York State Penal Law, Section 400.00, 11[6]; NYS Office of Mental Health, New York Mental Hygiene Law, Section 9.46; see NY Mental Hygiene Law, Section 9.01, NYS Office of Mental Health; Ollove 2013). As of 2013, mental health professionals are required to notify local officials of patients whom they deem "likely to engage in conduct that will cause serious harm to self or others." Because this reporting standard is consistent with the standard used for emergency hospital detention in New York, the law seems to trigger this reporting requirement whenever emergency hospitalization is initiated. Other states also have enacted reporting laws intended to dispossess of their firearms mentally ill persons thought to be at risk. Thoughtful analysis of such legislation and the ethics of psychiatric compliance with such regulations have been discussed and can be referenced for practice guidance.

Regardless of the gun control laws that exist in the state where one practices, inquiry should be made about possession of and access to firearms whenever a patient presents a risk of suicide or homicide. Even without reporting requirements such as those in New York, the clinician should initiate measures to ensure that firearms are securely removed from and inaccessible to a patient who is at risk for suicide or homicide. This can be accomplished with assistance from the patient's family or friends, law enforcement, and/or the patient.

ASSESSMENT OF THE RISK OF VIOLENCE TO A TARGETED INDIVIDUAL

As with assessment of risk for suicide, assessment of risk of violence toward others begins with the history of the present illness (e.g., recent violent thoughts, acts, and preparatory acts) and mental status examination (e.g., anger, hostility, resentment, and violent thoughts). If after initial assessment there is reason to be concerned about violence toward others, further assessment is in order. For purposes of this discussion, emphasis is placed on assessment of risk toward one or more targeted individuals, not the risk of violence in general, which is addressed in Section 7 of this book.

Felthous (1999) proposed an algorithm to help psychiatrists in dichotomous decision making for warnings and hospitalization as measures to prevent violence to third parties. This algorithm requires the psychiatrist to attempt to answer the following four questions: (1) Is the patient dangerous to others? (2) If yes, is the patient's dangerousness due to serious mental illness? (3) If not due to serious mental illness, is the dangerousness imminent? and (4) Are potential victims of the patient's violence reasonably identifiable? We would add to these questions the importance of always asking a patient who has thought about homicide about firearm access. If the patient has firearm access, reasonable measures should be taken to make the firearm(s) inaccessible to the patient. Weinstock and colleagues (2014) would add additional questions related to determining whether warning the potential victim would increase the risk of violence.

Assessment of dangerousness is a dynamic process because dangerousness itself ebbs and flows with internal changes and interactions with the environment, which can include therapeutic and other interventions that are less intrusive than warnings and less restrictive than hospitalization. Protective intervention, like the prediction of violence, is more art than science; the critical question is whether an appropriate attempt was made at assessment and appropriate intervention.

The potential for homicide and serious assault can be evaluated much like suicide potential. There are many helpful writings on the clinical assessment and safe management of potentially violent patients. Forensic psychiatrists should be familiar with the recommendations in the literature for assessing the risk associated with verbal threat, but they must exercise caution in assigning new standards of practice with corresponding liability. Borum and Reddy (2001), for example, provide a reasoned approach for assessing a patient's threat to harm a specific person.

The psychiatric profession has not settled on a standard for warning victims and notifying police. Even the American Psychiatric Association's model code for protecting third parties does not advocate a duty to protect, much less a specific duty to warn, though this code lists warnings as one of the protective actions the psychiatrist might choose to select (Appelbaum et al. 1989). Warnings and reports have long been allowed by ethical standards designed to prevent violence but have not been ethically prescribed (American Psychiatric Association 1989). The expert may point to a legal duty to warn if it is prescribed by law. Otherwise, in jurisdictions where the duty is not yet firmly imposed, the expert who feels compelled to opine that a victim should have been warned probably should qualify this conclusion as the expert's own judgment and not insist that it is a practice to which most of the psychiatric profession would adhere. A failure to warn is more clearly in error if it is in violation of case or statutory law, rather than if it is a perceived deviation from a nonexistent clinical standard.

In many duty-to-protect cases, the most serious and patent errors are clinical ones, not the failure to take extra-clinical measures such as warning a victim and reporting to a law enforcement agency. For example, the potentially violent patient was not evaluated carefully, not diagnosed accurately, not admitted to the hospital, not medicated properly, not observed closely enough, or the patient was discharged from the hospital prematurely and without adequate planning.

CONSULTATION ON DUTY-TO-PROTECT CASES

The forensic psychiatrist who consults on duty-to-protect cases already should be familiar with landmark cases in duty to protect jurisprudence. Some knowledge of recent legislative trends and familiarity with writings of clinicians on the topics of evaluating and managing potentially violent patients, risk assessment (e.g., Simon and Tardiff 2008), and algorithmic decision making is useful. Finally, it is recommended that the consultant continue to treat violent patients and remain well-practiced in the field.

If the referral comes from another state, the forensic psychiatrist should enlist the referring attorney's assistance in procuring pertinent jurisdictional law from state and federal courts, any protective disclosure statute, any privileged and confidential information statutes, and the state's mental health code. If the clinician–defendant was employed by a hospital or institution, obtain policy statements pertaining to homicidal and violent patients. With regard to the instant case, obtain all medical and psychiatric records, transcriptions of all depositions and courtroom proceedings already held on the case, and all exhibits already submitted into evidence.

The consultant should have some basic questions in mind before starting to read the case materials. Was the clinical assessment adequate? Was the diagnosis appropriate? What, if any, signs of violent potential were there? If clinical findings warranted further assessment for violent potential, was this done? Was the treatment provided appropriate? If signs of violence were escalating, was hospitalization considered? If the patient was hospitalized, the consultant should assess information on the level of observation, control, and thoughtful discharge planning before releasing the patient. The presence of sufficient and accurate progress notes is always a consideration. Finally, the consultant must look for sufficient communication between treaters if several professionals have been involved in the patient's treatment.

Though relying on legal parameters, the consultant should endeavor to be more fair and practical than the law seems to be. Our colleagues can be sued for breach of confidentiality or for failure to warn or protect. If the stakes seem high for physicians, consider their patients and the patients' potential victims. Inappropriate disclosure of confidential information can cause a patient to lose a job or his or her most valued relationship. Failure to take preventive action may lead to homicide. Yet our abilities to accurately predict and prevent violence are extremely limited (Mossman 2010). The clinician walks on a precarious tightrope. Tilting to one side or the other can risk liability for oneself and harm others.

The fair consultant will grant the defendant some margin by which to exercise good-faith judgment before finding an error of committing a breach of confidence in the face of serious potential harm or of omitting such disclosure to take specific extra-clinical measures. Fault can be established more firmly where the defendant violated clear legal regulations or deviated from the clinical standard of care. If the consultant is to refrain from advancing novel duties and standards, the prudent expert must also have the courage and objectivity to identify violations of a clearly stated and unambiguous law or substandard clinical practice, where the dereliction of the clinician's duty proximately caused the patient to harm another person.

SUMMARY KEY POINTS

- Embedded in the *Tarasoff* Principle duty to protect is the option of warning the intended victim of the serious danger, not necessarily a verbal threat.
- The duty to warn or protect in a given jurisdiction arises from the courts, the legislature, or both. These bodies not infrequently have disharmonious views about many aspects of this duty.
- It is not clear whether the legal duty to warn, as a component of the duty to protect, actually saves lives.
- Inquiry about access to firearms is a prudent measure when assessing and managing a patient's risk of violence.
- When consulting on a professional negligence case in which failure to fulfill the duty to protect is claimed, the forensic psychiatrist should check the relevant jurisdictional law from both statute(s) and court decisions.

REFERENCES

Alpers P, A Rossetti, D Salinas, and M Wilson. 2015. *United States—Gun Facts, Figures and the Law.* Sydney School of Public Health, University of Sydney. GunPolicy.org, 26 February. http://www.gunpolicy.org/firearms/region/united-states, accessed March 10, 2015.

American Law Institute. Restatement (Second) of Torts. Author (1965).

American Psychiatric Association (APA). 1989. *The Principles of Medical Ethics and Annotations Especially Applicable to Psychiatry.* Section 9, annotation number 8, page 6. Washington, DC: APA.

Appelbaum PS, H Zonana, R Bonnie, and L Roth. 1989. Statutory approaches to limiting psychiatrists' liability for their patients' violent acts. Appendix 2: American Psychiatric Association model statue on the physician's duty to take precautions against patient violence. *American Journal of Psychiatry* 146(7):821–829.

Barker J, L Bazzi, R Binder, K Fisher, B Kelly, J Knoll, and S Noffsinger. 2013. Mass murder and mental illness. *44th Annual Meeting Program of the American Academy of Psychiatry and the Law,* San Diego, CA, October 24–27, #T29, 29–30.

Beck B, K Susan, and L Mulbry. 2013. Revisions in gun and mental health laws in the wake of Newtown (Poster Session). *44th Annual Meeting Program of the American Academy of Psychiatry and the Law,* San Diego, CA, October 24–27, #S10, 87–88.

Beck J. 1980. When the patient threatens violence: An empirical study of clinical practice after *Tarasoff. Bulletin of the American Academy of Psychiatry and the Law* 10:189–220.

Borum R and M Reddy. 2001. Assessing violence risk in *Tarasoff* situations: A fact-based model of inquiry. *Behavioral Sciences and the Law* 19:375–385.

Boynton v. Burgess, 590 So. 2d 446 (Fla. Dist. Ct. App.-3 Dist. 1991).

Brief of Amicus Curiae in Support of Petition for Rehearing of Tarasoff. *The Regents of the University of California* (a motion of American Psychiatric Association, Area VI of the Assembly of the American Psychiatric Association, Northern California Psychiatric Society, California State Psychological Association, San Francisco Psychoanalytic Institute and Society, California Society for Clinical Social Work, National Association of Social Workers, Golden Gate Chapter California Hospital Association to the Supreme Court of the State of California in support of petition for rehearing, January 7, 1975. Tarasoff v. Regents of the University of California, 551 P.2d (Cal. 1974).).

Buckner F and M Firestone. 2000. Where the public peril begins 25 years after *Tarasoff. Journal of Legal Medicine* 21:187.

Cal. Civil Code § 43.92 (1986).

Cal. Civil Code § 43.92 (2007).

Cal. Civil Code § 43.92 (2013).

Canon v. Thumudo, 422 N.W. 2d 688 (Mich. 1988).

Charleston v. Larson, 297 Ill. App. 3d 540, 696 N.E. 2d 793, 231. Ill. Dec. 497 (Ill. App. Ct. 1998).

Corcoran MH and J Cawood. 2003. *Violence Assessment and Intervention: The Practitioner's Handbook.* Boca Raton, FL: CRC Press.

Edwards GS. 2010. Doing their duty: An empirical analysis of the unintended effect of *Tarasoff v. Regents* on homicidal activity. Social Science Research Network. http://ssrn.com/abstract=1544574, accessed August 13, 2013.

Ewing v. Goldstein, 15 Cal. Rptr. 3d 864 (Cal. Ct. App. 2004).

Ewing v. Northridge Hospital Medical Center, 16 Cal. Rptr. 3d 591 (Cal. Ct. App. 2004).

Fair v. United States, 234 F. 2d 288 (1956).

Felthous AR. 1987. Liability of treaters for injuries to others: Erosion of three immunities. *Bulletin of the American Academy of Psychiatry and the Law* 15(2):115–125.

Felthous AR. 1989. *The Psychotherapist's Duty to Warn or Protect.* Springfield, IL: Charles C Thomas.

Felthous AR. 1999. The clinician's duty to protect third parties. In *Forensic Psychiatry*, edited by PJ Resnick, *Psychiatric Clinics of North America* 22(1):49–60.

Felthous AR. 2006. Warning a potential victim of a person's dangerousness: Clinician's duty or victim's right? *Journal of the American Academy of Psychiatry and the Law* 34(3):338–348.

Felthous AR and C Kachigian. 2001a. The *Fin de Millenaire* duty to warn or protect. *Journal of Forensic Sciences* 46:1103–1112.

Felthous AR and C Kachigian. 2001b. To warn and to control: Two district legal obligations or variations of a single duty to protect? *Behavioral Sciences and the Law* 19(3):355–373.

Fleming JG and B Maximov. 1974. The patient or his victim: The therapist's dilemma. *California Law Review* 62:1025–1068.

Fox PK. 2010. Commentary: So the pendulum swings—Making sense of the duty to protect. *Journal of the American Academy of Psychiatry and the Law* 38:474–478.

Gutheil TG. 2001. Moral justification for *Tarasoff*-type warnings and breach of confidentiality: A clinician's perspective. *Behavioral Sciences and the Law* 19(2):345–353.

Herbert PB. 2003. The duty to warn: A reconsideration and critique. *Journal of the American Academy of Psychiatry and the Law* 30:417–424.

Herbert PB and KA Young. 2003. *Tarasoff* at twenty-five. *Journal of the American Academy of Psychiatry and the Law* 30(2):275–281.

Kachigian CK and AR Felthous. 2004. Court responses to *Tarasoff* statutes. *Journal of the American Academy of Psychiatry and the Law* 32(3):263–273.

Khin Khin E, R Jesse, K Stephanie, and S Sexton. 2013. Firearm legislation: The good, the bad, the ugly (Poster Session with handout). *44th Annual Meeting Program of the American Academy of Psychiatry and the Law*, San Diego, CA, October 24–27, 2013, #F15, 53–54.

Kunz M, B Belfi, D Green, J Schreiber, and G Pequeno. 2013. Guns and the mentally ill (Poster Session). *44th Annual Meeting Program of the American Academy of Psychiatry and the Law*, San Diego, CA, October 24–27, #S14, 90–91.

McDowell v. County of Alameda, 88 Cal. App. 3d 321, 151 Cal. Rptr. 779 (1979).

Merchants National Bank and Trust Co. of Fargo v. United States, 272 F. Supp. 409, 417–419 (DND 1967).

Miss. Code Ann. 41-21-97 (e) (1991).

Mossman D. 2010. Understanding risk assessment. In *Textbook of Forensic Psychiatry*, 2nd edition, edited by RI Simon and LH Gold, Washington, DC: American Psychiatric Press, 563–586.

New York State Penal Law, Section 400.00, 11(6). http://public.leginfo.state.ny.us/LAWSSEAF.cgi?QUERYTYPE=LALOS+&QUERY, accessed November 24, 2013.

Ollove Mi. 2013. States tackle mental illness and gun ownership. *PEW*. http://www.pewstates.org/projects/stateline/headlines/states_tackle_mental_illness_and_gun_ownership, accessed November 24, 2013.

Perlin ML. 1992. *Tarasoff* and the dilemma of the dangerous patient: New directions for the 1990s. *Law and Psychology Review* 16:29–64.

Restatement (Second) of Torts, Sections 315, 319, and 320, The American Law Institute (1965).

Rosenhan DL, TW Teitelbaum, KW Teitelbau, and M Davidson. 1993. Warning third parties: The ripple effects of *Tarasoff*. *Pacific Law Journal* 24:1165–1232.

Simon RI and K Tardiff. 2008. *Textbook of Violence Assessment and Management*. Washington DC: American Psychiatric Publishing.

Slobogin C. 2006, personal communication to Robert I. Simon, cited in Robert I. Simon 2006–2007. The myth of "imminent" violence in psychiatry and the law. *University of Cincinnati Law Review* 75:631–644, 637. Note 49.

Slobogin C. 2006–2007. *Tarasoff* as a duty to treat? Insight from criminal law. *University of Cincinnati Law Review* 75:645–661.

Soulier MF, A Maislen, and JC Beck. 2010. Status of the psychiatric duty to protect, circa 2006. *Journal of the American Academy of Psychiatry and the Law* 38:457–473.

St. George v. State, 283 A.D. 245, 127 N.Y.S. 2d 147 (N.Y. App. Div. 1954).

Stone AA. 1976. The *Tarasoff* decision: Suing psychotherapists to safeguard society. *Harvard Law Review* 90:358–378.

Tarasoff v. Regents of the University of California, 529 P.2d 553, 118 Cal. Rptr. 129 (1974).

Tarasoff v. Regents of the University of California, 17 Cal. 3d 425 (1976).

Tilley v. Schulte, 70 Cal. App. 4th 79 (1999).

28 U.S.C.A. Sec. 2671 (West 1990).

Weinstock R, D Bonnici, A Seroussi, and GB Leong. 2014. No duty to warn in California: Now unambiguously solely a duty to protect. *Journal of the American Academy of Psychiatry and the Law* 42:101–108.

Weinstock R, G Vari, GB Leong, and J Arturo Silva. 2006. Back to the past in California: A temporary retreat to a Tarasoff duty to warn. *Journal of the American Academy of Psychiatry and the Law* 34:523–528.

Wise TP. 1978. Where the public peril begins: A survey of psychotherapists to determine the effects of *Tarasoff*. *Stanford Law Review* 31:165–190.

Wulsin LR, H Bursztajn, and TG Gutheil. 1983. Unexpected clinical features of the *Tarasoff* decision: The therapeutic alliance and the "Duty to Warn." *American Journal of Psychiatry* 140:601–603.

21

Treatment boundaries in psychiatric practice and sexual misconduct in the therapist–patient relationship

ROBERT I. SIMON

INTRODUCTION

The concept of treatment boundaries developed during the twentieth century in the context of outpatient psychodynamic psychotherapy. Treatment boundary issues arose from the very beginning of psychoanalysis, reflected in Freud's disputes with Ferenczi, Reich, and others. Ethical principles promulgated by the mental health professions and the legal duties imposed by courts and statutes have additionally defined treatment boundaries. For example, the clinician's maintenance of confidentiality derives from three distinct duties: professional (clinical), ethical, and legal. Treatment boundaries are set by the therapist that define and secure the professional relationship of the therapist with the patient for the purpose of promoting a trusting, working alliance.

The boundary guidelines listed below are generally applicable across the broad spectrum of psychiatric treatments. Nevertheless, considerable disagreement exists among psychotherapists regarding what constitutes treatment boundary violations. Appropriate technique for one therapist may be considered a boundary violation by another therapist. Much variability in defining treatment boundaries appears to be a function of the nature of the patient, the therapist, the treatment, and the status of the therapeutic alliance. For example, notable exceptions may exist in alcohol and drug abuse programs, in inpatient settings, and with certain cognitive-behaviorally based therapies. Regardless of the therapy used, however, every therapist must maintain basic treatment boundaries with all patients. If boundary exceptions are made, they should be for the benefit of the patient. Every effort must be exerted to therapeutically restore breached boundaries. Brief boundary crossings that are quickly rectified can provide useful insight into conflictual issues for both the therapist and patient (Gutheil and Gabbard 1993). Harm threatens the patient when boundary violations progress in frequency and severity over time.

Boundary guidelines maintain the integrity of therapy and safeguard both the therapist and the patient. Proponents of therapies that breach generally accepted boundary guidelines risk harming the patient and incurring legal liability (Simon 1990a). Psychiatry continues to be highly receptive to innovative therapies that offer the hope of more effective treatments for the mentally ill (Simon 1993). The maintenance of basic treatment boundaries should not be inimical to therapeutic creativity.

With regard to sexual misconduct, the sexual exploitation of patients by therapists is of serious professional, ethical, and legal concern for the mental health professions. The results of a nationwide survey of psychiatrist–patient sex revealed that 7.1% of male and 3.1% of female respondents acknowledged sexual contact with their patients (Gartrell et al. 1986). Of the sexual contacts that occurred, 88% took place between male psychiatrists and female patients, 7.6% between male psychiatrists and male patients, 3.5% between female psychiatrists and male patients, and 1.4% between female psychiatrists and female patients. Most surveys show a consistent gender difference that varies from approximately 2:1–4:1 male-to-female ratio of therapists who sexually exploit their patients.

Survey results of sexual misconduct may be inaccurate because of underreporting related to embarrassment, fear of civil liability, and potential or pending criminal investigations. A 2004 review article (Sarkar 2004) on boundary violations stated, "It is also possible that sexual boundary violations, like other types of sexual misdemeanour are underreported because of issues to do with shame and guilt; and it is also possible that false accusations are comparatively overreported." Not utilizing survey results, and instead using literature review, individual state and government agencies, Marshall et al. (2008) reported that "an estimated 6%–10% of psychiatrists have had inappropriate sexual relations with patients." It is difficult to report accurate current numbers regarding the incidence of sexual misconduct by mental health professionals because of the possible reporting issues mentioned above. Though the exact number of patients or therapists involved is not known with certainty, it is known that sexual misconduct by therapists unfortunately continues to occur.

PSYCHOTHERAPY: THE IMPOSSIBLE TASK

All psychiatric treatments, regardless of theoretical orientation, are based on the fundamental premise that the interaction with another human being can alleviate psychic distress, change behavior, and alter a person's perspective of the world (Simon and Sadoff 1992). Psychotherapy can be defined as the application of clinical knowledge and skill to a dynamic psychological interaction between two people for the purpose of alleviating mental and emotional suffering. This principle also applies to biological and behavioral therapies. Yet psychotherapy is an impossible task (Simon 1990a). There are no perfect therapies, and there are no perfect therapists.

Psychotherapy has been described as a mutually regressive relationship with shared tasks but different roles (Shapiro and Carr 1991). Boundary violations are therapist role violations that inevitably occur to some degree in every therapy. Although maintaining treatment boundaries is a major psychotherapeutic task, competent psychotherapy also requires recognition by the therapist that he or she has erred. Often, the work of psychotherapy involves the therapeutic restitution of breached boundaries. Treatment boundaries usually can be re-established if the therapist raises a boundary violation as a treatment issue. Because therapists use themselves as a primary therapeutic tool, sensitivity to boundary violations must be maintained at a high level.

From a clinical perspective, the therapeutic alliance is considered by many practitioners to be the single most critical factor associated with successful treatment (Marziali et al. 1981). The maintenance of treatment boundaries creates the foundation for the development of the therapeutic alliance and the subsequent work of therapy. Trust is the essential basis for a secure therapeutic relationship that permits patients to reveal their most intimate problems. The patient's trust is based on the conviction that the therapist will use professional skills in a manner that benefits the patient. The development of trust may be the sole treatment goal. The maintenance of consistent, stable, and enabling treatment boundaries creates a safe place for the patient to risk self-revelation. Fundamentally, the therapist's professional concern and respect for the patient ensure that treatment boundaries will be preserved.

Treatment boundary violations occur on a continuum, usually interfering with the provision of good clinical care to the patient. Boundary violations frequently result from the therapist's acting out of his or her personal conflicts. As a consequence, the patient's diagnosis may be missed or overlooked. Inappropriate or useless treatment may be rendered. Moreover, the patient's original psychiatric condition may be exacerbated.

BOUNDARY GUIDELINES

Treatment boundaries are established by the therapist according to accepted professional standards. It is the therapist's professional duty to set and maintain appropriate treatment boundaries in the provision of good clinical care. This duty cannot be relegated to the patient. Once treatment boundaries are established, *boundary* issues inevitably arise from the therapeutic work with the patient, and these form an essential aspect of treatment. *Boundary crossings* that arise from either the therapist or the patient are quickly addressed and rarely harm the patient (Gutheil and Gabbard 1993). *Boundary violations*, on the other hand, arise solely from the therapist and are often detrimental to treatment, particularly if unchecked and progressive. The therapist who creates idiosyncratic boundaries or sets no boundaries at all is likely to provide negligent treatment that harms the patient and invites a malpractice suit. A fundamental task for practitioners is the maintaining of constant vigilance against boundary violations and immediately repairing any breaches in a clinically supportive manner.

The following boundary guidelines for psychotherapy help maintain the integrity of the treatment process:

- Maintain relative therapist neutrality.
- Foster psychological separateness of patient.
- Protect confidentiality.
- Obtain informed consent for treatments and procedures.
- Interact verbally with patients.
- Ensure no previous, current, or future personal relationship with the patient.
- Minimize physical contact.
- Preserve relative anonymity of therapist.
- Establish a stable fee policy.
- Provide consistent, private, and professional setting.
- Define time and length of sessions.

Some of these basic guidelines have been considered by Langs (1990, 303–323) to form the necessary treatment frame for the conduct of psychodynamic psychotherapy. Although additional boundary rules could be elaborated, a general consensus exists concerning the basic rules listed above. For example, rules concerning the management of transference and countertransference could be included but might not find ready acceptance among some behaviorists, biological psychiatrists, and in "here and now" treatments such as Gestalt therapy. Nevertheless, all therapists, regardless of their theoretical orientation, must recognize that transference and countertransference play an important role in any therapy.

An absolutist position concerning boundary guidelines cannot be taken. Otherwise, it would be appropriate to refer to boundary guidelines as boundary standards. Treatment boundaries are not rigid, easily defined, static structures that separate the therapist from the patient like a wall. Instead, they delineate a fluctuating, reasonably neutral, safe space that enables the dynamic, psychological interaction between therapist and patient to unfold. Because treatment boundaries have a certain degree of flux, unanimity of professional opinion does not exist on a number of boundary matters. Moreover, clinicians may place greater emphasis on certain boundary guidelines.

UNDERLYING PRINCIPLES

Rule of abstinence

There are a number of fundamental, overlapping principles that form the bases for boundary guidelines. One of the foremost principles is the rule of abstinence that states that the therapist must refrain from obtaining personal gratification at the expense of the patient (Freud 1959). Extratherapeutic gratifications must be avoided by both therapist and patient (Langs 1990, 303–323).

A corollary of the rule of abstinence states that the therapist's primary source of personal gratification *derives* from professional involvement in the psychotherapeutic process and the satisfactions gained in helping the patient. The only material satisfaction directly obtained from the patient is the fee for the therapist's professional services. Treatment boundaries are violated when the therapist's primary source of gratification is received from the patient directly rather than through engagement in the therapeutic process with the patient. The rule of abstinence is fundamental to virtually all boundary guidelines.

Duty to neutrality

The rule of abstinence attempts to secure a position of neutrality for the therapist with the patient. Therapeutic neutrality is not defined in the psychoanalytic sense of equidistance between the patient's ego, superego, id, and reality. Rather, it refers to the therapist knowing his or her place and staying out of the patient's personal life (Wachtel 1987, 176–184). Therapeutic neutrality permits the patient's agenda to be given primary consideration. The relative anonymity of the therapist assures that self-disclosures will be kept at a minimum, thus maintaining therapist neutrality. The law also independently recognizes the therapist's duty of neutrality toward patients (Furrow 1980).

The concept of relative neutrality refers to the limitations placed on psychotherapists that prevent interference in the personal lives of their patients. Life choices involving marriage, occupation, where one lives, and with whom one associates, although grist for the therapeutic mill, are basically the patient's final choice (Wachtel 1987, 176–184). Therapists must be very careful about expressing their personal views in the treatment situation concerning, for example, politics, religion, abortion, and divorce.

If an otherwise competent patient is thinking about making a decision that appears foolish or even potentially destructive, the therapist's role is primarily limited to raising the questionable decision as a treatment issue. For example, the therapist can legitimately explore the psychological meaning of the decision as well as its potential adverse consequences for the patient's treatment and life situation. Clinical situations do arise when the psychotherapist must intervene directly. If a patient's decision-making capacity is severely impaired by a mental disorder, the therapist may need to actively intervene to protect the patient or others (Simon 1990b). For example, a psychotically depressed, acutely suicidal patient who refuses to enter a hospital voluntarily requires involuntary hospitalization. Under these circumstances, the clinician intervenes in the patient's life for valid clinical, not personal, reasons.

Patient autonomy and self-determination

Fostering the autonomy and self-determination of the patient is another major principle underlying boundary guidelines. Maintaining patient separateness by supporting the process of separation–individuation follows as a corollary. Of the over 450 current psychotherapies, none holds as a long-term treatment objective that patients remain dependent and psychologically fused with their therapists or others. Obtaining informed consent for proposed procedures and treatments also preserves patient autonomy (Simon 1992). Patient self-determination dictates that the therapist's clinical posture toward the patient should be expectant; that is, the patient primarily determines the content of his or her sessions. This is not the modus operandi, however, in cognitive-behavioral therapies or even with some forms of interpersonal therapy. Moreover, the assurances that physical contact with patients be essentially avoided and that the therapist stay out of the person's personal life (no past, current, or future personal relationships) derive in large measure from the principle of autonomy and self-determination.

Progressive boundary violations invariably constrict the patient's freedom of exploration and choice. Properly maintained treatment boundaries maintain the separateness of the patient from the therapist while also preserving the psychological relatedness of the patient to others.

Fiduciary relationship

As a matter of law, the doctor–patient relationship is fiduciary (*Omer v. Edgren* 1984). The knowledge and power differentials that exist between therapist and patient require the therapist, as a fiduciary, not to exploit the patient for his or her personal advantage. This responsibility is "implicit" in the therapist–patient relationship and is fundamental to the general "duty of care." The special vulnerabilities and dependence of the patient rather than the unique powers of a profession give rise to a fiduciary duty (Simon 1987).

A fiduciary relationship arises, therefore, whenever confidence, faith, and trust are reposed on one side, and domination and influence result on the other (Black 1990). All mental health professionals, not only psychiatrists, have a fiduciary responsibility to their patients. The maintenance of confidentiality, privacy, a stable fee policy, and consistent time and professional treatment settings are based in large measure on the fiduciary duties of the therapist.

Respect for human dignity

Moral, ethical, and professional standards require that psychiatrists treat their patients with compassion and respect. The dedication of physicians to their patients has a long and venerable tradition that finds expression in the Hippocratic Oath. *The Principles of Medical Ethics with Annotations Especially Applicable to Psychiatry* (2013, Section 1) instructs: "A physician shall be dedicated to providing competent medical care, with compassion and respect for human dignity and rights." On clinical grounds alone, the competent therapist always strives to maintain the patient's healthy self-esteem in the course of therapy. Exploitative therapists, however, engage patients as part objects to be used for their own personal gratification. Frequently, such therapists attack the self-esteem of their patients as a means of gaining control over them. All of the boundary guidelines are based on the principle of respect for human dignity.

TREATMENT BOUNDARIES: GENERAL ISSUES

Boundaries in small communities

Psychiatrists and other mental health professionals who practice in small communities and rural areas encounter unique situations and customs that may complicate the task of maintaining treatment boundaries (Simon and Williams 1999). Boundary problems are more likely to occur in maintaining confidentiality and a position of relative therapist neutrality and anonymity. Boundary guidelines must be adaptable to small community practice without endangering the therapeutic frame and the patient.

Exigent boundary settings

In the course of treatment, it may be necessary for the sake of the patient or the welfare of others for the therapist to cross accepted treatment boundaries. The observance of usual treatment boundaries may be interrupted by crises in clinical care, and by intervening, superseding ethical or legal duties. For example, an agoraphobic patient initially may be so incapacitated that he or she is unable to come to the psychiatrist's office. Home visits may be necessary. The potentially violent patient who threatens others creates a conflicting ethical position for the clinician related to the maintenance of confidentiality. The existence of legal requirements to warn and protect endangered third persons may necessitate a breach of the patient's confidentiality. If the patient's cooperation can be enlisted in the process of warning, the treatment boundaries may be maintained. Engaging the patient in the decision to readjust treatment boundaries that result from treatment exigencies may permit salutary boundary reshaping that can facilitate the treatment process. But, according to Gutheil (2005), "theoretically benign boundary crossings can be misconstrued or portrayed in a worse light in later litigation. Boundary crossings thus require circumspection, weighing of pros and cons, and obtaining consultation with a low threshold."

Defensive boundaries

Defensive psychiatry refers to any act or omission that is performed not for the benefit of the patient but to avoid malpractice liability or to provide a legal defense against a malpractice claim. Defensive practices that produce deviant treatment boundaries usually take the form of clinically unnecessary prohibitions that disturb the therapist's position of neutrality. Typical clinical issues that provoke defensive treatment boundaries include *treating* patients with sexual transferences and *managing* potentially violent patients that may require the therapist to warn and protect endangered third parties. Defensive boundaries are usually created by unrecognized or uncorrected therapists' countertransferences (Simon 2000).

Impaired therapists

Impaired therapists usually experience great difficulty in setting and maintaining acceptable treatment boundaries (Olarte 1991). Deviant, aberrant, idiosyncratic boundaries form the basis for patient exploitation. Severely character-disordered therapists tend to repeat boundary deviations with their patients. Predatory, exploitative therapists also belong to this group. Therapists who establish aberrant boundaries may also be incompetent; impaired by alcohol, drugs, and mental illness; situationally distressed by personal crises; or suffering from a paraphilia, particularly frotteurism. Frotteurs have great difficulty in maintaining appropriate physical distance from patients, frequently becoming involved in inappropriate touching.

Psychotherapists with malignant character disorders or paraphilias manifesting severe narcissistic, antisocial, or perverse character traits may simply sexually exploit patients. The mismanagement of transference and countertransference feelings is an epiphenomenon of character impairment.

Vulnerable patients

Every patient is vulnerable to psychological harm from therapists who violate treatment boundaries. Borderline patients are especially at risk for psychic injury (Gutheil 1991). Many of these patients have been physically and sexually abused as children, and their sense of appropriate relationships and boundaries may be seriously impaired.

Treatment boundaries are frequently tested through compulsive repetition of early childhood relationships where personal boundaries were not respected. Highly dependent patients or patients recently experiencing a personal loss are also particularly vulnerable to exploitation.

Although therapists set treatment boundaries, patients invariably test boundaries repeatedly, and in various ways. Healthier patients generally are able to stay within acceptably established treatment boundaries, using the treatment framework productively. More disturbed patients often act out their conflicts around boundary issues. For instance, a patient who was sexually abused as a child may test the integrity of the therapist by continually challenging treatment boundaries. With more disturbed patients, a considerable portion of the therapy may be devoted to examining the psychological meaning of the patient's efforts to gain exceptions to established treatment boundaries. Patients who cannot tolerate limit setting by the therapist may be untreatable (Green et al. 1988).

DISCUSSION OF BOUNDARY GUIDELINES

Neutrality and self-determination

The rule of abstinence and the therapist's position of relative neutrality empower patient separateness, autonomy, and self-determination. Therapists who abandon a position of neutrality and undercut the patient's independence through numerous boundary violations tend to promote a fusional relationship between psychiatrist and patient. In extreme instances, the therapist gradually gains control over the patient's life, making basic life decisions for the patient. Whether done consciously or unconsciously, boundary violations limit a patient's options for independent psychological functioning and recovery. The achievement of psychological independence is a goal of treatment. The maintenance of patient separateness that permits pursuit of this goal is a boundary requirement for the therapist.

Confidentiality

The maintenance of confidentiality is a fundamental boundary guideline that must be adhered to unless specific clinical, ethical, or legal exceptions arise (Simon 1992). Confidentiality must be maintained unless release of information is competently authorized by the patient. Breaches of confidentiality typically occur when therapists find themselves in dual roles (Simon 1987). Such roles usually occur when the therapist must serve simultaneously the patient and a third party. Clinicians working in managed-care settings often find themselves struggling with dual roles (The Hastings Center 1987).

Informed consent

The law requires informed consent for treatments and procedures. Incidental to legal intent, informing patients of the risks and benefits of a proposed treatment maintains patient autonomy and fosters the therapeutic alliance (Simon 1989a). In a number of sexual misconduct cases, drugs and even electroconvulsive therapy have been used to gain control over patients (Simon 1992). *Negligent* medication practices are especially prominent in these cases. Obviously, no effort is made to inform the patient of the risks and benefits of any prescribed medications. Frequently, addictive medications are given, particularly barbiturates and benzodiazepines.

Verbal interaction

The process of psychotherapy requires that the interaction between therapist and patient be essentially verbal. Engaging the patient verbally acts as a check against acting out behaviors by the therapist. In psychotherapy, the therapist must always be alert to the possibility of acting out emotional conflicts with the patient. Acting out may be manifested either by the therapist's behavior or by inducing the patient to act out.

There is, however, a fundamental difference between active interventions utilized by the therapist and therapist acting out. For instance, when somatic therapies or behavioral modification techniques are used, active interventions are made in the service of the treatment, not for the purpose of exploiting the patient (Goisman and Gutheil 1992). Moreover, therapists may find it necessary to actively clinically intervene on behalf of a patient in crisis. All therapies, including Rogersian therapy and even psychoanalysis, employ active interventions and reinforcement approaches (Wachtel 1987, 120–122). The danger to patients and their therapy does not arise from therapist activity *per se*, but rather from therapist acting out.

Bibring (1954) noted that all dynamic psychotherapies variously utilize catharsis, suggestion, manipulation, clarification, and insight in their therapeutic approaches to the patient. Irrespective of the methods favored, the patient should be engaged primarily on a verbal rather than on an action level. Therapists who act out verbally can also seriously harm their patients. However, the behavioral expression of emotional conflict by therapists is usually more damaging to patients.

Personal relationships

Most therapists accept the boundary guideline principle of no previous, current, or future personal relationship with the patient. Past and current personal relationships with patients can hopelessly muddle treatment boundaries and doom any therapeutic efforts. Social chit-chat is not psychotherapy.

Maintaining post-treatment relationships with patients remains controversial (Simon 1992). For a number of sound clinical reasons, post-termination relationships with patients should be avoided (Simon 1992). Transferences can be timeless, raising serious concerns about a former patient's ability for autonomous consent to a post-treatment relationship. A 1-year waiting period has been proposed that "should minimize problems and allow former patients and therapists to enter into intimate relationships" (Appelbaum and Jorgenson 1991). The vast majority of therapist–patient sexual relationships begin within 6 months of termination. If the therapist thinks about the patient as a future sexual partner, boundary violations likely may result that impair the patient's treatment. *The Principles of Medical Ethics with Annotations Especially Applicable to Psychiatry* (2013, Section 2, annotation 1) states that, "Sexual activity with a current or former patient is unethical."

Physical contact

The avoidance of physical contact with patients is also a controversial issue (Bancroft 1981). Situations may arise in treatment when a handshake or a hug is the appropriate human response. Inoffensive and necessary touching occurs in the course of administering some procedures or treatments. Therapists who work with children, the elderly, and the physically ill frequently find that a caring human touch is comforting and is clinically supportive. An absolute prohibition against touching patients would preclude such therapeutic, human responses.

Nevertheless, therapists must be extremely wary of touching patients. Hugging may seem innocuous, but when carefully scrutinized, may contain erotic messages. Gratuitously touching the patient is clinically inappropriate and may be a prelude to sexual intimacies (Holub and Lee 1990). Holroyd and Brodsky (1989) found that nonerotic hugging, kissing, and touching of opposite-sex patients, but not same-sex patients, was a sex-biased therapy practice associated with a high risk of leading to sexual intercourse with patients. Every patient has the right to maintain the privacy of his or her own body.

Some psychiatrists continue to do their own physical examinations of patients. The transference and countertransference complications of physical examinations performed by the treating psychiatrist are well known. It is important that a physical examination not become the first step to progressive personal involvement with the patient.

Anonymity

Therapist self-disclosure is also a complicated and controversial topic (Stricker and Fisher 1990). Patient and therapist shared regression is one of the obvious dangers of therapist self-disclosure. Some therapists have found the sharing of a past personal experience to be helpful for certain patients in especially supportive psychotherapy. However, the self-disclosure of current conflicts and crises in the therapist's life can induce a role reversal in the patient who then attempts to rescue the therapist. Details of the therapist's personal life, especially fantasies and dreams, should not be shared with patients (Gutheil and Gabbard 1993). Self-disclosures about relationship problems, sexual frustrations, fantasies about the patient, and feelings of loneliness are particularly troublesome for the patient. Therapist self-disclosures not only waste treatment time but also promote a caretaking role on the part of the patient. Therapist self-disclosures, especially about current personal problems and sexual fantasies about the patient, appear to be highly correlated with eventual sexual misconduct (Borys and Pope 1989; Schoener et al. 1989). But, self-disclosure may be necessary if the therapist is suffering from an illness that might negatively affect the treatment or may cause the therapist to be absent from practice for a significant period of time. For example, a therapist's prolonged absence due to illness may require that the patient see another therapist. A simple explanation to the patient would be in order.

The therapist's position of relative anonymity, however, does not require that he or she remain a blank screen. The therapeutic relationship between therapist and patient is essentially interactive (Wachtel 1987, 176–184). For example, the therapist's overt and covert reactions to the patient can be therapeutically valuable in pointing out to the patient the repetitive nature of the patient–therapist interaction as it plays out in other important relationships.

The concept of anonymity and the increased use of social media over the past decade can have many implications for mental health professionals. Information about one's personal and professional life can and is now shared by many people on social media sites such as Facebook, Twitter, LinkedIn, and Instagram. It is important to remember that information posted by a therapist on these sites can be accessed by patients, and vice versa. Mental health professionals should avoid accessing patient information in the social media forum, as there is potential for boundary crossings. Some mental health professionals do utilize social media for business purposes. However, there are risks of engaging in this practice. For example, it has been stated that "While Facebook can be used for professional purposes, the potential dilemmas created by the overlap and interface between friends, family, and professional aspects of your life make it less than ideal as a social media marketing tool for professional purposes such as a psychiatric practice" (Luo 2013a,b). Social media will continue to evolve, and continued caution should be exercised whenever mental health professionals utilize this mode of communication. Koh et al. (2013) propose that "Discipline-specific guidelines for psychiatrists' interactions with social media and electronic communications are needed."

Fees

A fee should be established between the therapist and the patient that is mutually acceptable. Fees may change over time according to economic conditions and the personal circumstances of the patient. Therapists' fees should be paid with money only. The pecuniary value of nonmonetary payments is difficult to establish and should not be accepted (Simon 1992).

Therapists who become sexually involved with patients frequently discontinue billing. Although this practice has a number of meanings, some therapists do so in the erroneous belief that not billing the patient terminates the treatment relationship and therefore the possibility of being sued. The establishment and continuance of the doctor–patient relationship is not dependent on the payment of a fee (King 1986).

Treatment setting

As Langs (1990) points out, a consistent, relatively neutral treatment setting provides the necessary physical constants that endeavor to maintain "a maximal degree of consistency, certainty, and stability" for the treatment experience to unfold. Because many patients have suffered from inconstancy and intrusiveness in their relationships and physical environments, maintaining a professional treatment setting is psychologically important.

Behavior therapists, however, do accompany phobic patients into threatening environments and situations as part of their legitimate treatment regimen. Therapists with religious orientations may attend a patient's house of worship. Under exceptional circumstances or in an emergency, the therapist may find it necessary to make a house call. Flexibility is necessary because of clinical exigencies and reasonable variations in treatment approaches.

Effective psychotherapy cannot ordinarily be conducted over a telephone. With obvious exceptions, the telephone should be used mainly for making or breaking appointments or for emergencies (Canning et al. 1991). On occasion, therapy may be temporarily conducted over the telephone when the patient cannot come to the office for reasons of work, travel, or physical illness. Medications may require adjustment over the telephone between sessions. Telephone contact may be required in emergencies, but nonemergency telephone interviews should be well-structured, prearranged, time-limited therapeutic engagements that are paid for at the regular rates.

The advent of telemedicine has created a different avenue for patients to obtain mental health treatment without entering a psychiatrist's office. According to the American Telemedicine Association (ATA), telemedicine is formally defined as "the use of medical information exchanged from one site to another via electronic communications to improve a patient's clinical health status. Telemedicine includes a growing variety of applications and services using two-way video, email, smart phones, wireless tools and other forms of telecommunications technology." The ATA offers guidelines regarding the practice of telemedicine. With regard to treatment setting, the ATA recommends, "Both the professional and the patient's room/environment should aim to provide comparable professional specifications of a standard services room." It also suggests, "All efforts shall be taken to use video conferencing applications that have been vetted and have the appropriate verification, confidentiality, and security parameters necessary to be properly utilized for this purpose." (ATA 2013). With the increase in society's use of email communications, psychiatrists should be careful not to become reliant on email to provide complex psychiatric treatment, and again, ensure that security parameters are in place to protect patient confidentiality.

Time

Sessions that are defined in time and length also add stability to the treatment relationship. In sexual misconduct cases, therapy sessions progressively lose time definition, both in scheduling and length. Therapists must always question their reasons for lengthening or shortening sessions. Longer sessions may cause certain patients to feel special and, potentially, more vulnerable to exploitation.

On the other hand, the length of some sessions may require sensitivity to the exigent clinical needs of the patient. Patients in crisis often need additional time during a session. Patients with dissociative *identity* disorders may require flexibility in the length of sessions. Some longer sessions may be needed as various mental states emerge (Putnam 1989).

MONETARY EXPLOITATION

Boundary violations involving money and insurance matters are quite common (Simon 1992). Irregularities concerning patient billing of insurance companies may be only one of a number of boundary violations in the treatment. Any hint of dishonesty in the therapist's dealings with third parties will likely disrupt the therapist's position of neutrality and create mistrust in the therapist–patient relationship. Becoming involved or involving the patient in an acrimonious battle with third-party payers can disrupt boundaries and harm treatment.

Practitioners who become involved in business dealings with patients may later be accused of undue influence when purchasing valuable goods or property from the patient at below-market value, or when the patient leaves the witting therapist a large amount of money in a will (Halleck 1980). The use of "insider information" obtained from the patient for the personal advantage of the therapist occurs with disturbing frequency (American Psychiatric Association 1990). An example of such a practice occurred when a psychiatrist used a stock tip obtained from a bank executive's wife during the course of therapy to turn a large profit (Northrup 1991). Once the Securities and Exchange Commission learned from the patient that "insider" information about a merger was provided, it charged the psychiatrist with profiting illegally. Profits of $26,933.74 were surrendered, and the psychiatrist was fined $150,000 and sentenced to 5 years of probation and 3000 hours of community service (*Washington Post* 1991).

Psychiatrists who work in managed-care settings may face major ethical concerns and potentially serious double-agent roles (Sabin 1989). "Negative incentives" that cut costs at the expense of diminished quality of care represent a significant threat to the therapist's fiduciary commitment to patients (May 1986). Money matters must be secondary to the clinician's professional, ethical, and legal duty to provide adequate clinical care.

BOUNDARY VIOLATIONS AND MALPRACTICE

In almost all cases of therapist–patient sex, progressive boundary violations precede and accompany the eventual sexual acts (Simon 1989b). Empirical and consultative experience reveals that damaging boundary violations begin insidiously and are progressive. Boundary violations foster malpractice suits by creating a misalliance between therapist and patient. Boundary violations, usually reflecting the personal needs of the therapist, set patient and therapist against one another. Langs observes that the failure to maintain treatment boundaries may lead to autistic, symbiotic, and parasitic relationships with patients (Langs 1990, 339). Langs explains that autistic relationships (severed link) between therapist and patient damage meaningful relatedness, symbiotic (fusional) relationships pathologically gratify the patient, and parasitic (destructive) relationships exploit the patient. Frequently, bad results combined with bad feelings set the stage for a malpractice suit (Gutheil 1989).

Patients usually are psychologically damaged by the precursor boundary violations as well as the sexual exploitation (Schoener 1989; Simon 1991a,b). Even if the therapist and patient stop short of an overt sexual relationship, precursor boundary violations often prevent adequate diagnosis and treatment of the patient. The patient's original mental disorder is often exacerbated and other mental disorders are iatrogenically induced. Thus, therapists may be sued not only for sexual misconduct but also for negligent psychotherapy. Boundary violations that represent deviations in the standard of care and are alleged to have harmed the patient may form the basis of a malpractice suit. In sexual misconduct cases where insurance coverage is excluded, a malpractice claim may be filed based on the numerous, *harmful* boundary violations that precede therapist–patient sex. The following sections in this chapter on civil liability, malpractice cases, and malpractice insurance will further discuss sexual misconduct and malpractice.

DOUBLE AGENTRY

The problem of conflicting loyalties is a major concern to many psychiatrists (Weinstein 1991). Double agentry refers to the psychiatrist's conflicting loyalties when simultaneously serving the patient and an agency, institution, or society (The Hastings Center 1978). In the case of a military psychiatrist, for example, the professional duty owed to the soldier (patient) versus loyalty to the military's best interests poses a potential double-agent role. Prison psychiatrists are frequently confronted with the conflict of having to serve the interests of their prisoner patients, prison officials, and society. School psychiatrists must consider the interests of the student, the parents, and the school administration.

Boundary violations—particularly those involving breaches of confidentiality—may occur when therapists find themselves serving both the patient and a third party. Dual roles often skew the therapist's maintenance of appropriate treatment boundaries. Therapists must inform patients from the very beginning about any limitations placed on the patient's treatment, and particularly limits on confidentiality because of dual responsibilities of the therapist.

Practitioners may hold personal agendas that create a conflict of interest, disturbing the therapist's position of neutrality and creating legal liability. For example, in *Roe v. Doe* (1977) a psychiatrist was sued by a former patient for publishing a book that reported verbatim information from the therapy, including the patient's thoughts, feelings, and fantasies.

SEXUAL MISCONDUCT

Standard of care

The Principles of Medical Ethics with Annotations Especially Applicable to Psychiatry unequivocally prohibits sex with a current or former patient (2013). This ethical position has a venerable tradition in medicine since the time of Hippocrates. Sex between the therapist and the patient is negligence *per se* (Simon 1992). Therapist–patient sex is a violation of those statutes that govern the licensing and regulation of mental health professionals, incorporating ethical codes adopted by the professions that specifically prohibit sexual contact between therapist and patient. It is also unequivocal evidence of professional incompetence. The psychiatrist holds himself or herself out to the public as having standard professional skill and knowledge. The psychiatrist "must have and use the knowledge, skill, and care ordinarily possessed and employed by members of the profession in good standing" (Keeton et al. 1984). Because a respected minority of psychiatrists does not exist who will state that sex with a patient falls within the standard skill and knowledge of psychiatrists, sex between psychiatrist and patient is an unquestioned and unchallenged deviation in the standard of care.

An increasing number of states are limiting by statute the period of time after treatment ends whereby psychotherapists may be held legally liable for sexual involvement with a former patient (Gartrell et al. 1986). Some state statutes provide immunity from legal liability for sex between therapist and a former patient that occurs after a prescribed period of time, usually 1–2 years following termination (Bisbing et al., 1995, 755–756). Appelbaum and Jorgenson (1991) have proposed a 1-year waiting period that "should minimize problems and allow former patients and therapists to enter into intimate relationships." Because approximately 98% of sexual contact with former patients occurs within a year of initial clinical contact, most statutory time limits prohibiting post-treatment sex more than adequately cover the time of maximal vulnerability of patients to sexual exploitation (Gartrell et al. 1986). But, if the therapist entertains the prospect of sex with the patient in the future, boundary violations likely may result that impair the patient's treatment.

Nevertheless, although it may not be illegal for psychotherapists to have sex with a former patient after expiration of a statutorily prohibited period, it is unethical for psychiatrists to do so. The patient may not have had a therapeutic termination but rather an interrupted therapy by the therapist who anticipates having sex with the patient. Post-treatment sex with the patient often signals the presence of earlier precursor boundary violations by the therapist. Frequently, therapists who entertain the possibility of post-treatment sex with a patient communicate this desire during the course of treatment.

Therapist sex with a former patient presents complex ethical and legal issues. Some therapists marry their former patients. Moreover, constitutional issues surrounding the right of association and the competence of the former patient to choose freely complicate the legal analysis of post-treatment sex (Schoener et al. 1989). Clinically, however, the matter is much simpler. The most credible policy is to avoid sex with former patients. A closed-door policy toward former patients should be considered. Once the patient enters the door of the psychotherapist's office, it is forever closed to the possibility of a sexual relationship. Aside from ethical and legal concerns, a number of sound clinical reasons exist for this position (Simon 1992).

Sexual relations between supervisor and trainee also raise ethical issues. *The Principles of Medical Ethics with Annotations Especially Applicable to Psychiatry* states the following:

> Sexual involvement between a faculty member or supervisor and a trainee or student, in those situations in which an abuse of power can occur, often takes advantage of inequalities in the working relationship and may be unethical because: (a) any treatment of a patient being supervised may be deleteriously affected; (b) it may damage the trust relationship between teacher and student; and (c) teachers are important professional role models for their trainees and affect their trainees' future professional behavior. (Section 4, annotation 14, 2013)

Therapist–patient sex: Clinical issues, boundary violations

The road to therapist–patient sex is littered with numerous boundary violations (Simon 1999). Sexual misconduct rarely happens suddenly, but rather is usually preceded by progressive, increasingly damaging precursor boundary violations (Simon 1989b). The precursor boundary violations usually psychologically harm the patient by interfering with appropriate diagnosis and treatment (Simon 1991a). Precursor boundary violations can cause serious psychological injury, even if the therapist and patient stop short of a sexual relationship.

Although every case of sexual misconduct is unique, a "typical" scenario can be derived from cases evaluated for litigation:

- Therapist's position of neutrality is gradually eroded in "little" ways.
- Therapist and patient address each other by first name.
- Therapy sessions become less clinical and more social.
- Therapist's self-disclosures occur, usually about current problems and sexual fantasies about the patient.
- Therapist begins touching patient, usually by hugs and embraces.
- Therapist gains control over patient, usually by manipulating the transference and by medications.
- Therapy sessions become extended in time.
- Therapy sessions are rescheduled at the end of the day.
- Therapist and patient have drinks/dinner after sessions; dating begins.
- Therapist–patient sex begins.

Because precursor boundary violations to therapist–patient sex usually occur gradually and incrementally, the therapist may have time to restore treatment boundaries. Empirical and consultative experience reveals that damaging boundary violations begin insidiously and are progressive. During the segment of the therapy session that occurs "between the chair and the door," patients and therapists are more vulnerable to committing boundary excursions and violations. Inchoate boundary violations with a potential for damaging progression usually first appear within this interval. This part of the session can be scrutinized for early warning of boundary violations and studied for its instructive value in risk management and prevention of sexual misconduct (Gutheil and Simon 1995).

Epstein and Simon (1990) have devised an Exploitation Index that can be used by therapists as an early warning indicator of treatment boundary violations. A survey of 532 psychiatrists using the Exploitation Index revealed that 43% found that one or more questions alerted them to boundary violations, while 29% were stimulated to make specific changes in treatment practices (Epstein et al. 1992).

TRANSFERENCE EXPLOITATION

Patients who come for psychiatric treatment are undergoing painful mental and emotional suffering that is often debilitating. As a consequence, their decision-making capacity and judgment usually are impaired. Moreover, the therapist is viewed as a critically important source of help and hope. Under these circumstances, a patient's transference of expectant beneficence may develop that is highly influenced by early, powerful wishes for nurture and care. The therapist is frequently idealized as the all-good, all-giving parent. Combined with the fear of losing the newly acquired idealized parental figure, the beneficent transference leaves the patient vulnerable to exploitation by the therapist. The beneficent transference is a common psychological reaction, experienced to varying degrees by practically all patients.

It should be distinguished from the transference neurosis that develops in a number of patients usually undergoing intensive, psychodynamic psychotherapy.

Unlike the physician who works intuitively within the gambit of a positive transference that provides hope and succor to the patient, psychiatrists and other mental health professionals frequently work directly with transference phenomena as a therapeutic tool. As a treatment strategy in intensive psychotherapy or psychoanalysis, the therapist may encourage development of the transference but then is expected to keep countertransference feelings in check for the benefit of the patient. Biologically or behaviorally trained psychiatrists and psychotherapists may not place much emphasis on transference issues in treatment. Nevertheless, the importance of transference is well known and must be recognized by all therapists, regardless of their training and theoretical background. The legal concepts of undue influence and breach of fiduciary trust may be utilized in place of the concept of transference in the civil litigation of sexual misconduct cases involving biologically or behaviorally trained therapists (Simon 1991b).

The issue of patient transference and the competence to consent to therapist–patient sex sometimes arises in the context of litigation (Simon 1994). However, the breach of fiduciary trust by the therapist who engages in sex with the patient should be the appropriate focus of wrongdoing (Simon 1992). Thus, "In sexual misconduct cases, the issue is never the patient's consent but always breach of fiduciary trust by the therapist" (Simon 2003).

Certain patients appear to be particularly vulnerable to sexual exploitation. Patients with borderline, dependent, and histrionic personality disorders are vulnerable to sexual exploitation because significant potential exists for developing intense erotic and dependent transferences. The borderline patient may attempt to live out her or his transference with the therapist. Exceptions to treatment boundaries may be sought constantly (Gutheil 1989).

Many patients who are victims of sexual misconduct have been physically and sexually abused as children. In therapy, formerly abused patients tend to constantly test treatment boundaries to assess the integrity of the therapist. Exploitative therapists take advantage of these patients' efforts to find a person in authority whom they can begin to trust. No matter how seductive the patient, the therapist is expected to maintain his or her treatment neutrality while attempting to understand the meaning of the seductive behavior with the patient. The therapist charged with sexual misconduct by the patient cannot complain that he or she was seduced.

Civil liability

Malpractice is the most common form of legal liability in sexual misconduct cases. Litigation is almost always sparked by a real or perceived rejection of the patient by the therapist that shatters the patient's sense of specialness. If it is just the plaintiff's word against the therapist's word that therapist–patient sex took place, proving the case against the therapist may be very difficult. In these cases, the forensic psychiatrist's position on either side of the litigation should be one of neutrality concerning the factual dispute. A tenable stance is that if the therapist did engage in a sexual relationship with the patient, then negligence did occur.

When it can be demonstrated that significant boundary violations have occurred, the plaintiff's case alleging sexual misconduct by the therapist is bolstered. Although the presence of typical precursor boundary violations makes it more likely that sexual misconduct occurred, it cannot be inferred with certainty that an actual therapist–patient sexual relationship took place. If the plaintiff can provide corroborating evidence to support the allegations of sexual misconduct, such as testimony from other abused (former) patients, letters, pictures, hotel or motel receipts, and identifying body marks, then the legal defense of the therapist becomes very difficult.

The psychiatrist evaluating psychological damages will be asked to distinguish the pre-injury from post-injury psychiatric status of the abused patient. Pope and Bouhoutsos (1986, 45–56) have described a "therapist–patient sex syndrome." This syndrome may not be distinct, but probably reflects the existence of comorbidity so often seen in victims of therapists' sexual misconduct. A study by Bouhoutsos et al. (1983) found that 90% of the patients were damaged by therapist–patient sexual intimacies. Pope and Bouhoutsos, in their review of the literature, state, "overall, the balance of the empirical findings is heavily weighed in the direction of serious harm resulting to almost all patients sexually involved with their therapists" (Pope and Bouhoutsos 1986, 63). Guidelines for the assessment of psychological harm caused by therapist-patient sex have been proposed (Pope 1989; Schoener et al. 1989, 133–145). A systematic approach to the evaluation of claims of therapist–patient sexual misconduct also requires considerations of false accusations in order to maintain a balanced forensic perspective (Gutheil 1992).

Malpractice cases

A few representative malpractice cases will illustrate the general position that courts have taken in undue familiarity litigation. For example, the injurious nature of precursor boundary violations was underscored in *Zipkin v. Freeman* (1968), one of the earliest sexual misconduct cases. The defendant psychiatrist was found to have manipulated the patient to his advantage by convincing the patient to become his mistress and to leave her husband. The patient alleged that she had sex with the psychiatrist and attended "group therapy" that involved nude swimming. She complained that the psychiatrist mishandled the transference, which a psychiatrist is expected to handle properly. The judge stated:

> Once Dr. Freeman started to mishandle the transference phenomena, with which he was plainly charged in the petition and which is overwhelmingly shown in the evidence, it was

> inevitable that trouble was ahead. It is pretty clear from the medical evidence that the damage would have been done to Mrs. Zipkin even if the trips outside the state were carefully chaperoned, the swimming done with suits on, and if there had been ballroom dancing instead of sexual relations.

The jury awarded the patient monetary damages of $17,000.

Before the *Roy v. Hartogs* decision in 1976, there was little significant litigation arising from sexual involvement between psychiatrists and patients. In *Hartogs*, for the first time, large monetary damages were awarded after Dr. Hartogs attempted to treat his patient's fear of being a lesbian by initiating a sexual relationship with her. The court held that the psychotherapist–patient relationship was a fiduciary relationship similar to a guardian–ward relationship. The court further stated, "there is a public policy to protect a patient from the deliberate and malicious abuse of power and breach of trust by a psychiatrist when the patient entrusts to him her body and mind."

In *Simmons v. United States* (1986), the court addressed the consequences of mishandling the transference:

> The impacts of sexual involvement with one's counselor are more severe than the impacts of merely "having an affair" for two major reasons: First, because the client's attraction is based on transference, the sexual contact is ordinarily akin to engaging in sexual activity with a parent, and carries with it the feelings of shame, guilt, and anxiety experienced by incest victims. Second, the client is usually suffering from all or some of the psychological problems that brought him or her into therapy to begin with. As a result, the client is especially vulnerable to the added stress created by the feelings of shame, guilt, and anxiety produced by the incestuous nature of the relationship, and by the sense of betrayal that is felt when the client eventually learns that she is not "special" as she had been led to believe, and that her trust has been violated.

Malpractice insurance

Most professional liability insurers will not insure for sexual misconduct, excluding it as an intentional tort or criminal action. The rationale for this is that because sexual misconduct is not practice, it cannot be malpractice. Some malpractice policies will cover the costs of litigation but not the cost of damages. Other insurers will only cover the therapist if the charge of sexual misconduct is denied.

The negligent management of transference and countertransference has been alleged as a cause of therapist sexual misconduct and is covered by some professional liability policies. Because this allegation may be self-serving on the part of the therapist, the testimony of an expert witness may be necessary in a legal action between the therapist and the carrier.

As previously stated, most cases of therapist–patient sex are preceded by progressive treatment boundary violations. As a result, patients are usually psychologically damaged by precursor boundary violations in addition to the eventual sexual misconduct of the therapist (Simon 1991a). The therapist's mismanagement of boundaries may fall under the negligence provisions of his or her professional liability policy. The trend of court decisions in undue familiarity litigation favors compensation of victims.

The statute of limitations may be invoked in sexual misconduct cases. For example, in *Decker v. Fink* (1980), a sexual misconduct case, the Maryland Special Court of Appeals ruled that the plaintiff's impaired judgment, presumably because of the effects of transference, was not "sufficient legal justification for failing to timely file [a] medical malpractice action, and evidence established that [the] plaintiff knew or should have known [of the] existence of her alleged cause of action." In *Riley v. Presnell* (1991), however, the Massachusetts Supreme Judicial Court invoked the discovery rule, which tolled (stopped) the statute of limitations from running. It rejected the defendant's defense that it was too late to bring a malpractice suit 7 years after the alleged sexual misconduct. The plaintiff successfully contended that he was unable to discover the psychological injuries resulting from the sexual misconduct because of the harm caused by the psychiatrist's behavior. In cases that involve exploitation of the patient, the therapist's negligence may impair the patient's ability to become aware of the psychological injuries that are produced (Jorgenson and Appelbaum 1991). In *Colburn v. Kopit* (2002), the Colorado Court of Appeals found that, according to Colorado law, "An action for negligence or outrageous conduct must be filed within two years after the cause of action accrues." The finding of the appellate court was that "the statute of limitations for plaintiff's claims of breach of fiduciary duty, negligence, and outrageous conduct had expired before plaintiff filed this action."

Idealization of the therapist may prevent the patient from discovering his or her injury, thus permitting the presence of transference to toll the statute of limitations. Fraudulent concealment of negligence by the therapist also may toll the statute; for example, it may occur in therapist–patient sex when the therapist informs the patient that sex is therapy, or when the therapist does not inform the patient that he or she is under the influence of transference.

Civil and criminal statutes

An increasing number of states have statutorily made sexual activity both civilly and criminally actionable. For instance, Minnesota has enacted legislation that states:

> A cause of action against a psychotherapist for sexual exploitation exists for a patient or former patient for injury caused by sexual contact with the psychotherapist if the sexual contact

occurred: (1) during the period the patient was receiving psychotherapy…or (2) after the period the patient received psychotherapy…if (a) the former patient was emotionally dependent on the psychotherapist; or (b) the sexual contact occurred by means of therapeutic deception. (Minn. Stat. Ann. §604.201, 2014)

Some states make therapist–patient sex *negligence per se* by statute, creating a nonrebuttable presumption concerning the therapist's duty of care (Simon 1992). To establish liability, the plaintiff need only prove that sexual contact occurred and caused damage.

In legislation prohibiting therapist–patient sexual exploitation, sexual behavior is defined in a variety of ways, some so vague as to invite constitutional challenges based on violation of the Due Process Clause in state constitutions and the U.S. Constitution (Jorgenson et al. 1991). Most statutes define sexual activity as intercourse, rape, the touching of breasts and genitals, cunnilingus, fellatio, sodomy, and inappropriate or unnecessary examinations and procedures performed for sexual gratification. Obviously, statutory definitions cannot possibly encompass the wide variety of sexual activities that constitute abuse of patients by a therapist.

Three basic types of remedies have been codified into reporting, civil liability, and criminal statutes (Appelbaum 1991; Strasburger et al. 1991). Reporting statutes require the disclosure to state authorities by a therapist who learns of any past or current therapist–patient sex. A few states have civil statutes proscribing sexual misconduct. The civil statutes incorporate a standard of care and make malpractice suits easier to pursue. For example, Minnesota has enacted a statute that provides a specific cause of action against psychiatrists and other psychotherapists for injury caused by sexual contact with a patient (Simon 1992). Some of these statutes also restrict unfettered discovery of the plaintiff's past sexual history. Criminal sanctions may be the only remedy for exploitative therapists without malpractice insurance, who are unlicensed, or who do not belong to professional organizations.

Sexual exploitation of a patient, under certain circumstances, may be considered rape or some analogous sexual offense and therefore criminally actionable. Typically, the criminality of the exploitation is determined by one of three factors: the practitioner's means of inducement, the age of the victim, or the availability of a relevant state criminal code.

Some states can, and do, prosecute sexual exploitation suits using their sexual assault statutes (Simon 1992). Sex with a current patient may be criminally actionable if the state can prove beyond a reasonable doubt that the patient was coerced into engaging in the sexual act. Typically, this type of coercion is limited to the use of some form of substance, such as medication, to either induce compliance or reduce resistance. Anesthesia, electroconvulsive treatment, hypnosis, force, and threat of harm all have been used to coerce patients into sexual submission (Schoener et al. 1989, 331). To date, claims of "psychological coercion" via the manipulation of transference phenomena have not been successful in establishing the coercion necessary for a criminal case. In cases involving a minor patient, the issue of consent or coercion is irrelevant, because minors and incompetents (including adult incompetents) are unable to provide valid consent. Therefore, sex with a child or an incompetent is automatically considered a criminal act.

Wisconsin and an increasing number of other states make sexual relations between a therapist and patient a statutory criminal offense (Bisbing et al. 1995). For example, the Wisconsin statute holds:

Any person who is or who holds himself or herself out to be a therapist and who intentionally has sexual contact with a patient or client during any ongoing therapist–patient or therapist–client relationship regardless of whether it occurs during any treatment, consultation, interview, or examination is guilty of a class F felony. Consent is not an issue in an action under this subsection. (Wis. Stat. Ann. §940.22[2], 2014)

Professional disciplinary action

In addition to civil and criminal liability, psychiatrists who engage in sex with patients also can become embroiled in ethics proceedings conducted by professional organizations. The statute of limitations does not apply in ethics proceedings. Moreover, for the purpose of adjudicating allegations of professional misconduct, licensing boards typically are granted certain regulatory and disciplinary authority by state statutes. As a result, state licensing organizations, unlike professional associations, may discipline an offending professional more effectively and punitively by suspending or revoking his or her license. Because licensing boards are not as restrained by the rigorous rules of evidence that exist in civil and criminal actions, it generally is less difficult for the patient to seek redress through this means. Published reports of sexual misconduct adjudicated before licensing boards generally reveal that if the evidence was reasonably sufficient to substantiate a claim of exploitation, the professional's license was revoked or the professional was suspended from practice for varying lengths of time, including permanent suspension. The Federation of State Medical Boards has published a report titled *Addressing Sexual Boundaries: Guidelines for State Medical Boards* that "provides recommendations to assist medical boards with the investigation process, preparation for formal hearings, crafting an appropriate disciplinary response, physician monitoring, and physician education" in cases of alleged physician sexual misconduct.

Reporting sexual misconduct

Reporting the alleged sexual misconduct of other therapists based on the statements of patients is fraught with complex clinical, ethical, and professional issues. Requiring mandatory reporting may create serious double-agent roles for the therapist that can undermine subsequent treatment interventions with the exploited patient. A few states require reporting of sexual misconduct by therapists (Bisbing et al., 1995, 168–169). In most states with reporting requirements involving therapist–patient sex, reporting may not proceed without the patient's consent.

Clinical flexibility regarding reporting is required in the treatment and management of sexually exploited patients. When the patient is a therapist who reports exploiting his or her patient, does a *Tarasoff* duty to warn and protect his or her other patients arise? Conflicting ethical issues exist surrounding breaching confidentiality versus potential *Tarasoff* duties arising from the discovery of a patient–therapist's continuing sexual exploitation (Eth and Leong 1990).

The requirement to report an impaired colleague or the allegation of sexual misconduct often conflicts with the duty to maintain patient confidentiality. Some abused patients do not want their sexual relationship with a therapist made public. If the patient is the offending therapist, the conflict between reporting and maintaining confidentiality is further heightened because reporting likely would doom the therapy and unilaterally expose the patient (therapist) to grave personal and professional consequences.

Second, the reports of therapist sexual misconduct by a patient may not be true. False allegations of therapist–patient sex are a relatively rare phenomenon. Nevertheless, the new therapist should withhold judgment upon hearing charges of sexual misconduct against another therapist. Furthermore, the patient should decide about bringing allegations of therapist sexual misconduct in the open, except where mandatory reporting by the therapist is required. Thus, the question of reporting is turned into a treatment issue.

Third, treatment may be the most pressing need for the patient who has been sexually abused. Unfortunately, the patient may have to choose between treatment and litigation. Psychotherapy and litigation do not mix. The emotional turmoil and the additional stress the patient may experience when involved in litigation are often too disruptive to the continuing conduct of psychotherapy. Nevertheless, some therapists believe that therapeutic value exists for the plaintiff in pursuing a suit in overcoming helplessness, expressing anger and revenge, and resolving trauma.

Fourth, a therapist's zeal to report another therapist's alleged sexual abuse without regard to the patient's clinical status can further psychologically damage the patient. Abused patients have been re-victimized by therapists who have attempted to undo the trauma caused by the initial sexual exploitation. A common scenario occurs when the therapist bends over backward to try to prove his or her own trustworthiness to the patient or to try to re-parent the patient. As a consequence, serious, damaging boundary violations have occurred (Simon 2001). The maintenance of therapist neutrality is critical in these cases and should not be construed as a conspiracy of professional silence.

The new therapist faced with a patient alleging sexual exploitation should consider consultation with a forensic psychiatrist familiar with the legal and ethical issues surrounding allegations of sexual misconduct. The therapist may be better able to maintain a treatment role while the forensic consultant handles the legal issues with the patient. The therapist's provision of detailed psychiatric testimony gleaned in the course of therapy may utterly destroy the treatment relationship and sorely vex the therapist (Strasburger 1987).

Prevention

The sexual exploitation of patients is not correlated with the level of training or the theoretical persuasion of the therapist. Gartrell et al. (1986) found offenders were more likely to have graduated from an accredited residency and to have undergone personal psychotherapy or psychoanalysis. Thus, all therapists must be educated about sexual misconduct and the devastating consequences for the patient and the therapist. In tutorials and seminars, therapists need to be taught that the principle of abstinence requires that the therapist's primary source of gratification arise from the treatment process with the patient. The therapist's position of neutrality demands that the patient not be exploited as a personal source of gratification for the therapist. Receiving a fee for professional services is the only material satisfaction provided directly by the patient.

Moreover, therapists must be sensitized to the boundary violation precursors to therapist–patient sex. Because precursor boundary violations occur over time, the alerted therapist may be able to restore treatment boundaries before the patient is harmed or progression to therapist–patient sex occurs (Simon 1995). Of course, therapists with severe character disorders who relate to patients through manipulation and exploitation cannot be expected to benefit very much from educational efforts.

Therapists who find themselves sexually attracted to patients and in danger of acting out their feelings must consider the following:

- Consultation with a colleague
- Referral of the patient (with no further contact)
- Personal therapy
- Acknowledging personal and professional limitations with certain patients
- All of the above

Feelings of sexual attraction by therapists toward patients are common. A survey of 575 psychotherapists found that 87% felt sexually attracted to their clients, but only 9.4% of men and 2.5% of women acted out such feelings (Pope et al. 1986). Unfortunately, countertransference feelings, particularly the erotic variety, have become associated with mismanagement of the patient's treatment and are viewed with shame and embarrassment by some therapists. Countertransference, however, when properly managed, can be used as an important therapeutic tool (Heimann 1950). Alternatively, ignorance of countertransference phenomena may harm the therapeutic process.

SUMMARY

Treatment boundaries fluctuate in response to the dynamic, psychological interaction between therapist and patient. As a consequence, boundary crossings and violations occur in almost every therapy. The boundary-sensitive therapist usually can re-establish treatment boundaries before the patient is psychologically harmed. Although "minor" boundary excursions initially may appear innocuous, they can represent inchoate violations along the progression to eventual exploitation of the patient.

A spot test can be applied by the boundary-sensitive therapist to determine whether he or she has committed a boundary violation: first, is the intervention in question done for the benefit of the therapist or for the sake of the patient's therapy? Second, is the intervention in question part of a series of progressive boundary violations? If the answer to either is "yes," the therapist is on notice to desist immediately and to take corrective action. If basic treatment boundaries are violated and the patient is harmed, therapists may be sued, may be charged with ethical violations, and may lose their professional license.

Malpractice suits against psychotherapists alleging undue familiarity continue. Unlike the aftermath of other malpractice actions, the consequences for the offending therapist go far beyond large monetary judgments. The professional and personal disgrace, ethical proceedings, criminal proceedings, loss of licensure, as well as the loss of income, friends, and family are just some of the disastrous consequences that can occur. Numerous efforts to address this serious problem continue through civil and criminal litigation, legislation of protective statutes, and education of laypeople and professionals alike.

SUMMARY KEY POINTS

- Boundary guidelines for psychotherapy, such as maintaining therapist neutrality and separateness, confidentiality, informed consent, no personal relationship with the patient, minimization of physical contact, preservation of therapist anonymity, fee and session length stability, and a professional setting can help maintain the integrity of the treatment process.
- *The Principles of Medical Ethics with Annotations Especially Applicable to Psychiatry* unequivocally prohibit sex with a current or former patient (2013). Therapist–patient sex is a violation of those statutes that govern the licensing and regulation of mental health professionals, incorporating ethical codes adopted by the professions that specifically prohibit sexual contact between therapist and patient. It is also unequivocal evidence of professional incompetence.
- It may not be illegal for psychotherapists to have sex with a former patient after expiration of a statutorily prohibited period of time, but it is unethical for psychiatrists to do so. Malpractice is the most common form of legal liability in sexual misconduct cases. Most professional liability insurers will not insure for sexual misconduct, excluding it as an intentional tort or criminal action.
- An increasing number of states have statutorily made sexual activity both civilly and criminally actionable. In addition to civil and criminal liability, state licensing organizations, unlike professional associations, may discipline an offending professional by suspending or revoking his or her license.

REFERENCES

American Psychiatric Association (APA). 2013. *The Principles of Medical Ethics with Annotations Especially Applicable to Psychiatry* Washington, DC: APA. Sections 1, 2, 4. https://psychiatry.org/File%20Library/Psychiatrists/Practice/Ethics/principles-medical-ethics.pdf, accessed June 30, 2016.

American Psychiatric Association Ethics Committee. 1990. Non-sexual exploitation of patients. *Ethics Newsletter* 6(2).

American Telemedicine Association 2012. http://www.americantelemed.org/about-telemedicine/what-is-telemedicine#.V3V8tkrn9ol, accessed June 30, 2016.

American Telemedicine Association. 2013. *Practice Guidelines for Video-based Online Mental Health Services*. http://www.americantelemed.org/docs/default-source/standards/practice-guidelines-for-video-based-online-mental-health services.pdf?sfvrsn=6, accessed June 30, 2016.

Appelbaum PS. 1991. Statutes regulating patient–therapist sex. *Hospital and Community Psychiatry* 41:15–16.

Appelbaum PS and L Jorgenson. 1991. Psychotherapist–patient sexual contact after termination of treatment: An analysis and a proposal. *American Journal of Psychiatry* 148:1466–1473.

Bancroft J. 1981. Ethical aspects of sexuality and sex therapy. In *Psychiatric Ethics*, edited by S Block and P Chodoff, New York: Oxford University Press, 160–184.

Bibring E. 1954. Psychoanalysis and the dynamic psychotherapies. *Journal American Psychoanalytic of the Association* 2:745–770.

Bisbing SB, LM Jorgenson, and PK Sutherland. 1995. *Sexual Abuse by Professionals: A Legal Guide.* Charlottesville, VA: Michie, 833–855.

Black HC. 1990. *Black's Law Dictionary,* 6th edition, St. Paul, MN: West.

Borys DS and KS Pope 1989. Dual relationships between therapist and client: A national study of psychologists, psychiatrists, and social workers. *Professional Psychology Research and Practice* 20:287–293.

Bouhoutsos J, J Holroyd, H Lerman et al. 1983. Sexual intimacy between psychotherapists and patients. *Professional Psychology* 14:185–196.

Canning S, M Hauser, and T Gutheil, 1991. Communications in psychiatric practice: Decision making and the use of the telephone. In *Decision Making in Psychiatry and the Law,* edited by T Gutheil, H Bursztajn, A Brodsky et al., Baltimore: Williams and Wilkins, 227–235.

Colburn v. Kopit, 59 P.3d 295 (Colorado Court of Appeals, Div. III. 2002). http://caselaw.findlaw.com/co-court-of-appeals/1377690.html, accessed June 30, 2016.

Decker v. Fink, 422 A.2d 389, 390 (Md. Ct. Spec. App. 1980).

Epstein RS and RI Simon, 1990. The exploitation index: An early warning indicator of boundary violations in psychotherapy. *Bulletin of the Menninger Clinic* 54:450–465.

Epstein RS, RI Simon, and GG Kay. 1992. Assessing boundary violations in psychotherapy: Survey results with the exploitation index. *Bulletin of the Menninger Clinic* 56:1–17.

Eth S and G Leong. 1990. Therapist sexual misconduct and the duty to protect. In *Confidentiality Versus the Duty to Protect. Foreseeable Harm in the Practice of Psychiatry,* edited by JC Beck, Washington, DC: American Psychiatric Press, 107–119.

Federation of State Medical Boards. 2006. *Addressing Sexual Boundaries: Guidelines for State Medical Boards.* https://www.fsmb.org/Media/Default/PDF/FSMB/Advocacy/GRPOL_Sexual%20Boundaries.pdf, accessed June 30, 2016.

Freud S. 1959. Further recommendations in the technique of psychoanalysis. In *Collected Papers.* 2 vols., edited by E Jones and J Riviere, New York: Basic Books, 121–138.

Furrow B. 1980. *Malpractice in Psychotherapy.* Lexington, MA: D.C. Heath, 31.

Gartrell N, J Herman, S Olarte et al. 1986. Psychiatrist–patient sexual contact—Results of a national survey, 1: Prevalence. *American Journal of Psychiatry* 143:1126–1131.

Goisman RM and Gutheil TG. 1992. Risk management in the practice of behavior therapy: Boundaries and behavior. *American Journal of Psychotherapy* 46:532–543.

Green S, R Goldberg, D Goldstein et al. 1988. *Limit Setting in Clinical Practice.* Washington, DC: American Psychiatric Press.

Gutheil T. 1989. Borderline personality disorders, boundary violations, and patient–therapist sex: Medicolegal pitfalls. *American Journal of Psychiatry* 146:597–602.

Gutheil TG. 1991. Patients involved in sexual misconduct with therapists: Is a victim profile possible? *Psychiatric Annals* 21:661–667.

Gutheil TG. 1992. Approaches to forensic assessment of false claims of sexual misconduct by therapists. *Bulletin of the American Academy of Psychiatry and Law* 20:289–296.

Gutheil TG. 2005. Boundaries, blackmail, and double binds: A pattern observed in malpractice consultation. *Journal of the American Academy of Psychiatry and Law* 33:476–481.

Gutheil T and G Gabbard. 1993. The concept of boundaries in clinical practice: Theoretical and risk management dimensions. *American Journal of Psychiatry* 150:188–196.

Gutheil TG and RI Simon. 1995. Between the chair and the door: Boundary issues in the therapeutic "transition zone." *Harvard Review of Psychiatry* 2:336–340.

Halleck S. 1980. *Law in the Practice of Psychiatry.* New York: Plenum, 38–39.

Heimann P. 1950. On countertransference. *International Journal of Psychoanalysis* 31:81–84.

Holroyd JC and AM Brodsky. 1989. Does touching patients lead to sexual intercourse? *Professional Psychology: Research and Practice* 11:807–811.

Holub EA and SS Lee. 1990. Therapists' use of nonerotic physical contact: Ethical concerns. *Professional Psychology: Research and Practice* 21:115–117.

Jorgenson L and PS Appelbaum. 1991. For whom the statute tolls: Extending the time during which patients can sue. *Hospital and Community Psychiatry* 42:683–684.

Jorgenson L, R Randles, and L Strasburger. 1991. The furor over psychotherapist–patient sexual contact: New solutions to old problems. *William and Mary Law Review* 32:645–732.

Keeton P, D Dobbs, R Keeton et al. 1984. *Prosser and Keeton on Torts,* 5th edition. Section 32, p. 187, St. Paul: West.

King J. 1986. *The Law of Medical Malpractice.* St. Paul, MN: West, 17.

Koh S, GM Cattell, DM Cochran, A Krasner, FJ Langheim, and DA Sasso. 2013. Psychiatrists' use of electronic communication and social media and a proposed framework for future guidelines. *Journal of Psychiatric Practice* 3:254–263.

Langs R. 1990. *Psychotherapy: A Basic Text.* Northvale, NJ: Jason Aronson, 303–323, 339.

Luo J. 2013a. How to use social media and when (part I). *Psychiatric Times* May 17. http://psychnews.psychiatryonline.org/newsarticle.aspx?articleid=1688791, accessed December 31, 2013.

Luo J. 2013b. How to use social media and when (part II). *Psychiatric Times* May 24. http://psychnews.psychiatryonline.org/newsarticle.aspx?articleID=1691711, accessed December 31, 2013.

Marshall R, K Teston, and W Myers. 2008. Psychiatrist/patient boundaries: When it's OK to stretch the line. *Current Psychiatry* 7(8):53–62.

Marziali EM, C Marmar, and J Krupnick. 1981. Therapeutic alliance scales: Development and relationship to psychotherapy outcome. *American Journal of Psychiatry* 138:361–364.

May WE. 1986. Patient advocate or secret agent? *Journal of the American Medical Association* 256:1784–1787.

Northrup B. 1991. Psychotherapy faces a stubborn problem: Abuses by therapists. *Wall Street Journal* October 29, 1.

Olarte SW. 1991. Characteristics of therapists who become involved in sexual boundary violations. *Psychiatric Annals* 21:657–660.

Omer v. Edgren, 38 Wash. App. 376, 685 P.2d 635 (1984).

Pope K. 1989. Therapist–patient sex syndrome: A guide for attorneys and subsequent therapists to assessing damages. In *Sexual Exploitation in Professional Relationships*, edited by G Gabbard, Washington, DC: American Psychiatric Press, 39–55.

Pope K and J Bouhoutsos. 1986. *Sexual Intimacy between Therapists and Patients*. New York: Praeger.

Pope KS, P Keith-Spiegel, and BG Tabachnick. 1986. Sexual attraction to clients. *American Psychologist* 41:147–158.

Putnam FW. 1989. *Diagnosis and Treatment of Multiple Personality Disorder*. New York: Guilford Press.

Riley v. Presnell, 565 N.E. 2d 780, Mass. (1991).

Roe v. Doe, 93 Misc2d 201, 400 N.S.Y2d, 668 (Sup Ct 1977).

Roy v. Hartogs, 85 Misc. 2d 891, 381 N.Y.S. 2d 587 (N.Y. Sup. Ct. 1976).

Sabin JE. 1989. Psychiatrists face tough ethical questions in managed care setting. *Psychiatric Times* 16(1):10–11.

Sarkar SP. 2004. Boundary violation and sexual exploitation in psychiatry and psychotherapy: A review. *Advances in Psychiatric Treatment* 10:312–320.

Schoener G. 1989. Assessment of damages. In *Psychotherapists' Sexual Involvement with Clients: Intervention and Prevention*, edited by G Schoener, J Milgrorn, J Gonsiorek et al., Minneapolis, MN: Walk-in Counseling Center, 133–145.

Schoener G, J Milgrom, J Gonsiorek et al. 1989. *Psychotherapists' Sexual Involvement with Clients*. Minneapolis, MN: Walk-In Counseling Center, 331.

Shapiro E and W Carr. 1991. *Lost in Familiar Places: Creating New Connections between the Individual and Society*. New Haven, CT: Yale University Press.

Simmons v. United States, 805 F.2d 1363, 1365 (9th Cir. 1986).

Simon RI. 1987. The psychiatrist as a fiduciary: Avoiding the double agent role. *Psychiatric Annals* 17:622–626.

Simon RI. 1989a. Beyond the doctrine of informed consent: A clinician's perspective. *Journal for the Expert Witness, the Trial Attorney, the Trial Judge* 4:23–25.

Simon RI. 1989b. Sexual exploitation of patients: How it begins before it happens. *Psychiatric Annals* 19:104–112.

Simon RI. 1990a. Legal liabilities of an "impossible" profession. In *American Psychiatric Press Review of Clinical Psychiatry and the Law*, 2 vols., edited by RI Simon, Washington, DC: American Psychiatric Press, 3–91.

Simon RI. 1990b. The duty to protect in private practice. In *Confidentiality Versus the Duty to Protect. Foreseeable Harm in the Practice of Psychiatry*, edited by JC Beck, Washington, DC: American Psychiatric Press, 23–41.

Simon RI. 1991a. Psychological injury caused by boundary violation precursors to therapist–patient sex. *Psychiatric Annals* 21:614–619.

Simon RI. 1991b. Legal liabilities of an "impossible" profession. In *American Psychiatric Press Review of Clinical Psychiatry and the Law*. 2 vols., edited by RI Simon, Washington, DC: American Psychiatric Press.

Simon RI. 1992. *Clinical Psychiatry and the Law*, 2nd edition. Washington, DC: American Psychiatric Press.

Simon R. 1993. Innovative psychiatric therapies and legal uncertainty: A survival guide for clinicians. *Psychiatric Annals* 23:473–479.

Simon RI. 1994. Transference in therapist–patient sex: The illusion of patient improvement and consent, Parts 1 and 2. *Psychiatric Annals* 24:509–515, 561–565.

Simon RI. 1995. The natural history of therapist sexual misconduct: Identification and prevention. *Psychiatric Annals* 25:90–94.

Simon RI. 1999. Therapist–patient sex: From boundary violations to sexual misconduct. *Psychiatric Clinics of North America* 22:31–47.

Simon R. 2000. Defensive psychiatry and the disruption of treatment boundaries. *Israel Journal of Psychiatry* 37:124–131.

Simon RI. 2001. *Concise Guide to Psychiatry and Law for Clinicians*, 3rd edition. Washington, DC: American Psychiatric Press.

Simon RI. 2003. The law and psychiatry. *Focus*. Fall 2003, I(4):360, http://focus.psychiatryonline.org/doi/pdf/10.1176/foc.1.4.349.

Simon R and R Sadoff. 1992. *Psychiatric Malpractice: Cases and Comments for Clinicians*. Washington, DC: American Psychiatric Press.

Simon R and I Williams. 1999. Maintaining treatment boundaries in small communities and rural areas. *Psychiatric Annals* 50:1440–1446.

Strasburger LH. 1987. "Crudely, without any finesse": The defendant hears his psychiatric evaluation. *Bulletin of the American Academy of Psychiatry and the Law* 15:229–233.

Strasburger LH, L Jorgenson, and R Randles. 1991. Criminalization of psychotherapist–patient sex. *American Journal of Psychiatry* 148:859–863.

Stricker O and M Fisher. 1990. *Self-Disclosure in the Therapeutic Relationship.* New York: Plenum Press.

The Hastings Center. 1978. *In the Service of the State: The Psychiatrist as Double Agent.* Special supplement. New York: Briarcliff Manor.

The Hastings Center. 1987. *New Mental Health Economics and the Impact on the Ethics of Psychiatric Practice.* New York: Briarcliff Manor, April 16–17.

Wachtel P. 1987. *Action and Insight.* New York: Guilford Press, 120–122, 167–175, 176–184.

Washington Post, January 8, 1991, D10.

Weinstein H. 1991. Dual loyalties in the practice of psychiatry. In *American Psychiatric Press Review of Clinical Psychiatry and the Law*, 3 vols., edited by RI Simon, Washington, DC: American Psychiatric Press.

Wisconsin Statutes and Annotations. Wis. Stat. Ann. § 940.22(2) (West Supp. 1992). https://docs.legis.wisconsin.gov/statutes/statutes/940/II/22.

Zipkin v. Freeman, 436 S.W.2d. (1968).

22

The law and the physician: Ill physicians

MICHAEL GENDEL AND PAUL D. COOPER

INTRODUCTION

This chapter will review how physicians suffering from mental illness, including substance use disorders and other illnesses, are affected by regulatory law, policies of hospitals and other workplaces, and reporting and certifying agencies. It also will discuss problems and protections in other areas of civil law that are posed by physician illness. Special issues in defending, assessing, treating, and monitoring ill physicians will be explored. The significant role of state physician health programs in modulating the workings of regulatory law and administrative policy, as they affect sick doctors, also will be discussed.

CONVERGING LEGAL AND HEALTH ISSUES

The development of legal mechanisms to address ill physicians: Limitations

That illness potentially could impair a doctor at work, and thus endanger patients, has been recognized in published literature since the nineteenth century. However, there was little published in the scientific literature about physician health matters until the last 40 years. The handling of ill physicians generally has been the purview of state licensing boards, under the concept of "regulation of physician practice." These boards were established and began functioning in the United States in the latter half of the nineteenth century. The laws, and the licensing boards that they created, were meant to protect the public by defining "professional" and "unprofessional" behavior. Beginning in the nineteenth century (and, in some jurisdictions, continuing to the present day), being addicted to drugs and/or alcohol (usually referred to as "habitual intemperance") was considered unprofessional behavior rather than illness. Under this legal doctrine, a doctor could/can be disciplined simply for being ill (i.e., addicted to drugs and/or alcohol), rather than while actually practicing in an impaired condition or unsafe manner (Walzer 1990).

When state medical boards take action against physicians, a "sanction-oriented" approach has significant practical consequences, which limit this approach's effectiveness. For example, when otherwise qualified and capable doctors lose their ability to practice, their patients experience significant consequences and the already-strained physician workforce is further depleted. As Dilts and Sargent wrote in an earlier edition of this textbook, "Simply weeding out detected offenders did not materially advance the safety of patients, was needlessly wasteful of valuable medical skills and, not least, was inhumane" (Dilts and Sargent 2003, 171). Improved regulatory practices have permitted doctors, whose practices are adversely affected by the symptoms and disability caused by illness, to enter into formal arrangements with their state's medical board to obtain appropriate treatment, while continuing to practice under specified conditions and limitations, rather than be sanctioned (e.g., be formally admonished, have their medical license suspended or revoked). These arrangements are called probationary agreements, stipulations, or consent agreements.

The difficulty for the legal system in addressing ill physicians is that neither discipline nor peer review is likely to affect or improve problematic, unskilled, or unprofessional behavior caused by illness. One of the basic tenets of Anglo-American legal systems is that those subject to the system will act with rational self-interest and therefore are likely to respond to actual or threatened sanctions. However, this tenet applies imperfectly to those with serious illness (either mental or physical) or substance use disorders. For example, in the case of substance use disorders, sufferers are notoriously resistant to entering treatment or remaining sober even when facing significant adverse consequences. In fact, according to the *Diagnostic and Statistical Manual of Mental Disorders*, 5th edition (*DSM-V*), five of the diagnostic criteria for a substance use disorder involve continuing to use the substance despite adverse consequences (American Psychiatric Association 2013, 4483–4484). Similar difficulties also are associated with many psychiatric disorders, because judgment, motivation, behavioral control, social functioning, and cognition are often affected.

Many medical disorders also impact these functions, either directly (in neurological disorders) or indirectly (in many or most serious medical illnesses in which downstream emotional consequences are significant). Therefore, if illness is a cause of problematic physician performance or behavior, treatment for the underlying condition is the most effective remedy, and the one most likely to provide protection to the public. Medical board-imposed or peer review-imposed sanctions are less likely to be effective.

Illness, impairment, fitness, and incompetence

"Impaired physician" was a term used to describe ill physicians in early regulatory law, public policy dialogue, and the scientific literature. This nomenclature continued until very recently. Indeed, only in 2013 did the Federation of State Medical Boards (FSMB) publish guidelines for the return to work of physicians who had been out because of illness (Federation of State Medical Boards 2013); in previous FSMB literature ill physicians were termed "impaired." As of 2014, based on the presumption of impairment, many member boards of the American Board of Medical Specialties (ABMS) will not allow physicians to retain their board certification or sit for board examinations if they are currently subject to a medical board action. This is true even if this action is related solely to their being ill, rather than their having exhibited any unprofessional conduct or impairment in the work setting. There is a fundamental distinction between the concepts of illness and impairment. An "ill physician" is one who suffers from any illness or injury. An "impaired physician" is one whose illness has so adversely affected their ability to practice medicine that they cannot do so safely. An evaluation of the relationship between a physician's illness/injury and the physician's ability to practice safely is called a "fitness-for-duty evaluation." Guidelines for conducting such an evaluation are published by the American Psychiatric Association and addressed in scientific journals (Anfang et al. 2005) and in this chapter.

Until the mid-1980s, the phrase "impaired physician" was synonymous with physicians who suffered only from substance use disorders (SUDs). It did not include other medical and psychiatric illnesses that potentially could cause impairment, and was used to describe doctors with SUDs even if they were never impaired at work. In part, this was because treatment centers that specialized in treating health professionals with substance use disorders had been established in the United States, and doctors recovering from substance use disorders were active in helping their similarly afflicted colleagues. This practice was in contrast to professional silence about other important physician health problems. In 1973, this silence was broken dramatically with the publication of "The Sick Physician" in the *Journal of the American Medical Association* (American Medical Association 1973). This article defined an impaired physician as one unable to "practice medicine with reasonable skill and safety to patients by reason of mental or physical illness, including but not limited to deterioration through the aging process, or loss of motor skills, or excessive use or abuse of drugs, including alcohol." This publication also suggested that doctors developed certain illnesses (e.g., heart disease and cancer) at higher rates than the general population, and were more likely to commit suicide. Although completed suicide is more common among physicians, particularly female doctors, than the general population (Center et al. 2003), most other illnesses appear to affect doctors at rates similar to the general population of the United States. This notwithstanding, the aim of "The Sick Physician" was to underscore the need for doctors' health to be addressed and to identify potential obstacles to doing so (e.g., personal obstacles [denial, fear of licensure problems] and professional obstacles [lack of knowledge about and skill in helping sick doctors, the "conspiracy of silence"]).

"Incompetence" is a term for physicians whose knowledge or skills are insufficient to practice safely. "Illness" refers to doctors suffering from a medical or psychiatric illness (including substance use disorders). "Impairment" is a term for doctors whose illness (or injury) leads to the inability to practice safely because the symptoms of their illness cause such substantial disability at work. There is not necessarily any relationship between incompetence, illness, and impairment. A doctor with competence problems is not usually ill, though both competent and incompetent doctors may become ill. Illness may affect competent functioning if it is severe or lengthy enough to interfere with ongoing learning (e.g., difficulty learning due to cognitive impairment by neurologic disease), impacts decision making (e.g., impulsive decision making associated with mania), or affects the exercise of the doctor's skills (e.g., tremor that affects a surgeon's performance). If this impact is substantial enough to render a doctor unsafe to practice medicine, then the doctor is impaired. "Impaired" is a better term than "incompetent" for describing such a physician because it speaks to causes and remedies that are distinct from the educational approach used in addressing a "primary" deficit in knowledge and/or skill. The assessment of competence and its remediation is a matter separate from the assessment of fitness and is generally performed by different individuals or organizations than those who assess fitness for duty (Grace et al. 2014).

The evolution and central role of physician health programs (PHPs)

In the 1970s, a movement to help ill physicians began to take shape. It was motivated largely by the medical profession's response to the publication of "The Sick Physician." "Impaired Physician Committees" were formed, usually under the aegis of a state medical society. These committees were staffed by volunteer physicians. These individuals assisted other physicians who came forward for help voluntarily and intervened involuntarily in fairly obvious cases of impairment. Generally, the committee's efforts were unstructured, and the committee had no specific relationship with that jurisdiction's medical licensing board. Most volunteers were physicians in recovery from substance use disorder(s), and their focus was, somewhat understandably, on substance use disorders. Most of those attempting to provide assistance had no formal training in treating substance use disorders, other than what they had gleaned from their own experience with that illness.

Over time, it became clear that informal committees were not sufficient to handle the number of ill doctors, the complexity of medical and psychiatric problems from which doctor's suffer, and the equally complex effects of illness on their professional and personal lives. The need to help these doctors was sufficiently compelling that the volunteer committees became programs, which subsequently developed increased structure, more comprehensive policies and procedures, and better defined, though widely varying relationships with licensing boards, medical societies, malpractice insurance carriers, hospitals, and practice groups (DuPont et al. 2009). Leaders in the field of physician health learned that not only did doctors need to be able to access care for a variety of health problems, but also that those who evaluated and treated ill doctors had acquired expertise in working with their special problems; this argued for the "professionalization" of PHPs (rather than relying on a volunteer workforce). Challenges of working with ill physicians include that they have a very educated form of "denial of illness" (Stoudemire and Rhoads 1983, 654; Gendel 2005, 49); problems asking for help even when they know they are ill; the belief that they can best diagnose and treat themselves; complex patterns of self-prescribing and self-treatment (Gendel et al. 2011); profound fears of loss of confidentiality (Schneck 1998); and a host of issues pertaining to their workplace, career path, and family.

In 1986, Colorado established the first physician health program that was designed to assist physicians in addressing every potential health problem they might face (Caspar et al. 1988), as well as a variety of personal and social problems. The program operated under the assumption that the earlier a health, personal, or social problem was addressed with an appropriate intervention, the less likely it was to cause serious personal and professional sequelae (including impairment). Therefore, the program targeted problems such as work stress, malpractice stress, distress about bad patient outcomes, and marital and family problems. The program also attended to problems with professional boundaries and other workplace behavior problems (Dilts et al. 1994; Gendel 2000). With time, programs in other states began to address a similar scope of issues, and currently, most programs in the United States and Canada address at least some health and behavior problems in addition to substance use disorders. However, the "problem areas" served by these programs still vary greatly from state to state. The same variability exists with regard to funding source, staffing, and confidentiality policies. Current information about each state program may be found at the website of the Federation of State Physician Health Programs (FSPHP) (http://www.fsphp.org/sites/default/files/pdfs/2005_fsphp_guidelines-master.pdf), a national organization of U.S. PHPs. This organization facilitates the work of state PHPs, conducts an annual national meeting, promotes physician health research, and develops and updates guidelines for PHP work.

Almost all PHPs are authorized by their state's licensing board to monitor the ill physician's health problems. This involves evaluating his or her clinical condition over time, adherence to recommended treatment interventions, and participation in tissue testing for addictive substances (if indicated). This relationship is defined by state law and/or medical board policy and by the structure of the PHP. In some states, physician participants are not known to the board unless the physician is determined by the PHP to be a risk to patients, is noncompliant with PHP recommendations, or had been referred initially to the PHP by the medical board. In some states, every physician participant is known to the board. In other states, some but not all medical board members know the identity of each participant. Similarly, PHPs may be an entity separate from the board and other medical institutions, may operate directly under the auspices of the board, or may be related to a medical society or a malpractice carrier. In all states, PHPs monitor ill physicians when directed to do so by their state's medical board. In order to understand the legal ramifications of a physician's participating in a PHP, those working with ill doctors must know the relationship between the PHP and the medical board in their state.

There is a growing body of research related to the outcomes of physician health programs. Recent studies of physicians with substance use disorders demonstrate extremely high success rates compared to other populations (McLellan et al. 2008). A universal definition of "success" has not been determined, however. Relapse rates may be less important than rates of sustained periods of work. In fact, physician relapse rates are poor predictors of long-term outcomes (Brooks et al. 2012a). The scientific literature related to PHPs and physicians with mental illness is less robust but tends to suggest similar success rates (Knight et al. 2007). Studies of outcomes related to PHPs and physicians with "physical illness" are more difficult to interpret because of the conditions' heterogeneity. A small body of research has shown PHPs to be effective in improving outcomes for physicians with "boundary" problems (Brooks et al. 2012b).

More recently, research has focused on the effectiveness of PHPs in improving patient safety by using malpractice claims as a proxy measure for dangerous physician behavior. One study by Brooks et al. (2013) examined whether physicians' involvement in a PHP reduced the number of "claims paid" by their malpractice carriers. The study found that claims were paid less often on behalf of physicians after a PHP intervention (compared to a control group with no history of problem behavior or PHP intervention). It also found that although PHP-involved physicians had been at higher risk of increased "claims paid" than a control group before PHP participation, their risk post-PHP intervention was statistically significantly lower than the controls.

Presently, there are several issues that are problematic in the field of physician health. Stress and the stress syndrome, "burnout," appear to be serious and almost ubiquitous problems among physicians, and recent evidence links symptoms of burnout to medical errors (Shanafelt et al. 2010). In helping physicians prevent and manage stress, PHPs eventually must include in the process the institutions in which physicians work. Although most physicians are naturally hard-working and somewhat compulsive (Gabbard 1985), unabated stress and overwork can lead to significant personal and professional difficulties. Suicide rates among doctors, particularly female doctors (who complete suicide at a much higher rate than females in the general population), remain a significant problem despite a growing awareness of and concern about this phenomenon (Center et al. 2003). Most doctors with suicidal ideation do not seek mental health treatment (Shanafelt et al. 2011), probably at least partially because of the stigma of mental illness and the fear of negative professional consequences. In order to address this problem, PHPs, as well as other involved organizations and institutions, must help change "the culture of medicine" so that physicians can more readily seek out and receive potentially life-saving assistance. Additionally, physicians, medical institutions, and licensing boards should collaboratively develop sensible guidelines for addressing age-related cognitive decline among physicians, though cognitive problems do not exist solely in older doctors (Gendel et al. 2014). If such guidelines, informed by physician health research, are not developed, doctors could be subject to public policy and evaluation strategies that are reactive and ill-considered.

REGULATORY LAW AND THE ILL PHYSICIAN

The state licensing board's power

Control of the ill physician's ability to legally practice has generally been established via state law and is augmented by hospital regulations and medical ethics. Although statutes vary from state to state, most justify modifying (or terminating) a physician's unrestricted ability to practice whenever "impairment" is found; that is, the physician suffers from an illness that creates a strong likelihood of misconduct that, in turn, endangers patients. In most states, the medical board may investigate a physician if there is "a reasonable suspicion" of the existence of a potentially impairing illness.

State authority to regulate medical practice comes from its "police power," a residual constitutional power (Article 11) conferred upon the state by the Tenth Amendment. This authority was designed to help the state preserve and promote the health, safety, and welfare of its citizens. In most states, this authority is codified in a medical practice act (MPA) that empowers the licensing board to determine the fitness of licensees, both at entry into practice and on an ongoing basis. Regulatory action can be initiated because of complaints to the board or by the board itself "for cause." The medical board's authority over the ill physician is a specific example of this general power.

Board procedures

After the medical board receives a complaint against a physician, it notifies the physician of the complaint and provides the physician an opportunity to address (and refute) the allegation, either in writing or at an informal meeting. The initial complaint is a critical stage of the regulatory process of physician practice. Many liability insurance carriers have recognized the benefit, and perhaps necessity, of providing legal counsel (at the carrier's expense) to its insured physicians at this early stage of the proceedings. By doing so, malpractice carriers have realized significant ultimate savings, often avoiding having to defend their insureds from subsequent malpractice complaints.

When a licensing board perceives or suspects that physician illness may be a contributor to or cause of the alleged misconduct, it may refer the matter to a PHP, which then evaluates the physician. Medical practice acts routinely require physicians to limit their practice to areas in which their illness will not compromise their ability to practice safely.

If a physician is alleged to be in violation of that state's MPA, the medical board's ultimate findings can include dismissal, nondisciplinary letters to the physician/licensee indicating that the matter is being dismissed despite the board's having certain concerns, letters of admonition, stipulations to limit practice (either by consent or board proceedings), full probationary stipulations, license suspension, and license revocation. Records of such sanctions are maintained by the board to guide its consideration of any future complaints. If the complaint is found to be without merit, it may be dismissed. If a complaint does not result in a finding of a violation of the MPA but gives the board information about the physician's practice that may be of concern about possible future practice issues, the board may issue a letter of concern (LOC). Such a letter is maintained for a short period of time (usually 6 months) in case the concerning conduct recurs. A dismissal or LOC need not be reported on future license applications. The other sanctions are required to be reported, and a failure to do so is a violation of the MPA.

The domino effect

Complaints to the medical board are often either the catalyst for or component of the cascade of events known as the "domino effect."

Physician conduct is subject to review by a myriad of agencies and entities. These include federal and state law enforcement authorities, state medical boards, the American Medical Association (AMA), local medical societies, hospitals (via granting or restricting of hospital privileges), the American Board of Medical Specialties (via board certification), insurance provider panels, practice groups (including HMOs), insurance malpractice carriers (via determinations of coverage), the civil courts (via malpractice litigation), and, in high-profile cases, the media. A complaint to any of these entities may lead to other reviewing authorities' initiating an investigation. This "domino effect" sometimes creates additional, significant problems for the practitioner, particularly when the physician is suffering from an illness that compromises his or her ability to cope with typical stressors of life, much less to deal with multiple, potentially public inquiries into the their conduct. Confusion on the part of any of the reviewing authorities related to the difference between illness, impairment, and incompetence can trigger this effect.

For instance, if a physician is found to be ill and in need of monitoring, the state medical board may enter into a license stipulation by which the physician must agree to be treated and monitored for a defined period of time. This stipulation is considered a license "restriction." This license restriction subsequently is reported by the state medical board to the Federation of State Medical Boards (FSMB). The FSMB then relays this information to the American Board of Medical Specialties (ABMS). The ABMS's member specialty boards generally do not permit a physician under a practice restriction by a medical board to maintain board certification (or to sit for the certification examination). In turn, this loss of board certification may jeopardize the physician's hospital privileges or membership on health insurance provider panels. In order to minimize the potential unfairness of this cascade effect, both the ABMS and the FSMB, in conjunction with the FSPHP, are developing a process by which each "restriction" would be reviewed carefully. This review would attempt to distinguish which stipulations reflected unprofessional conduct (and would continue to affect board certification) and which were based only on the physician's being ill. Such a process, carefully implemented and undertaken, presumably would minimize ill physicians' exposure to multiple, professionally crippling consequences.

In an effort to provide the public with information about impaired physicians, Congress enacted legislation establishing the National Practitioners Data Bank (NPDB), which gathers and makes available to select entities information about physicians' medical board sanctions, civil malpractice suit settlements, and criminal convictions, among other information. Unfortunately, the accessing entity often does not recognize the difference between illness, impairment, and incompetence. Also, once definitive sanctions are imposed, the physician's otherwise confidential health information may be available on the NPDB. Ultimately, physicians may be placed in the problematic position of having to choose between the confidentiality of their health information and the risk of having sanctions imposed and publicized because of conduct related to illness. By defending an allegation via attributing its etiology to an underlying illness, physicians risk losing their right to privacy regarding their diagnosis and medical care.

Physician health programs have proved effective in reducing the "domino effect" by decreasing the pressure on hospitals' (and other entities') peer review and privileging processes. Previously, these groups were required to determine whether or not an ill physician's practice was so affected by illness that a complaint should be made to the medical board, despite their not necessarily having the training or experience to make such a determination. If referred by reviewing authorities, PHPs are able to conduct or orchestrate the evaluation, and if need be, treatment of physicians without their being reported to the medical board. In cases in which a report must be made to the medical board (the legal criteria for which vary from state to state), the PHP can provide more nuanced information to the board regarding the nature and extent of illness and the relative roles of illness and impairment in causing the conduct under consideration; this can lead to less punitive board action. PHP-led evaluations also reduce the exposure of reviewing authorities (e.g., hospitals) to litigation over the correctness of their evaluations.

The "safe harbor" provision of some medical practice acts (Colorado Medical Practice Act 2014) is an extremely important safeguard against the "domino effect." Under this provision, physicians applying or re-applying for licensure may legally answer "no" to the health questions, provided their case is "known" to the PHP. "Known" means that the physician has been evaluated by a PHP and is currently in compliance with the PHP's recommendations. The benefit of such provisions to the physician and the public is the prevention of the domino effect during the period in which the physician and his treatment providers address the medical condition, without the distractions of defending their professional reputation against multiple investigations or reviews.

CIVIL LAW AND THE ILL PHYSICIAN

Malpractice

In virtually every state, tort laws provide remedies to patients who suffer damages because of negligent physician conduct. The legal theory underlying these laws is commonly referred to as medical malpractice. Ill physicians, particularly those with mental illness or cognitive impairments, may have difficulty understanding the proceedings against them, cooperating with their counsel, testifying in a coherent manner about their treatment and the reasons for it, and maintaining their energy level during these often arduous legal proceedings. Attorneys pursuing malpractice claims frequently attempt to introduce the physician's/defendant's confidential health information in an attempt to buttress the claim against the physician. Generally, courts have denied access to such information, noting that it is irrelevant to those proceedings. If the physician were ill but not negligent, it would be unfair to allow the evidence to be admitted, given the high risk of such evidence prejudicing the jury against the physician (*Watson v. Chapman*, 343 S.C. 471, 2000; *Griffin v. McKenney*, 2002-CA-00353-COA, 2003). Such prejudice could lead to verdicts or settlements favorable to the plaintiff, even if there had been no malpractice.

Americans with Disabilities Act

The Americans with Disabilities Act (ADA), which was enacted in 1990, also can impact an ill physician's practice and recovery. The ADA requires that a "disabled person" receive "reasonable accommodations" in order to permit them to perform the essential duties of their employment/job. In the past, physical disabilities, mental health conditions, cognitive impairment, and substance use disorders have been accommodated, and the physicians affected by them have proved able to practice safely. Regular shifts for emergency doctors suffering from bipolar disorder, reduced workloads for conditions that slow the physician's performance, and careful monitoring of physicians with substance use disorders are all accommodations that have been effective and allowed physicians to continue to provide valuable medical services. Courts have defined reasonable accommodation on a case-by-case basis, weighing the difficulty of applying the remedy against the benefit of the services provided. If the accommodation is expensive or lengthy, the courts may not enforce the requirement. If the necessary accommodation is minimal, such as allowing physicians to dictate medical records rather than requiring them to enter the data by hand, it is very likely to be granted.

Confidentiality

During the course of litigation, licensing proceedings, or other matters, an ill physician is frequently asked to disclose his or her own health information. A physician should only produce these otherwise confidential records after careful consideration and discussion with legal counsel. A physician's involvement in civil litigation (particularly as a defendant) or licensing proceedings themselves does not vitiate his or her right to withhold confidential health information. In such cases, this information is generally not sufficiently relevant to the issues litigated to justify its release. Even if the information is required to be disclosed, its use should be restricted to that particular proceeding.

PHPs provide an extremely important filter for an ill physician's personal health information and help protect the confidentiality of this information. With the physician's consent, the PHP can provide only relevant and necessary information to reviewing authorities; reviewers need not directly view health records. However, with the PHP's involvement, the reviewers can be confident that they have a clear picture of the physician's functioning, treatment, and prognosis. This mechanism has preserved an important degree of confidentiality for the doctor. Written reports of PHPs need not and should not be made public.

Corporate practice of medicine

The case of *Darling v. Charleston Hospital* (1965) 211 N.E.2d 253 (Ill.) has led to many claims against hospitals, essentially for providing the domain in which an ill or impaired physician may practice. Because doctors are not normally employees of hospitals but rather independent practitioners exercising their own clinical judgment in treating patients, courts have traditionally refused to hold hospitals liable for actions of hospital staff physicians. The *Darling* case raised the possibility of liabilities being imposed on hospitals as a result of a physician's misconduct. In cases in which the hospital has knowledge of a physician's misconduct but fails to take appropriate action, or misleads the public about the physician's relationship to the hospital, the hospital may be held responsible for physician conduct. As hospitals purchase more physician practices and employ more physicians on a full-time basis, they risk increased liability for their physician-employees' malpractice.

SPECIAL ISSUES FOR THE ILL PHYSICIAN

Legal defense of the ill physician

For an attorney, defending a competent and healthy physician (e.g., in a malpractice suit) is often challenging, even if the facts of the case support the physician's care. Defending an ill physician presents additional challenges. As an initial step, the physician's attorney must become educated about his or her client's health condition and its potential ramifications on the physician's delivery of medical care. In order to accomplish this goal, the attorney likely will need to communicate with the physician's health-care providers, PHP, or both, and the physician will need consent to this. This information should help the attorney ascertain the degree to which he and she can rely on the physician-client's assistance in the case, and the physician's ability to testify effectively. It also will help the attorney to determine whether and how the stress of extended litigation (e.g., malpractice) will negatively impact the physician's well-being. The physician will need education and reassurance about the legal process in order to withstand its rigors, and should actively engage the defense attorney regarding questions, concerns, and fears. Family issues often prevent full communication of these issues with spouses or partners. The physician is usually too embarrassed to discuss the case with colleagues. The physician's reliance on his or her attorney is often the difference between success and failure in legal proceedings; however, the attorney also relies on the physician for education about the medical facts and issues that will be crucial to a successful defense of the doctor. The attorney may make requests for medical articles pertinent to the case and may benefit from witnessing a procedure, being shown and educated about the use of medical instruments that were involved, and learning the complication rates for the procedure at other institutions or in other practices. The physician and attorney, and the case, will benefit from shared professional knowledge and experience.

In many cases, it is helpful for counsel to educate his or her client about the legal system and process, in order to minimize unrealistic fears. It also may be productive for the attorney to assign the physician tasks, the completion of which will assist in the physician's defense. This helps the physician gain some sense of control in the case and feel that he or she is actually defending himself or herself. In many cases, the attorney will be the doctor's most important social support. It is also important for the attorney to determine whether or not the physician's illness adversely impacted patient care, and if so, to proceed to defend the case with that in mind. Before the physician's deposition, the attorney must attempt to discern whether opposing counsel will try to inject the physician's illness into the legal proceedings. If so, the attorney should research legal authorities related to the relevance and admissibility of such information, and decide whether a waiver of confidentiality is needed in order to argue lack of relevance.

The role of forensic psychiatrists and fitness-for-duty evaluations

Forensic psychiatrists, either as PHP employees or independent consultants, often are asked to evaluate ill physicians and to relay their findings to and collaborate with a variety of the institutions and organizations previously discussed. Many of these assessments are "fitness-for-duty" evaluations, which in this context are designed to assess the severity of a physician's illness or injury and such illness's or injury's impact on the physician's ability to safely perform the duties of his or her job (Gendel 2006, 668). In such an examination, it is essential to note the presence or absence of an illness or injury, evidence supporting the diagnosis, the symptoms reported by the evaluee, the signs noted by the evaluator, and the effect of the signs and symptoms on the physician's functioning in specific domains. The forensic psychiatrist eventually will opine as to which, if any, workplace functions are impacted and whether, overall, the doctor is or is not impaired and can or cannot practice medicine safely. The forensic psychiatrist also may be asked to opine about potential treatment interventions, prognosis, specific functional domains that require remediation/restoration, and means for monitoring and assessing the treatment's efficacy in improving the physician's functioning. In addition to fitness-for-duty evaluations, forensic psychiatrists may be asked to evaluate other issues that require forensic expertise, such as disability insurance claims, or whether a doctor's condition may be appropriate for accommodations under the ADA.

Treating the ill physician

Confidentiality, though always an important consideration in psychiatric or medical treatment, is especially crucial in the psychiatric treatment of ill physicians. At the outset of treatment, the treating physician should explain to his or her patient that communication with spouses, family members, co-workers, PHPs, licensing boards, hospitals, and employers is often necessary in order to complete a comprehensive, accurate assessment and initiate appropriate treatment. The treating physician should clearly explain when and why communication with these sources may be necessary and obtain written consent from the patient. As at the beginning of any mental health treatment relationship, the treating physician should explain which situations would lead to a "breach" in confidentiality (e.g., suicidality, child abuse reporting, elder abuse reporting, credible threats against an identifiable victim).

In some states, the MPA may mandate that a treating physician report the physician to the medical licensing board if the treater has a reasonable suspicion that the physician/patient is impaired or has displayed unprofessional conduct that violates the law. For example, in Colorado (Colorado Medical Practices Act 2014), a nontreating physician is required to report another physician to the medical board if he or she has knowledge or belief that the physician has violated the MPA in any way. Treating physicians are not required to report their physician-patients to the medical board unless they have knowledge or belief that the physician-patient cannot practice safely.

Many treating psychiatrists and other physicians are inexperienced or untrained in providing treatment to doctors. Two common mistakes are made (Dilts and Gendel 2000, 126). In some cases, there is a tendency to "over-identify" with the doctor-patient, assume the doctor-patient knows more about his or her condition than he or she does, to consider the doctor-patient unlikely to be seriously ill, and to be hesitant to subject the doctor-patient to the rigors of a time-consuming or painful workup; this leads to undertreatment. In other cases, conversely, treating physicians may feel challenged and practice defensively, not demonstrating the flexibility required to help doctors feel sufficiently special (by virtue of their profession) to tolerate the patient role, and thus depriving them of the ability to be a partner in their care; this often leads to the physician-patient's leaving treatment. Additionally, many clinically oriented psychiatrists are reluctant to advise their physician-patients to suspend their practice, even if they are very ill and likely impaired, because they are understandably focused on their supportive role and may be inexperienced in and timid about confronting their patients' level of disability. Recommending that the physician-patient take time off also has implications for the patient's self-esteem and identity as a capable doctor, not to mention financial ramifications. Consultation with a forensic psychiatrist or other physician skilled in making these decisions is always useful.

Physician-patients often feel ashamed of being ill, and may think that their knowledge of medicine, psychiatry, or substance use disorders should have been protective against developing such problems. Keeping this possibility in mind helps improve empathy in the treating physician. To the extent that such patients are "under fire," or believe that they are, from the licensing board, hospital, employer, litigant-patient, or from themselves (because of a bad patient outcome), the injury to self-esteem can be profound. Such doctors require much support and are at high risk for completed suicide. Including the patient's spouse, family, friends, and colleagues in the treatment plan can be very important.

Monitoring the ill physician

PHPs do the bulk of the monitoring of ill physicians, either as a result of referral from the licensing board or other entity, or as a result of the physician voluntarily seeking assessment, treatment referral, and monitoring. As noted previously, the FSPHP has published guidelines for the monitoring of physicians with substance use disorders and some other mental health conditions (FSPHP 2005). "Monitoring" refers to a type of follow-up over time, during which a PHP (or occasionally a psychiatrist or physician in the community) that is not a treatment provider for the doctor but functions in an otherwise clinical role, provides periodic assessment of the course of a physician's treatment, clinical status, and, frequently, workplace functioning. This process involves meeting with the physician and gathering collateral information from those treating the physician and, potentially, the physician's spouse, family members, employer, supervisor, colleagues, and/or co-workers. Physicians with substance use disorders usually are asked to attend and complete their primary treatment in a residential or outpatient setting, and subsequently are asked to attend aftercare, remain abstinent, utilize 12-step programs, follow recommendations of treatment providers, and participate in tissue screening and other monitoring activities (e.g., face-to-face meetings). Tissues sampled may include urine, blood, hair, nails, breath, saliva, or sweat. Each tissue type has advantages and disadvantages for monitoring purposes (Verebey et al. 2005). The frequency, length, and means of monitoring vary by PHP. For other psychiatric and medical disorders, the monitoring process is similar, absent the requirements for abstinence and, typically, tissue screening. However, ongoing laboratory monitoring may be required, (e.g., lithium level). PHPs attempt to keep private as many details as possible of the participant-doctor's health information and treatment. Even if information needs to be disclosed to a licensing board or other entity, a PHP can distill the relevant material and keep confidential irrelevant, specific information. Because treatment providers are much less experienced in providing such information, they tend to reveal more information than is necessary to regulatory bodies and other reviewing agencies (e.g., hospital credentialing committees).

SUMMARY

Ill physicians may be subject to various laws and policies, particularly regulatory law. This regulatory law generally is interpreted and enforced by a medical licensing board, which may sanction the physician for behavior that it considers unprofessional. Sanctions are unlikely to remedy problematic behavior caused by illness; typically, only treatment and monitoring can maintain or restore the ill doctor's ability to practice safely. Physician health programs provide an environment in which an ill physician may receive assessment, treatment referral, and monitoring, either in coordination with a licensing entity or, in most cases, confidentially. Attorneys representing ill physicians should be aware of the special needs of these clients. Additionally, psychiatrists and other treaters should be aware of these patients' special treatment needs.

SUMMARY KEY POINTS

- Illness, impairment, and incompetence among physicians are separate concerns, though aspects of each overlap with one another.
- Forensic evaluation of fitness-for-duty addresses the relationship between illness and potential work impairment.
- Medical board sanctions will not necessarily remedy unprofessional behavior caused by mental illness, substance use disorders, or other medical conditions.
- Assessment, treatment, and monitoring can be instrumental in maintaining or restoring a doctor's ability to practice medicine safely.
- An ill physician may face unique legal questions and unusual confidentiality concerns.
- The ill physician requires legal representation and medical care by individuals skilled in the defense or treatment of ill physicians.

REFERENCES

American Psychiatric Association. 2013. *Diagnostic and Statistical Manual of Mental Disorders, 5th Edition*. Washington DC, London: American Psychiatric Publishing, 4483–4484

American Medical Association. 1973. The sick physician. Impairment by psychiatric disorders, including alcoholism and drug dependence. *JAMA* 223:684–687.

Americans with Disabilities Act, 42 USC § 12112 (2014).

Anfang SA, LR Faulkner, JA Fromson, and MH Gendel. 2005. The American Psychiatric Association's resource document on guidelines for psychiatric fitness-for-duty evaluations of physicians. *Journal of the American Academy of Psychiatry and the Law* 33:185–188.

Brooks E, SR Early, DC Gundersen, JH Shore, and MH Gendel. 2012a. Comparing substance use monitoring and treatment variations among physician health programs. *American Journal on Addiction* 21:327–334. doi:10.1111/j.1521-0391.2012.00239.x

Brooks E, MH Gendel, DC Gundersen, SR Early, R Schirrmacher, A Lembitz, and JH Shore. 2013.

Physician health programmes and malpractice claims: Reducing risk through monitoring. *Occupational Medicine (London)* 63:274–280. doi:10.1093/occmed/kqt036

Brooks, E, MH Gendel, SR Early, DC Gundersen, JH Shore. 2012b. Physician boundary violations in a physician's health program: A 19-year review. *Journal of the American Academy of Psychiatry and the Law* 40:59–66.

Caspar E, SL Dilts, JJ Soter, RB Lepoff, and JH Shore. 1988. Establishment of the Colorado Physician Health Program with a legislative initiative. *JAMA* 260:671–673. doi:10.1001/jama.1988.03410050091036

Center C, M Davis, T Detre et al. 2003. Confronting depression and suicide in physicians: A consensus statement. *JAMA* 289:3161–3166.

Colorado Medical Practice Act, C.R.S. § 12-36-101 (2014).

Darling v. *Charleston Hospital*, 211 N.E.2d 253 (Ill.). (1965).

Dilts SL and MH Gendel. 2000. Substance use disorders. In *The Handbook of Physician Health*, edited by LS Goldman, M Myers, LJ Dickstein. Chicago: American Medical Association, 126.

Dilts SL, MH Gendel, RB Lepoff, CA Clark, and S Radcliff. 1994. The Colorado Physician Health Program: Observations at seven years. *American Journal on Addictions* 3:337–345.

Dilts SL and DA Sargent, 2003. The law and physician illness. In *Principles and Practice of Forensic Psychiatry*, 2nd edition, edited by R Rosner, London: Arnold, 171–179.

DuPont RL, TM McLellan, G Carr, MH Gendel, and GE Skipper. 2009. How are addicted physicians treated? A national survey of physician health programs. *Journal of Substance Abuse Treatment* 37:1–7.

Federation of State Medical Boards. 2013. *Report of the Special Committee on Re-entry for the Ill Physician*. http://www.fsmb.org/Media/Default/PDF/FSMB/Advocacy/special_committee_reentry.pdf, accessed July 7, 2016.

Gabbard GO. 1985. The role of compulsiveness in the normal physician. *JAMA*. 254:2926–2929.

Gendel MH. 2000. Personality and boundary problems. In *The Handbook of Physician Health*, edited by L Goldman, L Dickstein, Chicago: American Medical Association, 138–160.

Gendel MH. 2005. Treatment adherence among physicians. *Primary Psychiatry* 12:48–54.

Gendel MH. 2006. Substance misuse and substance related disorders in forensic psychiatry. *Psychiatric Clinics of North America* 29:619–673.

Gendel MH, E Brooks, SR Early, DC Gundersen, SL Dubovsky, SL Dilts, and JH Shore. 2011. Self-prescribed and other informal care provided by physicians: Scope, correlations and implications. *Journal of Medical Ethics* 38:294–298. doi:10.1136/medethics-2011-100167

Gendel MH, E Brooks, DC Gundersen, SR Early, and JH Shore. 2014. Cognitive problems among physicians evaluated at the Colorado Physician Health Program: A review of cases 1986–2013. Paper presented at the *International Conference on Physician Health*, London, September.

Grace ES, EF Wenghofer, and EJ Korinek. 2014. Predictors of physician performance on competence assessment: Finds from CPEP, the Center for Personalized Education for Physicians. *Academic Medicine* 89:912–919.

Knight JR, LT Sanchez, LSLR Bresnahan, and JA Fromson. 2007. Outcomes of a monitoring program for physicians with mental and behavioral health problems. *Journal of Psychiatric Practice* 13:25–32.

MacKennon Watson, a Minor, by his Guardian ad Litem, Susan Watson, Respondent v. David Chapman, M.D., Appellant. And Susan Watson and Don Watson, Respondents v. David Chapman, M.D., Appellant, 540 S.E.2d 484 (S.C. App. 2000), 343 S.C. 471.

McLellan TA, GS Skipper, M Campbell, and RL DuPont. 2008. Five year outcomes in a cohort study of physicians treated for substance use disorders in the United States. *BMJ* 337:a2038.

Michael L. Griffin and Angela Griffin, Appellants/Cross-Appellees v. Jefferson C. McKenney, M.D., Appellee/Cross-Appellant, 877 So.2d 425 (Miss. App. 2003), 2002-CA-00353-COA.

National Practitioners Data Bank, 42 USC § 11101.

Schneck SA 1998. "Doctoring" doctors and their families. *JAMA*. 280:2039–2042.

Shanafelt TD, CM Balch, G Bechamps, T Russell, L Dyrbye, D Satele, P Collicott, PJ Novotny, J Sloan, and J Freischlag. 2010. Burnout and medical errors among American surgeons. *Shanafelt, Annals of Surgery*. 251:995–1000. doi:10.1097/SLA.0b013e3181bfdab3

Shanafelt TD, CM Balch, L Dyrbye et al. 2011. Suicidal ideation among American surgeons. *Archives of Surgery* 146:54–62.

Stoudemire A and JM Rhoads. 1983. When the doctor needs a doctor: Special considerations for the physician-patient. *Annals of Internal Medicine* 98:654–659.

Verebey KG, Meehan G, and Buchan BJ. 2005. Diagnostic laboratory: Screening for drug abuse. In *Substance Abuse: A Comprehensive Textbook*, 4th edition, edited by JH Lowinson, P Ruiz, RB Millman et al., Philadelphia: Lippincott Williams & Wilkins, 564–577.

Walzer RS 1990. Impaired physicians: An overview and update of the legal issues. *Journal of Legal Medicine* 11:131–198.

23

The law and physician prescribing of controlled substances

GREGORY SOKOLOV

INTRODUCTION

A forensic psychiatrist may be asked to evaluate a physician who is accused of illegally or negligently prescribing controlled substances in a variety of different contexts. These may include (a) criminal prosecution, in which the physician was illegally prescribing controlled substances for distribution or personal use; (b) civil litigation proceedings (e.g., malpractice suit), where the prescribing physician fell below a reasonable standard of care in prescribing controlled substances, leading to damages for or death of a patient(s); or (c) state medical board investigations/proceedings regarding a physician's prescribing of controlled substances and/or possible impairment because of abuse of controlled substances.

PRESCRIPTION OPIOID ABUSE

The use of "prescription painkillers," referring to opioid or "narcotic" pain relievers, including drugs such as hydrocodone, oxycodone, and hydromorphone, has steadily increased in the United States over the past 10 years. Healthcare providers wrote 259 million prescriptions for painkillers in 2012, enough for every American adult to have one. An increase in drug overdose deaths is associated with this rise in number of prescriptions. According to the Centers for Disease Control and Prevention (CDC), in 2012, there were 41,502 deaths due to drug poisoning (often referred to as drug-overdose deaths) in the United States, of which 16,007 involved opioid analgesics and 5925 involved heroin. A recent study showed that contemporary heroin users were older men and women living in less urban areas, who were introduced to opioids through prescription medications (Cicero et al. 2014).

In addition to drug overdose deaths and a rise in illicit opioid addiction rates, prescription opioids also have been associated with an increased rate of criminal behaviors (e.g., theft, illegal sales, and other forms of "drug diversion"). Drug diversion is defined as the intentional transfer of a controlled substance from an authorized to an unauthorized possessor (Cicero et al. 2011). Data from a set of selected states show that prescription controlled substances were diverted by theft almost 13,000 times from 2000 to 2003. In 2003 alone, two million doses of six opioid analgesics were reported stolen from the supply chain, mainly retail pharmacies (Joranson and Gilson 2005).

As a result of rampant prescription opioid abuse and related criminal activity, the Drug Enforcement Administration (DEA) increased its enforcement efforts to prevent abuse and diversion of OxyContin (oxycodone). This marked the first time the agency had targeted a specific brand-name product for monitoring. In 2006, the DEA reported that 71 physicians had been arrested for crimes related to "diversion," the leakage of prescription medication into illegal drug markets. In addition, in 2014, hydrocodone-containing products were re-scheduled by the DEA from Schedule III to Schedule II, allowing for stricter monitoring of prescriptions.

BACKGROUND LAWS

In 1970, the 91st U.S. Congress passed the Drug Abuse and Prevention Control Act, which was signed into law by President Richard M. Nixon. Title II of the Act is entitled "The Controlled Substances Act," which allows licensed medical professionals to prescribe, dispense, and administer controlled substances for legitimate medical purposes in the course of professional practice.

The Controlled Substances Act established schedules for controlled substances ranging from Schedule I (most restrictive) to Schedule V (least restrictive). Drugs on Schedule I have no currently accepted medical use in the United States and a high potential for abuse. Schedule I drugs are listed as the "most dangerous drugs of all the drug schedules," with potentially severe psychological or physical dependence; Schedule I drugs include heroin and marijuana. Schedule II drugs are defined as drugs with a high potential for abuse, though less abuse potential than Schedule I drugs. These drugs are also considered dangerous, and include the opioid pain medications oxycodone and hydromorphone, as well as psychostimulants. Schedule III drugs include buprenorphine and codeine-containing products. Schedule IV drugs include benzodiazepines and barbiturates, in addition to sedative–hypnotic agents (zolpidem, zaleplon).

The “control” portion of the Controlled Substances Act attempts to prevent diversion, establishes a system of secure manufacture and distribution, requires record-keeping procedures, and sets up penalties (including criminal prosecution) for violating its provisions. Civil and criminal sanctions for serious violations of the statute are part of the government’s control apparatus. The Code of Federal Regulations (Title 21, Chapter 2) implements the Controlled Substances Act.

In the 1975 ruling *United States v. Moore*, the U.S. Supreme Court confirmed that physicians who are licensed by the Drug Enforcement Agency to prescribe narcotics under the Controlled Substances Act “can be prosecuted when their activities fall outside the usual course of professional practice.”

It is imperative that physicians be thoroughly familiar not only with federal laws regarding the prescription of controlled substances but also with their own state’s laws and regulatory practice standards. Access to these laws, or summaries thereof, is available through the Federation of State Medical Boards (FSMB).

PRESCRIPTION DRUG MONITORING PROGRAMS

In response to the problems of diversion and abuse of prescription medications, the federal government and many states have created prescription drug monitoring programs (PDMPs). Typically, PDMPs collect prescribing and dispensing data from pharmacies, conduct reviews and analyses of the data, and disseminate the relevant data to appropriate regulatory and law enforcement agencies.

Following the lead of New York in the 1910s, California and Hawaii enacted PDMPs in the 1940s. By the 1980s, seven more states had added PDMPs. As of November 2014, all states (with the exception of Missouri and the District of Columbia) have enacted legislation creating PDMPs. However, only 40 states currently have operational PDMPs. The National Alliance for Model State Drug Laws (http://www.namsdl.org) provides links to each state’s statutes and regulations regarding PDMPs.

Certain characteristics of PDMPs can have a deterrent effect on potential criminal activities associated with controlled substance prescriptions. For example, some state authorities report that use of tamper-resistant prescription forms significantly reduces or eliminates prescription forgery. In addition, PDMPs that make prescribing information available to health-care professionals at the point of clinical care may be useful for identifying “doctor shopping.” An individual who is immediately identified with such a history should have the treatment plan re-evaluated, and a referral for substance abuse treatment should be considered.

In California, the state’s database, known as the Controlled Substance Utilization Review and Evaluation System (CURES), contains over 100 million entries of controlled substance medications that have been dispensed in California. Each year, the CURES program responds to more than 60,000 requests for information from practitioners and pharmacists.

In New York, effective August 27, 2013, most prescribers are required to consult the Prescription Monitoring Program (PMP) Registry when writing prescriptions for Schedule II, III, and IV controlled substances. The PMP Registry is also available to New York-licensed pharmacists. One of the unique aspects of New York law is the requirement that prescribers consult the PMP Registry when writing prescriptions for commonly prescribed psychiatric medications, including benzodiazepines and psychostimulants. In addition, prescribers in New York are required to have an individual Health Commerce System account to gain access to the PMP, and can designate others, including unlicensed office and ward staff, residents, and interns, as individuals who can check the database for the physician prior to the physician’s prescribing. Penalties for prescribers who do not review the PMP prior to prescribing include escalating fines for first, second, and subsequent violations.

Research has demonstrated significant benefits of PDMPs for practitioners. A study of emergency medicine clinicians conducted in Ohio in 2010 found that prescribing practices changed in 41% of encounters when PDMP data were provided to the physician prior to his or her prescribing. Study authors also reported that in some cases, access to PDMP data resulted in increased, rather than decreased, prescribing, indicating that access to PDMP information potentially could facilitate more individualized controlled substance prescribing (Baehren et al. 2010). In another review paper, Gugelmann et al. (2012) concluded that although more research on the immediate and downstream effects of PDMPs is needed, these databases show significant promise in stemming the tide of prescription opioid diversion, abuse, dependence, and overdose. If states heed current recommendations regarding design, implementation, maintenance, security protections, and user education, PDMPs could prove to be an essential component in curtailing the current epidemic of prescription opioid abuse (Gugelmann et al. 2012).

Model policy

The FSMB assists state medical boards in protecting the public and improving the quality and integrity of health care in the United States. In April 1998, the Federation adopted the *Model Guidelines for the Use of Controlled Substances for the Treatment of Pain*, which was widely distributed to state medical boards, medical professional organizations, other health-care regulatory boards, patient advocacy groups, pharmaceutical companies, state and federal regulatory agencies, and practicing physicians and other health-care providers. The *Model Guidelines* have been endorsed by the American Academy of Pain Medicine, the Drug Enforcement Administration, the American Pain Society, and the National Association of State Controlled Substances Authorities. In April 2003, the *Model Guidelines* were updated and revised to become *Model Policy*. The goal of the revision was to provide state medical boards with an updated template about the appropriate management of pain that was in compliance with applicable state and federal laws and regulations (FSMB 2004).

The *Model Policy* has adopted the following criteria, which should be used when evaluating whether a physician's treatment of a patient's pain with controlled substances was appropriate

1. *Evaluation of the patient*: A medical history and physical examination must be obtained, evaluated, and documented in the medical record. The medical record should document the nature and intensity of the pain, current and past treatments for pain, underlying or coexisting diseases or conditions, the effect of the pain on physical and psychological function, and history of substance abuse. The medical record also should document the presence of one or more recognized medical indications for the use of a controlled substance.
2. *Treatment plan*: The written treatment plan should state objectives that will be used to determine treatment success, such as pain relief and improved physical and psychosocial function, and should indicate if any further diagnostic evaluations or other treatments are planned. After treatment begins, the physician should adjust drug therapy to the individual medical needs of the patient.
3. *Informed consent and agreement for treatment*: The physician should discuss the risks and benefits of the use of controlled substances with the patient, persons designated by the patient, or with the patient's surrogate or guardian if the patient does not have medical decision-making capacity. The patient should receive prescriptions from one physician and one pharmacy whenever possible. If the patient is at high risk for medication abuse or has a history of substance abuse, the physician should consider the use of a written agreement between the physician and patient outlining the patient's responsibilities, including (a) submitting to urine/serum medication levels screening when requested; (b) knowing the number and frequency of all prescription refills; and (c) understanding the reasons for which drug therapy may be discontinued.
4. *Periodic review*: The physician should periodically review the course of pain treatment and consider any new information about the etiology of the patient's pain or the patient's state of health. Continuation or modification of controlled substances regimens for pain management depends on the physician's evaluation of progress toward treatment objectives. If the patient's progress is unsatisfactory, the physician should assess the appropriateness of continued use of the current treatment plan and consider the use of other therapeutic modalities.
5. *Consultation*: The physician should be willing to refer the patient as necessary for additional evaluation and treatment in order to achieve treatment objectives. Special attention should be given to those patients who are at increased risk for medication misuse, abuse, or diversion. The management of pain in patients with a history of substance abuse or with a comorbid psychiatric disorder may require extra care, monitoring, documentation, and consultation with, or referral, to an expert in the management of such patients.
6. *Medical records*: The physician should keep accurate and complete records including, but not necessarily limited to (a) medical history and physical examination; (b) diagnostic, therapeutic, and laboratory results; (c) evaluations and consultations; (d) treatment objectives; (e) discussion of risks and benefits; (f) informed consent; (g) treatments; (h) medications, including type, dosage, quantity, and date prescribed; (i) instructions and agreements; and (j) periodic reviews.
7. *Compliance with controlled substances laws and regulations*: To prescribe, dispense, or administer controlled substances, the physician must be licensed in the state in which the medications are prescribed and comply with applicable federal and state regulations.

RISK EVALUATION AND MITIGATION STRATEGIES (REMS)

The Food and Drug Administration (FDA) Amendments Act of 2007 gave the FDA the authority to require a Risk Evaluation and Mitigation Strategy (REMS) from manufacturers to ensure that the benefits of a drug or biological product outweigh its risks. A REMS can include a medication guide, a patient package insert, a communication plan, elements to assure safe use, and an implementation system. The first opioid to be subject to the new REMS requirement was the recently approved fentanyl buccal soluble film. The FDA plans to extend mandatory REMS to other opioids, including all rapid-onset formulations and, eventually, all long-acting opioids, whether or not they are already FDA approved. In one published survey, 50% of the responding physicians were willing to comply with the mandatory education component of the REMS, including the requirement to provide education to patients, in order to continue to be able to prescribe the medication. However, a significant minority of physicians seemed unwilling to prescribe opioids subject to the new REMS requirement. Therefore, REMS could have the unintended effect of decreasing access to opioid medications for legitimate medical purposes (Slevin and Ashburn 2011).

MEDICAL MARIJUANA

Approximately 40 years ago and beginning with Oregon in 1973, individual states began to decriminalize and legalize both the recreational and nonrecreational (i.e., "medicinal") use of marijuana. As of June 2014, 23 states have legalized cannabis for medical use, with legislation authorizing the same pending in three states.

The Controlled Substances Act of 1970 categorized marijuana and its derivatives as Schedule I substances, indicating that in the opinion of legislators, cannabis had "a high potential for abuse," "no currently accepted medical use in treatment in the United States," and "a lack of accepted safety [standards] for use of the drug ... under medical supervision." The case of *Gonzales v. Raich* (2005) involved DEA agents' destruction of medical marijuana plants. Two patients and two caregivers in California brought suit, arguing that in passing the Controlled Substances Act, Congress exceeded its constitutional authority under the Commerce Clause, which allows the federal government to regulate interstate commerce. In 2005, in reversing the Ninth Circuit's decision, the U.S. Supreme Court ruled that the DEA could continue to enforce the Controlled Substances Act "against" medical marijuana patients and their caregivers, even though these patients and their caregivers resided in states with authorized medical marijuana programs. In the light of this ruling, the role of physicians in recommending medical marijuana became exceedingly muddled, and physicians continue to face potential criminal prosecution for running foul of federal regulations. Also, because cannabis can impact negatively the physical and mental health of users and because there are few well-accepted medical indications for cannabis, physicians potentially are placed in the problematic situation of recommending a substance that has risks and benefits that are not understood fully.

In 2010, the American Society of Addiction Medicine (ASAM) published a series of findings, conclusions, and recommendations regarding medical marijuana in a "white paper." This paper assessed the therapeutic value of smoked marijuana and the role of physicians in the prescribing of marijuana for medicinal purposes. The ASAM paper asserted that physicians who were in a "gate-keeping role" in states where medical marijuana had been legalized should adhere to the "established professional tenets of proper patient care," including a history and good faith examination of the patient; the development of a treatment plan with objectives; the provision of informed consent, including discussion of risks, side effects, and potential benefits; a periodic review of treatment efficacy; consultation, as necessary; and proper record keeping that supports the decision to recommend the use of medical marijuana. In addition, the paper recommended that the physician have a "bona fide" physician–patient relationship with the patient, and that the physician have adequate training in identifying substance use disorders and addiction.

MALPRACTICE ISSUES

Malpractice complaints may allege that a physician's prescriptions for controlled substances have caused a patient's addiction or suicide attempt or that the patient was not adequately informed of the risks of the medications. Negligent (or nonexistent) assessment of a patient's substance abuse history or current status is one area of concern. Inappropriate treatment for substance abuse problems also may be alleged. Prescription of excessive amounts of controlled substances, or prescribing such medications to a known "addict," may result not only in medical board investigations and subsequent loss of licensure but also malpractice litigation against the physician. Therefore, it is crucial that physicians follow the previously discussed *Model Policy*'s criteria when treating high-risk patients.

Standards of care for prescribers of controlled substances are established both by case law and statute. In states such as New York, new statutory requirements generated by PDMPs will raise standards and expand potential bases for malpractice claims (e.g., negligence in failing to check PDMP database prior to prescribing controlled substances to a patient). The admissibility of information contained in PDMP databases in criminal or civil cases is currently unknown, however.

MEDICAL BOARD INVESTIGATIONS

Physicians with active substance use disorders may suffer impairments in reasoning and judgment that contribute to inappropriate diagnosis or treatment of patients or prescription of controlled substances to themselves. Sometimes, these physicians will prescribe controlled substances to patients with the understanding that the patient will then share the medication with or give the medication to the prescribing physician. Physicians engaging in such behavior also are more likely to engage in other boundary violations with patients, including sexual relationships, in order to obtain prescription drugs for personal use. Certain physicians with substance use disorders may come under investigation by a state medical board. Typically, a state medical board will receive a complaint regarding a possibly impaired physician from one of a variety of sources. Upon receiving the complaint, the medical board will conduct an initial investigation, which typically includes reviewing and possibly confiscating patient records, including prescriptions.

Some state medical boards may order an impaired physician into a "diversion" or "Physician Health Program" (PHP), with the goal of providing the physician with treatment for his or her substance use disorder (and monitoring his or her progress and ability to practice medicine), rather than meting out punitive sanctions. Typically, a physician's failure to comply with provisions of a PHP-mandated treatment plan would be reported to the state medical board for possible sanctions (e.g., license suspension or revocation). Perhaps because of the significant impact such sanctions can have on a physician's livelihood, PHPs have been remarkably effective in helping impaired physicians attain and maintain abstinence. McLellan et al. examined 16 PHPs in the United States from 1995 through 2001, and found that 5 years after entry into one of the programs, over 75% of physician were abstinent, still licensed, and still practicing medicine (McLellan et al. 2008).

SUMMARY

In order to effectively manage risk in their practices, physicians must keep abreast of not only the newest developments in medicine, but also of related changes in state and federal laws. To that end, the Federation of State Medical Boards is an excellent resource that can provide physicians with updated information on prescription drug regulations, including prescribing standards, for each state. Other sources of information include the DEA's requirements for prescribing controlled substances, Substance Abuse and Mental Health Services Administration (SAMHSA) resources (http://www.samhsa.gov), and FDA (http://www.fda.gov) resources.

In addition to remaining knowledgeable about current prescription standards and regulations, physicians should maintain practice policies and procedures consistent with the guidelines in the *Model Policy* in order to manage risk effectively and minimize the possibility of medical board sanctions, civil suits, or criminal prosecution.

SUMMARY KEY POINTS

- Prescription medication (particularly opioid) abuse is a growing problem in the United States and the source of many investigations and sanctioning of prescribing physicians.
- Practice standards (e.g., *Model Policy*) have been established to guide physicians in appropriate prescribing and management of patients on controlled substances.
- State medical board investigations may involve physicians being ordered to "diversion" programs, if personal substance use is involved in inappropriate prescribing claims.

REFERENCES

American Society of Addiction Medicine. 2010. *The Role of the Physician in "Medical" Marijuana*. Chevy Chase, MD: American Society of Addiction Medicine.

Baehren DF, CA Marco, DE Droz, S Sinha, EM Callan, and P Akpunonu. 2010. A statewide prescription monitoring program affects emergency department prescribing behaviors. *Annals of Emergency Medicine* 56:19–23.

Centers for Disease Control and Prevention. *Trends in Drug-poisoning Deaths Involving Opioid Analgesics and Heroin: United States, 1999–2012*. http://www.cdc.gov/nchs/data/hestat/drug-poisoning/drug-poisoning.html, accessed April 27, 2015.

Centers for Disease Control and Prevention. Vital Signs. 2014. *Opioid Painkiller Prescribing*. http://www.cdc.gov/vitalsigns/opioid-prescribing/index.html, accessed September 27, 2014.

Cicero TJ, SP Kurtz, HL Surratt, GE Ibanez, MS Ellis, MA Levi-Minzi, and JA Inciardi. 2011 Multiple determinants of specific modes of prescription opioid diversion. *Journal of Drug Issues* 41:283–304.

Cicero TJ, MS Ellis, HL Surratt, and SP Kurtz. 2014. The changing face of heroin use in the United States: A retrospective analysis of the past 50 Years. *JAMA Psychiatry* 71:821–826.

Drug Enforcement Administration. *Drug Scheduling 2014*. http://www.justice.gov/dea/druginfo/ds.shtml, accessed September 27, 2014.

Federation of State Medical Boards (FSMB). 2004. *Model Policy for the Use of Controlled Substances for the Treatment of Pain*. Washington, DC: The Federation.

Gugelmann H, J Perrone, and L Nelson. 2012. Windmills and pill mills: Can PDMPs tilt the prescription drug epidemic? *Journal of Medical Toxicology* 8:378–386.

Joranson DE and AM Gilson. 2005. Drug crime is source of abused pain medications in the United States. *Journal of Pain and Symptom Management* 30:299–301.

McLellan AT, GS Skipper, M Campbell, and RL DuPont. 2008. Five year outcomes in a cohort study of physicians treated for substance use disorders in the United States. *BMJ* 337:a2038.

Medical Marijuna Pros and Cons. 2014. *23 Legal Medical Marijuana States and D.C.* http://medicalmarijuana.procon.org/view.resource.php?resourceID=000881, accessed September 27, 2014.

National Alliance for Model State Drug Laws. 2014. *State PMP Administrator Contact List*. http://www.namsdl.org/library/C4A0F9C4-65BE-F4BB-A9F31B9A33A11FCE/, accessed September 27, 2014.

New York State Department of Health. 2014. *I-STOP/PMP-Internet System for Tracking Over-Prescribing-Prescription Monitoring Program*. http://www.health.ny.gov/professionals/narcotic/prescription-monitoring/

New York Times Magazine. 2007. *When Is a Pain Doctor a Drug Pusher?* http://www.nytimes.com/2007/06/17/magazine/17pain-t.html?_r=0, accessed September 27, 2014.

Slevin KA and MA Ashburn. 2011. Primary care physician opinion survey on FDA opioid risk evaluation and mitigation strategies. *Journal of Opioid Management* 7:109–115.

State of California Department of Justice. Office of the Attorney General. 2014. *CURES/PMDP*. http://oag.ca.gov/cures-pdmp, accessed September 27, 2014.

24

Court oversight of psychotropic prescribing in youth in state custody

CORY JAQUES

INTRODUCTION

Over the past two decades, there has been a steady rise in the use of psychotropic medications to treat children and adolescents with emotional and behavioral problems (Zito et al. 2000). Public concern, often driven by media accounts, over the high rates of psychotropic medication use among youth in foster care has led to increased scrutiny about its appropriateness in this vulnerable population. Studies show that youth in state custody, including those in foster care and the juvenile justice system, have higher rates of psychotropic medication use, singly and concomitantly, than do youth who are eligible for Medicaid through income or disability qualifications (dosReis et al. 2001; Zito et al. 2008). Recent federal legislation also imposes increased oversight of prescribers to youth in state custody. These facts have led many states to adopt legislation requiring state agencies to monitor the treatment of children in their care. Practitioners have responded to these evolving standards, which are intended to promote the best care for young psychiatric patients in state custody. (For the purposes of this chapter, "youth in state custody" refers generally to two main groups of youth: those in foster care and those who are in various stages of an adjudication process managed by the juvenile justice system.)

In the United States, parents typically are the "guardians" of their children, and are authorized to direct their medical care, which includes decision making regarding psychiatric treatment and providing informed consent to such treatment (Feigenbaum 1992). When a minor is taken into state or county custody, the state or county must provide for the youth's basic health-care needs, including mental health and substance abuse treatment. However, medical services cannot begin without obtaining the appropriate consent for care. Entry into the foster care or juvenile justice systems does not automatically remove a parent's right to consent to their child's health care. For purposes of this chapter, when referring to youth in foster care or the juvenile justice system, the assumption is that parental guardianship has been temporarily or permanently terminated, and that the state has been appointed the legal guardian of, and assumed all parental responsibilities and decision making related to, the child.

Determining who may consent to health care for youth in state custody involves considering many different factors, many of which will vary by jurisdiction. In California, for example, the juvenile court has the authority to suspend a parent's right to consent to medical care once a minor has been adjudicated a ward or dependent of the court (California Welfare and Institutions Code §725). If the minor is declared a ward, the court may place him or her in a county facility, a group home, or home under parent or guardian supervision. Foster care placements include relatives, foster families, group homes, shelters, and other placements. Youth in the juvenile justice system include those who are residing in a detention center or in a community placement but are still under state supervision.

Increased need for mental health treatment for youth in state custody

Given the disruption in family bonds and high rates of traumatic exposures, it is not surprising that youth in state custody (either via the dependency of delinquency process) commonly experience social, emotional, and behavioral problems. The National Survey of Child and Adolescent Well-Being (NSCAW) revealed that youth involved in the child welfare system have disproportionately high rates of mental health problems, with approximately one-third of youth in foster care scoring in the "clinical" range on the Child Behavioral Checklist, a tool that assesses both internalizing and externalizing behaviors (U.S. Government Accountability Office 2011).

Another study showed that 63% of youth in foster care between the ages of 14 and 17 met criteria for one or more mental health diagnoses at some point in their lives (White et al. 2007).

Several hypotheses have been put forward to attempt to explain the increase in psychotropic prescriptions in youth, and foster youth in particular. These include prescribers' utilizing flawed diagnostic methods, pathologizing normal behavior, succumbing to the influence of the pharmaceutical industry, failing to provide alternate psychosocial treatments, and not resisting financial incentives to medicate. Other possible contributing factors include poor access to therapists trained in evidence-based treatments, lack of coordination of available services, overall shortage of child psychiatrists, and insufficient state oversight of psychotropic prescribing to youth in state custody.

Concerns about the increased use of psychotropic medications for youth in state custody mirror emerging legal doctrine about standards of care required for these patients. As medical treatments evolved, with new and more sophisticated medications being developed, legal concerns about the rights of patients to refuse such treatment emerged, necessitating judicial involvement in those medical decisions.

Prevalence of psychotropic medication use among youth in foster care

Media accounts often conclude that youth in foster care are being "over-medicated" or inappropriately medicated (De Sa 2014). However, the disproportionately high rate of psychotropic medication use among youth in foster care likely reflects, at least in part, increased levels of emotional and behavioral distress in these youth. Although inappropriate prescribing certainly does occur, this can be minimized through careful medical implementation of the "best interests" standard.

Currently, there is no comprehensive source of data regarding psychotropic medication usage among youth in foster care. Most studies on the use of medications in this population utilize data from Medicaid claims and are often geographically specific. However, published studies consistently show higher rates of use among youth involved in the child welfare system than in socioeconomically matched youth in the general population.

The prevalence of psychotropic use for youth in foster care in community settings ranges from 14% to 30% (Zima et al. 1999; Raghavan et al. 2005; Zito et al. 2005), with significantly higher prevalence rates for youth in therapeutic foster care (67%) and group homes (77%) (Breland-Noble et al. 2004).

The U.S. Government Accountability Office (GAO) released a report in 2011, after examining the use of psychotropic medications in five states: Florida, Maryland, Massachusetts, Oregon, and Texas. This 2008 data, which include Medicaid claims for prescriptions of psychotropic medications, indicated that 21%–39% of youth in foster care received a prescription for a psychotropic medication compared to 5%–10% of youth not in foster care (U.S. Government Accountability Office 2011). Studies have identified several factors that influence the likelihood of psychotropic use among children in foster care (Raghavan et al. 2005):

- *Gender*: Males are more than two times as likely to receive psychotropic medications as females (19.6% versus 7.7%).
- *Age*: The likelihood that a child will receive psychotropic medication increases with age (3.6% of 2- to 5-year-olds, 16.4% of 6- to 11-year-olds, and 21.6% of 12- to 16-year-olds).
- *Placement type*: Youth in the most restrictive placement settings are the most likely to be taking psychotropic medications.
- *Behavioral concerns*: Youth scoring in the clinical range on the Child Behavioral Checklist are more likely to be taking psychotropic medications than those who score in the subclinical range.

The Agency for Healthcare Research and Quality (an agency within the U.S. Department of Health and Human Services) funded a study of antipsychotic prescribing based on Medicaid claims from 16 states. The study found that utilization of antipsychotics in 2007 was much higher among foster youth than among nonfoster youth—12.4% versus 1.4%, respectively (Rutgers Center for Education and Research 2010). Concomitant use of psychotropic medications (a.k.a., "polypharmacy") is also on the rise, with as many as 22% of youth prescribed two or more medications from the same class (Zito et al. 2008). Youth with autistic spectrum disorders in foster care are twice as likely to receive three or more medications than those eligible for Medicaid through a disability status (Rubin et al. 2009). Almost universally, of particular concern is the rapidly expanding use of second-generation antipsychotic medications, especially when they are prescribed to treat illnesses for which they are not usually indicated, including attention deficit hyperactivity disorder (ADHD) and conduct disorder (Crystal et al. 2009; dosReis et al. 2011).

Although Medicaid data provide abundant information about the use of psychotropic medications in foster youth, little data exist about the use of psychotropic medications among detained youth, who are generally not Medicaid-eligible while incarcerated. Existing studies analyze data from a particular state or local jurisdiction, and knowledge of general national trends in "juvenile justice" psychotropic prescribing is lacking.

Ideally, psychotropic medications are prescribed after a thorough assessment and, if appropriate, trials of psychotherapeutic or behavioral interventions. Such medications should decrease the frequency and severity of significant psychiatric symptoms and allow the youth to engage more fully in much needed psychotherapeutic treatment. However, for foster and detained youth (i.e., youth detained in juvenile justice facilities), information often is difficult to access and stepwise, algorithmic treatment may be neither pragmatic nor available. In these circumstances, government regulation of prescribing practices, typically via an independent consultation with another psychiatrist, can be helpful and important.

Appropriateness of psychotropic medication use among children in foster care

In a comprehensive study, the Tufts Clinical and Translational Science Institute examined policies and practices concerning state oversight of psychotropic medication for children in foster care (Leslie et al. 2010). This study identified several patterns that may signal a "red flag" that factors other than clinical need are impacting the prescription of psychotropic medications. The most common red flags include instances when a child is prescribed too much medication, too many medications, or medication at too young an age.

A potential outlier practice that may be cause for concern is the prescription for medication in dosages that exceed recommendations. The Food and Drug Administration (FDA) establishes dosage guidelines for all medications. However, the majority of pediatric psychotropic use is off-label, and very few of the medications utilized have research-based guidelines for dosages in this population (Roberts et al. 2003). In the absence of robust, evidence-based prescription guidelines, some jurisdictions have adopted "practice parameters" to define safe and effective use of psychotropic medications, using a consensus-based approach (Naylor et al. 2007). Other jurisdictions have implemented systems that require pharmacy-based prior authorization in an effort to ensure proper use and dosage of psychotropic medications.

Another potential "red flag" is the use of multiple psychotropic medications concomitantly. Youth in state custody often have significant histories of maltreatment and trauma, resulting in multiple co-morbid diagnoses and complex mental health needs that may require multiple medications—often from more than one class—to adequately address mental health symptoms. A 2008 study of children in foster care revealed that 21.3% were prescribed psychotropic medication from one class, 41.3% from three or more classes, 15.4% from four or more classes, and 2.1% from five or more classes (Zito et al. 2008). Patterns that may be cause for concern include prescribing youth three or more medications at a time, or prescribing two or more medications within the same class for more than 30 days. In addition, prescribing multiple medications prior to adequately evaluating the efficacy of a single medication should raise a red flag.

The use of psychotropic medication to treat very young children is of particular concern, because this population may be especially vulnerable to adverse effects (Gleason et al. 2007). The previously referenced GAO study found that 0.3%–2.1% of children in foster care under the age of 1 year were prescribed medications that were potentially psychoactive—most commonly antihistamines and benzodiazepines—compared to 0.1%–1.2% of children not in foster care (GAO 2011).

Of all the categories of psychotropic medications used to treat mental illness in youth, second-generation antipsychotic medications have come under the most scrutiny, likely due to their potential for inducing serious side effects, including tardive dyskinesia, dystonia, and metabolic syndrome (e.g., hyperlipidemia, diabetes, weight gain, etc.). Over the past 20 years, there has been a dramatic rise in the use of second-generation antipsychotic medications for youth with mental health problems. A 2009 study found that youth in foster care were almost nine times more likely to be prescribed antipsychotic medications than other youth covered by Medicaid (Crystal et al. 2009). Although antipsychotic medications may be a legitimate and necessary treatment option for some youth in foster care, the use of these medications should be monitored closely. Patterns that may be cause for concern include prescribing youth antipsychotic medications for more than 2 years or prescribing this class of medication for illnesses other than schizophrenia, other psychotic disorders, or bipolar disorder.

LEGAL BACKGROUND

The recognition of the due process rights of children, as they relate to delinquency proceedings, began in earnest in the 1960s. In 1967, the U.S. Supreme Court clarified due process rights for juveniles facing delinquency charges. Gerald Gault, a 15-year-old, was taken into custody for making an obscene telephone call, and was subsequently found delinquent and sentenced to an indeterminate term at a state industrial school. In the decision *In re Gault,* the Supreme Court held that Gault was denied due process of law and that juvenile proceedings must meet the constitutional standards of due process and fair treatment guaranteed by the Sixth and Fourteenth Amendments, and previously believed by some to apply only to adults (*In re Gault* 1967). In light of the new evocation of children's rights, psychiatrists and state lawmakers adopted new protocols to ensure that patients' rights were not violated when admitted for psychiatric treatment and evaluation.

The psychiatric treatment of adults and children is regulated in all states through legislation that establishes guidelines for both voluntary admission and involuntary psychiatric evaluation and treatment. Some states distinguish between adult and juvenile patients, and others make distinctions based on the presence or absence of specific mental illnesses or drug and alcohol abuse (e.g., different involuntary commitment procedures). Regardless of the way by which patients are distinguished, each jurisdiction typically provides for short-term, emergency admissions, with procedures for involuntarily evaluating or hospitalizing patients.

The U.S. Supreme Court has consistently ruled that the Due Process Clause protects a competent adult's fundamental right to refuse unwanted medical treatment (*Cruzan v. Dir.*, Mo. Dep't of Health 1990). This protection applies to persons with mental illness by allowing them to refuse "invasive" treatment, such as involuntary administration of psychotropic medication, even when the state may think such measures are in their best interest. When patients are children, their parents typically are authorized to direct their medical care, which includes making decisions regarding psychiatric treatment and providing informed consent to such treatments (Feigenbaum 1992). Informed consent is the process by which the treating health-care provider discloses appropriate information to a competent patient so that the patient may make a voluntary choice to accept or refuse treatment (Appelbaum 2007). In the United States, minor children are generally considered legally incompetent and thus unable to provide informed consent to accept or refuse most forms of medical treatment. In cases where an individual is deemed incompetent via judicial means, and thus incapable of giving informed consent as to their treatment, courts have developed two different standards that may be used in complying with informed consent; the substituted judgment standard and the "best interests" standard. These standards are discussed elsewhere in this textbook in more detail, but a brief examination of them here is informative.

These standards evolved out of new constitutional requirements relating to psychiatric care. In *Mills v. Rogers*, the U.S. Supreme Court held that, with respect to incompetent persons, a judicial determination of substituted judgment was required before the administration of drugs (*Mills v. Rogers* 1982). That substituted judgment required a court to balance differing interests; in other words, the substitution of the state's judgment for the individual's had to be based on specific facts. In applying the balancing test (i.e., balancing the individual interest versus state interest) the Court held that involuntarily committed patients had a liberty interest in refusing medications and that this interest could be superseded only when outweighed by the state's interests. In applying the substituted judgment standard, the decision maker is required to "ascertain the incompetent person's actual interests and preferences" and to attempt to make the decision that an incompetent person would make if he or she were competent (*Mills v. Rogers* 1982).

Substituted judgment does not apply to children because they have never been "competent." Instead, their parents' judgment is substituted. In those cases, a new standard was developed to determine the appropriateness of medical treatment. To protect the due process rights of children, Courts looked to the best interests of the child in making decisions about medical treatment, including treatment with psychotropic medications. This is especially true for youth in state custody, because in those cases, the state acts "in loco parentis." The "best interests" standard reflects the idea that the treatment decision made on a legally incompetent patient's behalf should advance that individual's best interests. Therefore, this standard requires that decisions about the administration of medication be made based on the patient's best interests. Unfortunately, the legal decision maker (i.e., judicial officer) is not equipped to make decisions about specific psychiatric treatment options and how a child's best interests are best served under this test. Consequently, courts increasingly rely on treating physicians to help guide their decisions.

STATUTORY BACKGROUND

In addition to the due process standard created by the courts, Congress and the states have provided both the means and regulations for some types of psychiatric treatment. The Social Security Act (SSA), enacted in 1935, is a social welfare legislative act that created the Social Security system in the United States (Social Security Act 1935). The *Stephanie Tubbs Jones Child Welfare Services Program* (Title IV-B, Subpart 1 of the Social Security Act) provides grants to state and tribal agencies to develop programs directed toward the goal of keeping families together. These funds, often combined with state and local governments, as well as private funds, are directed to accomplish the following purposes: protect and promote the welfare of all children; prevent the neglect, abuse, or exploitation of children; support at-risk families through services that allow children, where appropriate, to remain with their families or return to their families in a timely manner; promote the safety, permanence, and well-being of children in foster care and adoptive families; and provide training, professional development, and support to ensure a well-qualified workforce.

The *Fostering Connections to Success and Increasing Adoption Act of 2008* amended title IV-B, subpart 1 of the Social Security Act to require state and tribal title IV-B agencies to develop a plan for ongoing oversight and coordination of health-care services, including mental health care, for youth in foster care (*Fostering Connections to Success and Increasing Adoptions Act* 2008). The intent of this act was to ensure that youth in foster care receive quality health-care services, including appropriate oversight of prescription medications (§422(b)(15) of the Act).

The Child and Family Services Improvement and Innovation Act of 2011 amended the law by adding to the requirements for the health-care oversight and coordination plan (§422(b)(15)(A)(ii) and (v) of the Act). This Act expands the requirements of the previous federal code by mandating that states amend their Title IV-B state plan to identify appropriate use and monitoring of psychotropic medications. In addition, states are required to use both training and technical assistance to oversee psychotropic prescribing and to document these efforts in their strategic child welfare systems' plans. In these plans, each state must include an outline of procedures to monitor and treat "emotional trauma" associated with a child's maltreatment and removal from his or her home, and protocols for the appropriate use and monitoring of psychotropic medications. The Children's Bureau has instructed states to address the following areas: (1) comprehensive and coordinated screening, assessment, and treatment planning; (2) informed and shared decision making and methods for ongoing communication between the prescriber, the child, his or her caregivers, and all other service providers; (3) effective medication monitoring; (4) availability of consultation by a board-certified or board-eligible child and adolescent psychiatrist; and (5) mechanisms for accessing and sharing accurate and up-to-date information and educational materials related to mental health and trauma-related interventions.

In April 2012, the Administration on Children and Families (ACF) released the Information Memorandum, "Promoting the Safe, Appropriate, and Effective Use of Psychotropic Medications for Children in Foster Care," to serve as a resource to State and Tribal title IV-B agencies as they comply with requirements to develop protocols for the appropriate use and monitoring of psychotropic medications, which were established by the Child and Family Services Improvement and Innovation Act (U.S. Department of Health and Human Services 2012). To help states create and implement oversight protocols, ACF convened a summit in August 2012: "Because Minds Matter: Collaborating to Strengthen Management of Psychotropic Medications for Children and Youth in Foster Care." This summit brought together representatives/leaders from the child welfare, Medicaid, and mental health systems from all 50 states, the District of Columbia, and Puerto Rico.

In order to meet the new statutory requirements set forth in the Child and Family Services Improvement and Innovation Act of 2011, state agencies have utilized different approaches. One approach is to devise and implement parameters that automatically trigger a "prior authorization" process or require expert consultation before a prescription can be filled. Most states also have developed psychiatric consultation hotlines to assist primary care physicians in making their treatment decisions. Some states will not reimburse doctors who do not follow the recommendations of the psychiatric consultant. Another approach is to keep Medicaid prescription registries in order to analyze the prescribing patterns of physicians and determine the "top prescribers" of antipsychotic medications. As of the writing of this chapter, the states with the most comprehensive and collaborative plans appear to be Florida, Maryland, Massachusetts, Minnesota, and Texas, all of which have detailed websites to provide information to physicians prescribing psychotropic medications to children and adolescents (Medicaid 2012).

PRACTICE GUIDELINES

A variety of policy statements and practice guidelines have been developed to guide and inform physicians treating youth in the foster care and juvenile justice systems. Examples include policy statements developed by the American Academy of Pediatrics (2002) and the American Academy of Child and Adolescent Psychiatry (AACAP n.d.). In addition, the practice parameters developed by the Texas Department of State Health Services are often used as a model for agencies seeking to improve their monitoring and oversight practices (Texas Department of State Health Services 2007). The AACAP statement proposes several guidelines to assist state and county agencies in developing programs and procedures for monitoring the use of psychotropic medications for youth in state custody. The standards are categorized as Minimal, Recommended, and Ideal.

A "Minimal" standard recommended by AACAP is that state child welfare agencies, the juvenile court, or other state or county agencies empowered by law to consent for youth to treatment with psychotropic medications should design and implement effective oversight procedures that include guidelines for the use of these medications for youth in state custody. A "Recommended" standard includes implementing a program that provides consultation by child and adolescent psychiatrists to the agency or persons that is/are responsible for consenting for youth to receive treatment with psychotropic medications. An "Ideal" program would include, among other things, the following:

- An advisory committee to oversee a medication formulary and provide medication-monitoring guidelines to practitioners who treat children in the child welfare system.
- Monitoring the rate and types of psychotropic medication usage and the rate of medication adverse events among youth in state custody.
- A process to review nonstandard, unusual, and/or experimental psychiatric interventions with children who are in state custody.
- Collecting and analyzing data regarding the rates and types of psychotropic medication use. This data should be available to clinicians in the state to improve the quality of care provided.

STATE-SPECIFIC EXAMPLE OF COURT AUTHORIZATION

In California, when a dependent child has been removed from parental custody, only the court has the authority to consent to the administration of psychotropic medication and may do so only upon a physician's request (California Welfare and Institutions Code §369.5(a)). In emergencies, psychotropic medications may be administered without court authorization. Briefly, an "Application Regarding Psychotropic Medication" (JV-220) must be completed and filed with the court and proper notice provided to the relevant parties and their attorneys. This includes notice to the minor, the minor's current caregiver, and the minor's parent or prior legal guardian, among others.

When submitting a JV-220 to the court, the prescribing physician is required to include a statement that addresses all of the following:

- The diagnosis of the child's condition that the physician asserts can be treated through the administration of the medication.
- The specific medication recommended, with the recommended maximum daily dosage and length of time this course of treatment will continue.

- The anticipated benefits to the child of the use of the medication.
- A description of possible side effects of the medication.
- A list of any other medications, prescription or otherwise, that the child is currently taking, and a description of any effect these medications may produce in combination with the psychotropic medication.
- A description of any other therapeutic services related to the child's mental health status.
- A statement that the child has been informed, in an age-appropriate manner, of the recommended course of treatment, the basis for it, and its possible results. The child's response must be included.

Upon receiving the completed JV-220 application, the court has 7 court days to approve the medication request, deny it, or order a hearing on the issue. Because this is a particularly complicated and sensitive matter, many counties have implemented their own protocols and local court rules regarding the JV-220 process. For example, in Los Angeles County, Juvenile Court Mental Health Services' clinicians (including pharmacists and physicians) review requests for court authorization and make a written recommendation as to the propriety of the proposed treatment based on information submitted on the JV-220 and, if necessary, review of collateral information.

SUMMARY KEY POINTS

- Psychotropic medications can be an important component of a comprehensive treatment plan to address the often-complex mental health needs of youth in state custody, including those in the foster care and juvenile justice systems.
- Some clinicians' current psychotropic medication prescribing patterns to treat these youth may not comport with evidenced-based practice standards that are generally supported by empirical research. Therefore, these prescribing patterns may violate the "best interests" legal standard of youth under these psychiatrists' care.
- Increased oversight of psychotropic medication prescribing is necessary to safely and effectively treat the mental health needs of these youth.
- State oversight systems, such as those highlighted in the Tufts report, may include such components as access to up-to-date guidelines on clinical practices and appropriate medication monitoring for youth in foster care and juvenile justice.

REFERENCES

American Academy of Child and Adolescent Psychiatry (AACAP). 2014. *Position Statement on Oversight of Psychotropic Use for Children in State Custody.* http://www.aacap.org, accessed December 2014.

American Academy of Pediatrics. 2002. Health care of young children in foster care. *Pediatrics* 109(3):536–541.

Appelbaum PS. 2007. Assessment of patient's competence to consent to treatment. *New England Journal of Medicine* 357(18):1834–1840.

Breland-Noble AM, EB Elbogen, EMZ Farmer, HR Wagner, and BJ Burns. 2004. Use of psychotropic medications by youths in therapeutic foster care and group homes. *Psychiatric Services* 55(6):706–708.

California Welfare and Institutions Code § 369.5(a).

California Welfare and Institutions Code § 725.

Cruzan v. Dir., Mo. Dep't of Health (497 U.S. 261, 1990).

Crystal S, M Olfson, C Huang, H Pincus, and T Gerhard. 2009. Broadened use of atypical antipsychotics: Safety, effectiveness, and policy challenges. *Health Affairs* 28(5):w770–w781.

De Sa K. 2014. Drugging our kids. *San Jose Mercury News*, August 24.

dosReis S, Y Yoon, DM Rubin, MA Riddle, E Noll, and A Rothbard. 2011. Antipsychotic treatment among youth in foster care. *Pediatrics* 128(6):e1459–e1466.

dosReis S, JM Zito, DJ Safer, and KL Soeken. 2001. Mental health services for youths in foster care and disabled youths. *American Journal of Public Health* 91(7):1094–1099.

Feigenbaum MS. 1992. Minors, medical treatment, and interspousal disagreement: Should Solomon split the child? *DePaul Law Review* 41(3):841–884.

Fostering Connections to Success and Increasing Adoptions Act. 42 U.S.C. 1305 (2008).

Gleason MM, HL Egger, GJ Emslie, LL Greenhill, RA Kowatch, AF Lieberman et al. 2007. Psychopharmacological treatment for very young children: Contexts and guidelines. *Journal of the American Academy of Child and Adolescent Psychiatry* 46(12):1532–1572.

In re Gault (387 U.S. 1, 1967).

Leslie LK, T Mackie, EH Dawson et al. 2010. Multi-state study on psychotropic medication oversight in foster care. *Tufts Clinical and Translational Science Institute.* http://www.tuftsctsi.org, accessed December 2014.

Medicaid. 2012. Summary of State Programs to Address Psychotropic Medication Use in Children in Foster Care. https://www.medicaid.gov, accessed December 2014.

Mills v. Rogers. (457 U.S. 291, 1982).

Naylor MW, CV Davidson, DJ Ortega-Piron, A Bass, A Gutierrez, and A Hall. 2007. Psychotropic medication management for youths in state care: Pharmacoepidemiology and policy considerations. *Child Welfare* 86(5):175–192.

Raghavan R, BT Zima, RM Anderson, AA Leibowitz, MA Schuster, and J Landsverk. 2005. Psychotropic medication use in a national probability sample of children in the child welfare system. *Journal of Child and Adolescent Psychopharmacology* 15(1):97–106.

Roberts R, W Rodriguez, D Murphy, and T Crescenzi. 2003. Pediatric drug labeling. *Journal of the American Medical Association* 290(7):905–911.

Rubin DM, C Feudtner, R Localio, and DS Mandell. 2009. State variation in psychotropic medication use by foster care children with autism spectrum disorder. *Pediatrics* 142(2):e305–e312.

Rutgers Center for Education and Research on Therapeutics. 2010. *Antipsychotic Medication Use in Medicaid Children and Adolescents*. Medicaid Medical Directors Learning Network and Rutgers Center for Education and Research on Mental Health Therapeutics. http://rci.rutgers.edu/~cseap/MMDLNAPKIDS.html, accessed December 2014.

Social Security Act § 422 (b)(15)(A)(ii) and (v) (2011).

Social Security Act. 42 U.S.C. ch. 7 (1935).

Texas Department of State Health Services. 2007. *Psychotropic Medication Utilization Parameters for Foster Children*. http://www.dfps.state.tx.us/Child_Protection/Medical_Services/guide-psychotropic.asp, accessed June 2016.

The Child and Family Services Improvement and Innovation Act. 42 U.S.C. 1305 (2011).

U.S. Department of Health and Human Services. 2012. ACFY-CB-IM-12–03. *Administration for Children and Families*. http://www.acf.hhs.gov, accessed December 2014.

U.S. Government Accountability Office (GAO). 2011. Foster children: HHS guidance could help states improve oversight of psychotropic medications. *Publication No. GAO-12-270T*. Washington, DC: U.S. GAO.

White RC, A Havalchak, L Jackson, K O'Brian, and P Pecora. 2007. Mental health, ethnicity, sexuality, and spirituality among youth in foster care: Findings from the casey field office mental health study. *Casey Family Programs*. http://www.casey.org, accessed December 2014.

Zima BT, R Bussing, GM Crecelius, A Kaufman, and TR Belin. 1999. Psychotropic medication use among children in foster care: Relationship to severe psychiatric disorders. *American Journal of Public Health* 89(11):1732–1735.

Zito JM, DJ Safer, S dosReis, JF Gardner, M Boles, and F Lynch. 2000 Trends in the prescribing of psychotropic medications to preschoolers. *Journal of the American Medical Association* 283(8):1025–1030.

Zito JM, DJ Safer, D. Sai et al. 2008. Psychotropic medication patterns among youth in foster care. *Pediatrics* 121(1):e157–e163.

Zito JM, DJ Safer, IH Zuckerman, JF Gardner, and K Soeken. 2005. Effect of Medicaid eligibility category on racial disparities in the use of psychotropic medications among youths. *Psychiatric Services* 56(2):157–163.

PART 3

Forensic Evaluation and Treatment in the Criminal Justice System

ALAN R. FELTHOUS

25

Forensic evaluation and treatment in the criminal justice system: Introduction

ALAN R. FELTHOUS

INTRODUCTION

As the "collective institutions through which an accused offender passes until the accusations have been disposed of or the assessed punishment concluded" the criminal justice system has three components: "law enforcement (police, sheriffs, marshals), the judicial process (judges, prosecutors, defense lawyers), and corrections (prison officials, probation officers, parole officers)" (Garner 1999, 381). Criminal forensic psychiatry is most relevant to the second component, the judicial process. Accordingly, this section addresses jail diversion programs, criminal competence, treatment for restoration of competence, criminal responsibility, post-adjudication evaluations and disposition of insanity acquittees, and presentencing evaluations. Correctional psychiatry constitutes a separate section of this volume.

Criminal law, of course, deals with crimes, a crime being defined as "[a] social harm that the law makes punishable; the breach of a legal duty treated as the subject-matter of a criminal proceeding" (Garner 1999, 377). Specific crimes are codified into statutory law by state and federal legislatures, with most states codifying their penal laws only once or twice a century and amending specific sections in the interim (Glaser 1974).

Criminal forensic psychiatry, including each of the topics addressed by the chapters in this section, begins with several legal contexts: the development of criminal law apart from civil law, the moral and legal importance attached to criminal intent and *mens rea*, codification of the criminal law in the United States, and criminal procedures requiring psychiatric assessments. Finally some recent developments in criminal forensic psychiatry are highlighted, including the potential and actual relevance of the still evolving technologies of neuroimaging and the Internet.

THE EMERGENCE OF CRIMINAL AS DISTINCT FROM CIVIL LAW

In early English law today's distinction between crime of criminal law and tort of civil law did not exist. Historians of criminal law concluded that criminal law evolved from the desire for revenge of the blood feud (Sayre 1931–1932). In the era of trial by battle and ordeal, early laws to emerge were based on strict liability, and criminal intent was not an element of a criminal offense prior to the twelfth century (Sayre 1931–1932). Neither was the distinction between felonies and misdemeanors what it is today. Prior to Bracton in the twelfth century, minor offenses were punishable by corporal punishment or amercement, and the distinction between civil and criminal aspects of trespass, between the misdemeanors and torts of today, was obscure (Sayre 1931–1932).

Only killings in self-defense or "by misadventure" were considered for royal pardon. In the centuries that followed, those who killed without guilty intent would also be relieved of criminal responsibility. The first statutory requirement of "malice aforethought" appears to have been articulated in a decree by Richard II in the fourteenth century (1389), intended to curb too liberally granted royal pardons: "[N]o charter or pardon shall be henceforth allowed before any justice for murder, the death of a man killed by making assault or malice prepense (*ou malice purpense*)" (Stephen 1883, 43, original in French).

Some crimes came under jurisdiction of canonical law, whereas other more serious crimes were dealt with by the secular government. Statutes enacted at the end of the fifteenth and beginning of the sixteenth centuries specified which types of homicide were excluded from "benefit of the clergy" (p. 996). Felonious homicide with malice aforethought was not clergyable and was punishable by death; whereas felonious homicide without malice aforethought was clergyable, subject to no more than a year of imprisonment and branding of the thumb (Sayre 1931–1932), and became known as manslaughter.

Originally "malice" referred to the homicidal motive as a "general malevolence or cold-blooded desire to injure" (Sayre, 1931–1932, 997). Eventually the meaning was broadened such that it was no longer a purely psychological element. Coke, in his *Third Institute* (1669, defined murder as an unlawful killing "with malice fore-thought, either expreſſed by the party, or implied by law" (Coke 1669, 47). Malice aforethought came to be the qualities that distinguished more serious from less serious felony homicides, some but not all qualities of which actually pertained to *mens rea*.

Hale (1736) in the eighteenth century drew a distinction between sanity in civil and criminal wrongdoing, respectively. The particularization of *mens rea* into specific types of criminal offenses developed somewhat differently for crimes of homicide, larceny, burglary, and arson. At the beginning of the thirteenth century, murder and manslaughter and voluntary and involuntary homicide were not legally distinguishable (Sayre 1931–1932).

In the United States as in England, malice aforethought distinguished murder from homicide (Kadish et al. 2012). Unlawful or criminal homicide is graded in severity with different names, e.g., murder and manslaughter, and with different degrees, first-degree and second-degree murder. Each state further grades criminal homicide following this general scheme.

Crimes are either felonies or misdemeanors. In early English law, felonies were defined, by Blackstone for example, as "every species of crime, which occasioned at common law the forfeiture of lands or goods" (Blackstone 1979 [1769], 94). In contrast to misdemeanors, felonies are serious or major crimes and include arson, burglary, murder, and rape. Today a felony is considered to be a crime that is "punishable by imprisonment for more than a year or by death" (Garner 1999, 633), the imprisonment typically occurring in a state or federal prison. A misdemeanor, minor crime, or summary offense is in contrast to a felony usually "punishable by fine, penalty, forfeiture, or confinement [usually for a brief time] in a place other than prison [such as a county jail]" (Garner 1999, 1014).

CRIMINAL INTENT AND SPECIFIC *MENS REA*

The requirement for criminal intent in English law is traced back to a sermon by St. Augustine on James 5:12: "swear not neither by heaven neither by the earth, neither by any other oath" (Sayre 1931–1932, note 30, 984). Supporting the requirement of intent in the offense of perjury, St. Augustine declared that a man is a perjurer in the eyes of God if he testifies, out of self-interest, that it rained in a particular spot, when he believes it did not rain there (Sayre 1931–1932, note 30, 983–984). This principle of "*reum non facit nisi mens rea*" was recited in the *Leges* of Henry I: "A person is not to be considered guilty unless he has a guilty intention" (*Leges*, p. 94, *Henrici Primi*, c. 5, §28,95), even though elsewhere the text supported absolute criminal liability (88,6a, 270, -70, 126, 222, 90, 11a, 282). From this, Coke in the *Third Institute* (1669, p. 107) formulated the *mens rea* requirement as "*actus non facit reum nisi mens sit rea*" (the act is not criminal unless the intent is criminal), which he repeated as accepted law in the mid-seventeenth century (Sayre 1931–1932, note 51, 988).

Important in criminal law and forensic psychiatry is the dichotomy of specific versus general intent crimes. In a general intent crime, the individual simply did what he or she intended, i.e., the criminal act (Kadish et al. 2012). A specific intent crime is defined as one in which the actor had "the intent to accomplish the precise criminal act that one is later charged with" (Garner 1999, 814). Examples of specific intent crimes include assault, burglary, conspiracy, embezzlement, false pretenses, forgery, robbery, and solicitation. The specific intent is an element of the *mens rea* that the prosecution must prove beyond a reasonable doubt in order to gain a conviction. This type of *mens rea* requiring specific intent, also termed "special" or "positive" *mens rea*, pertains to the grading of offenses (Gilles Phillips and Woodman 2008). "[S]pecific intent crimes require proof of a particular mental state beyond the mere intent to engage in the proscribed conduct" (Gilles Phillips and Woodman 2008, 490).

The offense of burglary, as an example of a specific intent crime, requires not only unlawful entry but the intent to commit another felonious act once inside the building. Assault with intent to kill requires, as the name of the offense indicates, that the assault was committed with the specific intent of killing the victim (Kadish et al. 2012). If the specific intent is not proven, conviction of a lesser included offense such as a general intent crime, in these cases trespass and battery, respectively, can be the adjudicated outcome.

To prove beyond a reasonable doubt a defendant's specific purpose, in the same sense that the act is proven, would often be an insurmountable challenge for the prosecutor. The Supreme Court has addressed this issue with the distinction between mandatory and permissive presumptions. A mandatory presumption is one that the jury must accept unless there is evidence to the contrary. "A person of sound mind and discretion is presumed to intend the natural and probable consequences of his acts, but the presumption may be rebutted" (*Francis v. Franklin* 1985, 309). In some cases, however, inferences must constitutionally be permissive; the U.S. Supreme Court upheld the District Court's jury instruction: "[p]ossession of recently stolen property, if not satisfactorily explained, is ordinarily a circumstance from which [the jury] may reasonable draw the inference and find, in the light of the surrounding circumstances shown by the evidence in the case that the person in possession knew that the property had been stolen" (*Barnes v. United States* 1973, 839, 840).

CODIFICATION OF PENAL LAW

A most impactful development in the twentieth century has been the American Law Institute's (ALI) Model Penal Code (Official Draft, 1962, reproduced in Appendix of Kadish et al. 2012, 1191–1253). Committed to simplifying, clarifying, and improving the administration of justice, prominent academics, lawyers, and judges founded the ALI in 1923. The move away from common law toward "codification" had its roots in the values of Jeremy Bentham (1780, 2007) who coined the term and espoused a system of rational, deterrent rather than retributive law that maximized benefit for most people (Kadish 1987). Supported by the essays on positive law by John Austin (1832 and 1863, 1954), by mid-twentieth century the Benthamite tradition of replacing judicial law with legislation had become widely accepted and practiced. After 1950 a series of tentative model penal code drafts were produced under the leadership of Professors Herbert Wechsler and Louis B. Schwartz. The 1962 Official Draft had unprecedented effect, with 34 states adopting some elements of the Model Penal Code over the next 20 years (Kadish et al. 2012, 1191).

CRIMINAL JUSTICE PROCEDURAL CONTEXT OF FORENSIC EVALUATION

The criminal forensic psychiatrist will be well aided by a general knowledge of criminal justice procedures to appreciate contextual aspects and limitations of his role as well as sources of information for his evaluation of a defendant. The investigation of a criminal offense involves interviewing suspects, witnesses, and victims and gathering physical evidence. In most cases the only clue to an offender's identity is personal identification by a victim or witness. Only 39% of violent offenses (murder, aggravated assault, forcible rape, and robbery) are cleared by arrest in cities with a population exceeding one million, and only 13% of serious property crimes (Kadish et al. 2012, citing FBI crime statistics for 2009).

Of those cases cleared by arrest about one-half are dismissed. Reasons for dismissal include that the suspect was not guilty, guilt could not be proven, police and prosecutors were too busy with other cases, or the offender had emotional or social problems better handled by another agency. In some jurisdictions charges were dismissed after the defendant successfully completed a pretrial diversion program (Kadish et al. 2012).

After arrest the suspect is brought before the magistrate, and many are released within 24 hours of arrest. The magistrate decides whether to release the defendant before the trial. More than 90% of convictions in most jurisdictions are secured by the defendant's plea of guilty, often resulting from either a hurried or prolonged negotiation between prosecutor and defense counsel (Kadish et al. 2012).

By pleading guilty a defendant waives three principal rights: the privilege against self-incrimination, the right to a jury trial, and the right to confront one's accuser. These three waived rights, elements of the offense, and the potential sentence are made explicit in open court with the judge, who must determine that the choice to plead guilty was "knowing and intelligent" (*Brady v. United States* 1970; Kadish et al. 2012).

Only a small fraction, perhaps 4% of all cases filed, actually proceeded to trial, and in one series, only 1% were acquitted (Givelber 2005). Others are disposed of by guilty pleas, dismissal, or pretrial diversion (Kadish et al. 2012). Yet the outcomes of trials and appeals court hearings serve to establish standard procedures; practices in arresting, charging, dismissing, diverting pretrial, and plea bargaining, in other words, standards for many other cases that never reach trial (Kadish et al. 2012). Sentencing can seem quite informal compared with the high formality of the trial in chief to determine guilt. Figure 25.1 illustrates the potential routes by which cases move through the criminal justice system and points of potential intercession by forensic psychiatry.

If the main goal of the criminal judicial process is to prosecute and sanction, equally important goals are to ensure that the process is fair and the outcome is just. A number of protections have been adopted to ensure that the process is fair, for example, the exclusionary principle that excludes the use of evidence at trial that was obtained by the government in a manner that violated the defendant's constitutional rights (Stone 2003). Each of the themes addressed in this section is concerned with fairness for the defendant, ultimately the *raison d'être* for psychiatric involvement, fairness that is usually required by the Due Process Clause of the Fourteenth Amendment.

The primary basis for constitutional regulation of criminal procedure is the Bill of Rights, the first Ten Amendments to the U.S. Constitution (Goldstein 2003). Except for the prohibition against excessive bail and the right to a grand jury indictment in felony cases, all of the procedural rights of the first Ten Amendments have been applied to the states via the Due Process Clause of the Fourteenth Amendment. As specified by the U.S. Supreme Court, every state's criminal procedures must conform to the U.S. Constitution (Goldstein 2007).

Especially where the consequence for the defendant is state-imposed punishment, the government does not require a person to be able to do something for which he or she is incapable. Thus, a person should not be convicted and punished for committing a crime that he or she was incapable of committing (Felthous 2008). Neither should the person be tried, convicted, and punished if he or she lacked any of a number of adjudicative competencies (Felthous 2008, 2010), including competence to waive *Miranda* rights, to plead guilty, to waive representation by counsel, to represent oneself without counsel, to waive into adult court for juveniles, to waive a jury trial, to waive appeals, to be sentenced, to be executed (Miller 2003), and various other subspecies of adjudicative competence in the broad sense (Perlin 2003).

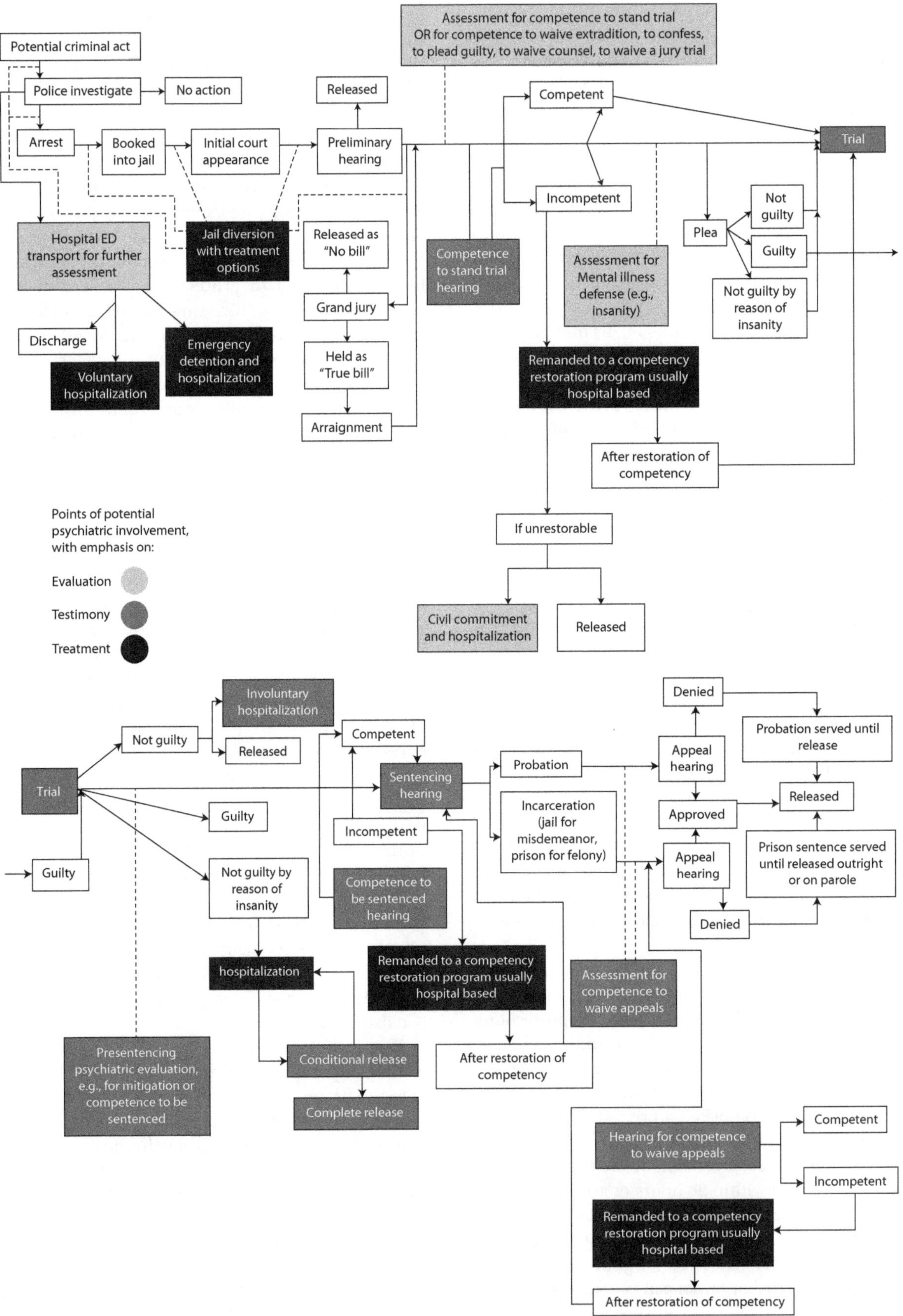

Figure 25.1 The pathways that a criminal defendant can progress through the criminal justice system with potential point of forensic psychiatric participation denoted.

It is the quest for fundamental fairness that brings psychiatric testimony into the criminal courtroom. The U.S. Supreme Court has based its most relevant holdings in this regard on the Due Process Clause of the Fourteenth Amendment. All of the following rights involving psychiatric expertise are based on the Due Process Clause: the defendant's right not to be tried or convicted while incompetent to stand trial (*Dusky v. United States* 1960; *Pate v. Robinson* 1966), reaffirmed in subsequent decisions addressing other aspects of the issue (e.g., *Drope v. Missouri* 1975); treatment for restoration of competence, i.e., the incompetent defendant must have his or her competence restored before he or she faces trial (*Drope v. Missouri* 1975); the standard of proof for the defendant to establish his or her incompetence can be no greater than preponderance of the evidence (*Cooper v. Oklahoma* 1996); a defendant's qualified right to refuse psychotropic medication prior to trial (*Riggins v. Nevada* 1992); the principle that involuntary treatment for restoration of competence must be medically appropriate and must be administered appropriately (*Riggins v. Nevada* 1992; *Sell v. United States* 2003); and treatment for restoration of competence to stand trial cannot be indefinite, also supported by the Equal Protection Clause (*Jackson v. Indiana* 1972). Conditions under which a defendant can be medicated involuntarily for restoration of competence are also regulated by the Due Process Clause (*Sell v. United States* 2003).

The Supreme Court has not ruled that the Due Process Clause requires availability of an insanity or other mental defense. Noting that the Supreme Court never supported abolition of the insanity defense, the Nevada Supreme Court determined that the insanity defense was so rooted in our notions of justice as to be a fundamental right protected by the Constitution (*Finger v. State* 2001). In a footnote in its *Clark* decision the High Court wrote "[W]e have never held that the Constitution mandates an insanity defense, *nor have we held that the Constitution does not so require*" (*Clark v. Arizona* 2006, note 20, 2722). Thus, although the Supreme Court has not interfered with state insanity jurisprudence, including abolition of the insanity defense, within this footnote it left the door open for future consideration. State law must nonetheless comport with the U.S. Constitution that provides defendants with the right to present evidence (*Crane v. Kentucky* 1986). Expressed more explicitly, "Whether rooted directly in the Due Process Clause of the Fourteenth Amendment or in the Compulsory Process or Confrontation Clauses of the Sixth Amendment," in his dissent in *Clark* Justice Kennedy stated, "the U.S. Constitution guarantees criminal defendants a meaningful opportunity to present a *complete* defense" (italics added, 2743, *Clark v. Arizona* 2006).

Throughout the various required competencies, especially the competency to commit a crime as defined by a jurisdictional insanity defense (Morse 1999) or adjudicative competencies best exemplified by the *Dusky* standard for competence to stand trial (*Dusky v. United States* 1960; see Felthous 2011), and competence to be executed (*Panetti v. Quarterman* 2007), rational thinking is required. It is true that most statutory CST standards and various less commonly applied competencies do not explicitly require rationality. Nonetheless, state CST standards would claim to comport with constitutionally required rationality (e.g., Dierker 2014, §11:12, 1., c., 138), and if a key mental element was lacking to achieve competency, such as the capacity to assist in one's defense, then the missing element was also missing in rationality. Specific standards require more than just rationality in defining the particular competence of concern, but rationality is certainly a theme in the various competencies required throughout the criminal justice process.

RECENT DEVELOPMENTS IN CRIMINAL FORENSIC PSYCHIATRY

Rosner (2003, p. 3), citing the Standards for Fellowship Programs in Forensic Psychiatry (Joint Committee on Accreditation of Fellowships in Forensic Psychiatry 1982) defined criminal forensic psychiatry so as to include "at a minimum, competence to stand trial, competence to enter a plea, testimonial capacity, voluntariness of confession, insanity defense(s), diminished capacity, sentencing considerations, release of persons who have been acquitted by reason of insanity."

Much has occurred in the realm of criminal forensic psychiatry since the Second Edition in 2003. First, tribute is well due to our friend and colleague Robert Miller who passed in the interim. His indefatigable and meticulous scholarship as editor of the criminal law section in the first and second editions (Miller 1994, 2003) provided an enduring, thorough, and well-referenced model for this section on forensic psychiatry.

It may not be hyperbole to suggest that the past decade has had the most substantive developments in the field of criminal forensic psychiatry of any other decade in the past. From the American Academy of Psychiatry and the Law (AAPL), forensic psychiatrists now have the benefit of the insanity practice guideline (AAPL 2014) complementing the earlier guideline on competency to stand trial forensic assessments (Mossman et al. 2007). Just published for the first time is the AAPL guideline for forensic assessments with subsections on gathering information on criminal cases, presentencing evaluations, and other topics relevant to both criminal and general forensic psychiatry (Glancy et al. 2015). The fifth edition of the American Psychiatric Association's *Diagnostic and Statistical Manual of Mental Disorders* was published in 2013. Additional landmark cases have shaped the law and provided further instruction for the proper practice of criminal forensic psychiatry. Considerable relevant scientific contributions are to be found in books and journals published over the past decade.

The digital technologies of neuroimaging and the Internet are gaining increasing relevance to criminal forensic psychiatry. Neuroimaging evidence is increasingly coming into evidence in criminal trials, but with considerable circumspection and reservation (Martell 2009). Magnetic resonance imaging (MRI), and computed tomography (CT) scans have routinely been admitted into evidence to demonstrate trauma and disease, whereas positron emission tomography (PET), single-photon emission computed tomography (SPECT) scans, and functional MRI (fMRI) studies are not so readily admitted (Moriarty 2008). In his review, Martell concludes that the use of structural brain imaging is empirically supported for providing evidence of brain lesions resulting from certain neurological disorders, traumatic brain injury, or stroke. Of the functional brain imaging techniques, PET can assist in the differential diagnosis of dementia, identification of brain tumors, and further assessment of temporal lobe epilepsy. SPECT is well established for the diagnosis of suspected brain trauma, epileptic foci, dementia, and cardiovascular disease. Martell (2009) cautions against using neuroimaging evidence to directly address violent or criminal behavior and to diagnose or confirm nonneurological psychiatric disorders such as disorders of mood, thought, or developmental disorders (Martell 2009).

In certain cases, PET has been admitted into evidence to show evidence of diminished impulse control and cognition as well as traumatic and toxic brain injury (Moriarty et al. 2013). As a brain imaging technique used to show impaired brain function, PET evidentiary application appears to have resulted in offense reduction through jury adjudication (*People v. Williams* 2004) or plea bargaining (*People v. Weinstein* 1992). Moriarty and colleagues (2013) conclude that courts are admitting neuroscientific evidence such as PET without an analysis of reliability, much like other behavioral science testimony.

Neuroimaging can be persuasive to a jury, as demonstrated empirically with mock jurors (Gurley and Marcus 2008). The relevant AAPL guideline cogently concludes that imaging procedures can be helpful in diagnosing certain brain disorders but not in establishing the functional criteria of the insanity defense (Giorgi-Guarnieri et al. 2014).

Today it behooves the forensic evaluator to inquire about a criminal defendant's computer literacy and particular uses of the Internet. As cataloged by Recupero (2010), there are a variety of criminal activities that one can engage in on the Internet. The Internet can also be used to facilitate criminal activity (McGrath and Casey 2002). Such activities can lead to specific charges and assessments for criminal responsibility. An emerging literature raises the possibility of computer or Internet psychopathology such as Internet Gaming Disorder, not an official *DSM* diagnosis at this time (American Psychiatric Association 2013). The defendant may have accessed the Internet in order to prepare for the forensic interview such as by Googling the evaluator. Of special relevance to evaluation for criminal responsibility are revelations that the defendant might have made on the Internet that reflected his or her violent fantasies and intentions. This is becoming better appreciated in the study of individual mass killers and terrorists, especially lone terrorists (Meloy and Yakeley 2014; Post et al. 2014), but this is also observed in more plebian offenders. What at first may appear to represent a bizarre delusional system woven together out of whole cloth can turn out to be "supported" by similar or identical fantasies and potential content for belief systems, which the defendant accessed on the Internet. In such cases the evaluator must consider whether the defendant's beliefs are delusional or represent a "subcultural" set of beliefs, perhaps entertained only by certain Internet users, a "virtual" subculture as it were.

A few changes in this section should be noted: as the section title indicates, treatment within the criminal justice system is as important as forensic assessments. Accordingly, chapters on jail diversion programs and the treatment and restoration of competence to stand trial are added. Also important to criminal forensic psychiatry are presentencing evaluations and post-adjudication dispositions. The chapters on competence to stand trial and criminal responsibility incorporate recent clinical, scientific, and legal developments with the aim of providing the most current, explanatory, and practical information.

REFERENCES

American Academy of Psychiatry and the Law (AAPL). 2014. AAPL Practice Guideline for Forensic Psychiatric Evaluation of Defendants Raising the Insanity Defense. *Journal of the American Academy of Psychiatry and the Law* 42(4):S3–S76 Supplement.

American Psychiatric Association (APA). 2013. *Diagnostic and Statistical Manual of Mental Disorders*. 5th edition. Washington, DC: APA.

Austin J. 1832 and 1863, 1954 by Weidenfeld & Nicholson. *The Province of Jurisprudence Determined* and *The Uses of the Study of Jurisprudence* reprinted in 1998 by Indianapolis, IN: Hackett.

Barnes v. United States, 412 United States 837 (1973).

Bentham J. 2007 (original 1780). *An Introduction to the Principles of Morals and Legislation*. Mineola, NY: Dover.

Blackstone W. 1979. *Commentaries on the Laws of England, Volume IV of Public Wrongs* 1769 [Facsimile of the first edition of 1765–1769]. Chicago: University of Chicago Press.

Brady v. United States, 397 U.S. 742 (1970).

Clark v. Arizona, 126 S. Ct. 2709 (2006), Kennedy J, dissenting.

Coke E. 1669. *The Third Part of the Institutes of the Laws of England: Concerning High Treaſon, and other Pleas of the Crown* and *Criminal Cauſes*. 4th edition. Fleetreet/Holborn, England: Bookfellers.

Cooper v. Oklahoma, 116 S. Ct. 1923 (1996).

Crane v. Kentucky 476 U.S. 683 (1986).

Dierker RH. 2014. *Missouri Criminal Practice Handbook, 2014 Edition Missouri Practice Series*. Vol. 28. Eagan, MN: Thomson Reuters.

Drope v. Missouri, 420 U.S. (1975).

Dusky v. United States, 362 U.S., at 402, 80 S. Ct. 788, 4 L. Ed. 2d 824 (1960).

Felthous AR. 2008. The will: From metaphysical freedom to normative functionalism. *Journal of the American Academy of Psychiatry and the Law* 36(1):16–24.

Felthous AR 2010. Introduction to the issue: Adjudicative competencies. *Behavioral Sciences and the Law* 28(5):581–584.

Felthous AR. 2011. Competence to stand trial should require rational understanding. *Journal of the American Academy of Psychiatry and the Law* 39(1):19–30.

Finger v. State, 27 P. 3d 66 (Nev. 2001).

Francis v. Franklin, 471 U.S. 307 (1985).

Garner BA. 1999. *Black's Law Dictionary*. 7th edition. St. Paul MN: West Group.

Gilles Phillips JK, and RE Woodman. 2008. The insanity of the mens rea model: Due process and the abolition of the insanity defense. *Pace Law Review* 28(3):455–494.

Giorgi-Guarnieri D, J Janofsky, E Keram, S Lawsky, P Merideth, D Mossman, D Schwartz-Watts, C Scott, J Thompson, and HV Zonana. 2002. Practice guideline: Forensic psychiatric evaluation of defendants raising the insanity defense. *Journal of the American Academy of Psychiatry and the Law* 30(2):S1–S40, Supplement 2002.

Givelber D. 2005. Lost innocence: Speculation and data about the acquitted. *American Criminal Law Review* 42:1167–1199.

Glancy GD, P Ash, EPJ Bath et al. 2015. Practice guideline: The forensic assessment. *Journal of the American Academy of Psychiatry and the Law* 30(2):S1–S53, Supplement 2015.

Glaser D. 1974. The classification of offenses and offenders. In *Handbook of Criminology*, edited by D Glaser, Chicago: Rand McNally College, 45–83.

Goldstein RL. 2007. Criminal law: Structure and procedures. In *International Handbook on Psychopathic Disorders and the Law: Volume II: Laws and Policies*, edited by AR Felthous and Henning Saß, Chichester, England: Wiley, 165–176.

Gurley JR and DK Marcus. 2008. The effects of neuroimaging and brain injury on insanity defenses. *Behavioral Sciences and the Law* 26(1):85–97.

Hale M. 1736. *Historia Placitorum Coronæ: The History of the Pleas of the Crown*. E. and R. Nutt and R. Gosling. London, England. Reprinted in 2003, Clark, NJ: Lawbook Exchange.

Jackson v. Indiana, 406 U.S. 715 (1972).

Joint Committee on Accreditation of Fellowship Programs in Forensic Psychiatry. 1982. A report by the Joint Committee on Accreditation of Fellowship Program in Forensic Psychiatry: Standards for fellowship programs in forensic psychiatry. *Bulletin of the American Academy of Psychiatry and the Law* 10(4):285–292.

Kadish SH. 1987. The model penal code's historical antecedents. *Rutgers Law Journal* 19:521–538.

Kadish SH, SJ Schulhofer, CS Steiker, and RE Barkow. 2012. *Criminal Law and Its Processes: Cases and Materials*, 9th edition. New York: Wolters Kluwer Law and Business.

Leges Henrici Primi. 1972. In *Leges Henrici Primic* (12th century), edited with Translation and Commentary by LJ Downer, Oxford: Clarendon Press, 80–303.

Martell DA. 2009. Neuroscience and the law: Philosophical differences and practical constraints. *Behavioral Sciences and the Law* 27(2):123–136.

McGrath MG, and E Casey 2002. Forensic psychiatry and the internet: Practical perspectives on sexual predators and obsessional harassers in cyberspace. *Journal of the American Academy of Psychiatry and the Law* 30(1):81–94.

Meloy JR and J Yakeley. 2014. The violent true believer as a 'Lone Wolf'—Psychoanalytic perspectives on terrorism. *Behavioral Sciences and the Law* 32(3):347–365. doi:10.1002/bsl.2109

Miller RD. 1994. Part 3: Forensic evaluation and treatment in the criminal justice system. In *Principles and Practice of Forensic Psychiatry*, edited by R Rosner, London: Arnold, 171–224.

Miller RD. 2003. Part 3: Forensic evaluation and treatment in the criminal justice system. In *Principles and Practice of Forensic Psychiatry*, edited by R Rosner, London: Arnold, 181–245.

Moriarty JC. 2008. Flickering admissibility: Neuroimaging in the U.S. courts. *Behavioral Sciences and the Law* 26(1):29–49.

Moriarty JC, Dd Langleben, and JM Provenzale. 2013. Brain trauma, PET scans and forensic complexity. *Behavioral Sciences and the Law* 31(6):702–720.

Morse SJ. 1999. Craziness and criminal responsibility. *Behavioral Sciences and the Law* 17(2):147–164.

Mossman D, SG Noffsinger, P Ash et al. 2007. AAPL practice guideline for the forensic psychiatric evaluation of competence to stand trial. *Journal of the American Academy of Psychiatry and the Law* 35(4):S1–S72.

Panetti v. Quarterman, 127 S. Ct. 2842 (2007).

Pate v. Robinson, 383 U.S. 375 (1966).

People v. Weinstein, 591 N.Y.S. 2d 715 (N.Y.S. Ct. 1992).

People v. Williams, 2004 WL 740049 (Cal. App. 4th Dist. 2004, (as modified/April 13, 2004), review denied (June 23, 2004).

Perlin MJ. 2003. Beyond *Dusky* and *Godinez*: Competency before and after trial. *Behavioral Sciences and the Law* 21(3):297–310.

Post JM, M Cody, and M Kristen. 2014. The changing face of terrorism in the 21st century: The communications revolution and the virtual community of hatred. *Behavioral Sciences and the Law* 32(3):306–334. doi:10.1002/bsl.2123

Recupero PR. 2010. The mental status examination in the age of the Internet--challenges and opportunities. *Journal of the American Academy of Psychiatry and the Law* 38(1):15–26.

Reeves R and R Richard. 2003. Education and training in forensic psychiatry. In *Principles and Practice of Forensic Psychiatry*, edited by R Rosner. London: Arnold, 52–55.

Riggins v. Nevada, 504 U.S. 127 (1992).

Rosner R. 2003. A conceptual framework for forensic psychiatry. In *Principles and Practice of Forensic Psychiatry*, edited by R. Rosner. London: Arnold, 3–6.

Sayre FB.1931–1932. Mens Rea. *Harvard Law Review* 45:974–1026.

Sell v. United States, 539 U.S. 166 (2003).

Stephen JF. 1883. *A History of the Criminal Law of England, Vol. 3*, New York: Cambridge University Press, 2014.

Stone HM, KO O'Leary, and RL Goldstein. 2003. An introduction to criminal procedure. In *Principles and Practice of Forensic Psychiatry*, 2nd edition, edited by R Rosner, London: Arnold, 796–803.

26

Jail diversion, specialty court, and reentry services: Partnerships between behavioral health and justice systems

DEBRA A. PINALS

INTRODUCTION

There is a growing recognition and discourse surrounding the high prevalence of individuals with mental illness and co-occurring substance use conditions in the criminal and juvenile justice systems. A 2006 report of the Bureau of Justice Statistics showed that at midyear 2005, more than half of those incarcerated in jails and prisons had some type of history of mental health problems, and of those with a mental health problem, approximately three-quarters had a co-occurring substance use problem (James and Glaze 2006). Numerous studies have examined these issues. It has generally been stated that approximately 10%–15% of jail and prison inmates have some form of mental disorder that requires treatment (Hoge et al. 2009). Additionally, men and women in the criminal justice system often have high prevalence of traumatic events in their lifetime. James and Glaze (2006) reported that just over 25% of individuals with mental health issues in jails and prisons had histories of physical or sexual abuse. Wolf and Shi (2012) described that among males incarcerated in prison, rates of childhood physical, sexual, and emotional trauma were high (physical trauma in childhood alone was noted in 44.7% of the population), and that trauma exposure was strongly associated with behavioral and clinical difficulties. Subpopulations, such as female and military veteran offenders present with histories of unique and specific traumatic exposure, with concomitant additional challenges and needs (Saxon et al. 2001; Messina et al. 2014). Criminal justice involvement and incarceration can itself be traumatizing (Miller and Najavits 2012; Pinals and Andrade 2015). It is estimated that between 7% and 9% of community-based offenders who are under the supervision of probation and parole have histories of serious mental illness (Feucht and Gfroerer 2011), and they are at particular risk of re-arrest and re-incarceration.

The reasons for these high prevalence rates of individuals with mental illness with and without co-occurring substance use challenges in correctional populations are multifactorial. Although deinstitutionalization—the downsizing and closing of state psychiatric facilities—has been cited as a main causative factor, there are actually many complicated policy, legal, economic, and other factors that led to the current status (Pinals 2014).

Regardless of the causes, remedies are increasingly being emphasized that include behavioral health and justice system partnerships for innovation in collaborative services (Council of State Governments 2014). For example, efforts have been building to establish what in broad-based terms can be called "jail diversion." Although this is a term that is evolving and shifting to more nuanced approaches and definitions, the general theme for this umbrella term encompasses programs that are designed to divert and redirect individuals from the justice system to alternative treatment-based programs as a more appropriate and effective strategy for their care. This chapter will review the evolution of the concepts related to jail diversion and describe specialty programs that have developed to redirect individuals with mental illness and co-occurring disorders, when appropriate and safe, into alternative services.

FROM JAIL DIVERSION TO SEQUENTIAL INTERCEPT MODELS

Overview of jail diversion

Jail diversion is not a new concept. A review of this topic indicated that the concept of diversion had been a major advocacy position as early as the 1970s to help address the growing population and challenges faced by individuals with mental illness in jails and prisons (Steadman et al.

1994). In that same review, jail diversion was defined as formal and informal programs that screened detainees for mental disorders and used mental health professionals to evaluate those individuals who screened positive. This was followed by a negotiation with justice system professionals to yield a reduction in charges or a disposition outside of a jail setting instead of further prosecution. Further, the definition included programs that focused on a variety of strategies such as linkages to identified community services to reduce pretrial jail time (Steadman et al. 1994). In a large survey of a national sample of jail diversion programs in the mid-1990s, key factors in jail diversion were identified for program development, including (1) integrated services, (2) regular meetings with stakeholders, (3) boundary spanners across systems, (4) strong leadership, (5) early identification of individuals who would benefit from the program, and (6) distinctive case management-type services (Steadman et al. 1995). Though they were not the focus under review in these early descriptions, the authors noted that there were also programs related to pre-arrest jail diversion that operated with police and mental health partnerships.

In a more recent summary of 10 years of experience with jail diversion programing, it was noted that overall, jail diversion programs reduce time in jail and link individuals with mental health and co-occurring substance use disorders to community-based services, all without apparent increase in public safety risk (CMHS National GAINS Center 2007). According to this same review by the National GAINS Center, types of jail diversion that exist include pre-booking and post-booking diversion (see Table 26.1). Pre-booking diversion takes place generally at the point of contact with law enforcement. Post-booking diversion occurs following the arrest and includes the screening, evaluation, negotiation, and linkages for individuals to receive services in the community in lieu of incarceration. These post-booking diversion programs include specialty courts and nonspecialty court models that utilize either a deferred prosecution strategy or a strategy of placing special conditions on the individual through probation. The nonspecialty court models do not require regular court appearances if the individual is adherent with the provisions set out at the initial hearing. Jail-based diversion programs that are also part of the post-booking model can include those initiated by pretrial staff or specialized jail staff that help screen individuals and refer them to community-based services (CMHS National GAINS Center 2007).

Table 26.1 Examples of programs that redirect individuals with behavioral health disorders from deep end justice system involvement to treatment

1. Pre-booking
   a. Police crisis intervention teams
   b. Police and mental health crisis clinician co-response
2. Post-booking
   a. Pretrial diversion programs with local jails
   b. Deferred prosecution programs pre- or post-arraignment
   c. Specialty courts
      i. Drug courts
      ii. Mental health courts
      iii. Veterans treatment courts
      iv. Homelessness courts

Jail diversion programs thus incorporate many types of designs and services linking behavioral health with criminal justice. Over the last several years, in addition to focusing on individuals with mental illness, there has been increased emphasis on co-occurring substance use disorders and, given the high prevalence of trauma in the correctional population, recognition that all diversion strategies must take into account trauma-informed approaches (Osher and Steadman 2007). With jail diversion programs increasingly recognizing the complex interaction of one's trauma history and downstream sequelae, targeted interventions have been successfully developed that include screening for trauma and then building program models that address these factors.

Of note, although the definitions described above can be used in many jurisdictions, refined concepts of diversion occur in local jurisdictions. For example, from a pure criminal justice lens, some criminal justice professionals articulate that true diversion is only diversion if at the end of the effort, the criminal case is disposed of so there are no criminal charges on the individual's permanent record. Programs operating under this principle would necessarily be those that attach prior to the arraignment or the filing of the criminal complaint. By diverting an individual early, none of the collateral consequences (such as difficulties obtaining housing, specific employment, etc.) of a criminal record follow the individual. Given these nuances, it is important when working on collaborative models to ensure that the language and meaning of diversion is well-understood and accepted by all stakeholders in any particular jurisdiction. In this chapter, the word "diversion" is used to refer to the general meaning of those programs and services that help decrease jail days or deeper end involvement in the justice system for a targeted group of individuals with behavioral health disorders.

The initial logic behind diversion approaches was that if one could identify and enroll appropriate individuals with mental illness and link them to comprehensive and appropriate services in the community, there could be improved mental health outcomes, which would directly lead to improved public safety (CMHS National GAINS Center 2007). Over the years, research has increasingly demonstrated the need to focus on more than just mental health outcomes to enhance public safety, and as noted above programs increasingly target substance use disorders and other criminogenic risk factors that have been demonstrated as being more contributory to public safety outcomes and recidivism than mental illness (Osher et al. 2012).

For many of the diversion programs, the focus on reduced recidivism is accomplished through efforts that align with the Risk–Need–Responsivity (RNR) model (Andrews and Bonta 2010). Because many people with mental illness commit crimes for the same reasons as people without mental illness (Fisher et al. 2014), the direct benefit of reduced recidivism from jail diversion programs seems most likely if the criminogenic factors are a focus of the intervention. Traditional clinical services have not embraced or incorporated these concepts yet. Although this model has been increasingly described relevant to jail diversion programs and seems promising, it has also been noted that there is more to learn and understand, and some caution needed, relative to its application to individuals with mental illness (Skeem et al. 2015). A more detailed discussion of the RNR framework is beyond the scope of this chapter but is noteworthy as this is an increasingly emphasized sorting approach to help determine who can benefit most from particular diversion strategies.

Introduction of the sequential intercept framework

As jail diversion programs have increased, collaborations and conversations between behavioral health systems and criminal justice systems have also become more common. An organizing framework to build these collaborations was described by Munetz and Griffin (2006) who conceptualized a public health-type framework that allowed for a parallel to primary, secondary, and tertiary prevention of further penetration of individuals with mental illness in the justice system. Specifically, they described what is known at the Sequential Intercept Model (SIM; see Figure 26.1). This framework depicts the criminal justice system along a continuum and describes how it can offer several potential points of interception at which individuals with serious mental illness could be identified and then linked to community services in lieu of incarceration.

Since its initial description, the SIM model has helped many jurisdictions build services in a fashion that is organized around these intercept points. Recently, SIM workshops have also become more common (Policy Research Associates 2014). The framework has been used also to focus on specific populations beyond those with serious mental illness. For example, certain veterans' services have been examined to ensure appropriate linkages for justice involved veterans across the criminal justice intercepts (Blue-Howells et al. 2013). Similar frameworks pointing out areas for intervention have been promoted to help redirect youth with mental health challenges into treatment services from the juvenile justice system (Skowyra and Cocozza 2006). The National GAINS Center, funded through the Substance Abuse and Mental Health Services Administration (referenced noted above), has promoted a pictorial representation of the SIM upon which behavioral health and other systems can map their services, and allow for further conversation related to gaps and needs. By fostering collaborative discussion, systems can enhance diversion strategies of all types across all points of the justice system. Next we turn to examine diversion strategies at specific intercept points.

POLICE-BASED DIVERSION

If one looks at the criminal justice system as a funnel, the most robust impact for diversion could be considered at the level of law enforcement. Fisher and colleagues examined data regarding consumers of state mental health services over 10 years and found that 28% had experienced at least one arrest (Fisher et al. 2006). Deane and colleagues (1999) found that about 7% of police contacts across numerous police departments and cities involved an individual with mental illness. For decades there has been the recognition that police play a critical role in decisions to arrest or to potentially help individuals with mental illness (Liberman 1969; Lamb et al. 2002) by directing them to treatment. Because of the high prevalence of arrest among individuals with mental illness, these decision points are critical. The degree of discretion an officer has with regard to the outcome of a particular encounter can vary greatly, and officers are often faced with choices with regard to what type of disposition may follow. Teplin and Pruett (1992) described the police as "streetcorner psychiatrists" and noted that there were numerous variables that contributed to officer decisions regarding the handling of particular encounters with individuals with mental illness. A more recent study out of Australia found that the severity of presenting symptoms and the officer's attitudes toward people with mental illness were most highly related to how officers would likely respond to a series of vignettes (Godfredson et al. 2010). Another study found that neighborhood factors were associated with decisions of police to refer individuals to services (Krishan et al. 2014).

Police-based diversion strategies have emerged as critical to decreasing the front door to the criminal justice system

Intercept 1	Intercept 2	Intercept 3	Intercept 4	Intercept 5
• Law Enforcement • Emergency Services	Booking and Initial Court Appearance	Jails and Courts	• Jail Reentry • Prison Reentry	• Community Corrections • Probation • Parole

Figure 26.1 Sequential Intercept Opportunities. (Adapted from Munetz MR and PA Griffin. 2006. *Psychiatry Services* 57(4):544–549; SAMHSA National GAINS Center 2014.)

when appropriate and safe. In some cases, these programs have been developed after highly publicized incidents of fatal shootings of an individual with mental illness by law enforcement. Others have evolved by interest in avoiding such circumstances or by the growing interest in developing community solutions to the challenges faced when persons with mental illness may have difficulty or reluctance in accessing services and then engage in behaviors that come to the attention of the police.

There are several main strategies related to law enforcement or pre-arrest diversion, which can be categorized based on the primary agency responsible for the response and based on the type of professional primarily responding to the situation (Borum 2000; Pinals and Price 2010). A police-based specialized police response involves a specially trained police officer who has specific knowledge regarding mental illness and mental health resources who responds to a scene. In a police-based specialized mental health response, there are mental health clinicians who are stationed within the police department to accompany the police for calls involving "emotionally disturbed persons" and to assist with follow-up visits and other activities. These events, when a clinician goes to a scene with the police, are often called "ride-alongs" or "co-responder" models. Finally, a mental health-based specialized mental health response includes services also known as mobile crisis services. These programs are generally funded through community-based mental health centers, Departments of Mental Health, or through providers that serve mental health needs of a region. These programs become familiar with the regional resources and often develop formal partnerships and memorandums of agreement with local police, so that they can develop the capacity for joint responses to specific crisis calls.

One of the critical areas in police-directed diversion is in providing officers with the training needed to best respond to situations involving individuals with mental illness. Crisis Intervention Team (CIT) training involves a 40-hour curriculum for a proportion of officers within a police department, who then become part of a specialized response team that can provide for improved recognition of the signs and symptoms of mental illness and the transition of individuals to treatment services instead of arrest. This model was developed in Memphis after a tragic incident involving a police officer's use of lethal force toward an individual who had mental illness. The goals of the program involve the training but also emphasize development of linkages to drop-off sites for immediate treatment access, as well as policies and procedures to better manage individuals in crisis and develop collaborations between police and treatment service agencies. The curriculum is broad and includes areas such as an overview of mental illness, direct lectures by persons with mental health challenges in recovery and tours to their living facilities, as well as training on de-escalation techniques (Schwarzfeld et al. 2008).

Studies of CIT have demonstrated its advantages in terms of decreased injuries to officers (Dupont and Cochran 2000; Reuland et al. 2009). Findings demonstrate the effectiveness in CIT officers making referrals to community services in lieu of arrest (Reuland et al. 2009; Compton et al. 2014). Hundreds of communities have initiated CIT development, and interest in the model continues to grow exponentially (Compton et al. 2008).

As noted, the model of specialized mental health response that partners with police is often referred to as the co-responder model. It was first formally developed as a way to enhance linkages of individuals with mental illness to appropriate services. The model evolved to include building pairs of specially trained officers who jointly responded to community crisis scenes with specialized mental health professionals (Reuland et al. 2009). Jurisdictions that utilize this model have shown success in diverting individuals who otherwise may have been arrested. Data from Massachusetts programs that have included both CIT and co-responder programs, for example, show a number of types of criminal charges that were averted or delayed to allow the individual to receive treatment intervention (Orr and Pinals 2014).

Lamb and colleagues (2002) articulated the value of police and mental health partnerships but also spoke of the importance of clarifying roles and responsibilities of mental health professionals and law enforcement as police responses were beginning to be examined. The Council of State Governments Justice Center, in partnership with the Police Executive Research Forum, carved out 10 essential elements to improving police responses for people with mental illness (Schwarzfeld et al. 2008). The elements range from collaborative planning and implementation, specialized training, and protocols related to information exchange, custodial transfer, disposition planning, and program evaluation, to name a few (Schwarzfeld et al. 2008). This type of roadmap has assisted with community development of these models. Several states now have such police diversion programs statewide (Reuland et al. 2012).

Although CIT and other pre-booking models of diversion were developed in large part to better redirect individuals with serious mental illness, additional focus has been on other populations. For example, CIT training most typically now includes training related to veterans and the trauma-informed approaches to utilize. In addition, a youth version of CIT, called CIT-Y, has also been promoted, and this can encompass training for school resource officers and line police, as well as partnerships with police, schools, and child-serving agencies, given the prevalence of arrests that seem to take place on school grounds, and the high proportion of youth with behavioral health conditions in the juvenile justice system (National Alliance on Mental Illness 2014; see also the National Center on Mental Health and Juvenile Justice at http://www.ncmhjj.com/). Additionally, police-based diversion programs are being built that also serve individuals with significant substance use issues, again in an effort to avoid arrest if treatment is needed and reasonable. At times, when the manifest behavior allows for police discretion, frustration with wait times in emergency rooms or a limited likelihood of retaining the patient in treatment can result in decisions to take someone into custody. Because of this, communities are also building alternatives that allow police options that maximize their efficiency as well as maximize the likelihood of the individual accessing treatment as soon as possible. For example, the San Antonio "Restoration Center" was created as an additional response to overcrowding in the local jail and the high prevalence of individuals with mental illness and co-occurring disorders among the population (National Public Radio 2014).

As more locales tackle better responses to individuals in the community who present with behavioral health crises, and more people are potentially diverted from arrest, it is important to address any service gaps to avoid repeated cycling. Creative collaborative models therefore catalyze community innovations making diversion programs meaningful to address the original goals of redirecting people away from the justice system and into treatment. Significant savings were reported related to the Restoration Center, both from the jail costs and from police overtime costs. More information over time will undoubtedly emerge about these types of cooperative diversion programs as community partnerships strengthen.

SPECIALTY COURTS AND OTHER COURT-BASED MODELS

Court-based interventions designed to decrease the jail usage and deeper end criminal justice involvement for individuals with mental illness and co-occurring disorders range in type as noted above. One such intervention is through what is referred to as "specialty courts." These consist of devoted court sessions where individuals, either pre-trial or post-adjudication, and as part of court-ordered probation, return to face the judge on a regular basis and work with others to help achieve better outcomes. Agreement to participate in a specialty court is generally done as a way to avert a jail sentence and minimize jail days.

In 1989, the first drug court was established in Miami–Dade County, Florida, and drug courts have increased in number ever since, currently numbering over 2700 across the country (National Association of Drug Court Professionals [NADCP] 2014). Drug courts operate on the model of therapeutic jurisprudence for a participant, who agrees to the terms of the drug court in lieu of incarceration. The "treatment" is delivered through the development of a drug court "team," most often consisting of treatment providers, probation, other courtroom personnel, and led by the presiding justice. Together the team members determine eligibility for drug court participation and then track progress through a series of advancing phases marked by sobriety and enhanced prosocial community engagement. Higher-risk offenders are generally the target population. Treatment phase advances are achieved by the rigorous use of sanctions (including anything from verbal admonishment up to and including brief periods of incarceration) and rewards (including anything from verbal praise to less frequent required appearances in court), leveraging the authority of the presiding judge and the overarching criminal case. There are key components of drug courts that are promulgated by the National Association of Drug Court Professionals (NADCP 2004). These components include a coordinated strategy that governs drug court responses to participant compliance, a nonadversarial approach whereby the participant's due process rights are protected and prosecution and defense promote public safety, as well as monitoring and evaluation to measure effectiveness.

Initial work related to drug court findings was largely anecdotal and qualitative but showed terrific promise, and organizations such as the NADCP and the National Drug Court Institute were born. Rigorous empirical drug court literature is still being produced, which is critically important but complex, especially given the methodological challenges in this body of research, where individual drug courts may vary in significant ways. One review of numerous studies across drug courts found that although arrests of participants may not have decreased, there was an overall reduction in re-conviction and re-incarceration for drug court participants across studies (Brown 2010). More recently, Larsen and colleagues demonstrated that there may be a way to more effectively assist drug court participants as we refine our understanding of subpopulations that may warrant specific interventions (Larsen et al. 2014).

Adult drug courts inspired a series of other specialty court programs, including mental health courts (discussed further below), juvenile drug courts (Henggeler 2007), veterans treatment courts (Pinals 2010), reentry courts, homelessness courts, and others. For each of these interventions, a target population or issue is identified, and the resources needed to assist this individual and to reduce the cycling through the justice system become targeted goals. For example, in a Veterans Treatment Court, on the day of the session, the courtroom is donned with military flags and will have among the observers representatives from veterans service agencies and formal veteran peer supports who stand ready to assist the veterans, screen referrals, and link the veterans to treatment services. Key components for these veterans treatment courts are also developed and promulgated, in large part through the NADCP.

As these models grow, there is recognition of the need to examine the challenges faced by the participants through a lens that encompasses attention to co-occurring substance use, mental health disorders, and trauma histories (Osher and Steadman 2007). For example, Steadman and colleagues helped articulate six steps to improve drug court outcomes for individuals with co-occurring mental health and substance use challenges (Steadman et al. 2013). The steps included understanding the needs of the drug court participants, adapting court structure according to the needs of participants, expanding treatment options to include mental health treatments, building in targeted case management and supervision, and expanding models for collaboration.

There are now hundreds of mental health courts in existence in the United States. These programs developed as another approach to the specialty court movement. These court sessions are viewed as targeting a wide range of individuals with a variety of mental health challenges. The Council of State Governments has produced a series of primers to help direct the field in the development of these programs. Following the theme of key guidelines, in one of their publications (Thompson et al. 2007) they provide the "Essential Elements" of a mental health court, including (1) planning and administration, (2) target population, (3) timely participant identification and linkage to services, (4) terms of participation, (5) informed choice, (6) treatment supports and services, (7) confidentiality, (8) court team, (9) monitoring adherence to court requirements, and (10) sustainability.

Recent literature on mental health courts reported their effectiveness in reducing jail days and increasing participation in community treatments and improved outcomes (Steadman et al. 2011; Goodale et al. 2013). The mental health court research has also examined a variety of nuanced issues about these programs. Studies have shown that programs can be effective even when they take in individuals who were charged with higher-level offenses (Reich et al. 2012), because early mental health courts focused on low-level offenses, though the RNR framework has not generally been the starting place for eligibility for mental health courts. Eligibility seems to rely on a selection process that uses formal and informal criteria, and is influenced by local available mental health services (Wolff et al. 2011). In this way, treatment planning is also somewhat more individualized than is seen in drug courts. In addition, perceived voluntariness and procedural justice were associated with greater program success, that participants receive more community-based mental health services but perhaps insufficient services to address criminal risk factors (Luskin 2013). Also, although participants do well in these types of diversion programs, there may be a high prevalence of them who are incompetent to stand trial, and this issue, along with competence to consent to treatment, likely warrants further attention (Stafford and Wygant 2005). With the growth of mental health courts as community-based alternatives to jails and other institutional settings, cost factors for their success will need to be examined. These programs have been thought of as opportunities for cost savings to the criminal justice system, and it is hoped that with greater stability there would be additional cost savings related to treatment services. However, one recent study showed that there may be additional treatment-related costs associated with them that will require further examination of how best to maximize their effectiveness and efficiencies (Steadman et al. 2014). Overall, however, specialty courts offer one important national approach to alternatives to incarceration that are meant to preserve individual rights and still protect public safety while providing a better service to society.

Additional court-initiated programs that do not require regular appearances in front of a judge can also be considered to fall under the array of "diversion" strategies. In particular, Osher and colleagues describe innovations working with the large number of individuals under community-based correctional supervision (Osher et al. 2012). These approaches include a framework for addressing a multitude of areas of need simultaneously by determining criminogenic needs, followed by ascertaining the level of substance use and mental health needs, and developing treatment programs that can address all three. Using this approach and embedding the RNR framework for planning for services could potentially then better achieve the reduction in recidivism as an outcome variable. One such model that is currently being applied to a variety of diversion services including probation-based court-mandated community services is MISSION-Criminal Justice (see Missionmodel.org; Pinals et al. 2014; Smelson et al. 2014), which incorporates several evidence-based practices using a peer and case management team to provide manualized community-based support and linkage interventions for those individuals with co-occurring disorders who are in the criminal justice system. Such models highlight the importance of decreased criminal recidivism as part of an overall holistic recovery strategy. Other models, such as the Veterans Administration-funded Veterans Justice Outreach program, is an attempt to offer support services for court-involved veterans who may be able to be diverted from jail with such support (Pinals 2010). Peer support services are also attached to specialty courts and other diversion programs.

REENTRY AND COMMUNITY-BASED JUSTICE–BEHAVIORAL HEALTH SERVICES

The transition from incarceration to community living is a period of tremendous stress and uncertainty. Although not considered jail diversion in the purest sense of the term, reentry programming and community-based interventions upon reentry aimed to keep individuals with mental illness and co-occurring substance use disorders from being re-arrested and returning to incarceration are viewed as important prevention strategies. In addition to the risk of re-arrest, morbidity and mortality for individuals with co-occurring disorders coming out of prisons is high (Binswanger et al. 2007). These factors taken together have contributed to a growing trend toward enhanced reentry services.

Over a decade ago, the APIC (Assess, Plan, Identify, Coordinate) model for reentry was asserted as a best practice model for inmates with these types of behavioral health challenges (Osher et al. 2002). This model encompasses necessary components for linking individuals to the right services upon custodial release. A period of in-reach and post-incarceration follow-up appears helpful in smoothing this transition for the individual. Specific service delivery models, such as Critical Time Intervention, a case management model that decreases in intensity over a period of increased stability and acceptance of the transition, has shown positive effects with reentry work with individuals with serious mental illness (Draine and Herman 2007). Community-based multidisciplinary treatment programs, such as Forensic Assertive Community Treatment, have shown a positive effect in decreasing revolving-door trends for individuals with serious mental illness who cycle through the criminal justice system (Lamberti et al. 2004; Cuddeback et al. 2008; Angell et al. 2014). MISSION-Criminal Justice, described above, has been used successfully in reentry services for male and female offenders with co-occurring disorders and trauma histories, and further studies of this are underway. Taken together, these types of programs and efforts recognize the importance of adding re-entry services and community-based behavioral health–criminal justice collaborations as part of the framework of strategies to decrease the criminalization of the participants.

SUMMARY

Police-based pre-booking jail diversion, specialty courts, and reentry services all have the goal of decreasing the involvement of individuals with mental illness and co-occurring substance use disorders in the criminal justice system and redirecting them to treatment. These efforts will undoubtedly continue to grow, and federal funding is rapidly attempting to push innovations to communities to establish enhanced behavioral health and criminal justice collaborative efforts. With these trends, the phenomenon of "decarceration" is likely to create shifts in where these individuals, especially those with criminogenic characteristics, are served. These trends will further inspire the need to have specialized programs available to assist the individuals who have benefitted from them (Lamb and Weinberger 2014). From a risk assessment and risk management perspective, these collaborative programs hold promise as individuals with criminal histories and possible violence history are released and in need of support. Forensic psychiatrists should be familiar with these opportunities to intervene, as they will likely be increasingly providing forensic assessments and treatment as part of these partnerships with criminal justice programs.

SUMMARY KEY POINTS

- Jail diversion can be construed as an umbrella term that encompasses a variety of programs designed to reduce jail days, defer prosecution, and link individuals with mental illness and co-occurring substance use disorders into treatment services.
- Police diversion strategies have shown promise in re-directing individuals to treatment prior to a criminal complaint moving forward.
- Specialty courts include a target population and regular appearances in front of a judge, as well as an array of staff that become part of the specialty court team to address and help reduce recidivism.
- As emerging models of police diversion, specialty courts, and reentry services develop, further research will be needed to understand their effectiveness, as well as cost factors that can inform policy planning.

REFERENCES

Andrews DA and J Bonta. 2010. *The Psychology of Criminal Conduct*. 5th edition. New Providence, NJ: Matthew Bender and Company.

Angell B, E Matthews, S Barrenger, AC Watson, and J Draine. 2014. Engagement process in model programs for community reentry from prison for people with serious mental illness. *International Journal of Law and Psychiatry* 37(5):490–500.

Blue-Howells JH, SC Clark, C van den Berk-Clark, and JF McGuire. 2013. The U.S. Department of Veterans Affairs Veterans Justice Programs and the Sequential Intercept Model: Case examples in national dissemination of intervention for justice-involved veterans. *Psychological Services* 10(1):48–53.

Borum R. 2000. Improving high risk encounters between people with mental illness and the police. *Journal of the American Academy of Psychiatry and the Law* 28(3):332–337.

Brinswagner IA, MF Stern, RA Deyo, PJ Heagerty, A Cheadle, JG Elmore, and TD Kopsell. 2007. Release from prison—A high risk of death for former inmates. *New England Journal of Medicine* 356(2):157–165.

Brown RT. 2010. Systematic review of the impact of adult drug-treatment courts. *Translational Research: The Journal of Laboratory and Clinical Medicine* 155(6):263–274.

CMHS National GAINS Center. 2007. *Practical Advice on Jail Diversion: Ten Years of Learnings on Jail Diversion from the CMHS National GAINS Center*. Delmar, NY: CMHS National GAINS Center.

Compton MT, M Bahora, AC Watson, and JR Olivia. 2008. A comprehensive review of extant research on Crisis Intervention Team (CIT) programs. *Journal of the American Academy of Psychiatry and the Law* 36(1):47–55.

Compton MT, R Bakeman, B Broussard et al. 2014. The police-based crisis intervention team (CIT) model: II. Effects on level of force and resolution, referral, and arrest. *Psychiatric Services* 65(4):523–529.

Council of State Governments Justice Center. Press Release. December 9, 2014. *New Efforts to Reduce the Number of People with Mental Disorders in Jails Set the Stage for Unprecedented Change*. http://csgjusticecenter.org/mental-health/press-releases/new-efforts-to-reduce-the-number-of-people-with-mental-disorders-in-jails-set-the-stage-for-unprecedented-change/, accessed December 12, 2014.

Cuddeback GS, JP Morrissey, and KJ Cusack. 2008. How many forensic assertive community treatment teams do we need? *Psychiatric Services* 59(2):205–208.

Deane MW, HJ Steadman, R Borum, BM Veysey, and JP Morrissey. 1999. Emerging partnerships between mental health and law enforcement. *Psychiatric Services* 50(1):99–101.

Draine J and DB Herman. 2007. Critical time intervention for reentry from prison for persons with mental illness. *Psychiatric Services* 58(12):1577–1581.

Dupont R and S Cochran. 2000. Police response to mental health emergencies-barriers to change. *Journal of the American Academy of Psychiatry and the Law* 42(3):338–344.

Feucht TE and J Gfroerer. 2011. *Mental and Substance Use Disorders Among Adult Men on Probation or Parole: Some Success Against Persistent Challenge*. Rockville, MD: Substance Abuse and Mental Health Services Administration.

Fisher WH, SW Hartwell, X Deng, DA Pinals, C Fulwiler, and KM Roy-Bujnowksi. 2014. Recidivism among released state prison inmates who received mental health treatment while incarcerated. Crime and Delinquency 60(6):811–832.

Fisher WH, KM Roy-Bujnowski, AJ Grudzinskas, JC Clayfield, SM Banks, and N Wolff. 2006. Patterns and prevalence of arrest in a statewide cohort of mental health care consumers. *Psychiatric Services* 57(11):1623–1628.

Godfredson JW, RP Ogloff, DM Thomas, and S Luebbes. 2010. Police discretion encounters with people experiencing mental illness: The significant factors. *Criminal Justice and Behavior* 37(12):1392–1405.

Gold J. 2014. National Public Radio, *Mental Health Cops Help Reweave Social Safety Net in San Antonio*. http://www.npr.org/blogs/health/2014/08/19/338895262/mental-health-cops-help-reweave-social-safety-net-in-san-antonio, accessed December 24, 2014.

Goodale G, L Callahan, and HJ Steadman. 2013. Law and psychiatry: What can we say about mental health courts today? *Psychiatric Services* 64(4):298–300.

Henggeler SW. 2007. Juvenile drug courts: Emerging outcomes and key research issues. *Current Opinion in Psychiatry* 20(3):242–246.

Hoge SK, AW Buchanan, BM Kovasznay, and EJ Roskes. 2009. *Outpatient Services for the Mentally Ill Involved in the Criminal Justice System: A Report of the Task Force on Outpatient Forensic Services*. Arlington, VA: American Psychiatric Association, Resource Document.

James DJ and LE Glaze. 2006. *Mental Health Problems of Prison and Jail Inmates*, Bureau of Justice Statistics Special Reports, NCJ 213600, U.S. Department of Justice, Office of Justice Programs, September 2006.

Krishan S, R Bakeman, B Broussard, SL Cristofaro, D Hankerson-Dyson, L Husbands, AC Watson, and MT Compton. 2014. The influence of neighborhood characteristics on police officers' encounters with persons suspected to have a serious mental illness. *International Journal of Law and Psychiatry* 37(4):359–369.

Lamb HR and LE Weinberger. 2014. Decarceration of U.S. jails and prisons: Where will persons with serious mental illness go? *Journal of the American Academy of Psychiatry and Law* 42(4):489–494.

Lamb HR, LE Weinberger, and WJ DeCuir. 2002. The police and mental health. *Psychiatric Services* 53(10):1266–1271.

Lamberti JS, R Weisman, and DI Faden. 2004. Forensic assertive community treatment: Preventing incarceration of adults with severe mental illness. *Psychiatric Services* 55(11):1285–1293.

Larsen JL, K Nylund-Gibson, and M Cosden. 2014. Using latent class analysis to identify participant typologies in drug treatment court. *Drug and Alcohol Dependence* 1(138):75–82.

Liberman R. 1969. Police as a community mental health resource. *Community Mental Health Journal* 5(2):111–120.

Luskin M. 2013. More of the same? Treatment in mental health courts. *Law and Human Behavior* 37(4):255–266.

Messina N, S Calhoun, and J Braithwaite. 2014. Trauma-informed treatment decreases posttraumatic stress disorder among women offenders. *Journal of Trauma and Dissociation* 16(1):6–23.

Miller NA and LM Najavits. 2012. Creating trauma-informed correctional care: A balance of goals and environment. *European Journal of Psychotraumatology* 3:17246. doi:10.3402/ejpt.v.20.17246

Munetz MR and PA Griffin. 2006. Use of the Sequential Intercept Model as an approach to decriminalization of people with serious mental illness. *Psychiatry Services* 57(4):544–549.

National Alliance on Mental Illness. 2014. *CIT for Youth Resource Center*. http://www.nami.org/template.cfm?section=CIT_for_Youth, accessed December 21, 2014.

National Association of Drug Court Professionals. 2014. *Drug Court History*. http://www.nadcp.org/learn/what-are-drug-courts/drug-court-history, accessed December 18, 2014.

National Association of Drug Court Professionals. Drug Court Standards Committee. 2004, October. *Defining Drug Courts: The Key Components*. U.S. Department of Justice, Office of Justice Programs, Bureau of Justice Assistance. NCJ 205621.

Orr K and DA Pinals. 2014. *Pre-arrest Law Enforcement-Based Jail Diversion Program Report: July 1, 2011 to January 1, 2014*. Massachusetts Department of Mental Health Forensic Services, http://www.mass.gov/eohhs/gov/departments/dmh/forensic-services.html, accessed December 21, 2014.

Osher FC, DA D'Amora, M Plotkin, N Jarrett, and A Eggleston. 2012. Adults with behavioral health needs under correctional supervision: A shared framework for reducing recidivism and promoting recovery. *Council of State Governments Justice Center, Criminal Justice/Mental Health Consensus Project*. Lexington, KY: Council of State Governments.

Osher FC and HJ Steadman. 2007. Adapting evidence-based practices for persons with mental illness involved with the criminal justice system. *Psychiatric Services* 58(11):1472–1478.

Osher FC, HJ Steadman and H Barr. 2002. *A Best Practice Approach to Community Re-Entry from Jails for Inmates with Co-Occurring Disorders: The APIC Model*. Delmar, NY: National GAINS Center, http://gainscenter.samhsa.gov/pdfs/reentry/apic.pdf, accessed December, 20, 2014.

Pinals DA. 2010. Veterans in the justice system: The next forensic frontier. Journal of the American Academy of Psychiatry and the Law 38(2):163–167.

Pinals DA. 2014. Forensic services, public mental health policy, and financing: Charting the course ahead. *Journal of the American Academy of Psychiatry and the Law* 42(1):7–19.

Pinals DA and JT Andrade. 2015. Recovery in correctional settings. In *The Oxford Textbook of Correctional Psychiatry*, edited by R Trestman, J Metzner, and K Appelbaum, New York: Oxford University Press, 217–222.

Pinals DA and M Price. 2010. Law enforcement and psychiatry. In *The American Psychiatric Publishing Textbook of Forensic Psychiatry*, 2nd edition, edited by R Simon and L Gold, Washington, DC: American Psychiatric Publishing, 413–452.

Pinals DA, DA Smelson, L Sawh, J Harter, and D Ziedonis. 2014. *Maintaining Independence and Sobriety through Systems Integration, Outreach, and Networking—Criminal Justice Edition. Treatment Manual*. Available at www.missionmodel.org, accessed July 17, 2016.

Policy Research Associates. *Sequential Intercept Mapping*. http://www.prainc.com/sequential-intercept-mapping/, accessed December, 21, 2014.

Reich WA, S Picard-Fritsche, L Cerniglia, and JW Hahn. 2012. *Predictors of Program Compliance and Re-arrest in the Brooklyn Mental Health Court*. New York: Center for Court Innovation. http://www.courtinnovation.org, accessed December 21, 2014.

Reuland M, L Draper, and N Blake. 2012. *Statewide Law Enforcement/Mental Health Efforts: Strategies to Support and Sustain Local Initiatives*. New York: Council of State Governments Justice Center for the Bureau of Justice Assistance, Office of Justice Programs, U.S. Department of Justice.

Reuland M, M Schwarzfeld, and L Draper. 2009. *Law Enforcement Responses to People with Mental Illness: A Guide to Research-Informed Policy and Practice*. New York: Council of State Governments, Justice Center.

Saxon AJ, TM Davis, KL Sloan, KM McKnight, ME McFall, and DR Kivlahan. 2001. Trauma, symptoms of Posttraumatic Stress Disorder, and associated problems among incarcerated veterans. *Psychiatric Services* 52(7):959–964.

Schwarzfeld M, M Reuland, and M Plotkin. 2008. *Improving Responses to People with Mental Illness: The Essential Elements of a Specialized Law Enforcement-Based Program*. New York: Council of State Governments Justice Center and the Police Executive Research Forum for the Bureau of Justice Assistance, Office of Justice Programs, U.S. Department of Justice.

Skeem JL, HJ Steadman, and SM Manchak. 2015. Applicability of the risk-need-responsivity model to persons with mental illness involved in the criminal justice system. *Psychiatric Services* 66(9):916–922.

Skowyra K and JJ Cocozza. 2006. *A Blueprint for Change: Improving the System Response to Youth*. Delmar, NY: National Center for Mental Health and Juvenile Justice.

Smelson D, DA Pinals, J Harter, L Sawh, and D Ziedonis. 2014. *Maintaining Independence and Sobriety through Systems Integration and Outreach Networking—Criminal Justice Edition. Participant Workbook*. http://www.missionmodel.org, accessed December 21, 2014.

Stafford KP and DB Wygant. 2005. The role of competency to stand trial in mental health courts. *Behavioral Sciences and the Law* 23(2):245–258.

Steadman HJ, SS Barbera, and DL Dennis. 1994. A national survey of jail diversion programs for mentally ill detainees. *Hospital and Community Psychiatry* 45(11):1109–1113.

Steadman HJ, L Callahan, PC Robbins, R Vesselinov, TG McGuire, and JP Morrissey. 2014. Criminal justice and behavioral health care costs of mental health court participants: A six-year study. *Psychiatric Services* 65(9):1100–1104.

Steadman HJ, SM Morris, and DL Dennis. 1995. The diversion of mentally ill persons from jails to community-based services: A profile of programs. *American Journal of Public Health* 85(12):1630–1635.

Steadman HJ, RH Peters, C Carpenter et al. 2013. *Six Steps to Improve Your Drug Court Outcomes for Adults with Co-occurring Disorders*. National Drug Court Institute and the SAMHSA GAINS Center for Behavioral Health and Justice Transformation. http://gainscenter.samhsa.gov/cms-assets/documents/200790-422255.r1-ndci-gains-six-steps-cod-2013.pdf, accessed July 7, 2015.

Steadman HJ, A Redlich, L Callahan, PC Robbins, and Vesselinov R. 2011. Effect of mental health courts on arrest and jail days: A multisite study. *Archives of General Psychiatry* 68(2):167–172.

Substance Abuse and Mental Health Services Administration (SAMHSA) National GAINS Center. 2014. Sequential Intercept Mapping model. Policy Research Associates, Inc., Delmar, New York.

Teplin, LA and NS Pruett. 1992. Police as street-corner psychiatrist: Managing the mentally ill. *International Journal of Law and Psychiatry* 15(2):139–156.

Thompson M, F Osher, and D Tomasini-Joshi. 2007. *Improving Responses with Mental Illness: The Essential Elements of a Mental Health Court*. New York: Council of State Governments Justice Center.

Wolff N and J Shi. 2012. Childhood and adult trauma experiences of incarcerated persons and their relationship to adult behavioral health problems and treatment. *International Journal of Environmental Research and Public Health* 9(5):1908–1926.

Wolff N, N Fabrikant, and S Belenko. 2011. Mental health courts and their selection processes: Modeling variation for consistency. *Law and Human Behavior* 35(5):402–412.

27

Criminal competencies

STEPHEN G. NOFFSINGER AND PHILLIP J. RESNICK

INTRODUCTION

An arrest sets in motion the events of criminal prosecution: booking, arraignment, discovery, plea negotiations, trial, sentencing (if convicted), and possible appeal. The recent arrest rate in the United States was 3888 arrests/100,000 persons, resulting in more than 12,000,000 arrests annually (Federal Bureau of Investigation 2012).

Mentally ill defendants are overrepresented in the criminal justice system (Skeem et al. 2011, 110), because they have a significantly greater chance of arrest (Teplin 1984, 800). Therefore, a substantial number of mentally disordered individuals are prosecuted through the criminal justice system in the United States. Mental disorders potentially impact defendants' ability to competently defend themselves from prosecution. Accordingly, forensic psychiatrists are frequently requested to evaluate criminal defendants' competence to participate in one or more phases of criminal prosecution.

CONCEPT OF COMPETENCE

Competence generally involves the ability to understand a body of knowledge and rationally apply that knowledge to a decision-making process. Competence refers to a mental state at a specific point in time. Mental illness can fluctuate over time; therefore, competence may also vary over time. Evaluating competence may be a present-state (e.g., competence for medical decisions) or a retrospective evaluation (e.g., competence to execute a will on a past date).

Assessing most criminal competencies involves evaluating the defendant's present mental state. Infrequently, a defendant's competence to stand trial, confess, plead guilty, or waive counsel is the basis of a post-conviction appeal—in these circumstances the evaluator retrospectively assesses the defendant's mental state and competence (*U.S. v. Bergmann* 2010; Kapalczynski and Noffsinger 2011, 581).

A mental disorder does not automatically indicate incompetence. Even a severely mentally disordered individual may be competent if his or her symptoms do not impair the mental functioning required for competence. However, a single delusion may render a well-appearing individual incompetent. An otherwise competent defendant with the single delusion that his or her attorney is demonic may be incompetent to stand trial, because the defendant's delusion may cause him or her to irrationally resist cooperating with the attorney.

Prior to the 1960s the concept of global incompetence was embraced—a person adjudicated incompetent in one area was deemed incompetent in all areas (Appelbaum and Gutheil 2007, 227). Many state laws indicated that civilly committed patients, based on their status as an involuntarily hospitalized patient, were incompetent to make decisions about their financial affairs, treatment, voting, and marrying. Beginning in the 1950s–1960s, courts, clinicians, and legislators realized that mental disorders may *selectively* impair functioning. With that realization the concept of specific competencies evolved, and more than 30 types of competence are now defined in law. Hence, an adjudication of incompetence in one area no longer means incompetence in other areas.

COMPETENCE TO STAND TRIAL

Criminal defendants have the right to be tried only if competent to stand trial (*Pate v. Robinson* 1966). Trying only competent defendants safeguards the accuracy of adjudication, ensures the fairness of the adversarial process, maintains the dignity of the court, and, if convicted, guarantees that the defendant knows why he or she is being punished (Ausness 1978, 666; Barnard et al. 1991, 367). Trials are more reliable when the defendant is competent (Bonnie 1990, 427). Fairness demands that the defendant know what is happening during the trial and contribute to his or her defense, and the dignity of the law is protected when a convicted defendant knows why he or she is being punished (Buchanan 2006, 458).

The U.S. Constitution guarantees defendants facing trial specific rights, including the Sixth Amendment's right to assistance of counsel and right to confront witnesses, and the Fourteenth Amendment's rights to substantive and procedural due process of law. Mental illness may impact a defendant's ability to exercise these rights. Mentally disordered defendants may be unable to cooperate with counsel and/or confront adversarial witnesses, effectively denying Sixth Amendment rights. Trying an incompetent defendant is fundamentally unfair, in violation of the substantive due process clause of the Fourteenth Amendment. Mentally disordered defendants may not be able to understand and exercise Fourteenth Amendment procedural due process rights.

History of competence to stand trial

The common law doctrine that defendants must be mentally competent to stand trial has been part of the criminal law for centuries (Ausness 1978, 666). The concept of trial competence began in thirteenth-century trials before the king's court in England. Defendants who failed to enter a plea were given three warnings by the court, and then confined and starved (*prison forte et dure*) or gradually crushed under increasing weights (*peine forte et dure*) (Statute of Westminster 1275) until they entered a plea or died (Grubin 1996). The phrase "to press someone for an answer" originated here. Before engaging such methods, the king's court investigated whether the defendant was intentionally withholding a plea (mute by malice), or whether, due to a mental defect, was unable to understand that a plea was required of him or her (mute by visitation of God). Defendants mute by visitation of God were spared the methods described above and a not guilty plea was entered for them. The difficulty in trying an incompetent defendant was recognized by courts as early as 1353 (Walker 1968, 219).

Legal standards for trial competence developed during subsequent centuries. In the Somervile trial (1583), the defendant was thought to be incompetent only if "absolutely mad." The Dyle trial (1756) specified a defendant's incompetence "if not of sound mind or memory." The most detailed early nineteenth-century competence standard came from Pritchard's trial (1836) that required that "the prisoner has sufficient understanding to comprehend the nature of the trial, so as to make a proper defence to the charge...sufficient intellect to comprehend the course of proceedings at trial, so as to make a proper defence—to know that he might challenge any of you to whom he may object—and to comprehend the details of the evidence."

Competence to stand trial standards

The U.S. Supreme Court articulated American trial competence standards in *Dusky v. United States* (1960), which inquires "whether the defendant has sufficient present ability to consult with his lawyer with a reasonable degree of rational understanding—and whether he has a rational as well as factual understanding of the proceedings against him." While *Dusky* did not require that mental illness be the basis for incompetence, the subsequently adopted federal Insanity Defense Reform Act (1984) required a present mental disease/defect as the cause of incompetence.

American states adopted trial competence standards similar to the *Dusky* standard. State and federal standards indicate that defendants are incompetent to stand trial if their mental illness makes them (1) unable to understand the nature and objectives of the proceedings and/or (2) unable to assist in their defense.

Evaluating competence to stand trial

Trying an incompetent defendant risks erroneous conviction; therefore, defense attorneys often request evaluation of their client's trial competence. Prosecutors and judges are also concerned about the mentally disordered defendant's trial competence. Trying an incompetent defendant may lead to an appeal of any conviction, and justice is not served by trying an incompetent defendant.

Defense attorneys question their client's trial competency in 8%–15% of felony prosecutions (Hoge et al. 1992, 389; Poythress et al. 1994, 439). Evaluations are sought due to a history of mental illness; behavior suggesting a mental disorder (currently or during the offense); and/or an uncooperative or irrational client (*Drope v. Missouri* 1975). The defense most often requests for a competence assessment, triggering the court to order the evaluation.

Competence to stand trial evaluations are among the most common court-ordered evaluations—approximately 60,000 are performed annually in America (Mossman et al. 2007, S3). Most are performed as an outpatient, although an inpatient evaluation may be arranged for the defendant who is uncooperative or suspected of malingering (Grisso et al. 1994; Soliman and Resnick 2010, 624). Approximately 20%–30% of defendants evaluated for trial competency are opined incompetent to stand trial (Cooper and Zapf 2003, 429).

The competence evaluation methodology includes the following:

1. Reviewing the defendant's relevant medical records.
2. Reviewing relevant collateral sources of information (school records, interview family members, etc.).
3. Personally interviewing the defendant, including:
    a. A psychiatric diagnostic interview and mental status examination. The defendant's orientation, memory, concentration, mood, affect and the presence of delusions, hallucinations and loose associations are especially relevant.
    b. Inquiring into the specific areas of competency to stand trial (see below).
4. Providing a written report with a well-reasoned opinion by applying the facts of the case to the competence standard in the relevant jurisdiction.

Most jurisdictions prohibit information obtained during a competence evaluation from being used to prove a defendant's guilt (e.g., O.R.C. 2945.371J). The defendant's confession made during a competency evaluation is inadmissible at trial.

The question sometimes arises as to whether the defendant is competent to consent to a competence to stand trial assessment. In the event that the examiner suspects that defendant lacks capacity to give informed consent for the competence evaluation, the evaluator should nevertheless proceed with the evaluation. The examiner is acting pursuant to a court order, and practically speaking, the court must be informed of the defendant's likely incompetence.

Specific inquiries are made during a competence to stand trial evaluation. The following areas should be examined (Resnick and Noffsinger 2004, 333):

1. Ability to Understand Nature and Objectives of Proceedings:
   a. Charges—The defendant must be able to understand the charges and the nature of the conduct alleged.
   b. Role as defendant—Defendants should be able to understand that they are charged with a crime and are facing prosecution (Bonnie et al. 1997, 250). A defendant delusionally believing that he is immune from prosecution is likely incompetent.
   c. Severity of charge—A defendant should be able to understand the severity of the charge and the possible range of penalties.
   d. Pleas—A defendant should be able to understand the pleas of Guilty, Not Guilty, No Contest, and Not Guilty by Reason of Insanity (and Alford pleas and Guilty but Mentally Ill, in some jurisdictions).
   e. Courtroom personnel roles—A defendant should be able to understand the roles of the defendant, defense attorney, judge, prosecutor, jury, witness, and victim.
   f. Adversarial nature of trial—A defendant should be able to understand which court personnel are acting adversely to their interests and demonstrate self-protective behavior.
2. Ability to Assist in Defense:
   a. Cooperate with defense attorney—A defendant must be able to have rational discussions and communicate relevant information to his or her defense attorney, and be free of paranoid ideas about the attorney. An incoherent or mute defendant is likely to be incompetent (Bonnie et al. 1997, 250).
   b. Understand plea bargaining—Approximately 85% of defendants plea bargain—pleading guilty in exchange for reduced charges, reduced sentence, or both. Defendants must understand the concept of plea bargaining and be able to rationally make decisions about plea bargaining.
   c. Willingness to consider mental-disorder defense—A defendant must possess sufficient insight into his or her illness to consider pleading Not Guilty by Reason of Insanity (Reisner et al. 2013, 88), Guilty but Mentally Ill, or seeking mitigation due to mental illness, if relevant. Otherwise competent defendants who irrationally refuse a mental-disorder defense may have such a defense imposed on them by the court and proceed to trial (*Frendak v. United States* 1979).
   d. Appraisal of evidence and estimate of likely outcome of trial—A defendant should be able to determine which evidence is helpful/harmful to the case; reasonably estimate the chances of conviction; and apply this information in deciding whether to accept a plea bargain.
   e. Attention, memory and concentration—A defendant should be able to pay attention during trial, and have sufficient memory to retain and apply the information during trial.
   f. Understand appropriate courtroom behavior—A defendant should be able to understand and exercise appropriate courtroom demeanor. It is important to differentiate between a defendant who (due to illness) is incapable of acting appropriately from a defendant who elects to act inappropriately.
   g. Rational account of offense—A defendant should be able to give a consistent and organized account of the offense. Such an account may help to achieve alibi, acquittal, insanity, or mitigation. However, a defendant with permanent amnesia for the offense is not categorically incompetent to stand trial (*Wilson v. United States* 1968).
   h. Formulate defense plan—A defendant should be able to work with his or her attorney to develop a basic plan of defense, working toward the goal of acquittal or mitigation.
   i. Make reasonable defense decisions—Using his or her knowledge of the information listed above, a defendant should be able to rationally apply that knowledge to his or her defense and make reasonable, logic-driven decisions (Morris et al. 2004, 243; Felthous 2011, 27).
   j. Freedom from self-defeating behavior—A defendant should be motivated to seek the best possible outcome for his or her trial. Defendants who seek an unfavorable outcome, due to mental illness, may be incompetent to stand trial.
   k. Testify at trial—A defendant should be able to give rational, organized, and logical trial testimony that may assist in his or her defense. A defendant should also be able to withstand the stress of testifying and being subject to cross-examination.

Competence to stand trial structured assessment instruments

Many structured instruments have been developed to assess trial competence: the Competency Screening Test (Lipsitt et al. 1971); Competency to Stand Trial Assessment Instrument (U.S. Department of Health 1973); Interdisciplinary Fitness Interview (Golding et al. 1984); Competence Assessment for Standing Trial for Defendants with Mental Retardation—CAST*MR (Everington 1990); and Georgia Court Competency Test (Nicholson et al.

1988). Some instruments are of limited utility, as they assess a defendant's factual understanding, but not reasoning ability (Hoge et al. 1997, 144). In recent years, additional competence assessment tools have been introduced, including the Computer-Assisted Determination of Competency to Stand Trial (CADCOMP) (Barnard et al. 1991); Evaluation of Competency to Stand Trial-Revised (ECST-R) (Rogers et al. 2004); and Inventory of Legal Knowledge (ILK) (Otto et al. 2011). Canadian researchers have developed the Fitness Interview test to address the Canadian competency standard (Zapf et al. 2001, 426).

The MacArthur Competence Assessment Tool—Criminal Adjudication (Mac-CAT-CA) assesses "adjudicative competence" that includes competence to enter a plea, stand trial, and participate in pretrial proceedings (Hoge et al. 1997). The Mac-CAT-CA assesses factual knowledge and decisional competence.

Structured competency assessment instruments are not diagnostic tests that decide whether a defendant is competent to stand trial. Rather, the instruments' designers recommend that clinicians consider test results as one source of information, interpreting those results in light of the clinical interview and other relevant data (Mossman et al. 2007, S43). The recent trend has been for examiners to increasingly utilize standardized assessments as one source of data when conducting competence evaluations (Rogers and Johansson-Love 2009, 459).

Outcome of competence evaluation

Competence to stand trial is addressed by the court in a competency hearing (*Pate v. Robinson* 1966; *Drope v. Missouri* 1975) and is a legal question adjudicated by a judge. There is a presumption of competence to stand trial. Preponderance of the evidence is the standard of proof required to prove incompetence (*Cooper v. Oklahoma* 1996). An incompetent defendant may not be convicted (*Pate v. Robinson* 1966). Clinical competency opinions are admitted into evidence at a competency hearing. Courts usually (up to 90%) base the adjudication of competence on the opinion of the court-appointed clinician (Reich and Tookey 1986; Freckelton 1996).

Most defendants examined for competence to stand trial are opined competent (Cooper and Zapf 2003, 429). A mental disorder is insufficient to conclude that a defendant is incompetent. In one study, almost one-third of defendants opined competent to stand trial had a psychotic disorder (Roesch et al. 1981, 151). In addition to a mental disorder, incompetence requires that the mental disorder impair the defendant's performance in the specific functional areas relevant to competence. Examiner decisions of competence appear to be unbiased and relate primarily to a defendant's functional ability (Cooper and Zapf 2003, 423).

Approximately 20%–30% of defendants evaluated for competence to stand trial are adjudicated incompetent (Nicholson and Kugler 1991; Cooper and Zapf 2003, 429; Pirelli et al. 2011, 13), although there is a wide range (4%–77%) of incompetency rates in different jurisdictions (Cochrane et al. 2001). Approximately 37%–50% of geriatric defendants are found incompetent (Heinik et al. 1994; Frierson et al. 2002). Males and females are equally likely to be found incompetent (Riley 1998, 229).

Younger adults are likely incompetent due to psychosis, mood disorder, or intellectual disability, while older defendants are likely incompetent due to dementia (Frierson et al. 2002). Positive psychotic symptoms, particularly conceptual disorganization and delusional thinking, are significantly associated with incompetence (James, 2001, 139; Lee et al. 2014, 1010). Preteens and young adolescents are frequently incompetent due to their inability to disclose relevant data to counsel, susceptibility to outside influence, inability to appraise the quality of legal representation, and difficulty making defense decisions (McKee 1998; Slovenko 2000).

Severity of the charge has little effect on incompetency rates, although recent authors suggest that complicated legal cases require a larger degree of mental capacity. Therefore, the competence required to stand trial on serious charges should be greater than for minor charges (Buchanan 2006, 459; Buchanan 2008, 352).

Feigning incompetence to stand trial is a legitimate concern. Defendants facing possible conviction may have a motive to avoid trial. Estimates of feigned incompetence range from 8% to 21% (Soliman and Resnick 2010, 614).

Clinicians opining that a defendant is incompetent to stand trial must make a prediction whether the defendant is likely to be restored to competence, given treatment. The U.S. Supreme Court ruled in *Jackson v. Indiana* (1972) that a defendant cannot be held for more than the reasonable period of time necessary to determine whether there is substantial probability that he or she will attain competency in the future.

Defendants adjudicated incompetent to stand trial are usually committed to a hospital for competency restoration treatment. Approximately 7000–9000 defendants are involuntarily committed to public hospitals annually for competency restoration (Steadman and Hartstone 1983; Davis, 1985), although that number is likely much higher in recent years. A growing number of incompetent defendants are unable to access needed mental health care because of shortages in state hospital psychiatric beds (Wortzel et al. 2007, 357).

Approximately 66%–90% of defendants referred for competency restoration are successfully restored to competency (Noffsinger 2001; Morris and DeYoung 2014, 87). Competency restoration rates vary, depending on illness severity and time allowed for competency restoration. Restoration to competence is accomplished by treating the defendant's mental illness and providing education about the trial process (Noffsinger 2001; Wall et al. 2003, 195). (See Chapter 28.)

Incompetent defendants who incompetently refuse antipsychotic medication may receive involuntary treatment to restore trial competency. The involuntary treatment must be the least intrusive treatment for restoration of competence and must be medically appropriate (*Riggins v. Nevada* 1992). A defendant adjudicated incompetent to stand trial who nevertheless competently refuses antipsychotic medication may still receive involuntary treatment, if the prosecution can prove that there is a compelling governmental interest at stake, such as bringing a defendant to trial on major charges (*Sell v. United States* 2003).

For defendants who cannot be restored to trial competency, charges are dismissed or held in abeyance. Common reasons for unrestorability include treatment-resistant psychosis, dementia, and moderate to severe intellectual disability. Factors associated with unrestorability include impairment in psycholegal ability and presence of severe psychotic symptoms (Advokat et al. 2012, 90). Characteristics of unrestorable defendants include more prior hospitalizations, more prior incarcerations, more previous findings of incompetence, lower-level charges, psychotic disorder, cognitive disorder, more medications prescribed, and lower global assessment of functioning scores (Colwell and Gianesini 2011, 297, Rotter and Greenspan 2011, 307). Unrestorable defendants may remain hospitalized only if civilly committed (*Jackson v. Indiana* 1972).

COMPETENCE TO WAIVE EXTRADITION

Defendants may be arrested in a jurisdiction different from where their charges originated and where they will be tried. Defendants can challenge extradition (transfer) to a requesting state. Only a handful of states have explicitly considered the issue of a defendant's right to be competent to proceed with an extradition hearing. In some states, competence to participate in an extradition hearing is similar to competence to stand trial, in that the defendant must understand factual material related to extradition under the Uniform Criminal Extradition Act and be able to assist defense counsel at the extradition hearing. Some states apply a more limited competency standard related solely to particular requirements of extradition (as to identity and fugitive status). Finally, a limited number of states have found that a fugitive has no right to be competent to proceed in an extradition hearing.

COMPETENCE TO CONFESS

The privilege against self-incrimination indicates that a defendant cannot be compelled to testify against himself or herself. The U.S. Supreme Court ruled in *Miranda v. Arizona* (1966) that the Fifth Amendment requires that police inform custodial defendants of their rights to remain silent; to counsel; and that any statements the defendant makes can be used against them. Defendants may waive *Miranda* rights and give a confession that may be introduced at trial by the prosecution as evidence of guilt. The standard for competence to waive one's *Miranda* rights (or any Constitutional right) is whether the defendant knowingly, intelligently (*Johnson v. Zerbst 1938*), and voluntarily waived that right.

With respect to the voluntariness of waiving *Miranda* rights, the U.S. Supreme Court ruled in *Colorado v. Connelly* (1986) that *police coercion* is necessary for a court to find that a defendant's confession was incompetently made. Evaluating the behavior of law enforcement officers to determine if police coercion occurred is usually beyond the expertise of the forensic mental health professional; however, the clinician may be asked to retrospectively evaluate the defendant's mental state during the confession and susceptibility to potentially coercive police behavior.

In addition, clinicians may retrospectively evaluate whether a defendant competently waived *Miranda* rights by determining whether the waiver of rights was made intelligently and knowingly. Intellectual disability, psychosis, mania, or severe depression may impair a defendant's ability to intelligently and knowingly make a decision to waive his or her *Miranda* rights. An incompetently made confession or incompetent waiver of *Miranda* rights may lead a court to rule a defendant's prior confession inadmissible at trial.

COMPETENCE TO PLEAD GUILTY

Many defendants plead guilty in exchange for a reduced sentence or dismissal of part of the indictment in the process known as plea bargaining. Pleading guilty involves waiving specific rights, including the privilege against self-incrimination; right to a jury trial; and the right to confront witnesses.

Clinicians may contemporaneously evaluate a defendant's competence who wishes to plead guilty, or (more frequently) retrospectively evaluate a defendant's competence to plead guilty as the basis of an appeal. At issue is whether the defendant had a mental disorder at the time that the decision to plead guilty was made, and whether the symptoms of the defendant's mental disorder impaired his or her ability to intelligently, knowingly, and voluntarily waive those rights (*Johnson v. Zerbst* 1938).

In *Godinez v. Moran* (1993) the Supreme Court rejected the notion that competence to plead guilty must be measured by a standard that is higher than (or even different from) the *Dusky* standard. The Court articulated that although a decision to plead guilty is undeniably a profound one, it is no more complicated than the sum total of decisions that a defendant may be called upon to make during the course of the trial.

COMPETENCE TO WAIVE COUNSEL

The Sixth Amendment affords criminal defendants the right to counsel. The purpose of counsel includes assisting the defendant through the adjudicative process and ensuring the validity of the plea and court process (*Faretta v. California* 1975). Defendants may waive counsel for numerous reasons, including mistrust of the legal system; financial reasons; assertion that they are innocent and do not need counsel; belief that they could represent themselves better than an attorney; belief they will earn sympathy by proceeding *pro se* against the government; or, any number of rational or psychotic beliefs.

In *Faretta v. California* (1975) the U.S. Supreme Court held that a criminal defendant has a Constitutional right to knowingly and intelligently refuse legal representation. Note that refusing counsel is not the same as representing oneself. The *Faretta* court added that a defendant's ability to represent himself or herself has no bearing on the defendant's competence to elect to represent himself or herself. In *Indiana v. Edwards* (2008), the Supreme Court ruled that courts may require a higher standard of competence for self-representation than that necessary for trial competence. The right to represent oneself is not absolute; courts have discretion in maintaining the validity of the court process.

Clinicians evaluating competence to waive counsel should familiarize themselves with jurisdictional law. Under *Faretta*, the clinician evaluating competence to waive counsel must assess whether the defendant understands that he or she is abandoning the right to representation by legal counsel and that there may be disadvantages of this decision. Although the evaluator may not agree with the defendant's rationale, the evaluator must be careful not to equate poor judgment with incompetence. Rather, the focus should hinge on whether the defendant has a mental illness that impairs the decision to intelligently waive counsel.

COMPETENCE TO WAIVE A JURY TRIAL

The U.S. Constitution guarantees the right to be tried by an impartial jury of one's peers but does not guarantee the right to waive a jury trial. Defendants may seek to be tried by the trial judge if they perceive that a bench trial is in their legal interests, which is frequently the case in contested insanity trials. There is not a specific legal standard to waive the right to trial by jury. Extrapolating from other legal standards, a defendant who waives trial by jury must make the waiver intelligently, knowingly, and voluntarily (*Johnson v. Zerbst* 1938).

The clinician assessing whether a defendant can competently waive trial by jury evaluates whether the defendant has a mental disorder that impairs the ability to understand the right to be impartially tried by a jury of one's peers, and investigates the rationality of the decision.

COMPETENCE TO BE SENTENCED

A defendant who is competent to stand trial or to plead guilty may experience an exacerbation of illness during the time between trial and sentencing, and subsequently become incompetent to be sentenced. Competence to be sentenced deals with evaluating the defendant's understanding that he or she has been convicted of a crime; the reason for the conviction; and the reasons that a sentence will be imposed. Competence to be sentenced requires that the defendant be able to rationally participate in a presentence investigation; to assist the defendant's defense attorney in minimizing the negative impact of their conviction; and to assist the attorney in offering mitigating factors that may cause the court to reduce their sentence.

COMPETENCE TO WAIVE APPEALS

Defendants who have been convicted may appeal their conviction. Defendants who are convicted and sentenced to death have numerous appeals filed automatically on their behalf. A mentally ill defendant may irrationally instruct his or her attorney to not file appeals, or may refuse to cooperate with his or her attorney in preparing appeals. In contrast, a defendant may rationally waive his or her appeals in the belief that pursuing further appeals is not likely to be fruitful or in his or her best interests.

Evaluating competence to waive appeals involves assessing the defendant's current mental state and understanding if current symptoms impair the defendant's ability to rationally make a decision whether to pursue appeals and to assist the defense counsel in that pursuit. A depressed defendant who, as a result of his or her depression, lacks energy/motivation to pursue appeals may be incompetent to waive appeals. A suicidal defendant seeking capital punishment may be incompetent to waive appeals, as is a defendant with paranoid delusions about his or her attorney or the court. In contrast, a defendant who prefers capital punishment compared to a life of imprisonment may be competent to waive appeals if his or her decision is rational and not the product of a mental disorder.

COMPETENCE TO BE EXECUTED

Presently, 31 states and the federal jurisdiction may impose the death penalty. In American jurisdictions, 15 years, on average, pass between when the defendant is sentenced to death and when the sentence is carried out. Defendants on death row may develop a mental disorder that may impair their competence to be executed.

The U.S. Supreme Court has ruled that executing a mentally retarded defendant is unconstitutional (*Atkins v. Virginia* 2002), as is executing a defendant who was under the age of 18 years at the time of the commission of the offense (*Roper v. Simmons* 2005).

In *Ford v. Wainwright* (1986), the U.S. Supreme Court ruled that it is cruel and unusual punishment, in violation of the Eighth Amendment, to execute an incompetent defendant, and that states must have sufficient procedures in place to allow a defendant to challenge his or her competence to be executed. The *Ford* Court held that the trial court should determine the defendant's competence to be executed by evaluating the defendant's understanding of the nature of the death penalty and the reason that the death penalty is being imposed.

In *Panetti v. Quarterman* (2007), the U.S. Supreme Court broadly interpreted their ruling in *Ford v. Wainwright*, indicating that a defendant's simple awareness of the state's rationale for the execution was insufficient to prove that the defendant is competent to be executed. Instead, a defendant must have a more substantive understanding of the nature of the death penalty and the reason for its imposition. Although not giving a bright-line definition of what a more substantive understanding of the death penalty constitutes, the Court held that simple "yes" or "no" responses by the defendant to a series of questions about the death penalty do not constitute a substantive understanding of the death penalty.

Forensic evaluators may be called upon to evaluate a defendant's competence to be executed. Such an evaluation should assess the defendant's mental state and the presence or absence of a mental disorder that may impact the defendant's understanding of:

1. The general concept of punishment
2. The nature of the death penalty
3. The nature of death row
4. The personnel present at the execution
5. The role of the defense attorney
6. What will happen when his or her execution is carried out
7. The reason that the death sentence has been imposed
8. Symptoms that may impact his or her perception of reality

SUMMARY KEY POINTS

- Competence to stand trial is one of the most common forensic mental health assessments.
- The clinician evaluating any of the criminal competencies must know the competence legal standard in the jurisdiction.
- Evaluating criminal competencies typically involves assessing the defendant's present mental state, although retrospective competence evaluations may be an issue.
- Mental illness does not equate with incompetence. Incompetence requires impairment of the specific mental functions operative for the specific competence.
- Incompetence to stand trial requires that a defendant either be unable to understand the nature and objectives of the court proceedings, be unable to assist in his or her defense, or both.

REFERENCES

Advokat CD, D Guidry, DMR Burnett, G Manguno-Mire, and JW Thompson. 2012. Competency restoration treatment: Differences between defendants declared competent or incompetent to stand trial. *Journal of the American Academy of Psychiatry and the Law* 40:89–97.

Appelbaum PS and Gutheil T. 2007. *Clinical Handbook of Psychiatry and the Law*, 4th edition. New York: Lippincott, Williams and Wilkins.

Atkins v. Virginia, 536 U.S. 304 (2002).

Ausness CW. 1978. Identification of incompetent defendants—Separating those unfit for adversary combat from those who are fit. *Kentucky Law Journal* 66:666–706.

Barnard GW, JW Thompson, WC Freeman, L Robbins, D Gies, and GC Hankin. 1991. Competency to stand trial: Description and initial evaluation of a new computer-assisted assessment tool (CADCOMP). *Bulletin of the American Academy of Psychiatry and the Law* 19:367–381.

Bonnie R. 1990. The competence of criminal defendants with mental retardation to participate in their own defense. *Journal of Criminal Law and Criminology* 81:419–446.

Bonnie RJ, SK Hoge, JP Monahan, EM Norman, and T Feucht-Haviar. 1997. The MacArthur Adjudicative Competence Study: A comparison of criteria for assessing the competence of criminal defendants. *Journal of the American Academy of Psychiatry and the Law* 25:249–259.

Buchanan A. 2006. Competency to stand trial and the seriousness of the charge. *Journal of the American Academy of Psychiatry and the Law* 34:458–465.

Buchanan A. 2008. Commentary: Facts and values in competency assessment. *Journal of the American Academy of Psychiatry and the Law* 36:352–353.

Cochrane RE, T Grisso, and RI Frederick. 2001. The relationship between criminal charges, diagnoses, and psycholegal opinions among federal pretrial defendants. *Behavioral Sciences and the Law* 19:565–582.

Colorado v. Connelly, 479 U.S. 157 (1986).

Colwell LH and J Gianesini. 2011. Demographic, criminogenic, and psychiatric factors that predict competency restoration. *Journal of the American Academy of Psychiatry and the Law* 39:297–306.

Cooper VG and PA Zapf. 2003. Predictor variables in competency to stand trial decisions. *Law and Human Behavior* 27:423–436.

Cooper v. Oklahoma, 517 U.S. 348 (1996).

Davis DL. 1985. Treatment planning for the patient who is incompetent to stand trial. *Hospital and Community Psychiatry* 36:268–271.

Drope v. Missouri, 95 S. Ct. 896, 980 (1975).

Dusky v. United States, 362 US 402 (1960).

Everington C. 1990. The Competence Assessment for Standing Trial for Defendants with Mental Retardation (CAST-MR): A validation study. *Criminal Justice and Behavior* 17:147–168.

Faretta v. California, 422 U.S. 806 (1975).

Federal Bureau of Investigation. 2012. *Crime in the United States 2012. Persons Arrested.* https://ucr.fbi.gov/crime-in-the-u.s./2012/crime-in-the-u.s.-2012/persons-arrested/persons-arrested, accessed July 22, 2016.

Felthous AR. 2011. Competence to stand trial should require rational understanding. *Journal of the American Academy of Psychiatry and the Law* 39:19–30.

Ford v. Wainwright, 477 U.S. 399 (1986).
Freckelton I. 1996. Rationality and flexibility in assessment of fitness to stand trial. *International Journal of Law and Psychiatry* 19:39–59.
Frendak v. United States, 408 A.2d 364 (D.C. 1979).
Frierson RL, SJ Shea, and MJ Craig-Shea. 2002. Competence-to-stand-trial evaluations of geriatric defendants. *Journal of the American Academy of Psychiatry and the Law* 30:252–256.
Godinez v. Moran, 509 U.S. 389 (1993).
Golding SL and R Roesch. 1984. Assessment and conceptualization of competency to stand trial: Preliminary data on the interdisciplinary fitness interview. *Law and Human Behavior* 9:321–334.
Grisso TJ, JJ Cocozza, HJ Steadman, WH Fisher, and A Greer. 1994. The organization of pretrial forensic evaluation services: A national profile. *Law and Human Behavior* 18:377–394.
Grubin D. 1996. *Fitness to Plead in England and Wales.* East Sussex, England: Psychology Press.
Heinik J, R Kimhi, and JP Hes. 1994. Dementia and crime: A forensic psychiatry unit study in Israel. *International Journal of Geriatric Psychiatry* 9:491–494.
Hoge SK, RJ Bonnie, N Poythress, and J Monahan. 1992. Attorney-client decision making in criminal cases: Client competence and participation as perceived by their attorneys. *Behavioral Sciences and the Law* 10:385–394.
Hoge SK, RJ Bonnie, N Poythress, J Monahan, M Eisenberg, and T Feucht-Haviar. 1997. The MacArthur Adjudicative Competence Study: Development and validation of a research instrument. *Law and Human Behavior* 21(2):141–179.
Indiana v. Edwards, 554 U.S. 164 (2008).
Insanity Defense Reform Act, 18 U.S.C. Section 4241 (1984).
Jackson v. Indiana, 406 U.S. 715 (1972).
James DV. 2001. Fitness to plead. A prospective study of the inter-relationships between expert opinion, legal criteria and specific symptomatology. *Psychological Medicine* 31:139–150.
Johnson v. Zerbst, 304 U.S. 458 (1938).
Kapalczynski PL and SG Noffsinger. 2011. Retrospective competency evaluations. *Journal of the American Academy of Psychiatry and the Law* 39:580–582.
Lee, E, R Rosner, and R Harmon. 2014. Mental illness and legal fitness (competence) to stand trial in New York State: Expert opinion and criminal defendant's psychotic symptoms. *Journal of Forensic Sciences* 59:1008–1015.
Lipsitt PD, D Lelos, and AL McGarry. 1971. Competency for trial: A screening instrument. *American Journal of Psychiatry* 128:105–109.
McKee GR. 1998. Competency to stand trial in preadjudicatory juveniles and adults. *Journal of the American Academy of Psychiatry and the Law* 26:89–99.
Miranda v. Arizona, 384 U.S. 436 (1966).
Morris DR and NJ DeYoung. 2014. Long-term competence restoration. *Journal of the American Academy of Psychiatry and the Law* 42:81–90.
Morris GH, AM Haroun, and D Naimark. 2004. Assessing competency competently: Toward a rational standard for competency-to-stand-trial assessments. *Journal of the American Academy of Psychiatry and the Law* 32:231–245.
Mossman, D, SG Noffsinger, PF Ash et al. 2007. Practice guideline: Forensic psychiatric evaluation of competence to stand trial. *Journal of the American Academy of Psychiatry and the Law* 35:S3–S72.
Nicholson RA, SR Briggs, and HC Robertson. 1988. Instruments for assessing competency to stand trial: How do they work? *Professional Psychology Research and Practice* 19:383–394.
Nicholson RA and KE Kugler. 1991. Competent and incompetent criminal defendants: A quantitative review of comparative research. *Psychological Bulletin* 109:355–370.
Noffsinger SG. 2001. Restoration to competency practice guidelines. *International Journal of Offender Therapy and Comparative Criminology* 45(3):356–362.
O.R.C. Section, 2945.371(J).
Otto RK, JE Musick, and C Sherrod. 2011. Convergent validity of a screening measure designed to identify defendants feigning knowledge deficits related to competence to stand trial. *Assessment* 18:60–62.
Panetti v. Quarterman, 551 U.S. 930 (2007).
Pate v. Robinson, 383 U.S. 375 (1966).
Pirelli G, WH Gottdiener, and PA Zapf. 2011. A meta-analytic review of competency to stand trial research. *Psychology, Public Policy and Law* 17:1–53.
Poythress NG, RJ Bonnie, SK Hoge, J Monahan, and LB Oberlander. 1994. Client abilities to assist counsel and make decisions in criminal-cases—Findings from three studies. *Law and Human Behavior* 18:437–452.
R. v. Dyle, O.B.S.P., 271 (1756).
R. v. Pritchard, 7 Carrington & Payne, 303 (1836).
R. v. Somervile (1583).
Reich J and L Tookey. 1986. Disagreements between court and psychiatrist on competency to stand trial. *Journal of Clinical Psychiatry* 47:29–30.
Reisner AD, J Piel, and M Makey. 2013. Competency to stand trial and defendants who lack insight into their mental illness. *Journal of the American Academy of Psychiatry and the Law* 41:85–91.
Resnick PJ and SG Noffsinger. 2004. Competence to stand trial and the insanity defense. In *Textbook of Forensic Psychiatry: The Clinicians Guidebook to Assessment*, edited by RL Simon and LH Gold, Arlington, VA: American Psychiatric Publishing, 329–347.
Riggins v. Nevada, 112 S.Ct. 1810 (1992).
Riley SE. 1998. Competency to stand trial adjudication: A comparison of female and male defendants. *Journal of the American Academy of Psychiatry and the Law* 26:223–240.

Roesch R, D Eaves, R Sollner, M Normandin, and W Glackman. 1981. Evaluating fitness to stand trial: A comparative analysis of fit and unfit defendants. *International Journal of Law and Psychiatry* 4:145–157.

Rogers R, CE Tillbrook, KW Sewell, and W Kenneth. 2004 *Evaluation of Competency to Stand Trial-Revised (ECST-R) and Professional Manual.* Odessa, FL: Psychological Assessment Resources.

Rogers R and J Johannson-Love. 2009. Evaluating competency to stand trial with evidenced-based practice. *Journal of the American Academy of Psychiatry and the Law* 37:450–460.

Roper v. Simmons, 543 U.S. 551 (2005).

Rotter M and M Greenspan. 2011. Commentary: Competency restoration research—Complicating an already complex process. *Journal of the American Academy of Psychiatry and the Law* 39:307–310.

Sell v. United States, 539 U.S. 166 (2003).

Skeem JL, S Manchak and JK Peterson. 2011. Correctional policy for offenders with mental illness: Creating a new paradigm for recidivism reduction. *Law and Human Behavior* 35(2):110–126.

Soliman S and PJ Resnick. 2010. Feigning in adjudicative competence evaluations. *Behavioral Sciences and the Law* 28:614–629.

Statute of Westminster of, 1275 (3 Edw. I).

Steadman HJ and E Hartstone. 1983. Defendants incompetent to stand trial. In *Mentally Disordered Offenders: Perspectives from Law and Social Science*, edited by J Monahan and HJ Steadman, New York: Plenum, 39–62.

Teplin LA. 1984. Criminalizing mental disorder—The comparative arrest rate of the mentally Ill. *American Psychologist* 39:794–803.

U.S. v. Bergmann, 599 F.3d 1142 (10th Cir. 2010).

U.S. Const. amend. VI.

U.S. Const. amend. XIV.

U.S. Department of Health. 1973. *Laboratory of Community Psychiatry: Competency to Stand Trial and Mental Illness.* Publication No. (AMD) 77–103. Rockville, MD: U.S. Department of Health.

Walker N. 1968. *Crime and Insanity in England.* Edinburgh: Edinburgh University Press.

Wall BW, BH Krupp, and T Guilmette. 2003. Restoration of competency to stand trial: A training program for persons with mental retardation. *Journal of the American Academy of Psychiatry and the Law* 31:189–201.

Wilson v. United States, 391 F.2d 460 (D.C. Cir. 1968).

Wortzel H, IA Binswanger, R Martinez, CM Filley, and CA Anderson. 2007. Crisis in the treatment of incompetence to proceed to trial: Harbinger of a systemic illness. *Journal of the American Academy of Psychiatry and the Law* 35:357–363.

Zapf PA, R Roesch, and JL Viljoen. 2001. Assessing fitness to stand trial: The utility of the fitness interview test (rev. ed.). *Canadian Journal of Psychiatry* 46:426–432.

28

Treatment for restoration of competence to stand trial

KELLY GOODNESS AND ALAN R. FELTHOUS

INTRODUCTION

Perhaps the largest forensic population requiring treatment consists of criminal defendants who have been found incompetent to stand trial (Torrey et al. 2010). Since the landmark case of *Jackson v. Indiana* (1972) that prevents individuals from being denied due process by holding them for unconscionably long time periods with no hope of attaining trial competence, a fair amount of attention has been directed to ascertaining the factors that are most associated with findings of incompetence, identifying who is likely to attain competence and in what period of time (Zapf 2013). Yet disturbingly little scholarly effort has been devoted to detailing model restoration programs or empirically deriving efficacious treatment modalities (Pinals 2005; Brinkley and DeMier 2009; Samuel and Michals 2011). Although much of competence restoration consists of the sound principles of mental health practices in general, there are aspects specific to competence restoration which require specialized training if the programs and interventions are to be effective, efficient, and adherent to legal requirements and ethical principles.

Competence to stand trial

There are two legal issues involved in the treatment for, and restoration of, incompetence to proceed. First, individuals who are incompetent to stand trial due to mental illness or defect can only enjoy a meaningful defense and due process if they are afforded treatment that allows them to meaningfully participate in their defense. Restoration to trial competence is the process of applying psychiatric and/or psychological treatment to those symptoms identified as barriers to a defendant's ability to legally proceed through the system. Second, the government has an interest in the prosecution and adjudication of criminal defendants, and thus has an interest in ensuring that incompetent defendants attain adequate competence. Although there is significant overlap between treating psychiatric patients in general and the treatment of incompetent defendants; there are important differences given the legally mandated goal of the treatment. The treatment may or may not serve the individual's best legal interests, and treatment providers may feel torn between meeting the legal mandate and addressing the full array of the patient's needs. Moreover, the government's interest in adjudicating an individual does not mean treatment is automatic, and ethical treatment providers must have an understanding of relevant case law.

WHAT DATA ARE RELEVANT TO THE LEGAL CRITERIA?

The data relevant to the legal criteria include the individual specific symptoms and deficits that negatively impact competence-related capacities, amenability to treatment, and the expected time required for treatment. Each of these can be impacted by the location in which treatment takes place as well as the defendant's desire to accept treatment.

The standard by which trial competency is judged was outlined in *Dusky v. United States* (1960) wherein the court concluded that "the test must be whether he has sufficient present ability to consult with his lawyer with a reasonable degree of rational understanding—and whether he has a rational as well as factual understanding of the proceedings against him" (p. 789). *Dusky* resulted in requiring a functional analysis of how symptoms of mental illness or defect impact competence-related capacities, and subsequently a number of jurisdictions have provided further guidance.

A mental disorder alone, or the mere presence of symptoms, does not equate to incompetence. The specific symptoms of mental illness or defect that negatively impact an individual's trial capacities must be identified. For example, some individuals will always have some level of hallucinations, but can be taught coping strategies, such as reality testing, in order that their hallucinations do not greatly interfere with trial capacities. Individuals with psychotic disorders are nearly eight times more likely to be found incompetent than individuals without a psychotic disorder, and those with a prior psychiatric hospitalization are nearly twice as likely to be found incompetent (Pirelli et al. 2011). As such, the use of antipsychotic medications has been the predominant treatment. However, several legal cases have addressed the issue of *voluntariness,* and have placed limits on the use of pharmacological interventions as the sole or primary intervention for competence restoration, making voluntariness relevant to the legal criteria.

Most jurisdictions place limitations on the available time for competence restoration, and many translate that to the amount of time the individual could have served if found guilty of his or her charges. Fortunately, available studies have found that overall competence restoration rates are high, with 75%–90% of individuals typically being restored in 6 months or less of inpatient restoration treatment (Pinals 2005; Mossman 2007). Zapf (2013) recently analyzed the average length of stay (LOS) for defendants admitted for competence restoration at Eastern State Hospital in Washington State over a 24-year period. She found an average LOS of 89.2 days for felony defendants who were restored to competency and a much quicker 29 day average LOS for misdemeanor defendants who attained competence. Morris and DeYoung (2014) studied 81 individuals who had failed restoration efforts after 6 months and found that the majority (64.2%) were eventually deemed restored to competence with extended restoration efforts. They found the utility of treatment maxed out at 3½ years, which suggests that there is a relatively small subset of individuals who are never able to attain competence. Individuals with organic dysfunction, severe cognitive impairment, or chronic psychosis are most likely to fall into the unrestorable category (Mossman 2007).

Competency to stand trial restoration overview

NO UNIFORM STANDARD OF PRACTICE

The fact that there is no uniform standard of practice for constructing treatment for competence restoration has been highlighted in multiple studies. In a recent study conducted by Samuel and Michals (2011) of 27 forensic programs, the need for standardization of programming and staff training was highlighted. Of the participating programs, only two of the 11 described themselves as well-organized with ongoing research, and they were the only two that distributed instructional handouts on a regular basis. Not surprisingly, only two programs provided any formalized training to staff who led competency training. Likewise, only two programs provided actual supervision of restoration staff through videotape or observation to ensure quality control. Only three programs utilized a standardized competency evaluation instrument. Interestingly, only three programs consulted with their patients' attorneys, even though all programs recognized doing so would be of "great importance." Though only a pilot study, Samuel and Michals' work highlights the need for greater standardization of practice, quality control, and importantly, the need for consistent training and supervision of restoration staff.

LOCATION OF TREATMENT

Since the deinstitutionalization of the mentally ill, more individuals with severe and persistent mental illness are becoming involved with the criminal justice system, and that system is increasingly bearing the responsibility for the care of our mentally ill citizens (Torrey et al. 2010). The mechanism through which many seriously mentally ill individuals ultimately receive psychiatric care is through a court's finding of criminal trial incompetence. The traditional location of competence restoration treatment has been psychiatric hospitals. Hospital-based treatment generally allows for more access to programs such as group and individual psychotherapy and more frequent contact with mental health providers. This treatment milieu is almost always more conducive to healing than a penal institution, and arguably the support staff should be better trained in dealing with mental illness. However, the need for bed space for incompetent patients has increased while resources have decreased, often making for long wait times before treatment. As a matter of necessity and in attempts to obtain more expeditious, humanitarian treatment, alternative treatment settings have been sought in jail-based and community-based programs.

Jennings and Bell (2012) detailed a comprehensive jail-based treatment program model entitled Restoration of Competency (ROC) that called for the provision of intensive psychiatric stabilization, forensic evaluation, and restoration and maintenance of competency within a local jail. The ROC model was developed as a pilot project in the 1990s and called for the transformation of a jail pod into a mental health facility that essentially mirrored many services usually provided in a hospital. Much like the Social Learning Diagnostic Program described by Goodness and Renfro (2002), the ROC program included team-based treatment in a therapeutic milieu that utilized a positive reinforcement management system to encourage and reward meaningful participation. Patients received active medication management and 3.5–5.5 hours daily of group-based rehabilitative activities aimed at both mental health issues and legal competence capacities. Jennings and Bell's 5-year outcome study showed that the program achieved an 83% overall competence restoration with an average treatment length of 77 days.

Depending on the extent of services, the benefits of jail-based competence restoration can include lower costs, reduced waitlists for hospital beds, decreased length of time to restore competence, elimination of incentives to malinger, seamless transition from competence restoration to adjudication, and assistance of local jail staff in better managing a population that requires specialized knowledge (Jennings and Bell 2012). The disadvantages of jail-based restoration include the general austerity of a penal institution, high noise levels, and the reality that jails are built to provide security versus the sort of supportive surroundings that are conducive to healing (Kapoor 2011). Moreover, not all jail-based programs are well organized or comprehensive, and some clinicians have questioned if restoration can be successfully accomplished in jail (Kapoor 2011). Additionally, jail medical staff may resist participating in competence restoration efforts as they face ethical quandaries when asked to set aside the patient's stated desires and potential best interest and focus on the goals of the justice system.

Some community-based competence restoration programs (CBCRPs) have begun to serve individuals who do not have violent charges. Programs are run by the state mental health agency and include case management that follows more of an intensive Assertive Community Treatment model wherein the patient is provided close medication oversight, transportation to medical appointments, individual instruction in legal rights and factual competence issues, and individually tailored interventions (Miller et al. 2009). Potentially destabilizing factors may be targeted, such as housing, unemployment, substance abuse, and the need for appropriate social activities. Community-based programming frees inpatient bed space, is less costly than inpatient restoration, and is more recovery oriented (Miller et al. 2009), which may offer at least some individuals an alternative that helps to address the reasons for the revolving door process between the criminal justice system and intermittent mental health treatment. Aside from budgetary barriers, CBCRPs have faced challenges through limited buy-in from courts, and some legal professionals may be attempting to circumvent *Jackson v. Indiana* through placement of neuropsychologically impaired individuals in nursing homes ostensibly for outpatient competence restoration.

Elements of competency restoration

Much of the scant literature regarding competence restoration treatment is descriptive in nature (Brown 1992; Noffsinger 2001). The studies meant to test treatment efficacy are often problematic due to methodological design issues, including lack of experimental control groups, small sample sizes, and poor outcome measures, making it impossible to draw firm conclusions. A case in point can be found in an often quoted study by Bertman et al. (2003) in which the authors made the first peer-reviewed efforts to evaluate what they asserted was the effectiveness of individualized treatment for the restoration of competency. Though prior authors have cited this study as an argument against individualized treatment plans, the reality is that Bertman's study included three groups of very small *n* of 10 or less, with little statistical difference between the groups. Moreover, their definition of six training sessions being individualized treatment is overreaching by generally accepted clinical treatment standards. This study simply does not allow for a global discarding of individual approaches. Indeed, most clinicians might support the notion that tailoring treatment for individual clinical concerns is paramount for effective intervention regardless of why a patient is in treatment.

Empirically examining psycholegal competency interventions poses many legal and clinical challenges (Scott 2003) and is a formidable task, especially as many who are best positioned to conduct such research are so busy with direct care services that little time is left to conduct research. However, this task should become a priority given the increasing number of individuals likely to enter treatment through the criminal justice system as incompetent to proceed. As demand increases and resources do not, resources should be expended on treatment efforts with statistically proven efficacy. Moreover, utilizing efficacious treatments is ethically incumbent upon clinicians, and "forensic clinicians engaged in competency restoration treatment need to be able to articulate the scientific basis for their interventions" (Brinkley and DeMier 2009, 388). Still, until time has allowed for greater empirical study, the legal push for alternatives to treatment based on medication only, our collective forensic clinical experience and, to a large extent, common sense, lead us to advocate for including all or some of the components described below in the treatment for and restoration of competence to stand trial. Many of these elements can be utilized regardless of whether treatment occurs in a community, jail, or hospital setting.

INITIAL ASSESSMENT AND TREATMENT PLANNING

The central goal of competence restoration treatment is to achieve an adequate level of factual and rational competence. Successful competence restoration does not require that treatment produce a perfect defendant, and the court's order does not generally authorize treatment to maximum personal benefit. Instead, treatment should be geared toward eliminating symptoms where possible and lessening residual symptoms that negate trial competence.

Generally, defendants are ordered into treatment after a relatively brief forensic examination of their competence-related capacities. These initial evaluations may be done under less than desirable conditions, including time pressures, noisy and chaotic jail environments, and little to no documentation of background information or prior treatment efforts. Thus, these evaluations may vary greatly in quality and may not provide a very good understanding of the patient's functioning. Moreover, by the time an individual actually enters treatment, his or her clinical presentation may be better or worse. Treating clinicians should consult the evaluations that formed the basis for commitment to treatment to ascertain what symptoms were identified as being of most concern to the court. However, we recommend treating clinicians conduct a comprehensive initial evaluation and devise a treatment plan to address the specific symptoms and deficits that negatively impact an individual's trial competence.

Deficits in factual competence are generally easy to identify. Factual understanding focuses on basic legal concepts such as the roles of attorneys and judges and the meaning of guilty and not guilty pleas, and deficits are often a matter of education or rote memorization. Deficits in rational competence can be more difficult to identify. Rational understanding is a higher-order ability than factual understanding because it requires that an individual have the capacity to understand, process, and logically apply information to his or her own case rather than simply memorize and parrot back facts.

A diagnostic interview and mental status evaluation will certainly inform the individual's overall mental health treatment. In addition, an objective, standardized trial competence assessment instrument should be administered when the defendant first arrives in order to guide treatment planning by systematically identifying deficits that contribute to the defendant's incompetence (Pendleton 1980; Noffsinger 2001). There are several such instruments from which to select, each having its own strengths and weaknesses (Pirelli et al. 2011). Indeed, "[n]ot all defendants are incompetent for the same reason, and therefore the underlying reason leading to each defendant's incompetence should be identified by an objective competence assessment upon admission to the program" (Noffsinger 2001, 360–361). Importantly, such instruments can be repeated throughout treatment to gauge progress.

Be it due to prior noted concerns, concerns that arise during the initial evaluation, or those that arise at some point in treatment, it may be necessary to place the patient on a malingering protocol as a part of his or her treatment plan to rule out (or in) the possibility of symptom exaggeration. Malingering protocols may include increased documentation by direct care staff, observation via closed-circuit cameras, and analysis of the consistency of behavior throughout the work shifts and over time so that a broad sample of the individual's behavior can be assessed. A malingering protocol can sometimes provide more useful information than administration of standardized malingering instruments.

Cultural barriers can impact mental health functioning and treatment engagement, which in turn can negatively impact competency capacities. At its most basic level, cultural issues can involve language barriers that affect the ability to communicate important facets of the person's life and background that may inform treatment (American Psychological Association and Jansen 2014). Clinicians must be sensitive to increased social stigma in some cultures regarding behavioral health problems or religious beliefs that impact treatment acceptance, treatment needs, and recovery (American Psychological Association and Jansen 2014). Appropriate provisions should be made for interpreters adequately trained in assisting mental health providers. Likewise, utilization of language-specific psycholegal materials aids the necessary acquisition of factual knowledge.

Treatment providers should not be hesitant to contact the involved attorneys or the court for information. Defense attorneys can provide important information regarding difficulties the patient may have had in consulting with counsel. It can be frustrating for treatment teams when an individual who they believe has been successfully restored is repeatedly court ordered into treatment as incompetent for reasons that may not have been well articulated to the hospital. By the same token, the court may repeatedly be mystified why the individual has been returned with a recommendation of competent to proceed if reports to the court were unclear, or in some cases because documentation had simply never been fully read. Increasing communication and collaboration with the stakeholders has been shown to resolve issues and improve outcomes and processes (Olley et al. 2009). "When the mental health and legal systems collaborate effectively, the entire competency process improves" (Finkle et al. 2009, 780).

PHARMACOTHERAPY

Research clearly indicates that successful restoration is often related to how well an individual's symptoms respond to psychotropic medications. Thus, an essential component of treatment for restoration of competence of most defendants who are found incompetent to stand trial is pharmacotherapy. Selecting the most appropriate medication and managing its administration is to a large extent simply a matter of accepted pharmacotherapy for mental disorders in general, which is well described in any current standard textbook of psychopharmacotherapy. Here we encourage currency in modern pharmacotherapy, but focus this discussion on consideration of special relevance to competence restoration.

Most defendants are incompetent due to schizophrenia or other psychotic or serious thought disorder. Proper treatment of the disorder, usually involving an antipsychotic, will at the same time improve the defendant's ability to think realistically and rationally such that his or her main incapacity for competence will be restored. The core symptoms resulting in incompetence are often the defendant's psychosis and disturbance of thought. However, extreme disturbance of mood or emotional and behavioral control can also impair the defendant's ability to assist in his or her defense and cloud the defendant's ability to think clearly and adaptively. However, even those conditions that cause suffering and other significant disability, such as nightmare disorder, ought to be treated while the defendant is in treatment, even if such disorders do not directly contribute to his or her incompetence. Humanitarian treatment and standard of care apply, even as the main goal of treatment is restoration of competence, and the main determinant for the defendant's readiness to be returned to court and trial is the restoration of his or her competence to stand trial.

Physically aggressive and violent behavior does not *per se* render a defendant incompetent to stand trial. Yet it must be addressed for safe and effective treatment management. Its efficacious pharmacotherapy, where indicated, can improve the defendant's psychological functioning such that it favorably strengthens abilities needed for competence. For safe, effective, and timely treatment of clinical aggression, it is recommended that the assessment of the nature of the aggression be initiated even before the defendant arrives at the hospital for admission (Felthous et al. 2009). A critical distinction must first be made between impulsive aggression which is often improved with appropriate pharmacotherapy and premeditated aggression, which without other mental disorders, is not (Felthous and Barratt 2003).

Once the aggression is determined to be impulsive, as most aggression in security hospitals appears to be

(Felthous et al. 2009), evaluators should determine whether the impulsive aggression is primary or secondary to another mental disorder (Felthous 2013). The specific drugs that have repeatedly demonstrated efficacy in the treatment of primary impulsive aggression include fluoxetine, lithium, phenytoin, carbamazepine, and valproate/divalproex (Felthous et al. 2013). Especially because no drug is U.S. Food and Drug Administration (FDA) approved for the treatment of primary impulsive aggression or intermittent explosive disorder (American Psychiatric Association 2013), an algorithm has been proposed to assist in selecting the most appropriate anti-impulsive aggressive agent (AIAA) for the individual patient (Felthous and Stanford 2015). Moeller and Swann (2007) developed an algorithm that is useful for the pharmacotherapy of secondary aggression, which has also been discussed in the context of correctional psychiatry (Felthous 2013).

Defendants who are remanded to a hospital for competence restoration typically have a serious mental disorder or defect, not impulsive aggression alone. In other words, if they show impulsive aggression this is often related to their primary mental disorder such as bipolar disorder or schizophrenia. Accordingly, the aggression will likely come under control with efficacious treatment of the primary disorder (Moeller and Swann 2007; Felthous 2013). If not, an AIAA can be added to the regimen with appropriate consideration (Felthous 2013) and the awareness that no AIAA is FDA approved for this use. Also to be borne in mind, risperidone (Moeller and Swann 2007) and olanzapine (Volavka et al. 2016) have been shown to help curb aggressive behavior, and clozapine has a remarkably anti-aggressive effect (Fava 1997) for mentally disordered individuals for whom such antipsychotics are otherwise indicated. Much of the evidence for clozapine's anti-aggressive efficacy derives from its use in treating schizophrenia (Volavka et al. 2004). Evidence suggests that clozapine may have anti-aggressive effects for other severe mental disorders, not just schizophrenia (Rabinowitz et al. 1996; Hector 1998).

Three landmark cases must be kept in mind when determining medically, ethically, and legally appropriate treatment in each case, as they underscore the need to explore alternative treatments for competence restoration versus solely relying on psychotropic medications. First, in *Washington v. Harper* (1990), the Supreme Court established that an individual has a constitutionally protected "liberty interest" in "avoiding the unwanted administration of antipsychotic drugs" (p. 221) and that those interests must be balanced against the state interests as the two may not be compatible. The importance of *Harper* was its attempt to define what criteria and procedures are constitutionally required to medicate a prisoner against his refusal. In *Harper*, the court found that under certain conditions, individuals could be involuntary medicated if they were dangerous to themselves or others, and medication was appropriate medical treatment. In *Riggins v. Nevada* (1992), the court found competency restoration did constitute "an important state interest" under certain conditions.

In *Sell v United States* (2003), the Court ruled that four criteria must be met before the government may override a "nondangerous" incompetent defendant's refusal of treatment with antipsychotic medication: important governmental interests are at stake; forced medications are substantially likely to render the defendant competent, while side effects are substantially unlikely to significantly interfere with the defendant's ability to assist counsel with his or her defense; there are no less intrusive treatments likely to achieve substantially the same results as medications; and administration of medication is medically appropriate.

EDUCATIONAL COMPONENT

Competence restoration generally should include educational components that can be delivered via a number of modalities. Although not all defendants will require psycholegal education, many need assistance in recognizing the application of legal concepts to their own situation. Requisite knowledge is both general, what any defendant should know, and specific, what individual defendants should know about their particular legal situation. General knowledge should include education about the elements of various types of charges, their severity, and the potential legal consequence associated with various charges; the standard pleas and the significance of each, the plea bargaining process; the roles of the principles in the courtroom; courtroom procedures and the nature of the adversarial trial process, and evaluating evidence (Davis 1985; Brown 1992; Noffsinger 2001).

Knowing what specific knowledge an individual needs to acquire requires some understanding of his or her legal case and how his or her symptoms negatively impact the defendant's ability to rationally work through the necessary decisions and issues. For example, it may not be clear that a defendant has delusions about individuals related to his or her case unless the defendant's specific case is discussed. Therefore, attending only to generalized knowledge may be insufficient to bring about trial competence or make continued incompetence clear. Pinals (2005) noted that clinicians who "are not familiar with competence or competence restoration may inadvertently ignore a significant issue in their patient's lives. When this occurs, by the time the patient's court case is slated for review, significant periods of time could have passed without any clinician speaking to the patient about the criminal charge" (p. 86). A decade later, her point is unfortunately still a matter of concern. It is not uncommon to find that during even lengthy hospitalizations, seemingly no clinician has addressed a particular defendant's understanding of the case, yet the patient was returned to the court with a recommended finding of competent to proceed.

Individual instruction for factual competence training is often accomplished through didactic groups. A competence education class may include written handouts or didactic lectures describing the legal process. Group problem-solving sessions utilizing issues that arise in participant's actual cases may be helpful (Siegel and Elwork 1990). Discussions regarding news stories involving criminal trials have also been utilized (Noffsinger 2001).

Some competency restoration programs have become more standardized or manualized than the available peer-reviewed literature reflects. This likelihood is reflected in the CompKit (2012) developed by Florida State Hospital with the assistance of multiple other agencies. The CompKit package includes separate written materials for instructors and consumers, a CD of the materials, and a DVD of movies involving mock hearings/trials and a competency training television game show. The CompKit has been updated several times and has been widely disseminated for use by interested providers.

A novel, potentially useful approach to teaching the knowledge needed for competence to stand trial is the Fitness Game developed by Cuneo and Owen (1990). It is a participatory game designed much like the board game Monopoly, where players learn about legal proceedings as the game progresses. The true effectiveness is in question, based on Meuller and Wylie's (2007) study of incompetent defendants in a state hospital. They found no significant difference on competency measures between the Fitness Game and a similarly designed game that targeted general mental health behavior such as symptom management, and treatment compliance (p. 897). Still, it may be helpful to utilize an engaging game as part of a multimodal treatment plan, and certainly could not cause harm.

EXPERIENTIAL COMPONENT

Noffsinger (2001) recommends competence restoration programming be multimodal, incorporating a broad selection of teaching methods that are delivered by multiple staff members in order to increase interest and retention. As such, adding experiential techniques may prove beneficial. Behavioral rehearsal through role-play or mock trials may assist in teaching interpersonal skills that allow the patient to better relate to and work with defense counsel while also increasing their understanding of expected courtroom behavior and procedures. Videotaped vignettes can teach basic legal procedures, add variety to training, and decrease anxiety regarding the legal setting (Noffsinger 2001). Mock trials can be conducted by treatment staff, though lawyers and judges have participated at some institutions. Staff may take on the major roles such as judge, prosecutor, or defense attorney, while patients participate as members of the jury, the bailiff, or the defendant (CompKit 2012). Best practices call for staff (paraprofessionals and licensed professionals alike) to be provided with specific training and ongoing supervision. Periodic quality checks to ensure that the interventions are being administered competently and as intended should be built into any program.

PSYCHOTHERAPY COMPONENT

Some patients would benefit from cognitive behavior therapy or other talk therapies in order to adequately uncover and work through irrational notions or excessive emotionality. Although anxiety reduction techniques (i.e., progressive relaxation, imagery) taught in a group setting may be sufficient for some patients, others may have psychological issues that appear to be interfering with competency restoration that would be better addressed through individual psychotherapy. An investment in individual psychotherapy could potentially go far in addressing the revolving door process between treatment noncompliance, legal charges, and court-ordered competence restoration treatment while also allowing for more intensive psychoeducation.

COGNITIVE REMEDIATION

Schwalbe and Medalia (2007) advocated using cognitive remediation as an adjunctive treatment in restoration programs. Cognitive remediation involves mental exercises that are meant to improve attention, memory, and problem solving, which may improve a patient's ability to retain information related to trial competence. Originally, cognitive remediation techniques were developed to assist individuals who had sustained neuropsychological injury, but have since been used with those with psychiatric illness such as schizophrenia. Schwalbe and Medalia advocate the use of the Neuropsychological Educational Approach to Cognitive Remediation (NEAR) model, as it was specifically designed for use with psychiatric patients who may, perhaps due to the illness itself, lack the intrinsic motivation necessary for repetitive drill exercises. The NEAR model is thought to be more stimulating, dynamic, and enjoyable because exercises are presented in real-life contexts in several different formats (via computer and verbal groups), and within a small group format that allows for interaction with others.

INDIVIDUALS WITH INTELLECTUAL DISABILITIES

Trial competence attainment can be particularly challenging, though not impossible, for individuals with developmental disabilities. The extent to which competency attainment efforts are successful with this group often depends on the severity and type of disability, which can be complicated by a comorbid psychiatric disorder. In general, one-third of individuals with developmental disabilities are believed to be able to attain competence to proceed (Zapf 2013). The Slater Method is a formal competency training tool specifically designed to address the difficulties encountered by persons with intellectual impairments (Wall and Christopher 2012). The Slater Method includes five modules: the purpose of the training, review of the charges, pleas, and potential consequences; courtroom personnel; courtroom proceedings, trial, and plea bargain; communicating with the attorney, giving testimony, and assisting in defense; and tolerating the stress of the proceedings. Each module is presented in sequential order a minimum of three times in order to engage in repetitious learning and improve retention. Wall and Christopher (2012) conducted a small retrospective study of mentally retarded or borderline intellectual functioning patients hospitalized for competence restoration. Patients treated through the Slater Method were more than 3½ times more likely to attain competence than those who were treated through traditional treatment alone. Their findings suggest systematic, programmed efforts at competence attainment are useful with those who have intellectual disabilities.

PERIODIC RE-EVALUATION AND DOCUMENTATION

The ethic of compartmentalizing forensic from therapeutic roles should not distract from the responsibility of measuring treatment progress and correspondingly documenting results in the health record. All treatment efforts, including observations made in group therapies (Pinals 2005), pharmacotherapeutic adjustments, and the patient's response, should be documented to accurately reflect the individual's daily physical and emotional functioning. This information is needed to track progress and inform treatment. Utilization of a standardized competence assessment instrument at periodic intervals is recommended to monitor progress toward attainment of competence to stand trial.

Pinals (2005, 85) wrote eloquently about some of the ethical struggles of clinicians who are charged with treating incompetent defendants in that clinicians "working as allies of their patients, ethical tensions arise in the notion that one of their jobs may be to help their patients regain competence to stand trial, which could culminate in an adjudication of guilt and possible incarceration or capital punishment for a particular patient." One of the primary mechanisms to deal with the ethical push/pull between the patient's treatment goals/needs and the goals of the criminal justice system is separating the roles of the patient's treating clinicians from that of their forensic evaluator who issues an opinion regarding competency to the court. All mental health professionals, regardless of professional affiliation, are ethically prohibited from entering into the dual roles. However, this does not mean that forensic treatment and forensic assessment should be completely compartmentalized, as such would mean the timing of restoration would lose efficiency and needlessly prolong treatment. There is a significant difference between assessing and documenting a patient's progress in meeting treatment goals and formally evaluating, articulating, and opining to the court whether or not an individual meets the standard for competence to proceed. Certainly, the latter evaluation should be conducted by an evaluator who is not involved in the patient's treatment.

Care should be taken to protect the individual's Fifth and Sixth Amendment rights to avoid unnecessary documentation of statements made by an incompetent defendant in the throes of illness. Care providers should remain mindful that the individual has been court ordered into treatment, and the records may ultimately be reviewed by legal professionals and used in ways that are difficult to anticipate. For example, documenting assertions of guilt or complicity would usually serve no clinical purpose.

SUMMARY KEY POINTS

It is our hope that by the next edition of this book, more empirically driven treatments will have been identified, and structured competency restoration programs will be the norm.

- Most individuals can successfully attain or be restored to competence to stand trial.
- Accurate and timely assessment and reassessment of symptoms and deficits are key to efficient treatment.
- Pharmacotherapy that follows the current state of the science is usually necessary but must be administered within the confines of the law.
- Nonmedication treatment modalities can be helpful and should address individual-specific symptoms and deficits.

REFERENCES

American Psychiatric Association. 2013. *Diagnostic and Statistical Manual of Mental Disorders*, Fifth Edition. Washington DC: American Psychiatric Publishing.

American Psychological Association and MA Jansen. 2014. *Reframing Psychology for the Emerging Health Care Environment: Recovery Curriculum for People with Serious Mental Illnesses and Behavioral Health Disorders*. Washington, DC: American Psychological Association.

Bertman LJ, JW Thompson, WF Waters, L Estupinan-Kane, JA Martin, and L Russell. 2003. Effect of an individualized treatment protocol on restoration of competency in pretrial forensic inpatients. *Journal of the American Academy of Psychiatry and the Law* 31(1):27–35.

Brinkley CA and RL DeMier. 2009. Implications of the *Sell* decision for treatment administration. *Journal of Psychiatry and Law* 37(4):373–412.

Brown DR. 1992. A Didactic Group program for persons found unfit to stand trial. *Hospital and Community Psychiatry* 43(7):732–733.

Cuneo DJ and BL Owen. 1990. *The Fitness Game*. Chicago: Illinois Department of Human Services.

Davis DL. 1985. Treatment planning for the patient who is incompetent to stand trial. *Hospital and Community Psychiatry* 36(3):268-271.

Dusky v. United States, 362 U.S. 402 (1960).

Fava M. 1997. Pharmacological treatment of pathologic aggression. *Psychiatric Clinics of North America* 20:427–451.

Felthous AR and ES Barratt. 2003. Impulsive aggression. In *Aggression: Psychiatric Assessment and Treatment*, edited by EF Coccaro, New York: Marcel Dekker, 123–148.

Felthous AR. 2013. The Ninth Circuit's *Loughner* decision neglected medically appropriate treatment. *Journal of the American Academy of Psychiatry and the Law* 41(1):105–113.

Felthous AR, SL Lake, BK Rundle, and MS Stanford. 2013. Pharmacotherapy of impulsive aggression: A quality comparison of controlled studies. *International Journal of Law and Psychiatry* 36:258–263.

Felthous AR, D Weaver, R Evans, S Braik, MS Stanford, R Johnson, C Metzger, A Bazile, and E Barratt. 2009. Assessment of impulsive aggression in patients with major mental disorders and demonstrated violence: Inter-rater reliability of rating instrument. *Journal of Forensic Sciences* 54:1470–1474.

Felthous AR and MS Stanford. 2015. A proposed algorithm for the pharmacotherapy of impulsive aggression. *Journal of the American Academy of Psychiatry and the Law* 43(4):456–467.

Finkle MJ, R Kurth, C Cadle, and J Mullan. 2009. Competency courts: A creative solution for restoring competency to the competency process. *Behavioral Sciences and the Law* 27:767–786.

Florida State Hospital. 2012. *CompKit, A Comprehensive Approach to Competency Restoration Training for Criminal Defendants*. Chattahoochee, FL: Florida State Hospital.

Goodness KR and NS Renfro. 2002. Changing a culture: A brief program analysis of a social learning program on a Maximum-Security Forensic Unit. *Behavioral Sciences and the Law* 20:1–12.

Hector RI. 1998. The use of clozapine in the treatment of aggressive schizophrenia. *Canadian Journal of Psychiatry* 43(5):466–472.

Jackson v. Indiana, 406 U.S. 715 (1972).

Jennings JL and JD Bell. 2012. The 'ROC' model: Psychiatric evaluation, stabilization and restoration of competency in a jail setting. In *Mental Illnesses—Evaluation, Treatments and Implications*, edited by L L'Abate. Rijeka: Intech, 75–88.

Kapoor R. 2011. Commentary: Jail-based competency restoration. *Journal of the American Academy of Psychiatry and the Law* 39:311–315. http://www.jaapl.org/content/39/3/311.full, accessed January 21, 2014.

Miller RK, N Gowensmith, S Cunningham, and K Bailey-Smith. 2009. Community based competency restoration. In *NASMHPD (National Association of State Mental Health Program Directors), Forensic Division Annual Meeting*, Virginia Beach, VA, September 28–30.

Moeller FG and AC Swann. 2007. Pharmacotherapy of clinical aggression in individuals with psychopathic disorders. In *International Handbook on Psychopathic Disorders and the Law, Volume I: Diagnosis and Treatment*, edited by AR Felthous and H Sass. Chichester, UK: Wiley, 397–416.

Morris DR and NJ DeYoung. 2014. Long-term competence restoration. *Journal of the American Academy of Psychiatry and the Law* 42(1):81–90.

Mossman D. 2007. Predicting restorability of incompetent criminal defendants. *Journal of the American Academy of Psychiatry and the Law* 35(1):34–43.

Mueller C and AM Wylie. 2007. Examining the effectiveness of an intervention designed for the restoration of competency to stand trial. *Behavioral Sciences and the Law* 25(6):891–900.

Noffsinger SG 2001. Restoration to competency practice guideline. *International Journal of Offender Therapy and Comparative Criminology* 45(3):356–362.

Olley MC, TL Nicolls, and J Brink. 2009. Mentally ill individuals in limbo: Obstacles and opportunities for providing psychiatric services to corrections inmates with mental illness. *Behavioral Sciences and the Law* 27(5):811–831.

Pendleton J. 1980. Treatment of persons found incompetent to stand trial. *American Journal of Psychiatry* 137(9):1098–1100.

Pinals DA. 2005. Where two roads meet: Restoration of competence to stand trial from a clinical perspective. *New England Journal on Criminal and Civil Confinement* 31(81):81–108.

Pirelli G, WH Gottdiener, and PA Zapf. 2011. A meta-analytic review of competency to stand trial research. *Psychology, Public Policy, and Law* 17(1):1–53.

Rabinowitz JM, M Avnon, and V Rosenberg. 1996. Effect of clozapine on physical and verbal aggression. *Schizophrenia Research* 22:249–255.

Riggins v. Nevada, 504 U.S. 127 (1992).

Samuel SE and TJ Michals. 2011. Competency restoration. In *Handbook of Forensic Assessment: Psychological and Psychiatric Perspectives*, edited by EY Drogin, FM Dattilio, RL Sadoff, and TG Gutheil. Hoboken, NJ: Wiley, 79–96.

Schwalbe E and A Medalia. 2007. Cognitive dysfunction and competency restoration: Using cognitive remediation to help restore the unrestorable. *Journal of the American Academy of Psychiatry and the Law* 35:518–525.

Scott CL 2003. Commentary: A road map for research in restoration of competency to stand trial. *Journal of the American Academy of Psychiatry and the Law* 31:36–43.

Sell v. United States, 539 U.S. 166 (2003).

Torrey EF, AD Kennard, D Eslinger, R Lamb, and J Pavle, Treatment Advocacy Center and National Sheriffs' Association. 2010. *More Mentally Ill Persons Are in Jails and Prisons than in Hospitals: A Survey of the States*. Arlington, VA: Treatment Advocacy Center and National Sheriffs' Association.

Volavka J, P Czobor, K Nolan et al. 2004. Overt aggression and psychotic symptoms in patients with schizophrenia treated with clozapine, olanzapine, risperidone, or haloperidol. *Journal of Clinical Psychopharmacology* 24:225–228.

Volavka J, P Czobor, L Citrome, and RA Van Dorn. 2016. Effectiveness of antipsychotic drugs against hostility in patients with schizophrenia in the Clinical Antipsychotic Trials of Intervention Effectiveness (CATIE) study. In *Violence in Psychiatry*, edited by KD Warburton and SM Stahl. Cambridge UK: Cambridge University Press, 177–186.

Wall BW and PP Christopher. 2012. A training program for defendants with intellectual disabilities who are found incompetent to stand trial. *Journal of the American Academy of Psychiatry and the Law* 40:366–373.

Washington v. Harper, 494 U.S. 210 (1990).

Zapf PA 2013. *Standardizing Protocols for Treatment to Restore Competency to Stand Trial: Interventions and Clinically Appropriate Time Periods*. Olympia: Washington State Institute for Public Policy.

29

Criminal responsibility

ALAN R. FELTHOUS

INTRODUCTION

This chapter begins with the historical development of the insanity defense, the M'Naghten Rule, and then explains the irresistible impulse test, contemporary insanity defense standards in the United States, including variations in the M'Naghten standard and judicial interpretations of wrongfulness. Other mental defenses include partial responsibility variants, heat of passion, extreme emotional disturbance, and guilty but mentally ill. Issues with relevance to criminal responsibility include voluntary and involuntary intoxication, settled insanity, impulse control disorders, disturbances in consciousness, the battered wife syndrome, and organized psychosis.

ORIGINS OF THE INSANITY DEFENSE

The insanity defense in the United States derives from English common law but also from Medieval and ancient theologies in Europe and the Middle East. Today the insanity defense is not only a central component of U.S. criminal jurisprudence, but a defense that has been incorporated into the criminal law in many other countries as well (Felthous and Saβ 2014; Taylor et al. 2014). Thus the insanity defense, though often criticized and diminished, reflects widespread concepts of procedural fairness and criminal responsibility that have endured for centuries.

The ancient origins of criminal responsibility have both theological and philosophical roots. The theological foundation for the insanity defense has been traced back to the disobedience of Adam and Eve who, by exercising their "free will," defied God by eating the forbidden fruit from the tree of knowledge. Within the Judeo-Christian framework, this account in Genesis led to the concept of free will and criminal responsibility. Aristotle formulated a concept of criminal responsibility in the fourth century BCE that influenced the Western church in the Middle Ages and remains consistent with and supportive of modern concepts of criminal responsibility. He distinguished between voluntary and involuntary acts with respect to their blameworthiness (Aristotle 2004).

In Roman law, specifically the Justinian Code (Justinian, Digest 48.8.12), perhaps the first written law in which insanity was codified as an excuse for crime (Walker 1985), which preceded canonical law of the Roman Church, insane offenders had been treated with leniency because, although a "madman has 'no will'" (Digest 1.18.14, 27), the offender's insanity was considered to be punishment enough ("*satisfurore ipso punitur*" Walker [1968] citing the Digest [1.18.14]).

Already early in the eleventh century, well before the Norman Conquest of 1066, English law distinguished between misdeeds that are intentional, voluntary, and of one's own free will, and those that are the result of coercion or accident (Felthous 2008). In mid-thirteenth century Henry de Bracton's familiar test of insanity, the first published insanity standard in England, emphasized understanding: "An insane person is one who does not know what he is doing, is lacking in mind and reason and is not far removed from the brutes" (de Bracton 1879, 1016). King Edward III recognized that insanity was a complete defense to a criminal charge in the fourteenth century (Simon and Aaronson 1988). By 1500 juries began to acquit offenders based upon insanity (Walker 1985, 25), with the earliest recorded insanity acquittal by a jury in England having occurred in 1505 (Simon and Aaronson 1988).

The maxim "*actus non facitreum nisi mens sit rea*" (an act does not make one guilty unless his mind is guilty) (Coke 1669, 107) had become embedded in English common law by the mid-seventh century (Gardner 1993). In the seventeenth and eighteenth centuries English jurists continued to emphasize the importance of the will and the intellect in criminal responsibility (Felthous 2008). Sir Matthew Hale, the foremost English jurist early in the eighteenth century, who maintained that criminal responsibility required the will which in turn required understanding, provided in 1736 the first published insanity test in English law:

> [I]f these *dementes*... are totally deprived of the uſe of reaſon, they cannot be guilty ordinarily of capital offenſes, for they have not the uſe of underſtanding, and act not as reaſonable

> creatures, but their actions are in effect in the condition of brutes. (Hale 1736, vol. 1, 31)

From the eleventh through the eighteenth centuries, the will gave meaning and coherence to criminal responsibility, but insanity standards were based on understanding, upon which the will depended to function properly (Felthous 2008). Reminiscent of de Bracton's insanity standard formulated almost five centuries earlier, Justice Tracy formulated what became known as the "wild beast test" in his instructions to the jury in the *Arnold Case* published in 1724. To be found insane, the defendant must be found to be

> totally deprived of his understanding and memory, and doth not know what he is doing, no more than an infant ... a brute, or a wild beast. (764–765)

Important in allowing insanity to be partial and not necessarily total (American Academy of Psychiatry and the Law 2014) was the delusion test of the *Hatfield* trial of 1800. That a criminal act could be excused if it were the product of a delusion without reference to awareness of the act's wrongfulness would later be related to the New Hampshire's and the short-lived District of Columbia's versions of the product tests.

In *Elements of Medical Jurisprudence* (Beck 1825), the first comprehensive American textbook on medical jurisprudence (Platt and Diamond 1966), Theodric Beck essentially approved the "right and wrong" test for insanity by favorably citing the use of this test in the English *Bellingham Case* (1812). By the early nineteenth century "right and wrong" had replaced "good and evil," and the former was the generally accepted test of insanity in U.S. courts during the first half of the nineteenth century.

THE M'NAGHTEN RULE

On January 20, 1843, a Scottish wood turner, Daniel M'Naghten, believed that he was being persecuted by the Tory Party of England and Sir Robert Peel, the prime minister and a Tory Party leader. M'Naghten shot and killed Edward Drummond, Peel's secretary. At trial he was acquitted based on insanity. Consternation over this verdict led Queen Victoria to summon 15 Law Lords in the House of Lords to respond to five questions about the insanity defense. Their response to two questions would become known as the M'Naghten Rule (American Academy of Psychiatry and the Law 2014):

> [E]very man is presumed to be sane...[T]o establish a defense on the ground of insanity, it must be proved that, at the time of the committing of the act, the party accused was labouring under such a defect of reason, from disease of the mind, as not to know the nature and quality of the act he was doing; or if he did know it, that he did not know he was doing what was wrong. (M'Naghten's Case 1843, 722)

The M'Naghten Rule of the House of Lords, serving as a model insanity standard, would eventually be adopted into law in England, most jurisdictions in the United States, and Commonwealth countries. It remains today the standard for the majority of states as well as the federal standard for the United States.

THE IRRESISTIBLE IMPULSE INSANITY STANDARD

Conceptually the irresistible impulse insanity standard had its historical psychopathological roots in the earliest studies of personality disorders. (For a fuller review see Saβ and Felthous 2007.) The first English case to use an irresistible impulse test was *Regina v. Oxford* in 1840, 3 years before the M'Naghten trial. In his successful insanity defense of Daniel M'Naghten, defense counsel Alexander Cockburn relied on the *Treatise on the Medical Jurisprudence of Insanity* by Isaac Ray, first published in 1838, in explaining M'Naghten's killing the Prime Minister's secretary as the result of an "irresistible impulse" (Diamond 1956). Almost immediately after the famous and influential M'Naghten Rule was announced, the Commonwealth of Massachusetts added the irresistible impulse rule (500, *Commonwealth v. Rogers* 1844).

Similarly, the District of Columbia would add an irresistible impulse test to its already in place M'Naghten rule cognitive test (*Smith v. United States* 1929). In *Fisher v. United States* (1946) the jury instructions further defined the irresistible impulse rule, wherein the mental illness overwhelmed or destroyed the defendant's will. By 1944, 17 states adopted the irresistible impulse test for insanity (Zilbourg 1944). Although some states combine a volitional or impulse-control disjunctively ("or") with a M'Naghten cognitive test for insanity, as of 1990 no state relies on irresistible impulse as its only test of insanity (American Academy of Psychiatry and the Law 2014).

THE MODEL PENAL CODE INSANITY STANDARD

Reminiscent of the dual cognitive/volitional pronged insanity standard of the Napoleonic concept of criminal responsibility (Felthous and Saß 2014), the American Law Institute (ALI) formulated its ALI standard in its Model Penal Code: "A person is not responsible for criminal conduct if at the time of such conduct as a result of mental disease or defect, he lacks substantial capacity either to appreciate the criminality (wrongfulness) of his conduct or to conform his conduct to the requirements of the law" (American Law Institute 1962). The Model Penal Code left to the states to decide whether to use "criminality" or "wrongfulness" in their insanity standards (*State v. Johnson* 1979). The "second paragraph" of the ALI test (Table 29.1) was intended to exclude a psychopathic personality disorder as a condition that would qualify for the insanity defense (*State v. Johnson* 1979).

Table 29.1 Insanity standards that contributed to insanity jurisprudence in the United States

Name of Standard	Year	Standard
Earliest Published Test in England	Thirteenth century	"An insane person is one who does not know what he is doing, is lacking in mind and reason and is not far removed from the brutes," de Braction, 1223/1224
"The Wild Beast Test"		"The defendant must be [found] to be '... totally deprived of understanding and memory and doth not know what he is doing, no more than an infant ... a brute, or a wild beast ...'" (Arnold's Case, 1724)
Good and Evil Test	1581	"If a mad man or a nautrallfoole, or a lunatic in the time of his lunacie, or a childe y apparently hath no knowledge of good or evil, do kil a ma, this is no felonious act nor any thing forfeited by it ... for they cannot be said to have any understanding wil." (Eirenarche Code, Lambard)
The M'Naghten Rule	1843	"[T]o establish a defense on the ground of insanity, it must be proved that at the time of the committing of the act, the party accused was labouring under such a defect of reason, from disease of the mind, as not to know the nature and quality of the act he was doing; or if he did know it, that he did not know he was doing what was wrong." (M'Naghten Case, 1843)
The Durham Rule	1954	The Product Test "[A]n accused is not criminally responsible if his unlawful act was the product of mental disease or defect." (Durham v. United States, 1954)
The ALI Test	1962	"A person is not responsible for criminal conduct if at the time of such conduct as a result of mental disease or mental defect he lacks substantial capacity either to appreciate the criminality of his conduct or to conform his conduct to the requirements of the law." (American Law Institute, 1962) "The terms 'mental disease or defect' do not include abnormality manifested only by repeated criminal or otherwise antisocial conduct."
The Federal Standard	1984	It is an affirmative defense to a prosecution under any federal statute that at the time of commission of the acts constituting the offense, the defendant, as a result of severe mental disease or defect, was unable to appreciate the nature and quality or wrongfulness of his acts. Mental disease or defect does not otherwise constitute a defense. (Insanity Defense Reform Act of 1984)
Criminal Justice Mental Health Standards	1989	1. A person is not responsible for criminal conduct if, at the time of such conduct, and as a result of mental disease or defect, that person was unable to appreciate the wrongfulness of such conduct. 2. When used as a legal term in this standard *mental disease or defect* refers to: a. "impairment of mind, whether enduring or transitory; or b. mental retardation, either of which substantially affected the mental or emotional processes of the defendant at the time of the alleged offense" (American Bar Association, 1989)

CONTEMPORARY INSANITY DEFENSE STANDARDS IN THE UNITED STATES

Within the past half century the greatest change in insanity jurisprudence in the United States took place soon after John Hinckley's attempted assassination of President Reagan and subsequent insanity acquittal in 1982. Several state and the federal ALI insanity standards were changed by dropping the volitional prong but leaving the cognitive prong of the ALI insanity standard in place. In such jurisdictions this effectively replaced the volitional component with the M'Naghten standard. However, even where the functional component of the ALI standard was amended or repealed, the second paragraph that originally limited application of the ALI standard was typically left in place.

Today most states have a M'Naghten or modified M'Naghten insanity standard, and most of the rest have an ALI or modified ALI insanity standard. Insanity laws for all 50 states' and federal jurisdictions are listed in the AAPL practice guideline on the insanity defense (American Academy of Psychiatry and the Law 2014). Especially useful, the Practice Guideline provides informative tables that go beyond just the insanity standard for each state.

ABOLITION OF THE INSANITY DEFENSE

Four states no longer have an insanity defense: Idaho, Kansas, Montana, and Utah. In *Clark v. Arizona* (2006) the Supreme Court held that due process does not require any "single canonical formulation of legal insanity" (2722). The

U.S. Supreme Court declined an opportunity to consider the constitutionality of abolishing the insanity decision when it denied *certiorari* in *Delling v. Idaho* (2012). Legal scholars argue that abolition of the insanity defense violates due process, because it disallows nullification of general *mens rea* (see Morse and Bonnie 2013).

THE MEANING OF "WRONGFULNESS"

The cognitive prong of most insanity tests in the United States typically requires that the defendant did not know or appreciate that the act he is accused of was "wrong" or "criminal." The meaning and interpretation of "wrongfulness" or "wrong" varies among states, however (Goldstein and Rotter 1988), and further clarification may be needed to determine whether this is based on a "subjective moral standard" or an "objective moral standard." The subjective moral standard refers to the defendant's subjective belief of whether the criminal act was wrong, whereas the objective moral standard is what the defendant believed to be other people's belief as to whether the act was morally right or wrong (Goldstein and Rotter 1988).

THE BURDEN AND STANDARD OF PROOF

All defendants are presumed to be innocent and sane, until proven otherwise in court. Because of the presumption of innocence, the prosecution has the burden of proving guilt—that is, all elements of the offense charged, including the mental elements—beyond a reasonable doubt (*Davis v. United States* 1895). At the time of Hinckley's acquittal in 1982, the prosecution in federal and most state courts also had the burden of proof that the defendant was not insane. Reforms that followed resulted in the defense assuming the burden of proving insanity in federal and most (75%) state courts (Steadman et al. 1993, 64). Although the standard of proof for the defendant in some states is "preponderance of the evidence," in the District of Columbia and all federal and other state jurisdictions, it is "clear and convincing evidence" (Slovenko 1995).

Involuntary imposition of the insanity defense

The lead landmark case on involuntary imposition of the insanity defense is *Frendak v. United States* decided by the Court of Appeals for the District of Columbia in 1979. Prior cases upheld the trial court's authority to impose an insanity defense on an unwilling defendant. According to *Frendak* a trial judge must first determine whether the defendant waived the insanity defense intelligently and voluntarily before proceeding to impose an insanity defense on an unwilling defendant. The jurisprudence on involuntary imposition of the insanity defense is not settled or uniform. One-third of the jurisdictions allow imposition of the insanity defense on an unwilling defendant. There is considerable variation on who may impose this defense and under what circumstances. Whether the defendant needs to be trial incompetent for involuntary imposition also varies widely (Miller 2002).

DEIFIC DECREE

A defendant, whose act was the fulfillment of a delusional commandment from God, cannot have known the act to have been wrong even if he or she knew the nature and quality of the act and knew that the act violated the law. Known as the *deific decree*, this version of the insanity defense has been adopted by jurisdictions in New York, Washington, and Colorado. The concept includes the moral standard of wrongfulness discussed above.

OTHER MENTAL DEFENSES

Partial responsibility, diminished capacity, and the *mens rea* defense

These three terms—partial responsibility, diminished capacity, and the *mens rea* defense—essentially denote the same principle. Not only for the insanity verdict but for all criminal convictions, the prosecution must prove each element of the offense, including each mental element, beyond a reasonable doubt (*Davis v. United States* 1895; *In re Winship* 1970, 364). If the defendant can defend against a mental element of the crime that the prosecution must prove in order for the defendant to be convicted of the crime, then the defendant can only be convicted of a lesser included crime that does not require this specific mental element. Typically this means reduction of the offense from murder to manslaughter or from first-degree to second-degree murder. Accordingly, the criminal punishment is reduced to correspond with the less serious offense (*Fisher v. United States* 1946).

Diminished capacity

Diminished capacity must be distinguished from the defense of diminished responsibility that originated in Scotland (*HM Adv. v. Dingwall*, 5 Irvine 466, 1867) and was adopted by the British Parliament within the English Homicide Act of 1957. The "diminished capacity" defense was first introduced in the United States by the California Supreme Court in 1949 (Miller 2003), which over several decades developed a remarkable jurisprudence of the doctrine (Bromberg 1979) until the California legislative replaced the diminished capacity with diminished actuality (Nair and Weinstock 2007). Although the classical principle of diminished capacity no longer exists in California, the pioneering jurisprudence that developed the doctrine in California served as a model for other states that would adopt and/or continue to allow a diminished capacity defense.

Heat of passion

Long used to reduce the criminal charge from murder to manslaughter or other less serious offense is the heat of passion defense. Three elements of this defense that must be proven are as follows: (1) when committing the act, the defendant was under the influence of heat of passion; (2) the sequence of events that led to the heat of passion would have caused a normal person to have acted similarly; and (3) from the provoking event to the act there was no time for the defendant to cool off (Goldstein 1989). Notice that the heat of passion defense does not presuppose a mental illness or defect (Felthous et al. 2001).

The heat of passion defense can negate criminal intent because a defendant who acted from a sudden, incendiary provocation could not at the same time be acting with premeditation. Because intent is an element of the crime of murder to be proven by the prosecution, the prosecution may have the burden of proving that the defendant lacked "heat of passion."

Extreme emotional disturbance

Several states have adopted a broader, formalized defense that can involve some measure of mental disturbance. New York, for example, enacted the "extreme emotional disturbance defense" in 1967 (New York Penal Law 1967). To establish this defense, the defendant must prove that he or she was under an extreme emotional disturbance (EED) when the act was committed. The defendant must as well prove that "there must be a reasonable explanation or excuse, the reasonableness of which is to be determined from the viewpoint of a person in the defendant's situation under the circumstances as the defendant believed them to be" (170). A defendant can put forth the defense if he or she had sustained a "significant mental trauma," according to New York State's highest court. This trauma can erupt inexplicably after remaining dormant, causing the defendant to commit homicide (*People v. Patterson* 1976); thus, in contrast to the classical heat of passion defense, a cooling off period is unnecessary for EED. In contrast to Maine's "heat of passion" defense, EED is a partial affirmative defense wherein the burden is placed on the defendant to prove emotional disturbance by a predominance of the evidence (*People v. Patterson* 1976). In contrast to the "heat of passion" defense, EED does not negate criminal intent, so the prosecution retains the burden of proving intent. The defendant has the burden of proving that the defendant was under the influence of extreme emotional influence when he formed intent.

ALCOHOL, DRUGS, AND CRIMINAL RESPONSIBILITY

In the first half of the eighteenth century Lord Chief Justice Matthew Hale enunciated what has become known as the voluntary intoxication exclusion of the insanity defense. A person who commits an offense while he or she is afflicted with *dementia affectata*, i.e., intoxication, "shall have no privilege by the voluntary contracted madness, but shall have the same judgment as if he were in his right senses" (Hale 1736, 32). Hale went on to describe two situations wherein the effects of an intoxicating substance can lead to exculpation; two potentially exculpatory situations that amount to prevailing law in the United States today (Slovenko 1995). Today the first of these exceptions is known as "involuntary or 'innocent' intoxication," and the second as "settled insanity."

The voluntary consumption of an intoxicating substance, even if causing psychotic symptoms that would meet the functional criteria of insanity, does not qualify as a mental disease or defect for purposes of the insanity defense. The voluntary intoxication exception has prevailed regardless how powerfully psychotomimetic the substance (Slovenko 1995).

Although not qualifying for the insanity defense with complete acquittal, depending on jurisdictional law voluntary intoxication can pertain to a diminished capacity or *mens rea* defense (Singh 1933), or to mitigation at sentencing (e.g., Texas Penal Code, §8.04). Voluntary intoxication can be used as a *mens rea* defense only for the *mens rea* of a specific intent crime: voluntary intoxication is never a defense, even a partial defense, for a general intent crime (Johnson 1994–1995). Montana law does not allow evidence of involuntary intoxication to establish a defendant's diminished capacity (*Montana v. Egelhoff* 1995, 1996) in contrast to the law in most states (Miller 2003). Because of variations in definition and application of diminished responsibility *vis à vis* voluntary intoxication, it behooves the examining psychiatrist to become familiar with the jurisdictional law (American Academy of Psychiatry and the Law 2014).

If consumption was not voluntary and if the resulting mental condition satisfied the functional criteria of the insanity defense, such intoxication could satisfy the insanity defense after all, sometimes termed "temporary insanity" (American Academy of Psychiatry and the Law 2014). Examples of involuntarily induced intoxication or psychosis include taking a mind-altering substance unknowingly or taking a lawfully prescribed medication that results in an unexpected, untoward mental change and the criminal act (American Academy of Psychiatry and the Law 2014). Involuntary intoxication can, according to jurisdictional law, result in complete negation of criminal responsibility because the offender was considered to have been "unconscious" at the time of the offense and incapable of *mens rea* or the formation of criminal intent. As Weinstock (1999) explained, however, the jurisprudence of *mens rea* defenses is "complex, differs from state to state, and is much more complicated than the insanity defense" (14).

Use of alcohol or a drug can result in a complete acquittal based on the insanity defense in jurisdictions that allow a defense of settled insanity. If it can be demonstrated that use of a substance caused or exacerbated psychotic symptoms that persisted after the acute effects of intoxication have passed, the defendant may have a recognized defense of settled insanity (Carter-Yamauchi 1998). The defense of settled insanity has been recognized by several but not all U.S. jurisdictions.

IMPULSE CONTROL DISORDERS

In jurisdictions with an irresistible impulse insanity rule or the ALI insanity standard with its volitional prong, one might expect that a disorder of impulse control (e.g., kleptomania, pyromania, intermittent explosive disorder) could qualify as a mental disorder. There is some evidence that once a pathological condition is recognized in the current edition of the *Diagnostic and Statistical Manual of Mental Disorders* (*DSM*), it can qualify as a mental disorder for the insanity defense, barring further explicit statutory exclusions. After Connecticut courts both allowed (*State v. Lafferty* 1981) and disallowed (*United States v. Torniero* 1984) pathological gambling as an insanity defense, the Connecticut legislature enacted law that excluded pathological gambling for an insanity defense (Conn. Gen. Sta. Ann. §53a-13(c)(2) [West, 1985]). Courts in some jurisdictions have allowed intermittent explosive disorder (e.g., Maryland, *Robey v. State* 1983; New York, *People v. Smith* 1995), whereas other courts have disallowed intermittent explosive disorder (U.S. Military, *United States v. Lewis* 1991).

UNCONSCIOUSNESS, AUTOMATISM, AND SOMNAMBULISM

In order for a criminal act to have been committed, the offender must have not only performed the physical act, but he or she must have done so voluntarily and consciously. Within the criminal law an "act" is "an intentional bodily movement (or intentional inaction) performed in a state of reasonably integrated consciousness" (Morse and Hoffman 2008, 1084–1085). If the *actus reus*, as so defined, was not committed, a crime was not committed. A defense of unconsciousness (*People v. Kelly* 1973) or automatism (Slovenko 1995) is therefore a complete defense.

Sleepwalking can negate the action requirement of a *prima facie* case or provide the "criteria for the affirmative defense of automatism" (Morse and Hoffman 2008). Not having legal authority in the United States, a leading decision by the Supreme Court of Canada may be the best-known sleepwalking case (*R. v. Parks* 1992). Although most cases of criminal acts committed while the defendant was asleep are attributed to sleepwalking (somnambulism), also to be included in the differential are REM sleep disorder and nocturnal dream-derived delusional behavior (Hempel et al. 2003).

POSTTRAUMATIC STRESS DISORDER

Posttraumatic stress disorder (PTSD) has been asserted in various mental defenses including the insanity defense (Jordan et al. 1986), diminished capacity defense (Slovenko 1995), unconsciousness defense, and imperfect self-defense (Berger et al. 2012). It has also been used for mitigation in plea bargaining and sentencing and to ask for a new trial based on failure to investigate for PTSD or ineffective counsel (Slovenko 1995). PTSD has been used successfully for a guilty but insane verdict in Oregon (McGuire and Cleak 2011). Juries have found defendants not guilty by reason of insanity due to PTSD (Appelbaum et al. 1993). The U.S. Supreme Court recognized the importance of a defendant's military history, combat experience, and related mental issues in effectively presenting evidence for mitigation in capital cases (*Porter v. McCollum* 2009). Possible PTSD from service in Operation Iraqi Freedom was the basis for a federal judge to depart downward from the Federal Sentencing Guidelines (*United States v. John Brownfield* 2009). A critical component to the success of a PTSD defense is establishing its clear and direct connection with the criminal act and by support for the traumatic exposure (Berger et al. 2012). The above cases and reviews were based on cases in which diagnostic criteria for PTSD predated *DSM-5* with its substantial changes. Levin et al. discuss the current criteria for PTSD (2014).

PERFECT AND IMPERFECT SELF-DEFENSE AND THE BATTERED WIFE SYNDROME

Psychiatrists do not usually receive referrals when the defense is self-defense, as this defense does not involve a question of abnormal psychology. For an imperfect defense of battered wife or spouse syndrome, however, mental health testimony can be essential. For such cases the consultant should be familiar with the evolution of perfect and imperfect self-defense (see Perkins 1969) as well as the scientific support for the battered wife syndrome.

Where a woman who is beaten repeatedly by her husband, eventually kills him and then claims self-defense, questions can arise such as whether the killing was motivated by revenge, whether she was "against the wall" (self-defense—that can result in acquittal) or could have fled from him, and whether at the time of the killing she believed that she herself was in such imminent danger of being killed or seriously harmed that she had to kill him to avert this danger (imperfect self-defense—that can reduce the grade of the offense). Particularly with recognition of the "battered wife syndrome" in the 1970s, expert testimony became increasingly admissible to establish the mental element of the self-defense defense.

Following *Ibn̄-Tamas v. United States* in 1979, some courts found testimony on the battered wife syndrome to be relevant in a self-defense defense against a charge of murder, even as they questioned the reliability of such testimony. In a New Jersey Supreme Court Case (*State v. Kelly* 1984), the court also left to the trial court to decide admissibility based on whether such evidence was sufficiently reliable. (For a different approach, a version of the duress defense taken by the Canadian Supreme Court, see *R. v. Lavellee* 1990.) In most jurisdictions courts admit expert testimony on how domestic violence can influence the behavior and perceptions of battered victims whether they be heterosexual women, nonheterosexual women, adult men, or children (American Academy of Psychiatry and the Law 2014).

PREMEDITATED BY PSYCHOTIC: DELUSIONALLY MOTIVATED OFFENSES

Where the defendant had carefully and purposefully planned and carried out his or her criminal act, but the act was motivated by delusion, the determination of psychosis and its influence on the defendant's behavior can be challenging. Yet in some such cases the defendant can be found to have met criteria for the insanity or other mental illness defense (Felthous et al. 2001). Some schizophrenic offenders show well-organized thought and behavior and yet can be quite dangerous because of delusionally driven behavior (Böker and Häfner 1973).

Once such disorder is diagnosed and the criminal act is thought to have been motivated by delusion, whether or not the defendant's condition satisfied the jurisdictional insanity standard, the defense can hinge on whether the defendant believed his or her act to have been wrong. Here there is the possibility of not only alternative, mutually exclusive motives, delusional and nondelusional, but also multiple "rational" motives for the same act that must be considered in formulating the relationship or lack thereof between delusion and the criminal act.

SUMMARY KEY POINTS

- The origins of criminal responsibility are both theological and philosophical.
- The M'Naghten Rule is the insanity standard for the majority of states and the federal government.
- Important in understanding the meaning of "wrongfulness" in a jurisdictional moral insanity standard is the distinction between subjective and objective moral standard.
- In most jurisdictions the standard of proof for the insanity defense is preponderance of the evidence, with the burden of proof belonging to the defendant.
- Where a mental defense is based on PTSD, of critical importance is the connection between PTSD and the criminal act.
- The imperfect self-defense in homicide cases involving the battered wife syndrome requires that the defendant spouse believed that she was in imminent danger of being killed or seriously harmed.

REFERENCES

American Academy of Psychiatry and the Law. 2014. AAPL practice guideline for forensic psychiatric evaluation of defendants raising the insanity defense. *Journal of the American Academy of Psychiatry and the Law* 42(4):S1–S76.

American Bar Association (ABA). 1989. *Criminal Justice Mental Health Standards*. Washington, DC: American Bar Association.

American Law Institute. 1962. *Model Penal Code*. Philadelphia: American Law Institute. 4.01.

American Medical Association. 1995. *Current Opinions of the Council and Ethical and Judicial Affairs*. Section 9.07. Washington, DC: American Medical Association.

Appelbaum PS, RZ Jick, T Grisso, D Givelber, E Silver, and H Steadman. 1993. Use of posttraumatic stress disorder to support an insanity defense. *American Journal of Psychiatry* 150:229–234.

Aristotle. 2004. *Nichomachean Ethics*. H Peters, trans. New York: Barnes and Noble, 39–64.

Arnold's Case, 16 Howell St. Tr. 695, 764 (1724).

Beck TR. 1825. *Elements of Medical Jurisprudence*. London: John Anderson, Medical Bookseller, West-Smithfield. Reprinted by Kessinger Publishing, Whitefish, MT.

Bellingham's Case. 1812. *The Proceedings of the Old Bailey. London's Central Criminal Court, 1674–1913*. http://www.oldbaileyonline.org/browse.jsp?id=t18120513-5&div=t18120513-5&terms=John Bellingham#highlights, accessed December 10, 2013.

Berger O, DE McNiel, and RL Binder. 2012. PTSD as a criminal defense: A review of case law. *Journal of the American Academy of Psychiatry and the Law* 40(4):509–521.

Böker W and H Häfne. 1973. *Gewalttaten Geistesgestörter* (German: The Violent Mentally Ill). Berlin: Springer.

de Bracton H. 1879. In *Angliãe Legibuseet Conseutubinibus 2*. Edited by T Twiss, London: Longman and Co. (Cited by Brombard W. 1979. *The Uses of Psychiatry in the Law: A Clinical View of Forensic Psychiatry*. Westport, CT: Quorum Books, 5.)

Bromberg W. 1979. *The Uses of Psychiatry in the Law: A Clinical View of Forensic Psychiatry*. Westport, CT: Quorum Books.

Carter-Yamauchi C. 1998. *Drugs, Alcohol and the Insanity Defense: The Debate over "Settled" Insanity*. Legislative Reference Bureau Report 7. Honolulu, HI: Legislative Reference Bureau, http:lrbhawaii.org/reports/legrpts/lrb/rpts98/settled.pdf, accessed July 4, 2016.

Clark v. Arizona, 126 S. Ct. 2709 (2006).

Coke E. 1669. *The Third Part of the Institutes of High Treason, and Other Pleas of the Crown, and Criminal Causes*, 4th edition, London, 107.

Commonwealth v. Abner Rogers Jr., 7 Metcalf 500 (Mass. 1844).

Conn. Gen. Stat. Ann. §53a-13(c)(2) (West 1985).

Davis v. United States, 160 U.S. 469 (1895).

Delling v. Idaho (Dissent Breyer, pp 1–3, No. 11–1515 (U.S. Nov 26, 2012) (Breyer J, dissenting). http://en.wikisource.org/wiki/Delling_v._Idaho/Dissent_Breyer, accessed January 17, 2014.

Diamond B. 1956. Isaac Ray and the trial of Daniel M'Naghten. *American Journal of Psychiatry* 112:651–656.

Durham v. United States, 214 F. 2d 862 (D.C. Cir. 1954).

English Homicide Act of 1957, 5 & 6 Eliz. 2, Ch. 2 Sec. 2. Esquirol, E.: *Des Maladies Mentales Considéreessousles Rapports Médical, Hygiéniqueet Médico-Legal* [Mental Diseases under Medical, Hygienic and Medico-Legal Aspects) Paris: Bailliéreé, 1839.

Felthous AR. 2008. The will: From metaphysical freedom to normative functionalism. *Journal of the American Academy of Psychiatry and the Law* 36(1):16–24.

Felthous AR, HL Kröber, and H Saβ. 2001. Forensic evaluation for civil and criminal competencies and criminal responsibilities in German and Anglo-American legal systems. In *Psychiatry for Today*, edited by F Henn, N Sartorius, H Helmchen, and H Lauter, Heidelberg, Germany: Springer-Verlag, 287–302.

Felthous AR and H Saβ. 2011. *Diagnostisches Prozess und Voreingenommenheit in der forensischenPsychiatrie* (German: The diagnostic process and bias in forensic psychiatry). *Forensische Psychiatrie, Psychologie, Kriminologie* 5(3):36–144.

Felthous AR and H Saβ. 2014. Forensic psychiatry. In *Handbook of Forensic Medicine*, edited by B Madea, Chichester, United Kingdom: Wiley, 813–828.

Fisher v. United States, 328 U.S. 463 (D.C. Cir., 1946).

Frendak v. United States, 408 A. 2d 364 (1979).

Gardner MR. 1993. The *Mens Rea* enigma: Observations on the role of motives in the criminal law past and present. *Ohio Law Review* 635–750.

Goldstein RL. 1989. New York's "Extreme Emotional Disturbance" defense: A hybrid creature of the law at the psycho-legal interface. In *Criminal Court Consultation*, edited by R Rosner and RB Harmon, New York: Plenum, 119–133.

Goldstein RL and M Rotter. 1988. The psychiatrist's guide to right and wrong: Judicial standards of wrongfulness since M'Naghten. *Bulletin of the American Academy of Psychiatry and the Law* 16(4):359–367.

Hale M. 1736, 2003. *Historia Placitorum Coronæ, The History of Pleas of the Crown*, Vol. I. London: Gosling, reprinted & copyrighted Clark, NJ: The Lawbook Exchange, Ltd., 2003.

Hempel A, AR Felthous, and JR Meloy. 2003. Psychotic dream-related aggression: A critical review and proposal. *Aggression and Violent Behavior* 8(6):599–620.

HM Adv. v. Dingwall, 5 Irvine 466 (1867).

Ibn-Tamas v. United States, 407 A. 2d 626 (1979).

Johnson LA. 1994–1995. Settled insanity is not a defense: Has the Colorado supreme court gone crazy? *Bieber v. People. University of Kansas Law Review* 43:259–274.

Jordan HW, GL Howe, J Gelsomino, and EW Lockert. 1986. Post-traumatic stress disorder: A psychiatric defense. *Journal of the National Medical Association* 78(2):119–126.

Justinian, Digest, circa 533 AD.

Levin AP, SB Kleinman, and JS Adler. 2014. DSM-5 and posttraumatic stress disorder. *Journal of the American Academy of Psychiatry and the Law* 42:146–158.

McGuire J and S Clark. 2011. PTSD and the law: An update. *PTSD Research Quarterly* 22(1):1–6.

Miller RD. 2002. *Hendricks v. People*: Forcing the insanity defense on an unwilling defendant. *Journal of the American Academy of Psychiatry and the Law* 30(2):295–297.

Miller RD. 2003. Criminal responsibility. In *Principles and Practice of Forensic Psychiatry*, edited by R Rosner, London: Arnold, 213–232.

M'Naghten's Case, 8 Eng. Rep. 718 (1843).

Montana v. Egelhoff, 272 Mont. 114 (1995).

Montana v. Egelhoff, 116 S. Ct. 2013 (1996).

Morse SJ and RJ Bonnie. 2013. Abolition of the insanity defense violates due process. *Journal of the American Academy of Psychiatry and the Law* 41(4):488–495.

Morse S and Hoffman MB. 2008. The uneasy entente between insanity and mens rea: Beyond Clark v. Arizona. *The Journal of Criminal Law and Criminology* 97(4):1071–1150.

Nair MS and R Weinstock. 2007. Psychopathy, diminished capacity and responsibility. In *The International Handbook of Psychopathic Disorders and the Law, Volume II: Laws and Policies*, edited by AR Felthous and H Saß, Chichester, England: Wiley, 275–301.

New York Penal Law §125.25, subd.L. par. [a]; §125.27 subd. 2 par. [a] (1967).

People v. Kelly, 10 Cal. 3d 565 (1973).

People v. Patterson, 383 N.Y.S. 2d 573 (1976).

People v. Smith, 217 A.D. 2d 221 (N.Y. App. Div. 1995).

Perkins RM. 1969. *Criminal Law*, 2nd edition. Mineola, NY: Foundation Press.

Platt A and BL Diamond. 1966. The origins of the 'Right and Wrong' test of criminal responsibility and its subsequent development in the United States: An history survey. *California Law Review* 54:1227–1259.

Porter v. McCollum, 130 S. Ct. 447 (2009).

R. v. Lavellee, 1 SCR 852, 1990. www.canlii.org/en/ca/scc/doc/1990/1990canlii95/1990canlii95.html, accessed December 27, 2013.

Ray I. 1838. *Treatise on the Medical Jurisprudence of Insanity*. Boston: Charles C. Little and James Brown.

Regina v. Oxford, 9 Car. & P. 525, 546 (1840).

Rex v. Arnold, 16 How. St., Tr. 695 (1724).

Rex v. Hadfield, 27 St. Tr. 1281 (1800).

R. v. Parks, 75 C.C.C. (3d) 287 (1992).

Robey v. State, 456A 2d 953 (Md. Ct. Spec. App. 1983).

Saβ H and Felthous AR. 2007. History and conceptual development of psychopathic disorders. In *The International Handbook of Psychopathic Disorders and the Law, Vol. I, Diagnosis and Treatment*, edited by AR Felthous and H Saβ, Chichester, England: John Wiley & Sons, Ltd., 9–30.

Singh RU. 1933. History of the defence of drunkenness in English Criminal Law. *The Law Quarterly Review* 49:528–546.

Simon RJ and DE Aaronson. 1994. The insanity defense 4–5, 1998, cited by Leslie A. Johnson "Settled Insanity is Not a Defense: Has the Colorado Supreme Court Gone Crazy?" *Bieber v. People. University of Kansas Law Review* 43:259.

Slovenko R. 1995. *Psychiatry and Criminal Culpability.* New York: Wiley.

Smith v. United States, 59 App. D.C., 144, 36 F. 2d 548 (1929).

State v. Johnson, 399 A. 2d 469 (1979).

State v. Kelly, 478 A. 2d 364 (N.J. 1984 [cited by Berger et al., 2012]).

State v. Lafferty, No. 44359 (Conn. Super. Ct. June 5, 1981).

Steadman HJ, MA McGreevy, JP Morrissey, LA Callahan, PC Robbins, and C Ciricione. 1993. *Before and After Hinckley: Evaluating Insanity Defense Reform.* London: Guilford Press.

Taylor PJ (ed.), E Dunn, AR Felthous et al. 2014. Forensic psychiatry and its interfaces outside of the UK: Comparisons across five continents. In *Forensic Psychiatry: Clinical, Legal and Ethical Issues*, 2nd edition, edited by J Gunn and PJ Taylor, Oxford, UK: Butterworth-Heinemann, 111–147.

Texas Penal Code. Section 8.04 Intoxication. Title 2, Chapter 8. http://www.statutes.legis.state.txus/Docs/PE/htm/PE.8.htm, accessed June 13, 2014.

Twiss T. 1879. *In Henrici De Bracton: legibuset Consuetudinibus Angliae.* London: Longman and Co.

United States v. John Brownfield, Jr. Memorandum Opinion and Order on Sentencing. Case No. 08-cr-00452-JLK United States District Court, District of Colorado, December 18, 2009, *nunc pro nunc.*

United States v. Lewis, 34 M.J. 745 (N.M. Ct. Crim. App. 1991).

United States v. Torniero, 735 F. 2d 725 (1984).

Walker N. 1968. *Crime and Insanity in England.* Edinburgh: Edinburgh University Press.

Walker N. 1985. The insanity defense, before 1800. *Annals of the American Academy of Political and Social Science* 477:25–30.

Weinstock R. 1999. Drug and alcohol intoxication: Mens rea defenses. *American Academy of Psychiatry and the Law Newsletter* 24(1):14–15.

In re Winship, 397 U.S. 358 (1970).

Zilbourg G.1944. Legal aspects of psychiatry. In *One Hundred Years of American Psychiatry*, edited by JK Hall, New York: Columbia University Press, 507–584.

30

Post-adjudication evaluations and disposition of insanity acquittees

LI-WEN LEE

INTRODUCTION

Although the insanity defense addresses issues of fairness in the law, the disposition of insanity cases involves consideration of multiple areas of concern, including protection of public safety, provision of appropriate clinical services, and respect for individual liberty interests, all within the constraints of available resources. Historically, insanity acquittees were indefinitely committed to inpatient settings for periods of time longer than the criminal sentence they would have received if they had been found guilty. Beginning in the 1960s, however, mental health advocacy efforts began to yield shorter commitments and deinstitutionalization for the psychiatric inpatient population as a whole. The change similarly impacted the commitment of insanity acquittees, and long-term commitment of defendants found not guilty by reason of insanity (NGRI) could no longer be assumed (Appelbaum 1982). With insanity acquittees returning to the community at a more rapid pace, the public began to perceive the insanity defense as overused (Steadman and Morrissey 1986). The attempted assassination of former President Ronald Reagan by John Hinckley in 1981 and his subsequent use of the insanity defense (*United States v. Hinckley* 1982) added to public perception of the insanity defense as misused and resulted in further public scrutiny of both the insanity defense and management of insanity acquittees (Hans and Slater 1983).

Public perception of the insanity defense as a legal loophole was related to a number of additional factors: mistrust of psychiatric testimony, lack of knowledge about the legal standard for insanity, and the misconceptions about the likely length of confinement subsequent to an insanity acquittal (Hans 1983). Contrary to persistent public perception that the insanity defense is overused (Silver et al. 1994; Perlin 1996), a study of eight states found that the insanity defense is only raised on 1% of felony cases, and when raised, a successful insanity plea occurs in only 26% of attempts (Callahan et al. 1991).

Against this backdrop of misperceptions about the insanity defense and insanity acquittees, the Hinckley case and other high-profile insanity defense cases provided the impetus for insanity defense reform (Borum and Fulero 1999). In some states, a verdict of guilty but mentally ill (GBMI) was added to reduce use of the insanity defense (Steadman and Morrissey 1986), and in a few states (Kansas, Montana, Idaho, and Utah), the insanity defense was abolished altogether.

In those states that retained the insanity defense, insanity defense reform redefined the insanity defense itself and instituted fundamental changes to the post-adjudication process. In many states, procedures were developed to allow the original hearing court to retain jurisdiction over an insanity acquittee's case as he or she moved toward community release. Another example of post-reform change was the provision to allow prosecutor participation in court hearings for community furloughs or release. Conditional release programs were developed to enhance public safety and ensure ongoing treatment (Borum and Fulero 1999).

This chapter focuses on state management of insanity acquittees. The structures of these systems, in the wake of insanity defense reform in the 1980s, reflect a shifting of attention to public safety as a counterbalance to the perception that the insanity defense serves as a mechanism for criminals to avoid punishment. As a result, insanity acquittee management involves numerous, and sometimes competing considerations, including public safety, clinical needs, and limited mental health resources. Clinicians who provide treatment to this patient population may find themselves in a dual role of both treating the patient's illness and addressing the potential dangerousness. They may be required to make disposition decisions based not only on clinical issues but also on public safety considerations. The role of forensic psychiatrists in the disposition of insanity acquittees typically requires some form of evaluation of risk.

Variations on insanity acquittee management systems will be reviewed, including the use of conditional release, degree of judicial oversight, and use of risk assessment. Descriptions of five state systems will be provided as illustrations of these variations.

OVERVIEW OF STATE MANAGEMENT OF INSANITY ACQUITTEES

After a finding of not guilty by reason of insanity, acquittees may be involuntarily committed for inpatient treatment. Commitment is often to hospitals operated by the state mental health agency, but some states also allow commitment to hospitals operated by the state corrections agency. As an example, Massachusetts allows commitment of insanity acquittees to Bridgewater State Hospital, which is operated by the Department of Corrections (MGL Chapter 123 §16(a) and (b)). Most states, but not all, have commitment procedures for insanity acquittees that are distinct from ordinary civil commitment. The Supreme Court, in *Jones v. United States* (1983) and *Foucha v. Louisiana* (1992), has upheld these commitment procedures for insanity acquittees. *Jones v. U.S.* involved a misdemeanor offense of petit larceny in Washington, DC. After successfully raising the insanity defense, the acquittee was automatically committed to St. Elizabeth's and eventually committed for a period of time exceeding the 1-year maximum penalty associated with his offense. In this case, the Supreme Court upheld the practice of automatic commitment on the grounds that an NGRI finding confirms both that a crime was committed and that mental illness was the cause. The Supreme Court held that an NGRI acquittee could be held in a mental institution until no longer mentally ill or dangerous, and therefore duration of commitment was not related to the length of the hypothetical criminal sentence.

Foucha v. Louisiana concerned the Louisiana statute requiring an NGRI acquittee to be held in the hospital until no longer dangerous, and which placed the burden on the acquittee to show in court that he or she was no longer dangerous. The Supreme Court, in a five-four decision, ruled that an NGRI acquittee could only be committed if still both mentally ill and dangerous.

More recently, in *State v. Klein* (2005), the Washington State Supreme Court reviewed the ongoing retention of an insanity acquittee whose conditional release had been revoked after she resumed using drugs and failed to report to her probation officer. The original offense leading to her status as an insanity acquittee had been related to psychiatric symptoms resulting from drug use, and she was diagnosed with polysubstance dependence and personality disorder, not otherwise specified. The court held that these diagnoses could constitute a mental illness for the purpose of ongoing commitment of an insanity acquittee, and further held that the illness justifying commitment did not need to be the same as that illness forming the basis for the insanity acquittal (Soliman and Resnick 2006). This decision expanded the definition of mental illness required to justify commitment of insanity acquittees in Washington State.

Mental illness and dangerousness are also both required for standard civil commitment, but for insanity acquittees, the seriousness of the instant offense has been found to be an important factor in the length of confinement, sometimes even overshadowing the mental disorder (Silver et al. 1994). In most states, the court that determines NGRI also determines commitment, but two states, Oregon and Connecticut, utilize a review board known as the Psychiatric Security Review Board (PSRB). As another variation on post-adjudication commitment procedures, there are states such as North Carolina where commitment is automatic for insanity acquittees (G.S. §122C-276), at least for an initial period.

In most, but not all, states the state mental health agency must obtain court approval prior to releasing an insanity acquittee into the community (Fitch 2014). In those states where court approval is necessary, opposition to the release from the court or the prosecutor was identified as the most common obstacle to release (Fitch 2014). In the adversarial court system, the prosecution has the opportunity to present evidence and testimony to counter the mental health agency's position that the acquittee is no longer dangerous or mentally ill.

Conditional release for insanity acquittees was introduced in the late 1970s and is utilized to maintain acquittees under court jurisdiction even after hospital discharge. Conditional release provides a least restrictive alternative while maintaining oversight intended to prevent recidivism. In both criminal and civil contexts, conditional release can be a cost-saving step, when compared to further incarceration or hospitalization (Weinstein 2014). Typical conditions of release include stipulations regarding treatment, housing, and supervision. By providing a mechanism for conditional release, rather than allowing for only unconditional release, public safety is enhanced. Most, but not all, states have some form of conditional release (Fitch 2014). In states that utilize a conditional release process, conditional release is viewed as a valuable interim step, during which time there are legal mechanisms by which an insanity acquittee could be removed from the community if safety concerns arise. In the absence of a conditional release system, there is no mandated mechanism to ensure follow-up or monitor outcomes. Clinicians, and courts, are forced to make all-or-nothing release determinations without the benefit of a more gradual transition to the community.

It has been suggested that key features of a successful conditional release program include centralized responsibility, a uniform system of treatment and supervision, and a network of community services (McGreevy et al. 1991), but there are many variations. In some states, the length of conditional release is indeterminate. In contrast, Ohio limits the length of conditional release to the length of the maximum criminal sentence (Callahan and Silver 1998).

Regarding the degree of centralization within state systems, Ohio uses decentralized process where release applications initiated by the treatment team are sent to the presiding judge (Callahan and Silver 1998), while under the

PSRB system, release recommendations historically originated with the PSRB rather than the treaters (Bloom and Buckley 2013). New York has a hybrid structure, with the recommendation to release initiated by the treatment provider but central office review and approval required before the application reaches court (NYCRR part 541).

The decision to release an insanity acquittee to the community entails consideration of several issues. The level of risk to the community must be understood, as well as the conditions of that release that would be necessary to maintain safety. A necessary accompanying consideration is whether the acquittee will comply with those conditions. Douglas (2014) argued that the HCR-20, as a structured professional judgment approach to risk assessment, is useful in informing conditional release decisions. Despite the development of actuarial risk assessment tools and structured professional judgment approaches, recent research regarding the process used to make recommendations for community release has found a great degree of variability. A survey of evaluators in nine states found that there was little uniformity in evaluator conceptualizations of the conditional release process, of how factors should be prioritized in making conditional release determinations, or in the use of structured assessment (Gowensmith et al. 2014).

This issue is not limited to the United States. In Canada, as in the United States, most insanity acquittees are initially hospitalized before returning to the community. A review board determines when an acquittee is ready for release. A study of the Canadian process found that structured risk assessment was not a standard component of information presented to the review board (Crocker et al. 2014). Certain factors influenced the review board significantly: violent behavior and compliance between review board hearings, seriousness of the instant offense, as well as static and dynamic risk factors similar to those found in the HCR-20. Crocker et al. (2014) suggested that the review board might be more cautious in their determinations in the absence of a comprehensive risk assessment.

Oregon

Since 1978, Oregon's system of insanity acquittee management has been based on the Psychiatric Security Review Board (PSRB). Prior to the institution of the PSRB system, there was no form of conditional release. The Oregon PSRB consists of five members of various backgrounds: an attorney, a psychiatrist, a psychologist, an individual familiar with probation and parole, and a lay citizen (Bloom et al. 2000). The PSRB is a centralized mechanism for monitoring insanity acquittees, and the membership reflects the board's role in bridging the mental health and criminal justice perspectives. Under the Oregon system, the trial court determines whether the acquittee remains mentally ill and a substantial danger to others. If determined to no longer suffer from a mental disorder and no longer be dangerous, the acquittee must be released without supervision. For those who are mentally ill or dangerous, the court also determines the maximum sentence possible, had the acquittee been found guilty. The length of this sentence is the maximum length of time the acquittee can be placed under the PSRB, after which time the individual must be discharged or civilly committed. The trial court also determines whether initial placement will be into a forensic hospital or on conditional release. After this point, the trial court is no longer involved in the management of the acquittee, and the PSRB determines movement from the forensic hospital to conditional release. The PSRB also has the authority to revoke conditional release and return an insanity acquittee to a forensic hospital (Bloom et al. 2000).

Data from 1978 to 2011 show that there were 2558 insanity acquittees committed to the PSRB, and 1974 were discharged. The number of insanity acquittees on inpatient status increased from 112 in 1978 to a peak of 405 in 2004, and then decreased to 328 in 2011. The largest category of inpatients in the state psychiatric hospital consisted of insanity acquittees. There was also a large number of acquittees on conditional release, with 400 individuals on this status in 2011 (Bloom and Buckley 2013).

In 2011, statutory modifications to the PSRB system (ORS §161) were prompted by a number of factors, including the increasing number of hospitalized insanity acquittees and fiscal problems, as well as a perception of the PSRB as risk-averse. Insanity acquittees charged with misdemeanors are no longer subject to PSRB oversight and are instead subject to a process similar to civil commitment. In addition, while the PSRB retains jurisdiction of more serious felony insanity acquittees, a parallel system for lower-level felony insanity acquittees was created. These lower-level acquittees are placed under the jurisdiction of the Oregon Health Authority (OHA). OHA created a State Hospital Review Panel (SHRP) to prioritize public safety concerns in rendering conditional release decisions. When acquittees return to the community under conditional release, they are transferred to the PSRB (Bloom and Buckley 2013).

Missouri

In Missouri, the statute concerning insanity acquittees dates to 1963, with additional amendments added in the 1980s and 1990s (Linhorst and Dirks-Linhorst 1997). These amendments increased the focus on public safety through key changes: (1) shifting the burden of proof in the insanity defense onto the defendant, (2) providing for automatic hospitalization of insanity acquittees who committed dangerous offenses, (3) raising release standards for insanity acquittees who committed dangerous offenses, (4) establishing roles for the prosecutor and the Attorney General's office in the release process, (5) requiring court-ordered conditional release, (6) monitoring conditionally released acquittees in the community, and (7) allowing inpatient commitment or community supervision to continue indefinitely (Linhorst 1997).

In 1996, the Missouri legislature tightened the NGRI system by requiring release applications to be filed in the original court of commitment and mandating notification to victims when release applications are filed. The legislature also added requirements that an acquittee proposed for release (1) not be likely "in the reasonable future to commit another violent crime against another person because of such person's mental illness," (2) understand "the nature of the violent crime committed against another person," (3) knows their behavior was criminal, and (4) is now able to conduct themselves lawfully (Dirks-Linhorst and Kondrat 2012).

In 1997, it was noted that half of long-term public psychiatric hospital beds were occupied by insanity acquittees (Linhorst and Dirks-Linhorst 1997). In 2012, a study of 1130 insanity acquittees concluded that the 1996 legislative amendments may have led to longer hospital stays for all insanity acquittees. Before 1996, insanity acquittees had mean inpatient commitment of 34.3 months prior to reaching conditional release. After 1996, the mean length of hospitalization before conditional release was 75.5 months (Dirks-Linhorst and Kondrat 2012). The 1996 legislative changes resulted in significant changes in practice, and a doubling of the length of stay before conditional release.

New York

New York is an example of a state where the original trial court can retain jurisdiction over post-acquittal process. Oversight of the mental health system is centralized, and conditional release is utilized. In New York, insanity defense reform slightly predated the Hinckley case. The impetus for New York's Insanity Defense Reform Act in 1980 was the highly publicized case of a New York City police officer, Robert Torsney, who shot and killed an unarmed teenager in 1976 (Steadman 1993). His defense claimed that he had suffered from a psychosis associated with epilepsy that caused his behavior (Barrett 2012) as the basis for the insanity defense. As an insanity acquittee, Torsney was then committed to a forensic psychiatric hospital, but no evidence of mental disease could be found. Torsney was recommended for community release less than a year after successfully pursuing the insanity defense. Public reaction to this decision was overwhelmingly negative, with the perception that the insanity defense system had been abused, thus prompting passage of the IDRA.

New York's IDRA resulted in a number of changes (McGreevy et al. 1991). First, the defense was made affirmative, shifting burden of proof from the prosecution to the defense. IDRA also mandates a process to evaluate and determine dangerousness of insanity acquittees, which then determines the degree of court oversight over an insanity acquittee's status and placement. As outlined in statute (CPL §330.20), the post-acquittal process begins with an initial dangerousness determination that dictates subsequent procedures for oversight and privileging. After a finding of nonresponsibility, an individual is evaluated for placement in one of three categories or "tracks": (1) dangerous mental disorder requiring a forensic hospitalization; (2) mentally ill but not dangerous, thus needing civil hospital commitment; or (3) neither dangerous nor suffering from symptoms of mental illness requiring hospitalization, and therefore appropriate for community placement without an initial period of commitment. This initial evaluation is conducted by two psychiatric examiners, but the trial court makes the ultimate determination. Dangerousness determinations require violence risk assessment and are not constrained to the current moment. Case law (*George L.* 1995) established criteria for assessing dangerousness and allows for inclusion of factors such as substance abuse history, need for medication, recency of the instant offense, and the need to prepare for a safe community transition.

Most insanity acquittees are initially found to have a dangerous mental disorder (categorized as Track I) and are placed in forensic psychiatric centers. When patients are deemed no longer dangerous, the treating clinician may apply for transfer to a civil psychiatric center. This application is first submitted to the hospital forensic committee (HFC). If approved by the HFC, the hospital clinical director must then grant approval, and the application is then approved at the central office level before being sent to court. Court hearings are adversarial, and the district attorney's office may oppose the application.

At the civil hospital, when patients are deemed clinically appropriate and safe for community access, they become eligible for increasing levels of privileges before reaching conditional release. Privilege levels off hospital grounds and conditional release status are subject to the same multilevel review and court hearing process as that described for transfer from the forensic to the civil hospital. For conditional release status, a typical order of conditions includes stipulations about compliance with treatment, monitoring by the state mental health agency, approval of place of residence, and prohibitions against substance use. Orders of conditions may be valid for up to 5 years and may be renewed as many times as necessary. Conditionally released patients may be unconditionally discharged after at least 3 years of successful community placement. Unconditional discharge applications are subject to the same application review and approval procedures.

Insanity acquittees found to be mentally ill but not dangerous (Track II) are treated in civil psychiatric centers, without an initial period of commitment to a forensic hospital. Their privilege levels are determined by the hospital in which they reside, without mandated external review, and decisions regarding community release are based on standard civil commitment standards. When released, they are also subject to an order of conditions. Those insanity acquittees who are found during the post-acquittal evaluation process to be neither dangerous nor to have symptoms of mental illness requiring civil commitment (Track III) are able to immediately return to the community, usually with an order of conditions. As with the other two categories of insanity acquittees, they may be unconditionally discharged after the minimum 3 years of community placement.

Insanity acquittees of any track who are in a civil hospital or under conditional release status and who become dangerous again, as defined by statute, may be recommitted to a forensic hospital. A study of patients recommitted within 10 years after transfer from a forensic facility found that high historical scores on the HCR-20 increased the risk of recommitment almost threefold. Specific risk factors associated with recommitment were prior supervision failure, negative attitude, problems with substance use, relationship problems, and either absent or less serious major mental illness (Green et al. 2014). Recommitment is not the only option; in instances of psychiatric decompensation of community-placed insanity acquittees, voluntary or involuntary civil commitment under mental hygiene law may be pursued.

The statute specifies that transfers, privileges, and releases must be "consistent with the public safety and welfare of the community and the defendant" (CPL §330.20), thus emphasizing the public safety mandate in insanity acquittee management. Centralized oversight provides some degree of statewide uniformity throughout the various facilities, and as described above, progress through the CPL §330.20 process is subject to a multilevel system of review. Perhaps resulting, at least partially, from the complexity of the system, the length of stay for insanity acquittees has increased over time, although the number of new insanity acquittees per year has gradually decreased. In the 1980s, 40% of insanity acquittees were released within 7 years of admission, but in the 1990s, this number decreased to 21%, and by the early 2000s, the number further dropped to only 8%. The number of insanity acquittee admissions dropped from a high of 77 in 1982 to a low of 22 in 2008 (Miraglia and Hall 2011).

South Carolina

Insanity acquittees in South Carolina are automatically hospitalized for a 120-day period. At the end of that time, the criminal court holds a hearing to determine whether continued hospitalization is necessary (S.C. Code §44-17-580). If the acquittee is determined to require further hospitalization, the acquittee remains in the hospital until the state mental health agency notifies the court that confinement is no longer necessary, at which time, the court will hold a release hearing. The original trial court may hold jurisdiction for a period of time equivalent to the maximum sentence for the instant offense, after which standard civil commitment procedures are followed. Considerations regarding the necessity of further hospitalization include sufficiency of insight, capacity to make treatment decisions, or likelihood of serious harm to self or others, but the statute does not speak to the use of therapeutic passes or to the conditions of confinement (Young et al. 2002). In the absence of statutory guidelines for the conditions of confinement, the South Carolina Department of Mental Health operated a seven-level insanity acquittee treatment program called the Allan Project, designed to offer increasing independence and decreasing supervision with each successive level (*State v. Hudson* 1999). Progression through the seven levels was a clinical determination made by the treatment team, and patients on higher levels could be granted passes for work or social activities in the community (Young et al. 2002).

South Carolina is another example of a high-profile case impacting the mental health system's autonomy in managing insanity acquittees. In this instance, Ui Sun Hudson attacked three children with a pair of scissors in 1995 and caused serious injury. She was found NGRI and hospitalized as statutorily required. The hearing regarding the need for further hospitalization did not occur until 18 months later, despite the 120-day time frame specified in statute. During this time, Hudson reached level four of the seven-level program, and the hospital granted her gradually increasing periods of unsupervised time in the community, including travel to employment. At her hearing, the attorney general and the judge expressed concern about unsupervised access to the community despite the lack of any adverse incidents. The judge found Hudson "in need of further hospitalization." Although the judge agreed to allow her to remain on her current level of privileges, he also ordered the hospital to obtain court approval prior to allowing her to advance to the next level or attain more privileges. The South Carolina attorney general (AG) remained unsatisfied with this ruling, and as a result of the AG's legal challenge, a consent order specified that the South Carolina Department of Mental Health (DMH) would obtain court approval prior to allowing unsupervised leave in any form from hospital grounds (*State v. Hudson* 1999).

Despite the decree, the AG appealed the original ruling. The South Carolina Court of Appeals determined that a committed NGRI patient could not have unsupervised leave from the hospital. As a result of this ruling, NGRI patients in the upper levels of the seven-level program and residing in the community under outpatient monitoring were abruptly returned to the hospital until court hearings could be scheduled, a process that took over a year (Young et al. 2002).

Maryland

Insanity acquittees in Maryland may be committed to the state Department of Health and Mental Hygiene or may be released to the community, either with or without conditions. As in other states, release from a secure facility may be either through conditional release or release without conditions, but in either situation, a formal hearing regarding dangerousness is required. Acquittees may petition for release annually, though the state may apply for release at any point in time (Md. Code Ann. 2006). Conditional release plans are reviewed by the state Community Forensic Aftercare Program (CFAP), and conditional release orders are usually 5 years in length but may be shorter or longer (Marshall et al. 2014). Acquittees on conditional release status are monitored by CFAP social workers, with information on the acquittee's mental status, compliance, substance use, and community functioning provided by caregivers, treatment providers, and family. Insanity acquittees in need of return to inpatient care can be voluntarily readmitted, but if the conditions of release have been violated, the court may revoke conditional release status.

Voluntarily readmitted insanity acquittees were found to have fewer arrests and fewer instances of treatment noncompliance than those insanity acquittees who were involuntarily readmitted. Those acquittees who were not readmitted at all had longer community duration prior to any psychiatric readmissions and fewer community psychiatric admissions. An interesting finding of Maryland's program was that acquittees residing with family members were more likely to be involuntarily readmitted than those living in community or structured residences, possibly because family members were more likely to notice problems or because the family was a destabilizing, rather than supportive, factor (Marshall et al. 2014).

PUBLIC SAFETY

Data published regarding conditional release programs generally show low re-arrest rates for insanity acquittees. Wiederanders et al. (1997) examined conditional release data from New York, Oregon, and California and found felony re-arrest rates ranging from 2.2% to 2.8% per year, and annual re-hospitalization rates from 14.5% to 20.4%. A 2011 study on New York insanity acquittees estimated that 2% of women and 14% of men were re-arrested within 2 years of release, with most re-arrests occurring within the first 5 years of release. Contrasted with the re-arrest rate from state prison, 42% for women and 56% for men, the re-arrest data for insanity acquittees were found to be favorable (Miraglia and Hall 2011). These statistics suggest that insanity acquittee management systems, as compared with incarceration, have been effective in reducing risk to the community.

With regard to risk factors, the New York study found that the factors associated with increased risk for any re-arrest were male gender, a diagnosis of antisocial personality disorder, and being in treatment for less than 2 years. The only predictor variables for re-arrest for violence were found to be the number of prior arrests for violence, age at release, and gender, as no women in this sample were re-arrested for violence in the New York study (Miraglia and Hall 2011). McDermott et al., in a 2008 study of insanity acquittees at Napa State Hospital in California, attempted to elucidate how clinicians make release decisions and found that three concerns appeared to be key considerations: responsiveness to and compliance with treatment, substance use, and risk of violence.

As mentioned earlier in this chapter, two responses to calls for insanity defense reform were to introduce the GBMI verdict to reduce the number of insanity acquittals and to abolish the insanity defense altogether. The Michigan experience with GBMI found that rather than decreasing the number of insanity acquittals, addition of GBMI resulted in relatively stable numbers of new insanity acquittees with an additional number of defendants found GBMI (Steadman 1986). A criticism of the GBMI verdict is that it may create expectations that a defendant found GBMI will receive specialized treatment, while in fact a finding of GBMI does not typically provide opportunities for treatment beyond what is ordinarily provided to other convicted state inmates.

In Montana, where the insanity defense was abolished, the impact of mental illness on criminal responsibility was not eliminated from consideration in the judicial system (Buitendorp 1996). Evidence that would have previously been submitted to support an insanity defense was instead used to support findings of incompetence to stand trial, *mens rea* considerations, and sentencing. The net effect of the redirected evidence regarding mental illness was to essentially allow a version of the insanity defense to continue despite abolition. One key difference with states allowing the insanity defense, however, is the post-adjudication process. Incompetence to stand trial could lead to dismissal of the charges, and hospitalization after that juncture was not necessarily the case. This raised the potential for a class of individuals who would previously have been committed for treatment but were instead able to avoid treatment.

Both the Michigan and Montana examples of attempting to avoid the insanity defense result in the possibility that defendants whose behavior was influenced by mental illness actually received less treatment than those defendants in other states who are able to receive the insanity defense. Given the conservative nature of many state conditional release programs and hospital services for insanity acquittees, this may have the unintended consequence of diminishing public safety rather than enhancing it.

USE OF LIMITED RESOURCES

In 1986, Steadman and Morrissey commented that insanity defense reforms resulted in a disproportionate investment of resources drawn from an already burdened mental health system. More recent studies have found that conclusion to remain valid. Even as the number of state hospital beds has steadily decreased from 500,000 in 1950 to 30,000 in 2010 (NASMHPD 2014), the percentage of state hospital expenditures on forensic services for insanity acquittees and competency restoration has increased over time. States have noted increasing numbers of forensic admissions to state psychiatric hospitals (Manderscheid et al. 2009). In 1983, state psychiatric hospitals expended 7.6% of their funds on forensic services, but by 2012, that figure had risen to 36%. In the setting of dramatically reduced state hospital bed availability, the utilization of inpatient beds for insanity acquittees can represent a significant use of resources. The extended length of stay of many insanity acquittees is an additional factor (NASMHPD 2012). On the other hand, as discussed earlier, research has found that insanity acquittee management systems can reduce re-offense rates. There are benefits that can be more elusive in terms of determining monetary value, including improved clinical outcomes and prevention of harm by avoidance of future offenses.

SUMMARY

Treatment and management of insanity acquittees must address clinical needs, but considerations for civil liberties are inevitably tied to issues of public safety and mental health resources. This is a delicate balance that can be tipped by a single, high-profile adverse event, as has been demonstrated in numerous states.

State management of insanity acquittees, when less centralized, can offer treatment providers greater flexibility to use clinical judgment, but centralized management offers the opportunity for more consistency in application of the relevant standards, and for assessing practice and tracking outcomes. Highly tiered review processes may be prone to more conservative decision making. Ultimately, the ideal would be to develop an insanity acquittee management system where risk assessment practices can be relevant for both public safety considerations as well as treatment planning.

SUMMARY KEY POINTS

- A finding of not guilty by reason of insanity typically triggers a process of assessment and review in which risk considerations impact clinical management options.
- States vary in the structure of insanity acquittee management in numerous ways, such as the process by which initial commitment is determined, and the complexity of mandatory review, availability of conditional release. Most states require court approval prior to community release.
- Release determinations in most jurisdictions involve assessment beyond current clinical status and behavioral stability. Additional considerations include understanding the level of risk to the community, the components of a release plan that would be necessary to maintain safety, and the likelihood of compliance to such a plan.
- Use of risk assessment tools is also variable but may be helpful in structuring assessments regarding readiness for community release or other related steps in insanity acquittee management.

REFERENCES

Appelbaum P. 1982. The insanity defense: New calls for reform. *Hospital and Community Psychiatry* 33:13–14.

Barrett CF. 2012. CPL § 330.20: Persons involuntarily committed pursuant to CPL entitled to procedural and substantive safeguards guaranteed involuntary civil detainees. *St. John's Law Review* 54:595–605.

Bloom JD and MC Buckley. 2013. The Oregon psychiatric security review board: 1978–2012. *Journal of the American Academy of Psychiatry and the Law* 41:560–567.

Bloom JD, MH Williams, and DA Bigelow. 2000. The forensic psychiatric system in the United States. *International Journal of Law and Psychiatry* 23:605–613.

Borum R and SM Fulero. 1999. Empirical research on the insanity defense and attempted reforms: Evidence toward informed policy. *Law and Human Behavior* 23:375–394.

Buitendorp RD. 1996. A statutory lesson from "Big Sky Country" on abolishing the insanity defense. *Valparaiso University Law Review* 30:965–1022.

Callahan LA and E Silver. 1998. Factors associated with the conditional release of persons acquitted by reason of insanity: A decision tree approach. *Law and Human Behavior* 22:147–163.

Callahan LA, HJ Steadman, MA McGreevy, and PC Robbins. 1991. The volume and characteristics of insanity defense pleas: An eight-state study. *Journal of the American Academy of Psychiatry and the Law* 19:331–338.

Crocker AG, TL Nicholls, Y Charette, and MC Seto. 2014. Dynamic and static factors associated with discharge dispositions: The national trajectory project of individuals found not criminally responsible on account of mental disorder (NCRMD) in Canada. *Behavioral Sciences and the Law* 32:577–595.

Dirks-Linhorst PA and D Kondrat. 2012. Tough on crime or beating the system: An evaluation of Missouri department of mental health's not guilty by reason of insanity murder acquittees. *Homicide Studies* 16:129–150.

Douglas KS. 2014. Version 3 of the historical-clinical-risk management-20 (HCR-20^{V3}): Relevance to violence risk assessment and management in forensic conditional release contexts. *Behavioral Sciences and the Law* 32:557–576.

Fitch WL. 2014. *White Paper: Forensic Mental Health Services in the United States (2014).* National Association of State Mental Health Program Directors. http://www.nasmhpd.org/sites/default/files/Assessment%203%20-%20Updated%20Forensic%20Mental%20Health%20Services.pdf, accessed December 3, 2014.

Foucha v. Louisiana, 504 U.S. 71 (1992).

Gowensmith WN, AE Bryant, and MJ Vitacco. 2014. Decision-making in post-acquittal hospital release: How do forensic evaluators make their decisions? *Behavioral Sciences and the Law* 32:596–607.

Green D, B Belfi, H Griswold, JM Schreiber, R Prentky, and M Kunz. 2014. Factors associated with recommitment of NGRI acquittees to a forensic hospital. *Behavioral Sciences and the Law* 32:608–626.

Hans VP and D Slater. 1983. John Hinckley, Jr. and the insanity defense: The public's verdict. *Public Opinion Quarterly* 47(2):202–212.

Jones v. United States 463 U.S. 354 (1983).

Laws of New York, Criminal Procedural Law §330.20.

Linhorst D. 1997. The legislative structuring of insanity acquittee policies. *Journal of Mental Health Administration* 24:166–177.

Linhorst DM and PA Dirks-Linhorst. 1997. The impact of insanity acquittees on Missouri's public mental health system. *Law and Human Behavior* 21:327–338.

Manderscheid R, J Atay, and R Crider. 2009. Changing trends in state psychiatric hospital use from 2002 to 2005. *Psychiatric Services* 60:29–34.

Marshall DJ, MJ Vitacco, JB Read, and M Harway. 2014. Predicting voluntary and involuntary readmissions to forensic hospitals by insanity acquittees in Maryland. *Behavioral Sciences and the Law* 32:627–640.

Massachusetts General Laws, c. 123 §16 (a) and (b).

Matter of George L, 648 N.E.2d 475 (N.Y. 1995).

McDermott BE, CL Scott, D Busse, F Andrade, M Zozaya, and CD Quanbeck. 2008. The conditional release of insanity acquittees: Three decades of decision-making. *Journal of the American Academy of Psychiatry and the Law* 36:329–336.

McGreevy MA, HJ Steadman, JA Dvoski, and N Dollard. 1991. New York state's system of managing insanity acquittees in the community. *Hospital and Community Psychiatry* 42:512–517.

Md. Code Ann., Crim. Pro. §3 (2006).

Miraglia R and D Hall. 2011. The effect of length of hospitalization on re-arrest among insanity plea acquittees. *Journal of the American Academy of Psychiatry and the Law* 39:524–534.

National Association of State Mental Health Program Directors Research Institute. 2012. *State Mental Health Agency Revenues and Expenditures Study*. Falls Church, VA: NRI.

New York Codes, Rules, and Regulations Title 14, Chapter 13, Part 541.

North Carolina General Statutes § 122C-276.

Perlin M. 1996. Myths, realities, and the political world: The anthropology of insanity. *Bulletin of the American Academy of Psychiatry and the Law* 24:5–22.

S.C. Code §44-17-580.

Silver E, C Cirincione, and HJ Steadman. 1994. Demythologizing inaccurate perceptions of the insanity defense. *Law and Human Behavior* 18:63–70.

Soliman S and P Resnick. 2006. Release of insanity acquittees. *Journal of the American Academy of Psychiatry and the Law* 34:555–557.

State v. Hudson, 519 S.E.2d 577 (S.C. Ct. App. 1999).

State v. Klein, 124 P.3d 644 (Wash. 2005).

Steadman HJ, MA McGreevey, JP Morrissey, and LA Callahan. 1993. *Before and After Hinckley: Evaluation Insanity Defense Reform*. New York: Guilford Press.

Steadman H and JP Morrissey. 1986. The insanity defense: Problems and prospects for studying the impact of legal reforms. *Annals of the American Academy of Political and Social Science* 484:115–125.

United States v. Hinckley, 672 F.2d 115 (D.C. Cir. 1982).

Weinstein NM. 2014. The legal aspects of conditional release in the criminal and civil court system. *Behavioral Sciences and the Law* 32:666–680.

Wiederanders MR, DL Bromley, and PA Choate. 1997. Forensic conditional release programs and outcomes in three states. *International Journal of Law and Psychiatry* 20:249–257.

Young SA, RL Frierson, R Gregg Dwyer, and A Shah. 2002. Commitment versus confinement: Therapeutic passes in the management of insanity acquittees. *Journal of the American Academy of Psychiatry and the Law* 30:563–567.

31

Presentencing evaluations

ALAN R. FELTHOUS

PRESENTENCING EVALUATIONS

Presentencing psychiatric evaluations can be requested by the defense or prosecuting attorney. The purpose of these evaluations is to assist the judge or jury in answering one or more of the following questions following criminal conviction: (1) Is the defendant competent to be sentenced? (Miller 2003, 203–204), (2) What treatment recommendations, if any, should be considered by the sentencing authority? and (3) How severe or lenient should the punishment be? (Felthous 1989). Pre-capital sentencing evaluations are addressed in Chapter 11 and so will not be discussed here.

In order to place the psychiatrist's role in sentencing into context, this chapter begins with a brief historical review of criminal punishment, followed by a discussion of the four purposes of punishment and the psychiatrist's role within each of these penal purposes. Finally the presentencing report itself will be described. This discussion will address the three main questions that concern psychiatric presentencing evaluations: competence, treatment recommendations, and mitigation.

Crimes, offenses against the king, were eventually defined as offenses "against the community at large." The criminal justice system regulated procedures for investigation, indictment, prosecution, and punishment for those convicted (Garner 1999, 381). Those convicted of a crime were subject to criminal sentencing, i.e., the imposition of a punishment. A court or jury pronounced and imposed the sentence.

As torture in the Middle Ages faded into disfavor, countries such as England, France, and tsarist Russia transported criminals to far-off places (Barnes 1930; Barnes and Teeters 1959). From 1597 until 1776 England transported criminals to the American colonies (Barnes and Teeters, 1959; Smith 1997). After 1776 and American independence, the English transported felons to Australia.

In the American colonies all punishment was corporal (Mattick 1974) and incarceration was not much used (Derschowitz 1978). Offenders who committed serious offenses were whipped, branded, mutilated, and put to death. Perpetrators of minor offenses were punished by public humiliation such as being subjected to the pillory, stocks, and dunking stool (Barnes and Teeters, 1959).

IMPRISONMENT

Meanwhile, by the sixteenth century in several European countries, bondage, meaning forced labor with restrictions in freedom, became an increasingly used alternative to the spectacle of the scaffold and physical punishments such as flogging (Spierenburg 1995). Upon breaking away from England, Americans also repudiated its severe punishments including execution for a variety of offenses. By the same token reducing such severe punishments was thought to better ensure conviction, and the increased certainty of punishment, it was hoped, would reduce crime (Rothman 1995). By the end of the seventeenth century, prisons intended for confinement began to replace work prisons (Spierenburg 1995). As execution became less available in the United States, this young country turned to long term imprisonment as the predominant punishment for most serious offenses (Rotman 1995).

CLASSIFICATION

As the penological goal of rehabilitation took hold, classification became a common practice in progressive correctional systems. Some prison units would be designed almost exclusively for security, maximum security, and eventually even supermaximum security. Other facilities devoted more resources toward rehabilitative programming. By the early twentieth century, state correctional departments began to include special institutions for the mentally ill or "defective delinquents," at Napanoch, New York, in 1921 and at Bridgewater, Massachusetts, in 1922 (Rotman 1995). Classification today typically takes place after sentencing and within the prison system. It has and can, however, occur in lieu of, or as part of, the sentencing process.

The four penalogical purposes of criminal punishment are retribution, deterrence, incapacitation, and rehabilitation. Expiation, of ecclesiastical and historical interest (Gardiner 1958), is no longer a consideration. Retribution is nonutilitarian, whereas each of the other purposes is intended to reduce or prevent crime. In *Traltato dei Delitti e Pelle Pene* (Essay on Crimes and Punishment) published in 1764, the Italian criminologist Cesare Beccaria first described the principles of *retributivism*. He argued against secret proceedings and torture and in favor of a humanitarian and a consistent legal system in which the punishment fit the crime (Barnes 1930). According to the classical school, punishment should be proportional to the crime for all offenders yet also humane and fair (Robinson 1922). Immanuel Kant (1965) asserted that society had a "categorical imperative to impose punishment fitting the crime." The ideal of *just taliones* was to be proportionate, not equivalent to the crime (p. 132).

Herbert Morris (1968) described punishment as a natural and inalienable right that respects an individual as a person. Premised on a person's capacity to freely choose his actions, including violation of society's most fundamental rules, proportionate punishment respects the person's choices *per se* as well as his choice in effect in deciding the sanctioning consequences of his offense conduct. This contrasts with a purely therapeutic or rehabilitative model that could result in tyrannical control over the individual with disregard of his freedom of choice of predictable outcomes. Nonetheless, the retributionists' punitive model is inappropriate for the mentally ill who because of their illness lack freedom of choice; respect for their personhood is better satisfied with the treatment model (Morris 1968), this exception to culpability falling within a contemporary retributionist system.

Culpability pertains to both adjudication of guilt and severity of punishment. Mental factors that might not have risen to the level to amount to a successful mental defense can nonetheless pertain to the comparative proportionality of punishment. The forensic psychiatrist can in effect assist the court in determining the appropriateness of retribution and setting the severity of punishment by conducting a presentencing evaluation that is similar to that for criminal responsibility (Appelbaum and Zaitchik 1995). Rarely, the discovery of new evidence in support of an insanity defense could lead to a new trial (*State v. King* 1989), but more typically the presentence evaluation can result in mitigation of sentence, leaving the original conviction in place. The presentencing evaluation can assess a broader range of factors than a responsibility evaluation (Appelbaum and Zaitchik 1995). As capital sentencing hearings especially welcome wide-ranging considerations addressed in Chapter 11, here the focus is on factors allowed in noncapital cases, with the realization that some factors may be equally relevant and admissible to both capital and noncapital sentencing.

Deterrence is a utilitarian theory of punishment wherein the punishment itself is intended to deter, prevent, or reduce the risk of future criminal behavior (Felthous 2007). Plato, the earliest philosopher to support primary and secondary deterrence as the justifying purpose of criminal punishment, maintained that offenders should not be punished because of their crimes but to prevent them and others from engaging in future criminal acts (Plato 2005, 196–197). With primary or specific deterrence, the individual offender should resist future criminal behavior because of the known penal consequences (Stetlerand and Goldstein 2003). With secondary or general deterrence, others in society should learn from the offender's consequential example and avoid making the same criminal mistake. Plato's concept of exemplary deterrence became a common purpose of criminal punishment in ancient and medieval systems of social control (Peters 1995). Consistent with this purpose, punishment was carried out as a public spectacle.

The psychiatric presentencing evaluation can relevantly address how the defendant's mental condition will affect the likelihood that punishment will deter his or her criminal conduct (Appelbaum and Zaitchik 1995). This can be a double-edged sword, however, in terms of sentencing severity. Although decreased likelihood of deterrence diminishes the justification for severe punishment, it could increase the justification for incapacitation resulting in longer, not shorter sentencing.

The separate question of general deterrence raises the possibility that severe punishment will serve to deter most individuals, but not necessarily individuals who themselves are mentally disordered (Appelbaum and Zaitchik 1995). The extent to which punishment of mentally disordered individuals deters others from criminal acts and the extent to which courts consider general deterrence when sentencing mentally disordered defendants are empirical questions with unknown answers. Appelbaum and Zaitchik (1995) suggest that in cases wherein the goal of sentencing is deterrence, the evaluator can assess the extent to which the defendant's mental condition would motivate future criminal conduct and the likelihood that deterrence would be lessened.

Just as the penological goal of deterrence can interact with incapacitation, so can it interact with rehabilitation. Diminished capacity for deterrence can be due not just to the impairment of the mental condition but to its resistance to treatment. Where the lack of deterrence is due to mental illness, but mental illness is improved with treatment, the defendant may regain the capacity to be deterred by punishment, even when imposed as a result of a criminal act committed while he or she was mentally disordered. Thus, if the evaluator addresses deterrence that could enhance punishment by contributing to the need to incapacitate, the evaluator should also attempt to address the alternative purpose of rehabilitation and the potential to be deterred by punishment by virtue of successful treatment. Although in many cases treatment can be provided within the correctional system, amenability to treatment and therefore deterrence ought not to be justification for a penal rather than a therapeutic disposition. Rather, where the defendant has already been convicted, treatable mental disorders with resultant deterrence ought to favor leniency in sentencing.

Incapacitation is the attempt to render the offender incapable of committing future crimes by making recidivism nearly physically impossible, at least during the period of incapacitation. Obviously execution is the most extreme and final form of incapacitation. Imprisonment always serves the purpose of incapacitation because at least while the offender is incarcerated he or she cannot victimize others in society.

In addressing whether, because of the risk of violence or recidivism, the defendant should be incapacitated, the court may turn to the psychiatrist's presentencing report. The court may be more likely to impose a lengthy prison sentence if the presentencing report suggests that the defendant is at high risk for reoffending (*Idaho v. Snow* 1991), or is not amenable to treatment and has a criminal history (*State v. Pryor* 1990; *State v. McNallie* 1994), whereas a mental condition that somehow reduces the risk of recidivism could favor leniency (*United States v. Studley* 1990). Thus, the presentencing evaluation is most relevant to the penological goal of incapacitation when dangerousness and criminal recidivism are addressed (Appelbaum and Zaitchik 1995).

More accurate, and in keeping with American Psychiatric Association (APA) recommendations, than declaring whether or not a defendant is dangerous, the evaluator can identify those factors that increase the risk of violent or criminal behavior (APA 1984). The presentencing report can also usefully identify protective factors that reduce the risk of violence or recidivism. Importantly the report can as well identify those factors that can reduce the intensity or likelihood of predisposing factors (Appelbaum and Zaitchik 1995). For example, if bipolar disorder increases the risk of assault when the patient becomes manic, this risk can be reduced by factors that support the defendant's compliance in taking an efficacious mood stabilizer.

The third utilitarian and fourth theoretical purpose of punishment is *rehabilitation*. Although Plato is most closely associated with deterrence, this early utilitarian also wrote in favor of rehabilitation. For those whose criminal propensities are amenable to reform, such as where the criminal acts result from ignorance, the proper intervention is correction and instruction (Peters 1995; Plato 2005). Cesar Lombroso, the Italian physician and anthropologist who founded the Italian school of criminology, argued that punishment should be determined by the nature of the offender, not the type of crime committed. In the late nineteenth century he published a pamphlet that catalyzed the rehabilitation movement as a major force in penology (Robinson 1922). An offender who steals for food could, for example, be taught a marketable skill so he or she can earn a living. Lombroso was not an absolutist, however, and would reserve incapacitation for offenders who were considered unchangeable by efforts at rehabilitation.

Rehabilitation can involve much more than simply psychiatric diagnosis and treatment. It can involve job training, for example, and successful job application. At least the evaluating psychiatrist should address mental conditions that can interfere with rehabilitation efforts and increase the risk of recidivism. The presentence report will be most useful if it identifies available treatment programs both inside and outside the correctional system (Appelbaum and Zaitchik 1995). The sentencing court may specify treatment measures as conditions of probation enforceable by revocation of probation and imprisonment when such measures are not followed by the mentally disordered offender (*United States v. Gallo* 1994).

STATUTES

Several states (e.g., California [Pre-sentence 1965], Kansas [Davis et al. 1971; Kan. Sentencing Code, 1969], Massachusetts [Mass 1970], Maryland [Smith 1976], New Jersey [Smith 1976], and North Carolina [Smith 1976]), and large metropolitan areas (e.g., Baltimore, Chicago, Cleveland, Detroit, New York City, Philadelphia, Pittsburgh, and Washington, DC [Felthous 1989]) enacted statutory provisions for psychiatric presentencing examinations. The goal of the Kansas State Reception and Diagnostic Center (KRDC), opened in 1961, was to promote effective rehabilitation of male felons (Davis et al. 1971). After conviction of a felony and sentencing, the defendant underwent a thorough multidisciplinary mental evaluation at KRDC. North Carolina's 1967 statutory enactment (Smith 1976; Jones 1969) served a similar purpose to that of Kansas. By this presentencing statute the judge could assign a multidisciplinary study group to gather information for the judge to use in sentencing (N.C. Gen. Stat. 1977).

This brief synopsis and the historical evolution of sentencing in the United States is intended to provide the psychiatrist with useful context for the specific task of conducting presentencing evaluations.

THE RELEVANCE OF PRESENTENCING EVALUATIONS TO THE PURPOSES OF PUNISHMENT

One might expect that retributivism would hold no place for presentence evaluations, because the severity of the punishment must correspond to the severity of the criminal offense, at least proportionately so. Modern retributivism, however, allows for a defendant's mental condition to be considered in assignment of criminal responsibility (Gray 2010; Johnston 2013, 2014) and in determining the nature and severity of punishment. Two retributive rationales support judicial authority in adjusting a defendant's sentence to meet his treatment needs or reduce the hardship of punishment that is caused by his mental disorder: to avoid violating human dignity and to support the principle of equal impact (Johnston 2014).

Harsh punishment, including deprivation of certain rights, is acceptable; inhumane punishment is not. Corporal punishment once acceptable is no longer because it is considered to be inhumane. Retributivist punishment is "[p]remised upon respect for the moral dignity and personhood of the offender" (Johnston 2014, 644). Thus, violation of human dignity is incompatible with retributivism. Like corporal punishment, any punishment that is intended to profoundly disturb a person's mental health is impermissibly inhumane. Johnston argues that prison sentencing, without allowance for a mentally disordered offender's reasonably foreseeable and serious vulnerabilities, results in an inhumane violation of his dignity. Therefore, the sentencing judge should be authorized to modify confinement conditions so as to be proportionately punitive yet not morally intolerable.

A related concept for considering the defendant's vulnerability to adverse effects of criminal punishment because of mental disorder is "the principle of equal impact" (Johnston 2013). Most legal scholars maintain that the just desserts theory of retributivism requires an objective standard (Gray 2010) that relates the punishment to the defendant's culpability from the nature and severity of the criminal act. Some commentators in contrast recognize that a given sanction such as incarceration can have a greater impact on defendants with vulnerabilities such as mental illness (Gray 2010; Johnston 2013). They recommend that the assessment of punishment take into account its differential, greater effect on such defendants (Gray 2010; Johnston 2013), a consideration referred to as the "equal impact principle." "The equal impact principle thus acknowledges the foreseeable, typical, and serious side-effects that certain penalties hold for vulnerable populations and seeks to adjust ordered sanctions so that members of vulnerable classes receive penalties of roughly equivalent severity as non-vulnerable individuals" (Johnston 2014, 646). Importantly, application of the equal impact principle in sentencing does not mean a reduction in punishment. Application realizes the principle of proportionality of retributivism and accordingly equalizes "the severity of penalties imposed on equally blameworthy offenders" (Johnston 2014, 646).

How these considerations are operationalized and put into sentencing practice is not clearly delineated. Courts have reduced or altered their customary sentencing out of concern for the harmful effect on vulnerable defendants. This has been justified by considering the mental disorder to have lessened the defendant's mental responsibility for the crime, even though such may not have resulted in a successful mental illness or defect defense. While accurate prediction of impact for mentally vulnerable defendants may be elusive, the forensic evaluation may be able to comment on recognized vulnerabilities and likelihood of improvement or deterioration under various sentencing conditions. Above all, the presentencing report should clearly state the defendant's treatment needs, including hospitalization if this level of care is required.

COMPETENCY TO BE SENTENCED

A presentencing evaluation assessment for competency to be sentenced does not fit well within the four theories of punishment, as this has more to do with procedural fairness and due process than punishment *per se* and so is more closely related to the criminal competencies discussed in Chapter 12. In some countries, e.g., Germany (Felthous et al. 2000), the central concern is the defendant's capacity to *serve* sentence in a prison setting.

U.S. jurisdictions differ in which standard for competence to be sentenced applies to noncapital sentencing. Some require that the defendant understand why he or she is being sentenced, whereas others apply the same standard as *Dusky* for trial competence (*Dusky v. United States*, 1960). Some but not all jurisdictions afford the defendant a right of allocution (Johnston EL, November 18, 2014, personal communication). According to the Ninth Circuit, a trial court is required to order a competency hearing if there is "reasonable cause to believe that the defendant may presently be suffering from a mental disease or defect rendering him mentally incompetent" (*United States v. Dreyer* 2012, 808). The threshold question was whether evidence would cause a "reasonable judge" to "experience genuine doubt" about the defendant's competence (*United States v. Dreyer* 2012, 808, citing *United States v. Mark* 2008, 814).

The question is whether the convicted defendant can protect his own rights throughout the sentencing procedure. The defendant must be able to provide relevant information to the person who is preparing his or her presentencing report. In order to ensure that information, conclusions, and recommendations are accurate, the defendant must be able to object when needed (Miller 2003). Allocution, the capacity to speak on one's own behalf during sentencing, has been considered an "elementary right" in assisting one's own defense (Peterson and Martinez 2014, 394–395; *United States v. Dreyer* 2012). Competency to be sentenced requires that the defendant know that he or she was convicted of a crime, reasons for the conviction, possible penalties, and why the court can sentence him or her to an appropriate punishment (Miller 2003).

Although seldom used in the United States, a functional approach has also been applied by the sentencing authority addressing whether the defendant has the capacity "to cope safely in a correctional setting" (Appelbaum and Zaitchik 1995, 681). A court might well consider whether imprisonment will aggravate the defendant's mental disorder (Sadoff 1988), increase the risk of suicide, or cause decompensation (Felthous 2008). A court's willingness to reduce the length of imprisonment because the defendant is mentally retarded may represent mitigation due to a mental condition (see below) more than a finding of incompetence, although the defendant's limited capacity to cope can be a consideration. (See, for example, *Illinois v. Watters* 1992.) In general sentencing a defendant with serious mental illness or mental retardation does not result in a finding of incompetence to be sentenced (Felthous 2008).

SEVERITY OF PUNISHMENT

Within the relevant sentencing guidelines, the court must decide where on the scale of leniency to severity a particular defendant should be sentenced. For this the court will consider various factors such as how heinous the crime was and how responsible the defendant was for his or her behavior.

Both of these factors contribute to the amount of moral turpitude attached to the defendant because of his or her crime and what corresponding degree of punishment would be most appropriate. Traditionally, when *mens rea* was shaped by ecclesiastical law, it was the free but errant exercise of the metaphysically free will that rendered the defendant criminally responsible (Felthous 2008). Through centuries of English common law, leading jurists maintained that it was the lack of rational thinking that crippled the will's capacity to function properly, so irrationality became a core defect to be identified by successive insanity tests.

According to the APA's Task Force on Sentencing (1984), psychiatrists should not make recommendations for disposition; rather they should strive for beneficence and nonmalfeasance in their recommendations. The psychiatrist who conducts a presentencing evaluation will therefore not contribute to the severity question by recommending for or against imprisonment. By conducting a thorough evaluation and full disclosure, his or her report can support public protection without a specific recommendation for imprisonment. The psychiatrist can comment on factors that affect the risk of violent behavior without attempting an accurate prediction.

Although these guidelines do not mention the will, i.e., the intentional, decisional faculty, or the question of criminal responsibility and moral turpitude, courts will consider these qualities when sentencing. Courts can be expected to apply presentencing evaluations to aspects of criminal responsibility, even though the defendant was already adjudicated guilty and therefore criminally responsible for the offense and even if the presentencing report did not address criminal responsibility in the broader sense, often framed as mitigating and aggravating factors. Indeed the hearing in question may be known as a "mitigation hearing."

MITIGATION

When psychiatric evidence is presented at the sentencing hearing, it is often referred to as a mitigation evidence or report. Here we consider several conditions for which psychiatric assessment may be requested before considering whether such conditions should result in mitigation or a reduced or more lenient sentence.

INTELLECTUAL DISABILITY

Several court decisions resulted in mitigation with reduced prison sentence due to mental retardation (now termed "intellectual disability" according to the *Diagnostic and Statistical Manual of Mental Disorders*, 5th edition (*DSM-5*, APA 2013). *Illinois v. Watters* (1992) was cited above. In *United States v. Chambers* (1995), the sentence of a borderline mentally retarded defendant was reduced from 188 months, the federal guideline minimum, to just 21 months based on "extraordinary family circumstances" and "diminished capacity" allowed by Federal Sentencing Guideline 5K2.13. In *United States v. Lewinson* (1993) the Ninth Circuit held that a mental disorder need not be a "'severe' impairment." Section 5K2.13 of the Federal Sentencing Guidelines (18 U.S.C. §1341) allows a downward departure from the Sentencing Guidelines if the mental disorder "significantly reduced [the] mental capacity [of the defendant] without qualification as to the nature or cause of the reduced capacity/except with respect to voluntary drug use" (p. 1006). Mental retardation may evoke a merciful response or effort to reduce prison time because of poor coping ability. The *Lewinson* case, however, clearly illustrates the concern about the offender's reduced criminal responsibility, termed "diminished culpability" (p. 1007) even if already found sufficiently responsible to be adjudicated guilty of the offense.

VOLUNTARY INTOXICATION

Evidence of voluntary intoxication is admissible at capital sentencing hearings for the purpose of mitigations. For noncapital offenders, in contrast, voluntary intoxication is typically mentioned in sentencing guidelines in order to limit or exclude its consideration. Marlowe, Lambert, and Thompson (1999) reviewed law in all U.S. jurisdictions and determined that jurisdictions follow one of the following ways in dealing with evidence of intoxication: (1) prohibition of such evidence; (2) admission of such evidence provided that it satisfies a substantive standard that is similar to wording in the insanity defense; (3) implicit inclusion in a "catch-all" sentencing provision; and (4) no published precedential guidance, leaving the matter to the trial courts.

The substantive standard inclusion provision varies widely among the few jurisdictions that follow this approach. In Arizona the standard is essentially its state's statutory insanity standard, i.e., intoxication must have "significantly reduced" the defendant's "capacity to appreciate the wrongfulness of the conduct or to conform it to the requirements of the law" (Ariz. Rev. Stat. §13-702). More broadly cast, in California and North Carolina the defendant must have "suffered" from a mental condition that "would [have] reduced his or her culpability (Cal. Rules of Court, Rule 423; N.C. Gen Stat. §15a-1340.16)" (Marlowe et al. 1999). In some extreme cases voluntary intoxication can pertain to "criminal responsibility" for purposes of punishment where it was not allowed as a defense against the criminal offense. For example in Texas where evidence supports temporary insanity caused by intoxication, such evidence may be introduced to mitigate the penalty and the court can instruct the jury accordingly (Texas Penal Code, Section 8.04).

A "catch-all" sentencing provision may, like that of Illinois law for example, permit evidence of "any other factors" that may be relevant to mitigation of punishment (Ill. Ann. Stat., Ch 730 §515-5.3.1). Marlowe et al. (1999) note that intoxication may be allowed into evidence without showing that the state of intoxication was actually connected to the criminal act. They caution against using intoxication that is unrelated to the offense, however, because it could be excluded as misleading or irrelevant, or if admitted, be considered as unconvincing by the fact finder.

Rehabilitation for an alcohol or drug use disorder can be a double-edged sword. Some courts have favored lighter sentences if the rehabilitation effort appeared to have been successful (*People v. Chen* 1991; *People v. Smith* 1995) and others have not supported leniency where rehabilitation failed (*State v. Wielkiewicz* 1993). In some federal cases wherein the defendant's effective use of rehabilitation was considered exceptional, it can serve as a basis for downward departure from sentencing guidelines (*United States v. Harrington* 1992; *United States v. Sally* 1997). Otherwise federal sentencing guidelines do not permit voluntary intoxication for downward departure (Marlowe et al. 1999, 204, note 4, citing *U.S. Sentencing Guidelines* §5K2.13). North Carolina exceptionally permits involvement in a rehabilitation program for mitigation (N.C. Gen. Stat. §15a-1340.16[E]). Without explicitly mentioning intoxication or substance abuse, some statutes consider "rehabilitative needs" to be relevant to sentencing (Marlowe et al. 1999).

Slobogin et al. (2009) note that state statutes that require proof of an aggravating or mitigating factor can result in sentencing at wide variance from the presumptive sentence. Arizona judges can increase the sentence by 25% or decrease it by 50% if requisite aggravating or mitigating factors are proven (Arizona R.S., §§13-502, 13-7-1, 13-7-2).

SENTENCING GUIDELINES

Federal and state sentencing guidelines set parameters and recommendations for judicial sentencing. Mandatory sentencing requirements must be based on facts found by the jury. Advisory guidelines, on the other hand, do not depend on such facts. Thus, the U.S. Supreme Court in *United States v. Booker* held in 2005 that the Federal Sentencing Guidelines were unconstitutional, i.e., in violation of the defendant's Sixth Amendment right to a jury trial, to the extent that these guidelines mandated enhanced sentences based upon facts that had not been found by the jury. In an earlier decision the Supreme Court had found similar state sentencing guidelines to be unconstitutional (*Blakely v. Washington* 2004).

Most of the seven general federal sentencing factors concern moral aspects of punishment and which sentencing options are available (18 U.S.C.A. §3553(a) [main ed. and supp.] 2004); most would not pertain to the psychiatric presentencing evaluation. The most relevant of these are the first two: the psychiatric evaluation includes the defendant's history and personal characteristics. The second category bears closer examination as the "need for the sentence imposed" ought

a. To reflect the seriousness of the offense, to promote respect for the Law, and to provide punishment for the offense
b. To afford adequate deterrence to criminal conduct
c. To protect the public from further crimes of the defendant
d. To provide the defendant with needed educational or vocational training, medical care, or other correctional treatment in the most effective manner

Of these, public protection is relevant to the forensic evaluation, as factors that increase the risk of relapse or recidivism such as medication noncompliance can usefully be included without making a prediction or suggesting a disposition. Especially important would be specific recommendations for mental health services and treatment for the defendant's mental disorder and related medical conditions.

A survey of contemporary state sentencing statutes by Johnston (2014) revealed a variety of factors for judges to consider in sentencing, including the offender's treatment needs such as hospital care, the defendant's capacity to cope in a correctional setting, vulnerability to harmful effects of imprisonment as a mitigating factor, and a defendant's need for specialized treatment. It behooves the evaluating psychiatrist to become familiar with the state's sentencing statute.

EVALUATION AND REPORT

The presentencing psychiatric evaluation and report is organized much like forensic evaluations and reports described in the respective chapters of this text. The approach is especially similar to that for criminal responsibility. Records to be reviewed include medical, school, mental health, substance abuse, and criminal records. Collateral interviews with friends and family must address "all known aspects of the defendant's life … regardless the level of personal sensitivity" (Atkins and Watson 2011, 56). Inquiries should be made about family history of mental illness, substance abuse, and childhood sexual, physical, and emotional abuse; as well as nonabusive trauma. In order to identify mitigating factors, the defendant's family and friends should be told of the importance of full disclosure (p. 56).

In felony cases a presentence investigation is prepared by a probation or parole officer. The resulting "sentencing assessment report" should include information about the defendant's personal and family history, his or her prior criminal record, and often proposed conditions for probation (Dierker 2013). The psychiatrist who conducts a presentencing evaluation should request any sentencing assessment report prepared by a probation/parole officer or other mental health professional with reference to the present or any prior cases of the defendant.

Psychological testing should be considered as a component of the psychiatric presentencing evaluation, particularly when cognitive impairments are suspected. In addition to the often used psychological tests, such as the Wechsler Adult Intelligence Scale, 4th edition (WAIS-IV) and the Minnesota Multiphasic Personality Inventory-2 (MMPI-2), instruments of special relevance to sentencing include measures of relevant risks and needs for planning supervision, such as the *Level of Service/Case Management*

Inventory (LS/CMI), and of risk for recidivism and violent recidivism. Several instruments have been designed to address recidivism for sexual offenders, such as the *Rapid Risk Assessment for Sex Offenders Recidivism* (RRASOR) and the *Sex Offender Risk Appraisal Guide* (SORAG) (Atkins and Watson 2011, 60–62), the *Hare Psychopathy Check List-Revised Second Edition* (PCL-R), and the *Historical/Clinical/Risk Management-20* (HCR-20: Version 2).

To be explored and incorporated as appropriate, Atkins and Watson (2011, 64–66) identify the following domains as especially relevant to sentencing: cultural background, military experience, gang involvement, socioeconomic status, circumstances of the index offense and defendant's state of mind at the time, the defendant's character, and victim-related variables.

The report should additionally include relevant jurisdictional law on sentencing that is being addressed, for example, Section 5K2.13 of the Federal Sentencing Guidelines, if the report is prepared for federal sentencing (Atkins and Watson 2011, 66–68). A useful presentencing report addresses those factors discussed here as particularly relevant to sentencing.

SUMMARY

Psychiatric presentencing evaluations can be requested to address competence to be sentenced, treatment consideration, mitigation, or a combination of these purposes where the offender has a mental disease or defect. Competence to be sentenced can be a type of adjudicative or procedural competence or, alternatively, competence to serve a particular sentence such as imprisonment. Psychiatric assessments can serve one or more of the four traditional legal purposes of punishment, even retribution. Accordingly, the psychiatrist should endeavor to understand how the evaluation can be used to assess punishment and to address the defendant's mental health needs, respectively.

SUMMARY KEY POINTS

- Psychiatric presentencing evaluations should not be recommended penal dispositions.
- Even without recommending specific criminal sentencing, the psychiatrist should anticipate that presentencing evaluations will be used to determine the nature and severity of punishment.
- Allowance for mental illness under the penological theory of retributivism can serve the legal principles of avoiding violation of human dignity and supporting the principle of equal impact.
- A need for the sentence imposed of special relevance to psychiatric presentencing reports is "to provide the defendant with needed educational or vocational training, medical care, or other correctional treatment in the most effective manner."
- Among the sources of information, the examining psychiatrist should request the sentencing report prepared by a probation/parole officer, as well as other forensic reports concerning the defendant.

ACKNOWLEDGMENT

Many thanks to E. Lea Johnston, Associate Professor of Law, University of Florida, Levin College of Law, for her useful suggestions in the finalization of this chapter.

REFERENCES

American Psychiatric Association (APA). 1984. Psychiatry in the sentencing process: A report of the Task Force on the Role of Psychiatry in the Sentencing Process. In *Issues in Forensic Psychiatry*, Washington, DC: APA, 185–215.

Appelbaum KL and MC Zaitchik. 1995. Mental health professionals play a critical role in presentencing evaluations. *Mental and Physical Disability Law Reporter* 19(5):677–684.

Arizona R.S. §§ 13-502, 13-7-1, 13-7-2.

Atkins EL and C Watson. 2011. Sentencing. In *Handbook of Forensic Assessment: Psychological and Psychiatric Perspectives*, edited by EY Drogin, FH Dattilio, RL Sadoff, and TG Gutheil, Hoboken, NJ: Wiley, 49–78.

Barnes HE. 1930. *The Story of Punishment: A Record of Man's Inhumanity to Man*. Boston: Stratford.

Barnes HE and NK Teeters. 1959. *New Horizons in Criminology*, 3rd edition. Englewood Cliffs, NJ: Prentice Hall.

Blakely v. Washington, 542 U.S. 296, 124 S. Ct. 2531, 159 L. Ed. 2d 403, 6 A.L.R. Fed 2d 619 (2004).

Davis VA, Jr., JM Hedden, SR Miller, and KE Witten. 1971. The Kansas State reception and diagnostic center: An empirical study. *Kansas Law Review* 19:821–845.

Derschowitz A. 1978. The role of psychiatry in the sentencing process. *International Journal of Law and Psychiatry* 1:63–78.

Dierker RH. 2013. *Missouri Criminal Practice Handbook*, 2013 edition. Section 33:8, 1, b., Eagan, MN: Thomson Reuters, 482–483.

Dusky v. United States, 362 U.S. 402 (1960).

Felthous AR. 1989. The use of psychiatric evaluation in the determination of sentencing. In *Criminal Court Consultation*, edited by R Rosner and RB Harmon, New York: Plenum Press, 189–208.

Felthous AR. 2007. Criminal sentencing: The role of mental health professionals with special consideration for psychopathic disorders. In *The International Handbook* of *Psychopathic Disorders and the Law, Volume II, Law and Policies*, edited by AR Felthous and H Saβ, Chichester, England: John Wiley & Sons, Ltd., 317–327.

Felthous AR. 2008. The will: From metaphysical freedom to normative functionalism. *Journal of the American Academy of Psychiatry and the Law* 36(1):16–24.

Felthous AR, Kröber S, and Saß H. 2000. Forensic evaluations for civil and criminal competencies and criminal responsibility in Germany and Anglo-American legal systems. In *Psychiatry for Today*, edited by F Henn, N Sartorius, H Helmchen, and H Lauter, Heidelberg, Germany: Springer-Verlag, 287–302.

Gardiner G. 1958. The purposes of criminal punishment. *Modern Law Review* 21(2):117–129.

Garner BA. (Editor-in-Chief). 1999. *Black's Law Dictionary*, 7th edition. St. Paul: MN: West Group.

Gray D. 2010. Punishment as suffering. *Vanderbilt Law Review* 63:1619–1693.

Idaho v. Snow, 815 P. 2d (475) (Idaho Ct. App. 1991).

Illinois v. Watters, 595 N.E. 2d 1369 (Ill. App. Ct. 1992) 16 MPDLR 597.

Johnston EL. 2013. Vulnerability and just desert: A theory of sentencing and mental illness. *Journal of Criminal Law and Criminology* 103:147–192.

Johnston EL. 2014. Conditions of confinement at sentencing: The case of seriously disordered offenders. *Catholic University Law Review* 63:625–678.

Jones NO. 1969. The presentence diagnostic program in North Carolina: Process and problems. *North Carolina Central Law* 9(2):133–157.

Kan. Sentencing Code §21-4603(3) at 355 (1969).

Kant I. 1965. *Metaphysical Elements of Justice.* Indianapolis: Bobbs-Merrill.

Marlowe DB, JB Lambert, and RG Thompson. 1999. Voluntary intoxication and criminal responsibility. *Behavioral Sciences and the Law* 17:195–217.

Mass. Gen. Laws. Ch 123 §15e (1970).

Mattick HW 1974. The contemporary jails of the United States: An unknown and neglected area of justice. In *Handbook of Criminology*, edited by D Glaser, Chicago: Rand McNally, 77–84.

Miller RD. 2003. Criminal competence. In *Principles and Practice of Forensic Psychiatry*, 2nd edition, edited by R Rosner, London: Arnold, 186–212, 203–204.

Morris H. 1968. Persons and punishment. *The Monist* 52:475–501.

N.C. Gen. Stat., Crim. Proc. Act. Ch. 15A, art.81, §15A-1332 (1977).

People v. Chen, 176 A.D. 2d 628 (1991) (575 N.Y.S. 2d 69).

People v. Smith, 222 A.D. 2d 738 (1995) (634 N.Y.S. 2d 578).

Peters EM. 1995. Prison before the prison: The ancient and medieval worlds. In *The Oxford History of the Prison: The Practice of Punishment in Western Society*, edited by N Morris and DJ Rothman, New York: Oxford University Press, 3–43.

Peterson G and R Martinez. 2014. Expanded responsibility of the court to order competency evaluations at time of sentencing. *Journal of the American Academy of Psychiatry and the Law* 42(3):394–395.

Plato, 525 AD, 2005. Gorgias. In *Essential Dialogues of Plato*, translated by Benjamin Jowett, trans. revised by Pedro de Blas, New York: Barnes and Noble, 119–199, 196–197.

Plato. 2005. Protagoras. In *Essential Dialogues of Plato*, translated by Benjamin Jowett, trans. revised by Pedro de Blas, New York: Barnes and Noble, 381–429.

1965. Pre-sentence diagnosis for California superior courts. *Correctional Review.* September-October:16–18.

Robinson LN. 1922. *Penology in the United States.* Philadelphia: John C. Winston.

Rothman DJ. 1995. Perfecting the prison: United States, 1789–1865. In *The Oxford History of the Prison: The Practice of Punishment in Western Society*, edited by N Morris and DJ Rothman, New York: Oxford University Press, 100–116.

Rotman E. 1995. The failure of reform: United States, 1865–1965. In *The Oxford History of the Prison: The Practice of Punishment in Western Society*, edited by N Morris and DJ Rothman, New York: Oxford University Press, 151–177.

Sadoff RL. 1988. *Forensic Psychiatry: A Practical Guide for Lawyers and Psychiatrists*, 2nd edition. Springfield, IL: Charles C Thomas.

Slobogin C, A Rai, and Reisner R. 2009. *Law and the Mental Health System: Civil and Criminal Aspects*, 5th edition. Thompson/West: St. Paul, MN.

Smith AE. 1997. *Colonists in Bondage: White Servitude and Convict Labor in America, 1607–1776.* Chapel Hill: University of North Carolina Press.

Smith CE. 1976. A review of the presentencing diagnostic study procedure in North Carolina. *North Carolina Central Law* 8:17–34.

Spierenburg P. 1995. The body and the state: Early modern Europe. In *The Oxford History of the Prison: The Practice of Punishment in Western Society*, edited by N Morris and DJ Rothman, New York: Oxford University Press, 44–70.

State v. King, 578 N.E. 2d 501 (Ohio Ct. App. 1989).

State v. McNallie, 870 P. 2d 295 (Wash. Sup. Ct., 1994).

State v. Pryor, 799 P. 2d 244 (Wash. Sup. Ct. 1990).

State v. Wielkiewicz, 123 Idaho 393 (1993) (848 P. 2d 451).

Stetler R and RL Goldstein. 2003. Punishment. In *Principles and Practice of Forensic Psychiatry*, 2nd edition, edited by R Rosner, London: Arnold, 804–810.

Texas Penal Code, Title 2, Section 8.04. codes.findlaw.com/tx/penal-code/penal-sect-8-04.html, accessed on July 15, 2015.

United States v. Booker, 543 U.S. 220 (2005).

United States v. Chambers, 885 F. Supp. 12 (D.D.C. 1995).

United States v. Dreyer, 693 F. 3d 803 (9th Cir. 2012).

United States v. Gallo, 20 F. 3d 7 (1st Cir. 1994).

United States v. Harrington, 808 F. Supp. 883 (D.C. 1992).

United States v. Lewinson, 988 F. 2d 1005 (9th Cir. 1993).

United States v. Marks, 530 F. 3d 799 (9th Cir. 2008).

United States v. Sally, 116 F. 3d 76 (3rd Cir. 1997).

United States v. Studley, 907 F. 2d (1st Cir. 1990).

PART 4

Civil Law

RICHARD L. FRIERSON

32

Specific issues in psychiatric malpractice

ROBERT WETTSTEIN

INTRODUCTION

In this chapter, several of the specific liability issues that concern mental health professionals—especially psychiatrists—will be discussed and reviewed. As space does not permit inclusion of all of the possible areas of psychiatric negligence that are not covered elsewhere in this volume, the present review is highly selective. The chapter will focus on negligence liability rather than liability for breach of contract, civil rights, intentional torts, or fraud, which can also be brought against the psychiatrist, whether based on the same conduct or otherwise. The present topics include error in medicine, law of negligence, tort reform, psychopharmacology, seclusion and restraints, suicide and attempted suicide, supervision of other health-care professionals, and consideration of the issues related to the use of electronic medical records.

ERROR IN MEDICINE

Error in medicine has attracted increasing attention from a variety of parties: physicians and their professional organizations, injured patients, plaintiff and defense attorneys, liability insurance companies, government agencies, researchers, public policy experts, and public health experts. Terminology in this field is complex and controversial, with the use of different definitions of error in medicine. Terms such as error, accident, inadvertent injury, complication, medical injury, therapeutic misadventure, iatrogenic injury, adverse drug event, and negligent adverse event are used in different accounts or studies of this issue. Errors in medicine are not necessarily equivalent to negligence and may or may not be necessarily preventable or harmful to the patient.

The true incidence and typology of medical errors in general medical populations are unknown, because studies have only been conducted in selected patient groups such as surgical or intensive care hospitalized patients or other subspecialized care populations. There is no national database of medical error, though some states compile and report more severe errors such as wrong-side surgery, and patient deaths. Research methods in this area include retrospective record review (Thomas et al. 2000; Hayward and Hofer 2001), computerized detection using electronic health records, physician self-reporting of incidents (O'Neil et al. 1993), patient self-reporting of incidents, or prospective observational studies (Andrews et al. 1997), some using standardized patients (Graber 2013). Of all medical errors, diagnostic errors are the most common, most costly, and most dangerous (Therani et al. 2013). Empirical research indicates that medical negligence is not rare, occurring in as many as 4% of hospital admissions, resulting in 44,000–98,000 deaths every year in American hospitals (Kohn et al. 2000), in addition to costly subsequent consequential medical care (Andrews et al. 1997). Operative complications and adverse drug effects are among the most common types of adverse events (Thomas et al. 2000).

Despite the considerable incidence of medical error, few injured patients actually file a legal complaint (Localio et al. 1991). Fewer than half of patient–plaintiffs receive any payment, and only about 10% of medical malpractice cases proceed to trial (Taragin et al. 1992). At trial, about one-fourth of medical malpractice plaintiffs prevail compared with one-half of plaintiffs in other tort cases (Litras et al. 2000). Thus, even though many malpractice cases are brought by patients who were treated negligently, these patients were infrequently compensated (Localio et al. 1991).

There is geographical variation in the incidence of medical malpractice litigation, its outcome, and liability insurance premiums, even from county to county within the same state. There is considerable variation in the annual prevalence of medical malpractice litigation across physician specialty; in one study, this ranged from 2.6% in psychiatry to 19.1% in neurosurgery (Jena et al. 2011). In psychiatry, the incidence of malpractice litigation against psychiatrists has ranged from 4% to 8% annually, since the 1980s. One national study found a decline in the frequency of medical liability paid claims, and a flat or declining level of compensation payments and insurance costs between 2004 and 2013 in five representative geographical areas, though the proportion of cases that resulted in compensation to the patient–plaintiff has been unchanged (Mello et al. 2014).

A public health and safety approach to medical error has been recommended, given contemporary advances in knowledge of human factors and injury prevention (Leape 1994; Kohn et al. 2000). This approach includes mandatory reporting of serious patient injuries or deaths due to medical error, which is not uniformly required in the United States. Effort is focused on the systematic identification and prevention of error through the proper design of the medical workplace, recognizing that injuries often result from failure of a complex, interdependent system rather than a single individual acting in isolation. Accompanying that cultural shift is an approach to error that is not blaming of the involved health-care professional but rather accepting and future oriented with regard to error prevention.

Handling medical error

A physician or associated health-care professional is faced with a dilemma when he or she becomes aware of an error in the patient's care, especially when the error is harmful to the patient and the patient and family are unaware. In one survey of internal medicine residents, only 54% discussed the mistake with their attending physicians, and only 24% informed the patient or families (Wu et al. 1991). Disclosing a serious error to a patient or family member is typically discouraged by risk management staff and legal counsel at hospitals and clinics, for fear of increasing the likelihood of a lawsuit for the error (Studdert et al. 2007). The presence of the National Practitioner Data Bank, though limited in its actual impact, also serves as a deterrent to spontaneous reporting of serious error (Baldwin et al. 1999).

The ethical theories of consequentialism and deontology each argue for a physician's duty to disclose significant medical error to patients and families, and professional medical associations have adopted policies favoring disclosure for ethical reasons (Wu et al. 1997). The Veterans Administration has adopted a system-wide policy of disclosing medical error to patients and family when that error has resulted in loss of a patient's function, earning capacity, or life, while providing assistance to them in filing a claim against the facility (Kraman and Hamm 1999). Empirical data pursuant to this practice at one facility demonstrated that claim frequency and severity data were moderate to those at comparable facilities (Kraman and Hamm 1999). Surveyed internal medicine patients at an outpatient facility indicated that they desired an acknowledgment from their physicians of even minor errors (Witman et al. 1996). Such honesty likely undercuts anger and vengefulness of patients and their families, the latter of which can prompt litigation demanding excess or even punitive damages (Hickson et al. 1992; Witman et al. 1996). Beyond being the "best defense," acknowledgements of medical error and apology also promote open communication between physicians and patients (Witman et al. 1996; Shuman 2000) and provide patients with information that they may need to make decisions regarding their subsequent health care. Such an approach contrasts with the earlier approach of "deny and defend" any professional misconduct. Yet, such a practice of disclosing one's own medical error does not necessarily extend to the situation of a psychiatrist who learns of a medical error made by another physician in the care of their joint patient.

To promote error disclosure and transparency, the majority of states in the United States have enacted "apology" statutes that immunize health-care professionals from disclosing the error to patients and families (McDonnell and Guenther 2008). In such jurisdictions apologies involving the expression of sympathy, regret, and condolence may not be admitted as evidence of negligence in subsequent litigation against the treatment provider. Statements of fault, however, are often not protected by these statutes (Mello et al. 2014). It is unclear whether such an approach by health-care professionals actually reduces litigation volume or cost (Studdert et al. 2007; Saitta and Hodge 2012; Mello et al. 2014).

LAW OF NEGLIGENCE

Medical malpractice litigation has been an important issue in the United States only in the last 150 years (Mohr 2000). Malpractice litigation has been driven by medical factors such as the promulgation of uniform accepted clinical standards of care in a social climate of professionalism. Legal factors such as the availability of professional liability insurance, presence of contingent plaintiff attorney fees, legal right to jury trial with use of citizen juries, and pleading of malpractice as a tort rather than a contract also contributed to sustaining malpractice litigation (Mohr 2000). The goals of medical malpractice litigation include compensating patients injured through negligence, deterring unsafe medical practice, and obtaining corrective justice (Studdert et al. 2004).

Tort law, the law of civil injury, is defined by state or federal statute and case law. By law, a physician has a duty to the patient to use that degree of skill and care that is expected of a reasonably competent physician in the same class to which he or she belongs, acting in the same or similar circumstances. A patient–plaintiff has the burden to prove that the physician had a duty to provide appropriate evaluation and treatment and that the physician failed to do so. Medical malpractice litigation is therefore fault based, and deviations in the standard of appropriate care occur by errors of omission or commission. The plaintiff must further prove that the defendant physician's failure to provide appropriate care and treatment to the patient was proximate cause of the physical or emotional harm to the patient. Harm to the patient that occurs through causes other than the defendant's negligence (e.g., the natural course of the underlying disease) is not the responsibility of the defendant. Liability can also be avoided if the defendant made an error in judgment in the assessment and care of the patient–plaintiff, despite the adverse outcome of the case.

Standards of medical care are predominantly national in origin, but some jurisdictions apply a local or regional standard of care. The standard of care is not that of the most highly skilled or even the average physician; it may be met if it is the standard used by a significant minority. In the litigation, the plaintiff and defendant attempt to establish the standard of care, and its breach, through the use of authoritative professional literature, practice guidelines, applicable government regulation, hospital and clinic policy, accreditation standards, and expert witness testimony (Ayers 1994; Hyams et al. 1995; Shuman 1997). However, even practice guidelines can widely differ in a particular medical specialty area, leading to uncertainty regarding the standard of care (Morreim 1997). Evidence-based medicine has been introduced as a principle to apply empirical knowledge to the practice of medicine and help identify what is appropriate care (Guyatt et al. 2000). However, alternate schools of thought, through a reputable minority of practitioners, can also set the acceptable standard of care in a given situation. Relevant evidence must pertain to the standard of care at the time of the alleged negligence and not at a subsequent time when medical advances may have occurred.

TORT REFORM

Tort reform has addressed the problems presented by the current legal approach to medical malpractice in the United States. These problems have included difficulty identifying negligent medical care, failure to compensate patients subjected to medical error, litigation-induced emotional and financial burden to the defendants (Bourne et al. 2015), failure to deter physician negligence, the cost of practicing defensive medicine by physicians when they order unnecessary and expensive tests and procedures, inefficiency in the system with long processing and litigation delays, and administrative or legal costs that occupy much of the insurance premium dollar. Federally sponsored tort reforms have not been enacted due to political reasons, although individual states have had variable success in this area.

More than half of the states have limited noneconomic damage awards to plaintiffs, and these have been repeatedly challenged in court as unconstitutional or otherwise illegal. State appellate courts have, however, upheld such statutory limits (e.g., *Chan v. Curran* 2015). These limits on pain and suffering and limits on plaintiff attorney fees have contributed to stabilization in the numbers of medical malpractice claims, pay outs, and insurance premiums. They have been a model for tort reform in other states (Mello et al. 2014).

Additional tort reforms include tightening of medical expert witness qualifications to those in the regular practice of medicine in the particular area in question, changing the medical standard of care from that of professional negligence to gross negligence, and pretrial screening with a certificate of merit requirement before the initiation of litigation. The most ambitious tort reform, adopting an administrative rather than judicial compensation system for medical injuries, has not occurred in the United States but has occurred in Sweden and New Zealand (Mello et al. 2014).

Reforms outside of the legal system, including open disclosure of medical errors, communication transparency, and early offers to settle claims out of court have been adopted by large health-care systems (Kachalia et al. 2010). Evaluating the impact of specific tort reforms in medicine has yielded inconclusive results, given methodological limitations of longitudinal research conducted without controlled studies (Kachalia et al. 2010; Mello et al. 2014; Waxman et al. 2014).

PSYCHOPHARMACOLOGY

Errors in prescribing and dispensing medications constitute a large proportion of medical errors and iatrogenic patient injuries in the United States (Bates et al. 1995; Classen et al. 1997). In nonpsychiatric hospitals, errors in prescribing and adverse medication events are relatively common and often preventable (Leape et al. 1995; Lesar et al. 1997). Such errors occur due to inadequate information about the patient, lack of knowledge of or experience with the medication, inadequate patient monitoring and name confusion, faulty interaction with other medical services, incorrect dosage calculation, drug–drug interaction, and packaging mix-ups, among others. Attempts to improve the systems by which medications are ordered, dispensed, and administered, such as bar coding in hospitals, have been frequently adopted to reduce adverse drug events (Bates et al. 1999). Computerized prescribing of medication, based on databases including the patient's drug and illness history, formulary guideline reference, and scientific drug information, enhances prescription efficiency and accuracy (Schiff and Rucker 1998).

Prescribing psychotropic medication increases the psychiatrist's exposure to professional liability claims (Brackins 1985; Wettstein 1985; Dukes and Swartz 1988; Slovenko 2000). It accounts for some of the excess professional liability claims that psychiatrists face relative to other mental health professionals. In addition to risking professional liability, psychiatrists—like all physicians—may be sanctioned by state and federal prosecutors in criminal actions, or state and federal licensing agencies (e.g., state medical board, U.S. Drug Enforcement Agency). These actions usually pertain to physicians who inappropriately administer, prescribe, dispense, or fail to keep proper records for controlled medications. Failure to obtain relevant history and conduct appropriate physical examinations before prescribing controlled medication can be considered negligent care and is often illegal.

Pharmaceutical manufacturers are often sued because of the manufacture, distribution, and marketing of psychotropic medications. The law of product liability requires that a manufacturer directly warn the ultimate consumers of the known risks of the use of the product. For most classes of prescription medication, however, the pharmaceutical manufacturers are governed by the "learned intermediary rule" that states that the manufacturer has a duty to inform the prescribing physician, but not the patient, of important drug information (Brackins 1985). The learned intermediary doctrine relieves manufacturers of tort liability when adequate warning has been provided to the prescribing physician. Professional (negligence) liability principles apply to prescribing physicians, but there is some uncertainty whether negligence or strict liability principles apply to pharmaceutical manufacturers (Brackins 1985; Ausness 1989–1990). Nevertheless, plaintiffs searching for the "deep pocket" often sue the manufacturer as well as the prescribing physician, health-care facility, and pharmacist.

Psychiatrists risk negligence liability in the following areas when they prescribe psychotropic medication (Wettstein 1983, 1988):

- Failure to take an adequate history prior to prescription
- Failure to obtain an adequate physical examination
- Failure to obtain an adequate laboratory examination
- Lack of indication for a prescription and off-label use
- Contraindication for a prescription
- Improper dosage
- Improper duration
- Failure to recognize, monitor, and treat side effects
- Failure to abate drug-drug or food-drug reactions and interactions
- Failure to consult with other physicians
- Failure to properly diagnose and treat the patient's disorder
- Failure to obtain informed consent to treatment
- Improper record-keeping

Typically, the plaintiff will allege several areas of negligence in the litigation against each defendant rather than a single cause of action. Litigation has been brought against physicians for prescribing all classes of psychotropic medications, so the following is a selective sample. Dispensing of medication in the office creates different obligations but will not be considered here due to its infrequency among psychiatrists.

Failure to take an adequate history

In *Leal v. Simon* (1989), an institutionalized intellectually disabled man was stabilized on haloperidol for self-abusive behavior. He was transferred to a community facility and began treatment with the defendant psychiatrist. The patient was stable for over a year, and the psychiatrist reduced his medication dose. The psychiatrist indicated that the medication withdrawal was necessitated by a state audit regarding medication use in the intellectually disabled, as well as the risk of tardive dyskinesia (TD). Within a month of the medication discontinuation, the patient deteriorated, requiring hospitalization and larger doses of haloperidol. He was returned to the state institution, developed contractures of his extremities, and became wheelchair-confined. The jury found that the psychiatrist was negligent in failing to review the patient's history, failing to obtain the patient's complete medical records from the transferring agency, and reducing the medication so abruptly.

Empirical data have been accumulating regarding the association between the use of psychotropic medication, particularly benzodiazepines and sedative-hypnotics, and automobile or other accidents such as falls (Barnas et al. 1992; Barbone et al. 1998; Thapa et al. 1998; Rapoport et al. 2011; Orriols et al. 2012; Kolla et al. 2013). In *Watkins v. United States* (1979), the prescribing physician was found negligent for prescribing diazepam to a patient without taking an adequate psychiatric history or reviewing the patient's psychiatric records, which led to a motor vehicle accident.

Lack of indication for a prescription

A psychiatrist prescribed diazepam for a man who, while driving his car the next day, collided head-on with a motorcycle. It was alleged that the patient was under the influence of beer and diazepam, which he had obtained for nonmedical purposes. The seriously injured plaintiff alleged that it was negligent to prescribe diazepam to a person who was likely to abuse drugs. A $410,000 out-of-court settlement was reached with the psychiatrist and other parties (*Munsell v. Lynk* 1983).

Contraindication for a prescription

Upon admission to a hospital, a male patient informed the staff that he was allergic to antihistamines because they caused urinary retention. He was nevertheless prescribed hydroxyzine and trifluoperazine. When urinary retention developed, the hydroxyzine was reduced and later discontinued, but complications developed, including a prostatic infection, the need for a catheter, and eventual prostatic resection. Expert testimony indicated that the hydroxyzine prescription was negligent given the patient's history, and that the hydroxyzine caused the bladder damage. A judgment for the plaintiff of $20,000 was awarded (*Miller v. U.S.* 1976).

More generally, off-label use of U.S. Food and Drug Administration (FDA)-approved psychotropic medications is common and a well-accepted form of medical practice, though with liability risk (Weiss et al. 2000). Off-label use consists of prescribing a medication for a medical condition not already FDA approved, or prescribing for a different patient population or in a different dosage than approved. Off-label use is not *per se* a deviation from the standard of accepted psychiatric care. In some cases, failure to prescribe a medication for an off-label use could be considered a deviation from the standard of care. Several professional medical associations have adopted specific policies on the use of off-label medications, typically noting that such use is appropriate when based on sound scientific evidence and medical opinion (Henry 1999). Case law generally has recognized the appropriateness of off-label prescribing (Kuntz 1998).

Failure to recognize, monitor, and treat side effects

In *Clites v. Iowa* (1980), the parents of a mentally retarded male at a state facility sued the state for negligence and failure to obtain informed consent. Several physicians had treated the patient with antipsychotic medication since age 18 for "aggressive behavior." After 5 years, tardive dyskinesia (TD) of the face and extremities was diagnosed. The trial court ruled that medication had been inappropriately prescribed, and that the patient was improperly monitored over the years. The trial court also ruled that the patient's parents, his legal guardians, "were never informed of the potential side effects of the use, and prolonged use, of major tranquilizers, nor was consent to their use obtained," thus violating the "standard that requires some form of informed consent prior to the administration of major tranquilizers." The parents had not been informed of the risks attendant to the treatment program, and the trial court rejected the defendant's argument that the parents had implicitly consented. The trial court awarded $385,165 for future medical expenses and $375,000 for past and future pain and suffering. This was subsequently upheld in the Iowa Court of Appeals (*Clites v. Iowa* 1982).

Prescription of an improper dose and duration

In *Hedin v. U.S.* (1985), the plaintiff was hospitalized for treatment of alcohol abuse and treated with thioridazine and then chlorpromazine as an outpatient. He continued to take chlorpromazine nearly 4 years before his physicians detected his TD and withdrew the medication. Though the patient had been aware of the movements involving the face, mouth, trunk, and extremities, he was unaware they were due to the medication. The defendant acknowledged having prescribed excessive amounts of medication over a prolonged period of time without proper supervision. Damages of nearly $2.2 million were awarded because the plaintiff had become functionally disabled from the dyskinesia.

Failure to diagnose and treat with medication

New psychotropic medications are continually being developed and released for disorders that were previously untreatable with medication, and new uses are being found for existing medications or combinations of medications. Cost-containment strategies in mental health care emphasize the need to provide effective treatment at the lowest expense, and somatic treatments can often fill this role. Slawson (1991) reported that patient complaints about the ineffectiveness or inappropriateness of medication far exceeded those about medication side effects. In cases of delayed or no improvement, liability can include the failure to obtain consultation from a clinician experienced with psychotropic medication and electroconvulsive therapy.

A related liability concern is the alleged failure to use psychotropic medication. A much-publicized case involving failure to treat depression with antidepressant medication was settled for an undisclosed amount after an arbitration panel awarded the plaintiff $250,000, without establishing a legal precedent (*Osheroff v. Chestnut Lodge* 1985). A similar action was brought by a patient who was treated for dysthymic disorder with psychoanalysis for 8 years after he had refused treatment with medication (*Cobo v. Raba* 1998). At trial, the jury found for the plaintiff, who was a physician specializing in infectious disease. On appeal, however, the North Carolina Supreme Court reversed and remanded, ruling that the defendant psychiatrist was entitled to a jury instruction on contributory negligence by the plaintiff, a legal doctrine in the state that permits a defendant to prove that the plaintiff's injuries were proximately caused by his or her own negligence.

Standard of care in psychopharmacology litigation

As in all medical negligence litigation, the plaintiff alleging negligence in prescribing must establish the relevant standard of care and prove that the defendant deviated from that standard. For several reasons, standards of care in psychopharmacology are often more elusive than they may seem. New psychotropic medications of all types are continually being introduced into the marketplace; for example, second-generation antipsychotic medications, with their lower incidence of movement disorders than conventional antipsychotic medications, have become a standard of care in the treatment of schizophrenia (Chiles et al. 1999; Slovenko 2000; Rabinowitz et al. 2001). However, second-generation antipsychotic medications carry their own potential sources of liability, including failure to recognize or manage the metabolic side effects that are frequently seen with their use (Mossman and Steinberg 2009).

Finally, decisions to treat patients with pharmacotherapy, especially in high-risk clinical situations such as pregnancy, are typically complex, risk–benefit processes dependent on factors related to the physician, patient, and family members (Wisner et al. 2000). In adverse drug reaction liability cases, the plaintiff may introduce the manufacturer's labelling (e.g., medication package inserts and the *Physicians' Desk Reference*) as evidence of the defendant's departure from the standard of care. In some jurisdictions, such evidence is considered *prima facie* evidence of negligence, though expert medical testimony will still be necessary to establish that the patient's injury resulted from the negligence (*Mulder v. Parke Davis & Co.* 1970; *Haught v. Maceluch* 1982). Other jurisdictions, however, have rejected the manufacturer's labelling as conclusive of negligence, and require expert testimony as well as the relevant medical literature to establish the standard of care (*Haven v. Randolph* 1972). Thus, compliance with the manufacturer's published recommendations will not invariably negate liability, and deviation will not necessarily impose liability (Yacura 1984).

SECLUSION AND RESTRAINTS

The use of seclusion and restraints in mental health or nursing home settings is highly regulated by state and federal regulations, state statutes, state and federal constitutional provisions, and standards set by The Joint Commission. Federal regulations were adopted by the Health Care Financing Administration in 1999 for Medicare-funded hospitals (HCFA 1999), and a federal statute was enacted in 2000 applicable to public or private general hospitals, nursing facilities, and residential treatment centers for children and youth (Public Law 106-310). The laws contain detailed rules about the definitions of seclusion and restraint, indications (e.g., patient age, diagnosis, symptoms), exceptions (e.g., time outs in a nonlocked setting to calm a patient), contraindications, role of physician and nursing staff, monitoring practices, need for consultation or review, need for patient consent, documentation of pertinent findings and decision making, and reporting of injuries or deaths resulting from their use. While burdensome to physicians and facilities alike, such rules are promulgated to protect patients from the emotional and physical harms that can occur from their use (Fisher 1994; Appelbaum 1999).

Although the use of seclusion and restraint is not a frequent source of litigation for psychiatrists and hospitals, liability can occur (Johnson 1990; Coffin 1999). In *Youngberg v. Romeo* (1982), a committed, mentally retarded person's constitutional right to be free from undue bodily restraint was recognized. Psychiatrists incur negligence liability for seclusion and restraints when overuse results in patient injury or death. The physicians in *Hopper v. Callahan* (1990), in which a female patient died in seclusion, were alleged to have failed to exercise professional judgment in ordering the seclusion and in failing to provide appropriate medical care.

Negligence liability can also occur for the failure to use appropriate restraints resulting in injury to staff, other patients, or the patient himself or herself. A hospitalized patient in an acute psychotic episode managed to escape from full leather restraints while unmonitored, and fled the hospital (*Rohde v. Lawrence General Hospital* 1993). He drove off in an unlocked automobile taken from the hospital parking lot and crashed into a fence, suffering serious injuries. Suit was brought against the hospital, nursing staff, and physician.

SUICIDE AND ATTEMPTED SUICIDE

Suicide and attempted suicide are among the most common and most expensive professional liability claims against mental health professionals and facilities (Bongar 2002). Damages for the survivor of a suicide attempt can exceed those for a completed suicide, due to the need for continuing medical and rehabilitative expenses for serious, disabling, but nonlethal injuries (e.g., paraplegia, burns, neuropsychological deficits). Income losses for middle- or upper-income individuals who commit suicide can reach into the millions of dollars.

Liability may occur for suicides during hospitalization, shortly after release from the hospital, and on an outpatient basis. Each situation presents different clinical and legal issues (Klein and Glover 1983). Liability is more likely with hospital suicides (Bongar et al. 1993), given the staff's greater control over the inpatient setting. Although the risk factors for hospital suicide are not empirically known, they may differ from those of outpatient suicide (Proulx et al. 1997; Powell et al. 2000).

Generally, liability is predicated on an inadequate assessment of suicide risk, and/or an inadequate response to that risk, which is proximately related to the suicide (Simon and Hales 2012). An assessment of suicide risk is ideally a comprehensive investigation of cognition, emotion, and behavior with regard to present and past self-destructiveness (Joiner et al. 1999). The clinician examines suicide ideation, suicide intention, suicide plan, availability of weapons, attitudes about suicide, past history of suicide attempts, and behavioral impulsivity. Additionally, clinical dimensions such as depression, hopelessness, and psychosis are assessed. The patient's ability to monitor his or her own suicidality and report it to the clinician should also be assessed (Gutheil et al. 1986). Repeated suicide assessments are typically necessary, especially when treating depressed or severely character-disordered hospital patients and those who are chronically suicidal, because suicide impulses can fluctuate in their presence and severity.

Once the suicide assessment has been completed, the clinician must respond in proportion to the level of risk identified. Both treatment and security/observation measures must be taken to reduce risk. This requires balancing treatment versus security needs, which may be mutually contradictory (e.g., prescribing higher medication doses with more lethality and potential for response versus lower doses; increasing hospital suicide precautions versus permitting more freedom to pursue treatment opportunities). Courts can be sympathetic to these conflicts; in *Topel v. Long Island Jewish Medical Center* (1981) an appellate court ruled that professional judgment determined whether a suicidal patient should be monitored continuously or at 15-minute intervals, and that it was proper for the defendant physician to evaluate the expected benefits and risks of constant surveillance. Suicides that occur upon release from the hospital raise questions about negligent release, either inadequate risk evaluation prior to release, or improper aftercare treatment plans.

No-suicide "contracts" and decisions to discharge a patient "against medical advice" are often used by clinicians under the erroneous belief that such practices will protect them from liability. Neither defensive measure reduces the likelihood of litigation, adverse legal outcome, or suicide (Devitt et al. 2000; Kroll 2000). Rather, contracting for safety can create a barrier to communicating intense emotional distress and can interfere with the therapeutic alliance. Staff may inappropriately reduce their attention to the patient's suicide potential, thereby deluding themselves that the patient is safe and creating a false sense of security (Miller et al. 1998). "No-suicide" contracts should not substitute for ongoing comprehensive risk assessment and treatment planning (Simon 1999).

NEGLIGENT SUPERVISION AND COLLABORATION

The psychiatrist incurs liability risks when he or she supervises or collaborates with other mental health professionals in the care of a patient. The nature and extent of the risk depend on the roles and responsibilities of the respective clinicians, the type and severity of the patient's mental disorder, the forms of psychiatric treatment that are provided to the patient, and the administrative system of clinical care in which the patient is seen. For present purposes, we can distinguish among supervision, consultation, and collaborative treatment—sometimes called "medical back-up," "dual treatment," "shared treatment," or "split treatment" (Sederer et al. 1998). In a supervisory relationship, the supervisee is expected to comply with the recommendations of the supervisor. In contrast, consultation involves two or more independently licensed or fully credentialed professionals. In a collaborative relationship, two or more licensed or credentialed professionals share the patient's care, with each of them independently responsible for particular aspects of that care.

Psychiatrists who supervise other clinicians bear considerable clinical and legal responsibility for that clinician's work. According to the legal doctrine of *respondeat superior*, the supervisor incurs vicarious liability for the supervisee. Thus, the physician in *Andrews v. United States* (1984) was found to have negligently supervised his assistant's counselling that eventuated in sexual intercourse. The presence of a supervisory relationship can be suggested by a system of care in which the psychiatrist signs or reviews team treatment plans, or billing claim forms for a patient, even though the psychiatrist has no formal supervisory role in the team. Similarly, the concept of the physician as "captain of the ship" is still prevalent, despite actual clinical practice to the contrary. And courts have held trainees to the same standard of care as fully trained professionals, so the supervisor does not entirely shoulder the liability.

In contrast, consultants should bear less clinical and legal responsibility for patient care than supervisors, especially if the consultant has not personally examined the patient and billed for the consultation. In that case, a court may rule that there is no physician–patient relationship, which is a predicate for professional liability (*Hill by Burston v. Kokosky* 1990). Depending on the clinical context, consultants may have clinical and legal responsibilities to perform adequate assessments of the patient, to coordinate care with the attending physician or psychotherapist, and to document their findings and decision making. To the extent that consultants participate in activities relating to treatment of the patient, they share the same liability exposure as treating psychiatrists. Malpractice claims against consulting psychiatrists have been litigated and settled out of court (Garrick and Weinstock 1994).

Psychiatrists who collaborate with nonmedical mental health practitioners in the care of a patient, whether at an agency or in private practice, might in theory have limited liability for patient care, given their restricted clinical activities such as infrequent and brief contact with a patient only for prescribing and monitoring psychotropic medication, and responding to emergency situations necessitating hospitalization (MacBeth 1999, 2001). In such a practice, the psychiatrist should not, in theory, have responsibility for the psychotherapist's errors and omissions. Yet, the legal system may not appreciate the critical distinctions between supervision, consultation, and collaboration, and consequently, split treatment arrangements may not minimize liability for collaborating psychiatrists. For instance, a plaintiff's attorney can attempt to distort a collaborative relationship into a supervisory one.

Liability exposure is also increased for the psychiatrist in clinical systems of care: (a) in which the psychiatrist is unable to see a patient in a timely manner to assess a patient's clinical change; (b) in which the psychiatrist is given medication responsibility for large numbers of patients; (c) when the psychotherapists are inadequately trained and supervised; (d) when mechanisms are inadequate to facilitate genuine collaboration and sharing of information between the psychiatrist and psychotherapist; and (e) when there are multiple therapists and multiple psychiatrists providing care to a single patient. Through the use of "joint and several liability," split treatment with multiple defendants can result in the well-insured psychiatrists having to provide most or all of the legal judgment against the defendants, especially when the nonphysician codefendants are uninsured or underinsured (Meyer 2012).

In collaborative treatment situations, the cotherapists need to clarify the nature of their relationship and their respective roles and responsibilities (Gutheil 1994; MacBeth 1999). A written contract or letter of agreement between the cotherapists can be useful for this purpose. It should be clear, for example, whether the psychiatrist is responsible in any way for the nonpsychiatrist's psychotherapy, or is only providing pharmacotherapy services. A judge or jury in a malpractice case could otherwise assume that the psychiatrist had supervisory authority over the psychotherapist. The psychotherapist's responsibility, if any, for monitoring medication response and side effects should also be clearly defined. There should be ample opportunities for interaction and coordination between the psychiatrist and psychotherapist, whether on a regular or crisis basis, to minimize miscommunication, splitting, and inconsistency in the treatment approach. Professional guidelines for such collaboration indicate that the patient should also be informed of each therapist's responsibilities and consent to the free sharing of information between the physician and nonphysician (American Psychiatric Association 1980; Gutheil 1994).

ELECTRONIC MEDICAL RECORDS

Clinical documentation serves a multitude of functions, including recording a patient's clinical condition and response to treatment, communicating the provider's findings and activity to other providers, and risk management (Kuhn et al. 2015). Providers are typically cautioned to document a particular clinical or historical finding or course of action to provide proof that this occurred. Providers are incentivized to overdocument rather than underdocument a patient's care and treatment (Sheehy et al. 2014).

Electronic health-care records (EHR) have been widely adopted by health-care systems and individual practitioners due to the implementation of financial incentives and the ongoing change to a patient-safety culture in medicine. In theory, EHRs could enhance the quality of patient care through improved communication among providers for a particular patient, increased efficiency, standardization of documentation of treatment, prevention of duplicate testing and treatment, reduction of malpractice liability, and research opportunities to investigate treatment efficacy and utilization. However, health-care providers have reported a mixed response to their use due to the increased time demand to complete a detailed menu-driven computerized record, distraction from attending to the individual patient at the time of the visit, and the human and financial cost of EHR adoption.

EHRs create novel clinical, administrative, financial, and legal risks (Hoffman and Podgurski 2009). It is unknown whether EHR adoption reduces or increases medical malpractice risk to individual providers (Virapongse et al. 2008). These new risks include errors from providers using the system, as well as "bugs," design flaws, "crashes" of the EHR system, and loss of information security and patient privacy. The provider, as before, remains responsible for the accuracy of the health-care documentation (Mangalmurti et al. 2010). The "copy and paste" or cloning function of EHR has drawn particular liability concern, especially related to the potential misuse of EHR to up-code a particular patient service to fraudulently increase billing for services (Sheehy et al. 2014). Copy and paste misuse includes the failure to update previously recorded information from the EHR into the current visit due to carelessness, honest error, time pressure, or intentional misrepresentation. Providers can create standardized text and improperly export it to the records of other patients. Similarly, providers may fail to enter medication discontinuation orders or notes in the system so that the record contains inaccurate current information about a patient's medications. EHR systems often provide "decision support" information to providers to guide health-care decision making, which providers ignore at their peril. Finally, patient access to their EHR presents new and additional challenges to providers, especially in psychiatry where patient access to psychiatric records has traditionally been limited.

SUMMARY

Though psychiatrists are less likely sued than other physicians in other specialties, there are still many practice risks deserving concern, especially in a managed care, split treatment, clinical environment. Psychiatry is practiced in an increasingly regulated and complex legal and financial environment. Systems of care issues that reduce the risk of error in the practice of psychiatric medicine are at the incipient stage of development. This chapter has considered some of the generic psychiatric issues likely to be brought to litigation. Though specific clinical practices may change in future years, with the development of new problem areas, similar liability concerns will no doubt be applicable.

REFERENCES

American Psychiatric Association. 1980. Guidelines for psychiatrists in consultative, supervisory, or collaborative relationships with nonmedical therapists. *American Journal of Psychiatry* 137:1489–1491.

Andrews v. United States, 732 F.2d 366 (4th Cir. 1984).

Andrews L, C Stocking, T Krizek et al. 1997. An alternative strategy for studying adverse events in medical care. *Lancet* 349:309–313.

Appelbaum P. 1999. Seclusion and restraint: Congress reacts to reports of abuse. *Psychiatric Services* 50:881–885.

Ausness RC. 1989–1990. Unavoidably unsafe products and strict products liability: What liability rule should be applied to the sellers of pharmaceutical products? *Kentucky Law Journal* 78:705–766.

Ayers J. 1994. The use and abuse of medical practice guidelines. *Journal of Legal Medicine* 15:421–443.

Baldwin L, L Hart, R Oshel et al. 1999. Hospital peer review and the National Practitioner Data Bank. *Journal of the American Medical Association* 282:349–355.

Barbone F, A McMahon, P Davey et al. 1998. Association of road-traffic accidents with benzodiazepine use. *Lancet* 352:1331–1336.

Barnas C, C Miller, G Sperner et al. 1992. The effects of alcohol and benzodiazepines on the severity of ski accidents. *Acta Psychiatrica Scandinavica* 86:296–300.

Bates D, D Boyle, M Vliet et al. 1995. Relationship between medication errors and adverse drug events. *Journal of General Internal Medicine* 10:199–205.

Bates D, E Miller, D Cullen et al. 1999. Patient risk factors for adverse drug events in hospitalized patients. *Archives of Internal Medicine* 159:2553–2560.

Bongar B. 2002. *The Suicidal Patient: Clinical and Legal Standards of Care*, 2nd edition. Washington, DC: American Psychological Association.

Bongar B, R Maris, A Berman et al. 1993. Inpatient standards of care and the suicidal patient (part I). *Suicide and Life-Threatening Behavior* 23:245–256.

Bourne T, L Wynants, and M Peters. 2015. The impact of complaints procedures on the welfare, health and clinical practise of 7926 doctors in the UK: A cross-sectional survey. *BMJ Open* 4:e006687.

Brackins LW. 1985. The liability of physicians, pharmacists, and hospitals for adverse drug reactions. *Defense Law Journal* 34:273–344.

Chan v. Curran, 237 Cal. App. 4th 601 (Cal.Ct.App. 2015).

Chiles J, A Miller, M Crismon et al. 1999. The Texas Medication Algorithm Project: Development and implementation of the schizophrenia algorithm. *Psychiatric Services* 50:69–74.

Classen D, S Pestotnik, R Evans et al. 1997. Adverse drug events in hospitalized patients. *Journal of the American Medical Association* 277:301–306.

Clites v. Iowa, Law #46274, Iowa District Court, Pottawattamie County, August 7, 1980.

Clites v. Iowa, 322 N.W.2d 917 (Iowa 1982).

Cobo v. Raba, 495 S.E.2d 362 (N.C. 1998).

Coffin C. 1999. Case law and clinical considerations involving physical restraint and seclusion for institutionalized persons with mental disabilities. *Mental and Physical Disability Law Reporter* 23:597–602.

Devitt P, A Devitt, and M Dewan. 2000. An examination of whether discharging patients against medical advice protects physicians from malpractice charges. *Psychiatric Services* 51:899–902.

Dukes M and B Swartz. 1988. *Responsibility for Drug-Induced Injury*. Amsterdam: Elsevier.

Fisher W. 1994. Restraint and seclusion: A review of the literature. *American Journal of Psychiatry* 151:1584–1591.

Garrick T and R Weinstock. 1994. Liability of psychiatric consultants. *Psychosomatics* 35:474–484.

Graber J. 2013. The incidence of diagnostic error in medicine. *BMJ Quality and Safety in Health Care* 22:ii21–ii27.

Gutheil T. 1994. Risk management at the margins: Less-familiar topics in psychiatric malpractice. *Harvard Review of Psychiatry* 2:214–221.

Gutheil T, H Bursztajn, and A Brodsky. 1986. The multidimensional assessment of dangerousness: Competence assessment in patient care and liability prevention. *Bulletin of the American Academy of Psychiatry and the Law* 14:123–129.

Guyatt G, R Haynes, R Jaeschke et al. 2000. Users' guides to the medical literature. *Journal of the American Medical Association* 284:1290–1296.

Haught v. Maceluch, 681 F.2d 291 (5th Cir. 1982).

Haven v. Randolph, 342 F.Supp. 538 (D.D.C. 1972).

Hayward R and T Hofer. 2001. Estimating hospital deaths due to medical errors. *Journal of the American Medical Association* 286:415–420.

Health Care Financing Administration. 1999. Interim final rule. 42 CFR 482.13(e). Available at: https://www.cms.gov/Regulations-and-Guidance/Guidance/Transmittals/downloads/R37SOMA.pdf, accessed July 24, 2016.

Hedin v. U.S., No. 5-83 CIV 3 (D. Minn. 1985).

Henry V. 1999. Off-label prescribing. *Journal of Legal Medicine* 20:365–383.

Hickson G, E Clayton, P Githens, and F Sloan. 1992. Factors that prompted families to file medical malpractice claims following perinatal injuries. *Journal of the American Medical Association* 267:1359–1363.

Hill by Burston v. Kokosky, 463 N.W.2d 265 (Mich. App. 1990).

Hoffman S and A Podgurski, A. 2009. E-health hazards: Provider liability and electronic health record systems. *Berkeley Technology Law Journal* 24:1523–1582.

Hopper v. Callahan, 562 N.E.2d 822 (Mass. Sup. Jud. Ct. 1990).

Hyams A, J Brandenburg, J Lipsitz et al. 1995. Practice guidelines and malpractice litigation: A two-way street. *Annals of Internal Medicine* 122:450–455.

Jena A, S Seabury, and D Lakdawalla. 2011. Malpractice risk according to physician specialty. *New England Journal of Medicine* 365:629–636.

Johnson S. 1990. The fear of liability and the use of restraints in nursing homes. *Law, Medicine, and Health Care* 18:263–273.

Joiner T, R Walker, M Rudd et al. 1999. Scientizing and routinizing the assessment of suicidality in outpatient practice. *Professional Psychology: Research and Practice* 30:447–453.

Kachalia A, S Kaufman, R Boothman et al. 2010. Liability claims and costs before and after implementation of a medical error disclosure program. *Annals of Internal Medicine* 153:213–221.

Klein J and S Glover. 1983. Psychiatric malpractice. *International Journal of Law and Psychiatry* 6:131–157.

Kohn L, J Corrigan, and M Donaldson. eds. 2000. *To Err Is Human: Building a Safer Health System*. Washington, DC: National Academy Press.

Kolla B, J Lovely, M Mansukhani et al. 2013. Zolpidem is independently associated with increased risk of inpatient falls. *Journal of Hospital Medicine* 8:1–6.

Kraman S and G Hamm. 1999. Risk management: Extreme honesty may be the best policy. *Annals of Internal Medicine* 131:963–967.

Kroll J. 2000. Use of no-suicide contracts by psychiatrists in Minnesota. *American Journal of Psychiatry* 157:1684–1686.

Kuhn T, P Basch, M Barr et al. 2015. Clinical documentation in the twenty-first century: Executive summary of a policy position paper from the American College of Physicians. *Annals of Internal Medicine* 162:301–303.

Kuntz R. 1998. Off-label prescribing of antidepressants and anxiolytics: An attorney's guide to psychoactive drugs. *Journal of Psychiatry and Law* 26:519–532.

Leal v. Simon, 542 N.Y.S.2d 328 (1989).

Leape L. 1994. Error in medicine. *Journal of the American Medical Association* 272:1851–1857.

Leape J, D Bates, D Cullen et al. 1995. Systems analysis of adverse drug events. *Journal of the American Medical Association* 274:35–43.

Lesar T, Briceland L, and Stein D. 1997. Factors related to errors in medication prescribing. *Journal of the American Medical Association* 277:312–317.

Litras M, S Gifford, C DeFrances et al. 2000. *Tort Trials and Verdicts in Large Counties, 1996*. Washington, DC: Bureau of Justice Statistics, US Department of Justice (NCJ 179769).

Localio A, A Lawthers, T Brennan et al. 1991. Relation between malpractice claims and adverse events due to negligence. *New England Journal of Medicine* 325:245–251.

MacBeth J. 1999. Divided treatment: Legal implications and risks. In *Psychopharmacology and Psychotherapy: A Collaborative Approach*, edited by M Riba and R Balon, Washington, DC: American Psychiatric Press, 111–158.

MacBeth J. 2001. Legal aspects of split treatment: How to audit and manage risk. *Psychiatric Annals* 31:605–610.

Mangalmurti S, L Murtagh, and M Mello. 2010. Medical malpractice liability in the age of electronic health records. *New England Journal of Medicine* 363:2060–2067.

McDonnell W and E Guenther. 2008. Narrative review: Do state laws make it easier to say "I'm sorry?" *Annals of Internal Medicine* 149:811–815.

Mello M, D Studdert, and A Kachalia. 2014. The medical liability climate and prospects for reform. *Journal of the American Medical Association* 312:2146–2155.

Meyer D. 2012. Split treatment. In *American Psychiatric Publishing Textbook of Suicide Assessment and Management*, 2nd edition, edited by R Simon and R Hales, Washington, DC: American Psychiatric Publishing, 263–279.

Miller v. U.S., 431 F.Supp. 988 (S.D. Miss. 1976).

Miller M, D Jacobs, and T Gutheil. 1998. Talisman or taboo: The controversy of the suicide-prevention contract. *Harvard Review of Psychiatry* 6:78–87.

Mohr J. 2000. American medical malpractice litigation in historical perspective. *Journal of the American Medical Association* 283:1731–1737.

Morreim E. 1997. Medicine meets resource limits: Restructuring the legal standard of care. *University of Pittsburgh Law Review* 59:1–95.

Mossman D and J Steinberg. 2009. Promoting, prescribing, and pushing pills: Understanding the lessons of antipsychotic drug litigation. Faculty Articles and Other Publications. Paper 18. http://scholarship.law.uc.edu/fac_pubs/18, accessed September 5, 2015.

Mulder v. Parke Davis & Co., 181 N.W.2d 882 (Minn. 1970).

Munsell v. Lynk, Genesee County (Mich.) Circuit Court, No. 80-58801-NI, June 1 (1983).

O'Neil A, L Petersen, E Cook et al. 1993. Physician reporting compared with medical-record review to identify adverse medical events. *Annals of Internal Medicine* 119:370–376.

Orriols L, R Queinec, P Philip et al. 2012. Risk of injurious road traffic crash after prescription of antidepressants. *Journal of Clinical Psychiatry* 73:1088–1094.

Osheroff v. Chestnut Lodge, 490 A.2d 720 (Md. App. 1985).

Powell J, J Geddes, J Deeks et al. 2000. Suicide in psychiatric hospital in-patients. *British Journal of Psychiatry* 174:264–272.

Proulx F, A Lesage, and F Grunberg. 1997. One hundred in-patient suicides. *British Journal of Psychiatry* 171:247–250.

Public Law 106-310, October 17, 2000. The Children's Health Act of 2000.

Rabinowitz J, P Lichtenberg, Z Kaplan et al. 2001. Rehospitalization rates of chronically ill schizophrenic patients discharged on a regimen of risperidone, olanzapine, or conventional antipsychotics. *American Journal of Psychiatry* 158:66–69.

Rapoport M, B Zagorski, D Seitz et al 2011. At-fault motor vehicle crash risk in elderly patients treated with antidepressants. *American Journal of Geriatric Psychiatry* 19:998–1006.

Rohde v. Lawrence General Hospital, 614 N.E.2d 686 (Mass. App. 1993).

Saitta N and S Hodge. 2012. Efficacy of a physician's words of empathy: An overview of state apology laws. *Journal of the American Osteopathic Association* 112:302–306.

Schiff G and T Rucker. 1998. Computerized prescribing. *Journal of the American Medical Association* 279:1024–1029.

Sederer L, J Ellison, and C Keyes. 1998. Guidelines for prescribing psychiatrists in consultative, collaborative, and supervisory relationships. *Psychiatric Services* 49:1197–1202.

Sheehy A, D Weissburg, and S Dean. 2014. The role of *copy-and-paste* in the hospital electronic medical record. *Journal of the American Medical Association* 174:1217–1218.

Shuman D. 1997. The standard of care in medical malpractice claims, clinical practice guidelines, and managed care: Towards a therapeutic harmony? *California Western Law Review* 34:9–113.

Shuman D. 2000. The role of apology in tort law. *Judicature* 83:180–189.

Simon R. 1999. The suicide prevention contract: Clinical, legal, and risk management issues. *Journal of the American Academy of Psychiatry and the Law* 27:445–450.

Simon R and R Hales. 2012. *American Psychiatric Publishing Textbook of Suicide Assessment and Management*, 2nd edition. Washington, DC: American Psychiatric Publishing.

Slawson P. 1991. Psychiatric malpractice: Recent clinical loss experience in the United States. *Medicine and Law* 10:129–138.

Slovenko R. 2000. Update on legal issues associated with tardive dyskinesia. *Journal of Clinical Psychiatry* 61(Supplement 4):L45–L57.

Studdert D, M Mello, and T Brennan. 2004. Medical malpractice. *New England Journal of Medicine* 350:283–292.

Studdert D, M Mello, A Gawande et al. 2007. Disclosure of medical injury to patients: An improbable risk management strategy. *Health Affairs* 26:215–226.

Taragin M, L Willett, and A Wilczek. 1992. The influence of standard of care and severity of injury on the resolution of medical malpractice claims. *Annals of Internal Medicine* 117:780–784.

Therani A, H Lee, and S Mathews. 2013. 25-year summary of US malpractice claims for diagnostic errors 1986–2010: An analysis from the National Practitioner Data Bank. *BMJ Quality and Safety in Health Care* 22:672–680.

Thapa P, P Gideon, T Cost et al. 1998. Antidepressants and the risk of falls among nursing home residents. *New England Journal of Medicine* 339:875–882.

Thomas E, D Studdert, H Burstin et al. 2000. Incidence and types of adverse events and negligent care in Utah and Colorado. *Medical Care* 38:261–271.

Topel v. Long Island Jewish Medical Center, 431 N.E.2d 293 (N.Y. 1981).

Virapongse A, D Bates, P Shi et al. 2008. Electronic health records and malpractice claims in office practice. *Archives of Internal Medicine* 168:2362–2367.

Watkins v. United States, 589 F.2d 214 (5th Cir. 1979).

Waxman D, M Greenberg, and M Ridgely. 2014. The effect of malpractice reform on emergency department care. *New England Journal of Medicine* 371:1518–1525.

Weiss E, M Hummer, D Koller et al. 2000. Off-label use of antipsychotic drugs. *Journal of Clinical Psychopharmacology* 20:695–698.

Wettstein R. 1983. Tardive dyskinesia and malpractice. *Behavioral Sciences and the Law* 1:85–107.

Wettstein R. 1985. Legal aspects of neuroleptic-induced movement disorders. In *Legal Medicine 1985*, edited by CH Wecht, New York: Praeger, 117–179.

Wettstein R. 1988. Informed consent and tardive dyskinesia. *Journal of Clinical Psychopharmacology* 8(Supplement):65S–70S.

Wisner K, D Zarin, E Holmboe et al. 2000. Risk-benefit decision making for treatment of depression during pregnancy. *American Journal of Psychiatry* 157:1933–1940.

Witman A, D Park, and S Hardin. 1996. How do patients want physicians to handle mistakes? *Archives of Internal Medicine* 156:2565–2569.

Wu A, T Cavanaugh, S McPhee et al. 1997. To tell the truth: Ethical and practice issues in disclosing medical mistakes to patients. *Journal of General Internal Medicine* 12:770–775.

Wu A, S Folkman, S McPhee, and B Lo. 1991. Do house officers learn from their mistakes? *Journal of the American Medical Association* 265:2089–2094.

Yacura M. 1984. Inside the PDR. *Trial* 20:64–67.

Youngberg v. Romeo, 102 S.Ct. 2452 (1982).

33

Psychiatric disability evaluations, workers' compensation, fitness-for-duty evaluations, and personal injury litigation

LIZA H. GOLD, JEFFREY L. METZNER, AND JAMES B. BUCK

INTRODUCTION

This chapter provides an overview of issues psychiatrists may face in disability determinations for the Social Security Administration (SSA), workers' compensation systems, private insurance policies, fitness-for-duty (FFD) examinations, and psychological damage claims in personal injury litigation.

PSYCHIATRIC ILLNESS, WORK IMPAIRMENT, AND DISABILITY

Functional impairment, with associated work disability, is one of the major consequences of mental illness (Gold and Shuman 2009; Schultz and Rogers 2010; Gold and Vanderpool 2011). Psychiatric disorders consistently rank in the top 10 leading causes of disability among adults in the United States and other parts of the world (World Health Organization 2008; Centers for Disease Control and Prevention 2011; National Institute of Mental Health 2014).

The SSA is the largest provider of disability insurance benefits in the United States, paying over $11.2 billion in disability benefits to approximately 10.2 million people in 2013 (SSA 2014a). Mental disorders rank among the highest percentages of long- and short-term claims among workers in private industry (Salkever et al. 2000; Dewa et al. 2002; Alpren and Bolduc 2010).

COMMON ISSUES IN DISABILITY EVALUATIONS

Disability evaluations and dual roles: "Wearing two hats"

Treating psychiatrists are drawn into providing disability documentation when a patient seeks disability compensation. SSA disability programs base decisions for eligibility for benefits primarily on information provided by treating clinicians. Workers' compensation systems typically rely on the treating clinician to provide ongoing reports regarding a patient's disability status. However, treating psychiatrists who become involved in their patients' disability claims face problematic implications of occupying these dual roles that can result in treatment dilemmas and disrupt the therapeutic relationship (Strasburger et al. 1997). Psychiatrists should consider referring to an independent psychiatrist under such circumstances (Gold and Davidson 2007; Gold and Shuman 2009; Vanderpool 2011).

The *Diagnostic and Statistical Manual of Mental Disorders, 5th edition* (*DSM-5*) and disability evaluations

The *DSM-5*'s (American Psychiatric Association 2013) changes in diagnostic and evaluation procedures are likely to have important consequences for disability evaluations (Gold 2014). The Global Assessment of Functioning (GAF) Scale has been removed, and a new rating methodology has not been endorsed. *DSM-5* has recommended that psychiatrists consider utilizing a new tool for assessment of global functioning and impairment, the World Health Organization Disability Assessment Schedule 2.0 (WHODAS 2.0) (Üstün et al. 2010). Unlike the GAF Scale, the WHODAS 2.0 is primarily a self-report instrument. However, government agencies and insurance systems are likely to continue requesting or requiring use of the GAF Scale in disability evaluations for some time (Gold 2014).

SOCIAL SECURITY DISABILITY INSURANCE

The SSA is responsible for administering the Social Security Disability Insurance (SSDI) Program (Title II) and the

Supplemental Security Income (SSI) Program (Title XVI). SSDI provides disability insurance coverage in the form of cash benefits for those disabled workers and their dependents who have contributed to the Social Security trust fund through the Federal Insurance Compensation Act (FICA) tax on their earnings. SSI provides a minimum income level for the needy, aged, blind, and disabled based on eligibility determined by statutorily defined need. Both SSDI and SSI programs require that individuals meet certain medical criteria to be eligible for benefits. The statutory definition of disability is the same in both programs; however, this discussion focuses only on impairment ratings for adults and the SSDI program.

Filing an SSDI claim and determining eligibility

SSDI was designed to provide replacement income for disabled workers. The SSA's process of determining disability emphasizes medical evidence that includes a signed report by the treating clinician concerning the applicant's medical history of impairment(s) that prevent work. If additional information is needed, the SSA may request a Consultative Examination (CE) from either the treating clinician or a nontreating mental health professional.

Each state's Disability Determination Service (DDS) makes the initial determination of eligibility for SSDI benefits. The DDS first assesses whether a claimant meets the SSA's definition of disability by sequentially addressing five threshold questions (SSA 2014b), specifically, whether a claimant

- Is engaged in substantial gainful activity
- Has a severe impairment or combination of impairments
- Meets or equals a "listed" or officially recognized impairment
- Is prevented by impairment(s) and residual functional capacity from engaging in relevant past employment
- Has the ability to engage in other gainful activity considering the claimant's education, past relevant experience, and residual functional capacity

There is a complicated appeal process for unfavorable DDS decisions (SSA 2014c).

Providing SSDI claim information

Information provided by treating clinicians is the cornerstone in the determination of eligibility for SSDI benefits. The SSA website provides a guide called "Medical/Professional Relations: Disability Evaluation Under Social Security," referred to as the "Bluebook," that helps clinicians understand and effectively document their findings for SSA review (SSA 2014b).

SSA defines total disability as the inability "to engage in any substantial gainful activity by reason of any medically determinable physical or mental impairment which can be expected to result in death or which has lasted or can be expected to last for a continuous period of not less than 12 months" (SSA 2014b). "Substantial gainful activity" (SGA) is considered to be any productive work of a nature generally performed for remuneration or profit, involving the performance of significant physical or mental duties or a combination thereof. This definition includes part-time work regardless of pay or similarity to an individual's former work. If jobs that the claimant could perform are available in substantial quantity somewhere in the country, then the claimant is not eligible for disability benefits (SSA 2014b). If claimants are earning over the statutorily prescribed level of income, SSA considers them to be engaged in SGA, and therefore not disabled. SSA will deny such claims no matter how serious the claimant's medical condition.

The SSDI claim analysis

The SSDI claim analysis begins with the diagnosis, based on "Paragraph A" criteria for a "listed" diagnosis. These are statutorily recognized diagnoses that the SSA has determined may meet the severity requirement of its definition of disability. The SSA lists nine categories of mental disorders, based on *DSM* diagnoses and their criteria (American Psychiatric Association 2013) (Table 33.1).

For each "listed" mental health diagnosis, there is first a description of the specific disorder. Second, paragraph "A" lists a set of medical findings that specify the symptoms needed to qualify for that diagnosis or listing. Third, paragraph "B" lists related functional limitations (Table 33.2).

Finally, for diagnostic categories statutorily defined as "chronic" (e.g., Intellectual Disability) paragraph C provides additional functional criteria that must be met for a claim to succeed.

Table 33.1 SSA listed categories of mental disorders

Organic mental disorders
Schizophrenic, paranoid, and other psychotic disorders
Affective disorders
Intellectual disability
Anxiety-related disorders
Somatoform disorders
Personality disorders
Substance addiction disorders
Autistic disorder and other pervasive developmental disorders

Table 33.2 SSA paragraph "B" functional limitations

Restriction of activities of daily living
Difficulty in maintaining social functioning
Deficiencies of concentration, persistence, or pace
Episodes of decompensation, each of extended duration

If the DDS deems that paragraph A criteria are satisfied, the SSA then assesses functional restrictions as delineated in paragraph B and, if necessary, paragraph C. The functional limitations and restrictions listed in paragraphs B and C must be the result of the clinical findings related to the mental disorder outlined in paragraph A.

Comprehensive definitions of Paragraph B functional limitations are provided by the SSA's "Bluebook." The SSA considers "C" criteria only if the "B" criteria in the relevant diagnostic groups are not met by the evidence. The paragraph C criteria recognize the significant impact of impairments related to certain chronic mental illnesses even when decreased by the use of medication or psychosocial factors such as placement in a structured environment.

The SSA recognizes that "listed" mental disorders do not encompass all types of clinical findings that may result in impairments severe enough to prevent work. Claimants may be found to be disabled based on reports indicating that they are experiencing medically equivalent impairments comparable to the impairments associated with the listed mental disorders (SSA 2014b). SSA also allows for consideration of the effects of a combination of impairments in determining disability for work.

Clinicians may also be asked to evaluate the elements of a claimant's "residual functional capacity" (RFC), defined by the SSA as "a multidimensional description of work-related abilities which an individual retains in spite of medical impairments" (SSA 2014b) (Table 33.3).

RFC is a description of what the claimant can still do in a work setting despite the limitations caused by impairments. If RFC is not sufficient to enable performance of work done previously, other factors will be considered in the assessment of ability to perform any other work, considering the claimant's age, education, work experience, and job availability in the national economy.

Information required for the psychiatric SSDI claim

The SSA's definitions and criteria for psychiatric disability translate into three key mental health concepts that must be present for an award of benefits:

1. Whether the claimant has a medically determinable impairment, referred to as a "listed" mental disorder
2. Whether the mental disorder has resulted in an inability to work
3. Whether the inability to work resulting from the mental disorder has lasted or will last for at least 12 months

Table 33.3 SSA definition of residual functional capacity (RFC)

Understanding and memory
Sustained concentration and persistence
Social interaction
Adaptation

SSDI reports should indicate whether a "listed" mental disorder or its equivalent is present. The SSA requires that clinicians provide information regarding

- The claimant's daily activities
- The location, duration, frequency, and intensity of symptom(s)
- Precipitating and aggravating factors
- The type, dosage, effectiveness, and side effects of any medication
- Treatments, other than medications, for the relief of symptoms
- Any measures the claimant uses or has used to relieve symptoms
- Factors concerning the claimant's functional limitations due to pain or other symptoms (SSA 2014b)

Clinicians should be certain to document whether the disorder interferes with the individual's ability to function in a work setting. They should comment on the degree and duration of functional limitation and indicate whether limitations have lasted or are expected to last at least 12 months, even if there may be some periods of time during the 12 months when the claimant may function well. These reports should contain a summary of the standard psychiatric examination, mental status examination, diagnosis, prognosis, treatment recommendations, and a description of limitations and remaining functional capacities regarding ability to perform ordinary activities. Lack of sufficient or relevant information in clinicians' reports can result in denial of a claim, a request for additional information from the treating clinician, or a request for a second opinion from a CE.

PRIVATE DISABILITY INSURANCE PROGRAMS

Various insurance companies offer individual or group disability policies designed to provide a disabled worker with greater financial benefits than those available through the workers' compensation system or SSA. Group policies are typically offered through employers as a benefit to employees; individual policies often attract self-employed professionals. Over time, the coverage offered by these policies has become more limited and more expensive (Anfang and Wall 2011).

Disability claims involve both forensic experts conducting independent medical examinations (IMEs) and treating clinicians. Treating clinicians are typically asked (with their patients' consent) to complete initial and ongoing claims forms certifying psychiatric impairment, provide copies of the treatment records, and perhaps speak with the claims adjustor or medical reviewer. If the insurance company has additional concerns or questions, they may request that the claimant undergo an independent psychiatric disability evaluation.

The psychiatric disability Independent Medical Examination (IME)

An insurance company or its designee may contact a psychiatrist to arrange an IME. Typically, an IME will include a clinical interview and a review of records. The referral letter should list the opinions the insurer is seeking in the form of questions and all relevant definitions (e.g., disability). Depending on the terms of the policy, the insurer may inquire whether claimants are disabled for any occupation (i.e., any gainful occupation for which the insured is reasonably fit by education, training, or experience) or disabled for their own occupation (i.e., the material and substantial duties of the individual's current occupation) or both. The psychiatrist should also be provided with all relevant psychiatric, medical, and insurance records, including previous IMEs. An IME may also include review or collection of additional data from the treating mental health providers regarding diagnosis, treatment, symptoms, and work impairment. Psychological testing may also be requested.

Insurers typically request opinions regarding

- Diagnosis
- Specific symptoms and related work impairment
- Adequacy of treatment provided, whether additional treatment or different treatment modalities, such as occupational rehabilitation or pain management services, are indicated
- Prognosis and likely length of disability
- Restrictions (e.g., activities in which an individual should not engage due to the possible exacerbation of his or her condition)
- Limitations (e.g., activities the individual cannot perform due to impairments)
- Motivation for recovery
- The possibility of malingering or the effects of primary or secondary gain

Psychiatrists should obtain informed consent, preferably in writing, before beginning the IME. This includes explaining the purpose of the evaluation, the limits of confidentiality, the fact that no treatment will be provided, and to whom the report will be forwarded (Anfang and Wall 2011; Vanderpool 2011). If the evaluee is unwilling or unable to give informed consent, the psychiatrist should terminate the examination and inform the referral source.

In addition to the standard elements of medical and psychiatric history and treatment, evaluators should also review

- Current sources of income, disability benefits, and policy terms
- Current symptoms, stressors, and related impairments
- Whether the claimant is working in any capacity
- Descriptions of a current "good" day and "bad" day, and a "typical day" before and after the onset of disability
- Social, academic, and any other area of functioning prior to disability
- Factors that may be contributing to disability
- Efforts at and responses to treatment
- Efforts at returning to work during or after treatment
- Future plans and self-prognosis

The claimant's work history should include job description, functioning up to the time of disability, what contributed to the disability, and what has changed in terms of functioning. Psychiatrists should obtain a detailed past work history (e.g., types of positions held in the past, length of jobs, and reason for leaving—termination, filed a workers' compensation claim, etc.). A detailed criminal and civil legal history should also be obtained (Wall and Appelbaum 1998).

Secondary gain, potential malingering, and motivation to return to work are particularly relevant and complex in the private disability insurance evaluation. Motivation to return to work may be impacted by economic and nonclinical factors. Evaluators should delineate symptoms that create impairment from factors, when present, affecting motivation or treatment.

The written report should reflect the nature of the referral, the history obtained, opinions listed as responses to the referral questions, and the bases for opinions (Gold and Shuman 2009; Anfang and Wall 2011). If there is insufficient information to provide an opinion, the IME psychiatrist should suggest what additional information would be required to provide an opinion (i.e., additional records, psychological testing, etc.).

IME psychiatrists should limit their opinions to those requested and should use the definition of disability supplied by the referral source. Sometimes a relevant and significant issue may be discovered in the course of the evaluation, and may require discussion even if no specific referral question addresses that issue. For example, if the psychiatrist finds that an individual whose disability claim is based on depression also has a substance use disorder of which the treating clinicians are unaware, the IME psychiatrist should raise this issue in the report.

Some referral sources provide a format for the written report, and psychiatrists should adhere to the requested format. IME psychiatrists should expect that other parties besides the referral source will review their reports, including the claimants themselves, their treating clinicians, and the claimants' attorneys. Examiners should always write reports using appropriate clinical language and avoid making judgmental or pejorative statements.

WORKERS' COMPENSATION

All states have workers' compensation programs, each differing in statutory requirements, case law, and administrative practices. Most federal employees are covered under the Federal Employees' Compensation Act, administered through the U.S. Department of Labor, Office of Workers' Compensation Programs.

Workers' compensation programs were intended to provide timely and efficient compensation to injured workers for work-related injuries while controlling employer's costs. These statutes represented a compromise, under which disabled employees receive a certain percentage of wages during the period of disability and medical care at the employer's (insurer's) expense, and the employer is liable only for limited and statutorily set awards. Workers' compensation is an exclusive remedy: claimants cannot make tort law claims regarding the same injuries. However, employers cannot utilize previously established defenses against liability such as contributory negligence or assumption of risk (Gold and Shuman 2009; Drukteinis 2011).

Eligibility for workers' compensation is determined by establishing a nexus between the injury and the employment. The worker only needs to show that the injury was the result of a work-related event. Generally, the injury must arise "out of and in the course of employment." This means that the employee was exposed to a risk in the place of employment greater than that encountered in everyday life and injury must have occurred within the time and place of employment (Warshaw 1988).

The American Medical Association's (AMA) *Guides to the Evaluation of Permanent Impairment* (AMA 2007) and state law provide definitions of relevant terms for psychiatrists involved in workers' compensation evaluations. Approximately 40 states and most federal workers' compensation programs either require or rely on the AMA's *Guides* to assess issues relevant to disability, although not all use the *Guides* in the same way or even require use of the most recent edition (Moss et al. 2012). However, programs typically share certain features:

1. Employees required to participate in workers' compensation program are entitled to benefits when they suffer an injury by accident arising out of and in the course of employment or occupational disease.
2. Negligence and fault are largely immaterial to the validity of a claim or the amount to which the claimant is entitled.
3. Benefits include cash-wage benefits, usually around one-half to two-thirds of the employee's average weekly wage, and hospital, medical, and rehabilitation expenses.
4. Employees and their dependents give up their right to sue the employer for damages for any injury covered by the workers' compensation program.
5. Rules of procedure and evidence are relaxed in the evaluation and adjudication of claims (Larson and Larson 2008).

Additionally, when psychiatric injury is claimed, claimants must demonstrate that they were placed at increased risk for exacerbation or injury, or that stress or trauma precipitated the effects of the condition (Larson and Larson 2008).

Differences between workers' compensation and other disability insurance systems

Tort law and workers' compensation differ with regard to liability, the nature of the injuries compensated, and the amount of compensation. Under tort law, liability is demonstrated by proving direct causation; under workers' compensation, liability is determined by the relationship of the injury to the workplace. Compensation in tort law is intended to restore that which the claimant has lost. In contrast, workers' compensation benefits tend to be statutorily fixed, modest, and time limited. Unlike SSDI, workers' compensation benefits may be awarded for disability that is partial or total, and temporary or permanent. Finally, pain and suffering, while compensable under tort law, are not compensable under workers' compensation (Gold and Shuman 2009; Drukteinis 2011).

Psychiatric claims in workers' compensation

Initially, workers' compensation statutes essentially excluded disability benefits for mental conditions (Tucker 2010). Concerns regarding the validity of claims of mental injury or trauma leading to a mental disorder have led many states to approach such claims by categorizing them as

1. Physical–mental injury claims
2. Mental–physical injury claims
3. Mental–mental injury claims

PHYSICAL–MENTAL AND MENTAL–PHYSICAL INJURY CLAIMS

Even after mental conditions became more widely recognized, they were required to have a physical connection. Physical injury leading to a mental disorder (i.e., physical–mental claim) and mental trauma leading to a physical disorder (i.e., mental–physical claim) reflect this concept (Larson and Larson 2008). All states allow claims for physical injuries that cause mental disorders and claims for injuries due to mental disorders that cause physical disorders.

In a mental–physical claim, stress or an emotional problem is claimed to have led to an objectively measured physical disorder, such as stress leading to heart attack (Larson and Larson 2008). In a physical–mental claim, a physical injury is alleged to have led to an emotional injury. An example of such a claim would be that of a firefighter who is burned in the course of duty, but whose impairments and subsequent disability result primarily from posttraumatic stress disorder rather than from physical problems.

MENTAL–MENTAL CLAIMS

The most controversial category of stress claim is the mental–mental claim: a claim that a psychological trauma has caused a psychiatric disorder (Gold and Shuman 2009; Tucker 2010; Drukteinis 2011). The most straightforward mental–mental claims are psychiatric disorders caused by an obvious traumatic event or limited sequence of events, such as a fire at a plant or a bank robbery (Gold and Shuman 2009; Drukteinis 2011). In contrast, attempts to evaluate the cumulative effects of exposure to work-related stress present a more difficult challenge. *Carter v. General Motors* (1960) established the legitimacy of an occupational stress claim under a workers' compensation statute.

Mental injury that results from a single or limited sequence of events, such as a fire, may be easier to identify as traumatic and potentially damaging. In contrast, chronic stress caused by a harsh supervisor resulting in depression is difficult to assess objectively. Moreover, even where mental–mental claims are allowed, statutory language frequently requires that such claims entail more than "ordinary" workplace stress, which all employees are assumed to experience (Drukteinis 2011).

Some jurisdictions have relaxed the realm of compensable emotional injury to include prolonged or cumulative work stress, and there has been a trend to compensate for many conditions, such as gastric ulcers, that are claimed to result from such stress (Gold and Shuman 2009). Some states still compensate mental injury leading to physical injury only when it can be traced to a specific traumatic workplace event. Because mental–mental claims are more difficult to demonstrate convincingly, recovery for them is limited (Lasky 1993; Larson and Larson 2008).

Psychiatric opinions in workers' compensation

One of the most common areas of dispute in workers' compensation claims is "causation," specifically, whether the mental disorder arose out of and in the course of employment. Absent a circumscribed traumatic event, the task of demonstrating a causal nexus to the workplace may be complicated by pre-existing mental disorders and other sources of stress in the claimant's life. A causal relationship between the workplace and the resulting psychiatric injury is more likely when the injury is severe and pre-existing psychiatric disorders or symptoms are few or absent (Gold and Shuman 2009; Drukteinis 2011).

Workers' compensation laws also recognize that exacerbation of a pre-existing injury can be causally related to the workplace. Psychiatrists may be asked to address apportionment to pre-existing disorders or other causes of impairment and disability (Larson and Larson 2008). Additionally, workers' compensation statutes specify four "subcategories" of disability that combine the evaluation of impairment with a prognostic assessment: temporary–partial, temporary–total, permanent–partial, and permanent–total. These categories are used to project loss and assess the benefit amount.

Under workers' compensation statutes, permanent disability benefits begin after the worker has reached maximum medical improvement (MMI) and has received an impairment rating. MMI generally means that the underlying condition causing disability has become stable and further medical treatment will not improve the condition, although treatment may still be needed to prevent further deterioration.

Psychiatric evaluation in workers' compensation

Psychiatrists are typically asked to provide opinions regarding one or more of the following questions (Brodsky 1987; Lasky 1993; Gold and Shuman 2009; Drukteinis 2011):

1. Does the claimant have a psychiatric disorder, and if so, what are the symptoms and the duration of the disorder?
2. Is the psychiatric disorder disabling, and if so, what are the functional impairments and how are they related to the claimant's occupation?
3. Was the psychiatric disorder caused by the workplace, and if so, how?
4. Is there apportionment to pre-existing disability or factors other than the workplace?
5. Is treatment indicated, and if so, what type, duration, and frequency?
6. What is the prognosis and duration of required treatment?
7. If treatment has been rendered, was it appropriate, considering type, duration, and frequency?
8. Would the claimant benefit from additional types of treatment, such as occupational or vocational rehabilitation treatment?
9. Has the claimant reached MMI? If not, when might the claimant reach MMI?
10. Is the claimant's disability temporary–partial, temporary–total, permanent–partial, or permanent–total?
11. Can the claimant return to the workplace, and if so, when?
12. If the claimant can return to the workplace, are limitations present or are restrictions recommended?

Psychiatrists should conduct a standard psychiatric examination with emphasis on issues pertinent to the referral questions. Psychiatrists should be familiar with the language in the state or federal statutes that applies to the case at hand and address their inquiries and opinions to the standards articulated by that language. Relevant medical, mental health, employment records, and performance evaluations should be reviewed. If the case is in litigation, psychiatrists should review legal complaints, depositions, responses to interrogatories, and investigative reports that often include statements from past employers, coworkers, and supervisors. Relevant legal history may also include any past arrests and prior litigation. Collateral sources of information will assist in the assessment of potential exaggeration, minimization, or malingering.

Evaluating psychiatrists should obtain an occupational history including a detailed work history both before and after the claimed injury, an assessment of pre-existing conditions, a summary of prior job experiences, whether the claimant has filed other workers' compensation or disability claims, and information about the evaluee's future plans for work. Emphasis should be placed on the worker's experience with the medical care system and the workers' compensation system due to issues related to entitlement and secondary gain. Depending on the opinions requested and the relevant jurisdictional statutes, psychiatrists may also need to provide a disability rating or percentage. If so, evaluating psychiatrists should utilize the statutorily prescribed rating system.

Generally speaking, a three-part analysis is used to adjudicate eligibility for benefits under workers' compensation:

1. The existence of a psychiatric disability that prevents work
2. That the disability is caused by psychiatric injuries
3. That the psychiatric injuries are work related (London et al. 1988)

The findings of the psychiatric evaluation should be presented in a written report that addresses these issues and should also provide specific answers to referral questions utilizing statutorily defined terms and ratings.

FITNESS-FOR-DUTY EVALUATIONS

The central purpose of a fitness-for-duty (FFD) evaluation is to determine whether employees whose psychological status is perceived as potentially unstable or threatening in some way that affects job performance or safety are able to safely and effectively perform their jobs. Concerns may involve performance issues or changes in behavior that are perceived to endanger the employee, coworkers, or the public. Evaluating clinicians should have a clear understanding of what event(s) precipitated the FFD referral, the employee's job requirements, and the employer's concerns.

Administrative and legal regulation of FFD evaluations

A variety of systems are in place to ensure continuing competence in safety-related occupations. Administrative bodies such as state medical review boards generally have a system of rules, including standards regarding job-related impairments and actions that may be taken if impairments are suspected or reported (Stone 2000). FFD evaluations are frequently mandatory if employees want to maintain licensure or continued employment.

Employees are potential vicarious liabilities for their employers (Schouten 2008). Employers are expected to monitor their employees' behavior and mental status, and they are required to intervene appropriately when that employee's performance or health status has reached a threshold of serious threat to the employee, others, or public safety. Employers are required to take steps to increase the probability that a workplace is protected from the danger presented by employees who have become unstable.

To meet the legal threshold for requiring an employee to undergo an FFD examination, an employer's referral should be based on the presence of both job-related performance or safety issues and an employee's known or suspected mental impairment. An individual with a mental impairment but no job-related performance or risk issues, or an individual with job-related performance or safety issues but without a known or suspected mental impairment, is not appropriate for a FFD evaluation (Stone 2000).

The psychiatric FFD evaluation referral

Referral sources often ask evaluators to complete FFD assessments on an urgent or emergent basis, and the need for a psychiatric FFD evaluation, particularly if a threat of violence is involved, may seem acute for both employee and employer. However, these complex assessments generally cannot be completed quickly for a variety of reasons, including the time required to obtain and review relevant documentation. Psychiatrists should carefully assess the appropriateness of the referral. Employees in a mental health crisis may require an emergency clinical assessment, often in an emergency room setting for safety purposes (Gold and Shuman 2009; Pinals and Price 2011; Wettstein 2011; Schouten 2011).

An independent evaluation is almost always necessary to address relevant forensic and treatment issues in FFD evaluations. Dual-agency relationships in FFD evaluations generally create insurmountable ethical, legal, and boundary problems. Additionally, individuals in occupations that impact public safety are subject to special scrutiny if they display poor judgment, signs of cognitive impairment, or disruptive behavior. They are also usually subject to higher standards of functioning to meet fitness requirements. FFD evaluations involving highly specialized or public safety jobs, such as those associated with weapons-carrying positions, often require forensically trained evaluators with additional expertise.

Informed consent

Prior to conducting the FFD evaluation, psychiatrists and referral sources should discuss the scope of evaluation, the inquiries that are permissible, and access to the FFD report, any of which might be limited by statute, policy, or contractual provisions. The evaluee should review and demonstrate understanding of these issues. Confidentiality issues are particularly complex in FFD evaluations due to the relationship between FFD evaluations and the workplace. Obtaining informed consent in writing, including the evaluating psychiatrist's role, a review of referral issues, the limits of confidentiality, and to whom the report will be forwarded, is essential (Gold et al. 2008; Gold and Shuman 2009). If the evaluee is unwilling to give informed consent for the evaluation, the evaluating psychiatrist should not proceed (Gold and Shuman 2009).

The psychiatric fitness-for-duty clinical examination

The FFD psychiatric examination should seek only information necessary to determine whether the employee can perform the job safely or presents a threat to self, others, or the public; if the employee cannot perform the job safely, are these occupational problems related to psychiatric illness? Prior to the clinical interview, psychiatrists should obtain a referral letter describing the work problems and stating the requested opinions. Documents provided for review should be relevant to issues of job performance, including a job description, safety, and psychiatric illness, and should include documentation of the concerns that have resulted in the evaluation.

In addition to the standard elements of a comprehensive psychiatric evaluation, evaluees should be encouraged to provide their perspective of the events leading to the FFD (Meyer and Price 2012). Evaluators should ask specific questions about the referral issues. Although some evaluees become angry when questioned, more often they want to explain why the employer's concerns are valid or invalid, and what may have led to misinterpretation or distortions in the reports of their behavior or functioning. These responses provide needed information regarding the evaluee's impulse control, cognition, insight, and judgment.

Finally, risk assessment and risk mitigation are an important part of all referrals for disruptive, threatening, or dangerous behavior. Evaluators should address any reported safety or danger concerns directly with the evaluee. Static and dynamic factors that indicate heightened risk of violence, if present, should be reviewed and discussed.

FFD evaluees frequently minimize psychiatric symptoms or impairments in order to return to the workplace. Minimization of symptoms may be due to lack of insight, denial, or intentional dissimulation. Psychiatrists should note and record discrepancies between the evaluees' report and those of the referral and collateral sources, as well as internal inconsistencies in the accounts of behavior, symptoms, or concerns.

The FFD report

A psychiatric FFD report should be limited to relevant job-related issues (Anfang et al. 2005; Gold et al. 2008; Pinals and Price 2011; Wettstein 2011). Psychiatric FFD reports typically provide opinions about the presence (or absence) of a psychiatric illness, and the extent, if any, to which the illness has interfered with the evaluee's ability to function effectively and safely in the specific work setting. Psychiatrists should describe how the mental illness affects job-related capacities and provide specific examples of impairments, including insight and judgment. The foundation for opinions should be discussed in detail in the report. If evaluators feel they do not have enough information to come to an opinion because of deficient documentation or lack of cooperation, the report should reflect these issues and what would be needed to reach an opinion.

If evaluating psychiatrists conclude that the evaluee has no psychiatric disorders or impairments that prevent return to the workplace, they should demonstrate that they understand the reasons that prompted the referral (Anfang et al. 2005; Anfang and Wall 2006). If such an evaluee presents ongoing safety or performance concerns in the workplace, employers or regulatory agencies will need to address these administratively. Alternatively, if evaluating psychiatrists conclude that a psychiatric disorder has caused an evaluee to become unfit for duty, this conclusion should be accompanied by supporting data relating symptoms to occupational impairments. FFD evaluations where dangerousness in the workplace or concerns of public safety has arisen also usually require an assessment of short- and long-term risk and suggestions for risk management.

PERSONAL INJURY

Historically, personal injury litigation has involved claims for damages caused by physical injuries. Courts have long recognized that psychological injuries often accompany physical injuries. When a causal connection between the physical and psychological injuries has been shown, damages for both types of injuries are recoverable.

Courts (and legislatures) have been more reluctant to compensate plaintiffs for mental suffering alone, because such claims are difficult to prove and distinguishing between serious emotional injury and feigned or exaggerated claims is often difficult. However, most states now recognize such claims.

When a person purposefully or recklessly engages in conduct with the intent of causing severe emotional distress, the claim is Intentional Infliction of Emotional Distress, also known as Outrageous Conduct. The conduct can be verbal (oral or written) or nonverbal, e.g., intending to induce panic by seemingly trying to run someone over. The common law in all states recognizes some form of the tort of Outrageous Conduct, and 23 states allow verbal conduct alone as sufficient, although verbal statements typically must be of sufficient virulence or offensiveness to be actionable (DiSabatino 2014). Outrageous Conduct is usually an ancillary claim to a primary claim, which is typically also an intentional tort, such as racial discrimination, defamation, or assault. Outrageous Conduct is rarely the only claim, because such claims can be viewed with suspicion by jurors, and causation and damages can be difficult to prove.

Recently, claims of cyberbullying or revenge porn have led to Outrageous Conduct litigation, as well as invasion of privacy or defamation. Due to highly publicized cases involving teen suicide, some states are considering whether to criminalize the misuse of social media, especially when minors are targeted (see, e.g., Colorado House Bill 14-1131, 2014).

As with other intentional torts, if the plaintiff can prove severe emotional distress, monetary damages including reasonable treatment costs are recoverable. Under the "thin skull" (or "eggshell") rule, if the plaintiff has pre-existing vulnerability, all damages are still usually recoverable. If the defendant is aware of the plaintiff's status and deliberately undertakes to exploit it, punitive damages may also be recoverable.

A less common claim is Negligent Infliction of Emotional Distress, where the victim is not specifically the "target" of the outrageous behavior but nonetheless experiences severe emotional distress as a result of offensive behavior directed toward another. This is sometimes referred to as "bystander" recovery. For example, if a mother witnesses her child killed in a crosswalk by a speeding driver, the mother may suffer severe emotional distress. In order to impose liability under such circumstances, courts construct a legal "duty" to act appropriately, then impose that duty on the defendant, then determine the defendant breached that duty with resultant damages to the plaintiff. The case law in this area has developed on a state-by-state basis.

States use one of three primary standards for evaluating claims of bystander recovery: (a) the impact rule, (b) the zone of danger rule, and (c) the foreseeability test (Ginsinger 2014). The impact rule requires the plaintiff bystander to sustain some physical contact or injury in the same accident that injures another. Five states have adopted this standard.

The zone of danger rule does not require physical contact, only proximity. If the plaintiff is close by the injurious event and experiences fear for his or her own safety, recovery is allowed. The proximity requirement entails inherent uncertainty and subjectivity. Ten states presently use this standard.

The most commonly used standard is the foreseeability test. Thirty-one states have adopted this rule, or a variant. In 1968, California first adopted this rule by imposing liability when the negligent defendant should have "foreseen" that his or her conduct would cause psychic injury to a bystander. The factors for imposing liability are (a) the plaintiff is near the scene of the traumatic event that injures another, (b) the plaintiff experiences shock from sensory and contemporaneous observation of the injury (as opposed to learning about it afterward), and (c) the plaintiff is closely related to the victim (*Dillon v. Legg* 1968). Although learning of a violent or accidental injury to a close family member or friend can form a basis for diagnosing PTSD (American Psychiatric Association 2013), the courts are unlikely to expand the criteria for "bystander" recovery in similar fashion.

Once the plaintiff can show liability (under the applicable standard for that jurisdiction), damages for severe emotional distress as well as treatment costs are generally recoverable. However, there are significant differences among the states as to what type and how severe the plaintiff's injuries must be. In addition, the thin skull rule is often rejected for bystander claims in favor of an objective standard, because a victim's idiosyncratic susceptibility or fragility creates difficulty proving causation and weeding out exaggerated claims.

The psychiatric examination for these types of tort claims should address the precipitating event(s), the accuracy and nature of alleged impairments, and whether the claimed impairments are proximately caused by the alleged intentional or negligent conduct at issue. A comprehensive assessment needs to address the following issues (Weissman 1985):

1. The extent to which the accident or exposure caused a new disorder or exacerbated a pre-existing disorder
2. Whether a disorder would have occurred at all but for the instant event(s)
3. The significance to the current disorder of proximate, pre-existing, and coexisting factors
4. The course of a pre-existing disorder with the focus on eventual impairments in the absence of the instant event(s)
5. The role of other factors including malingering, exaggeration, convenient focus, and secondary gain on the current problem(s)

General forensic principles previously described in this chapter apply equally to these evaluations. The medical–legal assessment of a personal injury case generally focuses on identifying the existence of a psychic injury, determining proximate cause, assessing credibility, and assessing prognosis. The nature and degree of impact of the specific event(s) on the life of the plaintiff should be described within the context of a biopsychosocial model (Hoffman and Spiegel 1989). The expert should describe findings and provide diagnostic formulations at a level of probative value. Although the focus and context of the expert opinions differ somewhat from disability examinations and reports summarized in other sections of this chapter, personal injury case reports, comprehensive psychiatric examinations, and ethical principles bear many similarities to those of disability evaluations (Gold et al. 2008).

SUMMARY KEY POINTS

- The Social Security Administration (SSA) administers two disability programs, SSDI and SSI. SSDI provides replacement income for disabled workers, whereas SSI provides a minimum income level for nonworking needy, aged, blind, and disabled persons.
- Psychiatric SSA claims rely primarily on information from treatment providers; initial determinations for eligibility depend on review of documents only.

- If possible, psychiatrists should avoid dual agency—that is, providing disability evaluations for their clinical patients. Dual-agency conflicts may disrupt treatment relationships and bias disability evaluations.
- Independent medical examinations (IMEs) for private disability insurers require a comprehensive psychiatric assessment with a focus on work history and should respond directly to specific referral questions.
- Workers' compensation is an exclusive remedy that provides monetary benefits for injured employees, if that injury is directly and causally related to employment. Psychiatric workers' compensation claims are either physical–mental, mental–physical, or mental–mental.
- Fitness-for-duty evaluations should focus on impairments in occupational functioning due to psychiatric illness. Information provided to employers should be limited to occupational functioning and related psychiatric issues.
- Psychiatrists should obtain informed consent before conducting disability evaluations, personal injury evaluations, or fitness-for-duty evaluations.

REFERENCES

Alpren H and L Bolduc. 2010. *Gen re Disability Factbook*, 6th edition. Portland, ME: Gen Re Life Corporation.

American Medical Association (AMA). 2007. *Guides to the Evaluation of Permanent Impairment*, 6th edition. Chicago: AMA.

American Psychiatric Association (APA). 2013. *The Diagnostic and Statistical Manual of Mental Disorders*, 5th edition. Washington DC: APA.

Anfang SA, LR Faulkner, JA Fromson, and MH Gendel. 2005. The American Psychiatric Association's resource document on guidelines for psychiatric fitness-for-duty evaluations of physicians. *Journal of the American Academy of Psychiatry and the Law* 33:85–88.

Anfang SA and BW Wall. 2006. Psychiatric fitness-for-duty evaluations. *Psychiatric Clinics of North America* 29:675–693.

Anfang SA and BW Wall. 2011. Long-term disability evaluations for private insurers. In *Clinical Guide to Mental Disability Evaluations*, edited by LH Gold and DL Vanderpool, New York: Springer, 241–257.

Brodsky C. 1987. The psychiatric evaluation in workers' compensation. In *Psychiatric Disability: Clinical, Legal, and Administrative Dimensions*, edited by AT Meyerson and T Fine, Washington DC: American Psychiatric Press, 313–332.

Carter v. General Motors, 106 N.W. 2d 105 (Michigan 1960).

Centers for Disease Control and Prevention. 2011. Mental illness surveillance among adults in the United States. *Morbidity and Mortality Weekly Report* 60(Supplement 3):1–32.

Colorado House Bill 14-1131. Available at http://extras.denverpost.com/app/bill-tracker/bills/2014a/hb_14-1131/, accessed July 16, 2016.

Dewa CS, P Goering, E Lin, and M Paterson. 2002. Depression-related short-term disability in unemployed population. *Journal of Occupational and Environmental Medicine* 44:628–633.

Dillon v. Legg 68 Cal. 2d 728 (1968).

DiSabatino MA. 2014. Civil liability for insulting or abusive language—Modern status. 20 *American Law Reports* 4th 773.

Drukteinis AM. 2011. Workers' compensation evaluations. In *Clinical Guide to Mental Disability Evaluations*, edited by LH Gold and DL Vanderpool, New York: Springer, 215–240.

Ginsinger DJ. 2014. Recovery under state law for negligent infliction of emotional distress under rule of *Dillon v. Legg*. 68 Cal. 2d 728, 69 Cal. Rptr. 72, 441 P2d 912 (1968) or Refinements Thereof, 96 *American Law Reports* 5th 107.

Gold LH. 2014. DSM-5 and the assessment of functioning: The World Health Organization disability assessment schedule 2.0 (WHODAS 2.0). *Journal of the American Academy of Psychiatry and the Law* 42:173–181.

Gold LH, SA Anfang, AM Drukteinis et al. 2008. AAPL practice guideline for the forensic evaluation of psychiatric disability. *Journal of the American Academy of Psychiatry and the Law* 36:S3–S50.

Gold LH and JE Davidson. 2007. Do you understand your risk? Liability and third-party evaluations in civil litigation. *Journal of the American Academy of Psychiatry and the Law* 35:200–210.

Gold LH and DW Shuman. 2009. *Evaluating Mental Health Disability in the Workplace: Model, Process, and Analysis*. New York: Springer.

Gold LH and DL Vanderpool. eds. 2011. *Clinical Guide to Mental Disability Evaluations*. New York: Springer.

Hoffman BF and H Spiegel. 1989. Legal principles in the psychiatric assessment of personal injury. *American Journal of Psychiatry* 146:304–310.

Larson LK and A Larson. 2008. *Workers' Compensation Law: Cases, Material, and Text*, 4th edition. Newark, NJ: Matthew Bender and Company.

Lasky H. 1993. *Psychiatric Claims in Workers' Compensation and Civil Litigation*. Vol. 1, New York: Wiley.

London DB, HV Zonana, and R Loeb. 1988. Workers' compensation and psychiatric disability. *Occupational Medicine* 3:595–609.

Meyer D and M Price. 2012. Peer review and psychiatric physician fitness for duty evaluations: Analyzing the past and forecasting the future. *International Journal of Law and Psychiatry* 35:445–451.

Moss R, D McFarland, CJ Mohin, and B Haynes. 2012. *Workers Compensation Legislative Research: Impact on Impairment Ratings from Switching to the Am erican Medical Association's Sixth Edition of the Guides to the Evaluation of Permanent Impairment*. Boca Raton, FL: NCCI.

National Institute of Mental Health. *Leading Categories of Diseases/Disorders*. http://www.nimh.nih.gov/statistics/index.shtml, accessed March 7, 2014.

Pinals DA and M Price. 2011. Fitness-for-duty of law enforcement officers. In *Clinical Guide to Mental Disability Evaluations*, edited by LH Gold and DL Vanderpool, New York: Springer, 369–392.

Salkever DS, H Goldman, M Purushothaman, and J Shinogle. 2000. Disability management, employee health and fringe benefits, and long term disability claims for mental disorders: An empirical exploration. *Milbank Quarterly* 78:79–113.

Schouten R. 2008. Workplace violence and the clinician. In *Textbook of Violence Assessment and Management*, edited by RI Simon and K Tardiff, Washington, DC: American Psychiatric Press, 501–520.

Schouten R. 2011. Workplace violence evaluations and the ADA. In *Clinical Guide to Mental Disability Evaluations*, edited by LH Gold and DL Vanderpool, New York: Springer Science + Business Media, 291–308.

Schultz IZ and ES Rogers. eds. 2010. *Work Accommodation and Retention in Mental Health*. New York: Springer.

Social Security Administration (SSA). 2014a. *Annual Statistical Report on the Social Security Disability Insurance Program, 2013*. Washington, DC: SSA.

Social Security Administration (SSA). 2014b. *Disability Evaluation under Social Security: Part I—General Information*. http://www.socialsecurity.gov/disability/professionals/bluebook/general-info.htm, accessed July 18, 2015.

Social Security Administration (SSA). 2014c. *Hearings and Appeals: Appeals Process*. http://www.socialsecurity.gov/appeals/about_odar.html, accessed July 18, 2015.

Social Security Administration (SSA). *Disability Programs: Medical/Professional Relations, Disability Evaluation under Social Security (Blue Book)*. http://www.socialsecurity.gov/disability/professionals/bluebook/14.00-Immune-Adult.htm, accessed July 18, 2015.

Stone AV. 2000. *Fitness-for-Duty: Principles, Methods and Legal Issues*. New York: CRC Press.

Strasburger LH, TG Gutheil, and A Brodsky. 1997. On wearing two hats: Role conflict in serving as both psychotherapist and expert witness. *American Journal of Psychiatry* 154:448–456.

Tucker A. 2010. A matter of fairness. *Journal of Legal Medicine* 31:467–484.

Üstün TB, N Kostanjsek, S Chatterji, and J Rehm. 2010. *Measuring Health and Disability: Manual for WHO Disability Assessment Schedule (WHODAS 2.0)*. Geneva, Switzerland: World Health Organization.

Vanderpool DL. 2011. Legal and ethical issues in providing mental health disability evaluations. In *Clinical Guide to Mental Disability Evaluations*, edited by LH Gold and DL Vanderpool, New York: Springer Science + Business Media, 37–74.

Wall BW and KL Appelbaum. 1998. Disabled doctors: The insurance industry seeks a second opinion. *Journal of the American Academy of Psychiatry and the Law* 26:7–19.

Warshaw L. 1988. Occupational stress. In *Psychiatric Injury in the Workplace*, edited by RC Larsen and JS Felton, Philadelphia: Hanley and Belfus, 587–593.

Weissman HN. 1985. Psycholegal standards in the role of psychological assessment and personal injury litigation. *Behavioral Sciences and the Law* 3:135–147.

Wettstein RM. 2011. Fitness-for-duty evaluations. In *Clinical Guide to Mental Disability Evaluations*, edited by LH Gold and DL Vanderpool, New York: Springer, 309–336.

World Health Organization (WHO). 2008. *The Global Burden of Disease—2004 Update*. Geneva, Switzerland: WHO.

34

Americans with Disabilities Act (ADA) evaluations

PATRICIA R. RECUPERO

INTRODUCTION

The Americans with Disabilities Act was passed by the U.S. Congress in 1990 and affords individuals with disabilities protections against discrimination that are similar to the Civil Rights Act of 1964. It protects against discrimination in a variety of ways, each of which is outlined in one of its Titles (Table 34.1).

Psychiatric evaluations for the Americans with Disabilities Act (ADA) most commonly involve employment cases (Title I). These employment cases are unique among other types of mental health disability evaluations. Often, the evaluee is hoping to remain working, whereas in many other disability assessments the evaluee seeks to establish proof of an inability to work (Gold and Shuman 2009). In the past decade the landscape of ADA evaluations and ADA cases has changed dramatically. The passage of the ADA Amendments Act in 2008 and the release of subsequent guidance from the Equal Employment Opportunity Commission (EEOC) (the agency charged with enforcing Title I of the ADA) have brought significant changes in the definitions and standards involved in ADA cases, particularly with respect to psychiatric disabilities (Regenbogen and Recupero 2012; Recupero and Harms 2013). Title II of the ADA, which covers Public Entities, has also impacted psychiatric practice through cases like *Olmstead v. L.C.* (1999), which protect the civil rights of psychiatrically disabled persons to be free from discrimination. This chapter discusses ADA evaluations in the context of the 2008 Amendments and subsequent EEOC guidance and focuses on Title I employment cases. Readers who plan to conduct ADA evaluations should review the EEOC documents and additional resources on ADA evaluations before agreeing to do so, as this chapter provides only a cursory introduction.

BASIC TERMS

It is important to understand the definitions of several legal terms for the purpose of conducting an ADA evaluation. As an attorney for the EEOC has noted, "practitioners who are aware of the different elements of proof at issue in an ADA case will be better equipped to address those issues, to conduct useful evaluations, and to provide relevant information helpful to employees and employers who seek their services" (Goodman-Delahunty 2000, 202). Because this chapter will refer to these terms throughout the discussion, they will be introduced here.

Impairment and disability

Under the ADA, "[a]n individual is considered to have a 'disability' if s/he has a physical or mental impairment that substantially limits one or more major life activities, has a record of such an impairment, or is regarded as having such an impairment" (EEOC 2008). The impairment does not rise to the level of a disability under the ADA if it does not meet the above requirements. Courts typically recognize most diagnosable disorders as *impairments*, but not necessarily as *disabilities* (Fram 2008).

Major life activity

As noted above, impairment must substantially limit at least one major life activity (MLA) in order for the impairment to be a disability under the ADA. The definition of an MLA has changed in recent years. Currently, the category is broad and includes a wide variety of daily activities. Whether an activity constitutes an MLA under the ADA depends on case law and guidance from the EEOC, which issues rules and opinions regarding the interpretation and implementation of the ADA.

Substantial limitation

To be a disability under the ADA, an impairment's effect on the performance of at least one MLA must be substantially limiting, relative to the general population (Hickox 2011;

Table 34.1 Titles of the Americans with Disabilities Act

Title I	Employment
Title II	Public Entities (including Public Transportation)
Title III	Public Accommodations (and Commercial Facilities)
Title IV	Telecommunications
Title V	Miscellaneous Provisions and Specific Exclusions

EEOC 2011b). This standard has been subject to debate and revision in recent years.

Reasonable accommodation

The ADA requires employers to provide reasonable accommodation to employees or job applicants with disabilities, as long as the accommodation does not pose "undue hardship" to the employer (Gold and Shuman 2009). Failure to provide "reasonable accommodations to the known physical or mental limitations of an otherwise qualified individual with a disability" constitutes discrimination under the ADA (42 U.S.C. §12112(b)(5)(A)). According to the EEOC, "[r]easonable accommodation refers to any change in the work environment or in the way things are customarily done that enables an individual with a disability to enjoy equal employment opportunities" (EEOC 2011a). Whether a particular accommodation is "reasonable" is a complex inquiry and dependent upon numerous factors.

Direct threat

An employer is not required to accommodate an employee if that employee poses a direct threat in the workplace, even if that threat is due to an ADA-related disability. A direct threat is defined as "a significant risk to the health and safety of others that cannot be eliminated by reasonable accommodation" (42 U.S.C. §12111(3)).

Essential job functions

Similarly, an employer is not required to retain an employee who is unable to perform the essential functions of his or her job with reasonable accommodations. Essential job functions (EJFs) are those functions that define the nature of a job but do not include incidental tasks.

DEVELOPMENT OF ADA LAW

Before the passage of the ADA, the rights of disabled persons in the United States were covered by the Rehabilitation Act of 1973, which used the term "handicapped" rather than "disabled" (42 U.S.C.A. §12101 note, September 25, 2008, §2(a)(3)). Under the Rehabilitation Act, courts' interpretations of the term "handicapped" were relatively broad in comparison to subsequent court decisions under the ADA of the 1990s and early 2000s (Center and Imparato 2003; Feldblum et al. 2008).

The ADA used the same definition for "disability" as the definition for a handicapped person under Section 504 of the Rehabilitation Act (Scott 2010). As stated previously, the ADA contains five Titles, but this discussion will focus on Title I, as it covers disability discrimination by private employers and is the most relevant to the majority of ADA evaluations performed by psychiatrists. Title II covers public services and may also be relevant in employment contexts because it applies to certain disciplinary and certification proceedings, such as the Bar in the legal profession and medical licensing boards (Timmons 2005).

Following the ADA's passage, the EEOC published regulations in 1991 for its interpretation and application (EEOC 1991). Subsequent case law significantly narrowed the class of persons who would be considered disabled under the ADA. Beginning in 1999, the U.S. Supreme Court, through a series of cases, further restricted the criteria by which someone could demonstrate that he or she was disabled under the ADA. For example, if one was able to use "mitigating measures" (such as glasses or medication) effectively, such that one's impairment no longer posed a substantial limitation, then one was not considered to be disabled under the ADA (*Albertson's Inc. v. Kirkingburg* 1999; *Murphy v. United Parcel Service, Inc.* 1999; *Sutton v. United Air Lines* 1999). Furthermore, the term "substantially limits" was interpreted to mean "prevents or severely restricts," and MLAs were defined as "activities of central importance to most people's daily lives" (*Toyota Motor Manufacturing v. Williams* 2002). As a result of these rulings, many individuals who had experienced discrimination in the workplace due to their impairments were unable to claim protection under the ADA. Furthermore, physicians treating disabled patients were placed "in the unenviable position of having to show what a patient was unable to do (that he or she was disabled), and then reverse course completely to extensively document that the patient could safely and effectively perform the job in question" (Thomas and Gostin 2009, 96).

Persons with psychiatric disabilities were often caught in what commentators have characterized as a "catch-22": if their disorder was severe enough to cause significant impairment, courts held that they were not qualified to perform the work; if their symptoms were manageable enough that they were able to work, then they were not "disabled" under the ADA and thus were not protected from employment discrimination (Hensel 2002; Center and Imparato 2003). Courts often found that plaintiffs with episodic impairments, such as bipolar disorder requiring temporary hospitalizations, were not sufficiently "disabled" to invoke the ADA's protection (Paetzold 2005). Around the beginning of the twenty-first century, somewhere between 90% and 97% of Title I ADA cases were either dismissed or decided in favor of the defendant employer, typically because the plaintiff was unable to meet the demanding standard for qualifying as "disabled" (Center and Imparato 2003; Ritchie and Zonana 2003; Hickox 2011).

THE ADA AMENDMENTS ACT OF 2008

In 2004, the National Council on Disability published a document criticizing the restrictive Supreme Court holdings and explaining the need to restore the ADA to its original intentions (National Council on Disability 2004). This report helped to speed the efforts of several stakeholders' groups to introduce amendments to the ADA (Feldblum et al. 2008). Efforts to amend and revise the ADA, to restore it to its original intent to protect disabled workers, began as a draft version called the "ADA Restoration Act" (Anderson 2009). The original draft was deemed by some commentators to contain too broad a protected class, and a revised set of amendments was developed with participation by civil rights activists, members of the disability community, and business leaders (Mitka 2008).

The Americans with Disabilities Act Amendments Act of 2008 (hereinafter ADAAA) became effective on January 1, 2009 (Pub. L. No. 110-325, 122 Stat. 3553, 2008). Mental health advocates praised the new amendments, predicting that they would rescue people with psychiatric disabilities from the Catch 22 in which the Supreme Court rulings left them. The overall effect of the new amendments was to broaden the class of persons whose impairments would qualify as "disabilities" under the ADA.

Specifically, the ADAAA implemented the following changes: (1) expanded the definition of MLAs, and a list of some examples of recognized MLAs was provided; (2) explicitly rejected the Supreme Court's holdings in *Sutton v. United Air Lines, Inc.* (1999) and *Toyota Motor Manufacturing v. Williams* (2002) as too restrictive; (3) broadened the class of individuals who were protected under the "regarded as" disabled category; and (4) clarified that employers need not provide accommodation for employees who are merely "regarded as" disabled but who are not, in fact, disabled (Fram 2008). The ADAAA also called for revision of the original EEOC guidelines in order to capture a broader class of disabled persons. The amendments emphasize that "[t]he definition of disability in this Act shall be construed in favor of broad coverage of individuals under this Act, to the maximum extent permitted by the terms of this Act" (42 U.S.C.A. §12101 note, September 25, 2008, §4(a)). In this respect, the ADAAA marked a return to a less restrictive standard for coverage like that of the Rehabilitation Act (Feldblum et al. 2008). Clinicians who conducted ADA evaluations prior to the passage of the ADAAA of 2008 may be familiar with the term "qualified individual with a disability"; however, the ADAAA removed this term from most of Title I, and the EEOC reduced use of the term as well in subsequent regulations (EEOC 2011b). Nonetheless, the *concept* is still relevant; a disabled person is not entitled to a particular job merely by nature of being disabled—one must still be qualified for the position, with or without reasonable accommodations.

The ADAAA specifically states that certain aspects of the EEOC's original ADA regulations were inconsistent with the congressional intent in enacting the ADA; consequently, the amendments directed the EEOC to revise the regulations (Siber 2009). The EEOC's final regulations (EEOC 2011b) were published in 2011, and psychiatrists who perform ADA evaluations today might find them helpful. Whereas the status of mental illness under the original ADA was often controversial, the final regulations stress that the ADAAA is intended to provide protection for persons with psychiatric disabilities (29 C.F.R. §1630 [Appendix]) (EEOC 2011b).

ADA EVALUATIONS AND PSYCHIATRIC DISABILITIES

Performing an ADA evaluation of a person with a psychiatric disorder can be a complicated process. The psychiatrist may be retained by an attorney for an employee–plaintiff in a discrimination lawsuit against an employer, but retention in the pre-litigation stage is also common (Gold and Shuman 2009). The purpose of the evaluation varies depending on the context. If serving as an expert witness, the forensic psychiatrist's role may be to determine whether the individual has an impairment, to assess and document the severity and impact of that impairment on the performance of major life activities (MLAs) and essential job functions (EJFs), and to offer information about treatment options and how they may affect work performance and prognosis. Alternative dispute resolution, such as mediation or arbitration, is common and encouraged in ADA cases, as it can minimize stress and cost for both sides in a dispute (Ritchie and Zonana 2003; Hickox 2011). In such cases, the psychiatrist's focus may be on helping the employer and employee to strategize possible accommodations for the disability. A mental health professional may also be asked to perform an evaluation or provide documentation and information about the nature of a claimed psychiatric disability, as well as any associated functional impairments, to an employer when an employee or job applicant discloses a disability and need for accommodation (EEOC 1997).

Establishing that an evaluee has an *impairment* may be as simple as determining that he or she has a diagnosable disorder of some kind. Under the ADAAA, the disorder need not be incapacitating in order to be deemed a disability. The EEOC specifically mentions conditions such as autism, major depressive disorder, bipolar disorder, posttraumatic stress disorder, obsessive–compulsive disorder, and schizophrenia as impairments that should easily meet the disability standard of substantial limitation in at least one MLA (EEOC 2011b). However, the ADA also specifically excludes certain diagnoses from coverage, including "various sexual behavior disorders, compulsive gambling, kleptomania, pyromania, and psychoactive substance use disorders resulting from current illegal use of drugs" (EEOC 1997). However, the individualized inquiry in an ADA evaluation is far more nuanced and complex than the mere question of whether an evaluee has a diagnosable disorder (Ritchie and Zonana 2003).

MAJOR LIFE ACTIVITIES (MLAs) AND ACTIVITIES OF DAILY LIVING (ADLs)

Under the newly amended ADA: "[M]ajor life activities include, but are not limited to, caring for oneself, performing manual tasks, seeing, hearing, eating, sleeping, walking, standing, lifting, bending, speaking, breathing, learning, reading, concentrating, thinking, communicating, and working… [A] major life activity also includes the operation of a major bodily function, including but not limited to, functions of the immune system, normal cell growth, digestive, bowel, bladder, neurological, brain, respiratory, circulatory, endocrine, and reproductive functions" (42 U.S.C.A. §12101 note, September 25, 2008, §4(a)). The lists are not intended to be exhaustive (Scott 2010). Under the ADAAA and the EEOC's final regulations, an activity does not have to be "of central importance to daily life" in order to be considered an MLA (Hickox 2011).

The EEOC has also provided guidance regarding what activities qualify as MLAs among persons with psychiatric or mental impairments:

> The major life activities limited by mental impairments differ from person to person. There is no exhaustive list of major life activities. For some people, mental impairments restrict major life activities such as learning, thinking, concentrating, interacting with others, caring for oneself, speaking, performing manual tasks, or working. Sleeping is also a major life activity that may be limited by mental impairments. (EEOC 1997)

Psychiatrists may recognize some similarities between the legal concept of MLAs and the clinical concept of activities of daily living (ADLs). Although the terms are not synonymous, understanding a disorder's impact on ADLs in a clinical sense "can provide a helpful starting point for an assessment of limitation in different MLAs" (Recupero and Harms 2013, 265). Through the final regulations (EEOC 2011b) as well as an earlier document about psychiatric disabilities (EEOC 1997), the EEOC has provided some guidance on evaluating MLAs in the context of mental illness.

Several possible MLAs to consider in the evaluation of a worker with a psychiatric disorder may include interacting with others, cognitive functions (such as thinking, concentrating, and learning), caring for oneself, sleeping, performing manual tasks, and communicating (Recupero and Harms 2013). Among these activities, there has been some controversy regarding the status of "interacting with others" as an MLA under the ADA (Hensel 2002; Hartman 2005). Some commentators had requested that the EEOC remove the term "interacting with others" from the list of MLAs in the post-ADAAA regulations, but the EEOC's final regulations retained the term as an example of a MLA (EEOC 2011b). Although employers might be concerned that persons with personality or character flaws (such as an argumentative or confrontational nature) might cite difficulty in "interacting with others" as *ipso facto* evidence of a disability, the ADAAA's intent was not to excuse workplace misconduct. As the EEOC notes:

> The definition of an impairment also does not include common personality traits such as poor judgment or a quick temper where these are not symptoms of a mental or psychological disorder. (EEOC 2011b, 17007)

EVALUATING AND DOCUMENTING SUBSTANTIAL LIMITATION

In an ADA evaluation, one of the psychiatrist's chief responsibilities is to assess and document the evaluee's level of functional impairment. Although not specifically required by the Supreme Court, legal scholars have suggested that expert medical testimony may be necessary in order to establish "substantial limitation" in post-ADAAA cases (Hickox 2011). The ADAAA specifies that, with the exception of eyeglasses, impairments should be considered in the absence of mitigating measures (42 U.S.C.A. §12101 note, September 25, 2008, §4(a)). Thus, to assess the severity of a person's impairment, the psychiatrist should assess the evaluee's level of functioning when a disorder is in its untreated form. However, it will often be necessary to provide information about an evaluee's expected level of functioning *with* mitigating measures such as psychotropic medication or psychotherapy. This latter inquiry is relevant to establishing whether an evaluee is able to perform the EJFs of the job in question, with or without reasonable accommodation.

Under the ADAAA and the new EEOC regulations, substantial limitation is a lower standard than previously required by courts under the original ADA:

> The term "substantially limits" is defined as "materially restricts" which is intended, on a severity spectrum, to refer to something that is less than "severely restricts," and less than "significantly restricts," but more serious than a moderate impairment which is in the middle of the spectrum. (Feldblum et al. 2008, 236)

The restriction imposed by a limitation need not be severe or outwardly obvious to casual observers in order to invoke ADA protection. For example, in *Overton v. Reilly* (1992), a chemist with depression objected to a new policy that would require him to have regular contact with the public. Although Overton's outward behavior may not have been perceived by others as pathological or problematic, his internal struggle and subtle psychiatric consequences of his disability were nonetheless significant. There are, however, cases in which an employee's disorder manifests as behavior or conduct that is noticeable and problematic in the workplace. In *Ray v. Kroger Co.* (2003), a grocery store employee with Tourette's syndrome was terminated after inappropriate outbursts and racial slurs in the workplace.

The evaluation of functional impairments for an ADA evaluation is otherwise similar to the assessment of functional impairment for other types of disability (see Chapter 31, this volume). When assessing limitations and functional impairments for an ADA case, the psychiatrist should consider whether, and how, a particular disorder or symptom cluster "materially restricts" the performance of one or more MLAs. The EEOC indicates that the evaluator may consider the nature and severity, expected duration, and long-term impact of a limitation in order to determine whether it is "substantial" (EEOC 2011b).

JOB DESCRIPTIONS AND EJFs

In all work-related disability evaluations, it is advisable to obtain a copy of the job description in question (Gold et al. 2008). The job description should list the major EJFs for the position in question. After performing a diagnostic evaluation, the psychiatrist may go through the EJFs one by one, analyzing the potential impact that the evaluee's disorder (and its treatment) may have on his or her performance of each EJF. Past job performance evaluations and an evaluee's vocational and educational history can also provide helpful information regarding an employee's ability to safely and effectively perform the EJFs of a position. When written job descriptions are brief and provide little information about the position, the psychiatrist may need to obtain further information from the employer, the evaluee, or other relevant parties.

In some cases, the evaluee's limitations in specific MLAs (e.g., impairment in interacting with others due to social anxiety or flat affect) may have some bearing on his or her ability to perform specific EJFs (e.g., cold-calling in sales jobs, contract negotiations, etc.). An evaluee's profession may also provide starting points for the evaluation of impairments or abilities in the performance of basic EJFs, such as the core competencies required in medicine (Regenbogen and Recupero 2012). The EEOC also provides guidance for the application of the ADA to specific professions; their resource document on reasonable accommodations for attorneys with disabilities, for example, has a wealth of helpful information that is applicable to a number of other fields and careers (EEOC 2011a).

A somewhat recent case that forensic psychiatrists should find informative is that of *Jakubowski v. The Christ Hospital, Inc.* (2010), in which a family medicine resident with autism spectrum disorder (Asperger disorder) sued his training program for being terminated due to errors and severe impairments linked to his disability. Although the resident was easily able to demonstrate that he was disabled, he was *not* able to demonstrate that he was otherwise qualified for his position as a family medicine resident. His deficiencies resulted in an inability to perform the EJFs of a resident in family medicine, and he had rejected the training program's attempts to accommodate his impairment by transitioning to a different medical specialty.

REASONABLE ACCOMMODATION

Depending on the context of the evaluation, the psychiatrist may be asked to provide recommendations of possible reasonable accommodations for the employer to consider. Although the employee bears the responsibility for disclosing the need for accommodation (Matejkovic and Matejkovic 2008/2009) and proposing an initial accommodation (*McKane v. UBS* 2010), the employer must engage in a meaningful interactive process to provide reasonable accommodation to the disabled employee (*EEOC v. Chevron Phillips* 2009; Valderrama 2010; Collins and Phillips 2011). The employee who discloses a disability and need for accommodation can make the request in plain English and need not use the phrase "reasonable accommodation" (EEOC 1997). Several cases have held that the submission of a note from a physician suggesting a change, e.g., transfer to a less stressful position, constitutes a request for accommodation (EEOC 1997; Gold and Shuman 2009). In some cases, impaired insight or judgment or other factors (such as severe social anxiety) may prevent an employee or job applicant from disclosing the need for accommodation until serious problems have arisen (Foote 2003). Unfortunately, the employee or applicant in such a case is not likely to succeed in an ADA suit; an employer is not required to provide accommodation if it is not aware that the employee's limitation requires accommodation.

An employer is not required to provide an accommodation that would pose an undue hardship (Collins and Phillips 2011), or to exempt a disabled employee from the EJFs associated with his or her position (Smith 2006). What constitutes an "undue hardship" varies from case to case, but often accommodations for employees with psychiatric disabilities are inexpensive and easily managed by the employer. Furthermore the EEOC, noting published research on this subject, has estimated that roughly half of requested accommodations have zero cost to the employer (EEOC 2011b). When considering options that have equivalent benefit or protection for the employee, the employer is usually free to select the accommodation carrying the least inconvenience or cost (Ritchie and Zonana 2003). The forensic mental health evaluator, therefore, would be well advised to consider suggesting accommodations that pose minimal hardship to the employer while still meeting the employee's or applicant's needs (Gold et al. 2008).

Examples of common accommodations for psychiatric disorders may include use of paid or unpaid leave (e.g., FMLA leave) for inpatient treatment or outpatient therapy appointments; a modified schedule to allow the employee to see a psychiatrist during the week; allowing the employee to come in to work later in order to minimize the impact of medications that cause somnolence; physical changes to the work environment to minimize distractions; policy changes, such as allowing frequent shorter breaks or allowing the use of headphones; providing a job coach or access to an Employee Assistance Program counselor during the work day; switching a position to part-time hours; or transferring the employee to a job better suited to his or her skills and needs, as long as that does not pose an undue hardship to the employer (Gold and Shuman 2009; Recupero and Harms 2013).

Organizations and resources such as the Job Accommodation Network (http://askjan.org/) and the documents available on the EEOC's website (http://www.eeoc.gov/) can help the psychiatrist, employer, and evaluee to learn more about possible accommodations that have worked for other employees. In formulating recommendations for specific accommodations, the mental health professional should be careful to provide a rational explanation for why and how a particular accommodation would be helpful (Ritchie and Zonana 2003). Courts have held that merely providing a list of possible accommodations, without explanation of why and how such accommodations would be helpful, is insufficient (Gold and Shuman 2009). Concerning post-ADAAA changes, the EEOC suggests that "accommodations such as break times, reduced hours, or job redesign ... are the more likely accommodations to be requested by those individuals whose coverage [under the ADA] has now been clarified [by the ADAAA]" (EEOC 2011b, 16992).

EVALUATION OF A DIRECT THREAT

The mental health evaluator may need to determine whether an employee's condition poses a direct threat in the workplace. This determination must be context specific. For example, a school bus driver may pose a direct threat if his or her condition requires treatment by medications that cause slowed reaction time or marked drowsiness. As other scholars have noted, the threshold for posing a direct threat may be lower in certain occupations (e.g., airline pilot) (Ritchie and Zonana 2003; Gold and Shuman 2009), and in such cases the employee may bear the responsibility for demonstrating that he or she does not pose a direct threat, once the direct threat issue has been raised (Collins and Phillips 2011). However, coworkers' or employers' irrational fears of mental illness are insufficient to demonstrate that an employee poses a direct threat. The psychiatrist's report or testimony may help to clarify that an employee's illness does not represent a direct threat (Smith 2007). The EEOC has offered detailed guidance on evaluating "direct threat" in persons with psychiatric disorders (EEOC 1997).

The case of *Jarvis v. Potter* (2007) concerned an employee whose symptoms of posttraumatic stress disorder were held to pose a direct threat that could not be accommodated in the workplace (Teitelbaum and Thomas 2009). The plaintiff was terminated from a job at the U.S. Postal Service after three incidents in which he reacted aggressively to being startled by coworkers; on two of these occasions he had responded with violent behavior toward the coworker. The Tenth Circuit upheld his termination, noting medical evidence that his disorder was chronic and severe and that it might pose a risk in the workplace. Although this case concerned the Vocational Rehabilitation Act and not the ADA, the standards and process for determining a violation are similar.

SUMMARY

Commentators have predicted that the ADAAA of 2008 may have the effect of increasing demand for ADA disability evaluations by forensic mental health professionals (Gold and Shuman 2009; Scott 2010). The observation that "[a] working knowledge of the ADA is increasingly important for mental health providers" (Ritchie and Zonana 2003, 273) is especially accurate in a post-ADAAA world. The performance of an ADA evaluation today may require less time spent in determining whether an evaluee is "disabled" and more time spent assessing the relationships between impairments, EJFs, and various possible accommodations for the evaluee's limitations (Regenbogen and Recupero 2012). Psychiatrists and other mental health professionals who will perform forensic evaluations in ADA cases are encouraged to review additional resources regarding the performance of ADA evaluations, especially guidance from the EEOC.

SUMMARY KEY POINTS

- The Americans with Disabilities Act (ADA) was passed in 1990 and was designed to afford individuals with disabilities protection against discrimination.
- Subsequent case law severely narrowed the class of persons who could be considered disabled under the ADA; persons with psychiatric disabilities had great difficulty proving they were disabled if their symptoms were manageable enough that they were able to work.
- The Americans with Disabilities Act Amendment Act of 2008 (ADAAA) broadened the class of persons whose impairments would qualify as disabilities, and the EEOC has further provided guidance related to mental impairments.
- Psychiatrists performing evaluations under the ADA should quantify impairment, determine how the impairment impacts major life activities, and analyze how the impairment impacts the evaluee's performance of essential job functions (EJFs).
- Finally, psychiatrists may be asked to provide recommendations regarding reasonable accommodations for employers to consider for the disabled employee.

REFERENCES

Albertson's, Inc. v. Kirkingburg, 527 U.S. 555 (1999).

Americans with Disabilities Act of 1990, Pub. L. No. 101-336, 104 Stat. 328 (1990).

Americans with Disabilities Act Amendments Act of 2008, Pub. L. No. 110-325, 122 Stat. 3553 (2008).

Anderson CL. 2009. Ideological dissonance, disability backlash, and the ADA amendments act. *Wayne Law Review* 55:1267–1326.

Center C and AJ Imparato. 2003. Redefining "Disability" discrimination: A proposal to restore civil rights protections for all workers. *Stanford Law and Policy Review* 14:321–345.

Collins GT and PJ Phillips. 2011. Overview of reasonable accommodation and the shifting emphasis from who is disabled to who can work. *Hamline Law Review* 34:469–502.

EEOC v. Chevron Phillips Chem. Co., L.P., 570 F.3d 606 (5th Cir. 2009).

Feldblum CR, K Barry, and EA Benfer. 2008. The ADA Amendments Act of 2008. *Texas Journal on Civil Liberties and Civil Rights* 13:187–240.

Foote WE. 2003. Forensic evaluation in Americans with Disabilities Act Cases. In *Handbook of Psychology*, edited by IB Weiner, New York: Wiley, 279–300.

Fram DK. 2008. Practitioners' note: The ADA Amendments Act: Dramatic changes in coverage. *Hofstra Labor and Employment Law Journal* 26:193–221.

Gold LH, SA Anfang, AM Drukteinis, JL Metzner, M Price, BW Wall, L Wylonis, and HV Zonana. 2008. AAPL practice guideline for the forensic evaluation of psychiatric disability. *Journal of the American Academy of Psychiatry and the Law* 36:S3–S50.

Gold LH and DW Shuman. 2009. *Evaluating Mental Health Disability in the Workplace: Model, Process, and Analysis*. New York: Springer.

Goodman-Delahunty J. 2000. Psychological impairment under the Americans with Disabilities Act: Legal guidelines. *Professional Psychology: Research and Practice* 31:197–205.

Hartman PA. 2005. "Interacting with Others" as a major life activity under the Americans with Disabilities Act. *Seton Hall Circuit Review* 2:139–173.

Hensel WF. 2002. Interacting with Others: A major life activity under the Americans with Disabilities Act? *Wisconsin Law Review* 2002:1139–1196.

Hickox SA. 2011. The underwhelming impact of the Americans with Disabilities Act Amendments Act. *University of Baltimore Law Review* 40:419–494.

Jakubowski v. The Christ Hospital, Inc., 627 F.3d 195 (6th Cir. 2010), cert. denied, 131 S. Ct. 3071 (2011).

Jarvis v. Potter, 500 F.3d 1113 (10th Cir. 2007).

Matejkovic JE and ME Matejkovic. 2008/2009. What is reasonable accommodation under the ADA? Not an easy answer; rather a plethora of questions. *Mississippi College Law Review* 28:67–96.

McKane v. UBS Financial Services, Inc., 363 Fed. Appx. 679, 22 Am. Disabilities Cas. (BNA) 1490 (11th Cir. 2010).

Mitka M. 2008. Federal government seeks to clarify the Americans with Disabilities Act. *JAMA* 300:889.

Murphy v. United Parcel Service, Inc., 527 U.S. 516 (1999).

National Council on Disability. 2004. *Righting the ADA*. http://www.ncd.gov/publications/2004/Dec12004, accessed July 30, 2016.

Olmstead v. L.C., 527 U.S. 581 (1999).

Overton v. Reilly, 977 F.2d 1190 (7th Cir. 1992).

Paetzold RL. 2005. Mental illness and reasonable accommodations at work: Definition of a mental disability under the ADA. *Psychiatric Services* 56:1188–1190.

Ray v. Kroger Co., 264 F. Supp. 2d 1221 (S.D. Ga. 2003), aff'd, 90 Fed. Appx. 384 (11th Cir. 2003).

Recupero PR and SE Harms. 2013. The Americans with Disabilities Act (ADA) and the Americans with Disabilities Act Amendments Act in Disability evaluations. In *Clinical Guide to Mental Disability Evaluations*, edited by LH Gold, and DL Vanderpool, New York: Springer, 259–289.

Regenbogen A and PR Recupero. 2012. The implications of the ADA Amendments Act of 2008 for residency training program administration. *Journal of the American Academy of Psychiatry and the Law* 40:553–561.

Rehabilitation Act of 1973, Pub. L. No. 93–112, 87 Stat. 355 (codified as amended in scattered sections of 15 U.S.C., 20 U.S.C., 29 U.S.C., 36 U.S.C., 41 U.S.C., and 42 U.S.C.).

Ritchie AJ and HV Zonana. 2003. Americans with Disabilities Act Evaluations. In *Principles and Practice of Forensic Psychiatry*, 2nd edition, edited by R Rosner, Boca Raton, FL: Taylor and Francis, 273–281.

Scott CE. 2010. The Americans with Disabilities Act Amendments Act of 2008: Implications for the forensic psychiatrist. *Journal of the American Academy of Psychiatry and the Law* 38:95–99.

Siber L. 2009. ADA Amendments Act of 2008: New hope for individuals with disabilities. *Rutgers Law Record* 33:65–73.

Smith DM. 2006. The paradox of personality: Mental illness, employment discrimination, and the Americans with Disabilities Act. *George Mason University Civil Rights Law Journal* 17:79–156.

Smith DM. 2007. Who says you're disabled? The role of medical evidence in the ADA definition of disability. *Tulane Law Review* 82:1–76.

Sutton v. United Air Lines, Inc., 527 U.S. 471 (1999).

Teitelbaum C and P Thomas. 2009. Post-traumatic stress disorder, employment discrimination, and direct threat claims. *Journal of the American Academy of Psychiatry and the Law* 37:109–111.

Thomas VL and LO Gostin. 2009. The Americans with Disabilities Act: Shattered aspirations and new hope. *JAMA* 301:95–97.

Timmons KC. 2005. Accommodating misconduct under the Americans with Disabilities Act. *Florida Law Review* 57:187–294.

Toyota Motor Manufacturing v. Williams, 534 U.S. 184 (2002).

U.S. Equal Employment Opportunity Commission (EEOC). 1991. Regulations to Implement the Equal Employment Provisions of the Americans with Disabilities Act. *Federal Register* 56:35726, codified at 29 C.F.R. § 1630.

U.S. Equal Employment Opportunity Commission (EEOC). 1997. *EEOC Enforcement Guidance: The Americans with Disabilities Act and Psychiatric Disabilities*. EEOC Notice No. 915.002.

U.S. Equal Employment Opportunity Commission (EEOC). 2008. *Americans with Disabilities Act: Questions and Answers*. February 2001, updated October 9, 2008. http://www.ada.gov/qandaeng.htm, accessed November 14, 2011.

U.S. Equal Employment Opportunity Commission (EEOC). 2011a. *Reasonable Accommodations for Attorneys with Disabilities*. Modified February 2, 2011. http://www.eeoc.gov/facts/accommodations-attorneys.html, accessed November 14, 2011.

U.S. Equal Employment Opportunity Commission (EEOC). 2011b. Regulations to Implement the Equal Employment Provisions of the Americans with Disabilities Act, As Amended. 29 C.F.R. Part 1630, RIN 3046-AA85. *Federal Register* 76(58):16978–17017.

Valderrama HK. 2010. Is the ADAAA a "quick fix" or are we out of the frying pan and into the fire?: How requiring parties to participate in the interactive process can effect congressional intent under the ADAAA. *Houston Law Review* 47:175–214.

35

Sexual harassment and gender discrimination

LIZA H. GOLD

INTRODUCTION

Sexual harassment and gender discrimination were non-issues prior to the end of the twentieth century. Media coverage of the Clarence Thomas Supreme Court confirmation hearings in 1991 and other highly publicized sexual harassment claims resulted in a sharp increase in workplace sexual harassment charges and lawsuits (Cunningham and Benavides-Espinoza 2008). Sex-based charges of discrimination filed with the Equal Employment Opportunity Commission (EEOC) and Fair Employment Practices Agencies (FEPA) increased by almost 40% between 1992 and 2012, and monetary awards have increased from $30.7 million to $138.7 million over the same time period. In addition, the percentage of men filing sexual harassment claims has steadily increased over time, from 9.1% in 1992 to 16.3% in 2011 (U.S. Equal Employment Opportunity Commission 2014).

DEFINING SEXUAL HARASSMENT AND GENDER DISCRIMINATION

Legal attempts to address gender disparities in pay and treatment in the workplace, including sexual harassment, began with the Equal Pay Act of 1963, which prohibited sex-based wage discrimination between men and women working for the same employer and performing jobs that require substantially equal skill, effort, and responsibility under similar working conditions. Title VII of the 1964 Civil Rights Act (CRA) prohibits discrimination on the basis of sex, race, color, religion, or national origin and established the EEOC to enforce its statutes.

Illegal sex-based discrimination, including sexual harassment, is not limited to behaviors motivated by sexual attraction or involving sexual activity. In addition, statutes, case law, and the legal system often use the words "sex" and "gender" synonymously, which has created confusion in understanding and identifying illegal behaviors. An individual's sex is a fact of biology; gender is a social construct associated with biological sex, but defined by cultural beliefs, values, and stereotypes. References to illegal "sex-based" discrimination encompass behaviors based on biological sex and on gender constructs associated with either biological sex.

A universally accepted definition of every behavior that might be considered sexual harassment does not exist. Illegal sexual harassment is a subset of all offensive types of gender-based or sexual behavior and a subset of illegal discrimination defined by administrative and case law. Illegal gender discrimination under Title VII of the 1964 CRA can encompass any type of disparate treatment in the workplace on the basis of biological sex: disparities in men's and women's pay for equal work, significant over-representation of men in leadership positions, pregnancy discrimination, and limited occupational choices for men or women. The scope of sexual harassment and gender discrimination behaviors also includes "gender policing," that is, targeting individual men or women for hostile, disparate, and adverse treatment because of failure to conform to gender stereotypes (Anderson 2006; Berdahl 2007).

The EEOC first defined sexual harassment in 1980 as "unwelcome sexual advances, requests for sexual favors, and other verbal or physical conduct of a sexual nature." The EEOC stated this conduct constitutes illegal sexual harassment when

1. Submission to such conduct is made either explicitly or implicitly a term or condition of an individual's employment.
2. Submission to or rejection of such conduct by an individual is used as the basis for employment decisions affecting such individual.
3. Such conduct has the purpose or effect of unreasonably interfering with an individual's work performance or creating an intimidating, hostile, or offensive working environment (EEOC 1980).

The essential component of sexual harassment is "unwelcome conduct" (i.e., conduct that lacks the elements of choice and mutuality) based on sex or gender. If overt or covert coercion is involved, it typically relies on the power of the perpetrator to affect a target's economic status. Sexual harassment may therefore include forms of gender discrimination that may not be motivated by sexual interest or attraction but that may nevertheless have personal and economic consequences.

The EEOC has defined two types of sexual harassment: *quid pro quo* and hostile environment. "*Quid pro quo*" harassment refers to situations in which work conditions or job benefits are explicitly or implicitly contingent upon or involve the exchange of sexual favors. "Hostile environment" sexual harassment refers to continuous, frequent, or repetitive patterns of offensive and unwelcome behavior that adversely affect the terms or conditions of employment. This category encompasses discrimination on the basis of gender alone, and can include behaviors such as sexually oriented joking or teasing, unwelcome display of sexual images or objects, unwelcome touching or propositions, or hostile treatment based solely on gender.

HISTORY OF SEXUAL HARASSMENT LAW

In *Williams v. Saxbe* (1976), the U.S. District Court for the District of Columbia first established that *quid pro quo* sexual harassment was a form of illegal sexual discrimination under Title VII. The U.S. Supreme Court first considered sexual harassment in *Meritor Savings Bank, FSB v. Vinson* (1986), and established that hostile environment sexual harassment was also a violation of Title VII. The Court stated that to prevail in a hostile environment claim, the behaviors must be so pervasive, repetitive, or severe that they alter the conditions of employment and create an abusive working environment. *Meritor* also established that voluntary participation on the part of the plaintiff did not legally establish that the defendant's actions were welcome.

In *Harris v. Forklift Systems* (1993), the Supreme Court unanimously held that a plaintiff is not required to have suffered psychological harm or prove that she was psychologically injured in order to win monetary damages. The Court stated that the presence of psychological harm is relevant to determining whether the plaintiff found the environment abusive, but is not necessary to establish illegal discrimination. The Court also stated that the frequency and severity of the conduct, whether it was physically threatening or humiliating, and whether it unreasonably interfered with an employee's work performance must be considered in examining sexual harassment claims.

In *Oncale v. Sundowner Offshore Services* (1998), the Supreme Court ruled that same-sex harassment could constitute an illegal form of sex discrimination under Title VII. The Court found that harassing conduct could be motivated by animus or hatred and did not need to be motivated by sexual desire in order to be discriminatory on the basis of sex. In *Burlington Industries, Inc. v. Ellerth* (1998) and *Faragher v. Boca Raton* (1998), the Supreme Court established that if no tangible employment action occurred, an employer might be able to avoid liability or limit damages by demonstrating that

1. The employer exercised reasonable care to prevent and promptly correct any sexually harassing behavior.
2. The plaintiff–employee unreasonably failed to take advantage of preventive or corrective opportunities provided by the employer.

Sex discrimination may also arise from employment actions or policies based on gender stereotypes. In *Price Waterhouse v. Hopkins* (1989), the Supreme Court held that gender stereotyping, in this case resulting in failure to promote a woman due to perceived nonconformity to a female stereotype, constituted a form of sex discrimination. Cases of same-sex harassment of men also have been successfully litigated on the basis of lack of conforming to traditional male stereotypes. In *EEOC v. Boh Brothers Construction Co., LLC* (2012), the Fifth Circuit Court of Appeals held that harassment based on lack of conformity to male gender stereotypes is a form of illegal discrimination.

FILING A SEXUAL HARASSMENT OR GENDER DISCRIMINATION CLAIM

The EEOC enforces federal statutes that prohibit discrimination and retaliation against individuals who have filed good faith complaints or participated in investigatory proceedings. Charges of retaliation, also illegal under Title VII, often form a related but separate basis of action in sexual harassment claims. Title VII requires that a plaintiff must exhaust EEOC administrative remedies for claims of discrimination and retaliation before being granted jurisdiction in federal district court.

After the EEOC investigates a claim, they may attempt to mediate or litigate the complaint. More commonly, the EEOC issues a "right to sue" letter, which allows a claimant to pursue private litigation. Legal action based on sexual harassment or gender discrimination may be brought in one or more legal or administrative contexts including Title VII (federal) complaints, state anti-discrimination laws, workers' compensation claims, and civil tort actions.

In practice, multiple causes of action are common in gender discrimination and sexual harassment cases. The facts of a case may support a variety of legal claims, alone or in conjunction with a Title VII action. The choice of complaint pursued usually involves consideration of issues relating to process, evidentiary requirements, and the recovery of damages. For example, many jurisdictions have laws prohibiting discrimination under Fair Employment Practices (FEP) statutes. Filing a claim under state law may be a more desirable option for someone who wants to expedite proceedings, because state law does not require exhausting EEOC remedies before litigating.

In addition, under federal law, compensatory and punitive damages for Title VII sexual harassment claims are capped at $300,000. Therefore, most Title VII claims are accompanied by additional claims, such as intentional infliction of emotional distress, or are brought in jurisdictions other than federal court where damages are not capped (Lindemann and Kadue 1992). Regardless of whether evidence of emotional injury is required in order to prevail, plaintiffs typically offer evidence of emotional harm in all types of actions, because the bulk of employer liability and damage awards in harassment and discrimination litigation is related to assertions of emotional distress and psychological injury (McDonald and Kulick 2001). Tort claims that may accompany harassment and discrimination claims include invasion of privacy, defamation, wrongful termination and wrongful discharge, intentional or (more rarely) negligent infliction of emotional distress, civil assault and battery, negligent retention or supervision, and loss of consortium.

PSYCHIATRIC ISSUES IN SEXUAL HARASSMENT CLAIMS

Psychiatrists retained in sexual harassment and gender discrimination cases may be asked to address causation of emotional injury, psychological symptoms and/or diagnoses, related functional impairment, and issues relating to treatment, treatment costs, and prognosis. These evaluations require the identification of psychiatric disorders, present and past level of functioning, and likelihood of recovery. Questions regarding prognosis, with and without treatment, require assessment of the plaintiff's motivation for recovery. Psychiatric factors that may affect claims of causation and damages should also be considered, such as possible alternate causation of claimed emotional distress and pre-existing mental health disorders or problems. Nonpsychiatric factors, such as adverse employment actions and workplace conflict, should also be examined.

A review of all relevant documents and a thorough psychiatric evaluation can provide information relevant to many of the psychiatric and legal issues raised in sexual harassment cases. Forensic experts should be familiar with the social science and psychological research that provides the scientific basis for opinions in sexual harassment and gender discrimination cases. The psychiatric outcome of such workplace experiences depends on multiple factors and circumstances.

A psychiatric evaluation of sexual harassment and gender discrimination claims requires an examination of many factors (Table 35.1). The issues of functional impairment, prognosis, and potential recovery are integral to damage assessments. Current level of impairment is assessed through evaluation of the claimant's history, behavior, and examination findings. The claimant's pre- and post-incident(s) functional capacities must be compared. Prognostic opinions should be based on an assessment of functioning, the effects of pre-existing and current psychiatric status, the natural history of the specific disorder, and the actual or potential effects of treatment.

Table 35.1 Relevant factors for consideration in sexual harassment and gender discrimination claims

Characteristics of the harassment (frequency, duration, magnitude)
Plaintiff's emotional, psychological, and workplace responses to the harassment
If the plaintiff complained, the employer's responses to the complaints and/or harassment
Availability of support for the plaintiff inside and outside the workplace
Plaintiff's resources, strengths, vulnerabilities, and past history
Effects of litigation, widely acknowledged to be stressful (Lenhart 1996; Strasburger 1999)
Emotional effects of retaliation, which may be clinically distinct from the effects of the claimed harassment
Effects of underlying medical conditions or medication that may cause psychological symptoms
Previous or concurrent trauma, sources of stress or distress
Use or abuse of drugs and alcohol
Effects of adverse employment actions or workplace conflict

Comparison of the plaintiff's personality, behavior, and functioning before and after the alleged harassment and discrimination is crucial in the determination of motivation for recovery and willingness to enter treatment (Gold 2004). Motivation to obtain treatment can be particularly problematic in the context of litigation. Plaintiffs are legally obligated to minimize their damages. Nevertheless, plaintiffs often become obsessively focused on legal issues rather than accessing treatment for psychiatric symptoms. In addition, even when plaintiffs obtain treatment, being a party in litigation often prevents resolution of psychiatric symptoms. Symptoms may become fixed and/or exacerbated when litigation becomes acutely stressful, for example, before a deposition or trial.

ASSESSING CLAIMS OF PSYCHIATRIC OR PSYCHOLOGICAL INJURY IN SEXUAL HARASSMENT AND GENDER DISCRIMINATION LITIGATION

Psychiatric evaluations in sexual harassment and gender discrimination cases are informed by research on the psychological effects of sexual harassment experiences, stress and trauma responses, and the legal issues unique to this litigation.

Sexual harassment and gender discrimination research

Social science research has confirmed that sexual harassment and gender discrimination are widespread phenomena, and has expanded understanding of their causes and outcomes (Fitzgerald et al. 1995; U.S. Merit Systems Protection Board 1995; Dansky and Kilpatrick 1997; Fitzgerald et al. 1997a,b; Fitzgerald et al. 1999a; Gutek and Koss 1996; Kabat-Farr and Cortina 2014). The majority of people reporting sexual harassment experiences are women, and the majority of alleged harassers are men. Women who work in historically male-dominated occupations report higher incidences of sexual harassment (Berdahl 2007).

Broadly speaking, sexual harassment and related forms of gender discrimination fall into three categories, described by three related but conceptually distinct dimensions of behavior (Fitzgerald et al. 1997a):

1. *Gender harassment*: A broad range of verbal behavior, physical acts, and symbolic gestures not aimed at sexual cooperation but which convey insulting, hostile, and degrading attitudes about women. Examples include sexual epithets, slurs, taunts, and gestures, the display or distribution of obscene or pornographic materials, gender-based hazing, and threatening, intimidating or hostile acts.
2. *Unwanted sexual attention*: Both verbal and non-verbal behavior that is unwelcome, offensive, and unreciprocated.
3. *Sexual coercion*: Extortion of sexual cooperation in return for job-related considerations.

Men and women experience different types of behavior as sexual harassment. Same-sex harassment of men by men, regardless of sexual orientation of either party, is typically based on deviation from gender stereotypes (Berdahl et al. 1996; Waldo et al. 1998; Magley et al. 1999; Kabat-Farr and Cortina 2014). Sexual harassment of women usually consists of a cumulative series of escalating and varied experiences causing the target to experience a chronic level of stress and affective arousal, most akin to a particularly noxious form of occupational stress (Fitzgerald et al. 1997b). The less severe forms of sexual harassment behaviors, such as offensive comments or jokes are the most prevalent; the most severe behaviors, such as physical or sexual assault, are the least frequent (U.S. Merit Systems Protection Board 1995; Schneider et al. 1997; Fitzgerald et al. 1999b; Leskinen et al. 2011).

The most common responses to sexual harassment are to ignore or avoid it; the least common response is to formally report it. Although studies consistently find individuals who report experiencing sexual harassment in the workplace, only 5%–30% file formal complaints and less than 1% subsequently participate in litigation (Fitzgerald et al. 1995; Schneider et al. 1997; Wayte et al. 2002; O'Connor 2007).

These social science data are often relevant in sexual harassment litigation. For example, "unwelcome conduct" is an essential element in the legal definition of sexual harassment. Defense attorneys typically interpret failure to immediately report harassment as evidence that the conduct was "not unwelcome," despite the plaintiff's later complaints. In addition, failure to report harassment, as noted above, can provide employers with an affirmative defense, a legal reality at odds with research that indicates failure to report is much more likely than formal reporting, and which may require expert testimony to explain to the finder of fact.

Exposure to sexual harassment can have significant work-related, psychological and physiological effects (Gold 2004; Foote and Goodman-Delahunty 2005; Bowling and Beehr 2006; O'Connor 2007; Street et al. 2007; Dionisi et al. 2012), even harassment that consists primarily of exposure to sexual behavior in the workplace (Berdahl and Aquino 2009). A meta-analysis of 49 studies (Chan et al. 2008) concluded that sexual harassment experiences are adversely related to a multitude of job-related, psychological, and physical outcomes.

The severity of the harassment, as indicated by objective factors such as its frequency and intensity, are primary predictors of psychological outcomes (Charney and Russell 1994; Lenhart 1996; Dansky and Kilpatrick 1997; Schneider et al. 1997; Fitzgerald et al. 1997a; Collinsworth et al. 2009; Rospenda et al. 2009; McGinley et al. 2011). Although even mild harassment can provoke significant emotional distress, women who experienced more severe sexual harassment have been found to have more severe psychological distress, including anxiety and depression. In addition, women who filed a formal complaint or sought legal services were also more likely to experience negative psychological outcomes, negative work-related outcomes, and more somatic symptoms than those who did not (Fitzgerald et al. 1995; Dansky and Kilpatrick 1997; Bergman et al. 2002).

Psychiatric and physiological symptoms caused by sexual harassment may rise to a level of prolonged or intense distress and/or functional impairment that meets criteria for a psychiatric diagnosis. Sexual harassment experiences do not necessarily result in the development of any specific psychiatric disorder. However, psychiatric diagnoses most commonly reported in association with sexual harassment experiences include adjustment disorders, depressive mood disorders, and anxiety disorders (Lenhart 1996; Dansky and Kilpatrick 1997; Gold 2004; Foote and Goodman-Delahunty 2005).

Sexual harassment and posttraumatic stress disorder

Posttraumatic stress disorder (PTSD) is a commonly claimed diagnosis in sexual harassment cases. PTSD is a preferred plaintiff's diagnosis in civil litigation (Gold 2003; Gold 2004), including sexual harassment cases (Long 1994; Gold 2004), because it implies single and external causation and focuses attention on the alleged event(s) rather than the plaintiff. The question of whether sexual harassment can be a form of trauma that may cause PTSD is a matter of continuing debate (Dansky and Kilpatrick 1997; Palmieri and Fitzgerald 2005; Stockdale et al. 2009).

The most common sexual harassment behaviors, such as verbal comments, are relatively minor and rarely traumatic. On the other end of the spectrum, the more uncommon and severe forms of sexual harassment, such as sexual assault, may clearly meet the *Diagnostic and Statistical Manual of Mental Disorders* (American Psychiatric Association 2013) criteria for a traumatic stressor. Questions arise when a plaintiff claims a diagnosis of PTSD directly caused by sexual harassment experiences that fall between these two extremes (Avina and O'Donohue 2002). Although some argue that moderate sexual harassment exposure is also more likely to result in PTSD (Holcomb and Holcomb 2008), a PTSD diagnosis or symptoms are most likely to be associated with more severe and/or more frequent sexual harassment (Dansky and Kilpatrick 1997; Gutek and Done 2001; Street et al. 2007; Stockdale et al. 2009).

Mental health professionals frequently and mistakenly diagnose any stress-related response or symptom as PTSD, particularly in the context of litigation (Rosen 1995). In fact, most people exposed to trauma do not develop PTSD (Kessler et al. 1995; Breslau et al. 1998; Breslau 2009). Exposure to the more common and less severe behaviors associated with sexual harassment can be distressing and stressful but is unlikely to result in the development of PTSD without a pre-existing vulnerability. This is consistent with research findings that indicate vulnerability factors play a significant role in individuals who develop PTSD (Breslau 2009; Raabe and Spengler 2013). An individual who claims or demonstrates symptoms consistent with PTSD as a result of exposure to less severe forms of sexual harassment should be carefully assessed for the possibility of malingering, individual susceptibility to psychiatric morbidity, pre-existing psychiatric disorders, or concurrent or prior traumatic exposure (Gold 2004).

Sexual harassment and personality disorders

Just as PTSD is a preferred plaintiff's diagnosis in sexual harassment litigation, Cluster C Personality Disorders, particularly borderline personality disorder (BPD), is a preferred defense diagnosis (Long 1994). The diagnosis of BPD in a plaintiff provides the defense opportunities to support legal arguments unique to sexual harassment litigation. One common defense strategy is to argue that PTSD claimed as damages in a sexual harassment case is likely to have been caused by a history of previous sexual abuse or victimization. These legal arguments take advantage of research that has found consistent and statistically significant associations between a history of childhood sexual abuse and diagnoses of BPD and PTSD (Ogata et al. 1990; Zanarini 1997; Zanarini 2000; Horwitz et al. 2001; Golier et al. 2003; Bandelow et al. 2005).

Features of BPD, such as dysfunctional coping, emotional reactivity, dysfunctional patterns of interpersonal behaviors, and perceptual distortions of self and others, are relevant to legal elements of a sexual harassment claim. By definition, sexual harassment must be "unwelcome" to be illegal. The legal standard applied to the question of whether behavior rises to an actionable level includes whether a "reasonable person" would have found the behavior offensive or distressing. Employers are not necessarily liable if plaintiffs demonstrate "hypersensitivity" to the comments or behaviors of others.

Defense attorneys may argue that prior sexual abuse, implied even if not proven by a diagnosis of BPD, renders abused individuals "hypersensitive"—that is, more likely to inappropriately interpret and label innocuous workplace behavior as sexual harassment. Defense attorneys may use a BPD diagnosis to claim that the plaintiff's perception of the alleged harassment is not credible due to cognitive distortion caused by BPD. Features of BPD may be invoked to argue that the plaintiff was an active participant in the events that she is now disavowing (playing on the gender stereotype of "a woman scorned"), thus undermining claims that the alleged harassment was unwelcome.

Psychiatric evaluation in sexual harassment cases should include consideration of behavioral patterns or cognitive processes that might affect interpersonal relationships or cause perceptual distortion. Determination of an individual's tendency to invite, misinterpret, distort, or overreact to the behaviors of others is a critical part of a sexual harassment assessment, whether due to BPD or any other psychological process, such as an underlying psychosis or paranoid thought disorder.

However, defense examiners often inappropriately assign a diagnosis of a personality disorder based on a plaintiff's current presentation. Women who have experienced sexual harassment, made a formal complaint, perhaps experienced retaliation, and experienced the stress of litigation can appear histrionic, angry, defensive, or reactive on evaluation, even in the absence of pre-existing psychiatric disorders (Lenhart 1996). This presentation may be exacerbated by the stress of undergoing a psychiatric evaluation, particularly by clinicians retained by the defendants, leading forensic examiners to assign a diagnosis of BPD in the absence of evidence that such a diagnosis was present prior to their examinations.

These psychiatrists may cite a narrow and outdated body of forensic literature, unsupported by research, asserting that individuals who have suffered childhood sexual abuse are both more likely to report sexual harassment and to claim the harassment has caused PTSD when compared to those without abuse histories (Feldman-Schorrig 1994; McDonald and Lees-Haley 1995; Feldman-Schorrig 1996). Moreover, methodologically sound research studies have shed considerable doubt on the assumption that claims of PTSD should be dismissed if evidence of prior trauma or prior psychological dysfunction is produced (Fitzgerald et al. 1999a; Stockdale et al. 2002; Stockdale et al. 2009).

Forensic evaluators should be cautious about making a personality disorder diagnosis based solely on the events in the case but in the absence of an adequate supporting longitudinal history. A diagnosis of a personality disorder should be based on lifelong, pervasive, and inflexible patterns of dysfunction and maladaptive coping. Individuals with personality disorders typically have histories of chaotic lives and problematic interpersonal relationships across all spheres of functioning. Evidence of such patterns and dysfunction requires review of previous employment history and records, prior and current interpersonal functioning in other areas of life, and even prior litigation history. Psychological testing can also provide valuable data in making this diagnostic determination.

SUGGESTED PRACTICES IN SEXUAL HARASSMENT AND GENDER DISCRIMINATION EVALUATIONS

1. *Maintain neutrality.* Psychiatric evaluators should avoid making assumptions about the facts of a case that can prejudice their opinions. The use of psychological testing with multiple validated measures as well as structured diagnostic interviews may help provide objective data to support opinions in sexual harassment evaluations (Lawson et al. 2013), but testing may not be indicated in all cases.
2. *Avoid the dual role of treating clinician and expert witness.* Sexual harassment cases present difficulties in occupying both roles beyond those usually associated with "wearing two hats" (Strasburger et al. 1997). Trying to occupy both roles can harm both the therapeutic relationship and the patient's litigation.
3. *Review all available documents.* This includes medical, legal, psychiatric, pharmacy, EEOC, investigative, and employment records. In cases where civil charges are filed in conjunction with or after the filing of criminal charges such as assault, battery, or rape, police records may be available.
4. *Conduct a complete assessment.* Clinicians should conduct a clinical interview of appropriate length, record review, and when possible, collateral interviews with third parties. In some cases, clinicians may need to conduct a site visit. Clinicians should also be aware that the evaluee's mental health history may not have begun with the alleged harassment. Obtain as extensive a history as possible, including review of past and current sources of trauma, and review of the claimant's litigation history, employment history, and history of interpersonal relationships.
5. *Decline to provide opinions outside areas of expertise or that are the purview of the court.* Attorneys will frequently exert pressure on experts to provide opinions beyond the boundaries of training and experience, and sometimes past the boundaries of the field of psychiatry. Psychiatrists should avoid providing opinions in areas in which they lack expertise, in which a scientific basis for opinions is lacking, or which are essentially legal arguments, not psychiatric conditions, such as "welcomeness," "reasonableness," and "credibility."
6. *Assess each case on its own merits.* Relevant research findings can be used to support opinions, but research findings cannot provide data about individual cases. Forensic clinicians should base their opinions on the case's specific facts and data, and should be prepared to defend those opinions on that same basis. Besides representing competent practice, familiarity with the specific facts of the case will help overcome legal arguments that an expert's testimony is not legally relevant (Gold 2004).

SUMMARY

A general definition of sexual harassment and gender discrimination does not exist. The complex nature of human relationships and behavior defies the development of social or legal formulas defining when conduct is offensive, and when offensive conduct is illegal. Fortunately, forensic psychiatrists are not tasked with providing universal definitions or legal determinations in sexual harassment and gender discrimination cases.

Nevertheless, forensic psychiatrists can offer expert opinions and testimony regarding the aspects of sexual harassment and gender discrimination that fall within psychiatric training and expertise. Credible opinions, based on professional expertise, guided by forensic and clinical psychiatric ethics and methodology, and informed by relevant social science are of value to all parties in sexual harassment cases. Forensic psychiatric expert testimony based on these fundamental practices and on relevant research can assist the court in clarifying the complex issues that arise in sexual harassment and gender discrimination litigation.

SUMMARY KEY POINTS

- Illegal sexual harassment in the workplace is a subset of gender-based workplace discrimination, defined by federal, state, and case law.
- The EEOC has defined two types of sexual harassment: *quid pro quo* and hostile work environment.
- Psychiatric evaluations in sexual harassment or gender discrimination should include characteristics of the harassment, premorbid functioning of the plaintiff, prior work history, the effects of retaliation, the effects of litigation, as well as other factors.
- Sexual harassment is adversely related to job-related, psychological, and physical outcomes, but the severity of the harassment is usually the

primary predictor of psychological outcome. More severe outcomes to less severe harassing behaviors raise issues of pre-existing psychological vulnerability.

- Personality disorder diagnoses should not be made in the absence of a longitudinal history consistent with these disorders.
- Psychiatric evaluators in sexual harassment litigation should maintain neutrality, avoid dual agency, review all documents, and conduct a complete assessment.

REFERENCES

American Psychiatric Association (APA). 2013. *Diagnostic and Statistical Manual of Mental Disorders*, 5th edition. Washington, DC: APA.

Anderson E. 2006. Recent thinking about sexual harassment: A review essay. *Philosophy and Public Affairs* 34:284–312.

Avina C and W O'Donohue. 2002. Sexual harassment and PTSD: Is sexual harassment diagnosable trauma? *Journal of Traumatic Stress* 15:69–75.

Bandelow B, J Krause, D Wedekind, A Broocks, G Hajak, and E Ruther. 2005. Early traumatic life events, parental attitudes, family history, and birth risk factors in patients with borderline personality disorder and healthy controls. *Psychiatry Research* 134:169–179.

Berdahl JL. 2007. The sexual harassment of uppity women. *Journal of Applied Psychology* 92:425–437.

Berdahl JL and K Aquino. 2009. Sexual behavior at work: Fun or folly? *Journal of Applied Psychology* 94:34–47.

Berdahl JL, VJ Magley, and CR Waldo. 1996. The sexual harassment of men? *Psychology of Women Quarterly* 20:527–547.

Bergman ME, RD Langhout, PA Palmieri, LM Cortina, and LF Fitzgerald. 2002. The (un)reasonableness of reporting: Antecedents and consequences of reporting sexual harassment. *Journal of Applied Psychology* 87:230–242.

Bowling NA and TA Beehr. 2006. Workplace harassment from the victim's perspective: A theoretical model and meta-analysis. *Journal of Applied Psychology* 91:998–1012.

Breslau N. 2009. The epidemiology of trauma, PTSD, and other posttrauma disorders. *Trauma, Violence, and Abuse* 10:198–210.

Breslau N, RC Kessler, HD Chilcoat, LR Schultz, GC Davis, and P Andreski. 1998. Trauma and posttraumatic stress disorder in the community: The 1996 Detroit Area survey of trauma. *Archives of General Psychiatry* 55:626–632.

Burlington Indus. Inc. v. Ellerth, 524 U.S. 742 (1998).

Chan DK-S, CB Lam, SY Chow, and SF Cheung. 2008. Examining the job-related, psychological, and physical outcomes of workplace sexual harassment: A meta-analytic review. *Psychology of Women Quarterly* 32:362–376.

Charney DA and RC Russell. 1994. An overview of sexual harassment. *American Journal of Psychiatry* 151:10–17.

Collinsworth LL, LF Fitzgerald, and F Drasgow. 2009. In harm's way: Factors related to psychological distress following sexual harassment. *Psychology of Women Quarterly* 33:475–490.

Cunningham GB and C Benavides-Espinoza. 2008. A trend analysis of sexual harassment claims: 1992–2006. *Psychological Reports* 103:779–782.

Dansky BS and DG Kilpatrick. 1997. Effects of sexual harassment. In *Sexual Harassment: Theory, Research and Treatment*, edited by W O'Donohue, Boston: Allyn and Bacon, 152–174.

Dionisi AM, J Barling, and KE Dupre. 2012. Revisiting the comparative outcomes of workplace aggression and sexual harassment. *Journal of Occupational Health Psychology* 17:398–408.

Equal Employment Opportunity Commission. Guidelines on Discrimination because of Sex. 1980:29 C.F.R. §1604.11(a).

EEOC v. Boh Brothers Construction Co., LLC, No. 11-30770 (5th Cir. 2013).

Faragher v. City of Boca Raton, 524 U.S. 775 (1998).

Feldman-Schorrig SP. 1994. Special issues in sexual harassment cases. In *Mental and Emotional Injuries in Employment Litigation*, edited by JJ McDonald and FB Kulick, Washington DC: Bureau of National Affairs, 332–390.

Feldman-Schorrig S 1996. Factitious sexual harassment. *Bulletin of the American Academy of Psychiatry and the Law* 24:387–392.

Fitzgerald LF, NT Buchanan, LL Collinsworth, VJ Magley, and AM Ramos. 1999a. Junk logic: The abuse defense in sexual harassment litigation. *Psychology, Public Policy, and Law* 5:730–759.

Fitzgerald LF, F Drasgow, CL Hulin, MJ Gelfand, and VJ Magley. 1997a. Antecedents and consequences of sexual harassment in organizations: A test of an integrated model. *Journal of Applied Psychology* 82:578–589.

Fitzgerald LF, F Drasgow, and VJ Magley. 1999b. Sexual harassment in the armed forces: A test of an integrated model. *Military Psychology* 11:329–343.

Fitzgerald LF, S Swan, and K Fischer. 1995. Why didn't she just report him? The psychological and legal implications of women's responses to sexual harassment. *Journal of Social Issues* 51:117–138.

Fitzgerald LF, S Swan, and VJ Magley. 1997b. But was it really sexual harassment?: Legal, behavioral, and psychological definitions of the workplace victimization of women. In *Sexual Harassment: Theory, Research, and Treatment*, edited by W O'Donohue, Needham Heights, MA: Allyn and Bacon, 5–28.

Foote WE and J Goodman-Delahunty. 2005. *Evaluating Sexual Harassment: Psychological, Social, and Legal Considerations in Forensic Examinations*. Washington, DC: American Psychological Association.

Gold L. 2003. Posttraumatic stress disorder in employment litigation. In *Posttraumatic Stress Disorder in Litigation: Guidelines for Forensic Assessment*, 2nd edition, edited by RI Simon, Washington DC: American Psychiatric Press, 163–186.

Gold LH. 2004. *Sexual Harassment: Psychiatric Assessment in Employment Litigation.* Washington, DC: American Psychiatric Publishing.

Golier JA, R Yehuda, LM Bierer, V Mitropoulou, AS New, J Schmeidler, JM Silverman, and LJ Siever. 2003. The relationship of borderline personality disorder to posttraumatic stress disorder and traumatic events. *American Journal of Psychiatry* 160:2018–2024.

Gutek BA and RS Done. 2001. Sexual harassment. In *Handbook of the Psychology of Women and Gender*, edited by RK Unger, Hoboken, NJ: Wiley, 367–387.

Gutek BA and MP Koss. 1996. How women deal with sexual harassment and organizational responses to reporting. In *Sexual Harassment in the Workplace: Psychiatric Issues*, edited by D Shrier, Washington DC: American Psychiatric Press, 39–57.

Harris v. Forklift Sys., Inc., 510 U.S. 17 (1993).

Holcomb WR and MG Holcomb. 2008. A victim typology of sexual harassment. *Psychological Reports* 103:819–826.

Horwitz AV, CS Widom, J McLaughlin, and HR White. 2001. The impact of childhood abuse and neglect on adult mental health: A prospective study. *Journal of Health and Social Behavior* 42:184–201.

Kabat-Farr D and LM Cortina. 2014. Sex-based harassment in employment: New insights into gender and context. *Law and Human Behavior* 38:58–72.

Kessler RC, A Sonnega, E Bromet, M Hughes, and CB Nelson. 1995. Posttraumatic stress disorder in the national comorbidity survey. *Archives of General Psychiatry* 52:1048–1060.

Lawson AK, CV Wright, and LF Fitzgerald. 2013. The evaluation of sexual harassment litigants: Reducing discrepancies in the diagnosis of posttraumatic stress disorder. *Law and Human Behavior* 37:337–347.

Lenhart S. 1996. Physical and mental health aspects of sexual harassment. In *Sexual Harassment in the Workplace and Academia: Psychiatric Issues*, edited by DK Shrier, Washington DC: American Psychiatric Press, 21–38.

Leskinen EA, LM Cortina, and DB Kabat. 2011. Gender harassment: Broadening our understanding of sex-based harassment at work. *Law and Human Behavior* 35:25–39.

Lindemann B and D Kadue. 1992. *Sexual Harassment in Employment Law.* Washington, DC: Bureau of National Affairs.

Long BL. 1994. Psychiatric diagnoses in sexual harassment cases. *Bulletin of the American Academy of Psychiatry and the Law* 22:195–203.

Magley VJ, CR Waldo, F Drasgow, and LF Fitzgerald. 1999. The impact of sexual harassment on military personnel: Is it the same for men and women? *Military Psychology* 11:283–302.

McDonald J and F Kulick. 2001. The rise of the psychological injury claim. In *Mental and Emotional Injuries in Employment Litigation*, 2nd edition, edited by JJ McDonald and FP Kulick, Washington DC: Bureau of National Affairs, xxxvi–xiv.

McDonald JJ and P Lees-Haley. 1995. Personality disorders in the workplace: How they contribute to claims of employment law violations. *Employee Relations Law Journal* 22:57–81.

McGinley M, JA Richman, and KM Rospenda. 2011. Duration of sexual harassment and generalized harassment in the workplace over ten years: Effects on deleterious drinking outcomes. *Journal of Addictive Diseases* 30:229–242.

Meritor Savings Bank, FSB v. Vinson, 477 U.S. 57 (1986).

O'Connor M. 2007. Expert testimony in sexual harassment cases: Its scope, limits and effectiveness. In *Expert Psychological Testimony for the Courts*, edited by M Costanzo, D Krauss, and K Pezdek, Mahwah NJ: Lawrence Erlbaum Associates, 119–148.

Ogata SN, KR Silk, S Goodrich, NE Lohr, D Westen, and EM Hill. 1990. Childhood sexual and physical abuse in adult patients with borderline personality disorder. *American Journal of Psychiatry* 147:1008–1013.

Oncale v. Sundowner Offshore Servs, Inc., 118 S. Ct. 998 (1998).

Palmieri PA and LF Fitzgerald. 2005. Confirmatory factor analysis of posttraumatic stress symptoms in sexually harassed women. *Journal of Traumatic Stress* 18:657–666.

Price Waterhouse v. Hopkins, 490 U.S. 228 (1989).

Raabe FJ and D Spengler. 2013. Epigenetic risk factors in PTSD and depression. *Frontiers in Psychiatry* 4:Art 80, 1–17.

Rosen GM. 1995. The Aleutian enterprise sinking and posttraumatic stress disorder: Misdiagnosis in clinical and forensic settings. *Professional Psychology: Research and Practice* 26:82–87.

Rospenda KM, JA Richman, and CA Shannon. 2009. Prevalence and mental health correlates of harassment and discrimination in the workplace: Results from a national study. *Journal of Interpersonal Violence* 24:819–843.

Schneider KT, S Swan, and LF Fitzgerald. 1997. Job-related and psychological effects of sexual harassment in the workplace: Empirical evidence from two organizations. *Journal of Applied Psychology* 82:401–415.

Stockdale MS, TK Logan, and R Weston. 2009. Sexual harassment and posttraumatic stress disorder: Damages beyond prior abuse. *Law and Human Behavior* 33:405–418.

Stockdale MS, M O'Connor, BA Gutek, and T Geer. 2002. The relationship between prior sexual abuse and reactions to sexual harassment: Literature review and empirical study. *Psychology, Public Policy, and Law* 8:64–95.

Strasburger LH. 1999. The litigant-patient: Mental health consequences of civil litigation. *Journal of the American Academy of Psychiatry and the Law* 27:203–211.

Strasburger LH, TG Gutheil, and A Brodsky. 1997. On wearing two hats: Role conflict in serving as both psychotherapist and expert witness. *American Journal of Psychiatry* 154:448–456.

Street AE, JL Gradus, J Stafford, and K Kelly. 2007. Gender differences in experiences of sexual harassment: Data from a male-dominated environment. *Journal of Consulting and Clinical Psychology* 75:464–474.

U.S. Equal Employment Opportunity Commission. 2014. *Enforcement and Litigation Statistics*. http://eeoc.gov/eeoc/statistics/enforcement/index.cfm, accessed August 1, 2014.

U.S. Merit Systems Protection Board. 1995. *Sexual Harassment in the Federal Workplace: Trends, Progress, Continuing Challenges*. Washington, DC: U.S. Government Printing Office.

Waldo CR, JL Berdahl, and LF Fitzgerald. 1998. Are men sexually harassed? If so, by whom? *Law and Human Behavior* 22:59–79.

Wayte T, J Samra, JK Robbennolt, L Heuer, and WJ Koch. 2002. Psychological issues in civil law. In *Taking Psychology and Law into the Twenty-First Century*, edited by JRP Ogloff, New York: Kluwer Academic/Plenum, 323–369.

Williams v. Saxbe, 413 F. Supp. 654 (D.D.C. 1976).

Zanarini MC. ed. 1997. *Role of Sexual Abuse in the Etiology of Borderline Personality Disorder.* Washington, DC: American Psychiatric Press.

Zanarini MC. 2000. Childhood experiences associated with the development of borderline personality disorder. *Psychiatric Clinics of North America* 23:89–102.

36

Civil competencies

J. RICHARD CICCONE AND JOSHUA C.W. JONES

INTRODUCTION

Western civil tradition assumes that adults have the capacity to make their own decisions. In specific instances courts are asked to intercede and abridge these rights. The courts are entrusted to protect a person from his or her own inability to make rational decisions, or to protect others from the same. Forensic psychiatrists, in turn, are often asked to provide an evaluation and opinion on whether and how mental illness impacts a person's ability to make decisions.

Because the right to make one's own decisions is held as fundamental, significant allowance is made for error, mistakes, and poor judgment. A person need not make excellent decisions to be considered competent; the threshold is usually quite low, just high enough to be considered rational. However, this threshold is a sliding scale with the definition of *rational* viewed in context of the decision's circumstance and potential for harm. Ultimately, a court makes the final decision as to whether a person is competent. The law is purposefully written in broad strokes that provide guidance, but not prescription, to the judicial fact-finder because laws cannot be written specifically enough to cover all situations.

DEFINITION AND COMPONENTS OF CIVIL COMPETENCY

In clinical settings, the evaluation of a person's ability to make decisions is called a "capacity evaluation." Forensic psychiatrists may provide an opinion on competency (i.e., capacity), but only the court can make a competency determination. Therefore, the forensic psychiatrist should be familiar with the legal standard for the competence being evaluated in the jurisdiction where the issue is to be adjudicated.

The essential abilities necessary to make a reasoned decision are surprisingly universal and applicable to many situations. In order to have the capacity to make a decision, a person must be able to understand the nature and consequences of the decisions to be made, rationally manipulate information that might influence that decision, and be able to communicate a choice. This basic decision-making analysis can be applied repeatedly, with differing specific parameters based on the competency being examined. Competence is decision specific; an individual may be competent in one area but not competent in another. Therefore, although the general steps necessary for the determination of competence provide a useful template, the specific questions to be answered are contextual. In this chapter we provide a general guide for conducting a forensic evaluation of civil competence and several examples that are illustrative of general and specific principles.

CONDUCTING THE CIVIL COMPETENCY EVALUATION

Before undertaking the evaluation, the forensic psychiatrist should first understand the context of the referral and clarify the question being asked. Frequently, the referral source (courts, attorneys, insurance companies, other physicians, etc.) may not have completely formulated a cogent question, and the forensic psychiatrist may help them frame the inquiry so that there can be an answer and a useful outcome. The evaluating psychiatrist should know who is seeking the evaluation, for what purpose, and how the findings will be used.

The role of the forensic psychiatrist is to determine whether the person in question suffers from a mental disorder. If there is no mental illness, the forensic psychiatrist's job may be finished after telling the court of this finding. If the individual does have a mental disorder, the task next becomes to determine whether or not the presence of the disorder impacts the individual's competency in question, and if so, to what extent. The presence of a mental disorder does not necessarily render a person incompetent. This concept is frequently foreign to referral sources, and the forensic psychiatrist will need to address this distinction in his or her report.

Generally, the forensic psychiatric evaluation is composed of three complementary components: (1) the psychiatric examination, (2) record review, and, when indicated,

(3) psychological testing. The psychiatric examination is the clinical diagnostic interview and observations as distinguished from the forensic psychiatric evaluation, which includes the integration of record review and testing. When a forensic psychiatrist is asked to render an opinion without one or more of these components, he or she should explain in the report how these conditions affect the outcome.

EXAMINATION

When performing a forensic psychiatric evaluation, the psychiatrist should endeavor to conduct a personal psychiatric examination whenever possible, although in some instances (e.g., contested wills, psychological autopsy, unwilling subject) it may not be possible. Informed consent should be obtained, including an explanation of the examiner's role and by which party he has been retained, how the examination will be used, and who may have access to the information gathered. The individual should be informed that the usual doctor–patient relationship is not created by the examination. The examinee retains the right to refuse to participate in the evaluation, and that refusal may be disclosed to the referring party.

The forensic psychiatrist may decide to record the examination (American Academy of Psychiatry and the Law 1999), and we support recording when feasible. The psychiatrist should inform the retaining party of the intent to record, allowing the party to make appropriate disclosures. Audio and/or video recording can be reviewed by others, can help refresh the memory of the examining psychiatrist, and can be helpful during trial. If consent for the examination is obtained prior to recording, we recommend that the evaluee re-consent during the recording.

The amount of time spent in evaluation is not the most important variable in the examination; sometimes the answer is obvious after a few minutes and sometimes the answer is obtuse, requiring multiple examinations. Time spent in the examination needs to be judiciously tailored to account for not only the intricacies of the examinee's clinical presentation but also the complexity of the competency question at hand. Accounting for outlying amounts of evaluation time in the forensic report will enhance the credibility of the final opinion.

Malingering is a universal concern in forensic psychiatry. In the criminal setting, the malingering subject is more likely to feign signs or symptoms of mental illness in order to escape or postpone consequences of his or her criminal charges. In the civil setting the impaired individual may attempt to disguise or minimize symptoms in order to retain rights that he or she fear may be limited. This should be investigated in the examination and addressed in the report.

RECORD REVIEW

Reviewing all pertinent, available records is an essential part of the forensic psychiatric evaluation. This allows the psychiatrist to corroborate or question the examinee's narrative and can give a more complete overview of the examinee's case. The psychiatrist should ask, usually in writing, for the referring party to send any and all relevant records relating to the case, and should specify any essential documents to avoid confusion. Acquisition and review of psychiatric and nonpsychiatric medical records is of utmost importance in establishing diagnoses. Legal documents pertaining to the matter at hand (e.g., wills, contracts) are also essential to review. Documents that can help a psychiatrist reconstruct the thought processes of the examinee, such as letters, journals, or social media posts, can give a contemporaneous window into an examinee's thought processes.

We recommend striving to review available records prior to the psychiatric examination to afford the psychiatrist the opportunity to ask the examinee to comment on inconsistencies, oddities, or other relevant points of interest found in the records. This can also help the psychiatrist structure the examination in more efficient and meaningful ways. If the complete record is not available before the examination, the forensic psychiatrist can inform the retaining party that additional examination time may be needed if the record review reveals previously unknown points of interest. While reviewing records, note taking is helpful in organizing voluminous amounts of information. Because such notes are discoverable and can be a source for cross-examination, they should be professional, factual, and without editorial commentary. This caveat holds true for notes taken during the psychiatric examination as well.

TESTING

The use of forensic assessment instruments may be a valuable adjunct to the forensic psychiatric examination and record review (Grisso 2003). Many instruments that have been created over the past 20 years have varying applicability to different circumstances and test populations, and vary widely in their validity and reliability. The evaluating forensic psychiatrist must select tests according to their reliability and appropriateness for each examinee. Often the use of psychological testing requires consultation with a psychologist.

Some tests, (e.g., Minnesota Multiphasic Personality Inventory-2 [MMPI-2] [Butcher 2011], Personality Assessment Inventory [PAI] [Morey 2015], and Millon Clinical Multiaxial Inventory [MCMI] [Choca and Grossman 2015]) provide insight into the individual's personality and psychopathology, identify critical risk items to be considered, and give an indication of how forthcoming the test taker has been (fake good/fake bad profiles). Although these instruments do not provide a functional evaluation, they can assist the forensic examiner with identifying the presence of a significant psychiatric disorder.

Frequently, civil competency evaluations question a person's cognitive abilities. Several screening instruments for cognitive dysfunction (e.g., Folstein Mini-Mental State Examination [MMSE] [Folstein et al. 1975], Montreal

Cognitive Assessment [MoCA] [Nasreddine et al 2005], Saint Louis University Mental Status [SLUMS] [Tariq et al. 2006], and Cognistat [Kiernan et al. 1987]) are widely used in the clinical realm and can be used to help the forensic psychiatrist determine if a full neuropsychological evaluation is indicated. Further neuropsychological testing can identify specific areas of impairment that may diminish an individual's ability to make a decision in the civil arena.

Other forensic assessment instruments gather data regarding the individual's functional capacity. These tests include the Adult Functional Adaptive Behavior Scale and the Multidimensional Functional Assessment Questionnaire (Grisso 2003). Some of these instruments may require the input of others (family, caretakers, etc.); therefore, the reliability of these instruments may be influenced by the accuracy of information provided by third parties. Forensic psychiatrists must be confident that the instruments utilized are appropriate and will withstand scrutiny. If a consultant is used, the psychiatrist should discuss with the consultant, prior to test commencement, which tests would be most appropriate to administer. Finally, forensic evaluators should understand their limitations of expertise. Some cases may be complex and require collaboration with other disciplines, such as neurology or psychology, or other psychiatrists with subspecialty expertise, such as child and adolescent psychiatry.

Some unusual cases may require the assembly of a multidisciplinary team.

WRITING THE CIVIL COMPETENCY REPORT

As experts, the forensic psychiatrists' task is to provide a clear explanation of the evaluation process, what was discovered, and the rationale behind the opinion regarding the individual's capacity to make the decision in question. The report is one way that the forensic psychiatrist communicates with the court and others in the legal system. The quality of report influences the weight given to the opinion. The report should include applicable psychiatric diagnoses, the opinion regarding the evaluee's competence, and the reasoning that links the two together. The written explanation of the reasoning is vital, adds credibility to the conclusions, and helps the fact-finder understand that the psychiatrist used a rational method for decision making.

Some have suggested that the forensic psychiatrist should not give an opinion on the ultimate question of competency, but simply lay the facts in front of the fact-finder (Bazelon 1989). We disagree, and remind the reader that the fact-finder is making the final decision regardless of the forensic psychiatrist's opinion, but that the forensic psychiatrist has the unique skill set to assist the court in linking the facts of the case with psychiatric knowledge to arrive at a reasoned opinion (Ciccone 1987).

The forensic psychiatrist should not write a report unless requested to do so by the retaining party. Once a report is requested, we recommend discussing the draft with the attorney verbally and never releasing a copy of a draft. Attorney suggestions on factual and grammatical errors and omissions can be considered while striving to maintain objectivity and fidelity to one's own psychiatric opinion.

SPECIFIC COMPETENCY EVALUATIONS

Guardianship

In most jurisdictions, there is a presumption of competency when adults enter into contractual arrangements or make decisions as they live their lives. Under the concept of *parens patriae*, the state has the authority to protect incompetent individuals and to preserve their property. A guardian is a person to whom the courts have given the power of managing the property and the personal interests of another person. These responsibilities may include the duty to make decisions regarding the physical needs of the person who, for defect of age, understanding, or self-control, is considered incapable of administering his or her own affairs. A guardian has a fiduciary responsibility to manage the affairs of the ward and may be held accountable for errors in transacting business affairs on the ward's behalf. A guardian does not have title to property that remains with the ward.

There are different types of guardians. A *testamentary guardian* is appointed for a child by a will and has responsibility for both the child and the child's estate until the child reaches the age of maturity. A *guardian ad litem* is appointed by the court to protect the interests of a minor, an incompetent, or a proposed conservatee in litigation. A *special guardian*, also known as a limited guardian or a conservator, has powers limited to managing a ward's financial affairs. A *general guardian* has the additional obligation to provide for the ward's personal needs including housing, clothing, food, health care, recreation, and education. These general definitions may have different names depending upon jurisdiction.

HISTORY

The tradition of protecting the property of an incompetent individual, integral to English Common Law, made its way to colonial America. In colonial times, it was expected that the immediate family would care for the incompetent individual. If necessary, the colony had the ability to act to protect the interest of the incompetent (Johns 1999). These efforts represent an attempt to preserve the estate of the incompetent so that those who have rightful claims against the estate, as well as those who could be expected to be supported by it, would be protected from having the estate dissipated by the incompetent.

An Associated Press report released in 1987, "Guardians of the Elderly: An Ailing System," found that the guardianship system in the United States had many weaknesses (Bayles 1987). The report stated that courts "routinely take the word of guardians and attorneys without independent checking or full hearings." The American Bar Association has responded and recommended more effective monitoring of the guardianship system, standardized training for judges and guardians, and robust periodic court review (Hurme and Emily 2001).

In 2010, the Government Accountability Office (GAO) identified hundreds of allegations of physical abuse, neglect, and financial exploitation by guardians, and found that potential guardians were not adequately screened or monitored, and courts and federal agencies did not communicate effectively about abusive guardians. Consequently, the forensic psychiatrist should understand the weaknesses and vulnerabilities of the guardianship system into which his or her evaluation might place an individual.

GENERAL GUARDIAN

A general guardianship, in some jurisdictions called a "committee of the person," involves a finding of global incompetence and is a drastic measure with far-reaching consequences. It is relatively difficult to accomplish because the courts have been reluctant to take an individual's right to manage his or her own affairs. The burden of proof is on the person bringing the petition. Appointment of a guardian requires evidence that the ward suffers a substantial impairment of his or her ability to manage property or has become unable to provide for himself or herself or dependents due to a specified disability. A showing that a person suffers from a mental disorder alone is insufficient. There must be clear and convincing proof of substantial impairment in the proposed ward's ability to manage his or her affairs (*In re Bailey* 1974). Expert testimony is not required but is usually employed. The physician—usually a psychiatrist—who undertakes a competency evaluation is not assessing competence in the abstract, but rather with respect to the ability to make specific informed decisions. The specific criteria used in the creation of a guardianship vary from jurisdiction to jurisdiction.

LIMITED GUARDIAN

In recent decades there has been a movement toward the establishment of specific guardianships for specific purposes (Brakel et al. 1985). In some jurisdictions the law provides for the creation of a *conservatorship* to ensure the financial well-being of an individual. A conservatorship does not require that the person be found globally incompetent, just that the person cannot manage his or her affairs as the result of physical and/or mental dysfunction.

Due process rights require that notice of the petition for conservatorship be served on the proposed conservatee, and the conservatee may be present and a guardian ad litem may be appointed to represent the proposed conservatee's interests. If a conservator is appointed, the court sets forth a specific plan as to the duration of the appointment and the frequency of reports to the court.

A family member is usually appointed as conservator, but a nonfamily member may be appointed, especially when there are family disagreements. When there is no family member available, the court may appoint a nonprofit corporation as conservator. It is possible for a Department of Social Services to act as conservator, even if the conservatee does not receive public assistance. A conservator looks after the ward's assets and supplies his or her needs but does not have legal decision-making capacity regarding consent to treatment; that usually requires the creation of a general guardianship.

TERMINATION OF GUARDIANSHIP

Wards who think that they have recovered the ability to manage their affairs can apply to have competence restored. Some jurisdictions call for periodic review of incompetence, and other jurisdictions have provisions for automatic restorations of competence. If there is a finding of restoration of competence, the individual regains his or her right to make personal and financial decisions, and the guardian is relieved. The termination of a guardianship also requires informing relevant individuals about the hearing. There is variation among jurisdictions regarding who should be notified and who must be present at the hearing.

CONDUCTING THE FORENSIC PSYCHIATRIC EVALUATION FOR GUARDIANSHIP

The psychiatric expert evaluating an individual for guardianship should be mindful of the potential abuses of guardianship. Information about who raised the issue of the individual's need for a guardian, why it is being sought, and the effects of a general or limited guardianship is important for a careful evaluation.

In addition to the general guidelines for record review stated above, recent bank statements and bills may provide information about the evaluee's functional financial ability. The evaluee also needs to have a reasonable understanding of his or her sources and amount of income, as well as expenses. An assessment of adaptive functioning is also important. Can the evaluee safely navigate through his or her day, not only providing for shelter and sustenance, but also for personal safety and well-being? Given the evaluee's possible wish to portray a more functional status than is reality, corroborating accounts or observations from family, friends, and other close associates can provide information, as can a visit to the person's home, especially observing the person in his or her home (Melton et al. 2007). Conversely, corroborating information can sometimes cast doubt on the petitioner's assertion that the evaluee needs guardianship, especially when potential financial gains are in play.

The psychiatric examiner should consider whether treatment or the introduction of social support services will allow a person to remain independent. In this way, the forensic psychiatrist provides the court with clinically relevant and legally useful information about an individual's ability to make and communicate decisions regarding one's self and property in varying contexts.

Testamentary capacity

The law presumes that an individual has testamentary capacity—that is, he or she is of sound mind when executing or altering a will. Testamentary capacity requires that a testator or testatrix has the ability to know and rationally understand (1) that he or she is making a will; (2) the natural objects of his or her bounty and claims upon them; and (3) the general nature and extent of his or her property (Garner 1999). In some jurisdictions, the testator must have a rational plan for the distributions of his or her property after death (Regan and Gordon 1997; Gutheil 2007).

HISTORY

In feudal times, fixed rules governed the inheritance of real property. Even when primogeniture, which gave the eldest son the right to inherit his father's estate, was the rule, there were significant exceptions where local customs prevailed. For example, in Kent, England, there was gavelkind tenure, which gave equal shares to sons (Friedman 2005). In 1572, the English Statute of Wills provided everyone with the right to make a will to dispose of real (immovable) and personal (movable) property. Over time the law was amended to exclude "idiots" or persons with "insane memory" (Brakel et al. 1985).

Colonial America used a variety of approaches to wills. New England colonies rejected primogeniture, except for Rhode Island, although Massachusetts and Pennsylvania gave a double share to the oldest son. Southern colonies used primogeniture until revolutionary times (Friedman 2005). American probate laws followed the English Statute of Frauds of 1677, which called for a written, witnessed will for real estate. By the time the nineteenth century ended, an increasing number of individuals left wills crafted by an attorney (Natale 1989).

WILL CONTEST

Less than 3% of wills are contested, and of those that are contested only 15% are successfully overturned (Slovenko 1973). There are a number of conditions that can invalidate a will, one of these being the effects of a person's mental condition at the time of the execution or alteration of the will. In a will contest there is the presumption of testamentary capacity, and the burden of proof rests with the party alleging incompetence. In most jurisdictions the "clear and convincing" standard must be met before the will is invalidated. A testator's suicide does not automatically invalidate a will. A previous adjudication of incompetency—such as the appointment of a guardian—also does not prevent establishing a valid will (Redmond 1987); however, the burden of proof is shifted (Bromberg 1980), and the proponent of the will must establish by clear and convincing evidence that the will was made during a "lucid interval" (*In re Will of Coe* 1900).

The concept of a lucid interval is based on the notion that an individual with a major mental disorder may have periodic remission of symptoms and during such an interval may have the minimal abilities to fulfill the legal criteria for testamentary capacity. Lucid intervals may be found in individuals who abuse alcohol or drugs, unless the substance use has led to some chronic, significant mental deterioration. At times this doctrine has been applied to the individual who is allegedly lucid for only a few minutes. However, "a few minutes" are usually insufficient for the individual to assess and comprehend the factors involved in the distribution of assets.

RETROSPECTIVE DETERMINATION

The evaluation of testamentary capacity frequently occurs after the testator's death. This precludes personal examination, an important source of information, and calls for a thorough examination of other sources. Essentially, retrospective evaluation is a psychological autopsy and can result in a useful description of the testator's mental status and functional ability at the time the will was created or altered. When undertaking a retrospective determination, the psychiatrist must rely on information from collaterals (friends, business partners, relatives, neighbors, hospital and nursing home staff, etc.) and a review of relevant records (school, military, work, medical, psychiatric treatment, etc.). It is also helpful to review letters and notes written by the deceased, especially around the time of the creation or alteration of the will. A visit to the residence or nursing home of the deceased may be useful (Perr 1981). An independent accounting of the nature and value of the testator's estate should be available. Despite the evaluator's best efforts, the unavailability of the testator may result in insufficient data to arrive at an opinion. The forensic psychiatrist must be confident in his or her diligence and be able to communicate this lack of a finding to the retaining party.

INSANE DELUSION

A delusional testator may appear well to the psychiatrically untrained. The court is interested in what is legally called an insane delusion; that is, a mistaken belief for which there is "no basis in reason, cannot be dispelled by reason, and can be accounted for only as the product of mental disorder" (Am. Jur. 1975). As with other instances of civil competence, the mere existence of a delusion does not invalidate a will, and most jurisdictions require proof that the delusional beliefs affected the creation or alteration of the will. Insane delusions often involve demented individuals who believe their spouse is having an affair.

The *Estate of Coffin* is frequently cited and involves the issue of insane delusion (*In re Estate of Coffin* 1968). Coffin married a woman who claimed that he had fathered her child, although she had been with other men. Shortly thereafter, they divorced and he had nothing to do with this child. Forty-one years later, Coffin met this child for the first time and, based on resemblance, decided that this was indeed his son. Before he could formally change his will, Coffin, Sr., died. His son went to court to challenge the validity of the will that had been written at a time when Coffin, Sr., did not believe he had a son. The lower court vacated the will because Coffin, Sr., wrote its provisions while under an insane delusion that this woman's child was not his son. The appellate court dismissed this argument and found Coffin, Sr., did not have an insane delusion when he wrote his will. There was sufficient information for him to believe that this woman's child was not his, and although he was mistaken, he was not insanely deluded. The court held that the petitioner has the burden to prove, by clear and convincing evidence, that there were not facts to support the testator's belief. The judgment invalidating the will was reversed.

In another case, Estoll left the bulk of her estate to her only child, a daughter. The codicil, executed 4 years later, left the bulk of her estate to her sister without mention of her daughter (*In re Estoll* 1968). The daughter opposed probate of the will and presented evidence that her mother had an insane delusion that "the person who would normally be the principal or only object of the testatrix's concern and bounty" was trying to poison her, as the decedent had told many people. She also would not accept pills or water from her daughter but accepted them from her sister. The codicil was set aside on the basis of the impact of this insane delusion.

UNDUE INFLUENCE

Undue influence involves manipulation or deception in engaging the affections of the testator, significantly impairing his or her ability to freely decide on the distribution of his or her property. By its nature, undue influence is often the result of concealed actions and may be difficult to determine. A noble purpose does not justify or legitimize undue influence, such as a physician convincing an elderly patient to leave the bulk of her estate to his research institute. Undue influence must constitute more than friendship or insincere praise. There must be evidence of coercion, compulsion, or restraint that led to a will that does not reflect the true desires of the testator. Some grounds for undue influence include harassment, threat of abandonment, and disaffecting lies about another potential heir (Perr 1981). The burden of proof is on the fiduciary heir to prove that no undue influence was exercised. A fiduciary relationship is one where an individual relies on and trusts another (e.g., attorney–client, doctor–patient, or guardian–ward). However, if the heir is not a fiduciary, the burden of proof falls to the party challenging the will.

The forensic psychiatrist can be asked to examine for undue influence after the testator is deceased, and should consider undue influence in testamentary capacity examinations requested around the time a testator is making or altering a will. The following circumstances provide reasons to consider the possibility of undue influence (Redmond 1987):

1. The psychiatrist is assured by the party requesting the examination that a competency statement is routine due to the testator's age.
2. The appointment is made by someone other than the testator or his or her attorney.
3. The testator is brought to the appointment by someone who answers most of the questions and is reluctant to allow the testator to be interviewed alone.
4. Specifics about the will are not given or the testator seems unclear about specific items in the will.
5. There is reluctance to give information about potential heirs and their relationship to the testator.

The psychiatrist must consider cognitive functioning, physical condition, and signs and symptoms of mental disorders that may reduce the testator's ability to resist undue influence. These same ailments may be so severe that the individual may also lack testamentary capacity.

When psychiatrists are not be able to arrive at an opinion as to whether or not there was undue influence, they may nonetheless opine if the individual's character structure—either alone or in combination with a physical or mental condition—made them particularly susceptible to the influence of others. The social environment of the testator may create the opportunity for undue influence on the cognitively impaired person by a cohabiting family member, a "helpful" neighbor, a "suitor," or professionals. A variety of social circumstances increase the possibility of undue influence: isolation from previously trusted family and friends, family conflict, or significant dependence on a caregiver (Peisah et al. 2009).

CONDUCTING AN EVALUATION FOR TESTAMENTARY CAPACITY

When the testator is available for examination, such as in the case of an anticipated challenge to the will, the customary psychiatric examination of an adult is appropriate (American Psychiatric Association 2006). If attorneys are to observe the interview, a one-way mirror allows for observation without undue intrusion; otherwise, the attorneys may be seated behind the examinee to minimize contact. It is useful to record this examination (Spar and Garb 1992), which may obviate the need for the attorneys' presence and provide compelling information for the court to consider.

If cognitive impairments are noted and are difficult to fully delineate on clinical examination, neuropsychological testing should be considered. The psychiatrist should be alert to psychological motivations that could include, but are by no means limited to, hostility toward heirs, fear, or "secrets" that the testator holds dear. The psychological and cognitive impact of nonpsychiatric medical problems cannot be ignored; disabilities secondary to physical problems must be factored into the decision-making process. Even if the presence of a significant mental disorder is obvious on examination, the evaluator must determine whether and how the signs and symptoms influence the decision-making process required to execute a valid will. For example, the testator with a mild dementia may have difficulty recalling new information, but may nonetheless know his children, the approximate size of his estate, and that he wishes to reward the child with whom he is living with a larger share of the inheritance.

The evaluator should ascertain whether the testator understands the purpose of a will. Testators should be asked to describe their property and estimate its value. They should also be asked to describe the division of their estate, their heirs, and the reasons underlying their decision to include or exclude potential heirs. This line of questioning is also an opportunity to assess for evidence of undue influence. Testamentary capacity requires comprehension of the overall size and components of one's estate. Although precise knowledge of the value of the estate is not required, the individual should have a reasonable approximation of its overall worth. An individual must also know the natural objects of one's bounty; generally, these are blood relatives, though at times they may include close friends, and occasionally a "faithful servant." The testator's denial that he has children based on the symptoms of a mental disorder may invalidate a will. However, ignorance of the existence of blood relatives (i.e., not due to delusion) does not constitute incompetency. The inability to read or write also would not, by itself, invalidate a will.

Competence to contract

Competence to contract, or contractual capacity, refers to an individual's capacity to enter into agreements. Society places a great deal of importance on the sanctity of the contract. Pettit (1999), in reviewing the evolution of contractual rights and the mentally ill, noted, "The most striking change is that the mentally disabled are now allowed to contract at all."

HISTORY

In a 1963 seminal case, *Faber v. Suite Style Manufacturing Corporation*, Faber contracted for land against the advice of his attorney. Faber planned to use the property to build a resort. Expert witnesses agreed that Faber was in the manic phase of his bipolar disorder at the time he entered into the contract. The court found Faber incompetent to enter into the contract because he acted "under the compulsion of a mental disease or disorder but for which the contract could not have been made."

In *Ortolere v. Teachers' Retirement Board* (1969), the court expanded the scope of mental incompetency that may void a contractual agreement. Ortolere, while under psychiatric care, changed her retirement option to a maximum allowance that extinguished all interests upon her death. Her husband sued, claiming she was not mentally competent to enter into this agreement. The court found that Mrs. Ortolere suffered from an involutional psychosis, melancholia type (major depressive disorder, severe with psychotic features) on the date she entered into the contract. Determining that the cognitive rules for incompetence were too restrictive, the court expanded the grounds of incompetence to include affectively driven behaviors resulting from a psychosis. The court found the contract void because she was laboring under a mental defect that prohibited her from acting in a reasonable manner, and the Board of Education knew of the impairment because Ortolere's mental illness led to her leave of absence.

CONTRACTUAL CAPACITY IN GUARDIANSHIP

Some have argued individuals who have a guardian, as a matter of law, have no ability to enter into a contract (Meiklejohn 1988). Those holding this view assert that the ward has been found incompetent, and in order for the guardian to protect the ward's estate, the guardian has to have control over it. The opposing view argues that the order establishing a guardianship creates a rebuttable presumption of incapacity to enter into a contract. They further argue that the state has an interest in upholding contracts, and those dealing with the ward may not have had constructive notice of the guardianship and may have acted in good faith. Most jurisdictions take a middle position, allowing for an individual to be found incompetent to enter into a contract but requiring the person requesting that the contract be voided to carry the burden of proof. To lack contractual capacity, the court must be convinced that the individual had a significant mental disability that impaired his or her capacity to understand the character of the transaction and act in a reasonable manner. In some jurisdictions, it must be shown that the other party knew of the incompetency or acted in bad faith. At times, the "fairness" of the contract will determine if it will be upheld by the court.

CONDUCTING THE FORENSIC PSYCHIATRIC EVALUATION FOR CAPACITY TO CONTRACT

As with the evaluations of other civil competence, the context of the request is important. The determination of the presence of a mental disorder and the resulting impairments is essential to determining an individual's capacity to enter into a contract. Although much of the case law and academic discourse in the literature focuses on commercial contracts, a contract is essentially any lawful agreement between two or more parties, and could include marriages and adoptions.

Capacity may vary over time depending on the nature, severity, and periodicity of a person's disorder. Additionally, in more complex contracts, a higher standard of capacity is required. Prior to the psychiatric examination, the psychiatrist should request a detailed explanation of the terms of the contract. During the psychiatric examination, the evaluee should be asked to explain the terms and his or her reasoning for deciding to enter into the contract.

SUMMARY KEY POINTS

- The forensic psychiatric evaluation of civil competencies is composed of three complementary components: the psychiatric examination, record review, and, when indicated, standardized testing.
- Appointment of a guardian requires evidence that the ward suffers a substantial impairment of his or her ability to manage property or has

become unable to provide for himself or herself or dependents due to a specified disability.

- Testamentary capacity requires that a testator or testatrix has the ability to know and rationally understand that he or she is making a will, the natural objects of their bounty and claims upon them, and the general nature and extent of his or her property.
- Undue influence involves manipulation in engaging the affections of the testator, which impairs the testator's ability to freely decide on the distribution of his or her property.
- The complexity of a contract is directly related to the capacity required to competently enter into it.

REFERENCES

79 Am. Jur. 2d Wills, 341, 1975.

American Academy of Psychiatry and the Law. 1999. Videotaping of forensic psychiatric evaluations (Task Force). *Journal of the American Academy of Psychiatry and the Law* 27:345–358.

American Psychiatric Association. 2006. Practice guideline for the psychiatric evaluation of adults. In *Practice Guidelines*, Washington, DC: American Psychiatric Association, 6–60.

Bayles F and S McCartney. 1987. *Guardians of the Elderly: An Ailing System*. Associated Press. http://www.apnewsarchive.com, accessed March 14, 2015.

Bazelon DL. 1989. *Questioning Authority: Justice*. New York: New York University Press.

Brakel SJ, J Parry, and BA Weiner. 1985. *The Mentally Disabled and the Law*. Chicago: American Bar Association.

Bromberg W. 1980. *The Uses of Psychiatry in the Law*. New York: Plenum.

Butcher JN. 2011. *A Beginner's Guide to the MMPI-2*, 3rd edition. Washington, DC: American Psychological Association.

Choca JP and SD Grossman. 2015. Evolution of the Millon Clinical Multiaxial Inventory. *Journal of Personality Assessment* July 7:1–9. [Epub ahead of print]

Ciccone JR and C Clements. 1987. The insanity defense: Asking and answering the ultimate question. *Journal of the American Academy of Psychiatry and the Law* 15:329–338.

Faber v. Suite Style Manufacturing Corporation, 242 N.Y.S.2d 763 (Sup. Ct. 1963).

Folstein MF, SE Folstein, and PR McHugh. 1975. "Mini-Mental State": A practical method for grading the cognitive state of patients for the clinician. *Journal of Psychiatric Research* 12:189–198.

Friedman LM. 2005. *A History of American Law*, 3rd edition. New York: Simon and Schuster.

Garner B. 1999. *Law Dictionary*, 7th edition. St. Paul, MN: West Group.

Grisso T. 2003. *Evaluating Competencies: Forensic Assessments and Instruments*, 2nd edition. New York: Kluwer Academic.

Gutheil TG. 2007. Common pitfalls in the evaluation of testamentary capacity. *Journal of the American Academy of Psychiatry and the Law* 35:514–517.

Hurme SB and W Emily. 2001. Guardian accountability then and now: Tracing tenets for an active court role. *Stetson Law Review* 31:867–940.

In re Bailey, 362 N.Y.S.2d 226 (Sup. Ct. 1974).

In re Estate of Coffin, 246 A.2d 489 (N.J. App. Div. 1968).

In re Estate of Estoll, 291 N.Y.S.2d 411 (App. Div. 1968).

In re Will of Coe, 62 N.Y.S. 376 (App. Div. 1900).

Johns AF. 1999. Ten years after: Where is the constitutional crisis with procedural safeguards and due process in guardianship adjudication? *Elder Law Journal* 7:33–152.

Kiernan RJ, J Mueller, JW Langston, and C Van Dyke. 1987. The neurobehavioral cognitive status examination, a brief but differentiated approach to cognitive assessment. *Annals of Internal Medicine* 107:481–485.

Meiklejohn AM. 1988. Contractual and donative capacity. *Case Western Reserve Law Review* 39:307–387.

Melton GB, J Petrila, NG Polythress, and C Slobogin. 2007. *Psychological Evaluations for the Courts: A Handbook for Mental Health Professionals and Lawyers*, 3rd edition. New York: Guilford Press.

Morey LC. 2015. Personality Assessment Inventory (PAI). *The Encyclopedia of Clinical Psychology* 1:1–10. http://onlinelibrary.wiley.com/doi/10.1002/9781118625392.wbecp284/full, accessed July 25, 2016.

Nasreddine ZS, NA Phillips, V Bédirian et al. 2005. The Montreal Cognitive Assessment, MoCA: A brief screening tool for mild cognitive impairment. *Journal of the American Geriatrics Society* 53:695–699.

Natale KR. 1989. A survey, analysis, and evaluation of holographic will statutes. *Hofstra Law Review* 17:159–202.

Ortelere v. Teachers' Retirement Bd., 250 N.E.2d 460 (N.Y. 1969).

Peisah C, S Finkel, K Shulman et al. 2009. The wills of older people: Risk factors for undue influence. *International Psychogeriatrics* 21:7–15.

Perr IN. 1981. Wills, testamentary capacity and undue influence. *Bulletin of the American Academy of Psychiatry and the Law* 9:15–22.

Pettit M, Jr. 1999. Freedom, freedom of contract, and the "rise and fall." *Boston University Law Review* 79:263–354.

Redmond FC. 1987. Testamentary capacity. *Bulletin of the American Academy of Psychiatry and the Law* 15:247–256.

Regan WM and SM Gordon. 1997. Assessing testamentary capacity in elderly people. *Southern Medical Journal* 90:13–15.

Slovenko R. 1973. *Psychiatry and Law.* Boston: Little, Brown.

Spar JE and SA Garb. 1992. Assessing competency to make a will. *American Journal of Psychiatry* 149:169–174.

Tariq SH, N Tumosa, JT Chibnall, MH Perry, and JE Morley. 2006. Comparison of the Saint Louis University mental status examination and the Mini-Mental State Examination for detecting dementia and mild neurocognitive disorder: A pilot study. *American Journal of Geriatric Psychiatry* 11:900–910.

37

Death, dying, and the law

M. CARMELA EPRIGHT AND RICHARD L. FRIERSON

INTRODUCTION

The "right-to-die" movement in the United States stems from the 1960s, an era that brought tremendous advances in medical technology such as the widespread use of mechanical ventilation, renal dialysis, and artificial nutrition. These interventions made it possible to preserve lives that would have been lost mere decades earlier, but they also had the capacity to prolong the dying process, often beyond limits found acceptable by the patients whose lives they were intended to preserve. Consequently, phrases such as "quality of life" and "death with dignity" have taken on political, social, and personal significance in the public sphere (Beauchamps and Childress 2009). Patients and families have since sought new laws, health-care policies, and rights, including the right to withdraw treatment, assign surrogate decision makers, and receive increased access to palliation, analgesics, and sedation. In some jurisdictions, patients and their caregivers have successfully argued for laws that promote a patient's choice to hasten death through physician-assisted suicide.

These overtures have been met with significant resistance. Religious groups argue that life itself must be preserved regardless of a patient's or surrogate's desires (Hains and Hulbert-Williams 2013). Human rights activists fear the potential abuse of euthanasia on members of vulnerable groups such as the indigent and the disabled (Van Norman 2014). Many medical providers prioritize cure and treatment over a strong conception of individual autonomy (Boudreau and Somerville 2013). Moreover, the drive toward patient-directed treatment at the end of life has been seen as a challenge to the traditional authority of physicians who are thought by some to be more qualified to make end-of-life decisions than persons without medical training (Filene 1998; Boudreau and Somerville 2013).

DONALD "DAX" COWART: TREATMENT WITHDRAWAL

The early 1970s brought several highly publicized cases that illustrate the conflict between preservation of life and the patient's right to refuse treatment. One of these high-profile cases involved 25-year-old Donald "Dax" Cowart who was critically injured in a 1973 explosion that killed his father. Cowart sustained second- and third-degree burns over 65% of his body. From the very beginning he clearly expressed a desire not to be treated for his injuries. His health-care providers continued to treat him, asserting that the pain associated with his treatment made him incompetent to make decisions about his care. Cowart's mother signed consent forms for any procedure deemed necessary by the health-care professionals (Kliever 1989). Because the accident rendered Cowart completely blind, partially deaf, fingerless, and unable to walk without assistance, he was not able to leave the hospital on his own accord and was thus forced to undergo whatever treatments his health-care providers recommended. During his hospitalization multiple psychiatrists concurred that Cowart was competent to make medical decisions. Cowart argued that his treatment should have been terminated when—as a competent adult—he asked to leave the hospital and return home to die from his injuries (Cowart and Burt 1998).

After Cowart was released from the hospital he became a successful attorney and advocate for the "right-to-die" movement. His case has since been considered one of the best examples of the importance of patient autonomy and the destructive power of physician paternalism (Kliever 1989). This case and others like it challenged the widely held view that because sick patients do not have as much information about their health as do their doctors, they are not rational enough to make health-care decisions on their own behalf. The overriding ethos prior to this time was that patients should be treated with paternalism and the benevolent protection provided by their wiser, more experienced physicians (Beauchamps and Childress 2009), but from this time forward both legal and medical decision making moved steadily toward a more patient-centered approach.

In the 40 years since cases like Dax Cowart's came to the public's attention, principles of patient autonomy and self-determination have become hallmarks of legal jurisprudence. These principles depend on the notion that if patients have the cognitive capacity to make their own decisions, such decisions must be protected. The legal and moral systems governing patient care were thus forced to determine the standards by which such capacity would be assessed (Strasser 1995). Cases like Cowart's challenged the notion that pain and illness rendered patients incapable of decision making, and legal mandates focused attention on the issue of informed consent (*Canterbury v. Spence* 1972). Informed consent shifted the burden of treatment decisions to the patient, while the responsibility to provide complete information was imposed upon the treating physician. *Canterbury v. Spence* held that physicians must reveal information that a "reasonable person" would likely find significant when determining whether or not to accept the proposed treatment. This ruling held that the standard for measuring the duty to disclose is that such disclosure must be reasonable but also as complete as possible under the circumstances. Although the physician was not required to disclose every conceivable risk, he or she was bound to provide information that might prevent the patient from pursuing the treatment in question, including potential risks, pain, and disability.

During the 1970s and 1980s questions regarding informed consent concerned the ways in which a patient's desires regarding his or her own treatment could be determined in cases in which the patient has lost the capacity to articulate such determinations on his or her own behalf. Given advances in medical technology, some unconscious patients could be kept on life support indefinitely. Decisions about withdrawal of treatment took on new significance and were more complicated when they involved an unconscious patient. Again, various high-profile cases sparked intense legal, personal, and public debates. One of the first of these media-fueled cases to gain public notoriety was that of Karen Ann Quinlan.

KAREN ANN QUINLAN: SURROGACY AND TREATMENT WITHDRAWAL

After Karen Ann Quinlan collapsed at a party, friends and fellow partygoers put her to bed but then found her unconscious and without respiratory function 15 minutes later. Emergency medical personal were able to restore her heartbeat and breathing, but she remained unconscious. Over the next several months Quinlan fell into a persistent vegetative state—a permanent unconsciousness characterized by irreversible cessation of cognitive functions of the cerebral cortex, although brainstem functions, such as breathing and heart rate, remain intact (Laureys et al. 2004). Quinlan's parents and appointed guardians, Joseph and Julia Quinlan, wanted to remove their daughter from the ventilator that was believed necessary to sustain her life. The Quinlan's argued that they knew Karen Ann's wishes better than any member of the hospital staff—none of whom had known Karen Ann in a conscious state. Her parents testified that their daughter would not wish to be artificially sustained using "extraordinary measures," and requested that she be removed from the ventilator (Angell 1993). Local officials threatened to bring homicide charges against the Quinlans and the hospital if the ventilator was removed (Cawthon 2004). The Quinlans sued.

Although the Quinlans lost in District Court, the New Jersey Supreme Court issued a ruling declaring that when the wishes of an adult regarding his or her care can be established, that individual's wishes must be upheld. However, the process to use in establishing those wishes—even with an advance directive—remained unclear. In Quinlan's case her parent's fight to remove Karen Ann's respirator became a pyrrhic victory; although the respirator was removed after the New Jersey Supreme Court ruling, Karen Ann was able to breathe on her own and survived in a vegetative state for nine additional years. The questions in this case were reintroduced to public debate through another tragic case involving another young woman.

NANCY CRUZAN: SURROGACY AND "CLEAR AND CONVINCING EVIDENCE"

In January 1983, 25-year-old Nancy Cruzan lost control of her car, overturned, and was discovered lying face-down in a ditch without detectable respiratory or cardiac function. She was estimated to be oxygen deprived for 12 to 14 minutes. Emergency medical technicians were able to restore her breathing and heartbeat. Cruzan remained in a coma for approximately three weeks and then progressed to an unconscious state in which she was able to orally ingest some nutrition. In order to ease her feeding and further her recovery, surgeons implanted a feeding and hydration tube, and she was admitted to a state hospital. However, subsequent rehabilitative efforts proved unsuccessful. It became apparent that Cruzan had virtually no chance of regaining her mental faculties. Her parents and appointed guardians, Lester and Joyce Cruzan, asked the hospital to terminate nutrition and hydration procedures. The hospital refused to honor the request without court approval.

The court decisions involving the Cruzans' battle with the State of Missouri are long and complex. Missouri argued that (1) although Cruzan was in a "persistent vegetative state," she was neither dead within the meaning of Missouri's statutory definition of death nor terminally ill, and thus her treatment was of "compelling interest" to the state; (2) Cruzan's right to refuse treatment did not outweigh Missouri's strong policy favoring the preservation of life; (3) conversations with her friends and family members concerning her desire to not "be placed on machines," unless she "could live at least halfway normally" were unreliable for the purpose of determining her intent, and were thus insufficient to support the parents' claim to exercise substituted judgment on her behalf; and (4) no person could terminate medical treatment for an incompetent person in the absence of "clear and convincing, inherently reliable evidence" of the incompetent's wishes, which they held was absent in Nancy Cruzan's case (Cawthon 2004).

The U.S. Supreme Court (*Cruzan v. Director, Missouri Department of Health* 1990) found that due process was not violated by Missouri's requirement that an incompetent person's wishes to withdraw life-sustaining treatment be *proved by clear and convincing evidence*, and that states were free to establish their own evidentiary standards regarding treatment withdrawal when patients are unable to articulate their own health-care decisions. In Cruzan's case, the testimony of additional witnesses ultimately satisfied Missouri's requirement that clear and convincing evidence of her wishes *did* exist, and medically assisted nutrition and hydration were terminated.

Although the ruling in *Cruzan v. Missouri* seemed to be a setback for the "Right-to-Die Movement," it resulted in a number of important precedents that ultimately benefited the movement. It also raised new questions. Most importantly, the Supreme Court determined that the standards for surrogacy are to be established by the state. Following *Cruzan*, nearly every state passed statutes that outlined the ways in which surrogates would be appointed and how decisions regarding patient care would be made. Following the Quinlan precedent, most states determined that the wishes of the patient—when they can be established—are paramount for surrogate decisions. Furthermore, most states determined that surrogate decision making ought to be performed by the people most likely to know the patient.

Another significant issue emanating from the *Cruzan* case was that the assisted nutrition and hydration was determined to be a form of health care, and like all other forms of health care, it can be refused and withdrawn if its delivery is against the will of the patient, whether this refusal or withdrawal request is issued by the patient or by the proper surrogate.

UNIFORM HEALTH-CARE DECISIONS ACT

Given that the Supreme Court had determined that questions concerning the identification of a surrogate decision maker and the standard of evidence used to determine the authority of these agents was a matter for states to decide, states sought a uniform means of answering these questions. In 1993, in an effort to assist states in adopting a clear standard, the National Conference of Commissioners on Uniform State Laws produced an act intended to address the problem of determining who has the authority to make health-care decisions (including the cessation of life-sustaining treatment) when the patient lacks this capacity. The resultant Uniform Health-Care Decisions Act (UHCDA) applies to health-care decisions for adults and emancipated minors. The act holds that any adult or emancipated minor with capacity may give oral or written instructions to a health-care provider, and these instructions remain in force in the event that the individual loses capacity. This act further provides for the appointment of a surrogate, either through a durable power of attorney for health care or other state-approved document signed while the patient has capacity. If the patient has not signed a formal document giving decision-making authority to a chosen individual, the act recommends a priority list of those authorized to assume this authority. The act recommends that this power first be given to a spouse, if one exists, then to an adult child, then a parent, and then to the patient's parents or to the patient's adult siblings. In the absence of such person(s), the act states that "an adult who has exhibited special care and concern for the patient, who is familiar with the patient's personal values, and who is willing and able to make a health-care decision for the patient," may assume the authority (National Conference of Commissioners on Uniform State Laws 1993). In the event nobody qualifies as a surrogate, the health-care provider may turn to an appropriate court for an appointment. Most states have adopted some version of this act, often with changes to the priority list. Nearly every state favors persons who are legally related to the patient.

Under this act, and in resulting laws adopted by most states, surrogate decision making is to be governed by the "substituted judgment standard." According to this standard, the decisions of surrogates must be in accord with the expressed preferences of the patient before becoming incapacitated (if these are known), and/or made by a surrogate who knows the patient well enough to determine what he or she would decide if he or she had the capacity to make the choice. The substituted judgment standard is to be used if the patient has ever had decision-making capacity. A second standard, "best interest standard," requires that when the wishes of the patient cannot be clearly determined, surrogates are to consider "what would a reasonable person choose" when determining what is best for this patient under these circumstances. It is the responsibility of a surrogate to first uphold the wishes and values of the patient rather than the surrogate's own wishes and desires, and to consider external factors such as community understandings of the patient's "best interest" only when the patient's own values and desires are impossible to establish. Finally, when it is impossible to ascertain the patient's own values, the UHCDA recommends a strong preference for life-sustaining procedures, and holds the preservation of life as central in determining "best interest."

The UHCDA clearly outlines procedures to follow when an individual lacks capacity to refuse or consent to medical treatment. The determination of incapacity, however, is usually left to treating physicians or consulting psychiatrists. These determinations require an assessment of four functional abilities: (1) the ability to express a choice, (2) the ability to understand information relevant to treatment decision making, (3) the ability to appreciate the significance of that information on one's own medical situation, and (4) the ability to reason with relevant information and logically weigh treatment options (Grisso and Appelbaum 1998). Quinlan and Cruzan (and Schiavo, below) clearly lacked an ability to express a choice. Dax Cowart retained this ability as well as an ability to understand medical information, to logically weigh options, and apply those options to his unique situation. The ability to understand information requires that information is received as presented by medical providers and that it is comprehended. This ability is most commonly impaired by cognitive disorders (e.g., dementia, intellectual disability, delirium). The ability to appreciate information in regard to one's situation requires a recognition and acceptance of one's medical condition(s). In end-of-life decisions, it requires understanding and acceptance of one's own impending death. Finally, the ability to reason and logically weigh treatment options requires that a patient is able to understand the benefits and risks of the possible treatment options, including consequences of possible failure of the proposed treatment, and to choose an option based on personal preference.

THERESA MARIE "TERRI" SCHIAVO: SURROGACY AND WITHDRAWAL OF NUTRITION AND HYDRATION

The public controversy over end-of-life decisions did not end with the UHCDA. Public misunderstanding of these issues was particularly evident in the Terri Schiavo case, which dominated the news in early 2005 until Terri's death on March 31, 2005. On February 25, 1990, Terri Schiavo suffered oxygen deprivation as a result of a cardiac arrest brought about by eating disorder-induced hypokalemia. Less than a year later, Terri's attending physician declared that she was in a persistent vegetative state. It was not until 8 years after Terri's collapse that her husband and surrogate, Michael Schiavo, requested the removal of the feeding tube that was sustaining Terri's life. He argued that Terri herself had made statements after seeing media coverage of the Karen Ann Quinlan case such as "I wouldn't want to be kept alive on machines."

The *Schiavo* case resulted in numerous trials and hearings; it was heard by the Supreme Court of Florida and considered, but ultimately rejected, as a suitable case by the U.S. Supreme Court. A Florida law was passed in response to her case ("Terri's Law") as was an act of Congress, Act for the Relief of the Parents of Theresa Marie Schiavo (Public Law 109-3); her feeding tube was withdrawn and reconnected twice. It was removed for the third and final time on March 18, 2005.

The controversy concerning Terri's case revolved around two issues: (1) whether her husband, Michael Schiavo, was her proper surrogate (as opposed to her parents, Robert and Mary Schindler, who wished to continue Terri's treatment) and (2) whether nutrition and hydration constitute "standard medical care" (rather than "basic care") and thus, like any other medical therapy, can be withdrawn by the proper surrogate decision maker. The Florida Supreme Court upheld the standards outlined in the UHCDA: the spouse of the patient was considered the rightful surrogate called on to interpret the patient's wishes; any treatment that violates the wishes of the patient receiving that treatment can be withdrawn; and while the preservation of life should be the preference in cases where the patient's wishes cannot be established, the patient's own wishes (even if interpreted through a surrogate decision maker) are the final arbiter of whether or not life-sustaining treatment should be continued.

WITHDRAWAL OF TREATMENT, EUTHANASIA, AND PHYSICIAN-ASSISTED SUICIDE (PAS)

Many who opposed the removal of Terri Schiavo's feeding tube charged that discontinuing nutrition and hydration was tantamount to euthanizing a patient; however, the court rulings in this and other cases consistently demonstrate that a bright line exists between euthanasia and treatment withdrawal, a line that is generally understood to be the distinction between letting die (in the case of treatment withdrawal) and killing (in the case of active euthanasia).

Euthanasia is derived from the Greek language; its definition involves a "good" or "easy" death. In its literal translation euthanasia has no relation to death involving another person. The shift in the meaning of the term to "assisted death" stems from 1969 Netherlands law that allowed doctors to assist in the suicide of terminally ill patients under prescribed and narrow conditions (Gomez 1991). In order to understand the various laws in the United States that govern assisted death, it is essential to understand the distinction between "active voluntary euthanasia," which requires a person other than the patient to participate in the delivery of a life-ending substance, and "voluntary passive euthanasia" (most often referred to as "physician-assisted suicide"), whereby the patient acquires a prescription for medications and then could choose or not choose to use to end his or her life without the active participation of a health-care provider or even the provider's knowledge of the time of death of the patient. Active euthanasia is illegal in all states, whereas physician-assisted suicide (PAS) is currently legal in five U.S. states (Oregon, Washington, Montana, Vermont, and California).

The first attempts to legalize assisted suicide through voter initiative were defeated in Washington State in 1991 and in California in 1992. In 1997, two landmark U.S. Supreme Court rulings reignited the controversy surrounding PAS by opening up the possibility that states could institute the practice. In *Vacco v. Quill* the court ruled that New York's ban on PAS was constitutional, that the state had the authority to ban the practice, and that there exists no constitutional guarantee of a "right to die." In *Washington v. Glucksberg* the court ruled that because assisted suicide is not a fundamental liberty, it is not protected under the Fourteenth Amendment. However, even though the Supreme Court ruled against a constitutional right to die in both cases, these rulings were a victory for those who favor assisted suicide, because although the court found that states could make assisted suicide illegal, the court also made it clear that states could legalize assisted suicide if they so choose. As a result, the question of the legality of assisted suicide was to be decided by the states.

In 1994, proponents of legalization successfully launched a referendum in Oregon to make PAS legal. For 3 years, the law was blocked by Oregon courts and did not take effect. In October 1997, following the rulings in *Vacco* and *Washington*, the Supreme Court refused to hear a case brought by groups who wished to challenge the constitutionality of Oregon's law, effectively upholding the law. In October 1997, opponents of the law launched a referendum to repeal the law, but voters rejected this attempt at repeal.

Following Oregon's lead, Washington State enacted nearly identical legislation in 2008, and Vermont followed suit in 2013. Montana also permits PAS as a result of a state Supreme Court ruling in *Baxter v. Montana* (2009) that held that terminally ill patients had a right to a lethal prescription from their physicians under the state's constitution. Although the details of Montana's law have not been carved out and will likely confront challenges in the form of proposed voter referendums, the restrictions and allowances for PAS are clearly outlined in Oregon's plan that was enacted nearly verbatim in both Washington and Vermont. Oregon's Death with Dignity Act requires that patients requesting a prescription capable of resulting in death must be terminally ill with a projected death within 6 months, the terminal diagnosis must be confirmed by two physicians, the patient must have informed his or her family, the patient must undergo screening for depression if medically indicated, and the patient must make two separate and documented requests (Oregon Death with Dignity Act 1994). The patient can withdraw the request at any time. Both Oregon and Washington State issue annual reports concerning the exercise of PAS in their state. The most recent information provided by these states indicates that far more requests are issued than acted on by the patients, and the patient demand for PAS has been consistently lower than original predictions (Oregon Public Health Division and Washington State Department of Health). According to the data provided by these states, patients requesting PAS have not been the poor and disabled as originally feared; most have been middle-class men. The majority have received a diagnosis of terminal cancer (Trice-Loggers et al. 2013). The most frequently stated reason for pursuing this intervention is a desire to exercise individual autonomy in the timing and method of their impending death (Oregon Public Health Division 2015).

PALLIATIVE CARE: SCOPE, LIMITATIONS, AND PAS

One of the central practical concerns raised by the medical community regarding laws that permit PAS is that this practice will limit the advancement of palliative care. Suffering manifested by pain, inability to pursue life goals, and isolation from social support are genuine concerns for patients and their families. Although the hospice movement and increasing support for palliative care programs at medical institutions has attempted to respond to these concerns, studies continue to demonstrate that intractable pain is poorly treated in the United States, and advocates for PAS suggest that such suffering necessitates the need for assisted suicide (Cantor and Thomas 2000). The doctrine of "double effect" (the notion that the use of analgesics is legitimate, even if such interventions shorten the life of the patient) is well supported in law. Physicians are not subject to malpractice liability, legal sanction, or professional discipline, provided their use of analgesics is within good faith practice guidelines. Although purposefully causing a patient's death through use of medications is considered active euthanasia and constitutes homicide, some risk taking in relieving patient suffering is considered acceptable medical practice. "The risk of death is justified, not because it is intended but because there is no alternative approach that makes the risk of death less likely and the alleviation of suffering possible" (originally quoted by Cantor and Thomas 2000; Fleischman 1998). Moreover, it is now widely accepted that pain itself shortens the life of the patient; thus, the relief of suffering is justified as a better alternative than allowing the patient both to bear pain and to permit the hastening of death as a result of that pain (Fohr 1998).

"Terminal sedation," sedation that results in unconsciousness through the remainder of the dying process, is more controversial and legally ambiguous (Quill et al. 1997). This practice walks a fine line between euthanasia and palliation and is widely seen as the palliative therapy of last resort (Quill and Byock 2000; Omipidam 2013). The use of analgesics to maintain a comatose state has some degree of legal protections. Physicians can prescribe analgesics for pain relief, even if the treatment poses some risk to the patient—ultimately there is little difference between doing so and performing a surgery that poses risk but simultaneously provides hope of recovery or pain relief. However, terminal sedation requires professional oversight, which calls for the risk associated with the practice to be in proportion to the intended benefit and demands that increased use of these medicines be titrated with great care and professionalism (de Graeff and Dean 2007).

WITHDRAWAL OF INEFFECTIVE TREATMENT

Perhaps the most controversial developing issue at the intersection of law and death is whether and when treatment may be considered "futile" or "ineffective" by the health-care provider such that it is acceptable to withdraw further treatment against the wishes of the patient or surrogate decision maker (Rubin 1998). Although many states are considering or instituting "futile care policies," Texas was the first state to formally institute legislation, the Advance Directives Act, in 1999. Since its institution, health-care providers can withdraw "futile treatment" once the patient or substitute decision maker is given a 10-day advance notice. However, controversies remain as to what constitutes futility, how the goals of treatment are to be determined, and who should decide these questions. Physicians can refuse to deliver treatment that does not serve to meet the medical needs of a patient, even if the patient or surrogate demands it. It may be considered malpractice to continue therapies that serve no medical purpose—indeed physicians have been sued for continuing expensive, ineffective treatments from which they profit. Nevertheless, physicians are more inclined to continue treatments such as dialysis or mechanical ventilation, even when these treatments have no hope of restoring the patient's function or helping that patient to meet his or her life goals. Families often contend that continuing the patient's life, even in a comatose, minimally conscious, or vegetative state, serves the patient's and family's goals.

The Texas law provides for the hospital and/or physician to refuse to continue treatment deemed medically ineffective, but only under narrow and prescribed conditions. Physicians and institutions must perform thorough reviews of the case, consult the hospital's standing ethics board, and attempt to reach a mutually agreeable treatment plan with the family. If the dispute continues after a waiting period, a second, ad hoc committee should be formed to review the case. If this second committee concurs that the treatment in question is indeed ineffective, the physician and institution must attempt to transfer the patient to another facility to deliver the requested treatment (Texas 1999). The final determination to withdraw treatment, despite the wishes of the patient or surrogate, can only be made if all of these options fail to mitigate the dispute. Furthermore, this law exempts the provider from criminal or civil prosecution.

BRAIN DEATH AND THE WITHDRAWAL OF TREATMENT

Unlike persistent vegetative states (PVSs) and other comatose states whereby part or all of the brain remains functional, brain death is the total and permanent cessation of the function of the whole brain. Simply put, brain death constitutes the death of the patient, whether or not other bodily functions such as breathing and cardiac function can be maintained artificially. The term *brain death*, used as a means to separate neurological death from death via cardiac arrest, was defined, in part, as a means of helping to identify potential organ donors whose cardiac and other functions may need to be maintained for the sake of organ procurement (Troug and Robinson 2003; Truog and Miller 2008). Because "the dead donor rule" requires that organ procurement cannot be the cause of the patient's death, a clarified notion of neurological death was necessary to determine the conditions under which organs can be procured despite the continuation of mechanical interventions intended to preserve perfusion of the organs until they can be harvested (Truog and Miller 2008; Sade 2014). Given that persons who have been declared dead according to neurological criteria are in fact dead, there is no legal obligation to continue to maintain their organ function via artificial means, regardless of the desires of the deceased's family. However, few people understand the criteria for neurological death. Most in the general public confuse brain death with PVS and do not understand that the person declared brain dead can never regain any form of neurological function (Truog and Miller 2008; Caplan et al. 2014).

Recent cases have fostered further confusion in the public sphere concerning this form of death. In the winter of 2013, 13-year-old Jahi McMath suffered brain death due to oxygen deprivation during an operation to remove her tonsils and trim her palate. Her family refused to accept her death and insisted that their daughter remain on respiratory and cardiac support. The hospital initially complied with this request, which reinforced the family's view that their daughter was not dead and that her life was being maintained on life support. The family sued Children's Hospital and Research Center in Oakland, California, contending that removing Jahi from mechanical support would result in her "death," despite the fact that the coroner had already issued a death certificate (Gostin 2014). The district court of San Francisco ordered a stay that required the hospital to continue treatment until a trial could be held. Ultimately, the court ruled that if the family could find a facility willing to admit the girl and perform the tracheotomy necessary to maintain her in her current state, Jahi would be transferred at the family's own risk. The family eventually moved her to an undisclosed facility in New Jersey, one of two states (the other being New York) that permit religious exceptions to the Uniform Declaration of Death. As of this writing Jahi McMath remains on mechanical support.

SUMMARY

The questions concerning death, dying, and the law seem to revolve in large part around the high-profile cases that bring the questions to public consciousness. Even questions that appear to be settled, such as the right to treatment withdrawal, the status of nutrition and hydration as medical treatment, and the definition of death, remain open to debate and will likely face future court and legislative challenges. PAS, in particular, will likely expand to additional states within the next decade.

Many jurisdictions are encouraging their citizens to identify a medical proxy and discuss their desires concerning end-of-life treatment with their loved ones. Legislation concerning the right of institutions to refuse to deliver ineffective treatment is also becoming increasingly attractive in some places, with several states considering bills to limit physician and institutional obligations to follow the mandates of family members when continued treatment is deemed to be medically ineffective and/or counterindicated. Thus questions concerning death, dying, and the law are continuingly evolving and seemingly constantly dependent on the individual cases that raise new concerns in the public imagination.

SUMMARY KEY POINTS

- The evolution of legal decisions regarding death and dying has been shaped by cases that have garnered widespread media and societal interest.
- Legislative actions have sought to prevent legal controversies by establishing procedures to be followed when a patient lacks the capacity to make treatment decisions regarding end-of-life care.
- There is a growing trend toward identifying surrogate decision makers for end-of-life care decisions, and these decision makers commonly utilize a substituted judgment model.
- Many jurisdictions are recognizing the right of a health-care provider to refuse to provide treatment that will be medically ineffective, even if such treatment is desired by the patient or a surrogate decision maker.
- The "right-to-die" movement has made significant gains in the last 20 years, culminating in the legalization of physician-assisted suicide in five of the United States.

REFERENCES

Act for the Relief of the Parents of Theresa Marie Schiavo. 2005 (Public Law 109-3).

Advanced Directives Act, TEX HS. Code Ann. § 166.046 (1999).

Angell M. 1993. The legacy of Karen Ann Quinlan. *Trends in Health Care, Law, and Ethics* 8:17–19.

Baxter v. Montana, 224 P.3d 1211 (2009).

Beauchamps T and J Childress. 2009. *The Principles of Biomedical Ethics*. Oxford: Oxford University Press.

Boudreau JD and M Somerville. 2013. Euthanasia is not medical treatment. *British Medical Bulletin* 106:45–66.

Canterbury v. Spence, 409 U.S. 1064, 93 S. Ct. 560 (1972).

Cantor NL. 1977. Quinlan, privacy, and the handling of incompetent dying patients. *Rutgers Law Review* 30:243–266.

Cantor NL and GC Thomas. 2000. The legal bounds of physician conduct hastening death. *Rutgers Law Review* 48:83–173.

Caplan A, DCL Magnus, and BS Wilfond. 2014. Accepting brain death. *New England Journal of Medicine* 370:891–894.

Cawthon E. 2004. *Medicine on Trial: A Sourcebook with Cases, Laws, and Documents*. Santa Barbara, CA: ABC CLIO.

Cowart D and R Burt. 1998. Confronting death: Who chooses, who controls. *Hastings Center Report* 28:14–24.

Cruzan v. Director, Missouri Department of Health, 497 U.S. 261 (1990).

de Graeff A and M Dean. 2007. Palliative sedation therapy in the last weeks of life: A literature review and recommendations for standards. *Journal of Palliative Medicine* 10:67–85.

Filene P. 1998. *In the Arms of Others: A Cultural History of the Right to Die in America*. Chicago: Ivan R. Dee.

Fleischman AR. 1998. Commentary: Ethical issues in pediatric pain management and terminal sedation. *Journal of Pain and Symptom Management* 15:260–261.

Fohr S. 1998. The double effect of pain medication: Separating myth from reality. *Journal of Palliative Medicine* 1:315–328.

Gomez CF. 1991. *Regulating Death: Euthanasia and the Case of the Netherlands*. New York: New York Free Press.

Gostin L. 2014. Legal and ethical responsibilities following brain death: The McMath and Munoz Cases. *JAMA* 311:903–904.

Grisso T and PS Appelbaum. 1998. *Assessing Competence to Consent to Treatment*. New York: Oxford University Press.

Hains CA and NJ Hulbert-Williams. 2013. Attitudes toward euthanasia and physician-assisted suicide: A study of the multivariate effects of healthcare training, patient characteristics, religion and locus of control. *Journal of Medical Ethics* 39:713–716.

Kliever LD. 1989. *Dax's Case: Essays in Medical Ethics and Human Meaning*. Dallas, TX: Southern Methodist University Press.

Laureys S, A Owen, and N Schiff. 2004. Brain function in coma, vegetative states, and related disorders. *Lancet Neurology* 3:537–546.

National Conference of Commissioners on Uniform State Laws. 1993. *Uniform Health-Care Decisions Act*. http://www.uniformlaws.org/shared/docs/health%20care%20decisions/uhcda_final_93.pdf, accessed July 20, 2015.

Omipidam BA. 2013. Palliative care: An alternative to euthanasia. *BMJ Supportive and Palliative Care* 3:229.

Oregon Death with Dignity Act, Public Law 127.800–995 (1994).

Oregon Public Health Division. 2015. *Oregon's Death with Dignity Act—2014*. http://public.Health.Oregon.gov/ProviderPartnerResources/EvaluationResearch/DeathwithDignityAct/Documents/year17.Pdf, accessed July 20, 2015.

Quill T and I Byock I. 2000. Responding to intractable terminal suffering: The tole of terminal sedation and voluntary refusal of food and fluids. *Annals of Internal Medicine* 132:408–414.

Quill TE, B Lo, and D Brock. 1997. Palliative options of last resort: A comparison of voluntarily stopping eating and drinking, terminal sedation, physician-assisted suicide, and voluntary active euthanasia. *JAMA* 278:2099–2104.

Rubin SB. 1998. *When Doctors Say No: The Battleground of Medical Futility*. Bloomington: Indiana University Press.

Sade R. 2014. Consequences of the dead donor rule. *Annals of Thoracic Surgery* 97:1131–1132.

Strasser M. 1995. Incompetents and the right to die: In search of consistent meaningful standards. *Kentucky Law Journal* 83:733–799.

Trice-Loggers E, H Starks, M Shannon-Dudley et al. 2013. Implementing a death with dignity program at a comprehensive cancer center. *New England Journal of Medicine* 368:1417–1424.

Truog R and F Miller. 2008. The dead donor rule and organ transplantation. *New England Journal of Medicine* 359:674–675.

Truog R and W Robinson. 2003. Role of brain death and the dead-donor rule in the ethics of organ transplantation. *Critical Care Medicine* 31:2391–2396.

Vacco v. Quill, 521 U.S. 793 (1997).

Van Norman G. 2014. Physician aid-in-dying: Cautionary words. *Current Opinion in Anaesthesiology* 27:177–182.

Washington v. Glucksberg, 521 U.S. 702 (1997).

Washington State Department of Health. 2009. *Release of Information Regarding the Death with Dignity Act.* http://www.Doh.Wa.gov/portals/1/Documents/5300/DWDADataRelease.Pdf, accessed July 20, 2015.

PART 5

Family Law and Domestic Relations

STEPHEN B. BILLICK AND BRADLEY W. FREEMAN

38

Role of the psychiatric evaluator in child custody disputes

STEVEN J. CIRIC AND STEPHEN B. BILLICK

INTRODUCTION

The role of the psychiatric evaluator in child custody cases is challenging and complex. There is high demand for competent psychiatric evaluators, given a substantial divorce rate in the United States, custody disputes arising between unmarried parties, and the frequency of litigation. Figures from the National Center for Health Statistics suggest a divorce rate above 50%, citing 3.6 divorces and annulments versus 6.8 marriages per 1000 population (Centers for Disease Control and Prevention 2014). The high number of divorces and separations affects more than one million children each year, and approximately 10% of divorces involve litigation over custody or visitation (Bernet 2002). Conflicts between unmarried parties include cohabiting, single, and noncustodial biological parents; grandparents; and the impact of reproductive technologies, surrogate childbearing, and DNA testing for paternity.

GOAL OF CHILD CUSTODY EVALUATIONS

The overall child custody goal for children in separation and divorce is to try to achieve 50%/50% or the optimal degree with their parental figures of attachment. When not initially possible, the evaluator should recommend approaches toward this goal. Child custody recommendations should never be punitive but made in the best interests of the child, e.g., supervised visitation. From the child psychiatric perspective, helping an inadequate or harmful parent to develop healthy interaction with both the children and the custodial parent is the ultimate goal, whenever possible.

IMPACT OF DIVORCE ON CHILDREN

The psychological impact of divorce on both children and parents can be far-reaching, so that a competent and thoughtful child custody evaluation may diminish future ill effects. While the divorce process on children is not automatically pathogenic, and most controlled research underscores the resilience of most children to "bounce back" from the stress of divorce (Emery and Coiro 1995; Hetherington and Stanley-Hagan 1999), other evidence possibly points to a greater risk for psychological problems. For instance, Wallerstein et al. (2000) cited national studies that demonstrate children from divorced families have more depression, learning, and interpersonal problems, and utilize more mental health services into adulthood.

Reanalyzing three decades of data from the New York Longitudinal Study of Chess et al. (1983), Shaw et al. (1993) conducted a prospective examination of parental functioning and children's adjustment *before* divorce, and found no consistent differences between children from to-be-divorced and always-married families. However, they did find a consistent predictor of the children's poor adjustment following divorce was parental conflict prior to divorce. Boys showed more post-divorce behavioral difficulties than girls, which was consistent with prior research (e.g., Zaslow 1988; Wallerstein 1991). The authors suggested this might involve the boys' loss of daily contact with their fathers. Wallerstein (1991) suggested the observed gender difference may involve a "sleeper effect" for girls, who go on to experience interpersonal problems in young adulthood. Emery et al. (2005), citing a meta-analysis in 1999 by Amato and Gilbreth, suggested the amount of contact between child and nonresident father is a poor predictor of the child's psychological well-being, and a father's payment of child support has greater impact. Lahey et al. (1988) reported a significantly higher incidence of parental Antisocial Personality Disorder in divorced families with boys who developed conduct disorder, giving rise to the consideration of a genetic vulnerability contributing to both parental marital discord as well as post-divorce maladjustment in the child. This viewpoint was supported in subsequent research (Jocklin et al. 1996).

The adverse effects of divorce on children have been discussed extensively by Wallerstein and Kelly (1980) and

Wallerstein et al. (2000). In 1971, Wallerstein and her colleagues embarked on a nonrandomized, noncontrolled study of 131 children going through separation and divorce with interval assessments between 18 months and 25 years post separation. Half of the children had difficulties during the first year after divorce and prolonged post-divorce maladjustment was associated with high levels of parental discord, parental mental illness, poor pre-divorce parenting, and a custodial parent burdened by emotional, physical, social, or economic stresses. Wallerstein et al. (2000) further observed that many of the post-divorce children from the longitudinal study, now adults, experienced relationship difficulties of their own.

Meta-analysis by Bauserman (2002) found that children in joint physical or legal custody were better adjusted than children in sole-custody settings, comparable to children in intact families. Stover (2013), citing Goldstein et al. (1996), noted that infants and younger children may benefit from more frequent contact with noncustodial parents. Evidence suggests that when a divorce is associated with a move to a less stressful situation, children in divorced families are similar in adjustment to intact families with nondistressed marital relations (Hetherington 1999). Emery et al. (2005) also discussed this "relief hypothesis" following parental separation in high-conflict marriages.

HISTORICAL PERSPECTIVE

Changes in custody decision making have evolved with recognition of the rights of children and women, shifting legal emphasis toward individual rights and equal protection, and given research in child development and attachment. Derdeyn (1976) wrote that in ancient times, "the father had absolute control over his children and could will or condemn them to death with impunity." For many years in England and the United States, children were considered to be chattels, the property of the father without their own rights (Sadoff and Billick 1981; Solnit and Schetky 1986).

The tender years

Following the British Act of 1839 advanced by Thomas Noon Talfourd, the "tender years doctrine" became the primary standard for determining child custody, concurrent with the women's rights movement of the late nineteenth and early twentieth centuries. This doctrine presumes a unique and optimal relationship between mothers and infants, consistent with infant attachment and psychoanalytic theory (Kelly 1994). Sadoff and Billick (1981) discussed how the doctrine introduced the psychiatrist and psychologist into the domestic relations court to present expert testimony regarding outcomes of parent–child relationships and child development. The "tender years doctrine" eventually expanded to include all children and led to mothers gaining custody in greater proportion to fathers.

The best interests of the child

The "best interests of the child" standard, which guides most custody decisions today, arose with increasing recognition of the rights of children and changing judicial attitudes. In the landmark case of *Painter v. Bannister* (1966), the Iowa Supreme Court held in a custody dispute between a child's father and maternal grandparents that "the primary consideration is the best interest of the child." The justices determined that the child, whose Iowa-born mother had died in a car accident, was to remain in the custody of his stable and Midwestern grandparents rather than return to his remarried, California-born, and "Bohemian" father. In *Watts v. Watts* (1973), a New York State Family Court held that maternal preferred custody statutes (embodiments of the "tender years doctrine") violated fathers' equal protection rights under the Fourteenth Amendment (Kelly 1994).

The model Uniform Marriage and Divorce Act, proposed by the American Bar Association in 1970, further established the "best interests of the child" standard as well as consideration of continuity in parenting, the quality of the parent–child relationships, the physical and emotional health of all parties involved, and a child's wishes if he or she is deemed to be of sufficient age and capacity to form an intelligent preference.

Goldstein et al. (1979) critiqued the "best interests" standard and suggested the less sanguine language of "least detrimental alternative" as a more realistic standard that appreciates the inevitable harm to a child in any divorce. Another criticism is that the standard is too vague, subjective, and prone to judicial bias and acrimonious litigation. Concern that the standard may force women to trade off spousal and child support to secure custody has not been demonstrated in research (Kelly 1994).

The "best interests" standard places the rights of the child above the rights of parents in custody determinations, and should theoretically eliminate judicial discrimination on the basis of a proposed custodian's gender, sexual orientation, and physical or psychiatric disability (to the extent that these factors do not bear on the individual's relationship to and ability to care for the child). Although potential for bias always exists, as in the study by Raub et al. (2013) suggesting court decisions around custody and visitation in high-conflict divorce correlate to parental income, courts rely ever more on psychological factors, and the "best interests" standard allows judges more flexibility.

WHEN AND HOW PSYCHIATRY BECOMES INVOLVED IN CUSTODY DISPUTES

Sources of requests for evaluations

The psychiatric evaluator in the separation/divorce process may be asked to give opinions on custody, visitation, and psychiatric treatment needs of parents or children. Waller and Daniel (2005) elucidated factors that may commonly prompt a custody evaluation, including sexual or physical

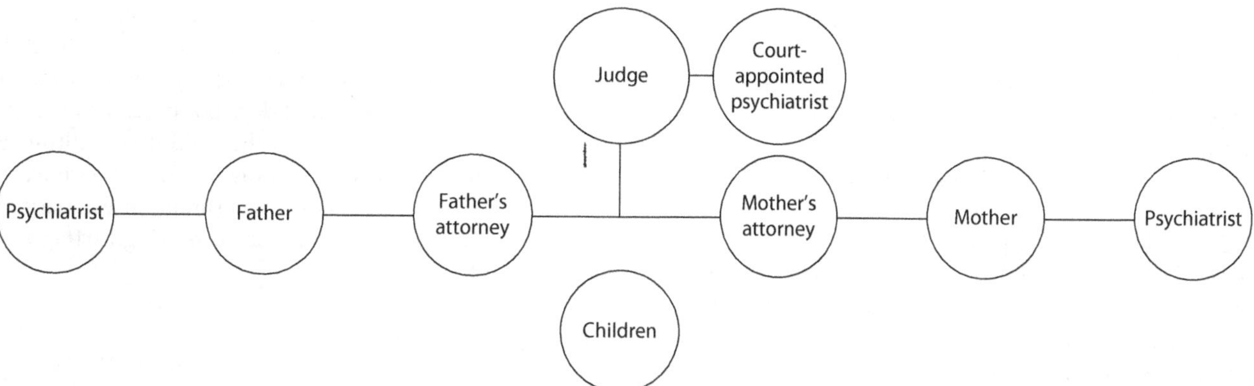

Figure 38.1 Traditional view.

abuse allegations, questions of parental fitness (e.g., mental illness or substance use), parental conflict, alienation issues, domestic violence, relocation, remarriage, parental sexual orientation, and grandparent or adoption issues.

An evaluator may respond to requests from both parties for a clinical consultation only, in an effort to reach a parenting agreement. Parents who favor the consultation room over the courtroom may be more amenable to reaching a mutual agreement (Levy 1985a), and courts in general acquiesce to parental agreement: the parents consent and the state assents (Despert 1953).

When only one party to a custody dispute pursues a psychiatric evaluation, the evaluator should request to interview both parties involved, though the other parent might be uncooperative out of fear the psychiatrist is biased. The evaluator should be aware of pressures for a favorable decision and remain "child-centered and child-oriented" rather than parentally driven, consistent with training in child and adolescent psychiatry.

When the court orders an independent evaluation, or when two opposing attorneys agree on one psychiatric evaluator, parents may be less amenable to a mutual decision, but it is easier for the psychiatrist to maintain parental neutrality, resist adversarial pressures, and represent the "best interests of the child" (see Figure 38.1).

A psychiatric evaluator may also be retained by a *guardian ad litem*, an attorney appointed by the court to represent the child and not one parent or the other. Judges and parents' lawyers sometimes pay more attention to parental concerns, so an active *guardian ad litem* is in the best position to utilize the psychiatrist's recommendations in court to advocate for the child's "best interests" (see Figure 38.2).

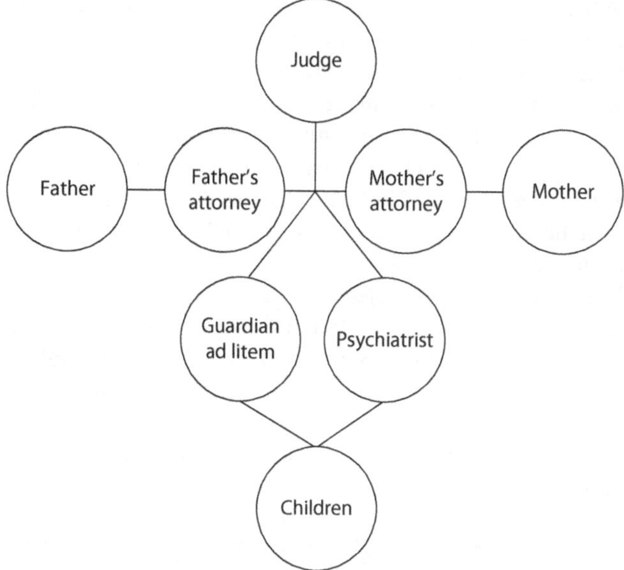

Figure 38.2 Preferred situation.

Mediation

Divorce mediation, an alternative to acrimonious and costly litigation, is a forum where all parties work together to reach mutual resolution (Ruman and Lamm 1985). Although the psychiatrist often has the same advantages as when providing clinical consultation, mediation is a legal process and usually involves one attorney and one psychiatric evaluator. Both are expected to be impartial to the needs of the parents, and the psychiatrist, of course, maintains the position of child advocate. California's Code of Civil Procedure (1984) marked the first state ruling mandating mediation attempts to resolve custody decisions before proceeding to litigation, and the federal government (e.g., Alternative Dispute Resolution Act of 1998) and other states subsequently adopted similar procedures. Mediation decreases burden on the judicial system and may be more sensitive to the emotional needs of parents and children. Dillon and Emery (1996) surveyed parents nine years after random assignment to mediation or litigation. The mediated families saw increased visitation, interparental communication, and noncustodial parent involvement. Emery et al. (1994) followed families for 1 year after similar random assignment and found fathers were more satisfied with mediation and more likely to cooperate with child support payments. Mothers were more satisfied with litigation, noting over 90% of the litigated custody cases ended in sole maternal custody. Maccoby and Mnookin's (1992) study of about 2000 divorcing California families found mandatory mediation to result in slightly higher instances of joint custody, though mediators were actively making this recommendation. In contrast,

Reynolds et al. (2007) analyzed all mandatory mediation outcomes in a North Carolina judicial district in 2002 and found no increase in the incidence of joint physical custody relative to litigation; in fact, mothers received sole custody more often. The authors suggested that mediators in North Carolina followed a best practice of refraining from a dual role of rendering custody recommendations to the court when mediation failed, and the mediation proceedings were confidential and privileged. Krauss and Sales (2000) commented that while some states require mediation efforts or favor joint custody, neither has been confirmed by empirical research to improve the outcomes of divorce for children and parents.

Visitation

When joint custody is not possible, visitation becomes especially important to minimize the child's sense of loss from divorce and encourage the natural affectionate bonds with both parents. Some researchers have suggested frequent overnight visitation with a nonresidential parent may result in attachment insecurity with the residential parent (Tornello et al. 2013), but this remains controversial. Warshak (2014) argues that valid and reliable research favors allowing children under 4 years old to be cared for at night by each parent, without jeopardizing the children's development. However, when visitation decisions are complicated by accusations of abuse or neglect, the psychiatric evaluator has the additional responsibility of assessing the validity and extent of the allegations, and considering restriction (e.g., daytime only or supervised) or denial of visitation when doing so would be in the child's best interests.

CONDUCTING THE PSYCHIATRIC EVALUATION

Training

In order to conduct a thorough and competent child custody evaluation, adequate training, ideally in child psychiatry and forensic subspecialty fellowships, is critical. The American Psychiatric Association (APA 1982) has recommended that the general psychiatrist undertaking custody evaluations consult with a child psychiatrist, when available, and that novice evaluators first sit in on several child custody cases to observe the process thoroughly before beginning their own evaluations. The psychiatrist should have knowledge of basic family law, including statutes and relevant case law in the jurisdiction of the evaluation (e.g., legal presumption in favor of joint custody) (AACAP 1997). Provided adequate training, any psychiatrist doing a competent and thorough psychiatric child custody evaluation, regardless of the source of payment, should arrive basically at the same final decision.

Role as evaluator

Solnit and Schetky (1986) reminded that the psychiatrist must always maintain the role of advocate for the child's best interests, parental neutrality, and not slip into role of therapist for a given party. As child advocate objectively applying the examination data to the appropriate legal standard, the forensic psychiatrist does not necessarily support what the child *wants*, but what the child *needs*. Ultimately, legal decisions of custody are always made by the court. The evaluator must try to conduct as prompt an evaluation as possible, as protracted evaluations can bring further stress on the child.

The interviews

A large part of the psychiatric evaluation in child custody cases consists of a series of interviews gathering careful parental and child histories from these primary sources. The evaluator first obtains a signed waiver of confidentiality from all parties to be interviewed, distinguishing the forensic evaluation from the psychiatrist's work of therapy, as it may become necessary to disclose findings to opposing attorneys and in court. Usually interviews include each parent individually, each child alone, the child with each parent individually, and sometimes the parents together without the child, the child together with both parents, or the child with his or her siblings. Conducting so many interviews can be time consuming, and the use of a team approach has been advocated (Ash and Guyer 1984; Weiner et al. 1985), but this is not always possible and many psychiatrists do successfully conduct the evaluation alone.

The examination

According to the American Psychiatric Association (1982), there are three major questions that should be addressed during the course of the evaluation:

1. What is the quality of the reciprocal attachment between parent and child?
2. What are the child's needs and the adults' parenting capacities?
3. What are the relevant family dynamics at play?

Levy (1985a) added a fourth primary question: What is the child's preference, if any, for custody?

To address these questions, the evaluator enquires about the extent of involvement each adult has with the child, directly observes interactions of parent with child, and attempts to establish who has the major role of "psychological parent" for the child (Goldstein et al. 1979; APA 1982). This person may not be the genetic parent. Indeed, current research in attachment theory suggests a child's early ties to a primary caregiver who is not the genetic parent result in a superior biological bond between that caregiver and child. Also, the role of "psychological parent" is usually shared by more than one person, for example, both genetic parents or one genetic parent and a step-parent or grandparent. The evaluator may use projective tests, such as drawings, or pose hypothetical questions to the child, to help determine whom the child relies on most and in what circumstances.

The evaluator may with great sensitivity ask the child directly about a preference for custody, but the reliability of the child's answer is age related. A younger child may express the preference of a parent that he or she is afraid of alienating, rather than express his or her own preference. Adolescent children are more capable of expressing their true desires, but they too may fear hurting the feelings of the parent not chosen. AACAP (1997) wrote that judges may give more weight to a stated preference when the child is 12 years of age or older, and some states actually require the evaluator to ask about a child's preference. Billick (1986) indicated the average 12-year-old has achieved the Piagetian stage of concrete operations and Kohlberg's stage of conventional morality, and suggested juveniles between the ages of 11 and 14 years should be accorded greater latitude in formulating decisions. One may also choose to infer the child's preference through observations.

The evaluator should assess parenting capacities in relation to the developmental needs of the child, including the capacity to provide support and nurturing, and allow appropriate separation and individuation. When joint custody is not possible and there is no clear-cut distinction as to who has the better parenting skills, the evaluator may be forced to make a value judgement, but must remain focused only on the child's development and avoid being swayed by irrelevant biases from attorneys or from within oneself, for example, given a nongenetic, mentally ill, or homosexual parent.

The psychiatrist also must analyze family dynamics and parental motives for seeking custody (e.g., anger, depression, revenge) as separate from parenting issues. The evaluator should also assess the potential custodial parent's ability to promote the relationship of the child with the noncustodial parent, which would favor a positive post-divorce outcome for the child. Finally, the evaluator should be aware of the child's potential involvement in family dynamics. A child may manipulate and influence his or her parents' behavior out of a wish for reunion.

The American Academy of Child and Adolescent Psychiatry (AACAP) *Practice Parameters for Child Custody Evaluation* (1997) detailed important examination factors, including the presence of parental alienation (i.e., where the child has notable, yet irrational, negative feelings toward one parent), each parent's parenting and disciplinary styles, parental physical and psychiatric health, finances, and each parent's family and marital history. The evaluator should explore allegations parents make against each other, but also note whether a parent spends most of the session attacking the other parent at the expense of focusing on the child.

The psychiatric evaluator should ensure the conditions of interviews are optimal, including scheduling of sufficient time for a thorough evaluation and breaks; the presence of attorneys, if required, without interference or uninvited participation; and participation of parents when evaluating a child. AACAP's *Practice Parameter for Child and Adolescent Forensic Evaluations* (2011) suggests the initial participation of a parent is helpful to provide historical information, allow for observation of parent–child interaction, and encourage the child's cooperation, after which it is beneficial to evaluate the child alone.

Collateral sources of information

When conducting the psychiatric evaluation, one may also use a variety of other sources of information, in addition to the previously described interviews. Home visits, where the evaluator can observe the behavior of the child and parents in a naturalistic setting, can be very informative and strikingly differ from the formal office interview setting. Both attorneys involved in the custody battle might have useful information. Other secondary sources of information include teachers, grandparents, pediatricians, or other mental health professionals working with the child or parents. The evaluator, however, should clearly document whether information is from secondary sources or direct observation, as the courts usually place more confidence in primary sources of clinical data.

Confidentiality issues

Malmquist (1994) examined the myriad and diverse ways in which courts regard the issue of confidentiality in custody disputes where one or both parents (or the child) have been, or are presently, in psychiatric treatment. For example, in some jurisdictions, simply entering into a custody dispute essentially puts a party's mental health at issue and automatically waives privilege. In other instances, the court remains guided by the best interests of the child standard and looks to a *guardian ad litem* or independent psychiatric expert to assess whether particular treatment records contain material potentially harmful to the child. Still other courts waive doctor–patient privilege only in cases where there is an allegation of parental unfitness, or rely on an independent psychiatric examination without delving into private treatment records. In the case of *In re Lifschutz* (1970), Malmquist noted the California Supreme Court held "the psychotherapist could be held to answer questions *directly relevant* to the subject of the suit (emphasis added)." Malmquist raised the impractical scenario of clinicians routinely providing quasi-*Miranda*-type informed consent warnings before treating patients who are, or may become, parents, and recommended the disclosure of private treatment records is limited to instances of alleged parental unfitness where the records sought bear directly on parental competency rather than the best interests standard.

The Maryland Court of Appeals, in *Laznovsky v. Laznovsky* (2000), upheld a parent's right to assert doctor–patient privilege in a child custody dispute, noting a constitutional right of privacy and the public policy benefit of protecting the psychotherapeutic process (Caracansi and Billick 2000). However, the court left open the possibility for family court judges to make exceptions in the case of a parent who claims fitness "without more" (albeit without clarifying the meaning of "without more" or the standard for waiver of privilege).

Children in therapy

This is a potentially wonderful source of additional material about the child. An adept therapist may be willing and able to testify on behalf of the child's best interests, though many are not comfortable with this. Above all, every attempt should be made to avoid disruption of the child's psychological support system and treatment.

Psychological testing

The psychiatrist may wish to consult with a psychologist who is experienced and capable in testing procedures in child custody disputes. AACAP (1997) suggested psychological testing might be most useful when the psychiatric health of a parent or child is a legitimate issue. The Minnesota Multiphasic Personality Inventory-2 (MMPI-2) is considered the most commonly used assessment instrument in the evaluation of child custody litigants (Ackerman and Ackerman 1997; Strong et al. 1999). Medoff (1999) cautioned that clinically significant elevations on MMPI-2 validity scales might indicate underlying psychopathology or empirically associated personality characteristics (e.g., neurotic defensiveness, unrealistic self-image, excessive reliance upon denial), and should not necessarily be explained away by common sense that parents want to present themselves in the best possible light when faced with custody matters. Consistent with normative data for the MMPI-2 in child custody litigation (e.g., Bathurst et al. 1997), Strong et al. (1999) described a method of data analysis that may help distinguish between deliberate attempts to create a positive social image (impression management) and the unintentional concealment of symptoms and areas of maladjustment (self-deceptive positivity).

Billick and Jackson (2007) reviewed psychological testing as an adjunct to the clinical evaluation of parents in child custody cases and favored the MMPI-2 given the high reliability of its validity and clinical scales. The authors noted the Hare Psychopathy Check List-Revised Second Edition (PCL-R) is the superior standard when assessing for antisocial personality defects, but is less practical to administer and importantly lacks validity scales.

Testing data should be used as an adjunct to the comprehensive clinical and forensic evaluation, and not be relied upon in a rote fashion when offering opinions about parental fitness and child custody. Although rating scales have been suggested to aid in the assessment of custody, these are not widely accepted as determinative and should also not be relied upon in making ultimate custody recommendations. Krauss and Sales (2000) cautioned that no actuarial prediction of a child's best interests is possible given the ambiguity of the standard and lack of operationalized outcome variables. Emery et al. (2005) recommended the use of these instruments should be limited to research.

Referrals for treatment

As part of the psychiatric evaluation in child custody cases, the evaluator is also usually obliged to assess the need for psychiatric treatment for parties involved. This is to help assure a favorable adjustment by the child after divorce. Referrals should be made to other therapists to keep the evaluator's role distinct, and treatment recommendations should be realistic.

MAKING RECOMMENDATIONS

The report

Usually the psychiatric evaluator is requested to prepare a report. The APA guidelines (1982) reminded that the content is not confidential and may be used as evidence in court. The report should clearly answer the basic questions addressed in the custody case, including description of the reciprocal attachment between parent and child, the child's needs and the adults' parenting capacities, and the relevant family dynamics. The evaluator should clearly state a recommendation for custody that the evidence in the report should decidedly support. In those cases where the evaluator finds it impossible to make a firm recommendation, he or she should state this and perhaps explore the advantages and disadvantages of different decisions, although this might be less useful to the court. The report should be free of professional jargon and theoretical discourse, though there may be need to discuss particular psychiatric diagnoses when they apply to an involved party and have an impact on the child.

Custody recommendation

Custody may be parsed into *legal* custody, relating to the rights and obligations to make major life decisions for the child, such as choice of school or medical care, and *physical* custody, relating to the rights of the custodian with whom the child resides. Custody may further be categorized as *primary, joint*, or *sole*, relating to the relative allocation of these rights to each custodian (or amount of time the child resides with the custodian).

When formulating an opinion on custody, it is recommended that joint custody be the first considered disposition. Several authors (Galper 1978; Ilfeld et al. 1982; Luepnitz 1982; Ware 1982) have written about the added benefits joint custody may provide. Wallerstein and Kelly (1980) emphasized the importance of a continuing relationship with both parents in helping children recover from post-divorce trauma. Less post-divorce conflict between parents in many ways is in the best interests of the child. The evaluator can emphasize to parents during the evaluation process that they will be brought together again and again in the future through their children at birthdays, graduations, confirmations, bar mitzvahs, or later, at similar events with grandchildren. Parents must be agreeable and capable of such negotiation, however, and when one parent significantly undermines the other parent, joint custody may not be in the best interests of the child. Krauss and Sales (2000) cited various studies that report on the exacerbation of adjustment problems for children with high-conflict parents where continued contact between parents was necessitated by joint custody arrangements.

The most common alternative to joint custody is single custody by one parent with visitation rights for the other parent. The evaluator usually considers the best fit between parent and child, but sometimes may be forced to choose the least harmful fit. When custody disputes are between a genetic (sometimes referred to as "biological") parent and a nongenetic parental figure, legal precedent has dictated the genetic parent has the right to custody unless proven unfit, despite research demonstrating that attachment behavior is also "biological." The "best interests" standard allows for questioning of this precedent for genetics, and the evaluator may wish to take advantage of this flexibility when it would benefit the child.

A review of visitation and custody state statutes in *Family Law Quarterly* (2013a) shows that, in some jurisdictions, statutes guide the courts to consider if the party claiming visitation or custody rights is a "psychological parent," stands "in loco parentis," or has an "equitable," "de facto," or "substantial" parental relationship with the child. Some states do not necessarily require a showing that a parent is unfit in order for the court to consider application by another party, whereas other states will tend to favor the "superior rights of natural parent," so that once a natural parent is deemed fit, the "custody is decided" (e.g., *Moore v. Moore* 1989, citing *Kay v. Rowland* 1985). In any case, the forensic psychiatrist must remain informed of all relevant statutes, in order to best apply data from the evaluation to the local standards, consistent with the four-step conceptual framework for forensic psychiatric practice advanced in this textbook.

Custody decisions can become more complicated in disputes between the state and a parent where allegations of abuse or neglect exist, given conflict between parents' rights and the state's responsibility to protect the child. The APA (1982) has cautioned custody evaluators involved in such cases to keep focus on the child's rights and needs, as opposed to addressing possible termination of parental rights.

Reynolds et al. (2007) discussed the "approximation rule" to resolve custody disputes (advanced by the American Law Institute in *Principles of the Law of Family Dissolution: Analysis and Recommendations*, 2002), by which judges allocate custody rights based on the approximate amount of time each parent spent taking care of the children before the divorce, as a concrete alternative to the indeterminate "best interests" standard. Obvious criticism is that this alternative standard is overly concrete, unfairly penalizes a breadwinner parent who had less contact with a child due to work obligations, and fundamentally favors an historical parenting arrangement without regard for whether this is in the best interests of the child.

Potential pitfalls

When making recommendations, evaluators need to be consciously aware of personal biases and remember that parents' characters, behaviors, and lifestyles are theoretically relevant only insofar as they affect the child. There is no empirical evidence that parental values affect post-divorce child adjustment, and evaluating parenting values or fundamental religious beliefs may represent an intrusion into constitutionally protected freedoms (Krauss and Sales 2000). Nevertheless, a few states have child custody laws that include consideration of the parents' "moral character" (Emery et al. 2005). The evaluator needs to choose the best or least disadvantageous custody option existing at the time of the evaluation, rather than focus on future possibilities. The evaluator should also try to be clinically flexible regarding alternative living arrangements for custody, for example, with a single parent, gay parent, or father versus mother. Last, it is possible in certain cases to make custody recommendations after having interviewed only one parent (e.g., when one parent refuses to be interviewed), though this is not ideal. AACAP *Practice Parameters* (2011) and the American Academy of Psychiatry and the Law *Ethics Guidelines for the Practice of Forensic Psychiatry* (1987, rev.1995, rev.2005) suggest, if this situation is unavoidable, being clear as to supporting data and qualifying expert opinions rendered without an interview. It is important to note that guidelines are "generally accepted" but are not intended to be rigid. It is important to note why this present evaluation is at variance and how "bias" was avoided in maintaining the "best interests of the child." A recommendation can be made if one can assume that the other parent is normal, and there is still compelling reason to recommend sole custody to the parent interviewed based on positive evidence from the child and the evaluation. It is also possible sometimes to infer aspects of the nonparticipating parent from the children's descriptions. Particularly with older children, they may be reliable reporters of pathology or destructive parenting in the nonparticipating parent.

Informing the parties involved

After making a recommendation and completing the written report, the evaluator may help to diffuse parental disappointment or anger by holding an interpretative interview with the parents (and possibly the attorneys) where the evaluator reviews the reasons behind the custody recommendation. The evaluator should also explain the recommendation to the child. During the interpretative interview, the evaluator can help the parents understand the reasons for the recommendation and may help them come to a negotiated agreement on custody. Ash and Guyer (1986) reported that in 71% of the cases, after hearing the evaluator's recommendation, parties either stopped litigation or negotiated an agreement. For example, the party for whom custody is not recommended may concede to this decision in exchange for a concession by the other party in a different area of dispute.

Testifying in court

This is not necessary in most cases. Ash and Guyer (1984, 1986) found evaluators were asked to testify in court in only 4%–5% of the cases. When the evaluator is called to testify in court, he or she should prepare by first discussing the recommendation and how it will be presented in court with the *guardian ad litem* or attorneys. One must prepare for the pressures of cross-examination, avoid being swayed by extraneous information, and attempt to testify only on what is relevant to the child's best interests. The best preparation for court is to have a firm recommendation and evidence that clearly supports that recommendation. Lawyers are trained and educated to manipulate, distort, confuse, and obfuscate on cross-examination. The psychiatrist needs to clarify, document, and be logical.

SPECIAL ISSUES IN CHILD CUSTODY DISPUTES

Joint custody and father custody

Levy (1985b) has advocated that fathers and mothers be considered equally for custody and has questioned whether sexism exists in child custody decision making. Ploscowe et al. (1973) have estimated the mother gains sole custody in 80% of cases, the father in 10%, and joint custody occurs in 10% of cases. Ash and Guyer (1984) cited in a random sample of cases from the local jurisdiction that fathers are granted custody in only 5% of cases. Meyer and Garasky (1993) suggested the figure for paternal custody might be closer to 15% based on survey and census data. Kelly (1994) reviewed that there has been a trend toward joint legal custody, and the most common arrangement in the United States is joint *legal* custody with sole maternal *physical* custody, usually with visitation by the other parent.

In the atmosphere of equal rights protections in the 1970s and 1980s, the provision of joint physical custody became an increasingly popular family court disposition. This shift also sprang from child development research into the importance of children's attachment to their fathers. In 1979, California (which adopted the nation's first "no-fault" divorce law in 1970) enacted the first joint custody statute, to be followed in over 40 states by 1991 (Kelly 1994). Some state laws specify a presumption for joint custody, not simply that it be considered (Derdeyn and Scott 1984). Joint custody has been regarded as a means to reduce the negative impact of divorce on the child, by maintaining the child's contact with both parents. However, AACAP (1997) noted for this arrangement to be successful, it likely requires parents who are psychologically healthy and cooperative. High conflict between divorcing parents, dramatic differences in approaches to discipline, and domestic violence might advise against joint physical custody (Reynolds et al. 2007).

Kelly (1994) noted some feminist groups have responded to the emphasis on joint custody by advancing the concept of a primary caretaker standard. The primary caretaker, usually the mother, spends the most time managing the daily needs of the child. This bears similarity to the "tender years doctrine" and to the "approximation rule" (see above). Kelly wrote that a primary caretaker standard, however, ignores the quality of the parent–child relationship and emotional attachment, in favor of counting childcare hours and concrete behaviors. This clearly does not meet the legally predominant standard of what is purely in the "best interests of the child."

Although it is still not usual, granting sole custody to a father is less uncommon than in the past. Lamb (1997) and Fitzgerald and McCread (1981) have discussed evidence that shows infants are strongly attached to both mother and father by the second half of the first year of life. Levy (1985b) also cited multiple other studies that describe the importance of the father throughout a child's development. An APA resource document on child custody issues indicated that the literature provides some evidence that boys tend to do better in father custody and girls in mother custody, all other factors being equal (Binder 1998).

When conducting a psychiatric evaluation for child custody, it is important to use the same criteria to evaluate men and women when assessing parenting capacities, and to recommend custody to the person who can best meet the child's needs. One should recommend custody to a single male if it is clinically indicated, rather than be moved by a sexist bias to recommend something that would not be in the child's best interests.

Gay and lesbian parents

Binder (1998) estimated that 6 to 14 million children have at least one gay or lesbian parent. Gates (2013) estimated that 37% of lesbian, gay, bisexual, and transgendered (LGBT)-identified adults in the United States have had a child at some point in their lives. In the past, when gay men and lesbian women were involved in child custody cases, they were generally denied custody based solely on their sexual orientation. The past several decades have seen slow changes in the way society (and psychiatry) views gays and lesbians. In 1973, the APA trustees voted to eliminate homosexuality *per se* as a mental disorder. After extensive scientific debate, the members of the APA upheld this decision by referendum in 1974. Since the *Diagnostic and Statistical Manual of Mental Disorders, 3rd edition, revised* (*DSM-III-R*, APA 1987), homosexuality has no longer been classified as a psychiatric disorder of any kind. Also, in *Lawrence v. Texas* (2003), the U.S. Supreme Court made a landmark 6–3 ruling against the sodomy law in Texas and effectively legalized same-sex sexual activity in the United States. Same-sex marriage is now legal in most states, following successful challenges to the 1996 Defense of Marriage Act, including the U.S. Supreme Court's holding in *United States v. Windsor* (2013). Despite these changes, unfortunately, sexual orientation is still a confounding issue in child custody cases today, and some attorneys may contest custody decisions based solely on this issue.

Hutchens and Kirkpatrick (1985) discuss three stereotypes that have led courts to hesitate to grant child custody to gay parents: that gays are psychologically or sexually maladjusted and not mentally fit to raise children; that children raised by gay men or lesbians will grow up to be gay or have gender identity problems; and that children raised by a gay parent will be stigmatized by the custodial parent's sexual orientation. The authors, however, cited numerous psychiatric and psychological studies that scientifically refute all three of these stereotypes, demonstrating that being raised by a gay parent does not compromise child development, and that gays' and lesbians' psychological functioning and parenting skills are not inferior to those of heterosexuals. Freedman (1971) has proposed that gay men and women may actually have better autonomous ego functioning because they were forced to be more independent minded when growing up.

The 1998 APA resource document prepared by the Subcommittee on Child Custody Issues reviewed the relevant literature (Binder 1998) and found no significant differences in parenting between divorced lesbian and heterosexual mothers, and no identifiable differences in the emotional and intellectual development and peer relationships between their children. Also, children of lesbian and gay parents show no statistical increase in the incidence of homosexuality, and there have been no reported cases of pedophilia committed by gay parents or their partners on their children (dispelling a prejudicial fear expressed by some courts). Farr and Patterson (2013) studied heterosexual, gay, and lesbian parents and their adopted children, and found that the quality of parenting behaviors, not family type, accounted for differences in the children's adjustment outcomes.

Hutchens and Kirkpatrick (1985), as well as others (Sadoff and Billick 1981; Herman 1990b), encourage psychiatrists to evaluate gay and lesbian parents the same as any other parent, in order to best ensure that a child custody decision is based on what is in the child's best interests and is not based on prejudice. The same principles of tolerance, objectivity, and neutrality should also apply when the psychiatric evaluator takes into account the rights and needs of youth who are the subjects of custody disputes, including consideration of parental support of the child to develop into a healthy and autonomous LGBT adult (Hulstein 2012).

The mentally ill parent

When evaluating parents who carry a psychiatric diagnosis, one should be aware that such a diagnosis does not automatically mean incompetence as a custodial parent. Herman (1990b) cited examples of psychotic parents who are either capable or incapable custodians. One first evaluates these parents as to their capacity to meet the best interests of the child. In addition, one needs to evaluate the parent's current psychiatric condition, insight, and compliance with and response to treatment. The psychiatric evaluator's recommendations of appropriate treatment for a parent with mental health issues, irrespective of the ultimate custody decision in court, may in the long run benefit both the parent and the children.

The decision for divorce is potentially a product of psychiatric illness. In one case example encountered by one of our authors (SBB), a mother sought divorce during the course of a psychotic depression, and the 14-year-old son told his mother's lawyer that his mother should be hospitalized rather than be divorced. She was, in fact, hospitalized, improved with treatment, and no divorce occurred.

Herman (1990b) noted that both true and false allegations of psychiatric or substance use disorders are common in child custody disputes. The evaluator always needs to verify these diagnoses and not accept them *a priori*. Also, personality-disordered parents, or even delusional parents, might have motives for custody influenced by their pathology, rather than the best interests of their child. Beaver and colleagues (2014) demonstrated a link between psychopathic character traits and negative parenting quality, an intuitive but not previously studied association.

Grandparents and other third parties

National statistics cite that 7.8 million children live in households headed by grandparents or other relatives, and 2.7 million children (or 3% of all U.S. children) are raised by grandparents or relatives (D.C. Child and Family Services Agency 2016). Although grandparent custody is usually a satisfactory arrangement (Schowalter 2000), the legal standpoint on this has varied

The U.S. Supreme Court, in *Troxel et vir. v. Granville* (2000) ruled unconstitutional a Washington State statute permitting visitation by any nonparental third party "at any time" if a court determines such visitation to be in the best interests of the child, noting the statute violated the Fourteenth Amendment Substantive Due Process liberty rights of a custodial mother, Ms. Granville, to make decisions concerning the care, custody, and control of her daughters. The Court cited precedent in a number of cases, including the landmark case *Parham v. J.R.*, 442 U.S. 584 (1979), where the U.S. Supreme Court held that parents should "retain a substantial, if not dominant, role in the decision [to civilly commit a minor], absent a finding of neglect or abuse." The Court also stated that there is a common law tradition to presume parental fitness and that in the case of Ms. Granville, there were no allegations to the contrary. The Court decried that the Washington statute actually weighed the visitation right of the grandparents as more important than "perhaps the oldest of the fundamental liberty interests recognized by this Court."

However, a review of state statutes pertaining to visitation in *Family Law Quarterly* (2013b) revealed that most states view grandparents as having standing to claim visitation rights, and many states also consider claims by step-parents, parents following termination of parental rights or adoption, or any interested party. The review identified that constitutional challenges to grandparent visitation have been made, so that in some jurisdictions visitation may only be imposed on showing that failing to do so would actually be harmful to the child, and is not merely in the child's "best interests" (e.g., *Burnett v. Burnett* 2011).

Allegations of child sexual abuse

Both true and false allegations of child sexual abuse occur in custody battles. The evaluator must be prepared to assess the validity of such allegations and discuss how they affect custody and visitation recommendations. Although Guyer and Ash (1986) reported an incidence for allegations of child sexual abuse of 33% in 400 court-ordered custody evaluations, a study of 9000 families in custody/visitation disputes by Thoennes and Tjaden (1990) yielded a figure of about 2%, replicated by McIntosh and Prinz (1993) who examined 603 family court cases. Thoennes and Tjaden found a similar incidence of false allegations in custody dispute and noncustodial dispute situations, whereas Green and Schetky (1988) emphasized that false allegations of child sexual abuse more commonly arise in the context of a custody battle. Gardner (1987) stated that the majority of children professing sexual abuse in custody situations are actually brainwashed to believe it, as part of the controversial Parental Alienation Syndrome (PAS). PAS was ultimately not included as a mental disorder in the *DSM-5*, because it has never been shown to be both reliable and valid. However, *DSM-5* contains a subtype of Relational Problem V code (not a mental disorder but a focus of clinical attention), *Child Affected by Parental Relationship Distress* (V61.29), which may be a relevant consideration in some custody disputes; and in some cases, the V code of *Child Psychological Abuse* may apply (American Psychiatric Association 2013).

Benedek and Schetky (1985), with a sample of 18 custody dispute cases, found an incidence of 55% for unfounded allegations. However, studies with larger sample sizes yielded more conservative figures. A survey of general child sexual abuse cases reported to a child abuse agency, found that 6% of allegations could not be substantiated (Goodwin et al. 1978). Jones and McGraw (1987) found that 8% of allegations were false, Thoennes and Pearson (1988) 14%, and McGraw and Smith (1992) 16.5%. Penfold (1995) remarked that some authors believe that child sexual abuse may actually be more frequent in divorce (e.g., the stress of the divorce triggering vulnerabilities in a parent, or ongoing abuse coming to light for the first time). She also wrote that some jurists believe virtually all such allegations in the custody context are false, a ploy on the part of the mother to besmirch the father. Raising an allegation of child sexual abuse (whether true or false) may actually jeopardize the accuser's chances of securing custody. The psychiatric evaluator needs to remain objective, but also aware of the importance of carefully examining the validity of these allegations. False allegations can have a potentially harmful impact on the child.

Green and Schetky (1988) have described how one can evaluate the child in such cases and assess the reliability of the child's disclosure. One must first assess the child's ability to separate reality from fantasy and his or her ability to verbally express and recall past events. Both will be a function of the child's developmental level. In general, according to these authors, false denials by children are relatively common, but false disclosures of sexual abuse by children are relatively rare. False disclosures may be seen in a child who has been "brainwashed" by a vindictive parent who seeks revenge or desires to end all contact between the child and the other parent; when a delusional parent has influenced a child; or, occasionally, when a child gives a false disclosure based on sexual fantasies, rather than reality. A child may also falsely accuse a parent for revenge or retaliation. False disclosures tend to be expressed more readily and without a significant change in affect than are true disclosures. Such children may appear outspoken, nondefensive, and may use adult terms, possibly learned from a coaching parent. True disclosures, however, usually are delayed, conflicted, and slow to be revealed, if revealed at all. They may be stated, retracted, and then restated again. They are usually accompanied by appropriate negative affect. The evaluator also should observe the interactions of the child with each parent. In cases of true allegations the child's behavior is usually more consistently fearful toward the accused parent. A young sexually abused child who does not understand the deviant nature of the molestation, however, may display learned seductive behavior toward the accused parent, rather than display fearful behavior. The evaluation may be further supplemented by play therapy with dolls or drawings, though children without a history of sexual abuse can demonstrate explicit sexual play.

When making recommendations for custody and visitation in cases where one is in doubt about allegations of sexual abuse, it is best to be conservative, yet constructive. The evaluator should be careful not to refuse visitation of any kind automatically, as this is rarely required without the consideration of further treatment.

Intimate-partner violence

In most cases, intimate-partner violence (IPV) will settle the matter of custody against the abusing partner, but the psychiatric evaluator may not be able to differentiate allegations from confirmed cases. Stover (2013) noted the psychiatric evaluator may consider the history, nature, and severity of the IPV, and whether the abusing partner still puts the children's best interests first; recommendations around custody and visitation should strongly take the abuse history into account and err on the side of the children's safety. As IPV may exist in the context of substance use and mental health problems, engagement in treatment by the abusing partner should be evaluated. Stover (2013) also cautioned that since the parent subjected to IPV may have consequent or exacerbated mental health, psychological trauma, and substance use issues, the psychiatric evaluator should exercise caution to not render a custody opinion against a parent who is struggling with the effects of IPV, and in favor of a potentially abusing partner.

Parental kidnapping

Parental kidnapping, the abduction or withholding of a child by one parent from the other parent, may occur in a variety of contexts related to divorce. Katz (1981) has described parental kidnapping to occur before a divorce is finalized by a parent who fears losing custody, or after divorce by the noncustodial parent, who flees to another state with the child to seek a new custody decision, or simply to hide from the custodial parent. Also, after a divorce is finalized, the custodial parent may disappear with the child in an attempt to deny the noncustodial parent visitation (Back and Buxton 1983). Other motives may include an attempt to protect the child from an abusing parent, a desire to blame and punish the left-behind spouse, a desperate effort to effect a reconciliation, or even paranoid delusions, sociopathy, and other mental disorders on the part of the abducting parent (Johnston et al. 1999).

Goodman (1976) estimated that between 25,000 and 100,000 cases occur annually. Lewis (1978) estimated that 60%–70% of cases occur before custody has been decided and go unreported. A national household survey conducted by Finkelhor et al. (1991) showed that over 350,000 families in 1988 saw one parent take unilateral action to deprive the other parent of contact with the child. About one-half of these cases involved actual concealing of the child or flight from the state or country.

Schetky and Haller (1983) have discussed the traumatic effects that parental kidnapping may have on the child, including difficulty in trusting others, withdrawal, poor peer relations, school problems, regression, anxiety, or depression. Johnston et al. (1999) described several risk factors for abduction cases, namely, allegations of child abuse, narcissistic/sociopathic personality traits, unmarried relationship status, low socioeconomic status and minority ethnic status. The latter two factors may be mediated by the reduced likelihood that these families will have the resources or cultural experience to settle their disputes in a legal forum. The authors proposed the courts need to have policies in place to effect rapid decisions or restrictive measures in high-risk situations.

Due to the potential harm to the child, strict criminal sanctions against parental kidnapping should be imposed. The legal system has been taking steps to try to decrease its occurrence, reflected in the prohibition on parental kidnapping in both United States federal law and the Hague Convention (Haller 1987). The National Conference of Commissioners on Uniform State Laws drafted the Uniform Child Custody Jurisdiction Act (UCCJA) in 1968. It has become law in nearly all states. According to Schetky and Haller (1983), this act has been helpful in reducing the likelihood of a kidnapping parent gaining custody of a child through a new custody decree in a different state. Prior to this act, one state was not obligated to honor a custody decision granted in another state. They have also described the addition of further legislation in the 1980s (e.g., the Parental Kidnapping Prevention Act of 1980), where an increasing number of states have made child kidnapping a felony. Even with implementation of these laws, however, parental kidnapping continues to be a significant problem. The Hague Convention on the Civil Aspects of Child Abduction (1980) governs international child abduction cases, calling for the prompt return of an abducted child to his or her habitual residence, unless it is demonstrated that his or her return would expose the child to grave risk of physical or psychological harm, or otherwise place the child in an intolerable situation.

Relocation

Relocation of the primary custodial parents may prompt a custody dispute and evaluation. The California Supreme Court held *In re Marriage of LaMusga* (2004) that a custodial parent does not have a presumptive legal right to relocate, and a court may re-evaluate a custody agreement if the noncustodial parent is able to show that the custodial parent's relocation will be detrimental to the child. Braver et al. (2003) found that maternal relocation is associated with negative impacts on children's long-term relationship with their fathers and their adjustment to the divorce. The authors suggest that their findings warrant reconsideration of Judith Wallerstein's controversial amicus curiae brief (1995) for *In re the Marriage of Burgess* (1996), which advocated that the best interest of the child is to allow the custodial parent to relocate to preserve the "centrality" of the well-functioning custodial parent–child relationship as paramount to positive adjustment of the child during the post-divorce years. However, Bruch (2005) argues that research supports the contention that it is the quality of relationship rather than quantity of visitation between child and noncustodial parent that is more beneficial to the child's adjustment, and that constraining the custodial parent's relocation may adversely impact the custodial environment (e.g., mothers moving to improve their financial situation). As with the debate about overnight visitation for infants and small children, the forensic psychiatrist is likely to provide the most tailored and objective evaluation by considering the particulars of each case at hand, taking research findings into account but refraining from uniformly imposing on every case his or her dogmatic position on the various professional debates.

Harassment of psychiatric evaluators

Of final note as a special issue that may be encountered which is the harassment of the psychiatric evaluator. The psychiatric evaluator should be warned that attorneys are trained to manipulate, coerce, confuse, intimidate, and distort as part of the adversarial system of the court. An attorney, if losing in court, may attack the evaluator professionally and personally in a vain attempt to discredit the logical or irrefutable facts of testimony. Some marriage/divorce attorneys may take the adversarial system to new extremes. They may attempt character assassination or other discrediting tactics, ignore the merits of the case, lodge ethical complaints, call regulatory agencies, or harass the evaluator in other ways, in order to persuade the evaluator either to come to a decision that favors their party, or to abandon the case entirely. There have even been instances where an attorney has lied over the phone, pretending to be someone else, in order to try to covertly get information from one of our authors who was involved in a custody battle for one of the attorney's clients. Because of the pressures placed on evaluators, many psychiatrists refuse to perform child custody evaluations, which unfortunately is detrimental to children who need their expertise.

Herman (1990a) pointed out that the psychiatrist also may receive personal threats from parents unhappy with the recommendations of the evaluator. Evaluators may be vindictively reported to state licensure boards or professional ethics boards by angry, hostile parents. Issues surrounding child custody elicit deep emotions within parents. Such feelings in a parent for whom custody is not granted may lead to unwarranted attacks on an evaluator, regardless of how well intentioned or reputable the evaluator may be. The evaluator should also be aware of the possibility even of violence when working with bitter, vengeful, dissatisfied parents. It is remarkable and fortunate that competent child psychiatrists subject themselves to this undeserving abuse, in order to guide and protect children from being further victimized by the divorcing process of their adult parents.

SUMMARY

Conducting a psychiatric evaluation in a child custody dispute is difficult, time consuming, and emotionally draining. The evaluator must do extensive interviews and effectively work with the child, parents, attorneys, and other adults significant to the child. The evaluator must make a recommendation that will have a profound effect on the rest of the child's life, even when there may be no clear-cut best recommendation. When formulating his or her recommendations, the evaluator must strive not to be biased by personal prejudice or the persuasive influence of attorneys. He or she must make a decision that is rooted in the evidence of the evaluation and is based only on what is in the best interests of the child. Throughout this process the evaluator needs to maintain his or her stance as advocate for the child's needs. The evaluation process may be painful for the child, the family, and the psychiatrist. The emotional and psychological rewards, however, are great. The evaluator may help provide the potential for a happy, healthy environment for the development of the child, a foundation for later life.

REFERENCES

Ackerman MJ and M Ackerman. 1997. Custody evaluation practices: A survey of experienced professionals (revisited). *Professional Psychology: Research and Practice* 28:137–145.

Alternative Dispute Resolution Act, 28 U.S. Code sect. 651–658 (1998).

American Academy of Child and Adolescent Psychiatry. 1997. Practice parameters for child custody evaluation. *Journal of the American Academy of Child Adolescent Psychiatry* 36(10 Supplement):57S–68S.

American Academy of Child and Adolescent Psychiatry. 2011. Practice parameter for child and adolescent forensic evaluations. *Journal of the American Academy of Child Adolescent Psychiatry* 50(12):1299–1312.

American Academy of Psychiatry and Law (AAPL). 2005. *Ethics Guidelines for the Practice of Forensic Psychiatry*. Bloomfield, CT: AAPL.

American Law Institute (ALI). 2002. *Principles of the Law of Family Dissolution: Analysis and Recommendations*. Newark, NJ: LexisNexis.

American Psychiatric Association (APA). 1974. *Diagnostic and Statistical Manual of Mental Disorders*, 2nd edition. Washington, DC: APA.

American Psychiatric Association (APA). 1982. *Child Custody Consultation*. Washington, DC: APA.

American Psychiatric Association (APA). 1987. *Diagnostic and Statistical Manual of Mental Disorders*, 3rd edition, rev. ed. Washington, DC: APA.

American Psychiatric Association (APA). 2013. *Diagnostic and Statistical Manual of Mental Disorders*, 5th edition. Arlington, VA: American Psychiatric Publishing.

Ash P and M Guyer. 1984. Court implementation of mental health professionals' recommendations in contested child custody and visitation cases. *Bulletin of the American Academy of Psychiatry and the Law* 12(2):137–147.

Ash P and M Guyer. 1986. The functions of psychiatric evaluation in contested child custody and visitation cases. *Journal of the American Academy of Child Psychiatry* 25(4):354–561.

Back S and J Buxton. 1983. The Denver Kidnapping Project: Resources for prevention and intervention in the Denver metropolitan area. Paper presented at the *Annual Meeting of the Colorado Interdisciplinary Committee on Child Custody*, September 11, Keystone, CO.

Bathurst K, AW Gottfried, and AE Gottfried. 1997. Normative data for the MMPI-2 in child custody litigation. *Psychological Assessments* 9:205–211.

Bauserman R. 2002. Child adjustment in joint-custody versus sole custody arrangements: A meta-analytic review. *Journal of Family Psychology* 16(1):91–102.

Beaver KM, C da Silva Costa, AP Poersch, MC Freddi, MC Stelmach, EJ Connolly, and JA Schwartz. 2014. Psychopathic personalty traits and their influence on parenting quality: Results from a Nationally Representative Sample of Americans. *Psychiatric Quarterly* 85:497–511.

Benedek EP and DH Schetky. 1985. Allegations of sexual abuse in child custody and visitation disputes. In *Emerging Issues in Child Psychiatry and the Law*, edited by DH Schetky and EP Benedek, New York: Brunner/Mazel, 145–146.

Bernet W. 2002. Child custody evaluations. *Child and Adolescent Clinics of North America* 11:781–804.

Billick SB 1986. Developmental competency. *Bulletin of the American Academy of Psychiatry and the Law* 14(4):301–309.

Billick SB and MB Jackson. 2007. Evaluating parents in child custody and abuse cases and the utility of psychological measures in screening for parental psychopathy or antisocial personality. In *The International Handbook of Psychopathic Disorders and the Law*. vol. 2, edited by AR Felthous and H Sass. West Sussex, England: Wiley, 95–112.

Binder RL. 1998. American Psychiatric Association resource document on controversies in child custody: Gay and lesbian parenting, transracial adoptions, joint versus sole custody, and custody gender issues. *Journal of the American Academy of Psychiatry and the Law* 26(2):267–276.

Braver SL, IM Ellman, and WV Fabricius. 2003. Relocation of children after divorce and children's best interests: New evidence and legal considerations. *Journal of Family Psychology* 17(2):206–219.

Bruch CS. 2005. Sound research or wishful thinking in child custody cases? Lessons from relocation law. *Family Law Quarterly* 40(2):281–314.

Burnett v. Burnett, 88 So.3d 887 (Ala. Civ. App. 2011).

California Code of Civil Procedure, Section 4607 (1984).

Caracansi A and SB Billick. 2000. Psychiatrist-patient privilege (legal digest). *Journal of the American Academy of Psychiatry and the Law* 28(3):366–368.

Centers for Disease Control and Prevention. 2014. *National Marriage and Divorce Rate Trends*. http://www.cdc.gov/nchs/nvss/marriage_divorce_tables.htm, accessed August 20, 2014.

Chess S, A Thomas, S Korn, M Mittleman, and J Cohen. 1983. Early parentla attitudes, divorce and separation, and early adult outcome: Findings of a longitudinal study. *Journal of the American Academy of Child and Adolescent Psychiatry* 22:47–51.

D.C. Child and Family Services Agency. 2016. *Grandparent Caregivers Program: Annual Status Report*, CY2015, released January 2016, Washington, D.C.

Derdeyn A, and E Scott. 1984. Joint custody: A critical analysis and appraisal. *American Journal of Orthopsychiatry* 54:199–209.

Derdeyn AP 1976. Child custody in historical perspective. *American Journal of Psychiatry* 133(12):1369–1375.

Despert J. 1953. *Children of Divorce*, citing a 1948 American Bar Association report, p. 189. Garden City, NJ: Doubleday.

Dillon PA and RE Emery. 1996. Divorce mediation and resolution of child custody disputes: Long-term effects. *American Journal of Orthopsychiatry* 66(1):131–140.

Elrod LD and Dale MD. 2008. Paradigm shifts and pendulum swings in child custody: The interests of children in the balance. *Family Law Quarterly* 42(3):381–418.

Emery RE and MJ Coiro. 1995. Divorce: Consequences for children. *Pediatrics in Review* 16(8):306–310.

Emery RE, SG Matthews, and KM Kitzmann. 1994. Child custody mediation and litigation: Parents' satisfaction and functioning one year after settlement. *Journal of Consulting and Clinical Psychology* 62(1):124–129.

Emery RE, RK Otto, and WT O'Donohue. 2005. A critical assessment of child custody evaluations. *Psychological Science in the Public Interest* 6(1):1–29.

Family Law Quarterly. 2013a. Chart 2: Custody Criteria. *Family Law Quarterly* 46(4):524–527.

Family Law Quarterly. 2013b. Chart 6: Third-Party Visitation. *Family Law Quarterly* 46(4):537–541.

Farr RH and CJ Patterson. 2013. Coparenting among lesbian, gay, and heterosexual couples: Associations with adopted children's outcomes. *Child Development* 84(4):1226–1240.

Finkelhor D, G Hotaling, and A Sedlak. 1991. Children abducted by family members: A national household survey of incidence and episode characteristics. *Journal of Marriage and the Family* 53:805–809.

Fitzgerald H and C McCread. 1981. Fathers and infants. *Infant Mental Health Journal* 2(4):214.

Freedman M. 1971. *Homosexuality and Psychological Functioning*. Belmont, CA: Brooks/Cole.

Galper M. 1978. *Co-Parenting: Sharing Your Child Equally, A Source Book for the Separated or Divorced Family.* Philadelphia: Running Press.

Gardner RA. 1987. *The Parental Alienation Syndrome and the Differentiation between Fabricated and Genuine Child Sexual Abuse*. Cresskil, NJ: Creative Therapeutics.

Gates GJ. 2013. *LGBT Parenting in the United States. Executive Summary of the Williams Institute*. http://williamsinstitute.law.ucla.edu/wp-content/uploads/LGBT-Parenting.pdf, accessed October 31, 2014.

Goldstein J, A Freud, and AJ Solnit. 1979. *Beyond the Best Interests of the Child*. New York: Free Press.

Goldstein J, AJ Solnit, S Goldstein et al. 1996. The Best Interests of the Child: *The Least Detrimental Alternative*. New York: The Free Press.

Goodman E. 1976. Child snatching. *Washington Post*, March 26, p. 27.

Goodwin J, D Sahd, and R Rada. 1978. Incest hoax: False accusations, false denials. *Bulletin of the American Academy of Psychiatry and the Law* 6:269–276.

Green AH and DH Schetky. 1988. True and false allegations of child sexual abuse. In *Child Sexual Abuse, A Handbook for Health Care and Legal Professionals*, edited by DH Schetky and AH Green, New York: Brunner/Mazel, 104–124.

Guyer M and P Ash. 1986. Child abuse allegations in the context of adversarial divorce. Paper presented at the *Annual Meeting of the American Academy of Psychiatry and the Law*, October 17, Los Angeles.

Haller LH. 1987. Kidnapping of children by parents. In *Basic Handbook of Child Psychiatry*, vol. 5, edited by J Noshpitz, New York: Basic Books, 646–652.

Herman SP. 1990a. Forensic child psychiatry. *Journal of the American Academy of Child and Adolescent Psychiatry* 29(6):955–957.

Herman SP. 1990b. Special issues in child custody evaluations. *Journal of the American Academy of Child and Adolescent Psychiatry* 29(6):969–974.

Hetherington EM. 1999. Family functioning and the adjustment of adolescent siblings in diverse types of families. *Monographs of the Society for Research in Child Development* 64:1–25.

Hetherington EM and M Stanley-Hagan. 1999. The adjustment of children with divorced parents: A risk and resiliency perspective. *Journal of Child Psychology and Psychiatry and Allied Disciplines* 40:129–140.

Hulstein MJ. 2012. Commentary: Recognizing and respecting the rights of LGBT youth in child custody proceedings. *Berkley Journal of Gender, Law and Justice* 27(2):171–197.

Hutchens DL and MJ Kirkpatrick. 1985. Lesbian mothers/gay fathers. In *Emerging Issues in Child Psychiatry and the Law*, edited by DH Schetky and EP Benedek, New York: Brunner/Mazel, 115–126.

Ilfeld F, Jr., H Ilfeld, and J Alexander. 1982. Does joint custody work? A first local look at outcome data of relitigation. *American Journal of Psychiatry* 62:139.

In re Lifschutz, 487 P.2d 557 (1970).

In re the Marriage of Burgess, 913 P.2d 473 (Cal. 1996).

In re Marriage of LaMusga, 88 P.3d 81 (Cal. 2004).

Jocklin V, M McGue, and DT Lykken. 1996. Personality and divorce: A genetic analysis. *Journal of Personality and Social Psychology* 71:288–299.

Johnston JR, LK Girdner, and I Sagatun-Edwards. 1999. Developing profiles of risk for parental abduction of children from a comparison of families victimized by abduction with families litigating custody. *Behavioral Sciences and the Law* 17:305–322.

Jones DPH and JM McGraw. 1987. Reliable and fictitious accounts of sexual abuse to children. *Journal of Interpersonal Violence* 2(1):27–45.

Katz S. 1981. *Child Snatching*. Washington, DC: American Bar Association Press.

Kay v. Rowland, 285 S.C. 516, 331 S.E. (2d) 781 (1985).

Kelly JB. 1994. The determination of child custody. *Future of Children* 4(1):121–142.

Krauss DA and Sales BD. 2000. Legal standards, expertise, and experts in the resolution of contested child custody cases. *Psychology, Public Policy, and Law* 6(4):843–879.

Lahey BB, SE Hartdagen, PJ Frick, K McBurnett, R Connor, and GW Hynd. 1988. Conduct disorder: Parsing the confounded relation to parental divorce and antisocial personality. *Journal of Abnormal Psychology* 97:334–337.

Lamb ME. 1997. *The Role of the Father in Child Development*, 3rd edition, edited by ME Lamb, New York: Wiley.

Lawrence v. Texas, 539 U.S. 558 (2003).

Laznovsky v. Laznovsky, 745 A.2d 1054 (Md. 2000).

Levy AM. 1985a. The divorcing family: Its evaluation and treatment. In *The Clinical Guide to Child Psychiatry*, edited by D Shaffer, A Ehrhardt, and L Greenhill, New York: Free Press, 353–368.

Levy AM. 1985b. Father custody. In *Emerging Issues in Child Psychiatry and the Law*, edited by DH Schetky and EP Benedek, New York: Brunner/Mazel, 100–114.

Lewis K. 1978. On reducing the child snatching syndrome. *Children Today* 7:19–21.

Luepnitz DA. 1982. *Child Custody: A Study of Families after Divorce*. Lexington, MA: Lexington Books.

Maccoby EE and RH Mnookin. 1992. *Dividing the Child: Social and Legal Dilemmas of Custody*. Cambridge, MA: Harvard University Press.

Malmquist CP. 1994. Psychiatric confidentiality in child custody disputes. *Journal of the American Academy of Child and Adolescent Psychiatry* 33(2):158–168.

McGraw JM and HA Smith. 1992. Child sexual abuse allegations amidst divorce and custody proceedings: Refining the validation process. *Journal of Child Sexual Abuse* 1:49–62.

McIntosh JA and RJ Prinz. 1993. The incidence of alleged sexual abuse in 603 family court cases. *Law and Human Behavior* 17:95–101.

Medoff D. 1999. MMPI-2 validity scales in child custody evaluations: Clinical versus statistical significance. *Behavioral Sciences and the Law* 17(4):409–411.

Meyer D and S Garasky. 1993. Custodial fathers: Myths, realities, and child support policy. *Journal of Marriage and the Family* 55:73–89.

Painter v. Bannister, 140 N.W.2d. 152 (1966).

Parham v. J.R., 442 U.S. 584 (1979).

Parham v. J. R., 445 U.S. 480 (1980).

Penfold PS. 1995. Mendacious moms or devious dads? Some perplexing issues in child custody/sexual abuse allegation disputes. *Canadian Journal of Psychiatry* 40(6):337–341.

People ex rel. Watts v. Watts, 77 Misc.2d 178 (NY Family Court 1973).

Ploscowe M, HH Foster Jr., and D Freed. 1973. *Family Law: Cases and Materials*, 2nd edition. Boston: Little, Brown.

Raub JM, NJ Carson, BL Cook, G Wyshak, and BB Hauser. 2013. Predictors of custody and visitation decisions by a family court clinic. *Journal of the American Academy of Psychiatry and the Law* 41(2):206–218.

Reynolds S, CT Harris, and RA Peeples. 2007. Back to the future: An empirical study of child custody outcomes. *North Carolina Law Review* 85(6):1629–1686.

Ruman M and MG Lamm. 1985. Mediation: Its implications for children and divorce. In *Emerging Issues in Child Psychiatry and the Law*, edited by DH Schetky and EP Benedek, New York: Brunner/Mazel, 76–84.

Sadoff RL and S Billick. 1981. The legal rights and difficulties of children in separation and divorce. In *Children of Separation and Divorce: Management and Treatment*, edited by IR Stuart and LE Abt, New York: Van Nostrand Reinhold, 4–16.

Schetky DH and LH Haller. 1983. Parental kidnapping. *Journal of the American Academy of Child Psychiatry* 22(3):279–285.

Schowalter JE. 2000. Grandparent visitation rights (editorial). *Journal of the American Academy of Psychiatry and the Law* 28:7–8.

Shaw DS, RE Emery, and MD Tuer. 1993. Parental functioning and children's adjustment in families of divorce: A prospective study. *Journal of Abnormal Child Psychology* 21(1):119–134.

Solnit AJ and DH Schetky. 1986. In the best interests of the child: An overview. In *Psychiatry Series: Vol. 6, Child Psychiatry*, edited by AJ Solnit, DJ Cohen, and JE Schowalter, Philadelphia: J. P. Lippincott, 517–522.

Stover CS. 2013. Commentary: Factors predicting family court decisions in high-conflict divorce. *Journal of the American Academy of Psychiatry and the Law* 41(2):219–223.

Strong DR, RL Greene, C Hoppe, T Johnston, and N Olesen. 1999. Taxometric analysis of impression management and self-deception on the MMPI-2 in child custody litigants. *Journal of Personality Assessment* 73(1):1–18.

Thoennes N and J Pearson. 1988. Summary of findings from sexual abuse allegations project. In *Sexual Abuse Allegations in Custody and Visitation Cases*, edited by B Nicholson and J Bulkley, Washington, DC: National Legal Resource Centre for Child Advocacy and Protection, 1–28.

Thoennes N and PG Tjaden. 1990. The extent, nature, validity of sexual abuse allegations in custody/visitation disputes. *Child Abuse and Neglect* 14:151–163.

Tornello SL, R Emery, J Rowen, D Potter, B Ocker, and Y Xu. 2013. Overnight custody arrangements, attachment, and adjustment among very young children. *Journal of Marriage and Family* 75(4):871–885.

Troxel et vir. v. Granville, 530 U.S. 120, 2054 (2000).

Uniform Marriage and Divorce Act § 402 H.N., In *Uniform Laws Annotated*. St. Paul, MN: West, 1991.

United States v. Windsor, 570 U.S. 12 (2013).

Waller EM and AE Daniel. 2005. Purpose and utility of child custody evaluations: The attorney's perspective. *Journal of the American Academy of Psychiatry and the Law* 33(2):199–207.

Wallerstein JS. 1991. The long-term effects of divorce on children: A review. *Journal of the American Academy of Child and Adolescent Psychiatry* 30:349–360.

Wallerstein, JS. 1995. Amica Curiae Brief of Dr. Judith S. Wallerstein, PhD, Filed in Cause No. S046116, *In re the Marriage of Burgess*, Supreme Court of the State of California, Dec. 7, 1995.

Wallerstein JS and JB Kelley. 1980. *Surviving the Breakup: How Children and Parents Cope with Divorce*. New York: Basic Books.

Wallerstein JS, JM Lewis, and S Blakeslee. 2000. *The Unexpected Legacy of Divorce: A 25 Year Landmark Study*. New York: Hyperion.

Ware C. 1982. *Sharing Parenthood after Divorce*. New York: Viking Press.

Warshak RA. 2014. Social science and parenting plans for young children: A consensus report. *Psychology, Public Policy, and Law* 20(1):46–67.

Weiner BA, VA Simons, and JL Cavanaugh Jr. 1985. The child custody dispute. In *Emerging Issues in Child Psychiatry and the Law*, edited by DH Schetky and EP Benedek, New York: Brunner/Mazel, 59–75.

Zaslow MJ. 1988. Sex differences in children's response to parental divorce: I. Research methodology and post-divorce family norms. *American Journal of Orthopsychiatry* 58:355–378.

39

Termination of parental rights and adoption

MEGAN M. MROCZKOWSKI AND STEPHEN B. BILLICK

HISTORICAL AND LEGAL PERSPECTIVES

The basic concepts of "parental rights" and the "interests of the child" have gone through evolutionary changes. Until the nineteenth century, the parental rights issue was relatively simple. Under Roman and early English law, the term "parent" referred to the biological (i.e., genetic) father, and children were treated as property of their parents, namely the father. Because wealth and property were considered an extremely important matter, the rights of inheritance were carefully protected and rigorously addressed in the legal system. This created an extreme imbalance between the rights of the parents and those of their offspring.

The term *parens patriae* had its origin in English Law where the king was considered the father or the parent of the citizens of the land. The U.S. government and its individual States function as a parent when it exercises its power of guardianship over persons with disability, such as minors, incompetents, and the mentally ill. Such power is not exercised by the States unless the person under disability has been deprived, for whatever reason, of nongovernmental protection and support of an adequate degree.

The twentieth century was the beginning of a new interest in delineating rights and the interests of the children over the rights and interests of the father, and of both parents. Child labor laws were enacted in the beginning of the twentieth century to further protect children. *In re Gault* (1967) is a pivotal landmark U.S. Supreme Court case regarding children's rights. The Supreme Court upheld a need for timely and adequately specific written notice, the right to counsel, the right to confrontation and cross-examination, and protection from self-incrimination. The need for a transcript and the right to appeal were not ruled on. The majority opinion written by Justice Fortas traced the long history of differences between juvenile and adult cases and offered juveniles many rights similar to those held by adults.

The social movement of the 1960s, with its emphasis on civil rights, influenced the parent–child law. Children were increasingly viewed as real people with specific rights, and society began to take interest in the well-being of minors; hence, the "best interest of the child" concept evolved. As the sociopolitical atmosphere changed again during the 1980s, various rights continued to be re-examined. The rights of parents and children were not viewed as equal by the law. The U.S. Supreme Court, in a series of cases, noted that the biological relationship, although not the exclusive consideration, is in fact, unique, and often prevailing.

Constitutional law holds that the rights of parents to raise their children in a manner they see fit constitutes "family privacy" (*Lochner v. New York* 1905). This suggests that the law allows great latitude to parental actions or inaction toward their children. However, parental rights are not infinite. In the U.S. Supreme Court case of *Prince v. Commonwealth of Massachusetts* (1944), the court stated, "the state, as *parens patriae*, has a wide range of power for limiting parental freedom and authority in things affecting the child's welfare." In *Roe v. Wade* (1973) the court pointed out that when the state intrudes upon a fundamental protected right (family privacy and parental rights), strict scrutiny must be observed by the court. Such a high level of review is mandated to ensure that fundamental constitutional rights have not been abridged.

Parental rights, as recognized by law, include the basic right to custody of their children unless the parents are proven unfit. Parents have authority to control their children until they reach majority, or are being emancipated. The child has no right to leave the parental home for another, although the law recognizes that parental control decreases with the child's increasing age, especially in later adolescence.

In the issue of discipline, the court gives parents wide latitude in the disciplining of children. The parent has the right, authority, and power to discipline the child, if it is viewed as being for the child's benefit. Corporal punishment is included, while abusive punishment is not. In general, if parental discipline is administered with good intent and there is no physical injury, the law will not intervene; however, if malice or serious physical injury results, the parental rights may have been exceeded (American Jurisprudence 22 §22, 1987).

Parents have the right to send their children to private, parochial, or the school of their choice. However, this is a limited right, because the schools must conform to guidelines and standards established by the state educational boards (*Pierce v. Society of Sisters* 1925). Home-based schooling programs following primary school were allowed in the Amish group, as illustrated in the Supreme Court case (*Wisconsin v. Yoder* 1972). Parents have a limited right to bring up their child in a reasonable religion, though inculcating Satanism and human sacrifice would be unacceptable. Religious practices that may affect a child's compulsory school attendance must be a part of an established religion to be acceptable, rather than a mere philosophy or a secular belief.

Parents have the right to hospitalize their children involuntarily for psychiatric evaluation and treatment. An independent medical authority must concur with the need for hospitalization. In many states, the minor child, however, has the right to a judicial review for involuntary hospitalization (*Parham v. J.R.* 1979). In other areas of medical care, the law gives parents broad discretion with limits. A child may be considered neglected if the parents fail to provide proper and necessary medical care (*In re Green* 1972). One of the prominent issues in this area has been the refusal by Jehovah's Witnesses to allow blood transfusion. All states that have ruled in this matter have ordered the blood transfusion if it has a reasonable likelihood of saving the life of the child. The courts have held that adults have the freedom to exercise full religious beliefs for themselves, but cannot exercise unlimited religious beliefs for their child.

In the *Matter of Faridah W.*, 1992, a New York case, the court declared a 16-year-old female who was born with spina bifida and had a neurogenic bladder to be a medically and emotionally neglected child, because her mother refused to permit her to undergo an enterocystoplasty. The court stated that, "A parent has a non-delegable affirmative duty to provide a child with adequate medical care, which has been determined to be that degree of care exercised by ordinary, prudent, loving parents who are anxious for the well-being of the child." The court further noted that the critical aspects of the parents' failure to obtain medical assistance must be to the extent that the child's mental, medical, or emotional health is adversely affected or in imminent danger of being adversely affected. In this case, the mother allegedly refused to comply with the medical expert's opinion and failed to provide a reasonable alternative to the proposed treatment. She also failed to visit her daughter during most of her lengthy hospitalization.

Parents have a right and the authority to determine their child's social activities and how best to meet their child's physical, emotional, and relationship needs. In parent–child relations, after granting custody to one parent, the other parent usually has the vested right to visitation. The Uniform Marriage and Divorce Act (1991) requires clear and convincing evidence that parental contact seriously endangers the child's physical, mental, or emotional well-being to justify termination of the right to visitation.

In many states, it was formerly assumed that an unmarried father had no claim to parental rights, and their permission, therefore, was not required for third-party adoption of their biological child. The Supreme Court, in the case of *Stanley v. Illinois* (1972), addressed a landmark *due process* case regarding parental rights. It was uncontested that Stanley was an unwed father who was seriously interested in his offspring. He had maintained a relationship, provided support payments, and held himself out as a father. The Illinois state law presumed an unwed father to be an unfit parent *per se*, with no opportunity to rebut the unfit determination. However, Illinois law required notice, hearing, and proof of unfitness before neglect proceedings could lead to termination of parental rights. Stanley had no hearing. The court found that Stanley's private interest involved companionship, care, custody, and management of the children he has "*sired and raised*." The court concluded, "It is cardinal that the custody, care, and nurturance of the child reside first in the parents, whose primary function and freedom include preparation [of the child] for obligations the state can neither supply nor hinder." The court went on to state that the integrity of the family unit was protected by the due process, equal protection, and "the rights retained by the people" clauses of the Constitution (*Griswold v. Connecticut* 1965), and that the law has not refused to recognize family relationships not legitimized by marriage. In *Stanley*, the court stated that while the state has a duty "to protect minor children through a judicial determination of their interest in a neglect proceeding," unwed fathers have a due process and equal protection right to have a hearing on fitness when state law declares a married, divorced, or unmarried mother to be presumed fit. Stanley was given a due process hearing and declared unfit to parent his child for other reasons.

TERMINATION OF PARENTAL RIGHTS (TPR)

The law does not view parenting as indigenous to the person, but rather something with which the family is vested by the state. The state assumes it is the parent's responsibility to understand, implement, and perpetuate the values of society. It assumes that a parent has the innate ability to balance rights and responsibilities, relinquish absolute power for the good of the developing child, and treat progeny in such a manner so as to maximize developmental potential. When a parent abdicates, neglects, or abuses this responsibility, the state engenders the doctrine of *parens patriae* to break into the delicate parent–child relationship, expose it to the legal and psychiatric community, and to ask the court's determination as to the appropriateness of terminating an assumed inalienable right of the individual—namely to parent one's own children (Mnookin 1978).

Out of the cruelty to animal laws and the child labor laws emerged early social legislation protecting children's rights. Then came the concept of "the best interest of the child" (Goldstein et al. 1973). The best interest standard is a well-established principle of law in areas of child custody and termination of parental rights (American Jurisprudence 2d §974, 1983). The concept of "best interests," however, tends to be vague. Some states have attempted to make the issue of best interest clearer and more specific. The District of Columbia (District of Columbia Code, 1981 §16-2353) has codified that the best interest of a child includes factors that consider the following:

1. The child's need for continuity of care and caretakers, and for timely integration into a stable, permanent home
2. The relationship of the physical, mental, and emotional health of all persons involved to the welfare of the child and his or her needs
3. The quality of the relationship of the child with his or her sibling, caretakers, foster parents, and natural parents
4. Whether a child has been left unclaimed in the hospital 10 days after a medical determination that he could be safely discharged
5. The child's opinion of his or her best interests to the extent he or she is able to express them
6. Evidence of continued drug-related activity in the parental home after interventional services have been provided (Armitage 1994)

In the state of California (California Civil Code 226(a) 1991), the court must consider the age of the child, the bonding or potential to bond with natural parents or the adoptive parents, and the ability of the parents to provide adequate and proper care and guidance to the child.

In the state of Michigan (Child Custody Act 1970), factors relating to determination of best interests in custody cases include

1. The love, affection, and other ties between the child and the parents competing for custody
2. Capacity and disposition of competing parents to give the child love, affection, guidance, and education
3. The capacity to provide necessary or any special medical care or remedial care required for the child
4. Length of time the child has lived in a satisfactorily stable environment
5. Permanence as a family unit of the proposed custodial home
6. The moral fitness of competing parties
7. The mental and physical health of the competing parties
8. Home, community, and school record of the child
9. Reasonable preference of the children if they are of sufficient age

In Connecticut (*In re Bernard Pecor* 1992), the court held that a child's best interest involving termination of parental rights cases must be met by considering

- The timeliness, nature, and extent of services offered by the state to help parents reunify (the presumption being that parental rights are important)
- The terms of any court order or agreement between an agency and the parents, and the extent to which the agreements were complied with
- Feelings or emotional ties between the parent and the child, related to the concept of psychological parent
- Age of the child
- Whether mental or behavioral disorders prevent the parents from changing their conduct, behavior, or circumstances that could be injurious to the child in the foreseeable future
- Whether any governmental agency or party prevented the parent from developing a relationship or that the lack of a relationship was based purely on economic circumstances

Congress determined that Native American parents and children were a special class requiring special protections. Federal law gives deference to the parental rights of Native Americans who are members of a recognized Indian tribe. The Indian Child Welfare Act of 1978 requires a finding by evidence "*beyond a reasonable doubt*" that allowing an Indian child to remain with the parent or parents would be likely to result in serious emotional or physical damage to the child. This law requiring a higher standard of proof was enacted because there was substantial evidence indicating that state social workers and others unfamiliar with Native American tribal child-rearing practices (including leaving the child for prolonged periods with other members of the tribe who are considered as "extended family"), inappropriately recommended termination of parental rights.

Schetky and Slader (1980) believe that the law must consider termination of parental rights as it relates to infringement of the rights of children: (a) the right to the maintenance of a parent–child relationship—that is, the right to have someone to call "parent"; (b) freedom from physical, sexual, or psychological mistreatment; and (c) the right to have "primary emotional needs for continuity, consistency and identity" met by being a part of a family.

Definition of TPR

Termination of parental rights means the adjudication that a child is free from the custody and control of either or both his or her living genetic parents by means of court order that completely severs and extinguishes the parent–child relationship (American Jurisprudence 2 & §34, 1987, pp. 172–173). It has, therefore, a profound and serious finality.

Termination of parental rights is governed by both federal and state statutes. The primary law on the federal level is the Adoption and Safe Families Act of 1997 (ASFA). ASFA amended the Adoption Assistance and Child Welfare Act (AACWA) by setting a strict deadline for implementing placement plans. States must comply with ASFA guidelines in order to receive federal funding, and therefore the federal requirements for ASFA have been adopted by all 50 states.

STANDARDS OF TERMINATION

The U.S. Supreme Court has recognized that "freedom of personal choice in matters of family life is one of the liberties protected by the Due Process Clause of the Fourteenth Amendment" (*Cleveland Bd. of Educ. v. LaFleur* 1974). Constitutional law provides minimal standards that must be met in order to terminate parental rights. In *Santosky v. Kramer* (1982), the U.S. Supreme Court held that before a state can completely and irrevocably sever parental rights, *due process* requires that evidence provided by the state be "*clear and convincing*" to support its allegation for termination (Haynes 2009).

The minimal constitutional standard must be met but can be exceeded by state law. Some states currently require "*beyond reasonable doubt*" standards of proof for termination of parental rights. *Due process* in termination proceedings requires fundamental fairness under the legal and factual circumstances of a case. The U.S. Supreme Court invoked the *Mathews v. Eldridge* (1976) elements as rules applicable to deciding what *due process* requires. These elements are (a) the private interest at stake; (b) the government's interest; and (c) the risk that the procedures used will lead to erroneous decisions.

Legal criteria or grounds for termination of parental rights vary among jurisdictions. However, the grounds/criteria must be supported by competent, relevant, clear, and convincing evidence. Common grounds for termination of parental rights include the following:

1. *Voluntary abandonment*: (NY SSL 384-b). A child is abandoned by his or her parent if such a parent evinces an intent to forego his or her parental rights and obligations as manifested by his or her failure to visit the child and communicate with the child or agency, although able to do so and not prevented or discouraged from doing so by the agency. In the absence of evidence to the contrary, such ability to visit and communicate shall be presumed.
2. *Permanent neglect*: This means a child who is in the care and custody of an authorized agency and whose parent or guardian has failed for a period of more than 1 year (after foster placement) to substantially and continuously or repeatedly and consistently maintain contact with or plan for the future of the child although physically and financially able to do so, notwithstanding the agency's diligent efforts to encourage and strengthen the parental relationship when such efforts will not be detrimental to the best interest of the child. It is important to note that a visit or communication by a parent with the child, which is of such character as to overtly demonstrate a lack of affectionate and concerned parenthood, shall not be deemed a substantial contact.
3. *Mental illness*: This means an affliction with a mental disease or mental condition that is manifested by a disorder or disturbance in behavior thinking, feeling, or judgment to a such an extent that if the child were placed in or returned to the custody of the parent, the child would be in danger of becoming a neglected child.
4. *Mental deficiency*: This means sub-average intellectual functioning, which originates during the developmental period and is associated with the impairment in adaptive behavior to such an extent that if the child were placed or returned to the custody of such parent, the child would be in danger of becoming a neglected child.
5. *Physical/sexual abuse.*
6. *Substance abuse*: When the parental substance abuse leads to danger of neglect or abuse of the child.

When the state interferes with parental rights as in involuntary termination of rights, it must carefully follow legal procedures and substantive law that reflects the grounds and criteria for termination. These procedures can vary among jurisdictions. In most cases, circumstances that take place in a child's life warrant interference by state agencies to take temporary custody of the child, as in cases of neglect, abandonment, or abuse by the parents or legal custodians. The child is initially removed on an emergency basis by a state agency such as child protective services. Hearings on this action are required and there must be substantive evidence of neglect or abuse based on *preponderance of evidence.*

The court then mandates the state agencies to make diligent efforts to assist the parent toward reunification with the child unless reunification is not possible, or is not indicated. All jurisdictions allow for waiver of reunification attempts under certain circumstances. When legal criteria and grounds for termination are met, a termination hearing is ordered following a petition by the state. The grounds for parental unfitness and termination must be stated and must be proved by *clear and convincing evidence.* The next procedural requirement is to prove that termination is in the best interest of the child by *clear and convincing evidence.*

Testimony of a child psychiatrist is frequently used in termination of parental rights cases. In addition to the prominently accepted principle of the "best interest of the child," the concept of "least detrimental alternative" has been applied in some cases.

STATISTICS OF TPR IN THE UNITED STATES

The U.S. Department of Health and Human Services, Administration for Children and Families publishes *Trends in Foster Care and Adoption.* The most recent publication in 2014 describes data from 2002 to 2013. During this time, there was a range of Parental Rights Terminated from 59,000 in 2013 to 82,000 in 2007.

CLINICAL ISSUES RELATED TO TPR

All clinical issues and evaluation must be viewed within the context of the legal grounds and criteria for termination.

MENTAL DISORDERS AND MENTAL ILLNESSES

Psychiatrists and psychologists are called to provide evidence in TPR proceedings when mental illness or deficiency is a proffered ground for termination. In New York, a parent's right can be terminated on the grounds of mental illness if the suffering parent is rendered incapable of caring for the children. The state is not required to make efforts to strengthen the parental relationship, and it is not required to show that efforts to strengthen the parental relationship would be detrimental to the child (*In re Demetrius F.* et al. 1991).

All clinical evaluations must be viewed within the context of the legal grounds for termination. Involuntary hospitalization for the mental disorders, combined with other factors that are offered as evidence that the hospitalized parent may be dangerous to the child, is a frequently recognized ground. A diagnosis of schizophrenia *per se* may not be accepted as evidence for unfitness. The schizophrenia must have an adverse impact on the ability to parent by interfering with the individual's thinking, perception, behavior, and judgment. Other associated problems such as poor or noncompliance with medication and recommended treatment, refusal to participate in parenting skills training and erratic parent–child interaction during visitation are also important areas of assessment.

A borderline personality disorder has been accepted as a diagnosis of "mental illness or disorder" and deemed by the court to be a long-term condition allowing for termination, if termination is in the best interest of the child, because such a parent was not considered capable of performing proper parental duties. The same parent did not comply with a court-ordered rehabilitation plan for reunification, which the court held as an independent reason, in addition to the mental disorder, to terminate parental rights (*In re the Interest of B.M. v. L.M.* 1991).

PARENTAL INCARCERATION

Criminal incarceration of a parent as a factor in TPR varies among jurisdictions. Parental incarceration is a growing problem that needs accommodation in the current time-driven model of permanency planning. Child welfare agencies need to recognize the importance of maintaining parent–child relationships, even when a parent is incarcerated, and to develop creative approaches for dealing with the unique challenges of parental incarceration.

Over the past 15 years, the population of female prisoners has increased by almost 400%, while the male prison population has increased by more than 200% (U.S. Department of Justice 1995). Two-thirds of the female prisoners in the United States had one or more children under the age of 18 years. In 1991, 72% of incarcerated mothers had minor children who had lived with them before entering prison. Approximately 50% of the incarcerated fathers had lived with their children prior to imprisonment (Snell 1994). In the survey of 1991, 71% of the children of incarcerated mothers and 13% of the children of incarcerated fathers were with grandparents or other nonparent relatives (Snell 1994). These data show that incarcerated mothers must rely on nonparent caregivers for childcare to a much greater extent than incarcerated fathers. Some 90% of the children of incarcerated fathers were cared for by their mothers (Johnston 1995), but only 25% of the children of incarcerated mothers were cared for by their fathers (Snell 1994).

Parental imprisonment does not change the basic legal requirement governing permanency planning. Agencies have a legal obligation to make "reasonable efforts" to preserve and strengthen the relationship between incarcerated parents and their children. The definition of reasonable efforts varies from jurisdiction to jurisdiction. For example, New York state law defines diligent efforts to incarcerated parents as including "making suitable arrangements with a correctional facility and other appropriate persons for an incarcerated parent to visit the child within the correctional facility, if such visiting is in the best interest of the child. … Such arrangements shall include, but shall not be limited to the transportation of the child to the correctional facility, providing social or rehabilitative service to resolve service to resolve or rectify problems which can impair the incarcerated parent's ability to maintain contact with the child other than incarceration itself" (NY SSL 384-b(7)(f)(5)). The most obvious challenge to the agency is the facilitation of a continued parent–child relationship relating to lengths of sentencing and distance.

The length of sentencing is likely to increase in the future as legislative efforts to eliminate or seriously limit parole result in more time served. At the same time, mandatory sentencing laws for certain crimes will lead to the imprisonment of even more parents. Distance is the other problematic issue affecting the ability of agencies to provide services to an incarcerated parent. Women's prisons are often located in rural areas, and inaccessible by public transportation. Despite these obstacles, the agencies must generally attempt to overcome them and assist the parent and child to maintain a meaningful relationship. Parental rights are not absolute, and in inappropriate cases, where diligent efforts are not in the best interest of the child, the state may go to court to seek TPR. To do so, the state must prove the parent is "unfit" (*Stanley v. Illinois* 1971; *Santosky v. Kramer* 1982).

The parent's "fitness" must be measured by the parent's ability to "maintain a place of importance in the child's life" (*In re Adoption of Sabrina* 1984). Recognizing the principle that parental incarceration does not automatically amount to unfitness, New Jersey's Supreme Court has articulated the factors that must be examined in TPR evaluations of incarcerated parents:

1. Parent's performance before incarceration
2. The extent to which children were able to rely on their parent
3. Parent's efforts to remain in contact with the children since incarceration
4. Parent's ability to communicate and visit with their children
5. The effect of parental communication and visitation on the children
6. The ability to provide nurturance and emotional support to their children
7. Risks posed to the children by the parent's criminal actions
8. The extent of the parent's rehabilitation during incarceration

9. The need of the children for permanency and stability and whether continuation of the parent–child relationships will undermine that need
10. The effect that the continuation of the parent–child relationship will have on the psychological and emotional well-being of the children

The trend toward incarceration of greater numbers of people for longer periods of time shows no signs of abating. As a result, increasing numbers of out-of-home caseloads will involve children of incarcerated parents. Effective family work in cases involving parental incarceration requires significant expenditure of time and resources. The child protective agencies should identify the cases where efforts would be successful in maintaining and strengthening viable parent–child relationships. In such cases, agencies must develop new permanency approaches, consistent with the requirements of the Adoption and Safe Families Act (ASFA 1997), for families in which a parent is incarcerated. For many children of incarcerated parents, the best permanency plan is one in which the parent continues to play a significant role in the child's life (Genty 1998).

CLINICAL ISSUES AND THE ROLE OF CHILD PSYCHIATRIST IN TPR EVALUATION

As numerous studies have documented, many children languish in foster care with little or no efforts being made to make permanent plans for them, in spite of the fact that their biological parents may be failing to progress toward the goal of reintegrating them into the family. Although foster care is thought of as a temporary placement, studies have shown that once a child is in placement, he or she has a 50% chance of remaining there for 3 years or longer (Wald 1976).

In terms of assessing the child's needs in this situation, there appears to be few clear-cut guidelines, and the available studies usually either relate to divorce (Malmquist 1968; Benedek 1972; Derdeyn 1976, 1978) or concentrate on legal aspects of such decisions (Foster and Freed 1964). Goldstein et al. (1973) introduced the concept of "psychological parent," and urged the court to make decisions based on the children's needs, interests, and the time perspectives. Schetky et al. (1979) directed their study toward a broader group of parents who failed to meet their children's needs and also had their parental rights terminated by the court. Their study of 51 parents whose rights were terminated revealed that the TPR cases were primarily cases of neglect rather than abuse. Most deal with abandonment or neglect. Less than 10% of all court cases involve physical abuse. In most cases, parents' backgrounds were notable for severe social, economic, and educational disadvantages, leading to family disruptions, problems with parent–child relationships, and out-of-home placements. Many were victims of neglect, physical, and sexual abuse. These parents were marginally functioning with interpersonal difficulties, unstable marriages, social mobility and isolation, and difficulty finding employment.

Many displayed low self-esteem, impulsivity, poor judgment, and difficulty planning ahead. The parents had serious deficiency in the capacity for empathy and an inability to put their children's needs before their own. They viewed their children as existing to satisfy their needs. Parents were deficient in their own role models for parents and had impaired object relations. Emotional illness in mothers often contributed to the neglect of the child. Mental illness in mothers was frequent: some 40% of mothers had psychiatric illnesses, were hospitalized for treatment, or sought outpatient treatment at some point. Fathers were notable for the absence of psychosis, but presence of *serious* personality disorders, antisocial personality disorder (ASPD) being most frequent. Neglectful parents are harder to reach and help than abusive parents. One possible reason is the fact that neglect is more insidious and more difficult to detect. A study of children languishing in foster care showed that many were experiencing developmental delays, had symptomatic behaviors, problems in response to visitation, and delays in academic performance.

In spite of the above findings, many children were doing well in long-term foster care and eventual adoptive homes. At the time of termination, all children had formed positive attachments to foster parents. It is important to stress that age, mixed race, presence of minor behavior problems, and duration of time in foster care were not barriers to finding adoptive homes for these children.

Fanschel (1976) noted that psychiatrists, in their evaluation of parents and children, and all parties pertinent to the case, should search for (a) covert aggression; (b) role reversal where the child has inappropriately become the parent of the parent, or is serving so many psychological needs of the parent that it amounts to serving in a parental role; (c) indications that the child is being drawn into the marital dysfunction; and (d) the existence of age-inappropriate expectations of the child often combined with little appreciation of the child's own feelings and needs as separate from the parents, or lack of knowledge of developmental norms. In addition to a variety of factors considered in light of the legal criteria, clinical issues such as the severity and duration of the parent's abnormal mental or emotional condition or conduct must be evaluated.

The likelihood of the parents changing their abnormalities, allowing reintegration of the child into the home within a reasonable period of time consistent with the current ASFA requirements, must be addressed. The issue of whom the child truly views as his or her parent—that is, who is the psychological parent of the child—must be assessed. Finally, the psychiatrist should also consider options for placement of the child and the "*least detrimental alternative*" when making a recommendation, bearing in mind the problems of children in prolonged foster placements.

Although the "best interest of the child" is a universally applied principle in most jurisdictions, the concept of "psychological parent" and the "least detrimental alternative" has also been heavily relied on as important in many jurisdictions.

CLINICAL CRITERIA FOR TPR

The information in this kind of evaluation must be weighed for and against termination of parental rights with a precision that exceeds the legal criteria, for the legal criteria in themselves are not very specific and not well defined to make an easy recommendation:

1. Basic aspects of the evaluation should include examination of the child individually, with both biological parents and foster parents. All participants should be informed of the limits of confidentiality or lack of confidentiality in the evaluation.
2. Review of all records from ancillary sources such as child's school, medical records, psychiatric treatment, child protective service, or agency records should be carried out to obtain history and factual information.
3. A thorough evaluation of the child's stated parental preference must be explored in the context of a child psychiatric evaluation.
4. The child's perception of the parent's abuse, neglect, and unavailability should be assessed.
5. Evaluation must be made of the child's development, including medical examinations, developmental milestones, and psychological testing.
6. Assessment should be made of parental attitudes, knowledge of parenting skills, and the parents' own development and emotional maturity (development).
7. Determination should be made of how parents coped with stressors/demands during their child's development.
8. Evaluation of the parents' perspective as to their own difficulties and alleged reasons for termination of parental rights should be conducted.
9. Psychiatric mental status examination of all parents should be conducted to assess psychopathology.
10. Assessment of child–parent interaction in an unstructured play setting is useful in detecting covert hostility, anger, and detachment.

Additional criteria or guidelines include the following:

1. The parental availability to provide continuity and consistency of care.
2. Parental empathy and their ability to recognize the child's needs as different from their own.
3. Parental affection, warmth, and nurturance toward their children. It may be helpful to explore the parent's own history of nurturance during his or her development if relevant, as many neglectful parents have a history of having been neglected or deprived themselves.
4. Parents' intelligence in terms of their ability to manage daily practical affairs in their own lives and its effects on their parenting availability.
5. Parental ability to utilize help from professional and personal supports, as well as community supports.
6. Parents' ability to successfully rehabilitate. Has there been parental improvement enough to keep pace with the child's developmental needs? Is the parent able to apply her or his knowledge of parenting skills to the child?
7. What special needs does the child have? Have they been met in order to foster satisfactory development?
8. The quality and intensity of the child's attachment to the natural parents as well as surrogate parents.
9. The parental ability to set limits with the child to help the child develop internal controls and effectively interact with her or his environment.
10. Long-term or permanent availability of surrogate parents as well as the adoptability of the child.
11. Evaluation of the parental separations or absences with appropriate comments on their implication on the child.
12. The parent's inability to take care of himself or herself either when the child was at home or placed out of the home.
13. The limitations of psychiatric treatment with certain psychiatric disorders (e.g., personality disorders, organic brain syndromes, severe developmental disorders).
14. The parent's refusal to use treatment that could be beneficial.
15. The gains made by children while living in foster care.

In summary, this comprehensive approach to evaluation involves a progression from assessment of the parental conduct or condition, to the parent–child relationship, to the effects of the parent's conduct on the child, to the child's relationship with the surrogate parent, and finally, the child's needs. This may also satisfy the court's need to protect parental rights and focus on parental fault in terms of the effects on the child and his or her development (Schetky et al. 1979).

Ethical issues and expert testimony in forensic child psychiatry

Termination of parental rights evaluation is a sensitive issue, and it is at this delicate interface of societal values, parental rights, and children's rights that the psychiatrist is asked to render an expert opinion.

The role of a psychiatrist in such evaluations is to assume the position of evaluating appropriate parenting skills and behavior rather than to make pure diagnostic and clinical statements. Weighing competing interest poses an ethical dilemma even when guided by the universally applied principle "best interest of the child." There is a terrible finality to termination of parental rights. Common ethical dilemmas that can potentially arise in TPR evaluations include

- Will the parent improve with giving him or her one more chance?
- How does termination affect the parent's mental health?
- Are there educational and social class biases that may affect our recommendations?

- How do we balance the interest of the child who is thriving well in foster care with the concern for the child's impoverished mother who has shown minimal improvement?

Therefore, a psychiatrist's participation in TPR evaluations runs headlong into the basic value system fundamentally ingrained in the teachings of psychiatry—namely professional neutrality, clinical tolerance to a wide range of lifestyles, the family's right to privacy, dependent decision making, and the belief that intact family is the cornerstone of our social, emotional, and developmental matrix. Finally, the ultimate decision of termination presents not only the parents' personal failure in adequately providing for their children, but also the failure of society's ability to rectify through all means, including psychiatric intervention, the basic flawed parenting styles that brought the family to professional attention in the first place. It is imperative that the courts understand the limit of our current expertise in defining appropriate or adequate parenting skills and our limits in facilitating these virtuous qualities in parents who are grossly inadequate or negligent in assuming parental responsibility (Schoettle 1984).

Psychiatrist's testimony on clinical issues of TPR evaluations should also include history of parental absences and separations from their child, the parent's failure to rehabilitate or change, even with professional assistance, and their inability to utilize help in planning for the return of their children. Limitations of psychiatric treatment for several diagnostic categories such as organic brain syndrome, mental retardation, and severe personality disorders must be acknowledged. It is important to document evidence that the child has made clear developmental gains while in foster care and/or any reversal of developmental delays or abnormalities which the child previously revealed while under the parent's care and custody.

PERMANENCY AND ADOPTION: FEDERAL REGULATIONS AND LEGAL PERSPECTIVES

Definition of adoption

The Child Welfare League of America defines adoption as the method provided by law to establish the legal relationship of the parent and child between persons who are not related by birth. Adoption is the legal proceeding whereby an adult person takes another adult or minor person into the relation of child and thereby acquires the rights and incurs the responsibilities of parent with respect to said adult or minor (Section 110 of the N.Y. Domestic Relations Law).

Statistics of adoption in the United States

It has been estimated that about two million children in the United States are adopted; this amounts to about 2% of all children in the United States (Kreider and Lofquist 2014).

1. One-quarter of these children were adopted by relatives (National Survey of Adoptive Parents 2007).
2. Of the children adopted, and not including step-parent adoptions,
   a. 37% were adopted from foster care.
   b. 38% were adopted through private domestic adoptions.
   c. 25% were adopted internationally (National Survey of Adoptive Parents 2007).

There are about four million stepchildren in the United States; this amounts to nearly 5% of all children in the United States (Kreider and Lofquist 2014). The exact number of adoptions occurring annually is unknown because there is no authority collecting this data.

The U.S. Department of Health and Human Services, Administration for Children and Families publishes *Trends in Foster Care and Adoption*. The most recent publication in 2014 describes data from 2002 to 2013. In 2013, there were 51,000 children adopted in the United States; there were 102,000 children waiting for adoption in the United States. The number of children awaiting adoption has been relatively stable during the period of 2002–2013; more specifically there have been between 50,000 and 57,000 adopted during this time. The number of children awaiting adoption has decreased from about 130,000 from 2002 to 2007 to closer to 100,000 from 2011 to 2013.

Legal aspects of adoption

Children are adopted through several different means. The most common method of adoption occurs through state foster care agencies, which are legal in all states. There are also licensed foster care agencies, licensed private adoption agencies, private independent adoption agents (facilitators), and the U.S. Department of State. In April 2008, the U.S. Department of State became the controlling representative of the United States to the Hague Convention of 1993 on Protection of Children and Co-operation in Respect of Intercountry Adoption, which then activated the U.S. Intercountry Adoption Act of 2000 (Public Law 106-287). In brief, the 1993 Hague Convention created safeguards to ensure that intercountry adoptions were in the best interest of the child and with respect to his or her fundamental rights (Hague Convention 1993).

Adoption can be "closed," with virtually no contact between biological and adoptive parents; or "open," with varying degrees of contact between parties. The court has power under the N.Y. Domestic Relations Law, Section 111, not only to grant an adoption but also to grant the natural parents visitation rights even after the adoption, if it is in the best interest of the child. This is referred to as an *open adoption*.

Adoptions today are not restricted to two-parent heterosexual couples. Single-parent and other nontraditional family structures such as homosexual couples also adopt children. Regardless of the route or type, the adopted child has the same legal status with respect to his or her adoptive parents, as do any biological children. Once adoption is final, the biological parents no longer possess legal rights to the child. However, statutory laws may vary on the timing and specifics of these legal issues.

Adoption through foster care

BILL OF RIGHTS FOR FOSTER CHILDREN

Ratified in Congress Hall, Philadelphia, on April 28, 1973, this is composed of the following points:

- *Even* more than for other children, society has a responsibility along with parents for the well-being of foster children. Citizens are responsible for acting to insure their welfare.
- *Every* foster child is endowed with the rights inherently belonging to all children. In addition, because of the temporary or permanent separation from and loss of parents and other family members, the foster child requires special safeguards, resources, and care.

Every foster child has the inherent right:

- *Article of the first*: To be cherished by a family of his or her own, either the child's family helped by readily available services and supports to reassume his or her care, or an adoption family, or by plan a continuing foster family.
- *Article of the second*: To be nurtured by foster parents who have been selected to meet his or her individual needs and who are provided services and supports, including specialized education, so that they can grow in their ability to enable the child to reach his or her potential.
- *Article of the third*: To receive sensitive, continuing help in understanding and accepting the reasons for his or her own family's inability to take care of him or her, and in developing confidence in his or her own self-worth.
- *Article of the fourth*: To receive continuing loving care and respect as a unique human being…a child growing in trust in himself or herself and others.
- *Article of the fifth*: To grow up in freedom and dignity in a neighborhood of people who accept him or her with understanding, respect, and friendship.
- *Article of the sixth*: To receive help in overcoming deprivation or whatever distortion in the child's emotional, physical, intellectual, social, and spiritual growth may have resulted from his or her early experiences.
- *Article of the seventh*: To receive education, training, and career guidance to prepare him or her for a useful and satisfying life.
- *Article of the eighth*: To receive preparation for citizenship and parenthood through interaction with foster parents and other adults who are consistent role models.
- *Article of the ninth*: To be represented by an attorney-at-law in administrative or judicial proceedings with access to fair hearings and court review of decisions, so that the child's best interests are safeguarded.
- *Article of the tenth*: To receive a high quality of child welfare services, including involvement of the natural parents and his or her own involvement in major decisions that affect his or her life.

June 20, 1972, was an important day for the foster child in New York State. It was the first day that a Section 392 foster care review hearing was held at family court, New York County, with Judge Edith Miller presiding. Prior to the enactment of Section 392 of the social service law, there was no court review of the thousands of children in foster care. It was thought that because of lack of court review many children in foster care remained in foster care needlessly and many more should have been adopted, while others should have returned home to their natural parents.

Section 392 of the SSL mandates that once a child has been in foster care for a continuous period of 18 months, the authorized agency charged with the care of the child must file a petition in family court seeking review of the child's status. The petition must set forth the disposition sought (that is, return of the child to his or her natural parents, continuing foster care, or initiating the proceedings to free the child for adoption), and the grounds or reasons for such disposition. All interested parties such as the authorized agency, the natural parents, and the foster parents are given notice by mail of the hearing. The court has the power to direct the agency to undertake diligent effort to encourage and strengthen the parent–child relationship when it finds such efforts will not be detrimental to the best interest of the child. Finally, the family court that has continuing jurisdiction may rehear the matter when it is deemed necessary but within 24 months (as in *Matter of Sheila G* [61 N.Y.S 2d 368, 474 N.Y.S 2d 421]). The family court is vested with continuing jurisdiction over the child until there has been a final disposition of custody. After the child is returned to the natural parent by the Social Service agency the family court loses its jurisdiction (as in *Matter of Lucinda G* [122 MISC 2d 416, N.Y.S 2d 736 (1983)]).

International adoption

The adoption of children born abroad began mainly after World War II when orphaned European children were adopted by U.S. parents (Alstein and Simon 1991). In the 1950s, after the Korean War, international adoption became more prevalent, especially children from Korea (Alstein and Simon 1991). In the late 1970s, adoption within the United States increased. In the 1990s, international adoption increased from Eastern Europe and China. The highest number of international adoptions occurred in 2004 when it is estimated that globally 45,000 children were adopted, 23,000 of those to parents in the United States. In 2008, the Intercountry Adoption Act (IAA) required that adoption agencies be accredited (Bailey 2009).

The overall decrease in international adoption is shown in the decline in immigrant visas issued to orphans coming to the United States for adoption. The number of adopted children coming to the United States decreased from 18,000 in 2000 to 11,000 in 2010 (Selman 2012a,b). In 2009–2011, about half (51%) of the internationally adopted children were born in Asia, one-fifth were born in Latin America, and one-quarter (25%) were born in Europe (U.S. Census Bureau, American Community Survey 2012). Of the adopted children from Asia, 57% were from China and 23% were from Korea; this is in contrast to before the 1990s when 71% of adopted children were from Korea (Selman 2012a,b). The majority of children adopted from Europe (73%) were from Russia and the majority of children adopted from Latin America (71%) were from Guatemala (Selman 2012a,b).

Transracial adoption

Based on the 2007 National Survey of Adoptive Parents, 40% of adopted children (not including those adopted by step-parents) were involved in a transracial, transethical, or transcultural adoption (Vandivere et al. 2009). In the past, transracial adoption has been opposed and restricted. The Multiethnic Placement Act of 1994 sought to eliminate these barriers. More specifically, the goals of this act were to decrease the length of time that children wait to be adopted, facilitate identification and recruitment of families that can meet the child's needs, and prevent discrimination based on race, color, or national origin (Multiethnic Placement Act 1994).

Historians of transracial placement in the United States generally agree that its occurrence, similar to international adoption, was extremely rare up to World War II (Silverman and Fiegelman 1990; Simon 1994). Initially, it occurred on a moderately large scale as a form of intercountry adoption from the 1960s to the mid-1970s. First, U.S. military involvement in the Far East was the background to the adoption of Japanese, Chinese, and subsequently Korean and Vietnamese children by Caucasian Americans. The adoption of Hispanic children from Latin America has also been considerable (Feigelman and Silverman 1983). Second, liberal child welfare regulations actively promoted transracial placement as a means of assisting disadvantaged African-American children by finding alternatives to institutionalization. Third, Caucasian families were willing to accept placement of African-American children and were then seen as progressive in being prepared to withstand stigma for the sake of principle, as many were motivated by the ideal of a more racially integrated society.

However, opposition arose against transracial placement. Concerns in both Native and African-American communities were based on the view that their culture was threatened with depletion if their children were placed away from home into Caucasian families. The rise of the civil rights and African-American consciousness movements took child welfare practice into the political arena, and the increasingly confident voice of some African-American professionals was raised in criticism of the adoption establishment. Transracial placement became emblematic of wider historical and political injustices. Such views were understandable in light of the lack of prior involvement and consultation with the African-American professionals and their community about the placement of African-American children in care. Hence, there followed a sharp decline in such placements after 1976.

Some reviewers have disputed that this opposition was justified and maintain that "transracial placement" is a viable means of providing stable homes for waiting children. Identity is one of the concepts most used by anti-transracialists. It is crucial to child development, but its meaning remains less resolved. Some authors present "a positive sense of racial identity" as a unified achievable goal (Maximé 1986), whereas others stress its fluidity and context dependency (Katz 1995). It has been defined as having overlapping parts such as personal identification and feelings about the self, as well as the degree of identification with various social groupings (Richards 1994). The process of transracial adoption seems to produce children whose self-esteem is at least as high as that of nonadopted children, and whose adjustment appears to be more than satisfactory (Silverman and Feigelman 1990, 199).

In 2009–2011, there were 438,000 transracially adopted children under the age of 18, which is 28% of all adopted children under 18. Compared to other children, transracially adopted children tended to be younger (Kreider and Lofquist 2014). A higher percentage of transracially adopted children lived with married parents, specifically 77% compared to 71% of other adopted children. Transracially adopted children lived in households with higher income, lower poverty rates, and with a higher percentage of advance education compared to children adopted by the same race of parent (Kreider and Lofquist 2014). These statistics make sense given the higher proportion of these children who are also internationally adopted (Child Welfare Information Gateway 2011; Ishizawa and Kubo 2014).

THE ADOPTION AND SAFE FAMILIES ACT (ASFA) OF 1997

The ASFA of 1997 amended the 1980 Adoption Assistance and Child Welfare Act (P.L.96-272), the federal statute that provided for partial federal reimbursement to states for child welfare and out-of-home care expenses (Adoption and Safe Families Act, Public Law 105-89). To qualify for reimbursement, state child welfare and out-of-home care plans must comply with the requirements of the 1980 statute, as amended by ASFA.

In the provisions of the 1980 act was the requirement that state child welfare agencies make reasonable effort to preserve families by avoiding unnecessary out-of-home care placements and, where out-of-home care placements could not be avoided, by reunifying families as quickly as possible. ASFA modifies this "reasonable efforts" requirement in some respects. First, the statute establishes "health and safety of the child" as the most important consideration in determining what family preservation and reunification efforts are required.

ASFA also sets forth three exceptions to the reasonable efforts requirement:

1. If the agency alleges that there are "aggravated circumstances" defined as severe or repeated child abuse, which may include abandonment, torture, or physical and sexual abuse
2. If the parent has been convicted of murder or manslaughter of a sibling or half-sibling of the child, or a felony assault resulting in serious physical injury to the child or another child of the parent
3. If the parental rights of the parent to a sibling have been terminated involuntarily via termination of parental rights proceeding, as opposed to a voluntary surrender (ASFA §101(a)(15)(D))

In addition to modifying the reasonable efforts requirement, ASFA also imposes new requirements for expedited filing of termination of the parental rights proceeding. The statute requires a state to file a petition for termination of parental rights for all children who have been in foster care for *15 of the most recent 22 months*, including all children already in care.

The TPR petition is to be immediately filed for children for whom "aggravated circumstances" (e.g., severe or repeated child abuse) has been found or whose parent or guardian has an enumerated serious criminal conviction (*Santosky v. Kramer* 1982, at 455).

U.S. 745 (1982) requires a higher burden of proof in a termination based on repeated abuse. The statute provides exceptions to the requirement to file termination of parental rights petition where

- The child is in kinship care.
- The agency documents "compelling reasons" which may include (a) a lack of sufficient grounds for a petition to terminate parental right; (b) inappropriateness because the child is in placement as a juvenile delinquent or person in need of supervision (PINS); (c) has a permanency goal other than adoption; and/or (d) refusal of a child over the age of 14 years to consent to adoption.
- The agency has not provided reasonable efforts to reunify the family, although legally required to do so.

The other significant amendments include criminal background checks for prospective foster and adoptive parents (42 USC 671(a)(20)(A)). The federal statute further provides that a prospective foster or adoptive parent must be denied placement of a child if the background check reveals

- A felony conviction at any time for child abuse or neglect, spousal abuse, or violent crimes, including homicide, sexual assault, or rape
- A felony conviction within the past 5 years for assault, battery, or a drug-related offense

The federal act additionally provides that the state must hold an initial permanency hearing for foster children within 12 months of the date the child entered foster care (42 USC 675(5)(c)). The date the child entered foster care is defined as the 60 days after the child was removed from his or her home. At this permanency hearing, the court determines the appropriateness of the child's permanency plan, including whether and when the child should be returned to the parent, placed for adoption, referred for legal guardianship, or placed in another planned permanent living arrangement.

These amendments were made to expeditiously transition foster-care children into suitable permanent homes. It was felt that foster care should serve mainly as a temporary safe haven for children—a secure setting where they can live while suitable permanent homes are being located for them.

The Adoption 2002 Report, a federal government undertaking in response to President Clinton's initiative on adoption and foster care, has outlined several important assumptions in its memorandum, including

1. Every child deserves a safe and permanent family.
2. Children's safety and health are of paramount concern and must guide all child welfare services.
3. Children deserve prompt and timely decision making as to who their permanent caregivers will be.
4. Permanency planning begins when a child enters foster care.
5. Adoptive families require support after the child's adoption is legalized.
6. The diversity and strengths of all communities must be tapped.
7. Quality services must be provided as soon as possible to enable families in crisis to address problems.

PERMANENCY AND ADOPTION: AN OVERVIEW

Family preservation beyond the best interest of the child

Family preservation should not compromise the well-being of children. When parents cannot be rehabilitated, or when parents' problems are too complex to be resolved in the short term, children bounce between the biological family and foster care, drifting from foster home to foster home. In such cases, the best interests of the children are not served.

The current foster-care system is overburdened, and the number of available, qualified foster parents has steadily diminished since the 1980s. This diminution is partly due to the increased needs of children traumatized by poverty, physical and sexual abuse, drug and alcohol exposure, and emotional maltreatment at the hands of both parents. Because traditional foster care was not designed to meet these special needs, specialized and therapeutic foster-care homes have become available. For many children, foster care remains a viable option for reducing risk. Kinship foster care also works in the interests of family preservation by allowing a relative to become a foster parent. The federal government has funded several projects to examine the practice elements in kinship adoptions. Evidence available suggests that the likelihood of kinship adoption of foster children depends, in great part, on the ethnicity of the children. Evidence also suggests that kinship adoptive families look vastly different than other adoptive families and are poorer, less educated, older, and more likely to be single than nonkinship adopting families (Barth 1994).

The foster-care system has provided invaluable assistance to children at risk. It deserves enhanced financial support, especially at a time when so many birth families are struggling to survive and may need to temporarily relinquish their child. Residential care facilities should be seen as positive alternatives for children in need. Residential facilities can fulfill a need for order, discipline, and rootedness in many young lives. They provide nonparental, well-qualified, and committed mentors who can turn around the lives of many youngsters who might wrongly be considered as hopeless cases. Residential care can be introduced into a child's life on a short-term basis at various points according to their needs, and can enhance family preservation, foster care, and adoption services. Young adolescents who can be taught fundamental principles such as "do no harm" and can benefit from the constructive adult guidance can experience the structure of residential care as liberating (Post et al. 1997).

Re-entry after reunification

Terling (1999) described the correlates of re-entry into child protective services for abused and neglected children reunited with their families. The correlates of re-entry included

1. *Type of abuse*: Neglect cases are the most common type of cases among both the family reunification cases and the re-entry cases. Among 59 cases of children who were examined after returning home, four had been repeatedly and severely physically and/or sexually abused, and previous documentation of risk of repeat abuse was present in those cases. Therefore, the mere presence of the severity of abuse warrants close attention during evaluation.
2. *Previous referrals*: The presence of previous referrals to a child protective agency is a strong indicator of the risk of re-entry. Also, inability of the parent to change after prior interactions with child protective services is a good indicator of the risk of re-entry. Of the re-entry cases, approximately 67% had previous referrals, versus 12% of non-re-entry.
3. *Substance abuse*: Some 50% of re-entry cases involved substance-abusing parents, as opposed to 20% for non-re-entry. Two important issues about substance abuse re-entry included (a) presence of a substance-abusing partner not in treatment; and (b) time allowed for recovery for the substance-abusing parent. Therefore in evaluating risk, importance should be given to perpetrators, partners, and their treatment, and the length of recovery in caregivers needs to be monitored for longer periods of time (months versus years).
4. *Parental competence* is the presence or absence of parental ability to provide an environment that is safe and healthy for the child to grow and develop. Parental competence can be impaired in (a) parents with low levels of intellectual functioning, thus possessing a deficit in their ability to process information and make decisions; and (b) parents who lack insight and do not understand or accept the agency's identification of their lifestyle and parenting as inappropriate. This lack of understanding interferes with their parenting skills and renders them incapable of changing their lifestyle/parenting to get their children back.
5. *Social isolation and negative relationships* such as an abusive spouse or a high level of family conflicts are significant predictors of re-entry.

There was less correlation of re-entry to parental income, child protective risk assessment by caseworkers, compliance, and family functioning assessment.

It is estimated that despite efforts by Child Protective Services to rehabilitate abusive and neglectful parents/families and make them suitable for the children, over one-third of these children return to the system due to additional maltreatment. The rate of children returning seems to be excessively high when dealing with the lives and future well-being of the children. Therefore, identifying for re-entry serves as a useful tool for practitioners and policy makers. Future research is needed to better understand the "whys" behind the successes and failures in order to develop policies and practices that do more than help some of these children, some of the time.

Research shows that although adopted children can have difficulties after placement, in the long run they progress well through their remaining childhood and into adult life. They tend to fare better than children brought up by their own parents in an abusive or neglectful environment, or in institutions, and are considerably better than children who have remained in long-term foster care. Several studies conducted in different countries to assess the effects of long-term foster care have all concluded that "Adoption, when available as an option, should be generally pursued rather than long-term foster care" (Mather 1999).

Mental health issues in adopted children

The emotional and behavioral adjustment of adopted children has received a great deal of attention as a result of the alleged over-representation of adopted children in mental health settings. The over-representation of adopted children and adolescents in clinical population research has varied widely. Several researchers have also suggested that the age of the child is an important factor; the older the child when placed in an adoptive home, the more likely the child is to have emotional and behavioral problems.

A study conducted by Borders et al. (1998), using a nationally representative sample of children in the United States, found no significant differences between adopted and nonadopted children on a range of adjustment variables. Brand and Brinich (1999) also concluded that a vast majority of adopted children showed patterns of behavior similar to those of nonadopted children.

The over-representation of adopted children in mental health settings found in earlier studies might be attributable to the presence of small groups of severely troubled adopted children in clinical samples. For the small group of severely troubled children and adolescents who had extensive behavior problems and were seen more frequently at the mental health centers, a better understanding of the factors that make these children vulnerable is an area of future research. Many factors such as (a) genetic predisposition to emotional and behavioral problems; (b) prenatal substance abuse by birth mothers; and (c) pre-adoption experiences such as neglect, abuse, or multiple placements may be contributing factors. This point needs to be emphasized because of the concerns that an error in interpretation could lead to pathologizing a very effective intervention for children. Most adopted children behave much like their nonadopted peers, and adoption remains a valuable and important social response to a complicated set of placement problems for children.

Role of child psychiatrist and medical practitioner in adoption assessment

Like all other parents, potential adopters need to have a thorough description of the children's past medical problems, their current health status, and their likely future needs. A comprehensive assessment of the child should be carried out to include the child's physical, emotional, developmental, and social status. Medical practitioners and child psychiatrists involved in adoption work assessments should have knowledge of the long-term consequences of child abuse and neglect. They should have an understanding of genetic illnesses that can be inherited from the birth parents, and of the long-term consequences of the parental lifestyles that may have involved exposure to alcohol, substance abuse, high-risk behaviors, and domestic violence. They should also be able to make recommendations on these children, and most often should be involved in considerable liaison with other health professionals, social services, foster parents, and adopters. It is important to recognize that if adoption is a real option for a group of very disturbed or disadvantaged children, then appropriately trained medical advisors with experience and knowledge in pediatrics and child mental health must be available to support this service.

SPECIAL ISSUES AND CONSIDERATIONS

Telling a child about being adopted

Telling a child about his or her unique route of entry into the family is a challenging process. In modern times it is recognized that children adapt more easily when they are aware of their birth circumstances. Therefore, parents are now advised openly to discuss adoption, not only with the child but also with relatives and friends. Then comes the question of when and how to discuss adoption. A 7- to 8-year-old child who possesses characteristics of logical thinking could more easily absorb and understand the adoption process than a younger child. Yet waiting until a child turns 7 years old is not recommended because

- Children ask questions earlier, and the parents would be forced to cover up or lie in some fashion.
- Sometimes children may inadvertently overhear comments about their adopted status from their relatives or friends.
- Children who look different from their parents often generate comments or questions from the public.
- Health-care providers ask questions regarding family history frequently in front of children.

The timing and substance of conversations about the child's adoption are challenging issues for both parents and providers. Most experts agree that open, life-long, and middle ground communication is the key to improving ego identity, smoothing the adaptation process, and building a child's positive self-image. One excellent method is to have a photo album of the child, beginning with the photographs of the adoptive mother and father going to the agency. It may be helpful to have another photograph of the parents' first contact with the child, along with a photograph of the mother carrying the child through the door into the new home. This provides a life-long continuity for the child's understanding of the adoptive "birthing" process into the adoptive home (Table 39.1).

The baby Byron case

This is a custody case that had considerable media coverage. This case highlights the problems most commonly raised in the transracial adoption debate.

> Byron, an African–American infant born addicted to heroin and cocaine, had been raised since July 1992—from the age of six days—by a Caucasian couple. This family had been selected to provide shelter for Byron on an emergency basis because his birth mother was unable to care for him. The foster family had their own biological child and two other adopted children. They were owners of a printing company. Byron's father was reportedly killed in an automobile accident in 1992. Byron's mother had four children who were cared for by two other families because she reportedly had neglected her children in the past. When Byron was a five-month-old, child protective officials tried to remove him from care of the Caucasian family and place him with an

Table 39.1 Stages of understanding adoption

Stage	Questions	Child's adoption related tasks	Goals for parent and child
Infants and toddlers (0–2)	"How do we begin?"	Adjusting to the transition to a new home Developing secure attachments	To become comfortable discussing adoption with others To use positive adoption language To become familiar with resources, support groups, books
Preschool (3–7)	"Where do babies come from?" "Where do I come from?" "Why or how did you choose me?" "Why don't I look like you?" "If you are in an adoptive family, can your birth parents or another family take you away?"	Learning about birth and reproduction Adjusting to initial information about adoption Recognizing physical differences within the family	To recognize child's egocentric thinking style To begin communicating about different ways children enter families To realize that despite the child's ability to parrot story, no abstract or conceptual understanding occurs yet To answer every question as faithfully as possible with positive adoption language To recognize physical differences but focus on similarities between child and the family To alleviate fears of losing adoptive parents by reassuring adoption is permanent
Middle childhood	"Why was I placed for adoption?" "Why didn't they keep me—didn't they like me?" "If you are adopted can you be un-adopted?" "If they didn't know how to take care of me, why didn't someone teach them?" "If they were poor why didn't someone give them money?" "Who do I look like?"	Understanding the meaning and implications of adoption Searching for answers regarding origin and reasons for relinquishment Coping with physical differences with the family Coping with the stigma of adoption Coping with peer reactions to adoption Coping with adoption related losses	To acknowledge sadness, anger, and grief associated with loss (7–11) of biological parents To assure child he or she is not bad or defective by offering actual reason for adoption To refrain from making negative comments about biological parents To offer factual information without embellishment To reassure that adoption is not a second choice To provide support groups and services for child
Adolescence	"Who am I?"	Exploring the implications and meanings of being adopted Connecting adoption to one's sense of identity Coping with racial identity Possibly searching for the biological family Coping with adoption related losses	To recognize child's abstract (12–17) thinking style To recognize identity difficulties of dealing with biological and adoptive parents To share adoption papers To continue use of support groups and services for child and parents
Young adult (18+)	"I want to meet my biological family"	Considering searching biological family Exploring implications of adoption as it relates to development of intimacy Coping with adoption related losses	To help child seek birth parents' To minimize parent's feelings of rejection To continue use of support groups and services for child and parents

Source: Adapted from Brodzinsky DM, LM Singer, and AM Braff. 1984. *Child Development* 55:869–878; Smit E. 1996. *Journal of Psychosocial Nursing and Mental Health Services* 34:29–36.

African–American foster family. The Caucasian family objected, and the judge left the child with them on a short-term basis. When Byron was eleven months old, the judge once again ruled that Byron should continue to stay with the Caucasian family who expressed desire to adopt him. When Byron was seventeen months old the judge ruled that he should be returned to his biological mother, which in the judge's opinion was in the best interest of the child. In referring to criticism of his decision, the judge felt it was racist to conclude that an African–American woman was no good, and then to give Byron to the "nice, white, suburban couple." Byron was then returned to his biological mother who was reported to have undergone treatment for her substance-abuse problems and was living in a residential drug treatment center. The foster family reportedly felt that race was very much an issue in this case. They suggested that if the court had considered only the child's best interest, had visited Byron, and considered the birth mother's history of drug addiction, the decision would have been different. Some commentators argued that children are best reared in families where they will be taught coping skills. Others suggested it was important for any baby to be kept with his or her own race. However, in June 1994, the judge removed Byron from his biological mother after she admitted using drugs.

It is important to be mindful of the concepts of bonding and psychological parenting in the context of many adoption disputes where there might be considerable bonding or a unique affective connection between the child and the caregiver.

Silverman (1993) reviewed transracial adoption research studies published in the past 10 years, focusing on outcome in adolescence and adulthood. This included a comparison group, and they had their subjects placed for adoption at an early age. These studies assessed family integration, self-esteem, school performance, racial identity, and overall adjustment of the transracial adoptees.

The first of the studies in this group carried out by McRoy et al. (1984) reported that family integration and general adjustment were successful, and their self-esteem and academic performance were satisfactory. Marked differences emerged in the area of racial identity. The in-racial adoptees referred to themselves as black, and 56% of the transracial adoptees referred to themselves as mixed or part white. McRoy and her colleagues saw this racial group orientation among the transracial adoption children as problematic.

Simon and Alstein conducted the longest-running study between 1971 and 1991 (Simon and Alstein 1981; Simon 1994). There were again no impressive differences among the groups in regard to family integration, academic performance, self-esteem, and general adjustment. Most children were under the age of 3 years at the time of adoption in this study. During adolescence and later as adults, the transracial adoptees were aware of, and comfortable with, their racial identity. There was clear variability in their reference group orientation, however, as many of them dated Caucasian and preferred Caucasian friends.

It is important, therefore, for forensic experts or evaluators who participate in the transracial adoption context to make clear to the court the limitation of scientific-based data in this area. At the same time, the expert should tell the court what is known about parent–child bonding and the outcome of transracial adopted children. Undoubtedly, there will continue to be considerable disagreement about whether the best way to assure a promising future for an African–American child needing a permanent home is to seek qualified adoptive parents without regard to race. A thoughtful framework needs to be kept in mind as psychiatrists participate in this passionate debate of transracial adoption, which is of national importance.

Subsidized adoptions

When financial aid is given to adoptive parents after the adoption of a child, it is called *subsidized adoption*. The intent of such adoptions is to ensure permanent homes for children who would otherwise remain in foster care until they were adults. The amount of monthly payments and the length of time the subsidy is granted are left to the discretion of the social services commissioner, and can vary. A voluntary agency that has a child in foster care and wishes to recommend to the local department of social services adoption by the foster parents, with subsidy, may do so. The social services department may accept such recommendations, which include the amount of subsidy to be provided in the first year. After the adoption, the family is like any other family and is independent of the agency, except for annual evaluations of the need for continued subsidy.

Parental visitation after adoption

Visitation with a natural parent after adoption should be considered:

1. If there is a solid parent–child relationship, visitation after adoption should be explored and, if beneficial, implemented with consent of all parties, including the child.
2. The court should not force visitation after adoption without the consent of the adoptive parents and the child.
3. If visitation is provided, the court should retain jurisdiction and modify or vacate visitation where appropriate.

Grandparent's visitation after adoption

The paramount concern of the court in making its final decision as to grandparent's visitation must be the "best interests of the child." The child's rights and wishes can be best considered if counsel represents them, and if the judge interviews the child as to his or her preferences. No petition for grandparent visitation should be dismissed without a hearing where the petition alleges that a relationship existed between the grandparent and the child. Prior to the hearing, a law guardian should be appointed to represent the interests of the child and his or her preferences, with the best interests of the child as a controlling factor. Several factors to be considered in the decision making include

1. The relationship between the grandparent and the child
2. The age of the child, and his or her wishes
3. The benefit to the child of a continued relationship with a grandparent
4. The recommendation of the law guardian
5. The contention and wishes of the adoptive parents
6. The extent to which visitation with grandparents could interfere with the new relationship of the child and the adoptive parents
7. In complex cases, the clinical assessment by a child psychiatrist

REFERENCES

Adoption and Safe Families Act of 1997. 1999. Changing welfare policies without addressing parental substance abuse. *Journal of Contemporary Health Law Policy* 16:243–271.

Adoption and Safe Families Act, Public Law 105-89, §101(b), 42USC, 675 (7).

Alstein H and RJ Simon. 1991. *Intercountry Adoption: A Multinational Perspective.* New York: Praeger.

American Jurisprudence 2 & § 34 (1987).

American Jurisprudence 2d 24, Generally §974, 960 (1983).

American Jurisprudence 2d 59, Discipline §22, 152 (1987).

Armitage DT. 1994. Parental competence and termination of parental rights. In *Principles and Practice of Forensic Psychiatry*, edited by R Rosner, London: Chapman and Hall, 282–308.

Bailey JD. 2009. Expectations of the consequences of new international adoption policy in the U.S. *Journal of Sociology and Social Welfare* 36(2):169–184.

Barth RP. 1994. Adoption research: Building blocks for the next decade. *Child Welfare* 73:625–638.

Benedek E. 1972. Child custody law. *American Journal of Psychiatry* 129:326–328.

Borders LD, LK Black, and BK Pasley. 1998. Are adopted children at greater risk for negative outcomes? *Family Relations* 47:237–241.

Brand AE and Brinich PM. 1999. Behavior problems and mental health contacts in adopted, foster, and non-adopted children. *Journal of Child Psychology and Psychiatry* 40:1221–1229.

Brodzinsky DM, LM Singer, and AM Braff. 1984. Children's understanding of adoption. *Child Development* 55:869–878.

California Civil Code §226(a), as found in West's annotated California Civil Code (main volume 1982; supplement 1991).

Child Custody Act of 1970, Michigan Comprehensive Law Annotated §722.23 (West supplement 1976).

Child Welfare Information Gateway. 2011. *Costs of Adopting.* Washington, DC: U.S. Department of Health and Human Services, Children's Bureau.

Cleveland Bd. of Educ. v. LaFleur, 414 U.S. 632, 639–40 (1974).

Derdeyn AP. 1976. A consideration of legal issues in child contests. *Archives of General Psychiatry* 33:165–171.

Derdeyn AP. 1978. Child custody conflicts in historical perspective. *American Journal of Psychiatry* 133:1369–1376.

District of Columbia Code 1981 §16-2353 (1991).

Fanschel D. 1976. Status change of children in foster care. Final results for the Columbia University Longitudinal Study. *Child Welfare* 55:143–171.

Feigelman W and AR Silverman. 1983. *Chosen Children.* New York: Praeger.

Foster H and D Freed. 1964. Child custody. *New York Law Review* 39:423–443.

Genty PM. 1998. Permanency planning in the context of parental incarceration: Legal issues and recommendations. *Child Welfare* 77:543–559.

Goldstein J, A Freud, and A Solnit. 1973. *Beyond the Best Interests of the Child.* New York: Free Press.

Griswold v. Connecticut, 381 U.S. 479 (1965).

Hague Convention of 29 May 1993 on Protection of Children and Co-operation in Respect of Intercountry Adoption.

Haynes JP. 2009. Parenting assessment in abuse, neglect, and permanent wardship cases. In *Principles and Practice of Child and Adolescent Forensic Mental Health*, edited by EP Benedeck, P Ash, and CL Scott, Arlington, VA: American Psychiatric Publishing, 157–169.

In re Adoption of Sabrina, 325 Pa. Super. 17, 472 A. 2d 624, 627 (Super. Ct. 1984).

In re Bernard Pecor, W.L. 10791 (CT 1992).

In re Demetrius F. et al. 575 N.Y.S. 2d 552 (1991).

In re Gault, 387 U.S. 1 (1967).

In re Green, 292 A. 2d 2387 (1972).

In re Interest of B.M. v. L.M., 475 N.W. 2d 909 (1991).

Ishizawa H and K Kubo. 2014. Factors affecting adoption decisions: Child and family parental characteristics. *Journal of Family Issues* 35:627.

Johnston D. 1995. Effects of parental incarceration. In: *Children of Incarcerated Parents*, edited by K Gabel and D Johnson, New York: Lexington Books, 59–88.

Katz I. 1995. Anti-racism and modernism. In *Learning and Teaching in Social Work: Towards Reflective Practice*, edited by M Yelloly and M Henkel, London: Jessica Kingsley, 120–135.

Kreider RM and DA Lofquist. 2014. *Adopted Children and Stepchildren: 2010. Population Characteristics*. Washington, DC: U.S. Census Bureau.

Lochner v. New York, 198 U.S. 45 (1905).

Malmquist C. 1968. The role of parental illness in custody proceedings. *Family Law Quarterly* 360:364–365.

Mather M. 1999. Adoption: A forgotten pediatric specialty. *Archives of Disability in Childhood* 81:492–495.

Mathews v. Eldridge, 96 S.Ct. 893 (1976).

Maximé JE. 1986. Some psychological models of black self-concept. In *Social Work with Black Children and Their Families*, edited by S Ahmed, X Cheetham, and J Small, London: Batsford/BAAF.F, 100–116.

McRoy RG, LA Zurcher, ML Lauderdale, and RE Anderson. 1984. The identity of transracial adoptees. *Social Casework* 65:34–39.

Mnookin R. 1978. *Child, Family and State: Problems and Materials on Children and the Law*. Boston: Little Brown.

Multiethnic Placement Act. P.L. 103-382 (1994).

New York Social Services Law § 384-b(7)(f)(5).

Parham v. J.R., 99 S.Ct. 2493 (1979).

Pierce v. Society of Sisters, 2689 U.S. 510 (1925).

Post SG, PR Frutig, and J Bennett. 1997. The moral challenge of children at risk: Protective policies and pediatrics. A report of the Children's Services, Inc. Task Force of Greater Cleveland. *Clinical Pediatrics (Phila.)* 36:625–633.

Prince v. Commonwealth of Massachusetts, 46 N.E. 2d 755 affn. 321 U.S. 158 without opinions; Reh. Den. 321 U.S. 804 (1944).

Richards B. 1994. What is identity? In *Culture, Identity and Transracial Adoption*, edited by I Gaber and J Aldridge, London: Free Association Books, 77–88.

Roe v. Wade, 410 U.S. 113 (1973).

Santosky v. Kramer, 102 S.Ct. 1388 (1982).

Schetky D and D Slader. 1980. Termination of parental rights. In *Child Psychiatry and the Law*, edited by E Benedek and D Schetky, New York: Brunner/Mazel.

Schetky DH, R Angell, CV Morrison, and WH Sack. 1979. Parents who fail: A study of 51 cases of termination of parental rights. *Journal of the American Academy of Child Psychiatry* 18:366–383.

Schoettle UC. 1984. Termination of parental rights-ethical issues and role conflicts. *Journal of the American Academy of Child and Adolescent Psychiatry* 23:629–632.

Selman P. 2012a. The rise and fall of intercountry adoption in the 21st century: Global trends from 2001–2010. In *Intercountry Adoption: Policies, Practices, and Outcomes*, edited by JL Gibbons and KS Rotabi, Southampton, UK: University of Southampton, 1–17.

Selman P. 2012b. Global trends in intercountry adoption: 2001–2010. *Adoption Advocate*, No. 44 (Feb), National Council for Adoption, Alexandria, VA.

Silverman AR. 1993. Outcomes of transracial adoption. *Future Child* 3:104–118.

Silverman AR and W Feigelman. 1990. Adjustment in interracial adoptees: An overview. In *Psychology of Adoption*, edited by DM Brodzinsky and MD Schechter, Oxford: Oxford University Press, 187–200.

Simon RJ. 1994. Transracial adoption: The American experience. In *In the Best Interests of the Child: Culture, Identity and Transracial Adoption*, edited by I Gaber and J Aldridge, London: Free Association Books, 1–124.

Simon RJ and H Alstein. 1981. *Transracial Adoption: A Follow Up*. Lexington, MA: Lexington Books.

Smit E. 1996. Unique issues of the adopted child: Helping parents talk openly and honestly with their child and the community. *Journal of Psychosocial Nursing and Mental Health Services* 34:29–36.

Snell TL. 1994. *Special Report: Women in Prison*. Washington, DC: U.S. Department of Justice, Bureau of Justice Statistics.

Stanley v. Illinois, 92 S. Ct. 1208 (1972).

Terling T. 1999. The efficacy of family reunification practices: Re-entry rates and correlates of re-entry for abused and neglected children reunited with their families. *Child Abuse and Neglect* 23:1359–1370.

Uniform Marriage and Divorce Act § 402 H.N. 1991. *In Uniform Laws Annotated*. St. Paul, MN: West.

U.S. Census Bureau. 2012. *American Community Survey*. Washington, DC: U.S. Census Bureau.

U.S. Department of Health and Human Services. 2007. *National Survey of Adoptive Parents (NSAP)*. Washington, DC: U.S. Department of Health and Human Services.

U.S. Department of Justice. 1995. *Sourcebook of Criminal Justice Statistics 1995*. Washington, DC: Bureau of Justice Statistics.

U.S. Intercountry Adoption Act of 2000 (Public Law 106–279).

Vandivere S, K Malm, and L Radel. 2009. *Adoption USA: A Chartbook Based on the 2007 National Survey of Adoptive Parents*. Washington, DC: U.S. Department of Health and Human Services, Office of the Assistant Secretary for Planning and Evaluation.

Wald M. 1976. State intervention on behalf of neglected children. *Stanford Law Review* 28:627–706.

Wisconsin v. Yoder, 406 U.S. 205 (1972).

FURTHER READING

Alstein H and R Simon. 1977. Transracial adoption: An examination of an American phenomenon. *Journal of Social Welfare*, winter.

Barth R and Berry M. 1988. *Adoption and Disruption: Rates, Risks and Responses*. New York: de Gruyter.

Barth RP. 1997. Effects of age and race on the odds of adoption versus remaining in long-term out-of-home care. *Child Welfare* 76:285–308.

Borgman R. 1981. Antecedents and consequences of parental rights termination for abused and neglected children. *Child Welfare* 60:391–400.

Brodzkinsky DM, D Smith, and A Brodzkinsky. 1998. *Children's Adjustment to Adoption: Developmental and Clinical Perspectives*. Newbury Park, CA: Sage.

Carrieri JR. 1991. *The Adoption. Child Custody, Foster Care and Adoptions*. New York: Lexington Books.

Diamond BL. 1990. The psychiatric expert witness; honest advocate or "hired gun"? In *Ethical Practice in Psychiatry and Law*. New York: Plenum Press, 75–84.

District of Columbia Code 1981 §16-2351 (1991).

Doe v. Commonwealth's Attorney, 403 F. Supp. 1199 (1976).

Doe v. Roe, 526 N.Y.S.2d 718 (1988).

Fialkov MJ. 1998. Fostering permanency of children in out-of-home care: Psycho-legal aspects. *Bulletin of the American Academy of Psychiatry and the Law* 16:343–357.

Griffith EE. 1999. Forensic and policy implications of the transracial adoption debate. *Bulletin of the American Academy of Psychiatry and the Law* 23:501–512.

Hall JG and BH Mitchell. 1982. The role of law in protecting the child. A critique of the English system. *Child Abuse and Neglect* 6:63–69.

Henry DL. 1999. Resilience in maltreated children: An implication for special needs adoption. *Child Welfare* 78:519–540.

Hollingsworth LD. 1998. Promoting same-race adoption for children of color. *Social Work* 43:10–17.

Holloway JS. 1997a. Foster and adoptive mothers' assessment of permanent family placements. *Archives of Disability in Childhood* 76:231–235.

Holloway JS. 1997b. Outcome in placements for adoption or long-term fostering. *Archives of Disability in Childhood* 76:227–230.

In Matter of Baby M, 538 A. 2d 1227 (1988).

In re Baby M, 525 A. 2d 1128 (NJ 1987).

In re Baby M, 537 A. 2d 1227 (NJ 1988).

In re Carmelata B., 579 P. 2d 518 (1978).

Kermani EJ and BA Weiss. 1995. Biological parents regaining their rights: A psycho-legal analysis of a new era in custody disputes. *Bulletin of the American Academy of Psychiatry and Law* 23:261–267.

Knight MR. 1985. Termination visits in closed adoptions. *Child Welfare* 64:37–45.

Lears MK, KJ Guth, and L Lewandowski. 1998. International adoption: A primer for pediatric nurses. *Pediatric Nursing* 24:578–586.

Lykken DT. 1997. Incompetent parenting: Its causes and cures. *Child Psychiatry and Human Development* 27:129–137.

Maas H. 1969. Children in long-term foster care. *Child Welfare* 48:321–333.

McRoy RG. 1994. Attachment and racial identity issues: Implications for child placement decision-making. *Journal of Multicultural Social Work* 3:59–74.

McRoy RG, LA Zurcher, ML Lauderdale, and RE Anderson. 1982. Identity of transracial adoptees. *Social Work* 27:522–526.

Nordhaus BF and AJ Solnit. 1998. Foster placement. *Child and Adolescent Psychiatric Clinics of North America* 7:345–356.

O'Flynn M. 1999. The Adoption and Safe Families Act of 1997: Changing child welfare policy without addressing parental substance abuse. *Journal of Contemporary Health and Law Policy* 16:243–271.

Proch K and J Howard. 1984. Parental visiting in foster care: Law and practice. *Child Welfare* 63:139–147.

Ritner B and CD Dozier. 2000. Effects of court-ordered substance abuse treatment in child protective services cases. *Social Work* 45:131–140.

Rosner R. 1994. *Principles and Practice of Forensic Psychiatry*. London: Chapman and Hall, Family Law Section.

Rushton A. 1994. Principles and practice in the permanent placement of older children. *Children and Society* 8:224–225.

Rushton A and H Minnis. 1997. Transracial family placements. *Journal of Child Psychology and Psychiatry* 38:147–159.

Schetky DH. 1992. Ethical issues in forensic child and adolescent psychiatry. *Journal of the American Academy of Child and Adolescent Psychiatry* 31:403–407.

Stanton AM. 1998. Grandparent's visitation rights and custody. *Child and Adolescent Psychiatric Clinics of North America* 7:409–419.

Vroegh KS. 1992. *Transracial Adoption: How Is It 17 Years Later?* Chicago: Chicago Child Care Society.

40

Child abuse and neglect

SUZANNE M. DUPÉE

INTRODUCTION

The maltreatment of children is not a new phenomenon. Empey et al. (1999) identified three periods in the history of childhood. In the pre-fifteenth century there was an *indifference to childhood.* From the fifteenth to eighteenth centuries there was a *discovery of childhood,* and in the nineteenth and twentieth centuries there was a *preoccupation with childhood.* The twenty-first century has accelerated the latter stage of *preoccupation with childhood.*

The Society for the Prevention of Cruelty to Children, the world's first child protective agency, was founded in 1874. Children were not offered protection by law until the late nineteenth century. Child abuse was mostly tolerated unless the case was extreme. The old saying, "spare the rod and spoil the child," validates parents who equate child abuse with good parenting. These parents often do not intend to damage the child but believe that corporal punishment will shape the child into a better adult. Many parents who engage in corporal punishment against their children might not be conscious of the cathartic benefit of letting out frustration (Averill 1983; Wolfe 1999; Averill 2012). Parents often justify their abuse by a false belief that corporal punishment is superior parenting. Other parents draw the line at some forms of corporal punishment such as spanking with objects.

The area of child abuse has evolved rapidly in the past 20 years. Cultural perceptions in the Western world regarding child maltreatment have changed dramatically. Parenting has become a highly valued skill for both mothers and fathers. The role of fathers has dramatically changed over the past 20 to 30 years, with today's father being more valued as an equal parenting figure. High levels of father involvement are associated with significant and highly desirable outcomes for children and families (Wilson and Prior 2011).

DEFINITIONS

The definition of child abuse encompasses physical abuse, emotional abuse, sexual abuse, and neglect. Several rare forms of child abuse occur in syndromes such as Munchausen by proxy and abuse of unborn children via intrauterine substance exposure—fetal abuse.

Physical abuse is defined as the nonaccidental physical injury of a child under 18 years old by a person who is responsible for the child's welfare (U.S. Department of Health and Human Services 2014). The injury is considered abuse regardless of whether the caregiver intended to hurt the child. Physical discipline such as spanking is not considered abuse as long as it is reasonable and causes no bodily injury (American Psychiatric Association 2013).

Child sexual abuse is defined as the use of the child as an object of gratification for adult sexual needs or desires. *Incest* refers to the sexual exploitation of a child by another family member. Sexual abuse includes noncontact exploitation of a child by a parent or caregiver, e.g., enticing or threatening the child to participate in sexual acts for the sexual gratification of others, even if there is no direct physical contact between the child and the abuser (American Psychiatric Association 2013).

Emotional or psychological abuse is defined as nonaccidental verbal or symbolic acts by a parent or caregiver that result or have potential to result in significant psychological harm to the child, e.g., humiliating, disparaging, belittling, scapegoating, abandoning, or threats of abandonment or harm or close confinement (the restriction of movement, e.g., binding the child's limbs to furniture or object, or confining the child to a small enclosed area, e.g., the closet). Other forms of emotional abuse include withholding basic needs such as food, shelter, sleep, or necessities as a form of punishment or coercing the child to inflict pain on himself or herself and disciplining the child excessively (i.e., at an extremely high frequency or duration even if it is not at the level of physical abuse) through physical or nonphysical means. Garbarino et al. (1986) identified five types of psychological maltreatment more likely to occur in families with atmospheres full of stress, tension, and aggression, and these are summarized in Table 40.1 (Garbarino et al. 1986).

Neglect is defined as any confirmed or suspected egregious act or omission by a child's parent or caregiver that

Table 40.1 Five types of psychological maltreatment

1. Rejecting—the child's legitimate need for a relationship with both parents is rejected.
2. Terrorizing—the child is bullied or verbally assaulted into being terrified by the target parent.
3. Ignoring—the parent is emotionally unavailable to the child, leading to feelings of neglect and abandonment.
4. Isolating—the alienating parent isolates the child from normal opportunities for social relationships.
5. Corrupting—the child is used as an agent of aggression against the target parent, with the child actively participating in deceits and manipulations for the purpose of harassing and persecuting the other parent.

deprives the child of basic age-appropriate needs and thereby results, or has reasonable potential to result, in physical or psychological harm to the child. Child neglect can be classified as physical, educational, and emotional neglect (U.S. Department of Health and Human Services 2014). Examples of physical neglect include abandonment, refusal of health care, delay in health care, expulsion from the home, custody-related issues, inadequate supervision, driving while intoxicated, or leaving a child unattended in a motor vehicle.

Munchausen syndrome by proxy is defined as a pattern of behavior in which a caregiver fabricates, exaggerates, or intentionally inflicts mental and/or physical health problems on the person in the caregiver's care. The American Professional Society on the Abuse of Children (APSAC) created the term "Pediatric Condition Falsification" (PCF) for the diagnosis of the abuse of the child. Factitious disorder by proxy (FDP) is used to diagnosis the caretaker who harms the child through PCF with the motivation of self-serving psychological needs (Schreier 2002). Munchausen syndrome by proxy is a descriptor for the disorder that contains both elements.

Fetal abuse is defined as the ingestion of substances during pregnancy that may have serious consequences to the developing fetus. The U.S. Supreme Court case *Ferguson v. City of Charleston* (2001) dealt with the question of the threat of criminal sanctions to deter a pregnant woman from using cocaine. Some states have passed laws mandating incarceration and rehabilitation of pregnant women using drugs during pregnancy. The question of prosecution and confinement has been criticized for a violation of the mother's rights (Fentiman 2006).

EPIDEMIOLOGY

Child maltreatment is a prevalent sociological problem as indicated by the millions of suspected reports of child abuse by the National Child Abuse and Neglect Data System (NCANDS) (U.S. Department of Health and Human Services 2012, 2014) through the Department of Health and Human Services. Despite the millions of reports to child protective agencies, the true statistics of child abuse are likely vastly underestimated due to nondisclosure within families.

In 2012, over 680,000 child abuse reports were made to Child Protective Services. Mandated reporters made 62% of reports. The most common form of child abuse was neglect. Figure 40.1 (U.S. Department of Health and Human Services 2014) provides a graphic overview of the percentage for each type of child abuse reported.

In 2012, an estimated 1640 children died from child maltreatment (2.2 per 100,000 children). Of those who died 70% experienced neglect, and 44% experienced physical abuse either exclusively or in combination with another form of maltreatment. Boys were at more risk of fatal outcome from child abuse than girls, with a rate of 2.5 per 100,000 and 1.9 per 100,000, respectively.

The youngest children were the most vulnerable, with 27% of reported victims under 3 years old and children under 1 year having the highest rate of victimization (21.9

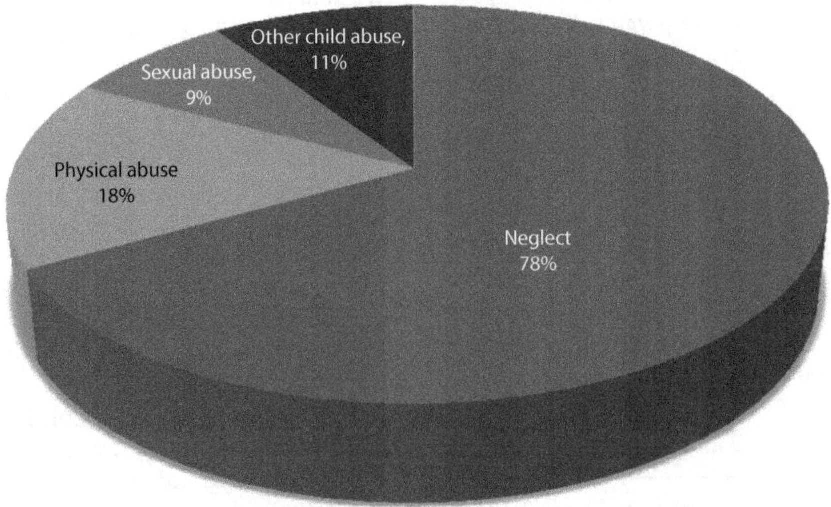

Figure 40.1 Types of child abuse and neglect.

per 1000 children). Children aged 3–5 years comprised 20% of victims. Racial differentiation of child abuse victims shows a high rate of abuse among native and Alaskan Indians. Parents dominate the most common perpetrators of child abuse, comprising 80%. Six percent were relatives other than parents, and 4.2% were unmarried partners of parents. Eighty-two percent of perpetrators were between 18 and 44 years old. Fifty-four percent were women, and 45% were men.

ETIOLOGY AND RISK FACTORS

The etiology of child abuse cannot be narrowed down to a specific causative factor; however, there are often similar combinations of risk factors common to child abuse victims, and these are noted in Table 40.2.

Interventions for treating family systems might involve interagency collaboration. It is critical to address the causes rather than the symptoms in order to effectuate long-term change and to break the cycle of violence and dysfunction in abusive families. Targeting one stressor (e.g., unemployment) could have a domino effect on improving other stressors (e.g., housing) and can lead to a more stable home environment for the child and decrease the risk of abuse. Prevention and education remain the stalwart of reducing the incidence of child abuse. Children in Early Head Start programs are at lower risk of being abused (Zhai et al. 2013).

PRESENTATION AND CLINICAL FINDINGS

Physical abuse

Physical abuse is often the most overt type of abuse. Bruises, cuts, burns, welts, and scars are frequently visible to others

Table 40.2 Factors increasing the risk of child abuse

- Poverty
- Lack of education
- Serious marital problems
- Frequent changes of addresses
- Violence between family members
- Lack of support from the extended family
- Loneliness and social isolation
- Unemployment
- Inadequate housing
- Very high expectations of the child and what the child should achieve
- Parent who was abused as a child
- Lack of knowledge and skills in bringing up children
- Low self-esteem
- Low self-confidence
- Depression, alcohol, and/or drug abuse
- Mental or physical ill health
- Work pressures

such as teachers, doctors, family members, and friends. Physical abuse results in a wide range of injuries that are characteristically more severe than could be reasonably attributed to the claimed cause (Ballin 1985). Bruises may be the first and only visible sign of physical abuse. It is true that most children sustain minor injuries and bruises in their normal play. Distinguishing whether a bruise is due to normal activity or child abuse is often very difficult, and dating of bruises has been shown to be highly inaccurate (Bariciak et al. 2003; Maguire and Mann 2013).

With rare exception, nonambulatory infants should not have any bruising (Sugar et al. 1999). The presence of a bruise in an infant should prompt further investigation for nonaccidental trauma or an underlying medical illness. Bruises over soft tissue areas in nonmobile infants that carry the imprint of an implement and multiple bruises of uniform shape are suggestive of abuse (Maguire et al. 2005). Pattern of burns specific to abuse include glove and stocking distribution, perineal and buttock burns due to submersion, absence of splash burns, and outlines of burns due to cigarette or an identifiable object (Andronicus et al. 1998). Kemp et al. (2014) found the majority of intentional non-scald contact burns are due to cigarettes, irons, hairdryers, and heaters. Single or multiple circular, deep-cratered burns are consistent with cigarette burns.

Fractures are common in both nonabused and abused children. Differentiation of fractures includes multiple fractures, bilateral long bone fractures, and fractures in different stages of healing or in developmentally disabled children. Leventhal et al. (2010) found an overlap between traumatic brain injuries and fractures attributable to abuse. Ravichandiran et al. (2010) found that 20% of abuse-related fractures are missed during the initial medical visit. Fractures of long bones such as the humerus, tibia, and fibula are commonly seen in abused children because the limbs are often used as a handle when young children are thrown or shaken.

Classic metaphyseal lesions (CMLs) or "bucket handle fractures" of the tibia, femur, and proximal humerus are thought to be caused by forceful shaking or twisting of a child. Other than children with rickets, these fractures carry a high predictor of child abuse during the first year of life (Kleinman et al. 1986, 2011). Buckle fractures of the fingers and toes indicate forced extension. Nonextremity fractures such as skull and ribs should alert the physician to the possibility of child abuse. However, no specific pattern of fractures is pathognomonic of abuse, and diagnosis is incomplete without a skeletal survey and investigating for other evidence of abuse (American Academy of Pediatrics 2009; Swoboda and Feldman 2013).

Abusive head trauma (AHT) or "shaken baby syndrome" is a leading cause of morbidity and mortality in infants and young children (Herman et al. 2011). These children present to the emergency department in subtle or dramatic ways with conditions ranging from lethargy, irritability, vomiting, rigidity, and decreased appetite, to seizures, altered consciousness, and respiratory distress due to subdural hematomas and/or retinal hemorrhages (Westrick et al. 2015). Missing the diagnosis of AHT can be fatal. Jenny (1999) found that 30% of AHT cases were missed, and 40% experienced medical complications due to the missed diagnosis. They found that four out of five deaths might have been prevented with earlier recognition. Abusive head trauma is 100% preventable with parent education about the risks to babies when they are shaken and with treating parental stress.

Emotional abuse

Unlike physical abuse and sometimes sexual abuse, emotional abuse leaves no visible scars. From a psychiatric perspective the signs and symptoms are even more obtuse and vague. The child might present with fear or anxiety related to or reluctance to return home to his or her caregiver. Child emotional abuse (CEA) is associated with serious and negative emotional and behavioral consequences (Hart et al. 1997; Egeland et al. 2000; Yates 2007). Research in the area of emotional child abuse has yielded more information related to neurodevelopment, psychological impact on children, and parent–child interactions.

Child emotional abuse had been ill defined and therefore efforts to identify and ameliorate its detrimental effects were hampered (Cicchetti 1991; Iwaniec 1995; Yates 2007). Slep et al. (2011) attempted to develop operationalized criteria for CEA to improve future research. Abusive parental behaviors such as humiliating, terrorizing, and scapegoating fell out of the scope of good caregiving. The researchers admitted some types of parental verbal aggression, such as yelling, would categorize the majority of parents as having engaged in acts of emotional aggression. The potential impacts were emotional rather than physical and included psychological harm, more-than-inconsequential fear reactions, and significant psychological distress. They found that it was difficult to capture every single important element of child emotional abuse that is being raised in the literature (Glaser 2002).

Egeland et al. (2000) demonstrated the relationship between CEA and insecure attachments to caregivers and declines in cognitive and motor competence in the first years of life in a high-risk poverty sample. By school age, CEA was associated with high levels of negativity, low academic achievement, impulsivity, low self-esteem, and difficulty forming friendships, depression, and suicidality (Maguire et al. 2015). CEA has been associated with not only behavioral and psychological sequelae but also changes to neurodevelopment. The understanding of the neurobiology of the stress responses in the developing brain has led to the discovery of relationships between parental caregiving, attachment, and the adverse effects of CEA. Research has consistently shown that early adversity interferes with the limbic–hypothalamic–pituitary–adrenal axis and the norepinephrine–sympathetic–adrenal–medullary system by altering stress responses (Teicher 2002; Bugental et al. 2003; Teicher et al. 2003; Martorell and Bugental 2006).

Maternal verbal abuse during childhood has been associated with a markedly higher risk for development of borderline, narcissistic, obsessive–compulsive, and paranoid personality disorders (Johnson et al. 2001). Verbal abuse may also have more long-lasting consequences than other forms of abuse (Ney 1987). The combination of verbal and other forms of abuse had the greatest impact on children by affecting their enjoyment for living and hope for the future.

Neglect

Neglect is the most common form of child abuse. Unlike physical or sexual abuse, neglect is often an act of omission by caregivers failing to fulfill the obligations of caring for the child. Child neglect can have long-term serious and deleterious effects on children's cognitive, socio-emotional, and behavioral development (Erickson and Egeland 2002; Hildyard and Wolfe 2002).

Three major subtypes of neglect identified are physical, psychological, and environmental. Examples of physical neglect include inadequate supervision, refusal or delay in seeking health care, exposure to avoidable hazards, and driving with the child while intoxicated. Psychological neglect includes a parent providing inadequate nurturance and affection or exposing the child to spousal abuse. Environmental neglect includes such behaviors as failure to enroll children in school, chronic truancy, or inattention to special educational or developmental needs.

Presentations of neglect can be obvious, such as malnutrition or inappropriate clothing or hygiene, or are subtle and insidious, such as fatigue, low self-esteem, depression and withdrawal, or failure to thrive and developmental delays. Children suffering from neglect are at risk of developing insecure attachments (Baer and Martinez 2006).

Munchausen syndrome by proxy

Munchausen syndrome by proxy is a rare entity. Although the term Munchausen syndrome by proxy is widely used, it has not been included as a diagnosis in the *Diagnostic and Statistical Manual of Mental Disorders*, 5th edition (*DSM-5*). Factitious Disorder Imposed by Another is the *DSM-5* diagnosis that encompasses the elements of Munchausen syndrome by proxy. In the United Kingdom, Munchausen syndrome by proxy is known as Fabricated or Induced Illness by Caregivers.

The American Professional Society on the Abuse of Children (APSAC) developed specific diagnostic criteria that encompass the term Pediatric Condition Falsification (PCF) as the diagnosis of the abuse of the child akin to Munchausen Syndrome by Proxy. Factitious Disorder by Proxy (FDP) is used to describe the diagnosis in the caretaker who harms his or her child through PCF with the motivation of self-serving psychological needs. Critical differentiating criteria from malingering include the absence of secondary gain, and ruling out of other mental and physical illnesses.

Mothers are the most common perpetrators of Munchausen syndrome by proxy (Meadow 1989; McClure et al. 1996; Malatack et al. 2006). About 10% of fathers are perpetrators (Shaw et al. 2008). Male perpetrators are more likely to kill their children than female perpetrators (Meadow 1982; Rosenberg 1987; Schreier 2004). Mothers frequently have nursing training and present as devoted, loving caregivers who often refuse to leave their child during procedures. The physician is an unknowing agent in unwittingly inflicting harm on the child through surgeries, medications, and procedures. Mothers are often so convincing that physicians defend against the mother. The perpetrating mother appears less concerned about the child's health than the medical staff and procedures. Female perpetrators often develop a good rapport or even close friendships with medical staff (Beard 2007; Shaw et al. 2008). Male perpetrators do not form close bonds with medical staff and might present as demanding, overbearing, or litigious (Shaw et al. 2008).

The abuse always occurs in the caregiver's presence, and there is no gender preference. The average age of the victim is 3 years old, and victims are rarely older than 6 years old (Fulton 2000). Presentation can involve almost every organ system and is often multisystem. The most common presentations of Munchausen syndrome by proxy are bleeding, diarrhea, seizures, apnea, fever, and rash. As an example, Munchausen syndrome by proxy should be considered in a child with apnea whose sibling died or if the apnea only occurs in the presence of one person (Forsyth 1996).

CHILD SEXUAL ABUSE

Child sexual abuse is an international problem. A plethora of research has evolved in the area of child sexual abuse over the past 30 years. Cases such as the multimillion dollar 6-year criminal trial of the McMartin preschool in Los Angeles in the 1980s prompted research about child witnesses, especially in the area of memory and suggestibility. The true incidence of child sexual abuse is unknown due to lack of or delay in reporting (London et al. 2008). Stoltenborgh et al. (2011) conducted a comprehensive meta-analysis of child sexual abuse cases reported in 217 publications between 1980 and 2008 including 331 independent samples with a total of almost 10 million participants. They found that the overall estimated child sexual abuse prevalence was 127/1000 in self-report studies by victims and 4/1000 in informant studies from professionals observing children such as doctors and teachers. Self-reported child sexual abuse was more common among females (180/1000) compared to males (76/1000). The lowest overall rate was found in Asia, and the highest rate for girls was in Australia and for boys in Africa. They found that child sexual abuse is a global problem.

Justice Powell of the U.S. Supreme Court stated in his opinion in the incest case of *Pennsylvania v. Ritchie* (1987), "Child abuse is one of the most difficult crimes to detect and prosecute, in large part because there often are no witnesses except the victim." There are often no injuries or physical evidence to prove the victim's allegations. Ultimately the verdict in most cases relies "heavily on a courts adoption of a particular story, one that makes sense, is true to what the listeners know about the world and hangs together" (Scheppele 1989).

Child sexual abuse encompasses a wide definition of sexual activities that are summarized in Table 40.3.

Table 40.3 Types of sexual abuse

- Verbal sexual propositions
- Sexual harassment
- Voyeurism
- Exhibitionism
- Fondling
- Masturbation
- Vaginal intercourse
- Oral intercourse
- Anal intercourse
- Penetration
- Child pornography
- Female genital mutilation

SPECIAL TOPICS IN CHILD SEXUAL ABUSE: CHILD SEX TRAFFICKING, CHILD PORNOGRAPHY, FEMALE GENITAL MUTILATION, AND SEXTING

Child sex trafficking, child pornography, and female genital mutilation are topics currently being discussed in the international forum. Child sex trafficking and child pornography are global public health problems. The 1996 Declaration and Agenda for Action for the First World Congress Against the Commercial Sexual Exploitation of Children (CSEC) provided a working definition of the commercial sexual exploitation of children (Adams et al. 2010). Commercial Sexual Exploitation of Children is defined as sexual abuse of a minor for economic gain. The National Human Trafficking Resource Center has a national hotline to report abuse. The U.S. Department of Justice estimated about 100,000 to 300,000 children entered the U.S. commercial child sex trade (http://www.traffickingresourcecenter.org). The American Professional Society on the Abuse of Children identified barriers to detecting child victims (Estes and Weiner 2001; Zimmerman 2006; Gragg et al. 2007; Clawson and Dutch 2008; Crane and Moreno 2011; Greenbaum et al. 2013).

Child pornography

Child pornography is a serious, prolific, multimillion dollar, worldwide business that almost invariably leaves a permanent, digital cyber record of child abuse. This is exacerbated by unfiltered and unmonitored circulation on the World Wide Web. The emotional damage to a child victim is extremely difficult to assess in monetary compensation due to the infinite reaches of distribution. Seto et al. (2006) found that child pornography offending is a stronger diagnostic indicator of pedophilia than is sexually offending against child victims.

In the U.S. Supreme Court case, *Paroline v. US* (2014) the victim was 8 years old when she was sexually abused by her uncle who produced child pornography of his niece which was sold and distributed on the Internet. He was ultimately prosecuted and sentenced to a lengthy prison sentence and ordered to pay $6000 to the victim. The victim initially benefitted from therapy and was deemed normal. Her emotional status, however, significantly declined as a teenager when she discovered trafficked images of herself on the Internet. The victim sought restitution against Petitioner *Paroline* under the Violence Against Women Act of 1994, §2259 (reauthorized in 2013) which requires District Courts to award restitution for certain federal criminal offenses, including child pornography possession. Paroline possessed child pornography images of the victim, but he never met the victim. The Court held that restitution is proper only to the extent the defendant's offense proximately caused a victim's losses and that defendants should only be liable for the consequences and gravity of their own conduct, not the conduct of others.

Sexting has become another new social phenomenon with the explosion of social media and smartphones among latency-aged children, tweens, and teens. Mitchell et al. (2012) conducted a study of 1560 youth Internet users, ages 10 through 17. They found that 2% of youth had appeared in or created nude or nearly nude pictures or videos but only 1% were sexually explicit. Seven percent of participants received nude or nearly nude images of others while 6% reported receiving sexually explicit images. Few youth distributed these images. They concluded that sexting is far from a normative behavior for youth. Further, teens should be educated about the legal consequences of sexting and what to do if they receive a sexting image, because the law can be punitive and harsh. Child pornography laws often intersect with adolescent sexting, occasionally resulting in catastrophic outcomes in which teens are convicted of sex offenses and required to register as sex offenders for decades to come (Calvert 2009; Richards and Calvert 2009; Judge 2012).

Female genital mutilation

The World Health Organization defines female genital mutilation (often referred to as female circumcision) as "includes procedures that intentionally alter or cause injury to the female genital organs for non-medical reasons" (http://www.who.int/mediacentre/factsheets/fs241/en/). Over 125 million women and girls have undergone the practice. Female genital mutilation has been defined as a violation of human rights in many countries, with laws being passed to outlaw the practice. In Senegal, about 20% of the female population is estimated to be circumcised. Female genital mutilation is practiced on the girls from infancy to 15 years old (http://www.WHO.int). Behrendt and Moritz (2014) found an increased prevalence of post-traumatic stress disorder and other psychiatric syndromes in women who underwent female genital mutilation.

CHILD SEXUAL ABUSE INTERVIEW GUIDELINES

Many organizations have set forth guidelines for forensic interviews of children. The American Academy of Pediatrics (AAP) published Guidelines for the Evaluation of Sexual Abuse in children in 2005. The American Academy of Child and Adolescent Psychiatry (AACAP) published Guidelines for the Clinical Evaluation of Children in 1988 (Bernet 1997) and a Policy Statement about Protecting Children in Abuse Investigations and Testimony in 1989.

Guidelines were also developed through nonmedical organizations or agencies. The National Children's Advocacy Center developed RADAR (Recognizing Abuse Disclosure types and Responding). CornerHouse developed the CornerHouse Forensic Interview Protocol—RATAC (Rapport, Anatomy Identification, Touch Inquiry, Abuse Scenario, Closure)—which is included in the Finding Words training curriculum. The RATAC protocol is the most widely used protocol in the United States (Faller 2014).

The American Professional Society on the Abuse of Children (APSAC) developed the Practice Guidelines for Psychosocial Evaluation of Suspected Sexual Abuse (APSAC 1990, 1997, 2012) , the Memorandum of Good Practice, and the revision, Achieving the Best Evidence. Many of these organizations also developed training programs for forensic interviewers. Additionally several states—Washington (Harborview Center for Sexual Assault and Traumatic Stress), Michigan (State of Michigan Governor's Task Force on Child Abuse), and Oregon (Oregon Department of Justice 2012)—developed interview guides.

In 2000, the *Eunice Kennedy Shriver* National Institute of Child Health and Human Development (NICHD), part of the National Institutes of Health (NIH) and the U.S. Department of Health and Human Services (USDHSS), developed a protocol for child sexual abuse allegations called the NICHD Investigative Interview Protocol. Due to the international collaboration in 1993, the NICHD has access to over 40,000 forensic interviews and has dramatically improved the quality of interviewing children in sexual abuse cases. The NICHD protocol has been translated into multiple languages and is available online. The NICHD investigative interview protocol technique is an 11- or 12-phase protocol as summarized in Table 40.4.

CHILD ABUSE AGENCIES

The Child Abuse Prevention and Treatment Act (CAPTA) provides federal funding to States to improve child protective services and interagency collaboration in the areas of investigation, prevention, assessment, mental health, education, prosecution, and treatment. CAPTA was originally enacted in 1974 and amended several times, most recently in 2010. Through CAPTA, reporting by mandated reporters was expanded to numerous professions and not just limited to medical professionals. CAPTA also expanded the types of abuse reported (Faller 2014).

Table 40.4 National Institute of Child Health and Human Development Protocol Phases

1. Systematic introductions
2. Rapport building
3. Training in episodic memory
4. Transition to substantive issues using open-ended to more closed-ended questions
5. Investigating the event
6. Break
7. Eliciting information not mentioned by the child
8. If the child fails to mention expected information
9. Information about disclosure
10. Closing
11. Ending on a neutral topic

Child Advocacy Centers (CAC) were developed in 1985 as a child-friendly place where sexual abuse victims and their families would undergo a single interview by forensically trained professionals. There are currently over 900 CACs in all 50 states and in 25 countries (National Children's Advocacy Center).

All states in the United States have child abuse reporting agencies with statutes mandating reporters such as health-care workers, teachers, and childcare providers. The operative legal term is "suspicion" of child abuse rather than "confirmation" or "investigation" of child abuse. Child abuse victims do not often reveal details or presence of abuse. Because child abuse is often kept behind closed family doors, identification by professionals such as teachers, physicians, and childcare workers is the first step toward intervention. Abusive families often do not welcome state agencies into their homes and become defensive about the allegations. Parents might influence children to lie to officials about abuse, thus leading victims to more reprisal if they confide family secrets. Children are often afraid of being separated from their parents and recant accounts of abuse.

Selph et al. (2013) found that risk assessment and behavioral interventions in pediatric clinics reduced abuse and neglect outcomes for young children. Common strategies for child maltreatment are parent education and home visiting programs. Research has found the most effective parent training programs provide families opportunities for practicing parental skills in their own home (Kaminski et al. 2008).

In 1993, an international meeting of experts on child sexual abuse was held to develop consensus about how child sexual abuse allegations could be investigated most productively (Lamb 1994). In the 1990s, a number of interview protocols were developed (Faller 2014). Several interview protocols have emerged ranging from scripted to semi-structured. Faller (1993) organized eight categories and key validation indicators to assess the veracity of sexual abuse allegations. Important criteria of each factor are identified to assess in child sexual abuse evaluations, and these are outlined in Table 40.5.

Table 40.5 Eight categories and key validation indicators assessing veracity of sexual abuse allegations

1. Timing and circumstance of disclosure
   a. Initial disclosure is spontaneous
   b. Absence of undue influence so ulterior motives to fabricate
   c. Anxiety or hesitancy regarding divergence of the sexual abuse
2. Language congruence with developmental level
   a. Description based on the child's point of view all prospective
   b. Use of age-appropriate vocabulary and speech
3. Quantity and quality of details
   a. Explicit, detailed account including contextual details, for example, where, when, what one was wearing, where others were during the abuse
   b. Unusual or superfluous details
   c. Idiosyncratic and sensorimotor details
   d. Increasingly progressive sexual acts
4. Appropriateness of sexual knowledge based on developmental level
   a. Sexual knowledge that exceeds the child's developmental level
   b. Precocious knowledge of sexuality
   c. Premature eroticization
5. Repetition over time: internal and external consistency
   a. Consistency of core elements
   b. Consistency of the reporting salient details
   c. Consistency with other statements
6. Description of offender behavior
   a. Coercion and tricks
   b. Bribes or rewards
   c. Element of secrecy
   d. Statements about telling or not telling
   e. What the offender said to obtain participation
   f. Pressure to recant
7. Plausibility of abuse
   a. Description recounted in a varied and rich manner as opposed to a rote recitation
   b. Circumstantially congruent description of being sexually abused
8. Emotional reaction of the child during the interview
   a. Emotional reaction consistent with accusations
   b. Emotional state consistent with the abuse

SPECIAL TOPICS: DOMESTIC VIOLENCE, PARENTAL ALIENATION, FALSE ALLEGATIONS

Domestic violence

Over 40 years of research regarding the relationships of children who are abused by their parents showed that there is a correlation between children exposed to domestic violence (also referred to as Intimate Partner Violence or IPV) and physical abuse against the children (Appel and Holden 1998). The U.S. Bureau of Justice statistics indicated the rate of IPV in 2010 was 3.6 per 1000 (United States Department of Justice Intimate Partner 2013). Children are present in many households where IPV occurs and, therefore, are exposed to witnessing their parents being injured or emotionally abused. Children in IPV households might not directly witness the violence but are aware of its existence in their home (Fantuzzo et al. 1997; Holden et al. 1998; Fantuzzo and Mohr 1999). Over 15 million children in the United States live in domestically violent households (McDonald et al. 2006). The relationship between IPV and child abuse has been a topic of research for many years. Moore (1975) discovered that 13% of children from 23 domestic violent families were hurt or threatened with violence. The U.S. Department of Justice reported children are present in about a third of domestically violent households (or one in 320 households). Fifteen percent of child fatalities were exposed to domestic violence with the caregiver being either the perpetrator of or the victim of the domestic violence (Margolin and Vickerman 2011).

Domestic violence in the household can lead to posttraumatic stress disorder (PTSD), especially if the violence is often repetitive and ongoing without a discrete precipitating traumatic event. The child's traumatic reactions may generalize to less serious demonstrations of anger and conflict and even verbal aggression (Margolin and Vickerman 2011). The child's sense of safety is continuously challenged as there is no escape from the trauma. Parents who engage in domestic violence also suffer increased stress that might adversely affect their parenting (Roberts et al. 2013). Mothers of young children in domestically violent relationships are at increased risk of depression and stress (Huth-Bocks et al. 2001), leading to impaired parenting. Often one salient traumatic domestic violent episode launches them into the child welfare system even if the pattern of domestic violence in the household is long term.

The cycle of domestic violence has been well documented over decades. Men who witness domestic violence in their families of origin are at increased risk for IPV (O'Leary et al. 2007). There is a known relationship between witnessing child abuse and neglect and the risk for IPV perpetration and victimization as an adult (Feerick et al. 2002; McKinney et al. 2009; Widom et al. 2014). Widom et al. (2014) found childhood neglect increases a person's vulnerability to domestic violence victimization in adulthood. The two most consistent predictors of domestic violence perpetration were child and adolescent abuse and family of origin.

The forensic mental health expert is called on to assess the effects of domestic violence in children, the relationship of the domestically violent parent with the child, or the parenting competency of the victim and perpetrators. Forensic evaluators should be familiar with local, state, and federal laws pertaining to domestic violence and child victims.

Parental alienation

Parental alienation syndrome (PAS) has been described as a form of emotional child abuse. PAS was a topic considered for inclusion in the *DSM-5* but ultimately was not included. PAS is a controversial phrase coined by Richard Gardner in 1985 (Gardner 1985) to describe the programming of a child in order to be alienated from the target parent. The term "parental alienation" has replaced "Parental Alienation Syndrome." Parental alienation is a simplified and descriptive term for the dynamic that frequents family court proceedings in high-conflict family law cases.

The primary manifestation of parental alienation is the child's unjustified campaign of denigration against a parent resulting from the combination of a programming (brainwashing) parent's indoctrinations and the child's own contributions to the vilification of the target parent. When true parental abuse and/or neglect is present, the child's animosity may be justified, and so the parental alienation syndrome explanation for the child's hostility is not applicable (Gardner 2002). The literature on parental alienation categorizes degrees of alienation, depending on the severity of the effect in terms of duration, magnitude, and intransigence of the child's rejection of the alienated parent (Baker 2006). The literature has moved away from using Gardner's labels of Parental Alienation Syndrome to using terms and phrases such as alienating behaviors, gatekeeping, alignments, and realistic estrangement (Fidler and Bala 2010). Realistic estrangement between parents occurs when the child's resistance or refusal might be the result of witnessing domestic violence, or experiencing abuse and/or neglect by the rejected parent.

Girls and boys experience alienation equally, although adolescents are more likely to become alienated than younger children (Kelly and Johnston 2001). Mothers or fathers can be alienated from their children (Bala et al. 2010). Most commonly, the primary custodian of the child is the perpetrator of alienation. However, it is difficult, but not impossible, for a parent with limited contact with the child to alienate the child from the primary custodial parent (Fidler and Bala 2010).

Raising parental alienation as an issue in Family Court usually corresponds with allegations of child abuse by the alienating parent. The wheels of justice slow down substantially when alienation and abuse are at issue. Strategically, this often gives the alienating parent more time and access to the children to perpetuate their alienating behaviors. Conversely the alienated parent becomes more marginalized with time until usually a series of mental health professionals evaluate, treat, and provide more guidance and education to the Court about the disturbed family dynamics. Forensic findings can include false allegations, underlying mental illness (of either parent), justifiable alienating behavior due to bona fide child abuse, or somewhere in between. The legal outcomes might range from a reversal of custody by placing the child with the targeted parent while the alienated parent seeks mental health treatment.

Whatever the findings, the effects of true alienation can last a lifetime and contribute to self-esteem problems, depressive disorders, a trend toward alcohol abuse, and insecure attachment styles as adults (Baker 2005a,b, 2006, a; Baker and Ben-Ami 2011; Ben-Ami and Baker 2012).

False allegations

False allegations of child abuse, unrelated or in combination with parental alienation, arise in several legal settings—family court, criminal court, and dependency court. In criminal cases and dependency cases, the risks to the family could be prosecution and foster care placement if the children are removed from their parents' custody. False allegations in Family Court might stem from innocent misperceptions and inaccurate interpretations (Perry 1995), such as a father bathing a young daughter who innocently reports touching of the genitals to a mother in a high-conflict custody case. Additionally, lack of child sexual development can lead to false child sexual abuse allegations that can halt the legal process and deny access of an innocent parent to his or her child. False allegations in Family Court are akin to throwing mud at the wall and seeing what might stick. Although the mud might not stick, the stain can be long-standing.

Recanting of allegations of child abuse is not as common as delaying reporting. In the U.S. Supreme Court case *Martinez v. Ryan* 2012, the 11-year-old female victim recanted accusations of sexual abuse (despite DNA evidence) due to the mother's reluctance to lend support to the victim's claims.

MULTIDISCIPLINARY INTERVENTION FOR EVALUATION AND TREATMENT

Maltreated children present with an extensive range of symptoms, behaviors, and disorders. Abused children are at risk of serious emotional, developmental, behavioral, and learning disorders. Comprehensive screening and evaluation of medical, developmental, educational, and psychiatric issues should be performed on all children suspected of abuse. Appropriate school placement, parental training, and education are part of a multidisciplinary approach. Children might present without current symptoms but still be at risk for developing psychiatric disorders in the future.

Psychological interventions have been shown in short-term clinical trials to ameliorate the consequences of CSA. Trauma-focused cognitive behavioral therapy for victims of child sexual abuse have demonstrated efficacy in decreasing negative psychological effects (Cohen et al. 2000; Macdonald et al. 2006; Scheeringa et al. 2011; Deblinger et al. 2012; Mannarino et al. 2012).

EMDR (eye movement desensitization and reprocessing) is another modality used to treat trauma victims. The majority of patients treated with psychotherapy and/or EMDR for PTSD recover or improve (Bradley et al. 2014). However, PTSD is often a chronic disorder, and the majority of patients continue to have residual symptoms. Psychopharmacologic interventions are used to target disorders related to trauma from abuse, e.g., selective serotonin reuptake inhibitors (SSRIs) are used to treat symptoms of depression, anxiety, and PTSD.

Forensic psychiatric evaluation of child abuse victims is dependent on the allegations and nature of the case, because there can be a broad range of symptomatology and presentations. In cases of child sexual abuse, a thorough and multidisciplinary approach is necessary to assess both the victims and perpetrators. Evaluations of child sexual abuse victims should be handled in a systematic manner by trained interviewers to minimize trauma to the child and the family. Ideally the victim should undergo only one mental health videotaped evaluation. The interviewer should possess solid knowledge of child sexual development and feel comfortable asking difficult questions of the child and the family. The interviewer should be aware of his or her own biases while interviewing and avoid assuming the abuse is all bad or painful, or that the victim is angry with the perpetrator (Schetky and Green 2014). According to Vizard (2013), an "assessment triangle," including the child's developmental needs, parenting capacity, and family and environmental factors are elements that provide for the framework of assessing the child victim.

ROLE OF THE FORENSIC PRACTITIONER

Forensic psychiatrists are often asked to assess victims and perpetrators of child abuse in legal settings—Dependency Court, Family Court, Criminal Court, and Civil Court. In Dependency Court the question posed to the evaluator might be the fitness of a parent accused of abuse. The evaluator opines about issues regarding visitation, reunification, and risks of further abuse. Additionally, the evaluator might be asked to assess the child victim for recommendations for mental health services and reunification. In Family Court, the child custody evaluator opines about the family dynamics to guide the court about the best interests of the child in various matters such as child abuse claims or domestic violence cases. In Criminal Court the evaluator might be asked to assess the perpetrator regarding potential for rehabilitation, the victim for assessment of abuse, or treatment of the victim or perpetrator. In Civil Court, the forensic evaluator is commonly asked to assess emotional damages due to alleged abuse. These cases are often difficult to assess due to the multifactorial nature of the specific case. The forensic evaluator is often asked to estimate present and future damages related to abuse. Making specific dollar-based predictions is not evidence based and fraught with problems and should be left to the triers of fact—judge and jury. A risk assessment model is best used to indicate future risk factors based on particulars of the case. Bernet and Corwin (2006) proposed using an evidence-based approach as a guide for estimating damages from child sexual abuse cases by asking four questions based on research and integration into the clinical evaluation (see Table 40.6).

Table 40.6 Evidence-based approach for estimating child sexual abuse damages

1. Was the child injured by sexual abuse?
2. Is the child at risk of psychological problems?
3. What treatment is currently recommended?
4. What treatment will be needed in the future?

Forensic practitioners are frequently involved in families where domestic violence is present. Child custody evaluators determine the best interests of the children in the context of exposure to domestic violence by evaluating the children's mental health, safety concerns of children and caregivers, and the dynamics between the domestically violent parent and the victim parent who often share custody. Complex dynamics often present in these high-conflict separations. Assessment of domestic violence in families with children requires a systematic, forensic approach that is evidence based. In family law cases, children are potentially exposed to a domestically violent parent even if they are not the direct victims of abuse. The victim of domestic violence, often one parent, is not always present to protect the children when custody is shared, thereby exposing the children to a potentially violent parent. In some cases, separation of parents is a safety factor and significantly reduces the risk of exposing the children to future violence.

LONG-TERM EFFECTS OF CHILD MALTREATMENT

The consequences of child maltreatment have been shown to affect victims throughout their life span from childhood to adulthood. Child abuse and neglect may affect a person's physical, cognitive, emotional, and behavioral development, thus disrupting the possibility of living a normal life. Goldman (2003) discussed three overlapping areas where the effects of child abuse and neglect lead to problems: health and physical well-being, intellectual and cognitive development, and emotional, psychological, and behavioral consequences.

Not all children are severely affected by abuse. The manifestation of abuse depends on their age and developmental status. McSherry (2011) found both abuse and neglect cause significant academic delays, poor school performance, and a higher incidence of disciplinary actions taken against these children. There are causal relationships between nonsexual child maltreatment and a range of mental disorders, drug use, suicidality, and promiscuity (Norman et al. 2012).

Children and adolescents are at risk of developing depressive disorders, conduct disorders, psychotic symptoms, suicidality, risky sexual behavior, substance abuse, and cigarette smoking (Norman et al. 2012; Arseneault et al. 2014; Kaplan et al. 2014). A history of abuse in childhood increases the likelihood of lifetime psychopathology. This association appears stronger for women than men (Macmillan et al. 2014). In adults abused as children, there is an increased risk of substance abuse, anxiety, depression, suicidality, dissociative disorders, and eating disorders (Herrenkohl et al. 2013; Chu et al. 2014; Johnson et al. 2014; McHolm et al. 2014).

Child sexual abuse is associated with 47% of all childhood-onset psychiatric disorders and with 26%–32% of adult-onset disorders (Wilsnack et al. 1997; Green et al. 2010; Pérez-Fuentes et al. 2013). Being raped, knowing the perpetrator, and a higher frequency of abuse are associated with increased risks of psychiatric disorders (Finkelhor and Browne 1985; Pérez-Fuentes et al. 2013). Abuse involving penetration and abuse by a father or stepfather carries greater risk of long-term harm (Beitchman et al. 1992).

There is no specific pathognomonic or psychopathological syndrome associated with child sexual abuse in adulthood. However, there is a plethora of long-term sequelae including increased probability of being widowed, separated, and divorced (Finkelhor et al. 1990), relationship problems, and psychiatric disorders, especially PTSD and mood disorders.

SUMMARY

Child maltreatment remains a serious and prevalent problem, with millions of children being abused worldwide. A proliferation of research, especially in the area of child witnesses and child sexual abuse, has led to the development of interview protocols and guidelines. Many agencies have devised their own protocols. Further research and revisions of the numerous protocols for interviewing are required to devise a uniform protocol to be used by all agencies. The NICHD protocol is a prime example of international collaboration, and training programs for the protocol are offered in over a dozen languages.

Victims of child sex trafficking and child pornography are difficult to identify due to the clandestine world in which the perpetrators dwell. Identifying the signs indicating these serious crimes is important. Children exposed to domestic violence often do not have visible scars, but their developmental trajectory is derailed. An emphasis on keeping children safe while repairing the damage from domestic violence is needed. Treatment protocols for child maltreatment victims, especially in the mental health arena, require further research.

Continued education of social services and medical personnel is needed to identify, evaluate, and treat victims of child maltreatment. Public awareness campaigns are important to educate the public about parenting and safe child-rearing practices. Many risk factors for child maltreatment are complicated sociological problems such as poverty, lack of education, and unemployment that ultimately perpetuate the cycle of abuse. Prevention rather than reaction is key in reducing the prevalence of child abuse.

REFERENCES

American Academy of Child and Adolescent Psychiatry (AACAP). 1988. *Policy Statement: Guidelines for the Clinical Evaluation of Child and Adolescent Sexual Abuse.* http://www.aacap.org/aacap/policy_statements/1990/Guidelines_for_the_Clinical_Evaluation_for_Child_and_Adolescent_Sexual_Abuse.aspx

Adams W, C Owens, and K Small. 2010. *Effects of Federal Legislation on the Commercial Sexual Exploitation of Children.* Washington, DC: U.S. Department of Justice, Office of Justice Programs, Office of Juvenile Justice and Delinquency Prevention.

American Academy of Pediatrics. 2009. Diagnostic imaging of child abuse. *Pediatrics* 123(5):1430.

American Professional Society on the Abuse of Children (APSAC). 1990. *Practice Guidelines: Psychosocial Evaluation of Suspected Sexual Abuse in Young Children.* http://www.apsac.org/practice-guidelines, accessed May 24, 2015.

American Professional Society on the Abuse of Children (APSAC). 1997. *Practice Guidelines: Psychosocial Evaluation of Suspected Sexual Abuse in Young Children*, 2nd edition. http://www.apsac.org/practice-guidelines, accessed May 24, 2015.

American Professional Society on the Abuse of Childaren (APSAC). 2012. *Practice Guidelines: Forensic Interviewing in Cases of Suspected Child Abuse.* http://www.apsac.org/practice-guidelines, accessed May 24, 2015.

American Psychiatric Association. 2013. *Diagnostic and Statistical Manual of Mental Disorders*, 5th edition. Arlington, VA: American Psychiatric Publications.

Andronicus M, RK Oates, J Peat, S Spalding, and H Martin. 1998. Non-accidental burns in children. *Burns* 24(6):552–558.

Appel AE and GW Holden. 1998. The co-occurrence of spouse and physical child abuse: A review and appraisal. *Journal of Family Psychology* 12(4):578.

Arseneault L, M Cannon, HL Fisher, G Polanczyk, TE Moffitt, and A Caspi. 2014. Childhood trauma and children's emerging psychotic symptoms: A genetically sensitive longitudinal cohort study. *American Journal of Psychiatry* 168(1):65.

Averill JR. 1983. Studies on anger and aggression: Implications for theories of emotion. *American Psychologist* 38(11):1145.

Averill JR. 2012. *Anger and Aggression: An Essay on Emotion.* New York: Springer Science and Business Media.

Baer JC and CD Martinez. 2006. Child maltreatment and insecure attachment: A meta-analysis. *Journal of Reproductive and Infant Psychology* 24(3):187–197.

Baker AJ and N Ben-Ami. 2011. To turn a child against a parent is to turn a child against himself: The direct and indirect effects of exposure to parental alienation strategies on self-esteem and well-being. *Journal of Divorce and Remarriage* 52(7):472–489.

Baker AJL. 2005a. Parent alienation strategies: A qualitative study of adults who experienced parental alienation as a child. *American Journal of Forensic Psychology* 23(4):41–64.

Baker AJL. 2005b. The long-term effects of parental alienation on adult children: A qualitative research study. *American Journal of Family Therapy* 33:289–302.

Baker AJL. 2006. Patterns of parental alienation syndrome: A qualitative study of adults who were alienated from a parent as a child. *American Journal of Family Therapy* 34:63–78.

Baker AJL. 2007a. *Adult Children of Parental Alienation Syndrome: Breaking the Ties That Bind.* New York: W. W. Norton.

Bala N, S Hunt, and C McCarney. 2010. Parental alienation: Canadian court cases 1989–2008. *Family Court Review* 48:162–177.

Ballin J. 1985. AMA diagnostic and treatment guidelines concerning child-abuse and neglect. *JAMA-Journal of the American Medical Association* 254(6):796–800.

Bariciak ED, Plint AC, Gaboury I, and Bennett S. 2003. Dating of bruises in children: An assessment of physician accuracy. *Pediatrics* 112(4):804–807.

Beard KV. 2007. Protect the children: Be on the lookout for Munchausen syndrome by proxy. *RN* 70:33–37.

Behrendt A and S Moritz. 2014. Posttraumatic stress disorder and memory problems after female genital mutilation. *American Journal of Psychiatry* 162:1000–1002.

Beitchman JH, KJ Zucker, JE Hood, GA DaCosta, D Akman, and E Cassavia. 1992. A review of the long-term effects of child sexual abuse. *Child Abuse and Neglect* 16(1):101–118.

Ben-Ami N and AJ Baker. 2012. The long-term correlates of childhood exposure to parental alienation on adult self-sufficiency and well-being. *American Journal of Family Therapy* 40(2):169–183.

Bernet W. 1997. Practice parameters for the forensic evaluation of children and adolescents who may have been physically or sexually abused. *Journal of the American Academy of Child and Adolescent Psychiatry* 36(10):37S–56S.

Bernet W and D Corwin. 2006. An evidence-based approach for estimating present and future damages from child sexual abuse. *Journal of the American Academy of Psychiatry and the Law Online* 34(2):224–230.

Bradley R, J Greene, E Russ, L Dutra, and D Westen. 2014. A multidimensional meta-analysis of psychotherapy for PTSD. *American Journal of Psychiatry* 162(2):214.

Bugental DB, GA Martorell, and V Barraza. 2003. The hormonal costs of subtle forms of infant maltreatment. *Hormones and Behavior* 43(1):237–244.

Calvert C. 2009. Sex, cell phones, privacy, and the first amendment: When children become child pornographers and the Lolita Effect undermines the law. *CommLaw Conspectus* 18:1.

Chu JA, LM Frey, BL Ganzel, and JA Matthews. 2014. Memories of childhood abuse: Dissociation, amnesia, and corroboration. *American Journal of Psychiatry* 156(5):749.

Cicchetti DP. 1991. *Development and Psychopathology.* Cambridge, UK: Cambridge University Press.

Clawson HJ and N Dutch. 2008. *Addressing the Needs of Victims of Human Trafficking: Challenges, Barriers, and Promising Practices.* Washington, DC: Department of Health and Human Services, Office of the Assistant Secretary for Planning and Evaluation.

Cohen JA, AP Mannarino, L Berliner, and E Deblinger. 2000. Trauma-focused cognitive behavioral therapy for children and adolescents an empirical update. *Journal of Interpersonal Violence* 15(11):1202–1223.

Crane PA and M Moreno. 2011. Human trafficking: What is the role of the health care provider? *Journal of Applied Research on Children: Informing Policy for Children at Risk* 2(1):7.

Deblinger E, E Pollio, and F Neubauer. 2012. 33 Treating trauma-related symptoms in children and adolescents. In *The Oxford Handbook of Traumatic Stress Disorders*, edited by JG Beck and DM Sloan, New York: Oxford University Press, 473.

Egeland B, NS Weinfield, M Bosquet, and VK Cheng. 2000. Remembering, repeating, and working through: Lessons from attachment-based interventions. In *WAIMH Handbook of Infant Mental Health*, edited by JD Osofsky and HE Fitzgerald, New York: Wiley, 35–89.

Empey L, M Stafford, and C Hay. 1999. *American Delinquency: Its Meaning and Construction.* New York: Wadsworth.

Erickson MF and B Egeland. 2002. Child neglect. *The APSAC Handbook on Child Maltreatment* 2:3–20.

Estes RJ and NA Weiner. 2001. *The Commercial Sexual Exploitation of Children in the US, Canada and Mexico.* Philadelphia: University of Pennsylvania, School of Social Work, Center for the Study of Youth Policy.

Faller KC. 1993. *Evaluating Young Children for Possible Sexual Abuse.* Paper presetented at the San Diego Conference on Responding to Child Maltreamtent, San Diego, CA.

Faller KC. 2014. Forty years of forensic interviewing of children suspected of sexual abuse, 74–2014: Historical benchmarks. *Social Sciences* 4(1): 34–65.

Fantuzzo J, R Boruch, A Beriama, M Atkins, and S Marcus. 1997. Domestic violence and children: Prevalence and risk in five major US cities. *Journal of the American Academy of Child and Adolescent Psychiatry* 36(1):116–122.

Fantuzzo JW and WK Mohr. 1999. Prevalence and effects of child exposure to domestic violence. *Future of Children* 9:21–32.

Feerick MM, JJ Haugaard, and DA Hien. 2002. Child maltreatment and adulthood violence: The contribution of attachment and drug abuse. *Child Maltreatment* 7(3):226–240.

Fentiman LC. 2006. The new "fetal protection": The wrong answer to the crisis of inadequate health care for women and children. *Denver University Law Review*, 84:537, 540.

Ferguson v. Charleston, 532 U.S. 67, 121 S. Ct. 1281, 149 L. Ed. 2d 205 (2001).

Fidler BJ and N Bala. 2010a, Children resisting postseparation contact with a parent: Concepts, controversies, and conundrums. *Family Court Review* 48:10–47.

Finkelhor D and A Browne. 1985. The traumatic impact of child sexual abuse: A conceptualization. *American Journal of Orthopsychiatry* 55(4):530.

Finkelhor D, G Hotaling, I Lewis, and C Smith. 1990. Sexual abuse in a national survey of adult men and women: Prevalence, characteristics, and risk factors. *Child Abuse and Neglect* 14(1):19–28.

Forsyth BWC. 1996. Munchausen syndrome by proxy. edited by Lewis M and Stubbe D. *Psychiatry: A Comprehensive Textbook.* 4th edition. Lippincott Williams & Wilkins, 1048–1054.

Fulton DR. 2000. Early recognition of Munchausen syndrome by proxy. *Critical Care Nursing Quarterly* 23(2):35–42.

Garbarino J, E Guttmann, and JW Seeley. 1986. *The Psychologically Battered Child.* San Francisco: Jossey-Bass.

Gardner RA. 1985. Recent trends in divorce and custody litigation. *Academy Forum* 29(2)3–7.

Gardner RA. 2002. Parental Alienation Syndrome vs. parental alienation: Which diagnosis should evaluators use in child-custody disputes? *American Journal of Family Therapy* 30(2):93–115.

Glaser D. 2002. Emotional abuse and neglect (psychological maltreatment): A conceptual framework. *Child Abuse and Neglect* 26:697–714.

Goldman J, MK Salus, D Wolcott, and KY Kennedy. 2003. *A Coordinated Response to Child Abuse and Neglect: The Foundation for Practice.* Washington, DC. U.S. Department of Health and Human Services, Office on Child Abuse and Neglect. Available from http://www.childwelfare.gov/pubs/usermanuals/foundation/foundation.pdf.

Gragg F, Petta I, Bernstein H et al. 2007. *New York Prevalence Study of Commercially Sexually Exploited Children: Final Report.* New York: New York State Office of Children and Family Services.

Green JG, KA McLaughlin, PA Berglund, MJ Gruber, NA Sampson, AM Zaslavsky, and RC Kessler. 2010. Childhood adversities and adult psychiatric disorders in the national comorbidity survey replication I: Associations with first onset of DSM-IV disorders. *Archives of General Psychiatry* 67(2):113–123.

Greenbaum J, N Kellogg, and I Reena. 2013. *APSAC Practice Guidelines: The Commercial Sexual Exploitation of Children: The Medical Provider's Role in Identification, Assessment and Treatment.* http://www.kyaap.org/wp-content/uploads/APSAC_Guidelines.pdf

Harborview Center for Sexual Assault and Traumatic Stress, and WA State Criminal Justice Training Commission. *Washington State Child Interview Guide.* depts.washington.edu/hcsats/PDF/guidelines/WA%20State%20Child%20Interview%20Guide%202009%202010.pdf

Hart SN, NJ Binggeli, and MR Brassard. 1997. Evidence for the effects of psychological maltreatment. *Journal of Emotional Abuse* 1(1):27–58.

Herman BE, KL Makoroff, and HM Corneli. 2011. Abusive head trauma. *Pediatric Emergency Care* 27(1):65–69.

Herrenkohl TI, S Hong, JB Klika, RC Herrenkohl, and MJ Russo. 2013. Developmental impacts of child abuse and neglect related to adult mental health, substance use, and physical health. *Journal of Family Violence* 28(2):191–199.

Hildyard KL and DA Wolfe. 2002. Child neglect: Developmental issues and outcomes. *Child Abuse and Neglect* 26(6):679–695.

Holden GW, RE Geffner, and EN Jouriles. 1998. *Children Exposed to Marital Violence: Theory, Research, and Applied Issues.* Washington, DC: American Psychological Association.

Huth-Bocks AC, A Levendosky, and MA Semel. 2001. The direct and indirect effects of domestic violence in young children's intellectual functioning. *Journal of Family Violence* 16:269–290.

Iwaniec D. 1995. *The Emotionally Abused and Neglected Child: Identification, Assessment and Intervention.* New York: Wiley.

Jenny C, KP Hymel, A Ritzen, SE Reinert, and TC Hay. 1999. Analysis of missed cases of abusive head trauma. *JAMA* 281(7):621–626.

Johnson JG, P Cohen, S Kasen, and JS Brook. 2014. Childhood adversities associated with risk for eating disorders or weight problems during adolescence or early adulthood. *American Journal of Psychiatry* 159(3):394–400.

Johnson JG, P Cohen, EM Smailes, AE Skodol, J Brown, and JM Oldham. 2001. Childhood verbal abuse and risk for personality disorders during adolescence and early adulthood. *Comprehensive Psychiatry* 42(1):16–23.

Judge AM. 2012. Sexting among US adolescents: Psychological and legal perspectives. *Harvard Review of Psychiatry* 20(2):86–96.

Kaminski JW, LA Valle, JH Filene, and CL Boyle. 2008. A meta-analytic review of components associated with parent training program effectiveness. *Journal of Abnormal Child Psychology* 36(4):567–589.

Kaplan SJ, D Pelcovitz, S Salzinger, M Weiner, FS Mandel, ML Lesser, and VE Labruna. 2014. Adolescent physical abuse: Risk for adolescent psychiatric disorders. *American Journal of Psychiatry* 155(7):954–959.

Kelly JB and JR Johnston. 2001. The alienated child: A reformulation of parental alienation syndrome. *Family Court Review* 39:249–266.

Kemp AM, SA Maguire, RC Lumb, SM Harris, and MK Mann. 2014. Contact, cigarette and flame burns in physical abuse: A systematic review. *Child Abuse Review* 23(1):35–47.

Kleinman PK, SC Marks, and B Blackbourne. 1986. The metaphyseal lesion in abused infants: A radiologic-histopathologic study. *American Journal of Roentgenology* 146(5):895–905.

Kleinman PK, JM Perez-Rossello, AW Newton, HA Feldman, and PL Kleinman. 2011. Prevalence of the classic metaphyseal lesion in infants at low versus high risk for abuse. *American Journal of Roentgenology* 197(4):1005–1008.

Lamb ME. 1994. The investigation of child sexual abuse: An international, interdisciplinary consensus statement. *Family Law Quarterly* 28:151–162.

Leventhal JM, KD Martin, and AG Asnes. 2010. Fractures and traumatic brain injuries: Abuse versus accidents in a US database of hospitalized children. *Pediatrics* 126(1):e104–e115.

London K, M Bruck, DB Wright, and SJ Ceci. 2008. Review of the contemporary literature on how children report sexual abuse to others: Findings, methodological issues, and implications for forensic interviewers. *Memory* 16(1):29–47.

Macdonald G, J Higgins, and P Ramchandani. 2006. *Cognitive-Behavioural Interventions for Children Who Have Been Sexually Abused.* London: The Cochrane Library.

MacMillan HL, JE Fleming, DL Streiner, E Lin, MH Boyle, E Jamieson, and WR Beardslee. 2014. Childhood abuse and lifetime psychopathology in a community sample. *American Journal of Psychiatry* 158(11):1878–1883.

Maguire S and M Mann. 2013. Systematic reviews of bruising in relation to child abuse—What have we learnt: An overview of review updates. *Evidence-Based Child Health* 8(2):255–263.

Maguire S, MK Mann, J Sibert, and A Kemp. 2005. Are there patterns of bruising in childhood which are diagnostic or suggestive of abuse? A systematic review. *Archives of Disease in Childhood* 90(2):182–186.

Maguire SA, B Williams, AM Naughton, LE Cowley, V Tempest, MK Mann, and AM Kemp. 2015. A systematic review of the emotional, behavioral and cognitive features exhibited by school-aged children experiencing neglect or emotional abuse. *Child: Care, Health and Development* 41:641–653.

Malatack JJ, D Consolini, K Mann, and C Raab. 2006. Taking on the parent to safe a child: Munchausen syndrome by proxy. *Contemporary Pediatrics* 23:50–63.

Mannarino AP, JA Cohen, E Deblinger, MK Runyon, and RA Steer. 2012. Trauma-focused cognitive-behavioral therapy for children sustained impact of treatment 6 and 12 months later. *Child Maltreatment* 17(3):231–241.

Margolin G and KA Vickerman. 2011. Posttraumatic stress in children and adolescents exposed to family violence: I. Overview and issues. *Professional Psychology, Research and Practice 38*(6):613–619.

Martorell GA and DB Bugental. 2006. Maternal variations in stress reactivity: Implications for harsh parenting practices with very young children. *Journal of Family Psychology* 20(4):641.

McClure RJ, PM Davis, SR Meadow, and JR Sibert. 1996. Epidemiology of Munchausen syndrome by proxy, non-accidental poisoning, and non-accidental suffocation. *Archives of Disease in Childhood* 75(1):57–61.

McDonald R, EN Jouriles, S Ramisetty-Mikler, R Caetano, and CE Green. 2006. Estimating the number of American children living in partner-violent families. *Journal of Family Psychology* 20(1):137.

McHolm AE, HL MacMillan, and E Jamieson. 2014. The relationship between childhood physical abuse and suicidality among depressed women: Results from a community sample. *American Journal of Psychiatry* 160(5):933–938.

McKinney CM, R Caetano, S Ramisetty-Mikler, and S Nelson. 2009. Childhood family violence and perpetration and victimization of intimate partner violence: Findings from a national population-based study of couples. *Annals of Epidemiology* 19(1):25–32.

McSherry D. 2011. Lest we forget: Remembering the consequences of child neglect—A clarion call to "feisty advocates." *Child Care in Practice* 17(2):103–113.

Meadow R. 1982. Munchausen syndrome by proxy. *Archives of Disease in Childhood* 57(2):92–98.

Meadow R. 1989. ABC of child abuse. Munchausen syndrome by proxy. *BMJ* 299(6693):248–250.

Mitchell KJ, D Finkelhor, LM Jones, and J Wolak. 2012. Prevalence and characteristics of youth sexting: A national study. *Pediatrics* 129(1):13–20.

Moore JG. 1975. Yo-Yo children—Victims of matrimonial violence. *Child Welfare* 54(8).

National Children's Advocacy Center. *History*. http://www.nationalcac.org/history/history.html, accessed May 24, 2015.

Ney PG. 1987. Does verbal abuse leave deeper scars: A study of children and parents. *Canadian Journal of Psychiatry* 32:371–378.

NICHD. *Protocol and Translated Versions*. http://www.nichdprotocol.com/the-nichd-protocol, accessed May 24, 2015.

Norman RE, M Byambaa, R De, A Butchart, J Scott, and T Vos. 2012. The long-term health consequences of child physical abuse, emotional abuse, and neglect: A systematic review and meta-analysis. *PLos Medicine* 9(11):e1001349.

O'Leary KD, AM Smith Slep, and SG O'Leary. 2007. Multivariate models of men's and women's partner aggression. *Journal of Consulting and Clinical Psychology* 75(5):752–764.

Oregon Department of Justice, Crime Victims' Services Division, Child Abuse Multidisciplinary Intervention (CAMI) Program. 2012. *Oregon Interviewing Guidelines*, 3rd edition. Salem, OR: Oregon Department of Justice.

Paroline v. US, 134 S. Ct. 1710, 572 U.S., 188 L. Ed. 2d 714 (2014).

Pennsylvania v. Ritchie, 480 U.S. 39, 107 S. Ct. 989, 94 L. Ed. 2d 40 (1987).

Pérez-Fuentes G, M Olfson, L Villegas, C Morcillo, S Wang, and C Blanco. 2013. Prevalence and correlates of child sexual abuse: A national study. *Comprehensive Psychiatry* 54(1):16–27.

Perry NW. 1995. Children's comprehension of truths, lies, and false beliefs. *True and False Allegations of Child Sexual Abuse: Assessment and Case Management*. Psychology Press, 73–98.

Ravichandiran N, S Schuh, M Bejuk, N Al-Harthy, M Shouldice, H Au, and K Boutis. 2010. Delayed identification of pediatric abuse-related fractures. *Pediatrics* 125(1):60–66.

Richards RD and C Calvert. 2009. When sex and cell phones collide: Inside the prosecution of a teen sexting case. *Hastings Communications and Entertainment Law Journal* 32:1.

Roberts YH, CA Campbell, M Ferguson, and CA Crusto. 2013. The role of parenting stress in young children's mental health functioning after exposure to family violence. *Journal of Traumatic Stress* 26(5):605–612.

Rosenberg DA. 1987. Web of deceit: A literature review of Munchausen syndrome by proxy. *Child Abuse and Neglect* 11(4):547–563.

Scheeringa MS, CF Weems, JA Cohen, L Amaya-Jackson, and D Guthrie. 2011. Trauma-focused cognitive-behavioral therapy for posttraumatic stress disorder in three- through six-year-old children: A randomized clinical trial. *Journal of Child Psychology and Psychiatry* 52(8):853–860.

Scheppele KL. 1989. Foreword: Telling stories. *Michigan Law Review* 87:2073–2098.

Schetky DH and AH Green. 2014. *Child Sexual Abuse: A Handbook for Health Care and Legal Professions*. New York: Routledge.

Schreier H. 2002. Munchausen by proxy defined. *Pediatrics* 110(5):985–988.

Schreier H. 2004. Munchausen by proxy. *Current Problems in Pediatric and Adolescent Health Care* 34(3):126–143.

Selph SS, C Bougatsos, I Blazina, and HD Nelson. 2013. Behavioral interventions and counseling to prevent child abuse and neglect: A systematic review to update the US preventive services task force recommendation. *Annals of Internal Medicine* 158(3):179–190.

Seto MC, JM Cantor, and R Blanchard. 2006. Child pornography offenses are a valid diagnostic indicator of pedophilia. *Journal of Abnormal Psychology* 115(3):610.

Shaw RJ, D Dayal, JK Hartman, and D DeMaso. 2008. Factitious disorder by proxy: Pediatric condition falsification. *Harvard Review of Psychiatry* 16:215–224.

Slep AMS, RE Heyman, and JD Snarr. 2011. Child emotional aggression and abuse: Definitions and prevalence. *Child Abuse and Neglect* 35(10):783–796.

State of Michigan Governor's Task Force on Child Abuse and Neglect and Department of Human Services. *Forensic Interviewing Protocol*, 3rd edition. Lansing, MI: Michigan Department of Health and Human Services.

Stoltenborgh M, MH van IJzendoorn, EM Euser, and MJ Bakermans-Kranenburg. 2011. A global perspective on child sexual abuse: Meta-analysis of prevalence around the world. *Child Maltreatment* 16(2):79–101.

Sugar NF, JA Taylor, and KW Feldman. 1999. Bruises in infants and toddlers: Those who don't cruise, rarely bruise. *Archives of Pediatrics and Adolescent Medicine* 153(4):399–403.

Swoboda SL and KW Feldman. 2013. Skeletal trauma in child abuse. *Pediatric Annals* 42(11):236.

Teicher MH. 2002. Scars that won't heal: The neurobiology of child abuse: Maltreatment at an early age can have enduring negative effects on a child's brain development and function. *Scientific American* 286(3).

Teicher MH, SL Andersen, A Polcari, CM Anderson, CP Navalta, and DM Kim. 2003. The neurobiological consequences of early stress and childhood maltreatment. *Neuroscience and Biobehavioral Reviews* 27:33–44.

U.S. Department of Health and Human Services. 2012. *Child Maltreatment* 2012. http://www.acf.hhs.gov/sites/default/files/cb/cm2012.pdf

U.S. Department of Health and Human Services. 2014. *Child Maltreatment 2014*. Washington, DC: U.S. Department of Health and Human Services. https://www.acf.hhs.gov/sites/default/files/cb/cm2014.pdf

U.S. Department of Health and Human Services. 2014. *The Child Abuse Prevention and Treatment Act (CAPTA) 2010*. Washington, DC: U.S. Department of Health and Human Services.

U.S. Department of Justice. 2013. *Intimate Partner Violence: Attributes of Victimization, 1993–2011*. Washington, DC: U.S. Department of Justice.http://www.ojp.gov/newsroom/factsheets/ojpfs_humantrafficking.html

Vizard E. 2013. Practitioner review: The victims and juvenile perpetrators of child sexual abuse—Assessment and intervention. *Journal of Child Psychology and Psychiatry* 54(5):503–515.

Westrick AC, M Moore, S Monk, A Greeno, and C Shannon. 2015. Identifying characteristics in abusive head trauma: A single-institution experience. *Pediatric Neurosurgery* 50(4):179–186.

Widom CS, S Czaja, and MA Dutton. 2014. Child abuse and neglect and intimate partner violence victimization and perpetration: A prospective investigation. *Child Abuse and Neglect* 38(4):650–663.

Wilsnack SC, ND Vogeltanz, AD Klassen, and TR Harris. 1997. Childhood sexual abuse and women's substance abuse: National survey findings. *Journal of Studies on Alcohol* 58(3):264–271.

Wilson KR and MR Prior. 2011. Father involvement and child well-being. *Journal of Paediatrics and Child Health* 47(7):405–407.

Wolfe DA. 1999. *Child Abuse: Implications for Child Development and Psychopathology*, Vol. 10. Thousand Oaks, CA: Sage Publications.

Yates TM. 2007. The developmental consequences of child emotional abuse: A neurodevelopmental perspective. *Journal of Emotional Abuse* 7(2):9–34.

Zhai F, J Waldfogel, and J Brooks-Gunn. 2013. Estimating the effects of head start on parenting and child maltreatment. *Children and Youth Services Review* 35(7):1119–1129.

Zimmerman C. 2006. *Stolen Smiles: A Summary Report on the Physical and Psychological Consequences of Women and Adolescents Trafficked in Europe*. London: London School of Hygiene and Tropical Medicine.

41

Juvenile delinquency

EILEEN P. RYAN

INTRODUCTION

Juvenile delinquency is a significant societal problem. Juveniles accounted for 13% of all violent crime arrests and 22% of all property crime arrests in 2011 (Puzzanchera 2013). The definition of juvenile delinquency varies depending on the local jurisdiction, but the traditional definition of a juvenile delinquent is someone under the age of 18 who is found to have committed a crime (adjudicated) in states in which it is declared by law that the minor's culpability is less than that of an adult, precluding sentencing as an adult.

This chapter will explore the history of juvenile justice in the United States, recent trends in our perceptions and treatment of juvenile offenders, risk factors for delinquency, mental health issues in this population, empirically based effective interventions, and prognosis for youthful offenders.

JUVENILE JUSTICE IN THE UNITED STATES

Juvenile courts deal with minors accused of violating a criminal statute, and the proceedings are civil as opposed to criminal. Therefore, instead of being charged with a crime, youth are accused of committing a delinquent act. The first juvenile court was established in Chicago in 1899, in large part due to the efforts of reformers such as Jane Adams, who also co-founded Hull House, a settlement house offering supportive services to the poor, especially the local immigrant population. Immigrant children living in poverty had higher involvement in criminal activity. Prior to the establishment of the juvenile court, young "hooligans" were subject to the same penalties as adult criminals and housed in adult jails.

In the name of *parens patriae* (*Prince v. Massachusetts* 1944), the state could act as a parent, and juvenile court judges were allowed to intervene in whatever manner was deemed by the court to be in the best interests of the child. The juvenile court offered none of the legal protections (e.g., right to an attorney, right to examine witnesses, etc.) offered to adults because its goal was not criminal, but rehabilitative. Judge Julian Mack, America's first juvenile judge, proposed in a *Harvard Law Review* article (Mack 1909) that the juvenile offender should be treated "as a wise and merciful father handles his own child." In keeping with the rehabilitative nature of the juvenile court, a different descriptive terminology was developed. Juveniles are not arrested; they are "taken into custody." They are not convicted at trials; they are "adjudicated" at hearings. Rather than sentenced, adjudicated delinquents are given "dispositions." Status offenses are those acts that would not be characterized as offenses if the perpetrator were an adult, for example, possession of tobacco products, truancy, and curfew violation.

LANDMARK CASES AND LEGISLATION IN JUVENILE JUSTICE

Unfortunately the promise of rehabilitation gave way to the reality of reform and training schools, many of which were not rehabilitative, and some of which were abusive. These facilities typically emphasized work and minimized the role of education or treatment. In *Kent,* the Supreme Court put an end to the unchecked powers of the juvenile court. Although it has been lamented that the Supreme Court decision in *Kent v. United States* (1966, 541) marked the beginning of the criminalization of the juvenile court (Quinn 2002, 719–730), juvenile courts had become small fiefdoms in which judges had extremely wide latitude.

In 1961 in Washington, DC, Morris Kent was 16 years old and already on probation for a variety of offenses when he was charged with rape and robbery. At that time, the Juvenile Court Act required a "full investigation" prior to waiving a juvenile to the adult system. The juvenile court judge did not rule on Kent's attorney's motion requesting a hearing and stated the court was waiving jurisdiction to adult criminal court after making a full investigation. However, the judge did not describe the nature of the investigation or the grounds for the waiver. Kent was found not guilty by reason of insanity (NGRI) for the rape, but guilty of housebreaking and robbery. He was subsequently sentenced to 30 to 90 years in prison. The Supreme Court ruled the waiver invalid, asserting that Kent was entitled to "the essentials of due process and fair treatment." In the majority opinion, Justice Abe Fortas observed that juveniles had "the worst of both worlds," getting "neither the protections accorded to adults, nor the solicitous care and regenerative treatment postulated for children."

The Supreme Court decision *In re Gault* (1967) followed closely on the heels of *Kent*. Gerald Gault was a 15-year-old boy in Arizona on probation for a minor property offense when he and his friend were accused by a neighbor of making an obscene phone call. Gault and his parents never saw the report filed by the probation officer, listing the charge as making lewd phone calls. At his hearing the neighbor was not present, no transcript of the hearing was made, and no one was sworn in to testify. For an offense for which as an adult the maximum sentence would have been a $50 fine or 2 months in jail, Gault was remanded to a training school for the remainder of his minority (ostensibly until age 21). The U.S. Supreme Court took the case, and writing for the majority, Justice Fortas noted, "Under our Constitution, the condition of being a boy does not justify a kangaroo court." The Court ruled juveniles have the right to notice of charges, an attorney, a hearing, and the privilege against self-incrimination, and the right to confront their accusers and cross-examine witnesses.

Given that juvenile court is not considered criminal court, prior to 1970 the standard of proof was preponderance of the evidence. The Supreme Court ruled in *In re Winship*, given the significant liberty interest at stake, the standard of proof should be beyond a reasonable doubt (*In re Winship* 1970). *Breed v. Jones* in 1975 established a juvenile's right to be free from double jeopardy (not to be tried in both juvenile and adult court for the same crime). However, in 1971, the Supreme Court refused to grant juveniles the right to a jury trial, noting the juvenile court remains at its core a tool for rehabilitation, and expressing a reluctance to turn it into a younger version of adult criminal court. The same rationale was used again in 1984, when the Supreme Court upheld pretrial preventative detention, indicating juveniles have no constitutional right to bail or to a speedy trial.

The Juvenile Justice and Delinquency Prevention Act passed in 1974 was designed to improve the handling of youth by the juvenile courts (Public Law No. 93-415, 1974) and has four core provisions. The Act: (1) focused on removing juveniles from adult lock-ups; (2) mandated the "sight-and sound" separation of incarcerated youth from adult inmates; (3) directed states to address the issue of disproportionate minority incarceration; and (4) directed de-institutionalization of status offenses. The Act was amended in 2002 and reflected the increased emphasis on "accountability" but was not substantively changed from the 1974 legislation (Juvenile Justice and Delinquency Prevention Act of 2002).

JUVENILE CRIME TRENDS

A sharp increase in juvenile crime in the late 1980s and early 1990s resulted in a shift in public opinion and public policy (Scott and Steinberg 2008, 4–13). State legislatures across the United States began to move away from the traditional emphasis on rehabilitation in the juvenile justice system and toward more harsh and punitive measures. By 2003, 31 states had enacted automatic transfer statutes requiring juvenile offenders with certain charges to be tried as adults (Steiner and Hemmens 2003). Also, the age at which juvenile court jurisdiction ended was lowered in 13 states to age 15 or 16 years (Snyder and Sickmund 2006).

Transfer laws were intended as a deterrent to juvenile crime and to effect a reduction in the rate of recidivism. Research on the specific deterrence effect of transfer laws has consistently indicated higher rates of recidivism for juveniles convicted in criminal courts versus their counterparts adjudicated for similar crimes in the juvenile courts; however, whether they deter potential juvenile offenders is less clear (Redding 2010).

Juvenile crime peaked in the early 1990s and has been falling since. According to national crime statistics reported by the Office of Juvenile Justice and Delinquency Prevention, the number of juvenile arrests for aggravated assault in 2011 was half of what it was in 1994. Between 1994 and 2010, the violent crime arrest rate decreased 55% to its lowest level since 1980 (Puzzanchera 2013). There is no consensus on the reasons for this decline, although a variety of explanations have been offered, including improved policing and youth initiatives, and a decrease in the demand for crack cocaine, which peaked in the 1990s (Sickmund and Puzzanchera 2014).

CAUSES AND RISK FACTORS FOR DELINQUENCY

Because delinquency is defined according to acts prohibited by law, including theft, violence, vandalism, and drug use, many delinquent acts are symptoms of conduct disorder. Conduct disorder according to the *Diagnostic and Statistical Manual of Mental Disorders*, 5th edition (*DSM-5*), is defined as a repetitive and persistent pattern of behavior in which the basic rights of others or major social norms or rules are violated, as manifested by at least three of fifteen criteria within the past 12 months, with at least one criterion present in the last 6 months. The criteria are divided into four categories: aggression to people and animals, destruction of property, deceitfulness or theft, and serious violations of rules. Childhood-onset type applies to individuals with onset of at least one symptom characteristic of conduct disorder prior to age 10; adolescent-onset type to those without symptoms characteristic of conduct disorder prior to age 10; and unspecified type in which the criteria for conduct disorder are met, but it is unclear as to whether the onset of the first symptom was prior to or after age 10 (American Psychiatric Association 2013). Callous–unemotional traits have been increasingly emphasized in theories regarding the etiology of conduct disorder (Frick et al. 2014), and in *DSM-5*, the specifier "with Limited Prosocial Emotions" (LPE) is applied to a minority of youth who display at least two of the following characteristics over at least 12 months and in multiple relationships and settings: lack of remorse or guilt; callousness/lack of empathy; lack of concern regarding poor performance at work, school, or other important activities; and shallow or deficient affect. This specifier is expected to guide further research and treatment and provide more information about the impairment and prognosis of children and adolescents with conduct disorder. It appears that the LPE specifier identifies a group of more severely antisocial youth for both genders, with younger age of criminal behavior and legal contact (Pechorro et al. 2015).

Symptoms of conduct disorder usually emerge in middle childhood to middle adolescence, and the delinquency peaks in middle to late adolescence. The majority of youth who meet criteria for conduct disorder will not meet criteria for antisocial personality disorder in adulthood and will desist in their criminal activity; however, the early onset type of conduct disorder has a worse prognosis and increased risk for adult criminal behavior.

The Pittsburgh Youth Study, a longitudinal study of 1517 inner-city boys, purposefully contained an oversampling of boys with disruptive behaviors and contributed significantly to our understanding of the development and evolution of delinquency in boys (Loeber and Farrington 2012) The Pittsburgh Youth Study identified three distinct developmental pathways to delinquency in boys: (1) Authority Conflict pathway characterized by stubbornness prior to age 12, then moving on to defiance; (2) Covert pathway characterized by minor acts such as lying and stealing, and progressing to more serious delinquent acts; and (3) Overt pathway characterized by minor aggression progressing to more serious fighting and violence. The researchers noted delinquency typically follows an orderly progression, with "problem behaviors" beginning long before major behavior problems and legal involvement. Early risk factors such as irritability and impulsivity were obvious between ages 3 and 6 years of age (Moffitt et al. 1996).

Among the cohorts in the Pittsburgh Youth Study, 30%–51% of boys by age 15 at various levels of risk had committed serious crimes. In their delinquency model, as the child aged, more risk factors accumulated and exerted an influence. Each risk factor added weight to previous risk factors, and the more risk factors, the greater the likelihood of delinquency. The more risk factors present, the more difficult it is to return to a normal developmental path without intervention. However, most antisocial children do not go on to become antisocial adults. Likewise, it is highly unusual for antisocial behavior to arise *de novo* during adulthood without a childhood or adolescent history of antisocial behavior.

Risk factors are variables that when present predict an increased probability of conduct disorder or delinquency. Risk factors for delinquency can be divided into individual risk factors, family risk factors, and social risk factors (Murray and Farrington 2010).

Individual risk factors

Numerous individual factors have been described as increasing one's risk for the development of conduct disorder and delinquency, including irritability and depression (Burke et al. 2005), low self-esteem (Kokkinos and Panayioutou 2004), trauma-related psychopathology (Steiner et al. 2011), and temperament (Caspi 2000; Caspi and Silva 1995). However, the most extensive research has consistently identified impulsivity, low IQ, and poor school achievement as the major individual risk factors (Murray and Farrington 2010).

The Pittsburgh Youth Study found low IQ was related to offending in boys independent of socioeconomic status, ethnicity, neighborhood, and impulsivity. Personality factors include having a low threshold for experiencing negative emotions such as anger, fear, and anxiety, as well as thrill-seeking and impulsivity. Additional risk factors include a lack of guilt, being older than one's classmates, and depression (Loeber et al. 1998).

Family risk factors

Poor parental supervision is one of the strongest risk factors for delinquency and conduct disorder (Loeber et al. 2009). Harsh and/or inconsistent parental discipline and child abuse, parental conflict, antisocial parents, and parental imprisonment are strong predictors of child antisocial behavior (Murray and Farrington 2008, 2010).

Social risk factors

Low socioeconomic status (SES) has been associated with delinquency, although what mediates the link is unclear. Poor child-rearing practices and family factors such as corporal punishment and maternal care/unresponsiveness have been implicated, but delinquent peers may be a mediating factor (Fergusson et al. 2004). It is well known that juvenile offending, more so than adult offending, occurs in groups. Delinquent acts tend to be committed in small groups (two to three persons) rather than alone or in large groups (Zimring 1981). There appears to be a reciprocal relationship between delinquency and delinquent peer bonding; that is, association with delinquent peers causes delinquency, and delinquency causes association with delinquent peers (Thornberry et al. 1994). In the Pittsburgh Youth study, among social risk factors, receiving public assistance was associated with the highest risk of delinquency. Having a broken family was the strongest demographic variable related to delinquency, and living in a high-crime neighborhood more than doubled the risk (Loeber et al. 1998). Poor attachment to parents is yet another identified risk factor in delinquency (Hoeve et al. 2012).

Childhood abuse is associated with changes in gene expression (Suderman et al. 2014), brain structure, and neural networks, and may influence neurotransmitter function and levels in a way that persists into adulthood (Teicher et al. 2014). However, not all children who are abused exhibit antisocial behavior. The interaction between genes and environment has been proposed as a mediating factor to explain the variability in the outcome of abused children. The monoamine oxidase A (*MAOA*) gene, which encodes the enzyme MAOA, plays a major role in the metabolism of the neurotransmitters dopamine, serotonin, and norepinephrine. A functional polymorphism in the *MAOA* gene in combination with self-reported maltreatment has been shown in some studies to impact delinquency (Caspi et al. 2002). Boys with a short variant of the polymorphism had a higher risk of delinquency when exposed to maltreatment; abused girls with at least one long variant of the polymorphism had a higher risk of delinquency (Aslund et al. 2011).

GENDER ISSUES AND THE DEVELOPMENT OF DELINQUENCY

Female juvenile delinquency has garnered increased research attention; however, overall there has been a paucity of research examining the causes and correlates of female delinquency relative to male delinquency. While overall, girls' delinquent acts are typically less chronic and severe than boys (Snyder and Sickmund 2006), it is a serious and growing problem. In 2011, girls accounted for one-third of juvenile arrests.

To date, there is no comprehensive theory of the development of delinquent behavior that is specific to girls; however, a number of large-scale studies have helped inform a better understanding of the development and maintenance of antisocial behavior in both males and females. The Pittsburgh Girls Study, a longitudinal community-based study of 2451 girls recruited when they were between the ages of 5 and 8 years, found that conduct disorder tended to have an insidious onset in girls, beginning with subsyndromal symptoms (Keenan et al. 2010).

In the landmark Dunedin Longitudinal Study, over 1000 boys and girls were followed from the ages of 3 to 21 using approaches and methods from developmental psychology, psychiatry, and criminology. The original taxonomy indicated two main types of antisocial behavior in youth (Moffitt 1993). The first type, life-course-persistent (LCP) antisocial behavior, is characterized by neurodevelopmental dysfunction (hyperactivity, central nervous system [CNS] dysfunction, learning disability [especially reading], and difficult temperament) along with social and familial deficits. LCP antisocial behavior has a significant male predominance, early onset in childhood, low prevalence (about 5%), and persistence into adulthood. The second type, adolescence-limited antisocial behavior, can be viewed as a social phenomenon. This type originates in the context of social relationships, has its onset during puberty, has a high prevalence, and has negligible sex differences, especially when drugs and alcohol are involved, and girls who are involved with antisocial males in intimate relationships (Moffitt and Caspi 2001; Moffitt et al. 2002). Risk factors include social and familial deficits such as poor supervision, broken homes, antisocial role models, and the perception of antisocial behavior as reinforcing. Girls are less likely to develop the more persistent developmental type of antisocial behavior because they more frequently lack the crucial risk factors for it (impulsivity, neurocognitive deficits, temperamental undercontrol). However, girls are as likely to develop the socially influenced form of antisocial behavior as boys with whom they share the same risk factors.

PSYCHOPATHOLOGY AND JUVENILE DELINQUENCY

Mental illness is prevalent among youth in the juvenile justice system. One study showed that among 1829 detained youth, nearly two-thirds of boys and nearly three-quarters of girls met diagnostic criteria for one or more psychiatric disorders. When conduct disorder was excluded, nearly 60% of boys and more than two-thirds of girls met criteria with impairment for one or more psychiatric disorders. Substance abuse disorders were found in half the boys and almost half of the girls (Teplin et al. 2002). Mood disorders are highly prevalent in this population. A study of 1024 incarcerated adolescents found that 60% had one or more psychiatric disorders; 25% had moderate depression, and 22% had severe depression as measured by the Beck Depression Inventory. From the Patient Health Questionnaire, 10% had major depressive disorder, 41% had drug abuse, 27% abused alcohol, and 29% had another major mental disorder. Comorbidity was especially common between depression and anxiety and drug and alcohol abuse. Sixty percent had one or more psychiatric disorders. Of those adolescents who were depressed, 20% had been previously diagnosed and treated compared to only 10% of youth with other disorders (Domalanta et al. 2003).

Abuse and trauma are strongly associated with risk-taking behaviors. Abuse is associated with alterations in the biological stress response system, which in turn can disrupt emotional and cognitive processes (Teicher et al. 2014), increasing the likelihood of risky behaviors in vulnerable youth. Girls in the juvenile justice system are more likely than non-juvenile-justice-involved girls to have experienced trauma, and were more likely to have experienced sexual abuse than boys (Wasserman and McReynolds 2011). In a large sample of detained inner-city youth, over 90% of the study participants had experienced at least one traumatic event, with 11% of the sample meeting full criteria for post-traumatic stress disorder (PTSD) within the past year (Abram et al. 2004). Among detained youth with PTSD, 93% met criteria for at least one other psychiatric disorder (Abram et al. 2007). Delinquent youth are more likely than nondelinquent youth to have experienced trauma and to report PTSD, major depression, and substance abuse. Even when accounting for the effects of demographics and trauma exposure, delinquency increases the likelihood of further traumatization and substance abuse in both genders, and increases the likelihood of major depression in girls (Adams et al. 2013). Other studies have found a higher prevalence of PTSD (30%), particularly among girls

Table 41.1 Overall prevalence of psychiatric disorders among incarcerated youth

Mental illness	Male %	Female %
Major depressive disorder	10.6	29.2
Psychotic disorders	3.3	2.7
Attention deficit hyperactivity disorder	11.7	18.5
Conduct disorder	52.8	52.8

Source: From Fazel S, H Doll, and N Langstrom. 2008. *Journal of the American Academy of Child and Adolescent Psychiatry* 47(9):1010–1019. With permission.

(Cauffman et al. 1998; Ariga et al. 2008). The results of a meta-analysis consisting of 25 studies on the prevalence of mental disorders in incarcerated juveniles are summarized in Table 41.1 (Fazel et al. 2008).

During the past decade, most states have enacted policies requiring at least mental health screening in their juvenile justice population. The Massachusetts Youth Screening Instrument-Version 2 (MAYSI-2) is a brief mental health screening tool that can be completed by nonclinicians at entry to a juvenile justice facility (Grisso et al. 2001, 541–548) in order to identify youth who may need immediate attention for suicidal risk and emergent mental health and substance abuse problems. Over 2000 juvenile detention or correction facilities in 44 states use a version of the MAYSI-2 for mental health screening (Grisso et al. 2012).

TREATMENTS FOR JUVENILE DELINQUENCY

There are a number of empirically validated interventions for delinquency, which are unfortunately unavailable to the majority of youth who could profit from them, in large part because of their cost and the inertia that is part and parcel of an entrenched system. Many delinquent youth receive no evidence-based treatment; many receive interventions that might be helpful or even necessary but require combination with appropriate wrap-around services. Unfortunately, psychopharmacology and some form of individual therapy or home-based services provided by persons with little specialized training remains the mainstay of treatment for most delinquents receiving care. Of course, psychiatric disorders must be treated aggressively and appropriately, but pharmacologic treatment is only one intervention. Evaluation and treatment of substance abuse are another important focus for many delinquent youth.

Evidence-based treatments typically involve a treatment "package" that must be delivered consistently over a sufficient period of time to be effective. The treatment modalities should be individualized and may involve individual, group, and family therapy; psychiatric evaluation and pharmacologic treatment; education- and school-based interventions; and effective and aggressive case management.

Psychodynamic psychotherapy is generally suitable for only a minority of delinquent youth with internalizing disorders, such as depression and anxiety, who are reflective, trusting, and willing to engage in a therapeutic relationship. However, given the nature and causes of delinquency, even youth who may profit from psychodynamic psychotherapy should receive other needed services that address the myriad of stressors and vulnerabilities in the juvenile's life. The last two decades have seen the rise of empirically validated interventions specifically geared toward delinquent youth, several of which are described below.

Multisystemic therapy (MST) has been one of the most extensively studied interventions in delinquent youth (Henggeler et al. 1996). MST has been studied and shown to have a positive effect over traditional supportive therapies in subsets of delinquent youth including those with substance abuse and sex offenses (Zajac et al. 2015). The MST model mandates attention to altering a variety of maladaptive and risk-sustaining factors in the youth's life and is essentially a family-based intervention. Adherence to the treatment model, which emphasizes that case managers take responsibility for the adherence of the youth and family to treatment, is quite different from the more traditional mental health model, which often tends to blame the patient and family for lack of efficacy. However, a multilayer meta-analysis of 22 international studies consisting of 4066 juveniles showed only a small positive effect on delinquency (van der Stouwe et al. 2014). The meta-analysis indicated larger effects were found in the U.S. studies, and that MST was most effective with nonethnic minority, sex-offending, younger juveniles (under age 15). The authors suggested the efficacy of MST for older juveniles might be improved by focusing on peer relationships and risks and protective factors in the educational domain/school setting.

Functional family therapy (FFT) and multidimensional treatment foster care (MTFC) are family-based treatments that include a variety of additional components individualized to the particular youth (individual, psychiatric, peer, school, and community). Functional family therapy focuses on modifying patterns of family interaction by modeling, prompting, and encouragement, in an effort to develop clear and direct communication and minimize conflict (Alexander and Parsons 1973). A long-term follow-up study of juvenile offenders found FFT to be superior to probation services (control), with FFT participants reporting a lower rate of rearrests compared to controls (Gordon et al. 1995). Multidimensional treatment foster care focuses on individual treatment including problem-solving skills and parent management training for families of adolescents in foster care (Chamberlain and Reid 1998). This therapy has been found to be more effective than services-as-usual group home care for adolescent males in the juvenile justice system, with the self-reported rates of violent offending four to five times higher in the group home population (Eddy et al. 2004).

The Stop Now and Plan (SNAP) program has shown promise as an intervention for antisocial behavior among boys between the ages of 6 and 11. A randomized controlled treatment effectiveness study showed improvements in aggression and other externalizing behaviors, as well as attention deficit hyperactivity disorder (ADHD) symptoms versus standard behavioral health services (Burke and Loeber 2014).

DELINQUENTS GROWN UP

What happens to juvenile delinquents in adulthood? The good news is the majority of juvenile offenders do not go on to develop antisocial personality disorder or become adult criminals. The bad news is juvenile delinquency exacts a significant price from the future of the individual child, and ultimately society. In their cohort of 1653 formerly detained youth, Abrams and colleagues found that 3 years after detention most youth struggled in one or more life domains, and more than one in five had marked impairment in functioning (Abram et al. 2009).

The boys and girls of the Dunedin study were assessed at age 32 years (Odgers et al. 2008). Four antisocial pathways were identified: (1) life-course persistent (LCP), which made up 10.5% of the males and 7.5% of the females; (2) adolescent-onset, which accounted for 19.6% of the males and 17.4% of the females; (3) childhood-limited (CL), which was 24.3% of the males and 20% of the females; and the largest group (4) antisocial low (AL), exhibiting low levels of conduct problems, which was 45.6% of the males and 55.1% of the females. The LCP males and females had the worst mental health, physical health, and economic outcomes, and early childhood antisocial behavior persisted into adulthood. The LCP pathway for both males and females was predicted by individual risk factors such a low IQ, reading disability, and hyperactivity, in combination with social and familial risk factors. The antisocial-low group had conduct problems that emerged in adolescence and persisted into adulthood (hence, the term "adolescence-limited" was not appropriate), but there was not an elevated risk of violence, and the mental health problems in these males and females were primarily restricted to substance abuse. The CL group had conduct problems that emerged during early childhood but desisted. The CL females at age 32 were not experiencing problems relative to their peers, but the males were behind in median household income and educational attainment.

SUMMARY KEY POINTS

- Juvenile crime peaked in the early 1990s and has steadily declined since that time; however, laws enacted in response to that increase remain in effect, resulting in harsher penalties for youth, including transfer to the adult system.
- The majority of youth who meet criteria for conduct disorder do not go on to become antisocial adults.
- Individual, family, and social risk factors for delinquency and persistent criminal behavior, including maltreatment, have an additive effect, and the more risk factors, the more likely a child will become delinquent.
- Mental illness, especially mood and anxiety disorders and substance abuse, is prevalent among youth involved in the juvenile justice system.
- There are a variety of empirically validated treatment interventions for juvenile delinquents.

REFERENCES

Abram KM, JY Choe, JJ Washburn, EG Romero, and LA Teplin. 2009. Functional impairment in youth three years after detention. *Journal of Adolescent Health* 44(6):528–535.

Abram KM, LA Teplin, DR Charles, SL Longworth, GM McClelland, and MK Dulcan. 2004. Posttraumatic stress disorder and trauma in youth in juvenile detention. *Archives of General Psychiatry* 61(4):403–410.

Abram KM, JJ Washburn, LA Teplin, KM Emanuel, EG Romero, and GM McClelland. 2007. Posttraumatic stress disorder and psychiatric comorbidity among detained youths. *Psychiatric Services (Washington, D.C.)* 58(10):1311–1316.

Adams ZW, MR McCart, K Zajac, CK Danielson, GK Sawyer, BE Saunders, and DG Kilpatrick. 2013. Psychiatric problems and trauma exposure in nondetained delinquent and nondelinquent adolescents. *Journal of Clinical Child and Adolescent Psychology* 42(3):323–331.

Alexander JF and BV Parsons. 1973. Short-term behavioral intervention with delinquent families: Impact on family process and recidivism. *Journal of Abnormal Psychology* 81(3):219–225.

American Psychiatric Association. 2013. *Diagnostic and Statistical Manual of Mental Disorders*, 5th Edition. Washington, DC: American Psychiatric Press.

Ariga M, T Uehara, K Takeuchi, Y Ishige, R Nakano, and M Mikuni. 2008. Trauma exposure and posttraumatic stress disorder in delinquent female adolescents. *Journal of Child Psychology and Psychiatry, and Allied Disciplines* 49(1):79–87.

Aslund C, N Nordquist, E Comasco, J Leppert, L Oreland, and KW Nilsson. 2011. Maltreatment, MAOA, and delinquency: Sex differences in gene-environment interaction in a large population-based cohort of adolescents. *Behavior Genetics* 41(2):262–272.

Breed v. Jones, 421, U.S. 519 (1975).

Burke JD and R Loeber. 2014. The effectiveness of the Stop Now and Plan (SNAP) program for boys at risk for violence and delinquency. *Prevention Science*. doi:10.1007/s11121-014-0490-2

Burke JD, R Loeber, BB Lahey, and PJ Rathouz. 2005. Developmental transitions among affective and behavioral disorders in adolescent boys. *Journal of Child Psychology and Psychiatry, and Allied Disciplines* 46(11):1200–1210.

Caspi A. 2000. The child is father of the man; personality continuities from childhood to adulthood. *Journal of Personality and Social Psychology* 78(1):158–172.

Caspi A, J McClay, TE Moffitt, J Mill, J Martin, IW Craig, A Taylor, and R Poulton. 2002. Role of genotype in the cycle of violence in maltreated children. *Science* 297(5582):851–854.

Caspi A and PA Silva. 1995. Temperamental qualities at age three predict personality traits in young adulthood: Longitudinal evidence from a birth cohort. *Child Development* 66(2):486–498.

Cauffman E, SS Feldman, J Waterman, and H Steiner. 1998. Posttraumatic stress disorder among female juvenile offenders. *Journal of the American Academy of Child and Adolescent Psychiatry* 37(11):1209–1216.

Chamberlain P and JB Reid. 1998. Comparison of two community alternatives to incarceration for chronic juvenile offenders. *Journal of Consulting and Clinical Psychology* 66(4):624–633.

Domalanta DD, WL Risser, RE Roberts, and JM Risser. 2003. Prevalence of depression and other psychiatric disorders among incarcerated youths. *Journal of the American Academy of Child and Adolescent Psychiatry* 42(4):477–484.

Eddy JM, R Bridges Whaley, and P Chamberlain. 2004. The prevention of violent behavior by chronic and serious male juvenile offenders: A 2-year follow-up of a randomized clinical trial. *Journal of Emotional and Behavioral Disorders* 12:2–8.

Fazel S, H Doll, and N Langstrom. 2008. Mental disorders among adolescents in juvenile detention and correctional facilities: A systematic review and meta-regression analysis of 25 surveys. *Journal of the American Academy of Child and Adolescent Psychiatry* 47(9):1010–1019.

Fergusson DM, N Swain-Campbell, and J Horwood. 2004. How does childhood economic disadvantage lead to crime? *Journal of Child Psychology and Psychiatry* 45(5):956–966.

Frick PJ, AH Cornell, SD Bodin, HE Dane, CT Barry, and BR Loney. 2003. Callous-unemotional traits and developmental pathways to severe conduct problems. *Developmental Psychology* 39(2):246–260.

Gordon DA, K Graves, and J Arbuthnot. 1995. The effect of functional family therapy for delinquents on adult criminal behavior. *Criminal Justice and Behavior* 22:60–73.

Grisso T, R Barnum, KE Fletcher, E Cauffman, and D Peuschold. 2001. Massachusetts youth screening instrument for mental health needs of juvenile justice youths. *Journal of the American Academy of Child and Adolescent Psychiatry* 40(5):541–548.

Grisso T, S Fusco, M Paiva-Salisbury, R Perrauot, V Williams, and R Barnum. 2012. The Massachusetts Youth Screening Instrument-Version 2 (MAYSI-2): Comprehensive research review. http://www.Nysap.Us accessed August 1, 2014.

Henggeler SW, PB Cunningham, SG Pickrel, SK Schoenwald, and MJ Brondino. 1996. Therapy: An effective violence prevention approach for serious juvenile offenders. *Journal of Adolescence* 19(1):47–61.

Hoeve M, GJ Stams, CE van der Put, JS Dubas, PH van der Laan, and JR Gerris. 2012. A meta-analysis of attachment to parents and delinquency. *Journal of Abnormal Child Psychology* 40(5):771–785.

In re Gault, 387 U.S. 1, 87 S.Ct. 1428, 1428 (S.Ct. 1967).

In re Winship. 1970. *In Re Winship*. 397:358.

Juvenile Justice and Delinquency Prevention Act of 1974. Pub. L. No. 93-415, 42 U.S.C. §5601 *et seq.*

Juvenile Justice and Delinquency Prevention Act of 2002. As amended, Pub. L. No. 93-415 (1974).

Keenan K, A Hipwell, T Chung, S Stepp, M Stouthamer-Loeber, R Loeber, and K McTigue. 2010. The Pittsburgh girls study: Overview and initial findings. *Journal of Clinical Child and Adolescent Psychology* 39(4):506–521.

Kent v. U.S., 383 U.S. 541 (1966).

Kokkinos CM and G Panayioutou. 2004. Predicting bullying and victimization among early adolescents: Associations with disruptive behavior disorders. *Aggressive Behavior* 30(6):520–533.

Loeber R, JD Burke, and DA Pardini. 2009. Development and etiology of disruptive and delinquent behavior. *Annual Review of Clinical Psychology* 5:291–310.

Loeber R and DP Farrington. 2012. Advancing knowledge about direct protective factors that may reduce youth violence. *American Journal of Preventive Medicine* 43(2 Supplement 1):S24–S27.

Loeber R, DP Farrington, M Stouthamer-Loeber, T Moffitt, and A Caspi. 1998. The development of male offending: Key findings in the first decade of the Pittsburgh youth study. *Studies in Crime and Crime Prevention* 7:141–172.

Mack J. 1909. The juvenile court. *Harvard Law Review* 23(1909):104.

Moffitt TE. 1993. Adolescence-limited and life-course-persistent antisocial behavior: A developmental taxonomy. *Psychological Review* 100(4):674–701.

Moffitt TE and A Caspi. 2001. Childhood predictors differentiate life-course persistent and adolescence-limited antisocial pathways among males and females. *Development and Psychopathology* 13(2):355–375.

Moffitt TE, A Caspi, N Dickson et al. 1996. Childhood-onset versus adolescent-onset antisocial conduct problems in males: Natural history from ages 3 to 18 years. *Developmental Psychopathology* 8(2):399–424.

Moffitt TE, A Caspi, H Harrington, and BJ Milne. 2002. Males on the life-course-persistent and adolescence-limited antisocial pathways: Follow-up at age 26 years. *Development and Psychopathology* 14(1):179–207.

Murray J and DP Farrington. 2008. Parental imprisonment: Long-lasting effects on boys' internalizing problems through the life course. *Development and Psychopathology* 20(1):273–290.

Murray J and DP Farrington. 2010. Risk factors for conduct disorder and delinquency: Key findings from longitudinal studies. *Canadian Journal of Psychiatry. Revue Canadienne De Psychiatrie* 55(10):633–642.

Odgers CL, TE Moffitt, JM Broadbent, N Dickson, RJ Hancox, H Harrington, R Poulton, MR Sears, WM Thomson, and A Caspi. 2008. Female and male antisocial trajectories: From childhood origins to adult outcomes. *Development and Psychopathology* 20(2):673–716.

Pechorro P, L Jimenez, V Hidalgo, and C Nunes. 2015. The DSM-5 limited prosocial emotions subtype of conduct disorder in incarcerated male and female juvenile delinquents. *International Journal of Law and Psychiatry* 39:77–82.

Prince v. Massachusetts, 321, 158 (United States 1944).

Puzzanchera C. December 2013. *Juvenile Arrests 2011.* Washington, DC: U.S. Department of Justice, Office of Justice Programs.

Quinn KM. 2002. Juveniles on trial. *Child and Adolescent Psychiatric Clinics of North America* 11(4):719–730.

Redding RE. 2010. *Juvenile Transfer Laws: An Effective Deterrent to Delinquency?* June edition, edited by Office of Juvenile Justice and Delinquency Prevention, Washington, DC: U.S. Department of Justice, Office of Justice Programs.

Scott E and L Steinberg. 2008. *Rethinking Juvenile Justice.* Cambridge, MA: Harvard University Press.

Sickmund M and C Puzzanchera. 2014. *Juvenile Offenders and Victims: 2014 National Report.* Washington, DC: U.S. Department of Justice, Office of Juvenile Programs.

Snyder HN and M Sickmund. 2006. *Junvenile Offenders and Victims: 2006 National Report.* Washington, DC: U.S. Department of Justice, Office of Justice Programs.

Steiner B and C Hemmens. 2003 (spring). Juvenile waiver 2003: Where are we now? *Juvenile and Family Court Journal* 54(2):1451–1477.

Steiner H, M Silverman, NS Karnik, J Huemer, B Plattner, CE Clark, JR Blair, and R Haapanen. 2011. Psychopathology, trauma and delinquency: Subtypes of aggression and their relevance for understanding young offenders. *Child and Adolescent Psychiatry and Mental Health* 5:21.

Suderman M, N Borghol, JJ Pappas, SM Pinto Pereira, M Pembrey, C Hertzman, C Power, and M Szyf. 2014. Childhood abuse is associated with methylation of multiple loci in adult DNA. *BMC Medical Genomics* 7:13. doi:10.1186/1755-8794-7-13

Teicher MH, CM Anderson, K Ohashi, and A Polcari. 2014. Childhood maltreatment: Altered network centrality of cingulate, precuneus, temporal pole and insula. *Biological Psychiatry* 76(4):297–305.

Teplin LA, KM Abram, GM McClelland, MK Dulcan, and AA Mericle. 2002. Psychiatric disorders in youth in juvenile detention. *Archives of General Psychiatry* 59(12):1133–1143.

Thornberry TP, AJ Lizotte, MD Krohn et al. 1994. Delinquent peers, beliefs, and delinquent behavior: A longitudinal test of interactional theory. *Criminology* 32(1):47–83.

van der Stouwe T, JJ Asscher, GJ Stams, M Dekovic, and PH van der Laan. 2014. The effectiveness of multisystemic therapy (MST): A meta-analysis. *Clinical Psychology Review* 34(6):468–481.

Wasserman GA and LS McReynolds. 2011. Contributors to traumatic exposure and posttraumatic stress disorder in juvenile justice youths. *Journal of Traumatic Stress* 24(4):422–429.

Zajac K, J Randall, and CC Swenson. 2015. Multisystemic therapy for externalizing youth. *Child and Adolescent Psychiatric Clinics of North America* 24(3):601–616.

Zimring FE. 1981. Kids, groups and crime: Some implications of a well-known secret. *Journal of Criminal Law and Criminology* 72(3):867–885.

42

Posttraumatic stress disorder in children and adolescents: Clinical and legal issues

FRANK K. TEDESCHI AND STEPHEN B. BILLICK

INTRODUCTION

References to what is now called posttraumatic stress disorder (PTSD) can be found in a wide range of historical texts spanning centuries, including the Bible, Homer, Herodotus, and Shakespeare. The symptoms that are recognized today as belonging to the well-defined psychiatric disorder that can result from exposure to trauma have also gone by other names, including "railway spine," "traumatic hysteria," "shell shock," and "combat fatigue" (Smith 2011). However, for much of its history PTSD has been referred to as a disorder of adults, with the initial *Diagnostic and Statistical Manual of Mental Disorders*, 3rd edition (*DSM-III*) criteria for PTSD being based primarily on studies of war veterans and adult rape victims (American Psychiatric Association 1980; March 1993). Despite this, there has long been recognition within the fields of psychology and psychiatry that children and adolescents develop posttraumatic symptoms as well, and may manifest these symptoms differently than adults depending on their age and developmental stage. Serious examination of the effects of trauma in children was first mentioned in literature during World War II (Dunsdon 1941; Brander 1943; Freud and Burlingham 1943), but it was not until 1987 that the *Diagnostic and Statistical Manual of Mental Disorders*, 3rd edition, revised (*DSM-III-R*) incorporated developmental specifiers for children and adolescents in the PTSD criteria (American Psychiatric Association 1987). Though the *Diagnostic and Statistical Manual of Mental Disorders*, 4th edition (*DSM-IV*) further expanded the developmental specifiers for PTSD (American Psychiatric Association 1994), the PTSD criteria in the *Diagnostic and Statistical Manual of Mental Disorders*, 5th edition (*DSM-5*) is the most developmentally informed to date, with a greater emphasis on the behavioral sequelae of trauma for children age 7 and above, and the creation of the first developmental subtype of a *DSM* disorder: posttraumatic stress disorder for Children 6 Years and Younger (American Psychiatric Association 2013a).

The uniqueness of PTSD in the forensic context is the ability to directly link the development of psychopathology to an exposure of a traumatic event. As a consequence, PTSD is becoming one of the most commonly litigated mental health disorders (Bottalico and Bruni 2012). The diagnosis can be used in court to illustrate tangible proof of loss of functioning, as evidence that an alleged crime occurred, as well as a means of determining civil compensation. In this context, as research on PTSD has progressed, courts have increasingly turned not only to the psychiatric interview as a means of establishing the diagnosis, but also neuroimaging and neurological manifestations of the disorder (Lubit et al. 2002). This is particularly important as courts have historically tended to award damages more commonly for injuries that are considered "physical," rather than purely "psychological" (Lubit et al. 2002). With children and adolescents the evaluation of PTSD has an additional layer of complexity, due to their different cognitive, emotional, language, and memory capacities. The expert must be well versed not only in specific *DSM-5* criteria, but also in models of pediatric development, neuroimaging research in juveniles, and forensic interviewing techniques for children and adolescents. The expert must also be prepared to perform evaluations and testify in an ever-expanding range of civil and criminal proceedings, including personal injury, medical malpractice, violent crime, physical and sexual abuse, neglect, custody evaluations, and the termination of parental rights.

POSTTRAUMATIC STRESS DISORDER IN THE *DSM-5*

Though the *DSM-IV* (American Psychiatric Association 1994) expanded the developmental specifiers for PTSD pertaining to the pediatric population that first appeared in the *DSM-III-R* (American Psychiatric Association 1987), it has been suggested that the *DSM-IV* criteria still lacked validity for younger children. In particular, it has been pointed out that the *DSM-IV* criteria were based on data for individuals only age 15 and above (Scheeringa et al. 2011, 2012), and that a number of the criteria required a verbal description of experiences and internal states beyond the language capabilities of younger children (Scheeringa et al. 1995). Additionally, the *DSM-IV* Cluster C criteria for avoidance and numbing have been criticized as far too difficult for children to meet, as numbing and a sense of foreshortened future are difficult for preschool and school-age children to describe (Scheeringa et al. 2011), and children have a lesser ability to engage in avoidant behaviors as their caretakers dictate their routine and location (Pynoos et al. 2009). As a result, largely because of the Cluster C criteria, fewer children with significant posttraumatic symptoms met *DSM-IV* criteria for PTSD, leading to underestimates of its prevalence (Scheeringa et al. 1995; Scheeringa 2003).

In the *DSM-5* (American Psychiatric Association 2013a), changes have been made to the PTSD criteria for individuals aged 6 years and above, which includes school-age children and adolescents. Specifically, whereas the *DSM-IV* had three symptom clusters (B, C, and D) that include 17 possible symptoms, the *DSM-5* now has four symptom clusters (B, C, D, and E) that incorporate a total of 20 symptoms. Cluster A is now clearer in what defines a traumatic event, and how it can be experienced. Criterion A2 has also been removed due to its poor ability to predict the onset of PTSD. The former *DSM-IV* Cluster C has now been divided into two new categories: Avoidance (Cluster C) and Negative Cognitions and Mood (Cluster D). The new Cluster D has introduced symptoms of persistent negative beliefs about oneself and negative emotional states. Cluster E (alterations in arousal and reactivity) has also added the new symptom of reckless or self-destructive behavior. This has led to the observation that the new *DSM-5* criteria place a greater emphasis on the "fight" aspects of PTSD, rather than just "flight" as previous *DSM* editions did (American Psychiatric Association 2013b).

More important to the evaluation of young children is the creation of the developmental subtype of PTSD applicable to children aged 6 years and younger: Posttraumatic stress disorder for Children 6 Years and Younger. In comparison to the criteria for individuals above age 6, there are three symptom clusters instead of four, which include re-experiencing (Cluster B), avoidance and negative cognitions (Cluster C), and arousal (Cluster D). In addition, rather than emphasizing verbal descriptions by the patient of internal phenomena, the criteria are more rooted in behavioral manifestations of exposure to trauma. Notable specifiers for Cluster B are that spontaneous and intrusive memories as well as dissociative reactions may both be expressed through play reenactment in young children. Cluster C combines symptoms of both avoidance and negative cognitions, and in acknowledgement of the challenges of detecting these symptoms in young children, requires that only one symptom from either category be present for the diagnosis to be made. In Cluster D it is also specified that children may manifest extreme temper tantrums as a consequence of trauma.

FORENSIC IMPLICATIONS OF CHANGES TO THE *DSM-5*

What impact will the more developmentally informed *DSM-5* criteria have on the evaluation of PTSD in children and adolescents? Several studies that employed developmentally appropriate PTSD diagnostic criteria similar to those in the *DSM-5* found the rates of cases meeting full diagnostic criteria significantly increased when compared to the rates of diagnosis using *DSM-IV* criteria (Scheeringa et al. 2006; Meiser-Stedman et al. 2008; Iselin et al. 2010). It is expected that the incidence and prevalence in young children will now increase, given the criteria for posttraumatic stress disorder for Children 6 Years and Younger are specifically tailored to this age group, symptoms from clusters B and C will be easier to detect due to a greater emphasis on behaviors that can be observed or reported on by caregivers, and less difficulty in meeting criteria for avoidance and negative cognitions. It is less clear what the impact of the *DSM-5* criteria will be for school-age children and adolescents. One study has found that the use of the updated criteria led the prevalence of the PTSD diagnosis to decrease in an adult sample, likely due to the removal of actual or threatened death from natural causes from Cluster A, as well as the requirement for one symptom of avoidance for diagnosis due to the split of the former Cluster C (Kilpatrick et al. 2013). However, a more likely scenario is that the *DSM-5* criteria will have greater sensitivity for older children and adolescents than the *DSM-IV*, as the removal of the former Criterion A2 will likely allow more school-age children to meet Cluster A criteria, the wording of Cluster B has been loosened to allow a wider array of intrusion symptoms, and the inclusion of "reckless or self-destructive behavior" in Cluster E allows for a wider breadth of externalizing behaviors that adolescents, in particular, may engage in.

If the incidence and prevalence of PTSD increase due to the greater sensitivity of the *DSM-5* criteria, it is reasonable to hypothesize that courts will see a sharp increase in PTSD-based litigation in cases involving juveniles. This raises questions for how courts will employ the *DSM-5* criteria. Despite the American Psychiatric Association's warnings of reliance on the *DSM* in forensic settings, will courts continue to rely on it in making the diagnosis of PTSD as they have in the past for rendering judgments and measuring damages (Lubit et al. 2002)? Or will courts also take note of the increasing body of research suggesting posttraumatic symptoms in children and adolescents which do not meet full criteria for PTSD may still cause significant distress and impairment in functioning (Carrion et al. 2002)? This is especially relevant due to continued inclusion of the delayed onset specifier in the *DSM-5*, which acknowledges what research has illustrated is the time course of developing posttraumatic symptoms in children and adolescents, but could be used in the court setting to argue that a youth is less impaired and suffering less than if the youth met full criteria.

Another question that has yet to be answered is what the specificity of the *DSM-5* criteria will be. Past criticism of the conceptualization of PTSD in the *DSM* has been that its symptoms overlap with multiple other diagnoses, including Major Depressive Disorder, anxiety disorders, disruptive behavioral disorders, and Attention Deficit/Hyperactivity Disorder. This is most true of the current Cluster D and to some degree in Cluster E. Data on the specificity of the new criteria for children and adolescents have not yet been published, and in the absence of this it is foreseeable that a common challenge to expert testimony will be whether another disorder can better account for symptoms in a juvenile than PTSD.

ADVANCES IN UNDERSTANDING POSTTRAUMATIC SYMPTOMS IN CHILDREN AND ADOLESCENTS

Epidemiology of exposure to trauma and PTSD

Research has demonstrated that many youth have been exposed to traumatic events. The Great Smoky Mountains Study demonstrated that in a community sample nearly 68% of children and adolescents ages 16 years and under surveyed had a lifetime exposure to a traumatic event, and that 37% had been exposed to more than one trauma (Copeland et al. 2007). Nearly 25% of the youth surveyed had been exposed to a violent trauma, while 11% had been exposed to sexual trauma. A further 33% of traumatic exposures were accounted for by physical illness, natural disasters, accidents, fire, and exposure to noxious agents. The National Child Traumatic Stress Network has additionally reported that 25% of youth have experienced a traumatic event by age 16 (Copeland-Linder 2008). Additionally, approximately 3 million cases of child abuse or neglect are reported in the United States each year (van der Kolk 2003), and national surveys have shown that 22% of adults have a childhood history of sexual abuse, and 30% have a history of physical abuse (Bremner 2003).

Though experiencing a trauma prior to the age of 16 is unfortunately not a rare event, it has been found that as in adults, it is a minority of children and adolescents who meet full diagnostic criteria for PTSD following a traumatic exposure—approximately 30% (Blom and Oberink 2012). Estimates of the prevalence of PTSD in the juvenile population have recently ranged from 0.5% to 9.2%, which is lower than the prevalence found in the adult population (Copeland et al. 2007; Cohen et al. 2010). However, in examining these data, it is important to keep in mind that the diagnosis of PTSD was made using *DSM-IV* criteria, and with more developmentally informed criteria of the *DSM-5*, prevalence rates will increase.

The likelihood of a child or adolescent developing posttraumatic symptoms and PTSD is also dependent on the type and severity of exposure. Natural disasters have been associated with lower PTSD rates of 0% to 5% in children (Salmon and Bryant 2002), though some studies have found that in more severe disasters rates can be as high as 95% (Gabbay et al. 2004). Physical injury has been associated with a rate of 23% (Aaron et al. 1999), while in cases of exposure to violent crime rates ranged from 27% to 33% (Arroyo and Eth 1985; Saigh 1991). A study of children in foster care found that 42% of those who had been physically abused developed PTSD (Dubner and Motta 1999). Among the highest rates of PTSD are those observed in children who have either witnessed their mother sexually assaulted or were exposed to parental homicide, estimated by one group to confer a PTSD rate of 100% (Pynoos and Nader 1988). Sexual abuse is also associated with high rates of PTSD, estimated by some to be as high as 90% (Salmon and Bryant 2002).

Developmental influences on posttraumatic symptoms

A cardinal feature of PTSD and posttraumatic symptoms in children and adolescents is that the manifestation of these symptoms is directly shaped by their age and developmental stage, including their capacity to encode and retrieve memories, their language capabilities, their ability to regulate their emotions, and their knowledge base (Salmon and Bryant 2002). In this context posttraumatic symptoms fall into four different age categories: preschool children, school-age children, adolescents, and adults.

The response of very young children to a traumatic event is primarily characterized by mood, behavioral, and anxiety symptoms, as they lack the language skills and emotional regulation of older children (Hagan 2005). Infants less than 12 months of age demonstrate increased crying, separation anxiety, irritability, an exaggerated startle response, and "freezing" (Veenema and Schroeder-Bruce 2002). In comparison, toddlers have greater disturbances of sleep, including nightmares and night terrors, show regression in behaviors and acquired skills, are more likely to have temper tantrums, and may demonstrate selective mutism (Veenema and Schroeder-Bruce 2002). Between the ages of 4 and 6 years, children may be more aggressive, can develop nocturnal enuresis, may regress in their use of language, and report somatic symptoms, such as headaches and stomachaches (Veenema and Schroeder-Bruce 2002). It has been suggested that younger children may be more susceptible to the posttraumatic symptom of re-experience (intrusive thoughts, images, or perceptions) because their memory is more visually and perceptually based (Fletcher 1996). The egocentrism found in young children can lead them to believe they were the cause of the traumatic event, which in turn can create stronger feelings of guilt than in older ages (Fletcher 1996; Rojas and Lee 2004). As mentioned earlier, preschool-age children also may not have the opportunity to engage in avoidant behaviors as their whereabouts and activities are determined by their caretakers (Pynoos et al. 2009).

School-age children (age 6 to puberty) have a greater ability to have empathy for others who were affected by a traumatic event, and exhibit more symptoms in their interactions with others, including a fear of novel situations, social phobia, and repetitious traumatic play (Beauchesne et al. 2002; Veenema and Schroeder-Bruce 2002). Children above the age of 6 years may not demonstrate avoidant symptoms like younger children, but can develop incident-specific fears resembling phobias (Pynoos et al. 2009). Their presentation may also be significant for a lack of visual flashbacks or numbing symptoms (Cohen 1998). School-age children can also exhibit extended periods of re-experiencing that alternate with periods of avoidance and numbing, instead of both occurring simultaneously (Schwarz and Kowalski 1991).

Posttraumatic symptoms in adolescents most closely resemble those of adults, though with more prominent aggressive and risk-taking behaviors (substance use, high-risk sexual behaviors). Oppositional behaviors at home and school are commonly seen, as are school avoidance, depression, and anxiety (Pine and Cohen 2002; Veenema and Schroeder-Bruce 2002). Loss of interest in previously enjoyed activities, social withdrawal, eating disorders, poor emotion regulation, personality changes, self-destructive and impulsive behaviors, and impaired interpersonal functioning are also frequent posttraumatic behaviors in this age group (Pelcovitz et al. 1994; March et al. 1997). Exposure to prolonged or multiple traumas may present with primarily dissociative symptoms, including depersonalization, derealization, self-injurious behaviors, and intermittent angry and aggressive outbursts (Cohen 1998).

Natural history of PTSD in children and adolescents

The development and progression of posttraumatic symptoms in the pediatric population is variable and can be influenced by a number of factors. Rather than simply stemming from a single traumatic incident, accumulated evidence suggests the pathogenesis of PTSD is multifactorial, with contributions from genetic, psychological, neurobiological, and social factors. Three factors that have been correlated with an increased risk of developing PTSD in multiple studies are the severity of the trauma exposure, the length of time of the exposure, and the level of parental distress (Foy et al. 1996). It has been asserted that the most important of these three factors in preventing negative outcomes following trauma is the ability of a parent or guardian to cope with that same trauma, and provide a sense of security and safety to a child (Lyons 1987). A previous history of exposure to trauma, having experienced multiple traumas, poor social support, a history of previous psychiatric disorders, and a parental history of psychiatric disorders have also each been found to confer a higher risk of developing PTSD (Cohen et al. 2010). There has been controversy in the field regarding differing vulnerability to developing PTSD between genders, though current evidence suggests girls are at a higher risk due to differences in the types of trauma and differing coping strategies (Olff et al. 2007; Langeland and Olff 2008).

For those youth who develop full PTSD, it has been found in multiple studies that a significant number will continue to demonstrate sustained symptoms for extended periods that can last up to years (McFarlane 1987; Nader et al. 1990; La Greca et al. 1996; Scheeringa et al. 2005; Cohen et al. 2010), even with community treatment (Scheeringa et al. 2005). Though it has been demonstrated in the adult population that symptoms of PTSD may decrease or remit with time, this appears to occur less frequently or more slowly in youth. This has led some to argue that posttraumatic symptoms may persist for longer periods in children and are not likely to remit spontaneously (Pine and Cohen 2002).

Posttraumatic symptoms from a dimensional perspective

Though many individuals who are exposed to significant trauma do not go on to meet full diagnostic criteria for PTSD, it is known from studies with adults that many will demonstrate at least some posttraumatic symptoms (Rothbaum et al. 1992). Research from the adult population also indicated that developing subsyndromal PTSD is more common than meeting criteria for full PTSD, is associated with similar rates of help seeking, and is correlated with higher rates of psychopathology and impaired functioning (Stein et al. 1997; Copeland et al. 2007). Children and adolescents can also develop subthreshold symptoms, which have been found to create levels of distress and impairment that do not meaningfully differ from cases of full diagnostic PTSD (Carrion et al. 2002). Children in a large community sample who developed posttraumatic symptoms but did not meet full criteria for PTSD showed significant impairments in multiple domains, including disruption of important relationships, school problems, physical problems, and exacerbation of emotional problems (Copeland et al. 2007).

"High magnitude" events such as physical or sexual abuse may be more predictive of the diagnosis of PTSD, but the majority of posttraumatic symptoms in the pediatric population are the product of "low magnitude" events that occur more commonly, such as deaths or losses (Costello et al. 2002; Copeland et al. 2010). Though resulting from less "severe" traumas, the symptoms that develop from low magnitude events may be no less distressing or impairing for a child than those from high magnitude events. With this in mind PTSD cannot be viewed as a categorical entity, but is more appropriately seen as existing on a continuum in children and adolescents. The importance of this in the forensic setting is that courts may have a tendency to rely solely on the category of PTSD as defined by the *DSM*, and thus risk underestimating a child's impairment and suffering when considering awards for damages.

Neurobiological effects of trauma in children

Numerous studies have found that psychological trauma can adversely affect normal neurodevelopmental processes and neurobiological functioning in children and adolescents. On a cellular level, trauma has been shown to affect multiple neurotransmitter systems. The norepinephrine system is a particularly important contributor to the autonomic stress response, with numerous studies demonstrating childhood abuse and neglect can lead to increased noradrenergic activity (De Bellis et al. 1999a,b; van der Kolk 2003). Children who have been exposed to trauma or diagnosed with PTSD have been found to have higher baseline epinephrine and dopamine levels than nonabused anxious children and controls (De Bellis et al. 1999b). It has also been shown that children with a history of traumatic exposure or PTSD have greater concentrations of urinary norepinephrine and dopamine than controls (De Bellis et al. 1999a,b). Additionally, alterations to serotonergic transmission may contribute to symptoms of hypervigilance, increased startle, impulsivity, and intrusive memories (Heim and Nemeroff 2009), while chronic stress is associated with decreased activity of gamma-aminobutyric acid (GABA) (Bremner et al. 2000; Bremner 2003). Finally, glutamate has also been suggested to play a role in the consolidation and maintenance of traumatic memories by mediating synaptic long-term potentiation, and may contribute to neuronal loss seen in the hippocampus and prefrontal cortex in adults with PTSD through excitotoxicity (Heim and Nemeroff 2009).

Genetic studies have identified several genes that are thought to be involved in the pathogenesis of PTSD. An excess of a polymorphism of a dopamine transporter gene, the SLC6A3 9 allele, has been found to be associated with an increased risk of PTSD (Segman et al. 2001), while specific haplotypes of the dopamine transporter (*DAT*) have been found to increase the risk of developing PTSD in preschoolers (Drury et al. 2013). Low expression of the S allele of the *5-HTTLPR* polymorphism in the *SLC6A4* serotonin transporter gene has also been associated with an increased risk of developing PTSD (Kilpatrick et al. 2007). A more recent study has also demonstrated that the S allele of the *5-HTTLPR* polymorphism is associated with a higher risk of developing PTSD secondary to childhood trauma in Americans of European descent (Xie et al. 2012). Investigation into the GABRA2 subunit of the $GABA_A$ receptor has pointed to an association between childhood trauma and GABRA2 single nucleotide polymorphisms (SNPs) in increasing the risk of developing PTSD, possibly through a greater posttraumatic anxiety response and facilitated traumatic memory encoding (Nelson et al. 2009).

The burgeoning field of epigenetics has increasingly illustrated the sustained functional changes to gene activity that exposure to trauma can create through DNA methylation. Animal models have found early life stressors can lead to methylation of genes that encode glucocorticoid receptors, leading to changes in hypothalamic–pituitary–adrenal (HPA) axis activity and observed behaviors (Yehuda and Bierer 2009). There is also evidence that epigenetic changes can be passed between generations, which has led to a hypothesis that maternal PTSD can increase the risk of PTSD in their children through epigenetic mechanisms (Yehuda and Bierer 2009). Higher cytosine methylation of the $NR3C1\text{-}1_F$ promoter for the glucocorticoid receptor gene has recently been reported to be found in individuals exposed to childhood abuse and early traumatic events (Yehuda et al. 2014). Additionally, the *FKBP5* glucocorticoid receptor co-chaperone has been found to predict the onset of adult PTSD symptoms following a trauma in patients with a history of childhood abuse, which more recently was determined to be associated with DNA demethylation of functional glucocorticoid response elements of *FKBP5* (Binder et al. 2008; Klengel et al. 2014). DNA methylation of the *ID3*, *GRIN1*, and *TPPP* genes following childhood trauma has also been correlated with an increased risk of depression in children (Weder et al. 2014).

Trauma also induces changes to the regions of the brain mediating the fear and stress response, including the HPA axis, amygdala, hippocampus, corpus callosum, and prefrontal cortex (Heim and Nemeroff 2009). The activation of the HPA axis by a stressor ultimately leads to a downstream release of glucocorticoids, specifically cortisol, which have been a source of controversy in the study of pediatric PTSD. Studies of adults with PTSD have shown decreased cortisol levels (Yehuda 2006), while most studies of traumatized children and adolescents have shown elevated levels of cortisol (De Bellis et al. 1999a; Cicchetti and Rogosch 2001; Gunnar et al. 2001). In reconciling these two seemingly disparate findings, it has been proposed that following a trauma, children and adolescents experience an increase in cortisol levels, which will gradually decrease as time passes due to a compensatory downregulation of an overly active HPA axis (van der Kolk 2003). It has also been posited that stress in early life may result in a persistent hypersecretion of corticotropin-releasing factor (CRF) in the central nervous system, which contributes to an increased reactivity to stress as an adult (Heim and Nemeroff 1999).

Neuroimaging

As the field of neuroradiology has advanced, courts have increasingly turned to neuroimaging as a means of illustrating observable neurological changes caused by trauma. The forensic importance of this lies in the observation that juries are more likely to award damages for physical disorders rather than those that are purely psychiatric (Lubit et al. 2002). Children and adolescents with a history of maltreatment have been observed on magnetic resonance imaging to have pituitary volumes that are significantly larger than controls (Thomas and De Bellis 2004). In contrast to imaging studies of traumatized adults which have demonstrated reduced volume of the hippocampus (Bremner 2003; Rinne-Albers et al. 2013), in youth exposed to trauma the majority of studies have shown no hippocampal volume changes (Rinne-Albers et al. 2013). This has led to the theory that prolonged and excessive exposure to glucocorticoids that results from trauma is neurotoxic and leads to a gradual reduction in the volume of the hippocampus over time, which becomes more prominent on imaging as the child ages (van der Kolk 2003; Carrion and Kletter 2012; Rinne-Albers et al. 2013). Multiple studies have also shown reductions in total cerebral volume in youth with a history of trauma, suggestive of diffuse neurological damage (Rinne-Albers et al. 2013). This is a finding that appears to be unique to children and adolescents and has not been reported in adult samples.

Specific types of trauma have been found to affect particular areas of the brains of children and adolescents, depending on the sensory modality of the trauma exposure. For example, in young adults who witnessed domestic violence or were sexually abused, changes in the visual pathways of the brain have been observed (Tomoda et al. 2009; Choi et al. 2012). In contrast, those subjects who were exposed to verbal abuse had observable changes in gray matter volume in areas of auditory processing (Tomoda et al. 2009). Seeing a trauma leads to changes in the visual cortex, while hearing trauma alters the auditory cortex.

One of the most replicated findings from structural imaging of PTSD in youth is a reduced cross-sectional area and connectivity of the corpus callosum (Rinne-Albers et al. 2013), not only in comparison to controls, but also to other psychiatric disorders (Teicher et al. 2004). Additionally, abnormalities in neuronal metabolism in the medial prefrontal cortex have been demonstrated on proton magnetic resonance spectroscopy (De Bellis et al. 2000), as have differences in the activity of the frontal and prefrontal cortex on functional magnetic resonance imaging in traumatized adolescents (Carrion et al. 2008).

COMORBIDITIES ASSOCIATED WITH PTSD

In addition to posttraumatic symptoms, traumatic exposure is associated with high rates of psychiatric comorbidity in children and adolescents. Community samples have demonstrated that traumatized children have rates of psychiatric disorders nearly twice that of nontraumatized counterparts (Copeland et al. 2007). Significantly higher rates of dysthymia and major depressive disorder have been found in youths with PTSD, as well as a high prevalence of generalized anxiety disorder, panic disorder, and specific phobias (Linning and Kearney 2004). Elevated rates of separation anxiety, attention deficit/hyperactivity disorder, and oppositional defiant disorder have also been demonstrated in abused children (Ackerman et al. 1998). Childhood sexual abuse has been found to be predictive of conduct disorder and adult substance abuse (Fergusson et al. 1996), and has additionally been associated with an increased risk of adolescent suicide attempts (Brown et al. 1999). It has been estimated that as many as 20% of all adolescent suicide attempts are related to sexual abuse (Brent et al. 2002). The development of borderline personality disorder has also been associated with a history of sexual trauma (Herman et al. 1992).

Psychiatric comorbidity is but one type of negative outcome of PTSD for children. Behavioral and cognitive deficits have been attributed to experiencing chronic trauma, including poor emotional regulation, deficits in learning and memory, and social difficulties (van der Kolk 2003). A poor sense of self, distorted body image, poor impulse control, and distrust and suspicion of others are also known sequelae of trauma (van der Kolk 2003). The hypervigilance against impending threats that children with PTSD manifest may lead to disturbances in attention that can be mistaken for ADHD (van der Kolk 2003). It has also been shown that children with PTSD perform worse academically than nontraumatized peers (Saigh et al. 1997). It has even been found that adults with a history of childhood trauma are at a higher risk of negative medical outcomes, including ischemic heart disease, cancer, liver disease, and chronic lung disease (Felitti et al. 1998).

FORENSIC EVALUATION OF PTSD IN CHILDREN AND ADOLESCENTS

The general purpose of the evaluation of trauma in a forensic setting is to evaluate, define, and determine the extent of psychological damage and suffering the person is experiencing due to a traumatic exposure, and to inform the court as to prognosis and recommendations for treatment. This does not necessarily mean the primary aim of the evaluation should be to diagnose or rule out PTSD, for as was previously discussed, subsyndromal posttraumatic symptoms are still quite impairing and are associated with high rates of psychiatric comorbidity. With children and adolescents in particular, there is a need to provide an evaluation that goes beyond the diagnosis of PTSD as defined by the *DSM-5*, and paint a broader picture of their functioning and developmental trajectory. In addressing these points, issues that must be resolved in the mind of the evaluator include whether the trauma in question was the immediate cause of distress and dysfunction, what the relative weight of comorbid psychiatric disorders is in affecting the individual's functioning and emotional state, and to what extent resilience factors or ongoing stressors may be modulating the presentation of posttraumatic symptoms. In addition to a full psychiatric history, necessary components of the evaluation are outlined in Table 42.1. It is vital that the evaluator assess the reliability of the information obtained, and the use of more sources of data and objective measures of symptoms may help to ensure that reliability.

Table 42.1 Components of the forensic psychiatric evaluation of trauma in children and adolescents

1. Diagnosis
2. Symptom severity
3. The causative trauma that led to psychopathology
4. Identification of any preexisting psychiatric conditions
5. Psychiatric comorbidity that developed following the trauma
6. Prognosis
7. Treatment recommendations

Source: From Lubit R. et al. 2002. *Child and Adolescent Psychiatric Clinics of North America* 11(4):823–857. With permission.

The forensic interview

THE PARENT INTERVIEW

With any pediatric forensic case it is recommended to interview the child's parents or guardians first when possible, with the notable exceptions of when it is the guardian that is accused of victimizing the child or there is suspicion that the guardian may be motivated to protect a perpetrator. Relevant past psychosocial, family, medical, psychiatric, and developmental history should be reviewed, and consent can be obtained to access previous records and to speak to collateral sources. A focus of the interview should be on the child's functioning prior to the stressor and subsequent changes (Lubit et al. 2002). In particular, questions about the quality of the child's play, the child's social interactions, and the child's academic performance must be asked. The evaluator should also explore the caretaker's perception of the child's ability to express positive emotions, the presence of negative beliefs, cognitions, and emotions, and reckless and self-destructive behaviors. With regard to this last point, the intent of reckless or self-destructive behavior must be understood in order to differentiate it from an act of impulsivity or rule-breaking behaviors, such as could be seen in ADHD or conduct disorder. For preschoolers, potential symptoms of avoidance, traumatic re-enactment in play, and frequency of temper tantrums must be investigated. The aforementioned finding that parental distress and support after a trauma have direct impacts on the course and outcome of posttraumatic symptoms also requires the evaluator to determine the caretaker's degree of functioning (Salmon and Bryant 2002).

It is vitally important to remember that parents have a tendency to under-report PTSD symptoms, and while they are good reporters of externalizing behaviors, they are known to be poor reporters of internalizing symptoms in their children (Lubit et al. 2002). Studies have demonstrated that when a parent's report of symptoms was used alone, it significantly underestimated the child's true symptom load (Scheeringa et al. 2006).

THE CHILD AND ADOLESCENT INTERVIEW

It is essential that the forensic interview be tailored to the emotional and cognitive developmental stage of the child. This has broad implications in determining their ability to relate details of the event, characterizing the developmental context in which their symptoms are occurring, discerning pathological from nonpathological behaviors, and estimating their ability to provide accurate testimony.

Children and adolescents may be reluctant to speak about their trauma for obvious reasons: difficulty describing what happened (particularly for younger children), feelings of embarrassment, shame, or guilt, and avoidance to prevent distress. Evaluators may avoid asking direct questions about the trauma for fear of upsetting the child (Lubit et al. 2002; Salmon et al. 2002). However, a necessary part of the interview is to engage with the child on aspects of the traumatic event in order to adequately evaluate and understand the child's symptoms and response to the incident (Pynoos and Eth 1986; Wolfe et al. 1994). This process can be made easier by forming a rapport with the child and helping the child feel at ease. This may include expressing empathy and regret for the discomfort the child may have, making efforts to minimize distress and fatigue from the interview, explaining the nature of the evaluation, and leaving time at the end of the interview to explore their impressions and thoughts about the evaluation (Lubit et al. 2002).

With young children, their ability to participate in an interview will not only be influenced by their reluctance to speak about the event, but also their developmental, cognitive, and language limitations. Establishing the child's understanding of the difference between truth, lies, and imagination is important for gauging the child's reliability.

With both children and adolescents, open-ended questions should generally be asked first, followed by more specific questions. Use of play, drawing pictures, storytelling, and sandwork are techniques that can be employed in enhancing communication with younger children (Pynoos and Eth 1986; Salmon et al. 2002). Traumatic play tends to be repetitive and simple and lacks the elaboration and imagination seen with children who have not experienced trauma. It is also often not enjoyable and does not relieve anxiety. The child may act out the trauma, taking the role of the aggressor, or incorporate undoing or denial into his or her retelling of the incident (Terr 1981). Drawing may help children give more detailed verbal reports by providing retrieval cues and structure to their narrative. Drawing may also reduce the social and emotional demands of the evaluation for the child (Gross and Hayne 1998).

The use of anatomical dolls in the evaluation of young victims of sexual abuse is controversial, and has been criticized as being overly suggestive and encouraging of fantasy (Ceci and Bruck 1995). The use of toys in the evaluation to re-create the trauma has also been described as a distraction that can prevent a young child from recalling or reporting details of the trauma, as they may associate more generally with play than with the details of an event (DeLoache and Marzolf 1995).

COLLATERAL REPORTS AND PSYCHOLOGICAL TESTING

The forensic evaluation of children and adolescents following an alleged trauma is recommended to involve multiple means of assessment and sources of collateral information in addition to the primary interview. What other individuals have said about the event to the child and what other interviews have been conducted must be examined to search for possible distortions of the child's account. In addition to the parent interview, collateral reports can be gathered from other family members (grandparents, siblings), teachers, school counselors, child protective services, the child's pediatrician, and past therapists or psychiatrists. Documents that should be reviewed include available medical, psychiatric, and therapy records, police reports, and media accounts (Lubit et al. 2002).

It has been asserted that evaluators often use unstructured assessments in forensic evaluations of PTSD that are not empirically supported, and therefore may be of limited reliability (Koch et al. 2005). Psychological testing may be beneficial at times for evaluating current cognitive functioning or comparing current functioning to previous cognitive baseline, as PTSD is known to affect memory, learning, and attention (Lubit et al. 2002). The Wechsler Intelligence Scale for Children, 4th edition (WISC-IV) is commonly used to assess intellectual functioning, and the Woodcock Johnson Tests of Achievement, 3rd edition, provides measures of math and language abilities, as well as visuospatial functioning. Memory can be tested with the Wide Range Assessment of Memory and Learning (WRAML), or the California Verbal Learning Test—Children's Version (CVLT-C) (Lubit et al. 2002). Tests to consider in assessing emotional and personality functioning include the Minnesota Multiphasic Personality Inventory-Adolescent Version (MMPI-A) and Personality Inventory for Children (PIC).

One rating scale that has been developed by the American Psychiatric Association (APA) using *DSM-5* criteria for assessing PTSD in school-age children is the National Stressful Events Survey PTSD Short Scale (NSESSS) (APA 2013c). It is a nine-item measure for children aged 11–17 years who have been diagnosed with PTSD or demonstrate clinically significant posttraumatic symptoms, and used as a self-report of symptoms in the prior 7 days. It is used to establish baseline symptoms as well as to track these symptoms over time. Further measures for PTSD symptoms in children and adolescents using *DSM-5* criteria are in development and are expected to be released in the near future.

Accuracy of testimony

An area of potential scrutiny in pediatric forensic cases is the accuracy of the child's report and testimony. Despite the cognitive, language, and memory limitations that children may possess, they have the ability to be reliable witnesses. It has been generally found that children perform as well as adults in recalling the core aspects of a memory, though they do less well on the peripheral details (Meyer 1997). When children make errors in their testimony, these are more likely to be a failure to report an event that did happen, rather than falsely report one that did not happen (Flin and Spencer 1995). Prior to middle childhood, children lack the cognitive strategies to retrieve memories spontaneously. They are reliant on prompts from adults including questions and repeating features of the event (Salmon and Bryant 2002). Without this structure provided by adults, the details are often not able to be accessed by the child. However, this also can be an avenue to the contamination of the memory, as repeated questions can compel a child to alter his or her response or confabulate.

The degree of suggestibility that a child or adolescent demonstrates is a frequent challenge to the child's testimony. There are unfortunately multiple examples of cases where suggestibility has led to false accusations of sexual abuse or trauma (Kulkofsky and London 2010). Age has been found to be the best predictor of suggestibility, with younger children consistently found to be more suggestible than older children or adults (Ceci and Bruck 1993). Fatigue and stress can also increase suggestibility (Goodman et al. 1999). Parents who are overly anxious or have histrionic traits may overreact to an innocent statement that a child made, which can lead to inaccurate recollections and false accusations (Lubit et al. 2002). Children can also unintentionally distort reality to avoid a feared punishment, avoid embarrassment, gain attention or sympathy, or even to be vindictive (Bernet 1993). Children and adolescents additionally may deny a trauma happened to protect an abuser, or to avoid feelings of embarrassment or guilt. Errors evaluators make while interviewing children that lead to distortions in testimony will be discussed further below.

Although there is a very real danger the recall of a suggestible child may be inadvertently altered, there is also evidence that children's memories can be resistant to making false accusations, even after leading questions have been posed. In studies in which children had undergone routine medical procedures, leading questions were asked. These children were not likely to make false reports of abuse even after a year (Goodman et al. 1991a,b; Saywitz et al 1991). Four-year-old children were also found to be resistant to alleging abuse, even when prompted by an evaluator to do so (Rudy and Goodman 1991; Flin and Spencer 1995).

Evaluation of malingering

In every forensic evaluation the issue of malingering should be examined. There is, however, little evidence that children will maintain symptoms in order to gain compensation (Kulkofsky and London 2010), and younger children are not motivated by financial rewards to change their account. Motivations change as a child ages, with adolescents more likely to present false information for secondary gain (Lubit et al. 2002). Parents may encourage their children to fabricate a traumatic experience for financial gain, or in cases of custody disputes to gain an advantage for their petition or for revenge. Symptoms that raise suspicion for malingering include those that draw attention, are exaggerated, or may not fit in a particular diagnostic category. There may be inconsistency between the child's reported loss of function and what the child is actually able to do, pointing to the value of observing the child in numerous settings, if possible. For example, claims may be made that the child is unable to function in school, despite continued participation in sports and other activities without difficulty. Additional presentations that are suggestive of malingering include an eagerness to discuss past trauma, an attitude of entitlement, low observed anxiety and depression in the context of high reported symptoms, and unrealistic claims of what constituted a trauma (Ingram et al. 2012). In testing the hypothesis that a child or adolescent may be malingering, Lubit et al. have suggested techniques such as asking about symptoms that are not part of PTSD, mentioning an atypical symptom in ear shot to see if it is reported by the patient, and making a loud noise to gauge the startle response (Lubit et al. 2002). Caution must be employed in pursuing a diagnosis of malingering. Children may have difficulty with sequences of events, details of an incident, or differentiating between episodes of a repeated event. This can resemble attempts to fabricate information, when, in actuality, the response may be developmentally appropriate.

Pitfalls to avoid

It has been suggested that the greatest errors forensic evaluators of pediatric PTSD tend to make include a failure to consider other stressors, misuse of psychiatric diagnoses, failure to consider other diagnoses, inattention to the credibility of reports of trauma, and ignoring the subjective nature of PTSD (Kulkofsky and London 2010). A full history may not be taken, which may lead the evaluator to overlook past traumas that occurred prior to the one in question as the source of posttraumatic symptoms. A poor history may also lead an evaluator to miss preexisting psychopathology unrelated to trauma. Malingering is also often not considered in children. Psychiatrists additionally often fail to appreciate that courts hesitate in accepting the diagnosis of PTSD based on the interview alone, and do not sufficiently use psychological testing and collateral reports. Finally, evaluators may not strictly follow *DSM* criteria, and may attempt to attribute PTSD to stressors that do not meet Criteria A.

With regard to contaminating a young child's testimony, the primary means by which children's accounts have been altered is through an evaluator's use of leading questions, which presume certain events occurred ("That's when he touched you in your private parts, right?"). Interviewer bias plays a key role in suggestibility as well, and can be expressed through positive and negative reinforcement, creating negative or accusatory emotional tone in the evaluation, repeating questions until a desired answer is given, and using peer or parental pressure in the interview (Kulkofsky and London 2010). Repeatedly asking the same question in the absence of interviewer bias can also unintentionally lead a child to change his or her answer as the child may fear that his or her previous answer may be "wrong " (Lubit et al. 2002). Specific and direct questioning in young children may lead them to feel that they must respond, and increases the risk that they will not report accurate information (Poole and Lamb 1998). Use of drawing can be of help in attaining a description of events but can also potentially introduce errors into children's accounts, as evaluators can inadvertently suggest inaccurate information during the interview (Bruck et al. 2000).

To guard against suggestive interviews with young children, using open-ended questions and avoiding the repetition of questions is recommended. An effort should be made to maintain a neutral emotional tone during the evaluation. In addition, the child should be allowed to describe the trauma in his or her own words. Finally, a structured interview protocol has been created by the National Institute of Child Health and Human Development (NICHD) for forensic evaluators, which is specifically designed to reduce suggestibility (Orbach et al. 2000).

Though neuroimaging can be a powerful and persuasive tool in the courtroom, there are clear limitations to what information it can convey. As it is a rare occurrence that a child or adolescent will have previous imaging to compare post-trauma studies to, the opposing side may assert that abnormalities seen on imaging may not be related to a stressor at all, and instead are due to a pre-existing condition (Bottalico and Bruni 2012). Due to the high rates of comorbidity of PTSD with other disorders, it may be difficult to differentiate between neuroanatomical changes caused by an anxiety or mood disorder from those that are associated with PTSD. Additionally, as findings from neuroimaging studies are from aggregate data compiled from multiple subjects, each with differing brain activity, a challenge can be whether a particular research finding is applicable to a specific individual. The field of neuroimaging is simply not yet at a stage where a definitive answer can be given to that question.

SUMMARY

Alan Stone has asserted that "No diagnosis in the history of American psychiatry has had a more dramatic and pervasive impact on law and social justice than posttraumatic stress disorder" (Stone 1993). Though it is a minority of youth who will develop full diagnostic PTSD following exposure to trauma, we now know how harmful and debilitating subthreshold symptoms can be, and that posttraumatic symptoms as defined by the *DSM* are but one type of sequelae children may experience. In approaching evaluations of traumatized and abused youth, child and forensic psychiatrists must incorporate knowledge of development, neurobiology, family dynamics, updates to the *DSM-5*, and the nature and course of PTSD in different age groups. The evaluation must involve not only forensic interviews of the youth and their caretakers, but also collateral sources of information from schools, legal authorities, psychological testing, and past psychiatric and medical records. Though there is a danger of contaminating a youth's recollection of events through improper interviewing, a well-prepared and careful evaluation and application of appropriate interviewing techniques are known to mitigate this risk, allowing a child to provide accurate and reliable testimony. For the large proportion of children and adolescents who are exposed to trauma prior to adulthood, the forensic evaluator plays an integral role not only in helping them receive the justice and compensation they deserve, but also in guiding them toward treatment, and educating attorneys and the courts as to the effects of trauma in this vulnerable population.

SUMMARY KEY POINTS

- The *DSM-5* criteria for posttraumatic stress disorder is most developmentally appropriate to date for children and adolescents.
- The incidence and prevalence of PTSD in young children in particular is expected to increase using the new criteria, which in turn is likely to increase PTSD-based litigation.
- Posttraumatic symptoms that do not meet full criteria for PTSD may still cause significant distress and impairment for many youth.
- Children will manifest posttraumatic symptoms differently depending on their age and developmental stage.
- Forensic evaluations of traumatized youth must incorporate information from multiple sources, outside of child and caretaker interviews, which may include psychological testing, medical and psychiatric records, and school reports.
- Care must be taken to acknowledge and avoid multiple pitfalls that are specific to performing forensic evaluations in the pediatric population.

REFERENCES

Aaron J, H Zaglul, and RE Emery. 1999. Posttraumatic stress in children following acute physical injury. *Journal of Pediatric Psychology* 24(4):335–343.

Ackerman PT, JEO Newton, WB McPherson, JG Jones, and RA Dykman. 1998. Prevalence of post traumatic stress disorder and other psychiatric diagnoses in three groups of abused children (sexual, physical, and both). *Child Abuse and Neglect* 22(8):759–774.

American Psychiatric Association (APA). 1980. *Diagnostic and Statistical Manual of Mental Disorders*, 3rd edition. Washington, DC: APA.

American Psychiatric Association (APA). 1987. *Diagnostic and Statistical Manual of Mental Disorders*, 3rd edition, Revised. Washington, DC: APA.

American Psychiatric Association (APA). 1994. *Diagnostic and Statistical Manual of Mental Disorders*, 4th edition. Washington, DC: APA.

American Psychiatric Association (APA). 2013a. *Diagnostic and Statistical Manual of Mental Disorders*, 5th edition. Washington, DC: APA.

American Psychiatric Association (APA). 2013b. *Posttraumatic Stress Disorder*. http://www.dsm5.org/Documents/PTSD%20Fact%20Sheet.pdf, accessed October 18, 2014.

American Psychiatric Association (APA). 2013c. *Severity of Posttraumatic Stress Symptoms—Child Age 11–17*. https://www.psychiatry.org/File%20Library/Psychiatrists/Practice/DSM/APA_DSM5_Severity-of-Post-Traumatic-Stress-Symptoms-Child-Age-11-to-17.pdf, accessed July 19, 2016.

Arroyo W and S Eth. 1985. Children traumatized by Central American warfare. In *Post-Traumatic Stress Disorder in Children*, edited by S Eth and RS Pynoos. Washington, DC: American Psychiatric Press, 103–120.

Beauchesne MA, BR Kelley, CA Patsdaughter, and J Pickard. 2002. Attack on America: Children's reactions and parents' responses. *Journal of Pediatric Health Care* 16(5):213–221.

Bernet W. 1993. False statements and the differential diagnosis of abuse allegations. *Journal of the American Academy of Child and Adolescent Psychiatry* 32(5):903–910.

Binder EB, RG Bradley, W Liu et al. 2008. Association of FKBP5 polymorphisms and childhood abuse with risk of posttraumatic stress disorder symptoms in adults. *Journal of the American Medical Association* 299(11):1291–1305.

Blom M and R Oberink. 2012. The validity of the DSM-IV PTSD criteria in children and adolescents: A review. *Clinical Child Psychology and Psychiatry* 17(4):571–601.

Bottalico B and T Bruni. 2012. Post traumatic stress disorder, neuroscience, and the law. *International Journal of Law and Psychiatry* 35(2):112–120.

Brander T. 1943. Psychiatric observations among Finnish children during the Russo-Finnish war of 1939–1940. *Nervous Child* 2:313–319.

Bremner JD. 2003. Long-term effects of childhood abuse on brain and neurobiology. *Child and Adolescent Psychiatry Clinics of North America* 12(2): 271–292.

Bremner JD, RB Innis, SM Southwick, L Staib, S Zoghbi, and DS Charney. 2000. Decreased benzodiazepine receptor binding in prefrontal cortex in combat-related posttraumatic stress disorder. *American Journal of Psychiatry* 157(7):1120–1126.

Brent DA, M Oquendo, B Birmaher et al. 2002. Familial pathways to early-onset suicide attempt: Risk for suicidal behavior in offspring of mood-disordered suicide attempters. *Archives of General Psychiatry* 59(9):801–807.

Brown J, P Cohen, JG Johnson, and EM Smailes. 1999. Childhood abuse and neglect: Specificity of effects on adolescent and young adult depression and suicidality. *Journal of the American Academy of Child and Adolescent Psychiatry* 38(12):1490–1496.

Bruck M, L Melnyk, and SJ Ceci. 2000. Draw it again Sam: The effect of drawing on children's suggestibility and source monitoring ability. *Journal of Experimental Psychology* 77(3):169–196.

Carrion VG, A Garrett, V Menon, CF Weems, and AL Reiss. 2008. Posttraumatic stress symptoms and brain function during a response-inhibition task: An fMRI study in youth. *Depression and Anxiety* 25(6):514–526.

Carrion VG and H Kletter. 2012. Posttraumatic stress disorder: Shifting toward a developmental framework. *Child and Adolescent Psychiatric Clinics of North America* 21(3):573–591.

Carrion VG, CF Weems, R Ray, and AL Reiss. 2002. Toward an empirical definition of pediatric PTSD: The phenomenology of PTSD symptoms in youth. *Journal of the American Academy of Child and Adolescent Psychiatry* 41(20):166–173.

Ceci SJ and M Bruck. 1993. Suggestibility of the child witness: A historical review and synthesis. *Psychology Bulletin* 113(3):403–439.

Ceci SJ and M Bruck. 1995. *Jeopardy in the Courtroom: A Scientific Analysis of Children's Testimony.* Washington, DC: American Psychological Association.

Choi J, B Jeong, A Polcari, ML Rohan, and MH Teicher. 2012. Reduced fractional anisotropy in the visual limbic pathway of young adults witnessing domestic violence in childhood. *Neuroimage* 59(2):1071–1079.

Cicchetti D and FA Rogosch. 2001. Diverse patterns of neuroendocrine activity in maltreated children. *Development and Psychopathology* 13(3):677–693.

Cohen JA. 1998. Practice parameters for the assessment and treatment of children and adolescents with posttraumatic stress disorder. *Journal of the American Academy of Child and Adolescent Psychiatry* 37(10):4S–26S.

Cohen JA, O Bukstein, J Hamilton, H Keable, J Kinlan, U Schoettle, M Siegal, and S Stock. 2010. Practice parameter for the assessment and treatment of children and adolescents with posttraumatic stress disorder. *Journal of the American Academy of Child and Adolescent Psychiatry* 49(4):414–430.

Copeland WE, G Keeler, A Angold, and EJ Costello. 2007. Traumatic events and posttraumatic stress in childhood. *Archives of General Psychiatry* 64(5):577–584.

Copeland WE, G Keeler, A Angold, and EJ Costello. 2010. Posttraumatic stress without trauma in children. *The American Journal of Psychiatry* 167(9):1059–1065.

Copeland-Linder N. 2008. Posttraumatic stress disorder. *Pediatrics in Review* 29(3):103–104.

Costello EJ, A Erkanli, JA Fairbank, and A Angold. 2002. The prevalence of potentially traumatic events in childhood and adolescence. *Journal of Traumatic Stress* 15(2):99–112.

De Bellis MD, AS Baum, B Birmaher, MS Keshavan, CH Eccard, AM Boring, FJ Jenkins, and ND Ryan. 1999a. Developmental traumatology part I: Biological stress systems. *Biological Psychiatry* 45(10):1259–1270.

De Bellis MD, MS Keshavan, DB Clark, BJ Casey, JN Giedd, AM Boring, K Frustraci, and ND Ryan. 1999b. Developmental traumatology part II: Brain development. *Biological Psychiatry* 45(10):1271–1284.

De Bellis MD, MS Keshavan, S Spencer, and J Hall. 2000. N-Acetylaspartate concentration in the anterior cingulate of maltreated children and adolescents with PTSD. *American Journal of Psychiatry* 157(7):1175–1177.

DeLoache JS and DP Marzolf. 1995. The use of dolls to interview young children: Issues of symbolic representation. *Journal of Experimental Child Psychology* 60(1):155–173.

Drury SS, ZH Brett, C Henry, and M Scheeringa. 2013. The association of a novel haplotype in the dopamine transporter with preschool age posttraumatic stress disorder. *Journal of Child and Adolescent Psychopharmacology* 23(4):236–243.

Dubner AE and RW Motta. 1999. Sexually and physically abused foster care children and posttraumatic stress disorder. *Journal of Consulting and Clinical Psychology* 67(3):367–373.

Dunsdon MI. 1941. A psychologist's contribution to air raid problems. *Mental Health* 2(2):36–41.

Felitti VJ, RF Anda, D Nordenberg, DF Williamson, AM Spitz, V Edwards, MP Koss, and JS Marks. 1998. Relationship of childhood abuse and household dysfunction to many of the leading causes of death in adults. The adverse childhood experiences (ACE) study. *American Journal of Preventative Medicine* 14(4):245–258.

Fergusson DM, LJ Horwood, and MT Lynskey. 1996. Childhood sexual abuse and psychiatric disorder in young adulthood: II. Psychiatric outcomes of childhood sexual abuse. *Journal of the American Academy of Child and Adolescent Psychiatry* 35(10):1365–1374.

Fletcher KE. 1996. Childhood posttraumatic stress disorder. In *Child Psychopathology*, edited by EJ Mash and RA Barkley. New York: Guilford Press, 242–276.

Flin R and JR Spencer. 1995. Annotation: Children as witnesses—Legal and psychological perspectives. *Journal of Child Psychology and Psychiatry, and Allied Disciplines* 36(2):171–180.

Foy DW, BT Madvig, RS Pynoos, and AJ Camilleri. 1996. Etiologic factors in the development of posttraumatic stress disorder in children and adolescents. *Journal of School Psychology* 34(2):133–145.

Freud A and DT Burlingham. 1943. *War and Children.* Westport, CT: Greenwood Press.

Gabbay V, MD Oatis, RR Silva, and G Hirsch. 2004. Epidemiological aspects of PTSD in children and adolescents. In *Posttraumatic Stress Disorder in Children and Adolescents: Handbook*, edited by RR Silva, New York: Norton, 1–17.

Goodman GS, BL Bottoms, BM Schwartz-Kenney, and L Rudy. 1991a. Children's testimony about a stressful event: Improving children's reports. *Journal of Narrative and Life History* 1(1):69–99.

Goodman GS, JE Hirschman, D Hepps, and L Rudy. 1991b. Children's memory for stressful events. *Merrill-Palmer Quarterly* 37(1):109–157.

Goodman GS, AD Redlich, J Qin, S Ghetti, KS Tyda, JM Schaaf, and A Hahn. 1999. Evaluating eyewitness testimony in adults and children. In *The Handbook of Forensic Psychology*, edited by AK Hess and IB Weiner. New York: Wiley, 218–272.

Gross J and H Hayne. 1998. Drawing facilitates children's verbal reports of emotionally laden events. *Journal of Experimental Psychology: Applied* 4(2):163–174.

Gunnar MR, SJ Morison, K Chisholm, and M Schuder. 2001. Salivary cortisol levels in children adopted from Romanian orphanages. *Development and Psychopathology* 13(03):611–628.

Hagan JF. 2005. Psychosocial implications of disaster or terrorism on children: A guide for the pediatrician. *Pediatrics* 116(3):787–795.

Heim C and CB Nemeroff. 1999. The impact of early adverse experiences on brain systems involved in the pathophysiology of anxiety and affective disorders. *Biological Psychiatry* 46(11):1509–1522.

Heim C and CB Nemeroff. 2009. Neurobiology of posttraumatic stress disorder. *CNS Spectrums* 14(1 Suppl 1):13–24.

Herman JL. 1992. Complex PTSD: A syndrome in survivors of prolonged and repeated trauma. *Journal of Traumatic Stress* 5(3):377–391.

Ingram TA, JS Dowben, KD Froelich, and NL Keltner. 2012. Biological perspectives: Detecting malingering of Post-Traumatic Stress Disorder (PTSD) in adults. *Perspectives in Psychiatric Care* 48(2):70–75.

Iselin G, R Le Brocque, J Kenardy, V Anderson, and L McKinlay. 2010. Which method of posttraumatic stress disorder classification best predicts psychosocial function in children with traumatic brain injury? *Journal of Anxiety Disorders* 24(7):774–779.

Kilpatrick DG, KC Koenen, KJ Ruggiero, R Acierno, S Galea, HS Resnick, J Roitzsch, J Boyle, and J Gelernter. 2007. The serotonin transporter genotype and social support and moderation of posttraumatic stress disorder and depression in hurricane-exposed adults. *American Journal of Psychiatry* 164(11):1693–1699.

Kilpatrick DG, HS Resnick, ME Milanak, MW Millar, KM Keyes, and MJ Friedman. 2013. National estimates of exposure to traumatic events and PTSD prevalence using DSM-IV and proposed DSM-5 criteria. *Journal of Traumatic Stress* 26(5):537–547.

Klengel T, D Mehta, C Anacker et al. 2014. Allele-specific FKBP5 DNA demethylation mediates gene-childhood trauma interactions. *Nature Neuroscience* 16(1):33–41.

Koch WJ, M O'Neill, and KS Douglas. 2005. Empirical limits for the forensic assessment of PTSD litigants. *Law and Human Behavior* 29(1):121–149.

Kulkofsky S and K London. 2010. Reliability and suggestibility of children's statements. In *Principles and Practice of Child and Adolescent Forensic Mental Health*, edited by EP Benedek, P Ash, and CL Scott, Washington, DC: American Psychiatric, 217–228.

La Greca AM, WK Silverman, EM Vernberg, and MJ Prinstein. 1996. Symptoms of posttraumatic stress in children after Hurricane Andrew: A prospective study. *Journal of Consulting and Clinical Psychology* 64(4):712–723.

Langeland W and M Olff. 2008. Psychobiology of posttraumatic stress disorder in pediatric injury patients: A review of the literature. *Neuroscience and Biobehavioral Reviews* 32(1):161–174.

Linning LM and CA Kearney. 2004. Post-traumatic stress disorder in maltreated youth: A study of diagnostic comorbidity and child factors. *Journal of Interpersonal Violence* 19(10):1087–1101.

Lubit R, N Hartwell, WG van Gorp, and S Eth. 2002. Forensic evaluation of trauma syndromes in children. *Child and Adolescent Psychiatric Clinics of North America* 11(4):823–857.

Lyons JA. 1987. Posttraumatic stress disorder in children and adolescents: A review of the literature. *Journal of Developmental and Behavioral Pediatrics* 8(6):349–356.

March JS. 1993. What constitutes a stressor? The Criterion A issue. In *Posttraumatic Stress Disorder: DSM-IV and Beyond*, edited by JRT Davidson and EB Foa, Washington, DC: American Psychiatric Press, 37–54.

March JS, L Amaya-Jackson, R Terry, and P Costanzo. 1997. Posttraumatic symptomatology in children and adolescents after an industrial fire. *Journal of the American Academy of Child and Adolescent Psychiatry* 36(8):1080–1088.

McFarlane AC. 1987. Posttraumatic phenomena in a longitudinal study of children following a natural disaster. *Journal of the American Academy of Child and Adolescent Psychiatry* 26(5):764–769.

Meiser-Stedman R, P Smith, E Glucksman, W Yule, and T Dalgleish. 2008. The posttraumatic stress disorder diagnosis in preschool- and elementary school-age children exposed to motor vehicle accidents. *American Journal of Psychiatry* 165(10):1326–1337.

Meyer JF. 1997. *Inaccuracies in Children's Testimony: Memory, Suggestibility, or Obedience to Authority?* Binghamton, NY: Haworth Press.

Nader K, R Pynoos, L Fairbanks, and C Frederick. 1990. Children's PTSD reactions one year after a sniper attack at their school. *American Journal of Psychiatry* 147(11):1526–1530.

Nelson EC, A Agrawal, ML Pergadia et al. 2009. Association of childhood trauma exposure and GABRA2 polymorphisms with risk of posttraumatic stress disorder in adults. *Molecular Psychiatry* 14(3):234–235.

Olff M, W Langeland, N Draijer, and BPR Gersons. 2007. Gender differences in posttraumatic stress disorder. *Psychological Bulletin* 133(2):183–204.

Orbach Y, I Hershkowitz, ME Lamb, KJ Sternberg, PW Esplin, and D Horowitz. 2000. Assessing the value of structured protocols for forensic interviews of alleged child abuse victims. *Child Abuse and Neglect* 24(6):733–752.

Pelcovitz D, S Kaplan, B Goldenberg, F Mandel, J Lehane, and J Guarrera. 1994. Post-traumatic stress disorder in physically abused adolescents. *Journal of the American Academy of Child and Adolescent Psychiatry* 33(3):305–312.

Pine DS and JA Cohen. 2002. Trauma in children and adolescents: Risk and treatment of psychiatric sequelae. *Biological Psychiatry* 51(7):519–531.

Poole DA and ME Lamb. 1998. *Investigative Interviews of Children*. Washington, DC: American Psychological Association.

Pynoos RS and S Eth. 1986. Witness to violence: The child interview. *Journal of the American Academy of Child and Adolescent Psychiatry* 25(3):306–319.

Pynoos RS and K Nader. 1988. Children who witness the sexual assaults of their mothers. *Journal of the American Academy of Child and Adolescent Psychiatry* 27(5):567–572.

Pynoos RS, AM Steinberg, CM Layne, EC Briggs, SA Ostrowski, and JA Fairbank. 2009. DSM-V PTSD diagnostic criteria for children and adolescents: A developmental perspective and recommendations. *Journal of Traumatic Stress* 22(5):391–398.

Rinne-Albers MAW, NJA van der Wee, F Lamers-Winkelman, and RRJM Vermeiren. 2013. Neuroimaging in children, adolescents and young adults with psychological trauma. *European Child and Adolescent Psychiatry* 22(12):745–755.

Rojas VM and TN Lee. 2004. Childhood vs. adult PTSD. In *Posttraumatic Stress Disorders in Children and Adolescents*, edited by RR Silva. New York: Norton, 237–256.

Rothbaum BO, EB Foa, DS Riggs, T Murdock, and W Walsh. 1992. A prospective examination of post-traumatic stress disorder in rape victims. *Journal of Traumatic Stress* 5(3):455–475.

Rudy L and GS Goodman. 1991. Effects of participation on children's reports: Implications for children's testimony. *Developmental Psychology* 27(4):527–538.

Saigh PA 1991. The development of posttraumatic stress disorder following four different types of traumatization. *Behaviour Research and Therapy* 29(3):213–216.

Saigh PA, M Mroueh, and J Bremner. 1997. Scholastic impairments among traumatized adolescents. *Behaviour Research and Therapy* 35(5):429–436.

Salmon K and RA Bryant. 2002. Posttraumatic stress disorder in children: The influence of developmental factors. *Clinical Psychology Review* 22(2):163–188.

Saywitz KJ, GS Goodman, E Nicholas, and SF Moan. 1991. Children's memories of a physical examination involving genital touch: Implications for reports of child sexual abuse. *Journal of Consulting and Clinical Psychology* 59(5):682–691.

Scheeringa MS. 2003. Research diagnostic criteria for infants and preschool children: The process and empirical support. *Journal of the American Academy of Child and Adolescent Psychiatry* 42(12):1504–1512.

Scheeringa MS, L Myers, FW Putnam, and CH Zeanah. 2012. Diagnosing PTSD in early childhood: An empirical assessment of four approaches. *Journal of Traumatic Stress* 25(4):359–367.

Scheeringa MS, MJ Wright, JP Hunt, and CH Zeanah. 2006. Factors affecting the diagnosis and prediction of PTSD symptomatology in children and adolescents. *American Journal of Psychiatry* 163(4):644–651.

Scheeringa MS, CH Zeanah, and JA Cohen. 2011. PTSD in children and adolescents: Toward an empirically based algorithma. *Depression and Anxiety* 28(9):770–782.

Scheeringa MS, CH Zeanah, MJ Drell, and JA Larrieu. 1995. Two approaches to the diagnosis of post-traumatic stress disorder in infancy and early childhood. *Journal of the American Academy of Child and Adolescent Psychiatry* 34(2):191–200.

Scheeringa MS, CH Zeanah, L Myers, and FW Putnam. 2005. Predictive validity in a prospective follow-up of PTSD in preschool children. *Journal of the American Academy of Child and Adolescent Psychiatry* 44(9):899–906.

Schwarz ED and JM Kowalski. 1991. Malignant memories: PTSD in children and adults after a school shooting. *Journal of the American Academy of Child and Adolescent Psychiatry* 30(6):936–944.

Segman RH, R Cooper-Kazaz, F Macciardi, T Goltser, Y Halfon, T Dobroborski, and AY Shalev. 2001. Association between the dopamine transporter gene and posttraumatic stress disorder. *Molecular Psychiatry* 7(8):903–907.

Smith DM. 2011. Diagnosing liability: The legal history of post-traumatic stress disorder. *Temple Law Review* 84(1):1–70.

Stein MB, JR Walker, AL Hazen, and DR Forde. 1997. Full and partial posttraumatic stress disorder: Findings from a community survey. *American Journal of Psychiatry* 154(8):1114–1119.

Stone AA. 1993. Post-traumatic stress disorder and the law: Critical review of the new frontier. *Bulletin of the American Academy of Psychiatry and the Law* 21(1):23–36.

Teicher MH, NL Dumont, Y Ito, C Vaituzis, JN Giedd, and SL Anderson. 2004. Childhood neglect is associated with reduced corpus callosum area. *Biological Psychiatry* 56(2):80–85.

Terr LC. 1981. "Forbidden games": Post-traumatic child's play. *Journal of the American Academy of Child and Adolescent Psychiatry* 20(4):741–760.

Thomas LA and MD De Bellis. 2004. Pituitary volumes in pediatric maltreatment-related posttraumatic stress disorder. *Biological Psychiatry* 55(7):752–758.

Tomoda A, H Suzuki, K Rabi, Y-S Sheu, A Polcari, and MH Teicher. 2009. Reduced prefrontal cortical gray matter volume in young adults exposed to harsh corporeal punishment. *Neuroimage* 47(2):66–71.

van der Kolk BA. 2003. The neurobiology of childhood trauma and abuse. *Child and Adolescent Psychiatry Clinics of North America* 12(2):293–317.

Veenema TG and K Schroeder-Bruce. 2002. The aftermath of violence: Children, disaster, and posttraumatic stress disorder. *Journal of Pediatric Health Care* 16(5):235–244.

Weder N, H Zhang, K Jensen et al. 2014. Child abuse, depression, and methylation in genes involved with stress, neural plasticity, and brain circuitry. *Journal of the American Academy of Child and Adolescent Psychiatry* 53(4):417–424.

Wolfe DA, L Sas, and C Wekerle. 1994. Factors associated with the development of posttraumatic stress disorder among child victims of sexual abuse. *Child Abuse & Neglect* 18(1):37–50.

Xie P, HR Kranzler, L Farrer, and J Gelernter. 2012. Serotonin transporter 5-HTTLPR genotype moderates the effects of childhood adversity on posttraumatic stress disorder risk: A replication study. *American Journal of Medical Genetics. Part B, Neuropsychiatric Genetics* 159(6):644–652.

Yehuda R. 2006. Advances in understanding neuroendocrine alterations in PTSD and their therapeutic implications. *Annals of the New York Academy of Sciences* 1071(1):137–166.

Yehuda R and LM Bierer. 2009. The relevance of epigenetics to PTSD: Implication for the DSM-V. *Journal of Traumatic Stress* 22(5):427–434.

Yehuda R, JD Flory, LM Bierer, C Henn-Haase, A Lehrner, F Desarnaud, I Makotkine, NP Daskalakis, CR Marmar, and MJ Meaney. 2014. Lower methylation of Glucocorticoid Receptor Gene Promoter 1_F in peripheral blood of veterans with Posttraumatic Stress Disorder. *Biological Psychiatry* E-published ahead of print. http://www.biologicalpsychiatryjournal.com/article/S0006-3223(14)00100-0/abstract, accessed October 26, 2014.

43

Forensic aspects of suicide and homicide in children and adolescents

PETER ASH

INTRODUCTION

Homicide and suicide are, respectively, the second and third leading causes of death for adolescents aged 15–19 (National Center for Health Statistics 2014). Society often expects psychiatry to be able to accurately predict and effectively prevent suicide and homicide, despite realistic limitations in these areas. In a treatment context, clinicians must recognize the children and adolescents most at risk for violence and take appropriate steps. In a forensic context, cases of homicide and suicide are frequently the focus of court scrutiny, and forensic psychiatrists frequently play a role in the adjudication of such cases.

SUICIDE

Epidemiology and demographics

Adolescent suicide rates have been quite variable, tripling from 1955 to 1979 (Brent et al. 1988), then increasing slowly to a peak in 1991, before falling back to the rates of the 1980s, although rates have been increasing slowly since 2007 (Centers for Disease Control and Prevention 2015). It is unclear why adolescent suicide rates increased through the early 1990s and then declined, although these changes roughly parallel the directions of changes in youth homicide rates and firearm-related deaths (see Figure 43.1).

The Centers for Disease Control and Prevention (CDC) maintains a number of publicly accessible online databases, some of which can be very useful for forensic psychiatrists. The CDC's WISQARS database (CDC 2015) contains national data regarding fatal injury, including accidents, suicide, and homicide. Querying WISQARS reveals a 2013 suicide rate of 8.6/100,000 for 15- to 19-year-olds representing 1748 suicides in the United States (CDC 2015). Rates for younger adolescents were much lower, averaging about one-sixth of the older adolescent rates, and rates for preadolescents are much lower still, with an average of only five deaths per year in children under age 10 classified as suicides in the decade ending in 2013. In 2013, male adolescents were about three times as likely to commit suicide as females. This difference is explained, in part, by the means of suicide employed: teenage males tend to use more lethal methods, such as firearms and hanging, rather than less dangerous methods often used by females, such as poisoning (e.g., carbon monoxide or pill overdose) or wrist cutting. By contrast, the most common method among unsuccessful attempts is overdose, followed by wrist cutting (Holinger 1990; Low and Andrews 1990).

Historically, white adolescents have been about twice as likely as African Americans to commit suicide. In a study comparing adolescent suicide victims to a control group of nonsuicidal adolescents, there was no significant difference found in socioeconomic status (Shaffer and Craft 1999). Gay and lesbian youth are at increased risk for suicide (Stone et al. 2014), but this appears to be a consequence of increased risk for mood disorder and other mental health problems which are risk factors for suicide, rather than related directly to stressors of stigmatization (Shaffer et al. 1995).

In adolescents, suicidal ideation and attempts are fairly common. The Youth Risk Behavior Survey (YRBS) is an annual survey of adolescent risky behavior conducted by the CDC. The 2013 YRBS found that 17% of high school students had seriously considered suicide in the previous 12 months, 13.6% had made a plan, 8% had made a suicide attempt, and 2.7% had made an attempt of sufficient severity as to receive medical attention (Kann et al. 2014). Girls had about double the rates of boys in each of these categories. Although completed suicide is rare in prepubertal children, self-destructive thoughts and behavior are frequent in this young age group, and those that express suicidal ideation are more likely to have symptoms of psychiatric illness and are more likely to evidence suicidal behavior later in adolescence (Dervic et al. 2008; Pfeffer 2003).

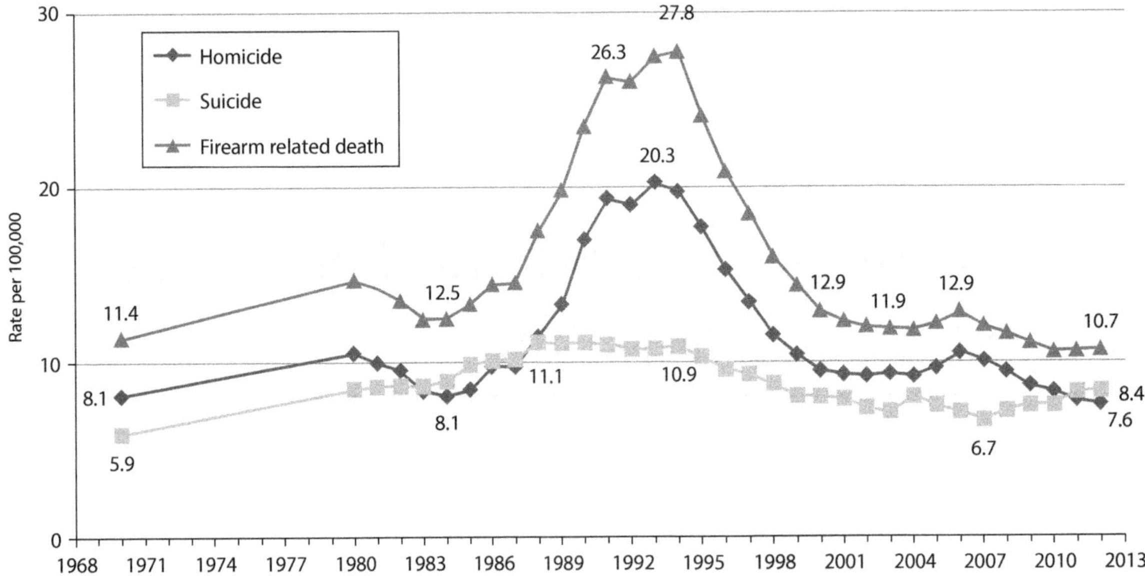

Figure 43.1 Rates (per 100,000) for homicide, suicide, and firearm-related deaths of youth ages 15–19, selected years 1970–2012. (Data for 1970–1980: National Center for Health Statistics. [2002] *Health United States, 2002 With Chartbook on Trends in the Health of Americans*. National Center for Health Statistics. Tables 46, 47, and 48; data for 1995–2012: Centers for Disease Control and Prevention. *Web-based Injury Statistics Query and Reporting System [WISQARS]* [Online]. [2014]. National Center for Injury Prevention and Control, Centers for Disease Control and Prevention [producer]. Available at www.cdc.gov/injury/wisqars/fatal.html. Modified from chart source: Child Trends Databank [2015]. With permission.)

Risk factors and precipitants

Predicting suicide in an individual case is clouded by the fact that completed suicide is rare when compared with clinical presentations of suicidal ideation and suicide attempts. The rate of suicidal ideation in the 2013 YRBS discussed above is over 2000 times the rate of completed suicide (17% ÷ 0.008%). This high ratio indicates the low specificity of using ideation as a risk factor for completed suicide, which very much complicates risk assessment. Similar to the adult population, there are no studies that identify factors that allow a clinician to accurately predict which adolescents will commit suicide. Research has therefore focused on risk factors; those characteristics that appear at greater frequency in the population of those who have completed suicide when compared to other groups. Because many youth who complete suicide were not previously in treatment, research assessment of those who have committed suicide is most commonly done utilizing psychological autopsy. The 1990s saw a great deal of research elucidating risk factors for adolescent suicide. The suicide risk factor literature is complex, reflecting changing rates and patterns of suicide, significant age and sex differences, and different sample populations, comparison groups, and statistical methods. Many different factors have been identified as increasing risk when compared to normal subjects (American Academy of Child and Adolescent Psychiatry 2001; Gould et al. 2003; Dervic et al. 2008; Cash and Bridge 2009). Risk factors commonly cited in the literature appear in Table 43.1.

Table 43.1 Summary of leading risk factors

- Individual factors
  - Previous suicide attempt
  - High intent/lethality of method
  - Psychopathology
    - Major depression
      - Helplessness and hopelessness
    - Bipolar disorder
    - Substance abuse comorbid with other psychopathology
    - Schizophrenia
    - Conduct or personality disorder, especially with impulsive characteristics
- Demographic factors
  - Over age 14, risk increases with age
  - Male
  - White
  - Unwed adolescent with unwanted pregnancy
- Family and environmental factors
  - Firearm in the home
  - Family pathology/discord
  - Abuse (physical or sexual)
  - History of violence
- Recent stressors
  - Separation
  - Arrest/legal problems

Clinically, suicidal ideation, especially when coupled with a plan involving lethal means, or a recent attempt, is most often the trigger to a judgment of imminent danger requiring hospitalization. In psychological autopsy studies, previous attempts have long been found to be the strongest risk factor for boys, increasing the risk about 30 times over the normal population (Shaffer et al. 1996; Brent et al. 1999).

Two well-controlled studies (Brent et al. 1993b; Shaffer et al. 1996) both found high rates of psychiatric disorder, around 90%, in suicide completers, a finding that has held up in later studies (Cash and Bridge 2009). Major depressive disorder was the most prominent finding and poses the most risk. In the absence of clear psychopathology, suicide is associated with recent legal or discipline problems, interpersonal loss or conflicts, and the presence of firearms (Brent et al. 1993c; Cash and Bridge 2009). Axis II psychopathology is also found in many suicide completers. Some biological factors have been implicated, including the serotonergic system (Zalsman et al. 2011) and brain structure (Lippard et al. 2014). Family stressors listed in Table 43.1 constitute a second domain of risk factors for suicide. Beyond the family, environmental factors can influence suicidality. Personal contact with a suicide victim can lead to increased suicidal behavior, such as a cluster of incidents in a single community.

Many, but by no means all, suicides have a clearly identified precipitant, although a stressor in the absence of preexisting vulnerability likely does not cause suicide. Marttunen et al. (1993) identified a precipitant in 70% of a series of cases. Of those, half the precipitants occurred in the 24 hours preceding the suicide. Interpersonal problems, particularly separations, were the most common stressor. Of particular interest to forensic psychiatrists, arrest is a risk factor as a precipitant for suicide. In one study (Brent et al. 1993a), among the minority of adolescents who did not appear to have a psychiatric disorder, 43% had legal problems or discipline in the prior year.

Firearms are the most common method of committing suicide, and firearm access is an independent risk factor for adolescent suicide (Simonetti et al. 2015).

Assessment

Asking about depressive feelings and symptoms, suicidal ideation, and a history of attempts of self-harm should be a routine part of the initial evaluation of an adolescent or depressed child. In a malpractice case arising from a suicide, liability often turns on the adequacy of the suicide assessment. The assessment of suicidality generally focuses on the risk and protective factors identified above, and information from collateral sources such as parents and prior psychiatric records, when available, should be sought. Information from sources other than the identified patient should be considered seriously, as many youth with suicidal ideation may be reluctant to reveal their true feelings. A patient with a constellation of risk factors that does not include moderate to high intent or a recent suicide attempt generally does not require hospitalization on the grounds of suicidality because of the low power of such risk factors to predict the short-term future (although the youth's condition may warrant hospitalization on other grounds). The threshold issue is generally the presence of thinking about suicide or a recent attempt. Characteristics of attempts with high intent include lethality of method, gestures of saying "goodbye," such as giving away belongings, leaving a note, writing a will, and efforts to minimize or prevent discovery and rescue. The American Academy of Child and Adolescent Psychiatry has developed practice parameters for the assessment and treatment of suicidal behaviors (American Academy of Child and Adolescent Psychiatry 2001). Assessing the severity of suicidal ideation involves evaluating the nature of the youngster's thinking, whether the youngster has formulated a plan, the lethality of the plan, access to means, the youth's level of helplessness and hopelessness, and the details of any recent attempts. Interviews with family members and reviewing medical and school records may provide useful additional data. Once suicidal thinking has been identified, other risk factors take on added significance. It is important to pay attention to the dynamic factors, including which stressors have precipitated suicidal thinking or past attempts, and to assess the likelihood of such stressors recurring.

In evaluating protective factors, the clinician needs to look to the nature of available social support, especially from the family, internal resistances to suicide, such as religious objections, the extent to which stressors in the environment can be ameliorated, and the usefulness of the family in monitoring the youngster's thinking and behavior.

Treatment

Once significant suicide risk has been identified, treatment encompasses four major components: protection of the patient, continuing assessment of risk, ameliorating risk factors, and enhancing protective factors.

Protection of the patient is the first consideration. In outpatient treatment, it is important to involve the family in monitoring and supporting the patient, making firearms and lethal medications unavailable to the patient, and forging an alliance for supporting continuing treatment. The family must feel comfortable with the outpatient plan and agree to accept some of the responsibility for the patient's safety. One important method of assessing a patient's capacity to be treated as an outpatient is to simply ask what he or she would do if stressors recurred. No-suicide contracts are often used in treatment, but there is little evidence that such contracts provide much protection. If the outpatient plan does not appear likely to manage the suicide risk, the youth is generally hospitalized. Involuntary hospitalization may be required if parents refuse voluntary admission of their child. While hospitalized, an appropriate level of observation should be maintained. During periods of active suicidal or self-destructive ideation, patients may require continual monitoring until such impulses have resolved.

Treatment should include addressing and diminishing those characteristics that constitute dynamic risk factors, including the treatment of underlying psychopathology. In the past 10 years, several multisite studies have provided evidence that a combination of psychotherapy and medication is the preferred approach in treating suicidal adolescents. The Treatment for Adolescents with Depression Study (TADS) showed that a combination of fluoxetine and cognitive behavioral therapy (CBT) resulted in significant improvement in 71% of moderately to severely depressed adolescents (March et al. 2004). Drug treatment alone and CBT alone also showed positive, although somewhat weaker, effects. Suicidal thinking was also significantly reduced in all groups, including the placebo group, although treatment effects in comparison to placebo were weak for this symptom. The Treatment of Adolescent Suicide Attempters Study (TASA) suggested that adolescent suicide attempters treated with psychotherapy and medication improved at about the same rate as nonsuicidal depressed adolescents (Vitiello et al. 2009).

Psychotherapy plays an important role in treatment in providing information about continuing risk, delineating how the youth thinks about suicide, addressing underlying psychopathology, helping the adolescent cope with such stressors as may be present, and enhancing protective factors such as more adaptive defenses or coping strategies. Some factors are best dealt with in a family context, including ameliorating disruptive or stressful family patterns and eliminating access to firearms. Unfortunately, parental compliance with a recommendation to remove firearms is fairly low, even when parents are provided with considerable information about the risks and strong recommendations (Brent et al. 2000). Working to increase family support is an important component of enhancing protective factors.

Legal considerations

In an outpatient treatment context, when the clinician determines the adolescent is at serious suicide risk, the clinician will probably want to hospitalize the patient. In most jurisdictions, the consent of a parent is sufficient for hospitalizing a minor, even over the minor's objections. State law varies as to the age at which an adolescent may object, the procedures available to an objecting minor, and whether certain youths, such as "mature minors" are able to give consent as though they were adults. If the parents do not consent to hospitalization or are unavailable, then involuntary hospitalization is available, provided the youth meets the state's civil commitment criteria. In treating a child or adolescent depressed patient, one dilemma that can arise is the extent to which the adolescent's confidentiality should be broken and the parents informed of the patient's status. It is useful at the outset of treatment to discuss with the minor patient the conditions under which the therapist will communicate information to the parents. When the clinician feels the need to discuss his or her patient's condition, for example, if a youth becomes more depressed and the therapist wishes to advise the parents to remove firearms from the home, it is preferable, when possible, to raise the need to talk to the adolescent's parents with the adolescent and obtain his or her assent. If the adolescent objects, but the therapist has significant concerns about the youth's safety, the therapist generally may discuss these issues with the parents over the adolescent's objections. This is allowable because in most cases the parents legally speak for the child and control access to information about treatment. In rare instances, such as when the minor is an emancipated minor or has "mature minor" status in a state that recognizes such a status, such a breach may not be possible, and the clinician then has fewer options. If the opportunity to involve the adolescent's support system is limited, the threshold for hospitalization is decreased.

Forensic psychiatrists are sometimes involved in determining the manner of death—whether the death was an unintended suicide, an accident such as unintended autoerotic asphyxiation (Sheehan and Garfinkel 1988), or suicide. The techniques employed in such analyses are similar to those utilized for adults.

A completed suicide by a patient in treatment may give rise to a malpractice action against the treating psychiatrist. When an outpatient commits suicide, a central question is likely to be whether the suicide was reasonably foreseeable, under the theory that if so, there was a duty to protect the patient, generally by hospitalizing him or her. The question of whether the suicide was foreseeable turns on the adequacy and documentation of the suicide risk assessment. Other issues that may come into play include whether appropriate informed consent was obtained for certain components of the treatment, whether the parents were sufficiently informed and involved in managing the patient, and whether the psychiatrist made available the means for suicide, as when an adolescent overdoses on antidepressant medication (much less common now with reduced use of tricyclic antidepressants), or any other defects that rendered the care below the standard of practice.

In 2004, the Food and Drug Administration (FDA) mandated a black box warning for the entire class of serotonin reuptake inhibitors (SSRIs) for youth based on a concern that SSRIs increase the risk of suicide in young people. Data analyses (Hammad 2004; Hammad et al. 2006) showed a doubling of reported suicidal thinking and behavior in youth receiving an SSRI from 2% for those on placebo to 4% for those on an SSRI, although there were no completed suicides in the sample. In 2007 the FDA revised the black box warning, limiting it to patients under 25 years of age and requiring appropriate monitoring, rather than a specific schedule implied in the previous black box warning (FDA 2007). The extent to which SSRIs cause suicide in youth remains controversial, in part because the data relied on for the black box warning included no completed suicides, that depression comes with a heightened risk of suicide so it is difficult in an individual case to determine whether the suicide resulted from the SSRI or from the underlying depression, and the data suggest the benefits of antidepressants in depressed youth outweigh the possible risks (Bridge et al. 2007). Nevertheless, the existence of the black box warning means a clinician who prescribes SSRIs to youth is well advised to inform parents of the potential for increased suicidal thinking, especially in the 2 months following a new prescription or increase in dose, and to carefully monitor side effects of the medication. In the event of a malpractice case involving suicide while a youth was taking an SSRI, the informed consent process and monitoring of reactions to the drug will be carefully scrutinized.

In malpractice litigation involving an adult who committed suicide, the degree to which the adult was responsible for his or her own acts, and thus a contributor to the outcome, is often important. When a minor commits suicide, the presumption that minors are not as competent as adults often reduces the responsibility of the minor for his or her actions. As is typical in malpractice cases, the psychiatrist's notes in the chart will be carefully reviewed. When assessing a suicidal youth who is going to be treated as an outpatient, it is therefore very important from a risk management perspective to document carefully the assessment process, noting which risk factors and protective factors were assessed. The assessment process is an ongoing one, and documentation of the continuing assessment of risk is useful. In those cases in which the patient is not hospitalized, it is useful to detail the clinician's reasoning about how the risk factors were weighed in devising the treatment plan. The most difficult patients from a risk management perspective are those who are at chronic risk for suicide, for whom long-term hospitalization is not a reasonable option, but where the clinician is aware there is significant risk that at some point an attempt may miscarry and result in a lethal outcome. In cases in which the clinician believes his or her treatment plan carries significant, but justified, risk, one of the best risk management strategies is "when in doubt, shout" (Rappeport 1984)—have another clinician evaluate the patient and document his or her findings. In the event of an unexpected adverse outcome, the test will be whether the psychiatrist acted reasonably, and having a second reasonable clinician evaluate the patient can strongly counteract the retrospective analysis of a plaintiff's expert.

In a malpractice case following an adolescent committing suicide on an inpatient psychiatric unit, the two most common issues are completeness of the assessment of the patient's suicidality by the doctor and hospital staff, and the adequacy of the measures to protect the patient. Again, the quality of the continuing assessments and the extent to which they are documented are very important. One common issue is whether the attending psychiatrist was aware of clinical findings by the staff. Managed care has increased the threshold of severity necessary to justify inpatient hospitalization, and a high percentage of inpatients are hospitalized because of concerns about their suicidality. Therefore, the presence of some risk factors is quite common among inpatients. Once suicidal risk is noted, a central issue will be the level of monitoring of the patient, and whether decreasing the level of monitoring was justified.

Matters of self-destructive and suicidal behavior are likely to heighten the anxiety of the patient's relatives, opening the door to questioning and scrutinizing the psychiatrist's treatment. One risk is that the psychiatrist's own reaction to a patient's suicidality will lead to neglect of basic good practice (Simon 2000). Psychiatrists need not be intimidated by the complexities and uncertainties of dealing with suicidality. It is helpful to keep in mind that courts, peer reviewers, and managed care agencies ordinarily accept clinical decisions that are in keeping with a community's general standard of care, based on a rational consideration of the documented facts, and made in the service of the patient's welfare and well-being.

HOMICIDE

Epidemiology

For most of the past 20 years, homicide was the second leading cause of death for adolescents after automobile accidents (National Center for Health Statistics 2014). However, youth homicide rates have been dropping, and youth suicide rates increasing, so that in 2013, the suicide rate for all teenagers was slightly higher (CDC 2015). Querying the CDC's public WISQARS database reveals that in 2013, the overall rate of homicide for 15- to 19-year-olds was 6.74 per 100,000 (CDC 2015). Homicide from ages 5–14 was about one-tenth the rate for older adolescents. The 2013 homicide rate for children under age 5 was 3.33 per 100,000, practically all due to child abuse. For adolescents, rates for males are much higher than rates for females, and, for African American males 15–19 years old, in 2012 homicide was the leading cause of death, at a rate approximately quadruple that of motor vehicle accidents, and almost 10 times the rate for white adolescents (CDC 2014). Death rates from homicide for 15- to 19-year-olds had been fairly flat at about 10–12 per 100,000 from 1976 until 1987 when, within the next 4 years, the homicide rate doubled reaching a peak of over 20 per 100,000 in 1993. The rate then declined by about two-thirds, back to the rates of the 1980s (see Figure 43.1). The cause of the decline remains controversial.

A similar pattern is seen in the Federal Bureau of Investigation (FBI) statistics pertaining to juvenile homicide offenders. In 2012, juveniles were determined to have committed approximately 725 of the 11,521 murders in the United States where the offender's age was known (National Center for Juvenile Justice 2015). This represents a decrease of about 74% from the peak in 1994. The vast majority (91%) of the known juvenile homicide offenders were male, and more than 60% were African American. While African Americans are involved in juvenile homicides more frequently than whites, most of these differences wash out if the comparisons are controlled for the effects of socioeconomic status (Griffith and Bell 1989; Ellis et al. 2009).

The 1980s increase in youth homicide was strongly associated with an increase in firearm use among youth (Snyder and Sickmund 1999). Rates of intrafamilial homicide and homicide with other weapons have stayed flat since the early 1980s. Blumstein and Cork (1996) hypothesized the increase followed a rapid increase of involvement of adolescents in the drug trade which led to increased gun carrying by youths. Why the rates subsequently declined, however, remains unclear (Blumstein and Wallman 2006). What is clear is that these changes in homicide rates mirrored a similar pattern of changes in rates of violent crime in the adult population, although the magnitude of increase was far greater among juveniles, and, interestingly, in youth suicide rates.

In previous years, acquaintances of the juvenile were more likely to be killed than strangers, but FBI statistics from 2012 involving juvenile offenders also reveal that murder victims were about equally likely to be acquaintances of the juvenile as strangers, and approximately 9% of victims were family members. Girls made up only 7% of the known juvenile homicide offenders, and girls were more likely than boys to use a knife or means other than a firearm than were boys, although firearms were the most common weapon used by both sexes (National Center for Juvenile Justice 2015).

Types of juvenile homicide

Homicide is a heterogeneous phenomenon among adolescents: the shooter who has been "dissed" outside a club, the adolescent girl who kills her stepfather because he has been sexually abusing her, and the psychotic adolescent who opens fire on his classmates at school represent very different pictures in terms of offenders, motivations, and victims. Studies of juvenile murderers have tended to be either interview studies of a convenience sample or analyses of FBI crime statistics. It is difficult to blend together these two different levels of analysis. There is a considerable literature on juvenile violence and its development, and homicide may present as the peak in severity of a violent career. Unlike suicide, it does not appear that juvenile homicide is primarily caused by mental health problems—although most offenders have psychiatric disorders—and many juvenile killers had not received psychiatric attention prior to offending. Findings over the past 14 years suggest it is useful to subdivide the conflict group into street confrontation, intrafamilial, and other, and to consider school shootings with multiple victims as a rare, but separate group. In addition, there are even less common subgroups, such as sexual homicide (Myers 1994), which have their own distinct characteristics.

Street homicides

Street violence is the most common form of juvenile homicide. Crime statistics often do not distinguish between street homicides occurring during the commission of another felony and street homicides arising out of conflict between youths. Gun carrying among adolescents is a major risk factor for homicide, as confrontations quickly escalate in lethality when one of the participants is armed. In many instances, the distinction between aggravated assault and homicide turns more on chance factors affecting the path of the bullet than on the intent of the shooter. When adolescents are asked about their reasons for carrying guns, keeping oneself safe is by far the most commonly cited reason (Ash et al. 1996). Although some adolescents report they derive an enhanced sense of power or self-respect from carrying a gun, few claim they carry a gun for the purpose of committing a crime. Most gun carrying by adolescents appears to be reactive in nature and is done because they fear harm on the street. Youths, particularly in minority groups, do face a much higher risk of victimization than the population at large. According to data from the CDC, in 2012, 17-year-old African American males were murdered at a rate more than eight times higher than their white peers and more than four times higher than the national average for all ages (CDC 2014). Adolescents who feel unsafe—especially those who live in inner-city neighborhoods where there is an "ecology of danger"—are more likely to arm themselves for protection, although the effectiveness of this strategy is debatable; handguns increase the likelihood of a violent confrontation. Whether fatal or nonfatal, street shootings heighten the overall level of fear in a community that, in turn, leads to rising levels of fear that encourage even more gun carrying (Blumstein and Cork 1996).

In those cities where gangs are prevalent, gang violence accounts for a substantial portion of youth homicides. Although there are difficulties in measuring levels of gang activity and whether a homicide is gang related, the CDC estimates that in Los Angeles, which has a high rate of gang activity, gangs are responsible for about three out of four youth homicides of 15- to 19-year-olds (CDC 2012).

There are three key points in the chain of events that precede almost every street shooting: first, the decision to acquire a handgun; second, the decision to carry it; and finally, the decision to use it. These are also the three key points for intervention. Most adolescents who become involved with guns acquire their first firearm in early adolescence (Ash et al. 1996; Brener et al. 1999). The majority receive their first gun from someone else, whether from a parent giving a child his first hunting rifle as a Christmas gift, or a teenager giving his best friend an illegally acquired handgun for protection. By middle to later adolescence, when delinquent boys are more likely to be arrested, they have begun to actively obtain handguns from a variety of sources, including buying from a drug dealer or an adult "straw purchaser," borrowing from a friend or acquaintance, or theft.

In an altercation between two inner-city youths, at least one of whom is armed, issues of respect and toughness—"being the man"—are very important, and perceived attacks on identity can rapidly escalate to lethal violence. In an analysis of transactions leading to inner-city street shootings, Fagan and Wilkinson (1998) emphasize the importance of a drug and alcohol context. Drug use worsens judgment, and the drug trade itself provides fertile ground for disputes over territory and payment. Fagan and Wilkinson emphasize the need to maintain hierarchy and respect in ways that feed into maintaining a violent identity. The threat of gun violence introduces new complexities for development of social identity, resulting in the paradox that creating a "safe" social identity may require the use of extreme forms of violence.

In Myers et al.'s (1995) series of juvenile murderers who were seen for mental health evaluation, those juveniles who committed homicide during the course of another crime were found to have very high (>95%) rates of family dysfunction, disruptive behavior disorders, previous violence toward others and prior arrests, and high (>70%) rates of school failure, family violence, and learning disabilities. Benedek and Cornell (1989) found consistent findings but generally lower rates of disorder. In both groups, fewer than 25% had received prior mental health treatment. Fendrich et al. (1995) found about one-third of juvenile murderers were using substances, primarily alcohol, at the time of the offense, a rate that was lower than all but the oldest group of adult offenders.

Intrafamilial homicide

Rates of killing a family member have been holding steady or decreasing since 1993, and in 2012 accounted for 9% of juvenile homicides (National Center for Juvenile Justice 2015). Parricide, killing the father, is the most common form (Heide and Petee 2007), generally found in the context of abuse and, when it occurs, is most often committed by older and depressed adolescents (Dutton and Yamini 1995). In many cases, unlike with street homicides, the adolescent does not exhibit a prior history of delinquency. The criminal defense of these youth often emphasizes the abuse victim status of the killer as a mitigating circumstance of the killing.

Psychotic motive

While psychotic motive overlaps the other categories, it is frequently dealt with separately, because it has different implications with regard to sentencing and treatment. In criminal justice statistics, psychotic motive is not broken out as a separate category, so overall rates are unclear, but in reports of cases referred to mental health professionals, psychosis is uncommon, accounting for less than 7% of cases (Benedek and Cornell 1989; Meloy et al. 2001). Myers et al. (1995) found no psychotic youth in their sample, although they found a history of psychotic symptoms in 71% of subjects. Psychotic juvenile defendants may be found not criminally responsible and referred for treatment of their psychosis.

School mass shootings

Statistically, schools are a safe place to be. About 1.3% of all youth homicides occur at school, a rate that has remained fairly stable over the past 20 years (Planty and Truman 2013). The first mass killing of students by a student in a U.S. K–12 school occurred in 1996 when a 14-year-old boy in the Frontier Middle School shot and killed a teacher and two students and wounded another in his algebra class. In the following 4 years, there were six additional incidents of mass killings by students in K–12 schools, the most deadly of which was the mass shooting at Columbine High School in Colorado, during which 12 students and 1 teacher were killed, 24 people were wounded, and the two student shooters committed suicide (for descriptions, see Verlinden et al. 2000; Wikipedia 2015). These shootings generated enormous amounts of media coverage and grave concerns about school safety. The clustering of the shootings in such a brief period strongly suggests a contagion effect. Such shootings, while fortunately very rare, nevertheless create a climate of fear in schools which has an impact on students' emotional well-being, their readiness to learn, and the hiring and retention of teaching staff.

Studies of school shootings (Verlinden et al. 2000; Reddy et al. 2001), the influential FBI report in 1999 (O'Toole 1999), and the reports of the U.S. Secret Service and the Department of Education's Safe School Initiative in 2000 and 2002 (Fein et al. 2002; Vossekuil et al. 2002), were consistent in finding that there was *no* profile of a school shooter that would prospectively identify the perpetrators. Except for the fact that all were male, the perpetrators were quite varied: few attackers had no close friends—only about a third were characterized as loners—and the majority had never been in disciplinary trouble at school or had a history of violence. Many attackers had felt bullied or persecuted at school. Of the 37 school shootings investigated by the Safe Schools Initiative, only one-third of the attackers had ever received a mental health evaluation, and only seven (17%) had ever been diagnosed with a mental health or behavioral disorder (Vossekuil et al. 2002). The most significant finding was that in almost all cases, the perpetrator had mentioned his plan to at least one peer, but there was a failure of peers to take the threats seriously and report the threats to school authorities. This finding led to an emphasis on encouraging students and staff to report all threats, even threats made as jokes, to school authorities, who would then institute a threat investigation.

Building on earlier work of the U.S. Secret Service in evaluating threats to the President (Fein and Vossekuil 1999), threat investigation of people with or without mental illness has moved away from profiling the subject to evaluating the pathways that lead to violent action (Borum et al. 1999). Put another way, threat assessment looks less at characteristics of the subject (such as stated intent, psychopathology, and access to weapons) and more at recent behavior that suggests the subject is moving on a path toward violence. This path typically begins with ideation, such as interest in mass killing or assassination, progresses through fantasies of killing, moves to a discreet planning stage (scouting out locations, selecting targets) and means acquisition (obtaining weapons), and culminates in offensive action. Because an individual in a psychiatric interview may deny many of these recent behaviors, a comprehensive evaluation involves obtaining collateral information (e.g., from peers and perhaps computer records, such as Internet browsing history).

A number of protocols have been developed to assist schools in implementing threat assessment protocols in the school environment (Fein et al. 2002; Cornell and Sheras 2006). These protocols emphasize developing multidisciplinary teams, and they detail the process of threat assessments. These multidisciplinary teams typically include school administrators, law enforcement personnel, and mental health professionals. Assessments begin with a triage process that considers the seriousness of the threat. Not all threats are serious. One study of the Virginia Student Threat Assessment program (Cornell et al. 2004) found that 70% of threats were transient and could be resolved quickly. The remaining substantive threats required more extensive evaluation and development of a safety plan to ensure the safety of the school and meet the educational needs of the threatening student.

The approach of encouraging students and staff to report threats, and then to actively investigate such threats, appears to have been effective in significantly reducing mass shootings in K–12 schools. In the 15 years since the Columbine shootings, there have been only four instances of mass shootings by students at K–12 schools that resulted in two or more deaths, not including the suicide of the shooter. Although no national statistics regarding the number of attacks thwarted by threat investigations are available, numerous anecdotes and news reports of interventions that have prevented planned attacks have been reported.

Legal issues

When a therapist is aware that a patient is dangerous to others because of mental illness, he or she will most commonly hospitalize the patient, involuntarily if necessary. In many states, therapists now have a *Tarasoff*-type duty to protect third parties, though the precise nature of the duty varies from state to state. The laws with respect to civil commitment and protection of third parties embody the same principles for adolescents as for adults.

Many states responded to the wave of juvenile violence in the early 1990s by passing laws that make it easier to try an adolescent in adult court, either by enacting discretionary waivers, which give the prosecutor discretion as to whether to waive the adolescent defendant, or mandatory waivers, laws that require that adolescents over a certain age and charged with certain crimes be tried in adult court. Homicide, being the most serious offense, heads the list of crimes for which waivers are invoked. Therefore, most youth arrested for homicide are tried as adults. In adult court, issues of competency to stand trial and insanity defense can be considered. Although many middle-to-late adolescents make decisions similar to adults, the determination of a younger adolescents' competency may turn on complex developmental issues, and so the techniques for evaluation are somewhat different than with adults (see, e.g., Mossman et al. 2007; Grisso 2013). The two strongest predictors of an adolescent's competency to stand trial are age and IQ (Ash 2003). Adolescents whose competency is seriously diminished will often be remanded to juvenile court. In addition to competency to stand trial, competency to confess may also be at issue. If a juvenile defendant is found incompetent to stand trial, the question of how his or her competence is to be "restored," when what may be needed is time for him or her to cognitively mature, poses knotty problems for interim disposition.

If the juvenile is not automatically waived to adult court on a murder charge, the issue of the judicial waiver to adult court needs to be considered. In many states, competency to stand trial is now required for a youth to be tried in juvenile court as well.

Insanity defenses for juveniles are relatively rare, largely because the incidence of psychosis is considerably less in minors than in adults. Only a small minority of states allow the insanity defense in juvenile court (Pollock 2001).

Psychiatric evaluations are sometimes sought to aid the court in sentencing adolescents. In the past decade, the U.S. Supreme Court has limited the punishments that can be given to adolescents (those under 18). In *Roper v. Simmons* (2005) the Court held that executing a person for a crime committed while an adolescent is cruel and unusual punishment and therefore unconstitutional. In *Graham v. Florida* (2010), the Court held that life without parole (LWOP) for crimes less than murder was unconstitutional, and in *Miller v. Alabama* (2012), the Court held that mandatory LWOP for adolescents convicted of murder was unconstitutional, although states could still allow a judge to hand down an LWOP sentence for murder following a hearing on its appropriateness in a specific case. Mental health testimony in sentencing hearings for murder convictions frequently focuses on issues of adolescent culpability (see Chapter 48).

Prevention

Psychiatry is fairly weak at predicting violence toward others, and most of the mental health research done has focused on adults, particularly psychiatric inpatients. It is unclear the extent to which the principles developed for adults generalize to adolescents, particularly because psychosis and substance abuse play a much smaller role in adolescent crime. If a patient expresses homicidal intent, a clinician has good grounds to intervene, but in the absence of expressed intent, risk factors such as a prior history of violence are so nonspecific as to be of little help in most individual cases. Homicide in adolescents frequently occurs impulsively, without prior threats or expressed ideation, which adds to difficulties in prediction. The widely fluctuating rates of juvenile homicide over the past decade and the difficulty in identifying prospective murderers suggest that interventions at the community level are likely to have the most effect in reducing mortality. Juvenile homicide is the tip of the iceberg of youth violence, and reducing youth violence generally is likely to reduce the juvenile homicide rate.

Given that most homicides are firearm related, reducing carrying of firearms appears among one promising strategy targeting juvenile homicide. While a sense of need for protection is the leading factor motivating gun carrying, fear of being caught with a gun is the strongest deterrent (Ash et al. 1996; Freed et al. 2001). The federal Youth Handgun Safety Act (1996) makes it illegal for juveniles to carry a handgun. Some pilot strategies that appear useful in deterring adolescents from carrying guns include enhanced prosecution of gun offenders (Seattle, Washington), directed police patrols aimed at deterring illegal gun carrying (Kansas City, Missouri), parental consent for police to search a juvenile's room and confiscate firearms found there (St. Louis, Missouri), and holding a gang responsible for the actions of individual members (Boston, Massachusetts). There is ample, albeit indirect, evidence that if an area is perceived as safe and well policed, young people are less apt to bring guns there. Schools are one clear example of this. A recent report from the U.S. Departments of Justice and Education finds that rates of gun carrying on school property have been falling and that youths feel safer in school than previously (Robers et al. 2014). It is unclear whether teens decline to carry guns to school because they feel they are unlikely to encounter an armed rival or because they fear detection by vigilant teachers, classmates, or school security technology and the penalties of "zero tolerance" policies. What is clear, however, is that the collective impact of these interventions has been positive. Schools are also promising sites for interventions with adolescents to build a sense of community and promote and teach nonviolent coping skills.

At a community level, a "rebuilding the village" approach involves collaborations between citizens, businesses, and government to promote a safer, healthier environment (Bell et al. 2001). A wide variety of techniques for promoting community health are available (see, e.g., Asset-Based Community Development Institute 2015).

SUMMARY

Adolescent violence, directed against self or others, exacts an enormous toll on its victims, their families, and society. Forensic psychiatrists are frequently consulted to assess cases involving youth, primarily adolescents, who are either thought to be at risk for killing themselves or others, or have already done so. Because of the high stakes involved, such cases generate great anxiety and concern for evaluators, patients, and families. Although a good deal of group data about these juveniles has been developed, our ability to predict accurately which individuals will carry out such violence remains severely limited. Clinical approaches for assessment and intervention have been developed. Psychiatric intervention has no doubt benefitted many at-risk patients, but rigorous research has so far not demonstrated a consequent significant decrease in death rates. This may in part reflect that many youth who kill themselves or others never see a mental health professional. Family and community interventions may have the most effect in reducing mortality.

REFERENCES

American Academy of Child and Adolescent Psychiatry. 2001. Practice parameter for the assessment and treatment of children and adolescents with suicidal behavior. *Journal of the American Academy of Child and Adolescent Psychiatry* 40:24S–51S.

Ash P. 2003. Commentary: Risk markers for incompetence in juvenile defendants. *Journal of the American Academy of Psychiatry and the Law* 31:310–312.

Ash P, AL Kellermann, D Fuqua-Whitley, and A Johnson. 1996. Gun acquisition and use by juvenile offenders. *JAMA* 275:1754–1758.

Asset-Based Community Development Institute. 2015. *Asset-Based Community Development Institute.* http://www.abcdinstitute.org, accessed January 4, 2015.

Bell CC, S Gamm, P Vallas, and P Jackson. 2001. Strategies for the prevention of youth violence in Chicago Public Schools. In *School Violence: Assessment, Management, Prevention*, edited by M Shafii and SL Shafii. Washington, DC: American Psychiatric Publishing.

Benedek EP and DG Cornell. eds. 1989. *Juvenile Homicide.* Washington, DC: American Psychiatric Press.

Blumstein A and D Cork. 1996. Linking gun availability to youth gun violence. *Law and Contemporary Problems* 59:5–24.

Blumstein A and J Wallman. 2006. *The Crime Drop in America.* New York: Cambridge University Press.

Borum R, R Fein, B Vossekuil, and J Berglund. 1999. Threat assessment: Defining an approach for evaluating risk of targeted violence. *Behavioral Sciences and the Law* 17:323–337.

Brener ND, TR Simon, EG Krug, and R Lowry. 1999. Recent trends in violence-related behaviors among high school students in the United States. *JAMA* 282:440–446.

Brent DA, M Baugher, B Birmaher et al. 2000. Compliance with recommendations to remove firearms in families participating in a clinical trial for adolescent depression. *Journal of the American Academy of Child and Adolescent Psychiatry* 39:1220–1226.

Brent DA, M Baugher, J Bridge et al. 1999. Age- and sex-related risk factors for adolescent suicide. *Journal of the American Academy of Child and Adolescent Psychiatry* 38:1497–1505.

Brent DA, JA Perper, CE Goldstein et al. 1988. Risk factors for adolescent suicide. A comparison of adolescent suicide victims with suicidal inpatients. *Archives of General Psychiatry* 45:581–588.

Brent DA, J Perper, G Moritz et al. 1993a. Suicide in adolescents with no apparent psychopathology. *Journal of the American Academy of Child and Adolescent Psychiatry* 32:494–500.

Brent DA, JA Perper, G Moritz et al. 1993b. Psychiatric risk factors for adolescent suicide: A case-control study. *Journal of the American Academy of Child and Adolescent Psychiatry* 32:521–529.

Brent DA, JA Perper, G Moritz et al. 1993c. Firearms and adolescent suicide. A community case-control study. *American Journal of Diseases of Children* 147:1066–1671.

Bridge JA, S Iyengar, CB Salary et al. 2007. Clinical response and risk for reported suicidal ideation and suicide attempts in pediatric antidepressant treatment: A meta-analysis of randomized controlled trials. *JAMA* 297:1683–1696.

Cash SJ and JA Bridge. 2009. Epidemiology of youth suicide and suicidal behavior. *Current Opinion in Pediatrics* 21:613–619.

Centers for Disease Control and Prevention (CDC). 2012. Gang homicides—Five U.S. cities, 2003–2008. *MMWR—Morbidity and Mortality Weekly Report* 61:46–51.

Centers for Disease Control and Prevention (CDC). 2014. *WISQARS Fatal Injury Reports, National and Regional, 1999–2012* [Author analysis of online database]. http://www.cdc.gov/injury/wisqars/fatal_injury_reports.html, accessed December 13, 2014.

Centers for Disease Control and Prevention (CDC). 2015. *WISQARS Fatal Injury Reports, National and Regional, 1999–2013* [Author analysis of online database]. http://www.cdc.gov/injury/wisqars/fatal_injury_reports.html, accessed July 1, 2015.

Child Trends Databank. 2015. *Teen Homicide, Suicide and Firearm Deaths*. http://www.childtrends.org/?indicators=teen-homicide-suicide-and-firearm-deaths, accessed May 23, 2015.

Cornell DG and P Sheras 2006. *Guidelines for Responding to Student Threats of Violence*. Longmont, CO: Sopris West.

Cornell DG, PL Sheras, S Kaplan et al. 2004. Guidelines for student threat assessment: Field-test findings. *School Psychology Review* 33:527–546.

Dervic K, DA Brent, and MA Oquendo. 2008. Completed suicide in childhood. *Psychiatric Clinics of North America* 31:271–291.

Dutton DG and S Yamini. 1995. Adolescent parricide: An integration of social cognitive theory and clinical views of projective-introjective cycling. *American Journal of Orthopsychiatry* 65:39–47.

Ellis L, KM Beaver, and J Wright. 2009. *Handbook of Crime Correlates*. San Diego, CA: Academic Press.

Fagan J and DL Wilkinson. 1998. Guns, youth violence, and social identity in inner cities. *Crime and Justice* 24:105–188.

Fein R, B Vossekuil, WS Pollack et al. 2002. *Threat Assessment in Schools: A Guide to Managing Threatening Stiuations and to Creating Safe School Climates*. Washington, DC: U.S. Secret Service and U.S. Department of Education.

Fein RA and B Vossekuil. 1999. Assassination in the United States: An operational study of recent assassins, attackers, and near-lethal approachers. *Journal of Forensic Sciences* 44:321–333.

Fendrich M, ME Mackesy-Amiti, P Goldstein et al. 1995. Substance involvement among juvenile murderers: Comparisons with older offenders based on interviews with prison inmates. *International Journal of the Addictions* 30:1363–1382.

Freed LH, DW Webster, JJ Longwell et al. 2001. Factors preventing gun acquisition and carrying among incarcerated adolescent males. *Archives of Pediatrics and Adolescent Medicine* 155:335–341.

Gould MS, T Greenberg, DM Velting, and D Shaffer. 2003. Youth suicide risk and preventive interventions: A review of the past 10 years. *Journal of the American Academy of Child and Adolescent Psychiatry* 42:386–405.

Graham v. Florida, 560 U.S. 48 (2010).

Griffith EE and CC Bell. 1989. Recent trends in suicide and homicide among blacks. *JAMA* 262:2265–2269.

Grisso T. 2013. *Forensic Evaluation of Juveniles*, 2nd edition. Sarasota, FL: Professional Resource Press.

Hammad TA. 2004. Results of the analysis of suicidality in pediatric trials of newer antidepressants. Presentation at the *FDA Center for Drug Evaluation and Research (CDER)*, Bethesda, MD. September 13, 2004. http://www.fda.gov/ohrms/dockets/ac/cder04.html#PsychopharmacologicDrugs, accessed March 26, 2005.

Hammad TA, T Laughren, and J Racoosin. 2006. Suicidality in pediatric patients treated with antidepressant drugs. *Archives of General Psychiatry* 63:332–339.

Heide KM and TA Petee. 2007. Parricide: An empirical analysis of 24 years of U.S. data. *Journal of Interpersonal Violence* 22:1382–1399.

Holinger PC. 1990. The causes, impact, and preventability of childhood injuries in the United States. Childhood suicide in the United States. *American Journal of Diseases of Children* 144:670–676.

Kann L, S Kinchen, SL Shanklin et al. 2014. Youth risk behavior surveillance—United States, 2013. *Morbidity and Mortality Weekly Report Surveillance Summaries* 63:1–172.

Lippard ETC, JAY Johnston, and HP Blumberg. 2014. Neurobiological risk factors for suicide: Insights from brain imaging. *American Journal of Preventive Medicine* 47:S152–S162.

Low BP and SF Andrews. 1990. Adolescent suicide. *Medical Clinics of North America* 74:1251–1264.

March J, S Silva, S Petrycki et al. 2004. Fluoxetine, cognitive-behavioral therapy, and their combination for adolescents with depression: Treatment for Adolescents with Depression Study (TADS) randomized controlled trial. *JAMA* 292:807–820.

Marttunen MJ, HM Aro, and JK Lonnqvist. 1993. Precipitant stressors in adolescent suicide. *Journal of the American Academy of Child and Adolescent Psychiatry* 32:1178–1183.

Meloy JR, AG Hempel, K Mohandie et al. 2001. Offender and offense characteristics of a nonrandom sample of adolescent mass murderers. *Journal of the American Academy of Child and Adolescent Psychiatry* 40:719–728.

Miller v. Alabama, 567 U.S. __, 132 S.Ct. 1733 (2012).

Mossman D, SG Noffsinger, P Ash et al. 2007. AAPL practice guideline for the forensic psychiatric evaluation of competence to stand trial. *Journal of the American Academy of Psychiatry and the Law* 35:S3–S72.

Myers WC. 1994. Sexual homicide by adolescents. *Journal of the American Academy of Child and Adolescent Psychiatry* 33:962–969.

Myers WC, K Scott, AW Burgess, and AG Burgess. 1995. Psychopathology, biopsychosocial factors, crime characteristics, and classification of 25 homicidal youths. *Journal of the American Academy of Child and Adolescent Psychiatry* 34:1483–1489.

National Center for Health Statistics. 2014. *Health, United States, 2013, with Special Feature on Prescription Drugs*. Hyattsville, MD: U.S. Dept. of Health and Human Services.

National Center for Juvenile Justice. 2015. *Easy Access to the FBI's Supplementary Homicide Reports: 1980–2012* [author analysis of online database]. http://www.ojjdp.gov/ojstatbb/ezashr/, accessed January 5, 2015.

O'Toole ME. 1999. *The School Shooter: A Threat Assessment Perspective*. Washington, DC: U.S. Department of Justice.

Pfeffer CR. 2003. Suicide in mood disordered children and adolescents. *Child and Adolescent Psychiatric Clinics of North America* 11:639–647.

Planty M and JL Truman. 2013. *Firearm Violence, 1993–2011* (NCJ 241730). Washington, DC: Bureau of Justice Statistics.

Pollock ES. 2001. Those crazy kids: Providing the insanity defense in juvenile courts. *Minnesota Law Review* 85:2041–2078.

Rappeport JR. May 1984. *Malpractice Prevention*. Catonsville, MD: Spring Grove State Hospital Center.

Reddy M, R Borum, J Berglund et al. 2001. Evaluating risk for targeted violence in schools: Comparing risk assessment, threat assessment, and other approaches. *Psychology in the Schools* 38:157–172.

Robers S, J Kemp, A Rathbun, and RE Morgan. 2014. *Indicators of School Crime and Safety, 2013* (NCES 2014-042/NCJ-243299). Washington, DC: National Center for Education Statistics, U.S. Department of Education, and Bureau of Justice Statistics, Office of Justice Programs, U.S. Department of Justice.

Roper v. Simmons, 543 U.S. 551 (2005).

Shaffer D and L Craft. 1999. Methods of adolescent suicide prevention. *Journal of Clinical Psychiatry* 60:70–74.

Shaffer D, P Fisher, RH Hicks et al. 1995. Sexual orientation in adolescents who commit suicide. *Suicide and Life-Threatening Behavior* 25:64–71.

Shaffer D, MS Gould, P Fisher et al. 1996. Psychiatric diagnosis in child and adolescent suicide. *Archives of General Psychiatry* 53:339–348.

Sheehan W and BD Garfinkel. 1988. Adolescent autoerotic deaths. *Journal of the American Academy of Child and Adolescent Psychiatry* 27:367–370.

Simon RI. 2000. Taking the "Sue" out of suicide: A forensic psychiatrist's perspective. *Psychiatric Annals* 30:399–407.

Simonetti JA, JL Mackelprang, A Rowhani-Rahbar et al. 2015. Psychiatric comorbidity, suicidality, and in-home firearm access among a nationally representative sample of adolescents. *JAMA Psychiatry* 72:152–159.

Snyder HN and M Sickmund. 1999. *Juvenile Offenders and Victims: 1999 National Report*. Washington, DC: Office of Juvenile Justice and Delinquency Prevention.

Stone DM, F Luo, L Ouyang et al. 2014. Sexual orientation and suicide ideation, plans, attempts, and medically serious attempts: Evidence from local Youth Risk Behavior Surveys, 2001–2009. *American Journal of Public Health* 104:262–271.

U.S. Food and Drug Administration. 2007. *Revisions to Product Labeling*. http://www.fda.gov/downloads/Drugs/DrugSafety/InformationbyDrugClass/UCM173233.pdf, accessed January 21, 2012.

Verlinden S, M Hersen, and J Thomas. 2000. Risk factors in school shootings. *Clinical Psychology Review* 20:3–56.

Vitiello B, DA Brent, LL Greenhill et al. 2009. Depressive symptoms and clinical status during the Treatment of Adolescent Suicide Attempters (TASA) Study. *Journal of the American Academy of Child and Adolescent Psychiatry* 48:997–1004.

Vossekuil B, R Fein, M Reddy et al. 2002. *The Final Report and Findings of the Safe School Initiative: Implications for the Prevention of School Attacks in the United States*. Washington, DC: U.S. Department of Education, Office of Elementary and Secondary Education, Safe and Drug-Free Schools Program and U.S. Secret Service, National Threat Assessment Center.

Vossekuil B, M Reddy, R Fein et al. 2000. *Safe School Initiative: An Interim Report on the Prevention of Targeted Violence in Schools*. Washington, DC: U.S. Secret Service National Threat Assessment Center and U.S. Department of Education.

Wikipedia. 2015. *List of School Shootings in the United States*. http://en.wikipedia.org/wiki/List_of_school_shootings_in_the_United_States, accessed July 5, 2015.

Youth Handgun Safety Act, 18 U.S.C. 922(x) (1996).

Zalsman G, M Patya, A Frisch et al. 2011. Association of polymorphisms of the serotonergic pathways with clinical traits of impulsive-aggression and suicidality in adolescents: A multi-center study. *World Journal of Biological Psychiatry* 12:33–41.

44

The child as a witness

SUZANNE M. DUPÉE

INTRODUCTION

Children can be called as witnesses in various different legal proceedings: as a perpetrator in juvenile cases, as an eyewitness or victim in a criminal case, as a victim in a child abuse case against the child's parents or other caregiver, in a custody battle between feuding and divorcing parents, or as a witness or victim in a civil matter. Despite the setting or context, the courtroom or other legal venues are usually out of the normal realm of children's environment. The courtroom is not a familiar playground for children, and litigation is by definition a contentious process. Child witnesses are thrust into highly contentious legal dilemmas, often with high stakes at issue, e.g., capital cases, child abuse cases, criminal cases, or custody cases. Depending on the age of the child, the child often has little to no understanding of court proceedings. The child's voice might be important, such as voicing custodial preferences in child custody disputes, but the child has little to no knowledge, limited rights, and often little protection in highly adversarial settings.

Before testifying as a witness, it is likely that a child has been prepped in some way—either by the child's own parent, law enforcement, a social worker from child protective services, a lawyer representing the child, or the child's parents. Sometimes the child is on the witness stand with little preparation or briefing. Often the child's testimony holds weight that can influence the outcome of the litigation. Sometimes the child's testimony holds little value. Sometimes the absence of the child's testimony can lead to the inability to prosecute child sexual molesters or sway a family judge to make decisions that are not in their own best interests. Depending on the type of litigation, children are likely to have no legal representation. Depending on the nature of the preparation, children might be adversely influenced or suggestible in their testimony that in turn might affect the outcome of the case. The legal system is a daunting place for children.

An intricate understanding of child development is optimal to obtain pertinent and accurate information from children and for justice to be served for all participants. Child psychiatrists and forensic psychiatrists can play an important role in the legal system in many different arenas. They can educate attorneys, judicial officers, and law enforcement about child development and interviewing children. They can consult with attorneys about child-related cases. They can be called upon to opine about competency to stand trial in juvenile delinquency cases.

History of child witnesses

Children are the most dangerous of all witnesses.

A. Baginsky

EARLY ENGLISH AND AMERICAN HISTORY

Children have been involved in legal cases for thousands of years dating back to Cain and Abel. In the seventeenth century judges were skeptical of child witnesses in sexual molestation trials, and they reduced sentences for convictions of child sexual perpetrators (Steenburg 2005). The 1692 Salem witch trials are the most famous and most referenced in regard to leading questions. Hundreds of 5- to 12-year-old children testified to observing bizarre witchcraft and wizardry. Much has evolved since the Salem witch hunt trials.

In England in 1779 the decision in *Rex v. Brasier* held that there is no age below which children are automatically disqualified from testifying (*Rex v. Brasier* 1779). In Jewish history, child witnesses had to be "of full age"—more than 13 years old (Whipple 1911). In the Antebellum Period before the American Civil War, the notion that children needed sheltering from the responsibilities and realties of adult life emerged in law and policy (Tanenhaus 2007). The "best interests" doctrine emerged as early as the mid-nineteenth century (Grossberg 1996). The twentieth century saw an explosion of research about child and adolescent development that has paved the path for more understanding about present-day child witnesses.

Landmark cases and laws pertaining to child witnesses

The evolution of cases involving child witnesses dates back centuries. After an outcry over failed prosecution in sexual abuse cases in the 1980s, hearsay exceptions for child witnesses is widely employed (Raskin 1989). Federal Rules of Evidence (Fed. R. Evid. 1984) established guidelines regarding child witness testimony and hearsay. Child witnesses are not excluded as witnesses irrespective of their age. Federal courts and most states allow hearsay evidence of children. Federal Rules of Evidence 801 (Fed. R. Evid. 801) defines hearsay as "a statement, other than one made by a declarant while testifying at the current trial or hearing offered in evidence to prove the truth of the matter asserted in the statement." Federal Rules of Evidence 803 lists 23 hearsay exceptions. Children's statements made to nonforensic professionals might be deemed hearsay and therefore are inadmissible (McGough 1996) but may qualify for the hearsay exception through Federal Rules of Evidence 803(4) (Fed. R. Evid. 803), which provides that the following statements are admissible as hearsay if they are made for purposes of medical diagnosis or treatment and describing medical history, pertinent to diagnosis or treatment. Another exception is Federal Rules of Evidence 803(2) (Fed. R. Evid. 803), which relates to "the excited utterance"—"a statement relating to a startling event or condition, made while the declarant was under the stress of excitement that it caused." The U.S. Supreme Court case *Ohio v. Clark* (2015) further extended issues regarding hearsay by protecting mandated reporters' initial questioning of possible child abuse victims.

Over the past two decades various evidentiary and procedural innovations have been introduced to reduce the barriers associated with children as participants in legal proceedings. Victims of Child Abuse Act of 1990 extended special accommodations to children, such as the presence of a support person during the child's testimony and a closed courtroom to the general public (Whitcomb et al. 1991). These accommodations include hearsay exceptions, videotaped testimony, and closed-circuit television (CCTV) (McAuliff and Kovera 2002; McAuliff et al. 2013).

Most states have taken steps to institute closed-circuit testimony to codify standards articulated in *Maryland v. Craig* (1990) to reduce the trauma to child abuse victims. CCTV testimony is more common in other countries such as Australia (Cashmore and De Haas 1992), and Britain (McAuliff and Kovera 2002) than in the United States (McAuliff et al. 2013).

Distinction between clinical or treating and forensic evaluations is a critical element in the legal process and attempts to minimize hearsay exceptions, because expert opinions may rely on hearsay (Fed. R. Evid. 703). Appeals of criminal convictions regarding admissibility of hearsay are common. Table 44.1 summarizes landmark English and American cases related to child witness testimony.

Children in court

Many court systems involve children directly or indirectly. Common settings for child witnesses are

1. Family court
2. Dependency or child protection courts
3. Civil court
4. Juvenile delinquency courts
5. Adult criminal courts

The first three settings are civil arenas where the child is often the primary subject of the litigation, whereas in juvenile court children are defendants or adjudicates, and in adult criminal court children are witnesses whose testimony might be the critical deciding factor influencing the outcome of the criminal trial. In child sexual abuse cases, multiple court systems are often involved: criminal, family, and dependency. The stakes, rules of evidence, and burden of proof are highest in criminal cases. Often the outcome of one case dictates the direction and outcome of another if cases span several systems.

Children are not experienced legal system participants. The concern that children will be traumatized or revictimized has been paramount for many decades. Children are often asked details about personal and often incriminating information about an important person in their lives (Tedesco and Schnell 1987). Berliner and Conte (1995) found that children reported primarily favorable experiences following disclosure of sexual abuse with increased distress related to more contacts with intervention professionals. Subsequently, a national movement to streamline the process of coordinated interviews and children advocacy centers was spawned (Henry 1997).

FAMILY COURT

In family court, the best interest of the child is the prevailing standard across the United States in custody battles. Many family court judges decide on custody of children in divorce without having the child testify. Children can find themselves involved in family court proceedings directly or indirectly as the focus of child custody disputes or as potential witnesses in their parents' legal cases of divorce or separation. If a custody evaluation is ordered or stipulated by the parties, children are always interviewed by a mental health professional or in some states by a guardian ad litem to determine the best interests of the child. The length of time spent on interviewing children ranged from 1.6 to 3.6 hours (Ackerman and Pritzl 2011). Evaluators are ethically bound not to provide custody recommendations without observing children with their parent or guardian (American Academy of Child and Adolescent Psychiatry 1997; Association of Family and Conciliation Courts 2006; American Psychological Association 2009; Martindale and Task Force for Model Standards of Practice for Child Custody Evaluation 2006).

Table 44.1 Landmark English and American cases

Case name	Description	Ruling	Significance
Rex v. Brasier (1779)	England	There is no age below which children are automatically disqualified from testifying.	Age of children to testify was addressed.
Wheeler v. US (1895)	Competency of children in a murder case involving a 5-year-old witness testifying against his father	There is no precise age that determines competency. Admissibility depends upon their ability to understand telling truth versus lies.	Age is not an exclusive witness determinant. Assessment of ability to tell the truth is critical.
Kentucky v. Stincer (1987)	Child sexual abuse case of 8-, 7-, and 5-year-olds. The defendant did not attend the competency hearing and appealed under the Confrontation Clause of the Sixth Amendment and Due Process under the Fourteenth Amendment.	The defendant's rights were not violated by not attending the competency hearing. The defendant's presence would not contribute to the fairness of the proceedings because neither girl was honest about substantive testimony.	Ratified procedures for evaluating competency of child witnesses.
Coy v. Iowa (1988)	Coy charged with sexual assault of two 13-year-old girls who were camping in the backyard of his neighbor. Neither girl could describe his face when they were assaulted. Trial court approved use of a large screen to be placed between the accused and witnesses. Defendant objected to use of screen based on Sixth Amendment Right to Confrontation and Fourteenth Amendment Right to Due Process.	Trial court rejected constitutional claims but instructed jury to draw no inference of guilt from screen. Defendant convicted of two counts of lascivious acts with a child(ren). U.S. Supreme Court held that the defendant's Sixth Amendment rights were violated.	Criminal defendants have the right to confront their witnesses to ensure fairness and integrity of the fact-finding process and make it more difficult for the witness to lie. The child's protection against facing the defendant was trumped by the Confrontation Clause of the Sixth Amendment.
Globe Newspaper v. Superior Court (1982)	Trial involved male accused of raping three minors. MA statue excluded members of the press and public from sexual offense and testimony of victims less than 18 years old. Globe challenged statue based on First Amendment violation.	U.S. Supreme Court held that the Globe Newspaper's constitutional right to face-to-face confrontation was violated. U.S. Supreme Court reversed and remanded the lower court's findings.	Exclusion of the press and public from child sexual offences cases violates the First Amendment apart from a caveat that child witnesses needed special protection.
Commonwealth v. Corbett (1989)	Defendant was charged with indecent assault and battery on a child under 14. Alleged 4-year-old victim was due to testify as the only percipient witness.	Judge found the child incompetent to testify.	Difficulties in assessing children's competency in criminal cases.
Idaho v. Wright (1990)	Female accused was charged with lewd conduct with minor, her 5-and-a-half and 2-and-a-half daughters.	Holdings of U.S. Supreme Court upheld that of the State Supreme Court and found that the pediatrician's interview techniques were unreliable and conducted in a suggestive manner.	Interviews conducted of children without video- or audiotaping and with leading questions lack trustworthiness and are not admissible.

(Continued)

Table 44.1 (*Continued*) Landmark English and American cases

Case name	Description	Ruling	Significance
Maryland v. Craig (1990)	Kindergarten owner and operator charged with first- and second-degree sexual offense of perverted sexual practice and assault and battery against a 6-year-old girl. State requested testimony via one-way closed-circuit television. Court found that courtroom testimony of the children would cause them serious emotional distress and they would stop talking and withdraw. Defendant was convicted.	The State has an interest in protecting child witness from the trauma of testifying in a child abuse case if sufficiently important to justify the use of a special procedure to avoid confrontation of the defendant. The distress must be more than *de minimis*, i.e., more than mere nervousness or reluctance. Decided on a case-by-case basis.	Child witnesses' protection to avoid confrontation of the defendant due to severe distress.
Tome v. U.S. (1995)	Divorced father charged with sexually abusing his 4-year-old daughter when she was in his custody.	Supreme Court reversed the Court of Appeals decision and held that the conditions of admissibility of some out-of-court statements where not established.	Addressed the question of whether out-of-court consistent statements made after be alleged fabrication or after alleged improper influence or motive are admissible under Federal Rules of Evidence.
Ohio v. Clark (2014)	Allegations of physical abuse of young children physically abused by their mother's boyfriend. A preschool teacher inquired about the injuries and made a child abuse report naming Clark as the perpetrator. Can a reporter become an agent for law enforcement for purposes of the Confrontation Clause and whether a child's out-of-court statements to a teacher in response to the teacher's concerns about potential child abuse qualify as "testimonial" statements subject to the Confrontation Clause?	Supreme court of Ohio reversed the lower court's conviction holding that the teacher was acting as a law enforcement agent when enquiring about the injuries. Out-of-court statements could only be admitted if the primary purpose of the teacher's questioning was to address ongoing emergency as opposed to establish past events.	Mandated reporters do not act as law enforcement agents. Out-of-court statements admitted if mandated reporter questions address immediate emergency.

Some children of divorcing parents receive therapy from mental health professionals, while the majority has no personal mental health support. Many courts appoint either a guardian ad litem or minor's attorney in complicated or high-conflict family law cases. In some jurisdictions children frequently testify in family law or criminal cases either as witnesses to domestic violence between their parents and/or to express their custodial preference.

In January 2012 California adopted Rule 5.250 allowing children to participate in family law matters on a case-by-case basis. If the child 14 years or older expresses an interest in addressing the court, the judicial officer must hear from that child unless the court makes a finding that addressing the court is not in the child's best interest and states the reasons on the record (California Rules of Court 2012). The judicial officer must consider whether the child is of sufficient age and capacity to reason to form an intelligent preference as to custody or visitation, to understand the nature of testimony. The court must determine if the child might be at risk of emotional harm or may benefit if he or she is permitted or denied the opportunity to address the court. Further the child must address issues relevant to decision making. Finally, the court must assess other factors related to the child addressing the court.

Interviews in child custody evaluations are by definition less formal, often more extensive, and follow a different format than child testimony in family court. Evaluators are trained to focus on building rapport with the child, not directly ask questions of preference (e.g., which parent do you want to live with) in order to illicit information helpful to make their recommendations to the court, whereas child witnesses are subject to formal testimony and cross-examination in an unfamiliar setting of the courtroom. Most courts close child witness testimony to the general public in family court hearings.

DEPENDENCY COURT

Children in dependency court cases are often extensively interviewed by forensic professionals: police, social workers, mental health professionals, child advocates, attorneys, and/or judges. Children in dependency court do not fare well on many indicators compared with the overall population and desire a voice in decision making (Bessell and Gal 2009).

Block et al. (2010) interviewed children in dependency court who attended their juvenile detention hearings. They found that lack of understanding and negative attitudes were common. They concluded that maltreated children may profit from greater understanding of dependency court. They also found that children often wish to have greater influence in dependency court decisions.

Runyan et al. (1988) implemented a structured psychiatric inventory of 75 sexual abuse victims at referral and 5 months later. They found that all children demonstrated a high degree of distress at the referral to Child Protective Services. They found that the anxiety in children who testified in juvenile and dependency courts improved 42% or 20 times on the Child Assessment Schedule Anxiety subscale. They concluded that testimony in juvenile court might be beneficial for the child, whereas they found that protracted criminal proceedings may have an adverse effect on the children's mental health.

In a subsequent multisite study by Whitcomb (1994) through the National Institute of Justice, they found that children showed distress at the initial interview but improvements on follow-up interviews. However, they found that repeated testimony and harsh cross-examination were found to be related to significant adverse effects.

CIVIL COURT

Children involved in civil proceedings are either witnesses or more commonly plaintiffs in civil tort actions. Legal civil cases involving children include personal injury, e.g., a motor vehicle accident or other accident, or a child sexual abuse case filed against a defendant. Children in civil cases are at the behest of their parents or guardians who have filed the action on their behalf. They are often subjected to depositions, evaluations by numerous retained experts on both sides, and testimony in court regarding the issue being litigated. Depositions can be stressful to children in different ways than testifying in open court, where they are often protected by the judge, with stricter protocols than in an attorney's office, often with many people and video cameras on. The exposure to the legal system often causes litigation stress and causes the child to relive the trauma expressly for litigation purposes.

JUVENILE DELINQUENCY COURT

Children and adolescents can also be involved in the legal system as delinquents. Teen or youth courts provide alternate early intervention dispute disposition for youths. They are staffed by youth volunteers who act in the roles of court personnel. This informal setting where a youth is judged by his or her peers might assist the delinquent in giving more informal testimony than adult court settings. Little research exists on the impact of children as witnesses in teen court.

ADULT CRIMINAL COURT

Quas et al. (2005) completed a long-term study of 174 of the original 218 child victims/witnesses involved in a short-term study 12 years prior. They found that being young at the outset of the legal case was associated with poorer later adjustment. Testifying repeatedly in cases involving severe abuse, and not testifying when the perpetrator received a light sentence, predicted poorer current mental health. When the perpetrator received a lenient sentence, more negative feelings about the legal system were felt by older children. Additionally, not having testified when the perpetrator received a light sentence predicted more negative attitudes. Greater distress predicted poorer adjustment. Older children spent more time on the witness stand (Whitcomb et al. 1991). Other forms of distress include facing and accusing the defendant (Goodman et al. 1992; Plotnikoff and Woolfson 2004).

Andrews and colleagues (2015) reviewed 120 transcripts of 6- to 12-year-old children testifying in sexual abuse trials. They found that neither prosecutors nor defense attorneys question children in developmentally appropriate ways and that children were more unresponsive to defense attorneys than to prosecutors.

Modern research on children's development and memory

Unlike most adults who are witnesses in forensic cases, children present a wide range of important factors to consider if they are called as witnesses. The child's stage of development with regard to the child's cognitive skills and memory is a critical factor to assess when the child is a witness. A 5-year-old child's ability to perceive, remember, organize, process, store, retrieve, and recall events will be vastly different from that of a 15-year-old and also different from children aged two or three.

COGNITIVE DEVELOPMENT

Children perceive the world differently than adults. A child's development is a sequential increase in the structural and/or functional complexity of a system (Yates 1996). According to Piaget's theory of cognitive development, memory constantly increases in complexity over a child's life.

Toddlers and very young children are egocentric, i.e., they are unable to perceive events and experiences from any point of view other than their own. They use *transductive reasoning*—a faulty type of logic involving making inferences from one particular to another in an illogical manner. They lack the ability to understand cause and effect. Logical contradictions are not important or appreciated. This type of thinking can easily lead to incorrect conclusions and serious ramifications in the justice system (Powell 2013).

Preschoolers (3- to 6-year-olds) become increasingly more cognitively sophisticated, and their language allows them to express themselves verbally and in writing. At around 4 years old, children enter a substage of *decentration* where they become increasingly accommodated to reality, and their own perception and interests decenter and they become aware of their own capacities. They acquire better understanding of time and space—important elements in many forensic evaluations. By this age, children's thinking becomes more logical.

Elementary school-aged children develop the ability to consider different variables. They enter the phase of concrete operations. They can distinguish between fantasy and reality, apply logic to their concrete experiences without interference of their perceptions, and put their feelings more into context. They often operate under *assumptive realities*, assumptions based on limited facts, which they do not alter in the face of contradictory evidence (Elkind 1970). In forensic settings *assumptive realities* might be the difference between conviction and acquittal.

Six or seven years old is a critical turning point in terms of a child's thinking, corresponding with entering first grade. A 6-year-old can distinguish between real and imagined events. A 3-year-old cannot. When children enter the formal operational stage (11 years old to adulthood), they develop the ability to abstract and construct.

The concept of time is often a critical issue in many forensic cases, especially in criminal cases. The ability to make accurate chronological judgments improves gradually across development (Friedman 1977, 1986, 1991, 2000; Carni and French 1984). A toddler has a relative absence of the meaningful sense of time. When toddlers are asked time frames, dates, or other time-sensitive information as part of their interview or testimony, they are unlikely to be able to describe the sequence, length, or details of events that might be out of their daily routine. Preschoolers do not comprehend relational terms (before, after, if, so, because, or, and but) until several years later, even though they spontaneously and correctly use these terms (Carni and French 1984).

Language is an important aspect with children in forensic settings. Children are not credible if they cannot communicate effectively. They might be required to offer testimony on concepts that are developmentally beyond their developmental stage (Segovia and Crossman 2012). Evans and colleagues (2009) analyzed 46 child sexual abuse case transcripts and concluded that attorneys' language influenced the accuracy of a child's testimony. Complex questions asked by defense attorneys predicted convictions rather than acquittals.

Lawyers and judges are rarely experts or even educated in the area of child development and psychology. Their jargonistic language is confusing to many adults and a foreign language to children. Young children's articulation is often not mastered in preschool children, therefore leading them to be misunderstood when interviewed. Their vocabulary is limited, thereby limiting their ability to provide details and descriptions of important facets of a case.

Competency, honesty, and credibility are critical factors in any forensic evaluation. In the courtroom a witness can only testify if he or she is sworn in. Children's competency to understand the oath is essential for the legal process. Evans and Lyon (2012) conducted a study with 164 child witnesses in criminal child sexual abuses cases tried in Los Angeles County and 154 child witnesses in U.S. State and Federal Appellate cases. They found that judges almost never found children incompetent to testify, but children exhibited substantial variability in their performance based on question type, and the children's truth–lie competency is underestimated by courtroom questioning.

Cognitive development encompasses the process of moral development. Children learn to lie very early in their development; however, children under the age of 3 have difficulty carrying out more sophisticated deceit. To understand the concept of a lie, children must understand the concept of truth. A child's ability to lie is related to his or her specific stage of cognitive development. Additionally, social and motivational factors affect their honesty (Talwar and Crossman 2012). Bussey and Grimbeek (2000) studied children's knowledge about and evaluation of lies and truths and concluded that 4-year-olds have sufficient understanding of lying and truth-telling competence to participate effectively in the legal system.

Memory of events and information is a critical element in forensic cases. There is a plethora of research about memory development and suggestibility with regard to children as witnesses in forensic settings. Most commonly children in legal proceedings are asked and expected to describe events that occurred in the past—it could be the immediate past in cases where children are interviewed within hours or days of the event, or years later, e.g., when a criminal or civil case goes to trial.

Memory is a complicated flow of information through a system that stores, organizes, encodes, and retrieves. Information can be lost at any stage. Memory can be divided into procedural, episodic, and semantic memory storage. Procedural memory involves remembering how to accomplish learned tasks such as tying one's shoelaces. Episodic memory stores up autobiographical memory (recalling oneself in an event). Semantic memory stores knowledge representations or general knowledge (Williams et al. 2008). Information gathered in testimony relies on declarative memory or episodic memory. Until about 3 years of age, autobiographical memory rarely persists to allow recall and reporting of an experienced event (Fivush 1994, 1997). Humphries et al. (2012) found that children as young as 5 years old can still be accurate in identifying culprits from video lineups. However, age was also significantly associated with accuracy. Testimony mostly relies on declarative-type memory or episodic memory, i.e., information linked to occurrences and, even more specifically, autobiographical memory. The development of autobiographical memory marks the emergence at which children can be expected to give testimony (Gordon et al. 2001).

SUGGESTIBILITY

Suggestibility is the ease of influence and persuasiveness to questions in a leading interview in which one accepts and changes his or her own judgments, opinions, or patterns of behavior (Drukteinis 2001).

A pivotal case of widespread suggestibility in young children was the California McMartin case in which over 350 preschoolers were interviewed with highly suggestive methods of questioning and led to false allegations of widespread child sexual abuse that were widely fanciful and bizarre, such as flying witches, secret tunnels under the school, orgies, children being flushed down toilets, and naked movie star games. The multimillion-dollar trial devastated the accused but ultimately led to reform of research of childhood sexual abuse. Not all children are suggestible though. Even in the McMartin case, some children were resistant to suggestive questioning.

Most of the research regarding suggestibility in children has focused on interview techniques. Principe et al. (2006) found that peer and family conversations were a common source of influence of child witness testimony. They studied how an erroneous rumor circulated among preschoolers can influence their memory. They found that naturally occurring conversations and interactions with classmates were as likely to report experiencing rumored events that they did not experience as were those who actually experienced it. Further, most of the reports of the rumored but nonexperienced events were in children's free recall, and were accompanied by high levels of fictitious elaboration. This finding is a powerful tool for attorneys in a wide range of cases including child custody, sexual abuse, and child neglect and physical abuse cases to discredit child witnesses.

FACTORS INFLUENCING CHILDREN'S MEMORY

Children's testimony is dependent on many variables including their age, exposure to trauma, traumatic reaction related to the event or events in question, time elapsed from the event to the testimony or interview, repeated interviews, prior knowledge, race and socioeconomic status, gender, interview aids, influence from authority figures, and interviewer bias.

Children as young as 3 or 4 years old can remember and report events with enough clarity and accuracy to assist triers of fact in rendering a verdict (Hershkowitz et al. 2012; Powell 2013). Three year-olds can provide information about experienced events; however, the ability to provide narrative responses to open-ended recall prompts only becomes reliable later in development. Even very young children can provide rich accounts of their experiences (Bahrick et al. 1998) that can endure for long periods of time (Schwartzmueller et al. 1996; Howard et al. 1997; Peterson 1999; Gordon et al. 2001).

When children have to testify about numerous events and not one single event, the accuracy of their recollection can be questionable depending on their age. Roberts et al. (2015) found that older children were more able than younger children to judge relative order of occurrences and that they remembered the first and last occurrences compared to the middle occurrences in older children, while younger children only remembered the first occurrence.

Older children are able to reconstruct a narrative in response to simpler prompts such as "what happened?" Several researchers studied the effect of free recall. Dent and Stephenson (1979) found that the free report produced highly accurate but incomplete recall. Further, Poole and Lindsay (2001), Goodman et al. (1994), and Greenhoot (2000) found that contrary to urban myth, children's spontaneous statements and free recall statements are not error free. Children's free-recall and spontaneous statements are generally more accurate than their responses to directed questions.

Our past experiences shape our perception of events. For children, their experiences in the world are exponentially limited compared to those of adults. Every day adds a new experience to their repertoire and therefore shapes their memory and subsequently their perceptions of the world. In legal proceedings the accuracy of children's memories is influenced by their experiences in the world and also is dependent on culturally based stereotypes (race, sex, mental illness) developed during preschool years (Corrigan and Watson 2007). Leichtman and Ceci (1995) conducted a study about delays in reporting events, stereotypes, and suggestibility. They found that children's stereotypes and influence by others can result in inaccurate memory of an event.

MEMORY AND TRAUMA

Children's memory for recalling traumatic incidents has been the subject of debate for many decades. Highly traumatic events are imprinted more than everyday routine events due to the level of emotionality and often the drama surrounding the event e.g. police involvement, injuries, removal of children from their parents. However, live courtroom testimony can be an emotionally traumatic experience for many children.

There is also a curvilinear relationship between very stressful events and less optimal memory performance. The risk of increased stress or recalling trauma is high. Low levels of stress illicit low levels of attention to memory. Moderate levels of stress can enhance recall. Higher levels of stress are predictive of lower levels of remembering (Ornstein 1995; Pezdek and Taylor 2002). The correlation between increased cortisol levels during stressful events is well documented. High levels of cortisol affect the hippocampus, thereby affecting memory retrieval (Quesada et al. 2012). However, stressful events can also cause imprinting due to the high emotionality of the event and therefore lead to stronger memories due to the personal meaning of the event.

Memory of public events, such as the September 11 terrorist attacks, are described as flashbulb memories. Memories are also anchored to events with high levels of trauma and stress. These memories are embedded like a photograph and are thought to be highly accurate and fixed due to overstimulation of the event (Segovia and Crossman 2012). Research has shown that retrospective accounts of traumatic events for persons with higher levels of posttraumatic stress disorder (PTSD) symptoms may be associated with amplified recollections of the precipitating events and may be more prone to alteration over time (Engelhard et al. 2008). Therefore, stress and trauma, especially if PTSD is present, can greatly affect the accuracy of a child's testimony in forensic settings. Alexander et al. (2005) found that the severity of PTSD symptomatology was positively associated with memory accuracy in adults recalling their past childhood sexual abuse.

Research in the area of child witnesses is limited to post-testimony reporting because randomized controlled studies are not possible or ethical. Tedesco and Schnell (1987) studied the effects of litigation based on the assumption that involvement in the court process further victimizes children. The authors sent questionnaires to victims of child sexual abuse and revealed that only 21% of the victims perceived that the questioning and investigation were harmful while 53% found it helpful. Court testimony and repeated interviews revealed more negative ratings.

The Academy of Child and Adolescent Psychiatry (AACAP) released a position paper in 1989 warning of the serious potential for trauma and serious stress to children involved in court proceedings. The position paper recommends modifications to allow children a safe way to participate in the legal system, such as limiting the number of interviews of child victims, coordinating court proceedings by single thorough, investigation shared between investigators and prosecutors, expedient court proceedings, modifications to hearsay and other evidentiary and courtroom restrictions, and assessment of child witnesses by forensic examiners.

REPEATED INTERVIEWS

There has not been consensus on the issue of repeated interviews of child victims. A study conducted by Bruck (2002) concluded that repeated interviews lead to errors in the forensic process. Other studies revealed that repeated interviewing increased the accuracy of testimony or had no adverse effect (Goodman et al. 1991; Baker-Ward et al. 1993). Pipe (1999) found that whereas information repeated across interviews was highly accurate, information reported for the first time after long delays was not.

INTERVIEWER BIAS

According to Bruck and Ceci (2002), the concept of interviewer bias (Ceci and Bruck 1995) is a defining feature of suggestive interviews. Interviewer bias is described as those interviewers who hold a priori beliefs about the occurrence of certain events and who mold the interview to maximize disclosures that are consistent with those prior beliefs. One hallmark of interviewer bias is the single-minded attempt by an interviewer to gather only confirmatory evidence and to avoid all avenues that may produce disconfirmatory evidence. Inconsistent or bizarre evidence is either ignored or interpreted within the framework consistent with the interviewer's hypothesis. Authenticity of statements is not challenged when it aligns with the interviewer's beliefs. Inconsistent statements are subject to repeated questioning designed to align the child's subsequent reports with the interviewer's initial beliefs.

RACE AND SOCIOECONOMIC

The research is lacking in considering race or socioeconomic status influencing suggestibility and false memory. Bruck (2004) synthesized 69 studies and found that language ability and creativity are consistently related to suggestibility. Race is often associated with intelligence and language. Given the disproportionate number of minority children in criminal proceedings (Vernon-Feagans 2002), child witness language skills is a concern when children are forensically interviewed.

GENDER

Bruck (2004) analyzed the result of 20 studies examining the possible link between gender and suggestibility. Only four studies found significant differences and the results were inconsistent. No definitive consensus has been reached answering questions of gender relationship of witnesses to suggestibility.

KNOWLEDGE ABOUT LEGAL SYSTEM

In international legal settings, studies have shown that children experience more distress when they lack knowledge of the legal system. Ben-Arieh (2007) found that adolescents in the Israeli legal system were subsequently more willing to cooperate with police when they had victim support through the legal process.

ANATOMICAL DOLLS

The use of anatomical dolls in child sexual abuse forensic evaluations continues to stir debate. Most research has led to negative and critical reviews for anatomical dolls for decades (Bruck 1995, 2000, 2009; Salmon 2001, 2011; Willcock 2006; Brown 2007, 2011; Poole 2011; Poole and Dickinson 2011; Otgaar 2012). Few authors support the use of anatomical dolls (Faller 2005; Anderson 2010; Hlavka 2010). Despite the long-standing controversy over the use of anatomical dolls in sexual abuse investigations, they continued to be used and are the subject of numerous appeals *Lee v. Lampert* (2011), *Kraus v. Taylor* (2013), *US v. Chaco* (2011), and *Spencer v. Peters* (2013). Due to the lack of consensus of the use of anatomically correct dolls, California has barred the admissibility of evidence collected through the use of anatomically correct dolls.

The use of non-verbal aids in forensic interviews has met with similar disagreements as the use of anatomically correct dolls. Several studies, Salmon (2012), Barton (2014),

Brown et al. (2012b) have cautioned against the use of non-verbal aids such as diagrams. Lyon (2012) recommended the use of non-verbal aids as a last resort after the disclosure section of the NICHD protocol and only when a subsequent interview is not practical or when delay endangers the child.

Special needs in child witnesses

INTELLECTUAL DISABILITIES

Children with intellectual disabilities are more vulnerable to abuse (Crosse 1993; Sedlak 1996a; Randall 2000; Balogh 2001; Hershkowitz et al. 2007; Reiter 2007) and are less likely to report the abuse or have their complaints investigated (Goldman 1994; Sharp 2001; Reiter 2007). Children with intellectual disabilities are also more suggestible than typically developing children (Henry 1999; Michel 2000).

Henry (2011) found lower perceptions of credibility for child witnesses with intellectual disability compared to typically developing child witnesses. Brown et al. (2012a) found that children with mild intellectual disabilities were as able as their mental age matches, but even though children with more severe cognitive impairments had qualitatively different competencies, they could be highly accurate in a supportive interview forensic setting. Further, more detailed responding is expected by mainstream children than those with intellectual disabilities (Gordon et al. 1994; Henry 2007, 2011).

Court testimony of children

PREPARATION

Lipovsky (1997) recommended the following goals to prepare children for court experiences: "to improve the child's ability to answer questions in court in the most accurate, complete, and truthful manner; to maximize the child's ability to be perceived as a credible witness; to minimize the likelihood that the child will suffer negative court-related consequences." Preparing a child does not mean coaching the child about how they should respond on the witness stand. Court preparation can include group classes in which the children might realize they are not alone in the process or individualized preparation by court personnel, mental health professionals, and volunteers (Finnegan 2002).

JURY PERCEPTION

Buck et al. (2014) studied the knowledge of jury-eligible college students, investigative interviewers, forensic psychologists, and public defenders with regard to interviewing children. Jury-eligible students were the least knowledgeable. Both investigative interviewers and public defenders performed better than jury-eligible students, but lacked substantial knowledge about the research on interviewing children on certain topics (e.g., using anatomically detailed dolls); forensic psychologists were the most knowledgeable.

CROSS-EXAMINATION

Most courts prefer to protect children from testifying in court because of the inherent risks and stress of court proceedings. Cross-examination is a stressful experience for even a seasoned expert witness. The effect of cross-examination-style questioning of child witnesses was studied by O'Neil and Zajac (2013a) concluded that cross-examination-style questioning is particularly detrimental to obtaining accurate event reports from children. Fogliati and Bussey (2015) found that cross-examination led children who were not coached to recant their initial true allegations and reduced children's accuracy for neutral events. In another study by Fogliati and Bussey (2014) they found that cross-examination may not be the most effective procedure for eliciting truthful testimony from children aged between 5 and 8 years. Stolzenberg (2013) found that pressing child witnesses to answer questions they are initially reluctant to answer is not an effective practice.

Children also risk losing credibility because they often change their incorrect and correct answers in response to cross examination. Zajac (2003) found that child witnesses rarely asked for clarification and often attempted to answer questions that were ambiguous or did not make sense, and 75% changed at least one aspect of their testimony. Cross-examination-style questioning is inappropriate for young children.

Special considerations for child sexual abuse

Most of the research of children's testimony in court has focused on child sexual abuse victims. Children's testimony often involves traumatic and intimate experiences which they have witnessed or been a victim of. Whitcomb (2003) found that children have multiple fears about testifying in court, and identified four factors as most frightening:

1. Facing the defendant
2. Describing details of the abuse
3. Testifying in front of strangers
4. Not understanding all the questions asked

There are typically two types of expert testimony challenged in child sexual abuse cases: (1) general testimony describing behaviors and other characteristics commonly observed in sexually abused victims ("profile" testimony); and (2) particularized testimony concerning the alleged victim's credibility. Numerous courts have ruled in favor of expert witness admissibility in child abuse cases: *State v. Sloan* (1995), *Barlow v. State* (1998), *State of Ohio v. Gersin* (1996).

Child witness interview techniques and guidelines

There are many risks to the forensic process if children are not interviewed in formal forensic settings such as police interviews, or by forensically trained medical or mental health professionals. Mandated reporters of child abuse are legally required to report reasonable suspicion of child abuse. This low threshold is meant to ensure that the baton for further investigation is handed to government agencies specializing in forensic investigations of child abuse. In reality the majority of initial disclosures of child abuse are to a medical professional as part of a routine evaluation or treatment (Suddath 2003) or schoolteachers. Pediatricians who are the first witness to the disclosure of child abuse are rarely forensically trained. By nature they are inquisitive and attempt to gather more details about the abuse. However, the information they gather is often not recorded in a manner compatible with the rigors of the legal system and interviews are rarely documented that include exact quotes of the questions and responses.

Comprehensive pretrial interventions utilizing a practice–feedback approach help children to give more accurate testimony when cross-examined (O'Neil and Zajac 2013b). Many elements need to be in place to prepare children for forensic interviews and maximize the utility of the information collected. Ideally, the timing of the interview is best done as proximate to the events or events, especially since children's memories are fluidly changing and developing. Additionally, the risk of contamination by external influences such as peer or family pressure increases. In reality there is often a significant time lag between the event in question and forensic interviews. Selecting age-appropriate interview procedures requires developmental sensitivity (Saywitz 1998, 2013).

In order to limit the number of interviews, it might be possible to gather questions from different sources such as defense attorneys and prosecutors before proceeding with the interview. McGough (1996) suggested an extension of this interview process in which the defense and prosecuting attorneys observe the interview and interject their questions during breaks. The setting of the forensic interview might also help alleviate anxiety and maximize factual information gathering to optimize the forensic process.

The American Professional Society on the Abuse of Children Practice Guidelines Series (2002) recommend interviewing children in Child Advocacy Centers. Traditionally child interviews have been conducted at police stations, child protective services offices, homes, and schools. All of these settings have inherent problems that might increase the anxiety or compromise evidence gathering. Although the presence of an adult support person might alleviate anxiety, it is recommended that forensic interviews are conducted alone with the child (Poole and Lamb 1998). In the courtroom the presence of a support person, transitional object, such as a stuffed animal or toy, and closed-circuit testimony might be beneficial for the child witness.

Forensic interviews are part of the evidence in many cases. A record of the interview by audiotaping, videotaping, or both, provides optimal evidence (Bertel 2012). Some states, such as Idaho and Utah, mandate that all investigative interviews of suspected child abuse must be audio or video recorded (Idaho Code 2011; Utah Code 2011). At least 12 states have statutes that discuss the admissibility of video-recorded forensic interviews as evidence in criminal cases of child abuse (Kellogg 2005).

GUIDELINES

The area of child sexual and physical abuse has been well researched over the past 30 years. Many organizations have set forth guidelines for forensic interviews of children. In 2000, The *Eunice Kennedy Shriver* National Institute of Child Health and Human Development (NICHD) developed a protocol for child sexual abuse allegations called the NICHD Investigative Interview Protocol. The NICHD protocol has been translated into multiple languages and is available online.

Court testimony of a child: Role of the mental health professional

Mental health professionals are often experts or consultants at many levels of the legal system when children are involved. Their roles are varied, from treatment provider to court-appointed expert to consultants and educators to attorneys, families, judges, and law enforcement. They might provide expert testimony about children's testimony in court or give opinions about the psychological impact on the child with respect to the event or events they witnessed, experienced, or are living, as in child custody disputes.

Experts can opine on the competency of a child to testify, e.g., in juvenile delinquency cases as defendants or in civil or criminal cases as witnesses. If the child is deemed competent to provide testimony, the mental health professional might be used as a consultant to the attorneys examining or cross-examining the witness. They might evaluate whether the child should testify in court or through closed-circuit television. They might prepare the child for testimony and treat anticipatory anxiety prior to and after testimony.

Competency is determined by the judicial officer in most cases. However, forensic mental health experts are often asked to evaluate on competency issues for children in court. The standards for competency to testify are similar to those of adults and involve perception, memory, and truth–lie competency; the understanding of the difference between the truth and a lie and the duty to tell the truth (Myers 1993; Lyon 2011).

Competency is different than credibility. Only the triers of fact (judge and/or jury) make the ultimate determination of the credibility of a witness. Experts might opine as to the consistency of statements made by a child in an investigation and relate them to the multiple developmental facets of child witnesses. In all forensic settings the expert's role is to give neutral, balanced opinions based on evidence. They should describe strengths and weaknesses of the child's testimony with respect to the aspects of the case, supported by research if applicable. The expert might opine on whether the method of forensic interviewing met standards and was valid or describe the flaws in the interview technique (Poole et al. 2015).

The importance of expert testimony in child sexual abuse cases was studied by Buck et al. (2011). They found that mock jurors were more likely to render guilty verdicts if the interview quality was good versus poor. Further expert testimony increased mock jurors' knowledge about child witnesses. Expert testimony on proper interview techniques may bolster the prosecution in cases where the child was interviewed in a high-quality manner.

SUMMARY

Children can be effective witnesses in forensic investigations. Research is consistent that even very young children have accurate recall of events and can assist authorities in making accurate determinations of the truth in the justice system. The general core difference between adult and child witnesses is the developmental trajectory of children compared to the relatively static cognition of adults. Research has primarily centered on very young or young children under 6 or 7 years old. There is far less research material on latency-aged children or adolescents as witnesses, most likely due to the rapid upward gradient of cognitive and memory changes in very young and young children. Studies of older children are often compared to adults and have found less variability in their suggestibility than with younger children. The social influences during adolescence such as peer pressure, emerging sexuality, and views on authority figures are areas for future research. Additionally, in the rapidly changing era of social media in which adolescents are almost universally ensconced, the influences from numerous media are a potential area for studies of adolescents in the legal system.

The area of interviewing techniques and protocols has gained greater definition over the past 20 years. Numerous protocols have been developed, all of them with a common goal of obtaining valid, uncontaminated, admissible evidence by trained forensic evaluators to assist in the pursuit of justice. Further refinement and possibly merging of the numerous interview protocols is likely. However, it is possible that all the protocols and guidelines have validity and are the result of the mission of the respective legislative bodies, associations, agencies, and academies.

The subject of witness in child sexual abuse cases overwhelms the research data. While child sexual abuse is a serious and sensitive issue, children are often involved in legal proceedings in many other arenas: civil litigation, dependency, and other nonsexual abuse criminal matters such as domestic violence. There is little research on child witnesses in many of these areas.

Children are now more protected in court settings with the advent of closed-circuit television to provide testimony, but also by more refined investigative interviewing techniques. In 2012, California introduced rules of court to allow evidence from children in family law cases if they wanted their voice to be heard. Given this recent change, there is little research available studying the pros and cons of children being more intricately involved in their parents' divorce.

There is plentiful data about child witnesses with intellectual disabilities, but there is little research available regarding the effects on child witnesses with mental illnesses when they are in the legal system. Children with mental illness are also a vulnerable group and are at risk of abuse.

Further, the long-term effect on children involved in the legal system is an area that is often overlooked and poorly researched. In civil litigation, literally the million-dollar question is the long-term effects of trauma (personal injury or abuse) and how that relates to damages. Such studies are often difficult and long term, making it almost impossible to conduct due to ethical considerations, but also due to the infinite number of variables that might affect a person's path through life after experiencing trauma as a child.

REFERENCES

Ackerman MJ and TB Pritzl. 2011. Child custody evaluation practices: A 20-year follow-up. *Family Court Review* 49(3):618–628.

Alexander KW, JA Quas, GS Goodman, S Ghetti, RS Edelstein, AD Redlich, and DP Jones. 2005. Traumatic impact predicts long-term memory for documented child sexual abuse. *Psychological Science* 16(1):33–40.

American Academy of Child and Adolescent Psychiatry (AACAP). 1986. *Policy Statement: Protecting Children Undergoing Abuse Investigations and Testimony.* https://www.aacap.org/aacap/policy_statements/1986/Protecting_Children_Undergoing_Abuse_Investigations_and_Testimony.aspx, accessed November 1, 2015.

American Professional Society on the Abuse of Children. 2002. *Investigative Interviewing in Cases of Alleged Child Abuse.* Charleston, SC: APSAC Practice Guidelines Series.

Anderson J, J Ellefson, J Lashley et al. 2010. The cornerhouse forensic interview protocol: RATAC. *Thomas M. Cooley Journal of Practical and Clinical Law* 12:193–332.

Andrews SJ, ME Lamb, and TD Lyon. 2015. Question types, responsiveness and self-contradictions when prosecutors and defense attorneys question alleged victims of child sexual abuse. *Applied Cognitive Psychology* 29(2):253–261.

Bahrick L, JF Parker, R Fivush, and M Levitt. 1998. The effects of stress on young children's memory for a natural disaster. *Journal of Experimental Psychology: Applied* 4(4):308–331.

Baker-Ward L, BN Gordon, PA Ornstein, DM Larus, and PA Clubb. 1993. Young children''s long-term retention of a pediatric examination. *Child Development* 64(5):1519–1533.

Balogh R, K Bretherton, S Whibley, T Berney, S Graham, P Richold, and H Firth. 2001. Sexual abuse in children and adolescents with intellectual disability. *Journal of Intellectual Disability Research* 45:4–201.

Barlow v. State, 507 S.E.2d 416 270 GA 54 (1998).

Barton R. 2014. *Using Photographs and Human Body Diagrams as Visual Aids to Help Children Talk About Bodily Touch.* http://hdl.handle.net/10063/3335, accessed November 2,2015.

Ben-Arieh A and V Windman 2007. Secondary victimization of children in Israel and the child's perspective. *International Review of Victimology* 14(3):321–336.

Berliner L and J Conte. 1995. The effects of disclosure and intervention on sexually abused children. *Child Abuse and Neglect* 19(3):371–384.

Bertel O. 2012. Let's to the videotape: Why the forensic interviews of children in child protective cases should be video recorded. *Family Court Review* 50(2):344–356.

Bessell S and T Gal. 2009. Forming partnerships: The human rights of children in need of care and protection. *International Journal of Children's Rights* 17(2):283–298.

Block SD, H Oran, D Oran, N Baumrind, and GS Goodman. 2010. Abused and neglected children in court: Knowledge and attitudes. *Child Abuse and Neglect* 34(9):659–670.

Brown D, M Pipe, C Lewis, M Lamb, and Y Orbach. 2007. Supportive or suggestive: Do human figure drawings help 5- to 7-year-old children report touch. *Journal of Consulting and Clinical Psychology* 75:33–42.

Brown D, ME Pipe, C Lewis, ME Lamb, and Y Orbach. 2012a. How do body diagrams affect the accuracy and consistency of children's reports of bodily touch across repeated interviews? *Applied Cognitive Psychology* 26(2):174–181.

Brown DA. 2011. The use of supplementary techniques in forensic interviews with children. In *Children's Testimony: A Handbook of Psychological Research and Forensic Practice*, 2nd edition, edited by ME Lamb, D La Rooy, LC Malloy, and C Katz, New York: Wiley, 217–249.

Brown DA, CN Lewis, ME Lamb, and E Stephens. 2012b. The influences of delay and severity of intellectual disability on event memory in children. *Journal of Consulting and Clinical Psychology* 80(5):829–841.

Bruck M. 2009. Human figure drawings and children's recall of touching. *Journal of Experimental Psychology: Applied* 15:361–374.

Bruck M and SJ Ceci. 2002. Reliability and suggestibility of children's statements: From science to practice. In *Comprehensive Textbook in Child and Adolescent Forensic Psychiatry*, edited by D Schetky and E Benedict, Washington, DC: American Psychiatric Association, 137–148.

Bruck M, SJ Ceci, and Francoeur E. 2000. Children's use of anatomically detailed dolls to report genital touching in a medical examination: Developmental and gender comparisons. *Journal of Experimental Psychology: Applied* 6(1):74.

Bruck M, SJ Ceci, E Francouer, and A Renick. 1995. Anatomically detailed dolls do not facilitate preschoolers' reports of a pediatric examination involving genital touching. *Journal of Experimental Psychology: Applied* 1(2):95.

Bruck M, SJ Ceci, and H Hembrooke. 2002. The nature of children's true and false narratives. *Developmental Review* 22(3):520–554.

Bruck M and L Melnyk. 2004. Individual differences in children's suggestibility: A review and synthesis. *Applied Cognitive Psychology* 18(8):947–996.

Buck JA, K London, and DB Wright. 2011. Expert testimony regarding child witnesses: Does it sensitize jurors to forensic interview quality? *Law and Human Behavior* 35(2):152.

Buck JA, AR Warren, M Bruck, and K Kuehnle. 2014. How common is common knowledge about child witnesses among legal professionals? Comparing interviewers, public defenders, and forensic psychologists with laypeople. *Behavioral Sciences and the Law* 32(6):867–883.

Bussey K and EJ Grimbeek. 2000. Children's conceptions of lying and truth-telling: Implications for child witnesses. *Legal and Criminological Psychology* 5(2):187–189.

California Rules of Court 5.250, effective January 1, 2012.

Carni E and LA French. 1984. The acquisition of before and after reconsidered: What develops? *Journal of Experimental Child Psychology* 37(2):394–403.

Cashmore J and N De Haas. 1992. *The Use of Closed-Circuit Television for Child Witnesses in the ACT (Vol. 1).* Sydney, Australia: Australian Law Reform Commission.

Ceci SJ and M Bruck. 1995. *Jeopardy in the Courtroom: A Scientific Analysis of Children's Testimony.* Washington, DC: American Psychological Association.

Commonwealth v. Corbett, 533 N.E.2d 207, 26 Mass. App. Ct. 773, 26 Mass App 773 (App. Ct. 1989).

Corrigan PW and AC Watson. 2007. How children stigmatize people with mental illness. *International Journal of Social Psychiatry* 53(6):526–546.

Coy v. Iowa, 487 U.S. 1012, 108 S. Ct. 2798, 101 L. Ed. 2d 857 (1988).

Crosse SB, E Kaye, and AC Ratnofsky. 1993. *A Report on the Maltreatment of Children with Disabilities*. Washington, DC: National Center on Child Abuse and Neglect.

Dent HR and GM Stephenson. 1979. An experimental study of the effectiveness of different techniques of questioning child witnesses. *British Journal of Social and Clinical Psychology* 18(1):41–51.

Drukteinis AM. 2001. The role of suggestibility in mental damage claims. *American Journal of Clinical Psychiatry and Law* 26:15–35.

Elkind D. 1970. *Children and Adolescents: Interpretive Essays on Jean Piaget*. New York: Oxford University Press.

Engelhard IM, MA van den Hout, and RJ McNally. 2008. Memory consistency for traumatic events in Dutch soldiers deployed to Iraq. *Memory* 16(1):3–9.

Evans AD, K Lee, and TD Lyon. 2009. Complex questions asked by defense lawyers but not prosecutors predicts convictions in child abuse trials. *Law and Human Behavior* 33(3):258–264.

Evans AD and TD Lyon. 2012. Assessing children's competency to take the oath in court: The influence of question type on children's accuracy. *Law and Human Behavior* 36(3):5.

Faller KC. 2005. Anatomical dolls: Their use in assessment of children who may have been sexually abused. *Journal of Child Sexual Abuse* 14:1–21.

Federal Rules of Evidence 703.

Federal Rules of Evidence 801.

Federal Rules of Evidence 803(2).

Federal Rules of Evidence 803(4).

Federal Rules of Evidence, Title 28 U.S.C.A. 601–615 (1984).

Finnegan MJ and S Gothard. 2002. Preparing children for court. In *The Handbook of Juvenile Forensic Psychology*, edited by NG Ribner, San Francisco: Jossey- Bass, 454–469.

Fivush R. 1994. Young children's event recall: Are memories constructed through discourse. *Consciousness and Cognition* 3:356–373.

Fivush R. 1997. Event memory in early childhood. In *The Development of Memory in Childhood*, edited by N Cowan. Hove, England: Psychology Press, 139–161.

Fogliati R and K Bussey. 2014. Effects of cross-examination on children's reports of neutral and transgressive events. *Legal and Criminological Psychology* 19(2):296–315.

Fogliati R and K Bussey. 2015. The effects of cross-examination on children's coached reports. *Psychology, Public Policy, and Law* 21(1):10–23.

Friedman WJ. 1977. The development of children's understanding of cyclic aspects of time. *Child Development* 48:1593–1599.

Friedman WJ. 1986. The development of children's knowledge of temporal structure. *Child Development* 57:1386–1400.

Friedman WJ. 1991. The development of children's memory for the time of past events. *Child Development* 62(1):139–155.

Friedman WJ. 2000. The development of children's knowledge of the times of future events. *Child Development* 71(4):913–932.

Globe Newspaper Co. v. Superior Court, County of Norfolk, 457 U.S. 596, 102 S. Ct. 2613, 73 L. Ed. 2d 248 (1982).

Goldman R. 1994. Children and youth with intellectual disabilities: Targets for sexual abuse. *International Journal of Disability, Development and Education* 41:89–102.

Goodman GS, BL Bottoms, BM Schwartz-Kenney, and L Rudy. 1991. Children's testimony about a stressful event: Improving children's reports. *Journal of Narrative and Life History* 1(1):69–99.

Goodman GS, JA Quas, JM Batterman-Faunce, MM Riddlesberger, and J Kuhn. 1994. Predictors of accurate and inaccurate memories of traumatic events experienced in childhood. *Consciousness and Cognition* 3:269–294.

Goodman GS, EP Taub, DP Jones, P England, LK Port, L Rudy, and GB Melton. 1992. Testifying in criminal court: Emotional effects on child sexual assault victims. *Monographs of the Society for Research in Child Development* 57(5):1–142.

Gordon BN, L Baker-Ward, and PA Ornstein. 2001. Children's testimony: A review of research on memory for past experiences. *Clinical Child and Family Psychology Review* 4(2):157–181.

Gordon BN, KG Jens, R Hollings, and TE Watson. 1994. Remembering activities performed versus those imagined: Implications for testimony of children with mental retardation. *Journal of Clinical Child Psychology* 23:239–248.

Greenhoot AF. 2000. Remembering and understanding: The effects of changes in underlying knowledge on children's recollections. *Child Development* 71(5):1309–1328.

Grossberg M. 1996. *A Judgement for Solomon: The D'Hauteville Case and Legal Experience in Antebellum America*. New York: Cambridge University Press, 163–164.

Henry J. 1997. System intervention trauma to child sexual abuse victims following disclosure. *Journal of Interpersonal Violence* 12(4):459–512.

Henry L, A Ridley, J Perry, and L Crane. 2011. Perceived credibility and eyewitness testimony of children with intellectual disabilities. *Journal of Intellectual Disability Research* 55:385–391.

Henry LA and GH Gudjonsson. 1999. Eyewitness memory and suggestibility in children with mental retardation. *American Journal on Mental Retardation* 104:491–508.

Henry LA and GH Gudjonsson. 2007. Individual and developmental differences in eyewitness recall and suggestibility in children with intellectual disabilities. *Applied Cognitive Psychology* 21:361–381.

Hershkowitz I, ME Lamb, and D Horowitz. 2007. Victimization of children with disabilities. *American Journal of Orthopsychiatry* 77:629–635.

Hershkowitz I, ME Lamb, Y Orbach, C Katz, and D Horowitz. 2012. The development of communicative and narrative skills among preschoolers: Lessons from forensic interviews about child abuse. *Child Development* 83(2): 611.

Hlavka HR, SO Olinger, and JL Lashley. 2010. The use of anatomical dolls as a demonstration aid in child sexual abuse interviews: A study of forensic interviewers' perceptions. *Journal of Child Sexual Abuse* 19(5):519–553.

Howard AN, HL Osborne, and L Baker-Ward. 1997. Childhood cancer survivors' memory of their treatment after long delays. Poster presented at the *Biennial Meeting of the Society for Research in Child Development*, Washington, DC.

Humphries JE, RE Holliday, and HD Flowe. 2012. Faces in motion: Age-related changes in eyewitness identification performance in simultaneous, sequential, and elimination video lineups. *Applied Cognitive Psychology* 26(1):149–158.

Idaho Code Ann. § 16-1618 (West 2011).

Idaho v. Wright, 497 U.S. 805, 110 S. Ct. 3139, 111 L. Ed. 2d 638 (1990).

Kraus v. Taylor, 715 F.3d 589 (6th Cir. 2013).

Kellogg N. 2005. The evaluation of sexual abuse in children. *Pediatrics* 116(2):506–512.

Kentucky v. Stincer, 482 U.S. 730, 107 S. Ct. 2658, 96 L. Ed. 2d 631 (1987).

Lee v. Lampert, 653 F.3d 929 (9th Cir. 2011).

Leichtman MD and SJ Ceci. 1995. The effects of stereotypes and suggestions on preschoolers' reports. *Developmental Psychology* 31(4):568–578.

Lipovsky J and P Stern. 1997. Preparing children for court: An interdisciplinary view. *Child Maltreatment* 2(2):150–163.

Lyon TD. 2011. Assessing the competency of child witnesses: Best practice informed by psychology and law. In *Children's Testimony: A Handbook of Psychological Research and Forensic Practice*, edited by ME Lamb, DJ La Rooy, LC Malloy, and C Katz, Chichester, UK: Wiley, 69–85.

Lyon TD. 2012. Twenty-five years of interviewing research and practice: Dolls, diagrams, and the dynamics of abuse disclosure. *APSAC (American Professional Society on the Abuse of Children) Advisor* 24(1–2):14–19.

Martindale D and Task Force for Model Standards of Practice for Child Custody Evaluation. 2006. *Models Standards of Practice for Child Custody Evaluations*. Association of Family and Conciliation Courts. http://www.afccnet.org/Portals/0/ModelStdsChildCustodyEvalSept2006.pdf?ver=2013-08-21-071826-000

Maryland v. Craig, 497 U.S. 836, 110 S. Ct. 3157, 111 L. Ed. 2d 666 (1990).

McAuliff BD and MB Kovera. 2002. The status of evidentiary and procedural innovations in child abuse proceedings. In *Children, Social Science, and the Law*, edited by BL Bottoms, MB Kovera, and BD McAuliff, New York: Cambridge University Press, 412–445.

McAuliff BD, E Nicholson, D Amarilio, and D Ravanshenas. 2013. Supporting children in US legal proceedings: Descriptive and attitudinal data from a national survey of victim/witness assistants. *Psychology, Public Policy, and Law* 19(1):98–113.

McGough LS. 1996. *Child Witnesses: Fragile Voices in the American Legal System*. New Haven, CT: Yale University Press.

Michel MK, BN Gordon, PA Ornstein, and M Simpson. 2000. The abilities of children with mental retardation to remember personal experiences: Implications for testimony. *Journal of Clinical Child Psychology* 29:453–463.

Myers JEB. 1993. The competence of young children to testify in legal proceedings. *Behavioral Sciences and the Law* 11:121–133.

NICHD Protocol and Translated Versions. http://nichdprotocol.com/the-nichd-protocol, accessed November 1, 2015.

Ohio v. Clark, 135 S. Ct. 2173, 576 U.S. 1, 192 L. Ed. 2d 306 (2015).

O'Neil S and R Zajac. 2013a. The role of repeated interviewing in children's responses to cross-examination-style questioning. *British Journal of Psychology* 104(1):14–38.

O'Neil S and R Zajac. 2013b. Preparing children for cross-examination: How does intervention timing influence efficacy? *Psychology, Public Policy, and Law* 19(3):307.

Ornstein PA. 1995. Children's long-term retention of salient personal experiences. *Journal of Traumatic Stress* 8(4):581–605.

Otgaar H, R Horselenberg, R van Kampen, and Lalleman. 2012. Clothed and unclothed human figure drawings lead to more correct and incorrect reports of touch in children. *Psychology, Crime and Law* 18(7):641–653.

Peterson C. 1999. Children's memory for medical emergencies: 2 years later. *Developmental Psychology* 35(6):1493–1506.

Pezdek K and J Taylor. 2002. Memory for traumatic events in children and adults. In *Memory and Suggestibility in the Forensic Interview*, edited by ML Eisen, JA Quas, and GS Goodman, Mahwah, NJ: Erlbaum Associates, 165–183.

Pipe ME, S Gee, JC Wilson, and JM Egerton. 1999. Children's recall 1 or 2 years after an event. *Developmental Psychology* 35(3):781–789.

Plotnikoff J and R Woolfson. 2004. *In Their Own Words: The Experiences of 50 Young Witnesses in Criminal Proceedings*. London: National Society for the Prevention of Cruelty to Children.

Poole DA, SP Brubacher, and JJ Dickinson. 2015. Children as witnesses. In *APA Handbook of Forensic Psychology*, edited by L Brian and PA Zaph, Washington, DC: American Psychological Association.

Poole DA, M Bruck, and M Pipe. 2011. Forensic interviewing aids: Do props help children answer questions about touching? *Current Directions in Psychological Science* 20(1):11–15.

Poole DA and ME Lamb. 1998. *Investigative Interviews of Children: A Guide for Helping Professionals*. Washington, DC: American Psychological Association.

Poole DA and DS Lindsay. 2001. Children's eyewitness reports after exposure to misinformation from parents. *Journal of Experimental Psychology, Applied* 7:27–50.

Poole OA and JJ Dickinson. 2011. Evidence supporting restrictions on uses of body diagrams in forensic interviews. *Child Abuse and Neglect* 35:659–669.

Powell MB. 2013. Overview of current initiatives to improve child witness interviews about sexual abuse. *Current Issues in Criminal Justice* 25(2):711–720.

Principe GF, T Kanaya, SJ Ceci, and M Singh. 2006. Believing is seeing how rumors can engender false memories in preschoolers. *Psychological Science* 17(3):243–248.

Quas JA, GS Goodman, S Ghetti, KW Alexander, R Edelstein, AD Redlich, and JJ Haugaard. 2005. Childhood sexual assault victims: Long-term outcomes after testifying in criminal court. *Monographs of the Society for Research in Child Development* 70(2):vii. 1–139.

Quesada AA, US Wiemers, D Schoofs, and OT Wolf. 2012. Psychosocial stress exposure impairs memory retrieval in children. *Psychoneuroendocrinology* 37(1):125–136.

Randall W, R Parrila, and D Sobsey. 2000. Gender, disability status and risk for sexual abuse in children. *Journal on Developmental Disabilities* 7:1–15.

Raskin DC and JC Yuille. 1989. Problems in evaluating interviews of children in sexual abuse cases. In *Perspectives on Children's Testimony*, edited by S Ceci, DF Ross, and MP Toglia. New York: Springer, 184–207.

Reiter S, DN Bryen, and I Shachar. 2007. Adolescents with intellectual disabilities as victims of abuse. *Journal of Intellectual Disabilities* 11:371–387.

Rex v. Brasier, 1 Leach 199, 168 Eng. Rep. 202 (1779).

Roberts KP, SP Brubacher, D Drohan-Jennings, U Glisic, MB Powell, and WJ Friedman. 2015. Developmental differences in the ability to provide temporal information about repeated events. *Applied Cognitive Psychology* 29(3):407–417.

Runyan DK, MD Everson, GA Edelsohn, WM Hunter, and ML Coulter. 1988. Impact of legal intervention on sexually abused children. *Journal of Pediatrics* 113(4):647–653.

Salmon K. 2001. Remembering and reporting by children: The influence of cues and props. *Clinical Psychology Review* 21:267–300.

Salmon K, ME Pipe, A Malloy, and K Mackay. 2012. Do non-verbal aids increase the effectiveness of "best practice" verbal interview techniques? An experimental study. *Applied Cognitive Psychology* 26(3):370–380. [Published online September 27, 2011.]

Saywitz K and L Camparo. 1998. Interviewing child witnesses: A developmental perspective. *Child Abuse and Neglect* 22(8):825–843.

Saywitz KJ and LB Camparo. 2013. *Evidence-Based Child Forensic Interviewing: The Developmental Narrative Elaboration Interview*. New York: Oxford University Press.

Schwarzmueller A, P Boyle, and FR March. 1996. Autobiographical memory from age 3 through 8. Poster presented at the *Conference on Human Development*, Birmingham, AL.

Sedlak AJ and DD Broadhurst. 1996a. *Executive Summary of the Third National Incidence Study of Child Abuse and Neglect (NIS-3)*. Washington, DC: U.S. Department of Health and Human Services, Administration for Children and Families, Administration on Children, Youth and Families, National Center on Child Abuse and Neglect.

Segovia DA and AM Crossman. 2012. *Cognition and the Child Witness: Understanding the Impact of Cognitive Development in Forensic Contexts*. INTECH Open Access Publisher. doi: 10.5772/53938

Sharp H. 2001. Steps towards justice for people with learning disabilities as victims of crime: The important role of the police. *British Journal of Learning Disabilities* 29:88–92.

Spencer v. Peters, No. C11–5424 BHS (W.D. Wash. Aug. 21 2013).

State of Ohio v. Gersin, 76 Ohio St.3d 491 (1996).

State v. Sloan, 912 S.W.2d 592 (Mo. Ct. App. 1995).

Steenburg NH. 2005. Children and the criminal law in Connecticut 1635–1855. In *Changing Perceptions of Childhood*, edited by J Nadelhaft. New York: Psychology Press, 161–182.

Stolzenberg S and K Pezdek. 2013. Interviewing child witnesses: The effect of forced confabulation on event memory. *Journal of Experimental Child Psychology* 114(1):77–88.

Suddath R. 2003. The child as a witness. In *Principles and Practice of Forensic Psychiatry*, 2nd edition, edited by R Rosner, Boca Raton, FL: CRC Press, 419–440.

Talwar V and AM Crossman. 2012. Children's lies and their detection: Implications for child witness testimony. *Developmental Review* 32(4):337–359.

Tanenhaus DS and W Bush. 2007. Toward a history of children as witnesses. *Indian Law Journal* 82:1059.

Tedesco JF and SV Schnell. 1987. Children's reactions to sex abuse investigation and litigation. *Child Abuse and Neglect* 11(2):267–272.

Tome v. United States, 513 U.S. 150, 115 S. Ct. 696, 130 L. Ed. 2d 574 (1995).

US v. Chaco, 801 F. Supp. 2d 1200 (D.N.M. 2011).

Utah Code Ann. § 62A-4a-414 (West 2011).

Vernon-Feagans L, CS Hammer, A Miccio, and E Manlove. 2002. Early language and literacy skills in low-income African American and Hispanic children. In *Handbook of Early Literacy Research*, edited by SB Neuman and DK Dickinson. New York: Guilford Press, 2–210.

Victims of Child Abuse Act. 1990. (§3266).

Wheeler v. United States, 159 U.S. 523, 16 S. Ct. 93, 40 L. Ed. 244 (1895).

Whipple GM. 1911. The psychology of testimony. *Psychological Bulletin* 8:307, 308. (paraphrasing A. Baginsky).

Whitcomb D. 2003. Legal interventions for child victims. *Journal of Traumatic Stress* 16(2):149–157.

Whitcomb D and National Institute of Justice, U.S. 1994. *The Emotional Effects of Testifying on Sexually Abused Children*. Washington, DC: U.S. Department of Justice Office of Justice Programs National Institute of Justice.

Whitcomb D, DK Runyan, E Devos, WM Hunter, T Cross, MD Everson, and C Cropper. 1991. *Final Report: Child Victim and Witness Research and Development Program*. Office of Juvenile Justice and Delinquency Prevention, Office of Justice Programs, U.S. Department of Justice.

Willcock E, K Morgan, and H Hayne. 2006. Body maps do not facilitate children's reports of touch. *Applied Cognitive Psychology* 20(5):607–615.

Williams HL, MA Conway, and G Cohen. 2008. Autobiographical memory. In *Memory in the Real World*, 3rd edition, edited by G Cohen and MA Conway. Hove, UK: Psychology Press, 21–90.

Yates T. 1996. Theories of cognitive development. In *Child and Adolescent Psychiatry a Comprehensive Textbook*, edited by M Lewis, Philadelphia: Williams and Wilkins, 3–16.

Zajac R and H Hayne. 2006. The negative effect of cross-examination style questioning on children's accuracy: Older children are not immune. *Applied Cognitive Psychology* 20(1):3–16.

45

Neuropsychological assessment of children and adolescents: Clinical and forensic considerations

LAURA J. PHILLIPS AND ANN C. MARCOTTE

INTRODUCTION

Neuropsychology is the branch of psychology devoted to the scientific study of brain–behavioral relationships and their clinical applications. Neuropsychology emerged as a distinct discipline within psychology in the 1950s (Benton 2000), although it was not until 1996 that the American Psychological Association recognized clinical neuropsychology as an official subspecialty in psychology (Barr 2008). Similar to psychiatry and neurology, research and clinical practice in neuropsychology fall within two broad domains: adult and pediatric. Pediatric neuropsychology is the branch of neuropsychology focusing on the applied understanding of neurobehavioral functions of the infant, child, and adolescent (Baron 2004). The number of neuropsychologists who self-identify as specializing in pediatrics, either solely or in combination with adult work, has also grown steadily over time, yet represents less than 40% of the neuropsychology community (Yeates et al. 2010; Sweet et al. 2011).

Most of what was known about human brain–behavior relationships was initially derived from studies of adult brains. Over the past several decades, the scientific community has come to recognize that children's brains are anatomically and functionally distinct from those of adults (Waber et al. 2007, 2012), and brain–behavior relationships in developing children are qualitatively and quantitatively different (Baron 2004). Understanding the pattern of normal brain development and its relationship to the emergence and regulation of complex behaviors and cognition in typically developing children and adolescents has been a focus of research in pediatric neuropsychology, as well as in developmental and cognitive psychology. Advances in medicine have contributed to increased rates of survival and improved outcomes for children with specific brain insults and neurological diseases, allowing for more in-depth study of genetic, congenital, and acquired brain abnormalities and their relationships to cognition and behavior. Similarly, technological advances in brain imaging have provided increasingly more sophisticated methods for studying brain development and understanding the negative influences of injury, disorder, and disease on a child's neurological functioning (Baron 2010).

As the field of neuropsychology has continued to expand, so has the reach of pediatric neuropsychologists, who now contribute to research and theoretical formulation, test development, and clinical evaluation and treatment/educational planning for patients. Pediatric neuropsychologists work in a range of settings, including university teaching and research settings, inpatient and outpatient medical settings, and private practices. The forensic arena is yet another area in which pediatric neuropsychologists are becoming increasingly involved. In this chapter, we outline the purpose and content of pediatric neuropsychological evaluations, both in clinical and forensic practice. We will then describe the contributions such evaluations can offer civil and criminal forensic cases involving children and adolescents.

THE CLINICAL PEDIATRIC NEUROPSYCHOLOGICAL EVALUATION

The seminal book, *Neuropsychological Evaluation of the Child* (Baron 2004), provides an excellent, in-depth overview of the pediatric clinical neuropsychological evaluation. In the broadest sense, clinical neuropsychological evaluations of children and adolescents are typically sought to delineate underlying neuropsychological factors affecting a child's behavior, social/emotional functioning, and/or pattern of learning, with an emphasis placed on defining the child's unique profile of strengths and weaknesses. The results are then used to guide future treatment and/or educational planning. A clinical pediatric neuropsychological evaluation includes direct behavioral observation of the child during testing as well as the administration of objective test measures. The evaluation process also includes a review of provided medical and academic records. A parent(s) or caretaker interview is performed to obtain the child's developmental, medical, behavioral, social/emotional, and educational histories, as well as the family medical, psychiatric, and educational histories. Such ancillary information plays a vital role in case conceptualization in child and adolescent neuropsychological evaluations.

As noted by Brooks and Iverson (2012), "No other specialty has developed, normed, and validated measures of cognitive ability in the same manner as neuropsychologists" (p. 66). This speaks to the strong scientist–practitioner tradition of clinical neuropsychology. A detailed review of principles of psychometric theory and issues pertaining to neuropsychological test development, test selection and use, and factors that can affect the interpretation of neuropsychological tests is beyond the scope of this chapter; the interested reader is referred to Bush, McAllister, and Goldberg (2012) and Brooks and Iverson (2012) for reviews on these topics. Measures selected for inclusion in the clinical neuropsychological battery to assess and quantify brain–behavioral relations vary as a function of the child's age and the specific referral question(s) of the case. Testing measures have been developed and normed for a range of ages, and tests are selected to allow for interpretation of a child's performance in the context of development through the use of age-based normative data. A clinical pediatric neuropsychological examination most typically includes measures of intelligence, academic functioning, receptive and expressive language, sensory and motor functions (including visual perception, visual–spatial organization, and fine motor dexterity and speed), learning and memory, attention and concentration, and executive functions. Intellectual and academic measures are included in pediatric neuropsychological evaluations to allow for a determination of possible learning disorders, which is a common referral question for testing. Depending on the case, a testing battery may also include objective measures of psychological and behavioral functioning that can include self-ratings completed by the child, in addition to standardized parent and teacher rating measures of the child. For cases in which a diagnosis of intellectual disability is being considered, standardized measures of adaptive behavioral functioning must also be included in the testing battery.

Referrals for clinical pediatric neuropsychological evaluations are sought for a number of reasons and from varying sources. School personnel may refer a student for a comprehensive clinical neuropsychological evaluation when learning and/or behavior problems are observed in the academic setting. Such referrals often come after a school district has completed its own series of special educational evaluations, from which questions pertaining to the specific nature of the student's difficulty with success in the academic setting remain to be answered. The clinical neuropsychological evaluation can explore possible neurocognitive, psychological, and behavioral factors affecting a child's school functioning in greater depth, in a more integrated manner, and with a greater appreciation for child development than is typically undertaken in school-based evaluations.

Parents are yet another common referral source for clinical pediatric neuropsychological evaluations. Children can present differently in the home environment than they do in school due to different demands being placed on them; thus, behaviors that could potentially signal a problem may be seen at home but not at school (and vice versa). Parent-based referrals also arise when parents seek an independent neuropsychological evaluation of a child when they are dissatisfied with the conclusions drawn and services put into place after a school district has completed its own evaluations or when a school district denies a parent's request for testing.

Medical personnel in a range of disciplines refer children and adolescents to a neuropsychologist to examine the acute or long-term sequelae of disease, disorder, or injury on brain functioning and to assist with treatment and/or educational planning. The past several decades have seen increasingly more sophisticated and sensitive means of understanding the negative impact of neurological insult. Although the site and extent of a brain lesion can be identified on imaging, the image does not clarify the nature of residual behavioral and cognitive strengths and accompanying areas of weakness, whereas a clinical neuropsychological evaluation can provide such important information (Lezak et al. 2012). Researchers in pediatric neuropsychology have studied the neurocognitive sequelae of many different pediatric medical conditions (i.e., premature birth, genetic disorders, spina bifida, brain tumors, epilepsy, acute lymphoblastic leukemia, head injuries), and there is a growing body of literature that provides some of these disorders and diseases a specific context within which a child's neuropsychological testing results can be conceptualized. (See Yeates et al. 2010 for reviews of the neuropsychological correlates and developmental sequelae of several of these medical conditions.) Challenges related to medical referral questions arise given the developing nature of the child and adolescent brain. Neuropsychologists may be asked to monitor and predict a child's recovery from a neurological insult, but such recovery can be heavily affected by many factors, such as age of insult, premorbid functioning, socioeconomic, family, and other environmental conditions. The evolving state of a child's brain further means that some areas of potential cognitive and/or behavioral impairment, especially those associated with the frontal lobes, such as executive functioning, may not be evident until later when the child enters that phase of brain development (Dennis 2000).

THE FORENSIC PEDIATRIC NEUROPSYCHOLOGICAL EVALUATION

Neuropsychologists increasingly play a role in the forensic arena. Since the 1980s, the value of clinical neuropsychologists in the courtroom has become more widely appreciated (Hartlage and Stern 2010), and the number of litigated cases involving neuropsychological experts has increased dramatically over time (Taylor 1999; Sweet and Giuffre Meyer 2012). Evaluations sought for clinical purposes initially can later evolve into forensic cases, with the treating neuropsychologist sometimes placed into the role of an expert fact witness in later legal matters. Alternatively, neuropsychologists can be retained for the specific purpose of examining an individual as part of a forensic case, thereby performing the evaluation as an expert witness to answer a legal question (Sweet and Westerveld 2012). In all forensic neuropsychological evaluations, as in forensic psychiatric evaluations, professional ethical issues including competency and scope of practice, consent and assent for testing, and limits of confidentiality differ from those of clinical evaluations and must be addressed (Bush et al. 2012).

There are similarities between clinical and forensic pediatric neuropsychological evaluations. In a forensic case, the neuropsychologist is typically provided with extensive records gathered by the legal team about the case, which are reviewed and considered in rendering an opinion. As part of the forensic neuropsychological evaluation process, the child's parent(s) or caretaker is also typically interviewed to obtain information about the child. The forensic neuropsychological evaluation frequently assesses the same areas of functioning as examined in a clinical neuropsychological evaluation, described above.

There is a critical need in forensic evaluations, however, to evaluate the examinee's effort toward testing directly (Heilbroner et al. 2009). Conclusions drawn from a neuropsychological evaluation depend on the validity of the data collected, and that validity is largely dependent on the examinee's honesty and effort in test taking. A negative response bias, noncredible effort, "faking bad," and feigning of symptoms can arise in the context of forensic pediatric evaluations, as examined children may perform in a suboptimal manner knowingly or unknowingly (Sweet and Westerveld 2012). Bush et al. (2012) have identified several reasons children may give less than perfect effort in testing, including anxiety about being evaluated, the presence or absence of a parent or other familiar adult in the room, possible oppositional behavior, a lack of understanding or appreciation of the testing and of the importance of trying one's best, instruction by others to do poorly, and a poor fit between the child and the examiner.

Tests specifically designed to measure testing effort, referred to as symptom validity tests, have been developed for use with adults, and the use of symptom validity tests with children has been the topic of recent research (Kirkwood 2012). As reviewed by Kirkwood, some "stand-alone" adult-based symptom validity tests with preliminary research support for use in pediatric populations include the Test of Memory Malingering (Tombaugh 1996), Word Memory Test (Green 2003), Medical Symptom Validity Test (Green 2004), and the Rey Fifteen Item Test (Rey 1964). See Table 45.1 for a description of these measures. Several self-report measures used with children and adolescents in evaluations were developed with embedded internal reliability and validity indices, allowing other ways to examine these behaviors. Examples of such tests include the Minnesota Multiphasic Personality Inventory (MMPI)-Adolescent, Personality Assessment Inventory—Adolescent, Personality Inventory for Youth, Behavior Rating Assessment System for Children—Third Edition, and the Trauma Symptom Checklist for Children.

Table 45.1 Examples of stand-alone symptom validity tests used in pediatric populations

Test and brief description	Time required (minutes)	Age effects minimal by
Fifteen Item Test: 15 items shown briefly and then drawn from memory	5	≥11 or 12 years
Medical Symptom Validity Test: Computerized forced-choice 10 word-pairs verbal memory test	5	≥8 years or ≥third grade reading level
Test of Memory Malingering: 50-item forced-choice visual recognition test	15	≥5 or 6 years
Word Memory Test: Computerized forced-choice 20 word-pairs verbal memory test	15	≥11 years or ≥third grade reading level

Source: Adapted from Kirkwood MW 2012. Overview of tests and techniques to detect negative response bias in children. In *Pediatric Forensic Neuropsychology*, edited by EMS Sherman and BL Brooks, New York: Oxford University Press, 136–161.

PEDIATRIC NEUROPSYCHOLOGY IN THE FORENSIC SETTING

Pediatric neuropsychologists can make meaningful contributions to both civil and criminal proceedings involving children and adolescents. Neuropsychologists often provide evaluations independent of other professionals who may also examine the same examinee, such as a forensic psychiatrist. In addition to their own evaluations, the results of the forensic pediatric neuropsychological evaluation may be of assistance to forensic psychiatrists in aiding case conceptualization and forming opinions. Some examples of civil and criminal cases in which a pediatric neuropsychologist may be asked to participate are described below.

Examples of pediatric forensic neuropsychological evaluations in civil cases

MEDICAL MALPRACTICE

When central nervous system (CNS) dysfunction is alleged to have resulted from medical error or negligence, pediatric neuropsychologists are well suited to rendering opinions about the cognitive and behavioral status of such children, as well as about possible causes of impairments given their understanding of brain–behavior relationships and knowledge of the range of effects CNS impairment can pose on normal development (Baron and Morgan 2012). Medical malpractice cases that are referred to a forensic pediatric neuropsychologist for evaluation can involve injuries allegedly sustained during and/or shortly after birth. For example, hypoxia, or oxygen deprivation during the perinatal period has been associated with neurodevelopmental sequelae that range from subtle language and learning difficulties to more severe motor impairment and mental retardation (Armstrong-Wells et al. 2010). Premature birth can also be associated with a range of cognitive and behavioral sequelae (Taylor 2010a, 2015; O'Shea et al. 2013). While motoric difficulties associated with birth or perinatal injuries tend to be evident sooner in a child's development, associated cognitive and behavioral deficits, such as learning or attention disorders, may not become apparent until the child is older. Malpractice suits can also arise from alleged negligent medical care provided to children after birth that can affect CNS functioning. For example, CNS problems can arise from surgical complications, such as problems during surgery with the administration of anesthesia such that the flow of oxygen to a child's brain was disrupted.

Prenatal exposure to prescription medications taken during pregnancy can be the basis for other medical malpractice lawsuits, particularly if it becomes known that the prescribing physician was aware of a medication's risk to the developing fetus. Attention is now being given to possible long-term neurodevelopmental effects associated with in utero exposure to certain prescription medications, such as neuroleptic medications (Meador et al. 2007) and antidepressant medications (Casper et al. 2003; Galbally et al. 2011).

TRAUMATIC BRAIN INJURY (TBI)

Another common context in which a forensic pediatric neuropsychologist becomes involved in civil legal proceedings arises when a child or adolescent has sustained an acquired brain injury that was the alleged result of trauma from an accident (e.g., motor vehicle accident, negligent fall) for which an unrelated party is responsible. There is an extensive and growing body of research on the neuropsychological consequences of pediatric TBI by age of insult, as well as across injury severity gradients (for reviews, see Babikian and Asarnow 2009; Taylor 2010b; Yeates 2010, 2012; Gioia et al. 2012). TBI, particularly of moderate to severe impairment, can produce long-term deficits in a variety of cognitive and motor domains, and such injuries can be related to declines in school performance with associated increased risk of grade retention, placement in the special education system, and other indicators of academic difficulties (Ewing-Cobbs et al. 1998; Taylor et al. 2003). TBI can also result in problems with social, emotional, and behavioral functioning, and children and adolescents who have incurred a TBI are at higher risk for psychiatric disorders, especially attention deficit/hyperactivity disorder (ADHD; Max et al. 2012). A TBI sustained in childhood can also affect a variety of functional outcomes in later life. For example, children who sustained moderate to severe TBI exhibit lower educational attainment, lower employment and reduced occupational status, increased risk for psychiatric disorder, and reductions in functional independence and perceived quality of life (Cattelani et al. 1998; Nybo et al. 2004; Anderson et al. 2009; Anderson et al. 2010).

Discerning post-TBI changes in a child's ability to function requires knowledge of normal development, the nature of the TBI, cognitive sequelae that are characteristic of the particular brain insult, and appropriate measurement of behavioral, cognitive, and academic functioning (Max et al. 2012). Pre-TBI cognitive and behavioral levels of functioning must be ascertained to determine if the child shows deviations from previous functioning due to the injury. Such information can sometimes be gleaned from a review of educational records, as well as retrospective information provided by the patient, family members, and teachers. A thorough developmental history can also provide the neuropsychologist with important information about the child's premorbid functioning that includes premorbid learning, attentional, psychiatric, or behavioral disorders; family risk factors; and the family environment (Gioia et al. 2012). Neuropsychologists may further be able to use a variety of current information to estimate a child's premorbid functioning. (See Max et al. 2012 for a review of such factors.)

CHILD CUSTODY CASES

There can be a role for a forensic pediatric neuropsychological evaluation in some child custody legal cases. Although it is more typical for the parents involved in such cases to undergo psychiatric, psychological, and/or neuropsychological evaluations to determine their ability to parent, neurocognitive and/or behavioral characteristics of the child involved in such cases may also have direct bearing on such cases. A child may present with suspected or known cognitive and/or behavioral conditions that may affect the ability of a parent to care for the child. A forensic pediatric neuropsychological evaluation can provide important information about a child involved in a custody battle, which can be considered by the court in determining custody arrangements that are in the best interest of an affected child or adolescent.

DUE PROCESS/IMPARTIAL HEARINGS IN THE SPECIAL EDUCATION SYSTEM

Forensic pediatric neuropsychologists can also play a role in due process hearings under the auspices of special educational laws. (See Hahn and Morgan [2012] for a review of special educational laws and due process hearings.) Psychiatrists can become involved in such school-based legal actions when a student's psychiatric and/or behavioral functioning affects learning and behavior in the school setting, and requires the provision of special educational services. Due process refers to the specific set of procedures used to resolve disagreements between families and a school system about decisions regarding a student's identification, evaluation, educational placement, and/or the provision of a free, appropriate, public education as delineated by special educational laws. Neuropsychologists may become involved in such matters when parents seek an independent pediatric neuropsychological evaluation to assist in a due process hearing, where, based on the findings of the independent evaluation, the neuropsychologist renders professional opinions as to the educational needs of the student.

Pediatric forensic neuropsychological assessment in criminal cases

The issue of competence refers to one's capacity to distinguish right from wrong and to control one's actions accordingly. Historically, psychiatrists and clinical psychologists have been the mental health professionals rendering opinions in court proceedings regarding the competency of a defendant. Factors considered in determining mental competency can include maturity of thought, the capacity for forethought, the capacity for problem solving, the ability to anticipate the outcome of one's action, the ability to identify and distinguish between multiple choices, and whether a person was reacting to a threat (Rosado 2000). Each of these factors is considered in determining competency; however, each can be affected by other factors. One mitigating factor is age at the time of the offense or time of trial. The emergence of many of the behaviors considered in determining competence parallel brain development, particularly that of the frontal lobes, which is the region of the brain responsible for our capacity to think abstractly, anticipate consequences, plan, and control our impulses. The frontal lobes continue to develop into young adulthood (Sowell et al. 1999; Sowell et al. 2001).

Another factor affecting competence is limited intellectual functioning. By definition, an individual with intellectual disability has deficiencies in reasoning, problem solving, planning, abstract thinking, judgment, academic learning, and learning from experience, as well as limitations in adaptive functioning (APA 2013). Evaluation of intellectual and adaptive functioning is required to render such a diagnosis, and documentation of intellectual disability can have a significant effect on court proceedings.

With an increasing understanding of the role brain function plays in determining behaviors, attorneys have increasingly turned to neuropsychologists to address the specific issue of limited competence based on impaired cognitive function (Hartlage and Stern 2010; Sweet and Westerveld 2012). It has been recognized that brain injuries can be associated with higher incidence of juvenile delinquency and the commission of violent crimes (Williams et al. 2010; Davies et al. 2012). Children with some types of learning disabilities and other neurodevelopmental disorders, such as ADHD, have been described as being at increased risk for involvement in the juvenile justice system (Gordon and Moore 2005; Gordon et al. 2012). Thus, delineating how an acquired or congenital brain disorder may affect behavior and learning through a forensic pediatric neuropsychological assessment can provide additional important information to assist in rendering determinations of the competence of a juvenile in the legal system; in some cases, this information can also serve as a mitigating factor in determining sentences (Hartlage and Stern 2010). Specific neuropsychological conditions that might be the focus of a forensic pediatric neuropsychological evaluation in criminal cases include neurodevelopmental disorders and traumatic brain injury.

NEURODEVELOPMENTAL DISORDERS

Studies estimate that children with severe emotional disturbance, learning disability, intellectual disability, and ADHD are overrepresented in the juvenile justice system. Reported estimates of such neurodevelopmental disorders in the juvenile justice system range from 30% to 70% (Rutherford et al. 1985; Murphy 1986; Casey and Keilitz 1990; Quinn et al. 2005), as compared to roughly 13% of the general school-aged population (U.S. Department of Education, National Center for Education Statistics 2013). As reviewed by Malmgren et al. (1999) and Mallett (2011), several theories have been proposed to account for the higher risk of juvenile court involvement for students with learning disorders, which include the school failure hypothesis, the differential treatment hypothesis, and the susceptibility hypothesis. The susceptibility hypothesis posits that youths with learning disabilities have cognitive, neurological, and intellectual difficulties that contribute to delinquent and antisocial behavior, and place them at risk for involvement in the juvenile justice system. Students with ADHD are also overrepresented in the juvenile court system. Inattention and impulsivity are the defining observable criteria for ADHD, but children and adolescents with ADHD can also show significant impairment in executive functioning skills (Barkley 1997), which include the ability to brainstorm multiple solutions to problems, plan effectively, reason abstractly about the consequences of actions, and self-monitor behavior. Thus, problem-solving capabilities can be limited in children and adolescents diagnosed with ADHD, and this may contribute to their being more likely to engage in criminal behavior than neurotypical peers (Brier 1989). Children and adolescents with language impairments have been reported to be more likely to engage in delinquent behaviors (Brier 1989). It has been proposed that the link between language deficits and delinquent behavior is due to immature "private speech" (defined as speech spoken to oneself with the purpose of self-guidance and behavioral regulation), which may in turn result in deficiencies in self-regulation (Camp 1977; Camp et al. 1977) and social problem solving (Kazdin 1987).

TRAUMATIC BRAIN INJURY

Several research studies have suggested a link between TBI and violent and nonviolent criminal behavior (Grafman et al. 1996; Sarapata et al. 1998; Freedman and Hemenway 2000). The prevalence rate of self-reported TBI of any severity among violent offenders has been reported to range from 60% to 87% (Slaughter et al. 2003; Schofield et al. 2006; Williams et al. 2010). Studies have suggested that individuals with histories of TBI are at increased risk for engaging in violent or aggressive behavior (Rosenbaum and Hoge 1989; Grafman et al. 1996) and for committing crimes that lead to arrest following the injury (Brooks et al. 1986; Hall et al. 1994). From a neurological perspective, the link between TBI and criminal behavior is often hypothesized as related to impairment in the frontal lobes of the brain. Injury to the frontal lobes has been associated with loss of control over subcortical and limbic structures that are involved in primitive impulses (Grafman et al. 1996). Lesions in these areas can therefore affect one's reasoning, judgment, impulse control, and social perception, and they can also affect mood and emotional regulation. Adults who have had a TBI with frontal lobe involvement may misperceive social interactions, make poor social judgments, overreact to provocative stimuli, or lash out impulsively (Damasio et al. 1990; Grafman et al. 1996; Turkstra et al. 1996, 2003).

A link between TBI and criminal behaviors in youth has been suggested as well (Williams et al. 2010; Davies et al. 2012). Williams and colleagues (2010) conducted a study that involved collecting the self-reported histories of TBI, criminal behavior, mental health, and substance use of 147 male offenders ages 11–19 years old. TBI with loss of consciousness was reported by 46% of the sample, while possible TBI was reported by another 19.1% of the sample. A recent study using meta-analysis methods was undertaken to examine the relationship between TBI and juvenile offender status (Farrer et al. 2013). Analyzing nine published studies, approximately 30% of the juvenile offenders were found to have had a history of TBI. Of the five studies included in the meta-analysis that included a control group, analyses suggested that the juvenile offenders were significantly more likely to have sustained a TBI as compared to controls, suggesting a relationship between TBI and juvenile criminal behaviors.

SUMMARY

As the field of pediatric neuropsychology continues to grow, both in science and practice, it will continue to provide a unique perspective to child and adolescent forensic cases. Knowledge gained in pediatric neuropsychological research on normal brain development, as well as the cognitive and behavioral profiles associated with congenital and acquired neurological conditions, will allow for a greater understanding of complex brain–behavioral relationships and their emergence in childhood and adolescence. This information can help to improve the quality of forensic work conducted in the context of civil legal actions, including medical malpractice, cases involving pediatric brain injuries, and school-based legal hearings. Such knowledge may further broaden our understanding of factors associated with juvenile criminal actions that may be of importance in forensic neuropsychology and psychiatry in criminal cases. Advances in testing methods, especially with regard to symptom validity testing in children and adolescents, will also serve to improve the validity of clinical and forensic evaluations.

REFERENCES

American Psychiatric Association. 2013. *Diagnostic and Statistical Manual of Mental Disorders*, 5th edition. Washington, DC: American Psychiatric Publishing.

Anderson V, S Brown, H Newitt, and H Hoile. 2009. Educational, vocational, psychosocial, and quality-of-life outcomes for adult survivors of childhood traumatic brain injury. *Journal of Head Trauma Rehabilitation* 24:303–312.

Anderson V, S Brown, and H Newitt. 2010. What contributes to quality of life in adult survivors of childhood traumatic brain injury? *Journal of Neurotrauma* 27:863–870.

Armstrong-Wells J, TJ Bernard, and M Manco-Johnson. 2010. Neurocognitive outcomes following neonatal encephalopathy. *NeuroRehabilitation* 26:27–33.

Babikian T and R Asarnow. 2009. Neurocognitive outcomes and recovery after pediatric TBI: Meta-analytic review of the literature. *Neuropsychology* 23:283–296.

Barkley R 1997. Behavioral inhibition, sustained attention, and executive functions: Constructing a unifying theory of ADHD. *Psychological Bulletin* 121(1):65–94.

Baron IS. 2004. *Neuropsychological Evaluation of the Child.* New York: Oxford University Press.

Baron IS. 2010. Maxims and a model for the practice of pediatric neuropsychology. In *Pediatric Neuropsychology: Research, Theory, and Practice*, 2nd edition, edited by KO Yeates, MD Ris, HG. Taylor, and BF Pennington, New York: Guilford Press, 473–499.

Baron IS and J Morgan 2012. Independent neuropsychological evaluations of children in medical malpractice cases. In *Pediatric Forensic Neuropsychology*, edited by EMS Sherman and BL Brooks, New York: Oxford University Press, 275–287.

Barr WB. 2008. Historical development of the neuropsychological test battery. In *Textbook of Clinical Neuropsychology*, edited by JE Morgan and JH Ricker, New York: Taylor and Francis, 3–17.

Benton A. 2000. Foreword. In *Pediatric neuropsychology: Research, Theory, and Practice*, edited by KO Yeates, MD Ris, and HG Taylor. New York: Guilford Press, xv.

Brier N. 1989. The relationship between learning disabilities and delinquency: A review and reappraisal. *Journal of Learning Disabilities* 22:546–553.

Brooks N, L Campsie, C Symington, A Beattie, and W McKinlay. 1986. The five year outcome of severe blunt head injury: A relative's view. *Journal of Neurology, Neurosurgery, and Psychiatry* 49:764–770.

Brooks BL and GL Iverson. 2012. Improving accuracy when identifying cognitive impairment in pediatric neuropsychological evaluations. In *Pediatric Forensic Neuropsychology*, edited by EMS Sherman and BL Brooks, New York: Oxford University Press, 66–88.

Bush SS, WS MacAllister, and AL Goldberg. 2012. Ethical issues in pediatric forensic neuropsychology. In *Pediatric Forensic Neuropsychology*, edited by EMS Sherman and BL Brooks, New York: Oxford University Press, 24–40.

Camp BW 1977. Verbal mediation in young aggressive boys. *Journal of Abnormal Psychology* 86:145–153.

Camp BW, WJ Van Doornick, SG Zimet, and NW Dahlem. 1977. Verbal abilities in young aggressive boys. *Journal of Educational Psychology* 69:129–135.

Casey P and I Keilitz. 1990. Estimating the prevalence of learning disabled and mentally retarded juvenile offenders: A meta-analysis. In *Understanding Troubled and Troubling Youth*, edited by PE Leone, Newbury Park, CA: Sage, 82–101.

Casper RC, BE Fleisher, JC Lee-Ancajas, A Gilles, E Gaylor, A DeBattista, and HE Hoyme. 2003. Follow up of children of depressed mothers exposed or not exposed to antidepressants during pregnancy. *Journal of Pediatrics* 142:402–408.

Cattelani R, F Lombardi, R Brianti, and A Mazzucchi. 1998. Traumatic brain injury in childhood: Intellectual, behavioural, and social outcome into adulthood. *Brain Injury* 12:283–296.

Damasio AR, D Tranel, and H Damasio. 1990. Individuals with sociopathic behavior caused by frontal damage fail to respond automatically to social stimuli. *Behavioral Brain Research* 41:81–94.

Davies RC, WH Williams, D Hinder, CNW Burgess, and LTA Mounce. 2012. Self-reported traumatic brain injury and postconcussion symptoms in incarcerated youth. *Journal of Head Trauma and Rehabilitation* 27:E21–E27.

Dennis M. 2000. Developmental plasticity in children: The role of biological risk, development, time and reserve. *Journal of Communication Disorders* 33:321–332.

Ewing-Cobbs L, JM Fletcher, HS Levin, I Iovino, and ME Miner. 1998. Academic achievement and academic placement following traumatic brain injury in children and adolescents: A two-year longitudinal study. *Journal of Clinical and Experimental Neuropsychology* 20:769–781.

Farrer TJ, RB Frost, and DW Hedges. 2013. Prevalence of traumatic brain injury in juvenile offenders: A meta-analysis. *Child Neuropsychology* 19(3):225–234.

Freedman D and D Hemenway. 2000. Precursors of lethal violence: A death row sample. *Social Science and Medicine* 50:1757–1770.

Galbally M, AJ Lewis, and A Buist. 2011. Developmental outcomes of children exposed to antidepressants in pregnancy. *Australian and New Zealand Journal of Psychiatry* 48:393–399.

Gioia GA, CG Vaughan, and PK Isquith. 2012. Independent neuropsychological evaluation of children with mild traumatic brain injury. In *Pediatric Forensic Neuropsychology*, edited by EMS Sherman and BL Brooks, New York: Oxford University Press, 205–228.

Gordon JA and P Moore. 2005. ADHD among incarcerated youth: An investigation on the congruency with ADHD prevalence and correlates among the general population. *American Journal of Criminal Justice* 30:87–97.

Gordon JA, RL Diehl, and L Anderson. 2012. Does ADHD Matter? Examining attention deficit and hyperactivity disorder on the likelihood of recidivism among detained youth. *Journal of Offender Rehabilitation* 51:497–518.

Grafman J, K Schwab, D Warden, A Pridgen, HR Brown, and AM Salazar. 1996. Frontal lobe injuries, violence, and aggression: A report of the Vietnam head injury study. *Neurology* 46:1231–1238.

Green P 2003. *Manual for the Word Memory Test.* Edmonton, AB: Green's Publishing.

Green P 2004. *Manual for the Medical Symptom Validity Test.* Edmonton, AB: Green's Publishing.

Hahn LG and JE Morgan. 2012. Neuropsychological contributions to independent educational evaluations: Forensic perspectives. In *Pediatric Forensic Neuropsychology*, edited by EMS Sherman and BL Brooks, New York: Oxford University Press, 288–317.

Hall KM, P Kazmark, M Stevens, J Englander, P O'Hare, and J Wright. 1994. Family stressors in traumatic brain injury: A two-year follow-up. *Archives of Physical Medicine and Rehabilitation* 75:876–884.

Hartlage LC and BH Stern. 2010. Historical influences in forensic neuropsychology. In *Handbook of Forensic Neuropsychology*, 2nd edition, edited by LC Hartlage and AM Horton, New York: Springer, 33–55.

Heilbroner RL, JJ Sweet, JE Morgan, GJ Larrabee, and SR Millis. 2009. American Academy of Clinical Neuropsychology Consensus Conference Statement on the neuropsychological assessment of effort, response bias, and malingering. *Clinical Neuropsychologist* 23:1093–1129.

Kazdin AE 1987. *Conduct Disorders in Childhood and Adolescence*, Vol. 9. Beverly Hills, CA: Sage.

Kirkwood MW 2012. Overview of tests and techniques to detect negative response bias in children. In *Pediatric Forensic Neuropsychology*, edited by EMS Sherman and BL Brooks, New York: Oxford University Press, 136–161.

Lezak M, D Howieson, E Bigler, and D Tranel. 2012. *Neuropsychological Assessment*, 5th edition. New York: Oxford University Press.

Mallett CA. 2011. *Seven Things Juvenile Courts Should Know About Learning Disabilities*. Reno, NV: National Council of Juvenile and Family Judges.

Malmgren K, RD Abbott, and JD Hawkins. 1999. LD and delinquency: Rethinking the "link." *Journal of Learning Disabilities* 32(3):194–200.

Max JE, RJ Schacher, and TJ Ornstein. 2012. Preinjury and secondary Attention-Deficit/Hyperactivity Disorder in pediatric traumatic brain injury forensic cases. In *Pediatric Forensic Neuropsychology*, edited by EMS Sherman and BL Brooks, New York: Oxford University Press, 258–274.

Meador KJ, G Baker, MJ Cohen, E Gaily, and M Westervled. 2007. Cognitive/behavioral teratogenetic effects of antiepileptic drugs. *Epilepsy and Behavior* 11(3):292–302.

Murphy DM. 1986. The prevalence of handicapping conditions among juvenile delinquents. *Remedial and Special Education* 7:7–17.

Nybo T, M Sainio, and K Muller. 2004. Stability of vocational outcome in adulthood after moderate to severe preschool brain injury. *Journal of the International Neuropsychological Society* 10:719–723.

O'Shea TM, C Downey, and KKC Kuban. 2013. Extreme prematurity and attention deficit: Epidemiology and prevention. *Frontiers in Human Neuroscience* 7:1–5.

Quinn MM, RB Rutherford, PE Leone, DM Osher, and JM Poirier. 2005. Youth with disabilities in juvenile corrections: A national Survey. *Exceptional Children* 71:339–345.

Rey A. 1964. *L'examen clinique en psychologie*. Paris: Presse Universitaires de France.

Rosado LM. 2000. *Understanding Adolescents: A Juvenile Court Training Program*. Washington, DC: American Bar Association.

Rosenbaum A and SK Hoge. 1989. Head injury and marital aggression. *American Journal of Psychiatry* 146:1048–1051.

Rutherford RB, CM Nelson, and BL Wolford. 1985. Special education in the most restrictive environment: Correctional/special education. *Journal of Special Education* 19:59–71.

Sarapata M, D Herrmann, T Johnson, and R Aycock. 1998. The role of head injury in cognitive functioning, emotional adjustment, and criminal behaviour. *Brain Injury* 12:821–842.

Schofield PW, TG Butler, SJ Hollis, NE Smith, SJ Lee, and WM Kelso. 2006. Traumatic brain injury among Australian prisoners: Rates, recurrence, and sequelae. *Brain Injury* 20:499–506.

Slaughter B, RJ Fann, and D Ehde. 2003. Traumatic brain injury in a county jail population: Prevalence, neuropsychological functioning, and psychiatric disorders. *Brain Injury* 17:731–741.

Sowell ER, PM Thompson, CJ Holems, TL Jernigan, and AW Toga. 1999. *In vivo* evidence for post-adolescent brain maturation in frontal and striatal regions. *Nature Neuroscience* 2:859–861.

Sowell ER, PM Thompson, KD Tessner, and AW Toga. 2001. Mapping continued brain growth and gray matter density reduction in dorsal frontal cortex: Inverse relationships during postadolescent brain maturation. *Journal of Neuroscience* 21:8819–8829.

Sweet JJ and D Giuffre Meyer. 2012. Trends in forensic practice and research. In *Forensic Neuropsychology: A Scientific Approach*, 2nd edition, edited by GJ Larrabee, New York: Oxford University Press, 501–506.

Sweet JJ, D Giuffre Meyer, NW Nelson, and PJ Moberg. 2011. The TCN/AACN 2010 "salary survey": Professional practices, beliefs, and incomes of U.S. neuropsychologists. *Clinical Neuropsychologist* 25:12–61.

Sweet JJ and M Westerveld. 2012. Pediatric neuropsychology in forensic proceedings: Roles and procedures in the courtroom and beyond. In *Pediatric Forensic Neuropsychology*, edited by EMS Sherman and BL Brooks, New York: Oxford University Press, 3–23.

Taylor HG 2010a. Children with very low birth weight or very preterm birth. In *Pediatric Neuropsychology: Research, Theory, and Practice*, 2nd edition, edited by KO Yeates, MD Ris, HG Taylor, and BF Pennington, New York: Guilford Press, 26–70.

Taylor HG 2010b. Neurobehavioral outcomes of pediatric traumatic brain injury. In *Pediatric Traumatic Brain Injury: New Frontiers in Clinical and Translational Research*, edited by VA Anderson and KO Yeates, New York: Cambridge University Press, 145–168.

Taylor HG 2015. Multiple risks for long-term cognitive impairments following pre-term births. *Acta Paediatrica* 104:218–220.

Taylor HG, KO Yeates, SL Wade, D Drotar, T Stancin, and M Montpetite. 2003. Long-term educational interventions after traumatic brain injury in children. *Rehabilitation Psychology* 48:227–236.

Taylor JS. 1999. The legal environment pertaining to clinical neuropsychology. In *Forensic Neuropsychology: Fundamentals and Practice*, edited by JJ Sweet, New York: Taylor and Francis, 421–424.

Tombaugh TN. 1996. *Test of Memory Malingering (TOMM)*. North Tonawanda, NY: Multi Health Systems.

Turkstra L, D Jones, and HL Toler. 2003. Brain injury and violent crime. *Brain Injury* 17:39–47.

Turkstra L, S McDonald, and P Kaufman. 1996. Assessment of pragmatic communication skills in adolescents after traumatic brain injury. *Brain Injury* 10:329–345.

U.S. Department of Education, National Center for Education Statistics. 2013. *Digest of Education Statistics.* http://nces.ed.gov/fastfacts/display.asp?id=64, accessed September 2013.

Waber DP, C DeMoor, PW Forbes et al. 2007. The NIH MRI study of normal brain development: Performance of a population based sample of healthy children aged 6 to 18 years old on a neuropsychological battery. *Journal of the International Neuropsychological Society* 13(5):729–746.

Waber DP, PW Forbes, CR Almli, EA Blood, and the Brain Development Cooperative Group. 2012. Four-year long longitudinal performance of a population-based sample of healthy children on a neuropsychological battery: The NIH MRI Study of Normal Brain Development. *Journal of the International Neuropsychological Society* 18:179–190.

Williams H, G Cordan, AJ Mewse, J Tonks, and CNW Burgess. 2010. Self-reported traumatic brain injury in male young offenders: A risk factor for re-offending, poor mental health, and violence? *Neuropsychological Rehabilitation* 20:801–812.

Yeates KO. 2010. Traumatic brain injury. In *Pediatric Neuropsychology: Research, Theory, and Practice*, 2nd edition, edited by KO Yeates, MD Ris, HG Taylor, and BF Pennington, New York: Guilford Press, 112–146.

Yeates KO. 2012. Independent neuropsychological evaluation of children with moderate to severe traumatic brain injury. In *Pediatric Forensic Neuropsychology*, edited by EMS Sherman and BL Brooks, New York: Oxford University Press, 229–257.

Yeates KO, MD Ris, H Taylor, and BF Pennington. eds. 2010. *Pediatric Neuropsychology: Research, Theory, and Practice*, 2nd edition. New York: Guilford Press.

46

Assessment and treatment of adolescent sex offenders

LISA MURPHY, J. PAUL FEDOROFF, AND GREGG DWYER

INTRODUCTION

Despite crime statistics that indicate adolescents play a significant role in sexual offense rates and can vary psychopathologically from adult offenders, research on adolescents who sexually offend (often referred to in the literature as an adolescent sex offender or ASO) is largely limited in comparison to studies of adult sex offenders. Available data reveal a wide range of estimates about ASO's incidence and prevalence. For example, one study estimated that approximately one-third to one-half of known sexual assaults against a child are committed by an adolescent offender (Prentky et al. 2000; Finkelhor et al. 2009). Official statistics have indicated that 12.5% of all arrests for sexual assault and 14% of arrests for other sex offenses involve ASOs (U.S. Department of Justice 2009). According to Snyder (2000), juveniles account for 23% of all sex offenders. When broken down by victim age, adolescents are reported to account for 4% of sex offenses against adults and 33% of sex offenses against children. When examining child victims, 40% of adolescent perpetrated sex offenses are against victims under age 6 (Snyder 2009). In Ybarra and Mitchell's online survey study (2013) of 1058 youth aged 14–21 years old, 1 in 10 (9%; $n = 108$) self-reported sexual perpetration ranging from unwanted kissing, touching, or other unwanted sexual contact (8%; $n = 84$) to completed rape (2%; $n = 18$).

Research on age at first offense has indicated a range up to 50% for the number of convicted adult sex offenders reporting that their first sexual offense occurred in adolescence (Abel et al 1985; Abel et al. 1993; Rasmussen 2004). Recidivism is addressed later in the chapter, and those rates vary from self-reporting data. Another study reported people under age 20 years account for nearly 50% of all incidents of sexual aggression in the United States (Lowenstein 2006). In addition, some adolescent sex offenders have reported initially engaging in problematic sexual behaviors in early childhood (Burton 2000). Another study estimated one out of eight sex offenders are under the age of 12 (Finkelhor et al. 2009). Ybarra and Mitchell (2013) found age 16 was the most common age of first offence.

Adolescents who sexually offend are an important subgroup of offenders providing important information about the onset and early course of problematic sexual interests and behaviors. As addressed elsewhere in this text, the sexual abuse of children, whether perpetrated by adults or adolescents, can cause severe physical and psychological trauma to the victim. Research on the characteristics and offense patterns of ASOs will contribute to our understanding of the onset and course of the paraphilias and to improved assessment, management, and treatment of sex offenders and potential sex offenders of all ages. Of particular importance is the need for a preventative approach in which adolescents with sexual interests in criminal activities are successfully identified and treated prior to the commission of any real-life offenses. By identifying the characteristics of people in danger of becoming ASOs, the field may move from offering correction and rehabilitation to offering primary prevention and treatment to enhance noncriminal, healthy, and fulfilling sexual interests and behaviors (Lowenstein 2006; Fedoroff 2016).

This chapter reviews ASO behavior and addresses associated characteristics and offending patterns. Similar to adult sexual offenders, it has been widely noted that ASOs are a heterogeneous group, with many potential factors contributing to their problematic sexual interests and nonconsensual behaviors (Vandiver 2006; Van Wijk et al. 2006; Robertiello and Terry 2007). Like other adolescent offenders, ASOs often have varied familial problems including a history of neglect, physical abuse, and sexual victimization (Seto and Lalumière 2010). They have been noted to have higher rates of behavioral problems and difficulties in school, various psychopathologies, increased feelings of social isolation, and a tendency toward offending in general (Lowenstein 2006; Vandiver 2006). These factors are examined along with information on sentencing patterns, the utilization of treatment approaches, and recidivism rates associated with ASOs.

DEFINITIONS AND CONCEPTS

Table 46.1 provides the authors' definitions for terms used in this chapter. These definitions may not be the same as those used in other publications. This fact highlights the caution needed when reviewing studies involving ASOs, because even the definition of what an "adolescent" is can vary.

LIMITS TO NORMALITY IN ADOLESCENT SEXUAL BEHAVIOR

When examining the issue of adolescent perpetrated sexual abuse, it is important to acknowledge that there is a wide range of sexual experience and exploration that is part of healthy adolescent experience. Cultural influences play a significant role in the determination of "normal" healthy sexual interests and activities. Behaviors that are considered atypical or problematic in some cultures may be commonplace in others. Within a given culture, familial and social factors also impact the context. Research has shown that in most stages of childhood, children exhibit some degree of sexual curiosity but adolescents as a group exhibit much more sexually motivated exploration than children (Murrie 2012).

However, there are children and adolescents who exhibit deviant sexual interests and behaviors that fall outside of the socially accepted range of normality and if acted upon can constitute a criminal offense. The determination of what exceeds acceptable adolescent behavior is most clearly understood through the legal definitions of abuse and age requirements for consent in a given jurisdiction. In Canada, for example, the Canadian Criminal Code defines the age of consent to sexual activity as 16 (Canadian Criminal Code 1985). However, in cases where an individual is in a position of trust over the consenting adolescent, such as a coach, teacher, or employer, the age of consent increases to 18. Also, the age of consent is raised to 18 in cases where digital media depicts nudity or sexual activity of the adolescent. In the United States, state law governs variation in age of consent to engage in sexual behavior with another. Determinations are made on a state-by-state basis except when there is photographic or video recording of the behavior, in which case the federal law takes precedence and the age is a minimum of 18 years regardless of the state (Sexual Exploitation and Other Abuse of Children, 18 USC §2256, 1984 amended 1986).

OFFENDER CHARACTERISTICS

Similar to their adult counterparts, ASOs are a heterogeneous population and differ on many important dimensions, including age at first offense, gender, and social and developmental characteristics. The following are some findings from the literature that provide general demographics. Although preadolescent children are known to commit abusive sexual acts, the dynamics are typically different, less clearly sexually motivated, and less frequent. The following is focused on adolescent-aged youth.

Onset and average age of offending

During adolescence, concern about appearance and self-image typically increases, together with an increase in frequency of sexual fantasies and masturbation (Saleh and Vincent 2004). Exploratory relationships, which can be exploitive, often occur during middle adolescence (Saleh and Vincent 2004). By late adolescence, the development of secondary sexual physical characteristics concludes, and ideally, sexual behaviors and interests become less solipsistic (Saleh and Vincent 2004). Consequently, sexual behaviors should be assessed within a developmental context rather than in absolutes. Although, taken out of this context, a behavior might seem exploitive and even abusive, it might be consistent with the person's developmental stage and as such warrant less significant or intrusive correctional measures, if any.

The average age for onset of sexual offending is the early teens; varying between 13 and 16 years of age for males (Bumby et al. 1997; Shaw 1999; Zolondek et al. 2002; Vandiver 2006) and 11 and 15 years for females (Bumby et al. 1997; Vandiver 2006). Retrospective data from adult sex offenders indicate that paraphilias typically first develop as deviant fantasies around puberty, followed by deviant behaviors 2 to 3 years later. Without treatment, by the time the adolescent reaches early adulthood, patterns of sexually deviant behavior are typically established (Saleh and Vincent 2004). Although there is no dispute that sexual interests develop and are modified from puberty to adulthood, there is controversy about when or if the modifiability of sexual interests stops. John Money and others have argued that sexual interest is like sexual orientation and becomes immutable (Money 1986; Cantor 2012). Others have suggested there is no evidence that sexual interest and behaviors are not continually and naturally modifiable throughout the life span (Fedoroff 2016).

Despite variation in the onset of sexual offending behavior, the age of first arrest for male and female adolescent sex offenders is similar. On average, adolescent females are first arrested at age 14 and males are first arrested at age 15 years. Age and risk of recidivism in adolescent sex offenders is inversely related (Vandiver 2006). That is, the younger the offenders are at the time of first arrest for a sexual offense, the more likely they are to be re-arrested for a nonsexual or sexual offense (Vandiver 2006). One explanation for this finding is that adolescents who begin offending earlier often also have more criminogenic factors and/or a lifestyle conducive to criminality compared to those who begin offending later in adolescence. For example, Seto and Lalumière (2010) did not find a significant difference between the age of first arrest for sexually offending adolescents and adolescents with nonsexual offending histories.

Table 46.1 Chapter definitions

Term	Definition
Adolescent	A person between the ages of 12 and 17 years inclusive, regardless of degree of physical or psychological maturity.
Child molester	A person who commits a sexual offense against a child. It is important to understand that not all individuals who have a sexual interest in children act on these interests and become child molesters. Some individuals suffer from deviant sexual fantasies or urges but never act on their interests. Conversely, not all child molesters have a persistent sexual interest in children, nor would they meet *DSM* or *International Classification of Diseases* (*ICD*) diagnostic criteria for pedophilia or pedophilic disorder.
Deviant sexual interest	The concept of being "deviant" is a statistical term referring to a quantifiable variable that diverges from an average score. Sexual interests are said to be deviant when they are outside the "norm" of a given population. This includes adults, adolescents, or children who have a sexual interest that is not in line with social prescriptions and, in some cases, legal definitions. Research on sexual offenders and those with problematic sexual interests are defined according to the laws and social norms of the jurisdiction and time period in which the research takes place. Regarding children and adolescents, little objective information regarding normal sexual development and exploration exists. Significant variation exists in what is considered "normal" child sexual exploration. It is unfortunate that the term "deviant" has become a derogatory label and is often falsely equated with immutability. By analogy, both people with genius and people with intellectual disability are deviant.
Juvenile sexual offenders (JSOs) or Adolescent sexual offenders (ASOs)	Refers to youth between ages 12 and 18 years who meet either of these criteria: (a) officially charged with a sexual crime or (b) committed an act that could be subject to legal charges. A juvenile is a person who is under an age fixed by jurisdictional law at which the person would otherwise have been charged as an adult. Some jurisdictions have an earlier cutoff period with adult charges being made once an individual turns 16 or 17. When convicted of a sexual offense, adolescents are subject to penalties less severe than if charged and convicted as an adult. There is also frequently an increased focus on rehabilitation over punishment. It should be noted that although the abbreviation ASOs is used in this chapter, in practice it is better to refer to "adolescents who have sexually offended" rather than the label ASO that implies being an offender is a permanent identity rather than a description of a past behavior.
Paraphilic disorders	Derived from the Greek "para" meaning around or beside and "philos" meaning love. Paraphilias involve arousal from sexual stimuli or acts that are outside the standard range of socially acceptable behaviors. However, for the individual with the paraphilia, this interest or behavior is persistent, often preferred, and in some cases necessary for sexual excitement and orgasm. Paraphilic disorders exist on a continuum from less conventional behavior to violent, harmful, or destructive behavior. Paraphilias are persistent sexually arousing fantasies, interests, or behaviors that involve nonhuman objects, suffering or humiliation of oneself or partner, or children or other nonconsenting people. To be considered a disorder, they must cause distress or harm to someone. Paraphilic disorders themselves are not illegal; however, acting in response to paraphilic urges may be illegal (sex offense), and in some cases, it could result in severe legal sanctions as is frequently observed in the case of pedophilic disorder. Patients with paraphilic disorders usually come to medical or legal attention by committing an act against a child or a nonconsenting adult because most of them, especially adolescents, do not find their sexual fantasies distressing or sufficiently ego-dystonic to voluntarily seek treatment. In addition, they may feel too ashamed to ask for medical advice prior to acting on their sexual interests. For some individuals, paraphilic fantasies or stimuli are obligatory for erotic arousal and are always included in their sexual activity (exclusive paraphilic disorders). In other cases, the paraphilic preferences occur only episodically, whereas at other times, the person is able to function sexually without deviant stimuli or fantasies.

(*Continued*)

Table 46.1 (*Continued*) Chapter definitions

Term	Definition
Pedophilia	A paraphilia that consists of persistent sexual interest and fantasies involving prepubescent children. In *DSM-5* the person must be at least 16 years of age and must be at least 5 years older than the victim. However, for younger people no age is specified and clinical judgment must be used (i.e., sexual maturity of the child and age difference between the victim and the perpetrator).
Sexual offense or sex crime	Criminal laws prohibiting sexual assaults are enacted in order to protect the right to autonomy and personal determination of involvement in sexual activities. Particular definitions vary among jurisdictions; however, within Western societies, the prohibition of nonconsenting or coerced sexual activity remains the constant. Attempts to protect children from sexual victimization by adolescents and adults remain consistent throughout Western cultures

Social and developmental characteristics

Research indicates ASOs are more likely than nonoffending peers to have learning deficits and conduct disorders that contribute to difficulties in the school setting (Zgourides et al. 1997). One study of ASOs in Canada found that nearly half of adolescent sex offenders experienced difficulty with educational activities and self-awareness, and had limited sexual knowledge. In addition, two-thirds of ASOs have limited social skills, experience difficulty making friends, and are often socially rejected by peers (Gal and Hoge 1999). One explanation for why some ASOs sexually assault younger children is because ASOs who sexually offend against children report closer social ties to younger children than to same-age peers (Timms and Goreczny 2002).

These findings are replicated in other studies in which ASOs were found to share characteristics such as loneliness, lack of suitable sexual education, lack of empathy or remorse for their victims, and limited self-esteem. Furthermore, ASOs are more likely to come from dysfunctional families in which abuse, inadequate supervision, and limited social support are common (Lakey 1994; Prentky et al. 2000). Although the sexually offending youth had more general and heterosocial skills deficits, they were statistically more likely to experience social isolation than the nonsexual offending youth (Seto and Lalumière 2010). In their study comparing alleged ASOs and nonsexual violent offenders in Germany, Driemeyer and colleagues (2013) found the former group were less sexually experienced, were less confident in their relationship skills, had a lower rate of victimization, and had more sexual deviance.

As a group, ASOs often display limited impulse control, judgment, and problem-solving skills (Kahn and Chambers 1991). Dwyer and Jerrell (2011) found oppositional defiant disorder (ODD) and disruptive behavior disorder (DBD) to be prevalent diagnoses within their sample of ASOs. A significant number of these adolescents were identified especially as having difficulties in the school setting. More than half of ASOs behave disruptively at school, 39% have been diagnosed with a learning disability, and 30% are frequently absent from school (Kahn and Chambers 1991; Bourke and Donohue 1996). When examining antisocial behavior by gender, female sex offenders tend to exhibit significantly fewer characteristics of antisocial behavior than their male counterparts. Other characteristics of female sex offenders may include use of drugs and/or alcohol, and physical fights with peers (Prentky et al. 2000; Lowenstein 2006). Brown and Burton (2010) found alcohol use to be the most robust predictor of a higher rate of nonsexual violence in their study of 290 male youths. However, Seto and Lalumière (2010) found nonsexual offenders had more substance use problems than the sexual offending adolescents.

Like their adult counterparts, many ASOs describe "cognitive distortions" they use to legitimize deviant sexual interests and which contribute to the commission of sexual offenses (Timms and Goreczny 2002). These errors in thinking manifest when offenders adopt beliefs about ways to behave consistent with their deviant sexual interests. According to Goocher (1994), some offenders sexually victimize others in order to regain personal control that they believe was taken from them when they were victimized themselves. For others, the rationalization or denial of deviant behavior works to reinforce offense facilitating thought patterns.

As a group, ASOs do not suffer from serious mental health issues, with less than 3% meeting *Diagnostic and Statistical Manual of Mental Disorders* (*DSM*) criteria for a serious mental illness or a severe personality disorder (Madsen et al. 2006). However, in another sample, 42% of adolescent sex offenders were found to meet the criteria for Major Depression (Poortinga 2009). Seto and Lalumière (2010) reported a higher rate of anxiety and low self-esteem but not depression, psychosis, or suicidal ideations in ASOs compared to nonsexual adolescent offenders. Dwyer and Jerrell (2011) examined the prevalence of mental health issues among juveniles with a history of sexual offending who were receiving treatment in a state mental health system. Based on the then current *Diagnostic and Statistical Manual of Mental Disorders*, 4th edition, text revision (*DSM-IV-TR*), the following diagnoses were found to be the most prevalent: attention deficit/hyperactivity disorder, oppositional defiant disorder, disruptive behavior disorder, adjustment disorder, mixed emotions and conduct, posttraumatic stress disorder, physical and sexual abuse of a child-victim, and parent–child relational problem. In another sample, youth who sexually offended were found to have higher anxiety ratings than the comparison group. However, the authors cautioned that these data were collected after arrest (Fanniff and Kimonis 2014).

Some themes have been noted when examining intellectually disabled ASOs. As a group these individuals have been found to be more susceptible to the social influences of their peer group, especially if they live together. Their offenses have been described as more "opportunistic" (Timms and Goreczny 2002). Others have explained these observations as "counterfeit deviance" due to observer's misinterpretations of the true motivations for the behaviors (Hingsburger 1991). For example, a person raised in a group home in which nudity was common may be falsely diagnosed with exhibitionism if the person's behavior in a new context is misunderstood as sexually motivated. A history of previous victimization is also more prevalent in this subgroup. Intellectually disabled offenders are also more likely to have victims who are in close physical proximity, tend to use less "grooming" behaviors, and often use comparatively unsophisticated strategies to commit offenses or to avoid being caught. They are also more likely to say there was a genuine reciprocated intimate relationship with the victim (i.e., to say they were in love) (Timms and Goreczny 2002).

Childhood victimization

A history of abuse among ASOs has been suggested to play a role in offending behavior. A history of personal sexual abuse is common in juveniles who sexually offend (Ryan et al. 1996; APA 1999; Myers 2001; Morris et al. 2002; Shaw 1999; Hunter et al. 2003; Salter et al. 2003; Seto and Lalumière 2010). Robertiello and Terry (2007) suggest that ASOs typically report a history of childhood victimization. Results for this sample indicated that up to 70% of ASOs had a history of childhood neglect, 60% reported physical abuse, and 50% reported a history of sexual abuse. Dwyer and Jerrell (2011) found mental health system records for their study sample indicated 51% of males and 100% of females had experienced sexual abuse. Additionally, 31% of males and 90% of females had been physically abused.

Interestingly, Fanniff and Kimonis (2014) found that physical and emotional abuse were *not* predictive after controlling for sexual abuse in their sample. Fanniff and Kimonis (2014) also reported a higher rate of sexual abuse among juveniles who sexually offended compared to those with delinquent, but nonsexual, behaviors. Brown and Burton (2010) found higher levels of trauma, including abuse and neglect, in youth who engaged in nonsexual and sexual violence than those who were only sexually violent. Seto and Lalumière (2010) also found a higher rate of physical (but not sexual) abuse victimization among the sexually offending than the nonsexual offending youths.

The observed rates of sex offenders who have been sexually victimized in their childhood have led to speculation that the experience of sexual abuse may make individuals more likely to sexually assault others when they reach adolescence or adulthood. This speculation should be interpreted with caution. It is important to note that despite evidence that some victims of child sexual abuse do go on to offend sexually in adolescence and adulthood, the majority of victims never go on to sexually offend later in life. For example, while there is evidence of a high prevalence of victimization, including sexual abuse, among female children, relatively few subsequently commit sex offenses.

As a group, ASOs with a history of personal abuse are also more likely to experience family instability, have parents with alcohol and/or substance abuse issues, have parents with limited education, and experience interparental violence (Kobayashi et al. 1995; Veneziano and Veneziano 2002; Van Wijk et al. 2006). It has been speculated that since less than one-third of ASOs reside with both birth parents, this may result in less support and supervision (Hunter and Figueredo 1999).

Notable differences have been observed in the abuse histories of male and female ASOs. Surveys have found that females tend to have their first experience of sexual victimization at a younger age than their male counterparts. Approximately 64% of female sex offenders were found to have been victimized before age 6, whereas 26% of males reported being victimized by that age. In addition, females also reported having a higher average number of molesters than did male offenders, 4.5 and 1.4, respectively (Vandiver and Teske 2006). Adolescent sex offenders have a significantly higher prevalence of childhood sexual victimization than nonoffending adolescents (Burton et al. 2002; Veneziano et al. 2004).

ARREST RATES AND SENTENCING PATTERNS

Child victims and their families are generally more reluctant to report sexual victimization when the offender is an adolescent compared to when an offender is an adult. Presumably, this is because the offender is so young and is usually known to the family (Davis and Leitenberg 1987). Consequently, this likely results in a misrepresentation of the true rate of sexual offending committed by adolescent offenders. Sexual acts may also be labeled as an act of sexual exploration or experimentation, rather than an offense requiring police involvement. Moreover, only a small minority of incidents that are actually reported to the police result in charges or a conviction (Davis and Leitenberg 1987).

When examining the cases that do result in a conviction, it is important to look at sentencing patterns by gender and the nature of the offense committed. Research conducted by Vandiver and Teske (2006) found that female adolescent sex offenders receive a sentence involving probation in approximately three-quarters of cases, with the remaining cases concluding in sentences involving residential treatment. Generally, noncustodial sentences for male and female adolescent sex offenders tend to be similar. One survey found that 77% of male adolescent sex offenders received a sentence of probation, and 22% were sentenced to "residential treatment" (Vandiver and Teske 2006).

However, the average sentence length of those in residential treatment was 2.8 years. Among those sent to residential treatment, 83% were given sentences less than 5 years, 12% were sentenced to 5–9 years, and only 5% received a sentence of 10 years or more. Differences emerge when comparing the average length of female sentences (2.8 years) to the average length of male sentences (5.5 years) (Vandiver and Teske 2006).

Only 50% of males received custodial sentences between 1 and 4 years, whereas 83% of females received an in-custody sentence of this length. Lengthier sentences of 10 years or more are given to males significantly more often than females, 27% and 5%, respectively (Vandiver and Teske 2006). It is possible that the coercive nature of some of the offenses committed by males may result in longer sentences than those of female offenders. Another possibility is that male sex offenders who receive residential sentences are viewed more harshly among judges than female sex offenders.

OFFENSE CHARACTERISTICS AND VICTIMIZATION PATTERNS

Early attempts to classify ASOs examined the contrast between offenders who strictly targeted children and those who offended against same-aged peers or adults. One study reviewed police records to identify characteristics that differentiated the two groups. Those with peer or adult victims were more likely than those with only child victims to have female victims (94% versus 68%) and to assault victims unrelated to the offender (84% versus 60%). This group also exhibited more gratuitous violence when committing the offense and showed higher rates of criminality in general (Hunter et al. 2000). This pattern is similar to adult sex offenders, in which those with pedophilia are less violent than nonpedophilic sex offenders (Motiuk and Brown 1996).

Victimization patterns have also been examined by comparing male and female ASOs. Although the majority of ASOs have victims who are younger than they are (Saunders and Awad 1988; Gilby et al. 1989; Greenfield 1997; Dwyer and Jerrell 2011), research generally suggests that female ASOs begin offending earlier than males. Females are also more likely than males to have younger victims ranging from infancy to 5 years of age (Veneziano and Veneziano 2002; Vandiver and Teske 2006). This may be due to their increased access to young children due to role-playing mother–child interactions as part of typical North American childhood play in which girls are given dolls and boys are given toy machines. In addition, male ASOs were significantly more likely to victimize someone of the opposite sex, whereas females tended to victimize both male and female victims equally (Fromuth and Conn 1997; Vandiver and Teske 2006).

RISK FACTORS

Similar to research on adult sex offenders, the literature on risk factors associated with ASOs focuses primarily on male offenders. One factor that increases the difficulty of accurate risk assessment in this population are the low recidivism base rates (Rich 2015), which range in the literature from 8% to 14% (Schram et al. 1991; Hagan et al. 1994; Rasmussen 1999; Miner 2002). The ongoing development and maturation of adolescents also need to be considered when examining risk factors in this population.

Traditional assessment of risk for sexual recidivism focuses on static factors that reflect past behaviors and experiences. Dynamic risk factors, however, involve variables that are amenable to change and are often used as treatment targets. How ingrained and persistent risk factors are in adolescent offenders is disputed. For example, Money claimed that "love maps" are established around age 8 and do not change, although unknown aspects of the love map may be discovered in later life (Money 1986). Cantor has claimed that pedophilia is "hardwired" due to a presumed abnormality of brain development and is therefore unchangeable (Cantor et al. 2008). Others have noted the fact that sexual interest changes in normal development (Fedoroff 2016). The literature on this crucial issue has been complicated by the conflation of variables such as gender identity and orientation with sexual interest and sex drive (Fedoroff 2016). It is generally agreed that some characteristics may be less resilient and more amenable to treatment than others, especially given the ongoing development of adolescents. Deviant sexual interest and psychopathic personality traits, for example, may be less static in adolescents than in their adult counterparts (Hunter 2012), and the *DSM-5* does not allow diagnosis of pedophilia in a person under age 16. As noted earlier, behavior and risk factors associated with ASOs must be examined through the lens of the social environment and in the context of child and adolescent development.

There are two general models of risk assessment with this population. The actuarial model involves statistical and mechanical assessment of risk based on comparison of static risk factors. Clinical risk assessment models are based on observation and professional judgment using defined risk factors. This model compares static and dynamic risk factors, while also taking into consideration protective factors (Rich 2015). Although each approach has its advantages, actuarial assessment has been found to be a more accurate predictor of risk overall, due to the fact that clinicians tend to "over-predict" recidivism (Hanson and Thornton 2000; Steadman et al. 2000; Harris and Rice 2007).

Research has identified some risk factors that are more strongly correlated to recidivism among ASOs. An empirical review of the literature by Worling and Långström (2003, 2006) identified five factors most strongly correlated with increased risk: deviant sexual arousal, previous sexual offense, multiple victims, social isolation, and failure to complete sex offender treatment programs. They also noted that problematic parent–child relationships and attitudes supportive of sexually abusive behavior were possible predictors of risk, but were not as strongly correlated as the other five.

Self-reported sexual interest in children or in sexual violence was found to be highly correlated with risk of sexual recidivism (Worling and Curwen 2000). Similarly, adolescent sexual recidivists were more likely to report sexual fantasies involving children or the use of force than adolescents who had not recidivated. Interestingly, despite the consistent use of Penile Plethysmography (PPG) as a measure of deviant sexual arousal for risk determinations in adult sex offenders (Hanson and Bussiere 1998; Murphy et al. 2015a,b), research has not found a strong correlation between PPG and risk of sexual recidivism among adolescent sex offenders (Gretton et al. 2001). PPG assessments are generally not recommended for ASOs due to the uncertain reliability of this measure in the population and the ethical issues involved in presenting individuals who are still developing with deviant sexual stimuli.

A number of offense-related characteristics are associated with increased risk of sexual recidivism. Research on both adult and adolescent sex offenders has found a significant correlation between sexual offense charges or convictions, prior to the index offense, and risk of sexual recidivism in the future (Hanson and Bussiere 1998). Additionally, the number of victims impacts an offender's propensity to commit more offenses. ASOs with two or more victims were more likely to go on to sexually re-offend than those with one victim (Langstrom 2002; Worling 2002). Most sexual offenses are committed by someone who is known to the victim; and this is true for ASOs as well (Myers 2001; Morris et al. 2002; Zolondek et al. 2002; Dwyer and Jerrell 2011). These offense-related factors are often noted in measures aimed at identifying risk in this population (Worling and Långström 2006).

Inability or lack of interest in developing close social ties with age-appropriate peers has also been associated with repeat sexual offending. ASOs with limited social skills were found to be three times more likely to sexually recidivate than ASOs with secure social ties and without other identified risk factors (Langstrom and Grann 2000). Inability to develop and maintain strong social relationships and general social isolation are factors that contribute to increased risk of offending in both adult and adolescent populations (Hanson 2000).

Research on effectiveness of sexual offender treatment programs suggests that integrating approaches to help build strong social and familial bonds, while also offering offender-specific interventions, increases the likelihood of successful reintegration (Worling and Curwen 2000). Conversely, individuals who fail to complete treatment or are unwilling to participate are statistically at an increased risk of sexual recidivism. A review of literature on the risk of recidivism in adult and adolescent populations identifies a positive treatment effect (Hanson et al. 2002; Worling and Långström 2006). For example, in the Hanson et al. (2002) meta-analysis, treated persons had a rate of 12.3% and untreated ones a rate of 16.8%.

Although not found as consistently, problematic parental relationships and attitudes supportive of offending have also been associated with increased risk of sexual recidivism. A moderate correlation with sexual recidivism has also been identified with perceived parental rejection. This in turn has also been associated with strength of parental bonds (Worling and Curwin 2000). Cognitive distortions and attitudes that blame the victim or minimize responsibility have been linked to increased risk of recidivism. Helmus et al. (2013) in their meta-analysis found a small but significant value in predicting recidivism for what they termed attitudes supporting sexual offending. Please see Risk Assessment below for further comments on this topic.

APPROACHES TO TREATMENT

Traditionally, treatment programs for adolescent sex offenders have been modeled after treatment programs created for adult sex offenders. However, research has not established whether or not such treatment approaches work for the adolescent sex offender population (Veneziano and Veneziano 2002). Recently, treatment programs for adolescents have been more frequently delivered within the community setting and have been tailored to suit the specific treatment needs of the adolescent population (Veneziano and Veneziano 2002).

Treatment approaches for adolescent sex offenders are often composed of various offense-specific and offense-related treatment targets. Such targets often include deviant sexual interests, poor parental attachment, cognitive distortion, pro-offending attitudes, and impulsivity (Hunter et al. 2004; Worling and Långström 2006). Adolescent sex offenders who receive cognitive-behavioral treatment that emphasizes family intervention have been shown to be significantly less likely to recidivate (Center for Sex Offender Management [CSOM] 2006). When the language style and avoidance goals used within an adult-oriented relapse prevention framework are altered to fit the needs of youth, results have shown promise (Murphy and Page 2000; Hunter and Longo 2004). Some suggest that the emphasis on incurability (inherent in relapse prevention approaches) is likely to negatively impact the offender's self-esteem, motivation, and confidence. By reframing this component, adolescents are able to make more positive life changes while in treatment (Hunter and Longo 2004).

Treatment for ASOs often includes group and individual sessions. Group treatment is advantageous as it increases efficacy and also facilitates the sharing of common experiences. However, it can be limiting if used as the sole treatment approach with sex offenders, as individual treatment targets may not be comprehensively explored within a group setting (Rich 2003; Worling 2004). Individual therapy can be used to address personal issues relating to the sex offending behavior and to promote the practical application of concepts learned in group sessions (CSOM 2006).

Pharmacological treatment approaches are also used among sex offender populations but are rarely utilized without concurrent therapy sessions. Anti-androgen treatments work to reduce testosterone levels and decrease the offender's overall sex drive. Due to ethical issues this type of treatment tends to be used more with adult sex offenders than adolescent sex offenders (Prentky 1997). Conversely, treatment for adolescent sex offending frequently involves techniques that are not specific to the sexually offending behavior but are deemed important in preventing future sex offending. Treatment targets and behavioral training among adolescent sex offenders usually focus on social skills and development, anger control, and substance abuse counselling rather than the use of drug therapy (Ertl and McNamara 1997).

Treatment outcomes among this population vary depending on the specific treatment targets and the general delivery of the program. Findings indicate when sex offender management strategies include a rehabilitative focus, the outcomes have been significantly more promising (Cullen and Gendreau 2000; Aos et al. 2006). In their review of the empirically supported treatment models, Dwyer and Letourneau (2011) recommended a family focused approach that focuses on healthy development without stigma. They also suggested use of treatment plans customized to the individual and taking into consideration that adolescents are still developing.

Guidelines for the treatment of male adolescent sex offenders between the ages of 12 and 18 have recently been published by the World Federation of Societies of Biological Psychiatry (WFSBP) (Thibaut et al. 2015). These guidelines are based on a systematic review of the literature and include discussion of 13 studies involving cognitive behavior therapy (CBT) and three studies involving multisystemic therapy (MST). Pharmacologic treatments involving selective serotonergic reuptake inhibitors (SSRIs), naltrexone (an opioid antagonist), medroxyprogesterone acetate (MPA) and cyproterone acetate (CPA), which are anti-androgens, and leuprolide (a gonadotropin hormone analogue, GNRHa) are also reviewed. The review is correctly cautious about advocating for any specific treatment due to the methodologic limitations of the published research. It notes that the levels of evidence as defined by Soyka et al (2008) are not good. Nevertheless, the WFSBP presents a treatment algorithm that begins with a recommendation for motivational interviewing, MST, CBT, and "psycho-social–educational" interventions (evidence level C or D). These psychological treatments are recommended for all adolescents regardless of level of assessed risk. Adolescents engaging in sexual behaviors with "low or moderate levels of violence" are recommended to receive SSRIs at the same dosages used to treat obsessive–compulsive disorder (evidence level D) with the caution that SSRIs have been associated with suicidal ideation in adolescents. The algorithm recommends that adolescents assessed as "high risk of violent sexual offending" should be treated with anti-androgens of increasing dosages followed by GnRHa's (evidence level D).

In addition to the low evidence levels in support of the recommended treatments in the above algorithm, there are additional levels of concern about following the algorithm as presented. The first is that the recommended treatments are based on sexual behaviors independent of diagnosis. A patient with major depression is more likely to benefit from treatments that also target depression than a patient with the same risk level but no mood disorder. The second is that SSRIs in the doses recommended in the WFSBP algorithm are associated with pharmacologically induced inhibited orgasm. Individuals with paraphilic interests are more likely to resort to their paraphilic fantasies if they have inhibited orgasm, making the treatment counterproductive. A third problem is the WFSBP focus on sex drive rather than paraphilic interest. For example, the WFSBP reviews and endorses treatment to reduce frequency of masturbation in adolescents who masturbate more than three times a day. There are many adolescents (and adults) who masturbate more frequently with absolutely no ill effects. Finally, the WFSBP recommends that antiandrogens be prescribed only by pediatric endocrinologists who likely have less experience with adolescent sex offenders than the average psychiatrist.

The WFSBP has attempted to provide some guidance for the assessment and treatment of adolescent sex offenders based on limited evidence. Some of the recommendations seem contradictory. For example, the WFSBP treatment guidelines for adolescent sexual offenders with paraphilic disorders state "we are unable to treat paraphilic disorders or sexual deviant (sic) behaviour specifically" (p. 21). Fortunately, the best evidence indicates that adolescents do well regardless of the specific treatment offered (Hanson et al. 2002; Reitzel and Carbonell 2006). According to the WFSBP article, only 15% of adolescent sex offenders are known to reoffend as adults (Worling and Långström 2006; Worling et al. 2010; Worling and Langton 2015). The most parsimonious explanation for this observation is that adolescent sex offenders recover from the factors that contributed to the index offence(s). We therefore recommend treatment be tailored to the individual needs of the adolescent, with algorithms being followed with extreme caution, if at all. For example, the WFSBP incorrectly states "pharmacotherapy cannot be a first-line treatment" (p. 27). The WFSBP correctly notes that motivation and willingness to follow treatment recommendations are important factors contributing to treatment efficacy. However, it also states, without reference, "In general, adjudicated youths are more motivated for treatment." In our experience, the reverse is true. This is because the aim of effective treatment is to enhance satisfaction from fully consensual sex. Treatment offered within adjudicated parameters is difficult to present as respectful of consensuality. Adolescents are quick to pick up on hypocrisy.

We recommend adolescent sex offenders be treated primarily as adolescents and with the expectation that they will develop consensual sexual interests. They should be told so, repeatedly. They should be educated about sex and especially that their problems are not due to sex itself, but rather due to sexual interest in nonconsensual themes (some paraphilias) and/or resorting to criminal acts. Efforts to facilitate healthy consensual sexual interests are almost always successful and easy to motivate.

RECIDIVISM RATES

A central theme in the literature on adolescent offenders is their propensity to re-offend and the likelihood that offending behavior will continue into adulthood. Studies on ASOs have found that rates of sexual recidivism tend to hover around 8%–14% (Schram et al. 1991; Hagan et al. 1994; Rasmussen 1999; Miner 2002). Studies examining the prevalence of nonsexual re-offending over an 8- to 10-year period reveal rates between 31% and 54% (Waite et al. 2005; Vandiver 2006). The most substantial point of this research is that a significant number of adolescent sex offenders continue to exhibit delinquent behavior and recidivate nonsexually, but relatively few continue patterns of sexual offending into adulthood.

Research by Sipe et al. (1998) followed a group of 164 juveniles convicted of a sexual offense for a period of up to 14 years after turning 18. At the time of the juvenile offense, the sample ranged from 11 to 18 years old. Results indicated that 10% of the juvenile sex offenders were arrested again in adulthood for a sexual offense and 33% recidivated with a nonsexual offense in adulthood. Interestingly, research has revealed that individuals with a high score on the Psychopathy Checklist: Youth Version (PCL: YV) and deviant sexual interests as measured by penile plethysmographic testing were more likely to recidivate sexually and nonsexually (Gretton 2001). Such findings suggest the presence of psychopathy in adolescent sex offenders may have much of the same implications from a criminal justice perspective as it does for adult sex offenders (Gretton 2001).

Risk factors that increase the likelihood an ASO will sexually re-offend include deviant sexual interests, prior criminal sanctions for hands-on sexual offenses, past criminal offenses with two or more victims, stranger victims, and social isolation from peers (Poortinga et al. 2009).

In order to understand the recidivism rates of ASOs in context, it is important to examine the relative recidivism rates of adult sex offenders. Bonta and Hanson (1995) performed a study on adult male offenders who were released from Correctional Services Canada between 1983 and 1984. The researchers examined recidivism within this group of males as measured by reconviction of any offense recorded. Findings indicated the base rate of sexual recidivism is significantly less than the general recidivism rate. For sexual offenders 10%–15% were reconvicted of another sexual offense over a 5-year period. When the follow-up period was extended to 10 years, the sexual recidivism rates increased to 20%. On a 15-year follow-up the rates rose to 25%.

The sexual recidivism rate in a group of mixed sex offenders was examined in a data set of 10 individual samples. Sexual recidivism was defined as new charges in the first five samples and by new convictions in the other five samples. The sexual recidivism rates for those who sexually assaulted adult women where similar to the rates of those who had sexually assaulted children (Webster et al. 1994). Although, it was found that rapists were much more likely than child molesters to re-offend in a nonsexual violent manner. Among the sample of child molesters, those who sexually offended against unrelated boy victims were most likely to sexually recidivate. This group was followed by those who offended against unrelated girl victims and by incest offenders (Hanson et al. 1993).

Although data support the fact that a large proportion of sexual offenders do not go on to sexually re-offend, it is important to note that many sex offenses go undetected by the police and official reports (Webster et al. 1994). According to Hanson et al. (1993), a reasonable estimate of actual rates of recidivism would be at least 10%–15% higher than the actual observed rates. As a result of these hidden figures of offending, it is difficult to accurately place the exact base rate of sexual recidivism. However, for the time being, such base rates are widely accepted and used in determining risk for sexual recidivism among adult sex offenders.

Concerning ASOs, two factors seem particularly important. The first is that risk of sexual recidivism decreases as age increases. The second is that risk of sexual re-offense decreases the longer the offender does not re-offend (Hanson et al. 2014). These two facts reinforce the likelihood that early interventions, especially if they precede commission of any crimes, are likely to be effective not only by preventing initial sex offenses but also by taking advantage of the fact that adolescents are developing and therefore, by definition, changing. It seems reasonable to expect successful interventions early on will pay off. Hopefully, ongoing research and treatment delivered with optimism about the outcome will show these statements are true.

SUMMARY KEY POINTS

- Almost half of sexual offenses are committed by adolescents
- Culture and context are factors of what is considered “normal” during early sexual exploration and development
- ASOs are a heterogeneous population and differ on many variables
- Although ASOs do not typically suffer from serious mental health issues, they are however more likely to have learning deficits, inadequate social skills, and conduct disorder
- Generally, families are more reluctant to report sexual offenses when the offender is an adolescent compared to if they were an adult
- Sentencing patterns for male and female ASOs are significantly different
- Treatment approaches often target offense-specific and offense-related treatment targets
- Treatment outcomes depend on the specific treatment targets set and on program delivery
- The risk of sexual recidivism decreases as age increases and the longer the offender does not reoffend

REFERENCES

Abel G, J Becker, and M Mittleman. 1985. Sex offenders: Results of assessment and recommendations for treatment. In *Clinical Criminology: Current Concepts*, edited by H Ben-Aaron, S Hunter, and C Webster. Toronto: M and M Graphics, 207–220.

Abel GG, CA Osborn, DA Twigg. 1993. Sexual assault through the life span: Adult offenders with juvenile histories. In *The Juvenile Sexual Offender*, edited by HE Barbaree, WL Marshall, and DR Laws. New York: Guilford Press, 104–116.

American Psychiatric Association Task Force on Sexually Dangerous Offenders. 1999. *Dangerous Sex Offenders: A Task Force Report of the American Psychiatric Association*. Washington, DC: American Psychiatric Association.

Aos S, M Miller, and E Drake. 2006. *Evidence-Based Adult Corrections Programs: What Works and What Does Not*. Olympia, WA: Washington State Institute for Public Policy.

Bonta J and R Hanson. 1995. Violent recidivism of men released from prison. Paper presented at the 103rd Annual Convention of the American Psychological Association, New York.

Bourke ML and B Donohue. 1996. Assessment and treatment of juvenile sex offenders: An empirical review. *Journal of Child Sexual Abuse* 5:47–70.

Brown A and DL Burton. 2010. Exploring the overlap in male juvenile sexual offending and general delinquency: Trauma, alcohol use, and masculine beliefs. *Journal of Child Sexual Abuse* 19(4):450–468.

Bumby KM, N Halstenson, and NH Bumby. 1997. Adolescent female sexual offenders. In *The Sex Offender: New Insights, Treatment, Innovations, and Legal Developments*, edited by BK Schwartz and HR Cellini. Kingston, NJ: Civic Research Institute, 1–16.

Burton DL. 2000. Were adolescent sexual offenders children with sexual behavior problems? Sexual Abuse: A Journal of Research and Treatment 12(1):37–48.

Burton DL, DL Miller, and TS Chien. 2002. A social learning theory comparison of the sexual victimization of adolescent sexual offenders and nonsexual offending male delinquents. *Child Abuse & Neglect* 26(9):893–907.

Canadian Criminal Code, 1985, SC 1892, c.29.

Cantor JM. 2012. Is homosexuality a paraphilia? The evidence for and against. *Archives of Sexual Behavior* 41:237–247.

Cantor JM, N Kabani, BK Christensen, RB Zipursky, HE Barbaree, R Dickey, and R Blanchard. 2008. Cerebral white matter deficiencies in pedophilic men. *Journal of Psychiatric Research* 42:167–183.

Center for Sex Offender Management (CSOM). 2006. *Understanding Treatment for Adults and Juveniles Who Have Committed Sex Offenses*. Silver Spring, MD: Offices of Justice Programs, 1–16.

Cullen FT and P Gendreau. 2000. Assessing correctional rehabilitation: Policy, practice and prospects. In *Criminal Justice 2000: Policies, Processes, and Decisions of the Criminal Justice System*, edited by J Horney, Washington, DC: U.S. Department of Justice, 109–176.

Davis GE and H Leitenberg. 1987. Adolescent sex offenders. *Psychological Bulletin* 101:417–427.

Driemeyer W, A Spehr, D Yoon, H Richter-Appelt, and P Briken. 2013. Comparing sexuality, aggressiveness, and antisocial behavior of alleged juvenile sexual and violent offenders. *Journal of Forensic Sciences* 58(3):711–718.

Dwyer RG and JM Jerrell. 2011. Use of mental health services by youths who have sexually offended. *Adolescent Psychiatry* 1(3):245–250.

Dwyer RG and EJ Letourneau. 2011. Juveniles who sexually offend: Recommending a treatment program and level of care. *Child and Adolescent Psychiatric Clinics of North America* 20(3): 413–429.

Ertl M and J McNamara. 1997. Treatment of juvenile sex offenders: A review of the literature. *Child and Adolescent Social Work Journal* 14(3):199–221.

Fanniff AM and ER Kimonis. 2014. Juveniles who have committed sexual offenses: A special group? *Behavioral Sciences and the Law* 32(2):240–257.

Fedoroff JP. 2016. Managing versus successfully treating paraphilic disorders: The paradigm is changing. In *Handbook of Clinical Sexuality for Mental Health Professionals*, 3rd edition, edited by S Levine, New York: Routledge, 345–361.

Finkelhor D, R Ormrod, and M Chaffin. 2009. Juveniles who commit sex offenses against minors. *Juvenile Justice Bulletin*, NCJ 227763. Washington, DC: U.S. Department of Justice. Office of Justice Programs.

Fromuth ME and VE Conn. 1997. Hidden perpetrators: Sexual molestation in a non-clinical sample of college women. *Journal of Interpersonal Violence* 12(3):456–465.

Gal M and R Hoge. 1999. A profile of the adolescent sex offender. *Youth and Corrections* 11(2):7–11.

Goocher B. 1994. Some comments on the residential treatment of juvenile sex offenders. *Child Youth Care Forum* 23:243–250.

Greenfield LA. 1997. *Sex Offenses and Offenders: An Analysis of Data on Rape and Sexual Assault, NCJ-163392*. Washington, DC: U.S. Department of Justice Office of Justice Programs Bureau of Justice Statistics, 1–39.

Gretton HM, M McBridge, RD Hare, O'R Shaughnessy, and G Kumka. 2001. Psychopathy and recidivism in adolescent sex offenders. *Criminal Justice and Behavior* 28(4):427–449.

Hagan MP, RP King, and RL Patros. 1994. Recidivism among adolescent perpetrators of sexual assault against children. *Journal of Offender Rehabilitation* 12:127–137.

Hanson RK. 2000. *Risk Assessment*. Beaverton, OR: Association for the Treatment of Sexual Abusers.

Hanson RK and MT Bussiere. 1998. Predicting relapse: A meta-analysis of sexual offender recidivism studies. *Journal of Consulting and Clinical Psychology* 66:348–362.

Hanson RK, A Gordon, AJ Harris, JK Marques, W Murphy, VL Quinsey, and MC Seto. 2002. First report of the collaborative outcome data project on the effectiveness of psychological treatment for sex offenders. *Sexual Abuse: A Journal of Research and Treatment* 14:169–194.

Hanson RK, A Harris, L Helmus, and D Thorton. 2014. High-risk sex offenders may not be high risk forever. *Journal of Interpersonal Violence* March:1–22.

Hanson RK, R Steffy, and R Gauthier. 1993. Long term recidivism of child molesters. *Journal of Consulting and Clinical Psychology* 61:646–652.

Hanson RK and D Thornton. 2000. Improving risk assessments for sex offenders: A comparison of three actuarial scales. *Law and Human Behavior* 24:119–136.

Harris G and M Rice. 2007. Characterizing the value of actuarial violence risk assessments. *Criminal Justice and Behavior* 34:1638–1658.

Helmus L, RK Hanson, KM Babchishin, and RE Mann. 2013. Attitudes supportive of sexual offending predict recidivism: A meta-analysis. *Trauma, Violence, and Abuse* 14(1):34–53.

Hingsburger D, DM Griffiths, and V Quinsey. 1991. Detecting counterfeit deviance: Differentiating sexual deviance from sexual inappropriateness. *Habilitative Mental Healthcare Newsletter* 10:51–54.

Hunter JA. 2012. Patterns in sexual offending in juveniles and risk factors. In *Juvenile Sex Offenders: A Guide to Evaluation and Treatment for Mental Health Professionals*, edited by EP Ryan, JA Hunter, and DC Murrie, New York: Oxford University Press.

Hunter JA, AJ Figueredo, NM Malamuth, and Becker JV. 2003. Juvenile sex offenders: Toward the development of a typology. *Sexual Abuse: A Journal of Research and Treatment* 15(1):27–48.

Hunter JA, SA Gilbertson, D Vedros, and M Morton. 2004. Strengthening community-based programming for juvenile sex offenders: Key concepts and paradigm shifts. *Child Maltreatment* 9:177–189.

Hunter JA, RR Hazelwood, and D Slesinger. 2000. Juvenile-perpetrated sex crimes: Patterns of offending and predictors of violence. *Journal of Family Violence* 15(1):81–93.

Hunter JA and AJ Figueredo. 1999. Factors associated with treatment compliance in a population of juvenile sexual offenders. *Sexual Abuse: A Journal of Research and Treatment* 11(1):49–67.

Hunter J and RE Longo. 2004. Relapse prevention with juvenile sexual abusers: A holistic and integrated approach. In *The Handbook of Clinical Intervention with Young People Who Sexually Abuse*, edited by G O'Reilly, WL Marshall, A Carr, and RC Beckett, New York: Brunner-Routledge, 297–314.

Kahn TJ and HJ Chambers. 1991. Assessing re-offense risk with juvenile sex offenders. *Child Welfare* 70:333–345.

Kobayashi J, BD Sales, JV Becker, AJ Figueredo, and MS Kaplan. 1995. Perceived parental deviance, parent-child bonding, child and abuse and child sexual aggression. *Sexual Abuse: A Journal of Research and Treatment* 7:25–43.

Lakey JF. 1994. The profile of treatment of male adolescent sex offenders. *Adolescence* 29(116):755–762.

Langstrom N. 2002. Long-term follow-up of criminal recidivism in young sex offenders: Empirical patterns and risk factors. *Psychology, Crime and Law* 8:41–58.

Langstrom N and M Grann. 2000. Risk for criminal recidivism among young sex offenders. *Journal of Interpersonal Violence* 15:855–871.

Lowenstein L. 2006. Aspects of young sex abusers—A review of the literature concerning young sex abusers (1996–2004). *Clinical Psychology and Psychotherapy* 13:47–55.

Madsen L, S Parsons, and D Grubin. 2006. The relationship between the five-factor model and DSM personality disorder in a sample of child molesters. *Personality and Individual Differences* 40:227–236.

Miner MH. 2002. Factors associated with recidivism in juveniles: An analysis of serious juvenile sex offenders. *Journal of Research in Crime and Delinquency* 39(4):421–435.

Money J. 1986. *Lovemaps*. New York: Irvington.

Morris RE, MM Anderson, and GW Knox. 2002. Incarcerated adolescents' experiences as perpetrators of sexual assault. *Archives of Pediatric and Adolescent Medicine* 156:831–835.

Motiuk L and S Brown. 1996. Factors related to recidivism among released federal offenders. Correctional Service Canada. http://www.csc-scc.gc.ca/research/r49e-eng.shtml, accessed December 27, 2015.

Murphy L, R Ranger, JP Fedoroff, H Stewart, G Dwyer, and W Burke. 2015b. Standardization in the use of penile plethysmography testing in assessment of problematic sexual interests. *Journal of Sexual Medicine* 12(9):1853–1861.

Murphy L, R Ranger, H Stewart, G Dwyer, and JP Fedoroff. 2015a. Assessment of problematic sexual interests with the penile plethysmograph: An overview of assessment laboratories. *Current Psychiatry Reports* 17(5):29.

Murphy WD and IJ Page. 2000. Relapse prevention with adolescent sex offenders. In *Remaking Relapse Prevention with Sex Offenders: A Sourcebook*, edited by DR Laws, SM Hudson, and T Ward, Thousand Oaks, CA: Sage, 353–368.

Murrie DC. 2012. Placing sexual behavior problems in context. In *Juvenile Sex Offenders: A Guide to Evaluation and Treatment for Mental Health Professionals*, edited by EP Ryan, JA Hunter, and DC Murrie, New York: Oxford University Press, 21–33.

Myers WC. 2001. Juvenile sex offenders. In the *American Academy of Child and Adolescent Psychiatry Task Force on Juvenile Justice Reform October 1999–October 2001. Recommendations for Juvenile Justice Reform*, edited by W Arroyo, W Buzogany, and G Hansen, Washington, DC: American Academy of Child and Adolescent Psychiatry, 56–59.

Poortinga E, S Newma, CE Negendank, and EP Benedek. 2009. Juvenile sex offenders: Epidemiology, risk assessment and treatment. In *Sex Offenders: Identification, Risk Assessment, Treatment and Legal Issues*, edited by FM Saleh, AJ Jr, Grudzinskas, JM Bradford, and DJ Brodsky, New York: Oxford University Press, 221–240.

Prentky R. 1997. Arousal reduction in sexual offenders: A review of anti-androgen interventions. *Sexual Abuse: A Journal of Research and Treatment* 9(4):335–347.

Prentky R, B Harris, K Frizzell, and S Righthand. 2000. An actuarial procedure for assessing risk in juvenile sex offenders. *Sexual Abuse: A Journal of Research and Treatment* 12(2):71–93.

Rasmussen LA. 1999. Factors related to recidivism among juvenile sexual offenders. *Sexual Abuse: A Journal of Research and Treatment* 11(1):69–85.

Rasmussen LA. 2004. Differentiating youth who sexually abuse: Applying a multidimensional framework when assessing and treating subtypes. *Journal of Child Sexual Abuse* 13:57–82.

Reitzel LR and JL Carbonell. 2006. The effectiveness of sexual offender treatment for juveniles as measured by recidivism: A meta-analysis. *Sexual Abuse: A Journal of Research and Treatment* 18:401–421.

Rich P. 2003. *Understanding, Assessing and Rehabilitation Juvenile Sexual Offenders.* Hoboken, NJ: Wiley.

Rich P. 2015. *The Assessment of Risk for Sexual Reoffense in Juveniles Who Commit Sexual Offenses.* Washington, DC: U.S. Department of Justice, Office of Sex Offender Sentencing, Monitoring, Apprehending, Registering, and Tracking.

Robertiello G and K Terry. 2007. Can we profile sex offenders? A review of sex offender typologies. *Aggression and Violent Behavior* 12(5):508–519.

Ryan G, TJ Miyoshi, JL Metzner, RD Krugman, and GE Fryer. 1996. Trends in a national sample of sexually abusive youths. *Journal of the American Academy of Child and Adolescent Psychiatry* 33:17–25.

Saleh FM and GM Vincent. 2004. Juveniles who commit sex crimes. *Annals of the American Society of Adolescent Psychiatry* 28:183–207.

Salter D, D McMillan, M Richards, T Talbot, J Hodges, A Bentovim, R Hastings, J Stevenson, and Skuse D. 2003. Development of sexually abusive behaviour in sexually victimized males: A longitudinal study. *Lancet* 361:471–476.

Saunders EB and GA Awad. 1988. Assessment, management, and treatment planning for male adolescent sexual offenders. *American Journal of Orthopsychiatry* 58(4):571–579.

Schram DD, DD Milloy, and WE Rowe. 1991. *Juvenile Sex Offenders: A Follow-Up Study of Reoffense Behavior.* Olympia, WA: Washington State Institute for Public Policy, Urban Policy Research and Cambie Group International.

Seto MC and ML Lalumière. 2010. What is so special about male adolescent sexual offending? A review and test of explanations through meta-analysis. *Psychological Bulletin* 136(4):526–575.

Sexual Exploitation and Other Abuse of Children, 18 USC § 2256; 1984; renumbered 1986.

Shaw JA, The Work Group on Quality Issues. 1999. Practice parameters for the assessment and treatment of children and adolescents who are sexually abusive of others. *Journal of the American Academy of Child and Adolescent Psychiatry* 38(12 Supplement):S55–S76.

Sipe R, E Jensen, and R Everett. 1998. Adolescent sex offenders grown up. *Criminal Justice and Behavior* 25(1):109–124.

Snyder HN. 2000. Sexual assault of young children as reported to law enforcement: Victim, incident, and offender characteristics. *A National Incident-Based Reporting System (NIBRS) Statistical Report.* http://www.bjs.gov/content/pub/pdf/saycrle.pdf, accessed December 27, 2015.

Soyka M, UW Preuss, V Hesselbrock, P Zill, G Koller, B Bondy. 2008. GABA-A2 receptor subunit gene (GABRA2) polymorphisms and risk for alcohol dependence. *Journal of Psychiatric Research* 42:184–191.

Steadman HJ, E Silver, J Monahan, PS Appelbaum, PC Robbins, EP Mulvey, T Grisso, LH Roth, and S Banks. 2000. A classification tree approach to the development of actuarial violence risk assessment tools. *Law and Human Behavior* 24:83–100.

Thibaut F, JMW Bradford, P Briken, F De La Barra, F Häßler, and P Cosyns. 2015. The World Federation of Societies of Biological Psychiatry (WFSBP) guidelines for the treatment of adolescent sexual offenders with paraphilic disorders. *World Journal of Biological Psychiatry* 17:1–37.

Timms S and AJ Goreczny. 2002. Adolescent sex offenders with mental retardation: Literature review and assessment considerations. *Journal of Aggression and Violent Behavior* 7:1–19.

U.S. Department of Justice. 2009. *Uniform Crime Report.* Washington, DC: U.S. Department of Justice.

Vandiver D. 2006. A prospective analysis of juvenile male sex offenders: Characteristics and recidivism rates as adults. *Journal of Interpersonal Violence* 21(5):673–688.

Vandiver M and R Teske. 2006. Juvenile female and male sex offenders. *International Journal of Offender Therapy and Comparative Criminology* 50(2):148–165.

Van Wijk A, R Vermeirer, R Loeber, L Hart-Karkhoffs, T Doreleijers, and R Bullens. 2006. Juvenile sex offenders compared to non-sex offenders. *Trauma, Violence, and Abuse* 7(4):227–243.

Veneziano C and L Veneziano. 2002. Adolescent sex offenders: A review of literature. *Trauma, Violence, and Abuse* 3(4):247–260.

Veneziano C, L Veneziano, S LeGrand, and L Richards. 2004. Neuropsychological executive functions of adolescent sex offenders and non-sex offenders. *Psychological Reports* 81:483–489.

Waite D, A Keller, EL McGarvey, E Wieckowski, R Pinkerton, and GL Brown. 2005. Juvenile sex offender re-arrest rates for sexual, violent nonsexual and property crimes: A 10-year follow-up. *Sexual Abuse: A Journal of Research and Treatment* 17(3):313–331.

Webster C, G Harris, M Rice, C Cormier, and V Quinsey. 1994. *The Violence Prediction Scheme: Assessing Dangerousness in High Risk Men.* Toronto, ON: Canadian Cataloguing in Publication Data.

Worling JR. 2002. Assessing risk of sexual assault recidivism with adolescent sexual offenders. In *Young People Who Sexually Abuse: Building the Evidence Base for Your Practice*, edited by MC Calder, Lyme, Regis Dorset, UK: Russell House, 365–375.

Worling JR. 2004. Essentials of a good intervention program for sexually abusive juveniles: Offense related treatment tasks. In *The Handbook of Clinical Intervention with Young People Who Sexually Abuse*, edited by G O'Reilly, WL Marshall, A Carr, and RC Beckett, New York: Brunner-Routledge, 275–296.

Worling JR and T Curwen. 2000. Adolescent sex offender recidivism: Success of specialized treatment and implications for risk prediction. *Child Abuse and Neglect* 24(7):965–982.

Worling JR and N Långström. 2003. Assessment of criminal recidivism risk with adolescents who have offended sexually. *Trauma, Violence, and Abuse* 4:341–362.

Worling JR and N Långström. 2006. Risk of sexual recidivism in adolescents who sexually offend. In *The Juvenile Sexual Offender*, 2nd edition, edited by HE Barbaree and WL Marshall, New York: Guilford Press, 219–247.

Worling JR and CM Langton. 2015. A prospective investigation of factors that predict desistance from recidivism for adolescents who have sexually offended. *Sex Abuse* 27:127–142.

Worling JR, A Littlejohn, and D Bookalam. 2010. 20-Year prospective follow-up study of specialized treatment for adolescents who offended sexually. *Behavioral Science and the Law* 28:46–57.

Ybarra ML and KJ Mitchell. 2013. Prevalence rates of male and female sexual violence perpetrators in a national sample of adolescents. *JAMA Pediatrics* 167(12):1125–1134.

Zgourides G, M Monto, and R. Harris. 1997. Correlates of adolescent male sexual offense: Prior adult sexual contact, sexual attitudes, and use of sexually explicit materials. *International Journal of Offender Therapy and Comparative Criminology* 41(3):272–283.

Zolondek SC, GG Abel, WF Northey, Jr, and AD Jordan. 2002. The self-reported behaviors of juvenile sexual offenders. In *Current Perspectives on Sex Crimes*, edited by RM Holmes and ST Holmes, Thousand Oaks, CA: Sage, 153–161.

47

Juvenile competency to stand trial, competency attainment, and remediation

ERAKA BATH AND SHAWN SIDHU

INTRODUCTION

Legal competence is a critically important cornerstone of the U.S. legal system, a system rooted in the principle of equal justice for all, and which prides itself on providing numerous procedural safeguards to maintain fairness. Legal competence is a core component of the "Due Process" provisions that are constitutionally protected by the Fifth and Fourteenth Amendments (LII/Legal Information Institute 2014a,b). In *Dusky v. US,* the U.S. Supreme Court set forth the constitutionally required test for competence to stand trial (Baerger et al. 2003). Being competent to stand trial as defined by the *Dusky* standard requires that the defendant has (1) sufficient present ability to consult with his lawyer with a reasonable degree of rational understanding and (2) a rational as well as factual understanding of the proceedings against him or her (Baerger et al. 2003). States vary in terms of including mental illness or developmental disability (or similarly worded predicates of competency) in their statutory definitions of competency to stand trial. In California, the *Dusky* standard is interpreted through Penal Code Section 1367, with incompetency to stand trial statutorily defined as being "a result of a mental disorder or developmental disability." In that sense, mental illness or developmental disability is considered necessary but not sufficient to be found incompetent to stand trial (IST). However, this statute does not mention the unique factors that arise in applying the competency issue to a juvenile population, namely, the impact of developmental maturity on competency to stand trial (CST).

Information about youths' competency to stand trial status is important for several reasons. First, states need guidance for the development of meaningful laws in this area. Basic research on cognitive and psychosocial development suggests that some youths will manifest deficits in legally relevant abilities similar to deficits seen in adults with mental disabilities, but for reasons of immaturity rather than mental disorders (Grisso et al. 2003). Unfortunately, nationally, the majority of states still do not have specific laws that address competency status in juveniles and default to the *Dusky* standard, a standard that was developed for adult defendants impaired by mental retardation and/or mental illness. Second, determination of a youth's competency to stand trial status may reveal important data about treatment and rehabilitative needs for highly vulnerable youth who may not otherwise be formally assessed or have had prior access to mental health treatment. For young offenders, all too often, psychiatric diagnoses, learning problems, and developmental and intellectual disabilities are first revealed *after* contact with law enforcement, and oftentimes during the course of a juvenile competency to stand trial evaluation. Nationally, many youth who come into contact with the juvenile justice system are racial and ethnic minorities.

JUVENILE OFFENDERS AND ADJUDICATIVE COMPETENCE

Once a youth enters the legal system, he or she is often placed in acute detainment until he or she receives a court date and can have a legal proceeding. Some youth may be on house arrest or other forms of holding during this time. If deemed competent to stand trial, the youth will then progress to trial and will undergo adjudication as determined by the judge. Common forms of adjudication in youth include a longer-term placement in a juvenile justice facility, placement on a forensic psychiatry unit or residential treatment center or home on probation, and possibly community service or another comparable punishment. Figure 47.1 provides a graphic illustration of a juvenile's pathway through juvenile court and where issues of competency may be raised.

The question of competence, in most states, may be raised by the judge, district attorney, or defense attorney (Grisso 2005a). Laws determine that these parties have an obligation to raise the question of competence whenever there is doubt that the defendant might have deficits in

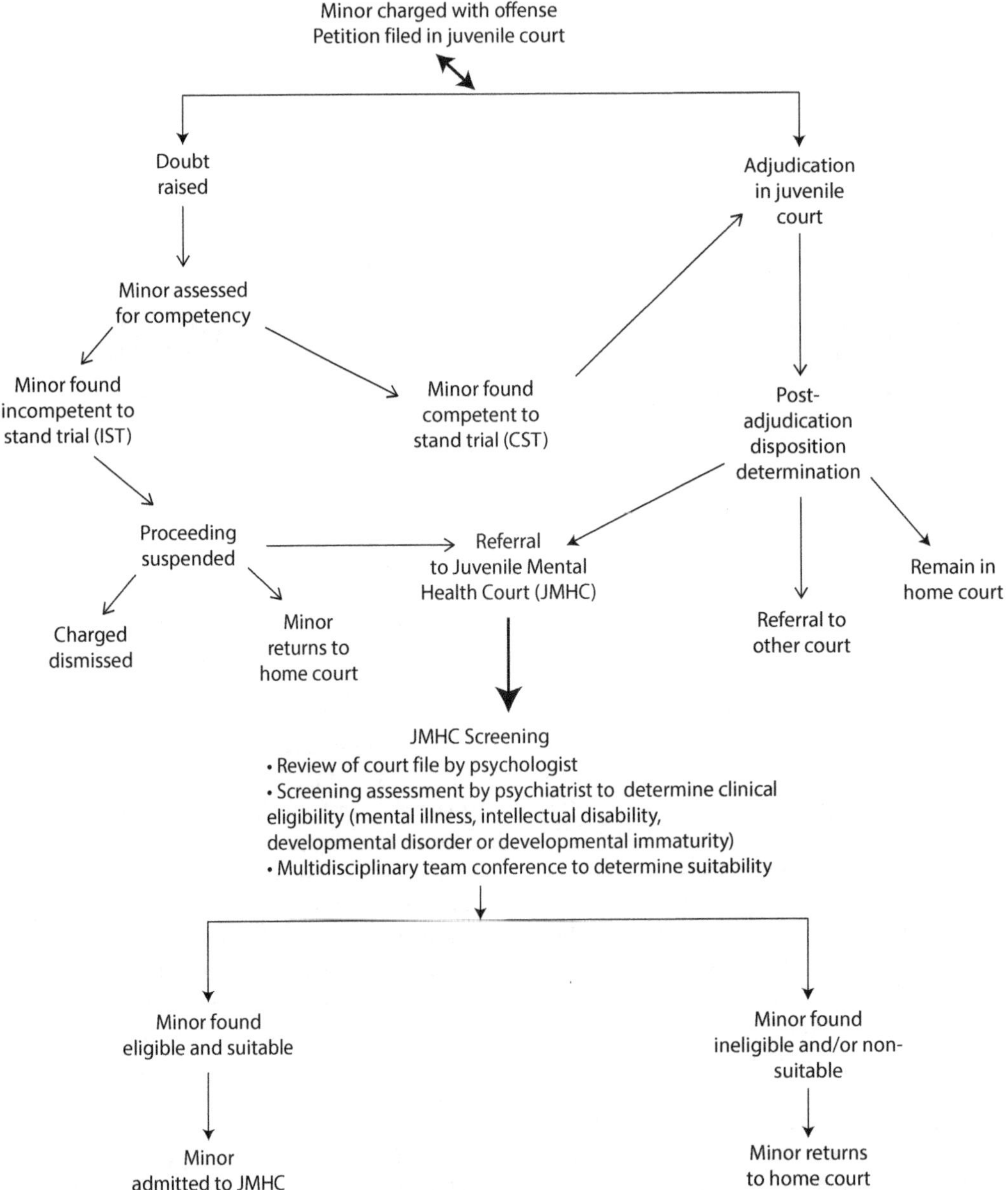

Figure 47.1 Minor charged with offense petition filed in juvenile court.

abilities related to competence to stand trial (Grisso 2005b). The court then orders a competency evaluation by a psychiatrist or psychologist with training and experience in juvenile forensic work. In many states, the competency evaluation must be completed, and results reported to the court, within a specified time period, with the potential for requesting an extension of the time period under extraordinary circumstances. The examiner then prepares a written report of competence evaluation. If deemed incompetent, in accordance with the Fourteenth Amendment of the U.S. Constitution and *Dusky v. United States*, the youth cannot legally proceed to trial for adjudication.

It is important that forensic examiners be familiar with the legal criteria for juvenile competency to stand trial (JCST). Examiners must possess a unique blend of expertise, including special training, knowledge, skill, and experience (Grisso 1998). It is also important to be familiar with the justice systems they are practicing in and the typical youth that are involved with those systems (Kruh and Grisso 2008). Expertise should be focused on forensic assessment and child development. Specifically, child clinical and developmental expertise should be in the following: normal development, developmental psychopathology, and developmentally appropriate assessment (Kruh and Grisso 2008).

In communities where professionals with these credentials are not available, other professionals can receive certification to perform competency evaluations through continuing education courses. In the most rural areas of the country, experts can be called in to perform evaluations, or less preferably mental health professionals without training can perform the evaluation. In rural communities or small ethno-cultural communities, there is often only one psychologist who is able to provide mental health services to a diverse-needs population (Fisher 2012). If a referral for competency to stand trial evaluation is made, and a forensic psychologist/psychiatrist is not available, any psychologist who has a background in clinical and/or assessment can conduct the evaluation. The Psychologists Code of Ethics Standard 2.01d (Standards of Competence) states that when psychologists are asked to provide services for which they have not obtained the competence necessary, psychologists who have closely related experience or prior training may provide such services if they make a reasonable effort to obtain the competence necessary by utilizing consultation, study, or relevant training and research. This standard provides two stipulations in which these services may be provided by a psychologist who does not have the education or experience required: (1) the psychologist's prior experience and training must be closely related to the service needed, and (2) agreeing to provide the service means that the psychologist must make reasonable efforts to obtain the skills and knowledge needed to effectively and efficiently conduct their work (Fisher 2012).

ASSESSMENT OF COMPETENCY TO STAND TRIAL IN JUVENILES AND REVIEW OF THE JCST SCALES

A variety of instruments have been developed to aid mental health professionals in the determination of competency to stand trial status. It is important to note that these instruments are only meant to be used as a supplement to a thorough clinical evaluation and do not definitively determine competency status independently. The majority of these instruments were developed originally for adults, and thus many were not standardized for use in children and adolescents. These tools vary in administration, structure, detail, objectivity of scoring criteria, empirical support, quality of concepts, domain detail, and generalizability (Mayzer et al. 2009). Examiners have the option to use standardized quantitative CST forensic assessment instruments (FAIs) or semistructured interviews that were developed specifically for use with the juvenile population (Juvenile Adjudicative Competence Interview, JACI) (Acklin 2012).

Juvenile adjudicative competence interview (JACI)

When a juvenile's competence is in question, the Juvenile Adjudicative Competence Interview (JACI) is considered the gold standard (Grisso 2005a). It provides the clinician with a structured set of questions to assess the understanding, appreciation, and reasoning in decisions about rights waiver as it pertains directly to the legal standard for competence to stand trial of the youth (Grisso 2005a; Kruh and Grisso 2008). Examiners are also provided with the definitions of the four dimensions of developmental maturity/immaturity and the various ways that these dimensions might present in an adolescent's responses to the JACI (Grisso 2005a; Kruh and Grisso 2008). The primary purpose of the JACI is to ensure that those conducting the examination are collecting relevant information to be considered when formulating an opinion about a youth's capacity for adjudicative competence (Kruh and Grisso 2008). All questions on the JACI should be presented to the youth in the order in which they appear on the form. At no time should the examiner rearrange the order or omit questions when administering the JACI.

The JACI is unique because if a youth fails to demonstrate an understanding, it provides a learning experience through "capacity checks." Capacity checks allow the examiner to teach the youth fact-related information pertaining to legal issues, and the opportunity to assess the youth's immediate and long-term retention of this information at a later time in the interview process.

Competence Assessment for Standing Trial for Defendants with Mental Retardation

The Competence Assessment for Standing Trial for Defendants with Mental Retardation (CAST-MR) is a highly structured interview including both multiple choice and open-ended questions designed to assess the competency of adult defendants who are intellectually disabled (Everington 1990; Kruh and Grisso 2008). The measure contains 50 items divided into three sections: Basic Legal Skills, Skills to Assist the Defense, and Understanding Case Events. These sections individually assess the defendant's knowledge of the adjudicative process, the defendant's understanding of the attorney–client relationship, and the defendant's ability to effectively discuss and communicate the facts of the case (Everington 1990; Kruh and Grisso 2008). Although the CAST-MR was not developed for juveniles, it was developed for defendants with limited cognitive abilities, and all items on the CAST-MR are set at a second-grade reading level, which makes it generalizable to youth (Kruh and Grisso 2008). The scoring criteria of this instrument are highly detailed and are provided for the open-ended questions; answers to the multiple choice questions are also provided (Kruh and Grisso 2008).

The CAST-MR is proven to have reliable scores, and demonstrate acceptable classification rates (Everington 1990; Kruh and Grisso 2008). However, it fails to assess for immature appreciation, which would require supplemental questioning. It also was not designed to assess psychosis-based threats to Competency to Stand Trial, which would eliminate it from being an appropriate choice if psychosis is of concern (Everington 1990; Kruh and Grisso 2008).

MacArthur Competence Assessment Tool—Criminal Adjudication

The MacArthur Competence Assessment Tool—Criminal Adjudication (MacCAT-CA) was developed by the MacArthur Foundation Research Network on Mental Health and the Law (Burnett et al. 2004; Acklin 2012). It is a highly standardized 22-item, measure that generally takes approximately 30–45 minutes to administer, and is known as the "queen" of competency to stand trial instruments. It has three different sections that assess the Understanding, Appreciation, Decision Making, and Assisting through the use of vignette methodology (Burnett et al. 2004; Acklin 2012). A benefit of using vignettes is that it helps the clinician determine the quality of the response through the production of ratings: 2 (adequate), 1 (questionable), or 0 (inadequate). Another benefit of the vignette methodology is its ability to remove the youth's emotionality of his or her case to assess the youth's true abilities (Acklin 2012). The MacCAT-CA has demonstrated significant reliability, and internal consistency improving classification accuracy. There has been some criticism of the vignette methodology because it provides little opportunity to thoroughly assess the Appreciation and Understanding as it pertains to the defendant's case (Burnett et al. 2004; Kruh and Grisso 2008; Acklin 2012). This is a limitation of this instrument, and as a result, it is critical that the clinician also asks case-specific questions.

The MacCAT-CA was not structured with the intent of comprehension by juveniles (Kruh and Grisso 2008), but there are studies that have validated the use of the MacCAT-CA with the juvenile population. However, it fails to address issues pertaining to developmentally based issues of Appreciation, and therefore may raise a question into the appropriateness of its use with juveniles (Burnett et al. 2004; Kruh and Grisso 2008).

Fitness Interview Test-revised (fit-r)

The Fitness Interview Test-revised (FIT-R) is a 16-question, semistructured clinical interview developed for assessment of competency to stand trial with Canadian adult defendants, and was designed to match the Canadian standard of Competency to Stand Trial (Roesch et al. 2006; Kruh and Grisso 2008). It is grouped into three sections to assess (1) Understanding, (2) Appreciation, and (3) Communication, and consists of four background questions and 16 other interview items that are presented in a standardized manner. Interviewers are given the flexibility to perform the interview with more of a conversational flow compared to the much more structured instruments above.

This test was not normed with the youth population, but studies show that there is good interrater reliability and construct validity with the juvenile population (Roesch et al. 2006), strong interrater reliability on total score and scale, and weak interrater reliability on clinical ratings (Roesch et al. 2006; Kruh and Grisso 2008). Lower scores were obtained on the FIT-R for those with low verbal ability.

Descriptions with the meaning of each item are provided; however, scoring criteria are not. After each section has been scored, they are scored against a 0–2 scale that contributes to the qualification of Unfit, Fit, or Questionable (Kruh and Grisso 2008). The simple wording in the FIT-R makes it suitable for use with youth. However, it does not assess issues related to developmental maturity, or psychosocial developmental threats to decision making (Roesch et al. 2006; Kruh and Grisso 2008). As a result, when utilizing the FIT-R for assessment of CST with juveniles, it is important to include questions pertaining to these specific issues when asking case-specific questions. Table 47.1 summarizes competency assessment instruments.

RISK FACTORS FOR BEING FOUND INCOMPETENT TO STAND TRIAL

The understanding of the impact from mental disorders, developmental disabilities, and developmental immaturity on JCST has increased substantially over the past decade, particularly, given the unique nature of these impairments relative to adult defendants (Bath and Gerring 2014). Like adults, many juveniles possess significant cognitive and psychiatric impairments that may render them incompetent to stand trial (IST) (Burrell et al. 2008). Prevalence estimates of psychiatric illness in the juvenile justice population have been found to range from 66% to 75%, and estimates of youth who meet the criteria for a developmental disability or intellectual impairment range from 30% to 70% (Quinn et al. 2005).

When performing a competency evaluation in youth, it is important to keep a few key components in mind. There are several risk factors for incompetency that serve as a "red flag" for mental health professionals and legal officials when evaluating for JCST. Such risk factors include age, intelligence, presence of mental illness, presence of developmental disorder, and developmental immaturity.

Age

A study by McKee compared matched youths and adults referred for competency evaluations, and found that 40%–58% of youth compared to 11% of adults met criteria for intellectual disability or borderline intellectual functioning (Ficke et al. 2006). McKee (1998) found that compared to juvenile pretrial youth defendants, adults were significantly more likely to have higher mean competency scores than youth. Furthermore, the percentage of youth found competent dropped off steeply with age. For example, 15- to 16-year-olds were not significantly different from adults, with both groups yielding competency scores above 90%. Yet, those youth less than 12 years of age scored significantly lower at approximately 50% for the measure. In other words, the younger the patients were in this study, the more likely they were to be found incompetent to stand trial. This finding has been replicated in several studies (Cross et al. 1989; Marsteller et al. 1997; Bonnie and Grisso 2000; Ryba et al. 2003; Grisso 2005b; Larson and Grisso 2011), and thus lower age is considered to be a highly significant risk factor for being found incompetent. A considerable number of studies have examined the impact of age and cognitive abilities on juveniles' adjudicative competence abilities including assertion of rights to silence and legal counsel (Savitsky and Karras 1984; Abramovitch et al. 1995; Cowden and McKee 1995; Grisso 1997; McKee 1998; Goldstein et al. 2002; Baerger

Table 47.1 Table of competency instruments

Abbreviated name	JACI	FIT-R	MacCAT-CA	CAST-MR
Type of assessment	Semistructured interview	Semistructured interview	Quantitative instrument	Quantitative instrument
Normed for	Youth only	Adults, good reliability and vailidity in youth but does not assess maturity	Adults only	Adults, but generalizable to youth (second-grade reading level)
Assesses	Understanding, Appreciation, and Reasoning	Understanding, Appreciation, and Communication	Understanding, Appreciation, Decision Making, and Assisting	Basic Legal Skills, Skills to Assist the Defense, and Understanding Case Events
Unique Aspect(s)	Built-in "capacity checks" when youth fails a section where tester can teach the youth information and then later re-test this information to assess recall	Canadian Sections are scored as Unfit, Fit, or Questionable	Includes vignettes, which some argue is preferable to using the patient's own case information as it allows a more objective assessment	Includes Multiple Choice Questions for clients with verbal expressive difficulties
Strengths	Gold standard in youth Takes into account developmental maturity	Format allows more flexibility, but some argue there is too much flexibility	Potentially the most reliable and consistent instrument Good in psychosis	Gold standard in intellectual disability
Limitations	Cannot use in Adults Not quantitative No Multiple Choice	May not be the best in low verbal ability clients	Vignettes do not allow thorough assessment of Appreciation and Understanding	Does not assess for immature appreciation or psychosis

et al. 2003). The most comprehensive study of this type was the MacArthur Juvenile Adjudicative Competence Study (Grisso et al. 2003). They found that on the MacCAT-CA, youths aged 15 and younger performed more poorly on average than did young adults, with a greater proportion manifesting a level of impairment consistent with that of adults in past research that had been found incompetent to stand trial (Grisso et al. 2003). In addition, about one-third of youths aged 13 and younger manifested this significant level of impairment, while 16- to 17-year-olds on average were no different from adults in their performance (Grisso et al. 2003). This study highlighted the fact that age can serve as a risk factor for juvenile CST evaluation, which can guide forensic examiners on their assessment.

Cognitive functioning and learning problems

The second predicate factor for JCST is cognitive functioning. Several studies have documented that juveniles with lower intellectual functioning are more likely to have CST deficits. The literature on juvenile competency to stand trial dates back to the 1990s, when Cooper et al. studied juvenile detainees at a placement center (Baerger et al. 2003). They found that only Full Scale Intelligence Quotient (FSIQ) was significantly associated with youth who were ultimately found incompetent to stand trial, although a main effect was found for age. In most studies, with the exception of Burnett et al. (2004), intelligence estimates have been positively correlated and diagnoses of mental retardation have been negatively correlated with the performance of youth on all elements of broad competence assessment tools (Grisso et al. 2003; Ficke et al. 2006) and verbal abilities, but not some other cognitive skills (Viljoen and Roesch 2005). In a large-scale study by Grisso et al. (2003), the authors found that 40% of adolescents and young-adult participants with an IQ between 75 and 89 showed significant CST impairment. Furthermore, youth deemed incompetent to stand trial during CST evaluations tend to have lower intellectual functioning than competent youth (Evans 2003; Kruh et al. 2006), are more likely than competent youth to have diagnoses of borderline intellectual functioning and mental retardation (McKee and Shea 1999), and are more likely to be diagnosed with mental retardation than a mental illness (Baerger et al. 2003). Juveniles with seriously impaired intellectual abilities often have poorer understanding of the purposes, procedures, and participants in trials than juveniles the same age with better intellectual capacity (Grisso 2005a).

Another study by McKee et al. also found that a history of intellectual disability or borderline intellectual functioning was significantly correlated with an incompetent status (Grisso 2005b). Many studies have replicated this finding (Cross et al. 1989; Marsteller 1997; Bonnie and Grisso 2000; Ryba et al. 2003). However, as the literature began to progressively build on previous findings, the understanding of intellectual deficits in youth deemed incompetent became much more refined. The same study by McKee et al. demonstrated that 96% of detainees found incompetent had failed at least one grade in school (Grisso 2005b). Redlich et al. found that those who had poor overall grades and, more specifically, poor scores on vocabulary subscales were more likely to have a greater number of police contacts. They also found that those who had difficulty understanding their *Miranda* rights were also more likely to be deemed incompetent (Viljoen and Roesch 2005). A history of special education needs was significantly associated with an incompetent status in a study by Baergert et al. (Larson and Grisso 2011). Ficke et al. compared matched competent and incompetent youth in a study with lower IQ cutoff scores than previous studies, and found that an IQ less than 60 was highly predictive of being found incompetent (Ryba et al. 2003). They also found that lower Wide Range Achievement Test (WRAT) reading subscores correlated with a poorer performance on competency measures, such as the Mac-CAT. Kivisto et al. (2011) found that those with a higher score on the Wechsler Abbreviated Scale of Intelligence (WASI) were more likely to be competent (Cross et al. 1989), and data from Bath et al. (2015) suggest that those with a diagnosis of Intellectual Disability are more likely to be incompetent to stand trial (Marsteller et al. 1997). Thus, there is a substantial body of literature pointing to intellectual disability and a history of academic difficulties as legitimate risk factor for being found incompetent to stand trial.

Learning and academic functioning also seem to be associated with reduced adjudicative competence among juveniles, but results have been less consistent than with age and intelligence (Kruh and Grisso 2008). Some studies indicate that among juveniles referred for CST evaluations, it was generally found that youth found competent were less likely to have been in special education than incompetent juveniles (Cowden and McKee 1995; Baerger et al. 2003; Kruh et al. 2006; however, see McKee and Shea 1999, for a different result) but may be no less likely to be diagnosed with a learning disorder (Kruh et al. 2006). Although learning and academic functions are not as strong as predictors compared to those previously mentioned, it is something worth forensic examiners and legal authorities considering when adjudicating juvenile competence.

Mental illness

The third predicate factor for juvenile CST is mental illness, yet whereas there are significant data in the adult literature to support an association between mental illness and competency status, data on whether or not mental illness is a risk factor for incompetency in youth are mixed. McKee et al. found that 79% of youth referred for competency evaluations had utilized mental illness in the past (Grisso 2005b). Baerger et al. also found that prior mental health treatment was a risk factor for being found incompetent (Larson and Grisso 2011). Ficke et al. showed a correlation between younger detainees, externalizing symptoms on the Brief Psychiatric Rating Scale (BPRS), and lower Mac-CAT (competency) scores (Ryba et al. 2003). However, data from Grisso et al. suggest that Mac-CAT scores were unrelated to subject responses on the Massachusetts Youth Screening Instrument (MAYSI) mental health questionnaire (Bonnie and Grisso 2000). Kivisto et al. (2011) also showed minimal correlation between the MAYSI and competency status. Last, Bath et al. (2015) showed that those with an Axis I diagnosis of a mood, psychotic, or substance use disorder were in fact more likely to be found competent. Therefore, while data from some studies imply that mental illness is a risk factor for being found incompetent, other studies negate this finding.

Developmental maturity

The final predicate factor in CST is developmental immaturity. Developmental immaturity refers to specific deficits in neurological, intellectual, emotional, and psychological development. Intellectual development is another important aspect of developmental maturity in CST evaluations. Intellectual development in adolescence involves improvements in basic information processing skills, including organization of information, sustained attention, short- and long-term memory, and verbal fluency (Grisso 2005a). Gains in deductive reasoning and abstract thinking are important for participation in one's defense, which is an essential component in the adjudicative process (*Dusky v. U.S.* 1960). Two major areas of functioning highlight emotional development in adolescents: impulse control and emotional lability. This ability to delay responses in order to assess and consider consequences, and the quick changes in mood, can affect juvenile's decision making, making it more changeable and less stable (Grisso 2005a). Psychosocial development is important to consider because peer influences and negative risks of one's behaviors are approached differently in early and middle adolescence than in later adolescence and adulthood (Grisso 2005a). These psychosocial changes are important in regard to juveniles' participation in their trials and judgment in decision making. Psychosocial factors relevant to CST include the following: autonomy (conformity and compliance), perceptions, and attitudes about risk, temperance, and perspective taking (Kruh and Grisso 2008).

Research suggests that some youth will manifest deficits in legally relevant abilities for reasons of age alone (i.e., "developmental immaturity") rather than the presence of a mental or developmental disorder (Bonnie and Grisso 2000; Grisso et al. 2003). The often cited, large multisite study by Grisso et al. (2003), investigating correlates of CST in detained and nondetained participants aged 11–24, found that approximately one-third of 11- to 13-year-olds and one-fifth of 14- to 15-year-olds were impaired in capacities relevant to adjudicative competence akin to seriously mentally ill adults who would likely be considered IST; those aged 16–17 did not differ significantly from young adults in terms of CST status (Grisso et al. 2003). More specifically, in a sample of detained youth, close to 35% of 11- to 13-year-olds and 22% of youth 14–15 years old were impaired in the areas of understanding and reasoning of trial-related matters, and youth aged 11–13 years old demonstrated less ability to focus on the long-term consequences of their decisions (Ficke et al. 2006; Larson and Grisso 2011).

Previous legal history

There is limited data present on the correlation between prior legal system involvement and competency status, and the data that exist are mixed. McKee et al. found prior arrests to be a significant risk factor for being found incompetent to stand trial (McKee and Shae 1999), while Grisso et al. found that performance on the Mac-CAT was unrelated to prior juvenile justice system involvement (Grisso et al. 2003).

NEUROBIOLOGY OF THE DEVELOPING ADOLESCENT BRAIN

Our understanding of the developing brain is growing every day. Adolescent brains when compared to those of adults show decreased dopamine activity in the prefrontal cortex and increased dopamine receptors in the ventral striatum, resulting in increased impulsivity and risk-taking behaviors (Steinberg 2008). Impaired decision making in teenagers has been linked to decreased impulse control, increased reward motivation, exaggerated emotional responsiveness, and increased susceptibility to peer pressure (Pope et al. 2012). These data are supported by Grisso et al., who found teenagers compared to adults significantly underestimated the risks of illegal activity as well as future consequences of short-term decision making (Grisso et al. 2003). As implied above, younger age correlated with poorer decision making in the context of police questioning and plea arguments as well in this study. Similarly, Kivisto et al. (2011) found that competency strongly correlated with the Judgment in Legal Contexts Instrument (JILC), and that future orientation helped to mediate the relationship between age, intellectual ability, and Mac-CAT scores.

RESTORING YOUTH TO COMPETENCY

There is ongoing debate about the best dispositional approaches for youth who have been found to be incompetent to stand trial. Whereas adult defendants can be remanded to a forensic hospital for competency restoration and treatment, juveniles are in a different category altogether. Because many jurisdictions lack forensic hospitals and competency restoration, remediation, or attainment programs for juveniles, there are limited dispositional options for youth who are determined to be incompetent to stand trial. The literature on juvenile competency restoration is sparse, and there are only a handful of programs nationally. Additionally, the nomenclature in describing juvenile competency restoration is in flux, with many experts differing in their opinion around the best terminology to use. Many argue that restoration is not an appropriate term, as many youth have never attained competency, so how can you restore what they never had? Emerging terminology suggests that Remediation and Attainment are the preferred terms growing in favor. For this chapter, the terms "attainment," "remediation," and "restoration" will be used interchangeably.

When thinking about juvenile competency attainment, it is important to consider the landmark case of *Jackson v. Indiana*. In *Jackson*, the U.S. Supreme Court held that a defendant could not be held longer than the reasonable period of time necessary to determine if there is a substantial probability that he or she would attain competency in the foreseeable future. This landmark case is guiding the efforts on juvenile competency attainment both in determining which youth should receive competency attainment services and the length of time those services should be provided. In some jurisdictions with limited competency attainment resources, youth who have lower-level misdemeanor offenses may be diverted out of the system if found incompetent to stand trial, whereas those with more serious, violent, or felony offenses may be selected to participate in remediation programs, given the public safety concerns.

Warren et al. (2010) has one of the few published papers in the area of competency restoration, and recommends that a good remediation program be an individualized and integrative community-based, developmentally and culturally appropriate program that is consistent with appropriate legal standards. Two of the primary goals of attainment services are to (1) assist the youth in attaining competency and proceed to trial, or (2) determine that the youth is not likely to be restored to competency in the foreseeable future and therefore divert from the juvenile justice system (Warren 2009). Warren (2009) created an interactive learning tool to assist with attainment of juveniles. This interactive learning tool is mental-health based and presents two adolescents, DJ and Alicia, who must appear in court. Warren's program uses a variety of techniques including role-playing, matching games, bingo, crossword puzzles, and videos within 24 chapters to address legal issues such as legal capacities, reasoning and decision making, perceived autonomy, perceptions of risk, time perspective, and abstract thinking. Participating youth receive these restoration sessions two to three times per week with trained Restoration Intensive Case Managers (RICM). The RICMs serve as the primary liaison between the court system and the youth and caregiver. The RICMs also function in a supportive capacity and help facilitate the adolescent's adherence to attending outpatient appointments. Results from this program have been promising overall; of the 563 youth found incompetent to stand trial and ordered in the restoration program, 72% were found to be restored to competence within 90–120 days of remediation services. It should be noted that individual characteristics of the youth played a role in the restoration success rates, with the highest restoration rates occurring in youth without mental illness or intellectual disability (91%) and lowest restoration success in youth with intellectual disability (47%). These findings further underscore the importance of understanding clinical and demographics risks factors of incompetency, and how these may inform the ways in which attainment programs are provided to different groups, as well as correlate with restoration success rates.

FUTURE DIRECTIONS

The clinical relevance of juvenile adjudicative competency is multifold. We have already seen from some of the landmark cases in child psychiatry and the law, starting with *Roper v. Simmons* (2005), *Graham v. Florida* (2010), and recently with *Miller v. Alabama* (2012) that age matters (Bath et al. 2013). Adolescent brains are different than adult brains, and our evolving understanding of these differences demonstrates that there are behavioral correlates related to these neuroanatomical differences; these differences impact development, maturity, and decision making. These differences also result in adolescents being more likely to engage in impulsive and novelty-seeking behaviors without consideration of long-term consequences, and have an impact on their culpability as well as their legal capacities. Yet legislative and judicial responses to juvenile competency to stand trial have lagged behind the literature. Whereas the literature has consistently demonstrated over the last two decades that age is an important predicate of incompetency, most states do not have specific juvenile competency to stand trial legislation that recognizes developmental immaturity as a cause of incompetency (Bath and Gerring 2014).

SUMMARY

Although an emerging field within forensic psychiatry, juvenile competency to stand trial is an incredibly important and evolving area of mental health. Younger age, intellectual disability, and school difficulties have all consistently been shown to be risk factors for being found incompetent to stand trial, while the data on previous mental health and juvenile justice system remains mixed. An understanding of the complex needs of those youth referred for competency evaluation, and a deepening appreciation for the contributions of neuroscience have led to mental health professionals adopting a stance that favors treatment and rehabilitation. Mental health advocacy groups have had a significant influence on the legal system all the way up through the U.S. Supreme Court (Bath et al. 2013, 2015).

SUMMARY KEY POINTS

- Juvenile Competency to Stand Trial is a rapidly evolving, dynamic field in forensic psychiatry.
- A juvenile's right to be competent to stand trial relates to due process protections and the Fifth, Fourteenth, and Fourth amendments.
- The Juvenile Adjudicative Competency Interview (JACI) is considered the gold standard for competency assessment in juveniles.
- Juvenile competency assessment may reveal important data about a juvenile's psychosocial and learning needs. Risk factors for being found incompetent to stand trial include young age, the presence of intellectual and developmental disorders, and mental illness.
- Legislative changes in juvenile competency to stand trial have lagged behind the literature, which have long documented that developmental immaturity (young age) is increasingly being recognized as a predicate cause of incompetency.
- Mental health and legal professionals should be attuned to risk factors for incompetency, and when in doubt, refer defendants for competency evaluations if one or more risk factors are present.
- Juvenile competency restoration, remediation, and attainment remain an ongoing challenge and are the next frontier in the juvenile competency to stand trial debate.

REFERENCES

Abramovitch R, M Peterson-Dadali, and M Rohan. 1995. Young people's understanding and assertion of their rights to silence and legal counsel. *Canadian Journal of Criminology* 37:1.

Acklin MW 2012. The forensic clinician's toolbox I: A review of competency to stand trial (CST) instruments. *Journal of Personality Assessment* 94(2):220–222.

Baerger DR, EF Griffin, JS Lyons, and R Simmons. 2003. Competency to stand trial in preadjudicated and petitioned juvenile defendants. *Journal of the American Academy of Psychiatry and the Law Online* 31(3):314–320.

Bath E and J Gerring. 2014. National trends in juvenile competency to stand trial. *Journal of the American Academy of Child and Adolescent Psychiatry* 53(3):265–268.

Bath E, K Pope, R Ijadi-Maghsoodi et al. 2015. Juvenile life without parole: Updates on legislative and judicial trends and on facilitating fair sentencing. *Journal of the American Academy of Child and Adolescent Psychiatry* May;54(4):343–347.

Bath E, L Reba-Harrelson, R Peace et al. 2015. Correlates of competency to stand trial among youths admitted to a juvenile mental health court. *Journal of the American Academy of Psychiatry and the Law* 43(3):329–339.

Bath E, S Sidhu, and ST Stepanyan. 2013. Landmark legislative trends in juvenile justice: An update and primer for child and adolescent psychiatrists. *Journal of the American Academy of Child and Adolescent Psychiatry* 52(7):671–673.

Bonnie RJ and T Grisso. 2000. Adjudicative competence and youthful offenders. In *Youth on Trial: A Developmental Perspective on Juvenile Justice*, edited by T. Grisso and R. Schwartz, Chicago: University of Chicago Press, 73–103.

Burnett DMR, CD Noblin, and V Prosser. 2004. Adjudicative competency in a juvenile population. *Criminal Justice and Behavior* 31(4):438–462.

Burrell S, C Kendrick, and B Blalock. 2008. Incompetent youth in California juvenile justice. *Stanford Law and Policy Review* 19:198.

Cowden VL and GR McKee. 1995. Competency to stand trial in juvenile delinquency proceedings—Cognitive maturity and the attorney-client relationship. *University of Louisville Journal of Family Law* 33:629.

Cross T, B Bazron, K Dennis, and M Essacs. 1989. *Towards a Culturally Competent System of Care: A Monograph on Effective Services for Minority Children Who Are Severely Emotionally Disturbed.* Washington, DC: CASSP Technical Assistance Center, Georgetown University Child Development Center.

Dusky v. United States, 362 U.S. 402 (1960).

Evans TM. 2003. Juvenile competency to stand trial: Problems and pitfalls. *American Journal of Forensic Psychology* 21(2):5–18.

Everington CT. 1990. The competence assessment for standing trial for defendants with mental retardation (Cast-MR) a validation study. *Criminal Justice and Behavior* 17(2):147–168.

Ficke SLV, KJ Hart, and PA Deardorff. 2006. The performance of incarcerated juveniles on the MacArthur Competence Assessment Tool-Criminal Adjudication (MacCAT-CA). *Journal of the American Academy of Psychiatry and the Law Online* 34(3):360–373.

Fisher CB. 2012. *Decoding the Ethics Code: A Practical Guide for Psychologists*. Los Angeles, CA: Sage.

Goldstein NE, MR Thomson, D Osman, and L Oberlander. 2002. Advocating a functional approach to determining adjudicative competency in juveniles. *Journal of Forensic Psychology Practice* 2(2):89–97.

Graham v. Florida 560 U.S. 48 (2010).

Grisso T. 1997. The competence of adolescents as trial defendants. *Psychology, Public Policy, and Law* 3(1):3.

Grisso T. 1998. *Forensic Evaluation of Juveniles*. Sarasota, FL: Professional Resource Press/Professional Resource Exchange.

Grisso T. 2005a. *Clinical Evaluations for Juveniles' Competence to Stand Trial: A Guide for Legal Professionals*. Sarasota, FL: Professional Resource Exchange.

Grisso T. 2005b. *Evaluating Juveniles' Adjudicative Competence: A Guide for Clinical Practice*. Sarasota, FL: Professional Resource Press/Professional Resource Exchange.

Grisso T, L Steinberg, J Woolard, E Cauffman, E Scott, S Graham, F Lexcen, ND Reppucci, and R Schwartz. 2003. Juveniles' competence to stand trial: A comparison of adolescents' and adults' capacities as trial defendants. *Law and Human Behavior* 27(4):333.

Kivisto J, TM. Moore, PA Fite, and BG Seidner. 2011. Future orientation and competence to stand trial: The fragility of competence. *Journal of the American Academy of Psychiatry and the Law Online* 39(3):316–326.

Kruh I and T Grisso. 2008. *Evaluation of Juveniles' Competence to Stand Trial*. New York: Oxford University Press.

Kruh IP, L Sullivan, M Ellis, F Lexcen, and J McClellan. 2006. Juvenile competence to stand trial: A historical and empirical analysis of a juvenile forensic evaluation service. *International Journal of Forensic Mental Health* 5(2):109–123.

Larson KA and T Grisso. 2011. Developing Statutes for Competence to Stand Trial in Juvenile Delinquency Proceedings: A Guide for Lawmakers. Worcester, MA: National Youth Screening and Assessment Project.

LII/Legal Information Institute. *14th Amendment/Constitution/US Law*. http://www.law.cornell.edu/constitution/amendmentxiv, accessed December 8, 2014.

LII/Legal Information Institute. *Milton R. Dusky, Petitioner, v. United States of America*. http://www.law.cornell.edu/supremecourt/text/362/402, accessed December 8, 2014.

Marsteller FA, Brogan D, Smith I et al. 1997. *Prevalence of Substance Use Disorders Among Juveniles Admitted to Regional Youth Detention Centers Operated by the Georgia Department of Juvenile Justice*. Rockville, MD: Center for Substance Abuse Treatment.

Mayzer R, AR Bradley, H Rusinko, and TW Ertelt. 2009. Juvenile competency to stand trial in criminal court and brain function. *Journal of Forensic Psychiatry and Psychology* 20(6):785–800.

McCroskey J. 2006. *Youth in the Los Angeles County Juvenile Justice System: Current Conditions and Possible Directions for Change*. Los Angeles, CA: Children's Planning Council. Commissioned by the Los Angeles County Board of Supervisors.

McKee GR. 1998. Competency to stand trial in preadjudicatory juveniles and adults. *Journal of the American Academy of Psychiatry and the Law Online* 26(1):89–99.

McKee GR and SJ Shea. 1999. Competency to stand trial in family court: Characteristics of competent and incompetent juveniles. *Journal of the American Academy of Psychiatry and the Law Online* 27(1):65–73.

Miller v. Alabama 567 U.S. _____ (2012).

Pope K, B Luna, and CR Thomas. 2012. Developmental neuroscience and the courts: How science is influencing the disposition of juvenile offenders. *Journal of the American Academy of Child and Adolescent Psychiatry* 51(4):341–342.

Quinn MM, DM Osher, JM Poirier, RB Rutherford, and PE Leone. 2005. Youth with disabilities in juvenile corrections: A national survey. *Exceptional Children* 71(3):339–345.

Roesch R, PA Zapf, and D Eaves. 2006. *Fitness Interview Test-Revised (FIT-R): A Structured, Interview for Assessing Competency to Stand Trial.* Sarasota, FL: Professional Resource Press.

Roper v. Simmons 543 U.S. 551 (2005).

Ryba NL, VG Cooper, and PA Zapf. 2003. Juvenile competence to stand trial evaluations: A survey of current practices and test usage among psychologists. *Professional Psychology: Research and Practice* 34(5):499.

Savitsky JC and D Karras. 1984. Competency to stand trial among adolescents. *Adolescence* 19(74):348–358.

Steinberg L. 2008. A social neuroscience perspective on adolescent risk-taking. *Developmental Review* 28(1):78–106.

Viljoen JL and R Roesch. 2005. Competence to waive interrogation rights and adjudicative competence in adolescent defendants: Cognitive development, attorney contact, and psychological symptoms. *Law and Human Behavior* 29(6):723–742.

Warren JI, J DuVal, I Komarovskaya et al. 2010. Developing a forensic service delivery system for juveniles adjudicated incompetent to stand trial. *International Journal of Forensic Mental Health* 8(4):245–262.

48

Evaluating adolescent culpability

PETER ASH

INTRODUCTION

Criminal culpability, the degree to which a person can be held morally or legally responsible for a crime, is a necessary predicate for punishment. Forensic evaluations relevant to determining culpability may be used at many different stages of legal proceedings, including determinations of which charges a defendant will face, decisions about whether to waive a youth to adult criminal court, negotiations and plea bargaining, trials on the issue of guilt, and in sentencing and parole hearings. There is a range of defenses that involve culpability, from those that fully negate criminal responsibility, such as *mens rea* and insanity defenses, to those that reduce but do not negate responsibility. For adolescents, those defenses that negate responsibility are typically similar to those utilized by adults, whereas defenses that partially reduce responsibility are more common and differ significantly from evaluations of adults.

LEGAL BACKGROUND

Mens rea

Mens rea, or guilty mind, needs to be proved for a criminal conviction. Most commonly, *mens rea* can be inferred from the act itself, but in some cases, the defendant might argue that his or her actions were the result of an accident, self-defense, duress, or other reasons that would negate criminal intent. Some crimes include a specific intent in their definition: the difference between manslaughter and murder, for example, turns on a difference of intent (without malice afterthought, as opposed to with malice). In those states that allow for a diminished capacity defense, diminished capacity serves to reduce the culpability of specific intent, for example, to allow extreme emotional distress to negate premeditation and thus reduce a charge from murder to manslaughter. *Mens rea* defenses do not require that culpability be reduced by a mental illness.

Legal insanity

For those with a mental illness or mental defect, culpability may be negated by an insanity defense, which is available in all but a few states, but which varies in definition from jurisdiction to jurisdiction (AAPL Task Force 2014, S38–S76). The most common factors in insanity tests are that the act was connected to a mental illness and the defendant did not know (or appreciate) the act was wrong—the "cognitive test." Some states also have a version of a volitional test—that the defendant could not conform his or her conduct to the requirements of the law. There are other variations as well. For example, New Hampshire utilizes the "product of a mental illness" test. Insanity evaluations of adults are discussed more fully in Chapter 29 of this text.

Insanity pleas are far less common in cases involving adolescents than they are in adults, largely because psychotic disorders are less frequent in adolescents and because juvenile defendants who have a severe mental illness are less likely to be waived to adult criminal court. Only a small minority of states allow insanity pleas in juvenile court (Pollock 2001). Because one of the missions of juvenile court is rehabilitation, adolescents who suffer from a mental illness sufficient to substantiate an insanity plea typically have a treatment plan for their mental illness as part of their disposition. For adolescents tried in adult criminal court who would qualify for an insanity defense, the techniques and principles are similar to those used for adults (see Chapter 29 and AAPL Task Force 2014). A few adolescents may qualify for an insanity defense based on developmental delay or immaturity, such as an intellectually disabled early adolescent who does not know sexual exploration with a child is wrong, that may require the examiner to have expertise in interviewing intellectually disabled youth.

Reduced culpability of adolescents

In a series of U.S. Supreme Court cases since 2005, the court has found that minors—those under age 18—are less culpable than adults. In *Roper v. Simmons* (2005), the court found "evolving standards of decency that mark the progress of a maturing society" had changed to the extent that the death penalty for youth under 18 years of age was "cruel and unusual punishment" and thus violated the Eighth Amendment and was unconstitutional. A large part of the court's rationale turned on three psychological aspects of adolescents: (1) that adolescents are developmentally immature, which included finding that they were more impulsive and more prone to respond to peer pressure; (2) that adolescent criminal behavior is often affected by adverse environmental circumstances over which they had no control (such as where they lived and the circumstances of their families); and (3) that their personalities are still in flux and so their actions could not be seen as reflecting enduring character traits. Five years later, in the case of *Graham v. Florida* (2010), using similar reasoning about adolescent culpability, and also noting that new neuroscience evidence about the development of the adolescent brain supported an understanding of why adolescents think differently from adults, the court held that a sentence of life without parole (LWOP) was unconstitutional for all nonhomicide offenses committed by minors. The *Graham* court also said, "A State is not required to guarantee eventual freedom to such an offender, but must impose a sentence that provides some meaningful opportunity for release based on demonstrated maturity and rehabilitation." This statement leaves unclear whether by "meaningful opportunity" the court was implying the state had a duty to foster rehabilitation, or whether the "meaningful opportunity" was a parole hearing at which the defendant had an opportunity to demonstrate he was rehabilitated. Two years later, in *Miller v. Alabama* (2012), the Supreme Court, again using the *Roper* analysis of adolescent culpability, ruled that even for murder, a *mandatory* LWOP sentence for adolescents was unconstitutional. The court did allow for an LWOP sentence following a murder conviction after a sentencing hearing during which the individual factors of a particular defendant and his crime were taken into consideration. By limiting the punishment options for adolescents convicted of serious crimes, the court opened the door to considering adolescent culpability issues both in future sentencing cases and in resentencing of adolescents who previously received sentences that would now be deemed unconstitutional. In the follow-up case of *Montgomery v. Louisiana* (2016), the Supreme Court clarified that *Miller* was retroactive, which means that all adolescents who previously received a mandatory LWOP sentence need either to have their sentence reduced to life with parole or to be resentenced under the *Miller* guidelines. Because adolescent culpability turns in large part on psychological factors, forensic evaluations of these defendants have an important part in sentencing hearings where life and LWOP sentences are being considered.

FACTORS TO CONSIDER

Taken together, the factors of various insanity tests and the issues highlighted by the Supreme Court in its adolescent sentencing cases provide a conceptual framework for assessing adolescent culpability. These factors are listed in Table 48.1.

In evaluations for an insanity defense, the evaluator needs to consider the factors pertaining to the relevant jurisdiction's formal test for insanity. If the adolescent meets the test for insanity, then he or she is fully excused from criminal culpability. Culpability lies along a continuum from fully excused to full responsibility. Most evaluations of adolescent culpability attempt to place the evaluated defendant on this continuum so other dispositional questions (such as appropriate punishment, trial setting, or disposition) can be appropriately answered. The Supreme Court holdings make clear that adolescents as a class are less culpable than adults, but it is far less clear how much reduction in culpability from adult standards is necessary to justify various dispositions. In evaluations for partial culpability, where the defendant does not meet the formal test for insanity, the factors utilized in insanity tests are nevertheless useful as areas to

Table 48.1 Factors to consider in evaluating adolescent culpability

- Factors pertaining to insanity defenses
  - Mental illness or mental defect
  - Appreciation of wrongfulness
  - Ability to conform to law
- Factors pertaining to reduced culpability
  - Immaturity
    - Impulsivity
    - Susceptibility to peer pressure
    - Risk taking
    - Time sense, overweighting immediate rewards compared to long-term costs
    - Limited ability to empathize
    - Incomplete brain development
    - IQ and adaptive functioning
  - Environmental circumstances
    - Adverse environmental factors, history of abuse and neglect
    - Peer group norms
  - Personality factors
    - Incomplete personality development
    - Psychopathy
    - Out-of-character action
- Nature of the crime
  - Degree of fit with patterns of adolescent crime as opposed to patterns of adult crime
  - Seriousness of the crime and harm done
  - Reactive attitudes toward the offense
- Other prognostic factors
  - Future dangerousness
  - Amenability to rehabilitation
- Malingering

Source: Adapted from Ash P. 2012. *Journal of the American Academy of Psychiatry and the Law* 40:21–32.

examine to elucidate where on the continuum of culpability an adolescent defendant falls.

Mental illness

The rate of mental illness in juvenile offenders is very high (Marsteller et al. 1997; Teplin et al. 2002), about 60%, or about triple the rate in the general population, if conduct disorder is excluded. About 40% suffer from more than one disorder. Many delinquents meet criteria for conduct disorder, but because theft, lying, and serious violations of rules are considered symptoms of that disorder (American Psychiatric Association 2013), such a diagnosis is of little explanatory value. Although mental illness is common in this population, most studies of the causes of delinquency find mental illness to be a poor predictor of why a youth becomes delinquent (U.S. Department of Health and Human Services 2001; Grisso 2008). Mental disorder may well magnify the effects of other factors relevant to reducing culpability through such pathways as impairing judgment and increasing aggressiveness and impulsivity. There are some cases in which the offense appears to meet the "product of a mental illness" test that can serve to justify a finding of reduced culpability on the theory that mental illness reduces the ability to act freely and voluntarily. The presence of mental illness also has implications for rehabilitation.

Appreciation of wrongfulness

The M'Naghten rules, formulated by the British House of Lords in 1843, had as their central concept that the defendant was not culpable if he or she did not know what he or she was doing was wrong (M'Naghten's Case 1843). Variants of this concept are the most common prong in states' insanity laws. It is termed a "cognitive test" because it has to do with knowing. The most common situations meeting this test are that the defendant was psychotic and was acting either in accordance with a delusion (such as a paranoid person thinking he was acting in self-defense when no attack was in progress), or as a result of command hallucinations that would excuse the act (such as believing God was commanding the act). In some cases, not knowing the act was wrong might be a result of intellectual disability, as in the case of a severely intellectually disabled adolescent noncoercively molesting a younger child as a result of defects in social judgment. The evaluations of adolescents for an insanity defense generally follow the same principles as insanity evaluations of adults (see Chapter 29 and AAPL Task Force 2014), although experience in interviewing adolescents generally is helpful in using appropriate language and in forming rapport. Because the base rate of psychosis in adolescence is lower than in adults, and because psychotic youth are less able than adults to refuse treatment, evaluations of adolescents who meet the cognitive prong are uncommon. In most cases the offender knew his or her actions were wrong. A defendant either knew an action was wrong or did not; evaluations of partial culpability rarely focus on how wrong the defendant thought the act was.

Ability to conform to law

The insanity statutes of some states include a prong having to do with whether the defendant could conform his or her actions to the requirements of law, often termed a "volitional prong" because it has to do with free will. Evaluations of reduced culpability typically focus on factors discussed further below which reduce, but do not eliminate, an adolescent's ability to act lawfully.

Immaturity

A key issue in evaluation of partial culpability is the extent to which the adolescent's decision to engage in a crime was affected by developmental factors. Studies of adolescent decision making in contexts such as giving informed consent for health care, expressing preferences about custody when parents divorce, participating in decisions about educational planning, and making trial-related decisions (Lewis et al. 1977; Weithorn and Campbell 1982; Taylor et al. 1985; Garrison 1991; Grisso et al. 2003) are consistent in showing that adolescents 15 years old and older make decisions in these areas similar to adults. In those studies, which are all in contexts that allow time to reflect, about half of 13- and 14-year-olds had reasoning that was significantly worse than adults. These findings were used to argue for increased autonomy rights for adolescents over 14, especially in the context of arguing that adolescent girls over age 15 should be able to obtain an abortion without parental consent (American Psychological Association 1990).

The decision to commit a crime, however, is often made impulsively, and the Supreme Court in the series of cases beginning with *Roper* discussed above, has recognized adolescent impulsivity as one of the factors reducing culpability in adolescents. Impulsivity has a number of factors in addition to simply making a decision quickly. It has long been recognized that adolescents are much more susceptible to peer pressure than are adults. Unlike adults, who tend to commit crimes when alone, adolescents tend to offend in groups (Zimring 2005). Adolescents also tend to make riskier decisions than adults, and this tendency is increased when adolescents are in groups (Gardner and Steinberg 2005). These tendencies derive in part from the fact that adolescents tend to overweight immediate rewards when comparing them against long-term consequences. Finally adolescents show less empathy. All these interferences with judgment tend to improve through adolescence. Each of these factors can be assessed in evaluating an adolescent in terms of his or her maturity and in considering the circumstances of the crime itself (e.g., whether the crime was committed impulsively or after planning and whether the perpetrator was alone or in a group).

Recent research on adolescent brain development reveals structural changes in the brain through adolescence, helping us understand the development of adolescent judgment (American Medical Association and American Academy of Child and Adolescent Psychiatry 2012; Luna et al. 2013; Casey and Caudle 2013). Speaking broadly, the limbic system, which is thought to contain critical structures related to emotion, develops earlier than the prefrontal cortex, which is the central area for executive processing. In addition, the nerve fibers connecting those two areas continue to myelinate over the course of adolescence and up to approximately age 25. Although neuroscience is not yet at the point of being able to use an individual brain scan to determine the culpability of an individual adolescent, brain research often is a compelling factor that helps judges and juries appreciate that adolescent impulsivity is not under full conscious control.

Adverse environmental circumstances

A number of adverse environmental circumstances, including child abuse and neglect, low socioeconomic status, and living in a high-crime neighborhood, are statistically linked to higher crime rates. Nevertheless, for adults, such factors do not generally mitigate culpability except in death penalty cases. The presumption of autonomy for adults holds that adults are expected to rise above such circumstances, in part because in theory they are able to distance themselves from them. Adolescents, in contrast, who find themselves in such conditions cannot independently escape from them. The Supreme Court has held that since such conditions are imposed, their effects reduce adolescent culpability. Evaluating the existence of such factors is relatively straightforward, although it is often difficult to demonstrate a clear link between the circumstances and the adolescent's behavior in a particular situation.

The strongest risk factor for adolescent violence is a delinquent peer group. In particular, gang membership is a main risk factor for adolescent violence. Because an adolescent chooses his peers, however, joining a gang is generally seen as a voluntary, not an imposed, circumstance, and gang membership is often cited as an aggravating factor. Nevertheless, in high crime areas, being tough is often protective, because being known as a pushover increases one's chance of being victimized (Garbarino 1999). One theory of morality holds that immoral action represents deviance from group values, so if a youth lives in a subculture that accepts and justifies violence when it is used to maintain respect on the street, an argument can be made that this reduces culpability in certain situations.

Personality factors

The third psychological factor the Supreme Court recognized was that an adolescent's personality is not fixed, and so an antisocial act committed by an adolescent does not represent a depraved character in the same way it would for an adult. Traits of personality disorder tend to diminish over the course of adolescence (Cohen et al. 2005). The most worrisome personality constellation is that of psychopathy, and even though psychopathy measured in adolescence has a significant correlation with psychopathy measured as an adult, the reported correlation is about 0.31 (Lynam et al. 2007), which is not high enough to be useful in making an accurate prediction in an individual case. Only about 20% of violent adolescents continue their violence into adulthood (U.S. Department of Health and Human Services 2001), and no predictors have been identified that allow for accurate identification of which adolescents will persist in their offending.

Ash (2012) points out some of the complications of the character theory of culpability. If a convicted defendant behaved out of character, federal sentencing guidelines allow for mitigation of punishment if the behavior "represents a marked deviation by the defendant from an otherwise law-abiding life" (U.S. Sentencing Commission 2003), although the guidelines specifically exclude mitigation for violent offenses on this basis. Such mitigation typically turns on the presence of some identified excuse, such as the defendant was intoxicated, under extreme emotional distress, or suffering from mental illness. Mitigation on the basis of out-of-character action seldom applies in adolescent cases, however. Studies of adolescent crime indicate the average adolescent at the time of arrest has committed numerous previous offenses, for most of which he was not caught (U.S. Department of Health and Human Services 2001). Prior to committing a first violent offense, self-report studies reveal that adolescent offenders have committed numerous and varied nonviolent offenses (Elliott 1994). Nevertheless, the possibility the offense is out of character needs to be investigated.

Nature of the crime

The extent to which the above factors are relevant to a particular crime often turn on the nature of the crime itself. In general, crimes committed by adolescents fall into a different pattern than crimes committed by adults. Some salient differences are shown in Table 48.2.

Adolescents are impulsive, and adolescent crime tends to be committed impulsively. However, in those cases in which a crime was planned in advance, the impulsivity of the adolescent perpetrator is not relevant. Similarly, most adolescent crime is committed in groups (Zimring 2005), so when an adolescent offends alone peer pressure

Table 48.2 Differences between juvenile and adult crime

Juvenile	Adult
More common	
Done in groups	Alone
Diverse offenses	Specialized
Impulsive	Planned
Criminal career shorter	

is seldom relevant. It is important to integrate factors that may reduce culpability with the hard facts about the nature of the crime.

Sentencing authorities commonly look to the seriousness of the crime and the harm done in their consideration of appropriate sentencing. An adolescent defendant's intent while committing the crime is highly relevant to his or her culpability, but crimes that "go bad" are punished more severely than the crime the defendant initially intended. Adolescent offenders are seldom practiced marksmen, and the difference between an aggravated assault and murder often turns on the chance path of the bullet rather than the intent of the shooter.

The reactive attitude a sentencing authority has toward adolescent crime also plays a large role. If one considers a situation from the perspective of "do the crime, do the time," one will have a very different view of appropriate sentencing than if one approaches the same situation from a perspective of "they're just kids" who need rehabilitation rather than punishment. Ash (2012) argues that much of the persuasiveness of explicating the above factors turns on their moving the fact finder to see the adolescent in terms different from an adult. Once one considers an adolescent as different, then the attitudes toward adult punishment are no longer in control, and it becomes necessary to formulate an alternative view of appropriate punishment. Society is still far from a consensus on what that view should be, but the trend is toward seeing adolescent crime as deserving of less punishment than adult crime.

Future dangerousness

Future dangerousness does not bear directly on culpability, but sentencing authorities are often interested in assessments of future dangerousness, because incapacitation is also a goal of punishment. Although adolescent crime is common, continuing an adolescent criminal career into adulthood is not. Only about 20% of violent adolescent offenders continue their violent careers into their twenties (U.S. Department of Health and Human Services 2001), and no robust predictors have been identified that allow us to identify which individuals will continue to offend.

Amenability to rehabilitation

Evaluations for juvenile courts often focus on a youthful offender's amenability to rehabilitation, in line with the rehabilitative mission of the juvenile court. In juvenile court, a focus on rehabilitation is often used to identify rehabilitative services. Amenability to rehabilitation is not, strictly speaking, an element that reduces culpability, although it is often a factor considered in sentencing and post-sentence rehabilitative services. In adult criminal court, the court's mission is typically not to foster rehabilitation. Nevertheless, as discussed above, the U.S. Supreme Court in *Graham,* where the court held unconstitutional life without parole sentences for youth convicted of crimes less than murder, noted that a youth must be given the opportunity to demonstrate rehabilitation.

Malingering

The possibility of malingering or unconscious distortion needs to be considered and explicitly addressed in the report when evaluating a criminal defendant, especially when examining the defendant's account of his or her role in the offense. In general, adolescents are less skilled at malingering than are adults.

THE EVALUATION

Many of the general principles of evaluations of criminal responsibility, including such issues as obtaining appropriate consent, interviewing techniques, and reviewing collateral data, are similar to those in evaluating adults covered in Chapter 29 and will not be repeated here. Evaluations of youth do, however, have some special characteristics.

Despite the fact that minors generally are not deemed competent, in most jurisdictions minors facing criminal charges are able to consent to evaluations that are court ordered or requested by their attorneys. Consent of parents or guardians is generally not needed, assuming the youth has legal representation. It is therefore especially important that the evaluator take care to make sure the youth understands the evaluator's role and other parameters of the evaluation. This may require education at the outset of the evaluation to foster the youth's understanding. Interviewing an adolescent is somewhat different from interviewing an adult, particularly in that language needs to be used which is appropriate to the defendant's developmental level. Because developmental information is important in assessing a youth's background environment and developmental level, school records, medical records, parent reports, and other collateral information are especially important in assessing youth. Police reports and other investigative material are crucial in understanding the nature of the crime, so it can be integrated with factors affecting culpability. Because issues of brain development play a strong role in assessments of adolescent culpability for serious crimes, neuropsychological testing to assess intelligence and executive functioning is often helpful, especially if testing can be conducted shortly after the offense, before the adolescent ages further in jail.

Integrating the findings

Many of the factors noted above lie on a continuum and do not have established metrics. For example, gauging a particular individual adolescent's impulsivity with respect to a particular crime requires integrating the defendant's developmental history, general level of maturity at the time of the offense, and impairments due to mental illness, with the actual circumstances of the crime. Although the general principles of the report are similar to other forensic reports on criminal responsibility (see, for example, Chapter 29, AAPL Task Force 2014; Buchanan and Norko 2011), the relevance of developmental considerations usually requires a more complete discussion in order to educate the finder of fact as to why particular developmental considerations are relevant.

SUMMARY

Assessments of reduced culpability in adolescents challenge the evaluator to integrate a wide range of factors. U.S. Supreme Court holdings over the past decade have reduced the severity of punishments allowable for the most serious crimes committed by minors, and the court's underlying reasoning has found application to a wide variety of adolescent offenses. These principles are increasingly being used by defense attorneys to mitigate punishment for 18- and 19-year-olds, as well. As the legal landscape continues to evolve, evaluators of adolescent defendants increasingly have an opportunity to inform those who make decisions in these cases of a wide range of factors relevant to administering just punishment.

REFERENCES

American Academy of Psychiatry and the Law (AAPL) Task Force. 2014. AAPL practice guideline for forensic psychiatric evaluation of defendants raising the insanity defense. *Journal of the American Academy of Psychiatry and the Law* 42:S3–S76.

American Medical Association and American Academy of Child and Adolescent Psychiatry. 2012. *Brief for the American Medical Association and American Academy of Child and Adolescent Psychiatry as Amici Curiae in Support of Neither Party, in* Miller v. Alabama, *U.S. Supreme Court Cases Nos. 10-9646, 10-9646.*

American Psychological Association. 1990. *Brief for Amicus Curiae in Support of Appellees,* Hodgson v. Minnesota, *497 U.S. 417, No. 88-805,* Washington, DC: American Psychological Association.

American Psychiatric Association. 2013. *Diagnostic and Statistical Manual of Mental Disorders,* 5th edition (*DSM-5*), Arlington, VA: American Psychiatric Publishing.

Ash P. 2012. But he knew it was wrong: Evaluating adolescent culpability. *Journal of the American Academy of Psychiatry and the Law* 40:21–32.

Buchanan A and MA Norko, 2011: *The Psychiatric Report: Principles and Practice of Forensic Writing.* New York: Cambridge University Press.

Casey BJ and K Caudle 2013. The teenage brain: Self control. *Current Directions in Psychological Science* 22:82–87.

Cohen P, TN Crawford, JG Johnson, and S Kasen. 2005. The Children in the Community Study of developmental course of personality disorder. *Journal of Personality Disorders* 19:466–486.

Elliott DS. 1994. Serious violent offenders: Onset, developmental course, and termination—The American Society of Criminology 1993 Presidential Address. *Criminology* 32:1–21.

Garbarino J. 1999. A boys' code of honor: Frustrated justice and fractured morality. Chapter 7 in *Lost Boys: Why Our Sons Turn Violent and How We Can Save Them.* New York: Free Press.

Gardner M and L Steinberg 2005. Peer influence on risk taking, risk preference, and risky decision making in adolescence and adulthood: An experimental study. *Developmental Psychology* 41:625–635.

Garrison EG. 1991. Children's competence to participate in divorce custody decisionmaking. Special Issue: Child Advocacy. *Journal of Clinical Child Psychology* 20:78–87.

Graham v. Florida, 560 U.S. 48 (2010).

Grisso T. 2008. Adolescent offenders with mental disorders. *Future of Children* 18:143–164.

Grisso T, L Steinberg, J Woolard et al. 2003. Juveniles' competence to stand trial: A comparison of adolescents' and adults' capacities as trial defendants. *Law and Human Behavior* 27:333–363.

Lewis CE, MS Lewi, A Lorimer, and BB Palmer. 1977. Child-initiated care: The use of school nursing services by children in an "adult-free" system. *Pediatrics* 60:499–507.

Luna B, DJ Paulsen, A Padmanabhan, and C Geier. 2013. The teenage brain: Cognitive control and motivation. *Current Directions in Psychological Science* 22:94–100.

Lynam DR, A Caspi, TE Moffitt et al. 2007. Longitudinal evidence that psychopathy scores in early adolescence predict adult psychopathy. *Journal of Abnormal Psychology* 116:155–165.

M'Naghten's Case, 10 CL and F. 200, 8 Eng. Rep. 718 (H.L., 1843).

Marsteller FA, D Brogan, I Smith et al. 1997: *The Prevalence of Psychiatric Disorders among Juveniles Admitted to DCYS Regional Youth Detention Centers: Technical Report.* Atlanta: Georgia Department of Children and Youth Services.

Miller v. Alabama, 567 U.S. __ Docket 10-9646, 132 S.Ct. 2455 (2012).

Montgomery v. Louisiana, 136 S.Ct. 718 (2016).

Pollock ES. 2001. Those crazy kids: Providing the insanity defense in juvenile courts. *Minnesota Law Review* 85:2041–2078.

Roper v. Simmons, 543 U.S. 551 (2005).

Taylor L, HS Adelman, and N Kaser-Boyd. 1985. Minors' attitudes and competence toward participation in psychoeducational decisions. *Professional Psychology: Research and Practice* 16:226–235.

Teplin LA, KM Abram, GM McClelland et al. 2002. Psychiatric disorders in youth in juvenile detention. *Archives of General Psychiatry* 59:1133–1143.

U.S. Department of Health and Human Services. 2001. *Youth Violence: A Report of the Surgeon General.* Rockville, MD: U.S. Department of Health and Human Services.

U.S. Sentencing Commission. 2003. *United States Sentencing Guidelines Manual: Section 5K2.20(b)(3).* Washington, DC: U.S. Sentencing Commission.

Weithorn LA and SB Campbell 1982. The competency of children and adolescents to make informed treatment decisions. *Child Development* 53:1589–1598.

Zimring FE. 2005. *American Juvenile Justice.* New York: Oxford University Press.

49

Forensic aspects of childhood bullying

BRADLEY W. FREEMAN

INTRODUCTION

Bullying, a new topic in this text, has been becoming more visible in the social landscape for children and adolescents in and out of school. This, of course, is not a new phenomenon, but the increasing media coverage and social climate change have brought bullying behavior into the limelight. There have been television shows, movies, video games, and numerous editorials that surround this topic either directly or indirectly. The government has established an anti-bullying website for the public, and the Centers for Disease Control and Prevention (CDC) have begun collecting statistics about the behavior. In March 2011, President Barack Obama and First Lady Michelle Obama hosted the inaugural White House Conference on Bullying Prevention that exemplifies the newfound interest and concern about this age-old social phenomenon (Shepherd 2011).

Following the Columbine High School massacre in Colorado on April 20, 1999, bullying became a frequent topic of discussion among students, teachers, parents, and politicians. This incident sparked discussions about gun control, social cliques, adolescent subculture, and violent video game exposure, among other topics. The publicized suicides of tormented students continued to fuel the movement toward finding an answer for bullying behavior. This public movement has culminated in evoking new legislation. Most states have both policy and legislation regarding bullying, but there remains no federal legislation directly focused on bullying.

The assessment of bullying (either victims or bullies) is complicated for several reasons. The behavior is often not readily apparent to authority, and the victims may not be open to assistance. Additionally, the evaluation of the victim encompasses different concerns than the examination of the bully. For instance, the bully evaluation could involve delinquency issues and almost always has a violence risk assessment as part of the overall examination. Victims, however, could be evaluated in the context of a civil suit, and this evaluation likely involves an opinion concerning diagnosis, damages, cause of the damages, and prognosis. Experts can also provide opinions about the psychological implications of bullying, including potential long-term effects and the interventions shown to be helpful in preventing bullying behavior.

Bullying behaviors can affect an individual into adulthood. For instance, victims can develop mood disorders and anxiety conditions. Additionally, bullying can influence the way in which people interact with others in the future. Falb et al. (2011) reported that after adjusting for age, race, and educational attainment, frequent victims of bullying had a higher risk of perpetrating intimate partner violence as adults. Meltzer et al. (2011) found that adults who reported being bullied in childhood were more than twice as likely as controls to attempt suicide later in life, even after controlling for other suicide risk factors.

WHAT IS BULLYING?

Bullying is a pervasive, widespread, cross-cultural, cross-gender phenomenon that appears to peak in early to mid-adolescence (Smith et al. 2002; Craig et al. 2009) and affects approximately half of school-aged youth worldwide (Wang et al. 2009; Mishna et al. 2010). Bullying has been defined in several different ways, but most authorities agree that there are three distinct factors that need be present to identify the behavior as "bullying." The first factor includes the presence of a power differential between the bully and the victim. The power differential does not necessarily need to be the classic physical disparity, but could be an intellectual, racial, or other difference. For instance, a minority student could be bullied by others due to their race without the bully having a physical advantage. The salient point is that the bully has some form of dominance over the victim. The second factor is that the bullying behavior is intentional. Furthermore, the intent is to intimidate, ostracize, demean, humiliate, or otherwise harm the victim in a substantial way. The final factor is that the bullying behavior is repetitious. The behavior is repeated until the bully achieves his or her goal, loses interest, changes the target, or there is an intervention by someone of authority (i.e., school resource officer, teacher, principal).

Bullying behavior can be categorized in four distinct areas (Table 49.1). The first category is physical bullying

Table 49.1 Bullying terminology

Bullying: A repetitive behavior over an extended period of time in which an individual with greater power attacks, humiliates, or intimidates a less powerful individual with malicious intent.

Physical bullying: When physical contact or a significant threat of physical contact is used to bully a less powerful individual (i.e., a student threatening to fight a less powerful student after school hours).

Verbal bullying: The deliberate use of language to cause psychological distress in another individual for the purposes of humiliation, intimidation, or other malicious reason (i.e., a student continually calls another student names in front of their peers).

Social bullying: When an individual uses his or her social status and/or interpersonal relationships to cause intentional and harmful distress in another individual (i.e., a student intentionally spreads hurtful rumors/gossip about another student).

Cyberbullying: The use of technology by a person to repeatedly and intentionally humiliate, embarrass, degrade, or otherwise harm a specific individual or group of individuals. There does not need to be a power differential present between the bully and the victim (i.e., a student regularly sends hurtful text messages/pictures to another student).

Sexting: Uses technology to send sexually explicit communication. This encompasses all forms of digital media (i.e., text, pictures, video). Sexting involves unwanted communication.

in which the bully uses physical intimidation to get their desired effect. The second type of bullying is verbal bullying. This occurs when adolescents use language to inflict harm onto their victims. In these cases, the harm is psychological and does not need to include physical injury. The third category is social or relational bullying in which the victim is indirectly attacked by the bully through maneuvers such as spreading rumors, ostracizing the victim from social groups, and other behaviors that cause emotional harm and/or social isolation. The last identified category is cyberbullying. Although these categories are distinct, bullies can use combinations of these behaviors to harm their target (i.e., name calling and physical aggression).

Cyberbullying is the newest arena for bullying and involves the use of technology. This form of bullying is unique when compared to the previous three "classic" categories. For instance, cyberbullying does not require the bully or the victim to ever meet in person, they can be separated by great distances, the power differential is much less important, and the bullying can be anonymous. Cyberbullying also continues to evolve as technology changes. The advent of social networking has played a significant role in the cyberbullying landscape.

Importantly, bullying is not constrained to a particular setting, although most bullies prefer an audience. Bullying can occur in all social settings, whether at school, at church, on the soccer field, in the library, or elsewhere. Of note, if the bullying occurs between an adult and a minor, it may very well qualify as child abuse. Additionally, the term "bullying" does not appear in all the different states' legislation or even in all school policies. The behavior is commonly referred to as harassment in many legal doctrines. In some suits brought against school systems, the plaintiff argued that the bullying behavior was essentially a form of harassment that violated his or her civil rights. Section 1983 of the Civil Rights Act is a popular avenue for plaintiffs to seek recourse when bullied in a public school setting.

EPIDEMIOLOGY

Like many social behaviors, bullying is likely underreported. In a national study from the CDC, 20.1% of high school students were bullied in 2011 in the 12 months preceding the survey; 22% for females and 18% for males. Additionally, 16.2% indicated they were bullied electronically; 22.1% of females and 10.8% of males (CDC 2012). The National Center for Educational Statistics determined that for the school year 2010–2011, 28% of students reported being bullied. Of those students, 65% were victims of relational bullying, and 63% were victims of verbal bullying. Approximately a quarter of those students were victims of physical bullying. With regard to cyberbullying, 9% of students reported being victimized in this way with the majority (50%) getting unwanted contact through text messaging (U.S. Department of Education 2011). In addition to victimization statistics, the bullies and bystanders have also been studied. Approximately 30% of young people admit to bullying others (Bradshaw et al. 2007). For bystanders, approximately 70% of students and staff have witnessed bullying. Interestingly, when bystanders intervene, the bullying stops within 10 seconds—a little more than half the time (Hawkins et al. 2001).

CYBERBULLYING

The newest form of victimization involves the use of technology. Cyberbullying has been given various definitions by various entities. The National Crime Victimization Survey defines cyberbullying as "having another student post hurtful information about the respondent on the Internet; make unwanted contact by threatening or insulting the respondent via e-mail, instant messaging, text messaging, or online gaming; purposefully exclude the respondent from an online community; or purposely sharing private information about the respondent on the Internet or mobile phones" (U.S. Department of Education 2011). This definition will continue to evolve with advances in personal technology and social media. A 2014 review of state laws showed that 19 states have the term "cyberbullying" included in their policies and laws surrounding bullying, while 48 states describe electronic harassment. All states except Montana require schools to have a bullying/harassment policy in place (Hinduja and Patchin 2014). Physical bullying necessitates a face-to-face interaction, whereas cyberbullying requires the bully to utilize technology.

It has been reported that almost half of 12- to 17-year-olds viewed their online social network profile daily and 22% visited several times a day (Lenhart and Madden 2007). Other research has tried to determine how much time adolescents are spending using social networking sites. In a 2008 study, the youth surveyed spent an average of 33 minutes each day on social media, which subsequently increased to almost an hour the following year (Steinfield et al. 2008). It is estimated that 93% of adolescents are online, and of those, 39% are online frequently throughout the day. Being "online" covers many types of Internet access. Victims of cyberbullying have been targeted through various technological avenues such as social media, text messaging via smartphones, blogs run by other individuals, e-mail accounts, and online gaming. Schools have a difficult time policing cyberbullying because of the ease of access and due to jurisdictional restrictions. There has been debate about how far the school can reach outside the schoolyard and into the community with regard to its policies. This is evident in current state legislation that shows only 12 states have included off-campus behaviors as part of their policy.

Sexting is a relatively new phenomenon in which individuals will send others explicit communications through the use of technology. Sending adult-related material across the Internet is not new either; however, sexting typically refers to the use of mobile devices. Sexting is not constricted to text only. The advancement of technology has allowed individuals the ability to send any type of digitized media from one person to another. This, of course, includes audio, pictures, and video, which has permitted the distribution of sexually explicit material in all these forms.

Although sexting itself does not necessarily fall under the category of cyberbullying, this type of communication is often used to harass others. There are significant risks for adolescents who engage in sexting. Apart from issues of harassment, possession of indecent photos of minors could constitute a charge of possession of child pornography. In 2009, *Wired* magazine reported a 60-year-old veteran assistant principal was charged with such an offense. The assistant principal was charged with investigating sexting at the school and a boy he was questioning with the school resource officer sent a suspicious picture to the principal's cell phone. Although his defense was successful, the matter lasted a year and cost him $150,000 (Zetter 2009).

Adolescents are also not immune to prosecution. In 2013, the *Washington Post* reported on three high school students in Fairfax County, Virginia, who made cellphone videos of drunken sex acts with other teens and shared them among themselves. This behavior resulted in them facing charges of creating and distributing child pornography (Jouvenal 2013).

THE SCHOOL'S ROLE/RESPONSIBILITY

Whether public, private, or parochial, the school system enjoys a central role in many societies. The established common law doctrine of *in loco parentis* (Latin for "in the place of a parent") demands that the school be responsible for creating a safe environment for the students as well as for protecting their interests. The role of the school is becoming ever more scrutinized and increasingly important. State and federal legislatures continue to develop new policy and law to support equality and opportunity for students in our ever-changing social climate. The role of the school essentially establishes a *duty to care* for the safety of the student. Safety has become a pressing issue for schools in the post-Columbine era (i.e., after April 1999). It has been argued that the original *duty to care* has been superseded with a *duty to protect* (*Walton v. Alexander* 1997). Litigation against school systems and their officials is often due to this assumed duty.

The duty to care is embodied in either state law or from the Due Process Clause of the Fourteenth Amendment to the U.S. Constitution. This amendment protects citizens from state actions that result in loss of or injury to life, liberty, or property. Cases filed in federal court allege a constitutional violation of due process by the state (i.e., school officials) under Section 1983 of the Civil Rights Act. The Supreme Court ruling in *DeShaney v. Winnebago County Department of Social Services* indicated that when the state holds someone against his or her will, the Constitution demands that the state provide for the person's safety and well-being. Because of this ruling, some courts raised the level of responsibility of the school from *duty to care* to *duty to protect* because of the school's "functional custody" of the student (*Lichtler v. County of Orange* 1993). Still, most courts try to determine if a special relationship between the school and the student exists before raising the *duty to care* to the Constitutional *duty to protect*. Since the 1990s, courts have looked more closely at the elements of *imminent danger* to students and *deliberate indifference* by the school before imposing liability (*Walton v. Alexander* 1997). Under this lens, the plaintiff must prove the school intentionally ignored the behavior after being given notice or had knowledge of the injury risk.

In 1999, the Supreme Court determined in *Davis v. Monroe County Board of Education* that private actions could be levied against a school receiving federal funds in instances of harassment between students when it acts with "deliberate indifference" (*Davis v. Monroe County Board of Education* 1999). Justice Sandra Day O'Connor included in the majority opinion that the harassment must be so severe and pervasive that the educational opportunity for the victim is barred and the student harasser is under the school's disciplinary authority. The ruling in the *Davis* case promoted the development of a five-part harassment test to determine the presence of public school liability based on Title IX of the Education Amendments of 1972. The five parts include that (1) the student is a member of a statutorily protected class (gender, race, disability); (2) the peer harassment is based on the protected class; (3) the harassment is severe, pervasive, and objectively offensive; (4) a school official with authority to address the harassment has actual knowledge of it; and (5) the school is deliberately indifferent to the harassment.

In the case of *T.K. and S.K. v. New York City Department of Education* (E.D.N.Y. April 2011), the federal district court found that a disabled student had a valid claim under the *Individuals with Disabilities Education Act* (IDEA) (*T.K. and S.K. v. New York City Department of Education* 2011). The student stated she was denied a free appropriate education due to bullying from peers because of her known disability. The court opined that a school should take quick and necessary steps to remedy bullying that interferes with a special education student's appropriate education.

The protection of free speech as elucidated in the First Amendment has been used by defendants charged with harassment. In the cyberbullying case of *Kara Kowalski v. Berkeley County Schools et al.*, a student sued the school for limiting her First Amendment right to free speech. The school suspended her after learning she had created a hate website directed toward another student at the school. The Fourth Circuit held that the speech created actual or foreseeable "substantial disorder and disruption" that the school was not required to tolerate and the student did not merit protection from the First Amendment (*Kowalski v. Berkley County Schools* 2011). In similar cases, *J.S. v. Blue Mountain School District* and *Layshock v. Hermitage School District* (*J.S. v. Blue Mountain School District* 2011), students were disciplined by the school for creating fake social media profiles of their principals. The parents sued citing the students' behavior was protected under the First Amendment right to free speech. In *Layshock*, a unanimous three-judge panel found in favor of the student holding that the offensive profile created by the student of the principal was protected free speech under the First Amendment (*Layshock v. Hermitage School District* 2010). In *J.S. v Blue Mountain School District*, a different Third Circuit panel of judges found, by a 2:1 vote, that the parody profile of the principal created by the student was not protected free speech. The basis of the opinion was due to the belief that the profile would lead to substantial disruption within the school. Both cases, although arriving at seemingly opposite judgments, relied on several Supreme Court cases including the 1969 case *Tinker v. Des Moines Independent Community School District*. The ruling in the *Tinker* case held that a school may not suppress a student's expression unless it will "materially and substantially disrupt the work and discipline of the school" (*Tinker v. Des Moines Independent Community School District* 1969).

STATE BULLYING LAWS

In 1999, Georgia was the first state to pass anti-bullying legislation. Since that time, all states, with the exception of Montana, have legislation that speaks to bullying behaviors. Montana has, however, adopted a statewide policy (U.S. Department of Health and Human Services 2010). The timing of bullying legislation appears to have begun, at least significantly, in the post-Columbine era. Many of the states that enacted legislation had model policies that provided guidance to state agencies. In 2010, the U.S. Department of Education (USDE) recommended guidelines for anti-bullying legislation in a report to Congress. The recommendations included 11 elements that are divided in four separate sections:

1. Purpose and definition (Components 1–4). Purpose, scope, definition of prohibited behavior, and enumeration of protected groups.
2. District policy development and review (Components 5–6). Implementation of policies, and review for compliance.
3. School District Policy Components (Component 7). Assignment of responsibility to carry out the law.
4. Additional Components (Components 8–11). Communication of policies, monitoring and accountability, actions and interventions to prevent bullying behaviors, legal remedies for victims.

Because these guidelines were introduced in 2010 and because each state is autonomous with regard to how they conceptualize legislation, there is little conformity among the states' laws and policies. Only two states, Maryland and New Jersey, have fully incorporated the USDE guidelines.

FEDERAL BULLYING POLICY

At this time, there is no federal legislation that directly addresses bullying. There are, however, federal laws that protect citizens against harassment based on sex, race, and national origin. In 2015, Robert P. Casey, Jr. (D-PA) introduced the Safe Schools Improvement Act (SSIA) of 2015 (S. 311 2015). This bill was designed to amend the Elementary and Secondary Education Act of 1965 to address and take action to prevent bullying and harassment of students. The updated bill has been referred to a committee for further consideration. In January 2015, the SSIA was reintroduced and sent to a committee. There are currently 40 sponsors who are overwhelmingly democratic.

The SSIA, if re-enacted, would demand that schools receiving federal funds establish a code of conduct that explicitly prohibits bullying and harassment. Schools would also be required to implement prevention strategies and professional development programs. The programs would need to help school personnel address bullying and harassment in a meaningful way. Last, the bill would require individual states to collect data about incidents of bullying and submit that information to the USDE.

The bill addresses the disparities among the different states with regard to their bullying policies and legislation. With regard to cyberbullying, the bill includes "electronic communication" in its definition of bullying. The bill also denotes gay and lesbian students as a protected group as current federal law does not include sexual orientation as a protected group. Some people believe that the formation of this new protected group has been a barrier to the bill's passage.

ASSESSMENT

Forensic aspects

The forensic psychiatrist may become involved in cases of bullying or cyberbullying and may find himself or herself on either the left or right of the courtroom aisle. For plaintiffs, an expert may be hired to elucidate damages by way of determining a psychiatric diagnosis and/or associated constellation of symptoms that show the victim was damaged. Oftentimes, posttraumatic stress disorder, anxiety disorders, and mood disorders dominate the evaluations, for obvious reasons. Additionally, the connection between the youth's symptoms and functional impairments to the bullying behavior is a key concept, as the alleged bullying must be shown to have caused the damages. Without this link, the case has no merit.

The defense may also request the services of an expert to try and rebut the plaintiff's complaint of damages or scrutinize an opposing expert's opinion. Experts must remember to be blind to the party for which they are retained and remain as unbiased as possible in their evaluation. The court may also retain the expert. For instance, the court may ask the expert to evaluate the alleged bully, especially if the alleged bully has a history of delinquent behavior that has failed to improve despite previous court-ordered interventions. If the matter is being heard in juvenile court, the evaluator should provide a diagnostic assessment and treatment recommendations due to the rehabilitative focus of this venue. For youth evaluated in other courts, the expert may still provide a diagnostic assessment and treatment recommendations as part of the evaluation unless specifically instructed not to do so.

Oftentimes, the parties involved usually have a preferred outcome for the expert's assessment. This may be for the bully to escape punishment or for the victim to gain financial compensation or other resources. During the course of the evaluation, the expert must consider the potential bias of information provided and be vigilant with regard to malingering. Competent cross-examination will explore the weight placed on specific pieces of information that may, if not considered by the expert in formulating the opinion, confound the expert's conclusions.

Evaluations for the court are generally conducted with more rigor than what may occur in clinical practice. The opinions provided must be supported by data that are as objective and as valid as can be obtained. The assessments of victims and bullies are not identical as each has their own unique aspects. Before an assessment can begin, it is necessary that the expert understand several details about the referral. Most importantly, the expert must have a clear understanding of the referral question(s). It is often helpful to have the referring party send a letter detailing the particular question(s) that need to be addressed. It is fairly common for the referral source to have a limited understanding of an expert's services and how evaluations are undertaken. If the referral question(s) is unclear, the expert should certainly consult with the attorney or judge to better understand the issue at hand. The expert can also educate them about the possible areas in which the expert can, and cannot, provide an opinion. A clear and specific referral question will help guide the evaluation and provide a focused opinion. In addition to a clear referral, the expert will need other preliminary details such as the expected time frame for the report, if there are obvious conflicts of interest, payment for services, and other aspects that might influence the evaluation.

GENERAL ASSESSMENT OF VICTIMS AND BULLIES

Although the evaluation of the youth is not unlike a typical clinical evaluation, it contains aspects that are normally outside a clinical scope. The expert will need to inform the youth and their family that the report is not confidential and that it may be subject to public scrutiny. Additionally, they need to be made aware that a forensic evaluation is not for treatment purposes. The youth is then scheduled for an interview if he or she, and the family, agree to proceed.

During the interview, the youth is asked a comprehensive set of questions about his or her mental health and level of functioning in an age-appropriate manner. The expert may begin by asking the youth what the purpose of the evaluation is, what he or she has been told about the evaluation, if the expert was given "reminders" about what must be discussed or avoided, the youth's thoughts about the evaluation, and what the youth hopes the evaluation is going to accomplish. This type of questioning helps to assess for malingering, especially if the youth's responses seem scripted. Use open-ended questioning as much as possible as this approach provides the most reliable information (Oates and Shrimpton 1991). Begin by building rapport with the patient about neutral topics such as their family, their daily routine, and things they enjoy doing. As rapport develops and the interview continues, the questions become more focused on the issue(s) at hand. The evaluator may need to use more specific questions to complement the information obtained from the open-ended questioning approach.

The evaluation will need to explore psychosocial domains as well. Domains such as the youth's family life, school routine, peer socialization, and how the youth interacts with their environment should be ascertained. Depending on the complexity of the history, the expert may find that creating a timeline of significant events is helpful. Parents, family members, teachers, coaches, and others can be useful sources of information with regard to the youth's psychosocial functionality. Persons who have known the youth before, during, and after the alleged bullying behavior are in an especially good position to compare and contrast behavioral and functional issues. Additionally, a full mental status exam must be conducted.

Psychological testing may be helpful. Testing should be based on the presenting problem or constellation of symptoms. The child's parents can complete mental health screening tools, and the youth can submit to testing for anxiety, mood symptoms, posttraumatic stress disorder, or other potential areas of concern. Additionally, some of the tools can be used to uncover dissimulation, specifically those containing validity scales. Two of the best predictors of malingering are internal consistency within the particular source and the external consistency with the other data collected. The child must also be assessed for safety. Necessary precautions should be taken if there is risk of harm to self or others.

In formulating opinions, the evaluator gives more weight to the data that are the most credible and unbiased. Not all forensic evaluations result in report writing. Unless a report is explicitly requested, the evaluator should consult with the referral source about the findings prior to engaging in writing a report. This has implications for the attorney involved as to what information may be discoverable. If diagnoses are identified, the evaluator must be able to support each diagnosis with data collected and include the rationale in the report. Support for each diagnosis must conform to the current established criteria.

The expert's opinions are essentially only as good as the information collected. Collateral sources of information play an important role in substantiating, elucidating, and weighing the data collected. With regard to bullying cases, collateral information is often provided from the parents/family, the school, treating providers, other individuals involved in the matter, and sometimes from police reports, surveillance video, medical and mental health records, and other official documentation. The amount of potential bias needs to be considered with each source of information and weighed accordingly. The weight given is usually based on the source's connection to those involved and what, if any, interest the source has in the outcome of the matter.

Persons outside the mental health field may attempt to equate "no diagnosis" with "no damages." Experts may need to explain that a psychiatric diagnosis is simply a label for a constellation of symptoms. Experts also need to explain that a person can still suffer significantly even though he or she may not meet the specific criteria for a major psychiatric disorder. For this reason, a focus on functional impairments is needed in addition to explaining the diagnosis or diagnoses provided. Also, the expert will need to describe the etiology of the symptoms as this relates directly to the legal idea of causation. Again, without a direct link between the bullying behavior and the damages, there is no causation and thus, no case.

Family and juvenile courts are interested in interventions that might be helpful for the youths involved. The evaluator will need to provide the court with specific treatment recommendations for the youth. Although this is not necessarily the case with criminal court, the expert may choose to provide recommendations there as well. Some experts believe that this blurs the line between a forensic duty and clinical care; however, courts are looking for guidance, and treatment recommendations can be helpful for the youth and the court's disposition of the matter.

Psychological testing and screening tools can be useful in a forensic assessment. The CDC has published a collection of assessment tools that address the evaluation of victims, bullies, and bystanders (Hamburger et al. 2011).

ASSESSING THE ALLEGED VICTIM

Evaluating the alleged victim includes screening for a wide variety of psychiatric ailments rather than performing a limited trauma assessment. The evaluator must collect a lifetime trauma inventory of the youth to better understand what may be producing or effecting current trauma-related symptoms. Because some children may be reluctant to discuss their past trauma, it may be necessary to rely on collateral information. The youth's bullying history is also a necessary area to explore. A bullying history helps to determine what type(s) of bullying the child has been exposed to and what the child's historical responses were to those experiences. The details about bullying incidents are similar to those of traumatic incidents. The youth should be asked about the nature of the bullying; why the youth believed he or she was targeted; and the duration, intensity, location, and outcome of the bullying behavior. The outcomes include the youth's change in thoughts, feelings, emotions, and behaviors related to the bullying he or she endured.

It is important to understand the victim's perception about how the bullying has affected his or her functionality. The expert can ask broad questions such as "What is different since the bullying? How has being bullied affected you? What is it like to be bullied the way you were bullied? Have you been bullied like this before?" The expert can then use the youth's responses to obtain more detailed information by asking more specific questions.

When interviewing the alleged victim's parents, it is important to gain an understanding of the child's behavioral and emotional history prior to and after the bullying. It is best to interview the parents individually and ask similar, if not the same, questions. By interviewing the parents in this way, the expert is better able to gauge external consistency of the other data. This can help to support or refute symptomatology and functional deficits that may be associated with the bullying behavior. The child's functional

Table 49.2 Examples of psychological tests to consider in the evaluation of bullying matters

Client type	Psychological tool
Victim and bully	Minnesota Multiphasic Personality Inventory-Adolescent (MMPI-A)
	Personality Assessment Inventory-Adolescent (PAI-A)
	Structured Clinical Interview for *DSM* Disorders (SCID)
	Child Behavior Checklist
	Trauma Symptom Inventory-2 (TSI-2)
Particular for victim	UCLA PTSD Reaction Index (RI)
	Child PTSD Symptom Scale (CPSS)
	Peer Relations Assessment Questionnaires-Revised (PRAQ-R)
Particular for bully	Structured Assessment of Violence Risk in Youth (SAVRY)
	Hare Psychopathy Checklist: Youth Version (PCL:YV)
	Level of Service/Case Management Inventory (YLS/CMI)

impairments need to be assessed in all domains, such as in their family relationships, academic performance, socialization with peers, behavior, spirituality, and employment. The evaluator must also assess pre- and post-event domains such as sleep, appetite, energy level, anxiety, mood, and somatic symptoms. A complete mental status evaluation is also completed.

Psychological testing can be useful in assessing the victim. Persons trained in testing should interpret the data and provide a summary of the results. Testing, although not infallible, can provide more objectivity as well as assess for dissimulation (Table 49.2).

ASSESSMENT OF THE BULLY

The difference between evaluating the victim and the bully essentially rests with the referral question. In most instances, the role of the forensic evaluation is to assess the mental and behavioral health of a juvenile suspected of bullying and offer intervention recommendations for the court. Additionally, the defense may be interested in looking for mitigating factors that might decrease the punishment or exculpate the youth altogether.

The evaluation of the youth suspected of bullying is generally in line with a typical clinical evaluation for mental illness with sensitivity surrounding secondary gain of avoiding punishment. As with the victim evaluations, the youth and the family should be aware of the lack of confidentiality surrounding the evaluation. They also need to understand the evaluation is not for treatment purposes. Collateral sources need to be obtained to help substantiate, elucidate, or refute information. Psychological testing can help provide objective data.

SPECIAL CIRCUMSTANCES

Evaluation of the school's response

The expert must be cautious not to stray into unfamiliar territory. An expert may be asked to provide an opinion concerning the response by the school system with regard to the bullying or harassment. In this instance, it is best left alone even if the school's response was obviously egregious or appropriate. Mental health experts would be wise to leave the evaluation of the school's response to others who are more familiar and have a better working knowledge of school administration and school policy. Unless the expert has specific training and experience in school administration, it is highly unlikely that a court would qualify the expert to be able to provide opinions in this area. The expert, however, may be able to comment on issues such as normal adolescent behavior, group contagion, and the social dynamics of a student body, but getting involved with the policy and procedures of a school system is not advised.

Postmortem evaluation

There are also disastrous occasions in which a youth will complete suicide due to bullying. In these cases, an evaluator may be asked to do a psychological autopsy to determine the motivation for the suicide. Evaluators who work in this area rely on various sources of collateral information to arrive at an opinion as to the etiology of the suicidal behavior. The evaluator must be sensitive to the surviving family members and the youth's community when conducting such an evaluation.

In postmortem evaluations, making a diagnosis is an academic task. In generating the opinion, the evaluator will need to search for connections between the decedent's behaviors surrounding the suicide with bullying behaviors of which he or she may have been exposed.

Video recording the interviews

There is some debate with regard to audio and video recording interviews with juveniles. As technology has progressed, creating high-quality recordings of forensic interviews is relatively inexpensive and easily facilitated. Still, there are other factors that need to be considered. Parents should consent to the recording of their child, and the youth must be made aware of the recording. Some practitioners choose to record all interviews whether it be with a child or an adult. Some prefer only to record under certain circumstances (i.e., want to preserve the youth's own words to be introduced in court). Video recording also allows the evaluator to capture body language, which can be very helpful when evaluating young children or individuals with limited verbal ability. If recordings are made, they need to be kept in a secure location as with all forensic records. Despite concerns of recording interviews, this can provide a great deal of transparency, and it supports the notion that the report is objective and comprehensive.

Cyberbullying assessment and the use of a forensic computer investigator

Cyberbullying utilizes the newest frontier with regard to social interaction. This medium has the capacity to target victims without the bully having to be physically present. The bully can attack the target anonymously and can distribute the attack very quickly to a substantial number of people. Distribution of inflammatory or defaming material can easily be accomplished through the use of social media.

When assessing the victim of cyberbullying, the expert should follow a similar procedure as he or she would for a victim of other forms of bullying. With cyberbullying, the expert will also want to include a detailed history of the victim's computer use including the number of e-mail accounts the youth has, the youth's use of social networking, participation in online gaming, use of video communications, frequency of posting to online sites, and his or her online profiles. The expert may inquire as to the involvement of a computer forensic investigator who may be able to extract helpful data from the technology used in the bullying (Table 49.3).

Table 49.3 Online resources related to bullying

- StopBullying.Gov (http://www.stopbullying.gov)
- American Academy of Child and Adolescent Psychiatry (http://www.aacap.org/aacap/Families_and_Youth/Resource_Centers/Bullying_Resource_Center/Home.aspx)
- American Academy of Pediatrics (https://www.aap.org/en-us/advocacy-and-policy/aap-health-initiatives/resilience/Pages/Bullying-and-Cyberbullying.aspx?)
- American Psychological Association (http://www.apa.org/topics/bullying/)
- National Institutes of Health, MedlinePlus (http://www.nlm.nih.gov/medlineplus/bullying.html)
- Centers for Disease Control and Prevention (http://www.cdc.gov/violenceprevention/youthviolence/index.html)
- National Education Association (http://www.nea.org/home/neabullyfree.html)
- Gay, Lesbian, and Straight Education Network (http://glsen.org/search?keywords=bullying)
- Cyberbullying Research Center (http://www.cyberbullying.us)
- Wright's Law (http://www.wrightslaw.com)
- National Crime Prevention Council (http://www.ncpc.org)
- Pacer's National Bullying Prevention Center (http://www.pacer.org/bullying/)

SUMMARY

Bullying behavior is a social problem that will continue to exist in the world's societies. The behavior should not be tolerated due to the potential for severe outcomes to the victim and others involved. Schools deal with bullying behavior on a daily basis, and their response is encapsulated in their policies, procedures, and codes of conduct. Very few bullying incidents ever reach the level of legal intervention. Still, bullying-related lawsuits are on the rise. Mental health experts may find themselves presented with cases that involve all types of bullying behaviors. Experts must have a clear referral question in which to generate an opinion based on as much credible and unbiased information as possible. As with most forensic reports, the limitations of the evaluation should be discussed.

REFERENCES

Bradshaw CP, AL Sawyer, and LM O'Brennan. 2007. Bullying and peer victimization at school: Perceptual differences between students and school staff. *School Psychology Review* 36(3):361–382.

Centers for Disease Control and Prevention (CDC). 2012. *Youth Violence: Facts at a Glance, 2012.* http://www.cdc.gov/violenceprevention/pdf/YV-DataSheet-a.pdf, accessed April 11, 2014.

Craig W, Y Harel-Fisch, H Fogel-Grinvald et al. 2009. A cross-national profile of bullying and victimization among adolescents in 40 countries. *International Journal of Public Health* 54(Supplement 2):216–224.

Davis v. Monroe County Board of Education, 526 U.S. 629, 119 S. Ct. 1661 (1999).

Falb KL, HL McCauley, MR Decker et al. 2011. School bullying perpetration and other childhood risk factors as predictors of adult intimate partner violence perpetration. *Archives of Pediatric Adolescent Medicine* 165(10):890–894.

Hamburger ME, KC Basile, and AM Vivolo. 2011. *Measuring Bullying Victimization, Perpetration, and Bystander Experiences: A Compendium of Assessment Tools.* Atlanta, GA: Centers for Disease Control and Prevention, National Center for Injury Prevention and Control.

Hawkins DL, D Pepler, and WM Craig. 2001. Peer interventions in playground bullying. *Social Development* 10:512–527.

Hinduja S and JW Patchin. 2014. *State Cyberbullying Laws: A Brief Review of State Cyberbullying Laws and Policies.* http://www.cyberbullying.us/Bullying_and_Cyberbullying_Laws.pdf, accessed April 14, 2014.

Jouvenal J. 2013. Teen sexting case goes to trial in Fairfax County. *The Washington Post*, April 17. http://www.washingtonpost.com, accessed September 12, 2014.

J.S. v. Blue Mountain School District, No. 08-4138 2011 WL 2305970 (3rd Cir. 2011).

Kowalski v. Berkeley County Schools (U.S. Ct. App. 4th July 27, 2011).

Layshock v. Hermitage School District, No. 07-4465 (3d Cir. Feb. 4, 2010).

Lenhart A and M Madden. 2007. *Teens, Privacy, and Online Social Networks. Pew Internet and American Life Project Report*. http://www.pewinternet.org/2007/04/18/teens-privacy-and-online-social-networks, accessed April 11, 2014.

Lichtler v. County of Orange, 813 F. Supp. 1054 (S.D. N.Y. 1993).

Meltzer H, P Vostanis, T Ford et al. 2011. Victims of bullying in childhood and suicide attempts in adulthood. *European Psychiatry* 26(8):498–503.

Mishna F, C Cook, T Gadalla et al. 2010. Cyber bullying behaviors among middle and high school students. *American Journal of Orthopsychiatry* 80(3):362–374.

Oates K and S ShrimptonS. 1991. Children's memories for stressful and non-stressful events. *Medicine, Science and the Law* 31(1):4–10.

S. 311: Safe Schools Improvement Act of 2015. 2015. https://www.govtrack.us/congress/bills/114/s311, accessed October 26, 2015.

Shepherd S. 2011. White House conference tackles bullying. *CNN*, March 10. http://www.cnn.com/2011/POLITICS/03/10/obama.bullying/index.html, accessed August 20, 2014.

Smith P, H Cowie, R Olafsson et al. 2002. Definitions of bullying: A comparison of terms used, and age and gender differences, in a fourteen-country international comparison. *Child Development* 73(4):1119–1133.

Steinfield C, N Ellison and C Lampe. 2008. Social capital, self-esteem, and use of online social network sites: A longitudinal analysis. *Journal of Applied Developmental Psychology* 29:434–445.

T.K. and S.K. v. New York City Dept. of Educ., 56 IDELR 228 (E.D.N.Y. 2011).

Tinker v. Des Moines Indep. Cmty. Sch. Dist., 393 U.S. 503 (1969).

U.S. Department of Health and Human Services. 2010. *State Anti-Bullying Laws and Policies*. http://www.stop-bullying.gov/laws/index.html, accessed April 14, 2014.

U.S. Department of Education. 2011. *Student Reports of Bullying and Cyber-Bullying: Results from the 2011 School Crime Supplement to the National Crime Victimization Survey*. Washington, DC: National Center for Education Statistics.

Walton v. Alexander 20 F.3d 1350 (5th Cir. 1994).

Wang J, R Iannotti, and T Nansel. 2009. School bullying among adolescents in the United States: Physical, verbal, relational, and cyber. *Journal of Adolescent Health* 45(4):368–375.

Zetter K. 2009. "Sexting" hysteria falsely brands educator as child pornographer. *Wired*, April 3.

PART 6

Correctional Psychiatry

JAMES L. KNOLL

50

The history of correctional psychiatry in the United States

PETER N. BARBORIAK

INTRODUCTION

The number of incarcerated persons in the United States reached an all-time high in 2010. The U.S. Department of Justice estimated that federal, state, and municipal governments incarcerated a total of 2,279,100 individuals during 2010. The incarcerated population decreased by approximately 2.5% to 2,220,300 individuals by 2013. An additional 4,751,400 individuals received community supervision in 2013 (Glaze and Kaeble 2014). A significant proportion of these incarcerated individuals suffer from psychiatric disorders or substance abuse. In 2006 the U.S. Department of Justice estimated that over half of inmates suffered from mental problems and two-thirds of inmates had a substance abuse history at mid-year 2005 (James and Glaze 2006). Mental health services to mentally ill criminal offenders remain an urgent problem despite a long history of psychiatric service to prisoners (Metzner 1997a).

Correctional psychiatry refers to the practice of psychiatry in the correctional setting, including lock-ups, jails, detention centers, juvenile correctional institutions, prisons, and community corrections programs. Historically, correctional psychiatrists have engaged in treatment and rehabilitation of prisoners (Travin 1994). Prisoners with legally recognized emotional or mental disorders have been identified as mentally disordered offenders. Certain mentally disordered offenders, however, are not in the custody of a correctional institution (Halleck 1987; Wettstein 1998). This chapter focuses on the historical development of correctional psychiatry in the United States.

Much of the history of correctional psychiatry in the United States has been driven by a long-standing medical interest in explaining and treating criminal behavior. Social reformers, rather than physicians, played the most important roles in the origins of American correctional institutions. The beginnings of American penology and the invention of the prison arose from the same reform movements that gave rise to mental hospitals in the early nineteenth century. Historical developments that shaped psychiatric institutions exerted similar influences on the historical development of correctional institutions.

EVOLUTION OF THE PRISON

The modern system of correctional incarceration originated in the first half of the nineteenth century. Reformers in Great Britain and the American colonies sowed the seeds for this new system beginning in the eighteenth century. Georgian government authorities and moral reformers on both sides of the Atlantic sought to find a solution to the perceived problem of rampant lawlessness. Reformers attempted to find humane alternatives to the traditional punishments practiced in Great Britain and the American colonies, including branding, mutilation, flagellation, public ridicule, and death. Limited incarcerations in workhouses involving forced labor became a popular alternative to traditional punishments. In Great Britain, the existence of a large empire with areas ripe for settlement and forced labor suggested another solution. Beginning in the seventeenth century, but expanding significantly in the eighteenth century, British courts transported convicts to colonies in America, the Caribbean, and later, Australia. British reformers such as John Howard, and Quakers on both sides of the Atlantic, advocated a different approach. They suggested that criminals could be morally redeemed through reflection and repentance in a regularized, structured, and peaceful environment. They argued that penitentiaries would humanely redeem the fallen (McGowen 1995).

In a similar fashion Quakers and others advocated for and established asylums for the mentally ill beginning in the eighteenth century. They argued that "moral treatment" in asylums would humanely redeem the mentally ill. In addition, early nineteenth century mental health reformers were strongly motivated to provide adequate housing and treatment for the mentally ill, who were often confined in local jails in the absence of any other suitable place for them (Grob 1994). Some historians have characterized the asylum and prison reform movements as merely flip sides of the same coin. Rothman viewed the emergence of psychiatric institutions and correctional institutions as part of an overarching mechanism to control social deviance in the United States (Rothman 1971).

The beginnings of correctional reforms in the United States are generally dated to 1790, with the opening of the Walnut Street Jail in Philadelphia, Pennsylvania. This facility pioneered the use of the "Pennsylvania system," which used solitary confinement as a tool to force the inmate to reflect upon and repent of his criminal behavior. The system was further refined at the Eastern State Penitentiary in Philadelphia, completed in 1829. Architects designed the physical layout of Eastern State Penitentiary as the "ideal prison," by meeting specific requirements of the Pennsylvania system, in which inmates were not allowed to interact with each other in any way. Proponents of the Pennsylvania system believed that total isolation would allow inmates to reflect on and reform their morals while protecting them from the corrupting influences of other criminals (Johnston 1994).

In 1817, New York opened Auburn State Prison and established the "Auburn system" model to secure and rehabilitate prisoners. In contrast to the Pennsylvania system, advocates of the Auburn system isolated inmates at night, but relied on group meals and hard labor performed in groups to provide the impetus to moral change. Inmates under the Auburn system were severely punished for talking to or otherwise interacting with each other. Although both models stressed isolation, strict obedience, and steady labor, fierce competition between advocates of the two systems developed by the 1830s (Friedman 1993).

Prison reform and mental health reform continued to be closely allied during the antebellum period. For example, Dorothea Dix, confident in the curative power of asylums, worked actively to reform jails and prisons. She tirelessly visited houses of correction, jails, and prisons, where she interacted with the prisoners. She took part in the controversy between the Pennsylvania and Auburn systems by writing in favor of the Pennsylvania system (Dix 1845, Gollaher 1995). Few American prisons during this period attempted to care specifically for mentally disordered offenders. The first psychiatric hospital for the criminally insane was opened next to Auburn State Prison in 1855. Eventually, hospitals for the criminally insane were opened in Massachusetts, Michigan, and Illinois (Halleck 1965).

Despite idealistic efforts to reform and humanize the criminal justice system, the new models themselves drew criticism as cruel and inhumane institutions. For example, Charles Dickens criticized the Pennsylvania system after visiting the Eastern State Penitentiary in 1842. He characterized the system as "rigid, strict, and hopeless solitary confinement." He witnessed inmates who suffered "an anguish so acute and so tremendous that all imagination of it must fall short of the reality." He wrote, "I hold this slow and daily tampering with the mysteries of the brain, to be immeasurably worse than any torture of the body" (Dickens 1842). Multiple criticisms of the early penitentiary systems reflected similar criticisms aimed at the asylum movement.

Prisons during the second half of the nineteenth century underwent a progressive decline in faith in the ability of the established prison models to redeem inmates. The period between approximately 1870 and 1900 witnessed the rise of a new correctional philosophy called the reformatory model. This model stressed the use of education and vocational training, combined with indeterminate sentencing, to promote change in the prisoner (Friedman 1993).

THE RISE AND FALL OF PSYCHIATRIC CRIMINOLOGY

Biological and anthropological theories dominated explanations for criminality and other antisocial behaviors in the nineteenth century. For example, the work of the Italian criminologist Lombroso postulated the existence of hereditary physical criminal types. Theorists on the etiology of crime, including psychiatrists, during the late nineteenth century supported the concept of a "criminal brain" based on anatomical and physiological studies. The practical application of such ideas led to the eugenics movement and sterilization of criminals in the early twentieth century (Halleck 1965). Subsequently, psychiatrists and others found little empirical support for hereditary biological and anthropological theories of criminal behavior. Noted psychiatrist William Alanson White effectively argued against coerced sterilization in 1915 (White 1917).

The origins of psychiatry's interest in developing an alternative to moralistic, biological, or anthropological theories of criminal behavior began in the nineteenth century. Interest in studying and treating antisocial and other deviant behaviors can be traced back to the father of psychiatry, Benjamin Rush. Rush suggested that medical causes could account for deviant behavior in his psychiatric textbook of 1812 (Rush 1812). This intellectual movement only began gaining momentum in the late nineteenth century. Correctional psychiatrist H.E. Allison called for psychiatric examination of all offenders as early as 1894 (Allison 1894).

The early twentieth century witnessed the flowering of the Progressive Era. Progressives believed in the rational reformation of society by experts. Though generally considered to date from approximately 1900–1920, the influence of the Progressive Era on correctional psychiatry extended from the 1920s to the 1960s. During this period, psychiatrists strove to view crime through a medical model and to establish a psychiatric criminology. Ultimately, optimism in psychiatry's ability to understand and treat deviant behavior scientifically led to calls for alternatives to incarceration and outpatient approaches to treatment.

The rise of a juvenile justice system during the Progressive Era played an important role in the development of correctional psychiatry. In 1909, William Healy established the first court clinic in Chicago, where he conducted psychiatric evaluations for the court. His model for a court clinic was later copied in other juvenile courts, and in adult criminal courts in major jurisdictions. In conjunction with the young sciences of psychology and sociology, Healy fostered a psychiatric interest in the study of delinquency that laid the groundwork for the rise of a medical model of crime, and influenced studies of psychopathy and antisocial behavior (Healy 1915; Levine and Levine 1992).

Another source for the origins of psychiatric criminology came from the mental hygiene movement. Founded by Clifford Beers, a former patient, with support from psychiatrists and psychologists in 1909, the National Committee for Mental Hygiene aimed to protect the public's mental health. The mental hygiene movement advocated for preventive measures to curb delinquency and criminal behavior (Salmon 1920).

Caught up in the ideals of the Progressives during the 1920s, psychiatrists argued strongly that psychiatric expertise could solve the problems of criminals and crime. Excitement over new psychological insights provided by psychoanalysis also played a role in this movement, in which the state of Massachusetts played a pioneering role. In 1921, Massachusetts enacted the Briggs Law, which called for psychiatric examination of all defendants charged with a capital crime, or felons with prior felony convictions (Halleck 1965). Prominent psychiatrists such as William Alanson White, superintendent of St. Elizabeth's Hospital in Washington, DC, called for closer relationships among psychiatrists, attorneys, and the courts (White 1927). Prominent legal scholars such as Sheldon Glueck reflected the growing interest of progressive attorneys and judges by incorporating the latest psychiatric concepts in their work (S. Glueck 1925).

Psychiatric explanations for criminal behavior catapulted into the general public's attention during the sensational Leopold–Loeb trial, an early "crime of the century." Nathan Leopold and Richard Loeb, two 19-year-old sons of wealthy Chicago families, murdered a 14-year-old boy in 1924. Their attorney, Clarence Darrow, successfully used the psychodynamic expert testimony to avoid the death penalty. Defense experts included William Healy, William Alanson White, and Bernard Glueck, a psychiatrist at Sing Sing Prison in New York. Psychiatric aspects of the Leopold–Loeb trial further encouraged the development of psychiatric criminology (Diamond 1994).

Leading psychiatric reformers wished to apply the medical model to the correctional system. They criticized the traditional correctional approach of punishment as cruel and ineffective. They urged a scientific, individualized approach "which has rehabilitation and reconstruction as its end" (B. Glueck 1935). Despite the rhetoric suggesting a possible medical cure for crime, correctional psychiatrists engaged in little treatment. Psychiatrists working for the courts and correctional institutions concentrated on diagnostics and classification (Halleck 1965). The first survey of correctional psychiatrists conducted by Overholser in 1928 identified 29 correctional institutions with at least one full-time psychiatrist and 64 institutions with at least one part-time psychiatrist. Overholser found that 110 criminal courts out of a total of 1058 employed full- or part-time psychiatrists (Overholser 1928).

The Committee on the Legal Aspects of Psychiatry of the American Psychiatric Association played an important part in advocating for increasing psychiatric involvement in corrections and psychiatric criminology. Psychiatrists such as Karl A. Menninger and William Alanson White represented crime as a kind of failure in life adaptation that fell within the focus of psychiatry. They asserted that psychiatric study of individual criminals and their crimes would lead to "an efficient and scientific solution" to the problem of crime. The Committee on Legal Aspects of Psychiatry issued a report supporting these views in 1925 (Grob 1985).

The interest in developing a psychiatric criminology and applying that knowledge to the criminal justice system flourished in the 1930s. Leading psychiatrists, lawyers, and judges continued to foster the process of close cooperation. The beginning acceptance of psychoanalytic theories engendered a confidence in fledgling American psychoanalysts that they could unlock the unconscious and psychosexual origins of criminal behavior. American psychiatrists were strongly influenced by the translation and American publication in 1931 of the seminal German study of the psychodynamics of crime, *The Criminal, the Judge and the Public* (Alexander and Staub 1931). In 1931, the Forensic Psychiatry Committee of the American Psychiatric Association, including members William Alanson White, Bernard Glueck, and Winfred Overholser, proclaimed that psychiatry must play an important role in the problems of crime (American Psychiatric Association 1932).

During this period, psychiatric work with criminals earned prestige and respect from others in the field. The National Commission on Law Observance and Law Enforcement, in conjunction with the American Bar Association, recommended that larger courts routinely access psychiatric expertise by establishing court clinics (American Psychiatric Association 1931). The establishment of court clinics resulted in the routine evaluation and occasional treatment efforts toward defendants in major cities. The first psychiatric clinic attached to an adult court was founded in Detroit in 1919. Subsequent court clinics opened in Baltimore, Chicago, New York, Cleveland, Pittsburgh, and Philadelphia. The American Psychiatric Association formally recognized the growing importance of forensic and correctional psychiatry by organizing a Section on Forensic Psychiatry in 1934 with William Alanson White as its first chairman. This and similar developments led to "golden years of awakening in the field of criminal Jurisprudence" (Zilboorg 1944).

Psychiatric interest in the "sexual psychopath" developed in the 1930s. Public opinion feared an epidemic of sex crimes, and the criminal justice system viewed psychiatrists as a valuable resource. A number of psychiatrists voiced confidence that scientific study of sexual offenders could result in effective prevention and treatment. Many state legislatures passed sexual psychopath laws including Illinois in 1938, and Michigan and California in 1939.

Psychiatric criminology fueled an interest into psychiatric research involving in-depth analysis into the histories of individual criminals (Karpman 1933; McCartney 1934). In practice, psychiatric attempts to evaluate, treat, and research criminals fell short of the standards proclaimed by the leading psychiatric thinkers of the day (Bromberg 1982). Despite these problems, few psychiatrists heeded voices of caution, such as Menas Gregory who commented that "psychiatry might be over-sold" (Gregory 1935). Despite strong interest and prestige, few psychiatrists actually practiced correctional psychiatry. A survey conducted by McCartney in 1934 revealed 48 full-time and 35 part-time psychiatrists practicing in prisons (Halleck 1965).

Interest in psychiatric criminology waned during the 1940s, as psychiatrists turned their attentions to the psychiatric aspects of the Second World War. Correctional psychiatry services decreased, and efforts toward treatment of offenders became sporadic. Research efforts continued, especially studies in the psychodynamics of psychopathy, which bore fruit during the decade (Cleckley 1941; Wittels 1943; Greenacre 1945). In addition, specialized programs for specific offender populations, especially sex offenders, became established in a number of states. Indeterminate sentencing for sexual offenders became more popular. Psychiatrists generally favored indeterminate sentencing as an important component in a treatment program for criminal behavior using the medical model. However the Group for the Advancement of Psychiatry fiercely criticized indeterminate sexual offender sentencing in 1947, owing to fears regarding due process and the lack of treatment for those receiving indeterminate sentences (Halleck 1965).

The 1950s witnessed a renewed interest in correctional psychiatry and psychiatric criminology. The success of psychoanalytic explanations and treatments for war-related traumatic neuroses spurred a general interest in individual and group therapy. Founded in 1950, the Association for Psychiatric Treatment of Offenders encouraged large-scale individual and group psychotherapeutic treatment for prisoners. Massachusetts instituted an extensive outpatient evaluation and treatment program for probationers and parolees. As correctional psychiatrists engaged in more intensive treatment rather than diagnosis and classification, ethical concerns regarding dual agency became more common (Halleck 1965).

Interest in innovative treatment and reformation of the psychopath resulted in the establishment of the Patuxent Institution in Maryland in 1955. Maryland courts committed "defective delinquents" to the institution under a completely indeterminate sentence until they were rehabilitated, and safe to reenter society. "Defective delinquent" was defined as "an individual who by the demonstration of persistent aggravated antisocial or criminal behavior evidences a propensity towards criminal activity and is found to have either some intellectual deficiency or emotional imbalance or both as to clearly demonstrate an actual danger to society" (*Md.Ann.Code* 1951). Patients received group therapy and individual counseling. An institutional review board evaluated patients for release to the community, which was usually contingent on continued outpatient therapy (Guttmacher 1968).

Wisconsin established a similar program for sex offenders. California opened the Vacaville Medical Facility to provide innovative therapeutic approaches, especially group programming, for prisoners in 1955. The Federal Bureau of Prisons achieved a role as an innovator in correctional psychiatry during this period. Psychiatrists provided a full range of forensic evaluations and innovative treatment programs for the federal prisons during this period (Halleck 1965). Despite these developments, even fewer psychiatrists worked in correctional settings, relative to past periods. A survey by Warren Wille in 1957 found 43 full-time and 35 part-time psychiatrists working in correctional settings. Only 19 state prisons reported having a full-time psychiatrist on staff. Ten states reported no psychiatrists working in any capacity in their correctional systems (Wille 1957).

Correctional psychiatry continued to make a resurgence through the 1960s, and correctional psychiatrists continued to express confidence in their ability to rehabilitate individual prisoners using psychotherapy. In terms of numbers, however, correctional psychiatry during the 1960s remained a minor part of clinical psychiatry. An American Psychiatric Association survey in 1961 indicated that 65 psychiatrists reported spending over 30 hours a week in correctional institutions, with an additional 45 spending at least 15 hours of part-time work or consultation (Halleck 1965). Three years later the chief psychiatrist of the Federal Bureau of Prisons reported that only 56 full-time psychiatrists covered the nations' 230 correctional institutions (Smith 1964).

Leaders in both psychiatry and corrections still envisioned an important role for psychiatry. They believed that psychiatry could contribute "understanding, handling, and, hopefully, correction of socially unacceptable behavior" (Smith 1964). In addition, psychiatry was felt to have a role in modifying the "anti-therapeutic" aspects of incarceration. By the 1960s, some forensic psychiatrists raised doubt about the concept that all criminals suffered from some type of mental illness (Guttmacher 1968).

The optimism expressed early in the decade changed to criticism as the decade ended. Proposals for new innovative programs remained on paper while the real prisoners often received minimal mental health services. Conflicts between psychiatrists and correctional staff impeded the therapeutic mission of correctional mental health services (Stamm 1962). Voices for immediate remedies became prominent. Critics noted that correctional institutions continued to stress security over the psychological needs of prisoners, and they called for action to reform correctional mental health services. (Halleck 1967). Correctional psychiatrists continued to complain that evaluation and treatment of inmates with mental illness were too limiting. Advocacy for primary focus on rehabilitation and for prisons to become "centers for the study, diagnosis, and treatment of the criminal mind" continued the goals of the Progressive Era (Fink et al. 1969). The 1960s witnessed the beginnings of standards of health care for jails and prisons. In 1966, the American Correctional Association published standards for correctional institutions that included a section on the health care (American Correctional Association 1966).

CORRECTIONAL PSYCHIATRY IN TRANSITION

The 1970s proved to be a time of significant change in correctional psychiatry. Psychiatrists saw their influence in corrections wane, as the concept of rehabilitation came under strong attack. Psychiatrists lost enthusiasm for the coerced psychiatric cure for criminal behavior (Rappeport 1974). Critics of psychiatry questioned the effectiveness and therapeutic authority of correctional psychiatry. A number of prison riots, especially the Attica rebellion in 1971, shook the foundations of corrections. The correctional bureaucracy began to question the utility of correctional psychiatry, as faith in rehabilitation for prisoners faded. Prison and jail inmate populations exploded and placed severe pressures on correctional systems. Overall, psychiatrists became more modest in their therapeutic goals (Roth 1986). Correctional psychiatry lost prestige and appeared unappealing to many if not most clinicians (Cumming and Soloway 1973).

The Supreme Court and lower courts significantly increased constitutional protections for prisoners' rights. Prior to 1973, the courts allowed prison administrators a free hand in running prisons, including the restrictions of civil rights. For example, the Virginia Court of Appeals ruled in 1871 that "Prisoners have no more rights than slaves" (*Ruffin v. Commonwealth* 1871). A number of Supreme Court and Appeals Court rulings greatly expanded the basic constitutional rights of prisoners. In 1974 the Supreme Court clearly affirmed a basic set of prisoner rights (*Wolff v. McDonnell* 1974). The Fifth Circuit Court of Appeals ruled that lack of mental health care could violate a prisoner's eighth amendment protections (*Newman v. Alabama* 1974). The landmark case *Estelle v. Gamble* (1976) set a standard for the provision of medical care for prisoners. *Estelle v. Gamble* held that inadequate medical care constituted cruel and unusual punishment. The U.S. Supreme Court established a "deliberate indifference" standard of medical care. In 1977, the Fourth Circuit Court of Appeals ruled that the right to mental health care was equal to a prisoner's right to medical care in *Bowring v. Godwin* (1977). The Supreme Court ruled on a prisoner's due process rights when transferred from a prison to a psychiatric hospital in *Vitek v. Jones* (1980). The court ruled that such transfers required procedural safeguards, including an administrative adversarial hearing with available legal counsel due to stigmatization and other "curtailment of liberty."

Research into antisocial behavior continued, but the emphasis in jails and prisons was to treat mentally disordered prisoners. Commentators increasingly questioned psychiatry's attempts to treat antisocial behavior, even in those individuals with other mental illnesses. Critics asserted that psychiatrists and other mental health professionals could not demonstrate the effectiveness of coerced treatment on patients engaging in antisocial behavior, and that the mental health system perpetuated myths about the curability of this population. John Monahan, for example, complained of the "psychiatrization of criminal behavior" (Monahan 1973). Critics in and out of psychiatry questioned the effectiveness and moral basis of sexual psychopath laws. States progressively phased out commitment laws and traditional treatment programs (Group for the Advancement of Psychiatry 1977).

By the early 1970s, many psychiatrists feared that changes making involuntary commitment laws more stringent would force many individuals with mental illness into the criminal justice system. (Abramson 1972; Kirk and Therrein 1975; Rachlin et al. 1975). Steadman's research to address this question cautioned that perceptions of increasing numbers of mentally ill inmates in prisons and jails were not supported by statistics (Steadman and Ribner 1980).

For the most part, the 1980s represented a period of consolidation for correctional psychiatry. Turning from a focus on societal goals, correctional practitioners focused on dealing with particular problems of mental health service delivery in the correctional environment, and on evaluation and treatment of individual prisoners (Roth 1986). The prestige of correctional psychiatry remained low. Critics from within psychiatry pointed out a number of perceived problems with correctional psychiatry: isolation from mainstream clinical practice, collusion with correctional authorities, professional legitimization of dehumanizing, coercive institutions, and poor working conditions. Correctional psychiatry positions seemed dangerous, unpleasant, and poorly paid (Goldstein 1983).

Inmate populations continued to grow rapidly due to increased conviction rates and the gradual shift to determinate sentencing. Social critics continued to criticize the mental health care provided in jails and prisons. Criticisms included the lack of specialized mental health housing units, misuse of psychotropic medications, overuse of restrictive interventions, and general prison conditions that contributed to prisoner psychopathology (Kaufman 1980, Hollingsworth 1985, Schulte 1985).

The 1980s saw the beginning of concerted efforts to create standards for correctional mental health care and the progressive differentiation of correctional psychiatry from other branches of the profession. The National Commission on Correctional Health Care published a set of health-care standards for jails, prisons, and juvenile detention centers (National Commission on Correctional Health Care 1986a; National Commission on Correctional Health Care 1986b). These efforts were supplemented by standards published by the American Bar Association in 1989. In 1989 the American Psychiatric Association published suggested guidelines for mental health-care standards in jail and prisons (American Psychiatric Association 1989).

THE NINETIES

Jail and prison populations continued to escalate during the 1990s, which fueled demand for more mental health services. Correctional mental health services, however, lagged behind (Manderscheid 2004). State legislatures and departments of correction searched for a solution to rising prison populations, limited prison beds, class action lawsuits, and growing costs of incarceration. Reflecting developments in the community, managed mental health appeared to be an effective way to curb costs, yet provide mandated services (Patterson 1998).

In a related development, various state departments of correction and the federal government experimented with privatization of prisons. In addition a number of states privatized correctional health care and mental health care in a bid to decrease the burden on budgets imposed by state-operated services. Large, for-profit companies such as Corrections Corporation of American, Wackenhut Corrections Corporations, and Prison Health Services managed prisons and health services beginning in the 1980s. A number of state legislatures and departments of corrections viewed these companies as the solution to their problems.

Proponents argued that privatization provided significant cost savings by the mechanism of competition-driven private-sector efficiency and innovation. Private-sector companies promised to provide the equivalent quality of service and save money by avoiding the bureaucratic obstacles, staff costs, and entrenched practices of state-operated correctional services. Critics of privatization warned that the quality of services would be compromised by profit consideration. Some accused corporations of underbidding in order to get a foothold in the state contracts. Critics also charged that private mental health centers provided overly restrictive formularies, restricting diagnostic testing, and decreasing lengths of stay (Schneider 1999; Swanson 2002). Newspapers alleged significant problems with correctional mental health services (Hurst 1995; Kurkjian 1996; Corcoran 1999a,b). Overall, critics characterized the state of prison mental health as woefully inadequate, cruel, and the by-product of a corrupt "prison–industrial complex" (Kupers 1999).

Eventually pressures on managed care resulted in increased health-care costs, and the same trend became evident in correctional mental health services. According to critics, competition between managed care companies resulted in instability, as contracts switched from company to company. Private corrections companies and managed health service providers continued to merge. The departments of correction experienced increased need for mental health services and limited resources resulting in shortened lengths of stay on mental health units (Allen and Bell 1998; Marshall 2000).

The courts continued to clarify and tighten prisoner rights during the decade. The Supreme Court clarified the definition of deliberate indifference regarding cruel and unusual punishment in *Farmer v. Brennan* (1994). The court ruled that prison officials were liable for cruel and unusual punishment if they knew that the inmate faced a substantial risk of harm, but disregarded that risk. The Supreme Court ruled on the involuntary administration of psychotropic medications to prisoners in *Washington v. Harper* (1990) and *Riggins v. Nevada* (1992) based on Fourteenth Amendment rights. In *Washington v. Harper*, the court ruled that psychotropic medications could be involuntarily administered if the treatment arose from "legitimate penological interests" and if the prisoner received institutional due process protections. Two years later, the *Riggins v. Nevada* decision ruled that pretrial detainees could not be involuntary treated with psychotropic medications unless the government established a need for treatment.

Research efforts in the 1990s concentrated on epidemiological studies to determine mental health service requirements. In addition, research efforts analyzed the provision of mental health services in specific institutions in light of mental health-care standards. Such research led to a promising analytic approach to understanding and improving correctional mental health services by utilizing a systems approach (Metzner 1997a,b, 1998). Epidemiological studies continued to demonstrate a high prevalence of mental illness and substance abuse in populations of prisoners (Teplin 1990; Teplin et al. 1996; Lamb and Weinberger 1998).

THE TWENTY-FIRST CENTURY

The new century witnessed continuing demand for correctional mental health services. Although the total prison population peaked during the first decade of the century, the United States continued to lead the world in the use of incarceration. Mental illness in correctional populations continued to be viewed to be in crisis (Aufderheide and Brown 2005). Advocates and popular media criticized the apparent movement of mentally ill individuals from the mental health system to the criminal justice system; characterized as criminalization of the mentally ill (Slate et al. 2013; Ford 2015).

The turn of the century did not usher in major changes to the roles and responsibilities of correctional psychiatrists. Perhaps one substantive change to basic practice was the adoption of telepsychiatry by correctional psychiatrists (or those who employed them) (Antonacci et al. 2008). A number of controversial issues emerged (or re-emerged) that presented challenges to the field and other correctional health-care providers. Correctional psychiatrists actively contributed to ongoing debates regarding solitary confinement (Metzner 2010), supermax prisons (Dvoskin and Metzner 2006), administrative segregation (O'Keefe et al. 2013), seclusion and restraint (Appelbaum 2007), suicide prevention (Daniel 2006), professional boundary and ethical issues (Metzner 2008), transgender populations (Simopoulos and Khin 2014), and involuntary medication of inmates (Salem et al. 2015), among others.

Litigation remained the mainspring for correctional reform. In *Brown v. Plata*, decided in 2011, the Supreme Court ruled that the State of California violated the Eighth Amendment rights of California prison inmates by housing them in overcrowded conditions and failing to provide constitutional levels of health services. The Court upheld a U.S. District Court decision that ordered California to reduce its prison population to 137.5% of design capacity within 2 years. Psychiatrists with correctional expertise played roles in providing consultation to the courts and states (Metzner 2002).

Practice standards and guidelines for correctional mental health care continued to be actively updated (Hills 2004; Thienhaus and Piasecki 2007; National Commission on Correctional Health Care 2015a). Private corporations continued to grow their share of the correctional health-care market, both in private prisons and as contractors to state-operated facilities. These companies remained sources of employment for correctional psychiatrists but advertised cost savings by using physician extenders. Corporate mergers remained a characteristic of the industry. For example, Corizon Health was formed in 2011 when Correctional Health Services (CHS) joined with PHS Correctional Healthcare (Corizon Health 2011). Provision of correctional mental health services by contracted academic medical centers was proposed as an alternative to for-profit providers (Appelbaum et al. 2002). Several such partnerships, however, did not survive competition from private providers.

The twenty-first century witnessed the maturation of correctional psychiatry into a distinct subspecialty. Academic activity and research in the field became increasingly more prominent in journals such as the *Journal of the American Psychiatry and the Law*. Publication of handbooks, manuals, and texts devoted to correctional psychiatry further reinforced the distinctiveness of the field (Scott 2010; Trestman et al. 2015). Psychiatry training programs experimented with incorporating correctional psychiatry rotations into their curricula (Fuehrlein 2014). In addition to publishing practice guidelines and accrediting correctional facilities, the National Commission on Correctional Health Care added specialty certification for mental health professionals to existing certification programs for correctional health professionals and nurses in 2013 (National Commission on Correctional Health Care 2015b).

Correctional psychiatrists rightly continue to focus on providing better clinical service for their patients; however, the field is claiming a more prominent role in the public policy, litigation, and research aspects of corrections. Developments in corrections and correctional mental health systems continue to provide psychiatrists and other mental health professionals with opportunities for leadership and innovation (Halpern 1998).

SUMMARY KEY POINTS

- Much of the history of correctional psychiatry in the United States has been driven by long-standing interests in explaining and treating criminal behavior by social reformers and physicians which reached a peak during the first half of the twentieth century.
- During the 1970s, a consensus of U.S. policy makers lost faith in the ability of psychiatrists to treat criminal behavior and concluded that rehabilitation of prisoners did not work.
- The 1980s and 1990s witnessed the development of correctional psychiatry into a distinct subspecialty through the formation of professional organizations, institutional standards, and treatment guidelines. Simultaneously correctional mental health systems were forced to cope with a massive explosion in prison populations.
- Despite challenges, correctional psychiatry has continued to mature during the twenty-first century. The field has continue to strive for improved clinical services and taken a more prominent role in, public policy, litigation, and the research aspects of corrections.

REFERENCES

Abramson MF. 1972. The criminalization of mentally disordered behavior: Possible side-effect of a new mental health law. *Hospital and Community Psychiatry* 23:101–105.

Alexander F and H Staub. 1931. *The Criminal, the Judge, and the Public*, G. Zilboorg, trans. New York: Macmillan.

Allen W and K Bell. 1998. Death, neglect, and the bottom line, push to cut costs poses risks. *St. Louis Post-Dispatch* September 27.

Allison HE. 1894. Insanity among criminals. *American Journal of Insanity* 51:54–63.

American Bar Association. 1989. *ABA Criminal Justice Mental Health Standards*. Washington, DC: American Bar Association.

American Correctional Association. 1966. *Manual of Correctional Standards*. Washington, DC: American Correctional Association.

American Psychiatric Association (APA). 1931. Report of the committee on legal aspects of psychiatry. *American Journal of Psychiatry* 88:375–382.

American Psychiatric Association (APA). 1932. Psychiatry and prison problems. *American Journal of Psychiatry* 88:822–823.

American Psychiatric Association (APA). 1989. *Report of the Task Force on Psychiatric Services in Jails and Prisons*. Washington, DC: APA.

American Psychiatric Association (APA). 2016. *Psychiatric Services in Correctional Facilities*, 3rd edition. Washington, DC: APA.

American Public Health Association Jails and Prisons Task Force. 1976. *Standards for Health Services in Correctional Institutions*. Washington, DC: American Public Health Association.

Antonacci DJ, RM Bloch, SA Saeed, Y Yildirim, and J Talley. 2008. Empirical evidence on the use and effectiveness of telepsychiatry via videoconferencing: Implications for forensic and correctional psychiatry. *Behavioral Sciences and the Law* 26:253–269.

Appelbaum KL. 2007. Commentary: The use of restraint and seclusion in correctional mental health. *Journal of the American Academy of Psychiatry and the Law* 35:431–435.

Appelbaum KL, TD Manning, and JD Noonan. 2002. A university-state-corporation partnership for providing correctional mental health services. *Psychiatric Services* 53:185–189.

Aufderheide DH and PH Brown. 2005. Crisis in corrections: The mentally ill in America's Prison. *Corrections Today* 67:30–33.

Bowring v. Godwin 551 F.2d 44 (1977).

Bromberg W. 1982. *Psychiatry between the Wars, 1918–1954: A Recollection*. Westport, CT: Greenwood Press.

Brown v. Plata, 134 S.Ct. 436 (2011).

Cleckley H. 1941. *The Mask of Sanity*. St. Louis, MO: Mosby.

Corcoran K. 1999a. Help for mentally ill prisoners in jeopardy; state officials threaten to scuttle $98 million outsourcing deal for psychological services *The Times [Indiana]*, January 18.

Corcoran K. 1999b. Mental health for inmates faces problems. *The Times [Indiana]*, January 18.

Corizon Health. 2011. Corizon launches from correctional healthcare merger [News Release], June 13.

Cumming RG and HJ Soloway. 1973. The incarcerated psychiatrists. *Hospital and Community Psychiatry* 24:631–633.

Daniel AE. 2006. Preventing suicide in prison: A collaborative responsibility of administrative, custodial, and clinical staff. *Journal of the American Academy of Psychiatry and the Law* 34:165–175.

Diamond BL. 1994. Psychoanalysis in the courtroom. In *The Psychiatrist in the Courtroom; Selected Papers of Bernard L. Diamond, M.D.*, edited by JM Quen, Hillsdale, NJ: Analytic Press, 1–18.

Dickens C. 1842. *American Notes for General Circulation*. Vol. 1. London: Chapman and Hall.

Dix D. 1845. *Remarks on Prisons and Prison Discipline in the United States*. Boston: Munroe and Francis.

Dvoskin J and J Metzner. 2006 An overview of correctional psychiatry. *Psychiatric Clinics of North America* 69:761–772.

Estelle v. Gamble, 429 U.S. 97, 97 S.Ct. 285 (1976).

Farmer v. Brennan, 114 S.Ct. 1970 (1994).

Fink L, WN Derby, and JP Martin. 1969: Psychiatry's new role in corrections. *American Journal of Psychiatry* 126:542–546.

Ford M. 2015. America's largest mental hospital is a jail. *The Atlantic*. http://www.theatlantic.com/politics/archive/2015/06/americas-largest-mental-hospital-is-a-jail/395012, accessed August 17, 2015.

Friedman LM. 1993. *Crime and Punishment in American History*. New York: Basic Books.

Fuehrlein BS, MK Jha, AM Brenner, and CS North. 2014. Availability and attitudes toward correctional psychiatry training: Results of a national survey of training directors. *Journal of Behavioral Health Services and Research*. 4:244–250.

Glaze LE and D Kaeble. 2014. *Correctional Populations in the United States, 2013*. Washington, DC: U.S. Department of Justice, Bureau of Justice Statistics.

Glueck B. 1935: Psychiatry and the criminal law. A. The psychiatric aspect. *Journal of Nervous and Mental Diseases* 81:192–194.

Glueck SS. 1925. *Mental Disorder and the Criminal Law; a Study in Medico-Sociological Jurisprudence, with an Appendix of State Legislation and Interpretive Decisions*. Boston: Brown, Little.

Goldstein N. 1983. Psychiatry in prisons. *Psychiatric Clinics of North America* 6:751–765.

Gollaher D. 1995. *Voice for the Mad: The Life of Dorothea Dix*. New York: Free Press.

Greenacre P. 1945. Conscience in the psychopath. *American Journal of Orthopsychiatry* 15:495–509.

Gregory MS. 1935. Psychiatry and the problems of delinquency. *American Journal of Psychiatry* 91:773–781.

Grob GN. ed. 1985. *The Inner World of American Psychiatry, 1890–1940: Selected Correspondence*. New Brunswick, NJ: Rutgers University Press.

Grob GN. 1994. *The Mad among Us: A History of the Care of America's Mentally Ill*. New York: Free Press.

Group for the Advancement of Psychiatry, Committee on Psychiatry and the Law. 1977. *Psychiatry and Sex Psychopath Legislation, the 30s to the 80s*. Vol. 9. New York: Group for the Advancement of Psychiatry, 831–956.

Guttmacher MS. 1968. *The Role of Psychiatry in Law*. Springfield, IL: Charles C Thomas.

Halleck SL. 1965. American psychiatry and the criminal. *American Journal of Psychiatry* 121(Supplement):i–xxi.

Halleck SL. 1967. *Psychiatry and the Dilemmas of Crime*. Berkeley: University of California Press.

Halleck SL. 1987. *The Mentally Disordered Offender*. Washington, DC: American Psychiatric Press.

Halpern A. 1998. Psychotherapy in American prisons: Prospects for the 21st century. *Abstract. Seventh Annual Meeting of the International Association of Forensic Psychotherapy*. Copenhagen, Denmark, May 15–17, 1998.

Healy W. 1915. *The Individual Delinquent*. Boston: Little, Brown.

Hills H, C Siegfried, and A Ickowitz. 2004. *Effective Prison Mental Health Services: Guidelines to Expand and Improve Treatment*. Washington, DC: National Institute of Corrections.

Hollingsworth JB. 1985. Overview of correctional psychiatry. *American Journal of Forensic Psychiatry* 6:23–28.

Hurst J. 1995. Appointment of "special master" is ordered to oversee psychiatric reforms. State claims system has improved. *Los Angeles Times*, September 15.

James DJ and LE Glaze. 2006. *Mental Health Problems of Prison and Jail Inmates*. Washington, DC: U.S. Department of Justice, Bureau of Justice Statistics.

Johnston N. 1994. *Eastern State Penitentiary: Crucible of Good Intentions*. Philadelphia: Philadelphia Museum of Arts.

Karpman B. 1933. *Case Studies in the Psychopathology of Crime*. 2 vol. Washington, DC: Mineoform Press.

Kaufman E. 1980. The violation of psychiatric standards in prisons. *American Journal of Psychiatry* 137:566–570.

Kirk SA and ME Therrein. 1975. Community mental health myths and the fate of former hospitalized patients. *Psychiatry* 78:209–217.

Kupers TA. 1999. *Prison Madness: The Mental Health Crisis Behind Bars and What We Must Do about It*. San Francisco: Jossey-Bass.

Kurkjian S. 1996. Lawsuit calls Plymouth inmates' mental care inadequate, officials deny claim finances drive policies. *Boston Globe*, September 10.

Lamb HR and LE Weinberger. 1998. Persons with severe mental illness in jails and prisons: A review. *Psychiatric Services* 49:483–492.

Levine M and A Levine. 1992. *Helping Children: A Social History*. New York: Oxford University Press.

Manderscheid RW, AW Gravesande, and ID Goldstrom. 2004. Growth of mental health services in state adult correctional facilities, 1988–2000. *Psychiatric Services* 55:869–872.

Marshall T. 2000. Prison health care called "snake pit." *Houston Chronicle*, May 4.

McCartney JL 1934. An intensive psychiatric study of prisoners: The receiving routine in the classification clinic Elmira Reformatory. *American Journal of Psychiatry* 90:1183–1203.

McGowen R 1995. The well ordered prison. In *The Oxford History of the Prison: The Practice of Punishment in Western Society*, edited by N Morris and DJ Rothman, New York: Oxford University Press, 79–109.

Md.Ann.Code, Art. 31B (1951).

Metzner JL. 1997a. An introduction to correctional psychiatry: Part I. *Journal of the American Academy of Psychiatry and the Law* 25:375–381.

Metzner JL. 1997b. An introduction to correctional psychiatry: Part II. *Journal of the American Academy of Psychiatry and the Law* 25:571–579.

Metzner JL. 1998. An introduction to correctional psychiatry: Part III. *Journal of the American Academy of Psychiatry and the Law* 26:107–115.

Metzner JL. 2002. Class action litigation in correctional psychiatry. *Journal of the American Academy of Psychiatry and the Law* 30:19–29.

Metzner JL. 2008. Commentary. Correctional mental health: The ethical, medical, and system-related obstacles to providing care for prisoners with severe mental illness and the considerations that should guide decisions about isolating them. *Virtual Monitor* 10:92–95.

Metzner JL. 2010. Solitary confinement and mental illness in U.S. prisons: A challenge for medical ethics. *Journal of the American Academy of Psychiatry and the Law* 38:104–108.

Monahan J. 1973. The psychiatrization of criminal behavior: A reply. *Hospital and Community Psychiatry* 24:105–107.

National Commission on Correctional Health Care. 1986a. *Standards for Health Services in Jails*. Chicago: National Commission on Correctional Health Care.

National Commission on Correctional Health Care. 1986b. *Standards for Health Services in Prisons*. Chicago: National Commission on Correctional Health Care.

National Commission on Correctional Health Care. 2015a. *Certified Correctional Health Professional Mental Health: Candidate Guide*. Chicago: CCHP Board of Trustees.

National Commission on Correctional Health Care. 2015b. *Standards for Mental Health Services in Correctional Facilities*. Chicago: National Commission on Correctional Health Care.

Newman v. Alabama, 503 F.2d 1320–24 Fifth Circuit (1974).

O'Keefe ML, KJ Klebe, J Metzner, J Dvoskin, J Fellner, and A Stucker. 2013. A longitudinal study of administrative segregation. *Journal of the American Academy of Psychiatry and Law* 41:49–60.

Overholser W. 1928. Psychiatric service in penal and reformatory institutions and criminal courts in the United States. *Mental Hygiene* 12:801–838.

Patterson RF. 1998. Managed behavioral healthcare in correctional settings. *Journal of the American Academy of Psychiatry and Law* 26:467–473.

Rachlin S, Pam A, and A Milton. 1975. Civil liberties versus involuntary hospitalization. *American Journal of Psychiatry* 132:189–191.

Rappeport JR. 1974. Enforced treatment—Is it treatment? *Bulletin of the American Academy of Psychiatry and Law* 2:148–158.

Riggins v. Nevada, 112 S.Ct. 1810 (1992).

Roth LH. 1986. Correctional psychiatry. In *Forensic Psychiatry and Psychology: Perspectives and Standards for Interdisciplinary Practice*. Philadelphia: F.A. Davis.

Rothman DJ. 1971. *The Discovery of the Asylum: Social Order and Disorder in the New Republic*. Boston: Little, Brown.

Ruffin v. Commonwealth 62 Virginia 790 (1871).

Rush B. 1812. *Medical Inquiries and Observations upon the Diseases of the Mind*. Philadelphia: Kimber and Richardson.

Salem A, Kushnier A, Dorio N, and Reeves R. 2015. Nonemergency involuntary antipsychotic medication in prison: Effects on prison inpatient days and disciplinary charges. *Journal of the American Academy of Psychiatry and the Law* 43:159–164.

Salmon TW. 1920. Some new problems for psychiatric research in delinquency. *Mental Hygiene* 4:29–42.

Schneider AL. 1999. Public-private partnerships in the U.S. prison system. *American Behavioral Scientist* 43:192–208.

Schulte JL. 1985. Treatment of the mentally disordered offender. *American Journal of Forensic Psychiatry* 6:29–36.

Scott CL. ed. 2010. *Handbook of Correctional Mental Health*, 2nd edition. Washington, DC: American Psychiatric Association.

Simopoulos EF and EK Khin. 2014. Fundamental principles inherent in the comprehensive care of transgender inmates. *Journal of the American Academy of Psychiatry and the Law* 42(1):26–36.

Slate RN, JK Buffington-Vollum, and WW Johnson. 2013: *The Criminalization of Mental Illness: Crisis and Opportunity for the Justice System*. 2nd edition. Durham, NC: Carolina Academic Press.

Smith CE. 1964. Psychiatry in corrections. *American Journal of Psychiatry* 120:1045–1049.

Stamm RA. 1962. Relationship problems between correctional and psychiatric staffs in a prison hospital. *American Journal of Psychiatry* 118:1031–1035.

Steadman HJ and Ribner SA. 1980. Changing perception of the mental health needs of inmates of local jails. *American Journal of Psychiatry* 137:1115–1116.

Swanson M. 2002. The private prison debate: A look into the efficiency of private prisons vs. public prison. *Major Themes in Economics* Spring 2002:97–113.

Teplin LA. 1990. The prevalence of severe mental disorder among male urban jail detainees—Comparison with the epidemiological catchment area program. *American Journal of Public Health* 80:663–669.

Teplin LA, KM Abram, and GM McClelland. 1996. Prevalence of psychiatric disorders among incarcerated women: I. Pretrial jail detainees. *Archives of General Psychiatry* 53:505–512.

Thienhaus OJ and M Piasecki. 2007. *Correctional Psychiatry Practice Guidelines and Strategies*. Kingston, NJ: Civic Research Institute.

Travin S. 1994. History of correctional psychiatry. In *Principles and Practice of Forensic Psychiatry*, edited by R Rosner, New York: Chapman and Hall, 369–374.

Trestman R, K Appelbaum, and J Metzner. eds. 2015. *Oxford Textbook of Correctional Psychiatry*. New York: Oxford University Press.

Vitek v. Jones 445 U.S. 480 100 Supreme Court 1254 (1980).

Washington v. Harper, 494 U.S. 210, 110 Supreme Court 1028 (1990).

Wettstein RM. ed. 1998. *Treatment of Offenders with Mental Disorders*. New York: Guilford Press.

White WA. 1917. Sterilization of criminals. *Journal of the American Institute of Criminal Law and Criminology* 8:499–500.

White WA. 1927. The need for cooperation between the legal profession and the psychiatrist in dealing with the crime problem. *American Journal of Insanity* 84:493–505.

Wille WS. 1957. Psychiatric facilities in prisons and correctional institutions in the United States. *American Journal of Psychiatry* 114:481–487.

Wittels F. 1943. Kleptomania and other psychopathic crimes. *Journal of Criminal Psychopathology* 4:205–216.

Wolff v. McDonnell, 418 U.S. 539 (1974).

Zilboorg G. 1944. Legal aspects of psychiatry. In *One Hundred Years of American Psychiatry*, edited by JK Hall, New York: Columbia University Press, 507–584.

51

Overview of correctional psychiatry

CHARLES L. SCOTT

INTRODUCTION

The U.S. correctional system is one of the largest providers of mental health care to its citizens. According to E. Fuller Torrey (1999), the Los Angeles County Jail houses 3400 inmates with mental illness, making it the largest psychiatric inpatient facility in the United States. In some jurisdictions more mentally ill receive treatment in the local jail or prison than in the community. What might explain this dramatic shift? The deinstitutionalization of individuals with chronic and severe mental illness from hospitals into the community has been cited as one of the most significant contributors to the rising population of offenders with mental illness behind bars. With the closure of many psychiatric facilities and limited community resources to treat individuals with chronic and severe mental illness, it is not surprising that many of these same persons have found their way into the criminal justice system (Lamb and Weinberger 2013).

Correctional environments are significantly different than hospital and community treatment settings. This chapter provides a definition of "corrections," highlights purposes of punishment, describes types of correctional settings, reviews stages of the criminal justice system, explains inmate classification schemes, and outlines the process governing the return of inmates to society.

DEFINITION OF CORRECTIONS

The term "corrections" includes those agencies and programs at the local, state, and federal level that oversee individuals who have been either accused of crimes or convicted of them. Police, prosecutors, and courts play an integral role in determining whether an individual enters the legal system and is subject to imposed controls from a correctional agency (Silverman 2001). Correctional settings are wide ranging and include lockups, jails, and prisons. Correctional mental health includes the provision of mental health assessment and treatment in a correctional setting.

The criminal justice system was created to address those actions committed by individuals that violate laws against society. These violations of laws are generally referred to as crimes. According to the 2013 National Crime Victimization Survey (NCVS), 10.2% of U.S. households have experienced at least one violent or property crime (Truman and Langton 2014). Each state and the federal government have a criminal code that defines specific crimes and associated sentences. In general, charges are likely to be filed in federal court when there is either: (1) an alleged violation of federal, as opposed to state law; or (2) if the alleged crime took place on federal property. The most common crimes referred to federal court include controlled substance violations, immigration law violations, mail or wire fraud, gun laws, postal offenses, child pornography, counterfeiting, and crimes that occur on federal property or in federal buildings (Federal Crime Cases 2015). Charges are filed in state court when an individual has violated a specific state statute and the alleged crime is not covered under federal jurisdiction.

THEORIES OF PUNISHMENT

For centuries, societies have established basic rules that govern how their citizens live with similarly established punishments for violating those rules. Why does society punish its citizens for their wrongdoing? Four classic theories of punishment help answer this question and include retribution, deterrence, rehabilitation, and incapacitation.

Retribution

Retribution involves the use of punishment in response to a law-violating act simply because the offender deserves it. This approach emphasizes that those who cause harm should be subject to punishment as a result. Early legal systems used retribution almost exclusively as the primary principle to punish offenders. This approach was referred to as *lex talionis*, or "the law (lex) of retaliation." Under the law of *lex talionis*, equal and exact retribution was exacted, as demonstrated in the words of the Hebrew scripture, "an eye for an eye, a tooth for a tooth, an arm for an arm, a life for a life" (Hooker 1997).

The concept known as "just desserts" is the modern equivalent of *lex talionis.* Although the individual is punished because his or her act deserves punishment, the "just deserts" approach allows consideration of punishment proportional to the severity of the crime, whereas this is not typically considered under strict retribution theory. It is important to note that the retribution principle is nearly entirely retrospective.

Deterrence

Under the theory of deterrence, punishment is imposed to deter or prevent individuals from committing a future criminal act. The concept of deterrence involves both specific and general deterrence. The concept of specific deterrence theorizes that imposing sanctions on an individual who has broken the law will make that individual less likely to violate the law in the future. In contrast, general deterrence theorizes that when citizens who have never offended become aware that other people are punished for illegal behavior, they will be less likely to commit an offense due to their fear of legal consequences.

The effectiveness of specific deterrence in preventing individuals in committing future offenses is questionable. In particular, nearly 70% of state prisoners released in 2005 were arrested within 3 years of release, and over 75% were arrested within 5 years of release (Durose et al. 2014). At the same time, nearly a quarter of all offenders did not reoffend, suggesting that a significant minority are deterred from future criminal acts. Other studies indicate that in some situations, punished individuals are specifically deterred from future offenses. For example, arrested drunk drivers (Shapiro and Votey 1984), first-time offenders (Smith and Gartin 1989), and spouse abusers (Sherman and Berk 1984) who received severe punishment were less likely to violate the law upon release when compared to those who received more lenient sentences. Three factors that are believed to affect the success or failure of criminal sanctions include the severity, the certainty, and the swiftness of punishment (Silverman 2001).

Rehabilitation

According to the rehabilitative theory of punishment, individuals are incarcerated in order to learn socially appropriate behaviors to replace their deviant actions. Correction, therefore, is designed to treat those traits that result in criminal behavior. The rehabilitative model argues that the purpose of incarceration is to reform inmates through educational, training, and counseling programs. The rehabilitative approach to managing criminal offenders was prominent following World War II until the 1960s (Silverman 2001). However, as the majority of released prisoners reoffended despite this rehabilitative approach, Americans became increasingly skeptical about the rehabilitative model of punishment. A published review of rehabilitation programs for inmates by New York sociologist Robert Martinson and colleagues contributed to the belief that rehabilitation programs for offenders had minimal benefit. This research reviewed 231 studies of offender rehabilitation programs conducted between 1945 and 1967 (Lipton et al. 1975). In his famous 1974 article titled "What Works? Questions and Answers about Prison Reform," Martinson interpreted the results from the above research. In this article he concluded, "with few and isolated exceptions, the rehabilitative efforts that have been reported so far have had no appreciable effect on recidivism." He emphasized, "Our present strategies… cannot overcome, or even appreciably reduce, the powerful tendencies of offenders to continue in criminal behavior" (Martinson 1974).

Martinson's article was widely read, and his published findings on rehabilitation were quickly renamed, "Nothing works!" His persuasive arguments had far-reaching effects and played a significant role in the American penal system moving away from the rehabilitative approach for offenders. Subsequent reviews of rehabilitation programs did not replicate Martinson's findings and utilized statistical analysis of treatment outcome not available to Martinson. In their survey of 200 studies on rehabilitation conducted from 1981 to 1987, Gendreau and Ross (1987) concluded that successful rehabilitation of offenders was possible and up to 80% reduction in recidivism had been noted in research studies examining effective programs. Despite these more encouraging results, the pendulum had already moved away from rehabilitation as a purpose for punishment. As a result, a harsher theory of punishment, known as incapacitation, became increasingly popular throughout the United States.

Incapacitation

Under the incapacitation principle, individuals are prevented from committing future criminal acts by holding them against their will in a secure environment. A sentence of life without the possibility of parole represents a more extreme form of incapacitation. The ultimate form of incapacitation is the imposition of the death penalty. With public concern increasing alongside the rising crime rate during the late 1980s and 1990s, many state legislatures passed laws that resulted in longer sentences. But not all incapacitation is the same. In general, there are three forms of incapacitation. Under a schema known as *collective incapacitation,* all offenders convicted of the same crime receive the same sentence. The anticipated effect of collective incapacitation is a substantial increase in the prison population as there is no attempt to distinguish between high- versus low-risk offenders (Cohen 1983; Silverman 2001). In contrast, *selective incapacitation* incarcerates only those offenders who are predicted to be at higher risk for reoffending. Legislative efforts to increase the length of incapacitation for higher-risk offenders have resulted in significant sentencing reform over the last three decades. These reforms include "truth in sentencing" (TIS) schemes and the passage of "three strikes you're out" statutes. TIS laws require offenders to serve a substantial portion of their prison sentence with restrictions on both parole eligibility and good-time credits (Ditton and Wilson 1999). Under "three strikes you're out" statutes, felons found guilty of a third serious crime can be incarcerated for 25 years to life, even if the felonies themselves were relatively minor. A third incapacitation approach is called *criminal career incapacitation*. Under this scheme, classes of criminals (rather than all criminals) with known high rates of crime receive longer sentences (Silverman 2001).

The increasing use of incapacitation as punishment resulted in a corresponding increased prison population between 1990 and the mid-2000s. Although there has been a slight downward trend in the total U.S. correctional population since 2007, nearly 1 in 35 adults in the United States remained under some form of correctional supervision as of December 2013 (Glaze and Kaeble 2014).

TYPES OF CORRECTIONAL FACILITIES

The U.S. correctional system is complex and includes a federal system, 50 separate state systems, and thousands of local systems. Each individual state determines its own criminal justice and correctional system with resulting differences in how crimes are defined, who is arrested, and what consequences are imposed for law violating behavior (Silverman 2001). Correctional housing facilities vary and are broadly classified into three types of facilities: lockups, jails, and prisons.

Lockups and jails

Lockups are local temporary holding facilities that constitute the first level of detention in many jurisdictions. The lockup is the most common type of correctional facility with an average stay usually lasting less than 48 hours. Lockups are often located in the local police station where only temporary detainment (e.g., arrestees charged with driving under the influence) is required. Approximately 30% of local police departments operate at least one lockup facility for adults separate from a jail. In jurisdictions with 500,000 or more residents, local lockups can detain up to 70 individuals, whereas lockups in jurisdictions with fewer than 10,000 residents typically house about three persons (Reaves and Goldberg 2000). In those jurisdictions that do not have a lockup facility, the individual arrested is detained in the local jail.

Jails are locally operated correctional facilities that hold persons before or after their trial. Individuals who are convicted of a misdemeanor (minor crime) receive a sentence of a year or less and complete their sentence in a jail, not a prison. Jails serve the following functions: holding detainees awaiting trial; holding those convicted of a misdemeanor who are serving their sentence; detaining violators of probation, parole, or bail; temporary detention of juveniles pending transfer to juvenile authorities; holding of mentally ill persons pending their movement to appropriate health facilities; transfer of inmates to federal, state, or other authorities; holding of individuals for the military, protective custody, contempt, or for the courts as witnesses; and sometimes operating community-based programs as alternatives to incarceration.

In some situations, individuals facing federal charges may also be detained in a local jail. For example, the U.S. Citizenship and Immigration Services (USCIS) have the authority to detain certain categories of noncitizens. The Marshals Service assumes custody of persons arrested by all federal agencies and is responsible for the custody of more than 220,000 federal prisoners. In jurisdictions where detention space is limited, the Marshals Service utilizes Cooperative Agreement Program (CAP) funds to improve local jail conditions in exchange for guaranteed space for federal prisoners (U.S. Marshals Service 2014).

Of the total incarcerated population in the United States, approximately one-third are held in local jails (Glaze and Kaeble 2014). At midyear 2013, 731,208 persons were held in local U.S. jails (Minton and Golinelli 2014). Of individuals detained in jail, approximately 60% are awaiting some type of court action on their current charge while the remaining inmates are serving time for their conviction (Minton and Golinelli 2014). The following findings characterize the U.S. jail inmate population: nearly half (46%) are on probation or parole at the time of their arrest; half have been using drugs or alcohol at the time of their offense; half are held for a violent or drug offense; over half grew up in a single-parent household; and nearly half (46%) had a family member who had been incarcerated (James 2004). Of jail inmates identified as mentally ill, over 30% were homeless in the year prior to the arrest compared to 17.3% of jail inmates without an identified mental disorder (Ditton 1999).

Prisons

Prisons are confinement facilities that maintain custodial authority over inmates who have been convicted of felonies. A felony is a more serious crime than a misdemeanor. The imposed sentence for a felony is greater than 1 year at a minimum. Prisons are operated by both state and federal governments and are typically large facilities, often with over 500 beds. More inmates serve their time in prisons when compared to jails. In particular, approximately one-third of all correctional inmates are incarcerated in jails, whereas two-thirds serve their time in a prison (Glaze and Kaeble 2014). The Federal Bureau of Prisons (BOP) was established in 1930. The federal prison system includes a nationwide system of 116 detention facilities responsible for the custody and care of nearly 210,000 federal offenders (About the Federal Bureau of Prisons 2011).

Thirty states and the federal system contract with private agencies to hold prisoners in privately operated facilities. An increase in private contracting of correctional beds has arisen to alleviate overcrowding in the state and federal system and to quickly obtain beds as the incarcerated population increases (McDonald et al. 1998). In 2013, private facilities housed 133,000 inmates, and this number represents 7% of all prisoners under state or federal jurisdiction (Carson 2014).

Prison demographic data demonstrate inequalities based on ethnicity, age, and gender. For decades, minority males have been overrepresented among prison inmates. At year-end 2013, Hispanic males comprised 22% of sentenced males, white males comprised 32% of sentenced males, and black males comprised 37% of sentenced males (Carson 2014). Men continue to dominate the prison population and are nearly 13 times more likely than women to be incarcerated in a state or federal prison. However, the face of the typical prison inmate as one of a young male is slowly changing. Between 2012 and 2013, female prisoners sentenced to more than a year in state or federal prison grew by nearly 3%, while male prisoners increased only 0.2% (Carson 2014).

Prison inmates are also getting older. Between 1995 and 2010, the number of state and federal inmates age 55 or older nearly quadrupled (Old Behind Bars 2012). The increasing length of sentences under mandatory sentencing schemes has contributed to the aging of the correctional population. Because inmates have a constitutional right to medical care, states and counties will likely face substantial financial burdens related to aging inmates who will require increasingly costly medical interventions.

OVERVIEW OF THE CRIMINAL JUSTICE PROCESS

Although the U.S. system of justice originates from English common law, there is no uniform criminal justice system in the United States. Often criminal actions are not discovered or reported to law enforcement agencies (The Justice System 2015). The majority of crimes are not solved. Under the Uniform Crime Report (UCR) Program, once a crime is reported to law enforcement, it is designated as "cleared" if at least one person is arrested, charged with the commission of an offense, and turned over to the court for prosecution. In 2013, law enforcement agencies cleared 48.1% of violent crimes (murder, forcible rape, robbery, and aggravated assault), 19.7% of property crimes (burglary, larceny-theft, and motor vehicle theft), and 20.7% of arson offenses (Federal Bureau of Investigation 2014).

Despite some variation in the handling of criminal cases between various jurisdictions, the most common sequence of steps in response to known criminal behavior is as follows. An individual becomes a suspect in a crime following reports from victims, other witnesses, discovery by a police officer, or from investigative work. For most crimes, especially minor crimes, police officers serve as gatekeepers in determining which persons will formally enter into the justice system. This discretionary arrest authority provides officers options other than taking the person into custody. For example, officers can warn offenders and release them or divert an offender to a mental health treatment program. In dealing with juveniles, the officer can bring the youth home and informally discuss the juvenile's behavior with the family (Finn and Sullivan 1988).

An arrest involves the taking of an individual into custody under the legal authority granted by the government. Law enforcement practices regarding who is arrested and why they are arrested vary according to the jurisdiction. In 2013, law enforcement made approximately 11.3 million arrests in the United States. Drug abuse violations represented the most common offense type for which individuals were arrested followed by larceny-theft and driving under the influence (Federal Bureau of Investigation 2014).

Individuals who are arrested or charged with an offense are usually taken to the police station or local jail for booking. The booking process has many administrative steps. This process includes taking the individual's mug shot, recording personal information, fingerprinting, assigning identifying case numbers, conducting medical and psychiatric screening, and beginning a new file for first time arrestees. Nearly half of those individuals who are arrested will leave the jail within 24–48 hours after they are booked. Inmates who are not released are thoroughly searched, their property is removed, and they are issued standard jail clothing (Silverman 2001).

Following the individual's arrest and subsequent booking, law enforcement agencies provide information regarding the accused to the prosecutor. Prosecutors have broad discretionary authority. They play a significant role in determining whether to initiate prosecution and what specific charges will be filed with the court. If no charges are filed, the accused must be released. At this stage, there are several alternatives to a formal filing of charges. The prosecutor may request that the judge enter a *nolle prosequi. Nolle prosequi* is defined as a formal entry upon the record by the prosecuting officer in a criminal action, by which he declares that he "will no further prosecute" the case, either as to some of the defendants, or altogether. This is commonly referred to as "Nol Pros" (Silverman 2001; The Justice System 2015).

Second, for individuals already involved in the criminal justice system, the prosecutor may decide to revoke probation or parole rather than initiate new charges. Third, the suspect may be civilly committed to a mental health treatment facility. Fourth, a decision to invoke civil sanctions, such a revocation of a person's license, may substitute for processing the arrestee through the criminal justice system. Charges may also be reduced or dismissed in those situations where the victim is unwilling to cooperate with prosecution or for suspects who agree to testify for the prosecution or act as an informer (Silverman 2001).

If a suspect is charged with a crime, he or she is taken before a judge or magistrate. At this initial appearance, the judge must inform the accused of the charges and decide whether there is probable cause to detain the individual. Probable cause exists when there is a reasonable belief that a crime has or is being committed and is the basis for all lawful searches, seizures, and arrests. For nonserious offenses, the judge or magistrate may determine guilt and assess a penalty at this stage. Defense counsel may also be assigned at this initial appearance. All suspects charged with serious crimes have a right to be represented by an attorney. The court assigns an attorney for indigent suspects who cannot afford their own counsel (The Justice System 2015).

Following the assignment of a defense attorney, the accused has an initial appearance, where the court may decide to release the accused prior to trial. For individuals released prior to trial, the court may set bail (The Justice System 2015). Bail is money that a defendant must provide up front (often through a contract with a bail bondsman) that must be forfeited if the accused fails to appear in court for trial. The amount of bail set is governed by multiple factors including the seriousness of the charges, the risk of flight from the governing jurisdiction, past legal history of the defendant, and the financial status of the defendant.

Depending on the locality, a preliminary hearing may follow the initial appearance of the defendant in court. The primary purpose of this hearing is for the court to determine if there is sufficient evidence of probable cause that the accused committed a crime. In situations where the judge does not find probable cause, he or she must dismiss the case. If probable cause is found or if the accused waives his or her right to a preliminary hearing, then the case may be forwarded to a grand jury (The Justice System 2015).

During the hearing before the grand jury, the prosecutor presents the evidence against the accused and the grand jury decides whether the evidence warrants the accused being brought to trial. If the grand jury determines there is sufficient evidence, then they submit an indictment to the court. An indictment is a written summary of the facts of the offenses charged against the accused. In some jurisdictions, both misdemeanor and felony cases move forward after a document known as the "issuance of information" is provided. The issuance of information is a formal written accusation that the prosecutor submits to the court. The accused may choose to waive a grand jury indictment and accept the service of information (The Justice System 2015).

Following an indictment or filing of an issuance of information with the court, the accused is then scheduled for an arraignment. An arraignment is a hearing where the accused is informed of the charges, advised of their rights, and requested to enter a plea. In some situations, the defendant may choose to enter either a plea of guilty or *nolo contendere*. A plea of *nolo contendere* indicates that the defendant accepts his or her penalty without admitting guilt. If the judge accepts a guilty or *nolo contendere* plea, a trial is not held and the case proceeds to the sentencing phase (The Justice System 2015).

In situations where the defendant pleads not guilty or not guilty by reason of insanity, a trial date is scheduled. In serious crimes, the defendant is guaranteed a right to trial by jury, though may choose to have a "bench trial" where the judge, rather than a jury, hears the case and determines guilt. At the trial, the defense and prosecution both present evidence, and the judge decides on issues of law. At the conclusion of the trial, a finding of guilty or not guilty is made. Next, the defendant is scheduled for a sentencing hearing where both mitigating and aggravating factors are presented.

Courts often review presentence investigations, completed by probation agencies, along with victim impact statements, in deciding the appropriate sentence for the convicted offender. Mental health professionals are frequently called on to present information regarding the defendant's psychiatric history as part of the sentencing process. Following the trial, the defendant may appeal his or her conviction or sentence. All states with a capital punishment provision provide an automatic appeal for defendants who receive the death penalty (The Justice System 2015).

The range of sentencing options include incarceration in a prison, jail, or other confinement facility, or release into the community on probationary status. Probation allows those convicted to remain in the community under specified restrictions such as drug testing or required treatment programs. At year-end 2013, 4,751,400 men and women were on probation (Herberman and Bonczar 2014). The court may also require the convicted offender to pay a fine or make restitution through financial compensation to a victim. Certain jurisdictions provide other alternatives to incarceration that are more intense than regular probation requirements though do not require actual incarceration. Such programs include boot camps, house arrest with electronic monitoring, intense supervision with mandated drug and/or psychiatric treatment, and community service.

INMATE CLASSIFICATION

Classification attempts to match inmates with the appropriate level of security, custody supervision, and services necessary to meet their needs. Appropriate classification is important for the following five reasons: protection of inmates; protection of the public; maximizing efficient use of resources; controlling inmate behavior; and providing planning information for budgets, staffing, and program development (Silverman 2001).

For individuals who are serving time in jail, the classification procedure typically occurs in the jail in which they are housed. As a result of this process, the inmate may be placed in a particular housing unit within the jail based on security, medical, and/or mental health needs. For those individuals sentenced to prison, the location of the classification process depends largely on the inmate's jurisdiction. In some areas, inmates are sent to a central reception and diagnostic center after they are sentenced. After an evaluation of the level of security and special services required, the inmate is transferred to the most appropriate matched facility. In other jurisdictions, the inmate undergoes the classification process in a prison reception unit where they are kept until this process is completed. The inmate is then placed in general population or transferred to another facility if needed.

Classification involves determination of both the security and custody level appropriate for the inmate. Facility security level has been defined as "the nature and number of physical design barriers available to prevent escape and control inmate behavior" (Henderson et al. 1997). Jurisdictions vary regarding how they define security levels for their correctional institutions. The Federal Board of Prisons (BOPs) guidelines provide one example of how a security-level system is determined. The BOPs security classification scheme includes four recommended security levels. Level I prisons are referred to as minimum security facilities or federal prison camps. These facilities are characterized by dormitory housing without a surrounding fence and a relatively low staff-to-inmate ratio. Level II facilities are termed "low-security institutions" and are typically surrounded by double fenced perimeters. These facilities have strong work and program components with a higher staff-to-inmate ratio when compared to a minimum security facility. Level III facilities, i.e., medium-security institutions, have more secure perimeters with electronic detection systems, cell-type housing, and greater staff-to-inmate ratios compared to level I and II facilities. Level IV facilities are considered high-security institutions. Their perimeters are often significantly reinforced and may consist of walls with towers at each corner manned by armed correctional officers. Housing in a level IV facility is primarily single- or multiple-occupant cell housing and close staff supervision, and movement control is characteristic (Silverman 1991).

Whereas the security level refers to the number of environmental barriers to prevent escape or manage behavior, an inmate's custody level is determined by the degree of staff supervision necessary to provide adequate control of the inmate (National Institute of Corrections 1987). Under the Federal Bureau of Prison classification scheme, inmates noted as "out custody" have a relatively greater degree of freedom of movement compared to higher-level-custody inmates. For example, such inmates may be assigned to less secure housing as they are eligible for work detail outside the secure perimeter of the institution, with decreased levels of staff supervision. Inmates classified as "in custody" are typically assigned to regular quarters, may have work assignments under normal levels of supervision, and are not allowed to participate in work programs outside the confines of the institution. A "maximum custody" classification label is the highest custody level assigned and requires intense control and supervision. This classification is generally given to those inmates who demonstrated violence, who had disruptive behavior, or who pose a serious escape risk (Silverman 2001).

Prison environments vary regarding the type of inmate received, and the level of security and staffing. Traditionally, inmates who have received the death penalty have been segregated into separate housing areas known as death row. Because persons who receive the death penalty have been viewed as dangerous and/or an increased escape risk, separate secure housing pods with increased supervision and correctional officer staffing were deemed necessary.

With the increasing financial burdens associated with longer periods on death row, some states have developed opportunities for inmates who have received the death penalty to be mainstreamed into the general population and/or to participate in work programs while on death row. Benefits for correctional administration cited by these policies have included cost savings, reduction in legal expenses regarding defense of standard of care law suits, and greater flexibility with the use of bed space. Advantages for inmates resulting from these emerging policies include increased access to legal resources, recreation time, commissary, visitation, medical care, and work programs (Silverman 2001).

No longer do inmates have to be convicted of a capital crime to be housed on a special security unit. During the last few decades, several jurisdictions have built or modified existing prison facilities that create highly isolated environments for those inmates considered too dangerous to be maintained in a general prison population. These facilities are known by various names to include "extended control facility," "supermax," "maxi-max," or a "security housing unit" (SHU). Often labeled a prison within a prison, these tightly managed facilities provide control of inmates who have exhibited violent or seriously disruptive behavior while incarcerated and as a result cannot be maintained in a less restrictive environment. In 1963, the U.S. Penitentiary at Marion, located in southern Illinois, was opened to replace Alcatraz and was the highest maximum security prison in the United States. Inmates in these types of facilities are often kept in their cells for up to 23 hours a day with minimal, if any, interaction with other inmates.

RELEASE FROM PRISON

The exact amount of time an offender serves in prison depends on the type of sentencing scheme outlined in the reviewing jurisdiction. Each state's penal code provides sentencing guidelines, which are minimum and maximum time frames to be imposed for each offense. An indeterminate sentencing scheme provides a minimum time period the inmate must serve and a maximum time period after which the inmate must be released (Silverman 2001). Under an indeterminate sentencing scheme, a parole board (or other reviewing agency) considers whether it is appropriate for the individual to be released and placed into the community.

As a result of increasing public skepticism regarding the rehabilitative potential of inmates and appropriateness for early release, indeterminate schemes have lost their popularity over the last several decades. In their place, more jurisdictions are adopting determinate sentencing schemes. A determinate sentencing scheme outlines a specified number of years that the individual must serve based on the committing offense. Under a determinate sentencing scheme, the time sentenced cannot be increased or decreased. Although determinate sentences are fixed, an inmate may be granted an earlier release date through the accumulation of "good time." Depending on each jurisdiction's statutory provision, good time credits can be earned through either automatic or earned credits. Credits can be earned through participation in work or treatment programs (Silverman 2001).

Under both determinate and indeterminate sentencing schemes, a prisoner may be released prior to completing his or her sentence through the process known as parole. Parole represents the conditional release of the offender into the community. Under an indeterminate sentencing scheme, a parole board (or similarly designated authority) decides whether the inmate should be granted an early release. If the inmate is released, a separate process known as parole supervision begins, which provides support, monitoring and supervision, and services to the newly released offender. Two important components often considered when deciding the appropriateness of parole include the severity of the offense and the inmate's risk of reoffending.

Inmates who have been sentenced under a determinate sentencing scheme are required to serve out their full sentence less any credits for participation in programs (known as good time credits). Those convicted offenders who are released into the community under parole remain under the supervision of the parole officer. They must adhere to specified conditions of parole for the remainder of their unexpired sentence. Failure to adhere to the conditions of parole can result in the offender being returned to prison to complete his or her sentence.

SUMMARY KEY POINTS

Mental health practitioners play a variety of vitally important roles in the assessment, treatment, and management of offenders at virtually every point along their journey through this complex system. Key points from this chapter include the following:

- There are four theories of punishment: retribution, deterrence (specific and general), rehabilitation, and incapacitation.
- Individuals convicted of a misdemeanor serve their sentences in jail while individuals convicted of a felony serve their sentences in prison.
- With longer sentences, the inmate population is aging, and as a result more costly medical interventions will be required to meet their medical needs.
- The process of classification involves matching the level of supervision and treatment to the inmate's needs.

REFERENCES

Carson A. 2014. *Prisoners in 2013*. Washington, DC: U.S. Department of Justice, Office of Justice Programs, Bureau of Justice Statistics.

Cohen J. 1983. *Incapacitating Criminals: Recent Research Findings. National Institute of Justice, Research in Brief*. Washington, DC: U.S. Department of Justice.

Ditton P. 1999. *Mental Health and Treatment of Inmates and Probationers*. Washington, DC: U.S. Department of Justice, Office of Justice Programs, Bureau of Justice Statistics.

Ditton P and D Wilson. 1999. *Truth in Sentencing in State Prisons*. Washington, DC: U.S. Department of Justice, Office of Justice Programs, Bureau of Justice Statistics.

Durose M, A Cooper, and H Snyder. 2014. *Recidivism of Prisoners Released in 30 States in 2005: Patterns from 2005 to 2010*. Washington, DC: U.S. Department of Justice, Office of Justice Programs, Bureau of Justice Statistics.

Federal Bureau of Investigation. 2014. *Crime in the United States*. Washington, DC: U.S. Department of Justice.

Federal Bureau of Prisons. 2011. *About the Federal Bureau of Prisons*. Washington, DC: Federal Bureau of Prisons, Office of Communications and Archives.

Federal Crime Cases. 2015. http://www.gottrouble.com/legal/criminal/federal/federalcases.html, accessed January 30, 2015.

Finn P and M Sullivan. 1988. Police respond to special populations: Handling the mentally ill, public inebriate, and the homeless. *National Institute of Justice Reports* 209:2–8.

Gendreau P and R Ross. 1987. Revivification of rehabilitation: Evidence from the 1980's. *Justice Quarterly* 4:349–407.

Glaze L and D Kaeble. 2014. *Correctional Populations in the United States, 2013*. Washington, DC: U.S. Department of Justice, Office of Justice Programs, Bureau of Justice Statistics.

Henderson J, H Rauch, and R Phillips. 1997. *Guidelines for the Development of a Security Program*, 2nd edition. Lanham, MD: American Correctional Association.

Herberman E and T Bonczar. 2014. *Probation and Parole in the United States, 2013*. Washington, DC: U.S. Department of Justice, Office of Justice Programs, Bureau of Justice Statistics.

Hooker R. 1997. Lex talionis. In *World Cultures, General Glossary*. http://richard-hooker.com/sites/worldcultures/GLOSSARY/LEXTAL.HTM, accessed January 30, 2015.

Human Rights Watch. 2012. Old Behind Bars. The Aging Prison Population in the United States. https://www.hrw.org/sites/default/files/reports/usprisons0112webwcover_0.pdf, accessed January 31, 2015.

James DJ. 2004. Bureau of Justice Statistics Special Report July 2004, NCJ 201932, Profile of Jail Inmates, 2002 U.S. Department of Justice Office of Justice Programs.

Lamb R and L Weinberger. 2013. Some perspectives on criminalization. *Journal of the American Academy of Psychiatry and the Law* 41:287–293.

Lipton D, R Martinson, and J Wilks. 1975. *The Effectiveness of Correctional Treatment: A Survey of Treatment Validation Studies*. New York: Praeger Press.

Martinson R. 1974. What works? Questions and answers about prison reform. *The Public Interest* 35:22–54.

McDonald D, E Fournier, M Russell-Einhourn, and S Crawford. 1998. *Private Prisons in the United States, Executive Summary*. http://www.abtassociates.com/reports/priv-report.pdf, accessed January 31, 2015.

Minton T and D Golinelli. 2014. *Jail Inmates at Midyear 2013—Statistical Tables*. Washington, DC: U.S. Department of Justice, Office of Justice Programs, Bureau of Justice Statistics.

National Institute of Corrections. 1987. *Guidelines for the Development of a Security Program*. Washington, DC: National Institute of Corrections, Department of Justice.

Reaves B and A Goldberg. 2000. *Local Police Departments 1997*. Washington, DC: U.S. Department of Justice, Office of Justice Programs, Bureau of Justice Statistics.

Shapiro P and H Votey. 1984. Deterrence and subjective probabilities of arrest: Modeling individual decisions to drink and drive in Sweden. *Law and Society Review* 18:111–149.

Sherman L and R Berk. 1984. The specific deterrent effects of arrest for domestic assault. *American Sociological Review* 49:261–272.

Silverman I. 2001. The correctional process. In *Corrections: A Comprehensive View*, 2nd edition. Belmont, CA: Wadsworth/Thomson Learning.

Smith D and P Gartin. 1989. Specifying specific deterrence: The influence of arrest in future criminal activity. *American Sociological Review* 54:94–105.

The Justice System. 2015. http://www.bjs.gov/content/justsys.cfm, accessed January 31, 2015.

Torrey EF. 1999. Reinventing mental health care. *City Journal*. http://www.city-journal.org/html/9_4_a5.html, accessed January 24, 2005.

Truman J and L Langton. 2014. *Criminal Victimization, 2013*. Washington, DC: U.S. Department of Justice, Office of Justice Programs, Bureau of Justice Statistics.

U.S. Marshals Service. 2014. *Fact Sheet*. U.S. Marshals Service. https://www.usmarshals.gov/duties/factsheets/overview.pdf, accessed January 31, 2015.

52

The structure of correctional mental health services

JOEL A. DVOSKIN, MELODY C. BROWN, JEFFREY L. METZNER, ERIN M. NELSON, AND STEVEN E. PITT

INTRODUCTION

The rate of incarceration in the United States hit alarming levels between 1978 and 2009, peaking at approximately 2,300,700 incarcerated adults in jails and prisons by the end of 2008 (Glaze 2010). Small but consistent declines in the population have been the trend since (decreases of 0.7% in 2009, 1.3% in 2011, and 0.5% in 2012; Glaze and Herberman 2013) as the number of releases from state prisons has begun to exceed the number of admissions (Carson and Golinelli 2013). Despite these decreases, the Bureau of Justice Statistics (BJS) estimates the total incarcerated population at the end of 2012 to be 2,228,400, putting approximately one in every 108 adults in the United States in prison or jail (Glaze and Herberman 2013). When compared to the global community, the United States continues to be at the top of incarcerated population rates: approximately 716 prisoners per 100,000 people versus the global average of 144 prisoners per 100,000 people (Walmsley 2013).

Commensurate with the high rates of incarceration in the United States is the high number of imprisoned individuals who suffer from a mental illness. Research indicates that a disproportionate number of inmates and detainees experience mental illness; however, prevalence estimates vary. At the conservative end of the spectrum, roughly 6%–11% of inmates in jail and prison are deemed currently in need of psychiatric care for serious mental illness, while 10%–15% require treatment for general mental illness (American Psychiatric Association [APA], Task Force on Outpatient Forensic Services 2009). Based on the 2012 estimated incarcerated population from the BJS, there were between 222,840 and 334,260 offenders with mental illness requiring treatment in U.S. prisons and jails at the year end of 2012. Teplin and Swartz (1989) noted that even after adjusting for demographic differences, the prevalence rates of schizophrenia and major affective disorder are two to three times higher in jails than in the general population. Steadman and his colleagues (1987) found that the prevalence of severe or significant psychiatric disability among sentenced felons is at least 15%. When coupled with mental retardation or brain damage, at least 25% of the inmate population in the New York State Department of Correctional Services was found to have at least a significant psychiatric or functional disability. Other studies, using vague and overly inclusive criteria, have identified more than 60% of inmates as experiencing a "mental problem" (James and Glaze 2006).

Incongruities exist when looking at the disposition and sentencing of persons incarcerated with a mental illness. Axelson and Wahl (1992) found that psychotic detainees charged with misdemeanors were discriminated against in accessing various types of pretrial release, resulting in lengths of stay six-and-a-half times longer than nonpsychotic controls. Similarly, Valdiserri et al. (1986) determined that psychotic inmates were four times more likely than nonpsychotic inmates to have been incarcerated for less serious charges such as disorderly conduct and threats. In a larger follow-up study to Axelson and Wahl's (1992), Harris and Dagadakis (2004) did not find differences in length of incarceration time between severely mentally ill and nonmentally ill control groups. They did, however, similarly find that the severely mentally ill group, who had less severe and less frequent previous offenses, was often incarcerated for the same length of time as the nonmentally ill group with more frequent and severe offenses.

In correctional institutions, those inmates with serious mental illnesses or in psychiatric crisis present a host of problems to correctional administrators. One problem, of course, is the possibility of serious injury to staff and other inmates posed by those few inmates with serious mental illness whose behavior is uncontrolled and violent. Untreated, inmates with psychoses may be terrified by hallucinations and stay up all night screaming, thereby keeping other inmates awake, who in turn become angry and violent in response. Thus, housing assignments must take into account the mutual fears of inmates with and without mental illness.

Another problem posed by the occurrence of psychiatric crisis and severe mental illness in correctional facilities is related to liability. Suicides and restraint-related deaths may have dire legal consequences. Despite the stereotype of "guards" as tough and unfeeling, a completed suicide is often devastating to custody staff, who feel responsible for keeping inmates safe. Indeed, public opinion, so seldom sympathetic to inmates, nevertheless solidly expects correctional officials, at the very least, to keep their inmates alive. Even in the absence of adverse judgments or settlements, legal fees can be costly.

The diversity of American correctional facilities is extraordinary. Local correctional facilities range from one-person police lockups to large urban jails, which may house more than 15,000 inmates. Similarly, state prisons vary from very small field camps to prisons of more than 5000 inmates. Notwithstanding the differences between facilities, jails and prisons are alike in many ways. Both are viewed as correctional settings, with uniformed staff, secure perimeters (depending on custody level), and usually stark accommodations. Jails and prisons can also be very stressful environments, due to forced association, segregation by gender, and extremes of noise and temperature. However, the challenge of keeping their respective facilities safe is the most important similarity that jails and prisons share.

Despite such similarities, there are also important differences between jails and prisons. While prisons are self-contained environments that tend to house inmates for long periods of time, jails often hold detainees for only a matter of hours; thus, jails need to be treated as part of the larger communities in which they exist (Steadman et al. 1989). The goals of the two settings also differ. For pretrial detainees, jails exist predominantly to hold and process people until their case is resolved by the courts. Often, jail detention depends solely on external factors such as the ability of the defendant's family to raise money to post bond. For sentenced misdemeanants, jails serve as short-term (usually less than 1 year) punishment, with or without an effort at rehabilitation. Prisons, on the other hand, serve to punish the most serious offenders, and ostensibly to prepare them through various prison programs for their eventual return to society.

Over the past several decades, there have been important changes in community mental health philosophies, the most important being the Recovery Model and an emphasis on Trauma-Informed Services (Pinals and Andrade 2015; see also Substance Abuse and Mental Health Services Association [SAMHSA] 2014). The Recovery Model is a way of looking at mental illness with more hope and respect than had previously been the case. It encourages clinicians to pay attention to each person's strengths and assets instead of merely documenting pathology. It provides a more hopeful way of looking at each person's future, and encourages clinicians to help people acquire the skills that will allow them to live safely with their mental illnesses. This model is slowly being adopted by a few correctional facilities (SAMHSA 2014).

Trauma-informed care is a relatively simple but enormously important change in the way that clinicians look at the people they treat. Clinical training teaches each practitioner to ask each patient, "What is wrong with you?" Instead, a trauma-informed approach to mental health treatment asks an equally important question, "What has happened to you?" The prevalence of traumatic experiences among jail and prison inmates is well documented (Miller and Najavits 2012), and respect for these traumatic experiences can dramatically assist clinicians informing a therapeutic alliance with their clients.

Needless to say, the difficult and stressful correctional environment creates serious challenges to the formation of the therapeutic milieu or relationship (Pinals and Andrade 2015). Nevertheless, correctional mental health workers who understand these principles can provide a higher quality of service to their clients and to the institutions in which they work.

THE LEGAL REQUIREMENTS FOR CORRECTIONAL MENTAL HEALTH SERVICES

O'Leary (1989), Cohen and Dvoskin (1992), Cohen (1988, 1998), and Jones (2015) have written extensively about the legal bases for requiring mental health services in jails and prisons, in addition to the required components and standards that various courts have established for such services.

Pretrial detainees have a due process right not to be punished, while convicted inmates are prohibited from suffering cruel and unusual punishment. For pretrial detainees, the right to treatment stems from due process rights guaranteed by the Fourteenth Amendment. "Detainees are entitled to at least the same level of care as the convicted" (Cohen, 1998, pp. 2–14). A convicted inmate's right to medical and psychiatric treatment in prison, guaranteed by the Eighth Amendment, stems from the state's role as incarcerator. In *Estelle v. Gamble* (1976), the Supreme Court interpreted this responsibility as the duty to avoid "deliberate indifference" to the serious medical needs of inmates. Other federal and state courts specifically included psychiatric needs within the standard (e.g., *Bowring v. Godwin* 1977), and have required that treatment be greater than the provision of psychotropic medication (*Langley v. Coughlin* 1989). It was not until 1994, however, with *Farmer v. Brennan* (1994), that a clearer definition of this term was presented. The *Farmer* decision equated deliberate indifference with recklessness, and applied the criminal standard of "actual knowledge" of risk. It is not essential to prove that an official clearly believed that harm was imminent; only that an official possessed substantial knowledge of risk (Cohen 1998). Examples of the application of this standard can be found in cases such as *Coleman v. Wilson* (1995) and *Madrid v. Gomez* (1995), both of which speak to the necessity of providing adequate treatment to inmates with mental illness.

To incarcerate someone with deliberate indifference to his or her significant psychiatric needs is thus viewed as cruel and unusual punishment and may be remedied, often through class action lawsuits, by injunctive relief, or by compensatory and/or punitive monetary damages. The conservative turn in the federal judiciary, however, has made it far more difficult for plaintiffs to succeed in such actions (e.g., *Wilson v. Seiter* 1991; *Hudson v. McMillan* 1992).

Congress has also been conservative relevant to prison reform, as reflected in passage of the *Prison Litigation Reform Act* (PLRA; 1996). The PLRA established new procedural requirements for suits by prisoners and significantly limited the ability of the courts to order relief. Consent decrees now require a finding of unconstitutional conditions (i.e., admission of such conditions by the defendants), fees are limited for special masters and attorneys, and other restraints to remedies are present. The U.S. Supreme Court in *Miller et al. v. French et al.* (No. 99–224, decided June 19, 2000) upheld the constitutionality of this act that had been challenged on due process and separation of powers principles.

In addition to constitutional litigation, correctional administrators who ignore the mental health needs of at-risk inmates who go on to commit suicide may also be vulnerable to tort liability, such as wrongful death actions (O'Leary 1989). Injuries to staff and other inmates resulting from inadequate mental health services can also lead to tort liability, as well as great expense due to occupational injury leave and disability retirements. In addition, inadequate medical or psychiatric services can result in malpractice claims against both medical and mental health providers in the jail.

Evolving legal requirements

Lower courts, generally via class action litigation, have also dealt with specific programmatic aspects of correctional mental health systems that include the placement of inmates with a serious mental illness in long-term segregation housing units, discharge planning, and the quality improvement process.

Because it is common for inmates with a mental illness to be overrepresented in segregation housing units, especially in systems that have problematic or inadequate mental health services, courts have attempted to partially remedy this problem by requiring mental health screening during the time immediately surrounding transfer of inmates to such housing units and/or establishing a process for providing mental health input into the disciplinary process (*Coleman v. Wilson* 1995). The purposes of the screening process include triaging of an inmate's mental health needs and exclusion of inmates from segregation housing when clinically indicated (e.g., due to psychosis or significant suicide risk). Courts have also required ongoing "rounds" in segregation housing to provide ongoing assessment of segregated inmates (*Coleman v. Wilson* 1995).

Courts have also required that inmates with a serious mental illness housed in segregation units must have access to appropriate levels of mental health treatment based on their clinical needs (*Madrid v. Gomez* 1995; *Ind. Prot. & Advocacy Servs. Comm'n v. Comm'r, Ind. Dep't of Corr.* 2012). Such treatment should include both structured out-of-cell therapeutic programming and unstructured out-of-cell recreational time. For example, for inmates requiring a special needs level of mental health care (e.g., residential level of care), at least 10 hours per week of structured therapeutic activities and another 10 hours per week of unstructured recreational time have been recommended by Metzner and Dvoskin (2006).

Mental health input into the disciplinary process for inmates with a serious mental illness has also been a component of remedial plans designed to reduce the length of stays for inmates with a serious mental illness in locked down settings (*Disability Advocates, Inc. v. New York State Office of Mental Health* 2007). Mental health assessments are designed to answer the question of whether the inmate's rule infraction was related to symptoms of a mental illness and, if so, whether the disposition should be mitigated (e.g., reduced disciplinary housing time) by the hearing officer.

Discharge planning has been increasingly recognized by both mental health and correctional staffs to be an essential element of an adequate correctional mental health system related to both the obvious clinical purposes and due to the benefits from a perceived reduced recidivism rate. Although decided on the basis of state statute and case law, *Brad H. v. City of New York* (2000) is instructive regarding the risks from a legal perspective of not providing adequate discharge services. A settlement agreement was reached in which the city is to provide discharge planning services that include, depending on clinical indications, medications, assistance with housing and entitlements as well as linkage services.

Grubbs v. Bradley (1993), *Coleman v. Wilson* (1995). and *Madrid v. Gomez* (1995) emphasized the importance of a quality assurance/improvement (QI) process in remedying an inadequate correctional mental health system. A QI system has been increasingly recognized within the correctional health-care field as an essential component in order to continually improve the effectiveness and quality of health-care services provided.

DIVERSION PROGRAMS

There are a number of reasons why people with mental illness find their way into correctional settings despite efforts to divert them to alternative dispositions (Lamb and Weinberger 1998). For some, the offense will be severe and unrelated to their mental illness, thus ruling out the possibility of dismissing charges or negotiated insanity pleas. For others, coincidental onset of a serious mental illness, often exacerbated by the stress of their incarceration and the correctional environment may result in decompensation in some individuals who were mentally intact prior to their incarceration (Gibbs 1987; Muzekari et al. 1999). Finally, with the continuously high rate of illegal drug use and its well-documented relationship to criminal behavior (see, e.g., Petrich 1976; Mirsky 1988; O'Neil and Wish 1990; Office of National Drug Control Policy 2013), urban jails face high numbers of newly admitted inmates who suffer from drug-induced psychosis on arrest.

Diversion programs are essentially intended to shift offenders with mental illness and/or substance abuse problems away from the criminal justice system (The Center for Health and Justice at TASC 2013). This does not imply, however, that mentally ill offenders should not, or would not, ever be detained. Although diversion may prevent incarceration in some cases, it may also mitigate the time spent behind bars, as well as impose contingencies for aftercare upon release. For those offenders requiring detention, mental health services must be provided by the correctional facility. Generally speaking, however, nonviolent mentally ill offenders are not likely to have their ongoing mental health needs best met by serving jail time. Instead, the safety of the community is better served by providing a comprehensive, inclusive diversion program designed to meet the needs of the offender, as well as the mental health and criminal justice systems (Coleman 1998; GAINS Center for Behavioral Health and Justice Transformation [GAINS] 2010).

Mental health courts (MHCs) are a relatively recent development to further assist in diverting offenders with mental illness and/or substance abuse problems. Initially funded by an act of congress, America's Law Enforcement and Mental Health Project (2000), MHCs typically handle nonviolent offenders, diagnosed with a mental illness or a co-occurring diagnosis of mental illness and substance abuse, who agree to the terms of enrollment in the program. They are intended to coordinate all violations, mandated treatment, and connecting the offender with social services in the community, including employment, housing, education, health care, and relapse prevention (American's Law Enforcement and Mental Health Project 2000). Research has largely shown that MHCs are working to reduce recidivism (Moore and Hiday 2006; McNiel and Binder 2007; Hiday and Ray 2010; Hiday et al. 2013) and to connect mentally ill patients with needed treatment in their communities (Steadman et al. 2011). The largest and most comprehensive study to date has been the on-going, multi-site MacArthur Foundation study (Steadman et al. 2011). Results from this study have confirmed a reduction in recidivism rates for those who participated in the MHCs system and also found a shift from crisis treatments to intensive treatments as compared to the control group (Callahan and Wales 2013). These findings indicate that MHCs appear to be working to both reduce recidivism as well as to effectively link offenders with community-based treatments.

Despite widespread agreement about the need for effective jail diversion programs, existing programs share few similarities. Since their implementation in 1992, diversion programs have grown substantially in number, with more than 560 programs existing across 47 states (GAINS 2010). With many varieties of resources and leadership, as well as differing needs of each community, it is not surprising to find significant variations in program models used (Clark 2004). Subsequent disparate definitions of inclusion criteria, strategies, and objectives have resulted in limited meaningful data available to evaluate existing programs and/or to provide guidelines for the continued development of future programs (Steadman et al. 1994a,b, 1995; Draine and Solomon 1999). Steadman and Naples' (2005) multisite evaluation, the largest to date, determined that there is growing evidence in support of jail diversion programs as beneficial to individuals, systems, and the communities they serve. In conjunction with ongoing research regarding the effectiveness of jail diversion programs (see also Steadman et al. 1994a,b), Steadman et al. (1995, 1999) delineated six key elements common to the most successful programs. First, effective programs included interagency involvement (e.g., mental health, substance abuse, and criminal justice systems) beginning at the program's inception. Second, regularly scheduled interdisciplinary communication between representatives was built in to the structure. Third, service integration was orchestrated by a designated "boundary spanner" who served as a liaison between agencies. A fourth key element was the presence of strong leadership. The fifth key element was the early identification of detainees with mental illnesses who meet the criteria for a diversion program. Finally, effective diversion programs consistently employed nontraditional case management strategies.

Whether diversion occurs pre- or post-booking, "the best programs see detainees as citizens of the community who require a broad array of services, including mental health and substance abuse treatment, housing and social services" (APA 2000, 29). Program success has essentially depended on building new system linkages and holding the community responsible for the provision of services (Steadman et al. 1999). Policies providing for the selective diversion of specific mentally ill offenders, and/or their careful reintegration into the community following incarceration, are more desirable than existing alternatives (Cohen 1998). In sum, the development of comprehensive diversion programs may break the "unproductive cycle of decompensation, disturbance, and arrest" (APA 2000, 30) so familiar to many of our nation's citizens with serious mental illnesses.

SERVICE COMPONENTS OF CORRECTIONAL MENTAL HEALTH CARE

Due to the many differences between jails and prisons, the priorities for mental health services are somewhat different in each setting. For example, Steadman (1990) found that for jails, the priority services are screening, crisis intervention, and discharge-oriented case management. Prison environments, on the other hand, due to their typically longer lengths of stay, lend themselves to the possibility of longer-term psychotherapy and psychiatric rehabilitation rarely seen in jails. Despite these differences, the services themselves fall into generic categories that hold up rather well across the two settings. Nevertheless, it is important to be mindful of the inevitable differences, subtle or obvious, between the implementation of services, as they are adapted to each specific correctional environment.

Perhaps the most comprehensive description of essential correctional mental health programs can be found in the APA's Work Group Report on Psychiatric Services in Correctional Facilities (APA 2015).

Cohen (1998) lists six minimal essential elements underlying the service components, taken from a prison class action suit in Texas (*Ruiz v. Estelle* 1980), as providing a useful framework for planning mental health services (see also APA 1989, 2000, 2015; Hills et al. 2004):

1. Systematic screening and evaluation
2. Treatment that is more than mere seclusion or close supervision
3. Participation by trained mental health professionals
4. Accurate, complete, and confidential records
5. Safeguards against psychotropic medication prescribed in dangerous amounts, without adequate supervision, or otherwise inappropriately administered
6. A suicide prevention program

In addition, a quality improvement process has become an essential component of most remedial plans or Settlement Agreements during the past decade (Metzner 2012).

Screening

Screening is regarded as perhaps the most important service element in correctional mental health (Pogrebin 1985; Teplin and Swartz 1989; Maloney et al. 2015). Screening is not only a specifically required legal obligation (Cohen 1998) but is clinically and programmatically essential. It is impossible to appropriately treat inmates with serious mental illnesses or psychiatric crises without identifying the specific individuals affected. The APA's Work Group Report on Psychiatric Services in Correctional Facilities (2016) lists four levels of mental health screening and evaluation procedures to be conducted as soon as possible after intake:

> *(Receiving mental health) screening includes observation and structured inquiry into mental health history and symptoms, including questions about suicide history, ideation, and potential; prior psychiatric hospitalizations and treatment; and current and past medications, both prescribed and what is actually being taken….*
>
> *Intake mental health screening is defined as a more comprehensive examination of each newly admitted inmate within 14 days of arrival at an institution. It includes a review of the reception mental health screening, medical screening, behavioral observation, review of mental health history, assessment of suicide potential, and mental status examination….*
>
> A brief mental health assessment is defined as a mental health examination appropriate to the level of services needed…. Brief mental health assessments occur within 72 hours of a positive screening and a referral (in an office with sound privacy.) Urgent cases receive immediate evaluation after referral….
>
> *A comprehensive mental health evaluation consists of a face-to-face interview in an office with sound privacy and a review of available health care records and collateral information. It concludes with a diagnostic formulation and, at least, an initial treatment plan.*

The National Commission on Correctional Health Care (NCCHC 2014a,b) recommends similar procedures, with a brief mental health assessment and/or a comprehensive mental health evaluation being required only if positive results occur. Maloney et al. (2015) estimate a typical positive referral rate of 25%–33% for further assessment beyond the initial intake assessment. Although there are a number of acceptable ways to provide this screening, several specific elements must be present:

- *Trained staff.* Standardized screening tools can be successfully administered by line staff, nurses, or case managers, provided that they are adequately trained in the administration of each screening instrument and know where to refer inmates in need of services.
- *Documentation.* The results of the screening must be clearly and legibly documented and available to those responsible for medical care, housing assignment, and follow-up services. Records must be maintained in a manner that assures the privacy and confidentiality of each inmate, while facilitating communication between different mental health and medical providers.
- *Low threshold.* The screening must have a low threshold for referral for more extensive evaluation. That is, any indication of either a history or current evidence of mental illness or psychiatric problems must result in referral for a follow-up evaluation. Likewise, any unusual or eccentric mannerisms or behaviors observed must be specifically documented and referred for further evaluation.
- *Standardization.* By routinely utilizing a standardized screening process during booking and by training staff in the screening procedure, one avoids an idiosyncratic process where a mentally ill inmate's chances of being identified depend on who happens to be on duty when the inmate arrives.

Martin et al. (2013) and Gebbie et al. (2008) provide comprehensive reviews of multiple screening tools available for correctional facilities. Ford et al. (2007) suggest that screening instruments should be brief; contain clear definitions, thresholds, and criteria; have low false-negative rates; and have reasonable false-positive rates. Based on these elements, Maloney et al. (2015) recommend four specific scales as effective screening devices: variants of the New York instrument, a suicide prevention screening guidelines form developed by agencies in New York (Sherman and Morschauser 1989); the Brief Jail Mental Health Screen (Steadman et al. 2005) used in conjunction with the New York instrument or other suicide screening instruments; the Correctional Mental Health Screen (Ford et al. 2007); and "15 Questions," a screening instrument used in the Los Angeles County Sheriff's Jail system.

Follow-up evaluations

No matter who conducts screening for mental health service needs, it will be necessary to provide more extensive and detailed evaluations for those inmates identified as potentially in need of mental health services. These examinations must be timely and responsive to specific issues raised during the screening, and must result in treatment recommendations that are practical within the correctional setting.

Because psychiatrists are difficult to recruit and are a great deal more expensive than other mental health providers, it makes sense to have these "second-level" follow-up evaluations routinely conducted by psychologists, social workers, or psychiatric nurses with advanced degrees. However, as these evaluations will be primarily diagnostic in nature, they will optimally be conducted by at least master's-level staff (preferably licensed) with training in psychopathology (Dvoskin 1989).

It is important to limit these evaluations to issues that have immediate and feasible treatment implications. Given the generally limited treatment resources in correctional settings, full-scale psychological test batteries should be limited to inmates whose symptoms raise diagnostic questions that can only or best be answered by psychological testing (Dvoskin 1989). For inmates who appear to require psychiatric services such as psychotropic medication, a referral to a psychiatrist or licensed independent provider (e.g., Advanced Practice Nurse Practitioner) will then be in order. Of course, in cases where a detainee enters the jail with psychotropic medication, or a long history of such treatment, it may be cost-effective to bypass this step and have the person referred directly to a psychiatrist.

It is important to have some capacity for the emergency administration of medication during weekends and nights. On-call psychiatrists may provide telephone consultation with on-site nonpsychiatric physicians, registered nurses, or physician's assistants. Twenty-four-hour on-site psychiatric availability is a luxury likely to be found only in a few very large and well-funded settings. In smaller jurisdictions, mobile crisis teams from the local community mental health provider or nearby general hospital emergency rooms may be able to provide services at the jail.

Psychotropic medications

Psychiatrists who work in correctional settings must be aware of all of the usual issues surrounding emergency psychiatry (e.g., Anderson et al. 1976; Salzman et al. 1986; Dubin 1988; Allen 2002). There are several other considerations that are especially or even uniquely important in dealing with inmates who are being treated for a psychiatric condition. People who are put in jails or prisons have often failed or refused to take their psychotropic medications as prescribed. It should therefore not be surprising that inmates may be unwilling to take their medication exactly as ordered by physicians (Smith 1989). Inmates who feel oppressed by the criminal justice system sometimes view psychotropic medication ordered by an institutional physician as an instrument of that oppression. Other inmates, believing the correctional environment to be unsafe, prefer to remain as alert as possible, and decline to take medications that are designed to provide tranquilization. Alternately, it is possible that inmates who are not suffering from a mental disorder may seek psychotropic medication in hopes of alleviating some of the situational stresses associated with their incarceration, or in hopes of selling them for profit.

Limitations in psychiatric resources are a significant issue in the provision of psychotropic medications to inmates. Busy physicians may spend an inadequate amount of time explaining the need for medication, its value to the inmates, or what to do about side effects. It takes time to build trust and create a truly therapeutic relationship between psychiatric providers and their patients, and shortages of clinical staff often make it difficult to do so. Moreover, systemic constraints on the flow of information may create protracted time periods between an inmate's initial complaint of side effects and his or her appointment with a physician.

Case management

Active case management is invaluable, yet frequently underutilized, in correctional mental health care. Case managers benefit inmates during their period of incarceration, as well as serve an essential role in the discharge planning process. For inmates who are confused and anxious, regular and surprisingly brief visits can provide reassurance that the inmate has not been psychologically abandoned. Often, the simple provision of accurate information about the criminal justice process can relieve a tremendous amount of anxiety and need not always be supplied by mental health professionals.

Within the correctional setting, stressors may build up in the absence of supportive services. It therefore is important periodically to "check in" with identified psychologically vulnerable and mentally ill inmates even during periods of apparently good adjustment. The establishment of a tracking mechanism identifying those inmates who are not receiving active mental health services, yet have a history of mental illness, can be of great benefit toward the maintenance of the inmate's psychological fitness. Case managers are ideal providers of such a service. Even annual visits with a case manager will allow the inmate a sense of connectedness and security, while simultaneously providing the mental health department with an opportunity to monitor the inmate's status. These very brief contacts are a worthwhile investment, especially if they prevent more serious exacerbations of an inmate's condition, thereby forestalling more extensive and costly services. Therefore, the inclusion of case management services offers the facility a prophylactic tool, reducing financial burden as well as mediating the potential for crises that disrupt normal facility functioning.

Case management is even more effective in linking inmates to appropriate mental health services on their release (Griffin 1990). Prior to discharge, case managers can play an integral role in the building or nurturing of social supports, such as helping the inmate to contact family or friends. Such collateral contact can be particularly helpful toward improving an inmate's quality of life while incarcerated as well as upon return to the community (Jacoby and Kozie-Peak 1997). Perhaps most importantly, however, case managers serve as a bridge, linking inmates with providers in the community. Continuity of care is critical to appropriate mental health service and falls well within the venue of case management service. Even the most impressive correctional mental health-care program can be rendered futile if the inmate patient is not linked with appropriate services after discharge (Steadman et al. 1995). Lamb and Weinberger (1998) assert that appropriate implementation of mental health services (and use of case managers) "would mean tailoring mental health services to meet the needs of mentally ill offenders and not treating them as if they were compliant, cooperative, and in need of minimum controls." Unfortunately, the criminal justice system is largely unprepared to provide case management services to mentally ill offenders upon release (Lamb and Weinberger 1998), and if not carefully monitored and adjusted, the patient may experience a variety of unsettling, uncomfortable, and even dangerous side effects. As a result, correctional nurses need to take special care when administering medications in the jail to ensure that the inmates are not "cheeking" medications to appear compliant or to save for later sale. Minor tranquilizers are especially prone to abuse and black market sale within the jail, and therefore are often not included in correctional formularies.

Crisis intervention

In the correctional setting, psychiatric crises may arise at any time, and involve virtually any offender. Crisis services must be readily accessible at all points during the intake and incarceration process. Even where the very best screening and evaluation services are present, it will still be impossible to identify on admission all of the inmates who will require psychiatric services during their incarceration or detention. No screen is perfect, and even "cutting-edge" instruments will have some false-negative errors. Further, certain kinds of psychoses may allow the inmate to appear, at least temporarily, quite unimpaired even under stress. It is important to note, however, that there are a number of reasons why inmates will either be, or appear to be, psychologically intact upon intake, and later experience a psychiatric crisis within the jail setting.

Jails and prisons can be extraordinarily stressful environments. Overcrowding, extremes of cold or heat, noise, filth, and the fear of assault may all contribute to the psychological deterioration of even the most "mentally healthy" inmate. Jails may be even more distressing than prisons, because most jail inmates have recently arrived and have a great deal of uncertainty as to the outcome of their legal status. For first-time offenders especially, their expectations are likely to be colored by television or movie dramatizations stressing violence in jails. Perhaps most upsetting to first-time offenders is the simple truth that jail inmates are not always very nice to one another. Together, these various stressors can lead to psychiatric decompensation at any time during the course of incarceration.

Another risk factor is any pre-existing psychological condition that makes a person vulnerable to psychiatric crisis or mental illness. Family histories of an affective disorder appear to increase the risk of severe depression, which could be triggered by the stresses associated with incarceration. Certain personality disorders, especially borderline personality disorder, create a variety of risks for psychiatric crises, including suicide gestures, emotional hyper-reactivity, and acute psychoses, especially in response to being locked up (Metzner et al. 1998).

Administration of psychotropic medications in emergency situations can be dangerous, especially with newly admitted inmates whose urine and serum blood toxicology results are pending. As the incidence of illegal drug abuse has increased, the likelihood of a psychiatric crisis being due to illicit drug use has also increased. The safe prescription of medications in emergencies involving newly admitted inmates should thus include a physical examination. Since the time of day will often preclude such safeguards, many physicians will elect such nonpharmacological treatment interventions as constant observation to resolve the immediate crisis and keep the inmate safe until services can be obtained. Other facilities will elect to utilize local general hospital emergency rooms.

Every jail and police lockup that receives direct admissions from the street must have access to medically supervised alcohol and drug detoxification services. However, this detoxification is primarily medical in nature and is not a mental health service. Once detoxification has been safely accomplished, mental health staff should provide assessment of any needed mental health services. For inmates with both mental illness and substance use disorders, upon release there should be a referral to a community program that provides for integrated treatment of co-occurring mental illness and substance use disorders.

Consultation services, when provided by mental health staff to correctional staff, can vary extensively, from sophisticated suggestions for handling difficult inmates to simply suggesting a cell change. The mental health staff must be viewed as supportive of the correctional staff's mission to make the facility safe for everyone.

Special management precautions in response to psychiatric emergencies include moving the inmate to a different bed location, thereby separating violent inmates from others, possibly allowing for easier and more frequent observation or closer proximity to nursing or other services. Often inmates will be put on "special watches" such as constant observation or one-to-one, especially where suicidal intent is suspected.

The special management precautions are required for two reasons. Each facility has an overriding obligation to protect inmates or detainees from foreseeable and preventable harm. There is also a duty to provide medical or psychiatric treatment, although the two considerations will often overlap. In either case, the most important job in any correctional psychiatric crisis is to ensure the safety of all of the people who live and work there. Thus, crisis response is as much the responsibility of correctional staff as it is the mental health staff, even where 24-hour mental health staff are available.

Verbal counseling in crises is not only the least intrusive intervention available, but often it is the most effective—especially when the crisis is in response to a specific event or the novelty of the incarceration itself. For any inmate, with or without long-standing mental illnesses, these crises are often a response to fear. Inmates fear many things, some real and some imagined. Often, simply providing information, spiking rumors, or offering support can significantly improve an inmate's response to his or her situation.

As with nearly all jail-based mental health services, it is imperative that adequate documentation and communication of crisis responses be maintained. When off-hour providers are contractors or are from other agencies, it is imperative that essential aspects of the crisis and actions taken in response to it be communicated to the mental health, medical, and correctional staff. Likewise, facility correctional and medical staff should, as standard policy, have a mechanism in place by which they can alert mental health staff of concerns about a given inmate. For instance, a third-shift officer might observe idiosyncratic behavior and should have a routine method of documenting his or her observations and informing the mental health department.

Finally, the competent resolution of any crisis must include some reasonable effort to prevent its recurrence. While the provision of information itself can be effective, other steps may include supporting a psychologically fragile inmate through a crisis, or preventive steps such as ongoing supportive therapy or skill building (e.g., how to safely "do time").

Thus, correctional facilities, as a matter of law and sensible policy, must have some sort of ready access to crisis services. These services include psychotropic medication, special watch procedures, psychological or counseling services, detoxification (because drugs may be available inside the facility), information (such as when the inmate will get to see a lawyer or receive visits), and consultation with correctional staff about how to handle problematic inmates.

Suicide prevention

Although suicide is clearly one of many sources of potential crisis in the correctional setting, its impact demands special consideration. Suicides in jails and prisons are often preventable, and jail suicide rates are especially likely to exceed general population rates in the community. The likelihood of higher rates is especially great if a suicide prevention program is not established. Standards for suicide prevention programs or protocols did not, however, begin to formalize and adequately address suicide prevention until the mid to late 1980s (Hayes 1995). The NCCHC (2014a,b) currently provides standards required for suicide prevention programs to follow, in order to maintain accreditation, with the following key components:

- *Training* should be provided for all staff to recognize verbal and behavioral cues that indicate potential suicide.
- *Identification* of ongoing risk should be made through routine and continuous risk assessments, especially at intake.
- *Referral* procedures should be specified, for suicidal inmates, to mental health-care providers or facilities.
- *Evaluation* should be conducted by a qualified mental health professional to determine risk level and the need for treatment of underlying mental illnesses.
- *Treatment* should address the underlying reasons for the inmate's suicidality.
- *Housing* should be safe and as suicide resistant as possible, with special attention to potential anchoring devices such as door hinges/knobs, air vents, and window frames; suicidal inmates should also not be placed in isolation unless constant supervision can be maintained
- *Monitoring* should be conducted at three levels based on status of risk: constant observation, with 1:1 monitoring; intermediate observation at intervals no longer than 5 minutes; and close observation in staggered intervals no longer than 15 minutes
- *Communication* should be ongoing between arresting/transporting officers, correctional staff, facility staff (including medical and mental health staff), and the at-risk individual for any signs or behaviors that may indicate a risk for suicide.
- *Intervention* procedures should address how to handle a suicide in progress, including how to cut down a hanging victim and other first-aid measures.
- *Notification* procedures should be in place for notifying prison administrators, outside authorities, and family members of potential, attempted, or completed suicides.
- *Reporting* procedures should be followed for documentation of the identification and monitoring of potential or attempted suicides.
- *Review* procedures for medical and administrative review in the event a suicide does occur.

- *Debriefing* provides individuals with an opportunity to discuss their thoughts and feelings about an incident.

Especially in local correctional facilities, where suicide rates are typically higher, suicide prevention has received a great deal of attention over the past few decades (Atlas 1989; Cox and Landsberg 1989; Cox et al. 1989; Haycock 1989; Hayes 1989; O'Leary 1989; Rakis and Monroe 1989; Sherman and Morschauser 1989). The combination of increased awareness of the problem and changes in institutional policy and practice have reduced the rates of suicide in jails and prisons by more than half since 1983 (Hanson 2010; Hayes 2012). According to the BJS, jail suicide rates dropped to their lowest in 2007 at 36 per 100,000 detainees but have increased slightly since to 43 per 100,000 in 2011 (Noonan and Ginder 2013). The suicide rate in prisons has remained fairly consistent between 2001 and 2011 at a rate of 14 per 100,000 prisoners, which is only slightly higher than the suicide rate for the general population (Noonan and Ginder 2013).

A comprehensive statewide program in New York enabled sheriff and police departments to dramatically reduce jail suicides (Cox et al. 1989) and has since been replicated in jails across the country. Applying a public health model to suicide prevention, this state-funded program is a simple and locally implemented scheme of staff training and procedure development for identifying and managing inmates at high risk of suicide, and is described in greater detail in Chapter 56.

As suicide rates have decreased, other trends and challenges have emerged that will require increased awareness and a potential change in protocols. One such trend is the increase in length of time of confinement before suicide occurs. Previously, research indicated that more than 50% of victims had died in the first 24 hours of confinement (Hayes 1983, 1989). The current trend reflects a much larger range: anywhere from 2 days to 4 months of confinement (Hayes 2012). This change is encouraging, in that it demonstrates the effectiveness of initial screening and prevention efforts; however, it also means that correctional staff need to remain vigilant and aware of potential suicidal indicators for a much longer period of time. Nevertheless, the first 72 hours of incarceration remain the focus of attention, especially since these typically include hours during the evenings or weekends when no clinical professionals are present. Suicide prevention also demands consistent staff emphasis on assessments by qualified mental health professionals and taking necessary precautions in handling patients with increased risks of self-harm (Hayes 2012).

As will be discussed in a subsequent section, active training and involvement of correctional staff is an essential component of correctional mental health. This tenet is especially true of suicide prevention. All staff, administrative and/or security, that have contact with inmates should undergo specific training in suicide risk assessment and intervention. Although the most common recourse for correctional staff will be to alert mental health personnel about an at-risk inmate, it is vital that they are at least cognizant of both risk factors and intervention strategies in the event that they become involved in a suicidal crisis situation. Laypersons without mental health training may harbor false beliefs regarding suicide potential. For example, many people wrongly believe that a person who is truly suicidal would never talk about it. Dispelling myths about suicide, and adopting an all-inclusive training policy for correctional personnel, can have a substantial impact on the psychological well-being of staff and inmates alike.

In addition to screening, essential aspects of a suicide prevention program include (1) clear policies and procedures governing the actions of all staff, including health care, mental health care, and custody staff; (2) an interdisciplinary suicide prevention committee; (3) investigation and quality improvement analysis of all serious attempts and completed suicides; and (4) assurance that all suicide watches are accomplished in a diligent and timely manner.

External hospitalization

Although access to hospitalization for emergency psychiatric treatment is essential, it is often unavailable, especially to smaller jails. The ability to obtain brief psychiatric inpatient care when necessary is of tremendous importance not only to the inmate requiring the transfer but also to the other inmates and staff. The goal of emergency hospitalization is to reduce severe psychiatric symptoms and stabilize the patient. Follow-up treatment should continue either in the correctional facility or, if pretrial release can be obtained, in the community.

Jails often use inpatient hospitals by transferring the detainee to an outside psychiatric hospital or ward. However, some jurisdictions such as San Diego, California (Meloy 1985), Los Angeles County, and Westchester County, New York, provide inpatient treatment within the local jail itself. Prison systems may house psychiatric inmates (who are unable to function adequately in the general population) at an off-site correctional facility whose purpose is to provide inpatient psychiatric care. Such facilities are staffed with correctional officers specially trained in mental health issues or psychiatric technicians with some correctional or security training. Regardless of context or locale, both jail and prison systems must have access to inpatient psychiatric services ranging from brief crisis intervention to longer-term psychiatric hospitalization.

Telemedicine

Telemedicine is essentially the transmission of electronic information, such as voice data and teleimages across geographically distant communication facilities, thereby allowing for long-distance patient health care and/or diagnosis (Charles 2000). Telemedicine has been used to enhance treatment options for geographically remote patients for almost six decades (Stevens et al. 1999). More recently, however, the rising cost of health care, including mental health care, and the increasing difficulty in recruiting and retaining psychiatrists have generated heightened interest in telemedicine and its promise of increased accessibility coupled with decreased cost. Technological advances (Mair and Whitten 2000) and decreasing implementation expenses (Strode et al. 1999) have enhanced the appeal of telecommunication as a viable alternate treatment modality.

Complications surrounding geographic isolation and limited access to mental health professionals familiar with the correctional setting may, at times, compromise care for inmates (Magaletta et al. 1998). In the correctional setting, access to any extra-institutional health-care service (psychiatric or otherwise) often requires extraordinary transportation and security expenses. Through telemedicine, correctional facilities, frequently located in remote areas, can minimize costly inmate transport, while concurrently allowing even the most dangerous inmates access to services in a secure environment (Charles 2000). Additionally, when telemedicine allows an inmate more timely access to psychiatric care, the likelihood of agitation and volatility may be reduced, thereby creating a more secure institutional environment for all correctional staff and inmates (Magaletta et al. 1998).

Stevens et al. (1999) reported that nonincarcerated patients and their treating psychiatrists were able to develop rapport via televideo just as well as when they were in the same room. Similarly, Morgan et al. (2008) found no differences in treatment satisfaction or inmates' perceptions of the therapeutic relationship when comparing a group receiving only tele-mental health to a control group receiving psychiatric services face to face. Further, preliminary data from the Federal Bureau of Prisons (BOP) telehealth pilot program indicated that virtually all inmate–patient participants, as well as treating psychologists and psychiatrists, have expressed satisfaction with telehealth services (Magaletta et al. 1998). The BOP telemedicine and telepsychiatry programs have been successful to such an extent that the Bureau is in the process of implementing telehealth technology system-wide (I. Grossman, personal communication, August 29, 2000). As of 2004, telemedicine and telehealth programs were operating in about half of all state correctional institutions and approximately 39% of federal institutions in the United States (Larsen et al. 2004). The Texas Department of Criminal Justice, Institutional Division, in conjunction with the University of Texas Medical Branch (UTMB) and Texas Tech University Correctional Managed Care organizations, has likewise enjoyed a successful telemedicine program. The UTMB region telepsychiatry division alone serves over 200 inmates per month and has received overwhelmingly positive responses from inmates and psychiatrists alike (R. Stanfield, personal communication, August 23, 2000; P. Nathan, personal communication, September 7, 2000).

Discharge planning

Discharge planning, also known as transition or reentry planning (American Association of Community Psychiatrists 2001), has become an important topic in the past decade as a result of several class-action lawsuits in correctional systems. A settlement was reached in 2003, as part of the *Brad H. v. The City of New* York (2000) class-action lawsuit, which specifically outlined appropriate steps for discharge planning for mentally ill inmates. Several states have expanded upon those requirements to include issues such as general health concerns (see *Foster v. Fulton County, Georgia* 2002) as well as drug and alcohol rehabilitation (see *United States of America v. Nassau County* 2001). Both the NCCHC and the APA also discuss the importance of adequate discharge planning and provide standards of care.

The logistics of implementing adequate procedures can be different for jails versus prisons due to differences in the lengths of stay as well as the unpredictability of discharge dates. For example, high turnover rates and shorter stays in jails require mental health professionals to begin discharge planning as soon as offenders are admitted (Dvoskin and Brown 2015). Although a great deal of variance exists between facility practices and policies, the primary purpose of any discharge planning procedure is to provide necessary and adequate resources in order for prisoners or detainees to safely return to the community. Discharge planning should begin as soon as a prisoner or detainee is identified as mentally ill, and continue throughout his or her stay. La Vigne et al. (2008) identified eight essential elements for discharge procedures:

- *Transportation* should be provided upon release to their destination as well as arrangements to ensure access to other locations mandated in their release plan, including transportation to obtain necessary medications.
- *Clothing, food, and amenities* should be provided or discussed, including clean and seasonally appropriate clothing and information for accessing food resources in the community.
- *Financial resources* should be provided to cover bare necessities including subsidized food, transportation, and shelter for the first several days after release.
- *Documentation* should be confirmed or provided in the form of a state-issued identification card.
- *Housing* should be identified that is safe and affordable for the first several days after release, and it should be confirmed that bed space is available prior to release.
- *Employment and education* assessments and referrals should be completed to assist the person in finding and maintaining employment.
- *Health care* facility/provider information in the community should be provided after an assessment of the person's mental and physical health-care status and needs in order to ensure continuity of care, and the person should be provided with enough medications to last until he or she can be seen by a health-care professional in the community; individuals with substance abuse or mental health issues should also have appointments scheduled with counselors in the community prior to release.

- *Support systems*, including family members and/or community- or faith-based organizations, should be provided with the offender's release date and plan in order to provide support after release, and a handbook listing community resources should also be provided.

Despite the best efforts of staff, many challenges still exist in transitioning offenders successfully and safely back into the community. A lack of funding and community resources is a common problem that can significantly affect the ability for released inmates to have their needs met (La Vigne et al. 2008). Another challenge is getting the cooperation and compliance of the offender, which can become more difficult when the offender's ability to manage his or her affairs has deteriorated after adjusting to life in confinement (Nelson and Trone 2000). Especially important is connecting inmates with entitlement programs such as Medicaid that can provide health care for indigent offenders after they are released, at least until they can gain access to employment and health insurance.

PSYCHOLOGICAL THERAPIES

Individual therapy

Environmental pressures inherent to the correctional setting can engender mental distress (Lindquist and Lindquist 1997). Even the most mentally healthy inmates may periodically find themselves in need of psychological services while incarcerated. Often, brief therapeutic contact is sufficient to alleviate situational stresses and transient difficulties encountered in the correctional setting. As previously discussed, case managers or social workers can be an invaluable resource for inmates in need of emotional support, information, or assistance with negotiating the daily demands of incarceration. In fact, the type of "therapy" most valuable to jail inmates is often provided by staff who lack formal training but who have a natural ability simply to treat others with dignity and humanity. Often, jail and prison inmates report that they were most helped through a crisis by a particular correctional officer or nurse, a chaplain, or even a fellow inmate. However, for inmates not formally assigned to a mental health caseload, case managers can serve as the first line of intervention, referring the inmate onward if more extensive service is warranted. Moreover, for short-stay inmates, tenure in jail may be an important opportunity for case managers to ensure appropriate referral to the social service or mental health service delivery system in the community.

For more extreme psychiatric crises, intervention might consist of longer sessions with higher-level mental health professionals. These sessions should focus on identifying personal strengths, which will help the inmate cope with the experience. Often, providing an understanding that others have gone through similar crises and survived can be reassuring. During periods of extreme psychological stress, a real part of the value of a therapist or counselor is to be a nonthreatening source of company. It is comforting simply to be listened to, especially in the middle of what may be perceived as an abusive experience. Inmates who experienced physical or sexual abuse or torture as children may experience incarceration as a reenactment of this trauma (Dvoskin 1990), and may be especially responsive to such support.

For those inmates suffering from severe mental illnesses, the immediate focus of therapy is to protect the inmate from deteriorating in response to the correctional environment. People with schizophrenia especially seem to have trouble adapting to environmental change and may require a great deal of support. One benefit of psychotherapy is to provide the seriously mentally ill inmate with a touchstone to aid in reality testing, to avoid withdrawal into psychosis in response to both real and imagined fears of staff or other inmates.

Group therapy

Group psychotherapy is the most cost-effective method of mental health treatment in corrections (Metzner et al. 1998). It is an ideal modality for providing much-needed services to large numbers of inmates despite the common paucity of resources. Moreover, group therapy sessions may be conducted independently, or be co-facilitated by mental health staff with varying levels of professional training. Creative and thoughtful matching of mental health staff expertise with the subject matter of the therapy group can be of great benefit. For instance, practical and applied topics, such as anger and stress management, are ideal material for correctional group work. Utilizing a staff psychologist (Masters or Doctoral level) in combination with a social worker or case manager affords participants with complementary balance in perspective and feedback. Alternately, a psychiatric nurse may be the ideal candidate to run a medication education or life skills group.

In the correctional setting, group therapy presents a unique set of challenges for participants and practitioners. Particularly when nondoctoral level practitioners facilitate groups, it may be quite useful to engage in active consultation and supervision processes (Morgan et al. 1999). For the participants, confidentiality is often a primary concern. Inmates must be counseled during pre-participation screening as to the importance of maintaining confidentiality of disclosures in the group setting. Other potential problem areas include security constraints, volatility and possible safety issues, and scheduling difficulties inherent to an institutional setting (Metzner et al. 1998).

Substance abuse

As many as 75% of all prisoners can be characterized as having a history of alcohol abuse or illicit drug use (U.S. Department of Justice 1999; James and Glaze 2006). The high rate of comorbidity between substance abuse or dependence and mental illness (Carey 1989) may be nowhere more apparent than among the offender population (Abram and Teplin 1991; Edens et al. 1997; Swartz and Lurigio 1999; James and Glaze 2006). Abram (1990) demonstrated the high prevalence of inmates with co-occurring disorders, including substance abuse and depression, most often with antisocial personality disorder being the primary syndrome.

For inmates with co-occurring mental health and substance abuse disorders, accurate diagnosis and subsequent treatment planning are complex, primarily as a result of the complicated symptom picture presented (APA 2015). Symptoms of one syndrome often mask those of another, and abuse of alcohol and other drugs can exacerbate psychiatric symptoms and even bring about psychotic episodes that may persist after intoxication subsides. The unfortunate result is that the presence of co-occurring disorder is often missed during the screening process (Edens et al. 1997).

Indeed, these co-occurring disorders are a growing concern among virtually all segments of the mental health system. The needs of the multiply-disordered population continue to rise and clearly must be addressed (Abram and Teplin 1991). The greater the relevance of substance abuse in an inmate's criminal background, the more important it is to identify and treat the problem, and to continue services upon release (Rice and Harris 1997). However, despite a growing number of treatment options, correctional facilities do not appear to have kept up with the demand for services (Metzner et al. 1998; Swartz and Lurigio 1999; Mears et al., 2002; Chandler et al. 2009). Toward the goal of improving treatment programming, the APA (2015) offers the following strategies to address the issue of co-occurring disorders in the correctional setting:

1. Integration of substance abuse and mental health treatment
2. Treatment of each disorder as primary, while appreciating potential interactions
3. Comprehensive assessment and consultation, focused on individualized planning for treatment of psychosocial issues and skill development
4. Cautious use of psychotropic medication
5. Context-specific interventions
6. Extension of treatment services into the community

STAFF TRAINING AND CONSULTATION

"One of the biggest barriers to care for offenders is the mutual distrust that exists between mental health providers and the community correctional system" (Roskes and Feldman 1999, 1615). Ongoing communication between mental health and correctional staff is an essential feature of effective treatment and intervention programs. Mentally ill offenders present a unique set of concerns in the correctional setting, and management difficulties may arise when correctional officers receive minimal or insufficient training about mental health issues (Versey et al. 1997).

Screening is essential to identify inmates and detainees in need of clinical attention upon arrival, and their subsequent mental health depends in large part on the ability of correctional officers to identify inmates in psychiatric distress and make appropriate referrals. It is therefore important to provide officers with basic training in identifying some of the signs of emotional disturbances, in addition to training the officers how to convey their observations to clinicians. With the well-documented rise in the number of mentally ill inmates nationwide, correctional staff are increasingly likely to be confronted with issues surrounding mental illness in the course of their daily work.

All new employee orientation processes should include a mental health component, presented by a member of the mental health staff. This training is certainly not meant to make diagnosticians of correctional officers, although correctional officers can supplement the efforts of clinicians by learning to assist inmates in coping with the everyday stresses of incarceration (Lombardo 1985). As has been discussed elsewhere in this chapter, staff training can be beneficial for all parties, particularly in facilitating the early recognition of psychiatric decompensation, suicide risk, and crisis intervention. Perhaps the most influential feature of facility-wide staff training, however, is an understanding of how to access available mental health resources when they are needed.

The importance of maintaining an open discourse and rapport between mental health and correctional staff cannot be overstated. The development of a trusting working relationship with officers allows mental health professionals the opportunity to offer opinions and/or suggestions that may diffuse potential psychiatric crises, thereby saving precious time, energy, and resources. Consultation between security and mental health staff will often revolve around the correctional management of inmates or detainees (Brodsky and Epstein 1982). A simple decision to separate two inmates can often prevent a dangerous assault or a psychiatric crisis, and administrators who learn to trust their clinical staff come to value advice in such decisions. Other common topics of consultation include, but are not limited to, assignment to appropriate housing or work detail, and appropriateness for various facility programs or educational opportunities.

Mental health staff have much to offer security personnel in terms of consultation and information sharing, and the benefits of communication are far from unilateral. Ensuring correctional personnel that their opinions and observations are meaningful and important, and welcomed by mental health staff, allows for virtually constant observation of inmate patients. Mental health staff are in direct contact with inmates for only a very brief period of time. Even those inmates participating in frequent therapy sessions still spend the vast majority of their days under the watch of correctional staff. Officers who observe and/or work with inmates on a daily basis often become very familiar with a given inmate's regular presentation. Therefore, officers are likely candidates to note subtle or progressive deterioration in an inmate's functioning. Allowing officers an opportunity to comfortably inform mental health staff of their concerns about an inmate is an effective method of heading off potential crisis.

Correctional officers can also be extremely helpful in teaching mental health staff about the stresses of day-to-day correctional life in cell blocks and housing units, and how to contribute to a safe institution. When training between correctional and mental health staff members is truly reciprocal, it helps to alleviate some of the natural tensions that occur. On the other hand, if mental health staff present themselves as having all of the answers, it can bolster the long-held myth that security and treatment are competitors. In fact, the opposite is true. Security and treatment are interdependent; without a safe environment, it is very hard to provide meaningful treatment, and without meaningful treatment, the correctional environment becomes more dangerous and unpredictable.

Finally, in addition to treating inmates, mental health professionals can help to reduce job-related stress among correctional line staff (Dembo et al. 1986–1987). Employing an open-door policy for correctional staff, providing literature on stress management, and/or offering consultation and referral services, allows officers an avenue of recourse when work stress becomes overwhelming. But providing mental health services to fellow employees is not recommended, due to the high likelihood of conflicting relationships. Essentially, all persons who live and work in a correctional facility are faced with similar daily stresses in terms of danger, noise, temperature, and the like. Extreme stress in officers may inherently compromise officer–inmate relations, in turn leading to exacerbation of inmates' psychological issues. Once again, open and active discourse, and simple human support may be among the most vital components of a successful program.

SPECIAL HOUSING AND MANAGEMENT OPTIONS

The most common reason for referral of an inmate to mental health services is disruptive or violent behavior, either toward self or others. Frequently, mental health staff will be asked to make a judgment about the level of supervision required to keep the inmate and others safe. Alternatives include transfer to a psychiatric facility, one-to-one or constant observation status, movement to a safer or more isolated cell, or movement to a cell nearer to the observation post maintained by staff.

Other creative approaches include the use of multibed dormitories for suicidal inmates. Company can help alleviate depression, and inmates who are ambivalent about their own suicidality may watch each other far more diligently than staff. Also, it is easier to watch a group of people in one room than in individual rooms.

It is important to be realistic. It is unfair and clinically inappropriate to order a 5-minute watch when the clinician knows there are inadequate staff to perform it. These orders are perceived by staff as an attempt by clinicians to shift responsibility to less well-paid correctional staff. By working together, it is usually possible to work out an arrangement that is both reasonable and clinically appropriate. For example, an order for constant observation could require three staff to observe three inmates in adjoining cells. An order worded "observe every minute," on the other hand, would allow one officer to walk back and forth, and observe all three inmates quite frequently.

For the very small percentage of inmates with severe mental illnesses whose behavior is extremely dangerous, states are increasingly creating secure treatment environments to provide a modified residential level of care. These specialized mental health programs should offer each inmate at least 10–15 hours of out-of-cell structured therapeutic activities per week and another 10 hours of out-of-cell recreational time per week (Metzner and Dvoskin 2006). There are varieties of methods to provide such treatment in a safe manner, which include the use of therapeutic modules, which are stand-alone enclosures somewhat similar to old fashioned telephone booths.

SPECIAL NEEDS INMATES

Minorities

For some ethnic minorities and non-English-speaking inmates, jails can be frightening and oppressive places. For example, Foster (1988) reports that traditional psychiatric approaches may not work well with Native Americans in the federal prison system. Similarly, among inmates with serious mental illnesses, Black and Hispanic inmates are typically less often served by the mental health system (Steadman et al. 1991). This phenomenon may reflect an unwillingness to seek help from predominantly white providers, reflect difficulties in speaking English as a second language, or a cultural practice to avoid seeking mental health assistance, but may also reflect subtle and even unintentional racism among those same providers. Toch et al. (1987) found a number of ethnic differences in prison infractions, and concluded that subcultural and psychological predispositions may converge to produce prison adjustment problems.

Women

Female detainees may have a variety of special problems in adapting to correctional settings (Sobel 1980). These include the possibility of pre-existing pregnancies, which require prenatal medical care, as well as recent mothers whose forced separation from their infant children can contribute to severe postpartum depression or even psychosis (see, e.g., McGaha 1986). Further, many more women than men are custodial parents at the time of their incarceration, often causing severe anxiety over the welfare of their children.

For some women, being locked up in a very small space by intimidating male authority figures can be frighteningly reminiscent of childhood experiences. For female inmates, especially those who have survived traumas, being strip-searched and showering under observation can seem abusive. Incarcerated females in New York frequently reported long histories of sexual violence at the hands of fathers, husbands, boyfriends, and strangers (Browne 1987). This abuse is often directly linked to the instant offense, as in the case of women who kill abusive spouses to protect themselves or their children.

Older inmates

The number of older inmates has increased rapidly since 1990, with an estimated increase of 550% (Williams et al. 2012). In the correctional context, due to histories of poor health care and multiple traumatic injuries, it has been suggested that age 50 years (rather than 65 as is the general population) can be considered a useful criterion for identifying geriatric inmates (APA 2015). Generally speaking, the offender population is likely to have conducted their lives in a manner less conducive to good physical health, thereby lowering the threshold for common ailments associated with aging. The elderly inmate is subject to the normal stresses of growing old, along with numerous exacerbating factors such as physical vulnerability to other inmates, estrangement or isolation, and a greater likelihood that they will die behind bars (APA 2015). As this subset of incarcerated offender continues to grow, so too will the incidence of age-related psychiatric and medical disorders. Correctional mental health professionals should be aware of, and plan for, the special needs of the incarcerated elderly.

Physical disabilities

Regardless of age, inmates—much like the general population—present with myriad medical and physical disabilities. Mental health service providers must be mindful of the special challenges posed to inmates who are physically disabled, deaf, or blind. This population may be especially vulnerable in a correctional setting. In addition to predatory peers, the occupational and recreational opportunities may be limited, exacerbating the normal stresses of incarceration. Although it has become clear that jails and prisons are covered by the Americans with Disabilities Act (ADA), the exact requirements of the ADA in prisons are still emerging. Many jails and prisons are composed of very old buildings with poor accessibility; however, staff must ensure that inmates have access to needed mental health and medical services, their physical disabilities notwithstanding (*Pennsylvania Dept. of Corrections v. Yeskey* 1989).

CORRECTIONAL HEALTH-CARE STANDARDS

Numerous sets of standards and guidelines for correctional health-care programs have been promulgated by national organizations such as the International Association for Correctional and Forensic Psychology (formerly the American Association of Correctional Psychology; 2010), American Bar Association (1989), American Correctional Association (2003), American Nurses Association (2013), APA (2015), American Public Health Association (Dubler 2003), National Commission on Correctional Health Care (1996, 1997, 1999, 2008), National Institute of Corrections (Anno 2001), and the United Nations (1975). There is a clear trend that the various state Departments of Correction (DOC) are attempting to conform to some national set of standards (Hayes 1989; Metzner et al. 1990; Metzner 1993; Hayes 2012).

The most current and widely referenced standards and/or guidelines for correctional mental health services have been published by the APA (2015) and the NCCHC (2014a,b). The NCCHC evolved from a program within the American Medical Association that published its first health-care standards for prisons and jails in 1979. The NCCHC standards focus predominantly on general health-care issues, although they have increased their focus on mental health issues in recent years (NCCHC 2008, 2014a,b). The guidelines developed by the APA task force, which assume compliance with the NCCHC standards, provide more specificity relevant to mental health services.

The American Correctional Association (ACA), through an annual Standards Supplement (ACA 2000), has significantly improved recommendations relevant to health services in correctional facilities. Although the ACA standards are less than comprehensive, they are to be applauded for current efforts to upgrade them. The ACA is in the process of developing performance-based standards that will, hopefully, expand the current (ACA 1989, 2000) recommendations pertinent to health-care standards.

It is beyond the scope of this chapter to compare the various national standards and guidelines. Such a comparison has been carried out by Metzner (1993) and Cohen (1998). This section will highlight common areas that are found in these national guidelines with brief commentary relevant to particularly difficult issues.

Guidelines provide a structure for correctional mental health systems by requiring the development of written policies and procedures that are to be reviewed/revised at least annually. They should include, but are not limited to, descriptions of the following characteristics of the mental health system (Metzner 1997):

- Mission and goals
- Administrative structure
- Staffing (i.e., personnel and training)
- Reliable and valid methods for identifying and tracking inmates with severe mental illness (best done via a computerized management information system)
- Availability of treatment programs
- Involuntary treatment, including the use of seclusion, restraints, forced medications, and involuntary hospitalization
- Other medico-legal issues such as informed consent, right to refuse medications, and record release authorizations
- Limits of confidentiality during assessment evaluations and/or treatment sessions with relevant exceptions noted

- Mental health record requirements
- Quality improvement plan
- Training of mental health staff regarding security issues
- Training of correctional staff concerning mental health issues
- Research protocols

The APA guidelines recommend that the fundamental policy goal for correctional mental health care is to provide the same level of mental health services to each patient in the criminal justice center that *should* be available in the community.

APA and NCCHC both support a correctional health-care system that integrates the medical, mental health, and dental systems under a central health-care authority (at the DOC central office level for prison systems). However, it is clear that a variety of different administrative models are effective, depending on a variety of factors, including the size and type of correctional population to be served. The importance of establishing medical autonomy relative to clinical decisions (i.e., not compromised by security reasons) and having regular administrative meetings between the health-care authority and the warden, sheriff, or official legally responsible for the correctional facility is emphasized by these standards.

The NCCHC recommends that staffing levels include a sufficient number of health services staff of varying types to assure timely inmate access to evaluation and treatment consistent with contemporary standards of care. The APA recognizes the importance of a multidisciplinary mental health staff. The need for adequate staffing by psychiatrists is also emphasized due to the unique importance of psychotropic medication as a treatment modality. The APA suggests that in jails, for every 75–100 inmates with serious mental illnesses who are receiving psychotropic medications, there be one full-time psychiatrist or equivalent. In prisons, with fewer admissions, the caseload of each full-time psychiatrist equivalent can rise to a maximum of 150 patients on psychotropic medications.

The APA recommends three levels of mental health screening for purposes of identifying newly admitted persons to the correctional facility:

- *Receiving screening*, which is frequently performed by trained custody staff upon booking, is a process designed to ensure that every newly arrived person who may require mental health evaluation is appropriately referred and placed in the proper living environment.
- *Intake mental health screening* is performed by appropriately trained health-care staff as part of the comprehensive medical evaluation provided to every inmate entering a correctional system.
- *Mental health evaluation* is performed by mental health staff in response to a referral from the screening process, other staff, or by self-referral.

The APA guidelines define mental health treatment as the use of a variety of mental health therapies, including biological, psychological, and social. Mental health treatment is described as occurring in a number of different settings, including

- Acute care (e.g., crisis intervention, infirmary care)
- Longer-term care
- Transitional care (e.g., residential treatment within the correctional facility)
- Outpatient treatment
- Inpatient hospital treatment

Program priorities described by the APA include recognizing and providing access to treatment for each inmate with serious mental illness and consulting with other health-care staff and correctional staff. Both the NCCHC and the APA discuss the importance of adequate discharge planning, which has also recently been the focus of class action litigation in correctional systems.

The NCCHC standards require regular review of inmates placed in segregation units for purposes of determining any medical contraindication for such placements and assuring reasonable access to needed health care. The APA guidelines expand these recommendations to include regular rounds by qualified mental health clinicians in all segregation housing units.

Compliance with the guidelines recommended by the APA task force report and the NCCHC standards will help ensure that the correctional mental health system is able to obtain necessary resources in order to provide adequate mental health services to the inmate population.

Segregation

Over the years, there has been a dramatic increase in the use of long-term segregation (Browne et al. 2011). It is suggested to be the result of a philosophical change in the management of problem inmates, with the underlying purpose of removing troublesome inmates in order to improve the level of safety of the general population (Riveland 1999; Collins 2004). Although this may be the best and only choice for certain inmates, such as when the safety of staff is at risk or for the most dangerous members of prison gangs, segregation should be used much less frequently and with greater caution. Metzner and Dvoskin (2006) recommend several elements to consider as emerging standards of care for the responsible use of segregation for the benefit of the inmates, the staff who oversee them, and as required by law: first, medical and mental health care is legally required and must be continued; second, a suicide prevention plan should be in place and inmates should be consistently monitored by mental health staff during rounds to detect dangerous psychological deterioration as early as possible; and third, incentive programs should be included where segregated inmates have the opportunity to improve and/or gain more control over their living conditions based on pro-social behavior that is definable, measurable, and achievable. Perhaps most importantly, segregation must truly be used only as a last resort when there is no other reasonable way to mitigate a serious threat to life safety, escape, or the safe and orderly operation of the facility

Long-term segregation for inmates with serious mental illness should be especially avoided, except for extraordinary circumstances, due to the potential physiological harm created by the extreme environment of segregation (APA 2012). Segregation can be very stressful from a mental health perspective, as it typically involves as many as 23 hours in a cell per day, little contact with staff, highly unusual and infrequent social interactions, extremes of noise and silence, and an environment of maximum control. Additionally, the use of segregation can further incapacitate inmates, who may already struggle with atrophied life skills due to their mental illness, from being able to healthily and successfully return to the community. For unusual circumstances that require segregation or an extremely high level of security of a mentally ill inmate for the safety of staff or others, Metzner and Dvoskin (2006) recommend adjusting conditions to include "at least 10–15 hours per week of out-of-cell structured therapeutic activities in addition to at least another 10 hours per week of unstructured exercise or recreation time" (p. 764).

The use of segregation in jails and prisons is controversial, and research on the long-term effects of segregation on mental health is sparse, conflicting, and typically not adequately designed to provide control groups for more meaningful analyses (see Suedfeld et al. 1982; Grassian, 1983; Zinger et al. 2001; Haney 2003). Recently, O'Keefe et al. (2013) found that most inmates, with or without mental illness, placed in long-term segregation housing did not experience significant psychological decline during their stay in segregation. However, inmates in segregation generally experienced more psychiatric symptoms than inmates not housed in segregation, which was largely related to their pre-segregation baseline. Of note, mentally ill inmates generally did not clinically improve while in segregation, which was very concerning, because many were experiencing active symptoms. Despite a paucity of empirical evidence, caution, careful planning, and an exhaustion of other resources should be used when deciding to place an inmate into prolonged segregation.

QUALITY IMPROVEMENT

For many reasons, a robust quality improvement system is an essential component of an adequate correctional mental system. Each facility or administrative authority should prepare a regularly updated quality improvement (QI) plan that systematically sets out to review and improve the quality of mental health services (APA 2015). Important elements of a QI system include quality assurance, peer review, and suicide prevention. The QI process should involve health-care staff at all levels as well as key correctional staff. Without active involvement from custody staff, QI efforts to improve relevant processes will be minimally effective at best. QI assessments frequently demonstrate that what is thought to be occurring in a correctional mental health system is very different from what is actually occurring.

SUMMARY

Jails and prisons are saturated with human service need, and the resources will probably never be adequate. Thus, administrators must take into account which services are most costly and sparse and use these resources judiciously.

Although prisons require a broad array of "community" mental health services, in jails and lockups, resources must be focused on short-term crisis services designed to identify, protect, and treat those inmates who are most vulnerable to suicide, injury, or severe psychological distress. The boundaries between the mental health and criminal justice systems are rarely clear (Dvoskin and Patterson 1998). Nevertheless, each setting and discipline must focus on the necessary interface of services that relate to its population and mission. To this end, active interdisciplinary discourse and cooperation are essential to maintaining the integrity and goals of the mental health and criminal justice systems. This chapter outlines the basic legal requirements for correctional mental health, provides an overview of effective treatment delivery, and proposes a structure for meeting those requirements in a cost-effective manner. Above all, resources must be used efficiently, so that each inmate has timely access to the essential services that the law and human decency require.

REFERENCES

Abram K 1990. The problem of co-occurring disorders among jail detainees: Antisocial disorder, alcoholism, drug abuse, and depression. *Law and Human Behavior* 14(4):333–345.

Abram K and L Teplin. 1991. Co-occurring disorders among mentally ill jail detainees, implications for public policy. *American Psychologist* 46(10):1036–1045.

Allen M. 2002. *Emergency Psychiatry*. Washington, DC: American Psychiatric Association.

American Association of Community Psychiatrists. 2001. ACCP attachment. http://communitypsychiatry.org/documents.aspx, accessed August 31, 2016.

America's Law Enforcement and Mental Health Project. 2000. 42 U.S.C. § 3796ii.

American Bar Association. 1989. *ABA Criminal Justice Mental Health Standards*. Washington, DC: American Bar Association. http://www.americanbar.org/publications/criminal_justice_section_archive/crimjust_standards_mentalhealth_toc.html, accessed February 10, 2015.

American Correctional Association. 1989. *Certification Standards for Health Care Programs*. Laurel, MD: American Correctional Association.

American Correctional Association. 2000. *2000 Standards Supplement*. Lanham, MD: American Correctional Association.

American Correctional Association. 2003. *Standards for Adult Correctional Institutions*, 4th edition. Alexandria, VA: American Correctional Association.

American Nurses Association. 2013. *Correctional Nursing: Scope and Standards of Practice*, 2nd edition. Silver Springs, MD: American Nurses Association.

American Psychiatric Association (APA). 1989. *Psychiatric Services in Jails and Prisons: Report of the Task Force on Psychiatric Services in Jails and Prisons*. Washington, DC: APA.

American Psychiatric Association (APA). 2000. *Psychiatric Services in Jails and Prisons*, 2nd edition. Washington, DC: APA.

American Psychiatric Association (APA). 2012. Position Statement on Segregation of Prisoners with Mental Illness. http://www.dhcs.ca.gov/services/MH/Documents/2013_04_AC_06c_APA_ps2012_PrizSeg.pdf, accessed August 31, 2016

American Psychiatric Association (APA). 2016. *Psychiatric Services in Correctional Facilities*, 3rd edition. Arlington, VA: APA.

American Psychiatric Association, Task Force on Outpatient Forensic Services. 2009. *Outpatient Services for the Mentally Ill Involved in the Criminal Justice System*. http://www.psych.org/learn/library—archives/task-force-reports, accessed February 10, 2015.

Anderson W, J Kuelmle, and D Catanzano. 1976. Rapid treatment of acute psychosis. *American Journal of Psychiatry* 133(9):1076–1078.

Anno B. 2001. *Correctional Health Care: Guidelines for the Management of an Adequate Delivery System*. Washington, DC: U.S. Department of Justice, National Institute of Corrections. http://www.americanbar.org/publications/criminal_justice_section_archive/crimjust_standards_mentalhealth_toc.html, accessed February 10, 2015.

Atlas R. 1989. Reducing the opportunity for inmate suicide: A design guide. *Psychiatric Quarterly* 60(2):161–171.

Axelson G and O Wahl. 1992. Psychotic versus nonpsychotic misdemeanants in a large county jail: An analysis of pretrial treatment by the legal system. *International Journal of Law and Psychiatry* 15(4):379–386.

Bowring v. Godwin, 55 1 F.2d 44 (4th Cir.) (1977).

Brad H v. City of New York, 185 Misc 2d 420 (Sup. Ct. N.Y. County) (2000).

Brodsky C and L Epstein. 1982. Psychiatric consultation through continuing education in correctional institutions. *Comprehensive Psychiatry 23*(6):582–589.

Browne A. 1987. *When Battered Women Kill*. New York: Free Press.

Browne A, A Cambier, and S Agha. 2011. Prisons within prisons: The use of segregation in the United States. *Federal Sentencing Reporter* 24(1):46–49.

Callahan L and H Wales. 2013. Applying mental health court research to practice [webinar]. *Counsel of State Governments* March 28. http://gainscenter.samhsa.gov/grant_programs/adultmhc.asp, accessed February 10, 2015.

Carey K. 1989. Emerging treatment guidelines for mentally ill chemical abusers. *Hospital and Community Psychiatry* 40(4):341–342, 349.

Carson E and D Golinelli. 2013. *Prisoners in 2012: Trends in Admissions and Releases, 1991–2012* (Report No. NCJ 243920). U.S. Department of Justice, Office of Justice Programs, Bureau of Justice Statistics. http://www.bjs.gov/index.cfm?ty=tp&tid=13, accessed February 10, 2015.

Chandler R, B Fletcher, and N Volkow. 2009. Treating drug abuse and addiction in the criminal justice system: Improving public health and safety. *Journal of the American Medical Association* 301(2):183–190. http://www.courtinnovation.org/sites/default/files/documents/Treating_Drug_Abuse.pdf, accessed February 10, 2015.

Charles B. 2000. Telemedicine can lower costs and improve access. *Healthcare Financial Management* 54(4):66–69.

Clark J. 2004. *Non-specialty First Appearance Court Models for Diverting Persons with Mental Illness: Alternatives to Mental Health Courts*. Delmar, NY: Technical Assistance and Policy Analysis Center for Jail Diversion. http://gainscenter.samhsa.gov/pdfs/jail_diversion/pre_trial_nocover.pdf, accessed February 10, 2015.

Cohen F. 1988. *Legal Issues and the Mentally Disordered Prisoner*. Washington, DC: National Institute of Corrections.

Cohen F. 1998. *The Mentally Disordered Inmate and the Law*. Kingston, NJ: Civic Research Institute.

Cohen R and J Dvoskin. 1992. Inmates with mental disorders: A guide to law and practice. Part II. *Mental and Physical Disability Law Reporter* 16(3–4):339–346.

Coleman R. 1998. How to keep the mentally ill out of jail. *Corrections Managers' Report* 4(3):11–14.

Coleman v. Wilson, 912 F. Supp. 1282 (E.D. Cal.) (1995).

Collins W. 2004. *Supermax Prisons and the Constitution: Liability Concerns in the Extended Control Unit*. Washington, DC: National Institute of Corrections. https://s3.amazonaws.com/static.nicic.gov/Library/019835.pdf, accessed February 10, 2015.

Cox J and G Landsberg. 1989. Introduction to special issue on jail suicide. *Psychiatric Quarterly* 60(1):3–6.

Cox J, G Landsberg, and M Paravotti. 1989. The essential components of a crisis intervention program for local jails: The New York local forensic suicide prevention crisis service model. *Psychiatric Quarterly* 60(1):103–117.

Dembo R, L Williams, and B Stafford. 1986–1987. The impact of providing mental health and related services at a youth detention center on staff stress. *Journal of Prison and Jail Health* 6(1):23–39.

Disability Advocates, Inc. v. New York State Office of Mental Health, No. 1:02-cv-04002 (S.D.N.Y.) (2007).

Draine J and P Solomon 1999. Describing and evaluating jail diversion services for persons with serious mental illness. *Psychiatric Services* 50(1):56–61.

Dubin W. 1988. Rapid tranquilization: Antipsychotics or benzodiazepines? *Journal of Clinical Psychiatry* 49(Supplement):5–12.

Dubler N. 2003. *Standards for Health Services in Correctional Facilities*, 3rd edition. Washington, DC: American Public Health Association.

Dvoskin J. 1989. The Palm Beach County, Florida, forensic program. In *The Mentally Ill in Jail. Planning for Essential Services*, edited by HJ Steadman, DW McCarty, and JP Morrissey, New York: Guilford Press, 178–197.

Dvoskin J. 1990. Jail-based mental health services. In *Effectively Addressing the Mental Health Needs of Jail Detainees*, edited by HJ Steadman, Boulder, CO: National Institute of Corrections, p. 75.

Dvoskin J and M Brown. 2015. Jails and prisons. In *Oxford Textbook of Correctional Psychiatry*, edited by RL Trestman, KL Appelbaum, and JL Metzner, New York: Oxford University Press, 31–34.

Dvoskin J and R Patterson. 1998. Administration of treatment programs for offenders with mental disorders. In *Treatment of Offenders with Mental Disorders*, edited by R Wettstein, New York: Guilford Press, 211–264.

Edens J, R Peters, and H Hills. 1997. Treating prison inmates with co-occurring disorders: An integrative review of existing programs. *Behavioral Sciences and the Law* 15(4):439–457.

Estelle v. Gamble, 429 U.S. 97 (1976).

Farmer v. Brennan, 511 U.S. 825 (1994).

Ford J, R Trestman, F Osher, J Scott, H Steadman, and P Robbins. 2007. *Mental Health Screens for Corrections*. Washington, DC: National Institute of Justice (NIS).

Ford J, R Trestman, V Wiesbrock, and W Zhang. 2007. Validation of a brief screening instrument for identifying psychiatric disorders among newly incarcerated adults. *Psychiatric Services* 60:842–846.

Foster D. 1988. Consideration of treatment issues with American Indians detained in the Federal Bureau of Prisons. *Psychiatric Annals* 18(12):698–701.

Foster v. Fulton County, Georgia, 223 F.Supp.2d 1301 (N.D. Ga.) (2002).

GAINS Center for Behavioral Health and Justice Transformation, Substance Abuse and Mental Health Services Administration. 2010. Getting inside the black box: Understanding jail diversion programs. Delmar, NY. http://gainscenter.samhsa.gov/cms-assets/documents/93753–443918.getting-inside-the-black-box.pdf, accessed February 10, 2015.

Gebbie K, R Larkin, S Klein, L Wright, J Satriano, J Culkin, and B Devore. 2008. Improving access to mental health services for New York state prison inmates. *Journal of Correctional Health Care* 14:122–135.

Gibbs J. 1987. Symptoms of psychopathology among jail prisoners: The effects of exposure to the jail environment. *Criminal Justice and Behavior* 14(3):288–310.

Glaze L. 2010. *Correctional Populations in the United States, 2009* (Report No. NCJ 231681). U.S. Department of Justice, Office of Justice Programs, Bureau of Justice Statistics. http://www.bjs.gov/content/pub/pdf/cpus09.pdf, accessed February 10, 2015.

Glaze L and E Herberman. 2013. *Correctional Populations in the United States, 2012* (Report No. NCJ 243936). U.S. Department of Justice, Office of Justice Programs, Bureau of Justice Statistics. http://www.bjs.gov/content/pub/pdf/cpus12.pdf, accessed February 10, 2015.

Grassian S. 1983. Psychopathological effects of solitary confinement. *American Journal of Psychiatry* 140:1450–1454.

Griffin P. 1990. The back door of the jail: Linking mentally ill offenders to community mental health services. In *Jail Diversion for the Mentally Ill. Breaking Through the Barriers*, edited by HJ Steadman, Boulder, CO: National Institute of Corrections.

Grossman I. 2000. Personal Communication with I. Grossman, Chief, Psychology Service, Federal Correctional Institution, Federal Bureau of Prisons, Phoenix, Arizona.

Grubbs v. Bradley, 821 F.Supp 496 (M.D. Tenn.) (1993).

Haney C. 2003. Mental health issues in long-term solitary and "supermax" confinement. *Crime and Delinquency* 49:124–156.

Hanson A. 2010. Correctional suicide: Has progress ended? *Journal of the American Academy of Psychiatry and the Law* 38:6–10. http://jaapl.org/content/38/1/6.full, accessed February 10, 2015.

Harris V and C Dagadakis. 2004. Length of incarceration: Was there parity for mentally ill offenders? *International Journal of Law and Psychiatry* 27:387–393.

Haycock J. 1989. Manipulation and suicide attempts in jails and prisons. *Psychiatric Quarterly* 60(1):85–98.

Hayes L. 1983. And darkness closes in: A national study of jail suicides. *Criminal Justice and Behavior* 10:461–484.

Hayes L. 1989. National study of jail suicides: Seven years later. *Psychiatric Quarterly* 60(1):7–29.

Hayes L. 1995. *Prison Suicide: An Overview and Guide to Prevention.* National Institute of Corrections http://static.nicic.gov/Library/012475.pdf, accessed February 10, 2015.

Hayes L. 2012. National study of jail suicide: 20 years later. *Journal of Correctional Health Care*18(3):233–245.

Hiday V and B Ray. 2010. Arrests two years after exiting a well-established mental health court. *Psychiatric Services* 61:463–468. http://journals.psychiatryonline.org/data/Journals/PSS/3909/10ps463.pdf, accessed February 10, 2015.

Hiday V, H Wales, and B Ray. 2013. Effectiveness of a short-term mental health court: Criminal recidivism one year postexit. *Law and Human Behavior* 37:401–411.

Hills H, C Siegfried, and A Ickowitz. 2004. *Effective Prison Mental Health Services: Guidelines to Expand and Improve Treatment*. Washington, DC: U.S. Department of Justice, National Institute of Corrections. https://s3.amazonaws.com/static.nicic.gov/Library/018604.pdf, accessed February 10, 2015.

Hudson v. McMillan, 112 S. Ct. 995 (1992).

Ind. Prot. & Advocacy Servs. Comm'n v. Comm'r, Ind. Dep't of Corr., 2012 U.S. Dist. LEXIS 182974 (S.D. Ind.) (2012).

International Association for Forensic and Correctional Psychology. 2010. Standards for psychology services in jails, prisons, correctional facilities, and agencies, 3rd edition. *Criminal Justice and Behavior* 37(7):751–808.

Jacoby J and B Kozie-Peak. 1997. The benefits of social support for mentally ill offenders: Prison-to-community transitions. *Behavioral Sciences and the Law* 15(4):483–501.

James D and L Glaze. 2006. *Mental Health Problems of Prison and Jail Inmates* (Report No. NCJ 213600). Washington, DC: U.S. Department of Justice, Office of Justice Programs, Bureau of Justice Statistics. http://www.bjs.gov/content/pub/pdf/mhppji.pdf, accessed February 10, 2015.

Jones M. 2015. Formative case law and litigation. In *Oxford Textbook of Correctional Psychiatry*, edited by RL Trestman, KL Appelbaum, and JL Metzner, New York: Oxford University Press, 13–17.

La Vigne N, E Davies, T Palmer, and R Halberstadt. 2008. *Release Planning for Successful Reentry: A Guide for Corrections, Service Providers, and Community Groups*. Washington, DC: The Urban Institute. http://www.urban.org/UploadedPDF/411767_successful_reentry.pdf, accessed February 10, 2015.

Lamb H and L Weinberger. 1998. Persons with severe mental illness in jails and prisons: A review. *Psychiatric Services* 49(4):483–492.

Langley v. Coughlin, F. Supp. 522, 538, 540–541 (S.D.N.Y. 1989) aff'd, 888 F.2d 252 (2d Cir.) (1989).

Larsen D, B Stamm, K Davis, and P Magaletta. 2004. Prison telemedicine and telehealth Utilization in the United States: State and federal perceptions of benefits and barriers. *Telemedicine Journal and e-Health* 10(2):S81–S90.

Lindquist C and C Lindquist. 1997. Gender differences in distress: Mental health consequences of environmental stress among jail inmates. *Behavioral Sciences and the Law* 15(4):503–523.

Lombardo L. 1985. Mental health work in prisons and jails: Inmate adjustment and indigenous correctional personnel. *Criminal Justice and Behavior* 12(1):17–27.

Madrid v. Gomez, 889 F. Supp. 1146 (ND CA) (1995).

Magaletta P, T Fagan, and R Ax. 1998. Advancing psychology services through telehealth in the Federal Bureau of Prisons. *Professional Psychology: Research and Practice* 29(6):543–548.

Mair F and P Whitten. 2000. Systematic review of patient satisfaction with telemedicine. *British Medical Journal* 320:1517–1520.

Maloney M, J Dvoskin, and J Metzner. 2015. Mental health screening and brief assessments. In *Oxford Textbook of Correctional Psychiatry*, edited by RL Trestman, KL Appelbaum, and JL Metzner, New York: Oxford University Press, 57–61.

Martin M, L Colman, A Simpson, and K McKenzie. 2013. Mental health screening tools in correctional institutions: A systematic review. *BMC Psychiatry* 13:275.

McGaha G. 1986. Health care issues of incarcerated women. *Journal of Offender Counseling, Services, and Rehabilitation* 12(1):53–59.

McNiel D and Binder, R. 2007. Effectiveness of a mental health court in reducing criminal recidivism and violence. *American Journal of Psychiatry* 164(9):1395–1403. http://ajp.psychiatryonline.org/data/Journals/AJP/3830/07aj1395.PDF, accessed February 10, 2015.

Mears D, L Winterfield, J Hunsaker, G Moore, and R White. 2002. *Drug Treatment in the Criminal Justice System: The Current State of Knowledge*. Washington, DC: Urban Institute Press. http://www.urban.org/uploadedpdf/410618_NIDA1_KnowledgeRpt.pdf, accessed February 10, 2015.

Meloy J. 1985. Inpatient psychiatric treatment in a county jail. *Journal of Psychiatry and Law* 13(3–4):377–396.

Metzner J. 1993. Guidelines for psychiatric services in prisons. *Criminal Behavior and Mental Health*, 3(4):252–267.

Metzner J. 1997. An introduction to correctional psychiatry: Part I. *Journal of the American Academy of Psychiatry and the Law* 25(3):375–381.

Metzner J. 2012. Treatment for prisoners: A U.S. perspective. *Psychiatric Services* 63(3):276.

Metzner J and J Dvoskin. 2006. An overview of correctional psychiatry. *Psychiatric Clinics of North America* 29(3):761–772.

Metzner J, G Fryer, and D Usery. 1990. Prison mental health services: Results of a national survey of standards, resources, administrative structure, and litigation. *Journal of Forensic Sciences* 35(2):433–438.

Metzner J, F Cohen, L Grossman, and R Wettstein. 1998. Treatment in jails and prisons. In *Treatment of Offenders with Mental Disorders*, edited by RM Wettstein, New York: Guilford Press, 211–264.

Miller et al. v. French et al. (99–224), 178 F.3d 437 (2000).

Miller N and L Najavits. 2012. Creating trauma informed correctional care: A balance of goals and environment. *European Journal of Psychotraumatology* 3:17246.

Mirsky K. 1988. Antisocial personality, substance abuse disorders, and depression in an urban county jail. Doctoral dissertation. Chicago: Northwestern University.

Moore M and V Hiday. 2006. Mental health court outcomes: A comparison of re-arrest and re-arrest severity between mental health court and traditional court participants. *Law and Human Behavior* 30(6):659–674.

Morgan R, A Patrick, and P Magaletta. 2008. Does the use of telemental health alter the treatment experience? Inmates' perceptions of telemental health versus face-to-face treatment modalities. *Journal of Consulting and Clinical Psychology* 76(1):158–162.

Morgan RD, C Winterowd, and S Ferrell. 1999. A national survey of group psychotherapy services in correctional facilities. *Professional Psychology: Research and Practice* 30(6):600–606.

Muzekari L C Lonigan, A Hatton, and C Rowe. 1999. Mental health services in the county jail: A critical partnership? *Psychological Reports* 84(3c):1099–1104.

Nathan P. 2000. Personal communication with P. Nathan, M.D., Associate Division Director, Texas Department of Criminal Justice-Health Services, Huntsville, Texas.

National Commission on Correctional Health Care. 2008. *Standards for Health Services in Jails.* Chicago: National Commission on Correctional Health Care.

National Commission on Correctional Health Care. 2014a. *Standards for Health Services in Jails.* Chicago: National Commission on Correctional Health Care.

National Commission on Correctional Health Care. 2014b. *Standards for Health Services in Prisons.* Chicago: National Commission on Correctional Health Care.

Nelson M and J Trone. 2000. *Why Planning for Release Matters.* New York, NY: Vera Institute of Justice.

Noonan M and S Ginder. 2013. *Mortality in Local Jails and State Prisons, 2000–2011. Statistical tables* (Report No. NCJ 242186). Washington, DC: U.S. Department of Justice, Office of Justice Programs, Bureau of Justice Statistics. http://www.bjs.gov/content/pub/pdf/mljsp0011.pdf, accessed February 10, 2015.

Office of National Drug Control Policy. 2013. *Arrestee Drug Abuse Monitoring Program II: 2012 Annual Report.* Washington, DC. http://www.whitehouse.gov/sites/default/files/ondcp/policy-and-research/adam_ii_2012_annual_rpt_final_final.pdf, accessed February 10, 2015.

O'Keefe M, K Klebe, J Metzner, J Dvoskin, J Felner, and A Stucker. 2013. A longitudinal study of administrative segregation. *Journal of the American Academy of Psychiatry and the Law* 41(1):49–60. http://www.jaapl.org/content/41/1/49.long, accessed February 10, 2015.

O'Leary W. 1989. Custodial suicide: Evolving liability considerations. *Psychiatric Quarterly* 60(1):31–71.

O'Neil J and E Wish. 1990. *Drug Use Forecasting Research Update* (Report No. NCJ122564). Washington, DC: U.S. Department of Justice, Office of Justice Programs, National Institute of Justice. https://www.ncjrs.gov/pdffiles1/Digitization/122564NCJRS.pdf, accessed February 10, 2015.

Pennsylvania Dept. of Corrections v. Yeskey. 524 U.S. 206 (1989).

Petrich J. 1976. Rate of psychiatric morbidity in a metropolitan county jail population. *American Journal of Psychiatry* 133(12):1439–1444.

Pinals D and Andrade, J. 2015. Applicability of the recovery model in corrections. In *Oxford Textbook of Correctional Psychiatry,* edited by RL Trestman, KL Appelbaum, and JL Metzner, New York: Oxford University Press, 217–222.

Pogrebin M. 1985. Symposium: The crisis in mental health care in our jails: Jail and the mentally disordered: The need for mental health services. *Journal of Prison and Jail Health 5(1)*:13–19.

Prison Litigation Reform Act. 1996. 18 U.S.C. Section 3626 (b)(2).

Rakis L and R Monroe. 1989. Monitoring and managing the suicidal prisoner. *Psychiatric Quarterly* 60(2):151–160.

Rice M and G Harris. 1997. The treatment of mentally disordered offenders. *Psychology, Public Policy and Law* 3(1):126–183.

Riveland C. 1999. *Supermax Prisons: Overview and General Considerations.* Washington, DC: National Institute of Corrections. https://s3.amazonaws.com/static.nicic.gov/Library/014937.pdf, accessed February 10, 2015.

Roskes E and R Feldman. 1999. A collaborative community-based treatment program for offenders with mental illness. *Psychiatric Services* 50(12):1614–1619.

Ruiz v. Estelle, 53 F. Supp. 1265 (S.D. Texas) (1980).

Salzman C, A Green, F Rodriguez-Villa, and G Jaskiw. 1986. Benzodiazepines combined with neuroleptics for management of severe disruptive behavior. *Psychosomatics* 27(1):17–22.

Sherman L and P Morschauser. 1989. Screening for suicide risk in inmates. *Psychiatric Quarterly* 60:119–138.

Smith L. 1989. Medication refusal and the rehospitalized mentally ill inmate. *Hospital and Community Psychiatry* 40(5):497–502.

Sobel S. 1980. Women in prison: Sexism behind bars. *Professional Psychology* 11(2):331–338

Stanfield R. 2000. Personal communication with R. Stanfield, BS, CSWII, University of Texas Medical Branch Correctional Managed Care, Huntsville, Texas.

Steadman H. 1990. *Jail Diversion for the Mentally Ill: Breaking Through the Barriers.* Boulder, CO: National Institute of Corrections.

Steadman H, S Barbera, and D Dennis. 1994b. *Developing Effective Jail Mental Health Diversion Programs.* Delmar, NY: Policy Research Associate.

Steadman H, S Fabisiak, J Dvoskin, and E Holohean. 1987. A survey of mental disability among state prison inmates. *Hospital and Community Psychiatry* 38(10):1086–1090.

Steadman H, E Holohean, and J Dvoskin 1991. Estimating mental health need and service utilization among prison inmates. *Bulletin of the American Academy of Psychiatry and the Law* 19(3):297–307.

Steadman H, D McCarty, and J Morrissey. 1989. *The Mentally Ill in Jail. Planning for Essential Services*. New York: Guilford Press.

Steadman H, S Morris, and D Dennis. 1995. The diversion of mentally ill persons from jails to community-based services: A profile of programs. *American Journal of Public Health* 85(12):1630–1635.

Steadman H and M Naples. 2005. Assessing the effectiveness of jail diversion programs for persons with serious mental illness and co-occurring substance use disorders. *Behavioral Sciences and the Law* 23(1):163–170.

Steadman H, A Redlich, L Callahan, P Robbins, and R Vesselinov. 2011. Effect of mental health courts on arrests and jail days: A multisite study. *Archives of General Psychiatry* 68(2):167–172.

Steadman H, J Scott, F Osher, T Agnesa, and P Robbins. 2005. Validation of the brief mental health screen. *Psychiatric Services* 56:816–822.

Steadman H, S Steadman-Barbera, and D Dennis. 1994a. A national survey of jail diversion programs for mentally ill detainees. *Hospital and Community Psychiatry* 45(11):1109–1113.

Steadman H, M Williams-Deane, JP Morrissey et al. 1999. A SAMHSA research initiative assessing the effectiveness of jail diversion programs for mentally ill persons. *Psychiatric Services* 50(12):1620–1623.

Stevens A, N Doidge, D Goldbloom, P Voore, and J Farewell. 1999. Pilot study of televideo psychiatric assessments in an underserviced community. *American Journal of Psychiatry* 156(5):783–785.

Strode S, S Gustke, and A Allen. 1999. Technical and clinical progress in telemedicine. *Journal of the American Medical Association* 281(12):1066–1068.

Substance Abuse and Mental Health Services Administration (SAMHSA). 2014. *SAMHSA's Concept of Trauma and Guidance for a Trauma-Informed Approach*. HHS Publication No. (SMA) 14-4884. Rockville, MD: Substance Abuse and Mental Health Services Administration. http://store.samhsa.gov/shin/content/SMA14-4884/SMA14-4884.pdf, accessed February 10, 2015.

Suedfeld P, C Ramirez, J Deaton, and G Baker-Brown. 1982. Reactions and attributes of prisoners in solitary confinement. *Criminal Justice and Behavior* 9:303–340.

Swartz J and A Lurigio. 1999. Psychiatric illness and comorbidity among adult male jail detainees in drug treatment. *Psychiatric Services* 50(12):1628–1630.

Teplin L and J Swartz. 1989. Screening for severe mental disorder in jails. *Law and Human Behavior* 13(1):1–18.

The Center for Health and Justice at TASC. 2013. *No Entry: A National Survey of Criminal Justice Diversion Programs and Initiatives*. Chicago: Center for Health and Justice at TASC.

Toch H, K Adams, and R Greene. 1987. Ethnicity, disruptiveness, and emotional disorder among prison inmates. *Criminal Justice and Behavior* 14(1):93–109.

United Nations, Fifth United Nations Congress on the Prevention of Crime and the Treatment of Offenders. 1975. *Health Aspects of Avoidable Maltreatment of Prisoners and Detainees*. New York: United Nations.

U.S. Department of Justice. 1999. *Mental Health Treatment of Inmates and Prisoners* (Report No. NCJ-174463), Washington, DC: U.S. Department of Justice.

U.S. District Court, Eastern District Court of New York. 2001. Settlement Agreement, *United States of America v. Nassau County Sheriff's Department*. http://www.justice.gov/crt/about/spl/documents/Nassa_sher_agreem.php, accessed February 10, 2015.

Valdiserri E, K Carroll, and A Hartl. 1986. A study of offenses committed by psychotic inmates in a county jail. *Hospital and Community Psychiatry* 37(2):163–166.

Versey B, H Steadman, J Morrissey, and M Johnsen. 1997. In search of the missing linkages: Continuity of care in U.S. jails. *Behavioral Sciences and the Law* 15(4):383–397.

Walmsley R. 2013. *World Prison Population List*, 10th edition. London: International Centre for Prison Studies. http://www.prisonstudies.org/sites/prisonstudies.org/files/resources/downloads/wppl_10.pdf, accessed February 10, 2015.

Williams B, M Stern, F Mellow, M Safer, and R Greifinger. 2012. Aging in correctional custody: Setting a policy agenda for older prisoner health care. *American Journal of Public Health* 102(8):1475–1481.

Wilson v. Seiter, 111 S. Ct. 2321 (1991).

Zinger I, C Wichmann, and D Andrews. 2001. The psychological effects of 60 days in administrative segregation. *Canadian Journal of Criminology* 43:47–83.

53

The architecture of correctional mental health law

FRED COHEN AND JAMES L. KNOLL

CONSTITUTIONAL SOURCE FOR RIGHT TO MENTAL HEALTH CARE

There is no explicit mention of a right to health care in the U.S. Constitution. If there were it is doubtful that persons in penal confinement would be singled out as recipients when no other persons are accorded this valuable benefit. In *Estelle v. Gamble* (1976) the U.S. Supreme Court determined that within the confines of the Eighth Amendment's prohibition against Cruel and Unusual Punishment prisoners did have an implicit right to medical care. The court limited that right to *serious* medical conditions and avoidance of the unnecessary and wanton infliction of pain. There is a certain logic to the coupling of treatment and the avoidance of pain given the location of the right in the Eighth Amendment. The court has since included pretrial detainees within the scope of that right, relying on the Fourteenth Amendment's Due Process Clause. Detainees may not be punished at all, while prisoners may be punished, just not in a cruel and unusual fashion.

No generalized right to treatment for prisoners was provided by the court, only a right to not suffer *deliberate indifference* in the failure or delay in providing needed care or in how such care was offered for *serious* ailments. *Estelle v. Gamble* involved a claim to inadequate medical care for a back injury suffered by a Texas inmate. Oscar Gamble, in a sense, won the doctrinal battle but lost on his personal claim. The care might have been better, opined Justice Marshall, but it did not descend to the depths of deliberate indifference, the enigmatic culpable mental state fashioned by the court. Justice Marshal did not define deliberate indifference; that would await the 1994 decision in *Farmer v. Brennan* (1994). He did indicate that a claim of negligent care (or malpractice) was not the equivalent of the cruelty; the wanton and needless infliction of pain protected against by the Eighth Amendment (*Estelle v. Gamble* 1976).

With *Estelle v. Gamble*, and subsequently *Farmer v. Brennan*, U.S. corrections has witnessed the launching and then the propelling of a judicially discovered and now judicially policed and enforced constitutional (i.e., national) right of prisoners to correctional health care. Deliberate indifference as a culpable mental state is equated with recklessness, and thus is located between negligence (inadvertence) and intent (acting deliberately to achieve a proscribed result). Deliberate indifference as recklessness subscribes to the more difficult to prove version of recklessness in that it requires actual knowledge of a serious risk rather than the less demanding version that asks whether a defendant knew or should have known of the risk.

There are now thousands of judicial decisions involving the claims of pretrial detainees and convicted inmates that their serious mental health needs were in some fashion violated. Indeed, it is the case that "Inmate lawsuits and court rulings have been the impetus for change for inmate health care delivery and continue to be the principal source of corrections health policy" (Kinsella 2004). Persons in penal confinement may seek damages for failed care or join in a federal class action claim alleging systemic failure and the need for a systemic, curative remedy. The latter are the game-changing cases in the sense that broad, future-oriented relief is required, and it is often very expensive. Clinical staff is to be hired, training required, buildings renovated or constructed, segregation housing and practices altered, records refined, medication revised, and more depending, of course, on the individual case (Cohen 2008, 2011).

THE LIMITS OF CRUEL PUNISHMENT AS A SOURCE OF RIGHTS

The Eighth Amendment prohibits cruel and unusual punishment (U.S. Constitution Amendment VIII). It has been persuasively argued that the normative force of the Eighth Amendment derives from the word "cruel" (Dolovich 2009). Punishment of the convicted in the sense of the intentional infliction of pain *is* constitutionally permissible. It is *cruel* punishments that are condemned. The Eighth Amendment also has force where punishments are grossly disproportional to the offense, totally without penological justification, or involve the needless and wanton infliction of pain (Dolovich 2009).

The denial of medical, dental, and mental health care as cruel punishment must find its constitutional mooring in the needless and wanton infliction of pain and suffering. Consider for a moment the linguistic and operational differences of a hypothetical, constitutional right to health care for prisoners: *All persons in civil or penal confinement shall be guaranteed access to such health care as will preserve life, health, and dignity.* If enacted, there would, of course, be contentious debates regarding a particular diagnosis or whether a particular modality of care was best adapted to preserve life and dignity. Americans turn to the courts for the interpretation and enforcement of such claims relatively more than residents of other nations (U.S. Department of Human and Health Services 2008). The judicial battles to develop and enforce an affirmative source of the claim (or right), however, would likely be far different than the current situation, where correctional health-care law is extruded as a series of positive requirements derived from a negative injunction regarding cruel punishments.

Inmates with mental illness have had some success in the courts leading to prohibitions and limitations on their being confined in penal isolation (or segregation, solitary, restricted housing) (Cohen 2011). The foundation of such decisions is the recognition that inmates with mental illness suffer more acutely than others. Juveniles have gained similar victories with "special vulnerability" also at the basis of such decisions.

European prisons are also experiencing a significant increase in the number of prisoners with mental illness and share the difficulties experienced in American prisons in providing adequate care (World Health Organization [WHO] 2007). With mental health care viewed as a human right and as a protection for the community, the WHO posits the standard of care for prison treatment as the equivalent of that available in the community (WHO 2007).

The WHO narrative on the essentials of prisoner mental health care is not so different than similar narratives from the United States. The glaring difference is that needs are not expressed in terms of the avoidance of pain, and the standard of care bears no resemblance to the strictures of the United States' judicially invented culpable mental state of deliberate indifference. In addition, there is scarcely a mention of the judiciary in the European scheme of things, while for the United States the judiciary is the creator, interpreter, and enforcer of correctional mental health care (Gordon and Lindqvist 2007; Salize et al. 2007). In sum, the right to correctional health care in the United States, obviously including mental health care, was judicially created from a constitutional amendment prohibiting cruel punishment and as a judicial creation; its future contours and enforcement will also likely depend on the judiciary.

SPECIAL POPULATIONS IN PRISONS

Special population groups, with their varying special needs, are those prisoners who exhibit unique physical, mental, social, and programmatic needs that distinguish them from other prisoners, and for whom staff should respond in a therapeutic, rehabilitative, or supportive fashion (Stojkovic 2005). Recall that the constitutional right to correctional health-care treatment extends only to *serious* medical and mental health conditions. Thus, the constellation of special populations far exceeds the boundaries of the medical model of mandated treatment. Further, there is no constitutional right to rehabilitation (not even clearly so for juveniles). To the extent that certain special needs groups require rehabilitative or vocational help, there is simply no constitutional hammer to swing (Cohen 2008). As examples of special populations, female inmates, the elderly, and juveniles will be discussed.

Female inmates

Female inmates have certain relevant needs that stand out, primarily by way of contrast with males. Females, for example, enter prison with symptoms of clinical depression that far exceed the rate of males, they often are the mothers of young children and remain attached to them in ways many male inmates do not, and they also have a very high rate of involvement with drugs (Bloom et al. 2003; Ward 2003).

"Special needs" membership for females requires heightened attention to abuse factors and trauma during the intake screening phase, and also requires programs that are responsive to such needs. There is no constitutional right to such programs by virtue of gender (Cohen 2004). Females and males are governed by the same constitutional principles governing medical care, but those principles are significantly different operationally (*Monmouth Co. Correctional Institution Inmates v. Lanzaro* 1984). For example, the National Council on Crime and Delinquency reported that some 8649 pregnancies existed in the group of female inmates, or about 9% of the population. In addition, female jail detainees won a right to elective abortion in *Monmouth Co. Correctional Institution Inmates v. Lanzaro* (1984).

There were 111,300 females incarcerated in federal and state prisons as of December 2013 (Carson 2014). There has been a dramatic increase in arrests and incarceration of females since the mid-1970s. No single theory seems to explain this increase, especially at a time when overall crime rates are falling.

The high rate of presenting mental illness in female inmates supports an argument that there should be heightened concern about their needs at initial reception and classification. It seems possible, if not likely, that future litigation will import many of these needs where care is mandated, or through an argument that an anticipatory–preventive response is required.

Older inmates

Older (over age 55) prisoners, numbering 124,400 in state and federal prisons, are somewhat similarly situated to female prisoners. Age alone creates no prison-based constitutional entitlements, but age does present a variety of special needs as to housing and medical–mental health care. Attorney Nancy Dubler and Dr. Budd Heyman point out:

> Socioeconomic status and lack of access to preventive and acute medical and dental care may create as much as a 10-year aging differential to the prisoner. Nationally, the number of inmates 55 and older more than doubled from 1981 to 1990. Estimates are that the number of prisoners over age 50 will reach 125,000 by the year 2000 with 40,000 to 50,000 being over age 65. Given the hyperaging phenomenon of the inmate population, many of these prisoners will be aged and infirm with multiple medical problems. These problems, if they mirror the general population, will include kidney failure, diabetes, cancer, heart disease, dementias, and the other degenerative diseases that fill geriatric practices and long-term care facilities.
>
> Were these abstractions not sufficiently troubling, caring for geriatric inmates is likely to be extremely expensive. Estimates for the care of an elderly inmate range from $60,000 – $69,000 per year, in contrast to about $20,000 per year for non-elderly inmates without AIDS. The majority of these monies cover the costs of medical treatments and medications, special equipment for the handicapped, special education, recreation and work programs, prison hospital beds, and special facilities needed to protect the frail and elderly in the violent prison world. (Dubler and Heyman 2006)

Older prisoners as a group possess at least the same legal rights as other prisoners to medical and mental health care and safe housing. As a group, however, they will require much more, and specialized, care than others, and they are ripe for inclusion in the "special needs" category (Curran 2000). As a group, they also represent the type of problems that prison litigation can highlight and resolve on their behalf. At the policy level, there is the nagging question of why some very old, often infirm, inmates are kept in prison.

Juveniles

At the other end of the age spectrum are juveniles, persons under the age of 18, who constitute just 11,300 (Deitch et al. 2009; Sedlak 2010) inmates out of 2,266,800 total prisoners. Imprisoned juveniles, by virtue only of their age-based status, like females and older inmates, may not now actually have a separate category of legal rights, but their claims are quantitatively different and in a few instances—for example, psychological developmental needs, preventive dental care, large muscle exercise, dietary needs—they may be distinct. Knowledge of their special needs, then, sharpens the existing need to screen, diagnose, and then provide the special care and protection dictated by youth. The special developmental circumstances of youth dictate a far more protective and proactive style than is needed for adults.

Health services for juveniles also present a separate category of needs. Dr. Michael D. Cohen points out:

> The particular health needs of young adults are largely related to the physical, emotional, cognitive, and behavioral consequences of puberty. Impulsive behavior results in high incidence of trauma, sexually transmitted diseases, unintended pregnancy, and suicide among adolescents. Asthma is the most common chronic medical condition, but there are a wide variety of childhood chronic illnesses with a prevalence of one per thousand or less, which may be regularly found in youth served by juvenile justice programs. In addition, chronic problems often begin in adolescence, and health staff must be alert to the onset of a significant symptom to facilitate an early diagnosis and initiate treatment. (Cohen et al. 2006)

There will, of course, be special problems related to consent to medical procedures or medication, special claims to large-muscle exercise based on developmental needs, education on nutrition, concern for abnormal growth patterns, and the like. Given the phenomenon of juveniles being waived to adult criminal courts, it seems likely that the question must eventually be addressed regarding whether juveniles in the adult penal system have a particularized and unique legal right to treatment (or anything else) based on their youth. Juveniles confined within the "civil" juvenile justice system do not have a well-founded constitutional claim to treatment (*Miletic v. Natalucci-Persichetti* 1992; *Alexander S. By and Through Bowers v. Boyd* 1995). What is at best a legally anemic claim within the juvenile justice system will not likely gain in strength for juveniles in adult prisons. Advocates certainly may argue that without early intervention and preventive care, juveniles will likely develop mental and physical disorders. The claim has a ring of plausibility and perhaps should be judicially tested by legal advocates. For now, however, juveniles in adult correctional facilities must meet the serious medical need or deliberate indifference requirements for medical and mental health care. Recognizing the characteristics of adolescence noted above should give those claims a certain priority and lead to earlier interventions and a plausible legal claim to a preventive strategy.

A CONSTITUTIONAL SYSTEM OF CORRECTIONAL MENTAL HEALTH CARE

Extracting the affirmative duties required of custodians and the corresponding rights for the confined from a constitutional source that forbids cruel punishment carries with it inherent limitations on the nature and scope of the duties on government and rights of the confined.

Nevertheless, anchored to the threshold requirements of a serious illness, and limited by a highly restrictive standard for measuring compliance—deliberate indifference—the key elements of a system have emerged. It is important to keep in mind that penal custodians and care providers are held only to the deliberate indifference standard that requires *actual knowledge* of risks for constitutional liability to attach. Thus, it has been argued that the court has encouraged the practice of not seeking and pursuing facts related to risks (Thompson 2010).

The *Estelle* constitutional mandate for correctional health care is a blessing and a mild curse. The ruling carves out mental health and medical care but, as noted earlier, omits many other confined populations desperately in need of care and at the mercy of state legislators and correctional administrators. This leads, for example, to compartmentalizing substance abuse treatment from mental health care when it is perfectly obvious they coexist in a large percentage of prisoners and would benefit from coordinated treatment. *Estelle* does not inevitably create a divide between medical and mental health care, and there is a strong case for the institutional melding of such services (Burns 2016).

With "seriousness" as the constitutional threshold for mandated care, those diagnosed with personality or character disorders may be regarded as less deserving of treatment than those with serious mental illness (SMI) (Ader et al. 2012). Given an approach to treatment driven by legal norms that tend to fragment care, even mandated medical and mental health care typically are treated as separate entities. Here, of course, there is a shared mandate to treat the seriously ill, but compartmentalized thinking then separates two treatment constellations where an integrated approach would make much more sense. This division, analogous to silo compartments, becomes a way of thinking even when there is a shared mandate. For the elderly, women, and youthful offenders, the separation evolves from the legal boundaries that exist, and it will likely ultimately require different policy decisions to remedy their neglected needs.

CUSTODY AND RECEPTION

The constitutional obligation to provide correctional health care is welded to the requirement of actual, penal custody. In *DeShaney v. Winnebago County Dept. of Social Services*, the Supreme Court established actual physical custody as the beginning of the duty of care and also its termination (*DeShaney v. Winnebago* 1989). Without custody, whether it be pretrial detainee status in jail or convicted in prison, there is no obligation to provide care or protection. Although there are differences in the populations of those confined in jail versus those in prison, the legal principles for providing constitutionally mandated care are the same. Detainees derive their rights from the Due Process Clause of the Fourteenth Amendment, while the convicted inmates' rights derive from the Eighth Amendment. Further, whereas jail is a more crisis-oriented care facility, prison will have longer, chronic care obligations (Cohen 2008; Cohen 2011).

As for process, the custodial treatment obligation most clearly begins at the point of reception, with the focus on intake screening and evaluation for security, suicide risk information, and health care, including mental health care. With many detainees and prisoners entering the penal confinement system with mental illness, deliberate indifference may apply where a particular mentally ill individual goes undetected and untreated as a result of a failure to screen or evaluate. The risks from not screening are so high, and the potential consequences so significant, that these risks cannot be dodged by omission. In the same sense that actual knowledge may not be subverted by turning one's back to the obvious, to not hearing the scream for help by closing the door, no jail or prison system may constitutionally operate without screening and evaluation.

The following points are a distillation of the leading standards on reception and intake:

1. *Receiving mental health screening*: Done immediately on admission through brief observation and structured interview. At this point in the process, the screening necessarily casts a wide net. Any suicide ideation or history of hospitalization, for example, leads to further assessment.
2. *Intake screening*: Trained staff makes further inquiry into relevant factors, usually as part of the obligatory comprehensive medical evaluation. This is more extensive than the receiving stage but does not approximate the intensity and professionalism required in the next stage.
3. *Evaluation*: A comprehensive examination by a qualified mental health professional, using clinical interviews, histories, psychological testing, and clinical judgment. Usually conducted only if the inmate screens positive, a "positive hit" at stage 1 or 2 or if the inmate clearly presents with a major illness (Psychiatric Services 2002; American Correctional Association Standards 2003 and NCCHC 2003). Typically, correctional institution policy or legally driven mandates require that such evaluations be conducted within a specific time frame, most commonly within a 2-week period.

The importance of adequate screening and initial evaluation cannot be overstated. Inadequate or misleading information accompanies the inmate and increases the likelihood of an early adverse outcome. The risk of mental and physical deterioration begins at the front door and may remain uninterrupted by adequate care until a tragic outcome occurs (Dlugacz 2015).

ADEQUATE STAFF, BED SPACE, AND ACCESS

This triad of components may be considered the basic foundation of correctional mental health care. However, there is no specific number or an agreed upon formula for determining constitutionally adequate staff or bed space. Indeed, adequacy itself will likely be determined by the timely access to care component: Do inmates requiring mental health care gain ready access to persons properly trained and certified to diagnose and treat, and is there adequate bed (or treatment) space to accommodate the treatment and housing needs of treatment-eligible inmates?

If a lawsuit is to be settled, then the parties will agree, or the court likely will order, fixed numbers of staff and beds, usually with a time frame for compliance. One example of such an approach is *Dunn v. Voinovich*, where the parties agreed to suspend formal discovery until an independent examination of Ohio's prison mental health care could be completed and results provided to the court. The results of the independent evaluation became the basis for a settlement, and the settlement in the form of a Consent Decree included specific requirements as to staff and bed space. The parties used ratio formulas to arrive at the specifics and importantly agreed that the mental health needs of female inmates were significantly greater than those of males and that a significant upward adjustment was required (DeCou 2001). The parties agreed to a certain number of patient beds, treatment space, and mental health staff. The *Dunn* case illustrates how a lawsuit anchored to the generalities of the Eighth Amendment and the evolving standards of *Estelle v. Gamble* and *Farmer v. Brennan* can morph into a specific set of legally enforceable mandates. Staff and bed space aside, it is the dynamic concept of access to such care that ultimately determines the efficacy of proposed remedies. Where staff and beds may be counted and, thus, objectified, access can be evaluated only by studying the pathways an inmate must negotiate to obtain care.

ISOLATION OF INMATES WITH MENTAL ILLNESS

The Bureau of Justice Statistics (BJS) does not have data on the number of prisoners held in solitary confinement. However, it is clear that reliance on such confinement varies from state to state and that a significant number of the two-plus million people in our jails and prisons are held in such confinement. Isolation units exist within various prisons and may be called control units, special management units, high-security units, administrative segregation, or disciplinary segregation. A supermax prison, in turn, qualifies as an isolation entity unto itself (Cohen 2006). There is some variability in the degree of social and psychological isolation. The most extreme form of isolation, at times referred to as "dark cells," consists of inmates held in solitary confinement and subject to social isolation and near total sensory deprivation by lack of access to light, sound, or fresh air.

Such "first-degree isolation" is characterized by near complete sensory and social deprivation, and remains in scattered instances. What might be termed "second-degree isolation," similarly having roots in the early history of American corrections, is far more common. This form of isolation (often called "segregation") has inmates housed typically in single cells with solid doors for 23 hours a day, with limited access to outside light and air, able to hear some movements outside their cell, and even yell or "tap" (in code) as communication. Meals are taken alone in the cell; exercise is indoors and very restricted, as is access to programs, visits, telephone, radio, television, and showers, and reading material is substantially limited. This is characteristic of the isolation or segregation units noted above and the typical supermax units.

"Second-degree" isolation, or solitary confinement, thus conveys a set of circumstances beyond life in a single, quiet cell. It definitionally includes deprivation of social interaction, the rudimentary sights and sounds of life, and basic decision making in life's most mundane choices. As one moves from such isolation to the still deprived world of ordinary prison conditions, an uncertain line is crossed that divides isolation from the mere harsh conditions of penal confinement. The critical factors in this divide would be out-of-cell time, congregate activity, exercise or "yard time," and access to work and available programs. Put another way, the greater the social isolation and sensory deprivation, the more eligible the unit for being labeled as penal isolation (Cohen 2011). Whether approached as a human rights issue or empirically as the cause of needless, often serious harm, extreme social and sensory deprivation is the subject of contentious debate (Goode 2012). The issue becomes more clearly subject to condemnation where the issue of inmates with serious mental illness in isolation is concerned (Haney 2003; Grassian 2006).

There is no judicial decision finding segregation, even long-term segregation, unconstitutional per se. However, there are several decisions that bar, or severely limit, its use with the psychologically vulnerable and those with SMI (*Madrid v. Gomez* 1995; *Jones 'El v. Barge* 2001; *Austin v. Wilkinson* 2002; *Presley v. Epps* 2005). These decisions are not identical in their reasoning; however, they display common themes. Once the decision is reached that longer-term penal isolation is prohibited for inmates who are, or are at risk of becoming, SMI, there is typically a debate over what diagnostic categories warrant exclusion. What used to be considered Axis I disorders under the *Diagnostic and Statistical Manual of Mental Disorders*, 4th edition (*DSM-IV*) would be automatically included. Other populations typically considered for exclusion from longer-term penal isolation include

1. Inmates at high risk for suicide
2. Inmates diagnosed with an organic brain syndrome resulting in significant functional impairment
3. Inmates diagnosed with a severe personality disorder associated with frequent episodes of psychosis or depression and resulting in significant functional impairment
4. Inmates diagnosed with any other serious mental illness or disorder that is worsened by confinement at supermax or segregation

In *Jones' El v. Berge*, the Federal District Court Judge opined that the question of adequate treatment for the mentally ill at Wisconsin's supermax need not even be deliberated, because the conditions themselves were unconstitutional, and no amount of treatment would cure the deficit. A University of North Carolina School of Law study concluded that "The Constitutional protections against cruel and unusual punishment, when considered against the volume of expert findings, must be said to prohibit solitary confinement, as does the Due Process clause.... solitary confinement is ineffective at decreasing violence within prisons; it is ineffective at preserving public safety; it is ineffective at managing scarce monetary resources; and it violates the boundaries of human dignity and justice" (University of North Carolina School of Law 2014). American Bar Association standards have described the isolation of inmates with SMI as "simply inhumane" (ABA 2011). Various states (New York, Ohio, Illinois) have adopted exclusionary rules for the vulnerable populations, to include those with SMI, in their policy and procedures. However, in the authors' experience, such rules not uncommonly fall short of effective in real-world practice and conditions.

OTHER RELEVANT ISSUES

There are a host of other issues relevant to the evolving correctional landscape and commonly vetted by the courts.

Records

Is a modern electronic records system constitutionally required? An electronic record system clearly is desirable, but certainly not required. Regarding constitutionality, the determinative question is the impact on continuity of care. Records are often a significant factor in the concept of continuity of care. With inmate–patients constantly on the move and staff regularly in flux, having decent medical records available when required becomes essential. The significance of records relates most importantly to the quality and continuity of care, and legal challenges to records to be successful must link inadequacy to failure in care.

Consent

Prisoners have a liberty interest in the privacy and security of their bodies (*Washington v. Harper* 1990; *Doe v. Delie* 2001). As a general proposition, inmates must consent to the use of psychotropic medication, although in the case of a genuine emergency there may be room for involuntary medication either for treatment or, less likely, for control. In an emergency situation, in jail or prison, where a prisoner represents an acute danger to himself or herself or others, forcible medication on the spot with no prior hearing is permitted.

Consent is an aspect of personal autonomy, and a fundamental principle of medical ethics. Informed consent requires the individual possess (1) voluntariness of choice, (2) understanding and access to the relevant information, and (3) mental competence to make the decision at issue (Appelbaum 2007). The issue of consent most often arises in the setting of an inmate patient's refusal of psychiatric treatment. Many incidents of treatment refusal are not due to a lack of treatment capacity, but rather to a host of other clinical factors, such as poor therapeutic alliance, inadequate time spent with the patient, objection to specific medication side effects, previous bad experiences with treatment, and fear of the stigma of receiving psychiatric treatment (Buckley et al. 2003). It is when the patient's lack of treatment capacity is truly illness or symptom related that the option of involuntary treatment should be considered.

In this last resort option, many facilities will follow the *Washington v. Harper* (USSC 1990), internal administrative panel model of satisfying the patient's due process rights to refuse treatment. However, the clinician should be aware that individual states may require more stringent standards, such as New York State, which requires a full judicial hearing for inmate–patients who require involuntary treatment (*Rivers v. Katz* 1986). The legal criteria for treatment capacity vary by jurisdiction, and there are no widely accepted curricula on how to evaluate treatment capacity (Kim 2010). Current practice is typically guided and delimited by state laws.

The legal development of informed consent has stressed a functionalist model of competence—which holds that the individual's capacity is determined by demonstrable abilities, as opposed to diagnoses or other psychiatric labels. At the same time, researchers have developed a set of interpretations based on these laws over the past three decades. The "Four Abilities" model developed by Appelbaum and Grisso has seen widespread acceptance in practice (Grisso and Appelbaum 1998). This model is based on a review of statutes, case law, and research data, and requires careful assessment of the following abilities: (1) the ability to understand information relevant to the decision; (2) the ability to appreciate the individual's situation and its consequences; (2) the ability to manipulate the relevant information rationally; and (4) the ability to express a stable, voluntary choice (Grisso and Appelbaum 1998).

Disciplinary hearings

Disciplinary hearings (intra-facility hearings to determine the consequences of disciplinary infractions by inmates) are often conducted by a senior correctional officer in the presence of corrections staff and the inmate. Punishment for disciplinary infractions may involve a "sentence" of anywhere from 2 weeks in a disciplinary segregation unit to reclassification followed by months to years in a supermax unit. Disciplinary hearings have very serious consequences for mentally ill offenders (Knoll 2008). Inmates with mental illness are more likely to be charged with rule violations than inmates without mental illness, and therefore have an increased rate of disciplinary infractions and placement in punitive segregation (Toch and Adams 1986; Lovell et al. 2000; James and Glaze 2006). The mentally ill inmate charged with a disciplinary infraction may or may not be entitled to mental health consultation or expert testimony, owing to the fact that there is considerable variability in how hearings are conducted, as well as the criteria and procedure for placing inmates in administrative segregation.

In a nationwide survey, considerable diversity among states was found regarding the role of mental health staff in disciplinary hearings (Krelstein 2002). Most states had policies on the issue, but there was no clear consensus on whether mental health staff should offer "ultimate opinions" regarding competency or sanity in the disciplinary process. In addition, the role of the clinician in these hearings may raise concerns about the dual agency dilemma (Metzner 2002). According to the National Commission on Correctional Healthcare recommendations: "the services of outside providers or someone on the institutions staff who is not involved in a therapeutic relationship with the inmate should be obtained" for such proceedings (APA 2000). This is analogous to the ethical bind in which the psychiatrist acts as both treating physician *and* forensic evaluator, and is generally to be avoided (AAPL 2005). If at all possible, the clinician should make efforts to adhere to this policy to avoid harming the treatment relationship. Testimony by an uninvolved clinician may be critical, as the severely mentally ill patient is not likely to be able to effectively advocate for himself or herself or explain his or her mental state at the time of the offense with the same impact as a trained clinician.

Given the trend of large numbers of inmates with SMI, as well as the growing recognition that this population should be kept out of punitive segregation, it seems likely that the need for mental health testimony at disciplinary hearings will become an increasingly formalized process. As usual, legal mechanisms will drive most changes. For example, in *Anderson v. Coughlin* (1987), inmates in several New York Department of Corrections' Secure Housing Units (SHU) alleged, *inter alia*, that their due process rights had been violated by the way that disciplinary hearings were conducted. In 2002, a private settlement agreement regarding the disciplinary due process issue was reached, resulting in amendments to the New York Department of Corrections' SHU regulations. The agreement required specific criteria be used by hearings officers in determining when an inmate's mental state or intellectual capacity is at issue during a hearing. Further, testimony is required by correctional mental health staff to address (1) the extent to which the inmate's current mental health status affects his or her fitness to proceed with the hearing, (2) the extent to which the inmate's mental status at the time of the incident did or did not affect his or her responsibility for the offense, and (3) the extent to which the inmate's current mental health status or clinical history make him or her suitable or unsuitable for SHU placement.

A second example comes from the California Department of Corrections and Rehabilitation (CDCR) in the case of *Coleman v. Brown* (2013). In *Brown*, it was found that mentally ill inmates who acted out were treated with punitive measures without regard to their mental status, or whether the conduct was the result of mental illness. As a result, the CDCR agreed to implement policies and procedures concerning mental health input into the inmate disciplinary process. Part of the process involves an assessment by mental health staff to determine: (1) Are there any mental health factors that would cause the inmate to experience difficulty in understanding the disciplinary process and representing his or her interests in the hearing that would indicate the need for the assignment of a staff assistant? (2) Did the inmate's mental disorder appear to contribute to the behavior? (3) If the inmate is found guilty of the offense, are there any mental health factors that the hearing officer should consider in assessing the penalty? In both *Anderson* and *Coleman*, mental health staff who testify at inmate disciplinary hearings must be trained to do so, and their testimony is subject to review and quality assessment by senior mental health administrators. Although there are nuanced differences, mental health testimony at disciplinary hearings may be roughly analogized to a criminal forensic evaluative process into corrections. As mental health considerations increasingly require attention in disciplinary proceedings (and pre-hearing diversion decisions), the issue of enhanced training for hearing officers has already become a requirement in disciplinary hearing settlement agreements.

SUICIDE

Suicide is nearly always singled out from the larger package of issues related to correctional mental health (*Disability Law Center v. Massachusetts Department of Corrections* 2012). In jurisdictions where general mental health training for staff may be virtually nonexistent, there are almost always a couple of hours of training on suicide prevention, including signs, prevention, observation, cut-down tools, and resuscitation techniques.

In some facilities, suicide observation involves a form of punitive practice, such as placing the inmate with little to no clothing in a cold, dark cell for indeterminate periods. The inmate may be placed in a bare cell for observation, and kept there for days without any sort of treatment. This obviously punitive reaction should be condemned regardless of the clinical status of the inmate. Rather, endorsements of suicidal intent should be treated as occasions for clinical assessment and intervention as needed.

As for suicide attempts and self-injurious behavior, every jurisdiction should have policy and procedure that clearly delineate between a suicide attempt and a gesture and collect and analyze this data. A useful guide to addressing suicide prevention generally can be found in the American Psychiatric Association Handbook (Simon and Hales 2006), while suicide prevention in correctional settings is addressed in Chapter 56. Correctional suicide prevention policy and procedure must be informed by evidence-based research, current methods of clinical suicide risk assessment, and reliable communication between relevant corrections staff (Knoll 2010).

Theories of liability

There are three primary theories of liability available in constitutionally grounded custodial suicide cases:

1. Failure to provide appropriate medical or mental health care for a serious ailment
2. Failure to provide a non-life-threatening (or safe) environment, translated to a "failure to protect"; and,
3. Failure to train

The first two theories are by far the most popular and at their core represent very different conceptions of the cause of a suicide and the duties allegedly breached. In both instances, deliberate indifference must be shown (Cohen 2011). It should be kept in mind that such suits alleging constitutional violations may be brought in addition to state wrongful death or survival actions, the latter being grounded in ordinary tort law and based on negligence.

A serious mental illness calls for responsive treatment, and when such treatment does not occur or is rendered with deliberate indifference, liability may exist. The duty here, of course, is responsive treatment with a goal to at least ameliorate the illness and prevent the suicide. An inmate may not be known to be mentally ill; for example, an arrestee demonstrating odd or unusual behavior with no known history of mental illness. The jailers' duty in such a case is to act preventively and not necessarily provide treatment. This means a "safe cell" and observation with no immediate, concomitant duty to treat (*Taylor v. Wausau* 2006).

Custodial suicide cases brought in federal court are notoriously difficult for plaintiffs to win. The cases falter on the actual knowledge of risk aspect of deliberate indifference. There must be clear, unambiguous evidence of a serious risk, and where this exists, it still may fall short of deliberate indifference. For example, in *Freedman v. City of Allentown* (1988), arrestees with "hesitation marks" on their throat and who were known to have made an attempt at this same jail were found not to present an imminent serious risk. Litigating individual cases for damages has not had the impact on change that class action, structural injunction lawsuits have. The latter decisions invariably require enhanced training on the subject and require staff to screen and take seriously threats of suicide (Settlement Agreement in *Disability Law Center v. Massachusetts Department of Corrections*).

Another example of the difficult challenge faced by plaintiffs in correctional suicide cases is the U.S. Supreme Court case of *Taylor v. Barkes*, a *per curiam* decision by the Court (*Taylor v. Barkes* 2015). In this case, an intake nurse had learned of a recent suicide attempt by Barkes, as well as his history of psychiatric treatment. Her failure to request enhanced observation did not amount to deliberate indifference. The court held that, at least as of 2004, there was no violation of clearly established law applicable to Delaware detention officials who likely failed to employ adequate suicide screening procedures that could have prevented Barkes' custodial suicide. This legal predicate suggests that the government officials sued in this case may successfully plead qualified immunity as a defense to any supervisory failures regarding the private contractor employed to deliver mental health care. While this decision appears to lower the legal bar for suicide preventative measures, good practice would still dictate proper screening and observation–treatment measures in accord with any perceived risk.

PRISON OVERCROWDING AND INMATES WITH MENTAL ILLNESS

In *Brown v. Plata* (2011), the U.S. Supreme Court issued a five to four decision that is the court's most important decision impacting correctional health care at least since *Farmer v. Brennan* in 1994. Justice Kennedy, writing for the slender majority, noted that the plaintiffs, an inmate class, had convincingly shown that the excessive overcrowding in the California prison system was the primary cause of the unconstitutional denial of medical and mental health care. The decision rests importantly on the language of the Prison Litigation Reform Act (PLRA), which requires a finding of "overcrowding as primary cause" and that no other relief short of the population reduction actually ordered will remedy the violation of the federal right to adequate health care.

In addition, there had to be failed previous orders less intrusive than population reduction orders, and in the case of *Brown v. Plata*, there had been many such failed orders. The lawyers for the inmates made an overwhelming showing on each of these requirements. What some have labeled a "prisoner release" order is actually a prisoner population reduction order. That is, the court upheld the lower courts' decision to require a total prison population not to exceed 137.5% of rated capacity within a 5-year period of time. This involved a reduction of some 46,000 prisoners, but California was allowed to transfer some inmates to local jails, provide for enhanced good time credits leading to a somewhat earlier release, or even build new facilities. In sum, the doors to California's prisons were not suddenly opened.

The overcrowding was linked to the cause of inadequate health care. Its relief, then, simply cleared the path to hiring adequate numbers of treatment staff, creating an adequate number of beds that were varied as to the conditions treated, and assuring reasonable access by eligible inmates to staff and bed space. As Justice Kennedy pointed out, constitutional violation in cases of conditions of confinement rarely are susceptible to a simple or straightforward solution. He pointed to budget shortfalls, a lack of political will, and systemic administrative failures (*Brown v. Plata* 2011). The California prison dilemma can thus be likened to a spider web, such that when one pulls on a single thread, the entire web is redistributed in a new and complex pattern. Indeed, this is the case in many state prison systems.

California's prison reduction, which fell by 15,493 persons from 2010 to 2011, constituted the most significant prisoner reduction in the nation in that period. A "Realignment" plan, effective October 1, 2011, now promises to be the most ambitious correctional reform in the nation, and with a significant impact on health care. Realignment transfers significant numbers of convicted felons from the state prison and parole systems to the state's 58 counties. This includes nearly all drug and property crimes (Petersilia and Cullen 2014–2015). Jails accustomed to providing crisis care now house offenders serving as many as 10 years, which means chronic health care is on the agenda, and despite some state funding, the jails seem remarkably unprepared as to physical plant, staffing, training, and culture.

SUMMARY

A Council on State Governments Report notes, "Today the most widely accepted policy is to provide inmates with a community standard of care. The community standard of care is based on the level of care someone in the community would receive" (Kinsella 2004). This may be aspirational but it most certainly is not accurate. Indeed, in *Estelle v. Gamble* it was plain that injured inmate Gamble would (or should) receive much more in the way of diagnostic testing if his back injury occurred in the community. It may be accurate to state that a medical procedure or intervention will likely be measured by the "standard of practice," but as for level of care, there is great variation across the country, because the Eighth Amendment proscription against cruelty is a limiting verbal device for an expansive right to treatment. Further, federal courts vary greatly on the norms and enforcement measures for required mental health care. One solution may be to establish a Federal Commission to draft a Uniform Code of Correctional Mental Health Care—essentially a legislative approach to standardizing and subsidizing correctional health care through the federal government.

In sum, the right to correctional mental health care in the United States flows from the Eighth Amendment's proscription against cruel and unusual punishment. Both *Estelle v. Gamble* and *Farmer v. Brennan* establish the inmate's right to medical care—albeit for serious conditions and the avoidance of the unnecessary infliction of pain. Yet the subjective test of deliberate indifference specified in *Farmer v. Brennan* sets an exceptionally high bar, essentially undercutting any generalized right to treatment for prisoners.

SUMMARY KEY POINTS

- The right to correctional mental health care in the U.S. derives from the 8th Amendment's proscription against cruel and unusual punishment.
- The constitutional right to correctional healthcare extends only to serious medical and mental health conditions.
- No generalized right to treatment for prisoners was provided by Estelle v. Gamble, only a right to not suffer deliberate indifference in the failure or delay in providing needed.
- *Farmer v. Brennan* set forth a subjective test for the recklessness required for deliberate indifference—the 8th amendment is violated only if the defendant in question knows there is a substantial risk of harm, yet disregards this risk.
- Deliberate indifference represents a more difficult to prove version of recklessness because it requires actual knowledge of a serious risk.
- The subjective recklessness required by deliberate indifference may encourage a practice of not seeking and/or pursuing facts related to risks.
- A widely espoused policy is to provide inmates with a community standard of care; however, this may be more aspirational than actual.

REFERENCES

Ader M, R Cuthbert, K Hoechst, EH Simon, Z Strassburger, and M Wishnie. 2012. *Casting Troops Aside: The United States Military's Illegal Personality Disorder Discharge Problem.* Silver Spring: Vietnam Veterans of America. http://www.theveteran.org/PPD-Documents/WhitePaper.pdf, accessed July 27, 2016.

Alexander S. *By and Through Bowers v. Boyd*, 876 F. Supp 773 (D.S.C. 1995).

American Academy of Psychiatry and the Law. 2005. *Ethics Guidelines for the Practice of Forensic Psychiatry.* http://www.aapl.org/ethics/htm, accessed July 27, 2016.

American Bar Association. 2011. *ABA Standards for Criminal Justice, Treatment of Prisoners*, 3rd edition. Chicago: American Bar Association.

American Correctional Association. 2003. *American Correctional Association Standards. Standards 4–4368, 4–4370*, 4th edition. Alexandria, VA: American Correctional Association.

American Psychiatric Association (APA). 2000. *Psychiatric Services in Jails and Prisons: A Task Force Report of the American Psychiatric Association*, 2nd edition. Washington, DC: APA.

Anderson v. Coughlin, (N.D. N.Y.) (1987).

Appelbaum, P. 2007. Clinical Practice. Assessment of patients' competence to consent to treatment. *New England Journal of Medicine* 357(18):1834–1840.

Austin v. Wilkinson, no. 4:01-CV-71 (N.D. Ohio) (2002).

Bloom B, B Owen, and S Covington. 2003. *Gender-Responsive Strategies: Research, Practice, and Guiding Principles for Women Offenders*. US Department of Justice, National Institute of Corrections. Washington, DC: GPO. http://static.nicic.gov/Library/020418.pdf, accessed July 27, 2016.

Brown v. Plata, 131 S. Ct. 1910 (2011).

Buckley PF, SG Noffsinger, DA Smith, DR Hrouda, and J Knoll. 2003. Treatment of the psychotic patient who is violent. *Psychiatric Clinics of North America* 26:231–272.

Burns K. in press. Coordinating physical and mental health care—Why? why now? How? In *Correctional Health Care: Practice, Administration, and Law*. Kingston, NJ: Civic Research Institute.

Carson A. 2014. *Prisoners in 2013. Office of Justice Programs, Bureau of Justice Statistics*. Washington, DC: U.S. Department of Justice.

Cohen F. 2004. The limits of judicial reform of prisons: What works, what does not. *Criminal Law Bulletin* 1(40):19–22.

Cohen F. 2006. Isolation in penal settings: The isolation-restraint paradigm. *Washington University Journal of Law and Policy* 22:295–324.

Cohen F. 2008. *The Mentally Disordered Inmate and the Law*. Kingston, NJ: Civic Research Institute.

Cohen F. 2011. *Practical Guide to Correctional Mental Health and the Law*. Kingston, NJ: Civic Research Institute.

Cohen M, L Burd, and M Beyer. 2006. Health services for youth in juvenile justice programs. In: *Clinical Practice in Correctional Medicine*, 2nd Edition, edited by M Puisis. Philadelphia, PA: Elsevier, 120–143.

Coleman v. Brown, 938 F. Supp.2d 955, 974, n.35 (E.D.Cal.) (2013).

Curran N. 2000. Blue Hairs in the Bighouse: The rise in the elderly inmate population, its effect on the overcrowding dilemma and solutions to correct it, 26 New England. *Journal on Criminal and Civil Confinement* 225:261–264.

DeCou K. 2001. *Incarcerated Women and Self-Harm: Security or Sanity*. Kingston, NJ: Civic Research Institute.

Deitch M, A Barstow, L Lukens, and R Reyna. 2009. *From Time Out to Hard Time: Young Children in the Adult Criminal Justice System*. Austin: University of Texas at Austin, LBJ School of Public Affairs.

DeShaney v. Winnebago County Department of Social Services, 489 U.S. 189 (1989).

Disability Law Center v. Massachusetts Department of Corrections, Civ. Action, no. 07-10463-MLW (D. Mass.) (2012).

Dlugacz H. 2015. *Reentry Planning for Offenders with Mental Disorders*. Kingston, NJ: Civic Research Institute.

Doe v. Delie, 257 F.3d 309 (3d Cir.) (2001).

Dolovich S. 2009. Cruelty, Prison Conditions, and the Eighth Amendment 84 N.Y.U.L. Rev. 881, 883.

Dubler N and B Heyman. 2006. End-of-life care in prisons and jails. In: *Clinical Practice in Correctional Medicine*, 2nd Edition, edited by M Puisis. Philadelphia, PA: Elsevier, 538–544.

Estelle v. Gamble, 429 U.S. 97 (1976)

Farmer v. Brennan, 511 U.S. 825 (1994).

Freedom v. City of Allentown, PA, 833 F.2d 1111 (3d Cir.) (1988).

Goode E. 2012. Prisons rethink isolation, saving money, lives and sanity. *New York Times*, March 10.

Gordon H and P Lindqvist. 2007. Forensic psychiatry in Europe. *Psychiatric Bulletin* 31(11):421–424.

Grassian S. 2006. Psychiatry effects of solitary confinement, *Washington University Journal of Law and Policy* 325:22.

Grisso T and P Appelbaum. 1998. *MacArthur Competence Assessment Tool for Treatment*. Sarasota, FL: Professional Resource Exchange.

Haney C. 2003. Mental health issues in long-term solitary and "Supermax" confinement. *Crime and Delinquency* 49:124–132.

James D and L Glaze. 2006. *Mental Health Problems of Prison and Jail Inmates (NCJ 213600)*. Washington, DC: U.S. Department of Justice, Office of Justice Programs, Bureau of Justice Statistics.

Jones 'El v. Berge, 164 F. Supp.2d 1096 (W. D. Wis.) (2001).

Kim S. 2010. *Evaluation of Capacity to Consent to Treatment and Research*. New York: Oxford University Press.

Kinsella C. 2004. Trends alert: Corrections health care costs. Lexington, KY: The Council for State Governments, 1–34. http://www.csg.org/knowledge-center/docs/TA0401CorrHealth.pdf, accessed July 27, 2016.

Knoll J. 2008. Punishment for symptoms: Disciplinary hearings for mentally Ill inmates. *Correctional Mental Health Report* 9(5):65–66, 70–71.

Knoll J. 2010. Correctional suicide: Assessment, prevention, and professional liability. *Journal of Correctional Healthcare* 16(3):1–17.

Krelstein M. 2002. The role of mental health in the inmate disciplinary process: A national survey. *Journal of the American Academy of Psychiatry and the Law* 30(4):488–496.

Lovell D, K Cloyes, D Allen, and L Rhodes. 2000. Who lives in super maximum custody? A Washington state study. *Federal Probation* 64:33–43.

Madrid v. Gomez, 889 F. Supp. 1146 (N.D. Cal. 1995) (1995).

Metzner JL. 2002. The role of mental health in the inmate disciplinary process. *Journal of the American Academy of Psychiatry and the Law* 30(4):497–499.

Miletic v. Natalucci-Persichetti, 1992 WL1258522 (S.D. Ohio 1992) (1992).

Monmouth Co. Correctional Institution Inmates v. Lanzaro, 595 F. Supp. 1417 (D.N.J.1894), Order Modified, 695 F. Supp. 759 (D.N.J. 1988) Opinion Amended, 717 F. Supp. 268 (D.N.J. 1989) (1984).

National Commission on Correctional Health Care. 2003. *Correctional Mental Health Care: Standards and Guidelines for Delivering Services*. Chicago: National Commission on Correctional Health Care.

Petersilia J and F Cullen. 2014–2015. Liberal but not stupid: Meeting the promise of downsizing prisons. *Stanford Journal of Criminal Law and Policy* 2:1–224.

Presley v. Epps, no. 4:05 CV148-JAD (N.D. Miss.) (2005).

Rivers v. Katz, 67 N.Y.2d 485 (1986).

Salize H. 2007. *Mentally Disordered Persons in European Prison Systems—And Outcome*. Kingston, NJ: Civic Research Institute.

Sedlak A and K McPherson. 2010. *Conditions of Confinement: Findings from the Survey of Youth in Residential Placement*. Washington, DC: U.S. Department of Justice, Office of Justice Programs, Office of Juvenile Justice and Delinquency Prevention.

Simon R and R Hales. 2012. *The American Psychiatric Publishing Textbook of Suicide Assessment and Management*. Arlington, VA: American Psychiatric Publication.

Stojkovic S. 2005. *Managing Special Populations in Jails and Prisons*. Kingston, NJ: Civic Research Institute.

Taylor v. Barkes (135 S. Ct. 2042) (2015).

Taylor v. Wausau Underwriters Ins. Co., 423 F. Supp.2d 882 (E.D. Wis.) (2006).

Thompson J. 2010. Today's deliberate indifference: Providing attention without providing treatment to prisoners with serious medical needs. *Harvard Civil Rights-Civil Liberties Law Review* 45:635.

Toch H and K Adams. 1986. Pathology and disruptiveness among prison inmates. *Journal of Research in Crime and Delinquency* 23:7–21.

University of North Carolina School of Law. 2014. *Solitary Confinement as Torture*. Chapel Hill: University of North Carolina School of Law, 215–216.

U.S. Department of Health and Human Services. 2002. *Confronting the New Health Care Crisis: Improving Health Care Quality and Lowering Costs by Fixing Our Medical Liability System*. Washington, DC: Manhattan Institute for Policy Research, Civil Justice Report, 1–28.

Ward J. 2003. Confronting issues in criminal justice: Law enforcement and criminal offenders; snapshots: Holistic images of female offenders in the criminal justice system. *Fordham Urban Law Journal* 30:723.

Washington v. Harper, 494 U.S. 210 (1990).

World Health Organization (WHO). 2007. *Background Paper for Trencin Statement on Prisons and Mental Health: Towards Best Practices in Developing Prison Mental Health Systems*. October 18. Copenhagen, Denmark: WHO.

54

Correctional psychiatry research

BRUCE B. WAY AND PHILIP J. CANDILIS

INTRODUCTION

This chapter will review why correctional psychiatry research is of critical importance to improving treatment efforts in corrections, as well as to carrying out the mission of evidence-based research in forensic psychiatry (American Academy of Psychiatry and the Law 2015); briefly review research in the major areas of treatments/services provided to the mentally ill in prisons and jails; and discuss practical and ethical issues in conducting correctional research.

Research in the following treatment/service areas will be briefly reviewed: (a) Screening/Assessment Services, (b) Clinic Psychological Services, (c) Medications, (d) Inpatient Services, (e) Crisis Services (including observation cells), (f) Disciplinary Cells, (g) Special Mental Health Residential Units, (h) Discharge Planning, and (i) Telemedicine.

SIGNIFICANCE

More than 20 years ago, Condelli et al. (1994) wrote:

> Reviews of the literature indicate that, until recently, little was known about inmates with psychiatric disorder, and that many professionals working outside of the forensic psychiatry field believe they are untreatable. Adequate programs have been called "virtually nonexistent" for most mentally ill inmates. (p. 63)

There has been major growth in the number of prisoners since these words were written. From 1980 to 2009 jail populations have more than tripled and prison populations almost quadrupled (http://felonvoting.procon.org/view.resource.php?resourceID = 004353). Recent statistics show that on December 31, 2009, there were more than 1.6 million inmates in federal and state prison (West et al. 2010), while 2012 data indicate approximately 750,000 inmates in county or city jails (Minton 2013).

In concordance with overall census increases, mental health caseloads have been rising rapidly (Thigpen et al. 2001; James and Glaze 2006; Way et al. 2008). Beck and Maruschak (2001) reported in 2001 that 13% (151,000) of prison inmates received mental health therapy, 10% (115,000) received psychiatric medication, and 2% (19,000) received 24-hour care for their mental illness. It is now commonly reported that the largest concentrations of institutionalized Americans with mental illness are in correctional environments (Torrey 1996).

Further, unlike free citizens, prisoners have a constitutional right to adequate health care, including mental health treatment (*Estelle v. Gamble*, 429 US 97, 103, 1976; *Ruiz v. Estelle*, 503 F Supp 1256, 1323 [SD Tex 1980]; Cohen and Dvoskin 1996) which has led to an explosion in the number of lawsuits concerning correctional mental health services (Metzner 2002). These lawsuits have produced a dramatic increase and modification in the types of mental health services provided to prisoners.

One of the most useful data sources for enumerating and describing prisoners with mental illness have been the periodic surveys conducted by the Bureau of Justice Statistics (BJS) at the U.S. Department of Justice. Every 5 to 6 years they conduct a "Survey of Inmates in State and Federal Correctional Facilities" and a "Survey of Inmates in Local Jails" which includes sections on mental health. These are the only national sources of data on prison and jail inmates with mental health problems. Unfortunately many of these surveys are almost 10 years old and no new surveys of mental health services are planned (email April 2015 from BJS).

As of 2000, a large percentage of prisons provide mental health services. It is expected that these totals are larger in 2016. Beck and Maruschak (2001) report there were about 1600 U.S. prisons. Of these, 78% screened for mental illness at intake, 79% provided psychiatric assessments, 63% provided 24-hour care for the mentally ill, 84% provided therapy, 83% distributed drugs, and 72% assisted the mentally ill on release.

Although correctional mental health treatment has become a legal and clinical imperative, the research base is quite modest compared to psychiatric research in other settings. For example, hundreds of papers examine emergency room decisions to admit patients to inpatient services (e.g., Way et al. 1998), but there are only a handful of studies on the crisis services in jails and prisons. This lack of site-specific research is due partly to the reluctance of correctional authorities to permit research activities that may lead to litigation (Metzner 2002). Fortunately, this may be changing since litigation often requires correctional systems to maintain databases of outcome measures for mental health services. Wakai et al. (2009) are among those who report that "there now appear to be signs of interest in and support for research with inmates by correctional agencies, academia, and health care organizations" (p. 743).

This imperative leads directly to the importance of addressing the complex ethical concerns that arise within total institutions, as well as from the unique logistical difficulties in conducting potentially coercive research.

MENTAL HEALTH SERVICES IN JAILS AND PRISONS

Screening for mental illness

Most prison and larger jail systems have a separate unit dedicated to identifying the needs of incoming inmates. Prior records are often sought, structured assessments conducted, diagnoses established, and treatment plans initiated. Of course, this is not just for mental health needs, but for all inmate needs, including security classification. The risk inmates pose to themselves and others is a common consideration upon entry into the correctional system and is mandated by the body overseeing correctional health care, NCCHC.

Prevalence of mental disorders in prison and jail populations is one of the few areas that has been well studied. More than a hundred papers report prevalence of mental disorder (e.g., Goff et al. 2007), although it is difficult to reconcile the large variability in these estimates. This variability even exists within BJS studies. For example, James and Glaze (2006), using self-report data, found that 56% (705,600) of prison inmates, 45% of federal prisoners (78,800), and 64% (479,000) of jail inmates had a mental problem. These percentages are considerably larger than a previous BJS report (Beck and Maruschak 2001), also using self-report data that 16% of state prison inmates thought they were mentally ill.

Another focus of research is measuring "serious" mental illness (SMI); this results partly from the litigation in many states to remove SMI inmates from disciplinary units. For example, Steadman et al. (2009) and Ditton (1999) report that about 15% of jail and prison inmates are diagnosed with SMI. This is much higher than the community estimate of 5%. (Kessler et al. 1996). However, differing definitions of "serious" confound easy comparisons between studies.

There also have been dozens of studies that have found that mentally ill prisoners have numerous and more serious comorbidity compared to their non-mentally ill cohorts, from serious physical health conditions and substance abuse to homelessness and prior criminality. For example, James and Glaze (2006) report that mentally ill inmates have higher rates of prior arrest, incarceration, substance abuse, and homelessness in the year before arrest, as well as greater past physical or sexual abuse. Way et al. (2008), in a cohort study of incoming state prison inmates with SMI, found that 28% had four or more prior psychiatric inpatient hospitalizations, that almost all had a prior psychiatric hospitalization at least 20 years ago, that 62% had a prior suicide attempt, and that 59% had received prior inpatient treatment for substance abuse. Ditton (1999) found that mentally ill prison inmates were more likely to be under the influence of alcohol at the time of their arrest, to be incarcerated for a violent offense, to be homeless, and to have been subject to physical and sexual abuse.

Only a handful of studies provide information on the methods and effectiveness of routine jail and prison screening procedures. The evidence that does exist suggests that much improvement is needed. Trestman et al. (2007) found a considerable number of jail inmates with current and historical psychiatric illnesses had not been identified at intake. Treatment could not begin nor could services be arranged for individuals who slipped through institutional screening procedures. The authors state unequivocally that "high levels of psychiatric morbidity with associated functional impairment exist despite increases in institutional awareness of and attempts to identify inmates with past evidence of psychiatric illness… There is little evidence that these jail inmates had recovered from a past illness, and a greater likelihood that they were chronically impaired by undetected psychiatric illness" (p. 490). There is further evidence that screening procedures cannot simply rely on prior treatment records. James and Glaze (2006) report that 40% of jail inmates and 30% of prison inmates reported psychiatric symptoms without a recent history.

During the intake process a psychiatric diagnosis is assigned to initiate the development of a treatment plan. However, there is almost no research on the accuracy or reliability of these diagnoses, or if and how they account for an inmate's criminality. Way et al. (2008) describe the process of developing a psychiatric diagnosis during the intake process in New York state prison and measures consistency over time. A psychologist or social worker develops an initial diagnosis within a few days in prison basing the information on an interview and available records. This initial diagnosis is reviewed by a psychiatrist a few days later. The authors report that the psychiatrist's diagnosis is identical to the initial diagnosis 95% of the time. The authors then compared the psychiatrist's diagnosis created during intake with the diagnosis at 6 months: 80% were still identical. It was expected that there would be more change in diagnosis at 6 months because treatment and additional assessments had occurred. For example, a *Diagnostic and Statistical Manual of Mental Disorders*, 4th edition (*DSM-IV*) diagnosis of Psychotic Disorder NOS (not otherwise specified) could evolve into Schizoaffective Disorder or Schizophrenia, diverging from the initial categorization.

CLINIC AND PSYCHOLOGICAL SERVICES

Prisons and larger jails contain a mental health clinic, which is analogous to an outpatient clinic in the community. Inmate–patients are escorted to these clinics for psychological and psychiatric treatment. James and Glaze (2006) report that 156,000 state prison inmates received professional mental health therapy in 2004, up from about 130,000 in 1997.

There has been very little research on what kinds of therapy are provided and their relative effectiveness. This deficit persists despite numerous studies that suggest inmates have more complex comorbidity than their nonincarcerated cohorts. Further, numerous commentators (e.g., Ax et al. 2007) stress the need for research on a broad range of interventions provided by the correctional psychologist exactly because of inmates' complex and comorbid presentations.

A recent study has begun the process of describing the therapies provided in correctional environments and has developed a model for understanding the various goals of these treatments. Bewley and Morgan (2011) surveyed 230 mental health professionals across 165 state prisons and asked what psychotherapeutic services they provided, the amount of time spent on each, and their opinion on the relative effectiveness of the services. Almost all 230 respondents were psychologists or social workers. They spent 38% of their time on individual counseling, 36% on administrative duties, and 13% on group therapy. In a survey with 16 content areas and 38 therapeutic factors, a factor analysis produced six goals: (a) mental health recovery, (b) emotional management, (c) institutional functioning, (d) reentry (vocational needs), (f) risk need (criminal recidivism issues), and (g) personal growth. The survey respondents thought they were particularly effective with recovery from mental illness and skill development.

MEDICATIONS

In underscoring the increased needs of mentally ill inmates, James and Glaze (2006) report that 15.1% (185,000) of all state inmates received a psychiatric medication in 2004; an increase of 12.3% (130,000) from 1997. No studies on types of medications administered and their relative effectiveness are available, nor whether certain medication classes are even needed for correctional populations. This dearth of data is quite surprising given the high costs of medication and the common efforts to restrict formularies. Without adequate data on usage and effectiveness, policy efforts to reduce medication costs cannot succeed.

INPATIENT SERVICES

Way and colleagues (Way et al. 1990; Way et al. 1991) documented the numbers of forensic inpatient beds and their staffing almost 25 years ago. More recent data on number of inpatient beds for prisoners are not available, but James and Glaze (2006) report that in 2004, 3.1% (38,000) state prison inmates had an "overnight hospital stay" for mental health treatment compared to 3.8% (40,000) in 1997. Only Reed and Lyne (2000) report on the effectiveness of inpatient treatment for mentally ill prisoners. The authors concluded, based on their review of 13 prisons with 348 psychiatric inpatient beds in England, that "the quality of services for mentally ill prisoners fell far below the standards ....Patients' lives were unacceptably restricted and therapy limited" (p. 1031).

EMERGENCY SERVICES CRISIS OBSERVATION CELLS

Most correctional environments contain crisis cells where inmates are sent from the general population for short periods. In many ways these are analogous to emergency room services in general hospitals. They offer short-term stabilization, the initiation or adjustment of psychiatric medications, assessment for transfer to inpatient treatment, and suicide observation and prevention. These cells are frequently open on several sides to permit staff observation, and usually require removal of an inmate's personal property and clothing. Crisis cells are a frequent target of lawsuits (e.g., *DAI v. New York State Office of Mental Health* 2002) because of these conditions.

Research on crisis observation cells indicates that inmate–patient satisfaction with observation cells is low. Way et al. (2013) found that transfer to an observation cell was the least favorable option for dealing with suicidal ideation—better only than talking with a correctional officer. Skogstad et al. (2005) report a similar result for New Zealand prison inmates. However, Way et al. (2005) found that crisis cells are effective in preventing suicide while in the cell, although it is unknown whether crisis cells reduce the potential for suicide once the inmate is returned to the general population.

It is unknown how many U.S. correctional institutions use crisis cells, how long inmate patients stay, what conditions are like, and what, if any, therapeutic efforts are provided. To date, there exists no research on what treatment is provided in crisis cells, or their effectiveness.

SPECIAL LONG-TERM RESIDENTIAL CARE UNITS FOR INMATES WITH SERIOUS MENTAL ILLNESS

Many correctional settings have special long-term residential units for inmates with serious mental illness (SMI). Sometimes called "Intermediate Care," these units provide more care than clinic services, but less than inpatient settings. Inmates suffering from SMI are housed separately from other inmates, with most clinical, rehabilitative, and recreation services provided on the special housing unit itself. Correctional officers on such units are typically specially selected and trained. Advantages of such units include residents being protected from being exploited, assaulted, or harassed by non-mentally ill inmates. Special housing units for inmates suffering from SMI have seen significant expansion in the last decade, primarily as a response to lawsuits focusing on the removal of such inmates from punitive segregation (Kupers et al. 2009).

Studies from the mid-1990s in New York State (Condelli et al. 1994; Condelli et al. 1997) reported that residents with SMI housed in the special units experienced fewer admissions to crisis cells, fewer administrations of emergency medications, inpatient hospitalizations, suicide attempts, and correctional infractions and restrictions. In 2001, Lovell et al. (2001a) studied a residential program for mentally ill prison inmates in Washington state and found that inmate–patients experienced fewer symptoms, infractions, assaults on staff, and higher rates of participation in school and work. In 2009, Kupers et al. reported on the establishment of a "step-down" residential unit for inmates with SMI created in response to a lawsuit to remove them from administrative segregation. Findings included large reductions in rates of misconduct, violence, and use of force.

Way et al.'s (2008) study of treatment for suicidal ideation compared samples from general population and long-term mental health housing. Results suggest that there is in fact reduced stigma in the special residential unit. The special unit patients were much more willing to have suicide observation in their cell (73% versus 16%) and to have mental health staff visit their cells (76% versus 31%) than patients in the general population. The stigma and vulnerability conferred by staff visits and suicide watch remain an important challenge to forensic practitioners in the general correctional setting.

Long-term SMI housing units often set a goal to move inmate–patients back to general population housing. Only one study was found that assessed inmates after transfer. Lovell et al. (2001b) reported that patients were able to maintain decreased psychiatric symptoms after return to the general population from the SMI unit. More research is necessary, however, to determine whether this policy is preferable to retaining inmate–patients with SMI in special units for their entire prison stay.

DISCIPLINARY HOUSING

Studies have long found a strong relationship between mental illness and breaking institutional rules (Toch and Adams 1986). James and Glaze (2006) in their Bureau of Justice Statistics study, report that 58% of inmates diagnosed with mental illness versus 43% of those with no diagnosis violate prison rules. In jails the percentages are 19% versus 9%. Consequently, inmates diagnosed with mental illness are more likely than non-mentally ill inmates to be placed in disciplinary housing.

Disciplinary cells, or "segregation," separate inmates from others and restrict their privileges. Usually the inmate is restricted to his or her single cell for 23 or 24 hours each day and not permitted to work, attend programs, or interact with other inmates. These units vary widely, however, particularly in their degree of "sensory deprivation" and access to mental health services. Many disciplinary cells are "open-celled," which allows noise from other cells.

Placing persons diagnosed with serious mental illness in punitive segregation has been the subject of both correctional research and human rights advocacy. It has also been a leading cause of litigation (Metzner and Fellner 2010; Kapoor 2014). In a landmark publication in 2012, the American Psychiatric Association (APA) published a position paper stating that long-term isolation is harmful to prisoners with serious mental illness, either by directly causing clinical deterioration, or by depriving them of treatment that would have resulted in improvement (APA 2012).

In fact, research has found that punitive isolation is associated with suicide risk (Way et al. 2005; Patterson and Hughes 2008). Further, Way et al. (2007) found that inmate-patients who died by suicide in punitive isolation died soon after transfer. Time in disciplinary cell before suicide had a median of 63 days.

The question of whether punitive isolation actually causes clinical deterioration is far from settled however. Some prominent commentators (Grassian 1983; Haney 2003) argue that disciplinary housing environments deprive individuals of adequate sensory input and thereby directly cause deterioration of mental functioning. However, other reports indicate that no psychological deterioration occurs during short periods of isolation (Bonta and Gendreau 1995; Zinger and Wichmann 1999; Andersen et al. 2003).

There are numerous potential reasons for these conflicting results, and full reviews are available (Suedfeld et al. 1982; Zinger and Wichmann 1999; Haney 2003). One reason for these conflicting results is that the actual amount of sensory restriction varies among disciplinary cell blocks. Indeed, a number of differing constructs may qualify as "disciplinary housing." Some authors report that sensory input in solitary confinement may not be that much different from regular cells, because inmates in solitary still communicate with medical staff, mental health staff, correctional staff, and other inmates. In addition, inmates in solitary may have access to reading material, mail, and radio and television programs—depending on the facility's policy (Suedfeld et al. 1982).

Another confounding variable in the debate over isolation arises from studies that have documented the extreme disability of inmates prior to being placed there. For example, Cloyes et al. (2006) reported that 45% of residents of Washington State's super-maximum security unit had SMI. Kapoor (2014) reviewed the literature and concluded that "although some scholars debate whether isolation is the cause or effect of the dangerous behavior observed in prisoners housed in isolation, it is clear that, at the very least, isolation adds no benefit to the treatment of mental illness in prison" (p. 2).

DISCHARGE PLANNING

Many correctional systems (72% of state prisons according to Beck and Maruschak [2001]) have specific discharge planning services for mental health where counselors set up mental health, housing, and other services in the community. Some states have special discharge planning mental health treatment programs that include an even more enhanced array of services, such as a visit in prison from the community mental health provider.

Although discharge planning may become a new area of prison ligation (Metzner 2002), and there are numerous guidelines for effective discharge planning (Veysey et al. 1997; Lurigio et al. 2000; Draine et al. 2005; Blandford and Osher 2013), none have been tested empirically.

There have been a few studies of reentry mental health programs that show promising results. Hartwell and Orr (1999) reported on a Massachusetts program for inmates with mental illness which provides extra services 3 months before, and for 3 months after, their release. The authors found much lower recidivism for participants. Kesten et al. (2012) describe the Connecticut Offender Reentry Program (CORP) for mentally ill inmates which, beginning 9–12 months before release, includes "a corrections-based Life Skills Reentry Curriculum, collaborative reentry planning sessions to identify and prioritize life concerns, and implementation of the reentry plan through targeted community services and criminal justice supervision" (p. 22). These authors found that CORP participants were only half as likely to be rearrested as inmate–patients who received standard treatment planning services.

Rather than studies of effectiveness of discharge planning per se, a number of studies have examined the outcomes of mentally ill inmates after release (e.g., Lamb et al. 1999). Although both Feder (1991) and Adams (1983) did not find any difference in recidivism between mentally ill and non-mentally ill groups following adjustment for recidivism risk factors, Cloyes et al. (2010) report that serious mental illness (SMI) represents a major risk for repeated incarceration. They found that inmates with SMI had a much shorter median time before return (385 days versus 743 days) than non-SMI releasees. Castillo and Alard (2011) report that mentally ill offenders released from jail with an alcohol problem recidivate earlier. In a study of work release from state prison, Way et al. (2007) found that mentally ill women were more likely to fail than non-mentally ill women, but the difference among male groups was not significant. Further, prisoners transferred to civil inpatient hospitals upon discharge have much longer lengths of stay in civilian hospitals (Way et al. 2004), although differences in severity of illness were not detected between groups.

TELEMEDICINE

Mental health assessment and treatment via computer have been growing rapidly in correctional environments, although the exact rate of growth is not known. Even though more research has been conducted about telemedicine in community settings (e.g., Charles 2000), some groups have studied its use in prisons. Magaletta et al. (1998) report high patient acceptance of the technology, access to a larger range of psychology services, and greater access to inmate–patients for research purposes. They noted that security was easily maintained with telepsychiatry. Zaylor et al. (2001) reported that Symptom Rating Checklist-90-Revised scores improved among inmates treated via telemedicine, and that psychiatrists corroborated the improvement on the Clinical Global Impression Scale. Finally, Kaplan and Lilly (2012) found no difference between telemedicine and face-to-face treatment in the number of crisis admissions and number of inpatient hospitalizations.

DIFFICULTIES AND CHALLENGES OF CONDUCTING RESEARCH IN PRISON AND JAILS

Conducting research in correctional environments is difficult, especially because obtaining approval from correctional authorities and Institutional Review Boards (IRBs) can be time consuming. IRBs require special protections for prisoners entering research, and prison administrators fear the increased likelihood of litigation (Metzner 2002). Due to a history of abuse of prisoners as research subjects, there are enhanced regulations for conducting research with inmates, and prisoners are considered a vulnerable population. IRBs must have a prisoner-representative on the board during deliberation and pay close attention to the research participant's capacity to consent in the coercive prison environment. Consent forms must promise that participation does not affect personal treatment or legal outcomes in the inmate's case, but prisoners may nonetheless participate in order to gain favor.

Cornerstone events leading to this state of affairs include the landmark legal case of *Kaimowitz v. DMH of Michigan* (1973) in which an inmate consented to psychosurgery but was blocked by the district court because of a prison's inherently coercive environment. Further, the National Commission for the Protection of Human Subjects of Biomedical and Behavioral Research in its ground-breaking Belmont Report (1979) assumed that informed consent by prisoners was impossible.

Recruitment of research participants is also difficult because inmates are harder to engage than subjects in the community. Prison is not the place for self-disclosure, and inmates fear that information they provide will be used against them. Skogstad et al. (2005) reported that inmates did not trust that mental health information would be kept confidential. Way et al. (2013) found that 42% of mental health patients residing in general population housing were unwilling to tell their counselor that they were having suicidal thoughts. Inmates are commonly ostracized and ridiculed for showing weakness, so that participation in a research project on mental illness may increase stigma and vulnerability.

Some research groups, however, have found that this may be a function of the setting. Way et al. (2013), for example, found that patients in special mental health residential units welcomed cell-side visits from mental health staff, although inmate–patients in the general population did not. Conversely, although Appelbaum, Hickey, and Packer (2001) advocate the inclusion of correctional officers in mental health treatment teams, current findings suggest inmates frequently mistrust correctional officers. Way's group (2013) found that talking to correctional officers about suicidal thoughts was an inmate's least favored treatment option. It was even the least favored option for inmate–patients in special mental health residential units that used correctional officers specially trained in mental health.

Recruitment is also challenging because incentives for participation are rigorously controlled. Even incentives such as small quantities of money will have a disproportionate effect in correctional settings and are almost invariably prohibited by administrators or IRBs. Even small gifts can be stolen or used for illicit purposes. Clinical research with medications may similarly be curtailed because of concerns for diversion or misuse.

After recruitment, maintaining participants in a research protocol remains a challenge. Inmates in jails have short stays that can end unexpectedly as a result of court proceedings. Although prison inmates have longer sentences, they may be transferred to other prisons or housing units, forcing them to drop out of the research.

Most psychiatric research is conducted in the correctional mental health clinic, but getting inmate–patients to the clinic and keeping them there for lengthy treatments or assessments can be problematic. Movement within prison and jails is restricted and carefully choreographed, so that researchers must rely on correctional officers for escorting subjects and meeting schedules. Punctuality and no-shows are a persistent problem. Moreover, the inmate–patient can usually only remain in the clinic for a few hours at a time before security counts interfere.

Research outcomes may be affected by the conflicting goals of the researchers and the institution. For example, a common outcome measure in correctional treatment is the reduction of disciplinary infractions. Staff and correctional officers may affect the measure because of their support (or lack of support) for the intervention. Staff have considerable discretion in formally reporting a behavioral incident or managing it themselves. More broadly, focusing on infractions may detract from goals that foster independence, such as adjustment in the community after release.

Finally, correctional research is challenged by the lack of validation of many assessment tools in the correctional setting itself. Outcome measures are generally developed with and for patients in the community, and have not been adapted for use in jails and prisons. For example, Way et al. (2004) specifically modified a quality-of-life instrument for use in prison.

ETHICAL ISSUES IN CORRECTIONAL PSYCHIATRY RESEARCH

The many vulnerabilities of prison inmates create special ethical requirements for both researchers and institutions (Christopher et al. 2011). As overcrowding becomes the standard across the country, these vulnerabilities create obligatory areas of focus for correctional researchers. As of 2009, over 2.3 million persons are in U.S. jails or prisons (Bureau of Justice 2010), facing a lack of enthusiasm for the provision of medical services (Wilper et al. 2009) and a persistence in mandatory minimum sentences that extend their incarceration.

For a population that is already overburdened with mental illness, substance abuse, infectious disease, and other medical conditions (Greifinger 2007; Okie 2007), inmates are vulnerable to the vicissitudes of poverty, poor education, lack of opportunity, and prejudice that affect life-long access to health care and healthy living conditions. Although inmates make up only 0.8% of the country's population, the estimated 12-month prevalence of HIV, tuberculosis, and hepatitis C in jails and prisons ranges from 25% to 43% (Hammett et al. 2002, Weinbaum et al. 2005). Among inmates with mental illness, 75% are diagnosed with substance abuse as well (Karburg and Mumola 2006). Mental illness itself significantly surpasses community prevalence across the diagnostic spectrum (Dvoskin and Metzner 2006). These characteristics create a unique imperative to conduct research that improves conditions and health-care outcomes.

Engagement in treatment remains a challenge among those who enter the correctional system. Inmates have notoriously poor adherence to treatment both before and after incarceration (Farabee and Leukefeld 2001; Czuchry et al. 2006), with 82% of one classic cohort of over 6000 inmates at high risk for HIV never having seen a primary care provider (Conklin et al. 1998). The return to the community, or reentry, is itself difficult enough to interfere with the need for health care. The challenge of finding housing, employment, and transportation complicates the often anemic efforts of correctional systems to provide community services (Petersilia 2003), resulting in recidivism and even death (Binswanger et al. 2007; Coviello et al. 2010).

Moreover, prisons have often failed to provide adequate medical and mental health treatment (Human Rights Watch 2003; Belenko and Peugh 2005; CDC 2006, Clemmitt 2007; Wilper et al. 2009). Because inmates cannot seek or obtain their own medical treatment, institutions are legally obligated to meet certain minimal requirements, resulting in inmates being the only class of U.S. citizen that has a constitutionally protected right to health care (Candilis and Huttenbach 2015). This historical context adds to the ethical obligation to research individual and population-specific vulnerabilities.

The vulnerabilities of the correctional setting consequently create a unique obligation for investigators contemplating research on the issues facing prisoners. The Belmont

Report (1979), the cardinal guide to human subjects research in the United States, includes institutionalized subjects among those who must be protected from research participation by virtue of their dependent status and potentially compromised capacity to consent.

The federal regulations that codify many aspects of the Belmont Report do not prohibit correctional research, however, but include prisoners among its vulnerable populations, namely children, pregnant women, fetuses, and neonates (45 CFR 46, 2009). Research with prisoners must be reviewed by an Institutional Review Board unaffiliated with the prison involved, and include a prisoner or prisoner representative. The research cannot be conducted at all unless it is relevant to the medical, institutional, or situational conditions inmates face. Research with this vulnerable population, therefore, requires a number of protections that go beyond the common requirements of oversight and consent. The abuses of prisoners in medical research from Nuremberg to modern times are catalogued elsewhere (Harkness 1996; Hornblum 1997), but support the appropriateness of this protective approach.

This protective stance began to shift in recent years as advocates and public health experts recognized that inmates may benefit from access to investigational treatments that were otherwise unavailable (Gostin et al. 2007; Christopher et al. 2011). Others interpreted access to research as an extension of the constitutional right to health care protected by landmark legal cases such as *Estelle v. Gamble* (1976).

The Institute of Medicine (IOM) consequently took up the issue of access to research in 2004, at the direction of the U.S. Department of Health and Human Services (Gostin et al. 2007). Torn by the conflicting duties to protect voluntariness, consent, confidentiality, and access to health care, a committee of the IOM nonetheless recommended permitting more than minimal risk research that could improve the health of the subject. This standard, among those commonly found in pediatric research protocols, lowered the bar on the risk usually permitted in prisoner research.

At the same time, however, the IOM recognized that coercion and oversight remained active policy concerns. They extended the definition of "prisoner" to include those constrained by other requirements of the judicial system such as probation and parole, and endorsed improving overall research oversight. The IOM was concerned that federal oversight (namely through the Office of Human Research Protections, OHRP) may not extend sufficiently to oversee all prisoner research. The IOM therefore advocated extension of the OHRP oversight model to all funding agencies and private institutions conducting prisoner research, creation of a national registry of prisoner research, and appointment of a specific prison research support advocate or PRSA.

A more nuanced view of research risk assessment was recommended as well. Because current analysis of research risk by IRBs is categorical (viz., minimal risk, minor increase over minimal risk, more than minor increase over minimal risk), assessments do not adequately consider specific risks and benefits, or the specifics of the actual confinement or restriction. Therefore, the IOM proposed a risk–benefit analysis similar to the one found in regulations for children. Benefits to prisoners must be clear and outweigh related risks. Even for Phase III research, where effectiveness has been demonstrated, the ratio of prisoner-to-nonprisoner subjects was not to exceed 50%. This assured that prisoners are not merely a sample of convenience.

Finally, in calling for "collaborative responsibility" as an offshoot of the principle of justice that guided the Belmont Report, the IOM recognized the importance of the stakeholders' perspective. From prisoners and correctional officers to staff and administrators, the IOM recommended input at all stages of research. The hope is that any correctional setting can provide the appropriate context for ethical research. This final recommendation would resonate strongly with those who recognized that inmates' personal views of coercion were frequently based on being included in decision-making and being treated respectfully (Lidz 1997; Cusack et al. 2010; Munetz et al. 2014), rather than the restricted freedom of movement.

SUMMARY

Despite large numbers of inmates with mental illness, and serious mental illness, and substantial comorbidity with other disabilities, there has been and continues to be very little research on the effectiveness or even the monitoring, describing, and enumerating of mental health services for prisoners. It is disheartening that even the BJS, the primary national source of statistics, has no studies underway to update already out-of-date information. Although it is challenging to conduct research, it is imperative if we wish to improve outcomes of inmates with mental illness.

REFERENCES

Adams K. 1983. Former mental patients in a prison and parole system—A study of socially disruptive behavior. *Criminal Justice Behavior* 10:358–384.

American Academy of Psychiatry and the Law. 2015. *AIER—The AAPL Institute for Education and Research*. http://aapl.org/aier.htm, accessed April 23, 2015.

American Psychiatric Association (APA). 2012. *APA Position Statement on Segregation of Prisoners with Mental Illness*. Arlington, VA: APA. http://www.psychiatry.org/advocacy_newsroom/position-statements, accessed April 23, 2015.

Andersen HS, D Sestoft, T Lillebaek, G Gabrielsen, R Hemmingsen, and P Kramp. 2003. A longitudinal study of prisoners on remand: Repeated measures of psychopathology in the initial phase of solitary versus non-solitary confinement. *International Journal of Law and Psychiatry* 26:165–177.

Appelbaum KL, JM Hickey, and I Packer. 2001. Use of correctional officers. The role of correctional officers in multidisciplinary mental health care in prisons. *Psychiatric Services* 52:1343–1347.

Ax RK, TJ Fagan, PR Magletta, RD Morgan, D Nussbaum, and TW White. 2007. Innovations in correctional assessment and treatment. *Criminal Justice and Behavior* 34:893–905.

Beck AJ and LM Maruschak. 2001. *Mental Health Treatment in State Prisons, 2000*. Washington, DC: Bureau of Justice Statistics.

Belenko S and J Peugh. 2005. Estimating drug treatment needs among state prison inmates. *Drug and Alcohol Dependence* 77(3):269–281.

Bewley MT and RD Morgan. 2011. A national survey of mental health services available to offenders with mental illness: Who is doing what? *Law and Human Behavior* 35:351–363. doi:10.1007/s10979-010-9242-4

Binswanger IA, MF Stern, RA Deyo et al. 2007. Release from prison—A high risk of death for former inmates. *New England Journal of Medicine* 356(2):157–165.

Blandford AM and F Osher. 2013. *Guidelines for the Successful Transition of People with Behavioral Health Problems from Jail and Prison.* New York: Council of State Governments Justice Center, and SAMHSA's GAINS Center for Behavioral Health and Justice Transformation.

Bonta J and P Gendreau. 1995. Reexamining the cruel and unusual punishment of prison life. In *Long Term Imprisonment: Policy, Science, and Correctional Practice*, edited by TJ Flanagan, Thousand Oaks, CA: Sage, 75–94.

Bureau of Justice Statistics. 2010. *Bulletin: Correctional Population in the United States, 2009.* NCJ 231681. Washington, DC: Bureau of Justice Statistics.

Candilis P and F Huttenbach. 2015. Ethics in correctional mental health. In *Oxford Textbook of Correctional Psychiatry*, edited by RL Trestman, KL Appelbaum, and JL Metzner, Oxford: Oxford University Press, 41–45.

Castillo ED and LF Alard. 2011. Factors associated with recidivism among offenders with mental illness. *International Journal of Offender Therapy and Comparative Criminology* 55:98–117.

Centers for Disease Control and Prevention. 2006. Tuberculosis prevention and control in correctional and detention facilities. *Morbidity and Mortality Weekly Report* 55:1–54. http://www.cdc.gov/mmwr/PDF/rr/rr5509.pdf, accessed April 23, 2015.

Charles BL. 2000. Telemedicine can lower costs and improve access. *Healthcare Financial Management* 54:66–69.

Christopher PP, PJ Candilis, JD Rich, and CW Lidz. 2011. An empirical ethics agenda for psychiatric research involving prisoners. *AJOB-Primary Research* 2:18–25.

Clemmitt M. 2007. Prison health care. *Congressional Quarterly* 17:1–24.

Cloyes KG, B Wong, S Latimer, and J Abarca. 2010. Time to prison return for offenders with serious mental illness released from prison: A survival analysis. *Criminal Justice and Behavior* 37:175–187.

Cloyes KG, D Lovell, DG Allen, and LA Rhodes. 2006. Assessment of psychosocial impairment in a super-maximum security unit sample. *Criminal Justice and Behavior* 33:760–781.

Cohen F and J Dvoskin. 1996. Inmates with mental disorders: A guide to law and practice. *Mental and Physical Disability Law Reporter* 16:339–346.

Condelli W, B Bradigan, and H Holanchock. 1997. Intermediate care programs to reduce risk and better manage inmates with psychiatric disorders. *Behavioral Sciences and the Law* 15:459–467.

Condelli W, JA Dvoskin, and H Holanchock. 1994. Intermediate care programs for psychiatric disorders. *Bulletin of the American Academy of Psychiatry and the Law* 22:63–70.

Conklin TJ, T Lincoln, and TP Flanigan. 1998. A public health model to connect correctional health care with communities. *American Journal of Public Health* 88(8):1249–1251.

Coviello DM, JW Cornish, KG Lynch, AI Alterman, and CP O'Brien. 2010. A randomized trial of oral naltrexone for treating opioid-dependent offenders. *American Journal on Addiction* 19(5):422–432.

Cusack KJ, HJ Steadman, and AH Herring. 2010. Perceived coercion among jail diversion participants in a multisite study. *Psychiatric Services* 61:911–916.

Czuchry M, TL Sia, and DF Dansereau. 2006. Improving early engagement and treatment readiness of probationers: Gender differences. *Prison Journal* 86(1):56–74.

Disability Advocates, Inc. (DAI) v. New York State Office of Mental Health, 1:02-cv-04002-GEL, Complaint (S.D.N.Y 2002).

Ditton PM. 1999. *Mental Health and Treatment of Inmates and Probationers*. Washington, DC: Department of Justice.

Draine J, N Wolff, JE Jacoby, S Hartwell, and C Duclos. 2005. Understanding community re-entry of former prisoners with mental illness: A conceptual model to guide new research. *Behavioral Sciences and the Law* 23:689–707.

Dvoskin J and J Metzner. 2006. An overview of correctional psychiatry. *Psychiatric Clinics of North America* 29:761–772.

Estelle v. Gamble, 429 US 97, 103 (1976).

Farabee D and CG Leukefeld. 2001. Recovery and the criminal justice system. In *Relapse and Recovery in Addictions*, edited by FM Tims, CG Leukefeld, and JJ Platt, New Haven, CT: Yale University Press, 40–59.

Feder L. 1991. Comparison of the community adjustment of mentally ill offenders with those from the general prison population: An 18-month follow-up. *Law and Human Behavior* 15:477–493.

Goff A, E Rose, S Rose, and D Purves. 2007. Does PTSD occur in sentenced prison populations? A systematic literature review. *Criminal Behaviour and Mental Health* 17:152–162.

Gostin LO, C Vanchieri, and A Pope. eds. 2007. *Ethical Considerations for Research Involving Prisoners. Institute of Medicine (US). Committee on Ethical Considerations for Revisions to DHHS Regulations for Protection of Prisoners Involved in Research.* Washington, DC: National Academies Press.

Grassian S. 1983. Psychological effects of solitary confinement. *American Journal of Psychiatry* 140:1450–1454.

Greifinger RB. ed. 2007. *Public Health Behind Bars: From Prisons to Communities*. New York: Springer.

Hammett TM, MP Harmon, and W Rhodes. 2002. The burden of infectious disease among inmates of and releases from US correctional facilities, 1997. *American Journal of Public Health* 92(11):1789–1794.

Haney C. 2003. Mental health issues in long-term solitary and supermax confinement. *Crime and Delinquency* 49:124–156.

Harkness JM. 1996. Nuremberg and the issue of wartime experiments on US prisoners. The Green Committee. *Journal of the American Medical Association* 276(20):1672–1675.

Hartwell S and K Orr. 1999. The Massachusetts forensic transition program for mentally Ill offenders re-entering the community. *Psychiatric Services*, 50(9):1220–1222.

Hornblum AM. 1997. They were cheap and available: Prisoners as research subjects in twentieth-century America. *BMJ* 315(7129):1437–1441.

http://felonvoting.procon.org/view.resource.php?resourceID=004353.

Human Rights Watch. 2003. *Ill-equipped: U.S. Prisons and Offenders with Mental Illness*. http://www.hrw.org/sites/default/files/reports/usa1003.pdf, accessed April 23, 2015.

James DJ and LE Glaze. 2006. *Mental Health Problems of Problems of Prison and Jail Inmates*. Washington, DC: Bureau of Justice Statistics.

Kaimowitz v. Michigan DMH, 42 U.S.L.W. 2063 Civil No. 73-1934-AW (1973).

Kaplan J and S Lilly. 2012. *Video Teleconferencing in New York State Prisons. Oral [Research-in-progress] Presentation*. 43rd Annual Meeting of the American Academy of Psychiatry and the Law, Montreal, Quebec, Canada.

Kapoor R. 2014. Taking the solitary confinement debate out of isolation. *Journal of the American Academy of Psychiatry and the Law* 42:2–6.

Karburg JC and CJ Mumola. 2006. *Drug use and Dependence, State and Federal Prisoners, 2004*. NCJ 188215. Washington, DC: Bureau of Justice Statistics.

Kessler RC, CB Nelson, KA McGonagle, MJ Edlund, RG Frank, and PJ Leaf. 1996. The epidemiology of co-occurring addictive and mental disorders: Implications for prevention and service utilization. *American Journal of Orthopsychiatry* 66:17–31.

Kesten KL, E Levitt-Smith, DR Rau, D Shelton, W Zhang, J Wagner, and R Trestman. 2012. Recidivism rates among mentally ill inmates: Impact of the Connecticut Offender Reentry Program. *Journal of Correctional Health Care* 18:20–28.

Kupers TA, T Dronet, M Winter, J Austin et al. 2009. Beyond supermax administrative segregation: Mississippi's experience rethinking prison classification and creating alternative mental health programs. *Criminal Justice and Behavior* 36:1037–1050.

Lamb HF, LE Weinberger, and BH Gross. 1999. Community treatment of severely mentally ill offenders under the jurisdiction of the criminal justice system: A review. *Psychiatric Services* 50(7):907–913.

Lidz CW. 1997. Coercion in psychiatric care: What have we learned from research? *Journal of the American Academy of Psychiatry and the Law* 26(4):631–637.

Lovell D, D Allen, C Johnson, and R Jemelka. 2001a. Evaluating the effectiveness of residential treatment for prisoners with mental illness *Criminal Justice and Behavior* 28:83–104.

Lovell D, C Johnson, R Jemelka, V Harris, and D Allen. 2001b. Living in prison after residential mental health treatment: A program follow-up. *Prison Journal* 81:473–490.

Lurigio AJ, JR Fallon, and J Pincin. 2000. Helping the mentally ill in jails adjust to community life: A description of a postrelease ACT program and its clients. *International Journal of Offender Therapy and Comparative Criminology* 44:532–548.

Magaletta PR, TJ Fagan, and RK Ax. 1998. Advancing psychology services through telehealth in the Federal Bureau of Prisons. *Professional Psychology: Research and Practice* 29:543–548.

McCann RA and EM Ball. 2000. DBT with an inpatient forensic population: The CMHIP forensic model. *Cognitive and Behavioral Practice* 7:447–456.

Metzner JL. 1993. Guidelines for psychiatric services in prisons. *Criminal Behavior and Mental Health* 3:252–267.

Metzner JL. 2002. Class action litigation in correctional psychiatry. *Journal of the American Academy of Psychiatry and the Law* 30:19–29.

Metzner JL and J Fellner. 2010. Solitary confinement and mental illness in U.S. prisons: A challenge for medical ethics. *Journal of the American Academy of Psychiatry and the Law* 38:104–108.

Minton TD. 2013. *Jail Inmates at Mid-Year: 2012 Statistical Tables*. Washington, DC: Department of Justice.

Morgan RD, DG Kroner, JF Mills, RL Bauer, and C Serna. 2013. Treating justice-involved persons with mental illness: Preliminary evaluation of a comprehensive treatment program. *Criminal Justice and Behavior*, Published Online December 9, 2013, doi:10.1177/0093854813508553

Munetz MR, C Ritter, JL Teller, and N Bonfine. 2014. Mental health court and assisted outpatient treatment: Perceived coercion, procedural justice, and program impact. *Psychiatric Services* 65(3):52–58.

National Commission for the Protection of Human Subjects of Biomedical Research. 1979. *The Belmont Report*. http://www.hhs.gov/ohrp/regulations-and-policy/belmont-report/index.html, accessed August 1, 2016.

Okie S. 2007. Sex, drugs, prisons, and HIV. *New England Journal of Medicine* 356(2):105–108.

Patterson RF and K Hughes. 2008. Review of completed suicides in the California Department of Corrections and Rehabilitation, 1999 – 2004. *Psychiatric Services* 59:677–681.

Petersilia J. 2003. *When Prisoners Come Home: Parole and Prisoner Re-entry*. New York: Oxford University Press.

Protection of Human Subjects 45 CFR 46 (2009).

Reed JL and M Lyne. 2000. Inpatient care of mentally ill people in prison: Results of a year's programme of semistructured inspections. *BMJ* 320:1031–1034.

Ruiz v. Estelle, 503 F Supp 1256, 1323, SD Tex (1980).

Skogstad P, FP Deane, and J Spicer. 2005. Barriers to help-seeking among New Zealand prison inmates. *Journal of Offender Rehabilitation* 42:1–24.

Steadman HJ, FC Osher, PC Robbins, B Case, and S Samuels. 2009. Prevalence of serious mental illness among jail inmates. *Psychiatric Services* 60:761–765.

Suedfeld P, C Ramirez, J Deaton, and G Baker-Brown. 1982. Reactions and attributes of prisoners in solitary confinement. *Criminal Justice and Behavior* 9:303–340.

Thigpen ML, SM Hunter, and M Ortiz. 2001. *Provision of Mental Care in Prisons*. Washington, DC: National Institute of Corrections.

Toch H and K Adams. 1986. Pathology and disruptiveness among prison inmates. *Research Crime and Delinquency* 23:7–21.

Torrey EF. 1996. Editorial: Jails and prisons—America's new mental hospitals. *American Journal of Public Health* 85:1611–1613.

Trestman RL, J Ford, W Zhang, and V Wiebrock. 2007. Current and lifetime psychiatric illness among inmates not identified as acutely mentally ill at intake in Connecticut's jails. *Journal of the American Academy of Psychiatry and the Law* 35:490–500.

Veysey BM, HJ Steadman, JP Morrissey et al. 1997. In search of the missing linkages: Continuity or care in US jails. *Behavioral Sciences and the Law* 15:383–397.

Wakai S, D Shelton, RL Trestman, and K Kesten. 2009. Conducting research in corrections: Challenges and solutions. *Behavioral Sciences and the Law* 27:743–752.

Way BB, D Abreu, D Ramirez-Romero, D Aziz, and D Sawyer. 2007. Prison work release and mental illness: How do inmates with mental illness fare compared to inmates without mental illness in Prison Work Release Programs? *Forensic Sciences* 52:965–966.

Way BB, MH Allen, JL Mumpower, TR Stewart, and SM Banks. 1998. Inter-rater agreement among psychiatrists in psychiatric emergency services. *American Journal of Psychiatry* 155:1423–1428.

Way BB, C Buscema, and D Sawyer. 2004. Quality of life instrument in prison: Detecting disability, external validity, and factor structure. *American Journal of Forensic Psychology* 22:1–12.

Way BB, JA Dvoskin, and HJ Steadman. 1991. Forensic inpatients in the United States: Regional and system differences. *American Academy of Psychiatry and the Law* 19:405–412.

Way BB, JA Dvoskin, HJ Steadman, HC Huguley, and SM Banks. 1990. Staffing of forensic inpatient services in the United States. *Hospital and Community Psychiatry* 41:172–174.

Way BB, AR Kaufman, JL Knoll, and SM Chlebowski. 2013. Suicidal ideation among inmate-patients in state prison: Prevalence, reluctance to report, and treatment preferences. *Behavioral Sciences and the Law* 31:230–238.

Way BB, R Miraglia, DA Sawyer, R Beer, and J Eddy. 2005. Suicide risk factors in New York State prisons. *International Journal of Psychiatry and the Law* 28:207–221.

Way BB, DA Sawyer, S Barboza, and R Nash. 2007b. Inmate suicide and time spent in disciplinary housing in New York State prison. *Psychiatric Services* 58:558–560.

Way BB, DA Sawyer, SN Lilly, CE Moffitt, and B Stapholz. 2008. Characteristics of inmate-patients who received a serious mental illness diagnosis during reception into New York State prison. *Psychiatric Services* 59:1335–1337.

Way BB, HE Smith, and D Sawyer. 2004. Transfers to civil psychiatric inpatient services from a maximum security forensic hospital. *Behavioral Sciences and the Law* 22:253–259.

Weinbaum CM, KM Sabin, and SS Santibanez. 2005. Hepatitis B, hepatitis C, and HIV in correctional populations: A review of epidemiology and prevention. *AIDS* 19(S3):S41–S46.

West HC, WJ Sabol, and SJ Greenman 2010. *Prisoners 2009*. Washington DC: Department of Justice.

Wilper AP, S Woolhandler, JW Boyd et al. 2009. The health and health care of US prisoners: Results of a nationwide survey. *American Journal of Public Health* 99(4):666–672.

Zaylor C, E Nelson, and DJ Cook. 2001. Clinical outcomes in a prison telepsychiatry clinic. *Journal of Telemedicine and Telecare* 7:47–49.

Zinger I and C Wichmann. 1999. *The Psychological Effects of 60 Days in Administrative Segregation*. Ottawa: Correctional Service of Canada.

55

Psychopharmacology in correctional settings

KATHRYN A. BURNS

INTRODUCTION

Correctional facilities are obligated to provide psychotropic medication as part of treatment for inmates with serious mental illness, because such inmates have a constitutional right to treatment and the standard of psychiatric care dictates that psychotropic medications are a necessary component of treatment. This determination flows from the U.S. Supreme Court's logic that failure to treat a serious medical need is a violation of the Eighth Amendment's proscription of cruel and unusual punishment (*Estelle v. Gamble* 1976). A federal court then determined that serious mental illness constitutes a serious medical need (*Bowring v. Godwin* 1977). Subsequent federal court decisions have more specifically addressed the need for the "appropriate use of psychotropic medications" as one component of a minimally adequate correctional mental health treatment program (*Ruiz v. Estelle* 1980). The Ruiz Court acknowledged concern about past "inappropriate" use of psychotropic medications in corrections. The concern was reflected in the court's edict that appropriate use of psychotropic medication entails prescription and monitoring by appropriately trained and licensed staff to treat mental disorders, and not solely as a means of behavioral control.

Against this backdrop of judicial skepticism toward corrections and concern about "dangerous" and mind-altering psychotropic medication, correctional facilities and systems must provide constitutionally adequate mental health care (*Ruiz v. Estelle* 1980). This chapter provides recommendations for consideration of medications for inclusion in a correctional formulary and discusses some aspects of managing the use of psychotropic medication in correctional settings. In spite of the focus on psychotropic medication, this chapter does not imply or otherwise endorse the notion that treatment with psychotropic medication alone is sufficient mental health care. Medication is a significant and necessary component of treatment, but not the sole intervention. Other types of interventions to be included in a treatment program will not be discussed as they are outside the scope of this chapter. The discussion about psychotropic medication that follows also assumes that medication is prescribed as part of a treatment plan and, as such, is clinically indicated, and that there are appropriately trained staff in sufficient numbers to periodically monitor response and potential side effects, and adjust the treatment, including medication, as necessary.

FORMULARY CONSIDERATIONS

General considerations

FACILITY MISSION AND POPULATION-BASED CONSIDERATIONS

When considering medications for inclusion on a correctional formulary, the facility's mission and inmate population characteristics are of paramount importance. For example, there are different considerations for jails, with high population turnover and short stays, versus prisons, where stays are generally longer with fewer inmates entering the system annually. Jails must consider a very broad formulary so that medications that are prescribed to detainees entering the jail from the community are continued without interruption, because many detainees will be returning to their community clinic after a very short jail stay. Alternatively, jails could have a narrow or restrictive formulary as long as they provide immediate access to a psychiatrist or other mental health clinician with prescriptive authority to conduct an assessment and make a therapeutic substitution for the community medication if it is not contained in the jail's formulary. The size of most jails does not justify the expense of manning the booking process with a psychiatrist or other advanced clinician, particularly when detainees are received 24 hours a day. Prisons, on the other hand, generally receive inmates on weekdays during regular business hours and hold inmates for longer periods of time. This provides an opportunity to consider a more narrow psychotropic medication formulary as staffing is available to provide reception assessment, therapeutic substitution of medications when necessary, follow-up in the same correctional system using the same formulary, and adequate time to observe the effectiveness of the medication substituted and make changes as necessary.

Jails are also more likely to receive detainees directly from the community, and the prevalence of substance intoxication and withdrawal is generally higher than that found in prisons. Consequently, it is imperative that jails have immediate access to medications used to treat withdrawal and provide safe detoxification. Although inmates in prison also have a very high prevalence rate of substance use disorders, the likelihood of life-threatening withdrawal is lower than that which occurs in jails. (Most inmates entering prison have already undergone detoxification in jail, although prison clinicians should be prepared to treat withdrawal symptoms, and benzodiazepine use may be restricted for that purpose. Unrestricted access to benzodiazepines in prison settings can create serious problems that are discussed more fully below.)

The very high prevalence of substance use disorders among correctional populations must be considered when developing a correctional system formulary (Karberg and Mumola 2004). It does not provide an absolute ban on including controlled substances in the formulary, but there are correctional ramifications. There is significant risk that the medication would be diverted to someone other than the intended patient, either as part of the facility's black market in which medication and other items are routinely sold, or traded in exchange for cash, tobacco products, food, sexual favors, protection, or other items or services. Security concerns include having to deal with illicit trading, intoxicated inmates, inmate fights, and victimization, all of which present a risk of harm to other offenders as well as security staff who must respond to these challenges. Even if the patient does not intentionally misuse his or her prescribed medication, he or she is vulnerable to intimidation by others to surrender their prescribed medication under threat of, or actual use of, physical force (Burns 2009). The strength of the addiction is incredibly pervasive and consuming for some addicts. Inmates ferment their own alcoholic beverages and have learned which medications or combinations of medications, controlled and noncontrolled substances, can be used to achieve a high (Bartlett et al. 2014). The knowledge that a weaker inmate is routinely receiving a controlled medication on a daily basis can present an opportunity for a steady supply for an addict who threatens or extorts it out of the more vulnerable inmate. Nearly all psychotropic medications are directly administered by nursing staff in correctional facilities (as opposed to giving inmates a monthly supply to keep in their property and take as directed). This is particularly true of medications that have a potential for abuse, misuse, or lethality in overdose. The storage, inventory, handling, and administration of controlled substances add significant nursing time to an already time-consuming system. Also, nursing preparation time can be prolonged if there is a requirement to administer liquid preparations and/or crush the medication prior to administration. (Although crushing the medication and placing it in liquid before handing it to the intended patient may help reduce the likelihood of diversion, it does not preclude it among these populations.) The cost of additional nursing preparation and administration time must also be multiplied by the requirement for multiple daily dosing unless extended release preparations are used which cannot be crushed. Medical administrators must be judicious when considering whether or not to include medication that is not medically necessary, highly abused, and requires special handling to a generally already overburdened medication administration process (Burns 2010).

Notwithstanding the preceding discussion, correctional facilities housing juveniles have different formulary considerations than adult facilities based on the prevalence of certain disorders, specifically Attention Deficit/Hyperactivity Disorder. Juveniles often enter custody on prescribed stimulant medications for well-documented diagnoses of ADHD. In these instances, juvenile facilities may wish to include stimulants on the formulary for continuity of care as well as clinical efficacy. (This is not to imply that adult offenders do not have the disorder, but the prevalence is lower and most adults do not enter jail or prison on prescribed stimulant medication. If continued use is medically necessary, the stimulant can be assessed by way of a preauthorization process to access a nonformulary medication.)

The number of older offenders in custody is increasing rapidly as a result of sentencing, three strikes legislation, and the aging of the inmate population (American Civil Liberties Union 2012). Facilities housing geriatric offenders will have additional factors to consider in weighing medications for inclusion in the formulary. Older inmates are more likely to have comorbid chronic and progressive medical conditions that impact psychotropic medication choices to manage the population. For example, tricyclic antidepressants are inexpensive and effective for the treatment of depression but may be contraindicated in older patients given their potential cardiotoxicity and anticholinergic side effects creating or exacerbating confusion. In this case, stronger consideration should be given to including selective serotonin reuptake inhibitor antidepressants on the formulary and excluding tricyclic medications. Additionally, given the prevalence of dementia, and particularly Alzheimer disease, correctional facilities housing older inmates may consider inclusion of a cholinesterase inhibitor on the psychotropic medication formulary. Although none have been shown to reverse dementia, there is evidence that they stabilize current functioning and delay further cognitive loss (Gunther 2013). These are important goals in correctional facilities aiming to preserve independent functioning as long as possible to reduce the need for more intensive nursing and supportive services. In general, prisons were not built for, or are ready to accommodate, the special needs of older inmates—most facilities use bunk beds and require fairly long walks to meals and clinic appointments, which present challenges to mobility-impaired older inmates. There are also security issues related to giving inmates canes, walkers, and other mobility aids.

Specific formulary considerations

ANTIPSYCHOTIC MEDICATIONS

Psychotropic medications classified as antipsychotic medications must be available for use in the treatment of schizophrenia and other psychotic disorders. Both conventional antipsychotic medications (the older or first generation of medications) as well as the newer or next-generation medications should be represented on the formulary for reasons that are at least in part related to side effect profiles. The conventional or first-generation antipsychotic medications are efficacious in treatment of psychosis but carry the potential burden of significant side effects related to normal body movement. Dystonia (severe, involuntary, and painful muscle spasms), profound restlessness (akathisia), medication-induced Parkinsonism (tremors and rigidity), and tardive dyskinesia (involuntary, uncontrolled movement of the muscles, most often involving muscles of the face and mouth, including the tongue) are among the types of movement side effects that are seen with first-generation antipsychotic medications (Bezchlibnyk-Butler et al. 2013). Some of them are preventable or responsive to the simultaneous use of antiparkinsonian medications including benztropine, amantadine, and trihexyphenidyl. However, benztropine and trihexyphenidyl have been misused/abused in correctional settings because they produce a type of "high" when ingested, smoked, or snorted. (Liquid or crushing these medications can reduce the likelihood of misuse and diversion but carries the added burdens discussed in relation to controlled substances: different storage considerations, additional nursing preparation time, and additional administration time.) Additionally, neither akathisia nor tardive dyskinesia is responsive to treatment with these medications. Akathisia resolves with the discontinuation of the offending antipsychotic medication, while tardive dyskinesia may resolve completely or lessen in severity with discontinuation of the medication but may also persist permanently. Monitoring of inmate patients prescribed typical antipsychotic medications must include regular examination at periodic intervals for the development of movement disorders for the duration of treatment with the medication. Most correctional systems utilize the Abnormal Involuntary Movement Scale (AIMS) to regularly examine and document the presence or absence of involuntary movements (Munetz and Benjamin 1988).

The newer or next-generation antipsychotic medications have also been called "atypical" because of their chemical mode of action when compared to the older or "typical" antipsychotic medications. Medications in this group include aripiprazole, asenapine maleate, clozapine, iloperidone, lurasidone, olanzapine, paliperidone, quetiapine, risperidone, and ziprasidone. As a group, they are less likely to impact normal movement or lead to the development of irreversible movement disorders. (The exception being risperidone, which does have some dose-dependent effect on movement.) However, these newer agents have demonstrated an increased risk for the development of adverse metabolic effects in patients taking them, which include hyperglycemia, diabetes, hyperlipidemia, and significant weight gain (Bezchlibnyk-Butler et al. 2013). Prescribers must carefully monitor all patients for whom the medications are prescribed for symptoms of hyperglycemia, and use these medications very cautiously with patients with pre-existing diabetes or significant risk factors for the development of diabetes. Baseline measurements of weight, blood pressure, fasting blood glucose, and lipids are recommended for all patients at the initiation of treatment with atypical antipsychotic medications and at periodic intervals thereafter during treatment, in addition to regular monitoring for symptoms of hyperglycemia (e.g., polydipsia, polyuria, weight gain, weakness) (American Diabetes Association 2004). Although monitoring these parameters is not overly burdensome, it can present challenges in large correctional facilities or systems in which inmate movement is highly controlled and medical and mental health services are not well integrated or co-located, so that monitoring body weights, blood pressures, and blood sugars may be more difficult than in a community clinic.

Previously, correctional systems tended to limit their formularies to first-generation antipsychotic medications due to the considerable medication cost differential in purchasing the older, generic formulations of medication compared to the newer and thus patented, name-brand next-generation medications. However, with time, many of the "newer" medications have become available in generic preparations and cost is less a consideration. Other previous considerations included the availability of the older medications as tablets, oral liquids, and injectable preparations (short-acting and decanoate formulations). Having this degree of options in medication formulation is helpful in addressing medication compliance and useful in emergencies. However, this too is changing and the newer, next-generation antipsychotic medications are becoming increasingly available in multiple preparations as well.

Additional considerations regarding formulary inclusion of various antipsychotic medications include clozapine's demonstrated efficacy for treatment of symptoms that have been refractory to treatment with other medications. Inclusion, or at least ready access, to clozapine is therefore important to ensure continuity of care for persons who have been taking clozapine in the community, as well as for use in patients with treatment-resistant symptoms. Some of the atypical medications also have indications for use in the treatment of affective disorders, including depression and bipolar disorder. The capacity to use one medication to treat several types of disorders or symptoms is a cost-effective consideration for formulary inclusion. Last, unfortunately, quetiapine has been abused in correctional populations, and some systems and facilities have excluded it from their correctional formularies (Tamburello et al. 2012).

ANTIDEPRESSANT MEDICATIONS

Depressive illnesses are prevalent in correctional populations (James and Glaze 2006). A variety of antidepressant medications should be available in the correctional formulary to treat this serious psychiatric illness. Tricyclic antidepressants are inexpensive but potentially cardiotoxic and lethal in overdose, necessitating ongoing nurse administration of the medication for the duration of confinement. Selective serotonin reuptake inhibitors (SSRIs) are equally efficacious and have a better safety profile so they could be prescribed as an inmate self-carry or keep-on-person medication. This can reduce the time spent in medication administration activities for nurses as well as inmates, and may enhance compliance.

Typically, monoamine oxidase inhibitors are not included on correctional formularies due to the dietary restrictions and over-the-counter cold and flu medications' potential to interact and precipitate hypertensive crisis. Other biochemically distinct types of medication such as amoxapine, mirtazapine, venlafaxine, and duloxetine may also be considered for formulary inclusion based on good safety profiles and efficacy in treatment of depression and sustaining remission. Unfortunately, bupropion has been widely misused in correctional populations. It has been crushed and snorted to achieve a type of high and so is no longer on many correctional formularies. Trazodone has a small but serious side effect of priapism among men which sometimes requires rapid surgical intervention and may result in permanent sterility. Because prompt recognition of the seriousness of this side effect and rapidly accessing emergency surgical treatment are often hard to guarantee in correctional facilities (prisons particularly are often located in quite remote areas and distant from medical facilities), and due to the availability of many other, safer antidepressant medication alternatives, trazodone is not recommended for inclusion on correctional formularies.

Some antidepressant medications also have demonstrated efficacy in the treatment of anxiety disorders and posttraumatic stress disorder. Paroxetine, venlafaxine, and nefazodone are particularly helpful in this regard. The versatility of some medications in treatment of various types of disorders is another important consideration for medication inclusion on the correctional formulary. Use of these types of medications for treatment of anxiety provides symptomatic relief without having to resort to the use of benzodiazepines, with all of the inherent problems associated with them in correctional settings.

MOOD-STABILIZING MEDICATIONS

Medications typically described as mood-stabilizing medications must be included on the correctional formulary for treatment of bipolar disorder, schizoaffective disorder, and other disorders with a recurrent or cyclical affective component. They may also be prescribed for inmates exhibiting a high degree of impulsivity and aggression. As a group, these medications typically require the most frequent laboratory testing to monitor serum levels of the medication and surveillance for potential effects on other systems such as hepatic metabolism, thyroid and kidney function, and bone marrow production. Lithium is probably the oldest known and least expensive medication of demonstrated efficacy in the treatment of bipolar disorder. It is not always well tolerated. Several medications originally developed as anticonvulsants have been approved by the FDA for treatment of bipolar disorder, including divalproex, valproic acid, carbamazepine, and lamotrigine. Other anticonvulsants have been widely used "off label" in both the community and in correctional facilities for treatment of bipolar disorder (Bezchlibnyk-Butler et al. 2013). Correctional administrators, and ideally, a Pharmacy and Therapeutics Committee that includes representation of psychiatrists and pharmacists, should address whether or not to permit off-label uses of medications as a matter of institutional policy and practice.

OTHER CLASSES OF PSYCHOTROPIC MEDICATIONS

As previously mentioned, benzodiazepine inclusion on correctional formularies should most likely be limited for detoxification and withdrawal protocols, although time-limited use during a psychiatric emergency or when an inmate is experiencing an acute stressor could also be considered. This is due to the high prevalence of substance abuse in correctional populations, the development of tolerance and physical dependence, and the availability of other efficacious treatments for anxiety disorders and symptoms. Certain of the antidepressant medications, as well as buspirone and hydroxyzine, provide alternative and effective treatment of anxiety without the difficulties inherent in prescribing controlled substances.

Inclusion of which types of the various classes of psychotropic medications discussed in the preceding sections as well as any other psychotropic medication placement on the formulary should be based on an analysis of the correctional facility mission, length of stay, age of inmate population, type(s) of serious mental illnesses present in the population, and prevalence of substance use disorders. Additional considerations include continuity of care and direct and indirect costs, including medication procurement, preparation, and administration procedures. In addition to adoption of a standard psychotropic medication formulary, every facility or system must provide a mechanism that permits review and approval to access medications that are not on the formulary. This process must include that medical consideration be given on a case-by-case basis to assure that inmates are not denied appropriate treatment for their serious mental health needs.

INFORMED CONSENT

Although correctional facilities are inherently coercive environments, the principles of informed consent remain applicable, and the nature and purpose of the proposed psychotropic medication, the risks and benefits of the medication, treatment alternatives, and the risks and benefits of no treatment must be explained in a way that is understandable by the inmate so that he or she can make an informed choice. The discussion and consent to treatment should be documented in the medical record. Inmates do have a right to refuse treatment, and this should also be explained. Correctional policies regarding informed consent, the right to refuse treatment, and the circumstances under which refusals can be overridden should conform to the rules and procedures of the jurisdiction in which the facility is located (National Commission on Correctional Health Care 2014a,b).

DELIVERY/ADMINISTRATION MODELS

Correctional facilities have developed a number of procedural mechanisms to ensure that medications are administered appropriately to inmates. (Medication administration is the act in which a single dose of an identified medication is given to the inmate to whom it is intended.) Virtually all psychotropic medications are directly administered by nursing staff. This is in contrast to other types of medications that may permit an inmate to retain possession of a limited supply of medication to take as directed on his or her own initiative rather than receiving them from a nurse.

Nursing administration of medication is accomplished in a number of ways, including a central administration point such as the infirmary or clinic at which all inmates must line up at certain specified times to receive their medications. This is commonly known as "pill call" or "med line." In this model, the length of the line and whether inmates wait indoors or outside in inclement weather have grave effects on medication compliance rates. In facilities where security concerns or the physical plant itself do not permit inmate movement to a central location for medication administration, a nurse may carry and then administer medications on the inmate housing units. In this situation, there may be a short pill call line on each housing unit. Alternatively, the nurse may walk from cell to cell administering medication accompanied by correctional staff. Many large facilities utilize a combination of these delivery methods, and some systems permit a limited number of psychotropic medications to be self-administered, such as SSRI antidepressants or some of the mood stabilizers other than lithium.

Given the numbers of inmates prescribed psychotropic medication, medication administration can be a very labor-intensive and time-consuming process. This impacts the number of times per day that medications may be administered (some facilities have only two administration times) and seriously limits the ability to use prn medications except under certain circumstances such as specialized mental health housing units with on-site nursing coverage. Fortunately, most psychotropic medication may be taken only once or twice daily given their metabolism. Nevertheless, medication administration procedures and times impact prescribers' medication selection, format (liquid versus pill form), and dosing frequency (twice a day versus sustained release preparations and once a day dosing), so prescribers must be aware of them.

HEAT-RELATED COMPLICATIONS OF PSYCHOTROPIC MEDICATIONS

Some psychotropic medications, particularly antipsychotic and certain antidepressant medications, are associated with an increased sensitivity to sunlight and risk of heatstroke, hyperthermia, and heat prostration. This is believed due to anticholinergic and antidopaminergic activity of the medications. However, there is also evidence of abnormal thermoregulation in individuals with schizophrenia, placing them at increased risk of heatstroke separate from potential medication effects (Charder and Knoll 2014). The occurrence of heat-related problems for inmates taking psychotropic medications may be exacerbated in correctional facilities where living areas have very limited or no means of cooling air temperature and work details may involve being outdoors and engaging in physical exertion during the heat of the day. Sustained high body temperatures that occur in untreated heatstroke may result in brain or muscle damage, kidney failure, coma, and even death.

Institutional staff at all levels (administration, medical, mental health, and custody staff) must be aware of the increased sensitivity of inmates taking psychotropic medications to heat-related problems and develop policies and procedures that ensure recognition of potential heatstroke and permit actions designed to lower body temperature. Generally, these procedures include providing additional water and break times, monitoring indoor and outdoor temperatures, increasing ventilation and instituting cooling measures (additional access to ice and cool water showers), considering the transfer to a cooler area of the institution, and accessing emergency medical care when necessary.

INVOLUNTARY MEDICATION

Medication may be administered forcibly to a nonconsenting inmate during an emergency so long as it is administered for medically appropriate reasons, ordered by an appropriately licensed prescriber, and used for a limited duration of time. These conditions are often specified by state rules and regulations. An emergency is generally defined as an imminent threat to the life or safety of the inmate or others or significant property destruction (National Commission on Correctional Health Care 2014a,b). Emergency administration of medication may prevent the need for the application of physical restraints or be used to assist the inmate in regaining control of his or her behavior if physical restraint is utilized.

Correctional facilities also have the capacity to administer psychotropic medication to competent, but refusing inmates, provided that certain procedural requirements are followed. The U.S. Supreme Court upheld a policy and procedure of the Washington Department of Corrections that permitted the Department of Corrections to approve involuntary administration of psychotropic medication rather than seek such approval from an outside entity, such as a court. The Supreme Court reasoned that correctional facilities have an obligation to protect the safety of other inmates in their custody, their own staff, and visitors, and have an interest in maintaining order in the facility. Therefore, under certain circumstances, correctional facilities may override medication refusals in instances where an inmate has a mental disorder and poses a likelihood of serious harm to himself or herself or others or is gravely disabled. Washington's policy provided inmates facing involuntary medication the right to a hearing on the issue; the right to notice of the hearing; the rights to attend the hearing, present evidence, and cross-examine witnesses; representation by a lay advisor; the right to appeal the decision; and the right to periodic review of ongoing administration of involuntary medication. A small committee of medical/mental health professionals with no current treatment relationship conducts the hearing (*Washington v. Harper* 1990). The hearing committee may consider security factors, but the decision is primarily a medical decision regarding the necessity of treatment with medication (Cohen 1998). Individual state laws may impose additional procedural requirements beyond these rights that were accepted as adequate by the *Harper* court.

PRESCRIBING GUIDELINES

Correctional facilities and systems must adopt standard policy statements and practice guidelines that are applied consistently by all practitioners with respect to psychotropic medications. This is imperative from a number of standpoints, including that practice guidelines and medication algorithms are the evolving standard of care in modern psychiatric practice. They are typically evidence based, which provides both a scientific basis and clinical rationale for making treatment decisions (American Psychiatric Association 2006). Correctional practice must stay current with community care. It is also important that prescribers working in a particular facility or system are consistent in their medication interventions. This is helpful to inmate patients as it provides for continuity of care across prescribers within a given facility but also when transferring from one prison to the next. It is also helpful in managing psychiatric workloads and inmate expectations. For example, if two prescribers are working at the same facility and one prescribes clonazepam as a first-line treatment for bipolar disorder, it will not take long for the second prescriber's bipolar patients to ask for clonazepam or be switched to the clonazepam caseload. Eventually, many other inmates will present to the first prescriber with bipolar symptoms that were remarkably latent until a benzodiazepine first-line treatment became available at the facility.

Policy statements should also address expectations regarding the frequency of medication management appointments, laboratory studies, and other monitoring parameter expectations (e.g., AIMS exams, abdominal girth measurements). Direction regarding the authorization process for access to nonformulary medications should also be included in the policy.

SUMMARY

Appropriate use of psychotropic medication is a significant and necessary component of treatment for offenders with serious mental illness confined in correctional facilities. It should be prescribed only as clinically indicated and as part of a treatment plan. Correctional facilities must have trained and appropriately credentialed staff in sufficient numbers to prescribe psychotropic medication and periodically monitor inmate patients for their response to treatment and potential side effects, and adjust the treatment, including medication, as necessary. Given national data about the prevalence of serious mental illness in correctional facilities, it is certain that antipsychotic, antidepressant, and mood-stabilizing medication must be available on every correctional formulary, while other types of medication may be considered based on the facility's mission, inmate population characteristics (age, gender, and the types and prevalence of mental illnesses that occur in the population served), and lengths of stay.

The adoption of recognized practice guidelines and medication algorithms for the treatment of various types of mental illness provides evidence-based, medically accepted treatment rationales and uniformity in the provision of treatment. This is particularly important for correctional systems where care is under constant scrutiny and often called into question by inmates, families, advocacy groups, and the courts. Correctional procedures for medication administration may impact medication choice, dosing frequency, and inmate medication compliance. Other factors that are related to psychotropic medication use in correctional facilities that require some special consideration include informed consent for treatment in an inherently coercive environment, vigilance for the possibility of heat-related disorders given the physical environment and inmate work details, and procedures to override medication refusal when clinically appropriate and necessary.

SUMMARY KEY POINTS

- Psychotropic medication is an essential component of mental health treatment for offenders confined in correctional facilities though it must be prescribed in conjunction with other clinically indicated treatment interventions.
- The use of psychotropic medication in correctional facilities requires appropriately trained staff in sufficient numbers for the prescription of

medication, periodic monitoring for response to treatment and side effects and dose adjustment.

- All correctional formularies must contain antipsychotic, antidepressant and mood stabilizing medications given the prevalence of serious mental illness in correctional populations.
- Inclusion of other types of psychotropic medication on the correctional formulary is based on characteristics of the offender population in the facility such as offender age, gender, other types of mental disorders present and prevalence of substance use disorders in addition to clinical efficacy and cost considerations.
- There are some aspects of psychotropic medication use unique to practice in corrections that include medication delivery/medication administration models, informed consent in an inherently coercive environment and the types of processes utilized to permit involuntary administration of medication.

REFERENCES

American Civil Liberties Union. 2012. *At America's Expense: The Mass Incarceration of the Elderly.* New York: American Civil Liberties Union. http://www.aclu.org/criminal-law-reform/report-americas-expense-mass-incarceration-elderly, accessed August 8, 2016.

American Diabetes Association. 2004. Consensus development conference on antipsychotic drugs and obesity and diabetes. *Diabetes Care* 27(2):596–601.

American Psychiatric Association. 2006. *Practice Guidelines for the Treatment of Psychiatric Disorders: Compendium.* Arlington, VA: American Psychiatric Association. http://psychiatryonline.org/guidelines.aspx, accessed August 8, 2016.

Bartlett A, N Dholakia, R England et al. 2014. Prison prescribing practice: Practitioners' perspectives on why prison is different. *International Journal of Clinical Practice* 68(4):413–417.

Bezchlibnyk-Butler KZ, JJ Jeffries, RM Procyshyn, and AD Virani. 2013. *Clinical Handbook of Psychotropic Drugs,* 20th revised edition. Boston: Hogrefe and Huber.

Bowring v. Godwin, 551 F.2d 44 (4th Cir 1977).

Burns KA. 2009. Commentary: The top ten reasons to limit prescription of controlled substances in prisons. *Journal of the American Academy of Psychiatry and the Law* 37:50–52.

Burns KA. 2010. Pharmacotherapy in correctional settings. In *Handbook of Correctional Mental Health,* 2nd edition, edited by CL Scott, Arlington, VA: American Psychiatric Publishing, 321–344.

Charder N and Knoll J. 2014. Heatstroke and psychiatric patients. *Psychiatric Times,* July 15.

Cohen F. 1998. *The Mentally Disordered Inmate and the Law.* Kingston, NJ: Civic Research Institute.

Estelle v. Gamble, 429 U.S. 97 (1976).

Gunther CS. 2013. Current pharmacologic treatment of dementia. *Carlat Report Psychiatry* 11(10):1–8.

James DJ and LE Glaze. 2006. *Mental Health Problems of Prison and Jail Inmates. Bureau of Justice Statistics Special Report.* NCJ 213600. Washington, DC: U.S. Department of Justice.

Karberg JC and CJ Mumola. 2004. *Drug Use and Dependence, State and Federal Prisoners. Bureau of Justice Statistics Report.* NCJ 213530. Washington, DC: U.S. Department of Justice.

Munetz MR and S Benjamin. 1988. How to examine patients using the abnormal involuntary movement scale. *Hospital and Community Psychiatry* 39(11):1172–1177.

National Commission on Correctional Health Care. 2014a. *Standards for Health Services in Jails.* Chicago: National Commission on Correctional Health Care.

National Commission on Correctional Health Care. 2014b. *Standards for Health Services in Prisons.* Chicago: National Commission on Correctional Health Care.

Ruiz v. Estelle, 53 F Supp 1265, S.D. Texas (1980).

Tamburello AC, JA Lieberman, RM Baum, and R Reeves. 2012. Successful removal of quetiapine from a correctional formulary. *Journal of the American Academy of Psychiatry and the Law* 40(4):502–508.

Washington v. Harper, 494 U.S. 210 (1990).

56

Suicide in correctional settings: Epidemiology, risk assessment, and prevention

JAMES L. KNOLL AND ANDREW R. KAUFMAN

INTRODUCTION

Suicide prevention in correctional settings requires a well-coordinated effort by mental health staff, corrections officers, and correctional administrators. The correctional environment creates special challenges that must be considered in suicide prevention policy and procedure. The correctional psychiatrist must be familiar with the standard clinical suicide risk assessment process, as well as critical nuances of risk assessment particular to correctional settings. Many evidence-based correctional suicide risk factors are known and must be considered during the screening process, as well as at clinically relevant times. This chapter will cover correctional suicide risk assessment and prevention from a psychiatric perspective, as well as the basic elements of correctional suicide prevention efforts from a systems perspective. Special clinical challenges in suicide prevention will also be discussed.

CORRECTIONAL SUICIDE-OVERVIEW

Correctional settings have a heightened risk of suicide due to many factors, including the fact that they are "repositories for vulnerable groups that are traditionally among the highest risk for suicide, such as young males, persons with mental disorders, socially disenfranchised … [and] people with substance use problems" (World Health Organization 2007). Suicide is the leading cause of death in local jails (Noonan and Ginder 2014). For female prisoners, it was the most common cause of unnatural death from 2001 to 2012. The suicide rate for incarcerated juveniles is approximately two times higher than adult inmates. Prior to the 1980s, correctional suicide prevention efforts across the United States were underdeveloped and of inconsistent quality. Legal action and research resulted in more effective suicide prevention policy and procedure, leading to significant reductions in correctional suicide. Whereas suicide among jail inmates in 1983 occurred at a rate of 129 per 100,000 inmates, by 1993 the rate had been reduced by more than half (54 per 100,000 inmates) (Mumola 2005). In 2002, the jail suicide rate had fallen to a third of the 1983 rate (47 per 100,000). Although not as pronounced, a similar trend was observed in state prisons during the same time period. While suicide rates in state prisons have always been lower than rates in jails, the rate of state prison suicide dropped from 34 per 100,000 in 1980 to 14 per 100,000 inmates in 2002 (Mumola 2005).

Clearly, changes made by correctional facilities over the past 30 years have had a powerful effect. Yet because the risk of suicide in corrections remains elevated compared to the general population, suicide prevention efforts endure as a pressing obligation. Correctional suicide risk factors have been researched extensively, and a list of evidence-based risk factors is given in Table 56.1. Due to the special circumstances of the correctional environment, suicide risk factor analyses much reach beyond mere psychiatric pathology and consider a range of unique variables (Knoll 2010). Further, some risk factors apply more strongly to jail settings, while others apply more to prison settings (Mumola 2005). For example, jail suicides typically occur in the first week of custody. In contrast, most state prison suicides occur during the first year of confinement. One similarity shared by jails and prisons is the method of suicide. In both, hanging (or ligature strangulation) is the most commonly used method (Shaw 2004). Thus, suicide prevention efforts must consider architectural approaches to include eliminating ligature points. Regardless of the setting, deaths by suicide in correctional settings have a powerfully devastating impact emotionally, legally, and financially.

The majority of correctional suicide prevention program guidelines, including those of the NCCHC and World Health Organization (WHO), recommend building policy and procedure around the following core elements:

- Correctional staff suicide prevention *training*
- Intake *screening* procedures
- Observation and monitoring procedures

Table 56.1 Correctional suicide risk factors

Demographic Factors
- Male gender (Noonan and Ginder 2014)
- Age 55 and older (Noonan and Ginder 2014)
- White or Hispanic, African American (Hayes 2010)
- Juvenile/youthful status (Gallagher and Dobrin 2006; Roberts and Bender 2006; Noonan and Ginder 2014)

Historical Factors
- Past suicide attempts (Fruehwald et al. 2004; Suominen et al. 2004; Hayes 2010)
- Violent or serious past attempts (Giner et al. 2014)
- History of psychiatric treatment and/or mental illness (Green et al. 1993; He et al. 2001; Goss et al. 2002; Shaw et al. 2004; Way et al. 2005; Daniel and Fleming 2006; Patterson and Hughes 2008)
- History of substance abuse (Green et al. 1993; Gore 1999; Shaw et al. 2004; Way et al. 2005)
- History of traumatic life events: childhood physical or sexual abuse, abandonment (Blaauw et al. 2002)
- Family history of suicide
- Chronic physical illness
- Conviction for a violent crime against a person (especially homicide, rape, child molestation) (DuRand et al. 1995; Mumola 2005; Duthé et al. 2013)
- First incarceration (Daniel and Fleming 2006)

Clinical Factors
- Mood disorder (He et al. 2001)
- Suicidal ideas
- Hopelessness (Ivanoff and Jang 1991)
- Irritation, rage
- Psychotic disorder (He et al. 2001)
- Impulsive, aggressive traits (Dumais et al. 2005)
- Severe personality disorder (He et al. 2001; Black et al. 2007)
- Unwilling to accept help

Social Factors
- Recent harassment: bullying, humiliation, sexual assault, peer conflict (Blaauw et al. 2001; Way et al. 2005)
- Victim of sexual or physical violence (without also perpetrating it) in last 12 months (Encrenaz et al. 2014)
- Loneliness (Brown and Day 2008)
- Overcrowded conditions (Kovasznay et al. 2004; Opitz-Welke et al. 2013)
- Recent life crisis (e.g., loss, family conflict, bereavement, loss of support, recent bad news, recent punitive sanctions, new charges, unexpected sentence) (Kovasznay et al. 2004; Way et al. 2005; Patterson and Hughes 2008)
- Longer prison length of stay (Frottier et al. 2002)

Environmental Factors
- Jails and holding facilities: first 1–2 weeks of incarceration (Hayes 2010; Noonan and Ginder 2014)
- Secure housing unit/isolation/single celled (Fruehwald et al. 2004; Daniel and Fleming 2006; Duthé et al. 2013; Reeves and Tamburello 2014)
- First 2 months of SHU placement (Way et al. 2007)
- Death row (Lester and Tartaro 2002)
- Ligature points accessible

Acute Items
- Suicidal intent
- Suicidal plan
- Available means (e.g., lethal medications, ligatures, sharps)
- Acts of anticipation (e.g., suicide note, putting affairs in order, giving away belongings)
- Anxiety, agitation (Kovasznay et al. 2004)
- Recent substance use or intoxication (Hayes 2010)
- Dysphoric or agitated depression
- Psychosis with delusions of nihilism or doom
- Global insomnia

Other Considerations/Individual-Specific Risk Factors
- Consider vulnerabilities of the individual, and how they may be affected by demands of the correctional setting

(Continued)

Table 56.1 (*Continued*) Correctional suicide risk factors

Risk-Reducing Factors

- Receiving visits from family members (Duthé et al. 2014)
- Purposeful activity (Leese et al. 2006)
- Future-oriented thinking, behavior, plans
- Ability to cite reasons for living (Malone et al. 2000)
- Good social support (Eagles et al. 2003)
- Absence of suicidal ideas or intent
- Hopefulness
- Willingness to accept help and/or treatment
- Good therapeutic alliance with treatment provider
- Stable mood symptoms, low symptom severity
- Religious or moral prohibition (Eagles et al. 2003)
- Compliance with effective treatment (Baldessarini et al. 2006)

- Clinical risk *assessment* and psychiatric evaluation
- Risk management and *treatment*
- Effective correctional staff *communication*

These important program elements must be prioritized and vigorously supported by administrative and system-wide efforts.

SCREENING FOR SUICIDE RISK

Screening is the principle way to identify individuals with a potentially elevated suicide risk. There are several key times when inmates should be screened due to an association with increased risk. In jails and other facilities with unsentenced, pretrial detainees, 33% of suicides occur during the first 48 hours and an additional 27% between day 2 and 14 of confinement (Hayes 2010). Thus, it is critical to begin screening right away as part of the admission/booking process. Additional observation during the first 2 weeks in a reception housing area will help identify warning signs. Another critical period for pretrial detainees is upon returning from court after a verdict, sentencing hearing, or other critical adjudicatory outcome.

For inmates in any correctional setting, screening is important at times that have been associated with increased suicide risk, such as after receiving bad news, or after suffering a humiliation. Inmates in punitive segregation and isolation, such as a Secure Housing Unit (Way et al. 2007), are also at an elevated risk and should be screened more frequently and observed daily for warning signs. Punitive isolation consisting of single-cell status has been associated with a particularly high risk for suicide (Reeves and Tamburello 2014).

Another special population with a very high rate, five times the general public rate (Lester and Tartaro 2002), of suicide are death row inmates. Treating psychiatrists on death row may encounter inmates suffering from overwhelming fear, helplessness, recurrent depression, and self-mutilation (Blank 2006). Inmates who are highly antisocial can also be at risk for suicide, particularly when there is comorbid depression and anxiety (Pennington et al. 2014). Familiarity with the evolving research on correctional suicide is a must for proper risk assessment and formulating correctional suicide prevention policy and procedure.

As the evidence base for screening progresses, it is likely that homegrown screening instruments will be replaced by more reliable tools. For example, in a study of 1120 federal inmates, the Suicide Ideation Scale and the Suicide Potential Index on the Personality Assessment Inventory showed good validity (Patry and Magaletta 2015). In addition, Suicide Concerns for Offenders in Prison Environment (SCOPE) and the Suicide Potential Scale have shown promise when tested among adult offenders (Perry et al. 2010). The personality assessment inventory (PAI) has also been shown to have good clinical utility in correctional settings (Wang et al. 1997; Rogers et al. 1998).

Screening should be performed by trained staff. Checklists or validated questionnaires should be utilized to ensure consistent and thorough procedure to identify at-risk individuals. Upon completion of the screening process, there should be clear guidelines as to when and how an individual will be referred for further assessment, and whether the individual should be placed on suicide precautions in the interim. The WHO (2007) recommended a variety of factors to be assessed at screening. These include the following:

- Presence of thoughts of death or suicide, current and past
- Past suicidal behavior, including in the current facility
- Past placement on suicide precautions in a correctional setting
- Prior mental health treatment, including hospitalizations
- Concerns by the arresting officer about suicide in this person
- Family history of suicide
- Recent significant loss (job, relationship, death of family/friend, etc.)
- Recent substance use and/or intoxication
- Appearance or expressions of hopelessness or fear of the future

- No social support
- Very serious and/or violent criminal charge (e.g., homicide, rape)
- A position of respect or prestige in the community
- Bizarre or confused actions, such as in a psychotic or delirious state

SUICIDE RISK ASSESSMENT PROCEDURE

For mental health professionals, it is considered the standard of care to perform an adequate suicide risk assessment (Simon 2002). All inmates/detainees who have screened positive for some level of suicide risk should be urgently referred to a mental health professional. Failing to adequately assess an inmate patient's suicide risk when clinically necessary deprives the clinician of the ability to identify, treat, and manage a patient's suicide risk. A comprehensive psychiatric evaluation is the essential, core element of the suicide assessment process (APA 2003). A thorough evaluation enables the clinician to (1) identify risk factors, (2) assess the overall degree of suicidality, and (3) implement precautions and treatment interventions designed to reduce a specific inmate patient's suicide risk. The value of identifying risk factors goes beyond assessment of risk, in that it allows the clinician to target potentially modifiable risk factors with appropriate treatment interventions. The suicide risk assessment procedure can be taught to mental health staff in the form of a structured, evidence-based training program, resulting in improved patient care and documentation (McNiel et al. 2008).

The clinical assessment for correctional suicide risk should not rely only on a standardized screening instrument or questionnaire but should include a thorough clinical interview that "allows the inmate to express his own subjective experience" (Felthous and Holzer 2006). Suicide risk assessment is a continuous, dynamic process in which all mental health staff should be well trained and ready to perform at any clinical encounter (Daniel 2006). Circumstances in which a suicide risk assessment is clinically indicated include abrupt changes in clinical presentation, and a lack of improvement or gradual worsening despite treatment. In the absence of suicidal intent, it is still critical to assess the degree and intensity of a patient's suicidal ideation. Repeat suicide assessments over time will be required because of the waxing and waning nature of suicidality. Thus, the suicide risk assessment is similar to checking an inmate patient's temperature when clinically indicated to see if he or she has a fever.

An adequate suicide risk assessment does not rely solely on an inmate patient's denial of suicidal intent, but involves an assessment of both risk-enhancing *and* protective factors in the context of the individual's circumstances and clinical status. In one survey of prison inmates, more than 40% reported they were unwilling to tell staff if they had suicidal thoughts (Way et al. 2013). The overall assessment of risk is a clinical judgment call that is clinically informed and supported by information gathered (Simon 2002). The systematic suicide risk assessment procedure includes the following elements:

1. Perform a general clinical evaluation (mental status exam, differential diagnosis, etc.)
2. Review relevant records
3. Gather necessary collateral information
4. Carefully explore suicidal ideation, behavior, planning, desire, and intent
5. Identify risk-enhancing factors (acute, chronic, dynamic, and static)
6. Identify protective factors
7. Synthesize all of the above
8. Employ clinical judgment to assess overall risk level
9. Generate risk reduction plan targeting modifiable factors

It is possible to conceptualize risk factors as falling into two broad categories—dynamic or static (Meloy 2000). Dynamic risk factors are fluid and potentially modifiable. The clinical importance of dynamic risk factors lies in the clinician's potential ability to target him or her with interventions. Static risk factors do not change (e.g., gender, past suicide attempts) and have shown a statistical relationship with suicide risk. Risk assessment should include some form of analysis of risk factors, and a general estimate of overall risk level (low, moderate, or high). The risk level should be followed by a treatment plan that directly addresses each relevant dynamic risk factor, and the clinician's reasoning for choosing or rejecting options.

CORRECTIONAL SUICIDE RISK FACTORS

In the field of suicidology, there has been a shift toward identifying more precise, evidence-based, disease-specific risk factors (e.g., for bipolar disorder [Marangell et al. 2006]), as well as more proximate suicide warning signs such as hopelessness, rage, reckless behavior, feeling trapped, increased substance use, social withdrawal, anxiety/agitation, dramatic mood change, and a lack of sense of purpose in life (Rudd et al. 2006; Jobes et al. 2008). The same shift has occurred in correctional psychiatry, where many of the standard suicide risk factors seen in free society still apply, but where there are also important risk factors unique to corrections.

Correctional suicide research over the past several decades has identified important corrections-specific risk factors. In a review of completed suicides in the California Department of Corrections and Rehabilitation from 1999 to 2004, 154 suicides were examined (Patterson and Hughes 2008). The findings associated with completed suicide included having a history of psychiatric treatment (73%); being single celled (73%); and recent punitive sanctions (e.g., new charges, receiving an unexpected sentence). In addition to the importance of identifying risk factors, clinical experience suggests that it is equally important to consider individual-specific vulnerabilities and their interplay with the correctional environment (Ivanoff and Hayes 2002). This involves considering how a particular inmate's vulnerabilities are likely to interact with correctional environment demands, such as negative life events or noxious conditions. According to this stress–vulnerability–coping model, it is when the individual inmate's coping resources become overwhelmed that the risk of suicide is enhanced.

Simply asking the inmate about suicidal ideation does not ensure that accurate or complete information will be received (American Psychiatric Association 2003). Suicides may occur impulsively, so that a present state denial of suicidal ideas does not eliminate risk for suicide. Further, individuals seriously contemplating suicide may not report their thoughts (Resnick 2002). In a study of 112 veterans who completed suicide, 72% denied suicidal thoughts to their health-care provider during the last clinical contact before suicide (Denneson et al. 2010). A study of prison inmates found that a third or more of inmates would not report suicidal thoughts to mental health staff for various reasons, including aversion to being placed in an observation cell (Way et al. 2013). Thus, the absence of self-reported suicidal ideas in an inmate patient whose overall suicide risk is elevated must be considered in the totality of his or her clinical circumstances. Inquiring about suicidal ideas is an important part of an adequate risk assessment, but it is only one piece of the overall suicide risk assessment process (Jobes et al. 2008).

The process of eliciting risk factors and assessing suicide risk during the evaluation is both delicate and complex. In the correctional setting, the endeavor may be uniquely challenging due to a variety of correctional culture forces. It is important to be skillful, yet empathic during an evaluation of an inmate patient's suicide risk. The reliability of the suicide risk assessment will only be as good as the interviewer's skill and ability to actively listen and ask the right questions. Thus, it is helpful to be familiar with reliable interview techniques and lines of inquiry (Shea 2002; APA 2003; Shea 2004). It is important that the evaluation of the inmate be performed in a safe and confidential setting. The clinician should not allow convenience or other factors to result in a "cell-side" evaluation, or similar setting that would reduce the inmate patient's willingness to speak about sensitive issues.

MANAGING SUICIDE RISK IN CORRECTIONS

Correctional facilities have a custodial responsibility to provide for the safety of those being kept in custody. Custodial suicide cases turn on three primary theories of liability: (1) failure to provide care, (2) failure to protect, and (3) failure to train correctional staff in suicide prevention (Cohen et al. 2011). From a clinical standpoint, the management of an inmate patient's suicide risk typically involves three main approaches: (1) monitoring/safety, (2) ongoing risk assessment, and (3) interventions to reduce risk. Once screened individuals have been identified as having an elevated risk of suicide, the next steps involve providing safety, providing treatment, and managing the risk. Inmate patients who are at high or unknown risk are observed carefully in a safe environment until their risk diminishes. Simultaneously, a treatment and risk management plan should be crafted that addresses each modifiable suicide risk factor.

Many current methods used for the acutely suicidal inmate have a strong historical influence reflecting correctional policy and procedure. For example, the suicidal inmate may incur loss of privileges, removal of all clothing/bedding, and placement in a bare cell. Other forms of acute prevention include various types of monitoring. There is no substantive research on the effectiveness of these methods, and little is known about what is most helpful to the acutely suicidal inmate.

THE SUICIDE OBSERVATION CELL

The use of isolation for inmates at risk for suicide remains a prominent tool in correctional settings. Assignment to a suicide observation cell generally results in confinement for 23 hours a day. Often, access to family visits, phone calls, and even attorney visits are limited or prohibited. The inmate patient's clothing is usually removed and replaced with a smock made of material that cannot be easily torn or otherwise used to form a ligature. Bedding material is also removed and replaced with a Spartan mattress made of similar "strong cloth" material. Potentially dangerous items, such as razors or plastic bags, are removed from the inmate's possession. Beyond these measure, the presence of less dangerous items, such as reading materials, personal hygiene items (e.g., toothbrush), and writing instruments may vary according to facility practice and the inmate patient's clinical condition.

Some of these procedures may increase safety, but with a potential loss of therapeutic intervention. Further, experience suggests that inmate patients may simply begin denying suicidal thinking in order to leave the often harsh conditions of observation cells. Eighty percent of inmates characterized the observation cell as undesirable (Way et al. 2013). In fact, in order to avoid being placed in such a cell, Skogstad et al. (2005) and Way et al. (2013) have shown that inmates will purposely not report suicidal ideation to clinicians.

INTERVAL MONITORING

Interval observation by correctional or medical staff is a commonly used monitoring procedure. Interval times vary according to facility policy but generally include visual observation every 15, 30, or 60 minutes. Fifteen-minute checks are often used for inmate patients who are either high or moderate risk. Fifteen-minute checks became a standard interval, not as a result of scientific evidence, but out of convenience and tradition. One staff member can briefly observe a large number of individuals in a very short time while walking down tier hallways.

One potential problem with 15-minute checks is that they still leave enough unmonitored time for an inmate to die by suicide. Hanging/strangulation is by far the most common method of suicide in corrections. Permanent brain damage can occur within 4–5 minutes, and death may occur in 5–6 minutes (American Heart Association 1992). Thus, for some inmates at risk of suicide, the 15-minute interval is too long to prevent serious morbidity or mortality. More than one-fifth of jail suicide victims were found less than 15 minutes after last being observed, and over 6% of all jail suicides from 2005–2006 occurred while the individual was being observed every 15 minutes or more frequently (Hayes 2010). To prevent deaths by suicide in inmates on 15-minute checks, it has been recommend that checks be conducted at irregular and/or staggered intervals (WHO 2007; National Commission on Correctional Health Care 2013).

CONTINUOUS MONITORING

Continuous observation, or 1-to-1 monitoring, is reserved for the individuals who represent an acute or high risk of suicide. Inmate patients on 1-to-1 in correctional facilities are almost always isolated in special cells, where a staff member can sit in front of their cell to provide constant supervision. This is the most costly way to provide monitoring, requiring a staff member's undivided, full-time attention. Constant monitoring is very expensive, consumes disproportionate staff resources, and is unpopular among inmates due to lack of privacy and other concerns. It is used only when the risk is high and for as little time as necessary. The use of video surveillance may not be reliable, and in the case of an inmate with high or unknown risk, this method should not be reflexively accepted "simply because that is the option jail officials choose to offer" (Hayes 2010, 2013). Another strategy involves altering architectural structure so that a greater number of cells are in the line of sight of a staff member. Unfortunately, even with continuous monitoring, suicides still occur due to lapses of attention. Hayes (2010) reported that nearly 1% of jail suicide victims were on constant observation at the time of their death.

THE SUICIDE RISK REDUCTION PLAN

A risk management plan should be crafted immediately after the clinical risk assessment has been completed. Risk assessments should be done at clinically relevant or critical times, such as when the inmate patient experiences a significant clinical change, a change in precaution levels, a stressor, or upon admission and discharge to an inpatient unit. At such times, it may be necessary to obtain collateral data from mental health records, previous clinicians, or relevant social contacts.

The basic principle behind the risk reduction plan is to identify all those risk factors that are potentially modifiable or amenable to treatment, and target them with reasonable treatment interventions. Table 56.2 gives a sample suicide risk reduction plan for a 28-year-old man with depression, heroin abuse, personality disorder, and relationship problems. He was referred for outpatient treatment in the prison general population upon discharge from the prison inpatient psychiatric unit where he had been admitted after attempting to hang himself in his cell. Note how each dynamic risk factor is targeted with interventions that are reasonable and appropriate to the patient's clinical situation. It would be important for the clinical note to contain some clarification of the patient's comprehension and willingness to follow the treatment plan. Interventions may include utilizing evidence-based coping action plans, intensive outpatient treatment, crisis response planning, and other relevant psychosocial interventions (Jobes et al. 2008).

There is general consensus in the professional literature that the "suicide prevention contract" should not replace a comprehensive or systematic suicide risk assessment (Simon 2004; Lewis 2007). At the present time, there are many clear warnings in the literature about the misuse and unreliability of the suicide prevention contract (SPC) (Garvey et al. 2009). There may be many different designations for the SPC, such as, "No Harm" contract, "No Suicide" contract, "Contract for Safety," and others. They all have the putative goal of persuading the inmate patient to make a pact with the clinician not to harm himself or herself. The SPC remains a "questionable clinical practice intervention" (Edwards and Sachmann 2010).

The SPC and its substantial limitations have been well addressed for over a decade (Simon 1999). The main problems with the SPC include the fact that (1) the "contracts" do not protect against legal liability, (2) they are not considered contracts as understood by law, (3) there is no clinical research to support their use, and (4) there is an abundance of literature warning clinicians about their pitfalls. Some clinicians may use the SPC as a cursory or hurried way of documenting a patient's suicide risk. Some may use it as a way of "managing" the patient's suicide risk, failing to understand that it might help assess risk but cannot be

Table 56.2 Sample: Suicide risk reduction plan

Dynamic Risk Factors (Subject to Change)	Management Plans (Discussed with Patient)
1. Depression—moderate	1. Weekly psychiatric follow-up, selective serotonin reuptake inhibitor antidepressant
2. Impulsivity	2. Depakote, DBT program
3. Heroin abuse	3. Abstinence, Narcotics Anonymous (NA) groups, random toxicology screens
4. Life crisis—marital problems	4. Increased frequency of individual psychotherapy

relied on as an evidenced-based practice for preventing suicide. If an inmate patient refuses to contract for safety, this may provide some worthwhile clinical data. But more commonly, inmate patients will simply acquiesce to the contract, which results in a highly questionable intervention.

CORRECTIONAL SUICIDE RISK MANAGEMENT DOCUMENTATION

The primary purpose of documentation is clinical. Documentation is used to serve as a reminder of what has occurred so far in treatment, what has been helpful, and what interventions have not produced meaningful results. This data must be available not only for the primary clinician, but also for other treatment team members, consultants, and future caregivers. The issue of continuity of care is critical and commonly arises in malpractice suits where there occurred some form of communication breakdown between providers. Proper documentation helps ensure that information critical to the patient's continuing care is not disregarded. Documentation informs patient treatment and management and communicates this to other relevant staff so that they have this important data to consider when they are tasked with the patient's care. The record also serves to remind staff what has occurred so far in treatment, what has been helpful, and what interventions have not produced any meaningful results. Another important purpose of documentation involves administrative requirements, such as satisfying the requirements of various accrediting agencies and meeting the requirements of the correctional facility's administrative policies.

It is well known that post-suicide lawsuits account for the largest percentage of suits against psychiatrists (Baerger 2001; Packman et al. 2004). The American Psychiatric Association guidelines indicate that "Documenting the suicide assessment is essential" (APA 2003). Documentation is virtually always the centerpiece of post-suicide lawsuits. It is particularly critical to document the suicide risk assessment upon initial evaluation, significant changes in the patient's condition, or when there is a lack of improvement or worsening of the patient's condition. Risk assessment documentation should include some form of analysis of risk factors, and a general estimate of overall risk level (low, moderate, or high). This should be followed by a treatment plan (risk management plan as noted above) that directly addresses relevant dynamic risk factors, and the clinician's reasoning for choosing or rejecting options. When noting an action taken in furtherance of a risk management plan, it is essential to include a statement, however brief, of the rationale for the action. For example, the psychiatrist should document that he or she considered the option of inpatient hospitalization and the clinical basis for rejecting or proceeding with that option.

OTHER PREVENTION EFFORTS

Adequate correctional suicide prevention efforts go beyond screening and precautions for acute suicidal crises. Correctional administrators must develop and maintain comprehensive policies and practices (Hayes 2013). An array of programmatic interventions should be utilized, from immediate response to regular staff training and psychological autopsies of all fatalities by suicide. The immediate response to an inmate's suicidal cognitions or behavior should involve crisis intervention (Ivanoff and Hayes 2002). Crisis intervention procedures can be accomplished by both correctional and mental health staff. Crisis intervention consists of the following procedures carried out by trained correctional mental health staff: (1) establishing psychological contact with the inmate patient, (2) defining the precipitating problem, (3) encouraging exploration of the inmate patient's emotional conflict, (4) exploring and assessing past attempts to cope, (5) generating and examining alternative solutions, (6) taking action to restore cognitive and emotional functioning, and (7) dynamically reassessing suicide risk over time.

In terms of psychotherapeutic approaches, dialectical behavior therapy (DBT) has demonstrated effectiveness in reducing suicidal behavior in randomized clinical trials. DBT is a 1-year outpatient program composed of weekly group skills training and individual psychotherapy; however, modification may be made for specific correctional environments. Skills training targets include life-threatening behaviors, treatment-interfering behaviors, and quality of life behavior. Other skills commonly addressed include distress tolerance, emotion regulation, and interpersonal effectiveness. When compared to treatment as usual, DBT has shown significant decreases in suicidal behavior and self-mutilation. DBT has been modified for a correctional setting (DBT-Corrections Modified) and used to help inmate patients reduce impulsive–aggressive behaviors (Shelton et al. 2009).

In addition to the NCCHC recommendations for suicide prevention in corrections (http://www.ncchc.org/spotlight-on-the-standards-26-1), researchers have recommended the following prevention considerations (Patterson and Hughes 2008):

- Increased clinical monitoring of inmates in high-security units
- Follow-up monitoring regimens for suicidal inmates
- Group therapy for inmates in segregation who are on the mental health caseload
- Personal observation of inmates on suicide watch instead of video monitoring
- Improved CPR policy and practices
- Adequate confidential interviewing space
- Careful review of prior documentation by clinicians
- Timely completion of all documentation of the suicide assessment and management process

The NCCHC has recommended performing a review of all suicides as an important part of an overall suicide prevention program. In the authors' experience, forward-thinking institutions have formed "suicide prevention improvement teams" consisting of representative staff from mental health, security, medical, administration, and quality improvement. The team meets on a regular basis to focus on identifying opportunities for change and improvement. Traditional efforts at suicide prevention have often focused on retrospective analyses of inmates' individual risk factors. However, a process improvement project conducted in the Connecticut Department of Corrections found that suicides often occur "due to poor communication of past information from community to the corrections department for non-sentenced inmates; inability to communicate events that occurred in court for sentenced inmates; inability to assess contradictions for restrictive housing in a thorough and timely manner; interruptions in the orientation process and improper housing of inmates" (Helfand and Trestman 2008). These experts recommended performing a "root cause analysis" after sentinel events, using the FMEA (Failure Mode and Effects Analysis) process as a guideline (http://www.isixsigma.com/dictionary/failure-mode-and-effects-analysis-fmea/).

Every correctional institution should have an adequate suicide risk assessment training program for all correctional staff. When this training is done in a systematic way, using evidenced-based methods, there is an increased likelihood of improved communication around suicide prevention issues, as well as improved risk assessment skills and documentation (McNiel et al. 2008).

CLINICAL CHALLENGES

Managing suicidal patients' risk is one of the most stressful endeavors a psychiatrist can face. The challenge may be more complex in correctional settings that are subject to limited resources and increasing numbers of individuals in the midst of acute life crises. Some of the more commonly seen challenges will be addressed here, and include the problems of inmate patient deliberate self-harm and "manipulative" suicide threats.

Deliberate self-harm and suicide risk

Self-inflicted injuries may occur with or without suicidal intent. The term *deliberate self-harm* (DSH) has been used to describe the willful self-infliction of painful, destructive, or injurious acts without the intent to die (American Psychiatric Association 2003). However, there is substantial definitional ambiguity surrounding the concept of DSH, and no universally accepted definition has been agreed upon (Mangnall and Yurkovich 2008). This may result in a confusion of synonyms, such as self-mutilation, parasuicide, and repetitive self-injury. Acts of DSH are considered to increase one's risk of suicide (Favazza 1998; Hawton et al. 2014). It is not possible to reliably distinguish patients who engage in self-harm from those who will ultimately commit suicide. The reasons for this are, in part, due to the dynamic and ambivalent nature of suicidal cognitions. For example, the individual may possess *both* the desire to self-harm *and* to commit suicide at the same time. Furthermore, the desire to self-harm may progress (either slowly or rapidly) to suicide. Indeed, an individual's suicidal intent may shift over time, which is why follow-up risk assessments are important. Finally, there is also the risk of accidental or miscalculated death while the individual engages in acts of self-harm.

Self-mutilation and suicide attempts cannot be easily differentiated, even in cases where the inmate is questioned about suicide intent (Konrad et al. 2007). Taking an unconcerned or punitive view of an inmate's DSH may increase risk by prompting the inmate to take increasingly more dramatic risks to communicate his or her problems. The detection of malingering among inmates whose external incentive may be to seek inpatient admission or psychiatric treatment is fraught with controversy and uncertainty. Even with the use of structured, objective tests for detecting malingering, there remains uncertainty, and clinicians are advised to remain "exceedingly cautious about assertions that individuals in ...correctional settings are (or are not) feigning serious mental illness" given the rates of inaccuracy observed in well-designed studies (Edens et al. 2007).

There is a paucity of research on the prevalence of self-injurious behavior in corrections. A study of 51 state and federal prison systems found that a very small percentage (less than 2%) of inmates engage in self-injurious behavior each year. However, the acts occurred weekly in 85% of systems, disrupted correctional operations, and required a disproportionate amount of resources (Appelbaum et al. 2011). Self-injurious behavior in an inmate–patient can be very challenging to manage from both clinical and security standpoints. The behavior tends to raise concerns about suicide risk, personality disorder and manipulative intent. Thus, it is important to consider these possibilities very carefully before arriving prematurely at a conclusion of manipulative behavior or malingered suicidal intent.

Suicide attempts have been clearly shown to increase one's risk of ultimately dying from suicide. Although some studies have attempted to distinguish suicide attempters from suicide completers, correctional mental health staff would be ill advised to place too much weight on these findings in their clinical practice. There is no research to date suggesting that clinicians can reliably distinguish patients who use DSH as a form of "manipulation" from patients who pose a genuine suicide risk. The fact that both may be present, and that suicidal intent often shifts over time should suggest approaching this scenario with caution.

"Manipulative" is a popular but often misused description of behavior seen in some inmate patients who come to psychiatric attention. The literature suggests "that it would be a mistake to underestimate the risk of those with recent instrumental suicide related behavior, dismissing their behavior as manipulative or attention seeking" (Skeem et al. 2006). It is also important to keep in mind that "not all low-lethality suicidal behaviors are meant to manipulate another person," and that "defining a behavior as manipulative impels distancing rather than greater understanding that the patient lacks necessary skills to gain a sense of control in nonmanipulative ways" (Berman 2006).

It is a well-known clinical phenomenon that some inmate–patients who engage in either DSH or various forms of self-mutilation do not suffer from suicidal cognitions at all; rather, they cut themselves as a way to cope, reduce their anxiety level, and/or focus on the sense of control that such acts provide. The challenge arises when mental health professionals seek to discern which of these individuals will go on to attempt suicide. An illustrative study was conducted in England and Wales over a period of 5 years (Hawton et al. 2014). It looked at incidents of self-poisoning or self-injury irrespective of degree of suicidal intent or underlying motive. Of 26,510 prisoners who engaged in such behavior, 109 subsequently died by suicide in custody, half of which occurred within 1 month of nonlethal self-harm. In male prisoners, the risk of suicide after self-harm was associated with older age as well as a previous self-harm incident of moderate or high lethality potential. In female prisoners, engaging in more than five incidents of DSH within a year was associated with subsequent suicide.

SUMMARY

Suicide prevention in corrections is a pressing mandate that requires reliable, evidence-based methods. Correctional suicide prevention goes far beyond clinical risk assessment and must involve facility-wide efforts at screening, training, communication, and policy review. The correctional environment creates special nuances that must be anticipated by the correctional mental health professional when conducting suicide risk assessments. Many correctional suicide risk factors are known and should be carefully considered during the suicide risk assessment process. The standard of care does not require the correctional mental health clinician to predict inmate patients' suicide. Rather, there is a general expectation by the courts that clinicians will use reasonable professional judgment, based on a thorough consideration of the clinical data and circumstances.

Successful correctional suicide prevention programs are a collaborative team effort, where correctional staff from multiple disciplines participate and give input to improve policies and procedures. Performing and documenting an adequate correctional suicide risk assessment will be likely to result in good psychiatric care, as well as protection from legal claims of negligence. Clinical efforts must be prioritized and supported by equally vigorous administrative and system-wide suicide prevention efforts.

REFERENCES

American Heart Association, Emergency Cardiac Care Committee and Subcommittees. 1992. Guidelines for Cardiopulmonary Resuscitation and Emergency Cardiac Care. *Journal of the American Medical Association* 268:2172–2183.

American Psychiatric Association (APA). 2003. Practice guideline for the assessment and treatment of patients with suicidal behaviors. Washington, DC: APA. http://www.psych.org/psych_pract/treatg/pg/SuicidalBehavior_05-15-06.pdf, accessed July 27, 2016.

Appelbaum K, J Savageau, R Trestman, J Metzner, and J Baillargeon. 2011. A national survey of self-injurious behavior in American prisons. *Psychiatric Services* 62:285–290.

Baerger D. 2001. Risk management with the suicidal patient: Lessons from case law. *Professional Psychology: Research and Practice* 32:359–366.

Berman A. 2006. Risk management with suicidal patients. *Journal of Clinical Psychology* 62:171–184.

Blaauw E, E Arensman, V Kraaij, FW Winkel, and R Bout. 2002. Traumatic life events and suicide risk among jail inmates: The influence of types of events, time period and significant others. *Journal of Traumatic Stress* 15:9–16.

Blaauw E, F Winkel, and A Kerkhof. 2001. Bullying and suicidal behavior in jails. *Criminal Justice and Behavior* 28:279–299.

Blank S. 2006. Killing time: The process of waiving appeal: The Michael Ross death penalty cases. *Journal of Law and Policy* 14:735–749.

Cohen F, J Knoll, T Kupers, and J Metzner. 2011. *Practical Guide to Correctional Mental Health and the Law.* Kingston, NJ: Civic Research Institute.

Daniel A. 2006. Preventing suicide in prison: A collaborative responsibility of administrative, custodial, and clinical staff. *Journal of the American Academy of Psychology and the Law* 34:165–175.

Daniel A and J Fleming. 2006. Suicides in a state correctional system, 1992–2002: A review. *Journal of Correctional Health Care* 12:24–35.

Denneson L, C Basham, K Dickinson, M Crutchfield, L Millet, and S Dobscha. 2010. Suicide risk assessment and content of VA health care contacts before suicide completion by veterans in Oregon. *Psychiatric Services* 61:1192–1197.

Duthé G, A Hazard, A Kensey, and J Pan Ke Shon. 2013. Suicide among male prisoners in France: A prospective population-based study. *Forensic Science International* 233:273–277.

Edens J, N Poythress, and M Watkins-Clay. 2007. Detection of malingering in psychiatric unit and general population prison inmates: A comparison of the PAI, SIMS, and SIRS. *Journal of Personality Assessment* 88:33–42.

Edwards S and M Sachmann. 2010. No-suicide contacts, no-suicide agreements, and no-suicide assurances: A study of their nature, utilization, perceived effectiveness, and potential to cause harm. *Crisis* 31:290–302.

Encrenaz G, A Miras, B Contrand, C Galera, S Pujos, G Michel, and E Lagarde. 2014. Inmate-to-inmate violence as a marker of suicide attempt risk during imprisonment. *Journal of Forensic and Legal Medicine* 22:20–25.

Favazza A. 1998. Self-mutilation. In *The Harvard Medical School Guide to Suicide Assessment and Intervention*, edited by DG Jacobs, San Francisco: Jossey-Bass, 125–145.

Felthous A and C Holzer. 2006. Carceral suicides—Some exceptions and paradoxes. *Journal of the American Acaddmy of Psychiatry and the Law* 34:176–178.

Fruehwald S, T Matschnig, F Koenig, P Bauer, and P Frottier. 2004. Suicide in custody: Case-control study. *British Journal of Psychiatry* 185:494–498.

Gallagher C and A Dobrin. 2006. Deaths in juvenile justice residential facilities. *Journal of Adolescent Health* 38:662–668.

Garvey K, J Pen, A Campbell, C Esposito-Smythers, and A Spirito. 2009. Contracting for safety with patients: Clinical practice and forensic implications. *Journal of the American Academy of Psychiatry and the Law* 37:363–370.

Giner L, I Jaussent, E Olié et al. 2014. Violent and serious suicide attempters: One step closer to suicide? *Journal of Clinical Psychiatry* 75:e191–e197.

Gore S. 1999. Suicide in prisons. Reflection of the communities served, or exacerbated risk? *British Journal of Psychiatry* 175:50–55.

Goss J, K Peterson, L Smith, K Kalb, and B Brodey. 2002. Characteristics of suicide attempts in a large urban jail system with an established suicide prevention program. *Psychiatric Services* 53:574–579.

Green C, K Kendall, G Andre, T Looman, and N Polvi. 1993. A study of 133 suicides among Canadian federal prisoners. *Medicine, Science and the Law* 33:121–127.

Hawton K, L Linsell, T Adeniji, A Sariaslan, and S Fazel. 2014. Self-harm in prisons in England and Wales: An epidemiologic study of prevalence, risk factors, clustering, and subsequent suicide. *Lancet* 383:1147–1154.

Hayes L. 2010. National study of jail suicide 20 years later. *Journal of Correctional Health Care* 18:233–245.

Hayes L. 2013. Suicide prevention in correctional facilities: Reflections and next steps. *International Journal of Law and Psychiatry* 36:188–194.

He X, A Felthous, CE Holzer, P Nathan, and S Veasey. 2001. Factors in prison suicide: One year study in Texas. *Journal of Forensic Sciences* 46:896–901.

Helfand S and R Trestman. 2008. *Suicide Prevention PI in Corrections: The Six Sigma Method.* 39th Annual Meeting of the American Academy of Psychiatry and the Law, Seattle, Washington, October 23–26.

Ivanoff A and L Hayes. 2002. Preventing, managing, and treating suicidal actions in high-risk offenders. *Jail Suicide/Mental Health Update Summer* 11:1–11.

Ivanoff A and S Jang. 1991. The role of hopelessness and social desirability in predicting suicidal behavior: A study of prison inmates. *Journal of Consulting and Clinical Psychology* 59:394–399.

Jobes D, M Rudd, J Overholser, and T Joiner. 2008. Ethical and competent care of suicidal patients: Contemporary challenges, new developments, and considerations for clinical practice. *Professional Psychology: Research and Practice* 39:405–413.

Knoll J. 2010. Correctional suicide: Assessment, prevention, and professional liability. *Journal of Correctional Healthcare* 16(3):1–17.

Konrad N, M Daigle, A Daniel et al. 2007. Preventing suicide in prisons, part I. Recommendations from the International Association for Suicide Prevention Task Force on Suicide in Prisons. *Crisis* 28:113–121.

Kovasznay B, R Miraglia, R Beer, and B Way. 2004. Reducing suicides in New York State correctional facilities. *Psychiatric Quarterly* 75:61–70.

Leese M, S Thomas, and L Snow. 2006. An ecological study of factors associated with rates of self-inflicted death in prisons in England and Wales. *International Journal of Law and Psychiatry* 29:355–360.

Lester D and C Tartaro. 2002. Suicide on death row. *Journal of Forensic Sciences* 47:1008–1111.

Lewis L. 2007. No-harm contracts: A review of what we know. *Suicide and Life-Threatening Behavior* 37:50–57.

Malone K, M Oquendo, G Haas, S Ellis, S Li, and J Mann. 2000. Protective factors against suicidal acts in major depression: Reasons for living. *American Journal of Psychiatry* 157:1084–1088.

Mangnall J and E Yurkovich. 2008. A literature review of deliberate self-harm. *Perspectives in Psychiatric Care* 44:175–184.

Marangell L, M Bauer, E Dennehy, S Wisniewski, M Allen, D Miklowitz et al. 2006. Prospective predictors of suicide and suicide attempts in 1,556 patients with bipolar disorders followed for up to 2 years. *Bipolar Disorders* 8:566–575.

McNiel D, S Fordwood, C Weaver, J Chamberlain, S Hall, and R Binder. 2008. Effects of training on suicide risk assessment. *Psychiatric Services* 59:1462–1465.

Meloy J. 2000. *Violence Risk and Threat Assessment: A Practical Guide for Mental Health and Criminal Justice Professionals*. San Diego, CA: Specialized Training Services.

Mumola C. 2005. *Suicide and Homicide in State Prisons and Local Jails. Bureau of Justice Statistics Special Report*. Washington, DC: Bureau of Justice Statistics. http://www.bjs.gov/index.cfm?ty=pbdetail&iid=1126, accessed July 27, 2016.

National Commission on Correctional Health Care. 2013. *Prevention of Juvenile Suicide in Correctional Settings*. http://www.ncchc.org/

prevention-of-juvenile-suicide-in-correctional-settings, accessed July 27, 2016.

Noonan M and S Ginder. 2014. *Mortality in Local Jails and State Prisons, 2000–2012*. NCJ 247448. Washington, DC: U.S. Department of Justice. http://www.bjs.gov/content/pub/pdf/mljsp0012st.pdf, accessed July 27, 2016.

Opitz-Welke A, K Bennefeld-Kersten, N Konrad, and J Welke. 2013. Prison suicides in Germany from 2000 to 2011. *International Journal of Law and Psychiatry* 36:386–389.

Packman W, T Pennuto, B Bongar, and J Orthwein. 2004. Legal issues of professional negligence in suicide cases. *Behavioral Sciences and the Law* 22:697–713.

Patry M and P Magaletta. 2015. Measuring suicidality using the personality assessment inventory: A convergent validity study with federal inmates. *Assessment* 22:36–45.

Patterson R and K Hughes. 2008. Review of completed suicides in the California Department of Corrections and Rehabilitation, 1999 to 2004. *Psychiatric Services* 59:676–682.

Pennington C, R Cramer, H Miller, and J Anastasi. 2014. Psychopathy, depression, and anxiety as predictors of suicidal ideation in offenders. *Death Studies* 39:288–295.

Perry A, R Marandos, S Coutlon, and M Johnson. 2010. Screening tools assessing risk of suicide and self-harm in adult offenders: A systematic review. *International Journal of Offender Therapy and Comparative Criminology* 54(5):803–828.

Reeves R and A Tamburello. 2014. Single cells, segregated housing, and suicide in the New Jersey Department of Corrections. *Journal of the American Academy of Psychiatry and the Law* 42:484–488.

Resnick P. 2002. Recognizing that the suicidal patient views you as an "Adversary." *Current Psychiatry* 1:8.

Roberts AR and K Bender. 2006. Juvenile offender suicide: Prevalence, risk factors, assessment, and crisis intervention protocols. *International Journal of Emergency Mental Health* 8:255–265.

Rogers R, K Ustad, and R Salekin. 1998. Convergent validity of the personality assessment inventory: A study of emergency referrals in a correctional setting. *Assessment* 5:3–12.

Rudd, MD, AL Berman, TE Joiner et al. 2006. Warning signs for suicide: Theory, research, and clinical applications. *Suicide and Life-Threatening Behavior* 36(3):255–262.

Shaw J, D Baker, IM Hunt, A Moloney, and L Appleby. 2004. Suicide by prisoners. National clinical survey. *British Journal of Psychiatry* 184:263–267.

Shea S. 2002. *The Practical Art of Suicide Assessment: A Guide for Mental Health Professionals and Substance Abuse Counselors*, 2nd edition. Hoboken, NJ: Wiley.

Shea S. 2004. The delicate art of eliciting: Suicidal ideation. *Psychiatric Annals* 34:385–400.

Shelton D, S Sampl, KL Kesten, W Zhang, and RL Trestman. 2009. Treatment of impulsive aggression in correctional settings. *Behavioral Sciences and the Law* 27:787–800.

Simon R. 1999. The suicide prevention contract: Clinical, legal, and risk management issues. *Journal of the American Academy of Psychiatry and the Law* 27:445–450.

Simon R. 2002. Suicide risk assessment: What is the standard of care? *Journal of the American Academy of Psychiatry and the Law* 30:340–344.

Simon R. 2004. *Assessing and Managing Suicide Risk: Guidelines for Clinically Based Risk Management*. Washington, DC: American Psychiatric Publication.

Skeem J, E Silver, PS Aippelbaum, and J Tiemann. 2006. Suicide-related behavior after psychiatric hospital discharge: Implications for risk assessment and management. *Behavioral Sciences and the Law* 24:731–746.

Skogstad P, F Deane, and J Spicer. 2005. Barriers to help-seeking among New Zealand prison inmates. *Journal of Offender Rehabilitation* 42:1–24.

Suominen K, E Isometsa, J Suokas, J Haukka, K Achte, and J Lonnqvist. 2004. Completed suicide after a suicide attempt: A 37-year follow-up study. *American Journal of Psychiatry* 161:562–563.

Wang E, R Rogers, GL Giles, P Diamond, L Herrington-Wang, and E Taylor. 1997. A pilot study of the Personality Assessment Inventory (PAI) in corrections: Assessment of malingering, suicide risk, and aggression in male inmates. *Behavioral Sciences and the Law* 15:469–482.

Way B, A Kaufman, J Knoll, and S Chlebowski. 2013. Suicidal ideation among inmate-patients in state prison: Prevalence, reluctance to report, and treatment preferences. *Behavioral Sciences and the Law* 31:230–238.

Way B, R Miraglia, D Sawyer, R Beer, and J Eddy. 2005. Factors related to suicide in New York state prisons. *International Journal of Law and Psychiatry* 28:207–221.

Way B, D Sawyer, S Barboza, and R Nash. 2007. Inmate suicide and time spent in special disciplinary housing in New York State prison. *Psychiatric Services* 58:558–560.

World Health Organization. 2007. *Preventing Suicide in Jails and Prisons*. http://www.who.int/entity/mental_health/prevention/suicide/suicideprevent/en/, accessed July 27, 2016.

57

The right to refuse treatment in a criminal law setting

MICHAEL L. PERLIN AND NAOMI WEINSTEIN

INTRODUCTION

The question of the right to refuse antipsychotic medication remains the most important and volatile aspect of the legal regulation of mental health practice (Plotkin 1977; Gelman 1984; Brooks 1987; Perlin and Cucolo 2016, §8-2; Perlin 2000). The issues that are raised—the autonomy of institutionalized individuals with mental disability to refuse the imposition of treatment that is designed (at least in part) to ameliorate their symptomatology; the degree to which individuals subjected to such drugging are in danger of developing irreversible neurological side effects; the evanescence of terms such as *informed consent* or *competency*; the practical and administrative considerations of implementing such a right in an institutional setting; and the range of the philosophical questions raised (dealing with autonomy, freedom, self-governance, and utilitarianism) (Perlin 1990; Perlin 1991; Perlin and Dorfman 1996; Perlin and Cucolo 2016, §8-2)—mark the litigation that has led to the articulation of the right to refuse treatment as "a turning point in institutional psychiatry" (Rhoden 1980) and "the most controversial issue in forensic psychiatry" (Brant 1983).

The conceptual, social, moral, legal, and medical difficulties inherent in the articulation of a coherent right to refuse treatment doctrine have been made even more complicated by the U.S. Supreme Court's reluctance to confront most of the underlying issues (*Mills v. Rogers* 1982). As a result of the court's decision in *Mills* (a case involving involuntarily committed civil patients) to "sidestep" the core constitutional questions (Wexler 1982; Perlin and Cucolo 2016, §8-5.8.1, 8-87), and its concomitant articulation of the doctrine that a state is always free to grant more rights under its constitution than might be minimally mandated by the U.S. Supreme Court under the *federal constitution* (*Mills v. Rogers* 1982, 300; Perlin 1987a), two parallel sets of cases have emerged.

In one set, state courts have generally entered broad decrees in accordance with an "expanded due process" model, in which the right to refuse treatment has been read broadly and elaborately, generally interpreting procedural due process protections liberally on behalf of the complaining patient. These cases have frequently mandated premedication judicial hearings, and have heavily relied on social science data focusing on the potential impact of drug side effects, especially tardive dyskinesia (e.g., *Rivers v. Katz* 1986; *Riese v. St. Mary's Hospital and Medical Center* 1987; *State ex rel. Jones v. Gerhardstein* 1987; Perlin 1991; *Virgil D. v. Rock County* 1994; Perlin and Dorfman 1996; Perlin and Cucolo 2016, §8-6.3.2; *Myers v. Alaska Psychiatric Institute* 2006). Some cases have begun to explore "second-generation" issues, such as the right to a jury trial in medication refusal hearings (e.g., *In re Brazleton* 1993; *People v. Fisher* 2009), whether a joint hearing on involuntary civil commitment and medication refusal is appropriate (e.g., *In re Barbara H.* 1998; *In re Dennis H.* 2002), or the application of the right in other settings such as juveniles in state care (e.g., *Matter of Sombrotto v. Christiana W.* 2008).

In the other set, federal courts have generally entered more narrow decrees in accordance with a "limited due process model." These provided narrower administrative review and rejected broad readings of the Fourteenth Amendment's substantive and procedural due process protections, relying less on social science data, which were frequently ignored or dismissed as part of an incomprehensible system allegedly beyond the courts' self-professed limited competency (e.g., *United States v. Charters* 1988; Perlin 1990, 1991; Perlin and Cucolo, 2016, §8-6.4). Generally (but not always), the state cases involved civil patients; more frequently, the federal cases dealt with individuals originally institutionalized because of involvement in the criminal trial process (Perlin 1991).

Although the Supreme Court has not dealt squarely with a civil right to refuse treatment case since its 1982 remand decision in *Mills*, it has since decided a case involving the rights of convicted prisoners to refuse medication (*Washington v. Harper* 1990; Perlin and Cucolo 2016, §8-7.1); one on the question of whether an insanity-pleading defendant was denied a fair trial because he was involuntarily medicated at trial, thus depriving the jury of a fair presentation of his "natural demeanor" at the insanity stage (*Riggins v. Nevada* 1992; Perlin and Cucolo 2016, §8-7.2); and one on whether a state may involuntarily medicate a defendant in order to render him or her competent to stand trial (*Sell v. United States* 2003). These cases are discussed extensively in this chapter.

As this short overview should demonstrate, it is impossible to authoritatively articulate one doctrine to cover all rights to refuse treatment litigation. It is also impossible to state such a doctrine even for cases that arise in a "criminal law setting," because the simplest "unpacking" of that category (Perlin 1989–1990) reveals that there are at least seven major subcategories to which the right to refuse could be applied, to cases involving the following:

- Defendants awaiting incompetency to stand trial (IST) determinations
- Defendants found "permanently" IST in accordance with the Supreme Court's decision in *Jackson v. Indiana* (1972)
- Defendants otherwise awaiting trial in jails
- Defendants seeking to proffer a not guilty by reason of insanity (NGRI) defense
- Defendants who have been institutionalized following an NGRI finding
- Convicted defendants in prison
- Capital defendants whom state officials seek to medicate so as to make them competent to be executed
- Defendants committed as sexually violent predators

However, if each of these categories is considered briefly, it may better illuminate whether any strands of doctrinal coherency can be spelled out (cf. Perlin 1987b, 2000).

DEFENDANTS AWAITING TRIAL

Awaiting an IST determination

Prior to 1987, medication cases involving defendants awaiting IST determinations had "resulted in a series of apparently random decisions from which almost no doctrinal threads could be extracted," leading to "significant and genuine confusion" in this area (Perlin 1990, 963; Perlin 1989, §14.09; compare, e.g., *State v. Hayes* 1978 to *Whitehead v. Wainwright* 1978). Subsequently, though, two separate decisions in one case—with radically different opinions—have brought some measure of coherence to this area.

In 1987, a panel of the Fourth Circuit Court of Appeals issued the first decision in *United States v. Charters* (*Charters I*) on the right of a federal pretrial detainee to refuse psychotropic medication (*Charters* 1987). *Charters I* rejected the notion that the "exercise of professional judgment standard" (articulated by the Supreme Court in a case involving physical restraint of an individual with severe mental retardation [*Youngberg v. Romeo* 1982]) applied to antipsychotic medication cases, resurrected right-to-privacy and freedom-of-thought-process arguments that had been generally abandoned in the years since the Supreme Court's decision in *Mills v. Rogers*, established a right to be free from unwanted physical intrusion as an integral part of an individual's constitutional freedoms, and articulated a complex substituted judgment–best interests methodology to be used in right to refuse treatment cases (Perlin 1990; Perlin and Cucolo 2016, §8-5.6.1).

Upon an *en banc* rehearing, the full Fourth Circuit vacated the panel decision (*Charters* 1988) (*Charters II*), "suggesting that the panel was wrong, about almost everything" (Perlin 1990, 965). Although it agreed that the defendant possessed a constitutionally retained interest in freedom from bodily restraint that was implicated by the forced administration of psychotropic drugs, and the defendant was protected "against arbitrary and capricious action by government officials" (*Charters II* 1988, 306), it found that informal institutional administrative procedures were adequate to protect the defendant's due process interests. It applied the "substantial professional judgment" test of *Youngberg*, and limited questioning of experts to one matter: "Was this decision reached by a process so completely out of bounds as to make it explicable only as an arbitrary, nonprofessional one?" (*Charters II* 1988, 313; Perlin and Cucolo 2016, §18-3.2, 18-46).

The two views of the rights of pretrial detainees to refuse medication reflected in *Charters I* and *Charters II* could not be more diametrically opposed. Also, the ultimate *en banc* decision has led to some important strategic decision making for attorneys representing individuals who wish to resist the imposition of such medication. Although, as a federal detainee, Charters was forced to litigate in federal court, in cases where litigants do have an option of availing themselves of a state forum, the second *Charters* decision made it more likely they will choose the latter jurisdictional alternative. When *Charters II* was decided, it was seen to potentially "signal the death knell for the litigation of right-to-refuse treatment issues in the federal forum" (Perlin 1990, 994) in cases in which litigants retain discretion as to where to sue. In the immediate following years, at least two state courts—albeit in civil cases—adhered to their endorsements of *Charters I* even *after* the *Charters II* decision (e.g., *McConnell v. Beverly Enterprises-Connecticut, Inc.* 1989; *In re A. C.* 1990; Perlin and Cucolo 2016, §18-3.2); but, several post-*Charters II* state cases have not granted defendants broader rights in similar cases (e.g., Perlin and Cucolo 2016, §18-6, 18-64; *State v. Otero* 1989; *People v. Lopez* 1990).

Subsequently, the Sixth Circuit has held that the "strict scrutiny" standard of substantive due process review applied to this question (see e.g., Perlin 1993–1994; Perlin 1997), finding that the government must prove its case by clear and convincing evidence (*United States v. Brandon* 1998). The Second Circuit has held in *United States v. Gomes* that, as the "heightened scrutiny standard" was appropriate for determining when a nondangerous criminal defendant could be forcibly medicated with antipsychotic drugs for the purpose of rendering him competent, a four-part test was needed:

> We think that the government must show, and the district court must explicitly find, by clear and convincing evidence (1) that the proposed treatment is medically appropriate, (2) that it is necessary to restore the defendant to trail competence, (3) that the defendant can be fairly tried while under medication, and (4) that trying the defendant will serve an essential government interest. (*United States v. Gomes* 2002, 82)

The court stressed that the process of medicating a defendant is a "dynamic one" that can be evaluated over the course of treatment "to ascertain, with expert assistance, both its effectiveness and the nature of any side effects" (p. 82). In reaching its determination, the court looked closely at "recent advances in antipsychotic medication" that "reduce our concerns that the defendant's health interests and fair trial rights cannot be adequately protected when he is involuntarily medicated to render him competent to stand trial" (p. 83).

In 2003, the Supreme Court directly addressed the issue of whether a state may involuntarily medicate a defendant to render him or her competent to stand trial, holding that when a mentally ill defendant faces serious criminal charges, the government may only involuntarily administer antipsychotic drugs if the treatment was medically appropriate, substantially unlikely to have side effects that may undermine the trial's fairness, and necessary to significantly further important governmental trial-related interests (*Sell v. United States* 2003). In reaching its conclusion, the court recognized that under *Washington v. Harper* (1990) and *Riggins v. Nevada* (1992) Sell had a liberty interest in avoiding the involuntary administration of antipsychotic drugs, and this interest was protected by the Fifth Amendment's due process clause against all but "essential" or "overriding" state interests (p. 179).

Sell is an extremely important decision for several reasons. First, it elevates much of Justice Kennedy's concurring opinion in *Riggins* (see below) to majority status. Second, the decision italicizes many important phrases like "*important* governmental interests," "*significantly further* concomitant state interests," that involuntary medication is *necessary* to further those interests, that administration of the drugs in *medically appropriate,*" emphasizing the importance of these issues to the court. Third, the court stresses the need to engage in a "least restrictive alternative" analysis in every such case. By way of example, the Ninth Circuit held that due process did not require the Bureau of Prisons to specify the medication before it could involuntary medicate a defendant (*United States v. Loughner* 2012). Finally, in its discussion, the court makes clear that decisional incompetence and current danger are the only two acceptable overrides in civil cases (Perlin and Cucolo 2016, §8-7.3.2). Also, it needs to be stressed that all circuits that have considered this issue post-*Sell* have concluded that the government bears the burden of proof in such cases by clear and convincing evidence (see, e.g., *United States v. Bradley* 2005; *United States v. Grape* 2008; citing *United States v. Bush* 2009; *United States v. Ruiz-Gaxiola* 2010).

But, notwithstanding *Brandon, Gomes,* and *Sell* (and other post-*Charters* federal cases rejecting its methodology; see e.g., *Preston v. Gutierrez* 1993; *Kulas v. Valdez* 1998; *United States v. Weston* 2000), the second Fourth Circuit decision in *Charters* remains important "jurisprudentially, constitutionally, and symbolically" (Perlin 1999, §3B-8.1b, 312). The individual's interests in refusing treatment with antipsychotic medications is arguably greater in the pretrial context because the defendant has an interest not only in avoiding unintended side effects, but also in avoiding what may be potentially legally prejudicial effects of medication (Dlugacz and Wimmer 2013). This makes cases like *Brandon, Gomes,* and *Sell,* even more important jurisprudentially and constitutionally.

DEFENDANTS PERMANENTLY IST

In *Jackson v. Indiana*, the Supreme Court held that it violated due process to commit an individual for more than the "reasonable period of time" necessary to determine "whether there is a substantial chance of his attaining the capacity to stand trial in the foreseeable future" (*Jackson* 1972, 733). If there were to be no such chance, a defendant originally committed pursuant to an IST finding would either be subjected to the civil commitment process or released; once having been "Jacksonized" (that is, having had his or her criminal indictments dismissed but remaining in need of hospitalization), such a patient must be treated like other civil patients (Perlin 1991). However, a recent study indicates that nonrestorable "*Jacksonized*" committees are often treated differently once committed than "regular" civil commitment patients (Levitt et al. 2010), being subject to more involuntary medication; further this cohort of patients was less likely to meet usual statutory commitment criteria (Levitt et al. 2010).

There has been virtually no case law on the rights of "Jacksonized" patients to refuse medication; none of the three pertinent cases substantially illuminates the underlying doctrinal issues (*DeAngelas v. Plaut* 1980; *Mannix v. State* 1981; *Woodland v. Angus* 1993; Perlin and Cucolo 2016, §8-7.5.2). *Charters II* and *Sell* should not have a significant impact on this population, who should be treated like other civil patients (due to the dismissal of the underlying indictments that triggered their entry into the criminal trial process). Thus, it can be expected that future developments here will track similar developments involving involuntarily committed civil patients (Perlin 1991), and will more closely adhere to the "expanded due process" model. A recent comprehensive state-wide study has concluded that "too many people found not competent to stand trial are [still] unnecessarily locked in a secure setting for treatment and, on average, are confined for longer periods than research demonstrates is clinically reasonable" (Justice Policy Institute 2011).

OTHERWISE AWAITING TRIAL IN JAILS

Cases involving jailed pretrial detainees have generally interpreted the right to refuse treatment broadly. In *Bee v. Greaves*, the Tenth Circuit ruled that "less restrictive alternatives" should be ruled out before psychotropic medication is involuntarily administered to a jailed detainee (*Bee* 1984, 1396; Perlin and Cucolo 2016, §8-6.3.3); other courts have similarly ruled that the availability of a less intrusive alternative that could have been employed by defendants must be considered in the determination of such a case (*Osgood v. District of Columbia* 1983; *Harrison v. State* 1994; *State v. Kotis* 1999; Perlin and Cucolo 2016, §8-6.3). Later, courts have also chosen to follow the holding of *Sell* and apply it to pretrial detainees (*In re Mark W* 2004).

DEFENDANTS PLEADING INSANITY

At trial

In *Riggins v. Nevada*, the U.S. Supreme Court reversed the decision of the Nevada Supreme Court (on the involuntary administration of medication to a defendant at trial), holding that the use of antipsychotic drugs violated the defendant's right to fair trial (*Riggins* 1992; Perlin and Cucolo 2016, §8-7.2). The court cited language from its previous opinion in *Washington v. Harper* (1990) regarding the impact of drug side effects on constitutional decision making, and construing *Harper* to require "an overriding justification and a determination of medical appropriateness" prior to forcibly administering antipsychotic medications to a prisoner (*Riggins* 1992, 134–135).

The *Riggins* Court focused on what might be called the "litigational side effects" (Perlin 1994c, 251) of antipsychotic drugs, and discussed the possibility that the drug use might have "compromised" the substance of the defendant's trial testimony, his interaction with counsel, and his comprehension of the trial (*Riggins* 1992, 137). In a concurring opinion, Justice Kennedy (the author of *Harper*) took an even bolder position. He would not allow the use of antipsychotic medication to make a defendant competent to stand trial "absent an *extraordinary* showing" on the state's part, and noted further that he doubted this showing could be made "given our present understanding of the properties of these drugs" (*Riggins* 1992, 139).

Justice Thomas dissented, suggesting that (a) the administration of the drug might have *increased* the defendant's cognitive ability; (b) since Riggins had originally asked for medical assistance (while a jail inmate, he "had trouble sleeping" and was "hearing voices"), it could not be said that the state ever "ordered" him to take medication; (c) if Riggins had been aggrieved, his proper remedy was a §1983 civil rights action; and (d) under the majority's language, a criminal conviction might be reversed "in cases involving...penicillin or aspirin" (*Riggins* 1992, 150–155).

Riggins is the Court's most expansive reading of the effect of psychotropic drugs' side effects on an individual's functioning (Perlin 1999, §3B-8.3). Justice Kennedy's concurrence highlights the ways that such side effects could imperil a fair trial:

> Behavior, manner, facial expressions, and emotional responses, or their absence, combine to make an overall impression on the trier of fact, an impression that can have a powerful influence on the outcome of the trial. If the defendant takes the stand, as Riggins did, his demeanor can have a great bearing on his credibility, his persuasiveness, and on the degree to which he evokes sympathy. (*Riggins v. Nevada* 1992, 142)

This is the clearest articulation of this position in any opinion by any Supreme Court justice.

Kennedy's observations as to jurors' responses to defendants who fail to display the proper "remorse and compassion" is also telling:

> The prejudice can be acute during the sentencing phase of the proceedings, when the sentencer must attempt to know the heart and mind of the offender and judge his character, his contrition or its absence, and his future dangerousness. In a capital sentencing proceeding, assessments of character and remorse may carry great weight and, perhaps, be determinative of whether the offender lives or dies. (Ibid., 144)

Kennedy's reliance here on a law review article that reports on the experiences of real jurors in real cases (Geimer and Amsterdam 1987) reflects an important sensitivity to the ways that jurors process clues and cues about the *persona* of capital defendants, and his integration of that data into an analysis of the ways that jurors may potentially respond to medicated defendants demonstrates a similar sensitivity to the way that visual images of mentally disabled defendants may be dispositive of juror decision making on this question.

Justice Thomas's opinion raises grave issues for defense counsel (Perlin 1994a, 2000). Had his position prevailed, would concerned and competent defense lawyers feel as if they were assuming a risk in *ever seeking* psychiatric help for an awaiting-trial defendant (Perlin 1992)? His analogizing of antipsychotic drug side effects to penicillin or aspirin may be disingenuous, or it may be cynical. What is clear is that nowhere in the lengthy corpus of right to refuse treatment litigation is this position ever seriously raised (Perlin and Dorfman 1993; Perlin and Cucolo 2016, §8-7.2, 8-164).

Following an NGRI verdict

While individuals who had been previously adjudicated NGRI were members of some early class actions challenging institutional drugging practices (e.g., *Davis v. Watkins* 1974; compare *Rennie v. Klein* 1979; *Davis v. Hubbard* 1980), there has been remarkably little litigation on behalf of this population (Perlin 1991, 47). The most important case, a Maryland state decision, construed a U.S. Supreme Court case that limits the treatment refusal rights of *prisoners* (*Washington v. Harper* 1990) to guard against the arbitrary administration of antipsychotic drugs in the context of NGRI insanity acquittees, and declared unconstitutional a state statute that failed to provide such a patient with the rights for adequate notice, to be present, to present evidence, and to cross-examine witnesses at a drug refusal hearing, and to have the right to judicial review of an adverse decision at such a hearing (*Williams v. Wilzack* 1990). *Williams*, which relied on both state and federal constitutions, thus suggests that lower courts may limit *Harper* to the specific population in that case (convicted prisoners), even where the patient's original confinement stems from the criminal trial process (Perlin and Cucolo 2016, §8-7.5.3, 8-186 to 8-187).

More recently, a federal district court in Wisconsin struck down that state's statute governing the administration of antipsychotic medication to insanity acquittees, finding the law unconstitutional because it did not require the court to make a determination that the incompetent insanity acquittee was dangerous and that the medication was in his best interests (*Enis v. Department of Health and Social Serv.* 1996). On the other hand, the California Court of Appeals has held that an insanity acquittee was not entitled to a hearing on his competence to refuse antipsychotic medications (*In re Locks*, 2000).

CONVICTED PRISONERS

The Supreme Court's decision in *Harper* sharply limited the right of convicted felons to refuse treatment under the federal constitution. (For pre-Harper cases brought under constitutional law theories, see, e.g., *Keyhea v. Rushen* [1986]; *Large v. Superior Court* [1986].) While the court agreed that prisoners (like all other citizens) possessed a "significant liberty interest" in avoiding the unwanted administration of antipsychotic drugs (*Harper* 1990, 221, quoting *Vitek v. Jones* 1980, pp. 488–491), it found that the need to balance this interest with prison safety and security considerations would lead it to uphold a prison rule regulating drug refusals as long as it was "reasonably related to legitimate penological interest," even where fundamental interests were otherwise implicated (*Harper v. Washington* 1990, 222). Thus, a state policy—that provided for an administrative hearing (before a tribunal of mental health professionals and correctional officials) at which there was neither provision for the appointment of counsel nor regularized external review—passed constitutional muster (*Harper* 1990, 223–224).

In a sharply worded opinion, Justice Stevens dissented, arguing that the refusal of medication was "a fundamental liberty interest deserving the highest order of protection," especially where the imposition of such medications might create "a substantial risk of permanent injury and premature death" (*Harper* 1990, 237). But *Harper* clarifies an important strand of Supreme Court jurisprudence: "Prison security concerns will, virtually without exception, trump individual autonomy interests" (Perlin 1999, §3B-8.2, 320).

Post-*Harper* cases have construed the decision in a wide variety of substantive and procedural contexts, with some courts relying on it to order full hearings on right-to-refuse claims, and others citing it to limit the scope of the applicant's right to refuse (Perlin and Cucolo 2016, §8-7.1, 8-156 to 8-158, and cases cited at note 1229). Moreover, although the trend has been slowed down by the Supreme Court's subsequent decision in *Riggins v. Nevada* (1992), *Harper* was the first Supreme Court case to "point…claimants to the state court door, and steer…them away from federal courts" (Brian 1992, 282).

The interplay between *Harper* and *Sell* was addressed in *United States v. Kourey* (2003). There, the court denied the prison officials' application for forced medication, brought pursuant to *Sell*, on the basis that *Sell* was inapplicable because the offense was not a serious offense, the prison had not gone through a *Harper* proceeding that might present alternative grounds related to the individual's dangerousness or the individual's own interests where refusal to take drugs puts his health gravely at risk, and that the defendant had not been formally adjudicated incompetent.

COMPETENCY TO BE EXECUTED

Still undecided is the important question of whether a state can involuntarily medicate an individual under a death sentence so as to make him or her competent to be executed. After the Supreme Court determined that an incompetent defendant with mental illness cannot be executed (*Ford v. Wainwright* 1986) (a holding that was extended to cases involving individuals with mental retardation in *Atkins v. Virginia* 2002, which effectively overruled the court's earlier decision in *Penry v. Lynaugh* 1989, and which was later clarified and expanded on in *Hall v. Florida* 2014), it initially agreed to hear a case that posed this precise question (*Perry v. Louisiana* 1990a).

In *Perry*, the Louisiana state courts had found that any due process right the capital defendant might have was outweighed by two compelling state interests: the provision of psychiatric care, and the carrying out of a valid death penalty (*State v. Perry* 1989). After the Supreme Court originally decided to hear the case (to determine whether the Eighth Amendment's proscription against cruel and unusual punishment prohibits states from so medicating death-row inmates; *Perry* 1990a), it ultimately vacated the lower court's decision and remanded for further proceedings in light of its decision in *Harper* on the scope of a convicted prisoner's right to refuse (*Perry v. Louisiana* 1990b).

The Supreme Court's reasoning in this case is not clear. It may be that the justices felt, upon reflection, that the only issue presented was that of forcible medication (finding the execution consequences irrelevant), and it was thus necessary for the state court to consider, after *Harper*, whether the difference in long-term harm in a case such as *Perry* (his execution) outweighed the state's interest in involuntarily medicating him (Perlin and Cucolo 2016, §17-5; "Supreme Court Sidesteps Issue" 1990). Interestingly, the Supreme Court had decided *Harper* a week *before* it chose to grant *certiorari* in *Perry*; its decision to vacate and remand for consideration of *Harper* may thus mean that the court could not—or would not—resolve the difficult tensions presented by such a case (Perlin 1994b).

On remand, the Louisiana Supreme Court found, under *state* constitutional law, that the state was prohibited from medicating Perry to make him competent to be executed. The court concluded:

> For centuries no jurisdiction has approved the execution of the insane. The state's attempt to circumvent this well-settled prohibition by forcibly medicating an insane prisoner with antipsychotic drugs violates his rights under our state constitution. ... First, it violates his right to privacy or personhood. Such involuntary medication requires the unjustified invasion of his brain and body with discomforting, potentially dangerous and painful drugs, the seizure of control of his mind and thoughts, and the usurpation of his right to make decisions regarding his health or medical treatment. Furthermore, implementation of the state's plan to medicate forcibly and execute the insane prisoner would constitute cruel, excessive and unusual punishment. This particular application of the death penalty fails to measurably contribute to the social goals of capital punishment. Carrying out this punitive scheme would add severity and indignity to the prisoner's punishment beyond that required for the mere extinguishment of life. This type of punitive treatment system is not accepted anywhere in contemporary society and is apt to be administered erroneously, arbitrarily or capriciously. (*State v. Perry* 1992, 747–748)

The Supreme Court subsequently denied *certiorari* in *Singleton v. Norris* (2003), a case where the Eighth Circuit denied a writ of *habeas corpus* seeking a stay of execution for an inmate who had regained competency as the result of forced antipsychotic medication. In reaching its determination, the Eight Circuit noted that it was guided by both *Harper* and *Ford* and its task was to weigh the state's interest in carrying out a lawfully imposed sentence against Singleton's interest in refusing medication. The court rejected Singleton's claim, based on *State v. Perry*, that the Eighth Amendment prohibited execution of one who is made "artificially competent" (p. 1027). Several years later, in *Panetti v. Dretke*, the Fifth Circuit found that a medicated defendant was competent to be executed. The Fifth Circuit affirmed the decision of the district court finding that, although the defendant suffered from schizoaffective disorder, and had a "delusional belief system in which he viewed himself as being persecuted for his religious activities and beliefs," the defendant was aware that he was to be executed and that he committed murders. The Supreme Court granted *certiorari* and ultimately reversed, holding that the defendant was denied constitutional procedures to which he was entitled under *Ford* (*Panetti v. Quarterman* 2007). However, in *Panetti*, the court did not discuss the issue of involuntary medication (Perlin 2010).

The Supreme Court has not yet directly revisited this question, but it can be expected that the question will inevitably arise again in the future, and that the court will have yet another chance to weigh the competing values (Perlin and Cucolo 2016, §17-4.1.6).

DEFENDANTS COMMITTED AS SEXUALLY VIOLENT PREDATORS

The Wisconsin Supreme Court has ruled that the rights and procedures for the involuntary administration of antipsychotic medication established in the state mental health code apply to sex offenders involuntarily committed as sexually violent persons (*State v. Anthony* D.B. 2000).

By contrast, a California appeals court held that competent committees under the Sexually Violent Predator Act (SVPA) could be involuntarily medicated in nonemergency circumstances as long as the medication was used for therapeutic and not punitive reasons (*In re Calhoun* 2003). The court found that commitment under SVPA "impliedly authorized" such involuntary treatment, because commitment as an SVP required a judicial determination that the individual had a mental disorder that rendered him a danger to others (p. 52). The court rejected arguments that involuntary medication of competent committees violated federal due process rights and state constitutional privacy rights.

INTERNATIONAL LAW AND THE RIGHT TO REFUSE TREATMENT

International standards concerning involuntary medication of criminal defendants and prisoners set a higher bar for medication of inmates (Dlugacz and Wimmer 2013). The Convention on the Rights of Persons with Disabilities (CRPD), to which the United States is a signatory, but has yet to ratify, requires that states recognize that persons with disabilities enjoy legal capacity on an equal basis with others. The CRPD is "regarded as having finally empowered the 'world's largest minority' to claim their rights, and to participate in international and national affairs on an equal basis with others who have achieved specific treaty recognition and protection" (Kayess and French 2008, 4). Article 25(d) of the CRPD addresses informed consent and requires health professionals to "provide care on the basis of free and informed consent by, inter alia, raising awareness of the human rights, dignity, autonomy and needs of persons with disabilities through training and the promulgation of ethical standards for public and private health care." Article 14.2 of the CRPD extends the rights it guarantees to those incarcerated or awaiting trial on an equal basis.

SUMMARY

This issue remains one of the most volatile areas of mental disability law. The decisions in *Charters II* (1988) and *Harper* (1990) had made it appear that the federal courts would no longer be the voluntary forum of choice for persons seeking to assert their right to refuse medication. The Supreme Court's decision in *Riggins* (1992) and *Sell* (2003), however, made it appear as if the federal forum would not necessarily be a hostile one for plaintiffs bringing such actions. Post-*Riggins* and post-*Sell* cases have been brought in both state and federal forums and, although results have been mixed, it can now be said that the complete exodus to state courts—predicted following the *Charters* and *Harper* decisions—has been halted, and that *both* state and federal courts now remain responsive to right to refuse medication actions (Perlin 1999, §3B-8.4, 330). The growing conservatism of the federal judiciary will most likely result in more affirmative litigation being brought in state courts based on state constitutional theories. Many state courts appear willing to consider carefully the arguments of plaintiffs in right to refuse cases brought by individuals in the criminal trial process.

It is necessary that the precise status of the patient—e.g., jail detainee, prisoner, insanity acquittee; *Jacksonized* permanently incompetent—be "unpacked" so as to "decode" the operative, controlling legal principles (Perlin 1991). If this is done, it is possible that some harmony might be brought to this most contentious area of litigation (Gelman 1983–1984, 122) and that the dilemma at the heart of the controversy—"preserving patient dignity while maintaining allegiance to treatment needs" (Roth 1986, 161)—might yet be resolved.

REFERENCES

Atkins v. Virginia, 536 U.S. 304 (2002).

Bee v. Greaves, 744 F.2d 1387 (10th Cir. 1984), cert. den., 469 U.S. 1214 (1985).

Brant, J. 1983. Pennhurst, Romeo and Rogers: The Burger Court and mental health law reform litigation. *Journal of Legal Medicine* 4:323–348.

Brian J. 1992. The right to refuse antipsychotic drug treatment and the Supreme Court. *Buffalo Law Review* 40:251–282.

Brooks A. 1987. The right to refuse antipsychotic medications: Law and policy. *Rutgers Law Review* 39:339–376.

Convention on the Rights of Persons with Disabilties. 2007, G.A. Res. 61/106, U.N. Doc. A/RES/61/106, (Dec. 6, 2006).

Davis v. Hubbard, 506 F. Supp. 915 (N.D. Ohio 1980).

Davis v. Watkins, 384 F. Supp. 1196 (N.D. Ohio 1974).

DeAngelas v. Plaut, 503 F. Supp. 775 (D. Conn. 1980).

Dlugacz H and C Wimmer. 2013. Legal aspects of administrating antipsychotic medications to jail and prison inmates. *International Journal of Law and Psychiatry* 36:213–228.

Enis v. Department of Health and Social Serv., 962 F. Supp. 1192 (W.D. Wis. 1996).

Ford v. Wainwright, 477 U.S. 399 (1986).

Geimer W and J Amsterdam. 1987. Why jurors vote life or death: Operative factors in ten Florida death penalty cases. *American Journal of Criminal Law* 15:1–54.

Gelman S. 1983–1984. Mental hospital drugging—Atomistic and structural remedies. *Cleveland State Law Review* 32:221–261.

Gelman S. 1984. Mental hospital drugs, professionalism and the constitution. *Georgetown Law Journal* 72:1725–1784.

Hall v. Florida, 134 S. Ct. 1986 (2014).

Harrison v. State, 635 So.2d 894 (Miss. 1994).

In re A. C., 573 A.2d 1235 (D.C. 1990).

In re Barbara H., 183 Ill. 2d 482, 702 N.E. 2d 555 (1998).

In re Brazleton, 245 Ill. App. 3d 1028, 615 N.E. 2d 406 (1993).

In re Calhoun, 6 Cal rptr.2d 34 (Cal.App.2d 2003).

In re Dennis H., 255 Wis.2d 359, 647 N.W.2d 851 (2002).

In re Locks, 69 Cal. App.4th 890, 94 Cal. Rptr.2d 495 (2000).

In re Mark W., 348 Ill.App.3d 1065, 811 N.E.2d 767 (2004).

Jackson v. Indiana, 406 U.S. 715 (1972).

Justice Policy Institute. 2011. *When Treatment is Punishment: The Effects of Maryland's Incompetency to Stand Trial Policies and Practices*. Washington, DC: Justice Policy Institute.

Kayess R and P French. 2008. Out of darkness into light? Introducing the Convention on the Rights of Persons with Disabilities. *Human Rights Law Review* 8:1–34.

Keyhea v. Rushen, 178 Cal. App. 3d 526.223 Cal. Rptr. 746 (1986).

Kulas v. Valdez, 159 F. 3d 453 (9th Cir. 1998).

Levitt GA, I Vora, K Tyler, L Arenzon, D Drachman, and G Ramos. 2010. Civil commitment outcomes of incompetent defendants. *Journal of the American Academy of Psychiatry and the Law* 38:259–358.

Large v. Superior Court, 148 Ariz. 229, 714 P.2d 399 (1986).

Mannix v. State, 621 S.W.2d 222 (Ark. 1981).

Matter of Sombrotto v. Christiana W., 50 a.D.3d 63, 852 N.y.S.2d 57 (2008).

McConnell v. Beverly Enterprises-Connecticut, Inc., 209 Conn. 692, 553 A. 2d 596 (1989).

Mills v. Rogers, 457 U.S. 291 (1982).

Myers v. Alaska Psychiatric Institute, 138 P3d 238 (Alaska 2006).

Osgood v. District of Columbia, 567 F. Supp. 1026 (D.D.C. 1983).

Panetti v. Dretke, 448 f.3d 815 (5th Cir. 2006).

Penry v. Lynaugh, 492 U.S. 302 (1989).

Panetti v. Quarterman, 127 S.Ct. 852 (2007).

People v. Fisher, 172 Cal.App. 4th 1006,91 Cal.Rptr.3d 609 (2009).

People v. Lopez, 160 A.D.2d 335, 554 N.Y.S.2d 98 (1989), app'l den., 76 N.Y.2d 791, 559 N.Y.S.2d 996, 559 N.E.2d 690 (1990).

Perlin, M.L. 1987a. State constitutions and statutes as sources of rights for the mentally disabled: The last frontier? *Loyola of Los Angeles Law Review* 20:1249–1327.

Perlin ML 1987b. The Supreme Court, the mentally disabled criminal defendant, and symbolic values: Random decisions, hidden rationales, or "doctrinal abyss." *Arizona Law Review* 29:1–98.

Perlin ML. 1989 (and 1999 cumulative supplement). *Mental Disability Law: Civil and Criminal.* Charlottesville, VA: Michie.

Perlin ML. 1989–1990. Unpacking the myths: The symbolism mythology of insanity defense jurisprudence. *Case Western Reserve Law Review* 40:599–731.

Perlin ML. 1990. Are courts competent to decide competency questions? Stripping the facade from *United States v. Charters*. *University of Kansas Law Review* 38:957–1001.

Perlin ML. 1991. Reading the Supreme Court's tea leaves. Predicting judicial behavior in civil and criminal right to refuse treatment cases. *American Journal of Forensic Psychiatry* 12:37–67.

Perlin ML. 1992. *Riggins v. Nevada*: Forced medication collides with the right to a fair trial. *Newsletter of the American Academy of Psychiatry and Law* 17:81–83.

Perlin ML. 1993–1994. The ADA and persons with mental disabilities: Can sanist attitudes be undone? *Journal of Law and Health* 8:15–45.

Perlin ML. 1994a. Therapeutic jurisprudence: Understanding the sanist and pretextual bases of mental disability law. *New England Journal of Criminal and Civil Confinement* 20:369–383.

Perlin ML. 1994b. *The Jurisprudence of the Insanity Defense*. Durham, NC: Carolina Academic Press.

Perlin ML. 1994c. The sanist lives of jurors in death penalty cases: The puzzling role of "mitigating" mental disability evidence. *Notre Dame Journal of Law, Ethics and Public Policy* 8:239–279.

Perlin ML. 1997. "Make promises by the hour": Sex, drugs, the ADA, and psychiatric hospitalization. *DePaul Law Review* 46:947–985.

Perlin ML. 2000. *The Hidden Prejudice: Mental Disability on Trial*. Washington, DC: American Psychological Association.

Perlin ML. 2010. "Good and bad, I defined these terms, quite clear no doubt somehow": Neuroimaging and competency to be executed after Panetti. *Behavioral Sciences and the Law* 28:671–689.

Perlin ML and HE Cucolo. 2016. *Mental Disability Law: Civil and Criminal*, 3rd edition. Newark, NJ: Lexis Law Publishing.

Perlin ML and DA Dorfman. 1993. Sanism, social science, and the development of mental disability law jurisprudence. *Behavioral Sciences and the Law* 11:47–66.

Perlin ML and DA Dorfman. 1996. Is it more than "dodging lions and wastin' time"? Adequacy of counsel, questions of competence, and the judicial process in individual right to refuse treatment cases. *Psychology, Public Policy and Law* 2:114–136.

Perry v. Louisiana, 498 U.S. 38 (1990a).

Perry v. Louisiana, 498 U.S. 1075 (1990b), reh. denied, 498 U.S. 1075 (1991).

Plotkin R. 1977. Limiting the therapeutic orgy: Mental patients' right to refuse treatment. *Northwestern University Law Review* 72:461–525.

Preston v. Gutierrez, 1993 WL 280819 (W.D. Mo. 1993).

Rennie v. Klein, 462 F. Supp. 1131 (D.N.J. 1978), supplemental opinion, 476 F. Supp. 1294 (D.N.J. 1979), modified, 653 F.2d 836 (3d Circ. 1981) (en banc), vacated and remanded, 458 U.S. 1119 (1982), on remand, 720 F.2d 266 (3d Circ. 1983) (en banc).

Rhoden N. 1980. The right to refuse psychotropic drugs. *Harvard Civil Rights-Civil Liberties Law Review* 15:363–413.

Riese v. St. Mary's Hospital and Medical Center, 198 Cal. App. 3d 1388, 243 Cal.Rptr. 2431 (1987), app'l dismissed, 774 P.2d 698, 259 Cal.Rptr. 669 (1989).

Riggins v. Nevada, 504 U.S. 127 (1992).

Rivers v. Katz, 67 N.Y.2d 485, 495 N.E.2d 337, 504 N.Y.S.2d 74 (1986).

Roth L. 1986. The right to refuse psychiatric treatment: Law and medicine at the interface. *Emory Law Journal* 35:139–160.

Sell v. United States, 539 U.S. 166 (2003).

Singleton v. Norris 319 F.3d 1018 (8th Cir. 2003), *cert. den.*, 124 S. Ct. 74 (2003).

State v. Anthony D.B., 237 Wis.2d 1,614 N.W.2d 435 (2000).

State v. Hayes, 118 N.H. 458, 389 A.2d 1379 (1978).

State v. Kotis, 91 Hawai'l 319, 984 P.2d 78 (1999).

State v. Otero, 238 N.J. Super. 649, 570 A.2d 503 (Law Div. 1989).

State v. Perry, 543 So. 2d 487 (La. 1989), reheating den., 545 So. 2d 1049 (1989).

State v. Perry, 610 So. 2d 746 (La. 1992).

State ex rel. Jones v. Gerhardstein, 141 Wis. 2d 710, 416 N.W.2d 883 (1987).

Supreme Court sidesteps issue of restoring inmates' competency to allow execution. 1990. *Psychiatric News*, December 21.

United States v. Bradley, 417 f.3d 1107, 10th Cir. 2005.

United States v. Brandon, 158 F. 3d 947, 6th Cir. 1998.

United States v. Bush, 585 F.3d 806, 4th Cir. 2009.

United States v. Charters, 829 F.2d 479 (4th Cir. 1987) (Charters I), on rehearing, 863 F.2d 302 (4th Cir. 1988) (en banc) (Charters 9I), cert. denied, 494 U.S. 1016 (1990).

United States v. Gomes, 289 F.3d 71 (2d Cir. 2002).

United States v. Grape, 549 F.3d 591 (3d Cir. 2008).

Unites States v. Kourey, 276 F.Supp.2d 580 (S.D.W. Va. 2003).

United States v. Loughner, 672 F.3d 731 (9th Cir. 2012).

United States v. Ruiz-Gaxiola, 623 F.3d 684 (9th Cir. 2010).

United States v. Weston, 206 F. 3d 9 (D.C. Cir. 2000).

42 U.S.C. §1983 (1871).

Virgil D. v. Rock County, 189 Wis. 2d 1, 524 N.W. 2d 894 (1994).

Vitek v. Jones, 445 U.S. 480 (1980).

Washington v. Harper, 494 U.S. 210 (1990).

Wexler, D. 1982. Seclusion and restraint: Lessons for law, psychiatry, and psychology. *International Journal of Law and Psychiatry* 5:285–294.

Whitehead v. Wainwright, 447 F. Supp: 898 (M.D. Fla. 1978), vacated and remanded on other gds., 609 F.2d 223 (5th Cir. 1980).

Williams v. Wilzack, 319 Md. 485, 573 A.2d 809 (1990), reconsid. den. (1990).

Woodland v. Angus, 820 F. Supp. 1497 (D. Utah 1993).

Youngberg v. Romeo, 457 U.S. 307 (1982).

58

Hunger strikes by inmates

GEORGE DAVID ANNAS

INTRODUCTION

A hunger strike, while passive in nature, is one of the most dramatic forms of protest that a human being can express. Such an action comes about as a last resort when one has no other peaceful means of protest remaining and is willing to die for the cause at hand. The act has been carried out in human culture since the beginning of recorded history, examples include the text of one of the oldest epic poems, the Hindu *Ramayana,* dating somewhere from 500 to 200 BCE (Chaurasia 2002), and Ancient Rome (Simanowitz 2012). As a testament to how powerful the act can be, it is notable that some hunger strikers changed history with their protest. Famous cases include those of Mahatma Ghandi, Hugo Chavez, and the pioneers of the women's Suffrage movement.

In addition to hunger strikes that have occurred in free society, this practice occurs routinely among the incarcerated. One well-known hunger strike occurred in 1981 among Provisional Irish Republican Army (IRA) prisoners at the Maze Prison in Northern Ireland, which led to the starvation deaths of 10 IRA members (BBC 2015). Yet examples of hunger strikes among the incarcerated have been documented as far back as the first century AD, when Aulus Cremutius Cordus, a Roman historian, starved himself to death during his confinement (Coleman 2013).

When the lack of autonomy of the incarcerated individual is considered, the logic of the hunger strike becomes perceptible. One of the few things a prisoner can exert control over is choosing not to eat. The precise frequency of hunger strikes in corrections is unknown as little data exist. In addition, the U.S. Department of Justice's (DOJ) Bureau of Justice Statistics (BJS) does not keep records on their incidence or prevalence.

Studies in the United Kingdom suggest that hunger strikes are infrequent, there is no apparent correlation between the type of crime and food refusal, and motives caused by anorexia nervosa are rare (Larkin 1991). In addition, protests of a personal injustice were more likely to motivate longer fasting, but overall weight loss was not substantially different between those groups and other strikers (O'Connor and Johnson-Sabine 1988).

Data regarding the prevalence of mental illness among correctional hunger strikes (as well as the potential impact of said mental illness on capacity) are similarly sparse. The studies mentioned above suggested an association between mental illness and hunger strikes, but had little information regarding decision-making capacity among mentally ill hunger strikers. Another UK study noted a low prevalence of mental illness motivating a hunger strike (Brockman 1999). This chapter will address the issue of hunger strikes in correctional settings, the role a forensic psychiatrist may play in their assessment and management, the unique aspects of assessing competence to engage in a hunger strike, and the ethical dilemmas that can arise in these situations. For simplicity I will use the term "prisoner" and the male gender when discussing hunger strikes in this chapter, with the understanding that they can take place in any correctional setting and among both men and women.

HUNGER STRIKE DEFINITION

What is a hunger strike? It is not a simple task to cleanly answer this question. The World Medical Association (WMA) in its Declaration of Malta on Hunger Strikers, states, "A hunger striker is a mentally competent person who has indicated that he has decided to embark on a hunger strike and has refused to take food and/or fluids for a significant interval" (1991, 1992). This definition indicates perhaps the most important aspect of one engaging in a hunger strike—competence. The International Committee of the Red Cross (ICRC) defines a hunger strike as "voluntary fasting pursued for a specific purpose" (Reyes 1998). The ICRC definition indicates another important aspect in addition to competence, that of the striker expressing a specific purpose. The word "voluntary" denotes *de facto* competence, as well as indicating that such an act should only be considered a hunger strike if it is free from coercion.

Perhaps the multiple definitions of hunger strike are suggestive of the complexity of the phenomenon. The Federal

Bureau of Prisons (BOP) defines a hunger strike as occurring when the prisoner "communicates that fact to staff and is observed by staff to be refraining from eating for a period of time, ordinarily in excess of 72 hours" or "when staff observe the inmate to be refraining from eating for a period in excess of 72 hours" (Lappin 2005). The California Department of Corrections and Rehabilitation (CDCR) defines a hunger strike as an inmate missing nine consecutive meals (2013). Other definitions focus on the length of time someone refuses food and determines the initial intervention at that point—usually a medical examination. The problem with the common definition used by correctional facilities is that neither competence nor a stated purpose is routinely addressed prior to using the label.

Despite the fact that one can encounter any combination of factors, stated purposes, and degrees of mental capacity, the ICRC definition of a hunger strike (i.e., a competent individual refusing food for a stated purpose) provides a straightforward and rational guideline to use when attempting to differentiate between one who simply stops eating for any reason, and one who is engaging in a hunger strike. As demonstrated later in this chapter, keeping such a definition in mind can help guide an evaluating psychiatrist toward a valid assessment and beneficial contribution to the team charged with managing the welfare of the prisoner.

One often encounters the term "Hunger Strike" whenever a prisoner refuses food, likely based on the definitions put forth by correctional institutions. Such a liberal use of the term may simply lead to confusion. For example, consider the case of an inmate who was depressed and had refused food with the intent to die (Associated Press 2014). Such an individual whose mental illness led to suicidal intent should not be considered by any mental health or correctional professional as having been on a hunger strike, because he is not likely to be acting autonomously, raising critical issues of competence and need for medical and legal intervention.

Other terms may be helpful to further qualify a hunger strike. A hunger striker who refuses all food and all fluids is referred to as a "dry hunger striker," while one who refuses food but accepts some form of liquid intake supplement is considered a "total hunger striker" or engaging in a "voluntary total fast" (Reyes et al. 2013). Those who refuse both food and all fluids may be doing so in a reactionary way with no intention of continuing and therefore no risk of death by starvation (Reyes 1998), or do so when driven by significant mental illness or mental defect (Larkin 1991). The true hunger striker's goal is to have his demands met; therefore, the goal is to prolong a fast as long as possible; the goal is not death. Yet the hunger striker may be prepared to die, if necessary (WMA 2006).

It is logical to conclude that, in some cases, a consulting psychiatrist will not be able to determine if a fasting prisoner is on a hunger strike or not, until an assessment for capacity is performed. The psychiatrist may find himself or herself in many potential roles, however, both during and after the assessment is performed.

PSYCHIATRIC EVALUATION OF HUNGER STRIKES

The consult

Depending on the situation, a forensic psychiatrist who does not work for the correctional facility may be independently asked to evaluate a prisoner for competence to engage in a hunger strike (such as by the prisoner's attorney, the judge, or the correctional facility). Although not eliminated altogether, the risk of institutional bias is lessened in these situations. A potential disadvantage in these cases may be the timing of the evaluation. Although the consulting psychiatrist will likely have little control in this regard, the time that it takes an institution to set up an evaluation by an outside consultant may delay the evaluation to the point where an otherwise competent hunger striker may appear less so upon examination (Birchard 1997).

As with any psychiatric consultation, it is vital to determine with the requesting entity the specific and appropriate question(s) to address. Such questions may include the following: "Does the prisoner have the capacity to engage in fasting?" or "Does the prisoner have a mental illness and, if so, does the mental illness impair the decision-making capacity of the prisoner in regard to a hunger strike?" Less sophisticated questions may be encountered, such as "is the prisoner a true hunger striker?" However, it is important to avoid labels that may insult a reactive prisoner and lead to a detrimental "power of wills" (Reyes 1998).

Should the question involve recommendations about management as well, the wording of the question may be even more important. For example, it would be reasonable and appropriate to answer questions regarding recommendations for management of a fasting prisoner with a mental illness who has been opined to be incompetent by the examiner. However, if one is asked "do you recommend force-feeding," this would not be appropriate to address. Regardless of the final opinion on capacity or the final adjudication of such, force-feeding is widely recognized as unethical, and efforts should be made to prevent its practice (WMA 1991–1992, 2006; see also Legal and Ethical Issues in Managing a Hunger Strike, below). The correctional institution may frame the scenario as "either the prisoner starts eating again or we will have to force feed him." However, the psychiatrist should be mindful to avoid falling into the trap of this false dichotomy.

An ethical ban on force-feeding does not preclude the potential necessity for artificial feeding in an emergent situation if an incompetent prisoner prolongs a fast, putting his life at risk. But the important point is that there are other interventions that should be attempted first in situations where food refusal is deemed to be secondary to a mental illness and not a competent protest decision (see below, Management of the Incompetent Fasting Prisoner). When these avenues are taken, the dilemma is often moot (Reyes 1998).

Whether in a correctional treatment or an independent consultant setting, forensic psychiatrists possesses specialized expertise that is helpful in the situations where a prisoner begins to consistently refuse food. This may include educating the prisoner and medical team about possible mental status changes that will be expected during starvation, educating the team about how the personality structure of the prisoner may affect his or her behavior, as well as using the knowledge of interpersonal team dynamics to prevent or minimize negative staff countertransference reactions during the management of hunger strikes.

EVALUATION OF COMPETENCE

When a forensic psychiatrist is asked to form an opinion on the prisoner's competence to engage in a hunger strike, much of the approach is similar to that of assessing one's capacity to make treatment decisions. However, there are a few aspects of this evaluation that are unique. Unlike someone refusing artificial feeding (which would require a medical procedure and therefore constitute a refusal of treatment), someone refusing food is refusing basic nourishment that we all engage in daily in order to continue living. One's competence *to* eat is never questioned, and unlike refusing a medical intervention that may or may not result in death, ultimately starvation always will.

Prior to evaluating the prisoner's competence, pre-evaluation preparation is necessary. The following recommendations for preparation are based on the author's experience, as well as the relevant literature applied to hunger strikes:

- Meet with treatment staff regarding concerns, prisoner's condition, prognosis, and interventions utilized
- Review the prisoner's medical and psychiatric history, lab results, and relevant studies
- Review any past hunger strikes by the prisoner and their outcomes
- Review any recent emergency treatment orders and why given (Kim 2010)

A widely accepted model for approaching the evaluation of competence to make treatment decisions has been developed by Grisso and Appelbaum (1998). They write that an approach to assessing competence to accept or refuse treatment should address the domains of communicating choices, understanding relevant information, appreciating the situation and consequences, and manipulating information rationally. In addition, they note the importance of evaluating for psychopathology and taking into consideration context and personal behaviors (1998). Some of these items are addressed below in the context of evaluating capacity to engage in a hunger strike.

Communicating choices

This aspect of competence rarely would become an issue with a hunger striker. If someone is not consistent in regard to refusing meals, it will be unlikely to lead to a life-threatening situation. Furthermore, a psychiatrist would rarely be called in until someone began stopping meals consistently.

Understanding relevant information and appreciating the situation and consequences of fasting

Although it would be rare that someone would not know that the ultimate consequence of fasting is death (and if he did not, it would be rare that he was competent), an adequate demonstration of understanding goes beyond this. It is important that he be able to demonstrate knowledge of the relevance of pre-existing medical conditions that might risk permanent injury sooner that one might expect. For example, for a prisoner with a stomach ulcer it is important that he be able to demonstrate the understanding that the dangers of an ulcer (relevant facts) pertain to him (his situation) and may put him at risk for internal bleeding early on during the fast (consequences). A prisoner with bipolar disorder may understand the basic facts in regard to prolonged fasting leading to death, but voice the opinion that he is invincible and therefore such a rule of nature did not apply to him (i.e., failure to understand one's situation and consequences, despite the ability to understand relevant information).

Another aspect of appreciating one's situation and consequences include his perceived expectation about what he will accomplish with his strike. This brings up an important and related aspect of the evaluation—the stated reason for the hunger strike, which also touches on the ability to rationally manipulate information to come to the decision to engage in a hunger strike.

Manipulating information rationally

One of the most vital aspects of an evaluation for competence to engage in a hunger strike involves eliciting the stated reason for the strike. For example, a prisoner stating that he is fasting in order to rid the body of demonic spirits may indeed lack the ability to engage in a rational process of decision making about refusing nutrients. But like one's competence to refuse treatment, a stated purpose that appears illogical may not necessarily imply a lack of competence. In the absence of significant impairment in other domains, this aspect of the evaluation may be as simple as the prisoner being able to demonstrate that the strike is a form of protest that is meant to bring about some goal, assuming the goal is not incoherent or bizarre.

A prisoner who decides to fast in order to protest the United States' involvement in a foreign war may sound irrational. However, the stated purpose, itself, would not alone imply a lack of competence. The importance of this aspect of the evaluation is the person's rational manipulation of information to reach the decision—the latter of which, in itself, may not be required to be seen as rational.

In a case such as this, one would need to delve deeper and determine what (if any) aspects of potential psychopathology might be influencing him. For example, does he recognize the outcome he is hoping for is unlikely? In contrast, does he appear to have another motive (such as suicide)? Are his actions consistent with his prior ("baseline") behavior?

Assessing psychopathology

A vital part of the evaluation will be to determine if a mental illness is the primary driving force behind the decision to stop eating. In some cases this may not be difficult to determine, such as the case of a depressed prisoner who states that he deserves death for his crime, the delusional prisoner who reports that there are microchips in the food that will cause another to gain remote control of his bodily functions after ingestion, or the catatonic patient who is immobile and mute. In such cases, the motive or cause behind the food refusal would not be difficult to determine with a clinical interview or appropriate physical exam (e.g., a Bush–Francis screen for catatonia). Often cases are more complex, but sometimes initial "red flags" can help begin to guide the evaluator.

A study by O'Connor and Johnson-Sabine (1988) reviewed cases of hunger strikes in a female remand prison in London as well as Broadmoor Hospital and one additional case at a London Psychiatric Hospital. They determined that hunger strikes were highly correlated with mental illness, with 14 out of 25 (whose charts were available to review) being diagnosed with a mental illness. This study also pointed out that cases where a prisoner refused all oral fluids as well as food (i.e., "dry" hunger strikes) were correlated with psychosis. In a study of British inmates in Lincolnshire, England, from 1978 to 1986, mental illness was also highly prevalent among hunger strikers (Larkin 1991). Two aspects of behavior appeared to increase the likelihood of mental illness driving the decision to fast: (1) if they refused (or were unable) to state why they were fasting, or (2) if they refused all fluids as well as food (i.e., "dry" hunger strikes). The study reaffirms the importance of a thorough evaluation of the prisoner for psychopathology in either of these findings. A "dry" hunger striker will be at risk of death much sooner and may be seeking death, rather than only risking it for a cause (or be easily distinguished from a "reactionary" prisoner who will not put himself at risk). The prisoner who cannot state a reason for a hunger strike may not be able to manipulate information rationally in order to engage in rational decision making.

Despite the O'Connor and Larkin studies, food refusal and mental illness may not be as highly correlated as their results initially suggest. Both studies were retrospective, and either did not determine if the fasting prisoners with a history of mental illness lacked capacity at the time of their fasting (O'Connor and Johnson-Sabine 1988) or had limited information in this regard (Larkin 1991). In addition, in the O'Connor study only two of those diagnosed with a mental illness had expressed motives that were strongly suggestive of psychosis (i.e., food being poisoned and food causing brain damage), yet six of them had a psychotic disorder among their diagnoses. This suggests that the remaining four with a psychotic disorder may have had capacity at the time (suggesting that the diagnosis of a mental illness may not have been causative in the decision to fast). The Larkin study also included a personality disorder as qualifying one as having a mental illness, potentially making the association seem higher than it was. In a 1999 article by Dr. Beatrice Brockman, she noted that among the 15 evaluations she performed for assessing competence to engage in a hunger strike, she opined a lack of competence in only one (and the judge in that case disagreed). While her report was anecdotal, its value may lie in the fact that it was composed of cases that were all personally evaluated by a single psychiatrist (Brockman 1999).

As with competence in regard to refusing medications or medical intervention, each case must be considered within the context of its own unique set of clinical circumstances. For example, a prisoner with a diagnosis of schizophrenia may still possess competence to engage in a hunger strike. The challenge in instances such as these is to determine the degree to which the symptoms of mental illness affect the prisoner's motive for fasting. Or put another way, does the prisoner's motive for fasting flow from a mental illness, and, if so, to what extent? Situations in which comorbid mental illness is present along with a seemingly rational reason for a protest fast can be more complicated. For example, a depressed prisoner who states a protest over the conditions of his confinement may be using the pretense of a hunger strike in order to act upon suicidal intent.

The psychiatrist may encounter extremely complicated cases in which clarifying a prisoner's motives for a hunger strike becomes challenging. Consider a case in which the conditions of confinement appear to have caused the symptoms—such as prisoner abuse leading to posttraumatic stress disorder (PTSD) or depression. In such a situation the prisoner's baseline behavior will likely change and he will be symptomatic, express hopelessness, and may quite rationally conclude that a hunger strike is his only means of protest available. Dealing with suspected prisoner abuse is outside the scope of this chapter, but the issue brings up the importance of recognizing that the psychopathology present may be a factor in one prisoner's competence, while it could be the rational cause for a protest in another. In such a situation where prisoner abuse is suspected, it is the ethical duty of the psychiatrist (regardless of the role he or she is in) to report this to the higher authorities until such an allegation is adequately investigated (Knoll 2014). All steps toward the prisoner's safety, well-being, and dignity will be the most effective intervention in such cases (see also, Legal and Ethical Issues in Managing a Hunger Strike, below).

Additional considerations regarding the evaluation of hunger strikes

In addition to the above factors, it is important for the prisoner to demonstrate the knowledge that he will likely lose the ability to make decisions for himself, should the fast be prolonged. Such situations highlight the importance of the prisoner assigning a proxy decision maker or clearly delineating advanced directives (see below, the Management of the Competent Hunger Striker). Another challenging scenario may arise when a prisoner is undergoing a hunger strike as part of a group. On the surface, a group hunger strike may seem to be more likely to involve competent participants, due to the organization involved and because it would be unlikely that a mentally impaired leader would be followed by a group. However, there remains a risk that some peer coercion may be at play, which could impact a vulnerable prisoner. Should evidence of coercion come up during the evaluation, the psychiatrist has an obligation to determine an avenue for safely extricating the vulnerable prisoner from such coercive influences. This may involve moving the individual to another area of the prison.

In addition to assessing decision-making capacity, a psychiatrist may be asked to make recommendations for managing a prisoner who engages in a hunger strike. The potential recommendations will be guided by the opinion on competence itself—i.e., for recommending treatment (over objection if necessary) for those whose mental illness impairs their competence to engage in a hunger strike.

MANAGEMENT OF THE INCOMPETENT FASTING PRISONER

In the case of a fasting prisoner whose mental illness is driving the refusal of food, the management should be aimed at addressing the mental illness. Thus, an assessment of capacity should be done as early as possible, so that there is time to implement treatment strategies to avoid permanent damage from prolonged fasting. In some instances a prisoner's mental illness may cause him to pose a danger to himself, and a court order for treatment over objection may be needed. It is also notable that situations like these are often not as black and white as they seem, and often even a psychotic prisoner may consent to accept some forms of nutrition, which might buy enough time for him to respond to medications or other treatment.

MANAGEMENT OF THE COMPETENT HUNGER STRIKER

There are few studies examining the phenomenon of early mental status changes in hunger strikers. However, some data may be considered from the work of Anthropologist Daniel Fessler who studied fasting among eating-disordered patients. While he noted that some showed signs of abrupt early psychosis, many showed more subtle psychological changes in the face of starvation. One observation was that starvation caused patients to become more impulsive and obstinate, potentially due to a decrease in serotonergic activity (Fessler 2003). Although most of the early changes rarely appeared to affect competence, the results suggest a correlation with more cognitive flexibility earlier in the fasting process, and perhaps more hostility and rigidity later (i.e., a reasonable resolution or compromise to the hunger strike may be more likely to be reached early on, as opposed to later in the process).

In addition to the Fessler study, an earlier report from Israel noted that a pre-existing psychotic disorder (or personality disorder with a history of psychotic episodes), increased the risk of psychosis earlier on in the process of fasting (Robinson and Winnik 1973). Thus, a hunger striker with schizophrenia may be at higher risk for early psychosis, even if competent at the onset of the fast. Another important consideration to address involves the assignment of a substitute decision maker to serve in the instance that a prolonged fast causes a prisoner to lose his competence. On a long enough timeline, all hunger strikes will lead to incompetence, and it is important to ask the prisoner to assign someone to speak for him in those instances, or to set out a clear advance directive. Some hunger strikers may prophylactically consent to artificial feeding or intravenous nutrition in the instance that the fasting has led them to lose consciousness. In contrast, some may only consent to this if certain demands have been met. Regardless, the discussion of this issue should be made as early as possible to help ensure that those decisions are made when the prisoner is most lucid.

Should a hunger striker wish to end a fast but feel compelled to continue due to peer pressure from other prisoners (such as in a group hunger strike), he must have an avenue to express this to his treatment team without concern that it will get back to the other hunger strikers. His motives may range from simply avoiding the feeling of shame, to fear of retaliation. In these instances confidentiality must be assured, as well as an avenue to provide nourishment to the prisoner without concern for the others knowing he has decided to stop his fast. Medical management of hunger strikers will be largely performed by the internist on duty, and may involve convincing the prisoner to accept some supplementation to help prolong and delay permanent injury. Some prisoners will concurrently accept intravenous fluids and/or treatment for infection or pain. Some may accept nutritional supplements, and may benefit from vitamin B or other supplementation (Oguz and Miles 2005). Therefore, it is important to offer these, as they may delay or reduce the risk of permanent injury.

Regarding the management of a competent hunger striker, it is important to recognize that despite the fact that a hunger striker often leaves no doubt to his competence, the correctional institution will often be successful in obtaining a court order authorizing force-feeding. Although a psychiatrist would not typically be involved in a force-feeding procedure, forensic psychiatrists are often consulted (both formally and informally) when ethical dilemmas arise among the treatment team.

LEGAL AND ETHICAL ISSUES IN MANAGING A HUNGER STRIKE

When a competent individual in free society engages in a prolonged hunger strike, it would be rare that a life-threatening situation would lead to the person being force-fed (especially if a clear advance directive was documented). However, in the United States, when a prisoner engages in a hunger strike, the situation becomes complicated due to his being in the custody of the state. In such cases, the courts must weigh the prisoner's rights against the interests of the state. The prisoner's rights are often argued in regard to personal liberty interests/autonomy, the first amendment right to free expression, and the right to refuse treatment (common law doctrine of informed consent and the right to privacy). The state's interests are often argued in regard to prevention of suicide, maintaining order, duty to provide medical care, and the overall prevention of death (Ohm 2006).

When weighing the two party's interests, it is notable that some early cases in the United States sided with the prisoner's right to continue food refusal. In the 1982 case of *Zant v. Prevatte*, the Georgia Supreme Court upheld a hunger striking prisoner's right to continue his fast, based on his right to privacy, which the Court found outweighed the state's interest in keeping a prisoner safe from harm (Ohm, 2006; 248 Ga. 832, 286 S.E.2d 715, 1982). However, more commonly courts will authorize force-feeding when a prolonged hunger striker is at risk of death, if not well before that point (Ohm 2006). Jurisdictions vary widely in regard to the correctional facility's authority to initiate force-feeding, some even authorizing this at the discretion of the treating physician without a court order. For example, an Illinois statute authorizes a treating physician to initiate force-feeding "to prevent death, damage, or impairment to bodily functions" (Ill. Comp. Stat. 5/3-6-2, 2004).

Although seemingly at odds with rational logic, one state interest that has been successfully cited to supersede the individual interests of the prisoner is that of force-feeding the prisoner to prevent a "security" risk based on interference with the orderly administration of the prison. A group hunger strike may potentially put some security interests at risk, it is difficult to argue that one hunger striker puts anyone at risk of harm but himself. Nevertheless, courts often give broad latitude and deference to correctional administrator's concern over security risks. For example the Supreme Court of Connecticut in *Commissioner of Corrections v. William B. Coleman* (2012) affirmed a lower court's granting of a permanent injunction authorizing the force-feeding of a hunger striking inmate. The court stated its opinion in part noting that allowing the hunger strike to continue would present "an unacceptable risk to the safety, security and orderly administration of the prison system." A competent hunger striker is not seeking to end his life, but the state interest in preventing "suicide" is often also successfully cited in cases ruling in favor of correctional facilities. For example, the Washington State Supreme Court referenced, in part, the prevention of suicide as the justification for authorizing for a hunger striking inmate (*McNabb v. Dept. of Corrections* 2008).

Therefore, it is not uncommon that the correctional facility will be successful in requesting court authorization for force-feeding. Such situations often leave medical staff in uncomfortable situations. While a court may grant the legal authority for a correctional institution to force-feed a prisoner, such a practice may be regarded as unethical in many, if not all, circumstances (WMA, 2006; Arnold, 2008, Rubenstein and Annas 2009). While ethical practice is often supported with legal authority, the latter does not invariably ensure the former.

ETHICAL GUIDANCE

When attempting to determine guidance for the proper ethical course in managing hunger strikes among the incarcerated, the most authoritative guidelines have been developed by the WMA in its Declaration of Malta on Hunger Strikers in 1991, and later revised in 2006. The Declaration focuses on detained individuals (such as immigration detainees in addition to prisoners) and contains 7 ethical principles and 13 guidelines consistent with those principles. Among the guidelines are ways in which to approach the difficult—and usually rare—incident where a hunger striker has reached the point where he is at risk of death and has left clear directives against artificial feeding or other hydration:

> Physicians may consider it justifiable to go against advance instructions refusing treatment because, for example, the refusal is thought to have been made under duress. If, after resuscitation and having regained their mental faculties, hunger strikers continue to reiterate their intention to fast, that decision should be respected. It is ethical to allow a determined hunger striker to die in dignity rather than submit that person to repeated interventions against his or her will. (Guideline 11, WMA, 2006)

Other exceptions include the question of whether or not the purpose of the hunger strike has been addressed partially. For example, consider this case: if a person loses capacity during a hunger strike before he is informed that some, but not all, of his demands have been met. The Malta guidelines therefore provide steps to ensure that all other avenues have been explored prior to any physician making the ultimate decision to defer intervention.

It is also important that one not only focuses on the decision-making capacity assessment but also be receptive to a potentially larger picture emerging in some cases. For example, among hunger strikers at the detention facility at Guantanamo Bay, Cuba (GTMO), there has been evidence that prisoner abuse was a factor in their protest (testimony of Dr. Steve Miles, *Dhiab v. Obama* [transcript]; The Constitution Project 2013). A full analysis of this topic is outside the scope of this chapter, but it has been well documented that many GTMO prisoners gave credible statements about being tortured while in custody and experienced undiagnosed and untreated PTSD and depression (Clark 2006; The Constitution Project 2013). This demonstrates a potential situation where one is severely depressed, desperate, and hopeless, and may yet express a valid protest about mistreatment. Thus, it is important to be mindful that the stated purpose of a hunger striker may be legitimate, despite the presence of significant symptomatology.

OTHER POTENTIAL ROLES

A forensic psychiatrist may also contribute to the treatment team as a liaison to the medical staff to advise on approaches that may help a prisoner remain in optimal health, while allowing him to "save face" in the instance that the person may be expressing ambivalence about continuing the strike. On the one hand, there is the ethical duty of a treating physician to offer the prisoner whatever means will help him return to accepting adequate nutrition of some kind. On the other hand, unethical or coercive strategies should be avoided. And amid all of this, the psychiatrist and medical staff should remain mindful of their own personal biases, and countertransference. Although not immune from these issues, this suggests another area in which a psychiatrist can contribute, such as in promoting more positive team dynamics.

SUMMARY

Hunger strikes in correctional settings have the potential to become intensely dramatic episodes for both the correctional staff and the prisoner. Something seemingly as simple as knowing when and when not to apply the term "hunger strike," can be significantly important in these situations and can help guide the clinician toward a proper and effective management strategy. The psychiatrist can assist in many ways, including forming an opinion on a hunger striker's competence, assisting in the management of incompetent as well as competent prisoners who refuse food, and providing education to the treatment team.

Important aspects of the assessment and management of food refusal in prisoners include:

- Early examination for competency
- Determining the stated reason and ruling out motives driven by mental illness
- Avoiding or minimizing an adversarial situation with the inmate
- Application of the WMA Declaration of Malta for ethical guidance

REFERENCES

Arnold F. 2008. Clinical care of hunger strikers. *The Lancet* 372:1–7.

Associated Press. 2014. Timeline of events in Embry's hunger strike. *Courier-Journal*. http://www.courier-journal.com/story/news/local/2014/05/17/timeline-events-embrys-hunger-strike/9239267/, accessed November 30, 2015.

BBC. 2015. More about the hunger strikes. In *British Broadcasting Company (BBC)*. http://www.bbc.co.uk/history/events/republican_hunger_strikes_maze, accessed April 30, 2015.

Birchard K. 1997. Psychiatric assessment of hunger strikers must be prompt. *The Lancet* 350:648.

Brockman B. 1999. Food refusal in prisoners: A communication or a method of self-killing? The role of the psychiatrist and resulting ethical challenges. *Journal of Medical Ethics* 25(6):451–456.

California Department of Corrections and Rehabilitation (CDCR). 2013. *Fact Sheet*. http://www.cdcr.ca.gov/stg/docs/Fact%20Sheet-hunger%20strikes%20in%20CA%20prisons.pdf, accessed November 30, 2015.

Chaurasia RS. 2002. *History of Ancient India*. New Delhi, India: Atlantic.

Clark P. 2006. Medical ethics at Guantanamo Bay and Abu Ghraib: The problem of dual loyalty. *Journal of Law, Medicine and Ethics* 34:570–580.

Coleman M. 2013. Hunger strike. In *The Lokashakti Encyclopedia of Nonviolence, Peace, and Social Justice*. http://www.lokashakti.org/encyclopedia/concepts/955-hunger-strike, accessed November 30, 2015.

Commissioner of Corrections v. William B. Coleman, No. SC18721 (CT Sup Ct, 3-13-2012).

Fessler DMT. 2003. The implications of starvation induced psychological changes for the ethical treatment of hunger strikers. *Journal of Medical Ethics* 29(4):243–247.

Grisso T and P Appelbaum. 1998. *Assessing Competence to Consent to Treatment: A Guide for Physicians and Other Health Care Professionals*. New York: Oxford University Press.

Illinois Public Act 093-0928, Section 3-6-2 (Institutions and Facility Administration), e-5, ftp://www.ilga.gov/Public%20Acts/93/093-0928.htm, accessed November 30, 2015.

Kim SYH. 2010. *Evaluation of Capacity to Consent to Treatment and Research*. New York: Oxford University Press.

Knoll J. 2014. The correctional psychiatrist obligation: Same as it ever was. *Correctional Mental Health Report* 15(5):65.

Lappin HG. 2005. *Program Statement 5562.05: Hunger Strikes*. Washington, DC: United States Department of Justice Federal Bureau of Prisons (BOP): BOP Policies. https://www.bop.gov/policy/progstat/5562_005.pdf, accessed August 8, 2016.

Larkin E. 1991. Food refusal in prison. *Medicine, Science and the Law* 31(1):41–44.

Miles S. 2014. Testimony of Dr. Steve Miles, *Dhiab v. Obama*. United States District Court for the District of Columbia. Transcript of Motion Hearing Proceedings Before the Honorable Gladys Kessler, United States District Court Judge, Tuesday, October 7, 2014 10:00 a.m.

McNabb v. Dep't of Corr., 163 Wash 2d 393; 180 P3d 1257 (2008).

O'Connor A and E Johnson-Sabine. 1988. Hunger strikers. *Medicine, Science and the Law* 28(1):62–64.

Oguz NY and S Miles. 2005. The physician and prison hunger strikes: Reflecting on the experience in Turkey. *Journal of Medical Ethics* 31:169–172.

Ohm TM. 2006. What they can do about it: Prison administrators' authority to force-feed hunger-striking inmates. *Journal of Law and Policy* 23:151.

Reyes H. 1998. Medical and ethical aspects of hunger strikes in custody and the issue of torture. *Geneva: International Committee of the Red Cross*, https://www.icrc.org/eng/resources/documents/article/other/health-article-010198.htm, accessed August 8, 2016.

Reyes H, SA Allen, and GJ Annas. 2013. Physicians and hunger strikes in prison: Confrontation, manipulation, medicalization and medical ethics (part 1). *World Medical Journal* 59:27–36.

Robinson S and HZ Winnik. 1973. Severe psychotic disturbances following crash diet weight loss. *Archives of General Psychiatry* 29:559–562.

Rubenstein LS and GJ Annas. 2009. Medical ethics at Guantanamo Bay detention center and in the US military: A time for reform. *The Lancet* 374(9686):353–355.

Simanowitz S. 2012. The enduring power of the hunger strike. *The Africa Report*. http://www.theafricareport.com/Columns/the-enduring-power-of-the-hunger-strike.html, accessed November 30, 2015.

World Medical Association. Declaration on Hunger Strikers. 1991, 1992, 2006. World Medical Association. Last revised by the 57th World Medical Assembly, Pilanesburg in South Africa. http://www.wma.net/en/30publications/10policies/h31/, accessed August 8, 2016.

Zant v. Prevatte, 248 Ga. 832, 286 S.E.2d 715 (1982).

PART 7

Aggression and Violence

WILLIAM NEWMAN

59

Antisocial personality disorder and psychopathy

ANTHONY MADEN AND WILLIAM NEWMAN

INTRODUCTION

Antisocial personality disorder (ASPD) is the term in the *Diagnostic and Statistical Manual of Mental Disorders*, fifth edition (*DSM-5*). The preferred term in the *International Classification of Diseases*, 10th revision (*ICD-10*) is dissocial personality disorder. The main distinction is that ASPD requires a history of childhood conduct disorder. For most purposes, the terms can be considered synonymous, and ASPD will be used throughout this chapter. Antisocial personality disorder is fairly common, with a community prevalence of 2%–3% and a massive 60% among male prisoners (Moran 1999). The implication of the latter figure is that ASPD is statistically the norm in many correctional facilities and for individuals working with offenders.

Except where otherwise indicated, the term *psychopathy* denotes the condition as operationally defined by Hare and as measured by the *Psychopathy Checklist, Revised* (Hare 2003). The prevalence of psychopathy has been measured at about 0.6% in the general population (Coid et al. 2009). The prevalence of psychopathy in prison populations is in the range of 15%–20% (Hare 1991).

Of the personality disorders, psychopathy is most commonly linked to individuals meeting criteria for antisocial and narcissistic personality disorders (Blackburn et al. 2003). Though many conceptualize psychopathy as a severe subset of ASPD, that is an oversimplification. Many individuals meet criteria for ASPD without meeting criteria for psychopathy. Another group meet criteria for psychopathy without meeting criteria for ASPD. Babiak and Hare (2007) describe individuals they termed "snakes in suits," the psychopath who integrates into the workforce and can wreak havoc, often without developing a criminal record.

BRIEF HISTORY OF ASPD AND PSYCHOPATHY

The historical origins of ASPD and psychopathy are typically traced back to Prichard's (1835) concept of moral insanity, which he defined as a disorder of the "feelings temper and habits" in the absence of cognitive impairment, delusions, or hallucinations, such that the individual is "incapable of conducting himself with decency and propriety in the business of life" (p. 15). When Prichard wrote in 1837, his patients would have included many with organic conditions who would not today be regarded as having ASPD or psychopathy. However, his notion of a man lacking the usual signs and symptoms of mental illness but nevertheless being incapable of following normal social conventions is remarkably close to modern ideas of ASPD and psychopathy.

Whatever the term has been used to describe it over the years, the concept of psychopathy has inescapable moral overtones. The uneasy interface between medicine and morality was recognized by Maudsley in 1874 when he observed that moral insanity "has so much the look of vice or crime that many people regard it as an unfounded medical intervention." In other words, it is difficult or impossible to distinguish criminality from psychopathy.

Moral insanity was widely accepted by U.S. and European Courts of Law throughout the latter part of the nineteenth century. It was later supplanted by the concept of psychopathic inferiority, coined by Koch (1891), who attributed the problem to "a congenital or acquired inferiority of brain constitution." Despite the archaic terminology, Koch deserves a mention because he argued against punishment in favor of special institutions for such individuals, an argument that remains pertinent over 100 years later and was actually implemented by the United Kingdom in its Dangerous and Severe Personality Disorder (DSPD) program, discussed later in this chapter.

Henderson (1939) was influential in shaping the modern concept of ASPD by defining individuals who "throughout their lives exhibit disorders of conduct of an antisocial or asocial nature." At around the same time, Cleckley (1941) established the concept of a psychopathic personality with core criteria relating to antisocial behavior. Cleckley was particularly influential because of his emphasis on the fact that ASPD was not found only in criminals. Cleckley showed that, although there may be a massive overlap between ASPD and offending, the association is not absolute. Cleckley's views were particularly influential on *DSM* and *ICD* classifications of personality disorder. They also influenced Hare (1991) in his development of an operationally defined concept of psychopathy.

We continue to struggle with these issues because they are insoluble. Morality and science are different, but equally valid, ways of approaching the same problem. The funding of scientific research in the field is to a large extent driven by the social and moral ramifications of a condition that is associated with violence and other offending behavior. The World Health Organization (Krug et al. 2002) rightly describes violence as "a universal scourge that tears at the fabric of communities." ASPD and psychopathy are the mental disorders most strongly associated with violent offending. These disorders are of scientific interest partly because of their moral connotations and unfortunate legal outcomes.

MEASUREMENT AND THE PSYCHOPATHY CHECKLIST

Hare refined and operationalized Cleckley's notions of a psychopathic personality to construct the 20-item Psychopathy Checklist (Hare 1991, Hare 2003). Each item is scored between 0 and 2, giving a range of total scores of 0–40. A score of 30 and above (often modified to 25 and above outside the United States) is the most commonly used cut-off to establish psychopathy. Hare has presented a two-factor and four-factor model over the years to characterize the items on the Hare Psychopathy Check List-Revised (PCL-R) (Harpur et al. 1989; Neumann et al. 2007). The four-factor model was essentially derived from the two-factor model (Figure 59.1).

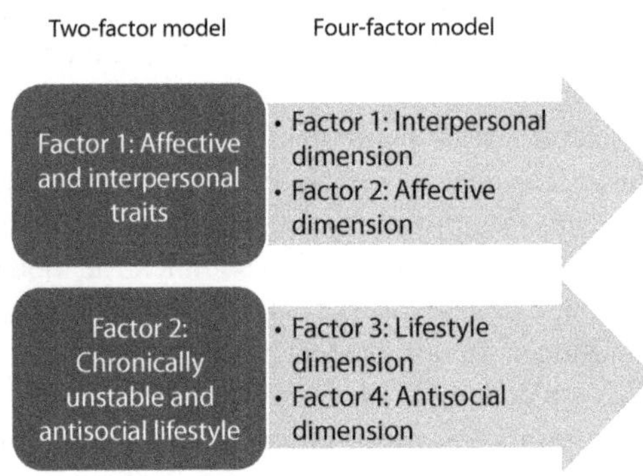

Figure 59.1 Transition from Hare's two-factor model to four-factor model of psychopathy.

Hare's work represented a major advance in the field because, for the first time, it was possible to reliably measure the degree or severity of psychopathy—and, by extension, some forms of ASPD. Before the advent of the PCL-R, the concept of psychopathy had become discredited because of the looseness of the definition and its pejorative overtones. The advent of a reliable, standardized measure rescued psychopathy from becoming no more than a lay term of abuse and rehabilitated it as a scientific concept.

At this point, psychiatric diagnoses are defined mainly by their symptoms. The problem in the case of psychopathy is that a large part of the symptomatology consists of aggressive and irresponsible behavior. The PCL-R has not solved this problem, but it has at least allowed us to measure and assess the symptoms more reliably. The first step in any process of scientific understanding is that of measurement.

The other major advance represented by the PCL-R was its recognition that, in individuals with ASPD, self-report will often be unreliable. Until the PCL-R came along, most standardized assessments of personality or personality disorder had relied on self-report. Hare argued that self-report was particularly unreliable in the case of an individual with psychopathy, so the PCL-R relies on the use of historical records as well as direct observations at interview.

The PCL-R has been extensively validated against various measures, and there are now norms for the general population as well as for offender and mental health populations. Table 59.1 lists some of the pertinent studies that have assessed the predictive utility of the PCL-R. Hare's website (http://www.hare.org) frequently updates a list of published studies pertinent to the PCL-R.

Table 59.1 Sample of pertinent studies that have established predictive utility of the PCL-R

Author(s)	Year	Publication	Brief summary
Hemphill et al.	1998	*Legal and Criminological Psychology*	Reported on utility of PCL-R compared to other predictive factors
Hare et al.	2000	*Behavioral Sciences and the Law*	Compared international samples to North American samples, where most of the early studies occurred
Skeem and Mulvey	2001	*Journal of Consulting and Clinical Psychology*	Removed nonspecific antisocial behaviors from analyses relating psychopathy and violence
Tengstrom et al.	2004	*Criminal Justice and Behavior*	PCL-R maintained predictive utility after controlling for variables
Weizmann-Henelius et al.	2015	*The Journal of Forensic Psychiatry and Psychology*	Assessed predictive validity of PCL-R for violent recidivism in female offenders

RECENT DEVELOPMENTS IN THE TREATMENT OF ASPD AND PSYCHOPATHY

The fundamental problem is that the concepts of psychopathy and ASPD apply to people who break the rules despite being fully aware of them. As a result, such people are often subject to censure or punishment. Mental health personnel have often held attitudes toward ASPD that are ambivalent at best and sometimes frankly hostile. It came to be known as a diagnosis of exclusion, at times reserved for patients considered unlikable for staff. In recognition of this phenomenon, the U.K. government developed a document titled: "Personality disorder: No longer a diagnosis of exclusion," as a sign of its determination to remedy the problem (Snowden and Kane 2003).

The origins of the negative attitudes toward the diagnosis of ASPD can be seen in the history of the concept, which from the beginning has had moral connotations. The diagnostic label can be viewed by some as an attempt to justify antisocial or aggressive behavior and provide offenders with a built-in excuse or mitigation. As noted above, that dilemma is not new and in some ways minimally changed since Maudsley's 1874 comment about the impossibility of distinguishing this particular medical diagnosis from bad behavior.

The challenge to clinicians is to develop pragmatic ways of negotiating these dilemmas. Mental health services often argue that individuals with ASPD would be better placed in correctional institutions, while the latter may expect psychiatry to relieve them of the burden of dealing with the most seriously personality disordered individuals. One of the issues to be addressed in treatment of personality disorder is how to judge the outcome. Some critics are dismissive of offending rates as a measure of success because many core features of the personality disorder may remain unchanged. This chapter considers an attempt in the United Kingdom to expand the role of mental health services in dealing with severe ASPD as an example of attempting to develop a system to address this issue.

OFFENDING BEHAVIOR PROGRAMS

Prisons and other correctional services can be characterized historically as swinging between the extremes of the rehabilitative ideal on one hand and therapeutic nihilism on the other. There is a tendency either to have unrealistic expectations of the extent to which offenders can be reformed, or to be unduly pessimistic and to reduce prisons to the function of locking up and counting their inmates.

The application of cognitive behavioral principles to the development of offending behavior programs (OBPs) represents one way forward. OBPs can be incorporated into an ordinary prison or probation regime, although most commentators suggest OBPs are more likely to be successful if the regime also fosters prosocial behaviors. There is now a vast literature on OBPs, which falls outside the scope of this chapter. McGuire (1995) serves as a good introduction to the field. Craig et al. (2013) is more up to date and includes a paper by McGuire on developments in the area since his original contribution.

OBPs are not framed in medical terms, so interventions primarily occur in response to types of repeated offending. Most of the program participants would probably meet criteria for ASPD (and possibly psychopathy), though the target of treatment remains offending behavior rather than personality.

Overall, the results from OBPs are encouraging, with significant reductions in recidivism rates. OBPs have proliferated because of their results and the fact that they are heavily manualized. Staff can be trained to deliver them in a fairly short time, and they can often be delivered partly or wholly to groups. All this increases efficiency in an area where the large number of potential candidates and tight budgetary constraints make cost a major issue.

There are several potential issues when enrolling individuals with ASPD and psychopathy in OBPs. The first problem is that because OBPs do not usually incorporate a diagnostic framework, it can be difficult to generalize findings. The encouraging figures for overall success rates may not apply to those with more severe personality disorders. A persistent question by some authors has been the extent to which such programs are effective in individuals with psychopathy (Wong et al. 2006).

In fact, we know that the higher the psychopathy score, the less likely it is that OBPs will succeed in reducing re-offending rates. Some colleagues have even suggested that treatment may increase re-offending rates in those with high PCL-R scores. That has not been confirmed, but these individuals are more likely to drop out of treatment, to subvert a program, or to fail to respond. As Wong and Hare (2005) noted, the wrong treatment is likely to make psychopaths worse.

Attempts to identify the right treatment have so far attempted to adapt the CBT principles of OBPs while making the delivery more intensive and safeguarding against attempts to subvert, divert, or otherwise undermine it. A good example is the U.K. Prison Service's Chromis Programme for high-risk offenders with high levels of psychopathy (Tew and Atkinson 2013). Motivation is also a central issue, with general agreement that any progress is likely to require collaboration. The principle of enlightened self-interest has been put forward as a way of encouraging narcissistic and self-centred individuals who may be encouraged to become more prosocial. The problem is that the principle only comes into play at a fairly late stage, when offenders have begun to suffer serious punishments in response to serious offending. In public health terms, there is a sense about such programs that they may offer too little, too late, and at too great a cost.

THE DUTCH TBS SYSTEM

The Dutch TBS system has a history of looking after violent and sexual offenders since 1928 (de Boer and Gerrits 2007). TBS is an acronym for a Dutch term that translates as "at the disposal of the government," which summarizes the position in which the offender–patients find themselves. The system is based on a legal provision that allows a court to order that certain categories of convicted offenders will serve the prison term warranted by their offence, before going on to a TBS institution for a mandated program of treatment. Detention within the TBS facility is indefinite, subject to regular review by a tribunal. The later stages of compulsory treatment and supervision will be in less secure facilities and eventually in the community, if and when suitable progress is made.

The TBS system seemingly overcomes the difficulties created by ASPD being used as an excuse for criminality because it allows the court first to deliver punishment before mandating treatment. Critics would argue that the additional period of detention in the TBS service amounts to further punishment, but the system is widely accepted in the Netherlands. In fact, most criticism is centered on the possibility that offenders may move through the system too quickly, rather than that their civil liberties are infringed upon. The ethical questions considered with the TBS system are similar to those considered with sexually violent predator (SVP) laws in the United States (Sreenivasan et al. 2010).

As with OBPs, the TBS system is based on offending and risk rather than diagnosis. Holland has no life sentence and TBS is part of the alternative. In practice, the TBS system treats offenders with a range of diagnoses, but many have ASPD or psychopathy. It uses a range of treatments, mostly delivered by psychologists or specially trained therapists. CBT has become the predominant psychological treatment in recent years. In addition, there is a strong vocational element, with workshops and other employment facilities of a comparable standard to those in the outside world. These vocational aspects are considered to be of at least equal importance, alongside psychotherapy, and they generally take up more of the patient's week. Medical input is largely restricted to prescribing antilibidinal or other medications, the latter including antidepressants and antipsychotics for the mentally ill.

The TBS system was not developed with a particular diagnosis in mind, but it highlights themes that emerge whenever services attempt to treat ASPD and psychopathy. First, it is a long-term endeavor; after 6 years' detention, 20% of patients are deemed unlikely ever to be discharged to the community. Second, the goal is safe management in the community rather than cure; those who are discharged remain subject to long-term, mandatory supervision. It may be that the service's successes owe as much, if not more, to prolonged supervision as to any intervention within the institution. Third, the treatment of comorbid disorders such as depression, substance misuse, and paraphilia is central to risk reduction.

U.K.'S DANGEROUS AND SEVERE PERSONALITY DISORDER (DSPD) INITIATIVE

The origins of the U.K.'s DSPD system reflect a major problem arising from a strict, dichotomous approach to punishment versus treatment as a response to offending by those with ASPD and psychopathy. The problem was that an approach that focused on punishment did not adequately address issues of continuing risk. The DSPD service grew out of a concern that mentally disordered offenders with severe ASPD or psychopathy were being released at the end of lengthy sentences with their problems unaddressed and their risks unchanged.

After a series of high-profile cases of re-offending in these circumstances (mainly a series of killings by predatory pedophiles who also met criteria for psychopathy) (Oliver and Smith 1993), the United Kingdom in 1999 allocated a substantial sum of money to setting up 300 high-secure beds for the treatment of men with a dangerous and severe personality disorder. The planning of the service was influenced by Hare's concept of psychopathy and used a PCL-R score as a guideline for admission, making DSPD similar to psychopathy. In effect, the program was an experiment in the treatment or management of psychopathy.

The most controversial aspect of the service was that half of the 300 beds were to be in highly secure hospitals, where patients would be detained for treatment under the U.K.'s Mental Health Act. The overwhelming weight of psychiatric advice was against the idea, which amounted to a heavy-handed attempt to legislate an instant solution to dilemmas about the management of psychopathy that had troubled clinicians for nearly 200 years.

The other essential ingredient of the government's strategy involved providing considerable resources. Each hospital bed cost around $600,000 per year and the minimum stay was predicted to be at least 2 years. With hindsight, it is apparent that the service was able to develop only because it came at the time of the credit-fueled bubble that preceded the 2008 financial crisis.

Treatment in psychiatric hospitals was particularly problematic. One of the major clinical issues is that hospitals operate according to a medical model that often involves taking away responsibility from a patient, particularly during the more severe phases of an illness. This removal of responsibility is recognized as problematic in all areas of psychiatry, hence the attempt to emphasize rehabilitation or recovery in patients with psychotic illnesses. The medical model is even more problematic in ASPD, where one of the basic problems is that the individual fails to accept responsibility for his actions. The problem is made worse by a system that further encourages the individual to give up responsibility. Patients within the hospitals rapidly develop the expectation that it was the hospital's job to make them better, rather than something they could achieve in collaboration.

The other problem involved deciding what treatment should be administered. The choice was cognitive behavioral therapy, similar to the OBPs. The reasons included a good evidence base for ethicacy; a tight, well-defined structure to the treatment that minimized problems when dealing with psychopathic individuals; and the fact that the treatments can be delivered (relatively) efficiently. The potential cost savings were negated by the massive costs of a highly secure bed.

At the beginning, there was a general concern about whether individuals with psychopathy could or would benefit from treatment. As in other attempts to treat high-risk individuals, these concerns were addressed by making the treatment intensive, giving a lot of emphasis to program integrity and staff supervision, and choosing the correct, tailored intervention. It was recognized, for example, that there is no point in teaching skills to those individuals who have no deficits in that area and would be likely to use any new skill in a manipulative and antisocial way.

In fact, a bigger problem proved to be the delivery of treatment rather than its content. An evaluation of the service showed that a relatively small amount of the time spent in an expensive institution involved meaningful therapeutic work. Burns et al. (2011) found that actual levels of treatment delivery were far below what was intended, whether because of the difficulties of working with these particular individuals, the difficulties of working in institutions not used to providing intensive psychological treatment, or both.

The service for DSPD opened in 2004 and closed soon thereafter, in 2010. Howells et al. (2007) described some of the challenges the program faced. Tyrer et al. (2009a,b) focused on the difficulties of selecting a tiny number of patients from a large pool of potential candidates. The DSPD program commissioned several evaluations of outcomes, with disappointing results. At best, the DSPD program was an expensive way of achieving a small amount of psychological change in a small proportion of the patients admitted to the service—who themselves composed only a small proportion of high-risk offenders.

The DSPD service was expensive because it involved a long stay in either a hospital or a high-security prison. It illustrates one of the dilemmas in treating ASPD and psychopathy. ASPD is common in offender populations. Correctional systems must therefore decide whether to devote resources to the intensive treatment of a small number of very high-risk individuals, or to give a less-intense treatment to a much greater number, including many who pose lower levels of risk.

As a general principle, there is much greater potential for achieving the benefit of risk reduction if one begins with higher-risk individuals. But even assuming the intended reductions can be achieved, the highest-risk individuals may not be able to make much progress through the system, largely because of the offences they have already committed. Deciding how to approach this problem remains a dilemma.

Closing the DSPD program was followed by a new emphasis on psychological treatment within the U.K.'s prisons, much more along the lines of conventional OBPs. The aim was to develop psychologically informed planned environments (PIPEs). They are specifically designed prison environments where staff members have additional training to develop an increased psychological understanding of their work. The units have activities with the potential to maintain gains made in other interventions, i.e., to support OBPs. The main aim is to get around the problem that confronts many treatment programs in prison. After leaving the therapy room, the individual has to return to an ordinary prison environment where attitudes and behavior are often the opposite of the prosocial standards taught during treatment. OBPs work partly by reducing the factors that lead to antisocial attitudes and behavior, but also by encouraging and facilitating prosocial behavior. Each arm of the treatment depends on the other.

TREATMENT OF ASPD AND PSYCHOPATHY

The DSPD project is largely considered a failure in terms of its stated objective of providing public protection by improving the treatment of dangerous offenders with severe personality disorders. It did, however, have a number of incidental benefits, one of which was to raise the general profile of personality disorder and personality disorder services in the United Kingdom. In turn, it led the National Institute for Clinical Excellence (NICE) to publish guidelines on the treatment, management, and prevention of antisocial personality disorder. NICE is a government body that produces guidance for clinicians in all fields of medicine. Just a few years earlier, it would have been unthinkable for NICE to produce a medical guideline in the field of ASPD.

The NICE guideline is divided into six sections, with one devoted to the treatment of ASPD and comorbidity and one devoted to psychopathy and severe personality disorders. The other four sections concern general principles in approaching ASPD: prevention; assessment and risk management; and the organization and planning of services. It reflects the state of our knowledge that a treatment guideline should have so much emphasis on aspects other than treatment. Unfortunately, there remains little to say about how to effectively "treat" the core features of ASPD and psychopathy.

As a result, the section on treatment emphasizes mainly the treatment of comorbid disorders such as drug and alcohol misuse or other psychiatric disorders such as depression. It is acknowledged that treatment of the core syndrome is problematic and may not be possible, but the overall situation, not to mention the associated risks, may be greatly improved by treating comorbid problems. Hence, despite the underlying pessimism about changing the personality disorder itself, there is some encouragement of an optimistic and positive attitude toward treatment. The rationale is that by successfully treating problems such as drug or alcohol misuse, the quality of life and risk of offending may be dramatically reduced. The point is often made that even more serious offenders spend most of their waking hours in activities other than offending. One aim of treatment is to increase the proportion of time spent not offending, and that can be achieved without actually treating the underlying personality deficits.

Current treatment recommendations in the literature for addressing ASPD and psychopathy are largely in line with the NICE guidelines described above. The greater the degree of psychopathy, the more difficult it is to deliver treatment and the lower the chances of success. There is no easy way around this problem, and most attempts focus on delivering intensive treatment; increasing motivation and compliance; and preventing subversion or drift in treatment. Once comorbid disorders have been addressed, management of the underlying personality disorder is often a long-term task in which the outcome is likely to depend as much on support and supervision in the community as on any specific intervention. The nature of the latter task has been nicely encapsulated by Tyrer and Bajaj (2005) in nidotherapy; it is acknowledged that the core aspects of the personality disorder will persist, and the task of the clinicians is to create an environment in which it is contained or cocooned so as to maximize quality of life and minimize risks to others.

Prediction is always difficult, but it seems unlikely that there will be any dramatic breakthrough in the social or psychological management of ASPD or psychopathy in the near future. The most likely scenario is that we will see greater refinement and extension of CBT techniques. So far, there is no sign of any pharmacological breakthrough either, except insofar as medication assists with comorbid disorders or provides symptomatic assistance in managing traits such as irritability and paranoia. It is not surprising, therefore, that when we look at future directions for research, the main focus is on the underlying organic abnormalities and early intervention.

RESEARCH INTO PSYCHOPATHY AND ASPD

A major problem is that psychopathy almost certainly encompasses a range of underlying conditions rather than a single entity. Studies of the brain have already found structural and functional correlates for impulsivity as well as for cold, calculating behavior.

A second issue is that much of the research in this area has been conceptualized not in diagnostic terms, but with reference to antisocial behavior or offending. The subjects may or may not meet the criteria for psychopathy, and it is not a straightforward matter to integrate the findings. When looking at the origins of antisocial behavior in childhood, the term *psychopathy* is avoided as a matter of principle, although studies are beginning to identify the importance of early deficits in empathy (Rowe et al. 2010; Blair et al. 2014).

In addition to the development of the PCL-R, there was an expansion of high-quality longitudinal studies, an early example being the Cambridge Study in Delinquent Development, the results of which are summarized in Farrington (1995). These cohort studies represent a massive commitment of time and resources, but they have gotten around the sampling problems that limited the usefulness of cross-sectional research. Some of the findings are stunning, such as a statistically significant continuity between behavior at the age of 3 and adult criminality (Stevenson and Goodman 2001).

DEVELOPMENTAL STUDIES

There is impressive continuity of antisocial behavior throughout the life span, yet at the same time the prevalence of offending changes dramatically with age. In the Cambridge study, three-quarters of juvenile offenders were convicted again between the ages of 17 and 24; and half were reconvicted between the ages of 25 and 32. At the same time, there was a dramatic decrease in offending after the peak age of 17. By the age of 32, a mere 6% of the Cambridge study's sample accounted for 50% of all the offending. Robbins (1966) found much the same in the United States.

The paradox was resolved by Moffitt (1993), who used the longitudinal Dunedin study to identify adolescence-limited and lifetime-persistent antisocial behavior. The latter group accounts for 5%–10% of the male juvenile offender population. They are more likely to have neurological problems. A detailed account of these studies falls outside the scope of this chapter, but there is bound to be considerable overlap between lifetime persistent offenders and adults with high psychopathy scores. Future research is likely to lead to greater integration between these areas.

PSYCHOPATHY AND THE NERVOUS SYSTEM

Much of the research on psychopathy and the nervous system has focused on demonstrating that parts of the brain are either under- or overfunctioning in psychopaths, or are under- or overdeveloped compared to the rest of the population. Raine's review (2013) makes it clear that the observed differences are many and varied.

For example, Raine et al. (1997) found evidence of reduced prefrontal function in murderers compared to controls. Soderstrom et al. (2000) found reduced blood flow in the hippocampal region in violent offenders with elevated psychopathy scores. Muller et al. (2003) reported similar findings. Reduced functioning in another brain region, the posterior cingulate gyrus, has been found in adult criminal psychopaths (Kiehl et al. 2001). Other brain regions with abnormal functioning include the superior temporal gyrus (Kiehl et al. 2004) and the amygdala (Glenn et al. 2009). A good case is made for structural and functional correlates of traits such as irritability, impulsivity, and aggression, although lacking any neat one-to-one correspondence.

The complexities in this area are perhaps best illustrated by Raine's (2013) discussion of the fact that his own brain scan resembles that of a serial killer, albeit a well-organized and careful man who planned his killings meticulously. Both show good frontal lobe function, consistent with planning and organizational abilities. Raine concludes that normal people may have abnormal scans, and that the killer may be the exception that proves the rule. Certainly, one message is that there are no simple answers, and perhaps none would have been expected given the complexity of the issues under consideration. It may also be, however, that the information available to us so far misses the point. Two people have similar brain scans because they are both methodical planners, but that does not explain why one devotes his talents to an academic career while the other becomes a sadistic, serial sexual killer.

The differences between psychopaths and others are not limited to the esoteric field of brain abnormalities. A consistent finding is that low resting heart rate correlates with antisocial behavior in children and adults. Prospective longitudinal studies have also shown that low heart rate in childhood is a reliable predictor of later delinquent, criminal, and violent behavior. Farrington (1997) reported that of 48 potential early predictors of later convictions for violence, only two were reliable predictors independently of all other risk factors: low resting heart rate and poor concentration. The relationship has been so reliably identified that it has even been proposed that low heart rate could be considered as a biomarker for the diagnosis of conduct disorder in children and adolescents (Moffitt et al. 2008).

The most plausible explanation is that the low heart rate is a proxy measure for a low level of autonomic arousal, leading to increased sensation-seeking behavior. Alternatively, the low heart rate may represent relative fearlessness, and it has also demonstrated that children with low heart rates are less empathic than those with high ones. In related work, Gao et al. (2010) demonstrated that early impairment in autonomic fear conditioning predicts adult criminality.

SUMMARY

This chapter presents a glimpse of the empirical work on the developmental and neurological correlates of antisocial behavior, ASPD, and psychopathy. Many of the findings are correlational rather than causal, and it is important to keep a sense of perspective. Nevertheless, it is interesting to juxtapose this work with that on treatment. The lack of progress in treatment of the more severe forms of ASPD contrasts starkly with the rapidity with which organic correlates are being identified. Perhaps this is no coincidence and the reason for the difficulty of treating psychopathy and severe ASPD is that it is so firmly embedded in developmental and other abnormalities of the nervous system.

SUMMARY KEY POINTS

- Hare's development of the PCL-R allowed an individual's degree of psychopathy to be reliably measured.
- Although we have learned a lot about psychopathy since the concept was first introduced, the mental health system still has few answers about beneficial treatment options.
- The National Institute for Clinical Excellence (NICE) published useful guidelines to help with the management of ASPD and psychopathy.
- Much of the ongoing research on psychopathy focuses on developmental factors and potential early interventions during childhood.

REFERENCES

Babiak P and RD Hare. 2007. *Snakes in Suits: When Psychopaths to Work*. New York: HarperCollins.

Blackburn R, C Logan, J Donnelly, and S Renwick. 2003. Personality disorders, psychopathy and other mental disorders: Co-morbidity among patients at English and Scottish high-security hospitals. *Journal of Forensic Psychiatry and Psychology* 14:111–137.

Blair RJR, E Leibenluft, and DS Pine. 2014. Conduct disorder and callous-unemotional traits in youth. *New England Journal of Medicine* 371:2207–2216.

de Boer J and J Gerrits. 2007. Learning from Holland: The TBS system. *Psychiatry* 6(11): 459–461.

Burns T, J Yiend, T Fahy, R Fitzpatrick, R Rogers, S Fazel, and J Sinclair. 2011. Treatments for dangerous, severe personality disorders. *Journal of Forensic Psychiatry and Psychology* 22:411–426.

Cleckley H. 1941. *The Mask of Sanity*. St. Louis: Mosby.

Coid J, M Yang, S Ullrich, A Roberts, and RD Hare. 2009. Prevalence and correlates of psychopathic traits in the household population of Great Britain. *International Journal of Law and Psychiatry* 32(2):65–73.

Craig LA, TA Gannon, and L Dixon. 2013. *What Works in Offender Rehabilitation: An Evidence-Based Approach to Assessment and Treatment*. Hoboken, NJ: Wiley-Blackwell.

Farrington DP. 1995. The development of offending and antisocial behavior from childhood: Key findings from the Cambridge study in delinquent development. *Journal of Child Psychology and Psychiatry and Allied Disciplines* 36:929–964.

Farrington DP. 1997. The relationship between low resting heart rate and violence. In *Biosocial Bases of Violence*. edited by A Raine, PA Brennan, DP Farrington, and SA Mednick, New York: Plenum, 89–106.

Gao Y, A Raine, PH Venables, ME Dawson, and SA Mednik. 2010. Association of poor childhood fear conditioning in adult crime. *American Journal of Psychiatry* 167(1):56–60.

Glenn AL, A Raine, and RA Schug. 2009. The neural correlates of moral decision-making in psychopathy. *Molecular Psychiatry* 14(1):5–6.

Hare RD. 1991. *The Hare Psychopathy Checklist-Revised.* Toronto, ON: Multi-Health Systems.

Hare RD. 2003. *The Hare Psychopathy Checklist-Revised.* 2nd edition. Toronto, ON: Multi-Health Systems.

Hare RD, D Clark, M Grann, and D Thornton. 2000. Psychopathy and the predictive validity of the PCL-R: An international perspective. *Behavioural Sciences and the Law* 18:623–645.

Harpur TJ, RD Hare, and AR Hakstian. 1989. Two-factor conceptualization of psychopathy: Construct validity and assessment implications. *Psychological Assessment* 1(1):6–17.

Hemphill JF, RD Hare, and S Wong. 1998. Psychopathy and recidivism: A review. *Legal and Criminological Psychology* 3:139–170.

Henderson DK. 1939. *Psychopathic States.* New York: Norton.

Howells K, G Krishan, and M Daffern. 2007. Challenges in the treatment of dangerous and severe personality disorder. *Advances in Psychiatric Treatment* 13:325–332.

Kiehl KA, AM Smith, RD Hare, A Mendrek, BB Forster, J Brink, and PF Liddle. 2001. Limbic abnormalities in affective processing by criminal psychopaths as revealed by functional magnetic resonance imaging. *Biological Psychiatry* 50:677–684.

Kiehl KA, AM Smith, A Mendrek, BB Forster, RD Hare, and PF Liddle. 2004. Temporal lobe abnormalities in semantic processing by criminal psychopaths as revealed by functional magnetic resonance imaging. *Psychiatry Research: Neuroimaging* 130:295–312.

Koch JLA. 1891. *Die Psychopathischen Minderwerigkeiten (Psychopathic Inferiorities).* Ravensburg: Dorn.

Krug EG, LL Dahlberg, JA Mercy, AB Zwi, and R Lozano. 2002. World report on violence and health. World Health Organization: Geneva.

Maudsley H. 1874. *Responsibility in Mental Disease.* London: Keegan Paul Trench.

McGuire J. 1995. *What Works: Reducing Reoffending: Guidelines from Research and Practice.* Hoboken, NJ: Wiley-Blackwell.

Moffitt TE. 1993. Adolescence-limited and life-course-persistent antisocial behavior: A developmental taxonomy. *Psychological Review* 100:674–701.

Moffitt TE, L Arsreneault, SR Jaffee, J Kim-Cohen, KC Koenen, CL Odgers, WS Slutske, and E Viding. 2008. Research review: DSM-V conduct disorder: Research needs for an evidence base. *Journal of Child Psychology and Psychiatry and Allied Disciplines* 49(1):3–33.

Moran P. 1999. The epidemiology of antisocial personality disorder. *Social Psychiatry and Psychiatric Epidemiology* 34(5):231–242.

Muller JL, M Sommer, V Wagner, K Lange, H Taschler, CH Roder, G Schuierer, HE Klein, and G Hajak. 2003. Abnormalities in emotion processing within cortical and subcortical regions in criminal psychopaths: Evidence from a functional magnetic resonance imaging study using pictures with emotional content. *Biological Psychiatry* 54(2):152–162.

Neumann CS, RD Hare, and JP Newman. 2007. The superordinate nature of the Psychopathy Checklist-Revised. *Journal of Personality Disorders* 21(2):102–117.

Oliver T and R Smith. 1993. *Lambs to the Slaughter.* London: Time Warner.

Prichard JC. 1835. *Treatise on Insanity and Other Disorders Affecting the Mind.* Philadelphia: Carey and Hart.

Raine A. 2013. *The Anatomy of Violence.* New York: Vintage Books.

Raine A, MS Buchsbaum, and L LaCasse. 1997. Brain abnormalities in murderers indicated by positron emission tomography. *Biological Psychiatry* 42:495–508.

Robbins LN. 1966. *Deviant Children Grown Up.* Baltimore: Williams and Wilkins.

Rowe R, B Maughan, P Moran, T Ford, J Briskman, and R Goodman. 2010. The role of callous and unemotional traits in the diagnosis of conduct disorder. *Journal of Child Psychology and Psychiatry and Allied Disciplines* 51(6):688–695.

Skeem JL and EP Mulvey. 2001. Psychopathy and community violence among civil psychiatric patients: Results from the MacArthur Violence Risk Assessment Study. *Journal of Consulting and Clinical Psychology* 69:358–374.

Snowden P and E Kane. 2003. Personality disorder: No longer a diagnosis of exclusion. *Psychiatrist* 11:401–403.

Soderstrom H, M Tullberg, C Wikkelsö, S Ekholm, and A Forsman. 2000. Reduced regional cerebral blood flow in non-psychotic violent offenders. *Psychiatry Research* 98(1):29–41.

Sreenivasan S, A Frances, and LE Weinberger. 2010. Normative versus consequential ethics in sexually violent predator laws: An ethics conundrum for psychiatry. *Journal of the American Academy of Psychiatry and the Law* 38(3):386–391.

Stevenson J and R Goodman. 2001. Association between behavior at age 3 years and adult criminality. *British Journal of Psychiatry* 179:197–202.

Tengstrom A, S Hodgins, M Grann, N Langstrom, and G Kullgren. 2004. Schizophrenia and criminal offending: The role of psychopathy and substance misuse. *Criminal Justice and Behaviour* 31:1–25.

Tew J and R Atkinson. 2013. The Chromis programme: From conception to evaluation. *Psychology, Crime and Law* 19:415–431.

Tyrer PJ and P Bajaj. 2005. Nidotherapy: Making the environment do the therapeutic work. *Advances in Psychiatric Treatment* 11:232–238

Tyrer PJ, S Cooper, D Rutter, H Seivewright, C Duggan, A Maden, B Barrett, E Joyce, B Rao, U Nur, D Cicchetti, M Crawford, and S Byford. 2009a. The assessment of dangerous and severe personality disorder: Lessons from a randomised controlled trial linked to qualitative analysis. *Journal of Forensic Psychiatry and Psychology* 20:132–146.

Tyrer PJ, S Cooper, D Rutter et al. 2009b. Critique of the assessment phase of the DSPD programme. *Journal of Forensic Psychiatry and Psychology* 20:151–154.

Weizmann-Henelius G, M Virkkunen, M Gammelgard, M Eronen, and H Putkonnen. 2015. The PCL-R and violent recidivism in a prospective follow-up of a nationwide sample of female offenders. *The Journal of Forensic Psychiatry and Psychology* 26:667–685.

Wong SCP and RD Hare. 2005. *Guidelines for a Psychopathy Treatment Programme*. Toronto, ON: Multi-Health Systems.

Wong SCP, TD Witte, A Gordon, D Gu, and K Lewis. 2006. Can a treatment program designed primarily for violent risk reduction reduce recidivism in psychopaths? *Canadian Psychology* 47:211.

60

Clinical assessment of aggression and violence

CHARLES L. SCOTT AND PHILLIP J. RESNICK

INTRODUCTION

The majority of those with mental illness are not violent. However, individuals with mental illness are at an increased risk for aggression compared to the general population (Swanson et al. 1990). With understandable concerns about the potential relationship of mental illness to violence, clinicians are increasingly asked to evaluate a person's risk of future dangerousness in various situations. These situations may include involuntary commitments, emergency psychiatric evaluations, seclusion and restraint release decisions, inpatient care discharges, probation/parole decisions, death penalty evaluations, domestic violence interventions, and fitness-for-duty evaluations.

Unfortunately, no interview or psychological test can predict future violence with high accuracy. Relatively infrequent events (e.g., homicide) are more difficult to predict than more common events (e.g., domestic violence) because they have a low base rate of occurrence. Despite this caveat, evaluators are generally expected to understand established factors and situations that are likely to increase a person's risk of future violence. This chapter summarizes important components of a structured clinical risk assessment to assist clinicians and forensic evaluators in the seemingly daunting task of evaluating future dangerousness.

DANGEROUSNESS AND DEMOGRAPHIC FACTORS

Dangerousness components

When conducting a violence risk assessment, the clinician may find it helpful to divide the concept of dangerousness into five components. The first component is the magnitude of threatened potential harm. Behavior may involve physical harm to persons or property, as well as psychological harm to others. In addition to identifying the likely target of violence, the degree of anticipated harm should be understood. For example, threatening to shoot someone in the face foreshadows a much greater risk of harm than threatening to kick someone on the leg.

The second component of dangerousness is the likelihood that a violent act will take place. Here it is important to clarify the seriousness of the person's intent to cause harm. A person's past history of acting on violent thoughts is the best predictor that violent intentions will be carried out. The third component is the imminence of the harm. For example, is the person threatening harm in the next 5 hours or the next 5 days? The fourth component examines the frequency of a behavior. Frequency is defined as the number of times a particular act has occurred over a specified period of time. The greater the frequency of an aggressive act, the higher the risk that the behavior will reoccur in the future. Situational factors constitute the fifth component of dangerousness. Situational factors that increase the risk of future violence include association with a criminally offending peer group, lack of financial resources and housing, easy access to weapons, or exposure to alcohol or illicit drugs (Scott et al. 2014).

Demographic factors

Demographic factors should be considered when assessing violence risk. First, data from the Epidemiologic Catchment Area study showed violent behavior was generally associated with younger age groups (Swanson et al. 1990). Second, males perpetrate violent acts approximately 10 times more often than females (Tardiff and Sweillam 1980). However, among people with severe mental disorders, men and women do not significantly differ in their base rates of violent behavior. In fact, rates are remarkably similar, and in some cases slightly higher for women (Lidz et al. 1993; Newhill et al. 1995). The MacArthur Foundation's Violence Risk Assessment Study monitored male and female psychiatric inpatients (aged 18–40) released in the community with mental disorders for acts of violence toward others

(Monahan et al. 2001). During the 1-year follow-up, men were "somewhat more likely" than women to be violent, but the difference was not large. Women were more likely than men to direct their aggression toward family members in the home environment. Violent acts by men were more likely to result in an arrest or need for medical treatment (Monahan et al. 2001). Finally, a person's socioeconomic status is relevant for assessing future dangerousness, as violence is nearly three times as common among individuals in lower income brackets (Borum et al. 1996).

Evaluating past violence history

A history of violence is the best predictor of future violent behavior (Klassen and O'Connor 1988). The evaluator can ask the individual to describe the most aggressive act they have ever committed, whether or not this resulted in a criminal arrest or conviction. Criminal and court records are particularly useful in evaluating the person's past history of violence and illegal behavior. For example, the age at first arrest for a serious offense is highly correlated with persistence of criminal offending (Borum et al. 1996). Each prior episode of violence increases the risk of a future violent act (Borum et al. 1996).

Prior criminal offending also increases the risk of future offending in individuals with mental illness. For example, in their study of over 15,000 people diagnosed with bipolar disorder, Webb et al. (2014) found that a history of criminal offending prior to a person being diagnosed with bipolar disorder was a strong independent predictor of criminality after the diagnosis was made.

Additional sources of information relevant in assessing a person's potential for violence include a military and work history. For those individuals who have served in the military, the clinician should review any history of fights, absences without leave (AWOL), disciplinary measures (Article XV in the Uniform Code of Military Justice), as well as the type of discharge. An evaluation of the work history should review frequency of job changes and reasons for each termination. Persons who are laid off from work are six times more likely to be violent than their employed peers (Catalano et al. 1993).

MENTAL DISORDERS AND VIOLENCE

Substance use and violence risk

Illicit drugs and alcohol are strongly associated with violent behavior (Monahan et al. 2001; Pulay et al. 2008). The majority of persons involved in violent crimes are under the influence of alcohol at the time of the act (Murdoch et al. 1990). Furthermore, nearly 90% of intravenous drug users have committed a violent offense (Darke et al. 2010). Stimulants, such as cocaine, crack, amphetamines, and PCP are of particular concern.

Research indicates that methamphetamine use is particularly problematic. Over 25% of methamphetamine users experience psychosis; clinically significant hostility was more common with severe psychotic symptoms that lasted longer than 2 days (McKetin et al. 2008). In their study of 278 methamphetamine users who did not meet criteria for schizophrenia or bipolar disorder, McKetin et al. (2014) found that violent behavior was over six times more likely when patients were using methamphetamine compared to when they were not. In addition, this increased risk was dose dependent, with heavier use (16 or more days in the past month) producing a 15-fold increase in violent behavior. For intravenous drug users, two factors are associated with future violent offending: having committed violence under the influence and having more impulsive personality traits (Torok et al. 2014).

Although persons with an alcohol or substance use disorder are more than twice as likely as those with schizophrenia to report violent behavior in the past year, substance use comorbid with a mental disorder poses an even greater risk of future violence than either condition alone (Swanson et al. 1990). Moreover, the comorbidity of substance use accounts for a significant portion of the violence committed by individuals with mental disorders (Monahan et al. 2001). Substance use may increase violence risk in individuals with mental illness through their acute pharmacological effects, the exacerbation of psychiatric symptoms, or resulting treatment nonadherence (Volavka and Swanson 2010). Evaluators should carefully review a person's substance use history and review any relationship of substance use to past mental health symptoms and/or aggressive behaviors. Screening questions to help evaluate the relationship of substances to aggression are provided in Table 60.1.

Psychosis and violence

Psychotic symptoms are particularly important to explore when conducting a violence risk assessment. In an analysis of 204 studies examining the relationship between psychopathology and aggression, Douglas et al. (2009) found that psychosis was the most important predictor of violent behavior. Recent research has indicated that even

Table 60.1 Substance use and violence screening questions

1. What effects does the substance have on you?
2. Has your substance use caused or worsened any type of mental health symptom?
3. Did you ever feel anger or aggression when using the substance?
4. Did you ever feel anger or aggression when withdrawing from the substance?
5. What is the most violent thing that you have done when using or withdrawing from the substance?
6. Do you have any legal charges related to your substance use?
7. Do you think it is likely you will continue to use alcohol or drugs?

individuals in the pre-psychotic states of their illness have a higher rate of criminal offending. For example, Purcell et al. (2015) determined that persons at risk for psychosis were significantly more at risk for being criminally charged and criminally convicted when compared to persons not identified as at risk for psychosis.

Delusions and command auditory hallucinations are among the most common psychotic symptoms that increase future dangerousness and therefore receive special attention in this chapter.

DELUSIONS AND VIOLENCE

The threat/control-override (TCO) type of delusions are characterized by the presence of beliefs that one is being threatened (e.g., being followed or poisoned) or that one is losing control to an external source (e.g., one's mind is dominated by forces beyond one's control) (Link and Stueve 1995). Swanson and colleagues (1996), using data from the Epidemiologic Catchment Area surveys, found that people who reported TCO symptoms were about twice as likely to engage in assaultive behavior as those with other psychotic symptoms.

In contrast, results from the MacArthur Study of Mental Disorder and Violence (Monahan et al. 2001) showed that the presence of delusions did not predict higher rates of violence among recently discharged psychiatric patients. In particular, a relationship between the presence of TCO delusions and violent behavior was not found. In a study comparing male criminal offenders with schizophrenia found not guilty by reason of insanity to matched controls of nonoffending individuals with schizophrenia, Stompe et al. (2004) also found that TCO symptoms showed no significant association with the severity of violent behavior. The prevalence of TCO symptoms also did not differ between the two groups. However, nondelusional suspiciousness, such as misperceiving others' behavior as suggesting hostile intent, has demonstrated a relationship with violence (Monahan et al. 2001).

Nederlof et al. (2011) conducted a cross-sectional multicenter study to further examine whether the experience of TCO symptoms is related to aggressive behavior. The study sample included 124 psychotic patients characterized by the following diagnostic categories: 70.2% paranoid schizophrenia; 16.1% "other forms" of schizophrenia; 3.2% schizoaffective disorder; 0.8% delusional disorder; and 9.7% psychosis not otherwise specified (NOS). These researchers developed the Threat/Control-Override Questionnaire (TCOQ), a 14-item self-report scale designed to measure both delusional threat and control-override symptoms in a more detailed manner than in previous research. The six *Threat* items specific to this instrument are as follows (Nederlof et al. 2011):

- Other people have tried to poison me or to do me harm.
- Someone has deliberately tried to make me ill.
- Other people have been secretly plotting to ruin me.
- Someone has had evil intentions against me.
- I have the thought that I was being followed for a special reason.
- People have tried to drive me insane.

The eight *Control-Override* items on the TCOQ are as follows (Nederlof et al. 2011):

- I am under the control of an external force that determines my actions.
- Other people control my way of movements.
- Other people can insert thoughts into my head.
- My thoughts are dominated by an external force.
- I have the feeling that other people can determine my thoughts.
- Other people can insert thoughts into my mind.
- I have the feeling that other people have control over me.
- My life is being determined by something or someone other than myself.

The authors determined that TCO symptoms were a significant correlate of aggression in their study sample. When the two domains of TCO symptoms were evaluated separately, only threat symptoms significantly contributed to aggressive behavior. In their attempt to reconcile conflicting findings from earlier research regarding the relationship of TCO symptoms to aggressive behavior, the authors suggested that various methods of measuring TCO symptoms may underlie the seemingly contradictory findings among various studies (Nederlof et al. 2011).

In addition to research examining the potential relationship of particular delusional content to aggression, Appelbaum et al. (1999) utilized the MacArthur–Maudsley Delusions Assessment Schedule to examine the contribution of non-content-related delusional material to violence. The seven dimensions covered by the MacArthur–Maudsley Delusions Assessment Schedule (with brief definitions) are as follows:

1. *Conviction*: The degree of certainty about the delusional belief.
2. *Negative affect*: Whether the delusional belief makes the individual unhappy, frightened, anxious, or angry.
3. *Action*: The extent to which the individual's actions are motivated by the delusional belief.
4. *Inaction*: Whether the individual has refrained from any action as a result of the delusional belief.
5. *Preoccupation*: The extent to which the individual indicates that his or her thoughts focus exclusively on the delusion.
6. *Pervasiveness*: The degree to which the delusional belief penetrates all aspects of the individual's experiences.
7. *Fluidity*: The degree to which the delusional belief changed frequently during the interview.

These authors found that individuals with persecutory delusions had significantly higher scores on the dimensions of "action" and "negative affect," indicating that persons with persecutory delusions may be more likely to react in response to the dysphoric aspects of their symptoms (Appelbaum et al. 1999). Other research has demonstrated that individuals suffering from persecutory delusions and negative affect are more likely to act on their delusions (Buchanan et al. 1993) and to act violently (Cheung et al. 1997).

COMMAND HALLUCINATIONS AND VIOLENCE

An evaluator should carefully assess if the person is experiencing auditory hallucinations when determining violence risk. Auditory command hallucinations are experienced by approximately half of psychiatric patients who experience auditory hallucinations (Shawyer et al. 2003). Because many patients do not report their command hallucinations to others, the frequency of these hallucinations is likely even higher (Zisook et al. 1995). The majority of command hallucinations are nonviolent in nature. Individuals are more likely to obey nonviolent commands than violent commands (Chadwick and Birchwood 1994). However, between 30% and 65% of individuals comply with commands to harm others (Shawyer et al. 2003; Fox et al. 2004).

Research establishing specific factors associated with persons acting on harm-other command hallucinations has been mixed. In a review of seven controlled studies examining the relationship between command hallucinations and violence, no study demonstrated a positive relationship between command hallucinations and violence; one found an inverse relationship (Rudnick 1999). In contrast, McNiel et al. (2000) found in their study of 103 civil psychiatric inpatients that 33% of patients reported having experienced command hallucinations to harm others during the prior year, and 22% of the patients reported that they complied with such commands. The authors concluded that study subjects who experienced command hallucinations to harm others were more than twice as likely to be violent than those without such commands.

Four factors have been described as increasing a person's willingness to comply with harm-other command hallucinations. First, persons are more likely to act on auditory hallucinations to harm others when they perceive the voice as powerful (Fox et al. 2004; Shawyer et al. 2008). Birchwood and Chadwick (1997) noted that persons who perceive a voice as powerful experience a subjective loss of control over the voice, with associated feelings of powerlessness and helplessness. Evaluators should ask the individual what he or she believes would be the consequence for failing to obey the voice, recognizing that direr perceived outcomes increase compliance (Barrowcliff and Haddock 2010). Second, individuals who have a positive appraisal of a harm-other hallucination are more likely to act when compared to individuals who interpret the voice as threatening. In other words, if the person believes that following the directive of the command hallucination will benefit him or her, that person is more likely to comply (Shawyer et al. 2008). Third, persons are more likely to follow harmful command hallucinations when they are associated with a congruent delusion (Shawyer et al. 2008). As an example, a person who hears a voice to kill his wife is more likely to act on this command if he has the delusional belief that his wife has been invaded by an evil alien who is preparing to kill him. Finally, Cheung et al. (1997) noted in their study of patients with schizophrenia that those whose hallucinations generated negative emotions (e.g., anger, anxiety, and sadness) were more likely to act violently than those individuals with voices that generated positive emotions.

When evaluating a patient with persecutory delusions, the clinician should also inquire if the patient has employed "safety actions." Safety actions are specific behaviors (such as avoidance of a perceived persecutor or escape from a fearful situation) that the individual has employed with the intention of minimizing a misperceived threat. In one study of 100 patients with persecutory delusions, over 95% reported using safety behaviors in the past month. In this study, individuals with a prior history of violence reported a greater ongoing use of safety behaviors (Freeman et al. 2007).

SCHIZOPHRENIA AND VIOLENCE RISK

Delusions and hallucinations are prominent symptoms of schizophrenia, and there is evidence that a diagnosis of schizophrenia is associated with an increase in criminal offending. In a retrospective review of 2861 Australian patients with schizophrenia followed over a 25-year period, Wallace, Mullen, and Burgess (2004) found that individuals with schizophrenia were significantly more likely to have been convicted of a criminal offense (including violent offenses) relative to matched controls. These authors noted that the criminal behaviors committed by individuals with schizophrenia could not be entirely accounted for by comorbid substance use, active symptoms, or characteristics of systems of care (Wallace et al. 2004). Fazel et al. (2014) determined that over 10% of men diagnosed with schizophrenia were convicted of a violent offense within 5 years of their diagnosis. In individuals diagnosed with schizophrenia, investigation of prior violent convictions is particularly important. In their study of nearly 14,000 individuals with two or more hospitalizations for schizophrenia treatment, Witt, Lichtenstein, and Fazel (2015) found that conviction for a violent crime prior to a diagnosis of schizophrenia was the strongest predictor of subsequent violence.

A typology of three groups indicates different pathways to violence among individuals with schizophrenia. The first group includes persons with a history of childhood conduct disorder who demonstrate aggressive behavior and antisocial acts before and after being diagnosed with schizophrenia. The second group becomes involved in aggressive behavior concomitant with the onset of their illness. The third group involves individuals with schizophrenia who engage in a physical assault after many years of their illness, i.e., a "late first offender" (Hodgins et al. 2014). Van Dongen et al. (2014) found that although persecutory delusions were associated with all three groups, they were more likely to be associated in the late first offender group.

Mood disorders and violence risk

Most studies examining the relationship between mood disorders and violence have not differentiated between bipolar disorder, mania, and depression (Graz et al. 2009). To evaluate if criminal behavior and violent crimes were more common in the diagnosis of depression versus mania, Graz et al. (2009) examined the national crime register for 1561 patients with an affective disorder who had been released into the community. The rate of criminal behavior and violent crimes was highest in the bipolar disorder group (15.7%) compared to patients in the major depressive disorder group (1.4%). The authors concluded that different mood disorders have different violence risk. Other studies have examined violence risk factors unique to different mood disorders, as summarized below.

DEPRESSION AND VIOLENCE

Depression may result in violent behavior, particularly in depressed individuals who strike out against others in despair. After committing a violent act, the depressed person may attempt suicide. Depression is the most common diagnosis in murder–suicides (Marzuk et al. 1992). Studies examining mothers who kill their children (filicide) have found that they were often suffering with severe depression. High rates of suicide following a filicide have been noted, with between 16% and 29% of mothers and 40% and 60% of fathers taking their life after murdering their child (Rodenburg 1971; Marzuk et al. 1992; Hatters-Friedman et al. 2005). In a study of 30 family filicide–suicide files, the most common motive involved an attempt by the perpetrator to relieve real or imagined suffering of the child, a category known as an altruistic filicide. Eighty percent of the parents studied had evidence of a past or current psychiatric history, with nearly 60% suffering from depression, 27% with psychosis, and 20% experiencing delusional beliefs (Hatters-Friedman et al. 2005).

In their analysis of 386 individuals from the MacArthur Violence Risk Assessment Study with a categorical diagnosis of depression, Yang et al. (2012) noted two important findings relevant to depression and future violence risk. First, violence that had occurred within the past 10 weeks was a strong predictor of violence by participants with depression, but not by participants with a psychotic disorder. This finding suggests that a past history of *recent* violence may represent a higher risk of future violence in depressed patients than in those with psychosis. Second, this risk of future harm by depressed patients was further increased with alcohol use.

BIPOLAR DISORDER AND VIOLENCE

Patients with mania show a high percentage of assaultive or threatening behavior, but serious violence is rare (Krakowski et al. 1986). Patients with mania most commonly exhibit violent behavior when they are restrained or have limits set on their behavior (Tardiff and Sweillam 1980).

Active manic symptoms have been suggested as playing a substantial role in criminal behavior. In particular, Fazel et al. (2010) compared violent crime convictions for over 3700 individuals diagnosed with bipolar disorder with general population controls and unaffected full siblings. This longitudinal study had two main findings. First, although individuals with bipolar disorder exhibited an increased risk for violent crime compared to the general population, most of the excess violent crime was associated with substance abuse comorbidity. Second, unaffected siblings also had an increased risk for violent crime, highlighting the contribution of genetics or early environmental factors in families with bipolar disorder.

Cognitive impairment and violence

The risk of violence increases for those with cognitive impairment (Quinsey and Maquire 1986; Borum et al. 1996). Brain injury has also been associated with aggressive behavior. After a brain injury, individuals may become verbally and physically aggressive (National Institutes of Health 1998). Characteristic features of aggression resulting from a brain injury include reactive behavior triggered by trivial stimuli, lack of planning or reflection, nonpurposeful action with no clear aims or goals, explosive outbursts without a gradual buildup, an episodic pattern with long periods of relative calm, and feelings of concern and remorse following the episode.

Epilepsy has also been described as having a relationship to violence. However, the evidence for this relationship has focused primarily on small samples of incarcerated individuals or children with epilepsy (Fazel et al. 2011). In their study of 22,000 individuals with traumatic brain injury and 22,000 individuals with epilepsy, Fazel et al. (2011) evaluated whether persons with either of these disorders were at an increased risk for violent crime compared with the general population or unaffected siblings. The authors reported several important findings. First, individuals with traumatic brain injury had a significantly increased risk of violent crime, particularly in cases involving focal brain injuries and injury after age 16. Second, after adjusting for familial factors, epilepsy was not associated with an increased risk of violent crime. Therefore, although evaluators should consider traumatic brain injury a risk factor for future violence, such causality does not appear to be established for epilepsy (Fazel et al. 2011).

PERSONALITY FACTORS AND VIOLENCE RISK

The most common personality disorder associated with violence is antisocial personality disorder (ASPD) (Monahan et al. 2001). The violence by those with antisocial personality disorder is often motivated by revenge, or occurs during a period of heavy drinking. Violence among these persons is frequently cold and calculated and lacks emotionality (Williamson et al. 1987). In addition to a *Diagnostic and Statistical Manual of Mental Disorders*, 5th edition (*DSM-5*) diagnosis of antisocial personality disorders or traits, the clinician should be familiar with the psychological construct known as psychopathy. The term *psychopath* was described by Cleckley (1976) as an individual who is superficially charming, lacks empathy, lacks close relationships, is impulsive, and is concerned primarily with self-gratification. Hare and colleagues developed the Psychopathy Checklist-Revised (PCL-R) (Hare 1991) as a validated measure of psychopathy in adults. Psychopathy is a strong predictor of general criminal behavior and violence among adults (Salekin et al. 1996). Psychopathy is more predictive of violence than a *DSM-5* diagnosis of ASPD.

ASSESSING CURRENT DANGEROUSNESS

When conducting an assessment of current dangerousness, play close attention to the individual's affect. Individuals who are angry and lack empathy for others are at increased risk for violent behavior (Menzies et al. 1985). In their meta-analysis of 610 individuals, Reagu et al. (2013) found a consistent and significant association between angry affect and violent behavior in the context of psychotic illness.

All threats should lead to clinicians attempting to gather additional details. An important line of inquiry involves understanding the exact relationship to an intended victim. Understanding how a violent act would be carried out and the expected consequences for the individual voicing the threat helps the clinician assess the degree of danger. In addition, fully considering the consequences of an act may help the individual elect an alternative coping strategy. For example, a man may be focused on revenge against his wife because of her infidelity. When confronted with the likelihood of spending many years in prison, he may decide to divorce his wife instead. Additional information that should be elicited includes potential grudge lists and an investigation of the subject's fantasies of violence (Monahan et al. 2001).

The clinician should also assess the suicide risk in any patient making a homicidal threat. One study found that 91% of outpatients who had attempted homicide also had attempted suicide and that 86% of patients with homicidal ideation also reported suicidal ideation (Asnis et al. 1997). In their study of 1460 adults with schizophrenia, Witt et al. (2014) found that suicidal threats were independently associated with violence risk in both males and females.

Inquiring about access to a weapon is particularly important in evaluating a person's risk for imminent dangerousness. A person who has used weapons against others in the past has an increased risk of future violence. The main difference between assault and homicide is the lethality of the weapon used. Loaded guns have the highest lethality of any weapon. An assault with a gun is five times more likely to result in a fatality than an attack with a knife (Zimring 1991). The recent movement of a weapon, such as transferring a gun from a closet to a nightstand, may be particularly ominous in a paranoid person. In general, the greater the fear, the more likely the paranoid person is to kill someone he misperceives as a persecutor.

Finally, the evaluator should ask the person to rate his or her own likelihood of future violence. Roaldset and Bjorkly (2010) asked 489 patients admitted to a psychiatric hospital to rate their risk of future threatening or violent actions toward others. Moderate or high-risk scores on self-ratings of future violence remained significant predictors of violence 1 year post-discharge. However, persons who rated themselves as "no risk" or refused to answer the question also had a considerable number of violent episodes, indicating that a self-report of low risk of violence may produce false-negatives.

When organizing strategies to decrease risk factors related to future violence, clinicians should distinguish static from dynamic risk factors. By definition, static factors are not subject to change by intervention. Static factors include such items as demographic information and past history of violence. Dynamic factors are subject to change with intervention and include such factors as access to weapons, acute psychotic symptoms, active substance use, and the person's living situation. Clinicians may find it helpful to organize a chart that outlines violence risk factors, management and treatment strategies to address dynamic risk factors, and the current status of each risk factor. This approach will assist in the development of a violence prevention plan that addresses the unique combination of risk factors for a particular patient and organizes interventions to manage those risks.

SUMMARY

Clinicians and forensic evaluators are requested to conduct violence risk assessments in a variety of situations. A structured clinical assessment approach is an important component of assessing future dangerousness.

SUMMARY KEY POINTS

- Although the majority of individuals with mental illness are not violent, specific interventions can be focused to help decrease violence risk.
- Alcohol and illicit drug use are among the greatest risk factors for aggression.
- Psychotic symptoms are associated with an increase in violence risk, particularly those with paranoia and suspiciousness.
- Individuals with mental illness who experience fear and anger are at a heightened risk of becoming violent.
- Identifying dynamic risk factors for future violence is important for developing a plan to help address and reduce violence risk.

REFERENCES

Appelbaum P, P Robbins, and L Roth. 1999. Dimensional approach to delusions: Comparison across types and diagnoses. *American Journal of Psychiatry* 156:1938–1943.

Asnis G, M Kaplan, G Hundorfean, and W Saeed. 1997. Violence and homicidal behaviors in psychiatric disorders. *Psychiatric Clinics of North America* 20:405–425.

Barrowcliff A and G Haddock. 2010. Factors affecting compliance and resistance to auditory command hallucinations: Perceptions of a clinical population. *Journal of Mental Health* 19:542–552.

Birchwood M and P Chadwick. 1997. The omnipotence of voices: Testing the validity of a cognitive model. *Psychological Medicine* 27:1345–1353.

Borum R, M Swartz, and J Swanson. 1996. Assessing and managing violence risk in clinical practice. *Journal of Practical Psychiatry and Behavioral Health* 4:205–214.

Buchanan A, A Reed, S Wessely, P Garety, P Taylor, D Grugin, and G Dunn. 1993. Acting on delusions, II: The phenomenological correlates of acting on delusions. *British Journal of Psychiatry* 163:77–81.

Catalano R, D Dooley, R Novaco, G Wilson, and R Hough. 1993. Using ECA survey data to examine the effect of job layoffs on violent behavior. *Hospital and Community Psychiatry* 44:874–879.

Chadwick P and M Birchwood. 1994. The omnipotence of voices: A cognitive approach to hallucinations. *British Journal of Psychiatry* 164:190–201.

Cheung P, I Schweitzer, K Crowley, and V Tuckwell. 1997. Violence in schizophrenia: Role of hallucinations and delusions. *Schizophrenia Research* 26:181–190.

Cleckley H. 1976. *The Mask of Sanity*. St. Louis, MO: Mosby.

Darke S, J Ross, M Teesson, R Ali, R Cooke, A Ritter, and M Lynskey. 2005. Factors associated with 12 months continuous heroin abstinence: Findings from the Australian Treatment Outcome Study (ATOS). *Journal of Substance Abuse Treatment* 28:255–263.

Darke S, M Torok, S Kaye, J Ross, and R McKetin. 2010. Comparative rates of violent crime among regular methamphetamine and opioid users: Offending and victimization. *Addiction* 105:916–919.

Douglas K, L Guy, and S Hart. 2009. Psychosis as a risk factor for violence to others: A meta-analysis. *Psychological Bulletin* 135:679–706.

Fazel S, P Lichtenstein, M Grann, G Goodwin, and N Långström. 2010. Bipolar disorder in violent crime. New evidence from population-based longitudinal studies and systematic review. *Archives of General Psychiatry* 67:931–938.

Fazel S, P Lichtenstein, M Grann, and N Långström. 2011. Risk of violent crime in individuals with epilepsy and traumatic brain injury: A 35-year Swedish population study. *PLOS Medicine* 8(12):e1001150. doi:101371/journal.pmed.1001150

Fazel S, A Wolf, C Palm, and P Lichtenstein. 2014. Violent crime, suicide, and premature mortality in patients with schizophrenia and related disorders: A 38 year total population study in Sweden. *Lancet Psychiatry* 1:44–54.

Fox J, N Gray, and H Lewis. 2004. Factors determining compliance with command hallucinations with violent content: The role of social rank, perceived power of the voice and voice malevolence. *Journal of Forensic Psychiatry and Psychology* 15:511–531.

Freeman D, P Garety, E Kuipers, D Fowler, P Bebbington, and G Dunn. 2007. Acting on persecutory delusions: The importance of safety seeking. *Behaviour Research and Therapy* 45:89–99.

Graz C, E Etschel, H Schoech, and M Soyka. 2009. Criminal behavior and violent crimes in former inpatients with affective disorder. *Journal of Affective Disorders* 117:98–103.

Hare R. 1991. *The Hare Psychopathy Checklist-Revised*. Toronto, ON: Multi-Health Systems.

Hatters-Friedman S, D Hrouda, C Holden, S Noffsinger, and P Resnick. 2005. Filicide-suicide: Common factors in parents who kill their children and themselves. *Journal of the American Academy of Psychiatry and the Law* 33:496–504.

Hodgins S, M Piatosa, and B Schiffer. 2014. Violence among people with schizophrenia: Phenotypes and neurobiology. *Current Topics in Behavioral Neuroscience* 17:329–368.

Klassen D and W O'Connor. 1988. A prospective study of predictors of violence in adult male mental health admissions. *Law and Human Behavior* 12:143–158.

Krakowski M, J Volavka, and D Brizer. 1986. Psychopathology and violence: A review of literature. *Comprehensive Psychiatry* 27:131–148.

Lidz C, E Mulvey, and W Gardner.1993. The accuracy of predictions of violence to others. *Journal of the American Medical Association* 269:1007–1011.

Link B and A Stueve. 1995. Evidence bearing on mental illness as a possible cause of violent behavior. *Epidemiologic Reviews* 17:172–181.

Marzuk P, K Tardiff, and C Hirsch. 1992. The epidemiology of murder-suicide. *Journal of the American Medical Association* 267:3179–3183.

McKetin R, D Lubman, J Najman, S Dawe, P Butterworth, and A Baker. 2014. Does methamphetamine use increase violent behaviour? Evidence from a prospective longitudinal study. *Addiction* 109:798–806.

McKetin R, J McLaren, D Lubman, and L Hides. 2008. Hostility among methamphetamine users experiencing psychotic symptoms. *American Journal on Addictions* 17:235–240.

McNiel D, J Eisner, and R Binder. 2000. The relationship between command hallucinations and violence. *Psychiatric Services* 51:1288–1292.

Menzies R, C Webster, and D Sepejak. 1985. The dimensions of dangerousness: Evaluating the accuracy of psychometric predictions of violence among forensic patients. *Law and Human Behavior* 9:49–70.

Monahan J, H Steadman, E Silver, P Appelbaum, P Robbins, E Mulvey, L Roth, T Grisso, and S Banks. 2001. *Rethinking Risk Assessment: The MacArthur Study of Mental Disorder and Violence*. New York: Oxford University Press.

Murdoch D, R Pihl, and D Ross. 1990. Alcohol and crimes of violence: Present issues. *International Journal of the Addictions* 25:1065–1081.

National Institutes of Health. 1998. *Rehabilitation of Persons with Traumatic Brain Injury* [Electronic Version]. http://consensus.nih.gov/1998/1998TraumaticBrainInjury109html.htm, accessed March 18, 2008.

Nederlof A, P Muris, and J Hovens. 2011. Threat/Control-Override symptoms and emotional reactions to positive symptoms as correlates of aggressive behavior in psychotic patients. *Journal of Nervous and Mental Disease* 199:342–347.

Newhill C, E Mulvey, and C Lidz. 1995. Characteristics of violence in the community by female patients seen in a psychiatric emergency service. *Psychiatric Services* 46:785–789.

Pulay A, D Dawson, D Hasin, R Goldstein, J Ruan, R Pickering, B Huang, P Chou, and B Grant. 2008. Violent behavior and DSM-IV psychiatric disorders: Results from the national epidemiologic survey on alcohol and related conditions. *Journal of Clinical Psychiatry* 69:12–22.

Purcell R, S Harrigan, N Glozier, P Amminger, and A Yung. 2015. Self reported rates of criminal offending and victimization in young people at-risk for psychosis. *Schizophrenia Research* 166:55–59.

Quinsey V and A Maquire. 1986. Maximum security psychiatric patients: Actuarial and clinical predictions of dangerousness. *Journal of Interpersonal Violence* 1:143–171.

Reagu S, R Jones, V Kumari, and P Taylor. 2013. Angry affect and violence in the context of a psychotic illness: A systematic review and meta-analysis of the literature. *Schizophrenia Research* 146:46–52.

Roaldset J and S Bjorkly. 2010. Patients' own statements of their future risk for violent and self-harm behavior: A prospective inpatient and post-discharge follow-up study in an acute psychiatric unit. *Psychiatry Research* 178:153–159.

Rodenburg M. 1971. Child murder by depressed parents. *Canadian Psychiatric Association Journal* 16:41–48.

Rudnick A. 1999. Relation between command hallucinations and dangerous behavior. *Journal of the American Academy of Psychiatry and the Law* 27:253–257.

Salekin R, R Rogers, and K Sewell. 1996. A review of meta-analysis of the psychopathy checklist and psychopathy checklist-revised: Predictive validity of dangerousness. *Clinical Psycholoyg–Science and Practice* 3:203–213.

Scott C, P Resnick, and W Newman. 2014. Violence: Psychiatric assessment and intervention. In *Violent Offenders: Understanding and Assessment*, edited by CA Pietz and CA Mattson, New York: Oxford University Press, 452–473.

Shawyer F, A Mackinnon, J Farhall, E Sims, S Blaney, P Yardley, M Daly, P Mullen, and D Copolov. 2008. Acting on harmful command hallucinations in psychotic disorders: An integrative approach. *Journal of Nervous and Mental Disease* 196:390–398.

Shawyer F, A Mackinnon, J Farhall, T Trauer, and D Copolov. 2003. Command hallucinations and violence: Implications for detention and treatment. *Psychiatry, Psychology and Law* 10:97–107.

Stompe T, G Ortwein-Swoboda, and H Schanda. 2004. Schizophrenia, delusional symptoms, and violence: The threat/control override concept reexamined. *Schizophrenia Bulletin* 30:31–44.

Swanson J, R Borum, and M Swartz. 1996. Psychotic symptoms and disorders and risk of violent behavior in the community. *Criminal Behaviour and Mental Health* 6:317–338.

Swanson J, C Holzer, V Ganju, and R Jono. 1990. Violence and psychiatric disorder in the community: Evidence from the Epidemiologic Catchment Area surveys. *Hospital and Community Psychiatry* 41:761–770.

Tardiff K and A Sweillam. 1980. Assault, suicide, and mental illness. *Archives of General Psychiatry* 37:164–169.

Torok M, S Darke, F Shand, and S Kaye. 2014. Violent offending severity among injecting drug users: Examining risk factors and issues around classification. *Addictive Behaviors* 39:1773–1778.

Van Dongen J, N Buck, and H Van Marle. 2014. Unravelling offending in schizophrenia: Factors characterizing subgroups of offenders. *Criminal Behaviour and Mental Health* 25:88–98. doi:10.1002/cmb.1920.

Volavka J. 2013. Violence in schizophrenia and bipolar disorder. *Psychiatria Danubina* 25:24–33.

Volavka J and J Swanson. 2010. Violent behavior in mental illness: The role of substance abuse. *Journal of the American Medical Association* 304:563–564.

Wallace C, P Mullen, and P Burgess. 2004. Criminal offending in schizophrenia over a 25-year period marked by deinstitutionalization and increasing prevalence of comorbid substance use disorders. *American Journal of Psychiatry* 161:716–727.

Webb R, P Lichtenstein, H Larsson, J Gedded, and S Fazel. 2014. Suicide, hospital-presenting suicide attempts, and criminality in bipolar disorder: Examination of risk for multiple adverse outcomes. *Journal of Clinical Psychiatry* 75:e809–816. doi:10.4088/JCP.13m08899

Williamson S, R Hare, and S Wong. 1987. Violence: Criminal psychopaths and their victims. *Canadian Journal of Behavioural Science* 19:454–462.

Witt K, K Hawton, and S Fazel. 2014. The relationship between suicide and violence in schizophrenia: Analysis of the Clinical Antipsychotic Trials of Intervention Effectiveness (CATIE) dataset. *Schizophrenia Research* 154:61–67.

Witt K, P Lichtenstein, and S Fazel. 2015. Improving risk assessment in schizophrenia: Epidemiological investigation of criminal history factors. *British Journal of Psychiatry* 206:424–430.

Yang S, E Mulvey, T Loughran, and B Hanusa. 2012. Psychiatric symptoms and alcohol use in community violence by person with a psychotic disorder or depression. *Psychiatric Services* 63:262–269.

Zimring F. 1991. Firearms, violence, and public policy. *Scientific American* 265:48–54.

Zisook S, D Byrd, J Kuck, and D Jeste. 1995. Command hallucinations in outpatients with schizophrenia. *Journal of Clinical Psychiatry* 56:462–465.

61

Clinical management of aggression and violence

WILLIAM NEWMAN AND KENNETH TARDIFF

INTRODUCTION

This chapter addresses the management of adults with aggressive and violent behaviors related to major psychiatric disorders. The chapter reviews many evidence-based treatment options, with a focus on particular diagnoses that are associated with aggression. The classifications of the disorders are consistent with diagnostic criteria in the *Diagnostic and Statistical Manual of Mental Disorders*, 5th edition (*DSM-5*, American Psychiatric Association 2013). The conditions are presented in the order addressed in the *DSM-5*, based on the order of development throughout the lifetime.

There is not currently a U.S. Food and Drug Administration (FDA)-approved pharmacological treatment of aggression. The treatments used to target aggression (beyond primary treatment of psychiatric disorders) are therefore off label and should be carefully considered after reviewing the available evidence. This chapter presents some of the existing evidence supporting off-label pharmacological treatments targeting aggression.

NEURODEVELOPMENTAL DISORDERS

Individuals with intellectual disability (formerly mental retardation in *Diagnostic and Statistical Manual of Mental Disorders*, 4th edition, text revision [*DSM-IV-TR*]) can display aggressive behaviors due to a variety of factors, including impaired impulse control, difficulty with long-term planning, and trouble handling stressful and emotional situations. Pharmacological treatments have shown some benefits in curbing aggressive behaviors in this population. Because much of the published evidence uses the *DSM-IV-TR* definition of "mental retardation," the term *cognitive impairment* will be employed throughout the remainder of this section for the sake of simplicity.

Treatment with lithium has proven beneficial in managing aggressive behaviors in this population, with suggested target lithium levels ranging from 0.5 to 1 mEq/L (Tyrer et al. 1984; Craft et al. 1987; Spreat et al. 1989). Treatment with valproate has also proven beneficial in managing aggression in individuals with cognitive impairment (Mattes 1992). Treatment with antipsychotic medications can also help manage aggressive behaviors (Amore et al. 2011). Risperidone in particular has displayed clear benefits in this population, generally at doses ranging from 0.5 to 4 mg/day (Hasler and Reis 2010). Beta blockers have also shown benefits in curbing aggression in patients with cognitive impairment (Ruedrich et al. 1990).

Nonpharmacological interventions have been employed to help curb aggressive behaviors in individuals with cognitive impairment, including psychotherapy and structured teaching. Behavioral skills training is one intervention that has especially shown promise (Travis and Sturmey 2013). Applied behavioral analysis (ABA) is another technique that has been tried in patients with cognitive impairment. However, the data to this point regarding the benefits of ABA for improving aggression have been equivocal (Aman et al. 1985; Hassiotis et al. 2011; Hassiotis et al. 2012).

SCHIZOPHRENIA SPECTRUM AND OTHER PSYCHOTIC DISORDERS

The primary pharmacological treatment of schizophrenia is with typical or atypical antipsychotic medications. In the management of acute agitation, antipsychotic medications can be administered orally or intramuscularly to address current or impending aggressive behaviors. Clozapine treats psychosis as well, but unlike other antipsychotic medications, clozapine has been shown to directly reduce long-term violence, even after controlling for sedation (Chiles et al. 1994; Citrome et al. 2001). Close, consistent laboratory testing is essential for following blood levels and monitoring for potential side effects of clozapine.

Table 61.1 Dosing information for common long-acting injectable antipsychotics

Name	Typical dosing range	Typical frequency	Half-life (t 1/2)	Other notes
Prolixin Decanoate	12.5–50 mg (increments of 6.25)	q2–3 weeks	15 days	Usually give test dose of 6.25 mg after patient tolerates oral Prolixin
Haldol Decanoate	25–300 mg (increments of 25)	q3–4 weeks	21 days	Usually dosed 10–15 times oral dose; max initial test dose of 100 mg
Risperdal Consta	25–50 mg (increments of 12.5)	q2 weeks	3–6 days	Usually does not reach steady state until 8 weeks after first injection
Invega Sustenna	39–234 mg (increments of 39)	q1 month	25–49 days	Initiation dose of 234 mg on day 1; maintenance dose on day 8 (±2 days)
Zyprexa Relprevv	150, 210, 300, 405 mg (see dosing recs)	q2–4 weeks	30 days	Requires monitoring for post-injection delirium/sedation syndrome (PDSS)
Abilify Maintena	400 mg (also comes in 300 mg)	q1 month	30–47 days	Single, 400 mg injection usually used for initiation and maintenance
Invega Trinza	273, 410, 546, 819 mg (see dosing recs)	q3 months	84–139 days	Initiated only after treatment with Invega Sustenna for at least 4 months
Aristada	441, 662, 882 mg (see dosing recs)	q1 month	29–35 days	Continue administering oral Abilify for 21 consecutive days

Some patients have a history of limited adherence to daily antipsychotic medications, which can result in untreated psychotic symptoms. In cases involving limited adherence, long-acting injectable medications can be administered periodically to ensure adherence and maintain therapeutic blood levels. Table 61.1 lists dosing instructions for commonly used long-acting injectable medications currently on the market. Depending on the location of the individual, the patient may voluntarily consent to treatment with long-acting injectable medications, have a substituted decision maker decide on his or her behalf, or be court ordered to continue receiving treatment.

Mood stabilizers can be used to treat residual aggressive behaviors for individuals with schizophrenia who do not respond to antipsychotic medications alone (McEvoy et al. 1999). Valproate (Dose et al. 1998) and carbamazepine (Okuma et al. 1989) have specifically been found to decrease aggressive behaviors by individuals who are also on antipsychotic medications. Lithium (Bender et al. 2004) and lamotrigine (Pavlovic 2008) prescribed in conjunction with clozapine have been shown to decrease aggression as well. However, the effects of lithium in combination with other antipsychotics have not been as well supported in the literature (Collins et al. 1991; Wilson 1993). Benzodiazepines can be used as adjunct treatment with antipsychotic medications to reduce aggressive behaviors, particularly in individuals who do not have a history of substance abuse (McEvoy et al. 1999).

In addition to medications, individuals with schizophrenia can be exposed to nonpharmacological treatment to assist them in adapting to their surroundings. Therapy should be aimed at both supporting the individual and helping to ensure medication adherence. Supportive therapy is one of the most commonly employed techniques with patients who have schizophrenia, though the outcomes are somewhat equivocal overall and have not shown direct benefits for aggression (Buckley et al. 2015). There is, however, evidence that cognitive behavioral therapy (CBT) may specifically improve aggression in patients with schizophrenia (Haddock et al. 2009; Rathod et al. 2010).

BIPOLAR AND RELATED DISORDERS

Aggressive behaviors by manic individuals are often impulsive and related to their elevated mood, grandiosity, or sense of invulnerability. The primary intervention is therefore treatment of the mania. Treatment involves the daily use of a mood stabilizer, such as lithium or valproate, with the potential addition of an antipsychotic when there are concurrent psychotic symptoms. Regarding combination treatment for individuals with mania and psychosis, the American Psychiatric Association (APA) Practice Guidelines note, "The *combination* [emphasis included] of an antipsychotic with either lithium or valproate may be more effective than any of these agents alone. Thus, the first-line pharmacological treatment for patients with severe mania is the initiation of either lithium plus an antipsychotic or valproate plus an antipsychotic" (APA 2002, 16).

Aggressive behaviors are often the precipitating factor leading manic patients to be hospitalized or arrested. Which outcome occurs frequently remains up to the discretion of the responding officer. Patients with bipolar disorder are at an overall increased risk of being arrested. In one study of individuals with bipolar disorder who had been arrested, the majority were manic (74.2%) and/or psychotic (59%) at the time of their arrest (Quanbeck et al. 2004). The presence of psychosis or comorbid substance use can further increase their risk of aggression (Asnis et al. 1997).

Nonpharmacological interventions center on educating the patient and the family about ways to help prevent, or at least recognize, manic episodes. Although early signs differ for individual patients, sleep changes are commonly noticed preceding a manic episode. Identifying warning signs can allow the patient or family to contact the treating provider and initiate changes to the treatment plan, as necessary. This exercise can improve communication, as well as the overall relationship between the provider, the patient, and the family (Perry et al. 1999).

DEPRESSIVE DISORDERS

Similar to bipolar disorder, the most important factor in preventing aggression in patients with major depressive disorder involves adequately treating the symptoms. Antidepressants are the first-line treatment. Most prescribers start with selective serotonin reuptake inhibitors (SSRIs) due to their favorable side effect profile. In patients experiencing psychotic symptoms as part of their depression, treatment with an antipsychotic should be added. According to the APA Practice Guidelines, "For patients who exhibit psychotic symptoms during an episode of major depressive disorder, treatment should include a combination of antipsychotic and antidepressant medications" (APA 2010, 20).

Some have suggested that taking SSRIs may itself be associated with violence (Mason 2002; Healy et al. 2006; Moore et al. 2010). The cases reported in those articles have involved extreme acts of violence, including homicide. Other authors have held that there is no association between violence and the use of SSRIs (Tardiff et al. 2002; Barber et al. 2008). In seemingly the most extensive study published thus far, Bouvy and Liem (2012) presented data from their 15-year analysis that tracked patients in the Netherlands. From their data, the authors reported a negative association between antidepressants and lethal violence. Based on the existing literature, there does not appear to be a clearly proven link between SSRIs and violent behavior.

There are relatively uncommon, though devastating, acts that are most often seen in the setting of depression. Murder–suicide is one act that is commonly linked to depression. Depending on the source, murder–suicide can be defined as committing suicide within 1 day to 1 week of killing another person (Marzuk et al. 1992; Bossarte et al. 2006). Marzuk and colleagues (1992) proposed a classification system for murder–suicide involving a combination of the perpetrator's relationship to the victim and the perpetrator's presumed motive. Of the five major types described by Marzuk and colleagues, the Consortial–Possessive type accounts for 50%–75% of murder–suicides (Marzuk et al. 1992). The Consortial–Possessive type involves ex-intimate partners seeking revenge. Depression is highly linked to the act of murder–suicide (Eliason 2009).

Another rare, though devastating, event associated with depression involves filicide, the murder of a child. More specific terms including neonaticide (murder of infant in first 24 hours) and infanticide (typically defined as murder of children under 1 year old) have been defined (Friedman et al. 2012). As with murder–suicide, there is a strong link between depression and filicide (Friedman et al. 2005; Razali et al. 2015; Shields et al. 2015). Screening and education have been proposed as measures to help prevent the potentially devastating effects of perinatal depression (Rhodes and Segre 2013).

Murder–suicide and filicide are both very rare events. Because both events are linked to depression, clinicians can best help prevent these tragedies through providing adequate treatment and thorough screenings of depressed patients for risk to others (in addition to asking about suicidality). In some instances, patients with depression may need to be hospitalized if there is concern about potential harm to others.

TRAUMA- AND STRESSOR-RELATED DISORDERS

Posttraumatic stress disorder (PTSD) is the trauma- and stressor-related disorder most often associated with aggression. Combat exposure and the level of PTSD symptoms have been associated with aggression and related legal problems in veterans (Wilson and Zigelbaum 1983; Miles et al. 2015). In one study, veterans hospitalized psychiatrically were seven times more likely to have committed an act or acts of violence in the preceding 4 months (McFall et al. 1999). Clinicians interacting with PTSD patients who either present agitated or have a known history of violence should consider asking questions relevant to violence risk assessment.

There are no specifically identified pharmacological treatments proven to effectively target aggression in PTSD. Schoenfeld and colleagues (2004) wrote a general overview presenting evidence for various pharmacological treatments of PTSD. The treatment of PTSD with benzodiazepines is worth specific mention. Studies have reported a range of 30.4%–73.7% of PTSD patients who are being prescribed benzodiazepines (Harpaz-Rotem et al. 2008; Lund et al. 2013). This fact is important because other reports have demonstrated an association between benzodiazepines prescribed for PTSD and related aggression (Kosten et al. 2000; Shin et al. 2012). One recent review concluded that benzodiazepines should be relatively contraindicated in patients with PTSD due to the worsening of aggression (Guina et al. 2015).

As with the pharmacological approaches, there is no psychotherapeutic modality that has been clearly demonstrated to specifically target aggression in patients with PTSD. CBT has proven most effective in addressing general symptoms of PTSD (Ursano et al. 2004). Virtual reality exposure therapy (VRET) is another emerging treatment option to address the general symptoms of PTSD (Goncalves et al. 2012). However, neither CBT nor VRET have been systematically studied regarding their impact on aggression in this population.

DISRUPTIVE, IMPULSE-CONTROL, AND CONDUCT DISORDERS

Intermittent explosive disorder (IED) by definition involves the patient exhibiting aggressive behavior. The violence is grossly out of proportion to any provocation or precipitating stressor. The violent episodes are generally not premeditated but rather are impulsive in nature. The patient may describe the violent episodes as spells or attacks in which the violence is preceded by a sense of tension or arousal and is followed by a sense of relief. The concept of IED as a separate entity has faced criticism over the years, particularly due to the ambiguities of the diagnosis and lack of diagnostic validity when using the *DSM-IV* criteria. However, recent studies have shown improved validity when applying *DSM-5* criteria (Coccaro 2012).

The first step of addressing IED involves excluding other potential diagnoses, including personality disorders, which are often associated with aggression. There are pharmacological interventions that have been reported as effective for decreasing the amount of aggression in patients with IED. Some of the medications found beneficial in select populations include fluoxetine, clozapine, and some mood stabilizers (Kant et al. 2004; Coccaro et al. 2009; Jones et al. 2011). CBT has been demonstrated as an effective intervention for individuals with IED (Gavolski and Blanchard 2002).

SUBSTANCE-RELATED AND ADDICTIVE DISORDERS

Substance use is often comorbid with conditions such as psychotic disorders, mood disorders, and personality disorders (particularly Cluster B). Substance use can considerably complicate the management of aggression, particularly when it is downplayed or not volunteered by individuals. Several studies have reflected the increased rates of aggression in individuals with comorbid mental health and substance use diagnoses (Swanson et al. 1990; Swanson et al. 1996; Johns 1997; Steadman et al. 1998). Targeting substance use treatment is a major aspect of managing aggressive patients. Many substances decrease the ability to plan actions and respond to dangerous situations. Addressing substance use issues can help limit the chance that individuals become victims or perpetrators of violent acts.

Alcohol has a very well-established association with violence. The number of establishments serving alcohol in a geographical region correlates highly with violence (Cameron et al. 2015). Studies have also shown that, on average, perpetrators of violent crimes have higher blood alcohol levels than perpetrators of nonviolent crimes (Langevin et al. 1982; Murdoch et al. 1990). This finding is consistent with the disinhibition resulting from acute alcohol intoxication. Alcohol impairs various regions of the brain, most importantly the prefrontal cortex, which results in individuals acting more impulsively and having a limited ability to make well-reasoned decisions.

Interestingly, evidence clearly linking other substances of abuse to violence is less apparent. Alcohol is the only substance of abuse clearly established to increase aggression in animal studies (Roth 1994). In humans, several substances of abuse are commonly associated with increased aggression, including phencyclidine, cocaine, opioids (primarily during withdrawal), and amphetamines (methamphetamine, "bath salts," etc.). This disparity seemingly stems from the fact that much of the violence related to substances of abuse occurs during the process of procuring or distributing the substances (Roth 1994).

Synthetic amphetamines (aka "bath salts") have received a lot of media attention over recent years. They have been linked with acts of extreme violence, including unusual "zombie" attacks (John et al. 2014; Vazirian et al. 2015). Evidence reflects that bath salts are highly addictive. In rat studies, the animals exerted nearly four times the effort to get bath salts than to get methamphetamine (Aarde et al. 2013). However, there are still no conclusive animal studies demonstrating that bath salts are directly linked to aggression. The combination of bath salts being highly addictive and potentially contributing to violent behavior makes them an important substance for clinicians to ask their patients about during clinical assessments.

NEUROCOGNITIVE DISORDERS

Neurocognitive disorder due to traumatic brain injury (TBI)

Aggression is an issue that clinicians frequently encounter when managing patients with acquired brain injuries. In the *DSM-5*, the condition is referred to as neurocognitive disorder due to traumatic brain injury. Various medications have been prescribed over the years attempting to target aggression in this population. Beta blockers present one effective strategy for specifically targeting aggression in patients with acquired brain injuries. The published research, though largely limited to small studies, has been encouraging. One research group published reports involving double-blind, placebo-controlled studies relating the benefits of beta blockers for individuals with acquired brain injuries (Greendyke and Kanter 1986; Greendyke et al. 1986, 1989).

Most of the published studies involving beta blockers for the management of aggression have used propranolol and pindolol. Many of the doses utilized in early studies were at higher doses than are even typically prescribed for antihypertensive effects. At the significantly higher doses, there were frequent reports of adverse events related to drops in heart rate and blood pressure. Recent studies have also found encouraging anti-aggressive effects using lower doses of beta blockers. For instance, Caspi et al. (2001) showed positive outcomes from treatment with pindolol 5 mg three times a day.

Some researchers have specifically chosen to study pindolol due to it displaying intrinsic sympathomimetic activity (ISA), a partial agonism seen particularly at higher doses. The ISA results in less problematic drops in heart rate and blood pressure than might be experienced with propranolol. Pindolol also comes in a generic formulation and can be easily titrated in patients whose vital signs and medical histories make them appropriate candidates.

Reports of other pharmacological treatment options for patients with acquired brain injuries have also appeared in the literature. Mood stabilizers are the other class that has shown significant benefits in this population. Multiple studies have reported the benefits of valproate to curb aggression in patients with acquired brain injuries (Geracioti 1994; Horne and Lindley 1995; Wroblewski et al. 1997). Another article discusses an open trial study showing benefits of carbamazepine to address agitation and aggression in individuals with severe closed-head injuries (Azouvi et al. 1999). One published case report alludes to beneficial effects of lithium in a patient with an acquired brain injury who had not responded to either propranolol or haloperidol (Haas and Cope 1985). However, due to the increased sensitivity to side effects of lithium in patients with acquired brain injuries, lower doses should be prescribed (Hornstein and Seliger 1989).

Major and mild neurocognitive disorder

The group of conditions previously referred to as dementias are now referred to as major and mild neurocognitive disorders in the *DSM-5*. In this section, the term *dementia* will be used because it is used in most of the studies cited in this section.

Aggressive behavior is a common problem encountered in patients with dementia, particularly as symptoms progress. One study reported that aggression had been a problem in over half (57.2%) of the subjects (Hamel et al. 1990). The aggressive behaviors can become a major burden for caregivers, both at home and at long-term facilities. Aggression also significantly increases the likelihood of individuals eventually being institutionalized (O'Donnell et al. 1992; Balestreri et al. 2000). Other psychiatric symptoms such as hallucinations, delusions, and depression can further complicate the management of patients with dementia.

For aggression that seems related to disease-related psychotic symptoms, low-dose antipsychotics should be prescribed. The typical antipsychotic haloperidol has been prescribed to patients with dementia diagnoses for decades. Low doses of haloperidol (1–5 mg daily) have been shown to decrease aggression in individuals with dementia (De Deyn et al. 1999; Allain et al. 2000). Low doses of the atypical antipsychotic risperidone (0.5–2 mg daily) have similarly been shown to decrease aggression in this population (De Deyn et al. 1999; Katz et al. 1999). The published results regarding the use of other antipsychotics for aggression in patients with dementia have largely been equivocal. However, clinicians should consider the FDA's 2005 black box warning regarding cerebrovascular events with atypical antipsychotic use for dementia in elderly patients. In 2016, the FDA approved Nuplazid, an atypical antipsychotic, specifically for the treatment of psychotic symptoms in Parkinson's disease.

Other medications have been suggested to target aggression that is primarily impulsive in patients with dementia. Benzodiazepines have proven effective, given either alone or in combination with antipsychotics (Yudofsky et al. 1990). However, clinicians must remember that elderly individuals are more likely to experience adverse effects such as delirium, paradoxical agitation, and the usual side effects associated with benzodiazepines. Mood stabilizers (lithium, valproate, carbamazepine) and beta blockers have also been reported as beneficial in patients with dementia (Mellow et al. 1993; Kunik et al. 1994; Lott et al. 1995).

There are a number of nonpharmacological approaches to managing patients with dementia and other major and mild neurocognitive disorders. Frequent reorientation is one strategy that helps limit agitation and related aggressive behaviors. A wealth of information about addressing additional factors such as pain, hearing deficits, misperceptions, and other issues are detailed in a document published by the Alzheimer's Society at https://www.alzheimers.org.

PERSONALITY DISORDERS

Individuals diagnosed with personality disorders sometimes display aggressive behaviors related to their personality structure. Antisocial and borderline personality disorders are the two personality disorders most commonly linked to aggression. The link is significant enough that aggressive behavior is a *DSM-5* diagnostic criterion for both antisocial and borderline personality disorder (APA 2013). Substance misuse is also common in both populations and can exacerbate the frequency and severity of aggressive behaviors.

Individuals with personality disorders have been the subjects of various studies involving the pharmacological management of aggression. One double-blind, placebo-controlled study presented the positive effects of using valproate to target impulsive aggression in patients with Cluster B personality disorders. The subjects in the study were prescribed average daily doses of 1400 mg, with average serum valproate levels of 65.5 (Hollander et al. 2003). Another double-blind, placebo-controlled study presented the positive effects of using lithium to target impulsive aggression in incarcerated individuals with "nonpsychotic personality disorders," with serum lithium levels typically under 1 mEq/L (Sheard et al. 1976). Yet another double-blind, placebo-controlled study presented the positive effects of using fluoxetine to target impulsive aggression in patients with personality disorders (Coccaro and Kavoussi 1997).

No pharmacological intervention has shown to be as effective in the overall management of individuals with antisocial personality disorder. These individuals are often prone to display planned, predatory acts of aggression, for which there is not a helpful pharmacological intervention. Contingency management and behavioral strategies are most effective for limiting planned aggression. Impulsive aggression is also a common issue encountered with antisocial personality disorder. Some case studies have reported benefits of addressing impulsive aggression in patients diagnosed with antisocial personality disorder using quetiapine, risperidone, and propranolol (Hirose 2001; Walker et al. 2003; Newman and McDermott 2011). Since the publication of the case report involving quetiapine, abuse of that antipsychotic medication in correctional settings and psychiatric hospitals has become more prevalent and therefore must be considered.

Similar to with antisocial personality disorder, multiple studies have been published about pharmacological interventions targeting the impulsivity and anger that often contribute to individuals with borderline personality disorder perpetrating acts of impulsive aggression. One double-blind, placebo-controlled study reported significantly decreased anger in subjects with borderline personality disorder placed on 15 mg of aripiprazole a day (Nickel et al. 2006). Other articles have reported decreased anger in patients with borderline personality disorder using mood stabilizers including lamotrigine, topiramate, and valproate (Hollander et al. 2001; Nickel et al. 2004; Tritt et al. 2005; Loew et al. 2006; Stoffers et al. 2010). In addition to anger, another common trait in borderline personality disorder is impulsivity that contributes to aggressive behaviors. The same four medications that have shown to impact anger in this population also improved impulsivity (Hollander et al. 2001; Nickel et al. 2004; Tritt et al. 2005; Loew et al. 2006; Nickel et al. 2006; Reich et al. 2009; Stoffers et al. 2010).

Psychotherapy also has an important role in addressing aggressive behaviors in patients with personality disorders, particularly individuals with Cluster B personality disorders or traits. The psychotherapeutic interventions must be tailored to each individual (Gerhart et al. 2013). A full discussion of psychotherapeutic interventions targeting patients diagnosed with personality disorders is beyond the scope of this chapter.

SUMMARY

There is not a single strategy to manage aggression using pharmacological or nonpharmacological interventions. Much of the existing evidence, particularly regarding pharmacological interventions, derives from case reports and small studies. Larger, controlled studies would improve our understanding of the effectiveness of the interventions. There remains much to be learned about the management of violence and aggression through future research.

SUMMARY KEY POINTS

- There is not currently an FDA-approved pharmacological treatment of aggression.
- Individuals diagnosed with conditions associated with aggression may benefit from a combined pharmacological and nonpharmacological treatment plan.
- Based on the existing literature, there does not appear to be a clearly proven link between SSRIs and violent behavior.
- Reports have demonstrated an association between benzodiazepines prescribed for PTSD and related aggression.
- Alcohol has a very well-established association with violence.
- Many individuals with Cluster B personality disorders behave aggressively.

REFERENCES

Aarde SM, PK Huang, KM Creehan, TJ Dickerson, and MA Taffe. 2013. The novel recreational drug 3,4-methylenedioxypyrovalerone (MDPV) is a potent psychomotor stimulant: Self-administration and locomotor activity in rats. *Neuropharmacology* 71:130–140.

Allain H, PHJ Dautzenberg, K Maurer, S Schuck, D Bonhomme, and D Gerard. 2000. Double blind study of tiapride versus haloperidol and placebo in agitation and aggressiveness in elderly patients with cognitive impairment. *Psychopharmacology* 148(4):361–366.

Aman MG, NN Singh, AW Stewart, and CJ Field. 1985. The aberrant behavior checklist: A behavior rating scale for the assessment of treatment effects. *American Journal of Mental Deficiency* 89:485–491.

American Psychiatric Association (APA). 2013. *Diagnostic and Statistical Manual of Mental Disorders*, 5th edition. Arlington, VA: APA.

American Psychiatric Association (APA). 2002. *Practice Guidelines for the Treatment of Patients with Bipolar Disorder* [Electronic Version]. http://psychiatryonline.org/pb/assets/raw/sitewide/practice_guidelines/guidelines/bipolar.pdf, accessed July 21, 2015.

American Psychiatric Association (APA). 2010. *Practice Guidelines for the Treatment of Patients with Major Depressive Disorder* [Electronic Version]. http://psychiatryonline.org/pb/assets/raw/sitewide/practice_guidelines/guidelines/mdd.pdf accessed July 21, 2015.

Amore M, M Bertelli, D Villani, S Tamborini, and M Rossi. 2011. Olanzapine vs. risperidone in treating aggressive behaviors in adults with intellectual disability: A single blind study. *Journal of Intellectual Disability Research* 55(2):210–218.

Asnis GM, ML Kaplan, G Hundorfean, and W Saeed. 1997. Violence and homicidal behaviors in psychiatric disorders. *Psychiatric Clinics of North America* 20(2):405–425.

Azouvi P, C Jokic, N Attal, P Denys, S Markabi, and B Bussel. 1999. Carbamazepine in agitation and aggressive behavior following severe closed-head injury: Results of an open trial. *Brain Injury* 13:797–804.

Balestreri L, A Grossberg, and GT Grossberg. 2000. Behavioral and psychological symptoms of dementia as a risk factor for nursing home placement. *International Psychogeriatrics* 12(Supplement):59–62.

Barber CW, D Azrael, D Hemenway, LM Olson, C Nie, J Schaechter, and S Walsh. 2008. Suicides and suicide attempts following homicide. Victim-suspect relationship, weapon type, and presence of antidepressants. *Homicide Studies* 12:285–297.

Bender S, T Linka, J Wolstein, S Gehendges, HJ Paulus, U Schall, and M Gastpar. 2004. Safety and efficacy of combined clozapine-lithium pharmacotherapy. *International Journal of Neuropsychopharmacology* 7(1):59–63.

Bossarte RM, TR Simon, and L Barker. 2006. Homicide-suicide: Characteristics of homicide followed by suicide incidents in multiple states, 2003–2004. *Injury Prevention* 12(Supplement):33–38.

Bouvy PF and M Liem. 2012. Antidepressants and lethal violence in the Netherlands 1994–2008. *Psychopharmacology* 222(3):499–506.

Buckley LA, N Maayan, K Soares-Weiser, and CE Adams. 2015. Supportive therapy for schizophrenia. *Cochrane Database of Systematic Reviews* Issue 4, Art. No.: CD004716. doi:10.1002/14651858.CD004716.pub4

Cameron MP, W Cochrane, C Gordon, and M Livingston. 2015. Alcohol outlet density and violence: A geographically weighted regression approach. *Drug and Alcohol Review* 35:280–288. Epub.

Caspi N, I Modai, P Barak, A Waisbourd, H Zbarsky, H Hirschmann, and M Ritsner. 2001. Pindolol augmentation in aggressive schizophrenic patients: A double-blind crossover randomized study. *International Clinical Psychopharmacology* 16(2):111–115.

Chiles JA, P Davidson, and D McBride. 1994. Effects of clozapine on use of seclusion and restraint at a state hospital. *Hospital and Community Psychiatry* 45:269–271.

Citrome L, J Volavka, P Czobor, B Sheitman, JP Lindenmayer, J McEvoy, TB Cooper, M Chakos, and JA Lieberman. 2001. Effects of clozapine, olanzapine, risperidone, and haloperidol on hostility among patients with schizophrenia. *Psychiatric Services* 52:1510–1514.

Coccaro EF. 2012. Intermittent explosive disorder as a disorder of impulsive aggression for DSM-5. *American Journal of Psychiatry* 169(6):577–588.

Coccaro EF, and RJ Kavoussi. 1997. Fluoxetine and impulsive aggressive behavior in personality-disordered subjects. *Archives of General Psychiatry* 54:1081–1088.

Coccaro EF, RJ Lee, and RJ Kavoussi. 2009. A double-blind, randomized, placebo-controlled trial of fluoxetine in patients with intermittent explosive disorder. *Journal of Clinical Psychiatry* 70(5):653–662.

Collins PJ, EP Larkin, and APW Shubsachs. 1991. Lithium carbonate in chronic schizophrenia—A brief trial of lithium carbonate added to neuroleptics for treatment of resistant schizophrenic patients. *Acta Psychiatrica Scandinavica* 84:150–154.

Craft M, IA Ismail, D Krishnamurti, J Mathews, A Regan, RV Seth, and PM North. 1987. Lithium in the treatment of aggression in mentally handicapped patients. A double-blind trial. *British Journal of Psychiatry* 150:685–689.

De Deyn PP, K Rabheru, A Rasmussen, JP Bocksberger, PL Dautzenberg, S Eriksson, and BA Lawlor. 1999. A randomized trial of risperidone, placebo, and haloperidol for behavioral symptoms of dementia. *Neurology* 53(5):946–955.

Dose M, R Hellweg, A Yassouridis, M Theison, and HM Emrich. 1998. Combined treatment of schizophrenic psychoses with haloperidol and valproate. *Pharmacopsychiatry* 31:122–125.

Eliason S. 2009. Murder-suicide: A review of the recent literature. *Journal of the American Academy of Psychiatry and the Law* 37(3):371–376.

Friedman SH, J Cavney, and PJ Resnick. 2012. Child murder by parents and evolutionary psychology. *Psychiatric Clinics of North America* 35:781–795.

Friedman SH, SM Horwitz, and PJ Resnick. 2005. Child murder by mothers: A critical analysis of the current state of knowledge and a research agenda. *American Journal of Psychiatry* 162(9):1578–1587.

Gavolski TE and EB Blanchard. 2002. The effectiveness of a brief psychological intervention on court-referred and self-referred aggressive drivers. *Behaviour Research and Therapy* 40(12):1385–1402.

Geracioti TD. 1994. Valproic acid treatment of episodic explosiveness related to brain injury. *Journal of Clinical Psychiatry* 55:416–417.

Gerhart JI, GF Ronan, E Russ, and B Seymour. 2013. The moderating effects of cluster B personality traits on violence reduction training: A mixed-model analysis. *Journal of Interpersonal Violence* 28(1):45–61.

Goncalves R, AL Pedrozo, ES Coutinho, I Figuera, and P Ventura. 2012. Efficacy of virtual reality exposure therapy in the treatment of PTSD: A systematic review. *PLoS One* 7(12):e48469.

Greendyke RM, JP Berkner, JC Webster, and A Gulya. 1989. Treatment of behavioral problems with pindolol. *Psychosomatics* 30(2):161–165.

Greendyke RM and DR Kanter. 1986. Therapeutic effects of pindolol on behavioral disturbances associated with organic brain disease: A double-blind study. *Journal of Clinical Psychiatry* 47:423–426.

Greendyke RM, DR Kanter, DB Schuster, S Verstreate, and J Wootton. 1986. Propranolol treatment of assaultive patients with organic brain disease. *Journal of Nervous and Mental Disease* 174:290–294.

Guina J, SR Rossetter, BJ DeRhodes, RW Nahhas, and RS Welton. 2015. Benzodiazepines for PTSD: A systematic review and meta-analysis. *Journal of Psychiatric Practice* 21(4):281–303.

Haas JF and DN Cope. 1985. Neuropharmacologic management of behavior sequelae in head injury: A case report. *Archives of Physical Medicine and Rehabilitation* 66:472–474.

Haddock G, C Barrowclough, JJ Shaw, G Dunn, RW Novaco, and N Tarrier. 2009. Cognitive-behavioural therapy v. social activity therapy for people with psychosis and a history of violence: Randomised controlled trial. *British Journal of Psychiatry* 194(2):152–157.

Hamel M, DP Gold, D Andres, M Reis, D Dastoor, H Grauer, and H Bergman. 1990. Predictors and consequences of aggressive behavior by community-based dementia patients. *Gerontologist* 30(2):206–211.

Harpaz-Rotem I, RA Rosenheck, S Mohamed, and RA Desai. 2008. Pharmacologic treatment of posttraumatic stress disorder among privately insured Americans. *Psychiatric Services* 58:1184–1190.

Hassiotis A, A Canagasabey, D Robotham, L Marston, R Romeo, and M King. 2011. Applied behaviour analysis and standard treatment in intellectual disability: 2-year outcomes. *British Journal of Psychiatry* 198(6):490–491.

Hassiotis A, D Robotham, and A Canagasabey. 2012. Brief report: Impact of applied behaviour analysis (ABA) on carer burden and community participation in challenging behavior: Results from a randomised controlled trial. *Journal of Intellectual Disability Research* 56(3):285–290.

Hassler F and O Reis. 2010. Pharmacotherapy of disruptive behavior in mentally retarded subjects: A review of the current literature. *Developmental Disability Research Reviews* 16(3):265–272.

Healy D, A Herxheimer, and DB Menkes. 2006. Antidepressants and violence: Problems at the interface of medicine and law. *PLOS Medicine* 3(9):1478–1487.

Hirose S. 2001. Effective treatment of aggression and impulsivity in antisocial personality disorder with risperidone. *Psychiatry and Clinical Neurosciences* 55(2):161–162.

Hollander E, A Allen, RP Lopez, CA Bienstock, R Grossman, LJ Siever, L Merkatz, and DJ Stein. 2001. A preliminary double-blind, placebo-controlled trial of divalproex sodium in borderline personality disorder. *Journal of Clinical Psychiatry* 62(3):199–203.

Hollander E, KA Tracy, AC Swann, EF Coccaro, SL McElroy, P Wozniak, KW Sommerville, and CB Nemeroff. 2003. Divalproex in the treatment of impulsive aggression: Efficacy in cluster B personality disorders. *Neuropsychopharmacology* 28(6):1186–1197.

Horne M and SE Lindley. 1995. Divalproex sodium in the treatment of aggressive behavior and dysphoria in patients with organic brain syndromes. *Journal of Clinical Psychiatry* 56:430–431.

Hornstein A and G Seliger. 1989. Cognitive side effects of lithium in closed head injury. *Journal of Neuropsychiatry and Clinical Neurosciences* 1:446–447.

John ME, C Thomas-Rozea, and D Hahn. 2014. Bath salts abuse leading to new onset psychosis and potential for violence. *Clinical Schizophrenia and Related Psychoses* 20:1–14.

Johns A. 1997. Substance misuse: A primary risk and a major problem of comorbidity. *International Review of Psychiatry* 9:233–241.

Jones RM, J Arlidge, R Gillham, S Reagu, M van den Bree, and PJ Taylor. 2011. Efficacy of mood stabilisers in the treatment of impulsive or repetitive aggression: Systematic review and meta-analysis. *British Journal of Psychiatry* 198(2):93–98.

Kant R, R Chalansari, KN Chengappa, and MF Dieringer. 2004. The off-label use of clozapine in adolescents with bipolar disorder, intermittent explosive disorder, or posttraumatic stress disorder. *Journal of Child and Adolescent Psychopharmacology* 14(1):57–63.

Katz IR, DV Jeste, JE Mintzer, C Clyde, J Napolitano, and M Brecher. 1999. Comparison of risperidone and placebo for psychosis and behavioral disturbances associated with dementia: A randomized, double-blind trial. *Journal of Clinical Psychiatry* 60(2):107–115.

Kosten TR, A Fontana, MJ Sernyak, and R Rosenheck. 2000. Benzodiazepine use in posttraumatic stress disorder among veterans with substance abuse. *Journal of Nervous and Mental Disease* 188:454–459.

Kunik ME, SC Yudofsky, JM Silver, and RE Hales. 1994. Pharmacologic approach to management of agitation associated with dementia. *Journal of Clinical Psychiatry* 55:S13–S17.

Langevin R, D Paitich, B Orchard, L Handy, and A Russon. 1982. The role of alcohol, drugs, suicide, attempts and situational strains in homicide committed by offenders seen for psychiatric assessment. *Acta Psychiatrica Scandinavica* 66:229–242.

Loew TH, MK Nickel, M Muehlbacher et al. 2006. Topiramate treatment for women with borderline personality disorder: A double-blind, placebo-controlled study. *Journal of Clinical Psychopharmacology* 26(1):61–66.

Lott AD, SL McElroy, and MA Keys. 1995. Valproate in the treatment of behavioral agitation in elderly patients with dementia. *Journal of Neuropsychiatry and Clinical Neurosciences* 7:314–319.

Lund BC, NC Bernardy, M Vaughan-Sarrazin, B Alexander, and MJ Friedman. 2013. Patient and facility characteristics associated with benzodiazepine prescribing for veterans with PTSD. *Psychiatric Services* 64(2):149–155.

Marzuk P, K Tardiff, and CS Hirsch. 1992. The epidemiology of murder-suicide. *Journal of the American Medical Association* 267:3179–3183.

Mason SE. 2002. Prozac and crime: Who is the victim? *American Journal of Orthopsychiatry* 72:445–455.

Mattes JA. 1992. Valproic acid for nonaffective aggression in the mentally retarded. *Journal of Nervous and Mental Disease* 180:601–602.

McEvoy JP, PL Scheifler, and A Frances. 1999. Treatment of schizophrenia 1999. The expert consensus guideline series. *Journal of Clinical Psychiatry* 60:S3–S80.

McFall M, A Fontana, M Raskind, and R Rosenheck. 1999. Analysis of violent behavior in Vietnam combat veteran psychiatric inpatients with posttraumatic stress disorder. *Journal of Traumatic Stress* 12:501–517.

Mellow AM, C Solano-Lopez, and S Davis. 1993. Sodium valproate in the treatment of behavioral disturbance in dementia. *Journal of Geriatric Psychiatry and Neurology* 6:205–209.

Miles SR, DS Menefee, J Wanner, A Teten Tharp, and TA Kent. 2015. The relationship between emotional dysregulation and impulsive aggression in veterans with posttraumatic stress disorder symptoms. *Journal of Interpersonal Violence* 31:1795–1816. Epub.

Moore TJ, J Glenmullen, and CD Furberg. 2010. Prescription drugs associated with reports of violence towards others. *PLOS Medicine* 5(12):1–5.

Murdoch D, RO Pihl, and D Ross. 1990. Alcohol and crimes of violence: Present issues. *International Journal of Addictions* 25:1065–1081.

Newman WJ and BE McDermott. 2011. Beta blockers for violence prophylaxis—Case reports. *Journal of Clinical Psychopharmacology* 31(6):785–787.

Nickel MK, M Mühlbacher, C Nickel et al. 2006. Aripiprazole in the treatment of patients with borderline personality disorder: A double-blind, placebo-controlled study. *American Journal of Psychiatry* 163:833–848.

Nickel MK, C Nickel, FO Mitterlehner, K Tritt, C Lahmann, PK Leiberich, WK Rother, and TH Loew. 2004. Topiramate treatment of aggression in female borderline personality disorder patients: A double-blind, placebo-controlled study. *Journal of Clinical Psychiatry* 65(11):1515–1519.

O'Donnell BF, DA Drachman, HJ Barnes, KE Peterson, JM Swearer, and RA Lew. 1992. Incontinence and troublesome behaviors predict institutionalization in dementia. *Journal of Geriatric Psychiatry and Neurology* 5:45–52.

Okuma T, I Yamashita, R Takahashi, H Itoh, S Otsuki, S Watanabe, K Sarai, H Hazama, and K Inanaga. 1989. A double-blind study of adjunctive carbamazepine versus placebo on excited states of schizophrenic and schizoaffective disorders. *Acta Psychiatrica Scandinavica* 80:250–259.

Pavlovic ZM. 2008. Augmentation of clozapine's antiaggressive properties with lamotrigine in a patient with chronic disorganized schizophrenia. *Journal of Clinical Psychopharmacology* 28(1):119–120.

Perry A, N Tarrier, R Morriss, E McCarthy, and K Limb. 1999. Randomised controlled trial of efficacy of teaching patients with bipolar disorder to identify early symptoms of relapse and obtain treatment. *British Medical Journal* 318:149–153.

Quanbeck CD, DC Stone, CL Scott, BE McDermott, LL Altshuler, and MA Frye. 2004. Clinical and legal correlates of inmates with bipolar disorder at time of criminal arrest. *Journal of Clinical Psychiatry* 65:198–203.

Rathod S, P Phiri, and D Kingdon. 2010. Cognitive behavioral therapy for schizophrenia. *Psychiatric Clinics of North America* 33(3):527–536.

Razali S, RM Salleh, B Yahya, and SH Ahmad. 2015. Maternal filicide among women admitted to forensic psychiatric institutions in Malaysia: Case series. *East Asian Archives of Psychiatry* 25(2):79–87.

Reich DB, MC Zanarini, and KA Bieri. 2009. A preliminary study of lamotrigine in the treatment of affective instability in borderline personality disorder. *International Clinical Psychopharmacology* 24(5):270–275.

Rhodes AM and LS Segre. 2013. Perinatal depression: A review of U.S. legislation and law. *Archives of Women's Mental Health* 16(4):259–270.

Roth JA. 1994. Psychoactive substances and violence [Electronic Version]. http://www.ncjrs.gov/txtfiles/psycho.txt, accessed July 29, 2015.

Ruedrich SL, L Grush, and J Wilson. 1990. Beta adrenergic blocking medications for aggressive or self-injurious mentally retarded persons. *American Journal of Mental Retardation* 95(1):110–119.

Schoenfeld FB, CR Marmar, and TC Neylan. 2004. Current concepts in pharmacotherapy for posttraumatic stress disorder. *Psychiatric Services* 55:519–531.

Sheard MH, JL Marini, CI Bridges, and E Wagner. 1976. The effect of lithium on impulsive aggressive behavior in man. *American Journal of Psychiatry* 133:1409–1413.

Shields LB, CM Rolf, ME Goolsby, and JC Hunsaker. 2015. Filicide-suicide: Case series and review of the literature. *American Journal of Forensic Medicine and Pathology* 36:210–215. Epub.

Shin HJ, CS Rosen, MA Greenbaum, and S Jain. 2012. Longitudinal correlates of aggressive behavior in help-seeking U.S. veterans with PTSD. *Journal of Traumatic Stress* 25:649–656.

Spreat S, D Behar, B Reneski, and P Miazzo. 1989. Lithium carbonate for aggression in mentally retarded persons. *Comprehensive Psychiatry* 30:505–511.

Steadman HJ, EP Mulvey, J Monahan, PC Robbins, PS Appelbaum, T Grisso, LH Roth, and E Silver. 1998. Violence by people discharged from acute psychiatric inpatient facilities and by others in the same neighborhoods. *Archives of General Psychiatry* 55:393–401.

Stoffers J, BA Völlm, G Rücker, A Timmer, N Huband, and K Lieb. 2010. Pharmacological interventions for borderline personality disorder. *Cochrane Database of Systematic Reviews* Issue 6, Art. No.: CD005653. doi:10.1002/14651858.CD005653.pub2

Swanson J, R Borum, M Swartz, and J Monahan. 1996. Psychotic symptoms and disorders and the risk of violent behavior in the community. *Criminal Behavior and Mental Health* 6:317–338.

Swanson JW, CE Holzer, VK Ganju, and RT Jono. 1990. Violence and psychiatric disorder in the community: Evidence from the Epidemiologic Catchment Area surveys. *Hospital and Community Psychiatry* 41(7):761–770.

Tardiff K, PM Marzuk, and AC Leon. 2002. Role of antidepressants in murder and suicide. *American Journal of Psychiatry* 159:1248–1249.

Travis RW and P Sturmey. 2013. Using behavioural skills training to treat aggression in adults with mild intellectual disability in a forensic setting. *Journal of Applied Research in Intellectual Disabilities* 26(5):481–488.

Tritt K, C Nickel, C Lahmann, PK Leiberich, WK Rother, TH Loew, and MK Nickel. 2005. Lamotrigine treatment of aggression in female borderline patients: A randomized, double-blind, placebo-controlled study. *Journal of Clinical Psychopharmacology* 9(3):287–291.

Tyrer SP, A Walsh, DE Edwards, TP Berney, and DA Stephens. 1984. Factors associated with a good response to lithium in aggressive mentally handicapped subjects. *Progress in Neuro-psychopharmacology and Biological Psychiatry* 8:751–755.

Ursano RJ, C Bell, S Eth et al. 2004. Practice guideline for the treatment of patients with acute stress disorder and posttraumatic stress disorder. *American Journal of Psychiatry* 161(Supplement):3–31.

Vazirian M, JM Jerry, J James, and RM Dale. 2015. Bath salts in the emergency department: A survey of emergency clinicians' experience with bath salts-intoxicated patients. *Journal of Addiction Medicine* 9(2):94–98.

Walker C, J Thomas, and TS Allen. 2003. Treating impulsivity, irritability, and aggression of antisocial personality disorder with quetiapine. *International Journal of Offender Therapy and Comparative Criminology* 47(5):556–567.

Wilson JP and SD Zigelbaum. 1983. The Vietnam veteran on trial: The relation of posttraumatic stress disorder to criminal behavior. *Behavioral Sciences and the Law* 1:69–83.

Wilson WH. 1993. Addition of lithium to haloperidol in non-affective, antipsychotic non-responsive schizophrenia: A double-blind, placebo-controlled, parallel-design clinical trial. *Psychopharmacology* 111:359–366.

Wroblewski BA, AB Joseph, J Kupfer, and K Kalliel. 1997. Effectiveness of valproic acid on destructive and aggressive behaviors in patients with acquired brain injury. *Brain Injury* 11:37–47.

Yudofsky SC, JM Silver, and RE Hales. 1990. Pharmacologic management of aggression in the elderly. *Journal of Clinical Psychiatry* 51:S22–S28.

62

Mass murder

JAMES L. KNOLL, WILLIAM NEWMAN, AND BRIAN HOLOYDA

INTRODUCTION

This chapter focuses on mass murder, a topic that has received considerable media attention of late. Mass murder is typically defined in the literature as a single event involving four or more victims at one location (Burgess 2006). Though rare, mass murder is catastrophic and impacts affected communities for years.

MASS MURDER OVERVIEW

Despite increased media attention over recent years, mass murder is not a new phenomenon. News media have suggested that mass killings became "a part of American life" after Charles Whitman climbed onto a tower at the University of Texas and killed 16 total people, including his wife and mother earlier that day in their homes (Mass public shootings 2007).

There are several challenges that make systematically researching mass murder difficult. For one, the base rate of mass murder is relatively low. According to Schenk and colleagues (2014), of the 9,776,094 emergency medical services (EMS) responses in the 2010 National EMS Database, 14,504 were categorized as mass casualty incidents. That amounts to 0.15% of the total responses. Because some responses involved multiple calls related to the same incidents, the 14,504 total calls involved 9913 unique incidents.

Furthermore, few perpetrators survive to explain their rationale. Perpetrators of mass murder generally differ from serial murderers, who kill a series of individual victims over an extended period. Unlike serial murderers, who can be very challenging for law enforcement to apprehend, mass murderers are more likely to be apprehended during or soon after commission of the crime (Burgess 2006). Many go into the situation expecting to be apprehended, be killed by law enforcement, or commit suicide (Fox and Levin 2003). Those who do survive may not be forthcoming about the thoughts that motivated their behavior, potentially driven by the desire to mitigate criminal responsibility (Declercq and Audenaert 2011).

Some data have been compiled about recent incidents involving "active shooters." The Federal Bureau of Investigation (FBI) published findings in 2014 designed to help prepare government agencies for active shooter incidents (Blair and Schweit 2014). To prepare the document, the authors reviewed all active shooter incidents in the United States between the years 2000 and 2013. They reviewed 160 total incidents, in which 486 individuals were killed and another 557 were wounded. These figures did not include the shooters. Of the 160 incidents, 64 (40%) fell within the federal definition of "mass killing"—defined as "three or more" victims killed. The FBI's findings showed that all but two incidents involved a single shooter. In 64 of the 160 incidents (40%), the shooters committed suicide either at the scene or soon thereafter. The majority of the incidents occurred at sites the FBI classified as areas of commerce (45.6%), educational environments (24.4%), or government properties (10.0%), accounting for a total of 80% (Blair and Schweit 2014).

Though the news media influenced the perception that the incidence of mass murder steadily increased from the 1960s to the 2000s, some reports suggested that this perception was based on distortion. Duwe (2005) evaluated FBI reports along with newspaper articles, network television stories, and magazine articles to suggest that the media's assertion at the time that mass murder was steadily on the rise was based on distortion. New data, however, suggest that there may indeed be a more recent trend of increased incidents. Although only 40% of the incidents in the 2014 FBI study described above met the federal definition of "mass killing," the data reflect a possible trend of increased incidents involving active shooters during the period studied. There were an average of 6.4 incidents per year in the initial 7 years studied and an average of 16.4 incidents per year in the next 7 years studied (Figure 62.1). It is unclear whether the same trend exists in incidents that would be strictly defined as mass murder.

A study of mass and school shootings occurring in the United States from 1998 to 2013 focused on whether temporal patterns indicated evidence of a contagion effect in

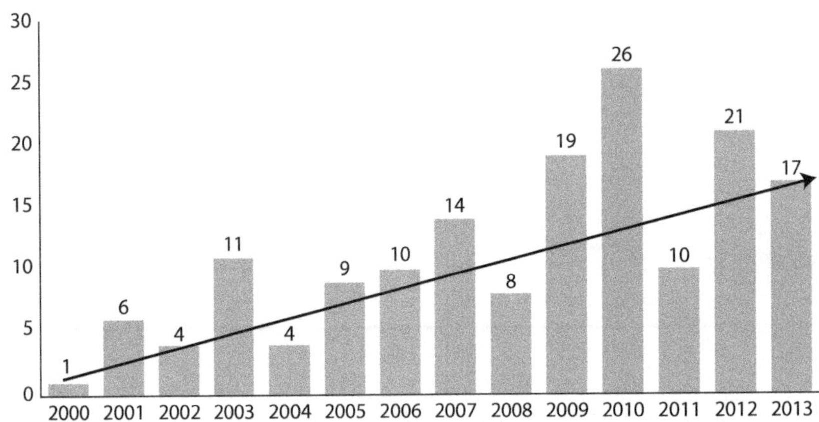

Figure 62.1 A study of 160 active shooter incidents in the United States between 2000 and 2013: Incidents annually. (From Blair JP and KW Schweit. 2014. *A Study of Active Shooter Incidents, 2000–2013*. Washington, DC: Texas State University and Federal Bureau of Investigation, U.S. Department of Justice.)

their immediate wake (Towers et al. 2015). The study suggested that mass shootings are incented by similar events in the immediate past, with a pattern of temporary increase in probability lasting 13 days. Mass shootings were found to occur, on average, approximately every 2 weeks, while school shootings occurred on average monthly. The authors suggested that certain individuals with inner mental turmoil might be inspired to act on previously suppressed urges by media exposure to mass shootings. No significant association was found between the rate of mass shootings and state prevalence of mental illness.

CLASSIFYING MASS MURDER

There is no exact profile of individuals who commit mass murder. However, studies looking into groups of mass murderers have produced a collection of commonalities. One detailed case study of five mass murderers found common traits and historical factors including the following: childhood bullying or isolation; turning into loners who felt socially isolated; demonstrating obsessional or rigid traits; being suspicious and holding grudges; externalization; narcissistic and grandiose personality traits; resentment; view of others being uncaring and rejecting; and fantasizing about violent revenge (Mullen 2004). Analysis of several individual mass murderers showed a common desire to leave a final message, typically through writings, audio recordings, photographs, and/or video recordings (Hempel et al. 1999; Knoll 2010). The contributing causes of mass murder events appear to involve a complex interplay of mental health issues, personality traits, and historical life events. Table 62.1 shows a biopsychosocial formulation of factors that may contribute to mass murder events.

There is not currently an established system for classifying mass murder. The literature contains vague descriptions of groups referred to as school shooters, disgruntled employees, pseudocommandos, and family annihilators. However, each group of mass murderer has characteristics that have been reported without tying them together into a usable system.

There is a classification system for evaluating the phenomenon of homicide–suicide (H-S), an incident involving one or more homicides followed by suicide, typically within a 24-hour period (Felthous and Hempel 1995; Bossarte et al. 2006). H-S events are typically well planned and differ from other forms of homicide. Fortunately, like mass murder, H-S is a rare event (Coid 1983; Bossarte et al. 2006).

One group proposed a classification system for H-S involving dual descriptions of the perpetrator's relationship to the victim(s) and the perpetrator's perceived

Table 62.1 Mass murder—contributing factors

Biological
- Psychosis
- Depression
- Brain pathology
- Personality disorders

Psychological
- Problems with self-esteem
- Persecutory/paranoid outlook
- Entitlement
- Antisocial traits
- Obsessional or rigid traits
- Narcissistic, grandiose traits
- Externalization—unable to take responsibility
- World seen as rejecting, uncaring
- Resentful with rumination on past humiliations
- Fantasize about violent revenge

Social
- Social alienation
- Being bullied
- Life stressors—marital, financial
- Access to and familiarity with firearms

Source: From Knoll J. 2012. *Psychiatric Clinics of North America* 35:757–780. With permission.

motive (Marzuk et al. 1992). Of the five primary H-S types described by this group, estranged intimate partners (consortial–possessive type) account for 50%–75% of incidents. The other four types are consortial–physically ailing, filicide–suicide, familicide–suicide, and adversarial homicide (extrafamilial)–suicide (Marzuk et al. 1992).

The H-S classification system provides a useful model for classifying mass murder incidents because there is likely a similar thought process with the two events. The perpetrator typically goes into the attack expecting to die, either committing suicide or forcing the police to kill him or her (Mohandie and Meloy 2000). Based on these similarities to H-S, Knoll (2012) suggested a classification system for mass murder based on similar dual descriptions of the perpetrator's relationship to the victims (family, school, workplace, specific community, pseudocommunity, indiscriminate, etc.) and perceived motive (depressed, resentful, psychotic, etc.). The following are case examples involving common combinations.

Familial: Depressed type

Between December 22 and December 28, 1987, Ronald Gene Simmons orchestrated the single largest familial massacre in U.S. history. Simmons experienced financial, legal, and occupational problems in the years leading to the massacre. In 1981, he fled New Mexico while being investigated for allegedly fathering a child with his 17-year-old daughter. He later quit a job as an accounts receivable clerk after reports surfaced of inappropriate sexual advances. Months before the killing spree, Simmons instructed family members to dig a hole in the yard for a family outhouse. He subsequently placed his victims' bodies in the shallow pit.

Simmons began by killing his wife, granddaughter, and five of his children on December 22. Over nearly a week, he proceeded to kill 14 total family members and two other individuals. Simmons was sentenced to death in 1989 and executed in 1990, the quickest sentence-to-execution period since the death penalty was reinstated in 1976 (Swanlund 2015). Although Simmons never discussed his motivation for the murders, evidence suggests that he was angry with several family members. In a letter to his daughter, who he had allegedly impregnated, Simmons wrote, "You have destroyed me, and you have destroyed my trust in you … I will see you in Hell." He wrote the letter after she reported him for molesting her. Simmons' wife also tried to leave him repeatedly and was openly hostile toward him (Clark Prosecutor n.d.). The Simmons case shows a typical example of a frustrated, angry individual channeling his misery toward family members. Although the number of victims in this case was unusually large for the Familial–Depressed type, the motivation seems typical.

School: Resentful type

On December 14, 2012, 20-year-old Adam Lanza shot his 52-year-old mother Nancy Lanza in the head with a rifle as she lay in bed in their Newtown, Connecticut, home. He then drove to Sandy Hook Elementary where, armed with his mother's rifle, he blasted his way through the locked front entrance doors. He then initiated a rampage that took the lives of 20 children and six staff (Vigdor 2013). Lanza stalked the school's classrooms, shooting teachers and students as they hid unarmed. He shot all but two of his victims multiple times. Though accounts differ slightly, teachers and students alike reported that Lanza called to and cursed at his victims while pursuing them. The incident ended after only 5 minutes, with Lanza shooting himself in the head (Connecticut State Police 2013). Lanza completed the deadliest mass shooting at a grade school or high school and the second deadliest mass shooting by a single person in U.S. history, second only to Seung-Hui Cho at Virginia Tech in 2007 (Effron 2012).

Lanza's history sheds little light on the motivation behind the attack. He attended Sandy Hook Elementary briefly, but later left to be homeschooled. After getting his GED, he attended college for 2 years. According to his father, Lanza was diagnosed with a sensory-integration disorder during elementary school and later diagnosed with Asperger disorder and obsessive–compulsive disorder. He was briefly treated at Yale with behavioral therapy and citalopram (Schwarz and Ramilo 2014). Some items identified in Lanza's room suggested that he had an interest in mass murder, such as newspaper clippings about the attacks at Columbine High School and Northern Illinois University (Curry 2013). Family members recalled odd behaviors such as cutting off communication with his brother and father for 2 years before the shooting and only communicating with his mother by e-mail, despite living in the same home. A document detailing Lanza's perspective on women's inherent selfishness was identified after his death (Solomon 2014). However, investigators identified no documents specifically alluding to the attack at the school. Although most school shooters are actively enrolled in the school they target, this case stood out because it horrified the nation and brought school shootings and gun control to the forefront of the news.

Workplace: Resentful type

On November 5, 2009, Army psychiatrist Nidal Hasan staged the largest mass murder at a domestic U.S. military base in history. He opened fire with a semiautomatic weapon at the Fort Hood Soldier Readiness Processing Center, where soldiers were being assessed for deployment. Hasan arrived at the scene dressed in Islamic garb, bowed his head in prayer, and then screamed "Allahu Akbar [God is the greatest]" before firing on unarmed soldiers. Hasan represented himself at trial. During his opening statements, he openly confessed to committing the shootings and explained his jihadi motives. Reports surfaced that Hasan had been presenting as increasingly radical since 2005 and felt ambivalent about remaining in the U.S. Army due to the military killing Muslims (Weiss 2013). Hasan cited religious motivations for the shootings. Hasan referred to himself as SoA, understood to represent shorthand for "Soldier of Allah." He wrote that there were irreconcilable differences between the belief systems of Islam and American democracy, and even renounced his U.S. citizenship (Herridge and Browne 2013). The Department of Defense officially classified the incident as "workplace violence" and did not mention terrorism in the report (Weiss 2013). Hasan was sentenced to death in August 2013 by a military court (Kenber 2013). Although this incident could also be classified as an act of terrorism, it is perhaps the most highly publicized workplace shooting in recent memory.

Specific community: Resentful type

On June 17, 2015, Dylann Roof opened fire at the Emanuel African Methodist Episcopal Church in Charleston, South Carolina. Roof spent about an hour at the church, participating in a prayer meeting, before starting the attack. He killed a total of nine victims. According to witnesses at the scene, Roof stood up and said he was there "to shoot black people" and made racially inflammatory statements to victims as he shot them. A friend of Roof indicated that he had alluded to a plan to "do something crazy" in hope of initiating a race riot (Sanchez and Payne 2015). Roof described himself as "awakened" by the situation involving Trayvon Martin, the African American teen who was shot and killed by George Zimmerman in 2012. On his personal website, Roof expressed frustration with the number of "black on white" crimes that he felt were not covered in the same detail by the media (The Last Rhodesian 2015). Roof posted a manifesto on his website (http://www.documentcloud.org/documents/2108059-lastrhodesian-manifesto.html) that summarized his racist stance and plan for an impending attack, as follows:

> I have no choice. I am not in the position to, alone, go into the ghetto and fight. I chose Charleston because it is [the] most historic city in my state, and at one time had the highest ratio of blacks to Whites [sic] in the country. We have no skinheads, no real KKK, no one doing anything but talking on the internet [sic]. Well someone has to have the bravery to take it to the real world, and I guess that has to be me.

Although the targets can differ, the unifying principle with the Specific Community–Resentful type is a group or groups that the perpetrator targets. In some cases, the act is racially based. In other cases, such as George Sodini, mass murderers of this type have targeted women based on the belief that they had been inappropriately rejected throughout their lifetime (Rubinkam 2009).

Pseudocommunity: Psychotic type

On April 3, 2009, Vietnamese immigrant Jiverly Wong burst into the Binghamton, New York, American Civic Association carrying two guns and wearing body armor. Wong had been taking English classes at the Civic Association. After blocking off the back exit using his father's car, Wong proceeded to kill 13 people before shooting himself. Although Wong's motivations initially seemed unclear, local police discovered that the incident was not entirely surprising to individuals close to him, including his father (Chief J. Zikuski, personal communication, April 4, 2009).

Soon after moving with his family from Vietnam to New York, Wong informed his father that somebody was trying to kill him. He stated, "They're in front of me and trying to capture me." Wong also complained of experiencing hallucinations involving people trying to harm him. He voluntarily went with his father to a hospital for treatment, but was released without being given treatment or a follow-up appointment. Wong's father later wondered whether their family's limited mastery of the English language contributed to his son not being treated (Huynh 2009).

After approximately 15 years in California, Wong returned to live with his parents in New York, at age 39. His family continued to notice concerning behaviors. For instance, Wong consistently wore long-sleeved shirts and pants, even during the heat of summer. He also behaved aggressively toward family members. He slapped his younger sister in the face and raised his voice toward his father over a minor household issue. Wong's father reported that in the weeks leading to the shooting, his son stopped eating, stopped watching television, and became increasingly isolative (Huynh 2009).

Witnesses at the scene indicated that Wong remained silent before opening fire. His motivation for the incident became more apparent after a local television station received a package from Wong, which included a two-page handwritten letter, photographs, and identification cards (Dowty 2009). The letter opens with the line, "I am Jiverly Wong Shooting [sic] the people" (Transcript of Letter 2009). He proceeded to explain that "undercover cop[s]" had been persecuting him for 18 years, which corresponded with the first time he discussed safety concerns with his father. In the letter, Wong described several classic paranoid ideas discussed by individuals with psychotic disorders. For instance, he mentioned "ultramodern" surveillance techniques employed by his persecutors. Upon returning to New York, Wong perceived the threats as more invasive and decided to take action. His fear and anger were driven primarily by his perceived interactions with a pseudocommunity of undercover law enforcement officers.

Indiscriminate: Resentful type

On July 18, 1984, James Huberty opened fire at a San Diego McDonald's, killing 21 (including five children) and injuring 19 others (Bosh 2014). He apparently chose the location based on familiarity with the restaurant (it was located only about 200 yards from his home) and his awareness that there were likely to be many people there. An angry, nonpsychotic Huberty explained to his wife immediately before the incident that, "society had their chance" (Knoll 2012). On the way out of his house on the day of the incident, Huberty told his wife and daughter, "I'm going hunting for humans and I won't be back" (Bosh 2014). He gave no hint either before or after the incident that he had a grievance directed toward that particular McDonald's (Knoll 2012). The Indiscriminate–Resentful type of perpetrator typically experiences prolonged rage directed at society in general and releases it in an arbitrary public location.

PSEUDOCOMMANDO

Before Knoll (2012) proposed the classification system for mass murder described above, the bulk of the literature on mass murder had focused on a specific group of perpetrators. Dietz (1986) first coined the term "pseudocommando" to describe a group of mass murderers driven by anger, resentment, and general paranoia. This group is characteristically paranoid and develops anger and resentment toward groups of individuals or society in general. They tend to plan out the attack in advance, practice their actions, and show up armed with a heavy arsenal designed to maximize casualties. In the classification system proposed by Knoll (2012), the pseudocommando would most often be described as Specific Community–Resentful or Pseudocommunity–Psychotic, depending on whether their targets were based on reality or psychosis.

Mullen (2004) presented his findings based on personal evaluations of five pseudocommando mass murderers who were apprehended before being killed or killing themselves. As opposed to the common public perception that mass murderers suddenly "snap" before becoming violent, Mullen indicated that the events were instead well planned and rehearsed. The individuals appeared to be pursuing vengeance related to a personal agenda. They often arrived with a heavy arsenal, wore some form of "warrior" gear, and had a detailed plan. Both Dietz (1986) and Mullen (2004) described pseudocommandos as paranoid, preoccupied with firearms, and focused on a particular group (or society at large) for injustices in their lives.

Pseudocommando psychology

The tendency to desire revenge has been aptly described as "a ubiquitous response to narcissistic injury" (Lafarge 2006, 447). In most developed countries not actively involved in war, humans face less daily threats to physical survival than did ancestors thousands of years ago. As a result, narcissistic injuries that threaten self-esteem have moved more to the forefront. Narcissistic blows are therefore treated "as though they were a threat to our survival" (Menninger 2007, 123). The hard-wired threat response, often no longer needed for physical survival, remains available for excessive use when reacting to ego threats.

The pseudocommando seemingly becomes driven by the "fight response" when dealing with ego threats. Vulnerable individuals with fragile egos can develop a need to avenge their damaged egos. They begin recognizing a degree of honor in retaliating to perceived injustices they have collected over time (Dietz 1986). Menninger (2007) compared the response to a child who responds to pain by desiring others to recognize that they hurt and wanting others to experience similarly hurt.

Pseudocommandos typically share traits. Dietz noted that all men who had killed 10 or more victims in a single incident shared some element of paranoia (Dietz 1986). Pseudocommandos tend to experience a degree of envy, particularly directed at enjoyment experienced by others. In response, they look to destroy others' ability to enjoy possessions or social status (Hyatt-Williams 1998). They also have a sense of entitlement and adopt the mindset that their struggles are related to the actions of others rather than of their own creation (Knoll 2012). Related to the pseudocommando's fixed paranoia, they often eventually develop nihilism. Their feelings of hopelessness can then manifest into suicidal ideation and other self-defeating acts (Edwards and Holden 2001). Ultimately, pseudocommandos develop a heroic revenge fantasy and begin formulating an incident of mass murder as their final act in an unfair life.

SCHOOL SHOOTINGS: OVERVIEW

Recently, school shootings have received considerable media attention. A school shooting is generally defined as an individual discharging a firearm in an educational institution. While some school shootings are limited to a single victim, some fall under the category of "mass murder" or "spree killing," with multiple victims. Despite the media attention they receive, school shootings—in particular, mass school shootings—are a relatively rare event (Harding et al. 2002). Due to their rarity, there are no commonly accepted criteria for defining a school shooting, let alone a mass school shooting. Researchers have instead utilized pattern matching to analyze this phenomenon (Verlinden et al. 2000).

In response to the highly publicized Columbine shooting in Littleton, Colorado, in April 1999, the U.S. Department of Education and the U.S. Secret Service launched the Safe School Initiative, an extensive examination of "targeted violence" in U.S. schools between 1974 and 2000 (Vossekuil et al. 2004). In the study, an incident of "targeted school violence" was defined as "any incident where (i) a current student or recent former student attacked someone at his or her school with lethal means (e.g., a gun or knife); and (ii) where the student attacker purposefully chose his or her school as the location of the attack" (Vossekuil et al. 2004, 7). The researchers identified 37 episodes of targeted school violence involving 41 attackers during the study period. In 73% of cases, the attacker(s) killed one or more students, faculty, or other individuals at the school; in 24% of cases, the attacker(s) used a weapon to injure at least one person at school; in the remaining case, a student killed his family before holding his class hostage. Regarding timing, 59% of cases occurred during the school day, 22% occurred prior to school, and 16% occurred after school. Ninety-five percent of the attackers were current students at the school, while 5% were former students. In the majority of incidents (81%), the attacker acted alone. Less commonly, there was a single attacker who received assistance in planning the attack (11%) or multiple attackers who acted together (8%).

Preti (2008) gathered data from Wikipedia to evaluate school shootings that occurred around the world between 1966 and 2008. He identified a total of 63 episodes of school shooting, 44 of which occurred in the United States, 7 in Canada, 7 in Europe, and 5 elsewhere. The United States had the greatest number of school shootings per year (1 per year), with a robust trend toward increasing episodes over time. Regarding timing, 24 of the documented events occurred between May 1999 and 2008, whereas 20 occurred between 1966 and April 1999. The number of individuals killed in the shootings ranged from 0 to 33; the number wounded ranged from 0 to 37. Preti noted that often a single perpetrator was responsible for the shooting and that it was more common for the shooting to end in suicide in Europe than in the United States, whereas more U.S. cases resulted in capture.

School shooters and their victims

Violence risk assessment is particularly challenging for rare events like school shootings (Mulvey and Cauffman 2001). Due to the infrequency and heterogeneity of school shootings, there is not currently a reliable profile for potential school shooters (Reddy et al. 2001). In the Safe School Initiative (SSI) report, all 41 identified attackers were males between the ages of 11 and 21, with 85% between the ages of 13 and 18 at the time of the attack. Social isolation and peer rejection have been associated with most incidents of school shooting in the United States (Band and Harpold 1999; Leary et al. 2003). Table 62.2 lists characteristics commonly associated with school shootings.

Table 62.2 School shootings—contributing factors

Individual
- Threatens violence
- Has detailed plan
- Blames others for problems
- History of aggression
- Uncontrolled anger

Family Factors
- Lack of supervision
- Troubled family relationships

School/Peer Factors
- Poor coping and social skills
- Feels rejected by peers
- Feels picked on and persecuted
- Socially isolated

Social/Environmental Factors
- Access to firearms
- Fascination with weapons/explosives
- Preoccupation with violent media/music

Attack-Related Behaviors
- Interest in targeted violence and weapons
- Organized for attack
- Communicated violent intentions
- Lacks prosocial supports

Source: Verlinden S, M Hersen, and J Thomas. 2000. *Clinical Psychology Review* 20(1):3–56. With permission.

The SSI report provided additional pertinent demographic data. Seventy-six percent of attackers were Caucasian, 12% were African American, 5% were Hispanic, and the remaining three were Native Alaskan, Native American, and Asian. In terms of family background, the majority (63%) came from two-parent homes, either with two biological parents (44%) or one biological parent and one stepparent (19%). Attackers' school performance varied considerably, with grades ranging from excellent to failing, though many (41%) were receiving As and Bs. Attackers had varied social relationships, ranging from socially isolated to popular among "mainstream students." The majority (63%) had experienced no or rare disciplinary action.

The SSI authors found that most (71%) of the attackers had felt bullied, persecuted, or injured by others prior to the attack. Though less than one-fifth of attackers had previously received a mental health diagnosis, the majority (78%) had a history of suicide attempts or suicidal thoughts. The majority of attackers (98%) had experienced a major loss before the incident, including a perceived failure or loss of status (66%), the loss of a loved one or a significant relationship (51%), and/or a major illness experienced by the attacker or someone close to them (15%). Most individuals demonstrated difficulty coping with the loss (83%).

Evidence from the SSI indicated that most school shootings are not impulsive, but rather are coordinated attacks. The attacker targeted at least one school administrator, teacher, or staff member in over half of the events (54%). The attacker targeted students in slightly fewer (41%). In the majority of incidents (73%), attackers had a grievance against at least one target prior to the event. The intended target became a victim in 46% of the attacks. Of nontargeted individuals injured or killed in the attacks, 57% were students and 39% were administrators, teachers, or staff.

Aftermath of school shootings

School shootings have deep emotional and political impacts on communities. Violent events in educational settings raise important questions involving gun control, school safety, bullying, and violent media. Following the Newtown attack, there was a flurry of gun control legislation. New York passed the Secure Ammunition and Firearms Enforcement (SAFE) Act of 2013; other states, such as Connecticut and Maryland, increased their firearms restrictions (Jackson 2013; Press 2013; Seiler 2013). The Assault Weapons Ban of

2013 was introduced to Congress, but defeated in the Senate (Weisman 2013).

Gun control laws focusing broadly on mental illness have been criticized as reactionary and unlikely to have an impact on preventing mass shootings or preventing firearm deaths (Appelbaum and Swanson 2010; Swanson 2013). Concurrently, concern has been expressed that such laws may overidentify persons as being at risk (false-positive identifications), as well as dissuade individuals from seeking needed treatment or making critical therapy disclosures (Swanson 2013).

THREAT ASSESSMENT

Over time, the mental health system has adopted a role with mass murder. Mental health professionals, particularly those with forensic training, are often asked to perform violence risk assessments. Fingers are also frequently pointed at the mental health system after mass murder incidents, whether the perpetrator was engaged in mental health treatment at the time or not (Firger 2014).

For over 50 years, the field of violence risk assessment has continued to grow. One of the important developments has involved the creation of structured violence risk assessment instruments (e.g., Historical Clinical Risk Management-20 [HCR-20], Violence Risk Appraisal Guide [VRAG], Classification of Violence Risk [COVR]) and the data that have derived from them (Monahan 2008). Mental health providers have historically been accused of overpredicting violence. In the case of mass murder, predicting relatively rare—though extremely tragic—events is a challenging endeavor.

Threat assessment on school and college campuses is a relatively new and rapidly evolving field. Expert consensus recommends a multidisciplinary threat assessment and management team whose priorities include a shared mission, regular communication, and networking (Hoffman and Zamboni 2014). Despite recent attention to threat management in school settings, establishing a rapport with school administrators about the need for collaboration and threat assessment teams remains a barrier.

Warning behaviors concerning for impending incidents of mass murder have begun to be described in the literature (Meloy et al. 2012). One group utilized existing research on targeted violence, experience with previous cases, and discussions with colleagues to propose eight warning behaviors to consider when conducting threat assessments (Meloy et al. 2012; Meloy et al. 2014). Those behaviors include behaviors suggesting planning, behaviors suggesting preoccupation, identification warning behaviors, novel aggression warning behavior, energy burst warning behavior, communication to a third party, increasing desperation or distress, and directly communicated threats. Meloy (2015) later published an article focused on the role of identification in threat assessment. Additional research will be essential in the continued effort to improve mental health professionals' threat assessments.

SUMMARY KEY POINTS

- Mass shootings are highly tragic, though extremely rare. Approximately six events on average occur per year.
- The majority of shootings occur in a place of business or an educational environment.
- A single individual who has planned and prepared for the incident carries out most shootings.
- Experience and research suggest that focusing media responsibility and encouraging third parties to report warning behaviors or leaked intent have the most potential for prevention.
- Policies and laws focusing on dangerous behaviors, as opposed to psychiatric diagnoses, are more likely to have a preventive effect.

REFERENCES

Appelbaum PS and JW Swanson. 2010. Law and psychiatry: Gun laws and mental illness: How sensible are the current restrictions? *Psychiatric Services* 61(7):652–654.

Band SR and JA Harpold. 1999. School violence: Lessons learned. *FBI: Law Enforcement Bulletin* 68:9–16.

Blair JP and KW Schweit. 2014. *A Study of Active Shooter Incidents, 2000–2013*. Washington, DC: Texas State University and Federal Bureau of Investigation, U.S. Department of Justice.

Bosh S. 2014. *Survivors Recount San Ysidro McDonald's Massacre after 30 Years*. http://www.kusi.com/story/26058350/survivors-recount-san-ysidro-mcdonalds-massacre-after-30-years, accessed June 30, 2015.

Bossarte R, T Simon, and L Barker. 2006. Characteristics of homicide followed by suicide incidents in multiple states, 2003–2004. *Injury Prevention* 12:ii33–ii38.

Burgess AW. 2006. Mass, spree and serial homicide. In *Crime Classification Manual*, edited by J Douglas, AW Burgess, AG Burgess, and RK Ressler, San Francisco: Wiley, 438–471.

Clark Prosecutor. *Ronald Gene Simmons*. http://www.clarkprosecutor.org/html/death/US/simmons131.htm, accessed July 4, 2015.

Coid J. 1983. The epidemiology of abnormal homicide and murder followed by suicide. *Psychological Medicine* 13(4):855–860.

Connecticut State Police Sandy Hook School Shooting Report. 2013. http://cspsandyookreport.ct.gov, accessed July 6, 2015.

Curry C. 2013. *Sandy Hook Report Offers Grim Details of Adam Lanza's Bedroom*. http://abcnews.go.com/US/sandy-hook-report-inside-gunman-adam-lanzas-bedroom/story?id=21009111, accessed July 6, 2015.

Declercq F and K Audenaert. 2011. Predatory violence aiming at relief in a case of mass murder: Meloy's criteria for applied forensic practice. *Behavioral Sciences and the Law* 29(4):578–591.

Dietz P. 1986. Mass, serial and sensational homicides. *Bulletin of the New York Academy of Medicine* 62(5):477–491.

Dowty D. 2009. *Binghamton Shooter in Letter to TV Station: "I Am Jiverly Wong Shooting the People."* http://www.syracuse.com/news/index.ssf/2009/04/binghamton_shooter_in_letter_t.html, accessed June 30, 2015.

Duwe G. 2005. A circle of distortion: The social construction of mass murder in the United States. *Western Criminology Review* 6(1):59–78.

Edwards M and R Holden. 2001. Coping, meaning in life, and suicidal manifestations: Examining gender differences. *Journal of Clinical Psychology* 57:1517–1534.

Effron L. 2012. *Mass School Shootings: A History.* http://abcnews.go.com/US/mass-school-shootings-history/story?id=17975571, accessed July 6, 2015.

Felthous A and A Hempel. 1995. Combined homicide-suicides: A review. *Journal of Forensic Sciences* 40:846–857.

Firger J. 2014. *Mental Illness in Spotlight after UC Santa Barbara Rampage.* http://www.cbsnews.com/news/mental-illness-in-spotlight-after-uc-santa-barbara-rampage, accessed July 4, 2015.

Fox JA and J Levin. 2003. Mass murder: An analysis of extreme violence. *Journal of Applied Psychoanalytic Studies* 5(1):47–64.

Harding DJ, C Fox, and JD Mehta. 2002. Studying rare events through qualitative case studies: Lessons from a study of rampage school shootings. *Sociological Methods and Research* 31(2):174–217.

Hempel A, J Meloy, and T Richards. 1999. Offender and offense characteristics of a nonrandom sample of mass murderers. *Journal of the American Academy of Psychiatry and the Law* 27(2):213–225.

Herridge C and P Browne. 2013. *Hasan Sends Writings to Fox News Ahead of Fort Hood Shooting Trial.* http://www.foxnews.com/politics/2013/08/01/hasan-sends-writings-ahead-fort-hood-shooting-trial, accessed June 29, 2015.

Hoffman J and K Zamboni. 2014. Building up a threat assessment process at universities. In *International Handbook of Threat Assessment*, edited by JR Meloy and J Hoffmann, New York: Oxford University Press, 351–359.

Huynh N. 2009. *Jiverly Wong's Father: What Prompted Mass Killing in Binghamton Remains a Mystery.* http://www.syracuse.com/news/index.ssf/2009/04/jiverly_wongs_father_our_son_w.html, accessed June 30, 2015.

Hyatt-Williams A. 1998. *Cruelty, Violence, and Murder: Understanding the Criminal Mind.* Northvale, NJ: Jason Aronson.

Jackson A. 2013. *Maryland Lawmakers Send Landmark Gun Control Bill to O'Malley's Desk.* http://www.capitalgazette.com/cg2-arc-0b697063-acf8-508e-adf9-b07ea4fb6c8d-20130405-story.html, accessed July 6, 2015.

Kenber B. 2013. *Nidal Hasan Sentenced to Death for Fort Hood Shooting Rampage.* https://www.washingtonpost.com/world/national-security/nidal-hasan-sentenced-to-death-for-fort-hood-shooting-rampage/2013/08/28/aad28de2-0ffa-11e3-bdf6-e4fc677d94a1_story.html, accessed June 30, 2015.

Knoll J. 2010. The pseudocommando mass murder: Part II, the language of revenge. *Journal of the American Academy of Psychiatry and the Law* 38(2):263–272.

Knoll J. 2012. Mass murder: Causes, classification, and prevention. *Psychiatric Clinics of North America* 35:757–780.

Lafarge L. 2006. The wish for revenge. *Psychoanalytic Quarterly* 75:447–475.

Leary MR, RM Kowalski, L Smith, and S Phillips. 2003. Teasing, rejection, and violence: Case studies of the school shootings. *Aggressive Behavior* 29:202–214.

Marzuk P, K Tardiff, and C Hirsch. 1992. The epidemiology of murder-suicide. *Journal of the American Medical Association* 267:3179–3183.

Mass Public Shootings on the Rise, but Why? 2007. Associated Press, http://www.nbcnews.com/id/18249724/ns/us_news-crime_and_courts/t/mass-public-shootings-rise-why/

Meloy JR, J Hoffmann, A Guldimann, and D James. 2012. The role of warning behaviors in threat assessment: An exploration and suggested typology. *Behavioral Sciences and the Law* 30(3):256–279.

Meloy JR, J Hoffmann, K Roshdi, J Glaz-Ocik, and A Guldimann. 2014. Warning behaviors and their configurations across various domains of targeted violence. In *International Handbook of Threat Assessment*, edited by JR Meloy and J Hoffmann, New York: Oxford University Press, 39–53.

Meloy JR, K Mohandie, JL Knoll, and J Hoffmann. 2015. The concept of identification in threat assessment. *Behavioral Sciences and the Law* 33(2–3):213–237.

Menninger W. 2007. Uncontained rage: A psychoanalytic perspective on violence. *Bulletin of the Menninger Clinic* 71(2):115–131.

Mohandie K and J Meloy. 2000. Clinical and forensic indicators of "suicide by cop." *Journal of Forensic Sciences* 45:384–389.

Monahan J. 2008. Structured risk assessment of violence. In *Violence Assessment and Management*, edited by RI Simon and K Tardiff, Arlington, VA: American Psychiatric Publishing, 17–33.

Mullen P. 2004. The autogenic (self-generated) massacre. *Behavioral Sciences and the Law* 222:311–323.

Mulvey EP and E Cauffman. 2001. The inherent limits of predicting school violence. *American Psychologist* 56(10):797–802.

Press TA. 2013. *Connecticut Governor Signs Gun Measures. New York Times*, http://www.nytimes.com/2013/04/05/nyregion/connecticut-lawmakers-pass-gun-limits.html.

Preti A. 2008. School shooting as a culturally enforced way of expressing suicidal hostile intentions. *Journal of the American Academy of Psychiatry and the Law* 36(4):544–550.

Reddy M, R Borum, J Berglund, B Vossekuil, R Fein, and W Modzeleski. 2001. Evaluating risk for targeted violence in schools: Comparing risk assessment, threat assessment, and other approaches. *Psychology in the Schools* 38:157–172.

Rubinkam M. 2009. *LA Fitness Center Shooting in Pennsylvania Leaves 4 Dead*. http://www.sandiegouniontribune.com/news/2009/aug/05/us-health-club-shooting-080509/.

Sanchez R and E Payne. *Charleston Church Shooting: Who Is Dylann Roof?* http://www.cnn.com/2015/06/19/us/charleston-church-shooting-suspect/

Schenk E, G Wijetunge, NC Mann, EB Lerner, A Longthorne, and D Dawson. 2014. Epidemiology of mass casualty incidents in the United States. *Prehospital Emergency Care* 18(3):408–416.

Schwarz H and M Ramilo. 2014. Sandy Hook shooter treated at Yale. Yale Daily News. January 22, 2014. http://yaledailynews.com/blog/2014/01/22/sand-hookshooter-treated-at-yale/, accessed February 4, 2016.

Seiler C. 2013. *New Gun Law Offers Reply to Mass Killings*. http://www.timesunion.com/local/article/New-gun-law-offers-reply-to-mass-killings-4195504.php, accessed July 6, 2015.

Solomon A. 2014. *The Reckoning: The Father of the Sandy Hook Killer Searches for Answers*. http://www.newyorker.com/magazine/2014/03/17/the-reckoning, accessed July 6, 2015.

Swanlund A. 2015. *Ronald Gene Simmons (1940–1990)*. http://www.encyclopediaofarkansas.net/encyclopedia/entry-detail.aspx?entryID=3731, accessed July 4, 2015.

Swanson J. 2013. Mental illness and new gun law reforms: The promise and peril of crisis-driven policy. *Journal of the American Medical Association* 309(12):1233–1234.

The Last Rhodesian. 2015. http://www.documentcloud.org/documents/2108059-lastrhodesian-manifesto.html

Towers S, A Gomez-Lievano, M Khan, A Mubayi, and C Castillo-Chavez. 2015. Contagion in mass killings and school shootings. *PLOS One*. http://dx.doi.org/10.1371/journal.pone.0117259

Transcript of Letter Purportedly Sent by Binghamton Shooter. 2009. http://www.syracuse.com/news/index.ssf/2009/04/transcript_of_letter_purported.html, accessed June 30, 2015.

Verlinden S, M Hersen, and J Thomas. 2000. Risk factors in school shootings. *Clinical Psychology Review* 20(1):3–56.

Vigdor N. 2013. *State Police: All 26 Newtown Victims Shot with Assault Rifle*. http://www.greenwichtime.com/newtownshooting/article/State-Police-All-26-Newtown-victims-shot-with-4220548.php, accessed July 6, 2015.

Vossekuil B, RA Fein, M Reddy, R Borum, and W Modzeleski. 2004. *The Final Report and Findings of the Safe School Initiative: Implications for the Prevention of School Attacks in the United States*. Washington, DC: U.S. Secret Service and U.S. Department of Education.

Weisman J. 2013. *Senate Blocks Drive for Gun Control*. http://www.nytimes.com/2013/04/18/us/politics/senate-obama-gun-control.html, accessed July 6, 2015.

Weiss D. 2013. *Fort Hood Trial: Don't Say the "t" Word*. http://www.frontpagemag.com/fpm/201585/fort-hood-trial-dont-say-t-word-deborah-weiss, accessed June 29, 2015.

63

Terrorism

WILLIAM H. REID, DANIEL J. REID, AND CHRIS E. STOUT

INTRODUCTION

This chapter will address several kinds of terror–violence and other acts that purposely create injury or fear in noncombatants. Not all terrorizing activity is physically violent. Although some discussions focus on transnational terrorism, we include activity that targets other large groups (such as religious believers or socioeconomic groups), private industry (e.g., large retailers, energy companies, and agricultural conglomerates), smaller civilian groups (communities, schools, public facilities, and gatherings), and cyber-communities. We include "cyberterrorism" and acts that, although not directly violent, nevertheless create damage or instill fear by virtue of widespread communication by perpetrators, other individuals, social media, or news media (Duarte et al. 2011; Peleg and Mass-Friedman 2013).

We generally separate "terrorism" topics from conventional criminal acts, acts of war, and victims of conventional crime or warfare, although the concepts overlap. Acts of war figure more prominently when addressing victims and victim care, although victims of terrorist acts often receive different (or combined) kinds of injuries, react differently in some ways, and should sometimes be treated differently, than most victims of war (Peleg et al. 2010; Miller 2011).

One's personal views affect whether or not one defines many acts as "terrorism." Professor J.K. Zawodny, a Polish underground combatant during World War II, wrote, "(O)ne man's terrorist is another man's freedom fighter" (JK Zawodny, personal communication, 1985). It is sometimes hard to tell whether a bombing is a political act or "senseless violence," or whether a military or police action meets common criteria for terrorism. Many would say that such distinctions matter little in the long run, especially to the victims.

Some have spoken of poverty or political repression as a fertile garden for the development of terrorism. It is now clear that poverty *per se* is not associated with increased violence, terrorism, or the "radicalization" of social protest. Some authors have noted that societies that move toward violence are very often those that are improving socioeconomically; internal group or terroristic violence routinely suggests a self-destructive societal trend (JK Zawodny personal communication, 1985; Alderdice 2009).

The U.S. Bureau of Counterterrorism has maintained a list of Foreign Terrorist Organizations (FTOs) since 1997. The list began with 20 large and small groups, including the Abu Nidal Organization, HAMAS, *Hezbollah* (*Hizballah*), Shining Path, and others, largely based in the Middle East, Asia, and South America. The "official" list grew slowly for a few years, starting with the addition of *al-Qa'ida* (*al-Qaeda*) in late 1999. By September 2012, the number had climbed to 57, with 34 added since September 11, 2001. Groups added after September 2001 are almost all associated with the Middle East and North Africa. Only six have been removed from the list since 2001 (Bureau of Counterterrorism 2015). It is a criminal offense for U.S. citizens or persons within U.S. jurisdictions to knowingly provide material support or resources to an FTO (U.S. Department of State 2000).

Truly valid and reliable studies of terrorism, its victims, and population responses to terrorism risk and events are difficult to separate from relatively useless surveys, anecdotes, and editorials, but there is a well-informed post-disaster and victim intervention literature. Many of the references herein derive from Israel, England, and the United States, with U.S. studies often focusing on the September 11, 2001, attacks and the April 19, 1995, bombing of the Alfred P. Murrah Federal Building in Oklahoma City.

TERRORISTS AND TERRORISM

Hacker, largely known for his work on skyjackings, differentiated terrorists into overlapping groups of "criminals, crusaders, and crazies" (Hacker 1977). *Criminal* activities were those based primarily on personal gain. *Crusading* referred to terrorism that attempts to support social or political causes. *Crazies* referred to perpetrators whose violence or extortion arises from highly personalized, often delusional, roots. Hacker's classification, with a few *caveats*, is still useful, and helps define some of the roles psychiatrists and other mental health professionals should attempt or avoid.

Post (2007) offered a more recent categorization of national and transnational terrorism. *National separatists* (such as the Irish Republican Army or Abu Nidal) are often the latest generation of a continuum. Idealistic or anarchist *social revolutionaries* tend to be youth and young adults rebelling against a status quo and clamoring for some version of what they purport to be social justice (cf. the Red Brigades, Shining Path, and the Revolutionary Armed Forces of Colombia [FARC]). For some, violence itself, irrespective of cause, effect, or consequence, seems to be a liberating or cleansing influence. *Religious extremists*, currently represented by many Middle Eastern groups (such as the Taliban and *al-Qa'ida*, which have existed for decades, and the relatively newer Islamic State) have become much more potent internationally over recent decades.

The terrorist's true purpose and avowed purpose are often different, but usually overlap. Activity purported to be altruistic may come from delusional roots or criminal intent. Criminal activity may generate money and other resources for some political or quasi-political goal. Embittered, distraught, or simply youthful rebels are often manipulated by experienced agitators to create media events and suggest much larger numbers than truly exist. Actions "for the people" may be based in revenge, narcissism, or merely love of violence or chaos. When terrorism represents legitimate protest, some faction of the protestors has often become radicalized and moved along a "developmental continuum" between social activism and terrorism (Reshetnikov 2008).

There is no single agreed-upon classification system for terrorism or terrorists. However, several systems have been proposed by previous authors, as summarized in Table 63.1. Reid and colleagues (2015) recently incorporated the concept of cyberterrorism into their classification system.

Cyberterrorism includes Internet-mediated damage to economic and monetary systems, finance mechanisms (such as credit card payment systems), communication systems, recordkeeping systems, power grids, and public confidence in all of those. Its effect on U.S. targets and/or people has become much greater during the past decade.

Table 63.1 Examples of terrorist/terrorism classifications

Hacker (1977)	"Criminals, Crusaders, and Crazies"
Trioni, general (1999)	Criminal, Irrational, Political, State, Religious, Ethnic/Cultural/Tribal
Trioni, state related (1999)	Resistance to Colonial Rule, Separatist, Internal-Political (to control a state or system), Anarchistic–Ideological (to destroy a state system), Support for External Takeover
Post (2007)	National Separatist, Social Revolutionary, Religious Extremist
Reid et al. (2015)	Wholly Domestic Violent, Violent from Foreign Sources, Cyberterrorism (foreign or domestic)

Its sources may lie anywhere in the world, with large groups or single hackers. Very small groups can wreak substantial damage and, sometimes, give the impression that they are much larger (or represent more people than they actually do). The consequences can be more destructive than those of traditionally defined terrorist organizations.

The overall success of a terrorist act is measured by its effect on the larger population. The act may preoccupy a government or large number of people and provoke substantial social response. Terrorism is thus useful to its perpetrators in many ways, including publicity, instilling fear, displaying power, demonstrating target weakness, manipulating governments and citizens, exacting revenge, effecting direct social damage such as economic collapse, and increasing repression (either directly or through government reaction).

EXTENT OF THE PROBLEM

The ancient adage "kill one, scare 10,000" still works and makes it easy to influence or control people with little expenditure by the terrorist. Much ongoing concern—as contrasted with "perceived" threat—comes from the availability, portability, affordability, and "import-ability" of nuclear and biochemical weapons, infrastructure vulnerability, and ubiquitous sensationalism by both news and social media.

The secondary and tertiary "scare" value (beyond physical damage and effects on specific targets) of real threats is enhanced exponentially by the speed and breadth of media coverage. Blends of factual reporting and editorializing, publicity on biased public media such as *Al-Jazeera* and many state-sponsored outlets, and the availability of social networks such as Facebook, Twitter, Instagram, *Weibo*, and *VKontakte* routinely expand and distort news.

Until the events of September 11, 2001, the great majority of U.S. civilians considered themselves insulated from transnational terrorism. Nevertheless, Americans in foreign countries have sometimes been part of a larger U.S. target (e.g., the 2012 bombing of the U.S. diplomatic mission in Benghazi, Libya; the 2000 bombing of the *USS Cole* in Yemen). Others may be caught coincidentally in non-U.S. targets (e.g., in the 2008 Mumbai bombings by *mujahedeen*, in which Americans and Britons were coincidentally present but singled out for additional violence [Sengupta 2008]).

Despite the relatively small number of directly injured Americans, terrorism has had a substantial effect on way of life in the United States. Millions of Americans and others worldwide who have not experienced physical injury are nonetheless affected by uninvited political change and abridgement of freedoms. In the United States, laws, rules and expectations about travel, food safety, communication, gatherings, and basic privacy have markedly changed daily routines. Huge portions of the U.S. population have become inured to those abridgements and inconveniences; entire generations now assume that searches and scans at airports, ever more tamper-resistant food and product packaging, government surveillance of mail and electronic communications, heavily armed police at public events, "hardening" strategically unimportant buildings to withstand attack, and closing off entire streets in front of government buildings and public monuments are "normal."

COPING WITH THE THREAT

Public perception of risk

With certain exceptions, *perceived* personal risk from terrorist threat tends to be higher—sometimes much higher—than actual risk, particularly in the United States. That perception extends from the generic to specific kinds of events, such as biological or radiological terrorism (Pearce et al. 2013). Public emotional and behavioral response to the 2001 attacks in New York and Washington, DC, had waned substantially a year after the events, but cognitive effects remained many years later (McArdle et al. 2012). Within a year of the 9/11 events, one of the authors (WHR) informally queried a number of psychiatrists practicing in Manhattan and the District of Columbia about their perceptions of continuing terrorism risk and their thoughts about remaining in those areas. Every person asked said that he or she believed the risk of another incident was high, but none planned to relocate.

There is evidence that both time without an event and constant threat itself are associated with lowered public concern. Israeli residents are very well studied in this regard. The effects of living in an industrialized (i.e., not "third-world") environment which is *per se* dangerous are significant to be sure, but one often sees a sort of community resilience and habituation to the constant risk of attack. Education and psychological-response-mitigation programs have been effective (cf. Farchi and Gidron 2010; Berger et al. 2012). Interestingly, the broad economic effects of risk from terrorism or war appear to be less than one might expect (Peleg et al. 2011).

One Australian study found a significant decrease in expressed public concern between 2007 and 2010, in spite of that country's proximity to volatile environments in Southeast Asia and Micronesia (Stevens et al. 2011). While a larger portion of Australians believe that the national threat of terrorism remains high and accept the possibility of future precautions, concern about being personally affected appears to have moderated over time. Subgroups of poorly educated people and migrants continued to be "disproportionately concerned."

One political consequence of external threat and perception of risk is increased public acceptance of authoritarianism (Asbrock and Fritsche 2013). People who are frightened, confused, or ambivalent generally welcome direction and are often indifferent to its source or potential consequences beyond their immediate security.

Role of the Internet and Web-based media

Separate from the important concept of cyberterrorism, the Internet and its contributions to rapid, uncensored, and unfiltered mass communication has increased both terrorism and its effects on large populations. Media accessibility in general, and Web-based media in particular, have made it easier and more efficient to develop and communicate within groups, including those associated with terror–violence. Some writers refer to "virtual communities of hatred" that contribute greatly to the radicalizing of people who otherwise would not actually participate in terrorism (Post 2010).

Terrorist "psychology"

It is a mistake to search for a single personality type or uniform "terrorist mindset," particularly without defining a specific kind of activity. There are many kinds of terrorist behaviors and motivations. Most terrorists do not demonstrate serious psychopathology, although (limiting our comments to organized, quasi-political groups and eliminating frankly psychotic, simply criminal, and/or revenge-motivated perpetrators) people with certain personality traits and tendencies are disproportionally drawn to terrorist roles.

Most of those traits are so generic that they are of limited utility for early prediction of terror–violence, but it may be helpful to monitor known suspects or groups for conditions that are correlated with destructive action. Those who are action oriented, aggressive, stimulus hungry, excitement seeking, and externalizing are statistically associated with a greater likelihood of overt action.

Other kinds of people often support terrorist group efforts, making eventual action possible but not participating directly in it. The personality traits most often seen are antisocial (including the truly psychopathic), narcissistic, borderline, and paranoid. That correlation can be established once the group is defined or terroristic behavior has taken place, but it is fruitless (and unfair) to surmise in the other direction (i.e., to try to predict terroristic behavior based on personality type).

The Japanese FTO United Red Army stated years ago that, "We intend to recruit young people who have lost hope in living, and their families, as well as in society. We want their explosive energy." One analysis of their known members indicated that 25% had lost one or both parents by the age of 14, with the loss of one's father being most disruptive. Of those whose parents were still living, 79% reported severe conflict with them. Over 33% had prior juvenile court convictions (Trioni 1999).

Members of FTOs—as contrasted with their leaders—often submerge their own identities into that of the group. Most organizations have little tolerance for differences of opinion about goals and actions. In addition, the group must commit terroristic acts to justify its existence. This group dynamic can press for the perpetuation, and often escalation, of violence.

There is a limited literature that describes the process of converting victims of war or terrorism into instruments of violence for terrorist leaders. Post (2000), discussing generational transmission of nationalist–separatist hatred and revenge, describes a former Palestinian refugee recruited by Abu Nidal to participate in bombing an Egyptian airliner.

Decades ago, Janis (1972) applied the old theory of "groupthink" to terrorist organizations. Not being caught, or being quickly released—such as through public outcry (cf. groups that press for release of *al-Qa'ida* combatants from U.S. detention facilities), extortion, or prisoner trades—can lead group members to illusions of invulnerability, which leads in turn to unreasonable optimism and terrorist risk taking. False presumptions of group "morality" are often added to propaganda and one-dimensional perceptions of the terrorist's "enemy" as evil, which subsidizes the perspective that violent behavior, even against innocent victims, is justified.

VICTIMS AND VICTIM RECOVERY

Work with victims is by far the largest terrorism-related role for mental health professionals. Much of the necessary skill and many of the syndromes encountered, such as anxiety, depression, and acute- and post-traumatic stress disorder, are already part of most clinicians' experience. Other situations require special training and sensitivity (such as working with teachers and students after attacks, child-victims, mass casualty situations, military personnel or civilians in danger zones chronically exposed to the threat of sudden violence, torture victims, first responders, and people preparing to travel or deploy to dangerous environments).

Individual victims

Victim response to terror–violence is not random. Understanding response patterns makes care more effective. Military and intelligence community professionals see value in incorporating critical incident debriefing and experienced mental health consultation when faced with terrorist acts, and integrating them into comprehensive counterterrorist programs (Applewhite and Dickins 1997). In the authors' experience, however, immediate "debriefing" (in the sense of intense questioning) is countertherapeutic and interferes with recovery. In dangerous situations, information may be a top priority, but victims fare better when simply provided unconditional support as they deal with trauma.

Victims of very recent violence require special understanding. A gentle approach, offering basic help such as food and a soft word, is the best place to start. Rapid-fire questioning, as frequently seen in movies or on television, should be avoided. Therapeutic actions that depend on the therapist's identifying with the victim are often ill advised. In mass casualties, efforts should be coordinated, which involves cooperating with local agencies and laying groundwork for lasting support.

The care of hostage victims and persons who have been tortured is particularly specialized. The authors strongly recommend special study and/or supervision for those working with such individuals, whether the trauma is recent or in the distant past (e.g., Holocaust survivors). Civilians who experience chronic anticipation of attack (such as many children in Israeli schools and *kibbutzim*, Nigerians living in fear of *Fulani* Muslim radicals, community victims of Mexican and South American drug wars, and many refugees) are also complex, especially when the terror is perceived—rightly or wrongly—as perpetrated by the State itself (Palmieri et al. 2010; Berger et al. 2012).

There is an expected correlation between severity of exposure to violent events and the extent and duration of posttraumatic symptoms (Desivilya et al. 1996; Henriksen et al. 2010; Scrimin et al. 2011). However, intensity of the trauma is not always directly related to the intensity and duration of its effects; severe trauma does not necessarily portend severe psychological symptoms. Tuchner et al. (2010) found no significant correlation between injury severity and quality of life for terrorist attack survivors after 2 years. Razik et al. (2013) found a similar lack of correlation in Pakistani emergency responders. Victims react differently to various combinations of trauma severity, chronicity, and type.

Expecting recovery is associated with *actual* recovery. Most victims have fairly good emotional recovery from terrorism-related sudden physical injury (North et al. 2011). Those who are chronically viewed as "victims" by family, associates, lawyers, and courts tend to respond less well to treatment, and sometimes deteriorate unnecessarily over time. This is consistent with older studies indicating that the majority of victims of ordinary disasters recover without long-lasting, substantial posttraumatic effects (Ursano et al. 1995), and that media exposure and personal injury litigation can exaggerate perceived symptoms and claims of distress.

PSYCHIATRIC PATIENTS

People with pre-existing serious psychiatric illness, as a group, develop proportionately worse acute and chronic posttraumatic symptoms than controls. Effects vary by individual and diagnostic category, and the syndromes seen are often not the same as subjective complaints (Franz et al., 2009). Caregivers should be alert for subtle presentations.

EMERGENCY RESPONDERS

A number of studies point out that emergency responders are emotionally vulnerable to repetitive exposure to tragedy, which is often mixed with immediate danger to themselves (Misra et al. 2009; Strand et al. 2010). In Pakistan, approximately 80% of first responders have been exposed to terrorist attacks, with prevalence rates of posttraumatic stress disorder (PTSD) and similar syndromes in the "high range" for similar workers in the West (Razik et al. 2013).

Modern Western first-responder teams often have sophisticated mental health support systems, including mandatory evaluations and offers of counseling. Nevertheless, a number of factors—including professional stigma, "macho" self-image, peer pressure, and perception of career blemishes—may interfere with individuals' use of available services.

Qualified post-shooting counseling for law enforcement officers, and other forms of intervention by experienced professionals, is sometimes as simple as good stress management. Military interventions are often most effective when provided in the field or near the current campaign, where they can occur without delay and in mission-relevant settings. One approach for military personnel returning from combat suggests returning them home by sea rather than by air, allowing for counseling to begin in transit and creating a gradual transition (Johnston and Dipp 2009).

SUICIDE AFTER TERRORIST EVENTS

The available studies, primarily of Western events and particularly the U.S. 9/11 attack and Oklahoma City bombings, indicate no general increase in suicide rates in either direct victims (including those with physical disabilities) or victimized regional societies (Pridemore et al. 2009; Weizman et al. 2009; Claassen et al. 2010). The Weizman (2009) study found some increase during one 11-month segment (December 2000 to October 2001) of a 6-year period.

Victims' families

Families of victims are victims as well (Dreman and Cohen 1990; Martin-Peña et al. 2011). Release of hostages who have been held for months or years brings a new and unexpected set of problems to the family, including guilt about some feelings and behaviors while the victim was away, disruption of the family equilibrium established in the victim's absence, and denial of the many issues that must be faced once release is secured. Divorce is extremely common after a hostage–spouse returns. The offspring of victims of war and concentration camps, including Holocaust victims, bear stigmata that may or may not be seen as symptoms (Dreman 1989).

Military families have been particularly well studied. Research on U.S. military deployments, especially to Iraq and Afghanistan, in which the concept of "terrorism" figures more prominently than in past campaigns, reflects the armed forces' progress in recognizing family reactions and needs. Military families generally tolerate deployments well. Most families restabilize without incident after the deployed person's return (Faber et al. 2008).

Community and societal victims

Large segments of the population who are not physically touched by terror–violence nonetheless bear peripheral effects (Reid 1989). Fears of airplane hijacking or bombing, travel restrictions, worry about privacy, eroded faith in financial institutions, bias against entire countries and cultures, and the like contribute to a general feeling that the world is dangerous.

The phrase *community resilience* is commonly used to describe good societal functioning (Butler et al. 2009; Ahmed et al. 2011; Ferrando et al. 2011; Johnson and Luna 2011). In spite of measurable—often inconvenient or repressive—social changes in response to terrorist threats, diagnosable psychopathology attributable to terrorism is not the rule in communities that are not under direct attack. Business tends to return quickly to normal or near normal. Relatively few people move away (unless the risk is very high). High-profile persons, such as politicians targeted for assassination, generally tolerate risk, employ security measures, and carry on (Nijdam et al. 2010).

Some community subgroups are more adversely affected. They include, depending on circumstances, migrant populations, those with less education, Holocaust survivors, persons with less effective prior functioning, women, persons with higher tested levels of neuroticism, those with lower tested extroversion, and those with "negative worldview changes" (Butler et al. 2009; Ahmed et al. 2011; Shmotkin and Keinan 2011; Stevens et al. 2011; Amital et al. 2012). Subgroups with relatively better outcomes tend to be those with the opposite characteristics.

Strong religious identification, regardless of culture or denomination, appears to provide substantial protection against the emotional effects of terrorism (Levav et al. 2008; Ahmed et al. 2011; Korn and Zukerman 2011). "Spirituality" has protective value as well, but should be considered separately from "religiosity" (McIntosh et al. 2011).

OTHER ROLES FOR MENTAL HEALTH PROFESSIONALS

Law enforcement training and support

Qualified mental health professionals can offer basic clinical training to law enforcement and military response teams that may be useful in crisis intervention, assessment of perpetrators and victims, victim support, stress management, department risk management, and a number of other areas. This does not mean clinicians should become field interveners or negotiators, or that police officers will acquire the skills and experience of clinicians. Experienced law enforcement, first responder, and military professionals routinely possess considerable intuition and psychological skill, but one should not mistake bravado or "street smarts" for deeper knowledge.

Some professional "profiling" teams, such as those trained and maintained by the FBI and a few private groups, have limited success in identifying perpetrators and assessing and predicting criminal behavior. The best profilers are typically experienced law enforcement specialists, not mental health professionals. Deducing perpetrator mindsets and predicting behavior based on limited information are primarily the stuff of fiction.

The issue of "agency" is very important when working with police or the military. Therapists who work within law enforcement and military organizations must be familiar with—and accept—their particular rules and expectations. It is easy to find oneself in an unethical position, or at least sliding down a "slippery slope."

PERPETRATOR EVALUATION AND TREATMENT

The few subspecialty-trained clinical professionals who deal with perpetrators, particularly in "field" situations of impending danger (such as unfolding terrorist activity), interrogation (military or civilian), or post-arrest evaluation should understand completely the broad implications of their activities. These include, but may not be limited to, what may happen to the perpetrator as a result of the clinician's involvement, ethical implications of such involvement, and effects on the clinician's own psyche and career. One should be aware of the uses to which evaluation findings may be put, and notify the evaluee (as appropriate to the situation and ethically required with law enforcement defendants) of one's intent, constraints on confidentiality, and the like. If the person has recently been arrested, the clinician should verify that defense counsel has been retained and the evaluee's rights as a criminal defendant have been appropriately protected.

Like other detainees, accused terrorists sometimes require psychiatric treatment in jails or prisons. Treatment of ill or injured perpetrators is a matter of clinical skill and clinical ethics. There is a small literature on the legal and bioethical dilemmas associated with treating terrorists, separate from the common roles of correctional physician or therapist (see e.g., Gesundheit et al. 2009).

Cases involving terrorism are often sensationalized. Evaluators should take pains to work professionally and to use appropriate forensic procedures, being careful not to step outside the bounds of their expertise and ethics.

Roles to avoid

Many clinicians legitimately participate in military, law enforcement, and civilian intelligence operations, but psychiatrists and psychologists are rarely trained combatants or law enforcement officers. Their roles must be clear and within carefully developed training and ethics guidelines. This is not merely a weighing of one ethic against another (such as confidentiality against danger), or of replacing traditional ethics with situational ones. If, for example, a police or military commander asks a psychiatrist about surreptitiously placing a drug in a hostage-taker's food to sedate him, that doctor (almost certainly inexperienced in hostage negotiation, lacking complete information about the situation, and acting in the heat of the moment) should not participate, even if tempted by a so-called "greater good" of protecting hostages. The "greater good" may or may not be truly greater, and the action may or may not really protect hostages. The only certainties are the immediate ethical breach and the slippery slope on which the professional will find himself or herself.

"Role confusion" is another reason to separate law enforcement from clinical activity. Consider the following example from the authors' experience:

Dr. A, a psychiatrist, introduced himself to one of the authors. He said, with some *braggadocio*, that he was a "member of the (city) SWAT (Special Weapons and Tactics) team," participated in anti-terrorism scenarios and drills, and was carrying a concealed handgun (implying that he had to be prepared for dangerous duty at all times). It soon became clear that he had been a police consultant and liked to view himself as part of the terror–violence and hostage response team. A local law enforcement executive later revealed that the clinician was not authorized to carry the weapon (that state had no concealed-carry permit statute at the time) and was considered something of a "kook" by area cops.

SUMMARY

Terrorism is a complex topic that, contrary to some published papers and many media stories, supports few absolutes and defies "unified" theories of cause or cure. Psychiatry and other mental health professions are irrelevant to many of its facets, but there are clinical and forensic roles for qualified clinicians.

SUMMARY KEY POINTS

- Terrorism has existed since social leaders—especially those of out-of-power groups—discovered the maxim "Kill one, scare 10,000." Broad perpetrator descriptions include Hacker's "criminals, crusaders and crazies" (1977), as well as more specific categories that recognize particular purposes in national and transnational groups, sometimes including internal revolutionaries and "freedom fighters."
- Despite the relatively small number of directly injured U.S. citizens, damage to Americans' way of life from terrorism has been substantial. Nonphysical damage in the United States and internationally includes general anxiety about safety, government or self-imposed restrictions, abridgement of freedoms, eroded faith in social and financial institutions, and overly broad bias against countries and cultures associated with terrorism.
- With certain exceptions, the public's *perceived* personal risk from terrorist threat tends to be much higher than *actual* risk, particularly in the United States.
- The Internet and rapid, uncensored, and unfiltered mass communication has had an enormous

role in the propagation of, and increased effects of, terrorism.

- Most terrorists do not demonstrate serious psychopathology. It is a mistake to search for one or two personality types or a uniform "terrorist mindset."
- Work with victims is by far the largest role for mental health professionals in the general field of terrorism. Victim response to terror-violence is not random; there are patterns that suggest avenues of effective care.
- Mental health professionals must avoid role confusion. Victim services, law enforcement training and support, and perpetrator evaluation and treatment are our most appropriate tasks.

REFERENCES

Ahmed AE, K Masood, SV Dean et al. 2011. The constant threat of terrorism: Stress levels and coping strategies amongst university students of Karachi. *Journal of Pakistan Medical Association* 61(4):410–414.

Alderdice JT. 2009. Sacred values: Psychological and anthropological perspectives on fairness, fundamentalism, and terrorism. *Annals of the New York Academy of Sciences* 1167:158–173.

Amital D, H Amital, G Shohat, Y Soffer, and Y Bar-Dayan. 2012. Resilience emotions and acute stress reactions in the population of Dimona and the general population of Israel two days after the first suicide bombing attack in Dimona. *Israel Medical Association Journal* 14(5):281–285.

Applewhite L and C Dickins. 1997. Coping with terrorism: The OPM–SANG experience. *Military Medicine* 162(4):240–243.

Asbrock F and I Fritsche. 2013. Authoritarian reactions to terrorist threat: Who is being threatened, the Me or the We? *International Journal of Psychology* 48(1):35–49.

Berger R, M Gelkopf, and Y Heineberg. 2012. A teacher-delivered intervention for adolescents exposed to ongoing and intense traumatic war-related stress: A quasi-randomized controlled study. *Journal of Adolescent Health* 51(5):453–461.

Bureau of Counterterrorism. 2015. *Foreign Terrorist Organizations* [Electronic Version]. http://www.state.gov/j/ct/rls/other/des/123085.htm, accessed November 21, 2015.

Butler LD, C Koopman, J Azarow et al. 2009. Psychosocial predictors of resilience after the September 11, 2001 terrorist attacks. *Journal of Nervous and Mental Disease* 197(4):266–273.

Claassen CA, T Carmody, SM Stewart, RM Bossarte, GL Larkin, WA Woodward, and MH Trivedi. 2010. Effect of 11 September 2001 terrorist attacks in the USA on suicide in areas surrounding the crash sites. *British Journal of Psychiatry* 196(5):359–364.

Desivilya HS, R Gal, and O Ayalon. 1996. Extent of victimization, traumatic stress symptoms, and adjustment of terrorist assault survivors: A long–term follow–up. *Journal of Traumatic Stress* 9(4):881–889.

Dreman S. 1989. Children of victims of terrorism in Israel: Coping and adjustment in the face of trauma. *Israel Journal of Psychiatry and Related Sciences* 26(4):212–222.

Dreman S and E Cohen. 1990. Children of victims of terrorism revisited: Integrating individual and family treatment approaches. *American Journal of Orthopsychiatry* 60(2):204–209.

Duarte CS, P Wu, A Cheung, DJ Mandell, B Fan, J Wicks, GJ Musa, and CW Hoven. 2011. Media use by children and adolescents from New York City 6 months after the WTC attack. *Journal of Traumatic Stress* 24(5):553–556.

Faber AJ, E Willerton, SR Clymer, SM MacDermid, and HM Weiss. 2008. Ambiguous absence, ambiguous presence: A qualitative study of military reserve families in wartime. *Journal of Family Psychology* 22(2):222–230.

Farchi M and Y Gidron. 2010. The effects of "psychological inoculation" versus ventilation on the mental resilience of Israeli citizens under continuous war stress. *Journal of Nervous and Mental Disease* 198(5):382–384.

Ferrando L, S Galea, E Sainz Cortón, C Mingote, E García Camba, A Fernandez Líria, and R Gabriel. 2011. Long-term psychopathology changes among the injured and members of the community after a massive terrorist attack. *European Psychiatry* 26(8):513–517.

Franz VA, CR Glass, DB Arnkoff, and MA Dutton. 2009. The impact of the September 11th terrorist attacks on psychiatric patients: A review. *Clinical Psychology Review* 29(4):339–347.

Gesundheit B, N Ash, S Blazer, and Al Rivkind. 2009. Medical care for terrorists—To treat or not to treat? *American Journal of Bioethics* 9(10):40–42.

Hacker FJ. 1977. *Crusaders, Criminals, Crazies: Terror and Terrorism in Our Time*. New York: Norton.

Henriksen CA, JM Bolton, and J Sareen. 2010. The psychological impact of terrorist attacks: Examining a dose-response relationship between exposure to 9/11 and Axis I mental disorders. *Depression and Anxiety* 27(11):993–1000.

Janis I. 1972. *Victims of Groupthink*. Boston: Houghton Mifflin Company.

Johnson K and JM Luna. 2011. Working toward resilience: A retrospective report of actions taken in support of a New York school crisis team following 9/11. *International Journal of Emergency Mental Health* 13(2):81–90.

Johnston SL and RD Dipp. 2009. Support of marines and sailors returning from combat: A comparison of two different mental health models. *Military Medicine* 174(5):455–459.

Korn L and G Zukerman. 2011. Affective and behavioral changes following exposure to traumatic events: The moderating effect of religiosity on avoidance behavior among students studying under a high level of terror event exposure. *Journal of Religion and Health* 50(4):911–921.

Levav I, R Kohn, and M Billig. 2008. The protective effect of religiosity under terrorism. *Psychiatry* 71(1):46–58.

Martin-Peña J, A Rodríguez-Carballeira, J Escartín, C Porrúa, and M Olff. 2011. Taxonomy of the psychosocial consequences caused by the violence of persecution of ETA's network. *Spanish Journal of Psychology* 14(1):172–182.

McArdle SC, H Rosoff, and RS John. 2012. The dynamics of evolving beliefs, concerns emotions, and behavioral avoidance following 9/11: A longitudinal analysis of representative archival samples. *Risk Analysis* 32(4):744–761.

McIntosh DN, MJ Poulin, RC Silver, and EA Holman. 2011. The distinct roles of spirituality and religiosity in physical and mental health after collective trauma: A national longitudinal study of responses to the 9/11 attacks. *Journal of Behavioral Medicine* 34(6):497–507.

Miller L. 2011. Psychological interventions for terroristic trauma: Prevention, crisis management, and clinical treatment strategies. *International Journal of Emergency Mental Health* 13(2):95–120.

Misra M, N Greenberg, C Hutchinson, A Brain, and N Glozier. 2009. Psychological impact upon London Ambulance Service of the 2005 bombings. *Occupational Medicine (London)* 59(6):428–433.

Nijdam MJ, BP Gersons, and M Olff. 2010. Dutch politicians' coping with terrorist threat. *British Journal of Psychiatry* 197(4):328–329.

North CS, B Pfefferbaum, A Kawasaki, S Lee, and EL Spitznagel. 2011. Psychosocial adjustment of directly exposed survivors 7 years after the Oklahoma City bombing. *Comprehensive Psychiatry* 52(1):1–8.

Palmieri PA, KJ Chipman, D Canetti, RJ Johnson, and SE Hobfoll. 2010. Prevalence and correlates of sleep problems in adult Israeli Jews exposed to actual or threatened terrorist or rocket attacks. *Journal of Clinical Sleep Medicine* 6(6):557–564.

Pearce JM, GJ Rubin, P Selke, R Amlôt, F Mowbray, and MB Rogers. 2013. Communicating with the public following radiological terrorism: Results from a series of focus groups and national surveys in Britain and Germany. *Prehospital and Disaster Medicine* 28(2):110–119.

Peleg K, DH Jaffe, and Israel Trauma Group. 2010. Are injuries from terror and war similar? A comparison study of civilians and soldiers. *Annals of Surgery* 252(2):363–369.

Peleg K, JL Regens, JT Gunter, and DH Jaffe. 2011. The normalisation of terror: The response of Israel's stock market to long periods of terrorism. *Disasters* 35(1):268–283.

Peleg O and M Mass-Friedman. 2013. Worry about terror among young adults living in ongoing security uncertainty. *International Journal of Psychology* 48(3):407–421.

Post JM. 2000. Terrorist on trial: The context of political crime. *Journal of the American Academy of Psychiatry and the Law* 28(2):171–178.

Post JM. 2007. *The Mind of the Terrorist: The Psychology of Terrorism from the IRA to al-Qaeda.* New York: Palgrave MacMillan.

Post JM. 2010. "When hatred is bred in the bone": The social psychology of terrorism. *Annals of the New York Academy of Sciences* 1208:15–23.

Pridemore WA, A Trahan, and MB Chamlin. 2009. No evidence of suicide increase following terrorist attacks in the United States: An interrupted time-series analysis of September 11 and Oklahoma City. *Suicide and Life-Threatening Behavior* 39(6):659–670.

Razik S, T Ehring, and PM Emmelkamp. 2013. Psychological consequences of terrorist attacks: Prevalence and predictors of mental health problems in Pakistani emergency responders. *Psychiatry Research* 207(1–2):80–85.

Reid WH. 1989. Terrorism and the social sciences. *Violence, Aggression and Terrorism (Israel)* 3:101–117.

Reshetnikov M. 2008. Visions of the future: Social processes and terrorism in Europe. *Journal of Analytical Psychology* 53(5):653–665.

Scrimin S, U Moscardino, F Capello, G Altoè, AM Steinberg, and RS Pynoos. 2011. Trauma reminders and PTSD symptoms in (school age) children three years after a terrorist attack in Beslan. *Social, Science and Medicine* 72(5):694–700.

Shmotkin D and G Keinan. 2011. Who is prone to react to coinciding threats of terrorism and war? Exploring vulnerability through global versus differential reactivity. *Community Mental Health Journal* 47(1):35–46.

Stevens G, K Agho, M Taylor, AL Jones, J Jacobs, M Barr, and B Raphael. 2011. Alert but less alarmed: A pooled analysis of terrorism threat perception in Australia. *BMC Public Health* 11:797.

Strand R, K Felices, and K Williams. 2010. Critical incident stress management (CISM) in support of special agents and other first responders responding to the Fort Hood shooting: Summary and recommendations. *International Journal of Emergency Mental Health* 12(3):151–160.

Trioni JE. 1999. *The Psychology of Terrorism. REQ 511 Counter-terrorism Policy and Intelligence Issues Course.* Washington, DC: Joint Military Intelligence College.

Tuchner M, Z Meiner, S Parush, and A Hartman-Maeir. 2010. Health-related quality of life two years after injury due to terrorism. *Israel Journal of Psychiatry and Related Sciences* 47(4):269–275.

Ursano RJ, CS Fullerton, and AE Norwood. 1995. Psychiatric dimensions of disaster: Patient care, community consultation, and preventive medicine. *Harvard Review of Psychiatry* 3(4):196–209.

U.S. Department of State. 2000. *Patterns of Global Terrorism*. Washington, DC: U.S. Department of State.

Weizman T, Y Yagil, and S Schreiber. 2009. Association between terror attacks and suicide attempts. *Suicide and Life-Threatening Behavior* 39(4):425–432.

64

Traditional stalking

KANG CHOI AND MOHAN NAIR

INTRODUCTION

Stalking has remained firmly fixed in the public eye. High-profile cases create the belief that erotomanic stalkers bent on murdering celebrities are the typical situation, despite evidence to the contrary. For a number of reasons, stalking has received increased attention and investigation over recent years. This chapter presents an overview of what has been learned about traditional, physical stalking.

Stalking has continued to be a significant forensic topic since the first stalking law was established in California in 1990. Stalking is defined as a pattern of intentional, unwanted, repeated behaviors directed at a person that cause fear or that would cause a reasonable person to feel fear (Spitzberg and Cupach 2007). Prior to 1990, the term *stalking* was primarily associated with psychiatric conditions considered relatively rare (e.g., erotomania and delusional disorders) and often involved celebrities and public figures. However, stalking arising from dysfunctional courtship behaviors and domestic conflict has now become the dominant focus. Research has shown consistently that most stalking situations arise out of ex-intimate situations. Ex-intimate stalkers are also the most violent. In contrast, stalkers of public figures and celebrities are among the least violent (Meloy et al. 2008).

Following the 1989 murder of actress Rebecca Schaeffer by an enraged, obsessed fan, and the killing of four Orange County women by ex-intimates, California became the first state to enact an anti-stalking law. The media's portrayal of stalking-related violence in conjunction with the efforts of domestic violence prevention advocates forced rapid (and in the opinion of some, hasty) legislation that made stalking a crime in all 50 states. Stalking across state lines is a federal offense.

THE CRIME OF STALKING

No single legal definition of stalking exists. Some states and the model anti-stalking code (National Institute of Justice 1993) have used component terms and concepts such as the requirement of threat, proximity, intent in the stalker, frequency of contacts, fear in the victim, and reasonableness of the victim's reaction. However, there is little legal consensus about these requirements. The inclusion of fear in the definition of stalking is used to distinguish stalking from harassment and to differentiate legal from illegal behavior. Individuals who did not report experiencing subjective or reasonable fear were less likely to consider behaviors stalking (Owens 2015).

California's anti-stalking law (Cal Pen Code §646.9) states: "Any person who willfully, maliciously, and repeatedly follows or willfully and maliciously harasses another person and who makes a credible threat with the intent to place that person in reasonable fear for his or her safety, or the safety of his or her immediate family…" The statute requires a "credible threat" but no requirement that the defendant had intent to carry out the threat.

States vary in their requirements of intent, threat, and resulting fear. Some states do not require intent on the part of the stalker. Florida considers the subjective reaction of the victim to be adequate. Some states require threatening behavior (e.g., Colorado), while others do not require credible threats (e.g., Arizona). Among states with credible threat requirements, some require an "apparent ability" to cause the harm, while others do not. In terms of fear, some states require actual fear, while other states use a reasonable person standard (a reasonable person would have felt fear). Some states require both a threat and fear (e.g., California), while others require only one of the two. Still other states do not require either (e.g., Hawaii) (Fox et al. 2011; Stalking Resource Center 2015). In 2007, 39 states required a fear element and 19 states required a threat component (Leiter 2007 in Fox et al. 2011). Stalking remains primarily a victim-defined crime. In some instances, individuals can be charged with stalking solely based on another's subjective feelings.

Federal regulation includes the 1996 Stalking Law, 18 U.S.C. 2261(A), which makes it a crime for any person to travel across state lines with the intent to kill, injure, harass or intimidate another person. The accused stalker must also place that person or a member of that person's family in a reasonable fear of death or serious bodily injury, or cause substantial emotional distress (Cornell Law 2015).

Some have criticized stalking laws as overriding constitutionally protected rights and not differentiating lawful from unlawful behaviors (McAnaney et al. 1993; Boychuk 1994; David 1994; Haas 1994; Guy 1993). This would include actions such as panhandling, the "normal" volatility of relationships, the right to travel, the right to be in public places, and "normal" attempts to communicate between ex-partners. Others feel that the laws have not been protective enough; they justify these statutes on the basis that it allows law enforcement and the judiciary to intervene more effectively and preemptively in potentially lethal domestic violence situations (Bradfield 1998; Radosevich 2000).

EPIDEMIOLOGY

There have been several large community surveys of stalking in the United States (Basile et al. 2006; Baum et al. 2009; Black et al. 2011; Catalano 2012; Breiding et al. 2014).

The 2011 National Intimate Partner and Sexual Violence Survey (n = 12,727) showed a lifetime prevalence of 15.2% in women and 5.7% in men, as well as a 12-month prevalence of 4.2% and 2.1%, respectively (Breiding et al. 2014). This is a slight change from the same survey's 2010 data (n = 16,507) showing prevalence rates of 16.2% in women and 5.2% in men; with 12-month prevalence of 4.3% and 1.3%, respectively (Black et al. 2011). However, these are higher rates than the 1998 National Violence Against Women Survey reporting a lifetime prevalence of 8.1% in females and 2.2% in males, with a 12-month prevalence of 0.4% and 1%, respectively (Tjaden and Thoennes 1998). Studies have generally reflected a range of lifetime prevalence from 2% to 13% in men and 8% to 32% in women (Spitzberg and Cupach 2007). The range in rates is partly affected by the definition of stalking used (stalking behaviors, type of resultant fears, etc.) and the population queried.

The range of behaviors used in questionnaires to assess rates of stalking go from the clearly benign and highly subjective (e.g., leaving unwanted messages, showing exaggerated expressions of affection, trying to be friends with the friend of the victim) to those that are clearly criminal and life threatening (e.g., rape, kidnapping, and using a weapon to subdue the individual). Wright et al.'s (1996) FBI sample of 30 stalking cases that resulted in seven homicides and six suicides is unlikely to have much in common with the 62% of young adults in the community who report being "repeatedly" stalked. Details of stalking studies in random and nonrandom populations are listed in Table 64.1.

Stalkers are mostly men who stalk women, usually an ex-intimate (Spitzberg and Cupach 2007). However, female stalking also occurs. According to the 2006 National Crime Victimization Survey, 43% of males were stalked by a female, and 24% of females were stalked by a female (Baum et al. 2009). These rates are higher than previous studies, and higher than studies in mental health settings (Meloy et al. 2011). In a study of 143 stalkers, Meloy et al. (2011) noted that female stalkers were mostly heterosexual, in their mid-30s, and were single, divorced, or separated. Mental illness was common in female stalkers, most commonly mood disorder, with a high prevalence of borderline personality disorder (Meloy and Boyd 2003). Unlike male stalkers, female stalkers were more likely to stalk male acquaintances, strangers, and celebrities, rather than ex-intimates.

Same-sex stalking is also common. In 1998, Tjaden and Thoennes noted that 60% of male stalking victims were stalked by another male. The 2006 Supplemental Victim Survey indicated that 23.5% of female stalking victims were stalked by a female, and 41.3% of males were stalked by a male (Baum et al. 2009). Based on prior studies, one-quarter of adult stalking may involve same-sex stalking (Strand and McEwan 2011), with higher rates in juveniles (Purcell et al. 2010). In a comparison of same-sex stalking cases (n = 94) and opposite-sex stalking cases (n = 160) from Sweden and Australia, Strand and McEwan (2011) noted that same-sex stalkers were more likely to have a "resentful" or "rejected" motivation. In contrast, opposite-sex stalkers were "intimacy seeking" or "incompetent suitors."

Juvenile stalking remains understudied, though may be different from adult stalking. In one of the first studies of juvenile stalkers (n = 299), a majority of stalkers were male (64%) and victims female (69%), similar to adult studies; however, with a higher proportion of female stalkers. Juvenile female stalkers mostly targeted other females; motivated commonly by bullying and retaliation for perceived injury. Juvenile male stalkers were most commonly motivated by rejection from a break-up (Purcell et al. 2010). Almost all juvenile stalkers knew their victims (98%). Juveniles used direct methods of stalking, including unwanted approaches (76%) and telephone calls (42%). Interestingly, stalking was most commonly seen as an extension of bullying, with 54% of victims being physically attacked (Purcell et al. 2009).

TYPOLOGY

There is no uniform classification of stalking. Stalking, like violence, is a common behavioral pathway that flows from diverse motivations. The sexual predator who follows the child with a well-rehearsed plan to torture, rape, and kill is a stalker; the high school student who simply cannot let go of his ex-girlfriend and insists on staying close to her in the cafeteria and hanging outside of her home in spite of being warned is a stalker; and the homeless individual with schizophrenia who keeps following a stranger in response to auditory hallucinations is a stalker.

Most relevant classifications of stalkers involve some combination of the relationship to the victim and the stalker's motivation. The most influential and known typologies are from Zona et al. (1998), Mullen et al. (2000), and Mohandie et al. (2006) (Racine and Billick 2014). Violence is directly related to intimacy and closeness (Schwartz-Ross and Morgan 1998).

Table 64.1 Stalking studies in random and nonrandom populations

Reference	Sample type	Percentage stalking	Remarks
Australian Bureau of Statistics (1996)	$n = 6300$ (females) Random community	15% lifetime prevalence	40% stalked months to more than 2 years Stalkers most often strangers. Two-thirds asymptomatic
Fremouw et al. (1997)	$n = 600$ college students	30% females 17% males	80% new stalkers 43% females and 24% males dated stalker
Kienlen et al. (1997)	$n = 341$	LAPD/Threat Management Unit	Simple obsessional 217 Love obsessional 87 Erotomanics 17
National Institute of Justice, Tjaden and Thoennes (1998)	$n = 8000$ females $n = 8000$ males Random community	8.1% female, 2.2% male lifetime prevalence	78% victims female 80% stalkers male 81% assaults 31% rapes
Harmon et al. (1998)	$n = 175$ Forensic clinic referrals		Affectionate/amorous 61% Persecutory/angry 31% Violent 46%
Mullen et al. (1999)	$n = 145$ stalkers Self/court referred		Typology: Rejected 58, Intimacy seeker 54, Incompetent 24, Resentful 24, Predatory 8
Tjaden and Thoennes (2000)	$n = 1785$ Domestic violence reports	18.3% females 10.5% males	One in six was stalked; protective orders frequent, stalking victims sustain less physical injury
	$n = 5910$ victims $n = 3842$ stalkers Police reports	69/100,000 female 20/100,000 male	78% victims female 87% stalkers male
Bjerregaard (2000)	$n = 788$ college students	25% females 11% males	96% females stalked by males One out of three males stalked by males Half ex-intimates; threat of violence: 23.8% females; 13.8% males
Fisher et al. (2000) National College Women Sexual Victimization (NCWSV) study	$n = 4446$	13.1% women reported being stalked since start of school year	Duration average 60 days Three out of ten reported emotional injury 10.3% had forced or attempted sexual contact
Sandberg et al. (2002)	$n = 62$ Adult psychiatric hospital clinical staff		52% harassed, 3% stalked
Spitzberg (2002)	Meta-analysis of 103 studies	Average prevalence: 23.5% women 10.5% men	Average length of stalking: almost 2 years 75% of victims are female
Purcell et al. (2005)	$n = 1844$ Random community		Stalking victims had higher caseness on GHQ-28 than nonvictims, and harassed victims 34.1% met caseness 1 year after stalking ended
Basile et al. (2006)	$n = 9684$ Random community ICARIS-2 phone survey	7% women and 2% men lifetime prevalence	
Baum et al. (2009) Supplemental Victimization Survey 2006	$n = 65,270$ Random community	In a 12-month period, 14/1000 persons age 18 or older were victims of stalking (1.4%)	11% stalked 5 years or more; divorced or separated had highest risk 34/1000

(Continued)

Table 64.1 (*Continued*) Stalking studies in random and nonrandom populations

Reference	Sample type	Percentage stalking	Remarks
Mohandie et al. (2006)	$n = 1005$ Nonrandom Three prosecutorial agencies, one police department, one corporate security department	81% of victims were female	73% in private context 27% in public context 28% physical assault 19% used weapons to harm or threaten victim or object of victim 58% of stalkers had precipitant (break-up of relationship or rejection)
Dressing et al. (2007)	$n = 2000$ (1000 women and 1000 men) Random community sample in Germany	11.6% lifetime incidence 17.3% women, 3.7% men	31% physical violence 19% sexual violence
Spitzberg and Cupach (2007)	$n = 175$ studies Meta-analysis	Lifetime: 8%–32% females 2%–13% males	Average stalking duration: 22 months Female victims 60%–80% 79% acquainted with stalker
MacKenzie et al. (2008)	$n = 122$ referred to forensic clinic	93% stalkers were men 69% of victims were women	Stalkers more likely to have insecure attachment styles, particularly fearful style
Purcell et al. (2009)	$n = 299$ juveniles Restraining order applications	64% stalkers were male 69% victims were females	98% pursued known victim 76% used phone calls 67% used text messaging
Dressing and Gass (2010)	$n = 300$ Admitted psychiatric patients	21.7% female, 21% male lifetime prevalence	Stalking course more difficult and violent 46.4% of victims had addictive disorder
Patton et al. (2010)	$n = 2783$ College students		Stalkers significantly higher on insecure-anxious scale, and lower on insecure avoidant scale
Black et al. (2011) National Intimate Partner and Sexual Violence Survey 2010	$n = 16{,}507$ Random community	16.2% women, 5.2% men lifetime prevalence	Two-thirds of female victims stalked by intimate partner More than one-half of female victims and more than one-third male victims stalked before the age of 25
Catalano (2012) Supplemental Victimization Survey-Revised	$n = 65{,}270$ Random community	In a 12-month period, 1.5% of persons age 18 or older were stalked	

By integrating concepts of delusional disorders and erotomania and nondelusional/borderline erotomania, Zona and colleagues (1998) divide stalkers into three types:

- *Simple obsessionals*: These individuals constitute the largest group, and form two-thirds of the 200 referrals to the LAPD/Threat Management Unit. Typically this involves the stalking of ex-lovers. Less frequently, obsessive attachments and resentments may involve the stalking of friend, roommates, co-workers, and acquaintances. This group carries the highest risk of violence.
- *Love obsessionals*: These individuals form one out of four of Zona's sample. They are characterized by the absence of any relationship with the victim. Involvement may occur through the media, i.e., star stalkers, but any chance contact may trigger a stalking episode.
- *Erotomanics*: These are predominantly females who believe, against all evidence to the contrary, that the victim loves them. Usually the victim is an individual in a higher station than the stalker.

Mullen and colleagues (2000) classify stalkers into five types:

1. Rejected
2. Intimacy seekers
3. Resentful

4. Incompetent suitors
5. Predatory

The rejected group is similar in composition to simple obsessives. The intimacy seekers are similar to love obsessors and erotomanics. The resentful group includes touchy and paranoid individuals for whom stalking and harassing becomes a way of getting back at co-workers, supervisors, or individuals from some system for perceived persecution. Incompetent suitors feel entitled to a relationship with their interest, regardless of that individual's preference. Predatory stalkers seek excitement from secretly observing their victims. For this group, stalking behaviors may be in preparation for an assault, usually sexual.

Mohandie et al. (2006) suggests a typology using two dimensions: prior relationship to victim and stalking context:

1. Previous relationship
   a. Intimate
   b. Acquaintance
2. No prior relationship or limited contact
   a. Public figure
   b. Private stranger

In a nonrandom study (n = 1005), Mohandie et al. (2006) reported that the largest group was the intimate category, at 50%. The intimate group includes cohabitants, married, and sexual intimates. This group was most violent, assaulting more than half of its victims, and one out of three used a weapon to threaten or harm.

BEHAVIORS ASSOCIATED WITH STALKING

Stalking involves intrusive attempts to make unwanted communication with the victim, or to intrude on or control the victim's life. The forms of communication and intrusion are only limited by the stalker's imagination. They include telephone contacts, following, writing letters, and increasingly e-mail and posting information on the Internet. As an example, Jake Baker, a University of Michigan student, was arrested by federal agents for sharing details of his fantasies and plans online to kidnap, rape, and torture a classmate (Branscomb 1995).

Stalkers may show up in places that they know the victim is expected to be, and/or make contact with or ingratiate themselves with the victims' family or acquaintances in an attempt to get close to them. Goods may be ordered on behalf of the victim, services such as the telephone and electricity turned off, and rumors started about the victim. For example, the disgruntled boyfriend of a physician complained to the Board of Medicine that she was improperly prescribing narcotic medications to addicts, compelling an investigation on her. In another case, a young man communicated to his ex-girlfriend's supervisor that the frequent phone calls she gets at work are from clients to whom she is offering her "call-girl" services.

More ominous intrusions include threats of violence, which are reported by 30%–80% of victims. Other examples include directly approaching the victim at his or her home, entering the victim's home to leave threatening mementos, initiating frivolous lawsuits, threatening the victim, threatening family members and friends, damaging property, and killing pets. Extreme cases can escalate to physically assaulting, kidnapping, and raping victims. Ex-intimate stalkers use the broadest range of surveillance and harassment techniques.

The form of communication may reveal something about the stalker and his or her relationship with the victim, real or imagined. Bizarre communication and gifts may suggest that the stalker is psychotic, but this may also be done with the conscious goal of "spooking" the victim. Letter writing is the most common technique employed by erotomanics and love obsessives.

Cupach and Spitzberg (2004) offer eight categories of stalking behavior: "hyper-intimacy, mediated contacts, interactional contacts, surveillance, invasion, harassment and intimidation, coercion and threat, and aggression." Mediated contacts involve the use of technology to communicate. It is unclear how much overlap there is between cyberstalkers and offline stalkers (Bocij and McFarlane 2003, in Spitzberg and Cupach 2007).

Stalking behavior can be prolonged. One-fourth of subjects in the study of Tjaden and Thoennes (1998) were stalked for an average of 1.8 years; delusional and erotomanic stalkers may continue as long as 5 or 10 years (Zona et al. 1998; Mullen et al. 2000). In a meta-analysis of 175 studies, Spitzberg and Cupach (2007) reported an average stalking duration of 22 months.

With advances in technology, the options for the stalker are many. However, stalkers are not abandoning more traditional means of stalking. In the 2006 Supplemental Victimization Survey, 73.2% of stalkers did not use cyberstalking or electronic monitoring (Baum et al. 2009). Similarly, the 2010 National Intimate Partner and Sexual Violence Survey reported that the dominant methods of stalking remained unwanted phones calls and physical approach.

MOTIVATION FOR STALKING

As with domestic violence, stalking is often associated with relationships that involve narcissistic or borderline personalities, pathologic rage (Edelson and Tolman 1992; Meloy 1998), enmeshment, and abandonment rage. The most common reason for stalking is the desire to be with a loved one (Mohandie et al. 2006; Spitzberg and Cupach 2007). Often this is coupled with or alternates with a need for revenge, control, and the desire to hurt or even kill the love object. Stalking behaviors may be maintained by revenge and hatred alone. This concept is neither new nor unusual in that pathologic jealousy and abandonment rage have always been the most common reason why men hurt or kill the women they claim to love (Stone 1989; White and Mullen 1989).

Individuals with paranoid, schizoid, and narcissistic personality disorders may be hypersensitive to or misconstrue communications from co-workers, neighbors, or casual acquaintances. A real or imagined slight becomes an obsession that then results in stalking behavior. Many have personality disorders that make it difficult for them to achieve real friendships, courtship behavior, and intimacy. Over half the stalkers in Mullen's sample (Mullen et al. 2000) had never been out on a date. Individuals who may have had a prior relationship may desperately try to hold on to it. Erotomanics and love obsessives typically have fantasy relationships as a substitute for a real one that they are not able to achieve.

Psychotic motivations may include affection, sexual desire, or the delusional belief that the other person loves them. The motivation may be driven by paranoid, grandiose, or religious delusions. Stalking may occur in response to auditory hallucinations. For example, a homeless individual may follow a jogger wearing a green sweatshirt to his door in response to auditory hallucinations and a delusion that the person is the messiah.

Individuals with intellectual disability and dementia can have trouble exercising appropriate control on their behavior. As a result, they may follow individuals to whom they are sexually attracted, feel affectionate toward, or are drawn by some curiosity or resentment.

Individuals with Autism Spectrum Disorder (ASD) have deficits in communication, social reciprocity, and socialization. ASDs have difficulty reading social cues and may have perseverative behaviors that interfere with social competency (Post et al. 2014). As a result, ASDs may attempt to initiate relationships with socially inappropriate conduct that unwittingly resembles stalking (Stokes et al. 2007). Romantic and sexual urges may be expressed in inappropriate and, at times, bizarre manners in individuals with ASD. ASDs may be over-represented in those who pursue unusual sexual lives, i.e., those whose choice of sexual expression tends to be viewed as "deviant or weird." Such individuals may be viewed as odd/eccentric, mentally disordered, or even criminal, depending on the crime, the period, and the surrounding culture.

Often lacking appropriate awareness of boundaries, ASDs may engage in inappropriate physical contact or attempts at closeness. Consider, for example, the student in high school who grabs the breasts or genitalia of a fellow student; exposing themselves hoping to attract another; or engaging in obsessional following. An indiscriminate approach can also lead to sexual and violent victimization of both males and females. Inappropriate attempts to gain the attention of a potential sexual partner may result in charges of sexual assault, sexual harassment, or stalking claims in the workplace, school, and other settings.

A 2007 study ($n = 25$) suggested that ASDs are more likely to have inappropriate touching and comments, belief that the person of interest must like them, and obsessive interest. They are also more likely to follow the person, pursue in a threatening way, make threats to the person, or threaten self-harm (Stokes et al. 2007).

Stalking sometimes represents a cover for underlying paraphilic disorders. Sexual predators and paraphiliacs, i.e., pedophiles, rapists, sadists, voyeurs, fetishists, and obscene phone callers, may engage in stalking-type behaviors (Lloyd-Goldstein 2000). The following three case examples demonstrate this principle:

- A 27-year-old male is repeatedly arrested and incarcerated for entering a female's home to acquire lingerie for sexual arousal. The prominent sexologist Havelock Ellis described a British soldier who was sexually aroused by the smell of menstrual blood; he was exquisitely sensitive to the smell, and would detect and follow women who were menstruating. On one occasion he was caught as he followed a woman into her tent and attempted to remove her menstrual pad while she was sleeping.
- A 31-year-old male would repeatedly follow women with a video camera, staying at a short distance from them, ultimately following them all the way up to their door. He was later convicted of following, overpowering, and raping a policewoman.
- A 16-year-old male would follow attractive young women on a jogging path while exposing his genitals. He then progressed to physical contact by brushing up against them. Eventually, he followed a woman and tried to rape her, leading to his arrest and incarceration.

PSYCHIATRIC DISORDERS AMONG STALKERS

The majority of stalkers have a mental illness, whereas a minority have a psychotic disorder (Meloy 2007). Cluster B personality disorders of the borderline, narcissistic, and histrionic types are predominant in ex-intimate stalkers. Less often, dependent, schizoid, and paranoid personality disorders may be noted. Substance abuse is common. Antisocial personality is uncommon; the presence of psychopathy should raise concerns about violence. There may also be interplay between psychotic disorder and typology of stalker. For instance, a resentful stalker with a psychotic illness with persecutory delusions may have increased risk of violence. However, an intimacy-seeking stalker with an erotomanic delusion may have decreased risk of violence (Mullen et al. 2006).

VICTIMS OF STALKING

Some 80%–90% of stalking victims are women. On the flip side, 80%–90% of stalkers are men. Stalking has been described in all ages, including adolescents (McCann 2001; Purcell et al. 2009).

The most common victims of stalking are young women in their reproductive years, who have had a sexual relationship with their stalker. As in other victims of domestic violence, some may have enmeshed, dependent, sadomasochistic relationships with the perpetrator. Often there is a history of childhood abuse (Bowlby 1979; Downs 1996; Gelles 1997; Goodyear-Smith and Laidlaw 1999). This group is at the highest risk of violence, including lethal violence. Physical assault, rape, and stalking often start even prior to the separation. Physical violence may occur in 20%–30% of stalking cases (Spitzberg and Cupach 2007).

Victims of nonintimate stalkers do not fit one particular profile. Those who are stalked by intimacy seekers and love obsessionals are often visible and appealing. Victims may include co-workers, roommates, casual acquaintances, and complete strangers. Therapists and physicians are especially prone to being stalked as a result of having to deal with emotionally needy people. In a meta-analysis of physician stalking studies, Nelson et al. (2015) noted a prevalence rate of 1.5%–25.1% (with one study showing 68.5%).

People with mental illness also seem to be vulnerable to stalking. In a German study of 300 patients admitted to a psychiatric hospital, 21% of the patients had been stalked, nearly twice as high of the German general population (11.6%). In addition, the course of their stalking was more difficult and violent (48.4% had been physically attacked and 83.9% had been struck) (Dressing et al. 2011).

Stalking can cause serious disturbances in emotional, social, interpersonal, and work functioning. Posttraumatic stress disorder has been reported in 37%–60% of stalking victims. Victims commonly report depression, anxiety, insomnia, somatization disorders, and substance abuse. A random community sample comparing victims of stalking, brief harassment, and nonvictims noted higher scores for severe depression in stalking victims, with 10% of victims endorsing recent SI (Purcell et al. 2005). Longer durations of stalking may be more damaging. Stalking lasting more than 2 weeks was associated with higher rates of anxiety, depression, and posttraumatic symptoms (Purcell et al. 2005). In addition, stalking victims who were threatened were significantly more likely to have PTSD symptoms than victims who were not. Victims who were physically harmed did have more PTSD symptoms, but the difference was not statistically significant.

Hall (1995) noted self-identified stalking victims as becoming aggressive, paranoid, and fearful. One-third of the females, and one-fifth of the men of domestic violence stalking victims sought psychiatric help (Tjaden and Thoennes 2000). As a result of stalking, victims may move, change jobs, stop working, change their usual routes, isolate, and, in some instances, arm themselves. The economic cost of stalking can be high. More than half of stalking victims lost five or more days at work (Baum et al. 2009). The negative emotional impact of stalking on the victim may persist even after the stalking has ended. Purcell et al. (2005) reported that more than one-third of stalking victims continued to have anxiety and depression a year after the stalking (34.1% met caseness for GHQ-28). The most common fear of stalking victims is the uncertainty of what would happen next (Baum et al. 2009).

Stalking victims often feel they have less power to address their stalking (Spitzberg and Cupach 2007). Cupach and Spitzberg (2004) noted five categories of victim coping: "moving with, moving against, moving away, moving inward, and moving outward." "Moving with" refers to efforts to negotiate with the stalker. "Moving against" refers to efforts to deter the stalker. While "moving inward" is coping by focusing on the self, including denial or buying a gun, "moving outward" is the seeking of outside help.

Self-identified victims recruited through the media (Hall 1995; Brewster 2000) or through support groups such as incest survivor groups (Kamphuis and Emmelkamp 2001) may be prone to exaggerate, fabricate, falsely attribute, or, in some instances, be delusional about being stalked.

FORENSIC ASPECTS OF STALKING

Stalking, like sex offending, is recognized as both a psychiatric and criminal problem. Many states and the model anti-stalking code specifically recommend mental health evaluations on those charged with the crime of stalking. Referring parties may request opinions on various aspects of stalking including the following:

- Assessment of criminal competency, i.e., insanity, diminished capacity, the ability to form specific intent
- Evaluation of stalking victims, i.e., mental state of victims who killed in self-defense (battered wife syndrome); claims of posttraumatic stress disorder and other psychiatric disorders as a result of stalking issues of false victimization
- Appropriateness of *Tarasoff* warning when clinicians become aware of a patient stalking a specific victim; issues to hospitalize or release stalkers
- Psychiatric worker's compensation evaluation of employees who claim to be stalked in the workplace; stalking and risk of workplace violence by disgruntled employees
- Violence risk assessment of stalkers
- Recommendations regarding civil commitment, rehabilitation, and treatment for stalkers
- Threat management consultations
- Stalking/child abduction and high-conflict child custody cases
- Assessment of paraphilic and predatory stalkers

Assessment

The assessment procedure includes the following:

- Psychiatric examination, including record review and collateral information, i.e., medical, psychiatric, police, work records
- Current psychiatric, chemical dependency, and medical problems
- Past history and response to treatment; motivations for stalking behavior; history of recent losses

- Psychological tests including Minnesota Multiphasic Personality Inventory-2 (MMPI-2)/ Minnesota Multiphasic Personality Inventory-2 Restructured Form (MMPI-2-RF), Millon Clinical Multiaxial Inventory-III (MCMI-III), Hare Psychopathy Check List-Revised (PCL-R)
- Violence risk assessment
- Family and social support
- Treatment recommendations, i.e., civil commitment, inpatient, outpatient
- Prognosis

Risk assessment

Stalking is a common behavior driven by various motives. Similar to a headache that may stem from mild sinus congestion or a life-threatening brainstem hemorrhage, some situations of stalking may represent grave danger. Therefore, there cannot be one risk assessment tool for stalking. Rather, the empirically tested and actuarial data available from different groups should be considered, i.e., the Danger Assessment Instrument for Batterers (Saunders 1995), Violence Risk Appraisal Guide (VRAG) (Quinsey et al. 1998), PCL-R (Hare 1991), the Stalking Risk Profile (SRP) (McEwan et al. 2011), Stalking Assessment and Management (SAM) (Kropp et al. 2011), and the Static-99 for sex offender recidivism (Hanson and Thornton 1999). General factors in violence risk assessment should also be noted (Monahan and Steadman 1994).

Mullen and colleagues (2006) suggest a "Stalking Risk Profile" that involves examining five domains: (1) the stalker and victim relationship; (2) motivation of the stalker; (3) characteristics of the stalker including psychology, psychopathology, and social context; (4) vulnerabilities of the victim; and (5) the general context of the stalking, including legal and mental health issues.

Factors likely to increase the risk of assault in stalkers (Palarea et al. 1999; Mullen et al. 2000; Rosenfeld and Harmon 2002; Rosenfeld 2004 in Meloy 2007; McEwan et al. 2009; McEwan et al. 2011) include the following:

- Substance abuse
- History of criminal offending including sexual and violent offending
- Male gender
- Making threats of violence and suicide
- The presence of personality disorder, especially borderline, narcissistic type
- Pursuing an ex-intimate
- Long-term preoccupation with victim
- Being unemployed or underemployed
- Being socially isolated
- Having high levels of anger directed at the victim
- Having an intense sense of entitlement
- Fantasizing about and planning assaults
- Possessing weapons and having a history of familiarity with weapons
- Access to victim; physical approaches to victim in multiple settings
- Sense of desperation to resolve situations; "crisis periods," e.g., protective disorders, police confrontation, threat of arrest or incarceration; current stressors such as death of loved one, job loss, loss of child custody/visitation
- History of noncompliance to treatment
- Explicit threats, current or prior (except for public figures)
- Less than 30 years old
- Less than a high school education

Mullen et al. (2006) suggested that stalking victims have three types of risks: (1) not knowing when the stalking will end or if it will start again; (2) whether the victim will have significant social or psychological damage; and (3) whether physical or sexual harm will occur.

In the 2006 Supplemental Victimization Survey ($n = 65{,}270$), most stalking occurred before the age of 25 (most frequent from ages 18–19 and 20–24) and declined with age (Baum et al. 2009). Stalking is also associated with income, with an increased risk with lower income.

Stalkers have a high rate of recidivism. In a 9-year study of 78 offenders, Eke et al. (2011) reported that 56% were charged with new stalking offenses and 33% of these stalkers committed physical violence. Predictors of violent recidivism included younger age at first offense, criminal history, prior failure on conditional release, and history of substance abuse problems. Similarly, in a study of 148 stalking and harassing offenders, Rosenfeld (2003) noted that 49% reoffended, with 80% reoffending during the first year. Stalkers with personality disorders (cluster B) and substance use disorders were at highest risk of recidivism.

Risk management

Meloy (1998) recommends the following risk management approach:

- Use a team approach including law enforcement, mental health professionals, and the courts, and personnel necessary to provide safety to the victim.
- Emphasize the victim's need to show responsibility for personal safety.
- Document specifics of contact so as to establish a course of conduct on the part of the perpetrator that defines stalking and the responses of fear in the victim.
- The victim should not initiate or have contact with the perpetrator, as it will reinforce the behavior.
- Obtain restraining orders to suppress approach behavior, also, to emphasize the continuity of the course of conduct and to document fear. Victims should be advised that restraining orders in some instances may provoke violence.
- Law enforcement and prosecution: File appropriately all police reports and take steps to help prosecute, even when it is troubling.
- Treatment of stalkers: For those with Axis I disorders, consider benefit from antipsychotic and mood stabilizers. Delusional disorders are difficult to treat.

Personality disorders likewise may be difficult to treat, but may benefit from the group therapy format, i.e., relapse prevention program similar to those used with sex offenders and domestic violence.

- Perform periodic violence risk assessment.
- Recognize, prevent, and contain situations ("dramatic moments"), which are expected to cause narcissistic injury in the stalker. This will result in increased risk of violence. Situations include protective orders, denied child custody visits, and police and judicial confrontations.

False victimization

False victimization often involves claims of physical illness, e.g., factitious disorder, factitious disorder by proxy, physical assault, sexual harassment, and sexual assault. Kanin (1994) noted false allegations of rape in about half of a sample of female college students. False claims of stalking are not uncommon, and have been reported in the law enforcement literature (Artingstall 1999). Mullen et al. (2000) reported 18 cases among their series of 145 victims, and Zona et al. (1998) reported six among a series of 341. These actions may be carried out for attention, malice, or from psychotic delusions. False victims tend to seek legal and psychiatric intervention earlier, and often show significant anger. Improbable stories, repeated episodes of stalking, and multiple stalkers—especially in individuals with a history of illness behavior, unsubstantiated disabilities, borderline personality, suspicious previous history of victimization, and litigious tendencies—should raise concerns regarding the authenticity of these claims.

Another form of false victimization is "paper abuse" or "paper stalking." This occurs by filing false and frivolous lawsuits with the intention to control the victim, to force contact, to financially drain, and to scare the victim (Miller and Smolter 2011 in Belknap et al. 2012). Miller and Smolter (2011) also note that once the legal system is recruited into the stalking, phone calls and e-mails from the stalker to the victim would be considered normal, or legal.

SUMMARY

Stalking continues to be seen by many as a crime of violence, enacted by mentally ill individuals who are obsessed with celebrities. Since 1990, there has been increased study, and more rigorous study, of stalking and stalking victims. From having been in the shadows as an exotic psychiatric condition, stalking has been re-cast as a terrifying "epidemic." Distortions of data and political agendas have made stalking out to be perhaps more pervasive and lethal than the data support. The risk of violence cannot be assessed on the basis of stalking alone, but on the traditional risk assessment instruments.

SUMMARY KEY POINTS

- Most victims are women and most perpetrators are men, usually ex-intimates.
- Cluster B personality traits (borderline, histrionic, narcissistic) predominate ex-intimate stalkers.
- Females more likely to stalk acquaintances, strangers, and celebrities.
- Posttraumatic stress disorder is common in stalking victims, as well as depression, anxiety, insomnia, somatization disorders, and substance abuse.
- Physical violence occurs in 20%–30% of stalking cases.
- Most stalkers have mental health diagnoses, but only a minority have psychotic disorders.

REFERENCES

Artingstall K. 1999. *Practical Aspects of Munchausen by Proxy and Munchausen Syndrome Investigation*. Boca Raton, FL: CRC Press.

Australian Bureau of Statistics. 1996. Women's Safety Australia. Canberra: Commonwealth of Australia. http://www.abs.gov.au/ausstats/abs@.nsf/mf/4128.0/, accessed July 23, 2016.

Basile KC, MH Swahn, J Chen, and LE Saltzman. 2006. Stalking in the United States: Recent national prevalence estimates. *American Journal of Preventive Medicine* 31(2):172–175.

Baum K, S Catalano, M Rand, and K Rose. 2009. *National Crime Victimization Survey: Stalking Victimization in the United States. Bureau of Justice Statistics Special Report*. http://www.victimsofcrime.org/docs/src/baum-k-catalano-s-rand-m-rose-k-2009.pdf?sfvrsn=0, accessed July 26, 2015.

Belknap J, AT Chu, and AP DePrince. 2012. The roles of phones and computers in threatening and abusing women victims of male intimate partner abuse. *Duke Journal of Gender Law and Policy* 19:373–405.

Bjerregaard B. 2000. Empirical study of stalking victimization. *Violence and Victims* 15(4):389–406.

Black MC, KC Basile, MJ Breiding, SG Smith, ML Walters, MT Merrick, J Chen, and MR Stevens. 2011. *The National Intimate Partner and Sexual Violence Survey (NISVS): 2010 Summary Report*. http://www.cdc.gov/violenceprevention/pdf/nisvs_report2010-a.pdf, accessed June 30, 2015.

Bocij P and L McFarlane. 2003. Cyberstalking: A matter for community safety—But the numbers do not add up. *Community Safety Journal* 2:26–34, in Spitzberg BH and WR Cupach. 2007. The state of the art of stalking: Taking stock of the emerging literature. *Aggression and Violent Behavior* 12(1):64–86.

Bowlby J. 1979. *The Making and Breaking of Affectional Bonds*. New York: Tavistock.

Boychuk KM. 1994. Are stalking laws unreasonably vague or over broad? *Northwestern University Law Review* 88:769–802.

Bradfield JL. 1998. Anti-stalking laws: Do they adequately protect stalking victims? *Harvard Women's Law Journal* 21:229–266.

Branscomb AW. 1995. Anonymity, autonomy and accountability: Challenges to the First Amendment in cyber spaces. *Yale Law Journal* 104:1639–1679.

Breiding MJ, SG. Smith, KC Basile, ML Walters, J Chen, and MT Merrick. 2014. *Prevalence and Characteristics of Sexual Violence, Stalking, and Intimate Partner Violence Victimization—National Intimate Partner and Sexual Violence Survey, United States 2011*. http://www.cdc.gov/mmwr/preview/mmwrhtml/ss6308a1.htm?s_cid=ss6308a1_e, accessed June 29, 2015.

Brewster MP. 2000. Stalking by former intimates: Verbal threats and other predictors of physical violence. *Violence and Victims* 15(1):41–54.

Catalano S. 2012. *Stalking Victims in the United States—Revised*. http://www.bjs.gov/content/pub/pdf/svus_rev.pdf, accessed June 30, 2015.

Cornell Law School, Legal Information Institute. https://www.law.cornell.edu/uscode/text/18/2261A, accessed July 14, 2015.

Cupach WR and BH Spitzberg. 2004. *The Dark Side of Relationship Pursuit: From Attraction to Obsession and Stalking*. Mahwah, NJ: Lawrence Erlbaum.

David JW. 1994. Is Pennsylvania's stalking law constitutional? *University of Pittsburgh Law Review* 56:204–244.

Downs DA. 1996. *More than Victims: Battered Women, the Syndrome Society, and the Law*. Chicago: University of Chicago Press.

Dressing H, K Foerster, and P Gass. 2011. Are stalkers disordered or criminal? Thoughts on the psychopathology of stalking. *Psychopathology* 44(5):277–282.

Dressing H and P Gass. 2010. Prevalence of stalking in a psychiatric hospital population. *Australian and New Zealand Journal of Psychiatry* 44(8):736–741.

Dressing H, P Gass, and C Kuehner. 2007. What can we learn from the first community-based epidemiological study on stalking in Germany? *International Journal of Law and Psychiatry* 30(1):10–17.

Edelson JL and RM Tolman. 1992. *Intervention for Men Who Batter: An Ecological Approach*. Newbury Park, CA: Sage.

Eke AW, NZ Hilton, JR Meloy, K Mohandie, and J Williams. 2011. Predictors of recidivism by stalkers: A nine-year follow-up of police contacts. *Behavioral Sciences and the Law* 29:271–283.

Fisher BS, FT Cullen, and MG Turner. 2000. *The Sexual Victimization of College Women*. Washington, DC: U.S. Department of Justice. https://www.ncjrs.gov/pdffiles1/nij/182369.pdf, accessed June 29, 2015.

Fox KA, MR Nobles, and BS Fisher. 2011. Method behind the madness: An examination of stalking measurements. *Aggression and Violent Behavior* 16(1):74–84.

Fremouw WJ, D Westrup, and J Pennypacker. 1997. Stalking on campus: The prevalence and strategies for coping with stalking. *Journal of Forensic Sciences* 42(4):666–699.

Gelles RJ. 1997. *Intimate Violence in Families*, 3rd edition. Thousand Oaks, CA: Sage.

Goodyear-Smith FA and TM Laidlaw. 1999. Aggressive acts and assaults in intimate relationships: Toward an understanding of the literature. *Behavioral Sciences and the Law* 17(3):285–304.

Guy RA. 1993. Note: The nature and constitutionality of stalking laws. *Vanderbilt Law Review* 46:991–1028.

Haas BB. 1994. The formation and viability of anti-stalking laws. *Villanova Law Review* 39:1387–1415.

Hall DM. 1995. The victims of stalking. In *The Psychology of Stalking: Clinical and Forensic Perspectives*, edited by JR Meloy, San Diego, CA: Academic Press, 113–160.

Hanson RK and D Thornton. 1999. *Static-99: Improving Risk Assessment for Sex Offenders*. (User report 99-02) Ottawa, ON: Department of the Solicitor General of Canada.

Hare RD. 1991. *The Revised Psychopathy Checklist*. Toronto, ON: Multi-Health Systems.

Harmon RB, R Rosner, and H Owens. 1998. Sex and violence in a forensic population of obsessional harassers. *Psychology, Public Policy and Law* 4:236–249.

Kamphuis JH and PMG Emmelkamp. 2001. Traumatic distress among support-seeking female victims of stalking. *American Journal of Psychiatry* 158(5):795–798.

Kanin EJ. 1994. False rape allegations. *Archives of Sexual Behavior* 23(1):81–92.

Kienlen KK, DL Birmingham, KB Solberg, JT O'Regan, and JR Meloy. 1997. A comparative study of psychotic and non-psychotic stalking. *Journal of the American Academy of Psychiatry and the Law* 25(3):317–334.

Kropp PR, SD Hart, DR Lyon, and JE Storey. 2011. The development and validation of the guidelines for stalking assessment and management. *Behavioral Sciences and the Law* 29(2):302–316.

Leiter RA. 2007. *National Survey of State Laws*, 6th edition. Farmington, MI: Thomson Gale, in Fox KA, MR Nobles, and BS Fisher. eds. 2011. Method behind the madness: An examination of stalking measurements. *Aggression and Violent Behavior* 16(1):74–84.

Lloyd-Goldstein R. 2000. Serial stalkers recent clinical findings. In *Serial Offenders: Current Thought, Recent Findings*, edited by LB Schlesinger, Boca Raton, FL: CRC Press, 167–186.

MacKenzie RD, PE Mullen, JRP Ogloff, TE McEwan, and DV James. 2008. Parental bonding and adult attachment styles in different types of stalker. *Journal of Forensic Sciences* 53(6):1443–1449.

McAnaney KG, LA Curliss, and CE Abeyta-Price. 1993. From imprudence to crime: Anti-stalking laws. *Notre Dame Law Review* 68(4):819–821.

McCann JT. 2001. *Stalking in Children and Adults: The Primitive Bond.* Washington, DC: American Psychological Association.

McEwan TE, PE Mullen, RD MacKenzie, and JRP Ogloff. 2009. Violence in stalking situations. *Psychological Medicine* 39(9):1469–1478.

McEwan TE, M Pathé, and JRP Ogloff. 2011. Advances in stalking risk assessment. *Behavioral Sciences and the Law* 29(2):180–201.

Meloy JR. 1998. The psychology of stalking. In *The Psychology of Stalking: Clinical and Forensic Perspectives*, edited by JR Meloy, San Diego, CA: Academic Press, 2–21.

Meloy JR. 2007. Stalking: The state of the science. *Criminal Behaviour and Mental Health* 17(1):1–7.

Meloy JR and C Boyd. 2003. Female stalkers and their victims. *Journal of the American Academy of Psychiatry and the Law* 31(2):211–219.

Meloy JR, K Mohandie, and M Green. 2008. A forensic investigation of those who stalk celebrities. In *Stalking, Threatening, and Attacking Public Figures: A Psychological and Behavioral Analysis*, edited by JR Meloy, L Sheridan, and J Hoffman, New York: Oxford University Press, 37–54.

Meloy JR, K Mohandie, and M Green. 2011. The female stalker. *Behavioral Sciences and the Law* 29(2):240–254.

Miller SL and NL Smolter. 2011. "Paper abuse": When all else fails, batterers use procedural stalking, *Violence Against Women* 17(5):637–650, in Belknap J, AT Chu, and AP. DePrince. 2012. The roles of phones and computers in threatening and abusing women victims of male intimate partner abuse. *Duke Journal of Gender Law and Policy* 19:373–405.

Mohandie K, JR Meloy, MG McGowan, and J Williams. 2006. The RECON typology of stalking: Reliability and validity based upon a large sample of North American stalkers. *Journal of Forensic Sciences* 51(1):147–155.

Monahan J and HJ Stedman. 1994, *Violence and Mental Disorder: Developments in Risk Assessment.* Chicago: University of Chicago Press.

Mullen PE, R Mackenzie, JR Ogloff, M Pathé, T McEwan, and R Purcell. 2006. Assessing and managing the risks in the stalking situation. *Journal of the American Academy of Psychiatry and the Law* 34(4):439–450.

Mullen PE, M Pathé, and R Purcell. 2000. *Stalkers and Their Victims.* Cambridge, UK: Cambridge University Press.

Mullen PE, M Pathé, R Purcell, and GW Stuart. 1999. Study of stalkers. *American Journal of Psychiatry* 156(8):1244–1249.

National Institute of Justice. 1993. *Project to Develop a Model Anti-stalking Code for States.* http://www.popcenter.org/problems/stalking/PDFs/NIJ_Stalking_1993.pdf, accessed November 12, 2015.

Nelson AJ, RS Johnson, B Ostermeyer, KA Sikes, and JH Coverdale. 2015. The prevalence of physicians who have been stalked: A systematic review. *Journal of the American Academy of Psychiatry and the Law* 43(2):177–182.

Owens JG. 2015. Why definitions matter: Stalking victimization in the United States. *Journal of Interpersonal Violence*, 1–31.

Palarea RE, MA Zona, JC Lane, and J Langhinrichsen-Rohling. 1999. The dangerous nature of intimate relationship stalking: Threats, violence, and associated risk factors. *Behavioral Sciences and the Law* 17(3):269–283.

Patton CL, MR Nobles, and KA Fox. 2010. Look who's stalking: Obsessive pursuit and attachment theory. *Journal of Criminal Justice* 38(3):282–290.

Post M, L Haymes, K Storey, T Loughrey, and C Campbell. 2014. Understanding stalking behaviors by individuals with autism spectrum disorders and recommended prevention strategies for school settings. *Journal of Autism and Developmental Disorders* 44(11):2698–2796.

Purcell R, B Moller, T Flower, and PE Mullen. 2009. Stalking among juveniles. *British Journal of Psychiatry* 194(5):451–455.

Purcell R, M Pathé, and PE Mullen. 2005. Association between stalking victimization and psychiatric morbidity in a random community sample. *British Journal of Psychiatry* 187(5):416–420.

Purcell R, M Pathé, and PE Mullen. 2010. Gender differences in stalking behavior amongst juveniles. *Journal of Forensic Psychiatry and Psychology* 21(4):555–568.

Quinsey VL, GT Harris, ME Rice, and CA Cormier. 1998. *Violent Offenders, Appraising and Managing Risk.* Washington, DC: American Psychological Association.

Racine C and S Billick. 2014. Classification systems for stalking behavior. *Journal of Forensic Sciences* 59(1):250–254.

Radosevich AC. 2000. Thwarting the stalker: Are anti-stalking measures keeping pace with today's stalker? *University of Illinois Law Review* 4:1371–1395.

Rosenfeld B. 2003. Recidivism in stalking and obsessional harassment. *Law and Human Behavior* 27(3):251–265.

Rosenfeld B. 2004. Violence risk factors in stalking and obsessional harassment: A review and preliminary meta-analysis. *Criminal Justice and Behavior* 31:9–36, in Meloy JR. 2007. Stalking: The state of the science. *Criminal Behaviour and Mental Health* 17(1):1–7.

Rosenfeld B and R Harmon. 2002. Factors associated with violence in stalking and obsessional harassment cases. *Criminal Justice and Behavior* 29:671–691, in McEwan TE, M Pathé, and JRP Ogloff. 2011. Advances in stalking risk assessment. *Behavioral Sciences and the Law* 29(2):180–201.

Sandberg DA, DE McNiel, and RL. Binder. 2002. Stalking, threatening, and harassing behavior by psychiatric patients towards clinicians. *Journal of the American Academy of Psychiatry and the Law* 30(2):221–229.

Saunders DG. 1995. Tradition of wife assault. In *Assessing Dangerousness: Violence by Sex Offenders, Batterers, and Child Abusers*, edited by JC Campbell, Thousand Oaks, CA: Sage, 68–95.

Schwartz-Watts D and DW Morgan. 1998. Violent versus non-violent stalkers. *Journal of the American Academy of Psychiatry and the Law* 26(2):241–245.

Spitzberg BH. 2002. The tactical topography of stalking victimization and management. *Trauma, Violence, & Abuse* 3(4):261–268.

Spitzberg BH and WR Cupach. 2007. The state of the art of stalking: Taking stock of the emerging literature. *Aggression and Violent Behavior* 12(1):64–86.

Stalking Resource Center. 2015. *Criminal Stalking Laws.* http://www.victimsofcrime.org/our-programs/stalking-resource-center/stalking-laws/criminal-stalking-laws-by-state, accessed July 14, 2015.

Stokes M, N Newton, and A Kaur. 2007. Stalking, and social and romantic functioning among adolescents and adults with autism spectrum disorder. *Journal of Autism and Developmental Disorders* 37(10):1969–1986.

Stone MH. 1989. "Murder" in narcissistic personality disorder. *Psychiatric Clinics of North America* 12(3):643–652.

Strand S and TE McEwan. 2011. Same-gender stalking in Sweden and Australia. *Behavioral Sciences and the Law* 29(2):202–219.

Tjaden P and N Thoennes. 1998. *Stalking in America: Findings from a National Violence against Women Survey.* https://www.ncjrs.gov/pdffiles/169592.pdf, accessed June 29, 2015.

Tjaden P and N Thoennes. 2000. The role of stalking in domestic violence crime reports generated by the Colorado Springs police department. *Violence and Victims* 15(4):427–441.

White GL and PE Mullen. 1989. *Jealousy: Theory, Research, and Clinical Strategies.* New York: Guilford Press.

Wright JA, AG Burgess, AW Burgess, AT Laszlo, GO McCrary, and JE Douglas. 1996. A typology of interpersonal stalking. *Journal of Interpersonal Violence* 11(4):487–502.

Zona MA, RE Palarea, and JC Lane. 1998. Psychiatric diagnosis and the offender-victim typology of stalking. In *The Psychology of Stalking. Clinical and Forensic Perspectives*, edited by JR Meloy, San Diego, CA: Academic Press, 70–83.

65

Cyberstalking and the Internet age

KANG CHOI AND MOHAN NAIR

INTRODUCTION

The rapid pace of technology and simultaneous life in both offline and online worlds increases our ability to express ideas and obtain information. However, the Internet age also increases our exposure, with increased risks to our personal information (including where we are, what we say, and to whom we communicate). As our identities expand into cyberspace, so too do the potential tools for use by stalkers.

EVOLVING TERMS: CYBERSTALKING/ CYBERHARASSING/CYBERBULLYING

Cyberstalking is often discussed in relation to, and sometimes interchangeably with, the terms *cyberharassing* and *cyberbullying*. Although there are no universally accepted definitions of these terms, there are general differences. Cyberstalking is the stalking of another person via the Internet, e-mail, and other electronic devices (Department of Justice 2001). Stalking generally refers to repeated, threatening behavior or conduct that causes actual or reasonable fear (Department of Justice 1998). The cyberstalker's motivation is often to control the victim, much like stalkers who employ offline techniques (Department of Justice 2001).

In contrast, cyberharassing refers to the use of electronic means to annoy, alarm, or cause substantial emotional stress for no legitimate purpose (Fukuchi 2011; Caplan 2013). Unlike cyberstalking, cyberharassing does not require a threat or resultant fear (although legal definitions vary). In addition, the motivation of the harasser may be to frighten or embarrass the victim.

Cyberbullying is the use of electronic communication to further aggressive, repeated behavior in a situation of unequal power, as well as to hurt or embarrass. Cyberbullying usually refers to behavior between minors but can also include adults (Ruedy 2008; Olweus 2011). In contrast to traditional bullying, cyberbullying is not limited to schools, can occur anywhere, and may have greater impact on the victim (Ruedy 2008). Cyberbullying can be divided into several categories: flaming, harassment, denigration, impersonation, outing, trickery, exclusion, and cyberstalking (Lexis 2012).

Cyberstalking, cyberharassing, and especially cyberbullying, have attracted increased media attention due to several well-publicized teen suicides. Intense harassment of teens in the wake of upsetting or embarrassing communications related to text messaging, sexting, e-mails, posting of videos, and social networking sites has also garnered considerable media attention.

In 2006, a 13-year-old Missouri teen, Megan Meier, hanged herself after she received disparaging posts on MySpace, including "the world would be a better place without you" and negative text messages from a boy she had befriended on MySpace, known to her as "Josh." "Josh" was actually a fictional character created by an adult neighbor, Lori Drew, her teenage daughter (former friend of Megan), and an employee. Lori Drew was charged with violating the MySpace terms of agreement, though was eventually acquitted on criminal charges related to violating the federal Computer Fraud and Abuse Act (CFAA) (Ruedy 2008).

In response to public outcry, Missouri passed Megan's Law in 2008, criminalizing any communication used to harass a person. In that same year, U.S. Representatives Kenny Hulshof (R-Mo) and Linda Sanchez (D-Ca) introduced the Megan Meier Cyberbullying Prevention Act. The federal measure included language criminalizing communications with the "intent to coerce, intimidate, harass, or cause substantial emotional distress to a person; using electronic means to support severe, repeated, and hostile behavior" (H.R. 6123, 110th Cong. §3(a) [2008]). The measure failed to pass because it was considered overbroad (Lipton 2012). Moreover, in 2012, the Missouri Supreme Court struck down a significant portion of Megan's Law as also being overbroad.

Cyberbullying

Cyberbullying is a significant problem. In many respects, the issue goes beyond school grounds with greater impact than traditional bullying due to the ever-present Internet and cell phones, ease of instantaneous and wide dissemination, anonymity emboldening bullies, and the permanence of items posted to the Internet (Ruedy 2008).

According to a recent survey, 92% of U.S. teenagers go online daily, and 89% of U.S. teenagers use at least one social networking site, primarily Facebook and Twitter (Lenhart 2015). Despite high participation online, cyberbullying is relatively low (with the caveat that some vulnerable groups underreport, such as gay students [Lexis 2012]). In a 2011 Pew Research Center study, 19% of teens surveyed were bullied in the past year, with the majority being bullied in person (12%). Nine percent were bullied with text messages, 8% bullied online, and 7% bullied over calls (Lenhart et al. 2011). Similarly, the 2009 School Crime Supplement to the National Crime Victimization Survey of 7,066,000 U.S. students (12 through 18 years old) found that 28% of students had been bullied at school, and 6% had been cyberbullied. However, other studies have reported rates as high as 40% (Hinduja and Patchin 2010).

As of 2011, 44 states had passed anti-bullying policies in public schools, 31 of which had laws addressing electronic harassment, and 6 directly addressing cyberbullying (Lexis 2012). By 2013, 49 states had anti-bullying laws with 9 states addressing cyberbullying (Hinduja and Patchin 2013). However, in a rush to protect children, there is the risk of criminalizing normal teenage behavior, such as "drama" acted out in cyberspace. Teenagers see drama as interpersonal conflicts played out in front of an audience, particularly social media sites. Unlike bullying, drama can occur without an imbalance of power, and can occur between friends; and may be an important part of teenage life and coping (Marwick and Boyd 2011). It is possible that "banter" between friends could be seen as cyberbullying (Lipton 2012). A real-world example of criminalizing teenage behavior is sexting.

SEXTING

Sexting involves sending suggestive nude or partially nude photos via text message to another person (Lenhart 2009). Cell phones have made this more common. In 2009, 75% of teens, 12 through 17 years old, owned a cell phone, with 66% of teens using text messaging. Of cell phone owning teens, 4% sent nude or nearly nude pictures, and 15% received nude or semi-nude pictures of someone they knew (Lenhart 2009). A 2008 online survey reported higher sexting rates: 20% of teens sent or posted nude or semi-nude pictures (mostly to a love interest or love relation). Thirty-nine percent of teens sent or posted sexually suggestive messages (The National Campaign to Prevent Teen and Unplanned Pregnancy 2008). By 2015, 88% of teens owned or had access to a cell phone or smartphone, with 90% using texting (Lenhart 2015).

Sexting can occur between two minors in a relationship. However, the images can easily be disseminated to other parties, often out of anger toward the other party. Sexting can be seen as part of sexual exploration, flirtation, and foreplay (Lenhart et al. 2011; Tang 2013). Those who are anxious or uncomfortable with face-to-face contact and physical proximity, or even talking to another person, are more likely to engage in this as part of courtship behaviors. Some states have prosecuted minors under child pornography laws, creating minor sex offenders, while other states have created lesser misdemeanors for minors. "Romeo and Juliet carve-outs" for minors in a relationship have been proposed to avoid prosecution of teens as sex offenders based on relatively typical teenage behaviors (Tang 2013).

CYBERSTALKING

Studies suggest that the prevalence of cyberstalking is 1%–43%, depending on the definitions used and the population studied (Cavezza and McEwan 2014). In a 12-month study of stalking, the 2006 Supplemental Victimization Survey found that one in four stalking victims had some form of cyberstalking (83% by e-mail, 35% by instant messaging) (Baum et al. 2009). In an online survey of 6379 members of a German social network, Dressing et al. (2014) reported a cyberstalking prevalence of 6.3%. Dressing suggests that the assumption that cyberstalking has higher prevalence than offline stalking may be due to less stringent definitions of stalking used in cyberstalking studies. In addition, there is likely crossover between online and offline stalking. In a comparison of offline and online stalkers, a majority of cyberstalkers used offline methods as well, suggesting that the Internet is an added tool for traditional stalkers (Cavezza and McEwan 2014). Details of selected random and nonrandom cyberstalking studies are listed in Table 65.1.

Similar to traditional stalking, most cyberstalkers are male ex-intimates. The victims are mostly women (Department of Justice 2001; Dressing et al. 2014). Victims of cyberstalking suffer negative emotional impacts similar to offline stalking victims (Dressing et al. 2014). However, the harms may be greater due to the ease of stalking in cyberspace (e.g., frequent contacts, wide dissemination, recruitment of other stalkers) and the permanent nature of its content. In a forensic sample ($n = 72$), Cavezza and McEwan (2014) did not find major differences between characteristics of offline and online stalkers. Cyberstalkers were not more likely to have multiple victims and not more violent (actually had lower rates of physical violence). Dressing et al. (2014) argues that cyberstalking is a "variant" of offline stalking rather than being a distinct entity. Most states have treated cyberstalking as an extension of traditional stalking. Forty-six states have expanded their offline stalking legislation to include "electronic forms of communication" (Baer 2010).

However, there are some significant differences between offline and online stalking, suggesting that cyberstalking may be distinct (Goodno 2007; Baer 2010). The ability to stalk in cyberspace creates advantages and incentives for the stalker, while complicating legislative efforts. Internet and wireless communication greatly reduce the amount of effort, cost, and energy required to stalk, which may induce more people to stalk. Technology allows for instantaneous and wide dissemination of information. In addition, the cyberstalker can be anyplace in the world and can even remain largely anonymous, which may embolden the stalker (Goodno 2007).

Table 65.1 Cyberstalking studies in random and nonrandom populations

Study	Sample size	Prevalence	Comments
Sheridan and Grant (2007)	$n = 1051$ Self-identified stalking victims	47.5% reported being harassed on the Internet 7.2% were deemed to be cyberstalked	No significant difference between online and offline stalking
The National Campaign to Prevent Teen and Unplanned Pregnancy (2008)	653 teens (ages 13–19) 627 young adults (ages 20–26) Random community		20% of teens sent or posted nude or seminude pictures (22% girls, 18% boys) 39% of teens sent or posted sexually suggestive posts (37% girls, 40% boys) 71% of girls and 67% of boys sent sexually suggestive content to boyfriend or girlfriend
2009 School Crime Supplement to the National Crime Victimization, Department of Education (2011)	$n = 7{,}066{,}000$ U.S. students (12–18 years old) Random community		28% of students had been bullied at school 6% had been cyberbullied
2006 Supplemental Victimization Survey, Baum (2009)	$n = 65{,}270$ (ages 18 and older) Random community	One in four victims stalked subjected to cyberstalking	Of those cyberstalked, e-mail used in 83%, instant messaging in 35%, with electronic monitoring in 1 in 13 victims (spyware, cameras, bugs, GPS)
Pew Research Center, Lenhart et al. (2011)	$n = 799$ teenagers (12–17 years old), telephone survey		95% of teens are online 80% of online teens use social media 69% of teens felt that peers were mostly kind on social network sites 19% bullied in the last 12 months (12% in person, 9% via text message, 8% via online, 7% via voice calls)
Dressing et al. (2014)	$n = 6379$ members of German social network site	Cyberstalking prevalence of 6.3%	69.4% of cyberstalkers were male 35% involved ex-partner stalking 32% of cyberstalking lasted up to 1 month
Cavessa and McEwan (2014)	$n = 72$ (36 cyberstalking offenders, 36 offline stalkers)		Both groups targeted women with primary motivation to get revenge for a break-up or to continue a relationship
Pew Research Center, Lenhart (2015)	$n = 1060$ parents $n = 1060$ teens (13–17 years old) Random community		92% of teens go online daily 88% of teens have or have access to a cell phone or smartphone (90% send texts)

Importantly, the cyberstalker can impersonate his or her victim online, writing inflammatory comments, distributing inappropriate content, or sending invitations for sex or violence that are attributed to the victim. In addition, the Internet allows for the incitement of third-party harassers, or an avenue to request that others do the stalking (Goodno 2007; Ruedy 2008). For example, in the 1999 *State of California v Dellapenta* case, the first case prosecuted under the 1998 California Cyberstalking law, a female victim rejected the romantic advances of an older male. The male stalker impersonated the female victim online in websites and chat rooms, posting advertisements for sex—stating that the victim had a rape fantasy and wished to be raped. In addition, the cyberstalker posted the victim's actual phone number and home address. Several men knocked on her door late at night wishing to rape her, causing the victim severe emotional distress (Miller and Maharaj 1999; Zeller 2006).

The incitement of third-party stalkers can also be achieved through inflammatory websites, such as the "Nuremberg Files." In the 2002 Ninth Circuit Court case, *Planned Parenthood of the Columbia/Willamette, Inc. v. American Coalition of Life Activists*, an anti-abortion group made a poster, "Dirty Dozen," including the names and addresses of abortion doctors with a $5000 reward for information that would result in the arrest, conviction, or loss of medical license for these physicians. This poster grew to a website called the "Nuremberg Files" which listed the names of physicians, abortion supporters, and noting who on the list had been murdered or injured. The court ruled that the website was a "true threat" and not protected by the First Amendment (Ruedy 2008).

The incitement to harass or stalk can also be unintentional. For example, a Quebec teenager, Ghyslian Raza, filmed himself in a pretend light saber battle imitating a movie, *Star Wars: Episode I—The Phantom Menace*. Fellow students uploaded the video, which was then picked up by the general media. He was dubbed the "Star Wars Kid" and became the target of mockery in the media and intense harassment at school, causing him to finish his high school semester in a psychiatric facility (Wired.com 2003). Also, proxy stalkers, such as friends or family, can be used when the primary stalker is not able to stalk (Melton 2004; Belknap et al. 2012). The case below provides an example of how cyberstalking can progress to actual physical stalking behavior.

The day after she was seen by a dentist, a 23-year-old female started receiving prodigious amounts of e-mail from him; the e-mails, which started at 3 o'clock in the morning the day after her visit, provided extreme personal information, made requests for similar information from her, and expressed sexual fantasies. Following the messages, the dentist started showing up in places that he expected her to be, based on conversations they had in the office. He began to show up at her workplace, telling her that he just happened to be in the area. At one point he visited her at home, allegedly to follow up on a dental problem, and attempted to make physical contact with her at the time she was there, leading her ultimately to seek legal help.

Free speech and cyberstalking

The biggest challenge to cyberstalking laws is the First Amendment. Cyber communications (texts, images, videos) are considered speech. Any restriction of speech content is subject to First Amendment analysis and must be narrowly tailored to avoid being overbroad (impinging on existing protected speech) or vague (must be clear what is being prohibited) and must meet a compelling government interest, or strict scrutiny (Major 2012; Young 2013). Freedom of speech is not absolute. Unprotected speech includes things such as obscenity, defamation, fraud, incitement, true threats, or speech integral to criminal conduct (Shimizu 2013; Young 2013).

Another argument used to curtail speech is the "captive audience" doctrine, which argues that a person cannot be forced to listen to undesired speech (Young 2013). However, the assumption in a public space, including the Internet, is that the individual can choose not to see or hear the message (Major 2012). Some argue that technology and the omnipresence of phones and Internet may create a sense of inescapability or of being held captive.

In 2006, Congress amended the Interstate Stalking Statute (18 U.S.C. §2261A) to include stalking behavior through the Internet (Interstate Stalking Act 1996). Congress also criminalized conduct with the intent to harass, broadening the initial requirement of causing a reasonable fear of death or serious injury. As a result, causing substantial emotional distress would now violate the Cyberstalking Statute (Young 2013).

In the 2012 case of *U.S. v. Sayer*, Sayer created fake social media accounts and advertisements in his ex-girflriend's name that requested sex with men. Sayer uploaded private sex videos they had made when dating and published her phone number and address. The District of Maine Court held that Sayer had violated the federal Cyberstalking Statute and did not have a First Amendment defense because his speech fell into the exception of "true threats" (Young 2013). In May 2014, the U.S. Court of Appeals, First Circuit, upheld the decision. The federal Cyberstalking Statute is likely to be upheld when there is a threat that includes specific identifying information and instructions on how to do the harm (Smolla and Nimmer 1989; Young 2013).

Most recently, in a June 2015 opinion, the U.S. Supreme Court addressed the question of Internet threats in *Elonis v. United States*. Elonis posted rap lyrics on Facebook describing violence against his separated wife, co-workers, a kindergarten class, and law enforcement. Elonis, under the pen name, "Tone Dougie," wrote disclaimers that his writings were "fictitious." However, both his wife and former employer felt threatened by these posts, which resulted in Elonis being fired from his job and his wife filing a restraining order. Elonis was convicted of violating five counts of the federal Interstate Communication Act (18 U.S.C. §875(c)), which makes it criminal to transmit in interstate commerce "any communication containing any threat…to injure another person."

After appeal, the Third Circuit Court upheld Elonis's conviction on grounds that "intent" only required what the defendant understood and if a reasonable person would have seen the communication as a threat. The U.S. Supreme Court overturned the ruling, opining that although intent is not explicitly required in 875(c), criminal statutes are presumed to have an intent requirement. In other words, the prosecution had to demonstrate that Elonis intended to threaten his wife, or that he would know that his wife would feel threatened. The court appeared to consider the nuances of written communication, as well as First Amendment implications. This decision may impact current and future cyberstalking statutes that solely rely on a victim's subjective perception of threat or a reasonable person standard of fear.

SUMMARY

Cyberstalking has received increased media attention as technology has permeated almost every aspect of our lives. The harms caused by cyberstalking are significant and can potentially be more damaging than their offline counterparts. However, the increase in cyberstalking has not resulted in a parallel increase in violence, despite public perception. In a drive to protect against these harms, society runs the risk of restricting protected speech, as well as criminalizing common human behavior.

SUMMARY KEY POINTS

- Cyberstalking is the stalking of another person using the Internet, e-mail, and other electronic devices.
- The prevalence of cyberstalking ranges from 1% to 43%; cyberbullying prevalence ranges from 6% to 40%.
- Sexting is common (20% of teens sent or posted nude or semi-nude photos of themselves), with the majority directed toward a boyfriend, girlfriend, or love interest; sexting has at times been prosecuted as a sex crime.
- Similar to traditional stalking, most cyberstalkers are male and the victims are mostly female; cyberstalkers are usually ex-intimates.
- Technology greatly reduces the effort, cost, and energy required to stalk, and offers greater anonymity and reach of the stalker (who can be anywhere in the world).
- Anti-cyberstalking legislation must not impinge on Free Speech and has most frequently been upheld on the ground of "true threats," which is unprotected speech.

REFERENCES

Azriel JN. 2009. Social networking as a communications weapon to harm victims: Facebook, MySpace, and Twitter demonstrate a need to amend Section 230 of the Communication Decency Act. *John Marshall Journal of Computer and Information Law* 26:415–429.

Baer M. 2010. Cyberstalking and the Internet landscape we have constructed. *Virginia Journal of Law and Technology* 15:153–172.

Baum K, S Catalano, M Rand, and K Rose. 2009. *National Crime Victimization Survey: Stalking Victimization in the United States. Bureau of Justice Statistics Special Report.* http://www.victimsofcrime.org/docs/src/baum-k-catalano-s-rand-m-rose-k-2009.pdf?sfvrsn = 0, accessed July 26, 2015.

Belknap J, AT Chu, and AP DePrince. 2012. The roles of phones and computers in threatening and abusing women victims of male intimate partner abuse. *Duke Journal of Gender Law and Policy* 19:373–405.

Caplan AH. 2013. Free speech and civil harassment orders. *Hastings Law Journal* 64:781–861.

Cavezza C and TE McEwan. 2014. Cyberstalking versus off-line stalking in a forensic sample. *Psychology Crime and Law* 20(10):955–970.

Department of Education. 2011. *Student Reports of Bullying and Cyber-Bullying: Results from the 2009 School Crime Supplement to the National Crime Victimization Survey.* http://nces.ed.gov/pubs2011/2011336.pdf, accessed June 30, 2015.

Department of Justice. 1998. *Stalking and Domestic Violence: Report to Congress, July 1998.* https://www.ncjrs.gov/pdffiles1/ovw/172204.pdf, accessed June 30, 2015.

Department of Justice. 2001. *Stalking and Domestic Violence: Report to Congress, May 2001.* https://www.ncjrs.gov/pdffiles1/ojp/186157.pdf, accessed June 30, 2015.

Dressing H, J Bailer, A Anders, H Wagner, and C Gallas. 2014. Cyberstalking in a large sample of social network users: Prevalence, characteristics, and impact upon victims. *Cyberpsychology, Behavior, and Social Networking* 17(2):61–67.

Elonis v. United States, 575 U.S. ____ 2015. http://www.supremecourt.gov/opinions/14pdf/13-983_7l48.pdf, accessed June 30, 2015.

Fukuchi, A. 2011. A balance of convenience: Burden-shifting devices in criminal cyberharassment law. *Boston College Law Review* 52:289–330.

Goodno NH. 2007. Cyberstalking, a new crime: Evaluating the effectiveness of current state and federal laws. *Missouri Law Review* 72:125–158.

Hinduja S and JW Patchin. 2010. *Fact Sheet: Cyberbullying Identification, Prevention, and Response.* http://www.cyberbullying.us/cyberbullying_identification_prevention_response.php, accessed June 30, 2015.

Hinduja S and JW Patchin. 2013. *State Cyberbullying Laws: A Brief Review of State Cyberbullying Laws and Policies.* http://www.meganmeierfoundation.org/cmss_files/attachmentlibrary/Bullying_and_Cyberbullying_Laws.pdf, accessed June 30, 2015.

Interstate Stalking Act. 1996. 18 U.S.C. 2261A. https://www.law.cornell.edu/uscode/text/18/2261A, accessed July 1, 2015.

Lenhart A. 2009. *Teens and Sexting: How and Why Minor Teens Are Sending Sexually Suggestive Nude or Nearly Nude Images via Text Messaging.* http://www.pewInternet.org/files/old-media//Files/Reports/2009/PIP_Teens_and_Sexting.pdf, accessed June 30, 2015.

Lenhart A. 2015. *Teens, Social Media and Technology Overview.* http://www.pewinternet.org/2015/04/09/teens-social-media-technology-2015, accessed June 30, 2015.

Lenhart A, M Madden, A Smith, K Purcell, K Zickuhr, and L Rainie. 2011. *Teens, Kindness and Cruelty on Social Network Sites.* http://www.pewinternet.org/files/old-media//Files/Reports/2011/PIP_Teens_Kindness_Cruelty_SNS_Report_Nov_2011_FINAL_110711.pdf, accessed June 30, 2015.

Lexis Law Review Insight. 2012. *Bullying and Cyberbullying: What Is Being Done to Stop It?* pp. 1–7.

Lipton JD 2012. Cyberbullying and the first amendment. *Florida Coastal Law Review* 14:99–130.

Major JB 2012. Cyberstalking, Twitter, and the captive audience: A First Amendment analysis of 18 U.S.C. § 2261A(2). *Southern California Law Review* 86(1):117–161.

Marwick AE and D Boyd. 2011. The drama! Teen conflict, gossip, and bullying in networked publics. Paper presented at *A Decade of Internet Time: Symposium on the Dynamics of the Internet and Society*, Oxford, UK.

Melton HC 2004. Stalking in the context of domestic violence: Findings on the criminal justice system. *Women and Criminal Justice* 15(33):46.

Miller G and D Maharaj. 1999. N. Hollywood man charged in 1st cyber-stalking case. *LA Times*. http://articles.latimes.com/1999/jan/22/news/mn-523, accessed July 10, 2015.

Olweus Bullying Prevention Program. 2011. *What Is Bullying? Definition, Statistic and Information on Bullying*. http://www.olweus.org/public/bullying.page, accessed February 12, 2014.

Ruedy MC 2008. Repercussions of a MySpace teen suicide: Should anti-cyberbullying laws be created? *North Carolina Journal of Law and Technology* 9(2):323–346.

Sheridan LP and TD Grant. 2007. Is cyberstalking different? *Psychology, Crime and Law* 13(6):627–640.

Shimizu A. 2013. Recent development: Domestic violence in the digital age: Towards the creation of a comprehensive cyberstalking statute. *Berkeley Journal of Gender, Law and Justice* 28:116–137.

Smolla RA and MB Nimmer. 1989. Smolla and Nimmer on freedom of speech §3:5 (citing *Ward v. Rock Against Racism*, 491 U.S. 781, 791 (1989)) in Young C. 2013. A First Amendment defense to the federal cyberstalking statute in the age of Twitter. *Washington Journal of Law, Technology and Arts* 9(1):53–67.

Tang X. 2013. The perverse logic of teen sexting prosecutions (and how to stop it). *Boston University Journal of Science and Technology Law* 19:106–126.

The National Campaign to Prevent Teen and Unplanned Pregnancy. 2008. *Sex and Tech: Results from a Survey of Teens and Young Adults*. http://thenationalcampaign.org/sites/default/files/resource-primary-download/sex_and_tech_summary.pdf, accessed June 22, 2015.

United States v. Sayer, Nos. 2:11-CR-113-DBH, 2:11-CR-47-DBH, 2012 WL 1714746 (D. Me. May 15, 2012). http://www.leagle.com/decision/In%20FDCO%2020120515D37, accessed July 1, 2015.

WIRED.COM, June 24, 2003. *Star Wars Kid Files Lawsuit*. http://archive.wired.com/culture/lifestyle/news/2003/07/59757, retrieved November 12, 2015.

Young C. 2013. A First Amendment defense to the federal cyberstalking statute in the age of Twitter. *Washington Journal of Law, Technology and Arts* 9(1):53–67.

Zeller Jr. T. 2006. A sinister web entraps victims of cyberstalkers. *New York Times*, http://www.nytimes.com/2006/04/17/technology/a-sinister-web-entraps-victims-of-cyberstalkers.html, accessed July 23, 2016.

66

Mental illness and firearms

AMY BARNHORST

INTRODUCTION

The relationship between mental illness and firearm violence has long been a contentious topic. The Second Amendment to the U.S. Constitution protects the right to bear arms. However, over time, legislation has restricted that right in the interest of public safety. Often this legislation passes in the wake of tragic (but statistically anomalous) events, reflecting the challenges associated with predicting and preventing violent behaviors. People with mental illness are one group whose Second Amendment rights have been limited in the name of safety. However, in practice, this intervention has been fraught with complexity and resulted in equivocal benefits.

STATISTICS OF FIREARM DEATHS IN THE UNITED STATES

According to Centers for Disease Control and Prevention (CDC) data, in 2013, 11,208 homicides occurred by firearms (CDC Fast Stats). The majority of homicides by firearm are single-victim crimes, related to gang activity or interpersonal arguments, or occurring during the commission of other felonies (Federal Bureau of Investigation 2012). In contrast, mass shootings account for a fraction-of-a-percent of firearm homicides. In 2013, there were four public mass shootings (four or more homicides during a single event) with 27 fatalities (*USA Today* 2013). This represents less than 0.001% of the firearm-related deaths in the United States that year.

While homicides garner more public and media attention, suicides compose the majority of U.S. firearm fatalities. In 2013, there were 21,175 firearm suicides in the United States, accounting for 65% of firearm fatalities (CDC Fast Stats 2015).

Not only are the majority of firearm deaths suicides, the majority of suicides are committed with firearms. More adults successfully complete suicide in the United States with guns than with all other methods combined (CDC Fast Stats 2015). This may be attributable to the fact that over 90% of suicide attempts with a firearm are fatal (Miller et al. 2004).

Multiple case-control studies have shown that having a gun in the home is a substantial risk factor for completed suicide (Brent et al. 1991; Kellerman et al. 1992; Wiebe 2003). One meta-analysis of 14 studies showed an adjusted odds ratio of 3.24 (95% CI, 2.41 to 4.40), indicating that people with firearm access are over three times more likely to complete suicide than those without (Anglemyer et al. 2014). Although this correlation does not necessarily imply causation, restricting the public's access to firearms has been shown to be an effective strategy in reducing suicides in both the District of Columbia and Switzerland (Loftin et al. 1991; Reisch et al. 2013).

MENTAL ILLNESS AND VIOLENCE

The public often presumes that people with mental illness are violent, and media coverage of public shootings tends to perpetuate this belief (Angermeyer and Matschinger 1996). However, research indicates that people with severe mental illness are more likely to be victims of violent crime than perpetrators (Choe et al. 2008). They are also more likely to be victims of violence than are other members of the population (Hiday 1999).

Rates of violence by mentally ill people appear elevated in many studies, but concomitant substance abuse consistently emerges as a confounding factor. Data from the MacArthur Research Network on mental illness and violence show that people discharged from psychiatric hospitals who do not have a history of substance abuse commit violent acts at the same rate as matched community controls. People with substance abuse issues, with or without concomitant mental illness, demonstrate higher violence rates than matched community controls. However, people with mental illness are more likely to have substance abuse disorders than people without mental illness. This confounding variable leads to an overall increase in the prevalence of violent acts perpetrated by mentally ill people (Steadman et al. 1998). Multiple other studies have corroborated that substance abuse is a more significant risk factor for violence than mental illness, and that higher rates of substance abuse among the mentally ill may artificially inflate the correlation between violence and mental illness (Elbogen and Johnson 2009; Martone et al. 2013).

Even among people with severe mental illness who commit acts of violence, there is little evidence that interventions by mental health professionals would have prevented the act. In the retroactive study of homicide defendants, 37% had any prior psychiatric contact; however, only 8% had been seen in an outpatient psychiatric setting in the 3 months preceding the act (Martone et al. 2013). This suggests that relying primarily on the intersection of these individuals and the mental health system is not sufficient.

Nonetheless, the mental health system is often identified as the solution for preventing mass shootings. In the wake of the Aurora movie theater shooting, CBS News ran a story entitled, "Theater attack prompts new Colorado mental health law" (CBS News 2013) After the 2014 Isla Vista shooting, an *SF Gate* headline read, "Isla Vista rampage adds urgency for mental illness laws" (*SF Gate* 2014). Implied in these headlines is a failure of the mental health system to take adequate measures to prevent such events.

However, putting the onus of violence prevention on the mental health system may have an unforeseen negative impact on people's civil liberties. Prospective attempts to identify potential attackers lack specificity, and incidents of violence, especially mass violence, are statistically rare. Research-borne actuarial tools lose their potency when applied by clinicians to patient populations whose background risk is low. Therefore, large numbers of people would need to be involuntarily detained and their civil liberties revoked in order to prevent one mass casualty incident (Buchanan 2006).

Legislation often passes in the wake of public shootings that specifically restricts firearm access by people with mental illness. The public perception of the causal role of mental illness in mass shootings may redirect the legislative focus away from violence prevention policies that rely on evidence-based risk assessment (Appelbaum 2006). Instead, specific restrictions may be targeted at persons with mental illness as a broad category, despite the vagueness of this descriptor and the fact that the majority of gun deaths in the United States are not perpetrated by persons with known mental illness (Applebaum and Swanson 2010).

In addition to misguiding legislation, reinforcing the perception of a strong link between mental illness and gun violence can increase the stigma of mental illness. One study examined public perceptions of violence potential in the mentally ill as influenced by media coverage of mass shootings. Researchers assigned a group of 1797 people either to read a fictional news story about a mass shooting perpetrated by a person with serious mental illness, or to a control group that did not read the article. Both groups were then asked to answer questions about perceived dangerousness of persons with mental illness and their level of support for legislative proposals to restrict firearm access in that population. Participants who read a news stories about the mass shooting were less likely to be willing to have someone with severe mental illness as a neighbor or a co-worker. They also endorsed a higher perceived level of dangerousness of people with mental illness than those who did not read one of the articles. In addition, they were more likely to support firearms restrictions targeted at the mentally ill (McGinty et al. 2013).

The public stigma resulting from perpetuating the perceived link between mental illness and violence likely creates obstacles to stable housing and employment for people with mental illness. In addition, this stigma becomes internalized by patients and inhibits people with mental illness from seeking and engaging in necessary treatment (Ritsher and Phelan 2004). Therefore, misguided attempts to increase public safety by restricting the freedoms of mentally ill people may not only have a minimal effect on overall violence reduction, but may also paradoxically worsen public mental health (Cole 2007).

THE SECOND AMENDMENT AND FEDERAL FIREARMS LEGISLATION

The right of citizens to bear arms was included in the Second Amendment to the U.S. Constitution in 1791. Theoretically, the Second Amendment allows people to maintain the force to organize a militia, rise up against government oppression, defend themselves and their communities, and assist in enforcing local laws. However, over 200 years later, the practical applications of Second Amendment rights have led to difficult questions. One question is who, if anyone, should be denied their Second Amendment rights. Determining who meets that threshold for dangerousness requires balancing individual freedoms with public safety.

The Gun Control Act of 1968 was the first federal statue to limit potentially dangerous individuals' access to firearms. Its inception came on the heels of the assassination of President John F. Kennedy, which raised public awareness of the relative lack of firearm regulations. The Gun Control Act specifically prohibited eight categories of people from purchasing or owning guns, including individuals legally determined to be "adjudicated as a mental defective" and those who had been "committed to any mental institution." Also prohibited were unlawful users or addicts of controlled substances, felons, fugitives from justice, individuals dishonorably discharged from the armed services, individuals who have been convicted of domestic violence or had a restraining order filed against them, people who have renounced their citizenship, and illegal aliens (Gun Control Act 1968). However, no guidance was given regarding enforcing these restrictions.

In 1981, the assassination attempt of Ronald Reagan again brought firearm regulation to the foreground. Reagan and his White House Press Secretary, James Brady, were shot and wounded by John Hinckley Jr., who later revealed that his actions were an attempt to impress the actress Jodie Foster. Though Hinckley had a history of psychiatric treatment, he had never met the criteria laid out in the Gun Control Act and was therefore able to legally obtain the gun used in the shooting. Out of this event, the Brady Handgun Act was eventually passed in 1993, establishing a federally mandated 5-day waiting period for handgun purchases, and requiring all federally licensed dealers to perform a background check on individual purchasers to ensure that the sale would not violate federal or state law (Brady Handgun Act 1993).

The Brady Handgun Act also laid the groundwork for the eventual development of the National Instant Criminal Background Check System (NICS) in 1998. NICS is a federal database of records maintained by the Federal Bureau of Investigation (FBI). It contains information compiled from multiple sources about disqualifying criminal and mental health records of potential buyers. Federally licensed gun dealers are required to access the database prior to a transfer of a firearm to determine if the buyer meets any of the exclusionary criteria. However, nonlicensed dealers, which comprise up to 25% of sellers at gun shows, are not required to utilize the NICS background check system prior to selling guns (Brady Handgun Act 1993).

In 1997, a law enforcement officer named Printz challenged the interim provisions of the Brady Act that required law enforcement officers to enact them on a state level. In *Printz v. U.S.*, the U.S. Supreme Court decided that under the Tenth Amendment, it was unconstitutional for the federal government to require state officials to implement or enforce federal mandates. Thus, state reporting of relevant information to the federal NICS database remains voluntary, allowing large gaps in the system's data and compromising its effectiveness (Price and Norris 2010).

In 2007, Seung-Hui Cho killed 38 people on the campus of Virginia Tech before shooting himself. Two years prior to the shooting, he was found by a Virginia court to be dangerous to himself and was mandated to outpatient psychiatric treatment (*New York Times* 2007). While assisted outpatient treatment may have qualified him as "adjudicated as a mental defective," no records had been uploaded to the NICS system and Cho was able to legally purchase firearms (Price and Norris 2010).

The federal government passed the NICS Improvement Act in 2008 on the heels of the Virginia Tech shooting to assist states in communicating relevant information to the central database. It also provided financial support for records transfer, and incentives for those who maintain above a minimum level of information sharing (NICS Improvement Act 2007). However, states are only able to report to the NICS database to the level at which they themselves collect data, if they elect to report at all.

Initially, no provision existed allowing individuals disqualified on the basis of mental illness to regain their eligibility to have firearms (though this did exist for felons). This discrepancy was rectified in the 2007 NICS Improvement Act, which allowed individuals to petition for reconsideration. If the designated legal authority determines that the person is unlikely to act in a dangerous manner in the future and that his or her possession of a firearm is not contrary to public interest, that person's right to purchase and possess a firearm can be restored (NICS Improvement Act 2007).

Some confusion remained regarding the criteria for "adjudicated as a mental defective" or "committed to a mental institution." In 1997 the Bureau of Alcohol, Tobacco, Firearms, and Explosives (ATF) clarified the terms, stating that "adjudication as a mental defective" required some degree of "danger[ousness] to himself or others" or "a lack of mental capacity to contract or manage his own affairs," and included people found incompetent to stand trial or not guilty by reason of insanity. The ATF also specified that voluntary admission to a psychiatric institution or admission for observation only did not qualify for firearm purchase disqualification (ATF 1997). In 2013, an executive order further clarified that assisted or involuntary outpatient commitment qualified as "committed to a mental institution" and therefore met the criteria for firearm prohibition (Office of the Press Secretary 2014).

CASE LAW

In 1975, the District of Columbia passed a law banning ownership and registration of new nonservice handguns and requiring guns at home to be kept locked and unloaded. Heller, a law enforcement officer, sued for his right to have his service weapon at home. In *District of Columbia v. Heller* (2008), the Supreme Court struck down this law as unconstitutional. The court opined that the Second Amendment granted individuals the right to keep and bear arms, even in the home for self-defense and absent affiliation with a militia. Though the ruling upheld the prohibitions put forth in the Gun Control Act, it effectively curtailed the passage of new firearm prohibitions outside of those categories (Gould 2009).

Many other relevant cases have questioned what is meant by "committed to a mental institution" or "adjudicated as a mental defective." The groundwork for this scrutiny was laid out in the class action suit *Lessard v. Schmidt* (1972). Lessard had been detained by Wisconsin police at her home after a reported suicide attempt and was involuntarily hospitalized. Her initial detention period was extended without her knowledge, and a hearing did not take place until 24 days later. Wisconsin's commitment statutes allowed, under certain circumstances, for a patient to remain in the hospital for an "observation" period for up to 145 days without a hearing. The Wisconsin District Court found that Wisconsin's commitment procedures violated due process rights. Though the decision did not address the Second Amendment directly, it laid the groundwork for questioning the due process of involuntary commitments that would later result in firearm disqualifications (Remington 1973).

In *U.S. v. Hansel* (1972), Hansel was convicted of purchasing a firearm illegally because of his prior psychiatric hospitalization. However, the Eighth Circuit Court reversed this conviction, citing that it was not technically a "commitment" because the hospitalization was deemed to be "observational" and legal commitment procedures had not been followed. Similarly, in *U.S. v. Giardina* (1988), Giardina was hospitalized in Louisiana for 14 days, one day short of the point at which a judge's commitment order is required.

Like Hansel, his conviction for illegal firearm purchase was overturned by a court of appeals based on the lack of formal judicial commitment (Lewis 2011).

In 2012, *U.S. v. Rehlander* upheld the decision in *Hansel.* Rehlander had been hospitalized involuntarily for 5 days, but had neither an adversarial hearing nor a judicial commitment. Therefore, the First Circuit Court concluded that due process had not occurred for a formal commitment and that he did not meet the criteria for a firearm disqualification (McCreary 2013). In these cases, admission to a psychiatric hospital without a judicial commitment did not suffice to prohibit firearm purchase.

However, in both *U.S. v. Waters* and *U.S. v. Chamberlain*, the circuit courts determined that the states had followed procedure sufficiently to meet the requirements for a firearms ownership disqualification, despite the lack of an adversarial hearing and a judicial order. Waters was hospitalized in New York, where statute allowed for up to a 60-day hospitalization under the certification of two physicians and a third applicant. Waters did not request the hearing available to him during that 60 days to contest the hospitalization, then requested his status be changed to voluntary. Thus, no judicial certification took place. However, in 1994, the Second Circuit determined that formal statutory commitment requirements had been met, and that this disqualification was in line with the intentions behind the Gun Control Act: to keep guns out of the hands of potentially dangerous people with mental illness (Lewis 2011).

Chamberlain was involuntarily hospitalized on an emergency basis in Maine and, like Waters, his status changed to voluntary before the hospital had to obtain a judicial order for further commitment. The First Circuit determined in 1998 that state commitment procedures had been followed, and that his hospitalization counted as a "commitment." In *Chamberlain*, the court elaborated on the intent of the Gun Control Act, explaining that had Congress intended that a full adversarial hearing be required to merit a commitment, it would have specifically said so (Lewis 2011).

In *U.S. v. Vertz* (2000), the exclusionary criterion of "adjudicated as a mental defective" also came under scrutiny. Vertz had been treated by a variety of mental health professionals for decades, and had at one point been court-ordered to obtain outpatient treatment. He was never determined to be either dangerous or incapable of managing his own affairs, the two specific requirements for "adjudicat[ion] as a mental defective." Thus, a Michigan court ruled that he did not meet the federal standards of "mental[ly] defective" that would prohibit him from buying a gun (McCreary 2013). Of note, this ruling occurred prior to the 2013 Executive Order specifying that outpatient commitment did qualify as "committed to a mental institution."

STATE LEGISLATION

While federal legislation prohibits firearm purchase by people who have been adjudicated as mentally defective or committed to an institution, state-level legislation varies widely. Some states exclude those with any mental illness from firearm ownership, without addressing their level of dangerousness, or what, exactly, qualifies as "mental illness." Alabama and Pennsylvania prohibit firearm sales to those who are of "unsound mind." In Montana, firearm purchase can be denied to those believed with reasonable cause to be "mentally ill, defective, or disabled." In Hawaii, South Dakota, Maryland, and Oklahoma, merely being diagnosed as having a mental or behavioral disturbance suffices (Norris et al. 2006).

Other states give more concrete guidelines. In Illinois, Arkansas, and the District of Columbia, voluntary admission to a psychiatric facility triggers a prohibition. Other states, such as Kentucky, Oklahoma, and Michigan, align with the federal government and specify that this commitment must be involuntary. The federal guideline of adjudication as mentally incompetent or not guilty by reason of insanity is shared among most, but not all, states (Norris et al. 2006).

Alaska, New Hampshire, Vermont, and Colorado place virtually no restrictions on firearm purchases in cases of mental illness. Twelve other states restrict people with mental illness from obtaining a concealed weapon permit, but not from obtaining a weapon legally (Norris et al. 2006).

In California, mental health-based restrictions are more directly tied to violence potential than to psychiatric history. Admission to a psychiatric facility for danger to self or to others triggers a firearm prohibition. This differs from federal standards, by which the prohibition would not be triggered until a commitment was certified. Involuntary holds for grave disability in California (inability to provide for one's food, clothing, or shelter), by contrast, follow the federal standard (California Department of Justice 2009).

State-level prohibitions and NICS background checks prohibit the purchase or register of new guns to people with certain mental health histories or criminal records. However, they do little to remove the guns already in circulation. California, New York, Connecticut, and Indiana have developed legislation not just to prevent future firearm purchases, but to remove existing firearms during a crisis, regardless of whether or not the person has met federal or state prohibition criteria. California has also piloted a unique program to remove guns already in the possession of prohibited persons (NPR 2013).

In 1999, Connecticut became the first state to pass gun removal legislation that was based on acute potential for violence without being tied to mental illness. Under this statute, the state's attorney or two law enforcement officers can petition the courts for a warrant for gun removal from individuals perceived to pose an "imminent risk" of harm to themselves or another. Within 14 days, a hearing must occur, at which time the guns may be returned, or their removal may be authorized for 1 year (Conn. Gen. Stat. §29-38c).

In 2005, Indiana passed legislation allowing police officers to seize weapons from a person with "a propensity for violent or emotionally unstable conduct" or with mental illness, without obtaining a warrant. The legislation followed the 2004 fatal shooting of a police officer by a man with paranoid delusions, a recent history of mental health evaluation for violence, and a large cache of weapons in his home. Though police knew he had firearms, they were unable to legally remove them at the time, because the man had never met any threshold for firearm prohibition. Interestingly, although the law was developed in response to a violent incident, the majority of the confiscations in the first two years were related to concerns for suicidality (Parker 2015).

In response to the Sandy Hook shootings in Connecticut, Governor Cuomo of New York signed the New York Secure Ammunition and Firearm Enforcement (SAFE) Act on January 15, 2013. The law prohibits possession of high-capacity magazines, tightens restrictions on gun sales, requires ammunition dealers and private firearm dealers to perform background checks, creates a registry for all semi-automatic weapons, and requires safe storage of assault weapons. Perhaps most relevant for mental health practitioners, it requires those privy to a patient's threat of violence to report that threat to the director of their facility, who in turn reports it to state authorities. Like the Indiana Dangerous Persons Law, the New York SAFE Act allows for law enforcement to remove that individual's weapons with no warrant, and without requiring other criminal or mental health history (*Huffington Post* 2013).

The 2014 Isla Vista shooting provided another situation where family members saw warning signs of violence and expressed concern to authorities. However, absent any disqualifying mental health or criminal history, police were powerless to intervene with the shooter, who had legally amassed multiple weapons. Largely in response to this event, California passed a Gun Violence Restraining Order in 2014 that was modeled closely after domestic violence restraining orders. This new law allows family members or police to petition the court when they believe there is a "substantial likelihood" that the respondent "poses a significant danger of harm to self or others in the near future by having access to a firearm." The court may then issue a warrant for gun removal with an ex-parte order, which may be converted to a 1-year order after a court hearing. Additionally, the person is prevented from owning firearms for the duration of the order via reporting to the NICS system. This legislation is another example of gun removal tied directly to acute risk of violence, rather than to mental health criteria (California Legislative Information: AB1014; Frattaroli et al. 2015).

California's Armed Prohibited Persons System (APPS) program, developed in 2007, allows the removal of weapons from prohibited persons, regardless of whether there is an elevated acute risk of violence. California Department of Justice officials cross-check disqualifying legal and psychiatric records with gun ownership records in the state firearm database. APPS agents then go to the home of firearm owners whose history prohibits ownership and confiscate any guns in their possession. In 2013, the state expanded funding for this program. A bill in Congress proposed allocating funds for other states to adopt this unique model (NPR 2013).

NICS REPORTING

The NICS database of disqualifying information is the checkpoint on which enforcement of national firearm prohibitions relies. Unfortunately, NICS is missing the names of millions of people who should be disqualified from gun ownership by their mental health or substance abuse histories (Mayors Against Illegal Guns 2011).

The efficacy of the NICS system is entirely dependent on the data supplied by individual states, which report to NICS voluntarily. As of 2012, 30 states had not uploaded any mental health records (Government Accountability Office 2012). Myriad factors contribute to this lack of participation.

Because of variations in state legislation, the disqualification data collected for transmission to NICS may not align with the federal restriction criteria. Funds provided by the NICS Improvement Act have facilitated the de-aggregation of state-level prohibitions from federal (Mayors Against Illegal Guns 2011). Other states report no information, and there is little to prevent disqualified individuals in those states from buying guns in neighboring states.

In addition, many states lack the technological infrastructure to synthesize the necessary records from law enforcement, psychiatric institutions, and courts. The NICS Improvement Act helped to address these deficiencies by providing funding and incentives to states for building functional databases that could be used for collecting and transmitting data to NICS (NICS Improvement Act 2015).

Privacy concerns are another potential barrier to NICS reporting. The Health Insurance Portability and Accountability Act (HIPAA) prohibits sharing protected patient information without permission, except under defined circumstances. Exceptions include disclosure to aid in law enforcement, protect the public against violence, and where otherwise superseded by state or federal law. Nonetheless, in 2012, officials in half the states surveyed expressed concerns about reporting patient records in the absence of a specific statute mandating reporting (Government Accountability Office 2012).

EFFECT OF NICS REPORTING ON GUN VIOLENCE

Despite attempts to address gun safety through policy changes, there have been few opportunities to examine the results. A 2000 study analyzed vital statistics of homicides and suicides by firearm before and after NICS implementation. They compared a "treatment" group of states (those who, prior to NICS, had no firearm-disqualification reporting system) and a "control" group of states (those who, prior to NICS, had an equivalent reporting system in place). They found that after the implementation of NICS, there was no difference in the change in firearm homicides and suicides between the two groups, with one notable exception: suicides by gun in people 55 and older decreased by 0.92 per 100,000 people. Additionally, this reduction was greater in states that implemented background checks and a waiting

Table 66.1 Significant U.S. firearm legislation

Year	Legislation	Content
1791	Second Amendment to the Constitution of the United States	Declares that "a well-regulated militia, being necessary to the security of a free state, the right of the people to keep and bear arms, shall not be infringed"
1968	Gun Control Act	Describes eight categories of "prohibited persons" who are not allowed to purchase or possess firearms
1993	Brady Handgun Act	Establishes waiting period for handgun purchases, required licensed dealers to perform background checks, lays groundwork for NICS
1997	*Printz v. United States*	Rules it is unconstitutional for states to be mandated to enforce federal law, effectively preventing mandatory record-sharing
1998	NICS Development	Establishes centralized database by which records of prohibited persons can be shared between states
2007	NICS Improvement Act	Incentivizes states to upload records to NICS, provides mechanism for restoration of Second Amendment rights
2008	*District of Columbia v. Heller*	Reaffirms the right of individual citizens to keep and bear arms at home in the absence of affiliation with a militia, effectively curtails future federal legislation restricting Second Amendment rights

period for gun purchase than in states that implemented background checks alone (Ludwig and Cook 2000).

Another study looked at 2002–2009 data from Connecticut to determine whether increased reporting of disqualifying mental health histories to NICS reduced gun violence. Connecticut began reporting to the NICS system in 2007. By merging data from multiple state organizations, researchers examined the incidence of gun violence and suicide in people with and without disqualifying mental health histories. The researchers reviewed records of 23,292 people with severe mental illness (defined as schizophrenia, bipolar disorder, or major depression plus at least one hospitalization). These people were categorized as having no disqualifying mental health or criminal history, having a disqualifying criminal history, or having a disqualifying mental health history. For those with a gun-disqualifying mental health history and no disqualifying criminal history, the likelihood of their committing a violent crime was reduced by 53% (6.7%–3.2%) after implementing NICS reporting. There was also a 34% decline (5.9%–3.9%) in violent crimes by people who had no disqualifying history. In contrast, those with a disqualifying criminal history were 1.6 times more likely to commit a violent crime after the 2007 reporting began. The increase in this population equalized any small reduction in overall crime contributed by the mental health disqualifications (Swanson et al. 2013).

Only 5% of people studied were disqualified from firearm purchase solely on the basis of their mental health history, and this group committed only 4% of the violent crimes in the study. Because the contribution to violent crime in this sample prior to NICS reporting was very small, even the 53% reduction in violent crime committed by this group had minimal impact on violent crime overall. In other words, even if state-level NICS reporting were done thoroughly for people with disqualifying mental health histories, and those people were successfully prohibited from purchasing firearms, the overall reduction of gun violence would likely remain small (Swanson et al. 2013). Table 66.1 summarizes significant firearm legislation in the United States.

PREVENTION STRATEGIES AND FUTURE DEVELOPMENTS

The issue of access to guns by people with real or perceived risk of violence raises the question of how to protect civil liberties while minimizing public risk. The challenge lies in determining which groups pose sufficient danger to merit targeted firearm restrictions. New policy is shifting away from focusing prohibitions on people with mental illness. Instead, groups like the Consortium for Risk-Based Firearm Policy are recommending a more evidence-based approach that looks at factors independently associated with a risk of violence. Their 2013 publication recommends increasing state-level firearm prohibitions for people who meet evidence-based criteria for an increased risk of violence, including people with substance use disorders, people with mental illness in the time period surrounding hospitalizations for violence, and people who have evoked concern for impending violence from family members or police. The report also advocates for an expansion of programs that remove firearms already in the possession of disqualified persons, and for legal mechanisms to restore Second Amendment rights after a prohibition has been triggered (Consortium for Risk-Based Firearm Policy 2013).

Finally, improved communication between states and the federal NICS database is crucial in minimizing firearm sales to potentially violent persons. Technological improvements, as well as incentives to collect and transmit more data will contribute to increased interstate communication. In order for the NICS database to be effective, gun dealers would need to be universally required to perform background checks by accessing it for every transaction. Closing the holes that currently compromise the system will help it function more effectively to help keep firearms out of the hands of potentially dangerous people.

SUMMARY KEY POINTS

- Though the media and public often assume acts of violence, especially mass shootings, are related to mental illness, the role of mental illness in violence is small.
- Much of the federal and state legislation in the United States limiting access to firearms is tied to mental illness, and many of these laws were passed in reaction to highly publicized shootings.
- The current system to keep firearms from prohibited persons has many vulnerabilities.
- There is little evidence to show that current firearm legislation has been effective in reducing overall violence or firearm homicide, though it has likely reduced firearm suicides.
- Future legislative efforts are focusing on restricting firearm access by people at a known increased risk of violence, rather than by people with mental illness. This may not only be a more effective approach to violence prevention but may also decrease stigma of mental illness.

REFERENCES

Angermeyer M and H Matschinger. 1996. The effect of violent attacks by schizophrenic persons on the attitude of the public towards the mentally ill. *Social Science and Medicine* 43(12):1721–1728.

Anglemyer A, T Horvath, and G Rutherford. 2014. The accessibility of firearms and risk for suicide and homicide victimization among household members: A systematic review and meta-analysis. *Annals of Internal Medicine* 160(2):101–110.

Appelbaum P. 2006. Violence and mental disorders: Data and public policy. *American Journal of Psychiatry* 163(8):1319–1321.

Applebaum P and J Swanson. 2010. Law and psychiatry: Gun laws and mental illness: How sensible are the current restrictions? *Psychiatric Services* 61(7):652–654.

Brady Handgun Act. 1993. http://www.gpo.gov/fdsys/pkg/BILLS-103hr1025enr/pdf/BILLS-103hr1025enr.pdf, accessed May 8, 2015.

Brent D, J Perper, C Allman, G Moritz, M Wartella, and J Zelenak. 1991. The presence and accessibility of firearms in the homes of adolescent suicides: A case-control study. *Journal of the American Medical Association* 266(21):2989–2995.

Buchanan A. 2006. Risk of violence by psychiatric patients: Beyond the "actuarial versus clinical" assessment debate. *Psychiatric Services* 59(2):184–190.

Bureau of Alcohol, Tobacco, Firearms, and Explosives. 1997. Definitions for the categories of persons prohibited from receiving firearms. https://www.atf.gov/file/84311/download, accessed July 27, 2016.

CBS News. 2013. Theater attack prompts new Colorado mental health law. http://denver.cbslocal.com/2013/05/16/theater-attack-prompts-new-colorado-mental-health-law, accessed May 8, 2015.

California Department of Justice. 2009. Mental health firearms prohibition report. http://ag.ca.gov/firearms/mhorfaqs.pdf, accessed May 8, 2015.

California Legislative Information: AB 1014 gun violence restraining order. http://leginfo.legislature.ca.gov/faces/billNavClient.xhtml?bill_id=201320140AB1014&search_keywords, accessed May 8, 2015.

Centers for Disease Control and Prevention. 2015. Fast stats, suicide. http://www.cdc.gov/nchs/fastats/suicide.htm, accessed April 22, 2015.

Centers for Disease Control and Prevention. 2015. Chart ten leading causes of death by age group. http://www.cdc.gov/injury/images/lc-charts/leading_causes_of_death_by_age_group_2013-a.gif, accessed April 22, 2015.

Choe J, L Teplin, and K Abram. 2008. Perpetration of violence, violent victimization and severe mental illness: Balancing public health concerns. *Psychiatric Services* 59(2):153–164.

Cole TB. 2007. Efforts to prevent gun sales to mentally ill may deter patients from seeking help. *Journal of the American Medical Association* 298(5):503–504.

Connecticut General Statute §29–38c. Gun seizure law (1999).

Consortium for Risk-Based Firearm Policy. 2013. Guns, public health and mental illness: And evidence-based approach for state policy. http://www.jhsph.edu/research/centers-and-institutes/johns-hopkins-center-for-gun-policy-and-research/publications/GPHMI-State.pdf, accessed December 14, 2015.

District of Columbia v. Heller, 554 US 570. 2008.

Elbogen E and Johnson S. 2009. The intricate link between violence and mental disorder: Results from the national epidemiologic survey on alcohol and related conditions. *Archives of General Psychiatry* 66(2):152–161.

Federal Bureau of Investigation. 2012. Crime in the United States. Expanded Homicide Data Table 10. https://ucr.fbi.gov/crime-in-the-u.s/2012/crime-in-the-u.s.-2012/offenses-known-to-law-enforcement/offenses-known-to-law-enforcement, accessed July 27, 2016.

Frattaroli S, E McGinty, A Barnhorst, and S Greenberg. 2015. Gun violence restraining orders: Alternative or adjunct to mental health-based restrictions on firearms? *Behavioral Sciences and the Law* 33(2–3):290–307.

Gould A. 2009. The hidden Second Amendment framework within *District of Columbia v. Heller*. *Vanderbilt Law Review* 62(5):1534–1575.

Government Accountability Office. 2012. Sharing promising practices and assessing incentives could better position justice to assist states in providing records for background checks. http://www.gao.gov/products/GAO-12-684, accessed May 8, 2015.

Gun Control Act. 1968. http://www.gpo.gov/fdsys/pkg/STATUTE-82/pdf/STATUTE-82-Pg1213-2.pdf, accessed May 8, 2015.

Hiday VA, M Swartz, J Swanson, R Borum, and H Wagner. 1999. Criminal victimization of persons with severe mental illness. *Psychiatric Services* 50(1):62–68.

Health Insurance Portability and Accountability Act (HIPAA) Privacy Rule and the National Instant Criminal Background Check System. 2013. http://www.regulations.gov/#percent21documentDetail;D=HHS-OCR-2013-0002-0001, accessed May 8, 2015.

Huffington Post. 2013. Cuomo signs NY SAFE Act: 13 provisions of the new gun control law. http://www.huffingtonpost.com/2013/01/16/cuomo-signs-ny-safe-act-new-gun-control-laws_n_2487966.html, accessed May 8, 2015.

Kellerman A, F Rivara, G Somes, D Reay, J Francisco, J Gillentine, J Prodzinski, C Fligner, and B Hackman. 1992. Suicide in the home in relation to gun ownership. *New England Journal of Medicine* 327(7):467–472.

Lessard v. Schmidt 414 U.S. 473 (1974).

Lewis L. 2011. Mental illness, propensity for violence and the Gun Control Act. *Houston Journal of Health Law and Policy* 11:149–174.

Loftin C, D McDowall, B Weirsema, and T Cottey. 1991. Effects of restrictive licensing of handguns on homicide and suicide in the District of Columbia. *New England Journal of Medicine* 325(23):1615–1620.

Ludwig J and P Cook. 2000. Homicide and suicide rates associated with implementation of the Brady Handgun Violence Prevention Act. *Journal of the American Medical Association* 284(5):585–591.

Martone C, E Mulvey, S Yang, A Nemoianu, R Shugarman, and L Soliman. 2013. Psychiatric characteristics of homicide defendants. *American Journal of Psychiatry* 170(9):994–1002.

Mayors Against Illegal Guns. 2011. How missing records in the federal background check system put guns in the hands of killers. http://prtl-sitea-maigs.nyc.gov/downloads/pdf/maig_mimeo_revb.pdf, accessed May 8, 2015.

McCreary J. 2013. "Mentally defective" language in the Gun Control Act. *Connecticut Law Review* 45(3):813–864.

McGinty E, D Webster, and C Barry. 2013. Effects of news media messages about mass shootings on attitudes toward persons with serious mental illness and public support for gun control policies. *American Journal of Psychiatry* 170(5):494–501.

Miller M, D Azrael D, and D Hemenway. 2004. The epidemiology of case fatality rates for suicide in the northeast. *Annals of Emergency Medicine* 43(6):723–730.

New York Times. 2007. Virginia Tech criticized for action in shooting. http://www.nytimes.com/2007/08/30/us/30school.html?pagewanted=all, accessed May 8, 2015.

NICS Improvement Act. 2007. https://www.cfda.gov/?s=program&mode=form&tab=step1&id=0530a2676199a6781bfa03d967a3dbc8, accessed May 8, 2015.

Norris D, M Price, T Gutheil, and W Reid. 2006. Firearm laws, patients, and the roles of psychiatrists. *American Journal of Psychiatry* 163(8):1392–1396.

NPR. 2013. One by one, agents track down illegally owned guns. http://www.npr.org/2013/08/20/213546439/one-by-one-california-agents-track-down-illegally-owned-guns, accessed May 8, 2015.

Office of the Press Secretary. 2014. Fact sheet: Strengthening the federal background check system to keep guns out of potentially dangerous hands. https://www.whitehouse.gov/the-press-office/2014/01/03/fact-sheet-strengthening-federal-background-check-system-keep-guns-out-p, accessed May 8, 2015.

Parker G. 2015. Circumstances and outcomes of a firearm seizure law aimed at dangerous persons: Marion County, Indiana 2006–2013. *Behavioral Sciences and the Law* 33(2–3):308–322.

Price M and D Norris. 2010. Firearm laws: A primer for psychiatrists. *Harvard Review of Psychiatry* 18(6):326–335.

Reisch T, T Steffen, A Habenstein, and W Tschacher. 2013. Change in suicide rates in Switzerland before and after firearm restriction resulting from the 2003 "Army XXI" reform. *American Journal of Psychiatry* 170(9):977–984.

Remington M. 1973. *Lessard v. Schmidt* and its implications for involuntary civil commitment in Wisconsin. *Marquette Law Review* 57(1):65–101.

Ritsher J and J Phelan. 2004. Internalized stigma predicts erosion of morale among psychiatric outpatients. *Psychiatry Research* 129(3):257–265.

SF Gate. 2014. Isla Vista rampage adds urgency for mental illness laws. http://www.sfgate.com/crime/article/Isla-Vista-rampage-adds-urgency-for-mental-5508371.php, accessed May 8, 2015.

Steadman H, E Mulvey, J Monahan, P Robbins, P Appelbaum, T Grisso, L Roth, and E Silver. 1998. Violence by people discharged from acute psychiatric inpatient facilities and by others in the same neighborhoods. *Archives of General Psychiatry* 55(5):393–401.

Swanson J, A Robertson, L Frisman, M Norko, J Lin, M Swartz, and P Cook. 2013. Preventing gun violence in people with serious mental illness. In *Reducing Gun Violence in America: Informing Policy with Evidence and Analysis*, edited by DW Webster and JS Vernick. Baltimore: Johns Hopkins University Press, 62–80.

U.S. v. Giardina 861 F.2d 1335 (1988).

U.S. v. Hansel 474 F.2d 1120 (1973).

U.S. v. Vertz 102 F.2d 787 (2002).

USA Today database of mass shootings. 2013. http://www.usatoday.com/story/news/nation/2013/09/16/mass-killings-data-map/2820423, accessed April 22, 2015.

Wiebe D. 2003. Homicide and suicide risks associated with firearms in the home: A national case-control study. *Annals of Emergency Medicine* 41(6):771–782.

67

Women and violence

JESSICA FERRANTI

INTRODUCTION

The vast majority of the literature on violence involves acts perpetrated by men. While much has been written about violence *against* women, relatively little consideration has been given to violence perpetrated by women. Studies of violence and violence risk assessment have primarily focused on violence perpetrated by high-risk male offenders with mental health problems who end up in the forensic system. This has led to the development of violence risk assessment instruments that attempt to help identify and reduce the violence risk within forensic systems, treatment settings, and in the community. However, there has been debate about whether such studies based on male violent offender data can be extrapolated to women (Nicholls et al. 2004; Skeem et al. 2005b; Logan and Blackburn 2009; Weizmann-Henelius et al. 2010).

There is no doubt that women who commit acts of externalized violence are violating social and psychological norms more so than their male counterparts (Coontz et al. 1994). Studies have suggested that when dealing with life's stressors, provocations, and anger, women are more likely than men to use nonviolent, noncriminal, and inward coping strategies (depression, anxiety, and substance misuse) (Yourstone et al. 2008). Numerous studies have shown that the behavioral profiles associated with stress coping differ in men and women, showing higher levels of aggressive behaviors in men (Verona and Kilmer 2007; Verona et al. 2007).

Traditionally, women are seen as nurturers and men are seen as combatants. In American society, young females are routinely regarded as "less criminal" than young males, and their crimes are perceived as less serious (Freiburger 2010). However, there are now many more role models for aggression in women. Women are increasingly participating in armed forces combat on the frontlines of conflicts, movies now commonly portray female heroines who wield weapons, and female participation in aggressive contact sports such as boxing is becoming more accepted. As society evolves in its acceptance of strong females who exhibit what would traditionally be regarded as "male" traits, recent crime statistics suggest that the rate of women perpetrating violence is also increasing (Friedman et al. 2013). In 2011, U.S. law enforcement made 534,704 arrests for violent crimes; women accounted for 19.6% of the violent offenders (Federal Bureau of Investigation 2011). Although women currently account for less than 10% of the incarcerated population in the United States, the number of incarcerated women is increasing (Carson and Sabol 2012). Women are the fastest-growing segment population in jails and prisons.

Studies suggest that regarding gender differences in violence risk, mental illness may substantially shift the balance in the direction of gender parity. Recent literature on risk of violence in mentally ill individuals indicates that women with mental illness have the potential to be as violent as mentally ill males (Maden 2007). Hodgins (1992) found that women with a major mental disorder were about 27 times more likely than non-mentally ill women to be convicted of a violent crime.

Studies suggest that clinicians are limited in their ability to accurately assess female patients' violence risk and tend to underestimate the level of risk in women (Skeem et al. 2005a,b). Some research suggests that women with psychiatric problems may display different biopsychosocial risk factors and antecedents compared to men. The motivation for most violence perpetrated by women seemingly differs in typology. (See Table 67.1).

TYPOLOGY OF VIOLENCE AND GENDER DIFFERENCES

Barratt et al. (1991) established a classification of aggression in humans: medically related (i.e., psychotic) aggression; premeditated (predatory) aggression; and impulsive (reactive or affective) aggression. Studies have consistently shown that accurate characterization of aggressive acts helps clinicians understand, treat, and prevent violence (Nolan et al. 2003; Quanbeck et al. 2007). Women tend to engage primarily in acts of impulsive violence and psychotic aggression (Krakowski and Czobor 2004). Women commit acts of

Table 67.1 Gender differences in typology of violence and victim characteristics

	Men	Women
Type of violence	Primarily impulsive, some predatory, some psychotic	Primarily impulsive, some psychotic, less frequent predatory/premeditated
Adult victims	Victims are usually known; vast majority of stranger violence carried out by men	Typically a family member or close social contact; extremely rarely engage in stranger violence
Child victims	Victims are most often adults	Victims are most often children
Site of violence	Often outside of the home	Most often in the home

premeditated or predatory aggression much less commonly than men (Frei et al. 2006; Katsavdakis et al. 2011). Women commit very few acts of violence toward strangers or against individuals whom they do not know within the social fabric of their lives (Harrell 2012).

IMPULSIVE VIOLENCE

Studies indicate that impulsive violence is often the result of interpersonal conflict within the social framework of the woman's life, including parents, husbands, and romantic partners, as well as children (Monahan and MacArthur Violence Risk Assessment Study 2001; Weizmann-Henelius et al. 2003; Yourstone et al. 2008). Compared to men, women are more likely to commit impulsive violent crimes at home (Meloy 2006).

Intimate partner violence

Women are far more often victims of intimate partner violence than perpetrators. While the physical and other power disparities between men and women are incontrovertible, studies have reported that both sexes admit to using violence against their partners (Frieze 2005). Women who are battered within relationships may use violence to defend themselves, to express anger, or to retaliate, but they are significantly more likely than men to sustain serious injuries from the ensuing violence (McHugh and Frieze 2006). Although alcohol use has been found to be a consistent risk factor for violence by men toward a female partner (Watkins et al. 2014), the same has not been clearly shown in violence by women toward their partners (Cunradi et al. 1999; Cogan and Ballinger 2006; Cunradi et al. 2011). Personality traits in the antisocial, borderline, and narcissistic domains occur at higher rates in male batterers (Fernandez-Montalvo and Echeburua 2008). These Cluster B personality traits that are characterized by poor frustration tolerance, instability of affect, aggressiveness, and impulsivity, are also pervasive in women who commit acts of interpersonal violence (Ross 2011; Maneta et al. 2013; Sijtsema et al. 2014).

Violence by women against children

The victims of violence perpetrated by women are most often children. Women who engage in impulsive physical maltreatment of their children often have higher rates of substance misuse and depression (Chemtob et al. 2013; Easterbrooks et al. 2013). Once again, Cluster B personality traits increase risk. Some studies indicate that women who are physically violent toward children have often been victims of physical abuse (Lang et al. 2006; Chemtob et al. 2013). Mothers who react to their children with violence tend to be overly reactive to their children's misbehavior (Bradley and Peters 1991; Caselles and Milner 2000). In one study of a nonpsychiatric population, 70% of mothers of colicky infants had explicit aggressive thoughts toward their infants, and 26% of these mothers had infanticidal thoughts (Levitzky and Cooper 2000).

Stranger violence

Impulsive violence by women against strangers is rare. In crimes against strangers by women, the perpetrators often have substance use problems, psychosis, and/or personality disorders. Impulsive violence by women against strangers may also spontaneously occur in the commission of other crimes.

Female gangs

For females with socioeconomic hardships and dysfunctional homes, gang membership has increasingly become an option. Traditionally, females involved in gangs were seen as ancillary associates of male groups and were defined by their relation to male members (Molidor 1996). Today, females are increasingly involved in gangs in one of three ways:

1. Membership in an independent female gang
2. Membership in a male gang as an ancillary member
3. Membership in a female offshoot of a male gang

Most researchers estimate that about 10% of all gang members are female (Hess et al. 2013). Physical fighting with peers to secure territory and resolve disputes with rival gangs makes violence directed toward strangers far more common in young females who are involved in gangs (Wingood et al. 2002).

PSYCHOTIC VIOLENCE

The risk of violence that is motivated by psychosis in women is associated with personality disorders (antisocial and borderline prominently), substance use disorders, psychiatric medication noncompliance, and poor clinical status/active symptoms (Dean et al. 2006). There is growing evidence that psychosis, especially delusional thinking, confers a disproportionate risk of violence on women compared to men (Hodgins et al. 1996; Dean et al. 2006). However, the association between certain types of psychotic symptoms and violence in both sexes is not entirely clear. Some studies have found that delusions are associated with serious violence (Humphreys and Johnstone 1993), while other studies have failed to find a clear association between delusions and violence (Teplin et al. 1994; Appelbaum et al. 2000; Stompe et al. 2004). There is some evidence of special patterns in the relationship between psychosis and violence in women. Because delusions are expressed through the filter of an individual's psychosocial experience and psychology, women suffering from psychosis may exhibit gender differences in the thematic content of their psychotic symptoms. In a study comparing 47 male and female homicide offenders found not guilty by reason of insanity (NGRI), Ferranti et al. (2013) reported that religious delusions were more common in female homicide offenders who killed infants and children. In addition, the male homicide offenders did not have any victims under the age of 18, and religious delusions were less frequently present, regardless of the victim's age. These results were consistent with other recent research on child murder by female homicide offenders found NGRI. In a study of women found NGRI for filicide, Friedman et al. (2005) found that the women frequently had mood problems, experienced auditory hallucinations, and almost all perpetrators had altruistic or acutely psychotic (delusional) motives.

Women who are motivated to violence by religious delusions often have self-preservation or the altruistic preservation of their children as the goal. Altruistically motivated filicide has been described by Resnick (1969) in his seminal work on motives in women who kill their children. The finding that many female perpetrators of psychotically motivated homicide against children have been found to have religious delusions at the time of the homicide is a red flag for clinicians who are evaluating women at risk of engaging in violence against their children. The presence of a psychotic disorder in women, particularly when paired with personality disorders and traits that confer high aggressivity, fearlessness, and externalized behaviors, is a mental health constellation that warrants a high degree of clinical surveillance for violence risk.

PREDATORY FEMALE OFFENDERS

Compared to men, acts of predatory violence by women are rare (Maden 2007). As with men, women who commit acts of predatory violence do so when motivated by an external goal, i.e., the intention to do the violence as revenge, primitive drive (aggressive or sexual) gratification, as an instrumental action to achieve personal or political profit, or to facilitate some other criminal intent such as robbery. Table 67.2 summarizes differences between men and woman in predatory homicides.

Table 67.2 Gender differences in predatory serial killing and mass murder

	Men	Women
Most common motivation for serial killing	Sadistic pleasure, sexual gratification	Personal profit
Victims	Strangers	Individuals within social environment
Method	Blunt force, use of sharp weapons	Most commonly poisoning
Mass murder	Men with firearm (more than 90% of all U.S. reported cases)	Very rarely commit mass murder (less than 10% of all U.S. reported cases)

SERIAL MURDER

Serial murder is rare in general, and serial murder by women is extremely infrequent. Hickey (1997) analyzed 35 cases of female serial killers in the United States who were active between 1795 and 1988. In about 75% of the cases, personal profit was seemingly the motive. In contrast, male perpetrators of serial killings commonly had sadistic and/or sexual gratification as primary motives (Frei et al. 2006). Of female serial killers, poisoning was the most common method of killing, and women primarily killed people they knew (Hickey 1997). In another study reporting on 105 female serial killers in 18 countries, poisoning was also the most common method of killing (Wilson and Hilton 1998). The findings that women tend to use more covert methods of killing, target individuals within their social environment, and exhibit less sadistic gratification in the killings are all important gender differences in serial murder.

MASS MURDER

Based on criminal databases, 72 mass murders occurred between 2000 and 2012 in the United States and 94% of the perpetrators were male (Federal Bureau of Investigation 2014). Choice of weapon may be factor as women appear less likely to use firearms in homicidal acts and are more likely to use knives, poisoning, or other methods that make killing multiple people at one time unfeasible (Wilson and Hilton 1998; Ferranti et al. 2013). In a series of two articles, Knoll discusses the militaristic nature of some mass murders using the term "pseudocommando" (Dietz 1986) to describe a type of offender who attacks in broad daylight, plans the attack, and carries out the offense with a large arsenal of weapons (Dietz 1986; Knoll 2010a,b). Knoll discusses the psychology of revenge and the "warrior" archetype (Knoll 2010a).

Traditional gender roles have dictated that, in times of military conflict, women's involvement in U.S. military forces centered on caretaking tasks such as nursing and cooking. In our history, women have only recently begun to have a role as "warriors" in contemporary armed forces combat. It is anticipated that women will be increasingly engaging in direct combat in positions on the frontlines of the armed forces. Once again, society's shifting conceptualization of gender roles and changing social conditioning of females may be an important influence in increasing the prevalence of violence perpetrated by women.

FILICIDE

Children are most often the victims of lethal violence perpetrated by women. In his review of the world literature on filicide, Resnick (1969) identified five major motives of maternal filicide:

1. Altruistic
2. Acutely psychotic
3. Fatal maltreatment
4. Unwanted child filicide
5. Spouse revenge filicide

In an altruistic filicide, a mother kills her child out of love, believing death to be in the child's best interest. In an acutely psychotic filicide, a psychotic or delirious mother can kill her child without any comprehensible motive as a result of disorganized behaviors or as a result of following command hallucinations. In mothers who physically abuse their children, fatal maltreatment filicide occurs, but murder is neither the intention of the act nor the anticipated outcome. In unwanted child filicide, a mother kills a child who is not wanted. Spouse revenge filicide is the rarest classification of filicide, and it occurs when a mother kills her child to inflict punishment via emotional harm to the child's father.

In studies looking at serious maternal violence against children, the risk of a fatality from maternal child abuse increases substantially when the mother has a major psychiatric illness (Husain and Daniel 1984; Friedman et al. 2005; Friedman and Resnick 2011). The filicide risk increases relative to other psychiatric disorders for children whose mothers have schizophrenia or mood disorders (Friedman and Resnick 2011). Based on U.S. Bureau of Justice Statistics reporting on homicide trends in the United States between 1980 and 2008, for children under the age of 5 killed by a parent, the homicide rate for biological fathers was only slightly higher than for biological mothers (Cooper and Smith 2011). However, of children under the age of 5 killed by someone other than their parent, 80% were killed by males (Cooper and Smith 2011).

POSTPARTUM VIOLENCE

Postpartum problems are generally categorized into two major categories: postpartum depression (including the less severe "baby blues") and postpartum psychosis. Studies have indicated that milder depressive symptoms, aka "baby blues," occur in as many as 70% of new mothers (Halbreich 2005). Major depressive disorder affects about 15% of new mothers (Friedman and Resnick 2009b). Women in situations of intimate partner violence have increased rates of postpartum depression (Lobato et al. 2012). In homes with intimate partner violence, there is a powerful confluence of risk factors for violence toward infants, including a climate of externalized violence as a means of resolving conflict.

Postpartum psychosis is the most severe postpartum mental disorder. Postpartum psychosis occurs in about 1–2 per 1000 childbirths (Spinelli 2009). The rate is 100 times higher in women with bipolar disorder or a past history of postpartum psychosis (Spinelli 2009). The psychotic symptoms typically present in the first 3–14 days postpartum, although some women may present several months later, usually with psychotic depression (Rhode and Marneros 1993). Women with postpartum psychosis are more likely to commit acts of violence toward themselves and to commit infanticide.

In 1970, Resnick coined the term "neonaticide" to denote the murder of a child within the first 24 hours of life, the period of highest risk for maternal violence (Resnick 1970). Almost all neonaticides are committed by women (Friedman and Resnick 2009a). Mothers who commit filicide are more frequently married compared with mothers who commit neonaticide. They also have a high frequency of substance use, unemployment, and a personal history of being abused (Friedman et al. 2005).

VIOLENCE RISK FACTOR PROFILES IN WOMEN

Psychosocial factors

Negative family environment, physical abuse, sexual abuse, and neglect by early caretakers are factors common in women who commit violent acts (Molidor 1996; Dean et al. 2006; Yourstone et al. 2008; Taylor and Bragado-Jimenez 2009; Ferranti et al. 2013; Tripodi and Pettus-Davis 2013). Maternal neglect in particular has been shown to be especially harmful to girls' development. In one study by Raine et al. (1994), maternal rejection at age 1 was shown to predict violent crime at age 18. Psychiatric illness is common in the parents of violent females (Yourstone et al. 2008). Violent parental modeling in the home, including exposure to intimate partner violence, contributes to intergenerational transmission of antisocial behavior in both males and females (Logan et al. 2009; Ehrensaft and Cohen 2012). Compared with men, women are more commonly married, living with an intimate partner, and/or have children at the time of the violent act (Table 67.3). While close social infrastructure is a protective factor for men, in women it is associated with a heightened risk of violence. The victims of women are

Table 67.3 Gender differences in violence risk profiles of violent offenders

	Men	Women
Social structure	Less commonly married or partnered	Commonly married or partnered and have children
Past history of violence	Often have past history of violence	Lethal act may be first and only crime
Juvenile history	May have a history of Conduct Disorder, juvenile offenses	Less commonly have juvenile offense history
Criminal history	May have longitudinal history of criminality	Less commonly have history of criminality
Mental illness	May or may not have mental illness; in psychiatric inpatient populations may commit violent acts at rate *equal* to women	May or may not have mental illness; however, 27 times more likely to commit a violent act if mental illness is present; violence rates for men and women in inpatient psychiatric populations have often been shown to be *equal*
Substance use disorder	Associated with violence	Associated with violence; impulsive violence against strangers more likely with alcohol intoxication
Personality disorder	More likely to have antisocial personality disorder diagnosis; commonly score higher on psychopathy measures	More likely to have borderline personality disorder diagnosis; commonly score lower on psychopathy measures

typically close to them, both in social relationship and in environmental proximity.

Every clinician learns the mantra that the best predictor of future violence is a history of violence. However, research suggests that there may be important exceptions in women. Some studies have shown that for women who have committed extreme acts of violence, i.e., homicide, the lethal act of violence was commonly their first and only crime (Yourstone et al. 2008; Ferranti et al. 2013). In women with major mental illness, violent recidivism rates are similar to cases of violent men with mental illness (Eronen et al. 1996; Putkonen et al. 2003).

Juvenile history

Conduct disorder in childhood is known to be a pathway to adult violent offending. For women, the lack of juvenile and longitudinal criminality may contribute to lower scores on measures of psychopathy such as the Hare Psychopathy Checklist-Revised (PCL-R), which may lead to underestimation of violence risk when utilizing structured violence risk assessment instruments. Psychiatric disorders appear to weigh more heavily in the violence risk potential of women. Societal perceptions of girls' aberrant behavior as less threatening than boys' behaviors may contribute to girls falling below the detection of law enforcement. Gender differences in delinquency risk factors have been observed. Early onset of puberty, sexual abuse, and problems with depression and anxiety had a higher correlation with delinquency in girls (Zahn et al. 2008). Rhoades and colleagues (2015) found that for men, involvement in the juvenile justice system alone predicted risk of adult arrest; however, for women, juvenile justice system referral was not a significant predictor of adult arrest. Instead, for women, family violence, parental divorce, and cumulative childhood risk factors were significant predictors of adult arrest.

Mental disorder

Studies consistently demonstrate high rates of psychiatric illness in women who are violent (Teplin et al. 1996; Robbins et al. 2003; Nicholls et al. 2009; Taylor and Bragado-Jimenez 2009). Substance use disorders and posttraumatic stress disorder (PTSD) are highly prevalent in population samples of incarcerated women (Wolff et al. 2011; Tripodi and Pettus-Davis 2013; Lynch et al. 2014). Studies indicate that there is a high prevalence of PTSD in women who commit violent crimes, supporting the association between the victimization of females and later perpetration of violence (Teplin et al. 1996).

In psychiatric inpatients, the risk of violence for men and women has been reported as equal in multiple studies (Binder and McNiel 1990; Lam et al. 2000; Robbins et al. 2003; Krakowski and Czobor 2004; Skeem et al. 2005b). When inpatient violence does occur, men commit more acts of violence that lead to serious injuries (Lam et al. 2000; Krakowski and Czobor 2004). In the general population being male *is* one of the most important static risk factors for violence, but once the parameters change to the acute inpatient psychiatric population, female patients can be equally violent. This relative absence of core gender differences in inpatient psychiatric populations has also been shown in forensic inpatients (Robbins et al. 2003; Nicholls et al. 2009). However, a 2015 meta-analysis investigating factors associated with violence by psychiatric inpatients found that studies with higher proportions of male patients reported higher rates of violence (Iozzino et al. 2015).

Borderline personality disorder

Borderline personality disorder is most correlated with externalized and self-directed violence in women (Logan and Blackburn 2009). Logan et al. (2009) reported that women incarcerated for a major violent offense were four times more likely to have a diagnosis of borderline personality disorder. Kuo and Linehan (2009) investigated biologic vulnerability to high emotional reactivity in individuals with borderline personality disorder and found higher reactivity to evocative stimuli. The tendency to form unstable and/or chaotic emotional attachments with others may help account for the frequency of violence in women with borderline personality disorder.

Antisocial personality disorder and psychopathy

Research suggests that the rate of antisocial personality disorder is lower in women compared to men across a range of institutional, forensic, and community settings (Dolan and Vollm 2009). In community samples, twofold to fivefold higher rates of antisocial personality disorder are typically found in men. Violent women are more likely to have been given a diagnosis of a mood disorder or borderline personality disorder and are less likely to have been given a diagnosis of conduct disorder or antisocial personality disorder (Rutherford et al. 1995; Beck 2004; Weizmann-Henelius et al. 2010; Ferranti et al. 2013).

Whether the diagnosis of borderline personality disorder and the psychopathy construct contain gender biases is an important question to consider. There may be sociological biases that cause mental health practitioners to more readily view affective dyscontrol problems as "female" disorders and more readily define antisocial tendencies as synonymous with a criminality. Research on psychopathy is often conducted on incarcerated populations; however, there are gender biases in sentencing that lead to fewer incarcerated female psychopathic individuals than male psychopathic individuals (Freiburger 2010).

Substance use and violence

Studies of violent female offenders have shown a strong association with substance use disorders (Sacks 2004). Alcohol, methamphetamine, and cocaine are the most commonly abused substances by women who commit acts of violence. In a study by Collins et al. (2007), women who committed acts of impulsive violence in bars most commonly did so against strangers. Acts of violence by women against strangers are exceedingly rare, but it appears that the social environment and the consumption of alcohol were able to override the typical patterns of violence by women. When the violence was directed at a stranger in the bar, the opponent was most often another woman of similar age, height, and physical build. The investigators found that the major precipitants of the incidents were predominantly either perceptions of obnoxious behavior or a conflict over a romantic partner. The women reported high alcohol intake before the incidents. The number of drinks consumed in the bar prior to the incident was positively correlated to violent acts. The authors concluded that the act of stranger violence was perhaps related to the gender and physical match between perpetrator and opponent. This finding has interesting implications for an evolutionary model for women's violence against other women in social settings, which may spur competitiveness for traditional resources such as environmental space and romantic partners.

Some studies suggest important gender differences in the association of aggressive responding with alcohol use. Alcohol use has been found to be a consistent risk factor for violence by men toward a female partner (Watkins et al. 2014). However, alcohol has not been clearly shown as a risk factor for violence by women toward a male partner (Cunradi et al. 1999; Cogan and Ballinger 2006; Cunradi et al. 2011).

SUMMARY

Although much has been written about violence perpetrated by men, relatively little consideration has been given to violence perpetrated by women. Research in the area of women and violence is growing and yielding important information about gender differences. The recent literature on violence indicates that certain populations of women with mental illness have the potential to be equally as violent as their male counterparts. These data offer an opportunity for improved interventions and treatment for women at risk.

SUMMARY KEY POINTS

- The criminal and psychological variables of violent women are often different than violent men.
- Women with mental illness may have the potential to be equally as violent as men with mental illness.
- Children are most often the victims of violence perpetrated by women.
- Women may score lower on structured violence risk assessment instruments.
- Being aware of gender differences in the risk factor profiles of women is essential to accurate detection and prevention of violence.

REFERENCES

Appelbaum PS, PC Robbins, and J Monahan. 2000. Violence and delusions: Data from the MacArthur Violence Risk Assessment Study. *American Journal of Psychiatry* 157(4):566–572.

Barratt ES, MS Stanford, L Dowdy et al.1991. Measuring and predicting aggression within the context of a personality theory. *Journal of Neuropsychiatry and Clinical Neuroscience* 3(2):S35–S39.

Beck JC. 2004. Delusions, substance abuse, and serious violence. *Journal of the American Academy of Psychiatry and the Law* 32(2):169–172.

Binder RL and DE McNiel. 1990. The relationship of gender to violent behavior in acutely disturbed psychiatric patients. *Journal of Clinical Psychiatry* 51(3):110–114.

Bradley EJ and RD Peters. 1991. Physically abusive and nonabusive mothers' perceptions of parenting and child behavior. *American Journal of Orthopsychiatry* 61(3):455–460.

Carson EA and WJ Sabol. 2012. *Prisoners in 2011*. NCJ 239808. Washington, DC: U.S. Department of Justice, Office of Justice Programs, Bureau of Justice Statistics.

Caselles CE and JS Milner. 2000. Evaluations of child transgressions, disciplinary choices, and expected child compliance in a no-cry and a crying infant condition in physically abusive and comparison mothers. *Child Abuse and Neglect* 24(4):477–491.

Chemtob CM, OG Gudino, and D Laraque. 2013. Maternal posttraumatic stress disorder and depression in pediatric primary care: Association with child maltreatment and frequency of child exposure to traumatic events. *Journal of the American Medical Association Pediatrics* 167(11):1011–1018.

Cogan R and BC Ballinger. 2006. Alcohol problems and the differentiation of partner, stranger, and general violence. *Journal of Interpersonal Violence* 21(7):924–935.

Collins RL, B Quigley, and KE Leonard. 2007. Women's physical aggression in bars: an event-based examination of precipitants and predictors of severity. *Aggressive Behavior* 33:304–313.

Coontz PD, CW Lidz, EP Mulvey. 1994. Gender and the assessment of dangerousness in the psychiatric emergency room. *International Journal of Law and Psychiatry* 17(4):369–376.

Cooper A and EL Smith. 2011: *Homicide Trends in the United States, 1980–2008*. Washington, DC: U.S. Department of Justice, Bureau of Justice Statistics.

Cunradi CB, GM Ames, and M Duke. 2011. The relationship of alcohol problems to the risk for unidirectional and bidirectional intimate partner violence among a sample of blue-collar couples. *Violence and Victims* 26(2):147–158.

Cunradi CB, R Caetano, CL Clark et al. 1999. Alcohol-related problems and intimate partner violence among white, black, and Hispanic couples in the U.S. *Alcoholism: Clinical and Experimental Research* 23(9):1492–1501.

Dean K, E Walsh, P Moran et al. 2006. Violence in women with psychosis in the community: Prospective study. *British Journal of Psychiatry* 188:264–270.

Dietz PE. 1986. Mass, serial and sensational homicides. *Bulletin of the New York Academy of Medicine* 62(5):477–491.

Dolan M and B Vollm. 2009. Antisocial personality disorder and psychopathy in women: A literature review on the reliability and validity of assessment instruments. *International Journal of Law and Psychiatry* 32(1):2–9.

Easterbrooks MA, JD Bartlett, M Raskin et al. 2013. Limiting home visiting effects: Maternal depression as a moderator of child maltreatment. *Pediatrics* 132(Supplement 2):S126–S133.

Ehrensaft MK and P Cohen. 2012. Contribution of family violence to the intergenerational transmission of externalizing behavior. *Prevention Science* 13(4):370–383.

Eronen M, P Hakola, and J Tiihonen. 1996. Mental disorders and homicidal behavior in Finland. *Archives of General Psychiatry* 53(6):497–501.

Federal Bureau of Investigation (FBI). 2014. Active Shooter Events from 2000 to 2012. *Law Enforcement Bulletin*,, January 7.

Federal Bureau of Investigation (FBI). 2011. *Uniform Crime Reports: Crime in the United States 2011*. Washington, DC: Federal Bureau of Investigation. https://ucr.fbi.gov/crime-in-the-u.s/2011/crime-in-the-u.s.-2011/fbi-releases-2011-crime-statistics

Fernandez-Montalvo J and E Echeburua. 2008. Personality disorders and psychopathy in men convicted for severe intimate partner violence. *Psicothema* 20(2):193–198.

Ferranti J, BE McDermott, and CL Scott. 2013. Characteristics of female homicide offenders found not guilty by reason of insanity. *Journal of the American Academy of Psychiatry and the Law* 41(4):516–522.

Frei A, B Vollm, M Graf et al. 2006. Female serial killing: Review and case report. *Criminal Behavior and Mental Health* 16(3):167–176.

Freiburger TL. 2010. The effects of gender, family status, and race on sentencing decisions. *Behavioral Sciences and the Law* 28(3):378–395.

Friedman SH, RC Hall, and RM Sorrentino. 2013. Commentary: Women, violence, and insanity. *Journal of the American Academy of Psychiatry and the Law* 41(4):523–528.

Friedman SH, SW Horwitz, and PJ Resnick. 2005. Child murder by mothers: A critical analysis of the current state of knowledge and a research agenda. *American Journal of Psychiatry* 162(9):1578–1587.

Friedman SH and PJ Resnick. 2009a. Neonaticide: Phenomenology and considerations for prevention. *International Journal of Law and Psychiatry* 32(1):43–47.

Friedman SH and PJ Resnick. 2009b. Postpartum depression: An update. *Womens Health (London)* 5(3):287–295.

Friedman SH and PJ Resnick. 2011. Child murder and mental illness in parents: Implications for psychiatrists. *Journal of Clinical Psychiatry* 72(5):587–588.

Frieze IH. 2005. *Hurting the One You Love: Violence in Relationships*. Belmont, CA: Thomson Wadsworth.

Halbreich U. 2005. Postpartum disorders: Multiple interacting underlying mechanisms and risk factors. *Journal of Affective Disorders* 88(1):1–7.

Harrell E. 2012. *Violent Victimization Committed by Strangers, 1993–2010. Special Report.* NCJ 239424. Washington, DC: U.S. Department of Justice, Office of Justice Programs, Bureau of Justice Statistics.

Hess KrM, CMH Orthmann, and JP Wright. 2013: *Juvenile Justice.* 6th edition. Belmont, CA: Wadsworth, Cengage Learning.

Hickey EW. 1997: *Serial Murderers and Their Victims.* Belmont, CA: Wadsworth.

Hodgins S. 1992. Mental disorder, intellectual deficiency, and crime. Evidence from a birth cohort. *Archives General Psychiatry* 49(6):476–483.

Hodgins S, SA Mednick, and PA Brennan. 1996. Mental disorder and crime. Evidence from a Danish birth cohort. *Archives of General Psychiatry* 53(6):489–496.

Humphreys M and EC Johnstone. 1993. Dangerous behaviour preceding first admissions for schizophrenia. *British Journal of Psychiatry* 163:547.

Husain A and A Daniel. 1984. A comparative study of filicidal and abusive mothers. *Canadian Journal of Psychiatry* 29(7):596–598.

Iozzino L, C Ferrari, M Large et al. 2015: Prevalence and risk factors of violence by psychiatric acute inpatients: A systematic review and meta-analysis. *PLoS One* 10(6):e0128536.

Katsavdakis KA, JR Meloy, and SG White. 2011. A female mass murder. *Journal of Forensic Science* 56(3):813–818.

Knoll JL, 4th. 2010a. The "pseudocommando" mass murderer: Part I, the psychology of revenge and obliteration. *Journal of the American Academy of Psychiatry and the Law* 38(1):87–94.

Knoll JL, 4th. 2010b. The "Pseudocommando" mass murderer: Part II, the language of revenge. *Journal of the American Academy of Psychiatry and the Law* 38(2):263–272.

Krakowski M and P Czobor. 2004. Gender differences in violent behaviors: Relationship to clinical symptoms and psychosocial factors. *American Journal of Psychiatry* 161(3):459–465.

Kuo JR and MM Linehan. 2009. Disentangling emotion processes in borderline personality disorder: Physiological and self-reported assessment of biological vulnerability, baseline intensity, and reactivity to emotionally evocative stimuli. *Journal of Abnormal Psychology* 118:531–544.

Lam JN, DE McNiel, and RL Binder. 2000. The relationship between patients' gender and violence leading to staff injuries. *Psychiatric Services* 51(9):1167–1170.

Lang AJ, CS Rodgers , and MM Lebeck. 2006. Associations between maternal childhood maltreatment and psychopathology and aggression during pregnancy and postpartum. *Child Abuse and Neglect* 30(1):17–25.

Levitzky S and R Cooper. 2000. Infant colic syndrome—Maternal fantasies of aggression and infanticide. *Clinical Pediatrics* 39(7):395–400.

Lobato G, CL Moraes, AS Dias et al. 2012. Alcohol misuse among partners: A potential effect modifier in the relationship between physical intimate partner violence and postpartum depression. *Social Psychiatry and Psychiatric Epidemiology* 47(3):427–438.

Logan C and R Blackburn. 2009. Mental disorder in violent women in secure settings: Potential relevance to risk for future violence. *International Journal of Law and Psychiatry* 32(1):31–38.

Logan JE, RT Leeb , and LE Barker. 2009. Gender-specific mental and behavioral outcomes among physically abused high-risk seventh-grade youths. *Public Health Reports* 124(2):234–245.

Lynch SM, DD Dehart, JE Belknap et al. 2014. A multisite study of the prevalence of serious mental illness, PTSD, and substance use disorders of women in jail. *Psychiatric Services* 65(5):670–674.

Maden T. 2007. *Treating Violence: A Guide to Risk Management in Mental Health.* Oxford: Oxford University Press.

Maneta EK, S Cohen, MS Schulz et al. 2013. Two to tango: A dyadic analysis of links between borderline personality traits and intimate partner violence. *Journal of Personality Disorder* 27(2):233–243.

McHugh MC and IH Frieze. 2006. Intimate partner violence: New directions. *Annals of the New York Academy of Sciences* 1087:121–141.

Meloy JR. 2006. Empirical basis and forensic application of affective and predatory violence. *Australian and New Zealand Journal of Psychiatry* 40(6–7):539–547.

Molidor CE. 1996. Female gang members: A profile of aggression and victimization. *Social Work* 41(3):251–257.

Monahan J. 2001: *Rethinking Risk Assessment: The MacArthur Study of Mental Disorder and Violence.* New York: Oxford University Press.

Nicholls TL, J Brink, C Greaves et al. 2009. Forensic psychiatric inpatients and aggression: An exploration of incidence, prevalence, severity, and interventions by gender. *Journal of Law and Psychiatry* 32(1):23–30.

Nicholls TL, JR Ogloff, and KS Douglas. 2004. Assessing risk for violence among male and female civil psychiatric patients: The HCR-20, PCL:SV, and VSC. *Behavioral Science and the Law* 22(1):127–158.

Nolan KA, P Czobor, BB Roy et al. 2003. Characteristics of assaultive behavior among psychiatric inpatients. *Psychiatric Services* 54(7):1012–1016.

Putkonen H, EJ Komulainen, M Virkkunen et al. 2003. Risk of repeat offending among violent female offenders with psychotic and personality disorders. *American Journal of Psychiatry* 160(5):947–951.

Quanbeck CD, BE McDermott, J Lam et al. 2007. Categorization of aggressive acts committed by chronically assaultive state hospital patients. *Psychiatric Services* 58(4):521–528.

Raine A, P Brennan, and SA Mednick. 1994. Birth complications combined with early maternal rejection at age 1 year predispose to violent crime at age 18 years. *Archives of General Psychiatry* 51:984–988.

Resnick PJ. 1969. Child murder by parents: A psychiatric review of filicide. *American Journal of Psychiatry* 126:325–334.

Resnick PJ. 1970. Murder of the newborn: A psychiatric review of neonaticide. *American Journal of Psychiatry* 126(10):1414–4120.

Rhoades KA, LD Leve, JM Eddy et al. 2015. Predicting the transition from juvenile delinquency to adult criminality: Gender-specific influences in two high-risk samples. *Criminal Behavior and Mental Health* April 28. doi:10.1002/cbm.1957

Rhode A and A Marneros. 1993. Postpartum psychoses: Onset and long-term course. *Psychopathology* 26(3–4):203–209.

Robbins PC, J Monahan, and E Silver. 2003. Mental disorder, violence, and gender. *Law and Human Behavior* 27(6):561–571.

Ross JM. 2011. Personality and situational correlates of self-reported reasons for intimate partner violence among women versus men referred for batterers' intervention. *Behavioral Sciences and the Law* 29(5):711–727.

Rutherford MJ, AI Alterman, JS Cacciola et al. 1995. Gender differences in diagnosing antisocial personality disorder in methadone patients. *American Journal of Psychiatry* 152(9):1309–1316.

Sacks JY. 2004. Women with co-occurring substance use and mental disorders (COD) in the criminal justice system: A research review. *Behavioral Sciences and the Law* 22(4):449–466.

Sijtsema JJ, L Baan, and S Bogaerts. 2014. Associations between Dysfunctional Personality Traits and Intimate Partner Violence in Perpetrators and Victims. *Journal of Interpersonal Violence* 29(13):2418–2438.

Skeem JL, EP Mulvey, C Odgers et al. 2005a. What do clinicians expect? Comparing envisioned and reported violence for male and female patients. *Journal of Consulting and Clinical Psychology* 73(4):599–609.

Skeem J, EP Mulvey, C Odgers et al. 2005b. Gender and risk assessment accuracy: Underestimating women's violence potential. *Law and Human Behavior* 29(2):173–186.

Spinelli MG. 2009. Postpartum psychosis: Detection of risk and management. *American Journal of Psychiatry* 166(4):405–408.

Stompe T, G Ortwein-Swoboda, and H Schanda. 2004. Schizophrenia, delusional symptoms, and violence: The threat/control override concept reexamined. *Schizophrenia Bulletin* 30(1):31–44.

Taylor PJ and MD Bragado-Jimenez. 2009. Women, psychosis and violence. *International Journal of Law and Psychiatry* 32(1):56–64.

Teplin LA, KM Abram, and GM McClelland. 1994. Does psychiatric disorder predict violent crime among released jail detainees? A six-year longitudinal study. *American Psychology* 49(4):335–342.

Teplin LA, KM Abram, and GM McClelland. 1996. Prevalence of psychiatric disorders among incarcerated women. I. Pretrial jail detainees. *Archives of General Psychiatry* 53(6):505–512.

Tripodi SJ and C Pettus-Davis. 2013. Histories of childhood victimization and subsequent mental health problems, substance use, and sexual victimization for a sample of incarcerated women in the US. *International Journal of Law and Psychiatry* 36(1):30–40.

Verona E and A Kilmer. 2007. Stress exposure and affective modulation of aggressive behavior in men and women. *Journal of Abnormal Psychology* 116(2):410–421.

Verona E, A Reed, and JJ Curtin. 2007. Gender differences in emotional and overt/covert aggressive responses to stress. *Aggressive Behavior* 33(3):261–271.

Watkins LE, RC Maldonado, and D Dilillo. 2014. Hazardous alcohol use and intimate partner aggression among dating couples: The role of impulse control difficulties. *Aggressive Behavior* 40(4):369–381.

Weizmann-Henelius G, H Putkonen, M Gronroos et al. 2010. Examination of psychopathy in female homicide offenders—Confirmatory factor analysis of the PCL-R. *International Journal of Law and Psychiatry* 33(3):177–183.

Weizmann-Henelius, GV Viemero, and M Eronen. 2003. The violent female perpetrator and her victim. *Forensic Science International* 133(3):197–203.

Wilson W and T Hilton. 1998. Modus operandi of female serial killers. *Psychological Reports* 82(2):495–498.

Wingood GM, RJ DiClemente, R Crosby et al. 2002. Gang involvement and the health of African American female adolescents. *Pediatrics* 110(5):e57.

Wolff N, BC Frueh, J Shi et al. 2011. Trauma exposure and mental health characteristics of incarcerated females self-referred to specialty PTSD treatment. *Psychiatric Services* 62(8):954–958.

Yourstone J, T Lindholm, and M Kristiansson. 2008. Women who kill: A comparison of the psychosocial background of female and male perpetrators. *International Journal of Law and Psychiatry* 31(4):374–383.

Zahn MA, SR Hawkins, J Chiancone et al. 2008: *The Girls Study Group—Charting the Way to Delinquency Prevention for Girls.* http://www.ncjrs.gov/pdffiles1/ojjdp/223434.pdf, accessed December 28, 2014.

PART 8

Psychological and Neuroimaging Assessments

BARBARA McDERMOTT

68

Use of psychological assessment tools in forensic psychiatric evaluation

SANJAY SHAH AND RANDY K. OTTO

INTRODUCTION

Forensic examination by psychiatrists and psychologists is predicated upon the assumption that, because of their expertise, these mental health professionals can provide the legal decision maker with information about the examinee's psychiatric and psychological functioning that are relevant to some legal issue in dispute, resulting in more informed, and presumably more accurate, decisions. Thus, the goal of forensic psychiatric assessment and forensic psychological examination is to assess and describe those aspects of the examinee's emotional, behavioral, and/or cognitive functioning that are relevant to some legal issue in dispute. Of course, forensic psychiatrists and forensic psychologists can only provide legal decision makers with helpful information if they employ valid assessment techniques. In this chapter we discuss the potential value of psychological assessment tools in a forensic psychiatric evaluation.

A MODEL FOR FORENSIC ASSESSMENT

Grisso (1986, 2003) proposed a model for forensic mental health assessment that can be applied to essentially any legal matter in which questions about an individual's emotional, behavioral, or cognitive functioning are at issue (see Figure 68.1). First, the examiner must be familiar with the relevant law. Thus, if evaluating a criminal defendant whose competence to stand trial is in dispute, the examiner must know what the law requires of a defendant when participating in the legal process. Next, the examiner distills from this what legal matters may be impacted by the examinee's emotional, behavioral, and/or cognitive functioning. By doing this, the examiner identifies the "psycholegal capacities" of relevance. In the case of a criminal defendant whose competence to stand trial is in dispute, the examiner would assess the defendant's emotional, behavioral, or cognitive functioning and how it affected his or her rational and factual understanding of the legal proceedings, and his or her ability to consult with counsel (*Dusky v. U.S.* 1960). Finally, the examiner selects the assessment techniques that best aid in assessment of these identified psycholegal capacities. Figure 68.1 provides a model for the forensic mental health evaluation.

DISTINGUISHING BETWEEN DIFFERENT TYPES OF ASSESSMENT TOOLS

There is no clear definition of what is meant by a psychiatric or psychological test. The *Standards for Educational and Psychological Testing* (Joint Committee on the Standards for Educational and Psychological Testing of the American Educational Research Association, the American Psychological Association, and the National Council on Measurement in Education 2014; hereinafter Joint Committee 2014) notes, "A test is a device or evaluative procedure in which a sample of an examinee's behavior in a specified domain is obtained and subsequently evaluated and scored using a standardized process. Whereas the label *test* is sometimes reserved for instruments on which responses are evaluated for their correctness or quality, and the terms *scale* and *inventory* are used for measures of attitudes, interest, and dispositions, the *Standards* uses the single term tests to refer to all such evaluative devices…[T]ests standardize the process by which test takers' responses to test materials are evaluated and scored" (Joint Committee 2014, 2, emphasis in original).

In this chapter we consider psychiatric and psychological assessment techniques broadly. The assessment tools psychiatrists and psychologists use can be categorized with respect to the constructs they assess and how they perform.

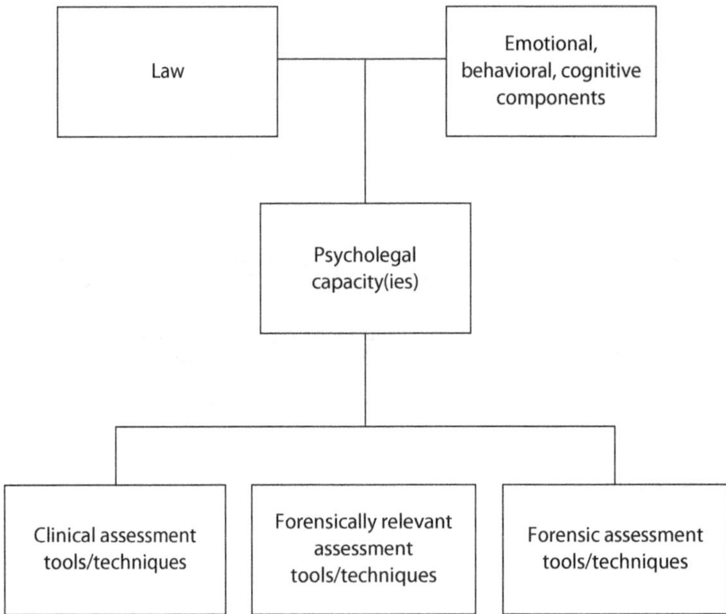

Figure 68.1 A model for forensic mental health evaluation. (Adapted from Grisso T. 1986. *Evaluating Competencies: Forensic Assessments and Instruments*. New York: Plenum Press.)

CLASSIFYING ASSESSMENT TOOLS ACCORDING TO THE CONSTRUCTS THEY ASSESS

Clinical assessment techniques

When conducting forensic evaluations psychiatrists typically employ assessment techniques that they also rely on when providing therapeutic services (e.g., the clinical interview; tests that aid in assessment of central nervous system structure, functioning, and metabolism such as magnetic resonance imaging [MRI], positron emission tomography [PET], and electroencephalogram; and tests that aid in assessment of more general health and functioning such as blood panels). Similarly, when conducting forensic evaluations psychologists often employ many of the same assessment tools they use in therapeutic settings (e.g., clinical interview, measures of emotional and behavioral functioning such as the Minnesota Multiphasic Personality Inventory-2 Restructured Form [MMPI-2-RF], measures of intellectual functioning such as the Wechsler Adult Intelligence Scale-4th edition [WAIS-IV]). All of these assessment tools, only some of which are "tests," can be classified as clinical assessment techniques (CATs) insofar as they assess clinical constructs or phenomena. Heilbrun, Rogers, and Otto (2002), in their discussion of assessment techniques that are employed in forensic psychiatric and psychological evaluations, distinguished these tools from two other types—forensically relevant assessment techniques (FRATs) and forensic assessment techniques (FATs).

Most CATs employed by psychiatrists and psychologists assess constructs that are fairly far removed from the questions the legal decision maker has about an examinee's functioning (see Table 68.1). For example, results of brain magnetic resonance imaging or the WAIS-IV provide little information about a defendant's understanding of the legal process and capacity to work with counsel, and results of a PET scan or the MMPI-2-RF tell us little about the likelihood the examinee will engage in violent behavior if her civil commitment is terminated. These measures are not without any value, however. Rather, they can be quite helpful with respect to identifying and/or describing clinical conditions underlying observed deficits in psycholegal capacities. Thus, results of MRI or the WAIS-IV may assist in identifying *why* a defendant demonstrates a limited understanding of the legal process and compromised ability to consult with his attorney. Similarly, results of PET and the MMPI-2-RF may identify clinical conditions that are associated with an increased risk for violent behavior in the community. Noteworthy is that the most commonly employed CAT—the clinical interview—not only assists in assessment of an examinee's general emotional, behavioral, and cognitive functioning, but it can also be tailored to focus on psycholegal abilities such as a defendant's mental state at the time of the offense or a child's understanding of the oath and need to tell the truth when testifying.

Forensically relevant assessment techniques

Like CATs, FRATs aid in assessment of clinical constructs, but clinical constructs that typically are of more relevance or interest in forensic contexts or settings. Thus, assessment tools that inform or structure judgments about risk for violence (e.g., Historical Clinical Risk Management-20, Version 3 [HCR-20]), response style (e.g., Word Memory Test [WMT]), and psychopathy (e.g., Psychopathy Checklist-Revised) are

Table 68.1 Examples of clinical assessment tools

	Norm based	Structured professional judgment	Checklist/ criterion referenced	Construct examined
Medical				
Clinical interview				Relevant history and functioning
Magnetic resonance imaging	✓			Measure of structure
Electroencephalograph	✓			Brain function
Blood panels	✓			Metabolism
Psychological				
Clinical interview				Relevant history and functioning
Millon Clinical Multiaxial Inventory-III (MCMI-III)	✓			Psychopathology and personality
Minnesota Multiphasic Personality Inventory-2-Restructured Form (MMPI-2-RF)	✓			Psychopathology and personality
Personality Assessment Inventory (PAI)	✓			Psychopathology and personality
Wechsler Adult Intelligence Scale-4th edition (WAIS-IV)	✓			Intelligence
Adaptive Behavior Assessment System-II (ABAS-II)	✓			Adaptive behavior
Wechsler Memory Scale-IV (WMS-IV)	✓			Memory functions
Wide Range Achievement Test 4 (WRAT4)	✓			Academic achievement
Folstein Mini-Mental State Examination	✓			Cognitive functioning

considered FRATs (see Table 68.2). Examples of forensically relevant assessment tools are provided in Table 68.2.

Forensic assessment techniques

In contrast to CATs and FRATs, FATs are specifically developed to aid in assessment of psycholegal capacities. Thus, tools specifically designed to structure or inform judgments about psycholegal capacities such as trial competence (e.g., MacArthur Competence Assessment Tool–Criminal Adjudication [MacCAT-CA]), mental state at the time of the offense (e.g., Roger's Criminal Responsibility Assessment Scales [R-CRAS]), and capacity to make treatment decisions (e.g., MacArthur Competence Assessment Tool–Treatment [MacCAT-T]) qualify as FATs (see Table 68.3). Of some historical interest is that one of the first FATs—a checklist

Table 68.2 Examples of forensically relevant assessment tools

	Norm based	Structured professional judgment	Checklist/ criterion referenced	Construct measured
Inventory of Legal Knowledge (ILK)	✓			Response style
Miller Forensic Assessment of Symptoms Test (M-FAST)	✓			Response style
Test of Memory Malingering (TOMM)	✓			Response style
Level of Service Inventory-Revised (LSI-R)	✓			Offense risk and intervention needs
Historical Clinical Risk Managment-20 (HCR-20)		✓		Violence risk
Violence Risk Appraisal Guide (VRAG)	✓			Violence risk
Structured Assessment of Violence Risk in Youth (SAVRY)		✓		Violence risk
Psychopathy Checklist-Revised (PCL-R)	✓			Psychopathy
Static-99	✓			Sex offender recidivism risk
Sexual Violence Risk-20 (SVR-20)		✓		Sexual offense risk
Spousal Assault Risk Assessment (SARA)		✓		Spousal assault risk

Table 68.3 Examples of forensic assessment tools

	Norm based	Structured professional judgment	Checklist/ criterion referenced	Construct measured
Evaluation of Competency to Stand Trial-Revised (ECST-R)	✓			Competency to stand trial
Fitness Interview Test-Revised (FIT-R)		✓		Competency to stand trial
MacArthur Competence Assessment Tool–Criminal Adjudication (MacCAT-CA)	✓			Competency to stand trial
Rogers' Criminal Responsibility Assessment Scales (R-CRAS)	✓			Criminal responsibility
Static-99/Static-2002	✓			Sex offender recidivism risk
Instruments for Assessing, Understanding, and Appreciating *Miranda* Rights	✓			*Miranda* rights comprehension

designed to structure assessments about criminal defendants' competence to proceed with the legal process—was developed by a psychiatrist, Robey (1965).

Comparing CATs, FRATs, and FATs

Generally speaking, the best validated assessment techniques are CATs, followed by FRATs and FATs (Heilbrun et al. 2002). Because of their broader application, most CATs like the WAIS-IV, MMPI-2-RF, and PAI, have larger normative samples and greater research bases examining their reliability and validity than more focused assessment tools. This presents forensic examiners with an interesting challenge insofar as the best validated tools examine constructs that are most removed from the psycholegal capacities about which the legal decision maker is concerned and the forensic examiner is attempting to assess.

CLASSIFYING ASSESSMENT TOOLS ACCORDING TO HOW THEY FUNCTION

Another way that assessment tools can be classified is with respect to how they function.

Norm-based assessment tools (tests)

Many assessment tools that psychiatrists and psychologists employ gain their utility because they provide normative data about examinees. The rationale underlying and value of norm-based assessment techniques—which are typically described as tests—are the same, whether they are medical tests such as MRI or psychological tests such as the WAIS-IV. The examiner draws conclusions about an examinee based on how his or her performance compares to a relevant comparison or norm group. Thus, the psychiatrist reviewing results of a brain image forms opinions about the examinee's brain functioning based on how the size of her ventricles compare to some normative comparison group. Similarly, the psychologist reviewing results of the WAIS-IV forms opinions about the examinee's intellectual and cognitive functioning by comparing his or her performance to same-aged peers on which the test was normed.

Although many CATs gain their utility from their norms-based approach, some FRATs and FATS provide such data as well. For example, the Psychopathy Checklist-Revised (PCL-R), a FRAT, informs an examiner's judgments about the psychopathic personality traits of an examinee by comparing the examiner's ratings of the examinee on 20 different items to the ratings of persons in various normative groups, including prison and forensic hospital samples. Similarly, the MacCAT-CA provides normative data about a criminal defendant's understanding of and ability to participate in the legal process by comparing his or her scores on the measure to the scores of various normative groups including defendants who were adjudicated incompetent to proceed, defendants with mental disorders for whom competence to proceed was not an issue, and defendants without any indications of mental disorder.

Structured professional judgment tools

Structured professional judgment tools (SPJTs) ensure a comprehensive assessment of factors that are relevant to understanding the phenomenon or construct of interest. They are not tests but are best conceptualized as checklists or memory aids that ensure consideration of all factors that are important when trying to understand a particular matter. SPJTs are typically developed by reviewing the empirical literature devoted to a topic area, and identifying those factors that should be considered when making decisions about the matter. For example, the HCR-20 is a SPJT that structures inquiries and judgments about violence risk for persons with mental disorders. Use of the tool involves conducting a clinical evaluation that is sure to consider the 20 items/factors the instrument authors determined were related to violence risk in this population based on their review of the literature (e.g., history of violent behavior, substance use, attitudes toward treatment). Similarly, the Fitness Interview Test–Revised (FIT-R), a SPJT designed for use when evaluating criminal defendants' competence to proceed with the legal process, requires the examiner to address 16 areas the instrument authors determined to be relevant to considering a defendant's understanding of and ability to participate in the legal process (e.g., understanding the nature and severity of the charge, appraisal of likely outcomes, capacity to relate to lawyer, capacity to plan legal strategy). In contrast to the HCR-20, however, in additional to considering the psychiatry and psychology literatures regarding trial competence, the FIT-R authors also considered statutes and case law that shape the legal construct of competence to proceed with the legal process.

SPJTs typically replace unstructured clinical judgment that, at least historically, describes much of what psychiatrists and psychologists have done in therapeutic and forensic settings. As compared to unstructured clinical judgment, professional judgments that are structured by empirically and/or legally grounded tools are more reliable and valid. As a result, there has been a clear movement to this approach in both medicine and psychology.

Actuarial assessment tools

A little more than a half-century ago Meehl (1954) published his treatise on the value of actuarial classification and assessment approaches. The actuarial method "uses an equation, formula or graph, or an actuarial table to arrive at a probability, or expected value, of some outcome" (Grove and Meehl 1996, 294). Actuarial assessment involves the mechanistic combination of select variables to classify or predict.

When actuarial assessment is discussed, it is routinely assumed that the variables that are included in the actuarial formula are derived empirically. However, strictly speaking, this need not be the case. Thus, one could describe the diagnostic approach employed in the *Diagnostic and Statistical Manual of Mental Disorders*, 5th edition (*DSM-5*; American Psychiatric Association 2013) as an actuarial one insofar as examinees are determined to have or not have a particular disorder based on what and how many diagnostic criteria (i.e., signs and symptoms) are observed. Typically, however, the items used to classify or predict are derived empirically, and the weight or significance assigned to any item is determined empirically as well. As an example, in their development of the Violence Risk Appraisal Guide (VRAG), Quinsey and his colleagues (1998) compared two groups of male incarcerated offenders in Canada who had been released to the community and followed for a number of years, some of whom were rearrested for a violent offense, and some of whom were not. Upon comparing the two groups on a large number of variables the investigators identified 12 that differentiated them (e.g., elementary school problems, history of alcohol abuse, level of psychopathy, age at time of index offense, marital history, criminal history). Finally, the investigators developed a formula in which the 12 items were weighted so as to maximally separate the two groups of offenders. They subsequently proposed that mental health and correctional professionals faced with making judgments about offenders' risk for violent reoffending use this tool.

As suggested by the above discussion of the VRAG, actuarial assessment is typically considered in the context of prediction in mental health applications (e.g., predicting whether someone will reoffend, abuse her child, or attempt suicide). However, it can be used for nonpredictive purposes as well. For example, the Rogers Discriminant Function and the Cashel Index are two actuarial formulas within the Personality Assessment Inventory (PAI) that are not used for prediction but are used to identify whether the examinee was feigning impairment when responding to items on the PAI.

Despite a convincing argument for the superiority of actuarial classifications and predictions when compared to unstructured clinical judgment in health care and other settings, mental health professionals have been slow to adopt actuarial classification methods, presumably for a number of reasons. In some cases, actuarial tools do not exist. For example, valid actuarial tools have not been developed to classify a defendant as competent or incompetent to stand trial, or to identify whether the best interests of a child are better met by living with a specific parent. Second, mental health professionals sometimes do not use existing tools because they have concerns about differences on important characteristics between the individuals with whom they are working and the individuals in the groups on which the tools were developed (e.g., Is it appropriate for an Australian psychologist to use the VRAG—a tool developed and validated in North America—to make a judgment about the likelihood that an Aboriginal offender will reoffend if returned to the Outback?). Finally, some commentators (e.g., Hilton et al. 2006) have offered that mental health professionals are reluctant to adopt these tools because they threaten their professional identity and prestige.

RESPONSIBLE USE OF PSYCHOLOGICAL ASSESSMENT TOOLS IN FORENSIC PSYCHIATRIC EVALUATIONS

How and in what way psychiatrists might use psychological assessment tools when conducting forensic evaluations are affected by a number of factors. These are addressed below.

Need and value

The first matter to consider is need and value. Are there some forensic evaluation contexts in which psychological testing may prove of assistance in addressing issues before the legal decision maker? The obvious answer is yes. Use of psychological assessment instruments can improve the utility of forensic psychiatric and forensic psychological evaluations assuming the instruments relied upon are valid assessments of behaviors or capacities that are in some way relevant to issues before the legal decision maker, or if they work in a way that ensures that the evaluation is more relevant, reliable, and valid.

For example, making a decision about whether a person who has been convicted of first-degree murder is ineligible for the death penalty as a result of intellectual disability will be informed by psychological testing. Judgments about the genuineness of psychotic spectrum symptoms reported by a Social Security Disability Income applicant will be more accurate if they are based on the results of psychological tests that are designed to identify people feigning such impairment (rather than the general impressions of an examiner). And an examiner's evaluation of and judgment about a defendant's ability to understand and participate in the criminal justice process will be more reliable and valid if he or she employs a tool that ensures a comprehensive inquiry into all psychiatric/psychological factors and legal factors that can affect trial competence. Use of psychological assessment tools is not always necessary, however, or without its problems.

Podboy and Kastl (1993) asserted that confirmatory bias (a tendency to seek and focus on data that confirm or are consistent with initial hypotheses and ignore or disregard disconfirming data) may operate with forensic examiners who use tests insofar as they reference test data that are consistent with their clinical impressions and ignore those data that run contrary. They also expressed concern that examiners who use tests could overly emphasize test results and fail to consider their limitations. Along similar lines, Wakefield and Underwager (1993) warned against overinterpretation of test results in forensic examination contexts.

Overreliance on the same test battery in all forensics evaluation can be problematic as well. Selection of tests and tools requires judgment and thoughtfulness. Greenberg et al. (2003), for example, described how using the same battery of tests and measures in all personal injury evaluations could be problematic. Tests of cognitive functioning, for instance, would not automatically be advised when the person being evaluated is not asserting cognitive impairment. Similarly, a forensic examiner should be less inclined to use an intelligence test in a competency to stand trial evaluation of a defendant who has a college degree, stable employment history, appropriate verbal skills, and no history of head injuries. Here, testing intelligence offers low incremental value, as this particular defendant would likely have at least minimal intellectual capacity to stand trial. If, however, this defendant has recently begun to exhibit disorganized speech and reported delusions and hallucinations with no prior history of mental health treatment, tests of personality and response style could offer additional diagnostic clarity.

Competence

Use of an assessment tool can only prove helpful if the user is competent in its administration and interpretation. The American Medical Association Code of Medical Ethics and licensing laws of all states obligate physicians to practice competently. Similarly, the Ethics Guidelines for the Practice of Forensic Psychiatry (American Academy of Psychiatry and the Law 2005) require that forensic psychiatrists claim expertise "only in areas of actual knowledge, skills, training, and experience" (p. 4).

The most authoritative reference for requirements of tests and test users are the *Standards for Educational and Psychological Testing* (Joint Committee 2014), which were developed by an interdisciplinary committee representing the American Educational Research Association, the American Psychological Association, and the National Council on Measurement in Education (Joint Committee 2014). Now in their third iteration, the purpose of the standards is to provide criteria for sound test development and use, and they are intended for use by "professionals who specify, develop, or select tests and for those who interpret, or evaluate the technical quality of, test results" (Joint Committee 2014, 1).

As a joint statement of three major professional organizations, the standards wield considerable authority. Regulatory authorities and courts have recognized them as establishing generally accepted standards for test use and development. Furthermore, "[c]ompliance or noncompliance with the Standards may be used as relevant evidence of legal liability in judicial and regulatory proceedings" (Joint Committee 2014, 2).

Considerable attention is paid in the standards to the issue of test user competence. Standard 9.0 directs that, "Test users are responsible for knowing the validity evidence in support of the intended interpretations of scores on tests that they use, from test selection through the use of scores, as well as common positive and negative consequences of test use" (Joint Committee 2014, 142). Standard 9.2 directs that, "Prior to adoption and use of a published test, the test user should study and evaluate test materials provided by the test developer. Of particular importance are materials that summarize the test's purpose, specify the procedure for test administration, define the intended population(s) of test takers, and discuss score interpretations for which validity and reliability/precision data are available" (Joint Committee 2014, 142).

Additional discussion of competence is included in Section 10 of the standards, which is devoted to psychological testing and assessment. Standard 10.2 directs that professionals who use psychological tests "should be familiar with the relevant evidence of validity and reliability/precision for the intended uses of the test scores and assessments, and should be prepared to articulate a logical analysis that supports all facets of the assessment and the inferences made from the assessment" (Joint Committee 2014, 164).

Competence to administer psychological assessment measures presumably varies considerably among psychiatrists. There are certainly some psychiatrists who have a sophisticated understanding of psychometric theory and a number of the assessment tools that are often employed in forensic evaluation contexts, just as there are some psychologists who have a sophisticated understanding of the actions and mechanisms of many psychoactive medications. It is likely, however, that few psychiatrists have completed formal training in psychological assessment and measurement that is required to administer, score, and interpret many psychological assessment tools.

Using assessment tools for which one does not have the requisite knowledge and skills certainly constitutes incompetent practice—for both psychiatrists and psychologists. The risks associated with incompetent test use are significant. Perhaps most importantly, inaccurate opinions may be formed and offered about the examinee's functioning. In addition, opinions that are anchored—in full or in part—in testing that has been incompetently administered, scored, or interpreted may be barred or, at the very least, challenged. And finally, psychiatrists and psychologists may be subject to malpractice or licensing actions (see, e.g., *Texas State Board of Examiners of Psychologists v. Denkowski* 2011).

THE ALLURE OF COMPUTERIZED PSYCHOLOGICAL TEST ADMINISTRATION, SCORING, AND INTERPRETATION

Largely facilitated by development and regular use of the personal computer, computerized psychological test administration, scoring, and interpretation has become increasingly common. Whereas some tests still must be administered by an examiner but can be scored and interpreted via computer (e.g., measures of intelligence such as the WAIS-IV), others can be computer administered, scored, and interpreted (e.g., measures of emotional and behavioral functioning such as the MMPI-2-RF, PAI, and Trauma Symptom Inventory-Revised [TSI-R]).

The value of computer-based test administration and scoring primarily lies in the reduction of scoring errors associated with "hand scoring." This application is significant because scoring errors are not uncommon (Allard et al. 1995; Allard and Faust 2000; Simons et al. 2002). Although computerized interpretive programs have considerable potential value, they also can prove dangerous insofar as they tempt mental health professionals to use tests about which they are not sufficiently knowledgeable. Although this challenge applies to all mental health professionals, psychologists are presumably at less risk given their formal training in psychometric theory and test administration, scoring, and interpretation.

The intricacies of computerized test interpretation are reflected in the ethics code of the American Psychological Association (American Psychological Association 2010). Section 9.06 of the Ethical Principles of Psychologists and Code of conduct directs that, "When interpreting assessment results, including automated interpretations, psychologists take into account the purpose of the assessment as well as the various test factors, test-taking abilities and other characteristics of the person being assessed, such as situational, personal, linguistic and cultural differences, that might affect psychologists' judgments or reduce the accuracy of their interpretations" (American Psychological Association 2010, 13). More directly addressing the challenge of computerized test interpretation, Section 9.09 of the ethics code directs, "[p]sychologists select scoring and interpretation services (including automated services) on the basis of evidence of the validity of the program and procedures as well as on other appropriate considerations… Psychologists retain responsibility for the appropriate application, interpretation and use of assessment instruments, whether they score and interpret such tests themselves or use automated or other services" (American Psychological Association 2010, 13).

The Standards for Educational and Psychological Testing (Joint Committee 2014) include language indicating that use of computerized psychological test administration, scoring, and interpretive programs by professionals not trained in psychometric theory and psychological assessment is problematic. In addition to the general knowledge and competence requirements discussed above, Standard 9.10 directs, "Test users should not rely solely on computer-generated interpretations of test results" (Joint Committee 2014, 145). Associated commentary in the Standards describes the potential for automated narrative reports to be misleading and references the need for professional judgment. Standard 10.17 directs that professionals who use computer-generated interpretations of psychological test data "should verify that the quality of the evidence of validity is sufficient for the interpretation" (Joint Committee 2014, 168). Associated commentary notes that computer-generated interpretations may result in misleading or oversimplified analyses of the meanings of psychological test scores.

Put bluntly, mental health professionals who use computers to administer, score, and/or interpret psychological tests must (1) have an adequate foundation in psychometric theory, (2) be knowledgeable about the development and appropriate use of the test, and (3) understand the basis for administration, scoring, and/or interpretive process. Without such competence, the professional cannot adequately judge the validity of the product and results, and the professional cannot speak to their meaning.

In response to the above, a reasonable question is whether, for psychiatrists who do not meet the requirements above, there is a meaningful difference between (1) using a computer to administer, score, and interpret a psychological test, and (2) referring the examinee to a psychologist who administers, scores, and interprets the same psychological test. There is a significant difference in these practices insofar as, in the latter case, the referral makes clear the psychiatrist's (1) lack of expertise in test administration, scoring, and interpretation, and (2) reliance on a consultant to provide opinions upon which the psychiatrist may rely when forming his or her own expert opinions. In the former case the psychiatrist can and should be held to answer questions about the psychometric properties of the test and any associated matters regarding its administration, scoring, and interpretation. In the latter case the psychiatrist could not be held to answer questions about these matters, any more than he or she could be held to answer questions about the properties of a PET scan machine that was used to produce a brain image upon which a consulted neurologist relied.

As an example, we equate a psychiatrist selecting and, via computer, administering, scoring, and interpreting tests like the MMPI-2-RF or PAI to a psychiatrist not qualified in neurology selecting the type of neurologic scan and contrast that will be run, and then reading and interpreting a computerized interpretation of the results. We think few, if any forensic psychiatrists would consider doing the latter. Rather, they would contact a neurologist, share with the consultant their challenge, and rely on the neurologist's expertise with respect to test selection, administration, and interpretation.

Psychiatrists should tread cautiously when considering use of assessment tools, keeping in mind the above considerations. That being said, there is considerable variability with respect to the knowledge and skills required to employ various assessment tools. As a result, from our perspective, there are two primary ways in which psychiatrists may employ psychological assessment tools in forensic evaluation. We discuss each below.

PSYCHIATRISTS' USE OF PSYCHOLOGICAL ASSESSMENT TOOLS

There are a considerable number of psychological assessment tools that are appropriate for psychiatrists to use when conducting forensic evaluations. Psychiatrists appear well situated to employ most, if not all, SPJTs when conducting forensic evaluations. Given that a purpose of SPJTs is to increase the reliability and validity of clinical judgments, psychiatrists (and psychologists) would do well to routinely use SPJTs for those forensic assessment tasks for which they exist. Recent research indicates that even evaluations that appear relatively straightforward such as competence evaluations, may be less reliable (and valid) than initially claimed (Murrie et al. 2008). Structured professional judgment tools that direct the examiner to consider legally relevant or empirically valid factors have the potential to improve the reliability and validity of judgments about diverse matters of concern to forensic psychiatrists and forensic psychologists such as competence to proceed with the legal process, competence to be executed, risk for general reoffending, risk for violence, and risk for domestic violence.

Perhaps most importantly, given the format and structure of SPJTs, advanced training in or understanding of psychometric theory and assessment are not required. Rather, all that is required for their use is an understanding of the construct that any particular tool is designed to assess or assist in assessing (e.g., violence risk, competence to stand trial), as well as the strategy employed by the developers when selecting tool items. Critical to using SPJTs is understanding and communicating to the legal decision maker that they are not tests, but rather tools that structure professional, clinical judgments to ensure a comprehensive consideration of factors that are relevant to understanding a particular psycholegal issue that is in dispute.

Indeed, that SPJTs are appropriate for use by psychiatrists is suggested in the manuals of many SPJTs, a sampling of which is offered in Table 68.4.

Table 68.4 Sample language describing qualifications for use of various structured professional judgment tools

Tool	Sample language
Fitness Interview Test-Revised (FIT-R)	"Evaluations of competence to stand trial should be conducted by mental health professionals, typically psychologists and psychiatrists but also social workers and nurse practitioners in some jurisdictions...The FIT-R is, we believe, well-suited to assist any professional qualified to conduct [competence to stand trial] evaluations" (Roesch et al. 2006, 23–24).
Spousal Assault Risk Assessment (SARA) Guide	"The SARA is not a test or scale in the usual sense of these terms...Because the SARA is not a controlled psychological test and is intended for use in many different contexts, there is no single set of qualifications for users. When the SARA is used to evaluate and make decisions about an individual, users are responsible for ensuring that their evaluation conforms to relevant laws, regulations and policies. In addition, users should meet the following minimum qualifications: (1) Expertise in individual assessment...(2) Expertise in the area of spousal assault" (Kropp et al. 1995 3, 12–13).
Structured Assessment of Violence Risk in Youth (SAVRY)	"The SAVRY is designed for use by professionals in a variety of disciplines who conduct assessments and/or make intervention/supervision plans concerning violence risk in youth...At a minimum, those who use the SAVRY should have expertise (i.e., training and experience) in conducting individual assessments, child/adolescent development, and in youth violence. In general, psychologists, psychiatrists, trained juvenile probation officers and social workers with requisite expertise would be qualified to use the SAVRY" (Borum et al. 2000, 15).

Table 68.5 Sample language describing qualifications for use of various psychological tests

Inventory of Legal Knowledge (ILK)	"In accordance with the Standards for Educational and Psychological Testing...ILK results should only be interpreted by professionals with sufficient coursework and training from an accredited college or university in psychological assessment and in the use and interpretation of psychological tests" (Otto et al. 2010, 7).
MacArthur Competence Assessment Tool-Criminal Adjudication (MacCAT-CA)	"Consistent with guideline offered in the Standards for *Educational and Psychological Testing*...clinical interpretation of the MacCAT-CA also requires professional training in psychological assessment and psychopathology" (Poythress et al. 1999, 5).
Minnesota Multiphasic Personality Inventory-2-RF (MMPI-2-RF)	"The Standards for Educational and Psychological Testing require that 'prior to the adoption and use of a published test, the test user should study and evaluate the materials provided by the test developer...At a minimum, these include the manual provided by the test developer. Ideally the user should be conversant with relevant studies reported in the professional literature' (AERA et al., p. 113). This includes reviewing and evaluating psychometric data on the reliability and validity of scale scores. To conduct a competent review of the MMPI-2-RF documentation and literature and this conform to this standard, the user must have graduate-level training in psychological testing and assessment and be familiar with the means by which basic psychometric functioning of test scores—such as reliability, measurement error, the various facets of validity, classification statistics and accuracy analyses, norms, and the derivation of standard scores—are evaluated. In summary, competent use of the MMPI-2-RF requires graduate-level training in psychological testing and assessment with a specific emphasis on basic psychometric, graduate-level training in the areas of personality and psychopathology, graduate and/or continuing education training on the MMPI instruments, supervised experienced in the administration, soring, and interpretation of the test, and familiarity with the current professional literature on the instrument" (Ben-Porath and Tellegen 2013, 10).
Personality Assessment Inventory (PAI)	"Interpretation of PAI profiles and test score patterns is solely the province of qualified professionals and requires training in the basics of psychometric assessment as well as descriptive psychopathology" (Morey 2007, 7).

PSYCHIATRISTS' RELIANCE ON PSYCHOLOGICAL CONSULTATION

As suggested previously, a comprehensive understanding of measurement theory addressing matters such as test construction, test reliability (inter-rater, split half, test–retest, alternative forms), test validity (e.g., face, discriminant, convergent), and test classification (e.g., sensitivity, specificity, positive predictive power, negative predictive power) is necessary to administer, interpret, and score many psychological measures. Thus, few psychiatrists will have the requisite knowledge and skills. Indeed, the complicated nature of many of these assessment techniques and the need for this knowledge are reflected in the administration manuals of many psychological tests.

There are many psychological tests that psychiatrists should not administer or interpret given their complexity. Rather, they would do well to refer forensic examinees for whom such testing is necessary to a psychologist competent to administer the construct at issue—much like they do with their medical specialist colleagues. Ideally, the psychiatrist would describe the matter in question and, with the psychologist, come to an agreement about the best tools to use.

Provided in Table 68.5 are excerpts from the manuals of a number of tests, all of which make reference to specialized knowledge about and training in psychometric theory and psychological assessment that is probably not possessed by many psychiatrists. An aggressive cross-examination regarding the development of the tool, its limitations, and the competencies required of someone administering, scoring, and interpreting these tests may prove damaging.

SUMMARY

Forensic psychiatrists and forensic psychologists can provide legal decision makers with helpful information if their evaluations of litigants are structured or informed by valid assessment techniques. Forensic assessment can be enhanced by implementing assessment tools when appropriate.

SUMMARY KEY POINTS

- A model for forensic assessment (Grisso 1986, 2003) applies the following steps: be familiar with the relevant law, understand what legal matters may be impacted by the examinee's emotional, behavioral, and/or cognitive functioning, and select the assessment technique(s) that best aid in assessment of identified psycholegal capacities.
- Assessment tools can be classified as the following: clinical assessment techniques (CATs), forensically relevant assessment techniques (FRATs), and forensic assessment techniques (FATs).
- Assessment tools can also be classified according to how they function: norm-based assessment tools (tests), structured professional judgment tools, and actuarial assessment tools.
- Responsible use of psychological assessment tools in forensic psychiatric evaluations requires forensic psychiatrists and psychologists to consider the following: need and value of assessment tools; competence in administering, scoring, and interpreting assessment tools; and special considerations when using computerized test administration, scoring, and interpretation.
- Psychiatrists may benefit by using psychological assessment tools, such as SPJTs, that increase the reliability and validity of clinical judgments.
- Psychiatrists may rely on psychological consultation such as when a comprehensive understanding of matters such as test construction, test reliability, test validity, and test classification is needed.

REFERENCES

Allard G, J Butler, D Faust, and TM. Shea. 1995. Errors in hand scoring objective personality tests: The case of the personality diagnostic questionnaire—Revised (PDQ-R). *Professional Psychology: Research and Practice* 26:304–308.

Allard G and D Faust. 2000. Errors in scoring objective personality tests. *Assessment* 7:119–129.

American Academy of Psychiatry and Law. 2005. Ethics Guidelines for the Practice of Forensic Psychiatry. http://www.aapl.org/docs/pdf/ETHICSGDLNS.pdf, accessed October 21, 2014.

American Psychiatric Association (APA). 2013. *Diagnostic and Statistical Manual of Mental Disorders*, 5th edition. Washington, DC: APA.

American Psychological Association. 2010. Ethical Principles of Psychologists and Code of Conduct. http://www.apa.org/ethics/code/principles.pdf, accessed October 21, 2014.

Ben-Porath Y and A Tellegen. 2013. *Minnesota Multiphasic Personality Inventory-2-RF: Manual for Administration, Scoring, and Interpretation*. Minneapolis: University of Minnesota Press.

Borum R, P Bartel, and A Forth. 2000. *Manual for the Structured Assessment of Violence Risk in Youth, Version 1.1*. Tampa: University of South Florida.

Dusky v. United States, 362 U. S. 402 (1960).

Greenberg SA, RK Otto, and AC Long. 2003. The utility of psychological testing in assessing emotional damages in personal injury litigation. *Assessment* 10:411–419.

Grisso T. 1986. *Evaluating Competencies: Forensic Assessments and Instruments*. New York: Plenum Press.

Grisso T. 2003. *Evaluating Competencies: Forensic Assessments and Instruments*, 2nd edition. New York: Kluwer/Plenum.

Grove W and P Meehl. 1996. Comparative efficiency of informal (subjective, impressionistic) and formal (mechanical, algorithmic) prediction procedures: The clinical-statistical controversy. *Psychology, Public Policy, and Law* 2:293–323.

Heilbrun K, R Rogers, and RK Otto. 2002. Forensic assessment: Current status and future directions. In *Taking Psychology and Law into the Twenty-First Century*, edited by JRP Ogloff, New York: Kluwer/Plenum, 119–146.

Hilton NZ, GT Harris, and ME Rice. 2006. Sixty-six years of research on the clinical versus actuarial prediction of violence. *Counseling Psychologist* 34:400–409.

Joint Committee on the Standards for Educational and Psychological Testing of the American Educational Research Association, the American Psychological Association, and the National Council on Measurement in Education. 2014. *Standards for Educational and Psychological Testing*, 3rd edition. Washington, DC: American Educational Research Association.

Kropp PR, SD Hart, CD Webster, and D Eaves. 1995. *Manual for the Spousal Assault Risk Assessment Guide*, 2nd edition. Vancouver: British Columbia Institute on Family Violence.

Meehl P. 1954. *Clinical Versus Statistical Prediction: A Theoretical Analysis and Review of the Evidence*. Minneapolis: University of Minnesota Press.

Morey LC. 2007. *Professional Manual for the Personality Assessment Inventory*, 2nd edition. Lutz, FL: Professional Assessment Resources.

Murrie DC, MT Boccaccini, PA Zapf, JI Warren, and CE Henderson. 2008. Clinician variation in findings of competence to stand trial. *Psychology, Public Policy, and Law* 14:177–219.

Otto RK, JE Musick, JE, and CB Sherrod. 2010. *Professional Manual for the Inventory of Legal Knowledge*. Lutz, FL: Professional Assessment Resources.

Podboy JW and AJ Kastl. 1993. The intentional misuse of standardized psychological tests in complex trials. *American Journal of Forensic Psychology* 11:47–54.

Poythress NG, R Nicholson, RK Otto, JF Edens, RJ Bonnie, J Monahan, and SK Hoge. 1999. *Professional Manual for the MacArthur Competence Assessment Tool-Criminal Adjudication.* Lutz, FL: Professional Assessment Resources.

Quinsey VL, GT Harris, ME Rice, and CA Corner. 1998. Violent offenders: Appraising and managing risk. Washington, DC: American Psychological Association.

Robey A. 1965. Criteria for competency to stand trial: A checklist for psychiatrists. *American Journal of Psychiatry* 122:616–623.

Roesch R, PA Zapf, and D Eaves. 2006. *Fitness Interview Test-Revised: A Structured Interview for Assessing Competency to Stand Trial.* Sarasota, FL: Professional Resource Press.

Simons R, R Goddard, and W Patton. 2002. Hand-scoring error rates in psychological testing. *Assessment* 9:292–300.

Texas State Board of Examiners of Psychologists v. Denkowski. 2011. SOAH Docket No. 520-09-2882. http://s3.amazonaws.com/static.texastribune.org/media/documents/Denkowski_Settlement.pdf, accessed November 1, 2014.

Wakefield H and R Underwager. 1993. Misuse of psychological tests in forensic settings: Some horrible examples. *American Journal of Forensic Psychology* 11:55–75.

Wechsler D and X Zhou. 2011. *WASI-II Manual.* Bloomington, MN: NCS Pearson.

69

Violence risk assessment: The state of the science

JENNIFER L. SKEEM AND JOHN MONAHAN

INTRODUCTION

Forensic psychiatry and psychology have grown tremendously over recent years as assessment-focused specialties. A variety of forensic assessment instruments have been developed to help mental health clinicians evaluate legally relevant questions about individuals involved in the civil-, criminal-, or juvenile-justice systems. Many of these instruments improve clinicians' ability to forecast the likelihood that an individual will behave violently. Increasingly, these instruments are being applied in response to statutes and regulations that require specialized assessments to identify "high-risk" individuals for initiating some form of preventive intervention, or "low-risk" individuals for eschewing (or terminating) such intervention.

In this chapter, we provide a current snapshot of the field of violence risk assessment. After highlighting the contexts in which risk of violence is assessed, we describe a framework for understanding alternative approaches to risk assessment and then compare the utility of these approaches in predicting violence. Before considering possible future developments in the field, we draw attention to two recent debates, i.e., whether group-based instruments are useful for assessing an individual's risk, and whether the pursuits of risk assessment and risk reduction should be separated.

We wish to be clear at the outset about our terminology and scope. We endorse the general definition of risk assessment given by Kraemer et al. (1997, 340): "The process of using risk factors to estimate the likelihood (i.e., probability) of an outcome occurring in a population." These authors define a risk factor as a correlate that precedes the outcome in time, with no implication that the risk factor and the outcome are causally related (e.g., past violence is a robust risk factor for future violence). Our outcome of focus is physical violence to others.

LEGAL DEVELOPMENTS

The populations in which violence risk is assessed vary across many disparate legal contexts. In the mental health system, civil commitment on the ground of "dangerousness," commitment as a sexually violent predator, and the tort liability of psychiatrists and psychologists for their patients' violence often turn on issues of risk assessment. In the justice system, risk assessment is increasingly being used to inform decisions about sentencing and parole. Risk assessment for violent terrorism is also becoming increasingly common.

The law regulating the process of violence risk assessment has become much more developed in the United States in recent years. Some laws specify risk factors that may and may not be used to estimate risk (e.g., race is constitutionally proscribed as a risk factor, whereas gender and age are generally permitted; see Monahan, 2013). Other laws allude to specific likelihoods of violence necessary to trigger preventive actions. For example, a Virginia statute allows for the civil commitment of a person with mental illness if there is a "substantial likelihood" that the person will cause serious physical harm to himself or herself or others in the near future, as a result of mental illness. The material used to train professionals in the law elaborates on the meaning of substantial likelihood: "a 'one-in-four' estimated risk of serious harm in the near future is sufficient, particularly when the harm being threatened is potentially fatal... A 'substantial risk' is *not* meant to mean 'more likely than not' (51%)" (Cohen et al. 2009, 133).

ASSESSMENT ALTERNATIVES

No distinction in the history of risk assessment has been more influential than Meehl's (1954) cleaving the field into "clinical" and "actuarial" (or statistical) approaches.

Subsequent research is fairly characterized in a comprehensive review by Ægisdóttir et al. (2006, 368): "one area in which the statistical method is most clearly superior to the clinical approach is the prediction of violence." In recent years, however, a plethora of instruments has been published that are not adequately characterized by a simple clinical–actuarial dichotomy. Rather, the risk assessment process now exists on a *continuum of rule-based structure*, with completely unstructured ("clinical") assessment occupying one pole of the continuum, completely structured ("actuarial") assessment occupying the other pole, and several forms of partially structured assessment lying between the two (Skeem and Monahan 2011).

The violence risk assessment process, in this regard, might usefully be seen as having four components: (1) identifying empirically valid (and legally acceptable) risk factors, (2) determining a method for measuring ("scoring") these risk factors. (3) establishing a procedure for combining scores on the risk factors, and (4) producing an estimate of violence risk. It is possible to array five current approaches to violence risk assessment according to whether the approach structures (i.e., specifies rules for generating) none, one, two, three, or all four of these components of this process. Purely "clinical" risk assessment structures *none* of the four components. The clinician selects, measures, and combines risk factors, and produces an estimate of violence risk, as his or her clinical experience and judgment indicate.

Performing a violence risk assessment by reference to a standard list of risk factors that have been found to be empirically valid (e.g., age, past violence, substance abuse), such as the lists provided in psychiatric texts structures *one* component of the process. Such lists function as an *aide memoir* to identify the risk factors the clinician should attend to in conducting his or her assessment, but they do not further specify a method for measuring these risk factors. As Tardiff (2008, 5) has stated, "Some factors may be more important than others for the individual patient."

The "structured professional judgment" approach exemplified by the HCR [Historical Clinical Risk Management]-20 (Webster et al. 1997) structures *two* components of the violence risk assessment process: the identification and measurement of risk factors, which may be scored as 0 if absent, 1 if possibly present, or 2 if definitely present. A revised version of this instrument—HCR-20 (Version 3)—has recently been released (Douglas et al. 2013). Structured professional judgment instruments do not go further and structure how the individual risk factors are to be combined in clinical practice (Douglas et al. 2014). Approaches to risk assessment that structure *three* components of the risk assessment process are illustrated by the Classification of Violence Risk (COVR) (Monahan et al., 2001). This instrument structures the identification, measurement, and combination of risk factors (via a classification tree design). But those who developed this instrument do not recommend that the final risk assessment reflect *only* the combined scores on the assessed risk factors. Given the possibility that rare factors influence the likelihood of violence in a particular case—and that, precisely because such factors rarely occur, they will never appear on an actuarial instrument—a professional review of the risk estimate is advised (while realizing that clinicians may overidentify "rare" factors). This professional review "would not revise or 'adjust' the actuarial score produced by the COVR, but would likely be of a more qualitative nature (e.g., 'higher than' or 'lower than' the COVR estimate)" (Monahan 2010, 195). A validation of the COVR in Sweden has recently been published (Sturup et al. 2013).

The best-known forensic instrument that structures all *four* of the components of the violence risk assessment process—i.e., that is *completely* actuarial—is the Violence Risk Appraisal Guide (VRAG). This instrument not only structures the identification, measurement, and combination of risk factors, it also specifies that once an individual's violence risk has been actuarially characterized, the risk assessment process is complete. As Quinsey et al. (1998, 197) have stated, "What we are advising is not the *addition* of actuarial methods to existing practice, but rather the *replacement* of existing practice with actuarial methods." A revision of the VRAG has recently been published (Rice et al. 2013).

DOES ONE ASSESSMENT APPROACH PREDICT BETTER THAN ANOTHER?

Of these five approaches, the unstructured ("clinical") one rests upon the least empirical support. In one major study of this approach, Lidz, Mulvey, and Gardner (1993, 1010) concluded that "clinical judgment has been undervalued in previous research. Not only did the clinicians pick out a statistically more violent group, but the violence that the predicted group committed was more serious than the acts of the comparison group. Nonetheless, the low sensitivity and specificity of these judgments show that clinicians are relatively inaccurate predictors of violence."

We know of no research that systematically compares the predictive utility of strategies that structure none, one, two, three, or all four components of the process. Relevant data are available, however, on approaches that structure two or more components. Recent debates about whether it is more appropriate to structure clinical judgment (e.g., HCR-20) or replace it altogether (e.g., VRAG) has prompted a number of horse races that compare the predictive efficiency of one risk assessment instrument against another.

Taken together, these studies provide little evidence that one validated instrument predicts violence significantly better than another. In a recent meta-analysis of 28 studies that controlled well for methodological variation across studies, Yang et al. (2010) found that the predictive efficiencies of nine risk assessment instruments (including the HCR-20 and VRAG) were essentially "interchangeable," with point estimates of accuracy falling within a narrow band (i.e., AUC = 0.65–0.71). Although most of these studies used total scores on the HCR-20 rather than structured clinical judgments (low/medium/high risk), there is some evidence that those judgments both predict violence and add incremental predictive utility to scores derived by actuarially combining items (see Heilbrun et al. 2009). But this latter claim is contested (Hanson and Morton-Bourgon 2009).

The results of the meta-analysis by Yang et al. (2010) are consistent not only with other syntheses of risk assessment research (e.g., Campbell et al. 2009; Olver et al. 2009), but also with the dominant message that has emerged from meta-analyses of alternative psychotherapy techniques. As pronounced by the Dodo bird at the end of the race in Lewis Carroll's *Alice's Adventures in Wonderland* (2011, 80), "*Everybody* has won, and *all* must have prizes."

Why might different instruments perform equally well in predicting violence? One persuasive explanation is that they tap "common factors" or shared dimensions of risk, despite their varied items and formats. In an innovative demonstration, Kroner, Mills, and Reddon (2005) printed the items of several leading instruments on strips of paper, placed the strips in a coffee can, shook the can, and then randomly selected items to create four new tools. The authors found that the "coffee can instruments" predicted violent and nonviolent offenses as well as the original instruments. In a recent extension of this approach to sex offenders, Buttars and Huss (2014) found that "coffee can instruments" predicted *better* than original instruments. Based on a factor analysis of the tools' items, Kroner et al. (2005) found that the instruments tap four overlapping dimensions: criminal history, an irresponsible lifestyle (e.g., poor engagement in school/work), psychopathy and criminal attitudes (e.g., entitlement), and substance abuse-related problems. Despite surface variation, then, instruments may generally tap "a longstanding pattern of dysfunctional and aggressive interpersonal interactions and antisocial and unstable lifestyle that are common to many perpetrators of violence" (Yang et al. 2010, 743).

The strongest risk factors for violence seem to be shared not only among risk assessment instruments, but also across key groups (e.g., Bonta et al. 2013). In particular, an increasing body of research suggests that only a small proportion of violence committed by people with mental illness—perhaps as little as 10%—is directly caused by symptoms (Skeem et al. 2011). Most people with mental illness share leading risk factors for violence with their relatively healthy counterparts.

ARE EMPIRICALLY BASED INSTRUMENTS USEFUL FOR INDIVIDUALS?

One issue that has generated much recent controversy is Hart, Cooke, and Michie's (2007, S60) argument that the margins of error surrounding individual risk assessments of violence are so wide as to make such predictions "virtually meaningless." As stated by Cooke and Michie (2010, 259), "on the basis of empirical findings, statistical theory, and logic, it is clear that predictions of future offending cannot be achieved, with any degree of confidence, in the individual case" (see also Hart and Cooke 2013).

This position has been vigorously contested, both with respect to the overall argument and application of statistics to make it. For example, Hanson and Howard (2010) demonstrate that the wide margin of error for individual risk assessments is a function of having only two possible outcomes (violent or not violent) and therefore conveys nothing about the predictive utility of a risk assessment tool, which must be judged by other criteria. Because all violence risk assessment approaches, not just actuarial approaches, yield some estimate of the likelihood that a dichotomous outcome will occur, none are immune from Hart et al.'s argument (as they recognize). Indeed, their argument "if true, . . . would be a serious challenge to the applicability of any empirically based risk procedure to any individual for anything" (Hanson and Howard 2010, 277).

Our view is that group data theoretically can be, and in many areas empirically are, highly informative when making decisions about individual cases (Scurich et al. 2012). Consider two examples from other forms of risk assessment. In the insurance industry, "until an individual insured is treated as a member of a group, it is impossible to know his expected loss, because for practical purposes that concept is a statistical one based on group probabilities. Without relying on such probabilities, it would be impossible to set a price for insurance coverage at all" (Abraham 1986, 79). In weather forecasting, "extensive statistical data are available on the average probability of the events [meteorologists] are estimating" and therefore when meteorologists "predict a 70 percent chance of rain, there is measurable precipitation just about 70 percent of the time" (National Research Council 1989, 46). In addition, consider the revolver analogy of Grove and Meehl:

> Suppose you are a political opponent held in custody by a mad dictator. Two revolvers are put on the table and you are informed that one of them has five live rounds with one empty chamber, the other has five empty chambers and one live cartridge, and you are required to play Russian roulette. If you live, you will go free. Which revolver would you choose? Unless you have a death wish, you would choose the one with the five empty chambers. Why? Because you would know that the odds are five to one that you will survive if you pick that revolver, whereas the odds are five to one you will be dead if you choose the other one. Would you seriously think, "Well it doesn't make any difference what the odds are. Inasmuch as I'm only going to do this once, there is no aggregate involved, so I might as well pick either one of these two revolvers; it doesn't matter which"? (Grove and Meehl 1996, 305–306)

The probabilities associated with risk assessment clearly are less certain than those associated with the number of bullets in a six-chamber revolver. Nevertheless, we find compelling Grove and Meehl's basic point that group data can powerfully inform individual assessments of risk.

We agree with Mossman (2015) that "something in the Hart-Cooke-Michie argument must be wrong." Mossman uses a medical rather than a ballistic analogy to make the same point as Grove and Meehl: "A 50-year-old individual who learns that half of people with his diagnosis die in five years will find this information very useful in deciding whether to purchase an annuity that would begin payouts only after he reached his 65th birthday."

Similarly, if all one knew about an individual was his or her Static-99R score and that he or she came from a population to which the Static-99R data and rates were relevant, the individual's Static-99R score would be the best and the only basis for making a probabilistic judgment about his or her behavior. This is true despite our belief that many factors not considered by the Static-99R (e.g., the person's employment status, substance use, or family relationships) affect sex offenders' likelihood of recidivism.

Finally, Faigman et al. (2014) have recently analyzed how the law deals with what they refer to as group-to-individual ("G2i") inference in scientific expert testimony, including scientific expert testimony on violence risk. They conclude:

> It is customary in the ordinary practice of medicine and related fields (e.g., clinical psychology) for professionals to make individual... judgments derived from group-based data. Likewise, it is *not* customary in the ordinary practice of sociology, epidemiology, anthropology, and related fields (e.g., cognitive and social psychology) for professionals to make individual... judgments derived from group-based data. (Faigman et al. 2014)

In the view of these authors, evidence-based scientific expert testimony on an individual's violence risk when offered by qualified psychiatrists or clinical psychologists should have no trouble being admitted in court.

SHOULD RISK ASSESSMENT AND REDUCTION BE SEPARATED?

Risk assessment has become big business in the U.S. justice system, principally because "the fiscal condition of most American jurisdictions is so dire that maintaining what is by international standards an absurdly bloated prison population is simply not a sustainable option" (Monahan and Skeem 2014, 158). Risk assessment can facilitate prison downsizing directly, by identifying for release those inmates who are least likely to return.

Risk assessment can also be used in the service of risk reduction. Correctional agencies that manage a staggering number of youth and adults are increasingly endorsing structured risk assessment approaches and treatment programs that reduce reoffending by targeting risk factors like anger, poor self-control, and antisocial attitudes. In this context, companies have begun marketing complex (and poorly validated) assessment systems that explicitly include treatment-relevant variables in their risk estimates and ostensibly serve the risk reduction enterprise better than simple actuarial tools. Fundamental requirements for developing, (cross-)validating, and applying risk assessment tools are "routinely ignored or violated" (Gottfredson and Moriarty 2006; see also Skeem and Eno Louden 2007).

This has sparked debate about whether the pursuit of risk assessment and risk reduction should be separated or integrated. Baird (2009) favors separation, arguing that the addition of treatment-relevant variables to otherwise parsimonious risk equations that emphasize past (mis)behavior will dilute their predictive utility. Andrews (2012), on the other hand, argues that some treatment-relevant variables are risk factors and should be integrated in risk estimates. His view is that efficient prediction can be achieved by statistically selecting and combining a few highly predictive risk factors, but tools that sample risk domains more broadly and include treatment-relevant risk factors can be equally predictive. Andrews' (2012) view is consistent with evidence that tools that differ in their inclusion of such factors yield similar predictive efficiencies (Campbell et al. 2009; Olver et al. 2009; Yang et al. 2010).

Monahan and Skeem (2014, 160) observed that this debate has been exacerbated by confusion about what a treatment-relevant risk factor is, exactly. They differentiated among the four different types of risk factors for violent reoffending or recidivism shown in Table 69.1. A *fixed marker* is a risk factor that cannot be changed (e.g., early onset of antisocial behavior). In contrast, both *variable markers* and *variable risk factors* can be shown to change over time. Variable markers (like age) cannot be changed through intervention, unlike variable risk factors (like employment problems). *Causal risk factors* are variable risk factors that,

Table 69.1 Four types of risk factors

Type of risk factor	Definition	Example
Fixed marker	Unchangeable	Gender
Variable marker	Unchangeable by intervention	Age
Variable risk factor	Changeable by intervention	Employment status
Causal risk factor	Changeable by intervention; when changed, reduces recidivism	Substance abuse

Source: Adapted from Kraemer HC et al. 1997. *Archives of General Psychiatry* 54:337–343; Monahan J and J Skeem. 2014. *Federal Sentencing Reporter* 26:158–166.

when changed through intervention, can be shown to change the risk of recidivism.

All four types of risk factors are relevant to *risk assessment*, but only causal risk factors are relevant to *risk reduction*. Put simply, treatment-relevant risk factors are causal risk factors. Unless a variable risk factor has been shown to be causal, there is little reason to assume that reducing the risk factor will reduce violence.

This fact is rarely recognized in current discourse. Instead, variable risk factors have been confused with causal risk factors under the rubric of "dynamic risk factors" or "criminogenic needs." Although the latter phrases typically reference a variable risk factor that *theoretically* can be changed through intervention to reduce risk, these phrases tend to be misused as synonyms for causal risk factors.

The most compelling form of evidence that a risk factor was causal would be a randomized controlled trial in which a targeted intervention was shown to be effective in changing one or more variable risk factors, and the resulting changes were shown to reduce the likelihood of post-treatment recidivism. As Monahan and Skeem (2014) observe, it is nearly impossible to locate such randomized controlled tests.

Although little is known about causal risk factors, there is increasing evidence that some risk factors are variable—that they change over time, and that change predicts re-offending (e.g., Howard and Dixon 2013). Variable risk factors have been shown to predict proximate violence and are the best point of reference the field presently has to offer for risk reduction. For example, in a randomized controlled trial, Bonta et al. (2012) found that, compared to untrained probation officers, specially trained probation officers spent more time discussing variable risk factors with their probationers (e.g., procriminal attitudes, antisocial associates), and their probationers manifested greater reductions in recidivism risk. Although little is known about which variable risk factors are causal, variable risk factors can be repeatedly assessed to monitor ebbs and flows in an offender's risk, and adjust levels of supervision and services accordingly.

PURPOSE-BASED CHOICE AMONG VALID INSTRUMENTS

Given a pool of instruments that are well-validated for the groups to which an individual belongs, our view is that the choice among them should be driven by the ultimate purpose of the evaluation. If the ultimate purpose is to characterize an individual's likelihood of future violence relative to other people, then choose the most efficient instrument available. This is appropriate for a single event decision in which there is no real opportunity to modify the risk estimate based on future behavior (Heilbrun 1997). If the ultimate purpose is to manage or reduce an individual's risk, then value may be added by choosing an instrument that includes treatment-relevant risk factors. (Although an integrated instrument would do, Mills and Gray [2013] demonstrate the utility of a two-stage process in which a risk assessment step is followed by a risk management step.) This choice is appropriate for ongoing decisions where the risk estimate can be modified to reflect ebbs and flows in an individual's risk over time. Beyond focusing risk-reduction efforts, these instruments could provide incentive for changing behavior (a parole board cannot advise an inmate to "undo" his past commission of an assault but can advise him to develop employment skills).

This view comes with three important caveats. First, techniques that include treatment-relevant risk factors will add no value to simpler approaches unless the risk assessment is followed by a period of control over the individual during which those factors are translated into an individual supervision and treatment plan (rather than simply filed away) and systematically targeted with appropriate services (rather than ignored in resource allocation). Risk reduction cannot be achieved through risk assessment alone, regardless of the approach applied. Second, treatment-relevant variables can and do appear in statistically derived risk assessment instruments (Monahan 2010); an instrument's degree of structure cannot be equated with its relevance to risk reduction. Third, even well-validated instruments offer little direct validity data for the treatment-relevant variables they include. It is not enough to demonstrate that a variable is a risk factor for violence; here, it must further be shown that the variable reduces violence risk when deliberately changed by treatment (i.e., is a *causal* risk factor; Kraemer et al. 1997). Causality is not a given: In one of the few studies to address this topic, Kroner and Yessine (2013) found that change in a treatment-targeted risk factor did *not* explain reduced risk of reoffending. This is a crucial issue to address in future research, if tools continue to be sold on the promise of informing risk reduction.

FUTURE DIRECTIONS

The violence risk assessment field may be reaching a point of diminishing returns in instrument development. It has long been argued that there may be a "sound barrier" to predictive validity in this area, such that the effect size of risk estimates for predicting criterion measures rarely exceeds a correlation of 0.40 (Menzies et al. 1985) or an AUC of .72 (Rice and Harris 2005). In this regard, Appelbaum (2011) has stated that "predictive assessments are the most challenging evaluations performed by mental health professionals." He speculates that a principal driver of this great challenge is the unknowable contingencies of life. Will a person's spouse leave or will the person lose his or her job or home? As a consequence, will the person return to drinking, stop taking medication, or reconnect with friends who have continued to engage in criminal behaviors? At best, predictive assessments can lead to general statements of probability of particular outcomes, with an acknowledgment of the uncertainties involved.

"The contingencies of life" will place an upper limit on what can be achieved in many risk assessment settings—especially those that approach risk assessment as a one-time diagnostic enterprise that focuses on individual characteristics. The upper limit may prove to be somewhat higher than it is now if contingencies and contextual factors are systematically embedded in risk appraisals and appraisals are updated over time (Mulvey and Lidz 1995; see also Dickson et al. 2013; Kroner et al. 2013).

There are other promising candidates for incremental advances in violence risk assessment. These include violent victimization (Sadeh et al. 2013), implicit measures (Nock et al. 2010), patient self-perceptions (Skeem et al. 2013), and the incorporation of risk factors from the neurosciences (Aharonia et al. 2013; Poldrack 2013).

If we are approaching a "sound barrier" in the *risk assessment* domain (Coid et al. 2011), there clearly are miles to go before we can rest on the *risk reduction* front. We hope that in the future psychology and psychiatry shift more of their empirical attention from predicting violence to understanding its causes and preventing its (re)occurrence.

SUMMARY KEY POINTS

- Laws regulating the process of violence risk assessment have become more developed over recent years. Increasingly, risk assessment tools are being applied in response to statutes and regulations that require specialized assessments to characterize individuals' risk of violence.
- Risk assessment tools may be aligned along a *continuum of rule-based structure*, with completely unstructured ("clinical") assessment occupying one pole of the continuum, completely structured ("actuarial") assessment occupying the other pole, and several forms of partially structured assessment lying between the two.
- Despite variation among tools, there is little evidence that one validated instrument predicts violence significantly better than another.
- Although some argue that empirically based risk assessments are too inaccurate to be useful in individual cases, we believe that group data theoretically can be, and in many areas empirically are, highly informative when making decisions about individuals.
- All types of risk factors (fixed markers, variable markers, variable risk factors, and causal risk factors) are relevant to *risk assessment*, but only causal risk factors are relevant to *risk reduction*. This is rarely recognized in current discourse, where imprecise terminology abounds. Treatment-relevant risk factors are causal risk factors—and little is known about them. Variable risk factors—despite their clear limitations—are the best the field currently has to offer, to guide risk monitoring and reduction efforts.
- Given a pool of well-validated tools, the choice among them should be driven by the ultimate purpose of the evaluation. If the ultimate purpose is to characterize an individual's likelihood of future violence relative to other people, then choose the most efficient instrument available. If the ultimate purpose is to manage or reduce an individual's risk, then value may be added by choosing an instrument that includes variable risk factors.
- The violence risk assessment field may be reaching a point of diminishing returns in instrument development. Future efforts should shift focus from predicting violence to understanding its causes and preventing its (re)occurrence.

REFERENCES

Abraham KS. 1986. *Distributing Risk: Insurance, Legal Theory, and Public Policy*. New Haven, CT: Yale University Press.

Ægisdóttir S, MJ White, PM Spengler et al. 2006. The meta-analysis of clinical judgment project: Fifty-six years of accumulated research on clinical versus statistical prediction. *Counseling Psychologist* 34:341–382.

Aharonia E, GM Vincent, CL Harenski, VD Calhoun, W Sinnott-Armstrong, MS Gazzaniga, and KA Kiehl. 2013. Neuroprediction of future rearrest. *Proceedings of the National Academy of Sciences* 110:6223–6228.

Andrews D. 2012. The risk-need-responsivity (RNR) model of correctional assessment and treatment. In *Using Social Science to Reduce Violent Offending*, edited by J Dvoskin, J Skeem, R Novaco, and K Douglas, New York: Oxford University Press, 127–156.

Appelbaum P. 2011. Reference guide on mental health evidence. In *Reference Manual on Scientific Evidence*, 3rd edition, edited by Committee on Science, Technology, and Law; Policy and Global Affairs; Federal Judicial Center; National Research Council, Washington, DC: National Academies Press, 813–896.

Baird C. 2009. *A Question of Evidence: A Critique of Risk Assessment Models Used in the Justice System*. Madison, WI: National Council on Crime and Delinquency. http://www.nccdglobal.org/sites/default/files/publication_pdf/special-report-evidence.pdf.

Bonta J, J Blais and H Wilson. 2013. The prediction of risk for mentally disordered offenders: A quantitative synthesis. User Report 2013-01. Ottawa, ON: Public Safety Canada. http://www.publicsafety.gc.ca/cnt/rsrcs/pblctns/prdctn-rsk-mntlly-dsrdrd/index-eng.aspx, accessed August 1, 2016.

Bonta J, G Bourgon, T Rugge, T-L Scott, AK Yessine, L Gutierrez, and J Li. 2012. An experimental demonstration of training probation officers in evidence-based community supervision. *Criminal Justice and Behavior* 38:1127–1148.

Buttars A and M Huss. 2014. Sex offender risk assessment: A re-examination of the coffee can study. Paper presented at the annual meeting of the American-Psychology Law Society, New Orleans, Louisiana, March.

Campbell MA, S French, and P Gendreau. 2009. The prediction of violence in adult offenders: A meta-analytic comparison of instruments and methods of assessment. *Criminal Justice and Behavior* 36:567–590.

Carroll L. 2011 (Original work published 1865). *Alice's Adventures in Wonderland*, 2nd edition, edited by R Kelly, Buffalo, NY: Broadview Press.

Cohen BJ, RJ Bonnie, and J Monahan. 2009. Understanding and applying Virginia's new statutory civil commitment criteria. *Developments in Mental Health Law* 28:127–139.

Coid JW, M Yang, S Ullrich, T Zhang, S Sizmur, D Farrington, and R Rogers. 2011. Most items in structured risk assessment instruments do not predict violence. *Journal of Forensic Psychiatry and Psychology* 22:3–21.

Cooke DJ and C Michie. 2010. Limitations of diagnostic precision and predictive utility in the individual case: A challenge for forensic practice. *Law and Human Behavior* 34:259–264.

Dickson SR, DLL Polaschek, and AR Casey. 2013. Can the quality of high-risk violent prisoners' release plans predict recidivism following intensive rehabilitation? A comparison with risk assessment instruments. *Psychology, Crime and Law* 19:371–389.

Douglas KS, S Hart, J Groscup, and T Litwack. 2014. Assessing violence risk. In *The Handbook of Forensic Psychology*, 4th edition, edited by IB Weiner and RK Otto, Hoboken, NJ: Wiley, 385–442.

Douglas KS, SD Hart, CD Webster, and H Belfrage. 2013. HCR-20: *Assessing Risk for Violence, Version 3*. Vancouver, Canada: Mental Health, Law, and Policy Institute, Simon Fraser University.

Faigman D, J Monahan, and C Slobogin. 2014. Group to individual (G2i) inference in scientific expert testimony. *University of Chicago Law Review* 81L417–480.

Gottfredson SD and LJ Moriarty. 2006. Statistical risk assessment: Old problems and new applications. *Crime and Delinquency* 52:178–200.

Grove WM and PE Meehl. 1996. Comparative efficiency of informal (subjective, impressionistic) and formal (mechanical, algorithmic) prediction procedures: The clinical–statistical controversy. *Psychology, Public Policy, and Law* 2:293–323.

Hanson RK and PD Howard. 2010. Individual confidence intervals do not inform decision-makers about the accuracy of risk assessment evaluations. *Law and Human Behavior* 34:275–281.

Hanson RK and KE Morton-Bourgon. 2009. The accuracy of recidivism risk assessments for sexual offenders: A meta-analysis of 118 prediction studies. *Psychological Assessment* 21:1–21.

Hart SD and DJ Cooke. 2013. Another look at the (im)precision of individual risk estimates made using actuarial risk assessment instruments. *Behavioral Sciences and the Law* 31:81–102.

Hart SD, C Michie, and DJ Cooke. 2007. Precision of actuarial risk assessment instruments: Evaluating the margins of error of group v. individual predictions of violence. *British Journal of Psychiatry* 190:S60–S65.

Heilbrun K. 1997. Prediction versus management models relevant to risk assessment: The importance of legal decision-making context. *Law and Human Behavior* 21:347–359.

Heilbrun K, KS Douglas, and K Yasuhara. 2009. Violence risk assessment: Core controversies. In *Psychological Science in the Courtroom: Consensus and Controversy*, edited by J Skeem, K Douglas, and S Lillienfeld, New York: Guilford, 333–357.

Howard PD and L Dixon. 2013. Identifying change in the likelihood of violent recidivism: Causal dynamic risk factors in the OASys violence predictor. *Law and Human Behavior* 37:163–174.

Kraemer HC, AE Kazdin, DR Offord, RC Kessler, PS Jensen, and DJ Kupfer. 1997. Coming to terms with the terms of risk. *Archives of General Psychiatry* 54:337–343.

Kroner DG, AL Gray, and B Goodrich. 2013. Integrating risk context into risk assessments the risk context scale. *Assessment* 20:135–149.

Kroner DG, JF Mills, and JR Reddon. 2005. A coffee can, factor analysis, and prediction of antisocial behavior: The structure of criminal risk. *International Journal of Law and Psychiatry* 28:360–374.

Kroner DG and AK Yessine. 2013. Changing risk factors that impact recidivism: In search of mechanisms of change. *Law and Human Behavior* 37:321–336.

Lidz CW, EP Mulvey, and W Gardner. 1993. The accuracy of predictions of violence to others. *Journal of the American Medical Association* 269:1007–1011.

Meehl PE. 1954. *Clinical versus Statistical Prediction: A Theoretical Analysis and a Review of the Evidence*. Minneapolis: University of Minnesota Press.

Menzies RJ, CD Webster, and D Sepejak. 1985. Hitting the forensic sound barrier: Predictions of dangerousness in a pre-trial psychiatric clinic. In *Dangerousness: Probability and Prediction, Psychiatry and Public Policy*, edited by CD Webster, MH Ben-Aron, and SJ Hucker, New York: Cambridge University Press, 115–142.

Mills JF and AL Gray. 2013. Two-tiered violence risk estimates: A validation study of an integrated-actuarial risk assessment instrument. *Psychological Services* 10:361–371.

Monahan J. 2010. The Classification of Violence Risk. In *Handbook of Violence Risk Assessment*, edited by RK Otto and KS Douglas, New York: Routledge, 187–198.

Monahan J. 2013. The inclusion of biological risk factors in violence risk assessments. In *BioPrediction, Biomarkers, and Bad Behavior: Scientific, Legal and Ethical Implications*, edited by I Singh, W Sinnott-Armstrong, and J Savulecu, New York: Oxford University Press, 57–76.

Monahan J and J Skeem. 2014. Risk redux: The resurgence of risk assessment in criminal sanctioning. *Federal Sentencing Reporter* 26:158–166.

Monahan J, HJ Steadman, E Silver, PS Appelbaum, PC Robbins, EP Mulvey, LH Roth, T Grisso, and S Banks. 2001. *Rethinking Risk Assessment: The MacArthur Study of Mental Disorder and Violence*. New York: Oxford University Press.

Mossman D. 2015. From group data to useful probabilities: The relevance of actuarial risk assessment in individual instances. *Journal of the American Academy of Psychiatry and the Law* 43:93–102.

Mulvey EP and CW Lidz. 1995. Conditional prediction: A model for research on dangerousness to others in a new era. *International Journal of Law and Psychiatry* 18:129–143.

National Research Council. 1989. *Improving Risk Communication*. Washington DC: National Academy Press.

Nock MH, JM Park, CT Finn, TL Deliberto, HJ Dour, and MR Banaji. 2010. Measuring the suicidal mind: Implicit cognition predicts suicidal behavior. *Psychological Science* 21:511–517.

Olver ME, KC. Stockdale, and JS Wormith. 2009 Risk assessment with young offenders: A meta-analysis of three assessment measures. *Criminal Justice and Behavior* 36:329–353.

Poldrack RA. 2013. How well can we predict future criminal acts from fMRI data? http://www.russpoldrack.org/2013/04/how-well-can-we-predict-future-criminal.html, accessed August 1, 2016.

Quinsey VL, GT Harris, ME Rice, and CA Cormier. 1998. *Violent Offenders: Appraising and Managing Risk*. Washington, DC: American Psychological Association.

Rice M and GT Harris. 2005. Comparing effect sizes in follow-up studies: ROC Area, Cohen's d, and r. *Law and Human Behavior* 29:615–620.

Rice ME, GT Harris, and C Lang. 2013. Validation of and revision to the VRAG and SORAG: The Violence Risk Appraisal Guide-Revised (VRAG-R). *Psychological Assessment* 25:951–965.

Sadeh N, RL Binder, and DE McNiel. 2013. Recent victimization increases risk for violence in justice-involved persons with mental illness. *Law and Human Behavior* 38:119–125.

Scurich N, J Monahan, and RS John. 2012. Innumeracy and unpacking: Bridging the nomothetic/idiographic divide in violence risk assessment. *Law and Human Behavior* 36:548–554.

Skeem J and J Eno Louden. 2007. *Assessment of Evidence on the Quality of the COMPAS*. http://www.cdcr.ca.gov/adult_research_branch/Research_Documents/COMPAS_Skeem_EnoLouden_Dec_2007.pdf, accessed June 13, 2013.

Skeem JL, SM Manchak, CW Lidz, and EP Mulvey. 2013. The utility of patients' self-perceptions of violence risk: Consider asking the person who may know best. *Psychiatric Services* 64:410–415.

Skeem JL, S Manchak, and JK Peterson. 2011. Correctional policy for offenders with mental illness. *Law and Human Behavior* 35:110–126.

Skeem JL and J Monahan. 2011. Current directions in violence risk assessment. *Current Directions in Psychological Science* 20:38–42.

Sturup J, J Monahan, and M Kristiansson. 2013. Violent behavior and gender of Swedish psychiatric patients: A prospective clinical study. *Psychiatric Services* 64:688–693.

Tardiff K. 2008. Clinical risk assessment of violence. *Textbook of Violence Assessment and Management*. edited by R Simon and K Tardiff, Washington, DC: American Psychiatric Press, 3–16.

Webster CD, KS Douglas, D Eaves, and SD Hart. 1997. HCR-20: *Assessing Risk for Violence, Version 2*. Vancouver, Canada: Mental Health, Law, and Policy Institute, Simon Fraser University.

Yang M, SCP Wong, and J Coid. 2010. The efficacy of violence prediction: A meta-analytic comparison of nine risk assessment tools. *Psychological Bulletin* 136:740–767.

70

Sex offender risk assessment

AMY PHENIX

EVALUATION OF SEXUAL OFFENDERS

Evolution of contemporary risk assessment

Sex offender commitment laws are not new in the United States. The nation's sexual psychopath laws from the early twentieth century required that psychiatrists make a determination of whether or not an individual met often vague criteria based solely on clinical judgment. Although most of these sexual psychopath statutes have been overturned or repealed, the sexually violent predator laws of the 1990s require that clinicians determine risk of re-offending as one component for commitment. Findings from the classic Hanson and Bussiere meta-analysis (1998) identified static or historical risk factors that predicted sexual re-offense, which allowed for the development of actuarial instruments. These instruments evidenced improved predictive accuracy over clinical judgments regarding sex offender risk. Increasingly, courts are requiring these actuarial instruments when making decisions about the civil commitment of sex offenders.

As with violence risk assessment, three generations of risk assessment for sexual offenders can be identified. The first involved unstructured methods not based on empirical data. Unfortunately, this method's accuracy was no better than chance, and clinicians were wrong as often as they were right. Today it is broadly accepted that evaluations based on unstructured professional judgment are not as accurate as structured risk assessments (Janus and Prentky 2003; Andrews et al. 2006; Quinsey et al. 2006; Monahan 2007). In the late 1990s the second generation of risk assessment evolved with the creation of actuarial risk scales composed of static, historical factors (Bonta and Wormith 2007). The third generation of risk assessment involves the evaluation of dynamic needs, identifying risk factors amenable to change. These dynamic risk factors, also called long-term vulnerabilities or psychological risk factors, have been incorporated into structured instruments to assess relevant risk factors for sexual re-offending (e.g., Fernandez et al. 2012; Helmus et al. 2012a; McGrath et al. 2012).

Currently, the question is not whether risk assessments should be completed for sex offenders, but what methodology should be used. To evaluate this question Hanson and Morton-Bourgon (2009), using meta-analyses, examined 118 studies to determine the accuracy of each method of prediction. For all outcomes, the actuarial method was superior (Cohen's $d = 0.67$ [a measure of the strength of the effect]). Unstructured professional judgment was significantly less accurate than actuarial methods ($d = 0.42$). The accuracy of structured professional judgment was slightly better than unstructured professional judgment ($d = 0.46$). It is now standard practice to use one or more actuarial instruments to evaluate static, or historical, risk factors, which rarely change and provide a baseline of risk for a sexual offender. These data suggest that contemporary risk assessment should include the use of validated actuarial instruments as well as a structured review of relevant dynamic risk factors. In this chapter, the development of current sex offender risk assessments is discussed, including information on reliability and validity as available, and guidelines for how to conduct a comprehensive sexual offender risk assessment are provided.

DETERMINING RISK OF SEXUALLY OFFENDING: ACTUARIAL INSTRUMENTS

The most commonly used and best validated actuarial measures for assessing sexual recidivism risk are the Static-99R and the Static-2002R (Hanson and Thornton 2000; Hanson et al. 2010). Following is a discussion of the development of these instruments.

Static-99 and Static-99R

The Static-99 was developed by Karl Hanson and David Thornton (2000) to assess risk of sexual and violent recidivism with sexual offenders. The Static-99's historical risk factors were derived from earlier tools, the Rapid Risk Assessment for Sex Offender Recidivism (RRASOR) and the Structured Anchored Clinical Judgment (SACJ-Min;

Grubin 1998; Hanson and Bussiere 1998; Hanson and Thornton 2000). The Static-99 measures the risk of sexual or violent reconviction. Because most sex offenses go undetected, the resulting risk estimates should be considered an underestimate of the true risk of recidivism (Bonta and Hanson 1994). The 10-item Static-99 included variables such as prior offenses, prior convictions (both sexual and nonsexual), and characteristics of the victim(s) as well as the offender. The original Static-99 has had over 65 validations on a wide variety of samples and in different jurisdictions (Helmus 2009).

STATIC-99R DEVELOPMENT AND VALIDATION SAMPLES

The Static-99 Revised (Static-99R) was released for clinical use in 2009 (Hanson et al. 2009; Helmus et al. 2012b). The Static-99 was revised for two reasons. First, the Static-99 did not adequately account for reductions in recidivism with advancing age at release (Hanson 2002; Helmus et al. 2012b). Second, more contemporary samples showed substantially lower base rates of sexual recidivism compared to those in the Static-99 development samples. The Static-99R development team has recommended the Static-99R replace the use of Static-99. The Static-99R (Helmus et al. 2012b) was developed and validated with 24 samples drawn from eight different countries. Eleven samples were from Canada, six were from the United States, two were from the United Kingdom, and one each was drawn from Austria, Denmark, Germany, Sweden, and New Zealand. A total of 8390 sexual offenders were included in these samples. For recoding age at release, the sample was divided into construction and validation subsamples. All offenders with a follow-up period less than 10 years were included in the construction sample ($n = 5714$). Offenders with a longer follow-up period were included in the validation sample ($n = 2392$). The entire sample was used to re-norm the Static-99R and to analyze variability of sexual recidivism base rates across the samples. Details of the samples are available in Helmus et al. (2012b). As noted previously, the only change in the Static-99R was the age at release item. Analyses indicated age was not fully accounted for in Static-99; as such, the age item was revised to include four age categories with decreasing risk points for increased age (Helmus et al. 2012b). This new scoring reflects increased risk for younger offenders and decreased risk with advancing age.

VALIDITY OF THE STATIC-99R

The accuracy of the risk assessment in the validation sample (AUC of 0.72) was statistically significant but only nominally higher than that for the Static-99 (AUC = 0.71; Helmus et al. 2012b). In a separate cross-validation of the Static-99R in California, Hanson et al. (2014) reported high relative risk validity (discrimination) and good absolute risk validity (calibration) in a prospective field study of 475 randomly selected adult males released from California prisons in 2006–2007 and followed for 5 years. The resulting AUC = 0.817 (95% CI 0.716–0.919) demonstrated strong relative predictive accuracy.

Ethnic variability was examined by Hanson et al. (2014) in a 5-year follow-up study. The predictive accuracy was statistically significant ($p < 0.05$) for Blacks and Whites, but not for Hispanics (Black [AUC = 0.765], Hispanic [AUC = 0.734], and White [AUC = 0.850]. That nonsignificant finding was at least in part due to the small sample size of Hispanic sexual recidivists ($n = 5$). Logistic regression equations for Black, Hispanic, and White sexual offenders revealed no significant differences in the adjusted base rate (predicted value for a Static-99R score of 2) or in the rate of change in relative risk for a one-unit increase in Static-99R score. Performance of the Static-99R with Black, Latino, and White sexual offenders was also examined in a large Texas study (Varela et al. 2013). The Static-99R did not perform well overall in this study, but its sexual recidivism predictive accuracy for relative risk was similar with Blacks (AUC = 0.65), Latinos (AUC = 0.57), and Whites (AUC = 0.59). Only the AUC for Blacks was statistically significant. In a sample of 319 Canadian Aboriginals and 1269 Canadian non-Aboriginals across five independent samples, Babchishin et al. (2012) found similar, statistically significant levels of predictive accuracy for the Static-99R with both groups, AUC = 0.698 and AUC = 0.726, respectively. However, with a smaller sample of Australian Aboriginals ($n = 67$) and non-Aboriginals ($n = 399$) and a relatively short follow-up period ($M = 29$ months), Smallbone and Rallings (2013) reported statistically significant sexual recidivism predictive accuracy for the Static-99R with Australian non-Aboriginal sexual offenders (AUC = 0.79) but not for Australian Aboriginal sexual offenders (AUC = 0.61). These results indicate that the variability of results based on ethnicity of the sample should be a consideration when using the Static-99R.

In 2015, new norms were released for the Static-99R that included two groups: larger routine correctional samples and high-risk/high-needs samples. The *Routine Norms* are based on correctional samples composed of sexual offenders selected at random. The *High-Risk/High-Needs Norms* are based on sexual offenders selected on the basis of perceived risk for relatively "rare or infrequent measures or interventions or sanctions, such as psychiatric commitments and being held past their release date" (Hanson et al. 2009; Phenix et al. 2012). The routine norms group has the lowest recidivism rates for scores under 7 on the Static-99R. For a score of 7 and above, the two normative groups merge, having similar probabilities of sexual reconviction.

Recent research confirms that the variability in sexual recidivism base rates in the Static-99R samples is due to differences in the presence of unmeasured risk factors external to Static-99R (Hanson and Thornton 2012). These external risk factors are often referred to as long-term vulnerabilities, psychological needs, or dynamic risk factors. Offenders with low to moderate dynamic needs are most similar to offenders in the routine norms; offenders with high dynamic needs are most similar to offenders in the high-risk/high-needs norms. Sexual offenders with identical scores on the

Static-99R have different rates of sexual recidivism based on the density of dynamic needs, with the higher-needs group exhibiting greater rates of sexual recidivism (Hanson and Thornton 2012; Thornton and Knight 2013). Clearly, evaluating dynamic risk factors is necessary when conducting a comprehensive sex offender risk assessment. Measures to assess these needs will be discussed later in this chapter.

RELIABILITY OF THE STATIC-99R

Hanson et al. (2014) assessed the reliability of Static-99R scores from 55 corrections and probation officers in California scoring 14 actual redacted parole cases. Overall inter-rater reliability was acceptable (ICC = 0.78). There was a substantial difference in the reliability of scores from experienced scorers (ICC = 0.85) and less-experienced scorers (ICC = 0.71), pointing to the importance of recent practice. Experienced scorers were defined as those who had scored 26 or more sexual offenders on the Static-99R in the previous 12 months. McGrath, Lasher, and Cumming (2012) reported very high reliability for the Static-99R (ICC = 0.89).

Static-2002 and Static-2002R

The Static-2002 was developed by Hanson and Thornton (2003) to create a risk assessment tool with improved predictive accuracy, conceptual clarity, and coherence. Like Static-99, the Static-2002 was designed to be a brief actuarial measure of relative and absolute risk for sexual recidivism that could be scored from commonly available information in correctional files.

The Static-2002 Revised (Static-2002R) was developed to better reflect decreasing risk with advancing age and to adjust for decreasing base rates of sexual recidivism and variability in those base rates in generating absolute risk estimates. The analyses and results were similar to those reported earlier for the Static-99R (Helmus et al. 2012a,b). The differences between the Static-99R and Static-2002R analyses and results are described here.

Static-2002R was developed on only seven available samples ($n = 2609$) compared to the larger number of samples for Static-99R. With these seven samples, the relative predictive validity for 5-year sexual recidivism was slightly higher on Static-2002R (AUC = 0.713) than the Static-2002 (AUC = 0.709). As with other actuarial tools, relative risk can be reported as nominal risk categories, percentiles, or relative risk ratios. Currently the Static-2002R has the same two normative groups as Static-99R, *Routine Norms* and *High-Risk/High-Needs Norms*.

RELIABILITY

Five studies reporting inter-rater reliability for the Static-2002 scores have been conducted, and all reported high indices of reliability (Haag 2005; Knight and Thornton 2007; Langton et al. 2007; Bengtson 2008). There are no published reports of reliability for the Static-2002R, although the only difference between the two is the age item.

CROSS-VALIDATIONS

Hanson et al. (2010) performed meta-analyses on samples from eight studies ($n = 3034$), both published and unpublished, to assess the predictive accuracy of the Static-2002 in comparison to the Static-99. Across the eight studies, the AUCs for sexual recidivism ranged from 0.64 to 0.79, and all 95% CIs excluded 0.50, reflecting statistically significant predictive accuracy in each of the studies. A similar pattern was evident for violent recidivism. (AUCs ranged from 0.64 to 0.77, and all were statistically significant.) Across all eight studies, the predictive accuracy for sexual recidivism was slightly higher for the Static-2002 (AUC = 0.685) than the Static-99 (AUC = 0.665), differences that were statistically significant. Babchishin et al. (2012) compared the predictive accuracy of the RRASOR, Static-99R, and Static-2002R for 7491 offenders (20 samples from the Static-99R re-norming project) primarily from Canada and the United States. Total scores of Static-2002R (AUC = 0.686) predicted sexual recidivism, similar to that for the Static-99R (AUC = 0.684). In a recent meta-analysis (Tully et al. 2013) of 43 studies and 31,426 sexual offenders, all of the reviewed tools produced at least a moderate effect size in predicting sexual re-offense including the Static-2002 (AUC = 0.70) and the Static-99 (AUC = 0.69).

Babchishin et al. (2012) examined the predictive accuracy of the Static-2002 and the Static-2002R with three samples of Canadian Aboriginals ($n = 209$) and non-Aboriginals ($n = 955$). Predictive accuracy for sexual recidivism was statistically significant in the total sample for the Static-2002 (AUC = 0.740) and the Static-2002R (AUC = 0.733) and in the non-Aboriginal sample for the Static-2002 (AUC = 0.763) and the Static-2002R (AUC = 0.759). In contrast to the Static-99 and Static-99R, there was a significant decrease in predictive accuracy in the Aboriginal sample for both the Static-2002 (AUC = 0.617) and the Static-2002R (AUC = 0.608), though the accuracy for the Static-2002 remained statistically significant.

Use of multiple actuarial instruments

The incremental validity of risk instruments is key to deciding what combination of instruments to use. Incremental validity is defined as the extent to which new information improves the accuracy of a prediction above and beyond that of the previous instrument(s) used.

Seto (2005) examined the incremental validity of several commonly used scales (i.e., RRASOR, Static-99, SORAG, and VRAG) and found the scales did not add incrementally to each other in the prediction of sexual recidivism. Evaluators were advised to choose the "best" instrument, the RRASOR. However, this study was limited by a small sample size. Babchishin et al. (2012) examined the incremental validity of the RRASOR, Static-99R, and Static-2002R in a large cohort of 7491 sex offenders from 20 samples in the Static-99 re-norming project. Contrary to Seto's (2005) prior findings, all three scales provided incremental validity to the prediction of sexual recidivism, despite the similarity in items on the scales. Decision rules for combining static, actuarial risk instruments for sexual offenders in the overall evaluation of risk were examined by Lehmann et al. (2013). In this study, the RRASOR, Static-99R, and Static-2002R all predicted sexual recidivism (AUCs of 0.69 to 0.71) and provided incremental validity to each other. The authors examined whether choosing the highest, the lowest, or averaging absolute risk estimates (probabilities) optimized accuracy. Their findings supported averaging the probabilities obtained on Static-99R and Static-2002R for the follow-up period of interest (5 or 10 years) for the best absolute estimate of risk to re-offend. In light of recent research on the use of multiple instruments, it is not necessary to choose between them, unless time or resources limit options to one or the other, because risk estimates may be more accurate if they are averaged across the two tools.

Regardless of which tool(s) is used, a number of best practices have emerged from the evolving work on developing actuarial instruments. The first is that relative risk should always be reported because it is consistently stable over time, as reflected in various temporal cohorts. Relative risk should be presented in multiple ways, including nominal risk categories (low, medium, and high rankings), percentiles, and relative risk ratios when available. In some cases, particularly high-stakes evaluations such as sexually violent predator (SVP) and sexually dangerous person (SDP), absolute risk estimates are informative and they should be based on contemporary local norms, if available, and/or the appropriate contemporary norm group estimates provided by the authors. Historically, for Static-99R and Static-2002R some degree of clinical judgment was required in determining which norm group is most appropriate for an individual offender based on the degree of pre-selection for treatment and/or high-risk/high-needs interventions. More recent research has allowed cutoffs on measures of dynamic risk factors/needs to inform the selection of the appropriate normative group. Research on the three actuarial instruments discussed in this chapter is ongoing. As such, normative information and recommendations may change. Thus, professionals using the Static tools should periodically check the static99.org website to ensure that current normative information and language is being used and that they are using the most appropriate methods for selecting absolute risk norm groups.

PSYCHOLOGICALLY MEANINGFUL RISK FACTORS (DYNAMIC RISK FACTORS)

Although the static risk factors have long been established, the changeable risk factors that predict sexual re-offense have been subject to more recent research (Mann et al. 2010). Psychologically meaningful risk factors, also called dynamic risk factors and long-term vulnerabilities, are frequently the targets of treatment because of their amenability to interventions that presumably will decrease risk. Assessment of these risk factors is an integral part of a contemporary risk assessment. Although static risk cannot change, dynamic risk can lower overall risk. Although there are many single sample studies identifying potential changeable risk factors, the Mann et al. (2010) meta-analysis categorized potential risk factors according to the strength of the evidence of their relationship with offending. This group made recommendations for which factors to use in current risk assessments.

Like static risk factors for sexual re-offense, many of the dynamic risk factors have low to moderate effect sizes, so evaluating them collectively will increase predictive accuracy. Currently there are four validated instruments that have been developed to assess psychologically meaningful risk factors in a structured way.

Stable-2007

The Stable-2007 measures sex offender risk factors that are changeable over time and can be used to formulate case management and identify treatment/supervision targets. This instrument can also inform treatment providers and supervision officers when offenders are becoming more or less dangerous over time. Because the Stable-2007 was developed and validated on a community sample, it is the most appropriate instrument to be used for offenders on community supervision.

The Stable-2007 is an outgrowth of the Dynamic Predictors Project (DPP; Hanson and Harris 1998) which included a retrospective file review and interviews with probation, police, and parole officers supervising sexual offenders in the community. The DPP identified a list of the most likely dynamic risk factors, which was used to create the Stable-2007's predecessors, the Sex Offender Need Assessment Rating (SONAR, Hanson and Harris 2000), the STABLE-2000, and the ACUTE-2000 (Hanson and Harris 2004). The Dynamic Supervision Project (DSP) was launched to develop an instrument on prospective data. The DSP followed approximately 1000 sexual offenders in Canada for an average of 43 months. Community supervision officers and law enforcement were trained in risk assessment instruments (Static-99, STABLE-2000, ACUTE-2000) and followed offenders on their caseload until the offenders recidivated or the study period ended. The officers were instructed to score the Static-99 once at the beginning of the project, the Stable-2000 every 6 months, and the ACUTE-2000 every supervision visit. Data were collected across Canada and in the states of Iowa and Alaska (Hanson et al. 2007). These data informed the revision from STABLE-2000 to Stable-2007. The Stable-2007 contains five categories of risk factors; three of the items have multiple factors. The items on Stable-2007 include (1) significant social influences, (2) intimacy deficits, (3) sexual self-regulation, (4) general self-regulation, and (5) cooperation with supervision.

Inter-rater reliability was measured for the Stable-2007 in a maximum security penitentiary (Fernandez 2008) and resulted in an ICC of 0.92 for the total score on the

Stable-2007. The Stable-2007 was cross-validated by Eher et al. (2012) who found that Stable-2007 was significantly related to sexual recidivism, violent recidivism, and general re-offense (AUC of 0.67–0.71). However, in this small sample of 261 rapists and child molesters, the Stable-2007 did not add incrementally above the Static-99. In a subsequent validation by Eher et al. (2013) with a larger sample ($n = 370$) incremental validity was found for the Stable-2007.

Structured risk assessment-forensic version (SRA-FV)

The SRA-FV was developed by David Thornton on a sample from the Massachusetts Treatment Center (MTC, Thornton and Knight 2013). This instrument was developed and validated on incarcerated offenders from the former sexual psychopath program in Massachusetts. As such, it is particularly suited for SVP/SDP evaluations and evaluations on high-risk sex offenders in adversarial conditions. The SRA-FV is based on previous research using the SRA framework (Thornton 2002). According to Thornton's Structured Risk Assessment (SRA), long-term risk factors can be divided into static risk indicators and enduring psychological risk factors that he refers to as *needs* or *long-term vulnerabilities*. The SRA model proposes that these long-term vulnerabilities can be organized into four domains: sexual interests, distorted attitudes, relational style, and self-management. The SRA-FV Need Assessment contains three of the four domains identified in the SRA framework. It has items measuring sexual interests, relational style, and self-management. Distorted attitudes were omitted, as it is difficult to measure such attitudes in adversarial circumstances when offenders may be inclined to provide a socially appropriate response, despite their true beliefs.

All offenders in the construction and cross-validation samples were sexual offenders who had been evaluated between 1959 and 1984 at the Massachusetts Treatment Center for Sexually Dangerous Persons in Bridgewater, Massachusetts, and released from MTC in or before 1984. The instrument was developed on 93–96 offenders and cross-validated on 365–444 offenders with five or more years follow-up. The validation produced an AUC for a 5-year follow-up of 0.72 which was unchanged at a 10-year follow-up.

The SRA-FV has a comprehensive coding manual (Version 1.55) that provides directions to score each item 0 (absent), 1 (some presence), and 2 (fully present). Additionally, the total score on SRA-FV can be used to select the appropriate norms for Static-99R, another advantage for SVP/SDP evaluations

Violence risk scale-sexual offender version (VRS-SO)

The VRS-SO (Olver et al. 2007) is a rating scale designed to assess risk and predict sexual recidivism, to measure and link treatment changes to sexual recidivism, and inform the delivery of sexual offender treatment. The VRS-SO assesses and measures change in treatment by using a modified application of the transtheoretical "model of change" (TTM). The TTM presumes that individuals in sex offender treatment progress through a series of stages known as precontemplation, contemplation, preparation, action, and maintenance, stages that are measured by VRS-SO.

The instrument was developed on 321 male federal Canadian offenders who had participated in a high-intensity sex offender treatment program at a maximum-security forensic mental health facility in Canada between 1983 and 1997. The VRS-SO is modeled closely after the Violence Risk Scale (Wong and Gordon 2006), which is designed to assess nonsexual violence risk and needs. The VRS-SO is a 24-item scale comprising 7 static and 17 dynamic items. The static items were developed with statistical–actuarial procedures on a randomly selected approximately half of the sample ($n = 152$) and cross-validated on the remaining portion of the sample ($n = 169$). A collection of 24 static variables identified from the literature were initially coded and correlated with sexual recidivism. Items with the strongest univariate relationships to outcome were retained and rescaled to a four-point scoring format. The static items can be summed to derive a total risk score. The dynamic items were developed through a review of sex offender prediction and treatment literature.

The dynamic items are potentially changeable by varying degrees. Change on the dynamic items is assessed and quantified through the assessment of a modified TTM. Each of the five stages of change has been operationalized for each of the 17 dynamic items. The advancement in the stages of change (e.g., from contemplation at pretreatment to action at post-treatment) provides evidence of the extent to which the offender has developed positive coping skills and abilities with respect to each dynamic factor. Baseline ratings and ratings as the offender progresses through treatment provide an assessment of positive treatment progress. A factor analysis of the dynamic items of VRS-SO revealed three factors labeled Sexual Deviance, Criminality, and Treatment Responsivity. Inter-rater reliability for VRS-SO for the dynamic items was assessed on 35 randomly selected cases and produced an ICC of 0.74 for pretreatment dynamic items and 0.79 for post-treatment dynamic items. After a 10-year follow-up, predictive accuracy of the VRS-SO static factors was 0.74; for pretreatment dynamic factors, 0.66; and for dynamic post-treatment items, 0.67. The extent to which the dynamic items made unique contributions to the prediction of sexual recidivism after Static-99 and the static items of the VRS-SO were controlled for was examined through Cox regression survival analysis. Significant independent contributions were made by the VRS-SO static item total and dynamic item total. Independent contributions were also observed when these analyses were repeated for Static-99 and the dynamic items, indicating the total dynamic score made significant incremental contributions to predicting sexual recidivism above that of the Static-99.

The VRS-SO has been subject to one independent cross-validation by Beggs and Grace (2010) on a sample of 218 child molesters who received treatment at a prison-based program in New Zealand. The VRS-SO showed good inter-rater reliability for 23 cases on pretreatment scores (ICC = 0.90) and for post-treatment items (ICC = 0.92) concurrent validity and high predictive accuracy for the static and dynamic risk factors both pre- and post-treatment. (AUCs = 0.70–0.81). The dynamic scale made significant incremental contributions after controlling for static risk. The manual provides measures of relative risk (Low, Moderate–Low, Moderate–High, and High) and absolute probabilities of sexual re-offense for the four risk groups at 3, 5, and 10 years.

SEX OFFENDER TREATMENT AND INTERVENTION PROGRESS SCALE (SOTIPS)

McGrath et al. (2012) developed SOTIPS, a new rating scale to assess dynamic risk among adult male sex offenders. SOTIPS predicted sexual, violent, and any criminal recidivism, as well as returns to prison, across time. However, combined SOTIPS and Static-99R scores predicted all recidivism types better than either instrument alone. These results bolster previous sexual offender studies examining the incremental validity of layering assessments of dynamic risk factors onto assessments of static risk factors (Hanson et al. 2007; Knight and Thornton 2007; Olver et al. 2007; Beggs and Grace 2010; Thornton and Knight 2013). These findings collectively indicate that a comprehensive risk assessment should include multiple actuarial instruments, including measures of both static and dynamic risk factors. This practice can also make the selection of Static-99R and Static-2002R norms more empirically based.

ADDITIONAL RISK FACTORS NOT CONTAINED IN STRUCTURED RISK ASSESSMENT INSTRUMENTS

There are no actuarial instruments or measures that assess dynamic risk factors that include all known risk factors for sexual re-offense. Consequently, there are several empirically supported or logically inferred risk factors to consider in overall risk. A contemporary risk assessment should consider psychopathy (as measured on the Hare Psychopathy Checklist Revised, Hare 2003), advanced age, level of community supervision, and sex offender treatment completion and treatment drop out.

SUMMARY

Contemporary risk assessment for sex offender evaluations should include the use of multiple validated actuarial instruments and the most appropriate validated dynamic risk assessment instrument as outlined in this chapter. Evaluators need to avail themselves of formal training prior to use of these instruments to ensure the reliability and validity of scores. Because these instruments do not contain all relevant risk factors and contextual factors, additional empirically related factors may be considered. Risk assessment should be individualized to the offender although the evaluator is discouraged from overriding empirically validated assessments with risk factors not related to sexual recidivism. Finally, evaluators are encouraged to remain current on the research that supports instruments they use and on new, evolving research that informs sex offender risk assessment. As with all of the static and dynamic instruments, the evaluator is advised to participate in formal training before using the instruments.

SUMMARY KEY POINTS

- Actuarial instruments are superior to unstructured clinical judgment when evaluating sex offender risk.
- The use of multiple actuarial instruments can provide enhanced predictive ability.
- Relative risk is stable over time and should be reported as nominal risk categories and percentiles.
- Instruments that assess dynamic risk factors are critical in determining the appropriate normative group and can also be used to develop treatment interventions aimed at risk reduction.
- Sex offender risk assessment should be individualized, but should not rely on idiosyncratic factors unrelated to sexual recidivism.

REFERENCES

Andrews DA, J Bonta, and JS Wormith. 2006. The recent past and near future of risk and/or need assessment. *Crime and Delinquency* 52:7–27.

Babchishin KM, J Blais, and L Helmus. 2012. Do static risk factors predict differently for Aboriginal sex offenders? A multi-site comparison using the original and revised Static-99 and Static-2002 Scales. *Canadian Journal of Criminology and Criminal Justice* 54:1–43. doi:10.3138/cjccj.2010.E.40

Babchishin KM, RK Hanson, and L Helmus. 2012. Even highly correlated measures can add incrementally to predicting recidivism among sex offenders. *Assessment* 19:442–461. doi:10.1177/1073191112458312

Beggs SM and R Grace. 2010. Assessment of dynamic risk factors: An independent validation study of the violence risk scales: Sexual offender version. *Sexual Abuse: A Journal of Research and Treatment* 22:234–251.

Bengtson S. 2008. Is newer better? A cross-validation of the Static-2002 and the Risk Matrix 2000 in a Danish sample of sexual offenders. *Psychology, Crime and Law* 14:85–106. doi:10.1080/10683160701483104

Bonta J and RK Hanson. 1994. *Gauging the Risk for Violence: Measurement, Impact and Strategies for Change*. (User Report No. 1994-09). Ottawa, ON: Department of the Solicitor General of Canada.

Bonta J and S Wormith. 2007. Risk and need assessment. In *Developments in Social Work with Offenders*, edited by G McIvor and P Raynor, London and Philadelphia: Jessica Kingsley, 131–152.

Eher R, A Matthes, F Schilling, T Haubner-MacLean, and M Rettenberger. 2012. Dynamic risk assessment in sexual offenders using STABLE-2000 and the STABLE-2007. An investigation of predictive and incremental validity. *Sexual Abuse: A Journal of Research and Treatment* 24:5–28. doi:10.1177/1079063211403164

Eher R, M Rettenberger, K Gaunersdorfer, T Haubner-MacLean, A Matthes, F Schilling, and A Mokros. 2013. Über die Treffsicherheit standardisierter Risikoeinschätzungsverfahren bei aus der Maßregel entlassenen Sexualstraftätern [About the accuracy of standardized risk assessment procedures for the evaluation of discharged sex offenders]. *Forensische Psychiatrie, Psychologie, Kriminologie* 7:264–272. doi:10.1007/s11757–013-0212-9

Eher R, F Schilling, T Haubner-MacLean, Tanja Jahn, and M Rettenberger. 2012. Ermittlung des relativen und absoluten Rückfallrisikos mithilfe des Static-99 in einer deutschsprachigen Population entlassener Sexualstraftäter. *Forensische Psychiatrie, Psychologie, Kriminologie* 6:32–40.

Fernandez Y. 2008. An examination of the inter-rater reliability of the STATIC-99 and STABLE-2007. Poster presentation at the 27th Annual Research and Treatment Conference of the Association for the Treatment of Sexual Abusers, Atlanta, GA.

Fernandez Y, AJR Harris, RK Hanson, and J Sparks. 2012. STABLE-2007 coding manual—Revised 2012. Unpublished report. Ottawa, ON: Public Safety Canada.

Grubin D. 1998. *Sex Offending Against Children: Understanding the Risk. Police Research Series Paper 99*. London: Home Office.

Haag AM. 2005. Do psychological interventions impact on actuarial measures: An analysis of the predictive validity of the Static-99 and Static-2002 on a re-conviction measure of sexual recidivism. Unpublished doctoral dissertation. Department of Applied Psychology, University of Calgary, Calgary, Alberta.

Hanson RK. 2002. Introduction to the special section on dynamic risk assessment with sex offenders. *Sexual Abuse: A Journal of Research and Treatment* 14:99–101.

Hanson RK and M Bussiere. 1998. Predicting relapse: A meta-analysis of sexual offender recidivism studies. *Journal of Consulting and Clinical Psychology* 66:348–362. doi:10.1037/0022–006X.66.2.348

Hanson RK and A Harris. 1998. *Dynamic Predictors of Sexual Recidivism. Corrections Research*. Ottawa, ON: Department of the Solicitor General Canada.

Hanson RK and AJR Harris. 2000. *The Sex Offender Need Assessment Rating (SONAR): A Method for Measuring Change in Risk Levels*. User Report No. 2000–1. Ottawa, ON: Department of the Solicitor General of Canada.

Hanson RK and AJR Harris. 2004. *STABLE-2000/ACUTE-2000: Scoring Manuals for the Dynamic Supervision Project. Unpublished Scoring Manuals*. Ottawa, ON: Corrections Research, Public Safety Canada.

Hanson RK, AJR Harris, T-L Scott, and L Helmus. 2007. *Assessing the Risk of Sexual Offenders on Community Supervision: The Dynamic Supervision Project*. Ottawa, ON: Department of the Solicitor General of Canada.

Hanson RK, L Helmus, and D Thornton. 2010. Predicting recidivism among sexual offenders: A multi-site study of STATIC-2002. *Law and Human Behavior* 34:198–211. doi:10.1007/s10979-009-9180-1

Hanson RK, A Lunetta, A Phenix, J Neeley, and D Epperson. 2014. The field validity of Static-99/R sex offender risk assessment tool in California. *Journal of Threat Assessment and Management* 1:102–117. doi:10.1037/tam0000014

Hanson RK and K Morton-Bourgon. 2005. The characteristics of persistent sexual offenders: A meta-analysis of recidivism studies. *Journal of Consulting and Clinical Psychology* 73:1154–1163. doi:10.1037/0022-006X.73.6.1154

Hanson RK and KE Morton-Bourgon. 2009. The accuracy of recidivism risk assessments for sexual offenders: A meta-analysis of 118 prediction studies. *Psychological Assessment* 21:1–21. doi:10.1037/a0014421

Hanson RK, A Phenix, and L Helmus. 2009. *Static-99 and Static-2002: How to Interpret and Report Scores in Light of Recent Research*. Workshop presented at the ATSA 28th Annual Research and Treatment Conference on September 30, Dallas, TX.

Hanson RK and D Thornton. 2000. Improving risk assessments for sex offenders: A comparison of three actuarial scales. *Law and Human Behavior* 24:119–136. doi:10.1023/A:1005482921333

Hanson RK and D Thornton. 2003. *Notes on the Development of Static-2002. User Report 2003–01*. Ottawa, ON: Department of the Solicitor General of Canada.

Hanson RK and D Thornton. 2012, October. Preselection effects can explain group differences in sexual recidivism base rates in Static-99R validation studies. Paper presented at the 31st Annual Research and Treatment Conference of the Association for the Treatment of Sexual Abusers, Denver, CO.

Hare RD. 2003. *Manual for the Revised Psychopathy Checklist*, 2nd edition. Toronto, ON, Canada: Multi-Health Systems.

Helmus L. 2009. *Renorming STATIC-99 Recidivism Estimates: Exploring Base Rate Variability Across Sex Offender Samples* (Unpublished master's thesis). Carleton University, Ottawa, ON, Canada.

Helmus L, RK Hanson, D Thornton, KM Babchishin, and AJR Harris, 2012a. Absolute recidivism rates predicted by Static-99R and Static-2002R sex offender risk assessment tools vary across samples: A meta-analysis. *Criminal Justice and Behavior* 39:1148–1171. doi:10.1177/0093854812443648

Helmus L, D Thornton, RK Hanson, and KM Babchishin. 2012b. Improving the predictive accuracy of Static-99 and Static-2002 with older sex offenders: Revised age weights. *Sexual Abuse: A Journal of Research and Treatment* 24:64–101. doi:10.1177/1079063211409951

Janus ES and RA Prentky. 2003. Forensic use of actuarial risk assessment with sex offenders: Accuracy, admissibility and accountability. *American Criminal Law Review* 40:1443–1499.

Knight RA and D Thornton. 2007. Evaluating and improving risk assessment schemes for sexual recidivism: A long-term follow-up of convicted sexual offenders. Unpublished report to the U.S. Department of Justice, Washington, DC.

Langton CM, HE Barbaree, MC Seto, EJ Peacock, L Harkins, and KT Hansen. 2007. Actuarial assessment of risk for re-offense among adult sex offenders. *Criminal Justice and Behavior* 34:37–59. doi:10.1177/0093854806291157

Lehmann RJB, RK Hanson, KM Babchishin, F Gallasch-Nemitz, J Biedermann, and K-P Dahle. 2013. Interpreting multiple risk scales for sex offenders: Evidence for averaging. *Psychological Assessment* 25:1019–1024. doi:10.1037/a0033098

Mann RE, RK Hanson, and D Thornton. 2010. Assessing risk for sexual recidivism: Some proposals on the nature of psychologically meaningful risk factors. *Sexual Abuse: A Journal of Research and Treatment* 22:191–217. doi:10.1177/1079063210366039

McGrath RJ, MP Lasher, and GF Cumming. 2012. The sex offender treatment intervention and progress scale (SOTIPS): Psychometric properties and incremental predictive validity with Static-99R. *Sexual Abuse: A Journal of Research and Treatment* 24:431–458. doi:10.1177/1079063211432475

Monahan J. 2007. Clinical and actuarials predictions of violence. In *Modern Scientific Evidence. The Law and Science of Expert Testimony*, edited by D Faigman, D Kaye, M Saks, and J Sanders, St. Paul, MN: West, 122–147.

Olver ME, SCP Wong, T Nicholaichuk, and A Gordon. 2007. The validity and reliability of the violence risk scale—Sexual offender version: Assessing sex offender risk and evaluating therapeutic change. *Psychological Assessment* 19:318–329. doi:10.1037/1040-3590.19.3.318

Phenix A, L Helmus, and RK Hanson. 2012. *Static-99R and Static-2002R Evaluators' Workbook*. http://static99.org, accessed July 28, 2016.

Poole D, D Liedecke, and M Marbibi. 2000. *Risk Assessment and Recidivism in Juvenile Sexual Offenders: A Validation Study of Static-99*. Austin, TX: Texas Youth Commission.

Quinsey VL, TH Grant, ME Rice, and C Cormier. 2006. Violence Risk Appraisal Guide (VRAG). In *Violent Offenders: Appraising and Managing Risk*, 2nd edition. The Law and Public Policy, edited by VL Quinsey et al. Washington, DC: American Psychological Association.

Seto MC. 2005. Is more better? Combining actuarial risk scales to predict recidivism among adult sex offenders. *Psychological Assessment* 17:156–167. doi:10.1037/1040-3590.17.2.156

Smallbone S and M Rallings. 2013. Short-term predictive validity of the Static-99 and Static-99-R for indigenous and nonindigenous Australian sexual offenders. *Sexual Abuse: A Journal of Research and Treatment* 3:302–316. doi:10.1177/1079063212472937

Thornton D. 2002. Constructing and testing a framework for dynamic risk assessment. *Sexual Abuse: A Journal of Research and Treatment* 14:137–151. doi:10.1077/107906320201400205

Thornton D and RA Knight. 2013. Construction and validation of the SRA-FV Need Assessment. *Sexual Abuse: A Journal of Research and Treatment*. Published online December 30, 2013. doi:10.1177/1079063213511120

Tully RJ, S Chou, and KD Browne. 2013. A systematic review on the effectiveness of sex offender risk assessment tools in predicting sexual recidivism of adult male sex offenders. *Clinical Psychology Review* 33:287–316. doi:10.1016/j.cpr.2012.12.002

Varela JG., M Boccaccini, D Murrie, J Caperton, and E Gonzalez, Jr. 2013. Do the Static-99 and Static-99R perform similarly for Black, White, and Latino sex offenders? *International Journal of Forensic Mental Health* 12:231–243. doi:10.1080/14999013.2013.846950

Wong SCP and AE Gordon. 2006. The validity and reliability of the violence risk scale: A treatment-friendly violence risk assessment tool. *Psychology, Public Policy, and Law* 12:279–309. doi:10.1037/1076-8971.12.3.279

71

Structured approaches to assessing malingering

MICHAEL J. VITACCO AND HOLLY E. TABERNIK

INTRODUCTION

The consideration and evaluation of malingering is one of the cornerstones of forensic evaluations. Rendering an accurate opinion and appropriately evaluating the examinee often require an investigation into the possibility the examinee is feigning a disability or deficit for the purposes of gaining an external inducement. The *Diagnostic and Statistical Manual of Mental Disorders*, 5th edition (*DSM-5*; American Psychiatric Association [APA] 2013) defines malingering as the "intentional production of false or grossly exaggerated physical or psychological symptoms, motivated by external incentives such as avoiding military duty, avoiding work, obtaining financial compensation, evading criminal prosecution, or obtaining drugs" (p. 726). The *DSM-5* acknowledges that malingering may be viewed as adaptive in certain circumstances. Beyond a clinical diagnosis used to describe behavior, some jurisdictions and courts consider malingering to be a criminal behavior. For example, the Uniform Code of Military Justice (UCMJ) Article 115 indicates any person malingering for the purpose of avoiding work, duty, or service can be subject to a court martial. In *United States v. Greer* (1998) the Fifth Circuit Court of Appeals held it was constitutional to enhance Mr. Greer's sentence due to obstruction of justice after it was concluded he was continually malingering in an attempt to avoid trial (see Knoll and Resnick 1999). It should be pointed out that Mr. Greer was provided an abundance of opportunities to modify his behavior before "earning" his sentence enhancement.

As this background demonstrates, the accurate assessment of malingering-related response styles is critical. False positives can result in individuals with bona fide mental illnesses proceeding to trial before they receive appropriate mental health treatment. Additionally, false positives can and often do result in bona fide mental health symptoms continuing unabated due to clinicians' reticence to treat symptoms viewed as potentially fabricated. False negatives result in the unnecessary allocation of scarce mental health resources to individuals more interested in avoiding trial or improperly gaining financial compensation, who may not be in need of the treatment provided. Given the ramifications associated with a diagnosis of malingering, its accurate assessment is of paramount importance to ensure just legal findings across judicial proceedings. To that end, forensic mental health professionals have an ethical responsibility to rely on the most reliable and valid methodologies available in order to provide accurate information to the trier of fact.

One such methodology is clinical judgment, whereby clinicians rely on their experience, which can be extensive, in evaluating the veracity of an evaluee's self-report. Bell and Mellor (2009) described several errors accompanying clinical judgment, including misuse of heuristics, potential clinician biases, limitations of information processing, and overemphasis of data obtained during clinical interviews. Unfortunately, clinicians relying on such impressionistic data are prone to committing more errors, regardless of the referral question or the scientific domain. As presented by Dawes, Faust, and Meehl (1989) actuarial methods are superior to clinical judgment. Thus, it should come as no surprise that, when it comes to accuracy, actuarial methodologies yield Cohen's *ds*, a measure of differences between two means, approximately 0.12 higher than decisions based strictly on clinical judgment (Spengler 2013). We believe that given the evidence outlining the strength of instrumentation over clinical judgment in clinical sciences, forensic mental health practitioners should rely on empirically based instruments when considering feigning/malingering.

The use of structured instruments provides another advantage for mental health practitioners. The *Frye* standard relies on determining whether a technique has gained "general acceptance" in the field, which is often predicated on peer review publication. The *Daubert* standard is more sophisticated in its approach to evidentiary admissibility, and provides four prongs. Those prongs include (a) determining whether the theory or methodology is testable and falsifiable, (b) if the technique has been subject to peer review and has achieved some indicia of general acceptance, (c) the known or potential error rate of the test or methodology, and (d) the existence and/or maintenance of standards concerning the test or methodology. Even a cursory review of evidentiary admissibility underscores the legal problem when relying on clinical judgment in determining feigning. Clinical judgment is highly susceptible to *Frye (Frye v. United States* 1923) or *Daubert* (*Daubert v. Merrell* Dow Pharmaceuticals 1993) challenges and clinicians' methodology should be vigorously questioned in court.

The purpose of this chapter is to encourage clinicians to relinquish reliance on clinical judgment when evaluating malingering in an effort to improve accuracy, validity, and defensibility of their diagnoses. In the first part of the chapter we present a comprehensive analysis on how to accurately assess malingering and related-response styles. The second half of the chapter focuses on the strengths and limitations of various structured clinical instruments designed to detect feigning. The chapter concludes with an approach to assessing malingering that relies on multi-methods and review of several data sources.

DSM-5, MALINGERING, AND BEYOND

Clinicians diagnosing malingering rely on the *DSM-5* (APA 2013) suggestions for when to consider malingering. Unfortunately, the newest addition of the manual failed to incorporate relevant research, leaving the same criteria from the last several editions. This limitation is noteworthy given the 80% false positives associated with the *DSM* criteria (Rogers and Vitacco 2002). Even if the *DSM-5* criteria were simply used as a screening tool designed to cue the clinician when a more extensive evaluation was required, this level of error is unacceptable. In the *DSM-5*, three of the four criteria provide no actual information that adds to understanding malingering. For instance, the mere fact that a medicolegal evaluation (i.e., forensic evaluations, disability evaluations) is occurring is not indicative of malingering. A second criterion is the presence of antisocial personality disorder. In criminal forensic work, many individuals we evaluate have lengthy legal histories and warrant this diagnosis. Yet, the proposed relationship between antisocial personality disorder or psychopathy and malingering has not been supported in multiple studies (cf., Gacono et al. 1995; Poythress et al. 2001; Kucharski et al. 2006). Rogers (1990) perceptively noted that the *DSM* criteria for malingering overrelied on criminogenic factors. A third criterion is lack of cooperation with the evaluation procedures. Individuals are uncooperative for multiple reasons, many unrelated to malingering. As seen by a simple analysis, the *DSM* indicators of malingering are ineffectual and provide the clinician meager guidance to understanding the construct.

The final criterion, "Discrepancy between claimed disability and objective findings" may prove useful in diagnosing malingering. The fact that the criteria for when to consider malingering have not fundamentally changed, even though there have been multiple revisions of the *DSM*, represents a failure to integrate relevant empirical strategies proven effective at detecting malingering. Instead of relying solely on the *DSM* to identify malingering, Rogers (1990) proposed empirical criteria for evaluating malingering. These criteria include (a) a pattern of self-reported symptoms that include an unusually high number of rare, blatant, preposterous, or absurd symptoms, or nonselective endorsement of any symptoms in a high number; (b) contrary evidence in the form of collateral interviews (e.g., interviews with an individual who knows the defendant and provides contrary evidence to their presentation), differences in current presentation, and past documentation of presentation, or strong evidence from psychological testing; and (c) evidence that spurious presentation was not merely attention-seeking behavior.

A SYSTEMATIC APPROACH TO ASSESSING MALINGERING: SIX RECOMMENDATIONS

This chapter presents evidence for the inclusion of specific malingering instruments and scales when assessing an examinee's response style. Clinicians should rely on a standard methodology. This type of structured approach to the evaluation provides a manner to safeguard against diagnostic errors that are common in forensic evaluations. Such errors in forensic evaluations include the following:

1. Overreliance on one type of data when formulating a clinical opinion during a forensic evaluation. In our own clinical work, we have frequently encountered forensic reports where the entire clinical opinion was buttressed by the defendant's version of events. This is not to say the defendant's self-report should be ignored. To the contrary, the defendant's self-report and abilities are critical to developing one's opinion; however, this self-report should be evaluated against independent collateral information and observations.
2. Underreliance or failure to use psychological testing, by default, leads to reliance on clinical judgment. Reid (2000) strongly cautioned against using a general clinical interview to detect and report malingering. Reid stated, "Some psychiatrists and psychologists believe that a good interview and sensitive clinician can see through malingering most of the time. That's just not true" (p. 226). As a field, forensic psychology and psychiatry should be opposed to strict reliance on clinical judgment due to its inaccuracy and tendency to lead to idiosyncratic judgments. When ruling out or ruling in malingering, clinicians are advised in the strongest terms to employ empirically based strategies, like those found in structured instruments designed for detecting feigning.
3. Using psychological testing in the absence of collateral information leads to errors in the accurate assessment of malingering. Psychological testing is frequently employed in evaluations of response style, but there are at least two instances where mistakes could be made on

the basis of psychological testing. The first would be to automatically discount malingering when psychological testing is negative for malingering. Savvy evaluees may have studied psychological testing or have been coached by unethical attorneys on how to avoid being detected. The converse is also true in that results consistent with feigning are not dispositive of malingering. Clinicians must consider alternative explanations for positive results on malingering testing. Even if the clinician ultimately concludes his or her examinee is feigning, there must be other factors taken into account in addition to psychological testing. For instance, the lead author has been involved in several cases where psychological testing was consistent with malingering, but collateral information pointed to a factitious disorder.

4. Clinicians must remain cognizant of potential biases that could lead them away from an impartial finding. The process whereby clinicians ignore, either consciously or unconsciously, information that is contrary to their initial hypothesis is a phenomenon known as confirmatory bias. This process leads clinicians to favor information that supports their initial clinical conceptualizations and ignores divergent information. Either way, not considering all the information related to an evaluee's clinical presentation is antithetical to a fair diagnostic conceptualization. One way to avoid confirmatory biases when evaluating response style is to actively search for evidence supporting the opposing view. We posit that in addition to decreasing the likelihood of inaccuracies, this process also improves credibility as a forensic practitioner.
5. Clinicians often err in their conceptualizations about the rarity or commonality of malingering. Clinicians create unneeded and problematic errors when they undertake forensic evaluations with the idea that "everybody lies." Equally problematic are clinicians who never formally diagnose malingering because they associate malingering with labeling someone as nefarious or a liar. We view both approaches as antithetical to empirical, structured approaches of assessment. Failing to accurately diagnose response style interferes with the aim of presenting accurate and impartial information to the court. Presenting accurate information to the court should be one of the primary goals of the forensic clinician, even if this portrays the client in a less than positive light. Clinicians should be mindful that malingering in forensic criminal cases averages between 15% and 18% (Rogers et al. 1998), although some studies have found slightly higher rates of around 21% (Boccaccini et al. 2006; Vitacco et al. 2007). In civil and correctional settings that rate is often substantially higher.
6. Ignoring explanatory models when conceptualizing malingering may reinforce improper decisions to not diagnose malingering. Clinicians may believe that saying an individual is malingering is equivalent to calling them a "liar." The *DSM* considers malingering to stem from criminological processes, which has clear negative connotations. While some individuals malinger for criminological reasons, others may do so for adaptive reasons. For example, a person may malinger in an attempt to receive mental health medications, move to a quieter unit, avoid a military assignment, or avoid an adverse court finding, including the death penalty. Understanding the underlying reason for malingering may remove the stigma associated with the diagnosis, but it does not abdicate the responsibility of the clinician to provide an accurate diagnosis, even one disadvantageous to the evaluee's case.

INSTRUMENTS USED FOR DETECTING MALINGERED PSYCHOPATHOLOGY

This section focuses on the armamentarium designed to detect malingering. To that end, we focus on several classes of measures. The first are traditional psychological measures designed to assess for psychopathology, which also have specialized scales developed to detect malingering and related response styles. For the purposes of this chapter we focus on the Minnesota Multiphasic Personality Inventory-2 Restructured Form (MMPI-2-RF; Ben-Porath and Tellegen 2008) and the Personality Assessment Inventory (PAI; Morey 2007). In addition, clinicians have an array of specialized measures to detect malingering. In this section our focus is on the Miller Forensic Assessment of Symptoms Test (M-FAST; Miller 2001), the Structured Interview of Reported Symptoms-2nd edition (SIRS/SIRS-2; Rogers 2012), and the Structured Inventory of Malingered Symptomatology (SIMS; Windows and Smith 2005). Finally, we focus on two instruments designed to assess malingering as it specifically relates to competency to proceed to trial examinations: the Inventory of Legal Knowledge (ILK; Otto et al. 2010) and the Atypical Presentation Scales from the Evaluation of Competency to Stand Trial (ATP; Rogers et al. 2004). Table 71.1 provides an overview of each of the reviewed instruments.

Minnesota Multiphasic Personality Inventory-2 Restructured Form

The MMPI-2-RF consists of 338 true/false items designed to assess for psychopathology and several scales designed to evaluate response styles, including malingering. As noted by Rogers and colleagues, "the MMPI-2 RF represents a major departure from the MMPI and MMPI-2 in its development of clinical and validity scales" (Rogers et al. 2011, 355). An earlier meta-analysis of the MMPI-2 demonstrated large to very large effect sizes in detecting malingering with scales incorporating endorsement of rare and infrequent symptoms (Rogers et al. 2003). Similar to the original versions of the MMPI, the response style scales of the MMPI-2-RF are designed to identify evaluees endorsing rare and infrequent symptoms at high levels. Scales for detecting malingering include the following: F-r (infrequent responses),

Table 71.1 Summary of feigning instruments

Instrument	Take home messages
MMPI-2 RF	1. The MMPI-2 RF malingering scales are fairly effective at incorporating empirically based strategies into their scales. 2. Clinicians are on the strongest empirical ground when they rely on the Fp-r and F-r scales in detecting feigned mental disorders. 3. Utilizing high cut-scores on the Fp-r and F-r scales (T > 90) leads to minimized false positives.
PAI	1. The NIM scale appears particularly useful in the classification of malingering. 2. Clinicians should not rely on the results of the RDF due to lack of consistent empirical support. 3. The PAI also can be used as an effective screen for malingering when used in conjunction with comprehensive measures of malingering, like the SIRS-2.
SIRS-2	1. The SIRS-2, like the SIRS, utilizes multiple empirically based detection strategies for detecting feigning. 2. For evaluating the feigning of psychosis or other severe psychopathology the SIRS-2 is the premiere instrument, but there appear to be limitations related to indeterminate classification on the SIRS-2. 3. The SIRS-2 should not be used to assess feigning of cognitive disorders, and there appear to be limitations for assessing individuals with significant trauma histories where there is objective evidence of dissociation.
M-FAST	1. The M-FAST produces large effect sizes in both civil and criminal forensic examinations when using the recommended cut-score. 2. Despite its strong psychometric properties, the M-FAST is designed as a screen. Using the M-FAST for something beyond a screen is antithetical to its intended use. 3. Like the SIRS, the M-FAST encompasses multiple detection strategies that appear to work optimally at distinguishing malingered from bona fide psychotic symptoms and other significant psychopathology.
SIMS	1. The SIMS demonstrated the ability to differentiate individuals with bona fide mental illness from those feigning mental illness. 2. The SIMS has a variety of scales, but the ones designed for cognitive feigning have not been as consistently validated. 3. The SIMS, although designed as a comprehensive measure of malingering, likely works best a screen for malingering.
TOMM	1. The TOMM has been normed with both clinical and experimental populations and has strong psychometric properties in the evaluation of cognitive malingering. 2. A below chance score on the TOMM may be indicative of malingering, but scoring below the recommended 45 cut-score warrants additional evaluation. 3. Given the unacceptable likelihood of false positives with individuals functioning in the moderate or severe range of intellectual disability, clinicians should be especially cautious about using the TOMM in these populations.
VIP	1. The VIP is considered groundbreaking because it contains indices measuring both motivation and effort (Denny 2008). 2. The VIP is particularly useful when an individual is claiming cognitive difficulties in the absence of a history of such deficits. 3. The VIP has not been adequately validated on individuals with legitimate cognitive dysfunction. Similar to the TOMM, we do not recommend use of the VIP with individuals with bona fide histories of moderate or severe intellectual disabilities.

Fp-r (infrequent psychopathology responses), Fs (infrequent somatic responses), FBS-r (symptom validity), RBS (response bias), L-r (uncommon virtue), and K-r (adjustment validity).

Research studies have demonstrated the effectiveness of the MMPI-2-RF response-style scales. In an experimental paradigm, undergraduate students were instructed to feign and their results were compared to patients with legitimate psychopathology. Out of the MMPI-2 RF validity scales, the Fp-r scale was the only style scale to demonstrate discriminant validity and to manifest incremental validity compared to the other RF validity scales (Sellbom and Bagby 2010). Sellbom et al. (2010) evaluated the effectiveness of the RF validity scales in a known-groups design using the Structured Interview of Reported Symptoms (SIRS, Rogers et al. 1992) with 125 forensic patients. The Fp-r and the F-r were most successful at differentiating feigners from non-feigners. These scales rely on the presence of rare symptoms to detect atypical responding. As noted by the authors, the Fp-r and F-r scales appear complementary to each other in the accurate detection of feigned presentations. In another known-groups design, Rogers et al. (2011) analyzed the effectiveness of the RF validity scales in a large sample of individuals ($n = 645$) undergoing disability evaluations. For feigned mental disorders, Fp-r and F-r scales produced very large effect sizes and an extremely low rate of false positives in contrast to individuals with an actual mental disability.

Personality Assessment Inventory

The PAI is a 344-item instrument that is designed to assess general psychopathology. As with the MMPI, the PAI has several scales designed for detecting malingering, including CDF (Cashel's Discriminant Function), NIM (Negative Impression Management), MAL (Malingering Index), and RDF (Rogers Discriminant Function). Additionally, Gaines et al. (2013) developed the MFI (Multiscale Feigning Index) for the PAI. As described by the scale name, this index relies on detecting feigning by considering elevations on several PAI scales. Although the MFI demonstrated good results compared to the SIRS, without cross-validation, clinicians are advised to rely on empirically supported indices of feigning that have undergone extensive cross-validation.

With regard to malingering, the PAI does not have the comprehensive research base as does the MMPI; however, a 2009 meta-analysis completed by Hawes and Boccaccini (2009) reported high effect sizes for malingering scales on the PAI showing differences between individuals classified as malingering compared to individuals' feigning psychopathology. Boccaccini, Murrie, and Duncan (2006) reviewed the ability of the PAI (and MMPI-2) to act as screens for malingering in 166 males undergoing pretrial forensic evaluations under the federal system. Using various cut scores, the authors found the NIM scale possessed the greatest level of accuracy for evaluating malingering; however, the RDF scale performed poorly. In a 2007 study, Hopwood et al. (2007) evaluated the ability of the PAI to detect feigning specific disorders. The NIM scale was effective across diagnostic classifications at ascertaining malingering.

Structured Interview of Reported Symptoms

The SIRS/SIRS-2 (see Rogers et al. 1992, 2010) is a structured clinical interview consisting of 172 items yielding eight primary scales. The eight scales encompass a variety of empirical strategies for detecting feigned presentation. These strategies consist of evaluating for the presence of rare symptoms, combinations of symptoms that do not go together, absurd symptoms, extremely high severity of symptoms, reporting symptoms across multiple diagnostic categories, differences in reported versus observed symptoms, presence of blatant symptoms, and presence of subtle symptoms. Since its publication in 2002, the SIRS has been cited as the most valid and used measure for evaluating feigning (Lally 2003; Archer et al. 2006). Specifically, the SIRS has demonstrated a high level of effectiveness with adolescent (Rogers et al. 1996) and adult offenders (Kucharski and Duncan 2006; Edens et al. 2007), as well as mental health patients (Edens et al. 2007; Vitacco et al. 2007).

The SIRS-2 was developed with the same basic structure as the SIRS, but with added steps to protect against false positives. The reader is advised to refer to the SIRS-2 manual for specifics on the newly developed steps. Yet, these changes have been met with criticism. Two reviews in the Open Access Journal of Forensic Psychology have been critical of the SIRS-2, while still touting some of its psychometric properties (Rubenzer 2010; DeClue 2011). Rubenzer (2010) indicated "the SIRS-2 is a strong choice for assessing feigned psychosis and severe psychopathology" (p. 273). Rubenzer discusses the use of the SIRS-2 for feigning cognitive impairment or somatic complaints, concluding with the recommendation that no single test, including the SIRS-2, should be relied on as a "gold standard." DeClue (2011) reported on potential legal admissibility issues with the SIRS-2, and expressed concern that the raw data from the SIRS-2 were not readily accessible. We concur with the warning proffered by Green et al. (2013), "The limited settings in which the SIRS-2 has been validated, coupled with differences between sensitivity rates observed in the current study versus those published in the manual, raises concerns for both the reliability and validity of the SIRS-2 scoring algorithms" (p. 216). As a final note, the SIRS-2 manual advises against using the instrument with individuals with substantial trauma histories who are actively dissociating.

Miller Forensic Assessment of Symptoms Test

The M-FAST is a structured clinical interview that consists of 25 items that load on seven scales. However, three scales are composed of a single item. Similar to the structure of the SIRS-2, the M-FAST relies on multiple, empirically based detection strategies. These strategies include atypical symptoms, unusual symptom combinations, unusual hallucinations, unusual symptom course, overly negative self-image, susceptibility to endorsing unusual symptoms, and differences in reported versus observed symptoms. However, the M-FAST was designed to be used as a screening tool to identify individuals in need of a more comprehensive evaluation of response styles. As such, when looking at the psychometric properties of screening instruments like the M-FAST, false positives are not only more acceptable, they are expected. In screening instruments, false negatives are much more problematic. If the individual's score does not reach the cut-score on the screen, they are generally ruled out from further assessment and malingering may go undetected. For this reason, most screening tools are designed to minimize false negatives.

The M-FAST appears most adept at detecting the presence of overt feigning (Vitacco et al. 2008). As a screen, the M-FAST has evidenced strong discriminant validity in both civil and forensic evaluations (Guy and Miller 2004; Veazey et al. 2005; Alwes et al. 2008). In a known groups design with pretrial forensic patients, using the SIRS as the classification standard, the M-FAST produced a strong alpha coefficient (how the items are related to one another) for the total sample and very large effect size between the nonmalingering and malingering groups (Cohen's $d = 2.69$). Using the recommended cut score of 6, the M-FAST produced perfect sensitivity and negative predictive power (Vitacco et al. 2007). Similar results were found for the M-FAST with 308 individuals undergoing evaluation for workers' compensation or disability (Cohen's $d = 3.0$; Alwes et al. 2008).

Structured Inventory of Malingered Symptomatology

The SIMS is a 75-item self-report test designed to evaluate feigning across five diagnostic domains. These domains include Low Intelligence (LI), Affective Disorders (Af), Neurological Impairment (N), Psychosis (P), and Amnesia (Am). Based on the manual, a total score of greater than 14 is suggestive of feigning, and produced an overall correct classification rate of 94.96%. It is important to note the final SIMS sample "was empirically validated at four different universities and community colleges in an analogue simulation study" (p. 12), but the validation samples lacked individuals undergoing forensic evaluations. As such, external validity is lacking due to the use of simulation designs.

The authors of the SIMS primarily relied on nonclinical samples in its initial validation, but several subsequent studies (Lewis et al. 2002; Vitacco et al. 2007; Alwes et al. 2008) have tested the efficacy of the SIMS with clinical populations. In a sample of 64 men undergoing pretrial forensic evaluations, Lewis et al. (2002) used the MMPI-2 and the SIMS as screening tools to assess for feigning. Effect sizes for all SIMS scales ranged from large to very large (*Cohen's ds* ranging from 1.1 to 3.0) between honest responders and feigners. Likewise, Vitacco and colleagues (2007) found very large effect sizes between the nonmalingering and feigning groups (Cohen's d ranging from 1.51 to 3.07), but the recommended cut score produced a moderate hit rate (0.72). Additionally, if employed as a screening tool, the SIMS produced strong results with excellent negative predictive power.

Competency-specific malingering instruments

In addition to the broad measures of malingered psychopathology, the Inventory of Legal Knowledge (ILK; Otto et al. 2010) and the Atypical Presentation Scales of the Evaluation of Competency to Stand Trial-Revised (ATP; Rogers et al. 2004) are both designed to detect competency-specific feigning.

The ILK is a 61-item instrument designed "to assist forensic examiners in the assessment of response styles of defendants undergoing evaluations of adjudicative competence" (Otto et al. 2010, 7). The ILK has demonstrated moderate correlations with other measures of malingering (Otto et al. 2011) and evidenced good discrimination in both college students and mental health populations instructed to feign (Guenther and Otto 2010). Yet, there have been concerns about the efficaciousness of the recommended cut-scores (Gottfried and Carbonell 2014a,b), which may be resultant from the relatively high rates of feigning (47%) in the validation sample (p. 19). Based on extant research the ILK has potential as a screening tool in competency to proceed to trial evaluations; however, only scores significantly lower than chance demonstrate feigning. Further research is needed to clarify cut scores on the ILK and test their ability to evaluate feigning.

The ATP scales of the Evaluation of Competency to Stand Trial-Revised (ECST-R, Rogers et al. 2004) are administered to assess for feigned presentation during competency to proceed to trial evaluations. The ATP consists of 28 items specifically crafted to assess for competency-specific impairment. The 28 items load onto three scales (Rational, Psychotic, and Nonpsychotic). In addition there is an Impairment scale and a scale named Both (sum of Psychotic and Nonpsychotic). The items are scored on a three-point scale (no, sometimes, and yes), except for the Impairment Scale, which is scored categorically (no or yes). Two additional scales are created by summing two of the aforementioned scales. For the sake of malingering, the Rational scale is not included, as these are items that represent legitimate concerns shared by most defendants. Two studies have demonstrated the effectiveness of the ATP scales to detect feigning. In a known-groups design (Vitacco et al. 2007), the ATP scales demonstrated very large effect sizes differentiating malingerers from nonmalingerers. In research using both simulation and actual competency cases, Rogers et al. (2004) reported the scales yielded large effect sizes for malingering in both simulation (Cohen's $d = 2.50$) and actual forensic (Cohen's $d = 1.83$) samples.

DETECTING MALINGERED COGNITIVE DEFICITS

In addition to feigning severe psychopathology in order to achieve a desired outcome, forensic mental health practitioners should be aware of the potential for individuals to feign memory or cognitive deficits. For example, individuals who have been charged with serious offenses may feign a head injury, asserting memory deficits that lead to an inability to recall critical aspects of their case. However, even in cases where an individual has actual amnesia, it is not enough to render them not competent to proceed to trial. As noted in *United States v. Wilson* (1966) and *United States v. Andrews* (2006) memory loss needs to be evaluated on a case-by-case basis, and the mere presence of amnesia is not an automatic bar to competency. Nonetheless, the stakes can be extremely high when considering intellectual deficits. For example, a diagnosis of Intellectual Disorder is a barrier to the death penalty (see *Atkins v. Virginia* 2002). Considering response styles in these assessments is critical to support the veracity of the clinician's opinion and reported test findings.

Mental health practitioners have a wide variety of measures at their disposal to evaluate cognitive malingering. In a survey of 188 neuropsychologists, the Test of Memory

Malingering (TOMM; Tombaugh 1996), MMPI-2, Rey 15-item test (Rey 1964), and the California Verbal Learning Test (Delis et al. 2000) were most frequently used to detect malingering; however, the TOMM, Validity Indicator Profile (VIP; Frederick 2003), Victoria Symptom Validity Test (Slick et al. 1997), Word Memory Test (Green 2006), and Computerized Assessment of Response Bias (Allen et al. 2002) were rated as most accurate.

Psychologists using structured approaches for detecting feigned cognitive impairment are encouraged to be aware of the Slick criteria. The Slick criteria consist of a set of criteria clinicians can rely on when making informed decisions on cognitive malingering (Slick et al. 1999). The criteria are relatively straightforward and are as follows: Criterion A: one identifiable, substantial external incentive; Criterion B: evidence from test data; and Criterion C: evidence from self-report. Finally, as a rule out, it is important that the behavior not be fully accounted for by psychological, neurological, or developmental factors.

In considering detection strategies for cognitive malingering, Rogers et al. (1993) set forth some strategies that can be integrated into empirically based measures of this type of malingering, including the following:

- Floor effect is a strategy where individuals who are feigning cognitive deficits miss even the most basic of questions, for instance, an individual with a high school diploma and no history of head injury who indicates he or she is unable to sum one plus one. The floor effect strategy is incorporated in several instruments designed to detect cognitive feigning. These instruments include the Rey 15-item test and the Test of Memory Malingering (TOMM; Tombaugh 1996), and the Hiscock Digit Memory Test (Hiscock and Hiscock 1989).
- Symptom validity testing specifically relies on below-chance levels of responding. This is a strong approach to detecting malingering because an individual who achieves a score significantly below chance has a very strong probability of feigning intellectual impairment. It should be pointed out that below-chance scoring on multiple choice items is highly unusual, as even unsophisticated feigners typically perform at better than chance.
- Forced-choice testing is a broad term that typically refers to achieving less than expected results when having to pick the correct choice from two options. This technique can also be incorporated into both symptom validity testing and floor effect strategies. Forced-choice testing evaluates an individual's performance against individuals with neurocognitive deficits with little motivation to feign (Berry and Schipper 2008). This approach can identify "probable" feigners who require a more in-depth evaluation of their response style.
- Magnitude of error refers to evaluating incorrect responses against what are considered typical responses. Magnitude of error responses refer to atypical and unusual responses, generally not given by individuals with bona fide cognitive disorders. Individuals suspected of feigning are much more likely to select a response with a low probability of occurring as compared to individuals with true impairment (Martin et al. 1998).
- Performance curve is a strategy focusing on which items on a measure are failed. Individuals who are feigning often will routinely miss easy questions, while answering more difficult questions correctly. This strategy is employed in the Validity Indicator Profile (VIP; Frederick 2003), discussed below.

Instruments used to detect cognitive malingering

This section reviews two of the most widely used instruments in the evaluation of cognitive and memory malingering. Given the relatively large number of instruments commercially available (Sweet and King 2002), we focus on two of the most used and validated: the Test of Memory Malingering (TOMM) and the Validity Indicator Profile (VIP).

According to the manual, the "TOMM is a 50-item recognition test for adults that includes two learning trials and a retention trial" (Tombaugh 1996, 1). The individual is shown 50 line drawings, and then presented with 50 cards with two line drawings on each card. The individual is simply asked to pick which of the two drawings he or she saw previously. The TOMM has several strengths; one of the primary strengths of the TOMM is that it is sensitive to malingering; the TOMM, however, is relatively insensitive to neurological and cognitive impairments. Any score below chance is indicative of malingering and a score of lower than 45 on Trial 2 or the retention trial indicates possible malingering. There have been concerns raised about the TOMM's classification of individuals with intellectual disabilities, although the results have been conflicting. The professional manual of the TOMM (see also Simon 2007) reported individuals with lower intellectual functioning score generally above the recommended 45 cut-score; however, Shandera et al. (2010) found individuals with more severe forms of cognitive dysfunction (e.g., moderate mental retardation) scored below the cut-score, and thus would be falsely categorized as malingering. As such, clinicians should be extremely cautious regarding using the TOMM with individuals manifesting moderate to severe intellectual disabilities until subsequent research can provide a more solid foundation for using the TOMM with this unique population.

The VIP is a paper and pencil test designed to detect cognitive malingering. The VIP evaluates consistency of responding as well as overall effort. Invalid profiles fall into one of three categories: (a) poor effort or carelessness, (b) random responding, or (c) malingering, high effort to appear impaired. Consistent with many intellectual tests, the VIP contains both a Verbal and Nonverbal subtest, so effort can be evaluated across both areas. The validation sample consisted of 944 nonclinical participants and

104 adults undergoing neuropsychological evaluation. The cross-validation sample consisted of 152 nonclinical participants, 61 brain-injured adults, 49 individuals considered to be at risk for malingering, and 100 randomly generated VIP protocols (see Frederick et al. 2000). The overall classification accuracy for the nonverbal test was 79.8%, with 73.5% sensitivity and 85.7% specificity. The verbal subtest of the VIP was similar, with an overall classification rate of 75.5%, 67.3% sensitivity, and a specificity rate of 83.1%.

SUMMARY

Structured approaches to evaluating malingering provide significant advantages over clinical judgment. The primary goal of this chapter was to present a structured methodology for appropriately evaluating malingering that goes significantly beyond the basic *DSM* criteria. Moreover, structured approaches to malingering require more than the administration of a malingering test (or several). A structured approach to the evaluation of malingering consists of (a) a close review of records in order to assess previous functioning and make analytic comparisons to current functioning, (b) an evaluation of the veracity of self-report in combination with observations and a review of records, and (c) use of psychological testing to make empirically based comparisons to normative groups. By taking the time to complete this structured step-by-step approach, clinicians place themselves in good position to make accurate statements regarding response style. In addition, by using structured approaches, clinicians are likely to be viewed as more credible when discussing their findings with the trier of fact.

SUMMARY KEY POINTS

- Clinical judgment in the determination of malingering is outdated and results in errors.
- An individual who is malingering may also have a mental illness; careful, structured approaches consider both.
- Forensic examiners should not place too much weight on one data point and instead consider an array of factors when evaluating response styles, like malingering.
- Considering explanatory models of malingering allows the clinician to understand the individual's motive for feigning.
- The evaluation of malingering should remain a cornerstone of forensic evaluations.

REFERENCES

Allen LI, GL Iverson, and P Green. 2002. Computerized Assessment of Response Bias in forensic neuropsychology. *Journal of Forensic Neuropsychology* 3:205-225. doi:10.1300/J151v03n01_02

Alwes YR, JA Clark, DR Berry, and RP Granacher. 2008. Screening for feigning in a civil forensic setting. *Journal of Clinical and Experimental Neuropsychology* 30(2):1–8. doi:10.1080/13803390701260363

American Psychiatric Association (APA). 2013. *Diagnostic and Statistical Manual of Mental Disorders,* 5th edition. Washington, DC: American Psychiatric Press.

Archer RP, JK Buffington-Vollum, R Stredny, and R Handel. 2006. A survey of psychological test use patterns among forensic psychologists. *Journal of Personality Assessment* 87(1):84–94. doi:10.1207/s15327752jpa8701_07

Atkins v. Virginia, 536 U.S. 304 (2002).

Bell I and D Mellor 2009. Clinical judgments: Research and practice. *Australian Psychologist*, 44(2):112–121. doi:10.1080/00050060802550023

Ben-Porath YS and A Tellegen. 2008. Empirical correlates of the MMPI-2 Restructured Clinical (RC) scales in mental health, forensic, and nonclinical settings: An introduction. *Journal of Personality Assessment* 90:119–121. doi:10.1080/00223890701845120

Berry DR and LJ Schipper 2008. Assessment of feigned cognitive impairment using standard neuropsychological tests. In *Clinical Assessment of Malingering and Deception,* 3rd edition, edited by R. Rogers, New York: Guilford Press, 237–252.

Boccaccini M, DC Murrie, and SA Duncan. 2006. Screening for malingering in a criminal-forensic sample with the Personality Assessment Inventory. *Psychological Assessment* 18(4):415–423. doi:10.1037/1040-3590.18.4.415

Daubert v. Merrell Dow Pharmaceuticals, 509 U.S. 579 (1993).

Dawes RM, D Faust, and PE Meehl. 1989. Clinical versus actuarial judgment. *Science* 243(4899):1668–1674. doi:10.1126/science.2648573

DeClue G. 2011. Harry Potter and the structured interview of reported symptoms? *Open Access Journal of Forensic Psychology* 3:1–18.

Delis DC, JH Kramer, E Kaplan, and BA Ober. 2000. *The California Verbal Learning Test*? 2nd edition. San Antonio, TX: Psychological Corporation.

Denny RL. 2008. Negative response bias and malingering during neuropsychological assessment in criminal forensic settings. In *Clinical Neuropsychology in the Criminal Forensic Setting*, edited by RL Denney and JP Sullivan, New York: Guilford Press, 91–134.

Edens JF, NG Poythress, and M Watkins-Clay. 2007. Detection of malingering in psychiatric unit and general population prison inmates: A comparison of the PAI, SIMS, and SIRS. *Journal of Personality Assessment* 88(1):33–42. doi:10.1207/s15327752jpa8801_05

Frederick RI. 2003. *Validity Indicator Profile, Professional Manual.* Minneapolis, MN: NCS Pearson.

Frederick RI, RD Crosby, and TF Wynkoop. 2000. Performance curve classification of invalid responding on the Validity Indicator Profile. *Archives of Clinical Neuropsychology* 15(4):281–300. doi:10.1016/S0887-6177(99)00002-5

Frye v. United States, 293 F. 1013 (D.C. Cir. 1923).

Gacono CB, J Meloy, K Sheppard, and E Speth. 1995. A clinical investigation of malingering and psychopathy in hospitalized insanity acquittees. *Bulletin of the American Academy of Psychiatry and the Law* 23(3):387–397.

Gaines MV, CL Giles, and RD Morgan. 2013. The detection of feigning using multiple PAI Scale elevations: A new index. *Assessment* 20(4):437–447. doi:10.1177/1073191112458146

Gottfried E and J Carbonell. 2014a, March. Improving the detection of feigned factual knowledge deficits in defendants adjudicated incompetent to proceed. *Poster Presented at the International Conference of the American Psychology-Law Society (AP-LS)*, New Orleans, LA.

Gottfried E and J Carbonell. 2014b, March. Optimizing the cut-score of the Inventory of Legal Knowledge (ILK) with defendants adjudicated incompetent to proceed. *Poster Presented at the International Conference of the American Psychology-Law Society (AP-LS)*, New Orleans, LA.

Green P. 2006. *The Nonverbal Symptom Validity Test. MS, Windows Computer Program.* Alberta, CA: Green's Publishing.

Green D, B Rosenfeld, and B Belfi. 2013. New and improved? A comparison of the original and revised versions of the Structured Interview of Reported Symptoms. *Assessment* 20(2):210–218. doi:10.1177/1073191112464389

Guenther CC and RK Otto. 2010. Identifying persons feigning limitations in their competence to proceed in the legal process. *Behavioral Sciences and the Law* 28(5):603–613. doi:10.1002/bsl.956

Guy LS, and HA Miller. 2004. Screening for Malingered Psychopathology in a Correctional Setting: Utility of the Miller-Forensic Assessment of Symptoms Test (M-FAST). *Criminal Justice and Behavior* 31(6):695–716. doi:10.1177/0093854804268754

Hawes SW and MT Boccaccini. 2009. Detection of overreporting of psychopathology on the Personality Assessment Inventory: A meta-analytic review. *Psychological Assessment* 21(1):112–124. doi:10.1037/a0015036

Hiscock M and CK Hiscock. 1989. Refining the forced-choice method for the detection of malingering. *Journal of Clinical and Experimental Neuropsychology* 11:967–974.

Hopwood CJ, LC Morey, R Rogers, and K Sewell. 2007. Malingering on the personality assessment inventory: Identification of specific feigned disorders. *Journal of Personality Assessment* 88(1):43–48. doi:10.1207/s15327752jpa8801_06

Knoll JL and PJ Resnick. 1999. *U.S. v. Greer*: Longer sentences for malingerers. *Journal of the American Academy of Psychiatry and the Law* 27:621–625.

Kucharski L and S Duncan. 2006. Clinical and demographic characteristics of criminal defendants potentially misidentified by objective measures of malingering. *American Journal of Forensic Psychology* 24(4):5–20.

Kucharski L, DM Falkenbach, SS Egan, and S Duncan. 2006. Antisocial personality disorder and the malingering of psychiatric disorder: A study of criminal defendants. *International Journal of Forensic Mental Health* 5(2):195–204. doi:10.1080/14999013.2006.1047 1243

Lally SJ. 2003. What tests are acceptable for use in forensic evaluations? A survey of experts. *Professional Psychology: Research and Practice* 34(5):491–498. doi:10.1037/0735-7028.34.5.491

Lewis JL, AM Simcox, and DR Berry. 2002. Screening for feigned psychiatric symptoms in a forensic sample by using the MMPI-2 and the Structured Inventory of Malingered Symptomatology. *Psychological Assessment* 14(2):170–176. doi:10.1037/1040-3590.14.2.170

Martin RC, MD Franzen, and S Orey. 1998. Magnitude of error as a strategy to detect feigned memory impairment. *Clinical Neuropsychologist* 12(1):84–91. doi:10.1076/clin.12.1.84.1722

Miller H. 2001. *Manual for the Miller Forensic Assessment of Symptoms Test.* Odessa, FL: Psychological Assessment Resources.

Morey LC. 2007. *Manual for the Personality Assessment Inventory.* Odessa, FL: Psychological Assessment Resources.

Otto RK, J Musick, and C Sherrod. 2010. *Manual for the Inventory of Legal Knowledge.* Odessa, FL: Psychological Assessment Resources.

Otto RK, JE Musick, and C Sherrod. 2011. Convergent validity of a screening measure designed to identify defendants feigning knowledge deficits related to competence to stand trial. *Assessment* 18(1):60–62. doi:10.1177/1073191110377162

Poythress NG, JF Edens, and M Watkins. 2001. The relationship between psychopathic personality features and malingering symptoms of major mental illness. *Law and Human Behavior* 25(6):567–582. doi:10.1023/A:1012702223004

Reid WL 2000. Malingering: Law and psychiatry. *Journal of Psychiatric Practice*, July: 226–228.

Rey A. 1964. *L'examen clinique en psychologie*. Paris: Presses Universitaires de France.

Rogers R. 1990. Development of a new classificatory model of malingering. *Bulletin of the American Academy of Psychiatry and the Law* 18(3):323–333.

Rogers R, RM Bagby, and SE Dickens. 1992. *Structured Interview of Reported Symptoms, Professional Manual.* Odessa, FL: Psychological Assessment Resources.

Rogers R, ND Gillard, DR Berry, and R Granacher. 2011. Effectiveness of the MMPI-2-RF validity scales for feigned mental disorders and cognitive impairment: A known-groups study. *Journal of Psychopathology and Behavioral Assessment* 33(3):355–367. doi:10.1007/s10862-011-9222-0

Rogers R, EH Harrell, and CD Liff. 1993. Feigning neuropsychological impairment: A critical review of methodological and clinical considerations. *Clinical Psychology Review* 13(3):255–274. doi:10.1016/0272–7358(93)90023-F

Rogers R, JD Hinds, and KW Sewell. 1996. Feigning psychopathology among adolescent offenders: Validation of the SIRS, MMPI-A, and SIMS. *Journal of Personality Assessment* 67(2):244–257. doi:10.1207/s15327752jpa6702_2

Rogers R, RL Jackson, KW Sewell, and KS Harrison. 2004. An examination of the ECST-R as a screen for feigned incompetency to stand trial. *Psychological Assessment* 16(2):139–145. doi:10.1037/1040-3590.16.2.139

Rogers R, RT Salekin, KW Sewell, A Goldstein, and K Leonard. 1998. A comparison of forensic and nonforensic malingerers: A prototypical analysis of explanatory models. *Law and Human Behavior* 22(4):353–367. doi:10.1023/A:1025714808591

Rogers R, KW Sewell, and ND Gillard. 2010. *Structured Interview of Reported Symptoms, Professional Manual*, 2nd edition. Odessa, FL: Psychological Assessment Resources.

Rogers R, KW Sewell, MA Martin, and MJ Vitacco. 2003. Detection of feigned mental disorders: A meta-analysis of the MMPI-2 and malingering. *Assessment* 10(2):160–177. doi:10.1177/1073191103010002007

Rogers R, C Tillbrook, and KW Sewell 2004. *Manual for the Evaluation of Competence to Stand Trial-Revised.* Odessa, FL: Psychological Assessment Resources.

Rogers R and MJ Vitacco. 2002. Forensic assessment of malingering and related response styles. In *Forensic Psychology: From Classroom to Courtroom*, edited by B. Van Dorsten, New York: Kluwer Academic/Plenum, 83–104. doi:10.1007/0-306-47923-0_5

Rubenzer S. 2010. Review of the structured interview of reported symptoms-2 (SIRS-2). *Open Access Journal of Forensic Psychology* 2:273–286.

Sellbom M and R Bagby. 2010. Detection of overreported psychopathology with the MMPI-2 RF form validity scales. *Psychological Assessment* 22(4):757–767. doi:10.1037/a0020825

Sellbom M, JA Toomey, DB Wygant, L Kucharski, and S Duncan. 2010. Utility of the MMPI–2-RF (Restructured Form) validity scales in detecting malingering in a criminal forensic setting: A known-groups design. *Psychological Assessment* 22(1):22–31. doi:10.1037/a0018222

Shandera AL, DR Berry, JA Clark, LJ Schipper, LO Graue, and JP Harp 2010. Detection of malingered mental retardation. *Psychological Assessment* 22(1):50–56. doi:10.1037/a0016585

Simon MJ. 2007. Performance of mentally retarded forensic patients on the Test of Memory Malingering. *Journal of Clinical Psychology* 63(4):339–344. doi:10.1002/jclp.20351

Slick DJ, G Hopp, E Strauss, and GB Thompson. 1997. *California Verbal Learning Test Version 1.0 Professional Manual.* Odessa, FL: Psychological Assessment Resources.

Slick DJ, ES Sherman, and GL Iverson. 1999. Diagnostic criteria for malingered neurocognitive dysfunction: Proposed standards for clinical practice and research. *Clinical Neuropsychologist* 13(4):545–561. doi:10.1076/1385-4046(199911)13:04;1-Y;FT545

Spengler PM. 2013. Clinical versus mechanical prediction. In *Handbook of Psychology, Vol. 10: Assessment psychology*, 2nd edition, edited by JR Graham, JA Naglieri, and IB Weiner, Hoboken, NJ: Wiley, 26–49.

Sweet JJ and JH King. 2002. Category test validity indicators: Overview and practice recommendations. *Journal of Forensic Neuropsychology* 3:241-274. doi:10.1300/J151v03n01_04

Tombaugh TN. 1996. *Professional Manual for the Test of Memory Malingering (TOMM).* Toronto, ON: Multi-health Systems.

Uniform Code of Military Justice, 915, Article 115.

United States v. Andrews, 469 F.3d 1113 (7th Cir. 2006).

United States. v. Greer, 158 F.3d 228 (5th Cir. 1998).

United States Code of Military Justice, Article 115.

Veazey CH, J Hays, AL Wagner, and HA Miller. 2005. Validity of the miller forensic assessment of symptoms test in psychiatric inpatients. *Psychological Reports* 96(3):771–774. doi:10.2466/PR0.96.3.771–774

Vitacco MJ, RL Jackson, R Rogers, CS Neumann, HA Miller, and J Gabel. 2008. Detection strategies for malingering with the Miller Forensic Assessment of Symptoms test: A confirmatory factor analysis of its underlying dimensions. *Assessment* 15(1):97–103. doi:10.1177/1073191107308085

Vitacco MJ, R Rogers, J Gabel, and J Munizza. 2007. An evaluation of malingering screens with competency to stand trial patients: A known-groups comparison. *Law and Human Behavior* 31(3):249–260. doi:10.1007/s10979-006-9062-8

Windows MR, and GP Smith. 2005. *Manual for the Structured Inventory of Malingered Symptomatology.* Odessa, FL: Psychological Assessment Resources.

72

Forensic neuropsychology

KYLE BRAUER BOONE

INTRODUCTION

Neuropsychology originally developed in the mid-1900s as a method of using assessment of various cognitive skills to identify which areas of the brain (primarily cortex) were damaged and dysfunctional. That is, language deficits would point to damage to the left hemisphere in most individuals, while dysfunction in visual perceptual/spatial abilities would implicate injury to the right hemisphere. Likewise, losses in verbal versus visual learning and memory would suggest damage to left and right medial temporal lobe structures, respectively. Disturbances in sequencing, problem solving, mental flexibility, multitasking/divided attention, and response inhibition would be consistent with dysfunction of frontal and subfrontal structures. Weaknesses in motor dexterity and strength of the hands/fingers could signal disruption of motor strips of the contralateral hemispheres. However, with advent of sophisticated brain imaging techniques, the use of testing to localize brain damage became less important. Instead, the focus of neuropsychological testing came to emphasize objective quantification of cognitive abnormalities for the prediction of function in daily life activities.

Concurrently, neuropsychological assessment began to be important within civil litigation as a method to document "damages," or losses in function associated with acquired brain injury. The types of cases in which neuropsychologists typically provide assessments in civil injury include traumatic brain injury, medical malpractice, toxic exposures, etc. Concurrently, neuropsychological assessment has assumed a critical role in criminal litigation contexts. Neuropsychologists provide test data relevant to such questions as to whether defendants have the cognitive capacity to understand right and wrong, the impact of their actions on others, societal laws, and their rights as a defendant and whether they are able to meaningfully collaborate with defense counsel. Neuropsychologists are unique in providing carefully quantified data regarding extent of cognitive loss and dysfunction for juries as they make decisions regarding extent of damages and criminal responsibility.

ASSESSMENT OF PERFORMANCE VALIDITY

Neuropsychologists have an obligation to ensure that the data they report to triers of fact accurately reflect a test taker's true level of neurocognitive function. Plaintiffs in a personal injury lawsuit have motive to inflate symptoms and level of dysfunction because this can increase damage awards. Likewise, individuals seeking disability benefits have incentive to feign or exaggerate symptoms because this may enhance compensation amounts. Criminal defendants have motive to feign cognitive deficits in the service of excusing themselves from responsibility for criminal acts, while individuals seeking accommodations for learning difficulties and attention deficit disorder have impetus to feign or exaggerate such disorders to insure they receive extra test administration time or other educational supports.

Neuropsychological assessment reports in the latter half of the 1900s typically would include a statement indicating that test takers appeared to be performing to true ability and that test results were judged to be an accurate reflection of true skill level. However, these assertions were based only on "gut" impressions, and whether these conclusions were accurate was unknown. In retrospect, it is now appreciated that the error rate was likely high. For example, Larrabee et al. (2009) concluded that the average prevalence of noncredible neurocognitive test performance in populations with motive to feign is 40% ± 10%.

Prior to the 1990s, research on techniques to identify noncredible performance on neurocognitive testing was sparse. Since that time there has been an explosion of publications addressing the development and validation of such techniques. Initially the field focused on creating tests that had a single purpose in identifying failure to perform to true ability, so-called "dedicated" or "free-standing" measures (originally referred to as "symptom validity tests" [SVTs], but now termed "performance validity tests" [PVTs] in recognition that test takers are asked to "perform" neurocognitive tasks; the label "SVT" is now used to refer to symptom overreport scales on objective personality inventories, such as the MMPI-2-RF; Larrabee 2012). However, more recently the field has moved toward validating performance validity techniques derived from standard neurocognitive tests ("embedded" measures) in that this reduces test battery administration length and provides an evaluation of performance validity in "real time" (i.e., during actual administration of standard neurocognitive tests, rather than extrapolating conclusions regarding validity of test scores from dedicated performance validity tests that may have been administered up to hours before or after the other tests). Additionally, the field of neuropsychology is now beginning to appreciate that performance validity is not a "unitary construct," and that test takers can elect to feign at different times during a neuropsychological exam, and in particular skill areas that they think are most impacted by the disorder they are claiming (Boone 2009). In fact, it is atypical for a noncredible test taker to feign on every type of task administered (Boone 2009), reflecting the perception that it would appear implausible if he or she could not perform any tasks. "Embedded" performance validity indicators best allow continuous measurement of performance validity across a neuropsychological exam.

In evaluating the suitability and appropriateness of various performance validity measures, the examiner must consider test *sensitivity* and *specificity*. *Sensitivity* refers to the percentage of noncredible test takers who are correctly identified as noncredible using the technique, while *specificity* refers to the percentage of credible patients who are correctly identified as credible. Test cut-offs are traditionally selected to maintain specificity of at least 90%, reflecting the view within the field that it is particularly important to ensure a low test false-positive rate to protect credible patients from being incorrectly determined to be noncredible. Resulting test sensitivity can be found to be low (<40%), moderate (40%–69%), or high (≥70%). There is likely a ceiling on performance validity test sensitivity because noncredible test takers are hetereogeneous and feign in differing ways. Low to moderately sensitive PVTs can be used to "rule in" noncredible test performance, but cannot be used to "rule out" malingering. That is, a positive finding is highly suspicious for noncredible performance because scores beyond cut-offs are relatively rare in credible populations (i.e., <10% false-positive rate), but a passing score on low to moderately sensitive PVTs is not unusual in noncredible populations; therefore, passing scores cannot necessarily be used to conclude that the test taker was performing to true ability.

Most "dedicated" performance validity tests involve recognition memory, in particular, "forced choice" paradigms in which the test taker is presented with a series of items (primarily words or pictures), and then several trials (often a total of 50) in which each previously seen stimulus is paired with a new stimulus, with test takers instructed to identify which item was previously seen (e.g., Test of Memory Malingering [Tombaugh 1996], Warrington Recognition Memory Test—Words [Bell-Sprinkel et al. 2013], Portland Digit Recognition Test [Binder 1993], Victoria Symptom Validity Test [Slick et al. 1996], Word Memory Test [Green 2005], Medical Symptom Validity Test [Green 2004], and Nonverbal Medical Symptom Validity Test [Green 2008]).

Additional dedicated performance validity tests involve speeded counting (Dot Counting Test; Boone et al. 2002a), rapid letter identification (b Test; Boone et al. 2002b; Roberson et al. 2013), recognition of words in a list (Rey Word Recognition Test; Bell-Sprinkel et al. 2013), and drawing of simple pictured items (e.g., letters, numbers, shapes) and circling of items recognized from a larger array (Rey 15-item plus recognition; Boone et al. 2002c). Dozens of "embedded" performance validity indicators have been validated, and the interested reader is referred to Boone (2007, 2013) and Victor et al. (2013a,b) for listings and discussion.

Current practice recommendations in the field indicate that performance validity measures should be administered throughout the neuropsychological exam (National Academy of Neuropsychology; Bush et al. 2005) and that both dedicated and "embedded" techniques should be employed (American Academy of Clinical Neuropsychology; Heilbronner et al. 2009).

CURRENT CONTROVERSIES REGARDING INTERPRETATION OF DATA FROM MULTIPLE PVTS

Although individual PVT cut-offs are set to allow few false positives, questions have been raised regarding overall specificity rates when multiple PVTs are employed. The concern has been that use of multiple PVTs may raise false-positive rates to well over 10%. However, multiple "real-world" studies of clinical populations have shown that although it is not unusual for credible patients to fail a single PVT, very few fail more than one. For example, Victor et al. (2009) reported that only 5% of their credible sample failed two PVTs (out of four), Schroeder and Marshall (2011) observed that 5%–7% of psychiatric patients failed two PVTs (out of seven), and Larrabee (2003) found that 6% of his credible moderate to severe traumatic brain injury sample failed two validity measures (out of four PVTs/one SVT). Victor et al. (2009) further documented that only 1.5% of their sample failed three PVTs, and zero failed four, while Larrabee (2014a) reported that 4% of his sample failed three measures (out of 6 PVTs/1 SVT), with no false-positive identifications after three failures. Other researchers have documented that two to three PVT failures are associated with 100% specificity (Meyers and Volbrecht 2003; Sollman et al. 2010; Chafetz 2011; Schroeder and Marshall 2011; Davis and Millis 2014a; Meyers et al. 2014). Larrabee (2008) demonstrated that, using posterior probabilities, the probability that a test taker who fails three PVT cut-offs is in fact noncredible is essentially 99%, a finding recently confirmed by Meyers et al. (2014).

Berthelson and colleagues (2013), citing results from a statistical simulation, argued that the false-positive rate for two PVT failures (with cut-offs set to 90% specificity) in a credible population is 11.5%. They concluded that when three PVT failures are required to document performance invalidity, only eight should be administered, because if more are given, the false-positive rate will rise above 10%. Silk-Eglit and colleagues (2015) subsequently examined false-positive rates in use of multiple "embedded" PVTs, and concluded that to maintain a false-positive rate of ≤10% when analyzing data from 3, 7, 10, 14, and 15 performance validity indicators, noncredible performance would be indicated by failing of ≥1, ≥2, ≥3, ≥4, and ≥5 indicators, respectively.

To check the accuracy of Berthelson et al. (2013) simulation, Davis and Millis (2014a) examined PVT false-positive rates in a neurologic population with no motive to feign impairment, and observed that when six to eight PVTs are administered (with cut-offs set to 90% specificity), the actual occurrence of one or two failures was lower than that predicted by Berthelson et al. (2013). They further documented that there was no significant relationship between number of PVTs administered and number failed ($r = 0.10$). Similarly, Larrabee (2014a), in examining scores in a "real-world" clinical sample, found that the actual occurrence of at least three PVT failures (out of seven) was only 4% (as compared to 7.3% for Berthelson et al.). Larrabee (2014a) suggested that the Berthelson et al. simulation overestimated the rate of multiple PVT failures in credible populations, likely because PVT data do not have normal score distributions required for use of the simulation model.

The Silk-Eglit et al. (2015) examination of false-positive rates with use of multiple embedded PVTs likely also overestimated false-positive rates but for different reasons. All subjects had motive to feign (i.e., were mild traumatic brain injury litigants), and the subjects assigned to the credible group were allowed to fail one PVT; using these criteria, noncredible subjects were likely included in the credible group. Further, some of the PVT cut-offs had lowered sensitivity (e.g., Rey 15-item recall ≤9 = 59% sensitivity, Boone et al. 2002c; TOMM Trial 2 or retention <45 = 48% sensitivity; Greve et al. 2008), additionally raising the likelihood that noncredible test takers were inadvertently assigned to credible group. Also, many of the "embedded" PVT scores were from the same tests; scores from the same test would likely be failed "as a group," falsely giving the appearance that the test taker had failed multiple PVTs. Finally, sample sizes in the Silk-Eglit study were very small (24 credible, 25 noncredible), raising questions regarding the reliability and stability of the findings.

Subsequently, Bilder et al. (2014) raised questions regarding the Larrabee (2014a) and Davis and Millis (2014a) critiques of the Berthelson et al. (2013) study, asserting that research in fact shows an impact of number of PVTs administered on number failed, although the data they provide indicate that failure on three out of up to eight PVTs is associated with an acceptably low false-positive rate (except in patients with severe neurologic compromise and functional limitations). Bilder et al. (2014) also argued that studies that exclude individuals with low IQ and dementia from credible samples artificially lower PVT false-positive rates. The authors appeared to recommend that before data on multiple PVTs can be used clinically, empirical data are needed on various combinations of PVTs because of differing probabilities of joint failure.

Davis and Millis (2014b) responded to the Bilder et al. (2014) paper, highlighting statistical limitations and pointing out that the psychometric standards that Bilder et al. are requiring of PVTs are not met by other neuropsychological instruments. Davis and Millis also noted that the apparent "huge" increase in PVT failures claimed as a function of increasing numbers of PVTs administered is actually small; that is, the predicted number of PVT failures when five are administered is 0.55, and the predicted number failed when nine PVTs are administered is 1.01, which while a "doubling" of error, in absolute numbers represents an increase from one-half to one PVT failed.

Finally, Larrabee (2014b), in critiquing the Bilder et al. (2014) paper, agreed that some patients are falsely identified as noncredible due to failed PVT performances, but research indicates that these false-positive identifications are limited to patients with severe impairment, often requiring supervised living arrangements, such as patients with dementia, moderate to severe traumatic brain injury involving structural brain imaging abnormalities and prolonged coma, stroke with aphasia, mental retardation, and severe psychiatric disturbance. Larrabee argues that in the absence of these conditions, PVT failures would not represent false-positive errors.

A further concern not yet adequately addressed by available literature on interpretation of data from multiple PVTs is the fact that performance validity is not a "unitary" construct and that many noncredible test takers are highly selective regarding the cognitive areas in which they attempt to feign deficits (Boone 2009). For example, a recent personal injury litigant evaluated by this author who was claiming unverified central nervous system (CNS) toxic injury failed four PVTs checking for veracity of performance in processing speed while passing the remaining 11 PVTs assessing for performance validity in memory, attention, visual perception/constructional skill, tapping speed, and sensory function. In another recent case involving a mild traumatic brain injury litigant, the test taker failed 4 of 12 PVTs, but the failures were confined to verbal and visual memory. In the latter case, some of the failed PVT scores were the most extreme ever observed by this examiner. Rather than reflecting "borderline" evidence of performance invalidity (i.e., failure on 4 of 15 PVTs, and 4 of 12 PVTs, respectively), the data from these cases provided compelling evidence that the patients were not performing to true ability, but only in specific cognitive domains. These illustrations raise concerns regarding the simple "summing" of abnormal PVT scores, and instead argue for tabulation of the number of PVT failures within each cognitive domain. As with interpretation of standard neurocognitive measures, "false-positive" PVT findings would be more likely those reflecting isolated failures "scattered" across the various domains. In addition, the second case illustrates that PVT failures are not necessarily comparable in "weight," in that extreme failures provide strong evidence of noncredible performance regardless of the number failed.

PROTECTING CREDIBLE POPULATIONS AT RISK FOR PVT FAILURE

The flurry of publications addressing the important issue of interpretation of data from multiple PVTs reveals an emerging consensus that multiple PVT failures are unusual in most clinical populations. However, there are two patient groups for whom this is not true: patients with dementia and patients with low intelligence. For example, Dean et al. (2009) observed that in a dementia sample with no motive to feign, patients with Mini-Mental State Examination (MMSE) scores of 15–20 failed an average of 47% of PVTs administered, and in patients with MMSE scores of ≤15, 83% of PVT cut-offs were exceeded. In a separate publication, Dean et al. (2008) showed that in a sample with no motive to feign, patients with IQ scores from 70 to 79 failed 17% of administered PVTs, while patients with IQs from 60 to 69 failed 44% of PVTs. Keary et al. (2013) observed that PVT scores declined as IQ decreased, but association with IQ disappeared as IQ rose. As discussed above, Larrabee (2014b) asserted that some additional patient groups may fail PVTs at a high rate (e.g., stroke with aphasia, moderate to severe traumatic brain injury with brain imaging abnormalities and prolonged coma, severe psychiatric disturbance), but the likely moderator is low IQ and/or dementia. For example, psychotic patients who fail PVTs are those who meet criteria for dementia (MMSE scores ≤24; Back et al. 1996).

The best solution for the problem of PVT cut-off high false-positive rates in individuals with low IQ is to remove these subjects from primary validation samples, and to examine them separately, developing cut-offs that are tailored for the determination of actual versus feigned intellectual disability. We tested this method in a recent publication (Smith et al. 2014) which included 55 credible patients (no motive to feign) with IQ ≤75 ($n = 55$) and noncredible patients ($n = 74$) assumed to be feigning low IQ (IQ scores ≤75). The credible group scored better than the noncredible group on virtually all domains (attention, visual perceptual/spatial tasks, processing speed, verbal learning/list learning, and visual memory). With cut-offs set to maintain approximately 90% specificity in the credible group, sensitivity rates in identifying noncredible subjects were highest for verbal and visual memory and select attentional scores. When failure rates were tabulated across seven most sensitive scores (>40% sensitivity), two or more failures were associated with 85.4% specificity and 85.7% sensitivity, and three or more failures resulted in 95.1% specificity and 66% sensitivity. Thus, failure on three of the seven cut-offs was unusual in truly low IQ individuals, but use of these cut-offs still identified two-thirds of noncredible subjects who were feigning global cognitive dysfunction.

These results are promising and suggest a viable approach to protecting groups at risk for PVT failure despite performing to true ability: First, adjust individual PVT cut-offs to achieve approximately 90% specificity in the target credible group, and then tabulate the number of failures; increasing numbers of failures will be most likely due to symptom misrepresentation. The following case illustrates use of this technique.

DIFFERENTIAL DIAGNOSIS OF ACTUAL VERSUS FEIGNED LOW IQ

Case vignette

This 24-year-old patient sustained massive injuries when he ran in front of a car in an apparent suicide attempt during an acute psychotic episode. In the hospital emergency department the patient was noted to be awake and moaning with eyes open; Glasgow Coma Scale (GCS) was rated at 10. Neurologic exam was grossly nonfocal with movement in all extremities. The patient was found to have sustained multiple facial fractures and a fracture at the base of the skull, as well as several orthopedic fractures. Brain computed tomography (CT) did not show intracranial lesions but did reveal a small amount of blood in the posterior horns of the lateral ventricles. During his hospitalization the patient was described as making "steady improvement" and that he "recovered his mental status." Six weeks after injury he was transferred to a subacute facility for ongoing physical therapy and occupational therapy; discharge diagnoses included paranoid schizophrenia and cerebral concussion.

The patient had never lived independently from his family. At the age of 14 months he was observed to have episodes of briefly "passing out," and the differential diagnosis included absence seizures. He performed very poorly in school, began receiving special education services in the fourth grade, and did not begin reading until fifth or sixth grade. He reportedly had difficulty playing sports because "he didn't understand the rules." He had never held employment, obtained a driver's license, or been in a romantic relationship, and he was described as socially isolated throughout his schooling. His first documented psychotic episode began approximately 4 months prior to the injury. He was psychiatrically hospitalized, during which time he was described as confused and disoriented, responding to internal stimuli, selectively mute, and aggressive toward staff and patients, and with numerous bizarre behaviors (holding his ears while screaming, taking off his clothes, banging his head and punching himself, displaying waxy flexibility and posturing, and urinating and defecating on himself). With treatment his acute symptoms resolved, and he was released to home; however, shortly afterward his psychotic symptoms returned at which time the suicide attempt occurred.

The patient underwent neuropsychological evaluation at request of defense counsel three and a half years after the injury. On exam the patient presented as "young" and immature. He did not appear to be acutely psychotic; however, on one task he stopped responding and appeared possibly to either have had an absence seizure or to be reacting to internal stimuli. Responses were slowed. Thought processes were grossly within normal limits, but the patient displayed a knowledge deficit (e.g., for aspects of his medical history, symptoms, and treatment) which appeared to be

Table 72.1 Neuropsychological test scores

Intellectual scores (WAIS-III)			
Full Scale IQ:	75; 5th %		
Verbal IQ:	80; 9th %		
Verbal comprehension index:	80; 9th %		
Performance IQ:	74; 4th %		
Perceptual organization index:	80; 9th %		
Information processing speed		PVT	
b Test			Roberson et al. (2013)
E-score	70	Passed	
Omissions	9	Passed	
Commissions	0	Passed	
Time	15′02 ″	*Failed*	
Dot counting test			Boone et al. (2002)
E-score	20	*Failed*	
Grouped dot time	7.5″	*Failed*	
Errors	1	Passed	
Trails A	64″; <1st %	*Failed*	Iverson et al. (2002)
Stroop A			Arentsen et al. (2013)
Word reading	76″; <1st %	*Failed*	
Color naming	126″; <1st %	*Failed*	
Digit symbol			Kim et al. (2010)
ACSS	3; 1st %	*Failed*	
Recognition equation	–98	*Failed*	
Recognition total	5	*Failed*	
Attention			
Digit span			Babikian et al. (2006)
ACSS	6; 9th %	Passed	
Reliable digit span	7	Passed	
Mean 3-digit time	1″	Passed	
Mean 4-digit time	2″	Passed	
Language			
Vocabulary (ACSS)	6; 9th%		
Visual perceptual/spatial skills			
WAIS-III picture completion			Solomon et al. (2010)
ACSS	4; 2nd %	*Failed*	
Most discrepant index	2	*Failed*	
WAIS-III block design (ACSS)	6; 9th %		
WAIS-III matrix reasoning (ACSS)	10; 50th %		
Rey complex figure			Reedy et al. (2013)
Copy	26; <1st %	*Failed*	
Memory—verbal			
WMS-III logical memory			Bortnik et al. (2010)
I (raw)	34; 25th %	Passed	
II (raw)	17; 9th %	Passed	
Recognition	19	*Failed*	
Effort equation	45.5	Passed	
Rey auditory verbal Learning Test			Boone et al. (2005)

(Continued)

Table 72.1 (*Continued*) Neuropsychological test scores

Total	27	*Failed*	
Trial 5	7; 1st %	*Failed*	
Short delay	3; <1st %	*Failed*	
Long delay	2; <1st %	*Failed*	
Recognition	8(1 FP) < 1st %	*Failed*	
Effort equation	10	*Failed*	
Rey word recognition	9	Passed	Bell-Sprinkel et al. (2013)
Warrington recognition words			Kim MS et al. (2010)
Total correct	49	Passed	
Recognition time	173″	Passed	
Memory—visual			
Rey complex figure			Reedy et al. (2013)
3-minute delay	9.5; <1st %	*Failed*	
Effort equation	32	*Failed*	
Rey 15-item			Poynter et al. (2014)
Recall	12	Passed	
Recognition correct	14	Passed	
Combination score	26	Passed	
Test of memory malingering			
Trial 1	48	Passed	Denning (2012)
Executive			
Wisconsin card sorting test	6 categories; WNL		
Similarities (ACSS)	8; 25th %		
Stroop Interference	174″; <1st percentile	Passed	Arentsen et al. (2013)
Trails B	210″; <1st percentile	*Failed*	Iverson et al. (2002)
Academic skills			
WRAT-4 Word Reading (SS):	77; 6th %		
WRAT-4 Spelling (SS):	82; 12th %		
WRAT-4 Math (SS):	74; 4th %		

related primarily to low intelligence. Further, he counted on his fingers when solving math problems.

Neuropsychological scores for this patient are reproduced in Table 72.1, including performances on PVTs.

The patient failed PVTs from 9 of 14 separate tests using published cut-offs, which normally would suggest that he was not performing to true ability. However, overall IQ score was low (FSIQ = 75), and judged accurate (rather than as reflecting negative response bias) because it was consistent with very poor premorbid academic function. As shown in Table 72.2, when cut-offs adjusted for low IQ were employed for seven tests found to be most sensitive in the differential of actual versus feigned low IQ per Smith et al. (2014), the patient passed all measures.

A neuropsychological evaluation in a forensic context involves two main steps: (1) determination as to whether obtained scores reflect valid and accurate data, and if this criterion is passed, (2) ascertainment of the nature, extent, and cause of any neurocognitive compromise. If concerns regarding test score veracity are encountered on step 1, the examiner cannot move on to step 2. In the patient's case, it was concluded that he was most likely performing to his

Table 72.2 Cut-off scores considering adjusted IQ

b test Omissions (cut-off ≥46)	= 9 (passed)
Digit Span four-digit time (cut-off ≥4″)	= 2″ (passed)
Digit symbol recognition correct score (cut-off ≤4)	= 5 (passed)
RAVLT trial 5 (cut-off ≤6)	= 7 (passed)
RAVLT effort equation (cut-off ≤7)	= 10 (passed)
Rey Word total correct (cut-off ≤7)	= 9 (passed)
Warrington total score (cut-off ≤38)	= 49 (passed)

true ability level and that the remaining standard neurocognitive scores were usable. Those latter scores were interpreted as showing substantial impairments in processing speed and visual memory; impaired to average skills in visual perceptual/spatial skills, verbal memory, and executive functions; borderline to low average academic skills (word reading, spelling, math); and low average vocabulary range and basic attention.

The patient was considered not likely to have any current cognitive sequelae related to the injury three and a half years earlier. The available data suggested that the patient most likely met criteria for a mild traumatic brain injury at that time. Records from his hospitalization referred only to a "cerebral concussion," and brain imaging was essentially normal. It is unclear whether the patient was rendered unconscious; in the emergency department he was described as awake and moaning with eyes open, and was trying to sit up. He had GCS of 10, which normally would fall within the moderate traumatic brain injury category, although it is unclear whether the patient's extensive orthopedic injuries contaminated the ratings. Further, he was described as "confused/disoriented" (score of 4 on verbal response section of the Glasgow Coma Scale), but this was also likely true prior to the suicide attempt due to his severe psychosis. Anterograde amnesia could not be reliably assessed due to sedation after the injury.

Reviews of the literature on neuropsychological function in mild traumatic brain injury (see Carroll et al. 2004, 120 studies; Dikmen et al. 2009, 33 studies), including six meta-analyses involving dozens of studies and thousands of patients in the aggregate (133 studies, $n = 1463$, Belanger et al. 2005; 21 studies, $n = 790$, Belanger and Vanderploeg 2005; 8 studies, Binder et al. 1997; 17 studies, $n = 634$, Frencham et al. 2005; 25 studies, $n = 2828$, Rohling et al. 2011; 39 studies, $n = 1716$, Schretlen and Shapiro 2003) show that patients who experience mild brain trauma have returned to baseline by weeks to months post-injury.

It was concluded that the patient had a long-standing, developmental intellectual disability as well as a psychotic disorder that were unchanged by the suicide attempt and related injuries three and a half years prior to exam, and that the patient had no current cognitive or psychiatric conditions stemming from that event. Of note, at the time of testing the patient was more functional than prior to the suicide attempt; for example, the patient's sister reported that he was now responding verbally to the family member's questions, whereas prior to the injury he did not.

SUMMARY

A critical goal within clinical neuropsychology is to quickly develop methods that assess for performance validity while adequately protecting credible patient subgroups who are at risk for being inaccurately determined to be malingering or otherwise not performing to true ability. One such method for protecting patients with low IQ is described in this chapter. Memory (especially recognition) and attentional PVT measures were found in the Smith et al. (2014) study to be most robust to low intelligence, and these are likely to show the most promise in differentiating actual versus feigned low IQ. Further, qualitative aspects of some memory recognition tasks may reveal error types that are not found in individuals with low IQ and would therefore be specific to noncredible performance; for example, Marshall and Happe (2007) indicated that it was rare for subjects with low IQ to produce "dyslexic" false-positive errors on the Rey 15-item recognition trial. Likewise, significantly below chance performance on forced choice measures would not be explainable on the basis of low IQ. Novel techniques may be worth pursuing, such as developing measures that assess for a "yes" response bias (exhibited by individuals with low IQ, but not necessarily adopted by noncredible individuals attempting to feign low IQ), such as on the Logical Memory recognition trial (Marshall and Happe 2007).

SUMMARY KEY POINTS

- Neuropsychologists have an obligation to carefully and comprehensively assess for performance validity during forensic neuropsychological exams through use of validated performance validity tests (PVTs).
- Performance validity is not a unitary construct, i.e., test takers may elect to underperform at differing timepoints during the exam and on differing types of neurocognitive tasks—there is no one noncredible profile.
- Adequate assessment of performance validity requires use of multiple PVTs interspersed throughout the neuropsychological exam to check for performance validity in "real time."
- Use of multiple PVTs does not result in substantially increased risk of false-positive identifications, except in the context of very low intelligence and dementia.
- Individuals with true low intelligence can be protected from inaccurate identification as noncredible through (1) setting PVT cut-offs to maintain less than 10% false-positive rates in low IQ populations, and (2) requiring multiple failures using these adjusted cut-offs.

REFERENCES

Arentsen TJ, K Boone, TT Lo, H Goldberg, M Cottingham, T Victor, E Ziegler, and M Zeller. 2013. Effectiveness of the Comalli Stroop test as a measure of negative response bias. *Clinical Neuropsychologist* 27:1060–1076.

Babikian T, KB Boone, P Lu, and G Arnold. 2006. Sensitivity and specificity of various Digit Span scores in the detection of suspect effort. *Clinical Neuropsychologist* 20:145–159.

Back C, KB Boone, C Edwards, C Parks, K Burgoyne, and B Silver. 1996. The performance of schizophrenics on three cognitive tests of malingering: Rey 15-item, Rey Dot Counting, and Forced Choice method. *Assessment* 3:449–458.

Belanger HG, G Curtiss, JA Demery, BK Lebowitz, and RD Vanderploeg. 2005. Factors moderating neuropsychological outcomes following mild traumatic brain injury: A meta-analysis. *Journal of the International Neuropsychological Society* 11:215–227.

Belanger HG and RD Vanderploeg. 2005. The neuropsychological impact of sport-related concussion: A meta-analysis. *Journal of the International Neuropsychological Society* 11:345–357.

Bell-Sprinkel TL, KB Boone, D Miora, M Cottingham, T Victor, E Ziegler, M Zeller, and M Wright. 2013. Cross-validation of the Rey word recognition symptom validity test. *Clinical Neuropsychologist* 27:516–527.

Berthelson L, SS Mulchan, AP Odland, LJ Miller, and W Mittenberg. 2013. False positive diagnosis of malingering due to the use of multiple effort tests. *Brain Injury* 27:909–916.

Bilder RM, CA Sugar, and GS. Hellemann. 2014. Cumulative false positive rates given multiple performance validity tests: Commentary on Davis and Millis (2014) and Larrabee (2014). *Clinical Neuropsychologist* 28:1212–1223.

Binder LM. 1993. Assessment of malingering after mild head trauma with the Portland Digit Recognition Test. *Journal of Clinical and Experimental Neuropsychology* 15:170–182.

Binder LM, ML Rohling, and GJ Larrabee. 1997. A review of mild head trauma: Part I. Meta-analytic review of neuropsychological studies. *Journal of Clinical and Experimental Neuropsychology* 19:421–431.

Boone KB. ed. 2007. *Assessment of Feigned Cognitive Impairment: A Neuropsychological Perspective.* New York: Guilford Press.

Boone KB. 2009. The need for continuous and comprehensive sampling of effort/response bias during neuropsychological examinations. *Clinical Neuropsychologist* 23:729–741.

Boone KB. 2013. *Clinical Practice of Forensic Neuropsychology: An Evidence-based Approach.* New York: Guilford Press.

Boone KB, P Lu, and D Herzberg. 2002a. *The Dot Counting Test.* Los Angeles: Western Psychological Services.

Boone KB, P. Lu, and D Herzberg. 2002b. *The b Test.* Los Angeles: Western Psychological Services.

Boone KB, P Lu, and Johnny Wen, J. 2005. Comparison of various RAVLT scores in the detection of noncredible memory performance. *Archives of Clinical Neuropsychology* 20:310–319.

Boone, KB, X Salazar, P Lu, K Warner-Chacon, and J Razani. 2002c. The Rey 15 -Item recognition trial: A technique to enhance sensitivity of the Rey 15-Item Memorization Test. *Journal of Clinical and Experimental Neuropsychology* 24:561–573.

Bortnik KE, KB Boone, SD Marion, S Amano, M Cottingham, E Ziegler, TL. Victor, and M Zeller. 2010. Examination of various WMS-III Logical Memory scores in the assessment of response bias. *Clinical Neuropsychologist* 24:344–357.

Bush SS, RM Ruff, AI Troster, JT Barth, SP Koffler, NH Pliskin, CR Reynolds, and CH Silver. 2005. Symptom validity assessment: Practice issues and medical necessity: NAN Policy and Planning Committee. *Archives of Clinical Neuropsychology* 20:419–426.

Carroll LJ, JD Cassidy, PM Peloso, J Borg, H von Holst, L Holm, C Paniak, and M Pepin. 2004. Prognosis for mild traumatic brain injury: Results of the WHO Collaborating Centre Task Force on Mild Traumatic Brain Injury. *Journal of Rehabilitation Medicine* 43 (Supplement):84–105.

Chafetz M. 2011. Reducing the probability of false positives in malingering detection of Social Security disability claimants. *Clinical Neuropsychologist* 25:1239–1252.

Davis JJ and SR Millis. 2014a. Examination of performance validity test failure in relation to number of tests administered. *Clinical Neuropsychologist* 28:199–214.

Davis JJ and SR. Millis. 2014b. Reply to commentary by Bilder, Sugar, and Helleman 2014 on minimizing false positive error with multiple performance validity tests. *Clinical Neuropsychologist* 28:1224–1229.

Dean AC, TL Victor, KB Boone, and G Arnold. 2008. The relationship of IQ to effort test performance. *Clinical Neuropsychologist* 22:705–722.

Dean AC, TL Victor, KB Boone, L Philpott, and R Hess. 2009. Dementia and effort test performance. *Clinical Neuropsychologist* 23:133–152.

Denning JH. 2012. The efficiency and accuracy of the Test of Memory Malingering trial 1, errors on the first 10 items of the Test of Memory Malingering, and five embedded measures in predicting invalid test performance. *Archives of Clinical Neuropsychology* 27:417–432.

Dikmen S, JD Corrigan, HS Levin, J Machamer, W Stiers, and MG. Weisskopf. 2009. Cognitive outcome following traumatic brain injury. *Journal of Head Trauma Rehabilitation* 24:430–438.

Frencham KAR, AM Fox, and MT Maybery. 2005. Neuropsychological studies of mild traumatic brain injury: A meta-analytic review of research since 1995. *Journal of Clinical and Experimental Neuropsychology* 27:334–351.

Green P. 2004. *Green's Medical Symptom Validity Test (MSVT) for Microsoft Windows: User's Manual.* Edmonton, Canada: Green's Publishing.

Green P. 2005. *Green's Word Memory Test for Microsoft Windows: User's Manual.* Edmonton, Canada: Green's Publishing.

Green P. 2008. *Green's Nonverbal Medical Symptom Validity Test (NV-MSVT) for Microsoft Windows: User's Manual.* Edmonton, Canada: Green's Publishing,

Greve KW, J Ord, KL Curtis, KJ Bianchini, and A Brennan. 2008. Detecting malingering in traumatic brain injury and chronic pain: A comparison of three forced choice symptom validity tests. *Clinical Neuropsychologist* 22:896–918.

Heilbronner RL, JJ Sweet, JE Morgan, GJ Larrabee, S Millis, and Conference Participants. 2009. American Academy of Clinical Neuropsychology Consensus Conference Statement on the neuropsychological assessment of effort, response bias, and malingering. *Clinical Neuropsychologist* 23:1093–1129.

Iverson GL, RT Lange, P Green, and MD Franzen. 2002. Detecting exaggeration and malingering with the Trail Making Test. *Clinical Neuropsychologist* 16:398–406.

Keary TA, TW Frazier, CJ Belzile, JS Chapin, RI Naugle, IM Najm, and RM Busch. 2013. Working memory and intelligence are associated with Victoria Symptom Validity Test hard item performance in patients with intractable epilepsy. *Journal of the International Neuropsychological Society* 19:314–323.

Kim MS, KB Boone, TL Victor, SD Marion, S Amano, ME Cottingham, E Ziegler, and M Zeller. 2010. The Warrington Recognition Memory Test for words as a measure of response bias: Total score and response time cutoffs developed on real world and noncredible subjects. *Archives of Clinical Neuropsychology* 25:60–70.

Kim N, KB Boone, T Victor, P Lu, C Keatinge, and C Mitchell. 2010. Sensitivity and specificity of a Digit Symbol Recognition trial in the identification of response bias. *Archives of Clinical Neuropsychology* 25:420–428.

Larrabee GJ. 2003. Detection of malingering using atypical performance patterns on standard neuropsychological tests. *Clinical Neuropsychologist* 17:410–425.

Larrabee GJ. 2008. Aggregation across multiple indicators improves the detection of malingering: Relationship to likelihood ratios. *Clinical Neuropsychologist* 22:666–679.

Larrabee GJ. 2012. Performance validity and symptom validity in neuropsychological assessment. *Journal of the International Neuropsychological Society* 18:625–631.

Larrabee GJ. 2014a. False positive rates associated with the use of multiple performance and symptom validity tests. *Archives of Clinical Neuropsychology* 29:364–373.

Larrabee GJ. 2014b. Minimizing false positive error with multiple performance validity tests: Response to Bilder, Sugar, and Hellemann 2014. *Clinical Neuropsychologist* 28:1230–1242.

Larrabee GJ, SR Millis, and JE Meyers. 2009. 40 plus or minus 10, a new magical number: Reply to Russell. *Clinical Neuropsychologist* 23:841–849.

Marshall P and M Happe. 2007. The performance of individuals with mental retardation on cognitive tests assessing effort and motivation. *Clinical Neuropsychologist* 21:826–840.

Meyers JE, RM Miller, LM Thompson, AM Scalese, BC Allred, ZW Rupp, ZP Dupaix, and AJ Lee. 2014. Using likelihood ratios to detect invalid performance with performance validity measures. *Archives of Clinical Neuropsychology* 29:224–235.

Meyers JE and ME Volbrecht. 2003. A validation of multiple malingering detection methods in a large clinical sample. *Archives of Clinical Neuropsychology* 18:261–276.

Poynter K, KB Boone, A Ermshar, D Miora, ME Cottingham, T Victor, E Ziegler, M Zeller, and M Wright. 2014. A re-examination of the Rey 15-item Memorization Test: There's a baby in that bathwater! *Paper Presented at the American Academy of Clinical Neuropsychology*, New York, June.

Reedy S, KB Boone, M Cottingham, DF Glaser, P Lu, T Victor, E Ziegler, M Zeller, and M Wright. 2013. Cross-validation of the Lu et al. 2003 Rey-Osterrieth Complex Figure effort equation in a large known groups sample. *Archives of Clinical Neuropsychology* 28:30–37.

Roberson CJ, KB Boone, H Goldberg, D Miora, M Cottingham, T Victor, E Ziegler, M Zeller, and M Wright. 2013. Cross-validation of the b Test in a large known groups sample. *Clinical Neuropsychologist* 27:495–508.

Rohling ML, LM Binder, GJ Demakis, GJ Larrabee, DM Ploetz, and JL Rohling. 2011. A meta-analysis of neuropsychological outcome after mild traumatic brain injury: Re-analyses and reconsiderations of Binder et al. (1997), Frencham et al. (2005), and Pertab et al. (2009). *Clinical Neuropsychologist* 25:608–623.

Schretlen DJ, and AM Shapiro. 2003. A quantitative review of the effects of traumatic brain injury on cognitive functioning. *International Review of Psychiatry* 15:341–349.

Schroeder RW and PS Marshall. 2011. Evaluation of the appropriateness of multiple symptom validity indices in psychotic and non-psychotic psychiatric populations. *Clinical Neuropsychologist* 25:437–453.

Silk-Eglit, GM, JH Stenclik, AS Miele, JK Lynch, and RJ McCaffrey. 2015. Rates of false-positive classification resulting from the analysis of additional embedded performance validity measures. *Applied Neuropsychology, Adult* 22:335–347.

Slick DJ, G Hopp, E Strauss, and FJ Spellacy. 1996. Victoria symptom validity test: Efficiency for detecting feigned memory impairment and relationship to neuropsychological tests and MMPI-2 validity scales. *Journal of Clinical and Experimental Neuropsychology* 18:911–922.

Smith K, K Boone, T Victor, D Miora, M Cottingham, E Ziegler, M Zeller, and M Wright. 2014. Comparison of credible patients of very low intelligence and noncredible patients on neurocognitive performance validity indicators. *Clinical Neuropsychologist* 28:1048–1070.

Sollman MJ, JD Ranseen, and DTR Berry. 2010. Detection of feigned ADHD in college students. *Psychological Assessment* 22:325–335.

Solomon RE, KB Boone, D Miora, S Skidmore, M Cottingham, T Victor, E Zeigler, and M Zeller. 2010. Use of the WAIS-III Picture Completion subtest as an embedded measure of response bias. *Clinical Neuropsychologist* 24:1243–1256.

Tombaugh TM 1996. *Test of Memory Malingering (TOMM)*. North Tonawanda, NY: MultiHealth Systems.

Victor TL, AD Kulick, and KB Boone. 2013a. Assessing noncredible attention, processing speed, language and visuospatial/perceptual function in mild TBI cases. In *Mild Traumatic Brain Injury: Symptom Validity Assessment and Malingering*, edited by DA Carone and SS Bush, New York: Springer Publishing Company, 231–268.

Victor TL, KB Boone, and AD Kulick. 2013b. Assessing noncredible sensory-motor function, executive function, and test batteries in mild TBI cases. In *Mild Traumatic Brain Injury: Symptom Validity Assessment and Malingering*, edited by D Carone and SS Bush, New York: Springer, 269–302.

Victor TL, KB Boone, JG Serpa, J Beuhler, and E Ziegler. 2009. Interpreting the meaning of multiple effort test failure. *Clinical Neuropsychologist* 23:297–313.

73

Neuroimaging and forensic psychiatry

ROBERT A. SCHUG AND LEIDY S. PARTIDA

INTRODUCTION

Practitioners in forensic psychiatry stand to gain tremendously from an empirical understanding of the initiation, maintenance, and potential desistance from criminality. Neurobiological crime research (i.e., neurocriminology) has contributed extensively to criminological study for over 100 years (i.e., Lombroso 1876) and has offered a unique understanding of the etiological mechanisms underlying antisocial behavior. Neuroimaging (the application of technologies and techniques that generate visual representations of brain structure and functioning in living persons), one of the branches of neurocriminology (and the forensic neurosciences), has been an effective methodology in identifying structural and functional deficits in frontal, temporal, and subcortical regions in antisocial children and adults—findings that are largely supported by neurological studies of brain trauma in antisocial populations, and congruent with neuropsychological investigations revealing verbal, spatial, and executive dysfunction in antisocial adults and children. Findings from neuroimaging research have recently begun to impact criminal justice systems in various arenas, including applications in lie detection and judicial processes; and may enhance forensic psychological assessment and inform policies and procedures regarding the identification, management, and treatment of various types of individuals in forensic psychiatric settings.

Two crucial bases of knowledge are of value in informing the forensic clinical practitioner regarding neuroimaging applications to forensic psychiatric work: (1) an understanding of brain imaging studies to date, examining relationships between brain structure and function and various forms of psychiatric symptomatology (including thoughts, affects, and behaviors that may lead to clinically significant impairment); and (2) an understanding of how brain imaging evidence has been applied to criminal legal proceedings in the past (including the reasons why it may or may not have helped the defendant—which often relate to standards of admissibility of evidence). This chapter serves as an integrative review of findings in both of these areas. It provides a summary of key areas of neuroimaging research on criminal, violent, and antisocial behavior, as well as an overview of previous criminal cases in which neuroimaging evidence was incorporated into the adjudication process. Although the scope of forensic work may include both criminal and civil proceedings, the focus of this chapter is on the application of neuroimaging to criminal cases. As such, it first covers the growing body of work on brain imaging studies of criminal, violent, and antisocial behaviors, as well as the history of criminal cases in which an attempt was made (whether successful or not) to utilize brain imaging evidence in order to aid criminal defendants.

LEGAL ISSUES RELATED TO NEUROIMAGING

The practitioner in forensic psychiatry stands to benefit from an understanding of both the clinical and legal applications of neuroimaging. Recent years have shown a heightened emergence of neuroimaging techniques in the contemporary court system. Defense attorneys have introduced the lion's share of neuroimaging evidence, and judges to date have admitted the use of brain imaging techniques such as computerized axial tomography (CAT or CT), positron emission tomography (PET), single-photon emission computed tomography (SPECT), electroencephalography (EEG), and magnetic resonance imaging (MRI). The admittance of these types of scans has occurred in different phases of the trial. Although most research suggests neuroimaging evidence is typically introduced in the sentencing (or penalty) phase of a trial, it has also been introduced in the guilt and post-trial phases. Despite the interest and growing body of research on this topic, debates and criticisms indicate further research and testing are necessary. Some critics have indicated the use of brain scans during penalty phases of death penalty cases can be productive. One reason is that federal and state laws label mental impairment as a form of mitigating evidence, which can be considered by a jury when deciding on capital punishment as a penalty. Another reason is that judges prefer to err in admitting the evidence, rather than negating it, in cases in which it could have reversed a death penalty sentence. Others believe neuroscience techniques to be too novel for appropriate use in courtrooms in criminal cases. Research findings suggest a bias in favor of the defense, commonly resulting in a verdict of not guilty by reason of insanity (Batts 2009, 261). Additionally, the novelty of neuroimaging techniques is associated with several key risks. For example, interpretations of neuroimaging scans may produce *false positives*—indications of brain abnormalities when the brain is actually normal, or *false negatives*—failure to elucidate abnormalities when the brain is in fact not normal (Moriarty 2008, 29). Researchers generally believe neuroimaging techniques are more efficient when utilized to mitigate charges. However, many have expressed the opinion that neuroimaging should not be introduced in a capital defense setting. Others have opined that neuroimaging techniques should be used to support other evidence of brain dysfunction (e.g., from a comprehensive social history investigation, neuropsychological testing, and evaluation by a neuropsychiatrist or neurologist), not utilized as the sole predictor of whether or not a defendant is guilty of a crime (Blume and Paavola 2011, 909; Moriarty 2008, 29).

Various legal issues have been identified in the literature related to neuroimaging. In criminal cases, neuroimaging evidence may have applications in insanity defenses (e.g., *People v. Weinstein*, 1992), as an indicator of criminal intent, in detecting deception by witnesses or defendants, and during the sentencing phases of trials in which the appropriateness of the death penalty must be determined (Yang et al. 2008, 65). Others have suggested its usefulness in predicting recidivism and future dangerousness, explaining the effects of trauma and mental illness, and predicting whether a person has a general propensity for violence (Blume and Paavola 2011, 909). Its (questionable) role as evidence of a defendant's past mental state has even been noted (Brown and Murphy 2010, 1119). For criminal proceedings, applications might include (1) demonstrating that a criminal defendant's brain is vulnerable to violence or aggression, based on similarities to the brains of other individuals characterized by violence or aggression in research studies; (2) diminished culpability—demonstrating that a criminal defendant lacked the behavioral controls to prevent him or her from acting in a criminal/violent manner, based on structural or functional deficits in brain regions associated with impulse control, response inhibition (prefrontal cortex), or aggression and violence (limbic system—see below); and (3) demonstrating that a criminal defendant's brain is marked by characteristics consistent with others with criminogenic mental illnesses such as psychopathy. Other legal issues related to neuroimaging data center on its admissibility for evidentiary purposes in court.

LEGAL CRITERIA FOR ADMISSIBILITY OF NEUROIMAGING EVIDENCE

For the forensic psychiatrist utilizing neuroimaging data, an understanding of the standards for its admissibility in court is paramount. Similar to other forms of evidence, neuroimaging data are subject to specific criteria in order to be admitted for evidentiary purposes in legal proceedings. According to Moriarty (2008), the state and federal court systems in the United States are required to abide by certain admissibility standards, though these standards are different. For example, the federal system utilizes the Federal Rules of Evidence (FRE) when deciding whether evidence should be admitted. Specifically, the U.S. Supreme Court identifies three court cases as precedents in the admission of expert evidence: *Daubert v. Merrell Dow Pharmaceuticals, Inc.*, *General Electric Co. v. Joiner*, and *Kumho Tire Co., Ltd. v. Carmichael*. The states also abide by evidentiary rules, which mostly follow the FRE template; however, each state has different variations of it. These variations usually follow Rule 401 (evidence must be relevant), Rule 702 (which regulates admission of expert testimony), and Rule 403 (which modulates confusion and unfair prejudice).

The *Frye* general acceptance standard originated from a 1923 D.C. Court of Appeals decision, which stated that use of the polygraph for evidentiary purposes was relatively novel. Therefore, its high rate of unreliability and inconsistency prevented it from attaining scientific general acceptance and validity. This case served as the precedent for subsequent cases attempting to introduce novel scientific evidence in the court system, requiring courts to determine whether the given novel evidence has reached general admissibility or not. Currently, some states continue to follow the *Frye* general acceptance standard. The federal courts ceased using the *Frye* standard because of the belief it was incompatible with FRE. The *Daubert* standard arose when the U.S. Supreme Court subsequently heard the scientific case of *Daubert v. Merrell Dow Pharmaceuticals, Inc.*, and held that all scientific evidence should be tested for the minimal standard of evidentiary reliability. This minimal standard of evidentiary reliability was determined by referring to the scientific method. Specifically, the court required that (1) the scientific theory or technique can be or has been tested, (2) the theory or technique has been subjected to peer review and publication, (3) there is knowledge of the potential or known rate of error of the theory or technique when applied, (4) the standards controlling the technique's operation exist and are maintained, and (5) the technique or theory has been generally accepted in the relevant scientific community. The subsequent cases of *General Electric Co. v. Joiner*, and *Kumho Tire Co., Ltd. v. Carmichael* also helped shape the general admissibility standard. In *Joiner*, the court ruled that methodology and conclusions are not entirely different from one another. Instead, a court could hold too much of an analytical gap exists between the data and expert opinion. In *Kumho Tire*, the court held that all expert evidence (not just scientific) should follow the *Daubert* requirements (Moriarty 2008, 29).

Several key weaknesses in the legal treatment of neuroimaging evidence have been identified in the empirical literature—including those related to its admissibility. For example, some authors (e.g., Feigenson 2006, 233 and Moriarty 2008, 29) have noted the inconsistencies among states regarding the standards of admissibility of neuroimaging evidence to prove specific kinds of facts. Although the federal courts are required to follow the Supreme Court's reliability standard, the states are not. While most states follow *Frye* or *Daubert* standards, there are variations from state to state in the applications of these standards (with some states even having their own unique standards). Overall, states following the *Frye* standard place emphasis on reliability, whereas those utilizing *Daubert* emphasize determining the acceptance and reliability of the evidence. Feigenson (2006, 233) also noted that the admissibility and persuasiveness of neuroimaging evidence (i.e., PET and SPECT in particular) depend greatly on the case-specific context.

Finally, it has been observed that on more than two-fifths of the instances in which neuroimaging evidence (i.e., PET and SPECT specifically) has been an issue in court, its proponents have presented or sought to present it to judges alone (e.g., before administrative law judges or relating to non-jury issues, such as competency to stand trial or injunctive relief), not juries. This is significant in that concerns about the courtroom use of fMRI data are often focused on their use by jurors, yet more often than not judges (not jurors) will be the decision makers on issues related to the offering of neuroimaging evidence. In fact, a high rate of admissibility for PET and SPECT evidence (82% as of 2006) has been noted, due possibly to the large proportion of bench proceedings where juries are not present and do not need to be protected from insufficiently reliable evidence (Feigenson 2006, 233). Egan (2007, 62) notes that the *Daubert* rule makes the trial judge responsible for the initial determination of relevance and reliability of evidence, and the trial judge must have a reasonable understanding of the science itself in order to do so. Given the technically complex information associated with neuroimaging, this can be a heavy burden. Ultimately, the admissibility of neuroimaging evidence in court as a whole remains to date nuanced and contextually variable, and it is critical for the practitioner in forensic psychiatry to understand the limitations of neuroimaging's potential evidentiary value in the eyes of the court.

DATA RELEVANT TO THE LEGAL CRITERIA

The steadily increasing body of scientific literature related to neuroimaging and criminal, violent, and antisocial behavior is directly relevant to the legal criteria for admissibility outlined by the Daubert standard—speaking to its testability, peer review and publication, potential/known error rate, operational standards, and acceptance by the scientific community. Neuroimaging data also have significant utility in informing the forensic psychiatric opinion. Given the growing number of studies in this area, along with the level of technical expertise needed to interpret and synthesize results, an organized understanding of the current and recent studies of neuroimaging and antisocial behavior can be challenging for the forensic psychiatric practitioner. One useful organizational framework for understanding this material is via the classification of studies by anatomical regions of the brain, as specific brain structures and areas have consistently demonstrated relationships with various forms of antisocial behavior. Previous empirical investigations have targeted specific regions of interest (ROIs) including whole-brain or right and/or left hemispheres, different areas of the cerebral cortex (e.g., frontal and temporal lobes), subregions within these lobes (e.g., the prefrontal cortex of the frontal lobe—which itself may be sectioned into subvolumes including the orbitofrontal cortex [OFC], and dorsolateral prefrontal cortex [DLPFC]), and specific subcortical structures such as the hippocampus and amygdala of the limbic system (discussed elsewhere—see Glenn and Raine 2014, 54; Raine et al. 2005, 185; and Yang et al. 2010, 9). Traditionally, these studies have examined gray matter (composed predominantly of neuronal cell bodies) and/or white matter (consisting chiefly of myelinated axon tracts, and representing connectivity between various brain areas).

A second useful organizational approach for the forensic practitioner is classifying previous research according to the imaging technique used. Neuroimaging studies of antisocial behavior may be structural or functional in nature. Structural technologies focus on the length, thickness, shape, volume, density and other physical properties of a particular brain area or component, using tools such as computed tomography (CT) scanning, diffusion tensor imaging, and structural magnetic resonance imaging (sMRI). Functional approaches examine the amount of neural activity present in any given brain region, utilizing tools such as positron emission tomography (PET), single photon emission computed tomography (SPECT), and functional magnetic resonance imaging (fMRI). Finally, a third useful organizational approach is organizing research according to the type of antisocial population examined. Participants recruited for neuroimaging studies of antisociality may be classified by specific crime type (e.g., murderers) or antisocial characteristics/behaviors (e.g., violence, aggression, gambling, or substance use). Participants may also be characterized by psychiatric disorders demonstrating associations with antisocial attributes (e.g., conduct disorder, oppositional defiant disorder, substance abuse disorders, bipolar disorder, schizophrenia, antisocial personality disorder, and psychopathy).

Most neuroimaging studies of antisocial behavior are undertaken with the overarching goal of making precise structural or functional measurements of ROIs in individuals characterized by crime, antisociality, or violence, and comparing these measurements to those of individuals without these characteristics (i.e., normal, healthy controls). Any identified between-groups differences in these measurements may be considered as potential brain-based neurobiological correlates of the various forms of antisocial behaviors and traits of study. What follows is a review of current, recent, and foundational neuroimaging research on antisocial behavior, using the aforementioned organizational frameworks (i.e., investigations of frontal and temporal lobes, the structural and functional findings from studies of these brain areas, and—to some degree—findings from studies of various antisocial populations).

FRONTAL LOBE AND PREFRONTAL CORTEX

The frontal lobe region constitutes roughly one-third of the cerebrum—far and away the largest quantity of cortical volume in humans compared with other animal species. Nearly two centuries of scientific inquiry have identified associations between frontal lobe damage and behavioral control problems, and investigations from the more-recent past have suggested the frontal lobe's role in the perception and appraisal of emotional stimuli, and the regulation of emotion responses (Schug et al. 2009, 326). In recent decades, neuroimaging studies have continued to suggest that deficits in structural and functional aspects of the frontal lobe play a critical role in the neurobiological processes underlying antisociality and violence. Earlier imaging studies of antisocial individuals often reported on more macro-level analyses of brain structure and functioning—understandable, given the spatial resolution limitations of the imaging techniques available at that time (although whole-brain volume analyses have been conducted in more-recent studies, e.g., Barkataki et al. 2006, 239). Nonetheless, these studies often implicated the frontal lobe in associations with various forms of offending. For example, an earlier meta-analysis of 20 structural and functional imaging studies found frontal lobe deficits to be associated with violent offending and temporal lobe deficits with sexual offending, and violent sexual offending to be associated with dysfunction in both lobes (Mills and Raine 1994, 145). Findings from diffusion tensor imaging research have also indicated frontal lobe white matter structural defects associated with violence (e.g., Hoptman et al. 2005, 133; Li et al. 2005, 184). Additionally, several PET studies have reported significantly reduced glucose metabolism in the frontal cortex, particularly the anterior medial frontal region and left white frontal matter, in individuals characterized by violent behavior (e.g., Goyer et al. 1994, 21; Raine et al. 1997, 495; Soderstrom et al. 2000, 29).

Several subregions comprise the surface of the frontal lobes, which have distinctive patterns of connectivity with other areas of the cerebral cortex, along with structures deep below the brain's surface. A number of these cortical subregions are believed to be involved in *executive functioning*, an umbrella term referring to the cognitive processes facilitating future, goal-oriented behavior (Morgan and Lilienfeld 2000, 113), including abilities such as maintaining an appropriate problem-solving set for future goal attainment (Luria 1966). Executive functioning is broadly composed of four distinct cognitive domains: volition (i.e., capacity for intentional behavior), planning (i.e., identification and organization of the steps and elements needed to carry out an intention or achieve a goal), purposive action (i.e., translation of an intention or plan into productive, self-serving activity), and effective performance (i.e., self-monitoring and self-correction; Lezak et al. 2004). Each of these domains is required for socially and contextually appropriate behavior and successful self-serving conduct (Spreen and Strauss 1998; Lezak et al. 2004), which intuitively make executive functioning and associated brain regions promising areas for studying the etiology of crime, violence, and antisociality.

The prefrontal cortex (i.e., the prefrontal region of the frontal lobe) eventually became a primary region of investigation for earlier neuroimaging research on antisocial behavior. In terms of structural findings, Raine and colleagues (2000, 119), using sMRI, found reductions in prefrontal gray volumes in individuals with antisocial personality disorder (ASPD) (who were significantly more violent) compared to controls and individuals with substance dependence. In fact, individuals in the ASPD group were characterized by 11% less prefrontal gray matter volume compared to controls, and nearly 14% less prefrontal gray matter volume compared to those in the substance dependent group. However, white matter volume in the prefrontal area did not differ significantly across the three groups. More recently, reduced prefrontal volumes were identified in violent schizophrenia patients compared to controls, and increased scores on an impulsivity measure were associated with reduced prefrontal volumes (Kumari et al. 2009, 39).

Raine et al. (1997, 495) conducted one of the classic functional imaging studies in this area, examining 41 murderers pleading not guilty by reason of insanity, and 41 age- and sex-matched controls. For this study, PET imaging was used during a continuous performance challenge task. Results indicated murderers demonstrated reduced glucose metabolism in lateral and medial prefrontal cortical regions (i.e., left and right medial superior frontal cortex, left anterior medial cortex, and right OFC). In a subsequent study (Raine et al. 2008), these authors found murderers characterized by affective (i.e., reactive and emotionally based) aggression demonstrated reduced lateral and medial prefrontal functioning when compared to controls, whereas those characterized by predatory (i.e., purposeful and goal driven) aggression had reduced medial prefrontal but not lateral prefrontal functioning relative to the control group. Another study (Volkow et al. 1995, 243) also found reduced glucose metabolism bilaterally in prefrontal regions in violent psychiatric patients with intermittent explosive disorder (IED; an illness defined by repeated unplanned outbursts of aggression which are disproportionately intense relative to situational factors and result in harm to property and person) compared to healthy controls. Finally, a meta-analysis of 43 structural and functional neuroimaging studies (Yang and Raine 2009) reported significantly reduced structure and function in prefrontal regions in antisocial individuals.

Dorsolateral prefrontal cortex

Researchers have come to recognize the prefrontal cortex as a composite of anatomically distinct subsystems, rather than a unitary structure (Dinn and Harris 2000, 173), and differentiations have been made between the functional properties of the orbitofrontal/ventromedial and dorsolateral prefrontal sectors (Damasio 1994; Lapierre et al. 1995, 139). These subvolumes may have critical yet differential associations with the emotional and behavioral components of antisocial behavior and violence. For example, multiple sources of evidence suggest that the dorsolateral prefrontal cortex (DLPFC) mediates executive functions (Dinn and Harris 2000, 173) and is involved with the temporal integration of behavior (Lapierre et al. 1995, 139). The DLPFC also plays a critical role in inhibitory control, which is necessary for the development of moral conduct and moral cognition (Kochanska et al. 1997, 1).

Structural deficits in the DLPFC have been identified in antisocial boys with substance dependence (Dalwani et al. 2011, 295); they have also been associated with emotional deficits in psychopathic individuals (Zamboni et al. 2008; Yang et al. 2009, 736), and aggressive symptoms of conduct disorder (Fairchild et al. 2013, 86). Functional deficits in the DLPFC have been identified in antisocial substance-dependent boys (Crowley et al. 2010) and have also been associated with behavioral inhibition and impulsivity in individuals with ASPD (Völlum et al. 2010, 123), impaired decision-making ability in young offenders (Syngelaki et al. 2009, 1213), and alcoholism in ASPD patients with a history of violent behavior (Laasko et al. 2002). van Holst et al. (2012) found that gamblers showed increased DLPFC and ACC in response to gambling-related cues compared to controls. Other researchers failed to identify functional deficits in psychopaths when performing DLPFC tasks (Basoglu 2008, 72; Blair et al. 2006, 153; Roussy and Toupin 2000, 413). Interestingly, an fMRI study of community individuals (Glenn et al. 2009, 909) found increased psychopathy scores to be related to increased activity in the right DLPFC during an emotional moral decision-making task.

Orbitofrontal cortex

The orbitofrontal cortex (OFC; also known as the ventromedial prefrontal cortex) is critical in guiding behavior by processing the reward–punishment value of stimuli, and thus plays a key role in controlling violent acts (Damasio et al. 1994). The OFC, however, modulates sensitivity to reinforcement contingencies (see Dinn and Harris 2000, 173 for a review), and is involved with inhibiting inadequately motivated actions and modulating aggressive behavior and autonomic reactivity (see Lapierre et al. 1995, 139 for a review). In humans, this system contributes more to social and self-awareness than the DLPFC (Damasio 1994; see also Lapierre et al. 1995, 139 for a review). Pathologies of the OFC/VMPFC appear similar to psychopathy, whereas clinical DLPFC syndromes appear somewhat incompatible (Lapierre et al. 1995, 139).

Structural deficits in the OFC have been identified in violent males diagnosed with ASPD and type 2 alcoholism (Laasko et al. 2002), violent offenders with substance abuse disorders (Schiffer et al. 2011, 1039), men with ASPD (Raine et al. 2011, 227), aggressive and impulsive psychiatric inpatients (Antonucci et al. 2006, 213), and boys diagnosed with conduct disorder (CD) (Huebner et al. 2008, 540); and have been associated with gender differences (i.e., girls more so than boys) in children characterized by aggression and behavioral problems (Boes et al. 2008, 677). Additionally, gray matter volumetric increases in the OFC have been associated with increases in callous–unemotional traits in girls with CD (Fairchild et al. 2013, 86). Functional deficits in the OFC have been reported in violent individuals relative to nonviolent controls (e.g., Mathews et al. 2005, 287; Kumari et al. 2006, 159; Joyal et al. 2007, 97); in boys with antisocial behavioral and substance abuse problems (Crowley et al., 2010); in adolescents with behavioral problems (White et al. 2013, 315); in children with CD, oppositional defiant disorder (ODD), and psychopathic traits (Finger et al. 2011, 152), and individuals with borderline personality disorder or ASPD (Völlum et al. 2004, 39); and have been associated with increased lifestyle and antisocial psychopathic traits in violent patients with schizophrenia (Dolan and Fullam 2009, 570). Structural and functional studies have also identified abnormalities in the connectivity between the OFC and amygdala in psychopathic individuals and adolescents with CD (Marsh et al. 2011, 279; Passamonti et al. 2012).

TEMPORAL LOBE

The temporal lobe is associated with several different brain functions: namely, memory retention and storage, organization of sensory input, language production, visual perception, and emotional responses. The temporal lobe has been a popular region of interest in neuroimaging studies of antisocial behavior, which have foundations in the classic investigations of murderers using electroencephalography (EEG) that noted functional abnormalities in this region (Stafford-Clark and Taylor 1949; Hill and Pond 1952, 23; Mundy-Castle 1953, 103). Both structural and functional neuroimaging investigations have identified temporal lobe deficits that have been related to various forms of antisocial, aggressive, and violent behavior (Dolan 2010, 199).

Structural deficits, including various forms of volume reductions, have been identified in the temporal lobe regions of antisocial individuals. For example, Dolan and colleagues (2002, 105) found 20% reductions in volume in frontal and temporal lobes in impulsive–aggressive men with ASPD compared to controls. Similar studies examining reduced gray matter have found consistent results in individuals diagnosed with ASPD, CD, and psychopathy (Kruesi et al. 2004; Pridmore et al. 2005, 856; Muller et al. 2008; Gregory et al. 2012). Barkataki and colleagues (2006, 239) used structural MRI to compare volumes of numerous brain structures among 13 men with ASPD, 13 men with schizophrenia and a history of violence, 15 nonviolent men with schizophrenia, and 15 healthy nonviolent male controls. Results indicated ASPD men were characterized by reduced whole brain and temporal lobe volume, as well as increased putamen volume, relative to controls. Using a cortical thinning approach, Yang and colleagues (2009) found that cortical gray matter in the right frontal and temporal cortices was significantly thinner in psychopaths compared to nonpsychopathic controls. Finally, using sMRI, Huebner et al. (2008, 540) identified reduced bilateral (i.e., on both sides of the brain) temporal lobe volumes in a sample of 23 boys diagnosed with CD compared to age- and IQ-matched controls.

Several literature reviews of functional imaging studies have consistently indicated aggressive and violent individuals tend to be characterized by functional deficits in the temporal lobe (Bufkin and Luttrel 2005, 176). In terms of PET findings, Volkow and colleagues (1995, 243) found reduced rates of glucose metabolism in medial temporal regions in eight violent psychiatric patients relative to eight normal comparison subjects, while Raine and colleagues (1996) found an abnormal asymmetry in glucose metabolism in the medial temporal lobe (reduced activity in the left hemisphere compared to the right) in murderers compared to controls. Wong and colleagues (1997, 49) also found that patients with schizophrenia who committed single or minor offenses demonstrated reduced activity in anterior temporal lobe structures compared to normal controls. Furthermore, Soderstrom and colleagues (2000, 29) examined several ROIs in an sMRI and SPECT study of 21 impulsive violent offenders referred for pretrial forensic evaluations and 11 healthy controls. Although results indicated no structural deficits among violent offenders, reduced regional blood flow in the right medial temporal and right angular gyri was noted in the violent offender group when compared to controls. Another study (Goethals et al. 2005, 187) found that patients with either borderline personality disorder or ASPD demonstrated reduced rCBF in both right temporal and prefrontal regions compared to controls, but that those characterized by violence also showed structural deficits. Finally, an earlier fMRI investigation (Kiehl et al. 2001, 677) reported criminal psychopaths were characterized by overactivation in the bilateral fronto-temporal cortex when processing emotional stimuli. In sum, consistent evidence from structural and functional neuroimaging studies continues to implicate the temporal lobe in various forms of criminality, violence, and antisocial behavior.

To summarize, the growing number of neuroimaging investigations to date speaks to the "state of the science" of neuroimaging and its application to forensic psychiatric practice, and may be relatable—in the eyes of the court—to its testability, peer review and publication, potential/known error rate, operational standards, and acceptance by the scientific community. As such, this body of empirical work is useful to those in the criminal justice system tasked with determining the evidentiary value of neuroimaging, particularly as it may measure up to admissibility standards such as *Daubert.*

REASONING PROCESS: PREVIOUS FORENSIC APPLICATIONS OF NEUROIMAGING EVIDENCE

The reasoning process leading to the forensic psychiatry opinion may be best understood by examining previous criminal cases in which neuroimaging evidence was introduced and accepted in order to inform the opinion of the court. The exact number of these cases, however, is somewhat difficult to ascertain. For example, in 2006, Feigenson noted there were approximately 130 court cases involving PET and/or SPECT evidence, and only two involving fMRI evidence (Feigenson 2006, 233; Yang et al. 2008, 65). Subsequently, Farahany (2012) noted the number of cases in which judges acknowledged neuroscience evidence (though not necessarily *neuroimaging* evidence specifically) in their opinion increased from 112 in 2007 to more than 1500 in 2011. Farahany also noted a significant limitation to these figures: the actual number of cases in which neuroscience evidence is presented is likely much higher because trial data are notoriously incomplete. A sizable number of criminal cases are settled outside of court, and Westlaw (the database utilized in this particular research) does not contain every criminal case (Farahany 2012).

Table 73.1 lists 27 such cases, in chronological order, separated according to whether the criminal defendant was aided by the evidence or not, or (in two cases) when subsequent evidence was identified which would have aided the defendant if admitted. While it serves as a qualitative review of sorts, it is not a comprehensive or exhaustive list of such cases, as the present cases were culled from the empirical literature and reflect only those garnering the attention of scholars in forensic neuroscience. As such they do not constitute a representative "sample," but rather a sample of convenience. Nonetheless, many of these cases were noteworthy in some way and offer an opportunity to discern some initial patterns regarding the use of brain imaging evidence in the courtroom.

First, of the 25 cases reported in the empirical literature in which neuroimaging evidence was admitted, it can be noted that there are more than double the number of cases in which neuroimaging evidence did not actually aid the defendant ($n = 17$ or 68%) compared to those in which it did ($n = 8$ or 32%). Second, these cases appear to be more commonly from California ($n = 6$ of 25 or 24% of the total), particularly so in the cases in which the defendant was aided ($n = 3$ of 8 or 37.5%). Cases from New York were the second-most common among all of the cases ($n = 4$ of 25 or 16% of the total), and the most common among cases in which the defendant was not aided ($n = 3$ of 17 or 17.6%). Third, among these cases it appears that

Table 73.1 Criminal cases involving neuroimaging evidence

Cases in which evidence was accepted and aided defendant							
Case	Year	Location	Case type	Imaging technique	Imaging outcome	Legal outcome	Source
U.S. v. Hinckley	1982	Washington, DC	Capital case (attempted assassination of President Ronald Regan): Guilt phase	CAT	Showed widened sulci (associated with schizophrenia)	Not guilty under reason of insanity	Moriarty (2008)
McNamara v. Borg	1991	California (9th Circuit)	Capital case: Guilt phase	PET	Introduced in support of the defendant's mitigation claim that he was suffering from schizophrenia.	Defendant sentenced to life imprisonment rather than execution. Jurors later acknowledged they were significantly influenced by the neuroimaging evidence in their decision to spare the defendant's life.	Moriarty (2008), Snead (2006)
Hoskins v. State	1999	Florida	Capital case: Sentencing phase	PET	Results indicated abnormality (unspecified)	Florida Supreme Court reversed imposition of death penalty, and remanded case for a new penalty proceeding so defendant could present a PET scan showing a brain abnormality (failure to allow neuroimaging evidence at the sentencing phase of trial was held to be reversible error).	Moriarty (2008), Snead (2006)
U.S. v. Aramony	2001	New York	53 charges (embezzlement, misappropriation of funds): Guilt phase	MRI	MRI scan used to argue a shrinking brain defense: showed widened sulci (associated with schizophrenia)	Shortly after brain imaging evidence determined admissible, entered into plea bargain that resulted in substantially reduced 7-year prison sentence.	Batts (2009), Snead (2006)

(*Continued*)

Table 73.1 (*Continued*) Criminal cases involving neuroimaging evidence

Cases in which evidence was accepted and aided defendant							
Case	**Year**	**Location**	**Case type**	**Imaging technique**	**Imaging outcome**	**Legal outcome**	**Source**
State v. Marshall	2001	Washington	Capital case: Sentencing phase	MRI, EEG, SPECT	Court noted that MRI, EEG, and SPECT evidence indicated defendant's brain had severe atrophy, electric brain activity far slower than that of a normal person, and abnormal blood flow.	Death penalty sentence reversed	Moriarty (2008)
People v. Williams	2004	California	Sentencing phase	PET	Defendant's expert testified that the PET scan showed decreased activity in the frontal lobe, basal ganglia, and thalamus, and stated that this pattern is often visible with traumatic brain injuries or psychotic disorders, and was associated with impaired judgment and an inability to regulate aggression.	Jury convicted defendant on a lesser charge of second-degree murder, rather than first-degree murder.	Moriarty (2008)
Peter J. Chiesa	2004	California	Capital case: Sentencing phase	SPECT	Introduced to show that the murder was not calculated, but rather the result of a poorly functioning brain	Evidence admitted at trial along with expert testimony and the jury found for two counts of second-degree murder.	Snead (2006)
Commonwealth v. Pirela; Commonwealth v. Morales	2004	Philadelphia	Capital case (two separate death sentencing proceedings for Simon Pirela [aka, Simon Morales]): Sentencing phase	MRI, PET	In first case, introduced to support mitigating factors of diminished capacity, brain damage, and mental impairment; in subsequent case, introduced to show mental retardation	Admitted in each case; in both cases, based on neuroimaging evidence, death sentences vacated and life imprisonment imposed	Snead (2006)

(*Continued*)

Table 73.1 (*Continued*) Criminal cases involving neuroimaging evidence

Cases in which evidence was accepted but did not aid defendant							
Case	**Year**	**Location**	**Case type**	**Imaging technique**	**Imaging outcome**	**Legal outcome**	**Source**
People v. Herbert Weinstein	1992	New York	Charged with second-degree murder (accused of strangling his wife and throwing her body from their 12th-story Manhattan apartment to make her death appear as a suicide): Sentencing phase	PET	Large cyst located in the membranous casing of the brain (the arachnoid membrane) had increased the pressure on defendant's frontal cortex, creating metabolic imbalances in the region.	Judge ruled that jury could hear defendant had a brain cyst, but not that such cysts or abnormal brain metabolism increase violent tendencies. Defendant pled guilty to the reduced charge of manslaughter.	Batts (2009)
People v. Holt	1997	California	Capital case: Sentencing phase	PET, EEG	PET scan images and an EEG showing abnormalities in both temporal lobes and damage to the cingulate gyrus region of the brain, which experts testified was consistent with aberrant sexual behavior	Evidence admitted, but the jury was not persuaded by this mitigation evidence and sentenced the defendant to death.	Snead (2006)
United States v. Gigante	1997	New York	Racketeering, RICO, conspiracy to murder, an extortion conspiracy, and a labor payoff conspiracy: Sentencing phase	PET	According to defense expert's interpretation, defendant was suffering from organic brain dysfunction, possibly due to Alzheimer disease or multi-infarct dementia.	The court held the PET scan evidence was unreliable, and furthermore neither credible nor persuasive. They also found his abnormalities could be a result of drug use.	Moriarty (2008)
Robinson v. State	1999	Florida	Capital case: Sentencing phase	SPECT	Petitioner had suffered brain damage to his frontal lobe (given little weight because of insufficient evidence that brain damage caused petitioner's conduct)	Trial court did not abuse discretion in denying the motion for the evidence in this case where petitioner did not show need for the additional test.	Snead (2006)

(*Continued*)

Table 73.1 (*Continued*) Criminal cases involving neuroimaging evidence

Cases in which evidence was accepted but did not aid defendant							
Case	**Year**	**Location**	**Case type**	**Imaging technique**	**Imaging outcome**	**Legal outcome**	**Source**
People v. Kraft	2000	California	Capital case: Sentencing phase	PET	Experts testified images were consistent with obsessive-compulsive disorder.	Evidence admitted, but the jury was unmoved by this evidence and sentenced defendant to death.	Snead (2006)
People v. Protsman	2001	California	First-degree murder: Sentencing phase	PET	Decrease in frontal lobe activity	The California Court of Appeal, following the general acceptance standard as mandated by their state supreme court, upheld the trial court's decision that the proposed use of the PET scan (as opposed to the PET scan itself) testimony did not meet the general acceptance standard. Sentenced to life in prison without the possibility of parole, plus one year for the weapon enhancement.	Moriarty (2008)
Rogers v. State	2001	Florida	Capital case: Sentencing phase	PET, MRI	MRI scan revealed no impairment.	Expert testimony did not posit that a PET scan would be essential in this particular case and that any impairment was sufficiently demonstrated with evidence already admitted.	Snead (2006)

(*Continued*)

Table 73.1 (*Continued*) Criminal cases involving neuroimaging evidence

Cases in which evidence was accepted but did not aid defendant							
Case	Year	Location	Case type	Imaging technique	Imaging outcome	Legal outcome	Source
United States v. Mezvinksky	2002	Pennsylvania	Defendant charged with federal fraud crimes and attempted to raise a mental health defense, alleging bipolar disorder, frontal lobe organic brain damage, and Lariam-induced toxic encephalopathy: Guilt phase	PET	Abnormal scan with frontal lobe decrease consistent with Alzheimer disease, toxic encephalopathy, or Pick disease.	PET scan was permitted in court. Neuroimaging was not enough for which defendant offered such testimony.	Moriarty (2008)
Harrington v. State	2003	Iowa	Capital case: Sentencing phase	Computer-based brain testing measuring P300 wave patterns of brain activity (i.e., brain fingerprinting)	Petitioner's brain did not contain information about the murder, but evidence confirmed his brain contained information consistent with his alibi.	Court did not rule on the admissibility of this evidence because it found resolution of this issue unnecessary to resolution of the appeal. (Due process claim was dispositive.)	Snead (2006)
Ex Part Simpson	2004	Texas	Capital case: Sentencing phase	MRI, EEG	An MRI and an EEG were introduced in the sentencing phase at trial, but the court concluded that the expert testimony did not establish mental retardation for the defendant.	The imaging and expert testimony were admissible, but unpersuasive as to preventing death sentence.	Snead (2006)
People v. Goldstein	2004	New York	Murder in the second degree: Sentencing phase	PET	Reduction in metabolism in the frontal lobe and the basal ganglia	Neuroimaging was not enough to convince the jury.	Moriarty (2008)

(*Continued*)

Table 73.1 (*Continued*) Criminal cases involving neuroimaging evidence

Cases in which evidence was accepted but did not aid defendant							
Case	**Year**	**Location**	**Case type**	**Imaging technique**	**Imaging outcome**	**Legal outcome**	**Source**
Roper v. Simmons	2005	Missouri	Capital case: Sentencing phase	Research based on anatomical brain scans, including fMRI	Neuroimaging showing that the adolescent brain was insufficiently developed to support functions such as long-term planning, impulse control, risk assessment, etc.	Finding that juveniles are more prone to violent behavior and to peer pressure, the court cited the amicus briefs relying on the neurological evidence.	Snead (2006)
Slaughter v. State	2005	Oklahoma	Capital case: Sentencing phase	Brain fingerprinting based on MERMER effect	Introduced as new evidence supporting innocence. When asked salient details of the crime scene, petitioner's brain response to that information indicated "information absent," indicating he did not have knowledge of "salient features of the crime scene."	Court found insufficient evidence to support a conclusion that brain fingerprinting would meet Daubert evidence standard.	Snead (2006)
Smith v. Anderson	2005	Sixth Circuit	Capital case: Sentencing phase	CAT, MRI	Evidence offered did not actually prove an organic brain disorder.	Court found evidence introduced not compelling enough to sustain the motion	Snead (2006)
State v. Reid	2006	Tennessee	Capital case: Penalty phase	PET	PET scan admitted as evidence, indicating shrinkage or atrophy of the left temporal lobe of the defendant's brain, that the damage had likely been caused by a head injury when the defendant was 7 or 8 years old, and that such injury was associated with psychotic disorders producing delusional states.	Tennessee Supreme Court noted without critique that trial court admitted PET scan evidence during penalty phase of a capital murder. Defendant was nonetheless found competent to stand trial.	Moriarty (2008)

(*Continued*)

Table 73.1 (*Continued*) Criminal cases involving neuroimaging evidence

Cases in which evidence was accepted but did not aid defendant							
Case	**Year**	**Location**	**Case type**	**Imaging technique**	**Imaging outcome**	**Legal outcome**	**Source**
State v. Mercer	2009	South Carolina	Capital case: Charged with armed robbery and shooting: Penalty phase	SPECT	SPECT scan showed questionable abnormality which did not prove dementia, poor judgment, etc.	Defendant sentenced to death	Blume and Paavola (2011)
United States v. Semrau	2012	Tennessee	Charged with three counts of health-care fraud: Penalty phase	fMRI (lie detection)	Two scans indicated he was telling the truth; one indicated he was lying.	Judge decided it would not be admitted as a defense; Defendant found guilty.	Shen and Jones (2011)
Cases in which evidence was obtained post-verdict, which could have aided defendant							
Case	**Year**	**Location**	**Case type**	**Imaging technique**	**Imaging outcome**	**Legal outcome**	**Source**
State v. South	1993	South Carolina	Capital case: Prior to trial	CAT	CAT scan was admitted, but was read as normal.	Convicted of murder and sentenced to death for a drive-by shooting of a police officer. Six years later, and MRI revealed a brain tumor that the radiologist had previously failed to discover.	Blume and Paavola (2011)
Zachary Short v. South Carolina	2005	South Carolina	Murder: Post conviction	MRI, PET	MRI and PET scans revealed significant abnormalities in defendant's brain structure and function. He also demonstrated poor performance on tests of verbal and abstract reasoning, impulsivity, and tactual memory-functions—largely associated with prefrontal and central cortex areas of the brain.	Tried and convicted for murdering police officer in Aiken, South Carolina.	Blume and Paavola (2011)

neuroimaging evidence was predominantly introduced during the sentencing phase of the criminal proceedings. For cases in which the evidence did not aid the defendant, this discrepancy is much more pronounced (i.e., $n = 16$ of 17 or 94.1% of cases) relative to cases in which neuroimaging evidence aided the defendant (i.e., $n = 5$ of 8 or 62.5% of cases).

Regarding imaging techniques, PET evidence was used most often in these cases ($n = 13$ of 25 or 52%), followed by MRI ($n = 8$ of 25 or 32%). For cases in which the defendant was aided, PET was used in four cases (50%), as the sole technique in three cases (75% of the cases it was used), and in conjunction with MRI in one case. On balance, MRI was utilized in three cases (37.5%), as the sole technique in one case and in conjunction with other methods in two cases (including the aforementioned case with PET). For cases in which the defendant was not aided, PET was used in nine cases (52.9%), as the sole technique in seven cases (77.8% of the cases it was used), and in conjunction with MRI in one case. On balance, MRI was utilized in five cases (29.4%), as the sole technique in one case and in conjunction with other methods in four cases (including the aforementioned case with PET). This may reflect the relatively high rates of admissibility of PET and SPECT (related to their use more so in proceedings before judges rather than juries) discussed by Feigenson (2008, 233—see above), or perhaps a reflection of technological advances in neuroimaging procedures, with the courts' willingness—over the time frame indicated—to admit evidence from a more established "tried and true" method such as PET (an older neuroimaging method) rather than a more-recent, less-proven technology (such as MRI). In fact, the long-standing conflict the law has between innovative science and reliability has been noted in the literature (Egan 2007, 62). In summary, while PET appears to have been the most prevailing technique among these cases, the proportion of cases using PET and MRI appears largely similar across cases in which the defendant was and was not aided by neuroimaging evidence. As such, the neuroimaging technique per se may not have played a substantive role in the effectiveness of the assistance to the defendant in each case.

Regarding neuroimaging outcome and how imaging data were applied (e.g., informing the forensic psychiatric opinion), eight of the cases (32% of overall cases) reported imaging findings to be associated with actual psychiatric or medical disorders (i.e. schizophrenia, psychotic disorders, Alzheimer disease, dementia, obsessive–compulsive disorder, toxic encephalopathy or Pick disease). Schizophrenia was the disorder most commonly referred to in the cases that aided the defendant ($n = 3$ or 37.5%), and this disorder was not mentioned in the cases in which the defendant was not aided. On balance, Alzheimer disease was the condition most-often mentioned in cases in which the defendant was not aided ($n = 2$ or 11.8%), and this disease was not mentioned in cases in which the defendant was aided. Only eight cases (32% of overall cases) mentioned structural or functional deficits in specific brain regions empirically associated with crime, violence, or antisociality (i.e., related to findings from the studies reviewed above); these cases were overwhelmingly among those in which the defendant was not aided (i.e., $n = 7$ of 8 or 87.5%).

It is noteworthy that while a modest number of cases, Table 73.1 listed psychiatric or medical disorders in their applications of neuroimaging evidence, none appear to have spoken to the putative relationships between these specific disorders and crime, violence, or antisocial behavior (see Schug and Fradella 2015)—in other words, *why* these disorders would have played a role in the defendants' criminal acts. Now, it is clear that the potential value of neuroimaging data in informing the diagnostic process—particularly for the forensic psychiatrist—cannot be overstated. The diagnostic capabilities of current neuroimaging techniques must be closely scrutinized, but it stands to reason that the effectiveness of these techniques in diagnosing various psychiatric and medical disorders will increase as more advanced technologies become available. Several recent studies have demonstrated the utility of various neuroimaging methods in diagnosing neuropsychiatric disorders such as ADHD, schizophrenia, Tourette syndrome, obsessive–compulsive disorder, major depression, bipolar disorder, borderline personality disorder, and Alzheimer disease (Tebartz van Elst et al. 2003, 163; Pearlson and Calhoun 2007, 158; Borairi and Dougherty 2011, 155; Bansal et al. 2012, 1; Klöppel et al. 2012, 457). In terms of the reasoning process, it is important for the forensic psychiatric practitioner, however, to go beyond utilizing neuroimaging techniques merely for diagnostic purposes, and instead be able to conceptualize the forensic client diagnostically and legally in terms of how these disorders or their symptoms may specifically contribute to criminal, violent, and antisocial behavior.

SUMMARY

Ongoing neuroimaging research has contributed to a greater empirical understanding of the initiation, maintenance, and potential desistance from criminal behavior; and this body of research can be of significant value to the field of forensic psychiatry. Organizational frameworks for this research related to brain regions of study, neuroimaging methods, and types of antisocial populations can be of tremendous benefit to the forensic psychiatry practitioner; as well as an appreciation for legal issues related to neuroimaging, criteria for its admissibility in court, and how existing data contribute to its evidentiary value. It must be remembered that neuroimaging as a practice is still in its infancy, and applications to psychiatry in general and forensic psychiatry in particular (i.e., in areas of the criminal justice system such as criminal proceedings) must be made with caution. The forensic psychiatrist should note that neuroimaging research and forensic psychiatric applications are inextricably bound, with each serving both to inform and benefit from the other. It is hoped that this interdependence of research and practice will contribute to a growing base of evidence from which the causes and cures of criminality will eventually be revealed.

SUMMARY KEY POINTS

- The forensic psychiatric practitioner may most effectively understand neuroimaging evidence to date using organizational frameworks related to anatomical regions of the brain, imaging technique used, or type of antisocial population studied.
- Structural and functional neuroimaging studies of criminal, violent, and antisocial persons to date have largely focused on the frontal lobe and its subvolumes, the temporal lobe, and subcortical structures found within the limbic system.
- Brain imaging evidence is subject to Frye and Daubert standards in terms of admissibility to court, though these standards are not consistently applied in the United States from state to state or at the federal level.
- A review of criminal cases reported to date in the empirical literature indicates neuroimaging evidence is most often introduced during the sentencing phase, and more often consists of PET scan data. Criminal cases in which this evidence actually aided the defendant appear markedly less common.

REFERENCES

Antonucci AS, DA Gansler, S Tan, R Bhadelia, S Patz, and C Fulwiler. 2006. Orbitofrontal correlates of aggression and impulsivity in psychiatric patients. *Psychiatry Research: Neuroimaging* 147:213–220.

Bansal R, LH Staib, AF Laine, X Hao, D Xu, J Liu, M Weissman, and BS Peterson. 2012. Anatomical brain images alone can accurately diagnose chronic neuropsychiatric illnesses. *PLoS One* 7:1–21.

Barkataki I, V Kumari, M Das, P Taylor, and T Sharma. 2006. Volumetric structural brain abnormalities in men with schizophrenia or antisocial personality disorder. *Behavioral Brain Research* 169:239–247.

Basoglu C, U Semiz, O Oner, H Gunay, S Ebrinc, M Cetin, O Sildiroglu, A Algul, A Ates, and G Sonmez. 2008. A magnetic resonance spectroscopy study of antisocial behaviour disorder, psychopathy and violent crime among military conscripts. *Acta Neuropsychiatrica* 20:72–77.

Batts S. 2009. Brain lesions and their implications in criminal responsibility. *Behavioral Sciences and the Law* 27:261–272.

Birbaumer N, R Veir, M Lotze, M Erb, C Hermann, W Grodd, and H Flor. 2005. Deficient fear conditioning in psychopathy: A functional magnetic resonance imaging study. *Archives of General Psychiatry* 62:799–805.

Blair KS, C Newman, DG Mitchell, RA Richell, A Leonard, J Morton, and RJ Blair. 2006. Differentiating among prefrontal substrates in psychopathy: Neuropsychological test findings. *Neuropsychology* 20:153–165.

Blume JH and EC Paavola. 2011. Life, death, and neuroimaging: The advantages and disadvantages of the defense's use of neuroimages in capital cases: Lessons from the front. *Mercer Law Review* 62:909–931.

Boes AD, D Tranel, SW Anderson, and P Nopoulos. 2008. Right anterior cingulate: A neuroanatomical correlate of aggression and defiance in boys. *Behavioral Neuroscience* 122:677–684.

Borairi S and DD Dougherty. 2011. The use of neuroimaging to predict treatment response for neurosurgical interventions for treatment-refractory major depression and obsessive-compulsive disorder. *Harvard Review of Psychiatry* 19:155–161.

Brown T and E Murphy. 2010. Through a scanner darkly: Functional neuroimaging as evidence of a criminal defendant's past mental states. *Stanford Law Review* 62:1119–1207.

Bufkin J and V Luttrel. 2005. Neuroimaging studies of aggressive and violent behavior current findings and implications for criminology and criminal justice. *Trauma, Violence, and Abuse* 6:176–191.

Crowley TJ, MS Dalwani, SK Mikulich-Gilbertson, YP Du, CW Lejuez, KM Raymond, and MT Banich. 2010. Risky decisions and their consequences: Neural processing by boys with antisocial substance disorder. *Plos ONE, 5*(9). doi:10.1371/journal.pone.0012835

Dalwani M, JT Sakai, SK Mikulich-Gilbertson, J Tanabe, K Raymond, SK McWilliams, LL Thompson, MT Banich, and TJ Crowley. 2011. Reduced cortical gray matter volume in male adolescents with substance and conduct problems. *Drug and Alcohol Dependence* 118:295–305.

Damasio A. 1994. *Descartes' Error: Emotion, Reason, and the Human Brain*. New York: GP Putnam's Sons.

Dinn WM and CL Harris. 2000. Neurocognitive function in antisocial personality disorder. *Psychiatry Research* 97:173–190.

Dolan MC. 2010. What imaging tells us about violence in anti-social men. *Criminal Behavior and Mental Health* 20:199–214.

Dolan MC, W Deakin, N Roberts, and I Anderson. 2002. Seratonergic and cognitive impairment in impulsive aggressive personality disordered offenders: Are there implications for treatment? *Psychological Medicine* 32:105–117.

Dolan MC and RS Fullam. 2009. Psychopathy and functional magnetic resonance imaging blood oxygenation level-dependent responses to emotional faces in violent patients with schizophrenia. *Biological Psychiatry* 66:570–577.

Egan EA. 2007. Neuroimaging as evidence. *American Journal of Bioethics* 7:62–63.

Fairchild G, CC Hagan, ND Walsh, L Passamonti, AJ Calder, and IM Goodyer. 2013. Brain structure abnormalities in adolescent girls with conduct disorder. *Journal of Child Psychology and Psychiatry* 54:86–95.

Farahany N. 2012. *2012 Annual Meeting of the International Neuroethics Society*. http://vimeopro.com/vcube/neuroethicssociety

Feigenson N. 2006. Brain imaging and courtroom evidence: On admissibility and persuasiveness of fMRI. *International Journal of Law in Context* 2:233–255.

Finger EC, AA Marsh, KS Blair, ME Reid, C Sims, P Ng, and JR Blair. 2011. Disrupted reinforcement signaling in the orbitofrontal cortex and caudate in youths with conduct disorder or oppositional defiant disorder and a high level of psychopathic traits. *American Journal of Psychiatry* 168:152–162.

Glenn AL and A Raine. 2014. Neurocriminology: Implications for the punishment, prediction and prevention of criminal behavior. *Nature Reviews Neuroscience* 15:54–63.

Glenn AL, A Raine, and RA Schug, L Young, and M Hauser. 2009. Increased DLPFC activity during moral decision-making in psychopathy. *Molecular Psychiatry* 14:909–911.

Goethals I, K Audenaert, F Jacobs, F Van den Eynde, K Bernagie, A Kolindou, M Vervaet, R Dierckx, and C Van Heeringen. 2005. Brain perfusion SPECT in impulsivity-related personality disorders. *Behavioural Brain Research* 157:187–192.

Goyer PF, PJ Andreason, WE Semple, and AH Clayton. 1994. Positron-emission tomography and personality disorders. *Neuropsychopharmacology* 10:21–28.

Hill DH and DA Pond. 1952. Reflections on one hundred capital cases submitted to electroencephalography. *Journal of Mental Sciences* 98:23–43.

Hoptman MJ, J Volavka, EM Weiss, P Czobor, PR Szeszko, G Gerig, M Chakos, J Blocher, LL Citrome, J-P Lindenmayer, B Sheitman, JA Lieberman, and RM Bilder. 2005. Quantitative MRI measures of orbitofrontal cortex in patients with chronic schizophrenia or schizoaffective disorder. *Psychiatry Research: Neuroimaging* 140:133–145.

Huebner T, TD Vloet, I Marx, K Konrad, G Fink, S Herpertz, and B Herpertz-Dahlmann. 2008. Morphometric brain abnormalities in boys with conduct disorder. *Journal of the American Academy of Child and Adolescent Psychiatry* 47(5):540–547.

Joyal CC, A Putkonen, A Mancini-Marie, S Hodgins, M Kononen, L Boulay, M Pihlajamaki, H Soininen, E Stip, J Tiihonen, and HJ Aronen. 2007. Violent persons with schizophrenia and comorbid disorders: A functional magnetic resonance imaging study. *Schizophrenia Research* 91:97–102.

Kiehl KA, AM Smith, RD Hare, A Mendrek, BB Forster, J Brink, and PF Liddle. 2001. Limbic abnormalities in affective processing by criminal psychopaths as revealed by functional magnetic resonance imaging. *Biological Psychiatry* 50:677–684.

Klöppel S, A Abdulkadir, CR Jack, N Koutsouleris, J Mourão-Miranda, and P Vemuri. 2012. Diagnostic neuroimaging across diseases. *Neuroimage* 61:457–463.

Kochanska G, K Murray, and KC Coy. 1997. Inhibitory control as a contributor to conscience in childhood: From toddler to early school age. *Child Development* 68:263–277.

Kruesi M, M Casanova, G Mannheim, and A Johnson-Bilder. 2004. Reduced temporal lobe volume in early onset conduct disorder. *Psychiatry Research: Neuroimaging* 132:1–11.

Kumari V, I Barkataki, S Goswami, S Flora, M Das, and P Taylor. 2009. Dysfunctional, but not functional, impulsivity is associated with a history of seriously violent behaviour and reduced orbitofrontal and hippocampal volumes in schizophrenia. *Psychiatry Research: Neuroimaging* 173:39–44.

Kumari V, M Das, S Hodgins, E Zachariah, I Barkataki, M Howlett, and T Sharma. 2005. Association between violent behavior and impaired prepulse inhibition of the startle response in antisocial personality disorder and schizophrenia. *Behavioral Brain Research* 158:159–166.

Lapierre D, CMJ Braun, and S Hodgins. 1995. Ventral frontal deficits in psychopathy: Neuropsychological test findings. *Neuropsychologia* 33(2):139–151.

Lezak MD, DB Howieson, DW Loring, JH Hannay, and JS Fischer. 2004. *Neuropsychological assessment*, 4th edition. New York: Oxford University Press.

Li T-Q, VP Mathews, Y Wang, D Dunn, and W Kronenberger. 2005. Adolescents with disruptive behavior disorder investigated using an optimized MR diffusion tensor imaging protocol. *Annals of the New York Academy of Sciences* 1064:184–192.

Lombroso C. 1876. *Criminal Man*. Milan: Hoepli.

Luria A. 1966. *Higher Cortical Functions in Man*. New York: Basic Books.

Ly M, JC Motzkin, CL Philippi, GR Kirk, JP Newman, KA Kiehl, and M Koenigs. 2012. Cortical thinning in psychopathy. *American Journal of Psychiatry* 169(7):743–749.

Marsh AA, EC Finger, KA Fowler, CJ Adalio, IT Jurkowitz, JC Schechter, DS Pine, J Decety, and RJ Blair. 2013. Empathic responsiveness in amygdala and anterior cingulate cortex in youths with psychopathic traits. *Journal of Child Psychology and Psychiatry* 54(8):900–910.

Marsh AA, EC Finger, KA Fowler, IT Jurkowitz, JC Schechter, HH Yu, DS Pine, and RJ Blair. 2011. Reduced amygdala–orbitofrontal connectivity during moral judgments in youths with disruptive behavior disorders and psychopathic traits. *Psychiatry Research: Neuroimaging* 194(3):279–286.

Mathews VP, WG Kronenberger, Y Wang, JT Lurito, MJ Lowe, and DW Dunn. 2005. Media violence exposure and frontal lobe activation measured by functional magnetic resonance imaging in aggressive and nonaggressive adolescents. *Journal of Computer Assisted Tomography* 29:287–292.

Mills S and A Raine. 1994. Neuroimaging and aggression. *Journal of Offender Rehabilitation* 21(3–4):145–158.

Morgan AB and SO Lilienfeld. 2000. A meta-analytic review of the relationship between antisocial behavior and neuropsychological measures of executive function. *Clinical Psychology Review* 20(1):113–136.

Moriarty JC. 2008. Flickering admissibility: Neuroimaging evidence in the U.S. courts. *Behavioral Sciences and the Law* 26(1):29–49.

Mundy-Castle AC. 1955. The EEG in twenty-two cases of murder or attempted murder. Appendix on possible significance of alphoid rhythms. *Journal of the National Institute for Personnel Research* 6:103–120.

Passamonti L, G Fairchild, A Fornito, IM Goodyer, I Nimmo-Smith, CC Hagan, and AJ Calder. 2012. Abnormal anatomical connectivity between the amygdala and orbitofrontal cortex in conduct disorder. *Plos One* 7(11). doi:10.1371/journal.pone.0048789

Passamonti L, G Fairchild, I Goodyer, G Hurford, C Hagan, J Rowe, and A Calder. 2010. Neural abnormalities in early-onset and adolescence-onset conduct disorder. *Archives of General Psychiatry* 67(7):729–738.

Pearlson GD and V Calhoun. 2007. Structural and functional magnetic resonance imaging in psychiatric disorders. *Canadian Journal of Psychiatry* 52(3):158–166.

Pridmore S, A Chambers, and M McArthur. 2005. Neuroimaging in psychopathy. *Australian and New Zealand Journal of Psychiatry* 39(10):856–865.

Raine A, M Buchsbaum, and L LaCasse. 1997. Brain abnormalities in murderers indicated by positron emission tomography. *Biological Psychiatry* 42(6):495–508.

Raine A, SS Ishikawa, E Arce, T Lencz, KH Knuth, S Bihrle, L LaCasse, and P Colletti. 2005. Hippocampal structural asymmetry in unsuccessful psychopaths. *Biological Psychiatry* 55:185–191.

Raine A, T Lencz, S Bihrle, L LaCasse, and P Colletti. 2000. Reduced prefrontal gray matter volume and reduced autonomic activity in antisocial personality disorder. *Archives of General Psychiatry* 57(2):119–127.

Raine A, Y Yang, KL Narr, and AW Toga. 2011. Sex differences in orbitofrontal gray as a partial explanation for sex differences in antisocial personality. *Molecular Psychiatry* 16(2):227–236.

Roussy S and J Toupin. 2000. Behavioral inhibition deficits in juvenile psychopaths. *Aggressive Behavior* 26(6):413–424.

Schiffer B, BW Müller, N Scherbaum, S Hodgins, M Forsting, J Wiltfang, ER Gizewski, and N Leygraf. 2011. Disentangling structural brain alterations associated with violent behavior from those associated with substance use disorders. *Archives of General Psychiatry* 68(10):1039–1049.

Schug RA and HF Fradella. 2015. *Mental Illness and Crime.* Thousand Oaks, CA: Sage.

Schug RA, Y Gao, AL Glenn, Y Yang, and A Raine. 2009. Role of the frontal lobe in violence. In *McGraw-Hill Yearbook of Science and Technology*, edited by McGraw-Hill Education Editorial Staff, Hightstown, NJ: McGraw-Hill, 326–328.

Shen FX and OD Jones. 2011. Brain scans as evidence: Truths, proofs, lies, and lessons. *Mercer Law Review* 62(3):861–883.

Snead CO. 2006. *Neuroimaging and the Courts: Standards and Illustrative Case Index*. Emerging Issues in Neuroscience Conference for State and Federal Judges. http://www.google.com/url?sa=t&rct=j&q=&esrc=s&source=web&cd=1&cad=rja&uact=8&ved=0ahUKEwj1taC6oJTOAhUP8GMKHUV1DSEQFggcMAA&url=http%3A%2F%2Fwww.ncsc.org%2F~%2Fmedia%2FFiles%2FPDF%2FConferences%2520and%2520Events%2FAAAS%2FNeuroimaging%2520and%2520the%2520Courts%2520Standards%2520and%2520Illustrative%2520Case%2520Index.ashx&usg=AFQjCNGPhls_ZrD7ar2ehXRwn1Zzty9emA, accessed July 29, 2016.

Soderstrom HMT, C Wikkelsö, S Ekholm, and A Forsman. 2000. Reduced regional cerebral blood flow in nonpsychotic violent offenders. *Psychiatry Research: Neuroimaging* 98(1):29–41.

Stafford-Clarke D and FH Taylor. 1949. Clinical and electro-encephalographic studies of prisoners charged with murder. *Journal of Neurology, Neurosurgery, and Psychiatry* 12:325–330.

Syngelaki EM, SC Moore, JC Savage, G Fairchild, and S Van Goozen. 2009. Executive functioning and risky decision making in young male offenders. *Criminal Justice and Behavior* 36(11):1213–1227.

Tebartz VEL, B Hesslinger, T Thiel, E Geiger, K Haegele, L Lemieux, and D Ebert. 2003. Frontolimbic brain abnormalities in patients with borderline personality disorder: A volumetric magnetic resonance imaging study. *Biological Psychiatry* 54(2):163.

Van Holst RJ, JN van der Meer, DG McLaren, W van den Brink, DJ Veltman, and A Goudriaan. 2012. Interactions between affective and cognitive processing systems in problematic gamblers: A functional connectivity study. *Plos ONE* 7(11):e49923. doi:10.1371/journal.pone.0049923

Van Holst, RJ, M van Holstein, B van den, V Wim, J Dick, and AE Goudriaan. 2012. Response inhibition during cue reactivity in problem gamblers: An fMRI study. *Plos ONE* 7(3):e30909.

Volkow ND, LR Tancredib, C Grant, H Gillespie, A Valentine, N Mullani, and L Hollister. 1995. Brain glucose metabolism in violent psychiatric patients: A preliminary study. *Psychiatry Research: Neuroimaging* 61(4):243–253.

Völlum B, P Richardson, S McKie, R Reniers, R Elliott, IM Anderson, S Williams, M Dolan, and B Deakin. 2010. Neuronal correlates and serotonergic modulation of behavioural inhibition and reward in healthy and antisocial individuals. *Journal of Psychiatric Research* 44(3):123–131.

Völlum B, P Richarson, J Stirling, R Elliott, M Dolan, I Chaudhry, C Dil Ben, S McKie, J Anderson, and B Deakin. 2004. Neurobiological substrates of antisocial and borderline personality disorder: preliminary results of a functional fMRI study. *Criminal Behaviour and Mental Health* 14(1):39–54. doi:10.1002/cbm.559

White SF, K Pope, S Sinclair, KA Fowler, SJ Brislin, CW Williams, and RJR Blair. 2013. Disrupted expected value and prediction error signaling in youth with disruptive behavior disorders during a passive avoidance task. *American Journal of Psychiatry* 170(3):315–323.

Wong MTH, J Lumsden, GW Fenton, and PBC Fenwick. 1997. Neuroimaging in mentally abnormal offenders. *Issues in Criminological and Legal Psychology* 27:49–58.

Yang Y, AL Glenn, and A Raine. 2008. Brain abnormalities in antisocial individuals: Implications for the law. *Behavioral Sciences and the Law* 26:65–83.

Yang Y and A Raine. 2009. Prefrontal structural and functional brain imaging findings in antisocial, violent, and psychopathic individuals: A meta-analysis. *Psychiatry Research: Neuroimaging* 174:81–88.

Yang Y, A Raine, P Colletti, AW Toga, and KL Narr. 2009. Abnormal temporal and prefrontal cortical gray matter thinning in psychopaths. *Molecular Psychiatry* 14(6):561–562.

Yang Y, A Raine, CB Han, RA Schug, AW Toga, and KL Narr. 2010. Reduced hippocampal and parahippocampal volumes in murderers with schizophrenia. *Psychiatry Research: Neuroimaging* 182:9–13.

Yang Y, A Raine, KL Narr, P Colletti, and AW Toga. 2009. Localization of deformations within the amygdala in individuals with psychopathy. *Archives of General Psychiatry* 66:986–994.

Zamboni G, ED Huey, F Krueger, P Nichelli, and J Grafman. 2008. Apathy and disinhibition in frontotemporal dementia: Insights into their neural correlates. *Neurology* 71(10):736–774.

PART 9

Special Topics in Forensic Psychiatry

SUSAN HATTERS-FRIEDMAN

74

Malingering

PHILLIP J. RESNICK

INTRODUCTION

Malingering is defined in the *Diagnostic and Statistical Manual of Mental Disorders*, 5th edition (*DSM-5*) as "the intentional production of false or grossly exaggerated physical or psychological symptoms, motivated by external incentives such as avoiding military duty, avoiding work, obtaining financial compensation, evading criminal prosecution, or obtaining drugs" (American Psychiatric Association [APA] 2013, 726). In contrast, *factitious disorders* involve the intentional production of false symptoms in the absence of obvious external rewards. Both disorders require a deceitful state of mind. Feigning is the deliberate fabrication or gross exaggeration of symptoms without any assumptions about its goals.

Malingering can be categorized into (1) pure malingering, (2) partial malingering, and (3) false imputation. When an individual feigns a disorder that does not exist at all, this is referred to as *pure malingering*. When an individual has actual symptoms but consciously exaggerates them, it is called *partial malingering*. *False imputation* refers to the attribution of actual symptoms to a cause consciously recognized by the individual as having no relationship to the symptoms. For example, a claimant who is aware that he is suffering from posttraumatic stress disorder (PTSD) due to an earlier trauma may falsely ascribe the symptoms to a car accident in order to receive compensation.

Wooley and Rogers (2014) tested this model by assessing whether various types of malingerers were able to fake PTSD without being classified as feigning. The partial malingering group proved to be the best feigning group in achieving these two goals. Surprisingly, the partial malingering group was no more successful than the false imputation group in eluding detection. Although the false imputation feigners simply needed to attribute their current PTSD symptoms to a different trauma, they added additional symptoms and distress. They took a "more is better" approach.

Persons usually malinger mental illness for one of the following five purposes: First, criminals may seek to avoid punishment by pretending to be incompetent to stand trial, insane at the time of the crime, or worthy of mitigation at sentencing. Second, malingerers may seek to avoid conscription into the military or to avoid combat. Third, malingerers may seek financial gain from social security disability, veterans' benefits, workers' compensation, or damages for alleged psychological injury. Fourth, prisoners may malinger to obtain drugs, or to be transferred to a psychiatric unit in order to facilitate escape or do "easier time." Finally, malingerers may seek admission to a psychiatric hospital to obtain free room and board, known colloquially as "three hots and a cot."

CLINICAL METHODS FOR DETECTING MALINGERING

Clinicians should utilize multiple sources of data including interviews, collateral sources, and psychometric tests in detecting malingering (Resnick 2008; Zapf and Grisso 2012). Reliance on clinical interviews alone will not allow the examiner to diagnose malingering in any but the most obvious cases. When a litigant is suspected of malingering, the clinician must look carefully for evidence of inconsistency in symptoms:

1. There may be inconsistency in the subject's report itself. For example, a malingerer may articulately explain that he or she is confused and unable to think clearly.
2. There may be inconsistency in what a person reports and the symptoms that are observed. For example, a malingerer may state that he or she is hearing voices during the interview but shows no evidence of being distracted.
3. There may be inconsistency in observation of the symptoms themselves. For example, a hospitalized patient may behave in a befuddled manner with a psychiatrist, but then play excellent poker on the ward with other patients.
4. There may be inconsistency between performance on psychological testing and a malingerer's report of his or her level of performance. For example, a litigant may

state on an intelligence test that he or she does not know how many legs are on a dog, but be performing well as an investment banker.

5. There may be inconsistency between what the malingerer reports and how genuine symptoms manifest themselves. For example, a defendant may report visual hallucinations are seen in black and white, whereas genuine visions are seen in color.

APPROACHES TO DETECTING MALINGERING

Clinicians should be particularly careful to ask open-ended questions of suspected malingerers and let evaluees tell their complete story with few interruptions. Details can be clarified later with specific questions. Inquiries about hallucinations should be carefully phrased to avoid giving clues about the nature of true hallucinations. The examiner should try to ascertain whether the subject has ever had the opportunity to observe psychotic people (e.g., during prior employment or in a family member). Clinicians may feel irritation at being deceived, but any expression of irritation or incredulity is likely to make the malingerer more defensive.

Clinicians may modify their interview style when defendants are suspected of malingering psychosis. The interview may be prolonged because fatigue diminishes the malingerer's ability to maintain a counterfeit account (Anderson et al. 1959). Rapid firing of questions increases the likelihood of getting contradictory replies from malingerers, but it may also create confusion among intellectually disabled persons. The clinician may get additional clues by asking leading questions that emphasize a different illness than the malingerer is trying to portray. Questions about improbable symptoms may be asked to see if the malingerer will endorse them. Another device is to mention, within earshot of the suspected malingerer, some easily imitated symptom that is not present. The sudden appearance of the symptom suggests malingering.

Inpatient assessment should be considered in difficult cases of suspected malingering. Feigned psychotic symptoms are difficult to maintain 24 hours a day. After completing a detailed examination, clinicians may decide to confront an evaluee with their suspicions. The suspected malingerer should be given every opportunity to save face. Once malingering is denied, there is a risk that it will be harder to admit later. It is better to say, "You haven't told me the whole truth," than, "You have been lying to me" (Inbau and Reid 1967).

Detailed knowledge about actual psychiatric symptoms is the clinician's greatest asset in recognizing simulated illness. Therefore, the phenomenology of genuine hallucinations, delusions, and other syndromes will be reviewed in this chapter.

MALINGERED HALLUCINATIONS

Before distinguishing genuine from true hallucinations, the clinician needs to differentiate between psychotic and nonpsychotic hallucinations. About 10%–15% of the healthy population sometimes experience auditory hallucinations (Sommer et al. 2010). Nonpsychotic hallucinations usually have a childhood onset with a median age of 12, whereas psychotic hallucinations begin at a median age of 21. Nonpsychotic hallucinations are often attributed to family members, spirits of dead people, or guardian angels, rather than real people such as Secret Service, police or malevolent neighbors (Laroi et al. 2012). Nonpsychotic hallucinations contain very little negative content, whereas almost all schizophrenic patients report some negative content. Nonpsychotic voices do not cause distress or disturbance in the daily life of the individual (Laroi 2012).

Persons reporting hallucinations with any atypical features should be questioned in great detail about the nature of their symptoms. Both psychotic patients (Goodwin et al. 1971) and patients with schizophrenia (Mott et al. 1965; Small et al. 1966) show a 76% rate of hallucinations in at least one sensory modality. The reported incidence of auditory hallucinations in patients with schizophrenia is 66% (Mott et al. 1965; Small et al. 1966). Eighty-two percent of hallucinating patients describe hallucinations in more than one modality (McCarthy-Jones et al. 2014). The incidence of visual hallucinations in persons with psychosis is estimated at 24% (Mott et al. 1965) to 30% (Small et al. 1966). Hallucinations are usually (88%) associated with delusions (Lewinsohn 1970).

Auditory hallucinations

Goodwin et al. (1971) described the following characteristics of auditory hallucinations. Both male and female voices were heard by 75% of the patients in their study. About two-thirds of hallucinating subjects could identify the person speaking (Goodwin et al. 1971; Kent and Wahass 1996; Leudar et al. 1997; McCarthy-Jones et al. 2014). The content of hallucinations was accusatory in over one-third of the cases.

Auditory hallucinations usually consist of single words or phrases, especially early in the disease process (Nayani and David 1996; Leudar et al. 1997). Hallucinated voices tend to become more complex over time, from single words to entire sentences. The number of voices heard also increases (Leudar et al. 1997). The syntax of long-standing auditory hallucinations is usually in complete sentences, and mirrors the syntax typically used by the evaluee (Nayani and David, 1996). In affective disorders, the content of the hallucination is usually mood-congruent and related to delusional beliefs (Asaad 1990).

Schizophrenic hallucinations tend to consist of personal insults, abuse, and derogatory comments about the patient or the activities of others (Goodwin et al. 1971; Oulis et al. 1995; Leudar et al. 1997; Laroi et al. 2012). Nayani and David (1996) reported that the most commonly encountered hallucinations were simple terms of abuse. Female subjects described insults conventionally directed at women suggesting promiscuity. Men described male insults such as those imputing homosexuality.

About one-third of persons with auditory hallucinations reported that voices asked them questions. Voices never sought information such as, "What time is it?" or "What is the weather like?" Instead they asked chastising questions, such as "Why are you smoking?" or "Why didn't you do your essay?" (Leudar et al. 1997).

Leudar et al. (1997) found that most patients in their study engaged in an internal dialogue with their hallucinations. Many were able to cope with chronic hallucinations by incorporating them into their daily life as a kind of internal advisor. Interestingly, sometimes their hallucinated voices would insist on certain actions after the patient refused to carry them out. The voices would rephrase their requests, speak louder, or curse the patient for being noncompliant. In contrast, malingerers are more likely to claim that they were compelled to obey commands without further consideration. Some malingerers describe voices in a stilted manner, such as "Go commit a sex offense." Other malingerers describe far-fetched commands, such as a robber who alleged that (malingered) voices kept screaming, "Stick up, stick up, stick up!"

Hallucinated voices are usually perceived as benign, benevolent, or malevolent. In a study by Chadwick and Birchwood (1994), patients commonly said that evil commands were evidence that the voice was bad, and kind protective words were evidence that the voice was good. Malevolent voices evoke negative emotions (anger, fear, depression, anxiety). Patients often respond by arguing, shouting, noncompliance, and avoidance of cues that trigger malevolent voices. Benevolent voices usually provoke positive emotions (amusement, reassurance, calm, happiness). Patients often respond by elective listening, willing compliance, and doing things to bring on their benevolent voices.

A common myth in detecting faked hallucinations is that if someone replies that they hear their voices in one ear or the other, they are faking. This myth is belied by the fact that when asked to place a finger on the part of the head that they could locate their voices, 71% of genuine hallucinators selected a place close to one ear (Hoffman et al. 2008). In persons with genuine auditory hallucinations, 71% were able to recall the first time they heard voices (Hoffman et al. 2008).

Persons suspected of feigning auditory hallucinations should be asked what they do to make the voices go away or diminish in intensity. Genuine patients are often able to stop auditory hallucinations when their schizophrenia is in remission, but not during the acute phase of their illness (Larkin 1979). Frequent coping strategies among persons with genuine schizophrenia are as follows: (1) specific activities (working or watching TV); (2) changes in posture (e.g., lying down or walking); (3) seeking out interpersonal contact; (4) taking medication; and (5) prayer (Falloon and Talbot 1981; Kanas and Barr 1984). Schizophrenic hallucinations tend to diminish when patients are involved in activities (Goodwin et al. 1971; McCarthy-Jones and Resnick 2014). Patients with genuine malevolent hallucinations usually develop some strategies to decrease them (McCarthy-Jones and Resnick 2014).

The suspected malingerer may be asked what makes the voices worse. Eighty percent of persons with genuine hallucinations reported that being alone worsened their hallucinations (Nayani and David 1996; McCarthy-Jones and Resnick 2014). Voices were also made worse by listening to the radio and watching television (Leudar et al. 1997). News programs were particularly hallucinogenic.

Atypical features were reported in less than 5% of patients with auditory hallucinations (McCarthy-Jones et al. 2014). Atypical voices included having a voice whose normal speaking tone is yelling, hearing only female voices, hearing only children's voices, and never hearing the same voice twice. Stephane et al. (2006) identified other atypical content of auditory hallucinations: "I hear voices of animals." "The voices sound robotic." "The voices refer to me as Mr. or Mrs." "I hear voices whenever I open a window."

Some malingerers may allege that their hallucinations went away after 1 or 2 days of treatment with antipsychotic medication. The first time a psychotic patient is given antipsychotics, the median length of time it takes for hallucinations to completely clear is 27 days (Gunduz-Bruce et al. 2005). In persons treated for schizophrenic hallucinations after 1 month, their voices became less loud and less distressing (Schneider et al. 2011). After 6 months of antipsychotics, they heard their voices less frequently and felt that they had more control of them. They also recognized they were self-generated (Schneider et al. 2011).

COMMAND AUDITORY HALLUCINATIONS

Command hallucinations are auditory hallucinations that instruct a person to act in a certain manner. Command hallucinations are easy to fabricate in order to support an insanity defense. The majority of commands to commit dangerous acts are not obeyed. Thus, the examiner must be alert to the possibility that a defendant may fake an exculpatory command hallucination or lie about an inability to refrain from a genuine hallucination. Knowledge of the frequency of command hallucinations and the factors associated with obeying commands are helpful in looking at the authenticity of such claims.

Hellerstein et al. (1987) found in a retrospective chart review that 38% of all patients with auditory hallucinations reported commands. Studies of schizophrenic auditory hallucinations found that 30%–67% included commands (Mott et al. 1965; Small et al. 1966; Goodwin et al. 1971; Hellerstein et al. 1987; McCarthy-Jones et al. 2014). Command hallucinations occurred in 30% (Goodwin et al. 1971) to 40% (Mott et al. 1965) of alcoholic withdrawal hallucinations. Patients with affective disorders reported that 46% of their hallucinations were commands (Goodwin et al. 1971).

Hellerstein et al. (1987) reported that the content of command hallucinations was 52% suicide, 5% homicide,

12% nonlethal injury of self or others, 14% nonviolent acts, and 17% unspecified. The research method of reviewing charts, rather than making direct inquiries, probably increased the relative proportion of violent commands since these are more likely to be charted.

Earlier research suggested that hallucinatory commands are generally ignored by patients (Goodwin et al. 1971; Hellerstein et al. 1987). McCarthy-Jones et al. (2014) found that 76% of their patients said they were able to resist their command hallucinations. However, Junginger (1990) reported that patients with hallucination-related delusions and hallucinatory voices that they could identify were more likely to comply with the commands. Kasper et al. (1996) reported that 84% of psychiatric inpatients with command hallucinations had obeyed them within the last 30 days. Among those reporting command hallucinations in a second forensic population, 74% indicated that they acted in response to some of their commands during the episode of illness (Thompson et al. 1992).

Junginger (1995) studied the relationship between command hallucinations and dangerousness. He found that 43% of the subjects reported full compliance with their most recent command hallucination. People are more likely to obey their command hallucinations if the voice is familiar, there are hallucination-related delusions (Junginger 1990), and the voice is perceived as powerful (Fox et al. 2004; Shawyer et al. 2008). Compliance with commands is less likely if the commands are dangerous (Junginger 1995; Kasper et al. 1996). A defendant alleging an isolated command hallucination in the absence of other psychotic symptoms should be viewed with suspicion. Noncommand auditory hallucinations (85%) and delusions (75%) are usually present with command hallucinations (Thompson et al. 1992).

Visual hallucinations

Persons with genuine visual hallucinations report that they are humanoid 70% of the time. A minority of visual hallucinations are animals or objects. Ninety-five percent of the time the visions are not something that the hallucinator has actually seen before. Over 80% of persons with visual hallucinations report that their response to their first visual hallucination was to be overwhelmed or fearful (Gauntlett-Gilbert and Kuipers 2003).

Visual hallucinations are usually of normal-sized people and are seen in color (Goodwin et al. 1971). Alcohol-induced hallucinations are more likely to contain animals (Goodwin et al. 1971). Visual hallucinations in psychotic disorders appear suddenly and typically without prodromata (Asaad and Shapiro 1986). Psychotic hallucinations do not usually change if the eyes are closed or open. In contrast, drug-induced hallucinations are more readily seen with the eyes closed or in darkened surroundings (Asaad and Shapiro 1986).

Occasionally, small (Lilliputian) people are seen in alcoholic, organic (Cohen et al. 1994), or toxic psychoses (Lewis 1961), especially anticholinergic drug toxicity (Asaad 1990; Contardi et al. 2007). The little people are sometimes 1 or 2 inches tall; at other times up to 4 feet in height. Lilliputian hallucinations are rarely seen in schizophrenia. Only 5% of visual hallucinations in the Goodwin study (1971) consisted of miniature or giant figures.

Visual hallucinations are volunteered much more often (46% versus 4%) by malingerers than by genuinely psychotic individuals (Cornell and Hawk 1989). Dramatic, atypical visual hallucinations should definitely arouse suspicions of malingering (Powell 1992).

MALINGERED DELUSIONS

Delusions are not merely false beliefs that cannot be changed by logic. A delusion is a false statement made in an inappropriate context and most importantly, with inappropriate justification. Normal people can give reasons, can engage in a dialogue, and can consider the possibilities of doubt. Persons with true delusions cannot provide adequate reasons for their beliefs.

Delusions vary in content, theme, degree of certainty, degree of systemization, and degree of relevance to the person's life in general. The more intelligent the person, the more elaborate his or her delusional system will usually be. According to Spitzer (1992), most delusions involve the following general themes: disease (somatic delusions), grandiosity, jealousy, love (erotomania), persecution, religion, being poisoned, and being possessed. Delusions of nihilism, poverty, sin, and guilt are commonly seen in depression. Technical delusions refer to the influence of such items as telephone, telepathy, and hypnosis. Delusions of technical content occur seven times more often in men than in women (Kraus 1994).

A malingerer may claim the sudden onset of a delusion. In reality, systematized delusions usually take several weeks to develop. As true delusions are given up, they first become somewhat less relevant to the everyday life of the patient, but the patient still adheres to the delusional belief. A decrease in preoccupation with delusions may be the first change seen with adequate treatment. In a later stage, the patient might admit to the possibility of error, but only as a possibility. Only much later will the patient concede that the ideas were, in fact, delusions (Sachs et al. 1974). The median length of time for delusions to fully clear after the first initiation of antipsychotic medication is 73 days (Gunduz-Bruce et al. 2005). Thus, malingering should be suspected if a person claims that a delusion suddenly appeared or disappeared.

In assessing the genuineness of delusions, the clinician should consider their content and the person's associated behavior. Malingerers' behavior usually does not conform to their alleged delusions, whereas acute schizophrenic behavior usually does. However, patients with schizophrenia may no longer behave in a manner consistent with their delusions after several months. Table 74.1 summarizes suspect hallucinations and suspect delusions.

Table 74.1 Suspect hallucinations and delusions

Auditory Hallucinations
Voices are unbearably distressing
Lack of strategies to diminish malevolent voices
Hearing voices of animals
Never hearing the same voice twice
Voice only yells
Voice sounds robotic
Hearing only children's voices
Hearing only female voices
Hallucinated questions seeking information
Allegation that all command hallucinations were obeyed
Hallucinations not associated with delusions
Stilted language reported in hallucinations
Visual hallucinations
Black and white rather than color
Dramatic, atypical visions
"Schizophrenic" hallucinations that change when the eyes are closed
Only visual hallucinations in "schizophrenia"
Miniature or giant figures
Visions unrelated to delusions or auditory hallucinations
Delusions
Abrupt onset or termination
Eagerness to call attention to delusions
Conduct not consistent with delusions
Bizarre content without disordered thinking

CLINICAL INDICATIONS OF MALINGERED PSYCHOSIS

All malingerers are actors who portray their psychoses as they understand them. Malingerers often overact their part. Malingerers sometimes mistakenly believe that the more bizarrely they behave, the more psychotic they will appear.

Malingerers are eager to call attention to their illnesses in contrast to schizophrenic patients, who are often reluctant to discuss their symptoms (Ritson and Forest 1970). One malingerer stated that he was an "insane lunatic" when he killed his parents at the behest of hallucinations that "told me to kill in my demented state." Malingering defendants may try to take control of the interview and behave in an intimidating manner. The clinician should avoid the temptation to terminate such an interview prematurely. Malingerers sometimes accuse clinicians of regarding them as faking. Such behavior is extremely rare in genuinely psychotic persons.

It is more difficult for malingerers to successfully imitate the form than the content of schizophrenic thinking (Sherman et al. 1975). Derailment, neologisms, and incoherent word salads are infrequently simulated. Positive symptoms of schizophrenia are faked more often than negative symptoms.

Malingerers give more approximate answers to questions than schizophrenic patients, such as "there are 53 weeks in the year" (Bash and Alpert 1980; Powell 1992). Persons malingering psychosis often fake intellectual deficits also (Bash and Alpert 1980; Schretlen 1988; Powell 1992). For example, a man who completed 1 year of college alleged he did not know the colors of the American flag. Malingerers are more likely to answer "I don't know" to detailed questions about psychotic symptoms, such as hallucinations. This response may simply mean that they do not know how to answer because they have never actually experienced the symptoms.

PSYCHOMETRIC TESTS FOR MALINGERING

The detection of malingering by standardized psychometric testing has been the focus of considerable research in recent years. The Structured Interview of Reported Symptoms (SIRS) was designed by Rogers et al. (1992) specifically to detect malingered psychiatric illness. The Minnesota Multiphasic Personality Inventory-2 (MMPI-2) is the most validated psychometric test for evaluating suspected malingering of psychopathology. Readers are referred to the Rogers (2008) book for details of detection of malingering with psychological testing, and to Chapter 71 of this book for psychological testing specific to evaluating malingered psychosis.

CLINICAL INDICATORS OF MALINGERED INSANITY DEFENSES

A crime without apparent motive, such as killing a stranger, lends credence to the presence of true mental disease. Genuine psychotic explanations for rape, robbery, or check forging are unusual. Another indicator of malingered psychosis is evidence from family members and collateral sources that the Global Assessment of Functioning (GAF) for the preceding year is inconsistent with the evaluee's current presentation (Kucharski et al. 1998).

In assessing defendants for criminal responsibility, clinicians must determine whether they report malingered symptoms at the time of the act, and/or malinger symptoms at the time of the examination. Some malingerers mistakenly believe that they must show ongoing symptoms of psychosis in order to succeed with an insanity defense. When defendants report psychiatric symptoms at the time of their examination, the clinician has the opportunity to see whether the alleged symptoms are consistent with genuine illness and current psychological testing results.

Defendants who have true schizophrenia may malinger an exculpatory symptom to escape criminal responsibility. These are the most difficult cases to accurately assess. Clinicians have a lower index of suspicion for malingering because of the history of psychiatric hospitalizations and the presence of residual schizophrenic symptoms. These defendants are able to draw upon their prior experience with hallucinations and their observations of other psychotic people in hospitals. They know what questions to expect from clinicians. If they spend time in a forensic psychiatric hospital, they may learn how to modify their story to fit the exact criteria for an insanity defense. Clinicians should not think of malingering and psychosis from an "either/or" perspective (Rogers et al. 1994).

Several clues can assist clinicians in the detection of fraudulent not guilty by reason of insanity (NGRI) defenses (Table 74.2). A psychotic explanation for a crime should be questioned if the new offense fits the same pattern as the defendant's previous convictions. Malingering should be suspected in defendants pleading insanity if a partner was involved in the crime. In a study at the Michigan Center for Forensic Psychiatry, 98% of successful NGRI acquittees acted alone (Thompson et al. 1992). Most accomplices of normal intelligence will not participate in psychotically motivated crimes.

Malingering defendants are more likely to present themselves as blameless within their feigned illness (Resnick 2008). This conduct was demonstrated by a man who pled NGRI to a charge of stabbing an 11-year-old boy 60 times with an ice pick. He stated that he was sexually excited and intended to force homosexual acts on the victim, but abandoned his plan when the boy began to cry. When he started to leave, 10 faces in the bushes began chanting, "Kill him, kill him, kill him." He yelled, "No," and struck out at the faces with an icepick. The next thing he knew, "the victim was covered with blood." The autopsy showed a cluster of stab wounds in the victim's head and neck—which was inconsistent with the defendant's claim that he struck out randomly at multiple faces in the bushes. His version showed a double avoidance of responsibility: (1) the faces told him to kill, and (2) he claimed to have attacked the hallucinated faces, not the victim. In other words, if even half of his story was believed, he hoped to avoid criminal responsibility. After his conviction, he confessed to six unsolved sadistic homosexual murders.

Table 74.2 Clues to malingered insanity defenses

Malingering should be suspected if any of the following are present:

1. A nonpsychotic, alternative rational motive for the crime
2. Suspicious hallucinations or delusions (see Table 74.1)
3. Current crime fits an established pattern of prior criminal conduct
4. Absence of any active or subtle signs of psychosis during the evaluation
5. Presence of a partner in the crime
6. Double denial of responsibility (e.g., disavowal of the crime plus attributing the crime to psychosis)
7. Alleged intellectual deficit coupled with alleged psychosis
8. Alleged illness inconsistent with documented level of functioning

MALINGERING IN POSTTRAUMATIC SITUATIONS

The types of psychiatric disorders that most commonly occur after a traumatic experience are posttraumatic stress disorder (PTSD), depressive disorders, post-concussion syndromes, and, occasionally, psychoses. Plaintiffs' attorneys strongly favor the diagnosis of PTSD because the diagnosis itself includes evidence that the symptoms are due to the litigated event. In contrast, depression after a traumatic event could be attributed to multiple other causes.

Posttraumatic stress disorder

ASSESSMENT OF PTSD SYMPTOMS

The diagnosis of PTSD is based almost entirely on the claimant's self-report of subjective symptoms. Accessibility on the Internet of specific *DSM-5* criteria permit the resourceful malingerer to report the "right" symptoms. The assertion that individuals dream or think about a traumatic event should be verified by others who have heard them talk about it in situations that are not related to the litigation. In addition, the clinician must obtain a detailed history of living patterns preceding the stressor. For example, symptoms such as difficulty concentrating or insomnia may have been present before the traumatic event. The clinician must carefully examine the reasonableness of the relationship between the symptoms and the stressor, the time elapsed between the stressor and symptom development, and the relationship between any prior psychiatric symptoms and current impairment.

Clinicians who simply inquire about specific symptoms of PTSD and other diagnostic criteria in the *DSM-5* will be easily fooled. Lees-Haley and Dunn (1994) found that 97% of untrained college students were able to endorse symptoms of checklists to meet the diagnosis of major depression, while 86% were able to meet the criteria for PTSD.

The clinician should insist on detailed illustration of PTSD symptoms. Coached claimants may know which PTSD symptoms to report but may not be able to elaborate on them with convincing personal life details. Invented symptoms are more likely to have a vague or stilted quality (Pitman et al. 1996). The examiner should see if litigants minimize other causes of their symptoms or exaggerate the severity of the compensable accident. Clinicians should also look for actual evidence in the mental status exam of irritability, difficulty concentrating, and an exaggerated startle response.

CLUES TO MALINGERED PTSD

Malingerers may depict themselves and their prior functioning in exclusively complementary terms (Layden 1966). Persons with PTSD insomnia compared to others with insomnia are more likely to have fear of the dark, fear of going to sleep, waking up with the covers torn apart, talking during sleep, waking up confused, and waking up from a frightening dream and then finding it hard to return to sleep (Inman et al. 1990).

Traumatic dreams occur in about 70% of persons with PTSD. About 50% of genuine nightmares in PTSD show variations on the theme of the traumatic event. For example, a woman who was raped may have dreams in which she feels helpless and is tortured without being raped. Posttraumatic nightmares, as contrasted with lifetime nightmares unrelated to trauma, are almost always accompanied by considerable body movement (van der Kolk et al. 1984). Body movement may be confirmed by the sleeping partner or disarray of sheets and covers. PTSD patients often awaken with the affect of the original trauma (Mellman et al. 1995).

Postconcussion syndromes

SYMPTOMS OF POSTCONCUSSION SYNDROME

Approximately 1.7 million traumatic brain injuries occur each year in the United States (APA 2013). Epidemiological studies indicate that a considerable number of minor head trauma patients report memory impairment, difficulty concentrating, a low threshold for fatigue, and abnormal levels of irritability (Wrightston and Gronwall 1980). Mild dysphoria, general psychological discomfort, and problems returning to previous employment were associated with this cognitive dysfunction. Neuropsychological assessment, with its focus on attention and concentration skills, visuomotor functioning, and memory abilities is particularly useful in the differential diagnosis of head injury and PTSD.

ASSESSMENT OF MALINGERED POSTCONCUSSIVE SYNDROME

Approximately 25%–50% of claimants of cognitive dysfunction are found to use suboptimal effort when given neuropsychological assessment (Guilmette et al. 1994; McAllister 1994; Youngjohn et al. 1995). The examiner must also not assume that symptoms reported after an accident are caused by the accident. It is common for symptoms reported by head-injured claimants to be present before their head injury. Table 74.3 shows the percentage of head-injured patients and control patients who alleged symptoms on a checklist.

Table 74.3 Frequency of symptoms reported after head injury

	Claimants (%)	Controls (%)
Anxiety or nervousness	93	54
Sleeping problems	92	52
Headaches	88	62
Back pain	80	48
Fatigue (mental or physical)	79	58
Dizziness	44	26

Source: Modified from Lees-Haley PR and JT Dunn. 1994. *Journal of Clinical Psychology* 50:252–256.

Considerable research has been done regarding faked memory loss. Although actual retrograde amnesia is characteristically brief in mild head injury, malingerers tend to overplay their memory loss. They may give implausible answers to questions regarding overlearned autobiographic data, such as their own name, age, gender, and social security number (Levin et al. 1992; Rogers and Correa 2008).

Several clues may be helpful in distinguishing faked from genuine ongoing memory problems. Brain injury does not impair procedural memory, such as driving a car or riding a bicycle. If memory is impaired for new learning, recollection of the head injury itself suggests faking. If a litigant volunteers several examples of memory failure, the degree of recollection itself suggests faking. Malingering is also suggested if the subject scores more poorly on questions labeled "memory testing" than on other questions that require similar memory. Another strategy to detect feigned cognitive impairment is the "floor effect." Some questions are so easy that an incorrect response is evidence of malingering. For example, the sum of two plus two or the number of legs on a dog are questions that even individuals with significant impairment can answer correctly (Rogers and Correa 2008).

Forced-choice tests are useful in assessing faked memory impairment. Forced-choice testing for memory is based on (1) presenting a large number of items in a two-choice format and (2) comparing the person's performance to the likelihood of success based on chance alone (i.e., no ability). The probability of purely guessing the correct response is 50%. The compelling conclusion is that the evaluee who scores below probability is deliberately motivated to perform poorly (Frederick et al. 1994; Soliman and Resnick 2010). Two of the more commonly used forced-choice memory tests are the Portland Digit Recognition Test (PDRT) and the Test of Malingered Memory (TOMM) (Bass and Halligan 2014).

MALINGERED AFFECTIVE DISORDERS

Depression may be malingered by defendants pursuing an insanity defense and by civil litigants seeking compensation. The Beck Depression Inventory (BDI) and the Hamilton Depression Rating Scale (HDRS) rely solely on self-report and thus are quite easy to malinger. Although malingerers of depression will claim depressed mood, they are less likely to report more subtle symptoms such as early morning awakening, diurnal variations in mood, psychomotor retardation, or loss of interest in sex. Malingerers may report difficulty falling asleep, while sleep disturbances in genuine depression more typically involve multiple awakenings, especially in the early morning hours.

In assessing whether a person is genuinely depressed, clinicians should look for a sad facial expression. Alleged weight loss should be verified in medical records. This is one of the best ways to show whether an evaluee is giving false information. Severe depression is often characterized by slow movements, slow speech, and difficulty concentrating. Assessment of difficulty concentrating can be made by seeing how attentive the evaluee is during a lengthy interview and whether he or she can spell a five-letter word backward.

Clinicians should be concerned about malingering when persons seeking hospital admission make conditional threats (Lambert and Bonner 1996). Statements such as "If you don't admit me to the hospital, I will hurt myself or someone else" or "I will sue you if you don't admit me to the hospital" are more consistent with personality disorders than severe depression (Reccoppa 2009).

Malingering of mania is unusual. Litigants may claim a history of manic symptoms, but it is difficult to sustain the flight of ideas, pressured speech, grandiose mood, increased psychomotor activity, and decreased need for sleep seen in true mania. Inpatient evaluation of suspected malingerers will usually reveal that these symptoms are not sustained.

SUMMARY

The detection of malingered mental illness is sometimes quite difficult. The decision that an individual is malingering is made by assembling all of the clues from a thorough evaluation of a litigant's past and current functioning with corroboration from clinical records, psychological testing, and other people. Clinicians must be thoroughly grounded in the phenomenology of the mental disease being simulated. Although the identification of a malingerer may be viewed as a distasteful chore, it is critical in forensic assessments. Indeed, clinicians bear a heavy responsibility to assist society in differentiating true disease from malingered madness.

SUMMARY KEY POINTS

- Knowing the detailed phenomenology of genuine symptoms helps the clinician to identify faked symptoms.
- Nonpsychotic genuine hallucinations should not be mislabeled as faked hallucinations.
- Malingered hallucinations are often described as more intense than genuine hallucinations.
- Genuine delusions usually do not start or stop suddenly.
- Having genuine schizophrenia does not preclude faking an exculpatory hallucination.

REFERENCES

American Psychiatric Association. 2013. *Diagnostic and Statistical Manual of Mental Disorders* (DSM-5), 5th edition.

Anderson EW, WH Trethowan, and J Kenna. 1959. An experimental investigation of simulation and pseudo-dementia. *Acta Psychiatrica et Neurologica Scandinavica* 34:132 (whole issue).

Asaad G. 1990. *Hallucinations in Clinical Psychiatry: A Guide for Mental Health Professionals*. New York: Brunner/Mazel.

Asaad G and B Shapiro. 1986. Hallucinations: Theoretical and clinical overview. *American Journal of Psychiatry* 143:1088–1097.

Bash IY and M Alpert. 1980. The determination of malingering. *Annals of the New York Academy of Science* 347:86–99.

Bass C and P Halligan. 2014. Factitious disorders and malingering: Challenges for clinical assessment and management. *Lancet* 383:1422–1432.

Chadwick P and M Birchwood. 1994. The omnipotence of voices: A cognitive approach to auditory hallucinations. *British Journal of Psychiatry* 164:190–201.

Cohen MAA, CA Alfonso, and MM Haque. 1994. Lilliputian hallucinations and medical illness. *General Hospital Psychiatry* 16:141–143.

Contardi S, G Rubboli, M Giulioni, R Michelucci, F Pizza, E Gardella, F Pinardi, I Bartolomei, and CA. Tassinari. 2007. Charles Bonnet syndrome in hemianopia, following antero-mesial temporal lobectomy for drug-resistant epilepsy. *Epileptic Disorders* 9:271–275.

Cornell DG and GL Hawk. 1989. Clinical presentation of malingerers diagnosed by experienced forensic psychologists. *Law and Human Behavior* 13:375–383.

Falloon IRH and RE Talbot. 1981. Persistent auditory hallucinations: Coping mechanisms and implications for management. *Psychological Medicine* 11:329–339.

Fox JRE, NS Gray, and H Lewis. 2004. Factors determining compliance with command hallucinations with violent content: The role of social rank, perceived power of the voice and voice malevolence. *Journal of Forensic Psychiatry and Psychology* 15:511–531.

Frederick RI, SD Sarfaty, DJ Johnston, and J Powel. 1994. Validation of a detector of response bias on a forced-choice test of nonverbal ability *Neuropsychology* 8:118–125.

Gauntlett-Gilbert J and E Kuipers. 2003. Phenomenology of visual hallucinations in psychiatric conditions. *Journal of Nervous and Mental Disease* 191:203–205.

Goodwin DW, P Alderson, and R Rosenthal. 1971. Clinical significance of hallucinations in psychiatric disorders. A study of Il6 hallucinatory patients. *Archives of General Psychiatry* 24:76–80.

Guilmette TJ, W Whelihan, FR Sparadeo, and G Buongiorno. 1994. Validity of neuropsychological test results in disability evaluations. *Perceptual and Motor Skills* 78:1179–1186.

Gunduz-Bruce H, M McMeniman, DG Robinson, MG Woerner, JM Kane, NR Schooler, and JA Lieberman. 2005. Duration of untreated psychosis and time to treatment response for delusions and hallucinations. *American Journal of Psychiatry* 162:1966–1969.

Hellerstein D, W Frosch, and HW Koenigsberg. 1987. The clinical significance of command hallucinations. *American Journal of Psychiatry* 144:219–225.

Hoffman RE, M Varanko, J Gilmore, and AL Mishara. 2008. Experiential features used by patients with schizophrenia to differentiate "voices" from ordinary verbal thought. *Psychological Medicine* 38:1167–1176.

Inbau FE and JE Reid. 1967. *Criminal Interrogation and Confessions*, 2nd edition. Baltimore: Williams and Wilkins.

Inman DJ, SM Silver, and K Doghramji. 1990. Sleep disturbance in post-traumatic stress disorder: A comparison with non-PTSD insomnia. *Journal of Traumatic Stress* 3:429–437.

Junginger J. 1990. Predicting compliance with command hallucinations. *American Journal of Psychiatry* 147:245–247.

Junginger J. 1995. Command hallucinations and the prediction of dangerousness. *Psychiatric Services* 46:911–914.

Kanas N and MA Barr. 1984. Self-control of psychotic productions in schizophrenics. *Archives of General Psychiatry* 41:919–920.

Kasper E, R Rogers, and P Adams. 1996. Dangerousness and command hallucinations: An investigation of psychotic inpatients. *Bulletin of the American Academy of Psychiatry and the Law* 24:219–224.

Kent G and SH Wahass. 1996. The content and characteristics of auditory hallucinations in Saudi Arabia and the UK: A cross-cultural comparison. *Acta Psychiatrica Scandanavica* 94:433–437.

Kraus A. 1994. Phenomenology of the technical delusion in schizophrenia. *Journal of Phenomenological Psychology* 25:51–69.

Kucharski LT, W Ryan, J Vogt, and E Goodloe. 1998. Clinical symptom presentation in suspected malingerers: An empirical investigation. *Bulletin of the American Academy of Psychiatry and the Law*, 26:579–585.

Lambert MT and J Bonner. 1996. Characteristics and six month outcome of patients who use suicide threats to seek hospital admission. *Psychiatric Services* 47:871–873.

Larkin AR. 1979. The form and content of schizophrenic hallucinations. *American Journal of Psychiatry* 136:940–943.

Laroi F. 2012. How do auditory verbal hallucinations in patients differ from those in non-patients? *Frontiers in Human Neuroscience* 6:25.

Laroi F, IE Sommer, JD Blom et al. 2012. The characteristic features of auditory verbal hallucinations in clinical and nonclinical groups: State of the art overview and future directions. *Schizophrenia Bulletin* 38:724–733.

Layden M. 1966. Symptoms separate hysteric malingerers. *Psychiatric Progress* 1:7.

Lees-Haley PR and RS Brown. 1993. Neuropsychological complaint base rates of 170 personal injury claimants. *Archives of Clinical Neuropsychology* 8:203–209.

Lees-Haley PR and JT Dunn. 1994. The ability of naïve subjects to report symptoms of mild brain injury, post traumatic stress disorder, major depression, and generalized anxiety disorder. *Journal of Clinical Psychology* 50:252–256.

Leudar I, P Thomas, D McNally, and A Glinski. 1997. What voices can do with words: Pragmatics of verbal hallucinations. *Psychological Medicine* 27:885–898.

Levin HS, MA Lilly, A Papanicolaou et al. 1992. Posttraumatic and retrograde amnesia after closed head injury. In *Neuropsychology of Memory*, edited by LR Squire and N. Butters, New York: Guilford Press, 290–308.

Lewinsohn PM. 1970. An empirical test of several popular notions about hallucinations in schizophrenic patients. In *Origin and Mechanisms of Hallucinations*, edited by Wolfram Keup, New York: Plenum Press, 401–403.

Lewis DJ. 1961. Lilliputian hallucinations in the functional psychoses. *Canadian Psychiatric Association Journal* 6:177–201.

McAllister TW. 1994. Mild traumatic brain injury and the postconcussive syndrome. In *Neuropsychiatry of Traumatic Brain Injury*, edited by JM Silver, SC Yudofsky, and RE Hales, Washington, DC: American Psychiatric Press, 357–392.

McCarthy-Jones S and PJ Resnick. 2014. Listening to voices: The use of phenomenology to differentiate malingered from genuine auditory verbal hallucinations. *International Journal of Law and Psychiatry* 37:183–189.

McCarthy-Jones S, T Trauer, A Mackinnon, E Sims, N Thomas, and DL Copolov. 2014. A new phenomenological survey of auditory hallucinations: Evidence for subtypes and implications for theory and practice. *Schizophrenia Bulletin* 40:225–235.

Mellman TA, R Kulick-Bell, LE Ashlock, and B Nolan. 1995. Sleep events among veterans with combat-related posttraumatic stress disorder. *American Journal of Psychiatry* 152:110–115.

Mott RH, IF Small, and JM Andersen. 1965. Comparative study of hallucinations. *Archives of General Psychiatry* 12:595–601.

Nayani TH and AS David. 1996. The auditory hallucination: A phenomenological survey. *Psychological Medicine* 26:177–189.

Oulis P, VG Mavreas, JM Mamounas, and CN Stefanis. 1995. Clinical characteristics of auditory hallucinations. *Acta Psychiatrica Scandinavica* 92:97–102.

Pittman RK, LF Sparr, LS Saunders, and AC McFarlane. 1996. Legal issues in posttraumatic stress disorder. In *Traumatic Stress* edited by BA van der Kolk, AC McFarlane, and L Weisaeth, New York: Guilford Press, 378–397.

Reccoppa L 2009. Mentally ill or malingering? 3 Clues cast doubt. *Current Psychiatry* 8(12).

Resnick PJ. 2008. Malingered psychosis. In *Clinical Assessment of Malingering and Deception,* edited by RR Richard, New York: Guilford Press, 51–68.

Ritson B and A Forrest. 1970. The simulation of psychosis: A contemporary presentation. *British Journal of Psychology* 43:31–37.

Rogers R. ed. 2008. *Clinical Assessment of Malingering and Deception*, 3rd edition, New York: Guilford Press.

Rogers R, RM Bagby, and SE Dickens. 1992. *Structured Interview of Reported Symptoms (SIRS) and Professional Manual*. Odessa, FL: Psychological Assessment Resources.

Rogers R and AA Correa. 2008. Determinations of malingering: Evolution from case-based methods to detection strategies. *Psychiatry, Psychology, and Law* 15:213–223.

Rogers R, K Sewell, and AM Goldstein. 1994, Explanatory models of malingering: A prototypical analysis. *Law and Human Behavior* 18:543–552.

Sachs MH, WT Carpenter, and JS Strauss. 1974. Recovery from delusions. *Archives of General Psychiatry* 30:117–120.

Schneider SD, L Jelinek, TM Lincoln, and S Moritz. 2011. What happened to the voices? A fine-grained analysis of how hallucinations and delusions change under psychiatric treatment. *Psychiatry Research* 188:13–17.

Schretlen DJ. 1988. The use of psychological tests to identify malingered symptoms of mental disorder. *Clinical Psychology Review* 8:451–476.

Shawyer F, A Mackinnon, J Farhall, E Sims, S Blaney, P Yardley, M Daly, P Mullen, and D Copolov. 2008. Acting on harmful command hallucinations in psychotic disorders. An integrative approach. *Journal of Nervous and Mental Disease* 196:390–398.

Sherman M, P Trief, and R Sprafkin. 1975. Impression management in the psychiatric interview: Quality, style and individual differences. *Journal of Consulting and Clinical Psychology* 43:867–871.

Small IF, JG Small, and JM Andersen. 1966. Clinical characteristics of hallucinations of schizophrenia. *Diseases of the Nervous System* 27:349–353.

Soliman S and PJ Resnick. 2010. Feigning in adjudicative competence evaluations. *Behavioral Sciences and the Law* 28:614–629.

Sommer IEC, K Daalman, T Rietkerk, KM Diederen, S Bakker, J Wijkstra, and MaPM Boks. 2010. Healthy individuals with auditory verbal hallucinations; Who are they? Psychiatric assessments of a selected sample of 103 subjects. *Schizophrenia Bulletin* 36:633–641.

Spitzer M. 1992. The phenomenology of delusions. *Psychiatric Annals* 22:252–259.

Stephane M et al. 2006. Computerized binary Scale of Auditory Speech Hallucinations (cbSASH). *Schizophrenia Research* 88:73–81.

Thompson JS, GL Stuart, and CE Holden. 1992. Command hallucinations and legal insanity. *Forensic Reports* 5:29–42.

van der Kolk B, R Blitz, W Burr, S Sherry, and E Hartmann. 1984. Nightmares and trauma: A comparison of nightmares after combat with lifelong nightmares in veterans. *American Journal of Psychiatry* 141:187–190.

Wooley CN and R Rogers. 2014. The effectiveness of the personality assessment inventory with feigned PTSD: An initial investigation of Resnick's model of malingering. *Assessment* 22(4):449–458.

Wrightson P and D Gronwall. 1980. Time off work and symptoms after minor head injury. *Injury* 12:445–454.

Youngjohn JR, L Burrows, and K Erdal. 1995. Brain damage or compensation neurosis? The controversial post-concussion syndrome. *Clinical Neuropsychologist* 9:112–123.

Zapf PA and T Grisso. 2012. Use and misuse of forensic assessment instruments. In *Coping with Psychiatric and Psychological Testimony*, 6th edition, edited by David Faust, New York: Oxford University Press, 488–510.

75

Amnesia, hypnosis, and brainwashing

GIOVANA DE AMORIM LEVIN, JOHN BRADFORD, A.G. AHMED, AND SANJIV GULATI

INTRODUCTION

Research on memory has led to important advances on the characterization of amnesia in neurological conditions, such as traumatic brain injury, dementia, epilepsy, delirium, and other conditions. Other types of amnesia, such as dissociative amnesia, are less well understood. Dissociative amnesia and malingering are likely the most common presentation of amnesia in forensic psychiatric settings (Cima et al. 2002). The incidence of true amnesia in this type of setting is not clear in the scientific literature. Malingered amnesia is also seen frequently in forensic patients, and arguably is the most common manifestation of all types of malingering (Grondahl et al. 2009). Often, there is insufficient evidence to provide an expert opinion on the subject of malingered amnesia or the role of true amnesia. The true incidence of amnesia in specific forensic psychiatric clinical situations such as homicide and in other clinical situations seen in forensic psychiatry is insufficiently researched, which makes it difficult to provide an evidence-based expert opinion (Bourget and Whitehurst 2007). To complicate this further, it is very difficult to design studies and to apply tests to determine the presence of true amnesia, as well as to answer some of the complex forensic psychiatric issues related to claimed amnesia.

Research into the biological aspects of memory has shown its fundamental role in cognitive functioning. There are three recognized components to memory: registration of information (encoding), storage, and retrieval. Personality development and response to life events are based largely on experiences that are memorized. Associated emotions are also processed and combined in a dynamic fashion, resulting in integration of memory and learning.

BIOLOGICAL ASPECTS OF MEMORY

There have been extensive studies on memory and its mechanism, as well as the classification of types of memory. Memory (or amnesia) in the context of a forensic setting has been much less explored and remains an area of controversy (Bourget and Whitehurst 2007).

The most commonly accepted types of memory are short-term and long-term memory. Short-term memory holds a small amount of information to be used readily (working memory). Most of this information dissipates quickly, but a fraction of this information becomes part of long-term memory, usually by a conscious effort, repetition, or association with previously acquired knowledge. Long-term memory is further divided into declarative (episodic and semantic) memory and nondeclarative (procedural, such as skills and habits, priming and perceptual learning, simple classical conditional, and nonassociative learning) memory.

Brain areas associated with memory include the medial temporal lobe, hippocampus and related structures in the parahippocampal gyrus, amygdala, striatum, cerebellum, and the neocortex. The Papez circuit has been recognized as the key anatomical region for registration and storage of memory. The Papez circuit goes through the following pathway: hippocampal formation, fornix, mammillary bodies, mamillothalamic tract, anterior thalamic nucleus, cingulus, entorhinal cortex, and the circuit completes by connecting with the hippocampal formation (Papez 1934). The original concept of the Papez circuit (American Psychiatric Association [APA] 2000) in 1937, was later reconceptualized by Maclean in 1952 to include structures like the amygdala. He also coined the term the *limbic system*, earlier referred to by Broca as the limbic lobe (Newman and Harris 2009). The limbic system is involved in both memory and emotions. Review of the brain structures and biochemical pathways involved in memory is beyond the scope of this chapter, and the following segments will focus on amnesia, hypnosis, and brainwashing in clinical forensic practice (Squire and Kandel 2009; Squire and Dede 2015).

AMNESTIC DISORDER (NEUROCOGNITIVE DISORDER) AND DISSOCIATIVE AMNESIA

Amnesia is the term used to describe any loss or impairment of memory for facts, information, and experience. Amnesia results as a failure of some components of the memory process. In a simplified way, it can be classified as follows:

1. Failure of registration: For example, amnesia, secondary to delirium, epilepsy, intoxication, concussion
2. Failure of creating new memories: For example, Korsakoff dementia (alcohol-induced major neurocognitive disorder)
3. Failure to recall: For example, dissociative amnesia, malingered amnesia, dementias

The *Diagnostic and Statistical Manual of Mental Disorders*, 4th edition (*DSM-IV*) recognized delirium, dementia, amnestic disorder, and other cognitive disorders in a single group of disorders, for which an underlying pathological process and etiology could explain the cognitive deficit. Dissociative amnesia, a disorder of memory for which no underlying medical cause can be determined, was also recognized in *DSM-IV* under dissociative disorders (APA 2000). In the *DSM-IV*, amnestic disorder was defined as due to a general medical condition, substance-induced persisting amnestic disorder, and amnestic disorder not otherwise specified. In the *Diagnostic and Statistical Manual of Mental Disorders*, 5th edition (*DSM-5*), the term *amnestic disorder* is no longer used and is now represented by the neurocognitive disorders (APA 2013). Under neurocognitive disorders, the *DSM-5* includes delirium, followed by syndromes of major neurocognitive disorders, mild neurocognitive disorder, and their etiological subtypes (such as Alzheimer, Huntington, Prion disease, and others), which include the dementias. Individuals with neurocognitive disorder have deficits primarily in cognitive functioning, and this is an acquired condition, rather than developmental. The cognitive functioning is a decline from previous level of performance in one or more cognitive domains, interferes (major neurocognitive disorder) or not (mild neurocognitive disorder) with independence in everyday activities, does not occur exclusively in the context of a delirium, and is not better explained by another mental disorder. The etiology is specified after the diagnostic criteria (APA 2013).

Psychogenic amnesia, initially described by Abeles and Schilder in 1935, was known as dissociative amnesia in the *DSM-IV*. Dissociative fugue was a separate diagnosis, also under dissociative disorders. In the *DSM-5*, dissociative amnesia continues to appear under dissociative disorders, with the difference that a dissociative fugue appears as a specifier (dissociative disorder with or without dissociative fugue). It is characterized by an inability to recall autobiographical information, usually of a traumatic or stressful nature, that is inconsistent with normal forgetfulness. Dissociative amnesia most often consists of localized or selective amnesia for a specific event or events, but it can manifest as generalized amnesia for identity and life history. The symptoms cause significant impairment in social, occupational, and other areas of functioning and are not attributable to the effects of a substance or a neurological or other medical condition. It is not better explained by dissociative identity disorder, posttraumatic stress disorder, acute stress disorder, somatic symptoms disorder, or major or mild neurocognitive disorder. It is a reversible memory impairment in which memories of personal experience cannot be retrieved in a verbal form (or, if temporarily retrieved cannot be wholly retained in consciousness).

AMNESIA IN THE FORENSIC PSYCHIATRIC SETTING

In the forensic psychiatric population, it is important to differentiate neurocognitive disorders, dissociative disorder, and malingering in the context of claims of amnesia. Medical history and laboratory and imaging studies are essential in determining possible organic causes of amnesia prior to considering dissociative amnesia and malingering (Rayel et al. 1999; Sommerlad et al. 2014).

As mentioned earlier in this chapter, it is estimated that there is a high prevalence of dissociative amnesia and malingering in forensic cases. The clinician should also be attentive to mixed amnesias, in which both a neurocognitive disorder and a dissociative amnesia or malingering coexist. For example, there's a strong association between violent crimes and states of acute intoxication. Acute intoxication may cause amnesia for the event, but in dissociative amnesia, it is the violent crime itself that is most likely to be associated with the dissociative amnesia as the individual dissociates from the traumatic event, usually the crime committed by the individual. The clinician should also strongly consider that the motivation for malingering amnesia is also the highest under the circumstances, as the individual hopes to escape criminal responsibility.

Amnesia claimed in the forensic psychiatric setting is usually retrograde, for the period of the alleged crime, but it can extend for minutes and even hours after the event, as described by Bradford and Smith in their study of amnesia in 30 cases of homicide (Bradford and Smith 1979). The prevalence of claimed amnesia for homicide and other violent offences varies between 20% and 70% in various studies, and it has been suggested that amnesia is more commonly claimed in serious charges (O'Connell 1960; Bradford and Smith 1979; Cima et al. 1984; Taylor and Kopelman 1984; Parwatikar et al. 1985; Schacter 1986). A study involving sexual offenders who claimed amnesia for the offense showed that these individuals had high degrees of violence and also fulfilled diagnostic criteria for potentially more harmful paraphilias (Bourget and Bradford 1995).

The mechanisms proposed to explain claims of amnesia for violent crimes in the absence of a neurocognitive disorder are summarized in Table 75.1.

The first proposed mechanism involves high levels of emotions, and it is not uncommon to have a spouse as the victim—that is, in cases of domestic homicide and domestic violence (Bradford and Smith 1979; Dalgleish and Cox 2002; Swihart et al. 1999). It has also been postulated that high levels of glucocorticoids may be responsible for impairment in retrieval in high stress situations. Glucocorticoid receptors have been found to mediate long-term memory formation (Joseph 1999; Chen et al. 2012; Osborne et al. 2015). With regard to the second proposed

Table 75.1 Common mechanisms of claims of amnesia in the forensic setting

Type of amnesia	References
Dissociative amnesia	Allen (1999), Holmes et al. (2005), Spitzer et al. (2006)
Substance-induced amnesia	Bradford and Smith (1979)
Malingered amnesia	Cima et al. (1984), Cima et al. (2002), Van Impelen et al. (2014)

mechanism, there are reports of height and frequency of alcohol abuse/intoxication in individuals claiming amnesia, for violent offences (Hopwood and Snell 1933; Lennox 1943; Bradford and Smith 1979). It appears that alcohol intoxication is only partially responsible for the claim of amnesia, because in some cases the alcohol level was shown to be too low to produce the clinical picture of amnesia. However, the effect of alcohol on the formation of memory is well established, and it is associated with high peak levels and chronicity of alcohol intake (Hopwood and Snell 1933; Lennox 1943; Bradford and Smith 1979; Goodwin 1995; Holmes et al. 2005). Recent evidence suggests that many of ethanol's effects on learning and memory stem from altered cellular activity in the hippocampus and related structures, and involve the NDMA receptor (Hicklin et al. 2011; White et al. 2000).

The third mechanism, malingering or malingered amnesia, is prevalent in the forensic population and is obviously expected to be even more prevalent when the motivation to avoid criminal responsibility is high, such as with serious violent crimes. Although in theory, these scenarios seem distinct, it is extremely difficult to clinically distinguish between the three mechanisms outlined above. It has been suggested that in addition to the clinical forensic interview, some tests may be helpful in diagnosing malingered amnesia, but it appears that the consensus among forensic psychiatrist is that establishing malingering in relation to amnesia is a difficult task (Cima et al. 1984; Cima et al. 2002; van Impelen et al. 2014).

Additional mechanisms/clinical presentations involving amnesia include the presence of schizophrenia, which although it does not fall into the categories of neurocognitive disorder or dissociative amnesia, can cause amnesia. Schizophrenia is often considered in criminal responsibility in forensic psychiatric settings. Further, amnesia in the context of sleep disorders, although less prevalent, may also have to be considered in criminal responsibility evaluations. Individuals suffering from schizophrenia have been reported to claim amnesia for serious crimes (Taylor and Kopelman 1984; Mafullul et al. 2001; Nolan et al. 2003). Nolan et al. (2003) suggest that confusion and disorganization as part of the psychosis may contribute to aggressive behavior in patients with schizophrenia, who also claim amnesia for the violent behavior (Nolan et al. 2003). Given the high prevalence of patients with schizophrenia in forensic psychiatric evaluations for criminal responsibility, clearly this is an area of research that warrants further attention in forensic mental health research.

Violent behavior has been described in sleep disorders, primarily in sleepwalking and sleep terrors (Bonkalo 1974). Ohayon and Schenck (2010) described violent behavior during sleep occurring in 1.6% of a large random stratified sample (n = 19,961) in an epidemiological study. Violent behavior during sleep was mostly found in individuals less than 35 years of age. In 72.8% of the cases of violent behavior during sleep, there was an association with parasomnias and sleep disorders (Ohayon and Schenck 2010). Sexual behavior during sleep has also been described and the term *sexsomnia* has been suggested for inclusion as a type of parasomnia (Shapiro et al. 2003). Several cases of sexsomnia associated with serious criminal charges have been reported (Ingravallo et al. 2014). An overview of sexsomnia and its medicolegal implications has been recently published by Organ and Fedoroff (2015).

A guide to evaluate amnesia in the forensic context has been proposed by Scott (2012). The recommendations are summarized in Table 75.2.

Table 75.2 Guide for evaluating amnesia in criminal behavior

Conduct a relevant medical and psychiatric examination	Include neurological examination and imaging when appropriate
Characterize the type of amnesia	Include type and extent of the memory deficit reported
Examine the possible role of substance use in the claimed amnesia	Special attention if the alcohol/drug level could produce amnesia
Evaluate degree of offense planning	Planning and premeditation should enhance an offender's memory of the event
Obtain collateral information	Medical, police reports and statements (offender and witnesses), alcohol/drug levels, jail records, others
Conduct appropriate psychological testing	SIRS, MMPI, Test of Memory malingering, Word memory test, SIMS, others, including symptoms validity testing
Potential psychophysiological tools	Guilt Knowledge Test (GKT), ERPs (evoke-related potential), others
Not recommended (due to vulnerability to suggestion)	Amytal interview, hypnosis

Source: Adapted from Scott CL. 2012. *Psychiatric Clinics of North America* 35(4):797–819.

HYPNOSIS AND THE AMYTAL INTERVIEW

The amytal interview was introduced in the 1930s as a treatment for patients suffering from psychosis and then subsequently used in nonpsychotic persons as a diagnostic tool in catatonia and hysterical states with muteness and stupor (Stoudemire 1982; Tollefson 1982). It was also used in abreaction to recover memory in dissociative amnesia and fugue states (Steinberg 2000). Amytal interviews are not recommended in the forensic psychiatric evaluation, as they may create distorted memories and/or implanted memories based on suggestion occurring during the procedure, which means that it is of very limited use in the forensic context (Kavirajan 1999). Sodium amytal also carries the risk of respiratory depression, and lorazepam has been suggested as a safe alternative in the treatment, and investigation of dissociative disorders, but for similar reasons, it would also be of very limited use in a forensic evaluation (Kavirajan 1999; Lee et al. 2011). Lynch and Bradford (1980) in a study to differentiate alcohol- or drug-induced amnesia from dissociative or malingered amnesia found that polygraphy was useful in making this differentiation. Although this was promising, no further research has been completed further evaluating this technique. Although this technique may be clinically relevant, the limitations on the use of polygraphy in a legal context would prevent its acceptance in court, according to decisions in *Frye v U.S.* (1923) and *Daubert v. Merrell Dow Pharmaceuticals Inc.* (1993). Similarly, hypnosis has been used to facilitate recall in clinical situations and also has been used by various police forces, but is not scientifically valid for use in court proceedings.

Hypnosis, which is based on suggestion, has also been rejected as a tool to recover memories in forensic psychiatric situations by the American Medical Association in 1985 (Council on Scientific Affairs 1985). The Council of Scientific Affairs found that recollections obtained during hypnosis can involve confabulations and pseudo-memories, and not only failed to be more accurate, but actually appeared to be less reliable than nonhypnotic recall. Further, the use of hypnosis with witnesses may have serious consequences for the legal process when testimony is based on material obtained from a witness under hypnosis for the purpose of refreshing recollection (Council on Scientific Affairs 1985). Recovered memories, with or without hypnosis or amytal have been controversial for many years, and their credibility is limited (Kihlstrom 1997; Kavirajan 1999; Loftus and Davis 2006; Lee et al. 2011; Cox and Barnier 2015). A comprehensive forensic psychiatric assessment is the best approach, although the consensus is that amnesia and expert testimony on the subject of amnesia remain a challenge in the forensic psychiatry arena.

LANDMARK CASES RELATED TO HYPNOSIS

People v. Shirley 1982

The Supreme Court of California excluded hypnotically refreshed testimony per se from witnesses. However, it explicitly excepted such testimony by an accused. The concern was three general characteristics of hypnotically enhanced recall that may lead to inaccurate memories. The subject becomes suggestible and may try to please the hypnotherapist with answers; the subject is likely to confabulate; and the subject experiences "memory hardening" that results in both true and false memories being held with great confidence and conviction making cross-examination more difficult.

State v. Hurd (Superior Court of New Jersey 1980)

In this case the victim, Ms. Jane Sell, was attacked in her own home early one morning but was unable to identify her attacker. Under hypnosis by a psychiatric expert Dr. Herbert Speigel, approximately 3 weeks after the attack, she stated while in a hypnotic state that her ex-husband, Mr. Paul Hurd was the assailant. This hypnotic trance was characterized by questioning by Dr. Speigel and a police detective involved in the investigation. In the post-hypnotic session Ms. Sell reported to be uncertain of the identification of the assailants, specifically her ex-husband. In this post-hypnotic session she was encouraged by both Dr. Speigel and the detective to "accept" the identification of the assailant. The legal issues in the case were as follows:

1. Whether the victim could be allowed to make an identification in court after she had not been able to do this prior to hypnosis
2. Whether hypnosis was a reliable tool the enhancement of memory
3. Whether the type of hypnotic interview in this particular case was unnecessarily suggestive so that the identification of the assailant from the hypnotic trance should be suppressed

In court, the defense motion, under the Fourteenth Amendment, was granted specifically to suppress the identification of the defendant by the victim who had undergone pretrial hypnosis. Dr. Martin Orne, an expert in hypnosis, testified at length about the inability to distinguish fact from fiction after hypnotic refreshment of memory, and that it was essential that the subject's statements be independently verified before they could be accepted as being reliable. He also testified that after hypnotic enhancement of memory, the subject of the memory enhancement would often report that the memory was clear and consistent and held with conviction, which was very different prior to memory enhancement. Dr. Orne recommended that the court adopt six safeguards related to memory enhancement. The safeguards were that the hypnosis should only be conducted by a licensed psychiatrist or psychologist trained in the use of hypnosis; that the qualified professional should be completely independent of either the defense or the prosecution; any information given to the qualified professional by law enforcement should be in writing; prior to the hypnosis, the qualified professional should obtain a detailed description of the facts as the subject remembered them (in order to avoid adding new elements to the witness' recall by suggestion); all sessions between the hypnotic subject and the qualified professional had to be audiotaped at a minimum and videotaping would be preferable but not mandatory; and during the hypnotic session only the qualified professional should be present.

The decision of the court was that hypnotically refreshed memory should only be admissible on a case-by-case basis, and that the safeguards outlined by Dr. Orne should be used to decide whether hypnotically induced memory enhancement should be admissible.

Rock v. Arkansas (U.S. Supreme Court 1987)

Mrs. Vickie Rock was charged with manslaughter as a result of the homicide of her husband by shooting. This occurred against a background of marital discord, and there was a fight immediately prior to the shooting where Mrs. Rock told the police investigators that her husband had choked her and thrown her against the wall. As she could not remember the exact details of the shooting, her defense attorney recommended that she undergo hypnosis in order to refresh her memory. A psychologist was retained and made notes of her recollection in an interview prior to the hypnosis. This session and the hypnotic trance session were recorded. Mrs. Rock did not relate any new information during the hypnotic session, but after the hypnotic session she was able to recall that the gun misfired without her finger on the trigger. A firearms expert was retained by her defense counsel and found that the firearm was defective. The prosecutor objected to the hypnotically enhanced memory recall, and the judge ruled that Mrs. Rock held to limited testimony to what she remembered and stated to the examiner prior to being placed under hypnosis. Mrs. Rock was convicted of manslaughter and she was sentenced to 10 years of imprisonment. The case was appealed to the U.S. Supreme Court.

The court held that Arkansas' per se ruling excluding all hypnotically refreshed testimony infringed on the criminal defendant's right to testify on his or her own behalf, and this violated the defendant's Fifth, Sixth, and Fourteenth Amendment rights. The reasoning was that the majority of the U.S. Supreme Court pointed out that the right to present testimony is not unlimited, but restrictions imposed by the state may not be "arbitrary or disproportionate to the purposes they are designed to serve." Further, the state has an obligation to weigh the interest served by its rule (e.g., preventing erroneous evidence) to justify the limitations imposed on the defendant's constitutional rights. Further, the veracity of hypnotically refreshed testimony can be tested by cross-examination, which is an additional safeguard for the judicial process. The Arkansas rule failed because it did not allow the trial court even to consider the hypnotically refreshed recall, and therefore effectively prevented Mrs. Rock from describing the events of the shooting. In addition, the unreliability of hypnotically enhanced recall can be subject to verification by corroborating evidence and other methods of assessing the accuracy of testimony. The dissenting justices believed that the constitution should be construed so as not to intrude upon the administration of justice by individual states. The minority also noted that the majority opinion was equally sensible but did not believe it should be imposed on Arkansas.

BRAINWASHING

The *Oxford English Dictionary* records the earliest known English language usage of brainwashing by Edward Hunter, in *Miami News*, published on October 7, 1950. Brainwashing is defined as a forcible indoctrination to induce someone to give up basic political, social, or religious beliefs and attitudes and to accept contrasting regimented ideas (*Merriam-Webster Dictionary*). Brainwashing is also known as coercive persuasion. The term initially referred to the thought reform method used by Mao Tse-tung to eliminate "wrong thinking" from the Chinese people and instead convert them to communism. Torture was not part of this thought reform process, but the term gained wider usage later to include any methods used to change beliefs by force. Brainwashing is traditionally associated with extreme levels of physical torture and also psychological abuse, but the term has also been used in the context of individuals who join cults (West 1989).

Amnesty International was founded in London in 1961. It is a nongovernmental organization focused on human rights. The objective of the organization is to conduct research and generate action to prevent and end grave abuses of human rights, and to demand justice for those whose rights have been violated. Amnesty International regularly identifies nations that are engaging in torture of prisoners, even before these individuals are charged or sentenced. These methods are not necessarily related to brainwashing in its original meaning. These abuses range from general neglect to extreme physical torture. In recent years, Amnesty International has been involved in broader causes of human rights violation (retrieved from https://www.amnesty.org/en/). Although the term *brainwashing* is at times used almost interchangeably with torture, its original meaning involved the goal of changing one's beliefs and did not involve obtaining information from the individuals subjected to its methods. One of the most prominent examples in history is the Nazi indoctrination, considered one of the most effective brainwashing techniques, with a single focus on racial hatred (Voigtländer and Voth 2015).

SUMMARY KEY POINTS

- Amnesia is a common presentation in the forensic setting. Dissociative amnesia, substance-induced amnesia, and malingering are the most common causes of amnesia in the forensic setting.

- Although relatively uncommon, medical causes of amnesia, including neurocognitive and sleep disorders, should always be considered.
- Hypnosis and amytal interviews are not recommended in forensic psychiatric evaluations as they may create distortions in recollection as well as create implanted memories, and are of very limited use in a court setting.
- Brainwashing is a form of coercive persuasion to changes one's basic beliefs, usually to accept a different set of values. The term has been broadened and has been used to describe certain aspects of cults as well as situations with extreme physical and psychological torture.

REFERENCES

Abeles M and P Schilder. 1935. Psychogenic loss of personal identity, amnesia. *Archives of Neurology and Psychiatry* 34(3):565–567.

Allen JG, DA Console, and L Lewis. 1999. Dissociative detachment and memory impairment: Reversible amnesia or encoding failure? *Comprehensive Psychiatry* 40(2):160–171.

American Psychiatric Association (APA). 2000. *Diagnostic and Statistical Manual of Mental Disorders*, 4th edition, text revision (*DSM-IV-TR*). Washington, DC: American Psychiatric Publishing.

American Psychiatric Association (APA). 2013. *Diagnostic and Statistical Manual of Mental Disorders*, 5th edition (*DSM-5*). Washington, DC: American Psychiatric Publishing.

Bonkalo A. 1974. Impulsive acts and confusional states during incomplete arousal from sleep: Criminological and forensic implications. *Psychiatric Quarterly* 48(3):400–409.

Bourget D and JM Bradford. 1995. Sex offenders who claim amnesia for their alleged offense. *Bulletin of the American Academy of Psychiatry and the Law* 23(2):299–307.

Bourget D and L Whitehurst. 2007. Amnesia and crime. *Journal of the American Academy of Psychiatry and the Law* 35(4):469–480.

Bradford JM and SM Smith. 1979. Amnesia and homicide: The *Padola* case and a study of thirty cases. *Bulletin of the American Academy of Psychiatry and the Law* 7(3):219–231.

Chen DY, D Bambah-Mukku, G Pollonini, and CM Alberini. 2012. Glucocorticoid receptors recruit the CaMKIIα-BDNF-CREB pathways to mediate memory consolidation. *Nature Neuroscience* 15(12):1707–1714.

Cima M, H Merckelbach, H Nijman, E. Knauer, and S Hollnack. 2002. I can't remember your honour: Offenders who claim amnesia. *German Journal of Psychiatry* 5:24–34.

Cima MN, H Nijman, H Merckelbach, K Kremer, and S Hollnack. 1984. Claims of crime-related amnesia and forensic patients. *International Journal of Law and Psychiatry* 27:251–221.

Council on Scientific Affairs, American Medical Association. 1985. Scientific status of refreshing recollection by the use of hypnosis. Council on Scientific Affairs. *Journal of the American Medical Association* 253(13):1918–1923.

Cox RE and AJ Barnier. 2015. A hypnotic analogue of clinical confabulation. *International Journal of Clinical and Experimental Hypnisis* 63(3):249–273.

Dalgleish T and SG Cox. 2002. Memory and emotional disorder. In *Handbook of Memory Disorders*, second edition, edited by AD Baddeley, MD Kopelman, and BA Wilson. West Sussex, England: John Wiley and Sons, 437–449.

Daubert v. Merrell Dow Pharmaceuticals, Inc. In 113 S. Ct. 2786 (1993).

Frye v. U.S. In 293 F. 1013, 1923: U.S. Supreme Court.

Goodwin DW. 1995. Alcohol amnesia. *Addiction* 90(3):315–317.

Grondahl P, H Vaeroy, and AA Dahl. 2009. A study of amnesia in homicide cases and forensic psychiatric experts' examination of such claims. *International Journal of Law and Psychiatry* 32(5):281–287.

Hicklin TR, PH Wu, RA Radcliffe, RK Freund, SM Goebel-Goody, PR Correa, WR Proctor, PJ Lombroso, and MD Browning. 2011. Alcohol inhibition of the NMDA receptor function, long-term potentiation, and fear learning requires striatal-enriched protein tyrosine phosphatase. *Proceedings of the National Academy of Sciences USA* 108(16):6650–6655.

Holmes EA, RJ Brown, W Mansell, RP Fearon, EC Hunter, F Frasquilho, and DA Oakley. 2005. Are there two qualitatively distinct forms of dissociation? A review and some clinical implications. *Clinical Psychology Review* 25(1):1–23.

Hopwood JS and HK Snell. 1933. Amnesia in relation to crime. *Journal of Mental Science* 79:27–41.

Ingravallo F, F Poli, EV Gilmore, F Pizza, L Vignatelli, CH Schenck, and G Plazzi. 2014. Sleep-related violence and sexual behavior in sleep: A systematic review of medical-legal case reports. *Journal of Clinical Sleep Medicine* 10(8):927–935.

Joseph R. 1999. The neurology of traumatic "dissociative" amnesia: Commentary and literature review. *Child Abuse and Neglect* 23(8):715–727.

Kavirajan H. 1999. The amobarbital interview revisited: A review of the literature since 1966. *Harvard Review of Psychiatry* 7(3):153–165.

Kihlstrom JF 1997. Hypnosis, memory and amnesia. *Philosophical Transactions of the Royal Society of London B: Biological Sciences* 352(1362):1727–1732.

Lee SS, S Park, and SS Park. 2011. Use of Lorazepam in drug-assisted interviews: Two cases of dissociative amnesia. *Psychiatry Investigation* 8(4):377–380.

Lennox WG. 1943. Amnesia, real and feigned. *American Journal of Psychiatry* 99:732–742.

Loftus EF and D Davis. 2006. Recovered memories. *Annual Review of Clinical Psychology* 2:469–498.

Lynch BE and JMW Bradford. 1980. Amnesia: Its detection by psychophysiological measures. *Bulletin of the American Academy of Psychiatry and the Law* 8:288–297.

Mafullul YM, OA Ogunlesi, and OA. Sijuwola. 2001. Psychiatric aspects of criminal homicide in Nigeria. *East African Medical Journal* 78(1):35–39.

Newman JD and JC Harris. 2009. The scientific contributions of Paul D. MacLean (1913–2007). *Journal of Nervous and Mental Disease* 197(1):3–5.

Nolan KA, P Czobor, BB Roy, MM Platt, CB Shope, LL Citrome, and J Volavka. 2003. Characteristics of assaultive behavior among psychiatric inpatients. *Psychiatric Services* 54(7):1012–1106.

O'Connell BA. 1960. Amnesia and homicide. *British Journal of Delinquency* 10:262–276.

Ohayon MM and CH Schenck. 2010. Violent behavior during sleep: Prevalence, comorbidity and consequences. *Sleep Medicine* 11(9):941–946.

Organ A and JP Fedoroff. 2015. Sexsomnia: Sleep sex research and its legal implications. *Current Psychiatry Reports* 17(5):34.

Osborne DM, J Pearson-Leary, and EC McNay. 2015. The neuroenergetics of stress hormones in the hippocampus and implications for memory. *Frontiers in Neuroscience* 9:164.

Papez JW. 1934. A proposed mechanism of emotion. *Archives of Neurology and Psychiatry* 38(4):725–743.

Parwatikar SD, WR Holcomb, and KA Menninger 2nd. 1985. The detection of malingered amnesia in accused murderers. *Bulletin of the American Academy of Psychiatry and the Law* 13(1):97–103.

People v. Shirley, California Supreme Court (1980).

Rayel MG, WB Land, and TG Gutheil. 1999. Dementia as a risk factor for homicide. *Journal of Forensic Sciences* 44(3):565–567.

Rock v. Arkansas,483 U.S. 44, 107 S.Ct. 2704 (1987).

Schacter DL. 1986. On the relation between genuine and simulated amnesia. *Behaviour Sciences and the Law* 4:47–64.

Scott CL. 2012. Evaluating amnesia for criminal behavior: A guide to remember. *Psychiatric Clinics of North America* 35(4):797–819.

Shapiro CM, NN Trajanovic, and JP Fedoroff. 2003. Sexsomnia—A new parasomnia? *Canadian Journal of Psychiatry* 48(5):311–317.

Sommerlad A, J Lee, J Warren, and G Price. 2014. Neurodegenerative disorder masquerading as psychosis in a forensic psychiatry setting. *BMJ Case Reports* June 13. doi:10.1136/bcr-2013-203458

Spitzer C, S Barnow, J Armbruster, S Kusserow, HJ Freyberger, and HJ Grabe. 2006. Borderline personality organization and dissociation. *Bulletin of the Menninger Clinic* 70(3):210–221.

Squire LR and AJ Dede 2015. Conscious and unconscious memory systems. *Cold Spring Harbour Perspective on Biology* March, 2(3):7.

Squire LR and ER Kandel. 2009. *Memory: From Mind to Molecules*, 2nd edition. Greenwood Village, CO: Roberts & Company.

State v. Hurd, 173 N.J. Super.333, 414 A.2d 291 (1980).

Steinberg M. 2000. Dissociative amnesia. In *Comprehensive Textbook of Psychiatry*, 7th edition, edited by BJ Sadock and VJ Sadock, Philadelphia: Lippincott, Williams & Wilkens, 425–436.

Stoudemire A. 1982. The differential diagnosis of catatonic states. *Psychosomatics* 23(3):245–252.

Swihart G, J Yuille, and S Porter. 1999. The role of state-dependent memory in "red-outs." *International Journal of Law and Psychiatry* 22(3–4):199–212.

Taylor PJ and MD Kopelman. 1984. Amnesia for criminal offences. *Psychological Medicine* 14(3):581–588.

Tollefson GD. 1982. The amobarbital interview in the differential diagnosis of catatonia. *Psychosomatics* 23(4):437–438.

van Impelen A, H Merckelbach, M Jelicic, and T Merten. 2014. The structured inventory of malingered symptomatology (SIMS): A systematic review and meta-analysis. *Clinical Neuropsychologist* 28(8):1336–1365.

Voigtländer N and HJ Voth. 2015 (epub). Nazi indoctrination and anti-Semitic beliefs in Germany. *Proceedings of the National Academy of Sciences USA* 11:7931–7936.

West LJ 1989. Persuasive techniques in contemporary cults. In *Cults and the New Religious Movements*, edited by M. Gallanter, Washington, DC: American Psychiatric Association Press, 165–192.

White AM, DB Matthews, and PJ Best. 2000. Ethanol, memory, and hippocampal function: A review of recent findings. *Hippocampus* 10(1):88–93. https://www.amnesty.org/en/

76

Culture and forensic psychiatry

ALEXANDER I.F. SIMPSON AND SUSAN HATTERS-FRIEDMAN

INTRODUCTION

We live in complex societies. There is great variety of income, race, ethnicity, and culture within them. The problems that forensic psychiatry is focused on, mental disorder and crime, are not evenly distributed within our societies. These problems afflict communities in different ways, and to varying degrees.

We often do not perceive these differences, or do not regularly reflect on why they might exist. We are immersed in our own values, patterns of life, patterns of behavior, and assumptions about the world. We are aware of difference but do not necessarily understand it. We can make assumptions about others, and about the meaning of thoughts, behaviors, or attitudes. We call people "individuals," "clients," "defendants," "evaluees," "patients," or "the accused."

Because of the diversity of our societies, many forensic assessments are cross-cultural, whether across economic or cultural difference. We commonly assess or treat people from other cultural groups. Further, adopting the same approach to all people ("color blindness") may not appreciate the subtle variances in need or biases that may manifest. For instance, pathways for people into forensic care may be different between ethnic groups (Flora et al. 2012). There is much evidence that race and culture may impact the needs people present with (Leese et al. 2006), how "dangerous" they are rated (Vinkers et al. 2010), or their access to services (Simpson et al. 2003). Are these observed differences due to differing socio-demographic experience because of structural or historical differences in society? Or do they stem from erroneous assumptions by mental health institutions and practitioners? These questions are too complex for this chapter to answer. But we consider how forensic practitioners may address these questions in their own practice.

In essence, forensic psychiatry is a process of understanding another person: understanding his or her disease, illness, disability, motivations, behavioral patterns, and the likelihood that he or she may behave in particular ways in the future. It is also about opining, recommending, offering, providing, or overseeing treatment. Treatment is aimed at making things "better." We assume that we share a similar understanding of "better," but this may not always be so.

The purpose of this chapter is to assist the forensic practitioner in understanding the impact of culture on his or her individual practice. This includes both forensic evaluation and treatment. It describes how cultural formulation can improve and inform forensic practice. It introduces clinically relevant concepts of culture and race, and looks at the application of tools to assess the impact of the cultural meanings and differences on a person's assessment and treatment in forensic practice.

WHAT DO WE MEAN BY CULTURE?

Culture was a term first coined by a German scholar in the late eighteenth century to describe the achievements of particular civilizations. The definition of culture has developed through time to encompass the myriad behaviors, attributes, practices, rituals, traditions, and their attached meanings for different social groups (Tseng et al. 2004). The National Institute of Mental Health's (NIMH) Culture and Diagnosis Group described culture as the "meanings, values and behavioral norms that are learned and transmitted in the dominant society and within its social groups. Culture powerfully influences cognition, feelings and self-concept as well as the diagnostic process and treatment decisions" (see Lu et al. 2008, 118; Aggarwal 2012).

Race, on the other hand, was originally conceptualized one dimensionally as a biological construct, referring only to the phenotypic traits of groups of people who may have shared similar physical features, such as the same color skin, eyes, or hair. Society responds to people of certain "racialized minorities" or "people of color" in stereotypic or prejudiced ways, making, as Henry Louis Gates noted, race "a lived experience." Race-as-experience therefore is more an artefact or by-product of socio-economic and political circumstances (Tseng et al. 2004).

Ethnicity acknowledges the critical roles of language, culture, and history as part of the formation of identity (Fernando 2003) and refers to shared belief systems and cultural practices among groups that are learned. Ethnicity also refers to the way people perceive themselves, therefore influencing self-concept and identity formation (Fabrega 2004).

Indigeneity, that is, being an indigenous person, is a particular cultural/ethnic experience, an epistemic class of its own. For indigenous people, identity is fundamentally interwoven in the relationship to their particular place, land, spirituality, and history. As a cultural group they have no other home than the place they live in. They are the people of the land whose identity has often been threatened grievously by colonization and economic development. They are overrepresented in forensic populations.

Culture can affect the symptoms a person presents with and may shape the form of illnesses such as schizophrenia (Myers 2011). Social context may make it easier or harder to engage in social supports. Cultural change brought about by colonization, development, or migrancy affects populations and individuals. For instance, while first-generation migrants may be at greater risk of developing a psychotic illness, there is clear evidence that second-generation immigrants are at highest risk of psychosis. This is rather than pre-immigration issues or diagnostic bias as being of greatest relevance. The reason for one's migrancy may play a role, with refugees recently shown to be at greater risk of developing a psychotic illness than other migrants (Anderson et al. 2015). Context is also important; remarkably, if one migrates but lives in a community with more than 25% of one's own ethnic group, then one's risk of psychosis is lowered. Some evidence of diagnostic misunderstanding may play a part in some settings (e.g., Lewis-Fernández et al. 2009). Cultural practices or rituals that may help deal with distress may be lost in the migration or assimilation processes. The new institutions that people encounter frequently fail to help people integrate and manage their distress or their psychotic experiences into their personal narrative and cultural worlds (Kirmayer 2012). The *Diagnostic and Statistical Manual of Mental Disorders*, 5th edition (*DSM-5*) has recognized these issues in moving away from the outdated concept of "cultural-bound syndromes" to "cultural concepts of distress." Cultural concepts of distress are described as including syndromes, idioms of distress, and their explanations (or perceived causes). Symptom clusters co-occurring among a cultural group would be included in syndromes. Cultural idioms of distress are shared ways of discussing and experiencing distress, such as discussing "nerves." Finally, cultural explanations or perceived causes are attributions and explanatory models with a recognized meaning behind symptoms. The authors of *DSM-5* note that all distress is "locally shaped" (American Psychiatric Association 2013).

CULTURE OF PSYCHIATRY AND LAW

Discussion of culture is often framed in terms of the difference between the assessor and the assessee, but discussion of culture *in* law and psychiatry must mention the culture *of* the law and psychiatry. Law and systems of justice are themselves cultural paradigms. We recognize that attorneys, probation officers, judges, experts, witnesses, or jurors all bring their own preconceived notions, attitudes, and value systems to the process of justice (Tseng et al. 2004). These preconceived notions affect their relatedness to others, their understanding about why people may behave in certain ways, and the culpability of people for that behavior. The fact that such people come together in this way is a cultural construct: that people must be held accountable for their actions, that they are innocent until proven guilty, and that they have a right to remain silent, etc. Further, the cultural idiom of McNaughton's rules is a very good example: as a culture we exempt some people who have performed an act from culpability, because we recognize something called a disease for which a person is not morally accountable. This is not a universal human understanding. A psychiatrist must try to "fit" a person's experience into such a set of rules (Fabrega 2004), but is also a participant in this culturally defined and sanctioned paradigm. Further, many players in the forensic process (judges, counsel, psychiatrists, psychologists) tend to come from privileged parts of society, whose experience of race and discrimination is very different than that of the poor evaluee of minority ethnicity from an educationally and socially deprived background.

The culture of the forensic assessor is likely to at least in part include the cultural influences of the dominant society; the cultural identity and background of the assessor; the institutional culture of the clinic, hospital, or organization, and the professional association with which the assessor is associated; and the professional cultures of biomedicine and psychiatry (Mezzich et al. 2009).

Psychiatry values that its learning is evidence based and is developed within the framework of a scientific or positivistic approach. Cultural understandings are formed differently from narrative and shared understandings of personal and community origins and beliefs. As Whitley (2007) states, both forms of understanding of people are ultimately aimed at the same thing: best outcomes for patients, but by different routes. Evidence-based approaches seek knowledge via the normothetic knowledge of science, while cultural or personal narratives do so via the idiographic understanding of the individual person's life, origin, and values. Care must be tailored to fit such values on the basis of best evidence. Norko (2005) has argued that forensic ethics are inextricably linked to compassion for the person under evaluation, including a comprehensive understanding of their life, narrative, and values. Griffith et al. (2010) construct the forensic report as a cultural narrative to give contextual meaning to the behavior and beliefs of the evaluee. They advocate that the understanding must then be related to the legal test in question. They argue that this idiographic narrative generates the possibility of empathic or imaginative understanding of the person not available in the more narrowly conceived forensic practice.

CULTURAL COMPETENCE AND FORENSIC PSYCHIATRY

We practice this work in the presence of diversity. To live effectively together, societies require shared rules to govern us all. Forensic psychiatry exists at the nexus between these forces: applying evidence-based knowledge, combined with an essential understanding of the narrative of the person being assessed or treated, appreciating who they are, and relating these themes to the shared sets of rules that govern societal responses to behavior (Fabrega 2004). What are the skills necessary for this task?

The ability to understand the person's own narrative is a skill that requires cultural sensitivity on the part of the forensic practitioner, and the proper questions and approaches to assist in exploring a person's experience comprehensively. The key skill that practitioners need to possess has been widely referred to as *cultural competence.*

Kirmayer (2012) defined "cultural competence" as a set of attributes that the practitioner possesses (see also Mezzich et al. 2009). These include self-awareness regarding one's own cultural beliefs and origins, and how those attributes may impact clinical interactions. Second, an evaluator requires some core knowledge about the socio-ethnic group of the person being assessed. If the evaluator is not knowledgeable in this area, he or she must recognize his or her limitations and seek the input of persons knowledgeable in those areas. Third is the area of skills competency, where one can successfully apply one's own knowledge and clinical skills in a culturally appropriate manner in an attempt to understand and formulate the relevant issues for the situation to be understood.

Kirmayer (2012) proposes that "cultural competence" may work at multiple levels, not only that of the individual practitioner, but also at an institutional and technical level. The ways law is structured and practiced may be examples of the institutional and technical aspects of interactions that may present challenges of cultural bias. Institutions may, for example, attempt to positively create roles to enhance "ethno-cultural matching," such as employing staff representative of the ethnic mix of the community being served or creating policies or processes to engage interpreters and cultural consultants to assist in care. Staff training and supervision, such as awareness, knowledge, and sensitivity training, are widespread and important steps to improve the cultural competence of a clinical program and individual staff members.

Mossman et al. (2007) in the American Academy of Psychiatry and the Law (AAPL) guidelines for competency to stand trial evaluations describe cultural competence explicitly as it is relevant to forensic practice and case formulation. They state that culturally competent evaluations require understanding of the context of the person and his or her life and acceptance of the person's cultural identity. They usefully underline the knowledge, skills, and attributes of the assessor with particular emphasis on the interactive style, bias, transference, and countertransference that can emerge in a forensic setting, citing the Stone, Appelbaum, and Griffith debates as a clear example of these competing forces.

APPLICATION OF CULTURAL COMPETENCE TO FORENSIC TASKS

Cultural competence is the first key skill a forensic practitioner must possess. To help construct a consistent and comprehensive approach to performing a culturally informed assessment, a few simple tools are of value. Indeed, tools to assist any practitioner in culturally sensitive interviewing and formulation are not new. Some of the most helpful and simple guidance came from Arthur Kleinman (1980) who suggested asking eight questions to gain access to the person's own understanding of why he or she is ill and what that means for that person (see Table 76.1).

The forensic assessor can see how these questions capture aspects of a person's beliefs about himself or herself and his or her situation, and get insight into the person's illness, its meaning, and factors relevant to treatment and future outcomes. Substituting risk or offending for illness in the questions clearly has useful application in considering a person's self-understanding about the issues being assessed.

The diagnostic nosologies of *DSM* and International Classification of Diseases (*ICD*) were developed to be "culture free," though both saw culture as very important in understanding the manifestations of distress of a person. Although *DSM-IV* rejected including a cultural axis (Mezzich 1995), it did give guidance about the development of a cultural formulation. It recommended that the following elements be addressed: the cultural identity of the individual, cultural explanations for the person's illness, cultural factors related to the psychosocial environment and levels of functioning, cultural elements in the relationship between the person and the clinician, and the overall cultural assessment for diagnosis and care.

Table 76.1 Kleinman's questions regarding the evaluee's understanding of illness and its meaning

1. What do you think has caused your problem?
2. Why do you think it started when it did?
3. What do you think your problem does inside your body?
4. How severe is your problem? Will it have a short or long course?
5. What kind of treatment do you think you should receive?
6. What are the most important results you hope to receive from this treatment?
7. What are the chief problems your illness has caused you?
8. What do you fear most about your illness/treatment?

Source: Adapted from Kleinman A. 1980. *Patients and Healers in the Context of Culture.* Berkeley: University of California Press.

Lewis-Fernández et al. (2014) describe how the cultural formulation structure of *DSM-IV* has been operationalized into a structured interview entitled the Cultural Formulation Interview (CFI). *DSM-5* published the CFI, a 16-question semi-structured assessment that can be used to obtain information about culture, including cultural definition, perceptions of cause, and the cultural factors affecting coping and help-seeking. The *DSM-5* argues that cultural concepts are important in clinical psychiatry to avoid misdiagnosis, obtain further clinical information, and improve rapport and efficacy. There are now a small number of studies giving modest support to the improvement in diagnosis and treatment understanding that can come from the use of the CFI in consultation or assessment services. For instance, Adeponle et al. (2012) found that when the CFI guided a consultation service assessment, misdiagnosis that had previously occurred in 60% of these referrals were much more clearly understood after the use of the CFI among immigrant groups. Aggarwal (2012) describes how the CFI can be applied in forensic settings, pointing out that this culturally informed interviewing is often absent in standard forensic texts.

The CFI lends itself very well to structured assessment or consultations. There is as yet no published evidence of its use in a forensic setting, though this is only a matter of time. Interestingly, Kapoor et al. (2013) have adapted the CFI for prison settings in the United States and describe it as being valuable in correctional psychiatric practice.

Mezzich et al. (2009) provide useful guidance for clinicians performing a culturally sensitive assessment. In addition to taking the usual care in the clinical interview, they emphasize the importance of taking care over expectations for greeting formalities, dress, and interpersonal distance. If using an interpreter or cultural broker, one must ensure his or her role is clear and acceptable to the person in advance. In the body of the interview itself, it should be ensured the interviewer shows appropriate respect for the cultural understandings and expectations of the person, and gives the person ample opportunity to express himself or herself. A very rote or rigid interviewing style may not communicate this level of interest or concern. It is often wise to seek clarification to ensure the person's perspective is properly understood.

The AAPL guidelines on fitness/competency to stand trial evaluations (Mossman et al. 2007) again deserve particular mention. The guidelines contain comprehensive guidance on cultural issues in fitness evaluations. They consider carefully the cultural values inherent in fitness to stand trial and the likely identification of the forensic assessor with those values. These values include the concept of procedural fairness, including the right to understand and confront one's accusers, to interact with counsel to assist with this, and the right of the defendant to express his or her own opinion and make a plea on the basis of his or her own interests. They point out that these are not necessarily shared in common by defendants of other cultures, who may not have a tradition of raising one's voice against authority or senior cultural or family leaders. Therefore, the defendant may not engage counsel in his or her defense, not because of problems of psychopathology, but because of cultural expression. The guidelines encourage the use of self-reflection by the clinician to assist in the avoidance of bias (including previously unrecognized bias).

CULTURE AND FORENSIC TASKS

Cultural assessment and formulation

Guided by the tools and questions described above, the psychiatrist must also know the limits of his knowledge, and when to seek consultation. Forensic psychiatrists need to identify the traditions, values, and culturally syntonic beliefs of the evaluee, and then consider their relevancy to the specific consultation questions (Glancy et al. 2015; Aggarwal 2012). Psychiatrists should ask defendants about how they self-identify rather than merely making assumptions, based on appearance (Aggarwal 2012). Cultural distinctiveness should be considered in forensic evaluations (Kirmayer et al. 2007); however, the risk of stereotyping evaluees rather than truly understanding their background must not be ignored. "Stereotyping provides a simplistic and distorted picture of the social and individual aspects of a person and in itself can have negative consequences for mental health" (Mezzich et al. 2009, 393).

Mezzich and colleagues note that "culture deeply informs every aspect of life and health" (Mezzich et al. 2009, 384), and they have offered an approach to the cultural formulation as part of clinical care. The intent was for the cultural formulation to coexist with a *DSM* formulation, and to be a narrative. The psychiatrist "should strive to describe the person as a cultural being identified with particular values, traditions and orientations....although culture and ethnicity identify groups this does not mean that all members of a group believe or behave in the same way; ideas and values associated with cultures and ethnicities may be highly variable owing to gender, age cohort, socio-economic class, geographic region (rural versus urban), religious factional differences and personal preferences" (Mezzich et al. 2009, 392). Ajaz et al. (2014) described the cultural formulations for forensic psychiatry as including an understanding of the following four factors: the evaluee's cultural identity, cultural explanation of illness, cultural factors relevant to psychosocial environment and functioning, and cultural elements of a physician–patient relationship.

Interpreters and cultural consultants

Interpreters are strongly recommended if the evaluee's primary language is not English, and if the evaluator is not fluent in the evaluee's primary language. Accuracy in evaluations is of great importance (Maddux 2010). Difficulties with interpretations of meaning across languages and cultures can lead to misinterpretations (Mossman et al. 2007). However, the use of an interpreter can be fraught.

Whenever possible, a court-approved interpreter with some background in mental health should be utilized in forensic evaluations (Maddux 2010; Tseng et al. 2004). The interpreter must understand the difference between linguistic and conceptual interpretation.

The psychiatrist should attempt to speak with the interpreter in advance, to explain the differences between forensic and general evaluations. Also in advance, the evaluation room should be set up such that the evaluator can have eye contact with the evaluee (Committee on Cultural Psychiatry, Group for the Advancement of Psychiatry [GAP] 2002). The interpreter should give verbatim translations, because other translation choices could cause distortion of meaning or loss of nuance (GAP 2002; Mossman et al. 2007; Glancy et al. 2015). Problematically, some subtleties of language and meaning can easily be lost in this process. Asking questions in different ways may assist in exploring an issue and checking out whether the correct understanding has been gained.

Mezzich et al. (2009) caution that while understanding of families increases cultural understanding, their perceptions "do not constitute the ultimate truth about the patient's condition, but provide a complementary perspective" (Mezzich et al. 2009, 389). Family members may offer to provide interpretations, but this could easily negatively impact the assessment—there are many reasons why an evaluee may not share the full story with a family member present (GAP 2002). Similarly, when performing an interview in a smaller community, it becomes more likely that the interpreter and evaluee may know each other from contexts other than the evaluation (Maddux 2010).

If the interpreter is knowledgeable not only about language and mental health, but also about culture (Tseng et al. 2004) then this is more ideal. For example, a Spanish interpreter from South America or Mexico or Puerto Rico may have a different cultural background than a Spanish interpreter from Spain, and it would be optimal in order to help situate the evaluee in terms of culture. Additionally, cultural consultants can be engaged in order to help the evaluator understand the meaning of specific actions to members of a specific culture. One must beware the risk of stereotyping. Cultural analysis with the assistance of a cultural consultant can help decrease misunderstandings and the evaluator's potential prejudged notions.

Describing the narrative

Forensic psychiatrists, as well as their evaluees, have had cultural and religious "personal experiences that have contributed to the shaping of [our] moral life" (Griffith 2005, 372) as Griffith highlighted in relation to the Stone/Appelbaum debate about the role of psychiatrists in the courtroom. This debate underlines that the forensic practitioner must be aware of cultural impact on transference and countertransference in approaching a forensic evaluation. Specifically, one must use caution not to overidentify with those from one's own cultural group, such that one may lose objectivity. Care should be taken that the goal of describing to the court the meaning of behavior within the evaluee's cultural context does not distort the truth. At the other end of the spectrum, one must use caution not to incorrectly diagnose those from other groups (Mossman et al. 2007).

Fabrega (2004) described the clinician as attempting to fit a cultural understanding of the defendant into the rules of law. He described that determining "culpability of homicide is entangled in questions about norms, values, competence, deception, responsibility, and blame" (Fabrega 2004, 179). However, the psychiatrist must also consider his or herown cultural beliefs. The psychiatrist too is part of the process of cultural understanding of the law.

Griffith (2005) has described that the forensic report should be a cultural narrative that helps give contextual meaning to behavior and beliefs. This can be tied in to legal test at issue. Narratives generate the possibility for greater empathic and imaginative understanding.

These debates have described that forensic psychiatrists' ethical tenets include striving for objectivity but also for understanding. When the evaluee is from another culture or holds different religious beliefs than the psychiatrist, it is particularly important to consider the potential for bias and countertransference that can affect the evaluation. One should consider cultural consultations in complex evaluations where culture is at issue (Hicks 2004; Boehnlein 2005). Further, even in "run-of-the-mill" cases in which the evaluee is of a different culture, it makes sense to examine one's own biases, unexplored fears, and the role of countertransference (Glancy et al. 2015; Mossman et al. 2007; Mezzich et al. 2009). To be culturally competent, one must not only respect cultural differences but also consider how these differences affect forensic evaluation, and frequently self-assess one's own assumptions. One must be aware of one's fears and prejudices. Forensic psychiatrists should strive to understand the evaluee's culture and values, how distress may be expressed within a culture, how culture may affect communication, and how racism and power dynamics impact relationships.

CULTURE IN SELECTED SCENARIOS

Fitness/competency to stand trial

AAPL's competence to stand trial guidelines provide an excellent discussion of cultural considerations in these evaluations (Mossman et al. 2007). They describe that most psychiatrists identify with the dominant culture's view, including that criminal proceedings are fair and just. The guidelines note: "competence to stand trial thus embodies a cultural notion that the legal system is reasonably fair, that accused persons will get fair treatment and a reasonable chance to defend themselves, and that the dignity and fairness of the criminal proceedings are vindicated when an accused person is a capable adversary of the prosecution" (Mossman et al. 2007, S29).

Some cultural values are inherent in competency assessments, and the forensic psychiatrist likely identifies with those values. These include procedural fairness (the right to confront one's accusers, to interact with counsel to assist with this, and the right of the individual to express their own opinion). These values are not necessarily shared by defendants of other cultures, who may not have a tradition of raising one's voice against those in authority, such as senior cultural or family leaders. For example, they may not engage others in their defense, not because of psychopathology, but because of cultural expression. Further, there are reasons other than mental illness why those from the nondominant culture may be suspicious of the legal process.

Insanity/criminal responsibility

Understanding culture allows us to understand how behaviors leading to legal charges originated and better understand their meaning. The *McNaughton* rules are embedded in Anglo-American society (Fabrega 2004). Whether one sees one's acts as wrong has cultural underpinnings as well (Tseng et al. 2004; Glancy et al. 2015), because what is considered wrong in one culture may not be considered wrong (or indeed may be considered right) in another culture. This difference may receive more weight in specific jurisdictions in which the "moral wrongfulness" is considered rather than merely the "legal wrongfulness."

One must attempt to grasp an understanding of the defendant's world view. Considering culture can help us understand personality prior to the offense, development, and meaning of education, as well as help conceptualize whether the offending was related to mental illness (Ajaz et al. 2014). The defendant's actions should be considered within the context of his or her own culture in attempts to understand the act. This can help the evaluator understand the defendant's reasoning (Kirmayer et al. 2007; Glancy et al. 2015; Aggarwal 2012). This in turn will help in assessing culpability and knowledge of wrongfulness (Boehnlein et al. 2005; Kirmayer et al. 2007; Aggarwal 2012). A cultural perspective in a sanity evaluation helps place the defendant's actions in context (Ajaz et al. 2014)

Kirmayer and colleagues noted, "In many cases, it is not whether the act was committed that is in question, or the level of intent or control, but what its meaning and significance is to the defendant. Culture frames problems and presents us with the categories and concepts through which we organize and understand our own actions" (Kirmayer et al. 2007, 100). It is important for the forensic psychiatrist to help the finder of fact (judge or jury) understand the role of culture in the offending. Cultural formulation may improve both understanding and empathy from the court.

The "cultural defense"

Each of our cultures shapes our identity, emotional reactions, thought processes, motives, and intentions. Debate exists about a cultural defense, regarding whether it is just to judge someone based on the values and laws of a society that is foreign to him or her (Ajaz et al. 2014). This is in contrast to the importance of maintaining integrity of the law. Cultural defenses can restrict the fundamental fairness of the law by introducing inconsistent rules for different groups of people (Kirmayer et al. 2007). Few groups have wanted the law to apply inconsistently to them and to so be excused of societal accountability, and thus the cultural defense is rarely raised, and likely properly rarely applied. Most groups desire to live by common values (Kirmayer et al. 2007).

Thus tension exists between understanding the person and his or her culture, and the universality of the rules against which people should be judged in our society. It is critical that we do not stereotype but still that we note cultural distinctiveness. Helping the court to understand the defendant's culture, through the cultural formulation, should lead to the fairest outcomes, without a change of the law depending on the defendant.

Culture and sentencing

Although a "cultural defense" is rarely used (and likely appropriately so), demands for culturally informed sentencing are much more common in international settings, particularly in relation to colonized indigenous peoples. Sentencing may be informed by cultural issues among New Zealand Maori (Mead 2003). For indigenous Canadians, this has been set out in a finding of the Supreme Court of Canada (in *R v. Gladue*), and now in the Criminal Code of Canada. In order to address historical overrepresentation of Canadian aboriginals in the justice system, CCC s718.2 e requires the sentencing court to pay particular attention to aboriginal offenders' circumstances. The unique background factors of the defendant (e.g., poverty, poor education, substance use, high crime communities) are considered along with the sentencing options given the index offending. Specifically, what is the right sentence for this offender committing this offense, harming this victim, within this community? Aboriginal status alone, however, should not be a mitigating factor. Restorative sentencing is encouraged, with an overall aim to reduce the use of incarceration. Traditional beliefs were strongly anchored in concepts including restitution and reintegration, but also taking responsibility for one's actions, and facing one's victims and the community. Restorative justice may be punitive as well as restorative. In *R v. Gladue*, the Supreme Court of Canada required that sentencing judges must consider the unique systemic and background factors of the aboriginal defendant in passing sentence. The court was clear that aboriginal communities did not reject the need for punishment and deterrence, but rather that a sentence should fit the needs of the person and his or her community. In sentencing, caution needs be used that culture is not a reason for discrimination either for or against a defendant.

Culture and risk assessment

Risk assessment requires both evidence-based (normothetic) analysis and risk formulation (ideographic) components. Cross-culturally, there are problems with both of these processes. There is very limited cross-cultural data on many of the risk tools commonly used. For instance, in noting this deficiency, Douglas and Reeves (2010) advise that caution must be exercised when using the Historical Clinical Risk Management-20 (HCR-20) for populations on which it has not been normed. They also state, though, that the core domains of risk being measured have been observed as relevant for violence prediction in many settings, so are likely to be of importance cross-culturally. The final risk judgement and risk formulation offer the opportunity to appropriately weight factors relevant to a particular cultural context. This requires the skills of cultural and risk formulation, to ensure that racial stereotyping does not bias the assessor because of a failure to understand this person, rather than seeing this person as representative of a particular group. Racial bias or inaccuracy had been noted in diagnosis (e.g., Adeponle et al. 2012) and in application of dangerousness criteria (Vinkers et al. 2010). Without cultural formulation being built into risk assessment and cross-cultural testing of the assumptions in risk assessment tools employed, similar risks of cross-cultural misinterpretation may confront the forensic practitioner.

Child protection and child custody

Similarly, the psychiatrist should examine his or her own potential biases and countertransference in civil cases. In cases of child protection, care must be taken about the meaning of actions within a certain cultural community. What is considered neglect in one situation may be appropriate parenting behavior in another. For example, while in many cultures, children may babysit other children by the time they are 12, in New Zealand, it is considered neglect to leave a child under 14 without supervision. In America, the Indian Child Welfare Act requires that different standards be met for native American children and families than other Americans. This includes before a Native American child can be placed with a non-Native American family, within various custody proceedings including foster care, adoption, and termination of parental rights (Wills and Norris 2010).

SUMMARY KEY POINTS

- Forensic psychiatric assessments often occur cross-culturally.
- Those of minority ethnicities are consistently overrepresented in the legal system and correctional populations around the world.
- Culture may affect the manifestation of symptoms that an evaluee presents with, and their meaning.
- Cultural formulation may improve both understanding and empathy. The cultural formulation can be narrative and coexist with *DSM* diagnoses.

REFERENCES

Adeponle AB, BD Thombs, D Groleau, E Jarvis, and LJ Kirmayer. 2012. Using the cultural formulation to resolve uncertainty in diagnoses of psychosis among ethnoculturally diverse patients. *Psychiatric Services* 63:147–153.

Aggarwal NK. 2012. Adapting the cultural formulation for clinical assessments in forensic psychiatry. *Journal of the American Academy of Psychiatry and the Law* 40:113–118.

Ajaz A, J Owiti, and K Bhui. 2014. Using a cultural formulation for assessment of homicide in forensic psychiatry in the UK. *International Review of Psychiatry* 26:607–614.

American Psychiatric Association (APA). 2013. *Diagnostic and Statistical Manual of Mental Disorders*, 5th edition. Washington, DC: APA.

Anderson KK, J Cheng, E Susser, KJ McKenzie, and P Kurdyak. 2015. Incidence of psychotic disorders among first-generation immigrants and refugees in Ontario. *CMAJ* 187(9):279–286.

Boehnlein JK, MN Schaefer, and JD Bloom. 2005. Cultural considerations in the criminal law: The sentencing process. *Journal of the American Academy of Psychiatry and the Law* 33:335–341.

Committee on Cultural Psychiatry, Group for the Advancement of Psychiatry. 2002. *Cultural Assessment in Clinical Psychiatry*. Washington, DC: American Psychiatric Press.

Douglas KS and KA Reeves. 2010. Historical-Clinical-Risk Management-20 (HCR-20) violence risk assessment scheme. In *Handbook of Violence Risk Assessment*, edited by RK Otto and KS Douglas, New York: Routledge, 147–186.

Fabrega H. 2004. Culture and formulations of homicide: Two case studies. *Psychiatry* 67:178–196.

Fernando S. 2003. *Cultural Diversity, Mental Health and Psychiatry, the Struggle against Racism*. New York: Brunner-Routledge, 11–25, 146–151.

Flora N, H Barbaree, Al Simpson, S Noh, and K McKenzie. 2012. Pathways to forensic mental health care in Toronto: A comparison of European, African-Caribbean, and other ethnoracial groups in Toronto. *Canadian Journal of Psychiatry* 57:414–421.

Glancy GD, P Ash, EPJ Bath et al. 2015. AAPL practice guideline for the forensic assessment. *Journal of the American Academy of Psychiatry and the Law* 43:S3–53.

Griffith EEH. 2005. Personal narrative and an African-American perspective on medical ethics. *Journal of the American Academy of Psychiatry and the Law* 33:371–381.

Griffith EEH, A Stankovic, and M Baranoski. 2010. Conceptualizing the forensic psychiatry report as performative narrative. *Journal of the American Academy of Psychiatry and the Law* 38:32–42.

Hicks JW. 2004. Ethnicity, race and forensic psychiatry: Are we color-blind? *Journal of the American Academy of Psychiatry and the Law* 32:21–33.

Kapoor R, C Dike, C Burns, V Carvalho, and EE Griffith. 2013. Cultural competence in correctional mental health. *International Journal of Law and Psychiatry* 36:273–280.

Kirmayer LJ. 2012. Rethinking cultural competence. *Transcultural Psychiatry* 49:149–164.

Kirmayer LJ, C Rousseau, and M Lashley. 2007. The place of culture in forensic psychiatry. *Journal of the American Academy of Psychiatry and the Law* 35:98–102.

Kleinman A. 1980. *Patients and Healers in the Context of Culture*. Berkeley: University of California Press.

Leese M, G Thornicroft, J Shaw, S Thomas, R Mohan, MA Harty, and M Dolan. 2006. Ethnic differences among patients in high-security psychiatric hospitals in England. *British Journal of Psychiatry* 188:380–385.

Lewis-Fernández R, NK Aggarwal, S Bäärnhielm et al. 2014. Culture and psychiatric evaluation: Operationalizing cultural formulation for *DSM-5*. *Psychiatry* 77:130–154.

Lewis-Fernández R, M Horvitz-Lennon, C Blanco, PJ Guarnaccia, Z Cao, and M Alegría. 2009. Significance of endorsement of psychotic symptoms by US Latinos. *Journal of Nervous and Mental Disease* 197:337–347.

Lu FG, RF Lim, and JE Mezzich. 2008. Issues in the assessment and diagnosis of culturally diverse individuals. In *Cultural Formulation: A Reader for Psychiatric Diagnosis*, edited by JE Mezzich and G Caracci, Lanham, MD: Jason Aronson, 115–148.

Maddux J. 2010. Recommendations for forensic evaluators conducting interpreter-mediated interviews. *International Journal of Forensic Mental Health* 9:55–62.

Mead HM. 2003. *Tikanga Maori: Living by Maori Values*. Wellington, New Zealand: Huia.

Mezzich JE. 1995. Cultural formulation and comprehensive diagnosis. *Psychiatric Clinics of North America* 18:649–657.

Mezzich JE, G Caracci, H Fabrega, and LJ Kirmayer. 2009. Cultural formulation guidelines. *Transcultural Psychiatry* 46:383–405.

Mossman D, SG Noffsinger, P Ash et al. 2007. AAPL practice guideline for the forensic evaluation of competency to stand trial. *Journal of the American Academy of Psychiatry and the Law* 35:S3–S72.

Myers NL. 2011. Update: Schizophrenia across cultures. *Current Psychiatry Reports* 13:305–311.

Norko MA. 2005. Compassion at the core of forensic ethics. *Journal of the American Academy of Psychiatry and the Law* 33:386–389.

Simpson AI, PM Brinded, N Fairley, TM Laidlaw, and F Malcolm. 2003. Does ethnicity affect need for mental health service among New Zealand prisoners? *Australian and New Zealand Journal of Psychiatry* 37:728–734.

Tseng WS, D Matthews, and TS Elwyn. 2004. *Cultural Competence in Forensic Mental Health: A Guide for Psychiatrists, Psychologists and Attorneys*. New York: Brunner-Routledge.

Vinkers DJ, SC De Vries, AWB Van Baars, and CL Mulder. 2010. Ethnicity and dangerousness criteria for court ordered admission to a psychiatric hospital. *Social Psychiatry and Psychiatric Epidemiology* 45:221–224.

Whitley R. 2007. Cultural competence, evidence-based medicine, and evidence-based practices. *Psychiatric Services* 58:1588–1590.

Wills CD and DM Norris. 2010. Custodial evaluations of native American families: Implications for forensic psychiatrists. *Journal of the American Academy of Psychiatry and the Law* 38:540–546.

77

Geriatric forensic psychiatry

BRIAN A. FALLS, GEN TANAKA, AND HAROLD J. BURSZTAJN

INTRODUCTION

As the subspecialty of forensic psychiatry continues to grow (Engstrom 2009), geriatric forensic psychiatry (also called "geroforensic psychiatry") will foreseeably become a field of ever-increasing import for two key reasons. First, the elderly population of developed nations is rapidly rising. In the United States, for instance, the elderly population will likely double between 2000 and 2050 (U.S. Census Bureau 2008). Second, medical and psychiatric knowledge are increasing at such a rate that by 2020, medical knowledge might double every 73 days (Denson 2011).

In this chapter, we discuss forensic psychiatric principles commonly encountered with a geriatric population; the geroforensic evaluation; capacity evaluations commonly performed with elderly evaluees; elder abuse; geropsychiatric malpractice issues; malingering of neurocognitive disorders; and older adults in the criminal justice system.

FORENSICALLY RELEVANT MEDICAL AND PSYCHIATRIC PROBLEMS IN OLDER ADULTS

Psychiatric disorders are more common among older individuals than younger individuals (Jeste et al. 1999). Substance use disorders appear to be increasing among older adults in the United States. Researchers forecast that substance use disorders in this population will increase by 70%, even when adjusted for overall growth of the elderly population segment (U.S. Census Bureau 2006; Han et al. 2008).

Even more forensically relevant to the older population than substance use disorders and noncognitive psychiatric disorders are *Diagnostic and Statistical Manual of Mental Disorders*, 5th edition (*DSM-5*) Neurocognitive Disorders (American Psychiatric Association [APA] 2013). Cognitive domains that can be impacted by these disorders include complex attention, executive functioning, memory, language, perceptual–motor skills, and social cognition. *DSM-5* taxonomy aside, forensic evaluators need to broadly consider "cognitive" impairment and avoid the artificial division between disorders of cognition and feeling (Bursztajn et al. 1991). About 30%–80% of patients with neurocognitive disorders can have behavioral and psychological symptoms of dementia (BPSD) (Margallo-Lana et al. 2001; Lyketsos 2002), which can include delusions, hallucinations (usually visual), agitation, aggression, and disinhibition (Taylor et al. 2012).

Neurocognitive disorders are often irreversible and tend to worsen over years. Yet there are some fairly common medical, affective, and social-context issues that can interfere with capacity that are potentially reversible. These factors include delirium; pseudodementia; medications/polypharmacy; isolation; and caregiver, family, and institutional dynamics relative to the increased dependency of the fragile elderly.

Pseudodementia refers to cognitive deficits that mimic dementia and are due to another condition, usually a psychiatric disorder. Some disorders that can impair cognition in such a manner include mood disorders, psychosis, dissociative disorders, conversion disorder, and Ganser syndrome (Dobie 2002). In particular, mood disorders can appear exquisitely similar to dementia, as the two types of conditions share symptoms of impaired concentration, apathy, anhedonia, amotivation, impoverished speech, changes in appetite, changes in sexual interest, and sleep disturbances. With the fragile elderly, affect-based impairment may be so difficult to disentangle from cognitive-based impairment as to highlight the limitation of the cognitive/affective distinction perpetuated when current diagnostic systems are mechanistically translated into formulations of capacity (Bursztajn et al. 1991).

Polypharmacy, along with medication use in general, is a common cause of cognitive problems in the elderly (Sergi et al. 2011). One out of six individuals age 65 or older is taking 10 or more medications (Guthrie et al. 2015). The sheer number of medications consumed by older adults is complicated by pharmacodynamic and pharmacokinetic inefficiencies that accompany aging (Taylor et al. 2012). Certain medical conditions, whose incidence increases with age, can also reversibly interfere with an individual's cognition.

SPECIAL CONSIDERATIONS FOR THE GEROFORENSIC EVALUATION

General considerations

As with any psychiatric interview, in the geroforensic evaluation, evaluators should ask open-ended questions and take time to genuinely listen. All forensic evaluees should be treated with respect (Appelbaum 1997) and, especially with larger evaluator–evaluee age discrepancies, a respectful approach can help build rapport (MacKinnon et al. 2006).

Forensic psychiatrists evaluating older adults should be mindful of hindrances to effective communication. Perceptual problems, such as hearing and visual impairments, can further complicate communication with evaluating psychiatrists by making elders feel embarrassed and disoriented. Especially in hearing-impaired evaluees, psychiatrists should use simple sentences and provide sufficient time for responses to inquiries. Evaluators should speak in a loud, clear voice; face evaluees so they can read lips; and sit close enough for evaluees to hear (Gerontological Society of America 2012; Blazer 2014, 13).

Older adults tend to have less positive attitudes toward mental health care than younger populations (Farberman 1997), which can also interfere with communication. Many older people experience relatively high anxiety levels yet do not complain about it. Older people may be more hesitant to reveal their affect verbally and more likely to be cautious in their responses (Blazer 2014, 12), so nonverbal communication may be especially important. Some other common reasons for guardedness include a desire to maintain independence, especially in capacity evaluations; reticence regarding finances or relationships; anxiety about or denial of mortality; and fear of loneliness or abandonment (Sprehe 2003).

Transference and countertransference

As with any psychiatric interview, countertransference and transference occur in the geropsychiatric forensic interaction. Forensic psychiatrists may misperceive older evaluees due to cultural ageist biases, their own fears of aging and mortality, or previous experiences with parents (Myers 1986; Blazer 2014, 12).

Similarly, evaluees may experience transference (Myers 1986). For those aged who are cognitively impaired, their perceptions of evaluating psychiatrists may be even more prone to distortion, based on prior experiences, than those of younger evaluees. Evaluees with mild neurocognitive impairment usually develop a transference consistent with their underlying lifelong character traits. Contrarily, individuals with major neurocognitive disorder may relate to psychiatrists in ways that have more to do with their organic illness than enduring personality patterns (MacKinnon et al. 2006).

Presence of third parties

Some frail elderly individuals will seek reassurance by requesting that family, friends, or other "familiar faces" be present during interviews. Family and friends may also insist on their being allowed to be present during evaluations. As with all forensic psychiatric interviews, evaluators should nonetheless resist temptation to include a third party. Doing so can distort and complicate interviews (Gavett et al. 2005). For instance, evaluees with neurocognitive disorders might seek clues in others' facial expressions and might, for example, confabulate based on this. Especially in undue influence evaluations or cases of suspected elder abuse/neglect, they may choose not to disclose certain information based on others' nonverbal cues, intimidating or otherwise. In clinical geriatric psychiatric evaluations, family or friends may provide much of the history while the patient is present in the room (Sadock and Sadock 2014). During a forensic evaluation, however, evaluators should not obtain collateral information with evaluees present (Simon 1996). Instead, collateral data should be gathered outside the setting of the forensic psychiatric examination.

The problem of dual agency

A frequent problem in general forensic practice, the "dual agency" issue is even more often encountered in geroforensic examinations and can result in serious bias (Strasburger et al. 1997). Treating physicians may have an interest in maintaining the therapeutic alliance with elderly patients and in avoiding a potential "shoot the messenger" reaction associated with the grief of decreased autonomy. For this reason, they are usually less likely to find examinees incapacitated, although the pendulum can also swing in the opposite direction.

CAPACITIES

Incapacity to make and articulate specific decisions is a problem that disproportionately affects older adults (Moye and Marson 2007). One group writes that "as our society ages, clinical assessment of higher order functional capacities has become increasingly important. In areas like financial capacity, medical decision making capacity, medication compliance, and driving, society has a strong interest in accurately discriminating intact from impaired functioning" (Marson et al. 2000). Below is a nonexhaustive list of commonly evaluated capacities in the elderly population. Most U.S. jurisdictions now legally recognize capacities as situation or task specific (Smyer 2007). Because the legal criteria differ between jurisdictions, here we offer only general legal definitions. It is important for geropsychiatric evaluators to familiarize themselves with their local laws.

Just because an evaluator diagnoses an individual with neuropsychiatric illness does not mean that the individual is incapacitated. Furthermore, there is no level of neurocognitive impairment that necessarily precludes any

Table 77.1 Some capacity assessment tools

Medical decision making	Advance directives	Independent living	Financial decision making
MacArthur Competence Assessment Tool–Treatment (MacCAT-T)	Competence Assessment Tool for Psychiatric Advance Directives (CAT-PAD)	Adult Functional Adaptive Behavior Scale (AFABS)	Financial Capacity Instrument (FCI)
Aid to Capacity Evaluation (ACE)	Hopkins Competency Assessment Test (HCAT)	Revised Direct Assessment of Functional Status (DAFS-R)	Hopemont Capacity Assessment Interview (HCAI)
Assessment of Capacity to Consent to Treatment (ACCT)		Multidimensional Functional Assessment Questionnaire (MFAQ)	
Capacity Assessment Tool (CAT)		Philadelphia Geriatric Center Multilevel Assessment Inventory (MAI)	

specific capacity. On the other hand, two different diagnoses, such as a neurocognitive disorder due to Alzheimer's disease dementia and neurocognitive disorder due to vascular dementia, may have overlapping areas of impairment. Therefore, it is important that evaluators approach each case individually.

For capacity evaluations, functional assessment is vital (Pfeiffer 1991). It is necessary to understand whether evaluees with memory problems can use memory aids, such as mobile devices, calendars, notes, and lists. It is important to elicit whether or not evaluees understand how to use professional help (e.g., bankers, attorneys, etc.) to compensate for their deficits, and whether they know someone they can trust. Evaluees should be able to describe how they know they can trust someone and to be able to recognize ambiguity and uncertainty in their relationships, because the fragile elderly, especially those with psychiatric illness, are more likely to be preyed upon (Lichtenberg et al. 2013). There are a number of tools that supplement, but do not replace, professional judgment in assessing the various capacities. These tools are summarized in Table 77.1.

Health-care consent capacities

As per *Jerry W. Canterbury v. William T. Spence* (1972), health-care decisional capacity is an important component in the triad of informed consent, the other two components being voluntariness and sufficient provision of information on the part of the health-care provider. Most state laws define the capacity to make medical decisions as the ability to communicate a health-care decision based on an understanding of significant benefits, risks, and alternative treatment options.

If individuals lack capacity to make their own health-care decisions, a previously appointed health-care proxy or durable power of attorney can make choices for them. If they had not designated a health-care proxy prior to their becoming incapacitated, many states allow for family members to make medical decisions for them.

In assessing patients' capacity to consent to treatment, evaluators examine their ability to understand relevant information, appreciate the current situation and its consequences, manipulate information rationally, and communicate a choice (Appelbaum and Grisso 1988). Some scholars have advocated for a capacity "sliding scale," wherein stringency of the utilized capacity standard is inversely proportional to the degree of risk of a medical procedure (Freedman 1981; Drane 1985).

Capacity to make an advance directive

An advance health-care directive (also known as a living will, advance decision, or personal directive) is a legal instruction in which a patient designates what actions should be taken for their health if they are no longer able to make decisions for themselves due to an incapacitating condition. An individual's capacity to execute an advance health-care directive is not the same as the capacity to make medical choices. The test of capacity to execute an advance directive is usually the same as that of the capacity to make a contract.

Capacity to consent to physician-assisted suicide

Five U.S. states now allow physician-assisted suicide (PAS), and others have considered permitting it. Oregon, Washington, and Vermont have statutes legalizing PAS, while New Mexico and Montana have set case law standards. If a forensic psychiatric evaluation finds that the patient has a mental disorder causing impaired judgment, treating physicians cannot prescribe lethal medication. Considering the irreversibility of the decision, a forensic psychiatric evaluation should be considered as indicated, even where not legally mandatory, given that primary care physicians do not recognize up to 90% of psychiatric disorders in their patients (Eisenberg 1992).

Several factors make these types of capacity evaluations very difficult. Foremost, as opposed to many other civil and criminal capacities, none of the states that allow PAS have a legal standard for capacity to consent to it.

Additionally, evaluators may be biased with respect to such an emotional topic as life-terminating treatment, especially in the absence of a standard "threshold" for capacity/incapacity (Ganzini et al. 1996; Zaubler and Sullivan 1996). Consequently, treating psychiatrists should not perform capacity evaluations because treating clinicians, as compassionate providers, may be more likely to either unwittingly enable incapacitated, depressed patients' desires to die. Clinicians may also automatically oppose these wishes, given the attachment that can form between treating clinicians and patients.

Although it has not been formally studied in patients requesting PAS, suicidal ideation is generally transient (Falls 2011), and patients with mental illness who want PAS may respond to treatments that are effective in other groups of suicidal persons (Ganzini and Lee 1997). A vital part of any capacity for PAS assessment is to consider whether patients have the capacity to change their mind, love themselves, and maintain a consciousness of time that differentiates transient, potentially treatable suffering from that which is permanent, certain, and intractable (Bursztajn et al. 1986). In summary, the stakes—human life—are enormous, and the potential for unintentional bias is high in these types of evaluations.

Capacity to live independently

The capacity to live independently is usually evaluated as part of determining whether an individual needs a guardian of person. Most states require that for a court to appoint a legal guardian, an individual must have a disabling condition, which usually includes a cognitive deficit; the condition must prevent the individual from performing basic functions necessary to live without assistance; and guardianship must be the least restrictive alternative (Zimny and Grossberg 1998).

Independent living capacity can be affected by a number of psychiatric diagnoses in the elderly, most commonly neurocognitive disorders, depression, or psychosis. When assessing the capacity for independent living, psychiatrists examine whether an individual is endangering himself or herself on account of problems with cognitive, psychiatric, or physical functioning. Functioning is typically conceptualized in terms of basic activities of daily living (BADLs), such as bathing, dressing, and feeding; and instrumental activities of daily living (IADLs), including shopping, taking medications, and managing finances. The ability to do these types of activities requires that a person understand the importance of the task and cognitively and physically be able to execute it. Individuals should also be able to exercise judgment regarding these activities, that is, to perform them consistently and to avoid dangerous behaviors (Zimny and Grossberg 1998; Moye and Braun 2007).

Financial capacities

GENERAL FINANCIAL CAPACITY

Financial capacity is an individual's ability to manage finances in a way that is consistent with personal values. In order to have financial capacity, individuals should be able to carry out financial tasks, such as adding/subtracting currency, managing bank accounts, and paying bills. Furthermore, they should be able to do these tasks in a manner consistent with personal interests and values. Values are particularly important, as individuals tend to differ greatly with regard to why, how, when, and to what degree they spend and invest money. If a court finds that an individual is not able to manage finances, it will appoint a conservator (or guardian of the estate, depending on the jurisdiction) to manage all or some of the finances (Hebert and Marson 2007).

TESTAMENTARY CAPACITY

The ability to execute a valid will, also known as testamentary capacity, is the most commonly contested type of capacity. Moreover, the number of will contests addressing testamentary capacity and undue influence has increased in recent years (Marson and Hebert 2008), as a result of an increase in mixed, nonnuclear families, the transfer of more wealth from the World War II generation (American Bar Association [ABA] and APA 2008), and the increasing prevalence of neurocognitive disorders associated with the aging population.

Most states require that for a finding of testamentary capacity, a testator (man making a will) or testatrix (woman making a will) know the following: what a will is; his or her potential heirs ("objects of bounty"); the nature and extent of his or her assets; and a general plan of distribution of assets to heirs (Roof 2012). (For simplicity, in this chapter we use the term *testator* to refer to both men and women.) If a testator does not understand at least one of these elements, the court may find that he or she lacks testamentary capacity. Consequently, the will, and any modifications to it, will be void. Yet legal standards for testamentary capacity vary greatly by state, so familiarity with the relevant laws of the jurisdiction is imperative.

For a finding of testamentary capacity, a testator must also be able to work with his or her attorney and not hold any delusional beliefs that impact the content of the will (e.g., revising a will to remove as an heiress a daughter who he believes is actually an impostor). Courts have historically applied a low legal threshold for finding testamentary capacity in the interest of honoring the testator's autonomy and freedom to distribute his or her assets. It is therefore important for evaluators to thoroughly understand a testator's lifelong financial values as well as relationships with prospective heirs. A striking departure from long-standing preferences about finances and property could indicate an "unnatural will," a legal term that signals an individual may lack testamentary capacity or be the victim of undue influence (described below).

Undue influence

Undue influence occurs when an influencer subverts a victim's free will, causing the victim to make a decision that inappropriately benefits the influencer. Additionally, such influence usually contradicts what the victim would have done in the absence of said influence. In forensic psychiatric practice, undue influence is most often encountered in evaluations of testamentary capacity, as it is alleged in over half of contested will cases (Shulman et al. 2005). Undue influence can also impact donative capacity, contractual capacity, and other capacities (Garner 2014).

To find that undue influence occurred, many courts require that a confidential relationship existed between the influencer and the victim; there was a way for fraud to occur; and the victim changed the financial arrangement so that it benefited the influencer. Perhaps most psychiatrically relevant is that the victim must be vulnerable to influence. The greater the neurocognitive and emotional impairment of the victim, the less influence is necessary for the court to find that he or she was unduly influenced (Shulman et al. 2005).

It should be noted that, especially in testamentary capacity cases, psychiatrists are often consulted after the victim has died (Gutheil 2007), and, accordingly, personal forensic evaluation of the victim is not possible. In evaluations in which the testator is deceased, previously administered cognitive instruments such as the Montreal Cognitive Assessment (MOCA) can provide helpful data in the context of all available information.

While reviewing records and performing interviews, geroforensic psychiatrists should consider tactics that perpetrators of undue influence utilize to procure money or goods from their victims. These include keeping victims isolated and unaware of the circumstances; being dishonest (e.g., lying, misrepresenting, or concealing of information for selfish gain); alienating victims from others; using intimidation (e.g., fostering dependency with fear of rejection if money or goods is not willed, or inducing fear by threatening to leave or emotionally/physically harm victims) and generally taking advantage of vulnerabilities; inducing shame and guilt and preying on insecurities; intermittently performing acts of kindness; and promising to care for victims in exchange for financial demands (Hall et al. 2005; ABA and APA 2008). Although there is no complete "profile" of an influencer, many influencers have sociopathic characters and antisocial behaviors, especially a parasitic lifestyle (e.g., living with or financially depending on victims), and/or have psychiatric illness themselves (Hall et al. 2005). When beneficiaries accompany elderly examinees to evaluations, evaluators cannot perform a comprehensive examination for the presence of undue influence.

Additionally, geroforensic psychiatrists should look for several factors that increase the risk of elderly individuals becoming victims of undue influence (Peisah et al. 2009). Demographic factors include advanced age, female gender, and unmarried status. Financial factors include financial independence with no designated money managers and mid- to upper-income bracket. Medical factors include organic brain damage; taking multiple medications; increasing frailty; physical, mental, or emotional illness (especially depression); and cognitive impairment, especially semantic memory deficits. Psychosocial factors include dependent personality traits; recent divorce or spousal death; living with the influencer; fear of change in the living situation (e.g., being placed in a nursing home); dependence on the influencer; and physical and/or social isolation, including estrangement from children (Hall et al. 2005; ABA and APA 2008; Peisah et al. 2009).

ELDER ABUSE

Elders, especially those residing in nursing homes, are particularly vulnerable to physical, sexual, and emotional abuse, as well as neglect and exploitation (Kleinschmidt 1997). Some states legally require clinicians to report suspected abuse or neglect. Federal legislation has also been enacted to combat elder abuse. For instance, the 2010 Elder Justice Act, among other provisions, allocated millions of dollars to establish and support specialized centers for developing forensic expertise on elder abuse, neglect, and exploitation and for providing services to victims (Public Act 111-148 Title VI Subtitle H—Elder Justice Act 2010).

Adult children, spouses, or other family members perpetrate in 90% of cases of elder abuse and neglect (Hildreth 2009). The number of victims is rising, with morbidity and premature mortality growing accordingly (Teaster and Otto 2006). Studies examining the prevalence of elder abuse report that approximately 7%–11% of cognitively intact older adults reported some form of abuse in the previous year (Teaster et al. 2004; Acierno et al. 2010; New York City Department for the Aging Elderly Crime Victims Resource Center 2011).

Unsettling as it may be, this percentage probably underestimates the actual prevalence because many cases of elder abuse go undetected and unreported. However, elder abuse can also be subject to overreporting, due to such misattribution factors as confabulation; paranoia in the face of helplessness; hopelessness and the ravages of time; and family dynamics such as scapegoating dynamics that can be perpetuated by bandwagon or "witch hunt" effects. Older individuals with neurocognitive disorders are especially susceptible because their impairments can render them incapable of reporting incidents.

Because elder abuse and neglect incidents typically happen in more isolated domestic settings, they are not discovered as often as those involving other vulnerable populations. Children, for example, are more often exposed to a wider variety of public areas, such as schools and playgrounds (Hafemeister 2013). Older individuals sometimes cannot make decisions about their living arrangements, and some with neurocognitive disorders do not fully understand or remember abuse or neglect for any meaningful period of time. Moreover, they often cannot reasonably improve their situation on their own. Silence, denial, fear of retaliation, and fear of the unknown can suppress reporting by victims or witnesses of abuse in a variety of care settings.

Risk factors for abuse and neglect include isolation, unfavorable caregiver qualities (particularly a history of antisocial behavior and/or substance use), and victim mental illness, especially neurocognitive disorders. Signs of elder abuse and neglect include atypical injuries; poor hygiene; unsanitary or hazardous living conditions; pressure ulcers; malnutrition and/or dehydration; expressed or apparent fearfulness around caregivers; and depression. Yet no combination of these signs is specific for abuse or neglect, so the presence of one or more of these potential indicators needs to be considered in the context of a broader inquiry (Kleinschmidt 1997).

Clinicians may consult forensic geriatric psychiatrists when elder abuse or neglect is suspected. Factors for forensic geropsychiatrists to consider in more detail include whether fact patterns are more consistent with abuse or neglect or other causes, such as, most commonly, the natural history of a medical or psychiatric disorder. It is also critical to consider whether informants—be they patients, family members, or staff members—are reliable historians. Reasons to question the accuracy of reports include motives such as primary (e.g., a better room in a nursing home) or secondary (e.g., attention seeking due to loneliness) gain. Furthermore, a number of impairments can accompany under- and overreporting, including avoidance of traumatic memories, as sometimes occurs in PTSD; undue influence or dependence on the abuser, which leads to avoidance of reporting of abuse; or patterns of confabulation, as seen in a variety of neurocognitive disorders which can lead to misattribution of abuse. Interviewing methods should avoid suggestion while simultaneously creating a safe environment for evaluees to disclose information that may humiliate and otherwise deeply upset them (Bursztajn 2000).

PSYCHIATRIC MALPRACTICE WITH RESPECT TO ELDERLY PATIENTS

In the general population, the most common type of psychiatric malpractice action arises from suicide of a patient (Simon and Sadoff 1992). Social, economic, and psychological factors increase the vulnerability of older adults to suicidal thoughts and behaviors, and suicide rates are five times higher among elderly males than in other segments of the population (Centers for Disease Control and Prevention [CDC] 2012). A neurocognitive disorder diagnosis further increases risk of completed suicide (Haw et al. 2009; Scocco et al. 2009; Seyfried et al. 2011). The larger number of malpractice suits after elderly patient suicide reflects the high rate of suicide in older adults.

Another common area of geriatric psychiatric malpractice is harm allegedly caused by medications. Polypharmacy in the elderly increases the risk of psychiatric malpractice allegations. As mentioned above, one out of six people age 65 or older is taking 10 or more medications (Guthrie et al. 2015). Despite the U.S. Food and Drug Administration's (FDA) caution in 2005 that atypical antipsychotics increase risk of all-cause mortality by 60%–70% with daily administration over a short period of time (FDA 2005), clinicians continue to prescribe these medications for psychotic and behavioral symptoms. This is particularly true in nursing homes, where residents are more severely cognitively impaired on average than their peers in the general community (Taylor et al. 2012).

Obtaining informed consent from patients, or their legally authorized medical decision makers, is critical when treating elderly individuals, especially with antipsychotics. As with all informed consent evaluations, and even more so with the fragile elderly who may be experiencing great fear or demoralization that may compound information processing impairments, effective, meaningful informed consent is not *pro forma* and does not rely solely on paper forms, which could contain either excessive or insufficient information. Instead, informed consent becomes more of a therapeutic alliance-based process. This process can have therapeutic and risk management benefits for patients, families, and clinicians. A geroforensic psychiatric consultant can aid this process and manage risk associated with treating marginally competent elderly patients (Gutheil et al. 1984; Gopal et al. 2012).

ASSESSMENT AND DETECTION OF MALINGERED NEUROCOGNITIVE DEFICITS

In almost any forensic evaluation, malingering should be ruled out. Dissimulation is an especially relevant consideration in capacity evaluations. Evaluees may "put on their best face" in an effort to persuade psychiatrists that they are not incapacitated, in order to maintain their independence. Cognitive deficits have historically been considered easy to feign, likely due to the presumed ease with which a person can convincingly feign deficits, as opposed to positive symptoms. One of the simplest strategies for detecting malingering is to identify discrepancies between reported symptoms and objective data on cognition found in the mental status examination, written records, and collateral interviews. Yet clinical assessment and collateral data alone often do not sufficiently exclude the possibility of malingering. Several strategies can be useful to assess suspected malingered cognitive problems. These include comparing performance on psychological instruments to that of test-takers with known cognitive impairment, overreporting detection, symptom validity testing (SVT), and the floor effect.

CRIMINAL AND CORRECTIONAL ISSUES IN THE ELDERLY

Criminal behavior in older adults

Older individuals commit far fewer crimes of every type than do their younger counterparts (Barak et al. 1995). Approximately 15% of older individuals apprehended are arrested for serious felonies (Aday and Krabill 2006). Research shows that elders tend to receive less harsh sentences than their younger counterparts for many different crime types (Steffensmeier and Motivans 2000).

Violent offenses committed by the elderly

International studies have shown that 11%–14% of indictable offenses committed by older offenders were violent ones (Barak et al. 1995; Home Office 2000). Most risk assessment instruments were not developed using groups of older individuals, nor have they been studied in such populations to date. For instance, the MacArthur Violence Risk Assessment study data that were used to design the Classification of Violence Risk (COVR) excluded individuals over 40 years old (Monahan et al. 2000). Additionally, the average age of the 618 offenders studied in the development of the Violence Risk Appraisal Guide (VRAG) was 28 at the time of the offense (Harris et al. 1993).

Geriatric sexual offenders

The majority of sexual offenders and sexual offense recidivists are younger men. Lower overall rates of offending and recidivism among older men are likely due to the fact that they tend to have better self-control (Hanson and Thornton 2003) and poorer sexual functioning (Barbaree et al. 2003) than younger men. Yet nearly 4% of all people arrested for sex crimes in 2006 were 60 or older (Hart 2008). Older sexual offenders are more likely to commit "nonviolent" offenses such as exhibitionism than "violent" offenses such as rape (Alston 1986; Flynn 2004), and are more likely to select children as victims than are younger sex offenders (Hucker 1984).

In terms of sexual recidivism risk factors, having a stranger victim was the strongest risk factor in those over 55, whereas it was not associated with recidivism in those under 25 (Fazel et al. 2002). The age of individuals who have committed rape is inversely correlated to sexual recidivism rates, which is not true of other sexual offense types (Hanson and Thornton 2003).

Psychiatric disorders among the incarcerated elderly

Up to half of older prisoners have a psychiatric illness (Fazel et al. 2001; Fazel and Danesh 2002), whereas only about one in seven prisoners of all ages have a treatable mental illness (Fazel and Danesh 2002). Rates of psychosis and depression each represent about a third of psychiatric illness in older prisoners, which is higher than in prisoners of all ages (Fazel and Danesh 2002).

Despite such high prevalence rates, older individuals are less likely than younger ones to receive treatment. This may be due to the fact that they are not as inclined to acknowledge psychiatric symptoms, even when treatments are available (Vega and Silverman 1988; Yorston and Taylor 2006; Sterns et al. 2008). Similar to the nonincarcerated general population, older incarcerated individuals are more likely to attempt and commit suicide than younger cohorts (Kuhlmann and Ruddell 2005). Additionally, as with younger inmates (James and Glaze 2006), psychiatric illness is far more common in incarcerated women than men (Aday and Krabill 2011).

Substance use disorders among the incarcerated elderly

Like the general incarcerated population, the elderly incarcerated are more likely to use substances than their nonincarcerated cohorts. In an Iowa survey, 71% of prisoners age 55 and older reported a history of substance use consistent with a substance use disorder, compared with more than 90% of younger prisoners. Among elderly offenders who report substance use disorders, alcohol use disorder is most common. Its prevalence of 85% in aged offenders is higher than in younger age groups. Elderly prisoners are also more likely to be arrested for alcohol-related crimes than younger prisoners (Arndt et al. 2002).

SUMMARY KEY POINTS

- As the elderly live longer and medical knowledge increases, geroforensic psychiatry has become a rapidly growing field, one that requires sensitive and comprehensive evaluation.
- Increasing prevalence of neurocognitive disorders with age results in older individuals being more likely to have their capacities evaluated.
- Treating clinicians may consult geroforensic psychiatrists in suspected elder abuse cases.
- Elder patient suicide and adverse drug reactions are common causes for medical malpractice lawsuits against geropsychiatrists.
- Geroforensic evaluators should always consider malingering, particularly malingering of neurocognitive symptoms.
- The prevalence of psychiatric and substance use disorders is higher among older inmates than younger inmates, yet this group is less likely to receive treatment than younger inmates.

REFERENCES

Acierno R, MA Hernandez, AB Amstadter, HS Resnick, K Steve, W Muzzy, and DG Kilpatrick. 2010. Prevalence and correlates of emotional, physical, sexual, and financial abuse and potential neglect in the United States: The National Elder Mistreatment Study. *American Journal of Public Health* 100:292–297.

Aday R and J Krabill. 2006. Aging offenders in the criminal justice system. *Marquette Elder's Advisor* 7(2):237–258.

Aday R and J Krabill. 2011. *Women Aging in Prison: A Neglected Population in the Criminal Justice System.* Boulder, CO: Lynne Rienner.

Alston L. 1986. *Crime and Older Americans.* Springfield, IL: Charles C Thomas.

American Bar Association and American Psychiatric Association. 2008. *Assessment of Older Adults with Diminished Capacity: A Handbook for Psychologists.* Washington, DC: American Bar Association and American Psychological Association.

American Psychiatric Association (APA). 2013. *Diagnostic and Statistical Manual of Mental Disorders*, 5th edition. Washington, DC: APA.

Appelbaum PS. 1997. A theory of ethics for forensic psychiatry. *Journal of the American Academy of Psychiatry and the Law* 25:233–247.

Appelbaum PS and T Grisso. 1988. Assessing patients' capacities to consent to treatment. *New England Journal of Medicine* 319:1635–1638.

Arndt S, C Turvey, and M Flaum. 2002. Older offenders, substance abuse, and treatment. *American Journal of Geriatric Psychiatry* 10:733–739.

Barak Y, T Perry, and A Elizur. 1995. Elderly criminals: A study of the first criminal offence in old age. *International Journal of Geriatric Psychiatry* 10(6):511–516.

Barbaree HE, R Blanchard, and CM Langton. 2003. The development of sexual aggression through the life span: The effect of age on sexual arousal and recidivism among sex offenders. *Sexually Coercive Behavior: Understanding and Management* 989:59–71.

Blazer D. 2014. The psychiatric interview of older adults. In *Clinical Manual of Geriatric Psychiatry*, edited by M Thakur, D Blazer, and D Steffens, Arlington, VA: American Psychiatric Publishing, 12–13.

Bursztajn HJ. 2000. Commentary on: Physicians indicated the need to frame questions and develop indirect approaches that foster patient trust in evaluating victims of domestic violence. *Evidence Based Mental Health* 3:63.

Bursztajn HJ, TG Gutheil, M Warren, and A Brodsky. 1986. Depression, self-love, time, and the "right" to suicide. *General Hospital Psychiatry* 8:91–95.

Bursztajn HJ, HP Harding, TG Gutheil, and A Brodsky. 1991. Beyond cognition: The role of disordered affective states in impairing competence to consent to treatment. *Bulletin of the American Academy of Psychiatry and the Law* 19:383–388.

Centers for Disease Control and Prevention (CDC). 2012. *Injury Prevention and Control: Data and Statistics (WISQARSTM) Fatal Injury Reports.* Atlanta, GA: CDC. http://www.cdc.gov/injury/wisqars/fatal_injury_reports.html, accessed October 22, 2014.

Denson P. 2011. Challenges and opportunities facing medical education. *Transactions of the American Clinical and Climatological Association* 122:48–58.

Dobie D. 2002. Depression, dementia and pseudodementia. *Seminars in Clinical Neuropsychiatry* 7:170–186.

Drane J. 1985. The many faces of competency. *Hastings Center Report* 15(2):17–21.

Eisenberg L. 1992. Treating depression and anxiety in primary care: Closing the gap between knowledge and practice. *New England Journal of Medicine* 326:1080–1084.

Engstrom E. 2009. History of forensic psychiatry. *Current Opinion in Psychiatry* 22(6):576–581.

Falls B. 2011. Legislation prohibiting physicians from asking patients about guns. *Journal of Psychiatry and the Law* 39(3):441–464.

Farberman R. 1997. Public attitudes about psychologists and mental health care: Research to guide the American Psychological Association public education campaign. *Professional Psychology: Research and Practice* 28:128–136.

Fazel S and J Danesh. 2002. Serious mental disorder in 23,000 prisoners: A systematic review of 62 surveys. *Lancet* 359:545–550.

Fazel S, T Hope, and I O'Donnell. 2001. Hidden psychiatric morbidity in elderly prisoner. *British Journal of Psychiatry* 179:535–539.

Fazel S, T Hope, I O'Donnell, and R Jacoby. 2002. Psychiatric, demographic and personality characteristics of elderly sex offenders. *Psychological Medicine* 32(2):219–226.

Flynn E. 2004. Elders as perpetrators. In *Elders, Crime, and the Criminal Justice System: Myth, Perceptions, and Reality in the 21st Century*, edited by ME Rothman, New York: Springer, 43–86.

Freedman B. 1981. Competence, marginal and otherwise: Concepts and ethics. *International Journal of Law and Psychiatry* 4(1–2):53–72.

Ganzini L, D Fenn, M Lee, R Heintz, and J Bloom. 1996. Attitudes of Oregon psychiatrists toward physician-assisted suicide. *American Journal of Psychiatry* 153:1469–1475.

Ganzini L and M Lee. 1997. Psychiatry and assisted suicide in the United States. *New England Journal of Medicine* 336:1824–1826.

Garner B. 2014. *Black's Law Dictionary.* Eagan, MN: Thomson West.

Gavett B, J Lynch, and R McCaffrey. 2005. Third party observers: The effect size is greater than you might think. *Journal of Forensic Neuropsychology* 4(2):49–64.

Gerontological Society of America. 2012. *Communicating with Older Adults: An Evidence-Based Review of What Really Works.* Washington, DC: Gerontological Society of America. http://aging.arizona.edu/sites/aging/files/activity_1_reading_1.pdf, accessed June 27, 2016.

Gopal A, L Cosgrove, I Shuv-Ami, E Wheeler, M Yerganian, and HJ Bursztajn. 2012. Dynamic informed consent processes vital for treatment with antidepressants. *International Journal of Law and Psychiatry* 35(5–6):392–397.

Gutheil TG. 2007. Common pitfalls in the evaluation of testamentary capacity. *Journal of the American Academy of Psychiatry and the Law* 35(4):514–517.

Gutheil TG, Bursztajn HJ, and A Brodsky. 1984. Malpractice prevention through the sharing of uncertainty: Informed consent and the therapeutic alliance. *New England Journal of Medicine* 311:49–51.

Guthrie B, B Makubate, V Hernandez-Santiago, and T Dreischulte. 2015. The rising tide of polypharmacy and drug-drug interactions: Population database analysis 1995–2010. *BMC Medicine* 74(13):1–10.

Hafemeister T. 2013. Financial abuse in the elderly in domestic setting. In *National Research Council (US) Panel to Review Risk and Prevalence of Elder Abuse and Neglect*, edited by R Bonnie and R Wallace, Washington, DC: National Academies Press, 403.

Hall RCW, RCW Hall, and M Chapman. 2005. Exploitation of the elderly: Undue influence as a form of elder abuse. *Clinical Geriatrics* 13(2):28–36.

Han B, JC Gfroerer, JD Colliver, and MA Penne. 2008. Substance use disorder among older adults in the United States in 2020. *Addiction* 104:88–96.

Hanson RK and D Thornton. 2003. Notes on the development of Static-2002. (Corrections Research User Report No. 2003-01). Ottawa, ON: Department of the Solicitor General of Canada.

Harris G, M Rice, and V Quinsey. 1993. Violent recidivism of metnally disordered offenders: The development of a statistical prediction instrument. *Crimnial Justice and Behavior* 20:315–335.

Hart M. 2008. The geriatric sex offender: Senile or pedophile? *Law and Psychology Review* 32:153–162.

Haw C, D Harwood, and K Hawton. 2009. Dementia and suicidal behavior: A review of the literature. *International Psychogeriatrics* 21(3):440–453.

Hebert K and D Marson. 2007. Assessment of financial capacity in older adults with dementia. In *Changes in Decision-Making Capacity in Older Adults: Assessment and Intervention*, edited by S Qualls and M Smyer, Hoboken, NJ: Wiley, 237–270.

Hildreth CJ. 2009. Elder abuse. *Journal of the American Medical Association* 306(5):568.

Home Office. 2000. *Prison Statistics England and Wales 1999.* London: Stationery Office.

Hucker S. 1984. Psychiatric aspects of crime in old age. In *Elderly Criminals*, edited by ES Newman, DJ Newman, and ML Gewirtz, Boston: Oelgeschlager, Gunn and Hain, 67.

James D and L Glaze. 2006. *Mental Health Problems of Prison Jail Inmates.* Washington, DC: U.S. Department of Justice, Bureau of Justice Statistics.

Jerry W. Canterbury v. William T. Spence 464 F.2d 772 (D.C. Cir. 1972).

Jeste D, G Alexopoulos, and SE Bartels. 1999. Consensus statement on the upcoming crisis in geriatric mental health: Research agenda for the next two decades. *Archives of General Psychiatry* 56:848–853.

Kleinschmidt K. 1997. Elder abuse: A review. *Annals of Emergency Medicine* 30:463–472.

Kuhlmann R and R Ruddell. 2005. Elderly jail inmates: Problems, prevalence and public health. *Californian Journal of Health Promotion* 3(2):49–60.

Lichtenberg P, L Stickney, and D Paulson. 2013. Is psychological vulnerability related to the experience of fraud in older adults? *Clinical Gerontologist* 36(2):132–146.

Lyketsos C. 2002. Prevalence of neuropsychiatric symptoms in dementia and mild cognitive impairment: Results from the cardiovascular health study. *Journal of the American Medical Association* 288:1475–1483.

MacKinnon R, R Michaels, and P Buckley. 2006. *The Psychiatric Interview in Clinical Practice*, 2nd edition. Washington, DC: American Psychiatric Publishing.

Margallo-Lana M, A Swann, and J O'Brien. 2001. Prevalence and pharmacological management of behavioural and psychological symptoms amongst dementia sufferers living in care environments. *International Journal of Geriatric Psychiatry* 16:39–44.

Marson DC and T Hebert. 2008. Testamentary capacity. In *Encyclopedia of Psychology and the Law*, edited by B Cutler, New York: Sage, 798–801.

Marson DC, SM Sawrie, B McInturff, S Snyder, A Chatterjee, T Stalvey, A Boothe, T Aldridge, A Chatterjee, and LE Harrell. 2000. Assessing financial capacity in patients with Alzheimer's disease: A conceptual model and prototype instrument. *Archives of Neurology* 57:877–884.

Monahan J, HJ Steadman, PS Appelbaum, PC Robbins, EP Mulvey, E Silver, LH Roth, and T Grisso. 2000. Developing a clinically useful actuarial tool for assessing violence risk. *British Journal of Psychiatry* 176:312–319.

Moye J and M Braun. 2007. Assessment of medical consent capacity and independent living. In *Changes in Decision-Making Capacity in Older Adults: Assessment and Intervention*, edited by S Qualls and M Smyer, Hoboken, NJ: Wiley, 205–236.

Moye J and DC Marson. 2007. Assessment of decision-making capacity in older adults: An emerging area of practice and research. *Journal of Gerontology* 62B(1):P3–P11.

Myers W. 1986. Transference and countertransference issues in treatment involving older patients and younger psychiatrists. *Journal of Geriatric Psychiatry* 19:221–239.

New York City Department for the Aging Elderly Crime Victims Resource Center. 2011. *Under the Radar: New York State Elder Abuse Prevalence Study. Elderly Crime Victims Resource Center, New York City Department for the Aging.* Rochester, NY: Lifespan of Greater Rochester.

Peisah C, S Finkel, K Shulman et al. 2009. The wills of older people: Risk factors for undue influence. *International Psychogeriatrics* 21(1):7–15.

Pfeiffer E. 1991. Comprehensive geriatric assessment. *Southern Medical Journal* 84(Supplement 1):433–441.

Public Act 111-148 Title VI Subtitle H—Elder Justice Act. 2010. Patient Protection and Affordable Care Act.

Roof JG. 2012. Testamentary capacity and guardianship assessments. *Psychiatric Clinics of North America* 35(4):915–927.

Sadock B and V Sadock. 2014. *Kaplan and Sadock's Synopsis of Psychiatry: Behavioral Sciences/Clinical Psychiatry*, 11th edition. Philadelphia: Lippincott, Williams, and Wilkins.

Scocco P, G Fantoni, M Rapattoni, G de Girolamo, and L Pavan. 2009. Death ideas, suicidal thoughts, and plans among nursing home residents. *Journal of Geriatric Psychiatry and Neurology* 22(2):141–148.

Sergi G, M De Rui, S Sarti, and E Manzato. 2011. Polypharmacy in the elderly: Can comprehensive geriatric assessment reduce inappropriate medication use? *Drugs and Aging* 28:509–519.

Seyfried L, H Kales, R Ignacio, Y Conwell, and M Valenstein. 2011. Predictors of suicide in patients with dementia. *Alzheimer's and Dementia: Journal of the Alzheimer's Association* 7(6):567–573.

Shulman K, C Cohen, and I Hull. 2005. Psychiatric issues in retrospective challenges of testamentary. *International Journal of Geriatric Psychiatry* 20(1):63–69.

Simon R. 1996. "Three's a crowd": The presence of third parties during the forensic psychiatric examination. *Journal of Psychiatry and Law* 24:3–25.

Simon R and R Sadoff. 1992. *Psychiatric Malpractice: Cases and Comments for Clinicians*. Washington, DC: American Psychiatric Publishing.

Smyer M. 2007. Aging and decision-making capcity: An overview. In *Changes in Decision-Making Capacity in Older Adults: Assessment and Intervention*, edited by S Qualis and M Smyer, Hoboken, NJ: Wiley, 3–24.

Sprehe D. 2003. Geriatric psychiatry and the law. In *Principles and Practice of Forensic Psychiatry*, edited by R Rosner, Boca Raton, FL: CRC Press.

Steffensmeier D and M Motivans. 2000. Sentencing the older offender: Is there an age bias? In *Elders, Crime, and the Criminal Justice System: Myth, Reality and Perception in the 21st Century*, edited by M Rothman and B E Dunlop, New York: Springer, 185–205.

Sterns A, G Lax, S Sed, P Keohane, and R Sterns. 2008. Growing wave of older prisoners: A national survey of older prisoners' health, mental health, and programming. *Corrections Today* 70(4):70–76.

Strasburger L, TG Gutheil, and A Brodsky. 1997. On wearing two hats: Role conflict in serving as both psychotherapist and expert witness. *American Journal of Psychiatry* 154(4):448–456.

Taylor D, C Paton, and S Kapur (Eds). 2012. Use of psychotropic drugs in special patient groups. In *The Maudsley Prescribing Guidelines in Psychiatry*, West Sussex, UK: Wiley-Blackwell, 419–585.

Teaster P, T Dugar, M Mendiondo, E Abner, K Cecil, and J Otto. 2004. *The 2004 Survey of Adult Protective Services: Abuse of Adults 60 Years of Age and Older.* Washington, DC: National Center on Elder Abuse.

Teaster P and J Otto. 2006. *The 2004 Survey of State Adult Protective Services: Abuse of Vulnerable Adults 18 Years of Age and Older.* The National Adult Protective Services Association and the National Committee for the Prevention of Elder Abuse. http://www.ncea.aoa.gov/Resources/Publication/docs/APS_2004NCEASurvey.pdf, accessed October 22, 2014.

U.S. Census Bureau. 2006. *Population Estimates Vintage 2006: National Tables*. Washington, DC: U.S. Census Bureau. http://www.census.gov/popest/data/historical/2000s/vintage_2006/, accessed October 22, 2014.

U.S. Department of Commerce and U.S. Census Bureau. 2008. *Population Projections, 2008*. Washington, DC: U.S. Department of Commerce.

U.S. Food and Drug Administration (FDA). 2005. *Public Health Advisory: Deaths with Antipsychotics in Elderly Patients with Behavioral Disturbances.* Silver Spring, MD: FDA. http://www.fda.gov/drugs/drugsafety/postmarketdrugsafetyinformationforpatientsandproviders/ucm053171, accessed October 22, 2014.

Vega W and M Silverman. 1988. Stress and the elderly convict. *International Journal of Offender Therapy and Comparative Criminology* 32(2):153–162.

Yorston G and P Taylor. 2006. Commentary: Older offenders—No place to go? *Journal of the American Academy of Psychiatry and the Law* 34(3):333–337.

Zaubler TS and MD Sullivan. 1996. Psychiatry and physician-assisted suicide. *Psychiatric Clinics of North America* 19(3):413–427.

Zimny G and G Grossberg. 1998. *Guardianship of the Elderly: Psychiatric and Judicial Aspects*. New York: Springer.

78

Gender issues in forensic psychiatry

RENEE M. SORRENTINO AND SUSAN HATTERS-FRIEDMAN

INTRODUCTION

This chapter explores the impact of gender on forensic psychiatry. The first section addresses gender issues related to evaluees and expert witnesses. The second section focuses on special topics in gender bias. In reviewing these subjects, it is important to keep in mind the role of stereotypes in gender biases. There is no question that gender differences exist in many areas of forensic psychiatry. The relevant question—whether these differences are correct or whether they are inaccurate and translate into a distorted understanding of forensic issues—remains elusive. The answer to this question will help us to understand whether males and females should be treated differently, or rather whether differences are the product of stereotypes that would be best addressed through education.

GENDER ISSUES RELATED TO EVALUEES

Gender differences in legal outcomes

When the role of gender in the determination of legal outcomes is examined, often studies conclude that female defendants receive more lenient sentencing than male defendants. For example, for charges resulting from death, a woman is more likely than a man to be incarcerated for manslaughter rather than murder (Carson and Sabol 2012). Less studied, however, is whether gender bias is present across all types of offenses, or whether the bias is more substantial for certain criminal behaviors. Rates of incarceration of women in the United States are on the rise. Incarcerated women are more likely to be mentally ill. The two most common Axis I diagnoses among incarcerated women are posttraumatic stress disorder (PTSD) and substance use disorders (Friedman et al. 2013; Friedman et al. 2016). Bipolar disorder may also increase criminality in women (Friedman et al. 2005).

Studies that evaluate the role of gender in competency to stand trial adjudications have largely found no association between gender and competency findings (Riley 1998; Cooper and Zapf 2003; Kois et al. 2013). Gender differences in not guilty by reason of insanity (NGRI) acquittees indicate that women found NGRI are older, more often married, less often substance abusers, and less often have criminal histories than the male counterparts (Tonana et al. 1990; Seig et al. 1995). Women were more likely than men to have a diagnosis of borderline personality disorder or a mood disorder (Ferranti 2013; Friedman et al. 2013).

Specific crimes have gender differences in outcomes. For the crime of filicide (child murder by the parent), fathers are far more likely than mothers to be incarcerated (Friedman et al. 2012). Mothers are more likely than fathers to be found NGRI (Friedman et al. 2005).

McKelvie (2002) studied the effect of the sex of the judge and sex of the victim on sentencing in hypothetical vignettes of a male murderer. Female judges gave longer sentences in cases of female victims, whereas male judges gave longer sentences in cases of male victims (McKelvie 2002).

The presence of gender disparity in criminal sentencing raises the question of whether men and women should be treated equally when it comes to punishment. Are there evidence-based reasons for the disparity? For example, do women receive more lenient sentences because they are less likely to engage in future violent criminal acts? Or, is the disparity based on the bias of our society, culture, and media that depict men as violent and women as docile? How do these biases affect our ability to recognize and evaluate female offenders? The answers to these questions are tied with our further understanding of the differences between male and female offenders.

Women prisoners have higher rates of mental illness than female community counterparts, and perhaps higher rates than male offender counterparts as well. Women prisoners have often faced multiple life stressors and have elevated rates of substance use disorders. Lewis noted: "The portrait of the female offender that emerges from existing literature is of a polysubstance-dependent minority single-mother in her child-bearing years with a history of psychiatric treatment, physical or sexual abuse often dating to childhood, and socioeconomic hardship" (Lewis 2006, 782).

Gender issues related to expert witnesses

Surveys of courtroom experts suggest that women more frequently experience gender discrimination (Price et al. 2004). Research on how the gender of the expert is perceived by judges and juries is variable. The gender of the expert may be perceived as positive, negative, or neutral depending on the study. Neal et al. (2012) found the gender of an expert was relevant only when the expert was not high in likability and knowledge. In this setting, males were viewed more favorably than females. Schuller et al. (2005) investigated whether the influence of the gender of an expert witness on jurors varied with the complexity of the expert's testimony in a simulated civil trial. They found that gender impacted on the jurors' receptivity to the testimony. More specifically, Schuller et al. (2005) found that the male expert was more persuasive then the female expert when the testimony presented was complex. In contrast, female experts were at an advantage in the low-complexity cases. A study by Couch and Sigler (2002) found individual mock juror response measures indicated no significant effect of gender on the effectiveness of the expert witness. The conflicting findings in these studies may be related to the specific type of case (Couch and Sigler 2002; Price et al. 2004; Schuller et al. 2005; Neal et al. 2012). For example, an expert's gender may be a major factor in the selection of an expert in cases of sexual harassment, "battered woman syndrome," or sexual offenses. In a survey of 94 forensic psychiatric members of a professional organization, 80% of women believed that gender was a consideration, whereas only 41% of men believed male gender to be relevant in the acquisition of cases (Price et al. 2004). In the same survey, 60% of female experts reported attorneys expressed a preference for the gender of an expert on a particular case. Only one-quarter of male experts had such an experience. Female experts were considered desirable in cases of sexual harassment and in sexual offenses.

SPECIAL TOPICS WITH POTENTIAL GENDER BIAS

The role of gender bias varies depending on the specific topic. In this section the impact of gender bias is explored in the following areas: sexual offenses, sexual harassment, transgenderism, stalking, and domestic violence. Understanding gender disparities in these areas is necessary to the pursuit of objective evaluations.

Sexual offenses

Little is known about female sex offenders due to a scarcity of research. Additionally, the cultural and societal perceptions of females as maternal and altruistic influence the objective investigation of females as perpetrators of sexual offenses. Female sex offenders are often misperceived of as rare and harmless. As an illustration of this cultural bias toward females, an Internet search for female sexual offenders identified sites such as "hottest females sex offenders," "teacher appreciation week: hottest female sex offenders," and "hot for teacher." A sexual act between a boy and an adult woman may even be viewed by some as a rite of passage. In contrast, male sexual offenders tend to be viewed as violent and dangerous with intent to inflict harm. Without more research in this area, the appropriate treatment and management of female offenders remain in question.

In the United States, women perpetrators account for approximately 2% of sexual assaults reported by victims (Greenfield and Snell 1999). The arrest rate (defined as arrests/100,000 persons) for forcible rape in the United States in 2012 was 13.2 for men and 0.1 for women (U.S. Census Bureau 2010).

It is difficult to understand the true prevalence of female sexual offending due to the likelihood of underreporting when the offender is female (West et al. 2011). In fact, self-report studies in which victims are asked to identify the gender of the perpetrator suggest that female sexual offenders are not rare. Petrovich and Templar (1984) found that 59% of 83 prisoners convicted of rape had been molested by a female in childhood. Mendel (1995) studied 121 sexually abused males receiving therapy in both private and community mental health clinics. The majority (60%) of his sample reported childhood sexual activity with females. Demaré et al. (1993) examined self-reported sexually aggressive behavior among men and found that sexually abused men were more likely to report having pressured women into sexual intercourse. Among the sexually abused men who reported sexual aggression against women, 80% had been sexually abused during childhood by a female perpetrator.

If self-report studies indicate female sexual offending is not rare, how do we reconcile the low rate of charged sexual offenses committed by females? Gender bias may be the answer. Authors Mendel (1995), Allen (1990), and Denov (2001) suggest that sexual abuse by females is not recognized as a result of traditional sexual scripts that depict women as incapable of committing sexual offenses. Studies of the general population have provided empiric evidence for the notion that female sexual offending is not recognized (Finkelhor 1984; Broussard et al. 1991). Gender bias is also apparent in the language of the laws that govern sexual offenses. Several American states have laws that define rape as perpetration by a male against a female. In Missouri, females can be found guilty of rape where she aids a male in committing the rape, but cannot commit a rape on her own (Denov 2003). Professionals' responses to sexual abuse by females may also be subject to gender bias. The *Diagnostic and Statistical Manual of Mental Disorders*, 5th edition (*DSM-5*), indicates the paraphilic disorders are substantially fewer in females compared with males (American Psychiatric Association [APA] 2013). Finkelhor et al. (1988) found police and prosecutors' responses to female sexual offenders were more ambivalent when compared with male offenders. Without gender-sensitive studies and gender neutrality of governing laws, society is at risk of ignoring female sexual offending and thereby creating a risk to the community. Forensic psychiatrists must guard against perpetuating similar gender misconceptions in evaluations.

Most studies investigating the differences between male and female sexual offending are limited by small samples. Research suggests substance abuse, psychological diagnoses, and criminal histories are more severe among male sex offenders (Johansson-Love and Fremouw 2009; West et al. 2011). Williams and Bierie (2014), utilizing a large sample, compared male and female sex offenders among 802,250 incidents of sexual assault reported to authorities over a 20-year period. Similarities between genders included the following: the home was the most common offense location; the most common victim-offender relationship was acquaintance; and a rarity of injuries or drug abuse during crimes. The differences between the genders included the following: the females were more likely to have male accomplices (30% versus 2% of males) and were more likely to offend against a victim of the same sex (50% versus 10% of males) (Williams and Bierie 2014). With regard to victim selection, female sexual offenders are described as less discriminating toward the gender of victims than male sexual offenders (Denov 2004), offending against both males and females (West et al. 2011). Women tend to know the victims, and to victimize children (West et al. 2011).

There is little empirical evidence about treatment efficacy or sex offender recidivism in females. In contrast, there are many studies investigating recidivism in male sex offenders and treatment outcomes. Female sex offenders have an estimated 5-year recidivism rate of 1%–3% compared to the 10%–15% recidivism rate of males (Cortoni and Hanson 2005; Poels 2007). However, it remains possible that recidivism is missed because of gender bias in reporting arrests. Sandler and Freeman (2009) found some important distinctions between female and male sex offender recidivists. In a study of 1466 females convicted of a sexual offense in New York State, the authors found an opposite relationship between age and likelihood of sexual recidivism for female and male sex offenders—with the likelihood of sexual recidivism actually increasing with age for females (Sandler and Freeman 2009). They also found a prior history of violent crime was not significantly related to likelihood of sexual recidivism for female sex offenders—unlike male sex offenders (Sandler and Freeman 2009).

Research on sentencing differences as a function of sex offender gender consistently finds women receive more lenient sentences (Koons-Witt 2002; Jeffries et al. 2003). Embry and Lyons (2012) examined the sentencing discrepancies between male and female sex offenders reported in the National Corrections Reporting Program data for the years 1994–2004. The authors found a significant difference in sentence length between men and women. The mean sentence length for men was longer than for women indicating a harsher penalty for the same or similar offenses (Embry and Lyons 2012). They did not find any instances in which women were sentenced to longer or more severe sentences with regard to any sex offense (Embry and Lyons 2012).

Vandiver et al. (2008) studied the effect of the sex offender registry on female sex offenders in two states. They found all nine female sex offenders reported at least one negative effect on her life as a result of being identified on the public registry (Vandiver et al. 2008). Tewksbury (2004) evaluated the attitudes of 227 women who were registered sex offenders. Approximately one-third of the women reported losing a job, being denied a place to live, losing a friend, experiencing in-person harassment, or being treated rudely in public due to registration (Tewksbury 2004). Similarly, negative consequences of registration have been reported in male offenders (Levenson and Cotter 2005). It is unknown whether the outcomes of registries and public notification differ by gender. For further information about sex offender registry legislation, see Chapter 80.

Females comprise a small minority of those designated as sexually dangerous persons. In general, civil commitment of female sexual offenders presents a challenge. The treatment programs developed for sexual offenders are specific to males, and there is a general lack of gender-specific programming for females within the criminal justice system and the community (Bloom et al. 2003; Schafer 2003). The absence of gender-specific programming and treatment is explained by the lack of research specific to female sexual offenders. As a result, the evaluation, management, and risk assessment for females are largely based on the male sex offender literature and therefore are not evidence based. The repercussions include treatment programs and legal decisions that do not rehabilitate female offenders, or worse, have no impact on stopping sexual offending.

Sexual harassment

In 2011, the U.S. Equal Employment Opportunity Commission (EEOC) reported receiving 11,364 claims of sexual harassment, of which 84% were filed by women (EEOC 2011). The number of claims filed by men has risen from 12% in 1997 to 16% in 2010 (EEOC 2011).

Ellison v. Brady was a landmark sexual harassment case in 1990 that set the "Reasonable Woman" standard in sexual harassment law (Profio 1992). *Ellison* marked a change from such cases as *Rabidue v. Osceola Refining Co.*, which utilized a "reasonable person" standard in adjudicating the plaintiff's sexual harassment claim (Profio 1992). In making its decision, the *Ellison* court stated by requiring the use of the reasonable woman standard in sexual harassment cases, the court attempted to bridge the gap between male and female perceptions of what conduct constitutes workplace sexual harassment (Profio 1992). In years following the *Ellison* ruling, the "Reasonable Woman" standard was renamed the "Reasonable Worker" standard and generalized to include any type of harassment or stalking regardless of the gender of the victim or harasser.

Gold (1998) identifies gender bias as one component of bias in the forensic assessment of sexual harassment claims. The first type of gender bias derives from the traditional view of psychological teaching that focuses on the intrapsychic features of a claimant. Gold (1998) suggests that this focus results in the scrutiny of a claimant's contribution to her problem, rather than evaluating the totality of events including external events. Second, Gold (1998) identifies an inherent gender bias in sexual harassment claims due to the societal and cultural perceptions of gender roles. Gold (1998) suggests that these gender biases be addressed by adherence to the forensic ethical guidelines and familiarity with research related to these issues.

Gender differences in the experience of sexual harassment are not well known. Street et al. (2007) compared the experiences of sexual harassment among men and women in the military. Consistent with previous research, women reported a higher frequency of sexual harassment, and both men and women who experienced sexual harassment reported negative mental health impact. However, more severe sexual harassment was associated with stronger negative mental health symptoms for men than for women (Street et al. 2007).

Gender dysphoria

Among the changes in the *DSM-5* is the change in name from "Gender Identity Disorder" to "Gender Dysphoria." This change reflects an attempt to destigmatize the condition by replacing the word "disorder" with "dysphoria." For a person to be diagnosed with Gender Dysphoria, there must be a marked difference between the individual's expressed/experienced gender and the gender others would assign him or her which leads to clinically significant distress or impairment in social, occupational, or other important areas of functioning for at least 6 months (APA 2013).

Before reviewing gender differences in the transgender population, it is important to define terminology. "Gender non-conforming" is used to refer to individuals whose gender expression is different from societal expectations related to gender. "Transgender" is a term referring to individuals whose gender identity, expression, or behavior is different from those typically associated with the assigned sex at birth. An older term, "transsexual," describes individuals whose gender identity is different from the assigned sex at birth who seeks to transition from male to female or female to male (Coleman et al. 2012).

The prevalence of transgenderism is unknown. Studies have relied on reviews of community samples of the following: individuals who are diagnosed with Gender Identity Disorder (GID), parental endorsement of behavioral items pertaining to GID, or the number of adult patients seeking contra-sex hormonal treatment or sex-transformative surgery at hospital- or university-based gender clinics (Zuker and Lawrence 2009). The prevalence figures reported in 10 studies in eight countries range from 1:11,900 to 1:45,000 for male-to-female individuals (MtF) and 1:30,400 to 1:200,000 for female-to-male (FtM) individuals (Zucker and Lawrence 2009).

As the public has become more aware of transgendered individuals and the unique legal challenges facing this population, legal protections have evolved. Today, legal protection in the areas of employment discrimination, marriage, child custody, health care, prison safety, hate crimes legislation, and asylum have been afforded in varying degrees to transgendered individuals (Transgender Law and Policy Institute 2010). However, transgendered individuals have not been afforded equal legal protection in all areas. Both the Rehabilitation Act of 1973 and the Americans with Disabilities Act (ADA) explicitly exclude both "transsexualism" and "gender identity disorders not resulting from physical impairments" from protection (Civic Impulse 2014). States have varied in interpretation of transsexualism as a disability. Some state laws include explicit exemptions for transsexual people while others have found that transsexualism is a protected disability under state laws.

Discrimination and general ignorance surrounding transgendered individuals has led to marginalization affecting access to housing, employment, and competent health care (Wall 2014). Although the overall prevalence of transgendered individuals in the correctional setting is low, approximately 14% of transgendered individuals in San Francisco reported having been incarcerated at least once (Minter and Daley 2003). Findings from the Bureau of Justice Statistics' third National Inmate Survey, from 2011 and 2012 show that inmates who self-identified as gay, lesbian, bisexual, or other reported higher rates of both being sexually victimized by another inmate and being sexually victimized by staff (Beck et al. 2013).

The legal challenges arising when transgendered individuals are incarcerated include the right to treatment and protection of an individual's Eighth Amendment rights. The 1976 landmark legal decision in *Estelle v. Gamble* established the legal precedence that "deliberate indifference to serious medical needs of prisoners constitutes the unnecessary and wanton infliction of pain" is in violation of the Eighth Amendment. The application of *Estelle v. Gamble* to the transgender population relates to whether incarcerated transgendered individuals have a right to the standard treatment available in the community for this population. The right to medical treatment for transgendered individuals has been widely litigated, and court opinions on this subject have changed over time. In *Meriwether v. Faulkner* (1987) the U.S. Court of Appeals for the Seventh District Circuit opined that "a transsexual inmate is constitutionally entitled to some type of medical treatment, however, the inmate does not have a right to any particular type of treatment, such as estrogen therapy" (*Meriwether v. Faulkner* 1987). Many cases that exclude hormonal therapy or sex reassignment surgery cite private and public medical insurances, such as Medicare and Medicaid, which have denied such treatments (*Maggert v. Hanks* 1997).

However, in cases in which a transsexual prisoner's hormonal treatment was discontinued due to incarceration, the courts ruled that such abrupt termination of treatment qualified as "deliberate indifference" (*South v. Gomes* 2000; *Wolfe v. Horn* 2001). These cases together with the 2005 U.S. Bureau of Prisons Program Statement on Patient Care established the guidelines of approving treatment for transsexual prisoners if the treatment predated incarceration. The Federal Bureau of Prisons' policy on hormonal treatment of transsexuals was coined the "freeze-frame" policy, referring to the "freeze" on treatment once an individual is incarcerated (Simpopoulos and Khin Khin 2014). This freeze-frame policy has been modified as a result of the 2010 *Adams v. Federal Bureau of Prisons* settlement. In the settlement, the Federal Bureau of Prisons agreed to implement an official policy memorandum stating that individuals in custody with a possible diagnosis of GID will receive an individualized assessment and evaluation and that treatment plans will be developed based on current accepted standards of care for GID and will not depend on the individual having received GID treatment prior to incarceration (*Adams v. Federal Bureau of Prisons* 2010). In *Kosilek v. Spencer* (2012) a U.S. District Judge in Massachusetts ruled that the Department of Corrections (DOC) had violated Kosilek's, a transgendered inmate, constitutional rights under the Eighth Amendment by denying sex reassignment surgery. The DOC was ordered to provide Kosilek with sex reassignment surgery. The DOC has appealed the case.

Incarcerated transgendered individuals have typically been classified and housed according to the external genitalia. Some facilities have addressed the housing of transgendered individuals by placing them in segregation. Litigation in the housing and classification of transgendered individuals is similarly based on the Eighth Amendment. In *Farmer v. Brennan* (1994) a transgender female inmate filed action against the prison claiming the prison officials were responsible for her being beaten and raped by another inmate because they placed her in a vulnerable environment. The Supreme Court ruled that a prison official's "deliberate indifference" to a substantial risk of serious harm to an inmate violates the cruel and unusual punishment clause. The Supreme Court further defined "deliberate indifference" as "the official must both be aware of facts from which the inference could be drawn that a substantial risk of serious harm exists, and he must also draw that inference" (*Farmer v. Brennan* 1994). As the knowledge and understanding of the transgender population grows, both with the support of advocacy organizations and case law, some jurisdictions have developed policies addressing the management and housing of transgender individuals.

Stalking

Depending on the study, women represent somewhere between 9% and 32% of stalkers (Zona et al. 1993; Strand and McEwan 2012). Yet, women are rarely prosecuted for stalking when compared to men. In fact, if a man reports that he is being stalked by a woman, he may have the experience of being told he is "lucky" and should be "flattered." One study found that women who stalked were physically violent in one-quarter of cases, though injuries usually did not require medical care (Meloy and Boyd 2003). Violence was more likely in cases where there had been previous sexual intimacy. An Australian study of referrals to a community forensic team specializing in stalking found half of the women had a personality disorder, and 30% had a delusional disorder (Purcell et al. 2001). Women were likely to stalk someone they had known, and 40% stalked professional contacts, such as doctors. Female stalkers are more likely than male stalkers to stalk victims of the same gender (West and Friedman 2008).

Purcell et al. (2001) found that the rates of threats and assaults by female compared to male stalkers were not significantly different. However, female stalkers were less likely to proceed from threats to assaults. Female stalkers were less likely to follow the victim and less likely to have a history of substance abuse or arrests. A study of Swedish and Australian female stalkers found that women were more likely than male stalkers to have borderline personality disorder (Strand and McEwan 2012). Women were more likely to stalk by telecommunication/email while men were more likely to follow. For both genders, there was an 80% chance of violence if the stalker: had a prior intimate relationship with the victim, used approach behavior, and was making threats (Strand and McEwan 2012). This implies that being stalked by a woman rather than a man does not predict a lack of violence. Female and male stalkers may have more in common than they have differences. Stalking by women should be taken just as seriously as stalking by men, and women's risk of violence in stalking should not be underestimated (Friedman 2015).

Domestic violence

Intimate partner violence (IPV) includes physical, sexual, and emotional abuse. The U.S. lifetime prevalence of physical assault by a partner is 9%–30%, and of rape is 8% (Friedman et al. 2008). The forensic psychiatrist must be aware that not only is violence perpetrated by male partners on female victims, but also perpetrated by women on men, can be bidirectional in relationships, and occurs in homosexual relationships as well. Mutual violence ("bidirectional reciprocal aggression"), violence out of anger, violence seeking revenge and control, as well as violence that the violent partner considers as self-defense (paranoid or not) may occur (Friedman et al. 2011). In addition to physicians failing to inquire about domestic violence, patients may not report victimization due to shame, or due to acceptance of the abuse. Women with severe mental illness may be particularly vulnerable to IPV victimization, perhaps related to low self-esteem, planning issues, and impaired judgment (Friedman and Loue 2007). Physicians should consider routinely screening for IPV, which can begin with a discussion about decision-making and anger in relationships. Symptoms of PTSD may also be screened for, because the prevalence of PTSD in victims of IPV has been found to be as high as 63.8% (Golding 1999).

Personality characteristics of batterers vary. Hamberger and Hastings (1988) described male batterers as moody and emotional, cold and calculating, or insecure and jealous. Similarly, female batterers may be compulsive, histrionic, and/or narcissistic (Buttell and Carney 2005). Courts often mandate participation in domestic violence intervention programs. However, the effectiveness has been questioned.

Forensic psychiatry's involvement in IPV cases includes reporting issues, risk assessments, court reports for mitigation of penalty and treatment recommendations, as well as potential evaluations for "battered women's syndrome" defenses. Therefore, the evaluator must have an understanding of patterns and motives in IPV. While states require reporting of child abuse, laws about reporting of IPV are more disparate. Many states, however, require reporting of injuries that occur due to crime—and IPV is a crime (Friedman et al. 2008). Arguments against reporting, however, include confidentiality issues, risk for abuse in retaliation, and deterrence of victims seeking treatment. Furthermore, in completing a risk assessment, it is important to consider that in some cases, legal sanctions and separation can increase risk. Restraining orders (civil protection orders) do not guarantee safety and are often violated.

"Battered women's syndrome" (BWS) is not a *DSM*-defined disorder. BWS has been described as related to the concept of "learned helplessness" related to chronic abuse victimization, symptomatology, and patterns of thought that arise. BWS may be correlated with PTSD symptoms. BWS is used in the legal arena as part of an affirmative defense, of imperfect self-defense. Therefore, this requires that the woman admit to the crime, but offer an explanation as to why it occurred. If a woman in an abusive relationship subjectively believes that her life is in acute danger, then the BWS defense might be used to help explain to the jury why her action of killing her partner was understandable in the context of her life circumstances. The forensic psychiatrist's role in a BWS case may be to help describe the context of the violence, use of excessive force, and impact of violence on symptomatology, as well as to explain to the court about the model of "learned helplessness" (Friedman et al. 2008). Criticisms of BWS include the lack of definition in the scientific literature, the use of BWS only in situations involving murder of a partner, and the expectation that learned helplessness is the only model—and that a woman is merely a passive abuse victim.

SUMMARY KEY POINTS

- Women may be more leniently sentenced than men for various crimes.
- Incarcerated women have higher rates of mental illness than their community counterparts.
- Gender of the expert witness may be a factor in expert choice.
- More research is needed about gender issues in sex offenders, sexual harassment, transgenderism, stalking, and partner violence.
- The forensic psychiatrist should guard against potential gender bias by critically analyzing whether perceived gender differences are based on data or assumption.

REFERENCES

Adams v. Federal Bureau of Prisons, 716 F. Supp. 2d 107 (D. Mass. 2010).

Allen C. 1990. Women as perpetrators of child sexual abuse: Recognition barriers. In *The Incest Perpetrator: A Family Member No One Wants to Treat*, edited by AL Horton, BL Johnson, LM Roundy, and D Williams, Newbury Park, CA: Sage, 108–125.

American Psychiatric Association (APA). 2013. *Diagnostic and Statistical Manual of Mental Disorders*, 5th edition. Washington, DC: APA.

Beck A, M Berzofsky, R Caspar, and C Krebs. 2013. *Sexual Victimization in Prisons and Jails Reported by Inmates, 2011–12: National Inmate Survey 2011–12.* Washington, DC: U.S. Department of Justice, Bureau of Justice Statistics.

Bloom B, B Owen, and S Covington. 2003. *Gender-Responsive Strategies: Research, Practice, and Guiding Principles for Women Offenders.* Washington, DC: U.S. Department of Justice, National Institute of Corrections.

Broussard S, W Wagner, and R Kazelskis. 1991. Undergraduate students' perceptions of child sexual abuse: The impact of victim sex, perpetrator sex, respondent sex, and victim response. *Journal of Family Violence* 6:267–278.

Buttell FP and MM Carney. 2005. *Women Who Perpetrate Relationship Violence: Moving beyond Political Correctness.* New York, NY: Haworth Press.

Carson AE and WJ Sabol. 2012. *Prisoners in 2011.* U.S. Department of Justice, Office of Justice Programs. Washington, DC: Office of Justice Programs, NCJ 239808, 1–33.

Civic Impulse. 2014. H.R. 8070—93rd congress: Rehabilitation act, https://www.govtrack.us/congress/bills/93/hr8070

Coleman E, W Bockting, M Botzer et al. 2012. Standards of care for the health of transsexual, transgender, and gender-nonconforming people. *World Professional Association for Transgender Health (WPATH)*, http://www.wpath.org/uploaded_files/140/files/Standards%20of%20Care,%20V7%20Full%20Book.pdf

Cooper VG and P Zapf. 2003. Predictor variables in competency to stand trial decisions. *Law and Human Behavior* 27:423–436.

Cortoni F and RK Hanson. 2005. *A Review of the Recidivism Rates of Adult Female Sexual Offenders* (Research Report R-169). Ottawa, ON: Correctional Service of Canada.

Couch J and J Sigler. 2002. Gender of an expert witness and the jury verdict. *Psychological Record* 52:281–287.

Dean K, E Walsh, P Moran, P Tyrer, F Creed, S Byford, T Burns, R Murray, and T Fahy. 2006. Violence in women with psychosis in the community: Prospective study. *British Journal of Psychiatry* 188:264–270.

Demaré D, HM Lips HM and J Briere. 1993. Sexually violent pornography, anti-women attitudes, and sexual aggression: A structural equation model. *Journal of Research in Personality* 27:285–300.

Denov M. 2001. A culture of denial: Exploring professional perspectives on female sex offending. *Canadian Journal of Criminology* 43:303–329.

Denov M. 2003. The myth of innocence: Sexual scripts and the recognition of child sexual abuse by female perpetrators. *Journal of Sex Research* 40:303–314.

Denov M. 2004. *Perspectives on Female Sex Offending: A Culture of Denial.* Surrey, UK: Ashgate.

Embry R and P Lyons. 2012. Sex-based sentencing: Sentencing discrepancies between male and female sex offenders. *Feminist Criminology* 7:146–162.

Estelle v. Gamble, 429 U.S. 97 (1976).

Farmer v. Brennan, 511 U.S. 825 (1994).

Ferranti J, B McDermott, and C Scott. 2013. Characteristics of female offenders found not guilty by reason of insanity. *Journal of the American Academy of Psychiatry and the Law* 41:516–522.

Finkelhor D. 1984. *Child Sexual Abuse: New Theory and Research.* New York: Free Press.

Finkelhor D, L Williams, and N Burns. 1988. *Nursery Crimes: Sexual Abuse in Daycare.* Beverly Hills, CA: Sage.

Friedman SH. 2015. Realistic consideration of women and violence is critical. *Journal of the American Academy of Psychiatry and the Law* 43:273–276.

Friedman SH, J Cavney, and P Resnick. 2012. Mothers who kill: Evolutionary underpinnings and law. *Behavioral Sciences and the Law* 30:585–597.

Friedman SH, S Collier, and R Hall. 2016. PTSD behind bars: PTSD among female inmates. In *The Comprehensive Guide to Post-Traumatic Stress Disorders*, edited by C Martin, VR Preedy, and VB Patel, New York: Springer, 1–14.

Friedman SH, R Hall, and R Sorrentino. 2013. Women, violence and insanity. *Journal of the American Academy of Psychiatry and the Law* 41:523–528.

Friedman SH, D Hrouda, C Holden, S Noffsinger, and P Resnick. 2005. Child murder committed by severely mentally ill mothers: An examination of mothers found not guilty by reason of insanity. *Journal of Forensic Sciences* 50:1–6.

Friedman SH and S Loue. 2007. Incidence and prevalence of intimate partner violence by and against women with severe mental illness: A review. *Journal of Women's Health* 16:471–480.

Friedman SH, S Loue, E Heaphy, and N Mendez. 2011. Intimate partner violence perpetrated by and against Puerto Rican women with severe mental illness. *Community Mental Health Journal* 47:156–163.

Friedman SH, M Shelton, O Elhaj, E Youngstrom, D Rapport, S Bilali, K Jackson, K Packer, H Sakai, P Resnick, R Findling, and J Calabrese. 2005. Gender differences in criminality: Bipolar disorder with comorbid substance abuse. *Journal of the American Academy of Psychiatry and the Law* 33:188–195.

Friedman SH, J Stankowski, and S Loue. 2008. Intimate partner violence and the clinician. In *The American Psychiatric Press Textbook of Violence Assessment and Management*, edited by RI Simon and KT Tardiff, Arlington, VA: American Psychiatric Publishing, 483–500.

Gold L. 1998. Addressing bias in the forensic assessment of sexual harassment claims. *Journal of the American Academy of Psychiatry and the Law* 26:563–578.

Golding J. 1999. Intimate partner violence as a risk factor for mental disorders: A meta-analysis. *Journal of Family Violence* 14:99–132.

Greenfeld L and T Snell. 1999. *Women Offenders* [Special report]. Washington, DC: U.S. Department of Justice, Bureau of Justice Statistics. http://www.bjs.gov/content/pub/pdf/wo.pdf.

Hamberger LK and J Hastings. 1988. Characteristics of male spouse abusers consistent with personality disorders. *PS Psychiatric Services* 39(7):763-770.

Harvard Law Review. 2014. Classification and housing of transgendered inmates in American prisons. *Harvard Law Review* 6:1746–1766.

Jeffries S, G Fletcher, and G Newbold. 2003. Pathways to sex-based differentiation in criminal court sentencing. *Criminology* 41:329–353.

Johansson-Love J and W Fremouw. 2009. Female sex offenders: A controlled comparison of offender and victim/crime characteristics. *Journal of Family Violence* 24:367–376.

Kois L, J Pearson, P Chauhan, M Goni, and L Saraydarian. 2013. Competency to stand trial among female patients. *Law and Human Behavior* 37:231–240.

Koons-Witt B. 2002. Gender and justice: The effect of gender and gender-related factors on the decision to incarcerate before and after sentencing guidelines. *Criminology* 40:297–328.

Kosilek v. Spencer 889 F.Supp.2d 190. (2012).

Larson B and S Brodsky. 2010. When cross-examination offends: How men and women assess intrusive questioning of male and female expert witnesses. *Journal of Applied Social Psychology* 40:811–830.

Levenson J and L Cotter. 2005. The effect of Megan's Law on sex offender reintegration. *Journal of Contemporary Criminal Justice* 21:49–66.

Lewis C. 2006. Treating incarcerated women: Gender matters. *Psychiatric Clinics of North America* 29:773–789.

Logan C and R Blackburn. 2009. Mental disorder in violent women in secure settings: Potential relevance to risk for future violence. *International Journal of Law and Psychiatry* 32:31–38.

Maggert v. Hanks, 131 F.3d 670 (7th Cir. 1997).

McKelvie S. 2002. Effects of sex of judge and sex of victim on recommended punishment of a male murderer in a mock scenario. *Psychological Reports* 91:533–536.

Meloy JR and C Boyd. 2003. Female stalkers and their victims. *Journal of the American Academy of Psychiatry and the Law* 31(2):211–219.

Mende M. 1995. *The Male Survivor: The Impact of Sexual Abuse*. London, UK: Sage.

Meriwether v. Faulkner, 821 F.2d 408 (7th Cir. 1987).

Minter S and C Daley. 2003. Trans Realities: A Legal Needs Assessment of San Francisco's Transgender Communities. San Francisco, CA: National Center for Lesbian Rights and the Transgender Law Center.

Neal T, R Guadagno, C Eno, and S Brodsky. 2012. Warmth and competence on the witness stand: Implications for credibility of male and female expert witnesses. *Journal of the American Academy of Psychiatry and the Law* 40:488–497.

Petrovich M and D Templar. l984. Heterosexual molestation of children who later become rapists. *Psychological Reports* 54:810.

Poels V. 2007. Risk assessment of recidivism of violent and sexual female offenders. *Psychiatry, Psychology and the Law* 14:227–250.

Price M, P Recupero, D Strong, and T Gutheil. 2004. Gender differences in the practice patterns of forensic psychiatry experts. *Journal of the American Academy of Psychiatry and the Law* 32:250–258.

Profio DA. 1992. *Ellison v. Brady*: Finally, a woman's perspective. *UCLA Women's Law Journal* 2:249–263.

Purcell R, Pathé M, and PE Mullen. 2001. A study of women who stalk. *American Journal of Psychiatry* AJP 158(12):2056–2060.

Riley S. 1998. Competency to stand trial adjudication: A comparison of female and male defendants. *Journal of the American Academy of Psychiatry and the Law* 26:223–240.

Samuels C. 2014. Patient care. *Program Statement 6031.01*. Washington, DC: U.S. Department of Justice, Federal Bureau of Prisons. https://www.bop.gov/policy/progstat/6031_004.pdf

Sandler J and N Freeman. 2007. Topology of female sex offenders: A test of Vandiver and Kercher. *Sexual Abuse* 19:73–89.

Sandler J and N Freeman. 2009. Female sex offender recidivism: A large-scale empirical analysis. *Sexual Abuse* 21:455–473.

Schafer N. 2003. *Gender Specific Programming: Bibliography (JRRSA 98-JN-FX-0112). Report to the Justice and Statistics Research Association.* Washington, DC: Office of Juvenile Justice and Delinquency Prevention, Office of Justice Program, U.S. Department of Justice.

Schuller R, D Terry, and B McKimmie. 2005. The impact of expert testimony on jurors' decisions: Gender of the expert and testimony complexity. *Journal of Applied Social Psychology* 35:1266–1280.

Seig A, E Ball, and J Menninger. 1995. A comparison of female versus male insanity acquittees in Colorado. *Bulletin of the American Academy of Psychiatry and the Law* 23:523–532.

Simopoulos E and E Khin Khin. 2014. Fundamental principles inherent in the comprehensive care of transgender inmates. *Journal of the American Academy of Psychiatry and the Law* 42:26–36.

South v. Gomez, 211 F.3d1275 (2000).

Strand S and TE McEwan. 2012. Violence among female stalkers. *Psychological Medicine* 42:545–556.

Street A, J Gradus, J Stafford, and K Kelly. 2007. Gender differences in experiences of sexual harassment: Data from a male-dominated environment. *Journal of Consulting and Clinical Psychology* 75:464–474.

Tewksbury R. 2004. Experiences and attitudes of registered female sex offenders. *Federal Probation* 68:30–33.

Transgender Law and Policy Institute. 2010. *Litigation: Case Law*. http://www.transgenderlaw.org/cases/index.htm, accessed November 5, 2014.

U.S. Census Bureau. 2010. *Statistical Abstract of the United States, 2010*, 129th edition. Washington, DC: U.S. Census Bureau.

U.S. Equal Employment Opportunity Commission. 2011. *EEOC—Employment Discrimination, Diversity, Harassment, Gender and Labor Issues*. http://www.eeoc.gov/index.cfm, accessed November 5, 2014.

Vandiver D, K Dial, and R Worley. 2008. A qualitative assessment of registered female sex offenders: Judicial processing experiences and perceived effects of a public registry. *Criminal Justice Review* 33:177–198.

Wall B. 2014. Commentary: Gender nonconformity within a conformist correctional culture. *Journal of the American Academy of Psychiatry and the Law* 42:37–38.

Warren J, M Burnette, S South, P Chauhan, R Bale, R Friend, and I Van Patten. 2003. Psychopathy in women: Structural modeling and comorbidity. *International Journal of Law and Psychiatry* 26:233–242.

West SG and SH Friedman. 2008. These boots are made for stalking: Characteristics of female stalkers. *Psychiatry* 5(8):37–42.

West S, SH Friedman, and KD Kim. 2011. Women accused of sex offenses: A gender-based comparison. *Behavioral Sciences and the Law* 29:728–740.

Williams K and D Bierie. 2014. An incident-based comparison of female and male sexual offenders. *Sexual Abuse* 27:235–257.

Wolfe v. Horn, 130 F.3d Supp. 2d 648 (E.D. Pa. 2001).

Zona, MA, KK Sharma, and JC Lane. 1993. A comparative study of erotomanic and obsessional subjects in a forensic sample. *Journal of Forensic Sciences* 38:894–903.

Zucker K and A Lawrence. 2009. Epidemiology of gender identity disorder: Recommendations for the standards of care of the World Professional Association for Transgender Health. *International Journal of Transgenderism* 11(1):8–18.

79

Substance abuse and addiction

GREGORY SOKOLOV

INTRODUCTION

Substance abuse and addiction issues may present in a variety of medico-legal contexts. Examples in the civil law include personal injury and wrongful death actions alleging negligent prescribing practices or use of a manufactured product, malpractice allegations of physician impairment due to substance use, state medical board actions, denial of life-insurance benefits, termination of parental rights, child custody, employment, and disability. Examples in criminal law include diversion treatment as an alternative to incarceration and mitigation of mental state for specific intent crimes (i.e., premeditated murder).

ADDICTION: DEFINITIONS

A long-standing definition of addiction is that it is "a primary, chronic, neurobiologic disease, whose development and manifestations are influenced by genetic, psychosocial, and environmental factors" (American Academy of Pain Medicine 2001). In this group's definition, addiction often is characterized by behaviors that include impaired control over drug use, craving, compulsive use, and continued use despite harm.

A newer definition describes addiction as "a primary, chronic disease of brain reward, motivation, memory, and related circuitry. Dysfunction in these circuits leads to characteristic biological, psychological, social, and spiritual manifestations." It also states that addiction is characterized by "inability to consistently abstain, impairment in behavioral control, craving, diminished recognition of significant problems with one's behaviors and interpersonal relationships, and a dysfunctional emotional response" (American Society of Addiction Medicine 2011).

EPIDEMIOLOGY OF SUBSTANCE USE DISORDERS

The National Survey on Drug Use and Health (NSDUH) is an annual survey sponsored by the Substance Abuse and Mental Health Services Administration (SAMHSA). The survey is the primary source of information on the use of illicit drugs, alcohol, and tobacco in the civilian, noninstitutionalized population of the United States aged 12 years old or older. Approximately 67,500 persons are interviewed in NSDUH.

According to statistics from the 2012 NSUDH, an estimated 22.2 million persons aged 12 or older (8.5%) were classified with substance dependence or abuse in the past year based on criteria specified in the *Diagnostic and Statistical Manual of Mental Disorders*, 4th edition (*DSM-IV*). Of these, 2.8 million were classified with dependence or abuse of both alcohol and illicit drugs, 4.5 million had dependence or abuse of illicit drugs but not alcohol, and 14.9 million had dependence or abuse of alcohol, but not illicit drugs. The specific illicit drugs with the largest numbers of persons with past-year dependence or abuse in 2012 were marijuana (4.3 million), prescription pain relievers (2.1 million), and cocaine (1.1 million). The number of persons with marijuana dependence or abuse did not change between 2002 and 2012. Between 2004 and 2012, the number with prescription pain reliever dependence or abuse increased from 1.4 million to 2.1 million, and between 2006 and 2012, the number with cocaine dependence or abuse declined from 1.7 million to 1.1 million. The number of persons with heroin dependence or abuse in 2012 (467,000) was approximately twice the number in 2002 (214,000) (National Survey on Drug Use and Health 2012).

NEUROBIOLOGY OF ADDICTION

A number of different neuronal circuits and neurotransmitters have been implicated in the complex neurobiological process of addiction. Positron emission tomography (PET) imaging of brain functioning indicates that dopamine is significantly associated with substance use, specifically in that drugs that are abused by humans increase dopamine in the "reward circuit" of the brain (ventral tegmental area, nucleus accumbens, and prefrontal cortex). This neuronal circuit is believed to underlie their rewarding effects

(Goldstein and Volkow 2011). In addition to dopamine, the neurotransmitters glutamate, gamma-aminobutyric acid (GABA), and opioid neuropeptides are important in this circuitry. Prominent brain structures include the amygdala, nucleus accumbens, and prefrontal cortex (Kalivas and Volkow 2005). Powerful new techniques (e.g., optogenetics and designer drug receptors) are starting to give researchers the potential to systematically investigate all genes, epigenetic markers, and neuronal circuits in better understanding the neurobiological processes leading to addiction. These advances combined with imaging technologies (both for preclinical and clinical studies) have spurred an unlimited growth of datasets transforming the research into the neurobiology of substance use disorders and the factors that modulate risk and resilience (Volkow and Baler 2014).

DIAGNOSES: *DIAGNOSTIC AND STATISTICAL MANUAL OF MENTAL DISORDERS*, FIFTH EDITION (*DSM-5*)

Among the major changes, the *Diagnostic and Statistical Manual of Mental Disorders*, 5th edition (*DSM-5*, American Psychiatric Association 2013) has eliminated the *DSM-IV* diagnoses of substance abuse and substance dependence; these were collapsed into one diagnosis named "substance use disorder." More specifically, three of the four substance abuse criteria were added to the substance dependence criteria, "legal problems" was eliminated, and "craving" was added, yielding a total of 11 criteria for the new diagnosis.

Among the rationale for these changes was that while *DSM-IV* substance dependence has been demonstrated to have excellent reliability and validity, *DSM-IV* substance abuse has much lower reliability and validity (Hasin et al. 2013). Furthermore, the *DSM-IV* hierarchical relationship between dependence and abuse created incorrect assumptions that Abuse is a milder form of dependence; all cases of dependence also meet criteria for abuse; and/or abuse is the prodrome of dependence (Hasin et al. 2013). Psychometric research indicated improvement of test–retest reliability of Abuse with removal of the hierarchy; latent class analysis of the combined abuse and dependence criteria suggested that the criteria correlated with a single factor or two closely related factors; item response theory model analysis of the combined criteria indicated "undimensionality"; and there was intermixing of the various criteria across the severity spectrum, with the exception of the "legal problems" criterion (Hasin et al. 2013). A diagnostic threshold of two criteria out of the total of eleven criteria was chosen specifically to achieve close approximation between the prevalence of the new single diagnosis of substance use disorder and the combined prevalence of the two diagnoses of *DSM-IV* abuse and dependence, in order to "avoid a marked perturbation in prevalence without justification" (Hasin et al. 2013, 841). In addition, the diagnosis for a particular substance use disorder has a severity specifier: As a general estimate of severity, a mild substance use disorder is suggested by the presence of two to three symptoms, moderate by four to five symptoms, and severe by six or more symptoms.

Critics have opposed the elimination of Substance Dependence, viewing it as a "helpful unifying heuristic for clinicians, scientists and sufferers for more than 30 years, and has strong empirical support" (Drummond 2011, 892). Additionally, it has been argued that from a prevention perspective, there is a need for a diagnostic category that recognizes problematic and hazardous substance use, as was the intent of *DSM-IV* abuse (Babor 2011). Concern has been expressed about the diagnostic threshold for *DSM-5* substance use disorder, specifically that it being "away from mainstream neurobehavioral theory regarding what constitutes a mental 'disorder' and 'addiction'"; and would allow "so much heterogeneity that the clinical and research utility of the diagnostic category would be greatly compromised" (Martin et al. 2011).

In previous editions of the *DSM*, the dependence diagnosis was considered to be the equivalent of addiction. The collapse of the *DSM-IV* abuse and dependence diagnoses into one diagnosis implies that the new *DSM-5* substance use disorder diagnosis is not equivalent to "dependence" or "addiction." In fact, the *DSM-5* states: "Some clinicians will choose to use the word *addiction* to describe more extreme presentations" (p. 485). It appears that the reader is left to infer that the *DSM-5* diagnosis closest to "addiction" is "severe substance use disorder," which would be a "more extreme presentation." Consistent with this, research in patients in treatment for alcohol, cocaine, or heroin addiction found that of the 11 possible *DSM-5* criteria, the modal number present was 10 (Hasin et al. 2012).

In judicial and legislative contexts, the diagnostic and conceptual discontinuity between *DSM-IV* and *DSM-5* approach to substance use disorders is likely to present challenges, given that the previous *DSM* editions, such as *DSM-IV*, have been cited in court opinions over 5500 times and in legislation over 320 times (Slovenko 2011). Unlike the *DSM-IV* diagnosis of substance dependence, which has been demonstrated by previous research to have excellent reliability and validity, the same is not yet true for *DSM-5* substance use disorder. Therefore, regardless of choice, the forensic psychiatric expert may need a working knowledge of the issues relevant to *DSM-IV* and *DSM-5*, including the changes, rationale, research, criticisms, and relationship of the new substance use disorder to "dependence" and "addiction."

In the "non-substance-related disorders" section of *DSM-5*, which is classified as behavioral conditions that do not involve ingestion of substances but have similar symptoms as substance use disorders, gambling disorder is included. Previously in *DSM-IV*, pathological gambling was included in the "impulse control disorders" rather than in "substance related disorders." Gambling disorder criteria include overlap with substance use disorders, including need to gamble with increasing amounts of money to achieve the desired excitement, repeated unsuccessful efforts to control or stop gambling, symptoms of restlessness and irritability upon cessation of gambling, and loss of employment or relationships due to gambling. In one recent study, subjects who met *DSM-5* diagnostic criteria for gambling disorder, as compared to those who were classified as "sub-threshold gambling disorder" or "recreational gambling," were at the highest risk for the new onset of co-morbid conditions, including mood, anxiety, or substance use disorders (Parhami et al. 2014).

In the "conditions for further study" section of *DSM-5*, caffeine use disorder and internet gaming disorder are listed. Proposed criteria sets are presented for these conditions on which future research is encouraged, and they are not recognized diagnoses.

ASSESSMENT

There is a large societal stigma against people with substance use disorders, and defendants may be quite averse to acknowledging the full extent or accurate histories of substance use–related problems. As such, all available records and collateral sources of information are especially crucial when performing a forensic evaluation involving an issue directly related to substance use disorders.

The American Psychiatric Association (APA) Practice Guidelines for Treatment of Patients with Substance Use Disorders outline the basic components of a substance use disorder evaluation and suggest the following: a systematic inquiry into the mode of onset, quantity, frequency, and duration of substance use; the escalation of use over time; the motivation for use; the specific circumstances of the individual's substance use (e.g., where, with whom, how much, by what route of administration); the desired effect of the substance used; the most recent dose of each substance used; the time elapsed since the most recent use; the degree of associated intoxication; the severity of associated withdrawal syndromes; and the subjective effects of all substances used, including substances other than the individual's "drug of choice" (APA 2006, 20).

In addition, the APA Practice Guidelines suggest that the evaluator address the following areas: a history of any prior treatment for a substance use disorder, including the characteristics of the treatment such as setting; context (e.g., voluntary or involuntary); modalities used; duration and, if applicable, dose of treatment; adherence to treatment; and short-term (3-month), intermediate (1-year), and longer-term outcomes as measured by subsequent substance use, level of social and occupational functioning achieved, and other outcome variables. Previous efforts to control or stop substance use outside of a formal treatment setting should also be discussed. For individuals who had previous treatment or periods of abstinence, additional history may include the duration of abstinence, the factors that promoted or helped sustain abstinence, the impact of abstinence on psychiatric functioning, the circumstances surrounding relapse (e.g., whether the relapse was related to withdrawal symptoms, exacerbation of a psychiatric disorder, or psychosocial stressors), the individual's attitude toward prior treatment, nontreatment experiences, and expectations about future treatments (APA 2006, 20).

TESTING

A forensic psychiatrist who is assessing suspected current or recent substance use in an individual should also be familiar with current laboratory tests to detect substance use, especially if making specific recommendations regarding monitoring. Blood has the shortest window of detection; most drugs are cleared from the blood at measurable levels in 12 hours or less. Urine has a detection window of about 1–3 days, as most drugs are cleared within this time after the most recent use of the drug, while other substances, such as cannabinols, may have longer detection periods up to several weeks. A standard 1.5-inch sample of head hair contains drug residuals from the prior 90 days, minus the week immediately before sample collection. A sweat patch test can detect substance use for a period of 1–21 days. Carbohydrate-deficient transferrin (CDT) is elevated in 80% of people who drink five or more drinks daily for 1 week or longer (DuPont 1999, 523–524).

INTOXICATION SEQUELAE

A defendant's or victim's loss of memory for events involved in an alleged crime presents significant problems for both the prosecution and defense, and for the forensic psychiatrist who is evaluating mental state at the time of an alleged offense. Amnesia for events during alcohol intoxication involves impairment of episodic memory. Episodic memory, by definition, includes the time, place, and other interrelated circumstances in which the event occurred. This contextual information is a prerequisite for formation of episodic memories. Alcohol's effect on encoding may disrupt the processing of context for the formation of an episodic memory. Alcoholic blackouts have been reported to be most closely associated with rapid rises in an individual's alcohol blood level (Lee et al. 2009).

Cannabis use has been associated with acute (toxic) psychosis, and exacerbation and causation of chronic psychotic disorders (including schizophrenia). A recent large-scale study has provided the first conclusive evidence that cannabis use significantly hastens the onset of psychotic illnesses during the critical years of brain development—with possible lifelong consequences. The first ever meta-analysis of more than 20,000 patients shows that smoking cannabis is associated with an earlier onset of psychotic illness by up to 2.7 years (McGrath et al. 2010).

An evaluation of the criminal responsibility of an offender who has consumed cannabis necessitates knowledge of the effect of the product on the offender's mental state at the time of the alleged offense. However, as the effects induced by cannabis are numerous and vary with individuals, the forensic psychiatrist should base the diagnosis and his or her evaluation on facts that are as objective as possible. Published guidelines have been proposed for the evaluation of criminal responsibility with relation to cannabis psychosis (Niveau 2002).

Methamphetamine, particularly smoked crystal methamphetamine, has become a major drug of abuse in the United States, where it is manufactured domestically and is relatively inexpensive. Users experience euphoria from this psycho-stimulant, which lasts longer than crack cocaine and does not require repeated re-dosing to maintain the high. However, methamphetamine is perhaps the most neurotoxic drug of abuse. Methamphetamine may cause agitation, confusion, irritability, and impulsivity. Methamphetamine also causes prolonged insomnia. Paranoid psychosis is a complication of chronic heavy methamphetamine use. Delusional thinking may lead to reactive violence aimed at those believed to be threatening harm toward the substance-using individual (National Institute on Drug Abuse 2006). Methamphetamine use in a defendant poses challenges to the forensic evaluator of an insanity defense, due to the fact that the drug may produce sustained psychotic symptoms, even after acute use has subsided, leading some to suggest methamphetamine-induced psychosis has the potential to reinforce "sanist" attitudes and practices among evaluators and courts (Thom et al. 2011).

TREATMENT RECOMMENDATIONS

A forensic psychiatrist may be asked to make specific treatment recommendations for substance use disorders, and may also identify the current stage at which an individual is in his or her recovery. The "Stages of Change" model is useful for conceptualizing an individual's motivation to address substance use problems (Prochaska and DiClemente 1983). The model, derived from research on tobacco cessation, divides the recovery process into sequential stages, with stage-specific goals to achieve before progression. The stages of change are precontemplation, contemplation, preparation, action, and maintenance. The recommended treatment interventions may be matched to the individual's current stage in recovery to enhance commitment to change and to increase the probability of successful change in substance use.

An individual with a substance use disorder should be enrolled in a treatment program of intensity commensurate with his or her level of problems. The Patient Placement Criteria algorithm developed by the American Society of Addiction Medicine assigns a patient within five levels of care (with sublevels): early intervention; outpatient treatment, intensive outpatient/partial hospitalization; residential/inpatient treatment; and medically managed intensive inpatient unit. Individuals are assigned to these levels of care based on six dimensions: intoxication/withdrawal potential; medical conditions and complications; emotional, behavioral, or cognitive conditions and complications; readiness to change; relapse, continued use, or continued problem potential; and recovery environment (Mee-Lee et al. 2001). Individuals matched to treatment placements based on this algorithm have been shown to have better outcomes than mismatched patients (Magura et al. 2003).

SUBSTANCE USE AND VIOLENCE

Active substance use substantially increases the risk of violence for any individual, and particularly by persons with psychiatric disorders. Research findings have shown such dually disordered individuals are more violent as a group than individuals with a psychiatric illness alone; and those with a psychiatric disorder but without substance abuse are no more violent than the general population (Monahan et al. 2001). In addition to an elevated general violence risk, substance use associated with psychiatric disorders with impulse control problems places individuals at a greater risk for threatening violence using firearms (Casiano et al. 2008). As such, it is imperative that a forensic psychiatrist performing a risk assessment for future dangerousness completes a thorough assessment of substance use disorder problems, and offers recommendations, if applicable, to mitigate risk factors for relapse and potential future violence.

CORRECTIONAL SETTINGS

Substance use disorders are rampant in correctional settings, and frequently co-occur with other mental health disorders. Among jail inmates, 76% of all inmates who reported a mental health history also met criteria for a substance use disorder (James and Glaze 2006). The term *substance use disorder* refers to either substance abuse or dependence (using *DSM-IV* criteria).

Substance use disorders increase the risk of criminality, incarceration, re-offense, and poor institutional adjustment (White 1997). Substance-addicted offenders also can present challenges to public safety, public health, and public policy. With the shift toward increased utilization of incarceration (especially for drug offenders) and longer sentences, a major push to expand treatment services has occurred in various correctional settings: prisons, jails, and community corrections agencies. Research confirms that treatment is one of the most effective tools for reducing drug use and recidivism. In fact, the majority of evidence-based practices (EBPs) for addressing drug-involved offenders involve various treatment modalities (Taxman and Belenko 2012, 1–8).

SUBSTANCE USE AND CRIMINAL RESPONSIBILITY

In American and English common law, voluntary intoxication does not fully excuse an individual who has committed a crime and is not a defense under a not guilty by reason of insanity (NGRI) plea in a general intent crime, although it may result in a diminished verdict or sentence (Slovenko 1995). In the case of *Montana v. Egelhoff*, the United States ruled on the issue of voluntary intoxication, in which the appellant was convicted of premeditated murder and argued he should have been allowed to present evidence of voluntary intoxication to negate the premeditation. The court ruled against the appellant, stating that allowing evidence of voluntary intoxication is not a founded principle of American law that would constitute a violation of the defendant's Fourteenth Amendment rights under the Constitution (*Montana v. Egelhoff* 1996).

In some jurisdictions, chronic substance use leading to psychosis may be the basis for an insanity defense under the concept of "settled insanity." In one paper, Feix and Wolber discuss specific areas that forensic evaluators should consider exploring when evaluating a possible insanity defense associated with substance use. These areas of inquiry include, but are not limited to, (a) whether the defendant exhibited psychotic symptoms only during intoxication or the symptoms seemed to persist after the typical time had passed during which the substance is known to be in its active phase; and (b) evidence of psychotic symptoms or episodes of mental illness before or at times other than when the defendant was intoxicated during the index offense (Feix and Wolber 2007, 181).

Under the concept of diminished capacity, a *mens rea* defense, voluntary intoxication may negate the capacity of an individual to form a specific intent required by the definition of the criminal charge in a specific intent crime (Weinstock et al. 1996). If the requisite specific intent were nullified, guilt could be found for a lesser included crime that does not require the specific intent (e.g., manslaughter instead of second-degree murder).

ASSESSMENT OF ADDICTED PROFESSIONALS

Forensic evaluations of an addicted physician may be part of any of the following: fitness-for-duty evaluation for employer or insurance carrier, state medical board evaluation, malpractice case, or disability evaluation.

Physicians are as likely to experience drug and alcohol addiction as anyone in the general population. Although alcohol is the primary problem in nearly half of all cases, physicians are more likely than others to abuse prescribed medications. In a study of 16 state physician health programs that examined 904 physicians who had been placed under monitoring for drug abuse, more than half of the physicians were in five medical specialties, with family medicine representing the highest number at 20% (McLellan et al. 2008); however, anesthesiologists make up 5.2% of physicians nationwide, and therefore, they are remarkably overrepresented in physician health programs, and most likely to be addicted to intravenous opioids (Kintz et al. 2005).

The following characteristics have been identified as predisposing factors associated with substance abuse in physicians: obsessive–compulsive personality style; family history of substance use disorders or mental illness; childhood family problems; personal mental illness history of sensation-seeking behaviors; denial of personal and social problems; perfectionism; and idealism (Talbott et al. 1998).

Signs that should raise concerns for active substance abuse by a physician may include any of the following: frequent tardiness and absences; unexplained disappearances during working hours; inappropriate behaviors in workplace, affective lability or irritability, interpersonal conflict, avoidance of peers or supervisors; keeping odd hours; disorganization and forgetfulness; diminished chart completion and work performance (Baldisseri 2007).

Attorneys in the United States demonstrate a significant prevalence of substance abuse and other psychiatric disorders, and these often lead to impairment in their professional functioning. One study showed that overall, 33% of attorneys had depression, problem drinking, or cocaine abuse, twice the rates of the general population (Benjamin et al. 1990). Started in the 1980s, Lawyer Assistance Programs (LAPs) exist in most states and usually provide both voluntary and involuntary (discipline-related) services. Similar to Physician Diversion Programs, the goal is to provide clinical monitoring and treatment for mental illness and/or substance use disorders.

SUMMARY KEY POINTS

- An understanding of the basic issues of substance use disorders, including intoxication and withdrawal symptoms, is crucial for forensic psychiatrists, as these disorders may be relevant in many forensic evaluations, both criminal and civil.
- In *DSM-5*, addictive disorders no longer exist as "abuse" or "dependence" but are now combined into "use disorders," with varying degrees of severity.
- The American Psychiatric Association (APA) Practice Guidelines for Treatment of Patients with Substance Use Disorders outline the basic components of a substance use disorder evaluation.
- In American and English common law, voluntary intoxication does not fully excuse an individual who has committed a crime and is not a defense under a not guilty by reason of insanity plea.

REFERENCES

American Academy of Pain Medicine, American Pain Society, and American Society of Addiction Medicine. 2001. *Definitions Related to the Use of Opioids in the Treatment of Chronic Pain.* Glenview, IL: American Pain Society.

American Psychiatric Association (APA). 1994. *Diagnostic and Statistical Manual of Mental Disorders*, 4th edition (*DSM-IV*). Washington, DC: American Psychiatric Publishing.

American Psychiatric Association (APA). 2006. *Practice Guideline for the Treatment of Patients With Substance Use Disorders*, 2nd edition. Alexandria, VA: APA.

American Psychiatric Association. (2013). *Diagnostic and Statistical Manual of Mental Disorders*, 5th edition (DSM-5). Washington, DC: American Psychiatric Publishing.

American Society of Addiction Medicine. 2011. *The Definition of Addiction.* Chevy Chase, MD: The Society.

Babor TF. 2011. Substance, not semantics, is the issue: Comments on the proposed addiction criteria for DSM-V. *Addiction* 106:870–872.

Baldisseri MR. 2007. Impaired healthcare professional. *Critical Care Medicine* 35:S106–S116.

Benjamin GA, EJ Darling, and B Sales. 1990. The prevalence of depression, alcohol abuse, and cocaine abuse among United States lawyers. *International Journal of Law and Psychiatry* 13:233–246.

Casiano H, B Shay-Lee, BJ Cox, JC Waldman, and J Sareen. 2008. Mental disorder and threats made by noninstitutionalized people with weapons in the national comorbidity survey replication. *Journal of Nervous and Mental Disease* 196:437–445.

Drummond C. 2011. The end of the dependence syndrome as we know it? *Addiction* 106:892–894.

DuPont RL. 1999. Diagnostic testing—Laboratory and psychological. In *Textbook of Substance Abuse Treatment*, 2nd edition, edited by M Galanter and HD Kleber. Washington, DC: American Psychiatric Press, 523–524.

Feix J and G Wolber. 2007. Intoxication and settled insanity: A finding by not guilty by reason by insanity. *Journal of the American Academy of Psychiatry and the Law* 35:172–182.

Goldstein RZ and ND Volkow. 2011. Dysfunction of the prefrontal cortex in addiction: Neuroimaging findings and clinical implications. *Nature Reviews Neuroscience* 12:652–669.

Hasin DS, MC Fenton, C Beseler, JY Park, and MM Wall. 2012. Analyses related to the development of DSM-5 criteria for substance use related disorders: 2. Proposed DSM-5 criteria for Alcohol, Cannabis, cocaine and heroin disorders in 663 substance abuse patients. *Drug and Alcohol Dependence* 122:28–37.

Hasin DS, CP O'Brien, M Auriacombe, G Borges, K Bucholz, A Budney, WM Compton, T Crowley, W Ling, and NM Petry. 2013. DSM-5 criteria for substance use disorders: Recommendations and rationale. *American Journal of Psychiatry* 170:834–851.

James DJ and LE Glaze. 2006. Mental health problems of prison and jail inmates. NCJ 213600. Washington, DC: U.S. Department of Justice, Office of Justice Programs, Bureau of Justice Statistics.

Kalivas PW and ND Volkow. 2005. The neural basis of addiction: A pathology of motivation and choice. *American Journal of Psychiatry* 162:1403–1413.

Kintz P, MV Marion, V Dumestre, and V Cirimele. 2005. Evidence of addiction by anesthesiologists as documented by hair analysis. *Forensic Science International* 153:81–84.

Lee H, S Roh, and DJ Kim. 2009. Alcohol-induced blackout. *International Journal of Environmental Research and Public Health* 6:2783–2792.

Magura S, EL Knight, HS Vogel, D Mahmood, AB Laudet, and A Rosenblum. 2003. Mediators of effectiveness in dual-focus self-help groups. *American Journal of Drug and Alcohol Abuse* 29:301–322.

Martin CS, DL Steinley, A Verges, and KJ Sher. 2011. The proposed 2/11 symptom algorithm for DSM-5 substance-use disorders is too lenient. *Psychological Medicine* 41:2008–2010.

McGrath J, J Welham, J Scott, D Varghese, L Degenhardt, MR Hayatbakhsh, R Alati, GM Williams, W Bor, and JM Najman. 2010. Association between cannabis use and psychosis-related outcomes using sibling pair analysis in a cohort of young adults. *Archives of General Psychiatry* 67:440–447.

McLellan AT, GS Skipper, M Campbell, and RL DuPont. 2008. Five year outcomes in a cohort study of physicians treated for substance use disorders in the United States. *British Medical Journal* 337:a2038.

Mee-Lee D, GD Schulman, M Fishman, DR Gastfriend, and JH Griffith. 2001. *ASAM Patient Placement Criteria for the Treatment of Substance-Related Disorders*, 2nd edition-Revised (ASAM-PPC-2R). Chevy Chase, MD: American Society of Addiction Medicine.

Monahan J, HJ Steadman, E Silver, and P Appelbaum. 2001. *Rethinking Risk Assessment: The MacArthur Study of Mental Disorder and Violence.* New York: Oxford University Press.

Montana v. Egelhoff, 518 U.S. 37, 57 (1996).

National Institute on Drug Abuse. NIDA Research Report. 2006. Methamphetamine Abuse and Addiction (NIH Publication No. 06–4210). Rockville, MD: National Clearinghouse on Drug and Alcohol Information.

National Survey on Drug Use and Health: Summary of National Findings. 2012. [Electronic Version]. http://www.samhsa.gov/data/sites/default/files/NSDUHresults2012/NSDUHresults2012.pdf, accessed November 22, 2015.

Niveau G. 2002. Criminal responsibility and cannabis use: Psychiatric review and proposed guidelines. *Journal of Forensic Sciences* 47:451–458.

Parhami I, R Mojtabai, RJ Rosenthal, TO Afifi, and TW Fong. 2014. Gambling and the onset of comorbid mental disorders: A longitudinal study evaluating severity and specific symptoms. *Journal of Psychiatric Practice* 3:207–219.

Prochaska JO and CC DiClemente. 1983. Stages and processes of self-change of smoking: Toward an integrative model of change. *Journal of Consulting and Clinical Psychology* 51:390–395.

Slovenko R. 1995. *Psychiatry and Criminal Culpability.* New York: Wiley.

Slovenko R. 2011. The DSM in litigation and legislation. *Journal of the American Academy of Psychiatry and the Law* 39:6–11.

Substance Abuse and Mental Health Services Administration (SAMHSA). 2013. *Results from the 2012 National Survey on Drug Use and Health: Summary of National Findings*, NSDUH Series H-46, HHS Publication No. (SMA) 13–4795. Rockville, MD: SAMHSA.

Talbott GD, KV Gallegos, and DH Angres. 1998. Impairment and recovery in physicians and other health professionals. In *Principles of Addiction Medicine*, 2nd edition, edited by WG Allen and KS Terry, Chevy Chase, MD: American Society of Addiction Medicine, 1263–1277.

Taxman FS and S Belenko. 2012. *Implementing Evidence-Based Practices in Community Corrections and Addiction Treatment.* Springer Series on Evidence Based Crime Policy. New York: Springer.

Thom KA, F Mary, and M Brian. 2011. Insanity, methamphetamine and psychiatric expertise in New Zealand courtrooms. *Journal of Law and Medicine* 18:749–758.

Volkow ND and RD Baler. 2014. Addiction science: Uncovering neurobiological complexity. *Neuropharmacology* 76:235–249.

Weinstock RW, GB Leong, and JA Silva. 1996. California's diminished capacity defense: Evolution and transformation. *Bulletin of the American Academy of Psychiatry and the Law* 24:347–366.

White HR. 1997. Alcohol, illicit drugs, and violence. In *Handbook of Antisocial Behavior*, edited by DM Stoff, J Breiling, and JD Maser, New York: Wiley, 511–523.

80

Sexually violent predator laws

DOUGLAS E. TUCKER AND SAMUEL JAN BRAKEL

INTRODUCTION

Sexually violent predator (SVP) commitment laws are the latest phase in the long history of legislation in the United States seeking to legally process and clinically treat sex offenders in a manner distinct from other criminal offenders. Washington was the first state to enact an SVP commitment law in 1990 (Wash. Rev. Code. Ann. 1992), with more than a dozen states following within the decade. These laws provide for continued (civil) confinement and involuntary treatment for the most serious and high-risk sexual offenders at the end of their criminal incarceration. The laws have been surrounded by controversy from the beginning, as they try to achieve societally necessary and legally proper results in a conceptually underdeveloped and politically polarized area where the overlap between criminal behavior and psychiatric illness has proven to be especially confounding. In addition to focusing discussion about proper management of criminal behavior in mentally ill individuals, these laws have provided a new arena for the central debate in criminal law over the relative value of public safety versus individual liberty.

It has been noted that laws of the SVP type have a typical life course, beginning with their birth in a state of public fear and outrage over one or more highly publicized sex crimes, subsequent ad hoc legislative committee recommendations and laws created under intense political pressure, and ultimate revision or repeal when the public furor diminishes and the financial and legal repercussions become evident (Sutherland 1950). Part of the reason for this repeated pattern may be the lack of integration between mental health and criminal justice systems in our society. Every time a serious problem is identified in the overlapping area between these two fields, society is surprised anew, and our conceptual confusion in the context of strong emotion leads to yet another policy lurch. Research has indicated that punishment is not as effective as rehabilitation at reducing criminal recidivism for many offenders (Cullen et al. 2000; Birgden 2004), but this has not translated into effective delivery of sex offender–specific treatment, either inside or outside of correctional settings (D'Orazio et al. 2009).

The SVP laws have been subject to repeated legal challenges since their first enactment a decade and a half ago, and while three U.S. Supreme Court forays into this arena (*Kansas v. Hendricks* 1997; *Kansas v. Crane* 2002; *U.S. v. Comstock* 2010) have definitively disposed of some of the major issues, others continue to be subject to litigation, especially at the state level. These include (1) the matter of what treatment is actually being provided under the programs; (2) the issue of confidentiality/privilege in sex offender treatment; (3) the significance and measurement of the subjects' (lack of) control or volitional capacity; (4) the accuracy of estimations regarding sexual recidivism risk at the time of initial commitment as well as at conditional release; (5) the "conditions" of conditional release, including monitoring and treatment procedures; and (6) revocation and recommitment standards and procedures.

Although paraphilic disorders have long been officially recognized as mental disorders, having been listed as such since the earliest classifications of the *Diagnostic and Statistical Manual of Mental Disorders* (*DSM*, published by the American Psychiatric Association), they are typically ego-syntonic in that affected individuals often do not see themselves as ill or in need of treatment. These disorders are generally agreed to be biopsychosocial in nature. They affect emotional development, relationships, and behavior, but those so diagnosed typically do not manifest the deficits in reality testing and daily functioning that psychiatrists and others associate with "real" mental illness. The criminal behavior often associated with paraphilic disorders has historically led to a greater measure of involvement by the criminal justice system than the mental health system, and while psychologists and other mental health professionals have developed programs of research and treatment for this population, the field of psychiatry appears thus far to have avoided engagement to any significant extent.

Psychiatrists (and others) have difficulty agreeing on whether or not sex offenders are mentally ill, despite official *DSM* recognition of various paraphilias, and many are uncomfortable with coerced inpatient treatment even if there is agreement on pathology. Involuntary treatment has been accepted by most psychiatrists as appropriate and necessary for individuals suffering from a variety of mental disorders which involve reduced insight and ability to control behavior, such as dementias, psychoses, and addictive disorders, but there has been reluctance to extend this to those with dangerous paraphilic disorders. Many psychiatrists have joined in critiquing the SVP commitment laws as medicalizing a "social problem," and for misusing psychiatry as an agent of social control instead of applying it toward legitimate therapeutic ends, with the implication that the pathology involved in dangerous paraphilias is more "social" than "psychiatric." However, the "social" use of psychiatry is endemic to, if not the essence of, the law/psychiatry interface, and psychiatrists have long been responsible for the care and treatment, as well as custodial management, of sexual as well as other criminal offenders, particularly when it appears that a mental disorder has contributed to the offending behavior. In fact, the differentiation between "criminal" and "mentally ill" behavior is of relatively recent vintage, operationally. For most of recorded history, society's rejects—the poor, the criminal, the mentally ill—were housed in the same facilities. As for paraphilic sex offenders in particular, there has been much debate about whether they are "mad" or "bad," and where they "belong," but by reasonable, defensible standards they are both, and will require integrated legal and mental health interventions in order to effectively address the problems they raise.

What follows is a brief review of the history of laws in the United States governing societal management of sexual offenders, a discussion of the SVP laws in particular, the current treatment being provided for committed SVPs, and some thoughts regarding the implications and future evolution of the legal and clinical management of these complex patient-offenders.

HISTORY OF SEX OFFENDER ADJUDICATION AND TREATMENT

It is important to appreciate that the SVP laws seeking to civilly commit mentally ill sex offenders do not operate in either historical or legal isolation. In response to the same social pressures that led to SVP legislation, other recent legal developments have included sex offender registration and notification statutes as well as laws and ordinances aiming to restrict where these offenders may reside or be employed.

Registration and notification

One does not have to be a student of sex offender legislation to have heard of Megan's Law, named after a young victim of a sexually motivated killing. Megan's Law is often associated with the SVP commitment movement, but it is primarily a registration/notification mandate for sex offenders, initially enacted by the New Jersey legislature in 1994. Subsequent federal legislation, passed by Congress in a 2-year period between 1994 and 1996 (a 1996 part of which is also known as Megan's Law; the others are the Jacob Wetterling Act and the Pam Lychner Act, named after other victims), provides incentives to the states to pass similar legislation in order to create a national database of such offenders, to be implemented in such a manner "as necessary to protect the public." A federal commitment law, the Adam Walsh Act, was enacted in 2006.

The underlying purpose of registration is dissemination and notification—to provide information regarding the identity and whereabouts of sex offenders to relevant groups of citizens and officials. State statutes reflect different ways of providing notification and determining whom to notify—from broad notification of the public at large via postings on the Internet (32 states), to narrow notification of police or other law enforcement agencies only. An intermediate approach involves notification of other "need to know" groups beyond law enforcement, in particular those who work with children or adolescents such as school officials, operators of parks and recreation areas, and staff of various other community organizations. There is substantial variation among the states regarding who is subject to the registration mandate. It can range from all persons convicted of certain statutorily enumerated sex crimes ("offense driven"), to a more discretionary "offender-driven" approach whereby an assessment of the offender's dangerousness (offense severity and likelihood of recidivism) is derived from specific data about the offender and victims. These "dangerousness" assessments may be subject to adversarial argument in a formal hearing. Under the discretionary approach, the length of time that an offender must remain on the registry as well as the availability of the information to outside sources is typically tiered according to a ranking of lower versus higher risk levels.

All 50 states today have sex offender registration and notification laws, which have been supported by several waves of Congressional legislation enacted during the 1990s. The fact that less than half the states have SVP commitment laws shows the extent to which the legal responses of registration and involuntary treatment are separated. Like commitment, registration has a history that well predates the 1990s, and during the twentieth century both have been applied to "habitual criminals" other than just sex offenders. The first registration statute specifically targeting sex offenders was passed by California in 1947. Registration mandates have often commingled sex offenders with other offenders, and it is interesting to note that both sexual and nonsexual offenders have occasionally complained about the relative stigma burdens associated with such lack of differentiation.

Residence and employment restrictions

In addition to sex offender registration requirements, many jurisdictions seek to enhance public safety by restricting residence and employment options. Recent research indicates that 20 states have state-wide statutory restrictions of this kind, while other states have local municipal or county ordinances in place (Hamilton 2011). These restrictions are categorically aimed at individuals convicted of sexual crimes, and are independent of any probation, early release, or parole conditions that might be imposed in specific cases.

Just as some of the objectives of residence and employment restrictions are the same as those of registration and notification statutes, so are many of the corresponding criticisms. These include insufficient differentiation among offenders subject to the restrictions, questionable legislative motivation (protective versus punitive), inadequately identified societal need, and unproved success in furthering the public safety goals. Critics point to the harm done to ex-offenders who wish to resume productive life, given their near-banishment from viable living or working opportunities, which in itself may contribute to criminal and sexual recidivism. For example, research has indicated that residency restrictions have increased homelessness among paroled sex offenders by 800%, which, apart from any humane concerns, is unlikely to promote the public safety objective (D'Orazio et al. 2009). Thus far, however, these alleged punitive motives and consequences have not been deemed sufficient to invalidate the laws for lack of procedural or substantive due process. The courts that have ruled on such constitutional challenges have, analogous to decisions on commitment, been content to honor the declared civil/regulatory purpose of the restrictions.

Commitment laws

Until the late 1930s, sexual offenders in the United States were dealt with by incarceration and punishment like all other offenders. A new era of interest in medical explanations for criminal behavior and an orientation toward treatment goals over punishment began to develop in the early twentieth century. Indeterminate sentencing was introduced, in which release decisions were determined by the offenders' demonstrated rehabilitation rather than by preset sentence limits. Eventually, "sexual psychopath statutes" began to appear in progressive jurisdictions, which provided for civil commitment and treatment of repeat sex offenders who were deemed to be suffering from a mental disorder associated with volitional impairment (i.e., inability to control one's impulses). Michigan and Illinois enacted the first such statutes in 1937–1938, with California and Minnesota following shortly thereafter. The Minnesota statute generated the first constitutional test of this type of legislation before the U.S. Supreme Court, in *Minnesota ex. rel. Pearson v. Probate Court* (1940). The challenge to the statute was on substantive due process grounds, notably the vagueness of the description of those susceptible to the statute's application. The Supreme Court, however, approved the legislation, noting that the key statutory term "psychopathic personality" was adequately defined as involving a "habitual course of misconduct in sexual matters," and an "utter lack of power to control sexual impulses." Between 1940 and 1976, sexual psychopath legislation modeled on the Minnesota statute was passed in 30 other states and the District of Columbia, and it was used to a substantial degree. The rehabilitative ideal behind these laws was widely shared, and the procedural shortcuts permitted by most of these statutes were considered acceptable given the benign intentions and predicted good outcomes (Brakel and Cavanaugh 2000).

Over time, the optimistic consensus among doctors and lawyers that the sexual offenders singled out by the law would benefit from treatment began to erode. Attorneys were the first to turn against these laws, consistent with legal concerns about liberty and autonomy. Eventually, however, mental health practitioners began to realize as well that treatments for this population were not as effective as had been hoped, and withdrew their support for the sexual psychopath laws. The Group for Advancement of Psychiatry (GAP) concluded in its 1977 report that the statutes were "social experiments that have failed and that lack redeeming social value" (GAP 1977). Complementary social trends that undermined support for the laws included the civil rights movement in the 1960s, the rise of the women's movement somewhat later (to the extent it promoted a desire to deal punitively rather than therapeutically with perpetrators of violence against women), and toward the 1980s, the general societal turn to more punitive "law and order" rather than rehabilitative policies. In the 6-year period between 1975 and 1981, more than half of the sexual psychopath statutes were repealed. By the mid-1980s, only 13 states still had these laws, and only five states applied them with any frequency (Massachusetts, Nebraska, New Jersey, Oregon, and Washington). The leading U.S. Supreme Court case of this era is *Specht v. Patterson* (1967), in which the court mandated the application of most criminal procedural safeguards to sexual psychopath commitments. These included a full judicial hearing, assistance of counsel, the right to confront and cross-examine adverse witnesses, the right to present one's own witnesses and evidence, and a final decision sufficiently articulated to permit meaningful review on appeal. In a subsequent case (*Allen v. Illinois* 1986), the U.S. Supreme Court held that the Fifth Amendment's self-incrimination privilege did not necessarily extend to the psychiatric examination in sexual psychopath commitments. By this point, however, such commitments were procedurally encumbered in every other way and quite rare. U.S. jurisprudence regarding sex offenders was close to where it was before the whole sexual psychopath law experiment began, with criminal incarceration of sex offenders undifferentiated from any other offenders.

SEXUALLY VIOLENT PREDATOR LAWS

In 1989, Earl Kenneth Shriner was released from a 10-year prison sentence in Washington State for kidnapping and sexually assaulting two teenage girls. He had been found not to be committable under the state's civil commitment statute, and on the day of his release from prison proceeded to rape a 7-year-old boy, cut off his penis, and leave him to die. This case caused widespread outrage, and in 1990 Washington passed the first of a new generation of sex offender laws known as Sexually Violent Predator Acts. Soon other states passed laws modeled on the Washington statute, and by the end of the millennium 16 states had enacted laws of this kind, including Arizona, California, Florida, Illinois, Iowa, Kansas, Massachusetts, Minnesota, Missouri, New Jersey, North Dakota, South Carolina, Texas, Virginia, Washington, and Wisconsin. Today the number stands at 20, including Pennsylvania (2003), Nebraska (2006), New Hampshire (2007), and New York (2007). The two atypical states include Texas, where SVP commitments are limited to outpatient treatment, and Pennsylvania, which allows only for the civil commitment of offenders who perpetrated their sexual offenses as juveniles and are "aging out" of the juvenile justice system at age 21. In addition, as mentioned, a federal SVP commitment law was passed in 2006 (the Adam Walsh Child Protection and Safety Act) and was sustained by the U.S. Supreme Court 4 years later in the *Comstock* case (*U.S. v. Comstock* 2010). Although the challenge to the law in this case initially duplicated many of the arguments settled in the 1997 *Hendricks* case (see below), the only surviving question by the time the case came before the U.S. Supreme Court was whether the enactment of a federal commitment law was a constitutional exercise of Congress' power under the Necessary and Proper Clause. The court ruled that it was. The Necessary and Proper Clause is a famous open-ended phrase in the Constitution that forms the basis for innumerable laws passed, for good or ill, by the federal legislature to implement its limited enumerated powers.

The central elements of the SVP laws are (1) legal authority for continuing to detain sex offenders with diagnosed mental disorders who are already in custody and likely to re-offend if released; and (2) implementation of the goal of continued confinement via civil commitment to a treatment facility The vast majority of this designated population are offenders convicted of any of a series of enumerated serious sexual crimes, but the laws also apply to those found Incompetent to Stand Trial or Not Guilty by Reason of Insanity (NGRI) for such crimes. Except for Texas, the laws and practices of the states aim to confine those found eligible under the SVP statutes to secure inpatient institutions. Even so, the laws provide for conditional release either as an alternative to initial placement in a secure facility, or more commonly, as a final phase of supervision and rehabilitation following inpatient treatment.

The laws uniformly require proof of four general conditions for civil commitment: (1) one or more charges (if found NGRI or Incompetent to Stand Trial) or convictions for sexually violent offenses; (2) a qualifying "mental abnormality"; (3) a specified likelihood of engaging in further acts of predatory sexual violence; and (4) a causal link between the mental abnormality and the risk of sexual recidivism. "Sexually violent offenses" are described by the SVP statutes as those found in the criminal code that involve forcible contact such as rape or, in its absence, physical contact with an underage victim. "Mental abnormality" is defined in the original Washington statute (and that of most other states with only minor differences in wording) as "a congenital or acquired condition affecting the emotional or volitional capacity which predisposes the person to commit criminal sexual acts in a degree constituting such person a menace to the health and safety of others" (Wash. Rev. Code. Ann. 1992).

As evident from the description above, SVP laws are explicitly focused on sexually violent behavior, which may be caused by any type of broadly defined mental condition or disorder. As a result, these laws have been interpreted to permit nonsexual and personality disorders as the qualifying mental abnormality, including Antisocial Personality Disorder (APD). Nonetheless, the vast majority of commitments have been for paraphilic disorders, usually with comorbid conditions. Pedophilic Disorder and "Paraphilia Not Otherwise Specified—Nonconsensual" (i.e., paraphilic rape, which is termed "Other Specified Paraphilic Disorder" in *DSM-5*) are the most common paraphilic disorders diagnosed in the SVP commitment population, although other paraphilic disorders are often present as well. Diagnoses of Pedohebephilic Disorder and Paraphilic Coercive Disorder were proposed for *DSM-5*, but rejected in large part out of concerns that they might facilitate SVP commitments (Tucker and Brakel 2012). These disorders of sexual deviance usually occur in conjunction with a variety of disinhibiting conditions including APD, other personality disorders, substance use disorders, intellectual disabilities or borderline intellectual functioning, other neurodevelopmental disorders (e.g., Autism Spectrum Disorder and Attention Deficit/Hyperactivity Disorder), psychotic disorders, mood disorders, minor and major neurocognitive disorders, and traumatic brain injuries. As might be expected, research has indicated that these associated disinhibiting conditions may increase the risk for sexual recidivism in paraphilic offenders (e.g., Alden et al. 2007; Hildebrand et al. 2004; Phenix and Sreenivasan 2009).

An array of biological and psychosocial treatments have been developed over the last few decades for paraphilic disorders and many of the most frequently co-occurring conditions (see Chapter 81). These treatments are roughly equivalent in their efficacy to the treatments that are commonly employed for other chronic mental illnesses, although they are only rarely utilized by psychiatrists. The goal is to achieve a level of workable symptomatic (emotional and behavioral) control rather than "cure," similar to the treatment objectives for most other chronic medical and psychiatric disorders.

The assessment of risk for sexually violent recidivism generally involves obtaining a baseline statistical risk estimate by using one or more of a number of actuarial instruments that have been developed for this purpose (e.g., Static-99R, Static-2002R, MnSOST-R, SORAG, etc.—see Chapter 70). Clinical judgment is then applied to this baseline estimate, with adjustment of the risk level made by considering the limitations of the actuarial instruments. For example, most sex offenses are not detected or reported, nor end in the perpetrator's arrest or conviction, and sexual recidivism risk persists beyond the finite time limits specified by the instruments (CSOM 2001; Hanson and Morton-Bourgon 2004). Additional research-proven risk-enhancing and risk-reducing factors not included in the instruments are also considered, as well as specific factors relevant only for the individual evaluee (e.g., debilitating physical illnesses of various kinds). This application of statistically validated risk factors in an individualized, clinically appropriate manner has been termed the clinically adjusted actuarial approach to risk estimation (Hanson 1998) (see Chapter 69). There are varying political and scientifically grounded ideas about what should constitute acceptable false-positive rates (commitment of nonrecidivists) and false-negative rates (release of recidivists). Likewise, there is variability among SVP laws in the statistical threshold for legal commitment, with most SVP laws requiring a "likelihood" or "substantial likelihood" of sexually violent recidivism for commitment, and little agreement on what these differential terms mean in application.

The process of commitment in most states involves a series of steps, and provides a variety of procedural safeguards. First, correctional staff screen those sexual offenders who are approaching their release, in order to select those who have committed statutorily designated sexually violent crimes. These individuals are then referred for comprehensive evaluation by clinicians who ideally have appropriate training and experience in sex offender evaluations. Those who are found to meet all of the statutory criteria (appropriate offense history, qualifying mental abnormality, and likelihood of sexually violent recidivism due to mental abnormality) are then referred to the prosecuting attorney's office, where further filtering occurs. This order is reversed in some states where, usually after an initial correctional screening, SVP candidates are reviewed by a prosecutor for legal viability before being referred to the state's mental health evaluators. A probable cause hearing is then held to determine whether sufficient evidence exists to proceed to the full trial, followed by the trial itself. The minimum standard of proof for mental health commitments was established in 1979 by the U.S. Supreme Court (*Addington v. Texas* 1979) as "clear and convincing evidence," although a majority of states have adopted the more stringent standard of "beyond a reasonable doubt" for SVP cases, i.e., the level of proof required for criminal conviction. Constitutionally, there is no right against self-incrimination in SVP proceedings (as per *Allen v. Illinois*), and the laws of some states provide for the possibility of penalizing an SVP commitment candidate for noncooperation with the state's evaluator by barring evidence offered by the candidate's own expert(s). However, in most states it appears that no penalty is exacted for refusing to cooperate. Commitments are generally for renewable periods of a year or two, or for an indefinite period, with the burden on the state to periodically justify continued commitment. Release is mandated when the offender has improved to the point where he or she can safely be managed in the community with appropriate treatment and supervision, and no longer meets the SVP criteria as determined by the court. Some states require a person committed under the SVP law to furnish a DNA sample, similar to criminally convicted felony sex offenders—an identification tactic increasingly used by law enforcement officials for many other kinds of convicted felony offenders as well.

Figure 80.1 illustrates the path of the commitment process in California, one of the biggest users of SVP civil commitment, as of December 31, 2013. There are more than 90,000 registered sexual offenders living in California communities and institutions, and more than 20,000 sexual offender inmates in the California Department of Corrections and Rehabilitation (CDCR) (CASOMB Report 2008). Each year, approximately 8000 sexual offenders are convicted of a felony sex offense, and roughly 39% of those convicted are sent to prison. Since the enactment of California's SVP statute in 1996, the CDCR has screened an average of about 250 convicted sex offenders per month who are eligible for release. This amounts to 53,927 inmates screened over the 18 years from 1996 to 2013, of which 14,335 (about 27%, or one-quarter of the total) were referred to the Department of Mental Health for further evaluation. Only 1983 individuals (3.7%) were evaluated as meeting the commitment criteria by state psychologists, and cases were filed by the District Attorney in 1736 instances (3.2%). Probable cause was found in 1431 cases (2.7%), and there have been 806 commitments after trial (1.5%), with 386 cases pending. As can be seen, only a small subset of all sex offenders have actually been committed under this law, i.e., about 1.5% of all released sex offenders.

In the United States as of 2014, a total of 4658 individuals were residing in inpatient facilities as civilly committed, and 829 individuals were in detention prior to commitment hearings, among the 17 programs who responded to a Sex Offender Civil Commitment Programs Network (SOCCPN) annual survey. Only 6 of 17 states (California, Illinois, Minnesota, New Jersey, Virginia, Washington) reported having civilly committed female clients, and these had very few (SOCCPN 2014). Five of the 20 states with SVP laws were holding civilly committed sex offenders separately in special facilities designated for such offenders, as opposed to mixing them with pre-commitment detainees (D'Orazio et al. 2009). In the 2014 SOCCPN survey, the states with the highest number of detained and/or committed SVP inpatients were California (929), Minnesota (701), Florida (633), Illinois (538), and New Jersey (484), while the lowest numbers were from New Hampshire (10), Pennsylvania (40), North Dakota (56), Federal BOP (62), and Arizona (94).

Despite early predictions that committed SVPs would never be released given the laws' announced intent to target only the worst of the worst (the typical statutory language speaks of "a small but extremely dangerous group of sexually violent predators...unamenable to existing treatment modalities"), this has not proven to be the case. Currently, among 17 responding programs in the SOCCPN survey,

California Dept. of State Hospitals - Sex Offender Commitment Program Summary Statistics Report

Summary Statistics Report 1/1/1996 Through 12/31/2013

1. Total Cases Referred	2. Total Offenders:	3. Deceased While in Custody:
53,927	26,008	178

4. Administrative Record Review and Clinical Screen Summary:				
(a) Suspended	(b) Stopped	(c) Returned	(d) Evaluate	(e) Pending
152	249	39,185	14,335	6

5. Referral Outcome Summary:					
(a) Positive	(b) Negative	(c) Pending	(d) Returned	(e) Suspended /Stopped	(f) Turner Decision
1,983	12,081	12	39,241	605	4

6. District Attorney Summary:			
(a) Referred to DA	(b) Petition Filed	(c) Withdrawn	(d) Pending
1,991	1,736	243	11

7. Probable Cause Summary:			
(a) Yes	(b) No	(C) Withdrawn	(d) Pending
1,431	65	156	64

8. Trial Outcome Summary:			
(a) Commit	(b) Release	(c) Withdrawn	(d) Pending
806	136	130	386

9. Commitment Summary:					
(a) DSH Admissions	(b) Out to Court	(c) Discharged	(d) Deceased	(e) 2 Yr Term	(f) Indeterminate Term
567	17	213	45	141	426

Figure 80.1 California Department of State Hospital: Sex offender commitment program summary statistics report.

769 individuals have been conditionally released, 1592 have been unconditionally released, and there are currently 344 conditionally released SVP outpatients (SOCCPN 2014). These same programs reported that 168 individuals had been returned to a facility following full discharge or conditional release for a variety of new violations and/or crimes. SVP treatment costs are an important concern. Average annual SVP treatment program costs in 2006 (the most recent data available) were $94,000 per person, ranging from a high of $166,000 in California to a low of $17,391 in Texas (where treatment is delivered in the community rather than an inpatient institution). Outpatient costs are not always lower than inpatient costs, however, and in some states with high-intensity conditional release monitoring and treatment programs may be substantially higher, well exceeding $100,000 per capita. This is generally equivalent to the cost of treating mentally disordered offenders in state hospitals, but represents more than three times the cost of incarcerating these individuals in prisons (Gookin 2007). Consideration of these costs of incarceration and treatment for sex offenders, however, should be weighed against the incalculable societal costs and harms associated with rape and child sexual abuse crimes (Heil and English 2007).

The first constitutional test to the U.S. Supreme Court of the new SVP laws occurred in 1997 in the case of *Kansas v. Hendricks* (1997). Leroy Hendricks had been molesting children for many years, including his own stepdaughter and stepson, and he himself admitted that he would stop only when he died. His attorneys appealed his commitment under Kansas' SVP law on the grounds of (1) substantive due process, (2) double jeopardy, and (3) the *ex post facto* doctrine. The substantive due process argument was that the commitment criterion of "mental abnormality" failed to satisfy the requirement that an individual be mentally ill and dangerous before he or she can be committed to a mental facility. There is a long history of legal doctrine (and philosophical tradition) in American jurisprudence that the state cannot confine someone for dangerousness alone (i.e., for *potential* misconduct) without some accompanying mental condition or impairment, as this would constitute an impermissible form of preventive detention (e.g., see *Foucha v. Louisiana* 1992). Justice Thomas, writing for a narrow 5–4 majority, rejected Hendricks' contention that "mental abnormality" failed to qualify, noting that the definition of medical terms for legal purposes is a legislative task, and that the diagnosis of pedophilia is classified by the psychiatric profession itself in *DSM-IV* as a serious mental disorder (Tucker and Brakel 2012). In particular, the majority opinion stated that the "mental abnormality" involves an inability to control sexually violent impulses. It also noted that the claims of double jeopardy (one can be tried only once for violation of the law) and *ex post facto* (one cannot be held to account under laws made after the fact) apply to the criminal law only. Relying on the prior *Allen v. Illinois* decision, the majority found that despite various criminal law-style safeguards, the SVP law described a legitimate civil procedure. In addition, the opinion noted that the law would be valid even if treatment were not medically available (based on the long history in this country of permitting detention and segregation of dangerous individuals with untreatable contagious diseases or mental disabilities), as well as if treatment were available but only secondary to the primary goal of continued confinement (so long as some form of treatment is prescribed).

SVP TREATMENT

Until the 1980s–1990s there was no standard treatment for sex offenders, and a variety of unvalidated psychotherapeutic, behavioral, and pharmacological approaches were used. However, a number of treatments have recently been developed and shown to be effective in reducing sexual recidivism (Hanson et al. 2002; Ward et al. 2008; Thibaut et al. 2010) (see Chapter 81). As a result, there has been significant upgrading of treatment provided for all sex offenders, including committed SVPs. Nearly all states have clearly defined stages and/or phases of their programs, with specific groups at each phase that the resident must meaningfully participate in or complete. The vast majority of programs require patients to participate in cognitive-behavioral group psychotherapy that emphasizes the identification of relapse prevention and risk management plans, with a focus on management of dynamic (changeable) risk factors, behavioral management of sexual arousal (e.g., masturbatory satiation), and intervention in the sexual reoffense cycle. These programs generally offer content for special-needs groups such as psychiatrically impaired or developmentally disabled offenders, and most also use individual psychotherapy as well as polygraph and penile plethysmography (PPG) assessment. These practices reflect a standard of treatment service structure and content that is generally consistent with recommendations made by Marques (2001) and by the Association for the Treatment of Sexual Abusers (2001). Currently, although 8 out of 15 responding programs say they contemplate [or permit] antiandrogen treatment on a voluntary basis, such treatment is in fact only rarely prescribed (0.43%–6% of resident population) (SOCCPN 2014).

The importance of a conditional release phase has been demonstrated by research indicating that poor community reintegration planning for child molesters released from prison is a risk factor for sexual recidivism (Willis and Grace 2008). This final phase in which qualified residents are conditionally released to the community has been called central to the credibility and effectiveness of these programs (Marques 2001). Nonetheless, only 10 of 16 responding states with inpatient SVP programs currently report having some form of conditional release arrangement (SOCCPN 2014). These programs provide assistance with community living arrangements, obtaining outpatient treatment services, case management, monitoring, and crisis intervention services.

FUTURE DIRECTIONS

SVP laws are the latest effort in the United States to devise a combined incapacitation-focused (via confinement) and therapeutic approach for the most dangerous, repeat sexual offenders. These laws may ultimately have the beneficial effect of forcing psychiatry to face sex offenders as treatable patients, and in so doing to expand training, to fund and conduct research, and to refine methods of assessments and treatment for this challenging population. The following is a list of suggestions for improvement in SVP legal and clinical policy, adapted from D'Orazio et al. (2009):

1. Start sex offender treatment in the correctional setting, as this could reduce the need for SVP commitments, enhance treatment gains, mitigate risk of reoffense, and save money while enhancing community safety.
2. Do not house probable-cause (pre-commitment) SVP individuals together with committed SVPs in the regular inpatient program, particularly if they decline to enroll in treatment, as they generally have a disruptive effect on the treatment milieu.
3. Enhance public education with information about SVP individuals, their treatment, and supervision in order to decrease misperceptions and increase the likelihood of safe reintegration.
4. Provide state-sponsored transitional housing for conditionally released SVPs to help reduce the widespread public fear and confusion regarding where these individuals are to be placed in the community.
5. Establish and fund research on treatment processes and outcomes for SVPs, including post-release recidivism data, so that future policy can be more data driven than crisis driven.
6. Improve collaboration among state agencies providing SVP treatment, particularly regarding the development of specific standards of treatment for this population. For example, the Sex Offender Civil Commitment Programs Network (SOCCPN) has

existed officially since 2006, with the stated mission of providing a forum to share information related to the effective management, assessment, and treatment of individuals held under civil commitment laws (SOCCPN 2014).

7. Redefine sexual offending as a public health problem that requires comprehensive cross-agency collaboration, involving both the correctional and mental health systems. A greater proportion of resources could then be expended toward primary prevention, i.e., preventing sex offenses in the first place by facilitating early intervention with at-risk individuals and families, and making community treatment available for paraphilic individuals.
8. Conduct a cost–benefit financial analysis with recommendations for best practice, including primary prevention and potentially less costly forms of sexual offense containment than SVP commitment.
9. Revise state laws that mandate reporting of individuals who in the course of treatment describe a history of sexual offending, as this unduly interferes with the treatment process and prevents individuals from coming forward to participate in it.
10. Develop risk assessment instruments that are specific to discrete paraphilic and sex offender populations, as recidivism base rates and the accuracy of the actuarial instruments vary across clinical samples and legal jurisdictions.
11. Change the designation for this group of dangerous sex offenders from "sexually violent predators" to something less stigmatizing, because this label yields extremely negative responses and gravely diminishes the released offenders' opportunities for housing, employment, interpersonal relations, and successful reintegration into the community.

SUMMARY KEY POINTS

- SVP laws have existed in the United States since 1990, and provide for the civil commitment of a small proportion (about 1%–2%, typically those convicted of dangerous contact offenses) of sexual offenders at the end of their criminal sentences.
- The U.S. federal government and 20 states currently have SVP statutes, and while there is no centralized database, recent surveys indicate a national census of approximately 5000 currently committed. Over the course of the programs' respective lives, surveys count 769 individuals who have been conditionally released, and at least 1592 who have been unconditionally released.
- SVP treatment programs strive to conform to a best-practices model of sex offender treatment, consisting of a cognitive–behavioral orientation with a focus on relapse prevention, phased progression, modification of dynamic risk factors for reoffense, and programming for special-needs groups, though only about half have a conditional release phase, and only about 1%–5% of committed individuals receive (voluntary) antiandrogen treatment.
- Statutory registration and notification requirements exist in all 50 states and are independent of SVP status, while employment and residency restrictions exist in some 20 states (not counting additional states with local municipal and county ordinances to this effect).

ACKNOWLEDGMENT

The authors are indebted to Steven Arkowitz, Psy.D. for his review of the manuscript and valuable feedback.

REFERENCES

Addington v. Texas, 441 U.S. 418 (1979).

Alden A, P Brennan et al. 2007. Psychotic disorder and sex offending in a Danish birth cohort. *Archives of General Psychiatry* 64(11):1251–1258.

Allen v. Illinois, 478 U.S. 364 (1986).

American Psychiatric Association (APA). 2013. *Diagnostic and Statistical Manual of Mental Disorders*, 5th edition (*DSM-5*). Washington, DC: APA.

Association for the Treatment of Sexual Abusers (ATSA). 2001. *Public Policy Statement: Civil Commitment of Sexually Violent Offenders*. http://www.atsa.com/civil-commitment-sexuallyviolent-predators, accessed June 28, 2016.

Birgden A. 2004. Therapeutic jurisprudence and sex offenders: A psycho-legal approach to protection. *Sexual Abuse* 16(4):351–364.

Brakel S and J Cavanaugh. 2000. Of psychopaths and pendulums: Legal and psychiatric treatment of sex offenders in the United States. *New Mexico Law Review* 30(1):69–94.

California Sex Offender Management Board (CASOMB). 2008. Report to the Legislature and Governor's Office: An assessment of current management practices of adult sex offenders in California. *Initial Report*, January, 2nd edition.

Center for Sex Offender Management (CSOM). 2001. Recidivism of sex offenders. http://www.csom.org/pubs/recidsexof.html, accessed June 28, 2016.

Cullen B, P Smith et al. 2000. A matched cohort comparison of a criminal justice system's response to child sexual abuse: A profile of perpetrators. *Child Abuse & Neglect* 24(4):569–577.

D'Orazio D, S Arkowitz et al. 2009. The California sexually violent predator statute: History, description and areas for improvement. https://ccoso.org/sites/default/files/

CCOSO%20SVP%20Paper.pdf, accessed June 28, 2016.

Foucha v. Louisiana, 504 U.S. 71 (1992).

Gookin K. 2007. *Comparison of State Laws Authorizing Involuntary Commitment of Sexually Violent Predators: 2006 Update, Revised.* Washington State Institute for Public Policy, Document No. 07-08-1101.

Group for the Advancement of Psychiatry. 1977. *Psychiatry and Sex Psychopath Legislation: The 30s to the 80s*, Rep. No. 98.

Hamilton M. 2011. Public safety, individual liberty, and suspect science: Future dangerousness assessments and sex offender laws. *Temple Law Review*, 83:697.

Hanson RK. 1998. What do we know about sex offender risk assessment? *Psychology, Public Policy and Law* 4(1/2):50–72.

Hanson R, A Gordon et al. 2002. First report of the collaborative outcome data project on the effectiveness of psychological treatment for sex offenders. *Sexual Abuse* 14(2):169–194.

Hanson RK and K Morton-Bourgon. 2004. *Predictors of Sexual Recidivism: An Updated Meta-Analysis* (User Report No. 2004-02). Ottawa, ON: Public Safety and Emergency Preparedness.

Heil P and K English. 2007. Prison sexual offender treatment: Recommendations for program implementation. Prepared on behalf of the *California Department of Corrections and Rehabilitation*. Sacramento, California.

Hildebrand M, C de Ruiter, and V de Vogel. 2004. Psychopathy and sexual deviance in treated rapists: Association with sexual and nonsexual recidivism. *Sexual Abuse* 16(1):1–24.

Kansas v. Crane, 534 U.S. 407 (2002).

Kansas v. Hendricks, 521 U.S. 346 (1997).

Marques J. 2001. Professional standards for civil commitment programs. In *The Sexual Predator: Legal Issues, Clinical Issues, Special Populations*. Vol. II., edited by A Schlank, Kingston, NJ: Civic Research Institute, 2-1–2-15.

Minnesota ex. rel. Pearson v. Probate Court, 309 U.S. 270 (1940).

Phenix A and S Sreenivasan. 2009. A practical guide for the evaluation of sexual recidivism risk in mentally retarded sex offenders. *Journal of the American Academy of Psychiatry and the Law* 37(4):509–524.

Sex Offender Civil Commitment Programs Network (SOCCPN). 2014. Annual Survey of Sex Offender Civil Commitment Programs.

Specht v. Patterson, 386 U.S. 605 (1967).

Sutherland EH. 1950. The diffusion of sexual psychopath laws. *American Journal of Sociology* 56:142–148.

Thibaut F, F de la Barra et al. 2010. The World Federation of Societies of Biological Psychiatry (WFSBP) guidelines for the biological treatment of paraphilias. *World Journal of Biological Psychiatry* 11:604–655.

Tucker D and S Brakel. 2012. DSM-5 paraphilic diagnoses and SVP law. *Archives of Sexual Behavior* 41(3):533.

U.S. v. Comstock, 560 U.S. 126 (2010).

Ward T, T Gannon, and P Yates. 2008. The treatment of offenders: Current practice and new developments with an emphasis on sex offenders. *International Review of Victimology* 15:183–208.

Wash. Rev. Code. Ann. §71.09.020(8) (West, 1992).

Willis G and R Grace. 2008. The quality of community reintegration planning for child molesters: Effects on sexual recidivism. *Sexual Abuse* 20(2):218–240.

81

Clinical assessment and treatment of sex offenders

JOHN BRADFORD, A.G. AHMED, AND SANJIV GULATI

INTRODUCTION

Although sexual behavior, partly expression of a basic biological drive (sex drive), is normal in most humans, it becomes problematic and criminal in nature in certain individuals. When this occurs, some of the most heinous crimes take place, and clinicians are often called on to provide opinions on the probable reason for and treatment of such aberrant behavior. Generally sex offenders are a complex and heterogeneous group of mostly male offenders, with varying types and severity of personality disorders and mental disorders including paraphilias and paraphilic disorders (American Psychiatric Association [APA] 2013) or more commonly multiple paraphilias (Bradford et al. 1992). A number of sex offenders do not have any paraphilia or paraphilic disorder or psychiatric diagnosis, but are convicted of sex crimes where they have failed to control their impulses or simply committed a crime categorized as a sexual offense by their culture or legal jurisdiction. This chapter examines the key aspects of clinical assessment and treatment available to both adult and adolescent sex offenders.

Sex offenders are individuals who commit sexual offenses and largely suffer from a sexual deviation or paraphilia. There are a number of sex offenders who do not have a paraphilia/paraphilic disorder but fail to control their sexual impulses for other reasons. Their sexual offending behavior may be opportunistic or impulsive, and most commonly is the result of serious personality disorders. Sexually deviant behavior can also occur secondary to various Axis 1 psychiatric conditions. The deviant sexual behavior in this instance would occur as a result of disinhibited behavior caused by the primary psychiatric condition (e.g., bipolar disorder). In these cases, the treatment of the sexual deviant behavior is through the treatment of the primary psychiatric disorder. Where the primary psychiatric problem is a serious personality disorder, the prognosis would be poor because of the inherent problems in the treatment of serious personality disorders. At the same time, there is a possibility that the symptoms of serious personality disorders such as impulsivity may respond to psychopharmacological treatment (Lee and Coccaro 2001). As there are these diagnostic issues to be resolved prior to a diagnosis of a paraphilia being made, a careful psychiatric evaluation needs to be completed.

For the first time in *Diagnostic and Statistical Manual of Mental Disorders*, 3rd edition (*DSM III*) the concept of erotic or sexual preference was recognized, and the sexual deviations were classified as paraphilias as opposed to personality disorders. This accepted the empirical evidence that individuals who were sexually deviant had an abnormal sexual or erotic preference.

The essential features of *Diagnostic and Statistical Manual of Mental Disorders*, 4th edition (*DSM IV*) diagnosis of a paraphilia are retained in *Diagnostic and Statistical Manual of Mental Disorders*, 5th edition (*DSM-5*) and include recurrent, intense sexually arousing fantasies, sexual urges, or behaviors generally involving (1) nonhuman objects, (2) the suffering or humiliation of oneself or one's partner, or (3) children or other nonconsenting persons, that occur over a period of at least 6 months (Criterion A). For some individuals, paraphilic fantasies or stimuli are obligatory for erotic arousal and are always included in sexual activity. In other cases, the paraphilic preferences occur only episodically (e.g., perhaps during periods of stress), whereas at other times the person is able to function sexually without paraphilic fantasies or stimuli. The behavior, sexual urges, or fantasies cause clinically significant stress or impairment in social, occupational, or other important areas of functioning (Criterion B) (APA 1994).

The *DSM-5* distinguishes paraphilia, a recurrent and intense sexual arousal to atypical objects or activities manifesting in the form of sexual fantasies, urges, or behavior, from paraphilic disorders (which is paraphilia accompanied by clinically significant distress or impairment). Consequently, establishing a diagnosis of paraphilia is not sufficient to diagnose paraphilic disorders.

DSM-5 described eight specific types of paraphilias: voyeuristic disorder (spying on unsuspecting strangers in normally private activities), exhibitionistic disorder (exposing the genitals to unsuspecting stranger), frotteuristic disorder (touching or rubbing against unconsenting person), sexual masochistic disorder (experiencing humiliation, bondage, or suffering), sexual sadism disorder (inflicting humiliation, bondage, or suffering), pedophilic disorder (preference for prepubescent children), fetishistic disorder (nongenital body parts or nonliving objects), and transvestic disorder (cross dressing). Other rare paraphilias are classified as other specified paraphilic disorder if the atypical sexual focus is known, or unspecified paraphilic disorder if the symptoms are characteristic of paraphilic disorder but the focus is unknown or the clinician chose not to specify.

A simple way of considering the spectrum of the paraphilias is to consider them as "hands-on" and "hands-off" paraphilias. The "hands-on" paraphilias involve some physical contact with either a consenting or a nonconsenting partner, and would include pedophilic disorder, sexual sadism, sexual masochism, and frotteurism. Zoophilia and necrophilia classified under the section "Other Specified Paraphilic Disorder" of *DSM-5* would also be included in this group. The "hands-off" paraphilias are the remaining paraphilias and include exhibitionism, voyeurism, fetishism, transvestitic fetishism, and the remaining paraphilias in the "Other Specified Paraphilic Disorder and Unspecified Paraphilic Disorder" grouping. There was an idea in the past that the presence of a "hands-off" paraphilia meant less concern than the presence of a "hands-on" paraphilia, but this is now rejected because of the well-documented crossover between the various paraphilias (Firestone et al. 2006). The primary paraphilia is simply to be regarded as a presentation of one aspect of a spectrum of paraphilic behaviors in any individual. Most often, this would overlap between "hands-on" and "hands-off" paraphilias.

ASSESSMENT

The treatment of sexual offenders therefore has to take all this into consideration, and means that a detailed and extensive assessment of sexual behaviors is necessary. As with other psychiatric conditions, the success of treatment is dependent on a detailed assessment to establish the correct psychiatric diagnosis. Most frequently, sexual offenders and others with paraphilias are evaluated in specialized sexual behaviors clinics (Bradford 1988, 2001). The comprehensive multimodal sexual behaviors clinic evaluation typically would consist of

1. A full psychiatric evaluation
2. A medical evaluation as necessary
3. A sex hormone profile and general biochemistry
4. Sexual questionnaires
5. Objective measures of sexual interest, specifically penile plethysmography and visual reaction time
6. Recidivism Risk Assessment

Table 81.1 describes the essential components of the evaluation and their purpose.

This baseline evaluation can be used to measure treatment outcome. The measures that are most sensitive to treatment outcome are the level of deviant arousal, the type and level of sexual fantasies, the levels of sex hormones in treatment with an anti-androgen medication, as well as cognitive distortions. There are sets of variables that are associated with an increased risk of recidivism (Hanson and Bussiere 1998). Positive treatment outcome with a reduction of sex offense recidivism is clearly the aim of the treatment.

The recidivism risk would be based on actuarial instruments such as the Psychopathy Checklist Revised Edition (Hare 1990); the Rapid Risk Assessment of Sexual Offender Recidivism (RRASOR) (Hanson 1997); Static 99 (Hanson and Thornton 1999); and various other actuarial instruments used to estimate the probability of recidivism. These instruments must be used with caution because of their limitations. Combining risk assessment tools does not improve accuracy of prediction in sex offender population. It may give the false impression that more is better. However, combining actuarial/static measure of risk with a dynamic measure (e.g., Static-99R with Stable 2007) may be complementary because each of the two measure different risk domains (Seto 2005).

TREATMENT

The treatment of sexual offenders includes both psychological and pharmacological treatments. Psychological treatments usually use a cognitive behavioral model and most commonly a relapse prevention approach. The two approaches complement each other and should be offered jointly.

Although there is no clear evidence that sexual offenders or paraphilic males have an increased sexual drive, in theory the principal aim of psychopharmacological treatment is the reduction in sexual drive (Turner et al. 2014). It is assumed that a reduction in sexual drive will result in a reduction in deviant sexual behavior (Bradford 1985; Kingston et al. 2012). Sexual drive is multidimensional and consists of sexual fantasies, sexual urges, and sexual behavior. In the case of a sexual deviation, the sexual fantasies and urges are mostly deviant in line with whatever paraphilia is present, although nondeviant fantasies are also present. The sexual urges and fantasies are in the direction of the erotic preference of the individual (for example, these would be toward young children in the case of pedophilia). The sexual drive can be eliminated to create an asexual individual who would have almost no sexual fantasies or sexual urges. With the increase in sophistication of psychopharmacological agents that can be used in the treatment of sexual offenders, it is now possible to titrate the level of sexual drive. At the same time, the sexual drive can be objectively monitored by sexual arousal testing, hormonal levels, and levels of sexual fantasies and measures of sexual behavior. This means that in most instances the sexual drive would be lowered only

Table 81.1 Purposes and essential elements of comprehensive evaluation of sex offenders

Elements	Purpose	Content/examples

Full psychiatric evaluation
• General psychopathology
  • Clinical history
  • Measure of comorbidity
• Specific psychopathology
  • Sexual history and functioning
  • Paraphilias
	Symptoms/criteria diagnostic clarification
	Sexual interests/fantasies
	Cognitive distortions and paraphilic interests
		• Symptom review
		• Paraphilia or paraphilic disorders
		• Co-occurring mental disorder
		• Co-occurring physical health
		• Forensic history including motives
		• Collateral history
		• Strengths/weakness/protective factors
		• Mental State Examination
		• Screening for substance use (e.g., MAST and DAST)
		• Personality assessment (e.g., MMPI)
		Self-rating/inventories:
		• Bradford Sexual History Inventory (BSHI)
		• Multidimensional Inventory of Development, Sex, and Aggression (MIDSA)
		• Clarke Sex History Questionnaire for Males-Revised (SHQ-R)
		• Multiphasic Sex Inventory (MSI)
		• Sexual Experience Survey (SES)
		• Severe Sexual Sadism Survey (SSSS)
		• Kurt Freund Paraphilia Scales
		Clinician rating:
		• Screening Scale for Pedophilic Interests (SSPI)

Biological evaluation
• General
  • Baseline workup
• Specific
  • Hormones
	Comorbidities and baseline status
	Sex hormones
		• Establish baseline Liver function test, thyroid function test, etc.
		• Establish a baseline for pharmacotherapy
		• Establish abnormal hormone levels are present and follow up

Psychophysiological evaluation • Phallometry • Viewing Time	Response to sexual stimuli	• Relative sexual arousal to atypical sexual focus or foci (children in pedophilia, sexual coercion and violence in rapists, sexual sadism, biastophilia)
Risk assessment • Clinical risk • Actuarial risk • Psychopathy	Measure of recidivism Measure of psychopathy	**High-risk recidivism clinical factors** • Youth, past sex offenses, extrafamiliar victims, stranger victims, noncontact offenses, male victims, multiple victims, past criminal records, anti-sociality, violation of parole, abnormal phallometrics • Static 99R/Static 2002R • Violent Risk Appraisal Guide-Revised (VRAG-R) • Violent Risk Appraisal Guide (VRAG)/Sex Offender Risk Appraisal Guide (SORAG) • Rapid Risk Assessment of Sexual Offender Recidivism (RRASOR) • Minnesota Sex Offender Screening Tool-Revised • Stable 2007 • HCR-20 • Child Pornography Offender Risk Tool (CPORT) (Child Pornography Offender only) • Hare Psychopathy Checklist-Revised (PCL-R)

partially to reduce deviant arousal and fantasies while enabling the individual to perform sexually in nondeviant situations. Ideally if a treatment were to be successful, the sexually deviant behavior would be completely suppressed while the normophilic (nondeviant behavior) would remain intact or even be enhanced (Bradford and Pawlak 1993a).

The pharmacological treatments of the paraphilias are well established (Bradford 2001), and this approach has been shown to be successful in all types of paraphilias. It is also arguably an economical approach to treatment as the paraphilias are usually present in multiple forms and a psychopharmacological treatment would suppress all of those paraphilias present. The psychopharmacological treatment of sexual offenders is focused on the paraphilias that are present.

BIOLOGY OF SEXUAL BEHAVIOR

Sex is a basic biological drive, and the psychopharmacological approach to the treatment of the paraphilias is based on this understanding.

Sexual behavior is affected by two types of hormones:

- Steroid hormones (e.g., estradiol, testosterone, and androstenedione) (Bancroft 2002, 2005; Krueger et al. 2009)
- Peptide hormones (e.g., gonadotropin-releasing hormone [GnRH],.gonadotropins, and prolactin) (Rubinow and Schmidt 1996; Owens et al. 2000; Bradford and Fedoroff 2009)

TREATMENT ALGORITHM

A treatment algorithm was developed by Bradford (Bradford 2000, 2001) based on the psychopharmacological effect on human sexual behavior by various drugs, as well as a clinical classification of the severity of the paraphilias. Sexual offenders with a paraphilia, (or a paraphilic disorder in *DSM-5*), would be eligible for psychopharmacological treatment based on this clinical algorithm. Paraphilia severity varies according to type, but it is clear that when victimization of third parties occurs, the condition is more serious than when there is no such victimization. As most sexual offenders have paraphilias/paraphilic disorders that involve the victimization of third parties, such a situation applies to this patient group. Clinical experience in evaluating and treating the paraphilias/paraphilic disorders is important in order to use this classification successfully, with primary paraphilia severity being classified as

- *Mild*: Exhibitionism, voyeurism, fetishism, "hands-off" paraphilias (with the proviso that comorbid paraphilias were also of a "hands-off" type), and mild cases of pedophilia (where deviant sexual fantasies and urges are present but no victimization). Deviant sexual preference as measured by sexual arousal tests would show pedophilic arousal, but not arousal to coercive or sexually sadistic stimuli.
- *Moderate*: "Hands-off" paraphilias where the control over sexual urges was poor and the risk of "hands-on" paraphilias was a concern. Exhibitionism where the target of the exhibitionistic behavior was a child would be an example. In "hands-on" cases such as pedophilia, there would be a low number of victims (less than three) and the level of victimization would be confined to fondling (no penetration). Sexual arousal testing would show a deviant sexual preference to pedophilia, but there would not be arousal to coercive stimuli or sexual sadism or clinical evidence of sadism being a problem.
- *Severe*: Only the "hands-on" paraphilias. This would be pedophilia with more than three victims and an increased level of intrusive sexual behavior beyond simple fondling, where there has been sexual penetration of the victim. There would be deviant sexual arousal to pedophilia on testing and there may be mild coercive arousal but no explicit evidence of sexual sadism in either testing or the clinical history.
- *Catastrophic*: Only "hands-on" paraphilias would be classified in this way. There would be clear evidence of sexual sadism, in terms of fantasies, urges, and behavior directed toward victims. There may not have been victimization, or victimization is denied but the consequences of victimization would be extreme such as death, or severe injury, and the level of control over deviant sexual impulses would be weak. If no victimization was present, there would be evidence of predatory stalking with homicidal urges and homicidal and torture fantasies. If victimization has occurred it would be severe in its degree of sexual and associated physical violence. Sexual arousal shows sexually sadistic arousal and high levels of coercive arousal toward either adults or children.

In order to use this classification guideline correctly, training in the paraphilias/paraphilic disorders is essential. This is because paradoxical situations arise where it would be difficult to classify sexual offenders. For example, a pedophile who only engaged in minor fondling (only outside of the clothes in a way that was made to look accidental) would be pedophilic toucherism (a variant of frotteurism). Although the numbers of victims may be higher than three, the condition would still be classified as moderate.

The algorithm of psychopharmacological treatment follows the classification of severity of the paraphilia in order to select the degree of intervention. The degree of psychopharmacological intervention would increase according to the severity of the paraphilia, with the highest level being equivalent to surgical castration. The aims of psychopharmacological treatment would be to

1. Suppress deviant sexual fantasies
2. Suppress deviant sexual urges and behavior
3. Reduce sexual offense recidivism

The algorithm for psychopharmacological treatment of the paraphilias is

- *Level 1*: Cognitive behavioral treatment; relapse prevention treatment would be always given regardless of the severity of paraphilia.
- *Level 2*: Pharmacological treatment would always start with selective serotonin reuptake inhibitors (SSRIs).
- *Level 3*: If SSRIs are not effective at adequate dose, then low dose of oral anti-androgen would be added (e.g., sertraline 200 mg p.o. daily and 50 mg MPA daily).
- *Level 4*: Full oral anti-androgen treatment (e.g., 50–300 mg MPA daily or 50–300 mg cyproterone acetate [CPA] daily).
- *Level 5*: Full anti-androgen treatment given intramuscularly (e.g., 300 mg MPA IMI every 1 to 4 weeks, or 200 mg CPA IMI every 2 weeks).
- *Level 6*: Complete androgen suppression due to CPA i.m. 200–300 mg per week, or a LHRH agonist (e.g., leuprolide acetate or goserelin acetate).

The impact of psychopharmacological intervention on sexual behavior at the various levels of the algorithm is as follows:

- *Level 2*: Suppression of deviant sexual fantasies, urges and behavior would occur, with a minor impact on overall sexual drive, allowing normal sexual activity to occur.
- *Level 2–3*: Suppression of deviant sexual fantasies, urges and behavior with a moderate reduction in sexual drive would be expected. Normal sexual behavior would occur, but at low level. A dose-dependent response would be expected.
- *Level 4–5*: Suppression of deviant sexual fantasies, urges and behavior with a severe reduction of sexual drive would be expected. Normal sexual behavior may occur, but at a very low level.
- *Level 6*: Complete suppression of sexual drive would be expected.

Subsequently, a Task Force of the World Federation of Societies of Biological Psychiatry published guidelines for the biological treatment of the paraphilias, specifically focusing on adult males (Thibaut et al. 2010). These guidelines were based on review of the scientific literature from 1969 to 2009 related to the pharmacological and biological treatment of sexual deviation, and also classified the literature according to an evidence-based scheme.

Each treatment was evaluated with respect to the strength of evidence for its efficacy, safety, tolerability, and feasibility. The described level of evidence was Level A, Level B, Level C, and Level D which were defined as the generally accepted definitions of an evidence-based approach to treatment (Thibaut et al. 2010).

The critical importance of the World Federation of Societies of Biological Psychiatry is that the pharmaceutical industry, in general terms, is not committed to having drugs approved for the treatment of paraphilias/paraphilic disorders (Bradford 1998). This means that most of the pharmaceutical agents used in their treatment are prescribed "off label." The World Federation review of the pharmacological treatment of sex offenders and people with paraphilias/paraphilic disorders based on evidence-based criteria is critical because it provides a justification for using these medications "off label."

The task force also in a more limited way reviewed the evidence for using general psychotropic medications, which is important when it comes to treating sexually deviant behavior associated with major psychiatric illness such as schizophrenia or bipolar disorder. The treatment of mentally abnormal sexual offenders would fall into this category. Unfortunately the level of evidence for the use of psychotropic drugs to reduce sexual drive is limited, with a lack of controlled studies, and would fall into a category of "No level of evidence or Good Clinical Practice." Nonetheless, using basic principles, the appropriate psychopharmacological treatment for psychosis can be modified to enhance sexual drive, reducing effects while still providing effective treatment for psychosis (Thibaut et al. 2010). Lithium carbonate, tricyclic anti-depressants, and anti-psychotics (thioridazine, haloperidol, and risperidone) have all been used in the past to suppress sex drive (Thibaut et al. 2010). Atypical anti-psychotics with activity at serotonin receptors could be selectively used in conjunction with the treatment of a major psychiatric illness with some degree of sex drive suppression indicated.

The Task Force also developed an algorithm of pharmacological treatment of the paraphilias/paraphilic disorders based on the review.

The algorithm is as follows:

Level 1:

- Aim: control of paraphiliac sexual fantasies, compulsions, and behaviors without impact on conventional sexual activity and on sexual drive
- Psychotherapy (preferentially cognitive behavioral therapy is available [Level C]: no level of evidence for other forms of psychotherapy)

Level 2:

- Aim: control of paraphiliac sexual fantasies, compulsions, and behaviors with minor impact on conventional sexual activity and on sexual desire
- May be used in all mild cases ("hands-off" paraphilia is with lower risk of sexual violence, i.e., exhibitionism without any risk of rape or pedophilia)
- No satisfactory results at Level I
- SSRIs: increase the dosage at the same level as prescribed in OCD (e.g., fluoxetine 40–60 mg/day or paroxetine 40 mg/day (Level C)

Level 3:

- Aim: control of paraphiliac sexual fantasies, compulsions, and behaviors with a moderate reduction of conventional sexual activity and sexual desire
- "Hands-on" paraphilias with fondling but without penetration

- Paraphiliac sexual fantasies without sexual sadism
- No satisfactory results at Level 2 after 4–6 weeks of SSRIs at high dosages
- Add a low dose of anti-androgen (e.g., cyproterone acetate 50–100 mg/day) to SSRIs (Level D)

Level 4:

- Aim: control of paraphiliac sexual fantasies, compulsions, and behaviors with a substantial reduction of sexual activity and desire
- Moderate and high risk of sexual violence (severe paraphilias with intrusive fondling with limited number of victims)
- No sexual sadism fantasies and/or behavior (if present: go to Level 5)
- Compliant patient, if not use IM form or go to Level 5
- No satisfactory results at Level 3
- First choice: full dosage of cyproterone acetate (CPA): oral, 200–300 mg/day or IM 200–400 mg once weekly or every 2 weeks; or medroxyprogesterone acetate: 50–300 mg/day if CPA not available (Level C)
- Possibility of comorbidity with anxiety, depressive, or obsessive-compulsive symptoms, then SSRIs might be associated with cyproterone acetate

Level 5:

- Aim: control of paraphiliac sexual fantasies, compulsions, and behaviors with an almost complete suppression of sexual desire and activity
- High risk of sexual violence and severe paraphilias
- Sexual Sadism fantasies and/or behavior or physical violence
- No satisfactory results at Level 3
- Long-acting GnRH agonists, i.e., triptorelin or leuprolide acetate 3 mg/month or 11.25 mg IM every 3 months (Level C)
- Testosterone levels measurements may be easily used to control the GnRH agonist treatment observance if necessary
- Cyproterone acetate may be associated with GnRH agonist treatment (1 week before and during the first month of GnRH) to prevent flare-up effects and to control the relapse risk of deviant sexual behavior associated with the flare-up effect

Level 6:

- Aim: control of paraphiliac sexual fantasies, compulsions, and behaviors with a complete suppression of sexual desire and activity
- Most severe paraphilias (catastrophic cases)
- No satisfactory results at Level 5
- Used anti-androgen treatment, i.e., cyproterone acetate (50–200 mg/day per os or 200–400 mg once weekly or every 2 weeks IM) or, medroxyprogesterone acetate (300–500 mg/week IM if CPA not available) in addition to GnRH agonists (Level D)
- Also may add SSRIs (No level of evidence) (Thibaut et al. 2010)

The psychopharmacological and psychological treatment of sexual offenders can fail or be undermined by the abuse of substances, disturbances in mood or the development of a concurrent psychiatric disorder, and noncompliance with the psychopharmacological treatment and associated cognitive behavioral treatment. As a result, close monitoring of the patient should be carried out, including

- Sex hormone monitoring in hormonal and anti-androgen treatment
- Random urine screening for substances; random breathalyzer monitoring for alcohol and possibly alcohol sensitization medication in high-risk cases
- Close psychiatric monitoring with fantasies checklists, sexual arousal tests
- Close psychiatric monitoring for the development of depression or other psychiatric disorders

SEXUAL OFFENDER RECIDIVISM

Historically, surgical castration had been used for the treatment of severe paraphilias, mostly sexual sadism and pedophilia, with those individuals who were castrated being high-risk, highly recidivating sexual offenders. Surgical castration resulted in a reduction of recidivism from over 60% to less than 5% in the majority of cases, as reported in several studies. Ultimately, it was the understanding of the biological mechanism by which surgical castration impacted deviant sexual behavior that drove the development of anti-androgen treatment for paraphilias.

A full review of sexual offender recidivism is beyond the scope of this chapter. However, a meta-analysis by Alexander (1997) reported that exhibitionists and pedophiles treated with psychological treatments had lower rates of recidivism than untreated controls. Studies of recidivism using the anti-androgen CPA over one to five years (when corrected for compliance and dosage) showed results similar to those achieved with surgical castration (Bradford 1995).

SELECTIVE SEROTONIN REUPTAKE INHIBITORS (SSRIS)

The treatment of paraphilias/paraphilic disorders has used drugs that affect serotonin (5HT) Basically, an increase in brain levels of 5HT reduces sexual drive and behavior. Although sexual behavior in humans is always regarded as being much more complicated than in animals, drugs affecting 5HT levels were regarded as useful to treat sexually deviant behavior by suppressing sexual drive (Greenberg and Bradford 1997).

A series of case reports starting in 1990 showed that SSRIs had an effect on deviant sexual behavior. Bradford et al. (1995) reported on a 12-week open-label dose-titrated study of pedophilia ($n = 20$) using sertraline, with the mean effective dosage being 131 mg/day. Some 86% of patients completed the study, and no patient was discontinued due to inadequate treatment response. A high proportion (86%)

of patients were rated as responders, with various sexual behaviors being significantly reduced during the duration of the study, while heterosexual coitus actually showed a small increase. Physiological measures of sexual arousal showed decreases in pedophilic arousal and improved or maintained normophilic arousal. This study showed evidence of improvement of normophilic behavior measured as both self-report and sexual arousal.

Greenberg et al. (1996) completed a retrospective comparison study with 3 serotonin reuptake inhibitors and found all of them had an effect on sexual drive, sexual fantasies and urges and none of them were superior to the other drugs. The drugs involved were fluoxetine, fluvoxamine, and sertraline. Later, Greenberg and Bradford (1997) compared paraphilic males ($n = 95$) treated with SSRIs to a control group ($n = 104$) who only received psychological treatment over a 12-week period. The SSRI-treated subjects showed a significant reduction in deviant sexual fantasies compared to those who received only psychotherapy.

The effectiveness of SSRIs in the treatment of sexual offenders requires further investigation, including the use of double-blind treatment. At the same time, the role of serotonin in sexual behaviors has been well established. As both the paraphilias and obsessive–compulsive disorder respond to SSRIs, it has been speculated that these two psychiatric conditions might have a similar basis, as well as certain similarities in their clinical characteristics. Indeed, it has been hypothesized that the paraphilias may be part of an obsessive–compulsive spectrum of disorders (Bradford 1999).

The SSRIs offer an approach to treatment that is useful for most paraphilic disorders of mild or moderate severity. The low side-effect profile and the lack of any hormonal effects, mean that they can be used to treat adolescent sexual offenders. This is important, as most paraphilias begin in adolescence with deviant sexual fantasies and urges, while the actual sexual acting starts later, mostly from the age of 20 years onward. Early diagnosis and treatment of the condition during adolescence can have a major impact on future victimization, and the SSRIs are playing an increasing role in this treatment approach.

HORMONAL AGENTS

The first psychopharmacological agents used to reduce sexual drive were estrogens, and clinical studies showed the treatment to be successful via the reduction of circulating testosterone. However, the adverse side effects of nausea, vomiting, and feminization were problematic and limited the use of estrogens.

Medroxyprogesterone acetate (MPA) has been the most widely used psychopharmacological agent for treatment of sexual offenders in the United States. Most studies have shown a positive treatment response of sexually deviant behavior to MPA.

The mechanism of action of MPA is via the induction of testosterone-alpha-reductase in the liver. This increases the metabolic clearance of testosterone, thereby reducing its plasma levels. MPA also has a progestinic effect that leads to a reduction in the secretion of gonadotropins. Moreover, MPA does not compete with androgen receptors at the receptor level, and so by definition is not a true anti-androgen (Southren et al. 1977). Treatment with MPA results in side effects, including weight gain, decreased sperm production, a hyperinsulinic response to a glucose load that might lead to potential problems in patients with diabetes mellitus, headaches, deep vein thrombosis, hot flushes, nausea, and vomiting—all of which can be managed medically. At the same time, a significant impact on sexual behavior was observed, including a reduction in sex drive, sexual fantasy, and sexual activity (Berlin and Meinecke 1981; Gagne 1981; Walker and Meyer 1981).

Clinic studies with MPA are mostly open trials. Initially, MPA was used in the treatment of paraphilic males. The two best-known open clinical studies were completed by Berlin and Meinecke (1981) and Gagne (1981). The two studies included about 70 patients, and each showed MPA to be effective treatment provided that the subjects were compliant with dosing as there was a tendency toward significant relapse rate if treatment was discontinued. Meyer et al. (1992) studied 40 men (mostly pedophiles) treated with MPA (400 mg per week, intramuscularly), and group and individual therapy followed-up for up to 12 years. A control group of 21 persons who were treatment refusers was included, and they were treated with psychotherapy over the same follow-up period. Some 18% reoffended while on MPA, and 35% reoffended after MPA was discontinued. In the control group, 58% relapsed, with raised baseline testosterone levels, head injury, and alcohol and substance abuse being factors associated with relapse.

MPA is a widely used psychopharmacological treatment with few reported serious side effects that could be a barrier to treatment, and the impact on recidivism has been shown in a number of studies, provided that the sexual offender remains on MPA. However, in long-term treatment with MPA with concomitant low levels of plasma testosterone, it is important to monitor for osteoporosis; at the earliest signs of osteopenia, both calcium and vitamin D supplements should be added to the treatment regimen.

LUTEINIZING HORMONE-RELEASING HORMONE AGONISTS

Luteinizing hormone-releasing hormone (LHRH) agonists have a specific treatment role in the paraphilias in that they produce a pharmacological "castration." The hypothalamic pituitary axis is overstimulated and is exhausted, and there is a significant inhibition of gonadotropin secretion. LHRH agonists have a prolonged action and may potentially be important in the future treatment of severe paraphilias. The potential use of these drugs to treat paraphilias was first described by Bradford (1985); since then limited clinical studies have been conducted on the use of LHRH agonists in this population.

The most important study to date in relation to the treatment of paraphilias with LHRH agonists was reported by Rosler and Witztum (1998). This was an uncontrolled open study of the treatment of 30 men who suffered from long-standing severe sexual deviation; 25 of the men experienced pedophilia. They were treated with monthly injections of 3.75 mg triptorelin and supportive psychotherapy for a follow-up period of 8–42 months, with treatment outcome being evaluated monthly by questionnaire. All of the men had a decrease in the number of deviant sexual fantasies and urges; quantitatively during therapy, this was reduced to zero. There was also a significant decrease in the number of deviant sexual interests to zero while receiving triptorelin. These effects were observed for at least 1 year in all ($n = 24$) who continued treatment for a year. The plasma testosterone levels fell to castration levels. Side effects were erectile failure, hot flushes, and decrease in bone mineral density. Briken et al. (2001) used leuprolide acetate over a 12-month period to treat sexually deviant males. There was a significant impact on sexually aggressive behavior as well as other sexual behavior. As with surgical castration, the risk of osteoporosis with treatment using a LHRH agonist is significant, and bone density studies should be conducted on an annual basis. Prophylactic treatment with vitamin D and a calcium supplement should be considered.

It is clear that LHRH agonists are going to play an increasingly important role in the treatment of sexual offenders in the future, and further research is needed when using these psychopharmacological agents. Although no outcome studies are available, the effects on available androgen are similar to what is seen in surgical castration. As a result, the outcome of long-term LHRH agonist treatment on sexual offender recidivism should be similar—if not identical—to the surgical castration studies, provided that the treatment is continuous.

LHRH analogues available for clinical use include leuprolide acetate, triptorelin (not available in the United States, but available shortly in Canada), and goserelin acetate.

ANTI-ANDROGENS

Cyproterone acetate (CPA) is a powerful anti-androgen that has been widely used in Canada and Europe, but is not available in the United States. It has anti-androgen, anti-gonadotropic, and also progestinic effects, and has a principal mode of action at androgen receptors throughout the body. It is a true anti-androgen as its mode of action is to block intracellular testosterone uptake and intracellular metabolism of the androgen (Liang et al. 1977). The effects of this medication are largely dose dependent, with sexual behavior decreasing because of a reduction in plasma testosterone as well as receptor blockade. This includes erections, masturbation, sexual intercourse, and deviant sexual behavior (Bradford 1985, 1995). CPA has strong progestational action (Schering 1983), and also blocks or reduces LHRH secretion (Neumann and Schleusener 1980). The full anti-gonadotropic effect of CPA is only seen in females, as in males the anti-androgen and anti-gonadotropic effects balance. The specific mode of action of CPA is competitive inhibition of testosterone and dihydrotestosterone at the androgen receptors. When given orally, CPA is 100% bioavailable and has a plasma half-life of 38 hours. In the intramuscular depot form, maximum plasma levels are typically reached in 82 hours (Neumann 1977; Schering 1983).

The side effects of CPA treatment are similar to those seen with MPA, and there is also a possibility of liver dysfunction and adrenal suppression (Bradford 1995). CPA is the most extensively studied pharmacological agent used to treat paraphilias, with the first clinical studies being conducted in Germany in 1971 in over 100 sexually deviant men (Laschet and Laschet 1971). The subjects were about 50% sexual offenders, and the duration of treatment in an open clinical trial ranged from 6 months to over 4 years. It was documented in 80% of cases that CPA (100 mg per day) eliminated sexual drive, erections, and orgasms, whereas a dose level of 50 mg per day caused a reduced libido but allowed erections to occur and some heterosexual and homosexual sexual behavior to continue weekly. In about 20% of exhibitionists, there was a complete elimination of all deviant sexual behavior, even after treatment was discontinued. This is not completely understood but could be the result of down-regulating androgen receptor sensitivity. Undesirable side effects documented in this study were fatigue, transient depression, weight gain, and some form of feminization including slight gynecomastia. In a subsequent study, Laschet and Laschet (1975) reported on 300 men treated for up to 8 years with an excellent treatment response, with minimal side effects in long-term management being reported. A number of other studies have all shown CPA as effective in reducing deviant sexual behavior. A double-blind placebo-controlled crossover study was completed by Bradford and Pawlak (1993a), while a similar study using CPA and evaluating the effect on the sexual arousal patterns of pedophiles was also reported by the same authors (Bradford and Pawlak 1993b). A single case study was also reported (Bradford and Pawlak 1987) that showed CPA to be an effective agent in the treatment of severe paraphilia—specifically sadistic sexually motivated homicide. In the double-blind, placebo-controlled crossover study of Bradford and Pawlak (1993b), 19 subjects (mostly pedophiles) were studied; all had high pre-treatment recidivism rates with a mean of 2.5 previous convictions per subject, and all met the *Diagnostic and Statistical Manual of Mental Disorders*, 3rd edition, revised (*DSM-III-R*) criteria for a paraphilia. CPA was administered orally in 3-month active treatment phases. There was a reduction in sexual arousal of responses by active drug, but this did not reach statistical significance. Self-report measures of arousal were all significantly reduced, while psychopathology measured by rating scales showed significant reductions, and self-reported sexual activity was significantly reduced. Other objective measures of sexuality including fantasies and masturbation were all significantly decreased by CPA (Bradford and Pawlak 1993a).

CPA is the only pharmacological intervention that has been subjected to research into treatment outcome and recidivism. A number of studies have shown CPA to be effective in reducing post-treatment recidivism rates (Bradford 1995).

Pre-treatment rates of recidivism ranged from 50% to 100%, and the post-treatment rate was 0% in follow-up periods ranging from 1 to 5 years, when adjusted for treatment compliance.

ADOLESCENT SEX OFFENDERS

Although adolescent sex offenders (ASOs) are estimated to account for 12.5% of all arrests for rape and 14% of all arrest for other sex offenses in the United States, there is a dearth of empirical research in this sex offender population (U.S. Department of Justice, Uniform Crime Report 2009). Pullman and Seto (2012) summarize the two perspectives to explain adolescent offending, namely, generalist (sexual offending as manifestation of generalized delinquency therefore not different from non-sex offenders) and specialist perspectives (they differ from other offenders), and therefore required specific assessment and treatment. Meta-analytic study of 3855 male adolescent sex offenders suggests both general anti-social orientation (criminal history anti-social personality, anti-social attitude and beliefs) and sexual deviance (atypical sexual interests, excessive sexual preoccupation, etc.) play similar roles among adolescent sex offenders, while the latter sets them apart from other adolescent offenders (Seto and Lalumiere 2010). Based on this they argue that evaluation of ASO recidivism risk should take into consideration both dimensions and, in keeping with the *Risk Needs Principles* (Andrews and Bonta 2010), this information should inform treatment and supervision intensity. As shown in Table 81.2, the assessment and treatment of adolescent sex offenders must be comprehensive and based on Risk-Need-Responsivity (RNR) principle for effective and efficient overall risk reduction, offender rehabilitation, and safe community.

The report of the World Federation of Societies of Biological Psychiatry Guidelines (WFSBP) for the treatment of adolescent sexual offenders with paraphilic disorders (Thibaut et al. 2016) concluded that in adolescents with paraphilic disorders, cognitive behavioral or multisystemic approaches to treatment should always be the first line of treatment. Furthermore, pharmacological interventions, when deemed necessary, should always be part of a more comprehensive treatment plan including psychological treatments. There are no medications approved for the treatment of adolescent sexual offenders, either in Europe or in North America, which means all pharmacological treatments

Table 81.2 Essential elements in ASO assessment and treatment

Elements	Indications
Elements of ASO assessment:	
Step 1: Assessing risk dimensions	
• Juvenile Sex Offender Protocol II (JSOAP) (Prentky and Righthand 2003) • Estimate of Risk of Adolescent Sexual Offense Recidivism (ERASOR) (Worling and Curwen 2001)	These two scales assess the General Antisocial Orientation and the Sexual Deviance risk dimensions.
Step 2: Evaluation of atypical sexual interests	
• Ask about atypical sexual interests (history or self-report questionnaire) • Sexual Fantasy Questionnaire and Sexual History Form for adolescents (Daleiden et al. 1998)	Identify • Risk to reoffend • Potential critical treatment needs
Step 3: Psychophysiological evaluation	
• Phallometry	• Limited but promising empirical data to support phallometry in the ASOs • Ethical concerns • Limited access
Elements of ASOs treatment	
• Multi Systemic Therapy (MST) (Bordin et al. 2009) • Community services • Functional family therapy	Family oriented, targeting multiple domains: • Family functioning • Social skills • Problem solving • Peer intervention • Academic achievement • Childhood adverse experience (e.g., sexual abuse, etc.) Usually include • Individual Cognitive Behaviour Therapy targeting atypical sexual arousal pattern, excessive sexual preoccupation • Substance use treatment

would be used off label. In general, the main-line treatment approaches for this age group would be cognitive behavioral treatments, family interventions, psychoeducational interventions, and the use of SSRIs. The use of anti-androgens is discouraged prior to age 17. The reason for this is that they could delay the onset of puberty or of bone growth. In fact adolescent sexual offenders need to be considered broadly in two groups based on age: those 18 years of age and older, and those 18 years of age and under (by implication, stage of puberty). For adolescents 18 years or older, the previously published guidelines would apply. For adolescents less than 18 years of age, two groups should be considered: Group I between 12 and 16 years of age; and Group II, 17 and 18 years of age. Group I would still be in an active developmental stage of puberty (between Tanner stages III and V). As part of the psychiatric evaluation, prior to pharmacological treatment, the assessment of the stage of puberty needs to be completed through hormonal levels, x-rays looking at epiphyseal closure, and consultation with a pediatric endocrinologist. This group could be treated with SSRIs taking into consideration the U.S. Food and Drug Administration safety warnings, indicating that the use of anti-depressants may increase the risk of suicidality in youths. In Group II (Tanner stage V) psychological treatments must always be the first line of treatment. If the Tanner V stage is reached, then the adolescent should go through the same evaluation of severity in the WFSBP adult guidelines, and if pharmacological treatment is necessary, the adult guidelines could be followed (Thibaut et al. 2010, 2016). In cases of Tanner IV or below considerations may be given to anti-androgen treatment, but this would have to be at the advice of an expert in adolescent endocrinology. It would also depend on the severity of the risk.

SUMMARY

The psychopharmacological treatment of sexual deviation has a sound basis in the neurobiology of sexual behavior. Compared to other psychopharmacological treatments in psychiatry, more is known of the actual mechanisms of action in these psychopharmacological agents used in the treatment of paraphilias/paraphilic disorders. There is considerable knowledge of the effects of serotonin on sexual behavior in both animal research and clinical studies in men with paraphilias and hypersexuality, as well as treatment of other psychiatric conditions. The anti-androgen and hormonal treatments (CPA, MPA, and LHRH agonists) also have a sound scientific basis in the neuroendocrinology and endocrinology of sexual behavior. The differential effect on sexual arousal patterns documented with CPA and sertraline is a fascinating research finding in both practical and neurobiological terms (Bradford and Pawlak 1987, 1993a,b; Fedoroff et al. 2015). The ideal treatment outcome with a normalization of sexual preference in sexually deviant males is supported by this research finding. The major problem when using the psychopharmacological treatment approach in sexual offenders has been the lack of government and pharmaceutical industry support for research, and this has led to there being a lack of double-blind placebo-controlled studies. Further significant ethical barriers exist because of the risk to third parties, and this has made double-blind, placebo-controlled studies very difficult to complete in sexually deviant men. Moreover, most psycho-pharmacological agents are used in off-label indications. Nonetheless, despite these difficulties, this is an important treatment approach and, when combined with cognitive behavioral treatment and relapse prevention, provides a very powerful tool for the treatment and rehabilitation of sexual offenders.

Further research is clearly needed in all the pharmacological agents, but particularly in the case of SSRIs and LHRH agonists. Interesting future research opportunities are likely to arise when drugs that are highly specific to serotonin subreceptors are developed (e.g., the 5HT1a receptor). This could mean a clinical "mapping" of the behaviors associated with pharmacological activity at a specific receptor, and would mirror research that has been carried out in animals, where sexual behavior is subreceptor-specific in some species.

SUMMARY KEY POINTS

- Very detailed sexual behaviors assessment protocols are available which include objective measures of sexual interest.
- The neurobiology/neurochemistry of sexual behavior is relatively well established in humans and well understood in animal research.
- There is considerable research available into many aspects of deviant sex behavior including assessment, treatment, recidivism, and treatment outcome.
- Well-established, evidence-based pharmacological treatment is available for the treatment of paraphilias/paraphilic disorders in adults. This includes the World Federation of Societies of Biological Psychiatry Task Force Report.
- Recently, treatment guidelines for the treatment of adolescent sexual offenders have been published by the World Federation of Societies of Biological Psychiatry.
- Further research is necessary in the neurochemistry of sexual behavior and the pharmacological treatment of deviant sex behavior.

REFERENCES

Alexander MA. 1997. *Sexual Offender Treatment Probed ANGW.* Madison: Wisconsin Department of Corrections Sex Offender Treatment Program.

American Psychiatric Association (APA). 1994. *Diagnostic and Statistical Manual of Mental Disorders*, 4th edition. Washington, DC: APA.

American Psychiatric Association (APA). 2013. *Diagnostic and Statistical Manual of Mental Disorders*, 5th edition. Washington DC: APA.

Andrews DA and J Bonta. 2010. Rehabilitation through the lens of the risk-needs responsibly model. In *Offenders Supervision: New Directions in Theory, Research and Practice*, edited by F McNeil, P Raynor, and C Trotter. Cullompton, UK: Willan Publishing, 19–40.

Bancroft J. 2002. Biological factors in human sexuality. *Journal of Sex Research* 39(1):15–21.

Bancroft J. 2005. The endocrinology of sexual arousal. *Journal of Endocrinology* 186(3):411–427.

Berlin FS and CF Meinecke. 1981. Treatment of sex offenders with antiandrogenic medication: Conceptualisation, review of treatment modalities and preliminary findings. *American Journal of Psychiatry* 138:601–607.

Bradford JM. 1988. Organic treatment for the male sexual offender. *Annual New York Academy of Science* 528:193–202.

Bradford JMW. 1985. Organic treatments for the male sexual offender. *Behavioral Sciences and the Law* 3:355–375.

Bradford JMW. 1995. Pharmacological treatment of the paraphilias. In *Review of Psychiatry.* Vol. 14., edited by JM Oldham and M Riba, Washington, DC: American Psychiatric Press, 755–778.

Bradford JMW. 1998. Treatment of men with paraphilia. *New England Journal of Medicine* 338:464–465.

Bradford JMW. 1999. The paraphilias, obsessive-compulsive spectrum disorder and the treatment of sexually deviant behaviour. *Psychiatric Quarterly* 70:209–220.

Bradford JMW. 2000. The treatment of sexual deviation using a pharmacological approach. *Journal of Sex Research* 37:248–257.

Bradford JMW. 2001. The neurobiology, neuropharmacology and pharmacological treatment of the paraphilias and compulsive sexual behaviour. *Canadian Journal of Psychiatry* 46:26–34.

Bradford JM and JP Fedoroff. 2009. The neurobiology of sexual behaviour and the paraphilias. In *Sex Offenders: Identification, Risk Assessment, Treatment, and Legal Issues*, edited by FM Saleh, AJ Grudzinkas, Jr, JM Bradford, and DJ Brodsky, New York: Oxford University Press, 36–48.

Bradford JMW and A Pawlak. 1987. Sadistic homosexual pedophilia: Treatment with cyproterone acetate. A single case study. *Canadian Journal of Psychiatry* 32:22–31.

Bradford JMW and A Pawlak. 1993a. Effects of cyproterone acetate on sexual arousal patterns of pedophiles. *Archives of Sexual Behavior* 22:629–641.

Bradford JMW and A Pawlak. 1993b. Double-blind placebo crossover study of cyproterone acetate in the treatment of the paraphilias. *Archives of Sexual Behaviour* 22:383–402.

Bradford JMW, J Boulet, and A Pawlak. 1992. The paraphilias: A multiplicity of deviant behaviours. *Canadian Journal of Psychiatry* 37:104–108.

Bradford JMW, D Greenberg, J Gojer, JJ Martindale, and M Goldberg. 1995. *Sertraline in the Treatment of Pedophilia: An Open Label Study.* New Research Program Abstracts #441; American Psychiatric Association Meeting, Florida, May 24, 1995.

Briken P, E Nika, and W Brener. 2001. Treatment of paraphilias with luteinizing hormone-releasing hormone agonists. *Journal of Sex and Marital Therapy* 27:45–55.

Daleiden EL, KL Kaufman, DR Helliker, and JN O'Neill. 1998. The sexual histories and fantasies of useful males: A comparison of sexual offending, nonsexual offending, and non-offending groups. *Sexual Abuse: A Journal of Research and Treatment* 10:195–200.

Fedoroff JP, S Curry, K Muller, R Ranger, and J Bradford. 2015. Evidence that arousal to pedophilic stimuli can change: Response to Bailey, Cantor and Lalumière. *Archives of Sexual Behavior* 44(1):259–263.

Firestone P, DA Kingston, A Wexler, and JM Bradford. 2006. Long-term follow-up of exhibitionists: Psychological, phallometric and offence characteristics. *Journal of the American Academy of Psychiatry and the Law* 34(3):349–359.

Gagne P. 1981. Treatment of sex offenders with medroxyprogesterone acetate. *American Journal of Psychiatry* 138:644–646.

Greenberg DM and JMW Bradford. 1997. Treatment of the paraphilic disorders: A review of the role of the selective serotonin reuptake inhibitors. *Sexual Abuse: A Journal of Research and Treatment* 9:349–361.

Greenberg DM, JMW Bradford, S Curry, and A O'Rourke. 1996. A comparison of treatment of paraphilias with 3 serotonin reuptake inhibitors: A retrospective study. *Bulletin of the American Academy of Psychiatry and the Law* 24(4):525–532.

Hanson RK. 1997. *The Development of a Brief Actuarial Scale for Sexual Offence Recidivism* (User report 97–04). Ottawa, ON: Department of the Solicitor General of Canada.

Hanson RK and MT Bussiere. 1998. Predicting relapse: Meta-analysis of sexual offender recidivism studies. *Journal of Consulting and Clinical Psychology* 66:348–362.

Hanson RK and D Thornton. 1999. *Static 99: Improving Actuarial Risk Assessment for Sex Offenders*

(User report 99–02). Ottawa, ON: Department of the Solicitor General of Canada.

Hare RD. 1990. *The Hare Psychopathy Checklist—Revised.* Toronto, ON: Multi-Health Systems.

Kingston DA, MC Seto, AG Ahmed, P Fedoroff, P Firestone, and JM Bradford. 2012. The role of central and peripheral hormones in sexual and violent recidivism in sex offenders. *Journal of the American Academy of Psychiatry and the Law* 40(4):476–485.

Krueger RB, MH Wechsler, and MS Kaplan. 2009. Orchidectomy. In *Sex Offenders: Identification, Risk Assessment, Treatment, and Legal Issues*, edited by FM Saleh, AJ Grudzinskas Jr, JM Bradford, and DJ Brodsky, New York: Oxford University Press, 171–188.

Laschet U and L Laschet. 1971. Psychopharmacotherapy of sex offenders with cyproterone acetate. *Pharmakopsychiatrie Neuropsychopharmakologic* 4:99–104.

Laschet U and L Laschet. 1975. Antiandrogens in the treatment of sexual deviations of men. *Journal of Steroid Biochemistry* 6:821–826.

Lee R and E Coccaro. 2001. The neuropsychopharmacology of criminality and aggression. *Canadian Journal of Psychiatry* 46:35–44.

Liang T, JL Tymoczko, and KMB Chan. 1977. Androgen action: Receptors and rapid responses. In *Androgens and Antiandrogens*, edited by L Martini and M Motta, New York: Raven Press, 77–89.

Meyer WJ, C Collier, and E Emory. 1992. Depo Provera treatment for sex offending behavior: An evaluation of outcome. *Bulletin of the American Academy of Psychiatry and the Law* 20:249–259.

Neumann F. 1977. Pharmacology and potential use of cyproterone acetate. *Hormone and Metabolic Research* 9:1–13.

Neumann F and A Schleusener. 1980. Pharmacology of cyproterone acetate with special reference to the skin. In *The Pharmacology of Cyproterone Acetate, Combined Antiandrogen–Estrogen Therapy. Dermatology Proceedings of Dianne Symposium*, edited by R Vokoer and D Fanta, Brussels, 19–51.

Owens MJ, CB Nemeroff, and G Bissette. 2000. Neuropeptides: Biology and regulation. In *Comprehensive Textbook of Psychiatry*, edited by BJ Sadock and VA Sadock, Philadelphia: Lippincott Williams and Wilkins, 60–71.

Prentky RA and S Righthand. 2003. Juvenile Sex Offender Assessment Protocol-II (J-Soap-II). Manual. NCJ 202316. Office of Juvenile Justice and Delinquency Prevention's Juvenile Justice Clearinghouse, USA. https://www.ncjrs.gov/pdffiles 1/ojjdp/202316.pdf.

Pullman L and MC Seto. 2012. Assessment and treatment of adolescent sexual offenders, implications of recent research on generalist versus specialist. *Child Abuse and Neglect* 36(3):203–239.

Rosler A and E Witztum. 1998. Treatment of men with paraphilia with a long acting analogue of gonadotropin-releasing hormone. *New England Journal of Medicine* 338:416–465.

Rubinow DR and PJ Schmidt. 1996. Androgens, brain and behavior. *American Journal of Psychiatry* 153:974–984.

Schering AG. 1983. *Androcur.* Berlin, Germany: Berlin/Bergkamen.

Seto M. 2005. Is more better? Combining actuarial risk scales to predict recidivism among adult sex offenders. *Psychological Assessment* 17:156–167.

Seto MC and ML Lalumière. 2010. What is so special about male adolescent sexual offending? A review and test of explanations using meta-analysis. *Psychological Bulletin* 136:526–575.

Southren AL, GG Gordon, J Vittek, and K Altman. 1977. Effect of progestagens on androgen metabolism. In *Androgens and Antiandrogens*, edited by L Martini and M Motta, New York: Raven Press, 263–279.

Thibaut F, F de la Barra, H Gordon, P Cosyns, and JM Bradford, and the WFSBP Task Force on Sexual Disorders. 2010. The World Federation of Societies of Biological Psychiatry (WFSBP) Guidelines for the Biological Treatment of Paraphilias. *World Journal of Biological Psychiatry* 11(4):604–655.

Thibaut F, JMW Bradford, P Briken, F de la Barra, F Häßler, and P Cosyns, on behalf of the WFSBP Task Force on Sexual Disorders. 2016. The World Federation of Societies of Biological Psychiatry (WFSBP) Guidelines for the Treatment of Adolescent Sexual Offenders with Paraphilic Disorders. *World Journal of Biological Psychiatry* 17:2–38.

Turner D, D Schottle, J Bradford, and P Briken. 2014. Assessment methods and management of hypersexuality and paraphilic disorders. *Current Opinion in Psychiatry* 27(6):413–422.

U.S. Department of Justice, Uniform Crime Report. 2009. Crime in the United States – Federal Bureau of Investigation, September 2010. http://www2.fbi.gov.

Walker PA and WJ Meyer. 1981. Medroxyprogesterone acetate treatment for paraphiliac sex offenders. In *Violence and the Violent Individual*, edited by JR Hays, TK Roberts, and KS Solway, New York: SP Medical and Scientific Books, 353–373.

Worling JR and T Curwen. 2001. Estimate of risk of adolescent sexual offence recidivism (ERASOR; Version 2.0). In *Juvenile's and Children Who Sexually Abuse: Frameworks for Assessment*, edited by MC Calder. Dorset, UK: Russell House Publishing, 372–397.

82

Torture and psychiatric abuse: Definition, ethics, and assessment

RYAN C.W. HALL AND RICHARD C.W. HALL

INTRODUCTION

Premum non nocere ("first do no harm") has been a tenet of medicine since the days of antiquity. That tenet can become a gray area, especially during times of war, armed conflict, terrorism, and police investigations, where the line between appropriate information gathering/interrogation is crossed and torture begins. The Nuremberg trials of the mid-twentieth century clarified what is and is not the acceptable practice of medicine during times of war, and to whom the physician owes a duty (e.g., the individual, the population, the state) (Trial of War Criminals before the Nuremberg Military Tribunals Under Control Council Law No. 10, II; Vesti et al. 1998, 185). Unfortunately, post-9/11 conflicts have again raised ethical concerns about the physician's role in what is and what is not torture, legitimate interrogation, forensic interviewing, and psychiatric abuse (Pope 2011, 158).

Besides the ethical issues related to torture, there are practical implications of how a forensic psychiatrist might become involved in a legal case of an individual who has been tortured. It is estimated that more than half the countries in the world engage in some form of torture, which results in accusations of torture being raised in many legal settings, such as immigration/asylum cases, human rights cases, civil compensation for acts committed, and the production of false confessions (Istanbul Protocol 2004, 3; Campbell 2007, 628; Carinci et al. 2010, 73; Hall 2012, 446; Pope 2012, 418). Conducting an evaluation on an individual who has been tortured produces its own challenges and implications separate and distinct from those seen in the usual criminal or civil forensic assessment. The examiner needs to understand the common forms of torture, the regional politics where the event occurred, and the unique transference issues such cases produce (Boehnlein et al. 1998, 173; PHR 2001; 35, 75–78; Istanbul Protocol 2004, 25, 50; IRCT 2012, 17–22; Pope 2012, 419, 422).

PSYCHIATRIC ETHICS AND PSYCHIATRIC ABUSE

A brief review of general psychiatric ethics and potential abuse is important because concerns that a psychiatrist encounters in clinical practice, such as confidentiality, agency, inappropriate relationships, interactions with colleagues, and appropriateness of a diagnosis, take on a new significance in the context of torture. (See Table 82.1.)

In general, the American Psychiatric Association (APA) refers psychiatrists to the American Medical Association's (AMA) Medical Code of Ethics as the primary source of medical ethics. The APA also maintains an addendum to the AMA code of ethics entitled, "The Principles of Medical Ethics with Annotations Especially Applicable to Psychiatry." As noted in the preamble, "A [Psychiatrist] must recognize responsibility to patients first and foremost, as well as to society, to other health professionals, and to self" (APA 2013, 2). Critical elements of psychiatric ethics are providing competent professional medical care with compassion and respect for human dignity and rights; not engaging in professionally dishonest or fraudulent behavior; reporting those who do engage in professionally dishonest or fraudulent behavior; respecting the law while at the same time "seek[ing] changes" in those requirements which run contrary to patients' best interests; and an ethical need to "safeguard patient confidences and privacy within the constraints of the law" (APA 2013, 2).

Ideally, physicians should be able to self-regulate/monitor to prevent abuses, but physicians have to also acknowledge that they may have blind spots for when a boundary crossing or violation has occurred or is occurring. General suggestions to reduce the risk of occurrence are maintaining healthy professional relationships (e.g., professional society involvement, supervision, relationship with trusted confidante); avoiding occupational burnout (e.g., maintaining healthy lifestyle, time away, variation in work patterns); being aware of vulnerable times in one's life (e.g., divorce or unhappy marriage

Table 82.1 Types of psychiatric abuse

Types of psychiatric abuse
Violating confidentiality
Inappropriate publishing of information for psychiatrist's benefit
Inappropriate release of information to family, third party, government, or press
Conducting inappropriate relationships with patients
Sexual relationship with current or former patient
Sexual relationship between supervisor/trainee, which can affect supervision of patient
Exploitative for psychiatrist's personal gain
Not informing patient of potential conflicts of interest at start of treatment or when conflict arises
Entering into therapeutic supervisory relationship with other professionals' (e.g., counselor) without actually performing appropriate supervision or review
Conducting evaluations under false pretenses
To obtain a confession
To obtain information for nontreatment purposes such as reprisals
To conduct research without appropriate informed consent
Violating fiduciary responsibility to patient
Treatment decisions for third-party payers' interest rather than patient's
Inappropriately using psychiatric knowledge
Intentionally misdiagnosing a patient to result in confinement, loss of job, discrediting of the individual, loss of rights, limiting of compensation, or to protect others
Intentionally misdiagnosing a patient to benefit the patient, such as disability assessment, civil litigation, avoidance of military service, avoidance of punishment
Making public statements about public/private figures without evaluation and release
Engaging in evaluations that one is not qualified for based on training, education, and experience
Participating in a legally authorized execution
Participating in torture
Providing treatment based on psychiatrist's personal political motivation
Diagnosing and treating to silence political dissent

potentially resulting in higher likelihood of sexual boundary violation); recognizing signs of transference (e.g., strong emotions elicited by a patient); and periodically trying to self-assess potential personal biases (e.g., cultural, religious, political) and how those affect interactions with their patients.

When psychiatric abuse occurs, depending on the severity and clarity of the situation, there may be several avenues to obtain ethical guidance both for the individual who recognizes he or she has committed an abuse and for the observer who has witnessed it, such as institutional committees or professional organizations. As noted in many ethics guidelines, abuses are to be reported to appropriate authorities—which may include professional organizations, state or national medical boards, or governmental departments. In cases of systemic or governmental sanctioned abuses, nongovernmental organizations (NGOs) such as Amnesty International or world governing bodies such as the United Nations or the International Court may also be appropriate avenues for reporting.

DEFINING TORTURE

In the post-9/11 world, various definitions and interpretations of what is or is not torture exist. Common to most definitions is that the act is intentional, that there is an imbalance of power, and that there is the infliction of pain and suffering to a severe degree (Campbell 2007, 630; BCRHHR 2013, 14). This creates a sense of extreme helplessness that leads to a decline in cognitive, emotional, and behavioral functioning (Istanbul Protocol 2004, 45).

Torture is defined by the 1984 UN Convention Against Torture (CAT) as

> [A]ny act by which severe pain or suffering, whether physical or mental, is intentionally inflicted on a person for such purposes as obtaining from him or a third person information or a confession, punishing him for an act he or a third person has committed or is suspected of having committed, or intimidating or coercing him or a third person, or for any reason based on discrimination of any kind, when such pain or suffering is inflicted by or at the instigation of or with the consent or acquiescence of a public official or other person acting in an official capacity. It does not include pain or suffering arising only from, inherent in, or incidental to lawful sanctions. (CAT 1984, Article 1 part 1)

The UN further clarifies that "Torture constitutes an aggravated and deliberate form of cruel, inhuman, or degrading treatment or punishment" as well as being based on all other relevant international instruments (Table 82.2),

Table 82.2 National and international declarations regarding torture that provide definitions and legal frameworks

- Nuremberg Trials (Law No. 10 International Military Tribunal) (1946–1949)
- Article 55 of the Universal Declaration of Human Rights (1948)
- Geneva Convention (1949)
  - Wounded and sick in the field
  - Wounded, sick, and shipwreck at sea
  - Prisoners of war
  - Civilians under foreign power during time of war
- European Convention for the Protection of Human Rights and Fundamental Freedoms (1953)
- UN Article 7 International Covenant on Civil and Political Rights (1966)
- UN Declaration on the Protection of All Persons from Being Subjected to Torture and Other Cruel, Inhuman or Degrading Treatment or Punishment (1975)
- [Intra]American Convention on Human Rights (1978)
- African Charter of Human and Peoples' Rights (1981)
- UN Convention Against Torture [CAT] (1984)
- European Convention for the Prevention of Torture and Inhuman or Degrading Treatment or Punishment (1989)
- Rome Statute of the International Criminal Court (1998)
- U.S. Government Torture Victims Relief Act (1998)

and that "It does not include...lawful sanctions to the extent consistent with the Standard Minimum Rules for the Treatment of Prisoners" (Istanbul Protocol 2004, 1).

Torture committed with the intention of destroying national, ethnic, racial, or religious groups may also be considered an act of genocide (BCRHHR 2013, 15). Under these conditions, the 1998 Rome Statute of the International Criminal Court gives the international court jurisdiction over potential torture cases committed as part of a widespread or systematic attack on a group, or as a war crime under the Geneva Conventions of 1949 and Law Number 10 of the International Military Tribunal used at Nuremberg (Istanbul Protocol 2004, 3, 10). The international court can also claim jurisdiction in cases where the state/government is unable or unwilling to prosecute individuals responsible for torture (Istanbul Protocol 2004, 10).

The United States, in 18 U.S.C. §2340, defines torture as "an act committed by a person acting under the color of law, specifically intended to inflict severe physical or mental pain or suffering (other than pain or suffering incidental to lawful sanctions) upon another person within his custody or physical control" (18 U.S.C. Chapter 113c, Torture). Specifically important to psychiatrists is the further definition of "severe mental pain or suffering," which is defined as the prolonged mental harm caused by or resulting from:

> (A) the intentional infliction or threatened infliction of severe physical pain or suffering; (B) the administration or application, or threatened administration or application, of mind-altering substances or other procedures calculated to disrupt profoundly the senses or the personality; (C) the threat of imminent death; or (D) the threat that another person will imminently be subjected to death, severe physical pain or suffering, or the administration or application of mind-altering substances or other procedures calculated to disrupt profoundly the senses or personality. (18 U.S.C. Chapter 113c, Torture)

ENHANCED INTERROGATION

After 9/11, the wording in 18 U.S.C. §2340 was debated, especially as applied to techniques that became known as "enhanced integrations." A legal justification for use of enhanced interrogation techniques such as waterboarding, sleep deprivation, sensory deprivation, sensory overload, and stress positions was put forth by Jay Bybee in 2002 in a document that became known as the "interrogation opinion" and is part of a larger body of communication known as the "torture memos" (Bybee 2002; Bradbury 2009). In the interrogation opinion, it was argued that although enhanced integration may "generally intend," it did not "specifically intend" to inflict severe physical pain (e.g., equivalent in intensity to the pain accompanying serious physical injury, such as organ failure, impairment of bodily function, or even death) or mental pain (significant psychological harm of significant duration) (Bybee 2002; Bradbury 2009). In 2009, by executive order and a Department of Justice review, opinions issued by the Office of Legal Counsel in regard to interrogations between 2001 and 2009 were withdrawn, superseded, and revoked (Bradbury 2009; Executive Order 13491).

THE PROHIBITED ROLE OF PHYSICIANS IN TORTURE

The World Medical Association (WMA) Declaration of Tokyo 1975 states "physicians shall not countenance, condone or participate in the practice of torture or other forms of cruel, inhuman or degrading procedures" (WMA 2006). This is similar to the World Psychiatric Association's position in the 1977 declaration of Hawaii, which prohibits the misuse of psychiatric skills as stated:

> The psychiatrist must never use his professional possibilities to violate the dignity or human rights of any individual or group and should never let inappropriate personal desires, feelings, prejudices or beliefs interfere with the treatment. The psychiatrist must on no account utilize the tools of his profession, once the absence of psychiatric illness has been established. If a patient or some third party demands actions contrary to scientific knowledge or ethical principles, the psychiatrist must refuse to cooperate. (WPA 1983)

In the United States, the AMA's position on torture is "Physicians must oppose and must not participate in torture for any reason" (AMA Opinion 2.067 Torture). Participation in torture includes, but is not limited to, "providing or withholding any services, substances, or knowledge to facilitate the practice of torture. Physicians must not be present when torture is used or threatened." The withholding of services becomes a potential double bind for physicians, since treatment may lead to a reduction of suffering, but at the same time can result in someone being made strong enough to undergo additional torture. The AMA acknowledges this with the statement that "Physicians may treat prisoners or detainees if doing so is in their best interest, but physicians should not treat individuals to verify their health so that torture can begin or continue." The AMA further encourages that "Physicians who treat torture victims should not be persecuted," which supports physicians who, in good faith, work in confinement situations and also those who treat the victims of torture after release.

The American Psychiatric Association and the American Psychological Association issued a joint position statement against torture in 1985 (Joint Resolution 1985). In 2006, the American Psychiatric Association issued an additional Position Statement on Psychiatric Participation in Interrogation of Detainees (APA 2006). As used in this statement, "interrogation" refers to a deliberate attempt to elicit information from a detainee for the purposes of incriminating the detainee, identifying other persons who have committed or may be planning to commit acts of violence or other crimes, or otherwise obtaining information that is believed to be of value for criminal justice or national security purposes. It does not include interviews or other interactions with a detainee that have been appropriately authorized by a court or by counsel for the detainee or that are conducted by or on behalf of correctional authorities with a prisoner serving a criminal sentence.

Much like the AMA, WMA, and WPA, it is stated, "Psychiatrists should not participate in, or otherwise assist or facilitate, the commission of torture of any person." It is stipulated that "Psychiatrists who become aware that torture has occurred, is occurring, or has been planned must report it promptly to a person or persons in a position to take corrective action." In addition, sections that are particularly important for a forensic psychiatrist to be aware of include the following:

> No psychiatrist should participate directly in the interrogation of persons held in custody by military or civilian investigative or law enforcement authorities, whether in the United States or elsewhere. Direct participation includes being present in the interrogation room, asking or suggesting questions, or advising authorities on the use of specific techniques of interrogation with particular detainees. However, psychiatrists may provide training to military or civilian investigative or law enforcement personnel on recognizing and responding to persons with mental illnesses, on the possible medical and psychological effects of particular techniques and conditions of interrogation, and on other areas within their professional expertise. (APA 2006)

Although the American Psychological Association is against "torture," there was debate regarding what was permissible involvement in activities such as "enhanced interrogations" (Vasquez 2011). In 2008, the American Psychological Association clarified its statement on torture to be, "Any direct or indirect participation in any act of torture or other forms of cruel, degrading, or inhuman treatment or punishment by psychologists is strictly prohibited" (Kazdin 2008; American Psychological Association 2013). The American Psychological Association specifically identified acts such as waterboarding, sexual humiliation, stress positions, and exploitation of phobias as torture (Kazdin 2008; American Psychological Association 2013).

INAPPROPRIATE WAYS IN WHICH PHYSICIANS CAN BE INVOLVED IN TORTURE

The UN's Manual on Effective Investigation and Documentation of Torture and Other Cruel, Inhuman, or Degrading Treatment or Punishment (AKA Istanbul Protocol) defines physicians' "participation in torture" as follows:

> Evaluating an individual's capacity to withstand ill-treatment; being present at, supervising, or inflicting maltreatment; resuscitating individuals for the purposes of further maltreatment or providing medical treatment immediately before, during, or after torture on the instructions of those likely to be responsible for it; providing

> professional knowledge or individuals' personal health information to torturers; and intentionally neglecting evidence and falsifying reports, such as autopsy reports and death certificates. (Istanbul Protocol 2004, 12)

In general, the fundamental ethics of health care are that actions taken to evaluate, protect, and improve a prisoner's/detainee's health are permissible and encouraged (Istanbul Protocol 2004, 12). Action taken to protect a detainee's health, even if it goes against his or her wishes, such as reporting suicidality, is ethical, but action taken to facilitate punishment or torture is not ethical (Istanbul Protocol 2004, 14–15). Steps physicians can take, especially if they are in a dual-agency situation (e.g., doctor working in a detention facility), to reduce potential ethics violations are as follows: (1) Identify themselves and the potential dual-agency role with the detainee (e.g., detainee's health and safety but also health and safety of others, such as staff and other detainees). (2) Clearly explain the purpose of an evaluation or treatment. (3) Contractually try to maintain professional independence and clinical judgments. (4) Maintain the confidentiality of medical records. (5) Identify and report abuse at the time it occurs or at the earliest time one becomes aware of it and it is safe to do so (e.g., delayed reporting to avoid reprisals against the individual already tortured) (Istanbul Protocol 2004, 13–15).

PHYSICAL ASSESSMENT OF TORTURE

Torture is subdivided into physical, mental, or sexual categories; however, classifying the type may be an academic exercise because many victims suffer multiple forms (Table 82.3) (Carinci et al. 2010, 74; Pope 2012, 419; BCRHHR 2013, 18).

The two most common forms of torture are beatings and threats (Carinci et al. 2010, 74–75; BCRHHR 2013, 18). Depending on the situation under which torture occurs, there may or may not be physical marks. Some who engage in the act will want to leave scars and permanent reminders as warnings to the victims and others. Some who engage in torture may want to inflict pain without leaving physical evidence, which may later result in unwanted investigations (BCRHHR 2013, 18). This may result in beatings taking place with wide blunt objects such as the proverbial rubber hose, or with cloth covering the sites such as thin-soled shoes when beating the feet to limit lacerations (Istanbul Protocol 2004, 31; BCRHHR 2013, 18). These methods may become important factually when conducting the interview of a victim of torture in order to try and determine if the perpetrators were brazen in their conduct and potentially to understand the victim's mentality of being marked or worried if others will believe their accounts without physical marks. In addition, they highlight the need for investigators to understand the common forms of torture, such as water or electrical methods, and ways to maximize the discomfort

Table 82.3 Common forms of torture

- Trauma
  - Beatings (truncheon, sticks, blunt objects)
  - Whippings (wire, cords, whips)
  - Blunt force injuries (punches, kicks, forced falls/drops)
  - Falanga (aka Falaka, Bastinad) beating bottoms of feet
  - Crush injuries (use of hammer on joints/fingers/bones, pliers on genitals)
- Penetrating injuries/disfigurement
  - Cuts
  - Amputations
  - Scarring
  - Items under fingernails
- Burns
  - Heated instruments (cigarettes, hot metal)
  - Fire
  - Scalding liquid
  - Caustic substance (acid, pepper extract)
- Forced positions
  - Suspensions/stretching
    - Cross suspension (tying hands to horizontal bar)
    - Butchery suspension (hanging hands above head)
    - Reverse butchery suspension (feet tied upward/head downward)
    - "Palestinian" suspension (forearms behind the back, with elbows flexed 90° tied to a horizontal bar or tied around the elbows or wrists with the arms behind the back
    - "Parrot perch" suspension (flexed knees from a bar passed below the popliteal region
  - Prolonged constraint
  - Subject to extreme conditions (hot/cold)
- Electrical shocks
- Asphyxiation
  - Strangling
  - Dry asphyxiation (plastic bag over head, smothering)
  - Wet asphyxiation (drowning)
  - Chemicals making it difficult to breathe
- Sexual torture
  - Rape
  - Genital mutilation
  - Irritants (pepper extract, chemicals) on mucus membranes
  - Forced nakedness
- Mental torture
  - Sensory deprivation (isolation, forced bonding with abuser)
  - Direct threats
  - Watching or forced participation in torturing others (family, friends, other detainees)
  - Mock executions
  - Humiliation
- Medical torture
  - Medications (sedation, paralytics)
  - Enucleation
- Violation of social taboos (e.g., sex, violation of dietary laws)

while minimizing the apparent damage by using conducting gels or wet towels (Istanbul Protocol 2004, 40; Carinci et al. 2010, 75). This is why many experts on torture recommend that resources such as the Istanbul Protocol are consulted prior to doing interviews and that one receives training on the topic and familiarizes oneself with common forms of regional tortures. For a more detailed discussion on types of tortures, injuries produced, and marks left, the reader is referred to the Istanbul Protocol, Chapter 5 (Istanbul Protocol 2004, 33–44).

PSYCHIATRIC EFFECTS OF TORTURE ON THE INDIVIDUAL

Torture has numerous physical and psychological effects not only on the individual who experienced it but also on his or her family (e.g., elevated rate of divorce, higher familial rates of mental illness) (Istanbul Protocol 2004, 45; Campbell 2007, 634). The common psychiatric conditions that occur in people who have been tortured include posttraumatic stress disorder (PTSD), depression, and anxiety disorders (Basoglu 1993, 609; PHR 2001, 65; Campbell 2007, 633; Wenzel 2007, 491; NMA 2014). These patients often present with symptoms of diminshed affect, insomnia, avoidance, and memory difficulties (Istanbul Protocol 2004, 45–58; Campbell 2007, 633; Błaż-Kapusta 2008, 5). International literature on torture also refers to the International Classification of Diseases (*ICD*) *10* (2004) diagnosis of Enduring Change of Personality after Catastrophic Experience (F62.0), which is a definite, significant, and persistent change in an individual's pattern of perceiving, relating to, or thinking about the environment and oneself associated with inflexible and maladaptive behaviors not present before the traumatic experience (Norwegian Medical Association 2014). In addition, some of the literature on torture also refers to "complex PTSD" and "Disorders After Extreme Stress NOS" (DESNOS), which are both concepts not currently recognized in *Diagnostic and Statistical Manual of Mental Disorders*, 5th edition (*DSM-5*), but are thought to be a special form of stress sequellae or subset of PTSD (Błaż-Kapusta 2008, 5–6; Carinci et al. 2010, 76; NWA 2014).

Although PTSD and depression are the two most frequent psychiatric disorders found in suvivors of torture, not everyone who has experienced torture will necessarily develop a psychiatric disorder (Basoglu 1993, 609; PHR 2001, 64; Istanbul Protocol 2004, 45). Debate sometimes occurs if certain behaviors are symptoms of mental illness versus being appropriate adaptive/protective responses (e.g., increased vigilance or social isolation during confinement) (Istanbul Protocol 2004, 45; McHugh and Treisman 2007, 212). Poor coping mechanisms such as substance use develop in many victums of torture (PHR 2001, 80). In addition, many people who have been tortured suffer from neurocognitive disorders such as traumatic brain injury and trauma-induced epilepsy (PHR 2001, 86–88; Istanbul Protocol 2004, 55–56; Williams and Amris 2007, 6). This may make it difficult to determine the exact cause of common symptoms such as impaired concentration, memory, executive function, and/or apathy. Neurological damage and deficits can also occur from malnutration (e.g., vitamin B_1, B_6, B_{12} deficiency), forced ingestion of toxic substances, and hypoxia caused by suffocation or drowning (PHR 2001, 43; Istanbul Protocol 2004, 55; Williams and Amris 2007, 6).

In addition, many individuals who have been tortured also present with somatic symptoms including headaches, gastrointestinal complaints, back/muscle pain, and sexual dysfunction (PHR 2001, 68; Istanbul Protocol 2004, 34; Wenzel 2007, 491; Williams and Amris 2007, 5; Carinci et al. 2010, 76; Williams et al. 2010, 718–719; NMA 2014). At times, it may be difficult to tell if these symptoms are due to actual physical trauma (e.g., physical damage to genitalia, chronic pain syndrome related to nerve plexis damage from suspension) or are psychosomatic in origin (Carinci et al. 2010, 75; Williams et al. 2010, 719). Depending on the geographic origin of the person who has been tortured, symptoms may be due to causes such as endemic parasitic infections (e.g., tapeworms, brain parasites) that the evaluator may not normally consider (Pope 2012, 422).

CONDUCTING AN INTERVIEW

Most forensic interviews of individuals who have been tortured seek to obtain specific information related to the torture. (See Table 82.4.) This information can be used for determining compensation, immigration status, future health-care needs, and as the basis for criminal prosecution of others. For that reason, information that should be included in the report includes the circumstances of the interview (e.g., where it occurred, who was present, its purpose), the specifics of the maltreatment (e.g., methods of torture or ill treatment, triggers for the maltreatment, the time when torture or ill treatment was alleged to have occurred, and who was involved or responsible for the maltreatment), and the examinee's physical and psychological symptom/exam findings including supporting documentation (e.g., lab results, x-rays, photos) (PHR 2001, 95–102; Istanbul Protocol 2004, 49–54; Pope 2012, 421; BCRHHR 2013, 62).

It needs to be noted that individuals who have been tortured may have limited knowledge or ability to recount information about their experiences for a multitude of reasons including sensory deprivation (blindfolds), being drugged, loss of consciousness during the torture, or brain damage. Therefore, it may be helpful to ask about all sensory modalities including smell, touch, and taste to help aid in memory retrieval (Istanbul Protocol 2004, 21). They may also lack trust in the evaluator or be fearful that revealing information might jeopardize their safety or the safety of others (Williams and Amris 2007, 6). Psychological factors such as memory loss related to PTSD or coping mechanisms such as denial or avoidance can also limit the amount of information discussed (Campbell 2007, 631). Cultural factors may also limit evaluees from discussing sensitive topics such as sexual abuse (PHR 2001, 33, 54; Istanbul Protocol 2004, 29).

Table 82.4 General information to obtain in an interview regarding torture

1. Circumstances leading up to detention/torture (activities, how detained)
2. Circumstances of detainment facility (food, water, toilets, showers, isolation/crowded, access to family or others outside)
3. Dates and times of the torture including first and last event
4. If exact dates not known, ways individual used to keep track of time and events
5. Locations (may be more than one) where occurred (e.g., detention center, jail/prison, unknown location)
6. Number of times or frequency of torture
7. Types of torture
8. Number and type of people present (e.g., guards, soldiers, police, unknown) including other detainees
9. Objects used and if so how (restraints, car battery, chairs, sticks, medical equipment)
10. Duration of time for which each event occurred (hours, until passed out)
11. Condition at end of session (able to walk, needed to be carried, passed out, how long was affected)
12. Any routine or changes in the routine (new types of experiences, new people)
13. Injuries received at time and current affects
14. Any medical treatment received and by whom
15. Information person was told (no one knows you are here, no one will believe you) or asked about
16. Description of people involved at any stage (e.g., name, rank, organization, sex, distinguishing marks, or mannerisms)

When doing a forensic evaluation on an individual who has been tortured, many of the tenets of a standard forensic psychiatric evaluation still apply, such as identifying oneself, revealing who requested the evaluation, explaining the purpose of the interview, defining the limits of confidentiality, and conducting the interview in as confidential a manner as possible (e.g., no guards in the room or out of earshot at the very least) (PHR 2001, 19–25; Istanbul Protocol 2004, 45–46; IRCT 2012, 14–16; Pope 2012, 419). These interviews can take place under two very broad conditions, either while the person is still confined or post-confinement. If done during periods of confinement, it is highly recommended that individuals performing these types of evaluations have additional training, supervision, and engage in such evaluations as part of a sanctioned team or organization (PHR 2001, 21; Istanbul Protocol 2004, 19, 27; IRCT 2012, 20; BCRHHR 2013, 41). These precautions may protect both the evaluators' and evaluees' safety. If evaluations are done during periods of confinement, the evaluator should plan for multiple interviews if possible to develop rapport, obtain more complete information, and help verify the safety of the evaluee after the initial contact (PHR 2001, 23–25; Istanbul Protocol 2004, 9; IRCT 2012, 24; NMA 2014).

The evalvator may need to make some changes from his or her usual style of interview to help gain the trust of the evaluee and to put him or her at ease. For example, when conducting an interview with someone who has been tortured, extra care needs to be taken to ensure that the individual does not feel like he or she is being "re-interrogated" (PHR 2001, 34–35; Istanbul Protocol 2004, 50; IRCT 2012, 19). To prevent this feeling, standard courtesies are a good place to start but may take on even more significance. For example, starting on time is more important than for most interviews, because many victims of torture are left waiting before a torture session to increase their sense of helplessness, uncertainty, and fear (Istanbul Protocol 2004, 25–27, 50; Pope 2012, 421). Allowing the evaluee to have some control of the interview such as being able to take breaks when he or she wants, stopping the interview to be continued another day, and being able to decline answering questions is important to help distinguish between past interrogations and the current interview (Istanbul Protocol 2004, 50–51). Traditional "emotionally neutral" styles of psychotherapeutic interviews should generally be avoided with survivors of torture, because it may remind evaluees of being interrogated by a cold authority figure, or alternatively that he or she is not being believed (Istanbul Protocol 2004, 50). The interview should not be rushed to avoid recreating past interview scenarios where rapid questions or other pressure techniques were used. Use of open-ended questions that allow the person to tell his or her story is important, as well as allowing the person some latitude in the intial topics discussed, such as superficial or seemingly unrelated topics (e.g., sports, holidays, happier times) to gain comfort. The evaluator should try to avoid leading questions, where possible. For example, an open-ended nonleading question would be "what happened to you?" or "what was your experience at xxx location?" rather than "were you tortured at XXX location?" (Istanbul Protocol 2004, 34).

At times, evaluators may need to ask questions in a tactful or face-saving way. For example, some people may be ashamed of what they did, admitted to, or for having implicated others. For that reason, it may be better to approch topics from a positive perspective, such as asking, "How did your release come about?" instead of "How did you stop the torture?" Other open-ended questions include, "Why do you think you were detained?" or "Why do you think it happened?" This approach may allow the evaluator to obtain information about what activity the individual was involved in, such as political causes, without asking about ideology.

Some individuals who have been tortured may find it difficult to talk about the torture, but may be more willing to indicate what happened to them in writing or using a checklist/questionnaire. Depending on the nature and location of the interview, an evaluator may want to use these types of instruments (Istanbul Protocol 2004, 53; Campbell 2007, 631; IRCT 2012, 20).

It is important to remember that, although the subject of the interview may be different from a standard forensic evalution, it should still be an objective forensic interview (Istanbul Protocol 2004, 18, 26, 50; IRCT 2012, 15, 17). Some guidelines suggest that the evaluator present himself or herself as an advocate for the evaluee. Care needs to be taken with this approach because it may result in the evaluee becoming suspicious of the evaluator's motives or fearful that he or she will overexpose himself or herself. In addition, the evaluee may assume a greater degree of safety than the evaluator can actually provide after the interview ends (PHR 2001, 23, 24; Istanbul Protocol 2004, 50–52; IRCT 2012, 19).

The evaluator should not overidentify with the individual who is alleging torture. Overidentification can result in important fact-finding questions not being asked, inconsistencies not being identified or addressed, and the alleged version of events not being carefully evaluated (PHR 2001, 31–32, 75–78; Istanbul Protocol 2004, 51; IRCT 2012, 20; Pope 2012, 419). In addition, overidentification can lead to countertransference issues, resulting in the evaluator becoming emotionally distraught or detached (Boehnlein et al. 1998, 174–175; PHR 2001, 75–78; Istanbul Protocol 2004, 51; IRCT 2012, 26; Pope 2012, 419). Either reaction can affect the quality of the forensic interview.

Although torture does occur, false allegations of torture and abuse also occur (Hall and Hall 2001, 343; Istanbul Protocol 2004, 53–54). Evaluators should try to determine if the physical and psychological findings are consistent with the alleged torture. False allegations of torture or exaggerations of minor incidents (e.g., circumstances under which pepper spray or forced extraction from cell was used) may be borne out of a desire for personal gain (e.g., gaining asylum), for political reasons, for revenge, and/or to hide crimes committed by the evaluee (Hall and Hall 2001, 345; Istanbul Protocol 2004, 54). In addition, especially with individuals with psychotic symptoms, it is important to confirm that claims being made are not just paranoid delusions. This is why, when possible, it is useful to confirm information using multiple sources (e.g., State Department reports, UN reports, Amnesty International reports, Human Rights Watch, other victims from same location) (Allodi 1998, 97; PHR 2001, 37, 100; Istanbul Protocol 2004, 25; IRCT 2012, 17; Pope 2012, 422).

Professional interpreters should be used when the evaluee speaks a different language (PHR 2001, 32; Istanbul Protocol 2004, 30; IRCT 2012, 20). Family should not be used to translate because victims may diminish their experiences to prevent loved ones from being exposed to the details (IRCT 2012; 20; Pope 2012, 420). In addition, families may not report accurately what happened in an attempt to preserve family honor. The evaluator needs to inform the interpreter of the unque challenges of this type of interview (IRCT 2012, 20). It is also important to assess the evaluee's comfort with the interpreter or if the evaluee is worried that information given could lead to reprisals. This is often more of a concern when the interpreter comes from the evaluee's native geographic region. It is usually best to use someone who is not native to where the alleged events took place, but at the same time is familiar with the dialect and customs.

For more in-depth references or general information on how to conduct an examination of an individual who has been tortured, the reader is referred to the Resources in Table 82.5.

Table 82.5 Resources

1. A Health Professional's Guide to Medical and Psychological Evaluations of Torture. Physicians for Human Rights (PHR) 2001
2. Boston Center for Refugee Health and Human Rights (BCRHHC)
3. National Consortium of Torture Treatment Providers
4. The International Rehabilitation Council for Torture Victims (IRTC)
5. United Nations: Istanbul Protocol (1999, updated 2004): Manual for the Effective Investigation and Documentation of Torture
6. The Center for Victims of Torture
7. Canadian Center for Victims of Torture
8. Amnesty International
9. Human Rights Watch
10. The Office of the United Nations High Commissioner for Human Rights (OHCHR)
11. The Norwegian Medical Association (NMA) Doctors Working in Prison: Human Rights and Ethical Dilemmas free course

SUMMARY KEY POINTS

- The act of torture violates domestic and international laws.
- Physician participation in acts of torture violates professional ethics and is a form of medical/psychiatric abuse.
- Forensic psychiatrists may be asked to conduct an evaluation on a survivor of torture for various legal/forensic concerns, such as asylum hearings, criminal investigations, and civil compensation actions.
- Special accommodations and style of questioning may need to be used when interviewing an alleged victim of torture to obtain needed information and limit or prevent retraumatization.
- Although special considerations may be needed for the interview, it still needs to be objective in nature, and the evaluator needs to be aware of potentially negative countertranference, which can be harmful to the evaluator and the evaluee.

REFERENCES

18 U.S.C. Chapter 113C, TORTURE. https://www.law.cornell.edu/uscode/text/18/part-I/chapter-113C, accessed June 27, 2016.

Allodi F. 1998. The physician's role in assessment and treatment of torture survivors. In *Caring for Victims of Torture*, edited by J Jaranson and M Popkin, Washington, DC: American Psychiatric Press, 89–106.

American Medical Association (AMA). 1999. *Opinion 2.067 Torture. Code of Medical Ethics and Current Opinions.* http://www.ama-assn.org//ama/pub/physician-resources/medical-ethics/code-medical-ethics/opinion2067.page, accessed September 6, 2014.

American Psychiatric Association (APA). 2006. *Position Statement on Psychiatric Participation in Interrogation of Detainees.* https://www.psychiatry.org/File%20Library/About-APA/Organization-Documents-Policies/Policies/Position-2014-Interrogation-Detainees-Psychiatric-Participation.pdf, accessed June 27, 2016.

American Psychiatric Association (APA). 2013. *The Principles of Medical Ethics with Annotations Especially Applicable to Psychiatry, 2013 edition.* https://www.psychiatry.org/File%20Library/Psychiatrists/Practice/Ethics/principles-medical-ethics.pdf, accessed June 27, 2016.

American Psychological Association (APA). 2013. *Position on Ethics and Interrogations.* http://www.apa.org/ethics/programs/position/, accessed September 7, 2014.

Basoglu M. 1993. Prevention of torture and care of survivors: An integrated approach. *Journal of the American Medical Association* 270:606–611.

Błaż-Kapusta B. 2008. Disorders of extreme stress not otherwise specified (DESNOS)—A case study. *Archives of Psychiatry and Psychotherapy* 2:5–11.

Boehnlein JK, DJ Kinzie, and PK Leung. 1998. Countertransference and ethical principles for treatment of torture survivors. In *Caring for Victims of Torture*, edited by J Jaranson and M Popkin, Washington, DC: American Psychiatric Press, 173–184.

Boston Center for Refugee Health and Human Rights (BCRHHR). 2013. *Caring for Torture Survivors Online Course.* http://media.wix.com/ugd/074eac_37bc4160e7e045e7adc1422bf1183672.pdf, accessed June 27, 2016.

Bradbury SG. 2009. *Memorandum for the Files from Steven G. Bradbury, Principal Deputy Assistant Attorney General, Re: Status of Certain OLC Opinions Issued in the Aftermath of the Terrorist Attacks of September 11, 2001.* http://www.justice.gov/opa/documents/memostatusolcopinions01152009.pdf, accessed September 8, 2014.

Bybee J. 2002. *Memorandum for Alberto R. Gonzales Counsel to the President Re. Standards of Conduct for Interrogation under 18 U.S.C. §§ 2340-2340A. August 1, 2002.* http://fl1.findlaw.com/news.findlaw.com/wp/docs/doj/bybee80102mem.pdf, accessed September, 7, 2014.

Campbell T. 2007. Psychological assessment, diagnosis, and treatment of torture survivors: A review. *Clinical Psychology Review* 27:628–641.

Carinci AJ, P Mehta, and PJ Christo. 2010. Chronic pain in torture victims. *Pain Headache Reports* 14:73–79.

Convention against Torture (CAT) and Other Cruel, Inhuman or Degrading Treatment or Punishment Adopted and Opened for Signature, Ratification and Accession by General Assembly Resolution 39/46 of 10 December 1984 Entry into Force 26 June 1987, in Accordance with Article 27 (1). http://www.ohchr.org/Documents/ProfessionalInterest/cat.pdf, accessed September 6, 2014.

Executive Order 13491—Ensuring Lawful Interrogations. http://www.whitehouse.gov/the-press-office/ensuring-lawful-interrogations, accessed September 6, 2014.

Hall RCW. 2012. Civil war. In *Encyclopedia of Immigrant Health*, edited by S Loue and M Sajatovic, New York: Springer, 445–447.

Hall RCW and RCW Hall. 2001. False allegations: The role of the forensic psychiatrist. *Journal of Psychiatric Practice* 7:343–346.

ICD 10. 2004. *"Chapter V. Mental and Behavioral Disorders (F00-F99)" in Disorders of Adult Personality and Behavior (F60-F69).* Geneva: World Health Organization. http://apps.who.int/classifications/apps/icd/icd10online2004/fr-icd.htm?gf60.html, accessed September 7, 2014.

International Rehabilitation Council for Torture Victims (IRCT). 2012. *Forensic Examination Missions by Medical Teams Investigating and Documenting Alleged Cases of Torture.* http://www.irct.org/Admin/Public/DWSDownload.aspx?File=%2fFiles%2fFiler%2fpublications%2fOperational-Manual-EN-10.02.12.pdf, accessed September 8, 2014.

Joint Resolution Against Torture of the American Psychiatric Association and the American Psychological Association Approved by the Board of Trustees, December 1985, Reaffirmed, 2007. https://www.psychiatry.org/File%20Library/About-APA/Organization-Documents-Policies/Policies/Position-2014-Torture.pdf, accessed June 27, 2016.

Kazdin A. 2008. *APA Letter to Bush: New Policy Limits Psychologist Involvement in Interrogations: Prohibits Psychologist Participation in Interrogations at Unlawful Detention Sites October 2, 2008.* http://www.apa.org/news/press/releases/bush-interrogations.pdf, accessed September 7, 2014.

Manual on the Effective Investigation and Documentation of Torture and Other Cruel, Inhuman or Degrading Treatment or Punishment ["Istanbul Protocol, Rev 1"]. 2004. UN Office of the High Commissioner for Human Rights, New York and Geneva. http://www.ohchr.org/Documents/Publications/training8Rev1en.pdf, accessed September 6, 2014.

McHugh PR and G Treisman. 2007. PTSD: A problematic diagnostic category. *Journal of Anxiety Disorders* 21:211–222.

Norwegian Medical Association (NMA). Updated 2014. *Doctors Working in Prisons Human Rights and Ethical Dilemma. Chapter 10: Medical Signs of Torture.* https://nettkurs.legeforeningen.no/mod/lesson/view.php?id=1447, accessed March 14, 2015.

Physicians for Human Rights (PHR). 2001. *Examining Asylum Seekers: A Health Professional's Guide to Medical and Psychological Evaluations of Torture.* http://www.capda.ca/docs/resources/physicians-for-human-rights-examining-asylum-seekers-a-health-professional's-guide-to-medical-and-psychological-evaluations-of-torture.pdf?sfvrsn=4, accessed June 27, 2016.

Pope KS. 2011. Are the American Psychological Association's Detainee Interrogation Policies Ethical and Effective?: Key Claims, Documents, and Results. *Zeitschrift für Psychologie* 219:150–158.

Pope KS. 2012. Psychological assessment of torture survivors: Essential, avoidable errors, and helpful resources. *International Journal of Law and Psychiatry* 35:418–426.

Trial of War Criminals before the Nuremberg Military Tribunals under Control Council Law No. 10. Volume II. Nuremberg October 1946–April 1949. http://www.loc.gov/rr/frd/Military_Law/pdf/NT_war-criminals_Vol-II.pdf, accessed September 7, 2014.

Vasquez M. 2011. *APA Response to Letter from Psychologists for an Ethical APA.* http://www.apa.org/news/press/statements/ethical-psychologist.pdf, accessed September 7, 2014.

Vesti P, K Helweg-Larsen, and M Kastrup. 1998. Preventing the involvement of physicians in torture. In *Caring for Victims of Torture*, edited by J Jaranson and M Popkin, Washington, DC: American Psychiatric Press, 185–202.

Wenzel T. 2007. Torture. *Current Opinions in Psychiatry* 20:491–496.

Williams AC and K Amris. 2007 Pain from torture. *Pain* 133:5–8.

Williams AC, CR Peña, and AS Rice. 2010. Persistent pain in survivors of torture: A cohort study. *Journal of Pain Symptom Management* 40:715–722.

World Medical Association (WMA). 1975, Updated 2006. *World Medical Association Declaration of Tokyo: Guidelines for Physicians Concerning Torture and other Cruel, Inhuman or Degrading Treatment or Punishment in Relation to Detention and Imprisonment.* http://www.wma.net/en/30publications/10policies/c18/index.html, accessed September 7, 2014.

World Psychiatric Association (WPA). 1977, Updated 1983. *The Declaration of Hawaii. Adopted in 1977 at the Sixth World Congress of Psychiatry in Honolulu, Hawaii.* http://www.codex.vr.se/texts/hawaii.html, accessed September 7, 2014.

83

Health care and the courts

GREGORY DAVIS

INTRODUCTION

On March 23, 2010, the Patient Protection and Affordable Care Act (ACA), commonly known as "Obamacare," was signed into law. The law was aimed at providing a form of universal health care in the United States by increasing access to coverage, improving quality and affordability of health insurance, and controlling health-care costs. The ACA sought to achieve these goals through a combination of employer and individual mandates, state and individual subsidies, expansion of public programs, and insurance exchanges. It represents the most significant legislative overhaul of the U.S. health-care system since the passage of Medicare and Medicaid in 1965. With the provisions of the ACA taking effect gradually from 2010 to 2020, outcome measures will be closely scrutinized by the public as well as both major political parties.

This chapter focuses on the provisions of the ACA itself, arguments for why universal health care is thought to be needed in the United States, an overview of the history of universal health care and politics leading to the passage of the ACA, legal challenges, and ramifications as the ACA is implemented throughout the United States.

ARGUMENTS FOR UNIVERSAL HEALTH CARE

Most industrialized countries have some form of universal health care. Canada and the United States had similar health-care systems in the early 1960s; however, Canada now has a universal single-payer health-care system. The Canadian government is committed to providing public funding support if their provinces abide by the guidelines of the Canada Health Act of 1984, which requires universal coverage for medically necessary care of all insured persons. In the United Kingdom necessary health care is provided for free to all permanent residents (NHS Constitution of England 2013). Together with Turkey, the United States is one of two members of the Organization for Economic Co-operation and Development (OECD) that do not have some form of universal health-care coverage (Carey et al. 2009).

The World Health Organization (WHO) ranked the health-care systems of 191 member states in their World Health Report in 2000 (Musgrove et al. 2000). The United States ranked 37th while its expenditure per capita was ranked first. The rankings were based on an index of life expectancy, fair financial contribution, and responsiveness of the health-care system. The OECD has also compared life expectancy versus spending. Data from 2008 indicated that the United States was grossly disproportionate in regard to per capita spending when compared to other member countries. For example, in 2008 the United States spent over \$7000 per capita on health care with a life expectancy of around 78 years. In contrast, Canada spent over \$4000 per capita with a life expectancy of almost 81 years. Despite a variety of health-care delivery systems, all OECD countries group near Canada on a predictable cost versus life expectancy curve, with the United States as the sole outlier with significantly higher expenditure and little increased life expectancy in return (OECD 2010).

According to the U.S. Census Bureau, 15.3% of U.S. citizens or 45.7 million were uninsured in 2007 (DeNavas-Walt et al. 2007). When compared to Canada, a study in 2006 estimated that U.S. residents were significantly less likely to have a regular medical doctor and more likely to forgo needed medications and have unmet health needs. Uninsured Americans were even less likely to receive needed care (Lasser et al. 2006, 1). Delaying medical care increases illness and costs overall. One study estimated that half of personal bankruptcies involved medical bills (Himmelstein et al. 2005, 63). In 2011, health care consumed 11.2% of the gross domestic product (GDP) in Canada compared with 17.7% of the GDP in the United States (OECD 2013).

Proponents of a universal health-care system in the United States argue that a substantial proportion of the U.S. population is not insured at any one time, increasing illness and cost. Despite spending significantly more money on health care, life expectancy is similar and in some cases decreased when compared to other OECD countries. Despite having disparate systems, most other OECD countries have some form of universal health care, which proponents argue could increase access to care, improve quality of care, and reduce costs if implemented in the United States.

HISTORY OF UNIVERSAL HEALTH-CARE COVERAGE IN THE UNITED STATES: FROM TRUMAN TO THE ACA

Prior to the 1900s the government did not involve itself in health insurance, leaving the states to allow private and voluntary programs to provide funds. There was not support in the working class for broad socialized insurance. In 1915 the American Association of Labor Legislation led the campaign for health insurance by drafting a model bill offering limited coverage to the working class and those making less than $1200 a year. The ideas in the bill drew debate but failed to create legislation. The discussion resumed during the Great Depression in the 1930s and Franklin D. Roosevelt's presidency. While several bills were created pushing for national health insurance, unemployment took top priority. A conservative resurgence in 1938 made further social innovations difficult (Starr 1982b, 81).

During Truman's presidency in the 1940s, health care received full support from the president and became a focus in national politics. In contrast to previous proposals for national health care, Truman included all classes of society, not just the working class. Truman proposed "the right to adequate medical care and the opportunity to achieve and enjoy good health" in his Economic Bill of Rights. Opponents entangled "socialized medicine" with the Cold War and part of the crusade against the communist influence in America. The American Medical Association (AMA) was against Truman's proposal as members believed that compulsory health care would limit physician autonomy. The AMA spent $1.5 million on lobbying efforts in 1945, which at the time was the most expensive in history. Truman's plan died in congressional committee (Schremmer and Knapp 2011, 400).

After WWII, private insurance systems expanded, providing coverage for union members and other groups that held influence in American politics, undermining a movement for universal health care. In 1958 a proposal was introduced to cover hospital costs for the elderly population already receiving social security. The AMA and various insurance companies were initially against the proposal, arguing that it was compulsory, would reduce quality of care, represented socialized medicine, and was un-American. The public pushed the issue onto the national agenda as care for the elderly was a universal issue that in time would come to affect everyone. The AMA countered with their own insurance proposal, an "eldercare plan" that was voluntary with broad benefits and physician services. The U.S. government broadened its proposed legislation to cover physician services. Hence, Medicare and Medicaid were created as President Johnson signed the legislation into law as the Social Security Amendments of 1965 (Starr 1982a).

In 1974 President Nixon proposed his Comprehensive Health Insurance Plan requiring employers to offer full-time employees broad health coverage. Nixon's proposal included an employer mandate to offer private health insurance. Medicaid was to be replaced with state health insurance plans for all with income-based premiums and cost sharing. Nixon's plan also included coverage for behavioral and mental health. After Nixon's resignation, subsequent presidents and congressmen advanced various bills and proposals for health insurance reform without significant success (Nixon 1974).

The Consolidated Omnibus Budget Reconciliation Act (COBRA) was passed by Congress in 1986. COBRA mandates insurance providers to provide health insurance coverage to individuals leaving employment via their previous employers. COBRA includes the Emergency Medical Treatment and Active Labor Act (EMTALA) as well as amendments to ERISA. EMTALA requires any hospital participating in Medicare to provide emergency health-care treatment to all in need, regardless of citizenship, legal status, or ability to pay (COBRA 1985). With very few hospitals that do not accept Medicare, EMTALA applies to nearly all hospitals. The cost of EMTALA is not covered by the federal government and created fears of a "free rider" problem, where individuals intentionally would go without health insurance knowing that hospitals would be required to treat them under the law (Roy 2012).

President Clinton expanded on Nixon's ideas in 1993 through a health-care reform bill that included a mandate for employers to provide health insurance to all employees through managed competition. Concerns included omission of insurance for the unemployed. Clinton's bill ultimately failed secondary to concerns about increasing complexity, overabundance of government regulation, and a barrage of negative press and advertising from the health insurance industry and conservative groups. Clinton negotiated a compromise with the 105th Congress in 1997 to enact the State Children's Health Insurance Program (SCHIP, now known as CHIP), a federal program that provides matching funds to states for health insurance to families with children.

Critics of an employer mandate argue that a mandate to employers drives up the costs of new hires, discourages new hires, increases unemployment, and increases the cost of running a business overall. With an employer mandate for full coverage, consumers would not be aware of health-care costs, removing any incentive to economize and increasing costs overall. An employer mandate does not address insurance concerns for the unemployed and may make individuals fearful to leave a job if they fall ill, as if they switch plans they could pay higher premiums or be denied coverage altogether (Roy 2012).

Conversely, an individual mandate would address the "free rider" problem created by the EMTALA by requiring individuals to buy their own insurance. An individual mandate could encourage competition and drive costs down by involving individuals directly benefiting from a plan. In 1989, Stuart Butler proposed a plan that included a provision to mandate all households to obtain adequate insurance. Butler argued that health-care protection is a responsibility of individuals, not businesses. He contrasted the inherent difference between insurance for health care and other material goods. He explained that if a man wrecks his Porsche and does not have insurance, society feels no obligation to repair his car. However, if a man has a heart attack, society will want to care for him regardless of his insurance status. Butler said that a mandate on individuals recognizes this implicit contract and moral obligation from society (Butler 1989).

In contrast to Clinton's proposal, in 1993 congressional Republicans created their own health reform bill using the concept of an individual mandate. They introduced the Health Equity and Access Reform Today (HEART) Act (Senate Bill 1770 1993), which proposed an individual mandate with a penalty provision together with health insurance vouchers for low-income individuals. The individual mandate was eventually removed from the bill.

In 2006 an insurance expansion bill was enacted in Massachusetts with an individual mandate and an insurance exchange under Republican Governor Mitt Romney. The law, officially titled An Act Providing Access to Affordable, Quality, Accountable Health Care, but informally known at "Romneycare," also contained an employer mandate requiring businesses with more than 10 full-time employees to provide health insurance (An Act Providing Access to Affordable, Quality Accountable Health Care 2006). Massachusetts since went from 90% of its residents insured to 98%, the highest in the nation (Massachusetts 2010).

Massachusetts provided a template for subsequent health-care reform bills introduced in Congress, eventually leading to the ACA. In 2007, the Healthy Americans Act (Senate Bill 334 2007) was introduced in Congress and also featured an individual mandate and regulated state-based insurance plans. It died in committee, but many of the sponsors and co-sponsors were involved in the 2008 health-care debate.

As part of the 2008 Democratic presidential primaries, both Hillary Clinton and Barack Obama presented plans to reform health care and to cover the 45 million Americans estimated not to have health insurance at some point in the year. Clinton's initial plan included an individual mandate requiring all Americans to obtain coverage, while Obama's plan involved a subsidy but stopped short of requiring all individuals to purchase insurance.

Obama identified universal health care as one of the stated goals of his administration, and after his inauguration both houses of Congress developed health reform bills. Obama initially did not support an individual mandate, but he was persuaded by congressional Democratic health policy experts that guaranteed issue of insurance to all Americans would require an individual mandate and a community rating of insurees. An individual mandate would also prevent "free riding" as well as adverse selection, where more ill individuals would selectively purchase insurance and increase costs. The drafters also hoped that drawing on bipartisan ideas, such as an individual mandate previously supported by Republicans, would increase the chances of the bill obtaining the necessary votes to pass. Bipartisan support would also increase positive public perception. However, Republican support for the bill and an individual mandate began to wane (Cohn 2010, 16).

In the senate, the ACA began as a revision of H.R. 3590, a bill regarding housing tax breaks for service members. The Republican minority vowed to filibuster any bill that they did not support, meaning 60 votes would be required to obtain passage. During the fall of 2009, a series of political circumstances gave Senate Democrats their sought-after votes and supermajority. The Senate passed the ACA by 60–39 on December 24, 2009. The bill was endorsed by a variety of advocacy groups including the AMA and the AARP. On January 19, 2010, Massachusetts Republican Scott Brown was elected to replace the late Democrat Ted Kennedy. The democratic supermajority in the Senate was lost, complicating the legislative strategy of further reform. The Patient Protection and Affordable Care Act was passed in the House on March 21, 2010, with President Obama signing the bill on March 30.

PROVISIONS OF THE PATIENT PROTECTION AND AFFORDABLE CARE ACT

An individual mandate requires all U.S. citizens and legal residents to have qualifying health coverage. In addition to an approved private insurance policy, qualifying health coverage includes Medicaid, Medicare, or other public insurance programs. Previous individual and group plans prior to March 23, 2010, were "grandfathered" with respect to new benefit standards provided grandfathered plans met minimum requirements such as extending dependent coverage to adult children up to age 26, prohibiting rescissions of coverage, eliminating annual limits on coverage by 2014, eliminating pre-existing condition exclusion by 2014, and eliminating waiting periods of greater than 90 days by 2014.

Those choosing not to have coverage pay a variable tax penalty. For a family this would be up to the greater of $2085 per family or 2.5% of household income by 2016. The mandate penalty will be adjusted for cost of living thereafter. Exemptions from the fine include those with religious objections, American Indians, undocumented immigrants, individuals who have been uninsured for less than 3 months, those for whom the lowest-cost health-care plan would exceed 8% of their income, and those whose income is below the tax filing threshold. In 2013, pursuant to the Supreme Court decision in *National Federation of Independent Business v. Sebelius* (2012), Medicaid-eligible individuals would not have to pay a penalty if their state chose not to expand Medicaid coverage.

The ACA includes an employer mandate where employers with 50 or more full-time employees will pay a penalty if they do not provide affordable and comprehensive health insurance. A full-time employee is considered an individual who works at least 30 hours per week. Part-time employees are partially counted in order to determine the size of an employer's workforce. Employers with more than 200 employees are required to automatically enroll individuals into offered health insurance plans, with the employee able to opt out if desired. As of 2014, implementation of the employer mandate was delayed 1 year.

The ACA offers a sliding scale of tax credits for individuals and families with incomes between 100% and 400% of the federal poverty level when purchasing insurance through an exchange. For example, those with an income of 150%–200% of the federal poverty level would contribute 4%–6.3% of their income. In 2013 a family with an income of up to $94,200 would qualify for a subsidy. Small businesses with no more than 25 employees and average annual wages of less than $50,000 will receive a tax credit.

Health insurance exchanges will be created as an online marketplace where individuals and small businesses can compare policies and purchase coverage. Health insurance policies are to meet minimum standards. Competition and regulations are intended to create transparency, reduce prices, and guarantee a variety of options. Access to coverage through exchanges is limited to U.S. citizens and legal immigrants who are not incarcerated. Four benefit categories—bronze, silver, gold, and platinum—will be offered representing increasing percentage coverage of benefit costs. For example, a silver plan will cover 70% coverage of the benefit costs of the plan.

A catastrophic plan with minimum catastrophic insurance coverage will be offered to those up to age 30. States will be allowed to prohibit plans participating in the exchange from providing coverage for abortions. Medical screenings and preventative care are considered an essential health benefit and cannot be subject to co-payments or deductibles. Examples of such services covered include vaccinations and immunizations, mammograms, colonoscopies, HIV screening, and wellness visits. Contraceptive coverage is also mandated for employers and educational institutions with the exception of religious organizations.

With the exception of "grandfathered" plans, new insurance plans are mandated to adhere to a variety of new regulations aimed at expanding access to coverage. In March 2010 the ACA required all individual and group health plans to allow children or dependents to remain on their parent's health insurance plan until they reach age 26. Children up to age 19 with pre-existing conditions would not be able to be excluded from a plan. From June 2010 to January 2014 a temporary national high-risk pool was created to provide coverage for those with pre-existing medical conditions, prior to a universal ban on restricting coverage in 2014. In September 2010 the ACA restricted the practice of rescission, which refers to the practice of canceling medical coverage after the covered individual becomes sick or injured.

In 2014, new individual and group insurance plans are required to accept all applicants. Pre-existing condition exclusions, meaning excluding a policyholder based on a medical condition present prior to insurance enrollment, will be prohibited. Insurers are required to renew policies as requested. Individual and small group plans are prohibited from basing premiums on an enrollee's health status. Individual and small group plans are able to vary premiums based on an enrollee's age, geographic location, and tobacco use up to certain limits. Annual dollar limits on coverage are eliminated, and coverage waiting periods are limited to 90 days.

Limits on open enrollment in the ACA are aimed at preventing healthy people from postponing obtaining health insurance until they became ill, which could lead to a smaller, more ill population of insured individuals and could cause premium costs to consumers to increase. Insurers are required to spend 80%–85% of dollars on health-care costs rather than administrative costs and profits. Insurance companies are required to issue refunds if this requirement is not met.

Beginning January 2014 the ACA provides funding for states to expand Medicaid coverage to all persons with incomes up to 133% of the federal poverty level. This covers individuals or a family of four with an income of up to $15,521 or $31,721, respectively, in 2014. The federal government will reimburse states for 100% of additional expansion costs from 2014–2016, with a gradual decrease in reimbursement to 90% by 2020 and beyond.

Through the ACA, funding is increased to various grants, scholarships, and loan repayment programs, and increased loan repayment tax relief is aimed at increasing the number of primary care physicians and other needed health professionals (Patient Protection and Affordable Care Act 2010).

LEGAL CHALLENGES TO THE PATIENT PROTECTION AND AFFORDABLE CARE ACT

In the *National Federation of Independent Business v. Sebelius* (2012), the Supreme Court decided on the constitutionality of the individual mandate and Medicaid expansion contained in the ACA.

As background, in 2011 Florida challenged the constitutionality of the ACA by bringing a lawsuit against the U.S. Department of Health and Human Services. As a plaintiff, Florida was joined by 26 other states as well as the National Federation of Independent Business and two individuals. The plaintiffs argued that the Medicaid expansions were coercive, the individual mandate exceeded Congress' powers as defined under the Commerce Clause, and the employer mandate interfered with state sovereignty. The U.S. District Court ruled that the individual mandate provision exceeded Congress' enumerated powers and was not removable from the ACA, invalidating the entirety of the law. They upheld the Medicaid expansion and dismissed the states' challenge to the employer mandate.

In an appeal to the 11th Circuit Court of Appeals, a three-judge panel reversed 2:1 in part the District Court's holding, finding that the individual mandate could be separated from the ACA, leaving the rest of the law intact. Several other federal court cases in 2010 and 2011 upheld the individual mandate as constitutional and, although not directly reviewed by the Supreme Court, represented a countrywide divide (*Thomas More Law Center v. Obama* 2012).

In November 2011, the Supreme Court granted *certiorari* to portions of three cross appeals to the Eleventh Circuit's opinion, with the decision commonly known by the name of one of the cases, *National Federation of Independent Business v. Sebelius.* On June 28, 2012, in an opinion by Chief Justice Roberts, the Supreme Court upheld the individual mandate of the ACA in a 5:4 vote as the imposition of a tax, hence a constitutional exercise of Congress' powers. He explained that Congress' choice of language, stating that individuals "shall" obtain insurance or pay a "penalty" to the Internal Revenue Service can be read as imposing a tax on those who go without insurance. The individual mandate could not be justified as a part of Congress' power under the Commerce Clause (power to regulate commerce among states) and the Necessary and Proper Clause (power to create laws for executing foregoing powers). Justice Roberts argued that the federal government is only able to regulate commercial activity through the Commerce Clause, while instead the individual mandate penalizes economic inactivity. He said that the distinction between doing something and doing nothing would not have been lost on the framers of the Constitution.

In regard to the expansion of Medicaid, the majority of the court found the expansion in some form unconstitutional. Seven justices agreed that Congress had exceeded their constitutional authority by threatening states with removal of Medicaid funding if they did not participate with the expansion. The court said that the ACA's requirement was unduly coercive and narrowed the Medicaid penalty provision by ruling that the federal government could not withhold funding if a state chose not to participate with the expansion in the ACA, essentially removing an "all or nothing choice" and allowing states to choose between participating in Medicaid expansion while receiving additional funding or rejecting Medicaid expansion and retaining existing payments (*National Federation of Independent Business v. Sebelius* 2012).

In time, *National Federation of Independent Business v. Sebelius* could be seen as a landmark decision in federalism jurisprudence (Weissmann 2012). The court's ruling against removal of Medicaid funding if a state did not participate with expansion set new limits on the federal regulation of commerce and on money that the government gives the states. Some experts argued that the Supreme Court ruling could change the relationship between the federal government and states, and could be a worrisome development as many programs are built on the government's spending power (Katyal 2012). Many long-standing laws contain clauses that condition money based on the states meeting certain expectations, making these laws possibly unconstitutional. Several important civil rights statutes condition receiving federal funds for programs based on abiding by nondiscrimination principles and could now be seen as unduly coercive (Russell 2012).

IMPLICATIONS OF THE PATIENT PROTECTION AND AFFORDABLE CARE ACT

In 2012 the Congressional Budget Office estimated that the ACA would reduce federal deficits by $84 billion in its first 10 years when the Supreme Court ruling was taken into account. Savings were estimated to be the result of reductions in spending for Medicare, Medicaid, and through additional tax revenues. Estimates of cost have varied with the American Action Forum suggesting that the deficit would actually increase by $554 billion in the first ten years and $1.4 billion in the succeeding 10 years (Holtz-Eakin and Ramlet 2010, 1136). Debates of cost have been highly politicized and part of the national conversation about the ACA.

Concerns remain that the ACA could actually create incentives for employers to drop insurance coverage. The American Action Forum estimated that in 2010 about 163 million workers and their family receive health insurance through their employers. With the ACA and resulting subsidies, there now exists an alternative subsidized source of insurance for workers that can be accessed if employers do not offer coverage. A simple calculation for businesses focuses on the trade-off between company savings for not providing insurance and the $2000 penalty per employee imposed by the ACA. In 2010 large companies were at least considering the trade-off. However, the calculation is more complex as reducing health insurance benefits may decrease employee satisfaction, making valuable labor more difficult to attract. But with new government subsidies, offering health insurance may not be as important for employee happiness as it was in the past. The American Action Forum estimated that it could make financial sense for employers to drop insurance for 43 million workers (Holtz-Eakin and Smith 2010). However, most micro simulation models for the Congressional Budget office, the RAND Corporation, and the Lewin Group estimate a range of 1.8% decrease to a 2.9% increase in Americans covered by employer-sponsored health insurance (Buchmueller et al. 2013, 1526). In one 2012 survey of employers, 9% of large firms currently offering insurance said that they anticipated dropping coverage in the next 3 years (Keckley et al. 2012). In another 2013 survey, 98% of firms with more than 1000 employees said that they expected health benefits to be an important component of compensation in 3 to 5 years (Towers Watson and National Business Group on Health 2013).

One of the major goals of the ACA and universal health care was to extend coverage to those previously uninsured. By the end of the first open enrollment period in March 2014, more than 7.1 million individuals had signed up for private plans with more than 3.5 million newly insured under Medicaid, meeting the Obama administration's goals (Shear and Pear 2014). However, it was unclear how many of these individuals were previously uninsured and 10%–15% had not paid their premiums. The Congressional Budget Office estimates that enrollment in exchanges will increase to 22 million in 2016. Coverage varies widely throughout the states with some states having a flourishing of health-care plans and competition while other states have hardly any choices at all. Roughly three dozen states have decided not to establish their own exchanges, relying instead on the federal exchange through HealthCare.gov.

Certain states with opposition have enacted strong restrictions on who can serve as counselors to guide consumers through the enrollment process. Negative press has also been thought to be discouraging consumers from enrolling in plans. At the beginning of the first open enrollment period in October 2013, there was a well-publicized shutdown of the federal health-care exchange website when healthcare.gov received 4.7 million visitors in the first 24 hours. The website failure raised concern from the public about how prepared the government was to implement the ACA. Outreach was variable by states. Some states such as Rhode Island and Colorado created pop-up stores to increase awareness in areas with lack of enrollment. This led to large discrepancies in health-care enrollment between states. In March 2014, an analysis from health economists at the University of Pennsylvania found that in Vermont 54% of eligible individuals had signed up for private insurance, while in South Dakota only 6% had done so (Polsky et al. 2014). In general states that have their own exchanges have reached more of the eligible population than those that have used the federal exchange.

As of 2014, about 25% of those enrolled in health-care plans are between the ages of 18 and 34. This is in contrast to the estimated 40% of total potential enrollees who are in that age group. Experts have argued that an increased number of young enrollees would be ideal to keep premiums down, as young people would have less illness and would help pay for the cost of insuring older, sicker individuals. It is unclear whether or not enough young people have enrolled (Andrews et al. 2014).

As a result of *National Federation of Independent Business v. Sebelius*, many states have opted out of Medicaid expansion. By 2014, 27 states and the District of Columbia had decided to expand Medicaid and receive additional funding from the federal government (Pear 2014). As a result an estimated 4.8 million low-income American fall into what experts call "the gap," where individuals earn too much to qualify for traditional Medicaid but are under the 138% of the FPL needed to qualify for tax credits as part of the ACA.

Public perception and awareness have remained a challenge. By the end of the first open enrollment period in March 2014, the majority of the public unfavorably viewed the ACA, and a significant percentage of the uninsured were unaware of key provisions of the ACA. In a March 2013 poll from the Kaiser Family Foundation, half of uninsured individuals planned to remain uninsured. Half of the uninsured were unaware that the ACA gives states the options of expanding their Medicaid programs, and 4 out of 10 did not know that government subsidies were available to help low- to moderate-income individuals purchase insurance. Approximately 46% of the public viewed the ACA unfavorably with 38% having a favorable view (Hamel et al. 2014).

SUMMARY KEY POINTS

Passed in 2010, the Patient Protection and Affordable Care Act is a monumental piece of legislation that aims at providing universal health care and reducing the number of uninsured through individual and employer mandates, Medicaid expansion, and competitive insurance exchanges. With the majority of the law taking effect starting in 2014, the full ramifications of the ACA have yet to be seen.

- The United States is one of the few industrialized countries without universal health care, and spends nearly twice as much per capita, with little to no benefit in life expectancy.
- Nearly 46 million Americans were estimated to be uninsured in 2007.
- Key provisions of ACA include an individual mandate, where individuals are required to purchase qualifying health insurance, in addition to an employer mandate for sizable companies to provide insurance to their employees.
- The ACA provides funding for states to expand Medicaid to all persons with incomes up to 133% of the poverty level.
- In 2012 the Supreme Court upheld most provisions of the ACA. They ruled against compulsory Medicaid expansion, finding the federal government's withholding of funding to states choosing not to participate in the expansion "unduly coercive."

REFERENCES

An Act Providing Access to Affordable, Quality Accountable Health Care. 2006. Chapter 58 of the Acts of 2006, Massachusetts.

Andrews W, H Park and A Tse. 2014. Ten key questions on health care enrollment. *New York Times,* March 27.

Buchmueller T, C Carey, and HG Levy. 2013. Will employers drop health insurance coverage because of the Affordable Care Act? *Health Affairs* 32(9):1522–1530.

Butler SM. 1989. Assuring affordable health care for all Americans. *The Heritage Lectures* 218.

Carey D, B Herring, and P Lenain. 2009. *Health Care Reform in the United States.* OECD Economics Department Working Paper No. 665.

Cohn J. 2010. How they did it. *New Republic* 241(9):14–25.

Consolidated Omnibus Budget Reconciliation Act of 1985. Pub.L. No. 99–272, 100 Stat. 82. http://www.legisworks.org/GPO/STATUTE-100-Pg82.pdf, accessed May 12, 2015.

DeNavas-Walt C, BD Proctor, and JC Smith. 2007. *Income, Poverty and Health Insurance Coverage in the United States: 2007. Current Population Reports*. P60-235. U.S. Census Bureau. Washington, DC: U.S. Government Printing Office.

Hamel L, J Firth, and M Brodie. 2014. *Kaiser Health Tracking Poll: March 2014*. Publication #8565-T. Menlo Park, CA: The Henry J. Kaiser Family Foundation.

Himmelstein DU, E Warren, D Thorne, and S Woolhandler. 2005. MarketWatch: Illness and injury as contributors to bankruptcy. *Health Affairs* W5:63–73.

Holtz-Eakin D and MJ Ramlet. 2010. Health care reform is likely to widen federal budget deficits, not reduce them. *Health Affairs* 29(6):1136–1141.

Holtz-Eakin D and C Smith. 2010. Labor markets and health care reform: New results. *American Action Forum*, May 27.

Katyal NK. 2012. A pyrrhic victory. *New York Times*, June 29.

Keckley PH, S Coughlin, S Wiley, J Girzadas, B Copeland, and E Reuss-Hannafin. 2012. *Deloitte Survey of U.S. Employers: Opinions about the U.S. Health Care System and Plans for Employee Health Benefits*. New York: Deloitte Center for Health Solutions.

Lasser KE, DU Himmelstein, and S Woolhandler. 2006. Access to care, health status, and health disparities in the United States and Canada: Results of a cross-national population-based survey. *American Journal of Public Health* 96(7):1–8.

Massachusetts Health Insurance Surveys. 2010. *Division of Health Care Finance and Policy*. http://chiamass.gov/assets/docs/r/pubs/10/mhis-fact-sheet-12-2010.pdf, accessed May 12, 2015.

Musgrove P, A Creese, A Preker, C Baeza, A Anell, and T Prentice. 2000. *The World Health Report 2000: Health Systems: Improving Performance*. Geneva, Switzerland: World Health Organization.

National Federation of Independent Business v. Sebelius, 132 S.Ct. 2566 (2012).

Nixon R. 1974. Special message to the Congress proposing a comprehensive health insurance plan. Speech presented to Congress, February 6.

Organization for Economic Co-operation and Development (OECD). 2010. *Health Care Systems: Getting More Value for Money. OECD Economics Department Policy Note No. 2*. Paris: OECD.

Organization for Economic Co-operation and Development (OECD). 2013. *OECD Health Data 2013*. Paris: OECD.

Patient Protection and Affordable Care Act. 2010. Pub.L. No. 111–148.

Pear R. 2014. Is the Affordable Care Act working? *New York Times*, October 26.

Polsky DE, J Weiner, C Colameco, and N Becker. 2014. Deciphering the data: Health insurance marketplace enrollment rates by type of exchange. *Leonard Davis Institute of Health Economics Data Brief*, March. http://ldihealtheconomist.com/media/health-insurance-marketplace-enrollment-rates-by-type-of-exchange.original.pdf, accessed May 12, 2015.

Roy A. 2012. The tortuous history of conservatives and the individual mandate. *Forbes*, February 7.

Russell K. 2012. Civil Rights Statutes Put at Risk by Health Care Decision. *SCOTUSblog* (blog), June 29. http://www.scotusblog.com/2012/06/civil-rights-statutes-put-at-risk-by-health-care-decision/, accessed May 12, 2015.

Schremmer RD and KF Knapp. 2011. Harry Truman and health care reform: The debate started here. *Pediatrics* 127(3):399–401.

Shear MD and R Pear. 2014. Obama claims victory in push for insurance. *New York Times*, April 2.

Starr P. 1982a. *The Social Transformation of American Medicine: The Rise of a Sovereign Profession and the Making of a Vast Industry*. New York: Basic Books.

Starr P. 1982b. Transformation in defeat: The changing objectives of national health insurance, 1915–1980. *American Journal of Public Health* 72(1):78–88.

Thomas More Law Center v. Obama, 133 S.Ct. 61 (2012).

Towers Watson and National Business Group on Health. 2013. Health Employer Survey on Purchasing Value in Health Care. March. http://www.towerswatson.com/en-US/Insights/IC-Types/Survey-Research-Results/2013/03/Towers-Watson-NBGH-Employer-Survey-on-Value-in-Purchasing-Health-Care, accessed May 12, 2015.

United Kingdom Department of Health. 2015. The NHS Constitution.

Weissmann J. 2012. The most important part of today's health care ruling you haven't heard about. *The Atlantic*, June 28.

84

Social media and the Internet

CATHLEEN A. CERNY, DELANEY SMITH, AND SUSAN HATTERS-FRIEDMAN

The Internet could be a very positive step towards education, organization, and participation in a meaningful society.

Noam Chomsky

It's been my policy to view the Internet not as an "information highway," but as an electronic asylum filled with babbling loonies.

Mike Royko

INTRODUCTION

For many people, the Internet is indispensible and inescapable. It has infiltrated every aspect of our lives. One can pay bills, shop, find a romantic partner, take college courses for credit, research medical conditions, watch television, and share every moment of life online. Through the Internet, one can learn how to do anything from ride a bike to build a bomb. Plus, social media allows someone to become anyone he or she wants to be without the pesky constraints of reality. It only makes sense that the Internet has become an indispensible tool for forensic psychiatrists.

Globally, there are 2.5 billion people online, which is about one-third of the world's population (We Are Social 2014). Four-fifths (81%) of North Americans are online and more than half (56%) are using social networks. Facebook is the largest online social networking site, with over a billion users worldwide. About 48% of all registered Facebook users log in on any given day (Statistic Brain 2014). Google, a web search engine and much more, does over a billion searches daily, 15% of which are novel (Chung 2013). Mobile devices like iPhones and web-enabled tablets allow people to be online anytime, anywhere. As of 2012, 116 million Americans owned smartphones, and in 2014 mobile use is predicted to overtake desktop Internet use (Warden 2013).

The practice of psychiatry, like the practice of all medical specialties, has been altered in a myriad of ways by the Internet and social media. This chapter specifically examines how the practice of forensic psychiatry has been impacted by the Internet. It discusses the importance of the Internet when it comes to doing thorough evaluations. The chapter further comments on how the Internet can be used in forensic psychiatry research and teaching, as well as to promote both individual forensic experts and the field. Importantly, the chapter looks at how the Internet can influence public perception of forensic psychiatry. Finally, the chapter will conclude by looking at Internet-related sources of liability.

THE INTERNET AND FORENSIC EVALUATIONS

Recupero wrote "to a psychiatrist conducting a forensic evaluation, the evaluee's Internet use can be relevant in nearly all aspects of the analysis" (Recupero 2010a, 15). In this day and age when Americans spend an average of 16 minutes out of every hour on social networks (Gaudin 2013), an evaluee's digital footprint can give important insights into their lives. Some potential online sources of digital collateral evidence include personal websites, social networking pages, profiles or tweets, web browser search histories, personal blogs, video sharing sites like YouTube, chat rooms, and other web discussion groups.

What is the benefit of knowing an evaluee's Internet habits and presence? First, forensic evaluators have always used collateral information to supplement, corroborate, or even refute evaluee self-reports. Evaluees can consciously or unconsciously shape the information they disclose during an evaluation to present themselves as they want to be seen. Digital evidence, similar to evidence provided by friends and family, can result in revelations about the evaluee that are not subject to the same type of conscious or unconscious self-editing that takes place in a one-on-one interview. To be clear, digital evidence dating from a point in time prior to the situation triggering the evaluation may give unguarded glimpses of evaluees; however, online representations can also be edited versions of the evaluees' true selves. Second, gathering information about an individual's web presence may uncover problematic Internet use (PIU). Examples of PIU include pathological gambling, excessive use of pornography, child pornography, self-injury chat sites, and excessive online gaming. PIU can be damaging to relationships and responsibilities. Some PIU, for example cyberbullying, can result in criminal charges. Child pornography is illegal PIU. Third, the evaluee's Internet activities may include explicit threats of harm to self or others. Fourth, a person's web history may show associations with or interests in dangerous fringe groups. Finally, looking at an individual's "digital footprint" can show a forensic evaluator how the evaluee views himself or herself. These areas are discussed in more detail below.

As indicated above, collateral information has long been used to addend, confirm, and/or counter an evaluee's self-report. In the past, psychiatrists had to rely on information from family, friends, police reports, school reports, and other first-hand observers. Now, with the Internet and social media, one can obtain collateral data generated directly by the evaluee. The data are "pure" in the sense that the data were generated at a time when the individual did not know he or she would be forensically evaluated. Search histories and Internet activity may be obtained through attorneys and police cyber experts.

There are many forms of problematic Internet use to explore with evaluees. Recupero offers some excellent opening questions that might help uncover PIU in evaluees (Recupero 2010b). Cyberbullying is one type of PIU, defined as the use of information technology to harm or harass other people in a deliberate, repeated, and hostile manner (U.S. Department of Health and Human Services 2014). Cyberbullying has gotten a lot of attention in the media due to bullying-related teen suicides around the world. Examples include Megan Meier who hung herself after a boy she "met" on MySpace told her that "the world would be a better place without you." It was later discovered that the boy was the online creation of Lori Drew, mother of one of Megan's former friends. The Cyberbullying Research Center has been collecting data from middle and high school students since 2002. In their most recent nine studies, about 26% of the students said that they have been the victims of cyberbullying at some point in their lifetimes. On average, about 16% of the students admitted to cyberbullying others at some point in their lifetimes (Patchin 2015). They also found a lifetime cyberbullying offending rate of 16%. Although most people think of cyberbullying as an adolescent and teen phenomenon, it is not limited to young people; Cyberstalking is the more commonly used term when adults are harassed via technology. Moving beyond cyber-harassment, PIU has sometimes been referred to as "Internet Addiction Disorder" to describe individuals whose activities of daily life are negatively impacted by excessive time spent in online gaming, gambling, pornography, chatting, blogging, pinning, shopping, etc. Although Internet Addiction Disorder is not included in the *Diagnostic and Statistical Manual of Mental Disorders*, 5th edition (*DSM-5*), researchers have attempted to define diagnostic criteria with mixed success. Screening scales such as the "Problematic and Risky Internet Use Screening Scale (PRIUSS)" for adolescents and young adults (Jelenchick et al. 2014) have been developed and can help identify key areas for further exploration. At least one inpatient unit treats PIU.

Examining the Internet activities of evaluees can also give insight into their belief systems and behaviors. Where the evaluee searches, shops, posts, and chats can tell the examiner a great deal that the evaluee may not choose to reveal himself or herself. The Internet search history of an evaluee needs to be put into context (see cautions when using the Internet as collateral below) but can be a goldmine of information. Did the evaluee do research on mental health diagnoses and symptoms prior to the evaluation? Did the evaluee look up information on a topic with negative implications such as bomb building or chloroform poisoning? Online shopping can also be telling. Does the evaluee purchase mind-altering medications/drugs via the Internet? If yes, are the purchases made legally or through legal loopholes? Did they purchase materials online that would help them learn about or engage in dangerous activities? Regarding social networking, is the evaluee part of any online groups that could be considered negative or extremist? For example, there are chat rooms for self-mutilators and anorexia suggestion sites. Has he or she posted or blogged about self-harm or violence against others? It is well known now that Eric Harris, one of the Columbine High School shooters, posted the results of explosive experiments on his websites prior to the massacre. Harris is not the only school shooter to have posted online clues about tragic future plans. In recent school shootings and mass murders, there are additional examples of Internet activity prior to the actual events. (Semenov et al. 2010). There are chat rooms and blogs for any interest under the sun, no matter how dark or deadly.

In addition, data from the Internet can tell us how an evaluee views himself or herself. The content, implied tone, and word choice of a person's post may convey grandiosity, self-importance, or righteous indignation. Conversely, one may learn that an evaluee has a very low opinion of himself or herself.

There are a few cautions when using the Internet as a collateral resource. Context is important when analyzing a person's search history. Was the person looking up information on Neo-Nazis for a research paper or because he or she is interested in that ideology? An evaluee might look up mental health information in order to malinger convincingly during an evaluation. Alternately, the evaluee may simply want to use correct terminology for real symptoms when talking to an intimidating evaluator. Evaluators need to consider generational differences in Internet use and communication styles when examining digital data. The forensic evaluator also needs to understand that an individual's

Table 84.1 Follow-up questions related to online child pornography

- Describe the security you use to protect your computer.
- Do you look at material daily? How many hours a day?
- What is your password for _____ and what does it mean to you?
- Where do you keep your computer? How many other people have access to it?
- Do you back-up/save the material you view online? How? Where do you store the back-ups? How many back-ups do you have?
- Do you have scrubbing software on your computer?
- What do the photos/videos you view have in common?
- Describe the type of material you like to view.

Internet use patterns can change over time for a wide variety of reasons. As indicated above, people can be whomever they want to be online. A person's digital footprint might be revelatory as to how he or she sees himself or herself and how the person interacts with others; however, some peoples' online personas are completely manufactured. There is a spectrum of how accurately someone's online persona reflects reality and also variation in how consciously individuals distort their Internet identities. Interestingly, there are about 81,000,000 fake Facebook profiles (Statistic Brain 2014). As with traditional forms of evidence, digital evidence needs context to be understood correctly.

The biggest obstacle a forensic evaluator faces when investigating the Internet habits of an evaluee may be knowing what to ask about, how to ask about it, and how to interpret the information gathered. Although Recupero has excellent suggestions for opening interview questions (Recupero 2010b), they are the tip of the iceberg. The Internet has its own language, with each site adding new terminology. No single forensic evaluator could possibly know all the ins and outs of every social media site, chat room, news feed, and blog he or she uncovers in the course of an evaluation. Due to lack of familiarity, there is the potential for misinterpretation errors. Evaluators may also not know when they have uncovered something important, and they may lack the language for follow-up questions. Using online child pornography as an example, Table 84.1 provides some follow-up questions when the evaluator thinks he or she has uncovered possible PIU.

THE INTERNET AND FORENSIC PSYCHIATRY RESEARCH

Google scholar (available at http://www.scholar.google.com) and PubMed (available at http://www.ncbi.nlm.nih.gov/pubmed) are online search engines that allow searches for medical and legal terms, and link directly to some free articles. The Journal of the American Academy of Psychiatry and the Law is currently available online free of charge (http://www.jaapl.org) and has a searchable engine in order to access desired articles. Other journals are available at a cost online. Alternatively, sometimes authors of sought-after articles may be contacted directly through email in order to obtain reprints. A frequent benefit of a university teaching appointment is access to their library and resource librarians to aid in locating difficult to find articles. Colleagues can share resources, collect research survey data in particular (through SurveyMonkey), and create Facebook pages to share psychiatric information with the public.

Physicians have a duty to keep themselves up-to-date with medical literature and to ensure that they are practicing medicine based on modern standards (Smith et al. 2011). As new technologies evolve, the standard of care and expectations regarding knowledge about the now much easier-to-access medical literature may also evolve. It is possible, for example, that with the decreasing cost of computers and their easy accessibility, courts could view literature searches as appropriate professional custom, and find liability for those who do not engage in them (Smith et al. 2011).

This may happen whether forensic psychiatrists want it to or not, recalling the famous *TJ Hooper* tugboat case in 1932. Although most tugboats did not have radios at that point in time, having a radio on-board could have prevented a bad outcome in that case. The court found that professions may be held to a standard in which they must use available technologies to increase safety. This was whether or not the technology had been adopted by the field. Similarly, and more recently, in 1974, *Helling v. Carey* (Washington Supreme Court) found that an ophthalmologist was negligent for his failure to diagnose glaucoma when the test was cheaply available and safe. It did not matter that the testing was not standard of care because the patient suing was under age 40 and had a calculated risk of 1 in 25 thousand of having glaucoma. Following the same logic, it might be argued that electronic technologies are cheaply available and safe.

However, it is not only doctors using the Internet looking for medical information. One should be aware that patients may also be searching and making their own diagnoses, as may evaluees in order to make their self-report appear more realistic in malingering. Lists of symptoms of many common mental illnesses are widely available on the Internet, as are actual psychological tests. Even those tests that are used specifically to uncover malingering, the Test of Memory Malingering, the Victoria Symptoms Validity Test, and the Word Memory Test, all had some amount of information about them available on the Internet (Bauer and McCaffrey 2006).

THE INTERNET AND FORENSIC PSYCHIATRY EDUCATION

Modern students are digitally fluent, making the Internet a powerful tool for forensic psychiatry education. The possibilities are almost endless. The Internet allows for education innovations like "flipped classrooms" where students learn the material through online lectures and modules, reserving the precious classroom time for higher-level discussion,

Table 84.2 17 U.S.C. section 107, for factors to be considered in determining fair use

- The purpose and character of the use, including whether such use is of commercial nature or is for nonprofit educational purposes
- The nature of the copyrighted work
- The amount and substantiality of the portion used in relation to the copyrighted work as a whole
- The effect of the use upon the potential market for, or value of, the copyrighted work

Source: Adapted from U.S. Copyright Office. 2012. *Fair Use.* http://www.copyright.gov/fls/fl102.html, accessed June 28, 2016.

integration, and application of concepts. Lectures and presentations on forensic psychiatry topics can be recorded and put online to be viewed by residents, fellows, and colleagues. Instructional videos can be made to educate the general public on controversial and poorly understood topics, such as the Insanity Defense and guns in the mentally ill. Online journals and blogs can be informative and geared toward different audience types.

Many people have given up their televisions in favor of watching on-demand content via the Internet. Entire television series and thousands of movies are available online through services like Netflix and Amazon Instant Video. In addition, YouTube and the like offer up clipped scenes from popular fiction that are easy to access and can be utilized in teaching. Small clips of movies or television shows are permissible to use in teaching within the confines of the Fair Use Doctrine. Table 84.2 shows the four factors to be considered in determining whether or not a particular use is fair per section 107 of title 17, U.S.C. (U.S. Copyright Office 2012). Popular culture examples are useful forensic teaching tools because they grab attention, focus interest, stimulate creativity, and foster connections between students and teachers (Berk 2009). For example, Friedman and colleagues (2011, 2013) created a typology of forensic psychiatrists in fiction. They used the typology as a launching off point to teach about public perception of forensic experts, as well as biases in forensic work. Similarly, Cerny et al. (2014) used fictional women from television to teach about female psychopathy.

THE INTERNET AS A MEANS OF SELF-PROMOTION, ADVERTISING, NETWORKING

Websites exist for many medical and psychiatric practices. Websites may advertise a physician's areas of expertise, provide presentations and publications, and link to one's CV. They may even provide links to media appearances. However, they are not without risk. One important risk is that of impeachment during testimony, especially for example if exaggerations exist on the website (Recupero 2010b).

Recupero described the types of website based on the level of interaction with the consumer. Passive websites contain contact information and descriptions of services—consumers do not interact with these websites. This is considered similar to giving someone a business card or information about a practice. In distinction, business websites are interactive and allow establishment of a relationship—for example, by allowing business transactions or clinical question submission. Intermediate websites do not allow financial transactions but are more interactive—providing advice. The greater the possible interaction with consumers, the greater is the potential legal risk. For example, inadvertently, a doctor–patient relationship and duty may begin. Liability may also ensue from posting inappropriate guarantees on one's website, and breach of contract lawsuits have occurred in other specialties. One should discuss with one's malpractice carrier or attorney regarding website establishment, and consider licensing issues (Recupero 2006).

Similarly, emailing patients is more momentous than it may seem due to the potential expanding legal duty that arises. It is important to adhere to institutional policies when engaging in electronic patient contact. Like with computers and other electronic devices, it is important to have sufficiently strong passwords for email accounts, to avoid unauthorized access to the data contained in sent emails, or other unscrupulous use of an account. More of concern for the forensic expert is email exchanges with legal counsel. This is discussed further in the liability section below.

Medical blogs represent a new opportunity to educate the public about our field. But they also risk revealing confidential information. One needs to consider carefully the appropriateness of pictures and postings on Facebook, lest they fall into hands other than what was expected. Thinking before blogging is critical in order to maintain one's professional image, as well as our profession's collective image to the public. A recent study examined medical blogs (Lagu et al. 2008) from 2006. In that year, 271 medical blogs were found. Patients were individually described in 42% of the blogs, and were portrayed positively in 16% and negatively in 18%. When the researchers further examined blogs regarding interactions with specific patients, 17% included enough information for patients to be able to identify either themselves or their physician. This can raise serious doubts in the minds of the public regarding whether doctors keep their information private. As well, clinical judgment may be of concern (Appelbaum and Kopelman 2014). A famous legal example is that of Dr. Robert Lindeman, a pediatrician involved in a malpractice case, who blogged (under the name of "flea") about the legal strategy and other case participants. Dr. Lindeman was discredited in court for his blog and the case was settled the next day (Saltzman 2007).

THE INTERNET AND PUBLIC PERCEPTION OF FORENSIC PSYCHIATRY

Online content is easily re-watched and shared with others. Forensic mental health professionals need to be mindful about how depictions of mental illness and mental health professionals, real or fictional, shape public perceptions. As discussed above in the The Internet and Forensic Psychiatry Education section, popular culture is rife with examples of forensic psychiatry. The Internet and social media allow for all those examples to be shared widely and rapidly.

The suicide of beloved actor Robin Williams (August 11, 2014) is an unfortunate example of how quickly information (and misinformation) can spread across the Internet and social media. In the days and hours following Williams' death, there were endless Facebook tributes, celebrity tweets of remembrance, YouTube videos of his famous friends expressing their grief, and up-to-the-minute news posts. About a week after Williams' death, his Facebook page indicated that 7.3 million people were talking about "it." The page had 9.2 million likes, which was an increase of 75% from the week before, with 3.9 million new page likes. In addition to Internet traffic related to honoring and remember this comedic great, there were also many posts regarding treatment for mental illness and suicide prevention. There were efforts to increase awareness about stigma of mental illness and addiction. On the reverse side of things, not all information posted about suicide and treatment has been accurate. Some commentators have compounded the stigma of mental illness and suicide. Internet trolls (seeking to sow discord by starting arguments) reportedly drove Williams' daughter to delete her Twitter account and resign from Instagram. The Internet and social media response to Robin William's suicide shows the power the cyber-world has to shape perception of psychiatry.

THE INTERNET AND LIABILITY FOR FORENSIC PSYCHIATRISTS

While the Internet has created many advantages for forensic psychiatrists, it has also resulted in potential liability. In addition to the concerns for treating psychiatrists described above, use of email can have specific implications for forensic psychiatrists with relation to their interactions with attorneys on cases. In the digital age traditional client-privilege has become more convoluted, with an increasing emphasis on the intent and purpose of communication (*Baklid-Kunz v. Halifax Hospital Medical Center* 2012). Evaluators must use the utmost caution in what is communicated to counsel electronically. Specific areas of concern are appearing overly friendly with an attorney, comments that might be interpreted to convey a bias toward a side and undermine a jury's view of the evaluator as impartial, and appearing to defer opinions to the attorney. A good rule of thumb before sending an email is to read it aloud as an opposing attorney might do and think of potential negative ways it could be misinterpreted.

Evaluators should also be mindful of the volumes of metadata that are now produced as they complete forensic reports electronically. Metadata is the footprint of information generated as one uses technology. In days past, a report may have been dictated using a dictation service or administrative assistant, in which case the only data produced besides the final report may have been handwritten notes and perhaps an edited draft. Today many choose to type their own report manually or with the aid of a voice-to-type software program. Most word processing programs cache changes made in a document over time which can create numerous iterations of a single report that can be accessed electronically, which make up the metadata. This information could be used in court proceedings (Favro 2007). One way metadata about a document can become apparent to others is when a document is sent electronically. This can, at times, allow the recipient to go back through some of the historic versions of the report and see possible changes in opinions or errors that were later corrected (Hricik and Scott 2008). One potential way to address this issue is to transfer documents to a pdf format before sending, though even this is not without potential problems. Similarly, one can use a commercial software "scrubber" or, in the case of Microsoft Office, a document inspector to reduce metadata (Wallace 2008).

Forensic psychiatrists should also be wary of overreliance on Internet-based literature reviews, electronic medical decision supports, or medication information tools as an ultimate arbiter of standard of care. Many of these sites and applications ("apps") specifically state that they are not intended to replace clinical judgment. Similarly, it is the forensic psychiatrist's own knowledge of standards that should be the basis of opinions in malpractice cases and not those of a certain website or app. Just as an expert would hesitate to name a single source text as definitive on a subject, experts should not put themselves in a position of explaining why one website was chosen over another.

SUMMARY KEY POINTS

- Examination of an evaluee's Internet and social media use can be an important part of the evaluation.
- There are pros and cons to digital collateral evidence; context is key.
- The Internet is a powerful forensic psychiatry research tool.
- The Internet and social media can be used to creatively teach "digital natives" about forensic psychiatry.
- Forensic psychiatrists can use the Internet to network and advertise, as long as they keep certain cautions in mind.
- The Internet and social media websites have tremendous influence over public perception of mental illness, mental health professionals, and forensic psychiatry.
- The Internet opens up a whole new world of potential liability for mental health professionals and forensic experts.

REFERENCES

Appelbaum PS and A Kopelman. 2014. Social media's challenges for psychiatry. *World Psychiatry* 13:21–24.

Bauer L and RJ McCaffrey. 2006. Coverage of the Test of Memory Malingering, Victoria Symptom Validity Test, and Word Memory Test on the Internet: Is test security threatened? *Archives of Clinical Neuropsychology* 21:121–126.

Berk RA. 2009. Multimedia teaching with video clips: TV, movies, YouTube, and mtvU in the college classroom. *International Journal of Technology in Teaching and Learning* 5:1–21.

Cerny CA, SH Friedman, and D Smith. 2014. Television's "Crazy Lady" trope: Female psychopathic traits, teaching and popular culture. *Academic Psychiatry* 38:233–241.

Chung S. 2013. Search insights: A brand planning power tool. *Google Think Insights.* https://www.thinkwithgoogle.com/articles/search-insights-brand-power-tool.html, accessed June 28, 2016.

Favro PJ. 2007. A new frontier in electronic discovery: Preserving and obtaining metadata. *Boston University Journal of Science and Technology Law V. 1* 13:114–139.

Friedman SH and CA Cerny. 2013. From Hannibal Lecter to Alex Cross: Forensic mental health experts in popular fiction. *Academic Psychiatry* 37:345–351.

Friedman SH, CA Cerny, S West, and S Soliman. 2011. Reel forensic experts: Forensic psychiatrists as portrayed on screen. *Journal of the American Academy of Psychiatry and the Law* 39:412–417.

Gaudin S. 2013. Americans spend 16 minutes of every hour online on social nets. *Computerworld.* http://www.computerworld.com/article/2496852/internet/americans-spend-16-minutes-of-every-hour-online-on-social-nets.html, accessed June 28, 2016.

Hricik D and CE Scott. 2008. Metadata: The ghosts haunting e-documents. *Georgia Bar Journal* 13(5):16–25.

Jelenchick LA, J Eickhoff, DA Christakis, RL Brown, C Zhang, M Benson, and MA Moreno. 2014. The Problematic and Risky Internet Use Screening Scale (PRIUSS) for adolescents and young adults: Scale development and refinement. *Computers in Human Behavior* 35:171–178.

Lagu T, EJ Kaufman, DA Asch, and K Armstrong. 2008. Content of weblogs written by health professionals. *Journal of General and Internal Medicine* 23:1642–1646.

Patchin JW. 2015. *Summary of Our Cyberullying Research (2004–2015).* http://cyberbullying.org/summary-of-our-cyberbullying-research, accessed June 28, 2016.

Recupero PR. 2006. Legal concerns for psychiatrists who maintain websites. *Psychiatric Services* 57:450–452.

Recupero PR. 2010a. The mental status examination in the age of the internet. *Journal of the American Academy of Psychiatry and the Law* 38:15–26.

Recupero PR. 2010b. Forensic psychiatry and the internet. In *Textbook of Forensic Psychiatry,* edited by RI Simon and LH Gold, Washington, DC: APP Press, 581–616.

Saltzman J. 2007. Blogger unmasked, court case upended. *The Boston Globe.* 2007. http://www.boston.com/news/local/articles/2007/05/31/blogger_unmasked_court_case_upended/?page=full, accessed June 28, 2016.

Semenov A, J Veijalainen, and J Kyppo 2010. Analysing the presence of school-shooting related communities at social media sites. *International Journal of Multimedia Intelligence and Security* 1:232–268.

Smith D, C Cerny, S Soliman, and SH Friedman. 2011, April. Technology and forensic psychiatry: Recommendations for practice. *American Academy of Psychiatry and the Law Newsletter* 19:28.

Statistic Brain. 2014. *Facebook Statistics.* http://www.statisticbrain.com/facebook-statistics, accessed June 28, 2016.

U.S. Copyright Office. 2012. *Fair Use.* http://www.copyright.gov/fls/fl102.html, accessed June 28, 2016.

U.S. Department of Health and Human Services. 2014. *What Is Cyberbullying?* http://www.stopbullying.gov/cyberbullying/what-is-it, accessed June 28, 2016.

United States ex rel. Baklid-Kunz v. Halifax Hospital Medical Center, 2012 U.S. Dist. LEXIS 158944 (M.D. Fla. Nov. 6, 2012).

Wallace P. 2008. What every attorney needs to know about electronic technology. *Florida Bar Journal* 82(9):22.

Warden C. 2013. 7 Mobile marketing stats that will blow your mind. *Convinceandconvert.com.* http://www.convinceandconvert.com/mobile/7-mobile-marketing-stats-that-will-blow-your-mind/, accessed June 28, 2016.

We Are Social. 2014. *Global Digital Statistics 2014.* http://thenextweb.com/insider/2014/01/08/worldwide-Internet-social-media-and-mobile-statistics-dig-into-183-pages-of-data/#!zbohl, accessed June 28, 2016.

85

Working in private forensic practice

WILLIAM H. REID

INTRODUCTION

This chapter describes one approach to private forensic psychiatry or psychology practice. It assumes that the reader will be retained most of the time by an attorney in a contested ("adversarial") proceeding, though experts are sometimes retained directly by courts or agencies. Many, but not all, of the principles and procedures herein also apply to clinicians who perform forensic services through agency or facility contracts, and/or as employees of agencies or facilities. Readers in academic or agency environments may notice differences between the professional viewpoints implied here and those in their own settings; this should not be construed as suggesting any significant differences in duty or ethics.

Much of the material herein has been summarized or excerpted from the author's book *Developing a Forensic Practice: Operations and Ethics for Experts* (Reid 2013).

The material in this chapter is built on four postulates that underlie successful and rewarding forensic work:

1. Practice well.
2. Understand the point of the legal exercise.
3. Be serious about ethics.
4. Quality begets success.

Courts and lawyers need experts with clinical expertise and some understanding of the legal process, not doctors who act like attorneys. The forensic expert's task is to understand his or her clinical discipline and how it applies to the forensic topic at hand.

PRIVATE FORENSIC PRACTICE

Private forensic practice, as addressed in this chapter, is work (1) at the interface of mental health and the law that is (2) performed in a private, fee-for-service context, usually (3) at the behest of a retaining attorney (but sometimes another entity). It often includes being a forensic "expert" (e.g., an "expert witness," which simply implies being allowed by a court to offer opinions within the bounds of one's education, training, and experience). The kinds of cases in which one may become involved vary, and one should be sure of actual expertise before participating in them (see Table 85.1).

DUTIES

Just as a clinician has certain duties to patients, forensic experts have duties that must be fulfilled in order to meet professional practice standards and, in some cases, legal requirements. For example, the attorney or organization that retains the expert (the "retaining entity") is entitled to know of issues that may affect the expert's ability to do the work, or that may interfere in the future (such as when testifying). Those concerns include conflict of interest, professional problems, inadequate knowledge or experience, and scheduling availability.

There are duties of honesty and objectivity to any court or other judicial or arbitrating body to which opinions are offered. One is expected to articulate opinions well and defend them convincingly, but to be honest in the process.

There are duties to the retaining entity's client(s), including those of practice standards and good faith. One should not, however, advocate directly for the litigant, nor should the litigant or any interested party be one's patient.

There is a duty of honesty and good faith to the opposing side of the case.

Treating clinicians have some duties that forensic experts *do not* have. Experts' duties to evaluees and other litigants or complainants are limited by the fact that forensic consultation rarely creates a "doctor–patient" relationship. Evaluations done solely for a forensic or administrative purpose do not, in my opinion, incur the duties of a treating clinician or clinical consultant. It is a good idea to remind evaluees of that fact, and refrain from calling them "patients" or "clients."

Table 85.1 Some private practice forensic topics

Category (some overlapping)	Includes (but may not be limited to)
Negligence, personal injury	Broad categories of common civil litigation including malpractice, emotional damage, disability, harassment, and discrimination
Criminal	Criminal responsibility (sanity), trial and other criminal-related competencies, offense mitigation
Juvenile adjudication	"Criminal" allegations, juvenile waiver to adult court
Competencies and capacities	Civil or criminal
Guardianships, conservatorships	
Child custody, best interest	
Disability, impairment, fitness for duty	
Workers' compensation	
Consultations, second opinions	A broad category of (usually) nonlitigation topics including helping individuals or organizations with such things as risk management, assessment of dangerousness, and clinical activities involving forensic issues

TRAINING, CREDENTIALS, REPUTATION, AND ETHICS

The expert's usefulness to lawyers, courts, and other entities is almost always related to his or her clinical background. Clinical skill and experience should come first, then forensic expertise.

Approved post-residency forensic fellowships can be valuable preparation for a forensic career but are not necessary for most forensic practice. Forensic subspecialty certification by the American Board of Psychiatry and Neurology is less important than *clinical* certification when working with lawyers and courts.

Accredited continuing education activities on forensic topics can increase one's practice skills. Participating in recognized forensic organizations is a good way to get current professional information, communicate with colleagues, compare practices, and stay abreast of ethical issues and guidelines.

Reputation and credibility are crucial in private forensic practice. They are easy to lose, and very difficult to re-establish. One's clinical background should be free of serious criticism (such as license blemishes, privilege suspensions, ethics complaints, or multiple malpractice lawsuits).

TREATER VERSUS EXPERT WITNESS/ CONSULTANT

The purpose and goals of a treating clinician are fundamentally different from, and often conflict with, those of a forensic expert or consultant. The treater has "fiduciary" and ethical obligations to the patient that demand that the patient's interests be placed above all else. Forensic responsibilities, on the other hand, are largely to objectivity and the court. "Dual" relationships involving both clinical and forensic or administrative work in the same person raise important conflict-of-interest problems, and should be avoided in almost all instances. Acting as both treater and expert without very good reason (such as a genuine emergency) is at best imprudent, and at worst knowingly misleads the judicial process.

The above principles notwithstanding, some "routine" administrative assessments are commonly completed by treating clinicians (though a separate evaluator is often a better choice). In the simplest cases, agencies ask treaters to opine from their records about, for example, mental disability, fitness for duty, or civil commitment.

Things get a bit more complicated when one is asked for a separate assessment or opinion about a patient's condition. Patients and patient care are significantly affected by what clinicians say to others, such as employers or agencies. Patient relationships affect (often strongly and/or adversely) one's evaluations and reports, and vice versa. A separate evaluator is best.

OTHER PRACTICE PRINCIPLES

Advocacy is the lawyer's job, not the expert's. It's not "your case," and the lawyer isn't "your lawyer." With few exceptions (such as the complex area of retention by a *pro se* litigant, not recommended for forensically inexperienced clinicians), *the expert should not be directly retained by a litigant.* Similarly, one should advocate articulately for his or her *opinions* (e.g., in reports or testimony), but not for the litigant per se.

One should not express an opinion without sufficient objective review and/or evaluation, and sufficient and representative information. Any "opinion" attributed to the expert must have an adequate foundation.

One should not communicate directly with a litigant or potential litigant, the court, or an opposing lawyer except through, or with the knowledge of, the retaining attorney. In particular, if someone calls or emails about a personal (or family) forensic matter, the psychiatrist should not do anything that might form or imply a relationship with that person, such as discussing the potential case or recommending a lawyer.

One should not accept cases without having the requisite expertise and objectivity.

In general, one should not accept an expert role in cases involving friends, close colleagues, etc., for whom there is likely to be significant bias or conflict of interest. It is ethical and proper to offer honest opinions against colleagues; however, one may wish to avoid those in one's own geographic area.

Finally, one must understand the vocabulary of forensic psychiatry. Much of the forensic expert role involves translating clinical information into the language of lawyers and courts, and working in a context of common legal terms. I recommend getting an inexpensive law dictionary.

CASE PROCEDURES

Initial attorney contact

When talking with a lawyer for the first time about a case, one should ascertain possible conflicts of interest early, and discuss them. This includes asking for the litigants' names, to see whether or not any of them creates a conflict. The lawyer's description of the case may or may not be accurate, or entirely accurate. Some lawyers are more straightforward than others. Conversations with attorneys in civil cases are usually "discoverable." One should assume that any notes taken will eventually become available to the other side. No opinions should be formed or offered based on an initial call, and one should not represent that opinions reached later will support the lawyer's side.

One should expect the following from the lawyer or other retaining entity before proceeding:

- An accurate case description, with the name of the case ("styling") if it has been filed
- A clear understanding of the expert's role
- A clear and binding fee agreement
- An expectation of receiving all available relevant records
- Time and freedom to review the records completely
- A general schedule of case deadlines
- An understanding of the expected work procedure

Typical early case procedures

A great many cases should proceed roughly as follows:

1. Receiving an initial communication from a lawyer or other potential retaining entity. Time is spent talking about the matter, getting to know the attorney, answering his or her questions, deciding whether or not one can be useful, deciding whether or not one wishes to participate, and agreeing on retention details. One should take notes and get relevant identifying information. *I do not recommend that this step be completed by email.*
2. Establishing a *written* agreement/contract, including fees and billing procedures.
3. Receiving records. One should request, and expect, *all* available and relevant records, often including clinical, school, employment, legal, corrections, etc., records; others' forensic or clinical reports, and depositions. One should rely on the lawyer to get the records rather than trying to do it oneself. Obtaining records for forensic review requires time and specific legal procedures in order to be certain the records are accurate and complete.
4. Completing an initial review. One may choose to review only selected records at this point but should not offer written opinions without adequate information. Notes should be taken as needed, understanding that they will probably be supplied to the other side (especially in civil matters). One should not be bullied into expressing opinions without all the relevant information.

   Any notes created should be preserved. An expert's notes and other materials are rarely "work product" (a concept that applies to lawyers, rarely to experts). Destroying notes, records, emails, phone messages, etc., created during the case is inappropriate, and can be illegal.

   A somewhat inexperienced plaintiff's expert was being deposed in a particularly sensational case involving several defendants. Lawyers from several firms were in the room as he began to answer questions posed by the other side's lawyers:

   Opposing Lawyer: "Did you receive my *subpoena duces tecum*, doctor, asking you to bring all of your notes to the deposition?"
   Expert Being Deposed: "Yes."
   Lawyer: "And may I see those notes, please?"
   Expert: "They aren't available."
   Lawyer: "Really? May I ask why not?"
   Expert: "I shredded them after I received your subpoena."
   Lawyer (somewhat taken aback): "May I ask why you shredded your notes in this case after being specifically asked to produce them for this deposition?"
   Expert: "They were my private notes, and I thought they might be harmful to (the plaintiffs)."

   The deposing lawyer spent the next several minutes on the record explaining the concept of "spoliation of evidence" (a felony), and sarcastically asking, in front of several lawyers who would likely spread the story to others, why the doctor should not be charged with a crime for destroying his notes.
5. Oral communication with the lawyer or retaining entity about the preliminary review, any need for further records, and next steps (such as examination, report, or testimony). One should not communicate

in writing, or create any report, unless the attorney requests it.

Many cases end here. The great majority never get to trial; many are resolved one way or another before reports are written or expert depositions taken.

6. Examinations, interviews, and/or testing. Examining or interviewing litigants or others should not take place before case review and discussion with the lawyer (there are exceptions).

DISCUSSING FINDINGS WITH THE LAWYER

Regular communication is important. Discussions and updates should cover, in terms the attorney can easily understand, how the review findings may affect the case. One should avoid using lots of psychiatric terms or "psychobabble"; the lawyer wants to know what the expert thinks, wants a clear and concise summary, and wants to see that the expert can convey his or her findings to others (such as jury members) articulately. If the findings seem ambiguous or the expert's views are ambivalent, now is the time to talk them out and try to find clarity. Early discussion focuses one's thoughts, so that future reports or testimony can be as concise as the findings allow.

"Adverse" findings

Lawyers often benefit from expert findings that seem to go "against" their clients almost as much as they benefit from findings that "support" them. They need to know both the strengths and the weaknesses of their cases in order to evaluate case merits objectively, save time and money on frivolous litigation, promote reasonable negotiations and settlements, and help their clients accept the truth about their situations. In addition, if one finds few merits in the psychiatric issues of a case, expressing or (if asked) documenting that result may protect the attorney from later criticism for not pursuing them (e.g., for not pursuing an insanity defense in a criminal matter).

EVALUATIONS

Even "simple" evaluations usually require record review before interview or examination. They should be treated with the same professional routine as any other case. Two exceptions are assessments for acute dangerousness and examination of criminal defendants, which require record review, but examination should take place as soon as feasible.

One must know the clinical principles involved in the evaluation (such as for assessing children, dealing with substance abuse, or exploring clinical nuances such as suicide risk), and apply them in the subspecialty forensic context (addressed below). *Routine clinical procedures and attitudes alone are insufficient for forensic interviews.*

Although psychiatrists and clinical psychologists are accustomed to dealing with sensitive topics, forensic evaluations often involve situations rarely encountered in general clinical practice. The objectivity required in assessments, reports, and testimony suffers when the expert cannot adequately recognize and manage his or her personal feelings about, for example, particular tragedy or heinous behavior. One should decline cases in which he or she cannot remain objective.

What if the evaluee fails to appear or does not cooperate?

OPPOSING ATTORNEY REFUSAL

The opposing attorney may believe an evaluation would jeopardize his or her case, or not wish to expose the litigant to additional scrutiny. He or she may allege that the evaluee would be traumatized by the examination. Opposing lawyers may also try to place unreasonable restrictions on one's evaluation (see below). These are usually matters for the lawyers to work out between themselves. One might comment about (a) the extent to which not doing an evaluation may affect your ability to form opinions, (b) the extent to which not doing an evaluation may affect your credibility, (c) the disclaimer that must be added to any report or opinions that lack an appropriate examination, and (d) the fact that psychiatric evaluations are almost never particularly "traumatic" for evaluees.

EVALUEE REFUSAL

If an evaluee calls to cancel, or does not keep the appointment, one should contact the retaining lawyer (not the opposing one). One should not reschedule or "negotiate" directly with the evaluee unless it is simply a matter of scheduling a more convenient time (and in that case notify the retaining entity). If an evaluee balks after arriving or demands to leave after the interview has begun, one should be polite, encourage the evaluee to stay, and briefly try to address concerns that may be making him or her uncomfortable. One should not "negotiate" extensively or do things that might be construed as manipulation in return for completing the examination. If the evaluee actually ends the interview prematurely, he or she should be politely informed that the behavior will be noted in the evaluation record, and the retaining lawyer informed.

Differences between forensic and "patient" interview styles

- A forensic evaluee almost always has a nonclinical interest in the outcome of the evaluation and the case.
- A forensic evaluee often has good reason to fool or mislead the examiner, and most can do so to some extent. Examiners should not assume that they can tell whether or not the evaluee is telling the truth, or whether or not an answer is accurate.

- Forensic evaluations thus usually require extensive corroboration.
- Forensic evaluators generally have no duty of "patient" confidentiality or clinical care to an evaluee (see Consents and Notifications, below).
- Unless targeted to a specific topic (such as trial competency), forensic evaluations are routinely longer than clinical ones, and frequently more comprehensive (see below).

Examination principles

QUESTIONS FROM THE EVALUEE

The examiner has no obligation to answer every question an examinee asks during or after an interview (and often should not), but queries and concerns should be handled with sensitivity. I recommend against providing feedback to evaluees about the examination. One may simply acknowledge that the question is reasonable and refer the evaluee to his or her attorney or other relevant party.

Evaluees often ask for a copy of the evaluator's report. Although they may be entitled to a copy at some point, it should not come from the examiner, but from the evaluee's attorney or other party (insurance company, employer, etc.), as relevant.

OUTSIDE CONSULTATION

If outside consultation such as psychological testing, general medical examination, laboratory tests, or neuroimaging is necessary for a complete evaluation, one should talk with the retaining attorney before arranging it. That discussion should include whether the additional person will be the expert's consultant or separately hired by the lawyer, and how he or she will be paid.

SCHEDULING AND PROCEDURE

One should give the retaining attorney or agency interview specifications and explain why they are important. Everyone should understand the evaluating expert's role, expected procedures (including pre-examination review and post-examination communications), the kinds of results that may reasonably be expected, the likely number and durations of interviews and/or testing, the examination location and environment, recording procedures, and approximate cost. The court may dictate or limit some of these. One should resist procedures that might prevent a proper and complete workup. Except for simple things like verifying times or giving directions, communications should be through the retaining attorney or agency, not directly with the evaluee.

SETTING

A professional office should be used whenever feasible, either one's own or a colleague's (e.g., when evaluating someone in a distant community). Personal settings such as a home office, hotel room, or the evaluee's home should be avoided, although an evaluee's home may be appropriate for some child or family evaluations, or civil capacity assessments in which the person cannot travel. Assessments should not be performed in lawyers' offices.

JAIL/PRISON SETTINGS

Assessments should be during "contact" visits whenever feasible. The retaining lawyer or agency should arrange the visit in advance, understanding the examiner's requirements and preferences. One alternative is to ask for the kind of room in which lawyers talk with their clients. A face-to-face interview using shackles, even through bars, is better than one through glass, by intercom, or through a detail-obscuring screen.

EXAMINER SAFETY

The following apply to all evaluations and clinical settings:

- The examiner should never knowingly put himself or herself in danger. Inattention to—or overconfidence about—assault by evaluees and patients has gotten evaluators killed.
- Examiners must not believe they can predict, "sense," or "talk down" assaultive behavior in predatory, enraged, frightened, psychotic, or confused evaluees. "Sensing" danger is cause to act on that intuition, but *one must not rely on intuition to prevent assault.*
- One must not let anyone else put him or her in danger, or accept a setting that might be dangerous. If a correctional officer, nurse, or other person assigns a setting that may not be safe, one should demand a safer one, a monitor, and/or a chaperone, as needed. *Examiners must not be shy about this.*
- "Panic buttons" and advice such as "don't sit between the evaluee and the door" are woefully overrated (especially when the door is locked).

WHO MAY BE PRESENT DURING THE ASSESSMENT?

Alone is best, if it can be accomplished safely. Security or corrections staff may monitor through a window but should almost never be within earshot of normal conversation. Sometimes an attendant or chaperone is required. He or she should be unobtrusive, avoid interfering unnecessarily, and afford as much privacy as feasible. A parent or guardian may be necessary or recommended for children's interviews, and sometimes group or family interviews are important; otherwise, family and co-litigants should not be present without good reason.

Having a lawyer in the room compromises the evaluation. The evaluee may be entitled to have his or her attorney there, but one should not accept a lawyer's presence without careful consideration with the retaining person. An audio or video recording of the assessment, particularly with an unattended recorder or camera, may allay an opposing attorney's concerns (see below). If an attorney demands to be present, he or she must be out of the evaluee's vision and be silent. Examiners should not tolerate lawyer interference. If it occurs, it should be carefully documented and consideration given to terminating the assessment.

RECORDING (AUDIO OR VIDEO)

Recording most interviews and evaluations is highly recommended. Video is preferred. Concerns that recording will alter the atmosphere of the interview are unfounded. Properly done, the process is usually innocuous; experienced videographers know how to be unobtrusive (although an unattended camera may be preferred). Recording *should not* be surreptitious. Continuous recording provides accurate, usually unimpeachable, documentation. It decreases some evaluator liability (e.g., for alleged inappropriate behavior). It renders detailed note-taking unnecessary and is helpful when writing reports. Recording may also increase the evaluator's credibility, showing that one is not afraid of scrutiny. It may defuse attorney requests to be present in the interview, and reassure the evaluee that the examiner will be honest and objective.

EXAMINATION FORMAT AND BEHAVIOR

Format and content vary with the purpose of the evaluation and other factors. There is not space in this chapter for a complete discussion, but here are some principles:

- Forensic interviews are not mere extensions of patient interviews. One must know the purpose and context of the evaluation, and modify the format and style accordingly.
- The examination should not be limited by common time constraints of routine clinical assessments. Many forensic evaluations should take several hours, not including psychological testing and other procedures. It is often useful to schedule two or more interviews.
- The procedure should be as professional and friendly as is compatible with the circumstances. One should explain the process and format to the evaluee, and offer breaks as appropriate.
- One should be respectful, but not "sandbagged" by the evaluee. Persistence and follow-up to queries are important. One should watch for both conscious and unconscious evasiveness, and be very thorough.
- The examiner should be honest (just as one expects of the evaluee), and avoid "tricks" such as making a sudden noise to assess startle effect.
- One may consider inviting the evaluee to bring one or two other people to the interview to provide corroboration, expansion, support, and/or contradiction of the evaluee's statements. One should talk separately with them, avoiding opportunity for the parties to "compare notes" between interviews.

CONSENTS AND NOTIFICATIONS

It is rarely necessary to obtain written consent from forensic evaluees, although some professions recommend it. The evaluee has usually agreed, through a lawyer, by virtue of pursuing a claim or action, as part of an employer or agency requirement, and/or in following an attorney's instructions, to be evaluated for the purpose contemplated. In addition, many evaluations are required by a court order (although the evaluee may simply refuse to participate). The evaluee is free to stop the interview at any time.

The above do not mean that one should proceed without regard for the evaluee's feelings and need for information. One should provide simple, clear facts about the following, ideally in written form, with a copy kept for the file:

- The evaluator's name and profession (and those of others in the room)
- The general purpose of the examination
- The evaluator's role in the case and who has retained him or her
- The fact that the evaluation is being recorded (in writing, by video, etc.)
- The uses to which the information obtained may be put (attorney discussions, a report, testimony, etc.)
- The fact that the evaluation is not intended to be stressful and breaks may be taken at any time
- The fact that the interviewer will not ask about the legal strategies of the case except as relevant to the evaluation task
- An invitation to ask reasonable questions
- The need for the evaluee to be honest and frank

This introductory process will often set a tone of comfortable professionalism, with a minimum of adversarial stance.

EVALUEES WITH CLINICAL NEEDS

Absent an emergency, one *should not* treat or give specific clinical advice or referral names to an evaluee. Simple, generic encouragement is often nice (e.g., "I hope you feel better soon"), but if one believes care is necessary, it should be recommended through, or after discussion with, the retaining attorney.

Special note regarding criminal defendants

When criminal responsibility (criminal "sanity," generally the mental ability to form criminal intent) is an issue, it is important to interview the arrestee/defendant as soon as feasible after the alleged crime. Nevertheless, *one must not forensically interview an arrestee before defense counsel is appointed and notified.* It is ethical to evaluate and treat an unrepresented arrestee or defendant for *clinical* purposes, but one must not do any "forensic" evaluation or assume any expert role. If such a person blurts something out, it may be recorded along with an impression of the person's state of mind at the time (e.g., delirious, intoxicated, psychotic, or not). One should not pursue the topic with the person unless it is clinically necessary. An examiner who treats an arrestee/defendant should not become an expert witness in the same case.

REPORTS

Reports are lasting representations of one's opinions, abilities, expertise, and effectiveness. In most cases, they are the expert's most influential activity. Done right, they help the case and the expert's reputation. Done wrong (e.g., without adequate preparation, misunderstanding the purpose or audience, with poor writing skills, or in the wrong format), the case is likely to suffer and one's usefulness to the attorney or court becomes severely limited. Forensic reports are quite different in format and intent from clinical reports, and effective styles vary with cases. Some reports take the form of letters or affidavits. They often become part of a public record.

What do reports and affidavits accomplish?

- They formally convey one's opinions and other information to parties who are important to the case.
- They organize and clarify the expert's opinions.
- They are a tool for resolving cases.
- They often become the basis for later testimony.
- In some situations, they determine whether or not a civil lawsuit (e.g., malpractice suit) can proceed.

Lawyers sometimes ask for a quick, last-minute report. One should resist such requests, because supporting information may be inadequate, and hurried reports are often sloppy or incomplete. One should take the time to follow a standard routine rather than being pressured by the lawyer. *It is improper to allow a lawyer to write one's report or convey opinions that you have not genuinely rendered.* The expert may, however, accept some predetermined format or talk with the attorney about helpful ways to frame opinions once they have been formed.

Report format

Format and style vary with the case, jurisdiction, and expert.

Short is usually better than long, unless the important information is very complex. Long reports are tiresome, and the more voluminous the material, the more likely it will contain extraneous material that may be harmful to the case. Well-written brief reports generally take extra thought and care. Winnowing the important points from many hours of work, then concisely explaining and supporting them, is time consuming.

Reports must be clear for the reader. They should be written for lay readers rather than professional ones, with opinions stated early and easy to find. One should avoid extremely detailed clinical material, extended recitations of psychodynamics, and pseudo-legalistic prose, but remember that expert opinions must be accompanied by sufficient explanation. When there is doubt, one may ask the person who requested the report how much explanation is required.

Some reports require certain kinds of format and content. If such requirements are not followed, the report can be invalidated or the case threatened. The retaining attorney can clarify those needs.

Legal terms must be used correctly. One should know the applicable *legal* definitions of all terms used in reports (e.g., "reasonable medical certainty/probability," "standard of care," "foreseeability"), not simply dictionary definitions or common usage.

Relevant disclaimers and caveats are important

One of the most important caveats is that the report is predicated on the information available at the time it was written, and the writer reserves the right to amend it if additional information becomes available. Another is disclosure of whether or not relevant persons were examined (e.g., criminal defendants or civil plaintiffs), and if they were not examined, whether or not examination might change the opinions in the report.

Reports should be well written

The report is a lasting representation of the expert. It must be properly formatted, clearly organized, and contain excellent grammar and spelling.

TESTIFYING

Most cases do not go to trial, but one must assume that testimony of some kind will be required.

The expert should always have a pre-testimony conference with the retaining attorney

The lawyer should bring one up to date about the case, go over likely questions and what he/she thinks is important, and maybe discuss the opposing lawyer. He or she may give advice such as

- "Listen carefully to the question."
- "Don't answer too quickly. Think first."
- "It's not a memory test. If you need to look at records or notes, do so."
- "Give short, direct answers; don't answer more than you're asked."
- In depositions, "don't be misled by the informal setting."
- "Don't speculate."
- "Don't argue (but *do* correct misunderstandings)." Arguing usually weakens testimony.
- "Don't be flippant, disrespectful, or arrogant." The opposing lawyer already knows the answers to most of the questions you will be asked. Your sense of humor is easily misconstrued, weakening your credibility.

Experts should stick to forensic opinions, not philosophy

Verbose, off-the-cuff explanations usually weaken testimony.

"Just answer 'yes' or 'no', Doctor"

One should generally ignore a demand for "yes or no" if the question cannot reasonably be answered that way (or if the false dichotomy of "yes or no" would misconstrue one's meaning). Experts are entitled to explain their answers, or respond with something like "I don't know"; "I can't answer 'yes-or-no' as you've phrased the question"; "answering 'yes or no' would misconstrue my opinion"; or "I don't understand your question."

Questions should be answered only once

Lawyers sometimes ask the same question several times, and then choose the most advantageous answer. One should not be talked out of accurate answers.

Personal questions

One should politely set limits on irrelevant personal questions (the answers are public record), but whether or not something is relevant is the judge's decision, not the expert's. "How much have you charged in this case?" is fair. "What was your gross income last year?" is probably out of bounds.

Experts must be able to tolerate criticism

Testimony is neither a collegial nor a scientific exercise. It is *adversarial*. Experts must tolerate questioning from lawyers who vigorously oppose their testimony, and who may be very good at turning their words, opinions, and even behaviors to the other side's advantage. When one has solid and well-articulated opinions, the opposing attorney may attack the expert's qualifications. That is unpleasant, but it is not personal; one should not become defensive.

Testimony should generally be free of surprises

Both the expert and the lawyer who retained him or her should know the strengths and weaknesses of the expert's opinions, potential arguments against those opinions, and any controversial issues in the expert's background *before* testimony.

Depositions

It is common for experts in civil matters to be "deposed" by the opposing side, usually after submitting an expert report. Deposition is a questioning process, carried out under oath, designed to reveal one's opinions and what one would say at trial. The setting is relatively informal, perhaps an office (preferably not one's own) or conference room, but the rules are strict.

Once a deposition is scheduled, the expert probably receives a *subpoena duces tecum* from the opposing lawyer (a demand to bring case records, files, notes, billing materials, etc.). One may question, or even decline, some of the requests (e.g., for highly personal items or onerous demands), but that should be done through the retaining lawyer. Many depositions are video-recorded and may be shown to the jury. When this occurs, one must behave (and dress) as if he or she were actually in court, and direct answers to the camera.

Trials

In trial testimony, opinions and comments should be directed to the "factfinder" (usually a jury, but sometimes the judge), not to the lawyer asking the questions. One should speak clearly and simply, uncomplicating the issues if possible, with concise points of importance. Jurors usually like doctors, but they hate arrogance, pseudoprofessional "psychobabble," and being "talked down to."

FEES AND BILLING

Fees, billing, and collection procedures in forensic practice are quite different from those in clinical practice. Most forensic practices have far fewer clients; individual bills are larger, and collections are usually better. Resolving billing disputes is far more straightforward.

Understanding the practicalities and ethics of charging and billing for forensic services greatly simplifies practice management. One should be clear about rates and fees, responsibility for payment, expectation of payment, and schedule and method of payment. Lawyers understand hourly fees, retainers, deposits, and the value of professional time and expertise.

One should realize, but not overestimate, one's value. Forensic professionals usually charge more per hour for forensic services than for clinical ones. Rates vary with training, experience, reputation, location, and personal preference. Most charges should be time based (procedure based may be acceptable). "Contingency fees" (those related to case outcome or lawyer recovery) are unethical.

Requiring a retainer and/or deposit against billings is usual (especially for new clients, time-consuming reports and testimony—see below). As a practical matter, one should watch for early portents of fee and collection problems, and be cautious if the attorney does not agree to a retainer or is late with payment.

In general, the person or entity that retains the expert should receive the bills. The financial agreement should be with the attorney or retaining entity, *not* with a litigant or other lawyer's client, even though that person may be the ultimate source of funds. One should not be expected to bill litigants directly, or to bill an insurance company, unless the company itself is the retaining entity.

It is important to bill regularly, and not let debt get out of hand. *One should never wait to bill until the case has been decided.*

All agreements should be in writing. The attorney should receive a written description of expert fees and billing procedures. Exceptions to standard procedures increase the probability of fee and collection disagreements. The "fee sheet" should specify the person or entity responsible for charges and the services to be charged. Time spent reviewing, interviewing, talking with the attorney and others, preparing reports, and testifying are obvious, but the fee agreement should also address things like unkept appointments, travel, and waiting time.

The fee agreement should note that work may cease if bills are substantially in arrears or deposits are not received. This can include not releasing reports and not being available for deposition or trial. One should be reasonable but firm in these communications, and try to prevent problems by being clear and taking early action rather than letting payment problems build.

OFFICE PROCEDURES

A successful forensic practice does not need a very large administrative system, but it must have a very *good* administrative system. Private practice is a service business that requires an excellent interface with forensic clients and a reliable, efficient "back office."

Staffing

People are the backbone of the practice, even if one has only one assistant. One should employ the very best staff feasible: intelligent, polite, dedicated, efficient, and very good at interacting with others (upon whom one's livelihood depends). Staff should be chosen carefully, trained well, and treated right.

The practice exists for the benefit and convenience of clients

Return business and word-of-mouth referrals are almost always one's largest revenue sources.

Availability

The telephone is one's main interface with clients and potential clients. The person who answers the office telephone *must* be a well-trained, courteous, real person. Potential clients who get a voicemail message very often go somewhere else.

Email and texting do not replace telephone contact

New attorney–clients may first email, but detailed contact should be by phone or in person, not by email or text. One learns far more in a direct conversation, with fewer security concerns.

Practice and its files be kept secure

New staff should have background checks and be trained in basic security procedures. One must be aware of, and deal with, the substantial security risks associated with email. Employees and contract workers should sign a confidentiality agreement.

Records

Everything that enters or leaves the office should be logged, including phone calls, letters, records, deliveries, and visitors. All case-related telephone conversations, scheduling agreements, billing changes, and the like deserve a file memo. There should be a procedure for keeping track of current and past cases, deadlines, case types, past testimony, referral sources, and similar information. These seeming "details" help one analyze practice patterns, keep track of referral sources, and adhere to jurisdiction rules (e.g., federal court rules for supplying testimony information).

Client files and records must be kept secure but easily accessible. Records often must be located after months, even years, of quiescence. It is useful to create a very accessible summary file for each case, with notes, reports, and other frequently addressed information. One *should not* store client records in "the cloud" without the client's permission and a very reliable retrieval and security system. Closed case archives should be kept until the client says they may be destroyed; one may wish to keep personal notes, reports, and financial files for decades.

Billing and collections

Most lawyers pay promptly; a few make it very hard to collect. Most collection problems can be prevented before they arise. A specific billing procedure, understood in writing before providing services, is a big help.

Budgeting

Compensation in private forensic practice usually comes in fairly large amounts, but infrequently. Slack periods and payment delays are routine. Retainers and deposits do not belong to the expert until they have been earned. It is helpful to keep a separate account for retainers and client deposits, to facilitate prompt refunds.

SUMMARY

This chapter has outlined the basic topics and procedures that make up most private forensic consultations: attorney relationships and communication, expert roles, record review, forensic examinations, forensic reports, and testimony. It also addressed many of the practical aspects of forensic work, such as office procedures and differences between general and forensic practice.

SUMMARY KEY POINTS

- Successful forensic work demands a clear understanding of one's duties and ethical responsibilities.
- Contrary to clinical duties, which largely arise from a doctor–patient relationship, much of one's forensic responsibility is related to being honest and objective for others to whom one owes a duty (often a retaining lawyer and/or a court).
- "Hired guns" and "whores of the court," common topics of public and media criticism, have no place in our profession.
- Practitioners who choose to become involved in forensic cases should first be very good clinicians, then understand what the legal process requires of a forensic consultant or expert witness.
- Quality forensic practice recognizes the differences between a purely clinical approach and the additional procedures and objectivity expected by lawyers and courts.

REFERENCE

Reid W. 2013. *Developing a Forensic Practice: Operations and Ethics for Experts.* New York: Routledge; Taylor & Francis.

86

Social science, law, and psychiatry

EUGENE LEE AND ANN M. KILLENBECK

INTRODUCTION

In their pathbreaking work, *Social Science in Law: Cases and Materials*, John Monahan and Laurens Walker argue that the use of the social sciences in the law reflects a departure from the "classical belief that the application of logic could determine a single, correct solution for every [legal] case" to the more nuanced "view that the answer to legal problems varies according to the social context" within which they arise (Monahan and Walker 2014, 1). This approach treats "law as a means of establishing social policy" and stresses the importance of identifying and using information about how people, and society, actually function (Monahan and Walker 2014, 1).

The social sciences—generally understood as those disciplines that study human society and individual relationships in and to society—include, but are not limited to, psychology, sociology, criminology, anthropology, history, economics, and political science. These areas of inquiry focus on many of the same issues that interest psychiatrists, in particular, forensic psychiatrists, albeit from diverse angles. This is entirely understandable. "Forensic" comes from the Latin word, *forensis*, meaning: public; to the forum or public discussion; argumentative, rhetorical, belonging to debate or discussion (American Academy of Forensic Sciences 2015). Forensic psychiatrists accordingly share common concerns with social scientists, and their work may be informed by social science not only in criminal matters and civil disputes, but also in questions of public health and policy.

The social sciences and social science studies—including psychology—differ from the medical education and training of psychiatrists. Nevertheless, it has been suggested that psychiatry may be closer to social science than to physical science (Stone 2008, 170). The diagnosis of mental disorders, for example, factors in psychosocial context (American Psychiatric Association 2013, 16). Psychiatrists may generally be versed with individualized bio-psycho-social modeling of patients' symptoms, functioning, and quality of life (Engel 1977, 132). There is, accordingly, overlap between the clinical disciplines.

Opportunities for meaningful dialogue are especially pronounced with the legal arena. Social science has been accurately described as contributing a "massive amount of material" dealing with psychiatry and law (Malmquist 2004, 1144). Indeed, numerous decisions by the Supreme Court of the United States have incorporated insights gleaned from the social sciences, with profound implications for forensic psychiatrists. Comprehensively summarizing these materials falls outside the scope of this book.

The goal of this chapter is to illustrate how some of these disciplines—and the cases in which they have factored—bear relevance to forensic psychiatry. It begins with a discussion of two overarching considerations. The first is a brief discussion about scientific methodology. The second, an examination of the importance of contexts in the issues implicated. The balance of the chapter then discusses a small set of examples of social science applications pertinent to forensic psychiatry.

METHODOLOGY

Generally speaking, clinical and legal researchers may ask: how does one know what is thought to be known? Randomized, double-blinded, and placebo-controlled interventional studies (for instance, involving biomedical pharmaceuticals) present one form of evidence. Population-based, observational studies may provide similarly rigorous evidence of a different nature. Both approaches (interventional and observational) should invoke critical analysis of association before cause-and-effect might be inferred.

Theorists of causality in the social sciences must consider the argument made by a group described as "Emergentists," who hold "that *some* social phenomena (and indeed, some physical and biological phenomena), rather than *all* of them, are not amenable to scientific investigation insofar as such investigation is causal" (Rudner 1966, 71). They may focus on a "thesis of absolute emergence," a form of skepticism which "advances the belief that some events are, in *principle*, unpredictable (i.e., there are events the prediction of which is *logically impossible*), since they are not connected with other events in any lawlike fashion" (Rudner 1966, 71). A different variant suggests a "thesis of *relative* emergence," which posits that given "certain circumstances (e.g., our technology or knowledge, or the inaccessibility to observation of phenomena, at a given time), it is not *technically possible* to predict the occurrence of certain events" (Rudner 1966, 71).

Social science in particular might require familiarity with both qualitative and quantitative research methodologies. The former is especially pronounced in social science investigations, which may use qualitative techniques to gather information relevant to understanding human behaviors and factors relevant to such behaviors. In the latter, quantitative approaches require thoughtful distinction between statistical significance, clinical significance, and legal significance (Kraemer and Kupfer 2006, 990; Monahan and Walker 2014, 94). Additionally, even statistically significant results have limited applicability on individual case assessments without, for instance, adequate matching of control variables.

BEHAVIOR AND CONTEXT

Forensic psychiatrists and social scientists may study patterns in peoples' behaviors. For some, this includes questions of culpability and consequence. These are also central elements in the law, a system of rules that protects rights and governs behaviors. When individual behaviors conflict with those rules, prescribed directives are applied in ways that—at least theoretically—maximize consistency and fairness. Criminal law, for example, serves to punish (both as retribution on the criminal, and as restitution for the victim), to deter (incapacitating the criminal, and serving as an example to others from doing the same act), and to express values of society (Wilson and Herrnstein 1985, 492–498). As one great figure in American law wrote:

> What have we better than a blind guess to show that the criminal law in its present form does more good than harm? I do not stop to refer to the effect which it has had in degrading prisoners and in plunging them further into crime, or to the question whether fine and imprisonment do not fall more heavily on a criminal's wife and children than on himself. I have in mind more far-reaching questions. Does punishment deter? Do we deal with criminals on proper principles? (Holmes 1897, 470)

As they answer these questions, legal decision makers routinely incorporate expert clinical assessments of human behavior. Some obvious examples include evaluations for criminal responsibility, competence to stand trial (and restoration of fitness when incompetent), and managing the risks of self-injurious and violent behaviors, topics covered in detail elsewhere in this book. How though, do physicians treat patients suffering from mental disorders characterized by patterns of violating the rights of others?

For example, the diagnostic criteria for Conduct Disorder include "a repetitive and persistent pattern of behavior in which the basic rights of others or major age-appropriate societal norms or rules are violated" (American Psychiatric Association 2013, 469). Similarly, Antisocial Personality Disorder features "a pervasive pattern of disregard for and violation of the rights of others" (American Psychiatric Association 2013, 659). Such behavioral patterns themselves are typically neither exculpatory (e.g., the insanity defense) nor preclusive of treatment, rehabilitation, and recovery.

Understanding behavioral change for justice-involved persons is of natural interest to forensic psychiatrists. Are the causes of crime "buried deep in political economy, culture and social structure," and interventions "mere tinkering" (Andrews et al. 1990, 45)? Challenging reliance on models of psychopathology, one meta-analysis compared effect sizes for major predictors of recidivism, finding no significant difference between mentally disordered and non-disordered offenders (Bonta et al. 1998, 123). Here, criminal history variables were the best predictors for recidivism, and clinical variables had the smallest effect sizes (Bonta et al. 1998, 129–132).

More recently, a 2012 white paper from the American Council of State Governments Justice Center put forth a three-dimensional framework integrating criminogenic risk with behavioral health needs (e.g., substance abuse and mental illness), emphasizing that mental illness is not a core criminogenic risk factor (Osher et al. 2012, 33–34). The paper highlights risk factors predictive of future criminal activity, with numerous factors clearly outlining the justice-involved person's social context. These criminogenic risk factors include one's associates (who are potential sources of positive—and immediate—reinforcement for criminal behavior) and situations involving family and educational, vocational, and leisure-time pursuits (Osher et al. 2012, 23).

Psychiatric de-institutionalization also deserves mention with respect to social context, as the number of patients in American state and county mental hospitals peaked at 559,000 in 1955. This was followed by decades of consistent annual declines (Mechanic and Rochefort 1990, 307). By 2014, the census in state hospitals had dropped to 40,600 people (NASMHPD 2014, 6). De-institutionalization is understood in three separate domains. First, psychiatric medication rose to large-scale use (Brill and Patton 1957, 509). Second, courts examined civil rights for persons potentially living with mental illnesses. (See, e.g., *Baxstrom v. Herold* 1966.) Third, applied economic and political sciences created vehicles enabling hospitals to discharge patients to community settings, using then-novel programs such as Community Mental Health Centers, Medicare, Medicaid, and Social Security. With shrinking availability of psychiatric hospital beds, the potential for flux into jails and prisons (e.g., "trans-institutionalization") is questioned. At times, this debate references a study of European countries finding inverse associations between estimated numbers of psychiatric inpatients and (1) the numbers of prison inmates, and (2) the numbers of deaths attributed to murder (Penrose 1939, 12).

EVOLVING STANDARDS OF DECENCY

An example of the interplay between and among American law, social science, and forensic psychiatry can be seen in the use and value of the social sciences in cases implicating the Eighth Amendment prohibition of "cruel and unusual punishments." That limitation on government authority is important but, as is often the case with constitutional provisions, susceptible to many meanings. As Chief Justice Warren observed in the seminal case of *Trop v. Dulles*, 356 U.S. 86, 100–101 (1958), "the words of the Amendment are not precise, and ... their scope is not static. The Amendment must draw its meaning from the evolving standards of decency that mark the progress of a maturing society." The court's subsequent attempts to clarify and develop this "evolving standards of decency" test can be seen in two sets of cases in which social science offered critical insights. The first focuses on the punishment of individuals based on their status, as opposed to actual behaviors. The second concerns efforts to impose the death penalty.

Status versus behavior

Criminal sanctions are generally imposed in the wake of individually culpable conduct. Serious crimes require that the offender possess a particular state of mind, in legal terms, a *mens rea*. The conduct in question must, the law instructs, involve a particular type of decision or action. So, for example, the Model Penal Code speaks of the need for a complete criminal act to include mental states described as "willing," "knowing," "reckless," or "negligent." This raises an especially troubling concern: what should the law make of, and how should it assess, allegedly criminal acts where the "conduct" at the heart of the prosecution reflects an individual's status, rather than his or her actual behavior?

Two Supreme Court decisions illustrate both the problem and the value of social science research. In *Robinson v. California*, 370 U.S. 660 (1962), the Court held that a California statute criminalizing mere addiction to drugs, as opposed to usage, constituted cruel and unusual punishment. The court recognized that the individual being prosecuted may well have "actual[ly] use[d]... narcotics within the State's jurisdiction." That is, he may have engaged in criminally culpable conduct. However, the jury was instructed that it could convict "if they found simply that [Robinson's] 'status' or 'chronic condition' was that of being 'addicted to the use of narcotics'" (*Robinson v. California* 1962, 665).

The court rejected that approach. There was no proof that the defendant "touched any narcotic drug within the State or [was] guilty of any irregular behavior there." Rather, he was simply an addict, "an illness which may be contracted innocently or involuntarily" (*Robinson v. California* 1962, 667). Stressing the importance of "contemporary human knowledge," the majority recognized the problems posed by assigning criminal sanctions for simple status (*Robinson v. California* 1962, 666). Indeed, it declared that "[e]ven one day in prison would be a cruel and unusual punishment for the 'crime' of having a common cold" (*Robinson v. California* 1962, 667).

Further, in *Powell v. Texas*, 392 U.S. 514 (1968), the court considered a similar issue: if the state cannot punish a drug addict for addiction, then what about an alcoholic for public drunkenness? Here, the case hinged on whether public drunkenness was nothing more than an unavoidable consequence of a person's condition (here, alcoholism). If so, *Robinson* seemed to compel the conclusion that the Eighth Amendment prohibits any punishment.

The court did not, however, find a constitutional violation. Instead, it upheld a $50 fine against a man with a pronounced history of alcoholism after police found him publicly intoxicated. Writing for the court, albeit in a plurality opinion (which is not as authoritative as a true majority opinion), Justice Marshall looked carefully at the nature of alcoholism, including its definition(s), causes, status as a medical condition, impact on a person's culpability, and susceptibility to deterrence or rehabilitation. He stressed that, at least at that time, alcoholism remained a fairly new subject of academic inquiry that had not yet attained expert consensus, noting "the comparatively primitive state of our knowledge on the subject" (*Powell v. Texas* 1968, 526). Accordingly, the court was "unable to conclude ... on the current state of medical knowledge, that chronic alcoholics ... suffer from such an irresistible compulsion to drink and to get drunk in public that they are utterly unable to control their performance of either or both of these acts" (*Powell v. Texas* 1968, 535). More tellingly, he expressed the concern that a premature determination of an alcoholic's culpability for Eighth Amendment purposes would "freeze the developing productive dialogue between law and psychiatry into a rigid constitutional mold" and thereby "write the Constitutional formulas cast in terms whose meaning, let alone relevance, is not yet clear either to doctors or to lawyers" (*Powell v. Texas* 1968, 537).

In both cases, knowledge derived from the social sciences provided the frameworks within which the court made a determination about whether "evolving standards of decency" countenanced the imposition of punishment solely on the basis of status. Tellingly, the court was willing to fashion a rule when it was confident that the state of scientific knowledge supported that decision. However, when the information before it was not up to sufficient scientific standards, the court demurred.

Nature and conditions of punishment

The social sciences have been especially useful as a means for providing contexts in cases where guilt has been adjudicated and the focus is on the nature and scope of the resulting punishment. That process began with *Furman v. Georgia*, 408 U.S. 238 (1972), in which a sharply divided court found that the nation's death penalty practices violated the Eighth

Amendment. Notably, Justice Brennan, quoting from a report prepared for the American Law Institute as part of its formulation of the Model Penal Code, painted the debate over capital punishment as a clash between modernism and pre-modernism, with the behavioral sciences arrayed on the former's side:

> [T]he struggle about this punishment has been one between ancient and deeply rooted beliefs in retribution, atonement, or vengeance, on the one hand, and, on the other, beliefs in the personal value and dignity of the common man that were born of the democratic movement of the eighteenth century, as well as beliefs in the scientific approach to an understanding of the motive forces of human conduct, which are the result of the growth of the sciences of behavior during the nineteenth and twentieth centuries. (*Furman v. Georgia* 1972, 296)

Neither Justice Brennan nor his colleagues discussed in detail the behavioral sciences, nor their relationship to the death penalty. "Mainstream" social sciences did not, accordingly, play a determinative role in *Furman*. Nevertheless, the notion that they had a role was established.

One key question in subsequent cases was what part such studies would play. Are they evidence that sets the constitutional standard? Or are they simply evidence that may be applied to determine if the constitutional threshold has been met? In *Rhodes v. Chapman*, 452 U.S. 337 (1981), the court examined an Ohio penitentiary and found that the conditions within it were constitutional. Much of the discussion centered on the minimum square footage that a cell must have to ensure that a prisoner does not become overly cramped.

The majority criticized the lower court, stating that it "erred in assuming that opinions of experts as to desirable prison conditions suffice to establish contemporary standards of decency" and stressed that "such opinions may be helpful and relevant with respect to some questions, but they simply do not establish the constitutional minima; rather, they establish goals recommended by the organization in question" (*Rhodes v. Chapman* 1981, 348n13). Justice Brennan disagreed, concluding that "public health, medical, psychiatric, psychological, penological, architectural, structural, and other experts have proved useful to the lower courts in observing and interpreting prison conditions" (*Rhodes v. Chapman* 1981, 363). He further stated that "[a]lthough expert testimony alone does not suffice to establish contemporary standards of decency … such testimony can help the courts to understand the prevailing norms against which conditions in a particular prison may be evaluated" (*Rhodes v. Chapman* 1981, 364).

Justice Marshall, in turn, argued that while "[n]o one would suggest that a study, no matter how competent, could ever establish a constitutional rule … once the rule is established, it is surely the case that expert evidence can shed light on whether the rule is violated." More importantly, he indicated that the proper assessment of such evidence requires a sensitivity to those norms that typify the social sciences: "The majority … casts [this evidence] aside without even a token evaluation of the methodology, content, or results of any of the studies on which the District Court relied. If expert opinion is of as little value as the majority implies, then even plaintiffs with meritorious claims that their conditions of confinement violate the Eighth Amendment will have tremendous difficulty in proving their cases" (*Rhodes v. Chapman* 1981, 376).

Other Eighth Amendment cases have taken a different approach. In recent years, the court has concluded that a death sentence is per se unconstitutional when the defendant committed the offense while under age 18. In *Roper v. Simmons*, 543 U.S. 551 (2005), the majority made extensive use of expert opinion to reach three conclusions about minors: they have greater "immaturity and irresponsibility," are "more vulnerable or susceptible to negative influences and outside pressures," and possess a "character … not as well formed as that of an adult" (*Roper v. Simmons* 2005, 569–570). As a result, the court concluded that minors, as a class, cannot exhibit the especially heinous culpability necessary to deserve execution. The majority found particular significance in the diagnostic criteria for Antisocial Personality Disorder, as minors would not receive the diagnosis because of their age. According to the court, "[i]f trained psychiatrists with the advantage of clinical testing and observation refrain, despite diagnostic expertise, from assessing any juvenile under 18 as having antisocial personality disorder, we conclude that States should refrain from asking jurors to issue a far graver condemnation" (*Roper v. Simmons* 2005, 573).

The dissenting justices provided important perspectives. Justice O'Connor objected to the assumption that minors, as a class, all carry common psychological characteristics, arguing instead that trial courts should determine sufficient maturity "not by means of an arbitrary, categorical age-based rule, but rather through individualized sentencing in which juries are required to give appropriate mitigating weight to the defendant's immaturity, his susceptibility to outside pressures, his cognizance of the consequences of his actions, and so forth" (*Roper v. Simmons* 2005, 602–603). Justice Scalia, in turn, accused the majority of misusing "scientific and sociological studies, picking and choosing those that support its position" and of "never explain[ing] why those particular studies are methodologically sound" (*Roper v. Simmons* 2005, 617).

HUMAN MEMORY AND SUGGESTIBILITY: EYEWITNESS IDENTIFICATION

Another example of the interplay of social science on American law is in the area of eyewitness identification. Eyewitnesses can play important, pivotal roles in cases, bridging key players of the legal system (e.g., investigators, jurors, and judges) with events otherwise lost. An eyewitness's senses detect nearby, unfolding events and transform that sensory input into memories stored within the brain. The eyewitness later articulates those memories to third parties, thereby creating impressions of what originally occurred. The problem is that human brains preserve scenes neither fully nor perfectly, so eyewitnesses' later recollections are not always entirely accurate and complete.

Psychologists have developed a wealth of research demonstrating limitations of eyewitness testimony. (See, e.g., Faigman et al. 2014.) These studies establish that memory fades with time (Faigman et al. 2014, 587), that eyewitnesses sometimes mesh subsequent events back into earlier ones to create single memories of what were, in reality, multiple scenes (Faigman et al. 2014, 587), and extreme stress can diminish the memory's quality (Faigman et al. 2014; Sandi 2007, 12.1.3, 12.1.4). Likewise, observers' ability to recall oral statements verbatim can be weak, because the human brain tends to capture the "gist" of another's comments, and not the actual words (Faigman et al. 2014, 574). Further, research shows that observers may struggle to accurately recall observees' physical appearances. For instance, psychologists have demonstrated a phenomenon termed "weapons focus," in which eyewitnesses experience greater difficulty remembering the physical characteristics of a person holding a weapon, because the eyewitness's attention naturally gravitates toward the weapon itself (Faigman et al. 2014, 586). Research has also demonstrated that observers are generally more error prone when remembering the appearances of a person of a different race (Faigman et al. 2014, 559, 584).

These factors in eyewitnesses' accuracy raise a key question for the courts: when one side's eyewitness testifies, should the other side be able to offer a social scientist as an expert witness about memory? Courts have largely agreed that experts "limit their testimony to the general principles derived from sound empirical research. Unlike clinicians, for instance, social scientists in this area do not pretend to have specific insights into the accuracy of particular witnesses" (Faigman et al. 2014, 527–528). For instance, if an individual observes a bank robbery, an expert cannot testify about the quality of that exact memory. The more contentious question is whether an expert witness can testify about the reliability of a generic eyewitness who fits a particular demographic profile and observes a given kind of scene under specific circumstances. Here, the psychologist might discuss issues impacting the accuracy of a female of Race A observing for 10 seconds a male of Race B as he holds a gun while running out of a bank on a rainy day.

Historically, courts were reluctant to admit such testimony. In part, they reasoned that limits on memory were sufficiently self-evident that jurors did not require expert testimony. This reasoning changed with the rise of DNA evidence and ensuing high-profile exonerations. Of overturned convictions, a disproportionately high number had involved eyewitness testimony as central to prosecutors' arguments. This phenomenon caused an increasing number of courts to reconsider their rules, particularly in cases when guilt might hinge on an eyewitness's identification. A growing number of courts, meanwhile, do not categorically exclude such expert testimony and instead follow the same rules for admissibility as in other circumstances involving expert testimony, particularly today's dominant *Daubert* and *Frye* tests (Faigman et al. 2014, 538–539).

Wrongful convictions have also caused law enforcement to rethink the procedures officers employ when interviewing witnesses. A 1999 report from the U.S. Department of Justice recommended practices for the collection and preservation of eyewitness evidence, proposing principles, policies, and procedures for law enforcement and prosecutors to interface with eyewitnesses and to process their testimony (Table 86.1). Future considerations to improve the reliability of eyewitness evidence included sequential and "blind" lineups.

Historically, eyewitnesses observe lineups simultaneously, which has potential for relative judgment: the witness may transform the task from identification ("Do I see the perpetrator?") to comparison ("Which person looks most like the one I saw?"). As one individual in the lineup might most resemble the witness's recollection, so increases

Table 86.1 Recommendations for eyewitness evidence

Examples	Reasoning
Ask open-ended questions (e.g., "What can you tell me about the car?"), instead of leading ones ("Was the car red?").	Questions themselves may generate false memories.
Instruct witnesses to avoid discussing details of the incident with other potential witnesses.	Witnesses may incorporate each other's recollections into their own memories.
Compose lineups so that suspect(s) do not stand out.	Witnesses may identify suspects (if present) merely for looking unique within lineups.
Emphasize that the true perpetrator might not be in the lineup, and that it is just as important to clear innocent persons from suspicion as it is to identify guilty parties. Assure witnesses that, regardless of whether an identification is made, authorities will continue to investigate the incident.	These statements lower the chances of witnesses feeling pressured to make (potentially incorrect) identifications.

Source: Adapted from U.S. Department of Justice. 1999. *Eyewitness Evidence: A Guide for Law Enforcement.* https://www.ncjrs.gov/pdffiles1/nij/178240.pdf, accessed July 5, 2016.

the chances of incorrect identification. This error might decrease with the practice of sequential lineup, in which the eyewitness sees participants one at a time, thus diminishing the comparative emphasis.

Another consideration draws from "double-blinding" in scientific methodology. As investigators may bias research subjects with unintentional cues (e.g., body language, or tone of voice), so too officers may unintentionally suggest suspects' identities to eyewitnesses during lineups. If, during the lineup, officers are unaware of actual suspects' identities, this practice could, in theory, improve the accuracy of eyewitness testimony.

PROTECTION OF RIGHTS IN THE JURY SYSTEM

One key aspect of the American system of justice is its use of the jury in both criminal and civil trials. This is more than a simple matter of preference: the right to an assessment of the facts and evidence by an "impartial" jury was a central element in the Bill of Rights. Behavioral research offers valuable perspectives about key aspects of the jury system. For example, how might a juror's world view impact his or her vote? Does it affect others' votes? Can experts assist in the selection of jurors to provide an advantage to one party and/or a "fairer" jury?

Courts have considered these questions with the assistance of behavioral and psychological research. As the following examples show, this research has played key roles in both the composition of a jury and its selection.

Death qualified juries

Juror attitudes about the death penalty have created an intersection between social science and the criminal justice system. Historically, during *voir dire* in capital cases, courts have allowed prosecutors to excuse for cause any potential juror unwilling to render a death sentence. Great dispute surrounds how emphatic and unambiguous this unwillingness must be, but courts and researchers have identified three general categories of capital case venire (jury pool) members:

1. Death qualified: Those willing, if appropriate, to find a defendant guilty and to impose a death sentence, even if they personally oppose the death penalty
2. Those who would impartially vote during the trial's guilt phase but, if the jury found the defendant guilty, would be unwilling to consider death as a possible punishment
3. Those who would vote not guilty in order to avoid the possibility of a death sentence during the penalty phase

Of particular concern is the relationship between a venire member's death penalty views at the trial's penalty phase and his or her voting tendencies during the guilt phase. In other words, are members of any category predisposed to find a generic defendant guilty (or guilty of a more serious charge) in the first place? Courts and researchers have grappled with this, and clashed over the answer.

In *Witherspoon v. Illinois*, 391 U.S. 510 (1968), the Supreme Court held that a sentence of death could not be carried out if the jury that imposed the sentence was chosen by excluding veniremen for cause simply because they voiced general objections to the death penalty. Because the excused veniremen had not stated that they would in all cases refuse to impose the death penalty, the court held that the resulting jury was "uncommonly willing to condemn a man to die" (*Witherspoon v. Illinois* 1968, 521). The court refused, however, to hold that a properly constructed death qualified jury is unconstitutional, stating that the then-available studies showing that death qualified juries were more prone to convict were "too tentative and fragmentary" to justify their use in formulating such a rule (*Witherspoon v. Illinois* 1968, 517). This prompted social scientists to develop a larger body of research focused on whether jurors who are willing to impose a death sentence are inclined to convict.

The court took up this question in *Lockhart v. McCree*, 476 U.S. 162 (1986), a case in which the jury convicted the defendant of a capital crime but did not sentence him to death. The defendant argued that because the trial court excluded individuals unwilling to impose a sentence of death (category 2 above) from both the guilt and penalty phases, the jury was unconstitutionally predisposed toward guilt. Various social science studies played prominent roles in the case and the justices discussed them at some length. The majority found them inadequate, declaring that "we are constrained to point out what we believe to be several serious flaws in the evidence upon which the courts below reached the conclusion that 'death qualification' produces 'conviction-prone' juries" (*Lockhart v. McCree* 1986, 168), concluding that "[w]e have serious doubts about the value of these studies in predicting the behavior of actual jurors" (*Lockhart v. McCree* 1986, 171).

Lockhart provides an important example of law directly confronting and dissecting a body of social science research. The majority and dissent felt that the studies deserved detailed comment, and these comments provide insight into the justices' approach to such data. The time between *Witherspoon* and *Lockhart* also demonstrates social scientists' responsiveness to the court's perceived needs. In 1968, the *Witherspoon* court noted a dearth of evidence. By 1986, researchers had made more studies available for review. The majority found these new studies still inadequate, yet the two cases demonstrate a dynamic between the judiciary and social science academics being well aware of each other. Judicial concerns about inadequate studies can cause scientists to conduct further investigations; new research findings may then trigger judicial analyses, praise, and directions for further study. This cycle may continue, expanding the knowledge base on both sides.

Choosing a jury and managing a trial: Trial consultants

Trial consultants also create a point of intersection between law and social science. Increasingly in recent decades, attorneys have turned to outside specialists who are not themselves lawyers, but who possess expertise directly relevant to trial management. Such consultants may offer services ranging from audio-visual support during an attorney's multimedia presentation in the courtroom to public relations management. Their roles vary, as do opinions about the usefulness and propriety of their services. The American Society of Trial Consultants, however, states that its goals "lie at the very heart of the law's ability to deliver justice." As set out in their organization's mission, trial consultants help "litigators become better at persuading jurors and other fact-finders, and that makes the system work in a way that is more meaningful, more reliable, and ultimately more fair" (American Society of Trial Consultants 2015).

A common function of trial consultants is to assist in jury selection. For instance, consultants might conduct telephone surveys of local residents, correlating demographic information with lay opinions on hypothetical facts comparable to the case at hand. Consultants might observe venire members' body language, tone, and answers, opining on potential jurors' hidden biases concerning the litigants. During trial, consultants might observe jurors' reactions, and can even bring in paid observers who match the jury's demographics. During court recesses, consultants can meet with those observers, gauge their reactions, and help the attorney to manage these concerns once trial resumes. Post-verdict, consultants may interview former jurors and learn information that serves as a basis for appeal, or be useful information for future clients.

Of course, such activities may require substantial funds. Some might argue that trial consultants function essentially as platinum litigation plans for affluent clients. Nevertheless, trial consultants create an important gateway for social scientists to involve themselves in legal processes.

A more fundamental question is whether indigent criminal defendants enjoy the right to government-funded trial consultants. This question implicates a wide range of situations claiming that the government must provide expert assistance. In legal terms, this is a question of "due process"—that is, an examination of the manner in which government acts and whether it is fair in light of the issues involved. These claims are assessed within the framework provided by *Mathews v. Eldridge*, 424 U.S. 319, 335 (1976), within which the court focused on three factors: (1) the nature of "the private interest that will be affected by the official action," (2) "the risk of an erroneous deprivation … and the probable value … of additional or substitute procedural safeguards," and (3) the nature of "the Government's interest…." So for example, in *Ake v. Oklahoma*, 470 U.S. 68 (1985), the court held that a criminal defendant who raises the serious possibility of an insanity defense must have access to a psychiatrist, stressing the importance of the indigent defendant having access to "the basic tools of an adequate defense or appeal" (*Ake v. Oklahoma* 1985, 77) and the "the probable value" of psychiatric assistance (*Ake v. Oklahoma* 1985, 79).

This means that when a court decides whether to provide a defendant with a trial consultant, it must balance the defendant's risk (here, of empaneling an inappropriately pro-prosecution jury), the government's interest (of conserving public funds and not creating an inordinately pro-defense jury), and the value of desired assistance (the trial consultant's abilities, e.g., to identify bias in the jury pool). The Supreme Court has not taken up this specific issue of a right to trial consultants, and most courts that have evaluated such requests have rejected them. Two observations made in these cases are especially interesting. The first is that the Constitution does not require "the state to provide … a most-sophisticated defense" and that "all competent lawyers are endowed" with what the *Ake* court characterized as the "raw materials" of a constitutionally sound defense, the ability to "pick a jury fairly disposed toward doing substantive justice" (*Moore v. Johnson*, 225 F.3d 495, 503 (5th Cir. 2000)). The second is the contention that the goal of a "jury-selection expert" is not necessarily to produce a fair and impartial jury, but rather "to bias the jury in his employer's favor" (*United States v. Mikos*, 539 F.3d 706, 713 (7th Cir. 2008)).

Each of these considerations is superficially appealing. Each is, nevertheless, subject to the critical investigations that scientists may provide when examining for possible bias. This is especially pertinent in cases where the stakes are pronounced, for example, those where the prosecution is seeking the death penalty. If, as many judges and attorneys argue, jury selection is the most important phase of any trial, the considered application of scientific insights in that process seems eminently just.

SUMMARY

Forensic psychiatry and the social sciences share common goals: the development of insights into human behavior and the formulation of tools and techniques that assist individuals and society. Oliver Wendell Holmes famously observed that "[t]he life of the law has not been logic: it has been experience" (Holmes 1963, 5). The insights into experience gleaned from the social sciences have, accordingly, played crucial roles in the development of law, and can enhance the forensic psychiatrist's efforts to assist patients and to improve public policy.

SUMMARY KEY POINTS

- Social sciences include psychology, sociology, criminology, anthropology, history, economics, and political science.
- Creating law and policy can engage dialogue between courts, psychiatry, and social science.
- Relevant to this dialogue are scientific methodology, accuracy of findings, and context.
- Eyewitness testimony and jury systems have strengths and limitations.

ACKNOWLEDGMENTS

The authors thank Everett DePangher, J.D., for his assistance in preparing this chapter.

REFERENCES

Ake v. Oklahoma, 470 U.S. 68 (1985).

American Academy of Forensic Sciences. 2015. *What Is Forensic Science?* http://www.aafs.org/students/choosing-a-career/what-is-forensic-science/, accessed July 5, 2016.

American Psychiatric Association (APA). 2013. *Diagnostic and Statistical Manual of Mental Disorders*, 5th edition. Arlington, VA: APA.

American Society of Trial Consultants (ASTC). 2015. *The ASTC Mission*. http://www.astcweb.org/history_mission_statement, accessed July 5, 2016.

Andrews DA, J Bonta, and RD Hoge. 1990. Classification for effective rehabilitation: Rediscovering psychology. *Criminal Justice and Behavior* 17:19–52.

Baxstrom v. Herold, 383 U.S. 107 (1966).

Bonta J, M Law, and K Hanson. 1998. The prediction of criminal and violent recidivism among mentally disordered offenders: A meta-analysis. *Psychological Bulletin* 123:123–142.

Brill H and RE Patton. 1957. Analysis of 1955–1956 population fall in New York State mental hospitals in first year of large-scale use of tranquilizing drugs. *American Journal of Psychiatry* 114:509–517.

Engel GL. 1977. The need for a new medical model: A challenge for biomedicine. *Science* 196:129–136.

Faigman DL, JA Blumenthal, EK Cheng, JL Mnookin, EE Murphy, and J Sanders. 2014. *Modern Scientific Evidence: The Law and Science of Expert Testimony*. Eagan, MN: Thomson Reuters.

Furman v. Georgia, 408 U.S. 238 (1972).

Holmes OW. 1897. The path of the law. 10 Harv. L. Rev. 457. Cambridge, MA: Harvard Law School.

Holmes OW. 1963. Lecture I. In *The Common Law*, edited by MD Howe, Boston: Little, Brown and Company, 5–33.

Kraemer HC and DJ Kupfer. 2006. Size of treatment effects and their importance to clinical research and practice. *Biological Psychiatry* 59:990–996.

Lockhart v. McCree, 476 U.S. 162 (1986).

Malmquist CP. 2004. Book forum: Forensic psychiatry. *Principles and Practice of Forensic Psychiatry*, 2nd ed. *American Journal of Psychiatry* 161:1143–1144.

Mathews v. Eldridge, 424 U.S. 319 (1976).

Mechanic D and D Rochefort. 1990. Deinstitutionalization: An appraisal of reform. *Annual Review of Sociology* 16:301–327.

Monahan J and L Walker. 2014. *Social Science in Law: Cases and Materials*. St. Paul, MN: Foundation Press.

Moore v. Johnson, 225 F.3d 495 (5th Cir. 2000).

NASMHPD (National Association of State Mental Health Program Directors) Medical Directors Council. 2014. *The Vital Role of State Psychiatric Hospitals*. http://nasmhpd.org/Publications/The%20Vital%20Role%20of%20State%20Psychiatric%20HospitalsTechnical%20Report_July_2014.pdf http://nasmhpd.org/sites/default/files/The%20Vital%20Role%20of%20State%20Psychiatric%20HospitalsTechnical%20Report_July_2014%281%29.pdf, accessed July 5, 2016.

Osher F, DA D'Amora, M Plotkin, N Jarrett, and A Eggleston. 2012. *Adults with Behavioral Health Needs under Correctional Supervision: A Shared Framework for Reducing Recidivism and Promoting Recovery*. New York: Council of State Governments Justice Center, Criminal Justice/Mental Health Consensus Project.

Penrose LS. 1939. Mental disease and crime: Outline of a comparative study of European statistics. *British Journal of Medical Psychology* 18:1–15.

Powell v. Texas, 392 U.S. 514 (1968).

Rhodes v. Chapman, 452 U.S. 337 (1981).

Robinson v. California, 370 U.S. 660 (1962).

Roper v. Simmons, 543 U.S. 551 (2005).

Rudner RS. 1966. *Philosophy of Social Science*. Engelwood Cliffs, NJ: Prentice Hall.

Sandi C. 2007. Memory impairments associated with stress and aging. In *Neural Plasticity and Memory: From Genes to Brain Imaging*, edited by F Bermúdez-Rattoni, Chapter 12. Boca Raton, FL: CRC Press/Taylor & Francis. http://www.ncbi.nlm.nih.gov/books/NBK3914/, accessed January 15, 2016.

Stone AA. 2008. The ethical boundaries of forensic psychiatry: A view from the ivory tower. *Journal of the American Academy of Psychiatry and the Law* 36:167–174.

Trop v. Dulles, 356 U.S. 86 (1958).

U.S. Department of Justice. 1999. *Eyewitness Evidence: A Guide for Law Enforcement*. https://www.ncjrs.gov/pdffiles1/nij/178240.pdf, accessed July 5, 2016.

United States v. Mikos, 539 F.3d 706 (7th Cir. 2008).

Wilson JQ and RJ Herrnstein. 1985. *Crime and Human Nature: The Definitive Study of the Causes of Crime*. New York: Simon and Schuster.

Witherspoon v. Illinois, 391 U.S. 510 (1968).

87

Community-based interventions for justice-involved individuals with serious mental disorders

ROBERT L. WEISMAN, J. STEVEN LAMBERTI, AND J. RICHARD CICCONE

INTRODUCTION

Over the past 50 years the supply of inpatient psychiatric beds in the United States has largely vanished. In 1955, 560,000 patients were cared for in state psychiatric facilities; today less than one-tenth that number exists. Given the doubling of the U.S. population, this equates to a 95% reduction, bringing the per capita public psychiatric bed count to what it was in 1850–1914 per 100,000 individuals (Torrey et al. 2012). As state hospitals were downsized and closed, many individuals with chronic psychiatric disorders became homeless, frequenting hospital emergency services for care, food, and shelter. As deinstitutionalization progressed throughout the 1960s, 1970s, and 1980s, individuals with serious mental disorders also began entering correctional facilities.

By the 1990s and 2000s, a growing number of sources began reporting that persons with serious mental disorders were overrepresented within the criminal justice system—the new asylums. On March 5, 1998, the *New York Times* featured a front-page headline proclaiming "Prisons Replace Hospitals for the Nation's Mentally Ill" (Butterfield 1998). In 2003, a Human Rights Watch study reported that more individuals with serious mental illnesses reside in prisons than in hospitals (Human Rights Watch 2003). In addition, studies by Teplin and colleagues (Teplin 1984) and survey data from the U.S. Bureau of Justice Statistics (Ditton 1999) suggested that the prevalence of serious mental disorders in correctional facilities was two to four times higher than the general population rate. This problem is not limited to correctional facilities. Studies also found very high rates of serious mental disorders among the large population of individuals on probation in the community (Ditton 1999; Crilly et al. 2009).

Although some of these mentally ill individuals have committed violent acts, most have been arrested for relatively minor crimes such as theft, vagrancy, or disorderly conduct (Vladiserri et al. 1986). In addition, people with serious mental disorders are unlikely to receive adequate treatment they need while incarcerated. According to a Department of Justice report on treatment of mentally ill inmates and probationers, treatment is typically limited to medications, with approximately half of mentally ill individuals receiving no treatment at all (Ditton 1999). This lack of treatment contributes to disciplinary problems and to the high rate of suicides observed among mentally ill inmates (Hayes 1995; Human Rights Watch 2003; James and Glaze 2006). Once released from correctional facilities, mentally ill persons are left with little support, and reincarceration rates are two to three times higher than those prisoners without serious mental illness (Baillargeon et al. 2009). Overall, these reports highlighted the need for intervention strategies aimed at transitioning persons with severe mental illnesses out of jails and prisons, as well as preventing their recidivism.

As noted by Sisti et al., these concerns are not new: "Dorothea Dix, Moses Sheppard, Thomas Scattergood, and other 19th century reformers decried the poor treatment of the mentally ill in jails, poor houses, and asylums of the day. They called for a new kind of refuge in which mentally ill persons could live and heal, built on principles of humane and moral treatment." Sadly, disproportionate numbers of people with serious mental disorders today live in environments that are anathema to goals of treatment and recovery as they continue to cycle through jails, hospitals, and the streets (Sisti et al. 2015).

CURRENT INTERVENTIONS FOR JUSTICE-INVOLVED INDIVIDUALS WITH SERIOUS MENTAL DISORDERS

The term *justice-involved* describes mentally ill persons who are actively involved with the criminal justice system. This definition includes incarcerated individuals as well as those under community supervision by a judge, probation officer, or other criminal justice system representatives. The term may also be applied to individuals with histories of repeated arrest or incarceration because of their frequent contact with criminal justice authorities. Several approaches are currently in use for mentally ill individuals who are actively involved with or at high risk for involvement with the criminal justice system. Because these strategies are generally aimed at preventing incarceration, they are sometimes broadly referred to as "jail diversion" strategies. Jail diversion strategies are a diverse group of interventions that are based in jail, court, and community settings. Given their diversity, a helpful framework for understanding and organizing intervention strategies aimed at preventing criminal justice system involvement is called the *Sequential Intercept Model* (Munetz and Griffin 2006).

According to the model, individuals who are arrested will move through the criminal justice system in a series of five predictable steps or "intercepts." Each provides an opportunity to identify individuals with serious mental disorders and to divert them into necessary treatments and services. The intercepts and examples of corresponding interventions are as follows:

- *Intercept 1: Law Enforcement and Emergency Services.* This intercept represents the initial point of contact for mentally ill individuals who become involved with the criminal justice system. A variety of police-based diversion strategies have been developed at this intercept, the most widely disseminated being Crisis Intervention Teams (CITs) (Franz and Borum 2010). CIT utilizes a 40-hour curriculum to train police and emergency responders how to identify mentally ill persons, how to intervene nonviolently, and how to divert them to emergency rooms instead of to jail.
- *Intercept 2: Initial Detention and Initial Court Hearings.* This intercept encompasses jail and court-based activities that take place following arrest. The predominant approach to jail diversion at this intercept is Pre-Trial Diversion (Camilletti 2010). This strategy is an alternative to prosecution that involves early identification of mentally ill detainees, negotiation with the district attorney and public defender, and diversion into treatment.
- *Intercept 3: Courts and Corrections.* The third intercept encompasses an array of specialized court-based approaches that include mental health court, drug court, and veterans' court. Specialty courts utilize a judge to oversee a mentally ill defendant's outpatient treatment progress in partnership with the individual's treatment providers. In addition, conditional release statutes are used by nonspecialty courts to engage mentally ill individuals in treatment and services by offering them as a condition of release from jail.
- *Intercept 4: Re-Entry from Jails and Prisons.* This intercept represents the critical period of transition from correctional facilities back into the community. A common approach to helping individuals make this transition is called Transitional Case Management (Ventura et al. 1998). This approach utilizes jail-based case managers who prepare clients for release by arranging for insurance re-instatement, medication provision, housing, and follow-up treatment appointments.
- *Intercept 5: Community Corrections.* The last intercept encompasses the activities of probation and parole officers. Probation is the most common correctional disposition, and it functions to prevent recidivism by ensuring compliance with court-ordered conditions. Other community-based approaches to preventing incarceration include assisted outpatient treatment (AOT) programs such as those operating under Kendra's Law in New York and Laura's Law in California, and forensic assertive community treatment (FACT) programs (Lamberti and Weisman 2010).

A central characteristic shared by these intervention strategies is the use of legal authority to direct mentally ill individuals to treatment. Although published reviews suggest that authority-based strategies improve adherence to psychiatric care, evidence that they prevent criminal recidivism among justice-involved adults with serious mental disorders is lacking. A 2009 review of 21 published jail diversion studies "revealed little evidence of the effectiveness of jail diversion in reducing recidivism among persons with serious mental illness" (Sirotich 2009). Also, two large randomized controlled trials of AOT (also called outpatient commitment) have been conducted, and neither found a significant effect on reducing criminal involvement (Steadman et al. 2001; Swartz et al. 2001). In addition, a recent Cochrane Review of various forms of mandated treatment concluded, "We found little evidence that compulsory treatment was effective" (Kisely et al. 2011).

In considering how to prevent criminal recidivism among justice-involved adults with serious mental disorders, it is necessary to understand why mentally ill persons become involved with the criminal justice system. The conventional wisdom has been that deinstitutionalization and lack of access to psychiatric treatment are the primary causes (Torrey 1997; Daly 2006) and, therefore, the solution is simply to divert justice-involved individuals into existing psychiatric treatment programs. However, this approach fails to recognize why some people with serious mental disorders become involved with the criminal justice system, while others do not. What is different about justice-involved individuals?

UNDERSTANDING THE CYCLE OF RECIDIVISM

The failure of deinstitutionalization as an explanatory model has recently led researchers and policy makers to seek a criminologically informed framework for understanding and preventing criminal recidivism (Fisher et al. 2006; Lamberti 2007). Though separate from psychiatry and mental health, the field of criminology is relevant to the question of criminal justice involvement because criminology is the study of crime, the causes of crime, and crime prevention. Within the field, the predominant framework for understanding and preventing criminal behavior is the Risk–Needs–Responsitivity (RNR) Model (Andrews et al. 2006; Taxman and Marlowe 2006). This model states that preventing crime requires targeting specific risk factors that drive criminality with interventions that are matched to each individual's level of motivation, learning style, and circumstances. Based on decades of research, eight main risk factors have been identified that are predictive of criminal behavior whether or not a person has a mental disorder (Andrews and Bonta 2010). Standardized risk assessment tools such as the Level of Service Inventory—Revised (LSI-R), the Wisconsin Risk and Needs (WRN), and the Psychopathy Checklist—Revised (PCL-R) have incorporated these risk factors to varying degrees. These tools are commonly used to predict risk of criminal re-offense and probability of rehabilitation for individuals within high-security psychiatric wards or prison settings with the aim of determining who should be detained or released.

Also known as "criminogenic risk factors," the eight major risk factors are listed below:

- *History of Antisocial Behavior*: An individual's criminal record as well as past antisocial behaviors that may not have resulted in arrest. Risk increases with having a large number of prior offenses, being arrested at a young age, and having violations while on conditional release.
- *Antisocial Personality Pattern*: A pervasive and long-standing pattern of disregard for and violation of the rights of others (American Psychiatric Association 2013). Antisocial personality is characterized by failure to abide by the law, impulsivity, irresponsibility, lying, lack of remorse, and callous disregard for safety of self or others.
- *Antisocial Cognition*: Thoughts, rationalizations, beliefs, and attitudes that are favorable to crime. These can include rationalizations that justify crime (e.g., "the victim deserved it," "it's OK to steal from rich people," etc.), beliefs that crime will yield benefits, and negative attitudes toward law enforcement and the criminal justice system.
- *Antisocial Associates*: Also called "social support for crime," this risk factor includes both association with criminal companions as well as relative isolation from friends, family, and others who are law-abiding citizens.
- *Substance Abuse*: Problems with alcohol and drugs excluding tobacco and caffeine. Risk applies both to history of abuse and current abuse, and it is highest when active abuse is present.
- *School/Work*: Lack of educational and vocational achievement as well as history of interpersonal conflicts and lack of satisfaction within those environments. This risk factor can include history of truancy and disciplinary problems, failure to graduate from high school, unemployment, or a pattern of unstable employment.
- *Family/Marital Circumstances*: Quality of relationships with family members, including spouses if married. For young people, the risk factor can include a lack of nurturing by and/or a lack of caring toward parental figures. For married individuals, it can include lack of mutual caring, respect, and interest.
- *Leisure/Recreation*: Low levels of participation and satisfaction in prosocial leisure pursuits. This risk factor can include lack of hobbies, interests, club memberships, or other constructive pastime activities.

It is noteworthy that mental illness has largely been viewed by the field of criminology as noncontributory to criminal justice system involvement (Bonta et al. 1998). This perspective is at odds with the experience of clinicians, who have observed their patients being arrested for what amounts to being psychotic in the wrong place at the wrong time. Research within the mental health field has provided considerable evidence that untreated psychotic symptoms are, in fact, a risk factor for arrest and incarceration (McNiel et al. 2000; Swanson et al. 2006). Behaviors related to manic episodes such as driving recklessly, risky sexual encounters, and other forms of impulsivity can also lead directly to arrest and incarceration. In addition to symptoms of psychosis and mania, people with serious mental disorders have higher prevalence rates of the eight established risk factors. For instance, individuals with schizophrenia and related disorders have approximately five times the rate of substance abuse (Regier et al. 1990) and 10 times the rate of unemployment compared to the general population (Rosenheck et al. 2006). These findings provide a clear rationale to understanding why disproportionate numbers of mentally ill individuals enter the criminal justice system, along with implications for how their criminal recidivism might be prevented.

Consistent with the Risk–Needs–Responsivity model, the key to preventing criminal recidivism among justice-involved adults with serious mental disorders is to engage them in interventions that target the risk factors driving their recidivism. With the exception of history of antisocial behavior which cannot be changed, criminogenic risk factors among adults with serious mental disorders are potentially modifiable with appropriate intervention strategies. In recent years, evidence-based interventions have emerged that can be used to address modifiable risk factors among justice-involved adults with serious mental disorders in community settings. Examples include integrated dual diagnosis treatment for co-occurring substance use disorders (Drake et al. 2001), individual placement and support for unemployment (Bond 1998), and family therapy and support to address family problems (Marsh 1998). In addition, promising new cognitive behavioral approaches have been developed for antisocial cognitions (Little and Robinson 1988; Ross and Fabiano 1991; Hornsveld et al. 2008; Bush et al. 2011). Despite the recent emergence of effective interventions that target criminogenic risk factors, however, engaging individuals with serious mental disorders in the community with necessary treatments and services is easier said than done.

Nonadherence is common among justice-involved individuals with serious mental disorders in community settings. Research suggests that half of all outpatients with schizophrenia are nonadherent with medications (Barkhof et al. 2012), and that approximately 90% of all mentally ill inmates were nonadherent with treatment prior to their arrest (Lamb et al. 2007). Persons with serious mental disorders may refuse needed treatments and services for several reasons, including paranoia, cognitive impairments, impaired judgment due to drug addiction, negative family influences, and fear of stigma. Some mentally ill individuals are unaware that they are ill and, as a result, see no need for treatment. These individual risk factors for nonadherence interact with well-documented deficiencies in our service delivery system. In the first state-by-state report on the nation's mental health system in 2009, the United States received a "D" grade due to multiple deficiencies (Aron et al. 2009). These deficiencies in our mental health system, or systemic risk factors, include lack of outreach, limited hours, lack of appropriate housing, cultural and language barriers, fragmentation of care, and financial barriers. When a person with multiple individual risk factors encounters a system with multiple deficiencies, the likelihood of treatment nonadherence increases dramatically. The relationship between individual and systemic risk factors, nonadherence, and jail and hospital recidivism is called the *cycle of recidivism*. This cycle is illustrated in Figure 87.1.

Justice-involved individuals with serious mental illness are often labeled as nonadherent or "noncompliant" by care providers when they fail to engage in treatment. However, it is more useful to view nonadherence as a mismatch between people and systems of care. Consider the example of a homeless man with bipolar disorder and alcoholism whose case was closed due to nonadherence because of his repeated failure to show for scheduled outpatient clinic appointments. If the outpatient clinic had provided the man with outreach along with hot coffee and sandwiches, he may have engaged in care.

If high-risk individuals with serious mental illness are not engaged in necessary treatments and services, they are likely to behave in ways that can lead to hospitalization or incarceration. Such behaviors may include public intoxication, trespassing, agitation, verbal harassment, and/or physical assaultiveness. Whether problem behaviors result in an individual being jailed or hospitalized can depend on who intervenes and the surrounding circumstances. For example, a young man who smashes a television in response to hearing voices would probably be arrested and sent to jail if this behavior occurred at a shopping mall. However, the same young man would probably be sent to a hospital if the event happened at his mother's house. Once released from jail or discharged from the hospital, however, such individuals remain at risk for continuing the cycle of recidivism unless engaged in effective interventions to break the cycle.

ENGAGING JUSTICE-INVOLVED INDIVIDUALS WITH SERIOUS MENTAL DISORDERS

The first step in engaging justice-involved individuals is to optimize treatments and services, with the understanding that nonadherence has both individual and systemic causes. Many individuals with serious mental disorders who are nonadherent in the context of lack of outreach, lack of transportation, drug side effects, treatment ineffectiveness, financial barriers, or cultural and language barriers can eventually be engaged once those issues have been addressed. Strategies to optimize care through establishing rapport, providing education, offering choices, minimizing drug side effects, utilizing long-acting injectable medications, providing outreach visits, and promoting cultural competence are cornerstones of promoting adherence. However, sometimes optimizing care is not enough. Some justice-involved adults with serious mental disorders remain unwilling or unable to engage with community-based treatments and services despite optimization. When such individuals engage in criminal activity or prove dangerous to themselves or others, they become candidates for intervention strategies involving the use of legal leverage.

Legal leverage is the process of using legal authority to engage justice-involved individuals with serious mental disorders and/or chemical dependency into necessary treatments and services (Lamberti et al. 2014). Legal authority can originate from several sources within the criminal justice system, including judges, probation and parole officers,

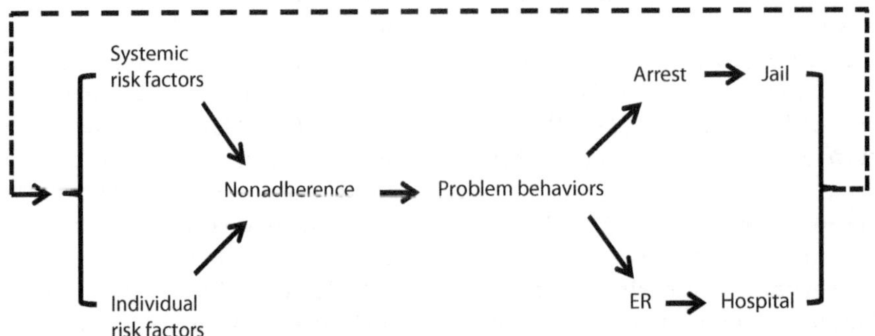

Figure 87.1 The cycle of recidivism

pretrial service officers, and police officers. In addition, legal authority can originate from "civil" sources such as forensic case monitors within the forensic system. The effectiveness of legal leverage-based strategies to prevent criminal recidivism among persons with serious mental disorders is likely to depend on several factors. Consistent with risk–needs–responsivity theory, one key factor is the effectiveness of those interventions to which individuals are being leveraged. Legal leverage is unlikely to prevent recidivism if an individual is leveraged to receive standard psychiatric treatment that fails to address the risk factors driving that individual's recidivism. Given that justice-involved individuals are involved in both service systems, another crucial factor is the willingness of mental health and criminal justice professionals to work together.

Collaboration between criminal justice and mental health professionals can prove challenging because of their different work environments, priorities, and goals. Mental health professionals typically work within clinics and hospitals that are geographically separate from courts, jails, and prisons. While criminal justice professionals fight crime and protect public safety, mental health professionals fight disease and promote personal health. And while mental health professionals work within a collaborative culture and utilize a relational style of communication with patients, criminal justice professionals work within an adversarial culture and utilize an authoritarian communication style with defendants. In addition to having different cultures and priorities, regulations surrounding information sharing can present barriers to collaboration. Mental health service providers are bound by Health Insurance Portability and Accountability Act (HIPAA) law and protecting patient confidentiality. Attorneys are bound by attorney–client privilege and laws and policies governing interagency communication. In addition to federal and state laws, local or agency-level policies and administrative rulings may bear consideration. Despite these potential challenges and barriers, effective mental health–criminal justice collaboration may hold the key to preventing criminal recidivism among mentally ill persons who straddle both systems.

To appreciate the importance of mental health and criminal justice collaboration, one must recognize that optimal use of legal leverage involves a process rather than a single event of "diverting" an individual from one system into another. Whenever mentally ill individuals enter probation, parole, or a mental health court, criminal justice and mental health professionals will go through a similar series of steps in serving them. Both must engage and assess each mentally ill individual, and both must generate a plan based on their assessments. Likewise, both monitor each individual for adherence to the plan, and both must address behavioral problems that emerge during the course of plan implementation. Unfortunately, these processes typically occur in a parallel, disconnected manner that can result in a person with serious mental illness falling through the cracks. The following example illustrates some of the pitfalls that can occur in the absence of active collaboration between mental health and criminal justice professionals who work with justice-involved individuals in community settings.

Case vignette—Diego, part 1

Diego is a 25-year-old homeless Hispanic man with schizoaffective disorder and alcohol use disorder who is arrested for indecency after urinating on a public sidewalk. Recognizing that he is mentally ill, police take Diego to an emergency room instead of jail. There his blood alcohol level is found to be three times the legal limit. The following morning he is assessed by the emergency room psychiatrist who finds him to be paranoid but not a danger to himself or others. Diego is subsequently discharged to a homeless shelter, and to the local mental health clinic where he fails to show for his appointments. A month later he is arrested after punching a convenience store attendant, and he is jailed for 7 months. His release plan includes treatment at the local mental health clinic and probation. Diego reluctantly attends his first mental health appointment at the insistence of his probation officer, but he has difficulty understanding the clinic psychiatrist due to hearing voices and his limited English. The psychiatrist writes a prescription for antipsychotic medication, but Diego discards it and subsequently reports to his probation officer in a psychotic state. When the probation officer calls the clinic to schedule an urgent appointment, Diego is given the next available appointment in 3 weeks. Diego starts drinking heavily and fails to show for his follow-up clinic appointments. The mental health clinic closes his case due to treatment nonadherence.

PRINCIPLES OF MENTAL HEALTH–CRIMINAL JUSTICE COLLABORATION

Collaboration is generally defined as the action of working with another person to achieve a common goal. It can also be defined as traitorous cooperation with an enemy (Merriam-Webster.com 2007). Given the substantial differences that exist between mental health and criminal justice professionals, it is necessary to share common principles in order to prevent criminal recidivism among individuals with serious mental disorders. Prospective collaborators should adopt the principle that promoting client health and protecting public safety are complementary rather than competing goals. Justice-involved individuals with serious mental disorders are members of society, and targeting the health-related and social issues that drive their criminal behavior will ultimately benefit society. Although specific decisions about when to err on the side of health or safety must be made on a case-by-case basis, acknowledging the complementary nature of these goals can provide a foundation for effective collaboration.

Offering treatment to mentally ill individuals as an alternative to punishment is a controversial issue, and some suggest offering treatment alternatives to incarceration is being "soft on crime." If the goal of intervention is to prevent crime, however, then it must be recognized that many of the factors driving criminal behavior of the mentally ill may be modifiable with appropriate treatments and services. Offering necessary interventions in combination with careful monitoring should therefore be seen as a strategy for preventing crime rather than enabling it. The perspective that effective treatment can be considered as a legitimate alternative to punishment has recently emerged within legal circles as "therapeutic jurisprudence," the study of law as a therapeutic agent (Wexler 1990).

Community-based care of justice-involved adults with serious mental disorders rarely proceeds smoothly. Typically this treatment course involves a backward step for every two steps forward. Problematic behaviors should be expected when working with this high-risk population. As a result, problem-solving approaches should be used to address behavioral problems whenever possible. Depending on the seriousness of the behaviors and applicable laws, problem-solving approaches can include offering new treatments and services as well as promoting adherence to existing treatments and services through motivational enhancement strategies. Persons with serious mental disorders may also benefit from having second chances, particularly in instances where they had limited control or when they self-report and acknowledge their problem behaviors. When sanctions are necessary, least restrictive alternative should be considered, such as increased monitoring, work assignments, community service assignments, writing assignments, curfew restrictions, and loss of privileges for those in residential programs.

Another important principle of mental health and criminal justice collaboration is that legal decisions about how to manage behavior problems should be clinically informed. Criminal justice authorities are clearly "the deciders" in determining how to respond to problematic behaviors from a legal standpoint. However, mental health professionals bring a wealth of knowledge about mental illness, effective treatment options, and availability of services and supports in the community. In addition, treating clinicians generally have a high degree of familiarity with each individual under their care. As such, mental health professionals are positioned to enhance the legal decision-making process by sharing their knowledge and experience. Shared decision making involves active discussion and sharing of opinions and ideas between mental health and criminal justice professionals, rather than a simple reporting relationship. In reporting relationships, mental health professionals essentially become extensions of the criminal justice system by serving only to report patient infractions such as illegal drug use to the authorities. Research has suggested that such relationships can actually serve to increase rather than decrease criminal justice system involvement (Solomon and Draine 1995).

THE ROCHESTER FORENSIC ASSERTIVE COMMUNITY TREATMENT (R-FACT) MODEL

The search for effective intervention strategies to help individuals who repeatedly cycle through jails and prisons has led clinicians and researchers to consider the assertive community treatment (ACT) model. ACT emerged in the 1970s as a means of bridging the gap between state hospitals and the community during the deinstitutionalization era by using mobile treatment teams to provide outreach for those with serious mental disorders who were in need. As the ACT model developed, it incorporated additional elements to meet the special needs of these individuals, including addiction treatment, employment assistance, and housing assistance. ACT teams also provide around-the-clock availability and include a half-time psychiatrist for every 50 enrollees to ensure optimal treatment. Although the model addressed mental health system deficiencies as well as some of the known recidivism risk factors, research showed that ACT had little or no effect on reducing rates of arrest and incarceration (Mueser et al. 1998; Bond et al. 2001). Despite publication of these findings in academic journals, frontline care providers continued adapting the ACT model in different ways to manage justice-involved individuals. These various adaptations of the ACT model became generally known as forensic assertive community treatment (FACT) programs (Lamberti and Weisman 2010).

The first FACT programs recognized by the American Psychiatric Association were Project Link in 1999, in Rochester, New York (Gold Award 1999), followed by Chicago's Thresholds Jail Linkage Project in 2001 (Gold Award 2001). Unlike traditional ACT programs, these emerging FACT programs had a strong criminal justice orientation and were designed to serve individuals involved with the criminal justice or forensic service systems. Their referrals usually arose from jails, courts, probation or parole officers, forensic hospitals, or other sources within the criminal justice or forensic systems. Although standard ACT teams typically enroll some individuals with criminal histories, such persons are admitted more by default than by design. FACT team staff are informed about the criminal justice system, and educated regarding criminal justice procedures and the roles and responsibilities of criminal justice staff members. Despite these similarities, however, national survey studies subsequently demonstrated great variability between existing "FACT" programs in terms of their structure, function, and daily operation (Lamberti et al. 2004; Lamberti et al. 2011).

The Rochester Forensic Assertive Community Treatment (R-FACT) model was developed at the University of Rochester through a National Institute of Mental Health (NIMH)-funded research project aimed at standardizing and testing the FACT intervention. Funding enabled the Rochester research team to travel to FACT programs across the country, to conduct focus groups with service providers and recipients, and to consult with national experts and program stakeholders. This process led to identification and incorporation of two key elements that distinguish the R-FACT model: targeting of criminogenic risk factors and use of legal leverage. R-FACT is designed to break the cycle of recidivism by utilizing legal leverage derived from a court, assisted outpatient treatment, and probation to promote engagement in evidence-based treatments and services that target recidivism risk factors. This process involves combining risk assessment with standard clinical assessment for early identification of criminogenic risk factors, and active collaboration with criminal justice partners for optimal use of legal leverage to engage individuals in necessary treatment and service interventions. A randomized controlled study of 70 justice-involved adults with schizophrenia and related disorders compared R-FACT to community mental health treatment as usual with case management. Individuals receiving usual treatment spent twice as much time in jail and half as much time engaged in outpatient treatment as those receiving R-FACT (Lamberti and Weisman 2014). Further research is needed to determine critical elements of the model, to identify which justice-involved individuals are most appropriate for this intervention, and to examine the model's generalizability to different geographic regions.

Case vignette—Diego, part 2

Diego is arrested after swearing at pedestrians while panhandling. He is again taken by police to the emergency room instead of jail. There he is briefly hospitalized for treatment of his psychosis with an oral antipsychotic medication. Because of his history of multiple arrests, he is discharged back to the homeless shelter along with follow-up by an R-FACT team. The team transports Diego to the shelter on his day of discharge, and he is relieved to learn that one of the team members is bi-lingual in Spanish. Diego and the team member chat in Spanish on their way to the shelter, and they discover that they had attended the same high school. One week later Diego gets into a loud verbal altercation at the homeless shelter after accusing another resident of staring at him. The shelter calls the R-FACT team who evaluate Diego later that day. The team determines that he has stopped his antipsychotic medications and that he has started drinking again. They call Diego's probation officer who agrees to a joint meeting. After discussing treatment options with the R-FACT team psychiatrist, the probation officer offers Diego a choice: either accept a long-acting injectable form of antipsychotic medication and alcoholism treatment, or receive a violation for failure to adhere to his conditions of probation. Faced with the possibility of re-incarceration and feeling comfortable with his new treatment team, Diego agrees to accept the proposed plan.

SUMMARY

The reduction of beds and closure of psychiatric hospitals, along with the expansion of correctional facilities across the United States have together created a new clinical entity—the "justice-involved" patient. Increasingly large numbers of serious mentally ill patients are now being referred from local jails and state prisons to community mental health agencies. This new population of "justice-involved" patients requires new treatment approaches in order to prevent recidivism and promote recovery in the community.

SUMMARY KEY POINTS

- Persons with serious mental disorders are overrepresented within the criminal justice system and, once released, they experience rates of reincarceration two to three times that of persons without mental illness.
- The key to preventing criminal recidivism among justice-involved adults with serious mental disorders is to engage them in treatments and services that target the criminogenic risk factors driving their recidivism.
- Although many individuals with serious mental disorders can be engaged by optimizing treatments and services, some will be caught in the cycle of recidivism because they remain unwilling or unable to engage in necessary care.
- Legal leverage is the process of using legal authority to engage justice-involved individuals with serious mental disorders into necessary treatments and services.
- Optimal legal leverage for justice-involved patients in community settings requires active and ongoing collaboration between mental health professionals and criminal justice authorities that is based upon shared goals and principles.
- R-FACT is an example of an intervention strategy designed to break the cycle of recidivism by utilizing legal leverage to engage justice-involved individuals in interventions that target the risk factors driving the cycle.

REFERENCES

American Psychiatric Association. 2013. *Diagnostic and Statistical Manual of Mental Disorders*, 5th edition. Arlington, VA: American Psychiatric Publishing.

Andrews DA and J Bonta. 2010. *The Psychology of Criminal Conduct*, 5th edition. New Providence, NJ: Matthew Bender & Company.

Andrews DA, J Bonta, and J Wormith. 2006. The recent past and near future of risk and/or need assessment. *Crime and Delinquency* 52:7–27.

Aron L, R Honberg, and K Duckworth. 2009. *Grading the States 2009: A Report on America's Health Care System for Adults with Serious Mental Illness*. Arlington, VA: National Alliance on Mental Illness.

Baillargeon J, IA Binswanger, JV Penn, BA Williams, and OJ Murray. 2009. Psychiatric disorders and repeat incarcerations: The revolving prison door. *American Journal of Psychiatry* 166:103–109.

Barkhof E, CJ Meijer, LMJ de Sonneville, DH Linszen, and L de Haan. 2012. Interventions to improve adherence to antipsychotic medication in patients with schizophrenia—A review of the past decade. *European Psychiatry* 27:9–18.

Bond G, R Drake, K Mueser, and E Latimer. 2001. Assertive community treatment for people with severe mental illness: Critical ingredients and impact on patients. *Disease Management and Health Outcomes* 9:141–159.

Bond GR. 1998. Principles of the individual placement and support model: Empirical support. *Psychiatric Rehabilitation Journal* 22:11–23.

Bonta J, M Law, and K Hanson. 1998. The prediction of criminal and violent recidivism among mentally disordered offenders: A meta-analysis. *Psychological Bulletin* 123:123–142.

Bush J, Glick B, and Taymans J. 2011. *Thinking for a Change: Integrated Cognitive Behavior Change Program*. Washington, DC: National Institute of Corrections. http://static.nicic.gov/Library/025057/Documents/_Complete%20T4C%203.1.0.pdf, accessed June 28, 2016.

Butterfield F. 1998. Prisons replace hospitals for the nation's mentally ill. *New York Times*, March 5:1.

Camilletti C. 2010. *Pretrial Diversion Programs: Research Summary*. Contract No. GS-10F-0114L, Number 2008-F_0815. Washington, DC: U.S. Department of Justice, Bureau of Justice Assistance.

Crilly JF, ED Caine, JS Lamberti, T Brown, and B Friedman. 2009. Mental health service use and symptom prevalence in a cohort of adults on probation. *Psychiatric Services* 60:542–544.

Daly R. 2006. Prison mental health crisis continues to grow. *Psychiatric News* 41:1.

Ditton PM. 1999. *Mental Health Treatment of Inmates and Probationers* [Special Report]. Washington, DC: U.S. Department of Justice, Bureau of Justice Statistics.

Drake RE, SM Essock, A Shaner et al. 2001. Implementing dual diagnosis services for clients with severe mental illness. *Psychiatric Services* 52:469–476.

Fisher WH, E Silver, and N Wolff. 2006. Beyond criminalization: Toward a criminologically informed framework for mental health policy and services research. *Administration and Policy in Mental Health and Mental Health Services Research* 33:544–557.

Franz S and R Borum. 2010. Crisis intervention teams may prevent arrests of people with mental illnesses. *Police Practice and Research*, First published on October 21 (iFirst).

Gold Award Article. 1999. Prevention of jail and hospital recidivism among persons with severe mental illness. Project Link, Department of Psychiatry, Rochester New York. *Psychiatric Services* 50:1477–1480.

Gold Award Article. 2001. Helping mentally ill people break the cycle of jail and homelessness: The Thresholds, State, County Collaborative Jail Linkage Project, Chicago, Illinois. *Psychiatric Services* 52:1380–1382.

Hayes LM. 1995. *Prison Suicide: An Overview and Guide to Prevention*. Washington, DC: U.S. Department of Justice.

Hornsveld RH, HL Nijman, CR Hollin, and FW Kraaimaat. 2008. Aggression control therapy for violent forensic psychiatric patients: Method and clinical practice. *International Journal of Offender Therapy and Comparative Criminology* 52:222–233.

Human Rights Watch. 2003. *Ill-Equipped: U.S. Prisons and Offenders with Mental Illness*. New York: Human Rights Watch. http://www.hrw.org/reports/2003/usa1003/, accessed June 28, 2016.

James DJ and LE Glaze. 2006. *Mental Health Problems of Prison and Jail Inmates*. NCJ 213600. Washington, DC: U.S. Department of Justice.

Kisely SR, LA Campbell, and NJ Preston. 2011. Compulsory community and involuntary outpatient treatment for people with severe mental disorders. *Cochrane Database of Systematic Reviews*, Issue 12, Art. No. CD004408. doi: 10.1002/14651858.CD004408.pub4

Lamb HR, LE Weinberger, JS Marsh, and BH Gross. 2007. Treatment prospects for persons with severe mental illness in an urban county jail. *Psychiatric Services* 58:782–786.

Lamberti JS. 2007. Understanding and preventing criminal recidivism among adults with psychotic disorders. *Psychiatric Services* 58:773–781.

Lamberti JS, A Deem, RL Weisman, and C LaDuke. 2011. The role of probation in forensic assertive community treatment. *Psychiatric Services* 62:418–421.

Lamberti JS, A Russ, K Cerulli, R Weisman, D Jacobowitz, and G Williams. 2014. Perceptions of autonomy and coercion among recipients of legal leverage. *Harvard Review of Psychiatry*. 22:222–230.

Lamberti JS and RL Weisman. 2010. Forensic assertive community treatment: Origins, current practice and future directions. In *Reentry Planning for Offenders with Mental Disorders: Policy and Practice*, edited by H Dlucacz, Kingston, NJ: Civic Research Institute, Chapter 7:1–24.

Lamberti JS and RL Weisman. 2014. *The Rochester FACT (R-FACT) Model*. Data presented at the National Council of Behavioral Health meeting in Washington, DC. May 7.

Lamberti JS, RL Weisman, and D Faden. 2004. Forensic assertive community treatment (FACT): Preventing incarceration of adults with severe mental illness. *Psychiatric Services* 55:1285–1293.

Little GL and KD Robinson. 1988. Moral reconation therapy: A systematic, step-by-step treatment system for treatment resistant clients. *Psychological Reports* 62:135–151.

Marsh D. 1998. *Serious Mental Illness and the Family: The Practitioners Guide. Wiley Series in Couples and Family Dynamics and Treatment*. Hoboken, NJ: Wiley.

McNiel DE, JP Eisner, and RL Binder RL. 2000. The relationship between command hallucinations and violence. *Psychiatric Services* 51:1288–1292.

Merriam-Webster online dictionary. 2007. http://www.merriam-webster.com/dictionary/collaboration, accessed April 4, 2015.

Mueser K, G Bond, R Drake, and S Resnick. 1998. Models of community care for severe mental illness: A review of research on case management. *Schizophrenia Bulletin* 24:37–74.

Munetz MR and PA Griffin. 2006. Use of the sequential intercept model as an approach to decriminalize people with serious mental illness. *Psychiatric Services* 57:544–549.

Regier D, M Farmer, D Rae et al. 1990. Comorbidity of mental disorders with alcohol and other drug abuse: Results from the Epidemiologic Catchment Area (ECA) Study. *Journal of the American Medical Association* 264:2511–2518.

Rosenheck R, D Leslie, R Keefe et al. 2006. Barriers to employment for people with schizophrenia. *American Journal of Psychiatry*, 163:411–417.

Ross R and E Fabiano. 1991. *Reasoning and Rehabilitation. A Handbook for Teaching Cognitive Skills*. Ottawa, ON: T3 Associates.

Sirotich F. 2009. The criminal justice outcomes of jail diversion programs for persons with mental illness: A review of the evidence. *Journal of the American Academy of Psychiatry and the Law* 37:461–472.

Sisti DA, AG Segal, and JE Ezekiel. 2015. Improving long-term psychiatric care: Bring back the asylum. *Journal of the American Medical Association* 313:243–244.

Solomon P and J Draine. 1995. Jail recidivism in a forensic case management program. *Health and Social Work* 20:167–173.

Steadman HJ, K Gounis, D Dennis, K Hopper, B Roche, M Swartz, and PC Robbins. 2001. Assessing the New York City involuntary outpatient commitment pilot program. *Psychiatric Services* 52:330–336.

Swanson JW, MS Swartz, RA Van Dorn et al. 2006. A national study of violent behavior in persons with schizophrenia. *Archives of General Psychiatry* 63:490–499.

Swartz M, J Swanson, V Hiday, H Wagner, B Burns, and R Borum. 2001. A randomized controlled trial of outpatient commitment in North Carolina. *Psychiatric Services* 52:325–329.

Taxman F and D Marlowe. 2006. Risk, needs, responsivity: In action or inaction? *Crime and Delinquency* 52:3–6.

Teplin LA. 1984. Criminalizing mental disorder: The comparative arrest rate of the mentally ill. *American Psychologist* 39:794–803.

Torrey EF. 1997. *Out of the Shadows: Confronting America's Mental Illness Crisis*. New York: Wiley.

Torrey EF, JJ Geller, C Jacobs, and K Rogasta. 2012. *No Room at the Inn: Trends and Consequences of Closing Public Psychiatric Hospitals*. Arlington, VA: Treatment Advocacy Center.

Ventura LA, CA Cassel, JE Jacoby, and B Huang. 1998. Case management and recidivism of mentally ill persons released from jail. *Psychiatric Services* 49:1330–1337.

Vladiserri EV, KR Carroll, and AJ Hartl. 1986. A study of offenses committed by psychotic inmates in a county jail. *Hospital and Community Psychiatry* 37:163–166.

Wexler DB. 1990. *Therapeutic Jurisprudence: The Law as a Therapeutic Agent*. Durham, NC: Carolina Academic Press.

88

Employee Retirement Income Security Act (ERISA)

J. RICHARD CICCONE

INTRODUCTION

On Labor Day 1974, President Gerald Ford signed the Employee Retirement Income Security Act (ERISA) into law (29 U.S.C. §§1001–1046). This law played a significant role in the restructuring of health care, and made health-care reform more difficult. The purpose of this chapter is to provide (a) a brief background of the events that led to enactment of the law; (b) an overview of the relationship of ERISA to health-care plans; and (c) a review of some attempts to have the courts remedy impediments to health care that managed care companies constructed by using ERISA as a shield.

ERISA'S ORIGINS

In order to understand the development and structure of ERISA and how it bears on health care, one must trace the development of retirement plans, which was (and is) the primary subject of ERISA. The U.S. pension system grew rapidly during the 1940s and 1950s in part because employers increased retirement benefits when wage freezes were imposed during World War II. Participation in pensions by union workers was boosted in 1948 when the U.S. Court of Appeals (7th Circuit) held that pensions are a form of remuneration for labor under the National Labor Relations Act (*Inland Steel Company v. NLRB* 1948). As a form of pay, pensions were a mandatory subject of collective bargaining and, therefore, an issue employers could not avoid.

Regulations had failed to keep up with the growth of pension assets and, in 1958, after learning of extensive abuses in pension plans, Congress enacted the Welfare Pension Plans Disclosure Act (29 U.S.C. §§301–308). The law was an attempt to protect the pension assets of employee participants and beneficiaries against companies that would use the money for operating costs.

Despite the protections provided under this Disclosure Act and other laws, abuses continued, and in March 1962 President Kennedy established the cabinet-level Committee on Corporate Pension Funds. Although the committee was working, significant abuses of pension funds continued. In December 1963, the Studebaker automobile plant in South Bend, Indiana, shut down. When the plant closed, the single-employer pension plan that had been negotiated between the United Automobile Workers and the Studebaker company did not have the funds to provide benefits for all its vested employees. Retirees and workers who had reached age 60 years at the time of the company's closure received full lifetime annuities; however, about 4000 employees who were vested received lump sum payments equal to only 15% of the actuarial value of their accrued pension.

In 1965, the Kennedy Committee on Corporate Pension Funds issued a report that reaffirmed the value of private pension programs and severely criticized government regulation of pension plans for not providing adequate protection of the pension funds. It recommended that to ensure the continued development of the private pension system, Congress should enact more substantive legislation to protect the pension plan participants and beneficiaries.

Accounts of older workers losing pension benefits they had earned over decades because of plan terminations, lay-offs, or misuse (stealing) of pension funds captured the media's attention and rallied public support in favor of reform. During a 1966 Senate hearing held in the wake of the Studebaker incident and the Kennedy Committee, Nolan Miller, a 60-year-old former Studebaker employee who worked at the company for 38 years, testified that the news that he did not reach the age of 60 in time to be given a full pension was bitter news indeed (Reilly 1994).

In May 1972, the Chairman of the Senate Labor and Public Welfare Committee, Harrison Williams, and ranking Minority Member Jacob Javits, introduced a bill intended to remedy the problems with existing pension plan law. In September 1972, the Senate Labor Committee approved the bill. The bill, which as enacted became ERISA, was designed to protect pension plans by establishing national standards for funding and payment. To minimize administrative and financial burden of maintaining a pension plan, ERISA would preempt all state laws on the subject. This preemption permitted employers whose operations crossed state lines to have one employee benefit plan that applied to all its employees, despite the employees being in various states. At the eleventh hour, the House Committee extended ERISA's scope to include all employee benefit plans. This extended ERISA's preemption to state laws governing health plans as well as pension plans. Preemption affects not just state statutes but also common law remedies such as actions in tort, of which malpractice is a subcategory.

ERISA's primary purpose was to provide a scheme for the protection of employees' pension funds. As an afterthought, all employee benefit plans were added to the ERISA legislation. ERISA is a complicated, multifaceted law. Stone has written that "ERISA as it relates to health benefits, presents an array of technical legal rules and distinctions that test the comprehension of seasoned attorneys" (Stone 1999). ERISA came to have a profound effect on the health-care system, including the provision of inpatient and outpatient psychiatric care.

ERISA PLANS

Definitions

Prior to describing ERISA's impact on health-care plans, it is necessary first to understand those parts of the statute that are especially relevant. ERISA restrictions, protections, and regulations apply generally to ERISA plans. ERISA plans include "pension benefit plans" and "welfare benefit plans." Health-care plans are considered welfare benefit plans. The definition of welfare benefit plan includes the following elements:

- It is established or maintained by an employer, employee organization, or both
- It provides medical coverage
- The benefits may be provided through the purchase of commercial insurance or a self-insurance fund

ERISA has a number of components that affect health-care plans, hospitals, and physicians. If a health-care plan is a "governmental plan" or "church plan" it is not subject to ERISA; therefore, ERISA applies only to private-sector health-care plans. States cannot require ERISA self-insured plans to cover particular benefits. ERISA provides compensation for care that is wrongly denied but does not provide a remedy for beneficiaries who are harmed by a prospective denial of benefits. Also of note is that ERISA does not protect hospitals or physicians that provide care from liability.

Remedies under ERISA

When a plan participant has a grievance, ERISA does provide remedies, though such remedies are limited. In particular, under Section 502(a)(1)(B) of ERISA, plaintiffs may not recover extracontractual damages such as those sought in typical malpractice claims. This restriction has protected ERISA health-care plans from being sued for malpractice in state courts. A plaintiff who has been denied benefits may not recover compensatory damages. Even when the denial of benefits leads to disastrous consequences, the plaintiff may not be granted punitive damages. This restriction may be reasonable for a pension plan. For example, assume the pension plan has $1000, and each of 10 participants is to receive $100. If a participant is improperly denied the $100, the remedy is to award the $100; to award more than the $100 would be to take money away from other retirees. It is unclear that this restriction is reasonable for a health-care plan, where compensatory and punitive damages can encourage the provision of non-negligent care.

ERISA usually preempts state claims for damages. This preemption is based on two provisions in ERISA. Section 502 describes complete preemption, and Section 514 describes conflict preemption. Each of these sections is described below:

- *Section 502: Complete Preemption*: Complete preemption is derived directly from the statute and comes into play when a participant attempts to bring a lawsuit based on state law against an ERISA plan where the subject matter of the claim is within the scope of ERISA's enforcement provision. The state law claim is "completely preempted," and the case is moved from state court to federal court. For example, a lawsuit based on the denial of a benefit is completely preempted and will be removed from state court to federal court.
- *Section 514: Conflict Preemption*: Conflict preemption, derived from U.S. Supreme Court decisions, is at issue when states try to regulate health care and their efforts affect ERISA plans. The provisions of Section 514 of ERISA indicate Congress' intent to have a uniform body of laws in order to minimize the burdens of employers' having to comply with conflicting directives from state to state.

The preemption provisions found in Section 514 are often referred to as the "preemption clause," the "saving clause," and the "deemer clause." The preemption clause, Section 514(a), is written broadly and provides that ERISA "supersedes any and all state laws insofar as they…relate to any employee benefit plan." The phrase "relate to" has been interpreted broadly to include state laws that have a connection or reference to an employee benefit plan. The saving clause, Section 514(b)(2)(A), limits this ERISA preemption stating that "any law of any state which regulates insurance" is "saved" from preemption. However, the deemer clause, Section 514(b)(2)(B), limits the saving clause, stating that an employee benefit plan may not "be deemed to be an insurance company…or to be engaged in the business of insurance." Since employee benefit plans may not be deemed to be insurers, and therefore are subject to the preemption clause, large employers may escape state regulation by self-insuring (accumulating funds for health care) rather than purchasing insurance from state-regulated insurance companies. Of 163 million employees and dependents with employer-based health plans, 127 million are covered by ERISA plans, which can be divided into two groups. Seventy-two million employees and dependents are covered by ERISA plans that purchase insurance that follows state insurance law but are not subject to liability. Fifty-five million employees and dependents have ERISA plans that escape all state regulation.

ERISA's limited remedies and its preemption of state remedies made it difficult to deal with ERISA's negative effects in the health-care system and the provision of health care. As discussed in the next sections, states and patients have tried to use the courts to deal with the perceived inequities and barriers to health care, e.g., denial of benefits. These court cases have included issues involving attempts to tax ERISA plans, to limit the denial of benefits, to identify vicarious liability, and to challenge conflicts of interest that may exist.

SIGNIFICANT COURT CASES DEALING WITH ERISA AND HEALTH CARE

ERISA must be understood in the context of market forces. A discussion of the increasing cost of health care in the 1960s and 1970s and the problems faced by U.S. corporations that had to compete in a world economy against foreign industries that had a lesser health-care burden is beyond the scope of this chapter. However, it is important to note that managed care was seen as the answer to containing health-care costs, even if it meant decreasing coverage and lowering the standard of care. ERISA, as it turned out, would allow this to happen beyond the control of state laws and without risk of liability (Stone 1995).

Taxing ERISA plans

Some states have attempted to regulate health care through taxation. Of special note is the case *New York State Conference of Blue Cross and Blue Shield Plans v. Travelers Insurance Company*, which was decided by the U.S. Supreme Court in 1995. In the circumstances leading up to this case, New York State had imposed a scheme of variable surcharges on hospital bills. Commercial insurers and private insurers, including self-insured plans, other than the Blue Cross Blue Shield plans, were assessed a surcharge of 13% of the hospital bill. The proceeds from this tax were kept by the treating hospital. A further 11% surcharge was imposed and turned over to the state's general fund. In addition, health maintenance organizations (HMOs) were assessed up to a 9% surcharge, based on the number of Medicaid patients enrolled, and were to pay this amount to the state's general fund. The Blue Cross Blue Shield plans were exempted from these surcharges because their open enrollment policies resulted in their having higher medical costs than commercial insurers. Through this system of surcharges, New York was shoring up the Blue Cross Blue Shield plans, thereby assuring that through the Blues open enrollment, marginal and high-risk individuals would be able to obtain health insurance. HMOs were encouraged to enroll Medicaid recipients at lower costs to the state. Finally, the revenues retained by the hospitals allowed them to shift the costs of care of uninsured or underinsured patients to commercial insurers and HMOs.

Justice Souter, writing for a unanimous court in *Travelers*, stated that the surcharges do not "relate to" employee benefit plans within the meaning of ERISA's preemption provision and, therefore, are not preempted by ERISA. The surcharges made the Blues less unattractive as an insurance alternative and, therefore, had an indirect economic effect on choices made by buyers. The Supreme Court acknowledged that it is possible a state law might have such an acute economic effect, even though its effect was indirect, so as to effectively force an ERISA plan to adopt certain substantive coverage or effectively restrict its choice of insurers, which would lead to the state law being preempted under Section 514. However, the court held that New York State's statutory surcharges did not force substantive coverage or restrict the choice of insurers. Instead, the court found that the surcharges merely indirectly affected the relative price of insurance policies, which is no different from many state laws in areas that have traditionally been subject to local regulation which Congress could not have intended to eliminate through ERISA.

ERISA preemption litigation suits

Suits against ERISA plans asserting that decisions to limit care or to deny benefits directly harmed the plaintiff have failed. To illustrate this point, in *Corcoran v. United Healthcare, Inc.* (1992), the plaintiffs brought a state law malpractice claim against an ERISA plan alleging that negligent utilization review resulted in the death of their unborn child. During Florence Corcoran's first pregnancy, she was put on bedrest and fetal monitoring. When fetal distress occurred, a Caesarean section was performed, and her child survived. After Mrs. Corcoran became pregnant again, her obstetrician recommended complete bedrest and, later in the pregnancy, ordered hospitalization of Mrs. Corcoran so that the fetus could be monitored around the clock. However, her ERISA plan had instituted managed care utilization review since her previous pregnancy. While her same obstetrician recommended the same bedrest and fetal monitoring, United Healthcare ("United") determined that hospitalization was not necessary and instead authorized the less expensive 10 hours per day of home nursing care. Mrs. Corcoran was hospitalized from October 3–12, 1989, but, because United had not precertified her stay, she returned home. On October 25, 1989, when the home care nurse was not on duty, the fetus went into distress and died.

In *Corcoran*, the U.S. Court of Appeals, Fifth Circuit, noted that although United did indeed make medical decisions and give medical advice, "it does so in the context of making a determination about the availability of benefits under the plan." Thus, the court ruled that Section 514 of ERISA preempted a state court malpractice action, and Section 502 of ERISA did not compensate a plaintiff for damages. The plaintiffs, who alleged that coverage decisions were wrongly made, were limited to recovery of their contractual benefits as provided in Section 502 and therefore were not permitted damages for emotional distress.

Theory of vicarious liability and managed care entities

There have been many attempts to sue managed-care entities on the basis of state law theories of vicarious liability. The doctrine of "ostensible agency" has been a part of vicarious liability in many jurisdictions; this doctrine imposes liability if a reasonable person would conclude that the clinician is an employee or agent of the health-care facility even if he or she is not. For example, health-care plans that direct patients to a list of preferred providers are closed panel HMOs and presumably would meet the requirements for vicarious liability in many states.

In *Dukes v. U.S. Healthcare* (1995), the U.S. Court of Appeals, Third Circuit, ruled that a vicarious liability action against an HMO did not fall within the scope of Section 502 of ERISA. The *Dukes* case was a consolidation of two cases filed in state court against HMOs organized by U.S. Healthcare. Each of the two consolidated cases alleged medical malpractice of HMO-affiliated hospitals and medical personnel. In the *Dukes* case, Darryl Dukes' primary care physician discovered a problem with Mr. Dukes' ears. Surgery was performed and Mr. Dukes was given a prescription for blood studies. However, when Mr. Dukes gave the prescription to the hospital's laboratory, the hospital refused to perform the blood studies for a reason not discussed in the record.

The following day, Mr. Dukes saw another physician who also ordered a blood test, which was performed. However, Mr. Dukes' condition continued to worsen, and he died. At the time of his death, Mr. Dukes' blood sugar level was very high—a condition that allegedly would have been found through a timely blood test.

Mr. Dukes' wife brought suit in state court alleging medical malpractice, among other claims. The HMO removed the case to federal court based on the HMO's being part of an ERISA plan, and the theory that Mrs. Dukes' claims "relate to" a welfare plan and are therefore preempted under Section 514 of ERISA. Mrs. Dukes moved that the case be remanded to state court, and the HMO moved that it be dismissed. The district court dismissed Mrs. Dukes' claims against the HMO and remanded to state court the claims against other defendants that Mrs. Dukes had brought.

The Third Circuit found that there was "no claim that the plans erroneously withheld benefits." The *Dukes'* court noted "the plaintiffs...complain about the low quality of the medical treatment that they actually received and argued that U.S. Health Care HMO should be held liable under agency and negligence principles." Yet, Congress did not create ERISA Section 502 as a remedy for medical malpractice. The net result of *Dukes* was that the Third Circuit returned the lawsuit to state court for trial. However, the Third Circuit did not reach the question of whether Section 514 of ERISA would preempt the malpractice actions in the state courts. The *Dukes* case was ultimately settled out of court.

ERISA fiduciary duties

As stated above, ERISA does not protect from liability doctors or hospitals that provide care to patients. ERISA insulates from liability those who make benefit determinations even when they depart from accepted medical standards of care. *Pegram v. Herdrich* (1999) deals with the application of ERISA fiduciary duties to HMO decisions about what care is needed and, therefore, what will be paid for.

In March 1991, Cynthia Herdrich, a part-time legal secretary, experienced pain in her lower abdomen that she thought might be appendicitis. She went to see Dr. Lori Pegram, a physician at her managed-care HMO, Carle Care in Bloomington, Illinois. Six days later, Dr. Pegram identified a 6 × 8 centimeter inflamed mass in Herdrich's abdomen. Dr. Pegram did not order an ultrasound at a local hospital, but instead referred Herdrich to a facility staffed by Carle Care, which was more than 50 miles away and could not perform the ultrasound for 8 days. Before the 8 days elapsed, Herdrich's appendix ruptured causing peritonitis that required emergency surgery.

Herdrich sued Dr. Pegram and Carle Care in state court for medical malpractice, and charged that the tests were delayed because the plan's doctors had financial incentives to hold costs down. Carle Care was providing health-care services as part of an ERISA plan. Carle Care and Dr. Pegram asserted that ERISA preempted the two counts of state law fraud and moved the case to federal court. Herdrich alleged that provision of medical services under the terms of the Carle Care HMO—rewarding its physician owners for limiting medical care—entailed a breach of its ERISA fiduciary duty, because these terms created an incentive to make decisions in the physicians' self-interest rather than the exclusive interest of plan participants.

The original malpractice counts were tried by a jury in state court, and Ms. Herdrich prevailed on both, receiving a total of $35,000 in damages. A Federal District Court rejected her ERISA claim that the HMO had breached its fiduciary duty. A three-judge panel of the U.S. Court of Appeals for the Seventh Circuit voted two to one that when

HMO physicians delay providing needed medical treatment to increase their bonus, they may breach a fiduciary duty, an impermissible conflict of interest. The full Appeals Court declined to review the three-judge panel's ruling. The refusal to review the decision *en banc* was appealed to the U.S. Supreme Court. The U.S. Supreme Court granted *certiori*.

The *Pegram* suit challenged the common type of "mixed" eligibility determination. Mixed eligibility decisions are those that involve elements of both "eligibility decisions" (whether the ERISA plan covers a particular condition or course of treatment) and "treatment decisions" (the appropriate medical response to the patient's condition).

With this important health-care case—one that could have a direct effect on the provision of care to psychiatric patients—coming before the U.S. Supreme Court, the American Psychiatric Association (APA) decided to write an amicus brief. The APA reviewed the trade-off between ERISA coverage and state law coverage. In general, if a particular matter is subject to ERISA, then it is not subject to state law; however, liability under state law (with damages) provides a stronger remedy, because ERISA damages only allow recovery of the cost of the denied benefit.

The APA brief stressed two points: (a) the real harm that can be caused by certain kinds of incentives to withhold or delay or re-direct treatment; and (b) the need for such incentives to be subject to the same legal coverage whether under ERISA or state law. The theme of the amicus brief was that if state law does not apply, then ERISA must apply so that no gap in legal coverage results.

The Supreme Court heard oral argument on the case in February 2000 and issued its opinion in June 2000. The Supreme Court held unanimously in favor of the HMO. Justice Souter wrote, "no HMO organization could survive without some incentive connecting physician reward with treatment rationing." The Supreme Court held that ERISA duties do not apply to the decisions challenged, because Congress did not mean for mixed determinations to be ERISA fiduciary decisions. The Supreme Court did not say, however, what limits, if any, there are on the application of state law to HMO structures and the harm caused by the mixed determinations made by ERISA plans. This critical issue will now be played out in the state courts.

Rather than resulting in a major setback for those trying to hold managed care accountable for its mistreatment of patients, *Pegram* contained language that some viewed as potentially helpful to patients. The Supreme Court's opinion in *Pegram* indicated that it does not believe that Congress, in passing ERISA, ever intended to supplant state medical malpractice laws. But *Pegram* did not address the accountability issue, and it may have opened the door to state courts holding managed care companies accountable for their negligent medical necessity determinations.

SUMMARY

When ERISA was passed to protect employee pensions and benefits, few, if any, could have foreseen that ERISA preemption and limited remedies would allow managed care companies to reduce professional standards of care while protecting the managed care company from liability. It is ironic that a law passed to protect the rights of employees has been used to deny patients who have been damaged appropriate recourse, and encourages managed care companies to deny care, confident that they are legally beyond reach.

SUMMARY KEY POINTS

- ERISA's primary purpose was to provide a scheme for the protection of employee pension funds. All employee benefit plans, including healthcare, were added as an afterthought.
- ERISA does not provide a remedy for beneficiaries who are harmed by prospective denial of benefits.
- ERISA does provide limited remedies but usually preempts state claims for damages with Section 502 describing complete preemption and Section 514 describing conflict preemption.
- Attempts to tax ERISA plans have met with limited success, *Blue Cross and Blue Shield Plans v. Travelers* (1995).
- ERISA does not shield doctors or hospitals from malpractice liability.
- In *Pegram v. Herdrich* (1999) the Supreme Court held that ERISA duties do not apply to "mixed" eligibility determinations, i.e., decisions that involve deciding if the ERISA plan covers the treatment and if the treatment is appropriate for the patient.

ACKNOWLEDGMENT

The author wishes to thank Louis M. Ciccone, Esq., for his assistance.

REFERENCES

29 U.S.C. §§1001–1046.

29 U.S.C. §§301–308.

Corcoran v. United Healthcare, Inc., 965 F.2d 1321 (5th Circuit 1992) cert. denied 506 US 1033 (1992).

Dukes v. U.S. Healthcare, 57 F.3d 350 (3rd Cir. 1995).

Inland Steel Company v. NLRB, 170 F.2d 247, 7th Cir. 1948 cert. denied 336 U.S. 960 (1949).

New York State Conference of Blue Cross and Blue Shield Plans et al. v. Travelers Insurance Company et al., 514 U.S. 645 (1995).

Pegram v. Herdrich, 530 U.S. 211 (1999).

Reilly MM. 1994. ERISA 1974–1994. *Twenty Years of Pension Reform and Beyond.* Tax Notes, November 7, 749–750.

Stone AA. 1995. Paradigms, preemptions and stages: Understanding the transformation of American psychiatry by managed care. *International Journal of Psychiatry* 18:353–387.

Stone AA. 1999. Managed care, liability and ERISA. *Psychiatric Clinics of North America* 22:17–29.

PART 10

Basic Issues in Law

ROBERT LLOYD GOLDSTEIN

89

Philosophy of law: Classic and contemporary jurisprudence

ROBERT LLOYD GOLDSTEIN AND SANFORD L. DROB

Laws are the sovereigns of sovereigns.

Louis XIV

Law and justice are not always the same.

Gloria Steinem

INTRODUCTION

Since Stone called into question the ethical boundaries of forensic psychiatry (Stone 1984), a number of leaders in the field have drawn on the principles of moral philosophy (the branch of philosophy concerned with ethical theories) to conceptualize and implement ethical guidelines and operational principles; in the process, an ethical framework for forensic psychiatry has gradually evolved (Appelbaum 1997). Although few of our colleagues are as knowledgeable in philosophical matters as Stone and Appelbaum, nonetheless, an appreciation of the basic concepts of legal philosophy will serve to enhance every forensic psychiatrist's understanding of the history, development, and purposes of the legal institutions and practices that operate at the interface between psychiatry and the law. This process of exploring and charting the *terra incognita* of the law is bound to promote a greater degree of intellectual stimulation and satisfaction for the forensic practitioner, who applies psychiatric expertise to a rather specialized set of issues within the context of a system whose conventions and procedures may seem alien and mysterious to the nonlawyer.

WHAT IS LAW?

The philosophy of law applies the discipline of philosophy to study the issues raised by the existence, nature, and practice of law. This basic overview of the subject is intended as an introduction for the forensic psychiatrist and does not begin to address the full scope of legal philosophy dating back "twenty-four hundred years—from the Greek thinkers of the fifth century BC, who asked whether right was right by nature or only by enactment and convention, to the social philosophers of today, who expound on the ends, the ethical basis, and the enduring principles of social control" (Pound 1954). The quintessence of legal philosophy, simply stated, is "What is law?" The first step in studying this question involves analyzing the socio-cultural antecedents in prelegal societies of the rules and regulations from which law originates. Before formal rules or laws had been enunciated and certain individuals were accorded privileged status in the community (e.g., as "judges" of others), even the most primitive societies had norms that evolved from the particular needs of that society. For example, on the most simplistic level, it is apparent that *revenge* played a major role in creating the norms in early societies. The instinct of an aggrieved or injured party to take revenge and the evolution of social conventions to control the expression of that instinct served as the basis of customary norms that underlie the civil and criminal law of more complex societies. With more complex interrelationships among the people in a community, norms developed and resulted in codifications in law, regulations, and systematized mechanisms, such as courts, judges, and juries, for resolving conflicts (Elliott 1985).

Golding (1975) set forth a lucid and concise analysis of the elements of a legal system within any society. He addressed the question of what it means to say that a legal system exists in society (any given society). Golding proposed that the statement that a legal system exists in society is true if

1. There are laws in society.
2. There exists in society an agency for making and changing the laws.
3. There exists in society an agency for determining infractions of the laws.
4. There exists in society an agency for enforcing the laws.
5. There exists in society an agency for settling disputes between individuals.

These five conditions set forth the general conditions for all legal systems. The first condition—that is, the existence of laws—is a necessary element of any society that claims to have a legal system, because it is inconceivable to have a "lawless" legal system. Golding classified conditions (2) through (5) as *jural agencies* and reached the conclusion that a society possesses a sufficient degree of what he terms *jural complexity* to permit us to assert that it has an actual legal system, if it has both a set of laws and any two of the four enumerated *jural agencies*. *Jural agencies* are viewed in terms of the type of *jural activities* they perform. In the course of analyzing these terms and concepts, Golding offered an example based on the major role of revenge in creating the norms in early societies, which was alluded to above:

> Suppose that we come across two separate cases of one man killing another. Suppose further that in all behavioral and psychological respects the two acts are perfectly alike: each actor, with venom in his heart, kills his enemy with a sword. Now, it does not follow that there can be no difference between the two cases; in fact, one is a pure case of murder, while the other is not. This is possible because one of the killers (the latter) is the state executioner who is carrying out the sentence of a court. His act is the act of an *official*—he is a jural agent—acting in an official capacity, and it is an instance of a jural activity. (Golding 1975, 22)

Jural agents have an authoritative status within a society to carry out appropriate jural activities (e.g., settling a dispute, making or changing a law, or enforcing a law). Laws of competence (or power-delegating laws) regulate and establish when a particular jural agent is acting in an appropriate official capacity. The *authoritative* status of a society's jural agencies and the jural acts they perform derive from certain characteristics or qualities inherent in its laws: its laws are perceived as *valid* both behaviorally and psychologically (i.e., most members of the society conform their behavior to the rules or laws most of the time and view them as normative guides to action). Laws are binding on a society (1) when they are enforced (by sanctions), (2) when they are recognized as binding because they are legitimate (i.e., enacted in accordance with the formal procedures that have been established for making laws in the society), and (3) when they are perceived as imposing a moral obligation or duty to obey them.

THEORIES OF LAW

It is a truism that law serves as a device for social control; yet law differs from other methods of social control, for example, mere force or morality (Murphy and Coleman 1990). The forensic psychiatrist should be familiar with the two main traditions in legal philosophy, Natural Law and Legal Positivism.

NATURAL LAW

According to the theory of Natural Law, legal validity requires a corresponding moral validity as an absolute logical and conceptual prerequisite. At the very least, laws must be morally permissible. The classical version of natural law theory dates far back to the ancient Greeks and their doctrine of the *Logos*, i.e., the invisible pattern or principle that governs the transactions of the cosmic order. In *Summa Theologiae*, St. Thomas Aquinas emphasized the essence of natural law theory:

> As Augustine says, that which is not just seems to be no law at all. Hence the force of a law depends on the extent of its justice...Every human law has just so much of the nature of law as it is derived from the law of nature. But if at any point it departs from the law of nature, it is no longer a law, but a perversion of law. (Aquinas 1954, 784)

According to Aquinas, natural law is the "participation of the eternal law (i.e., the Divine law for the governance of the universe) in the rational creature" (Aquinas 1954, 787). Lawmaking is grounded on reason in order to promote the common good of the community. One is obligated to obey the law (which has a coercive force, backed up by sanctions) not because of the threat of force, but only under circumstances when the content per se of the law is itself moral. The eternal verities of the moral order, expressed as a part of the order of nature in the view of medieval Christian theology, provide the rationale for laws and their attendant legal obligations.

Contemporary legal philosophers have carried on the tradition of natural law theory, albeit reformulated in the more acceptable idiom of our own age, divested of the metaphysical and theological trappings of the classical natural law system of Aquinas. Hart (1961) articulates a "minimum content" theory of natural law, which he views as the "core of good sense" in natural law theory. Hart believes that because society is concerned with the survival in proximity of its members (it is not a "suicide club"), natural law provides a meeting ground for the minimal overlap between morality and law that serves this aim. The nature of the *human condition* (e.g., that humans are vulnerable to harm, limited in their powers of self-control and foresight, limited in their altruism, and by necessity attempting to cooperate in order to survive in a world of scarce, limited resources) mandates that the major social institutions of law and morality will overlap somewhat in dealing with these basic human concerns.

Fuller (1964) has written about legal systems and the central importance of "the internal morality of the law." In order to qualify as a legitimate legal system, the overwhelming majority of its rules must be seen to satisfy procedural demands of a moral nature, compatible with justice and fairness, for example, treating "like cases *like*," not applying rules after the fact, giving fair notice, and impartially enforcing the rules. Fuller wrote extensively about the legal pathology inherent in Nazi Germany, where the entire system of secret, arbitrary laws, based on the whims of those in power, failed to meet the minimal standards of morality that make law possible. Fuller's approach focuses on the moral requirements of formal legal *procedure* only, and imposes no moral limitations on the *content* of laws.

Dworkin (1977) advanced a theory of judicial decision making, the "rights thesis," which stands for the proposition that principled judicial action involves a search for the right answer to the question "who has the right to win?" Protection of rights that are based on the moral values of our legal order would outweigh utilitarian considerations of policy or the collective welfare. In arguing that Japanese Americans had a *right* not to be interned after the attack on Pearl Harbor, Dworkin writes:

> Individual rights are political trumps held by individuals. Individuals have rights when, for some reason, a collective goal is not a sufficient justification for imposing some loss or injury upon them. (Dworkin 1977, xi)

LEGAL POSITIVISM

Legal Positivism derives its name from the fact that law is *posited* by human authority. The compendium of Roman law compiled by order of the Emperor Justinian I in the sixth century captured the concept of Legal Positivism in admirably pithy terms: "What pleases the Prince has the force of law." John Austin, the nineteenth century English legal philosopher, is generally regarded as the Father of Legal Positivism. Austin rejected Natural Law theory and its essential connection between law and morality. He held that the existence of law is one thing; its merit or demerit is another (Austin 1954). Austin's theory of law is often referred to as the *Command* theory. The *command of the sovereign* (or supreme political authority) constitutes the law governing a given society. The sovereign is defined as that individual (or group) who receives the obeisance of the society on a habitual basis and who in turn is not in the habit of obeying others in the society. Once a law has the *imprimatur of the sovereign*, indicating the will or desire to be obeyed, there is a nonoptional condition imposed in the form of a legal duty or obligation. The law is a coercive device for social control, a "command backed by a threat" to enforce compliance (whether or not the threatened sanction is actually carried out). Punitive sanctions, in the criminal law, entail punishment by the appropriate jural agency. Privative sanctions, in the civil law, deprive the individual of the state's jural enforcement authority (regarding transactions such as making a will) if he or she fails to follow the relevant legal rules. The *command of the sovereign* is the legitimate law of the society in question. The pedigree test for legal validity, according to Austin, is simply that the law's enactment can be traced to the sovereign whose actions define legality for that society.

Hart (1961) significantly refines Austin's "command-of-the-sovereign" model of the law by emphasizing the importance of overall legal systems and legal rules (e.g., a pedigree test that defines legal validity for a particular society by specifying that laws must be enacted according to agreed-upon rules for generating binding laws). Hart further distinguishes between *primary rules*, which are the rules that impose legal duties and obligations on individuals, and *secondary rules*, which are "rules about rules." The secondary rules involve the primary rules themselves, how to recognize them (i.e., how to determine if they possess the proper pedigree to constitute a valid law); how to initiate, modify, or repeal them altogether (e.g., by establishment of legislatures); how to determine conclusively whether they have been violated; and how to settle legal disputes (e.g., through the establishment of courts and rules of adjudication). A succinct statement of Hart's theory of the law is that "Law [is best regarded] as a system of primary and secondary rules" (Hart 1961, 107). Many regard Hart's work as the definitive exposition of the basic philosophical question, "What is law?"—essentially settling the issue once and for all. Others, including adherents of Legal Realism and Critical Legal Studies, criticize Hart for achieving uniformity at the price of distortion (Twining 1973; Unger 1986).

SOCIAL CONSTRUCTION OF LAW AND PSYCHIATRY

Several contemporary issues at the interface between jurisprudence, social science, and the mental health professions are worthy of the forensic practitioner's attention. The continuing controversy between Natural Law theory and Legal Positivism is reflected in similar debates regarding the "natural" status versus social construction of mental illness (Schaffner and Tabb 2014). Each of these debates is embedded in broader philosophical questions regarding the nature of ethics and morality and, especially, the problem posed by philosophical relativists and ethical emotivists who hold that values and morality are themselves individually or communally subjective (Wilks 2002). This issue is in effect duplicated within psychiatry itself, where it has been argued that the entire mental health profession, with its focus upon *evaluating* mental health, intelligence, adaptation, identity, insight, reality testing, interpersonal relations, and various other psychological functions, is itself value laden. On what basis are such evaluations made? Are they grounded in trans-temporal and trans-cultural "science," or do they simply reflect the current attitudes of the community or mental health professions. Given these complexities, the forensic psychiatrist cannot uncritically cloak himself or herself in a veneer of "scientific objectivity." How to recognize the place of values within the mental health professions without losing scientific perspective on "truth" is itself a profound philosophical challenge for both the courts and the forensic specialist (Appelbaum 1997).

FREE WILL, DETERMINISM, AND CRIMINAL RESPONSIBILITY

One significant jurisprudential issue that can result in a conflict between the values of the law and the forensic specialist's understanding of human behavior arises in connection with conceptualizations of human agency and the determinants of an individual's behavior. The issue of the place of free will in law and ethics is at least as old as Kant, who noted that the demands of morality and ethics, which assume the possibility of freely chosen, responsible action, conflict with the tenets of natural science, which assumes that all events, including all human behavior, are a function of a chain of antecedent causes. The problem has not gone unnoticed in the recent literature on jurisprudence, which has raised questions regarding the "myth of free will" in the criminal law. Matthew Jones (2002), for example, has argued that the law has always assumed that an individual has the capacity to freely choose between behavioral alternatives. Jones has pointed to the fact that the Supreme Court explicitly acknowledged this axiom by stating that a "belief in freedom of the human will [is] universal and persistent in mature systems of law" (*Morissette v. United States* 1952). This *legal fiction* that has direct bearing on both the notion of criminal responsibility and the rationale for punishment, has been directly challenged by social scientists. For example, the neuropsychologist Sam Harris has argued that both the belief in and the subjective experience of free will is an illusion and that the rationale for holding criminal defendants "responsible" and "punishing" them for their actions rests upon an outmoded, pre-scientific mindset. According to Harris (2015), if we examine our own experience closely, we realize that everything we think of, feel, and intend simply arises from an unconscious source and is in no way dependent on our own will and decision. This proposition, which has received (albeit controversial) support in the experimental literature (Libet et al. 1999) accords with the basic scientific principle of universal causality and is in opposition to the assumptions of virtually all systems of ethics and law. As Jones points out, the future of criminal law will in many ways be impacted by scientific findings that strongly suggest that human behavior has genetic and environmental causes that place limits on the presumed free, responsible human subject. Courts and forensic specialists may, in effect, adopt a form of *philosophical compatibilism* (Dennett 2003), which regards those actions as free that are compatible with an individual's desires and therefore not obviously "compelled." However, the problem remains, for example, with respect to offenses such as pedophilia, regarding the origins of one's desires, which few would argue are freely chosen. Jurisprudentially, the question is whether courts, with the prodding of the social science and mental health fields, will expand their conception of behaviors that are regarded as ill or dysfunctional, as opposed to criminal, and adjust sanctions accordingly. While some have called for such reform, others, such as Jones, have argued that the criminal law is flexible enough to retain its current conceptions of punishment by changing from a punitive to a more utilitarian rationale for its implementation.

PSYCHOLOGICAL JURISPRUDENCE

Darley and colleagues (2002) have argued that a field of "Psychological Jurisprudence" can aid the law in securing the public's acceptance of and compliance with law and judicial decisions, as well as alter the behavior of those who have previously failed to comply with legal requirements. Others (Birgden 2004) have called for a "Therapeutic Jurisprudence" that will employ psychological principles to motivate offenders to refrain from future criminal acts and participate in rehabilitation. Such authors have argued that the law can greatly benefit from a "conception of the person [that is] based upon research about people's motivation, cognition, and decision-making" (Darley et al. 2002, 37). Darley et al. criticize the deterrence model of criminal sanctions on the grounds that at least for certain offenses an individual's estimate of the likelihood of being apprehended and punished has little impact on his or her behavior. Laws, they argue, must be adjusted to be commensurate with human motivation, so that the vast majority of individuals feel motivated to comply with the law regardless of any governmental sanction or punishment. When laws (e.g., those prohibiting the sale and possession of substances like marijuana) do not accord with such motivations, a legal and social crisis ensues. This analysis, of course, raises the question of the relativity of values—whether law can or should be subject to presumed "natural" or objective values, or should simply reflect the consensus of the people who are subject to its sanctions.

FEMINIST JURISPRUDENCE

The values, rights, and modes of thought of previously suppressed or "different" (Minow 1991) segments of the population raise a variety of issues and problems for the law. Contemporary feminist jurisprudence, for example, involves both a broad-ranging critique of the foundations of legal thought and a focus on specific substantive issues that have limited the rights, freedom, and economic status of women in the eyes of law and society.

Feminist jurisprudence is quite varied in its outlook, and several models have emerged; these include the *liberal model*, which focuses on equal rights and the effort to assure that women attain meaningful equality; the *dominance model*, which critiques existing models of law on the grounds that they are vehicles to extend practices of male domination; and the *difference* model, which holds that equal treatment under the law is only achieved when differences between the sexes are recognized and taken into account. Each model, however, appeals to (and at times critiques) certain fundamental moral or axiological principles, such as the equality of all human beings, and seeks to rectify those situations where the law unjustly deviates from (or in some instances *should* deviate from) these principles (Francis and Smith 2015). In addition, feminist critics argue that certain established *legal principles*, such as adherence to legal precedent, have the effect of maintaining and legitimizing a status quo in which women and other minorities are diminished in worth, status, and power.

An important issue for feminist jurisprudence relates to the real and purported differences between the sexes. For example, it has been argued that because women become pregnant and bear children, simple "equality under the law" can effectively result in gender discrimination in which women are denied jobs and economic advancement. This occurs, for example, when the law does not grant rights for family, pregnancy leave, and part-time employment (Minow 1991). It is argued that simple "equal treatment under the law" in such cases effectively results in gender discrimination. Such "equal treatment," it is said, is only equal under a patriarchal, male-dominated conception of legal justice.

According to some feminist thinkers, a further (and conservative) implication of gender difference is that aspects of a patriarchal or at least "paternalistic" jurisprudence may need to be retained, in order to achieve social and economic equality for women. These thinkers have raised questions regarding the dismantling of "protectionist" laws, e.g., alimony and child support, which have been limited under the rubric of "gender equality," but which may actually contribute to what has been termed the "feminization of poverty" (Francis and Smith 2015).

Another important jurisprudential issue for feminist thinkers involves the distinction between public and private domains. Typically, the latter is regarded as largely outside the law's reach. An important question relates to the state's interest in "voluntary" behavior within private economic arrangements that involve the human body. Questions regarding "voluntary and consensual prostitution" and participation and distribution of gender-oppressive pornography exemplify this issue. With regard to prostitution, for example, no single "feminist" voice has emerged; liberal feminists advocate its legalization, while "dominance" feminists argue that it is essentially repressive (Hung 1999). Feminist scholars have also raised questions regarding whether the law should permit women to engage in paid surrogate pregnancies and gamete donation; some have argued that doing so legitimizes power inequalities within which women cannot effectively act voluntarily (Andrews 1988).

The question of public versus private domains also arises in connection with marriage and cohabitation situations in which women are physically, emotionally, or economically abused in a manner that would never be tolerated within a public arena. Women living in "traditional" marriage or other "consensual" co-habitation arrangements, in which they are not paid for domestic work and child-rearing, may continue to be subject to such abuse in a manner that is beyond the reach of the law (Dempsey 2009). Of particular interest to mental health professionals is the feminist critique of the family therapy model of domestic abuse, which tends to view such abuse exclusively as an individual or family problem, rather than a social and legal one as well (Hansen and Harway 1993).

Feminists are also concerned with issues relating to the subtle and often unrecognized infiltration of traditional religious notions into the legal arena. This, they argue, has long been evident in efforts to restrict the scope of *Roe v. Wade* (1973) and more recently in arguments over the Defense of Marriage Act and gay marriage. While many feminists recognize that the question of abortion, for example, raises deep moral questions and conflicts, they argue that these conflicts must be balanced against a woman's right to control her own body and destiny and should not, on the principle of the separation of church and state, be dictated by religious notions of "life" and "personhood" (Francis and Smith 2015).

REFERENCES

Andrews L. 1988. Surrogate motherhood: The challenge for feminists. *Journal of Law, Medicine and Ethics* 16:72–80.

Appelbaum PS. 1997. A theory of ethics for forensic psychiatry. *Journal of the American Academy of Psychiatry and Law* 25:233–247.

Aquinas T. 1954. Human law. In *Basic Writings of St. Thomas Aquinas*, Vol. 2, edited by AC Pegis, New York: Random House, 782–789.

Austin J. 1954. *The Province of Jurisprudence Determined.* New York: Noonday Press.

Birgden A. 2004. Therapeutic jurisprudence and responsivity: Finding the will and the way in offender rehabilitation. *Psychology, Crime and Law* 10:283–295.

Darley J, S Fulero, C Haney, and T Tyler. 2002. Psychological jurisprudence: Taking psychology and law into the twenty-first century. *Perspectives in Law and Psychology* 14:35–59.

Dempsey M. 2009. *Prosecuting Domestic Violence.* Oxford: Oxford University Press.

Dennett D. 2003. *Freedom Evolves*. London: Penguin Books.
Dworkin R. 1977. *Taking Rights Seriously*. Cambridge, MA: Harvard University Press.
Elliott ED. 1985. The evolutionary tradition of jurisprudence. *Columbia Law Review* 85:38–97.
Francis L and P Smith. 2015. Feminist philosophy of law. In *The Stanford Encyclopedia of Philosophy*, Summer 2015 edition, edited by EN Zalta. http://plato.stanford.edu/archives/sum2015/entries/feminism-law/, accessed June 5, 2015.
Fuller L. 1964. *The Morality of Law*. New Haven, CT: Yale University Press.
Golding MP. 1975. *Philosophy of Low*. Englewood Cliffs, NJ: Prentice Hall.
Hansen M and M Harway. 1993. *Battering and Family Therapy: A Feminist Perspective*. Thousand Oaks, CA: Sage.
Harris S. 2012. *Free Will*. New York: Free Press.
Hart HLA. 1961. *The Concept of Law*. Oxford: Oxford University Press.
Hung L. 1999. A radical feminist view of prostitution: Towards a model of regulation. *University of College London Jurisprudence Review* 6:123–145.
Jones M. 2003. Overcoming the myth of free will in criminal law: The true impact of the genetic revolution. *Duke Law Journal* 52:1031–1053.
Libet B, A Freeman, and J Sutherland J. eds. 1999. *The Volitional Brain: Towards a Neuroscience of Free Will*. Exeter, UK: Imprint Academic.
Minow M. 1991. *Making All the Difference: Inclusion, Exclusion and American Law*. Cambridge, MA: Harvard University Press.
Morissette v. U.S., 342 U.S. 246, 250 (1952).
Murphy JG and Coleman JL. 1990. *Philosophy of Law: An Introduction to Jurisprudence*. Boulder, CO: Westview Press.
Pound R. 1954. *An Introduction to the Philosophy of Law*. New Haven, CT: Yale University Press.
Roe v. Wade, 410 U.S. 113 (1973).
Schaffner K and K Tabb. 2014. Varieties of social constructivism and the problem of progress in psychiatry. In *Philosophical Issues in Psychiatry, III: The Nature and Sources of Historical Change*, edited by K Kendler, Oxford: Oxford University Press, 85–106.
Stone AA. 1984. *Law, Psychiatry and Morality: Essays and Analysis*. Washington, DC: American Psychiatric Press.
Twining W. 1973. *Karl Llewellyn and the Realist Movement*. Norman: University of Oklahoma Press.
Unger RM. 1986. *The Critical Legal Studies Movement*. Cambridge, MA: Harvard University Press.
Wilks C. 2002. *Emotion, Truth and Meaning*. Dordrecht: Kluwer Academic.

90

Foundations of American law: The court system and the legislative process

ROBERT LLOYD GOLDSTEIN

INTRODUCTION

The common law is a distinctive legal system that originated in medieval England, grew and developed in the courts of the king, and during the twelfth and thirteenth centuries came to be applied throughout the English realm. Hogue (1985) distinguishes it from other legal systems of that period (e.g., local customary law, canon law administered by church courts, rules of feudal custom applied by courts of baronial overlords) "by calling it simply the body of rules prescribing social conduct and justiciable in the royal courts of England" (Hogue 1985, 5). In time, three royal courts (three superior courts of common law) emerged: the Court of Exchequer (with jurisdiction over controversies pertaining to the king's property and revenue), the Court of King's Bench (with jurisdiction over criminal cases and civil cases involving a breach of the peace), and the Court of Common Pleas (with jurisdiction over all other civil disputes between the king's subjects).

In addition, there was another system, rivaling that of the common law, which also originated in the Middle Ages: the Court of Chancery, which exercised jurisdiction over suits in equity. Judges in equity, originally ecclesiastical dignitaries, intervened to correct the harshness or inflexibility of the common law on grounds of morality or conscience (Scott and Kent 1967). An excellent exposition of the origins, development, and complexities of the common law, which does not assume professional legal training, can be found in the slim volume *Origins of the Common Law* (Hogue 1985). The reception of the common law of England in the United States was characterized by a process of selective adoption, providing for the continuity of English and American legal principles, but transforming them for American use by specific legislative enactment or judicial decision. In other words, the principles of English common law were drawn on as sources of guidance, but did not always find acceptance. As Justice Story said in a leading case:

> The common law of England is not to be taken in all respects to be that of America. Our ancestors brought with them its general principles, and claimed it as their birthright; but they brought with them and adopted only that portion which was applicable to their condition. (*Van Ness v. Pacard* 1829)

The most prominent characteristic of early American law was the strong tendency toward codification. Although the common law served as a fundamental subsidiary law, there was a paucity of lawyers trained in the English tradition and few law books available to transmit the corpus of English common law doctrine. Historically, this was the pragmatic basis for the adoption of elaborate and rather complete codes of law, which constituted most of the law under which the American colonists lived (Walsh 1932). A century ago, case law was the dominant ingredient in American law, and legislation was of lesser importance. Today, with the enormous growth of the federal regulatory agencies and the tendency toward comprehensive law codification (e.g., the Uniform Commercial Code), "legislation has fully come of age as a form of American law" (Jones et al. 1980, 3).

The following sections outline the present-day organization of the American court system (at both the federal and state levels), the nature and authority of case law, and the legislative process. Finally, the meeting ground is examined where case law and legislation come together—that is, statutory interpretation and construction by the courts.

The organization of court systems in the United States is rather complex and reflects the historical realities of our federal system of government. There is a dual system of state and federal courts, each with its own system of legal doctrine and practices. However, to complicate matters further, each system of courts is routinely called on to confront and decide issues of law originating within the other system. For example, federal issues regularly come to the fore in state trials (e.g., the exclusionary rule in a state criminal proceeding) and are decided by the state court in accord with guiding federal precedents. Conversely, lawsuits governed by state law are often brought in federal courts (under "diversity" jurisdiction) and then the federal trial court will generally be bound to apply state substantive law in the case before it (although it will continue to follow federal procedural law).

FEDERAL COURTS

Article III of the Constitution provides, in pertinent part, as follows:

> Article III, Section 2. The judicial Power of the United States shall be vested in one Supreme Court and in such inferior Courts as the Congress may from time to time ordain and establish.

Thus, the Supreme Court is the only federal court directly created by the Constitution. Congress has the power to create, modify, abolish, and establish the composition and jurisdiction of all other federal courts.

The Supreme Court is the court of last resort for the federal system and, in cases containing federal questions, for the state judicial systems as well. It has broad discretion to refuse to hear the vast majority of cases for which review is sought. The court must be persuaded that the issues involved in the case are sufficiently important, as questions of federal law that must be decided with finality, to grant *certiorari* for hearing and decision on the merits. The Supreme Court is nothing less than the "umpire of the federal system, authoritative guardian of constitutional liberties and final overseer of the consistency and substantial justice of the general law administered in the courts of the United States" (Jones et al. 1980, 48). While the Constitution does not expressly give the Supreme Court the power to determine the constitutionality of acts of Congress or state legislation, the court itself, in a series of opinions, held that it had the power to review and invalidate federal and state legislation it determines to be unconstitutional (*Marbury v. Madison* 1803; *Fletcher v. Peck* 1810).

Courts of appeals have final jurisdiction over all cases arising in the lower federal courts in their district or circuit (except those reviewed by the Supreme Court). There are 13 such circuits, 11 comprising geographical divisions among the states, a 12th for the District of Columbia, and a 13th that reviews cases from specialized federal courts (e.g., the Tax Court).

There are currently 91 district courts, at least one in every state, up to four in the more populous states. These are the major trial courts of the federal system and have jurisdiction over cases within the judicial power of the United States, as defined in the Constitution. Procedure in the district courts is uniform throughout the United States for civil and criminal cases. There are a number of special courts in addition to the foregoing, including the Court of Military Appeals, the Court of International Trade, the Tax Court, and the Court of Appeals for the Federal Circuit (created from the merger of the Court of Claims and the Court of Customs and Patent Appeals).

STATE COURTS

Each of the 50 states has its own system of courts, with a triple-layered hierarchical structure. At the bottom of the hierarchy are the "inferior" or "petty" trial courts, whose jurisdiction is limited to civil suits involving small amounts of money (e.g., small claims court) or minor criminal violations. At the next level are trial courts of general jurisdiction, usually referred to as superior courts. (New York State, confusingly, calls its trial courts of general jurisdiction the Supreme Court, which in most other states is the name given to the highest appellate court.) Their principal function is to hear civil and criminal cases generally. They are courts of record (i.e., detailed records of the proceedings are made), and their procedure is strictly formal. Specialized trial courts exist separately or are part of the trial court of general jurisdiction, for example, probate courts and family courts.

At the top of the judicial hierarchy are the appellate courts, which hear appeals from the judgments of the trial courts of general jurisdiction. These state courts of last resort are usually called the Supreme Court of the state but may have other names (e.g., Supreme Judicial Court, Court of Appeals). In over half of the states, there are intermediate appellate courts as well, which serve to screen out and make final authoritative disposition of the bulk of appellate litigation. This allows the highest appellate court broad discretion to focus on cases that raise novel, difficult, or socially important issues.

NATURE AND AUTHORITY OF CASE LAW

All systems of law employ case law to some extent, but it is especially authoritative and influential in a common law system such as our own. Case law has its origin in the judicial decisions judges reach in deciding disputes between particular parties. It is a "by-product of the ongoing process of settling particular controversies" (Jones et al. 1980, 3). Law exists in two authoritative forms, legislation and case law. How does dispute settlement of a particular case become a potential source of authoritative and generally applicable case law? The answer lies in the doctrine of *stare decisis* ("to stand by precedents and not to disturb settled points"). The doctrine declares that once a judicial decision settles a particular controversy or a disputed point of law, that decision becomes binding and will be followed in all subsequent factually similar cases. The authoritative force of precedent was firmly established at the dawn of the common law era in the royal courts of England. The meritorious features of this principle have been described as follows (Bodenheimer et al. 1980):

1. The doctrine of *stare decisis* enhances the social values of predictability, calculability, and certainty in the planning of private and business activities. Legal rights, duties, and obligations are relatively stable and ascertainable as a result.

2. Attorneys have a settled basis for legal reasoning and dispensing advice to clients, knowing that courts are generally bound by legal authority and precedent. The probable outcome of potential litigation may often be forecast and the total caseload of litigation may be presumably drastically diminished thereby.
3. Judges are forced to follow established precedents and thereby potential arbitrariness, favoritism, and bias are curbed. Otherwise, mere whims and idiosyncratic notions of right and wrong might be applied with the detrimental effect of erosion of public confidence in the integrity of the judiciary and loss of respect for the law. The public is more likely to accept judicial decisions as binding, in the knowledge that they are based on precedent, an objective body of law, and impartial reasoning free from bias or subjective concerns.
4. Following precedents promotes judicial efficiency and reduces the costs of litigation. Judges do not have to examine each legal issue *de novo* every time and each past decision need not be reopened in every case.
5. The doctrine of *stare decisis* is more consistent with a sense of justice, in that all individuals are more assured of being "treated alike in like circumstances." Order, stability, and continuity of the law satisfy our reasonable expectations that justice will be done.

Judicial decisions serve as precedents only within the same judicial system or jurisdiction: for example, a decision of New York's highest state court (the Court of Appeals) is binding precedent only in that court and in New York's lower courts. It has no binding authority for future cases adjudicated in the courts of New Jersey, California, or any other state system. Even decisions of the U.S. Supreme Court are not binding on state courts unless a federal question or constitutional interpretation was at issue. The higher a court stands in the hierarchy of its own jurisdiction, the greater force as precedent its decisions are accorded. (For example, decisions of the Supreme Court of California are binding on all lower California courts, whereas decisions of the intermediate appellate courts have much less precedential authority and are liable to be overruled at some future date by the higher tribunal. Subordinate courts must always adhere to precedents of higher courts with supervisory jurisdiction over them.)

American courts have never regarded the doctrine of *stare decisis* as absolutely binding, as have English courts until quite recently. Sometimes legal rules become antiquated or obsolete and innovation and responsiveness to social change call for the abandonment of an established precedent. In such cases, the highest courts have reserved the authority to overrule or set aside their own past decisions, when public policy considerations and the proper development of the law require a change. Courts do not lightly make use of their prerogative to overrule their own clear precedents. Generally they agree with Cardozo that "adherence to precedent should be the rule and not the exception" (Bodenheimer et al. 1980, 68).

LEGISLATION

Legislation, as a source of the law, has been compared to a proverb, while case law has been likened to a parable. The latter is composed of principles inferred from decisions handed down in particular cases that decided concrete disputes between parties. The former is an authoritative, prescribed general rule, promulgated by a lawmaking body. According to Patterson,

> A proposition of case law may be correctly stated in several different ways, each of which is equally official. A statute (proposition of legislation) is stated as an exclusive official wording of the rule. Case law is flexible; legislation is (textually) rigid. (Jones et al. 1980, 12)

In the United States, the Constitution of 1789, in Article 1, Section 1, created a bicameral legislature, the Congress of the United States, composed of the Senate and the House of Representatives. All legislative powers of the federal government are conferred on the Congress and its organization, procedures, and enumerated powers are set forth in other sections of the Constitution. Likewise, the constitutions of the several states also establish authoritative lawmaking bodies (the state legislatures). Rules of legislative law are promulgated as formalized legal documents in authoritative textual form (statutes or codes) that are prospective in application—that is, the legislative acts are rules of law or precepts to be followed in the future. Legislation, as described by Oliver Wendell Holmes, "looks to the future and changes existing conditions by making a new rule to be applied thereafter to all or some part of those subject to its power" (*Prentis v. Atlantic Coast Line Co.* 1908).

Legislation is generally more authoritative than case law and supersedes prior judicial decisions, unless the enactments exceed the legitimate powers of the legislature (i.e., unless they are unconstitutional). Judges are bound by the statute as it is enacted and cannot rewrite it or revise it. When a particular statutory law governs the resolution of a case before the court, the judge's role is merely to apply it to the controversy to be decided.

STATUTORY CONSTRUCTION (INTERPRETATION)

Chung Fook v. White, 264 U.S. 443 (1924)

Certiorari to a judgment of the Circuit Court of Appeals that affirmed a judgment of the District Court denying a petition for a writ of *habeas corpus*. Mr. Justice Sutherland delivered the opinion of the Supreme Court:

> Chung Fook is a native-born citizen of the United States. Lee Shee, his wife, is an alien Chinese

> woman, ineligible for naturalization. In 1922 she sought admission to the United States, but was refused and detained at the immigration station, on the ground that she was an alien, afflicted with a dangerous contagious disease [chlonorchiasis]. No question is raised as to her alienage or the effect or character of her disease; but the contention is that nevertheless, she is entitled to admission under the proviso found in §22 of the Immigration Act of February 5, 1917, c. 29,39 Stat, 891. A petition for a writ of habeas corpus was denied by the Federal District Court for the Northern District of California, and upon appeal to the Circuit Court of Appeals, the judgment was affirmed.

The pertinent parts of the proviso are as follows: "That if the person sending for wife or minor children is naturalized, a wife to whom married or a minor child born subsequent to such husband or father's naturalization shall be admitted without detention for treatment in hospital." The measure of the exemption is plainly stated and, in terms, extends to the wife of a naturalized citizen only.

But it is argued that it cannot be supposed that Congress intended to accord to a naturalized citizen a right and preference beyond that enjoyed by a native-born citizen. The court below thought that the exemption from detention was meant to relate only to a wife who by marriage had acquired her husband's citizenship, and not to one who, notwithstanding she was married to a citizen, remained an alien under §1994 Rev. Stats…We are inclined to agree with this view; but, in any event, the statute plainly relates only to the wife or children of a naturalized citizen and we cannot interpolate the words "native-born citizen" without usurping the legislative function… The words of the statute being clear, if it unjustly discriminates against the native-born citizen, or is cruel and inhuman in its results, as forcefully contended, the remedy lies with Congress and not with the courts. Their duty is simply to enforce the law as it is written, unless clearly unconstitutional.

Affirmed

Courts are not always able to apply statutory law mechanistically or formalistically for a variety of reasons inherent in the legislative process. Even though the drafters of legislation strive to be precise and minutely specific in their phraseology, words are often imperfect symbols to communicate intent, sometimes resulting in vague or ambiguous meanings. Further uncertainties in legislative intent may be superimposed in the course of the legislative process of enactment (e.g., by the amendments added to the original bill). Unforeseen circumstances or unthought-of cases are bound to arise. As Hart observed,

> Human legislators can have no such knowledge of all the possible combinations of circumstances which the future may bring…. We have not settled, because we have not anticipated, the question which will be raised by the unenvisaged case when it occurs…. When the unenvisaged case does arise, we confront the issues at stake and can then settle the question by choosing between the competing interests in the way which best satisfies us. In doing so we shall have rendered more determinate our initial aim, and shall incidentally have settled a question as to the meaning, for the purposes of this rule, of a general word. (Hart 1961, 125–126)

There are a number of traditional judicial formulas for the resolution of doubts as to the legal effect of statutes, such as the plain meaning rule ("where the act is clear upon its face, and when standing alone, it is fairly susceptible of but one construction, that construction must be given to it" [*Hamilton v. Rathbone* 1899]) or the ascertainment of the legislative intent or purpose in enacting the legislation. *Chung Fook* is an example of the former approach (Llewellyn 1950; Murphy 1975). The following case excerpt considers legislative intent or purpose.

United States v. American Trucking Associations, 310 U.S. 534 (1940)

Mr. Justice Reed delivered the opinion of the Supreme Court:

> In the interpretation of statutes, the function of the courts is easily stated. It is to construe the language so as to give effect to the intent of Congress. There is no invariable rule for the discovery of that intention. To take a few words from their context and with them thus isolated to attempt to determine their meaning, certainly would not contribute greatly to the discovery of the purpose of the draftsmen of the statute…. (*United States v. American Trucking Association* 1940)

There is, of course, no more persuasive evidence of the purpose of a statute than the words by which the legislature undertook to give expression to its wishes. Often these words are sufficient in and of themselves to determine the purpose of the legislation. In such cases we have followed their plain meaning. When that meaning has led to absurd or futile results, however, this court has looked beyond the words to the purpose of the act. Frequently, however, even when the plain meaning did not produce absurd results but merely an unreasonable one "plainly at variance with the policy of the legislation as a whole," this court has followed that purpose, rather than the literal words…. The interpretation of the meaning of statutes is exclusively a judicial function. This duty requires one body of public servants, the judges, to construe the meaning of what another body, the legislators, has said. Obviously there is danger that the courts' conclusion as to legislative purpose will be unconsciously influenced by the judges' own views or by factors not considered by the enacting body. A lively appreciation of the danger is the best assurance of escape from its threat, but hardly justifies an acceptance of a literal interpretation dogma… Emphasis should be laid, too, upon the necessity for appraisal of the purposes as a whole of Congress in analyzing the meaning of clauses or sections of general acts.

There is a substantial catalogue of judicial maxims or canons of statutory construction, formulated by the courts, to resolve interpretive questions. Judicial creativity is especially called for in those cases where the legislative issue to be determined was totally unforeseen by the lawmakers and the judge must assign a legal effect to the statute that it did not originally possess:

> Interpretation is often spoken of as if it were nothing but the search and the discovery of a meaning which, however obscure and latent, had nonetheless a real and ascertainable preexistence in the legislator's mind. The process is, indeed, that at times, but it is often something more. (Cardozo 1921)

When judges sometimes, under the guise of statutory interpretation, exceed the proper limits of their authority and go beyond or override the intent of the legislature in order to remake the law according to their own views (to achieve what they regard as a "good result"), they draw criticism that the courts are usurping legislative prerogatives and undermining the rule of law.

REFERENCES

Bodenheimer E, JB Oakley, and JC Love. 1980. *An Introduction to the Anglo-American Legal System.* St. Paul, MN: West.

Cardozo BN. 1921. *The Nature of the Judicial Process.* New Haven, CT: Yale University Press.

Chung Fook v. White, 264 U.S. 443 (1924).

Fletcher v. Peck, 10 U.S. (6 Cranch) 87 (1810).

Hamilton v. Rathbone, 175 U.S. 414 (1899).

Hart HLA. 1961. *The Concept of Law.* Oxford: Oxford University Press.

Hogue AR. 1985. *Origins of the Common Law.* Indianapolis, IN: Liberty Press.

Jones HW, JM Kernochan, and AW Murphy. 1980. *Legal Method.* Mineola, NY: Foundation Press.

Llewellyn KN. 1950. Remarks on the theory of appellate decision and the rules or canons about how statutes are to be construed. *Vanderbilt Law Review* 3, 395–443.

Marbury v. Madison, 5 U.S. (1 Cranch) 137 (1803).

Murphy AW. 1975. Old maxims never die: The "plain meaning" rule and statutory interpretation in the "modern" federal courts. *Columbia Law Review* 75:1299–1328.

Prentis v. Atlantic Coast Line Co., 211 U.S. 210 (1908).

Scott AW and RB Kent. 1967. *Cases and Other Materials on Civil Procedure.* Boston: Little, Brown.

United States v. American Trucking Associations, 310 U.S. 534 (1940).

Van Ness v. Pacard, 27 U.S. (2 Pet.) 137 (1829).

Walsh WF. 1932. *A History of Anglo-American Law*, 2nd edition. Indianapolis, IN: Bobbs-Merrill.

91

Judicial review of the constitution: Search and seizure, smartphones, and protecting digital privacy

ROBERT LLOYD GOLDSTEIN

INTRODUCTION

Modern cell phones are not just another technological convenience. With all they contain and all they may reveal, they hold for many Americans "the privacies of life." The fact that technology now allows an individual to carry such information in his or her hand does not make the information any less worthy of the protection for which the Founders fought. Our answer to the question of what police must do before searching a cell phone seized incident to an arrest is accordingly simple—get a warrant (*Riley v. California* 2014, 28).

Frequently, a police officer, in a reflective mood, will say "Judge, you know this Fourth Amendment makes my job a lot tougher and more difficult." What does one respond, except to say: "Officer, that's precisely what a Bill of Rights is for. Even in service, you are not permitted the efficiency permitted a counterpart in a Gestapo or an NKVD. From day to day, that is your burden; but from decade to decade and century to century, that is your glory...Yes, Officer, it makes your job a lot more difficult. It's supposed to!" (*Zimmerman v. State* 1989).

Democracy means that if the doorbell rings in the early hours, it is likely to be the milkman (Winston Churchill).

CONSTITUTIONAL JUDICIAL REVIEW

The Constitution of the United States has endured for over two centuries. It is the supreme Law of the Land, the ultimate legal authority in the complex hierarchy of our legal system. The Constitution establishes the norms that govern the distribution of law-making powers and their exercise within our system of authoritative sources of law, encompassing case law derived from court decisions, federal and state, and legislative enactments by the U.S. Congress and the 50 state legislatures. The Constitution proclaims its own supremacy and overriding authority in the Supremacy Clause of the Constitution (Article VI, Clause 2):

> This Constitution, and the Laws of the United States which shall be made in Pursuance thereof; and all Treaties made, or which shall be made, under the Authority of the United States, shall be the supreme Law of the Land; and the Judges in every State shall be bound thereby, any Thing in the Constitution or Laws of any State to the Contrary notwithstanding.

In 1803, the epic decision by Chief Justice John Marshall, in the seminal case of *Marbury v. Madison* (1803), declared that "It is emphatically the province and duty of the judicial department to say what the law is." This cornerstone doctrine of American constitutional law declared the basic principle that the U.S. Supreme Court had the authority to review acts of Congress and declare them void if they are in conflict with the Constitution ("repugnant to the Constitution"). This power of judicial review established the U.S. Supreme Court as the supreme arbiter and ultimate authority in the interpretation of the U.S. Constitution, the "final, formal interpreter of the words of the Constitution" (Mason and Beaney 1959). According to Mr. Justice Jackson, addressing the finality of the court's authority to interpret the Constitution: "We are not final because we are infallible, but we are infallible only because we are final" (*Brown v. Allen* 1953, 540). Later Supreme Court decisions extended the court's power to review and invalidate state court decisions and state legislation it determines to be unconstitutional. Although there is no explicit provision in the U.S. Constitution that confers the power of constitutional judicial review on the court, nevertheless, its supremacy in this regard has been legitimized by popular acquiescence and approval over the course of American history and is generally respected by the country as a permanent and indispensable feature of our entire constitutional system (Tepker 2004).

SEARCH AND SEIZURE

The Fourth Amendment to the U.S. Constitution is the part of the Bill of Rights that prohibits unreasonable searches and seizures of property by the government. It protects against arbitrary arrests and is the basis of the law regarding arrest and search warrants, stop-and-frisk, wiretaps, and other forms of surveillance. It requires that any warrant issued be supported by "probable cause." Probable cause to search requires a fair probability that contraband or evidence of a crime will be found in a particular place (Emanuel 2014). Adoption of the Fourth Amendment was in response to the many abuses associated with writs of assistance, a type of general search warrant issued by the British government during the colonial era. Writs of assistance gave British officers of the Crown virtually unbridled authority to conduct raids and rummage through homes, in an unrestrained search for evidence of criminal activity. The authorities possessed almost unlimited power to search for anything and seize personal property (such as charts, pamphlets, personal effects, and any other items, as well as contraband) at any time, with very little oversight. These abusive and unreasonable British colonial policies were viewed at the time by future U.S. President John Adams as "the spark which originated the American Revolution" (Adams and Adams 1856). The Fourth Amendment, which has been the subject of more Supreme Court decisions than any other area of criminal procedure (Goldstein 2007), holds that

> The right of the people to be secure in their persons, houses, papers, and effects against unreasonable searches and seizures, shall not be violated, and no Warrants shall issue but upon probable cause, supported by Oath or affirmation, and particularly describing the place to be searched and the persons or things to be seized. (U.S. Constitution, Amendment IV)

The ultimate touchstone of the Fourth Amendment is reasonableness. Most arrests are warrantless but must be made on probable cause to make the arrest. Probable cause to make an arrest requires a reasonable likelihood that a violation of the law has been committed by the individual to be arrested (Emanuel 2014). Warrantless searches incident to a lawful arrest occur with far greater frequency than searches conducted pursuant to a warrant. In a long line of cases, the Supreme Court has refined the constitutional contours of the search incident to arrest doctrine and crafted a number of rules to assess the reasonableness of these exceptions to the warrant requirement (*Chimel v. California* 1969; *U.S. v. Chadwick* 1977; *New York v. Belton* 1981; *Virginia v. Moore* 2008). The court has long recognized that it is reasonable to search the person arrested and the area "within his immediate control" in order to seize any weapons (that might be used to resist arrest, escape, or endanger the officer's safety), as well as to search and seize any evidence on his or her person to prevent its concealment or destruction. In *U.S. v. Robinson* (1973), the court took it one step further by concluding that since the custodial arrest of a suspect based on probable cause was already a reasonable and legal intrusion under the Fourth Amendment, a warrantless search incident to the arrest of the personal property of the arrestee, for example, a crumpled pack of cigarettes found to contain heroin, was permissible and required no additional justification. The court explained that "the authority to search the person incident to a lawful custodial arrest, while based upon the need to disarm and to discover evidence, does not depend on what a court may later decide was the probability in a particular arrest situation that weapons or evidence would in fact be found upon the person of the subject" (*Robinson* 1973, 235). In other words, any privacy interests a suspect retained after a full-custody arrest were significantly diminished by virtue of the arrest itself. Other warrantless searches that the court has upheld as reasonable include the "protective sweep" of the premises incident to an arrest in the suspect's home (*Maryland v. Buie* 1990) and the search of a vehicle's passenger compartment, under certain circumstances, when it was reasonable to believe evidence relevant to the crime of arrest might be found in the vehicle (*Arizona v. Gant* 2009).

Katz v. United States: Fourth Amendment protection of the "reasonable expectation of privacy"

The first wiretap case decided by the Supreme Court was *Olmstead v. United States* (1928). The court's ruling allowed the government to obtain private wiretapped telephone conversations without a warrant and place them into evidence. The court held that the Fourth Amendment's protection against unreasonable searches and seizures only applied to *places* and *things*. It did not apply to intangible conversations passing over telephone wires. Moreover, the court pointed out that the tap had been placed on wires outside the premises; a violation of the Fourth Amendment required a physical trespass on the subject's property.

In a famous (and prophetic) dissent, Mr. Justice Brandeis wrote:

> The progress of science in furnishing the Government with means of espionage is not likely to stop with wire-tapping. Ways may some day be developed by which the Government, without removing papers from secret drawers, can reproduce them in court, and by which it will be enabled to expose to a jury the most intimate

occurrences of the home. Advances in the psychic and related sciences may bring means of exploring unexpressed beliefs, thoughts and emotions. "That places the liberty of every man in the hands of every petty officer"... Can it be that the Constitution affords no protection against such invasions of individual security? (*Olmstead v. United States*, 1928, 474)

Nearly 40 years later, in 1967, the Supreme Court rejected *Olmstead* and extended Fourth Amendment protection to all areas where an individual has an actual (subjective) reasonable expectation of privacy and society is prepared to recognize that this expectation is (objectively) reasonable. In *Katz v. United States* (1967), the court rejected the traditional notion that only private property was protected by the unreasonable search and seizure clause of the Fourth Amendment. Katz, a bookmaker, had used a public pay phone booth to transmit long-distance illegal bets. The FBI, acting without a warrant, recorded his incriminating conversations via an electronic recording device attached to the exterior of the phone booth. There was no physical intrusion into the booth itself. Prior to *Katz*, the standard had been that the police must have physically intruded into a constitutionally protected area, such as the private property of the suspect. The Fourth Amendment was generally meant to protect "things" from intrusive physical search and seizure; it was not meant to protect personal privacy. The court, in holding that government wiretapping was subject to the Fourth Amendment's warrant requirements, wrote that "One who occupies [a telephone booth], shuts the door behind him, and pays the toll that permits him to place a call is surely entitled to assume that the words he utters into the mouthpiece will not be broadcast to the world" (*Katz v. United States* 1967, 353). The court determined that immaterial intrusion with technology violated Katz's reasonable expectation of the right to privacy. Even though Katz made the phone calls on public property and the FBI did not physically trespass in installing the device, the court held that the Fourth Amendment protected his justifiable reliance on the expectation of privacy, even in a place accessible to the public. The court emphasized that "the Fourth Amendment protects people, not places" (*Katz* 1967, 352), and therefore, physical intrusion is not necessary to constitute a "search."

TECHNOLOGY ON AN ACCELERATING EXPONENTIAL CURVE: A CHALLENGE FOR THE LAW

I am not an advocate for frequent changes in laws and constitutions, but laws and institutions must go hand in hand with the progress of the human mind. As that becomes more developed, more enlightened, as new discoveries are made, new truths disclosed, and manners and opinions change with the change of circumstances, institutions must advance also, and keep pace with the times.

Thomas Jefferson, excerpt from letter to Samuel Kercheral, July 12, 1816

It has become something of a truism that the law faces great difficulties keeping pace with the social repercussions of technology (Wadhwa 2014). This is hardly surprising. In the first two decades of the twentieth century, there was more technological advancement than in the entire nineteenth century. Ours is a world of exponential technological progress. Kurzweil has predicted that we will not experience 100 years of progress in the twenty-first century—it will be more like 20,000 years of progress. In his "Law of Accelerating Returns," he refers to change of this magnitude as *the Singularity*—"change so rapid and so profound that it represents a rupture in the fabric of human history" (Kurzweil 2006). Other futurists, such as Moravec and Hawkins, point to the emergence of increasingly sophisticated technologies over the course of human history (e.g., the invention of imagery, writing, mathematics, printing, the telescope, flight, rockets, radio, television, the computer, and on and on), separated by shorter and shorter intervals, until a point beyond human comprehension will be reached (Moravec 1990; Hawkins 2002). The law has struggled to keep up with the proliferation of advances in technology in recent years, such as clandestine government surveillance programs, genome testing, cloning, self-driving cars, drones, robots, Google, Facebook, and, of course, the ubiquitous smartphone.

Riley v. California (2014) was a landmark case involving the unique privacy interests at stake when police conduct a warrantless search incident to arrest of the digital contents of a suspect's smartphone. Chief Justice Roberts noted that the sale of cell phones has topped 1.2 billion worldwide. In the United States, 64% of adults now own a cell phone of some kind. There are more than a million "apps" (mobile application software on a cell phone) available at each of the two major app stores. The average cell phone owner has installed over 30 apps, "which together can form a revealing montage of the user's life" (*Riley v. California* 2014, 20). The court observed that these phones "are now such a pervasive and insistent part of daily life that the proverbial visitor from Mars might conclude they were an important feature of human anatomy" (*Riley v. California* 2014, 9). Privacy advocates heralded the decision for striking a major blow in favor of digital privacy rights and reaffirming the principle that technological advances should not result in an erosion of "the protection for which the Founders fought."

RILEY V. CALIFORNIA: THE NEW *KATZ* FOR THE DIGITAL ERA

A San Diego police officer stopped David Riley for a traffic violation, which eventually led to his arrest on weapons charges after firearms were discovered under his car's hood.

While searching Riley incident to his arrest (without a warrant), the police seized a smartphone from his pants pocket. A warrantless search of his smartphone's data uncovered evidence of Riley's ties to the "Bloods" street gang and records that placed his phone at a shooting some 3 weeks earlier. They also found photographs of Riley standing in front of a car they suspected had been involved in the earlier shooting incident. Riley was ultimately convicted of assault with a semiautomatic firearm, shooting at an occupied vehicle, and attempted murder. The California Court of Appeal affirmed his conviction.

The Supreme Court held that warrantless searches of a cell phone incident to arrest were unreasonable and constituted a violation of the Fourth Amendment. The court established a bright line rule: "Our answer to the question of what police must do before searching a cell phone seized incident to an arrest is accordingly simple—get a warrant" (*Riley v. California* 2014, 28). Writing for a unanimous court, Chief Justice Roberts held that cell phones store uniquely private information. He resoundingly rejected the government's argument that searching an arrestee's smartphone was comparable to a search of the contents of a physical item, such as a crumpled pack of cigarettes found on his person, while looking for contraband.

> That is like saying a ride on horseback is materially indistinguishable from a flight to the moon. Both are ways of getting from point A to point B, but little else justifies lumping them together. Modern cell phones, as a category, implicate privacy concerns far beyond those implicated by the search of a cigarette pack, a wallet, or a purse. A conclusion that inspecting the contents of an arrestee's pockets works no additional intrusion on privacy beyond the arrest itself may make sense as applied to physical items, but any extension of that reasoning to digital data has to rest on its own bottom. (*Riley v. California* 2014, 17)

The court went on to emphasize that although an arrestee has diminished privacy interests, it "does not mean that the Fourth Amendment falls out of the picture entirely" (*Riley v. California* 2014, 16). The court noted that in today's world, smartphone users "keep on their person a digital record of nearly every aspect of their lives—from the mundane to the intimate" (*Riley v. California* 2014, 19). The *Harvard Law Review* analyzed the court's reasoning as follows:

> Where cell phones are concerned, privacy interests are at their apogee. Quantitatively, cell phones have an "immense storage capacity" that houses a vast array of information moored far into the owner's past. Qualitatively, cell phones may reveal detailed information about all aspects of a person's life through browsing history, geolocation data, and apps...Cell phone searches implicate privacy interests that are not only substantial, but also ubiquitous. (Harvard Law Review 2014)

The historic English common law dictum that "an Englishman's home is his castle" (which was adopted by the American colonists as the *Castle Doctrine*) is reflected in the special protections that a person's home and property receive under the Fourth Amendment. The King did not have unbridled authority to intrude on his subjects' dwellings: "The house of every one is to him as his castle and fortress, as well as for his defense against injury and violence as for his repose" (*Semayne's Case* 1604). As noted above, the Fourth Amendment was a response to the British government's reviled writs of assistance, which served as a general type of search power giving officers of the Crown arbitrary and unbridled authority to search any home without cause. The court, in this regard, argued that the privacy interests at issue in the search of a smartphone's digital contents are paramount even to those at stake in the search of a home, traditionally regarded as the most sacrosanct and inviolable place under American law. The court observed that ransacking an individual's home, in an exhaustive search for everything that might be incriminating, would actually be less intrusive than searching the individual's smartphone. The court explained that a smartphone "not only contains in digital form many sensitive records previously found in the home; it also contains a broad array of private information never found in a home in any form—unless the phone is" (*Riley v. California* 2014, 20–21).

In *Katz*, the court rejected the traditional approach that the Fourth Amendment protected only private property from unreasonable government intrusion. It extended that protection to government infringement on the individual's reasonable expectation of privacy ("The Fourth Amendment protects people, not places"). "*Riley* is the new *Katz*... [a landmark decision that] marks the beginning of increased protections for privacy in the digital age" (Lamparello and MacLean 2014, 4). It is an auspicious sign that the court has successfully kept pace with the times and remains steadfastly committed to safeguarding "the protection for which the Founders fought."

REFERENCES

2014. The Supreme Court—Leading cases. *Harvard Law Review* 128:251–260.

Adams CF and J Adams. 1856. *The Works of John Adams, Second President of the United States, With a Life of the Author*, Vol. I. Boston: Little Brown and Company.

Arizona v. Gant, 556 U.S. 332 (2009).

Brown v. Allen, 344 U.S. 443 (1953).

Chimel v. California, 395 U.S. 752 (1969).

Emanuel SL. 2014. *Criminal Procedure*, 30th edition. New York: Wolters Kluwer Law and Business.

Goldstein RL. 2007. Criminal law: Structures and procedure. In *International Handbook of Psychopathic Disorders and the Law*, edited by A Felthous and H Sass, West Sussex, UK: John Wiley & Sons.

Hawkins GS. 2002. *Mindsteps to the Cosmos*. New York: World Scientific.

Katz v. U.S., 389 U.S. 347 (1967).

Kurzweil R. 2006. *The Singularity Is Near: When Humans Transcend Biology*. New York: Penguin Group.

Lamparello A and CE MacLean. 2014. *Riley v. California*: The New Katz or Chimel? *Richmond Journal of Law and Technology* 21:1–19.

Letters of Thomas Jefferson, edited by F Irwin, Tilton, NH: Sanbornton Bridge Press, 128.

Marbury v. Madison, 1 Cranch 137 (1803).

Maryland v. Buie, 494 U.S. 325 (1990).

Mason AT and WB Beaney. 1959. *The Supreme Court in a Free Society*. Englewood Cliffs: Prentice Hall.

Moravec H. 1990. *Mind Children: The Future of Robot and Human Intelligence*. Cambridge, MA: Harvard University Press.

New York v. Belton, 453 U.S. 454 (1981).

Olmstead v. U.S., 277 U.S. 438 (1928).

Riley v. California, 134 S. Ct. 2473 (2014).

Semayne's Case, 5 Coke Rep. 91 (1604).

Tepker HF. 2004. *Marbury's* legacy of judicial review after two centuries. *Oklahoma Law Review* 57:127–142.

U.S. Constitution, Article III, Clause 2 or the Supremacy Clause.

U.S. Constitution, Amendment IV.

U.S. v. Chadwick, 433 U.S. 1 (1977).

U.S. v. Robinson, 414 U.S. 218 (1973).

Virginia v. Moore, 553 U.S. 164 (2008).

Wadhwa V. 2014. Laws and ethics can't keep pace with technology. *MIT Technology Review*. https://www.technologyreview.com/view/526401//laws-and-ethics-cant-keep-pace-with-technology/, accessed July 16, 2015.

Zimmerman v. State, 552 A.2d 47 (1989).

92

Tort law and the psychiatrist

J. MICHAEL HEINLEN

INTRODUCTION

Psychiatrists today face a broad range of potential liabilities as a result of their professional activities. Consider the following scenario. A former patient has accused her psychiatrist of engaging in sexual activity with her during the course of treatment. As a result, (1) the psychiatrist faces criminal sexual assault charges; (2) he is being sued by the former patient for battery and malpractice; (3) the hospital with which he had been affiliated has terminated his privileges; and (4) his insurance carrier says it will not bear the costs of his defense or pay any damages assessed against him at trial. This example illustrates the three types of practice-related legal disputes a psychiatrist is most likely to encounter: criminal, tort, and contract.

Criminal law involves the state asserting its interest in maintaining public order. It does not seek to resolve private disputes; rather, its goals are to punish or reform offenders and to deter crime (Holmes 1881, 41–51). In a criminal trial, the prosecutor, acting as the state's agent, brings charges against a defendant and must prove beyond a reasonable doubt (i.e., with 90%–95% certainty) that the defendant committed the crime. At the end of the trial, the fact finder, often a jury, decides whether the defendant is guilty or innocent. In the present example, the state's interest is in preventing sexual assault. In most jurisdictions, the prosecutor in such a case must convince a jury that the sex acts occurred and were not consensual (Simon 2001, 221–223). The use of drugs, hypnotism, or threats of harm to induce compliance can be presented as evidence that the acts were involuntary, and lack of consent is assumed if the patient was a minor or incompetent. Several states go further and ban any sexual contact between psychiatrists and their patients. In those states, the prosecutor need only prove that the sexual conduct occurred and that it was intentional.

Civil law, as opposed to criminal law, comprises contract law and tort law and has evolved to settle disputes. *Contract law* comes into play when parties to an agreement disagree about the terms of the agreement (Farnsworth 1999, 3–26). Typically in a contract suit, one party believes the other has failed to fulfill its obligations under the agreement. The aggrieved party, the plaintiff, sues the other, the defendant, for breach of contract. Each presents its evidence and arguments at trial, and the fact finder finds for either the plaintiff or the defendant. If it finds for the plaintiff, the defendant can be forced to comply with the terms of the contract or be compelled to pay money damages to the plaintiff for losses incurred as a result of the breach. Our example presents two possible contractual disputes. First, the psychiatrist might bring an action against the hospital for terminating his privileges. Second, if he is found liable in the malpractice suit, he may claim that his insurance policy binds the insurer to pay any damages assessed against him. In either case, the result will depend on an analysis and interpretation of the terms of the pertinent contract.

Tort law seeks to resolve disputes over attribution of blame and responsibility for harm (Prosser 1971, 1–7). Like criminal law, it comes into play when someone's actions violate social norms. But unlike criminal law, where the state brings charges against defendants, the injured parties, themselves, assert tort claims against those who injured them. At trial, the fact finder must decide by a preponderance of the evidence (i.e., greater than 50% certainty) whether a defendant is liable. If the defendant is found liable, the fact finder can assess damages to be paid to the plaintiff.

In the example, battery and psychiatric malpractice are tort claims. To prevail on her battery claim, the patient, like the prosecutor in the criminal trial, will need to convince the fact finder that the psychiatrist coerced her into engaging in the sexual activity. Unlike the prosecutor, however, she need only prove this by a preponderance of the evidence, not beyond a reasonable doubt. Further, the patient can win in the tort action even if she consented to the sexual conduct. If she can prove that having sex with a patient falls below the requisite standard of care for psychiatrists and that the sexual activity aggravated her underlying condition, the fact finder can find the psychiatrist liable for malpractice.

WHY HAVE TORT LAW?

Before tort law as we know it now existed, private vengeance was a sacred duty. If your neighbor mistook your father for a wild boar and shot him with an arrow, you did not bring a wrongful death action. Rather, you and your family undertook a moral obligation to kill a member of the offender's family. This was the blood feud. Though it came to be regulated—the types of wrongs that could be expiated by blood were ultimately limited, as were the days and locations on which revenge could be exacted—private wrongs were settled privately throughout most of the Middle Ages (Bloch 1961, 125–130). Since that time, tort law has evolved as an alternative means of dispute resolution.

Justifications for tort law

In common-law jurisdictions, such as England and the United States, tort law has developed into a system that assigns responsibility for harm to wrongdoers and compensates injured parties for their losses. It is a judge-made collection of rules to impose liability for damages. Theorists justify tort law primarily on four grounds: (1) it maintains public order; (2) it alleviates the hurt suffered by victims of wrongdoing; (3) it compensates victims for their losses; and (4) it deters harmful behavior (Prosser 1971, 1–7; Shuman 1994, 3–8). As to the first, one of the reasons tort law originally developed was to constrain the mayhem inherent in a legal system based on the blood feud. Today, it remains a tool for channeling angry conflicts into (relatively) peaceful confrontations. Further, insofar as it imposes moral and financial responsibility for harm on wrongdoers, tort law helps appease the need for vengeance satisfied by the blood feud.

On a more tangible level, the award of money damages in tort judgments is justified on the ground that it restores victims to their pre-harm state. In other words, tort law compensates people who have been injured by unsafe behavior. If you wreck my car, for example, I am entitled to an award of damages to cover both the cost of repairing or replacing the car and any expenses and losses incurred as a result of the accident. In addition, forcing wrongdoers to pay for their mistakes may deter harmful behavior. These are the two most common justifications for tort law—restitution and deterrence. It compensates people harmed as a result of unsafe behavior that society wants to prevent.

There are, however, significant problems with these justifications. On the most basic level, there is no proof that fear of potential tort liability alters people's behavior (Shuman 1993, 165–166). And even if there were such proof, liability insurance and government compensation programs, along with the time and expense of litigation, minimize the deterrent effects of tort law. Studies show that 90% of accident victims who recover for their losses are paid by third-party insurers or compensation plans, not through tort actions. In addition, the high emotional and monetary cost of taking a case to trial discourages many victims from making claims (Hensler et al. 1991, 107–108, 175). In practice, only insured or wealthy wrongdoers who have caused serious—i.e., costly—injuries get sued. As a result, much harmful behavior escapes the tort system.

The time, expense, and emotional upheaval of litigation also make clear that tort law is not the most effective means of compensating injury victims. Indeed, the costs of obtaining tort compensation are higher than for other compensation systems. A further problem is that many damage awards include sums to compensate for pain and suffering. But unlike tangible losses, pain and suffering cannot readily be valued in monetary terms. Though it is relatively easy to compute the money needed to replace a car or to pay hospital expenses, how does one appraise the value of pain endured as a result of a car accident? Simply put, "tort damages cannot 'buy out' the pain in the same way they can 'buy out' the hospital bill" (Shuman 1994, 46). Insofar as money damages cannot restore victims to a pain-free state, an alternative theory has been offered to justify them; namely, that damages for pain and suffering serve as offsetting substitute pleasures (Ingber 1985, 784). Even though someone might suffer from chronic pain, that pain can be offset, for example, by the ability to buy a fancy house or to relax on a beach in Hawaii. Unfortunately, there is no empirical evidence to support the contention that damage awards can, in fact, mitigate a victim's pain (Shuman 1994, 47 n.37).

There are, thus, numerous unsettled issues regarding the policies and rationales underlying tort law. Despite such theoretical debates, it remains, without question, a body of law that functions in practice to make people who engage in unsafe conduct subject to liability to their victims when that conduct results in injury.

VARIETIES OF TORT

Historically, tort law has been concerned with two types of injury-causing behavior: negligent and intentional. In the modern era, most tort actions have been based on negligence; the law holds people responsible when their careless behavior harms others. Tort law, however, also compensates victims of intentionally bad acts. Someone who commits assault and battery may not only have to answer to the state in a criminal trial, he or she can also be sued by the victim in a civil trial and be the subject of an award of damages. Although tort claims against psychiatrists are limited to claims of negligent and intentional tort actions, there is a third variety of tort, strict liability, which is confined almost solely to cases involving the marketing and distribution of dangerous products. This is an unusual tort because a defendant can be found liable even without a showing of fault. In a strict-products-liability action, the plaintiff need only prove that a seller or manufacturer of dangerously defective goods placed those goods into the stream of commerce and that those goods caused harm (*Restatement [Second] of Torts* 1965, §402A).

Negligent torts

A plaintiff must prove four essential elements to prevail in a tort suit based on negligence: duty, breach, cause, and harm (Prosser 1971, 143–144). The first element requires proof that the defendant owed the plaintiff a duty of care. Next, the plaintiff must show that the defendant breached the duty and that the breach caused harm. The general standard by which the defendant's duty is measured is reasonable care under the circumstances (Terry 1915). The issue is whether a reasonable person in the defendant's position would have acted as the defendant did.

As an example, a store owner has a duty to the public to maintain the sidewalk in front of his store in a safe, passable condition. This duty arises from the fact that whenever someone engages in behavior that will foreseeably have an impact on other people, such as exploiting a public sidewalk for the purpose of attracting customers, he has a duty to behave in a manner that will not harm those people. If the store owner allows the concrete on the walk to become so worn and cracked that people might trip when passing by, he risks a negligence action if someone falls and hurts herself. By neglecting to maintain the walk, the store owner breached his duty and any injury caused by that breach is compensable in tort. Note that a plaintiff need not prove intent in a negligence action. It is irrelevant that the store owner did not mean to hurt anyone. The question is simply whether he failed to use reasonable care in fulfilling his duty. If so, and if that failure caused harm, the plaintiff is entitled to recover damages for her injury.

The shop owner in such a case may have a number of defenses. For instance, he can deny that he breached a duty, arguing that it would have been unreasonable to expect him to maintain the walk in better condition than he did. He can dispute causation, arguing that the plaintiff's injuries occurred because someone pushed her, not because she tripped on the defective sidewalk. Or he can question the harm, for instance, by claiming that no damage was done. If the plaintiff waited too long to file the lawsuit, the shopkeeper can even bar the claim on procedural grounds. Every state has a statute of limitations that requires tort suits to be brought within a specified period after discovery or occurrence of the allegedly negligent act.

Psychiatric malpractice

Medical malpractice refers to negligent torts committed by health-care professionals acting in the course of their professional duties. A psychiatrist whose unreasonable care harms a patient or a third party to whom a duty is owed may be liable for malpractice. In the context of malpractice claims, the duty element of the tort is normally established by showing the existence of a doctor–patient relationship (Rigelhaupt 1982; Simon 2001, 20–22; Simon and Shuman 2007, 17–36). As soon as a psychiatrist agrees, either explicitly or implicitly, to diagnose or treat a patient, duties arise. Whether such an agreement was made is a fact question, and when this is in dispute, the court must decide. Generally, however, it is not difficult for plaintiffs to prove the element of duty. Giving advice to friends and neighbors, providing sample medications, or prescribing medication during the course of independent medical evaluations can give rise to a doctor–patient relationship. The psychiatrist's duty to the patient then remains until the doctor–patient relationship is terminated, either by a unilateral act of the patient, mutual agreement that services are no longer required, or by a unilateral act of the psychiatrist (in the latter case, termination should be accompanied by reasonable notice to the patient and assistance in providing a new therapist).

Psychiatrists have a duty to exercise reasonable care in treating their patients. Failure to do so is a breach of the duty to the patient (Simon and Shuman 2007, 6, 9–10). This does not mean the treatment must be perfect or extraordinary; rather, it means that the psychiatrist must "possess and exercise the degree of skill and learning possessed and exercised, under similar circumstances, by the members of his or her profession in good standing, and to use ordinary and reasonable care and diligence, and his or her best judgment, in the application of his or her skill to the case" (*Corpus Juris Secundum* 2005, 556: Physicians and Surgeons §83). The question of whether a defendant exercised the requisite standard of care in any given case is an issue to be decided by the fact finder based on the testimony of expert witnesses. Indeed, this is where most of the action in malpractice suits lies.

Courts have found that psychiatrists also owe duties to third parties in at least three contexts. *First*, when a psychiatrist recognizes, or reasonably should recognize, that a patient poses an imminent threat of serious harm to an identifiable third party, in many states the psychiatrist has a duty to protect that individual from injury. Failure to warn the intended victim or notify the police may be a breach of the duty (Simon 2001, 179–182; Simon and Shuman 2007, 165–168, 182–185). *Second*, in cases involving recovered memory of sexual abuse or ritual satanic abuse, some states have found that therapists owe a duty to individuals who could potentially be misidentified as playing roles in such abuse. Thus, if, as a result of treatment, the patient falsely accuses someone of abuse, the psychiatrist has breached a duty to that individual and may be liable for damages (Simon 1998, 132–136; Berger 2000; Simon and Shuman 2007, 95–96). *Third*, some states allow the victims of a psychiatrist's patients to bring third-party malpractice claims against the psychiatrist. Such states recognize that when, as a result of negligent treatment, a patient injures another, the psychiatrist owes a duty to the victim of the patient's violent acts (Kussmann 2012, 575–578).

Once duty and breach have been established, a plaintiff must still prove that the breach caused injury. Tort law divides the causation element into two categories: cause-in-fact and proximate cause (Simon and Shuman 2007, 6–7). The cause-in-fact analysis considers whether the injury would have happened regardless of the psychiatrist's bad act. This is often expressed as a "but for" analysis, which asks, "but for the wrongful quality of the therapist's conduct, would the plaintiff have suffered the same harm?" (Robertson 1997). If the injury would have occurred regardless of the wrongful conduct, the causation requirement is not satisfied. But if the wrongful conduct was a cause-in-fact of the injury, the plaintiff must also prove that there is a reasonably close, proximate, connection between the injury and the wrongful act. The standard used in making this determination is a reasonable foreseeability. When a reasonable person would have foreseen the risk of harm, the proximate cause element is met (Kelley 1991).

If the plaintiff can prove that she suffered harm as the result of a breach of the defendant's duty to her, she is entitled to an award of compensatory damages intended to restore her to the position she would have been in if there had been no negligent act. In extreme cases, involving willful, malicious, or reckless behavior, punitive damages may also be awarded. Negligence alone will not merit punitive damages, which are intended to punish the defendant, rather than to compensate the victim (Prosser 1971, 9–14, 313–323; Simon and Shuman 2007, 7–8).

Major areas of liability for psychiatric malpractice

NEGLIGENT TREATMENT

The law does not demand successful treatment, it merely requires that a psychiatrist perform in a manner consistent with the way an average reasonable psychiatrist would perform under similar circumstances. Although this is a rather nebulous standard, courts consider a number of specific practices as essential elements of the standard of care psychiatrists owe their patients. These include, for example, the duty to obtain a complete clinical history, to disclose adequate information to gain informed consent for treatment, to document all decisions made during the course of treatment, to supervise the patient's progress—both during and after treatment—and to monitor reactions to medication. Failure to comply with any of these duties can subject a psychiatrist to liability if the patient suffers harm as a result of treatment (Sarno 1981; Simon and Shuman 2007, 79–100; Simon 2001, 87–88).

CONFIDENTIALITY

Psychiatrists owe their patients a duty to maintain the privacy of all confidential communications (Zelin 1986; Shuman and Weiner 1987; Simon 2001, 41–44, 53–54). The issue of confidentiality actually involves two related concepts: confidentiality, per se, and testimonial privilege (Simon and Shuman 2007, 37–56). The duty of confidentiality is an ethical obligation that protects a patient's privacy by preventing disclosure of confidential information to third parties. Testimonial privilege refers to the patient's right to prevent a physician from disclosing information in a judicial proceeding. Testimonial privilege is most often established by statute or court rule, and it purports to resolve the ethical dilemmas on the part of a physician faced with conflicting duties—one to the patient to maintain confidentiality, and another to the court to tell the truth. Statutes or court rules resolve the dilemma by giving the patient the right to prevent the physician from testifying. In effect, they codify a public policy judgment that it is more important to safeguard patient privacy generally than to ascertain the truth in specific trial situations.

Absent an exemption, a psychiatrist who breaches the duty to maintain patient confidentiality risks a malpractice action. There are, however, several exemptions; the duty of confidentiality is not absolute. In certain circumstances it may be both legally and ethically permissible, even necessary, to divulge patient confidences. A patient, for example, may waive the right to confidentiality by requesting that medical records be sent to potential employers or insurers. Similarly, there is no right to confidentiality when a patient consents to be examined at the request of a third party, as for example in a disability hearing or litigation. There are also a number of contexts in which a psychiatrist may divulge patient information without the patient's consent. For instance, if the psychiatrist determines that a patient poses a risk of committing violence to self or others and the violence can only be prevented by intervention, the psychiatrist may intervene. Likewise, if the patient's judgment is markedly impaired and other people's lives depend on his or her sound judgment, as for example, an airline pilot or police officer, the psychiatrist may choose to divulge that information. In such cases, disclosure is a matter of choice; the psychiatrist has the option of maintaining the patient's confidence or disclosing the information. In other instances, there is no choice. Statutes define certain situations that mandate disclosure. Though these vary from state to state, statutory disclosure requirements typically apply in the following scenarios: when there is evidence of child abuse; on the initiation of involuntary hospitalization; when an identifiable third party has been threatened; where there is evidence of a past treasonous act; and where there is intention to commit a future crime.

There are also exceptions to the testimonial privilege. For instance, it generally does not apply in criminal proceedings, child custody disputes, child abuse proceedings, or civil commitment proceedings. Significantly, when a patient-litigant's claim or defense rests on his or her mental state, the patient loses the right to prevent the psychiatrist from testifying. Thus, there will be no privilege in malpractice suits brought by patients against their therapists.

NEGLIGENT RELEASE AND SUICIDE

As discussed, one of the general rules of tort liability is that a defendant's negligent act must be the proximate cause of the plaintiff's injury. If someone carelessly spills gasoline on the street, he or she will not necessarily be liable for the damage that follows when someone else intentionally throws a cigarette into the spill and causes a fire. The act of intentionally throwing the cigarette was an intervening cause of the fire, which arguably superseded or broke the chain of causation between the careless spill and the damage. Ordinarily, only if the intervening act is careless or negligent are courts likely to find that the person who spilled the gasoline should have foreseen that a cigarette would be thrown into the spill (Prosser 1971, 270–289).

This is important to keep in mind with respect to the most common psychiatric malpractice claim—failure to prevent a patient from harming himself or herself (Kussman 2000; Simon 2001, 143–147; Simon and Shuman 2007, 131–163). Normally, suicide constitutes an intervening cause; regardless of anyone else's careless behavior, the suicide victim's own acts ultimately caused the harm. Psychiatrists, however, have a duty to protect their patients from themselves. The standard of care owed to all patients, regardless of the initial complaint, includes suicide risk assessments. If there is a perceived risk, the psychiatrist must take affirmative action to protect the patient. Failure either to diagnose the risk or to take adequate precautionary measures can result in liability when the patient commits or attempts to commit suicide. In either event, the reasonableness standard applies. The plaintiff must show that the suicide was reasonably foreseeable or that, in view of the perceived risk, the precautions taken were unreasonable.

Generally, the risk of liability is greater for inpatient than for outpatient suicides. Courts assume that it is easier to anticipate and manage suicidal patients in the controlled setting of a hospital. Typical claims involving inpatient suicides include charges of failure to supervise, failure to restrain, premature release, and negligent discharge. Limitations of control help shield psychiatrists from liability in cases involving outpatient suicides. In those situations, as noted, courts consider whether the treatment was reasonable. Claims might include charges of improper diagnosis, inadequate supervision, abandonment, lack of proper referral, or failure to hospitalize.

DUTY TO PROTECT

Psychiatrists do not only have a duty to prevent patients from harming themselves (Simon and Shuman 2007, 165–199; Kussmann 2012, 575–578). This is counter to the conventional rule, which holds that people have no duty to prevent one person from harming another (*Restatement [Second] of Torts*, §315A). Indeed, psychiatrists traditionally had only a limited duty to exercise control over institutionalized patients. Since 1976, however, with the decision in *Tarasoff v. Board of Regents of the University of California*, a California malpractice case, the psychiatrist's duty to third parties has expanded dramatically. *Tarasoff* involved a therapist who knew his patient was obsessed with another person. When the patient killed that person, the victim's family sued, claiming the therapist had breached a duty to warn the victim about the threat to her life. The California Supreme Court ultimately agreed, holding:

> [O]nce a therapist does in fact determine, or under applicable professional standards reasonably should have determined, that a patient poses a serious danger of violence to others, he bears a duty to exercise reasonable care to protect the foreseeable victim of that danger. While the discharge of this duty of due care will necessarily vary with the facts of each case, in each instance the adequacy of the therapist's conduct must be measured against the traditional negligence standard of the rendition of reasonable care under the circumstances. (*Tarasoff v. Board of Regents of the University of California* 1976, 345)

In reaching its decision, the court recognized that a duty to warn already existed in the context of certain, special relationships. Specifically, in some cases, a person who has the *right* to control another person also has a *duty* to control the other person's conduct. A physician, for example, could be liable for harm done by a patient on temporary leave from a mental hospital. *Tarasoff* expanded the existing law by designating the therapist–patient relationship as one of the special relationships that gives rise to such a duty. Since *Tarasoff*, a majority of states have established rules requiring psychiatrists to act affirmatively to protect third parties from a patient's violent acts. Though the laws vary, the general rule is that a duty to protect arises when a therapist determines, or by the standards of the profession should have determined, that a patient poses an imminent threat to an identifiable third party. The key issues are whether the violent act was foreseeable, whether there was an identifiable victim, and whether the psychiatrist warned the victim or notified appropriate authorities (Perlin 1992; Simon 2001, 179–182; Kussmann 2012, 520–531).

SEXUAL EXPLOITATION

Psychiatrists have a duty to refrain from having sex with their patients, and the states have been particularly resolute in enforcing this duty. Indeed, sexual contact with a patient subjects a psychiatrist to a host of legal and professional consequences, ranging from criminal prosecution on charges of sexual assault or rape; to civil suits alleging negligence, loss of consortium, or battery; to ethical sanctions; and to license revocation (Flaherty 1988; Simon 2001, 219–226). In the context of a malpractice claim, a plaintiff generally must prove that sexual contact took place in breach of the duty, and that harm, typically a degeneration in psychological condition, resulted. Several states have made it easier for plaintiffs to prevail by enacting statutes that make any sex between a therapist and patient both criminally and civilly actionable. Such laws create a statutory presumption of harm whenever a therapist engages in sex with a patient. Some states even allow the patient's spouse to bring an independent claim of loss of consortium (interference with the marital relationship) against the offending therapist. Though there are several potential defenses, including claims that the patient consented or that treatment had ended, once the court finds that sexual activity took place, it is exceedingly difficult for the defendant to prevail.

Intentional torts

The general rule regarding intentional torts is that a person is liable for harmful or offensive contact if he or she engages in a willful act with either: (1) the intent to harm or offend; or (2) substantial certainty that harmful or offensive contact will result (Prosser 1971, 31–34). Whether contact is offensive is determined on the basis of a reasonableness standard (contact is offensive if it offends a reasonable sense of personal dignity). Thus, a plaintiff bringing an intentional tort claim must prove that the defendant intentionally did something harmful or offensive or that the defendant knew with substantial certainty that his or her actions would result in harm or offense (Jung and Levine 1987). Characteristic intentional torts include assault, battery, false imprisonment, and defamation.

Because a plaintiff must prove what was in the defendant's mind when he or she acted, it is generally more difficult to prove intent than negligence. Once intent has been shown, however, it is much easier to prove causation. In contrast to negligent torts, there is no foreseeability requirement in intentional torts. The intent element applies only to the decision to engage in the harmful or offensive contact, not to the consequences of that conduct. If the defendant did a wrongful act, he or she is responsible for the consequences of that act even if the consequences were not foreseeable. Likewise, there is no probability standard. If the defendant meant to do something harmful or offensive, there is no requirement that success be highly likely. This means, for example, that someone who intentionally shoots a rubber band at a bus driver will be liable for all damages that accrue when the rubber band hits the driver in the eye, knocks her contact lens out, and causes a multivehicle accident. It makes no difference that the shooter only meant to annoy the driver and never intended to cause a catastrophic accident.

A defendant in an intentional tort action can claim that he or she acted in self-defense or that the plaintiff consented to the allegedly harmful act (Prosser 1971, 101–112). In a self-defense claim, the defendant must concede that he or she intended to harm the plaintiff. But the defendant will also argue that his or her acts were reasonable responses to the plaintiff's own threatening behavior. Another defense to an intentional tort action is consent. If the plaintiff willingly consented to the conduct, the defendant will prevail. To be effective, consent must be competent, knowing, and voluntary. That is, the plaintiff must have had sufficient information and mental capacity to make an informed decision, and his or her consent must not have been coerced or fraudulently obtained.

Major areas of psychiatric liability

BATTERY

The two most common intentional tort claims brought against psychiatrists are battery, brought when a patient alleges that treatment was provided without informed consent, and false imprisonment, typically in cases involving involuntary commitment. As to the first, patients must consent to treatment on the basis of information regarding the nature and consequences of the proposed medical regimen (Simon and Shuman 2007, 57–78). This requirement protects the patient's autonomy by preserving his or her right to determine what happens to his or her body.

As noted, informed consent must be competent, knowing, and voluntary (Moldoff 1961; Twerski and Cohen 1988; Simon 2001, 63–74). Competence is not something that can be calculated scientifically. It is context specific and involves considerations of a patient's ability to understand treatment options, make treatment choices, and communicate those choices. A patient's incompetence will not foreclose the ability to go ahead with treatment, it merely means that the psychiatrist will have to obtain substitute consent from someone authorized to provide it (e.g., a parent, guardian, or spouse). The knowing element of the consent requirement is met by providing the patient with sufficient information to make an informed choice. Traditionally, the amount of information necessary to fulfill this requirement has been measured on a professional standard. That is, the psychiatrist must provide the amount and kind of information a reasonable psychiatrist would disclose under the circumstances or that is customarily provided in his or her community. Many states, however, now have adopted a standard based on the patient's perspective, requiring the psychiatrist to provide all material information a reasonable person in the patient's position would want to know to be able to make an informed decision. Though there are no absolute rules regarding what kind of information is material, courts have looked favorably on the following: assessments of the patient's condition; the nature and purpose of the proposed treatment; risks and benefits of the treatment; viable alternatives to that treatment, along with the risks and benefits of the alternative treatments; and projected outcome with and without treatment. Finally, there are four limited exceptions to the consent requirement:

1. When emergency treatment is necessary to save a patient's life or to prevent imminent bodily harm, the law presumes consent if the patient cannot give consent and there is not adequate time to seek substitute consent.
2. If the patient is deemed incompetent, his or her consent is not required; nevertheless, consent must be obtained from a substitute decision maker.
3. If a psychiatrist believes that full disclosure would harm the patient's health, in a narrow set of circumstances full disclosure may not be required.
4. If the patient competently, knowingly, and voluntarily waives his or her right to information, the consent need not be informed.

If inadequate information was provided and none of these exceptions applies, a psychiatrist who begins treatment without obtaining informed consent risks liability for negligence or, in the worst-case scenario, battery.

FALSE IMPRISONMENT

Under certain limited conditions, states grant psychiatrists the authority to hospitalize patients against their will under civil commitment schemes (Simon and Shuman 2007, 115–129). The requirements and procedures involved are provided in statutes, which vary from state to state. Although there are differences, three criteria underlie all involuntary commitment statutes. The patient must be mentally ill, he or she must present a threat to self or community, and he or she must be unable to provide for his or her own basic needs. If these conditions are met, the statutes generally insulate the committing psychiatrist from liability. A patient suing on the basis of false imprisonment must prove that the psychiatrist acted in bad faith in seeking commitment (Chase 1970; Simon 2001, 125–130).

PSYCHIATRIST AS WITNESS

Two types of witnesses offer testimony at trial: fact witnesses and expert witnesses. A fact witness, as the term implies, provides the court with the facts of the case—who did what, when, and where. The fact witness is limited to testifying about things that he or she directly witnessed or performed, and is generally limited in offering any personal opinions, drawing conclusions, or relating the opinions or reports of others. Whereas a fact witness need not have any special expertise, an expert witness is a person whose knowledge of a particular field is beyond the understanding of the average layperson. Experts appear in court to help jurors or judges understand the case by clarifying points about specialized topics. While an expert may testify as to facts, he or she is further permitted to offer opinions. Indeed, that is the main function of an expert witness.

A psychiatrist involved in a tort suit might appear in either capacity (Gutheil 1998a, 226–229; Gutheil 1998b; Gutheil 2010). Like anyone else, a psychiatrist might testify as a fact witness in a trial in which he or she is the plaintiff, but such a case would only rarely center on his or her professional role as a psychiatrist. Conversely, as a defendant in a malpractice action, the therapist would take the stand to report the facts of the case as he or she had observed them. Additionally, a treating psychiatrist might be called to testify in a suit involving a patient and a third party, as, for example, when the patient claims psychological injury as the result of an allegedly traumatic accident. In any event, when the therapist appears as a fact witness, he or she may only identify the patient's symptoms, the diagnosis applied, and the treatment prescribed. He or she may not take the additional step of testifying that the treatment met the requisite standard of care in the malpractice suit or of positing an opinion as to the causal link between the allegedly negligent act and the diagnosis of emotional distress in the patient's claim against a third party.

As a properly qualified expert witness, the psychiatrist may offer opinions regarding causation and standard-of-care issues. In tort cases alleging psychological harm, for instance, a psychiatrist/expert may be called to establish both the extent of such damages and the link between them and the traumatic event. In a malpractice suit, she may review the facts of the case at issue and offer opinions about how they relate to the elements of a negligence claim. Thus, she may give opinions as to whether a doctor–patient relationship had been established, whether the defendant's performance met the required standard of care, the extent of any damages, and whether there was a causal link between any negligence and the damage suffered.

SUMMARY

Tort law seeks to deter harmful conduct and compensate victims of such conduct. It is generally concerned with two types of injury-causing behavior: negligent and intentional. As applied to psychiatrists, this means that psychiatrists have a duty to exercise reasonable care in treating their patients. Failure to provide such care is *negligent*, and a psychiatrist whose unreasonable care causes foreseeable harm may be liable for malpractice. Tort law also bars psychiatrists from *intentionally* harming their patients. A patient who is harmed by a psychiatrist's negligence or intentional acts may be entitled to recover damages to compensate for the harm.

SUMMARY KEY POINTS

The following are examples of acts or omissions that may result in liability for malpractice if they cause foreseeable harm:

- Failure to provide treatment in manner consistent with the way an average reasonable psychiatrist would perform under similar circumstances
- Failure to maintain the privacy of confidential patient communications
- Failure to prevent a patient from harming himself or herself
- Failure to prevent a patient from harming others
- Engagement in sexual activity with a patient

The following are examples of intentional acts that may result in tort liability:

- Providing treatment without informed consent
- Seeking involuntary commitment in bad faith

REFERENCES

Berger JM. 2000. Comment: False memory syndrome and therapist liability to third parties for emotional distress injuries arising from recovered memory therapy: A general prohibition on liability and a limited liability exception. *Temple Law Review* 73:795–827.

Bloch M. 1961. *Feudal Society*. LA Manyon, trans. Chicago: University of Chicago Press.

Chase RF. 1970. Annotation: Liability for false imprisonment predicated upon institution of, or conduct in connection with, insanity proceedings. *American Law Reports Annotated, 3rd Series* 30:523–560.

Corpus Juris Secundum. 2005. Eagan, MN: West.

Farnsworth EA. 1999. *Contracts*, 3rd edition. New York: Aspen.

Flaherty MR. 1988. Annotation: Improper or immoral sexually related conduct toward patient as ground for disciplinary action against physician, dentist, or other licensed healer. *American Law Reports Annotated, 4th Series* 59:1104–1132.

Gutheil TG. 1998a. Witnesses, depositions, and trials. In *The Mental Health Practitioner and the Law: A Comprehensive Handbook*, edited by LE Lifson and RI Simon, Cambridge, MA: Harvard University Press, 225–236.

Gutheil TG. 1998b. *The Psychiatrist as Expert Witness*. Washington, DC: American Psychiatric Press.

Gutheil TG. 2010. The expert witness. In *Textbook of Forensic Psychiatry*, 2nd edition, edited by RI Simon and LH Gold, Arlington, VA: American Psychiatric Publishing, 93–110.

Hensler DR, MS Marquis, AF Abrahamse et al. 1991. *Compensation for Accidental Injuries in the United States*. Santa Monica, CA: Rand.

Holmes OW. 1881. *The Common Law*. Boston: Little, Brown.

Ingber S. 1985. Rethinking intangible injuries: A focus on remedy. *California Law Review* 73:772–856.

Jung DJ and DI Levine. 1987. Whence knowledge intent? Whither knowledge intent? *University of California Davis Law Review* 20:551–584.

Kelley PJ. 1991. Proximate cause in negligence law: History, theory, and the present darkness. *Washington University Law Quarterly* 69:49–105.

Kussman PC. 2000. Annotation: Liability of doctor, psychiatrist, or psychologist for failure to take steps to prevent patient's suicide. *American Law Reports Annotated, 5th Series* 81:167–244.

Kussmann PC. 2012. Annotation: Civil liability of psychiatrist arising out of patient's violent conduct resulting in injury to or death of patient of third party allegedly caused in whole or part by mental disorder. *American Law Reports Annotated, 6th Series* 80:469–598.

Moldoff WM. 1961. Annotation: Malpractice: Physician's duty to inform patient of nature and hazards of disease or treatment. *American Law Reports Annotated, 2nd Series* 79:1028–1035.

Perlin ML. 1992. *Tarasoff* and the dilemma of the dangerous patient: New directions for the 1990s. *Law and Psychology Review* 16:29–63.

Prosser WL. 1971. *Handbook of the Law of Torts*, 4th edition. St. Paul, MN: West.

Restatement (Second) of Torts. 1965. St. Paul, MN: West.

Rigelhaupt JL. 1982. Annotation: What constitutes physician-patient relationship for malpractice purposes. *American Law Reports Annotated, 4th Series* 17:132–160.

Robertson OW. 1997. The common sense of cause in fact. *Texas Law Review* 75:1765–1800.

Sarno GG. 1981. Annotation: Civil liability for physical measures undertaken in connection with treatment of mentally disordered patient. *American Law Reports Annotated, 4th Series* 8:464–518.

Shuman DW. 1993. The psychology of deterrence in tort law. *Kansas Law Review* 42:115–168.

Shuman DW. 1994. The psychology of compensation in tort law. *Kansas Law Review* 43:39–77.

Shuman DW and MF Weiner. 1987. *The Psychotherapist-Patient Privilege: A Critical Examination*. Springfield, IL: Charles C Thomas.

Simon RI. 1998. Litigation hot spots in clinical practice. In *The Mental Health Practitioner and the Law: A Comprehensive Handbook*, edited by LE Lifson and RI Simon, Cambridge, MA: Harvard University Press, 117–139.

Simon RI. 2001. *Concise Guide to Psychiatry and Law for Clinicians*, 3rd edition. Washington, DC: American Psychiatric Press.

Simon RI and DW Shuman. 2007. *Clinical Manual of Psychiatry and the Law*. Arlington, VA: American Psychiatric Publishing.

Tarasoff v. Board of Regents of the University of California, 551 P.2d 334 (Cal. 1976).

Terry HT. 1915. Negligence. *Harvard Law Review* 29:40–54.

Twerski AD and NB Cohen. 1988. Informed decision making and the law of torts: The myth of justiciable causation. *University of Illinois Law Review* 1988:607–655.

Zelin JE. 1986. Annotation: Physician's liability for unauthorized disclosure of confidential information about patient. *American Law Reports Annotated, 4th Series* 48:668–713.

93

An introduction to civil procedure

ROBERT LLOYD GOLDSTEIN

CIVIL PROCEDURE AND PROCEDURAL JUSTICE

Civil procedure establishes an orderly continuum of rules of litigation in the civil justice system. It is best defined as "the sum total of rules, forms, doctrines, and devices" that govern the formal activities of a technical nature in the adjudication of civil disputes (Grilliott 1979, 223). The principal objective of procedural rules is to provide a fair process for ascertaining the truth and delivering substantive justice in civil lawsuits. Procedural rules "should be construed and administered to secure the just, speedy, and inexpensive determination of every action and proceeding" (Federal Rules of Civil Procedure [FRCP] Rule 1 2015). A number of research studies involving the social psychology of the dispute resolution process have demonstrated the central importance of a litigant's perception of fundamental fairness in procedure (even when the litigant is disappointed by the substantive outcome) (Tyler 1998; Lind and Tyler 1998). Adherence to the standards of "procedural justice" is crucial to maintain confidence in the institutions of dispute resolution. Procedural justice implements the substantive law and provides litigants with a sense of receiving fair treatment before an unbiased and impartial tribunal. Golding has set forth the basic standards of procedural justice as follows:

- *Neutrality*: No man should be the judge in his own cause; the dispute settler should have no private stake in the outcome; the dispute settler should not be biased in favor of or against any party.
- *Persuasive conflict*: Each party should be given fair notice of the proceedings; the dispute settler should hear the argument and evidence of both sides; the dispute settler should hear a party only in the presence of the other party; each party should be given a fair opportunity to respond to the arguments and evidence of the other party.
- *Settlement*: The terms of the settlement should be supported by clearly articulated reasons; the reasons should refer to the arguments and evidence presented (Golding 1975, 113).

The Federal Rules of Civil Procedure (FRCP) govern court procedure for civil lawsuits in the 94 U.S. Federal District Courts (which are the trial courts for federal cases). The FRCP were established in 1938 and are revised and amended periodically. (The most recent amendments went into effect on December 1, 2010.) Most of the states have adopted rules of civil procedure for use in their own state courts that are based on the FRCP. (A nationwide dual system of federal and state courts exists side by side.) The FRCP are grouped into 11 titles (which comprise 86 rules), as follows:

Title I—Scope of Rules; Form of Action
Title II—Commencing an Action; Service of Process; Pleadings, Motions, and Orders
Title III—Pleadings and Motions
Title IV—Parties
Title V—Disclosures and Discovery
Title VI—Trials
Title VII—Judgment
Title VIII—Provisional and Final Remedies
Title IX—Special Proceedings
Title X—District Courts and Clerks; Conducting Business; Issuing Orders
Title XI—General Provisions

Perusal of the 11 FRCP titles attests to the immense breadth and purview of the subject matter of civil procedure. It is well beyond the scope of this modest introduction to the topic for a readership of forensic mental health professionals to undertake more than a superficial overview of modern-day civil procedure. A brief survey cannot do justice to a subject of such enormous complexity. For those who wish to explore more fully any particular aspect of civil procedure, a number of casebooks and hornbooks are available that provide an exhaustive, in-depth exposition of this fundamental cornerstone of the law (Wright and Kane 2011; Friedenthal et al. 2013). In the following sections, a necessarily condensed sample of selected topics is presented, to attempt to convey the flavor of some of the issues that shape procedural law within our adversarial judicial system.

CIVIL PROCEDURE AND THE ADVERSARIAL SYSTEM

The adversarial system is observed primarily in countries where the Anglo-American common law system predominates. The American judicial system is based on the adversarial model (except for Louisiana, whose civil code derives predominantly from a version of the French Code Napoleon) (Kagan 2003). The various stages of a civil lawsuit, from filing to final judgment, are governed by the applicable rules of civil procedure, whether federal or state. Lawyers master the intricacies of the rules of procedure to promote their cases and gain a competitive advantage over their opponents, within the constraints of the rules, at each stage of the proceedings. The adversarial system is *lawyer centered.* The lawyer-advocates for each party shape and control the litigation. "The central precept of the adversary system is that the sharp clash of proofs presented by opposing lawyers, both zealously representing the interests of their clients, generates the information upon which a neutral and passive decision maker can most justly resolve a dispute" (Asimow 2007, 653).

Most of the pretrial and trial decisions, the most critical tactical decisions, are made and carried out by the lawyers for each party, who frame the issues, undertake investigations and discovery, present the evidence, decide which witnesses to call, select expert witnesses, present the evidence, examine witnesses, conduct cross-examinations, and make their arguments to the jury. At trials, the judge plays a more passive role, acting as an impartial moderator and referee on points of law, and seeing to it that the rules are followed to ensure fair play. (Nevertheless, it should be noted that judges play a very active role in many aspects of the cases over which they preside, for example, deciding motions for summary judgment, aggressively trying to settle cases, and acting as gatekeepers in deciding questions regarding the admissibility of proffered expert testimony) (Asimow 2007).

JURISDICTION

The adjudicatory authority of the court, whether it has the power or competence to decide a given controversy, is known as *jurisdiction.* The term generally denotes the requisite authority of the forum court to decide the particular matters involved in the case before it (subject matter jurisdiction) and the requisite power over a given defendant and/or his or her property (*in personam* jurisdiction and/or *in rem* jurisdiction), to enable it to enforce the legal obligations owed by the defendant. *In personam* jurisdiction gives the court the power to hold the defendant personally liable, issue a judgment against him or her, and seize his or her assets. *In rem* jurisdiction empowers the court to decide claims relating to a piece of property or a legal status (e.g., marriage). In addition to meeting all the requirements for jurisdiction, considerations of procedural due process require that the forum court must ensure that the party whose rights will be affected is provided adequate notice and an opportunity to be heard in conjunction with any assertion of *in personam* or *in rem* jurisdiction (Weinstein 1992).

JURISDICTION OVER THE PARTIES

Originally, the chief basis for personal jurisdiction was premised on notions of state sovereignty. The actual presence of the individual within the state was the basis of personal jurisdiction, because the court could exercise power over those within the territorial or geographic boundaries of the government (of which the court was a part) and render binding judgments against that individual. In the early cases, physical presence within the state was the primary, if not the sole, basis for personal jurisdiction. In the leading case, *Pennoyer v. Neff* (1877), the Supreme Court held that if a defendant voluntarily ventured into the forum state and was personally served with process while present there, that would be sufficient to exercise personal jurisdiction over him or her.

Physical presence is still a valid method of getting jurisdiction. *Pennoyer* is still good law: when an out-of-state resident, if only briefly, voluntarily travels to the forum state (with which he or she has no other contacts) and is served with process while there, then the local court has personal jurisdiction over him or her. In *Burnham v. Superior Court* (1990), a New Jersey man, subsequent to separating from his wife, traveled to California for a short visit on business and to see his children (who had moved there with their mother after the marital separation). While he was in California, his wife served him with process for a divorce lawsuit to be tried in that state. The Supreme Court held that in-state service was a constitutionally valid basis for California to exercise personal jurisdiction.

Another basis of jurisdiction premised on state sovereignty is *domicile.* A state can exact reciprocal duties and obligations from its citizens in return for the protection and privileges it accords them. Thus, the courts of a state may constitutionally exercise *in personam* jurisdiction over an individual domiciled in that state, who is temporarily absent from the jurisdiction, when service of process takes place out of state. (Domicile has been defined as the place where a person has his or her permanent principal home; the place to which, even if he or she were temporarily absent, they intend to return.) Domicile is roughly equivalent to state citizenship. Even if a person has a number of residences, he or she can have but one domicile at a time. The leading case allowing *in personam* jurisdiction on the basis of domicile within the forum state is *Milliken v. Meyer* (1940). The Supreme Court held that "domicile in the state is alone sufficient to bring an absent defendant within the reach of the state's jurisdiction for purposes of a personal judgment" (provided that the individual was given actual notice of the proceedings and an opportunity to be heard by extraterritorial service of process). Under modern jurisdictional theories, a further basis of jurisdiction is recognized when a state exercises jurisdiction over a nonresident motorist who is involved in a motor vehicle accident within the forum state. In such a situation, the state has the right, premised on its police power, to protect its citizens who are injured by an inherently dangerous instrumentality, namely, the motor vehicle. (However, only "specific jurisdiction" is conferred, i.e., jurisdiction is allowed only for any lawsuit based on the in-state accident itself.) In these cases, in-state service of process may be made on a designated official of the forum state, e.g., the Director of the Bureau of Motor Vehicles, with service by registered mail on the nonresident defendant (Wright and Kane 2011).

These nonresident motorist cases are only one example of modern-day jurisdictional theories and doctrines, designed to keep pace with the realities of the twentieth and twenty-first centuries. The rapid technological advances of the modern age, which have resulted in the emergence of our more progressively mobile and interconnected society, have challenged the law to keep up with the social repercussions of technology since the time of *Pennoyer*'s antiquated physical presence rule. In response to the changing times, all states have enacted "long-arm statutes" that confer extraterritorial jurisdiction over nonresident individuals or corporations who are physically absent from the state, provided that the prospective defendants have sufficient "minimum contacts" with the forum state.

Long-arm statutes have adopted specific standards for personal jurisdiction, based on certain kinds of activity within the forum state, including the transaction of any business in the state, the commission of a tortious act within the state, the commission of tortious acts outside the state that cause injury within the state (provided that the defendant conducts business activities in the state), the ownership, use, or possession of real estate within the state, or entering into contracts to insure any person, property, or risk located in the state.

The basis of jurisdiction that underlies the long-arm statutes, and that has come to provide the theoretical underpinning of modern-day jurisdictional doctrine, was set forth by the Supreme Court in the landmark case *International Shoe Company v. State of Washington* (1945). In this modern era of increasing interstate mobility of individuals, as well as the growth of corporate business activities nationwide, the law needed to keep pace. Courts needed to craft new, more flexible standards for the assertion of personal jurisdiction over nonresidents and out-of-state corporations by a forum state in which they operated, transacted business, or with which they otherwise had significant contacts. Consequently, the Supreme Court went beyond the physical power theory of jurisdiction established in *Pennoyer* (which had come to be viewed as rather anachronistic) and established the new "minimum contacts" test. The court explained:

> Historically the jurisdiction of courts to render judgments in personam is grounded on their de facto power over the defendant's person...But now...due process requires only that in order to subject a defendant to a judgment in personam, if he be not present within the territory of the forum, he have certain *minimum contacts* with it such that the maintenance of the suit does not offend "traditional notions of fair play and substantial justice." (International Shoe Company 1945, 316)

The minimum contacts test provides a local forum for local plaintiffs to bring a lawsuit against nonresident individuals or corporations. However, plaintiffs can do so only if it seems sufficiently fair to impose the burden on the out-of-state defendants to have to travel to the forum state to defend the action. For example, it would be considered fair for a court to exercise jurisdiction (and would satisfy the minimum contacts test) "if a corporation...is continuously and systematically entering the state" to market its products there. The Supreme Court has placed increased emphasis on due process considerations in adopting its minimum contacts doctrine, as a limit on the power of courts to assert *in personam* jurisdiction. In a long line of cases, the court has attempted to refine the requisite standards for "the kind and sufficiency of contacts needed to bring a defendant within the threshold of *International Shoe*" and has extended the minimum contacts requirement to jurisdiction over property as well as person (*Buckeye Boiler v. Superior Court of Los Angeles County* 1969; *Shaffer v. Heitner* 1977; *Kulko v. Superior Court* 1978).

With technology on an accelerating exponential curve, and with changes so rapid, unique, and profound in this Internet era, long-arm statutes have been seriously challenged in cases involving Internet commercial and defamation disputes. A key issue involves whether an individual may bring an action and enforce a judgment in his or her own state, or whether the action must be brought in the state where the defendant resides or where the business is located. Jurisdictional disputes of this nature have resulted in the adoption of new standards. In *Zippo Manufacturing v. Zippo Dot Com* (1997), the defendant, based in California, had electronically entered into online contracts with thousands of paying customers in Pennsylvania, the plaintiff's state of incorporation. The plaintiff brought suit in Pennsylvania for a variety of trademark offenses. The Pennsylvania court announced a new standard based on the presumption that the exercise of personal jurisdiction is "directly proportionate to the nature and quality of commercial activity that an entity conducts over the Internet." The court held that in a case wherein a defendant enters into contracts involving the "knowing and repeated transmission of computer files over the Internet, personal jurisdiction is proper."

SUBJECT MATTER JURISDICTION

In addition to the requirement that a court have jurisdiction over the parties, it must also have the power to adjudicate the kind of controversy before it. This is referred to as *Subject Matter Jurisdiction*. Jurisdiction over the subject matter, in state and federal courts, is limited by the requirements of constitutional provisions, as well as by specific state and federal statutes. For example, state statutes may authorize particular courts to adjudicate only certain types of litigation, such as probate and domestic relations matters. Perhaps the most common method of distributing judicial power is according to the dollar amount in controversy (e.g., in California, most matters in which the dollar amount involved is less than $25,000 are restricted to the municipal courts; most matters involving a greater amount are assigned to the superior courts). These courts are said to have "original jurisdiction" over the lawsuit. Other specialized tribunals are given appellate jurisdiction to review the decisions of the trial courts (Friedenthal et al. 2013).

Federal courts exercise subject matter jurisdiction over two basic types of controversies: Diversity of Citizenship cases and Federal Question cases. Diversity of Citizenship jurisdiction is based on Article III, Section 2 of the Constitution, which confers subject matter jurisdiction on the federal courts in regard to 'Controversies…between Citizens of different states," subject to many qualifications. Historically, the rationale underlying Diversity Jurisdiction was the avoidance of actual prejudice to out-of-state litigants in state courts (as well as the elimination of out-of-state litigants' apprehensions about potential prejudice, whether justified or not) by offering them the alternative of a presumably more unbiased federal forum. In all diversity cases, the amount in controversy must exceed $75,000. (The party seeking to invoke federal diversity jurisdiction does not have to prove that the amount in controversy exceeds that amount but only has to make a good faith claim to that effect.) This provision serves to limit access to the federal courts to the more significant cases, in an attempt to control the caseload of an already overloaded system. Federal Question jurisdiction involves jurisdiction by the federal courts over a substantial claim founded directly on federal law. For example, a claim for copyright or trademark violation derives from federal law, namely, the federal copyright or trademark statutes. Other examples of Federal Question cases are actions against federal officials and cases arising under the securities laws or antitrust laws. In Federal Question cases, there is no amount in controversy requirement (Emanuel 2014).

RULE 26 EXPERT REPORTS

Forensic mental health professionals who testify in federal court are well advised to acquaint themselves with the provisions of Federal Rule 26, which is the basic rule of the FRCP dealing with experts, covering a broad range of issues, from expert compensation (Goldstein and Laskin n.d.) to trial preparation protection for communications between a party's attorney and expert witnesses (*Republic of Ecuador v. Bjorkman* 2012). The rule provides that each party must automatically furnish a list (at least 90 days before trial) that identifies any experts it intends to call at trial. Rule 26(a)(2)(B) requires that the party who will call a retained expert must have the expert prepare and sign a report containing all of the expert's opinions and the basis for them, the facts or data considered by the expert in forming the opinion, any exhibits to be used by the expert, the expert's qualifications (including a list of all publications authored within the preceding 10 years), the compensation the expert is receiving, and a list of any other cases in which he or she has testified as an expert (at deposition or trial) within the preceding 4 years. Treating physicians are generally not required to submit a report (but disclosure must be provided setting forth the subject matter on which the witness is expected to present evidence and a summary of the facts and opinions to which the witness is expected to testify). By requiring full disclosure, Rule 26 serves to prevent the tactic of unfair surprise at trial from affecting the outcome of the case (Rocco 2008).

The Supreme Court, in *Daubert v. Merrell Dow Pharmaceuticals, Inc.* (1993), determined that federal trial judges should be the "gatekeepers" whenever the admissibility of scientific or technical evidence is challenged. The judges' preliminary task is to ensure that scientific evidence is not only relevant, but that it rests on a reliable foundation. "The inquiry envisioned by the Court is viewed as a flexible one, with its overarching subject the scientific validity (and thus the evidentiary relevance and reliability) of the principles and methodology of the proposed testimony (as distinguished from the conclusions that it generates)" (Goldstein 2003, 794). Pretrial *Daubert* hearings are frequently used by trial courts to fulfill their gatekeeping responsibility, in deciding questions of the admissibility of proffered expert testimony. "Rule 26 reports are perhaps the single most important piece of evidence in a *Daubert* hearing" because "the court will have before it a complete statement of all the opinions to which the expert will testify and their factual basis." Accordingly, the Rule 26 report "often serves as the cornerstone of reliability analysis under *Daubert*" (Rocco 2008, 2234).

REFERENCES

Asimow M. 2007. Popular culture and the adversary system. *Loyola of Los Angeles Law Review* 40:653–685.

Buckeye Boiler Co. v. Superior Court of Los Angeles County, 71 Cal. 2d 893 (1969).

Burnham v. Superior Court, 495 U.S. 604 (1990).

Daubert v. Merrill Dow Pharmaceuticals, Inc., 509 U.S. 579 (1993).

Emanuel SL. 2014. *Emanuel Law Outlines: Civil Procedure*, 25th edition, New York: Wolters Kluwer Law and Business.

Federal Rules of Civil Procedure [FRCP] Rule 1 (2015).

Friedenthal J, A Miller, J Sexton, and H Hershkoff. 2013. *Civil Procedure*. St. Paul, MN: West Academic.

Golding MP. 1975. *Philosophy of Law*. Englewood Cliffs, NJ: Prentice Hall.

Goldstein RL. 2003. An introduction to civil procedure. In *Principles and Practice of Forensic Psychiatry*, 2nd edition, edited by R Rosner, London: Arnold, 789–795.

Goldstein RL and AM Laskin AM. n.d. [Unpublished manuscript]. When Rule 26 imposes a "reasonable" deposition fee for the expert: Pitfalls for the forensic psychiatrist.

Grilliott HJ. 1979. *Introduction to Law and the Legal System*. Boston: Houghton Mifflin.

International Shoe Company v. State of Washington, 326 U.S. 310 (1945).

Kagan RA. 2003. *Adversarial Legalism: The American Way of Law*. Cambridge, MA: Harvard University Press.

Kulko v. Superior Court, 436 U.S. 84 (1978).

Lind EA and TR Tyler. 1988. *The Social Psychology of Procedural Justice*. New York: Springer Science and Business Media.

Milliken v. Meyer, 311 U.S. 457 (1940).

Pennoyer v. Neff, 95 U.S. 714 (1877).

Republic of Ecuador v. Bjorkman, 2012 WL 12755, at *4 (D. Colo Jan. 4, 2012).

Rocco KA. 2008. Rule 26(a)(2)(B) of the Federal Rules of civil procedure: In the interest of full disclosure. *Fordham Law Review* 76:2227–2260.

Shaffer v. Heitner, 433 U.S. 186 (1977).

Tyler TR. 1998. Justice and power in civil dispute processing. In *Justice and Power in Sociolegal Studies*, edited by BG Garth and A Sarat, Evanston, IL: Northwestern University Press, 313–315.

Weinstein J. 1992. The early American origins of territoriality in judicial jurisdiction. *St. Louis Law Journal* 37:1–47.

Wright CA and MK Kane. 2011. *Law of Federal Courts*. St. Paul, MN: West Academic.

Zippo Manufacturing v. Zippo Dot Com, 952 F. Supp. 1119 (W.D. Pa. 1997).

94

An introduction to significant issues in criminal procedure

ROGER J. BERNSTEIN AND ROBERT LLOYD GOLDSTEIN

The tendency of those who execute the criminal laws of the country to obtain convictions by means of unlawful seizures and enforced confessions, the latter often obtained after subjecting accused persons to unwarranted practices destructive of rights secured by the Federal Constitution, should find no sanction in the judgments of the courts, which are charged at all times with the support of the Constitution, and to which people of all conditions have a right to appeal for the maintenance of such fundamental rights.

The efforts of the courts and their officials to bring the guilty to punishment, praiseworthy as they are, are not to be aided by the sacrifice of those great principles established by years of endeavor and suffering which have resulted in their embodiment in the fundamental law of the land.

***Weeks v. United States*, 232 U.S. 383, 392, 393 (1914)**

INTRODUCTION

The adoption of the U.S. Constitution was conditioned on simultaneous approval of the 10 amendments constituting the "Bill of Rights." Reflecting the colonists' concern with arbitrary exercises of government power and with protection of individual rights, 4 of these 10 amendments impose significant limits on the procedures that governments can use to investigate crime and to try individuals accused of crimes. Moreover, within these 10 amendments at least 16 distinct limitations on government conduct can readily be discerned.

Because these protections in the Bill of Rights are broadly phrased, they have been held to apply to modern-day law enforcement techniques, such as wiretaps, that were unknown when the amendments were adopted. In the last hundred years these protections have been held to apply to police lineups and other identification procedures, to custodial interrogations of suspects, to police seizure and examination of cell phones, and to many other aspects of modern-day criminal procedure.

The need to solve crimes often creates significant pressure on judges to give the broad phrases in the Bill of Rights a constrained interpretation, in the name of apprehending the guilty and protecting the public. Judges have often expressed concern that an expansive interpretation of the Bill of Rights "would … reduce the efficiency of crime prevention and detection to a degree which would seriously endanger public safety" (*United States v. Robinson* 1966, 114–115). This law enforcement imperative has frequently led the U.S. Supreme Court—or at least a majority of its justices—to adopt a narrow view of the constitutional protections against law enforcement overreach. This pressure has also caused the court to carve out exceptions to these protections. The pressure to relax these constitutional protections is particularly acute because evidence that the government has obtained by conduct that violates these protections is often excluded from prosecutor use at trial to convict even where the most serious crimes are charged.

The U.S. Supreme Court has plenary authority to determine how federal and state courts shall interpret and apply the protections in the Bill of Rights. However, a number of state constitutions also contain their own protections for the accused in the criminal justice process. Some state courts have interpreted their state constitutions as providing protections significantly greater than those required by the federal Bill of Rights.

This chapter presents an overview of the U.S. Supreme Court decisions concerning conflicts between individual rights and law enforcement in some of the most heavily litigated areas of criminal procedure. Because case law varies in different jurisdictions and is constantly evolving, this discussion is necessarily general; it is at most a starting point for further analysis in any individual case.

FOURTH AMENDMENT LIMITATIONS ON ARREST, SEARCH, AND SEIZURE

The basic purpose of the Fourth Amendment "is to safeguard the privacy and security of individuals against arbitrary invasions by governmental officials" (*Camara v. Mun. Court of City and County of San Francisco* 1967, 528). This amendment, which governs all searches and arrests conducted by government agents, contains two grammatically independent but closely related clauses. The first clause provides the following:

> The right of the people to be secure in their persons, houses, papers, and effects against unreasonable searches and seizures, shall not be violated, ...

The second clause provides:

> [A]nd no Warrants shall issue, but upon probable cause, supported by Oath or affirmation, and particularly describing the place to be searched and the persons or things to be seized.

The first clause, which sets out a reasonableness test for searches and seizures, does not require that a warrant be issued for a search or arrest. It has been up to the Supreme Court to determine when the second clause applies so that a warrant is required for a search or arrest. Many of the Supreme Court's cases express a general preference for warrants; however, in a large number of cases the court has approved warrantless searches.

The second clause only applies to those searches that require a warrant. It sets out requirements for probable cause and particularity that govern not only the issuance of search and arrest warrants by judges and magistrates but also their execution. In practice the standard for probable cause is not exacting. Probable cause to search has been defined by the Supreme Court as "a fair probability that contraband or evidence of a crime will be found in a particular place" (*Illinois v. Gates* 1983, 238). The probable cause standard is a "practical, nontechnical conception" that is "not readily, or even usefully, reduced to a neat set of legal rules" (*Illinois v. Gates* 1983, 231–232).

Preference for warrants for searches or arrests inside a suspect's home

The judicial preference for requiring a warrant is strongest for searches of an individual's home. Because "the very core" of the Fourth Amendment protection against unreasonable searches and seizures is considered to be freedom from governmental intrusion within one's own home, a warrantless search of a home is presumptively unreasonable and therefore unconstitutional. Accordingly, the Supreme Court has held that police officers may not park outside a house and use a thermal imaging device to ascertain whether high-intensity lamps are being used inside to grow marijuana plants (*Kyllo v. United States* 2001, 31). The police may not place a beeper in a private residence without first applying for and securing a warrant, because placing such a device inside a home constitutes "a threat to privacy interests in the home…." (*United States v. Karo* 1984, 716). Moreover, because the "curtilage" surrounding a house is subject to the same privacy protection as the house itself, the police may not stand on the porch of a house with a narcotics-sniffing dog in order to detect possible narcotics activity inside the house (*Florida v. Jardines* 2013, 1413). On the other hand, the "curtilage" concept does not extend into the navigable airspace over a house. The police may operate an aircraft at 1000 feet over a house in order to see whether marijuana plants are growing in the backyard, even if the backyard is protected by a high fence (*California v. Ciraolo* 1986, 210). The rationale is that there is no valid expectation of privacy with respect to aerial observation of open-air activity, regardless of where it takes place.

Similarly, a high level of Fourth Amendment protection applies to a police entry into a home to effect an arrest. Unless the police can point to exigent circumstances, a warrant is required before police officers may enter a home to make "a routine felony arrest" (*Payton v. New York* 1980, 591). Moreover, the gravity of the offense will govern the degree to which exigent circumstances will excuse a failure to obtain a warrant for entering a home to effect an arrest. Even when "exigent circumstances" are present, the police may not enter a suspect's home to make an arrest for a minor, noncriminal traffic offense if they do not have a warrant authorizing the entry. The Supreme Court has held that the state's interest in prosecuting minor offenses is too slight to overcome the presumption of unreasonableness that attaches to warrantless entries into a home. But if there are exigent circumstances at the level of imminent destruction of evidence, or hot pursuit of a fleeing felon, or immediate threats to the safety of the public or the officers, the police may make a warrantless entry into a home to make a felony arrest (*Welsh v. Wisconsin* 1984, 750–753).

Electronic surveillance and privacy

Fourth Amendment protection has gradually been held to extend to electronic communications outside the privacy of one's home. In a 1967 decision the Supreme Court considered whether the warrantless placing of a listening device on the outside of a public telephone booth to record the user's telephone calls violated the Fourth Amendment. Significantly, the court declared for the first time that "the Fourth Amendment protects people, not places." A concurring opinion held that a search governed by the Fourth Amendment is deemed to have occurred when government officers violate a person's "reasonable expectation of privacy" (*Katz v. United States* 1967, 360–362). The "reasonable expectation of privacy" approach, which often appears in subsequent Supreme Court cases, is inherently subject "to a degree of circularity" (*United States v. Jones* 2012, 962).

Some Supreme Court decisions have reflected a view that technological advances diminished a person's justified expectation of privacy. In 1983 the court held that the warrantless use of a "beeper" in a drum of chemicals to track the movement of the drum to a suspect's cabin did not transgress the Fourth Amendment. The court endorsed "augmenting the sensory facilities bestowed upon [the police]...with such enhancement as science and technology afforded them" (*United States v. Knotts* 1983, 282). Moreover, while *Katz* applies to communications by telephone, it does not apply to a pen register that only records the telephone numbers dialed from a telephone. The court reasoned that there is no reasonable expectation of privacy in the numbers dialed on a telephone because that information is voluntarily conveyed to telephone company personnel (*Smith v. Maryland* 1979, 739).

As technology has advanced further, however, the Supreme Court has increasingly found the Fourth Amendment's warrant clause to be applicable as a privacy protection. In 2012 the court considered whether government agents acting without a search warrant could install a GPS tracking device on the undercarriage of a car and track the vehicle's movements over the next 28 days. Employing divergent rationales, the court unanimously held that the installation and use of a GPS device to track a vehicle without prior judicial approval violated the Fourth Amendment. A number of the justices considered warrantless use of a GPS device to be a violation of individual privacy rights; others considered it to be a physical trespass upon property (*United States v. Jones* 2012).

Inevitably, police searches of cell phones have been the subject of a Fourth Amendment ruling. In 2014 the U.S. Supreme Court considered two cases in which police officers searched a "smartphone" and a "flip phone" post-arrest without a warrant. The prosecutors attempted to justify the warrantless searches of the seized phones as a permissible search incident to arrest that was necessary to prevent the destruction of evidence. However, noting "the immense storage capacity" of "modern cell phones" for personal and private information, the Supreme Court unanimously held that a warrantless search of a seized cell phone or smartphone is unreasonable (*Riley v. California* 2014, 2489). Among other things, it noted the inability of an arrested person to delete incriminating evidence from a properly secured cell phone that has been taken by the police. It did not credit prosecution fears of "remote wiping" of data from seized cell phones.

Case law is divided, thus far, as to whether there is a privacy interest in cell tower information that reveals the location of users of cell phones. Law enforcement is now able to use information from cell tower sites to track an individual's movements in real time on public roads and in private residences alike, as long as the individual is carrying a cell phone that is on. The Florida Supreme Court has suppressed evidence obtained by law enforcement officers who tracked a drug dealer through his cell phone usage without obtaining a warrant. Answering the question of whether Fourth Amendment privacy rights applied, the court held: "Requiring a cell phone user to turn off the cell phone just to assure privacy from governmental intrusion that can reveal a detailed and intimate picture of the user's life places an unreasonable burden on the user to forego necessary use of his cell phone, a device now considered essential by much of the populace" (*Tracey v. State* 2014, 523). Currently police departments and FBI agents are engaged in surreptitious warrantless use of devices that mimic a cell phone tower and provide the exact location of all cell phones using that tower, thereby sweeping up information about the cell phone usage and location not only of a suspect but also of every bystander using a cell phone in that vicinity. The constitutionality of this tactic has yet to be determined.

A significant amount of electronic surveillance in the form of eavesdropping on telephone calls is now regulated by statutes that generally require a warrant. In 1968 Congress passed a statute that specifically authorizes electronic eavesdropping and wiretapping of telephone calls by law enforcement officials, but only pursuant to a warrant based on probable cause (Omnibus Crime Control and Safe Streets Act 1968). The statute (which now applies to emails, text messages, and other electronic communications) requires several hurdles to be cleared before a warrant can be issued, such as demonstrating that other investigative methods have been tried and failed or reasonably appear unlikely to succeed. The statute contains exceptions to its warrant requirement for "an emergency situation" such as "conspiratorial activities threatening the national security interest." However, a warrant must be applied for within 48 hours after the eavesdropping begins, and if the application is not granted then the intercepted communications may be suppressed as a violation of the statute (Omnibus Crime Control and Safe Streets Act 1968). Although Congress did not explicitly authorize surreptitious break-ins into private premises to install and remove electronic listening devices, the Supreme Court has held that such authorization is implicit in the statutory authorization to wiretap (*Dalia v. United States* 1979, 247–255).

Subsequent statutes culminating in the 2001 Patriot Act have, ostensibly in the interest of national security, authorized warrantless electronic surveillance or surveillance supervised only by a secret court. In several pending criminal cases (e.g., *United States v. Mohamud* 2014), the defendants are challenging the constitutionality of the National Security Administration's indiscriminate "vacuuming" of domestic electronic communications where those communications appear to have led to the criminal prosecution. A Supreme Court ruling on whether the Fourth Amendment precludes mass interception of private communications is not likely for quite a few years after the publication date of this treatise.

Finally, the Fourth Amendment does not prevent "undercover" recording of conversations. Federal law enforcement officials, as well as law enforcement agents in most but not all of the states, are permitted to employ informants who unbeknownst to a suspect are "wired" to covertly record their telephone conversations without securing a warrant (*United States v. White* 1971, 750–754). Although the dissenting justices expressed concern about undermining "confidence and security in dealing with one another in individual relationships," the Supreme Court upheld the practice of secretly taping personal conversations. Its rationale is that an individual does not have a reasonable expectation of privacy in conversations with another person since that person may repeat from memory or from post-conversation notes what he or she has heard; therefore, a covert tape recording can be considered to be simply a memory aid. Instances of surreptitious electronic surveillance of forensic psychiatrists by patients have raised particular concerns regarding the erosion of trust in relationships that have traditionally depended on an expectation of privacy (Goldstein 1989).

Exceptions to the warrant requirement

As noted, the Supreme Court has deemed many types of warrantless arrests and searches to be permissible exceptions to the warrant clause of the Fourth Amendment. This is sometimes due to clearly exigent circumstances, but other times it rests on disputed premises about the actual needs of law enforcement. Moreover, when a warrant is not required, probable cause for a warrantless search is not invariably required (*Vernonia Sch. Dist. v. Acton* 1995, 653). The following categories of cases involve exceptions to the warrant and probable cause requirements. Some of these exceptions, such as the exception for "stop and frisk" searches by police officers, are applied in thousands of cases every year.

WARRANTLESS ARRESTS

In many circumstances officers may lawfully arrest an individual without an arrest warrant, provided that there is probable cause to believe that the person has committed or is committing a crime (*Gerstein v. Pugh* 1975, 111–114). Warrantless arrests are permitted for any felony offense that an officer has probable cause to believe a person has committed without regard to whether the officer was present when the felony occurred. Traditionally a law enforcement officer could only make a warrantless arrest for a misdemeanor if the misdemeanor was committed in the officer's presence. However, warrantless arrests for misdemeanors committed outside the presence of the arresting officer are now permitted by state statutes for an increasing number of misdemeanors and have not been held to violate the Fourth Amendment. In addition, as noted above, although a warrant is normally required to enter a dwelling to make an arrest, exigent circumstances can justify immediate entry into a dwelling to make a warrantless felony arrest.

After making a warrantless arrest, the arrested person must still be brought before a court for a judicial determination as to whether there was probable cause for the arrest. A delay of more than 48 hours between arrest and the court appearance can only be justified by "an emergency or some extraordinary circumstance" (*County of Riverside v. McLaughlin* 1991, 57).

INVESTIGATORY DETENTIONS ("STOP AND FRISK")

In *Terry v. Ohio* (1968) the Supreme Court held that "important government interests" can justify a brief investigatory police detention of a suspect on less than probable cause. If officers have "a reasonable, articulable suspicion" that someone is involved in criminal activity, they may stop him or her and question him or her briefly. They may also conduct a limited pat-down frisk for weapons if they reasonably believe that the individual poses a threat to the safety of the officers or others. If the brief investigative stop yields probable cause to believe that the stopped individual is engaging in criminal activity or has engaged in it, then arrest and prosecution can proceed without violating the Fourth Amendment. Not surprisingly, "*Terry* stops," often referred to with the phrase "stop and frisk," are a frequently used investigative method, one that is subject in a number of jurisdictions to issues of racially discriminatory deployment.

The grounds for upholding a claim of reasonable suspicion have been the subject of many decisions. A suspect's unprovoked flight upon seeing the police in an area of heavy narcotics trafficking can provide reasonable suspicion for an investigatory stop pursuant to *Terry* (*Illinois v. Wardlow* 2000, 124). However, an individual's simple presence in an area of expected criminal activity, standing alone, is not enough to support a reasonable, particularized suspicion that the person is committing a crime (*Illinois v. Wardlow* 2000, 124). While flight can provide reasonable suspicion, some courts have held that flight is not sufficient to find probable cause for an arrest. A lower court has held that "unprovoked flight, without more, cannot elevate reasonable suspicion to detain and investigate into the probable cause required for an arrest" (*United States v. Navedo* 2012, 474). Moreover, a number of state courts have declined to follow the U.S. Supreme Court's view that flight from police officers results in reasonable suspicion that criminal activity is afoot. For instance, the Tennessee Supreme Court has held that flight—even in areas of gang violence—is not sufficient grounds for an investigative stop (*State v. Nicholson* 2006, 661).

When reasonable suspicion is supported by police officer testimony, courts will not inquire whether the reason given by the police officer for a stop was pretextual. An automobile may be stopped where the police have probable cause to believe that a traffic violation has occurred, even if the actual motive of the police is to investigate drug activity (*Whren v. United States* 1996, 811–813).

The range of police activities permitted during an investigatory detention must be reasonably related to the circumstances that initially justified the detention (*United States v. Sharpe* 1985, 682). A state can require a suspect to disclose his or her name when a *Terry* stop has been made without violating either the Fourth or the Fifth Amendment

(*Hiibel v. Sixth Judicial Dist. Court of Nevada, Humboldt County* 2004, 187).

The involuntary transport of an individual to a police station for questioning is not considered to be a permissible "brief investigative stop" permitted under a *Terry* stop rationale (*Kaupp v. Texas* 2003, 630). Similarly, the police exceeded the limits of a "brief investigative stop" when they asked an airline passenger to accompany them to a small police room, retained his ticket and driver's license, and did not indicate that he was free to depart (*Florida v. Royer* 1983, 502–503). However, a 20-minute roadside stop does not fall outside the brevity requirement of *Terry* (*United States v. Sharpe*, 683). But, police officers who complete a stop of vehicle for a traffic infraction may not prolong the stop in order to investigate potential criminal activity unless there is a reasonable suspicion that a criminal offense is also occurring (*Rodriguez v. United States* 2015).

CONSENT SEARCHES

Government agents, without a warrant or probable cause, may conduct a search based on an individual's voluntary consent whether consent is express or implied (*Schneckloth v. Bustamonte* 1973, 219). The scope of a consent search may not exceed the scope of the consent given (*Florida v. Jimeno* 1991, 251).

A key issue for allegedly consented-to searches is voluntariness. Consent is not voluntary if given only because of a police officer's claim of lawful authority to conduct a search (*Bumper v. North Carolina* 1968, 548). Generally speaking, however, police officers may approach persons at random in most public places, ask them questions, and seek consent to a search. Even in a confined situation such as a bus or plane, a passenger's consent to a police officer's request to search his or her luggage is considered to be voluntary if "a reasonable person" would feel free to decline a police officer's request to search (*Florida v. Bostick* 1991, 436).

If there was an illegal arrest before consent is given, the subsequent consent to a search is generally invalid. In a 1983 case where the arresting officers lacked probable cause to make the arrest, the defendant's subsequent consent was "ineffective to justify the search" (*Florida v. Royer* 1983, 501–508).

Joint living arrangements have led to a complex body of law concerning the right of co-occupants of the same dwelling to give or withhold consent to a search. A co-tenant may validly give permission to a police officer to search jointly inhabited private premises when the other occupant is not present. The co-occupant may not subsequently object, because the co-occupant took the risk that his or her fellow occupant could admit visitors in his or her absence. However, when both occupants are present and one consents to the search while the other refuses to consent, the refusal to consent carries the day in order to protect the privacy interest in the home. The Supreme Court has held that a co-occupant's refusal to consent vitiates a search for which only one consent was obtained (*Georgia v. Randolph* 2006, 121–122). As the court observed, however, there is nothing to stop a consenting co-occupant from assisting the police in obtaining a search warrant and returning to the premises to conduct a court-authorized search.

SEARCHES INCIDENT TO A VALID ARREST

After making a valid arrest, police may conduct a warrantless search of the arrestee regardless of whether they have probable cause or reasonable suspicion to believe that the arrestee possesses weapons or prohibited substances or evidence pertaining to a crime (*New York v. Belton* 1981, 461). The rationale is the need to secure weapons that could be used to resist arrest or escape as well as the need to prevent the destruction of evidence. Generally, the scope of the permissible search incident to arrest is not limited to the arrestee's person but extends to the area within the arrestee's immediate control. A search incident to arrest is only valid if it follows the arrest; this exception "does not permit the police to search any citizen without a warrant or probable cause so long as an arrest immediately follows" (*Smith v. Ohio* 1990, 543). Nor does the issuance of a speeding citation, which does not involve an arrest, supply a basis for a search of the driver's car (*Knowles v. Iowa* 1998, 118).

Searches incident to the arrest of automobile occupants have been the subject of changing jurisprudence. The Supreme Court initially held that after arresting automobile occupants the police may search the passenger compartment of the automobile and any open or closed containers found therein without regard to the location of the arrested individual (*New York v. Belton* 1981, 460). This was intended to be a "bright line rule." However, in a 2009 case in which the arrested automobile occupants had been secured in patrol cars before their car was searched, a majority of the court held that the police officers could not search the vehicle because there was no valid concern about securing weapons or preventing escape. As a result, after arresting an automobile occupant, law enforcement may search the passenger compartment of a car "only when the arrestee is unsecured and within reaching distance of the passenger compartment at the time of the search" (*Arizona v. Gant* 2009, 343).

When individuals are arrested in a home, the police may search not only the area within the arrestee's immediate control, but also may search for weapons and confederates in "closed closets and other spaces immediately adjacent to the place of arrest from which an attack could be immediately launched." Since an arrest warrant only authorizes the seizure of the arrested person, after an in-home arrest the police may conduct a "protective sweep" beyond the spaces immediately adjacent to the arrest only if they have a "reasonable belief based on specific and articulable facts that the area to be swept harbors an individual posing a danger to those on the arrest scene" (*Maryland v. Buie* 1990, 334, 337). The protective sweep involves only a cursory inspection of those spaces where a person may be found and may last no longer than reasonably necessary to dispel a reasonable suspicion of danger (*Thompson v. Louisiana* 1984, 21–23). Items in plain view may be seized during a protective sweep.

SEIZURE OF ITEMS IN PLAIN VIEW

Whether or not a protective sweep is involved, police may seize evidence that is in plain view without a warrant, provided that (1) they did not violate the Fourth Amendment in arriving at the place from which the evidence can be plainly viewed; (2) the searching officer has a lawful right of access to the evidence itself; and (3) the incriminating character of the evidence seized is immediately apparent (*Horton v. California* 1990, 136–137). To establish the incriminating character of an item, police must show that on examining that which is already exposed to view, they have probable cause to believe that it is evidence or contraband; a reasonable suspicion that an object might be contraband is not sufficient (*Arizona v. Hicks* 1987, 328). The court has expanded the plain view doctrine to include items discernible by plain touch in a pat-down search, such as a weapon that bulges under a coat, but not items whose character cannot be determined on plain touch but only by squeezing and sliding them after touching them (*Minnesota v. Dickerson* 1993, 378).

EXIGENT CIRCUMSTANCES

Government agents may conduct a warrantless search or seizure when probable cause exists and exigent circumstances justify proceeding without a warrant. Exigent circumstances exist when evidence is in imminent danger of destruction (*Cupp v. Murphy* 1973, 296); the safety of law enforcement officers or others is threatened (*Warden, Md. Penitentiary v. Hayden* 1967, 298–299); the police are in hot pursuit of a suspect, whether on public streets or into a private dwelling (*United States v. Santana* 1976, 42); or a suspect is likely to flee before the pursuing officer can obtain a warrant (*Minnesota v. Olson* 1990, 100).

VEHICLE SEARCHES

Police are not required to obtain a warrant to search an automobile but must have probable cause to believe that the vehicle contains contraband or evidence of criminal activity. The inherent mobility of vehicles, including when parked and unoccupied, creates exigent circumstances that generally make obtaining a warrant impractical (*Pennsylvania v. Labron* 1996, 940). However, when a car is parked and the suspect has already been arrested and is therefore unable to gain access to the automobile, the normal mobility of an automobile is deemed absent, and a warrant to search the car is required (*Coolidge v. New Hampshire* 1971, 460–461).

CONTAINER SEARCHES

The use of a closed or locked container does not create a reasonable expectation of privacy where probable cause to search it otherwise exists. When there is probable cause to believe that a vehicle contains contraband, the entire vehicle, including any closed containers within it, may be searched without a warrant (*Wyoming v. Houghton* 1999, 302). Upon making an arrest, police may examine the contents of any container within the arrestee's reach (*New York v. Belton* 1981, 460). No warrant is necessary to search the contents of trash receptacles left for collection (*California v. Greenwood* 1988, 40–42).

INVENTORY SEARCHES

The police may conduct a warrantless search of property of which they have lawfully taken custody to prepare an inventory, according to standardized criteria, for the purposes of (1) protecting the owner's property; (2) protecting the police against claims of lost or stolen property; or (3) protecting the police from potential danger (*S. Dakota v. Opperman* 1976, 369). An inventory search of a vehicle lawfully in police custody—including a search of the passenger compartment, glove compartment, trunk, and any containers in the vehicle—is considered reasonable under the first clause of the Fourth Amendment and therefore does not require a warrant (*Colorado v. Bertine* 1987, 371–372). This is so even if the vehicle has been impounded for nothing more than parking violations (*South Dakota v. Opperman* 1976, 369). However, a supposed inventory search will not be upheld if it is "a ruse for a general rummaging in order to discover incriminating evidence" (*Florida v. Wells* 1990, 4).

BORDER SEARCHES

The Fourth Amendment is virtually inapplicable at any international border. Routine border stops and searches of persons, luggage, personal effects, and vehicles may be conducted at the border or at its "functional equivalent" (e.g., an inland international gateway airport) without reasonably articulable suspicion, let alone probable cause (*United States v. Montoya de Hernandez* 1985, 538). The government may also conduct warrantless searches for illegal aliens at the border (*United States v. Martinez-Fuerte* 1976, 556–562). However, at points removed from the border the Fourth Amendment requires probable cause before border patrol agents may search vehicles (*Almeida-Sanchez v. United States* 1973, 269). On the other hand, a roving border patrol may stop a vehicle in the general area of the border and question its occupants if "specific, articulable facts" give rise to reasonable suspicion that the vehicle may contain illegal aliens, whereupon information uncovered in the stop can provide probable cause for arrest (*United States v. Brignoni-Ponce* 1975, 881).

When a border patrol agent stops a car away from the border, "apparent Mexican ancestry of the occupants of the car, standing alone, is not reasonable grounds for concluding that the occupants of the vehicle are illegal aliens" (*United States v. Brignoni-Ponce* 1975, 885–886). However, at a border or at an established checkpoint apparent Mexican ancestry by itself is a basis for diverting individuals for questioning and for searches of vehicles and personal property (*United States v. Martinez-Fuerta* 1976, 563).

The foregoing cases date from the 1970s and 1980s. More recently a lower federal court has decided that because of the growth of the Hispanic population, Hispanic appearance cannot be considered at all when a police officer claims to have had reasonable suspicion that illegal activity is taking place (*United States v. Montero-Camargo* 2000, 1135). A lower federal court has also held that notwithstanding "the specter of 9/11," the Arab ethnicity and Arabic conversations of two airplane passengers could not be considered in determining whether there was probable cause to detain them as potential terrorists (*Farag v. United States* 2008, 460–468).

OTHER WARRANTLESS SEARCHES

Warrantless searches of businesses that are "pervasively regulated" because of public safety concerns are permitted where (1) there is a substantial state interest behind the regulatory scheme; (2) the search is necessary to further that scheme; and (3) the authorizing statute is an adequate substitute for the warrant requirement in giving notice to owners and limiting the discretion of those conducting the search. Moreover, government regulation can itself reduce an individual's reasonable expectation of privacy. For example, the court has held that an automotive junk dealer, who was required by statute to keep a record for police inspection of all automobiles and parts in his possession, had a reduced expectation of privacy in his business and could not have a Fourth Amendment objection to a warrantless (or suspicionless) search of his junkyard (*New York v. Burger* 1987, 702–711). Similarly, federally licensed gun dealers are subject to warrantless searches: "[w]hen a dealer chooses to engage in this pervasively regulated business and to accept a federal license, he does so with the knowledge that his business records, firearms, and ammunition will be subject to effective inspection" (*United States v. Biswell* 1972, 316). However, where an industry such as the hotel industry is not pervasively regulated, a warrantless search is impermissible. Obtaining evidence from a commercial concern that is not so regulated requires either a subpoena, that can be objected to before the compliance date, or a court-approved search warrant (*City of Los Angeles v. Patel* 2015).

Where a state program serves "special needs...beyond the normal need for law enforcement," the state may dispense with the warrant and probable cause requirements and have its searches judged solely by the reasonableness standard (*Chandler v. Miller* 1997, 314). For example, the Supreme Court has upheld warrantless random drug testing as justified by the special needs of public safety in the employment context (*Nat'l Treasury Employees Union v. Von Raab* 1989, 664; *Skinnery v. Ry. Labor Executives' Ass'n* 1989, 626–634). It has upheld warrantless searches of the offices or persons of public employees based on "reasonableness" rather than probable cause (*O'Connor v. Ortega* 1987, 713–714). It has upheld warrantless drug testing of public school students and warrantless searches of students by school authorities based on reasonableness rather than probable cause (*New Jersey v. T.L.O.* 1985, 341–342; *Vernonia Sch. Dist. 47J v. Acton* 1995, 653). It has also upheld warrantless searches of the homes of probationers and parolees on the premise that probationers only have conditional liberty and therefore reduced privacy expectations (*Griffin v. Wisconsin* 1987, 875–880).

THE FIFTH AMENDMENT, COERCED CONFESSIONS, AND OTHER SELF-INCRIMINATION ISSUES

The Fifth Amendment provides (in relevant part): "No person...shall be compelled in any criminal case to be a witness against himself." Police interrogation of a suspect in custody threatens the exercise of this Fifth Amendment privilege because the "inherently coercive" environment created by custodial interrogation can extract admissions against interest. For many years the courts focused simply on the voluntariness of in-custody confessions. However, as a result of "the coercion inherent in custodial interrogation" the Supreme Court's decision in *Miranda v. Arizona* (1968, 442, 479) laid down "concrete constitutional guidelines for law enforcement agencies and courts to follow" at the outset of interrogations. The police must warn a suspect "prior to any questioning" that "he has the right to remain silent, that anything he says can be used against him in a court of law, that he has the right to the presence of an attorney, and that if he cannot afford an attorney one will be appointed for him prior to any questioning if he so desires." As the court recently observed in an opinion reaffirming *Miranda*, "*Miranda* has become embedded in routine police practice to the point where the warnings have become part of our national culture" (*Dickerson v. United States* 2000, 430). Failure to give the *Miranda* warnings will result in the suppression of the un-warned statements in a prosecutor's case in chief under the "exclusionary rule" (discussed *infra*).

Miranda warnings are only required where a suspect is both in custody and subject to interrogation (*Illinois v. Perkins* 1990, 297). A number of Supreme Court rulings concerning these two requirements have circumscribed the application of *Miranda* fairly tightly.

Whether a suspect is in custody for purposes of *Miranda* warnings depends on the "objective circumstances," not on the subjective views of the interrogating officers or the person being interrogated (*Stansbury v. California* 1994, 321). A suspect is in custody if there is either a formal arrest or a restraint of movement to the degree associated with formal arrest. Outside the arrest context, however, the Supreme Court has held that custody "is a term of art" that applies only if there is a serious danger of coercion. In a number of situations involving questioning by law enforcement authorities, the court has held that the suspect was not in custody, and hence no warnings were required before incriminating statements could be sought. A prisoner moved to a prison conference room for questioning by detectives about an unrelated crime was not in custody for *Miranda* purposes because he had been told that he was free to return to his cell (*Howes v. Fields* 2012, 1189). Similarly, *Miranda* warnings were not required when an imprisoned suspect made incriminating statements to an undercover agent whom the suspect believed to be a cellmate, because the "essential ingredients" of a "police-dominated atmosphere" and "compulsion" were not present (*Illinois v. Perkins* 1990, 296–300). A routine meeting between an individual and a probation officer does not constitute custody (*Minnesota v. Murphy* 1984, 429–434). Nor does "informal" detention of a suspect during the execution of a search warrant or detention pursuant to a routine traffic stop constitute custody that requires prequestioning warnings (*Michigan v. Summers* 1981, 702; *Berkemer v. McCarty* 1984, 422).

The Supreme Court has defined interrogation for purposes of *Miranda* warnings as "words or actions on the part of the police…that the police should know are reasonably likely to elicit an incriminating response from the suspect" (*Rhode Island v. Innis* 1980, 301). In addition to express questioning, other tactics such as "psychological ploys" designed to elicit incriminating responses may amount to interrogation (*Arizona v. Mauro* 1987, 526). A court-ordered psychiatric examination of an in-custody defendant constitutes an interrogation that may not be the subject of testimony absent *Miranda* warnings (*Estelle v. Smith* 1981, 462–463). In some situations, evidence obtained through a *Miranda* violation is nonetheless admissible. For example, the court held that testimonial evidence obtained from a suspect interrogated in custody was admissible despite the failure to give *Miranda* warnings because a threat to public safety had necessitated immediate police action (*New York v. Quarles* 1984, 654).

Silence during interrogation is not sufficient to invoke the right to remain silent; that right must be invoked unambiguously. However, a waiver of the right to remain silent need not be express; a waiver of the right to remain silent may be inferred from circumstances. For instance, if a suspect in custody receives the required warnings, remains silent for a period of time, and then elects to answer questions, it is "presumed" that the suspect understood his or her rights and "made a deliberate choice to relinquish the protection those rights afford" (*Berghuis v. Thompkins* 2010, 381, 385). Moreover, officers are not required to clarify an ambiguous request for counsel. The court has found a valid waiver of the right against compulsory self-incrimination where the defendant initially waived his right to counsel and then, during questioning, said: "Maybe I should talk to a lawyer." The court held that this statement was not sufficiently clear to alert a reasonable police officer that the suspect was in fact requesting an attorney (*Davis v. United States* 1994, 459).

There are limits on police ability to secure a waiver of *Miranda* protections. Once an individual clearly invokes the right to have an attorney, police officers may not later approach him or her, re-warn him or her, and subject him or her to further interrogation, unless that individual himself or herself initiates further exchanges or conversations with the authorities (*Edwards v. Arizona* 1981, 484–485). However, this prophylactic rule does not apply if there has been a break in custody of at least 14 days before the police again seek to question the suspect. The rationale is that the person has not been isolated in police custody for that time frame; hence, the coercive effect of custody is considered to have worn off (*Maryland v. Shatzer* 2010, 110).

Moreover, the "question first, warn later" strategy used by many police departments to induce suspects to waive the right to remain silent has been held to be an unconstitutional method of securing a waiver of Fifth Amendment rights. Many police departments have been trained to question a suspect first, then give the *Miranda* warnings, then repeat the same questions while playing on the idea that the suspect has already told them everything. The Supreme Court has held this ploy to be unconstitutional because its patent objective "is to render *Miranda* warnings ineffective by waiting for a particularly opportune time to give them, after the suspect has already confessed" (*Missouri v. Seibert* 2004, 611).

Even though a defendant has invoked his or her right to counsel and a lawyer has been appointed to represent the defendant on a charged offense, if he or she is no longer in custody the police may interrogate him or her about another suspected offense, even a factually related one, provided *Miranda* warnings are administered again (*Texas v. Cobb* 2001, 173).

Voluntariness remains a Fifth Amendment issue post-*Miranda*. Whether a confession is voluntary depends entirely on the presence or absence of coercive police activity, not on a defendant's mental condition. Thus, the fact that a suspect was a chronic schizophrenic who—after receiving *Miranda* warnings—confessed while in an acute psychotic state following a divine command hallucination, did not invalidate his confession to murder charges. The court reasoned that *Miranda* protects defendants against government coercion leading them to surrender rights protected by the Fifth Amendment; it goes no further than that. It commented: "[The defendant's] perception of coercion flowing from the 'voice of God', however important or significant such a perception may be in other disciplines, is a matter to which the United States constitution does not speak" (*Colorado v. Connelly* 1986, 169–171). Thus, absent evidence of police coercion, the confession of a severely mentally ill suspect, however unreliable it may otherwise appear to be, is constitutionally valid once *Miranda* rights are waived.

The Fifth Amendment applies only to testimony; it does not protect a suspect from being compelled to submit to "fingerprinting, photographing, or measurements, to write or speak for identification, to appear in court, to stand, to assume a stance, to walk, or to make a particular gesture" (*Pennsylvania v. Muniz* 1990, 591). Even though the act may provide incriminating evidence, a suspect may be compelled to put on clothing (*Holt v. United States* 1910, 252–253); to provide a blood sample (*Schmerber v. California* 1966, 765); and to provide a handwriting exemplar or a voice exemplar (*Gilbert v. California* 1967, 266; *United States v. Wade* 1967, 222–223).

THE SIXTH AMENDMENT RIGHT TO COUNSEL: EYEWITNESS IDENTIFICATIONS; COUNSEL OF ONE'S CHOICE

The Sixth Amendment provides (in relevant part): "in all criminal prosecutions, the accused shall enjoy the right …

to have the Assistance of Counsel for his defense." However, the amendment does not specify the stages of a criminal case to which the right to counsel applies.

Criminal defendants who are required to appear in pretrial lineups and show-ups have a constitutional right to have legal counsel attend. In *United States v. Wade*, the court held that a post-indictment, pretrial lineup is a "critical stage" of a criminal proceeding where the defendant has the right to be represented because of "the innumerable dangers" involved in eyewitness identifications (*United States v. Wade* 1967, 224). The court recognized that:

> the vagaries of eyewitness identification are well-known; the annals of criminal law are rife with instances of mistaken identification. Mr. Justice Frankfurter once said: "What is the worth of identification testimony even when uncontradicted? The identification of strangers is proverbially untrustworthy. The hazards of such testimony are established by a formidable number of instances in the records of English and American trials. These instances are recent—not due to the brutalities of ancient criminal procedure. (*United States v. Wade* 1967, 228)

Due to the dangers of subtle and not-so-subtle suggestion during lineup procedures, the court held that counsel's presence at a post-indictment, pretrial lineup was constitutionally required. Nevertheless, the court declined to hold that a failure to have counsel present at a lineup automatically required exclusion of the identification of the defendant at trial by the witnesses who had earlier identified him at the lineup. The witness' courtroom identification of the defendant would still be admissible if the government "could establish by clear and convincing evidence that the in-court identifications were based upon observations of the suspect other than the lineup identification" (*United States v. Wade* 1967, 240).

When suggestive elements in an uncounseled identification procedure made it "all but inevitable" that an eyewitness would identify the defendant, a subsequent in-court identification was suppressed (*Foster v. California* 1969, 443). But when a trial court in a subsequent case found that a witness's courtroom identification rested on "an independent recollection of her initial encounter with the assailant, uninfluenced by the pretrial identifications," the Supreme Court held that failure to have counsel present at a post-arrest lineup did not preclude courtroom testimony identifying the defendant (*United States v. Crews* 1980, 473).

Although there have been recent efforts to demonstrate the unreliability of eyewitness identifications, the court has held that trial judges are not required to prescreen eyewitness evidence for reliability merely because a pretrial identification is made under suggestive circumstances (*Perry v. New Hampshire* 2012, 725).

The right to counsel established in *Wade* does not apply when a witness identifies a defendant following the arrest of that defendant and prior to the actual commencement of criminal proceedings without counsel present. This is so even though the identification procedure immediately post-arrest may be just as suggestive as one post-indictment (*Kirby v. Illinois* 1972, 689–690).

Other forms of post-arrest police contact with an individual who has counsel may violate the Sixth Amendment. Police officers may not use an informant to seek information or statements from a counseled defendant about the case for which the defendant has counsel (*Massiah v. United States* 1964, 204–206; *Maine v. Moulton* 1985, 176). But the right to counsel is not violated if the police use an informant to obtain information about another offense for which no charges have been filed (*Illinois v. Perkins* 1990, 299).

Another area of Sixth Amendment controversy concerns the right to counsel when a defendant's only source of funds for paying a lawyer is the proceeds of the alleged criminal activity. Many criminal statutes provide for forfeiture of funds derived from criminal activity. In 1989 the Supreme Court held that such funds may be forfeited at the outset of a case even if the forfeiture prevents a defendant from hiring counsel of his or her choice and remits him or her to a court-appointed attorney. The court stated that the Sixth Amendment right to "Assistance of Counsel" guarantees defendants in criminal cases "the right to adequate representation, but those who do not have the means to hire their own lawyers have no cognizable complaint so long as they are adequately represented by attorneys appointed by the courts" (*Caplin and Drysdale, Chartered v. United States* 1989, 624). As long as there is probable cause to believe that a defendant's assets are forfeitable, they may be frozen by court order as soon as he or she is charged (*United States v. Monsanto* 1989, 611–614). Moreover, if a court is concerned that a defendant's counsel has or may have a conflict of interest, the court may reject a defendant's proposed waiver of the conflict of interest and deny the defendant his or her choice of counsel (*Wheat v. United States* 1988, 163).

Exclusionary rule

As a presumed deterrent to government violations of the Constitution, a judicially crafted exclusionary rule provides that evidence obtained through most (not all) violations of the Fourth, Fifth, or Sixth Amendments cannot be used by the prosecution in a criminal trial. Not only is evidence seized in violation of the Fourth Amendment excluded from use at trial; evidence that is later obtained by exploitation of a Fourth Amendment violation is also excluded (*Wong Sun v. United States* 1963, 488). Statements obtained during in-custody interrogation without *Miranda* warnings are also inadmissible in a prosecutor's principal evidence at trial. However, if a suspect is interrogated without *Miranda* warnings and the un-warned statements lead the police to other evidence, that evidence is not subject to exclusion even though the unconstitutionally obtained statements led to its discovery (*United States v. Patane* 2004, 637).

There are numerous exceptions to this exclusionary rule. These are generally based on a precept that exclusion of evidence in certain contexts would not be a strong deterrent to the constitutional violation at issue. For instance, confessions obtained in violation of *Miranda* may be used to cross-examine a defendant who elects to testify. Because the principal need for a confession is in a prosecutor's case in chief, "sufficient deterrence" is achieved by excluding unwarned confessions only from a prosecutor's direct case. The Supreme Court majority also expressed the view that un-warned confessions should be available for the purpose of avoiding "perjury" by testifying defendants (*Harris v. New York* 1971, 224–225). However, at least one state court, applying a state constitution, has ruled that an illegally obtained confession may not be used to cross-examine a testifying defendant in a criminal case (*State v. Santiago* 1971).

The court has also held that the government may use illegally obtained evidence to refresh a witness's memory (*United States v. Kusek* 1988, 949); at a defendant's sentencing hearing (*United States v. Nichols* 2006, 441); in grand jury proceedings (*United States v. Calandra* 1974, 349–354); in habeas corpus proceedings (*Stone v. Powell* 1976, 489–495); in civil deportation proceedings (*I.N.S. v. Lopez-Mendoza* 1984, 1042–1051); and in parole revocation proceedings (*Pennsylvania Bd. of Probation and Parole v. Scott* 1998, 363–369).

In *United States v. Leon* (1984, 920), decided in 1984, the Supreme Court added a "good faith exception" to the exclusionary rule. It held that evidence obtained through objective good faith reliance by law enforcement agents on a facially valid search warrant that is later found to lack probable cause need not be suppressed. The good faith exception also applies when police obtain evidence (1) in reliance on a warrant later found to be technically defective (*Massachusetts v. Sheppard* 1984, 991); (2) in reliance on a statute authorizing warrantless searches that is later declared unconstitutional (*Illinois v. Krull* 1987, 349–350); (3) in reliance on a police record that erroneously indicates the existence of an outstanding arrest warrant for an individual (*Arizona v. Evans* 1995, 13–16); or (4) in reliance on a mistaken but reasonable assumption that the conduct forming the basis for a *Terry* stop violated the law (*Heien v. North Carolina* 2014).

Furthermore, even when law enforcement conduct is held to be unconstitutional under newly announced doctrines, the exclusionary rule is only applied prospectively. The Supreme Court has held that "if the law enforcement officers reasonably believed in good faith that evidence they had seized was admissible at trial, the imperative of judicial integrity is not offended by the introduction into evidence of that material even if decisions subsequent to the search or seizure have broadened the exclusionary rule to encompass evidence seized in that manner." The court also observed that retroactive application of the exclusionary rule would not serve to deter predecision violations (*United States v. Peltier* 1975, 537, 541).

However, the good faith exception does not apply where a law enforcement agent does not have reasonable grounds for believing that a search or arrest warrant was properly issued (*United States v. Leon*, 922–923). The Supreme Court has specifically identified four situations where police reliance on a warrant is not objectively reasonable:

1. When the warrant was issued in reliance on a deliberately or recklessly false affidavit of a law enforcement agent (*Franks v. Delaware* 1978, 155–156)
2. When the magistrate issuing the warrant failed to act in a neutral and detached manner, e.g., by participating in the search after issuing the warrant (*Lo-Ji Sales, Inc. v. New York* 1979, 326–328)
3. When the warrant was based on an affidavit "so lacking in indicia of probable cause as to render official belief in its existence entirely unreasonable"
4. When the warrant was so facially deficient that an officer could not reasonably have believed it to be valid (*United States v. Leon* 1984, 923)

Another exception to the exclusionary rule is attenuation. A court may admit evidence that would not have been discovered but for official misconduct if the causal connection between the illegal conduct and the acquisition of the evidence is sufficiently attenuated to purge the evidence of its taint (*Wong Sun v. United States* 1963, 488). The Supreme Court has set forth three factors for courts to consider in determining whether the causal chain has been sufficiently attenuated: (1) the time elapsed between the illegality and the acquisition of the evidence; (2) the presence of intervening circumstances; and (3) the purpose and flagrancy of the official misconduct (*Brown v. Illinois* 1975, 603). Similarly, even if police engage in illegal activity, evidence is admissible if it is discovered through a source independent of the illegality, or if the evidence inevitably would have been discovered through independent, constitutional means (*Murray v. United States* 1988, 537).

Speedy trial rights

The constitutional contours of the Sixth Amendment right to a speedy trial are exceptionally vague. Many factors go into a balancing test. A 5-year delay was not a denial of the speedy trial right where the prosecution had adequate justification for some of the delay, the defendant acquiesced in more than 10 trial continuances and quite clearly did not want a speedy trial, and no prejudice from the 5-year delay could be identified (*Barker v. Wingo* 1972, 533–536). On the other hand, an 8-1/2 year delay in bringing a defendant to trial was too long where the government's "egregious persistence in failing to prosecute" for six of those years was responsible for the delay (*Doggett v. United States* 1992, 657).

When there is a speedy trial violation, the only remedy is dismissal of the charges. As a result, the speedy trial statutes that have been enacted to provide some specificity in this area contain many grounds for excusing trial delay. Of interest here is that most of the state speedy trial statutes, as well as the federal speedy trial statute, specifically sanction trial delay in order to permit a psychiatric examination as to competency.

REFERENCES

Almeida-Sanchez v. United States, 413 U.S. 266 (1973).
Arizona v. Evans, 514 U.S. 1 (1995).
Arizona v. Gant, 556 U.S. 332 (2009).
Arizona v. Hicks, 480 U.S. 321 (1987).
Arizona v. Mauro, 481 U.S. 520 (1987).
Barker v. Wingo, 407 U.S. 514 (1972).
Berghuis v. Thompkins, 560 U.S. 370 (2010).
Berkemer v. McCarty, 468 U.S. 420 (1984).
Brown v. Illinois, 422 U.S. 590 (1975).
Bumper v. North Carolina, 391 U.S. 543 (1968).
California v. Ciraolo, 476 U.S. 207 (1986).
California v. Greenwood, 486 U.S. 35 (1988).
Camara v. Mun. Court of City and Cnty. of San Francisco, 387 U.S. 523 (1967).
Caplin and Drysdale, Chartered v. United States, 491 U.S. 617 (1989).
Chandler v. Miller, 520 U.S. 305 (1997).
City of Los Angeles v. Patel, __ U.S. __, 135 S.Ct. 2443 (2015).
Colorado v. Bertine, 479 U.S. 367 (1987).
Colorado v. Connelly, 479 U.S. 157 (1986).
Coolidge v. New Hampshire, 403 U.S. 443 (1971).
County of Riverside v. McLaughlin, 500 U.S. 44 (1991).
Cupp v. Murphy, 412 U.S. 291 (1973).
Dalia v. United States, 441 U.S. 238 (1979).
Davis v. United States, 512 U.S. 452 (1994).
Dickerson v. United States, 530 U.S. 428 (2000).
Doggett v. United States, 505 U.S. 647 (1992).
Edwards v. Arizona, 451 U.S. 477 (1981).
Estelle v. Smith, 451 U.S. 454 (1981).
Farag v. United States, 587 F. Supp.2d 436 (E.D.N.Y. 2008).
Florida v. Bostick, 501 U.S. 429 (1991).
Florida v. Jardines, 133 S. Ct. 1409 (2013).
Florida v. Jimeno, 500 U.S. 248 (1991).
Florida v. Royer, 460 U.S. 491 (1983).
Florida v. Wells, 495 U.S. 1 (1990).
Foster v. California, 394 U.S. 440 (1969).
Franks v. Delaware, 438 U.S. 154 (1978).
Georgia v. Randolph, 547 U.S. 103 (2006).
Gerstein v. Pugh, 420 U.S. 103 (1975).
Gilbert v. California, 388 U.S. 263 (1967).
Goldstein RL. 1989. Spying on psychiatrists: Surreptitious surveillance of the forensic psychiatric examination by the patient himself. *Bulletin of the American Academy of Psychiatry and the Law* 17:367–372.
Griffin v. Wisconsin, 483 U.S. 868 (1987).
Harris v. New York, 401 U.S. 222 (1971).
Heien v. North Carolina, 135 S.Ct. 530 (2014).
Hiibel v. Sixth Judicial Dist. Court of Nevada, Humboldt Cnty., 542 U.S. 177 (2004).
Holt v. United States, 218 U.S. 245 (1910).
Horton v. California, 496 U.S. 128 (1990).
Howes v. Fields, 132 S. Ct. 1181 (2012).
Illinois v. Gates, 462 U.S. 213 (1983).
Illinois v. Krull, 480 U.S. 340 (1987).
Illinois v. Perkins, 496 U.S. 292 (1990).
Illinois v. Wardlow, 528 U.S. 119 (2000).
I.N.S. v. Lopez-Mendoza, 468 U.S. 1032 (1984).
Katz v. United States, 389 U.S. 347 (1967).
Kaupp v. Texas, 538 U.S. 626 (2003).
Kirby v. Illinois, 406 U.S. 682 (1972).
Knowles v. Iowa, 525 U.S. 113 (1998).
Kyllo v. United States, 533 U.S. 27 (2001).
Lo-Ji Sales, Inc. v. New York, 442 U.S. 319 (1979).
Maine v. Moulton, 474 U.S. 159 (1985).
Maryland v. Buie, 494 U.S. 325 (1990).
Maryland v. Shatzer, 559 U.S. 98 (2010).
Massachusetts v. Sheppard, 468 U.S. 981 (1984).
Massiah v. United States, 377 U.S. 201 (1964).
Michigan v. Summers, 452 U.S. 692 (1981).
Minnesota v. Dickerson, 508 U.S. 366 (1993).
Minnesota v. Murphy, 465 U.S. 420 (1984).
Minnesota v. Olson, 495 U.S. 91 (1990).
Miranda v. Arizona, 384 U.S. 436 (1968).
Missouri v. Seibert, 542 U.S. 600 (2004).
Murray v. United States, 487 U.S. 533 (1988).
Nat'l Treasury Employees Union v. Von Raab, 489 U.S. 656 (1989).
New Jersey v. T.L.O., 469 U.S. 325 (1985).
New York v. Belton, 453 U.S. 454 (1981).
New York v. Burger, 482 U.S. 691 (1987).
New York v. Quarles, 467 U.S. 649 (1984).
O'Connor v. Ortega, 480 U.S. 709 (1987).
Omnibus Crime Control and Safe Streets Act of 1968, Title III, codified at 18 U. S. C. §§ 2510-21.
Payton v. New York, 445 U.S. 573 (1980).
Pennsylvania Bd. of Probation and Parole v. Scott, 524 U.S. 357 (1998).
Pennsylvania v. Labron, 518 U.S. 938 (1996).
Pennsylvania v. Muniz, 496 U.S. 582 (1990).
Perry v. New Hampshire, 132 S. Ct. 716 (2012).
Rhode Island v. Innis, 446 U.S. 291 (1980).
Riley v. California, 134 S. Ct. 2473 (2014).
Rodriguez v. United States, __ U.S. __, 135 S. Ct. 1609 (2015).
S. Dakota v. Opperman, 428 U.S. 364 (1976).
Schmerber v. California, 384 U.S. 757 (1966).
Schneckloth v. Bustamonte, 412 U.S. 218 (1973).
Skinner v. Ry. Labor Executives' Ass'n, 489 U.S. 602 (1989).
Smith v. Maryland, 442 U.S. 735 (1979).
Smith v. Ohio, 494 U.S. 541 (1990).
Stansbury v. California, 511 U.S. 318 (1994).
State v. Nicholson, 188 S.W.3d 649 (Tenn. S. Ct. 2006).
State v. Santiago, 53 Haw. 254 (1971).
Stone v. Powell, 428 U.S. 465 (1976).
Terry v. Ohio, 392 U.S. 1 (1968).

Texas v. Cobb, 532 U.S. 162 (2001).
Thompson v. Louisiana, 469 U.S. 17 (1984).
Tracey v. State, 152 So.3rd 504 (2014).
United States v. Biswell, 406 U.S. 311 (1972).
United States v. Brignoni-Ponce, 422 U.S. 873 (1975).
United States v. Calandra, 414 U.S. 338 (1974).
United States v. Crews, 445 U.S. 463 (1980).
United States v. Jones, 132 S. Ct. 945 (2012).
United States v. Karo, 468 U.S. 705 (1984).
United States v. Knotts, 460 U.S. 276 (1983).
United States v. Kusek, 844 F.2d 942 (2d Cir. 1988).
United States v. Leon, 468 U.S. 897 (1984).
United States v. Martinez-Fuerte, 428 U.S. 543 (1976).
United States v. Mohamud, 2014 WL 2866749 (2014), appeal pending as of December 31, 2015.
United States v. Monsanto, 491 U.S. 600 (1989).
United States v. Montero-Camargo, 208 F.3d 1122 (9th Cir.), cert. denied, 531 U.S. 889 (2000).
United States v. Montoya de Hernandez, 473 U.S. 531 (1985).
United States v. Navedo, 694 F.3d 463 (3d Cir. 2012).
United States v. Nichols, 438 F.3d 437 (4th Cir. 2006).
United States v. Patane, 542 U.S. 630 (2004).
United States v. Peltier, 422 U.S. 531 (1975).
United States v. Robinson, 354 F.2d 109 (2d Cir. 1965), cert. denied, 384 U.S. 1024 (1966).
United States v. Santana, 427 U.S. 38 (1976).
United States v. Sharpe, 470 U.S. 675 (1985).
United States v. Wade, 388 U.S. 218 (1967).
United States v. White, 401 U.S. 475 (1971).
Vernonia Sch. Dist. 47J v. Acton, 515 U.S. 646 (1995).
Warden, Md. Penitentiary v. Hayden, 387 U.S. 294 (1967).
Weeks v. United States, 232 U.S. 383, 392, 393 (1914).
Welsh v. Wisconsin, 466 U.S. 740 (1984).
Wheat v. United States, 486 U.S. 153 (1988).
Whren v. United States, 517 U.S. 806 (1996).
Wong Sun v. United States, 371 U.S. 471, 488 (1963).
Wyoming v. Houghton, 526 U.S. 295 (1999).

95

Theories of legal punishment and contemporary trends in sentencing

ROBERT LLOYD GOLDSTEIN AND ROGER J. BERNSTEIN

Well, I thought that modern penology has abandoned that rehabilitation thing, and they—they no longer call prisons reformatories or—or whatever, and punishment is the criterion now. Deserved punishment for crime.

Justice Antonin Scalia, during oral argument (*Miller v. Alabama* 2012)

In its function, the power to punish is not essentially different from that of curing or educating.

Michel Foucault (1975)

INTRODUCTION

Since the dawn of civilization, the institution of punishment has existed in every society. Over the centuries, philosophers and legal scholars have struggled to clarify the relationship between punishment and justice and attempted to justify the practice on both moral and rational grounds. The broad purposes of the criminal law are to prevent certain undesirable conduct and thereby protect the interests of society; it is framed in terms of imposing punishment for undesirable conduct (Bedau and Kelly 2010). When punishment is imposed by English-speaking courts, it is referred to as *sentencing*. In criminal cases, the state is the complaining party, "the initiating and enforcing agent" (Murphy and Coleman 1990), in contrast to cases in private or civil law, in which individuals seek redress for harm. In criminal cases, the state views itself as the injured party and, in order to protect the public interest, may choose to prosecute crimes even in cases where the victim prefers not to press charges. A discussion of why certain classes of acts are criminalized in order to prevent seriously harmful conduct, whereas other acts, perhaps equally harmful, are regarded as the province of civil law (e.g., tort actions providing for the award of monetary damages), is beyond the scope of this chapter and has been analyzed elsewhere (Simons 2008).

According to Hart (1968), the shared conception of punishment is defined in terms of five elements:

1. It must involve pain or other consequences normally considered unpleasant (e.g., incarceration).
2. It must be for an offense against legal rules.
3. It must be of an actual or supposed offender for his or her offense.
4. It must be intentionally administered by human beings other than the offender.
5. It must be imposed and administered by an authority constituted by a legal system against which the offense is committed (Hart 1968).

A society may be said to have an *institution of legal punishment* if it satisfies three conditions: (1) a set of criminal laws; (2) a procedure for determining who shall be punished as a way of enforcing the laws; and (3) an authoritative social mechanism for imposing the punishment (Golding 1975).

There are a number of rival theories of punishment, each with its enthusiastic adherents and critics, namely, Retributivism, Deterrence, Incapacitation, and Rehabilitation. Courts imposing sentences rely on a combination of these traditions, sometimes choosing that objective most likely to be achieved.

RETRIBUTIVISM

As Justice Scalia asserted, the retributive theory of punishment justifies legal punishment as just punishment for moral desert. "[D]oing justice [is] punishing offenders for the crimes they commit" (Robinson and Darley 1997). The equation *justice = retribution* has become axiomatic: that justice is giving offenders what they deserve in consequence of their deserts (Moore 2010). "[N]owadays, retributivism has arguably taken the lead as *the* justification of punishment among academics and—maybe more importantly—policymakers, and punishment is acknowledged to be an inherently retributive process" (Materni 2013, 265).

Immanuel Kant is regarded as the Father of Retributivism, the first to set forth a systematic philosophical rationale for the practice. In 1797, Kant promulgated an *absolute* concept of justice, asserting that "the penal law is a *categorical imperative*." Kant's measure of justice is the *lex talionis* ("the eye for an eye" principle), meaning that lawful retaliation is that in which the correct punishment corresponds in kind and degree to the wrong suffered. In Kant's world, in every case in which a crime has been committed, punishment *must be imposed* and the punishment *must fit the crime*. Accordingly, "whoever has committed Murder must die" (Kant 1965, 102). Kant provides the following hypothetical to emphasize society's duty to exact retribution:

> Even if civil society were to dissolve itself by common agreement of all its members (for example, if the people inhabiting an island decided to separate and disperse themselves around the world), the last murderer remaining in prison must be executed, so that everyone will duly receive what his actions are worth and so that the bloodguilt thereof will not be fixed on the people because they failed to insist on carrying out the punishment; for if they fail to do so, they may be regarded as accomplices in this public violation of legal justice. (Kant 1965 [trans.], 102)

According to Kant, this equalizing standard (when offense and punishment stand in equal relationship to each other) balances the cosmic scale, restores the moral balance to equilibrium, and vindicates justice. Failure to punish the culprit is an *unthinkable violation* of the duty of justice, and Kant warns that "If legal justice perishes, then it is no longer worthwhile for men to remain on this earth" (1965, 100).

Retributivism is said to differ from mere revenge or vindictiveness, in that the latter are personal responses to criminal wrongdoing, sometimes of an extralegal nature. Retribution, on the other hand, is based on a respect for the law and on a "cluster of moral concepts: rights, desert, merit, moral responsibility, and justice" (Murphy and Coleman 1990, 121). Retributive punishment signifies a condemnatory attitude expressed toward the guilty offender: the criminal is an enemy of society and the imposition of punishment is, according to Lord Denning, "the emphatic denunciation by the community of a crime" (Hart 1968, 2).

Critics of retributivism contend that the inconvenient truth is, it is no more than vengeance in disguise—*public vengeance* at the hands of the state (Dolinko 1992). It may be true that satisfying the public desire for vengeance—calling it "justice" and establishing institutions to achieve such justice—may at bottom reflect our instinctual, atavistic drive for revenge. It has been argued that the instinct of an injured party to take revenge played a significant role in creating the customary norms in early societies and served as the foundation of norms that underlie the institutions of criminal and civil law of more complex societies (Elliott 1985). This line of reasoning is supported by hypotheses based on the findings of experimental and evolutionary psychologists that we as a species are "hardwired to react punitively to crime...and natural selection has favored human beings with that hardwiring...Individuals with clear senses of right and wrong and a willingness to act on them...are better community members, fostering cohesion, increasing the odds of community survival, and perpetuating the gene pool that predisposed people to be retributive" (Tonry 2011, 8).

DETERRENCE

The utilitarian penologists (in a tradition extending from Plato and Protagoras to Beccaria, Bentham, and Mill) view deterrence as the paramount justification for legal punishment. According to this theory of punishment, members of a society are deterred from the commission of proscribed acts because of the possible consequences (i.e., the threat of punishment or the execution of punishment) that the criminal law mandates. This is a *forward-looking* theory (as opposed to the *backward-looking* rationale for criminal punishment of Retributivism), which rests on the empirical premise that the threat of punishment or its actual imposition in a particular case serves as an effective deterrent to others. The evil of punishment is justified, therefore, because it leads to the greater overall good of society by preventing future criminal behavior. Plato stated the "classical" theory of deterrence around 2400 years ago:

> Punishment is not retribution for a past wrong. What has been done cannot be undone; it is for the sake of the future and to secure that both the person punished and those who see him punished may either learn to detest the crime utterly or at any rate to abate much of their old behavior. (Plato 1975 [trans.], 934)

According to the utilitarian approach of Bentham (1961), the chief end of punishment is *general deterrence*—that is, the imposition of punishment on the offender promotes the greater good of deterring other members of society from committing similar acts, thereby resulting in an overall reduction of crime. Bentham sets forth a cost–benefit analysis to decide which acts need to be criminalized and to calculate the optimal amount of punishment for specific offenses (in order to satisfy utilitarian considerations of promoting the overall safety and happiness of society, the common good shared among the greatest number), which is necessary to prevent criminal activity at the "cheapest rate possible" (Golding 1975). Bentham's calculus serves to arrive at a balance where overall social benefits outweigh social costs, resulting in a net social gain.

Specific Deterrence refers to a related aim of criminal punishment: to deter the criminal himself or herself (rather than to deter others) from committing future offenses. (It goes without saying that in the event the criminal is executed, the punishment would be absolutely effective in deterring him or her from the commission of future crimes.) This is the basis of a famous gallows humor quip in a cartoon depicting the prisoner addressing the hangman: "This is certainly going to be a lesson to me!" The effectiveness of general deterrence has never been proven and "[f]or many convicted offenders—maybe even for most—however, prison ends up being a 'school of specialization in crime,' and the prison door turns out to be a revolving door. Thus, current prison practice casts serious doubts on the personal deterrence effect of criminal punishment" (Materni 2013, 291). Unsurprisingly, Kant rejected the deterrence theory categorically: "Judicial punishment can never be used merely as a means to promote some other good for the criminal himself or for society, but instead it must in all cases be imposed on a person on the ground that he has committed a crime" (Kant 1965, 102).

INCAPACITATION AND REHABILITATION

When criminals are deprived of their liberty and are isolated from society, they lose the capacity to commit further crimes against society. The mainstay of the system, incarceration, *incapacitates* the offenders and, if nothing else, protects the public from the crimes they would commit were they free to do so. The protective efficacy of incapacitation seems obvious. However, it has been strenuously argued by some scholars (Robinson and Darley 1997) that moral desert should be the *sine qua non* for the infliction of criminal punishment on the offender. In other words, "[w]e *need* to practice incapacitation. But we also *need* a criminal justice system which punishes people *for having done 'something bad'*" (Materni 2013, 300). Adoption of a purely utilitarian approach, taken to its logical conclusions in order to protect society, poses the danger of a slippery slope of unlimited preventive detention (beyond the completion of their sentence) of all individuals considered to be at risk of committing future crimes. In this regard, we have already witnessed the continuing controversy generated by laws that enable the post-sentence preventive detention of "dangerous" sex offenders, which raises difficult constitutional and human rights issues. A discussion of this topic is well beyond the scope of this chapter and is analyzed elsewhere (Cucolo and Perlin 2013).

The final theory of punishment is Rehabilitation. Many commentators believe that there has been a loss of faith in the scientific and philosophical rationale for making rehabilitation the paramount goal of sentencing (Wilson 2013). Rehabilitation aims to offer the offender effective therapeutic attention that would enable him or her to lead a more productive and successful life and be able to safely re-enter society without continuing to pose a threat to the community. This approach is viewed with suspicion by some as a discredited paternalistic reform theory (Moore 2010); others reject it as an indiscriminate attempt to impose the psychiatric–medical model on a heterogeneous population of criminal offenders without regard for scientific, moral, or political considerations. The latter believe that the overwhelming consensus of research in this area has resulted in the undermining of virtually all of the enduring mythology regarding prior optimistic assessments of corrective efficacy (Walker 1991). However, the literature falls short of establishing that nothing works. "Nothing works" may be an overstatement. Compared to a recidivism rate of 50%–75% in the United States and Europe, the recidivism rate in Sweden, Denmark, and Finland is 30%, and only 20% in Norway (Hernu 2011). The Scandinavian model of rehabilitation (particularly in Norway) has shown promise. It has been described as promoting a "focus on human rights and respect" for inmates' dignity as human beings (Hernu 2011; W.W. 2011). Another promising success attained through rehabilitation programs, with a corresponding reduction in the recidivism rate, has been reported in India's prison system (Bedi 2007).

LEGISLATIVE AND JUDICIAL APPROACHES TO PUNISHMENT

The major theories of criminal sentencing have had varying levels of influence on legislators and judges, and empirical research has rarely played a significant role. Rehabilitation was a dominant penological goal from the late nineteenth century until the last quarter of the twentieth century. During this period the "indeterminate" model of criminal sentencing was dominant. In the last 30 years rehabilitation and indeterminate sentences have been abandoned, and crime prevention and incapacitation have dominated criminal justice policy. To meet these goals, there has been a sharp increase in the use of rigid sentencing formulas and very long prison sentences. Sentences of life imprisonment are now imposed for noncapital crimes such as trafficking substantial quantities of narcotics. At the same time, however, the U.S. Supreme Court has begun to ameliorate highly punitive sentences imposed on juveniles in capital and noncapital cases.

Transition from indeterminate sentencing to determinate sentences

The indeterminate model of criminal sentencing was adopted in many jurisdictions in the time period between 1870 and 1910, and prevailed throughout the United States by 1950. In indeterminate sentencing a judge imposes a sentence consisting of the range of years set forth in the applicable statute, e.g., 8 to 25 years. A parole board is given wide discretion to determine when, after the minimum time is served, the convicted person will be paroled from prison. Rehabilitation is the principal premise of indeterminate sentencing, and the parole board is supposed to be guided by "prisoner reformation" (*Dreyer v. State* 1902).

A variation of this model prevailed in the federal system until 1987. Prior to 1987 federal criminal statutes also authorized sentencing within a broad range of years, but gave federal judges wide discretion to determine a specific sentence anywhere within that range. As a result, judges could decide for themselves the goals to be sought in each sentence. Some federal judges focused on rehabilitation, while others focused on "just deserts." Under this system different offenders could receive widely varying sentences for substantially the same criminal offense. Yet after the length of a prison sentence was set by the federal judge, the U.S. Parole Commission still had discretion to release an offender at any time after the offender had served at least one-third of the sentence that was initially imposed (*Mistretta v. United States* 1989). As a result a large number of sentenced federal prisoners actually served no more than a third of the judicially imposed sentence.

Indeterminate sentencing remained prevalent until the 1970s or 1980s, depending on the jurisdiction. Beginning in the 1970s public attention to significantly elevated crime levels and increasing drug use led to a perception that the indeterminate sentencing model was too lenient. Congress concluded that federal judges exercised too much discretion in sentencing, resulting in unacceptable sentencing disparities for the same offense as well as in sentences that were considered unacceptably low. The result was a transition to a determinate sentencing model that took discretion away from federal judges and eliminated parole in the federal sentencing system. As a result, the U.S. Parole Commission could no longer determine the actual amount of time served following the imposition of sentence. Reductions in prison time for good behavior were also minimized. These changes were intended to achieve a "truth in sentencing" system for federal sentences in which prisoners served out the actual sentence that the court imposed (less a small allowance for good behavior). The theoretical justifications for abandoning indeterminate sentencing in favor of determinate sentences were grounded in the punitive ideologies of retribution, incapacitation, and/or just deserts, together with the general belief that indeterminate sentencing had failed to control crime (Doherty 2013).

To cabin judicial sentencing discretion, Congress enacted a "Sentencing Reform Act" in 1984 that became effective for crimes committed after November 1, 1987. Under this legislation all federal sentences are to be determined by "Sentencing Guidelines" that assign a numerical "base offense level" to each kind of offense. The offense level is increased on a systematic basis for more serious iterations of an offense to derive a "total offense level." In practice the determination of the seriousness of an offense in a nationwide court system could only be accomplished by using a quantitative measure for offense severity. Therefore, the length of federal sentences is governed almost entirely by quantitative measures, such as the overall quantity of drugs in a narcotics distribution operation or the total amount of money lost in a Ponzi scheme or investment fraud. The theory is that the quantitative characteristics of a crime are the best way to measure the crime's severity and reduce sentencing disparities.

Prior convictions also increase the severity of a sentence according to a table, with greater weight given to prior felonies than to prior misdemeanors. The premise is that a lengthier criminal history best identifies those offenders who are mostly likely to recidivate. In this system an offender's actual role in an offense, no matter how minimal, may lower the offense level only a small amount. As a result, a minor player in a large narcotics operation that imports large drug quantities can receive a prison sentence of 30 years or even life imprisonment despite the minor role.

Once the "total offense level" for a given case is computed and the defendant's criminal history is ascertained, a narrow sentencing range, often no more than 6 months, is determined by using a nationally applicable sentencing table. This is a grid on which the "total offense level" increases on the vertical axis and criminal history severity increases on the horizontal axis. The intersection of the total offense level and criminal history in this table determines the sentencing range, which is often as little as 6 months. The judge's role is limited to deciding what sentence to impose within this narrow range (U.S. Sentencing Commission 2015). Judges may depart from the grid-determined sentence and grant a lower or higher sentence only in highly atypical circumstances (e.g., significantly diminished mental capacity or very unusual family circumstances). In practice the principal method of obtaining a sentence lower than the mathematically determined one has been to provide accomplice testimony to assist the government in prosecuting other offenders.

As noted, Congress gave this highly determinate federal sentencing model the Orwellian title of "Sentencing Guidelines." In 2005 the Supreme Court, responding to widespread dissatisfaction with the rigidity of this system, found the "Sentencing Guidelines" to be unconstitutional and decreed the federal Sentencing Guidelines to be "advisory" instead of mandatory (*United States v. Booker* 2005). In practice, as of this writing there are relatively few federal judges who vary their sentences far from the narrow sentencing ranges that are mathematically prescribed in the "Guidelines."

Similar sentencing models based on a sentencing table that measures offense severity and prior criminal record quantitatively have been adopted in 21 states. Only in a few of these 21 states is the application of the sentencing table sentencing range mandatory. In most states the sentencing table result is advisory, and in some it indicates a presumptive sentence. In most of the states that employ a sentencing table the judges retain significantly more discretion than federal judges have under the federal Sentencing Guidelines.

Substantial increases in criminal penalties

Concurrently with the transition to determinate sentencing, federal—and state—prison sentences have increased sharply in length since the federal "Sentencing Guidelines" were adopted. The principal reason is the shift in sentencing objectives away from rehabilitation and toward punishment, deterrence, and incapacitation.

The "War on Drugs" commenced by President Nixon in 1971 began a series of increases in sentence length in narcotics cases that culminated in Congressional adoption of extremely long narcotics sentences in the 1980s. Under current law the maximum statutory penalty even for relatively small amounts of narcotics is a 20-year prison term. Larger quantities of narcotics (whether possessed by a defendant or only by co-conspirators) carry a mandatory minimum sentence of 10 years and a maximum sentence of life imprisonment. Prosecutors have discretion to double these mandatory minimum sentences for a second felony narcotics trafficking offense. At the same time, the offense levels in the Sentencing Guidelines for narcotics offenses were set so that they would be parallel to the major increase in the severity of statutory narcotics penalties. Under the Sentencing Guidelines the offense levels for major narcotics crimes can result in a life sentence or in a sentence that is decades long, with practically no discretion available to federal judges to depart from these sentencing outcomes.

States also increased sentences for narcotics offenses as part of the "War on Drugs." In New York, for example, the mandatory penalty for sale of more than 2 ounces of cocaine or heroin was set at 15 years to life in prison in 1973. The quantities of drugs sold in the United States did not diminish after narcotics sentences were lengthened.

The most dramatic illustration of the sharp increase in criminal penalties is contained in the 1994 Federal Death Penalty Act. This statute created 60 new death penalty offenses under 41 federal statutes. As a result, a federal death penalty is now authorized for offenses that were previously subject only to state law, such as murder for hire, fatal drive-by shootings, sexual abuse crimes resulting in death, car-jacking resulting in death, and certain crimes not generally resulting in death such as the running of a large-scale drug enterprise (Capital Punishment in Context 2015). In practice, federal prosecutors, who are often aware of the public's reservations about the death penalty, have almost never sought the death penalty under these statutes. These statutes are essentially irrelevant to the administration of the death penalty in practice.

Responding to a view that punishments for white-collar crime were too low, for example, the "offense levels" for financial crimes were calculated so that they can readily result in a prison sentence for offenses involving a loss no greater than $30,000. The offense levels for financial crimes will almost always result in a prison sentence for fraud or embezzlement offenses involving losses greater than $400,000.

Habitual offender statutes

The length of prison sentences has also been dramatically increased since the 1970s by the adoption of habitual offender provisions in many state and federal statutes. A prominent example is the "three strikes and you're out" law adopted by referendum in California in 1994. In California a third felony conviction for any type of crime will automatically result in a prison sentence of 25 years to life. Faced with overflowing prisons, California amended this statute in 2012 so that a third conviction does not result in an automatic 25-year-to-life sentence, unless the third conviction is for a "serious or violent" felony. However, in a number of instances prosecutors can manipulate this system by electing to charge virtually the same offense either as a misdemeanor or as a felony, with the result that a prosecutor can control whether or not the "three strikes" law will apply simply by making a different charging decision (*Ramirez v. Castro* 2004).

Some 25 other states have habitual offender statutes that can result in long automatic sentences for successive convictions. These laws vary from state to state, primarily with respect to the seriousness of the predicate offenses. Most other states have less draconian habitual offender provisions than California. For instance, in Maryland only violent felony convictions are considered, and an automatic sentence of life imprisonment is only imposed in the event of a fourth violent felony conviction. In the federal system, beginning in 1987, two felony convictions in unrelated cases involving either a crime of violence or a narcotics offense will result in "career offender" status. That status requires a sentence of no less than 15 years and as high as life imprisonment, depending on the severity of the third offense.

The proponents of "three strikes and you're out" laws contend that a potential offender who knows that another arrest and conviction will automatically result in imprisonment for 25 years to life will avoid committing another offense to avoid such punishment. Whether or not there has been any deterrent effect is, of course, extremely difficult for social science to ascertain. Proponents of these statutes take the view that recidivism is unavoidable and lengthy incapacitation is necessary, despite the well-established correlation between increased age and lower recidivism rates.

Reaction to current sentencing regimes

Beginning around 2010, the vastly increased expense of providing prisons for a burgeoning corrections population, and the resulting state budgetary strains, has caused some re-thinking of highly punitive criminal sentencing policies, primarily in the states. A number of states have repealed mandatory minimum sentences for narcotics crimes and have begun to emphasize rehabilitation as a method of reducing overall corrections spending. In New York, for example, legislation passed in 2005 eliminated maximum life sentences for most drug offenses and lowered mandatory minimum sentences. Mandatory minimum sentences for some narcotics offenses were removed in 2009 and nonincarceration treatment alternatives were authorized (New York Division of Criminal Justice 2014). This transition is still in its infancy. Although "mass incarceration" has become a subject of political discourse in the 2016 presidential election campaign, very little change has taken place at the federal level, where budgetary concerns are less immediate. The only shift so far at the federal level is a slight amelioration of the narcotics guidelines for nonviolent offenders, and an increased willingness to consider executive clemency for prisoners serving long sentences for nonviolent crimes (usually narcotics offenses).

Juvenile offender sentencing

A small group of ground-breaking Supreme Court cases that draw extensively on psychological research about juvenile brain development have begun to cause significant changes in juvenile sentencing policy. The decisions in these juvenile sentencing cases—which have been decided by only the narrowest majorities of the court—run counter to the punitive philosophy that currently dominates sentencing of adult offenders.

In 2005 the Supreme Court held that the Eighth Amendment prohibition against cruel and unusual punishment barred capital punishment for children who had committed a capital crime while younger than 18 years of age (*Roper v. Simpson* 2005). It noted that "a lack of maturity and an underdeveloped sense of responsibility are found in youth more often than in adults and are more understandable among the young. These qualities often result in impetuous and ill-considered actions and decisions." The court also observed that juveniles "are more vulnerable or susceptible to negative influences and outside pressures, including peer pressure." And the court pointed out that the United States was the only country in the world that still imposed the death penalty on juvenile offenders. For these reasons, among others, the court concluded that sentencing a juvenile offender to death violated the Eighth Amendment.

In 2008 the Supreme Court held that imposing the death penalty on an adult offender for a nonhomicide crime violates the Eighth Amendment (*Kennedy v. Louisiana* 2008). Two years later, the court ruled that the Eighth Amendment prohibits imposition of a sentence of life without parole on a juvenile offender who did not commit a homicide offense (*Graham v. Florida* 2010). The court rejected the notion that a juvenile offender could be deemed incorrigible and bound to recidivate. It noted: "It is difficult even for expert psychologists to differentiate between the juvenile offender whose crime reflects unfortunate yet transient immaturity, and the rare juvenile offender whose crime reflects irreparable corruption." And the court again noted the comparative immaturity of juvenile offenders. It stated that "developments in psychology and brain science continue to show fundamental differences between juvenile and adult minds"—for example, in "parts of the brain involved in behavior control."

In 2012 the Supreme Court held that a mandatory sentence of life imprisonment without parole could not be imposed on a juvenile who committed a capital offense (*Miller v. Alabama* 2012). The court's reasoning built on the prior cases. First, the court held that the same "developments in psychology and brain science" that it had cited in 2010 as showing lack of neurological development required it to recognize the diminished culpability of juveniles in homicide and nonhomicide offenses alike. It reiterated its earlier conclusion that "transient rashness, proclivity for risk, and inability to assess consequences—both lessened a child's 'moral culpability' and enhanced the prospect that, as the years go by and neurological development occurs, his deficiencies will be reformed." The court also observed that "[l]ife without parole forswears altogether the rehabilitative ideal." It held that "[i]mprisoning an offender until he dies alters the remainder of his life by a forfeiture that is irrevocable."

Although mandatory sentences of life without parole are now unconstitutional, courts retain discretion to impose a sentence as long as life without parole on a juvenile offender who commits a capital offense. But a judge or jury must now have the opportunity to consider mitigating circumstances, specifically including immaturity, before imposing the harshest possible penalty of a sentence of life without parole on a juvenile offender. A state must now provide a juvenile offender with "some meaningful opportunity to obtain release based on demonstrated maturity and rehabilitation." Unfortunately, the Supreme Court has not yet decided whether this precept requires reconsideration at some later point (by either a parole board or a court) of a discretionary decision to sentence a juvenile offender to life imprisonment without parole.

There are thousands of juvenile offenders in the United States who are currently serving a sentence imposed of life without any possibility of parole (Amnesty International 2005; The Sentencing Project 2014). To date some state courts have held that retroactivity requires re-sentencing of juveniles who are serving a life sentence without parole (*Jones v. State* 2013; *Falcon v. State* 2015). Other states have rejected retroactive re-sentencing of juvenile offenders who have been earlier sentenced to life imprisonment without parole (*People v. Carp* 2014). A number of states have enacted laws requiring that sentences of not less than 25 years, 35 years, or even 40 years without parole be imposed on juvenile offenders in homicide cases. A lengthy minimum sentence without parole for a crime committed while a juvenile is arguably unconstitutional because of the psychological immaturity of juvenile offenders that the Supreme Court has now recognized.

REFERENCES

Amnesty International and Human Rights Watch. 2005. *The Rest of Their Lives: Life without Parole for Child Offenders in the United States*. New York: Amnesty International and Human Rights Watch.

Bedau HA and E Kelly. 2010. *Punishment, The Stanford Encyclopedia of Philosophy*. http://plato.stanford.edu/archives/spr2010/entries/punishment, accessed December 8, 2012.

Bedi K. 2007. *It's Always Possible: One Woman's Transformation of India's Prison System*. Lanham, MD: Himalayan Press.

Bentham J. 1961. *An Introduction to the Principles of Morals and Legislation*. New York: Hafner.

Capital Punishment in Context. http://www.capitalpunishmentincontext.org/issues/expansion, accessed July 2015.

Cucolo HE and ML Perlin. 2013. "They're planting stories in the press": The impact of media distortions on sex offender law and policy. *University of Denver Criminal Law Review* 3:185–246.

Doherty F. 2013. Indeterminate sentencing returns: The intention of supervised release. *New York University Law Review* 88:976–990.

Dolinko D. 1992. Three mistakes of retributivism. *University of California, Los Angeles Law Review* 39:1623–1655.

Dreyer v. State, 187 U.S. 71, 79 (1902).

Elliott ED. 1985. The evolutionary tradition of jurisprudence. *Columbia Law Review* 85:38–97.

Falcon v. State, 162 So.3d 954, 962 (Fla. 2015).

Foucault M. 1975. *Discipline and Punish: The Birth of the Prison*. New York: Random House.

Golding MP. 1975. *Philosophy of Law*. Englewood Cliffs, NJ: Prentice Hall.

Graham v. Florida, 560 U.S. 48 (2010).

Hart HLA.1968. *Punishment and Responsibility*. Oxford: Oxford University Press.

Hernu P. 2011. Norway's controversial 'Cushy Prison' experiment—Could It catch on in the U.K.? *Daily Mail* July 25.

Jones v. State, 122 So.3d 698 (Miss. 2013).

Kant I. 1965 [trans.]. *Metaphysical Elements of Justice*. Indianapolis, IN: Bobbs-Merrill.

Kennedy v. Louisiana, 554 U.S. 407 (2008).

Materni MC. 2013. Criminal punishment and the pursuit of justice. *British Journal of American Legal Studies* 2:263–304.

Miller v. Alabama, 132 S.Ct. 2455 (2012).

Mistretta v. United States, 488 U.S. 361, 363 (1989).

Moore MS. 2010. *Placing Blame: A Theory of the Criminal Law*. Oxford: Oxford University Press.

Murphy JG and JL Coleman. 1990. *Philosophy of Law: An Introduction to Jurisprudence*. Boulder, CO: Westview Press.

New York Division of Criminal Justice Services. 2014. *Criminal Justice Update*. New York: Division of Criminal Justice Services.

People v. Carp, 496 Mich. 440, 469-475 (Mich. 2014).

Plato. 1975 [trans.]. *The Laws*, TJ Saunders, trans. Aylesbury, England: Penguin Books.

Ramirez v. Castro, 365 F.3d 755 (9th Cir. 2004).

Robinson PH and JM Darley. 1997. The utility of desert. *Northwestern University Law Review* 453:453–498.

Roper v. Simpson, 543 U.S. 551 (2005).

Simons KW. 2008. The crime/tort distinction: Legal doctrines and normative perspectives. *Widener Law Journal* 17:719–732.

The Sentencing Project. 2014. *State Responses to 2012 Supreme Court Mandate on Life Without Parole*. http://sentencingproject.org/doc/publications/jj_State_Responses_to_Miller.pdf, accessed July 8, 2015.

Tonry M. 2011. *Retributivism Has a Past: Has It a Future?* Oxford: Oxford University Press.

United States v. Booker, 543 U.S. 220 (2005).

U.S. Sentencing Commission. 2015. Chapter 5: Determining the sentence. http://www.ussc.gov/guidelines-manual/2015/2015-individual-chapters-pdf, accessed July 8, 2015.

Walker N. 1991. *Why Punish?* Oxford: Oxford University Press.

Wilson JQ. 2013. *Thinking about Crime*. New York: Basic Books.

WW. 2011. Norwegian v. American justice: Plush and unusual punishment. *The Economist* July 28.

96

Forensic research on the Internet

PETER ASH AND PAUL J. O'LEARY

INTRODUCTION

The explosion of information on the Internet over the past several decades has changed how we get information. The types of information most relevant to the practice of forensic psychiatry include

- Legal documents such as statutes and court opinions
- Secondary source information, such as commentary on legal cases
- General information that may be relevant to a specific case
- Collateral information about an evaluee
- Information about the forensic psychiatrist that may be used by others

The advent of the smartphone has also increased the ways in which we obtain information. Previously, information on the web was available primarily on computers utilizing web browsers, but the advent of tablets and smartphones has brought with it a plethora of apps that assist in obtaining information.

OBTAINING LEGAL DOCUMENTS AND SECONDARY SOURCE INFORMATION ON THE WEB

Legal documents are highly suited to web presentation: government materials are public and not copyrighted, so anyone who wants to post or reference them is free to do so. Much legal material that was previously available only to those with fairly expensive subscriptions to such legal databases as Lexis or Westlaw, or to those who could physically travel to a law library, is now available to any forensic psychiatrist with an Internet connection or a smartphone.

Statutes of the federal government and all states are now available on the web, as well as a great deal of other regulatory and administrative material (the *Code of Federal Regulation*, manuals of civil and criminal procedure, treaties, etc.). One of the advantages of web information is that it is a fairly straightforward task to keep it up-to-date, so as new legislation is enacted or a new opinion is delivered, the addition is easily added to the existing body of information.

Court systems began to put appellate opinions on the web in the mid-1990s. The U.S. Supreme Court began its website in the year 2000, although a number of other sites had been posting selected Supreme Court opinions for several years prior to that. Most appellate decisions had previously only been available through pay sites such as Lexis and Westlaw, but currently most appellate decisions are available on the web for free.

A wide variety of secondary sources are also available. The federal government has done an excellent job posting government documents in a variety of fields, some of which are useful for forensic psychiatrists. For example, the publications of the U.S. Department of Justice, such as the FBI *Uniform Crime Reports* (UCR), are available. In addition, the federal government has put many of its databases online (e.g., the FBI *Uniform Crime Reports*, injury data, census data) together with tools to extract data of the user's specifications (see, for example, http://www.ucrdatatool.gov for extracting UCR data). Many legal periodicals and law reviews have moved to making the full text of all or some of their articles available for free, and the full text of all articles of the *Journal of the American Academy of Psychiatry and the Law* is available (http://www.jaapl.org). Finally, the characteristic of the web that anyone can publish information he or she finds interesting and/or wants to publicize leads to the posting of a great deal of information about forensic topics, from the American Psychiatric Association's position on capital punishment to militia sites containing instructions for small bomb construction.

GENERAL PRINCIPLES IN LOCATING WEB MATERIAL

With the improvement of search engines, finding material has become increasingly simple. Previously, one needed to pick search terms with great care. However, now using a general search engine such as Google, Yahoo, or Bing will often get one to available material without having to search on legal or organization websites. Remarkably, a search on Google that includes the organization name and the information sought is often more efficient than entering the terms in the search box of the organization's website. This is true because Google's ranking of results pulls from a larger pool of searches, whereas on the organization site, the result ranking algorithms are often dependent on the keywords entered by the organization. Most users generally start a search with the words and terms they associate with their expected results, and frequently, scanning the first page of search results leads to what they want. The more the user puts in information specific to what is being searched for, the more likely one will retrieve the information sought. For legal cases, searching on the citation is generally the most efficient way to locate the case.

Narrowing a search

If the original search returns too many results, the use of search operators can be very helpful in narrowing the search. Some of the most commonly used operators for Google searches are listed in Table 96.1. Other search engines utilize similar operators.

Expanding a search

If a Google search does not provide the information being sought, there are numerous sites that specialize in pointing to information that is of use to forensic psychiatrists. Table 96.2 lists samples of some of the types of sites available.

SMARTPHONE APPS

Apps are application designed to run on smartphones and tablet computers. As of May 2015, Android users were able to choose between 1.5 million apps, and Apple's App Store contained 1.4 million available apps (statista.com 2015). Considering the number of available apps, and the rate new apps are created, rather than reviewing a number of specific apps, Table 96.3 provides information about some sites that review legally relevant apps.

Though we are not reviewing a number of legal apps, there are a few apps that bear mentioning because they appear on each of the site's lists. Table 96.4 lists these apps along with a summary of their purpose.

OBTAINING COLLATERAL INFORMATION ABOUT AN EVALUEE

Obtaining collateral information about a person being evaluated, which includes searching the Internet for publicly available information relevant to a case, is becoming a standard aspect of a forensic evaluation (Glancy et al. 2015, S10). Although it is clearly legal to conduct an Internet search about one's patients, there is some controversy about whether a therapist should do so, because knowing information about a patient that the patient has not communicated

Table 96.1 Refining a Google search query

Notation	Find result	Example
+term	Search includes the term. Common terms like "The, A, and" are excluded from the search unless specifically requested.	+The King
term1 OR term2	With term1 or term2 or both	Tahiti OR Hawaii
term1|term2	Both term1 and term2	Tahiti|Hawaii
term1 -term2	The minus sign in front of a term filters term2 out of the search results.	AAPL -apple
"term"	Using quotation marks around a phrase will require that particular word order.	"no sharper than that between twilight and dusk"
"term1 * term2"	An asterisk within quotes signifies a variable, allowing searches for unknown terms.	"cruel and unusual punishment * amendment"
term1 AROUND(n) term2	Searches for terms that are separated from each other by *n* or less words.	court AROUND(2) psychiatrist
term site:website	Searches for the term only in the specified website	Meeting site:aapl.org
inurl:term	Returns results with term in the URL of the site	inurl: NGRI
allinurl:term1 term2	Searches for sites with all search terms in the URL	allinurl: psychiatrist malpractice
term filetype:file extension	Searches for a Specify a type of document. Examples of common file extensions include: PDF: Portable Document Format PPT: PowerPoint DOC: Word Document	Medical Exam filetype: PPT

Note: The notation column show the generic notation to use, with *term* being the search term. The Find Result column explains the function of the notation.

Table 96.2 Specialized search sites

Index of sites—Links to a variety of legal and forensic psychiatry information sites	
www.aapl.org	American Academy of Psychiatry and the Law
Legal sites—Capabilities for searching a variety of legal materials	
lp.findlaw.com	General legal search site
www.law.cornell.edu	Cornell University Law School's Legal Information Institute
www.oyez.org	A multimedia database: Hear oral arguments in some landmark supreme court case
www.justia.com	General legal search
scholar.google.com	Search for articles, cases, and statutes
www.casetext.com	Full text of law cases
Government information	
www.supremecourtus.gov	Homepage of U.S. Supreme Court
www.ncjrs.org	Justice Information Center (NCJRS)
www.gpo.gov/fdsys/search/home.action	Government Publishing Office index to all U.S. government publications
www.fbi.gov/ucr/ucr.htm	FBI's *Uniform Crime Reports*
ojjdp.ncjrs.org	Office of Juvenile Justice and Delinquency Prevention
canlaw.net	Canadian law information

Table 96.3 Sites that review law apps

Site summary	Site address
University of California, Los Angeles School of Law Library lists apps that focus on legal research and news. The site lists information about almost 70 current apps that might be of interest to law students and lawyers. However, it does not list them according to functionality.	*tinyurl.com/legalapps-ucla*
University of Wisconsin-Madison Law Library lists many of the same apps that might be of interest to law students and lawyers, and sorts the apps by functionality.	*tinyurl.com/legalapps-uw*
The American Bar website lists 10 apps for productive lawyers. The apps listed focus on the practice of law and courtroom aids.	*tinyurl.com/legalapps-AmBar*
The website LegalTechNews lists 12 apps for legal research, some of which are not listed on the other sites. The apps listed focus on the practice of law and courtroom aids.	*tinyurl.com/legalapps-LegTech*

Table 96.4 Selected well-reviewed legal apps

App name	Summary
Fastcase	Contains cases and statutes from all 50 states and from the federal government.
iSSRN	The Social Science Research Network is a resource for scholarly research in a number of disciplines, including law. With the iSSRN application, users may search more than 260,000 research papers in the SSRN library.
Black's Law Dictionary	The 10th edition contains more than 45,000 terms, alternate spellings or equivalent expressions for more than 5300 terms, and West key numbers. Hyperlinked cross-references make finding related terms quick and easy. Audio pronunciations for thousands of hard-to-say legal terms. Bookmark terms for quick reference. Featured Word of the Day.
ABA Journal	The app provides breaking legal news and articles featured in the ABA Journal.

to the therapist may feel to the patient like an intrusion of privacy and affect the therapeutic alliance (Gabbard et al. 2011; Kirschner et al. 2011; Kolmes and Taube 2014). However, in forensic evaluations, the role of the psychiatrist is not one of therapist, and there is no therapeutic alliance. If the evaluator is not aware of publicly available information, the thoroughness of his or her evaluation may be questioned. For example, consider an assessment of the mental state and intent of a defendant charged with a hate crime, and the evaluator is unaware of, and so did not take into account, the defendant's readily identifiable rants and threats on public Internet discussion sites.

The issue of an evaluator asking for access to nonpublic information on the web, such as asking an evaluee to provide access to an otherwise restricted Facebook page, is more problematic. Such material would ordinarily require a release from the evaluee, or having the retaining attorney obtain the information through the normal discovery processes.

Information obtained from a web search of an evaluee, like other collateral information, may be useful in a variety of ways, including either confirming or disconfirming evidence for what the evaluee reports in an interview. There are a variety of problems utilizing web search information. Recupero (2010) and Metzner and Ash (2010) have discussed strategies and problems involved in web searches for collateral information. These include searching at social media and blog sites in addition to general search engines. If the evaluee has a common name, a web search may reveal so many hits that it is difficult to hone in on the particular person. The famous New Yorker cartoon of two dogs looking at a computer monitor with the caption, "On the Internet, nobody knows you're a dog" (Steiner 1993), highlights the problem of the question of validity of information obtained from the web. Psychiatrists who are unfamiliar with social networking sites may have difficulty navigating those sites to search for information, may have little sense of what the norms are for posting, and may even have trouble deciphering the information itself. Scott and Temporini (2010) give an example of a text message exchange involving a 14-year-old boy, spacedude102, shortly before he committed suicide:

```
ohionetfin: whatup?
spacedude102: *) and :-Q~420
ohionetfin: :-O
spacedude102: #-)
ohionetfin: ?
spacedude102: :-C, want 8-#
```

An evaluator who is not familiar with emoticons and text abbreviations may not decipher that spacedude102 was saying that he was drunk [*)] and using marijuana [:-Q ~ 420], had partied all night [#-)], was extremely sad [:-C], and wanted death [8-#].

Digital evidence of a wide variety of sorts, including social media pages, text message and email exchanges, and logs of websites visited by the evaluee, has become quite common in litigation. Such material is typically provided by the retaining attorney, who may ask the forensic evaluator to interpret the information.

WEB INFORMATION ABOUT THE FORENSIC EVALUATOR

Information about the forensic psychiatrist is also readily available on the web, and it is common for evaluees and attorneys to Google forensic psychiatrists with whom they interact. Privacy is not what it used to be: not only are the postings and most publications of the psychiatrist available, but with a little investigation, such material as the psychiatrist's work history, ratings by patients, and approximate home value, is readily available. More diligent investigation, often purchased over the web relatively cheaply, will yield even more personal information. Attorneys in certain subspecialties may share materials including prior reports and deposition transcripts in restricted access sites. At a deposition, it is no longer rare to be confronted with, "But doctor, in a talk (or deposition or trial) you gave 6 years ago you said..." when a video or transcript of that talk has been uploaded to the web, or a summary of the talk was printed somewhere, or the expert has expressed an opinion on a bulletin board or in an Internet discussion group. Controversial experts may have negative information posted about them. Once material is on the web, it is very difficult to get it removed.

In order to deal effectively with this lack of privacy, a forensic psychiatrist is well advised to Google himself or herself with some regularity to keep abreast of what material is on the web. Professionals do change their opinions and views, and it is useful to know what changes are documented on the web or in testimony transcripts so the expert can anticipate what questions might be asked during testimony. The psychiatrist should also recall that he or she is not responsible for remembering everything he or she ever did: when being cross-examined by an attorney who appears to be relying on some web source, it is appropriate to ask to see the source, both to refresh the psychiatrist's memory, as well as to verify that the source is accurate, and the behavior being questioned actually occurred and is not being taken out of context.

FURTHER READING

As might be expected given the rapid rate of evolution of the web, it is hard for books that discuss legal research on the web to stay up to date. Those that have been published tend to go out of print quite rapidly. The most useful material is placed on the web itself, and revised or removed as technology changes. At the time of this writing, Googling the phrase "legal research on the internet" brought up 71,000 hits.

REFERENCES

Gabbard GO, KA Kassaw, and G Perez-Garcia. 2011. Professional boundaries in the era of the Internet. *Academic Psychiatry* 35:168–174.

Glancy GD, P Ash, EP Bath et al. 2015. AAPL practice guideline for the forensic assessment. *Journal of the American Academy of Psychiatry and the Law* 43:S3–S53.

Kirschner KL, R Brashler, BJ Crigger et al. 2011. Should health care professionals Google patients or family members? *PM and R: Journal of Injury, Function, and Rehabilitation* 3:372–376.

Kolmes K and D Taube. 2014. Seeking and finding our clients on the internet: Boundary considerations in cyberspace. *Professional Psychology: Research and Practice* 45:3–10.

Metzner JL and P Ash. 2010. Commentary: The mental status examination in the age of the internet—Challenges and opportunities. *Journal of the American Academy of Psychiatry and the Law* 38:27–31.

Recupero PR. 2010. The mental status examination in the age of the internet. *Journal of the American Academy of Psychiatry and the Law* 38:15–26.

Scott CL and H Temporini. 2010. Forensic issues and the internet. In *Principles and Practice of Child and Adolescent Forensic Mental Health*, edited by EP Benedek, P Ash, and CL Scott, Washington, DC: American Psychiatric, 253–261.

Statista.com. 2015. Number of apps available in leading app stores as of May 2015. http://www.statista.com/statistics/276623/number-of-apps-available-in-leading-app-stores/, accessed June 21, 2015.

Steiner P. 1993. On the Internet, nobody knows you're a dog. *New Yorker*, July 5. https://en.wikipedia.org/wiki/On_the_Internet,_nobody_knows_you%27re_a_dog#/media/File:Internet_dog.jpg, accessed June 1, 2015.

PART 11

Landmark Cases in Forensic Psychiatry

MERRILL ROTTER

97

Introduction: The case for landmark cases

MERRILL ROTTER AND HOWARD FORMAN

The cases that follow in this section are the landmark cases in forensic psychiatry. Most if not all of them will have been referenced and perhaps described in prior chapters. For example, the chapter on civil commitment would not be complete without noting the importance of such precedents as *Lessard v. Schmidt* and *O'Connor v. Donaldson*. The holdings in those cases are critical to both the understanding of involuntary commitment and implementing appropriate dispositions for patients. However, Landmark Cases hold more than holdings. Landmark Cases have intrinsic importance as an eye into the evolution of thinking about individual rights, theories of mental illness, views of psychiatric treatment, and public policy toward children and adults, rich and poor, those with and without mental illness, and/or histories of negligent, discrimination, or criminal behavior. Studying the specific facts of a case and the legal reasoning associated with a particular holding illuminates these social, clinical, ethical, and legal considerations in a way not possible through a limited review of the principle or precedent stands for which it is known (Appelbaum 1994).

Furthermore, it is our belief that forensic practice is enhanced when one understands how the law thinks in general. Broad considerations of federalism, activism, states' rights, and conservative vs. liberal ideology may all be mined from cases in which the narrow starting point is mental illness. In fact, Landmark Cases are often cited for reasons other than the narrow, forensic psychiatric-related holding.

As an example, consider the case of *Robinson v. California*, 370 U.S. 660 (1962) where Mr. Robinson was found guilty of a misdemeanor for violating California Health and Safety Code §11550 which criminalized addiction. The Supreme Court overturned this conviction through a majority opinion that held punishment for the status of having a disease violated the Eighth Amendment's prohibition on cruel and unusual punishment. *Robinson* is most famously compared and contrasted by the justices in *Powell v. Texas*, 392 U.S. 514 (1968). In *Powell*, the homeless defendant argued that he was being punished for a "status" crime like *Robinson* when he was arrested for being publicly intoxicated because he claimed (likely legitimately) that he was a "chronic alcoholic." The court did not change course and overturn its *Robinson* prohibition of punishing a status crime, but rather, decided that *Powell* was fundamentally a different situation. Although both defendants may be addicts, Powell was being punished for public intoxication, *actus reas*, not his status of being an alcoholic.

Robinson's impact though goes far beyond one decision in a case with a similar fact pattern. One can find *Robinson* cited in later landmark cases in supporting the application of the Eighth Amendment to the states through the Fourteenth Amendment in a child abuse case (*Deshaney v. Winnebago County Department of Social Services*, 489 U.S. 189), the justification for civil versus criminal confinement with reference to a debate about post-insanity acquittal procedures (*Foucha v. Louisiana*, 504 U.S. 71, 1992), and the need for proportionality between offense and punishment with reference to the death penalty (*Atkins v. Georgia*, 536 U.S. 304, 2002). *Robinson* is only one such example.

It is beyond the scope of this introduction and section to delineate the myriad streams of interpretation, citation, and interconnection. In the section that follows we blended a topic-by-topic based division, but within each topic the cases are organized chronologically to demonstrate the advance (or occasionally regression, perhaps) of the legal reasoning in that particular domain. This allows the reader to efficiently educate himself or herself on what the law is, and provides a historical perspective to see how it arrived to its current state. Although we have strived for coherent categorizations, many cases could belong in more than one chapter. *State v. Andring*, for example, is as much a case involving child abuse as it is about confidentiality, and thus could be placed within either case grouping. The categorization in this section maintains continuity with prior editions of this text. For reference purposes, we have included the official landmark case list collated by the American Academy of Psychiatry and the Law, with its somewhat differing divisions. Several of the more recent death penalty cases have not been included in this section, given their comprehensive review elsewhere in the book.

As noted above, there is no replacement for reading the actual court opinions themselves, so the authors have strived to give the reader something more than a list of skeletal takeaways. Each summary includes the information that is relevant, including who are the parties involved, the history of the case itself, the facts of the case (which surprisingly are often not under dispute), the constitutional or legal codes being weighed, the questions the court addressed, and often just as importantly, the questions not addressed, the scope of the ruling, and its applications. In certain cases, the dissenting opinions that hold no legal weight but can be brilliant and critical of the majority opinion will be commented upon. The authors hope that the summaries that follow will spark an interest to delve more deeply into the cases.

REFERENCE

Appelbaum P. 1994. *Almost a Revolution*. New York: Oxford University Press.

98

Civil, juvenile justice and family law cases

MERYL B. ROME AND ANDREW J. RADER

EMOTIONAL HARM

Carter v. G.M., 361 Mich. 577 (1960)

In this workers' compensation case, the Michigan Supreme Court upheld a ruling by the workers' compensation board that James Carter, a machine operator who worked on assembly line production at General Motors, was entitled to disability compensation because of psychosis caused by stress at his job. Significantly, Mr. Carter was under only the ordinary pressures of a machine worker, but suffered from an underlying personality disorder and a predisposition to the development of schizophrenia that made him more vulnerable to those pressures. Thus, in the words of the compensation board that had granted compensation, the work pressures were the "straws that broke the camel's back."

Carter's significance lies not only in the fact that the Michigan Supreme Court did not require Mr. Carter to prove that he was subject to pressures more extraordinary than those endured by his coworkers, but also in the court's acceptance of the premise that a compensable disability need not be caused by a single *physical* injury or a single *mental* shock to plaintiff. Instead, the disability can be caused by psychiatrically succumbing to the usual ongoing daily pressures encountered by him and other employees engaged in similar work. Competent medical evidence having established the causal link between the ordinary work pressure and the disability, Mr. Carter was found to be entitled to compensation.

In so holding, the Supreme Court focused on the *purpose* of the workers' compensation rule, to wit, to ameliorate the economic plight of an employee injured in the course of and on account of his employment by imposing on industry the obligation to pay him weekly payments at rates based on his wages during the period of disability. This is as opposed to focusing on the *cause* of the injury, to wit, the determination that the disability resulted from a sudden disabling event or, for that matter, was caused by the predisposition to the disability. So long as the precipitant to the injury was work related, the court ruled, the injury is subject to compensation under the workers' compensation framework.

Dillon v. Legg, 69 Cal. Rptr. 72, 441 P.2d 912 (1968)

At common law, a person could not bring suit for psychic injuries (e.g., posttraumatic stress) if he or she was not in personal danger from the acts he/she witnessed. *Dillon v. Legg* represents a break with judicial tradition by recognizing a cause of action based exclusively on the psychic injury of a claimant *not personally endangered* by the acts of the tortfeasor.

On September 27, 1964, infant Erin Lee Dillon, while crossing the street with her mother and sister, was hit and killed by an automobile operated by the defendant. Plaintiffs commenced suit, alleging a cause of action for the sister's fear and distress for her own safety (she was nearly hit by the automobile), and another cause of action demanding compensation for the mother who, while not personally endangered by the accident, suffered horror and fright as a result of witnessing the collision with Erin. Upon motion by the defendant, the trial court sustained the sister's cause of action because she was personally endangered by the defendant's automobile, but dismissed the mother's cause of action, holding that California law does not recognize a cause of action for people outside the "zone of danger."

The trial court relied on California precedent holding that claims for purely psychic injury by individuals not personally in danger were not legally cognizable because the tortfeasor owed a duty only to the individual in fear for *his own* safety—not for the safety of others. A person outside this "zone of danger" could not recover in court, and any pleadings made alleging fear, shock, or distress caused by witnessing harm to others were dismissed by the court for failing to state a cause of action. Consequently, the sister's cause of action was valid because she had been in the zone of danger, but the mother's cause of action failed.

The reasoning behind the refusal to recognize liability to those people not in fear for their own safety was that the imposition of duty would invite fraudulent claims and involve the court in the "hopeless task" of defining the extent of the tortfeasor's liability. In the court's words, "in substance, the definition of liability being impossible, denial of liability is the only realistic alternative."

On appeal, the California Supreme Court broke new ground, acknowledging and endorsing the commonsense notion of "natural justice" that "all ordinary human feelings are in favor of [the mother's] action against the negligent defendant." Eviscerating the "zone of danger" distinction, the court concluded that it could "hardly justify relief to the sister for trauma which she suffered upon apprehension of the child's death and yet deny it to the mother merely because of a happenstance that the sister was some few yards closer to the accident. The instant case exposes the hopeless artificiality of the zone of danger rule." Any fear of fraudulent claims, the court continued, does not warrant courts of law in closing the door to all such cases. Courts must depend on the efficacy of the judicial processes to ferret out the meritorious from the fraudulent in particular cases.

AMERICANS WITH DISABILITIES ACT

Bragdon v. Abbott, 118 S.Ct. 2198 (1998)

What physical and mental conditions does the Americans with Disabilities Act ("ADA") protect, and how is the analysis made as to whether a person suffers from such a condition? Does it protect people who carry a disease yet suffer no symptoms? *Bragdon* represents the Supreme Court's pronouncement that a person infected with the human immunodeficiency virus (HIV), even if asymptomatic, suffers from a "disability" under the ADA. The ADA seeks to eliminate discrimination against the disabled. Upon remand to the First Circuit Court of Appeals, it was held that HIV-positive status, in and of itself, had not been scientifically shown to "pose a direct threat to the health or safety of others," and therefore a dentist's refusal to fill the cavity of an asymptomatic HIV-positive patient in his office violated the ADA.

Respondent Sidney Abbott was infected with HIV when she presented for a dental appointment with the petitioner, Dr. Randon Bragdon. Although she was asymptomatic, she disclosed her HIV status to Dr. Bragdon, who performed a dental examination. During the examination, he found a cavity, which, because of Ms. Abbott's HIV status, he refused to fill outside a hospital. He offered to perform the work at a hospital at no additional cost for his services, but Ms. Abbott would be responsible for the cost of using hospital facilities. Ms. Abbott declined treatment and sued Dr. Abbott for violating her rights under the ADA.

The ADA states that "No individual shall be discriminated against on the basis of disability in the full and equal enjoyment of the goods, services, facilities, privileges, advantages, or accommodations of any place of public accommodation by any person who…operates a place of public accommodation."

The court first found that an HIV infection constitutes a "disability" under the ADA. The relevant section of the ADA defines disability as "a physical or mental impairment that substantially limits one or more of major life activities of such individual." The analysis of whether Ms. Abbott fit within that definition has three components: (1) whether her HIV infection was a physical impairment; (2) whether the activity on which she relied (reproduction and child bearing) constituted a major life activity; and (3) whether the physical impairment substantially limited the major life activity.

Addressing the first element, that the HIV was a physical impairment, the court found that because the virus immediately begins to damage the infected person's white blood cells and because of the severity of the disease, it is an impairment *from the moment of infection*. Moreover, because the disease is "invariably fatal," the court ruled that it is axiomatic that it impacts upon major life activities, including the one presented in this case, reproduction. Focusing on the third element, the court stated that Ms. Abbott's infection substantially limited her ability to reproduce in two ways: first, an infected woman who tries to conceive imposes a significant harm of infection on her male partner; second, the infected woman risks infecting her child during gestation and childbirth.

Having concluded that HIV infection is a disability under the ADA, the court next discussed whether Dr. Bragdon was permitted to refuse Ms. Abbott treatment in his office under the exception to the ADA in cases where the infectious condition poses a "significant risk to the health or safety of others that cannot be eliminated by modification of policies, practices, or procedures or by the provision of auxiliary aids or services." Here, the Supreme Court remanded the matter back to the U.S. Court of Appeals, which, after studying the state of scientific knowledge on the transmission of HIV, and being guided by the collective wisdom of professionals in the field of dentistry, determined that no proof of infection to health-care workers in the dental office existed and, further, that universally accepted methods of preventing infection were practicable and effective. Consequently, it was determined that the risk of infection could be eliminated.

Thus, the Supreme Court, in conjunction with the holding by the Court of Appeals after remand, held that HIV infection is, in and of itself, and even in the absence of symptoms, a disability within the meaning of the ADA and entitled to the protections the ADA affords.

Pennsylvania Department of Corrections v. Yeskey, 118 S.Ct. 1952 (1998)

Another question concerning the Americans with Disabilities Act is "to whom does it apply?" In *Yeskey*, the Supreme Court was asked whether it applies to prison inmates. The court answered that it does.

Ronald Yeskey was sentenced to 18–36 months in a Pennsylvania correctional facility but was recommended for placement in a Motivational Boot Camp for first-time offenders, the successful completion of which made him eligible for parole in just 6 months. However, he was refused admission to the program because he suffered from hypertension, and brought suit alleging that the exclusion from the program derogated his rights under the ADA. The State of Pennsylvania, on the other hand, argued that the ADA was not intended to apply to prison inmates.

In a concise opinion, the court looked to the clear wording of the statute, that proscribes any "public entity" from discriminating against any "qualified individual with a disability" on account of that disability. In this case, Mr. Yeskey was a qualified individual, as he was entitled to enter into the boot camp, and the Pennsylvania Department of Corrections is a public entity. The unambiguous language makes no exception for prison inmates, and the High Court will not imply one. Prison inmates are entitled to protection under the Americans with Disabilities Act.

Olmstead v. L.C. ex. rel. Zimring, 119 S.Ct. 2176 (1999)

In another decision lending broad interpretation of the ADA, the Supreme Court ruled that "discrimination" includes confining mentally ill patients in unnecessarily restrictive facilities. The ADA requires states to place persons with mental disabilities in community settings rather than in institutions when the state's treatment professionals have determined that community placement is appropriate, the transfer from institutional care to a less restrictive setting is not opposed by the individual, and the placement can be reasonably accommodated, taking into account the resources available to the state and the needs of others with mental disabilities.

L.C. and E.W. were mentally retarded women. L.C. had also been diagnosed with schizophrenia and E.W. with a personality disorder. They were confined to the Georgia Regional Hospital psychiatric unit, but in time became sufficiently stabilized to be treated in a community-based setting. Each woman wanted to leave the ward, and each woman's treating physicians agreed that they could be appropriately treated outside the hospital walls, with the goal of reintegrating them into mainstream society. Nonetheless, each woman remained confined because the state lacked sufficient resources to place them in a less restrictive environment.

The Americans with Disabilities Act states in pertinent part that

> No...individual with a disability shall, by reason of such disability, be excluded from participation in or be denied the benefits of the services, programs, or activities of a public entity, or be subjected to discrimination by such entity.

Congress instructed the Attorney General to promulgate regulations administering the ADA, which was done. One of the regulations requires public entities to "make reasonable modifications" to avoid discrimination on the basis of disability, unless those modifications would fundamentally alter the nature of the service, program, or activity.

The State of Georgia averred that the women were not being discriminated against by reason of their disability, but rather were being confined due to inadequate funding. The state sought to place this case into the exception to the ADA's nondiscrimination rules by claiming that, because it has the obligation to administer care to a wide variety of people with mental disabilities, the requirement that patients be placed in the least restrictive setting would unreasonably and fundamentally alter the services the state provides.

The first question the court answered was whether the continued confinement in a psychiatric unit, when the patient and the treatment team feel that a community-based program is appropriate, is a form of discrimination. Answering in the affirmative, and finding support in the positions of the Attorney General and various amici briefs (including one submitted by the American Psychiatric Association), the court held that unjustified institutional isolation discriminates in two ways: first, institutional placement of persons who can handle and benefit from community settings perpetuates unwarranted assumptions that persons so isolated are incapable or unworthy of participating in community life (i.e., stigma), and second, confinement in an institution severely diminishes the everyday life activities of individuals, including family relations, social contacts, work options, economic independence, educational advancement, and cultural enrichment.

Having thus concluded that unjustified isolation is a form of discrimination, the court turned to the state's concern that the provision of outside placement to some patients may impose financial strains that could affect the treatment afforded other patients. Here, the court returned to the language of the regulations: the state must make "reasonable modifications" to avoid discrimination, and need not make changes that fundamentally alter the state's programs. This, the court held, requires states to balance the equities of all patients in meting out the requirements of the state's mental health system as a whole. To that end, the states require wide latitude to fashion their own systems that minimize discrimination yet do so in a financially responsible manner.

United States v. Georgia, 546 U.S. 151 (2006)

Can a prison inmate sue the state for money damages under the civil claims portion of the ADA when the state has sovereign immunity protecting it from such suits? Or does the state's sovereign immunity override an individual's right to bring such claims? The answer, under *United States v. Georgia*, is that an individual has a right, under the Fourteenth Amendment, to bring such claims, notwithstanding the state's claim of immunity.

Tony Goodman, a paraplegic inmate confined to a Georgia prison, sued the State of Georgia under Title II of the Americans with Disabilities Act of 1990. The ADA provides that

> no qualified individual with a disability shall, by reason of such disability, be excluded from participation in or be denied the benefits of the services, programs, or activities of a public entity, or be subjected to discrimination by any such group.

In addition, the ADA authorizes suits by private citizens for money damages against public entities that violate this provision.

Mr. Goodman claimed that the prison conditions in which he was forced to live violated his rights under Title II of the ADA. In particular, he claimed that he was confined 23–24 hours a day in a 12- by 3-foot cell in which he could not turn his wheelchair around, that the toilet and shower facilities were not accessible by him, and that as a result, he was at times forced to sit in his own waste. He also claimed that this treatment violated his Eighth Amendment right to be free from cruel and unusual punishment, as applied to the states through the Fourteenth Amendment.

The case was dismissed at the trial level because, in part, Georgia law barred claims for money damages against the state under sovereign immunity statutes. The Eleventh Circuit affirmed.

The Supreme Court reversed. Writing for the Court, Justice Antonin Scalia found that Congress had clearly and unequivocally intended the money remedies contained in the ADA to be available against all states and that Congress has the authority to enforce the provisions of the Fourteenth Amendment by providing for money damages when states violate the amendment. But Justice Scalia left unanswered the question of whether money damages are recoverable in those circumstances where the state's conduct *does* violate the ADA but *does not* rise to the level of a constitutional violation.

Thus, despite Georgia's assertion of sovereign immunity, Mr. Goodman could recover money damages for violations of the ADA that also violate the Fourteenth Amendment.

SEXUAL HARASSMENT

Meritor Savings Bank v. Vinson, 477 U.S. 57 (1986)

Meritor supplies the Supreme Court's exposition of the meaning of "sexual discrimination" or "sexual harassment" under Title VII of the Civil Rights Act of 1964. The court emphasized that there are two distinct forms of such discrimination: quid pro quo sexual harassment, in which sexual favors are demanded in exchange for workplace retention or promotion, and hostile environment sexual harassment, in which the recipient is subjected to unwelcome sexual comments or advances. *Meritor* also holds that, within limits, a supervisory employee who harasses a subordinate employee does so as the agent of the employer, thereby subjecting the employer to liability for such harassment.

Title VII of the Civil Rights Act of 1964 makes it "an unlawful employment practice for an employer...to discriminate against any individual with respect to his compensation, terms, conditions, or privileges of employment, because of such individual's race, color, religion, sex, or national origin."

In 1974, respondent Michelle Vinson met Sidney Taylor, a vice president of Meritor Bank. Ms. Vinson worked her way up the bank ladder from teller-trainee, to teller, to head teller to assistant branch manager. It was undisputed that her advancement was due to merit alone. In September 1978, Ms. Vinson took an indefinite sick leave from the bank and was fired a month later for excessive use of her sick leave.

Following her discharge, she filed suit against Meritor Savings Bank, claiming that it was liable for sexual harassment perpetrated by Mr. Taylor, its employee. She averred that Mr. Taylor asked her out to dinner and suggested that they go to a motel. While at first she resisted his advancements, she ultimately acquiesced out of fear of losing her job. During the next 4 years, Ms. Vinson had sexual relations with Mr. Taylor approximately 40–50 times, and was subjected to demeaning sexual fondling and comments in front of other employees.

After a trial, the District Court held that because Ms. Vinson's relationship was a voluntary one having nothing to do with her continued employment or her advancement or promotions, she was not the victim of sexual discrimination while employed at the bank. Moreover, the District Court held that because the bank had an express policy against discrimination, and no one had ever lodged a complaint about sexual harassment by Taylor, the bank was not on notice and could not be held liable.

The U.S. Court of Appeals for the District of Columbia Circuit reversed. It found that there are two types of harassment: that which involves the conditioning of concrete employment benefits on sexual favors, and harassment that, while not affecting economic benefits, creates a hostile or offensive working environment. The court also found that the bank could be liable through an agency theory: a "supervisor" is an agent even if he or she lacks authority to hire, fire, or promote, because "the mere existence—or even the appearance—of a significant degree of influence in vital job decisions gives any supervisor the opportunity to impose on employees."

The U.S. Supreme Court heard the case and affirmed the rulings of the Court of Appeals. In the high court, the bank claimed that in enacting Title VII, Congress intended to prohibit discrimination with respect to economic, not purely psychological, damages. The court, through the pen of Justice Rehnquist, strongly disagreed, pointing out that not only did the plain language of the statute not so limit the damages, but the intent of Congress was "to strike at the entire spectrum of disparate treatment of men and women" in employment.

In support of its position, the court looked to the position taken by the Equal Employment Opportunity Commission (EEOC). That agency determined that the "hostile environment" (i.e., non quid pro quo) harassment violates Title VII, which affords employees the right to work in an environment free from discriminatory intimidation, ridicule, and insult. Recalling a precedent, the court stated:

> Sexual harassment which creates a hostile or offensive environment for members of one sex is every bit the arbitrary barrier to sexual equality at the workplace that racial harassment is to racial equality. Surely, a requirement that a man or woman run a gauntlet of sexual abuse in return for the privilege of being allowed to work and make a living can be as demeaning and disconcerting as the harshest of racial epithets.

This is not to imply that all workplace conduct of a sexual nature violates Title VII. The test is whether it is sufficiently severe or pervasive to alter the conditions of the victim's employment and create an abusive environment. Nor does the fact that the plaintiff had "voluntary" intercourse with Mr. Taylor conclusively prove there was no harassment. The test, according to the court, was not whether her participation was "voluntary," but rather whether Mr. Taylor's advances were unwelcome.

The court was more circumspect with respect to whether the failure of the bank to be on notice of the harassment, or the fact that it had a grievance procedure in place, absolved it of liability. While not placing strict liability on an employer for the harassment of its employees, the court did look to traditional agency theory to find that employers can be held liable, though not automatically, for the sexually harassing acts of their supervisors.

Harris v. Forklift Systems, Inc., 114 S.Ct. 367 (1993)

After the court's decision in *Meritor Savings Bank*, a dispute arose among the appellate courts as to what conduct created "abusive work environment" harassment. Was it necessary (as the district court in this case found) that the environment must "seriously affect [an employee's] psychological wellbeing" or lead the plaintiff to suffer injury? No, according to the Supreme Court's ruling in *Harris*.

Teresa Harris was a manager at Forklift Systems, Inc. Charles Hardy was Forklift's president. Throughout Ms. Harris' employment, Mr. Hardy frequently directed offensive remarks at Ms. Harris, often in the presence of other employees. These comments were not only of the sexual variety (e.g., he suggested that they "go to the Holiday Inn to negotiate [Harris'] raise"), but also discriminatory gender statements (e.g., she was a "dumb ass woman"). Harris complained, and Hardy apologized and explained that he was only kidding, but soon thereafter he returned to making frequent insulting utterances. Harris sued under Title VII.

The District Court found that some of Hardy's comments "offended [Harris], and would offend the reasonable woman," but it also found that the comments were not so severe as to be expected to seriously affect Harris' psychological well-being. The court did not believe that she suffered injury, because the working environment was not "so poisoned as to be intimidating or abusive." Therefore, the District Court ruled against Harris. The U.S. Court of Appeals for the Sixth Circuit affirmed.

Justice O'Connor, writing for the Supreme Court, reaffirmed the holding of *Meritor* that Title VII does not require "economic" or "tangible" discrimination; rather, it only requires that the discriminatory conduct be "sufficiently severe or pervasive to alter the conditions of the victim's *employment* and create an abusive working environment." This is an objective standard (i.e., the proverbial "reasonable person" would find the environment hostile). However, the Court added, even an environment that does not seriously affect employees' psychological well-being can detract from employees' job performance, discourage employees from remaining on the job, or keep them from advancing in their careers. In addition, even without these tangible effects, the discrimination offends Title VII's broad rule of workplace equality.

Because sexual harassment can affect the work environment even without harming the well-being of employees, the court found that an objectively abusive environment alone is sufficient to state a claim for violation of Title VII.

Oncale v. Sundowner Offshore Services, Inc., 118 S.Ct. 998 (1998)

In *Oncale*, the Supreme Court reaffirmed that an objectively sexually abusive environment always violates Title VII's proscription against discrimination based on sex. Whereas in *Meritor Savings Bank* the court laid out the general elements of a sexually harassing environment, and in *Harris* the court ruled that the victim's psychological well-being need not be harmed, in *Oncale* the court ruled that same-sex sexual harassment is equally actionable because it is still discrimination "because of...sex."

Joseph Oncale was a roustabout on an eight-man crew on an oil platform in the Gulf of Mexico. On several occasions, he was forcibly subjected to sexual abuse by co-workers in the presence of other crewmen. He had been threatened with rape and finally left the job because he felt that if he stayed, he would be raped. He filed suit, but the U.S. District Court of the Eastern District of Louisiana dismissed the case, holding that there was no cause of action for same-sex sexual harassment. The Court of Appeals affirmed.

The Supreme Court reversed. While it conceded same-sex sexual harassment was "assuredly not the principal evil Congress was concerned with when it enacted Title VII," at bottom Congress wanted to prohibit discrimination based on sex. Furthermore, not only does the statute protect men as well as women, but it also protects people from discrimination from people of the same protected class. For example, the court had in the past rejected any conclusive presumption that an employer will not discriminate against members of his own race. Quoting precedent, the court observed that "because of the many facets of human motivation, it would be unwise to presume as a matter of law that human beings from one definable group will not discriminate against other members of that group."

Taking the point one step further, Justice Scalia, writing for the court, noted that to be unlawful the discrimination need not be motivated by sexual desire. Thus, a woman who simply does not like other women to be present in her workplace, and creates an abusive environment to keep other women out, would be liable under the statute for sex discrimination. "The critical issue, Title VII's text indicates, is whether members of one sex are exposed to disadvantageous terms or conditions of employment to which members of the other sex are not exposed."

Justice Scalia rejected the argument that this expansive interpretation of Title VII transforms the statute into a general civility code. *Meritor* and *Harris* stood for the proposition that to be actionable the discrimination must be severe and pervasive enough to create an objectively hostile environment. The statute does not reach into innocuous differences between the sexes, just as it does not forbid male-on-male roughhousing or even intersexual flirtation. It requires neither asexuality nor androgyny in the workplace. Rather, it bans an objective level of abuse as a condition of employment.

JUVENILE JUSTICE

In re Gault, 387 U.S. 1, 87 S.Ct. 1428 (1967)

In re Gault represented a broad elucidation and expansion of the procedural due process rights enjoyed by juveniles under the U.S. Constitution. Gerald Gault, a 15-year-old Arizona boy, was taken into custody on June 8, 1964, for making obscene phone calls. His parents were not at home and were not notified of the detention, and only learned from people in the neighborhood that Gerald was in custody.

The arresting officer filed a petition with the court that resulted in a hearing being scheduled for the next day, June 9. The petition made no reference to the factual basis for the apprehension or the judicial action contemplated. Rather, it stated only that "said minor is under the age of eighteen years, and is in need of the protection of this Honorable Court; [and that] said minor is a delinquent minor." The petition requested a hearing and an order regarding the care and custody of Mr. Gault.

On June 9, Gerald, his mother, his older brother, and probation officers appeared before the Juvenile Judge in chambers. The complainant was absent, there was no sworn testimony, and no record or memorandum of the substance of the hearing was made. The arresting officer testified as to what the complainant had told him and to a confession made by Gerald, which had been obtained without parents or counsel being present and without any notification to Gerald or a parent of his rights. On June 15, another hearing was held, wherein a "referral report" was made by the probation officers and filed with the court, but was not disclosed to Gerald or his parents. Again, the complainant was not present nor was any record made. At the close of the hearing, Gerald was committed as a juvenile delinquent to the State Industrial School for 6 years.

No appeal of juvenile cases was permitted by Arizona law, so a federal writ of habeas corpus was filed. This writ was dismissed by the lower court. On appeal to the Arizona Supreme Court, the petitioners argued that the Arizona Juvenile Code violated Gerald's due process rights by not requiring that parents and children be apprised of the specific charges, by not requiring proper notice of a hearing, by not providing for an appeal, by allowing the use by the juvenile court of unsworn hearsay testimony, and by the failure to make a record of the proceedings. In addition to these due process arguments, the appellants also asserted the Arizona Juvenile Code abrogated the Gaults' right to confront witnesses against them and that the failure to *advise* appellants of their right to counsel and their privilege against self-incrimination violated those protections provided by the Constitution. It was also contended that the removal of Gerald from the custody of his parents without a finding of their unsuitability was improper.

The Arizona Supreme Court, while conceding that the constitutional guarantee of due process is applicable to such proceedings, held that such guarantees are "implied" in the Arizona Juvenile Code, and affirmed the dismissal of the writ.

The U.S. Supreme Court granted leave to appeal and in a far-reaching decision sought to eliminate the perceived distinction between adult "adversarial" criminal proceedings wherein the state stands as prosecutor, and juvenile proceedings, wherein the state is theoretically acting *in loco parentis*, i.e., acting in the child's best interest. By exposing the juvenile system as essentially a criminal system for the young, and upon reviewing the procedural sequence of events, the Supreme Court ruled that the constitutional protections affording due process to adults are, in large part, applicable to juvenile delinquency proceedings because the juvenile proceedings, just like felony proceedings against adults, involve a determination that may subject the juvenile to a loss of liberty for years. Thus, juveniles were held to be constitutionally entitled to timely notice of hearings, to be advised of their right to counsel, to actually have counsel, and to cross-examine witnesses against them. Moreover, the privilege against self-incrimination, which guarantees that no person shall be compelled to be a witness against himself when he is threatened with a deprivation of liberty, applies to juvenile delinquency proceedings.

In *In re Gault*, the U.S. Supreme Court decreed that juvenile delinquency proceedings are analogous to adversarial criminal proceedings, and imbued minors subject to delinquency proceedings with broad constitutional protection.

Fare v. Michael C., 442 U.S. 707 (1979)

Generally, under the Fifth Amendment, all interrogation of a person in the custody of the police must stop if the person indicates in any manner that he or she wishes to speak with an attorney or invokes his or her right to remain silent. But what of a young murder suspect who asks to speak with his probation officer whom he trusts as an advisor?

Michael C. was taken into custody of the Van Nuys, California, police on suspicion of murder. After being advised of his *Mirada* rights to remain silent and to have an attorney present during questioning, Michael asked to speak with his trusted probation officer. The request was refused, and Michael went on to make highly incriminating statements and sketches. Upon being charged with murder in Juvenile Court, he moved to suppress the statements and sketches based on violations of his right to remain silent and to have an attorney present during questioning.

The Juvenile Court detailed Michael's extensive past experience with the legal system and found that Michael had voluntarily waived his rights. Accordingly, the motion to suppress was denied. But the California Supreme Court reversed, holding that Michael's request for his probation officer, a guardian figure whom Michael had been instructed to call in case of encounters with the police, constituted a *per se* invocation of his rights. It was, thought the California Supreme Court, like asking to call one's parent.

The U.S. Supreme Court granted *certiorari* because California's invocation of the *per se* standard meant that rather than analyzing the issue under a "totality-of-the-circumstances" surrounding the waiver of the *Miranda* rights to determine whether the waiver was voluntary, the California court had held that, *as a matter of federal law,* a juvenile's request for his probation officer carried the same significance as a request for an attorney. This threatened a significant expansion of the *Miranda* doctrine and rights.

The U.S. Supreme Court reversed the California Supreme Court because requesting an attorney and requesting a probation officer are not alike. Instead, according to the court, only an attorney holds a "critical position" in the legal system because of his or her unique ability to guard the minor's Fifth Amendment privileges and to prevent overreaching by police officers. And, the *per se* rule applies only to attorneys because "the lawyer is the one person to whom society as a whole looks as the protector of the legal rights of that person in his dealings with the police and the courts." This differs from a probation officer, who is not so trained in the law as to be a legal advisor. To the contrary, the probation officer is allied with the prosecution and it is he or she who files the criminal petition against the accused. Whereas an attorney, in his or her best professional judgment, may tell an accused to remain silent to thwart an investigation, a probation officer is duty-bound to assist the police in their investigation.

Justice Scalia said that juvenile courts are perfectly capable of reviewing the "totality-of-the-circumstances" to determine whether a particular person has made a voluntary waiver. Given the enormous variety of claims of involuntary waiver of *Miranda* rights that confront the lower courts on a regular basis, and the lower courts' ability to take into consideration the juvenile's age, experience, education, background, intelligence, and capacity to understand the warnings given to him or her, the high court found that only the flexibility available in the totality-of-the-circumstances standard would suffice. Indeed, postulated Justice Scalia, the totality-of-the-circumstances may even result in a finding that a particular juvenile in calling for his or her parents or a probation officer was invoking his or her right to remain silent, whereas an older, more experienced juvenile, similarly calling for his or her parent or probation officer, was not invoking this right.

The Supreme Court held that the California Supreme Court wrongly applied a *per se* standard and went on to rule that, under the totality of the circumstances, Michael had not invoked his right to silence or his privilege against self-incrimination. Considering his extensive experience with the criminal justice system and the lack of proof of coercion or improper police tactics, there was no reason to believe that he did not understand his rights before making his statements. Therefore, he voluntarily and knowingly waived his rights and consented to interrogation, and his statements and sketches could be used against him in the murder prosecution.

Graham v. Florida, 130 U.S. 2011 (2010)

In *Graham v. Florida*, the U.S. Supreme Court held that the sentence of life imprisonment without the possibility of release on a juvenile offender in a *nonhomicide* case violates the defendant's Eighth Amendment right to be free of cruel and unusual punishment. All juveniles convicted of such crimes must be given the opportunity for (but not promise of) release.

At age 16, Petitioner Graham committed an armed robbery. He and some friends broke into a restaurant. One of Graham's accomplices struck the restaurant manager on the head with a metal bar causing a laceration that required stitches. Graham was caught and, under Florida law, was prosecuted as an adult for armed burglary with assault or battery, a first-degree felony carrying a maximum penalty of life imprisonment without the possibility of parole. Under a plea agreement, he was sentenced to probation. Soon after his plea, Graham was involved in two home invasion robberies, during one of which his accomplice was shot. Graham dropped his wounded accomplice off at the hospital but was apprehended after doing so. Three guns were found in his car.

Following a hearing, the judge, despite having the authority to sentence Graham to the 30 years requested by the prosecutor or the 4 years recommended by the Florida Department of Corrections, sentenced him to life in prison without the possibility of parole for violating his probation. Thus, the sentence punished the crime he committed at age 16.

Writing for the court, Justice Kennedy explained that the court addresses cruel and unusual punishment cases under two types of analysis. In the first, the court considers all the circumstances of the case to determine whether the sentence is unconstitutionally excessive. Under this analysis, the court begins by determining whether a sentence for a term of years is grossly disproportionate to the defendant's crime. Next, the court may review whether the sentence is out of proportion to sentences meted out by other jurisdictions for the same crime. If either is disproportionate, under the first analysis the sentence may be considered cruel and unusual.

The second classification of cases uses categorical rules to define the Eighth Amendment standards. Within this second classification are two subsets, one considering the nature of the offense, the other considering the characteristics of the offender.

In applying the second, categorical approach, the court first looks at nationwide standards to determine whether any consensus has arisen surrounding a particular issue. In reviewing national standards on the issue at bar, the court found that 37 states as well as the District of Columbia and the federal system permit life without parole for juvenile nonhomicide offenders. This, however, does not complete the analysis. The court must also look at the *de facto* sentences meted out. Reviewing these, the court found that while 37 states permit such sentencing, only 11 states have actually imposed it. And of the 123 juvenile serving such sentences in the entire United States, 77 were in Florida, and the rest scattered throughout the remaining 10 states. Moreover, the court observed that the mere fact that the sentence is *available* under a given state's statutes does not mean that the legislature in that state *desired* that it be imposed on juveniles being charged as adults. Based on this review of *actual* sentences imposed, Justice Kennedy determined that the imposition of life without the possibility of parole for nonhomicidal juveniles is quite rare and that there exists a consensus *against* the imposition of such sentence on juveniles.

Further exploring the issue, Justice Kennedy wrote that a given sentence must also meet penological goals. Compared to adults, juveniles are less mature, have an underdeveloped sense of responsibility, and are more vulnerable to negative influences. Therefore, they are less culpable than adults, and must receive a correspondingly lesser sentence. Simultaneously, a juvenile has greater capacity to change as he or she matures and this, too, distinguishes him or her from a mature adult.

It is also wrong to equate nonhomicidal crimes with homicides. While a nonhomicidal crime may be quite devastating to the victim, a life has not been taken and therefore the nonhomicidal crime is less depraved than the homicide. According to the court, a sentence of life without the possibility of parole, while not the same as a death sentence, carries some of the same punishments. It deprives the defendant of any hope, destroys the desire or purpose of self-improvement, and informs the convict that whatever the future may hold for his or her mind and spirit, he or she will nonetheless spend the rest of his or her days in prison. For a 16-year-old boy convicted of a nonhomicidal crime, the imposition of life in prison without the possibility of parole serves no penological goals.

For the same reasons that a juvenile is not as culpable as an adult for his or her wrongdoing (lack of maturity, etc.), the goals of reduced risk of recidivism, deterrence, and retribution for the crime are more poorly achieved when applied to a juvenile. Juveniles do not have the same mental or emotional maturity or responsibility as do adults. On the other hand, the possibility of rehabilitation, another penological goal, is greater in a juvenile, who may still grow and develop into a more responsible adult.

The State of Florida brought forth several other arguments, among them that judges should have the discretion to impose life without parole on juveniles for particularly heinous crimes. Justice Kennedy acknowledged the necessity for flexibility of sentencing, but observed that even a case-by-case approach is constricted by the Eighth Amendment.

The Supreme Court in *Graham* made the categorical ruling that juveniles deserve the opportunity to rehabilitate themselves and, while they are not *entitled* to release from prison, they are required to have the *chance* of release. Consequently, the imposition of a life sentence without the possibility of parole on a juvenile for a nonhomicide crime violates the Eighth Amendment.

Miller v. Alabama, 132 S.Ct. 2455 (2012)

In *Graham*, the Supreme Court took up the constitutionality of a sentence of life imprisonment without possibility of parole for juveniles who committed a *nonhomicide* offense. In *Miller v. Alabama*, the court addressed whether a mandatory life imprisonment without possibility of parole for convicts who were under the age of 18 at the time they committed a *homicide* violates the Eighth Amendment's prohibition on cruel and unusual punishment and determined, for many of the same reasons announced in *Graham*, that it does.

Miller involved two separate cases in which a 14-year-old boy was convicted of murder and sentenced under the state sentencing requirements to mandatory life imprisonment without possibility of parole. In one case, Kuntrell Jackson accompanied friends in an armed robbery during which one of Mr. Jackson's co-defendants killed a store clerk. Jackson was convicted of capital felony murder. In the other case, Evan Miller, after a robbery gone wrong, beat the victim to death with a baseball bat.

Reaching back to two lines of precedent, Justice Kagan, writing for the court, said that we first start with the idea from *Roper v. Simmons* (holding unconstitutional the imposition of the death penalty on juveniles) and *Graham v. Florida* (holding unconstitutional the imposition of mandatory life without possibility of parole for juveniles who commit a nonhomicide offense) that children are constitutionally different from adults for purposes of sentencing because they have diminished culpability and greater prospects of reform, and joining it with other cases requiring that the sentencing judge be permitted to consider the characteristics of a defendant before sentencing him or her to death.

Reviewing these lines of cases, the court recognized that the same factors that diminish a juvenile's culpability in nonhomicide cases and therefore may render a minimum harsh sentence disproportionate to the crime (e.g., immaturity, recklessness, lack of comprehension of consequences) are also present in homicide cases. Youth, itself, is a mitigating factor a sentencing court must consider. Moreover, because a youth sentenced to life without the possibility of parole will spend more years and a greater percentage of his or her life in prison than a similarly sentenced adult, the court considered life imprisonment without the possibility of parole to be, for the juvenile offender, on par with the death sentence for an adult and must be viewed accordingly.

Thus, the reasoning in *Graham* applies to any juvenile life without parole sentence, and the court ruled that the Eighth Amendment forbids a sentencing scheme that mandates life in prison without possibility of parole for juvenile offenders.

99

Criminal law and forensic psychiatry

HOWARD OWENS AND JEREMY COLLEY

COMPETENCE IN CRIMINAL CASES

Dusky v. United States, 362 U.S. 402 (1960)

The *Dusky* case provided the opportunity for the Supreme Court to define the test for competence to stand trial in a criminal case. The defendant, Milton Dusky, had been convicted in U.S. District Court in Missouri of kidnapping and interstate transport of a minor. Dusky asserted on appeal that the trial court erred in three ways: first, in finding him competent to stand trial; second, in submitting the question of insanity to the jury for decision; and third, in instructing the jury according to the *M'Naghten* test for insanity. The U.S. Court of Appeals upheld the lower court on all three issues.

Dusky was originally charged, along with two juvenile co-defendants, with abducting a 15-year-old girl and driving her across state lines, where the two boys raped her and Dusky attempted to rape her. His attorney raised the issues both of his competence and insanity, and he was hospitalized for examination at a federal medical center for 4 months. A psychiatric report gave a diagnosis of "Schizophrenic Reaction, chronic undifferentiated type," marked by visual hallucinations and complicated by alcoholism. A later report stated that the defendant was "unable to properly understand the proceedings" and "unable to adequately assist counsel." In support of this opinion, the report noted that Dusky felt he was being "framed." One of the experts testified that while the defendant did understand the charges and the basic elements of court procedure, he was "unable properly to assist in his own defense 'due to an inability to interpret reality from unreality,' and to 'suspicions' and 'confused thinking.'" In spite of this testimony, the trial court ruled that the defendant had sufficient mental capacity to stand trial, citing the fact that he was oriented and, "based on the limited evidence" available, that he was able to assist counsel. Dusky was then convicted at trial.

The Court of Appeals declined to overrule the verdict, holding that "how much mental capacity or alertness a defendant must have to be able to assist his counsel" was "a question of fact for the trial court." The court noted its policy that a trial judge not be required to believe evidence he or she found unconvincing and pointed out that, as a result, the judge was not bound by the conclusions of expert witnesses. The court also upheld the conviction on the other two issues presented.

In a brief *per curiam* decision, the Supreme Court overturned Dusky's conviction. It held that the record was insufficient to support the conclusion that the defendant was competent to stand trial in the first place; therefore, the court did not have to address the insanity issues. The case was remanded to the district court for a new hearing on the issue of Dusky's competence and for a new trial, if he was found competent.

Although the court did not spell out its rationale for the decision in any detail, it endorsed the position taken by the solicitor general that "the test must be whether [the defendant] has sufficient present ability to consult with his lawyer with a reasonable degree of rational understanding—and whether he has a rational as well as factual understanding of the proceedings against him." The court clearly believed that the trial judge needed more information than he had available to decide the issue of competence, and that he had relied on inadequate criteria—the mere facts that Dusky was oriented and had "some recollection of events"—without attending to the question of the defendant's rational understanding of the facts.

Wilson v. U.S., 391 F. 2d 460 (1968)

Robert Wilson was charged with five counts of assault and robbery in Washington, DC. Because of a head injury suffered in a car chase following this crime spree, Wilson had a permanent, retrograde amnesia with no recollection of the events charged in his indictment. He was admitted to St. Elizabeth's Hospital, where evaluation revealed that he had a normal mental status except for the amnesia. Psychiatric reports to the court, however, concluded that he was not competent to stand trial because of his amnesia. Although he was able to understand the charges against him, the defense argued that he could not assist his attorney by recalling any facts about events surrounding his arrest. The trial court found Wilson to be competent, pointing out that he had the capacity to understand the details of the case by relying on other sources of information; he could follow the proceedings in court and discuss the case with his attorney in a rational way. The court indicated that memory loss would bar prosecution of a criminal case only when the defendant's memory was in fact "crucial" to the presentation of a defense.

On appeal to the U.S. Court of Appeals, the issue was whether Wilson was denied due process and effective assistance of counsel when the government brought him to trial suffering as he did from amnesia. The court accepted the trial court's analysis of what was required for competence. It reiterated the *Dusky* standard (*Dusky v. U.S.*, 362 U.S. 402, 1960), stating that the defendant should be able to consult with his attorney "with a reasonable degree of rational understanding" and should have a "rational as well as factual understanding" of what went on in court. More specifically, the issue was whether the defendant had sufficient information available about the events for which he was indicted, without having to rely on his own memory, in order to present his defense fairly at trial. The court remanded the case for further post-trial consideration of this issue, i.e., whether Wilson's amnesia in fact deprived him of a fair trial.

In a concurring opinion, Judge Leventhal pointed out that it is a common occurrence for a person to be convicted of negligent homicide even though his memory is impaired by intoxication at the time of the crime. In dissent, Judge Fahy took a directly opposite point of view (and apparently conflated the concepts of memory and understanding), maintaining that to try a man suffering from amnesia was the same as trying someone "in absentia," because the defendant would have a "complete lack of factual understanding."

Sieling v. Eyman, 478 F. 2d 211 (1973)

Gilbert Sieling was charged by the state of Arizona with multiple counts of assault. He was examined by three psychiatrists, all of whom agreed that he was insane at the time of the crime according to the relevant *M'Naghten* test. Two of the doctors also found him to be competent to stand trial, while one doctor stated that he was incompetent. The trial court found the defendant to be competent. One month later he asked to change his plea to guilty. This plea was accepted, and Sieling was sentenced to a long prison term. Subsequently, Sieling appealed his conviction, contending that his plea should not have been accepted because he was mentally incompetent to make it. He argued that his competence to waive the right to stand trial was a separate issue from competence to stand trial and was therefore not given consideration when the trial court ruled on his competence.

The U.S. Court of Appeals for the Ninth Circuit accepted Sieling's argument and remanded the case to the state court to pursue a retrospective examination of Sieling's competence to waive his rights at the time that he pled guilty. The court cited *Westbrook v. Arizona*, 384 U.S. 150 (1966) in support of the distinction between competence to stand trial and competence to waive important rights. The court reasoned that when a defendant's competence has previously been raised as an issue, the trial court must make a further inquiry to determine specifically whether the defendant's waiver of rights is adequate. The defendant's capacity in this situation must be measured by a higher standard, i.e., a degree of competence that would enable him to make decisions of "very serious import." The court borrowed from *Schoeller v. Dunbar*, 423 F. 2d 1183 (1970), the language of "reasoned choice" to define such a higher standard. The court therefore remanded the case back to the state court so that it could resolve the issue as to Sieling's competence to plead guilty. The court suggested that because there were on record three psychiatric opinions about Sieling's state of mind only a month before his guilty plea, the trial court might well have sufficient basis to resolve the issue of his competence, even according to a higher standard.

Estelle v. Smith, 451 U.S. 454 (1980)

In response to the Supreme Court's constitutional restrictions on the death penalty, a number of states passed new death penalty statutes that delineated more precise criteria for when the death penalty could be applied. *Estelle v. Smith* dealt with the use of psychiatric testimony to predict future dangerousness as a criterion for a death sentence in Texas.

In 1973, Ernest Smith was indicted for the murder of a store clerk in a robbery. The trial court ordered a psychiatric examination to determine Smith's competency to stand trial. After a 90-minute jail interview, Dr. James P. Grigson reported that the defendant was competent. Subsequently, a jury convicted Smith. Texas law required a separate sentencing procedure before the same jury. One of the criteria that the jury had to consider was the question of whether the defendant was likely to commit further acts of violence in the future. The prosecutor sought to call Dr. Grigson to testify, and the judge denied a defense motion to prevent his testifying. Dr. Grigson had acknowledged at a hearing that he had not obtained permission from Smith's attorney to examine him. Dr. Grigson testified that Smith was a "very severe sociopath" who would continue his present behavior and that he was going to commit other similar criminal acts in the future. The jury heard this testimony and found that Smith satisfied the criteria for the death penalty.

Smith petitioned for a writ of habeas corpus in U.S. District Court, which vacated his sentence on the grounds that the trial court made a constitutional error in admitting the psychiatric testimony. The U.S. Court of Appeals affirmed, holding that "Texas may not use evidence based on a psychiatric examination of the defendant unless the defendant was warned, before the examination, that he had a right to remain silent, was allowed to terminate the examination when he wished, and was assisted by counsel in deciding whether to submit to the examination."

The issue before the Supreme Court was whether the state's use of the psychiatric testimony violated Smith's rights under the Fifth and Sixth Amendments. The court affirmed the Court of Appeals' conclusion.

Writing for the majority, Chief Justice Burger dismissed the state's arguments that the Fifth Amendment privilege against self-incrimination was not relevant to the penalty phase of a trial and that Dr. Grigson's observations were "nontestimonial." The opinion noted that the psychiatric diagnosis depended on Smith's statements about the crime. While the judge had ordered the examination for the "neutral" purpose of determining competence, the state had used the results for another objective adverse to the defendant without informing him that it could do so. Noting that the decision in *Miranda v. Arizona*, 384 U.S. 436, 467 (1966), applied to "custodial interrogation," the court also rejected the idea that a psychiatric interview in jail was clearly noncoercive. When Dr. Grigson testified for the prosecution, his role changed, and he became an agent of the state rather than the court. Therefore, the court reasoned, the state violated Smith's Fifth Amendment rights. The court concluded that the state cannot compel a defendant to respond to a psychiatrist where the defendant has not initiated a psychiatric examination or introduced psychiatric evidence and where the interview could be used against him.

The opinion pointed out that the Sixth Amendment applies to the states through the due process requirement of the Fourteenth Amendment. The court had held previously that the Sixth Amendment entitles a person to an attorney once an adversarial proceeding has begun. Because the psychiatric examination of Smith occurred at a critical point and because counsel was not notified that the interview would encompass the issue of future dangerousness—about which issues the defendant could not be expected to know his rights—the state was violating Smith's right to the advice of counsel. The opinion quoted the amicus brief of the American Psychiatric Association to the effect that clinical predictions of violence have a very low reliability, and that psychiatrists have no special qualifications for forecasting dangerousness.

In a concurring opinion, Justices Stewart and Powell indicated that because of the lack of notice to counsel, the use of Dr. Grigson's testimony was impermissible at any stage of the trial. For the same reason, Justice Rehnquist argued that the Fifth Amendment issue did not have to be addressed; he noted his disagreement with the idea that the psychiatric examination was coercive in the way intended by *Miranda*.

Colorado v. Connelly

In *Colorado v. Connelly*, the Supreme Court addressed the question of when the confession of a criminal defendant is voluntary: the case established a requirement that some coercive activity on the part of the police is necessary for a court to find that a confession was made involuntarily. The case thereby set a strict limit on when the defense could raise the issue of competence to confess or competence to waive procedural rights.

Francis Connelly had approached a Denver police officer and spontaneously reported that he had committed a murder. The officer immediately advised Connelly of his rights (under *Miranda v. Arizona*, 384 U.S. 436, 1966). Connelly said that he understood and wanted to talk because his conscience bothered him. The following day, however, he showed signs of serious mental disorder: he was disoriented, gave confused answers, and said that "voices" told him to confess. He was hospitalized, and only after 6 months of treatment was he found to be competent to proceed. At a hearing, a psychiatrist testified that Connelly was suffering from chronic schizophrenia at the time he confessed and that he had been "reluctantly" following hallucinatory commands. In this way his mental condition interfered with his capacity to exercise "free and rational" choice. The court then ruled that a confession was admissible "only if it is a product of the defendant's rational intellect and free will," and that Connelly's illness destroyed his volition and compelled him to confess.

The Colorado Supreme Court confirmed the decision, relying on the due process clause of the Fourteenth Amendment, which the court concluded would require the state to reject a confession that was not given of the defendant's "free will." The U.S. Supreme Court reversed the Colorado decision, holding that the admissibility of a confession is governed by state rules of evidence rather than by *Miranda* or other decisions involving police misconduct.

Writing for the majority, Chief Justice Rehnquist emphasized that the court's prior decisions in this area involved police coercion or "overreaching." Without a demonstration of police misconduct, Rehnquist found no basis for concluding that the state had deprived the defendant of due process of law. He rejected the idea that the defendant's mental condition alone rendered his confession "involuntary"; the Colorado Supreme Court had therefore erred in invoking the idea of "free will." Rehnquist thus restricted the concept of voluntary confession to mean only that the confession was made without intimidation, coercion, or deception.

Justice Stevens concurred with the majority in part but made a distinction between pre-custody and post-custody statements, arguing that placing a person in custody in itself introduced an inevitable element of coercion. He noted that it was undisputed that Connelly was not competent to stand trial after he was in custody and that he was therefore not competent to waive his rights at that point.

Justice Brennan dissented from the entire decision: he argued that the Constitution guarantees a "Fundamental right to make a vital choice with a sane mind." He quoted the *Miranda* decision itself to the effect that a "heavy burden rests on the government to demonstrate that the defendant knowingly and intelligently waived his privilege against self-incrimination." Brennan considered the majority opinion to be a step toward a system of law enforcement that would be inquisitional rather than adversarial, with the result that the process would be less reliable and more open to abuse.

Ford v. Wainwright, 106 S.Ct. 2595 (1986)

In *Ford v. Wainwright*, a divided Supreme Court addressed the issue of a mentally impaired person's competence to be executed. Alvin Ford had been convicted of murder in Florida in 1974 and was sentenced to die. Several years later he began to show signs of serious mental disorder, developing grandiose paranoid delusions and coming to believe that he had won a landmark case against the state, so that he could not be executed. A psychiatrist evaluated him over a period of 14 months and concluded that he was psychotic. Ford then refused to see this psychiatrist again, believing he was conspiring against him. A second psychiatrist examined him and concluded that he had no understanding of why he was to be executed and in fact did not believe that he would be, since he could control the state's governor through mind waves.

Florida law proscribed the execution of the insane and required the governor to determine if an apparently insane condemned person "has the mental capacity to understand the nature of the death penalty and the reasons why it was imposed on him." The state therefore appointed three psychiatrists who examined Ford together for a total of 30 minutes. The psychiatrists found him competent to be executed.

Ford's counsel filed a writ of habeas corpus in federal court, seeking a hearing on the issue of Ford's competence. The district court denied the request and was upheld by the Court of Appeals. The Supreme Court heard the case and focused on two issues: first, whether the Eighth Amendment itself barred the execution of the insane; and second, whether Florida's procedure satisfied the requirements of due process.

Writing for a plurality of four justices, Justice Marshall's opinion held that the Eighth Amendment did bar the execution of the insane and that Florida's procedure did not give Ford a fair hearing. The court reversed the Court of Appeals and remanded the case for a hearing on the evidence of Ford's competence.

Marshall reviewed a long history of opinion in common law (going back to Coke and Blackstone) that insanity barred execution. He quoted Coke to the effect that it "offends humanity" to execute the insane and argued that such executions neither make sense as retribution nor provide any example to others as a deterrent. He noted that no state allows the execution of the insane and concluded that to sanction it would be "cruel and unusual punishment."

On the procedural issue, Marshall argued that capital cases require a higher standard of reliability in fact finding and that "death is different" because it is irremediable. Marshall invoked the principle that the fact finder must have all the relevant information to make a decision. Florida failed to ensure Ford's fundamental right to be heard because the defense submission of two additional psychiatric reports was given no attention. The governor had an announced policy of excluding any "advocacy" on the issue of competence to be executed, and the entire determination of the issue was carried out within the executive branch. The denial of any opportunity for the defense to challenge state witnesses also resulted in an inadequate assurance of accuracy in the proceeding.

Justice Powell provided the fifth vote for the majority in concurring that executing the insane was "uniquely cruel" and in finding the Florida process defective. He agreed that the "essence of a 'court' is independence from the prosecutorial arm of government." He departed from Marshall only in his opinion that due process did not require a "full-scale" competency trial. A flexible concept of due process might be accommodated by another arrangement, such as an independent review board.

Justice O'Connor concurred in the result, but argued that the Florida statute and not the Eighth Amendment barred the execution. She agreed that the Florida procedure was constitutionally defective. Justice Rehnquist, joined by Chief Justice Burger, dissented and made the point that the same common-law tradition on which Marshall relied had always assigned to the executive the responsibility to determine the sanity of the condemned—the governor being the prisoner's custodian.

Godinez v. Moran, 113 S.Ct. 2680 (1993)

Godinez v. Moran established the principle that there is only a single standard for competence to stand trial. The decision effectively overruled *Sieling v. Eyman*, 478 F.2d 211 (1973). Richard Moran was arrested after a crime spree in which he killed three people and then shot himself in a suicide attempt. Two psychiatrists examined Moran and found him to be competent to stand trial. About two-and-a-half months later, Moran asked the trial court to dismiss his attorneys and allow him to plead guilty. He offered the explanation that he wanted to stop any presentation of mitigating evidence in his case. The court accepted Moran's guilty plea, and he was subsequently sentenced to death for the three murders.

Some 18 months later, Moran filed a claim with the court that he had been mentally incompetent to represent himself at the time of his guilty plea. After the state court rejected this claim, he filed a habeas corpus petition with the U.S. District Court, which denied his petition. On appeal, however, the Ninth Circuit Court of Appeals reversed the decision. The Ninth Circuit Court concluded that the record available to the trial court should have led that court to question Moran's competence to make a voluntary waiver of important rights. The court held that competence to waive constitutional rights requires a higher level of mental functioning than is required for competence to stand trial. The court reasoned that the "rational and factual" understanding required by *Dusky v. U.S.*, 362 U.S. 402 (1960) was not the same as having a capacity for "reasoned choice."

Justice Thomas, in his opinion for the majority in the Supreme Court, rejected the Ninth Circuit ruling and reaffirmed Moran's conviction. Thomas argued that there was no meaningful distinction between "rational and factual understanding" and "reasoned choice." He also concluded that there could be only one standard for competence in criminal cases. He pointed out that all criminal defendants are faced with important decisions, especially the decision whether to plead guilty or not guilty. While pleading guilty is undoubtedly an important decision, Thomas reasoned that it is no more complex than other decisions that defendants have to make. If the *Dusky* standard is adequate to allow a person to plead "not guilty," it logically must be adequate for the person to plead "guilty." The decision to waive the right to counsel like-wise demands no more mental capacity than other decisions. Thomas also emphasized the fact that, besides being competent, a waiver of rights must also be "knowing and voluntary." (This formulation parallels the standard formulation for informed consent, which requires a person to have capacity, knowledge, and voluntariness.) Thomas conceded that while this formulation could be construed as a higher standard for pleading guilty or waiving rights, it is *not* a higher standard for *competence.*

Justice Kennedy offered a concurring opinion, in which he emphasized the idea that the standard for competence should not be confused with the *occasion* for its application. He noted that the requirement for competence applies throughout all phases of the trial process and that the trial court has an obligation to address the issue of the defendant's competence at any point where significant doubts about it might arise. (Kennedy's opinion is curiously silent about the question of why Moran's desire to prevent any mitigating evidence from being presented did not constitute an occasion for further inquiry into his competence.)

Justice Blackmun, in dissent, accepted the Ninth Circuit requirement for a higher standard of competence to waive constitutional rights. Blackmun pointed out that the initial psychiatric reports that found Moran to be competent also contained a clear warning that he was filled with guilt and remorse and that he might not be disposed to make an effort to defend himself. Blackmun argued that the court had indeed disregarded evidence of Moran's disturbed mental state at the time he pled guilty. Blackmun concluded that it would not be an excessive burden on trial courts to require a specific inquiry about competence at the point where a defendant with a history of mental disorder seeks to waive the right to counsel.

Cooper v. Oklahoma, 116 S.Ct. 1923 (1996)

In *Cooper v. Oklahoma*, the Supreme Court addressed the issue of whether a criminal defendant's Fourteenth Amendment rights were violated by an Oklahoma statute that presumed a defendant to be competent unless he was able to prove his incompetence by clear and convincing evidence.

Byron Cooper was convicted of murdering an 86-year-old man in a burglary and was sentenced to death. During the course of these criminal proceedings, the issue of his competence to stand trial was raised five times. During the pretrial phase a state psychologist examined him and found him to be incompetent, and he was sent to a state mental health facility for treatment. After his hospitalization, two psychologists offered conflicting opinions about his competence. Having reviewed their evaluations, the court found Cooper to be competent. Subsequently, the defense attorney again raised the issue that Cooper was refusing to communicate, but the court declined to re-open the issue of his competence. During his trial the defendant showed signs of bizarre behavior: he was observed to be talking to himself and to "spirits," and he began to fear that his attorney wanted to kill him. A new competency hearing was held, at which a third psychologist testified that Cooper again was incompetent. The court, however, again ruled that he was competent. The judge noted that his "shirtsleeve opinion" was that Cooper was not "normal" but that "to say he's not competent is something else." The judge went on to suggest that it was possible for a client to be unable to help with his defense but still to be competent. He concluded that it would take "smarter people than me" to answer such a question, but he ruled that the defense had failed to prove by clear and convincing evidence that Cooper was incompetent. Finally the defense moved for a mistrial or a re-investigation of the defendant's competence, but these motions were denied.

Cooper's conviction was appealed to the Oklahoma Court of Criminal Appeals, where the defense argued that the clear and convincing standard of proof violated the Due Process clause of the Fourteenth Amendment. The court rejected this appeal, and the United States Supreme Court agreed to hear the case. The Supreme Court reversed the Oklahoma Court's decision, holding that the Oklahoma law did violate due process. In effect the law allowed the state to try a defendant who was more likely than not to be incompetent.

The court's reasoning was based on the premise that trying an incompetent person would violate due process. The state is allowed to presume that a person is competent and to put the burden on the defendant to prove his incompetence by a preponderance of the evidence. In this case, however, the defendant was put on trial after he had already shown that he was more likely than not incompetent. The court considered this error to amount to a matter of "fundamental fairness," where the risk to the defendant outweighed any interest the state could have in the efficient prosecution of the case. Although the risk of malingering justifies placing the burden of proof on the defendant, it does not justify a higher standard of proof beyond a preponderance of the evidence.

The court pointed to the case of *Medina v. California*, 505 U.S. 437 (1992) as the basis for placing the burden of proof on the defendant. It then observed that only four states have required proof of incompetence by clear and convincing evidence. Some states in fact require the prosecution to prove that the defendant is *competent*. The court rejected Oklahoma's attempt to invoke *Addington v. Texas*, which required a standard of clear and convincing evidence in civil commitment cases. The court reasoned that civil commitment and criminal competence were entirely different issues and that the ruling in *Addington* was designed to *protect* the individual's liberty interests, not to limit them.

Indiana v. Edwards, 554 U.S. 164 (2008)

In *Indiana v. Edwards*, the Supreme Court revisited whether or not the standard for competence to stand trial equals the standard for competence to proceed *pro se*. More specifically, the court entertained the question, "whether in these circumstances, the Constitution prohibits a state from insisting that the defendant proceed to trial with counsel, the State thereby denying the right to represent himself."

In 1999, Mr. Edwards entered a store and attempted to steal a pair of shoes; store security witnessed the attempted theft and pursued Mr. Edwards, who in turn pulled a gun and fired, wounding one of the security officers and a bystander. He was apprehended and charged with multiple felonies, including attempted murder, battery with a deadly weapon, criminal recklessness, and theft. Mr. Edwards suffered from schizophrenia, and underwent three evaluations of his fitness to proceed. In August 2000, he was found unfit; in March 2002, he had regained competence to stand trial. However, in November 2003 he was found unfit to proceed again. By June 2004, he was again fit, and in June 2005, on the eve of trial, Mr. Edwards requested to dismiss counsel and represent himself. The Indiana trial court refused his request, and Mr. Edwards proceeded to trial with counsel. He was convicted on charges of criminal recklessness and theft, but the jury could not reach a verdict on the attempted murder and battery charges.

In December 2005, the state retried Mr. Edwards on the attempted murder and battery charges, and again, Mr. Edwards requested to represent himself at trial. The court again denied his request, finding that Edwards continued to suffer symptoms of schizophrenia, and "[w]ith these findings, he's competent to stand trial but I'm not going to find he's competent to defend himself." Mr. Edwards again proceed to trial with counsel; the jury found him guilty of both charges.

Mr. Edwards appealed to the Indiana intermediate appellate court, arguing a deprivation of his Sixth Amendment right, and the appellate court agreed, and ordered a new trial. The state appealed the decision, and the Indiana Supreme court upheld the decision of the appellate court, citing the U.S. Supreme Court precedent cases *Faretta v. California* and *Godinez v. Moran*. The U.S. Supreme Court granted *certiorari*.

The majority held that the Constitution does not prohibit a state from insisting a defendant proceed to trial, or, stated differently, a state may limit a defendant's right to self-representation, if the court does so after "a realistic account of the particular defendant's mental capacities by asking whether a defendant who seeks to conduct his own defense at trial is mentally competent to do so." To reach this conclusion, the court addresses *Faretta* and *Godinez*, concluding that though these cases frame the question at hand, they do not answer it. The majority maintained that while *Faretta* found "a constitutional right to proceed without counsel" when a criminal defendant "voluntarily and intelligently elects to do so" rooted in the Sixth Amendment, the case did not address the issue of mental competence, and also acknowledged limits to this right in other circumstances. In *Godinez*, the court concluded, a related but distinct question was at issue: whether a defendant was competent to waive his right to counsel in order to enter a guilty plea, as opposed to represent himself at trial: "the competence that is required of a defendant seeking to waive his right to counsel is the competence to waive the right, not the competence to represent himself."

The majority went on to make three core arguments. First, the court argued that competence to consult with an attorney is different than performing as an attorney. Second, in support, the court cited briefs by the American Psychiatric Association, which state that "symptoms of severe mental illness can impair the defendant's ability to play the significantly expanded role required for self-representation even if he can play the lesser role of represented defendant." Third, the court maintained that allowing a defendant who is not competent to represent himself to do so is not fair, in reality and in appearance. Importantly, though, the court demurred from articulating a standard for competence for self-representation at trial. The dissent emphasized a citizen's right to self-representation as fundamental as captured in the Sixth Amendment, and stressed that "the defendant's choice must be honored out of 'that respect for the individual that is the lifeblood of the law'...What the Constitution requires is that a defendant be given the right to challenge the State's case against him using the arguments he sees fit." The dissent did not dispute that waiving counsel knowingly and voluntarily is most likely foolish, but argued "the dignity at issue is the supreme human dignity of being master of one's own fate rather than the ward of the state—that of individual choice." The dissent provided additional information to support a conclusion that though mentally ill, Mr. Edwards' requests to represent himself were not a product of his mental illness but rather sprang from disagreements with his counsel about the best defense to put forward at trial. The dissent also drew attention to the potential harms of the majority's decision to those who suffer from mental illness: "At a time when all society is trying to mainstream the mentally impaired, the Court permits them to be deprived of a basic constitutional right—for their own good."

HYPNOSIS

State v. Hurd, 414 A.2d 291 (1980)

Paul Hurd, the defendant in an assault case, filed a motion in a New Jersey superior court to suppress the victim's identification of him in court because she had been hypnotized. The defendant was divorced from the victim, who had later remarried. He was charged with having broken into her home at night and with stabbing her numerous times with a knife, while her current husband slept nearby. Immediately after the attack, the victim was unable to identify the perpetrator, and referred to him as a "stranger," but she also suggested to the police that they "check out" her ex-husband. The prosecutor arranged for the victim to be examined by a psychiatrist, who hypnotized her in the presence of police officers. Her current husband was meanwhile outside in the waiting room. Six days after hypnosis, the victim made a statement identifying Hurd as her attacker.

The issues in the case were (1) whether a victim could be allowed to make an identification in court after she had been unable to do so prior to hypnosis; (2) whether hypnosis was reliable enough to be used for memory enhancement; and (3) whether the method used in this particular case was unnecessarily suggestive, so that the identification should be suppressed.

The court granted the defendant's motion to suppress the identification, ruling that hypnotically induced recollection could only be admitted in testimony under strictly limited conditions, which the court enumerated:

1. Hypnosis must be done by a licensed M.D. or Ph.D. trained in hypnosis.
2. The hypnotist must be independent of the parties in the case.
3. Only written information should be given to the hypnotist prior to the hypnosis.
4. The hypnotist should independently obtain the subject's recollections of the facts prior to initiating hypnosis.
5. All contacts by the hypnotist with the witness should be recorded.
6. Only the hypnotist should be present during the interviews.

The court relied in its opinion on the expert testimony of Dr. Martin Orne. Dr. Orne indicated that hypnotic recall is often unreliable and that a hypnotized subject is highly vulnerable to suggestion, is likely to have diminished critical judgment, and may fill in gaps in memory by confabulation when pressed to give an answer. Once suggestions are made, Dr. Orne said, it is impossible to distinguish between confabulation and accurate details. Dr. Orne also testified that the procedure used in this case was in fact clearly suggestive of the identification of Hurd as the assailant. He also maintained that the presence at the doctor's office of police officers and the current husband (who had himself been a possible suspect) tended to point the finger at Hurd, and that the victim was in fact an unreliable witness, as indicated by her contradicting herself.

The court relied on *Frye v. United States*, 293 F. 1013 (1923), for the standard for judicial acceptance of scientific evidence: the reliability of a procedure must be shown to have received general acceptance in the scientific community for the procedure to be admitted in evidence. The court reasoned that the expert testimony made it clear that hypnosis did not receive such general scientific acceptance for the purpose of memory enhancement.

People v. Shirley, 181 Cal. Rptr. 243 (1982)

In *People v. Shirley*, the California Supreme Court addressed the question of whether the testimony of a witness should be admitted in a criminal trial after the witness had undergone hypnosis to enhance her memory. The court held that such testimony could not be admitted in California.

Catherine C. was the complaining witness in a rape trial. She testified that the defendant had threatened her with weapons and compelled her to submit to intercourse. The defendant in contrast testified that Catherine C. had invited him into her home and had willingly engaged in consensual sex. Prior to the trial, the prosecutor had had Catherine C. hypnotized for the purpose of "filling in the gaps" in her story. During the trial her performance was erratic: she gave self-contradictory testimony and had lapses of memory, even being unable to recall what she said on the witness stand one day previously. In spite of these inconsistencies, the jury convicted the defendant of rape. In overturning the conviction, the California Supreme Court ruled that it was an error to allow Catherine C. to testify after having undergone hypnosis.

The record indicated that the witness made different statements in her testimony at trial compared to her statements in a preliminary hearing. The defense had moved to exclude all testimony that resulted from the hypnosis. The trial court, however, ruled that the hypnosis only affected the weight that should be given to this evidence, not to its admissibility. At the trial, the defense called a psychiatrist to testify as an expert. He made several points about the unreliability of memories enhanced by hypnosis: first, that there is no assurance that the memory would be correct; second, that any motive to distort the truth could still operate under hypnosis; third, that hypnosis might give the witness implicit permission to believe in such a distortion; and finally that hypnosis can have the effect of making the witness more convinced that her memory was valid.

The California Supreme Court did an extensive review of court decisions regarding hypnosis and also reviewed the psychiatric literature regarding the validity of hypnotically enhanced memory. The court found a widespread consensus that hypnotically enhanced testimony is not reliable. It cited *Frye v. United States*, 293 F. 1013, as the standard for admissibility of scientific evidence. The *Frye* rule stated that evidence based on a scientific technique is admissible if the technique has gained general acceptance for reliability in the scientific community. In reviewing the record of court decisions in the preceding decade, the court found a gradual change in the approach of the courts. In early cases, the courts tended to follow the rule articulated by the trial court in *Shirley*, that hypnosis constituted an issue in weighing the evidence but not in its admissibility. In more recent cases, however, courts had become increasingly concerned about the dangers of introducing hypnotically refreshed testimony. The court noted the approach of *State v. Hurd*, 414 A.2d. 291, which it characterized as formulating "an intricate set of procedural prerequisites" for the use of hypnosis. The court concluded that even such a set of safeguards could not forestall the problems inherent in the use of hypnosis. The *Hurd* rules were largely aimed at avoiding the problem of suggestibility in the hypnotic interview, but these rules did not address the fact that the witness could lose critical judgment about her own memory or still confuse actual memory with confabulation or show unjustified confidence in the correctness of her memory. The court concluded that its review of scientific literature indicated that hypnosis as a memory enhancement technique did not meet the *Frye* test of general acceptability.

The court made one exception to its ruling, which anticipated the case of *Rock v. Arkansas*, 107 S.Ct. 2704. When the defendant is the witness who has submitted to hypnosis, his testimony remains admissible because of his fundamental right to testify in his own behalf.

Rock v. Arkansas, 107 S.Ct. 2704 (1987)

Vickie Lorene Rock was convicted of manslaughter in the death of her husband. She appealed her conviction, arguing that the state of Arkansas, in excluding her own hypnotically refreshed testimony from her trial, had infringed on her constitutional right to testify on her own behalf.

In the context of "simmering" marital disputes, Rock and her husband had a fight over his refusal to let her leave their apartment to get something to eat. The husband was shot, and when the police arrived, Rock told them that her husband had choked her and thrown her against the wall; that she picked up a pistol; that he hit her again; and that she shot him. Because she could not recall precise details of these events, her attorney arranged for her to be hypnotized, after which she remembered having her thumb on the hammer of the pistol but not having her finger on the trigger. She then stated that the gun discharged when her husband grabbed her. A firearms expert also offered an opinion that the gun was defective and prone to fire when struck.

The trial court, operating under an Arkansas rule that no hypnotically refreshed testimony was admissible, allowed the defendant to testify only to those details that she had recalled prior to hypnosis, as documented by the hypnotist's sketchy notes. As she testified the prosecutor repeatedly objected, and was sustained, when she mentioned anything that went beyond the doctor's notes. The defendant was then convicted.

On appeal to the Supreme Court, the issue was whether Arkansas' *per se* rule excluding hypnotically refreshed testimony was unconstitutional. The Supreme Court concluded that in this instance the rule did amount to a violation of the defendant's rights under the Fifth, Sixth, and Fourteenth amendments. The court held that the defendant's right to testify in her own behalf derived from several sources in the Constitution. The due process requirement of the Fourteenth Amendment includes the right to be heard. The choice to testify is also a necessary corollary of the Fifth Amendment, i.e., the defendant has the privilege of either testifying or refusing to do so. Finally the Sixth Amendment was designed to ensure that the testimony of witnesses on the defendant's behalf should be admissible. The court reasoned that the most important witness for the defense might be the defendant herself and therefore that any severe limits on her testimony could vitiate her ability to present a defense.

The majority pointed out that the right to present testimony is not unlimited, but that restrictions imposed by the state may not be "arbitrary or disproportionate to the purposes they are designed to serve." The state has an obligation to weigh the interests served by its rule (e.g., preventing erroneous evidence), to justify the limitations imposed on the defendant's rights. There are additional safeguards for the judicial process, however (e.g., the veracity of hypnotically refreshed testimony can still be tested by cross-examination). The Arkansas rule fails because it does not allow the trial court even to consider posthypnotic recollections and effectively prevented this defendant from describing the events of the shooting at all.

A dissent by four justices emphasized the unreliability of hypnosis as a technique for memory enhancement and suggested that the majority would require the trial court to make a scientific assessment of the reliability of the testimony in each case, an assessment that the dissenters implied was beyond the competence of the courts.

CRIMINAL RESPONSIBILITY

M'Naghten's Case, 8 Eng. Rep. 718, 722 (1843)

The *M'Naghten* case is by far the oldest case currently designated as a landmark. The furor surrounding M'Naghten's acquittal in this case during the reign of Queen Victoria was comparable to the more recent furor in this country regarding the Hinckley verdict. Because of her concern over the threat of assassination, the Queen was instrumental in having the case re-examined by the House of Lords.

Daniel M'Naghten suffered from a paranoid psychosis, in which he believed that he was being persecuted by the Tory party. Medical testimony in his trial indicated that he believed that he was being stalked and persecuted by Tories, who wanted to murder him. On January 20, 1843, he shot and killed Edward Drummond, who was the secretary to the Prime Minister, Robert Peel. The prosecution portrayed the case as one of deliberate political assassination, arguing that M'Naghten intended to shoot Peel and only killed Drummond by mistake. The defense portrayed M'Naghten as an insane person who had been in a state of terror, believing he was being threatened by the Tories, and who had not known whom he was shooting, believing that Drummond was only one of the conspirators against him. Defense experts testified that M'Naghten was delusional and that he was incapable of exercising control over acts connected to his delusions. After hearing the expert testimony, the jury acquitted M'Naghten on the ground of insanity.

The House of Lords directed several questions to Her Majesty's Judges (who served a function somewhat analogous to a Supreme Court in resolving issues of law). The crucial issue was to define the standard for insanity, where a person suffered from delusions but might also have known that he was acting contrary to the law. What if the defendant, acting on a delusion, was attempting to get revenge for some grievance or to produce some (delusional) benefit to society? Lord Chief Justice Tindal presented the conclusion of the judges, which constitutes the original formulation of the "M'Naghten Rule": for a defendant to be found insane, "it must be clearly proved that, at the time of the committing of the act, the party accused was laboring under such a defect of reason, from disease of the mind, as not to know the nature and quality of the act he was doing; or, if he did know it, that he did not know he was doing what was wrong." It must be left to the jury to decide, in a particular case, whether the defendant had a sufficient degree of reason to know that what he was doing was wrong. Tindal went on to explain that the answer to this question would depend on the nature of the delusion. The defendant must be judged "as if the facts with respect to which the delusion exists were real." Therefore, if the man believed his life to be threatened and acted in an effort to defend himself, he might be found not guilty; if he acted only from a sense of injury and sought revenge, he would still be culpable.

It is interesting to speculate as to whether the articulation of the "M'Naghten Rule" would actually have made any difference to the jury in judging M'Naghten. The trial court's actual instructions to the jury were in fact hardly distinguishable from the rule in its ultimate form: "The question to be determined is, whether at the time the act in question was committed, the prisoner had or had not the use of his understanding, so as to know he was doing a wrong or wicked act."

Durham v. United States, 214 F.2d 862 (1954)

Durham represented an effort by Judge David Bazelon and the U.S. Court of Appeals for the District of Columbia Circuit to redefine the test for insanity in a criminal case. The case is now mainly of historical significance: it reflects a conceptual development in judicial thinking about insanity but had only limited practical effect as a precedent. In 1972 the court overturned its *Durham* rule in deciding *United States v. Brawner* (471 F. 2d 969).

The Court of Appeals addressed two issues in *Durham*: first, whether the trial court had applied the rules on the burden of proof incorrectly, and second, whether the existing test of insanity was obsolete. Monte Durham had presented an insanity defense in his trial for housebreaking. He had a long psychiatric history that included, at different times, diagnoses of personality disorder and psychosis, with episodes of antisocial behavior, attempted suicide, and psychiatric hospitalization. At his trial, the court rejected his insanity defense on the grounds that Durham had failed to establish that he did not know the difference between right and wrong or that he was subject to an irresistible impulse (these two tests constituting the accepted rules in the District of Columbia Circuit at the time). The trial court found that because there was no testimony about his state of mind on the day of the offense, the usual presumption of insanity would therefore hold.

Bazelon's opinion rejected this logic, reversing Durham's conviction and remanding the case for a new trial. On the burden of proof issue, Bazelon pointed out that the prosecution is not required to prove the defendant's sanity until "some evidence of mental disorder is introduced." At that point, however, sanity had to be proved by the prosecution beyond a reasonable doubt. Although the trial court apparently did not see evidence of insanity, Bazelon found the testimony of the only expert witness to be "unequivocal" that Durham was of unsound mind at the time of the crime. (The prosecution had presented no expert testimony in rebuttal.) Bazelon criticized the trial court for restricting the psychiatric testimony to an all-or-nothing type of response: "The inability of the expert to give categorical assurance that Durham was unable to distinguish between right and wrong did not destroy the effect of his previous testimony that the period of Durham's insanity embraced" the day of the offense.

After reviewing the historical development and establishment of the right–wrong test in most American jurisdictions, Bazelon maintained that the rule must change with new scientific knowledge: modern psychiatry recognized the individual as an integrated personality from which "reason" cannot be abstracted as an isolated element that determines conduct. Bazelon concluded that the "fact finder should be free to consider all information advanced by relevant scientific disciplines." He went on to set out a deliberately broad rule: that a defendant was "not criminally responsible if his unlawful act was the product of mental disease or mental defect." Bazelon thus invited psychiatrists to testify expansively, while specifically reserving for the jury the ultimate questions of insanity and moral responsibility.

Washington v. United States, 390 F.2d 444 (1967)

In *Washington v. United States*, the U.S. Court of Appeals for the District of Columbia Circuit went beyond *Durham v. U.S.* (214 F.2d 862, 1954) in elaborating its critique of psychiatric expert testimony in insanity cases. The court criticized both lawyers and witnesses for over-reliance on medical jargon, and it offered specific suggestions for how experts should testify.

Washington had been convicted of rape, robbery, and assault after having presented an insanity defense. The Court of Appeals upheld the conviction, on the grounds that the jury did hear at least a minimum amount of information to be able to decide the issue of sanity. In writing the opinion, however, Chief Judge Bazelon suggested that the jury might have been "hindered" by the psychiatrists' use of jargon, and much of his opinion then dealt with this issue.

Judge Bazelon briefly reviewed the history of how the "product" test in *Durham* had been intended to widen the range of expert testimony in order to provide juries with more extensive scientific information. Bazelon observed that *Durham* had been mistakenly interpreted as excusing from criminal responsibility anyone classified by the psychiatric profession as mentally ill. He emphasized that psychiatrists have no such classification as to what is an excusing condition; therefore, expert opinion should not bind a jury in its conclusions. He pointed out that the Court of Appeals had given a legal definition of mental illness in *McDonald v. United States* (312 F.2d 851 1962)—that is, "any abnormal condition of the mind which substantially affects mental or emotional processes and which substantially impairs behavior control." (The word *any* made clear that the concept of insanity was not tied to particular diagnoses.)

Bazelon maintained that in Washington's trial the use of psychiatric labels without behavioral data gave the jury a very limited basis for its decision; psychiatrists testified as to their conclusions based on only single interviews, and the jury did not hear detailed data from hospital observation. What the jury did hear was a "confusing mass of abstract philosophical discussion" of legal and psychiatric labels, including confusing definitions of terms like "neurosis," "schizoid," "sociopath," and "irresistible impulse."

Part of the court's purpose in *Durham* and *McDonald* was to clarify the responsibility of expert witnesses for giving explanatory descriptions of mental conditions and to keep separate the legal question of culpability from the medical concept of illness. Bazelon instructed trial judges to limit the expert's use of labels and to ensure that their meaning was explained when they were necessary. He explicitly dropped his endorsement of *Durham's* "product" test, now concluding that the concept had no clinical meaning to psychiatrists, and that psychiatrists should not be testifying about the ultimate issue of sanity.

Bazelon's appendix included suggestions that many forensic psychiatrists might question: for example, that psychiatrists should not concern themselves with the legal meaning of "mental disease," and that they should give explanations in court in the same fashion as they would to the family of a patient.

People v. Patterson, 383 N.Y.S.2d 573 (1976)

In *People v. Patterson*, New York State's highest court had to deal with the distinction between "extreme emotional disturbance" and other, apparently similar, "diminished capacity" or "heat of passion" defenses. The specific issue in the case was whether New York violated due process rights by placing the burden of proof on the defendant in a murder case, requiring him to show that he acted under extreme emotional disturbance.

Gordon Patterson had killed a man whom he found with his estranged wife in a state of "semi-undress." The state tried and convicted Patterson under a statute that allowed, as an affirmative defense to the charge of murder, the argument that the defendant acted under the influence of "extreme emotional disturbance for which there was a reasonable explanation or excuse, the reasonableness of which is to be determined from the viewpoint of a person in the defendant's situation under the circumstances as the defendant believed them to be." Proof of this disturbance by a preponderance of the evidence meant that the defendant would be convicted only of manslaughter, not murder.

The New York State Court of Appeals held that Patterson's conviction did not violate due process. The court ruled that the state always has the burden of proving every element of a crime, including intent; as long as the state does so, the burden can be placed on the defendant to show that he formed that intent under the influence of extreme emotional disturbance.

The court reasoned that extreme emotional disturbance does not contradict intent but rather serves to *explain* the defendant's intentional action. The concept of such a disturbance includes more than sudden, spontaneous reactions: "it may be that a significant mental trauma has affected a defendant's mind for a substantial period of time, simmering in the unknowing subconscious and then inexplicably coming to the fore." The court distinguished this case from the Supreme Court's decision in *Mullaney v. Wilbur* (421 U.S. 684) where the court held that due process did require a prosecutor in Maine to prove the *absence* of "heat of passion" for a murder conviction. After making a detailed historical review of the differences between the statutory definitions of murder and manslaughter in Maine and New York, the New York Court of Appeals pointed out that the New York legislature had discarded the concepts of "premeditation" or "deliberation," requiring only proof of intent in its current definition of murder. In Maine, the "heat of passion" would by definition negate intent, because "malice" or "premeditation" was logically inconsistent with the "heat of passion"; if the defendant acted with premeditation, he could therefore not be responding to a sudden, inflammatory provocation. In New York, by contrast, the presence of extreme emotional disturbance does not make the act any less intentional.

Frendak v. U.S., 408 A.2d 364 (1979)

Paula Frendak was convicted of murder after a jury trial in the District of Columbia. Prior to her trial she had been given varying diagnoses (schizophrenia or borderline personality) and was found to be incompetent to stand trial on two occasions. After she was eventually found to be competent, the trial court held a hearing regarding her sanity at the time of the crime, and the court decided to impose the insanity defense over the defendant's objection. At trial, the jury found the defendant to be not guilty by reason of insanity (NGRI). The court had based its decision on *Whalem v. U.S.* (120 U.S. App. D.C. 331), where the Court of Appeals for the D.C. Circuit had held that a trial judge does have discretion to raise the insanity defense over the objection of the defendant, even if the defendant is competent to stand trial. Frendak challenged the validity of this ruling.

On hearing Frendak's appeal, the Court of Appeals for the D.C. Circuit re-interpreted *Whalem* and held that the trial judge may not force the insanity defense on a competent defendant as long as the defendant had waived the defense in an intelligent and voluntary manner. The court held that competence to stand trial was not sufficient in itself to allow such a waiver. The trial judge was required to make a further assessment into the intelligence and voluntariness of the decision. Because it was unclear as to whether Frendak had in fact made such a waiver, the case was remanded to the trial court for a decision on that issue.

In reaching its decision in Frendak's case, the court had to deal with the question of whether *Whalem* had been affected by two other Supreme Court decisions: *North Carolina v. Alford,* 400 U.S. 25 (1970) and *Faretta v. California,* 422 U.S. 806 (1975). These two cases stood for the proposition that the defendant has the right to make key decisions in her own case. *Alford* held that it was not unconstitutional for a judge to accept a guilty plea from a defendant who maintained that he was in fact innocent. The court reasoned that a defendant might have a valid reason for wanting to plead guilty, e.g., to get a shorter sentence, even while claiming to be innocent. In *Faretta*, the Court ruled that the Sixth Amendment gives the defendant the right to control his or her defense, including the right to represent himself or herself without a state-imposed attorney. The court pointed out that *Alford* does not give the defendant an absolute right to have a guilty plea accepted and that *Faretta* does not allow the defendant to control all aspects of the defense. Following these precedents, however, the court in *Frendak* reasoned that the defendant might have a valid interest in not wanting to make an insanity defense (e.g., not wanting to be confined in a hospital for a longer period of time than the potential prison sentence). This interest would outweigh the abstract concept of justice that is articulated in *Whalem*, i.e., the state's interest in protecting a morally blameless person from conviction. The court indicated that it was not abolishing *Whalem* but only limiting the discretion of the trial court, which must defer to the defendant's decision about the insanity defense as long it was intelligently and voluntarily made. The criteria for judging this decision would be whether the defendant was fully informed of her alternatives and understood the consequences of the choice.

Ibn-Tamas v. United States, 407 A.2d 626 (1979)

Ibn-Tamas v. United States expanded the scope of expert testimony about spousal abuse that could be considered relevant in a homicide trial. Beverly Ibn-Tamas had been convicted of the murder of her husband in the Superior Court of the District of Columbia. The defense alleged that her husband, a physician, was a violent man who had assaulted his wife on numerous occasions and had threatened her with a gun in the past. In 1976, while the defendant was pregnant, there was another argument and assault, during which she shot and killed him. She then asserted in her defense that she had felt in imminent danger due to his repeated threats and violence. She testified that prior to the shooting, her husband had again struck her and threatened her with a pistol. A witness for the prosecution provided a different account, which suggested that the husband had begged for mercy before the final shot. This testimony raised a serious question about the assertion of self-defense.

The defense offered the testimony of a psychologist on the subject of the battered wife syndrome and elicited her expert opinion as to whether Ibn-Tamas fitted the pattern of a battered woman. It argued that the testimony was relevant, because it would help the jury to determine the credibility of the claim that she perceived herself in imminent danger from her husband and shot him in self-defense.

The trial court excluded the testimony for three reasons: that it included past violent acts that the jury was not entitled to hear about; that it invaded the province of the jury in judging the facts and the credibility of the defendant; and that the expert necessarily concluded that the victim was a batterer.

The Court of Appeals for the District of Columbia reversed the decision and held that the expert testimony was not, in principle, inadmissible: the trial court should have been guided by the principle that the defense is free to introduce any expert testimony that is likely to aid the fact finder, as long as its probative value outweighs its prejudicial impact. The court concluded that the psychologist's testimony would not have invaded the province of the jury but rather could have supplied background information to help the jury determine the ultimate issue of guilt or innocence; and that she did not directly express an opinion on the ultimate issue. The court held that the expert testimony here was beyond the ordinary knowledge of the jury, so that its probative value did outweigh any prejudicial effect: it would be probative of Ibn-Tamas's perceptions at the time of the killing, a factor that was central to her claim of self-defense.

The court did not consider the trial record sufficient for it to decide that the expert testimony was actually admissible in this case. It remanded the case for further examination of the psychologist's credentials and for a determination as to whether her methods for evaluating the battered wife syndrome had achieved general scientific acceptance.

Ake v. Oklahoma, 470 U.S. 68 (1985)

In *Ake v. Oklahoma* the Supreme Court sanctioned a distinct expansion of the role of the psychiatric expert for the defense in insanity cases. Glen Burton Ake was arrested for murder in 1979. At his arraignment, a judge ordered a psychiatric examination because of bizarre behavior. A psychiatrist found him to be delusional and apparently schizophrenic, and the court committed him to a state hospital for examination of his competence to stand trial. Hospital psychiatrists initially advised the court that Ake was incompetent; subsequently he was found competent after being treated with 600 mg of Thorazine (chlorpromazine) per day. During his stay in the hospital, no examination was done with regard to his sanity at the time of the offense. When his attorney asked the court to arrange for such an examination, the judge denied the request. At trial, Ake presented an insanity defense, calling as witnesses the psychiatrists who had examined him. Because none of the doctors had examined him as to his mental state at the time of the offense, there was no expert testimony about that issue. The judge instructed the jury that Ake should be presumed sane unless he presented evidence sufficient to raise a reasonable doubt about his sanity. The jury convicted him and sentenced him to death. The Oklahoma Court of Criminal Appeals then upheld the trial court's denial of the services of a psychiatric expert for the defense.

On appeal to the Supreme Court the issue was whether the Constitution required that Ake should have had access to a psychiatric examination for sanity and the assistance of a psychiatrist in the preparation of an insanity defense. In an opinion written by Justice Marshall, the court held that when an indigent defendant makes a preliminary showing that his sanity is likely to be a significant issue, the Fourteenth Amendment does require the state to provide access to such psychiatric services. The guarantee of due process of law depends on the idea that justice is not equal when an indigent person is denied a meaningful opportunity to defend himself. (In *Gideon v. Wainwright* [372 U.S. 335, 1963] the court had held the state responsible for providing legal counsel for indigent defendants.)

Marshall made clear that the defense would not be entitled to all the assistance money could buy, or to an expert of its own choice, but only to "adequate opportunity to present their claims fairly." In weighing the competing interests in the case, he noted that the defendant had a "uniquely compelling" interest in the accuracy of the criminal proceeding, and that the court was concerned with the risk of erroneous conviction; at the same time he found it an exaggeration for the state to claim that it would be a "staggering burden" to provide what Ake had requested. He noted that most other states already provided such assistance.

Marshall spelled out various ways in which a psychiatrist might be crucial to the defendant's case: to gather facts to be presented in court; to analyze the information and draw conclusions about how the defendant's mental state affected him; to identify "elusive" signs of mental disorder that a layperson would miss; and to help in framing questions for the prosecution's experts in cross-examination. With a touch of irony, Marshall pointed out that *Barefoot v. Estelle* (463 U.S. 880, 1982) had upheld the use of psychiatric testimony to determine future dangerousness in capital cases, with an explicit assumption that both the prosecution and the defense could present expert testimony on the issue.

Chief Justice Burger wrote a concurring opinion in order to make the point that the ruling specifically applied only to capital cases. Justice Rehnquist dissented, arguing that the facts of the case, for example, Ake's having indulged in a long, organized, purposeful crime spree prior to his arrest, provided evidence as to his sanity, so that additional psychiatric examination was not warranted. He also rejected the idea of a court-appointed defense psychiatrist serving as a "consultant" or "advocate" as opposed to the traditional independent expert.

Foucha v. Louisiana, 112 S.Ct. 1780 (1992)

In a sharply divided five-to-four decision, the Supreme Court ruled in *Foucha v. Louisiana* that a defendant found to be NGRI could only be committed to a psychiatric hospital as long as he continued to be both mentally ill and dangerous. Louisiana law at the time required an NGRI acquittee to be held in the hospital until a review panel found him to be no longer dangerous to himself or others. Once the review panel recommended the person's release, a court hearing would be held in which the defendant had the burden of proof to show that he was no longer dangerous.

Foucha had been convicted of burglary and illegal discharge of a firearm. He was found NGRI at trial in 1984. In 1988, the superintendent of the hospital where he was confined recommended that he be released, because he showed no evidence of having any mental illness since the time of his admission. The hospital suggested that he had probably suffered from a drug-induced psychosis at the time of the crime, and that he had now recovered. He continued to show signs of an antisocial personality, and one psychiatrist testified that he would not be comfortable saying that Foucha was not a danger to others. The court ruled that Foucha had not shown that he was no longer dangerous, and he was retained in the hospital. The state Supreme Court affirmed the lower court's decision.

The Supreme Court relied on three prior decisions to reach its conclusion. In *Addington v. Texas* (441 U.S. 418) the court had held that civil commitment required a showing by clear and convincing evidence that a person was both mentally ill and required hospitalization for the protection of self or others. *Jones v. U.S.* (463 U.S. 354) had allowed the state to commit a defendant found NGRI without meeting the *Addington* burden, because the court had held that the NGRI verdict established the facts that the defendant was mentally ill and had committed a criminal act. The *Jones* court had inferred that the defendant, at the time of the verdict, must be mentally ill and dangerous. *Jones* still indicated, however, that the defendant should be released when he had either recovered his sanity or was no longer dangerous. As a result, the court reasoned that Foucha could not be kept in the hospital without a determination that he was both currently mentally ill and dangerous. The court also cited *Vitek v. Jones* (445 U.S. 480, 1980) which established a convicted felon's liberty interest in not being sent to a mental hospital without showing that he was mentally ill. The court concluded that an NGRI acquittee would be entitled to the same consideration as a convicted felon.

The court went on to point out that in some narrow circumstances a person who was a danger to the community might be detained for a limited period of time, as defined by *U.S. v. Salerno*, 481 U.S. 739. *Salerno*, however, involved pretrial detention and applied only to cases of serious crimes where there was an overwhelming government interest in confining the defendant. Furthermore, *Salerno* placed strict limits on the duration of confinement; if acquitted, the defendant would immediately go free.

The court also emphasized the fact that, in Foucha's case, no doctor had actually testified positively that he was dangerous. The state had placed the burden on him to prove he was not dangerous, rather than assuming the burden to prove by clear and convincing evidence that he was. The court concluded that the state's argument—that Foucha was an antisocial personality who could commit more crimes—would allow the state to detain any NGRI acquittee with such a personality disorder or indeed any convicted felon who had already served his maximum sentence.

Justice O'Connor wrote a concurring opinion in order to point out that the majority was only addressing the Louisiana statute and was not passing judgment on more narrowly formulated laws. It might therefore be acceptable to confine an NGRI acquittee if the nature and duration of the confinement had a medical justification and were tailored to a specific public safety concern. Justice Kennedy dissented, apparently out of concern that Foucha's initial insanity might have been malingered. He argued that the state had an interest in incapacitative incarceration, even though it was not considered to be punishment. Justice Thomas also wrote a dissent, which maintained that there was a legitimate distinction to be drawn between NGRI and civil committees, which justified different procedures for their commitment. The NGRI acquittee has been found to have committed a criminal act; because psychiatry is not an exact science, the decision to release the acquittee should not hinge on whether the person is thought to have regained his sanity. Thomas maintained that it was thus a reasonable legislative judgment to say that the NGRI acquittee should not be released as long as he remains dangerous.

Clark v. Arizona, 548 U.S. 735 (2006)

In *Clark v. Arizona,* the U.S. Supreme Court held that Arizona's test for insanity, which eliminated the cognitive component of the *M'Naghten* standard so that it hinged on a defendant's ability to tell whether an act charged as a crime was right or wrong, did not violate due process. The court also held that Arizona law excluding evidence of mental illness and incapacity due to mental illness on the issue of *mens rea* did not violate due process.

On June 21, 2006, a police officer on patrol responded to complaints of a pick-up driving the streets of a Flagstaff neighborhood blasting loud music. The officer, in a marked car with sirens and lights engaged, pulled over the truck, driven by the defendant Eric Clark. The officer exited his car, approached Clark, informing him to remain in his vehicle, after which Clark shot the officer, killing him. Clark was subsequently apprehended and charged with first-degree murder.

At trial, Clark did not dispute the events of the shooting, but he made two arguments: first, he was insane at that time of the shooting, which Arizona defined as "at the time of the commission of the criminal act [he] was afflicted with a mental disease or defect of such severity that [he] did not know the criminal act was wrong." Clark also disputed that he possessed *mens rea* required for a conviction of first-degree murder because, on account of his mental illness, he believed he was shooting an alien, not a law enforcement officer. The judge overseeing the case found Clark guilty of first-degree murder, determining, consistent with state law as articulated in *Mott v. Arizona,* that evidence regarding the effects of mental illness on capacity should be restricted to a determination of sanity only, and could not be used by a defendant to rebut *mens rea* as an element of the crime the prosecution need prove beyond a reasonable doubt. Clark appealed, and the U.S. Supreme Court granted *certiorari,* after the Arizona Court of Appeals confirmed the conviction and the Supreme Court of Arizona declined to review further Clark's due process claims.

With regard to Arizona's elimination of the cognitive component of the *M'Naghten* insanity test via legislative amendment in 1993, the majority first qualified the burden of Clark's claim, that this amendment "offends a principle of justice so rooted in the traditions and conscience of our people as to be ranked as fundamental," for the U.S. Supreme court to overrule how a state defines its criminal laws and procedure. The court found that it did not, citing that some states do not offer an insanity defense, and in those that do, the use of the full *M'Naghten* test is far from universal. Moreover, the court argued, on the basis of logic, that "cognitive incapacity is itself enough to demonstrate moral incapacity." In other words, the two incapacities are redundant, not additive—if you do not know that nature and quality of the act, then you cannot know its wrongfulness.

With regard to Clark's *mens rea* objection, the majority upheld the decision in *Mott v. State* as constitutional; in this case, the Arizona state court held that testimony of a professional psychologist or psychiatrist about a defendant's mental incapacity owing to mental disease or defect was admissible, but may be considered only for its bearing on an insanity defense, and that such evidence could not be considered on the element of *mens rea.* To do so, the court distinguished the presumption of innocence from the presumption of sanity, and the relevant burdens to overcome them. The prosecution bears the burden to overcome the presumption of innocence, and must prove their case beyond a reasonable doubt. However, the defendant bears the burden to overcome the presumption of sanity, and must do so with proof, in Arizona, by clear and convincing evidence, but the court emphasized that legislatures are given wide latitude to define "the strength of the presumption of sanity and the kind of evidence and degree or persuasiveness to overcome it."

Furthermore, the court argued, channelling expert (as opposed to lay) testimony on a defendant's capacities to the question of sanity only (as opposed to allowing such experts to cast doubt on *mens rea*) is not fundamentally unfair: "What counts for due process, however, is simply that a State wishes to avoid a second avenue for exploring capacity, less stringent for a defendant, has a good reason for confining the consideration of evidence of mental disease and incapacity to the insanity defense." Thus, the majority concluded that states are allowed under certain circumstances to limit what and how certain evidence is admitted if there is a compelling state interested to justify the restriction, and the state's interest in defining criminal responsibility with regard to lack of capacity related to mental illness is such a compelling interest. What's more, the majority cited concerns that "an expert's judgment in giving capacity evidence will come with an apparent authority that psychologist and psychiatrists do not claim to have. We think that this risk, like the difficulty in assessing the significance of mental-disease evidence, supports the State's decision to channel expert testimony to consideration on the insanity defense, on which the party seeking the benefit of this evidence has the burden of persuasion."

The dissent reframed the question at hand: "The issue is not, as the Court insists, whether Clark's mental illness acts as 'an excuse from customary criminal responsibility,' ... but whether his mental illness, as a factual matter, made him unaware that he was shooting a police officer." In this vein, the dissent argued that testimony from mental health experts on Clarke's diagnosis was relevant to answering this question, and disagreed with the majority's characterization of such testimony as unreliable, especially in the context of a first-degree murder trial: "While the State contends that testimony regarding mental illness may be too incredible or speculative for the jury to consider, this does not explain why the exclusion applies in all cases to all evidence of mental illness." The dissent, in closing, took another of the majority's argument to the absurd: "In sum, the rule forces the jury to decide guilt in a fictional world with undefined and unexplained behaviors but without mental illness. This rule has no rational justification and imposes a significant burden upon a straightforward defense: He did not commit the crime with which he was charged."

SUBSTANCE ABUSE AND CRIME

Robinson v. California, 370 U.S. 660 (1962)

Robinson v. California represents the Supreme Court's comment on a state's use of criminal procedures as a way of dealing with the problem of drug addiction. The California Health and Safety Code made it a misdemeanor for a person to "be addicted to the use of narcotics." A jury in Los Angeles convicted Robinson under this statute, basing its decision on a police officer's testimony that he had found "track" marks on Robinson's arms. The prosecution made no claim that the defendant engaged in any other illegal conduct at the time. A California appeals court upheld the conviction.

When the case reached the Supreme Court, the issue was whether the California statute was unconstitutional under the Eighth and Fourteenth Amendments. A majority opinion, written by Justice Stewart, held that it was unconstitutional. Stewart pointed out that the California statute allowed the state to find a person guilty of an offense continuously, regardless of whether he had ever actually used narcotics in the state. He relied heavily on the idea that addiction is an illness, analogous to mental illness or leprosy, arguing that it would universally be considered cruel to punish people for such illnesses. Justice Douglas wrote a concurring opinion, emphasizing the severity of the illness involved and the barbarity of punishing someone for it.

Justices Clark and White dissented separately. Clark accepted the use of a criminal penalty as part of a program of addiction control, where civil and criminal procedures were both "inherently" aimed at treatment. According to his analysis, California's criminal provisions applied to addicts who still had control over their drug use, while civil commitment was available to deal with those who had lost self-control. White, on the other hand, rejected the idea that Robinson had not engaged in illegal conduct, because addiction logically implies that a person must have committed the act of using drugs. To White, therefore, the conviction did not depend on Robinson's status as an addict.

Powell v. Texas, 392 U.S. 514 (1968)

Powell v. Texas, coming 6 years after *Robinson v. California* (370 U.S. 660, 1962), addressed a closely related issue: whether it was cruel and unusual punishment to convict an alcoholic for public drunkenness.

Powell had been convicted in the Corporation Court of Austin, Texas, for being intoxicated in public. He was retried on appeal in county court, where a medical expert testified that Powell was in fact a chronic alcoholic and that, while his taking his first drink was voluntary, Powell had also acted under a compulsion that was "not completely overpowering" but a "very strong influence." His counsel argued that it was a violation of the Eighth Amendment to arrest him for a disease, chronic alcoholism, since he did not appear in public of his own volition when he was drunk. The court rejected this argument and reinstated Powell's conviction and a fine of $50.

Powell appealed his case directly to the Supreme Court, which affirmed his conviction. Justice Marshall, writing for the majority, maintained that there was in fact no consensus among the medical profession about the "disease concept" of alcoholism. Distinguishing the case from *Robinson v. California*, Marshall reasoned that Powell was convicted not for the status of being an alcoholic but rather for the act of being in public while intoxicated. Marshall pointed out the potentially radical effect that accepting Powell's argument could have in criminal law: a psychiatrist could testify that an assaultive person suffered from an "aggressive neurosis" that he could control while sober but not while drunk; under Powell's claim, such a person could no longer be held accountable because he acted under an "exceedingly strong influence." The court, therefore, concluded that, given the present state of medical knowledge, an alcoholic could not be construed to suffer from an "irresistible compulsion" to drink and get drunk in public in a way that the person was "utterly unable to control."

Justice Fortas, in a dissent joined by three of his colleagues, pointed out the fact that Powell had been convicted one hundred times since 1949 for public drunkenness—evidence of the compulsive nature of his behavior. Arguing that such a "condition" is indeed a "status," the dissent considered that the sole question in the case, as in *Robinson*, was whether a criminal penalty could be imposed on a person for a disease.

Montana v. Egelhoff, 116 S.Ct. 2013 (1996)

After a night of heavy drinking, James Egelhoff was accused of shooting and killing two acquaintances. At the time of his arrest, his blood alcohol level was measured at 0.36%. Egelhoff was convicted at trial after offering the defense that his extreme intoxication had rendered him mentally incapable of committing murder. Montana's criminal code provided that voluntary intoxication could not be considered in determining the mental state of the defendant, and the trial court had instructed the jury accordingly. On appeal, the Montana Supreme Court overturned Egelhoff's conviction. The court ruled that the Due Process clause of the Fourteenth Amendment gave the defendant the right to present "all relevant evidence"; it held that intoxication was relevant to the issue of whether the defendant acted "knowingly and purposefully" in causing the victim's deaths.

The U.S. Supreme Court then agreed to review the case. The issue before the court was whether Montana's criminal code violated the Due Process clause of the Fourteenth Amendment in its provision that voluntary intoxication cannot be considered in determining the mental state of the defendant, which is an element of the charge of murder. The Supreme Court reversed the decision of the Montana Supreme Court. A divided court held that due process *does not* guarantee to the defendant the right to present all relevant evidence. (A plurality of four justices depended on the concurrence of Justice Ginsburg for the decision.) The court held that this right exists only where restrictions on the presentation of evidence would offend a principle of justice "so rooted in the traditions and conscience of our people as to be ranked as fundamental."

The court relied on historical practice as a guide, noting to begin with that there is a well-established rule in common law that voluntary intoxication provides no excuse for a crime. The court pointed out, however, that there are any number of evidentiary rules (e.g., the hearsay exclusion) that exclude relevant evidence, where the probative value of the evidence is outweighed by the risk of unfair prejudice. The court conceded that, by the end of the nineteenth century most American jurisdictions allowed the consideration of intoxication in determining whether a defendant was capable of forming the specific intent to commit a particular crime. The court was not persuaded, however, that this fact demonstrated a "deeply rooted" and "fundamental" right. The court pointed out that one-fifth of the states never adopted such a rule; although the rule had gained general acceptance, it was still too recent and not "sufficiently uniform" to be considered fundamental.

Justice Ginsburg's concurrence argued that the Montana statute represented a legislative judgment about the circumstances when a person can be held criminally responsible and therefore was a measure that redefined *mens rea*. The defendant in this case committed a killing under circumstances that would establish actual purposefulness but for his voluntary intoxication. She concluded that a legislative redefinition of *mens rea* does not offend any fundamental principle of justice.

In dissent, Justice O'Connor argued exactly the opposite. She maintained that the Montana statute was excluding an "essential element" of the crime in excluding evidence of intoxication. She argued that it was inconsistent to require proof of "knowing" behavior and "purpose," and yet to exclude evidence of intoxication. Justices Souter and Breyer also filed dissenting opinions that made the additional argument (against Justice Ginsburg) that the Montana Supreme Court had never understood the Montana statute to be a redefinition of the mental element of homicide.

SEX OFFENDERS

Specht v. Patterson, 386 U.S. 605 (1967)

The State of Colorado convicted Specht of a sex offense and then invoked its separate Sex Offenders Act in order to sentence him to an indefinite term of detention (which could be up to life). Under this act, a trial court could find that a person convicted of a sex crime represented a "threat of bodily harm" to the public or was a mentally ill habitual offender. The procedure for making this determination required only a psychiatric examination and written report that would make a recommendation as to whether the defendant was treatable as a sex offender. On appeal, the Colorado Supreme Court approved the procedure, and a federal appeals court rejected Specht's *habeas corpus* petition.

On appeal to the U.S. Supreme Court, the issue was whether Colorado could constitutionally convict the defendant under one statute and then sentence him under another, without a new hearing. The court held that Colorado's procedure was unconstitutional under the Fourteenth Amendment. The court reasoned that the Sex Offenders Act did not make a specific crime the basis of the sentence; it only made the conviction of that crime the basis for a new, separate proceeding to determine if the convicted fit the criteria for treatment as a sex offender. The latter would therefore constitute a new finding of fact and was equivalent to a criminal proceeding on a new charge. The court held that in this situation the Fourteenth Amendment required full rights to due process, including the right to counsel, to a hearing, to confront witnesses, to cross-examination, and to offer evidence in one's own defense.

Allen v. Illinois, 478 U.S. 364 (1986)

Terry Allen was arrested and charged with a sex offense, and the State of Illinois filed a petition under its Sexually Dangerous Persons Act to have him declared a sexually dangerous person. The court then ordered an examination of Allen by two psychiatrists. When the two psychiatrists testified in court, Allen objected that they had obtained information from him in violation of his Fifth Amendment privilege against self-incrimination. The psychiatrists were allowed to testify that Allen was mentally ill and that he had a propensity to commit further sexual crimes. On appeal the Appellate Court of Illinois reversed the lower court's decision, but the Supreme Court of Illinois reinstated it, holding that the court proceeding had been "essentially civil in nature," with the aim of providing treatment for Allen, not punishment. The court observed that the state's interests in treating him and in protecting the public would be stymied by allowing him to refuse to be interviewed by psychiatrists. Because the Fifth Amendment protects a person from being compelled to testify against himself in a criminal case, the crucial issue in *Allen* was whether the proceedings were criminal or civil.

The U.S. Supreme Court held that the proceedings under the Illinois Sexually Dangerous Persons Act were indeed civil. The court noted first that the statute expressly states that it is a civil proceeding. It then noted that the act requires the state to prove that the person has a mental disorder and is dangerous. The act also requires the state to provide treatment for the sexually dangerous person in a psychiatric facility. Unlike a convicted prisoner, the person might apply for release at any time and attempt to prove that he is no longer dangerous. The court concluded that the fact that a proceeding has some due process safeguards or the fact that it can result in a loss of liberty does not mean that the proceeding is criminal in nature.

Four justices dissented from the decision, concluding that the substance of the Illinois statute made it unlike the usual civil commitment: the proceeding only begins after the person is charged with a crime; the state has to prove that a sexual offense was committed; the act would authorize longer incarceration than a criminal conviction; and the act defines the sexually dangerous person as having "criminal propensities." Although the state argued that allowing the person a right to remain silent would make diagnosis impossible, the dissenters pointed out that Illinois commitment law actually protects a patient's right to silence. Thus, both the criminal defendant and the subject of civil commitment in Illinois have a right to remain silent. Only the sexually dangerous person can be required to give information that can be used to incarcerate him.

In re Young and Cunningham, 857 P.2d 989 (1993)

Andre Young and Vance Cunningham were committed as sexually violent predators by the State of Washington under its Community Protection Act. Their cases were joined in a challenge to the constitutionality of their commitments. Their appeal to the Supreme Court of Washington involved multiple issues and arguments, and they were each successful to some extent, even though the court upheld the constitutionality of the act itself. Among the issues raised by Young and Cunningham were the following: that the act was in effect a criminal law that violated the double jeopardy and *ex post facto* provisions of the Constitution; that the act amounted to preventative detention of dangerous individuals and that a finding of dangerousness required a demonstration of a recent, overt act of violence; that the act should take into account the principle of the least restrictive alternative; and that procedurally an involuntary commitment requires a probable cause hearing and a unanimous jury verdict, as well as according the subject the Fifth Amendment right to remain silent.

The court recognized that the purposes of the act were both to provide treatment for sex offenders and to protect the community by incapacitating persons who had an intractable condition and were particularly dangerous. The court accepted the need for a civil commitment scheme that was "specially tailored" to this population. The act defined sexually violent predators as individuals with antisocial personalities who were not amenable to ordinary psychiatric treatment but who were likely to engage in sexually violent behavior. The act explicitly recognized that their prognosis for cure was poor. Young and Cunningham had both been found to fit this definition. Young had six convictions for raping adult women over a period of 31 years. He had refused to participate in a psychiatric examination, even after being ordered to do so by the trial court. He had, however, been given a diagnosis of personality disorder with paranoid and antisocial traits as well as a diagnosis of paraphilia. Cunningham had three convictions for raping adult women and was also given a diagnosis of paraphilia. In his case the trial jury had voted 11–1 to find that he was a sexually violent predator. The Washington Supreme Court ruled on a number of issues:

1. *Double jeopardy and* ex post facto *prohibitions*: The court held that the act was a civil statute, so that these constitutional provisions did not apply. Relying on *Allen v. Illinois*, 478 U.S. 364, the court found that the act was not so punitive in nature that it warranted designation as a criminal law. The court pointed out that incapacitation has always been a recognized goal of civil commitment and that designation as a sexually violent predator was based on findings of mental abnormality, not culpability.
2. *Due process*: Again citing *Allen v. Illinois*, the court noted that mental illness and dangerousness are required as criteria for civil commitment, but ruled that the terms "mental illness" and "mental disorder" were in fact used interchangeably. Some experts had testified that the concept of "mental abnormality" is virtually the same as the concept of "mental disorder" as used in the APA's *Diagnostic and Statistical Manual of Mental Disorders*. Both Young and Cunningham had indeed been given diagnoses of Paraphilia.
3. *Preventative detention*: In *Foucha v. Louisiana*, 112 S. Ct. 1780, the committed individual had a diagnosis of antisocial personality. He was found by the Supreme Court not to be committable without a mental illness. Making

a fine distinction, the Washington Supreme Court noted that antisocial personality is not a mental disorder according to the APA. (It was a V-code in the *Diagnostic and Statistical Manual of Mental Disorders*, 3rd edition, revised [*DSM-III-R*].) Young and Cunningham by contrast had mental disorders. Further distinguishing the case from *Foucha* was the fact that Washington placed the burden of proof on the state to show beyond a reasonable doubt that a person was a sexually violent predator.

4. *Overt act requirement*: Although civil commitment law in Washington did require a recent overt act to prove dangerousness, the court ruled that for an incarcerated inmate such a requirement would be impossible for the state to meet. For a person released in the community, however, the court held that the recent overt act criteria did apply. Because Cunningham had been released four-and-a-half months prior to his commitment and had apparently committed no new acts of violence, the court held that the state had not demonstrated his dangerousness. The court therefore reversed Cunningham's commitment.
5. *Procedural issues*: Noting that Equal Protection does not require that all persons be dealt with equally, the court reasoned that the past behavior of convicted sex offenders differs significantly from the behavior of the mentally ill and therefore justifies different treatment. The court did rule, however, that a 45-day waiting period for a hearing was an unwarranted infringement on the liberty interests of the offender, and it required the state to hold a hearing within 72 hours of seeking commitment.
6. *Least restrictive alternative*: While dangerousness justifies the use of secure confinement, the court noted that the state's mental health statutes require the state to consider the least restrictive alternative. Because not all sex offenders are equally dangerous, equal protection requires the state at least to consider less restrictive alternatives before confining sex offenders.
7. *Unanimous verdict*: The standard of "beyond a reasonable doubt" usually requires a unanimous jury verdict. In Cunningham's case, one juror thought that the state had failed to meet its burden of proof. As a result, the court held that this verdict was insufficient to adjudicate Cunningham a sexually violent predator. The verdict in Young's case, however, was affirmed.
8. *The Fifth Amendment*: The court reiterated that the act was not a criminal statute, so that the right to remain silent did not apply.
9. *Expert testimony*: Young and Cunningham challenged the state's experts, claiming that they were operating on theories about prediction of behavior that were not generally accepted by the scientific community. The court rejected this argument, pointing out that to accept it would vitiate all civil commitment laws. The prediction of dangerousness does not violate due process, in spite of the uncertainty of psychiatric diagnosis.

In a dissenting opinion, Justice Johnson characterized the Community Protection Act as nothing but a scheme for the indefinite confinement of people who were not mentally ill and therefore as unconstitutional under the standard of *Foucha*. He pointed to the circular logic involved in using past sexual conduct as the basis for finding an "abnormality," which is then used to establish the likelihood of future dangerous sexual conduct.

Kansas v. Hendricks, 117 S.Ct. 2072 (1997)

In 1994 Kansas passed a Sexually Violent Predator Act, providing civil commitment for persons who were found to have a mental abnormality or personality disorder that predisposed them to commit violent sexual offenses. The state used this statute to commit Leroy Hendricks, a man with a long history of sexual abuse of children. Hendricks was approaching the end of a prison sentence for a sex crime and had been scheduled for release when he was committed. Hendricks challenged his commitment, claiming that it violated the Constitution's prohibition of double jeopardy and *ex post facto* laws. When the Kansas Supreme Court heard the case, it overturned Hendrick's commitment, holding that the concept of "mental abnormality" did not meet standard criteria for civil commitment, because due process required the finding that the person at issue suffered from a mental illness.

The Kansas Sexually Violent Predator Act stated that there is a small but very dangerous group of sex offenders who do not have a mental disease or defect that would make them eligible for ordinary involuntary commitment. These individuals instead have an antisocial personality disorder that is not amenable to standard psychiatric treatment. The act defined this type of mental abnormality as "a congenital or acquired condition affecting the emotional or volitional capacity, which predisposes the person to commit sexually violent offenses." To be subject to commitment under the act, a person had to be convicted of a sexual offense, charged with a sexual offense, or found NGRI regarding a sexual offense. Once determined by a court to be a Sexually Violent Predator, the person would be detained until his or her mental abnormality was improved to the extent that the person was "safe" to be in the community. Hendricks was found to qualify for commitment after he testified that the only sure way to keep him from abusing children would be for him to die.

The U.S. Supreme Court overturned the ruling of the Kansas Supreme Court, holding that the Sexually Violent Predator Act was constitutional. The court noted that Hendricks' double jeopardy and *ex post facto* arguments hinged on the contention that the act subjected him to additional punishment beyond his original sentence upon conviction at trial. Following *Allen v. Illinois* (478 U.S. 364) the court ruled that the act was genuinely a civil commitment and not a criminal statute. The court pointed out that the act required both a finding of dangerousness and of mental abnormality. It held that pedophilia, which was Hendrick's diagnosis, was indeed a mental disorder, but that furthermore the term "mental illness" has no unique legal significance. The court never required a state to use any particular terminology in civil commitment statutes. The court also concluded that the act was not so punitive as to render it effectively a criminal statute. If a person were found to be safe to be released, he could be released immediately. The court went on to find that the lack of effective treatment for sex offenders did not make the law unconstitutional. The court pointed out that it has long been recognized as a legitimate purpose for civil commitment laws to segregate from the general public certain people who represent a danger and are unable to control themselves. (The court cited the example of people with highly contagious diseases.)

In a dissent, Justice Breyer disagreed with the basic contention that the Sexually Violent Predator Act was not punitive. He agreed that the concept of "mental abnormality" could satisfy due process requirements for commitment. He argued, however, that the fact that Kansas did not provide any treatment for sex offenders in prison and only began to offer treatment after their sentences were served provided a telling indication that the act was primarily a mechanism for further incarceration. Otherwise, he reasoned, why would the state not bother to begin treating the sexually violent inmate while in prison?

McKune v. Lile, 536 U.S. 24 (2002)

In *McKune v. Lile,* the U.S. Supreme Court considered whether a Kansas law that leveraged felons convicted of sexual offenses to confess all prior deviant sexual behavior violated their Fifth Amendment right against self-incrimination.

Mr. Lile had been convicted in 1982 of rape; a few years before the completion of his criminal sentence, he was eligible to enroll in Kansas' Sexual Abuse Treatment Program (SATP), which consisted of 18 months of individual and group therapy to reduce an inmate's risk of sexual reoffending on release. To participate in the program, inmates had to complete an "Admission of Responsibility" form, via which they were expected to detail all prior sexual offenses and acknowledge their guilt. The information the inmates provided was not privileged, and per the statute, could be used against them in future prosecutions. Mr. Lile declined to complete the form, invoking his Constitutional guarantee against self-incrimination. As a result, per the SATP statute, he lost certain privileges for the remainder of his sentence. Specifically, he was relocated from a medium to a maximum security facility, his wage for prison labor was reduced, the amount of money he could spend on canteen items per month was lowered, and he lost access to a personal television. Mr. Lile's claim was initially upheld in federal district court and the Court of Appeals, and Kansas petitioned the U.S. Supreme Court for *certiorari*. The court, in a 5–4 decision, reversed and remanded.

The majority argued that while SATP required an inmate to confess his prior crimes, this requirement did not constitute compulsion, and, therefore, did not violate the Fifth Amendment. The privileges that inmates lost for refusing to participate in SATP, the majority argued, were not "atypical and significant hardships." As the majority stated, not all persuasion is compulsion: "It is well settled that the government need not make the exercise of the Fifth Amendment privilege cost free ... The Court likewise has held that plea bargaining does not violate the Fifth Amendment, even though criminal defendants may feel considerable pressure to admit guilt in order to obtain more lenient treatment." The majority also argued that goals of SATP represented a vital state interest in terms of rehabilitation of offenders and ensuring public safety, and this end justified its means, in terms of requiring inmates to confess.

The dissent argued that the loss of privileges for refusal to participate in SATP were identical to those imposed for violation of prison rules such as theft, drug abuse, assault, and possession of dangerous contraband, and, therefore, concluded that refusal resulted in punishment, not a mere loss of privileges. The dissent also distinguished between the certainty of the consequences of refusing to participate in SATP, compared to the probabilistic risk-versus-benefit calculation a defendant must consider when invoking his or her Fifth Amendment right to remain silent. With regard to balancing an individual's interest against self-incrimination versus the state interest in law enforcement, the dissent concluded, "The State's interests in law enforcement and rehabilitation are present in every criminal case. If those interests were sufficient to justify impinging on prisoners' Fifth Amendment right, inmates would soon have no privilege left to invoke."

Kansas v. Crane, 534 U.S. 407 (2002)

In *Kansas v. Crane,* the U.S. Supreme Court considered whether or not, and to what degree, the Kansas statute authorizing civil commitment of sexually violent predators (SVPs) required a finding of the individual's inability to control his or her dangerous sexual conduct.

Over the course of a single day, in 1993, Mr. Crane committed two acts of sexual battery—exposing his genitals to a tanning salon attendant, and later, entering a video store, exposing his genitals to the clerk and threatening to rape her unless she performed oral sex. He subsequently pleaded guilty, and the state sought to have him committed as a sexually violent predator. The statute in Kansas at the time allowed civil commitment of an individual "convicted of any of several enumerated sexual offenses, if it is proven beyond a reasonable doubt that he suffers from a 'mental abnormality'—a disorder affecting his 'emotional or volitional capacity which predisposes the person to commit sexually violent offenses'—or a 'personality disorder,' either of 'which makes the person likely to engage in repeat acts of sexual violence.'" Crane was committed on this basis at trial, and appealed to the state supreme court, which overturned the decision, arguing that the state SVP statute, deemed Constitutional in the prior 1997 U.S. Supreme

Court decision *Kansas v. Hendricks*, required that to ensure due process, the state was required to prove beyond a reasonable doubt that the individual lacked complete control over his dangerous sexual behavior, and had failed to do so in Mr. Crane's case. The state requested *certiorari* from the U.S. Supreme Court.

The court, relying on its prior decision, clarified that the state SVP statute did require an inquiry into an individual's inability to control his or her dangerous sexual behavior; however, the inability must not be total to justify civil commitment. The court argued that such a determination was necessary to distinguish those offenders with a mental disorder—who are subject to commitment—from those recidivists who do have control of their behavior, and are more appropriately managed via a criminal rather than therapeutic model. The court conceded that determinations of an individual's inability to control behavior would lack mathematical precision, and that in the area of mental illness, liberty interests are not always best enforced through "precise bright-line rules."

The dissent argued that requiring the fact finder to inquire about an individual's volitional capacity beyond establishing that an SVP suffers from a mental disorder that renders him likely to reoffend would be redundant, and, therefore, not required to ensure due process. In other words, by definition, a person suffering a mental disorder that predisposes him or her to deviant sexual behavior has diminished volutional capacity, and an independent inquiry is not needed. Given this impression, the dissent recommended not just remanding the case back to the state for reconsideration but urged reversal, as the facts of the case establish that Mr. Crane suffered from exhibitionism, a condition that predisposed him to commit sexually violent offenses, and, therefore, he could be committed civilly under Kansas state law.

THE DEATH PENALTY

Barefoot v. Estelle, 463 U.S. 880 (1982)

Barefoot was convicted of the murder of a police officer in Texas in 1978. Under the Texas death penalty statute (approved by the Supreme Court in *Jurek v. Texas* [428 U.S. 262, 1975]), a separate sentencing proceeding addressed two "special questions" (which had to be answered in the affirmative and beyond a reasonable doubt in order to sentence the defendant to death): first, whether Barefoot's conduct was deliberate in causing the death, and second, whether there was a probability that he would commit further violent criminal acts.

The prosecutor called as witnesses two psychiatrists, who had not examined Barefoot, and asked them hypothetical questions. Their answers suggested that Barefoot would commit more violent offenses—one of the psychiatrists testified that he was "100% sure" that a person with the given characteristics would be violent in the future. The jury decided against Barefoot and sentenced him to death.

The legal issues before the Supreme Court had to do with whether the lower federal appeals courts had erred in rejecting a *habeas corpus* petition and a stay of execution. The psychiatric–legal issues, however, were whether a psychiatrist could predict future acts of violence and whether a psychiatrist should be allowed to testify from hypotheticals without examining the defendant.

The Supreme Court ruled against Barefoot on both questions, that is, that the court would not bar psychiatrists from predicting future violence, nor would it bar hypothetical testimony without examination.

In his majority opinion, Justice White argued that to prohibit psychiatrists from testifying about dangerousness amounted to trying to "disinvent the wheel." Reasoning that it is "not impossible" for a layperson to assess the probability of future violence in a sensible way, White concluded that it would make no sense to prevent psychiatrists from doing the same. He quoted the *Jurek* case to the effect that the criminal justice system routinely requires such predictions to be made, for example, by judges and parole officers. He pointed out that the view of the American Psychiatric Association, which in its amicus brief cast doubt on psychiatrists' ability to predict danger, was not a "constitutional rule," and furthermore, that the defense could present its own witnesses to controvert inaccurate psychiatric testimony. White implied that it should be easy to impeach the testimony of a psychiatrist who claimed 100% certainty.

As to the second question, White pointed out that hypothetical questions are well established and commonly admitted. He reiterated the basic guideline that expert testimony should be admitted whenever it is "helpful" to the fact finder.

Justice Marshall dissented, arguing that because the death penalty is qualitatively different from other penalties, there is a corresponding need for a higher degree of reliability in death penalty decisions. Justice Blackmun also wrote a dissent, with which Justices Marshall and Brennan joined: Blackmun argued that "specious testimony" by a psychiatrist should not be allowed to color the decision of an "impressionable" jury. He noted that *Frye v. United States* (293 F. 1013, 1923) had held that unreliable scientific evidence was prejudicial because it could mislead the jury by the "aura" of scientific infallibility. He quoted the same APA amicus brief that the majority rejected, to the effect that psychiatrists cannot predict future violence correctly, and added that the state had not in fact demonstrated a pattern of repetitive assault or violent crime on Barefoot's part. He also invoked the APA opinion that it is unethical for a psychiatrist to offer a professional opinion about a person without conducting an examination. Blackmun characterized the majority opinion as accepting the admissibility of expert testimony that is "so unreliable and unprofessional that it violates the canons of medical ethics."

Payne v. Tennessee, 111 S.Ct. 2597 (1991)

Payne v. Tennessee revised an important principle in capital sentencing jurisprudence by allowing the jury in a capital case to hear evidence about the impact of a crime on the family of the victim.

Pervis Payne was convicted of the brutal murder of a 28-year-old woman and one of her small children. (One of the victims was found to have suffered 84 knife wounds in the attack.) In spite of the apparently overwhelming evidence against him, Payne had chosen to testify in his trial, claiming that another man had committed the murders immediately before he arrived at the scene. Payne was found guilty by the jury. In the sentencing phase of his trial, four character witnesses testified on his behalf, including a psychologist who reported that he had a low IQ and was "mentally handicapped." The prosecution presented the mother and grandmother of the victims, who testified about the severe impact of the crime on the small boy who survived the attack and who knew that his mother and sister had been killed. The jury then sentenced Payne to death.

The Supreme Court stated that it granted *certiorari* in this case in order to allow a reconsideration of its prior position that the Eighth Amendment prohibited a capital sentencing jury from hearing victim impact evidence related to the personal characteristic of the victim and the emotional impact of the crime on the victim's relatives. The court's previous approach (established in *Booth v. Maryland,* 482 U.S. 496 and *South Carolina v. Gathers,* 490 U.S. 805) was that a jury should decide a capital sentence based only on the character of the defendant and the circumstances of the crime; the characteristics of the victim were not considered relevant to the defendant's blameworthiness. In departing from this rule, the court noted that when judges have had discretion in sentencing, they have always been allowed to consider the degree of harm caused by the crime as an important factor. The court therefore reasoned that victim impact evidence is designed to inform the jury about the "uniqueness" of the victim as an individual and therefore about the specific harm caused by the murder. The harm caused is directly related to the defendant's moral culpability. The court also noted that the state has a legitimate interest in rebutting the mitigating evidence offered by the defense. The court concluded that Payne's sentencing did not violate the Eighth Amendment.

A dissenting opinion by Justices Marshall and Blackmun argued that this decision was based on no change in the law or the facts of the cases cited, but merely resulted from a change in the makeup of the Supreme Court. The dissent reiterated the idea that capital sentencing is supposed to involve an individualized decision about the defendant's responsibility for the crime and his moral guilt, in order to avoid arbitrary or capricious decision making. The dissenters argued that victim impact evidence is an invitation to prejudice, directing the jury to look at the character and status of the victim rather than simply at the character of the defendant. An additional dissent by Justices Stevens and Blackmun maintained that victim impact evidence serves no purpose except to appeal to the emotions of the jury, and that such evidence has never been admissible.

State v. Perry, 610 So.2d 746 (1992)

In *State v. Perry* the Supreme Court of Louisiana addressed the question whether the state could give anti-psychotic medication involuntarily to an incompetent death row inmate in order to render him competent to be executed. Michael Perry had been convicted of murdering his mother, father, nephew, and two cousins. He had a long history of mental illness, with a diagnosis of schizophrenia. Prior to his trial, Perry was found to be incompetent and was treated with anti-psychotic medications in a state hospital over a period of 18 months. He was then found to be competent and was allowed to withdraw his insanity plea and plead not guilty. He was convicted at trial and sentenced to death. His sentence was upheld by the Louisiana Supreme Court, but a new evaluation of his competence to be executed was ordered. Psychiatric experts then reported that Perry suffered from an incurable disorder, but that his psychotic symptoms could be diminished by giving him medication. The trial court found that he was competent to be executed while being maintained on anti-psychotic drugs and ordered that the state should continue to medicate Perry, by force if necessary. Perry appealed to the U.S. Supreme Court, which remanded the case for reconsideration in light of its decision in *Washington v. Harper,* 494 U.S. 210 (1990). The trial court held that *Washington v. Harper* was inapplicable, and renewed its order for forced medication. The Louisiana Supreme Court reversed this ruling, holding that it violated Perry's right to privacy and amounted to cruel and unusual punishment under the constitution of the state of Louisiana.

The court found that the Louisiana constitution contained a higher level of protection against cruel and unusual punishment than that provided by the Eighth Amendment to the U.S. Constitution. Even though he was a convicted felon, Perry still maintained some liberty interests, specifically with regard to the "invasion" of his body and mind by powerful drugs. The court concluded that involuntary medication, administered for the sole purpose of making him competent to be executed, was an unjustified invasion of his privacy and added a special and degrading indignity to his punishment that made it "cruel, excessive, and unusual." The court accepted as a matter of fact that Perry would only be competent to be executed as long as he was medicated. The forcible medication therefore was ordered solely in order to bring him to execution and not for the purposes that might be sanctioned under the standards of *Harper* (where the Supreme Court ruled that a prison inmate might be medicated involuntarily if the medication was medically indicated for his own good and where his safety or the safety of others around him was at issue). The court backed up its conclusions by quoting from the Hippocratic Oath, wherein physicians swear only to act in the best medical interests of patients. The court reasoned that Perry's forced medication was not meant to do him any good, in fact did not even constitute medical treatment, and therefore required a physician to act unethically.

Two dissenting justices marshalled a number of objections to the majority decision. Justice Marcus argued that the standard for competency to be executed required only that Perry be aware of his punishment and of the reason that it was being administered. Marcus concluded that the trial judge did not abuse his discretion in finding Perry competent under this minimal standard. Justice Marcus also argued that the state did have a legitimate penological interest in carrying out Perry's execution, and that *Harper* only required that it be shown that Perry's medication was reasonably related to this interest. Justice Cole questioned more fundamentally the assumptions of the majority, maintaining that involuntary medication was in fact a valid treatment, which was in Perry's best interest to relieve his suffering, and which should not be construed as doing him harm, even if it led eventually to his being executed.

Roper v. Simmons, 543 U.S. 511 (2005)

In *Roper v. Simmons,* the U.S. Supreme Court held that the execution of juveniles under the age of 18 at the time of their commitment offense was unconstitutional. This decision overturned the ruling of the court 16 years earlier in *Stanford v. Kentucky,* in which the 5–4 majority determined the execution of juveniles ages 16–18 was not a violation of the Eighth Amendment, applied to the states via the Fourteenth Amendment.

On September 8, 1993, defendant Christopher Simmons, age 17, planned and executed the murder of Shirley Crook. Simmons and two accomplices broke into Mrs. Crook's house, bound and gagged her, and tossed her body off a bridge, to her death. At school the next day, Simmons bragged about the murder to classmates; he was subsequently arrested, charged with first-degree murder, convicted, and sentenced to death.

In 2004, the Supreme Court ruled in *Atkins v. Virginia* that execution of the mentally retarded constituted cruel and unusual punishment and therefore was unconstitutional via the Eighth Amendment. The majority's reasoning in *Roper* parallels that in *Atkins.*

To reach its conclusion, the majority considered "'the evolving standards of decency that mark the progress of a maturing society,' to determine which punishments are so disproportionate as to be 'cruel and unusual,'" as articulated in *Trop v. Dulles.* The majority argued that since its decision in *Stanford,* a consensus had evolved among the states barring the execution of those under age 18. The court also relied on the rule, established in decisions preceding *Stanford,* that the Constitution contemplates that the court's own judgment can be brought to bear on the question of the acceptability of the death penalty, and with regard to the death penalty for those under 18, judged the punishment excessive.

To reach this conclusion, the majority relied on three main arguments. First, juveniles are susceptible to immature and irresponsible behavior, and therefore, their irresponsible conduct is not as morally reprehensible as that of an adult. Second, their own vulnerability and lack of control over their immediate surroundings mean juveniles are less culpable for failing to escape negative influences. Third, juveniles have not yet established a consistent identity and, therefore, and have a greater chance of rehabilitation compared to adult offenders.

The thrust of the dissent's argument was against a categorical exclusion of those under age 18 from the death penalty, saying that juries are equipped well enough to distinguish on a case-by-case basis those under 18 who deserve the death penalty and those who do not. The dissent noted that in most cases, juries would, and do, find the death penalty excessive for juveniles, but that they therefore can be relied on to render fair judgments. The dissent also took issue with the way the majority determines that a consensus exists among the states, concluding that it does not.

100

Legal regulation of psychiatry

JAMES W. HICKS

HOSPITALIZATION

Lake v. Cameron, 364 F. 2d 657 (1966)

In *Lake v. Cameron*, the U.S. Court of Appeals for the District of Columbia applied the principle of the "least restrictive alternative" to involuntary commitment of the mentally ill. The U.S. Supreme Court has not endorsed this requirement, but most jurisdictions now require the state to consider alternatives before seeking involuntary hospitalization.

In 1962, a policeman found Catherine Lake, a 60-year-old, senile woman, wandering about Washington, DC, and took her to the D.C. General Hospital, from which she was transferred to St. Elizabeth's Hospital. Lake filed a writ of *habeas corpus*, which was dismissed by the district court without a hearing. At the subsequent commitment hearing, two psychiatrists testified that she had a "chronic brain syndrome" with memory impairments and was unable to care for herself, and she was found to be of "unsound mind" and committed to St. Elizabeth's.

Lake appealed the summary dismissal of her writ, and the D.C. Court of Appeals remanded the case to the district court for a hearing. At the hearing, a psychiatrist testified that Lake was not intentionally dangerous to herself or others, but that she was prone to wandering and had in fact been injured after wandering away from the hospital for more than a day. Lake's husband and sister testified that they were eager for her release and would try to provide for her needs, but the court concluded that they were incapable of doing so. The court denied relief but allowed that Lake might be entitled to release if she were able to find another facility that could take care of her.

Lake appealed again, arguing that passage of new legislation (the D.C. Hospitalization of the Mentally Ill Act) after her hearing required her case be remanded for the court to consider "any other alternative course of treatment which the court believes will be in the best interests of the person or of the public." Plaintiff's court-appointed attorney clarified that Lake objected to total confinement in a mental institution but would accept treatment in a setting more appropriate to her needs.

Chief Judge Bazelon, writing for the D.C. Court of Appeals, applied the principle that a deprivation of liberty to prevent harm to a mentally ill person should be limited to what is necessary to protect that person. The court also reasoned that the state, rather than the indigent patient herself, should bear the burden of exploring alternative resources in the community more suited to the needs of the patient. The case was remanded to the district court for an inquiry into alternative placements, preferably one that Lake would be willing to accept.

Baxstrom v. Herold, 383 U.S. 107 (1966)

In *Baxstrom v. Herold*, the U.S. Supreme Court determined the due process rights of prisoners facing civil commitment at the end of their prison sentence.

Johnnie Baxstromn was committed to a New York prison in 1959 after being convicted of assault. In 1961, a prison physician certified him as "insane" (i.e., suffering from a mental illness), and he was transferred to Dannemora State Hospital, a psychiatric hospital for prisoners. When Baxstrom's penal sentence was about to end, the hospital director applied for civil commitment based on the opinion of two hospital physicians that Baxstrom was still mentally ill and in need of hospital care. Baxstrom appeared alone at the commitment hearing and was only permitted a brief opportunity to ask questions. He was retained at Dannemora State Hospital as a civilly committed patient.

Baxstrom sought a writ of *habeas corpus*, which was dismissed after an independent psychiatrist testified that he remained mentally ill. Baxstrom again applied for a writ of *habeas corpus* in 1963, arguing that he was sane, and that if he were insane, he should be transferred to a civil psychiatric hospital. He was unable to obtain psychiatric testimony on his behalf, and the writ was dismissed again. The appeals court affirmed the dismissal, and the Court of Appeals of New York (the state's supreme court) denied appeal. The U.S. Supreme Court granted *certiorari*.

The court found that New York's statute for civil commitment of a prisoner at the expiration of a penal sentence violated the Equal Protection Clause of the Fourteenth Amendment in two respects. First, all nonprisoners facing civil commitment have the right to a full jury trial to determine whether they are mentally ill. The court found no basis for distinguishing the psychiatric commitment of a prisoner from all other civil commitments. Second, no other person may be committed to a Department of Corrections facility without a judicial finding that they are too dangerously mentally ill to be treated safely in a civil hospital. The court rejected the director's argument that a prisoner's past criminal record was sufficient proof of dangerousness, and that placement should be an administrative matter.

The court reversed and ordered a new hearing to determine whether Baxstrom was mentally ill, and if so, whether he should remain at Dannemora State Hospital.

Jackson v. Indiana, 406 U.S. 715 (1972)

In *Jackson v. Indiana*, the U.S. Supreme Court determined that a person found incompetent to stand trial, but not yet convicted, may be committed only long enough to restore competence or to determine whether he or she will become competent in the foreseeable future.

In 1968, Theon Jackson was charged with two counts of robbery involving approximately $9 in property and cash. Jackson entered a plea of not guilty. The court ordered a competency assessment, because Jackson was mentally retarded, deaf, and mute and could communicate only through limited sign language. Two physicians concluded that Jackson was unable to understand the nature of the charges against him or to participate in his defense. One physician testified that Jackson was unlikely ever to learn to communicate more effectively, and that his "prognosis appears rather dim." The other physician testified that Jackson was likely to be incompetent on the basis of his intelligence alone, even if he were not deaf and mute.

The trial court found Jackson incompetent to stand trial and committed him to the Indiana Department of Mental Health until "the defendant is sane." Indiana law did not require periodic review by the court or by mental health authorities. Jackson's attorney filed a motion for a new trial, arguing that his client would never become competent to stand trial, and that his commitment amounted to a "life sentence" without being convicted of a crime. The trial court denied the motion. The Indiana Supreme Court affirmed the original commitment. The U.S. Supreme Court granted *certiorari*.

The court found that Indiana's indefinite commitment of a person as incompetent to stand trial violated both the Equal Protection and Due Process Clauses of the Fourteenth Amendment. In addressing equal protection, the court relied on the previous ruling in *Baxstrom v. Herold* (see above), which found that a prisoner approaching the end of his or her sentence could not be committed as mentally ill without the protections provided to all others facing civil commitment. If criminal conviction does not justify less protection during commitment, then "the mere filing of criminal charges surely cannot suffice." The court found that Jackson was subjected to a more lenient commitment standard and to a more stringent standard of release than if he had not been charged with an offense.

In addressing due process, the court noted that the nature and duration of commitment must bear some "reasonable relation" to the purpose of commitment. Federal law and the laws in several states do not permit the continued commitment of those found incompetent to stand trial unless they are likely to become competent or are found to be dangerous. The court concluded that a person found incompetent to stand trial "cannot be held more than the reasonable period of time necessary to determine whether there is a substantial probability that he will attain that capacity in the foreseeable future." If an incompetent person is likely to be restored to fitness, then his or her "continued commitment must be justified by progress toward that goal." If not, then he or she must be released or committed according to civil commitment procedures.

The court chose not to establish arbitrary time limits for restoring competency but noted that Jackson had been confined already for over 3 years even though he was unlikely to ever become competent. The court reversed, remanded, and recommended that the trial court consider dismissing the charges or holding a limited trial to establish innocence or insanity.

Lessard v. Schmidt, 349 F. Supp. 1078 (1972)

In *Lessard v. Schmidt*, the Wisconsin District Court established broad due process rights in civil commitment. Although these rights were subsequently incorporated into many state statutes, the U.S. Supreme Court has never ruled on the minimum constitutional standards for civil commitment.

In 1971, Alberta Lessard was picked up in front of her house by two police officers, who took her to the Mental Health Center in Milwaukee, Wisconsin. She was detained for 4 days on an emergency basis without a hearing. Her confinement was extended for 10 days following an appearance by the police officers before the judge. The Mental Health Center then requested that she be permanently committed as suffering from schizophrenia. Lessard was not informed of any of the proceedings. At the commitment hearing, which took place 24 days after her initial detention, the judge found her to be "mentally ill" and committed her for 30 days. Her commitment was subsequently extended every 30 days for nearly a year.

On her own initiative, Lessard retained an attorney, who filed a class action in federal district court under 42 U.S.C. Section 1983, which provides relief to any person deprived of their constitutional rights by state statute. Lessard argued that Wisconsin's involuntary commitment statute deprived her, and all others held involuntarily under its provision, of due process rights. The district court agreed to hear the case and agreed that the statute was unconstitutional.

The court emphasized that only a compelling state interest can justify denial of the fundamental "liberty to go unimpeded." Traditionally, the deprivation of liberty inherent in civil commitment has been justified both by the police power of the state (to protect the community from the dangerous actions of the mentally ill) and by the *parens patriae* role of the state (to provide treatment to those who would not willingly seek help). The court questioned the *parens patriae* role, noting that many mental illnesses are untreatable, the quality of institutional treatment may be inadequate and lengthy, and involuntary hospitalization may worsen health. The court quoted the famous pronouncement by Justice Brandeis: "Experience should teach us to be most on our guard to protect liberty when the government's purposes are beneficent.... The greatest dangers to liberty lurk in insidious encroachment by men of zeal, well-meaning but without understanding."

The stringent safeguards provided to arrested persons facing imprisonment had not been provided in civil commitment cases. The court observed that the deprivation of liberty in the civil and criminal contexts is comparable. Individuals civilly committed to a mental institution in Wisconsin lost numerous civil rights, including the presumption of competency, the right to make contracts and sue, the right to marry, the right to professional licenses, and the right to drive, vote, and serve on juries. The court observed that committed individuals were likely to face tremendous stigma and difficulties returning to life outside of the institution. The court referred to the U.S. Supreme Court decision in *In re Gault, 387 U.S. (1967),* in which adult criminal procedural safeguards were extended to juvenile court, which had historically been treated as civil in spite of the significant deprivations of liberty.

The district court established the following procedural safeguards constitutionally required for commitment of the mentally ill. The patient must be given timely notice of the "charges" and notice of all rights, including the right to a jury trial. A probable cause hearing must be held within 48 hours. The patient has the right to representation by an attorney. Hearsay evidence may not be admitted in the hearing. The patient retains the privilege against self-incrimination and must be informed that any information provided during examination may be used against him or her in the hearing. The state must prove beyond a reasonable doubt that the patient is both mentally ill and dangerous. Finally, the state must demonstrate that less restrictive alternatives to commitment are not available or not suitable.

Lessard was ordered released. Wisconsin was given 90 days to review its commitment procedures and determine whether all patients currently detained should be released, converted to voluntary status, or recommitted in conformity with the ruling.

O'Connor v. Donaldson, 422 U.S. 563 (1975)

In *O'Connor v. Donaldson*, the U.S. Supreme Court ruled against the involuntary custodial confinement of the nondangerous mentally ill without meaningful care or treatment. The court did not uphold the lower courts' articulation of a broad right to treatment (see *Donaldson v. O'Connor* below).

Kenneth Donaldson was committed to the Florida State Hospital at Chattahoochee in 1957 on the initiative of his father. Donaldson was diagnosed with paranoid schizophrenia and committed for "care, maintenance, and treatment." Donaldson repeatedly requested discharge during his nearly 15 years of hospitalization, claiming that he was not dangerous, not mentally ill, and not receiving treatment. The hospital superintendent, Dr. O'Connor, repeatedly refused Donaldson's request, even though Donaldson had never posed a danger to himself or others.

Almost immediately after O'Connor's retirement, Donaldson was released by the hospital. He immediately filed suit for damages in federal district court, alleging that O'Connor had intentionally and maliciously deprived him of his constitutional right to liberty. O'Connor countered that he had acted in good faith in his belief that state law authorized indefinite custodial confinement of the mentally ill. He also claimed that he believed Donaldson would have been unable to make a "successful adjustment outside the institution," though he gave no reason for this opinion. In fact, Donaldson had been successfully employed for many years before his confinement and obtained a job in hotel administration after his release. Responsible acquaintances had repeatedly promised to provide any needed support if he were released.

In federal district court, the jury returned a verdict against O'Connor and awarded compensatory and punitive damages. The court of appeals affirmed the judgment and delivered a broad opinion, finding in the Fourteenth Amendment a right to treatment for persons involuntarily committed (see *Donaldson v. O'Connor* below). The U.S. Supreme Court granted *certiorari* but chose not to address whether patients have a right to treatment.

The Supreme Court held that "a State cannot constitutionally confine without more a non-dangerous individual who is capable of surviving safely in freedom by himself or with the help of willing and responsible family members or friends." The phrase "without more" generally has been interpreted to mean "without further justification" rather than "without treatment." However, the court vacated the district court's judgment and remanded for a new trial in light of a recent ruling on the scope of immunity possessed by state officials.

Addington v. Texas, 441 U.S. 418 (1979)

In *Addington v. Texas*, the U.S. Supreme Court established "clear and convincing evidence" as the minimum standard of proof for civil commitment.

In 1975, the mother of Frank Addington petitioned the Texas trial court to commit her son to a mental hospital in accordance with Texas law. Addington requested a trial, at which the jury was instructed to determine by a standard of "clear, unequivocal, and convincing evidence" whether he was mentally ill and required hospitalization for his protection or the protection of others. The jury found for commitment, and Addington was committed to the Austin State Hospital for an indefinite period.

Addington appealed, and the court of appeals agreed with his contention that the standard for commitment should have been "beyond a reasonable doubt," the same standard required for criminal conviction. The Texas Supreme Court reversed, stating that the appropriate standard for civil commitment is a "preponderance of the evidence" (i.e., more likely than not). Because the higher standard used in the jury instruction was to Addington's advantage, the error was harmless, and the judgment was reinstated. The U.S. Supreme Court granted *certiorari.*

The U.S. Supreme Court reflected that the standard of proof serves to allocate the risk of error between the parties and to indicate the importance of the decision. In criminal cases, the consequences of criminal punishment are severe. The most stringent standard of "beyond a reasonable doubt" indicates that society should take nearly the entire risk of error upon itself. In most civil cases, fairness argues that neither party should be favored, unless a strong social policy is at stake. The least stringent standard of a "preponderance of the evidence" splits the risk of error between the two parties. In some civil cases, an intermediate standard of "clear and convincing evidence" has been employed where the interests at stake are "more substantial than mere loss of money." This intermediate standard is used in proceedings for deportation or removal of parental rights.

The court considered each of the three standards in turn. Civil commitment is a significant deprivation of liberty with adverse consequences for the committed individual. Because the individual should not share equally the risk of error with society, a standard of a "preponderance of the evidence" does not adequately protect the individual's rights. On the other hand, a standard of "beyond a reasonable doubt" should not be required. In civil commitment, the state does not exercise its power for punishment but for treatment. An individual who is erroneously released may suffer as a result. On a practical note, the court opined that, "Given the lack of certainty and the fallibility of psychiatric diagnosis, there is a serious question as to whether a state could ever prove beyond a reasonable doubt that an individual is both mentally ill and likely to be dangerous."

The court determined that an intermediate level of proof by "clear and convincing evidence" would fairly balance the interests of the state and the rights of the individual. Half of the states were already using this standard for civil commitment. States could choose to use an even higher standard, but this was not required. The case was vacated and remanded to the Texas Supreme Court to determine whether to continue to include the term "unequivocal" in the state's standard.

Parham v. J.R., 442 U.S. 584 (1979)

In *Parham v. J.R.*, the U.S. Supreme Court declined to extend to children the full gamut of procedural safeguards that had been established for adults facing civil commitment.

J. R. was one of two plaintiffs in a class action brought in federal court by all minors detained for psychiatric treatment in Georgia. (The other plaintiff, J. L., died before the case was decided.) The two boys had been admitted to Central State Regional Hospital on a voluntary basis by their parents due to uncontrollable disruptive behaviors. J. R. was admitted at the request of his seventh set of foster parents. J. L. was committed by his own parents, but he became a ward of the state when his parents relinquished their parental rights.

Georgia's statute for voluntary commitment of juveniles required that a parent or guardian sign an application. The hospital superintendent then must find "evidence of mental illness" and that the child is "suitable for treatment" in the hospital. J. R. argued that Georgia's commitment procedures for minors violated the Due Process Clause of the Fourteenth Amendment. The district court agreed, noting that commitment is a severe deprivation of liberty requiring, at a minimum, the right to receive notice and be heard before "an impartial tribunal." The court also determined that the state had failed to provide adequate resources for outpatient treatment and ordered Georgia to expend whatever resources necessary. The state appealed, and the U.S. Supreme Court granted *certiorari.*

The Supreme Court held that Georgia's procedure for the voluntary commitment of minors was constitutional. A due process claim should be tested by balancing three factors: the private interest of the individual, the potential consequences of an erroneous decision for the individual, and the government's interest. The court found that though a child has a liberty interest in not being committed, voluntary commitment of a child (by a parent) does not carry the same stigma as involuntary commitment of an adult. A child might be seriously harmed if he or she fails to receive needed treatment. The private interest at stake includes the interest of the parents, who are obliged for the welfare of the child. The court stressed the traditional presumption that the "natural bonds of affection lead parents to act in the best interests of their children." In the absence of abuse and neglect, the parents should "retain a substantial, if not the dominant, role in the decision… subject to a physician's independent examination and medical judgment."

The court noted that adversarial judicial proceedings would deter parents from seeking treatment for their children, would distract physicians from more important clinical duties, and would not improve the quality of the ultimate decision, which is a medical matter. The court found evidence that admitting psychiatrists had "acted in a neutral and detached fashion in making medical judgments in the best interests of the children." State psychiatrists, in fact, declined to admit many children brought in by their parents.

Justice Brennan wrote a minority opinion dissenting in part. Parents often do not have the best interest of their children in mind when they seek commitment, and children are particularly vulnerable to deprivation of rights. He argued for post-commitment judicial review with traditional due process safeguards.

Vitek v. Jones, 445 U.S. 480 (1980)

In *Vitek v. Jones*, the U.S. Supreme Court determined that a prisoner still serving a sentence is entitled to procedural protections before being transferred to a mental hospital.

In 1974, Larry Jones was sentenced to prison in Nebraska for a charge of robbery. In 1975, he was placed in solitary confinement, where he set his mattress on fire and suffered severe burns. After recovering, he was transferred pursuant to state law to the secure unit of the Lincoln Regional Center, a state mental hospital. The director of correctional services was authorized to transfer a prisoner to an outside institution for examination and treatment. The transfer could only occur when a designated physician or psychologist concluded that the prisoner suffered from a mental disease or defect and could not be given proper treatment in the prison facility. Jones challenged his transfer and the statute as a violation of procedural due process under the Fourteenth Amendment. The district court agreed. The state appealed.

Though Jones had been released on parole, the U.S. Supreme Court decided that the case was not moot and granted *certiorari*. The court agreed that Jones possessed a liberty interest in avoiding transfer to a mental hospital. A liberty interest was created by the statute, which required that a physician find a prisoner to be suffering from a mental disease or defect. This required proper procedures to ensure an accurate finding.

A liberty interest was also found to exist in the Fourteenth Amendment. A convicted prisoner has lost his right to freedom from confinement but retains "a residuum of liberty that would be infringed by a transfer to a mental hospital." The stigma and involuntary treatment that may result from transfer to a psychiatric hospital are "qualitatively different from the punishment characteristically suffered by a person convicted of crime."

The Supreme Court agreed with the district court's minimum required procedures, including written notice, an adversarial hearing with the opportunity to present testimony and cross-examine witnesses, an independent decision maker, notice of rights, and availability of legal counsel. A prisoner facing a finding of mental illness is entitled to independent legal assistance, but a licensed attorney is not required.

Jones v. United States, 463 U.S. 354 (1983)

In *Jones v. United States*, the U.S. Supreme Court chose not to extend the due process protections established in earlier cases to the category of individuals adjudicated not guilty by reason of insanity (NGRI).

In 1975, Michael Jones was arrested for attempting to steal a jacket from a department store. He faced a maximum prison sentence of 1 year. Following his arrest, he was committed to St. Elizabeth's Hospital in the District of Columbia for a determination of his competency to stand trial. He was diagnosed with schizophrenia but found to be fit. He entered an uncontested plea of not guilty by reason of insanity. At the subsequent hearing, he was recommitted to St. Elizabeth's on the basis of testimony that his illness was "still quite active." After more than 1 year in the hospital, he petitioned the court to be released unconditionally or recommitted pursuant to civil commitment standards including a jury trial and proof by clear and convincing evidence that he was currently mentally ill and dangerous. The superior court and court of appeals both rejected his argument. The U.S. Supreme Court granted *certiorari*.

Jones relied on the earlier decision in *Addington v. Texas* (see above) that established a minimum standard of "clear and convincing evidence" for commitment. He indicated that his commitment was based on a standard of a preponderance of the evidence. He also argued that the finding that he was currently mentally ill and dangerous had been based on the earlier finding that he was insane at the time of the offense. He argued that if the state automatically commits insanity acquittees, the commitment can be reasonably justified only for the length of the maximum prison sentence that the acquittee would have served if convicted. After that, civil commitment standards must be used.

The court observed that the finding of insanity at the time of the offense is highly probative of mental illness and dangerousness at the time of the subsequent commitment hearing. The court maintained that a finding beyond a reasonable doubt that a person has committed a criminal act "certainly indicates dangerousness." A nonviolent crime against property therefore could constitute dangerousness. The court also reasoned that a person who has committed a criminal act as a result of mental illness is likely to remain ill and in need of treatment for some time. In contrast to the situation in *Addington*, the insanity acquittee has acknowledged mental illness as a criminal defense, so a higher standard of proof is not required to reduce the risk of unfair stigma or unneeded treatment. A standard of a preponderance of the evidence is sufficient for due process purposes for commitment of insanity acquittees.

In his argument regarding the length of commitment, Jones had relied on the holding in *Jackson v. Indiana* (see above) that "the nature and duration of commitment bear a reasonable relation to the purpose for which the individual is committed." However, the purpose of commitment of an insanity acquittee is treatment, not punishment. There is no correlation between the severity of offense for which a defendant was charged and the length of time necessary for an insanity acquittee to recover from mental illness. The court concluded that "when a criminal defendant establishes by a preponderance of the evidence that he is not guilty of a crime by reason of insanity, the Constitution permits the government, on the basis of the insanity judgment, to confine him to a mental institution until such time as he has regained his sanity or is no longer a danger to himself or society."

In dissenting opinions, four justices argued that past criminal behavior and mental illness should not justify indefinite future commitment, particularly following a single, nonviolent misdemeanor. They argued that "at some point the Government must be required to justify further commitment under the standards of *Addington*."

Zinermon v. Burch, 494 U.S. 113 (1990)

In *Zinermon v. Burch*, the U.S. Supreme Court recognized a deprivation of liberty in the voluntary hospitalization of an individual who was not competent to consent to the admission.

In 1981, Darrell Burch was found wandering in a disoriented state along a Florida highway. When evaluated at a community mental health service in Tallahassee, he was found to be hallucinating and confused. He believed that he was "in heaven." He signed forms giving consent to admission and treatment. He was diagnosed with schizophrenia and treated with psychotropic medication. He was transferred to Florida State Hospital in Chattahoochee for further treatment. He signed additional forms requesting voluntary admission and treatment, including an "Authorization for Treatment" cosigned by his attending physician, Dr. Zimmerman. Progress notes from the hospital indicated that Burch was unable to state the reason for his hospitalization and continued to believe that he was in heaven. He was hospitalized for 5 months.

In 1985, Burch filed a complaint in district court under 42 U.S.C. Section 1983, which provides relief to any person deprived of his or her constitutional rights by state statute. He alleged that staff at the two hospitals "knew or should have known that Plaintiff was incapable of voluntary, knowing understanding and informed consent to admission and treatment at FSH." Burch argued that he had been involuntarily hospitalized without legally adequate consent, thus depriving him of his liberty without due process in violation of the Fourteenth Amendment. The district court dismissed the action, stating that there was no federal remedy for an alleged, random, unauthorized violation of Florida law. The court of appeals reversed, and the U.S. Supreme Court granted *certiorari*.

The court held that state hospital employees admitted Burch as a voluntary patient without determining whether he was mentally competent to sign the voluntary admission forms, and that this was sufficient to state a federal claim for damages. By statute, Florida required informed consent for voluntary psychiatric hospitalization. It is foreseeable that a person with mental illness might be unable to give a knowing consent to admission. Therefore, he or she was in danger of being confined indefinitely without the procedural safeguards of involuntary commitment. If Burch had undergone an involuntary commitment hearing, he might have been released. Even if he were confined, he would have gained certain protections, including the appointment of a guardian and periodic judicial review.

In a dissenting opinion, several justices argued that the state should not be held liable for the "unauthorized and wrongful… departure from established state practice" by particular state employees.

THE RIGHT TO TREATMENT

Rouse v. Cameron, 373 F. 2d 451 (1966)

In *Rouse v. Cameron*, Chief Judge Bazelon, writing for the Court of Appeals for the District of Columbia, extended the statutory right to treatment for civilly committed patients to an individual hospitalized after an acquittal by reason of insanity.

Charles Rouse was found not guilty by reason of insanity on a misdemeanor charge of carrying a dangerous weapon and was committed to St. Elizabeth's Hospital in the District of Columbia in November 1962. If he had been found guilty, he would have faced a maximum sentence of 1 year. He was later given a diagnosis of "Antisocial Reaction." He was confined as dangerously mentally ill for 4 years before he filed a writ of *habeas corpus* in district court. He argued, among other things, that the hospital was not providing him treatment for his mental illness.

The district court denied relief and refused to consider Rouse's argument that he had received no psychiatric treatment. The court concluded that its jurisdiction was limited to whether he remained mentally ill and dangerous. Rouse appealed.

The court of appeals observed that the purpose of involuntary hospitalization is treatment rather than punishment. Without treatment, a hospital is no better than a penitentiary. Civilly committed patients had a statutory right to treatment through the federal Hospitalization of the Mentally Ill Act of 1964, and many states recognized by statute a right to treatment. The court speculated that indefinite confinement without treatment might violate the Equal Protection Clause and might be considered "cruel and unusual punishment" under the Constitution.

The court acknowledged numerous practical limitations to the provision of treatment to committed mentally ill patients, including staff shortages and disagreement among professionals about appropriate treatments. The hospital must only show that "bona fide efforts" at treatment have been made, not that a patient has been cured or has improved with treatment.

The court concluded, "The patient's right to treatment is clear," and remanded to the trial court for a hearing on whether Rouse had received adequate treatment. In a dissenting opinion, one judge argued that Rouse himself had contended during the course of hospitalization that he was not mentally ill and needed no treatment, so his allegation that the hospital was providing him no treatment was simply a legal strategy.

Wyatt v. Stickney, 344 F. Supp. 373 (1972)

In *Wyatt v. Stickney*, Judge Johnson, writing for the Alabama District Court, established specific minimum standards for proper treatment and care in a state facility for the mentally retarded. Similarly extensive and detailed standards were subsequently incorporated into numerous state regulations regarding the care of the mentally ill.

Ricky Wyatt was a mentally retarded patient confined involuntarily at Bryce Hospital in Tuscaloosa, Alabama. In 1970, a class action suit was filed on his behalf alleging poor treatment and horrible conditions of confinement. In 1971, the district court agreed that patients at Bryce Hospital were subjected to brutal, unsanitary, and dangerous conditions. The court ruled that "to deprive any citizen of his or her liberty upon the altruistic theory that the confinement is for humane therapeutic reasons and then fail to provide adequate treatment violates the very fundamentals of due process."

The court found that Bryce Hospital failed to provide a safe and humane environment, a sufficient number of qualified staff, and individualized treatment. The court held that involuntarily committed patients "unquestionably have a constitutional right to receive such individual treatment as will give each of them a realistic opportunity to be cured or to improve his or her mental condition." Bryce Hospital was given 6 months to improve the level of care.

At a subsequent hearing, the court found that the hospital continued to be grossly deficient and had failed to satisfy minimum medical and constitutional standards. The court invited the various parties and *amici* to propose standards for constitutionally adequate treatment. After considering the submissions, Judge Johnson issued an Order and Decree of 1972 detailing the minimum constitutional standards for adequate treatment of the mentally ill. The court declined to appoint a master to oversee the implementation of the standards, to issue an injunction against further commitments, or to appropriate funding from the state's budget. However, the court said that "the very preservation of human life and dignity" were at stake, and that these measures would be taken if necessary.

The minimum standards included a "humane psychological and physical environment," "qualified staff in numbers sufficient to administer adequate treatment," and "individualized treatment plans." The standards included such details as the appropriate temperature for hot water and minimum staff-to-patient ratios.

Donaldson v. O'Connor, 493 F.2d 507 (1974)

Kenneth Donaldson was hospitalized for nearly 15 years at the Florida State Hospital at Chattahoochee before filing suit for damages in federal court in 1971. He argued that he had a constitutional right to receive treatment or be released. In its initial holding, the district court of appeals considered for the first time "the far-reaching question whether the Fourteenth Amendment guarantees a right to treatment to persons involuntarily civilly committed to state mental hospitals."

Donaldson was committed in 1957 upon the petition of his father, who believed he was experiencing delusions. Throughout his hospitalization, he refused to take any medication or receive electroconvulsive therapy. No other therapy was offered. He was denied ground privileges, occupational therapy, and the opportunity to speak at any length with a psychiatrist. His attending psychiatrist accorded him the same treatment that he provided to nine hundred other patients, even though Donaldson's condition appeared to be in remission. He was not given the opportunity for outpatient care, even though a variety of third parties offered to provide him assistance and supervision. Finally, there was no evidence in the record that Donaldson had ever been violent in any way.

The district court of appeals referred to an influential 1960 article in the *American Bar Association Journal* by Dr. Morton Birnbaum, who argued that treatment serves as a *quid pro quo* justification for hospitalization. In exchange for his or her loss of freedom, the patient receives treatment. The court also referred to *dicta* in the case of *Rouse v. Cameron* (see above) that a constitutional right to treatment might exist.

The court found that a right to treatment exists in the Due Process Clause of the Fourteenth Amendment. Civil commitment is a "massive curtailment of liberty" that cannot be justified except for some permissible governmental goal. When a person poses a danger to himself or others, the restriction is justified by the government's interest in preserving safety. When a nondangerous person is committed, only the provision of treatment can justify the deprivation of liberty. The court held that "minimally adequate treatment" must be provided, defined as "the provision of rehabilitative treatment, or, where rehabilitation is impossible, minimally adequate habilitation and care, beyond the subsistence level custodial care that would be provided in a penitentiary."

The court concluded, "We hold that a person involuntarily civilly committed to a state mental hospital has a constitutional right to receive such individual treatment as will give him a reasonable opportunity to be cured or to improve his mental condition."

His case was eventually heard before the U.S. Supreme Court (*O'Connor v. Donaldson*, 1975), which ruled against the involuntary confinement of a nondangerous, mentally ill individual, but did not endorse the lower court's ruling regarding a constitutional right to treatment.

Estelle v. Gamble, 429 U.S. 97 (1976)

In *Estelle v. Gamble*, the U.S. Supreme Court established "deliberate indifference" to an inmate's medical needs as a form of cruel and unusual punishment barred by the Constitution.

J. W. Gamble was an inmate in the Texas Department of Corrections when he claimed to have injured his back. In 1973, a bale of hay fell on him while he was performing a prison work assignment. He was seen by a medical assistant and prescribed pain medication. The following day, he was seen by a prison physician who diagnosed lower back pain and prescribed a muscle relaxant. Over the next

3 months, Gamble was seen by prison health personnel a total of 17 times. His treatment was complicated several times by staff failure. A prescription was not filled for 4 days because staff lost the prescription. Staff failed to carry out a doctor's order to move him to a lower bunk bed. Prison guards refused to allow Gamble to see a physician for chest pain, even though he had been diagnosed with an irregular cardiac rhythm. An x-ray of his back was never ordered.

Gamble was twice brought before the prison disciplinary committee due to his refusal to resume work. In both cases, prison health personnel testified that Gamble was capable of returning to work. Gamble filed suit against the director of the Department of Corrections, the prison warden, and the medical director under 42 U.S.C. Section 1983, which provides relief to any person deprived of their constitutional rights by state statute. The district court dismissed the complaint, and the court of appeals reversed. The Supreme Court granted *certiorari.*

Gamble claimed that he been subjected to cruel and unusual punishment in violation of the Eighth Amendment of the Constitution. The intent of the drafters of the Constitution was to prevent torture and other barbarous methods of punishment. However, courts have extended the protection consistent with "the evolving standards of decency that mark the progress of a maturing society." Since an inmate must rely on prison staff for all medical treatment, denial of medical care by prison staff "may result in pain and suffering, which no one suggests would serve any penological purpose."

The court held that "deliberate indifference to serious medical needs of prisoners" should be the standard for determining whether a violation of the Eighth Amendment exists. The court distinguished such actions from an accident or other inadvertent failure to provide treatment. A prisoner should seek tort relief, rather than a constitutional remedy, for inadvertent medical malpractice. The court noted that Gamble had been seen by medical personnel on 17 occasions and concluded that he had not stated a sufficient claim for violation of his constitutional rights.

In a dissenting opinion, Justice Stevens argued that the determination whether a constitutional right had been violated should be based not on the motivation of prison staff but on the nature of the harm done.

Youngberg v. Romeo, 457 U.S. 307 (1982)

In *Youngberg v. Romeo*, the U.S. Supreme Court established a right to "minimally adequate or reasonable training to ensure safety and freedom from undue restraint" for the mentally retarded in a state institution. The court also established a standard of professional judgment when evaluating the treatment provided.

Nicholas Romeo was a profoundly mentally retarded young man who was involuntarily committed to Pennhurst State School and Hospital by his mother. While hospitalized, Romeo was injured on many occasions, as a result of both his own violence and attacks by other residents. Romeo's mother filed suit in district court in 1976 seeking damages against Pennhurst for failing to protect her son. She claimed that Pennhurst violated his rights under the Eighth and Fourteenth Amendments.

After the suit was filed, Romeo was transferred to another hospital for treatment of a broken arm. He was physically restrained on a daily basis to prevent him from harming others. Pennhurst left Romeo in the hospital under those conditions pending settlement of the suit. In response, Romeo's mother filed a second suit claiming that he was restrained for prolonged periods on a routine basis and that the hospital had failed to provide him with appropriate treatment for his mental retardation. The jury returned a verdict for the defendants.

The court of appeals reversed and remanded for a new trial, holding that the Fourteenth Amendment, rather than the Eighth, was the appropriate source for the rights of a committed patient. The Fourteenth Amendment establishes a liberty interest in freedom of movement and personal security. The court also found a fundamental liberty interest in "habilitation" intended to treat mental retardation. In determining whether a hospital had violated this right, courts should defer to medical judgment. The Constitution only requires the courts to ensure that "professional judgment in fact was exercised" in administering treatment.

The U.S. Supreme Court granted *certiorari* in order to determine, for the first time, whether a patient has a "constitutionally protected liberty interest in safety, freedom of movement, and training within the institution." The court found that Romeo's claim to safe conditions must be valid, since even prisoners have such a right. The right to freedom from bodily restraint is "the core of the liberty protected by the Due Process Clause."

The court found Romeo's assertion of a "constitutional right to minimally adequate habilitation" more controversial. Generally, the state does not have a constitutional duty to provide services. Even when a person is wholly dependent on the state, the state is permitted considerable discretion. The court concluded that the Fourteenth Amendment does require the state to provide "minimally adequate or reasonable training to ensure safety and freedom from undue restraint." The court did not consider whether an involuntarily committed patient has a right to additional treatment.

The court acknowledged that the state has interests, such as the need to protect other residents, which compete with the patient's liberty interests. To balance these interests, the court upheld the "professional judgment" standard articulated by the court of appeals. A professional decision is presumed to be valid, and "liability may be imposed only when the decision by the professional is such a substantial departure from accepted professional judgment, practice, or standards as to demonstrate that the person responsible actually did not base the decision on such a judgment." A professional may be immune from liability in cases where budgetary constraints limit treatment.

The court vacated the decision of the court of appeals and remanded to the district court for further proceedings.

Farmer v. Brennan, 114 S.Ct. 1970 (1994)

In *Farmer v. Brennan*, the U.S. Supreme Court determined that a subjective standard should be used when evaluating claims of deliberate indifference in the care and custody of prisoners.

In 1989, Dee Farmer was beaten and raped by a cellmate within 2 weeks of her transfer to the federal penitentiary in Terre Haute, Indiana. Farmer was a transsexual (born male) who had undergone estrogen therapy, silicone breast implants, and unsuccessful surgical removal of testicles prior to her arrest. In prison, she continued to receive smuggled hormone treatment and to wear clothing in a feminine manner. She was sometimes housed in the general (male) prison population but was more often segregated because of safety concerns or violations of prison rules. She was transferred to Terre Haute for disciplinary reasons. Prior to her rape, she had raised no objection to prison officials regarding her transfer or placement in the general population.

Farmer filed suit in federal court, alleging that her Eighth Amendment rights had been violated when prison officials placed her in the general population "despite knowledge that the penitentiary had a violent environment and a history of inmate assaults, and despite knowledge that petitioner, as a transsexual who 'projects feminine characteristics,' would be particularly vulnerable to sexual attack by some USP-Terre Haute inmates." The district court granted summary judgment, concluding that there had been no deliberate indifference. Prison officials had no "actual knowledge" of danger and were not "reckless in a criminal sense." The court of appeals agreed. The U.S. Supreme Court granted *certiorari* in order to define the term "deliberate indifference."

The Eighth Amendment requires prison officials to provide food, clothing, shelter, and medical care and to take reasonable measures to guarantee safety. Permitting prisoners to be violently assaulted serves no "legitimate penological objective." The case of *Estelle v. Gamble* (see above) set the standard of "deliberate indifference" for determining whether the Eighth Amendment has been violated, and most courts had equated this with "recklessness," which lies somewhere between neglect and intent.

The court held that a subjective test must be applied to determine whether deliberate indifference exists, because the Eighth Amendment outlaws cruel and unusual "punishments" rather than "conditions." Therefore, "an official's failure to alleviate a significant risk that he should have perceived but did not, while no cause for commendation, cannot under our cases be condemned as the infliction of punishment." Likewise, a prison official who responds reasonably to a substantial risk will not be liable even if the harm occurs. On the other hand, the judge or jury can conclude that a prison official knew of a substantial risk from "the very fact that the risk was obvious."

Having defined the appropriate standard, the court remanded the case.

Brown v. Plata, 134 S. Ct. 436 (2011)

In *Brown v. Plata*, the Supreme Court upheld a district court order forcing California to drastically reduce its prison population in order to correct deficiencies in the provision of medical and psychiatric care that had been held to violate the Eight Amendment.

The case began as two separate class action suits that involved prisoners with serious mental illnesses (*Coleman v. Brown*, initiated in 1990) and medical conditions (*Plata v. Brown*, initiated in 2001). The state prisons at the time were operating with approximately twice as many inmates as the facilities had been designed to hold, and staffing was comparably inadequate. Overcrowding created unhealthy conditions (with, for example, more than 50 prisoners sharing a single toilet and suicidal inmates confined in cages the size of a telephone booth) as well as competition for medical evaluation and treatment. Only half the budgeted positions for psychiatrists were filled. The suicide rate was nearly 80% higher than the national prison average, and more than two-thirds of suicides were thought to be foreseeable or preventable. Sick inmates were held in congested cages for hours, and urgent medical care might be delayed for months due to long referral wait lists. Independent surveys found extreme departures from standard practice "widespread" and the proportion of preventable deaths "extremely high."

Separate district courts appointed receivers in 1995 (in *Coleman*) and 2005 (in *Plata*) to oversee the state's remedial plans, but overcrowding persisted, and conditions in the prisons continued to deteriorate. In 2006, the governor declared a state of emergency, announcing that "immediate action is necessary to prevent death and harm caused by California's severe prison overcrowding." Plaintiffs in the two actions asked the district courts to consolidate the cases and convene a three-judge court, in accordance with the federal Prison Litigation Reform Act of 1995, which stipulated that only such a court can compel a state to limit its prison population. The three-judge court ordered California to reduce the population to 137.5% of the prisons' design capacity, which would require the release of approximately forty thousand inmates over 2 years. The state appealed to the Supreme Court.

The Supreme Court found that inmates' constitutional rights were being violated, that overcrowding was the primary cause of the violations, that the state had been given sufficient time to correct the deficiencies, and that the order to reduce overcrowding was both necessary and narrowly drawn. The court rejected the state's argument that the need to release some prisoners who were healthy and thus not a party to the actions made the order overly broad, noting that even healthy inmates are not "remote bystanders [but] that system's next potential victims." The court also concluded that the prison population could be reduced while preserving, or perhaps even improving, public safety. For example, the state could divert low-risk offenders to community programs. The court upheld the district court's order in all respects.

Several justices dissented, arguing that judges should not meddle in policy or attempt to manage state institutions. In his dissent, Justice Scalia suggested that, given the enormity of an order to release forty thousand convicted felons, the court should "bend every effort to read the law in such a way as to avoid that outrageous result." He also argued that the violation of the rights of a "small proportion of prisoners [who] have personally received sufficiently atrocious treatment" could not justify an intervention aimed at all inmates in the system.

RIGHT TO REFUSE TREATMENT

Application of the President and Directors of Georgetown College, Inc., 331 F.2d 1000 (1964)

In *Georgetown College*, Judge Wright of the District of Columbia Circuit Court of Appeals explained his reasoning in issuing an order permitting a hospital to administer an involuntary blood transfusion in an emergency over a patient's religious objections.

Jesse Jones was a 25-year-old mother who was brought to the Georgetown University Hospital by her husband in 1963 after she had lost two-thirds of her blood from a bleeding ulcer. Because of their religious faith as Jehovah's Witnesses, Jones and her husband refused to authorize a blood transfusion to save her life.

As her death became imminent, the hospital applied to a district court judge for permission to administer blood. The judge refused to consider the application, and the hospital's attorney appealed to a judge of the circuit court of appeals. Judge Wright rushed to the hospital and spoke to the patient's husband and doctors. The treating physicians confirmed that Jones would die without blood. The judge interpreted Jones' only audible communication to him, "Against my will," as an indication that she would not feel responsible if the court ordered the transfusion. He signed an order permitting the hospital to administer such transfusions as were necessary to save her life.

In his opinion, the judge clarified that the emergency order was intended to maintain the *status quo*, to prevent the issues raised by the hospital's application from becoming moot through the death of the patient. After receiving the transfusion, the patient recovered, and no further transfusions were needed. The judge noted that there was strong precedent for a single judge to issue an emergency order when it would be impractical to convene a full court. He argued that it was appropriate for the court to consider the issue, because it was unlikely to attract the attention of legislators. If the court did not intervene, such legal issues would be settled only after the fact through civil suits for damages brought by the private parties.

The judge delineated several factors that played a role in his decision and that might be relevant to the full court in reaching a decision after the emergency had passed. When Jones went to the hospital to receive medical attention, she placed the hospital in the position of being legally responsible for her care. Jones was "*in extremis* and hardly *compos mentis* at the time in question" and therefore no more competent than a child would be to make treatment decisions. If she were not competent, her husband would not have the right to prohibit treatment that would save her life. The state has an interest in not allowing a parent to abandon an infant, in this case Jones' 7-month-old son. Jones did not want to die, and if the transfusion were forced upon her by the law, she would not be responsible for the violation of her religious beliefs. Treatment may be forced upon adults for certain contagious diseases, with no exemption for religious beliefs if the community is at risk. Finally, "a life hung in the balance," and there was no time for reflection; the judge chose to "act on the side of life."

The temporary order expired, and the hospital did not apply for another order, because Jones had recovered following the emergency transfusion. Jones later filed a petition for a rehearing by the court of appeals *en banc*, citing the rights of "free exercise of religion and… of a free citizen to have his body inviolate." The petition for a rehearing was denied. In dissenting opinions, judges questioned whether Judge Wright had exceeded his jurisdiction by intervening without the full court and whether the court has any role "when a legally competent adult refuses, on grounds of conscience, to consent to a medical treatment essential to preserve life."

Rennie v. Klein, 720 F.2d 266 (1983)

In *Rennie v. Klein*, the Third Circuit Court of Appeals established for civilly committed patients a right to refuse medication. This is the highest federal court to have ruled on this issue.

John Rennie had been involuntarily hospitalized for the twelfth time at the Ancora Psychiatric Hospital in New Jersey when he instituted a class action suit asserting a right to refuse antipsychotic medication. The district court recognized a constitutional right of involuntarily committed mentally ill patients to refuse antipsychotic medications and granted an injunction. Both parties appealed.

The court of appeals agreed that there exists a constitutional right to refuse treatment, but found that the procedures outlined in New Jersey's Administrative Bulletin 78-3 provided adequate protection of that right. According to the bulletin, a patient who protests the administration of antipsychotic medication must be permitted a meeting with the attending physician at which the reasons for prescribing the drug and the drug's risks and benefits are explained. If the patient continues to refuse treatment, then a meeting with the treatment team is required, and the physician must seek approval from the medical director of the hospital. The medication plan must be reviewed weekly.

The court ruled that the medication administered must be the "least intrusive means" of accomplishing the state's goals. While appeal was pending, the U.S. Supreme Court vacated the court's judgment in *Romeo v. Youngberg* (see above), which had also utilized a "least intrusive means" analysis. The Supreme Court remanded *Rennie* to the district court of appeals for reconsideration.

On remand, the court found that the decision to override the patient's right to refuse medication must be the product of the medical authority's professional judgment, which "will be presumed valid unless it is shown to be a 'substantial departure from accepted professional judgment, practice or standards.'" Even though its constitutional analysis of the case had changed, the court's holding remained the same: New Jersey's regulations provided sufficient due process protections "without the need for interposing external judicial requirements." The court limited its judgment to the case of mentally ill patients involuntarily committed to a hospital who constitute a danger to themselves or others.

Several members of the court were reluctant to abandon the "least intrusive means" analysis. In a concurring opinion, one judge also commented that the use of medications may not be justified "purely on economic or administrative grounds, as part of an attempt to 'warehouse' the patient."

Rogers v. Commissioner, 458 N.E.2d 308 (1983)

In *Rogers v. Commissioner*, the Supreme Judicial Court of Massachusetts established a broad right for involuntarily committed patients to refuse medication.

Ruby Rogers was one of seven patients committed to Boston State Hospital who filed a class action suit in 1975. They challenged the hospital's practice of secluding and medicating them against their will as a violation of the Constitution. After their complaint was filed, a federal district court judge issued a temporary restraining order prohibiting the use of seclusion or administration of antipsychotic medication to hospitalized patients in nonemergency situations without their consent. At trial, the judge denied damages, because the hospital's practices were in accordance with acceptable medical standards. However, the judge found a constitutional right to refuse treatment in nonemergency situations. This right extended to incompetent patients, for whom the treatment decision should be made by a guardian using a substituted judgment standard. Both parties appealed the decision.

The court of appeals affirmed the denial of damages but remanded on the injunction against involuntary medication. The court found that the physician should balance the interest of the incompetent patient and the state's interest in preventing violence. It did not require the appointment of a guardian for a decision to involuntarily treat an incompetent patient with antipsychotic medication.

The U.S. Supreme Court granted *certiorari*. The court vacated the judgment of the lower courts and remanded to the court of appeals to determine the patient's rights under Massachusetts law (rather than the U.S. Constitution).

The court of appeals looked to the recent Massachusetts case of *Guardianship of Roe* (1981) involving outpatient refusal of antipsychotic medication, in which the substituted judgment determination of a judge could not be delegated to a guardian. The defendants in the current case argued that the interests and needs of the hospital in treating an involuntarily confined patient should be sufficient to transfer the treatment decision from the judge to doctors. They were supported in this argument by *amici* briefs from the American Psychiatric Association and the Massachusetts Psychiatric Society. The court disagreed, noting that hospital physicians have conflicting interests with patients who wish to avoid medication.

The court held that "no State interest justifies the use of antipsychotic drugs in a non-emergency situations without the patient's consent." Involuntary commitment to a hospital for purposes of public safety does not reflect on the judgmental capacity of a patient. A patient may be competent to make some decisions but not others. The right to make decisions about treatment is an essential element of a patient's general right to manage his or her affairs. Therefore, a mentally ill patient committed to a hospital must be considered competent to refuse medication unless found incompetent before a judge. In such a case, the judge must make a substituted judgment decision, which is distinct from what is medically in the best interests of the patient. The judge must determine whether the patient would have consented to the treatment if competent.

In answering a separate question posed by the U.S. Supreme Court, the district court of appeals concluded that "only if a patient poses an imminent threat of harm to himself or others, and only if there is no less intrusive alternative to antipsychotic drugs, may the Commonwealth invoke its police powers without prior court approval to treat the patient by forcible injection of antipsychotic drugs over the patient's objection." Referring to the case of *Guardianship of Roe*, the court also found that, in rare circumstances, under its *parens patriae* powers, the state may medicate a patient in the absence of a threat of violence and without prior court approval to prevent the "immediate, substantial, and irreversible deterioration of a serious mental illness."

Washington v. Harper, 110 S.C. 1028 (1990)

In *Washington v. Harper*, the U.S. Supreme Court considered whether a prisoner is entitled to a judicial hearing when seeking to refuse psychiatric medication.

Walter Harper was sentenced to the Washington State Penitentiary in 1976 for robbery. He was treated with antipsychotic medication on the prison's mental health unit. He was paroled in 1980, but his parole was revoked in 1981 when he assaulted two nurses at the Harborview Medical Center in Seattle. Upon re-incarceration, he was sent to the Special Offender Center, a psychiatric hospital of the Department of Corrections. He was diagnosed with manic–depressive illness and voluntarily treated with antipsychotic medication.

In 1982, Harper refused to continue his medication. His treating psychiatrists sought approval to medicate him involuntarily pursuant to the hospital's policy. According to the policy, an inmate could be subjected to involuntary treatment with medication only if he suffered from a mental disorder and was either gravely disabled or posed a likelihood of serious harm to himself, others, or property. The inmate was entitled to a hearing before a committee composed of a psychiatrist, a psychologist, and an administrator at the hospital, none of whom were involved in his treatment. The inmate could only be medicated against his or her will if a majority of the committee, including the psychiatrist, agreed that the criteria were met. The inmate had to be given notice of the hearing, of the diagnosis, and of the reason for medication. The inmate had the right to attend, present evidence, and receive the assistance of a lay adviser. The inmate had the right to appeal the decision to the superintendent of the hospital as well as to judicial review in state court. The committee was required to review the case 7 days after the initiation of involuntary treatment, and the treating psychiatrist had to submit a report to the medical director every 14 days during the course of involuntary treatment.

In 1985, Harper filed suit under 42 U.S.C. Section 1983, which provides relief to any person deprived of his or her constitutional rights by state statute, claiming that the state had violated the Due Process, Equal Protection, and Free Speech Clauses of the Constitution. The trial court held that Harper had a liberty interest in refusing antipsychotic medication, but that the policy satisfied the requirements of due process. The Washington Supreme Court reversed, concluding that due process would require a judicial hearing, with the full protections of an adversarial proceeding, in which the state had to prove by "clear, cogent, and convincing" evidence that antipsychotic medication was necessary and effective to further a compelling state interest.

The U.S. Supreme Court granted *certiorari* and first determined that the case was not moot, even though Harper was no longer receiving antipsychotic medication. The court agreed that Harper possessed a liberty interest in refusing antipsychotic medication under the Due Process Clause of the Fourteenth Amendment as well as under state law, because the policy stipulated that medication be administered only under certain conditions. Under the Due Process Clause, however, this liberty interest must be balanced against the prisoner's medical interests and the state's legitimate interest in prison safety and security. The court concluded that "when a prison regulation impinges on inmates' constitutional rights, the regulation is valid if it is reasonably related to legitimate penological interests."

Referring to the prior decision in *Parham v. J.R.* (see above), the court concluded that the Constitution does not prohibit medical personnel, rather than judges, from serving as independent decision makers. The court opined that "prison authorities are best equipped to make difficult decisions regarding prison administration." The court also concluded that a standard of "clear, cogent and convincing" is neither required nor helpful for medical decision making and that it is not required for a lawyer to assist the inmate. The court held that the hospital policy satisfied both substantive and procedural due process requirements.

Riggins v. Nevada, 504 U.S. 127 (1992)

In *Riggins v. Nevada*, the U.S. Supreme Court extended the qualified right of a prisoner to refuse psychiatric medication to an individual facing trial but not yet convicted.

David Riggins was arrested for murder in 1987. Prior to his trial, Riggins was treated with thioridazine for complaints of hearing voices and trouble sleeping. The district court found him to be competent, and the trial proceeded. The defense requested an order to suspend administration of the antipsychotic until the end of trial. They argued that the Fourteenth Amendment and state constitution barred the involuntary administration of antipsychotic medication as an infringement on Riggins' freedom. The defense also argued that Riggins had a right to show jurors his "true mental state" as part of his insanity defense. The state denied the motion.

Riggins presented an insanity defense at trial and testified on his own behalf. The jury found him guilty of murder and sentenced him to death. Riggins appealed to the Nevada Supreme Court.

Among other claims, Riggins argued that the forced administration of antipsychotic medication had denied him the ability to assist in his own defense and prejudicially affected his demeanor at trial. He argued that the state had not demonstrated a need to administer thioridazine and had not explored less intrusive alternatives. The Nevada Supreme Court affirmed the conviction and sentence, holding that the denial of the request to terminate medication was neither an abuse of discretion nor a violation of Riggins' trial rights. The U.S. Supreme Court granted *certiorari* to decide whether forced administration of antipsychotic medication during trial violates the Sixth and Fourteenth Amendments.

The court referred to the previous decision in *Washington v. Harper* (see above) that found it impermissible to involuntarily administer antipsychotic medications to a prisoner without a finding of overriding justification and medical appropriateness. The Equal Protection Clause of the Fourteenth Amendment guarantees that a person detained for trial, but not yet convicted, be provided at least as much protection as a convicted prisoner. Therefore, the state was obligated to determine the need and medical appropriateness of continuing antipsychotic medication once Riggins requested that it be terminated. Due process would have been satisfied if the district court had determined that treatment with antipsychotic medication was medically appropriate and essential for the safety of Riggins and others. The state also might have argued that involuntary treatment was required to maintain Riggins' fitness to stand trial (though the court declined to decide whether this would be a constitutionally sufficient rationale).

The district court's decision presumably was based on weighing the risk that the jury would be swayed by Riggins' outward appearance against the risk that Riggins would become incompetent without medication. Such a decision did not acknowledge Riggins' liberty interest in freedom from involuntary medication. The U.S. Supreme Court concluded that there was "a strong possibility that Riggins' defense was impaired due to the administration of [thioridazine]." Permitting Riggins to present expert testimony on the effects of the antipsychotic on his demeanor did not resolve the possibility that the medication might adversely affect his testimony, his interaction with his attorney, and his comprehension of the trial proceedings. In the absence in the record of any evidence that the administration of antipsychotic medication was necessary to accomplish an essential state policy, the court reversed and remanded.

Hargrave v. Vermont, 340 F. 3d 27 (2003)

In *Hargrave v. Vermont*, the U.S. Court of Appeals ruled that the state could not discriminate against the mentally ill when pursing involuntary treatment by ignoring a patient's preferences expressed in a durable power of attorney (DPOA) for health care that had been properly executed while the patient was competent.

In 1998, Vermont passed legislation to supersede procedures established by a 1985 consent decree authorizing the involuntary medication of civilly committed individuals following an adjudicatory hearing in which the patient was found incompetent. The consent decree stipulated that the hearing must "ascertain and effectuate the decision that the patient would have made if competent." DPOAs had subsequently been used as evidence of such preferences. Under the new act, a court could override a patient's preferences as articulated in a DPOA if, after 45 days of such treatment, the patient had "not experienced a significant clinical improvement in his or her mental state, and remain[ed] incompetent."

Nancy Hargrave had been hospitalized numerous times for the treatment of paranoid schizophrenia and had been court ordered to take medication while at the Vermont State Hospital in 1997. In 1999, she executed a DPOA specifying that, in the event of becoming incompetent, she would refuse all psychotropic medications and electroconvulsive therapy. She then filed suit in federal court arguing that Vermont's new procedures for involuntary medication violated the federal Americans with Disabilities Act (ADA) and the federal Rehabilitation Act. The district court dismissed the state's claim that Hargrave did not have standing because she was not under imminent threat of involuntary medication. The court also allowed a class of all mentally ill individuals who have a DPOA to join in the suit. The district court then issued summary judgment that Vermont's act facially discriminated against the mentally ill "to the extent to which the provisions allow their lawfully executed DPOAs to be abrogated."

On appeal, Vermont argued that the ADA's exception for employees who pose "a direct threat" in the workplace would apply to Hargrave and the other plaintiffs, because they would be civilly committed at the time of any hearing for involuntary medication. The court of appeals rejected this, noting that the state would be required to perform an individualized determination of danger at the time the DPOA would be abrogated, and that in any case the ADA exception might not apply outside the context of employment. The court also rejected the state's argument that the act did not discriminate against the mentally ill because it would affect only "the small class of people who are mentally ill, dangerous, committed to State custody, and incompetent to make treatment decisions." The court observed that only mentally ill patients who had been civilly committed and found incompetent would have their treatment preferences overridden, in contrast to "equally incompetent patients who are physically ill or injured" and in contrast to patients committed to a hospital for other reasons, such as tuberculosis or drug addiction.

The court of appeals affirmed the district court's decision finding the act discriminatory and enjoining its implementation.

Sell v. U.S., 539 U.S. 166, 123 S. Ct. 2174 (2003)

In *Sell v. U.S.*, the Supreme Court ruled that in certain rare circumstances, psychotropic drugs may be involuntarily administered solely to render a defendant competent to stand trial, but that alternative legal justifications for involuntary treatment should be pursued first.

Charles Sell was a dentist who had been hospitalized and treated with antipsychotic medication for persecutory delusions involving the police and communists. In 1997, he told officers that God had told him that for "every [FBI] person I kill, a soul will be saved." Shortly thereafter, he was charged with several counts of insurance fraud, found competent to proceed by a federal judge, and released on bail. Bail was later revoked at a hearing in which Sell was "totally out of control" and spat in the judge's face. He then incurred new charges of attempting to murder the FBI agent who had arrested him and a former employee who planned to testify against him, and these were joined for trial with the fraud charges.

Following a new psychiatric evaluation, Sell was found incompetent to stand trial and hospitalized at the U.S. Medical Center for Federal Prisoners, where he refused recommended antipsychotic medication. The hospital conducted administrative hearings by a reviewing psychiatrist and a Bureau of Prisons official, both of whom concluded that Sell was delusional, dangerous, and likely to benefit from medication. Sell contested the hospital's decision at a hearing before the federal judge, who ruled that "anti-psychotic medications are the only way to render the defendant not dangerous and competent to stand trial."

Sell appealed to the federal district court, which affirmed the order for involuntary medication even though it found the judge's determination of dangerousness "clearly erroneous." The court opined that antipsychotic medications were "medically appropriate" and "represent the only viable hope of rendering defendant competent to stand trial." Sell and the government both appealed to the federal court of appeals, which affirmed both of the district court's findings. The U.S. Supreme Court granted *certiorari.*

The court referred to *Harper v. Collins* and *Riggins v. Nevada* (see both above), which had established that an inmate's liberty interest in avoiding unwanted medication could be overridden "only if the treatment is medically appropriate, is substantially unlikely to have side effects that may undermine the fairness of the trial, and, taking account of less intrusive alternatives, is necessary significantly to further important governmental trial-related interests." The court emphasized that an argument about the government's interest in restoring competence could be avoided if involuntary treatment were pursued instead with the less controversial aim of restoring the defendant's health or reducing dangerousness. The court also noted that prolonged confinement of a defendant resulting from his or her medication refusal might suffice to allay some of the government's concern.

The Supreme Court vacated the lower court's order, finding it had failed to consider whether involuntary medication was essential, in the absence of dangerousness, to further a governmental interest and whether it could impair Sell's ability to put forth a defense.

INFORMED CONSENT

Canterbury v. Spence, 464 F.2d 772 (1972)

In *Canterbury v. Spence*, the District of Columbia Court of Appeals established the doctrine of informed consent as the proper basis for a suit of malpractice involving a failure to warn a patient of all of the potential risks of a procedure that a reasonable patient would wish to know.

In 1958, Dr. Spence evaluated Jerry Canterbury for severe upper back pain. A myelogram revealed a filling defect, and Spence told the 19-year-old that he would require surgery for a ruptured disc. Canterbury did not object or inquire further. Spence spoke to Canterbury's mother over the phone and told her that the procedure was no more dangerous than "any other operation." Canterbury was recovering normally on the day after the operation when he suddenly fell at the side of his bed. He became paralyzed from the waist down. His condition improved little after a second, emergency operation. At the time of trial in 1968, Canterbury was incontinent and required crutches to walk.

Canterbury filed suit in the District of Columbia, alleging that Spence was negligent in his performance and in his failure to inform Canterbury of the risks of surgery. The district court gave a directed verdict against Canterbury, stating that there was no medical testimony to show causality for the paralysis. Canterbury appealed, and the court of appeals reversed and remanded for a jury trial.

The court noted that suits against physicians for failing to disclose risk were not new. The doctrine of informed consent rests on the common law notion, expressed in *Schloendorff v. Society of New York Hospital* (1914), that "every human being of adult years and sound mind has a right to determine what shall be done with his own body." When making decisions about treatment, the patient is in a fiduciary relationship with the physician, relying on information possessed only by the physician. The physician is therefore under a duty to communicate specific information about abnormal findings, diagnosis, recommended treatments and alternatives, and any risks that may be involved in treatment. Having received this information, it is "the prerogative of the patient, not the physician, to determine for himself the direction in which his interests seem to lie." Treatment that has not been approved by the patient constitutes battery by the physician.

The court observed that some jurisdictions evaluate the duty to disclose as a matter of physicians' customary practice. The court concluded that the trier of fact should use a standard of what is "reasonable under the circumstances" when determining what the patient needs to know to make a decision. Because full disclosure is obviously unreasonable, "the scope of the physician's communications to the patient… must be measured by the patient's need, and that need is the information material to the decision… all risks potentially affecting the decision must be unmasked." Even risks of a very low probability should be disclosed if they involve death or serious disability.

The court identified two exceptions to the duty to disclose. In an emergency, a physician may treat an unconscious patient (or one otherwise incapable of consenting) if the "harm from a failure to treat is imminent and outweighs any harm threatened by the proposed treatment." The physician still should attempt to obtain the consent of a family member. The second exception is when the disclosure of risk is medically contraindicated because the disclosure itself may do psychological harm or complicate treatment. This exception may not serve as an excuse for paternalistic behavior on the part of a physician who worries that the patient will decide against the procedure.

Finally, the court noted that a failure to disclose does not prove malpractice. A causal connection must exist, in that the disclosure would have resulted in a decision by the patient to decline the treatment. In determining this issue, some courts had used a subjective standard, inquiring of the patient whether he or she would have agreed to the treatment if informed of the risk. The court of appeals reasoned that this "places the physician in jeopardy of the patient's hindsight and bitterness." Instead, the court should use an objective standard to determine what "a prudent person in the patient's position would have decided if suitably informed of all perils bearing significance."

Kaimowitz v. Michigan Department of Mental Health, No. 73-19434-AW Mich. Cir. Ct., Wayne Co. (1973)

In *Kaimowitz v. Michigan Department of Mental Health*, a Michigan court acted on the petition of a third party in halting experimental psychosurgery on an involuntarily committed patient.

In 1955, John Doe was civilly committed to the Ionia State Hospital as a Criminal Sexual Psychopath under Michigan's Criminal Sexual Psychopathic Law. He had murdered and raped a student nurse while he was a patient at Kalamazoo State Hospital. In 1972, Doe signed an informed consent form to receive psychosurgery as part of a study of the treatment of uncontrollable aggression. The study was funded by the state of Michigan and had been approved by two separate review committees. Doe was found to be the only appropriate candidate for the surgical experiment and was scheduled to have depth electrodes inserted into his brain. A third party, Kaimowitz, became aware of the planned experimental psychosurgery and notified the press. Kaimowitz then filed a writ of *habeas corpus* on behalf of Doe, alleging that he was being illegally detained for the purpose of experimental psychosurgery. As a result of the publicity, the Department of Mental Health put a stop to the experiment.

The Michigan court first considered the constitutionality of Doe's detention and directed his release. The court determined that the issue of consent was not moot, since similar experiments could arise in the future. The court held that psychosurgery should never be undertaken upon involuntarily committed patients when there is a high-risk, low-benefits ratio because of the impossibility of obtaining truly informed consent. The court based this conclusion on the common law doctrine of informed consent and the Constitution.

The court noted that psychosurgery was a dangerous and irreversible procedure with no predictable benefits to the patient or to scientific knowledge. Therefore, the adequacy of the patient's consent must be closely scrutinized. Under the common law, a person has the right to the inviolability of the body, and a medical operation performed without the patient's informed consent is battery. Informed consent must be competent, knowing, and voluntary. The court referred to the Nuremberg Code of 1948 regarding the subject of medical experimentation: "The person involved... should be so situated as to be able to exercise free power of choice, without the intervention of any element of force, fraud, deceit, duress, overreaching, or other ulterior form of constraint or coercion.... The degree of risk to be taken should never exceed that determined by the humanitarian importance of the problem to be solved by the experiment."

After hearing testimony regarding life in a state hospital, the court concluded that "involuntarily confined mental patients live in an inherently coercive institutional environment" in which it is impossible to give truly informed consent. The patient is stripped of supports and self-worth and feels compelled to cooperate with the institutional authorities who control his or her freedom.

The court raised other constitutional concerns. By damaging a patient's creativity, psychosurgery may impinge on the First Amendment right to generate ideas. "Intrusion into one's intellect" may also violate the right to privacy found in the First, Fifth, and Fourteenth Amendments. The court also speculated that psychosurgery might implicate the Eighth Amendment right to be free from cruel and unusual punishment.

THE RIGHT TO DIE

Cruzan v. Director, 110 S.Ct. 2841 (1990)

In *Cruzan v. Director*, the U.S. Supreme Court for the first time considered the question whether a state may limit a patient's right to refuse life-sustaining treatment, in this case by requiring "clear and convincing" evidence of the incompetent patient's wishes.

Nancy Cruzan entered into a "persistent vegetative state" after a car crash in 1983. She required gastric tube feeding and hydration to stay alive. After several years, when it became clear that she had no chance of regaining her mental faculties, her parents asked that the artificial nutrition be terminated. The hospital refused to honor the request without court approval. The Missouri trial court found that Cruzan had a fundamental right, under the state and federal constitutions, to refuse "death prolonging procedures." The court relied upon statements Cruzan had made to a friend years earlier and determined that she would not wish to continue the life-sustaining procedures if she were currently competent to make the decision. Though agreeing with the finding, Cruzan's guardian *ad litem* believed he was obligated to appeal the decision.

The Missouri Supreme Court reversed the decision, refusing to find a broad constitutional "right of a person to refuse medical treatment in every circumstance." Missouri's Living Will Statute indicated a state policy strongly in favor of the preservation of life. The court rejected the idea that Cruzan's parents could choose for her in the absence of a formal living will or "clear and convincing, inherently reliable evidence" of her wishes. Cruzan's statements to her roommate did not meet this standard. The U.S. Supreme Court granted *certiorari* to consider whether Cruzan had a right under the Constitution that would require the hospital to withdraw life-sustaining treatment.

The court noted that advances in medical technology had led to an increase in the number of cases involving the right to refuse life-sustaining treatment. In the New Jersey case of *In re Quinlan* (1976), a father was given judicial approval to disconnect the respirator that was maintaining the life of his daughter, who was in a persistent vegetative state. The New Jersey Supreme Court based its decision on the constitutional right of privacy. The state's interest in prolonging life had to give way to the individual's right to privacy, particularly in light of the poor prognosis. The father was allowed to make the decision for his incompetent daughter. Most courts since *Quinlan* had based the right to refuse treatment on the common law right to informed consent.

The U.S. Supreme Court surveyed several other informed consent cases around the country and noted a variety of standards as well as methods for determining how an incompetent patient exercises the right to refuse medical treatment. The majority opinion confined itself to the narrow issue whether the Constitution prohibited Missouri from choosing its own method of dealing with the "right to die." The court held that the state's procedural requirement that evidence of the incompetent's wishes as to the withdrawal of treatment be proved by clear and convincing evidence did not violate the Constitution. A state may choose to accept the "substituted judgment" of close family members but is not required to do so.

The state has the right to assert an unqualified interest in the preservation of human life without consideration for the quality of any individual's life. The state also has an interest in safeguarding the individual's personal decisions regarding matters of life and death. Not all incompetent patients have family to make decisions for them, and not all family members act in a patient's best interest. The risk of error in continuing life-sustaining treatment is simply to maintain the *status quo*, whereas treatment withdrawal is irreversible.

In a concurrence, Justice O'Connor noted that "no national consensus has yet emerged on the best solution for this difficult and sensitive problem," which should be "entrusted to the 'laboratory' of the States." In a separate concurrence, Justice Scalia argued that the removal of life-sustaining treatment should be equated with assisted suicide, which most states forbid.

Four justices dissented in lengthy opinions arguing that "Nancy Cruzan is entitled to choose to die with dignity." They argued that there exists a fundamental constitutional right to refuse medical treatment. The fact that Cruzan was incompetent does not deprive her of this right, which can be exercised meaningfully only by others acting in her best interest. Since no third party's situation would be improved, and no harm to others would be averted, no state interest could outweigh the individual's right in this case. Justice Stevens argued that the majority's decision "permits the State's abstract, undifferentiated interest in the preservation of life to overwhelm the best interests of Nancy Beth Cruzan." He maintained that life, death, and faith are private matters, and Missouri's policy was designed to "define life, rather than to protect it."

Washington v. Glucksberg, 117 S.Ct. 2258 (1997)

In the case of *Washington v. Glucksberg*, the U.S. Supreme Court considered whether a state's ban on physician-assisted suicide violates the Due Process or Equal Protection clauses of the Fourteenth Amendment.

In 1994, four physicians and three severely ill plaintiffs, joined by the nonprofit organization Compassion in Dying, brought suit in district court arguing that the Washington statute criminalizing assisted suicide was unconstitutional. They argued that there exists "a liberty interest protected by the Fourteenth Amendment which extends to a personal choice by a mentally competent, terminally ill adult to commit physician assisted suicide." The district court agreed. The court also found that the statute violated the Equal Protection Clause by treating the terminally ill who choose physician-assisted suicide differently from terminally ill patients who choose to refuse life-sustaining measures.

The court of appeals affirmed the lower court holding, though without agreeing that the statute violated the Equal Protection Clause. The court concluded that "the Constitution encompasses a due process liberty interest in controlling the time and manner of one's death—that there is, in short, a constitutionally recognized 'right to die'." The U.S. Supreme Court granted *certiorari*.

The court observed that almost every democracy criminalizes assisted suicide. In America, suicide was a crime until legislatures decided that it was unfair to punish a suicide's family. In recent years, and in many states, prohibitions against assisted suicide had been reaffirmed. In 1991, voters in Washington State rejected a ballot initiative that would have permitted a form of physician-assisted suicide. In contrast, in 1994, voters in Oregon enacted a Death with Dignity Act that legalized physician-assisted suicide for competent, terminally ill adults. In 1997, the president signed federal legislation prohibiting the use of federal funds for physician-assisted suicide.

The court considered whether the Due Process Clause protects a right to commit suicide, which itself includes a right to receive assistance in committing suicide. Several fundamental rights have been recognized as protected by the Due Process Clause of the Fourteenth Amendment, including the right to marry, to have children, to direct the education of children, to privacy in marriage, to contraception, to abortion, and to refuse life-sustaining medical treatment (see *Cruzan v. Director* above). The court expressed reluctance to impose its own policy preferences by asserting new and open-ended liberties not "deeply rooted in this Nation's history and tradition." The court distinguished the right to assisted suicide from the right established in *Cruzan*, which was based on the common law rule that unwanted treatment is battery.

Even though the right to assisted suicide is not a fundamental liberty interest protected by the Fourteenth Amendment, the Washington statute must still relate to a legitimate government interest. The court observed that the state has an "unqualified interest in the preservation of human life," as noted in *Cruzan*. The state has an interest in preventing suicide, in treating and protecting depressed patients, and in protecting the integrity and ethics of the medical profession. The state also has an interest in protecting the poor, the elderly, and the disabled from abuse, neglect, and mistakes, including "the real risk of subtle coercion and undue influence in end of life situations."

Legalizing assisted suicide for competent, terminally ill adults could start the state down a slippery slope leading to the practice of euthanasia. Recent studies had indicated that in the Netherlands, where assisted suicide had been legalized, thousands of patients were administered lethal doses of morphine without their consent.

Several justices wrote concurring opinions. Justice Stevens noted that palliative care cannot alleviate all pain and suffering; situations will arise in which "an interest in hastening death is legitimate… [and] entitled to constitutional protection." The justices observed that the process of data gathering and experimentation is better suited to legislative bodies, who would strike the proper balance between state and individual interests.

CONFIDENTIALITY

In re Lifschutz, 487 P.2d 557 (1970)

In 1970, the Supreme Court of California ruled that psychotherapist–patient privilege was not absolute and belonged to the patient, not the therapist.

After being assaulted, Joseph Housek filed a civil suit for damages in a California court. He alleged that the assault caused him "physical injuries, pain, suffering, and severe mental and emotional distress." During deposition, Housek acknowledged that he had received psychiatric treatment from Dr. Joseph Lifschutz approximately 10 years earlier. The respondent subpoenaed Lifschutz and medical records relating to his treatment of Housek. At his deposition, Lifschutz refused to produce any medical records and refused to answer any questions relating to the treatment. Housek was not present and neither expressly claimed nor waived a psychotherapist–patient privilege.

A California superior court ordered Lifschutz to comply with the subpoena, reasoning that, in instituting litigation, Housek had tendered as an issue his mental and emotional condition. Therefore, California's statutory psychotherapist–patient privilege did not apply. Lifschutz continued to refuse. The court of appeals and U.S. Supreme Court declined to hear the case. The superior court found Lifschutz in contempt and had him confined. Lifschutz sought a writ of *habeas corpus*, which was denied by the court of appeals. The California Supreme Court agreed to consider the writ, noting the belief by many psychiatrists in an absolute privilege of confidentiality.

The court observed that psychotherapy is a profession "essential to the preservation of societal health and well-being." Legislatures in California and other states have recognized that psychotherapy must be conducted in an environment of confidentiality. However, the need for confidentiality must be balanced with society's need for determining truth in litigation. The court concluded that the patient, not the psychotherapist, has a constitutional claim to a "right of privacy." Housek, the holder of the privilege, waived his right to keep such information confidential when he disclosed in deposition that he had received treatment from Lifschutz.

The court dispensed with Lifschutz' argument that any compromise of confidentiality would have an adverse effect on the general practice of psychotherapy. Psychotherapy had flourished even though no state provided for absolute confidentiality. Lifschutz also argued that the existence of an absolute clergy–penitent privilege denied equal protection to psychotherapists in that the confidentiality of the clergy–penitent relationship was being unfair deference relative to that accorded a psychotherapist and his patient. The court observed that the relationship of clergy to a penitent serves a different purpose than the psychotherapeutic relationship; the California legislature did not act irrationally in granting the absolute privilege to clergy only.

In conclusion, the court recommended that trial courts carefully control compelled disclosures of psychiatric information, because of the potential invasion of a patient's constitutional privacy interests. Courts may take various steps to protect litigants from embarrassment, publicity, and prejudicial evidence.

Doe v. Roe, N.Y. Supp. 2d 668 (1977)

In *Doe v. Roe*, a New York court agreed that statute, professional regulations, professional ethics, and common law all support a right to confidentiality for patients.

In 1977, Dr. Jane Roe, a psychiatrist, and her husband, Peter Poe, a psychologist, published a book that described psychotherapeutic sessions conducted 8 years earlier with Jane Doe and her former husband. The book included extensive verbatim descriptions of the patients' thoughts, feelings, emotions, and sexual fantasies. It also described the disintegration of the marriage. Doe sued for damages for breach of privacy and for an injunction against publication.

Doe asserted several theories in support of a patient's right to confidentiality. New York State statute and licensing regulations both prohibit disclosure of information obtained from a patient by a physician. The physician-patient relationship is contractual and implies a promise by the physician to obey the Hippocratic Oath; the Oath includes a provision to keep secret all communications from the patient. Finally, courts have increasingly recognized "privacy actions" for unreasonably publicizing what should have been left in confidence.

The court reviewed the statutory and case law, public policy, the Hippocratic Oath, and the Principles of Medical Ethics of the American Medical Association. The court concluded that "a physician, who enters into an agreement with the patient to provide medical attention, impliedly covenants to keep in confidence all disclosures made by the patient concerning the patient's physical or mental condition as well as all matters discovered by the physician in the course of examination or treatment." The court found this to be particularly true in a psychiatric relationship, where a patient is expected to discuss "personal material of the most intimate and disturbing nature."

The defendants argued that Doe and her ex-husband had consented to the publication. The court rejected outright "the value of an oral waiver of confidentiality given by a patient to a psychiatrist during the course of treatment." The court also rejected the defendants' contentions that the book's contribution to scientific knowledge outweighed Doe's right to confidentiality. The court also rejected the claim that the identity of Doe and her ex-husband had been adequately disguised.

The court awarded damages of $20,000 and permanently enjoined the defendants from circulating or publishing the book. The court refused to award punitive damages, noting that "the defendants' acts were not willful, malicious, or wanton—they were merely stupid."

Jaffee v. Redmond, 116 S.Ct. 1923 (1996)

In 1996, the U.S. Supreme Court established a therapist–patient privilege under federal law that extends to therapy provided by licensed social workers, as well as to psychiatrists and psychologists.

Mary Lu Redmond had shot and killed Ricky Allen while working as a police officer at the Village of Hoffman Estates, Illinois, in 1991. Following the traumatic incident, Redmond received extensive counseling from a clinical social worker, Karen Beyer. Allen's family brought suit against Redmond and her employer, alleging that Redmond had violated Allen's constitutional rights by using excessive force. Allen's family sought access to the social worker's therapy notes for use in cross-examination. Redmond argued that the records were protected against disclosure by her psychotherapist–patient privilege.

The district court judge disagreed and ordered the disclosure. At deposition, and on the witness stand, both Redmond and Beyer refused to follow the judge's order. The judge advised the jury that the refusal was unjustified and that the jury could presume that the contents of the notes would have been unfavorable. The jury ruled in favor of the petitioner and awarded damages. The federal court of appeals reversed and remanded, recognizing a psychotherapist privilege under Rule 501 of the Federal Rules of Evidence. The U.S. Supreme Court granted *certiorari*, because the federal courts had not reached uniform opinions on the issue.

Rule 501 of the Federal Rules of Evidence allows federal courts to define new privileges by interpreting "common law principles… in the light of reason and experience." The court recognized the important role of psychotherapy: "The psychotherapist privilege serves the public interest by facilitating the provision of appropriate treatment for individuals suffering the effects of mental or emotional problems. The mental health of our citizenry, no less than its physical health, is a public good of transcendent importance." The court also recognized that effective psychotherapy depends on an atmosphere of confidence and trust. All states have enacted some form of psychotherapist privilege, and a state's promise of confidentiality would have little value if not honored by a federal court.

The court concluded that "confidential communications between a licensed psychotherapist and her patients in the course of diagnosis or treatment are protected from compelled disclosure under Rule 501 of the Federal Rules of Evidence." The privilege should extend to communications made to licensed social workers; social workers serve members of the public who cannot afford the assistance of a psychiatrist or psychologist, but whose interests in psychotherapy are no different. In a dissenting opinion, Justice Scalia argued that the extension of the privilege to licensed social workers ignored the difference in training and credentials.

MALPRACTICE LIABILITY

Roy v. Hartogs, 381 N.Y.S. 2d 587 (1976)

In 1976, a New York court of appeals held that sexual intercourse between a therapist and his patient constituted medical malpractice.

Julie Roy received psychotherapy from Dr. Renatus Hartogs from 1969 to 1970. Roy alleged that Hartogs induced her to have sexual intercourse with him as part of her therapy. She sued Hartogs, arguing that his improper treatment emotionally and mentally injured her to such an extent that she was required to seek hospitalization on two occasions in 1971. At trial, the jury awarded Roy $50,000 in compensatory damages and additional punitive damages. Hartogs appealed.

The New York Court of Appeals noted that, as a matter of public policy, seduction had been abolished as a cause of action. In this case, the court held that sexual intercourse constituted medical malpractice, a different cause of action. In a concurring opinion, the presiding justice observed that "all imminent experts in the psychiatric field including the American Psychiatric Association abjure sexual contact between patient and therapist as harmful to the patient and deviant from accepted standards of treatment of the mentally disturbed."

The court reversed, however, on the issue of damages. The court concluded that, in light of the plaintiff's pre-existing mental condition, an award of more than $25,000 would be excessive. The court also found no evidence that Hartogs' conduct was so wanton or reckless as to permit an award for punitive damages.

In a dissenting opinion, one justice observed that Roy was presumably competent to consent to a sexual relationship in the course of therapy and did not complain about the sexual relationship at the time. If Hartogs committed an ethical violation, as opposed to malpractice, he should suffer the sanctions of the appropriate medical authority rather than face civil damages for malpractice.

Clites v. Iowa, 322 N.W. 2d 917 (Iowa Ct. App. 1982)

In *Clites v. Iowa*, a state court considered a case in which tardive dyskinesia was an adverse outcome of antipsychotic treatment that constituted medical malpractice.

Timothy Clites was a mentally retarded young man who resided at the Glenwood State Hospital-School, a residential facility operated by the state of Iowa. In 1970, at the age of 18, Clites was prescribed major tranquilizers for aggression. After 5 years of treatment with multiple antipsychotics, Clites was diagnosed with tardive dyskinesia. In 1976, his father submitted a claim to the Iowa State Appeal Board for the negligent use of antipsychotic medication and physical restraints. The board failed to take action, and his father filed a claim in state court for negligence.

The trial court reached several findings of fact. There was no evidence in the record of severe aggression requiring major tranquilizers as treatment. No physician examined Clites over a 3-year period, even though patients who are prescribed major tranquilizers should be closely monitored. "Drug holidays" were not attempted to monitor Clites' progress and need for continued medication. Tardive dyskinesia should have been recognized and responded to with a change in medication or consultation. "Polypharmacy" was not the least intrusive means of treatment. Major tranquilizers were used for the convenience of staff rather than treatment; the use of physical restraints was "cruel and inhuman" and conducted for staff convenience.

Clites' expert testified that standard practice was to obtain a written informed consent from a patient or guardian before administering major tranquilizers. Clites' parents were never informed of the potential side effects and, therefore, could not have given informed consent. The court observed that Clites' condition worsened following the use of antipsychotics, in that he became increasingly aggressive and self-abusive. At the time of the suit, he was described as "only a fraction of his former self."

The court awarded damages of over $700,000 for past and future medical expenses and pain and suffering. The state appealed.

The court of appeals noted that the standard of care owed to patients by hospitals and physicians was not in dispute: "Doctors are held to such reasonable care and skill as is exercised by the ordinary physician of good standing under like circumstances." The court found substantial support in the record for the trial court's conclusion that Clites' condition was caused by tardive dyskinesia induced by the negligent administration of major tranquilizers, that the condition was permanent, and that the damages awarded were appropriate.

DUTY TO PROTECT

Tarasoff v. Regents of the University of California, 551 P.2d 334 (1976)

In 1976, the California Supreme Court ruled that therapists have a "duty to protect" third parties from foreseeable danger posed by a patient. Other jurisdictions have followed suit, either with case law or legislation imposing *Tarasoff*-like duties on therapists.

In 1969, Prosenjit Poddar, a student at the University of California at Berkeley, killed Tatiana Tarasoff. Two months earlier, he had informed his psychologist, Dr. Moore, that he intended to kill Tarasoff when she returned from summer vacation. Moore notified the campus police and requested that they confine Poddar for psychiatric evaluation. The campus police took Poddar into custody but found him to be rational, accepted his denial that he would harm Tarasoff, and released him. Moore's supervisor at the university health service directed that no further attempts be made to confine Poddar and that all notes from his therapy be destroyed. No one notified Tarasoff or her family that she was in danger.

Tarasoff's parents filed suit against Moore, his supervisor, the campus police, and the regents of the University of California. The superior court concluded that there was no cause for action against the defendants. The plaintiffs appealed to the California Supreme Court.

In 1974, the court issued a ruling establishing a therapist's "duty to warn" the potential victim of predictable danger. In 1976, following an outpouring of protest and the submission of an amicus brief by the American Psychiatric Association, the court took the unusual step of reconsidering the matter, at which time they established the broader "duty to protect." According to the court, "When a therapist determines, or pursuant to the standards of his profession should determine, that his patient presents a serious danger of violence to another, he incurs an obligation to use reasonable care to protect the intended victim against such danger."

The court noted that persons generally owe a duty of care to anyone foreseeably endangered by their conduct, if their conduct is unreasonably dangerous. The common law has traditionally excused persons from responsibility for harm caused by another person, unless they bear a "special relationship" to the dangerous person or to the third party at risk. The court found a "special relationship" to exist between therapists and patients. In analogous cases, physicians had been held liable for failing to diagnose or warn family members of a patient's infectious disease.

The court rejected the argument presented in the amicus brief that therapists are unable to predict violent acts. Therapists are not required to predict violence precisely; they must only exercise "that reasonable degree of skill, knowledge, and care ordinarily possessed and exercised by members of [the profession] under similar circumstances." The court also dispensed with the argument that therapy would be harmed by both the potential and actual violations of confidentiality. The court noted that the public interest in safety outweighs the right to privacy. The professional ethics of the American Medical Association and statutes defining patient confidentiality make exception for cases in which a patient is thought to pose a danger to others. The court concluded, "The protective privilege ends where the public peril begins."

The court found no cause of action against the police for failing to confine Poddar, because public employee laws provide immunity for such exercises of discretion. The court remanded the case to the lower court to determine whether the defendants were liable for failing to take other measures to protect the victim. The court explained that a therapist might be required "to warn the intended victim or others likely to apprise the victim of the danger, to notify the police, or to take whatever other steps are reasonably necessary under the circumstances."

Lipari v. Sears Roebuck, 497 F. Supp. 1985 (1980)

In *Lipari v. Sears*, the Nebraska District Court extended the duty to protect to third parties belonging to a class of foreseeable victims, rather than to a specifically identified individual.

In 1977, Ulysses Cribbs entered a nightclub in Omaha, Nebraska, and fired a shotgun into a crowded dining room. He killed Dennis Lipari and wounded his wife, Ruth. She filed a wrongful death suit against Sears Roebuck & Co. for negligence in selling a gun to Cribbs when they "knew or should have known [he] had been adjudged mentally defective or had been committed to a mental institution." Sears then filed a third-party complaint against the United States under the Federal Torts Claims Act. Cribbs had been a patient at the Veterans Administration at the time he purchased the gun, though he dropped out of day-care treatment against the advice of his doctors. Sears claimed that the Veterans Administration knew or should have known that Cribbs was dangerous to himself or others yet failed to take customary steps to treat him. The United States filed a motion to dismiss the action.

The district court denied the United States' motion to dismiss the claim. Noting that the Nebraska Supreme Court had never addressed the issue of the therapist's duty to third persons, the district court considered the decision in the related California case of *Tarasoff v. Regents* (see above). The court found that the relationship of a therapist to a patient gives rise to a duty to third persons in Nebraska as well. The court did not accept the argument of the United States that a therapist cannot accurately predict which patients will pose a danger to others. It found instead that the "standard of care for health professionals adequately takes into account the difficult nature of the problems facing psychotherapists" and that a therapist would not be held liable simply for making a mistake.

The United States also argued that a therapist's duty to third persons should be limited to warning identifiable potential victims. Referring again to *Tarasoff*, the court determined that "whatever other steps are reasonably necessary under the circumstances" might require more than warning. Foreseeability is more important than identifiability, and "the V.A.'s employees could have reasonably foreseen an unreasonable risk of harm to the Liparis or a class of persons of which the Liparis were members."

EXPERT WITNESS TESTIMONY

Frye v. U.S., 293 F. 1013 (D.C. Cir. 1923)

In 1923, the District of Columbia Court of Appeals established what would come to be known as the "*Frye* test" for admissibility of scientific evidence based on general acceptance of the methodology by the scientific community.

James Frye was convicted of murder. At trial, he offered an expert witness to testify on the results of a "deception test." The premise of the test (an early form of "lie detector") was that systolic blood pressure rises when a subject tells a lie. The trial judge excluded the testimony. Frye appealed. His attorneys argued that the grounds for exclusion of expert testimony was a novel question. They proposed that "when the question involved does not lie within the range of common experience or common knowledge, but requires special experience or special knowledge, then the opinions of witnesses skilled in that particular science, art, or trade to which the question relates are admissible in evidence."

The court of appeals noted that it is difficult to define the point at which a scientific principle or discovery becomes demonstrable rather than experimental. The court concluded that "while courts will go a long way in admitting expert testimony deduced from a well-recognized scientific principle or discovery, the thing from which the deduction is made must be sufficiently established to have gained general acceptance in the particular field in which it belongs." The court upheld the decision, noting that the systolic blood pressure deception test had not gained sufficient standing and scientific recognition to justify its admission as expert testimony.

Daubert v. Merrell Dow, 61 U.S.L.S. 4805, 113 S.Ct. 2786 (1993)

In *Daubert v. Merrell Dow*, the U.S. Supreme Court held that the *Frye* test had been superseded by the Federal Rules of Evidence, with the result that federal courts have a broader range of factors to consider when determining whether scientific evidence is relevant and reliable.

Jason Daubert and Eric Schuller were born with serious birth defects. Their parents sued Merrell Dow Pharmaceuticals, Inc., in California court, alleging that the birth defects resulted from the mothers' use of Bendectin, a prescription anti-nausea drug. The case was moved to federal court. After extensive discovery, Merrell Dow moved for summary judgment. Merrell Dow's expert submitted an affidavit stating that more than 30 published studies had concluded that there was no evidence that Bendectin causes birth defects. The petitioners offered the testimony of eight other experts who concluded the opposite based on pharmacological, *in vitro*, and animal studies and a re-analysis of previously published epidemiological studies.

The district court concluded that the petitioner's evidence was not "sufficiently established to have general acceptance in the field to which it belongs" and therefore not admissible under the *Frye* test. The re-analysis of data had not been published or subjected to peer review. The court granted summary judgment in favor of Merrell Dow. The court of appeals affirmed, citing the prior decision in *Frye v. U.S.* (see above). The U.S. Supreme Court granted *certiorari* in light of differing opinions among federal courts regarding the proper standard for the admission of expert testimony.

The court observed that the *Frye* test of "general acceptance" had been the dominant standard in determining the admissibility of scientific evidence at trial. The plaintiffs argued that the *Frye* test had been superseded by the adoption of the Federal Rules of Evidence. The court agreed. Rule 402 of the Federal Rules of Evidence establishes that "evidence which is not relevant is not admissible." Rule 702 provides that "if scientific, technical, or other specialized knowledge will assist the trier of fact to understand the evidence or to determine a fact in issue, a witness qualified as an expert by knowledge, skill, experience, training, or education, may testify thereto in the form of an opinion or otherwise."

The *Frye* test is not mentioned in the Rules, and "a rigid 'general acceptance' requirement would be at odds with the 'liberal thrust' of the Federal Rules and their 'general approach of relaxing the traditional barriers to opinion testimony'." The court observed that scientific knowledge is a process, rather than a certainty. To qualify as scientific knowledge, expert conclusions must be "derived by the scientific method." Under the Rules, the trial judge must ensure that all scientific evidence is not only relevant, but reliable.

The court proposed several factors, but not a "definitive checklist or test" that bears on the inquiry into whether the testimony is scientific and relevant. Trial judges may consider whether the theory or technique can be (and has been) tested, whether it has been subjected to peer review and publication, what its error rate is, what standards control its operation, and whether it has been generally accepted within the relevant scientific community. The court emphasized that the inquiry is flexible and that the focus must be solely on principles and methodology, not on the ultimate conclusion.

The court remarked on other rules that may apply. Rule 703 provides that otherwise inadmissible hearsay evidence may be admitted if it is "of a type reasonably relied upon by experts in the particular field in forming opinions or inferences upon the subject." Rule 706 allows the court to appoint an expert of its own choosing. Rule 403 permits the exclusion of relevant evidence if the danger of unfair prejudice or confusion outweighs its probative value. Finally, the court emphasized that the conventional devices of cross-examination, presentation of contrary evidence, and instruction on the burden of proof are appropriate safeguards for challenging admissible, but questionable, evidence.

Kumho Tire v. Carmichael, 119 S.Ct. 1167 (1999)

In *Kumho Tire v. Carmichael*, the U.S. Supreme Court extended to technical or other specialized knowledge the holding in *Daubert* (see above) regarding scientific knowledge.

In 1993, the rear tire blew out on a minivan driven by Patrick Carmichael. In the resultant accident, one of his passengers died and others were injured. The Carmichaels sued the tire maker and distributor, claiming that the tire was defective. Their case relied largely on the testimony in deposition of a mechanical engineer and expert in tire failure analysis, who inspected the tire and applied several premises to conclude that a defect in manufacture or design had caused the blow-out.

The district court examined the expert's methods in light of the factors suggested in *Daubert v. Merrell Dow* and excluded the testimony as not reliable. The court of appeals reversed, noting that the Supreme Court in *Daubert* explicitly limited its holding to cover only the "scientific context" rather than "skill- or experience-based observation." The U.S. Supreme Court granted *certiorari* in light of uncertainty among federal courts whether *Daubert* applies to expert testimony based on "technical" or "other specialized" knowledge.

The court conceded that the ruling in *Daubert* referred only to "scientific knowledge," since that was the issue at hand. The rationale for the decision, however, applies equally to other expert testimony. In practice, it would be impossible for judges to apply different rules, because technical and scientific fields use overlapping methodologies.

The court agreed that a trial judge may use the reliability factors discussed in *Daubert*, because engineering testimony "rests upon scientific foundations." The court noted that in other cases, "the relevant reliability concerns may focus upon personal knowledge or experience." The court emphasized that the *Daubert* factors were flexible and not definitive.

The court reviewed the trial judge's conclusion that the expert could not reliably determine the cause of the tire's separation using the methods to which he testified. He had applied rules that other experts in the field do not use, and he had disregarded the results of his own inspection. The court concluded that the district court had not abused its discretion in excluding the evidence.

101

American Academy of Psychiatry and the Law Landmark Cases by Category as of 2014*

CIVIL RIGHTS OF PSYCHIATRIC PATIENTS CASES

Right to treatment

- *Rouse v. Cameron*, 373 F.2d 451, 125 U.S. App. D.C. 366 (1966)
- *Wyatt v. Stickney*, 344 F.Supp. 387 (M.D. Ala. 1972)
- *Donaldson v. O'Connor*, 493 F.2d 507 (1974)[†]
- *Youngberg v. Romeo*, 457 U.S. 307, 102 S.Ct. 2452 (1982)

Right to refuse treatment

- *Application of President and Directors of Georgetown College Inc.*, 118 U.S. App. D.C. 80, 331 F.2d 1000 (1964)[†,‡]
- *Superintendent of Belchertown State School v. Saikewicz*, 370 N.E.2d 417 (1977)[§]
- *Guardianship of Roe*, 383 Mass. 415, 421 N.E.2d 40 (1981)[†]
- *Rennie v. Klein*, 720 F.2d 266 (1983)
- *Rogers v. Commissioner of Dept. of Mental Health*, 390 Mass. 489, 458 N.E.2d 308 (1983)
- *Washington v. Harper*, 494 U.S. 210, 110 S.Ct. 1028 (1990)
- *Hargrave v. Vermont*, 340 F.3d 27 (2003)
- *Sell v. U.S.*, 539 U.S. 166, 123 S.Ct. 2174 (2003)

Right to die

- *Vacco v. Quill*, 117 S.Ct. 2293 (1997)[§]
- *Washington v. Glucksberg*, 117 S.Ct. 2258 (1997) (including concurring opinion)

Civil commitment

- *Lake v. Cameron*, 364 F.2d 657 (1966)[¶,‡]
- *Lessard v. Schmidt*, 349 F.Supp. 1078 (1972)[†,‡]
- *O'Connor v. Donaldson*, 422 U.S. 563, 95 S.Ct. 2486 (1975)
- *Fasulo v. Arafeh*, 378 A.2d 553 (1977)[¶]
- *Addington v. Texas*, 441 U.S. 418, 99 S.Ct. 1804 (1979)
- *Parham v. JR*, 442 U.S. 584, 99 S.Ct. 2493 (1979)
- *In re Richardson*, 481 A.2d 473 (1984)[¶]
- *Zinermon v. Burch*, 494 U.S. 113, 110 S.Ct. 975 (1990)

Managed care

- *Wickline v. State*, 239 Cal. Rptr. 810 (1987)[¶]
- *Wilson v. Blue Cross of Southern California*, 271 Cal. Rptr. 876 (1990)[¶]
- *Corcoran v. United Healthcare, Inc.*, 965 F.2d 132 (15th Cir., 1992)[§]
- *Dukes v. United Healthcare, Inc.*, 57 F.3d 350 (3d Cir., 1995)[†]
- *NYS Conf. of Blue Cross & Blue Shield Plans et al. v. Travelers*, 115 S.Ct. 1671 (1995)[†]
- *Aetna Health Inc. v. Davila*, 542 U.S. 200, 124 S.Ct. 2488 (2004)[§]

PHYSICIAN–PATIENT RELATIONSHIP CASES

Informed consent

- *Natanson v. Kline*, 350 P.2d 1093 (1960)[¶]
- *Canterbury v. Spence*, 150 U.S. App. D.C. 263, 464 F.2d 772 (1972)
- *Kaimowitz v. Michigan DMH*, 1 MDLR 147 (1973)

* The Landmark Cases were developed by the Association of Directors of Forensic Psychiatry Fellowships, under the auspices of the American Academy of Psychiatry and the Law.

† Denotes cases on the Landmarks list from prior years but deleted in 2007.

‡ Denotes cases deleted from the Landmarks list from prior years but *re-added* in 2014.

§ Denotes cases on the Landmarks list from prior years but deleted in 2014.

¶ Denotes cases on the Landmarks list from prior years but deleted in 1999.

- *Truman v. Thomas*, 27 Cal. 3d 285, 611 P.2d 902 (1980)*
- *Cruzan v. Director*, Missouri DMH, 497 U.S 261, 110 S.Ct. 2841 (1990)

Confidentiality/privilege/privacy

- *In re Lifschutz*, 2 Cal. 3d 415, 467 P.2d 557 (1970)
- *Doe v. Roe*, 400 N.Y.Supp. 2d 668 (1977)
- *Whalen v. Roe*, 429 U.S. 589, 97 S.Ct. 869 (1977)†
- *Hawaii v. Ariyoshi*, 481F.Supp. 1028 (1979)‡
- *In re Zuniga*, 714 F. 2d 632 (1983)‡
- *Commonwealth v. Kobrin*, 395 Mass. 284, 479 N.E. 2d 674 (1985)*
- *Jaffee v. Redmond*, 116 S.Ct. 1923 (1996)

Liability to patients

- *Roy v. Hartogs*, 381 N.Y.S. 2d 587 (1976)
- *Clites v. Iowa*, 322 N.W. 2d 917 (Iowa Ct. App. 1982)
- *Aetna v. McCabe*, 556 F.Supp. 1342 (1983)*
- *Mazza v. Medical Mutual Insurance Co. of North Carolina*, 319 S.E. 2d 217 (1984)†

Duty to protect

- *Tarasoff v. Regents of University of California*, 17 Cal. 3d 425, 551 P.2d 334, 131 (Cal. Rptr. 14, 1976)
- *Lipari v. Sears*, 497 F.Supp. 185 (D. Neb. 1980)
- *Jablonski v. U.S.*, 712 F.2d 391 (1983)†
- *Petersen v. State of Washington*, 671 P.2d 230 (1983)‡
- *Naidu v. Laird*, 539 A.2d 1064 (Del. 1988)†
- *People v. Wharton*, 809 P.2d 290 (1991)‡
- *Menendez v. Superior Court*, 834 P.2d 786 (1992)‡

CRIMINAL PROCESS CASES

Competency to stand trial

- *Dusky v. U.S.*, 362 U.S. 402, 80 S.Ct. 788 (1960)
- *Wilson v. U.S.*, 129 U.S. App. D.C. 107, 391 F.2d 460 (1968)
- *Jackson v. Indiana*, 406 U.S. 715, 92 S.Ct. 1845 (1972)
- *Sieling v. Eyman*, 478 F.2d 211 (9th Cir. Ariz. 1973)*
- *Drope v. Missouri*, 420 U.S. 162 (1975)‡
- *Riggins v. Nevada*, 112 S.Ct. 1810 (1992)
- *Godinez v. Moran*, 113 S.Ct. 2680 (1993)
- *Cooper v. Oklahoma*, 116 S.Ct. 1373 (1996)
- *Indiana v. Edwards*, 128 S.Ct. 2379 (2008)

* Denotes cases on the Landmarks list from prior years but deleted in 2007.

† Denotes cases on the Landmarks list from prior years but deleted in 2014.

‡ Denotes cases on the Landmarks list from prior years but deleted in 1999.

Criminal responsibility

INSANITY DEFENSE

- *M'Naghten's Case*, 8 Eng. Rep. 718, SEng Rep. 722 (1843)
- *Durham v. U.S.*, 94 U.S. App. D.C. 228, 214 F.2d 862 (1954)
- *Washington v. U.S.*, 129 U.S. App. D.C. 29, 390 F.2d 444 (1967)
- *Frendak v. U.S.*, 408 A.2d 364 (1979)
- *Jones v. U.S.*, 463 U.S. 354, 103 S.Ct. 3043 (1983)
- *U.S. v. Torniero*, 735 F.2d 725 (1984)‡
- *Foucha v. Louisiana*, 112 S.Ct. 1780 (1992)
- *Clark v. Arizona*, 548 U.S. 735, 126 S.Ct. 2709 (2006)

DIMINISHED CAPACITY

- *People v. Patterson*, 39 N.Y.2d 288, 347 N.E.2d 898 (1976)*
- *Ibn-Tamas v. U.S.*, 407 A.2d 626 (D.C. 1979)
- *People v. Saille*, 820 P. 2d 588 (1991)‡
- *Montana v. Engelhoff*, 116 S.Ct. 2013 (1996)

Psychiatry and the death penalty

- *Estelle v. Smith*, 451 U.S. 454, 101 S.Ct. 1866 (1981)
- *Barefoot v. Estelle*, 463 U.S. 880, 103 S.Ct. 3383 (1983)
- *Ake v. Oklahoma*, 470 U.S. 68, 105 S.Ct. 1087 (1985)
- *Ford v. Wainwright*, 477 U.S. 399, 106 S.Ct. 2595 (1986)
- *Payne v. Tennessee*, 111 S.Ct. 2597 (1991)
- *State v. Perry*, 610 So.2d 746 (1992)
- *Atkins v. Virginia*, 536 U.S. 304, 122 S.Ct. 2242 (2002)
- *Roper v. Simmons*, 543 U.S. 551, 125 S.Ct. 1183 (2005)
- *Panetti v. Quarterman*, 127 S. Ct. 2842 (2007)

Prisoner's rights

- *Baxstrom v. Herold*, 383 U.S. 107, 86 S.Ct. 760 (1966)
- *Estelle v. Gamble*, 429 U.S. 97, 97 S.Ct. 285 (1976)
- *Vitek v. Jones*, 445 U.S 480, 100 S.Ct. 1254 (1980)
- *Farmer v. Brennan*, 114 S.Ct. 1970 (1994)
- *Brown v. Plata* 134 S.Ct. 436 (2011)

Defendant's rights

CONFESSIONS

- *Colorado v. Connelly*, 479 U.S. 157, 107 S.Ct. 515 (1986)

GUILTY PLEAS

- *North Carolina v. Alford*, 400 U.S. 25, 91 S.Ct. 160 (1970)

SEX OFFENDERS

- *Specht v. Patterson*, 386 U.S. 605, 87 S.Ct. 1209 (1967)
- *Allen v. Illinois*, 478 U.S. 364, 106 S.Ct. 2988 (1986)
- *In re Young*, 857 P.2d. 989 (1993)*
- *Kansas v. Hendricks*, 117 S.Ct. 2072 (1997)
- *Kansas v. Crane*, 534 U.S. 407, 122 S.Ct. 867 (2002)
- *McKune v. Lile*, 536 U.S. 24, 122 S.Ct. 2017 (2002)
- *U.S. v. Comstock*, 560 U.S. 126, 130 S.Ct. 1949 (2010)

Drugs/alcohol

- *Robinson v. California*, 370 U.S. 660, 82 S.Ct. 1417 (1962)
- *Powell v. Texas*, 392 U.S. 514, 88 S.Ct. 2145 (1968)

Hypnosis

- *State v. Hurd*, 173 N.J. Super. 333, 414 A.2d 291 (1980)
- *People v. Shirley*, 181 Cal. Rptr. 243 (1982)*
- *Rock v. Arkansas*, 483 U.S. 44, 107 S.Ct. 2704 (1987)

EMOTIONAL HARM/DISABILITY/ WORKPLACE CASES

- *Carter v. General Motors*, 361 Mich. 577, 106 N.W.2d 105 (1960)*
- *Dillon v. Legg*, 68 Cal. 2d 728, 441 P.2d 912 (1968)
- *Forrisi v. Bowen*, 794 F.2d 931 (1986)†
- *Nassau County v. Arline*, 480 U.S. 273 (1987)†
- *Thing v. La Chusa*, 771 P.2d 814 (1989)†

Americans with disabilities act

- *Bragdon v. Abbott*, 118 S.Ct. 2196 (1998)
- *Pennsylvania v. Yesky*, 118 S.Ct. 1952 (1998)*
- *Olmstead v. L. C. ex rei. Zimring*, 119 S.Ct. 2176 (1999)
- *Toyota Motor Mfg., Ky. v. Williams*, 534 U.S. 184, 122 S.Ct. 681 (2002)‡
- *U.S. v. Georgia*, 546 U.S. 151, 126 S.Ct. 877 (2006)

Sexual harassment

- *Meritor Savings Bank FSB v. Vinson*, 106 S.Ct. 2399 (1986)
- *Harris v. Forklift Systems, Inc.*, 114 S.Ct. 367 (1993)
- *Oncale v. Sundowner Offshore Services, Inc.*, 118 S.Ct. 998 (1998)

Expert witness testimony standards

- *Frye v. U.S.*, 293 F. 1013 (1923)
- *Daubert v. Merrell Dow Pharmaceuticals Inc.*, 61 U.S.L.W. 4805, 113 S.Ct. 2786 (1993)
- *General Electric Co. v. Joiner*, 118 S.Ct. 512 (1997)‡
- *Kumho Tire Co., Ltd. v. Carmichael*, 119 S.Ct. 1167 (1999)

CHILD CASES

Child abuse reporting

- *Landeros v. Flood*, 17 Cal. 3d 399, 551 P.2d 389 (1976)
- *People v. Stritzinger*, 34 Cal. 3d 505, 668 P.2d 738 (1983)
- *State v. Andring*, 342 N.W.2d 128 (Minn. 1984)
- *DeShaney v. Winnebago County Dept. of Social Services*, 489 U.S. 189, 109 S.Ct. 998 (1989)

Juvenile court

- *Application of Gault*, 387 U.S. 1, 87 S.Ct. 1428 (1967)
- *Fare v. Michael C.*, 442 U.S. 707 (1979)

Education-related services

- *Board of Education of Hendrick Hudson Central School Dist. Westchester County v. Rowley*, 458 U.S. 176, 102 S.Ct. 3034 (1982)
- *Irving Independent School District v. Tatro*, 468 U.S. 883, 104 S.Ct. 3371 (1984)

Custody

- *Painter v. Bannister*, 258 Iowa 1390, 140 N.W.2d 152 (1966)
- *Santosky v. Kramer*, 455 U.S. 745, 102 S.Ct. 1388 (1982)

Juvenile sentencing

- *Graham v. Florida* 560 U.S. 48, 130 S.Ct. (2011)
- *Miller v. Alabama*, 132 S. Ct. 2455 (2012)

* Denotes cases on the Landmarks list from prior years but deleted in 2007.

† Denotes cases on the Landmarks list from prior years but deleted in 1999.

‡ Denotes cases on the Landmarks list from prior years but deleted in 2014.

Subject Index

A

B

D

E

F

G

H

I

J

K

L

M

N

O

P

S

T

U

Y

Z

Case Index

C

D

M

N

O

P

T

U

V

W

Y

Z